THE
ENCYCLOPEDIA OF MISSIONS

THE
ENCYCLOPEDIA
OF
MISSIONS

DESCRIPTIVE, HISTORICAL, BIOGRAPHICAL, STATISTICAL

SECOND EDITION

Edited under the Auspices of the Bureau of Missions

BY

REV. HENRY OTIS DWIGHT, LL.D., REV. H. ALLEN TUPPER, JR., D.D.
AND REV. EDWIN MUNSELL BLISS, D.D.

25142

FUNK & WAGNALLS COMPANY
NEW YORK AND LONDON
1904
Republished by Gale Research Company, Book Tower, Detroit, 1975

COPYRIGHT, 1904, BY
FUNK & WAGNALLS COMPANY
(Registered at Stationers' Hall, London)
Printed in the United States of America. Published October, 1904

Library of Congress Cataloging in Publication Data

Main entry under title:

The Encyclopedia of missions.

    Reprint of the 1904 ed. published by Funk & Wagnalls Co., New York.
    1. Missions--Dictionaries. I. Dwight, Henry Otis, 1843-1917, ed. II. Tupper, Henry Allen, 1856-   , ed. III. Bliss, Edwin Munsell, 1848-1919, ed.
BV2040.E5   1975   266'.003   74-31438
ISBN 0-8103-4205-7

CONTENTS

	PAGE
PREFACE TO THE FIRST EDITION	vii
PREFACE TO THE SECOND EDITION	xi
LIST OF CONTRIBUTORS OF SPECIAL ARTICLES	xiii
ABBREVIATIONS USED IN THE ENCYCLOPEDIA	xiv

THE ENCYCLOPEDIA OF MISSIONS 1

APPENDICES:
  I. DIRECTORY OF FOREIGN MISSIONARY SOCIETIES 817
  II. CHRONOLOGICAL TABLE OF THE EXTENSION OF PROTESTANT MISSIONS FROM THE TIME OF CAREY 824
  III. LIST OF BIBLE VERSIONS 826
  IV. MISSIONARIES WHO HAVE MADE TRANSLATIONS OR REVISIONS OF HOLY SCRIPTURE 830
  V. STATISTICAL TABLES 835
  VI. ROMAN CATHOLIC FOREIGN MISSIONS 848

PREFACE TO THE FIRST EDITION

THE standpoint of this Encyclopedia is, primarily, that of one who, interested in foreign mission work, seeks to enlarge his vision and increase his knowledge; secondarily, that of one who, looking forward to a personal share in it, seeks to inform himself as to its various phases, that he may the more readily decide where he can probably labor to the best advantage. The basis is the Society in which each individual is more especially interested; its history, organization, development; its missions and stations. Then the view broadens to take in the countries, races, and religions in their relations to the work, not only of his own, but of other denominations. Special topics open up, individual workers stand out in prominence, and as one step after another is taken, it becomes apparent that the work is not divided, but is one; and all these with varied names are but portions of the one great army of the Church.

The plan thus includes two general departments: 1. The organized work—the societies, their origin and growth at home, and their work abroad; 2. The countries in which, the races for which, that work is carried on, and the religious beliefs that are encountered.

Accessory to these are: 1. A gazetteer of Mission Stations; 2. Biographical sketches of Missionaries; 3. Description and enumeration of Bible versions; 4. Articles on special topics closely related to the work of Foreign Missions; 5. Maps, appendices of bibliography and statistics, and indices.

It became early evident that to accomplish so much, minutiæ must give place to perspective. However fascinating the details might be, they must be constantly used merely as illustrations. To do more, would not only have so enlarged its extent as to make the book unwieldy, but have blurred the distinctness of the impression that it has been sought to give. Thus in the accounts of the societies and their work personal terms are few. The history of Missions, both at home and abroad, is largely the history of individual men and women. Those who have stood at the helm and guided these great organizations were and are no less missionaries than those who have gone to the foreign field, yet even to mention the names of all within the space allowed would have almost made the work a mere chronicle. So of the countries and stations, the races and religions. The effort has been to give so much geography, history, etc., as would serve as a framework for pictures of missionary work and spiritual need.

With regard to the biographical sketches, it became evident very early that it would be necessary to draw the line sharply to exclude the living, and that to mention all, even of the dead, would be impossible. The sketches, too, must be brief, indicating rather than describing the work each did. So of the Bible versions; brief paragraphs were all that could be attempted.

When the question of special topics came up, the scope seemed unlimited. There were city missions; home missions; missions in their relations to commerce, music, the liquor traffic, the slave-trade; early Christian and medieval missions; the various questions under discussion in regard to methods of missionary work,—the lay element, education, self-support of native churches, etc. To treat even a few of these thoroughly, tho eminently desirable, would be impracticable. As careful a selection as possible has been made, and as much space given as seemed proportionate to the general scope of the work.

The plan led also to the decision to embody statistics and general lists in the form of appendices, which could easily be changed in subsequent editions, as the work developed. These appendices include: (a) A bibliography; (b) Lists of Bible versions, arranged alphabetically and geographically, showing the languages and dialects, the number of people reached by them, the linguistic families to which they belong, the characters in which they are written, the amount of translation work done, and the society under whose auspices they have been prepared, and in the Index the page of the Encyclopedia where they are referred to; (c) A list of missionary societies with the addresses of their secretaries, the date of organization, and the page of the Encyclopedia where they are spoken of; (d) A list of missionary stations, giving their geographical location, the societies carrying on work in them, the number and sections of the maps where they are found, and the page of the Encyclopedia where they are described; (e) Tables of statistics: (1) By societies and missions; (2) By countries and societies; (3) A summary of the whole. The General Index includes names of persons mentioned, places referred to, and general subjects treated. The maps cover all important mission-fields with as much fulness as is practicable The effort has been made to locate every mission station of importance, and in some cases the outstations. The importance of political influence in Africa and of the languages of India has led to the furnishing of a map of each country specially designed to bring out those characteristics.

Specific statements as to the appendices will be found in prefatory notes to them.

Many questions came up for consideration. In the alphabetical arrangement of articles a difficulty arose in regard to the location of the societies. To place them under their corporate names would be confusing, and the effort has been made to designate each by the term by which it is most widely known, with cross-references wherever it seems necessary. If there is difficulty in finding any one, a reference to Appendix C will easily give the solution.

Then came the question of spelling. The spelling of foreign names is in hopeless confusion. No two societies agree. Often the same society is not consistent with itself. Governments have laid down rules, which few follow; and no two Governments make the same rules. Should we spell Beirut, Beyrout, or Beyroot; Maulmain or Moulmein; Harpoot, Harput, or Charput; Foochow or Fuhchau; Gurhwal or Garhwal; Punjab or Panjab; Hyderabad or Haidarabad; Assiout, Assyoot, or Siout; San Paulo or São Paulo; Otjimbenque or Otyimbingue?

But instances almost innumerable could be added. The reader will find a few of the perplexities noted in Appendix D. To be absolutely logical or consistent was impossible. In India names the spelling of Hunter's Encyclopedia has been adopted. In Africa, the Church Missionary Society and the ABCFM reports have been followed in the main; elsewhere the editor has done the best he could, and if in any instance some mission station eludes the patient search of the reader, let him make a note of his failure for the benefit of future workers in this line.

Numerous requests have come in for an indication of the pronunciation of the names of places. To do this, however, was so manifestly impossible that no effort has been made. Each reader is at perfect liberty to pronounce Kachchh or Njenhangli as he chooses.

Another difficulty arose from the recurrence of the same name. If one is perplexed to distinguish the Washingtons that occur in every State of the Union he will understand the danger of confounding the various Salems of Africa, the Bethels of the West Indies and India, or the Bijnaurs (Bijnours?) of the Northwest Provinces and Oudh.

The question of statistics was also a perplexing one. After much consideration it was decided to give the general statistics in the form of tables in an appendix, introducing into the body of the Encyclopedia only such as were necessary in order to indicate the general nature and scope of the work in the different stations. So far as practicable, these have been brought up to date of publication.

At the commencement of the work blanks were sent to every mission society and mission station that could be learned of. The societies in almost every case responded, and many of the stations. With these as a basis and the careful study of the reports of the societies, the various Encyclopedias, etc., the great majority of the statements were prepared. In a few instances the society statements came from outside parties. Thus the article on the American Baptist Missionary Union was furnished by Dr. L. P. Brockett; that on the Moravian Missions, by Rev. B. Romig of Herrnhut; and so of a few others. Whenever it was practicable these statements were referred to persons connected with or specially informed regarding the societies, with a view to their being free from inaccuracy. Some countries, etc., were described by writers specially acquainted with them. Thus the India articles were prepared by Rev. C. W. Park, of

Birmingham, Conn., formerly of Bombay; Japan, by Rev. W. E. Griffis, D.D.; Brazil, by Rev. J. Beatty Howells, long a missionary in that country. The subjoined list will indicate most of the writers. The biographical sketches are chiefly the work of Rev. Samuel Hutchings, D.D., whose eighty-three years of age have not dimmed his interest or dulled the keenness of his pen. For the lists of Bible versions we are indebted to the kind courtesy of R. N. Cust, LL.D., of London. The sketches of the versions have mostly been prepared by Dr. Bernhard Pick, of Allegheny, who has made the subject a special study. The Arabic version, however, has been described by its translator, Rev. Dr. C. V. A. Van Dyck, of Beirut; the Turkish version by Rev. H. O. Dwight, of Constantinople.

In seeking for any title look first in the Encyclopedia; also in the Index of Appendix B for Bible versions; in Appendix C for societies or faith missions; in Appendix D for Mission Stations; and in the general Index for all. The page references in the appendices refer only to articles, not to places where mention of any topic is made in other articles; e.g., the station of Allahabad will be found, by Appendix D, on page 41 of Vol. I. It will also be found, by the general Index, on page 250, Vol. II., etc. So of the versions. Any person desiring to look up the whole work of a Society will turn from the account of the Society itself to that of the country where it works, the stations it occupies, and the biographical sketches of its missionaries, as he finds them mentioned in the different articles. In giving accounts of stations only those have been included in the body of the work with regard to which some definite information is given beyond the mere fact of their being occupied by a certain society. The complete list appears in Appendix D.

It is a pleasant duty to acknowledge the kind courtesy of the many who have assisted in the work: of the publishers, who have furnished the means and have left the editor so free to carry out the plan as fully as was practicable; those who have worked in the office with an interest that has shown their task to be no mere perfunctory duty; the contributors, whose patience, consideration, and ability have done so much to make the work not merely instructive, but entertaining; the officers of the Missionary Societies, whose unfailing willingness to answer innumerable questions has been so often put to the test. To name each one would be to give the list of all with whom the editor has come in contact in his work; yet he cannot but make special acknowledgments to Dr. Dalman, of Leipzig, for his article on the Jews; to the Rev. S. M. Jackson, for the Bibliography; to Dr. Cust, of London, for his table of Bible versions; to the officers of the Church Missionary Society, for the free use of their atlases of India and Africa.

That errors and omissions, some apparently inexplicable, will be noticed, must be expected. Any report of such to the publishers will be gladly received.

The work in truth has been a labor of love, and the highest return that can come from it will be the consciousness that it has furnished a link in the chain that is to bind together the great divisions of the one great army of the Church, as they come through its pages to know and understand each other better.

EDWIN MUNSELL BLISS.

NEW YORK CITY, March, 1891.

PREFACE TO THE SECOND EDITION

NO long series of reasons need be given why The Encyclopedia of Missions demands revision after twelve years. Political changes have parceled out among the nations the islands of the Pacific, have brought one at least of the Asiatic nations into parity of influence with Western Powers in shaping the destinies of the Far East, and have marked all Africa with the familiar national colors of Europe and made her mysterious central regions a field for the personally-conducted tourist, and a participant in the privileges of the Universal Postal Union. The body of experience in the mission field has crystallized into what is sometimes called a "Science of missions," made up of more or less exact principles of labor, which are more and more widely accepted by missionaries of all nations as fundamental. The mere increase of missionary enterprises and the expansion of mission fields are notable facts, while above every other reason the growth of the Christian community in almost every non-Christian land requires the rewriting of every descriptive paragraph in the book. When the editors asked valued advisers in Europe and America what faults of The Encyclopedia of Missions most loudly called for correction in a Revised Edition, the answer, as unanimous as if the question related to some text-book of science written twelve years ago, was "Its antiquity."

It is with grave misgivings, nevertheless, that this revision is offered to the public. Rigorous compression has been required in order to keep the Revised Edition within limits of bulk and cost which permit a considerable reduction of price.

Articles dealing with the various Missionary Societies have most persistently rebelled against our limitations of space. The history of societies of the first magnitude, the story of their origin, development and expansion under providential leadings; the record of the stedfast faith which has been demanded for their support, together with hints of the reasons why they are now recognized as instruments of a Divine purpose to shape the destinies of the race, would demand several volumes of the size of the one now offered.

The editors have, therefore, had no option but to give mere sketches of the Societies, showing salient points of history and general characteristics of effort rather than details of labors. Even so it has been impossible to mention, except in the Directory, many Societies which are doing noble work with narrow means and with but a handful, perhaps, of missionaries in the field. It is merely an introduction to the study of the missionary movement in the various nations and denominations which can be offered in this work. The great characteristics belonging to all the Societies in common: their motive, aim, difficulties, methods, mutual helpfulness, general relations and influences, direct and indirect, are treated in separate articles, all of which should be read by the student of the work of any one Society who would comprehend the fulness of its might as an agency for Christian civilization and the dignity of its position before those who hope for the elevation of the race.

One important change in the plan of the book, which some may regret, is the omission of maps. None of the old maps could be republished without radical and expensive changes. It is hoped that the wide circulation attained by Dr. Beach's fine "Geography and Atlas of Protestant Missions" will go far to relieve inconveniences resulting from the absence of the maps in the Encyclopedia. As a further relief, an effort has been made, in describing mission stations, so to define their location that their approximate place can be found in any good atlas.

Descriptive notes of about 5,000 cities, towns, and villages are furnished in this work. Our aim has been to give some data concerning all places in non-Christian lands, which are of present importance in the missionary enterprise. In deciding what places to omit through lack of space for all, we have tried to limit such omissions to outstations, and to stations which have shown little growth in a number of years, and may be regarded as in a dormant condition. The task of describing places, hundreds of which are found in no existing atlas or gazetteer, invites errors which we cannot hope to have escaped, and for which we must crave the leniency of critics. The spelling of the names of these places has caused much perplexity owing to diversity and even inconsistency of usage among the Missionary Societies. In order to avoid adding to the confusion we have thought best to follow as a general rule the system adopted by Beach in his "Atlas of Protestant Missions."

Success in our undertaking could not be possible without the collaboration of the officers of Missionary Societies all over the world. This has been freely asked, and we gratefully realize that it has been most cordially given. Moreover, many missionaries and others have placed at our disposal their knowledge as experts, or have prepared for the Encyclopedia articles on special subjects. A list of these contributions to the value of the book we give below, indicating at the same time the names of those whose articles in the first edition we were able to use without important modification. We would also make special acknowledgment of our indebtedness to Dr. Beach's "Atlas of Protestant Missions," whenever his laborious research has served to correct or to supplement our own endeavors. The general information found in Dr. J. S. Dennis' "Centennial Survey of Foreign Missions" has also been of great value in preparing for the Appendix the Directory of Missionary Societies and the List of Bible Translators.

In sending out this new edition of The Encyclopedia of Missions we cannot refrain from mentioning the astonishment mingled with awe aroused in our own minds by our close study of the growth of the missionary enterprise since the first edition was issued. It is our belief that if any will study this rapid advance and growth they will find the conviction unavoidable that this enterprise and its present power in the non-Christian world is the fruit of more than a merely human impulse. This book presents again an illustration of the fact that the "stone which the builders rejected is become the head of the corner. It is the Lord's doing and it is marvelous in our eyes!"

LIST OF CONTRIBUTORS OF SPECIAL ARTICLES

*Andrus, Rev. A. N. ....Mardin, Turkey.
*Atterbury, Rev. W. W., D.D...New York City.
Barrows, Mrs. J. H...........Oberlin, Ohio.
*Barton, Rev. J. L............Boston, Mass.
Beach, Rev. H. P. ....New York City.
*Brockett, L. P., M.D........Brooklyn, N. Y.
Brown, Rev. A. J., D.D.......New York City.
Carroll, Rev. H. K., LL.D....New York City.
*Chambers, Rev. R...........Erzroom, Turkey.
Chester, Rev. S. H., D.D.....Nashville, Tenn.
*Cobb, Miss M. L............East Orange, N. J.
Coe, Rev. E. B., D.D.........New York City.
Condit, Rev. J., D.D.........San Francisco, Cal.
Conklin, Rev. J. W., D.D.....New York City.
Crawford, Rev. L. S., D.D....Trebizond, Turkey.
Cronkhite, Rev. L. W.........Greenwich, N. Y.
*Crowell, Miss K. R..........East Orange, N. J.
Cushing, Rev. J. N...........Rangoon, Burma.
*Cust. R. N., LL.D...........London.
Dennis, Rev. J. S............New York City.
Doremus, Miss S. B..........New York City.
*Eddy, W. W.................New York City.
*Ellinwood Rev. F. F., D.D...New York City.
Fletcher, Miss A. C..........Washington, D. C.
Gamewell, Rev. F. D.........New York City.
*Gates, Rev. O. H............Berlin, Germany.
*Gilman, Rev. E. W., D.D....
*Gracey, Rev. J. T., D.D.....President International Missionary Union.
Greene, Rev. F. D............New York City.
*Griffis, Rev. W. E., D.D.....Boston, Mass.
*Grout, Rev. Lewis (late of South Africa)..............
Haas, Rev. John A. W., D.D...New York City.
Hand, Chas. W., Esq.........New York City.
Haven, Rev. W. I., D.D......New York City.
*Howells, Rev. J. B..........Jaher, Brazil.
*Hulbert, Prof. H. B.........Seoul, Korea.
*Hulbert, Prof. H. W. (late of Beirut, Syria)............Marietta, Ohio.
*Hutchings, Rev. S., D.D. (late of Madras, India).........
*Jackson, Rev. S. M..........New York City.
*Kalopothakes, Rev. M. D.....Athens, Greece.
*Labaree, Rev. B., D.D.......Urmia, Persia.
*Laurence, Rev. E. A.........

*Laurie, Rev. T., D.D. (late of Mosul, Turkey)..........
*Loomis, Rev. S.............Newark, N. J.
*Lovett, Rev. R. ....London, England.
*Marshall, C. J..............Salvation Army, New York City.
*Martin, Rev. Chalmers (late of Bangkok, Siam).........Pittsburg, Pa.
Martin, Rev. Paul............Princeton, N. J.
*McFarland, Rev. H. H.......Woodhaven, L. I.
Mackay, Rev. R. P., D.D......Toronto, Ont.
*McLaurin, Rev. J...........Woodstock, Can.
*McLeman, Rev. D...........Akaroa, New Zealand.
*Morse, R. C................New York City.
Ohl, Rev. J. F. F., Mus.D......Philadelphia, Pa.
*Panaretoff, S., Prof.........Robert College, Constantinople.
*Park, Rev. C. W. (late of Bombay, India)...........
*Parsons, Miss E. C..........New York City.
*Pick, Rev. B., Ph.D., D.D....New York City.
*Romig, Rev. B..............Herrnhut, Germany.
*Russell, Rev. F., D.D........New York City.
Sailer, Mr. T. H. P., Ph.D.....New York City.
*Shedd, Rev. J. H., D.D......
Shedd, Rev. W. A............Urmia, Persia.
*Shelton, Rev. C. W..........Birmingham, Ct.
Smith, Rev. G. B.............New York City.
Speer, Mr. R. E..............New York City.
*Sproull, Rev. W. J..........Latakiyeh, Syria.
Starbuck, Rev. C. C..........
Steele, Rev. R., D.D..........Sydney, Australia.
*Taylor, Rev. J. Hudson......London, England.
*Thomson, Rev. A., D.D......
Tisdall, Rev. W. St. Clair, D.D..Bedford, England.
Turner, Mr. F. P..............New York City.
*Watson, Rev. A., D.D........Alexandria, Egypt.
Wells, Mr. Amos R...........Boston, Mass.
*Whitney, Rev. J. F. (late of Micronesia)..............
*Wilshere, Rev. D............Nassau, Bahamas.
Wishard, Mr. L. D...........Chicago, Ill.
*Wood, Rev. I. F. (late of Ceylon)....................
*Wood, Rev. J...............Ottawa, Can.
*Wright, Rev. W., D.D........

*Contributors to the First Edition whose work has been available for the present work.

ABBREVIATIONS USED IN THE ENCYCLOPEDIA

ABCFM	American Board of Commissioners for Foreign Missions.
ABHMS	American Baptist Home Mission Society.
ABMU	American Baptist Missionary Union.
ABS	American Bible Society.
ACM	Australian Church Missionary Society.
AFFM	American Friends' Board of Foreign Missions.
AMA	American Missionary Association.
AME	African Methodist Episcopal Missionary Society.
AWM	Australian Wesleyan Methodist Missionary Society.
B	Basel Missionary Society.
Ber	Berlin Missionary Society.
BFBS	British and Foreign Bible Society.
BMP	Foreign Mission Board of the Baptist Convention of the Maritime Provinces.
BMS	Baptist Missionary Society.
BOQ	Foreign Mission Board of the Baptist Convention of Ontario and Quebec.
BTS	Bible Translation Society.
BZM	Baptist Zenana Missionary Society.
CA	Christian and Missionary Alliance.
CC	Christian Church Missionary Society.
CEZ	Church of England Zenana Missionary Society.
CIM	China Inland Mission.
CMS	Church Missionary Society for Africa and the East.
CP	Cumberland Presbyterian Missionary Society.
CSFM	Church of Scotland Foreign Missions Committee.
CWBM	Christian Woman's Board of Missions (Disciples).
DBS	Danish Bible Society.
DMS	Danish Missionary Society.
DS	Danish Santal Mission.
EA	Evangelical Association.
ECS	Episcopal Church in Scotland Missionary Society.
ELGC	Evangelical Lutheran General Council Missions.
ELGS	Evangelical Lutheran General Synod Missions.
ELUS	Evangelical Lutheran United Synod of the South.
Erm	Ermelo Missionary Society.
FCMS	Foreign Christian Missionary Society (Disciples).
FCS	Free Church of Scotland Missions.
FFMA	Friends' Foreign Missionary Association.
FMS	Finnish Missionary Society.
GES	German Evangelical Synod of the United States.
GM	Gossner Missionary Society.
HEA	Hawaiian Evangelical Association.
Her	Hermannsburg Missionary Society.
Ind	Independent Missionary.
JB	Jamaica Baptist Missionary Union.
JU	Jerusalem Union of Berlin.
KIM	Kurku Inland Mission.
Leipz	Leipzig Missionary Society.
LMS	London Missionary Society.
MCC	Missions of the Methodist Church in Canada.
ME	Missionary Society of the Methodist Episcopal Church in the United States.
MES	Board of Missions of the Methodist Episcopal Church, South.
MM	Melanesian Mission Society.
Mor	Moravian Missions.
MP	Methodist Protestant Missionary Society.
MR	Mission Romande (French Switzerland).
NAM	North African Mission.
NBC	Foreign Mission Board of the National Baptist Convention of America.
NBS	National Bible Society of Scotland.
Neth	Netherlands Missionary Society.
Neth.B	Netherlands Bible Society.
Neth.M	Netherlands Mennonite Missionary Society.
Neuk	Neukirchen Missionary Institute.
NHM	New Hebrides Mission.
Nor	Norwegian Missionary Society.
NSM	Netherlands State Missionary Society.
OV	Old Version.
P	Paris Evangelical Mission Society.
PB	Christian Mission (commonly called the Brethren).
PCC	Foreign Mission Committee of the Presbyterian Church in Canada.
PCE	Foreign Mission of the Presbyterian Church in England.
PCI	Foreign Mission of the Presbyterian Church in Ireland.
PE	Protestant Episcopal Church of America Missionary Board.
PMMS	Primitive Methodist Missionary Society.
PN	Board of Foreign Missions of the Presbyterian Church in the U. S. A.
Pruss. BS	Prussian Bible Society.
PS	Presbyterian Church in the U. S. A. (South) Board of Foreign Missions.
RBMU	Regions Beyond Missionary Union.
RBS	Russian Bible Society.
RCA	Reformed Church in America (Board of Foreign Missions).
Rhen	Rhenish Missionary Society.
RP	Synod of Reformed Presbyterian Church in North America.
SA	Salvation Army.
SAMS	South American Missionary Society.
SBC	Southern Baptist Convention (Foreign Missionary Board).
Scand	Scandinavian Alliance of the U. S. A.
SDA	Mission Board of the Seventh Day Adventists.
SPCK	Society for Promoting Christian Knowledge.
SPG	Society for the Propagation of the Gospel.
SPGJ	London Society for the Propagation of the Gospel among the Jews.
Swed.M	Swedish Missionary Society.
Swed.N	Swedish National Missionary Society.
Swed.U	Swedish Missionary Union.
UB	United Brethren in Christ.
UE	United Evangelical Missionary Society.
UFS	United Free Church of Scotland.
UM	Universities' Mission to Central Africa.
UMFC	United Methodist Free Churches (Home and Foreign Missions).
UP	United Presbyterian Church of North America Board of Foreign Missions
UPS	United Presbyterian Church of Scotland Board of Foreign Missions.
Utr	Utrecht Missionary Union.
WCM	Welsh Calvinistic Methodist Missions.
WMS	Wesleyan Methodist Missionary Society.
WU	Woman's Union Missionary Society.
YMCA	Young Men's Christian Association.
YWCA	Young Women's Christian Association.
ZBM	Zenana Bible and Medical Mission.
ZIM	Zambesi Industrial Mission.

THE ENCYCLOPEDIA OF MISSIONS

A

AANA: A settlement in Upolu, Samoa; station of the LMS.

ABACO ISLAND. See GREAT ABACO.

ABADIYEH: A village in Palestine near the southern end of the Sea of Tiberias; mission station of the Friends' Foreign Mission Society, with a school and a dispensary.

ABASA: Village E. of Cape Coast Castle, Gold Coast, W. Africa; outstation of the WMS, with six village schools and about 600 professing Christians.

ABBOTABAD: Town in the district of Peshawar in the northwest frontier province of India; mission station of the CMS, and of the Church of England Zenana Missionary Society, with a dispensary and a number of pupils in the zenanas.

ABDUL MASIH (Servant of Christ): The new name which was adopted by Sheikh Saleh, converted through the influence of Henry Martyn in 1809; and soon afterward admitted to the Church at Calcutta. He was born at Delhi, was Persian and Arabic Moonshi of Lucknow, then became keeper of the King of Oudh's jewels and was for years a most zealous Mussulman. Just after he had been horrified by the atrocities of his coreligionists in the Rajput State of Jodhpur, he became deeply impressed by Martyn's preaching, and accepted Christ as his Savior. The Sheikh Saleh's conversion caused great excitement among his former associates; and he became an able and influential minister of Jesus Christ. He was the first native pastor under the Church Missionary Society in India.

ABEBIFY: Town in the Gold Coast Colony, W. Africa; 4,000 inhabitants using the Ashanti language and worshiping idols or fetishes; station of the Basel Missionary Society, having connected with it 17 outstations, in which are 15 village schools. The Christians of this place number 735. Name also given as Abetifi.

ABEEL, David: Born June 12, 1804, at New Brunswick, N. J. He accepted the position of chaplain of the American Seamen's Friend Society at Canton, with a conditional appointment as missionary of the American Board at the end of a year, and sailed with Mr. Bridgman, October 14, 1829, for China. In December, 1831, Mr. Abeel entered the service of the American Board, and sailed on the 27th for Batavia, partly for his health, but chiefly to visit the churches planted by the Dutch, two centuries before, in the islands of southeastern Asia. While visiting London, July 25, 1834, he told of the degradation of the women of the East, and presented an appeal to the Christian women of Great Britain, which resulted in the formation of the Society for Promoting Female Education in the East. October 17, 1838, he returned to Canton, but the "opium war" preventing his usefulness there, he visited Malacca, Borneo, and other places. On account of ill health he returned to New York, April 3, 1845, and died at Albany, N. Y., September 4, 1846, aged 42. He published *A Journal of a Residence in China; A Missionary Convention in Jerusalem; The Claims of the World to the Gospel.*
Williamson (G. R.), *David Abeel*, New York, 1849.

ABEIH: A village of the Lebanon district in Syria, 25 miles S. of Beirut. A mission station established by the ABCFM, but in 1870 transferred to American Presbyterian Board. The Theological Seminary which was founded there in 1869 was transferred to Beirut in 1874. Depending upon the 4 stations of the Lebanon district are 45 outstations, and as many primary schools, with about 650 church members. The missionary statistics of Abeih are included in those of the district thus described.

ABENAQUI: This is a dialect of the Micmac language of the North American family. It was first reduced to writing by missionaries of the American Board, and is written with Roman letters.

ABEOKUTA: Capital of the Yoruba district (Lagos Protectorate), W. Africa. It stands on the E. bank of the Ogun river, about 60 miles N. of Lagos, with which it is connected by railroad. It occupies the two highest of several detached hills which ascend gradually to the N. E., and terminate in a bluff surmounted by masses of smooth gray granite. This bluff gives the place its name, which means "under the rock." Wars ruined the Yoruba country in the early part of the 19th century and the fugitives from many towns gathered here, slowly forming the city which now has 150,000 inhabitants, and is an

1

important commercial center. The growth of the city was greatly stimulated about 1840 by the arrival there from Sierra Leone of freed and Christianized slaves, who were natives of the Yoruba country. These men set themselves against the human sacrifices and other cruelties of the fetishism, and the atrocities of the slave-trade of which this city was a center. They also prepared the way for the establishment of missions.

A mission was opened in the city by the CMS in 1846; by the WMS about the same time, and by the SBC (of America) in 1856-1876. Hostility of slave merchants and liquor dealers to the enlightening effect of Christianity has led to several fierce attempts to destroy a reform which opposed both. At last a general uprising against the English took place in 1867, during which all white men were driven from the city, and 400 native Christians fled for their lives; the churches were sacked, and Christian influence might have been destroyed for years had not Mr. Johnson, the able negro preacher, held to his post throughout the troubles. At present the four native chiefs who rule the city attend church regularly, and form a regular Council of Government. A Board of Education for the Yoruba region under these chiefs has taken the place of the savage councils of the fetish priests, which terrorized the land in the first half of the 19th century. Intemperance and polygamy are forces which still resist advances of spirituality among the people, and the influx of foreign traders facilitated by the railway is not an unlimited benefit to the city.

Paganism, Mohammedanism and Christianity are the prevailing religions at Abeokuta. There is a Roman Catholic mission there. The Protestant Christian community consists of about 5,000 souls, of whom 1,700 are communicants. There are 11 missionaries and 73 native workers, men and women, connected with the three missions. The CMS carries on, in connection with Abeokuta Station, 21 village schools, a theological class and a dispensary, besides maintaining a special work for lepers. The WMS has 22 outstations, and 3 village schools, and the SBC reports 2 outstations and 1 village school.

ABETIFI. See ABEBIFY.

ABKHASIANS: A warlike tribe, inhabiting the country between the Black Sea and the Caucasus. Under the Roman Emperor Justinian they became Christians, but subsequently adopted Mohammedanism, to which religion they still nominally belong, though their religion in fact consists of a barbarous mixture of Christian, Mohammedan and heathen notions and usages. The greater part of these people have been induced by the Turkish government to remove to Asiatic Turkey, where they form agricultural communities, living apart from the rest of the population.

ABOA: Town on the Rombi river in the German Colony of Kamerun; station of the German Baptist Missionary Society, opened in 1900. Also written Abo.

ABOKOBI. See AGBOGBA.

ABOMEY: The capital of Dahomey. It was captured by the French in 1892. It is not a mission station, but has been reached by the Wesleyan Missionary Society. It has about 20,000 inhabitants.

ABORIGINES PROTECTION SOCIETY: The tendency of colonists from the so-called civilized countries to disregard the rights of natives of territory which they desire to occupy has had many painful illustrations in Australia, the Pacific islands, and various parts of Africa, not to mention other better known regions. Feelings of revulsion from such injustice and of sympathy for its victims caused the formation of this Society in 1837. The Society aims steadily to champion the rights of tribes, especially in Africa, which are oppressed by the thoughtlessness, carelessness, or greed of white settlers. It seeks to prevent settlers from crowding natives off from lands actually in occupancy, and to secure just legislation regulating the distribution of land to white settlers, limiting or forbidding the sale of liquor to natives, and otherwise placing legal barriers in the way of injury to those who through ignorance or weakness cannot defend their own interests. The methods so far used by the Society have been by appeal to public sentiment through the press, and by direct application to the Government. This Society is not in any sense a missionary organization. Nevertheless its object is one which coincides with the purpose and wish of all missionaries, which fosters the spread of civilization among backward races and which attracts them toward the adoption of that Christian principle of good will to all on which the existence of the Society is based. Headquarters, Broadway Chambers, Westminster, London, S. W., England.

ABURAH: A town N. E. of Kumassi in the Gold Coast Colony, W. Africa; station of the WMS, with 1 missionary, 49 native workers, men and women, 75 outstations and 550 church members.

ABURI: A town of 6,500 inhabitants in the Gold Coast Colony, W. Africa. A station of the Basel Missionary Society, established in 1847. It has 6 missionaries and 18 native workers, men and women. It has 9 outstations, 10 village schools and 700 church members. Also station of the WMS, with 4 missionaries and 93 native workers, men and women. It has 14 village schools, 1 high school and 650 church members.

ABYSSINIA: The name is derived from Arabic "Habash"="mixed" population. The inhabitants call themselves Itiopavians—Ethiopians. The region now included under the common name Abyssinia has been called most appropriately the "Switzerland" of Africa. It consists, for the most part, of a mountainous plateau averaging 9,000 feet above sea level, precipitous on the east, and falling away more gradually in other directions, everywhere being intersected by profound ravines and dominated by lofty snow-capped peaks. A desert, stretching from the Red Sea to the base of the mountains, still further isolates this Alpine region. Abyssinia, made up of the provinces of Tigré, Lasta, Amhara, Gojam, Shoa, and adjoining lands, covers about 150,000 square miles. The average climate on this lofty plateau is delightfully temperate, the depths of the ravines being thoroughly tropical, while the higher mountain shoulders are decidedly Arctic. The soil is fertile, and supports a great variety of vegetable and animal life. Rich mines of great variety abound, and the country furnishes every necessity for a highly developed civilization.

The people of Abyssinia number about 3,500,000; they are much superior in every respect to their African neighbors.

The Introduction of Christianity: Abyssinia has been called the first and only mission field of the Coptic Church. It was converted to the Christian faith early in the 4th century, in this wise: Meropius, a philosopher of Tyre, went on a voyage for purposes of travel and observation to "India"—a much-abused title, supposed to designate in this case South Arabia. He had with him his two young nephews, Frumentius and Edesius. The ship put into a port on the west coast of the Red Sea and its passengers were promptly slain by the natives. Frumentius and Edesius alone were saved alive as slaves, and taken to Axum, the ancient capital of Abyssinia. Frumentius was instrumental in introducing some knowledge of Christianity among the people and, having asked help in his missionary labors from the Church in Egypt, he himself was consecrated bishop of Abyssinia. He is known in the church of that land as Abu Salama, "the Father of Peace."

The venerable translation of the Bible into Ethiopic dates from the 4th century and, if not finished by Frumentius, was doubtless set under way through his zealous foresight. Upon this book rests whatever power Abyssinia had in its best days.

The Abyssinian Christians are connected ecclesiastically with the **Coptic Church** of Egypt, but hold to certain observances of Judaism. The clergy being the only educated people and holding great power in their hands, conservative influences and deep suspicion of foreigners have ruled the policy of the kingdom up to the present time. In the new Africa, Abyssinia is destined to play an important part. That its Christianity should be revived and made to live in the hearts of its adherents is the most pressing duty of the Christian Church.

The Jesuit Episode: In 1490 A.D., the Abyssinian Christians were rediscovered by the naval officers of John II. of Portugal, who had sailed all the way around southern Africa. The Christian world thought that at last the famous "Prester John" was found away up in the Abyssinian Mountains. The King of Portugal sent Petro Cavilham, the Jesuit, to push the interests of Portugal in Africa. This interference was resented. The Abyssinians came to blows with the Portuguese soldiers, who worked under orders from the Jesuits. At one time these zealous churchmen were victorious, and 8,000 enemies lay dead upon the battle-field. As the young Abyssinian Prince Facilidas, whom the Jesuits had half won over, walked through the heaps of slain, he is reported to have come to this conclusion: "A religion which causes so much bloodshed cannot be good. We had better, tho victorious, return to the faith of the conquered and remain faithful, as they were." When he became king he expelled the Jesuits, and all further attempts on their part to get a footing in the country failed. The attempt, in 1621, when the Jesuits installed a patriarch in Abyssinia, was especially disastrous. Over a century later (1750-1754) a third attempt was unsuccessful. French influence now seems paramount in Abyssinia and the construction of a railroad to Harrar from the French seaport of Jibuti on the Red Sea has greatly strengthened this influence.

Protestant Missions in Abyssinia: In 1830 Bishop Gobat and Mr. Kugler were sent on a mission to Abyssinia by the CMS. The work began with bright prospects. Bishop Gobat traveled extensively and learned the Amharic, the common language of the people, a dialect of the ancient Ethiopic, which, though still used in church services, has become a dead language, even to many of the priests who go through the ceremonies. Bishop Gobat broke down in health, and had to leave the country. Mr. Kugler died. Later, Mr. Isenberg and Dr. Krapf took up the work. The Jesuit cloud again appeared on the horizon in the shape of Sapeto, who was sent out by the Propaganda. His intrigues aroused the old suspicions of foreign interference, and all foreigners were expelled the country in 1838. Krapf and Isenberg went to Shoa, and were received in a kindly manner by the king. There they compiled an Amharic dictionary, as well as a geography and prayerbook. Before this the Bible had been translated at Cairo, in 1808, into Amharic by an Abyssinian monk, Abu Rumi, assisted by the French Consul Asseline. In 1840 the MS. was bought and revised by the British and Foreign Bible Society. Altho the Protestant missionaries had been expelled, the work went on. The Protestant missionaries remained on the borders of Abyssinia until 1859, when they were allowed to return to the capital only to be imprisoned in 1862 through a Frenchman's intrigue with the ignorant and suspicious king Theodore. An English military force released the captives in 1868, and the CMS has not renewed its efforts for the Abyssinians. The Swedish Evangelical National Society in 1866 began a mission near Massaua on the Red Sea in what was Abyssinian territory, but is now the Italian colony of Eritrea. Its missionaries have gradually pressed toward the Abyssinian frontier and now they have 5 stations W. of Massaua manned by 18 missionaries and 13 native workers, both men and women, and with a printing house, schools, and about 300 communicants connected with their churches.

The Sacred City of the Ethiopians, Bent (T.), London, 1893; *The British Mission to Abyssinia,* Rassam (H.), London, 1869, 2 vols. *Wanderings Among the Falashas of Abyssinia,* Stern (H.), London, 1862; *Abyssinia,* Vivian (H.), London, 1901.

ACCA. See ACRE.

ACCRA: A town on the Gold Coast, W. Africa; station of the WMS, with 3 missionaries and 34 native workers, men and women. It has 30 outstations and 2 village schools. The National Baptist Convention (U. S.) also opened a station here in 1900. The number of professing Christians found at Accra is about 650. The name is also written Akra.

ACCRA, or Ga language: This language belongs to the negro family of African languages, and is spoken by about 100,000 people living in the region of the Volta river, Gold Coast Colony, W. Africa. It is written with Roman letters.

ACRE (St. Jean d'Acre): A seaport on the coast of Palestine, which was celebrated during the Crusades. It is a strongly Mohammedan town, surrounded by a wall and used as a place of detention for political prisoners. One of the recognized heads of the **Babis** resides here in banishment, and hence directs and encourages his followers in Persia and elsewhere. Acre is a station of the CMS, with 7 missionaries and 20 native workers, men and women; there is also a hospital with two dispensaries in the outstations, and there are 8 schools. Taking the town and its outstations together, the number of communicants is about 100, mostly from branches of the Oriental Church.

ADABAZAR: A town of Asiatic Turkey, about 60 miles E. of Nicomedia; a station of the ABCFM. Mission work resulted early in the establishment of a strong church, which supports its own pastor and schools and has become a center of great influence among the villages of that section. The church has taken upon itself responsibility for a girls' boarding school, the Board furnishing three unmarried women missionaries as its teachers.

ADALIA: A seaport on the southern coast of Asia Minor, the ancient Attaleia. The population is about 13,000 Mohammedans, with quite a number of Greeks. It is not occupied as a mission station, but is visited by colporteurs of the BFBS.

ADAMS. See AMANZIMTOTE.

ADAMSHOOP: Town in the Orange River Colony, S. Africa, founded by the son of a slave. Station of the Berlin Mission Society since 1867. One missionary and 20 native workers form the force at this station and 4 outstations and 500 church members.

ADANA: A city of 45,000 inhabitants, the seat of government of the province of the same name. S. of the Taurus Mountains in Asiatic Turkey. The people of the city are mostly Mohammedans, but there are a considerable number of Armenians, some Nusairiyeh and a small Greek community. The people of Adana are noted for energy and force of character. It is a station of the ABCFM, with a working force of 5 missionaries and 32 native workers, men and women. It has an excellent girls' boarding school, an orphanage, a fine church building with 650 church members.

Adana is also an outstation of the RP for work conducted in Arabic.

The ABS has a Bible depot and subagency there.

ADDA, or **Ada:** A town on the Gold Coast, W. Africa; station of the Basel Missionary Society, with several outstations and 6 village schools and a kindergarten. The number of professing Christians is about 250.

ADDYMAN, John: Born in Leeds, county of Yorkshire, England, on October 22, 1808. Converted at sixteen, he at once threw himself earnestly into evangelistic work, first in Leeds and then in London. He was at this time connected with the Wesleyan Methodists, but his views on the subject of church government having undergone some change, he left the Wesleyan community and united himself with the Methodist New Connexion. He was called into the ministry of that body in 1833. Just at this time the subject of commencing a mission in Canada was seriously occupying the members of the New Connexion and Mr. Addyman was chosen to be the pioneer of the movement in the Far West. His labors in Canada were very trying, involving great privations and dangers, and often attended by romantic experiences. During what is known as the Canadian Rebellion he was in great peril, his life being threatened; being suspected as a spy, he was arrested and kept for some time in prison. At length, through his arduous toils and trials, his health failed, and in 1845 he returned to his native land, having been the main instrument in establishing 177 churches, which contained more than 4,000 members, but which have since expanded into large and flourishing centers, and now form part of the Methodist Church of Canada. He died June 7, 1887.

ADELAIDE: A village of 1,200 inhabitants, on the left bank of the Koonap River, in Cape Colony, S. Africa. Religion, the denominations common in Britain and America; the native fetishism also exists. It is a mission station of the UFS, established in 1861, and has a working force of a missionary and his wife with a native worker. There are 185 church members.

ADEN: A fortified seaport at the southwestern corner of Arabia, belonging to Great Britain, having been bought from the Turks in 1839 by the British East India Company. The climate is hot and very trying to Europeans. The population is almost exclusively Mohammedan, but of several races and tribes who go to Aden for commerce from the interior of Arabia and from Africa. The UFS has a mission station at Shaikh Othman in the district of Aden. Three missionaries and 2 native workers, men and women, compose the force which carries on a high school, a hospital, and a dispensary.

ADMIRALTY ISLANDS: A group of islands lying N. E. of New Guinea, belonging to Germany and forming a part of Bismarck Archipelago.

ADOWA: Capital of Tigré, **Abyssinia**; a town of about 3,000 inhabitants. It has not now any missionary enterprises.

ADRIANOPLE: Capital of the Turkish province of the same name (Turkish Edirneh), on the Maritza (ancient Hebrus), in Thrace, 130 miles northwest of Constantinople. Population, 85,000 Mohammedans, Greeks, Armenians, Jews, with a few Roman Catholics and a small group of Protestants. The scenery of the city is beautiful, the gardens of the wealthy citizens delightful, and the appearance of the 40 mosques most picturesque. The trade, centered in a capacious bazaar, is considerable, and the city possesses strategic importance. Founded by Emperor Hadrian in 125. Mission station of British Society for Propagating the Gospel among the Jews; 1 Jewish missionary; also an outstation of Constantinople (ABCFM); it has a native Evangelical church, and a Bible depot of the ABS.

AFGHANISTAN: A country of Central Asia, N. E. of India, which it separates from Russia and Persia. It is a mountainous country, with lofty tables and deep ravines, few rivers, and a climate that presents a great variety, changing from intense cold to tropical heat. The population is estimated at about 5,000,000 Mohammedans of the Sunnite sect, divided into two classes, Durranes and Ghilzais. They are a fierce, turbulent people, constantly at feud and difficult to govern. No mission work can be attempted at present in Afghanistan, but the British and Foreign Bible Society have published the New Testament, Psalms, and historical books of the Old Testament in Pashtu, or Afghani.

AFRICA: The continent of Africa is equal in area to Europe and North America combined, comprising nearly 12,000,000 square miles. Its greatest length is 5,000 miles, and its greatest breadth, 4,600. Both tropics cross it, and the equator intersects it a little below the center. By far the largest portion of its territory is therefore intertropical. In its physical configuration Africa has been happily compared to an inverted saucer. It is rimmed on a great part of its seaboard by a narrow strip of low land; at a distance of from 50 to 200 miles from the coast the land rises rapidly to an average height of from 2,000 to 3,000 feet, and in some parts to lofty mountain ranges; then the whole interior is a vast table-land, sinking slightly in the middle. In this hollow lie the great lakes whence flow the mighty rivers that drain the whole country.

These rivers are the dominating features of African geography. The problems that have chiefly concerned the explorer have been to ascertain and locate the sources and the courses of the four great streams, the Nile, the Niger, the Congo, and the Zambesi; and the triumphs of modern African exploration are almost all connected with these four names. The Nile is by far the longest of the four, having a course extending over 37° of latitude; but the Congo exceeds it in volume and in the dimensions of its basin. Of the four great lakes of what is usually called Central Africa, Victoria Nyanza and Albert Nyanza belong to the Nile system; Tanganyika belongs to that of the Congo, and Nyasa to that of the Zambesi, one of whose tributaries, the Shiré, flows out of it.

I. *Geographical and Political Divisions:* The following table shows the divisions of Africa as constituted at the present time (1903). The process of delimitation is still going on in northern central Africa, but by consulting the latest maps in connection with this table it will be seen that the process of partition is practically completed. For areas, populations, missionary and other facts the different divisions should be studied under their respective heads. The abbreviations in parentheses after the names in the table indicate the government under whose influence or into whose possession the territory named has fallen, viz.: B—Great Britain; F—France; G—Germany; I—Italy; Ind—Independent State; P—Portugal; S—Spain; T—Turkey.

Abyssinia (Ind).
Algeria (F).
Angola (P).
Basutoland (B).
Bechuanaland Protectorate (B).
British East Africa (B).
Cape Colony (B).
Central African Protectorate or Nyasaland (B).
Congo Free State (Ind).
Dahomey (F).
Egypt (T & B).
Egyptian Sudan (T & B).
Eritrea (I).
French Congo (F).
French Guinea (F).
French Somaliland (F).
Gambia (B).
German East Africa (G).
German Southwest Africa (G).
Gold Coast Colony (B).
Italian Somaliland (I).
Ivory Coast (F).
Kamerun (G).
Lagos (B).
Liberia (Ind).
Natal (B).
Nigeria (B).
Orange River Colony (B).
Portuguese East Africa (P).
Portuguese Guinea (P).
Rhodesia (B).
Rio de Oro (S).
Rio Muni (S).
Senegal (F).
Senegambia and Niger (F).
Sierra Leone (B).
Somaliland Protectorate (B).
Togoland (G).
Transvaal Colony (B).
Tripoli (T).
Tunis (F).
Wadai (F).
Zanzibar (B).

The New International Encyclopedia gives the following approximate statistics of the division of the area and population of Africa among the various powers:

Country	Area Sq. miles.	Pop.
France	4,000,000	32,635,910
Great Britain	2,700,000	41,773,360
Germany	1,000,000	14,200,000
Portugal	800,000	8,197,790
Turkey	400,000	1,300,000
Italy	200,000	450,000
Spain	80,000	136,000

II. *Geographical Exploration:* The first of modern travelers was Bruce, who traveled through Nubia and Abyssinia in 1768-73, and traced the course of the Blue Nile. After that the Niger was for a half century the goal of successive explorers. Mungo Park reached its upper waters in 1796; Denham, Clapperton, and Laing followed; but it was not till 1830 that Lander, sailing down the stream, discovered its outlet in the Gulf of Guinea. In 1816 Tuckey attempted to explore the Congo, but fell a victim to the climate. Central Africa proper still remained untouched. In 1845 Sir Roderick Murchison, President of the Royal Geographical Society, said: "Our knowledge of Africa advances slowly, and is confined almost exclusively to the coast;" and in 1851 another president, Captain Smyth, said: "All beyond the coast of Central and Southern Africa is still a blank in our maps."

The wonderful discoveries of the last 60 years begin with the two missionaries of the Church Missionary Society, Ludwig Krapf and John Rebmann, who were the earliest explorers of Africa, from the eastern side (1844-46). Rebmann's discovery of Mount Kilima-Njaro, in 1848, was the first great step forward in what has been well called the Recovery of Central Africa. In the following year Livingstone made his first important journey, in the far south, and reached the small lake Ngami. In 1854 Baikie took the second Niger expedition (with which was **S. Crowther**) up the Benué branch more than 600 miles from the sea; and about the same time Barth was prosecuting his extensive journeys in the Sudan and around Lake Chad. Livingstone was then gaining his great reputation in the south, particularly by his journey across Africa from Loanda to the mouth of Zambesi, by which the course of that river was determined (1854-55). In 1857 Burton and Speke, stimulated by the researches of Krapf and Rebmann, which had for several years pointed to a great inland sea somewhere in the interior, made their great journey from the East Coast, and in the following year discovered Lake Tanganyika and the Victoria Nyanza.

In 1859 Livingstone discovered Nyasa, and, not knowing that the mystery of the inland sea, heard of by Rebmann, had been solved, wrote home: "This (Nyasa) must be what the Church Missionary Society has been thinking of for many years." (The Portuguese, however, knew of Nyasa; and Cazembe's capital, in the heart of the lake region, had been reached by Lacerda as far back as 1798, and by Monteiro in 1831.) In 1862 Speke, on his second journey with Grant, discovered Uganda, and the outflow of the Nile from the Victoria Nyanza, and sent home his famous message, "The Nile is settled." Meanwhile several Egyptian officers with Petherick had ascended the White Nile nearly to the Albert Nyanza, which, however, was first seen by Baker in 1864. In 1866 Livingstone, abandoning his southern fields, began his later travels in the lake regions, around Tanganyika, and on what are now known to be the headquarters of the Congo. The search for him, when his long absence caused anxiety, led to Stanley's first journey (1871), and to that of Cameron. The latter was the first to cross Africa from east to west (1874-75); but his too southern route missed the course of the Congo, which was determined by Stanley on his second journey in 1876-77. This was the journey in the course of which Stanley explored the Victoria Nyanza and visited Uganda. Meanwhile, the remarkable explorations in the Sudan of Schweinfurth, (1869-71) and Nachtigal (1869-74), particularly those of the former in the territories west of the Upper White Nile, revealed to the world countries and peoples utterly unknown before, notably the Monbuttu and Nyam-Nyam districts and races.

The Congo particularly, within eight years of the discovery of its course, became a comparatively familiar stream. The vast territories drained by it have, by European treaty, been formed (so far as commerce is concerned) into a **Congo Free State.**

Among the events and ongoings that in more recent years have contributed to the enlargement of our knowledge of Africa, may be mentioned the protectorate practically assumed over Egypt by Great Britain since 1883, the long continued troubles in the Sudan, and especially events that culminated in the overthrow of the Orange Free State and the South African Republic, and reduced them to British colonies. To these happenings should be added the activity manifested by Great Britain in pushing its African railway enterprises, aided by some other powers, a process that promises to bring into railway connection with the whole world the entire east coast and the eastern portion of the continent.

The more recent explorations have been undertaken less to discover new regions than to increase our knowledge of regions already reached. The best known of the expeditions since 1885 was that of Stanley, undertaken to discover the fate or whereabouts of Emin Pasha (Snitzer). This went up the Congo, traversed the vast forests of equatorial Africa, and crossed into Zanzibar. In 1899 an expedition led by E. S. Grogran and Arthur Sharp crossed the continent from north to south, investigating the feasibility of a "Cape to Cairo" railroad, and making many valuable discoveries. Donaldson Smith explored Somaliland with good results, Foureau crossed the Sahara to the Congo, and Marchand made his memorable "mission" to Fashoda within the period named. The future exploration of the continent will certainly be conducted from motives chiefly commercial and in a scientific manner, assuring to the next generation a knowledge of this vast continent as accurate and full as that which we now have of the better known regions of the earth.

III. *Races and Languages of Africa:* The missionary problem of this vast "dark continent" is intimately related to the character of the races and languages found within its boundaries. The population of Africa is estimated by the more recent authorities at 175,000,000, or about one-eighth of the entire population of the earth. Deniker, in his "Races of Men" (London, 1900), gives a complete classification of the African races from which we derive the following abstract:

1. *Arabo-Berber, or Semito-Hamites:* This stock is found in N. Africa to as far as 15° S. lat. It includes about three-fourths of the so-called Arabs of N. Africa, who in fact are Berbers speaking Arabic. There are four sub-races (1) Djerbas, the Berbers of the Tunisian coast (2) the Elles type, of Central Tunis, (3) the present Berber type of Algeria-Tunisia, and (4) the Jerid or Oasis type. The Fellahin of the Nile valley below the first cataract belong to this stock. The ancient Egyptian language preserved as the Coptic dialect is spoken by about 500,000 to 750,000 Berbers, and the Arabo-Berber tribes of the Nile valley between the first and fourth cataract number about 190,000.

2. *Ethiopians, or Kushito-Hamites, or Nubians:* This stock inhabits N. E. Africa from the 25th deg. to the 4th deg. S. lat. They occupy the coast of the Red Sea, and of the Indian Ocean from the Gulf of Aden to Madisha. The principal divisions of this stock are (1) Nubians, speaking the Amharinga and Tigrenga dialects, (2) the Gallas, or Oroma, who are nearly pure Ethiopians, (3) the Somalis, who are Gallas mixed with an Arab stock, and (4) the Afari, or Danakil.

3. *Fulah-Zandeh Group:* This comprises a whole series of populations of mixed Ethiopians and Nigritians, extending in a belt five or six degrees wide across the continent, including with many other tribes, the Masai, of the eastern section, the Nyam-Nyam, or Zandeh, and on the more westerly side, the Fulah-Zandeh.

4. *Nigritians:* These comprise all the negro populations that do not speak the Bantu dialects, and which are conveniently divided into four sections, viz: those of the Eastern, Central and Western Sudan, and the coast of Guinea, embracing many tribes and subdialects.

5. *Negrilloes:* These are a stock of pigmies, extending in a belt reaching in general three degrees on either side of the equator entirely across Africa.

6. *Bantu Group:* This group embraces numerous peoples of Central and S. Africa, whose dialects form the **Bantu** linguistic family, distinct from the Nigritian. They are conveniently divided into Western, Eastern and Southern sections, embracing many tribes and families. To the southern section of this group belong the well-known Zulu tribes.

7. *Bushmen-Hottentots:* A people reduced by the more warlike Bantu tribes to a few thousand families, many of them nomads and forest hunters.

The ethnological divisions have not been easy

to fix, but the best authorities are fairly agreed in arranging them by language, and the linguistic grouping has made such progress of late years that the above may be taken to be a fairly consistent outline grouping of the races of the continent.

IV. Religions of Africa: The missionary to Africa has the task of making himself acquainted with a greater variety of religious customs and superstitions than can be found in any other quarter of the world. These religions are characterized in general by a belief in some sort of surpeme being, in many quarters by the worship of ancestors, somewhat as in China, by **Fetishism** with its priests, sorcerers and groveling rites, and by superstitious fears, incantations, charms and barbaric ceremonials. Idolatry, in the sense of the making and worshiping of images, is not so widely diffused as might be supposed. There is nothing in Africa like the elaborate image-worship of India. Hideous idols are common among the West African Negroes; but in Central Africa, so far as is known, none are to be found. But what is called fetish worship is universal. A fetish is a charm; and almost any object—a tree, a stick, a stone, a shell, a plant, the limb of an animal, a vessel filled with some strange compound—in fact, anything whatever—may have power imparted to it by certain medicine-men—power to preserve the owner or bearer from danger, or power to injure his enemies. Particular fetishes fulfil particular purposes.

All these native religions may be comprised under the term pagan. Of the pagans on the entire globe, six-sevenths are in Africa, which is therefore emphatically the pagan continent. Of the imported religions of Africa the leading representative is Mohammedanism. Carried in the 7th century by fire and sword over North Africa, this faith has, in the last two centuries, advanced its borders considerably, and now prevails widely in both the Western and Eastern Sudan, in West Africa and along the east coast, and its missionaries are more or less actively spreading their faith among the populations of Central Africa.

The Christian populations of Africa comprise the Copts, descendants of the Monophysites of the 5th century, numbering about 750,000; the Abyssinians, whose ecclesiastical system depends upon that of the Coptic Church; Roman Catholics who have had missionaries in Africa continuously since the 16th century, and now aggregate about 2,450,000; and Protestants, numbering about 3,250,000, including the English and Dutch of South Africa.

Hindus, chiefly dwelling on the east coast of the continent, number about 250,000 in Africa; and according to varying estimates there are from 550,000 to 750,000 Jews, chiefly on the Mediterranean coast.

V. Missionary Work in Africa, General View: The first Protestants to undertake evangelizing work in Africa were the Moravians, who began in 1792. Since that time nearly every Protestant denomination has undertaken missionary work in some part of the "dark continent." For details of this work the reader should consult the articles upon the political and territorial divisions of the continent, and particularly the statistical tables found in the Appendix to this work.

Statistics naturally take no account of the great number of Christian men and women in Africa not directly related to missions, but who exercise evangelizing influences in innumerable ways. The established and self-supporting churches are naturally evangelizing agencies, and it is farther to be considered that very much work by Christians cannot be identified nor reduced to statistical form.

Obstacles and Difficulties encountered in Missionary Work in Africa: These are many, but not insurmountable. The first is the *climate* of many parts to which missionaries have undertaken to go. This is deadly to most Europeans or Americans who spend any time on the coast or in the lowlands.

The vast number of languages spoken by the 175,000,000 or more of the inhabitants of Africa is a very serious obstacle to missionary labor. Nowhere is a universal speech more of a desideratum.

Slavery and the appearance of the Arab slave-trader are still real terrors in many regions, and sadly interfere with the progress of the Gospel; but there is reason to hope that this great crime against humanity is permanently under restraint, so that its vitality will steadily fail.

The traffic in liquor is another obstacle to the missionary enterprise and the spread of the Gospel, particularly on the west coast of Africa. Steps have been taken to limit this evil.

Other difficulties and problems that confront the missionary in Africa can be only mentioned. The brutal animal nature of the natives in many regions makes the instilling of a pure religion seem nearly impossible. Polygamy and the degradation of women to the level of mere beasts are facts to be counted on. The influence of the sorcerer and wizard, based on the nearly universal belief in evil spirits, is encountered everywhere, and such men are the natural enemies of the missionary because they are the religious leaders of their tribes. The greed of commercial enterprise, resulting in age-long abuse of the natives, who have been wronged by the white man since the earliest times, also weighs in some parts of the continent to make entrance into the confidence of the African people more difficult.

Nevertheless, most Africans are hospitable to the foreigner, naturally docile under the influence of stronger minds, and especially curious and eager to learn new things. In this latter trait they are far more easily reached than are the Chinese with their fixed and retrogressive temperament. The Africans, moreover, are not naturally atheistic, and have many ideas and beliefs that prepare them to believe the Gospel. A history that shows individual Africans, like Bishop Crowther of Yorubaland, or national development, as in Uganda, promises like fruit from Christian teaching elsewhere.

Keane, *Africa* (Stanford's Compendium of Geography and Travel), London, 1895; White, *Development of Africa*, London, 1892; Brown, *Story of Africa and Its Explorers*, London, 1892–95; Keltie, *The Partition of Africa*, London, 1895; Johnston, *History of the Colonization of Africa by Alien Races*, Cambridge, 1899; Livingstone, *Missionary Travels and Researches in South Africa*, New York, 1858; *Last Journals of David Livingstone in Central Africa*, London, 1874; Cameron, *Across Africa*, New York, 1877; Stanley, *Through the Dark Continent*, New York, 1878; Drummond, *Tropical Africa*, New York, 1888; Stanley, *In Darkest Africa*, New York, 1890; Johnston, *Livingstone, and the Exploration of Central Africa*, London, 1891; Bryce, *Impressions of South Africa*, New York, 1897; Lloyd, *In Dwarf Land and Cannibal Country*, London, 1899.

AFRICA, German East. See GERMAN EAST AFRICA.

AFRICA, German Southwest. See GERMAN SOUTHWEST AFRICA.

AFRICAN METHODIST EPISCOPAL CHURCH; Parent Home and Foreign Missionary Society of the, (1847): The foreign mission work of the African Methodist Episcopal Church is found in Africa, South America, West Indies and Hawaii. The first foreign field of the church was Haiti (1824), where the society now reports 10 stations and 2,000 adherents. In British Guiana it reports 20 stations and 5,000 adherents. It reports 15 missionaries in the Windward Islands, and 3 missionaries in Cuba. Its missions in Africa include stations in Sierra Leone, Liberia, the Lagos Colony (on the West coast of the continent), in Cape Colony in South Africa, extending northward as far as Northern Rhodesia. In Africa it reports altogether 300 preachers and a membership of 11,000. The origin of the work of this organization in South Africa was the withdrawal, in 1894-95, of a number of native church members from the WMS churches in the Transvaal. The seceders formed a new body which adopted the name, "Ethiopian Church." The movement was in some measure a protest against a color line in the churches of Africa. In 1896 the Ethiopian church united with the African Methodist Episcopal Church of the United States, and the movement is spreading with some energy among native churches in Africa.

The Woman's Parent Mite Missionary Society (1872), and the Woman's Home and Foreign Missionary Society (1892), are auxiliaries, the last named having its chief support in the Southern States. The headquarters of the society are: 61 Bible House, New York City. Organ: *Voice of Missions*.

AFRICAN TRAINING INSTITUTE (Colwyn Bay, North Wales): This Institution was founded in 1889 by the Rev. W. Hughes for the purpose of giving a thorough English training to exceptionally gifted Africans. The plan was heartily approved by many of the African Christian clergy and others, and is supported by auxiliary committees established at several points in W. Africa. The Training Institute is located in a delightful part of Wales, at Colwyn Bay, and has already shown its usefulness. It has educated more than 200 Africans, who are now working at about 15 places in W. Africa, mainly in the Congo region, and who, by so much, become the direct channels of the influence of the Institute. The Institute teaches its pupils some of the arts which will find place for application in Africa and it has 8 auxiliary or preparatory schools in Africa, the most intelligent of whose graduates will be taken to complete their training in the mother institution. The number of students now in training is about 75.

AGARPARA: A village near Calcutta, India; station of the CMS, with one unmarried woman missionary in charge of a house for female orphans.

AGBOGBA, or ABOKOBI: A town N. of Accra in the Gold Coast Colony, W. Africa; station of the Basel Missionary Society, with 21 outstations and 15 village schools. The number of professing Christians is about 500.

AGNEW, Miss Eliza: Sailed from Boston to Ceylon, under the ABCFM, in 1839, and for forty-three years she labored as a missionary of the Cross, never returning to native land. She was the first unmarried woman sent as a missionary to Ceylon, and for forty years she was the efficient principal of the girls' school at Oodooville. In June, 1883, Miss Agnew received a paralytic shock, and during the same month she passed into her heavenly rest.

AGRA: A city of about 170,000 inhabitants, capital of the district of the same name in the United Provinces, British India. It has several magnificent architectural relics of the Mogul Empire, and is venerated by the Hindus as the scene of the incarnation of Vishnu. It is an important center of Mohammedanism. The climate is good except from April to September.

It is a station of the BMS, opened in 1811, and now carried on by 5 missionaries, men and women, and 24 native workers. There are 2 outstations and 9 village schools, an orphanage, and 70 church members.

It is also a station of the CMS, commenced in 1853, and now having a working force of 21 missionaries and 38 native workers, men and women, who carry on 7 village schools, 5 high schools and a fine college. There are 205 communicants connected with this mission.

The BZM commenced a station here in 1871 and has 5 missionaries and 11 native workers, all women, with 5 village schools and more than 400 women pupils in the zenanas.

The Edinburgh Medical Mission Society has a training class here.

The ME has a station here with a missionary and his wife and 32 native workers, 20 village schools, and 550 church members.

AGU: Town in the German colony of Togoland, W. Africa; station of the N. German Missionary Society, opened in 1900.

AGUADILLA: Town on the W. shore of Porto Rico; a flourishing station of the Presbyterian Home Missionary Society, with about 150 adherents.

AGUASCALIENTES: Capital of the smallest State in the Mexican Republic, 270 miles northwest of Mexico City. It takes its name from the hot springs which abound in the vicinity. It is surrounded by rich gardens abounding in olives, figs, vines, pears, etc. Climate, temperate; population, 32,000 Mexicans; language, Spanish; religion, Roman Catholic. Mission station of Cumberland Presbyterian Church (1888); 1 missionary and wife, 2 unmarried women, 7 native workers, men and women, a printing house, 2 industrial schools, 1 outstation, 3 common schools, and 105 church members.

AHMADABAD: The capital of the district of the same name, Bombay, British India. It was formerly one of the most magnificent cities of India, and its superb architectural monuments still testify to the fact. It is an important center of the Parsees. It is a mission station of the PCI, established in 1861; with 6 missionaries and 30 native workers, men and women, a theological seminary, 2 orphanages, a high school, and 11 common schools. There are 100 members in the church.

It is also occupied as a mission station by the ME, with 1 missionary and his wife and 5 native workers, and by the Christian and Missionary Alliance, and the Salvation Army, statistics in regard to which are lacking.

AHMADNAGAR: A city in the presidency of Bombay, British India, standing on the Deccan plateau and on a line of rail joining Dhond on the Bombay and Madras line, with Manmad on the Bombay and Calcutta line. It has 35,000 inhabitants, of whom 3,572 are Christians, for the most part connected with the mission of the ABCFM. This mission was commenced in 1831. Up to 1855 the whole number of converts amounted only to 78. But then a movement arose which spread to about 100 villages, and brought over 600 communicants into the church. A convert, Krishnarao, introduced, in 1862, the *Kirttan* at the meetings—songs on the life of Christ, sung with instrumental accompaniment. The present force of the mission consists of 17 missionaries, men and women, of whom 2 are physicians and 3 industrial instructors. It maintains 1 theological seminary, 1 training school for women workers, 2 high schools, 1 industrial school of great efficiency, 1 industrial school for women, 1 hospital, 1 dispensary. Connected with the mission are 2 churches in the city which pay the expenses of their own Christian work and contain 634 members. In the district superintended from the city are 17 other churches with 1,280 members and 18 common schools.

The SPG entered Ahmadnagar in 1870, and has its headquarters outside of the city with a somewhat extensive work in the district to the north.

The Christian Literature Society for India has a publishing house in the city and conducts a normal training-school.

The Industrial Missions Aid Society has a rug factory in the city which gives employment to boys trained in the industrial schools of the Mission.

It is a notable fact that while the population of the district decreased by 52,000 in 10 years, 1891-1901, the Christians of the district increased in the same time from 6,734 to 20,864.

AHOUSAHT: Village on the W. coast of Vancouver Id.; station of the Presbyterian Church in Canada, with 1 missionary and his wife, 1 missionary woman, 1 Sunday-school and 1 village school.

AIDIN: A city 57 miles southeast of Smyrna, Turkey. Population, 35,000, chiefly Mohammedans, but with a few Greeks and Armenians. It is picturesquely situated on the Mæander River, and built out of the ruins of the ancient city of Tralles, once occupying this site. Outstation of the ABCFM worked by the missionaries at Smyrna.

AILSA CRAIG: Village in West Shirè, Nyasaland, Africa; station of the Zambesi Industrial Mission, with an industrial school and 2 village schools.

AIM OF CHRISTIAN MISSIONS: The aim of foreign missions is not to be confused with the aim of the Christian Church in the world, or of the Christian nations of the world. There are many good and Christian things which it is not the duty of the foreign missionary enterprise to do. And we must not confuse the aim of foreign missions with the results—an easy confusion—because there is no other force so powerful to accomplish results accessory and indirect. It is misleading also to confuse the ultimate issues with the immediate aims; it is not only misleading, it is fatal. Some things can only be secured by those who do not seek them. Missions are powerful to transform the face of society, because they ignore the face of society, and deal with it at its heart. They yield such powerful political and social results, because they do not immediately concern themselves with them. Again, we must not confuse the aim of missions with the methods of missions. It is an easy thing to select a method with the view to the accomplishment of some given end, and then because the end is difficult of accomplishment, because the method is easy of operation, because its results, apart altogether from the main aim, are good and useful in themselves, it is easy to exalt the method into the place of the end.

Having cleared the ground so far, what is the aim of foreign missions? It is a religious aim. It cannot be stated too strongly in an age when the thought of men is full of *things*, and when the body has crept up on the throne of the soul, that the work is not immediately and primarily a philanthropic work, a political work, a secular work of any sort whatsoever. It is a spiritual and a religious work. Of course religion must express itself in life, but the missionary does not go into the world primarily as trustee of a better social life. He goes as the trustee of His life Who said of Himself, "Except ye eat the flesh of the Son of man, and drink His blood, ye have no life in you." "I came that they may have life, and may have it more abundantly." "The bread which I will give is my flesh, which I will give for the life of the world." President Seeley's lectures on Christian Missions have the great merit of laying chief emphasis on this predominance of the religious and spiritual character of the aim of missions.

The aim of missions, then, to borrow Dr. George Washburn's phrase, is to make Jesus Christ known to the world. Other phraseology may be used. We can say the aim of missions is the evangelization of the world. Or, we can say the aim of missions is to preach the Gospel to the world. And if we understand these terms in their Scriptural sense, they are synonymous with the phrase just quoted. But many persist in using them at less than their Scriptural value. It makes clear what the aim of missions is, to say: The aim of foreign missions is to make Jesus Christ known to the world.

And almost any method, almost any agency, may be recognized as legitimate which subjects itself with fidelity to this supreme aim. As Alexander Duff said in 1854, in the first Missionary Conference in New York City, "The chief means of divine appointment for the evangelization of the world are the faithful teaching and preaching of the pure Gospel of salvation, by duly qualified ministers and other holy and consistent disciples of the Lord Jesus Christ, accompanied with prayer, and savingly applied by the grace of the Holy Spirit; such means, in the providential application of them by human agency, embracing not merely instruction by the living voice, but the translation and judicious circulation of the whole written Word of God, the preparation and circulation of evangelical tracts and books, as well as any other instrumentalities fitted to bring the Word of God home to men's souls, together with any processes which experience may have sanctioned as the most efficient in raising up everywhere indigenous ministers and teachers of the living Gospel." This is fair and broad. It sets out openly a range of mission effort that will throttle and restrict no useful missionary enterprise, and it exalts to a predominant and singular place the supreme aim of making Jesus Christ known to His world. Philanthropy and education will have a large part among the methods of missionary work, but they are its methods and not its end. By these and all other agencies the enterprise seeks to plant in humanity the principle of the divine life itself, to live and bear fruit in a thousand fold more social amelioration and intellectual improvement than the missionary movement as such could accomplish.

This description of the missionary aim does not lift from our shoulders the burden of responsibility that we cannot escape, and it does not lay there a burden of responsibility that we cannot bear. We dare not say that we have done our duty when we have spoken Christ's name to the world; nor that we have made Jesus Christ known to the world when we have given the world such a proclamation of Christ as would suffice for us who already know Him to take in the full meaning of the message. Neither, on the other hand, are we left to struggle hopelessly under the burden of the world's spiritual conversion or moral regeneration. We cannot convert one single soul; how shall we convert the world? Midway between the position of no responsibility, and of all responsibility, the Church stands, sharing something with God, sharing also something with the world. We cannot sever ourselves from that link of loving sympathy which binds us to its death; we cannot sever ourselves from that link of sympathy which binds us to His life. We are meant to be between His life and its death, channels of the grace and salvation of God.

The aim of missions is to make Jesus Christ known to the world with a view to the salvation of men for that eternity which embraces alike the time that is to come and the time that now is. We cannot narrow salvation to but one world, this one or the next. And further we must not state the aim of missions in purely individualistic terms. Our duty lies certainly to our generation, but it does not stop there. We are bound to preach to every person in the world the Gospel of the only Savior; we are bound also to make known to the world that there is a body of Christ which is His Church, and to gather up all responsive men into visible churches, which shall be outward evidence of the body of Christ, and shall secure to the Gospel an influence and perpetuity which institutions and not individuals must supply. Henry Venn, Dr. Warneck and Rufus Anderson have given proper emphasis to this element in missionary policy and duty. We are to establish and foster native churches, self-extending, self-maintaining, self-directing, which shall carry out to their own people, whom we may not reach, the message that has come to them, and which shall carry down into the generations to come after them, the blessings which we have given them as their own. This is the aim of foreign missions, to make Jesus Christ known to the world, with a view to the full salvation of men, and their gathering into true and living churches to which the missionary enterprise may commit the larger and enduring Christian duty as it passes on to "regions beyond."

This is the supreme aim. It is a just thing to challenge the world to sympathy with missions, because of the philanthropic and social results that missions achieve, and the heroic spirit which they display. But their supreme aim is neither to establish republics or limited monarchies throughout the world, nor to lead Chinese or Hindu people to wear our dress, nor to remodel their social institutions, where these are already wholesome and clean. The supreme aim is to make Jesus Christ known. Any true view of the world must make room for other forces than missions. God is King, and so surely as His hand is upon the work of missions, it is upon all the great forces that are making the world. We cannot acknowledge that the force of political influence has escaped from His control, that He stands impotent before the commerce and civilization of the world. His hand is upon these things. They play at last into His almighty purposes. They are but part of His influence. They and all the forces of life run resistlessly on to the great goals of God. But these forces are only supplementary to the power that the missionary holds in his hands from His pierced hand Who died and rose again, and Who is King of them that reign as kings, and Lord of them that rule as lords.

This aim of missions should have determining authority. We sometimes allow ourselves to drift into methods of work that presuppose a quite contrary aim. When we lift off the shoulders of a new native church, for example, the burdens that it must bear if it is ever to grow, the act seems like kindness, while it is fatal to the Church and neglectful of the supreme missionary aim. It is easy to slip into indirect conceptions of duty, or to do what God can do through other agencies. Missions are to do their own work, and not the work of other agencies or other forces. Methods of work, in their proportion and in their perpetuation, should be ruled by the supreme and determining aim of the missionary movement.

And not alone the method of missions, but the spirit of the enterprise should be ruled by that aim. It proposes no promiscuous and indefinite project. It has its own clean-cut piece of work to do. To be sure it is often confused enough in the actual work among men, but the circumstances which confuse it show also how important its clear perception and prosecution are. If this is the aim of missions, the enterprise is not a miscellaneous and undefined task. It is a clear and practicable project, well justifying the words of Simeon Calhoun, the "Saint of the Lebanon:"

"It is my deep conviction, and I say it again and again, that if the Church of Christ were what she ought to be, twenty years would not pass away till the story of the cross would be uttered in the ears of every living man."

AIMARA LANGUAGE: In Bolivia nearly 400,000 people speak this language. It belongs to the South American family, but has been modified by the Spanish. It is written with Roman letters.

AINU LANGUAGE: Classed among the aboriginal languages of the Extreme Orient family, the Ainu has no literature and has been written for missionary purposes and in Roman letters only. It is spoken by about 150,000 people found in Japan.

AINUS: Tribes inhabiting Saghalien, Yezo, the Kurile islands and various adjacent regions, partly under Japanese and partly under Russian jurisdiction. As in the case of many aboriginal races the name of this race means simply *men*. Tradition says that the Japanese were originally Ainus, and only became a distinct race by intermarrying with the Chinese. The Ainus are different from other Mongolian tribes, and in their more vigorous physical formation resemble the Caucasian type. Tho armed and painted like savages, they are inoffensive and hospitable, but rather shy. They are pagans, and practise polygamy. Groups of 10 or 12 families live together in miserable huts, with a chief for each group. They support themselves by hunting and fishing. Those of them who have been converted to Christianity have shown sturdiness and enthusiasm.

AINTAB: A city of Asiatic Turkey, about 35 miles west of the Euphrates, in the province of Aleppo. It has 30,000 inhabitants, chiefly Mohammedans and Armenians. One of the most flourishing stations of the ABCFM, with a large female seminary and a college founded in 1874. There are 4 large churches, 2 of them having stone buildings, with accommodation for over 1,000 each. The Protestant community is one of the most influential in Turkey. The effort in 1863, to establish an Episcopal cathedral failed. The common schools are on the graded system, are supported entirely by the people, and are of very marked efficiency. The Central Turkey College at Aintab altho independent, is closely connected with the mission. The hospital and dispensary has been most efficient. The work of the station is carried on by 12 missionaries and 132 native workers, men and women. It has 27 outstations, 61 primary schools, 7 high schools and an orphanage. The number of church members in the field is about 3,500.

AIN-ZAHALTA: A village in the Lebanon district of Syria; station of the British Syrian Schools Society, with a dispensary, 6 outstations and 6 village schools.

AITUTAKI ID. See HERVEY ISLANDS.

AIYANSH: A station of the CMS in the diocese of Caledonia, British Columbia, founded in 1883. It is carried on by a missionary and his wife and 5 native workers, men and women. An industrial school and a publishing establishment are carried on, and the number of communicant Christians is 78.

AJERMANDIDI: A mission station of the Netherlands Missionary Society in the Minahassa Peninsula of **Celebes.**

AJMERE: A territory in Rajputana, India, governed by a Chief Commissioner, appointed by the Governor General of India. Its area, including the district of Merwara, which forms its southern portion, is only 2,711 square miles, and its population (1901), 476,912.

Hinduism is the prevailing religion. Mohammedans are also found and a small number of Christians. The language is Hindustani.

The province adjoins the Rajputana desert, has a limited rainfall and is subject to destructive famines.

Missionary work is carried on in Ajmere by the CMS, the UFS and the ME. The whole number of places occupied as stations by these societies is four.

AJMERE: Capital of the commissionership of Ajmere in British India. Its population numbers (1901) 73,839. The prevailing religions are Hinduism, Jainism and Mohammedanism. It has a very fine and old Mosque built on the site of a Jain temple. It is a mission station of the UFS (opened in 1862). The ME and the SPG also have native workers here. The UFS has a publishing establishment, a dispensary and a hospital in this place. The aggregate working force is 8 missionaries and 140 native workers of both sexes. The total number of communicant Christians is about 700.

AJNALA: A town in the district of Amritsar, Punjab, India; station of the CMS, with 21 native workers, and of the CEZMS, with 4 women missionaries, and 8 native women workers, 4 village schools, 1 high school and 1 hospital. There are 33 communicants.

AKABE: A town on the Benue river, Nigeria, W. Africa; station of the CMS, opened in 1897. The people are in the main fetish worshipers, with a few Mohammedans among them.

AKIDU: A village on Lake Kolar, Madras, British India. A flourishing station of the BOQ, established in 1880, and operated by 3 missionaries and 42 native workers, men and women. It has 9 outstations, a dispensary, a high school and 22 common schools, with 1,700 communicants in the field under its supervision.

AKITA: A city in the island of Hondo, Japan, with 30,000 inhabitants. A station of the FCMS, with 3 missionaries and 4 native workers, men and women. It has a dispensary, a nurses' training class, 9 outstations and 220 church members. It is also an outstation of the ME in charge of 2 native workers.

AKKAWAY, or **Acawaio:** This is a language of the South American family spoken by a limited number of the people of Guiana. For missionary purposes, it has been written with Roman characters.

AKROPONG: A town in the Gold Coast Colony. W. Africa, in the domain of the Ashanti language.

The religion of the people is Fetishism. The Basel Missionary Society opened a station here in 1835, which has been very successful. Ten missionaries and 38 native workers, men and women, form the corps of instructors for the people of the town and of 14 outstations. The total number of communicant Christians is 2,100.

AKWAPIM: A dialect of the Otshi language spoken in parts of the Ashanti country in W. Africa.

ALABA IS.: The northernmost group (commonly known as the Torres Is.), of the New Hebrides Islands. The Melanesian Mission has kept teachers in the Torres Islands since 1878.

ALASKA: The northwestern corner of North America, formerly known as Russian America, and purchased by the United States in 1867 for $7,200,000. It embraces all of the N. American continent W. of the 141st meridian of W. longitude, together with a narrow strip of land between the Pacific ocean and the British dominions, and also all islands near its coast, as well as the Aleutian archipelago. Including islands, its area is 590,883 miles; an area about equal to that of the Northern States east of the Mississippi, with the addition of the Virginias, Kentucky and Tennessee. The exact eastward bounds of the southern coast strip of Alaska are still unsettled. The population (1900) is 63,592, of whom 25,000 are Indians and Eskimos. The white population is rapidly increasing in consequence of the discovery of several very rich deposits of gold in the western and central part of the country. The native tribes of Alaska are pagans, mostly worshipers of departed spirits, cruel in their rites, and superstitiously subservient to their medicine men or religious leaders. The climate of Alaska in its southern coast regions and in its islands is much less severe than in the same latitude on the eastern coast of the continent. On the central plateau, 600 miles long from east to west and 400 miles wide from north to south, the summers are quite hot, altho the winters are very cold. Because of the hot summers the cereals and many vegetables of the temperate zone can be grown, and Alaska may yet prove to be an agricultural region with a large population. Access to the interior of the country is facilitated during the summer by the Yukon River, which is one of the great rivers of the continent, being navigable for 1,500 miles.

The Russian (Greek orthodox) Church had opened missions among the Aleutian islanders and at one or two points on the mainland before the cession of Alaska to the United States, and had made some converts. Since the country became a dependency of the United States, various Protestant denominations and the Roman Catholic Church have established mission stations in various places. The Protestant missions in Alaska have about 20 stations, occupied by 118 missionaries and 13 native workers, men and women, with places of worship, schools and hospitals. These missions are maintained by the Presbyterian Home Missionary Society, the Protestant Episcopal Domestic and Foreign Missionary Board, the Moravian Church, the Friends', the Methodist Episcopal, the Baptist, the Congregational, and the Lutheran Churches (Swedish and also Norwegian), the American Missionary Association and some smaller societies. Some of the mission stations occupied are within the Arctic circle, where daylight in winter is a sunless sort of twilight of but three hours duration. One station (Point Barrow), on the northernmost point of the territory, is reached by reindeer post. A considerable number of Indians and Eskimos have been drawn under the influence of these missions. In the southern part of the country, men engaged in the liquor traffic seduce and destroy a certain number of the simple-minded natives. But in all the stations education, especially industrial education, has been made an ally of religion in lifting the ideals and enriching the lives of the people. The total of Protestant Christian natives is (1900) 7,600 souls.

Alaska: Government Printing Office, Washington, 1900; *Missionary Review of the World*, Vol. XI, p. 513; Vol. XII, p. 500; Vol. XIV, pp. 481, 499; Jackson (S.), *Alaska and Missions on the North Pacific Coast*, New York, 1880; *Education in Alaska*, Washington, 1896; Knapp (F.), and Childe (R. L.), *Thlinkets of S. E. Alaska*, Chicago, 1897; Burroughs (J.), and others of Harriman Expedition, *Alaska*, 2 vols., 1901.

ALBANIA: The region called Albania includes the two provinces of Jannina and Skodra (Scutari) in European Turkey, stretching along the eastern shore of the Adriatic from 39° to 43° north latitude, and from 18° 24' to 21° 48' east longitude. Its extreme length is about 300 miles from Montenegro to the Gulf of Arta and the frontiers of Greece, while its breadth varies from 50 to 100 miles, from the Adriatic to an irregular line on the east, generally following lofty mountain ranges. It is a mountainous region throughout, being traversed by two or three elevated ranges which run parallel, in general, to the shore of the Adriatic Sea. It is also well watered, altho its rivers are not navigable. Its large lakes of Jannina, Castoria, Ochrida, and Scutari impart a peculiar interest to the country.

The earliest authentic notices of the country occur in connection with the Greek colonies of Epidamnus, or Dyrrachium (now Durazzo), the ancient port of transit from Brundusium (Brindisi) and Epidaurus, in Dalmatia, to which we may add the later colony of Jannina, which seems to have grown up almost unnoticed, not far from the ancient Oracle of Dodona, on the western shore of the lake of the same name.

The name Albania, first applied to this country in 1079, originated from Elbassan, the seat of the tribe of Albani in the center of the land. Anciently the region from Prevesa to the mouth of the Voyussa was called Epirus, and was considered more or less as a province of Greece, while all north of Voyussa was known as Illyricum. Hence we may conclude that the Apostle Paul himself preached the Gospel in Albania, when he tells us (Rom. 15: 19), that "from Jerusalem, and round about unto Illyricum, I have fully preached the Gospel of Christ." Albania is the least civilized of all the provinces of Turkey. Except at rare and short intervals, under honest and energetic Pashas, brigandage, with its cruel murders and atrocities, may be said to be an almost constant feature of the country; so much so, that the districts of Dibra, Jakova, Ipek have long been inaccessible to outsiders, while the Mirdites, southeast of Scutari, retain even now a barbarous semi-independence, to guard which all strangers are jealously excluded.

The soil is fertile, and in several districts is well cultivated; but much of it lies waste, partly from defective methods of agriculture, but also from the insecurity of life and property in consequence of the bands of robbers that so frequently infest the country and commit the most frightful excesses. It is difficult to form any reliable estimate of the population, but probably 2,000,000 may not be far from the truth.

There is no missionary station in Albania. The BFBS has colporteurs and book depots at various points, and the ABCFM has native workers who are Albanians teaching one or two schools in the borderland between Albania and Macedonia.

The Balkan Peninsula, Laveleye (E. A.), 2 vols., London, 1887.

ALBANIAN LANGUAGE: As the term "barbarian" was applied by the Greeks to all who spoke a different language from their own, we know that the Pelasgi in Greece itself, the Epirotes, and the Illyrians, with many of the Macedonians, spoke not Greek, but a different language, which there is every reason to believe is the same as the Albanian, now spoken by their descendants. The origin and character of the Albanian have been the subject of much discussion, some regarding it as belonging to the Indo-Germanic class, and others pronouncing it a Turanian language. In fact, like the Armenian, it partakes of the characteristics of both these classes; but from its undoubted analogy in its peculiar roots to the Greek, Latin, Sanskrit, Celtic, etc., it is classed by many scholars not as a derivative from any of these, but as a sister of equal antiquity. A great obstacle to the critical study of Albanian is the absence of any literature except of comparatively recent origin. No Albanian alphabet exists. The Gheg, or northern, dialect has been written with Roman letters, while the southern or Tosk dialect has been written with Greek letters. A modification of the Roman alphabet will probably prevail as the one mode of writing Albanian.

Not a little care is needed to distinguish the original terms and forms of the language from the many words adopted later from the Greek, Latin, Slavic, Turkish, and other languages. The subject has engaged much attention, and we may notice as preeminent in this department Dr. Hahn, who compiled an Albanian dictionary and grammar, with many characteristic specimens of the language, and Demetrio Camarda, who studied the language chiefly among the Albanian colonies of Calabria and Sicily, and has written largely on its structure and affinities. To promote these studies care is now taken to commit to writing such historical ballads as have been handed down to the present time, as well as other poems which have been preserved in various forms of writing. The publications also of the British and Foreign Bible Society and a few also by the Religious Tract Society, of London, have greatly aided these studies. Several grammars also have been published, among which we may mention that for the use of Greeks, by Mr. C. Christophorides, a native of Elbassan. It is worthy of note that the prelates of the Greek Church in Albania and the religious teachers of the Mohammedan body alike oppose with some violence every effort to transform the Albanian into a written language. The cause of this opposition seems to be the same in each case —political intolerance of independent growth in a subject people.

ALBANIANS: A people chiefly found in European Turkey, whose subordinate political existence, lack of literature, and tendency to wander abroad have arrested their national development and obscured their origin and racial affinities. Groups of Albanians are found in Sicily, in Calabria, in Greece, and in some islands of the Greek Archipelago. Traces of the Albanian language or of a tongue closely allied to it are also found in Southern Italy. These and other considerations have led some to conclude that the existence of isolated groups of Albanians points to their being the remnants of a people originally inhabiting Greece and Southern Italy, and retaining to this day their distinct language and racial peculiarities.

According to this view the Albanians are of one stock with the ancient Pelasgi. However this may be, they cling with an intense nationality to their language and their tribal organization and the wild diversities of physical surroundings which belong to Albania. Their strong clan feeling has prevented anything like cohesion to maintain a national unity. But their modern history offers instances of a temporary union of the clans to resist a common enemy. Such a general union took place in resisting the Bulgarian invasion of Albania in 517-550, and again under Prince George Castriotes in resisting the Turkish invasion in 1443-78. The military ability shown by Albanians in these episodes of their history and in such a case as that of Ali Pasha of Jannina, is a quality by which the Turks still profit. The flower of the Turkish army is composed of Albanians; and of the great Albanians who have risen to distinction in the service of the Sultan, it is only necessary to recall the name of Mehemmed Ali Pasha, the renovator of Egypt and founder of the present Khedival house, to see that Turkey does well to seek Albanians for positions requiring initiative and courage.

The Albanians are called "Arnaouts" by the Turks. They call themselves, however, "*Skipetar*,"—the Eagle People. They are divided into clans so sharply separated as to introduce dialects into the language. Their clan feeling the Turkish Government has used with skill to foment jealousies that shall prevent the Albanians from uniting to throw off a hated yoke.

Since the conquest of Albania by Turkey in 1478 the Albanians have been alternately harassed and tempted by appeals to their love for a military life, and about one-half of their number have become Mohammedans, still clinging to their own language, however, and not regarded as thoroughly orthodox in belief because still admitting the ties of race. Of the Albanians who have refused to accept Mohammedanism, those living in the southern part of Albania belong to the Greek Church, and those in the northern part, including the semi-independent Mirdites, are Roman Catholics. In each case the ineradicable love of the Albanians for their language has tended to keep the masses of the people in dense ignorance. The Roman Catholic Albanians are taught to read in Italian or in Servian. The Greek Church follows its usual policy, insisting that schools and churches among its Albanian adherents shall use the Greek language. As to the Mohammedan Albanians, their schools are conducted in Turkish, and their religious worship in Arabic. Whatever their religious connection, worship is an unintelligible pantomime, and education, an opportunity for culture in a foreign tongue from which a few may and do profit, but from which the masses derive little benefit because the women are wholly illiterate and the "bookless Albanian" is the sole language of the home-life.

Races of European Turkey, Clark (E. L.), New York, 1878; *Turkey in Europe*, by Odysseus, London, 1900; *Albania and the Albanians in* 1898, Callan (H.), Scottish Geog. Mag., Vol. 15, pp. 337-350, Edinburgh, 1899; *Roman Catholic Albania*, Nyon (R.), Blackwood's Magazine, Vol. 173 pp. 476-487, London, 1903.

ALBERNI: Town in Vancouver Id., British Columbia; station of the Canada Presbyterian Church, which has an industrial school there for the Indians.

ALBINA: A town on the Maroni river in Surinam; station of the Moravian Missions, opened in 1894 for East Indian coolies. It has 2 chapels and 2 village schools with about 40 professing Christians.

ALCHUKA-FU (A-she-ho): Town of some importance on the Transsiberian Railway, in Manchuria; station of the UFS. One of the resident missionaries is a physician. There are about 60 professing Christians there. (Also written Ashiho.)

ALEPPO: A city of Asiatic Turkey, on the borders of the Syro-Arabian Desert, and capital of the province of the same name. The city is encompassed by low, barren hills and irregular mounds, intersected by fertile valleys. It is a city of thoroughly Oriental type, with extensive bazaars, numerous mosques, and a people remarkable for their elegant bearing. The streets are unusually good for the East; and the stone houses are very well built. The city, being on the only safe route between Syria and Eastern Asia, is a center for the Damascus and Bagdad caravans. The inhabitants are noted for their shrewdness in trade. There has been a considerable European colony in Aleppo since the middle of the 16th century. It was the principal factory of the English Levant Company until Napoleon's Mediterranean enterprises broke up their trade. The city has about 120,000 inhabitants, chiefly Mohammedans. There is also a strong Roman Catholic element in the population besides Greeks, Armenians and Jews. The ABCFM has occupied Aleppo as a station at various times but has abandoned it on finding no extensive response to effort. The PCE opened a station there in 1895 for work among the Jews. It has 2 missionaries and 4 native workers, with a primary school and a dispensary.

ALERT BAY: A settlement of the Kwagutl tribe on the northern coast of Vancouver Island; station of the CMS, with 2 missionaries and their wives, 2 unmarried women and 2 native workers. There is a high school, an industrial school and a primary school. The communicants number 22.

ALEUTIAN: This language is spoken by the people of the Aleutian Islands, and belongs to the Arctic Coast branch of the North American family. It has been written with Russian letters.

ALEXANDER, Bishop Michael Solomon: Born in Prussian Poland, 1799. He was brought up in the strictest principles of Rabbinical Judaism. When he was 16 he was a teacher of the Talmud and the German language. At the age of 21 he went to England, having not the slightest acquaintance with Christianity, not even knowing the existence of the New Testament. He settled in a country town as tutor in a Jewish family. Whilst there the sight of a handbill of the London Society for the Conversion of the Jews aroused his curiosity, and he obtained and read the New Testament. Shortly afterwards he accepted the post of Rabbi at Norwich and subsequently at Plymouth. There in the providence of GOD, he became acquainted with the Rev. B. B. Golding, curate of Stonehouse, to whom he gave lessons in Hebrew, and through whom, after much inward conflict, he almost came to a conviction of the truth of Christianity. He used to steal silently down to Stonehouse Church on Sunday evenings, and, under the shadow of its walls, would stand riveted to the spot, while he listened to the songs of Christian praise, in which he dared not as yet take part. His congregation heard of his leanings towards Christianity, and he was suspended from his duties as Rabbi. Further trials awaited him, but the LORD strengthened his faith and on June 2, 1825, in St. Andrew's Church, Plymouth, he was baptized in the presence of 1,000 people. His wife's baptism followed six months later. In 1827 he was ordained deacon in Dublin, where he had settled in order to gain a livelihood as a teacher of Hebrew. Here, through his consistent Christian character, he made many friendships. Eventually he became a missionary of the Society, laboring first in Danzig and later in London, where he held the post of Professor of Hebrew and Rabbinical Literature in King's College, until 1841, when he was consecrated the first Anglican Bishop in Jerusalem. His work there was full of blessing, two prominent Jerusalem rabbis being baptized. It was a great blow to the Society's mission there when, in 1845, Bishop Alexander suddenly died, his last act being one of prayer, before he retired to sleep to awake in another world. One of his grandchildren is a CMS missionary in Japan.

ALEXANDER, T. T.: Born in Mt. Horeb, Tenn., October 8, 1850; sent by the Presbyterian Board (North) to Japan in 1877. Died at Honolulu, November 14, 1902. During his life in Japan he had been active in the opening of new stations, had taught theology in the Mejii Gakuin in Tokio, and just prior to his departure from Japan had been in charge of the evangelistic work in the city of Kioto, where also he was helping the Congregational missionaries in the Theological Department of the Doshisha.

Dr. Alexander was a man of great ability, one of the best Old Testament scholars in Japan; a man of rare openness of mind and beauty of character; a lover of peace; always forgetful of himself, modest and gentle in all his ways, yet a man of iron principle and of unswerving devotion to what he believed to be right. Few foreigners in the Empire were so highly valued as he by the Japanese, both for the purity and sweetness of his Christian character and for the value and solidity of his counsel and judgments in their perplexities. He did much at the time when the liberal movement was strong in Japan, to help many to find solid standing ground.

For the last seven or eight years of his life, Dr. Alexander was alone on the field, Mrs. Alexander and the children residing in Maryville, Tenn., for the education of the children. Happily, the eldest daughter, Miss Emma, under appointment as a missionary to Japan, had stopped in Honolulu for a brief visit with her father and was present with him at the time of his death.

ALEXANDER, William Patterson: Born in Paris, Ky., U. S. A., July 25, 1805; studied Latin and Greek at Bourbon Academy; taught school to obtain the means to go to college; entered Center College, Ky., 1826; graduated at Princeton Theological Seminary, 1830; ordained by Presbytery of Cincinnati, October 12, 1831; embarked November 26, 1831, as a missionary of the American Board for the Hawaiian Islands, reaching Honolulu, May 18, 1832. Soon after his arrival he was appointed one of a deputation from the Hawaiian Islands to go to the English Mission at the Society Islands, and also to visit the Marquesas Islands to ascertain if it would be expedient to establish a mission there. A favorable report having been made, it was decided at a meeting of the mission in April, 1833, to undertake a mission at the Marquesas Islands, and Messrs. Alexander, Armstrong, and Parker were appointed to commence the new mission. They reached Nukahiva, the largest island, November 10. After spending eight months among the cannibals, they left the Marquesas Islands to the LMS, whose missionaries were then on their way thither, and returned to Honolulu, arriving May 12, 1834. Mr. Alexander's first station in the Hawaiian Islands was at Waioli, on the island of Kauai, where he remained from 1834-43. A great revival occurred 1836-38, when the natives came incessantly from early in the morning till late at night to converse on religion. In 1837, Mr. Alexander translated Legendre's Geometry, and prepared a text-book on surveying and navigation for the Lahainaluna Seminary. His efforts, in conjunction with Dr. Armstrong, to establish a boarding-school for the missionaries' children, resulted in the founding of the Ponahue School (chartered in 1853 as Oahu College). Failure of health requiring a change to a drier climate, Mr. Alexander left the Waioli parish, and took charge of the seminary at Lahainaluna, on Maui, in 1843. This was a high-school established for the special purpose of educating teachers. Mr. Alexander's health having suffered from his sedentary employment, he was granted, in 1849, a year of respite from school-teaching. This year he spent in surveying land for the Hawaiian Government on East Maui. During this period the Hawaiian Government was changed from an absolute to a constitutional monarchy, and the poor serfs were granted their homesteads in fee simple. In this movement Mr. Alexander was greatly interested, and gave its leaders his earnest cooperation. Besides his labors in the Lahainaluna Seminary, he published a *Pastor's Manual*, common school and Sunday school books, two standard books on the *Evidences of Christianity*, and *A System of Theology*. He died at Oakland, Cal., in 1884.

ALEXANDRETTA: A seaport in the province of Aleppo, Asiatic Turkey, at the extreme north of the Syrian coast. It is the chief port of entry for the trade of Mesopotamia. It is low, marshy, and unhealthy, and most of those who do business there reside in the city of Beylan, on the mountains, about 12 miles distant. It is also called Iskanderun.

ALEXANDRIA: A city of Egypt, on the shore of the Mediterranean. Founded by Alexander the Great, 332 B.C. During the Roman Empire it was the capital of the country and a large and important city. It was the seat of a patriarch, and an important center of learning in early Christian history. During the Middle Ages it declined greatly in importance, and at the time of the Mameluke rule (1300-1800 A.D.) the inhabitants were reduced to about 5,000. Under the Turkish rule, however, and especially during the reign of Mohammed Ali (1811) Alexandria grew rapidly, and now the population numbers about 320,000. Of these 250,000 are natives (chiefly Mohammedans), speaking the Arabic language. The remainder are from every country in Europe and almost of the world, so that it is even more of a Babel than is Constantinople. The presence of a large number of Europeans resident there throughout the year has had a great influence in making the city one of the most attractive in appearance on the Mediterranean, with broad streets, fine buildings and pleasant drives. Being on the sea, the heat is not as intense as at Cairo, and there have grown up a number of suburbs, among which Ramleh is one of the most popular.

The general character of the people is very low, the natives having acquired most of the vices of the Europeans. Some of these foreign residents, however, are men who take an interest in the public welfare, and are liberal in sustaining hospitals and other benevolent and philanthropic undertakings.

The Mohammedans have acquired a very bitter feeling toward the Christians and the Jews, and are ever ready to join in any demonstration or insurrection against them, if they have any reason to suppose that such a movement is agreeable to the rulers of the city. This feeling found expression in a massacre during Arabi Pasha's rebellion, when the city was bombarded by the British fleet, June 11, 1882, and occupied by British troops the next day.

Next to the Mohammedans the Syrian Catholics are quite strong. The Greek Church is wealthy and influential, but the Coptic community is small and feeble.

Mission work is carried on chiefly by the Missions of the United Presbyterian Church of the United States, who maintain 2 schools, one for boys and a very flourishing and efficient one for girls.

The Kaiserswerth Deaconesses also have a fine school here, opened in 1857. The Bible distribution is under the care of the BFBS. The Church of Scotland has a mission to the Jews in the city carried on by 10 missionaries, men and women, who have 4 schools. The North Africa Mission, the Egypt Mission Band, and the WMS also have stations in this city.

ALGERIA: A colony of France in North Africa, lying on the Mediterranean between Morocco on the west and Tunis on the east, indefinitely bounded on the south by the Sahara. It has an area of about 184,474 square miles, and a population of 4,739,931 (1901). Of this the French population numbers 292,464, the Jews 57,132, Tunisians and Moroccoans 26,266, Spaniards 155,265, Italians 38,791, and about 25,000 other foreigners. The Algerian Sahara contains about 125,000 square miles and has about 50,000 inhabitants.

The native population is wholly Mohammedan, and consists mainly of Berbers (75 per cent.) and Arabs (15 per cent.). The Roman Catholic Church has 2 bishops and 386 priests. There are in the colony 21 Protestant pastors and 7 Jewish Rabbis. Government grants to the religious establishments are shared by the Protestants in proportion to their numbers. Oran, Algiers and Constantine are the capitals, respectively, of the three districts of the same names into which the colony is divided.

Laws of the colony protecting Mohammedanism as the prevailing religion restrict Christian missionary effort in Algeria. The Protestant missionary societies laboring there are the French Society for the Evangelization of the Jews, the Penny Collection Fund for Israel, the Algiers Spanish Mission, Miss Trotter's Mission, the Swedish Missionary Society, the NAM and the PB. Four central towns are the field occupied by these Societies.

Atterbury, *Islam in Africa*, New York, 1899; Bridgeman, *Winters in Algeria*, New York, 1899; Somerville, *Sands of Sahara*, London, 1901; Wilkin, *Among the Berbers of Algeria*, London, 1900.

ALGIERS: Capital of the French colony of Algeria, North Africa. Population (1901), 96,542, French, 20,000, including Jews, 6,000, who own most of the land in the city, and native Arabs. The town is built in the form of an amphitheater, on an elevation of 500 feet, and, seen from a distance, presents a very imposing appearance, heightened by the dazzling whiteness of its houses, which rise in terraces on the side of the hill. The climate is so equable as to make it a health resort. It is a strong Roman Catholic center. It is the seat of an agency of the BFBS with a Bible depot, colporteurs and Bible women. The North Africa Mission also has a station there with 6 missionaries, men and women. Several societies especially devoted to Jewish work also have missionaries there.

ALIGARH: City and railway station in the United Provinces, India, southeast of Delhi. Population of city and suburbs (1901), 70,434. The religions found here are Hinduism, Jainism, Mohammedanism. There are also a very few Christians. The climate is changeable and uncertain in temperature. The CMS established a station here in 1863 which has now an important work among the women, carried on by 3 unmarried missionaries. There is a dispensary here. The general work is under charge of a married missionary and his wife, with 31 native workers, both men and women. There are 3 outstations, 10 village schools and about 100 communicants.

ALI-ILLAHI: A sect existing among the Mohammedans of Persia and Turkey. They are known under different names, as Dawudi, Abdulbegi, etc. There is great resemblance between their religious beliefs and those of the **Nusairiyeh** of Syria, if indeed the sects are not one and the same. They hold their real opinions in secret, while professing before Mohammedans to be strict Muslims, and in their presence conforming to all the rites of Islam. But to Christians they declare their hatred of the Mohammedan prophet and law, and do not hesitate to violate the Mohammedan ritual. Nevertheless, even to Christians they will not reveal their secret doctrines or practices with any particularity. They have no books. The Dawudi division profess to have great respect for the Psalms of David. Apparently this strange religion is but a heathenish conglomeration of Pagan, Mohammedan, Jewish, and Christian superstitions. Its adherents number many hundred thousands in Persia. It is understood that many of them are becoming **Babis.** Considerable attempts have been made to lead them to Christianity, but with little success. Their gross superstitions and ignorance, with their great fear of the Mohammedan rancor of bigotry, hold them fast in their present deplorable condition.

ALIWAL NORTH: Town and railway station on the Orange river in Cape Colony, South Africa; mission station of the Primitive Methodist Society, with 4 missionaries of both sexes and 5 native workers. It has an industrial school, 2 theological classes, 2 village schools, and about 1,200 professing Christians.

ALLAHABAD: Seat of the Lieutenant Governor of the United Provinces, British India; situated at the confluence of the Ganges, Jumma, and Saraswati rivers; the stronghold of Hinduism, which for centuries has fought successfully in this region against Mohammedanism. The population is (1901) 172,032, Hindus, Mohammedans and Christians, with many less important religious groups. It was the first point in India occupied by the CMS (in 1813). It is now a station of the CMS, the PN, the ME, the Zenana, Bible and Medical Mission, and the Woman's Union Foreign Missionary Society of America. The total force stationed at Allahabad by these societies consists of 37 missionaries and 109 native workers, men and women. The various enterprises which they carry on include a Divinity school, a training school for women, 4 high schools, 3 orphanages, 43 village schools, a dispensary and a hospital. The Bible Societies and the YMCA also make this a center for their work in the Province. The total of communicants connected with the various missions is about 550.

ALLEN, David Oliver: Born in Barre, Mass., September 14, 1799; graduated at Amherst College, 1825; graduated at Andover Theological Seminary, 1827; ordained and sailed as a missionary of the American Board for India, June 6, 1827. There he was connected with the mission press for many years. In 1847 an edition of the whole Bible in Marâthi, translated by the members of the two missions, was revised by Mr. Allen, editorial superintendent of the American Mission Press, and member of the Committee of the Bombay Bible Society. Dr. Allen was a faithful worker and wise counselor. His services, especially in connection with the press and the translation of the Scriptures, were of great value to the missionary cause. Dr. Allen published a valuable work on *India, Ancient and Modern,* and was the author of several articles in periodicals. He resided at Lowell, Mass., from 1860 until his death, from congestion of the lungs, July 17, 1863.

ALLEPPIE: A seaport at the foot of the western Ghats, in Travancore, India. Population, 22,000. In 1816 the CMS founded a station there, principally for the purpose of redeeming the Syrian (Jacobite) community, which had been settled there since ancient times, but had utterly degenerated. In the beginning the undertaking seemed destined to succeed. The Syrians even allowed the missionaries to preach in their churches. But in 1836 a new bishop suddenly broke off all relations with the mission, and the missionaries addressed themselves to the heathen. The mission is now carried on by one missionary and his wife with 26 native workers, men and women. It has 8 schools and a special mission to lepers. The Mission to Lepers in India and the East also has a station and Leper Asylum here. A reform movement originating in the Jacobite Church now promises good results.

ALLGEMEINER EVANGELISCH-PROTESTANISCHER MISSIONSVEREIN. See GERMANY, MISSIONARY SOCIETIES OF.

ALLUR: Town in the Nellore district, Madras, India. It was occupied as a station by the ABMU in 1873, and has a missionary and his wife and 10 native workers, men and women. It has 5 outstations, 2 preaching places and about 300 church members.

ALMORA: Capital of the Kumaun district, United Provinces, India, situated among the Himalayas, 5,337 feet above the sea, near the frontier of Tibet. Climate temperate, making it a resort for invalids during the hot and rainy seasons. Population of the district, 493,599—Hindus, Muslims, Europeans. Language, Hindi (Kumauni dialect). Mission station LMS (1850), with 10 missionaries and 48 native workers, men and women. It has 10 outstations, a college, a hospital, 6 dispensaries, a leper asylum, a high school and 18 common schools.

ALVAY: Village near Point Pedro on the N. side of the Jaffna peninsula, Ceylon; occupied as a mission station by the WMS in 1880. It now has 1 missionary and 23 native workers, men and women, with 6 outstations and 8 primary schools.

ALWAR: A city of 53,000 inhabitants in Rajputana, India, and capital of the native state of the same name. A station of the UFS was established here in 1880. It is occupied by a missionary and his wife and 28 native workers, with 6 common schools and 2 outstations. Also called Ulwar.

ALWAYE: Village in Cochin, S. India, S. E. of Trichur. It is a station of the CMS since 1881 and is occupied by a missionary and his wife, and 21 native workers. There are 3 outstations and 4 village schools.

AMALAPURAM: Town in the delta of the Godavari river, Madras, India, occupied by the Plymouth Brethren as a station with a missionary and his wife and 3 unmarried women.

AMALIENSTEIN: A village in Cape Colony, S. Africa. Mission station of the Berlin Missionary Society (1853). The mission premises were originally presented to the mission by a German lady enthusiastically interested in missions, and her name is perpetuated by the name of the station. The work is carried on by 4 missionaries and 23 native workers, men and women. There is an outstation and there are more than 600 communicants, mostly Hottentots.

AMANZIMTOTE: Town in Natal, South Africa, S. W. from Durban; station of the ABCFM, which has founded there important educational institutions, including a girls' boarding school, an industrial school and a theological class. It is also called Adams.

AMARWARA: A village in the Chhindwara district in the Central Provinces, India. The Swedish National Missionary Society has a station there, opened in 1886, and now occupied by 4 missionaries and 4 native workers. There is a hospital there and 2 outstations.

AMASIA: A city of about 30,000 inhabitants in the province of Sivas, Asiatic Turkey. It was the birthplace of Strabo, and the capital of the last kings of Pontus, of whose tombs and defensive fortifications there are remains. It lies on the Yeshil Irmak River, about 60 miles from the Black Sea coast. It is an important trade center. There is a small German colony in the city and a Protestant Armenian community of some vigor connected with the ABCFM. The majority of the inhabitants are Mohammedans.

AMATOLE: A village S. of Stutterheim, Cape Colony, S. Africa, where there are 8 outstations and more than 400 church members under the care of native workers connected with the Wesleyan Missionary Society of South Africa.

AMBALA: City of (1901) 78,638 inhabitants on the Punjab Railway, and capital of the district of the same name in the Punjab, India. It is on the whole a healthy place of residence. The majority of the population are Mohammedans, but a little more than one-third of the inhabitants are Hindus. Both the Punjabi and Urdu languages are in use.
The PN Society has a station there occupied by 7 missionaries and 19 native workers. There are a hospital and dispensary, special work for lepers, 2 high schools and 4 village schools.
The WMS also has a station here under the care of a missionary and 2 native workers.
Also written Umballa.

AMBALANGODA: Town on the S. W. coast of Ceylon; station of the WMS with 1 missionary and 15 native workers, men and women. There are 3 outstations, 2 preaching places, 5 common schools and 25 church members.

AMBARAWA: Town S. of Samarang in Java; station of Neukirchen Mission, with a missionary and his wife, and 6 native workers and 6 outstations.

AMBATO: Town of Ecuador, South America, S. of Quito; station of the Gospel Missionary Union, with a missionary and his wife and one unmarried woman missionary.

AMBATOHARANANA: A town of Madagascar, near Antananarivo. Has a college founded in 1881 by the SPG and a community of nearly 700 Christians connected with that Society.

AMBATOMAKANGA: A district in the outskirts of Antananarivo, Madagascar; station of the LMS (1831) with 2 missionaries and their wives and 1 unmarried woman and 292 native workers; 1 high school and 48 village schools, and 3,116 church members.

AMBATOMANGA: A village S. E. of Antananarivo, Madagascar; station of the Paris Evangelical Society, with 1 missionary and his wife and 1 unmarried woman and 99 native workers, men and women. It has 40 outstations and 40 village schools, 1 high school, 1 industrial school, 1 dispensary and 900 church members.

AMBOHIBÉLOMA: A town in the province of Imerina, west of Antananarivo, Madagascar. Mission station of the Paris Evangelical Society, transferred from the LMS after the French occupation of the island. It has 1 missionary, 92 native workers, men and women, 32 outstations, 25 village schools, 1 high school, a dispensary and about 200 communicant Christians.

AMBOHIDRATRIMO: A village in Madagascar, situated about 10 miles N. W. of Antananarivo. Formerly capital of a petty kingdom. Station of the LMS (1901) formed by separating a portion of the Amparibe district, including 40 churches. It now has (1903) 1 missionary and his wife, 350 native workers, men and women, 58 day schools and 5,331 professed Christians, of whom 1,839 are church members.

AMBOHIMAHASOA: A town in the eastern part of Madagascar, north of Fianarantsoa; station of the LMS (1890), with a missionary and his wife and 119 native workers, 40 village schools, 1 dispensary and 1,200 church members.

AMBOHIMANDROSO: A town of south central Madagascar. The neighboring districts are thickly populated, the native population being Betsileo. The uneducated people are extremely dull, superstitious, and suspicious. Mission station of the LMS since 1875. There are 8 missionaries and 260 native workers, men and women. There is a dispensary, and a belt of 91 village schools in the surrounding region. The church members number about 1,000.

AMBOHIMANGA: A town N. of Antananarivo, Madagascar, station of the LMS (1862), with 2 missionaries and their wives and 242 native workers, 46 village schools and 2,063 church members. Station also of the SPG, with 1 native worker. Station also of the Norwegian Missionary Society; no statistics.

AMBOHIMIADANA: A town in the western part of Madagascar; station of the Friends Foreign Mission Association, with 1 unmarried woman missionary and 187 native workers, men and women, 18 outstations, 1 dispensary, and 475 church members.

AMBOHIPOTSY: A district S. W. of Antananarivo, Madagascar; station of the LMS (1863) with 1 missionary and his wife and 306 native workers, 42 Sunday-schools, 42 village schools, and 3,000 church members.

AMBOINA. See MOLUCCA ISLANDS.

AMBONIRIANA: A town in the central portion of Madagascar, near Betafo; station of the Friends Foreign Mission Association (1899), with 1 missionary and 54 native workers, men and women, 1 industrial school and 24 outstations, and 63 professing Christians.

AMBOSITRA: A city of South Central Madagascar; station of the LMS transferred in 1898 to the Paris Evang. Society. It has 5 missionaries and 150 native workers operating in about 100 outstations, with a dispensary, a Bible depot, 4 high schools, a training class for women workers, and 80 village schools. The number of professing Christians is 1,200.

AMBRYM. See NEW HEBRIDES.

AMBUR: Town of 10,000 inhabitants in the Eastern Ghats, not far from the border of Mysore, in the Madras Presidency, India; station of the mission of the German Evangelical Lutheran Synod of Missouri, Ohio, etc.; with a missionary and his wife and 2 native workers and 2 common schools.

AMEDSCHOVHE: A town in German Togoland, W. Africa; station of the North German Missionary Society (1889), with 4 missionaries, 3 married women, and 25 native workers, men and women, 7 outstations, 11 village schools, 1 college and 358 communicants.

AMERICAN AND FOREIGN CHRISTIAN UNION: The Society was formed in the city of New York in the year 1849, for the uniting of all Christian denominations in the work of the world's evangelization. Its early labors were among the so-called alien populations of our own country, especially in the large cities. It also wrought vigorously in foreign lands, with main reference to giving God's Word and the preaching of the Gospel to those who were in the territories of Roman Catholicism. Italy, Bohemia, Austria, France, Spain, the countries of South America, the West Indies and Mexico were included in its wide field.

As the denominations became more numerous and strong, there arose the not unnatural tendency to conduct their missionary labors through their own denominational agencies. Hence the Society found its resources gradually lessened, and was compelled to limit the field of its work. At present it devotes its energies to the evangelization of France.

The Union owns the site and building of the American Church, 21 Rue de Berri, Paris. The maintenance of that most important church is included in the Union's care. It also cooperates with the French missionary societies. At the same time the Union is trustee of the funds raised in this country for the building of an American church in Berlin.

Headquarters: The Chelsea, 222 W. 23d St., New York.

AMERICAN BAPTIST MISSIONARY UNION: The constituency of this society is composed of the Baptist Churches of the Northern and Western States. The Lott Carey Convention (colored), and the German Baptist Churches of North America cooperate with it in several missions.

A. History: The Baptists in America entered heartily into the missionary movement at the beginning of the 19th century, and as early as 1812 had afforded substantial assistance to the English Baptist Mission at Serampur, India. Many of the missionaries of that society had been obliged to go to India by way of America, because passage was denied them in the vessels of the East India Company. While their presence and addresses in the United States had aroused much enthusiasm, no organization to promote foreign missions was formed until, in consequence of their careful study of the Bible on the passage to India, Mr. and Mrs. Adoniram Judson, and Luther Rice, of the newly organized ABCFM, became Baptists and were baptized at Calcutta. Mr. and Mrs. Judson remained to establish a mission wherever Providence might indicate, while Mr. Rice returned to America in the hope of inducing the Baptists in this country to undertake their support. The conversion of these missionaries to Baptist views was regarded as a Providential indication of the will of God, and the work of collecting funds to support the enterprise thus thrown upon their hands was entered upon by the Baptist churches with enthusiasm. A meeting of delegates representing all sections of the country was called to meet at Philadelphia; and there, on May 18, 1814, was formed the "General Convention of the Baptist Denomination in the United States of America for Foreign Missions." This body was incorporated June 15, 1821, when the words "and other important objects relating to the Redeemer's Kingdom" were added to the title.

From its organization, in 1814, until 1845, this Triennial Convention was supported by the churches of the whole denomination in the Southern as well as the Northern States; but the period, 1840-45, had been one of great excitement and agitation on the subject of slavery, and in 1845, upon the appearance of divergences of view as to the eligibility of slaveholders to appointment as missionaries, the churches in all the Southern States withdrew from the Triennial Convention, and a separate association, with the title of the Southern Baptist Convention, was organized. This action necessitated a reorganization of the friends of missions in the Northern States, which was brought about at an extra session of the Triennial Convention, held in New York City in November, 1845, when a new constitution was adopted, and the new Convention went into operation in May, 1846, under the name of the American Baptist Missionary Union. The enthusiasm of both the November and May meetings was greatly increased by the presence of Dr. Judson, then visiting his native land for the first time since he left it, in 1813. Missions about to be abandoned were reinforced, upon Dr. Judson's earnest pleadings, and new work was entered upon. The debt of the Convention, amounting to $40,000, was paid, and contributions were largely increased.

B. Organization and Constitution: "The single object of the American Baptist Missionary Union is to diffuse the knowledge of Jesus Christ, by means of missions, throughout the world." The Union is composed of missionaries in service, life-members and honorary life-members. It meets annually the fourth Tuesday of May, when its officers—president, two vice-presidents, recording secretary, and the Board of Managers—are chosen by ballot. The Board of Managers is composed of 75 elective members, of whom not more than three-fifths shall be ministers, and not less than one-fifth shall be women. Immediately after the annual meeting, the Board of Managers elects its officers and an executive committee of 15 (not more than 8 ministers), whose duties comprise the management of the entire missionary work of the Union, and the control of the finances at home and abroad, the latter in accordance with the instructions and approval of the Board of Managers.

All the officers and members of the Board of Managers, the secretaries, and all missionaries employed by the Executive Committee must be members in good standing of regular Baptist churches.

C. Development of Work: 1. *Asiatic Missions:* Owing to the fact that, when Mr. and Mrs. Judson were compelled by the East India Company to leave Madras, the only vessel in which they could secure passage was bound for Rangoon, the missionary work of the Baptist Convention had its commencement in Burma rather than in India, as was the first intention. The mission thus started for the Burmese in Rangoon, in 1813, was gradually extended, and included, in addition to stations among the Burmese, the Sgau-Karen, Pwo-Karen, Shan, Kachin, and Chin races. In 1831 the mission to Siam was commenced.

In 1835 the Board of Managers were authorized by the Triennial Convention to "establish new missions in every unoccupied field where there was a reasonable prospect of success." Accordingly, that same year the Telugu Mission of India was established, and the following year work was begun in Assam at the request of the English Commissioner in that country. The same year the Bangkok Mission in Siam was removed to Hongkong, the work being chiefly among the Chinese. In 1872 a mission was commenced in Japan, a mission having been previously begun in the Lu Chu Islands. In 1884 the Livingstone Mission in Africa was transferred to the Union, and in 1900 work was begun in the Philippine Islands. The Society also supports or aids Baptist work in France (1832), Germany, Austria and Bohemia (1834), Denmark (1891), Sweden (1855), Finland (1889), Spain (1870), Russia (1887), and Norway (1892).

The Woman's Baptist Foreign Missionary Society, Tremont Temple, Boston, Mass., was organized in 1871 as the result of appeals from the wife of a missionary in Burma for single women to work among the women of that country. In response, a general meeting for women was convened in Boston, in April, 1871; a constitution was presented and endorsed by the two hundred women present; the object of the Society, as stated in the constitution, was "to furnish support, through the American Baptist Missionary Union, to Christian women employed by said Union as missionaries, native teachers or Bible women, together with the facilities needed for their work, such laborers being recommended by this Society." In December of the same year their first missionary was sent out, and at the end of the first year they had six missionaries in the field, while the home organization numbered 141 auxiliaries, and the receipts were $9,172.

The Home Department consists of a Board of Managers, meeting twice each month for an entire day to transact the business of the Society; this Board is divided into various committees which meet more frequently. State secretaries are appointed by the Board, and they in turn appoint Association secretaries. The Home Department includes (1902) 1,523 circles with 37,646 members; 419 young ladies' circles with 8,591 members; 452 junior organizations with 12,705 members. Total receipts, $121,771.26. There are 78 missionaries on the foreign field, 433 schools with 16,690 pupils, and 134 Bible women.

The Woman's Baptist Foreign Missionary Society of the West was organized in 1871 on the general lines of the other Woman's Society, working through the ABMU. The first missionary was sent to Burma in December, 1871, and the receipts for the first year were $4,245. Its Home Department (1902) reports 17,873 contributors in the senior circles; 62 young ladies' circles, and 134 junior organizations. Total receipts, $60,280. It now has 35 missionaries on the foreign field; 220 schools with 6,771 pupils; and 100 Bible women.

The Woman's Baptist Foreign Missionary Society of California was organized in 1875, in San Francisco, and the Woman's Baptist Foreign Missionary Society of Oregon was organized in 1878. In 1902 a joint committee of the Missionary Union and the Woman's Societies was appointed to consider the relation of the latter to the Union. This committee recommended that the Societies of California and Oregon be merged into the Society of the West. This was accordingly done in 1903.

D. The Fields: I. Burma (1813): On being driven from Bengal by the East India Company, Dr. and Mrs. Judson went to Madras intending to found a mission in the Penang Straits. Failing, however, to find a ship for Penang, they embarked for Burma, not wishing to wait at Madras lest the East India Company should compel their return to England. They landed in Rangoon July 13, 1813. In 1816 G. H. Hough and wife joined them, bringing a printing press given by the Serampur Mission. June 27, 1819, the first convert was baptized, and others soon following a church was formed. The Emperor of Burma having died, the brutal conduct of his successor brought on the first Burmese War with England (1824-26). On the capture of Rangoon by the English in 1824 Mr. Judson and Dr. Price were arrested and imprisoned by the Burmans, their captivity culminating in the horrors of Oung-pen-la, from which they were released only in January, 1826, when the king needed Mr. Judson's services as interpreter in the negotiations for peace. The mission was reinforced after the restoration of peace, and supplied with a skilled printer and all appliances for issuing books and tracts. In 1834 Mr. Judson completed the translation of the Scriptures into the Burmese language, and it as well as the other issues of the Mission Press were eagerly received. *The Religious Herald*, which is still continued, was founded in 1844. After the death of Dr. Judson in 1852, the extension of the British possessions in Burma gave opportunity for the enlargement of the mission. The station at Rangoon was reoccupied at once, and there the missionaries found a small group of 15 church members who had survived the 16 years of persecution. A general convention of the missionaries in Burma assembled at Maulmain in 1853, which decided that Burma missions should be at once permanently established in Rangoon, Bassein, Henzada, Prome, Taungngu and Shwegyin; constituted a publication committee for the control of the Mission Press; recommended increased attention to preaching in the native tongues, the ordination of a larger number of native pastors, and the missionary supervision of schools as a "means of Christian instruction rather than of imparting a secular education." The establishment in the principal stations of Normal schools for training teachers and preachers was approved; the founding of other boarding schools, and the teaching of English were discouraged. Some of the decisions of the Convention have been modified on subsequent experience, but this Convention must always be regarded as one of the most important events in the history of the Burma missions.

Since the overthrow of the Burmese Kingdom in 1885 and the incorporation of its territories in the Indian Empire, the prospects of the work among the Burmans have materially improved. Work for the **Karens** was commenced by Rev. and Mrs. George Dana Boardman at Tavoy in 1828. That year Ko-thah-byu, the first Karen convert, afterward known as "the Karen Apostle," was baptised. The first church was formed in 1830. In 1832 the Karen language was reduced to writing and the first book printed. In 1843 the New Testament was printed in Karen, and publication of the *Morning Star*, a Karen journal, was commenced. The Karen Theological Seminary was instituted in Maulmain in 1846, and in 1848 the Karen pastors in the Bassein district assumed self-support. In 1850 a Home Missionary Society was formed, entirely under the direction of the Karens. The jubilee of the Karen Mission was celebrated at Bassein, in 1878, by the dedication of the Ko-thah-byu Memorial Hall, paid for by the Bassein Karens, and set apart for the use of the Bassein Sgaw Karen Normal and Industrial Institute.

In 1883 the entire Scriptures were issued in Pwo Karen. This completed the work of giving the Scriptures to the Karens.

A mission among the **Shans,** who are very bigoted Buddhists, was established in 1860 by Dr. Bixby at Taungngu. Ten thousand Shans had settled in the district shortly before Dr. Bixby arrived there, they having fled from civil war in their own land. It being impossible to enter the Shan country, schools were established for them at Taungngu, where a small church was soon organized. In 1871 the Gospel of Matthew and a grammar of the Shan language were printed. In 1885 the first edition of the Shan New Testament was published and the entire Bible in 1891.

After the deposition of King Thibaw and the annexation of Burma by the English in December, 1885, Shanland itself was open to the missionaries. A station was opened at Hsipaw, in the Northern Shan states, in 1890, and at Mone, South of Mandalay, in 1892. In both stations medical work has an important part.

The *Chins* are allied to the Karens and are nominally Buddhists. They are found on both sides of the western Yoma range of mountains, stretching from Arkan to the Naga hills of Assam. Those to the south are divided into 4 tribes using different dialects; those of the north are less known. The first Chin convert was baptized by Dr. Francis Mason at Tavoy, in 1837. The Chin language was reduced to writing twenty years later by a Karen preacher from Bassein, who baptized 40 of these wild people. It was not until 1884 that an American missionary established himself in the Chin country.

The *Kachins*, also allied to the Karens, are found in northeastern Burma, their country extending into China and Assam and north to Tibet. They are a wild and savage people. Among these tribes work was opened by Rev. J. U. Cushing, in 1877. Several Karen teachers from Bassein were then sent into the Kachin mountain villages and since then Karens have been laboring among them, wholly supported by the Karens in Bassein. The first Kachin Church was formed in 1882 at Pumwai. The Kachin language was reduced to writing by the Rev. Ola Hansen, who also translated the Gospel of St. John, a catechism and some smaller works. Since then a system of applying the Roman letters to the Kachin language has been adopted by the missionaries and by the Government.

In 1894 Rev. and Mrs. W. F. Armstrong were especially set apart to work among the half million Telugus and Tamils, who have migrated to Burma. They have a large and self supporting church at Rangoon, Other missionaries are doing more or less work among them.

The ABMU has in Burma (1903) 27 stations and 640 outstations; 173 American missionaries and 1,756 native workers, men and women; 741 churches with 41,770 communicants; 2 theological schools, 33 boarding and high schools, and 511 elementary schools. The aggregate number of pupils in all these educational institutions is 19,430.

II. Assam (1836): Direct evangelistic work is done among the Assamese, Bengalis, Kols (imported from Nagpur to work in the tea-gardens) and the hill men such as the Garos, Nagas, Mikirs, etc. Rev. Nathan Brown and Rev. O. T. Cutter and their wives commenced the mission in Assam at Sadiya in 1836, being followed in 1837 by Rev. Miles Bronson, D.D., who was stationed at Jaipur. Both of these stations were given up later, in favor of Sibsagar and Nowgong. The Scriptures have been translated into Assamese and printed in Roman letters and schools have been opened. But the Assamese do not seem to have been deeply touched by the Gospel. The Assamese churches at these two stations number about 725 members, while the Garos and other hill men and the immigrants from Bengal are far more ready to receive Christianity with heart and soul. The first two Garo converts were baptized in 1863. They instantly began working among their own people, with such success that when Dr. Bronson visited the Garo country in 1867, a church of 40 members was formed at Rajasimla. Since then the missions among Garos have been most successful.

There are (1903) in Assam 12 stations and 147 outstations; 54 American missionaries and 238 native workers; 76 churches; 7,150 communicants; and 146 schools with 2,739 pupils.

III. India; Telugu Mission: The enterprise of the ABMU in India was begun by Rev. and Mrs. S. S. Day at Vizagapatam in 1836. In 1840 the force removed to Nellore. Schools were opened at various points; the first Telugu convert was baptized in 1840, and a second in 1843. But soon both missionaries broke down and returned to America. The mission prop erty, schools, and the little church of seven members, including the two Telugus, was left in the care of a Eurasian preacher, and the question of abandoning the Telugu Mission was seriously considered. Mr. Day, however, recovered his health and, with Rev. Lyman Jewett, returned in 1848. The next five years were full of struggle. In 1853 a deputation sent by the Society to examine the Asiatic Missions having visited Nellore, advised that the mission be either strongly reinforced or relinquished at once. The Board of Managers of the ABMU threw the responsibility on the denomination, as represented in the annual meeting, which decided to reenforce and continue the mission. Other difficulties having arisen, in 1862 the question of abandoning the mission was again raised. The missionary map, always in view at the annual meetings of the Union, had upon it a number of red marks to indicate the stations in Burma. These marks looked like a cluster of stars, while across the Bay of Bengal there was one lone star, indicating the only station of the Board in India; and at one of the meetings, when the question of abandoning or reenforcing this mission was under discussion, it was spoken of as the "Lone Star Mission." Dr. S. F. Smith, author of "My Country, 'Tis of Thee," wrote that night a poem picturing in place of the one star, a glorious constellation in that region. The prophecy has been fulfilled.

In 1864 the working force was increased by Rev. J. E. Clough, the "Missionary for Ongole." The following year four Telugus were baptized and from that moment fruit from the long period of seed-sowing began to appear. At the end of another decade there were nearly 4,000 baptized converts in that mission field. Then came a time of trial; famine, flood, cholera, and another and a terrible famine. Sorely were the new converts tried, but neither their faith nor the faith of the missionaries failed. During the period of famine the missionaries deemed it wise to put off all baptisms until the work of distributing relief was over. Then between June 15 and September 17, 1878, 9,147 were baptized, 2,222 in one day. The work went steadily on, and in December, 1890, another revival occurred, when 1,671 persons were baptized in one day and during the following five months nearly 10,000 were baptized at the various stations.

There are (1903) 26 stations and 388 outstations in the Baptist Telugu Mission, 99 American missionaries and 1,008 native workers; 116 churches with 54,995 communicants; 1 theological school with 149 students; and 549 other schools with 10,664 pupils.

IV. *Missions in China:* In 1833 Rev. J. T. Jones, of the Burma mission, in consultation with his associates went to Bangkok and turned his attention to the translation of the New Testament and the creation of a Christian literature. Altho his work was in the Siamese language, the first converts in Bangkok were three Chinese. From the first the work among the Chinese was more promising than that for the Siamese, and on the arrival of reenforcements one of the missionaries removed (in 1842) to Hongkong and another (in 1849) to Ningpo.

The mission at Bangkok has not been largely successful in itself. But through the Chinese converts in Bangkok an entrance to the people of China was secured before that Empire was open to foreigners. It is continued as a part of the enterprise of evangelizing China.

The first Baptist Church in China was formed in the Portuguese colony of Macao and the first convert was baptized in 1837. In 1843 the second Baptist Chinese Church was organized at Hongkong. In 1846 it was decided to remove the mission to the mainland and Swatow was chosen as the central station. In 1881 a branch of the Swatow mission took up work among the Hakkas of the highlands.

Stations have been established in several centers in the Swatow region. The work of the Baptist Southern China mission embraces 5 stations and among other enterprises it includes a biblical school for preachers; a training class for Bible women; Bible translation; elementary and high schools; general dispensary and hospital work and a medical class for students.

The *Eastern China Mission* of the ABMU was begun at Ningpo by J. D. Macgowan, M. D., in 1843. A hospital was opened and the good will of the people gained by the successful treatment of difficult cases. The first convert in this field was baptized in 1849. Gradually the force was increased until the mission now has 5 stations and about 800 church members.

Rev. Josiah Goddard did important work in translating the New Testament into the Ningpo dialect, and his son, Rev. J. R. Goddard, was the chief translator of the Old Testament, which was put into Roman letters in 1901.

A boys' boarding school was opened about 1880 by the native Christians. This has since been maintained without expense to the Union.

The *Western China Mission* was begun by W. M. Upcraft, formerly agent for the BFBS, and Mr. George Warner in 1889. The first station was Hsü-chau, in the province of Sze-chwan. During the first year seven converts were baptized. Medical work was begun by Mrs. Warner in 1891. Two new stations were opened in 1894. The following year the Sze-chwan riots occurred; the missionaries were obliged to flee, and the mission premises were totally destroyed. Operations were resumed in 1896 with increased vigor, and hope was large for continued expansion of the work, when the Boxer Movement of 1900 swept through the land and the missionaries were obliged to flee and the mission property was again destroyed. Many foreigners and native Christians were massacred. The work was resumed in 1901 and increased opportunities are everywhere manifest.

The *Central China Mission* was commenced in 1893 at Han-yang-fu by Rev. and Mrs. J. S. Adams and Rev. and Mrs. W. F. Gray. In 1895 the First Baptist Church was organized. Medical work was begun in 1897 by Rev. G. A. Huntley, M. D., and each year has witnessed a steady growth. In 1902 a mission hall and dispensary were erected and the new Metropolitan Tabernacle of the Baptists in mid-China was erected and dedicated.

There are (1903) in the southern, eastern, western and central China Missions 15 stations and 202 outstations; 77 American missionaries and 232 native workers; 85 churches with 3,870 communicants; 2 theological schools with 49 students; 6 boarding and high schools with 313 students and 35 other schools with 534 pupils.

V. *Missions in Japan:* Jonathan Goble was sent to Japan by the American Baptist Free

Mission Society in 1860, where he labored for his own support in part until 1872, when the Free Mission Society became a part of the ABMU, which assumed Mr. Goble's support and appointed Rev. Nathan Brown as their first missionary. To him the Japan mission largely owes its early development. The first Baptist Church in Japan was organized at Yokohama in 1873 with eight members, and the following year a station was opened in Tokio. In 1878 Kobe was occupied, and Sendai in 1882. In 1886 a station was opened in Shimonoseki, in Southern Japan, but the mission headquarters were later transferred to Chofu. In 1891 native helpers were sent from Kobe to work among the people of the Lu Chu Islands, locating in the city of Nafa. Osaka was occupied in 1892, Mito in 1899 and Otarun in 1902. The progress in all these stations has from the first been steady and substantial.

There are (1903) 9 stations and 86 outstations; 58 American missionaries and 137 native workers, 30 churches, with 2,157 communicants; 1 theological school with 19 students; 5 boarding and high schools with 332 students; 6 other schools with 313 pupils.

VI. *Missions to Africa; Liberia:* The Triennial Baptist General Convention was disposed very early to aid the African Baptist Missionary Society in planting a mission in Africa in the vicinity of the present republic of Liberia. That Society had sent missionaries to Liberia in 1821. But the unusual difficulties of the field and the mortality among its white missionaries led the ABMU to suspend its mission there in 1856.

Congo: Henry M. Stanley, after crossing Africa, appeared at Boma, near the mouth of the Congo, August 7, 1877. When news of his feat reached England, it aroused a desire to begin mission work in this hitherto untouched region. The responsible management of the new enterprise was placed in the hands of Mr. and Mrs. H. Grattan Guinness. The first missionaries of this "Livingstone Inland Mission" sailed for the Congo in 1878, and by 1883 six stations had been established, extending from the coast to the head of Livingstone Falls. A steamer for the navigation of the Upper Congo was launched on the Pool, in November, 1884. The staff then consisted of 26 missionaries; one of the languages had been reduced to writing; a grammar and dictionary had been published and a hopeful beginning made in various lines of missionary activity. At this time the mission was transferred to the care of the ABMU. In August, 1886, began the remarkable revival at Bansa Manteke, known as "the Pentecost on the Congo," and in November of that year the first church on the Congo was formed with 42 members by the Rev. Henry Richards, after seven years of apparently fruitless labors. A training school for native evangelists was opened at Bansa Manteke, and other stations speedily founded. At every point the success at Bansa Manteke has been duplicated in smaller degrees. From 1890-97 the progress of the work was hindered by difficulties between the natives and the Congo State officials. Largely through the intervention of the missionaries, however, the troubles were settled, and since then, with increased facilities for communication, openings for aggressive missionary work have steadily multiplied.

There are (1903) 8 stations and 98 outstations; 33 American missionaries and 217 trained Christian native workers; 8 churches with 3,104 communicants; 1 theological school with 20 students; 5 boarding and high schools with 36 students; 107 other schools with 3,249 pupils.

VII. *Philippine Islands Mission:* The interest of the American Baptists centers in the Visayan group of islands. Rev. Eric Lund, for 20 years a missionary of the ABMU in Spain, was chosen to open the work. Early in 1900 Mr. Lund arrived in Iloilo in the island of Panay, accompanied by Señor Branlio Manikan, a young Visayan who had been sent from the Philippine Islands to Spain to be educated for the priesthood, but had been converted at Barcelona, in the mission under the care of Mr. Lund. By an interdenominational agreement the district north from Iloilo on Panay and the western provinces of Negros became the distinctive field of the Baptists, and Jaro, which is an important trade center, was chosen as the headquarters for the work. Reenforcements were sent out, and in June, 1901, a church of 43 members was organized at Jaro. Tracts and leaflets were distributed by the thousand, a religious newspaper was founded, and the work continued with accelerating movement. In Negros, as in Panay, the work reached from the central station into the surrounding country. Already a remarkable company of native leaders has been raised up, and the work has everywhere developed with marvelous rapidity. While the educated classes are friendly, the work is mainly among the peasants. Medical work was begun in 1902 and proves an important factor in gaining all classes of the people. Persecution has been severe, and as a result some 8,000 people have left their villages and established a Protestant town on the mountain side, calling it Calvary. There are (1903) 2 stations and 5 outstations; 11 American missionaries and 7 native workers, and 3 churches with 372 communicants.

VIII. *European Missions:* European missions were not contemplated in the original purpose of the Triennial Convention. Aside from a few points on the western frontier of the United States, where domestic missions were maintained for a few years, and a mission to the North American Indians, the founders of the Convention thought of missions to the heathen as the only ones within their scope; and when the way was opened for missionary work in Europe, a distinction was soon established between missions to lands where the Greek or Roman Catholic is the State Church, and those where Protestantism prevails. Thus, missions to France (1832), Greece (1836), and, later, Spain (1870), were conducted as foreign missions, and missionaries were sent to them from the United States, their work to be supplemented, as in Asia, by native preachers; while the missions in Germany (1834), Sweden (1834), and in other Protestant countries were from the first prosecuted by native preachers, the Convention exercising only a general superintendence, and rendering counsel and financial aid when necessary.

The work of the ABMU in France dates from 1832, and was the result of the report of a committee sent by the Union to investigate the need and opportunity for missionary work in that country. Under Louis Philippe, the American preachers were not molested, tho native preachers were arrested. Progress was slow, altho the Rev. Reuben Saillens, associated with the McAll Mission, gave much assistance. Since 1891 Mr. Saillens has devoted himself specially to the work, and great advance has been made, and 31 preachers, 30 churches, and 2,409 members are reported (1903).

Baptist work in Germany was inaugurated by the baptism, by President Barnes Sears of Brown University, of seven men at Hamburg (1834). One of these, Johann Gerhard Oncken, then an agent of the Edinburgh Bible Society, and a bookseller, became the leader of the Baptist movement in Germany. Every effort was made by the ecclesiastical and civil authorities to stop the work. The leaders were imprisoned and fined, but the work progressed and extended into Denmark and Russia. There are reported (1902) in Germany, 203 preachers, 231 churches, 41,552 members; in Denmark, 40 preachers, 29 churches, 3,928 members.

The Missionary Union has had no American missionaries in Germany, tho Dr. Bickel and some others had been pastors here; but it has sustained a part of the missionaries, aided in building chapels and churches, helping the theological seminaries, etc., especially in their missionary work in Austria, Hungary, Rumania, Bulgaria and East Switzerland. Emigration has carried off large numbers of their members and will do so still, but they show a fair net increase.

The Baptist work in Russia was commenced as a mission enterprise from Germany in 1851, at the same time as work in Lithuania and the Silesian Mountains. Progress was rapid notwithstanding severe opposition, and in 1888 the Russian churches hitherto included in reports from Germany were set apart. There are (1902) 117 preachers, 108 churches, 22,244 members; and in Finland 12 preachers, 34 churches, 2,133 members.

On the ship that carried Messrs. Colman and Wheelock to Burma (1817) were several Swedes and Norwegians. Some of these were converted and commenced work in their homes. Other sailors were converted in New York and Hamburg. One was ordained and a church was organized in Gothenburg in 1848. Soon after the Rev. Andreas Wiberg, a well known scholar of the Lutheran church in Sweden, joined the Baptist community, others of influence were added, and, by the help of the American Baptist Publications Society and the ABMU, the work has grown until there are (1902) in Sweden 764 preachers, 568 churches, 42,011 members, and in Norway, 16 preachers, 35 churches, with 2,707 members.

In 1870 the ABMU adopted a work commenced in Spain a few years earlier by Prof. W. J. Knapp, an independent missionary. The work has not progressed rapidly. There are 4 preachers, 4 churches, and 135 members.

Summary: The Society was organized in 1814 with two missionaries in the foreign field, and with but a single convert from heathenism in 1819, had, in 1840, 97 missionaries, 68 churches, 44 schools, and more than 2,900 baptized believers; and an income of $56,948.42. In 1870 the number of communicants had grown to 48,763; the force of missionaries was 127, the income amounting to $217,510.56. In 1902 478 missionaries of the Union were laboring in 7 heathen countries and preaching the Gospel in more than 25 languages. The converts in heathen lands alone numbered 111,650, organized into 1,003 churches, of which 668 were entirely self-supporting. In heathen lands there were 1,473 schools of all grades with 37,356 pupils, 2 colleges and 7 theological and Bible schools for the training of a native ministry. The receipts from all sources (1902) reached $624,713.79 and the average annual income for the previous five years was $653,777.

PERIODICALS published by the Society and Auxiliaries: *The Baptist Missionary Magazine; The Helping Hand* (Woman's Societies); *Around the World* (for young people). GENERAL LITERATURE: Smith (S. F.), *Missionary Sketches,* Boston, 1879 and 1883; *Rambles in Mission Fields,* Boston, 1884; Downie (D.), *The Lone Star* (the Telugu Mission), Philadelphia, 1893; Saillens (R.), *Au Pays des Tenebres;* Histoire de la Premiere Mission au Congo, Paris, 1889; Titterington (Mrs. S. B.), *A Century of Baptist Missions,* Philadelphia, 1891; *Jubilee Conference of ABMU Mission in Assam,* Calcutta, 1887.

AMERICAN BIBLE SOCIETY: Headquarters, Bible House, Astor Place, New York City, U.S.A.

Undenominational, representing all the evangelical communities of the United States. Combines both home and foreign work.

History: Prior to the Declaration of Independence, the American colonies of Great Britain had been dependent on the mother country for all their English Bibles. The hostilities which ensued cut off the supply of books printed in London, and a memorial was addressed to the Continental Congress urging that body to undertake the publication of an edition of the Scriptures. The committee to which the matter was referred, after consultation with printers in Philadelphia, reported that the cost of an edition of the Bible would exceed £10,000, and that neither the type nor the paper could be procured in this country, but recommended the purchase, at the expense of Congress, of 20,000 copies in Holland, Scotland, or elsewhere. During the next thirty years private enterprise did much to meet the immediate wants of the nation, but failed of course to reach the homes of indifference and poverty.

The British and Foreign Bible Society was organized in 1804 at London, and its first foreign edition of the Scriptures was The Gospel of John (2,000 copies), in Mohawk and English. This was followed by efforts to secure an organization in America which resulted in the formation of the Philadelphia Bible Society in 1809. Similar societies were also formed in Connecticut, Massachusetts, New Jersey and New York, all with the well-defined object of putting the Scriptures into every destitute family within the immediate circle of their direct influence, and through the thinly settled regions on the frontier.

Samuel J. Mills, one of the four who, at the haystack prayer-meeting at Williams College, gave the impulse that resulted in the formation of the ABCFM, after his graduation from Andover Seminary in 1812 made two tours of investigation, and his report that the number of families found without the Bible far exceeded all expectations raised a deep conviction that some more efficient means must be found for meeting the want.

Early in 1816 Elias Boudinot, President of the New Jersey Bible Society made a public communication in favor of a national Bible movement. The New York Bible Society followed this with formal action, resulting in the calling of a convention, which met May 8, 1816, in the consistory of the Reformed Dutch Church in Garden Street, and organized the American Bible Society. Thirty-five local organizations united in this action, and eighty-four became auxiliary to it during the first year of its existence.

In the earlier years the offices of the Society were in the lower part of New York, but the great increase of work necessitated better accommodations, and in 1853 it took possession of its present quarters. The outlay involved in this building was provided for by individual subscriptions made for the purpose and by rentals received after its completion, no funds raised for publication and distribution being invested in it.

Constitution and Organization: The American Bible Society is incorporated under the laws of the State of New York for the sole purpose of publishing and circulating the Holy Scriptures without note or comment. It is required by its by-laws to put the prices of all its publications as low as possible, and practically sells them at lower prices than would be charged if all the ordinary elements of cost were taken into account.

The business of the Society is conducted by a Board of Managers consisting of thirty-six laymen, residents of New York or its vicinity, one-fourth of whom go out of office every year, but may be re-elected. Any minister of the Gospel who has been made a life-member by the contribution of thirty dollars is entitled to be present and vote at the monthly meetings of the Board, with all the power of an elected manager. The executive officers are three corresponding secretaries and a treasurer; district secretaries are employed in the United States, while the foreign work is chiefly under the care of specially appointed agents. A large number of Auxiliary societies are in close relation with the National Society. These are expected to see that their own districts are well supplied through depositories, colporteurs, or voluntary agents, and to donate any surplus to the National Society for the general work. Until 1874 the Society had only two special agencies, in the Levant and La Plata. That number has been increased, until now it has its own representatives in Brazil, Central America, China, Cuba, Japan and Korea, La Plata, The Levant, Mexico, Philippines, Porto Rico, Siam and Venezuela. These agencies are, some of them, quite large, and have the charge of the translation and manufacture of Bibles, as well as of their distribution, chiefly through colporteurs. It also acts through the various missionary societies that naturally look to it as an American organization for assistance in their Bible work, or through other local Bible societies—*e.g.*, the Bible Society of France. This action takes the form of grants of Scriptures when the versions used are published by the Society, and of sums of money for expense of colportage or printing or purchase of Scriptures not published by the Society.

In the foreign field the aim is always to work in complete harmony with other organizations of whatever kind that have the same end in view. Whether at home or abroad, it is the conviction of the Society that the best results are reached by *sale*, tho without profit, rather than by free distribution. This does not preclude special grants, but such are discouraged rather than encouraged.

Versions and Translations of the Bible Circulated: As early as 1818 plates of the New Testament in Spanish were procured for the Spanish-speaking nations of America, and at the same time provision was made for giving the printed Gospel to some tribes of North American Indians. Others followed, until the whole number comprises more than eighty languages and dialects. Many of these have been printed on the Society's own presses, or immediately at its own expense, while others have been printed or purchased by means of grants to missionary societies.

A large portion of these versions have been prepared by missionaries, the expense of publication having been assumed by the Bible Society. Within the first seven years $37,000 was thus expended. The establishment of distinct foreign agencies has lessened the amounts paid directly to the Missionary Boards, but the Society aways looks to the missionaries of every name for the hearty cooperation which it has received in the past, and tho "the Board will favor versions in any language which in point of fidelity and catholicity shall be conformed to the principles upon which the American Bible Society was originally founded," ordinarily no translation is printed and published until a committee of missionaries or other persons skilled in the language have given it their approbation.

Among the more important versions are the Chinese (Mandarin, classical, and a number of colloquials); Japanese; Siamese; Korean; Mongolian; Armenian; Bulgarian; Turkish; Arabic; several of the dialects of the Pacific islands, and a number in Africa. Conspicuous among them all stands the Arabic version, prepared at the sole expense of the American Society, and which is recognized by scholars everywhere as one of the finest versions of the Bible in existence.

Development of Foreign Work: It was natural that the attention of the Society should be directed to the Spanish colonies of America. In 1818 plates of the New Testament in Spanish were procured, and a few years later a special report in regard to Mexico led to the sending of supplies of Scriptures to that country. South America also was visited about the same time by an exploring expedition sent out by the American Board, and in 1833 the Bible Society sent a special representative to report on the conditions along the west coast. No continuous work was done, however, beyond the making of grants to the missionary societies, until 1864, when a regular agent, Mr. Andrew W. Milne, was placed in charge of the La Plata field.

The development of missionary work in other parts of the world was not overlooked, and grants in aid of versions and for the distribution of Scriptures were made in many countries. In 1836 the Rev. Simeon H. Calhoun was appointed to represent the Society in Syria, but he served only a few years, and it was not until 1854, when the Rev. C. N. Righter was sent to Constantinople, that the Levant Agency was fairly inaugurated. In 1876 there was a new impulse given to the work by the sending of the Rev. Luther Halsey Gulick, M.D., to China and Japan, and of the Rev. A. L. Blackford to Brazil. It was not long before Dr. Gulick realized that the field entrusted to him was too large for any one man, and he devoted himself to China, leaving Japan, with the subsequent addition of Korea, to form a separate agency. From that time the advance was rapid. Special agents were appointed in 1878 for Mexico; 1882 for Cuba; 1888 for Venezuela; to which Colombia has been added, 1890 for Siam and Laos; 1892 for Central America. The opportunities opened up by the war with Spain were promptly met; both as regards the needs of the army and of the newly acquired provinces; and special agents were commissioned to Porto Rico and the Philippines.

In this general development, as was inevitable, the Society's work has frequently come into close relations with that of the British and Foreign Bible Society. In some cases there has been arranged a division of territory; in others, a combination of forces; while in others the two great societies have worked side by side, each realizing that there was work enough for both.

Statement of Foreign Work: South America: The American Bible Society has three agencies in South America: the La Plata, Brazil, and Venezuela and Colombia. The La Plata agency covers all of South America not included in the other two, especially Argentina, Uruguay, Paraguay, Ecuador, Peru, Chile and Bolivia. The Rev. Andrew W. Milne is still in charge (1903) after nearly forty years of service, with his headquarters at Buenos Aires, Argentina. The language used is chiefly Spanish, though there are versions of portions of the Bible in some of the Indian dialects, notably the Quichua and Aimara. This Agency has had from its inception to contend not only with the bitter hostility of the Roman Catholic priesthood, but with the opposition of the new governments to every form of evangelical work, which, however, is changing to a more favorable attitude. The following summary by decades shows how vigorously the work has been prosecuted:

Decades.	Bibles.	Testaments.	Portions.	Totals
From 1864 to 1870	5,579	7,631	10,417	23,627
From 1871 to 1880	15,347	18,347	45,415	79,467
From 1881 to 1890	37,671	41,193	117,644	196,508
From 1891 to 1900	59,599	60,765	145,856	266,220
	118,196	127,936	319,332	565,822

The Brazil Agency is distinct from the rest of South America on account of the use of the Portuguese language. The work of Bible distribution from the headquarters at Rio de Janeiro is rendered easier than in the La Plata agency by the railways recently built and by the river navigation; but the general conditions are much the same: hostility on the part of most of the ruling class (with a few notable exceptions), as well as of the ecclesiastics; and absolute indifference on the part of the people. Each year, however, shows advance, and the total (1902) of 330,772 volumes distributed since 1876 shows the seed sown.

The Agency for Venezuela and Colombia, which has its headquarters at Bucaramanga, Colombia, is probably the most difficult field occupied by the Society. The continued revolutions, with the consequent disturbance of economic and social conditions; the rigid censorship, making it impossible for the agent to report fully and freely, have (1902) hampered severely. Yet, even under such conditions, more than 90,000 Scriptures were circulated in thirteen years; and with the establishment of peace and the opening of the Panama canal, great advance is looked for.

Central America: This agency covers all the States of Central America and has its headquarters at Guatemala City, Guatemala. The present agent (Rev. F. G. Penzotti) had a long and most trying experience in Bible work in South America, and the circulation of over 94,000 volumes in nine years, mostly in Spanish, is witness to his activity and success.

Mexico: From his headquarters at Mexico City, the agent of the Bible Society superintends the work both in Mexico and along the frontier in Texas. In no agency has there been more of individual labor, and special reference should be made to the work of Miss Melinda Rankin on the Texan border in 1852 and later. The circulation is chiefly in Spanish, and during the twenty-three years from the founding of the agency, numbered over 408,000 volumes.

Cuba and Porto Rico: The headquarters of these two agencies are at Havana and San Juan. The circulation in both is chiefly in Spanish and amounted in Cuba in nineteen years to 98,000 volumes, and in Porto Rico in three years to about 10,000, while in 1902, as many more were circulated.

The Levant: The prominent part taken by American missionary societies in the Levant has marked it from the first as a special field of the American Bible Society. The agency was at first somewhat undefined in extent, but included in general the entire Turkish Empire, in Europe, Asia, and Africa, with Greece and Persia, while a general superintendence of southern Russia and the Caucasus was conducted from the headquarters at Constantinople. Northern Africa, west of Egypt, was dropped; Greece was handed over to the British and Foreign Bible Society; Persia was for a few years made a separate agency, and the share of the American Society in Russia was confined to assistance rendered to the Russian Bible Society. At present the agency includes Bulgaria, European Turkey, Asia Minor, Mesopotamia, Syria, Egypt, and the Sudan. The agent's office is at the **Bible House,** Constantinople, and there are subagents at Beirut and Alexandria.

Few agencies reach so great a number of races and languages. The Scriptures are sold in Arabic, Turkish (printed in three characters—Arabic, Armenian, and Greek), Armenian (Ancient, Ararat, and Modern), Greek (Ancient and Modern), Kurdish, Persian, Syriac (Ancient and Modern), Hebrew, Judeo-Spanish, Bulgarian, Slavic, Rumanian, Croatian, Russian, besides all the languages of Europe.

One characteristic feature of this agency is that the great majority of the Scriptures distributed in it are manufactured at the Bible House, Constantinople, and the Presbyterian Mission Press at Beirut. The work done at both places compares very favorably with the best work in the United States. Special versions have been prepared, some of them of the whole Bible, as the Arabic, Turkish, Armenian, Bulgarian; others of portions in special dialects. These have been printed in numerous editions to suit the taste of every class of men, from the Turkish or Christian ecclesiastic to the poorest day laborer. The total circulation of nearly 2,000,000 copies has been almost entirely by sale, the prices, however, being placed within the reach of the people, with comparatively little regard to the cost of the book. Thus a Bible in plain binding, which costs the Society $2 for printing and binding alone, is sold for 60 cents.

In Persia the British and Foreign Bible Society occupies the southern portion of the field, and the American Society's work in Northern Persia is conducted through the Presbyterian Mission.

China: The first regular agent of the American Bible Society to China was Rev. Luther H. Gulick, M.D., who was appointed in 1876. A son of a veteran missionary to the Hawaiian Islands, and himself connected with mission work in Micronesia, and afterward in Italy and Spain, he proved admirably adapted to the work of organization that devolved upon him. Japan was also at first included with China under Dr. Gulick's care, but was, in 1881, made a distinct agency, and Siam was added, but was itself also made independent in 1889.

The flexibility that has marked the conduct of the Society's work is illustrated in China, where the entire agency is divided into six colporteur districts, each under the care of a foreign superintendent to whom the native colporteurs report, while the general agent has his headquarters at Shanghai.

As was natural, the first efforts of the agency were put forth in the line of Bible translation, and as fast as portions could be prepared they were offered for sale. The number of copies sent out from two of the three presses during the first year was 39,371, of which over 33,000 were portions. This number was nearly doubled the next year, and in 1901 the total circulation was 428,927, including 12,341 Bibles, 32,334 Testaments and 384,252 portions; and this was a considerable falling off from the previous year owing to the Boxer outbreak.

The work of translation still continues, the different missionary societies uniting with the British and Foreign, Scotch National, and American Bible Societies to secure as great uniformity and accuracy as possible. The manufacture is carried on chiefly at Shanghai, but also at Fuchau and at Yokohama, in Japan. A conception of the work will be gained from the following table of publications in 1901:

Place of Publication.	Dialect.	Book.	Volumes.	Pages.
Shanghai.	Mandarin	New Test..	5,000	2,750,000
"	"	Genesis....	20,000	2,160,000
"	"	Matthew...	40,600	2,764,000
"	"	Mark......	40,000	1,760,000
"	"	Luke......	40,600	3,008,000
"	"	John......	40,000	2,320,000
"	"	Acts.......	40,000	2,880,000
"	Classical	New Test..	2,000	580,000
"	"	Matthew...	500	25,000
"	Shanghai Colloq..	Gen.-Ruth	500	211,500
"	Soochow "	Gen.-Ruth	500	211,500
Fuchau.	Classical	Bible......	3,000	3,576,000
"	Fuchau Colloquial	New Test..	6,000	5,118,000
"	"	Mark......	3,000	228,000
Yokohama,	Mandarin	Bible......	5,000	5,410,000
"	"	New Test..	12,000	6,600,000
"	"	Psalms....	6,000	756,000
"	Canton Colloquial.	New Test..	2,000	1,136,000
"	Classical	New Test..	7,000	4,608,000
Total			273,700	46,102,000

An interesting and significant fact in Bible work in China was the interest taken in it by the young Emperor and the preparation and presentation to the Empress Dowager of a magnificent copy of the Scriptures in 1899.

Japan and Korea: On receiving information in 1872 that a Japanese version of some of the Gospels was nearly complete, the Society promptly made a grant to promote its publication. It subsequently assumed the support of Drs. S. R. Brown and D. C. Greene, and bore a considerable part of the expense of translating the New Testament, which appeared in parts and was completed in 1880. The next year Japan was made a separate agency, and was so conducted until 1890, when the narrowness of the field and the peculiar intermingling of interests led to an arrangement between the American Bible Society, the British and Foreign Bible Society, and the National Bible Society of Scotland to act in unison, apportioning the territory between them, and acting under a general Bible Society's Committee consisting of six missionaries appointed by the American Bible Society, four by the British and Foreign Bible Society and two by the National Bible Society of Scotland. The American Society is represented by an agent residing at Yokohama. The work done is indicated by the figures of circulation in 1901: 5,505 Bibles; 27,615 Tests.; 148,372 portions; total, 181,492. It is notable that nearly one-third of the Bibles and Testaments were in English. Of the total, about one-half was assigned to the American Society.

The work in Korea, under the general care of the agent at Yokohama, is as yet not fully organized. The work of translation is still going on and the distribution is for the most part under the care of the missionaries.

Siam and Laos: Bible work in Siam was for many years carried on by the missionaries of the PN under the general direction of Dr. Gulick; but as the work enlarged both in China and Siam, a division became necessary, especially as the advance included the Laos people on the north. The headquarters of the agent are at Bangkok, where also most of the printing is done. From the organization in 1890 to 1902 the circulation was 282,954, the last year showing 37,216, an advance of 5,484 over the previous year. Of these, the great majority, 32,521, were Siamese, 3,615 Chinese, 942 Laos, the remainder Tamil, Cambodian, Malay and English.

Philippine Islands: This latest agency of the Society was established in 1899, and covers the entire archipelago. The agent's office is in Manila. The circulation for the first year was, naturally, small, but the second year rose to 52,793, and in 1902 to 91,260. The New Testament in Tagalog has been completed by the BFBS, which had commenced the translation before the outbreak of the Spanish War. As yet only the Gospels have been translated into Pampanga and Ilocano, but the work is going on as rapidly as possible. The printing is done in Japan.

The total issues of the Society for the year 1902 were 1,993,558, of which 734,649 were distributed in the United States (including Porto Rico and Hawaii), and 1,258,909 copies in foreign lands. The total issues of the Society in 87 years amounted to 72,670,783 copies.

The Bible Society Record, an illustrated monthly, is the Society's official organ.

AMERICAN BOARD OF COMMISSIONERS FOR FOREIGN MISSIONS:

I. History: In 1806 Samuel J. Mills, with three other students of Williams College, fled for refuge from a thunder storm to the shelter of a hay-stack, and while waiting there pledged themselves to the work of foreign missions. Later they entered Andover Theological Seminary. In 1810 Samuel J. Mills, Gordon Hall, Adoniram Judson, Samuel Newell and Samuel Nott, students in the Seminary, conferred with the faculty, and a number of prominent ministers, in the home of Professor M. Stuart, and were counseled, "Go in the name of the Lord, and we will help." The next day two of these ministers, Drs. S. Spring and S. Worcester, outlined a plan for organizing the American Board of Commissioners for Foreign Missions, which three days later, on the twenty-ninth of June, was adopted by the General Association of Congregational Churches of Massachusetts at Bradford, Mass., and on September 5, 1810, at Farmington, Conn., a constitution was adopted and officers were elected. Dr. Worcester, the first secretary, prepared an address to the churches, and every effort was made to arouse interest in the new enterprise. The following year (1811) Judson was sent to England to confer with the London Missionary Society as to the advisability of cooperation, but the distance between the two organizations was deemed to make this inadvisable and he returned. In September of the same year Burma was selected as a promising field for the first enterprise of the Board. Owing to financial straits, it seemed unwise to attempt anything beyond what the actual cash on hand would warrant, and at a meeting of the Prudential Committee, January 27, 1812, there was at first but one vote—probably Dr. Worcester's—in favor of pledging the support of the men already appointed, but that one vote carried the day. It was decided to trust God, it was His work, and go forward, believing that the funds would be obtained. From this principle the Board has never departed.

By a special effort six thousand dollars was collected, and on February 6, 1812, Messrs. Judson, Hall, Newell, Nott and L. Rice were ordained at Salem, Mass., and before the end of the month Messrs. Judson and Newell, with their wives, sailed from Salem, and Messrs. Hall, Rice and Nott, with Mrs. Nott, from Philadelphia, for Calcutta.

The work thus being fairly inaugurated, the next step was to secure a charter from the Massachusetts Legislature. This met with some opposition, but at length on the 20th of June, the charter was granted, and the American Board had a legal existence.

It is doubtful whether the founders of the Board anticipated the support of other than Congregational churches, but at its second meeting in 1811, a proposition was made to the General Assembly of the Presbyterian Church for the organization of a similar society with which the Board might cooperate. The Assembly declined to do this, but recommended the Presbyterian churches to work through the American Board. Accordingly at the next meeting of the Board, in 1812, eight commissioners were added to represent the Presbyterian Church. In 1814 the number of Commissioners was increased by one number from the Associate Reformed Church, in 1816, by one from the Reformed (Dutch) Church, and later one from the Reformed German Church was added to the Board.

In 1825 a proposition was made by the United Foreign Missionary Society (Presbyterian), formed in 1817 for work among the Indians, for union with the American Board. This was cordially endorsed by the General Assembly, and for twelve years the Board represented officially the Presbyterian Church. In 1837, on the separation between the Old and New Schools, the former withdrew from support of the Board, and adopted the Western Foreign Missionary Society, formed in 1812, as their own organization. The New School branch of the Presbyterian Church continued to work with the American Board until 1870, when they withdrew to support the Board of Foreign Missions of the reunited Presbyterian Church. In 1857 the Reformed Dutch Church established its own Board; the next year the Associate Reformed Presbyterians became a part of the United Presbyterian Church, and took up a distinct work; and in 1865 the Reformed German Church did the same, so that since 1870 the Board has practically represented Congregationalists alone.

The ABCFM now (1902) has in the different fields an aggregate of 549 American missionaries, 3,581 trained Christian native workers, 524 churches with 55,645 communicants, 14 theological schools, 118 boarding and high schools, with 10,895 students, 1,134 other schools with 46,149 pupils. Contributions from missionary fields in the year ending in July, 1902, were $167,512; in America, $677,593.85; total receipts, $845,105.85.

Coordinate with the growth of the Board itself has been that of its great auxiliaries, the three Woman's Boards. As far back as 1812 several missionary associations of women aided the ABCFM, and these were gradually so systematized that in 1839 there were no less than 680 with nearly 3,000 local agents.

In 1868, the Woman's Board of Foreign Missions was organized, auxiliary to the American Board. At first the formation of an interdenominational society was contemplated. On the first Tuesday of January, 1868, about forty ladies met in Boston, and a proposition of the American Board for cooperation with it was submitted to them, and a resolution was adopted "to cooperate with the American Board in its several departments of labor for the benefit of our sex in heathen lands." Committees of ladies were appointed to prepare a constitution and list of officers; and on the ensuing week, at the same place, the New England Women's Foreign Missionary Society was organized.

By the special request of leading members of other denominational Boards, and in accordance with the original plan of union of evangelical sects, the first article of the constitution was adopted as follows:—

"The object of this Society is to engage the earnest, systematic cooperation of the women of New England, with the existing Boards for Foreign Missions, in sending out and supporting unmarried female missionaries and teachers to heathen women."

While there was to be union under the organization, in conference, prayer, and the home department of work, the treasurer was to keep a denominational account, crediting each religious body composing the union with the sums received from its constituents, and paying the aggregate amount to the Foreign Missionary Society with which it was connected.

In September of the same year the constitution was altered, and the work of the Society was limited to the fields of the American Board. The restriction of work to New England was also removed, by changing the name to The Woman's Board of Missions, whereby ladies in any part of the land in sympathy with the American Board could become auxiliary to its work.

The following year the Woman's Board was incorporated by the Legislature of Massachusetts. Auxiliaries were formed among the women of the churches, and these were gathered into "Branches" having regularly appointed officers, constitutions, etc., each comprising not less than 20 auxiliaries and mission circles.

During the first year the support of 7 missionaries and 11 Bible women was assumed. The field of work has been extended gradually until the support of all single and some married women, of girls' boarding and day schools, of primary schools in part, of kindergarten work and of all Bible women laboring in the fields of the ABCFM is now provided by the Woman's Boards, which also sustain an extensive medical work.

There are (1902) 24 branches with 1,136 senior and 573 junior auxiliaries and mission circles, and 221 cradle rolls, a total of 1,930 organizations, which hold, upon an average, as many as 12,000 meetings yearly. Christian Endeavor Societies, King's Daughters and Sunday Schools are affiliated. The Woman's Board of Missions now has 131 missionaries in 18 fields; 33 girls' boarding schools, 300 day schools, 200 Bible women. Its annual receipts are $139,607.22.

The Woman's Board of Missions of the Interior, also organized in 1868, and embracing the sixteen States of the interior and northwest, has its headquarters at 153 LaSalle Street, Chicago. It publishes a monthly magazine, *Mission Studies*, and provides a department in *Life and Light for Woman*. The whole number of societies contributing last year was 2,320, of which 1,154 were seniors, 102 young ladies, 542 Christian Endeavor societies, and 522 children's societies, including Junior Christian Endeavor, mission bands, Sunday-schools, and wee folks' bands.

It supports 72 missionaries, 70 native Bible women, 136 native teachers, 2 colleges, 17 boarding schools, 2 training schools for Bible women, a kindergarten training school, and a large number of village and day schools; also evangelistic and medical work. Receipts, $80,820.01.

The Woman's Board of Missions of the Pacific was organized in 1873, and has five branches—Northern California, Southern California, Oregon, Washington, and Utah. It supports five missionaries, and helps in educational and medical work in India, China, and Japan. Receipts, $6,090.83.

II. *Constitution and Organization:* The ABCFM is a company incorporated under the laws of the State of Massachusetts, U. S. A., "for the purpose of propagating the Gospel in heathen lands by supporting missionaries and diffusing a knowledge of the Holy Scriptures." It is composed of corporate members, of whom one-third are by law laymen, one-third clergymen, and the remaining third may be chosen from either of these two classes. It is self-perpetuating, having full and sole power to fill all vacancies in its own body, elect officers, and to gave final decision on all matters relating to the management of the missions under its charge. It has no ecclesiastical character or relations, no organic connections with any church or body of churches, and is legally amenable to no authority except that of the Legislature of the State of Massachusetts, and to that only if it violates the terms of its charter. There has been, however, of late years an increasing desire on the part of the Congregational churches for closer, if not organic relations with the Board, and this has been recognized and met by the Board itself. The number of corporate members was increased to 350, and again to 500.

Efforts have been made to secure uniform representation from the different parts of the country, based in general on the proportion of annual contributions from each section. Nominations to membership in the Board are made by the various State Conferences or Associations, the Board itself reserving the right of election. The regular meetings of the Board are held in different sections of the country, in the month of October of each year.

The actual business of the Board is entrusted to a Prudential Committee consisting of the President and Vice-president *ex officio*, and twelve members, six ministers and six laymen. The executive officers are three Secretaries, an Editorial Secretary, and a Treasurer. The offices occupied in the earlier years of the Board's history were generally small rooms in tenement houses, except in 1820-21, when they were in the basement of Lyman Beecher's Church in Hanover Street. For many years they were at 33 Pemberton Sq., the property of the Board. They are now in the Congregational House, 14 Beacon Street, Boston.

III. *Development of Foreign Work:* The two missionary parties that sailed for Calcutta in 1812 had Burma for their objective point, but the hostility of the East India Company and a change of views on baptism by Messrs. Judson and Rice resulted in the establishment of the Marâthi Mission at Bombay in 1813. The next step, in 1816, to Ceylon, where Newell and his wife had visited, was a natural one. Meanwhile the interest grew, and mindful of the need of the heathen nearer home, the Board sent an exploring committee through Georgia and Alabama, whose report resulted in missions to the Cherokees, in 1817, and to the Choctaws, in 1818. In 1825 several missions started by the United Foreign Missionary Society were transferred to the Board, and in 1830-35 several other tribes were brought within the scope of their work.

Attention was then turned to the Levant. In 1819, Pliny Fisk and Levi Parsons landed at Malta, then removed to Smyrna, and from there visited Palestine, Alexandria, Syria and Cyprus. These visits and the translation and press-work done at Malta and Smyrna laid the foundation for the missions to Syria, Egypt, Asia Minor, Persia, Greece and Bulgaria.

Simultaneously with the sailing of Fisk and Parsons for the Levant, Bingham and Thurston, with several associates, set sail for the Hawaiian Islands.

The ten years from 1819 to 1829 were chiefly spent in strengthening the work already commenced; but then again the impulse forward could not be resisted. Bridgman and Abeel sailed for Canton and Eli Smith and Dwight conducted a grand exploring tour through Asiatic Turkey and Persia, which resulted in the commencement, in 1831, of the station at Constantinople, the general enlargement of work among the Armenians throughout Asia Minor, and the establishment, in 1834, of the mission to the Nestorians at Persia. The struggle of the Greeks for national existence had attracted the attention of the Christian world, and in 1831 Jonas King commenced a station at Athens. Abeel's journey from Canton to Singapore and Bangkok resulted in the formal opening of mission work in those places two and three years later. The slavery question and the efforts of the colonization societies had excited much interest in Africa, hardly yet known even as the Dark Continent, and the Gaboon mission on the West Coast was started at Cape Palmas in 1834, and that to the Zulus in Southeastern Africa in 1835, but it was not until the bequest of Asa Otis, amounting ultimately to over a million dollars, that the ABCFM felt able to undertake work in other parts of Africa.

The early growth of the missions was rapid, new fields ever opening before the Board. In 1834 work was begun in Madura, India; in 1836, Eastern Turkey; in 1847, Central Turkey and Fuchau, China. Assyria was occupied in 1851; Micronesia in 1852; North China in 1854; European Turkey in 1859; Japan in 1869; Bulgaria in 1871. In 1872 the Board consented to undertake the care of the fields of the American and Foreign Christian Union in Papal Lands, and adopted the missions in Spain, Austria, Italy and Mexico. In 1880 it entered West Central Africa; in 1882 Shan-si, China; in 1883 East Central Africa; and in 1902 the Philippine Islands.

In 1857 the Amoy Mission in China and the Arcot Mission in India were transferred to the care of the Reformed Church in America, and in 1860 the Assyrian Mission was merged in that of Eastern Turkey; in 1870 the Persian, Syrian and Gaboon Missions, and two of the Indian Missions were transferred to the reunited Presbyterian Church; the other missions to the North American Indians were either developed into self-supporting churches or transferred to other societies; in 1871 the Hawaiian Islands practically assumed self-support.

IV. *The Missions of the Board;* 1. *Marathi Mission:* Driven from Calcutta, on their arrival in 1812, and deprived of their associates, Mr. and Mrs. Nott and Mr. Hall, after many trials, established themselves at Bombay in 1813 They found the Governor, Sir Evan Nepeau, a warm friend, a vice-president of the BFBS, and immediately began to preach, and set about the work of preparing a translation of the Bible and other Christian literature, and opened schools. Other missionaries were sent to join them and new stations were opened. The first convert was Kader Yar Khan, a Muslim, baptized in 1869. The first church was organized at Bombay in 1826 and the first pastor ordained in 1854. The mission has suffered from the famines 1876-8 and 1896-7 and from the bubonic plague

The mission has (1902) 8 stations and 124 outstations; 42 American missionaries; 553 native workers; 54 churches with 5,607 communicants; 185 Sabbath schools; 20 schools for higher education with 3,597 pupils; 156 common schools, and the grand total under Christian instruction in the mission is 9,093. Industrial and medical work are carried on; orphanages and widows' homes have been established; Christian Endeavor Societies flourish; the *Dnyanodaya,* a weekly paper, and the *Balbodh Mewa,* a monthly illustrated magazine for young people, are issued regularly.

2. *Ceylon:* In 1813 Mr. Newell had urged the occupation of Ceylon, and in 1816 Messrs. Richards, Meigs and Poor reached Jaffna, followed by Messrs. Spaulding, Woodward, Myron, Winslow and John Scudder. The Ceylon Mission began at Battycotta and Tillipally in the ruins of Portuguese churches older than the settlement of America, and at Oodooville in the residence of an ancient Franciscan friar. From the very first great attention was paid to education and the preparation of literature. In 1826 Battycotta Seminary and Oodooville Female Boarding School were established, and in 1872 Jaffna College, which in 1895 organized the first college Association in the mission field. The work in Ceylon has been among the Tamils, and from the first the spiritual development has been noticeable.

There are now (1902) in this mission 6 stations and 31 outstations; 13 American missionaries; 412 native workers; 18 churches with 2,100 communicants; 5 schools for higher education; 136 common schools, and the aggregate of those under Christian instruction is 11,039. Jaffna College with 108 pupils is independent of the mission, but is in close relations with it. It is affiliated to Calcutta University. The churches have a native Evangelical Society for Home Missions, while a Students' Foreign Mission Society and a Woman's Society each support a missionary in Madura. The Christian Endeavor and YMCA also do good work.

3. *Madura:* In 1834 the Ceylon Mission sent Levi Spaulding to learn the condition of the Tamils of Southern India and the result was the establishment of the American Board's Madura Mission. The population of over 2,000,000 was overwhelmingly Hindu and largely of the weaver caste. The bitter hostility to the missionaries as the "pariahs" of the white people was met by the marked courtesy of the English, and largely overcome by the vigorous educational policy carried through by Mr. Poor. The most important educational institution, Pasumalai College and Training Institute, was opened in 1842 at Tirumangalam, but three years later was moved to Pasumalai, near Madura City. It has steadily increased in grade and expects to be affiliated to Madras University. Medical work, industrial training and publication of literature are carried on effectively. The Madura Mission has (1902) 11 stations and 355 outstations; 35 American missionaries; 645 native workers; 38 churches with 5,036 communicants; 268 Sabbath schools with 7643 pupils; 16 schools for higher education; 192 other schools, and the aggregate under Christian instruction in the mission is 8,059. The Christian Endeavor and YMCA are flourishing institutions. The mission has a printing house at Pasumalai, from which two periodicals are issued.

4. *Madras:* In 1836 Messrs. Winslow and Scudder established at Madras a printing house for works in the Tamil language. There was cordial cooperation with the missionaries of the LMS and the work grew until, by 1842, 53,180,467 pages had been printed, and the press was able not only to refund the purchase money, but to pay all expenses and to aid the general mission work by its profits. The death of Dr. Scudder in 1855, the removal of Mr. Winslow in 1864, the entrance of other societies led to the transfer of the press to other hands and the close of the station in 1866.

5. *Arcot:* The Arcot Mission was commenced by Dr. H. M. Scudder in 1850, in connection with the Madras Mission of the ABCFM, but in 1858 was transferred to the care of the Reformed Church in America.

6. *Sumatra:* Messrs. Munson and Lyman with their wives sailed in 1833 to explore the East Indian Archipelago; they reached Batavia in September.

Leaving their wives they proceeded to Tapanuli in Sumatra, and from there went to visit the Battas of the interior, arriving at the village of Sacca in June, 1834. A petty war was in progress and both fell victims to the rage of the combatants. When it became known that the strangers were good men who had come to help the people, the neighboring villages leagued together and laid Sacca waste. A thick jungle covers the spot, and even the name has passed from the place. The mission was not resumed.

7. *Siam:* In 1831 David Abeel commenced work at Bangkok, finding a friendly reception from the Portuguese Consul, but great hostility on the part of the King. He was, however, compelled to leave by ill health. Three years later reenforcements were sent to carry on the work, but found Mr. Abeel's converts organized into a church by a missionary of the ABMU. They remained for a time, devoting themselves largely to education and the preparation of literature, but with the entrance of other societies the work of the ABCFM was dropped in Siam in 1850.

8. *Singapore:* Work was begun in 1834 as a central point from which to reach southeastern Asia and the adjacent islands, but the decision of the Government of the Dutch East Indies to exclude all but missionaries sent from Holland defeated the plan, and the mission was closed in 1844.

9. *Borneo:* This mission, undertaken in 1836, was composed of members of the Reformed (Dutch) Church of America and derived its support through the American Board from that denomination. Efforts were directed specially to the Chinese and Dyaks. Many difficulties were encountered, both from the nature of the field and from the objections of Dutch officials. The missionaries labored faithfully until 1848, when failure of health compelled those then in charge to withdraw, and the failure to find recruits caused the mission to be discontinued.

10. *Hawaiian (Sandwich) Islands:* In 1779 these islands were brought into notice through the murder of Capt. Cook, and again, in 1809, when Henry Obookiah came to New Haven with two other Hawaiian boys, who were converted in 1813. In 1819 Hiram Bingham, Asa Thurston and others were sent to Hawaii as missionaries of the ABCFM, arriving March 31, 1820. Their arrival was opportune. The people had revolted against the tabu, destroyed the idols and their temples, and discarded for the moment their old religion. Four years later the principal chiefs agreed to recognize the Sabbath, and the ten commandments were adopted as the basis of government. In eight years there were 445 native teachers connected with the mission and 26,000 pupils in mission schools. The Bible was circulated, high chiefs became Christians, and in 1828, simultaneously and without communication, a revival unexpectedly commenced in Hawaii, Oahu and Maui, and in 1838 one of the most remarkable revivals in history began, lasting six years, and resulting in about 27,000 conversions. In 1850 the Hawaiian Evangelical Association was formed for work in their own and other islands, and in 1863 Christianity was dominant in the islands; there were churches, schools and colleges, printing presses and Christian literature, while the native church was sending missionaries to Micronesia and the Marquesas. Accordingly, the American Board practically withdrew from the field in that year. Many of the missionaries remained in the islands as pastors, teachers, etc., and the North Pacific Missionary Institute, for the training of native pastors, is still in charge of a missionary of the Board as well as the work among the Japanese immigrants.

11. *Micronesia:* This name is applied to four groups of coral islands in the Pacific Ocean. In 1852 Messrs. Snow, Gulick and Sturges, with their wives and two Hawaiian helpers, were sent to these islands by the ABCFM in cooperation with the Hawaiian Evangelical Association. They occupied two stations, Kusaie and Ponapi in the Caroline Group. For four years they had no certain communication with the outside world, depending on the none too friendly trading vessels for mail and supplies. In 1856 a missionary ship, the Morning Star, was built by the Board for work in these islands, and Mr. and Mrs. Hiram Bingham were sent to the Gilbert Island Mission, while Messrs. Pierson and Doane, with their wives, were stationed in the Marshall group. Languages were mastered and reduced to writing, simple books were laboriously prepared, schools were started and preaching services held, though the latter were difficult, and more was accomplished in the day schools and house to house visiting. For the work in these islands a "Missionary Navy" is essential. After the Spanish-American war in 1901, work was begun in the Ladrone Islands, with a station in Guam.

There are 4 stations and 63 outstations; 24 American and 1 Hawaiian missionaries; 149 native pastors and teachers; 57 churches, with 5,953 communicants; seven training schools, with 205 students; 85 native schools, with 3,297 pupils.

Owing to political and financial difficulties the transfer of this mission by the ABCFM to some English or German Society seems possible.

12. *Palestine and Syria:* Pliny Fisk and Levi Parsons, appointed missionaries to Jerusalem in 1819, landed at Smyrna, where Mr. Fisk stopped to study the language, while Mr. Parsons went on. A Greek revolt drove Mr. Fisk to Alexandria, and the coming of associates, followed by exploring journeys, resulted in the conviction that Syria offered the best location, and Beirut was selected, in 1824, as a missionary station. A printing establishment, part of whose equipment was afterward removed to Constantinople and part to Beirut, was set up at Malta out of reach of the Turkish Government. At Beirut and vicinity hostility developed into persecution, and war and pestilence again and again broke up the work. The first native church was organized in 1848. In 1870 the Syrian Mission was transferred to the care of the Presbyterian Church in the U. S. A.

13. *Asiatic Turkey:* Mr. Parsons on his first visit to Jerusalem met some Armenian pilgrims who said they would rejoice if a mission could be sent to their people. An Armenian ecclesiastic secured and translated a letter written by Jonas King on leaving Syria in 1827, and it produced a wonderful effect in Constantinople. Two years later, Messrs. Eli Smith and H. G. O. Dwight made their long journey through Asiatic Turkey, the Caucasus and Northern Persia, which opened up the condition of the Oriental churches to the Christian world and brought it face to face with the needs in that whole section. The result was the establishment of the station at Constantinople in 1831 by Mr. Goodell (with Messrs. Dwight and Schauffler), who came north from Beirut, bringing with him some publications issued at Malta. In quick succession Smyrna, Brousa, Trebizond, and Erzerum were occupied as stations. For a decade the strength of mis-

sionary effort was given to consolidation, and then commenced a new era of extension until by 1863 the entire region of Asia Minor, Northern Syria and Mesopotamia was dotted with missionary establishments.

The great extent of territory covered, the poor means of intercommunication, and the variety of problems in different sections led to the division of the work into three missions, Western, Eastern and Central Turkey. Each is a separate unit for administrative purposes, yet there is a bond of union in the fact that Constantinople is the center for the publication work and the financial management, as well as the place to which go all the questions concerning the relations with the government. The work of the Western Turkey mission is chiefly among Armenians and Greeks; of the Eastern mission chiefly among Armenians, tho one station, Mardin, reaches the Jacobites, the legacy of the old Assyria Mission; the Central is almost entirely among Armenians who have the peculiarity that their language is Turkish. The Western mission embraces also that portion of European Turkey where Armenians are principally found. There have been efforts to reach other classes. W. G. Schauffler was commissioned first to the Jews and afterward devoted himself specially to the Turks, but the great work of the ABCFM in Turkey has been among Armenians and Greeks.

Education has always held a prominent place. The American College for Girls at Constantinople, Euphrates College at Harput, Anatolia College at Marsovan and Central Turkey College at Aintab, as well as the different theological schools and academies, are missionary institutions. There has been excellent literary work done in Bible translation, in general book publications and in the weekly and monthly periodicals. The missions suffered heavily during the massacres of 1894-5, but have to a considerable degree recovered themselves.

The missions of the ABCFM in Asiatic Turkey have 12 stations and 270 outstations; 145 missionaries; 811 native workers; 114 organized churches with 13,125 communicants; 132 high grade and 1,134 lower schools with a total of 60,964 under instruction.

14. *Persia:* One of the results of the tour of exploration by Messrs. Smith and Dwight was to attract attention to the Nestorians in northwestern Persia and in the mountains of the Turkish border. In 1833 Justin Perkins sailed for that work, and two years later he and Dr. Asahel Grant opened a station at Urmiya. They received a warm welcome from the Patriarch, Mar Yohannan, and the work prospered, especially that for girls and women under the care of Fidelia Fiske. In 1870 this mission was transferred to the Presbyterian Church in the U. S. A.

15. *European Turkey:* Work was commenced among the Bulgarians at Adrianople in 1858, in connection with the Western Turkey mission, but as new stations were formed, the European Turkey Mission was organized, the literary work of the new mission being carried on at Constantinople, however, until after the establishment of the Principality of Bulgaria. Various political disturbances have hampered missionary operations, but have never stopped them.

This mission has (1902) 4 stations and 56 outstations; 28 missionaries; 85 native workers; 16 churches with 1,415 communicants; 3 higher grade and 19 other schools, with a total of 787 under instruction.

16. *Greece:* The great interest felt in America in the Greek struggle for independence turned the attention of Christian benevolence to that country, and Jonas King was called from Beirut to Athens to disburse the gifts for the sufferers. He remained there as a missionary of the American Board until his death in 1869. A few other missionaries were sent to Greece by the Board, but the work farther east seemed more important and promising, and with his death the mission was discontinued.

17. *China, Canton* (1830): Elijah C. Bridgman and David Abeel, the latter under the American Seaman's Friend Society, sailed from New York October 14, 1829, and arrived in Canton, February 25, 1830. After two years study of the language Mr. Bridgman issued the first number of the *Chinese Repository*. In 1833 S. Wells Williams and Ira Tracy joined the mission, followed the next year by Dr. Peter Parker. Owing to the opium war of 1840, the work was suspended till 1845, when it was resumed under many restrictions. In 1847 Mr. Bridgman was transferred to Shanghai. A civil war in 1854 and a war with England in 1856 again interrupted the work; the missionaries were expelled and their houses, printing establishment and books destroyed by fire. The treaty of 1858 with the foreign Powers guaranteed the toleration of Christianity in all parts of the Empire, and the work was again resumed and continued till 1866, when, other societies coming in, and the working force becoming greatly depleted by death, the mission was discontinued.

18. *Amoy* (1842): Established by David Abeel, who was joined in 1844 by two missionaries, members of the Reformed Church in America, which then cooperated with the American Board. In 1857 the work of Amoy was transferred by the ABCFM to the Board of Missions of that church.

19. *Fuchau* (1847): Established by Stephen Johnson and Lyman B. Peet, who was transferred from the mission in Siam. Reenforcements were sent out in 1848, 1850 and in 1853, when a small boarding school for boys and girls was opened. In 1857 the first church was formed of 4 members. The New Testament was translated into the Fuchau dialect and the first edition published, in 1866, by the American Board and Methodist Episcopal Missions conjointly. Work on the Old Testament was begun, but not completed fully till 1888. The American Female College was dedicated in 1881. The first Christian Endeavor Society of the Mission, as well as of the country, was formed in 1885. In 1893 the native Woman's Missionary Society was formed. Evangelistic, Educational, Medical and Literary work are carried on, and the aim of the mission is self-support in all departments.

In the Fuchau Mission, there are 5 stations, 96 outstations, 38 American Missionaries with 210 native workers; 62 churches with 2,486 communicants, 2 theological schools, 2 colleges, 5 boarding schools, 90 common schools, 4 hospitals with 452 patients; 10 dispensaries with 30,857 outpatients; native workers contributed $4,844.59.

20. *North China Mission* (1860): Elijah C. Bridgman was transferred from Canton to

Shanghai in 1847, to assist in translating the Scriptures. In 1854 he was joined by Messrs. Atchison and Blodgett, thus forming the Shanghai Mission; in 1860 the Mission was transferred to Tientsin, the key to the surrounding country, and the name was changed to the North China Mission. A year later the first convert was baptized. In 1864 the famous Bridgman School was opened. In 1869 the only printing press under the control of Protestant Missions in North China was established. Besides the work of the Mission, it has done printing for the American Bible Society, the Church Missionary Society, the Russian Ecclesiastical Mission, and the North China Tract Society. The Boxer movement of 1900 temporarily interrupted the work of the Mission; Mission buildings were destroyed, and missionaries and native Christians were massacred or fled for their lives. Indemnities have since been promised, and in some instances paid, and the outlook is full of hope.

There are in this mission (1902) 7 stations, 50 outstations, 52 American missionaries and 56 native workers; 8 churches with 1,455 communicants; 1 theological seminary, 1 college, 8 boarding and high schools, 9 common schools; 3 hospitals, 3 dispensaries.

21. *Shansi Mission* (1882): Established at Tai-yuen-fu by Martin L. Stimson. Eleven millions of people inhabit Shan-si Province, of high natural ability but addicted to opium. Refuges have been established, and evangelistic and medical work is carried on. The first church was organized in 1888. The following year a boys' boarding school was opened. The work was interrupted by the Boxer movement of 1900, but has since been resumed, with added opportunities for usefulness.

There are (1902) 2 stations, 4 American missionaries, 9 native workers, 2 churches with 134 communicants, 1 orphanage, 1 common school, with 28 pupils.

22. *South China Mission* (1883): Formerly known as the Hongkong Mission, established by C. R. Hager; the American Board occupies the field at the earnest solicitation of Christian Chinese of California, the greater number of whom came from the Province of Canton. The field of this mission is inhabited by 2,000,000 people. For the first few years the work of the Mission was considered tentative. During 8 years there was but one missionary in the field, but in spite of hindrance the work has been successful. A building answering for church, missionary residence, station headquarters, etc., has been erected at a cost of $16,000, the larger part of this amount having been given by the natives. The people are as accessible as before the Boxer movement of 1900, while the obstacles are growing less. The Chinese Christians in California cooperate with the Mission in its outstation work. There are 2 stations and 20 outstations; 6 American missionaries, 37 native workers; 4 churches with 1,090 communicants; 1 boarding school and 10 common schools; 1 dispensary.

23. *Western Africa:* In November, 1833, Rev. J. L. Wilson and Mr. S. R. Wyncoop embarked at Baltimore in a vessel sent out by the Maryland Colonization Society, and reached Cape Palmas early in the following year. Having decided upon Cape Palmas as a favorable location, they returned to America. The mission was established in December, 1834, by Mr. Wilson and his wife, greatly to the joy of the natives. The negroes of the Guinea coast were found to be fearfully degraded. Schools were established, missionary reenforcements sent out and new stations opened. In 1836 there were 100 pupils in the schools, many of them from the far interior; a printing press was set up; a church with 6 members organized. In 1837 the Board was compelled to lessen its expenditures. It was a serious blow to this mission. Printing ceased, 2 schools were closed, the boarding school reduced, the natives discouraged and confidence was impaired. Then followed the inimical French occupation, and the abominations connected with the relations of foreign traders with Africa. In 1843 the mission was removed to the Gaboon, on account of the attitude of the American Colony from Maryland.

24. *The Gaboon Mission:* Was organized at Cape Palmas in 1835. The new location brought the mission into contact with nobler races, as the Mpongwes and Bakeles. Two dialects were reduced to writing, and many heard the Gospel gladly. Under great difficulties from the climate, the temper of the natives, and adverse foreign influences, it maintained itself and made a good record in school and church work during the thirty-five years of its connection with the Board. In 1870, this mission was transferred to the care of the Presbyterian Board.

25. *Zulu Mission* (1835): Established by Messrs. Lindsay, Venable, Wilson, Grout, Champion, and Dr. Adams. It was the first organized effort of any society in this region; the people were savage and their language unwritten and unknown. Dingaan, the chief of the Zulus, received the missionaries, and schools were opened and a printing press set up. Repeated conflicts between the Zulus and Dutch Boers hindered the work for the first years, and twice the missionaries were compelled to flee. The Board had decided to discontinue the attempt to labor amid such adverse conditions, when, in 1843, Natal became a British colony. From that time the work has gone steadily forward. The native population increased rapidly; Sabbath congregations and day schools became large and prosperous; churches were formed and schools established; government allotments of land for mission purposes and annual grants-in-aid for schools were secured. In 1846 the first convert, an old woman, was baptized. Her son afterward became pastor of the church of which she was the first member, and her grandson was the first Zulu to receive a full medical education. In 1870 began a decisive conflict between heathenism and Christianity, which resulted in a more intelligent and decided Christian living in the converts. In 1883 the translation and publication of the entire Scriptures was completed, and a hymn book has since been issued. The Umzumbe Home and Inanda Seminary are for the higher education of the girls, while the High and Normal School at Amanzimtote gives the boys a similar opportunity. In 1892 a hospital and dispensary were opened by Dr. Bridgman. A feature of the mission is the Zulu Home and Foreign Mission Society, which supports 5 evangelists. New opportunities have resulted since the close of the Boer War, and a larger field than ever before is open to the Zulu Mission. There are (1902) 11 stations and 13 outstations; 31 American missionaries; 397 native workers;

23 churches; 3,555 communicants; 1 theological seminary; 3 schools for higher education with 389 students; 50 common schools with 2,500 pupils; 1 hospital and a dispensary.

26. *East Central African Mission* (1883): This is at once the foreign mission enterprise of the Zulu Mission and an independent movement to reach the tribes in the interior. In 1880 Myron W. Pinkerton was sent by the Zulu Mission to examine the ground for a new mission, but died before accomplishing his object. The following year E. H. Richards was sent by the Mission to continue the work of exploration and reached the capital of Umzila's kingdom in October, 1881, when permission was given to open the new mission. In 1882 William C. Wilcox explored the region around Inhambane Bay, and the following year he established the mission. In 1884 he was joined by Mr. and Mrs. Richards and Mr. and Mrs. Ousley, the latter being graduates of Fisk University, and of the schools of the American Missionary Association. In 1887 Miss Nancy Jones joined the Mission, the first single woman of African descent to be commissioned by the American Board. Four Zulu Christian workers were added to the force, and the work went quietly on. The Gospels and Acts were translated and published, and schools were established. The coast region proving unhealthful in 1893, the Mission was moved to Mt. Silinda, in Gazaland. Schools have been opened, including an industrial school, and evangelistic and medical work is carried on. In January, 1897, the first Church of Christ in Gazaland was formed with 16 members, all on confession of faith. Title deeds to 27,000 acres of land have been secured, including the fine Silinda forest.

There are (1902) 3 stations, 6 outstations; 11 American missionaries, 11 native workers; 1 church with 41 communicants; 1 boarding school with 64 students; 2 common schools with 41 pupils; 2 dispensaries.

27. *West Central African Mission* (1880): Established by Messrs. Bagster, Sanders and Miller, at Bailundu and Bihé. The Portuguese authorities at first treated the missionaries with civility and rendered them important service, and the natives heartily welcomed them; the traders were prejudiced against them, and succeeded, in 1884, by bribes and false reports, in causing their expulsion, but the governor was appealed to, and they were allowed to return. The first church was organized in 1887, with 14 members all under 20 years of age; deacons were chosen from among them, and later one became their pastor. A printing press was established, schools opened and industrial and medical work was begun. In 1901 the Mission was seriously threatened by an uprising of the natives against the Portuguese authorities. Nevertheless steady growth and enlarged opportunities are reported.

There are 4 stations with 12 outstations; 24 American missionaries; 37 native workers; 4 churches with 163 communicants; 1 theological school with 13 students; 10 common schools with 1,146 pupils; 2 hospitals and 4 dispensaries.

28. *Japan:* About 1827, a company of Christian laymen of Boston and vicinity began to meet regularly to pray for the conversion of the world; their first contributions of $600 were devoted to Japan, which as yet had not been visited by Protestant missionaries. Forty years later, Dr. Neesima, a Japanese, then a student at Amherst, appealed to the American Board to send missionaries to Japan. At this time the original gift of $600 had increased to over $4,000, and it was decided to send Rev. D. C. Greene and his wife to open the new work. They landed in Yokohama November 30, 1869. Work was begun that same year in Tokio, but after a careful inspection of the field the mission was removed to Kobe in March, 1870. In February, 1873, the famous edict was issued which led to the withdrawal of the proclamations against Christianity posted during more than 250 years in every town and hamlet throughout Japan. Public preaching was immediately begun, and a church of 11 members was organized at Kobe, in April, 1874, and in May a church was organized at Osaka. Schools, hospitals and dispensaries were opened, and evangelistic tours begun. The same year Joseph Neesima and Paul Sawayama returned from America, the one to establish a Christian school, the other to become an eminently successful pastor. The Kioto Training School, now called Doshisha, was opened in 1876, and a school for girls, now Kobe College, was opened. In 1883 the northern Japan Mission was opened at Niigata and Sendai, but in 1890 was incorporated as a station of the Japan Mission. In 1891 an impetus was given to the work by the Union Evangelistic Movement, when work was carried on in 42 provinces, by 22 denominations, employing 536 foreign and Japanese workers representing 376 churches. Seventy-seven evangelistic bands were formed; over 2,000,000 handbills and posters were used; over 600,000 tracts were distributed; and over 10,000 yen was raised for the work. About 20,000 enrolled themselves, giving name and address, as converts, or as earnest inquirers after the truth.

There are (1902) 12 stations, 102 outstations; 68 American missionaries, and 119 native workers; 81 churches with 10,856 communicants; 1 theological seminary with 16 students; 2 colleges with 506 students, 5 boarding schools for girls with 384 pupils; 1 kindergarten training school and 4 kindergartens. Native contributions were $16,895.

29. *South America:* Messrs. J. C. Brigham and Theophilus Parvin arrived in Buenos Aires, October, 1823. They perfected themselves in the Spanish language; opened a school with some 20 pupils and a Sabbath-school for Protestant children, with a similar number; revived a Bible Society which had been previously formed, and gave an impulse to Bible distribution; established preaching services both on Sunday and week days at the house of an Englishman; held Bethel meetings on board ships in the harbor, and in various ways promoted the work. Mr. Marvin visited America in September, 1825, was ordained in Philadelphia, and returned to Buenos Aires the next year with a press, printer, and female teacher. He wished to labor on his individual responsibility; the income of the school was sufficient for his support, and at his own request he was honorably discharged from the service of the Board. Mr. Brigham left Buenos Aires in October, 1824, and after a tour of exploration, pursuing the original design of the mission, returned to the United States in 1826, was there invited to the domestic secretaryship of the American Bible Society, and was released from the service of the Board.

In 1833 an exploring expedition was sent out with a view to founding a mission on the western coast of Patagonia. The project was found impracticable and the missionaries returned.

30. *Mexico* (1872): The Mission to Mexico represents the only work the American Board is now conducting upon this continent. It is one of the Board's three missions in Papal Lands, the other two being in Spain and Austria. The object of these three missions in countries generally known as Roman Catholic is not to attack and disintegrate the dominant church, but to introduce the leaven of the simple Gospel of Christ, and to plant there gospel institutions which shall produce earnest, sincere Christian men and women. Work was begun in 1872 at Guadalajara by J. L. Stephens and D. F. Watkins, and the following year a church was organized with 17 members. In 1873 a work conducted by Miss Melinda Rankin at Monterey was transferred to the Board. In 1874 Mr. Stephens was killed while preaching at Ahualulco. The next years were full of trials and adversities. In 1877 the work at Monterey was transferred to the Presbyterian Board which was already working in that vicinity. Opposition on the part of the Roman Catholics, and a lack of harmony among the missionaries led the Board to reconstruct the mission on a new basis. In 1881 the missionary in charge was instructed to turn the work over to new missionaries on their arrival; instead, however, he transferred the mission to the Methodist Episcopal Church, South, and, when Messrs. Crawford, Howland, and Bissell arrived, in 1882, they began what was practically a new mission. Two churches were organized, one at Tlajamulco in 1883, and one at Guadalajara in 1884. The same year was commenced the publication of a weekly illustrated paper. In the meantime a new station was opened in 1882 at Chihuahua by Mr. and Mrs. J. D. Eaton. At this time Protestant Christianity was unknown in northwestern Mexico. In November, 1883, the first converts were baptized, and in April, 1886, the first church at Chihuahua was organized; the same year Hermosillo was occupied as a mission station. In 1890 the Rio Grande Congregational Training School was opened at Ciudad Juarez. In 1891 the various stations were united in one mission, having been given better facilities for communication by the building of railroads. There are (1902) 5 stations and 33 outstations; 16 American missionaries and 22 native workers; 21 churches with 1,121 communicants; 1 theological school with 8 students; 3 boarding and high schools with 177 pupils; 4 other schools with 133 pupils.

31. *Mission to Italy:* On the withdrawal of the American and Foreign Christian Union, and at the earnest invitation of the Free Church of Italy, the Board commenced a mission in Italy in 1872. The purpose was to aid certain churches and evangelistic agencies founded by the Union. In 1874 it was decided to suspend operations in that field because of the limited means and the limited number of men that the Board found itself enabled to employ in nominally Christian lands, and the difficulty of finding a clear field for the Board's methods of labor on account of the presence of so many other evangelical agencies at work in Italy.

32. *Mission to Spain:* When in June, 1869, Spain adopted a constitution guaranteeing full religious liberty to natives and foreigners alike, various evangelical bodies took advantage of the situation to commence Gospel work in that land. In 1872 the American Board established a mission, with Barcelona and Santander as stations. Two sons of the Hawaiian missionary, Rev. Peter J. Gulick, with Rev. Gustavus Alexy and Miss Blake, were sent out to this mission. A school, previously opened by Mr. Lawrence, connected with the Broadway Tabernacle Church, New York City, at once came under the care of the mission. Aid was given to feeble evangelical churches, literature was distributed, and regular preaching services sustained. In 1873 Barcelona was abandoned, and the first church was dedicated at Santander in the same year. Political disturbances and the reactionary tendencies of a new government interfered with the work during the next few years. In 1875 Zaragoza was occupied and the following year a church was organized with 75 members from an old Protestant body and 12 new converts. A school for girls was established at Santander, which has since developed into the International Institute for Girls, located at San Sebastian. During the Spanish-American war it was removed temporarily to Biarritz, France, and it is now to be located in Madrid.

In 1882 the mission assumed care of the work carried on in the province of Tara by the Evangelical Society of Geneva, so that since 1883 the field of the Board has extended from Santander along the line of railway to the Mediterranean. A monthly Christian Endeavor paper is published, and two National Christian Endeavor Conventions have been held.

There are (1902) 1 station with 17 outstations; 5 American missionaries and 24 native workers; 8 churches with 354 communicants; 1 boarding school with 34 pupils and 15 common schools with 772 pupils. The native contributions were $3,068.

33. *Mission to Austria:* Established in 1872 by Messrs. H. A. Schauffler, E. A. Adams and A. W. Clark and their wives, followed the next year by Rev. E. C. Bissell and wife. Prague, in Bohemia; Brünn, in Moravia, and Innsbruck, in Tyrol, were occupied; colporteurs and evangelists were employed and encouragement given to active Christian workers in the already existing Protestant churches. Violent opposition on the part of the Roman Catholic clergy and inimical interference by the government rendered the work very difficult. The action of the Reformed Consistory at Vienna for a time seriously crippled the work. In no field has opposition been more persistent, the difficulties greater, or the faithful labors of the missionaries more abundant.

The work among Bohemian immigrants in America has been greatly assisted by converts made in this mission. An important feature of the work has been the establishment of Christian Associations, both for young men and for young women. The only Rescue Home in all Bohemia and Austria is carried on by the mission.

There are now 1 station and 63 outstations; 4 American missionaries and 17 native workers; 13 churches with 1,297 communicants; 14 YMCA; 1 YWCA; 1 Rescue Home.

Besides the various missions above described the ABCFM carried on 15 missions among the North American Indians. Of this part of the work of the society the following presents a summary:

1. *Cherokees* (1816-60): 112 missionaries, mostly lay and female; 12 churches, with 248 members in 1860; schools; printing, 14,084,100 pages; mission given up because the Board's proper work was done.

2. *Choctaws* (1818-59): 153 missionaries; 12 churches, with 1,362 members in 1859, when nation was declared a Christian people; schools; printing, 11,558,000 pages; mission given up because of complications arising from existence of slavery; in 1872 1 missionary resumed labor, and withdrew in 1876, leaving 4 churches under the native pastor.

3. *Osages* (1826-37): Commenced by United Foreign Missionary Society in 1820; transferred to the Board in 1826; 26 missionaries; 2 churches of 48 members; schools with 354 pupils; their country ceded to the Cherokees.

4. *Maumees, or Ottawas* (1826-35): Commenced by Western Missionary Society in 1822; transferred that same year to the United Foreign Missionary Society, and to the Board in 1826; 6 missionaries; church with 25 members; given up because of changes in the population.

5. *Mackinaws* (1826-36): Commenced by the United Foreign Missionary Society, 1823; transferred to the Board, 1826; 17 missionaries; a church with 35 members; given up for the same reason as No. 4.

6. *Chickasaws* (1827-35): Commenced by Synod of South Carolina and Georgia, 1821, and transferred to the Board in 1827; 10 missionaries; a church of 100 members; schools with 300 pupils; given up for the above-mentioned reason.

7. *Stockbridge Indians* (1828-48): 8 missionaries; a church of 51 members; given up as above.

8. *Creeks* (1832-37): 6 missionaries; 80 church members; given up because of peculiar embarrassments.

9. *Pawnees* (1834-44): 10 missionaries; given up because of the roving character of the Pawnees and the hostile incursions of other tribes.

10. *Oregon Indians* (1835-47): 13 missionaries; broken up by the massacre of 1847.

11. *Senecas* (New York State) (1826-70): Commenced by the New York Missionary Society, 1801; transferred to the United Foreign Missionary Society, 1821, and to the Board in 1826; 47 missionaries; from first to last, about 600 church members; transferred to Presbyterian Board, 1870.

12. *Tuscaroras* (New York State) (1826-60): Commenced as above; 10 missionaries; church members gathered, 200; given up because the Board's work was done.

13. *Ojibways* (1831-70): 28 missionaries; converts not definitely known; transferred to Presbyterian Board in 1870.

14. *Abenaquis* (1835-56): 1 Indian missionary; 75 members; given up because of increasing discouragements.

15. *Sioux, or Dakotas* (1835-83): 40 missionaries; in part transferred to the Presbyterian Board in 1870; transferred to the American Missionary Association in 1883.

From the above statement it will be seen that two missions and a part of a third were transferred to the Presbyterian Board in 1870; one to the American Missionary Association in 1883; 5 were given up because of peculiar difficulties; 4, because of changes in the population; 1 because of massacre, and the remaining two because the tribes had become practically Christianized. The whole number of missionaries employed was 500; churches, 47; members, 3,800; Indians reached by these missions, about 100,000; 12 languages were reduced to writing, and besides the Scriptures much Christian literature was published and many schools established and conducted during the continuance of the missions.

The periodical publications of the ABCFM are *The Missionary Herald, Life and Light for Women* (by the Woman's Board), *The Mission Dayspring* (for children) and *Mission Studies.* These are all monthly publications. An *Almanac* is also issued every year. Bibliography: *History of the Missions of the ABCFM*, Anderson (R.), 5 vols., Boston, 1870-74; *The Hawaiian Islands*, Anderson (R.), Boston, 1864; *Memorial Volume of the First Fifty Years of the ABCFM*, Anderson (R.), Boston, 1861.

AMERICAN CHURCH MISSIONARY SOCIETY. See PROTESTANT EPISCOPAL DOMESTIC AND FOREIGN MISSIONARY SOCIETY.

AMERICAN CHRISTIAN CONVENTION. See CHRISTIAN CHURCH.

AMERICAN FRIENDS' Board of Foreign Missions (1871): There are 14 yearly meeting Foreign Mission Boards and 10 women's organizations in the Society of Friends, each of which carries on a distinct foreign mission work. The other Yearly Meetings have not opened separate missions, thinking it wiser to strengthen the existing missions than to begin weak ones of their own. In most cases they have some definite work in the missions which they assist. In the Quinquennial Conference of 1892 provisions were made for the formation of a central bureau, as a medium of communication between the boards of other denominations and the Friends', and as a bureau of information. This was formally organized in 1894, under the name of "The American Friends' Board of Foreign Missions."

In 1900 it was incorporated under the laws of the State of Indiana, and made preparations to take up work in the foreign field, following the plan laid down in the Uniform Discipline in its further organization for this class of work. Its income is derived from appropriations of the yearly meetings and other Boards, and from donations, legacies, etc.

Upon the organization of the Five-Years' Meeting in 1901, this central body became one of its organizations. It is made up of representatives appointed from the various Yearly Meetings.

The American Friends' Foreign Missions include the work of the Central Board and the Yearly Meetings and are carried on in China, Japan, India, Syria, Africa, Mexico, Alaska, Cuba and the West Indies. The total receipts (1903) were $58,268.00.

Missions; 1. *Mexico* (1871): The first foreign missionary work of the Friends was begun by the Indiana Yearly Meeting, at Matamoros and Ciudad Victoria, in the State of Tamaulipas, Mexico, in 1871. Schools were begun, and in 1872 a mission press was established at Ciudad Victoria, which issues a religious monthly paper as well as books, tracts, etc., which have a wide circulation throughout the Spanish speaking world.

In 1873 a girls' school was established at Matamoros, later known as the Hussey Institute. The Penn Institute at Ciudad Victoria, a boarding and day school for girls, was established and supported by the New York Yearly Meeting, which also supports two foreign missionaries and three native teachers. In 1902 the Juarez Evangelical Institute, a school of high grade, and a Bible Institute for young men was established at Ciudad Victoria. In 1888 the Western Yearly Meeting opened a station at Matehuala in the State of San Luis Potosi; a second station was established by them in 1889 at Cedral and a third in 1901 at Catorce Real, where medical work was begun, and has proved of great value. In 1902 a fourth station was established at La Paz, besides educational and evangelistic work. A paper called "*El Catolico Convertido* is published by the mission and has a wide circulation. There are (1903) 6 stations and 9 outstations; 16 American missionaries and 29 native workers; 11 churches, with 766 members; 3 boarding and high schools, with 133 pupils; 7 other schools, with 382 pupils.

2. *West Indies* (1883): The Iowa Yearly Meeting began work at Glen Haven, Jamaica, in 1883, among two distinct classes of people—the colored population born on the island and the coolies brought as laborers from the East Indies. These last are generally heathen. There is a well established training home for girls and another for boys, with a large attendance of day scholars.

In 1886 another station was established at Sea Side and a third, in 1889, at Amity Hall. All these stations are in good condition and the prospects encouraging.

There are (1903) 3 stations; 10 outstations; 9 American missionaries and 15 native workers; 3 churches, with 530 members; 2 boarding schools, with 34 students; 4 other schools, with 250 pupils.

3. *Japan* (1885): The Woman's Foreign Missionary Association of Friends of Philadelphia began work in Tokio, Japan, in 1885.

The work is mainly evangelistic and educational. A girls' boarding school has been successful. In 1899 a sub-station was opened at Mito by the Canada Yearly Meeting, Woman's Foreign Missionary Society, and outstations have been established.

At Tsuchiura a Meeting and First Day School are kept up by resident native Christians, with occasional visits from Japanese and foreign members of the Evangelistic Committee. At Ishioka, a Japanese evangelist has charge of the work. Since the disorganization of the Society of Friends in 1894, occasioned by Nationalist criticism of the Quakers during the whole Chinese war, the mission has not reorganized under the name of Friends, but the church work is carried on under the care of a committee of Japanese and missionaries who are Friends.

There are (1903) 2 stations and 2 outstations; 7 American missionaries; 22 native workers; 276 church members; 1 boarding school, with 23 pupils; 1 other school, with 140 pupils.

4. *Alaska* (1887): The Friends' Mission Board of the Kansas Yearly Meeting founded a mission at Douglas Island, Alaska, in 1887. Church services and First Day schools are held for both whites and natives, and a day school is taught during about seven months of the year. At the outstation of Takou preaching services are held and a school is carried on. A small steamer is used to follow the Indians to their outposts, but their absence from their homes a large part of the year greatly retards the work. The Kansas Board is investigating the question of getting the Indians settled in industrial colonies.

A second station was opened in 1894 on Kaak Island, by the Foreign Mission Board of the Oregon Yearly Meeting, on the same general lines as the Mission at Douglas Island. Here too they are confronted with the problem of the long absence of the Indians from their homes; and a home school for the native children is contemplated. In 1897 the Foreign Mission Board of the California Yearly Meeting opened a mission near Kotzebue Sound, looking out toward the Polar Sea, among the dwindling race of Eskimos. The Alaskan is accessible, teachable and responsive, and the outlook is encouraging. There are 4 outstations in the care of native helpers, who are said to have a good influence over the white miners and trappers as well as the natives.

There are (1903) 3 stations and 4 outstations; 9 American missionaries, and 15 trained Christian native helpers; 3 churches with 358 members; 3 day schools with 144 pupils.

5. *Palestine* (1888): This Mission was commenced in 1869 by Eli and Sybil Jones, and continued at their expense till 1874, when it became an independent mission under the name of the Friends' Syrian Mission (England). In 1888 the Ramallah station was transferred to the New England Yearly Meeting, which heretofore had contributed to the work through the English Friends. At the time of the transfer there was a school for boys, another for girls, and a cottage hospital and dispensary. A Training Home for Girls has been established, and in 1902 a much needed Training Home for Boys was opened. Both boys and girls receive industrial training in addition to the school and Bible work. There are (1903) 1 station; 4 American missionaries and 31 native workers; 1 church with 36 members; 2 boarding schools, with 49 students; and 7 other schools, with 225 pupils.

6. *China* (1890): The Ohio Yearly Meeting Foreign Mission Board dates the founding of its China Mission 1890, tho its pioneer missionary, Esther Butler, had been in the country for three years, learning the language and preparing for the work in the mission of another denomination. A station was established at Nanking, where land was purchased and buildings erected. In 1892 a church was organized; in 1896 a girls' boarding school and a hospital were opened. In 1898 a second station was opened at Liu-hohsien, a few miles north of Nanking, where evangelistic, educational and medical work is being pressed forward. There are (1903) 2 stations and 10 American missionaries; 2 churches; 1 boarding school with 27 students; 4 day schools.

7. *India* (1896): This Mission was established by the Ohio Yearly Meeting Foreign Mission Board at Nowgong, Central Provinces, in 1886. The work is conducted by four American women missionaries and is mainly evangelistic.

8. *Cuba* (1900): The American Friends' Board of Foreign Missions began work in the northeastern part of Cuba in 1900, sending out four missionaries who began work at Jibara. A second station was established in 1902 at Holguin, and early in 1903 Banes, Tanamo, and Puerto Padre were occupied. Church schools and colportage work are in successful operation. There are (1903) 5 stations and 2 outstations; 11 American missionaries; 1 native worker; and 1 school, with 20 pupils.

9. *Africa Industrial Mission:* A board was organized in 1902, composed of two members from each of ten American Yearly Meetings, and incorporated under the laws of the State

of Ohio, as the Friends' Africa Industrial Mission. Three missionaries were sent out to begin the work and establish themselves among the Kavirondo people in British East Africa, near Kisumu. The location chosen was on the banks of a river, with waterfalls that can be utilized for power, and several springs of the best water for household purposes. The soil proved fertile and the prospects are most encouraging. There is one station and ten American missionaries.

Woman's Foreign Missionary Union of Friends (1881): The first foreign missionary organization of women among Friends was formed in 1881 as a Yearly Meeting Society. In 1890 the ten independent societies organized in the yearly meetings were united in the Woman's Foreign Missionary Union of Friends. It has four departments of work: Interest and Organization; Literature; Juvenile and Junior; Proportionate and Systematic Giving, having a general secretary for each department.

In 1903 there were ten yearly meeting organizations in the Union, the greater number working through the AFFM. The missions in China, India and San Luis Potosi in Mexico are entirely supported by three of the women's societies. 18 missionaries are supported by them.

The Friends' Missionary Advocate, monthly.

AMERICAN MISSIONARY ASSOCIATION: The American Missionary Association was formed in Albany, N. Y., September 3, 1846. It was preceded by four recently established missionary organizations, subsequently merged into it, the result of the growing dissatisfaction with the comparative silence of the older missionary societies in regard to slavery, and as a protest against it. The first of these, the Amistad Committee, secured the liberation of forty-two negroes who had risen upon their captors in the Spanish slave schooner "Amistad" that was bearing them into slavery, and were finally sent by the Committee to their native land, accompanied by three missionaries. The other organizations were the Union Missionary Society, formed in Hartford, Conn., the Committee for West India Missions among the recently emancipated slaves of Jamaica, and the Western Evangelical Missionary Society for work among the American Indians.

In the Foreign field, in addition to the missions received from the societies named, it took under its care one missionary in the Hawaiian Islands, two in Siam, and a number of missionaries and teachers laboring among the colored refugees in Canada—so that in its Foreign Department in 1854 its laborers numbered seventy-nine, located in Africa, Jamaica, the Sandwich Islands, Siam, Egypt—among the Copts, Canada—among the colored refugees, and in North America among the Indians.

The Home department embraced two distinct fields, the west and the south, and the largest number of home missionary workers employed by the Association was 112 in 1860, 15 of them being located in the slave States and in Kansas.

In 1859, as the crisis in the slavery question approached, the Society closed its work among the Copts and Indians, and directed its attention distinctly to the colored people. As the war commenced, in 1861, the Association felt itself specially called and providentially prepared to work for negroes, and the first systematic effort for their relief was made by it. Large numbers of "contrabands," or escaping fugitive slaves, were gathered at Fortress Monroe and Hampton, Va., and were homeless and destitute. The Association sent Rev. L. C. Lockwood as a missionary, to make investigations. He reached Hampton September 3, 1861, and the next day arrangements were made for meetings in several places, the house of ex-President Tyler being one of them—a new use for that mansion, and a new era for the colored people.

But the great event in Mr. Lockwood's mission was that on the 17th of September, 1861, he established the first day school among the freedmen. The teacher of that humble school was Mrs. Mary S. Peake, an intelligent Christian woman. Her mother was a free colored woman, her father an educated Englishman. That little school laid the foundation for the Hampton Institute, and was the forerunner of the hundreds that have followed. The school-house stood on the coast where, two hundred and forty-one years before, the first slave-ship entered the waters of the American Continent. That first slave-ship and this first negro school will hereafter be contrasted as the initiators of two widely different eras—of barbarism and civilization. During the war the Society extended its work as rapidly as possible, and at its close was in the front rank of the various organizations at work among the freedmen, turning its attention specially to education and the establishment of a high grade of schools. As a result the Association founded Fisk University, Tennessee; Talladega College, Alabama; Tougaloo University, Mississippi; Straight University, Louisiana; and Tillotson College, Texas, together with forty-five normal and graded schools and twenty-seven common schools, scattered over the South.

Theological departments also were established in Howard University, Fisk University, Talladega College and Straight University, with an aggregate of 69 students. Industrial instruction first began in Southern mission schools in Talladega, Ala., and was early introduced into many other schools, and has been constantly extended. Talladega College and Tougaloo University have large farms. In all the larger institutions and normal schools, mechanical arts are taught to the boys, and household work, cooking, sewing, washing, nursing, etc., to the girls. From these schools go forth annually hundreds of well-qualified teachers and ministers.

When General Grant, in 1870, invited the religious and missionary bodies to assist in the work among the Indians, the Association took up again the department which it had dropped, and, in 1882, by an arrangement with the ABCFM it assumed the care of its missions among those people, withdrawing itself from the foreign field. It was also a pioneer in work among the Chinese in California as early as 1852. In 1875 a special superintendent was appointed, and the work was soon greatly enlarged. Parallel with these lines was the Society's work among the mountain whites of West Virginia, parts of Virginia, Kentucky, North Carolina, Tennessee, Georgia and Alabama. With the opening of Alaska, in 1890, it pressed to its westernmost limits at Cape Prince of Wales. After the war with Spain, by arrangement with the Congregational Home Missionary Society, it took Porto Rico as its field, leaving Cuba to the other Society.

The Bureau of Woman's Work, organized in

1883, conducts that part of the work of the Association, by direct appeals and through Women's State Missionary Unions.

A summary of the Society's work shows that in the southern States it has 79 schools with 480 teachers and 14,048 pupils, 230 churches, 139 ministers and missionaries, 12,155 members, and 17,311 Sunday school scholars; among the Indians 20 churches, 1,453 members, 2,661 Sunday school scholars, 6 schools, 342 pupils, 47 white and 41 Indian teachers and missionaries; among the Chinese 33 American and 11 Chinese teachers; in Porto Rico, 2 schools, 10 teachers, 343 pupils.

Official organ of the Society: *The American Missionary*, monthly, New York.

AMERICAN TRACT SOCIETY: This Society is undenominational, representing all the Evangelical communities of the U. S. It combines both home and foreign work, publishing Evangelical Christian literature in book and leaflet form in 155 languages or dialects. It has depositaries in principal cities, employs colporteurs, and makes grants to religious and benevolent institutions.

The possibilities of the printing press as an evangelistic agency were seen very soon after the invention of printing. At Basel, in Switzerland, there was virtually a Bible Society, a Colportage Association, and a Tract Society for France as early as 1524. The New Testament and, afterward, the Old Testament, in several portions, were very widely circulated. In many places, unreached by the reformers in person, the Reformation was inaugurated by the circulation of the writings of Luther and Melancthon. Indeed the press proved a most effective agency in scattering seeds of reform everywhere.

The influence of this idea was manifested in England by the organization of the Society for the Promotion of Christian Knowledge in 1698, followed after a century by the Religious Tract Society, in 1799, and the movement extended across the Atlantic. In 1812 "The New York Religious Tract Society" was formed, and in 1814 "The New England Tract Society," at Boston. In 1823 this latter society changed its name to the "American Tract Society," and in 1825 it became a branch of a national organization, which was then instituted, bearing the same name, and designed to constitute a great central society for the whole Union, inviting the cooperation of Christians of all denominations, and of other tract associations as auxiliaries, in publishing and circulating whatever would best "diffuse a knowledge of our Lord Jesus Christ as the Redeemer of sinners, and promote the interest of vital godliness and sound morality," provided only that such publications should be "calculated to receive the approbation of all evangelical Christians."

Organization: The Society, consisting of persons who have become members and Directors by the payment of not less than $30 at one time, elects a Board, consisting of President, Vice-President and 36 Managers. This Board appoints an Executive Committee of 18 Members which in turn appoints the Executive Officers, consisting (1903) of a Secretary, a Publishing, Secretary, an assistant Treasurer and Auditors. The Board of Managers also has authority to appoint Members, Directors, Honorary Vice-Presidents and to fill vacancies. The Executive Committee is divided into three Sub-committees on Publishing, Distribution and Finance. The Publishing Committee is not permitted to contain two members from the same ecclesiastical connection, and no tract can be published to which any member of the Committee objects. The headquarters of the Society are in the Tract Society Building in New York City. There are also depositaries in Boston, Cincinnati, and Chicago, and District Secretaries at Boston, Rochester, Cincinnati, and Chicago, with Superintendents of Colportage at Rochester and St. Louis.

Two of the organizations that were, for practical purposes, united with the American Tract Society of New York, still maintain a separate corporate existence; the American Tract Society instituted in Boston, and the Western Tract Society, with headquarters at Cincinnati. The former withdrew from the New York Society during the anti-slavery discussion of 1857-60, but again united with it in 1897, so far as active work is concerned. the District Secretary for New England of the New York Society acting as its Secretary, and the Manager of the Boston depository as its Treasurer. In Cincinnati the Western Tract Society has a separate Secretary.

Development: For two years after the Society's organization, only tracts were issued. In the third year volumes appeared, the first being Doddridge's *Rise and Progress, Saints' Rest, Baxter's Call, Pilgrim's Progress,* etc. Systematic tract distribution in New York, City and elsewhere began in the fourth year. In the sixth year prominence was given to the value of tracts in connection with faithful personal efforts to save souls, Harlan Page becoming eminent in this transcendent duty.

The volume enterprise was inaugurated in the eighth year by attempt to reach every family in the South Altantic States with one or more volumes. The West was included the next year. The work was so enlarged that in the seventeenth year nearly 100 works had been published, the *Evangelical Family Library* was issued, and some 2,000,000 volumes had been put into circulation, and 60,000,000 of tracts.

In 1841 the Society inaugurated its system of colportage, with special reference to the destitute, isolated settlements, unreached by the churches, and to the great numbers who refuse to enter the churches. The number of colporteurs increased rapidly until by 1860, over 600 were employed for the whole or a part of each year.

Another important feature in the publications of the Society has been its periodicals. The first to be established was *The American Messenger*, the official organ of the Society, founded in 1843. It is an illustrated religious monthly. There followed in 1847 the *Amerikanischer Botschafter*, similar in scope and purpose to the *Messenger*, designed for circulation among the German-speaking population; in 1852 *The Child's Paper*, now known as *Good Cheer*, an illustrated monthly paper for young folks; in 1871 a new German weekly, called the *Deutscher Volksfreund*, and the *Illustrated Christian Weekly*, which was afterwards sold (1888) to another house. Two new periodicals were added in 1879; *Morning Light*, for the younger scholars in the Sunday school, and *Apples of Gold* for the youngest readers. Besides all these, there is *Light and Life*, a monthly tract periodical consisting of a new eight-page tract each month. The new conditions occasioned by such exigencies as attended the Mexican War, the Civil War, and the Spanish War, have been met by the Society with special publications and arrangements for distribution. Especially has this been the case in regard to the opportunity furnished by the Spanish War. The Sunday School paper, *Apples of Gold*, has been issued in Spanish, under the title of *Manzanas de Oro*; hymnals have been prepared and a general literature as complete as possible, to all of which has been accorded a most enthusiastic reception from the missionaries of various denominations as well as from the pastors, teachers, and others in Cuba, Porto Rico, Mexico, and South America.

The flood of immigration to America has furnished another field for the Society's work. The great mass of these immigrants land at New York City, and the Tract Society employs a colporteur, sometimes with one or more assistants, to meet, encourage and advise them and to supply them with leaflets, papers, etc., in their own languages. The readiness of immigrants to receive these and the attention paid are remarkable, and many times thanks are returned to the Society by the new comers after they have reached their homes in various parts of the country. Special colportage work is also carried on among the Mormons, the negroes of the South, in the mining and lumber regions, and libraries are supplied to the army and navy and to merchant ships.

The foreign work of the Society is carried on through grants to the missions of the various denominations or to local Tract Societies. The general method is for a committee, representing the several mission Boards abroad, to request the issue of specific publications, original or translated. The American Tract Society then provides the needed funds or prints the tract or volume on its own presses. Frequently it appropriates a lump sum from year to year to be used by a committee or mission press, according to the principles and methods of the Society. Among the missions thus assisted during 1901-2 were those of the ABCFM in Austria, Turkey, South Africa and India; of the ABMU in Burma; of the SBC in China; of the Free Baptists India; of the PN in Africa, India, Persia, Syria and Siam; of the RCA in Arabia and India, etc. Among the Tract Societies aided were the Religious Tract Society of France, the Evangelical Tract Society of Geneva, the Italian Evangelical Publishing Society, the North India Christian Book and Tract Society, the Central China, North China, and Chinese Tract Societies, the Korean Religious Tract Society, the Japanese Book and Tract Society, etc.

The total number of volumes issued from the home office during the seventy-eight years (to 1903), is 32,743,752; of tracts, 449,554,252; and of periodicals, 264,278,668; making a grand total of 746,576,672 copies of publications printed. During 1902 new publications issued at foreign mission stations, by the aid of funds furnished by the Society, were 38, of which 24 were volumes and 14 tracts. The whole number of publications issued up to 1903 at foreign mission stations, with the approval of the Society's Publishing Committee, either wholly or in part with funds of the Society appropriated for this purpose, is 5,080, of which 1,018 are volumes and 4,062 tracts.

The regular catalog of the society includes, aside from a large number of books, tracts, hand bills, maps, etc., in English, publications in over 20 foreign languages, including German, French, Spanish, Italian, Welsh, Dutch, Norwegian, Danish, Swedish, Hungarian, Finnish, Bohemian, Polish, German-Hebrew, Lithuanian, Croatian and Chinese.

The foreign cash payments for publication (1902) were $4,928.08, making a total expenditure of $747,140.51. The total receipts (1902) were $383,983.06.

AMHARIC: This language belongs to the Semitic family of languages, is used in Abyssinia, and is related to the ancient Ethiopic or Giz. It is written with the Giz letters increased by some additional characters, and it has adopted words from the Galla and some other neighboring African tribes. The Amharic is modified into many dialects by the isolation of different sections of the country.

AMITY HALL: A town near the eastern extremity of Jamaica, W. I.; station of the American Friends' Foreign Missionary Society (1897) with 1 missionary and his wife, 1 unmarried woman missionary, and 4 native workers, men and women; 3 outstations, 4 Sunday schools, 2 young people's societies, 1 high school and 108 professing Christians.

AMKHUT: A village in the Malwa region, Central India; station of the PCC (1897), with a missionary physician and his wife and 1 native worker, an orphanage and a dispensary.

AMOY: A seaport on the southern coast of an island of the same name, belonging to the province of Fo-kien, China. It has an excellent harbor; the climate is cool in winter, wet in spring, and hot in summer; its inhabitants, in 1901, were 96,000.

Amoy was one of the earliest centers of European trade in China. The stream of emigration thence to Singapore, noticed by missionaries and by the chaplains of foreign seamen, at that point, led to the establishment of the first English and American missions at Amoy.

The RCA (commenced by ABCFM in 1842 and transferred in 1854) now has at Amoy 15 missionaries and 16 native workers, men and women, with 6 outstations. The PCE (opened 1850) has 11 missionaries, men and women, and the two societies together 11 preaching places, 5 village schools, 3 high schools, 1 theological class, 1 training class for women workers, 1 medical class, 1 dispensary, 1 printing house, 1 foundling asylum, 1 orphanage, and 425 church members.

The LMS has at Amoy (founded 1844) 14 missionaries and 59 native workers, men and women, with 65 outstations, 40 village schools, 1 high school, 1 theological class, 1 college, and 2,000 church members.

The missionary operations at Amoy show a good example of comity between the three societies engaged.

AMPAMARINANA: A town of Central Madagascar, near Antananarivo. Mission station of the LMS, opened in 1864 and carried on by a missionary and his wife, with 229 native workers. There are 25 village schools, and 2,622 communicants.

AMPARIBE: A town of Central Madagascar, a little northwest of Antananarivo. Mission station of the LMS opened in 1861, and now carried on by one missionary and his wife with 425 native workers. There are 59 village schools and 3,645 communicants.

AMRAOTI: Chief town of a district of the same name in E. Berar, Central Provinces, India. Its population is about 33,000. It is a station of the CA but no statistics are given. It is an outstation of the UFS (1871) with 22 native workers, men and women, 4 village schools, and 48 church members.

AMRITSAR: An important city and commercial center of the Punjab, India, and the chief seat of the Sikh worship. Population (1901), 162,429. It has a "pool of Immortality," on an island in which stands the chief temple of the Sikh religion. This holy place makes Amritsar a religious metropolis, and attracts to it great numbers of Pilgrims.

It is a station of the CMS, founded in 1851, and now carried on by 14 missionaries, and 24 native workers, men and women, with 4 outstations, 1 village school, 1 high school, 1 hospital, 5 dispensaries, and 1 printing house. There are 165 communicants.

It is also a station of the CEZMS with 16 missionaries and 45 native workers, all women, with 13 village schools, 3 high schools, 1 industrial school, 1 training class for women workers, 1 hospital, 2 dispensaries, and 400 pupils in zenanas.

The religious importance of the place gave a profound influence to the conversion here of one of the Sikh priests some years ago. A Mohammedan religious teacher converted here in 1866 became the Rev. Imad-ud-din, a Christian pastor of influence and preacher of great power.

AMROHA: A city of 35,000 inhabitants in the Rohilkhand division of the United Provinces, India. Occupied as an outstation by the ME with 13 native workers, men and women. It has 3 preaching places, 8 village schools, and the number of professing Christians is 570, chiefly Sikhs, but some of them converted Mohammedans.

AMSTERDAM FARM: A village in the Carolina district of the Transvaal Colony, S. Africa. Station of the SPG, with 2 missionaries.

AMURANG: A station of the Netherlands Missionary Society in the Minahassa peninsula of the island of Celebes.

ANAA. See TUAMOTU ISLANDS.

ANAKAPALLE: Town of 17,000 inhabitants (and railroad station), west of Vizagapatam, Madras, India; station of the BOQ (1898), with a missionary and his wife, 4 native workers, men and women, and 3 Sunday schools.

ANALAKELY: A town in the Imerina district of Madagascar; outstation of the LMS, founded in 1861; has 148 native workers, with 20 village schools, has 1,400 communicants.

ANAMABOE: A village near Cape Coast Castle in the Gold Coast Colony, W. Africa; station of the WMS, with 1 missionary and 46 native workers, men and women, 33 outstations, 4 village schools and 450 church members.

ANAMITIC: A mongrel dialect of Cochin China so far influenced by the Chinese as to have its nearest affinity with that language.

ANAND: A town in the Gujarat district, Bombay, India. A station of the PCI, opened in 1877. It is now occupied by 4 missionaries and 42 native workers, men and women, with 5 outstations, 15 village schools, a high school and an orphanage. There are 144 communicant Christians.

ANANDPUR: A town in the Punjab, British India; a station of the Basel Missionary Society, opened in 1856. There are now 3 missionaries and 4 native workers, men and women, with 109 communicants.

ANANTAPUR: A town in a district of the same name, Madras, India; station of the LMS (1890), with 1 missionary and his wife, 1 missionary woman, and 20 native workers, men and women, 12 outstations, 12 village schools, and 45 church members.

ANCESTOR-WORSHIP: The worship of deceased ancestors has been an important feature of the religious practises among widely separated peoples from remote ages. In modern times it has chiefly attracted popular attention in China, but it exists in Africa (See **Bantu Race**); traces of it are found among the American Indians; it is discovered among the Hindus, who have in the book of Vishnu a ritual for its proper performance; it can be noted in Western Asia in a reverence toward the graves of sages and heroes, which leads Mohammedans and others to pray with equal fervor at the tomb of Hannibal or at the mausoleums of forgotten Christian saints, and it appears in the early religious observances of Egyptians, Greeks and Romans. Its essential features are: (a) unshakable belief in the immortality of the soul (b) trust in the power of the dead to help or harm the living and (c) a sense of personal privilege through ties of kin to enjoy the protection of the deified or semi-deified ancestor. The mind of the man who worships his progenitors is in an attitude resembling that of those who appeal for help to patron saints in some branches of the Christian Church.

In China Ancestor-worship is a part of the Confucian system, but is older by centuries than the time of Confucius, and its claims are more binding on a Chinaman than those of any other form of worship. He may sneer at Buddhism, ridicule the outrageous claims of the Taouist exorcists, and may even be brought to see that the teachings of Confucius himself are but moral aphorisms incapable of changing the life and bettering the future of his disciples, but he will not give up the worship of the ancestral tablet, and the paying of that honor and reverence to deceased parents which is the outcome of filial piety, the root of all Chinese institutions, the bulwark of her government, the strong chain which has bound the people together as a nation. The worship of ancestors is the real religion of China, and as long as the incense is smoking on the ancestral altar, so long will Christianity find in this practise a formidable foe, founded as it is on the best and most natural instincts of the human heart.

When a man dies one of his three souls is supposed to go into the grave with the body, one goes to Hades, and one goes into the tablet which is prepared for its occupancy by his oldest son. The use of the tablet originated in the Chau dynasty, 350 B. C. Rev. Dr. J. Campbell Gibson thus describes this resting place for the soul:

<small>The tablet itself is a small block of wood eight inches to a foot in height and a few inches in breadth, on the front of which is written the name of the person whom it represents. It is sawn through its thickness into two portions, and on the</small>

inner surface thus exposed the inscription of the name is repeated, and usually the date of birth and of death is added. This tablet is prepared soon after death takes place, and it is retained during one or two generations in the home of the family. Offerings are made to it from time to time. As the tablets of successive generations take their places in the home, those of earlier date are removed to join those of past generations in the ancestral temple. Every clan and every section of a clan has its own ancestral temples, and few villages, however small, are without one at least.

On the new and full of every moon special offerings and worship are paid, and in the spring pilgrimages are made to the tomb, which is swept and put in repair. There is no need of priestly interference in this worship; the head of the family is the high-priest, and as the older ones die the younger ones take their places in this as in all other family matters. Ancestor-worship binds family ties, it perpetuates mutual interest, and is the least objectionable and therefore the most dangerous form of pagan worship. While it is founded on high principles—the reverence and love of parents—it is, in fact, a duty rendered from motives of self-protection and self-interest, for if the tablet is not erected, if the worship be not paid, it is believed that the wandering spirit will wreak its wrath on the offending descendant. The fear of this wrath is more real, more vivid than the fear of any of the other gods.

Each succeeding generation in bequeathing property assigns a portion to be used for the permanent maintenance of offerings on behalf of the dead. The practise affects the laws of land tenure; it modifies the laws of inheritance, giving a larger share of the property to the eldest son, because responsibility for keeping up the worship rests upon him. It also makes the birth of numerous daughters a calamity, because sons only can assure maintenance of that worship which is supposed to benefit the departed soul.

Ancestor-worship has been of benefit to China in this respect: it has preserved the reverence of parental authority, which reaching upward has caused national respect for the head of the nation as the father of his people, and it has preserved the position of woman more on an equality with man, and has defined the position of the mother of the family as *the* wife. Only one "illustrious consort" can be named on the tablet to father and mother, so there is but one wife, *tsih*, in the family. Concubines there may be, but they are not admitted into the worship of the ancestral hall, and this one fact has done much to preserve the legal, social and domestic position of woman. Moreover, the system not only forms a link between the living and the past generations of the clan, but it also unites all contemporary branches descended from a common stock. In fact it has been said that Ancestor-worship is the only point upon which all the Chinese unite.

This peculiarity of the effects of the worship of ancestors is seen wherever it is practiced. In ancient Greece and Rome, as among the wild tribes of Africa to-day, the tie of blood relationship to a common object of worship always tended to knit the clans or tribes together into a close corporation, admission to which was almost impossible. It also tended to cultivate an exclusiveness which regarded all who are not members of the tribe as barbarians without rights and to whom enmity is a duty. In Africa this natural enmity is sometimes set aside and a stranger is admitted to security by mingling his blood with that of a tribal chief. In this ceremony, intended to establish a sort of blood relationship between the foreigner and the savage tribe, there is ample reason for believing that its effect in requiring the foreigner to venerate the ancestors of the tribe is presupposed by those who accept him as a friend.

The barrier against Christianity formed by Ancestor-worship is solid and hard to pass. In China the people feel a shock of pain and revulsion on learning that Christians do not worship their deceased parents. When a Chinese becomes converted and abandons the practise he is regarded as having inflicted irreparable injury upon all of his ancestors. He has perhaps reduced them all to beggary. The stigma resting upon Christians is the more ineffaceable and painful to endure because at the spring "feast of All-souls", every person in the Chinese Empire *except* the Evangelical Christians takes part in the worship of the dead.

Under these circumstances many wise men have advised against a too rigid rejection of Ancestor-worship, which may after all be nearly akin to filial respect. But the attitude of Christianity to this form of worship can easily be determined when its true character is understood. Dr. E. Faber succinctly stated its position when the question was discussed in the Missionary Conference of 1890. In brief, "Ancestral worship presupposes disembodied souls to be subject to the same wants as living bodies; it demands real sacrifices to them; it makes the happiness of the living depend upon appeasing the desires of the dead; it is not merely commemorative, but it is a pretended intercourse with the world of spirits; it has developed an extreme view of paternal authority, placing it above the authority of God, and crushes individual liberty and it chains millions of people to the past and prevents sound progress."

Gibson (J. C.), *Mission Problems in S. China*, New York, Revell, 1900; Yates (M. T.), *Ancestral Worship*, Shanghai, 1867; Maine (H.), *Early Law and Custom*; Seebohm (H. E.), *Structure of Greek Tribal Society*, London; *Religious System of the Amazulu*; *Ancestor Worship*, Callaway (H.), London, 1870.

AN-CHIA-CHWANG: A town in the province of Shan-tung, China; station of the ME, with 6 native workers, men and women, 2 village schools, 2 outstations and 200 church members.

ANDAMAN ISLANDS: A long narrow group of small islands in the eastern part of the Bay of Bengal. Area, 2,000 square miles. They include the North, Middle, South and Little Andaman islands, with a number of islets, and all are densely wooded. They are used as a penal colony. The climate is very unhealthy. The population in 1901 was 17,500 of whom 11,465 were convicts and 1,882 native aborigines.

The natives are a diminutive and barbarous people, who seem to be distinct from all other known races in physical features, language, and customs.

The people of these islands are averse to intercourse with strangers. Their religion is little known but seems to consist of worship of good and evil deities.

Missionary effort has been mainly directed toward the convicts at Port Blair.

ANDOHALO: District E. of Antananarivo, Madagascar; station of the Paris Evangelical Society, with 1 missionary, 45 native workers, men and women, 16 outstations, 16 Sunday schools and 640 communicants.

ANDEVORANTO: A village of 2,000 inhabitants on the eastern coast of Madagascar, and an SPG station, founded in 1874. It now has 129 communicants under the care of one European missionary.

ANDREWS, Lorrin: Born April 29, 1795, at East Windsor (now Vernon), Conn.; graduated at Jefferson College, Pa.; Princeton Theological Seminary, 1825; sailed as a missionary of the ABCFM, November 3, 1827, for the Sandwich Islands, reaching Honolulu, March 31, 1828; was stationed at Lahaina with Mr. Richards. In 1831 he was appointed to establish the Lahainaluna Seminary, which was opened in September of that year with 25 pupils. During the succeeding ten years he exerted himself to found the institution on a permanent basis. He resigned his connection with the Board in 1842, because of conscientious differences of opinion. In 1845 he removed to Honolulu, and received the appointment of judge under the Hawaiian Government. For many years he sat upon the bench and officiated with ability and integrity. His services were highly appreciated by Judge Lee. For many years he acted as secretary of the Privy Council, keeping the records in English and Hawaiian. He resigned his office of judge in 1855, but an annuity of $1,000 was appropriated for his benefit and continued by successive legislatures to the very last. During the later years of his life his mind and pen were constantly occupied. His *Hawaiian Dictionary*, defining nearly 17,000 words, occupied him for many years. His research into the folk-lore of the Hawaiian people had been very extensive. He died at Honolulu, September 29, 1868.

ANEIKADU: A village of the district of Tanjore, S. India, occupied as an outstation by the Leipzig Missionary Society. It has 10 native workers, men and women, and 356 communicants.

ANEITIUM. See NEW HEBRIDES.

ANEITIUM LANGUAGE: It is of the Melanesian family and is used by the people of an island of the N. Hebrides. It is written with Roman letters.

ANGOLA: A possession of Portugal, also called Portuguese West Africa, bordering the Atlantic, with a coast line of more than a thousand miles from the borders of the French Congo to German Southwest Africa and extending back into the continent variable distances to the borders of the Congo Free State and British South Africa. It has an area of 484,000 square miles, and an estimated population of 4,119,000. That characteristic feature of the African coast, the line of cliffs approached by terraces, is continued northward through Angola. The country is well watered, especially in the north. In the south the rainfall is less, and many of the streams dry up. Great diversity of climate is experienced in such a length of coast line. There are also extreme local variations, due to accidental conditions. Vegetation becomes more abundant as you pass from south to north. The elephant and lion become scarce. Panthers and hyenas are numerous. Zebras and antelopes occur in the south. Insects are rare, but the rivers are well stocked with fish. Caoutchouc, orchilla moss (used in dyeing), gum copal, palm, acacia, baobab, etc., are chief sources of wealth. Manioc, maize, millet, sorgo, and European fruits and vegetables are cultivated. The country is also rich in minerals. The population of Angola is affected by the northward movement of Boers; also by immigration from Brazil, and by the intermingling of Portuguese with the natives. But north of Mossamedes acclimatization for Europeans is a difficult and dangerous process. There are about 6,000 of European descent in Angola.

Preto is the name given to the negroes who have been brought into direct contact with European civilization, and who are found chiefly in the coast towns and their vicinity, and on the lines of travel and trade. Among them are found many well-informed people, merchants, and colonial officials.

The tribes south of Benguela are supposed to belong to the primitive race, Bushmen or Hottentots, and partake of their general characteristics.

The Ganguelas occupy the Upper Kubango basin. A great variety of social condition is found in studying the different tribes. They are represented as savage, but intelligent and enterprising. In some tribes trial by ordeal of the poisoned cup is practised. Their headdress is wonderful, surpassing that of most African peoples; their dress is scanty.

On the Congo is found the Bafyote or Bacongo group. They were the founders of the ancient kingdom of Congo. That kingdom still exists, tho weak, as most the tribes have seceded. Roman Catholic influence was once apparently great, but evidently superficial. Fetishism is rampant, nearly every natural object being a fetish. The Bamba magicians have wonderful skill in feats of jugglery.

The principal centers of trade and general influence are San Salvador, capital of the old Congo kingdom, and the center of a flourishing Baptist mission; Ambriz; S. Paolo de Loanda, the capital and largest city for 3,000 miles on the west African seaboard; Dondo, at the head of navigation of the Quanza; Pamba, in the Ambaca district, terminus of the railway from Loando; and Bihé, the terminus of the southern trade route, 300 miles long, starting from Benguela.

Bihé is properly the name of the extremely fertile plateaus about 5,000 feet above the sea level occupied by rude and wholly uncivilized but shrewd people of mixed origin. It is the headquarters of a mission of the ABCFM. On the coast are Benguela, charmingly situated and Mossamedes, a well-sheltered port. Travel has been facilitated in recent years by the opening of new railroads. About 225 miles of railroad have been built, and other railways are projected, connecting the principal towns of the territory. There are also about 800 miles of telegraph in operation.

Apart from Roman Catholic missions under Portuguese protection, the missionary societies established in Angola are the BMS, ME, ABCFM, PB, and the FCMS. The BFBS also has an agency in Angola. The whole number of stations occupied by these societies is 14.

Monteiro, *Angola and the river Congo*, London, 1895, 2 vols.

ANGORA: A city of 36,000 inhabitants; capital of the province of the same name in Asiatic Turkey. It is a place of considerable commercial importance, as it was in ancient times under the name of Ancyra of Galatia. The majority of the population are Mohammedans. It is a strong center of the Armenian Catholics. There are also Armenians, a few Greeks, and some Protestants. At Istanos, a village a few miles from Angora, there is a Protestant church of influence and activity which affects all the region.

ANGRA PEQUEÑA: A town on a bay of the same name on the coast of German Southwest Africa. It is the seaport of Great Namaqualand, where the Rhenish Missionary Society has several stations and a colony of Europeans is slowly growing.

ANG-TAU: A village in the Fo-kien province, China, S. W. of Fuchau; station of the ME with 17 native workers, men and women, 4 outstations, 7 Sunday schools, 5 young people's societies, 5 common schools and 400 church members. Also written Tang-tau.

ANGULANA: A town S. of Colombo on the W. Coast of Ceylon; station of the WMS, with one missionary and 16 native workers, men and women, 3 outstations, 4 Sunday schools, 5 village schools and 65 church members.

ANHALT-SCHMIDT: A town in Cape Colony, South Africa. Mission station of the Berlin Evangelical Missionary Society (1860); with 2 missionaries, 12 native workers, men and women, 2 outstations, and 500 communicants.

ANIWA: A small island in the southernmost group of the New Hebrides. Population, 192, all Christians.

ANIWAN: This language belongs to the Melanesian family and is used by less than a thousand persons inhabiting Aniwa Island. It has been written for missionary purposes with Roman letters.

ANKLESWAR: A town of 11,000 inhabitants near Broach on the Narbada River, Bombay, India; station of the German Baptist Brethren Mission, with a missionary and his wife, an orphanage, and 25 church members.

AN-KO-CHUANG: A town in the Chi-li province of China; station of the ME, with 6 native workers, men and women, 1 high school, 1 village school, and 185 church members.

ANLO: A dialect of the Ewé language, q. v.

ANNAM: A kingdom under the protectorate of France, occupying the most eastern portion of the Indo-Chinese peninsula, east of Siam and southeast of Burma. Area, 30,000 square miles. Surface, irregular and mountainous. Rivers numerous, and, altho too shallow for navigation, most useful for irrigation. The country produces an abundance of rice, sugar, spices, and tropical fruits. The Annamese are somewhat akin to the Chinese in language and in many of their important customs, but they also partake largely of the Malay characteristics, and evidently form a link between the Mongolian and Malay races. They are generally quiet and inoffensive, indolent and fond of gayety. The women are much oppressed, but not obliged to live in seclusion. The religions are Buddhism, Confucianism, Spiritism, and Christianity. Annam is governed by an emperor, with a French resident to guide his policy. Mandarins appointed by the emperor govern the provinces and control the standing army, which is comparatively large. The capital of the country is Hué, on a river of the same name. The early history of Annam is involved in obscurity; it is only known that wars with the neighboring powers determined its boundaries, and that the empire was formerly entirely subject to China.

In the 17th century, when Annam was most prosperous, the Jesuits (among them the celebrated Jesuit missionary, Alexander von Rhodes, who came there in 1615) introduced Christianity, and in spite of much persecution propagated it with such energy that at the close of the 18th century French priests had converted the emperor and established a hierarchy of great influence. Later, however, these doctrines were rejected by the emperors, and the priests and converts persecuted. One emperor, Tu-Due, was especially opposed to Christianity, and the murder of several missionaries, between 1854 and 1858, served as pretext for the acquirement of a French colony in the East. In 1858 a French fleet was sent by Napoleon III., which succeeded in capturing several important towns, and, altho the Annamese made stout resistance, the French succeeded in dictating terms of peace by which they became possessors of three provinces. These remain in their possession under the name of Indo-China, the only important French colony in the East. By this treaty three ports in Tonquin were opened, and Christianity was permitted throughout Annam. An insurrection occurred in 1862, which was quelled by the French.

There are no Protestant missions in Annam, the only missionaries being of the Roman Catholic Church. In the entire kingdom of Annam, with a population numbering (1901) 6,124,000, there are 420,000 Catholics, under the care of 125 European and 264 native priests, in 7 apostolic vicariates.

Tonkin, or France in the Far East, Norman (C. B.), London, 1884; *Peoples and Politics of the Far East*, ibid., London, 1895.

ANNAMESE: The language spoken in Annam belongs to the Mon-Anam branch of the Indo-Chinese family of languages. It has its own written characters, but has been written in Roman letters in some Bible translations. It is spoken by about 10,000,000 people.

ANNFIELD: A village in the Dehra Dun district, United Provinces, India; station of the CMS (1859), with 3 missionaries and 7 native workers, men and women, a village school and 206 communicants.

ANOSIBE: District S. E. of Antananarivo, Madagascar; station of the Paris Evangelical Society (1899), with 1 missionary, 2 unmarried missionary women, 62 native workers, men and women, 30 outstations, 30 village schools, 1 high school, 1 industrial school, and 25 communicants.

ANTANANARIVO: Capital of Madagascar. Climate, temperate. Elevation, 4,500 feet. Population (1901), about 50,000; of Hova, Malagasy, Polynesian and Micronesian stock, each class speaking a separate language. Religion, fetishism; belief in charms and ordeals. Social condition, comparatively civilized. Occupations, metal and straw work, spinning, weaving, etc., in all of which skill is shown.

Station of the LMS and of the Paris Evangelical Society, to which the LMS transferred the most of its work after the French occupation of the island in 1896. Together the Societies have 29 missionaries and 24 native workers, men and women, 9 high schools, 1 college, and a printing house. There are 30,000 church members in the district.

Also station of the Friends Foreign Mission Society, with 6 missionaries and 31 native workers, men and women. It has 2 high schools, a printing house and a dispensary, and 300 professing Christians.

Also station of the SPG with 6 missionaries and 8 native workers, men and women, and 733 communicants.

The Norwegian Missionary Society also has a station here (since 1869), with a hospital.

ANTIGUA: An island in the British Colony of the Leeward Islands, W. I. Its population is about 36,000, chiefly negroes who are Christians. The Moravians have seven mission stations in the island.

ANTIOCH: A city of 17,500 inhabitants, in the province of Aleppo, Asiatic Turkey. It is situated on the Orontes River, about 20 miles from the Mediterranean Sea. The largest part of the population is Mohammedan. Greeks, Armenians, Roman Catholics, and a few Protestants make up the Christian part of the population. Altho the place has lost the importance of Apostolic days, it is still the seat of a Greek Patriarchate.

It is a station of the Reformed Presbyterian Churches of Ireland and Scotland, with 3 missionaries and 7 native workers, men and women, a dispensary, 2 village schools and 50 church members.

ANTIOKA: Station of the Swiss Romande Missionary Society, situated on the Komati River, N. of Lourenço Marques, Portuguese East Africa. It is occupied by 2 missionaries and their wives, 1 unmarried missionary woman, and 2 native workers: 2 preaching places, 2 village schools, a book depot, and 30 communicants.

ANTOFAGASTA: A seaport in Chile, S. America, the terminus of a railway across the Andes into Bolivia. Population about 8,000; station of the ME, with 1 missionary, 2 Sunday schools, and 80 church members.

ANTSIRABÉ: A district near Betafo, Madagascar; station of the Norwegian Missionary Society, with 2 missionaries, and a hospital.

ANUM: A town of the Volta, Gold Coast, West Africa. Population, 5,000. A station was founded here by the Basel Missionary Society in 1864, but in 1869 the city was destroyed by the Ashantis. In 1881, however, the station was rebuilt. There are now 5 missionaries and 31 native workers, men and women, with 21 outstations and 23 village schools. There are 740 communicants.

ANUPSHAHR: A town on the Ganges in the Bulandshahr district, United Provinces, India; station of the ME with 6 native workers, men and women, 8 Sunday schools, 5 village schools, a Young People's Society, and 600 church members.

AONLA: Town in the Rohilkhand district, United Provinces, India, S. W. of Bareilly; station of the ME, with 19 native workers, men and women, 8 Sunday schools, 4 village schools, and 750 church members.

AOMORI: A town of 15,000 inhabitants on the extreme northern coast of the island of Nipon, Japan.

It is a station of the RCA with 1 missionary woman, 2 native workers, man and woman, and 30 professing Christians. Occupied in 1891.

It is also a station, occupied in 1893, of the PE, with 2 women missionaries and 2 native workers, man and woman.

It is also an outstation of the ME with 1 native worker.

APAIANG. See GILBERT ISLANDS.

APAM: A town on the coast E. of Cape Coast Castle, Gold Coast Colony, W. Africa; station of the WMS, with 1 missionary, 51 native workers, 42 outstations, 6 Sunday schools, 5 common schools and 325 church members.

APAMANA. See GILBERT ISLANDS.

API. See NEW HEBRIDES.

API, or **BAKI LANGUAGE:** The Api or Baki, belongs to the Melanesian family of languages and is spoken in the island of Api, New Hebrides. It is written with Roman letters.

APIA: The principal seaport of Upolu, Samoan Islands, with an excellent and much frequented harbor. Mission station of the LMS (1836), with (1903) 4 missionaries, men and women, 38 native worders, and 1,525 communicants.

Mission station of the International Medical Mission Association, with 1 missionary and his wife, 1 hospital, and 1 dispensary.

Also mission station of the Seventh Day Adventist Missionary Society, with a missionary and his wife and 3 unmarried missionary women. A book depot is kept up.

APIZACO: Town in Tlaxcala, Mexico; station of the ME, with 8 native workers, 4 outstations, 5 common schools and 434 church members.

APPELSBOOSCH: Village in Natal, South Africa; station of the Church of Sweden Mission, with 6 missionaries and 6 native workers, men and women. Connected with it are 6 outstations, 4 preaching places and 4 village schools.

APPENZELLER, Rev. Henry G.: Born at Souderton, Pa., February 6, 1858. Died June 11, 1902. Graduated from Franklin and Marshall College, Lancaster, Pa., in 1882; attended Drew Theological Seminary two years; appointed by Bishop Fowler, in 1885, as one of the first Methodist missionaries to Korea, arriving at Chemulpo with his wife on April 5, 1885. During seventeen years he was one of the most faithful and efficient missionaries of the Methodist Episcopal Church and held, with honor, a number of responsible positions. He was president of the Pai Chai College at Seoul, principal of the Theological Department and pastor of three churches. As one of the translators of the Scriptures into the Korean language he made a permanent contribution to the cause of missions, and his linguistic services were highly esteemed by his associates of other denominations. The name of Pai Chai Hak Tang was given to the college by the King of Korea, who paid for the tuition of a number of pupils, and who showed the highest regard for the principal. On July 24, 1887, Mr. Appenzeller had the joy of hearing the testimony of the first convert in the mission; and Christmas day of that year he preached his first sermon in the Korean language, his text being: "Thou shalt call His name Jesus, for He shall save His people from their sins." In April and May, 1887, Dr. Appenzeller journeyed nearly 200 miles to Pyeng-yang, it being the first missionary journey taken in that direction, and during the following year he went to Wi-ju, the gateway to China, receiving eleven men into the Church on profession of their faith in Christ. In his exploring itineraries, at a later date, he visited eight provinces of the kingdom; and during these missionary journeys he left a deep and lasting impression for good. In 1890 he took part in the organization of the first Quarterly Conference in Korea at Seoul, and before his labors ceased he had the pleasure of seeing the number of communicants in Korea reach nearly 4,000. On the afternoon of June 11, 1902, Dr. Appenzeller set sail for Mokpo to attend a session of the Board of Bible Translators, which had been called to meet there. During the night of that day the steamer was run into by another steamer near Guelin Island, and with fourteen Koreans, three Japanese and eight of the crew, this devoted missionary lost his life.

APOSTOLIC AND EARLY CHRISTIAN MISSIONS: For the first three centuries of its life, the Christian Church was distinctively a missionary church. Its chief purpose was the spread of Christianity. It fought heresy bitterly, but for the great mass of the people, creeds were a secondary consideration. Preaching the Gospel took always the first place.

From the paucity of record, apart from the Book of Acts, and some references in the epistles, some have supposed that aside from Paul, Peter and John, and their immediate associates, there was little interest either in the Apostolic company or the great mass of believers, in the carrying of the Gospel message to remote sections. That this is incorrect, is manifest from the advance actually made (see Geography of Missions). It is impossible that a new faith should so rapidly have extended over so wide a territory and against such fearful odds, in comparatively so short a time without great effort. At the middle of the 2d century Justin Martyr wrote: "There is no people, Greek or barbarian or of any other race, by whatsoever appellation or manners they may be distinguished, however ignorant of arts or agriculture, whether they dwell in tents or wander about in covered wagons, among whom prayers and thanksgiving are not offered, in the name of the crucified Jesus, to the Father and Creator of all things."

Fifty years later Tertullian in his address to the heathen said: "We are but of yesterday, and yet we already fill your cities, its lands, camps, your palace, senate and forum; we have left you only your temples."

Already Abgar, claimed by the Armenians as their first leader in the faith, had been baptized, and even if St. Thomas himself never visited India, a Christian teacher from Alexandria visited Malabar in 190 and not long after it was reported that there were 350 strong churches in that land. Early in the 3d century twenty bishops from the Nile valley attended a council in Alexandria, while Tertullian's church at Carthage was but the leader among several in North Africa. It is to be remembered also that when Constantine made Christianity the religion of the Roman Empire, he accepted a situation already of remarkable character. It was no parallel to the conversion of some of the northern nations, where the ruler's will was all that was needed to insure a change of worship, regardless of a change of thought or of heart. No emperor, however mighty, could have made Rome Christian, had Christianity not already been woven into the very fiber of its national life.

In considering how this was brought about the agencies, methods and underlying purpose must be kept in mind.

Agencies: The great agency of the Apostolic Church in the missionary enterprise was the rank and file of its membership. During the first three centuries there were very few who like Paul and Barnabas, Silas, Timotheus and a few others, gave themselves to the work of preaching in new countries. Even the great leaders who followed the apostles, Polycarp, Justin Martyr, Ignatius, Origen, Tertullian, Cyprian, Clement and others, were not missionaries in the sense in which the term is used now. They were all located in the centers, and did valiant work in them, but they were seldom explorers, leaders in the outreaching of the Church. That was chiefly, almost entirely, the work of obscure men, for the most part laymen, and also for the most part not distinctively set apart for the work. The one supreme characteristic of the Apostolic Church in this respect is the missionary zeal and activity of the individual members. Women as well as men—merchants, miners, sailors, soldiers, craftsmen, voluntarily made it one of their chief objects, whether at home or abroad, in private or public life, to extend to others the Gospel message. Then, as in no period since, was it true that every individual Christian was a missionary, and it was to this individualistic evangelism that was due the marvelous extension of those three centuries.

Methods: In all this, then, there was little organization. Bishops gradually acquired control in their own cities and districts, but all were equal, and there seems to have been no concerted action. Each man, whether in the centers or on the outskirts of the Empire, was free to conduct his dioceses much as he pleased and this freedom extended to the specific action of his individual followers, who were free to teach as they judged best, so long as they kept clear of heresy and made manifest in their lives the principles they professed. It was in the combination and accord of precept and practise that lay the great power of that early Church.

Yet there was after all a certain method apparent in this individualism. The special efforts were made in the great centers, the cities of the Roman Empire, and along the lines of commercial activity. As fast as the community in one place became large enough a leader was found, placed there and expected to see that his diocese grew in numbers and influence. Thus Gregory Thaumaturgus was made bishop of his native city, Neo-Cesarea, in Pontus, when there were about twenty-seven Christians there. At the close of his ministry there were said to be but twenty-seven pagans left.

With the growth of the Church there developed also the aids to work. This is the period of the early versions—the Peshito and Curetonian Syriac for Syria and Mesopotamia; the Memphitic, Thebaic and Bashmuric for Egypt and the Upper Nile Valley; the North African and Italian Latin for Carthage and Rome. Alexandria, always a literary center, became, too, the seat of a catechumen's school, practically a missionary college from which trained workers were sent out to Africa, Europe and Asia.

Motive: In the earlier years of this period, the controlling motive in this missionary work appears to have been personal loyalty to the Savior and a desire that, as He had been rejected and crucified, so now He might be accepted and enthroned. There was indeed recognition of the need of men, but the impelling impulse was less that than their love for Christ and a desire that

He receive full honor. As the work continued the human element became more prominent. The risen Savior out of sight was to a degree replaced by the needy ones in sight. There was a better conception of the object of Christ's mission, in its relation both to the individual soul and to the multitudes who were without God and without hope. Human sympathy assumed a larger place, and the salvation of men became more distinctively the object and motive of missionary labor.

With the opening of the 4th century there came a change in almost every respect. The active missionary propaganda of the Apostolic Church gave place to an effort to assimilate the great mass of heathenism, which, when Constantine made Christianity the dominant faith, accepted its forms without entering into its spirit. At the same time the loose individualism of the preceding period was followed by a closer, more compact organization, due partly to the change in political conditions, partly to the necessity of better supervision to counteract the influences of heathenism, the growth of divergent and heretical creeds, and partly to incursions from the wild natives of the north. The Church had by a sudden bound become a nation, and the simpler forms possible in a community became inadequate to the new duties and responsibilities.

The result, so far as missionary work was concerned, was that the Church as a whole ceased to have any special interest in it, the immediate need filling the vision completely. It was the period of the great councils, and, to the leaders and the people generally, the conservation of the faith seemed more essential than its extension. There were, however, individuals who still felt the burden of the nations, and the incoming of the hordes of East Goths, Vandals and Huns, presented opportunities as well as needs that taxed to the full the fervor of ecclesiastics at home, and such apostles as Ulfilas, Honoratius and Patrick in Europe, Gregory the Illuminator in Armenia, Frumentius in Africa and the Nestorian missionaries who penetrated to Central and Eastern Asia, but left so little record that their achievements are clouded in obscurity. In agencies, methods and motive the movement changed entirely. The great mass of the Church gradually came to know nothing and care nothing about missions; the ecclesiastical leaders for the most part were content with their immediate duties, and individuals commissioned by the Church but scarcely supported by it were the sole agents. With this period began, too, a movement toward national rather than individual conversion. Whole communities and even races were brought into the church *en masse*. So too, in this period, the motive that became so prominent in the next, of loyalty to and ambition for the Church, began to gain its hold. It was no longer Christ, the Savior of the needy soul, that filled the vision, so much as the "body of Christ," the Church to be, enlarged, solidified, glorified.

In a very real sense, then, the proclamation by Constantine making Christianity the religion of the Roman Empire was the greatest calamity that ever befell the Christian Church. It practically suffocated the already waning energies, and laid the foundation for that period of inactivity during which the Eastern Church crystallized and the Western developed the ecclesiastical machinery of Papacy. That missionary activity did not disappear entirely was due to individuals rather than the Church, as will be evident in the record of the succeeding centuries until the Reformation, described in the article on Medieval Missions.

ARABIA: A peninsula at the southwestern extremity of Asia, lying within latitude 30° and 12° 45′ N., and longitude 32° 30′ and 60° E. Its land boundaries are Egypt on the northwest and Palestine and Syria on the northeast. Commencing at the northeast, the waters which successively surround it are: the Persian Gulf, Gulf of Oman, Indian Ocean, Gulf of Aden, and the Red Sea. Its total area is estimated at over 1,000,000 square miles. Arabia was formerly divided and described by foreigners as consisting of Arabia Petraea, the rocky mountainous region in the north; Arabia Deserta, the vast desert lands, and Arabia Felix, the "Happy" land, on the shores of the Red Sea and Indian Ocean. A study of the physical features of the country suggests a more rational division of the surface into equal thirds; one comprising the mountainous lands along the coasts; another the desert lands, which form almost a complete ring around the central plateau of tableland, which forms the third physical division.

Beginning with the coast district at the northwest, the principal districts are: 1. *The Sinaitic peninsula*, a triangle with the Red Sea as its apex, Palestine for its base, and the gulfs of Suez and Akabah for its sides, corresponds very nearly to Arabia Petraea. 2. *Hejaz* extends from latitude 28° to 21° N. along the shore, and for a distance inland varying from 60 to 150 miles. It is for the most part sandy and stony, with only a few fertile spots around Medina and Kholeys, a few days' journey north of Mecca. Around this holy city of the Mohammedan is the Haram, or Sacred Territory, at the southern extremity of the district. 3. *Yemen* occupies the remainder of the mountain coast as far south as Aden, and consists of two portions. That part lying along the shore is called Tehamah, and is flat and rocky, while the inland part, stretching sometimes 300 miles to the east, is mountainous, with precipitous hills and fertile valleys. The oasis of the southern Jowf is also included in this district. 4. *Aden*, a small peninsula on the coast, about 100 miles east of Bab-el-Mandeb, with the island of Perim, at the entrance to the Red Sea, is subject to Great Britain. It includes in its district a smaller peninsula, Little Aden, and the settlement and town of Sheikh Othman, ten miles from Aden, in all 70 square miles. Its population (1901) is 43,974. Aden is simply a coaling station, but its position makes it of great strategic importance. 5. *Hadramaut* and *Mahrah* occupy the 1,200 miles of coast between Aden and Cape Ras-el-Hadd. They have the same general features of the other coast districts—a sandy or rocky shore, behind which mountain ranges stretch back into the great desert—and little is known in regard to the interior, its inhabitants or products. 6. *Oman* and *Hasa* complete the line of coast districts, extending from Cape Ras-el-Hadd to the head of the Persian Gulf. The mountains in Oman are the highest on the coast, and the strip of coast land in Hasa has extensive fertile tracts. Mascat, the capital of Oman, is the only good harbor.

The central third of Arabia, especially Nejd, is the stronghold of the Arab nation. On the extreme north and northeast lies the desert, with the oasis of Jof and Teima, varying the monotony of the stony waste. South of the stony desert lie the Nefud, or sandy passes, between which and Nejd is the district of Shomer, with its two parallel mountain ranges running northeast to southwest. The principal provinces of the nine into which Nejd is divided are: Ared, the central province, containing the capital, Riadh; Sedeyr, or Sudeir, in the highlands of the Toweyk mountain range, which runs north and south through the heart of Nejd; Yemamah, south of Ared, a fertile district, celebrated in native history as the home of brave men and beautiful women; and Woshem, a small but important district west of Ared. Of the desert surrounding Nejd, that portion lying to the southward is called the Dahna, or "Crimson," from the color of the sand, and covers 50,000 square miles. Of it little is known; not even the Bedouins have traversed its full extent, and European travelers shrink from its heat and sterility.

Climate: In the Sinaitic peninsula the air is dry, clear, and, in the main, healthy, with winter rains. The summer temperature in the valleys is excessively high, but the nights are cool. In general the sandy slopes of the coast districts are hot and unhealthy, with a cooler, more healthy air in the mountains. In the desert the heat is intolerable, and in the Nefud district the deadly "simoom" blows. This is a storm of a cyclonic nature, carrying in its center a noxious gas, which is death if inhaled in any quantity. It lasts from two to ten minutes at any one point, and the only way to escape it is to cover the mouth with a cloth and lie down on the ground, where the heavier pure air is found. Camels instinctively bury their noses in the sand, but horses are often killed by the gas. The dwellers in Arabia are divided into the nomadic Bedouins, and the dwellers in towns.

1. The Bedouins are the shepherds and herdsmen, who wander about the deserts from one fertile valley to another. They have been called brigands, because they consider themselves the lords of the land, and, in the absence of constituted authority, take summary methods to punish the traveler, whom they regard as a trespasser. In lieu of official fees for passports, they take whatever property they can lay hold of. By paying a fee to the first sheikh whose territory is invaded, an escort is secured to the traveler, giving safety in that district; a similar payment to the successive sheikhs will insure like protection; but the neglect of such an acknowledgment of their rights will lead to loss of property and sometimes of life. The Bedouin is not murderous by nature, but of necessity, when his demands are resisted. There are northern and southern Bedouins. The southern or "pure" Bedouins are fewer in number and more savage in disposition. In all there are about 1,500,000 of the Bedouins. They recognize no authority save that of their chief, the sheikh, for they are thoroughly democratic, and consider every man equal. The chief may be such by the law of heredity, but is oftener chosen on account of his qualifications for the position. The Bedouin is nominally a Mohammedan, but he scorns the formalities of the Koran, and disregards its ceremonial requirements. Tho he be not far from Mecca, he does not mingle with the devout who go there, nor will he always spare the caravan of pilgrims that passes through his territory. Among some of the tribes a lower religious belief exists; all gradations between sun-worship, tree-worship and no worship at all, have been found.

Lying, perjury, sensuality, and theft are their vices, while fidelity and the observance of a promise to the extent which the romancers chronicle are not uncommon. With all their bad traits, they are to be admired for their shrewd common sense, allied with a sarcastic, humorous side of their character. Their dress is simple, and they carry staves provided with crooks, together with short knives and old matchlocks, with which they seldom fail to hit the mark.

2. The sedentary Arabs number about six-sevenths of the entire population of the peninsula of Arabia. The Koreysh are the noblest of the race, and claim direct connection with the Prophet. Their clan ties and national feeling are very strong, and they own allegiance to their tribal head, the Sheikh, Imam, or Sultan. Where the doctrines of the Wahabees prevail the Mohammedan religion is followed with all its strictness of ceremonial and observances. Fetishism is found in Mahrah and places on the borders of the great desert. With belief in one God and observance of the rules of the Koran as to dealings between man and man, one naturally supposes that the people of Arabia would make no difficulty about tolerating the advances of sincere Christians. The rules of the Koran, however, as to generous dealings with men are commonly understood as limited to Mohammedans, and the degraded type of Christianity known to the Arabs makes them the more inclined to give full scope to their religions principle of non-intercourse with people outside of Islam. Death would certainly smite any Christian discovered in the Sacred territory of Arabia, and the risk of death would attend travel in any part of the interior of the country. It is for this reason that Mohammedanism is the only religion professed in Arabia at any distance from the coast-line.

In person the Arab is tall, well formed, lithe, with dark hair and eyes. Physically and morally, the race compares favorably with any of the races of mankind; mentally, it is superior to most races. Special traits are found in the different provinces. The people of Hejaz are fickle; those of Yemen are noted for gentleness and pliability, together with revengefulness; the tribes in Nejd possess a reputation for tenacity of purpose and dignity of deportment. A love of sport and games is found among the races of Oman and Hasa which is absent elsewhere.

Arabic is spoken in its purity in Nejd and Shomer, more inelegantly in the other provinces, until in the southern provinces it is merged into an African dialect. Education is deficient; the teaching of the young is carried on mainly in the household, where the father teaches his sons to read and write and to practise that politeness which is notable among the Arab children.

The total number of inhabitants of Arabia proper is estimated at about 6,000,000. Of this number the people of Hejaz (300,000) and Yemen (900,000) are admittedly subjects of the Sultan of Turkey. The other districts of Arabia are governed by their own chiefs (*Emir* or *Imam*). Turkey claims the right to rule the whole peninsula but has not yet been able to make good the claim.

Missions have not found entrance to Arabia as yet, owing to the determined attitude of Mohammedanism toward dissent from its teachings wherever it has power to enforce the death penalty. Two noble efforts have been made by loving service to break through the barriers of fanaticism. One of these is the Keith-Falconer Mission at Aden (now carried on by the UFS), with its chief station at Sheikh Othman on the high land back of the seaport.

The other missionary effort for Arabia is that of the Arabian Mission of the RCA operating from Turkish and independent territory on the Persian Gulf, with three stations, of which the most effective and most hopeful form of work is that of the hospital and dispensary.

Kamil, by Jessup (H. H.), New York, 1898; *Arabia, the Cradle of Islam,* Zwemer (S. M.), New York. 1901; *Keith-Falconer, Memorials of,* Sinker (R.), *Arabia: Journey through Central and Eastern,* Palgrave, (W. G.), London, 1869.

ARABIAN MISSION. See REFORMED CHURCH IN AMERICA, BOARD OF FOREIGN MISSIONS.

ARABIC: The Arabic language is closely allied to the Hebrew and Syriac, of the Semitic family. This appears in Bible translation, where the Hebrew may be turned into good classical Arabic with comparative ease. Difficult and ambiguous passages can be translated word for word, often by the same word that is used in the Hebrew, leaving the ambiguity the same in the translation as in the original. It is rich and refined; has an abundant and valuable literature, and is spoken by 50,000,000, and used in worship (generally without knowledge) by more than 200,000,000 of the inhabitants of the globe.

ARABKIR: City of Eastern Turkey, on the caravan road from Aleppo to Trebizond, and 50 miles northwest of Harput. Population, 30,000. Mohammedans, Armenians and Protestants. The prosperity of the town is due to the caravan trade and the cotton industry. The vicinity is rich in fruit trees. It was formerly a station of the ABCFM, but is now an outstation of Harput. Its evangelical church has lost many members through emigration, due to the insecurity of the country.

ARAGUARY: Town in Minas Geraes, Brazil; station of the PS (1895) with a missionary and his wife and an unmarried missionary woman; 14 outstations, and 250 church members.

ARAKAN: For sixty years a British province of Farther India, now a part of the province of Burma, since the war of annexation of 1885-86. It is separated from Burma proper by the western Yoma range of mountains, which have many volcanoes, mostly quiescent, and rise from 4,000 to 10,000 feet above the level of the sea. The habitable portion is a narrow strip of alluvium, extending from the mountains to the Bay of Bengal. It extends from the westernmost of the delta branches of the Irawadi on the south to Chittagong on the north, and is bounded on the W. by the Bay of Bengal. Above Ramree Island the territory widens, and from 19° to 21° 30′ several short ranges of mountains are interposed between the Yoma range and the Bay of Bengal, and are inhabited mostly by the hill tribes. Its area is 16,500 square miles, and its population is 672,000.

The people are of the same Mongoloid stock as the Burmese, excepting the inhabitants of the northern mountainous region who are of the same stock as the Karens. The religion of the people of the towns and the lowlands is Buddhism, while that of the hill tribes is spiritism or *nat* worship.

Missionary operations were commenced by the BMS about 1826 and by the ABMU in 1835, both missions being abandoned after some years because of the deadly climate. The ABMU reestablished its mission in 1888 at Sandoway and has met with good success among the hill tribes and the Tamils and Telugus who go to Arakan for work. Also written Aracan and Arracan.

Comstock (G. C.), *Notes on Arakan,* in Journal Am. Oriental Soc., Vol. 1, 1847.

ARAWAK: This language belongs to the South American group, and is spoken in Dutch Guiana. It is written in Roman letters and is hardly one of the permanent languages since only a few thousand people are known to use it.

ARCHBISHOP'S MISSION to the Assyrian Christians: The interest of the Church of England in the Nestorians was especially aroused by the report of the Royal Geographical Society's expedition to the Euphrates Valley in 1837. This resulted in the sending out of a joint expedition by the Royal Geographical Society and the SPG. Their report supplemented by numerous appeals from the Nestorians occasioned another journey in 1876, and the sending out of a missionary in 1881, tho it was not until 1886 that the work was put on a permanent footing.

The mission has no regular organization or constitution, but is carried on under the auspices of the Archbishop of Canterbury. The mission priests, who are all unmarried, receive no regular stipends beyond £25 annually for personal expenses, but live from a common fund. The work carried on is largely educational. A college has been formed for priests and deacons, besides 5 high schools and 40 village schools, the total number of scholars being roughly estimated at 1,200. Besides the educational work, the mission clergy exercise the function of ecclesiastical and temporal judges, deciding disputes between the native Christians and divorce and other spiritual cases, according to the Canon Law of the ancient Chaldean Church.

The object of the Mission is stated to be "in the first place to train up a body of literate clergy; secondly, to instruct the youth generally in both religious and secular knowledge; and thirdly, to print the very early liturgies and service books, to which the Assyrians are much attached, which have never been printed in the original, and of which the very primitive character is shown by their freedom from doubtful doctrine. The Mission seeks in no way to anglicanize the Assyrians on the one hand; nor on the other to condone the heresy which separated them from the rest of Christendom or to minimize its importance." A committee connected with the Protestant Episcopal Church of the U. S., aids the mission.

ARECIBO: A seaport on the N. coast of Porto Rico. Population about 8,000; station of the ME (1901) with one missionary and his wife, and a Sunday school.

ARGENTINE REPUBLIC: One of the most important of the South American republics. It occupies that portion of the continent south of latitude 22° S., with the exception of the western slope of the Andes which forms Chile. It is bounded on the north by Bolivia and Paraguay and on the east by Brazil and Uruguay. Its southern boundary has long been a matter of dispute with Chile, but was settled by treaty in 1881, according to the terms of which Patagonia was ceded to the Republic as far south as the Straits of Magellan, along with the eastern portion of Tierra del Fuego. At the same time a line running along the crest of the Andes was defined as the western boundary. At present the country is divided into 14 provinces and 9 territories, with a combined area of 1,319,247 square miles and an estimated population, in 1900, of 4,659,067. The provinces are: Buenos Aires, Santa Fé, Entre Rios, Corrientes, Rioja, Catamarca, San Juan, Mendoza, Cordova, San Luiz, Santiago, Tucaman, Salta, Jujuy. With such an extent of latitude the climate is most varied, tho in general healthful. All gradations between a temperate cool climate and a moist, tropical one may be found in this Republic. In Northern Patagonia the climate resembles that of the British Isles, while Buenos Aires rivals in salubrity the south of France. A dry cool temperature prevails along the mountain slopes, but along the coast at the north a thoroughly tropical climate is found.

The most remarkable feature of the country is its great plains or pampas, which occupy about three-fourths of the surface, stretching 2,000 miles in length and 500 in width. On these plains great herds of cattle are raised, and within late years wheat has been grown. The population has a large percentage of foreigners (Italians, French, Spanish, Germans, English), and the remainder consists of descendants of the Spaniards and Guarani and Quichua Indians. Negro descendants are scarce, as few slaves were brought to this section. Spanish is the prevailing language, tho in Corrientes the Guarani language is spoken, and Quichua in Santiago. The government encourages immigration from the south of Europe.

Altho it has an area twenty times as large as that of the New England States, the Argentine Republic contains a population of less than three per square mile. The broadest religious liberty is recognized; and the agricultural settlement founded by the late Baron Hirsch for Jewish refugees is most flourishing.

The Argentine Republic was occupied as a Mission field in 1836 by the ME, which now has 5 stations there; and in stations and outstations about 2,000 communicants connected with its churches. The SAMS, the Seventh Day Adventist Missionary Society, the International Medical and Benevolent Society, the South American Evangelical Missionary Society, and the Missionary Pence Association have establishments at Buenos Aires. The BFBS and the YMCA also have agents in that city. The Christian and Missionary Alliance and the Plymouth Brethren carry on missionary operations in two or three places, but no published statistics give information as to its extent.

ARIVONIMAMO: Town situated west of Antananarivo, Madagascar; station of the Friends' Foreign Mission Association (1888) with 2 unmarried missionary women and 234 native workers, men and women; 60 outstations and preaching places and 550 professing Christians.

ARKONA: A small town in the Transvaal Colony, South Africa, situated on the Lepalule River, northeast of Pretoria. Mission station of the Berlin Evangelical Lutheran M. S. (1877), with 1 missionary and 18 native workers, men and women, and 2 outstations.

ARKONAM: A town in Madras, India. Mission station of Established Church of Scotland; 4 missionaries and 23 native workers, men and women; 7 outstations, 11 village schools, and 90 church members.

ARMENIA: In strict use of the term, there is no Armenia at the present day. The name is not used either politically or geographically with reference to a definite territory. When used, the name refers in general to a vaguely defined region centering about Lake Van in Eastern Turkey, and extending thence north and southwest. Ancient Armenia was also a country whose bounds continually changed with the fortunes of war. Its northern limit was sometimes the Kur River, now in Russia; its eastern boundary was once, at least, the Caspian Sea, and the western boundary was usually the Euphrates River. The greater part of the region thus described now lies within the Turkish Empire and is also called Kurdistan.

In order that misunderstandings may be avoided it should be remembered that this region contains only a fraction of the **Armenian Race**. It is inhabited by Turks, Armenians, Russians, Persians, Kurds, Circassians, Greeks, Nestorians, Yezidees, Syrians and Jews. These all have had long residence in the country, which is now divided between Turkey, Persia and Russia. The Armenians are scattered over the three empires.

ARMENIAN CATHOLIC CHURCH: Since the Council of Florence, A.D. 1439, a considerable body of Armenians have been connected with the Church of Rome. As is the case with members of other branches of the Eastern Church which have accepted the supremacy of the Roman pontiff, they are allowed to retain their own ancient liturgy and many of their peculiar usages. In Turkey, Armenian Catholics as a rule avoid using their own language in social life. On the whole they are more frequently given office under the Turkish Government than members of the Gregorian Armenian Church. The congregation of the Mechitarists, which was formed by the Abbot Mechitar, belongs to them. They possess a famous monastery on the Island of San Lazzaro, near Venice, from which center they have successfully labored since 1702 for Armenian literature and education in the interests of the Roman Catholic Church. The Orthodox Armenians are inflexibly opposed to these schismatics, as they call them.

ARMENIAN CHURCH: Its own writers claim that its history goes back to the time of Christ. One Abgar or Abgarus, King of Edessa, is said by Moses of Khorene, the Armenian historian, to have been converted by hearing of the wonderful works of Jesus and to have been baptized by Thaddeus, one of the seventy disciples first sent out as missionaries. This Abgar is held by the Armenians to have been their king, although Tacitus calls him King of the Arabs. It was not, however, until the 4th century that the Armenian nation, as a whole, accepted Christianity. At the beginning of that century

St. Gregory the Illuminator preached at the Court of Armenia with such effect that from that day to this Christianity has been the national religion of the Armenians. For this reason the Armenian Church is often called "the Gregorian Church." The Armenians themselves, however, call it "the Church of the Illuminator (*Lusavorchagan*)."

Persecution only served to endear the Church to the people, and from that time it has been identified with their nationality. Under Turkish rule each religious body is also a political organism. The Armenian Church is little more than that at present. It is therefore inseparably identified with the race, and is pervaded by much of the corruption of Oriental Christianity.

Church Doctrine: 1. By accident—some say purposely—the Armenians were not represented in the Fourth Ecumenical Church Council which met at Chalcedon in 451 A.D., and which condemned Nestorianism and Eutychianism. When the decisions of the Council were reported to them, owing possibly to the poverty of their language at that time, it not having proper words to distinguish the two ideas of *the nature of Christ* and *the person of Christ*, the decision was misunderstood. In a synod of Armenian bishops in 491 the decision of the Council of Chalcedon was rejected, and at one of the synods of Tivan, now in Russia, their capital at that time, they declared decidedly for the Monophysite doctrine. This doctrine is not made prominent in their modern creeds.

Other leading characteristics of the Armenians are:

2. They believe the Spirit proceeds from the Father only.

3. They accept seven sacraments, altho in practice, baptism, confirmation, and unction are intermingled.

4. They baptize infants eight days old or less by threefold immersion, immediately offering them the communion.

5. They accept transubstantiation, and worship the consecrated elements as God.

6. They use unleavened bread, which is dipped in the wine and given to the people, who receive it into the mouth from the hand of the priest.

7. They pray for the dead, but deny Purgatory.

8. They practice auricular confession to the priest, who imposes penance and grants absolution, but gives no indulgences.

9. They pray to the Virgin and to saints, and have great faith in their mediation. With the Greeks, they reject images and accept pictures.

10. They believe in the perpetual virginity of Mary "the Mother of God."

11. They regard baptism and regeneration as the same thing, and have no practical conception of a new birth. All are saved who partake of all of the sacraments, do proper penance, observe the fasts of the Church, and perform good works.

12. Original sin is removed by baptism, actual sin by confession and penance.

Services are held in the church each morning at sunrise and each evening at sunset throughout the year. The altar is invariably toward the east. The sacrament of the Lord's Supper is observed twice a week, but the people partake usually only twice a year. Mass is observed as one of the formal rites of the Church. Confession to the priest is a necessary preparation for participation.

Church Government.—Originally the Church was under one spiritual head, the Catholicos, who was the general bishop. He resided at first at Sivas but later contentions arose, and with them divisions, until now there are three who hold his office: one, recognized as the Supreme Catholicos, resides at Echmiadzin, their holy city, now in Russia; one at Aghtamar, upon an island in Lake Van, in Eastern Turkey; and one at Sis, in the ancient province of Cilicia. It is said that at the consecration of the Echmiadzin Catholicos the dead hand of Gregory the Illuminator is even now employed as a medium of succession. The Catholicos alone can ordain bishops and consecrate the sacred oil which is used in the various ceremonies of the Church.

Besides the Catholicos, there are in Turkey two patriarchs, one of whom resides at Constantinople and one at Jerusalem. These offices were established by Mohammedan authority for political purposes alone. The patriarch must have a bishop's office ecclesiastically, but to this is added considerable influence with the government and over all Gregorian Armenians in civil matters. The patriarch of Constantinople is, by virtue of his office, the recognized civil head of the Armenian Church in Turkey.

There are nine different grades of Armenian clergy, all of whom are consecrated by the laying on of hands. These, in the order of rank, are: Catholicos, bishop, priest, deacon, sub-deacon, candle-lighter, exorcist, reader, and porter. There is also a class called vartabeds, who are preaching monks. The priests are married, and must have a wife at the time of ordination, but can never remarry. The priest cannot become a bishop unless his wife dies.

Obstacles Peculiar to Missionary Work Among Armenians: 1. The idea that the Church is coextensive with the Armenian race, so that one who withdraws from the Church rejects his nationality. 2. The Church is already Christian, and consequently Christian life has little relation to the Christian profession. 3. The difficulty, from the side of the Turkish Government, in erecting buildings and in maintaining Christian and educational institutions. 4. The existing poverty and oppression, accompanied by Oriental penuriousness. 5. The turning of the attention of young men to the Western world, as a refuge from oppression and massacre, and the consequent emigration of large numbers.

Peculiar Encouragements: 1. The religious nature of the race, and the fact that they accept the Bible as the Word of God. 2. The desire for education. 3. The peculiar relation of the Armenians to the 14,000,000 of other races among whom they dwell, and who must be reached largely through the evangelized Armenian Church. 4. Since mission work began among the Armenians, there has been a gradual rejection of their superstitions and reliance upon rites, and a marked awakening in the line of education. 5. Of late years, owing to the urgent demands of the people for the Gospel preaching, the vartabeds, bishops, and sometimes the priests and teachers, preach, and their sermons are often evangelical in tone and full of wholesome advice.

In ecclesiastical matters the Armenian Church reckons A.D. 551 as the year 1. This is the point of departure for the dates found in nearly all old manuscripts of the Church.

Fortescue (E. F. K.), *The Armenian Church*, London, 1872, 8vo.; Bianchini (P.), *The Armenian Ritual* (with European musical notation); Venice, 1876, 4to; Lynch (H. F. B.), *Armenia*, London, 1901; Anderson (R.), *History of Missions to the Oriental Churches*, Boston, 1870, 2 vols.

ARMENIAN LANGUAGE: Belongs to the Iranic branch of the Aryan family of languages. It has two marked divisions, the ancient, written language, which is rich in vocabulary and inflection, and the modern, spoken, which has dropped many of the older forms and constructions, and contains Persian and Turkish roots and idioms. The difference between these two branches of Armenian is very marked; it is something the same as that between the Latin and Italian. The ancient language was the product of an age of learning, and was then embodied in literary works. The modern tongue is the result of centuries of ignorance, without books, literature, or education. The difference between these two branches is now so great that an uneducated person can understand little or nothing of the classical language.

There are two principal spoken Armenian dialects at the present time—the Ararat dialect, which is spoken by many of the Armenians in Russia and Persia, and the western dialect, which is used in Southern Russia, Western Armenia, and Eastern Asia Minor. The Bible has been translated into both these dialects. The difference between these two dialects consists mostly in forms and constructions.

Altho there was a language, there was no Armenian alphabet until the beginning of the 5th century. At that time Mesrop, one of the learned saints of the Church, invented 36 of the 38 characters; the two others were added later. The relation of Armenian to other languages is yet a question of discussion and doubt.

Perhaps one-third of the Armenians in Turkey, especially those in the southern and western parts, and in the Kurdish Mountains, have lost their vernacular, and speak only Turkish or Kurdish. An effort is being made in Russia to force Russian upon the Armenians in place of their own tongue.

ARMENIANS: It is probable that no country of the size of that anciently called Armenia now has so many separate races preserving their identity among its inhabitants. The early history of these peoples is so mixed with myth and legend that the truth is difficult to find. During the Assyrian and Median periods there was evidently a great organized monarchy, with a strong military power, in the Lake Van basin. The Van inscriptions show a line of kings who were, both in civilization and in military powers, far in advance of any of their contemporaries in neighboring kingdoms. At times they were formidable enemies to the Medes.

This country was well known to the Assyrians as early as the 9th century B. C. At that time three principal races occupied the territory. These were the Naïri, who were spread from the mountains west of Lake Van along both sides of the Tigris to the Euphrates, and even farther; the Urarda (people of Ararat), who dwelt to the north and east of the Naïri, on the Upper Euphrates, about Lake Van and possibly on the Araxes; and the Minni, whose country lay to the southeast of the Urarda, in the Urmia basin. The Naïri, Urarda, and the Minni were propably Turanian or, at least, non-Aryan, races. Their congeners in Western Asia were the early Babylonians, and not the Medes, the Persians, or the Phrygians.

Besides these three races, it is evident, according to Sayce, from inscriptions recently deciphered, that, even at the time of the Egyptian King Thotmes IV., there was a powerful race in the north called the Hittites, or Khiti. In the records of the conquests of Assur-nazir-pal mention is made of his conquests among the Hittites. As far as we can learn, nearly all of these conquests were made within the limits of Armenia or upon its borders. What became of this people is not known at the present day.

These races appear to have maintained their independence until the time of Assur-bani-pal, about 640 B. C., when the last king of this series succumbed to the Assyrian yoke.

But, at the time of Herodotus, everything seems to indicate that a strange people had entered the land, bringing with them a new language, new names and customs, and a new religion. The source from which they came is doubtful. Herodotus and Stephen believe they came from Phrygia, while their language and religion would indicate Media. One thing is certain: the old Turanians had ceased to rule, and the Armenian race had been formed, which is undoubtedly a mixture of the ruling Aryan tribes with the primitive Turanian populations. The word "Armenia," used in Isaiah xxxvii:38 and 2 Kings xix:37, is an incorrect translation for "the land of Ararat."

Armenian histories describe the events of some sixteen centuries respecting which contemporary evidence has not yet been found. According to them, the first ruler of Armenia was Haik, the son of Togarmah, the son of Gomar, the son of Japheth, the son of Noah. This Haik is said to have left Babylon to escape the tyranny of Belus, the King of Assyria. Belus pursued him to the land of Ararat, and there, in a great battle, was slain by Haik. This occurred some twenty-three centuries B. C. At this time the Armenian kingdom was set up. Even to this day the Armenians call themselves Haik, and their country Haiasdan. Several centuries later, they say, Aram, the seventh from Haik, having incurred the hatred of the Queen of Assyria, was slain in a battle with that nation, and his kingdom became an Assyrian province.

It may be mentioned in passing that the name Aram appears among the kings who left inscriptions upon the rocks at Van. But neither his race nor his language shows any affinity to the Armenian.

The Armenian histories narrate that at the time of the captivity of Israel a certain number of the Hebrews escaped to the mountains of Armenia and intermarriages took place. Later the Armenian King Dikran (Tigranes) was the friend and ally of Cyrus. His successor was Vahakn, celebrated in song and story for his great victories, and deified after death.

The last of the Haik dynasty was Vahe, who was an ally of Darius III. against the Macedonians, and was defeated and slain by them. From that time Armenia was trampled by conquering armies until 190 B. C., when the country was freed by two Armenian nobles, who divided it, one of them ruling over Armenia Major, and the other over Armenia Minor, which was north and west of the Euphrates. This division continued until 89 B. C., when Dikran II. (Tigranes), of the line of Ardashes (Artaxus), conquered Armenia Minor and united the two kingdoms.

In 67 B. C. Armenia became an ally of Rome, but rebelling, their king, Ardavaz, was captured by Pompey and beheaded in Alexandria by Cleopatra, 30 B. C., and the country became tributary to Rome. The country was in turmoil for two and a half centuries thereafter.

In 261 of the Christian era Armenia became again subject to Persia. All of the royal family were slain except Durtad, the young son of the king. He escaped to Rome, and in 286, by the help of Rome, was established upon the Armenian throne. It was through him that the Armenians as a nation accepted Christianity.

It was the constant effort of Persia to subvert Armenian Christianity and establish Magianism in its stead. To this end, cruel persecutions were undertaken, and frequent incursions were made. From 632 to 859 A. D. Armenia was the scene of almost incessant struggle between the Eastern Empire and the Mohammedans, and it became by turns subject to each.

In 859 the dynasty of the Pagratidae came into power, and was recognized by both the Caliph and the Emperor of Constantinople, but in 1079 the greater part of the country became dependent upon Constantinople.

A small kingdom remained in the Taurus Mountains, north of Cilicia, which allied itself with European monarchs during the crusades. It maintained its independence until 1375, when the last Armenian king, Leo VI., was captured by the Egyptians and banished.

From this time Armenia lost its separate national existence. The greater part of the country was annexed to Turkey, while the eastern section remained subject to Persia and the northeast to Russia. Russia took another large section of Armenia in 1878.

Personal Characteristics: As far as moral traits are concerned, the Armenian compares favorably with the other races of the East. Ages of subjection have generally disposed them to quiet submission. They have now little hope of political restoration as a nation, altho a constant agitation is carried on with that end in view. The Armenians are cultivators of the soil, artisans, merchants, and bankers. They are persevering and shrewd in financial dealings. In Asiatic Turkey the Greeks alone can compare with them in trades, professions, business ability, and general intelligence. The Greek is more speculative and the Armenian slower and more cautious. In the finances of the Turkish Government some Armenians hold high positions, and in many ways they have rendered themselves indispensable to the prosperity and life of the country. In spite of the general increase of poverty throughout Turkey, the Armenians, up to the period of the massacres of 1895-96, held their own better than the other races.

The number of Armenians who are now scattered throughout the world is estimated at from 2,000,000 to 3,000,000. Perhaps two-thirds of the race reside in Turkey. The rest are in Russia, Persia, India, China, Africa, Europe, North and South America, and in nearly every country of the world. Up to the present time the nation has preserved its individuality to a remarkable degree, resembling in this respect, as in others, the Jews. With their dispersal throughout the world, however, the Armenians intermarry with other races and a distinct tendency to race disintegration has appeared.

See also **Armenia, Armenian Language, and Armenian Church.**

Lynch (H. F. B.), *Armenia,* London, 1901, 2 vols, 8°.; Curzon (R.), *Armenia: A Year at Erzroom,* London, 1854, 8°.; Harris (J. R. & H. B.), *Letters from Armenia,* New York 1897. 12°.

ARMENO-TURKISH LANGUAGE: The Turkish language when written with Armenian letters. See TURKISH LANGUAGE.

ARMSTRONG, Richard: Born at McEwensville, Pa., April 13, 1805; graduated at Dickinson College, Pennsylvania, 1828, and at Princeton Theological Seminary, 1830; ordained by the Presbytery of Baltimore, and sailed as a missionary of the American Board for the Hawaiian Islands, November 26, 1831, reaching Honolulu, May 16, 1832, after a six months' voyage. At a meeting of the mission in April, 1833, it was decided to commence a mission at the Marquesas Islands, and he was appointed, with Messrs. Alexander and Parker, to that field. After they had resided several months on Nukahiva Island they were informed that English missionaries were on the way from the LMS to occupy those islands. It was, therefore, decided to relinquish the field and return to the Hawaiian Islands. Their residence for eight months among savages and cannibals was one of great danger and discomfort. Mr. Armstrong's first station after his return was at Haiku, then at Wailuku, on Maui, from 1835-40. Here he had a parish of 25,000, schools with 1,700 children to examine and supply with teachers, churches to build, and in various ways he identified himself with all public interests. In 1840 he was removed to Honolulu to take charge of Mr. Bingham's church, where he remained eight years. The large stone church left unfinished he completed, planning and superintending the work. While at Honolulu Mr. Armstrong was engaged for many months in translating the proceedings incident to the concession to the people of right to the fee of their homes, and even in making actual surveys of the lands subject to the new law. During the four years' absence of Mr. Richards (1842-46) Mr. Armstrong was really the head of the Department of Public Instruction, the whole work being devised and superintended by him. On the death of Mr. Richards, in 1847, the position was offered to Mr. Armstrong, which he finally accepted, remaining in this office until 1855. He then became President of the Board of Education. He died in consequence of injuries received in falling from his horse September 23, 1860.

The king, Liholiho, published in the native paper a sketch of his character and work, which describes Dr. Armstrong as Minister of Public Instruction, President of the Board of Education, member of the House of Nobles and of the King's Privy Council, Secretary of the Board of Trustees of Oahu College, Trustee of the Queen's Hospital, and executive officer of the Bible and Tract Society, and deeply interested in developing the agricultural resources of the kingdom. The king adds that Dr. Armstrong's accurate knowledge of the Hawaiian language, and the facility with which he wielded the pen, naturally imposed upon him an immense amount of toil;

that his immediate and appropriate duties were connected with the cause of education, all the schools of the kingdom coming under his supervision, and that no government officer or missionary was brought into such close intimacy with the nation. Tho his week-day duties were so abundant and onerous, Dr. Armstrong never spared himself as a minister of the Gospel. He was an eloquent preacher in the Hawaiian language, and always listened to with deep interest by the people.

ARNI: Town in the North Arcot district, Madras, South India. Climate, tropical. Population, Hindu, Muslim, with a few Christians. Language, Tamil, Telugu, and Hindustani. Mission station of the Reformed (Dutch) Church in America, established in 1854. It has 2 missionaries and 64 native workers of both sexes, a publishing house, 17 outstations, an industrial school, and 18 village schools. The professing Christians number 300.

ARNO. See MARSHALL ISLANDS.

ARNOT'S GARENGAUZE MISSION. See CHRISTIAN MISSIONS.

ARORAI. See GILBERT ISLANDS.

AROUCA: A town of Central Trinidad, east of Port of Spain and northeast of San Fernando. Mission station of the UFS, with 1 native worker and 185 church members.

ARU ISLANDS: A group of islands in the Dutch East Indies lying W. of New Guinea. The population numbers about 25,000. The Netherlands Missionary Society has a station on Wokan, the largest island of the group.

ARUPPAKOTAI: A town in the Madura district, Madras, India; station of the ABCFM, with a missionary and his wife, 94 native workers, men and women, 85 outstations, a high school, 42 village schools, a YMCA, and 965 church members. Also written Arrupukottai.

ARYALUR: A town of the Trichinopoli district, S. India; station of the SPG, opened in 1825; has 13 native workers, 6 preaching places, 4 village schools, and 320 native communicants.

ARYA SOMAJ: This body is one of several societies or organized bodies of Hindus which admit the spiritual and moral degradation of the people and seek to introduce reform. It originated in Northern India, and while it has made some growth in Central India, its chief strength is in the Punjab. It is far more antagonistic to Christianity than the Brahmo Somaj. Such antagonism is demanded by the appeal which it makes to the patriotism of Hindus, as exemplified in its watchword of "India for the Indians." In its view that man is a traitor to India who accepts Christianity. This political quality in its aims doubtless explains in some degree the vigor seen in the Arya Somaj.

Its religious ideas also contain elements of strength. It teaches that God is one God, the Creator of all things, and the kindly Well-wisher of all His creatures, who, however, has never revealed Himself by incarnation. This monotheistic teaching it claims to find in the four Vedas, which alone, by the way, it accepts out of all the Hindu religious literature.

Religion, according to the Arya Somaj, consists of obedience to God, study of the Vedas, contentment with one's lot, and the practise of truth and justice toward all men. The doctrine of the transmigration of souls is the true eschatology, for it rights all wrongs and at the same time assures, in time, the salvation of all from the condition commonly called Hell.

Some remarks on details will better show the bearings of its curious creed:

(a) Its testimony for the monotheism of the Vedas is clear and explicit. (b) It is inconsistent in adopting the schools of philosophy in general terms, at the same time that it differs from some of them so widely in its positive theism and in its theory of creation. (c) Its humane elements in respect to woman and child-marriage are evidently borrowed from Christianity and the higher sentiment which it has created. (d) Its doctrine in respect to caste is a virtual arraignment of the entire Indian cultus and civilization. (e) It strikes a blow at the all-prevailing pessimism of India in ascribing benevolence of design to the supreme and personal creator of all things. In this respect it approaches very nearly to the Christian view and to that of Plato and Aristotle. (f) It is less grossly anthropomorphic and more spiritual than the old Hindu faith in its conception of heaven and hell, which it looks upon, not as places, but as characters and conditions; on the same principle, caste is character and not an accident of birth. (g) It is elevated in its ethical standards, and it gives to ethics a godward side. Obedience to God is one of its foremost requirements. (h) Its denial of all incarnations of deity is a two-edged sword, which strikes at both Hinduism and Christiantiy. It is so far in accord with Islam. (i) Tho it approves of Yoga or asceticism in theory, yet its definition of true religion is as practical as that of the apostle James. It embraces the cardinal virtues of life, both active and passive—such as contentment, repression of the passions, the return of good for evil, knowledge of the Vedas, obedience to God, and truthfulness and just dealings toward all men. (j) Its positively missionary character is in sympathy with Buddhism and Christianity, rather than with Hinduism. (k) Its advocacy of female education is a proof that it has caught the spirit of Christian lands. In no one feature does the Arya Somaj strike more deeply at the root of old Hinduism than in its policy with respect to women. (l) It apparently attempts a compromise between true theism and the prevailing pantheism. It inspheres the human soul in the infinite soul, and apparently expects its absorption into deity; yet it speaks of the soul as a real entity, and maintains its free will, and therefore its moral responsibility. (m) Its doctrine of transmigration is exceedingly plausible. No better reasons could be given for such a theory of eschatology.

The relation of the Arya Somaj to Christianity and to Western thought is unique and full of interest. It is exceedingly hostile to Christian propagandism, and yet it is a far more efficient handmaid of Christianity than was the Brahmo Somaj in its most palmy days. It is more efficient, because its attitude toward all Hindus is more conciliatory, and therefore more persuasive and influential. It is less radical as to changes in doctrine, and yet not one more step radical with respect to those great social movements which Christianity is striving to promote. Moreover, the Arya Somaj is a real ally of Christianity against the various current phases of Western infidelity. It takes the side of truth against the agnosticism of Huxley and Herbert Spencer. It is strongly theistic. It believes in an intelligent and omnipotent First Cause, and a real creation of the world. It maintains benevolence of design in the creation and government of the world, which Tyndall and Darwin reject. It is in advance of Max Müller in the doctrine of a preternatural revelation of God to man. It brings all virtue and philanthropy within the domain of religion, and is a rebuke to all those who would dispense with God in the government of human affairs. It challenges all forms of pessimism, ancient or modern, Eastern or Western, and maintains that the one God of the universe is wise and good, and therefore worthy of all reverence and love.

Nevertheless, while modern Aryanism is in some sense an ally of Christian civilization, it must not be forgotten that it is more or less of the nature of an entrenchment of essential Hinduism. The more nearly it counterfeits the truth of God and shuns disgusting rites, the more plausible does it become. It considers that it has adjusted itself to modern science and progress, and needs no further change. Christian missionaries must bear in mind the fact that the Arya Somaj is an aggressive and bitter enemy of Christianity. It hopes to bar the extension of the teachings of Jesus Christ in India, just as it hopes to check Islam, or to overthrow the degrading superstitions of popular Hinduism. In order better to attack Christianity it is borrowing from Western scoffers at the Bible a logic and a vocabulary and from the missionaries, a carefully proven theory of the uses of school, pulpit and press for purposes of propaganda. Its enmity to Christian teachings is deliberate and permanent.

This enmity might be a source of dread to the missionary, were not the Arya Somaj fatally weak in risking its whole system upon the untenable claim that the four Vedas teach a pure monotheism. Because of this weakness which must some time be revealed, this active organization will serve its day, holding what light it has before the people, and then it will fall because it has no stable foundation.

ASANSOL: Town in Bengal, India; station of the Methodist Episcopal Church, North, with 3 missionaries and 4 native workers of both sexes, 3 village schools, an orphanage, young people's societies and about 325 professing Christians.

ASHANTI LANGUAGE: This language belongs to the Negro family of African languages, and is spoken in W. Africa by about 3,000,000 people along the Gold Coast. For missionary purposes it has been written with Roman characters. It is also sometimes called the Otshi language. It exists in two dialects, the Akwapim and the Fanti.

ASHTON, Rev. W.: Born July 13, 1817. Died March 29, 1897. He was a missionary of the LMS at Barkly West, South Africa, and during a service of fifty-four years in the mission field he, as a self-sacrificing, consecrated missionary of the cross, did much for the enlightenment of the Dark Continent.

ASIA MINOR: Originally confined to a small section on the border of the Ægean, the term has come to include that portion of Asiatic Turkey lying between the Black Sea on the north and the Mediterranean on the south, the Marmora and Ægean seas on the west, and the Euphrates Valley on the east. This last boundary is vague, as the Euphrates is tortuous in its course. It is, however, sufficiently accurate for practical purposes. See TURKEY.

ASIATICS IN THE UNITED STATES: The discovery of gold in California, in 1849, opened the way for the immigration of the Chinese to this country in large numbers. In the one year of 1852 there were 20,000 arrivals. Twenty-five years later, there were no less than 150,000 in the United States. Of these, 30,000 were in San Francisco, somewhat more than this number in other parts of California, and the remainder scattered elsewhere. In San Francisco, Chinatown embraces the greater part of fifteen blocks, in which Chinese life as seen in China is quite accurately reflected. The Chinese being so extremely conservative, they cling very tenaciously to their own modes of life. While learning our language, and observing our ways, they largely live in a world of their own; and most of them eventually to go back home and die among their own people. They bring their idolatry with them, and in San Francisco alone have eighteen temples.

The first Christian work was begun among the Chinese in 1852, by the Presbyterian Board of Foreign Missions, which sent the Rev. Wm. Speer, D.D., to San Francisco for this purpose. He labored with great zeal and earnestness until his health broke down, and for long years was remembered as "The Chinaman's Friend." He was succeeded in 1859 by the Rev. A. W. Loomis, D.D., who for thirty-two years was a devoted and successful laborer. In 1866 a Chinese church of twelve members was organized. In 1870 Dr. Loomis was joined by Rev. I. M. Condit, D.D., who still has charge of the Presbyterian work in California. The mission house built by Dr. Speer became too strait for the work, and in 1882 the First Presbyterian Church, being situated in close proximity to the encroaching Chinese quarters, was purchased and occupied as mission headquarters.

In 1868 Rev. Otis Gibson, D.D., established a mission of the M. E. Church. A commodious building was erected for chapel, school and rescue purposes, in which vigorous work has ever since been carried on. A Congregational mission was opened in 1870 by Rev. W. C. Pond, D.D., who has ever since been its efficient superintendent, with Rev. Jee Gam as native pastor. In 1898 this mission purchased a large building, which has been fitted up in a manner well adapted for work. The Rev. John Francis, of the Baptist Church, established a mission in 1870. Later a building for church and school purposes was built in a location well suited for its efficient work.

These missions, besides preaching services in the Chinese language, Sunday schools and other church work, have each evening schools, in which the rudiments of English are taught. They have also opened stations at many of the principal towns and cities of the State, where many Chinese have been instructed and brought to Christ.

Many Christian people in our American Churches were awakened to a sense of their responsibility to these heathens; but, with the barrier of an unknown tongue lying between, how could they do anything for them? The Chinese were anxious to learn English, and so the plan of *Chinese Sunday Schools* was adopted. These were opened in nearly all the prominent churches of San Francisco, and at other important points. As the Chinese went East, missions and schools were gradually opened, until now, more than seventy of them are found in the cities and towns of our broad land. In New York, Boston, Philadelphia, Pittsburg, Chicago, and Portland, Oregon, where Chinese are found in the largest numbers, many flourishing Sunday schools exist, connected with the various churches, and also several organized missions. All this has resulted in the conversion of hundreds of souls, among whom are found many devoted Christians.

In the first years of Chinese mission work there were not many families or children. But as these began to increase in San Francisco, schools were opened. These schools are now found in the principal missions, with an enrollment of 250 scholars. A Chinese public school has been in existence for several years, which has grown until now five American teachers are employed. A goodly number, too, of the native-born Chinese attend our American public schools; 2,600 in San Francisco are under eighteen years of age, and 2,000 of these are of school age. There are 1,700 native-born now here, besides many who have gone back to China. 3,000 women are estimated to be in San Francisco, of whom the largest share are of bad character. Slave girls have been imported in large numbers, who are bought and sold like chattels. There is no such thing as slavery known among men, but among females it is sadly prevalent.

Homes for the rescue of these slave girls were established in 1873 in connection with the Presbyterian and Methodist missions. During the thirty years of their existence probably 1,500 girls have been rescued. Each mission has a fine building for a home. Many of these rescued ones have become Christians, married Christian men, and gone out to set up Christian homes for themselves.

In 1870 Chinese branches of the YMCA were formed in different missions. Each has a central society in San Francisco, with branch societies at the various points where Christian work has been established. There are scores of these societies, to which from the beginning several thousand members have belonged. Entering the association is the first step toward giving up idolatry and learning the religion of Jesus. The Chinese are very social in their nature and this society is a power to draw them together and away from the dangers of bad resorts.

Approximate results of Chinese work in our country may be briefly stated in the following summary:

The number of Chinese in the United States, 100,000. Of these, in San Francisco, 20,000; on the Coast outside of San Francisco, 52,000; in other States and Territories, 28,000. The whole number of Christians in the United States from the beginning, divided between Presbyterians, Methodists, Congregationalists, and Baptists, with a few from other denominations, 4,000. The present number of Christian Chinese in the United States, 1,600. Of these in San Francisco, 600; in other parts of the coast, 500, and in other States, 500. The number of Sunday Schools, 75, with an attendance during the year of 2,500 scholars; children in schools, 500. The number of lay preachers converted in U. S., who have labored both here and in China, 60. Chinese ordained ministers who were converted in U. S., 12.

The influence of those converted here upon their homes in China as they return is one of the most hopeful phases of the work. All the Chinese who have emigrated, not only to this country, but to nearly all others, are from the one province of Canton, and from a few districts or counties of that province. While this is so, still they represent a population of probably ten or fifteen million souls. The reflex influence of the thousands of Christians converted here, and the thousands more who have been instructed in a knowledge of the truth, and seen with wondering eyes the prosperity of this Christian country, as they return home to dwell among these millions, is very great. It is mightily weakening the power of idolatry, as well as building up the constituency of a Christian community. A score or more of chapels have been built, some entirely and others partly, by these American Chinese Christians. One church in the heart of this region was built entirely by California Christians, costing six thousand Mexican dollars, and in which they support a native pastor. This is only *one* notable instance among many. Quite a number of the native preachers of this region were converted in the United States. More and more the hearts of the Chinese Christians among us are turning toward transplanting in China the seed which has been sown among them here. The contact of the Chinese with our Christian civilization is no mean power in helping to bring about the New China.

Mission work among the Japanese in the United States is a hopeful and growing one. On the Pacific Coast they are fast increasing in numbers, as they are free to come, while an exclusion law shuts out the Chinese. Dr. E. A. Sturge, who is the best of authority, says: "There are about 60,000 Japanese on this Coast, 40,000 in California and 4,000 or 5,000 in San Francisco. More than forty steamers are plying between this Coast and Japan, and every steamer arriving adds to the number of Japanese in our country. There are not many of these people in the East, as there is no employment for them there. There are about a hundred in Chicago, and perhaps two hundred in New York City. Most of those who come directly from Japan belong to the student class, and are here for the purpose of study, while the majority of those who come from Hawaii belong to the laboring class. The Japanese in this land are nearly all young men, and very few of them expect to remain in America more than five years. As they all wear the American dress, and reside in no special quarter, their presence is scarcely realized."

Mission work among this people was begun in a small way twenty-five years ago, but as they have rapidly increased in the last decade, the work has grown into two flourishing missions of the Methodist and Presbyterian Churches. Both of these missions have commodious buildings and are carrying on a most interesting and encouraging work. The Methodist mission, which is the largest, is under the superintendency of the Rev. M. C. Harris, D.D., and the Presbyterian is under E. A. Sturge, M.D. They both have the aid of native pastors. The Japanese readily accept Christianity, and a thousand Christians are now reckoned to be on the Coast. The work is spreading beyond San Francisco, as the people are scattering throughout the State in the fields and orchards. The Methodist mission has stations to the number of eight or ten, while the Presbyterians are also establishing stations at outlying points.

ASISIPI. See SANDY LAKE.

ASMARA: A village west of Massaua, in the Italian Colony of Eritrea, N. E. Africa; station of the Swedish National Missionary Society (1891), with 7 missionaries and 6 native workers, men and women; 3 village schools, an orphanage, a printing house and 51 communicants.

ASSAM: A province of British India ceded to the East India Company by the king of Burma in 1826. Until 1874 it was administered as a part of Bengal. It is now a separate province under a lieutenant-governor. It lies between the parallels of 24° 30' and 28° 15' N. latitude, and between the meridians of 89° and 96° 50' E. from Greenwich. It is the chief seat of tea-culture in India. Its area is 49,004 square miles and its population (in 1891) 5,476,833.

The country consists of two extensive river valleys and three ranges of mountains. At the north, Bhutan occupies the southern slope of the Himalaya Mountains, and the somewhat lower range which overlooks the wide and fertile valley of the Brahmaputra. The valley of this great river extends from Sadiya in the east to the foot of the Garo Hills, where the river turns to the south. The right bank is level, and has broad fertile lands, densely inhabited; the left bank is crowded by a range of hills named from the tribes that occupy them, the Garo, the Khasi, and Jaintia, Naga, and Singpho Hills. The comparatively level and broad valley extending from the right bank of the Brahmaputra is mostly occupied by Assamese, the ruling race. They have also several cities and towns on the left bank. Southwest of the hills of the left bank lies the valley of the Surma, a large tributary stream flowing into one of the delta branches of the Jumna or Brahmaputra. This valley is broad, well watered, and fertile. The Khasi and Jaintia hills overlook it. It was formerly claimed as a part of the Eastern Bengal plains, but the Indian Government has now transferred this whole valley to the Assam Province, to which it properly belongs.

The People: The ruling class, the Assamese, hold very similar relations to the hill tribes of Assam as the Burmans do to the hill tribes of that country. They are of different race, habits, and religion. The Assamese are believed to be allied to the Shans, tho, perhaps, remotely. They were formerly Buddhists, but about the middle of the 18th century, having sought the protection of Bengal, they adopted the entire Brahmanist system—divinities, caste, idol-worship, and all. Their language, tho originally of the Pali stock, has, by the adoption of Hinduism, and their intimate association with Eastern Bengal, acquired a large infusion of Bengali. The hill tribes, which in the aggregate outnumber the Assamese, are, beginning with the Chinese frontier on the northeast: the Mishmies; the Khamtis, said to be of the Tai or Shan family who are most numerous on the Chinese side of the mountains; the Singphos, who are found in large numbers also on the Burmese side of the mountains; the Aror, the Nagas, the Kacharis, or Kosaris, north of the Brahmaputra; the Mikirs, in the hills near Nowgong; the Garos, of several clans; and on the slopes of the Khasia and Jaintia Hills, looking toward the Surma Valley, the Khasi and Jaintia tribes, and still another tribe of Nagas, are found. To these must be added the Kols, a tribe from Chota Nagpur, in Central India, who have been brought by the Government into Assam to work in the tea gardens. It is said that there are over 250,000 of them now in Assam.

It is believed that some of the largest of these tribes are either closely affiliated to hill tribes in Burma, or, perhaps, identical with them; this is very probable in regard to the Singphos of Assam and Chittagong, and the Kachins of Upper Burma; also the Nagas of Assam and the Chins of Burma. The relationship of these tribes is a matter of some moment to those engaged in Bible translation for them.

Climate: Assam is wholly within the north temperate zone, tho in the subtropical part of it. Its location and the high hills and mountains which cover so large a portion of its surface should make it healthy, but do not. In the valleys there are marshy lands, and the fickle, moist, and variable temperature, with its terrible cold and its fervid heat, have rendered it particularly fatal to the Europeans and Americans who have spent much time there. It is frequently visited by the cholera, and both acute and chronic diseases of the liver prevail. Of late years the construction of good roads, and the drainage of the marshes for the establishment of tea gardens has somewhat improved the salubrity of the country.

Religions: The Assamese, as we have said, adopted **Hinduism** about 1760. They are rigid adherents to caste. One or two of the hill tribes on the north of the Brahmaputra, notably the Kacharis and several of the Bhutan hill tribes bordering on Assam at the north, are Mohammedans. The greater part of the hill tribes, including all those south of the great river—the Garos, Nagas, Khasis, Mikirs, Singphos, etc.— are demon worshippers, making offerings to the **Nats**, or demons, to induce them not to injure them. They believe in a living Supreme Being, the Creator, but think He is too much occupied with the vast affairs of the universe to care for human beings, and too merciful to punish them for anything they have done or may do; and so they do not offer Him any worship or reverence. They believe dimly in a future life, but not in a state of rewards or punishments. In general, their religious belief is the same as that of the hill tribes of Burma. The tribes nearest to the Chinese have adopted some ideas of ancestral worship.

Missions in Assam: The first mission commenced here was that of the American Baptist Missionary Union, established in 1836 at the solicitation of Captain Jenkyns, the British deputy commissioner, who offered of his own means a considerable sum toward the expense of such a mission to the heathen under his charge. The first missionaries were Rev. Nathan Brown, an eminent missionary and scholar, who had begun his missionary life in Burma, and Mr. O. T. Cutter, a printer. The first station was at Sadiya, near the northeast frontier of Assam, about 400 miles from the Burman capital, and about 200 from Yunnan, in China. The tribe to whom they were designated were the Khamtis, a hill tribe occupying both sides of the lofty range which separates Assam from China. The geography and ethnology of this region were not well understood, and the voyage up the tortuous Brahmaputra was exceedingly tedious, occupying over four months in the native boats. The missionaries, however, entered upon their work with a stout heart, and, finding that there was little to be done among the Khamtis, they turned their attention to the Assamese and Shans in and around Sadiya. In 1839 an insurrection of the Khamtis commenced with an attack on Sadiya, which necessitated the removal of the missionaries to Jaipur. Jaipur was abandoned from its unhealthiness and other causes, and Sibsagar, on a southern affluent of the Brahmaputra, was selected. This is now the chief town in Eastern Assam, and is still a station of the ABMU. The station at Nowgong was established in 1841. The first Assamese convert was baptized the same year. In 1842 a school was opened there, with 80 pupils, and in 1843 the Nowgong Orphan Institution was established, which for many years was the means of doing much good. It was given up in 1856. The station at Gauhati was commenced in 1843. There were very few converts, and these Assamese only, till 1846. From this time till 1853 there were frequent accessions to the churches in Sibsagar, Nowgong, and Gauhati, mostly Assamese, with a very few Kacharis and Nagas. In 1863 the first of the Garos, the fiercest of the hill tribes, was baptized, and soon became a missionary to his tribe. The same year one of the Mikirs was baptized. From these beginnings the good work spread with great rapidity till in the churches of the Garo Association, in 1877, there were 617 members.

The Kols from Chota Nagpur, who are employed in the tea gardens, began to attract attention in 1874. They are mostly in the district of Sibsagar. Some of them had heard of Christ from Lutheran missionaries in their home in Bengal, and in Assam they were ready to accept Him. There are now two or three large churches of these people. There have been some conversions among the Mikirs, who are best reached from Nowgong. Tho there was considerable promise among the Kacharis, north of the Brahmaputra, the accessions from that tribe have not been large. Work was commenced among the Nagas as early as 1840, but without much result till 1871, when Rev. E. W. Clark made a tour of the hills. There are at least three distinct tribes of Nagas in these hills.

There are now 21 mission stations in Assam, of which 8 belong to the ABMU and 1 to the SPG, the remaining 12 belonging to the Welsh Calvinistic Methodist Society. The census returns 35,000 Christians in Assam of all denominations.

ASSAMESE: A language spoken in Assam, belongs to the India branch of the Aryan family of languages. It is written with the Bengali character and is used by about 2,000,000 people.

ASSOCIATE REFORMED PRESBYTERIAN SYNOD OF THE SOUTH: The foreign missionary work of this denomination began in 1875, when a missionary was sent to Egypt to work in connection with the United Presbyterian Mission Society. Upon her death this connection ceased, and work was begun in Mexico. The field of operations is the State of Tamaulipas, with the central station at Tampico.

There are (1902) 17 outstations, 11 missionaries, 7 native workers, 330 communicants, 182 pupils in five schools. Income about $9,000.

ASSUAN: A town in Upper Egypt, situated on the Nile near the first cataract. It is celebrated for its granite, and for the great irrigation dam finished in 1902. A station on the so-called Apostles' route, established by the Moravian Brethren in Egypt in 1865, but afterward abandoned by them. Visited as an outstation by the United Presbyterian Mission of the United States of America. Station of the Sudan Pioneer Mission of Eisenach, opened in 1900. It is occupied by a missionary and his wife and 3 native workers. There are 2 village schools.

ASUNCION: The capital of Paraguay, S. America. Population 35,000; station of the ME, with one missionary and his wife, and one unmarried woman missionary, and 11 native workers, men and women; 3 village schools, 2 high schools, 1 college and 70 members of the church. Station also of the SDA with one missionary and his wife.

ASSYRIA: That portion of Asiatic Turkey extending from Diarbekir on the north to Mosul on the south, and comprising the northern part of the Mesopotamia plain. The word is now seldom used as a geographical term.

ASSYRIAN CHRISTIANS: A term sometimes used to designate members of the **Nestorian Church.**

ASYUT, or **SIUT:** A city on the Nile, 228 miles by rail south of Cairo. Population, 30,000, mostly Mohammedans. It was formerly a principal seat of the slave-trade, and an important military station. It is now noted for a great irrigation dam on the Nile, finished under English auspices in 1903, subsidiary to the great dam of Assuan. Ruins and catacombs abound in the neighborhood. It is a mission station of the United Presbyterian Church of the U. S., established in 1865, with 14 missionaries of both sexes, a hospital and dispensary, a high school for girls and a college.

ATAFU ISLAND: Also called Duke of York's Island, is one of the **Tokelau** group of islands, N. of Samoa.

ATHABASCA LANDING: Settlement on the Athabasca River in the district of Alberta, Canada; station of the CMS, with a missionary and his wife.

ATIU. See HERVEY ISLANDS.

ATRAULI: A town of 15,000 inhabitants N. E. of Aligarh, United Provinces, India; station of the ME, with 10 native workers, men and women; 11 Sunday schools, 7 village schools, and 900 church members.

ATTABARI: A town in the Darang district of Assam, India; station of the SPG, with one missionary and 10 native workers, 8 preaching places, 5 common schools and 800 communicants.

ATTANGAL: A town in Travancore, S. India; station of the LMS (1899), with 2 missionaries and their wives, and 34 native workers, men and women; 12 outstations, 14 Sunday schools, 21 common schools and 110 church members. Also written Attingal.

AUCKLAND: A city on the Hauraki Gulf, New Zealand. It has, including the suburbs, 57,000 inhabitants, chiefly English, Irish, Scotch, and Germans, engaged in working the gold and coal-mines near the town and in the manufactories whose products form the chief exports. Station of the CMS, with one missionary and 28 native workers, and 83 communicants.

AUER, John Gottlieb: Born at Neubulach, Wurtemberg, Germany, November 18, 1832. He was well trained by an earnest Christian mother. In 1854 he was admitted to the Missionary Training School at Basel, and in 1858 was sent as missionary to Akropong in W. Africa, and became a teacher in the seminary. In 1862 he dissolved his connection with the Basel Missionary Society, offered himself as a candidate for the ministry in the Episcopal Church, and was ordained by Bishop Payne at Cavalla. In 1863 his wife died, and shortly after he sailed for America. Returning to his field in 1867, he devoted himself to two definite objects—a higher education for the African Church and a systematic preparation for giving to the heathen the Gospel in their own tongue. Acceding to Bishop Payne's request, he became the head of the high school at Cavalla. He believed that the Bible should be given to the people in their vernacular. In addition to the work of teaching, he translated or composed books in the Kroo language and the Grebo. He prepared a Grebo primer and dictionary, and revised the translation of the Prayer-Book. He also devised a method of writing the Grebo with vocal marks, thus saving the use of multiplied vowels. He had a school of twelve students, whom he faithfully trained.

He was ordained bishop of Cape Palmas, at Georgetown, D. C., April 17, 1873. Returning to Germany, in July, he began at once to carry his work through the press, and by November he had prepared an elementary book and a Bible history in the Kroo language, a translation of the Psalms, and a book of hymns in metre in the Grebo, a revised edition of the Prayer-Book and a tune-book. To this he added a book of chants. The translation of parts of the Scripture and Church Services into Grebo, begun by Bishop Payne, he completed. On November 20, leaving his family, he started for Africa. Tho very feeble on arriving at Cape Palmas, December 29, he entered earnestly on his mission work. He died, February 16, 1874, at Cape Palmas.

AUKA NEGROES: Descendants of former runaway slaves in Surinam, who during a century and a half have become a large tribe inhabiting the forests at a distance from the white settlements. Moravian missionaries have labored among them since 1765 and have won about 30,000 of them to a profession of Christianity.

AULUA: A village on the island of Mallicollo, New Hebrides group, Polynesia; station of the New Hebrides Missionary Society, with a missionary and his wife and 17 native workers, men and women, 9 village schools, and 62 church members.

AURANGABAD: In the Nizam's Dominions, India, 180 miles northeast of Bombay. Its population is about 34,000. It is a station of the CMS, opened in 1860, and now occupied by 5 missionaries and 54 native workers, men and women. There are 14 village schools, and 800 communicants.

AUSTRAL ISLANDS: A group of small islands lying S. of Tahiti and belonging to France. The Paris Evangelical Mission Society has occupied five islands of this group, of which Rurutua is the largest, taking over the field from the LMS, after the islands passed under French control. There are 8 native workers and about 650 communicants in the group.

AUSTRALIA: When Australia was discovered the aboriginal race inhabiting it were found to be a nomadic people, very low in the scale of human life. Anthropologists have difficulty in classifying them and in tracing their origin. Their languages have also puzzled philologists, as "they have little or no connection with that stock to which the Malay, Polynesian, and Melanesian belong. Dr. Bleek, whose reputation gives weight to his opinion, believes them to be nearly allied to the languages of southeastern Africa."

This article will be limited to some mention of various efforts to evangelize these aborigines, and also those directed to the Asiatic immigrants in differents parts of Australia.

The first missionary effort for the aborigines was made at Lake Macquarie in 1825 by the LMS. Many of their agents passed through Sydney, and some of them had found an asylum there during times of peril at Tahiti. After six years of failure from the roving habits of the blacks, the London Missionary Society gave up the work, but the Colonial Government continued it. The missionary, Mr. L. E. Threlkeld, persevered amid many trials and discouragements, acquired the language, printed a spelling-book and translations of parts of Scriptures. But little impression was made upon the people and the tribes around Lake Macquarie having become almost extinct, the mission was closed in 1861.

In 1832 another mission was established at Wellington. The same difficulties were encountered there, but the missionaries did their best to acquire the language of the district, to teach the young, and to address the people. They composed a grammar and a vocabulary, and translated portions of Scriptures, chiefly St. Luke's Gospel, and a part of the Anglican Liturgy. But they had to admit that the supply of food existing at the mission was what drew the people to them. As the country became settled the influence of vicious whites rendered nugatory all efforts, and in 1847 the mission was broken up.

Through the influence of an eminent clergyman of New South Wales, Pastor Gössner of Berlin sent out several missionaries in 1840 to labor among the aborigines at Moreton Bay and Keppel Bay. But the enterprise came to nothing after eighteen years of continued effort. About 1850 Rev. William Ridley attempted missionary labor among the aborigines of New South Wales. He devoted his means and himself to the work, learned the language of the people among whom he lived on the Namoi River, prepared a grammar of the language and translated portions of the Gospel narrative. His labors were not entirely in vain, but the migratory habits of the people forced him to abandon his mission.

More recent efforts in New South Wales have been on the plan of forming reservations for the residence and work of the aborigines and for educating the children. In this the Government has become the protector of the tribes, and the Moravian Missionary Society and the various Christian denominations in Australia have worked perseveringly for their enlightenment and elevation. Missionary effort for the aborigines is carried on at 26 stations in the various parts of the Australian continent. But only a limited number of the tribes will submit to the restrictions of life on a reservation. A certain number of these degraded people have become Christianized, but the general result of all these years of effort is the discouragement resulting from dealing with a dull and unstable people.

The total number of the Aborigines now existing in Australia is about 55,000. Of these about 5,000 are classed as civilized in the census reports.

Attracted by the gold fields and by the encouragements to industry, many thousand Chinese emigrated to Australia. Numbers of them are engaged in merchandise, others in gold mining, many in market gardening and other industrial work. Some of them can read and write, and all are accessible to Christian influence. The numbers in 1888 in Australia were about 40,000, and even the restrictive legislation directed against them has not reduced their number below 30,000 (1901).

Attempts have been made by the different churches to establish missions among them in the chief centres where they have been located. The agents have been chiefly Chinese converts, but commonly superintended by European missionaries who know the Chinese language. A gratifying amount of success has attended this effort.

Sugar planting in Queensland led to a great demand for cheap labor, and vessels were sent to recruit among the New Hebrides and Solomon Islands for laborers under an engagement for three years. Many evils sprang up in this deportation, and statutes were passed by the Imperial Parliament and by the Parliament of Queensland to regulate the labor traffic. As a result, a large number of Polynesians have been brought to Queensland during twenty years. Some of these were recruited near mission stations, and had been instructed in Christian truth. Most of them were from heathen and cannibal islands. All of them, however, had heard of the missionary, and had been led to respect his efforts for their good. Unfortunately the languages of these islands are almost all different, and on one sugar plantation the laborers represented so many various tongues that missionary teaching in any one of them could only be very limited. But as there are more than 9,000 in Queensland the necessity for reaching them in some way has led to the use of the English language in missions among them. This they acquire very readily and encouraging results are reported.

AUX CAYES: A seaport town on the southwest coast of the island of Haiti, West Indies. Population, 8,000, chiefly negroes and mulattoes. The climate is unwholesome. The manufacture of rum is one of the principal industries. It is a mission station of the PE, which has a native worker and about 50 communicants. The Western Annual Conference of the West Indies Wesleyan Methodist Missionary Society, and the African Methodist Episcopal Church also have agencies here.

AVÉZA: Village on the island of Raiatea, Society Islands, Polynesia; station of the Paris Evangelical Society, with a native worker and 170 church members.

AWEMBA: A settlement to the S.W. of Lake Tanganyika in British Central Africa; station of the LMS (1900) with a missionary and his wife.

AXIM: A seaport on the coast of the Gold Coast Colony, W. Africa; station of the WMS, with a missionary and 52 native workers, men and women, 65 outstations, 12 Sunday schools, 10 village schools, and 360 church members.

AZAMOR: A town near Mazagan, Morocco; station of the Southern Morocco Mission, with a missionary and his wife, and a dispensary.

AZERBAIJAN TURKISH: See TURKISH.

AZIMGARH: A city sixty miles north of Benares, British India; station of the CMS since 1831. The Society has there 5 missionaries and 19 native workers, men and women, with a high school and 8 village schools. The religions of the people among whom they work are in general Hinduism and Mohammedanism. There are about 100 Christians connected with the mission

B

BA: A town on Viti Levu, Fiji Islands; station of the Australian Wesleyan Methodist Missionary Society, with 1 missionary and 628 native workers, 283 Sunday schools, 330 village schools, and 7,475 professing Christians.

BAAKLEEN: A village of the Lebanon district in Syria; station of the Palestine and Lebanon Nurses' Mission, with 4 missionary women, 2 native workers, 1 dispensary, and 1 hospital.

BAALBEC: A town of Syria, northeast of Beirut. It is celebrated for its ruins of the Temple of the Sun. It is a station of the British Syrian Schools' Committee, with 2 missionary women and 3 native women workers, 1 village school, a high school, and a dispensary.

BABIS (pron. **Babees**): A sect among the Mohammedans of Persia. In 1845 a young mollah of Shiraz, named Mohammed Ali, commenced to preach against the vices of his coreligionists. His bold invective against the corruption of the religious hierarchy won instant response from the common people and gave him great popularity as a preacher. It also aroused fierce anger among the men whose hypocrisy and luxurious living he attacked. He began to claim that he was divinely ordained to reform the religious faith and practise of the country, quoting from the Bible and the words of Christ as well as from the Koran in support of his teachings. As he diverged more and more from the doctrine that the teachings of the Koran have superseded all earlier revelations, he began to defy the mollahs of Shirez to harm him, declaring himself to be the *Bab*, that is to say, the "door" or forerunner of the Mahdi who is to come in the last days to reform religion. Threatened with punishment by the chief Mohammedan theologians of Teheran he answered by a ringing defiance of all efforts to lay hands on the messenger of God. Multitudes of all classes of the people became his followers; the Bab was regarded as supreme authority, the throne itself seemed to be endangered, and finally the Persian Government arrested him and put him to death.

His followers, who called themselves Babis (People of the Bab), included some eminent Mohammedan mollahs, and one remarkable and eloquent woman who continually stirred up the people to persevere in the new doctrine. When the authorities undertook to make further arrests, the Babis resisted, and serious battles occurred, particularly in the district of Shiraz, in some of which the Persian troops were defeated. In 1848 an attempt was made upon the life of the Shah by some of the Babis. An edict of proscription was then issued against the sect and thousands of its members were massacred. The leaders of the Babis escaped to Turkey and established themselves at Baghdad. The Persian Government, finding that Babism could not be eradicated while the successors of the Bab still lived, requested Turkey to surrender the refugees. This Turkey refused to do, but finally consented to place the leaders of the sect under surveillance at a point distant from the Persian frontier. All efforts were vain, however, and Babism still flourishes in Persia more or less openly.

The Bab left a volume of his teachings—an ambitious but illiterate production called "Bayan" (Exposition). The doctrines held by his followers seem to be of a progressive character, however, and are now a mixture of Mohammedanism, Indian Theosophy and Pantheism, in which they follow the lead of the Sufis. Certain texts and precepts taken from the New Testament and the Psalms of David are added to this eclectic body of doctrine. A principle of the sect held in common with some of the Dervish orders is that all Mohammedanism as taught to-day, and in fact all religions, are hopelessly corrupt, that the Mahdi will, therefore, shortly appear to reform the world and that then true religion will be found to include parts of the Mohammedan, Buddhist, and Christian teachings. The system of morals preached by the Babis is in marked contrast to that of Islam in laying stress on the brotherhood of all mankind and in stigmatizing polygamy. Like all Mohammedans, they hold the use of wine or spirits to be a sin.

Two rival disciples of the Bab, each claiming to be his divinely appointed successor, are now in exile under surveillance of the Turkish Government, the one in the Island of Cyprus, and the other at Acre, in Syria. The latter is named Beha-ed-din and has entered into relations with English and Americans with a view to uniting all religions. He claims 10,000 followers in Chicago and Baltimore, in the United States, who believe that he is the promised Messiah.

Babism is one of the results of the impact of Christianity upon Islam. It was thought at one time that the Babis were more open to Christian teaching than orthodox Mohammedans. So far, however, they are merely more tolerant and more ready to seek in the Bible support for their doctrines.

Missionary Review of the World, Vol. VII, N. S., pp. 362, 451, 529, 894; Vol. XV., N. S., pp. 771, 775; Vol. XVII. pp. 91. 207. *A Year among the Persians,* also, *Babism,* Browne (E. G.), (in "Religious Systems of the World"), London.

BACHELER, Rev. Otis Robinson, M.D.: Born in Antrim, N. H., January 17, 1817. In the spring of 1839 he was accepted as a medical missionary by the Free Baptist Mission Society; and after continuing his studies for another year, he sailed, with his wife, for India. He made Balasor the center of his work until 1851, when he returned to America. On his return to India, in 1863, he settled at Midnapur, where the rest of his missionary life was spent. His dispensary proved to be a great blessing to many, and through its influence hundreds were attracted to the Gospel message. When he returned to India from America he brought a printing press, which was of great use in his work; and in 1886 he became principal of the Midnapur Bible School, which position he held until he retired from the field. After spending 53 years as a missionary he retired in 1893, and passed into his rest at New Hampton, N. H., on New Year's morning, 1901.

BADAGA LANGUAGE: Belongs to the Canarese group of the Dravidian family of languages. It is spoken by the Badaga tribe, living in the Nilgiri Hills south of Mysore, India. It is written with the Canarese letters.

BADAGRI: A city near Lagos, W. Africa, formerly important as a trading center. It is a mission station, opened by the WMS in 1842, and transferred to the CMS in 1845; it has 5 native workers, men and women, with 2 outstations, 3 village schools, and 102 communicants.

BADULLA: A town and military post in the south central part of Ceylon. The climate is healthy because of the elevation, which is about 2,000 feet. It is a station of the WMS, with 3 missionaries and 37 native workers, men and women. There are 6 outstations, 19 village schools, 1 high school, 1 industrial school, 1 hospital, 2 orphanages, and a printing house. There are 80 church members.

BADDÉGAMA: A village N. of Galle in the southern part of Ceylon; station of the CMS, founded in 1819. At present the station is occupied by 4 missionaries and 56 native workers, men and women. It has 3 outstations, 35 village schools, and 1 high school. There are 220 communicants.

BAGHARA: Town in the north of the Santal Parganas, Bengal, India; station of the CMS (1875), with 2 missionaries and their wives, 18 native workers, men and women, 9 village schools, and a high school, and 75 communicants. Also written Bhagaya.

BAGHCHEJIK. See BARDEZAG.

BAGHDAD: A city of southern Mesopotamia, capital of the province of Baghdad, in Asiatic Turkey. It is situated on the Tigris, about 250 miles north of its confluence with the Euphrates. The population, numbering about 180,000, is composed chiefly of Arabs, tho there are large numbers of Persians, Kurds, Syrian Christians, and about 15,000 Jews. It was the favorite seat of the Abassid Caliphs, and under Haroun-al-Raschid became very famous. Under Turkish rule very much of its prosperity has been lost, tho it is still the most important city of Southeastern Turkey, both commercially and politically. Near it is the shrine of Kerbela, to which the Persians flock in pilgrimages in honor of the Shi'ite saints, Hassan and Hossein. There is thus constant communication with Persia and

Kurdistan. It was long the seat of a British resident, and it still ranks very high as a diplomatic post of Great Britain, Russia, and France. Baghdad has been the starting point for the various expeditions to explore the ruins of Babylon at Hilleh, on the Euphrates, 100 miles to the south, and of Seleucia and Ctesiphon. Since the University of Pennsylvania has been excavating at Niffer, Baghdad has been made the seat of an American consulate. Missionary work has been attempted at various times by the ABCFM and the CMS. The intense heat of the climate makes it very trying to Europeans. At present it is occupied as a station by the CMS, with 8 missionaries and 7 native workers, men and women, who have charge of 2 village schools and 1 hospital. There are 35 communicants here.

BAHAWA: A village in the Santal Parganas, Bengal, India; station of the CMS. It is occupied by a missionary and his wife and 41 native workers, men and women. There is 1 high school and 1 dispensary, and there are 545 church members. The name is also written Barhawa.

BAHIA: A city of Brazil, South America, on All Saints Bay, 800 miles northeast of Rio de Janeiro. Population, about 200,000, chiefly Portuguese; religion, Roman Catholic, the city being the seat of an archbishop. It is a mission station of the CA, of which no statistics are available; of the PN, which commenced operations here in 1871; and has 4 missionaries and 1 native worker, men and women, and 1 common school. It is also a station of the SBC, opened in 1882. There are now 3 missionaries and 15 native workers, men and women, with 27 outstations and 516 church members.

BAHIA BLANCA: Seaport in the Argentine Republic; station of the South American Evangelical Mission, with one missionary.

BAHRAICH: A town in the United Provinces, India; station of the ME, founded in 1867. It has 21 native workers, 10 Sunday schools, 3 common schools, and 182 church members.

BAHREIN: The largest island of the Bahrein group in the Persian Gulf, off the coast of El Hasa, in Arabia; station of the RCA Arabian Mission (1892), with one missionary and his wife and a dispensary.

BAHRWAL ATARI: A town in the Amritsar district, Punjab, India; station of the CMS (1889), with (1902) 8 native workers, and 200 baptized Christians, of whom 23 were baptized during 1901. Station also of the CEZMS (1890), with (1902) 9 native women workers, 2 common schools, 1 hospital, 1 dispensary, 700 Zenana visitations and 5 Zenana pupils.

BAIHIR. See BEHIR.

BAILUNDA: A region in the district of Benguela, Portuguese West Africa. It lies on the uplands about 200 miles from Benguela, its seaport. The climate is healthy and the temperature, altho hot, is even. A mission station of the ABCFM was opened there in 1881; occupied by 2 missionaries and their wives, 2 missionary women, and 5 native workers. There are 9 outstations, with 1 high school and 2 village schools. There are 25 church members. The station has been much harassed by the bad feeling of European traders which has excited the suspicions of the native tribes.

BALASOR: A seaport of Orissa, Bengal, India, 150 miles southwest of Calcutta. Population about 20,000, Hindus and Mohammedans. Language, Uriya, Santali, Hindustani. First mission station occupied by the American Free Baptist Missionary Society in 1838. It has now 2 missionaries and their wives, and 3 missionary women, with 74 native workers, men and women. There are 2 outstations, 8 village schools, 1 high school, 1 kindergarten, 2 orphanages, and 230 church members. Also written Balasore.

BALDWIN, Stephen Livingston: Born at Somerville, N. J., January 11, 1835. His ministerial life covered a period of forty-four years. One half of this time was spent as a missionary in Fuchau, China; eight years he was pastor of churches in the Newark and New England Conferences, and the last fourteen years of his life were devoted to the work pertaining to the office of Recording Secretary of the Missionary Society of the Methodist Episcopal Church. On October 4, 1858, Mr. and Mrs. Baldwin sailed for China. In 1861 he returned to America, on account of the failing health of Mrs. Baldwin, who died at sea; but the next year he was in Fuchau again, remaining there until 1870, when he was granted a year's furlough at home. The Fuchau Conference appointed him a delegate to the General Conference of 1880; and he was a member of the Ecumenical Conference held in London in 1881. While he was pastor of St. John's Methodist Episcopal Church, Boston, he was elected in June, 1888, Recording Secretary of the Missionary Society of the Methodist Episcopal Church, in which he continued until he died in Brooklyn, N. Y., July 28, 1902. Dr. Baldwin rendered important services as General Secretary of the Ecumenical Missionary Conference held in New York City in 1900. Under the strain of the work of organizing this Conference, his health gave way, and that important service to the cause of missions doubtless hastened his death.

BALI: An island situated E. of Java. The people are heathen, but a few Mohammedans and some Christians are found there. The language is allied to the Javanese.

The Utrecht Missionary Society has a station upon this island and seems, after many vicissitudes, to have gained a stable foothold.

BALIGE: A village on Lake Toba in the North Central part of Sumatra, East Indies. Station of the Rhenish Missionary Society, founded in 1881. It is occupied by a missionary and his wife, with 10 native workers, men and women. There are 5 outstations, 4 village schools, and 1,400 communicants.

BALL, Dyer, M.D.: Born at West Boylston, Mass., June 3, 1796; graduated at Union College, 1826; studied theology at New Haven and Andover; ordained, 1831; was agent in 1833 for Home Missionary Society in Florida. While at the South he was much engaged in labor for the colored population. In 1835-37 he studied medicine with reference to foreign mission work, and received the degree of M.D. from the medical institution in Charleston. He sailed in 1838, under the ABCFM, for Singapore. He was stationed there two years, teaching, preaching, healing the sick, and superintending the printing of Chinese books. In June, 1841, he went to Macao, and then to Hongkong. To him it was given to be the pioneer in opening the city of Canton for residence of missionary families, and to open the way for excursions into the country around. His medical services were of great assistance in conciliating the good-will of the people. His Almanac was for many years a most acceptable publication. He was most laborious in out-of-door work, mingling with the people on the banks of the river or on the ferries, and then extending his visits to the villages and market. In this way he became widely known and more and more respected as his true character and the nature of his labors were understood. In 1854 he visited the United States, returning, in 1857, to Macao. His constitution was much broken, and before his death he was confined to his house four months. During the last seven years of his life, the old man, bowed down by his infirmities, and leaning upon his cane would make his way downstairs and totter out to the little chapel opening on the street, and there, seated in an arm chair, he would distribute tracts or speak to passers who might drop in to look upon his gray hairs; for the Chinese venerate old age. He died March 27, 1866, after twenty-eight years' mission service.

BALLANTINE, Henry: Born at Schodack Landing, on the Hudson, near Albany, N. Y., March 5, 1813. He graduated at the University of Ohio, Athens, 1829; entered Theological Seminary, Princeton, but left on account of ill health; resumed his studies at Union Theological Seminary, Virginia; finished at Andover, 1834; ordained at Columbus, O., April, 1835; sailed same year as a missionary of the American Board for India. In 1837 he was stationed permanently at Ahmednagar. His health failing, he left, in 1850, for home, but returned in 1852. He labored with great zeal and without interruption as preacher and pastor, and as editor and translator until 1865. During the last five years of his life he gave much time to the theological education of young men. By medical advice he left India with his family, September 4, 1865. An accidental detention of the ship in the Red Sea aggravated his malady, and he died November 9, off the coast of Portugal, and his body was consigned to the ocean. His connection with the mission covered thirty years. An accurate knowledge of the Marâthi, added to an acquaintance with Sanskrit, prepared him to become a translator of the Bible, and he has left the impress of his idiomatic Marâthi on many parts of the sacred volume in that language. He translated or composed some of the best hymns in the Marâthi hymn book.

BALRAMPUR: Town in the Gonda district of the United Provinces, India; station of the ME, with 18 native workers, men and women, 9 Sunday schools, 1 village school and 170 church members.

BALUCHI LANGUAGE: Belongs to the Iranic branch of the Aryan family of languages, and is spoken in Baluchistan, by a population of about 1,500,000. It is written with Arabic letters with slight modifications.

BALUCHISTAN: A country of Asia, bounded on the north by Afghanistan, on the east by British India, on the south by the Indian Ocean, and on the west by Persia. Its area is about 130,000 square miles. The population is estimated at about 500,000, divided into two sections, the Baluchis and the Brahuis—which are sub-divided into tribes and again into families. The Baluchis have several points of resemblance to the Tartars and may perhaps have sprung from a commingling of Persian and Tartar stock. The Brahuis seem to have a linguistic affinity with some of the tribes of the Punjab. Mohammedanism is the religion of the general mass of the population.

Baluchistan is ruled by the Khan of Khelat under the direction of an English resident. For strategic purposes the British authorities have built a railway from India into the country, and an English garrison is maintained at Quettah.

Missionary operations are limited to one station of the CMS at Quettah. There have been a few conversions notwithstanding the fanaticism that would apply the sword to every man who abandons Islam. On the whole, the greatest encouragement is found in the steady circulation of the Scriptures from the Quettah depot.

Baluchistan, Hughes (A. W.), London, 1877.

BANDA: The capital of a district of the same name, United Provinces, India. It is situated on the Ken River and has about 24,000 inhabitants. It is a station of the SPG, opened in 1873, and is now occupied by 1 missionary and 2 missionary women with 8 native workers. It has a high school and 3 village schools. There are 32 communicants.

It is a station also of the ME with 10 native workers, men and women, and 7 village schools. There are 40 church members.

BANDAWE: A town on Lake Nyasa, Central Africa, in the W. Nyasaland Protectorate; station of the UFS, with 7 missionaries and 38 native workers, men and women. It has 22 outstations, 1 high school, 55 village schools, 1 dispensary and 450 church members.

BANDOENG: A town in the west central part of the island of Java, Dutch East Indies; station of the Netherlands Missionary Union, with 2 missionaries and 4 native workers, a hospital and a theological class. There are 50 communicants. Also written Bandung.

BANGALORE: A city of Mysore, India, 175 miles west of Madras. It is on an elevated site, a great resort for invalids; it has considerable trade, and is a military post. Population, 180,000, chiefly Hindus.

It is a station of the LMS (1820) with 7 missionaries and 22 native workers, men and women, 1 theological class, 2 high schools, and 12 village schools. There are 121 church members.

Station of the WMS with 9 missionaries and 174 native workers, men and women. It has a theological seminary, 3 high schools, and 37 village schools. The communicants number 630.

Station of the SPG (1837) with 7 native workers, men and women, 2 village schools and 405 communicants.

Station of the Church of England Zenana Missionary Society, with (1902) 5 women missionaries, 2 of them physicians) and 14 native women workers, a dispensary, a hospital, an orphanage, 3 elementary schools, and 6 zenana pupils.

Station of the Leipzig Missionary Society, with 7 native workers, 3 high schools and 400 communicants.

Station of the ME, with 3 missionaries and 7 native workers, men and women; it has 2 high schools, and 14 church members.

Station of the American Advent Missionary Society, with 1 missionary, 3 native workers and a printing house.

BANGKOK: Capital of Siam, on the Menam River, about 20 miles from its mouth. It is the chief commercial center of the country. Climate, intensely hot in summer. Population, 400,000—Siamese, Chinese, Burmans, Malays, Arabs, Hindus; nearly one-half of the entire population is Chinese and practically the whole of the commerce of Bangkok is in their hands. The approach of the city is very beautiful, and some of the temples are very fine specimens of elaborate decoration. A large number of the houses are built on rafts, and the internal traffic of the city is largely carried on by canals, altho streets and bridges have been built and electric cars introduced in some quarters.

Bangkok is occupied as a missionary station by the ABMU (1833), with 3 missionaries and 7 native workers, men and women, 4 outstations and 190 church members.

It is also a station of the PN (1840) with 16 missionaries, men and women and 2 native workers, 2 high schools, a common school and a printing house. There are also 187 church members.

The ABS has a Bible depot there in charge of an American agent.

BANJERMASSIN: Chief town of the Dutch Residency of the same name in S. E. Borneo, situated near the seacoast. It has about 45,000 inhabitants. It is a station of the Rhenish Missionary Society, with a missionary and his wife, 1 unmarried woman and 6 native workers, men and women. There are 2 outstations and 4 village schools. The communicants number 140.

BANKHERI: Town in the Gonda region, Central Provinces, India; station of the Friends' Foreign Missionary Association (1896), with 1 missionary and his wife, 2 native workers, 1 village school, 1 dispensary and 10 professing Christians.

BANKIPUR: A town in Bengal, India, a suburb of Patna. Mission station of the BMS (1818); 2 missionaries and their wives, with 12 native workers, men and women. It has 3 outstations and 5 village schools. The communicants number 26. Also written Bankipore.

BANKURA: Capital of the Bankura district, Bengal, India, 100 miles N. W. of Calcutta. Population, about 19,000. Mission station of the WMS; 4 missionaries and 36 native workers, men and women, 6 outstations, 2 high schools, 18 village schools, 97 church members.

BANNI: A town on the island of Fernando Po, in the Bight of Biafra, on the W. coast of Africa; station of the Primitive Methodist Missionary Society (1880), with a missionary and his wife, 1 native worker, a chapel, a Sunday school and 16 church members.

BANNU: A town in the Northwest Frontier Province of India, S. of Peshawar; station of the CMS (1864), 1 missionary physician and 4 native workers, 1 high school, 1 hospital, 1 dispensary and 33 communicants. Also called Edwardesabad.

BANSA MANTEKE: A town in the Congo Free State, West Africa, 160 miles from the mouth of the river; station of the ABMU (1879), with 7 missionaries and 48 native workers, men and women, 32 outstations, 34 village schools, a high school, a theological seminary, and 1,500 church members. This station is an instance of the pervasive power of the Gospel of Christ. When it was first occupied, the people were entirely unknown to the outside world and were living in gross darkness of paganism. Their language had never been reduced to writing. It was seven years before a single convert came forward for baptism, and he was threatened with death for becoming a Christian. Since that first conversion 2,000 of that Bantu tribe have been baptized; they have the beginnings of a printed literature; the people themselves have taken up the duty of evangelization, and everywhere within a radius of thirty miles of the station the pagans have the Gospel preached to them by their own countrymen.

BANSKO: A village in the Razlog district, European Turkey; outstation of the ABCFM; an independent self-supporting church has grown up in connection with the mission, composed of Bulgarians.

BANTING: A town in the district of Sarawak, Borneo; station of the SPG, founded in 1851; it has 1 missionary and 7 native workers, 2 outstations, 13 preaching places and a high school.

BANTU RACE: The preponderating element of the population of Africa from about the fifth degree of north latitude to Cape Colony (excepting the Hottentots, Bushmen and some smaller groups) is the Bantu race, numbering 60,000,000 or more. The name in almost all the languages of this region (Zulu, *Abantu;* singular *Umantu* person) means "the people."

Among the members of the Bantu race may be named the Zulus, the Amaxosa or Kafirs the Bechuana, Basuto, and kindred tribes on the south; the Ovaherero, Ovampo, Balunda, Bateke and Mpongwe, on the west; the Congo, Bayansi, Bangala, Babangi, Manyema; the people of Toro and Uganda, the Angoni, and others among the Great Lakes; the Rua, Bemba, Babisa, and other tribes near the Lesser Lakes and on the sources of the Congo; and the Wakamba, Swahili, Wanika, Mahenge, Wakonde, Makua, and other tribes to the number of two hundred or more.

The general kinship of these tribes is seen, to some extent, in their person, their hue, their features, their religious notions, their mental type, and their mode of life; but most of all in their language. Taking their language as our guide and proof, we are left with no doubt that these tribes belong to one and the same family, between which and all other known families or races there is a manifest and fixed difference. To be sure, the languages of the tribes differ from each other in many respects, especially in many of their words, or in the forms of their words, but the grammar is essentially the same in all.

The more the comparative philologist comes to know of this Bantu family of languages, the more does he find of beauty, compass, flexibility, and plastic power. All the best known dialects whether on the east, south, or west, or in the interior, are found to be soft, pliant, easy flowing, regular and systematic in forms, philosophical in structure and principle, and wonderfully rich in ability to express all the shades of thought and feeling of which the people who speak them have knowledge. And it is specially interesting to note that this great field of underlying, substantial oneness of speech is the one in which great Christian missions are being extensively planted, and are finding unexpected facilities in the wideness of the region where the **Bantu languages** prevail.

In respect to the origin of the Bantu race, and how, whence, or when they came into the part of Africa they now occupy, the people themselves can tell us nothing. Nor does ancient history throw light on the subject. And yet we are not without some good reasons for opinions in relation to it. Some hold, with plausible show of reasons, that the Hottentots of S. Africa are of the same race as the ancient Egyptians, or at least that the two families were one in origin, and if so, then the fact of their being so widely separated points to the probable incoming of another people, as from the east, by which they were divided, and a portion of them pushed on to the southern extremity of the continent.

Inquiring now to which particular branch of the great families of men such an incursive, immigrating race belonged, we can hardly doubt that it was Hamitic, having its origin probably in some branch of the Cushites. The descendants of this line were numerous, and some of them settled, for a time at least, in Asia. Others settled in Arabia, and doubtless many went at an early date to Africa. Herodotus speaks of two classes of Ethiopians, one in Asia, the other in Africa. Many of the former served as soldiers under Xerxes, tho their home is not easily determined. The historian, however, tells us that the Asiatic Ethiopians were black, like those of Libya, but differed from them in language, and had straight hair; whereas those of Libya had very curly hair. Now, between the Bantu tribes and the proper negro race, there is, to a certain extent, just this kind of difference at the present time. To be sure, the Bantu race is not white, and yet their hue is not so dark as that of the Nigritian negro, nor is their hair so woolly; and as to their language—that most decisive mark of an affinity or of a difference—there is a wide difference between the Bantu languages and those of the real negro of the Sudan. Taking, then, all these suggestive facts together, it does not seem improbable that the immigrants who pushed the Hottentots before them to the southward were from Asia. If this was the case, it is easy to see why the Bantu peoples should be found at this day more robust, taller, of a lighter color, with hair less woolly, with a nose more elevated, of a much greater facial angle, a higher forehead, and altogether of a more intelligent, Caucasian look than their Nigritian neighbors. At the same time we see in the whole Bantu race so much of the true negro type that we must come to the conclusion that, if the Bantu family originated in any wise other than the negroes of Nigritia, it mingled with these until it was largely fashioned after their type.

The appearance, color, and customs of the Zulu are so like those of the other tribes of the Bantu family that a description of the former will give a good idea of all. The better classes of these tribes, especially of the Zulu and the Kafir, are somewhat slender, erect, of good stature, and well proportioned; it is easy for them on occasion to be graceful, dignified, commanding. They are made to be agile and swift rather than strong; and yet their women often carry heavy burdens on their heads for long distances. Their color varies from a reddish copper or light bronze to a pure black. The latter, with just a little tinge of the red, pleases them best. A few have the regular features of the Caucasian; some, the pure negro; but most of them are of some grade between the two. Their black eyes often twinkle with merry humor, their beautifully white teeth are well set, their general expression is pleasant and confiding. Physically considered, the Bantu tribes are a well-built, fine-looking race.

In respect to natural affection, mental traits, and social life, the Bantu family afford an interesting study. Except when provoked to anger by insult or injustice, they are mild, gentle, kind, not wanting in either parental or filial affection; are helpful and sympathetic toward the suffering; and yet, under a sense of being wronged or in the excitements of war, they can be wild and fierce in the extreme. They are hospitable, fond of visiting, fond of society, cannot bear to work alone or be alone. They are proverbial for politeness, have numerous rules of etiquette, which are generally sensible. They are quick to see the difference between right and wrong, ever ready to decry injustice, and to submit gracefully to the suffering of deserved punishment. During the writer's residence of many years among the Zulus, with almost no lock and key in use, his grain, tools, cattle—everything they most desired—being ever open to access, he was not aware that anything was ever stolen from him. He once thought they had taken a hatchet, but after months had elapsed and the annual burning of the grass had occurred he found it in a field just where he had used and left it. And yet the common, social life of the Zulu is far from perfect. As one has said, "He is far from being as honest in word as he is in acts. He is prone to have very large reservations in his own mind when he is avowedly giving a full account of some occurrence, and manages to disguise and distort facts with exceeding cleverness and skill. A Zulu will excuse a fault with such ready plausibility that he will make an intentional act of wrong doing seem but an undesigned accident." He expects his hospitality to be reciprocated, his kindness to be rewarded. Indeed he is said to have it for a proverb that "it is better to receive than to give." It is easy for him to get very angry and try to settle his dispute with a club. And yet he can hardly be said to be vindictive in his resentments. If the storm of passion is quick to rise, it is also quick to abate and be forgotten.

It would take a volume to describe the superstitions of these people. Of all their superstitions, none have upon them a stronger or more hurtful hold than their belief in what is called witchcraft. They believe certain evil-minded men, whom they call *abatakati*, have it in their power to hurt, kill, or destroy anybody or anything, by the use of poisonous powder, incantation, or even by the force of mere will or purpose. Of these so-called witches the people have great fear. And so it is that any calamity, sickness, or death is often ascribed to some influence of this kind; whereupon some *inyanga*, witch doctor, is called to "smell out" the author of the evil. And inasmuch as all the possessions, wives, children and cattle of the man found guilty are to be confiscated and portioned out the chances are that the sentence will fall upon one of the more wealthy men, especially if he may happen to be unpopular.

The Zulu word *inyanga* is a term of wide import and use. It may denote one who has a trade, as a blacksmith, a basket-maker, or one whose business is to help others across a river. Its more proper use is to designate those who are skilled in higher pursuits, as a medical doctor, a witch doctor—*i.e.*, one qualified to find out the cause and cure of evil by communicating with the shades of the departed. A Zulu's mode of preparing himself for one of these higher professions is to go through a long-continued course of rigorous training, by means of fasting self-inflicted sufferings, diving and staying under water, wanderings in wild and weird places, that he may come into contact and communion with the *amahlozi*, or fall into a swoon and have strange visions of the spirits, about which he has been talking and thinking so long. Then he makes his appearance in public, all besmeared, perhaps with white clay, his hands full of snakes, his head covered with feathers, singing, dancing, reciting his visions, and so is prepared to be recognized as having attained to the degree of a medical priest, or a diviner.

The religious views and practises of the Zulus correspond, in a measure, to all the essential elements of the true faith; only on a false basis. They have their divinities, their sense of obligation and dependence, sense of guilt, belief in need of help, need of a Savior, need of sacrifices, even unto blood, need of prayer, the duty of worship and service, and a belief that the present life is to be followed by another. In their ignorance of the true God and in their search for some kind of divinity, they turn to the spirits of the departed, the shades of their ancestors, especially the ghosts of the great ones of their race. For here too **Ancestor-Worship** is practised. They call these shades by various names, as *ihlozi*, plural *amahlozi*; *itunga*, or *isitunzi*. Ask them about the end of man, where he goes when he dies, and they say he becomes an *ihlozi* and goes off to live somewhere underground, there to build and abide with his ancestral friends. Sometimes they say the dying man becomes an *isitunzi* (spirit) and reappears from time to time in a smoke; and so it is that they stand in awe of a serpent, and say, when it appears about their houses, that the spirit of their friend has come back to visit them, and see how they fare. Lions and leopards are sometimes looked upon as the embodiment of the spirit of a departed friend. To the shades of the dead, they look for help in time of trouble, confess their sins, pray, and offer sacrifices. Such for substances is the origin, kinship, appearance, and such are the religious ideas and superstitutions of the many tribes which form the Bantu race of Africa.

Zululand, Grant (L.), London, 1865; *Journal of the Anthropological Inst. of Great Britain and Ireland*, N. S., Vol. 1, pp. 37–47, London, 1898; *Globus* (German), Vol. 77, pp. 193–195, Vol. 80, pp. 384–386, Braunschweig, 1900, 1901.

BANTU LANGUAGES: Among all branches of the **Bantu** race in Africa, the existence of kinship seems to be shown by the peculiarities of their language. The resemblances between the speech of widely separated tribes have not as yet been studied and fully interpreted. But enough is known to lead to a supposition that the Zulu and the Kafir-Xosa languages may be the oldest and most fully developed of the whole family. The Zulu would seem, also, to have been least affected by abrasion or other modification through contact with other languages, having been developed, fixed, and kept, by its own indigenous, automatic principles. Hence the belief that the distinguishing grammatical features of the entire Bantu family are more manifest and clearly defined in the Zulu than in any other of its branches. In Zulu, the incipient element of the noun, the nominal "prefix" or preformative, is more complete than in most of the Bantu dialects. Thus the prefix *um*, as in *umfana*, boy, is simply *m*, *mfana*, in some branches. *Mpongwe*, the name of a country and tribe in the northwest part of the Bantu field, would be *Umpongwe* in the southeast among the Zulus and Kafirs. The Zulu plural prefix, *aba*, as in *abafana*, boys, becomes *ba*, as *bafana*, in some dialects. For *person*, the Zulus have *umuntu;* another tribe has *muntu;* another, *mutu;* another, *mtu;* another, *mundu*. For the Zulu plural of this word, *abantu*, people, some other tribes say *bantu;* some, *antu;* some, *atu;* some, *wantu;* some, *watu;* some, *wandu*, and some, *andu*. *Mtesa* (late king of Uganda) would be *Umteza* in Zulu, and the Lake Nyanza would be in Zulu, *Inyanza*. On the Lualaba, a branch of the Congo, the natives say *nyama*, meat; instead of which the Zulus say *inyama*, meat. Among the Zulus *bula amayte* means thresh or break stones. The Congo people called Stanley "*Bula Matadi*," "the Rock Breaker." The Zulu and Kafir tribal names, *Amazulu*, and *Amaxosa*, would be, in some dialects, *Mazulu*, *Maxosa*, just as other tribal names in other parts of the Bantu field, such as *Makua*, *Maravi*, *Manyema*, would begin with *a*, as *Amakua* among the Zulus.

Among the distinguishing grammatical features of the entire Bantu family of languages, one is what may be called a system of pronominal assimilations and repetitions. This mode is sometimes designated as the "alliterative," because of the frequent recurrence of some particular letter or syllable in a given sentence. Especially in the Zulu, nouns may be grouped into eight distinct classes, according to their "prefix" or incipient element. Each class of nouns has its own pronominal forms, all of which bear a striking resemblance to the initial element of the noun to which they refer, or for which they stand. Thus one class of nouns comprises all those whose incipient is *ili;* and for this class the relative is *eli*, the demonstrative *leli*, this; *lelo*, that; the personal pronoun, nominative, and accusative, *li;* oblique form, *lo;* definitive, *lona*, and fragmentary form, simply *l*. Another class of nouns comprises all those whose incipient is *isi*, as *isibaya;* and for this the relative pronoun is *esi;* the demonstratives, *lesi* and *leso;* personal, *si;* oblique, *so;* definitive, *sona*, and fragmentary, simply *s*. Each class and number has its own preformative letter to be used in forming the possessive; as, *u*, which passes over into its semi-vowel *w*, for the first class, singular; *b* fc, the plural; *l* and *a* for the second class; *y* and *z* for the third. Thus, for the possessive *my* or *mine*, we have, *wami*, *bami;* *lami*, *ami;* *yami*, *zami*, according to the class and number of the noun; as, *umfana wami*, my boy; *abafana bami*, my boys. For the possessive *his* or *her*, if the noun be of the first class, we have *wake*, *bake*, *lake*, etc., according to the class of the noun possessed; as, *umfana wake,* his boy; *ilizwi lake,* his word; *izinkomo zake,* his cattle. For the possessive *their,* referring to persons or to nouns in *aba,* as *abafana,* boys; *abantu,* people; we have *wabo, babo, labo, abo, yabo,* etc., as, *ilizwi labo,* their word; *izinkomo zabo,* their cattle. And for the possessive *their,* referring to nouns in *izin,* as *izinkomo,* we have, in like manner, *wazo, bazo, lazo, azo, yazo,* etc., as, *ilizi lazo,* their voice; *isibaya sazo,* their fold; *izimpondo zazo,* their horns.

One of the most important points in which the Bantu languages differ from the English and many others is found in the fact that, for the most part, the formative letters precede the root; that is, most of the inflections to which a word is subject, are made by changes in the beginning of the word; thus, *umfana,* boy; *abafana,* boys; *inkomo,* cow; *izinkomo,* cows; *izwi* or *ilizwi,* word; *amazwi,* words. So in the adjective: *umfana omkula,* large boy; *abafana abakula,* large boys; *inkomo enkulu,* great cow; *ilizwi elikulu,* great word. So in the possessive pronouns: *abafana bami,* my boys; *izinkomo zami,* my cows; *ilizwi lami,* my word.

This giving to the nominal incipient so much of molding influence over the pronouns and over the prefixes contributes largely to precision and the power of inversion. It is also thought by some to add to the euphony of the language. Indeed, some who at first failed to see that the principle really constitutes a vital feature of the language, were wont to regard it as nothing more than a kind of "euphonic alliteration."

From all this it will be seen that the Bantu languages allow great scope and variety in the arrangement of words in a sentence and at the same time preserve clearness and precision.

One of the greatest defects of these languages, as might be supposed, is the paucity of words, especially those needed for the expression of moral and religious thoughts. Yet, even here, the case is not so difficult as might be presumed. One root will often give a large stem, with a good number of branches, and no small amount of fruit. Thus, from the verb *bona,* see, we have *bonisa,* cause to see, show; *bonisisa,* show clearly; *bonela,* see for; *bonelela,* look and learn, imitate; *bonana,* see each other; *bonelana,* see for each other; *bonisana,* cause each other to see, show each other; *bonakala,* appear, be visible; *bonakalisa,* make visible; *umboni,* a seer; *umboneli,* a spectator; *umbonelo,* a spectacle; *umbonisi,* an overseer; *umboniso,* a show; *isibono,* a sight, curiosity; *isiboniso,* a vision; *isibonakalo,* an appearance; *isibonakaliso,* a revelation—and all this without going into the passive voice; as, *bonwa,* be seen; *boniswa,* cause to be seen; *bonisiswa,* cause to be clearly seen, etc. Perhaps no other language exceeds the Zulu in the scope and liberty which it gives for the formation of derivative words.

The liberty which it gives for combining two or more words, so as to form a significant compound, is another point worth mentioning. In this way we get *impumalanga,* east, from two words—*puma,* come out, and *ilanga,* the sun; *inchonalanga,* west—from *chona,* sink, and *ilanga,* sun. So, *inhlilifa,* an heir, comes from combining two words which signify "to eat the estate of the deceased;" while *inhlulanhlebe,* a bat, signifies "a long-eared animal;" and *ihlolenkosikazi,* the jasmine, "queen's eye."

Many of the names which the natives give to persons, places, rivers, mountains, are also compound terms; and, whether simple or compound, the most of them are significant.

Perhaps no language can lay a better claim than the Zulu to an exemption from two great faults—on the one hand, that superabundance of vowels and liquids which produces excessive softness; and on the other, that superabundance of consonants which produces excessive harshness. The happy mean which it has observed in its inter-mixture of mute consonants with vocalic and liquid sounds makes it both pleasing to the ear and easy to speak.

One of the striking peculiarities of several Bantu languages is that sharp, shrill sound called a "click." It constitutes an elementary part of the word in which it occurs, as much so as its vowels or consonants, and is never found in the formative part. Of these clicks there are three kinds, each of which takes its name from the manner in which it is made, as the dental, the palatal, and the lateral. The origin of these peculiar sounds may, doubtless, be found in the onomatopoetic effort to suit the sound of the word to the thing signified.

The indigenous literature of all the Bantu tribes is very scant, since no alphabet exists with which to write out thoughts, folk-lore, songs, royal eulogies, and common law. They have a variety of unwritten, simple songs: evening songs, domestic songs, hunting songs, heroic songs, and religious songs, or songs in which they give expression to a wish or prayer. With the singing of these, accompanied with the *gumbu,* a musical instrument of one string, they pass many an hour of leisure. Their language abounds in bold, figurative epithets and complimentary terms, of which they make great use in singing the praises of their kings. The royal court, upon grand festal occasions, offers ample field for the royal rhapsodist or bard to pour forth his poetic imaginings in a most profuse and fervid style, speaking of the king, to his face, as black and beautiful, tall and straight, a majestic elephant, a ravenous hyena, the merciless opponent of every conspiracy, the devourer, waster, smasher of all his foes; lovely as a monster of resistless might, "like heaven above, raining and shining."

BAPATLA: A town of the Kistna district, Madras, India, 40 miles east of Ongole. Healthful location. Population, chiefly Telugus; station of the ABMU (1883), with 2 missionaries and their wives, 1 missionary woman and 47 native workers, men and women, 20 outstations, 30 Sunday schools and 2,515 church members.

BAPTIST CONVENTIONS OF CANADA; Foreign Missionary Work of the: The first foreign missionary work of the Baptists of Canada was done in connection with societies in the United States. As early as 1838 a Society for the Maintenance of Foreign Missions was established at Chester, Nova Scotia. Seven years later the first representative of the Canadian Baptists on the foreign field was sent to Burma and later two others, to labor under the ABMU. The interest in foreign missions was not aroused in Ontario and Quebec till 1866, when a student in Woodstock College desired to go out as a missionary and there seemed no way to send him. Dr. Fyfe, the principal, then wrote to the Secretary of the

ABMU. The result was a meeting of six pastors, with Dr. Fyfe and Dr. Murdock of the ABMU, at the parsonage in Beamsville, Ontario, in October of that year. Here the Canadian Auxiliary to the ABMU was formed, and in October, 1867, just one year later, their first two missionaries were sent to the Telugu Mission of the ABMU. Two years later the Rev. John McLaurin, also a graduate of Woodstock College, and his wife were sent out.

Up to 1873 both sections of the Baptists of Canada worked in connection with the ABMU, supporting missionaries in Burma and among the Telugus of India, as well as a number of native helpers. In that year, however, both the eastern and western provinces established independent and separate foreign mission boards, while remaining in cordial sympathy with the ABMU.

The Foreign Mission Board of the Baptist Convention of the Maritime Provinces in 1873 sent out a party of seven missionaries to explore and, if deemed advisable, to establish a mission among the Karens of Siam; they failed to find Karens in Siam in sufficient numbers to warrant establishing a mission and the project was abandoned. At this juncture an invitation for them to cooperate with the new organization in the western provinces was accepted, and the missionaries were transferred to the Telugu country.

The Foreign Mission Board of the Baptist Convention of Ontario and Quebec, in 1873, were offered a mission of the ABMU, at Cocanada (Madras, India). The offer was accepted, and the Rev. John McLaurin was released from his connection with the ABMU to take charge of the new mission. He landed at Cocanada with his family in 1874. The following year he was joined by the missionaries of the Maritime Provinces, who were in Siam, and thus in 1875 was formed the Canadian Baptist Telugu Mission. There are two boards in the homeland, but their work in the foreign field is very closely united in interest, in method as well as in territorial relations. The work is carried on along evangelistic, educational and medical lines; a strong native church is steadily pressing toward self-support; Bible women and colporteurs are an especially effective evangelizing agency.

Missions of the Convention of the Maritime Provinces: District of Vizagapatam, Madras, India; 6 stations, 21 outstations, 21 Canadian missionaries, 49 native helpers, 8 churches, 495 communicants, 17 day schools, 1 hospital and dispensary.

Missions of the Convention of Ontario and Quebec: (1) Godavari and Kistna Districts, Madras, India; 8 stations, 111 outstations, 35 Canadian missionaries, 196 native helpers, 38 churches, 4,363 communicants, 18 day schools, 1,366 pupils, 9 boarding schools with 304 students, 4 physicians and 3 hospitals and dispensaries. (2) Bolivia, South America; 3 stations, 7 Canadian missionaries, 2 schools.

The organ of the Baptist Foreign Missionary Societies of Canada is *The Canadian Missionary Link*, monthly, Toronto.

BAPTIST MISSIONARY SOCIETY: The Baptist Missionary Society, founded October 2, 1792, was the first of the many missionary organizations which had their beginning in the closing years of the 18th and the opening of the 19th centuries. Since 1781 William Carey, the "Northamptonshire Cobbler," had been putting forth every effort to arouse his ministerial brethren to something of his own absorbing interest in the question of giving the Gospel to the heathen. His paper, "An Inquiry into the Obligations of Christians to use Means for the Conversion of the Heathen," published in 1792, was a most impassioned appeal, and with his two sermons, preached before the Baptist Association at Nottingham, May 30, and at Kettering, October 2, 1792, resulted in the formation of the Baptist Missionary Society. The two points deduced from the text of the latter have since become famous —"Expect great things from God; attempt great things for God." At the conclusion of this sermon twelve of the ministers who had heard it withdrew to a little white house, still to be seen from the Midland Railway, and passed the following resolutions:

"Desirous of making an effort for the propagation of the Gospel among the heathen, agreeably to what is recommended in Brother Carey's late publication, we whose names appear to the subsequent subscription, do solemnly agree to act in society for that purpose.

"As in the present divided state of Christendom it seems that each denomination, by exerting itself separately, is most likely to accomplish the great ends of a mission, it is agreed that this society be called 'The Particular (Calvinistic) Baptist Society for Propagating the Gospel among the Heathen.'

"As such an undertaking must needs be attended with expense, we agree immediately to open a subscription for the above purpose, and to recommend it to others.

"Every person who shall subscribe £10 at once, or 10s 6d annually, shall be a member of the Society."

The twelve ministers present subscribed £13 2s 6d. These "great things" were ridiculed by their fellows, but the event has proved that "the greatest things of God have quiet and small beginnings."

Carey became the first missionary of the Society, Andrew Fuller its first secretary, and Sutcliffe, Dr. Ryland, Jr., and Reynold Hogg formed with these two the first committee. Samuel Pierce, one of the first subscribers at Kettering, desired to be sent to the heathen, but his early death prevented.

Constitution and organization: The organization of the Baptist Missionary Society is very simple. Its membership comprises pastors of churches making an annual contribution; ministers who collect annually, and all Christian persons concurring in the objects of the Society who are donors of £10 or upward, or subscribers of ten shillings annually to its funds.

The affairs of the Society are conducted by a committee of forty-eight members, two-thirds of whom are residents beyond twelve miles of St. Paul's. The committee meets monthly, or oftener, in London, on a fixed day, for the despatch of business; seven members make a quorum. A public meeting of the Society is held annually, when the list of the committee is read, the accounts are presented, and the accounts of the previous year reported. The committee may summon public meetings in London or elsewhere whenever the interests of the Society require it.

All honorary and corresponding members of the committee, and all ministers who are members of the Society, and the secretary and treasurer of London auxiliaries are entitled to attend and vote at the meetings of the committee.

Statement of Missions; India: A mission to Tahiti, in the South Seas, was at first thought of by the Society, but this plan was changed by the accounts received from Mr. John Thomas, a surgeon in the employ of the East India Company at Bengal, of the great needs of India. Andrew Fuller, in his account of the meeting held to consider the matter, says, "We saw plainly that there was a gold mine in India, but it was as deep as the center of the earth. Who would venture to explore it? 'I will go down,' said Carey, 'but remember that you must hold the ropes.' We solemnly engaged to him to do so, nor while we live shall we desert him." In March, 1793, Carey and John Thomas sailed for India in a Danish vessel. They landed in Calcutta, November 10. Carey had told his society that he should require from it money sufficient to pay for his passage only, believing that once in India he could support himself. The years that followed were very trying. He found work in an indigo factory, perfected his knowledge of the Bengal language, wrote a grammar of it, translated the New Testament into it, learned Sanskrit, mastered the botany of the region, corresponded with the German missionaries, Schwartz and Guericke, in the far south, set up a printing-press, and planned new missions —all at his own cost. On his rude press, which, from his great devotion to it, the natives thought was an idol, he printed the New Testament as fast as he translated it. In 1797 Mr. John Fountain was sent out to reenforce Carey, and in 1799 Messrs. Ward, Grant, Brunsdon, and Marshman reached Calcutta. In this year the indigo factory was given up, and on account of the persistent opposition of the East India Company the little band of missionaries removed to the Danish settlement of Serampur, on the west bank of the Hugli, fourteen miles above Calcutta. Here they purchased house and grounds for church, home, and printing office. An income for the mission was secured from the boarding schools opened for Eurasian boys and girls, and conducted by Mr. and Mrs. Marshman. In December, 1800, Carey baptized the first Hindu convert, Krishnu Pal, a Brahman, who became a noted preacher, and from his own funds built the first house of Christian worship in Bengal.

Carey was appointed by Lord Wellesley, then Governor-General, first Bengali, afterward Sanskrit and Marathi, professor in the College of Fort William. The families of the little missionary community lived together, eating at the same table at a cost not much more than £100 a year.

The work of translating the Scriptures, teaching, preaching, printing, and establishing schools went actively on. Before Carey's death (1834) the whole Bible had been translated into forty different languages and dialects, and the sacred books of the Hindus translated into English. In addition, Dr. Marshman translated the Bible into Chinese, prepared a Chinese grammar and dictionary, and translated Confucius into English.

In 1812 the printing press at Serampur was destroyed by fire. The loss from this calamity was great, but the gain was perhaps greater, for the interest and sympathy of Christians at home, of all denominations, was aroused to a degree never felt before. The whole amount of the loss, £10,000, was raised within fifty days and sent to Serampur, where work was speedily resumed. This was the first instance of really large donations to the cause of missions.

The work extended to other parts of India, and many stations were established. In 1810 these stations were organized into five missions: the Bengal Mission, including Serampur, Calcutta, Dinajpur, etc.; the Hindustani Mission (Northern India), including Patna, Agra, etc., and the Burman, Bhutan, and Orissa Missions. In 1813 there were in all 20 stations, with 63 European and native laborers.

In 1827 the missionaries at Serampur and the Society at home became two distinct and independent missionary bodies, because of the refusal of the former, using in mission service a large amount of property which they had accumulated without the aid of friends at home, to render to the parent Society a strict account of their pecuniary transactions. In 1854 the Serampur Brotherhood had contributed to the mission £90,000. A friendly separation was therefore agreed upon, which continued for ten years. In 1837 the two bodies were reunited.

There are in Bengal, Orissa and the United Provinces of India (1892) 195 stations and outstations of the BMS, 112 missionaries, 239 native workers, 7,335 communicants, 7,482 pupils in schools. The educational work includes the Serampur College, founded by Carey in 1829; Training Institutions at Cuttack and Delhi, besides elementary schools and orphanages. The Society also carries on special work among English speaking students and has a printing press in Calcutta.

Ceylon: The work of the BMS in this field was commenced in 1812 and has been largely educational. There are (1902) 80 stations and outstations, 5 missionaries, 26 native workers, 1,033 communicants and 3,196 pupils in schools.

China: Several attempts were made by the BMS to commence mission work in this country, and since 1877 it has been carried on successfully. In 1902 there were 346 stations and outstations in the provinces of Shantung, Shensi and Shansi, with 43 missionaries, 122 native workers, 4,652 communicants and 1,312 pupils in schools. This mission suffered severely during the Boxer troubles but has rallied well. The fact that the Rev. Timothy Richard of Shanghai, Secretary of the Society for the Diffusion of Christian Knowledge among the Chinese, is enrolled among the missionaries of this Society is indication of the interest it takes in the supply of Christian literature for that Empire.

Palestine: This mission of the BMS has been carried on since 1880, with headquarters at Nablous. There were in 1902, 1 station and 5 outstations, 2 missionaries, 7 native workers, 129 communicants and 90 pupils in the schools.

Africa: From 1842-82 the Society had a most flourishing and hopeful mission on the West Coast of Africa. The West Indian churches, always desirous of sending the gospel to Africa, began, after their emancipation, to carry out their wishes. Generous contributions were made and the Society in England agreed to second their efforts. Two missionaries from Jamaica chose for the new mission the island of Fernando Po, near the mouth of the Kameruns River, in the Gulf of Guinea. Several missionaries from

England, with reenforcements from Jamaica, arrived there in 1842; the mission was firmly established, and soon extended to the coast of what is now the Kameruns; books were prepared and large portions of the Bible translated into the Dualla language by Mr. Saker, from Jamaica, who had reduced it to writing. The work at Fernando Po had, on account of Roman Catholic opposition, to be given up, and the settlement at Victoria, in the Kameruns, was transferred to the Basel Missionary Society when that region became a German colony.

In 1877 Mr. Robert Arthington, of Leeds, England, offered the committee of the Society £1,000 if they would at once undertake a mission to the Congo country, in Africa. This proposal, and succeeding generous gifts, enabled the Society to begin operations, and missionaries were immediately sent out. Settlements were soon formed on the Upper and Lower Congo. Many deaths have thinned the missionary ranks, but the places of those who fell were quickly filled and the work goes hopefully forward. In August, 1886, the mission premises at Stanley Pool were destroyed by fire; the missionaries were in great distress; but, as was the case at Serampur in 1812, the loss was quickly made good by friends of the mission at home. Mr. W. Holman Bentley, one of the pioneers, has done efficient work in reducing the language to writing, and supplying literature.

In the two missions at the Lower Congo, including Matadi, San Salvador, Wathen and Zombo, and the Upper Congo, including Arthington, Bolobo, Lukoleba, etc., there are (1902) 61 stations and outstations, 58 missionaries, 62 native workers, 607 communicants, 3,025 pupils in the schools. Most valuable auxiliaries to the work are the two river steamers, "Peace" and "Goodwill."

West Indies: About the beginning of the 19th century a colored man from Georgia, U. S. A., P. George Liele, organized congregations of slaves in Jamaica. After his death application was made (1813) to the BMS for assistance and on advice of Mr. Wilberforce a missionary was sent out. Others followed, chapels and schools were built, and at the outbreak of the insurrection (1831) there were 14 English missionaries, 24 churches and 10,838 communicants. The insurrection checked the work in the island, but the earnest appeals of the missionaries on their return to England helped much toward the abolition of slavery in the British Dominions. After order had been restored the work was again pressed with success until in 1842 the churches in Jamaica announced themselves as independent of the Society's funds. In the West Indies, including Jamaica, there are (1902) 286 stations and outstations of the BMS, with 38,345 communicants (of whom 32,208 are in Jamaica). Of the 10 missionaries and 619 native workers, all but two missionaries (in Jamaica) are independent of the Society. The Society also has 4 stations and 61 outstations in Italy and in France. A mission commenced in Japan in 1879 has been given up.

The Baptist Zenana Mission: This woman's organization for mission work is in connection with the BMS, and was organized in 1867. It is independent in its officers, committees, and funds. In India it supported, in 1900, 64 missionaries and 200 native workers in 20 stations; had 94 schools with 3,620 pupils, and 6 hospitals and dispensaries where 23,500 patients are treated. In China, it had (1900) 11 missionaries and 20 native workers in 4 stations, and 18 schools, with 180 pupils.

The medical work of the BMS is conducted as a special auxiliary formed in 1901, conjointly with that of the Baptist Zenana Mission.

The Young People's Missionary Association in aid of the Baptist Missionary Society was organized in 1848. The Annual Report of the BMS gives a list of individuals, schools, etc., supported by these various organizations.

Organ: *Missionary Herald,* monthly.
Marshman (J. C.), *Life and Times of Carey, Marshman & Ward,* 2 vols., London, 1859; Myers (J. B.), *Centenary Volume of the BMS,* London, 1893.

BAPTIST MISSIONARY SOCIETY (German): See GERMANY, MISSIONARY SOCIETIES IN.

BAPTIST SOUTHERN CONVENTION: See SOUTHERN BAPTIST CONVENTION.

BAPUJI APPAJI: A Brahman of Nasik, Western India. He made a public profession of faith in Christ after he was twenty-five years of age, and as native pastor at Bombay and missionary among his fellow countrymen he wrought faithfully and successfully. He was a member of the Translation Committee of the CMS, and translated several small books into Marâthi. He died at Poona, January 16, 1894.

BARAKA: A town on the Gaboon River, West Africa. Missionary work was commenced here by missionaries of the ABCFM in 1842. The station was transferred in 1870 to the PN. It now has 2 missionaries, 2 unmarried women missionaries, 8 native workers, men and women, 1 village school, 2 high schools and 226 church members.

BARAMA: A town in British Guiana, W. of the Essequibo River; station of the SPG, with 1 missionary, 2 native workers, and 2 village schools.

BARANAGAR: A town on the Hugli River near Calcutta, Bengal, India; station of the Church of England Zenana Missionary Society (1891), with (1902) 2 missionary women and 19 native women workers, 1 industrial home for converts, 11 common schools and 35 Zenana pupils. Also written Baranagore.

BARARETTA. See GALLALAND.

BARBADOS: An island of the Caribbean group, W. I., belonging to Great Britain. The population is 182,306, mostly negroes, with a number of Hindus brought there to work in the fields, and a few Chinese. The language is a jargon based on English. Missionary operations have been carried on in this island by the Moravians (since 1765) and the Seventh Day Adventist Mission Board (U. S.), the Salvation Army, the Brethren (PB), and the African Methodist Episcopal Church (U. S.).

BARBARY STATES: A general term designating that portion of North Africa stretching from the western boundary of Egypt to the Atlantic, and from the Mediterranean to the Sahara, and including **Tripoli, Tunis, Algeria,** and **Morocco.** The name is derived from the Berbers, the ancient inhabitants of the region, who still constitute a considerable portion of the population.

BARDEZAG: A large village on the hills bordering the Gulf of Nicomedia, S. of the city of Nicomedia, Asiatic Turkey. Its population, about 5,000, is entirely Armenian. The mission station of the ABCFM, formerly at Nicomedia, was transferred to this place largely on account of its greater healthfulness. There is a large Protestant community and a flourishing boys' school, where of late years the experiment of manual training has been made with great success. There is also an orphanage for boys whose parents were killed in the massacres of 1895-96. The Turkish name of the place is Baghchejik.

BARDWAN: Chief town of the district of the same name, Bengal, India. Population, 35,000. A station of the CMS with 3 missionaries, 1 with his wife, 5 native workers and 31 communicants, and 1 village school supervised by the Church of England Zenana Missionary Society. Also written Burdwan.

BARELI: A city of the United Provinces, India, on a branch of the Ganges, 122 miles southeast of Delhi. Population (1901), 131,208, chiefly Hindus. Station of the ME (1856) with 8 missionaries, men and women, 3 of them medical, 53 native workers, men and women, 1 hospital, 1 theological school, 1 orphanage, 1 high school, 27 village schools, 70 Sunday schools, Young People's Society, and 516 church members. Also written Bareilly.

BARHAWA. See BAHAWA.

BARINGA: A settlement in the Congo Free State situated on the Maringa River, about 200 miles from the Congo; station of the RBMU (1900), with 3 missionaries and 2 missionary women, 1 of whom is unmarried; 1 preaching place, a village school and a dispensary.

BARISAL: Capital of the district of Bakarganj, Bengal, India. Climate damp, but very healthful, and the coolest in all Bengal. Population, 16,000. Race, Bengali and Mugh. Language, Bengali, Arrakanese, and mixed Hindustani. Station of the BMS (1828), with 4 missionaries and 3 married missionary women, 15 native workers, 28 outstations, 52 Sunday schools, 60 village schools, Young People's Societies, 1,000 church members.

Also of the Baptist Zenana Mission (1871), with 3 unmarried missionary women, 12 native women workers, 3 Sunday schools, 8 village schools and 1 high school.

Also station of the Oxford Mission to Calcutta (1901), with 4 missionaries and a theological school.

Also station of the SPG (1869), with 19 native workers, 10 village schools and 234 communicants. Written also Burrisal.

BARKLY WEST: A town in Bechuanaland, South Africa, near the diamond fields. Mission station of the LMS (1842); 1 missionary and wife.

BARODA: Capital of Baroda, a native State in India, 231 miles north of Bombay. Population, 103,790. Formerly the town, which is a fairly well built and pleasant place, was a very important seat of trade and of various industries, and at present, tho its prosperity has declined, it carries on considerable commerce with the surrounding country. Station of the ME, with 3 missionaries and their wives, 2 unmarried missionary women, 122 native workers, men and women, 5 outstations,68 Sunday schools, 50 common schools, 1 high school, a Young People's Society and 1,550 church members.

BAROTSE TRIBES: The peoples occupying the valley of the Upper Zambesi, a vast and populous plain, 189 miles long by 30 to 35 broad, subject to periodical inundations and resultant fevers. The Barotse Empire was founded by a Basuto conqueror. The Barotse succeeded in throwing off the foreign yoke, but the kingdom was maintained. It has been described as including 18 large nations subdivided into over 100 tribes. Each tribe speaks its own dialect, but Lesuto, the tongue of the exterminated Basuto (Makololo) conquerors, is the common medium of communication. The region occupied by tribes subject to the Barotse kingdom covers an area of about 100,000 square miles, with a population of perhaps 1,000,000. Europeans were long excluded from the country. Grain, vegetables, and cattle abound. The villages are built on artificial mounds for protection against the inundations of the Zambesi. The people worship the sun and the new moon, and observe feasts at the graves of their ancestors. The missions of the French Protestants have been very successful among the Barotse, and the paramount chief is a professing Christian who has visited France and England.

BAROTSELAND. See RHODESIA.

BARRA: A town NW. of Rio de Janeiro in Brazil; station of the MES (1894), with a native worker, 1 outstation, 1 village school, 1 Sunday school and 171 church members. Also written Barra Mansa.

BARRACKPUR: A town and military station in Bengal, India, situated on the Hugli, 15 miles from Calcutta; station of the Church of England Zenana Missionary Society (1871), with (1902) 3 women missionaries and 22 native women workers, 11 common schools, 1 training home for converts and 43 Zenana pupils.

Station also of the WMS, with 1 missionary, 14 native workers, men and women, 5 outstations, 1 Sunday school, 1 high school, 2 common schools and 63 church members.

BARRANQUILLA: One of the important commercial cities of Colombia, S. America, situated on a cañon of the Magdalena River, about 20 miles from the sea. Population, about 40,000. It is a station of the PN (1888), with 2 missionaries and their wives, 3 unmarried women missionaries, 2 high schools, 1 common school, and 46 church members.

BARRIPORE: A town S. W. of Calcutta, Bengal, India; station of the SPG (1829), with 11 native workers, 15 chapel preaching places and 760 communicants.

BARROW POINT. See POINT BARROW.

BARROWS LECTURESHIP FOR INDIA: Lectureship on the Relations of Christianity to Other Religions founded at the University of Chicago, in 1894, by a donation of $20,000 from Mrs. Caroline E. Haskell, of Chicago. The lectures, six or more in number, are required by the terms of the foundation to be delivered in Calcutta, and, if deemed best, in Madras, Bombay, or other important cities of India.

Large numbers of educated Hindus and Muslims are now familiar with the English language. To these scholarly and thoughtful men the lectures are to be directed, setting forth, in a friendly, conciliatory way, the great truths of Christianity, their harmony with truths found in other religions and their claims upon men.

Mrs. Haskell expressed a wish that the Rev.

John Henry Barrows, D.D., the President of the Parliament of Religions, and afterwards President of Oberlin College, should be the first lecturer. Dr. Barrows inaugurated the lectureship during the winter of 1896-7, when he delivered more than one hundred lectures and addresses in Hindustan. These lectures were published in book form, both in India and America, under the title: "Christianity, the World Religion." The second lecturer on this foundation was Principal Fairbairn of Mansfield College, Oxford, who spent the winter of 1898-9 in India and there delivered a series of scholarly lectures afterward incorporated in his "Philosophy of Religion." In the winter of 1902-3, the third series of lectures on this foundation were delivered in India by the Rev. C. C. Hall, D.D., President of Union Theological Seminary, New York. The third series commanded the same respectful, not to say cordial, attention from Hindus and Muslims as the previous lectures. It is the judgment of competent observers that influence of considerable importance and value has been exerted already through this lectureship.

Mrs. Haskell named the lectureship from Dr. Barrows, who at the time of its establishment was her pastor (First Presbyterian Church, Chicago). It is frequently called the "Haskell Lectureship," however, from the giver of the fund which supports it.

BARTHELEMY: One of the Leeward Islands, West Indies. Mission station of the Moravians.

BASARUR: A town in S. Kanara, South India; station of the Basel Missionary Society (1876), with 2 missionaries (one of them married), 15 native workers, 3 outstations, 2 common schools and 45 communicants.

BASEL EVANGELICAL MISSIONARY SOCIETY (Evangelische Missionsgesellschaft, Basel): On August 30, 1730, the German Christian Society (Der Deutschen Christenthums Gesellschaft) was founded at Basel through the influence of Dr. Urlsperger, who had recently visited England. This society undertook, as a kind of union, to collect and impart information far and near respecting the kingdom of God. It corresponded to the London Missionary Society. In 1801 Friedrich Steinkopf, who since 1798 had been secretary of the Basel Society, went to London as preacher to the German Savoy Church, and, in 1802, became a director of the London Missionary Society. In 1804 he took part in founding the British and Foreign Bible Society. He was the connecting link between England and Basel, and largely through his influence the Basel Mission was founded.

C. F. Spittler, who had gone to Basel as successor of Friedrich Steinkopf (lay secretary), became so interested in foreign missions that he proposed to go to Berlin and enter a training mission school founded there, in 1800, by Johann Jänicke. Thereupon the Basel Society attempted to induce Jänicke to remove his school to their city. On his declining the offer, it became more and more evident that Basel must begin a work of her own. In May, 1815, just as the city was about to be bombarded from Hüningen, the Rev. Nicolaus Von Brunn, at a regular missionary meeting in his church, at which a young man presented himself for missionary service, suggested to Spittler that such young men should be educated at Basel and then be recommended to the English societies who sent out men to the field. Steinkopf arrived at Basel in September, 1815, and induced Spittler to form a special committee for this purpose. On the 25th of the same month this body (Rev. N. Von Brunn, President; Rev. Mr. Wenk, Secretary; and a merchant, Mr. Marian-Kuder, Treasurer) held its first meeting as a mission "collegium" in the parsonage of St. Martin's Church. Christian Gottlieb Blumhardt, who from 1803 to 1807 had been theological secretary of the German Christian Society at Basel, was invited to take up the work of the new venture. After a little delay, in the spring of 1816, Blumhardt went to Basel as "inspector" or manager of the Evangelical Missionary Society, and on August 26 of the same year opened a training school for missions. Under the management of Blumhardt, who was a very cautious man, the mission school slowly began to gather headway. For the first few years its students, when ready for serivce, were handed over to foreign missionary societies, especially to the Rotterdam and the Church Missionary Societies. But as early as 1821 it began to send out missionaries under its own direction. In that year Zaremba and Dittrich were ordained as the first Basel missionaries for Southern Russia.

From 1816 Blumhardt edited the *Evangelical Missionary Magazine*, in 1828 founded the *Heidenbote*, the special organ of the Society; wrote a history of missions in several volumes, and managed the Society so frugally that at his death the mission house (school) was supported by the income of the magazine and the *Heidenbote*, and an available fund was raised to the amount of 100,000 florins, with a reserve fund of 20,000 florins. The following missions were started during his era: (1) One in South Russia (1821), was suspended by an imperial ukase, and dissolved in 1839. Before the work was stopped, however, the Bible had been translated into Turkish-Tatar and the modern Armenian languages; Armenia and the regions toward Baghdad and Tabriz had been visited, and an evangelical congregation had been established among the Armenians at Shamakhi. (2) Eight men were sent to Liberia in 1827 and 1828, but four soon died, and the remaining four settled in other regions. (3) In 1828 the mission on the Gold Coast was founded, but during the first twelve years as many missionaries died without having seen the fruit of their labors. (4) In 1834 Hebich, Greiner and Lehner were sent to the west coast of India.

The second "inspector," William Hoffmann (1839-50), set the plan of his work more clearly before the public, and pressed home the obligation that rested on the whole Christian Church. He also provided a more efficient instruction in the seminary for missionary candidates. In ten years the income of the Society almost doubled; the number of stations had increased fivefold; new life was thrown into the mission on the Gold Coast, placing the work in Africa on an assured basis. In 1846 mission work was undertaken in China, at the suggestion of Gützlaff. In 1846-50 attempts were made to establish the work in East Bengal and Assam, but later on these fields were relinquished to other societies

Under Joseph Josenhans (1850-79) the work of the Society was systematized and organized; the *Missionshaus* was erected, schools were established and the industrial work that became so marked a feature of the Society's missions was put in operation. During the term of Otto Schott (1879-84) female and medical missionaries first went out.

Since then Inspector Oehlen, son of the well-known professor, has been a most efficient manager.

Constitution and Organization: The Basel Evangelical Missionary Society is strictly undenominational, being affiliated with no State Church, and having relations with nearly all the Protestant Churches of Central Europe. While essentially German, its location in Switzerland and its general character differentiate it from the German Societies. Its affairs are conducted by a committee of thirteen gentlemen (six clergymen and seven laymen). This committee is self-perpetuating, but manifests its sense of obligation to the public by the completeness of its reports and the care with which it conducts its business.

The Basel Mission House is far more than a mere headquarters for the Society. It contains a training school, a book department, library, refectory, dormitory, hospital and work-shops. The 80-100 students come chiefly from southern Germany and Switzerland and represent every class in life: agriculturists, artisans, clerks, mechanics, teachers, surgeons, etc. The general theory is that every man of good character and sincere Christian purpose can be utilized somewhere, and it is the business of the Society to find out where. The course of training covers six years, is thorough, and embraces all the different departments of value in mission work, including the classics, Bible study, history, science and the trades, but especially the development of character. The graduates from the theological seminary are ordained, through the courtesy of some church, Reformed, Lutheran, or Free, as the case may be, tho the ordination is not for European service. In view of the undenominational character of the Society, there was some question as to what ecclesiastical order should be adopted for the churches on the mission field. Finally the Presbyterian form was adopted and a simple liturgy is used.

Another distinctive feature of the Basel Society is *The Industrial and Commercial Commission*, first organized by Inspector Josenhans to meet the situation on the Gold Coast. The mission there was absolutely dependent upon direct commercial communication with Europe for all the necessaries of life. The native Christians had no method of earning an independent livelihood. The establishment of a depot of supplies and the instruction of the natives in agriculture and in the various crafts was the inevitable outcome of any attempt at missionary work. Vessels were purchased by the Society to navigate the various rivers of the territory occupied, and commercial houses sprang up at convenient points. In India the commercial development has been still more extensive, including weaving establishments at Mangalore and in the region about Cananore, large tile manufactories at Mangalore and Calicut and the employment of mechanics and joiners under mission auspices. The net income of the commission in 1900, all of which was handed over to the Society, was 203,996 francs ($40,799). This department has been a paying investment from the beginning. The total income of the Society amounted in 1902 to 1,626,116 francs ($325,223). Nearly one-half of this came from Southern Germany; Switzerland stands next. Contributions come from all parts of Europe, from Asia, Africa, America, and even Australia.

Statement of Missions; Africa: The first effort in Liberia (1827) failed entirely owing to the climate; a second (1828), on the Guinea coast, was almost entirely a failure, but in 1831 a band succeeded in maintaining themselves in the higher ground and established the station at Akropong. There was considerable difficulty with the Danish Governor, but that was overcome and the work placed on a firm foundation. Special attention has been paid to the school system, from the simplest elementary schools up to the theological seminary. The industrial department, too, has been most successful. With the German occupation of the Kameruns, the Basel Society took over the mission work of English and American Societies in that colony. On the Gold Coast there are (1902) 12 stations, 177 outstations, 77 missionaries, 270 native workers, 8,265 communicants, and 5,594 pupils in schools; in Kameruns 9 stations, 143 outstations, 55 missionaries, 142 native workers, 2,874 communicants, and 4,073 pupils in schools.

India: The Basel fields in India lie in Kanara (Coorg), Malabar, and the South Marâthi region. The first station occupied was Mangalore (1834). The work was extended and special attention was paid to education and industrial work, especially weaving, brick work and joiner work, giving employment to multitudes of Christians repudiated by their caste or otherwise suffering from want. There are 24 stations, 110 outstations, 148 missionaries, 653 native workers, 8,488 communicants and 11,054 pupils in the schools.

China: The Chinese mission of the Basel Society was commenced under advice from Gützlaff in 1846, and with special instructions to make it an "inland mission." Attention was directed to the Hakka people, extending from Canton to the borders of Kiang-si and Fo-kien. The work is divided in two districts, highland and lowland, and is carried on with the same care for education and general industrial training that is characteristic of Basel mission work elsewhere. There were (1902) 15 stations, 75 outstations, 44 missionaries, 151 native workers, 3,622 communicants and 1,640 pupils in the schools.

Periodical: *Der Evangelische Heidenbote*, Basel; monthly, *Evangelische Missions Magazine*, illust., monthly; *Le Missionaire*, in French, monthly.

BASIM: A town in the province of Berar, India. Population, 13,000. Station of the ME, with one missionary and his wife, 13 native workers, men and women, 2 common schools, 6 Sunday schools, a Young People's Society, and 64 church members.

BASRA: Capital of a province of the same name, adjoining the Persian Gulf at the S. E. extremity of Asiatic Turkey. The city is situated on the Euphrates below its junction with the Tigris, and is quite unhealthful. It is a station of the RCA (Arabian Mission), opened in 1891. It now has 4 missionaries, two of them married and one of them a physician, 2 outstations and 1 dispensary. Otherwise written Busrah and Bussora.

BASSA. See GREAT BASSA.

BASSEIN: The southwestern district of Burma, extending from the western Yoma range of mountains on the west to the main stream of the Irawadi and its principal outlet on the east, and from the Bay of Bengal on the south to the point on the north where the Yomas approach nearest to the great river. It includes four or five of the larger delta branches of the Irawadi. Area, 6,848 square miles. The soil is rich and fertile, tho subject to floods. The population somewhat exceeds 475,000, of which about 175,000 are Karens (Sgaus and Pwos in about equal numbers), over 225,000 Burmans, and the remainder Talaings, Telugus, Chinese and a few English. The district has been the seat of very thriving and successful missions since 1837. The ABMU has three missions there: a Burman mission, including also the Telugus; a mission to the Sgau Karens, with about 10,000 communicants and 50,000 adherent population and 85 Christian villages, the largest and most advanced of all the Karen missions in Burma; and a mission to the Pwo Karens, with about 1,375 communicants, and 22 Christian villages, with an adherent population of perhaps 7,000. The Roman Catholics have a flourishing mission among the Pwo Karens in Bassein, but with few converts from the Sgaus. The SPG has also a mission in Bassein, which is included in its diocese of Rangoon. Some efforts have been made by other denominations to plant missions here, but with little success. Education has been carried to a greater extent among the Karens of Bassein than in other district in Burma.

Story of the Karen Mission in Bassein, Brocket (L. P.), Philadelphia, 1891; *Self-Support in Bassein*, Carpenter (C. H.), Boston, 1884.

BASSEIN: Chief town of the district of Bassein, Burma. It is situated on the Bassein River, one of the delta branches of the Irawadi, and has an important trade in rice. Population, 30,000; about 20,000 of the people are Buddhists, and the remainder are Hindus, Mohammedans and Christians.

It has been a station of the ABMU since 1840. It is now operated by 12 missionaries and 300 native workers, men and women. It has 64 outstations, 157 preaching places, 123 village schools and 2 high schools, and there are 12,605 communicants.

BASSETERRE: Capital of the island of St. Kitts, W. I. Population, 9,900. Station of the Moravians (1777), with 1 missionary and his wife, 32 native workers, men and women, 2 Sunday schools, 3 common schools, and 570 communicants.

BASTA: A village in the Bijnaur district, United Provinces, India. Station of the ME, with 13 native workers, men and women, 6 Sunday schools, 3 village schools, a Young People's Society and 475 church members.

BASUTOLAND: A territory belonging to British South Africa, annexed to Cape Colony in 1871, but placed directly under the authority of the crown in 1894; lying between Natal and the Orange River Colony, with Cape Colony on the south. Its area is estimated at 10,293 square miles, with a population estimated in 1901 at 263,500, of whom 647 were Europeans. The country is an elevated plateau, well watered and with a fine climate. The Paris Evangelical Mission Society and the SPG carry on missions in this territory, occupying altogether 17 stations. The influence of these missions upon the whole Basuto people has been beneficent and profound.

Norris-Newman, *The Basutos and Their Country*, London, 1882; Widdicombe, *Fourteen Years in Basuto Land*, London, 1892; Barkley (Mrs.), *Among Boers and Basutos*, London, 1900; Casalis (E.), *My Life in Basutoland*, 1889.

BATALA: A town in the Punjab, India, 24 miles from Amritsar. Population, 26,000, Hindus, Muslims, Sikhs, etc. Mission station of the CMS (1878), with 3 missionaries (2 missionaries' wives), 22 native workers, 1 high school, 2 common schools and 72 communicants.

Also station of the CEZMS, with (1902) 4 missionary women, one of them being a physician, 7 native women workers, 1 hospital, 1 dispensary, 3 common schools and 70 Zenana pupils.

BATANGA. See GREAT BATANGA.

BATAVIA: Capital of Java, Dutch East Indies. Population (1900) 115,887, of whom about 9,000 are Europeans. Founded in 1519 by the Dutch, it is one of the most magnificent possessions of the crown of the Netherlands. In 1722 there were about 100,000 Christians in and about the city, and in 1728 the Bible was translated into the vernacular tongue, the High-Malayan. But at present the whole native pouplation of the city, with very insignificant exceptions, is Mohammedan. In 1842 the English missionaries were expelled, and only the Roman Catholics were tolerated. Of late, however, a change has taken place. The Java Comité, founded in Batavia in 1851, but since 1855 directed from Amsterdam, has a missionary and his wife there, with 3 native workers, 1 common school and 21 communicants. The Salvation Army has also a post here.

BATHURST: A town of 9,000 inhabitants on an island at the mouth of the Gambia River, W. Africa. It is the chief town of the Gambia (British) Colony. Station of the WMS, with 3 missionaries, 34 native workers, men and women, 4 outstations, 4 chapels, 4 common schools and 730 church members.

BATHURST: A village in Cape Colony, South Africa, 20 miles S. E. of Grahamstown; population 1,000; station of the South African Wesleyan Methodist Missionary Society, with 22 native workers, 14 outstations, 6 chapels, 3 common schools, a Young People's Society and 230 church members.

BATHURST: A village south of Freetown, Sierra Leone, W. Africa; station of the CMS (1822), with 6 native workers, men and women, 1 chapel, 1 Sunday school, 2 common schools and 318 communicants.

BATTA LANGUAGE: The Batta belongs to the Malayan family of languages and is spoken by more than three million of the inhabitants of Sumatra. It is written with its own alphabet. The Batta is found in at least three separate dialects. Of these, the Mandailing, or Southern Batta, is used by the more cultured people and is the language most used in literature. The Toba, or Northern Batta, has been printed in Roman letters for missionary purposes.

BATTALAGUNDU: A town northwest of Madura, Madras, India. Language, Tamil, Telugu. Station of the ABCFM (1872), with 1 missionary and his wife, 39 native workers, men and women, 16 outstations, 16 preaching places, 22 Sunday-schools, 19 common schools, 1 high school, a YMCA and 362 church members.

BATTICALOA: A seaport town in the Eastern Province of Ceylon; mission station of the SPG (1846), with 17 native workers, men and women, 3 chapels, 6 common schools and 140 communicants.

BATTLEFORD: A town in the district of Saskatchewan, Canada; station of the CMS (1876), with 2 missionaries, 2 native workers, 2 outstations, 3 common schools and 40 communicants.

BATTLE HARBOUR: A settlement on the eastern extremity of the coast of Labrador; station of the Labrador Medical Missionary Society (1892), with 5 missionaries, men and women (3 of them medical), an outstation and 2 hospitals.

BATTLE RIVER: A settlement in the district of Alberta, Canada; station of the Methodist Church in Canada (1881), with 1 missionary and his wife, 2 outstations, 1 high school, 1 Young People's Society and 135 church members.

BATTYCOTTA: A district in the west part of the peninsula of Jaffna, Ceylon, coincident with one of the parishes anciently formed by the Portuguese Government. There were also churches built in these parishes, which afterward fell into decay, and when (1817) the ABCFM occupied the place as a mission station the remaining buildings were put into their hands by the British Government for mission purposes.

This station now has 1 missionary and his wife, with 98 native workers, men and women, 10 outstations, 8 preaching places, 37 common schools, 1 high school and 450 church members, besides Jaffna College, independently supported but with a missionary at its head.

BAU: A town on the island of Viti Levu, Fiji Islands; station of the Australasian Wesleyan Methodist Missionary Society, with 1 missionary, 476 native workers, 18 outstations, 165 chapels and preaching places, 234 Sunday schools, 347 village schools and 5,146 church members.

BAURO. See SOLOMON ISLANDS.

BANZA MANTEKE. See BANSA MANTEKE.

BAVARIAN LUTHERAN MISSIONARY SOCIETY; Neuen Dettelsau. See GERMANY; MISSIONARY SOCIETIES IN.

BAYAMON: A village in the outskirts of San Juan, Porto Rico; station of the Christian Woman's Board of Missions (Disciples), with 1 unmarried woman and an orphanage.

BAZEIA: A town in the eastern part of Cape Colony, S. Africa, situated in a fertile, well-watered and thickly populated tract of land west of Umtata; station of the Moravians, occupied in 1862 on the invitation of the British Government agent for the Tembu people and the native chief of this especial tribe. The station was destroyed once by whirlwind and again by the Kafir war of 1881-82, yet the work here has been encouraging.

The present establishment consists of 2 missionaries and their wives, 13 native workers, men and women, 2 Sunday schools, 5 village schools and 98 church members. Also written Baziya.

BEACONSFIELD: A town in the diamond fields, Cape Colony, South Africa. Population, 10,500; mission station of the Berlin Missionary Society (1885), with 1 missionary, 1 unmarried woman missionary, 8 native workers, 1 outstation and 123 communicants. Also a station of the South African Wesleyan Methodist Missionary Society, with 41 native workers, 23 outstations, 3 chapels, 3 Sunday schools, 2 village schools, a Young People's Society and 502 church members.

BEAR'S HILL: A settlement in the northern part of Assiniboia, Canada; station of the Canadian Methodist Church Mission (1887), with 1 missionary and 107 communicants.

BEAUFORT: A village E. of Savanna La Mar, Jamaica, W. I.; station of the Moravian Mission (1834), with 13 native workers, men and women, 1 chapel, 1 village school and 370 communicants.

BEAVER LANGUAGE: Belongs to the central group of the North American family of languages and is spoken by Indians living in Athabasca, Canada. It is written with syllabic characters.

BEAWAR: A town in Rajputana, India, 300 miles south of Delhi. A pleasant town, well laid out, with broad streets planted with trees; the houses well built of masonry, with tiled roofs. Climate, unusually dry. Population, 21,000, Hindus, Muslims, Jains, Christians, Parsees, etc.

Station of the UFS (1860), with 3 missionaries and their wives and 5 unmarried missionary women, 2 of them medical, 55 native workers, men and women, 10 village schools, 2 high schools, 1 dispensary, 1 hospital and 176 church members.

BECHUANALAND: A territory of Great Britain in Africa, extending east and west through 9 degrees of longitude, from the Transvaal colony and Matabeleland on the east, to German Southwest Africa on the west, and bounded on the north by Rhodesia and on the south by Cape Colony. It naturally belongs to the general region called British South Africa. The area is about 213,000 square miles, with an estimated population of 200,000. Until November, 1895, Bechuanaland included the Crown Colony of British Bechuanaland, and the Bechuanaland Protectorate. At that time the Crown Colony was annexed to Cape Colony and the territory was about to be put under the administration of the British South Africa Company. In consequence of Jameson's raid, however, this was not done, and the Protectorate is governed by a resident commissioner, with headquarters at Mafeking. By these changes the boundaries and local sovereignty of the native tribes were altered, and fixed as at present.

These tribes are the Bamangwato, under chief Khama, the Bakhatla, under Lenchwe, the Bakwena, under Sabele, the Bangwaketse, under Bathoen, the Bamaliti, under Ikaneng, and some smaller tribes. Each chief rules his own people under the protection of the King. Licenses for the sale of intoxicants are forbidden. There is a native infantry-police. The railway from Cape Town northward traverses the Protectorate as far as Bulawayo, and the telegraph line to Fort Salisbury, in Mashonaland. Missionary work is carried on by the LMS, the Hermannsburg Missionary Society and the Missions of French Switzerland. The number of stations is seven. The character of the natives near these stations has been greatly modified and they have adopted to a considerable extent European costumes and European style of dwellings.

Hepburn, *Twenty Years in Khama's Country*, London, 1895; Mackenzie, *Life of John Mackenzie, South African Statesman and Missionary*, London, 1902; Lloyd, *Three African Chiefs*, London, 1895; *Bechuana of S. Africa*, Crisp (W.), London, 1896.

BEERSHEBA: A town east of Rustenburg, Transvaal Colony, S. Africa; station of the Hermannsburg Missionary Society (1873), with 6 missionaries, men and women, 4 native workers, 4 outstations, 5 chapels, 2 village schools, 1 theological school, and 1,170 communicants. Also written Berseba.

BEGORO: A town of the Gold Coast, West Africa, northwest of Akropong. Population, 4,000. Mission station of the Basel Missionary Society (1876); 3 missionaries, 1 missionary's wife, 47 native workers, men and women, 35 outstations, 13 village schools (1902), 621 communicants.

BEHAR: A province of Bengal, British India. It lies in the Ganges Valley, being divided into two nearly equal parts by that great river, which runs through it from west to east. For the most part the country is flat; its highest hill is only about 1,600 feet above sea-level. Besides the Ganges itself, several large tributaries of that river flow through the province. The area is 44,130 square miles and the population is about 24,000,000. There are small areas near Calcutta where the density of population is greater than in Behar; but, taken as a whole, this is the most densely peopled province in all India. Each square mile of its territory contains on an average 524 inhabitants; the lowest average being found among the hills in the southeastern part, where the population, of 287 to a square mile, consists chiefly of the aboriginal Santals. The highest average, of 869 per square mile, is found in the district of Saran, in the western part of the province. In this latter district, which is wholly agricultural, the density of population in one locality reaches the enormous average of 1,240. The prevailing religion is Hinduism, with a considerable number of Mohammedans. Nearly, or quite, a fifth of the entire population belong to classes that derive their living from the soil, chiefly by way of agriculture or the care of herds.

Few provinces of India possess more historical interest than Behar. Here, for nine hundred years, from the 4th century before Christ to our 5th century, flourished an ancient Hindu kingdom, known as that of Magadha, the rulers of which encouraged the arts and learning, built roads and sent fleets and colonists to islands as far east as Java. To Palibothra, the ancient capital of this kingdom (now identified with Patna, its chief town of modern days), Seleucus Nicator, one of the immediate successors of the great Alexander, sent his envoy, Megasthenes. At a period still earlier—five or six hundred years before Christ—Gautama Buddha lived as a devout ascetic in Behar, and it was at the spot now known as Buddh Gaya, in the southwestern part of the province, that he is said to have sat for five years under the sacred Pipul Tree wrapped in profound contemplation, until he had attained enlightenment, or Buddhahood. A spot so sacred in the estimation of millions could not fail of identification, and in recent years the intelligent care of the Indian Government has conducted researches there which have been rewarded by the discovery of most interesting relics of the early days of Buddhism. Ancient temples, dating back to 250 B. C., have been excavated; thrones, jewels, sacred images of Buddha, and other remains have been disinterred.

BEHIR: A town in the Gond region, Central Provinces, India; station of the Balaghat Mission (1898), with 1 missionary and his wife, 1 unmarried missionary woman, 2 native workers, 1 village school, 1 industrial school, 1 dispensary, a hospital, an orphanage and 10 communicants. Also written Baihir.

BEHRENS, Henry William: Born February 13, 1827, in Hermannsberg, Germany; died April 22, 1900, at Bethany, Transvaal, Africa. In early youth, through the influence of the village pastor, Ludwig Harms, he determined to be a foreign missionary. Many obstacles preventing, he did not sail for his field of labor in Africa until November 10, 1857, when he was sent out under the Hermannsburg Society.

At Ehlenzeni, Natal, Behrens labored six years among the Zulu Kafirs. He himself and six Kafirs built church, school, and home. No baptisms occurred, altho he preached regularly to three hundred natives.

In 1863 he was sent to work among the Bechuanas at Linokana (in what is now the Transvaal). After a year of faithful work, he saw no results. He sat weeping one day at his door when a negro inquired the cause of his trouble and begged him to visit his people in Magaliesberg. Mr. Behrens accepted this as a call, went to the region, and found a people ready to hear. Their hearts had been prepared by one of their number who while imprisoned with the Boers had heard the Gospel from an English missionary. Behrens began work there November 29, 1864. He soon founded the Christian village, Bethany, where he spent the rest of his life, preaching, composing hymns, and teaching. He was pastor of a congregation of nearly two hundred negroes. He organized a school for the training of native teachers and established nine schools for children. Besides carrying on the work at Bethany, Mr. Behrens supervised the entire work of the Society among the Bechuanas, and saw the work grow rapidly. Once every two years he visited every one of the twenty-nine stations and twenty-seven missionaries. This he did faithfully for thirty-six years.

BEIRUT: A city situated on the eastern coast of the Mediterranean, capital of the Turkish province of Syria (Suriyè). It is the commercial and literary center of Syria, and in its appearance and in the culture of its inhabitants more nearly resembles a European city than any other city in the land.

It is situated on a plain at the foot of the Lebanon, and in beauty of scenery rivals Naples, the shore here describing a graceful curve of several miles' radius, in the bosom of which the city lies, built on rising ground. It is adorned with many elegant buildings, public and private, rising one above another in a gentle slope, with a near background of mulberry, olive, and pine groves, and a more distant background of the terraced and vine-clad sides of Mount Lebanon, whose peaks, nearly 10,000 feet high, are snow crowned for several months of the year.

The climate is tropical. The rainy season is confined principally to the three winter months, when the thermometer rarely sinks below 50° Fahrenheit. A long summer reigns, with unbroken heat day and night, while the thermometer ranges from 80° to 90°, and occasionally rises to 100°.

The population numbers about 100,000, and is composed of Mohammedans, Druses, Christians of various sects, and Jews.

An English company has brought water to it from the mountain in an aqueduct six or eight miles long, and has also lighted its streets with gas.

There are carriage roads in the city and its suburbs, extending to the near points in the Lebanon, and one to Damascus (built by a French company). A railroad also connects Beirut and Damascus.

Mission work, vigorously conducted since 1823, first by the ABCFM, and since 1870 by the PN, has borne fruit not only in direct visible results of educational institutions established, youth educated and sent forth as teachers, physicians and preachers, books printed, a Protestant community gathered, congregations assembled, and converts enrolled, but indirectly by the uplifting of the whole community to a higher plane of social, intellectual, and moral life.

In self-defense and in rivalry the other religious sects have opened schools and colleges, printing-presses and hospitals. The Mohammedans have even so far run counter to their old tradition and practises as to open schools for girls, lest their Fatimas and Zobeides should learn in Christian schools too many verses of the Bible and too many Gospel hymns; and the Greek Church has been compelled to open Sunday schools, in imitation of the Protestants.

The PN has at Beirut (opened by the ABCFM in 1823) a station of which the working force consists of 4 missionaries and their wives, with 7 unmarried women and 13 native workers, men and women. There are 3 preaching places, 3 outstations, 1 high grade boarding school for girls, 1 theological school, 5 Sunday schools, 1 printing house which sends forth its issues wherever the Arabic language is spoken in three continents. It publishes about 25,000,000 of pages annually, about half of these being pages of Scripture. In "the Press" are steam-presses, with all the apparatus for type-casting, electrotyping, lithographing, and binding. From its doors go forth yearly about 60,000 bound volumes of scientific and religious books.

The Syrian Protestant College is auxiliary to the mission, and in closest sympathy with it. It occupies a splendid position on high ground overlooking the sea. It embraces preparatory, collegiate, medical and commercial departments, and is more fully described in a separate article.

There is also a station of the Kaiserswerth Deaconesses at Beirut, established in 1860. It has 26 deaconesses, who conduct a fine hospital, served by the Medical Department of the Syrian Protestant College. It also carries on a high school and 2 village schools.

Miss Taylor's orphanage, opened in 1868, is carried on by 2 unmarried women and 6 native workers, men and women. It has a dispensary.

The Church of Scotland has a mission to the Jews, with a missionary and his wife and 2 common schools.

The Jerusalem and the East Mission Fund also has a station here, but no statistics are given.

The British Syrian schools have a station at Beirut, with 5 women missionaries and 49 native workers, 19 outstations, 1 high school, 1 school for the blind, 1 dispensary and 18 common schools.

The BFBS has a Bible depot here, with 1 agent and 6 native workers.

BEIT MERI: A village in the Lebanon district of Syria; station of the Friends' Foreign Mission Association (1898), with 1 woman missionary, 2 native workers, 1 chapel, 1 Sunday school and 2 village schools.

BELGAUM: A city in the district of Belgaum, Bombay, India, 80 miles northeast of Goa. Population (including suburbs), 32,000, Hindus, Muslims, Jains, Christians, Parsees, etc.; station of the LMS (1820), with 3 missionaries and their wives, 14 native workers, men and women; 6 outstations, 6 Sunday schools 8 village schools and 61 church members.

BELIZE: A city of British Honduras, Central America, a place of considerable importance, containing several churches, a hospital, etc. Population, 9,113, including many negroes; station of the WMS (1825), with 3 missionaries, 27 native workers, men and women; 6 chapels, 7 Sunday schools, 7 village schools, 1 high school and 700 church members. Also station of the Jamaica Baptist Missionary Society (1887), with 1 missionary, 6 outstations, 6 chapels, 5 Sunday schools and 310 church members.

BELLA BELLA: A settlement on an island in Milbank Sound, British Columbia; station of the Canadian Methodist Missionary Society (1880), with 1 missionary physician and his wife, a chapel, a Sunday school, a dispensary, a hospital, and 90 church members.

BELLA COOLA: A settlement on Burke Channel, on the coast of British Columbia; station of the Canadian Methodist Missionary Society, (1881), with 1 missionary physician and his wife, a Sunday school, a dispensary and 20 church members.

BELLARY: Chief city of the district of the same name, Madras, India. Climate, hot; very dry. Population, 59,467, Hindus, Muslims, Christians. Language, Canarese, Telugu, Hindustani. Social condition, rather poor. Station of the LMS (1810), with 7 missionaries and 49 native workers, men and women, 10 outstations, 10 Sunday schools, 11 village schools, 2 high schools, 1 college, 1 orphanage and 175 church members. Also station of the SPG (1880), with 1 native worker, 1 village school and 162 communicants.

BELLESA: A village near Massaua, Eritrea, N. Africa; station of the Swedish National Evangelical Missionary Society (1890), with 3 missionaries and their wives, 3 missionary women (one a physician), 7 native workers, 6 village schools, a dispensary, an orphanage and 71 communicants.

BELOMBO. See BENITO.

BELOOCHISTAN. See BALUCHISTAN.

BENARES: Capital of the Benares Division, United Provinces, India, situated on the northern bank of the Ganges River, at the junction of the Ganges and Jumna. Population, 209,331, of whom about 155,000 are Hindus and 50,000 Mohammedans. In point of population Benares ranks sixth in India. It manufactures silks and shawls, cloth embroidered with gold and silver, jewelry, brass work, and lacquered toys—the last two being exported to England in considerable quantities.

That which gives to Benares its interest and importance, however, is the fact that it is to-day, and has been for more than twenty-five centuries, the religious capital of India, and the most sacred of all the sacred places of Hinduism. Its origin dates back to the remotest period of Aryan occupation of India. Its early name was Varanasi, whence the modern Vanarasi, or Benares. Another name by which it is often called by the people is Kasi. It had been for many years—probably for some centuries—renowned by Hindus for its sanctity, when, in the 6th century. Gautama, then just starting out on his mission of converting India to his new cult of Buddhism, fixed his residence at Sarnath, the site of the ancient Benares, only four miles from the modern city. It remained the headquarters of Buddhism until, after a period of 800 years, the forces of Brahmanism rose against their younger rival, overwhelmed the strongholds of Buddhism, and after a long struggle expelled it root and branch from the land. Benares then resumed its preeminence of sanctity in the minds of devout Hindus, which it has never since let slip. During the Mohammedan period, under the Mohammedan Empire (1200-1800) many of the old Hindu buildings were appropriated to Mohammedan uses, while many were destroyed, and the development of Hinduism and its architectural expression seem to have been kept in strict subjection; yet the city is said to contain to-day, besides innumerable smaller shrines, 1,454 Hindu temples, most of which are insignificant architecturally, and 272 Mohammedan mosques. The largest of these is the Mosque of Aurangzib, built by the Mogul emperor of that name from the ruins of a Hindu temple. It stands on the high bank of the Ganges, with minarets towering up 147 feet. The cliff which forms the river front, and on which the city now stands, is some 100 feet above the water level. Flights of stairs at convenient points lead down to the water's edge. These are known as "ghats," or descending places, and up and down are continually passing Hindu devotees and pilgrims, with their attendant priests, going to or returning from the sacred waters of the Ganges, which are supposed to be capable of washing away sin. The view of the city from the water is exceedingly imposing, but the streets are narrow and mean, dirty and crowded. Benares is thronged by pilgrims from all parts of India. To bathe in the Ganges here is the hope of every devout Hindu; and to die in its sacred embrace, or, failing that, to have one's bones after death transported thither and flung into the stream, is supposed to ensure the soul a speedy entrance into Paradise. Bottles and jars are filled by the pilgrims and carried by them to their homes, in order that their friends who are unable to make the journey in person may be anointed with a few drops of the holy water. Many wealthy Hindus, princes and others, swell the ranks of the pilgrims, and some even keep up residences in the sacred city. It is from this pilgrim trade that the prosperity of the city chiefly arises, as well as from the fees exacted by the Brahmans for the varied religious ceremonies.

At Benares is situated Queen's College, with a roll of many hundred students; also a normal school. These are government institutions. An observatory, where Hindu astronomers have pursued the study of astronomy, and which was erected in 1693, overlooks one of the ghats. There is a hospital, a town hall, a library and other literary institutions.

The central position of Benares in the estimation of Hinduism, gives it peculiar importance to the Christian missionary. Blows struck here are aimed at the very heart and center of the Hindu faith. "Humanly speaking," says the Rev. M. A. Sherring—himself for many years a missionary at Benares—"were the city to abandon its idolatrous usages and to embrace the Gospel of Christ, the effect of such a step upon the Hindu community would be as great as was produced on the Roman Empire when Rome adopted the Christian faith. The special sanctity and influence of Benares constitute a gigantic obstacle to all religious changes within it." The effect of education and of the dissemination of Christian ideas has been to modify profoundly the life of the better classes of native society in the city, altho ancient rites and usages are scrupulously maintained.

Missionary effort was commenced in Benares by the BMS in 1816. The city is now a station of the LMS (1820), with 8 missionaries and 28 native workers, men and women, with a high school and 12 common schools and 34 church members.

It is a station also of the CMS (1832), with 11 missionaries and 22 native workers, men and women. It has 3 outstations, 2 high schools, an orphanage and 6 village schools and 175 communicants.

The WMS has here 2 missionaries and 16 active workers, men and women, with 6 village schools and 30 church members.

The Baptist Zenana Mission has 3 women missionaries and 3 native women workers, with 119 Zenana pupils.

The Zenana Bible and Medical Mission has 15 women missionaries and 34 native women workers, with 1 hospital, 1 dispensary, 1 high school, 6 village schools and 225 Zenana pupils.

BENGA LANGUAGE: Belongs to the Bantu family of African languages and is spoken in the region of the Gaboon River, French Congo, W. Africa. It is written with Roman letters.

BENGAL: One of the Lieutenant-Governorships of British India, lying north of Madras and the Bay of Bengal and east of the Central Provinces and the United Provinces. It comprises (1) the territory often spoken of as Bengal Proper, through which the Ganges and Brahmaputra rivers describe the lower portion of their courses, including the deltas of those great streams; (2) the province of Orissa, which stretches along the coast of the gulf south of the delta; (3) the province of Behar, to the northwest of Bengal Proper, and (4) the district of Chota-Nagpur, south of Behar and west of Orissa. Its total area is 151,543 square miles and its population numbers (1901) 74,744,866. In no other part of British India is the average density of population so great, the average for the whole of Bengal being 470 per square mile, while in some parts of **Behar** the average is over 800 per square mile.

The population of Bengal exhibits great diversity of race, religion, language and civilization. About one-third of the whole population are Mohammedans, nearly two-thirds Hindus and a residue of about 3,000,000 is composed of the adherents of other religions, chiefly those professed by the half-savage aboriginal hill tribes. The Christian population of Bengal is (1901) 278,366, having increased 44 per cent. during the decade 1891-1901. The increase of population of Bengal during the same period was but little more than 4 per cent.

The prevailing language is the **Bengali.** In Behar and Chota Nagpur the Hindi is chiefly used, and in Orissa the **Uriye** is the language of Hindus and Christians. The aboriginal tribes called Kols, Santals and Gonds found in Chota Nogpur and other districts in the northwest part of Bengal are described in separate articles, to which the reader is referred.

The Mohammedans of Bengal are mostly descendants of converts made from the lower castes of Hindus centuries ago, but they still make many converts every year from Hinduism. Behar was once a center of Buddhism.

The missionary history of Bengal, as well as its political history, is one of the utmost interest. While this province was not the seat of the earliest Protestant missionary activity in India—an honor which belongs to Madras—it is ever associated in the minds of Christian people with the names of Carey, Marshman and Ward, who made Serampur the starting-point of widely diffused evangelistic influences; with that of the eccentric Thomas, who was the pioneer of the work afterward more effectively prosecuted by the Serampur band, and in more recent times with that of Duff, whose educational work at Calcutta and whose immense energy and missionary zeal were the means of lifting the work of Christian instruction to the prominence which it deserves as a factor of missionary success. At the present time Bengal is well occupied by the agents of many Protestant missionary societies. The English Baptists, still preserving the traditions and continuing the work of Thomas, Carey and their early associates, the SPG, the CMS, the CSFM, the UFS, the LMS, the WMS, the ME, the ABMU and many other societies and independent agencies, are conducting missionary operations in Bengal. The missionary societies cooperate with the government and with the people in their efforts to extend education, having many schools and colleges in connection with their work at nearly all mission stations. In the year just mentioned there were within the province 51 vernacular newspapers, 13 being sheets of some importance. Several papers, edited wholly in English, are also issued by natives, besides those conducted by European writers.

Bengal is sometimes called "Lower Bengal," since this term was applied to it when it formed a part of the **Bengal Presidency**.

BENGALI LANGUAGE: The Bengali belongs to the Indic branch of the Aryan family of languages. It is said to approach more nearly to the Sanskrit than any other of the modern languages of India. It is spoken by about 40,000,000 inhabitants of Bengal and Central British India. Among its various dialects the Musulmani Bengali is used by some 20,000,000 Mohammedans in lower and eastern Bengal and has been much changed by the introduction of Arabic and Persian words. The Sanskrit letters, with slight modification, are used for writing all or nearly all of the dialects of Bengali.

BENGAL PRESIDENCY: One of the former administrative divisions of British India. It comprised the northwest Provinces, Oudh, Assam, etc., besides the present lieutenant-governorship of Bengal. The name is still used in common language and in army circles, but it is no longer the name of an administrative division. See India.

BENGHAZI: A town of Tripoli, North Africa, on the eastern shore of the Gulf of Sidra. It stands on the verge of a large plain, sandy and barren for nearly a mile from the shore, but beyond that having a fertile but rocky soil to the foot of the Cyrenaic Mountains. Population, 9,000, many of whom are Jews and negro slaves. Chief occupations of the people are agriculture and cattle-raising. No mission work at present.

BENGUELA: A district of Angola, W. Africa, and a town in that district from which a railroad is to be constructed to the E. frontier of the colony, it being the seaport for trade with Bihè and the region in which missionary stations are established.

BENITO: A town on an island in the San Benito River, in the Spanish Colony of Cape San Juan, W. Africa; station of the PN (1864), with 1 missionary, 3 missionary women, 11 native workers, men and women, 10 outstations, 9 Sunday schools, 3 village schools, 2 high schools and 490 church members. Also mentioned as Belombo.

BENNETT, CEPHAS: Born at Homer, N. Y., March 20, 1804. Dr. Bolles, Secretary of the ABMU, advised him to offer himself to the Society to go out as its missionary printer. He was appointed in 1828 and sailed May 22, 1829, reaching Calcutta October 6, and Maulmain, January 14, 1830, with his printing presses. He commenced at once the printing of tracts, for which the demand in the early history of the mission was very great. In 1832 he began to print the Burmese Scriptures, and as superintendent of the mission press in Burma for more than half a century he was permitted to print the Bible in three languages—the Burmese, translated by Dr. Judson; the Sgau Karen, translated by Dr. Mason, and the Pwo Karen, by Rev. D. L. Brayton, and also the New Testament in the Shan language. From the press under his care were sent forth more than 200,000,000 of Scriptures, tracts, and religious and educational books in all the dialects of Burma. He was not only a printer, but a preacher of the Gospel, having been ordained to the ministry by his brethren of the mission, and in the intervals of his work as a printer he labored as an evangelist. The year 1834 he spent in Rangoon, then under Burman rule, preaching and distributing tracts. When in Tavoy, whither he went in 1837 to print the Karen Bible, and where he remained till his return in 1857, he spent much of the cold season in the jungles, among the heathen and the native Christians. In these tours he visited all the Tavoy and Mergui districts. His deep interest in the educational work of missions led him, in the early part of his residence in Maulmain, to take charge of the government school for two and a half years. To him chiefly is due the founding of the Burma Bible and Tract Society, and through his influence its operations were enlarged by the recent vernacular schoolbook departments. He was also much engaged in the English church in Rangoon. Mr. Bennett was taken seriously ill in July, 1885, but rallied. Early in November he had a relapse, and on the 16th he passed away, in the eighty-second year of his age, after fifty-six years of mission service.

BENSONVALE: A town in the Orange River Colony, N. E. of Aliwal North; station of the South African Wesleyan Missionary Society, with 1 missionary, 83 native workers, 33 outstations, 10 village schools, 1 high school, a Young People's Society, and 1,110 church members.

BERAR: A commissionership of Central India, consisting chiefly of a fertile valley lying east and west between the Satpura range on the north and the Ajanta range on the south. Its length from east to west is 150 miles, and its breadth, about 140. It touches the central provinces on the north and east, Bombay Presidency on the west, and the Nizam's dominions on the south. Area, 17,700 square miles. The population numbers 2,897,491 and is mostly composed of Hindus. Mohammedans, Parsees and Christians are also found in Berar in small numbers. Some aboriginal tribes, as the **Bhils** and **Gonds**, are also found in this region.

The language of the Hindus of Berar is Marâthi.

Berar has been entered by the UFS, and the Kurku and Central India Hill Mission. The Christian and Missionary Alliance also has, there is some reason to suppose, undertaken evangelistic work in this province. But Berar has not thus far been the scene of missionary operations to the extent which the density of its population and the opportunities which it affords for persistent and successful work would seem to demand.

BERBER LANGUAGES. See BERBER RACE; also KABYLE.

BERBER RACE: The Berbers are sometimes spoken of as descended from the Libyans, or at least as closely related to them. Arab writers represent them as having come from Canaan previous to the days of Joshua. From their language, customs, and physical type they are adjudged by some as affiliated with the Semites; though others prefer to group them as being originally Hamitic. Where they have come in contact with other races or tongues, they have been more or less affected by them; where they have been left in comparative seclusion, as in the oases of the desert, they have remained, in both race and speech, comparatively pure.

The present home of the Berber race has its center in the Barbary States, especially around the Atlas Mountains. Indeed, the Barbary States derive their name from the appellation used in Europe to designate this race. According to Dr. Cust, "The Berber or Amazirg is still at the present day in various shades and degrees of intermixture, ethnological, linguistic, and religious, with Arab and negro, the staple and principal stock of the whole population of North Africa from the Mediterranean to the extreme southern limit of the Sahara." The race may be divided into eight or ten tribes or groups, chiefly according to the shades of difference in the language or dialects they use; tho the parent of all these dialects, the old Libyan, as known to the Romans among the Numidians and their cognates, no longer exists. The old Guanch Berber, or Libyan as spoken by the original inhabitants of the Canary Islands, is also extinct. The Kabyles of Algeria are Berbers. They comprise a confederation of tribes and speak a variety of dialects, are given to agricultural pursuits, and dwell in villages. Those who dwell among the mountains have large flocks of sheep and goats, and because of their seclusion from Arab admixture have the purest dialect. They have, under the French, a sort of republican government. They are a fine race, hospitable and kind. The Mzab Kabyles occupy the extreme south of Algeria, but, having great commercial enterprise, are found everywhere. They are Mohammedan dissenters. The Shamba Kabyles, a predatory tribe, dwell on the oases of the Sahara. The Tuwarik, or Tuaregs, another group of Berbers, are nomadic in their habits, and extend from Algeria to Bornu and Timbuctu. Twenty years before the Christian era a governor of the Roman province of Africa led an army against this then, as now, unconquered tribe.

The aborigines of Morocco have been divided into the Arab-Berbers and the Shilus, or Shelloohs. The former inhabit the northern parts of the great Atlas range, live in a cheap kind of hut covered with mats, tho in the plains they build of wood and clay, and have villages. They live chiefly upon their cattle and sheep, and make use of mules and donkeys. Their complexion is light, the hair of many is fair, the beard scant. They are well-built, strong, active bold, and are often at war with their neighbors. These and the Shilus number about 4,000,000, forming half the population of the Moroccan Empire. Their dress is scant, consisting chiefly of a jacket and trousers, and sometimes a blanket. The other Morocco tribe, the Shilus, speaking the Shilha dialect, occupy the southern part of Morocco, together with the regions west of the Atlas range. These are of a smaller make and darker complexion. They are more civilized and powerful than the northern Berbers. They work at trades and cultivate the land, are patriarchal, hospitable, live in houses made of stone and mortar, and have villages and towns surrounded by walls and towers. They claim to be the aborigines of the country, and call themselves Amazirg.

There is a mixed tribe, Arab-Berber, called the Senegal, living on the north banks of the Senegal River. They are partly nomadic, partly settled, and make a living by collecting gum for the merchants at marts along the river.

The inhabitants of Ghadamis of Tripoli, at home and by themselves, speak the Ghadamsi, a dialect of the Berber; but with the Arabs, the Arabic; with the Tuwarik, the Tamaskeh, and with their negro slaves, the Hausa.

Another Berber tribe dwells at Siwah, the oasis of Jupiter Ammon, on the confines of Egypt. That their own home dialect should be found to have a clear affinity with the Berber helps to show how broad is the territory the Berbers have occupied; also how remarkable has been the resistance offered by the Berber language to the pressure of other tongues for more than three thousand years.

As to the origin and import of the name of this ancient North African race there is some diversity of opinion. It is said to have first been used by the Arab writers of the 2d century to designate the Libyans of Herodotus. Some suppose it to have been derived from Verves, as found in the ancient Roman geography of Mauritania. By others, with more reason, it is supposed to be but a modification of Barbari, a term denoting any one who was, to the Aryan or Greek, a foreigner, speaking a language to them unknown. This accords with the fact that the word Berber is not known to the Berbers as a national appellation. They call themselves Amazirg, the Free.

As to the religion of the Berbers, their pagan faith is nearly extinct. Some of them seem to have accepted the Jewish or the Christian religion in the centuries gone by, at least for a time. But at present they generally profess the Mohammedan faith, tho many of them know but little of it. And yet they are not lacking in bigotry and fanaticism, as the bitter opposition and persecution to which converts to the Christian faith are subject afford sad proof.

Missionary effort has not neglected these people. The North African Mission, the Swedish Missionary Society, the Gospel Missionary Union and others have used every means to come into contact with the Berber tribes.

BEREA: A settlement in Basutoland, S. Africa, E. of Maseru; station of the Paris Evangelical Mission Society (1843), with 1 missionary and his wife, 17 native workers, 6 outstations, 7 village schools, and 425 communicants. French form of name, Bérée.

BEREA: A settlement southwest of Gnadendal, Cape Colony, S. Africa. A station of the Moravians, occupied in 1865, when the overcrowding of Gnadendal made it necessary for some of the people to form a colony. Statistics given in combination with Gnadendal.

BEREN'S RIVER : A settlement on the E. shore of Lake Winnipeg, Manitoba, Canada; station of the Canadian Methodist Church (1871), with 1 missionary and his wife, 2 outstations, a chapel, a Young People's Society and 100 church members.

BERHAMPUR: A town in the Ganjam district, Madras, India; the principal town in the district of the same name. Climate, unhealthful. Population, 25,000, Hindus, Mohammedans, Christians. Station of the BMS (1825), with 3 missionaries and their wives, 10 native workers of both sexes, 4 Sunday schools, 3 village schools, and 220 church members. Also station of the Baptist Zenana Mission Society, with 3 women missionaries, 5 native women workers, and a dispensary. Also written Berhampore.

BERHAMPUR: A city and military station S. of Murshidabad, Bengal, India. Population (1891) 23,515; climate, unhealthful but improved by military sanitation. Station of the LMS (1824), with 2 missionaries and their wives, 4 women missionaries, 25 native workers, men and women, 9 Sunday schools, 6 village schools, 2 high schools, and 35 church members. Also written Burhampore.

BERLIN: A town east of King Williams Town, Cape Colony, S. Africa; station of the South African Baptist Missionary Society (1889), with 2 women missionaries, 3 native workers, 2 outstations, chapel, Sunday school, and 24 church members. Native name Tshabo.

BERLIN JERUSALEM UNION. See GERMANY, MISSIONS IN.

BERLIN MISSIONARY SOCIETY. See GERMANY, MISSIONARY SOCIETIES IN.

BERLIN WOMEN'S MISSIONARY SOCIETY for China. See GERMANY, MISSIONARY SOCIETIES IN.

BERSABA: A settlement in Surinam, South America, S. of Paramaribo. It is in the center of a district which has always been the darkest corner in Surinam, the stronghold of idolatry and sorcery. Idol temples and places of sacrifice are very numerous. The former are not imposing edifices, such as are found in India, but small structures only a degree above common pigsties, and located in out-of-the way corners behind the houses of the village. They are not used for worship, but only as repositories for the idols and their belongings, which are needful for heathen dances and the performances of the sorcerers. Station of the Moravian Missions (1858), with a missionary and his wife, 35 native workers, 3 chapels, 2 Sunday schools, 1 village school, and 190 church members.

BERSEBA. See BEERSHEBA, TRANSVAAL.

BERSHEBA: A station of the Rhenish Mission in Great Namaqualand, German S. W. Africa. Here the missionary Krönlein translated the New Testament into Nama. It has 1 missionary, 1 native worker, 1 village school, and 224 communicants.

BERU: One of the Gilbert Is. which has long been occupied by Samoan pastors under the LMS and was made a missionary station by that Society in 1901. There is now (1903) a training institution for evangelistics, and a woman's training institution for Christian workers. The church members number 450.

BETAFO: A town in Imerina, Madagascar. Mission station of the Norwegian Missionary Society.

BETERVERWACHTUNG: A settlement near Graham's Hall, in British Guiana, South America. Station of the SPG, with a missionary, 2 native workers, and 24 communicants. Also station of the Canadian Presbyterian Mission (1885), with 2 missionaries and their wives, 7 native workers, men and women, 4 Sunday schools, 3 village schools, and 110 church members. Also called Better Hope.

BETGERI. See BETIGERI.

BETHABARA: One of the most important of the Moravian mission stations in Jamaica, West Indies (1840) and the center of an extensive field of effort. It is situated in the southern part of the island, on the uneven surface of the lofty range of table-land known as the Manchester Mountains. It has a missionary and his wife, 15 native workers, men and women, 2 Sunday schools, 2 village schools, a Young People's Society, and 345 communicants.

BETHANIE: 1. A town and railway station S. of Bloemfontein, Orange River Colony, S. Africa; station of the Berlin Missionary Society (1834), with 3 missionaries, 17 native workers, 1 outstation, and 930 communicants.

2. A settlement W. of Pretoria, Transvaal Colony, S. Africa; station of the Hermannsburg Missionary Society (1864), with 1 missionary and his wife, 10 native workers, men and women, 3 outstations, 7 village schools, and 2,225 communicants.

BETHANIEN: 1. A settlement in German S. W. Africa; station of the Rhenish Missionary Society, with 1 missionary and his wife, 1 village school and 500 communicants.

2. A village in South Arcot, Madras, India; station of the Danish Missionary Society (1861), with a missionary and his wife, 3 native workers, 2 outstations, 1 village school and 45 communicants.

BETHANY: 1. (India) A village in the Santal Parganas, Bengal; station of the Bethel Santhal Mission (1890), with 1 missionary and his wife, 3 native workers, 1 chapel, 1 Sunday school, 1 village school, 1 high school, a dispensary, a hospital, an orphanage and 600 communicants.

2. (West Indies) A village in the Manchester Highlands of Jamaica; station of the Moravian Mission (1835), with 1 missionary and his wife, 15 native workers, men and women, 2 chapels, 2 Sunday schools, 2 village schools, and 370 communicants.

BETHEL (Africa): 1. A settlement N. of Stutterheim, Cape Colony, S. Africa; station of the Berlin Missionary Society (1837), with 2 missionaries, 7 native workers, and 140 communicants.

2. A settlement in the Usambara region, German East Africa; station of the German East Africa Mission (1893), with 2 missionaries, 1 missionary's wife, 2 chapels, 1 village school and 20 communicants. Called also New Bethel.

3. A village S. of Bonaberi on the coast of Kamerun, W. Africa; station of the Basel Mis-

sionary Society (1886), with 13 missionaries, men and women, 25 native workers, 22 outstations, 25 village schools, and 500 communicants.

4. A settlement in the Lichtenberg district of the Transvaal Colony, S. Africa, about 50 miles S. E. of Mafeking; station of the Hermannsburg Missionary Society (1872), with a missionary and his wife, 2 native workers, 4 outstations, 1 chapel, 1 village school and 1,250 communicants.

5. A settlement in Zululand (Natal) S. Africa, about 40 miles S. E. of Vryheid; station of the Hermannsburg Mission (1886), with 1 missionary, 4 native workers, 4 chapels, 4 village schools and 230 communicants. Also station of the Swedish Holiness Union (1894), with 1 missionary and his wife, 3 outstations, 1 village school, 1 training school for women workers, and 90 communicants.

BETHEL (Alaska): A station of the Moravian Mission in S. W. Alaska, situated on the River Kuskokwim (1885), with 2 missionaries and their wives (one a physician), 7 native workers, 1 chapel, 1 Sunday school, and 115 communicants.

BETHEL (India): A village in the Santal Parganas, Bengal, India; station of the Bethel Santhal Mission (1875), with 1 missionary physician and his wife, 8 native workers, 5 village schools, 2 high schools, 2 orphanages, 1 dispensary, 1 hospital, and 800 church members.

BETHEL (West Indies): A town in the N. W. of the island of St. Kitts, W. I.; station of the Moravian Missions (1832), with 15 native workers 1 chapel, 1 Sunday school, 1 village school and 130 communicants.

BETHEL TOWN: A village 20 miles S. of Montego Bay, Jamaica, W. I.; station of the Christian (Disciples) Woman's Board of Missions, with 1 missionary, 2 chapels, 2 Sunday schools, 1 village school, 2 Young People's Societies, and 120 church members.

BETHEL SANTHAL MISSION (1875): Evangelistic work among the Santals near Jamtara, Bengal, India, was begun in 1875 by Pastor A. Haegert, at his own expense. A mission house was built for a central station and the village which grew up about it was called Bethel. Schools were opened in neighboring sections of the Santal Parganas. Later Pastor Haegert added a hospital and training school to the equipment of the Mission.

There were (1900) 4 stations and 2 outstations, 5 missionaries and 20 native helpers, 1,500 communicants, 1 high school, with 25 students, 7 other schools with 150 pupils, 1 physician, 13 hospitals and dispensaries.

An auxiliary Society has been formed in England to collect funds for this Mission and is called The English Council of the Bethel Santhal Mission.

BETHESDA (Africa): 1. A settlement in the S. W. part of Basutoland, S. Africa; station of the Paris Society for Evangelical Missions (1843), with 1 missionary and his wife, 22 native workers, 12 outstations, 11 village schools, and 620 communicants.

2. A village about 40 miles W. of Kokstad, Griqualand, Cape Colony, S. Africa; station of the Moravian Missions (1877), with 2 missionaries and their wives, 27 native workers, men and women, 2 preaching places, 10 village schools and 390 communicants.

BETHESDA (India): 1. A village S. of Madhupur, Bengal, India; station of the Bethel Santhal Mission (1891), with 1 missionary, 3 native workers, 1 chapel, 1 Sunday school, 1 village school, 1 high school, 1 orphanage, a dispensary, a hospital and 30 communicants.

2. A town in South Arcot, Madras, India. See KALLAKURCHI.

BETHESDA (West Indies): A village on the E. coast of the island of St. Kitts, W. I.; station of the Moravian Missions (1820), with 16 native workers, men and women, 1 chapel, 1 Sunday school, 1 village school and 400 communicants.

BETHLEHEM: 1. A town in Palestine, near Jerusalem. The birthplace of Jesus Christ. Station of the CMS (1899), with 4 missionary women, a village school and a high school. Also station of the Jerusalem Union of Berlin (1861), with 8 missionaries, men and women, 13 native workers, men and women, 3 outstations, 1 chapel, 1 orphanage and 5 village schools.

2. A village in the Santal Parganas, Bengal, India; station of the Bethel Santhal Mission (1884), with 1 missionary woman (physician), 3 native workers, 1 chapel, 1 Sunday school, 1 village school, 1 high school, 1 orphanage, a dispensary, a hospital and 50 communicants.

BETIGERI: A village near Gadag, in the Dharwar district, Bombay, India. Population of Gadag-Betigeri (1891) 23,880. Station of the Basel Missionary Society (1841), with (1902) 2 missionaries and their wives, 20 native workers, men and women, 5 village schools, 1 Sunday school and 279 communicants. Also station of the SPG (1888), with 6 native workers, men and women, 3 village schools and 36 communicants. Also written Bettigeri and Betgeri.

BETO: A village in the southern part of Borneo, Malaysia; station of the Rhenish Missionary Society, with 1 missionary and his wife, 2 native workers, 1 Sunday school, 2 village schools, and 70 communicants.

BETTER HOPE. See BETERVERWACHTUNG.

BETUL: A town in the Central Provinces, India, 50 miles N. E. of Ellichpur. Population, 5,000, chiefly Gonds. Station of the Swedish National Missionary Society (1880), with 5 missionaries, men and woman, 2 native workers, 1 Sunday school, 1 village school and 15 communicants.

BEUSTER, Rev. C.: Missionary of the Berlin MS to Africa. He was the first preacher of the Gospel sent to the Bawendo tribe in North Transvaal, and for twenty-nine years, amidst the greatest difficulties, he labored among this benighted people. He rendered the tongue of this tribe into a written language, translated part of the Scriptures and other literature; taught untutored minds in the primary schools, and pursuing his long and tedious journeys on foot, he preached the Gospel to thousands who had never heard the Word of Life. For years he was the victim of the unhealthful climate of the North Transvaal; but without intermission he continued his labors of love until he passed from earth, in the year 1901.

BEYROUT. See BEIRUT.

BEZWADA: A town of 20,000 (1891) inhabitants on the Kistna River, S. W. of Ellore, Madras, India; station of the CMS (1858), with 5 missionaries, men and women, 47 native workers, men and women, 28 village schools, 1 high school and 780 communicants. Also station of the CEZMS (1881), with (1902) 2 missionary and

14 native women workers, 4 elementary schools and 298 Zenana pupils.

BHADRAKH: A town in the Balasor district, Orissa, Bengal, India; station of the Free Baptist General Conference (1890), with 1 woman missionary, 8 native workers, men and women, 1 chapel, 1 Sunday school, 1 village school and 25 church members.

BHAGALPUR: A city in the Bhagalpur district, Bengal, India, situated on the Ganges, with a population (1901) of 75,760, chiefly Hindus and Mohammedans. Station of the CMS (1850), with (1901) 2 missionaries, 1 with his wife, 8 native workers, 11 outstations, 2 elementary schools, 1 high school, 1 dispensary, 1 hospital, 1 orphanage and 288 baptized Christians. Also station of the CEZMS (1882), with (1902) 4 missionary and 14 native women workers, 11 elementary schools and 178 zenana pupils. Also station of the Mission to Lepers in India and the East (1887), with 1 chapel and 1 Leper asylum.

BHAGAYA. See BAGHARA.

BHAISDEHI: A town in the Central Provinces, India, N. E. of Ellichpur; station of the Kurku and Central India Mission (1889), with 2 missionaries and their wives, 3 native workers, 1 chapel, 1 Sunday school, 1 village school, 1 orphanage, a dispensary, a hospital and 6 church members.

BHAMO: A town and trading center and head of steam navigation of the Irawadi River, 180 miles north of Mandalay, Burma. Population about 7,000. It is but 40 miles from the Chinese frontier. It is a station of the ABMU, opened in 1877, and occupied by 8 missionaries and 12 native workers, men and women. It has 9 outstations, 10 preaching places and 2 common schools. There are 120 church members.

BHANDARA: A town of 13,000 inhabitants, east of Nagpur in the Central Provinces of India; station of the UFS, with 1 missionary physician, 20 native workers, men and women, 4 village schools, 1 orphanage, a dispensary, a hospital and 30 church members.

BHARTPUR: Chief city of the native state of Bhartpur, Rajputana, India. Population (1891) 68,033, chiefly Hindus. Station of the ME, with 21 native workers, 1 chapel, 15 Sunday schools, a Young Peoples' Society, 8 village schools and 550 church members.

BHERA: A town of about 17,000 inhabitants situated on the Jhelam River in the Punjab, India; station of the UP (1884), with 1 missionary and his wife, 2 missionary women and 2 outstations.

BHILS: An aboriginal Kolarian race of Central India. One of their typical men is about 5½ feet in stature, with short arms, prominent cheek bones, thick lips, black hair and heavy beard. Together with other Kolarian aborigines they were pushed back by an early Aryan invasion from the plains into the hill country, and are now found scattered over Rajputana, the hills of the Vindhya and Sappura ranges, the outlying portions of Indore and Gwalior provinces, the hills as far south as Poona, and eastward along the Godavari and Wand rivers. Their favorite abode is along the rugged, wooded banks of the Tapti, Mahi and Nerbada Rivers which flow into the Arabian Sea. Their estimated number is 3,000,000. Cruelly treated by the Marathi, they have lived apart, with their own chieftains and councils which settle disputes between individuals and communities, the British authorities maintaining a difficult supervision over them. Marauding expeditions into the cultivated country, brigandage, the chase with bow and arrows as weapons, the raising of sheep and goats, some rude agriculture, and some simple manufactures in bamboo have been their means of support. When at home, they dwell in little hamlets, called *pals*, each homestead, tolerably well built of loose stones and interwoven bamboo, located on a separate hillock so that an enemy may not surprise a whole town at once. Their clothing is meager. They have now no separate language. They are addicted to drink, and when intoxicated are quarrelsome. Polygamy is practiced, but more than two wives is unusual. Women are chaste after marriage.

Their religion is spirit worship, with additions from Hinduism. They are firm believers in ghosts and in witches. The latter they swing head downwards until they die or confess; but upon confession the witch is punished with death or banishment. Siva and other Hindu deities are worshipped and local deities are numerous. Gatamji, their patron saint, occupies a niche in most Bhil houses. A Brahman is usually called in to officiate at the naming of the child and at marriage. The dead are burned and the ashes cast into sacred streams, for unless they have such a resting place, their spirits are supposed to trouble surviving relatives.

Missionary work was begun among the Bhils by the Church Missionary Society in 1880. It was at first very difficult to get in touch with this scattered, secluded and suspicious highland folk, but persistent kindness at last won their confidence. The first converts were enrolled in 1889, but in 1900, after twenty years of labor, the mission numbered fourteen baptized and fifteen catechumens. The work of the missionaries in famine relief in 1901-2 proved the turning point in the history of the mission, and since the Gospel has been welcomed, thousands of children have been enrolled in the schools, and in the spring of 1903 fifty-four converts were baptized and the Bhils undertook the building of their own church. The Bhil Mission of the Church Missionary Society occupies four stations in Rajputana; Kherwara, Lusaria, where there is a girls' orphanage; Baulia, and Bilaria, with a boys' orphanage.

The history of other missions has been similar. The United Free Church of Scotland has an encouraging Bhil Mission in Rajputana with a "Bhil Home" at Udaipur. Amkhut is the field of the vigorous Bhil Mission of the Presbyterian Church of Canada, with educational, medical, orphanage, and industrial departments. The Christian Bhils have proved good mechanics. The baptisms in 1901-2 numbered 105.

The Bhils are at a crisis in their history, and before long will become either Hindus or Christians. Because of the absence of caste, they do not meet the opposition which the Hindus do from their own people when they try to improve their condition. They are now coming to know their need, and at present they seem peculiarly open to the Gospel.

Wild Races of S. E. India, Lewin (T. H.), London, 1870; *Brief History of the Indian Peoples*, Hunter (W. W.), London.

BHIMPUR: A town lying N. W. of Midnapur, Bengal, India; station of the Free Baptist General

Conference (1874), with 2 missionaries and their wives (physicians), 139 native workers, men and women, 2 outstations, 45 Sunday schools, 45 village schools, 2 orphanages, 1 industrial school, 1 dispensary, 3 Young People's Societies and 270 church members. Also written Bhimpore.

BHINGA: A village N. E. of Bahraich, in the United Provinces, India; station of the ME, with 11 native workers, men and women, 8 Sunday schools, 1 village, school, 4 Young People's Societies and 220 church members.

BHIWANI: A city of the Punjab, India, 60 miles W. of Delhi. Population (1891) 35,487. Station of the Baptist Zenana Mission (1887), with 4 missionary women, one a physician, 3 native women workers, 3 Sunday schools, 3 village schools, a dispensary, a hospital and 50 Zenana pupils.

BHOT: A village in the Almora district, United Provinces, India, situated near Chandag, north of Pithoragarh; station of the ME, with 1 missionary woman (physician), 14 native workers, men and women, 3 chapels, 4 Sunday schools, 23 village schools, 1 Young People's Society, and 25 church members.

BHUTAN: An independent native state on the southern slope of the eastern part of the Himalayan range, E. of Sikkim and separating British India from the frontier of Tibet. It has an area of about 13,000 sq. miles and a population estimated at about 30,000. The religion of the people is Buddhism of a degraded type. Their language is allied to the Tibetan. The people are called Bhutias.

BIBLE CHRISTIAN HOME AND FOREIGN MISSIONARY SOCIETY: This society was organized in 1821 for the purpose of sending missionaries into unchristianized portions of the United Kingdom and into heathen lands. In 1831 it sent two missionaries to North America, one of whom occupied a station in Canada, and the other in Prince Edward's Island. Their work was eminently successful, and in 1883, when the union of all the Methodist churches in Canada was effected, the membership of this mission was about 7,000.

In 1850 Messrs. James Way and James Rowe were sent to South Australia, and later several other missionaries settled in Victoria, Queensland, and New Zealand. The work here being carried on under favorable circumstances, soon grew independent and self-supporting, and now the principal work done in this mission is the planting of new churches in needy districts.

In 1885 the Society sent two missionaries to Yunnan, China, under the auspices of the China Inland Mission, whose repeated appeals for help had aroused much interest. At present the Society has three stations, Yunnan-fu, Chao-tung-fu, and Tung-Chawan-fu, 12 missionaries, 6 native evangelists, 41 church members and 200 scholars. The recent changes have brought large numbers of inquiries.

At home the Society has missionaries working among the lowest classes of people in London and other parts of England.

The Woman's Missionary League of the Bible Christian Missionary Society, was organized as an auxiliary to the Society in 1892 with special reference to the work in China.

BIBLE DISTRIBUTION: Its object is to bring knowledge of the Bible within reach of every person. The great Bible societies have adopted the principle that the end which they are to keep in view is not the possession of the Bible, but its proper use, and that any distribution which ignores this distinction is liable to do more harm than good. At different times certain persons have given away large numbers of Scriptures to the crowds that gather at such places as Jerusalem, or at fairs and expositions. The object was undoubtedly laudable, but the invariable result has been that the books thrown broadcast in this way exercised little or no influence for good, and even inspired a feeling of contempt.

In order to meet the requirement that the Bible shall be placed within the reach of every person, however poor, the societies have adopted the general principle of gauging prices by the ability of the people rather than by the cost of the book. In such lands as the United States, Great Britain and the larger part of the Continent the Bible societies as a rule ask cost price for their publications, reckoning in the cost the expense of printing and binding, but making no account of the outlay for editorial work. To this however, there are exceptions. In order to meet a special need, an' edition, usually of the New Testament, is sometimes placed at a figure even less than the cost, as in the case of the editions designed for use in the schools or for distribution among the poorer laborers.

In the mission fields the day's wage of a laborer is often taken as the gauge, and an edition of the whole Bible, in plain but substantial binding, is issued at such a figure as will be within the reach of the ordinary peasant or artisan. Editions of the New Testament, or of different portions of Scripture such as the Gospels, Psalms, Proverbs, the Pentateuch, etc., are made proportionate in price. Scriptures in finer binding are sold at actual cost, since they are of the nature of luxuries.

If the distributor is satisfied that a person is not able to give the price of the book, and that a copy will be well used, ordinarily a free grant is made. The plan of trying to secure the attention and interest of a person not especially interested in the Bible by the donation of a copy has not, as a rule, been successful. But no iron rule as to free distribution can be laid down. Much must be left to the judgment of the person engaged in the work.

For many years the Bible societies worked as auxiliary to the mission societies in distributing the Bible; making grants of books, giving money to pay colporteurs, etc. As the different denominations entered the field, and in not a few cases covered much the same ground, the work began to individualize, and at last the necessity for providing the Scriptures for many people whom the missionaries could not attempt to reach, led to the appointment of a class of agents quite distinct from those of the missionaries. Thus grew up the system of agencies much like those of any mercantile house. The Bible Society Agent is located at some central point, such as Berlin, Vienna, Constantinople, etc. He keeps informed as to the needs of the territory assigned to him, and seeks to improve every opportunity to increase the circulation of the Scriptures and to add to the popular understanding of their value. In Japan the Bible Society Agent has made a point of selling the Scriptures on railroad trains, with good effect.

As in the case of missionary societies, so with

the Bible societies, disadvantages have arisen from the presence of two or more in the same territory. This has often entailed needless expense, and has produced more or less of friction, if not between the Societies or their Agents, at least between their employees. (See **Comity**).

The subordinate agencies of distribution are:

1. *Bible Depots.* These do not serve merely or even principally as salesrooms or places of storage, but above all they are centers of influence The sales from a Depot seldom equal those by a colporteur and it has sometimes been a serious question whether the cost of maintaining them has been wisely incurred; yet where an effort to dispense with them has been made, they have been quickly reestablished as an essential feature of Bible work.

2. *Colporteurs.* The work of these men is the main stay of Bible distribution in the mission fields. By far the larger part of the Scriptures sold on mission ground pass through their hands and colporteurs have done and are doing quietly and unobtrusively a work unsurpassed in importance by that of any class of evangelistic laborers, because it is generally like the work of the pioneer. More than the missionary preacher or teacher, colporteurs come in contact with men. They seek people out in their homes, their shops, their fields, and find access to places which no one else could enter. Having as their aim the placing of the Bible in the hands of all who will read and study it, they have to be wiser than serpents. Their daily life abounds in incidents as thrilling as any in the history of the Church. They are commonly plain men, selected not because of education but for their initiative, their tactful methods of dealing with men, and their knowledge of the Bible as a practical guide to life rather than as a storehouse of doctrines. At present there are few lands where every city and town, or even every village and hamlet is not within the field assigned to some colporteur. This of course demands careful organization, and no one can read the annual reports of the Bible societies without realizing how gigantic is the work to which they are bending every effort.

3. *Bible Readers.* The work of the Bible society at the point of distributing the Scriptures is so nearly the same as that of the missionary society, that it is not always possible to draw the line sharply between their respective spheres. For many years the Bible societies did not consider it within their sphere to do more than actually distribute the Bible. Holding aloof from all preaching, they considered that Bible readers who must inevitably be in a great degree teachers, were more properly mission employees. Yet in many cases, when people were unable or unwilling to read themselves, it was found that the Bible reader, by arousing an interest in the Bible, became a very important factor in its distribution. Moreover the missionary societies have found it simply impossible to provide such laborers for all outlying regions. It has thus come about that the Bible societies have accepted the employment of Bible readers as a legitimate part of their work.

Every missionary in the foreign field, whether man or woman, preacher, physician, or teacher, also becomes a distributor of the Bible in the ordinary line of daily duty. Travelers, merchants and officials of many nations and many religious denominations have often gladly used their opportunities for giving to others the book which they most prized for themselves. Many a courier or dragoman in the East shows with pleasure the New Testament quietly put into his hands by the stranger whom he has served. The number of copies of Scriptures distributed in this unrecorded way is greater than is commonly imagined.

As to the results of Bible distribution, one might almost say that the history of missions throughout the world is the history of the wonderful influence of the Bible upon men of every race. All missionary literature teems with incidents illustrating the far-reaching results of inducing men to read the Bible. Sometimes it is a robber in the Armenian highlands, who has stolen the book from a traveler, sometimes it is a peasant in Mexico who has received it from an American soldier during the war of 1848; sometimes it is a Hindu peasant who has taken the book from the doctor who healed his disease, but the result in each case is the same—changed life and a desire to tell others of the wonderful book. Something of the magnitude of this influence of the Bible, may be judged from the fact that according to the conclusions of Rev. Dr. James S. Dennis, after a laborious study of the reports of the different Bible societies in order to avoid duplication of statistics, the number of Scriptures or portions of Scripture annually distributed in foreign mission fields by the Bible societies, is 3,286,834.

BIBLE HOUSE, CONSTANTINOPLE: One of the perplexing problems connected with mission enterprise is that of providing a place for the transaction of its secular affairs. Missions have many of the qualities of a great business. There is first the financial responsibilities for the different departments involving the expenditure of thousands of dollars annually. There is, too, a great amount of publication involving a stock of printed sheets, bound volumes, electrotype plates, etc. The treasurer must have a safe deposit for his money. The Bible society or Mission Publication Department needs storage room for its books, the more nearly fire proof the better. This problem early became a most serious one in Constantinople. That city was the center of four missions of the American Board, and of the agencies of the American, and the British and Foreign Bible Societies, and many other missions looked to it for the transaction of important business. At first a room was hired by each agency in one of the numerous khans; but this was soon too small. Then a whole building was rented for all together in the business section of the city, but that was insufficient. The existence of the Bible House in New York suggested a similar building in Constantinople; but when applied to, the American Bible Society did not feel justified in doing more than permit its agent, the Rev. Isaac G. Bliss, D.D. to raise the money for a Bible House. This he did in 1866 and secured a number of prominent New York business men to act as trustees of the property. There were the usual delays attending such an enterprise, but in 1872 the building was complete and ready for occupancy. It is excellently adapted to its purpose, providing for the different missionary organizations, office room, safe vaults, storage room for publications, editorial rooms for publication work, as well as for Bible revision committees. All these are supplied at a merely nominal rent. Other rooms are occupied by printing and binding establishments, and on the street are stores, the income from which has been applied to completing the property and to furnishing a Sunday service for the transient crowd always to be found in such a great city. Viewed simply as a business investment for the care of the secular part of missionary enterprise, the Bible House has been well worth all that it cost; but it has had another and even greater value, as a proof of the practical character of Protestant missions. It is known all through the city and indeed throughout the Empire as the "American Khan," and as the center of those influences which have done more than all else to arouse ambition for a better life. Enemies have recognized its influence and shaken their fists at it in impotent rage, and many a poor despised Christian has rejoiced in its simple beauty and strength as the token of the power that is yet to redeem the land. If ever there were sermons in stones they have spoken from the walls of the Bible House.

BIBLE LANDS MISSIONS AID SOCIETY: In 1853-4 Rev. C. G. Young, a minister in the North of England, traveling in the East, came into contact with missionaries of the American Board engaged in work among the Armenians in Constantinople, and was greatly impressed with their devotion and zeal. Returning to England he urged that an endeavor should be made to associate Christians of all the churches in an effort to cooperate with those already in the field. Circumstances contributed to awaken interest in the subject. It was just before the Crimean War and the Eastern question was assuming an acute phase. The Sultan was looking to Britain for support against Russia. Sir Stratford Canning (Lord Redcliffe) the astute and able English ambassador at the Porte, had sought to influence the Sultan in the direction of a policy of toleration in religious matters. For several years Christians in Britain had watched with sympathy the converts among the Armenians, who had been grievously persecuted. After one or two public meetings which increased interest in the scheme of an auxiliary agency in England, on the 3d of July, 1854, the Turkish Missions' Aid Society was organized, the Earl of Shaftesbury being elected president. The Society is entirely undenominational, both in its supporters and in the distribution of its funds. The first rule of its constitution describes its aim: "The object of this Society is not to originate a new mission, but to aid in the extension of gospel work in Bible lands, especially that carried on by the Americans."

The Society has been and is a most valuable helper to many branches of missionary work in Turkey, having furnished funds to the amount of $512,000 to various special objects of importance.

The name of the Society was changed a few years ago by substituting "Bible Lands" for the "Turkish" of the original name. Altho not so largely supported as formerly, the Society continues to work on the same lines, making its special province the assistance of Christian work in Greece, Bulgaria, Turkey, Persia, Syria, and Egypt.

The organ of the Society is "*The Star in the East*," published quarterly.

BIBLE TRANSLATION: "The Day of Pentecost was fully come" and the spirit of God worked great miracles, and the Galilean disciples were enabled to proclaim the gospel in the divergent tongues of the vast heterogeneous crowd of three continents. "We do hear them speak in our tongues the wonderful works of God."

What the spirit of God did on the day of Pentecost for fifteen or sixteen peoples, that are the translators of the Bible doing for all the peoples of the world. The end in view is that every man may hear in his own tongue the wonderful works of God. For such a work special gifts, graces, acquirements, and instruments are needed, and of these we proceed to speak in the following sections.

Qualifications Necessary for a Translator: The translator should be deeply conscious of the gravity of his work as well as of its importance. The man who enters on such work in a frivolous spirit will fail, like the general who enters on a great war with a light heart. Perfection in translation is unattainable, but it should be aimed at. Translation at best bears pretty much the same relation to the original that the wrong side of velvet bears to the right side. In the wrong side of the texture you may have all the material of the original: the warp and woof may be skilfully shot, all the weight and color may be in the piece, but the glossy pile is wanting. In translation the artistic touch which each author gives to his work, independent of the substance matter, can never be caught or transferred by another hand. If this be so in ordinary translation, it is still more applicable to Bible translation.

The original languages of the Bible constitute great difficulties. The Semitic Old Testament is full of perplexities. The language is archaic, the idioms are Oriental, the transitions are abrupt, the allusions are uncertain; the words thrown together in juxtaposition give little cue, by form or relation, to their exact meaning. Many passages are vague, and capable of several interpretations, and all passages have alliteration and play upon words which cannot possibly be reproduced in translation.

The original of the New Testament is Aramaic Greek, and the old Hellenic forms are filled with new ideas, like the new wine in the old bottles. The old Hellenic words had to be emptied of their old meanings before being dedicated to the new service, and they are often inadequate expressions of the fresh gospel thought. The translator will have to trace the Hebrew conception in the Greek form.

In both old and New Testaments there are many hands visible. The Holy Ghost, who inspired the men that wrote as they were moved did not interfere with their individuality or style of expression. Paul does not write like Luke nor John like James. The prophets are distinct from each other in thought and style, and immeasurably removed from the feeling and form of our exact metallic age. Taking into account the composite character of the book, ranging from simplest narrative to most flowing rhapsody, one cannot but recognize how ill-equipped a modern scholar is for translating right through the Bible. The man who would successfully reproduce this Holy Book must himself be under the influence of the Holy Spirit who inspired and guided the various authors. Purvey, in his prologue to Wickliffe's Bible, says: "He hath need to live a clean life, and be full of devout prayers, that the Holy Spirit, Author of wisdom, knowledge, and truth, dress him in his work, and suffer him not to err. . . . By this manner, with good living and great travail, men may come to true and clear translating, and true understanding of Holy Writ."

Faith in the Bible is absolutely essential to the translator. It is not desirable that he should have to take down all his beliefs from the shelf and reexamine them whenever a new hypothesis regarding the Bible makes its appearance. The translator should not only have a reasonable intellectual belief in the Word of God, but he should be a man who has tried and tested it, and found in it his own strength and joy. Having felt its power himself, he will know why he must be careful that none of its meaning is lost in passing through his hands. Having been blessed by it, he will do all that is in his power to make it the bearer of blessings to others. Every phrase, word, letter, mood, and tense will have due weight with him, and nothing will be slurred over or dealt with in a careless or slovenly manner.

A sound judgment is indispensable to a translator of the Bible. No matter how great his attachment and loyalty to the Bible, if he has an ill-balanced mind he is in danger of getting entangled with Biblical fads; and the Biblical faddist is always discovering things in the text of the Bible that have no existence, giving prominence to parts that are of no more importance than other parts, and unconsciously using the book to support his own whimsical opinions. The translator should know the Bible in the unity of its truth, and be able to see individual passages in the light of surrounding truth. He should be able to divest himself of the prejudices of the religious or philosophical school in which he has been brought up, and to cast aside all prepossessions in favor of even the venerable readings of his own Authorized Version.

Sound scholarship must be based on sound judgment. A liberal education, especially in languages, is a good groundwork for Biblical scholarship. The man who professes to know twenty or thirty or a hundred languages is to be avoided. None of the phenomenal linguists of the past ever did any work that has lived, and this rule is not likely to change in the future. The translator should concentrate his chief attention on a few languages, and leave large profession to people who wish to be wondered at. A good knowledge of the original languages of the Bible is requisite to a good translator, and if he has an opportunity of learning Arabic, he will be well rewarded. The Syriac version was one of the translations first made from the original after the writing of the New Testament—perhaps the very first, and a knowledge of the Peshito will be useful to the translator; but Syriac has little literature worth reading, and the time spent on it might more profitably be devoted to Arabic. The Latin Vulgate should also be at the side of the translator for consultation, and also the Septuagint; and of living versions the English Revised and Segond's French will be found useful and suggestive. The translator should be thoroughly acquainted with the manners and customs of Bible lands, and with all modern discoveries bearing on the Bible.

The translator should be thoroughly acquainted with the literature of the language into which he is to render the Scriptures. He should read its classics, and especially the poetry, in order to enrich his vocabulary with choice words, and to learn to pack them close with concentrated thought. He should read the newspapers, and converse with the people, until he is able to think in their language, without the intrusion of auxiliary words from other languages. Most languages have corresponding idioms, and by constant watchfulness and practice approximations may be found. If the language is foreign to the translator, he should employ a trustworthy native to accompany him as much as possible. He should be constantly composing in the language, and employing his native assistant to correct his compositions, and he should get by heart a choice specimen of the language daily.

Patience, in abundant measure, is a necessary endowment of a translator. Haste is the fruitful author of ill-done work. The student in a hurry will never be a scholar. The impatient translator will turn out crude and unfinished copy. There will doubtless be many influences drawing and pushing him forward at headlong speed. It may be that he is called to work for a bookless people, who have never had the Scriptures. Or he finds an imperfect version in the hands of the people, and by the help of a presumptuous native he hastens to improve the version, *currente calamo*.

Patience is an attribute of strength, and the translator requires firm moral fiber to resist the influences that would hinder patience from having her work perfect.

Bishop Steere of Zanzibar spent five years in completing his version of the Gospel of St. Mark into the Swahili tongue.

By this patient procedure with one Gospel he acquired facility in translation, and he had the joy of giving the New Testament to that great people before being taken home to his reward. The memorable words of the revisers of the Authorized Version should never be forgotten by translators: "We did not disdain to revise that which we had done, and to bring back to the anvil that which we had hammered; but having and using as great helps as were needful, and fearing no reproach for slowness, nor coveting praise for expedition, we have at length, through the good hand of the Lord upon us, brought the work to that pass that you see."

So in the translation of Luther's Bible. The scholars who aided Luther revised with him every line with patient care, and sometimes they returned fourteen successive days to the revision of a single line.

The English and German translators and revisers were rendering the Scriptures into their mother tongues, but the majority of translators and revisers are called upon to translate into tongues which are foreign to them, and which they are obliged to learn. The wise translator will always work with the assistance of native scholars, and this will necessitate patience in many respects. He will have to bear with the inaccurate and self-satisfied ways of the unmethodical natives. He will not be able to take renderings on trust, but must lead his helper round the idea until the exact point is reached. Sometimes, when engaged on languages which have no literature, and which have never been written, he will have to catch the words alive, and fix them as best he can on paper.

There is nothing, perhaps, which tries a translator's patience so much as having his work revised by others. It is never pleasant to have one's composition found fault with, and every correction made by a reviser assumes imperfect work on the part of the author. If the translator has the grace of patience when he first sees the work that has cost him so much pulled to pieces, he will soon come to appreciate the suggestions of men much inferior to himself. For all these things patience and Christian courtesy are absolutely necessary.

The translator should cultivate a simple, easily understood style. Very often first translations, made into a literary language, are cast in too lofty a style. The native helper is a scholar, generally proud of his native literature, in which he has been educated, and his aim will be to translate the Scriptures in accordance with high classical models. It is not the business of a translator to render a version in a language as the language ought to be, but as the language is. The common plain language of the people as used in commerce and in everyday life will be the victorious form of speech, and into this form, avoiding all vulgarisms and low expressions, the Scriptures should be translated.

When the proper standard has been reached another question of great difficulty will arise. The translator should strive to convey the meaning while remaining as faithful as possible to the letter of the text. The sense must be given whether the passage be rendered literally or not, but pains should be taken to transfer the sense by giving due weight to every word.

Translators of the Scriptures should, whenever practicable, carry out their work by committees. The general rule of the British and Foreign Bible Society on this subject is as follows: "That whenever it is practicable to obtain a board of competent persons to translate or revise a version of the Scriptures, it is undesirable to accept for publication the work of a single translator or reviser."

The first great version of the Old Testament takes its name, Septuagint, from the supposition that the translation into Greek was the work of seventy scholars. It was certainly the work of a large revision committee — hence its great value and permanence. The revision of the English Bible which resulted in the Authorized Version of 1611 was the work of many scholars. The Dutch version was the production of twelve translators and sixteen revisers. The Manx Old Testament was the work of twenty-four translators and two revisers.

The text to be followed is of primary importance in Bible translation. Up to 1881 the work of translation for the British and Foreign Bible Society was carried on in accordance with the following instructions:

"Whenever practicable, a version should be a direct translation from the Hebrew and Greek originals. For the Hebrew Bible, the edition of Van der Hooght is considered the standard; and in the use of this the translator is at liberty to follow either the *ketib* or the *keri;* but not to adopt any rendering which is not sanctioned by the Massoretic vowel-points, or the *keri*, or the English Authorized Version, or the marginal readings of this last. In the Greek Testament the Elzevir edition of the 'Textus Receptus' of 1633, and reprinted by the British and Foreign Bible Society, is considered the standard; but in cases where the Authorized Version differs from this, either in the text or in the marginal reading, the translator is at liberty to adopt a rendering which may agree with any one of these three; and if a translator or editor think it better to omit the subscriptions of the epistles, the insertion of these is not required."

As far as the Old Testament is concerned these instructions still hold good. Hebrew manuscripts of the Old Testament are of no great antiquity, dating only from A. D. 916. No doubt there are ancient readings preserved in such versions as the Septuagint, the Samaritan Pentateuch, the Syriac, and the Latin Vulgate. And there are doubtless previous readings of the old Hebrew preserved in quotations in the New Testament. Collations of such readings have been made with much labor and some skill; but nothing has been discovered or done to warrant the Bible Society in adopting a new text.

The case of the New Testament widely differs from that of the Old. Numerous ancient and important Greek manuscripts of the New Testament, in whole or in part, have been discovered in recent years. Enormous learning and pains have been bestowed on the collation and classification of these manuscripts, and on the investigation of early versions and quotations. Sufficient material has been accumulated for the substantial restoration of the Greek Testament of the fourth century.

Under these circumstances the Committee of the British and Foreign Bible Society in 1881 resolved to authorize missionaries and others engaged on behalf of the Society in the work of translation or revision to adopt such deviations from the "Textus Receptus" as are sanctioned by the text of the Revised English Version of 1881. The careful attention of translators was at the same time invited to the observations of the Company of Revisers on the revision of the Greek text in their preface, and to the caution suggested by their emphatic words: "Many places still remain in which for the present it would not be safe to accept one reading to the absolute exclusion of others." "In these cases," the revisers add, "we have given alternative readings in the margin, whenever they seem to be of sufficient importance or interest to deserve notice." These alternative readings should, therefore, be carefully studied before any change is adopted from the "Textus Receptus"; and, whilst the committee did not desire to control the conscientious judgment of translators or revisers, they suggested that where the marginal note in the English version indicates that ancient authorities support the Elzevir text, there would be safety in adhering for the present to the Elzevir text.

The same regulations substantially have been adopted by the American Bible Society, and thus far the two great societies have proceeded on the same lines in the work of translation and revision.

The Names for the Divine Being require special attention. The difficulty of finding any Supreme Being among the heathen is sometimes very great. Sometimes the gods are so numerous that the difficulty consists in making a proper selection. Sometimes there are no gods at all; but the translator's chief difficulty will be to find any name among the heathen associated with the ideas of reverence or worship. In this matter as in many others the translator will have to do the best he can. In the Septuagint and Greek Testament, Theos is substituted for Elohim, and Lord (Kurios) for Jehovah and Adonai promiscuously. The terms were not equivalents, but apostles and martyrs preached the gospel meanings into the names until they became expressive of the true gospel thoughts now associated with each. Every care should be taken to select the best word, but it must be remembered that in all countries the truth about God is gathered not so much from the name as from what is taught concerning Him who bears it. The translator in a heathen tongue must select the best term or name he can find. Tho he may be obliged to take the name of a false god, he will find that by degrees, through reading the Bible, the false meaning will disappear, and the true meaning assert itself. It might be possible to transfer the original names of God by transliteration, but in that case the names would, in themselves, be absolutely without significance when first introduced.

Translators will find it difficult to render the word *Baptizo* in a manner satisfactory to all. If translating for a non-denominational society which is supported by all denominations, they can not be expected to translate the word by a term which supports the views of one denomination. In versions made for the British and Foreign Bible Society the word *Baptizo* and its cognates are transliterated or transferred, as is done in the English Bible, unless it can be translated by some native word signifying sacred washing, without limiting the form to either dipping or sprinkling. An attempt has been made to get over the difficulty by placing the neutral term in the text, and the denominational term in the margin, with the words "some translate immerse"—which is simply the statement of a fact. Where the version is Baptist, it would be better that the difficulty should be got over by an alternative reading than that a rival version should be issued. These matters require to be dealt with on both sides in a spirit of mutual forbearance.

Translators should be careful to choose the central language in commencing versions, and to resist all pressure to undertake translations in insignificant and dying dialects. Many versions produced in local *patois* have led to considerable waste of Christian money. At first it may not be possible, with limited experience, to say which branch of a group of languages is the best vehicle for reaching the most people; but first editions should be tentative and small, and the second editions should be revised into the dominant form. Prince L. L. Bonaparte made versions of the Scriptures into more than a hundred languages, dialects, and *patois*, for linguistic purposes. These his Highness has handed over to the Bible Society, with permission to revise them for evangelistic purposes; but there are only a few of them on which the Society would be at all justified in spending funds.

The translator should be careful to mark in some distinctive way words inserted to make the sense complete, but which have no equivalents in the originals. Such words are marked in our English Bibles by being printed in italics. This is somewhat unfortunate, as in all other forms of English literature italics are used to give emphasis and prominence to words. The italics should be as few as possible. A great many in the Authorized Version are superfluous. In foreign languages the supplied words, when necessary, should be printed in type similar to the body of the text, but somewhat smaller. In preparing chapter and page headings only simple summaries should be given. In our English Bibles the chapter headings are printed in such small italics that they are seldom consulted, and they form an undesirable wedge between chapter and chapter. The British and Foreign Bible Society has long had a paragraph English Bible prepared by Canon Girdlestone, and it has begun to print foreign versions in paragraphs, with sectional headings which simply announce the subjects of the sections. The headings are simple summaries, such as "The Creation," "The Flood," "The Temptation," "The Fall," etc. Versions so arranged, well printed and accompanied by maps, have been published in Italian, Sesuto, Malagasi, French, and Dutch, and they have been well received. In China, too, the committee have agreed to publish summaries, sectional headings, and simple explanations of words and terms not likely to be understood by the Chinese.

The Scriptures can be read much more intelligently in the paragraph form. Much can be done by artistic printing, by proper spacing, and the arrangement of parallelisms to encourage the reading of the Scriptures. Lasserre's Gospels in paragraph form are so arranged that every page says "read me"; and Frenchmen, for the first time, read the gospel with pleasure. There are many additional considerations, and necessary conditions, and infinite details, which might be advanced with regard to Bible translation, but these will be best learned in the practical work of translation. As in preparing sermons, writing books, and public speaking, each worker reaches his own style by his own methods, so translators must be left to find out the lines within certain limitations on which they can best accomplish the sacred work entrusted to them; and in the matter of details, common sense and scrupulous conscientiousness will be the best guides.

The list of versions in the Appendix enables one to judge of the immense work already accomplished in Bible translation.

The Bible is the greatest of all the classics, and its importance may be judged in contrast with them. There are, at the present time, over a thousand philologists busied with Bible translation and revision, and wherever the living missionary goes he takes with him the living word. Versions of the classic masterpieces of Greece, Rome, and the Far East are few, and are found on the shelves of libraries and in the homes of learning. The versions of the Bible are for the people, and no sooner have they fallen from the press than they are taken up in such quantities by the missionaries, by the colporteurs, by the zenana women, and by all who wish the divine message made known, that the average circulation of the British and Foreign Bible Society alone is over four million copies a year. See **Bible Distribution**.

BIBLE VERSIONS: By far the larger proportion of existing versions of the Bible are used in foreign missionary operations. For the most part, also, they are the fruit of the patient toil of missionaries in the field. The missionary translator, unseen and almost forgotten in the isolation of his life work as he studies the sounds, the structure and the vocabulary of a strange language, and then uses his knowledge in translation of the Scriptures, renders a double service to mankind. He not only sets before savage and illiterate tribes the Book which is to lift them in the scale of humanity, but at the same time he gives to the people the idea of committing speech to paper, and provides them with the means of doing so. More than this, he has placed in a form accessible to students in the home land the essential data for studying and classifying the language in which he is working. He thus materially aids the extension of knowledge. As Dr. Cust has remarked, "It is a marvelous surprise to a scholar who has never left Europe to have a translation of a Gospel handed to him, of the genuineness and approximate accuracy of which there can be no doubt, in a language that is unprovided with scientific works or literary helps."

The list of known languages and dialects continually grows longer as the surface of the earth is more fully explored. It has been estimated that the total number of languages now rendering active service exceeds 2,000. Yet it is by no means this number of versions of the Bible which we must aim to provide. The list of languages which are dead, and that of other languages which are extinct, show that no version of the complete Bible should be undertaken without careful study of the place and the rank, as permanent or temporary, which that language holds in which the version is to be made. Such a fate as befell John Eliot's Indian Bible, serving only as a library curiosity because of the extinction of the language in which it is printed, is a warning on this point.

As at present conducted, the process of publishing a version is generally as follows: The opportunity or need of one being apparent, an arrangement is made between some one of the Bible societies and the missionary society occupying a certain field, by which one or more missionaries especially fitted for the work are instructed to devote either the whole or a part of their time to the preparation of the translation, their support and the incidental expense being, in many cases, assumed by the Bible society. When the translation is completed, preparations are made for publishing, either on the field, if good printing presses and binderies are available, or in America, England, or Continental Europe, according to circumstances. It was formerly the custom to do much of the publishing in London or New York, but since the establishment of the numerous foreign agencies it is very largely done at the great centers of those agencies, as Vienna, Constantinople, Shanghai, Tokio, etc.

The translation thus made is the property of the Bible society that incurred the expense, and, altho there is no regular copyright taken out, the rights of each society are carefully regarded. In some cases, as those of the Japanese, Chinese, and Turkish versions, two or more societies have combined to share the expense, and have equal rights of publication. Whenever one society has need of the publications of another the required copies are purchased, cost price rather than selling price being paid, on the principle that one society should not reap financial benefit from the benevolence of another. In certain cases permission is asked, and usually granted, for the use of plates for the reduplication of a version. In general the rule has been for each society to assist every other to the best of its ability, so far as convenience or cautious regard for mutual interest was involved, the aim being not to secure honor or glory to themselves, but to further by every possible means the great aim of the societies.

The number of living and effective versions of the Bible somewhat exceeds 400. All the languages of the "conquering" class now possess versions of the Bible. Substantially the same is true of the "permanent class of languages." As to the weak languages which cannot hold their ground, and the dialects which cannot all survive the diffusion of education, in general, portions only of Scriptures have been translated into them.

A list of existing Bible Versions, and a list of missionaries who have translated or revised the Bible for the Bible societies, will be found in the Appendix.

BIBLE WOMEN: Mission reports originally employed this term as the simplest expression for Christian service on the part of a native woman. A "Bible Woman" read the Bible to other women, went from neighbor to neighbor, repeating texts and explanations as she had heard them, or, if she could not read, she recited memorized passages of Scripture or sang a hymn. The phrase will always signify those who make the Bible known to others. The Bible woman ingeniously invents opportunity to introduce the Word of God to the heathen. She teaches women to read in order that they may study the Bible; she gathers children about her to teach them Bible verses and stories; she enforces her Bible teaching by the example of her own self-sacrificing, happy Christian life. In the progress of missions, however, the content of the term has expanded until it covers wide and varied activities. What does not the Bible woman do? She is equally ready to join in a husking-bee or a grape-gathering, to help a tired mother with her sewing or in the care of sick children. Groups of women before their doors knitting or spinning, tho they sometimes curse the woman and the Book, more frequently respond to her pleasant greeting with an invitation to stop. In 1901, when people were dying of plague in Bombay at the rate of four hundred daily, the Bible women kept at their posts, visiting segregation camps. They move with gentle ministration from one bedside to another in all the women's wards of mission hospitals in Asia, and conduct services in their waiting rooms for patients. The writer has seen them addressing rooms full of listeners in the Margaret Williamson Hospital, Shanghai, at Dr. Benn's dispensary in Tientsin, teaching convalescents at Canton Hospital. At Tooker Memorial Hospital, Su-chau-fu, patients, especially from the country, often begin to arrive early in the morning, and one of the Bible women has many precious opportunities to preach to these early comers as she sits in the gate-house with her sewing. These women also do a roadside work, conveying the first elementary notions of Christianity to their fellow passengers on the boat, or to the traveler resting, like themselves, in the tea-house or under a wayside tree. Taking advantage of the relations of kinship or clanship, they penetrate to remote country districts where the foreigner has never gone, and publish the name of Jesus where ear has never heard it. In wet and cold, more often in blazing heat, they thread narrow city lanes and teach the alphabet, perhaps, to the secluded women of India. They are leading spirits in the women's meetings, they explain the *bhajans*, they are a right hand to the pastor. It is they who arrange for the sick to be cared for, who advise mothers about their children, urge their education, discourage early marriage, warn against opium. "These Bible women in many ways prove a blessing. The other day, three of them heard a fierce quarrel going on at a village over distribution of the harvest. The women, who were farmers and Mahars in caste, had come to blows; with God's blessing the Bible women became peacemakers and all the belligerents were soon sitting together, listening to the word of Christ's love." "A class has been formed," (says the report of the American Marathi Mission) of old women, some of them blind and crippled; a Bible reader teaches them four times a week. The Bible women have been very faithful to the Dorcas Society; many garments have been made for the poor and money gathered for materials." "A staff of nineteen women are occupied in our Bible work (LMS in Calcutta). Men, also, welcome these modest Christian workers who often have an opportunity of delivering the Gospel message to men of rank and position."

The Bible woman is the link between missionary and native church. She clears up misunderstandings and interprets each to the other. She supplements the missionary's halting tongue with her fluent prayers. She is her escort to the high class house where rigorous etiquette must be observed, and she delicately chooses the proper moment in which to introduce her Gospel message. "Our efforts," wrote a missionary in Travancore, "would amount to comparatively little in such a climate had we not a band of native women to go forth under our direction to labor from day to day." "We must repeat ourselves in our Christian women," said another.

The superior natural equipment of the Bible woman was well expressed by Miss Ricketts at the Shanghai Conference in 1890:

"She has been in the exact condition of her hearers. She knows the depth of their ignorance, their habits, temptations, modes of thinking and feeling, and therefore she can appeal to them and carry home her appeal by illustrations drawn from their common life. She has at her command a store of proverbs which give point to what she says. She knows how much may be expected of them in coming regularly to worship, and can meet objections to keeping the Sabbath. One of our Swatow Bible women can almost always gain and keep the ear of her countrywomen. She carries with her a wholesome, sunny atmosphere which the people enjoy. When they ply her with irrelevant questions she replies, "I have only one little mouth and cannot answer so many things. What I am saying is of life and death concern to you."

The ideal Bible woman reflects the missionary's methods, and energy and, to a degree, absorbs her cultivation. Her eyes see what sort of instruction the country class needs and discern the secret of sudden coldness in the church. She is the missionary's indispensable helper, and, tho many times proving a disappointment, and often taxing that forbearance which is the price paid by superior endowment and training to less disciplined assistance, missionary and Bible woman mutually depend upon one another, and shut up together as they often are for weeks of itineration, sharing hardship and persecution, their relation in numberless cases is that of established trust and friendship. Every reader of missionary magazines will here and there come upon such testimony as the following, in a missionary's letter from Marsovan, Asia Minor: "Yeranouhi, the choicest of the Bible women, closed her lovely and most useful earthly life in November, 1901. Her loss seems irreparable, and was felt as keenly by the missionaries as by the poor people to whom she had so long, so wisely, and so tenderly ministered."

While the old type of uneducated Bible woman still obtains in places, there is a growing sentiment in favor of training. At least eleven of the leading British and American Societies report distinctive "Bible Training Schools" with an enrollment of 468 pupils. Thorough courses of Bible instruction characterize these schools, and, in most of them, at least music and physiology are taught, and out-door practice is required. The school of the Women's Union Society at Yokohama has a four years' course. Bible women generally work under missionary inspection and render reports. Conferences are occasionally held for their benefit. The women are often of good social position and genteel appearance, but blindness has not prevented some from great usefulness in this calling.

Location; Numbers: We rarely hear of Bible women in missions to Roman Catholic countries, to the South Seas or on the continent of Africa. They are employed in the Turkish Empire, in Persia, Egypt, Korea, Japan, China and especially all over India. "At least two thousand (in India), trained by American and English mission schools, have access to hundreds of thousands of Hindu homes."

When Miss Ellen Stone of Salonika was captured by brigands she had a band of nine Bulgarian Bible women associated with her. Of these it is said: "The women, distaffs in hand, spinning as they walk, not to lose a precious minute, Testament and hymn-book tucked in the girdle, often with babies on their backs, gather for the prayer hour. It is a sight to make believers in the work of the Bible woman, to see these hard-handed, labor-bowed mothers of many children able to read and sing, thanks to her patience and encouragement."

Certain cities are centers of extensive labors in this line. Jaffna, Ceylon, is worked by over fifty Bible women. In Madura, Madras Presidency, thirty-one have access to a thousand non-Christian homes of the city where Bible instruction is gladly received, and seventeen other women visit in seventy-two villages and instruct over a thousand pupils. At Ahmednagar, Bombay Presidency, ten classes, including 250 illiterate women, are taught by seventeen Bible women who also have pupils in private houses. Thirty-six women of the Union Society are laboring in and about Yokohama. Foochow, China, is another center, where three missions engage in training women for Bible work.

As to the number of Bible women employed in Protestant missions, only a very partial estimate is possible. In 1899 the British and Foreign Bible Society received returns from 552 women under its direction. The London Missionary Society, in 1902, reported a staff of 271 Bible women, the Church of England Zenana Society 242, the American Baptist Union 250, the Presbyterian Board (North) 225, the Congregational Woman's Board (Boston) over 200. The Zenana, Bible and Medical Society (London) reports 92, and the United Free Church of Scotland 36. The American Marâthi Mission employs 109 Bible women as against a total of 84 pastors, preachers and men Bible readers.

Those workers who appear on the pages of reports are usually paid, and by this method, a mission ensures to itself the advantages of consecutiveness and definite hours of labor. The wages of Bible women range from 25 to 50 dollars a year. In addition to this recognized force, there are many voluntary workers, the amount and value of whose services can never be tabulated. In some of the newer missions, it is aimed to develop this voluntary corps and to reduce the number of paid workers to a minimum. The Mission of the Presbyterian Church (North) in Korea is a marked example of this aim. Hundreds of Korean women are voluntarily doing the work of a Bible woman, as against a handful who are paid. The writer has seen one effectively preaching of her own free will to a miscellaneous crowd on a river bank. These Korean volunteer Bible women were met, night after night, in country meetings, where they found the Scripture passages for the slow, and set the example of quiet and order to the uninitiated. They were heard of, selling Testaments as they traveled about in the conduct of their own business, or led meetings with beginners in the Christian life. Their cleanliness, their pure language and their Gospel message, all were reenforced by the fact that no pecuniary reward had touched their hands.

BICKNELL, Henry: Missionary of the LMS to Tahiti, 1796-1820. In 1819 he baptized King Pomare, and also assisted him in the framing of a code of laws by means of which good government on the island was formally established. Died at Tahiti, August 7, 1820.

BICKERSTETH, Edward: Died August 5, 1897. M. A. Fellow Pembroke College, Cambridge. Ordained deacon in 1873; ordained priest in 1874. Chief station, Delhi, India, from 1877-81. Transferred to Japan in 1886. Consecrated in St. Paul's Cathedral in 1886, second English Bishop in Japan. Son of E. H. Bickersteth, Bishop of Exeter, and grandson of a former Secretary of the CMS. He was moved by the missionary Bishop French of Lahore to devote his life to a missionary career; and, influenced by French, he planned a brotherhood of Cambridge men, which should form a strong and concentrated mission at some central station, in affiliation with one of the established societies. Bickersteth's hereditary associations naturally led him to approach the CMS, but, difficulties arising, he concluded matters with the SPG, and Delhi was chosen for the new "Cambridge Mission."

Bishop Bickersteth arrived in Japan April 16, 1886, and at his request he was allowed to make his residence at Tokio. His great achievement is spoken of as the formation of the Nippon Sei-kokwai or "Japan Catholic Church". He felt that the peculiarly independent spirit of the Japanese and the tendency toward a latitudinarian development of Christianity among them, rendered it important that the ecclesiastical organization, with its doctrines and forms, should be positively recognized. He soon felt the value and importance of woman's work in Japan; and wrote to the Society these urgent words: "I feel strongly that the policy of working through clergy only, without the assistance of lady missionaries, has in the past crippled our Missions." And since then, Japan has always claimed and received a good share of SPG women.

In 1887 Bishop Bickersteth, accompanied by Bishop Scott, of North China, visited Korea, and their appeal to the Archbishop of Canterbury resulted in the establishment of the SPG Mission in this important field. In 1892 the Bishop set himself to visit every station and outstation of the Anglican Missions in Japan, and his study of this large diocese, with its extremities 2,000 miles apart, led him to the conviction that Japan now needed more bishops. His suggestions were accepted and acted upon. Bishop Bickersteth did much toward consolidating the Japanese Church under American, English and Canadian Episcopal Missions into the Nippon Sei-kokwai with its complete synodical organization, and his name will also be remembered as the founder of the two community missions of St. Andrew and St. Hilda, the former of which (for men) renewed its connection with the SPG in 1900. The Bickersteth Hall, in Delhi, India (built in 1891) affords a splendid opportunity for preaching the Gospel in the very heart of the Mohammedan quarter, and the Bickersteth Memorial Studentships for the maintenance of students studying for the ministry at St. Andrew's Divinity School, Tokio, supply a felt need.

BIHÈ. See ANGOLA.

BIJAPUR: Chief town of the district of the same name in the Bombay Presidency, India. Formerly an imposing city, it now has (1891) about 16,000 inhabitants. Station of the Basel Missionary Society (1885), with (1902) 1 missionary and his wife, 9 native workers, 4 village schools and 53 communicants. Name written by the Germans Bidschapur.

BIJNAUR: A town in the Rohilkhand division, United Provinces, India. Population (1891), 16,236. Station of the ME, with 1 missionary and his wife, 41 native workers, men and women, 4 chapels, 20 Sunday schools, 17 village schools, 1 high school, 1 Young People's Society and 1,216 professing Christians. Also written Bijnour.

BILASPUR: A town and railway station in the Central Provinces, India. Population (1891), 11,236. Station of the Christian (Disciples) Woman's Board of Missions (1893), with 7 missionary women, of whom one is a physician, 1 chapel, 1 Sunday school, 2 village schools, a dispensary, a hospital, an orphanage and 70 professing Christians.

BILIN: Name of a tribe inhabiting a part of the northern regions of Abyssinia. About half of the tribe are Roman Catholics, a part are Mohammedans, and the rest belong to the Abyssinian Church. The tribe is also called Bogos.

BILIN LANGUAGE. See BOGOS.

BILSI: A town in the Rohilkhand division, Central Provinces, India; station of the ME, with 23 native workers, men and women, 11 Sunday schools, 7 village schools, a Young People's Society and 960 professing Christians.

BIMLIPATAM: A town on the coast of the Vizagapatam district, Madras, India; station of the BMP (1876), with 2 missionaries and their wives, 1 missionary woman, 6 native workers, men and women, 2 outstations, 1 chapel, 1 Sunday school, 1 theological seminary and 22 church members.

BINA: A town and railway station in Central India, S. W. of Lalitpur; station of the FCMS (1894), with 1 missionary and his wife, 1 missionary woman, 3 native workers, 1 chapel, 1 Sunday school, 1 village school, 1 orphanage and 60 church members.

BINGHAM, Hiram: born at Bennington, Vt., October 30, 1789; graduated at Middlebury

College, 1816, at Andover Theological Seminary, 1819. A visit to the foreign mission school at Cornwall, Ct., while Henry Obookiah was there awakened in him a desire to carry the Gospel to the Sandwich Islands. He was ordained September 29, 1819; sailed October 23 of the same year as a missionary of the ABCFM and was stationed at Honolulu. His undaunted courage, inflexible will, combined with his good nature and cheerfulness, fitted him to meet the opposition in that stronghold of wickedness. He returned to the United States in 1841 on account of the ill health of Mrs. Bingham. Six years after his return he published *History of the Mission* down to 1845, in an octavo volume of 600 pages, a work of great historic value. He died in 1869 after a brief illness.

BING-YAE. See PING-YANG-HSIEN.

BIRD, Rev. William: Died August 30, 1901. On the 17th of August, 1901, Rev. William Bird celebrated the 79th anniversary of his birthday. He had entered on his fiftieth year of service in the Syria Mission.

He first came to Syria in 1823 as an infant. When his parents and their associates were obliged to flee from Syria, this child became treasurer of the Syria Mission, his bed and pillow being the safe deposit vaults for the cash, thus eluding the rapacity of the Turkish officials and the violence of a lawless populace.

Not long after, when he returned a second time, with his parents, to Beirut, the entire Protestant community came in a little boat to meet them. It consisted of two men.

In 1853 Mr. and Mrs. William Bird began their missionary career (under the ABCFM), the last twenty years of which was spent in the service of the Presbyterian Board (North). Having spent his childhood in Syria, the difficult Arabic language was practically his vernacular. His life was full of zeal and earnestness and self-denial. He preached with power and marked effect. He was loved and honored by the people. Wherever he went he was welcomed. He ate with the people and slept as they slept when on his missionary tours, winning their confidence and friendship by identifying himself with them, as few missionaries are able to do. He was particularly attractive in his school work and enthusiastically welcomed by all children. He was loved and honored by all who knew him, and is deeply mourned by all his associates and acquaintances.

BIRI SIRI: A village on the borders of Assam in Eastern Bengal, India, N. E. of Nasirabad; station of the Victorian Baptist Foreign Mission Society (1893), with 31 native workers, 20 outstations, 20 chapels, 18 Sunday schools, 20 village schools, 1 training school for women workers and 512 professing Christians.

BIRTLE: A town in the western part of Manitoba, Canada; station of the PCC (1883), with 1 missionary and his wife, 2 missionary women, and 1 high school.

BISAULI: A village in the Rohilkhand District, United Provinces, India, N. W. of Budaun; station of the ME, with 20 native workers, men and women, 2 chapels, 16 Sunday schools, 6 village schools, 1 Young People's Society, and 1,290 professing Christians.

BISHNUPUR: A town in Bengal, India, S. E. of Bankura; station of the WMS. Statistics included in those of **Bankura**. Name also written Bishenpore.

BISHOP, Artemus: Born at Pompey, N. Y., December 30, 1795; graduated at Union College, 1819, and Princeton Theological Seminary, 1822; sailed as a missionary of the ABCFM in the first reenforcements for the Sandwich Islands, 1822. He was stationed at Kailua, and was associated with Mr. Thurston in the translation of the Bible. After residing twelve years at Kailua, he removed to Ewa, on Oahu, where he labored twenty years with great success. Here he translated *Pilgrim's Progress* and many other books. He never left the islands except once, and that as a delegate to the Marquesas Mission, in 1858. He died at Honolulu, December 18, 1872.

BISRAMPUR: A town in Chota Nagpur, Bengal, India; station of the German Evangelical Synod Missionary Society, U. S. A. (1869), with 2 missionaries, 1 missionary's wife, 1 missionary woman (physician), 22 native workers, men and women, 9 outstations, 10 chapels, 1 Sunday school, 6 village schools, 1 high school, 1 industrial school, 1 theological seminary, 1 orphanage, a hospital, a dispensary, and 670 communicants.

BISTOPUR: A town E. of Calcutta, Bengal, India; station of the BMS (1844), with 4 native workers, 12 outstations, 14 village schools, 1 high school, 13 Sunday schools, 7 young people's societies, and 475 church members.

BITHYNIA: In ancient times a section of Asia Minor, bordering on the Sea of Marmora and the Gulf of Nicomedia. There is no present province of that name, but the term is still applied in general to the same region. It includes especially the cities of Brousa and Nicomedia, with no very well defined limits either to the north or east.

BITLIS: A city of Eastern Turkey, 150 miles southwest of Erzerum. Climate, healthy, dry. Population, 25,000, Mohammedan Kurds and Turks and Christian Armenians. Its situation among the mountains of Kurdistan is peculiarly beautiful, and surrounded as it is by high peaks, it served for a long time as the virtual capital of the Kurds. The rough, turbulent character of the people has often occasioned trouble and even danger; a massacre of Armenians occurred in the city in 1895.

Station of the ABCFM (1859), with 1 missionary and his wife, 3 missionary women, 29 native workers, men and women, 12 outstations, 9 chapels, 3 Sunday schools, 19 village schools, 2 high schools, 1 industrial school, and 250 church members.

BIZERTA: A seaport town and seat of a Roman Catholic bishop, in Tunis, Africa; station of the NAM (1898), with 2 missionary women and 1 Sunday school. Also station of the (Swedish) Women's Foreign Mission Work (1898), with 2 missionary women.

BLACKFOOT CROSSING: A station of the CMS (1883) on the S. Saskatchewan River, Alberta, Canada, with 3 missionaries (1 a physician), 1 missionary's wife, 2 native workers, 1 chapel, 1 high school, 1 dispensary and 94 baptized Christians.

BLACKFOOT LANGUAGE: Belongs to the central group of the North American family of languages. It is spoken by some 7,000 Indians in the Province of Alberta, Canada. It is written with Roman letters.

BLACKLEAD ISLAND: A station of the CMS among the Eskimos, on the W. coast of Cumberland Sound, north of Labrador (1894), with 2 missionaries (1 with his wife), 1 village school, and 5 baptized Christians.

BLANTYRE: Chief town of the Nyasaland (British) Protectorate, Central Africa, situated in the Shirè Hèglelands, S. of Lake Nyasa, at an elevation of 3,000 feet. Population, about 6,500. Station of the CSFM (1874), which has had many difficulties to overcome, some due to early inexperience, some to the intrigues of jealous merchants and some to inevitable collisions with Arab slave dealers. The place is now, however, prospering, has an appreciable commerce and offers safety for life and property. The Church of Scotland has, at Blantyre, 16 missionaries, men and women, of whom 3 are physicians, 22 native workers, 1 chapel, 13 village schools, 1 high school, 1 industrial school, special work among lepers, 4 dispensaries, 1 hospital, 1 printing house and 370 church members.

It is a station, also, of the NBC (1889), with 2 missionaries, 3 native workers, 1 chapel, 1 Sunday school, 1 industrial school, and 100 professing Christians.

BLAUBERG: A town in the northern part of the Transvaal Colony, South Africa. Station of the Berlin Evangelical Missionary Society (1868), with 1 missionary, 11 native workers, 3 outstations and 101 communicants.

BLEBY, Rev. Henry: Born in Winchcombe, England, March 16, 1809. Died May 22, 1882. Missionary under the WMS. He was received into the ministry in 1830 and sent out to the Jamaica district in the West Indies, where he rendered valuable services to the Church of God. He was prominent among a noble band of men who, in the midst of deadly persecution, counted not their lives dear to themselves if they could but mitigate the sufferings of their oppressed fellow creatures. On one occasion the enemies of missions to the slaves seized him, daubed his body with pitch, and took a lighted candle to set the pitch on fire. He was only saved by the brave interference of his wife. The experiment of Wesleyan missions in the West Indies owed much of its success to the courage and faithfulness of Mr. Bleby in the discharge of the difficult duties that devolved upon him.

He was the author of the following works: *Death Struggles of Slavery* (being a narrative of facts in Jamaica during the two years immediately preceding negro emancipation). *Scenes in the Caribbean Sea. Reign of Terror* (W. Indies). *Romance without Fiction; or, Sketches from the Portfolio of an old Missionary.*

BLIND OF THE FEMALE SEX IN CHINA; German Missions to. See GERMANY; MISSIONARY SOCIETIES IN.

BLIND; Missions to the: This is one of the works of general philanthropy for which non-Christian peoples are indebted to Christian missions. Pagan, and more especially Mohammedan, peoples give help to the blind as they do to other impotent folk. The emotion of pity is a characteristic of the human race, of which, happily, traces may be found even where self-seeking sometimes seems to have extinguished all other motives of action. But in the non-Christian countries that habit of thought for the welfare of others is lacking which Jesus Christ teaches His followers. As a rule, in such countries the helplessness of the blind is regarded as a natural calamity for which alleviation cannot be imagined, and which therefore separates them from any possible connection with the interests of social life. Pity for their condition is superficial and finds sufficient expression in occasional doles of food or pence, and only occasionally in the construction of shelters for them. The lot of a sightless one, at the best, if he is one of the common people, is that of a plaintive suppliant who suffers in ragged and lonely uncertainty until death releases him. Schemers for easy gain take advantage of the calamity in some of the Asiatic countries. A blind child is taken in hand and cared for, as a business investment by men who clutch as their due the proceeds of the beggar's appeal to the pitiful. In Turkey, men make it their profession to scour the country in search of such impotent folk in order to hire or buy them from their relatives, and then to exploit their miserable condition on the streets of the cities. In China, it was in past years generally, and in some places still is, the custom of similar harpies to gather up blind girls and house and feed and clothe them in order to make money by thrusting them into a life of debauchery. In such lands the best that can happen to a blind person who is of the poorer classes is to be left alone that people may toss him a beggar's dole and pass by on the other side. But let the Gospel enter such a land and the missionary who is charged to make it known cannot rest until he has devised means of giving the blind the power to read, to earn a living, and to feel, by means of this kindness which appreciates his deeper needs, the love of Jesus Christ for outcasts.

The work of missionaries for the blind cannot here be catalogd in detail. But it is a work which should not be passed by without reference. In China an unusually large per cent. of the population become blind through smallpox, leprosy, and ophthalmia. For neither disease is any sane medical treatment provided by the natives. Filthy and immoral habits, and the brutality of parents who wilfully blind their children through greed of gain, are also causes of blindness in China. As far back as 1857 the mission of the Protestant Episcopal Church (U. S.) at Shanghai established a school for the blind. In the northern part of the empire efforts to help the blind took a new development when William Murray, then a colporteur of the National Bible Society of Scotland, succeeded in applying the Braille system of raised dots to the Chinese characters. His Christian sympathy for the wretched Chinese blind drew the whole power of his mind to their relief, with the result that he solved the problem of enabling them to read books.

The system which Mr. Murray arranged is so simple that even Chinese who can see have found the Braille alphabet of dots more easy to master and use than the quaint but perplexing characters written by their own ancient scribes. Mr. Murray readily obtained money to open a school for the blind at Peking in 1881, which has not only taught blind beggars to read and write and to work for their own support, but has transformed some of these hopelessly dependent creatures into active missionary agents, as Scripture readers, singers of sacred songs, and organists in Christian chapels. The amazement of the natives on seeing a blind child read with his fingers arouses the deepest interest, and becomes a means of turning men's minds to study of the reasons for the intelligent humanity of the followers of Christ.

The Braille system has been adopted by some of the missionary societies, and as the children in the blind schools learn to write it, they also begin preparation of a stock of Bible verses and other useful matter which, once committed to paper, they can read again and again. The Bible societies have made this and the Moon system the means of publishing, in the Mandarin and three local dialects of Chinese, Gospels or other parts of Scripture for the blind.

What Mr. Murray did for the Chinese of the Peking region was done for the people of a good part of Turkey by the late Rev. Elias Riggs, D.D., aided by Mr. G. W. Moon. Some of the Gospels have been prepared for the blind in Armenian and in Turkish. One or the other of these two systems has been adopted for the uses of the blind in Arabic, in seven of the languages of India, in Burmese, in Sinhalese, in the Toba language of Sumatra, and in the language of Uganda, in Africa. Thus in many lands numbers whose case had been given up by their nearest friends as beyond human aid, have been taken in hand for Christ's sake by strangers from beyond the seas and have been caused to see the light.

There are now 12 institutions for the blind in China, maintained by the PN, the CMS, the PE, the CIM, the WMS, the PCE, the Berlin Ladies' Missionary Association, and the German Mission to the Chinese Blind, besides the Murray Mission and another independent mission expressly to the blind. In India 6 such institutions are carried on by the CMS, the CSM, the CEZ, the CP, and the ABCFM. In Japan there are 4 missionary institutions for the blind established by the CMS, the MCC, and an independent mission. Another independent organization carries on a school for the blind in Korea. The PCE has an outdoor mission to the blind in Formosa, and cooperates with the Japanese Government in giving permanent asylum to those who need it. The British Syrian Schools Committee has opened three schools for the blind in Syria, one of them on the ruins of Tyre—that ancient queen of the Mediterranean. In nearly all of these institutions there is provision to endow the pupils with simple industries which will give them occupation and support. But the number of asylums and schools for the blind does not represent the work of missions for these wrecked lives. In every mission field where no such schools exist, individual missionaries teach, and elevate, and comfort, and make happy individuals who but for them would never know the meaning of sympathy. Moreover, this humanitarian work has stirred non-Christians to imitate or support so far-reaching a charity. Even in Turkey, Mohammedans have been led in recent years to copy this part of the teaching of the Christians.

There is no point of comparison between the non-Christian religions and Christianity which reveals a sharper contrast than their idea of what constitutes kindly care for the feeble and helpless. The man who does not know Christ may probably feel pity, but his religion does not direct his pity to reach its proper goal. So he gives the sufferer a penny and leaves him as he was. But the man who has learned from Jesus Christ cannot leave the blind man when he has given him bread. He sees the profounder needs belonging to manhood—the needs of heart and soul and mind. He has to supply these needs by a continual and unflinching sacrifice of himself. But in doing it, he becomes the means of revolutionizing a hopeless and useless life by bringing it within touch of the springs of power in the eternal world. This work for the blind of non-Christian lands would not be done if it were not done by Christian missions.

BLISS, Edwin Elisha: Born at Putney, Vt., April 12, 1817; died at Constantinople, Turkey, December 20, 1892. Graduated at Amherst College in 1837, having for his college mates Henry Ward Beecher, Roswell D. Hitchcock, and Richard S. Storrs. Graduated at Andover Theological Seminary in 1842; sailed for Turkey March 1, 1843, as a missionary of the ABCFM assigned to the Nestorians living in the mountain region along the frontier of Persia. The Turkish Government having refused, on account of the disturbed state of the country, to let an American go to the Nestorian district, Mr. Bliss was temporarily assigned to Trebizond. The demands of other fields proving pressing, he never reached the field to which he was first assigned. Mr. Bliss studied the Turkish and Armenian languages. In 1851 he was sent to open a new station at Marsovan, in the eastern extremity of the province of Sivas, and through ignorance of the country and devotion to his duty he exposed himself to malaria, becoming subject to attacks of intermittent fever, from which he could not count himself free to the very end of his life. After having worked with great success in the Marsovan field, Mr. Bliss, in 1856, was transferred to Constantinople for literary work in the Armenian language. During thirty-six years he was occupied in the department of publication, part of the time in editing the *Avedaper* newspaper, and later in the preparation of books and tracts, many of which have been daily food to the Evangelical Churches of Turkey. During his whole missionary life he esteemed it a privilege and duty to preach when opportunity offered, altho a victim of ague, and working during the week like a slave of the printing-press. Dr. Bliss' influence in mission councils and in native churches alike was extraordinary. The simplicity and piety of his private life, the certainty with which his action was controlled by "common sense unbiased by passion or prejudice," to use the words of one of his associates, "and the mingled devotion, pathos, and humor which characterized his discussions of important matters," caused it to be remarked that while other missionaries of renowned power were at Constantinople at the same time with him they all recognized in Dr. Bliss a peer. Probably all admitted that for uniform soundness of judgment at times of crisis he stood first in the mission. Dr. Bliss preferred to spend time in doing his work rather than in calling attention to it. Hence he was not widely known outside of mission circles, altho his services in Turkey continued nearly fifty years.

BLISS, Isaac Grout: Born at Springfield, Mass., July 5, 1822; graduated at Amherst College, 1844, and studied at Andover and New Haven Theological Seminaries. He married Eunice B. Day, of West Springfield, and in 1847 was ordained a missionary of the ABCFM. Stationed at Erzerum, Eastern Turkey, he was a pioneer in opening up the valley of the Euphrates to missionary influence. Uninterrupted labor and continued traveling, at that time far more dangerous and fatiguing than now, broke down a naturally fine constitution, and in 1852 he was obliged to visit America, and later to resign his connection with the Board. Scarcely a year after his resignation an invitation came to him from the American Bible Society to go to Constantinople as agent for the Levant. The work being less confining, in the winter of 1857-58 he entered upon it with enthusiasm.

He found the agency without any organization at all. There were almost no rules as to the distribution of Bibles, and the greater part of the funds received from their sale was applied to general missionary work. With great tact and patience, and indomitable will, he set to work to bring order out of confusion. His field was very large, covering the whole Turkish Empire (including Egypt, Syria, and Mesopotamia), Persia and Greece. Located at Constantinople, the port by which most missionaries to those lands entered into their fields, and where for many years the annual meetings of the whole missionary force were held, his house was always open, and there were few of those who passed through that did not enjoy its hospitality. He traveled some, tho not as much as he felt essential, directing almost the entire work from the little office that he shared with the treasurer of the mission of the ABCFM at Constantinople. Their cramped and unhealthy quarters were a constant trial, and at last the resolution was formed to build a Bible House for Constantinople corresponding to that in New York. Called home in 1866 to attend the Jubilee of the Bible Society, he pressed the need of such a building. The Society was unwilling to take it up, but allowed him his time to raise the needed money, and in 1867 he returned with the requisite funds. The securing of a site and the erection of the building met with the most determined opposition, but in 1872 the edifice was complete and universally recognized as the handsomest business building in the city. It has since been enlarged as the work has grown. See **Bible House**, Constantinople.

While in the midst of superintending the erection of the Bible House, Dr. Bliss took the time, in 1870, to make a hurried visit to America, and secured the transference to Beirut of the great work of electrotyping and printing the Arabic Bible. This had hitherto been done at the Bible House in New York, and the change seemed to many hazardous, yet by dint of most earnest appeals he secured the endorsement by the Society of a step since recognized to be one of the most important in its history.

Then came the question of the Turkish versions. There were at that time three, in the Arabic, the Armenian, and the Greek characters, all made by different men, and with differences of meaning as well as of idiom. This had long been felt to be most unfortunate, yet there seemed to be no help for it. Dr. Bliss believed that the difficulty could be overcome, and even at the risk of offending some, he pressed for a union of the forces that were revising each version. At last he carried the day, and the Turkish version of to-day is scarcely less a monument to the men who made it than to him whose clear vision and earnest purpose made it possible for them to make it.

Meanwhile, he pressed colportage unceasingly. From 2,500 copies during the first year, the circulation ran up to 56,628 in the twenty-fifth year of the agency.

The winter of 1888-89 was a trying one, and he sought relief in the warmer climate of Egypt, but on February 16, 1889, he passed away in Assiout, Upper Egypt. He was buried by the side of a lifelong friend and fellow-laborer, Rev. John Hogg, D.D., at the very outpost of his agency, whence it had been his desire to push on the Bible work into the heart of Darkest Africa.

BLODGET, Rev. Henry: Born in Bucksport, Me., July 25, 1825. Died in Bridgeport, Conn., May 23, 1903. For forty years a missionary of the ABCFM in China, and for eight years a Corporate Member of the Board. He graduated from Yale College in the class of 1848, and was tutor there from 1850 to 1853. He studied in New Haven and Andover Theological Seminaries, and was ordained as missionary in January, 1854, sailing that same year for China. He arrived at Shanghai in September, 1854, and began to preach in the Chinese language a year later. Dr. Blodget was engaged at Shanghai and at Tientsin ten years, but in 1864 he located at Peking, where he remained until 1894, when, owing to the increasing infirmities of old age, he returned to America. He had a wide influence in Peking, being universally respected by representatives of the Government, missionaries of all societies and the Chinese Christians. For the last thirty years of his life in Peking Dr. Blodget gave his time largely to literary work. He gave his best strength for nearly ten years, with a company of five, to the translation of the New Testament into the Mandarin Colloquial of Peking. He translated 194 hymns and six doxologies, and, besides the New Testament and these hymns, Dr. Blodget translated several lesser works, as *Thomas à Kempis, The Reformed Church Catechism,* by Philip Schaff; *President Edwards' Consecration,* and *Henry and His Bearer.* He also carried from Shanghai a Catechism and Trimetrical Classic, which he rendered into Pekingese Colloquial, and which has been widely distributed in North China. But Dr. Blodget, while giving his time largely to literary work, possessed strongly the evangelistic spirit. Every morning he had a Bible class for helpers and inquirers, and he gave time to preaching in the street chapel in the afternoons. Once or twice in the year he made a tour into the country, and for sixty miles south of Peking these visits exerted great influence for good. His life and labors were a permanent contribution to the cause of missions.

BLOEMFONTEIN: Capital of the Orange River Colony, S. Africa. Population (1890), 3,459. Mission station of the Berlin Evangelical Missionary Society (1875), with 2 missionaries, 10 native workers, men and women, and 370 communicants. Also station of the SPG (1850), with 1 missionary woman. Also station of the South African Wesleyan Methodist Missionary Society, with 71 native workers, 1 Sunday school, 1 village school, 1 Young People's Society and 1,550 professing Christians.

BLORA: A town E. of Samarang, Java, Dutch E. Indies; station of the Neukirchen Missionary Society (1891), with 1 missionary and wife, 7 native workers, 1 chapel and 2 village school.

BLUEFIELDS: A town of 2,000 inhabitants on the Mosquito coast, Nicaragua, Central America.

Station of the Moravian Missions (1848), with 3 missionaries and their wives, 14 native workers, 2 chapels, 2 Sunday schools and 300 communicants.

BLYTHWOOD: A town in the Transkei district of Cape Colony, S. Africa; station of the UFS, with 5 missionaries, 2 of them with their wives, 4 missionary women, 5 native workers, men and women, 4 village schools and 1 theological seminary. Also written Blythswood.

BOARDMAN, George Dana: Born at Livermore, Me., February 8, 1801. In April, 1823, he offered his services to the Baptist Board of Missions, and was accepted. In June of that year he entered Andover Theological Seminary, where he remained two years, sailing for Calcutta July 16, 1825. Because of the Burmese war he remained in the vicinity of Calcutta, occupied with study of Burmese until 1827, when he removed to Maulmain, which became the seat also of the mission in Burma. Sir Archibald Campbell offered Mr. Boardman a fine, large spot of ground for a mission establishment. On this he built a bamboo house costing about $100. The mission and the Board in America, thinking that the field of operations should be widened by the establishment of new stations, Tavoy, about 150 miles from Maulmain, was selected as the site for the new station, and Mr. Boardman, by the unanimous choice of his associates, was appointed to commence it. He took with him Ko-Thah-Byu, the first Karen convert, a young Siamese lately baptized, and four of the boys from his boarding-school, and reached the city of Tavoy, April 9, 1828. He soon commenced public worship in Burman, and inquirers began to present themselves. On May 16 he baptized **Ko-Thah-Byu**, the Karen Christian who had accompanied him. As the result of the indefatigable labors of this remarkable man many of the Karens of the villages scattered over the mountains of Tavoy flocked in from the distant jungles to listen to the truths he taught. Mr. Boardman resolved to visit the Karens in the jungle, and on February 28, 1828, he set out on his first tour, accompanied by Ko-Thah-Byu and another Karen, a professed believer in Christ. So much encouraged was he by the readiness of the people to receive him and give attention to his instructions, that he determined to pursue a course of itinerary preaching among their villages. In these tours he was generally accompanied by Ko-Thah-Byu or some other convert, and some boys from the schools. He usually visited three or four villages a week, preaching in *zayats* or from house to house, and talking with those he met by the way. Some of his journeys were long and dangerous, and often on foot. He also made tours in the mission boat on the river. These labors were continued for three years in great physical debility, to which he was reduced by pulmonary disease. Tho unwilling to slacken his labors on account of his own health, he was obliged by Mrs. Boardman's very critical illness to leave his station and to remove to Maulmain. Soon after his return to Tavoy, Mr. F. Mason joined him as an associate, and on the 31st of January, 1831, they set out together on a visit to the Karens. They reached their destination on the third day, where they found a bamboo chapel erected on a beautiful stream and a hundred persons assembled, more than half of them applicants for baptism. Having lost strength, Mrs. Boardman advised her husband to return to Tavoy, but he replied, "The cause of God is of more importance than my health, and if I return now our whole object will be defeated. I want to see the work of the Lord go on." When, however, it was evident he could not live long, and it was thought best to return without delay, he consented, on condition that the candidates were baptized that evening, to return the day following. So just before sunset he was carried out in his bed to the water-side, and in his presence Mr. Mason baptized thirty-four persons. While being conveyed to the boat from the comfortless roof of the heathen Tavoyer which had sheltered them for the night, he died, February 11, 1831. He was buried on the mission premises, the funeral being attended by all the European gentlemen and officers of the station, with many natives. Tho but thirty years of age and but three years in the service, he had accomplished a great work. Within the last two months of his life 57 had been baptized, all Karens, and at the time of his death the mission church at Tavoy had 70 members.

King (A.), *George Dana Boardman*, Boston, 1875.

BOBBILI: A town of 15,000 inhabitants N. of Vizianagram, Madras, India; station of the BMP (1879), with 1 missionary and his wife, 8 native workers, men and women, 1 chapel, 3 Sunday schools and 85 church members.

BOCAS DEL TORO: A town on the N. coast of the isthmus of Panama, belonging to Panama, and situated at one of the entrances to the lagoon of Chiriqui. Population, 3,000.

Mission station of the UMFC (1865), with 1 missionary, 6 native workers, 3 chapels, 3 Sunday schools, 3 village schools, and 300 professing Christians. Also station of the Jamaica Baptist Missionary Society (1894), with 1 missionary and his wife, 1 village school and 161 church members.

BOCHABELO: A village in the Middelburg district of the Transvaal Colony, S. Africa, lying east of Pretoria; station of the Berlin Missionary Society (1865), with 5 missionaries, 26 native workers, and 1,800 baptized Christians. Also written Botschabelo.

BODINAYAKANUR: A village in the western part of the Madura district, Madras, India; station of the Leipzig Missionary Society (1892), with 13 native workers, 4 village schools, 1 high school, and 300 communicants.

BOELOEH HAWAR: A village S. of Medan, Sumatra, Dutch East Indies; station of the Netherlands Missionary Society (1890), with 3 missionaries and their wives, 6 native workers, 4 village schools and 15 communicants.

BOENISCH, Frederick: A missionary of the Moravians to Greenland (1734). A man of great courage and zeal, his arrival at a time of great discouragement was most opportune. After five years of privation and labor one Greenlander named Kaiarnak received the Gospel, and took up his residence among the missionaries, but was driven away for a time by a band of ruffians, afterward proving his steadfastness by returning. In 1740 Mr. Boenisch married Anna Stack. Their children and children's children have served as missionaries during 160 years, a sixth generation of the family having now entered upon missionary service. It was during Mr. Boenisch's term of service that the brethren ceased to preach the attributes of God, the fall of man, and the demands of the Law, and instead began to preach Jesus Christ. This change was what awakened the consciences of the benighted people, leading them to become true followers of Jesus.

BOGADJIM: A settlement in German New Guinea; station of the Rhenish Missionary Society, with a missionary physician and his wife.

BOGOS LANGUAGE: Belongs to the Hamitic family of languages and is spoken by the Bilin tribe in the North of Abyssinia. It is written with the Amharic letters.

BOGOTA: Capital of the republic of Colombia, on a picturesque and fertile plateau 9,000 feet above the sea. Climate, temperate. Population (1891), 100,000. Mission station of the PN (1856), with 3 missionaries and their wives, 1 missionary woman, 1 native woman worker, 1 village school, 1 high school, and 90 church members.

BOGUTU LANGUAGE: Belongs to the Melanesian family of languages and is spoken in some of the Solomon Islands. It is written with Roman letters, and is also called the Isabel Island language.

BOKHARA: A Russian vassal state in Central Asia, lying between north latitude 41° and 37° and between east longitude 62° and 72°, bounded on the north by the Russian province of Turkestan, on the east by the Pamir, on the south by Afghanistan, and on the west by the Kara Kum Desert.

The modern state was founded by the Usbegs in the 15th century, after the power of the Golden Horde had been destroyed by Tamerlane. The dynasty of the Manguts, to which the present ruler belongs, dates back to the beginning of the last century. The Emir of Bokhara, in 1866, proclaimed a holy war against the Russians, who thereupon invaded his dominions and forced him to sign a treaty ceding the territory now forming the Russian district of Syr Daria and to permit Russian trade. In 1873 a further treaty was signed, in virtue of which no foreigner was to be admitted without a Russian passport, and the state became practically a Russian dependency.

The Russian Trans-Caspian Railway runs through Bokhara from Chargui on the Oxus to a station within a few miles of the capital, and thence to Samarkhand.

The area of the country is about 92,000 square miles and the population is about 1,250,000, belonging mainly to various Turkish tribes. The religion is Mohammedanism, and missions are strictly forbidden, excepting those of the Russian (Greek Orthodox) Church.

Russia in Central Asia, Curzon (G.), London, 1889; *History of Bokhara*, Vambery, London, 1873.

BOHEMIA: A country of Central Europe, formerly an independent kingdom, now a part of the Austro-Hungarian Empire. It has a population of nearly 6,000,000, of whom about two-thirds are Bohemians (Czechs), the remainder being chiefly Germans. The capital and chief city is Prague. The language of the majority is Czech, one of the principal dialects of the western branch of the Slavic languages. Its alphabet is the Latin, and it bears a closer resemblance to the Polish than to any other Slavic language. Agitation for the official recognition of this language, with autonomy for the country, has been long-continued and disturbing. The religion is Roman Catholic, but the number of Protestants is increasing.

Mission work is carried on by the ABCFM among the Roman Catholics, and by the UFCS among the Jews.

BOHEMIANS: The Bohemians, or, as they call themselves, Czechs (Tchekhs), form one of the principal tribes of the Slavic race. They occupy the country of Bohemia in Austria, and number about four millions. They are all Catholics, with the exception of 150,000, who belong to the Protestant Reformed and Lutheran Confession. The first germs of Christianity were planted among them by Cyril and Methodius, missionaries to the Slavs in the 9th century, and the Bohemian Prince Borivoi was baptized by Methodius in 873-74. But Orthodox or Greek Christianity was unable to maintain itself long in Bohemia, and was soon supplanted by Catholicism. With the introduction of Catholic Christianity, Bohemia came under the influence of German civilization and feudalism, and gradually the German element grew stronger and stronger. Beginning with the year 1253 this German influence spread rapidly, so that the Bohemians were in danger of being entirely Germanized. The reign of Charles I., known also as Charles IV., Emperor of the Holy Roman Empire, is considered one of the brightest periods of Bohemian history. He founded the University of Prague in 1348, and thus helped to make the capital of Bohemia the center of a great intellectual and educational movement. The most important period, however, is undoubtedly the time of John Huss and the reformatory movement which he began. Born in 1368 in an obscure village of Bohemia, and educated at the University of Prague, Huss raised his voice against the corruption and depravity of the Roman Church, and demanded a purer form of religion. Almost the whole of Bohemia joined his movement, and the enthusiasm which his sermons and writings evoked was very great. Beguiled into the Council of Constance, where he was called to be heard, Huss was burned at the stake in 1415; but his death was the signal for the beginning of the terrible Hussite wars, which lasted for eighteen years, and the effects of which were felt through the succeeding generations, until 1620, when Bohemia lost her political independence and fell under the dominion of the Hapsburg dynasty of Austria. The Hussite movement in Bohemia cannot be satisfactorily explained by merely regarding it as a religious movement. To understand its full bearing, one ought to bear in mind that it was also a national movement directed against the encroachments of Germanism that threatened Bohemia. The religious element of Hussism did not give all the fruit that might have been expected from it. After the death of Huss his supporters split into two parties, the Taborites and the Utraquists, or Calixtins. The former, which may be considered as the extreme party, carried the principle of the free interpretation of the Scriptures to extremes. The Utraquists, forming the so-called moderate party, were not disinclined to come to terms with the Catholic Church. To the Hussite movement was due the formation of the Society of the Bohemian Brothers, known subsequently by the name of Moravian Brothers, distinguished for its piety, its good works, and the writers it contributed to Bohemian literature.

BOHTAN: A district of Eastern Turkey, S. W.

of Lake Van. It is inhabited chiefly by Kurds, Armenians, and Nestorians, and is a wild region, both in its physical aspects and the character of the people. Mission work is carried on chiefly by the ABCFM, tho sometimes preachers from the Nestorian mission of the Presbyterian Church (North) come among the Syriac-speaking Nestorians.

BOLENGE: A settlement in the Congo Free State, Africa; station of the FCMS (1896), with 2 missionaries and their wives, one of them a physician, 1 Sunday school, 1 village school, 1 dispensary.

BOLIVAR, Ciudad: Capital of the State of Bolivar, in Venezuela, situated on the Orinoco. Population (1891), 11,686. Station of the South America Evangelical Mission, with 1 missionary. Also station of the Venezuela Mission, with 1 missionary and his wife.

BOLIVIA, Republic of: One of the South American republics, lying just north of Chile and the Argentine Republic. Its constitution was adopted August 25, 1836. By the treaty of peace with Chile, in 1880, all the coast territory was lost, and there are now eight provinces, with a total area of 567,431 square miles. Including 1,000,000 Indians, the population numbers 2,300,000, of whom 500,000 are Mestizoes, or half-breeds, and 500,000 whites. La Paz, the capital, has about 65,000 inhabitants. Education is at a low ebb. The nominal religion is Roman Catholic, but the mass of the Indians are pagans. It is the least developed of the South American republics.

The Baptist Convention of Ontario and Quebec has established mission stations at Oruro and La Paz (1899), and the Plymouth Brethren have a station at Sucre.

BOLLOBHPUR: A village in the Nadiya district, Bengal, India; station of the CMS (1849), with 2 missionaries, one with his wife, 24 native workers, men and women, 1 chapel, 3 village schools and 130 communicants.

BOLOBO: A city in the Congo Free State, situated on the Congo River about 125 miles above Stanley Pool. Climate, tropical; population, 20,000; race, Bantu; language, Kibangi. Moral condition, low, owing to belief in witchcraft and to the practise of human sacrifice. Station of the BMS (1888), with 6 missionaries, 5 of them with their wives, 1 missionary woman, 10 native workers, 1 Sunday school, 1 village school, 1 dispensary, 1 printing house, 31 church members.

BOLONDRON: A town of 2,500 inhabitants in the province of Matanzas, Cuba; station of the American Church Missionary Society (1899), with 1· missionary and his wife, 3 native workers, 1 chapel, 1 Sunday school, 1 village school.

BOLPUR: A town S. E. of Suri, Bengal, India; station of the ME, with 1 missionary and his wife, 6 native workers, men and women, 6 Sunday schools, 9 village schools, 1 orphanage, and 30 professing Christians.

BOMA: Capital of the Congo Free State, Africa, situated on the right bank of the Congo River, about 70 miles from its mouth. Formerly it was the advance post of the Dutch and Portuguese traders in the Congo region; station of the CA, of which no statistics are obtainable.

BOMBAY: The capital of the presidency of the same name, and the chief seaport in India. It is situated on the Indian Ocean, at the southern end of the island of Salsette, which stretches along the shore of the continent from north to south for a distance of over twenty miles. At its southern extremity there was formerly a group of quite small islands, separated from each other and from the larger island by narrow channels. Upon these Bombay has been gradually built up; and now, by filling in the channels between the separate islands, these have all been consolidated with one another and with the larger island of Salsette itself. The harbor, which is the safest and most spacious in all India, and one of the finest in the world, lies between the city and the mainland. In 1661, the Portuguese, whose sway was then undisputed all along the western coast of India, ceded the island of Bombay to England as a part of the dowry of the Portuguese princess, Catherine, when she became queen. The population was then supposed to be 10,000. Soon after, Charles II. gave it over to the East India Company for an annual rental of £10. In 1673 its population was reported as 60,000—"a mixture of most of the neighboring countries, mostly rogues and vagabonds." The mixture of races then presented by its population has continued to be a feature of its life ever since. In 1773 Bombay became subject to the Governor-General of India, whose capital was at Calcutta, where it has continued to be ever since, tho the local presidency government was still retained. The growth of the city has been rapid and continuous. Its magnificent harbor has attracted the commerce of the world, and merchants and traders from all parts of the East have flocked to its bazaars. A series of wise and farseeing statesmen have guided its destinies, under whose direction the city has been adorned with fine buildings, connected first by wagon roads, and since 1850 by rail, with all parts of the Indian Empire, furnished with docks, and raised to a position of undisputed preeminence as the chief port of entry and commercial center for all India. Steamers sailing daily bring the city into close connection with Liverpool, London, and the Mediterranean ports. The mails between India and Europe arrive at and depart from Bombay. Steamers sail hence to all parts of the East, and sailing ships seek its harbor from all over the world. It presents more of the appearance of a European city to the traveler than almost any other city of the East. Here the proverbial conservatism and leisurely slowness of Orientals seem to have given place to the quicker and more energetic motions of Western nations.

In population Bombay ranks first of all Indian cities, and among those belonging to the British Empire is exceeded only by London itself. The census of 1901 gave a population of 776,006 souls—Buddhists and Jains, 17,387; Hindus (of all castes and races), 502,851; Mohammedans, 158,713; Parsees, 48,597; Jews, 3,321; Christians, 42,327. The European population by itself, which is mostly British, numbered nearly 10,500. This classification by religion is comparatively simple, but that by race and language is vastly more complex. It is said that Bombay probably contains among its population representatives from a larger number of nationalities than any other city. It is easy to believe that this is so. Nearly every Asiatic race has contributed its quota to the census; the diversity of race and language among the inhabitants of India alone is very great, and among the dwellers in Bombay are individuals from all parts of India, speaking all of the principal tongues which are used anywhere within the limits of India. Africans of many tribes, representatives from nearly every European country, from America, from China, and from widely separated islands of the sea, go to swell the diversity of the Bombay population. The number of languages actually used in Bombay is very great—doubtless a hundred, more or less. For the most part, however, the Mohammedans speak the Hindustani; Hindus are divided chiefly between the Marathi and the Gujarathi; the Parsees use a dialect of the latter tongue; while Hindustani, overstepping the limits of Mohammedan communication, has become in Bombay, as largely throughout India, a *lingua franca*, in low and colloquial forms of which Hindus of different races become intelligible to each other, and to the Europeans, whom some of them serve in divers capacities, and who often learn no other native language. For purposes of education and business, English itself is making rapid progress among all classes. It is now not only possible but easy for a European to live in Bombay, to employ servants, deal with tradesmen, purchase articles in the bazaars, engage in business, and converse on all subjects with intelligent natives, Hindu, Mohammedan, or Parsee, without knowing a single word of any other language than English.

The government supports in Bombay a college (known as the Elphinstone College), a medical college, a school of art, a high school, and many schools of lower grade. The Bombay University, existing not for the purpose of instruction, but merely for that of examination and the conferring of degrees, is accommodated in two elegant buildings on the esplanade, close to the imposing array of structures which give a home to other departments of governmental activity. Colleges and high schools all over the presidency are affiliated with the university, and send up hosts of students every year to pass the examinations prescribed by it and to receive the academic distinction of its degrees.

Hospitals for Europeans, for native patients, and for incurables have been built either by private munificence or public funds. A sailors' home near the principal landing dock affords accommodation to mariners. The Young Men's Christian Association pursues the activities usual to organizations of that name, including hostels for students connected with the different colleges. There is also a central office of the YWCA, with 4 young women in charge. The city has a number of European churches connected with the Church of England, the chief of which is St. Thomas' Cathedral, and several owned by the Established Church of Scotland, the Free Church, the American Methodists, and the Baptists. The Jews have several synagogs. The Roman Catholics, besides their churches, have two large schools for native youth in charge of Jesuit missionaries.

The character of Bombay is determined by its geographical and commercial relations. It is first and chiefly a business center. It is not the capital of a native dynasty and the center of the life and energies of a race, as the adjacent city of Poona was long the capital of the Maratha dynasty and people. It is not a great political center, tho it is the capital of the Bombay Presidency and the seat of the government, and for much of the year the residence of the governor.

It is certainly not a center of intellectual life, tho it contains several institutions of learning, and many newspapers, English and vernacular, are printed there. In the matter of intellectual activity it is easily outranked by Calcutta; nor is it, like Benares, the chief point of a vast religious development. Its life is commercial, and the intensity of its business energy somewhat detracts from the vigor which otherwise its people might throw into religious or intellectual matters.

Bombay has been the scene of Christian missions ever since 1813, in which year Messrs. Gordon Hall and Samuel Nott (joined soon afterward by Samuel Newell) began the first permanent mission in that city, and also the first mission of the ABCFM. The Church Missionary Society began work in 1820, the Scottish Missionary Society in 1823; but in 1835 the work of this organization was transferred to the Established Church of Scotland. In 1843, after the disruption, the missionaries of the Scotch establishment threw in their lot with the Free Church, leaving the mission property in the hands of the old Church. From that time there have been two Scottish missions in the city. The Society for the Propagation of the Gospel began in 1859, and the American Methodists in 1871, tho their work has been chiefly among Europeans and Eurasians (persons of mixed European and Indian parentage), of whom there are many in Bombay. The Bombay auxiliary to the British and Foreign Bible Society was founded in 1813, and the Bombay Tract and Book Society in 1827. Both of these societies have rendered inestimable aid to the cause of evangelism. The two Scottish missions from the first devoted their strength to educational efforts. Each of these missions has long sustained a collegiate institution; hundreds of Hindu, Parsee, and Mohammedan young men have received within the walls of these colleges a good secular education combined with biblical and religious training. The whole force of these various societies now at work in the city, including the Zenana Bible Mission and the BFBS, is 93 missionaries and 201 native workers, men and women, and the aggregate of native communicants reported by the different missions is 1,579.

BOMBAY PRESIDENCY: One of the chief administrative divisions of British India, of which the capital is the city of Bombay. Its territory lies in the western part of India, and its boundaries are on the northwest, Baluchistan and Khelat; on the north, the Punjab; on the northeast, the native states of Rajputana; on the east, the native states of Central India, the Central Provinces, West Berar, and the dominions of the Nizam of Haidarabad; on the south, the Presidency of Madras and the native state of Mysore, and on the west the Indian Ocean. It includes 24 districts in India, besides the little district of Aden, in Arabia, having altogether an area of 124,123 square miles, with a population (1901) of 18,559,561; within the territorial limits of the presidency are a number of native states under the general supervision of the Bombay Government. These include an additional area of 65,761 square miles, with a population of (1901) 6,908,648. The surface of the presidency presents three well marked types of physical appearance. In the northern part the regions of Gujerat and Sindh, with the peninsulas of Kathiawar and Cutch, are for the most part flat, and in their northern and western portions merge into sandy and arid deserts. South of the Narbada River, and for the most part about thirty miles from the sea, stretches the range of mountains known as the Western Ghats. Between them and the sea the narrow strip of land is known as the Konkan, and consists largely of detached ranges of hills, with fertile valleys between, through which flow numerous tidal creeks. East of the mountains is the great upland of the Deccan, nearly 2,000 feet above the level of the sea at its western edge, where it is buttressed by the Ghats. The prevailing religions are Hinduism and Mohammedanism. Christians and Parsees and a few Jews make up together hardly more than two per cent. of the population. It is worthy of note, however, that while during the decade 1891-1901 the whole population of the presidency decreased by 318,753 souls through famine and plague, the Christian population increased by 50,000—from 170,000 to 220,000.

The languages in use in the province of Bombay are Marathi, which is used by nearly one-half of the population; Hindustani or Urdu, used by the Mohammedans; Gujarathi, Kanarese, and Sindhi, which taken together are the speech of more than one-third of the population.

The missionary societies carrying on operations within the borders of this presidency are the following, named as far as possible in the order of their entrance into the province: ABCFM (1813); LMS (1820); CMS (1820); CSFM (1825); UFS (1843); Basel Missionary Society (1837); SPG (1825); PCI (1842); PN (1870); ME (1872); Poona and Village mission; the Christian and Missionary Alliance; the Ramabai Association; the Mission to Lepers; the Kurku and Central India Hill Mission; the Industrial Missions Aid Society; the Zenana Bible and Medical Mission, the Salvation Army, and some others which do not publish statistics.

BOMBE: A settlement about 20 miles N. of the seat of government of the Kamerun Colony, W. Africa; station of the Basel Missionary Society (1897), with 3 missionaries, one with his wife, 24 native workers, 15 outstations, 16 village schools, and (1902) 161 communicants.

BONABERI: A settlement near the mouth of the Kamerun River in the German Colony of Kamerun, W. Africa; station of the Basel Missionary Society (1889), with 5 missionaries, two of them having wives, 24 native workers, 23 village schools, and (1902) 540 communicants.

BONACA ISLAND: The easternmost of the Bay Islands, lying off the coast of Honduras, Central America; station of the SDA (1886), with 3 missionaries and their wives, 3 missionary women, 2 native workers, 10 outstations, 4 chapels, 10 Sunday schools, 3 village schools, and 126 church members.

BONAKU: A settlement on the Kamerun River in the German colony of Kamerun; station of the German Baptist Missionary Society (1891), with 2 missionaries, one with his wife, 1 missionary woman, 5 chapels, 1 village school, 1 industrial school, 1 dispensary and a YMCA. Station also of the Basel Missionary Society, with (1902) 21 outstations, 23 common schools, and 783 communicants.

BOND, Rev. Elias: Born, Hollowell, Maine; graduated at Bowdoin College, 1837; Bangor Seminary, 1840; arrived at Honolulu, May 21, 1841, and labored unremittingly at Mohala, Hawaii, until his death July 24, 1896. He labored under the Hawaiian Evangelical Association. Mr. Bond was distinguished for his successful establishment in Kohala of training schools for Hawaiian boys and girls, and for the personal interest he manifested in the educational, social, commercial, as well as moral and spiritual, life of this people. By a fortunate real estate investment, he was enabled to make munificent donations to missionary boards, and pursue somewhat independently his missionary and educational work.

BONDE LANGUAGE: Belongs to the Bantu family of African languages, and is spoken by an unknown number of people in the Usambara region in the northern part of German East Africa. It is written with Roman letters.

BONDOWOSO: A village in the eastern part of Java, Dutch East Indies, lying S. E. of Surabaya; station of the Java Committee, with 1 missionary and his wife and 1 common school.

BONGAUNDANGA: A settlement in the Congo Free State, W. Africa, situated on the Lopori River S. W. of Upoto; station of the RBMU (1889), with 5 missionaries, 1 with his wife, 1 missionary woman, 2 native workers, 1 chapel, 1 Sunday school, 1 village school, and 1 dispensary.

BONGINDA: A settlement in the Congo Free State, W. Africa, situated on the Lopori River; station of the RBMU (1889), with 3 missionaries, 1 with his wife, 1 native worker, 1 chapel, 1 Sunday school and 1 dispensary.

BONGU: A settlement on the E. coast of German New Guinea; station of the Rhenish Missionary Society, with 1 missionary and his wife, and 1 village school.

BONNY: A town and seaport at one of the mouths of the Niger, in British Nigeria, Africa; station of the CMS (1865), with 3 native workers. Climate, very unhealthy, due to the surrounding country being so flat and swampy. Population, 12,000. Race and language, Ibo, Idzo and Kwa.

BONTHE: A town on Sherbro Island, off the coast of Sierra Leone, W. Africa; station of the CMS (1863), with 10 native workers, men and women, 3 outstations, 1 chapel, 1 Sunday school, 4 village schools, and 270 communicants. Also station of the UB (1855), with 3 native workers, 1 chapel, 1 Sunday school, 1 village school and a Young People's Society.

BOOK AND TRACT SOCIETY OF CHINA. See CHRISTIAN LITERATURE SOCIETY FOR CHINA.

BOONE, William Jones: Born in South Carolina, July 1, 1805; graduated at the University of South Carolina; studied law under Chancellor de Saussure; pursued a theological course at the Seminary of the Protestant Episcopal Church at Alexandria, Va., and having studied medicine with reference to the missionary field, offered himself to the Board of Missions; was appointed and sailed July 8, 1837, reaching Batavia October 22. Here he studied the Chinese language, held an English service, distributed tracts, established schools and found his medical knowledge of great use. Consecrated missionary bishop to China, 1844. In 1846 Bishop Boone began the translation of the Prayer-Book, and engaged in the revision of the New Testament. In 1847 he was chosen one of the committee of delegates from the several missions to revise the translation of the Bible. His ability as a scholar was highly appreciated. He died at Shanghai, July 17, 1864.

Stevens (Bp.), *Memorial Sermon on W. J. Boone*, Philadelphia, 1865.

BORABORA: One of the Society Islands N. W. of Raiatea; station of the Paris Evangelical Missions Society, with 1 native worker, 1 chapel, 1 Sunday school and 315 professing Christians.

BORDA: A village S. of Hoshangabad, Central Provinces, India; station of the Swedish National Missionary Society (1894), with 1 missionary and his wife, 1 native worker, 1 Sunday school and 17 Christians. Also written Bordhai.

BORNEO: The largest island of the East Indian Archipelago, situated directly on the Equator. Area, 272,820 square miles, divided as follows: 1. Under British rule, North Borneo, 31,106; Brunei, 3,000; Sarawak, 35,000; total 69,106 square miles. 2. Under Dutch rule, West Coast, 58,926; South and East districts, 144,788; total, 203,714 square miles. Population: 1. British, 475,000; 2. Dutch, 1,073,289; total, 1,548,289. Of this about one-half—that covering the South and East districts—is mere conjecture. The climate is remarkably healthy for an equatorial island. The surface of a large part of the island is mountainous and well irrigated by rivers. The inhabitants of North Borneo are chiefly Mohammedan settlers; of Sarawak and the Dutch possessions, Malay, Javanese and Chinese settlers and aboriginal tribes, mostly Dyaks, of the Malay race. The Portuguese gained a temporary foothold in the 16th century, but were superseded by the Dutch, who have held permanent control.

British North Borneo is under the jurisdiction of the British North Borneo Company, being held under a grant from the Sultans of Brunei and Sulu.

Dutch Borneo was administered by the Dutch East India Company until its dissolution in 1798, since which time it is governed by a representative of the home government. Mission work is carried on in British Borneo by the SPG in 9 stations, connected with which are 49 workers, both native and foreign, and 13 schools and a Christian constituency of about 5,000, of whom 1,250 are communicants. In Dutch Borneo the Rhenish Missionary Society has 8 stations, with 45 workers of both sexes, 23 schools and about 1,000 communicants.

BORSAD: A town in Gujarat, Bombay, India, N. W. of Baroda; station of the PCI (1860), with 2 missionaries, 3 missionary women, 1 of them a physician, 80 native workers, men and women, 5 outstations, 4 chapels, 44 Sunday schools, 37 village schools, 1 high school, 3 orphanages, 1 dispensary and 191 church members.

BOTTLENOSE: A settlement on the W. coast of the island of Fernando Po, in the Bight of Biaffra, West Africa; station of the Primitive Methodist Missionary Society, with 1 missionary, 1 chapel, 1 Sunday school, 1 village school and 10 communicants.

BOWEN, George: Born at Middlebury, Vt., April 30, 1816. His conversion occurred in the spring of 1844. The May anniversaries of the great missionary societies just at the time, introduced him, as it were, into a new world of Christian enterprise. He at once devoted his life to this missionary work. He studied in the Union Theological Seminary of New York, was ordained by the Presbytery, July 4, 1847, and sailed soon after for India, under appointment of the ABCFM. In January, 1848, he arrived in Bombay, which was the scene of his labors, interrupted only by occasional tours of missionary service in other parts of India.

The social gap separating natives from missionaries led him to decline receiving a salary, and he supported himself, living in a simple way among the natives. Living a life of habitual self-abnegation, he was singularly free from asceticism, and altho uncompromising in his views of Christian principle, he was welcomed in the houses of high and low. It was by his personal ministry that he became known, at first despised and ridiculed, and then esteemed among the people of India. He became secretary of the Bombay Tract Society and editor of the Bombay *Guardian*, acquiring wide influence by the eminent ability and spirituality of his writings, selections from which have been published in America and Great Britain in three volumes severally entitled, *Daily Meditations*, *Love Revealed*, and the *Amens of Christ*.

After a brief illness, early on Sabbath morning, February 5, 1888, apparently while peacefully sleeping, he was not, for God took him. His death produced a deep sensation in Bombay and Western India. Those most competent to form a judgment concur in the estimate that he exhibited a degree of self-sacrificing devotion to which there is perhaps no existing parallel in the whole field of missionary labor.

BRADLEY, Dan Beach: Born at Marcellus, N. Y., July 18, 1804; graduated from a medical college in the city of New York, 1833; sailed July 2, 1834, as medical missionary of the ABCFM; arrived at Bangkok, Siam, July 18, 1835; was ordained by the members of the mission in Siam, November 5, 1838. In consequence of more hopeful calls elsewhere it was decided by the Board, in 1846, to withdraw its mission in Siam. Dr. Bradley and Rev. Jesse Caswell, unwilling to give up the work in which they had engaged, sought maintenance elsewhere. Dr. Bradley returned to the United States in 1847, and was released from the service of the Board, and went out in 1849 in connection with the AMA. He was the first educated physician and surgeon who had visited Siam, and his skill in the healing art seemed to the natives little less than miraculous. His mastery of Siamese was surprisingly accurate, and his translations of the Scriptures were of high value. His published writings, both in English and Siamese, were voluminous. Those relating to Siam and the Siamese, published in the Bangkok *Calendar* for successive years, form the mine whence much of the material of more recent books and articles upon Siam has been extracted. He died at Bangkok, June 23, 1893.

BRAHMANBARIA: A town on the borders of Assam, in Bengal, India. Population (1891) 18,006; station of the New Zealand Baptist Missionary Society (1891), with 1 missionary and his wife, 1 missionary woman, 2 native workers, man and woman, 1 chapel, 1 Sunday school, 1 village school and 7 communicants.

BRAHMO SOMAJ: A modern, reforming, Theistic sect in India, originated by Rammohun Roy, a high caste Brahman of character and scholarship, who from his youth declared that idolatry was contrary to the practice of the ancestors and who purposed to bring his people back to the monotheism of the ancient Vedas. He became so far interested in Christianity that he assisted in the educational work of Dr. Duff and in Bible translation. So far as he was a Christian, he was a Unitarian, and was eclectic toward all the great religions. His leading resulted in the first Hindu Theistic Church, opened in Calcutta in 1830 as the Brahmo Somaj (The Congregation of God). After his death (1833) the Somaj languished for some years until Debendranath Tagore, who had received a good English education, joined it in 1841, and proved an efficient leader and organizer. In 1844 he and twenty others signed the initiatory covenant he had prepared, pledging themselves to abstain from idolatry; to worship no created thing, but only the one God; to lead holy lives and to seek forgiveness through abandonment of sin. This organization, which came to be called the Adi (First) Brahmo Somaj, had by 1847 enrolled 767 covenanted members, and by 1850 the establishment of branches in other provinces had been begun.

With the increase in numbers, marked differences of opinion were developed, especially in regard to the authority of the Vedas. This agitation resulted in the issuing of a new statement by Debendranath called Brahma Dharma (The Theistic Religion). It stated the Four Fundamental Principles of Indian Theism as:

1. In the beginning before this universe was, the one Supreme Being (Brahma) was; nothing else whatever was; He has created all this universe.
2. He is eternal, intelligent, infinite, blissful, self-dependent, formless, one without a second, all pervading, all governing, omniscient, omnipotent, immovable, perfect, without parallel.
3. By worship of Him alone can happiness be secured in this world and the next.
4. Love toward Him, and performing the works he loves constitute his worship.

Subscription to these principles admitted to membership. It was further declared that intuition and the book of nature are the original basis of the Brahman's creed, but divine truth is to be gratefully received from any portion of the Hindu Scriptures or other good book containing it; God is the Heavenly Father, exercising providence and hearing prayer; repentance is the only way of salvation; good works, charity, knowledge, contemplation and devotion are the only religious rites; penance and pilgrimages are useless; the only sacrifice is that of self; there is no distinction of castes, no transmigration; the mission of the Brahma Somaj is to purify the old religion, not to destroy it.

The concessions made did not satisfy the more progressive element, who found a new leader in Keshab Chandar Sen (1838-1884). His faith in the Hindu superstition taught him in childhood had been shattered by a thorough English education in the Presidency College, and in 1858 he joined the Brahmo Somaj, but ere long outstripped Debendranath in advocacy of radical reform. He urged the abolition of all caste distinctions, including the sacred thread, the distinguishing badge of Brahmans. This Debendranath consented to for himself, but declined to impose upon others. Under his leadership rites for deceased ancestors and cremation were remodeled, and steps were taken toward the education and elevation of women, who were admitted to membership in the Society. Marriage reform, including the abandonment of polygamy, of child marriage, and of the permanence of widowhood, was advocated, and in a measure practised. But, having broken with Hinduism, he was not content with a society which purposed only to purify the old faith. With a large number of the younger members he seceded and in 1866 organized a new Theistic Society called The Brahmo Somaj of India, the purpose being to affiliate with it all the other somajes,—a plan which was never fulfilled. The creed of this Somaj included belief in God, the first cause; the immortality of the soul; the two-fold Scripture, nature and intuition; rejection of the incarnation of God, but belief in divinity dwelling in every man, and displayed more vividly in some, as in Moses, Jesus, Mohammed, and other great teachers; admission that the worship of Brahma is the essence of all religions. It declares the brotherhood of man, prescribes duties toward God, self, others, and the lower animals, proclaims the retribution of evil deeds in this world and the next, and urges the pursuit of holiness by worship, subjugation of the passions, repentance, study, good companionship and contemplation, describing salvation as the deliverance from the root of corruption, and unending growth in purity and happiness in Him who is the fountain of infinite holiness and joy. A simple form of service was prepared, consisting of prayer, hymns, reading from Hindu or other Scripture, and a sermon.

For some time the Adi Brahmo Somaj, led by Debendranath and Raj Narain Bose, secretary, and the Brahmo Somaj of India, under Keshab Chandar Sen and his cousin, Pratrap Chandar Mozoomdar, as Secretary, with "The Indian Mirror" as its organ, continued in not unfriendly rivalry. But the latter society was much perturbed by Keshab Chandar Sen's increasing mysticism, his assertion of his own special inspiration and authority, and finally by the marriage of his daughter of fourteen to a youthful Maharaja, contrary to the principles of the marriage reform and the Native Marriage Act of 1872, which he had championed. A considerable portion of the membership seceded and in 1878 organized at Calcutta the Sadharana (General) Brahmo Somaj, with Ananda Bose as president. After an effort to lead the Somaj movement Mozoomdar gave over the attempt and went into retirement.

As an organized movement the Brahmo Somaj was at its height about 1880, when 149 Somajes were reported throughout India. Latterly it has been much less in evidence. Its result is thus summed up by Gustav Warneck: "The movement originated from an apprehension of religious truth, but it degenerated more and more, either to an ordinary rationalistic liberalism, or to a mysticism rich in phrases and ceremonies, and spending its whole energy in words. Tho in language much inclined to Christianity it has not in the whole proved a bridge to Christianity, nor has it exerted any noteworthy reformatory influence in heathenism. Nevertheless it is a characteristic symptom of the religious ferment which the Christian leaven, along with Western education, has begun to stir among the Hindus."

Williams (M.), *Brahmanism and Hinduism;* Hopkins (E. W.), *The Religions of India;* Bose (Ram Chandra), *Brahmoism,* New York, 1884 (Funk & Wagnalls).

BRAINERD, David: Born at Haddam, Conn., April 20, 1718. His parents were cultivated as well as religious people. He himself was inclined from early childhood to take an interest in religious matters, but he considered that he did not really commit the guidance of his life to Jesus Christ until he was 20 years old. This once decided he was wholly and permanently committed to live for his Master.

He felt the duty of teaching Christianity to the Indians, and went to Long Island for that purpose. But later (1742) he was appointed, on behalf of the Scottish Society for the Promotion of Christian Knowledge, to work among the Indians living between Stockbridge, Mass., and Albany, N. Y. Later he was sent to the tribes on the Delaware River in Pennsylvania, and in New Jersey between the Delaware and the sea coast. During the time of this service he sent his journal regularly to Scotland, and the Society there published it in 1746, the first part under the title *Mirabilia Dei inter Indicos*, and the second part as *Divine Grace Displayed*.

It is hard to realize now the brave self-denial involved at that time in this young man's going alone into a dense and trackless forest to live among savages, many days' journey from any white settlement. As Brainerd wrote, he "had none to converse with but rude and ignorant Indians," except when he found himself obliged to plead the cause of the Indians against the avarice of conscienceless whites who wished to brutalize and rob them. But he found a reward in seeing some remarkable instances of changed lives produced by the power of the Holy Spirit among his Indian friends. He was more than content with his life, and worked on in increasing feebleness—often prostrated by sickness, but giving up only when his life was worn out. Then he painfully made his way back to New England to die. The end came October 9, 1747, at Northampton, Mass., when Brainerd was 29 years old.

This young missionary was not remarkable for learning; he accomplished no great and widespread results in the field which he had chosen. But his journals are full of life and power to this day. They are a true record of a simple life—a "human document" which shows mistakes, shortcomings and bitter regrets as faithfully as longings for a higher life, craving after God, and a consuming desire to glorify God by winning the souls of the savages to a godly life. So the man's character impresses the reader; his lofty principles and aims, his saintliness, his loyalty to Jesus Christ; and does not fail to arouse desires to follow his example. It is through this quality of his journals that Brainerd's greatest achievement is the lasting impression made by his character upon the Church in America and Europe. It was Brainerd's character which made Jonathan Edwards a missionary to the Indians of Stockbridge; it was to Brainerd's memoirs to which Henry Martyn traced his decision to become a missionary; to those simple records of a godly life, too, William Carey was indebted for much of that inspiration which shaped his decision to be a missionary tho he had to go alone. Brainerd was a true, noble man and a Christian hero of that small class of heroes whose lives seem to shape history.

David Brainerd, Wesley (J.), Bristol, 1768; Edwards (J.), revised by Dwight (S.), New Haven, 1822, and New York, 1884; Sherwood (J. M.), New York, 1887.

BRASS: A district in the Niger delta on the coast of W. Africa. The region is flat and touring can be done in the dry season only, the missionaries wearing long water boots and tramping through the thick black mud of the mangrove swamps. The people are fetish worshipers, paying chief worship to the great serpents which abound. The CMS has carried on two stations since 1868, called Brass Tuwon and Brass Nimbi. The missionaries are 7 men and women and the native workers 3. There are schools with an industrial department, a dispensary, and about 600 avowed Christians in the district, of whom 51 are communicants.

BRASS NIMBI. See NIMBI.

BRAYTON, Rev. Durlin L., D.D.: In the year 1837 Mr. Brayton went to Burma under the ABMU, and he labored in the Pwo Karen Mission until the year 1900, visiting America but twice during this long period of service. As the oldest missionary in Burma, as the leading missionary among the Pwo Karens for many years, and as the translator of the Bible into the Pwo Karen dialect, he was widely known and greatly honored on the mission field. During his service as a missionary he saw Burma develop from a province of little importance to the most prosperous province in India; and he lived to see the dominion of Great Britain increase from detached possessions to the control of the entire territory of the Hindus, and he heard the Queen of Great Britain and Ireland proclaimed the "Empress of India." Twice the degree of Doctor of Divinity was conferred upon him. Shortly before his death the Pwo Karen Association was held in Rangoon, in the compound of which he lived; and to his fellow workers this Father in Israel spoke this touching valedictory: "It has been my highest pleasure to seek first His Kingdom and do His Will. By His grace I have been enabled to fight the good fight and keep the faith. But when it shall please the loving Father He will call me to Himself to be with Christ forever. I know there is a crown of glory laid up for me that fadeth not away." He died at Rangoon April 23, 1900.

BRAZIL: The United States of Brazil lie between the 4th degree of north and the 33d of south latitude, and the 35th and 72d west longitude, including within their bounds about two-fifths of the whole South American Continent. This youngest born of the American republics measures from north to south 2,000 miles, and from east to west 2,500 miles, thus covering an area of about 3,200,000 square miles, but little less than the whole continent of Europe. It borders upon all the South American countries except Chile and from the vast extent of its territory and the immense value of its undeveloped natural resources is bound to play an important part in the history of the New World. The surface of the republic may be roughly divided into three great basins—one at the north, formed by the Amazon and its tributaries; another at the south, formed by the streams which united produce the Parana, one of the principal branches of the Rio de la Plata, and, lying between the two, the section drained by the São Francisco, the third river in size in South America.

Climate: In so vast a territory, with such great differences of altitude, there are, of course, many varieties of climate. On the whole, however, with the exception of some of the towns along the seacoast and the valley of the Amazon, the country in general is salubrious; even in the seaboard towns the mortality is not above, rather below, that of the large cities of Europe. In the greater part of the country the hot season is also the rainy season, which lasts for three or four months, when, altho the days of continuous rain are few, the afternoon showers fall with great regularity, lasting from ten minutes to an hour or two, and thus, lowering the temperature and refreshing the air, insure cool nights.

The most prevalent diseases are pulmonary consumption, intermittent fevers, and rheumatism. Leprosy and goiter are common. Epidemics of yellow fever occur only at intervals in some of the seacoast towns. The population, according to the last official census (1890), was 14,333,915, of whom 6,302,198 were whites, 4,638,495 of mixed blood, 2,097,426 negroes, and 1,295,796 Indians. The Indian element predominates in the northern states. A census was taken in 1900, but was rejected as tainted with error.

History: Brazil was discovered about the year 1500, and was soon after taken possession of by the Portuguese and continued to be a colony of Portugal till 1822, when its independence was proclaimed by the son of the King of Portugal, who was acting as prince-regent. He assumed the title of Pedro I., Emperor of Brazil, and in 1824 gave the country a constitution which in its main features was considered liberal. In 1831 he abdicated in favor of his son, the late Dom Pedro II., who was at that time only five years old. The government was by regents from that date till 1840, when the emperor's majority was proclaimed, altho he was but fourteen years of age. Dom Pedro II., after having occupied the throne for a half century, less one year, was deported in November of 1889, when the republic was proclaimed. As a natural result of its history the language of the country is Portuguese. It is a beautiful language, compact, expressive, flexible, and well adapted for oratory and literature. The literature is principally rich in fiction and poetry, the few scientific works being mostly translations from the French. As French is considered a necessary part of a liberal education, all the professional men read it, and generally more than half the books on their shelves are in that language, while French novels of all sorts form the staple literary diet of the ladies of the wealthier classes.

The established religion of the empire was Roman Catholic. Under the republic, equality between all forms of religion has been declared, but the government continues to provide for the maintenance of existing functionaries of the Roman Catholic Church.

Qualities of the People: The Brazilian people are, in general, hospitable, generous, charitable, gay, courteous, communicative, quick at learning, rather fond of show, somewhat ceremonious and proud, rather inclined to look down upon labor and laborers, but with a remarkable suavity and a native politeness which is as general in the lowest as the highest classes. Tho not as excitable as the Spanish, there is still a strong element of jealousy in their disposition, and a tendency to vindictiveness which gives rise to many homicides in the course of a year, tho crimes against property are much fewer than in most European countries.

The race as it exists to-day is the result of a combination of widely diverse ethnical elements, molded in a great degree by ecclesiastical influences. The typical Brazilian is small of stature, with elegantly diminutive feet and hands, slightly built frame, nervous and bilious temperament, bloodless and sallow complexion, and a generally anemic and wornout look—evidently wanting in the strength and energy to cope with the difficulties to be encountered in developing a new country.

The bloodless revolution in Brazil, by which a country nearly as large as the whole of Europe passed from a monarchical to a republican form of government, with no interruption of the function of government, no injury to its commerce, no interference with the regular march of business, no mobs or fighting, emphasized certain peculiarities of Brazilian character which merit attention on the part of those who expect to engage in missionary labor among them.

One element of Brazilian character which unquestionably had a great deal to do with the quiet advent of the republic, was the prevalent intellectual sluggishness, which indisposes the people in general to take the trouble to think out and decide any matter for themselves. In the great majority of cases the readiness with which they transferred their allegiance from one government to another was due not so much to want of fidelity to political convictions, as to the total absence of convictions on the subject.

The lower classes have been accustomed for so many centuries to leaving their consciences in the hands of the priests, and yielding them an unreasoning obedience, that the habit of blindly following their leaders has become a second nature to them; so when the republic came they did what was most natural, accepted it, because those whom they had been accustomed to follow accepted it.

Even among the educated classes there is an intellectual apathy which shows itself in all departments of intellectual activity—science, philosophy, politics and religion—and this is nothing more than the natural result of the policy persistently pursued by the Church of Rome to repress speculation and original thought, and to allow its votaries free exercise of their intellectual powers only along two lines of activity—money-making and amusement.

In view of these intellectual conditions of the rising generation in Brazil, the great importance of educational work there becomes evident. While confessedly an indirect evangelizing agency, it is, perhaps, one of the most important in the present crisis. There is almost no positive opposition to the Gospel; it is simply ignored by many who admit that it is a very good thing, but who are unwilling to make the intellectual effort necessary to investigate its claims, and to think the matter out for themselves.

The change of government, by throwing upon the people the management of their own affairs, will gradually force the people to think for themselves. It is of the first importance, therefore, that measures be taken at once to turn the newly awakened intellectual activity in the right direction, as well as to make accessible to the people the materials for a right judgment in science and religion.

The prominent moral characteristic of the Brazilian people is a very great lack of conscientiousness, an almost complete absence of the feeling that everything must give way to right and duty. The result of this has been referred to in speaking of their physical characteristics. It has also been prominent in their political history. One of the first measures of republican government was a general decree that all officeholders who gave in their adhesion to the new government within a certain time would be continued in office, while those who refused to do so would be immediately replaced by others. The result of this measure was a wholesale coat-turning, which would have been amusing had it not been so sad an indication of the utter lack of principle on the part of so large a portion of the best citizens. Altho many had just before been ardent monarchists, and nearly all had voted for the monarchical candidate in the recent elections, not one in a hundred declined to accept the offered conditions, and the State and municipal machinery moved on without the slightest hitch.

The police of Brazil are a military organization, wear soldier's uniform, carry guns, and in their ordinary patrol work use sword bayonets. As soon as these soldier-police, scattered all over the country, received orders from their superior officers to accept the republic, they tore the crowns from their caps and proclaimed a change of government. Outside of the large cities the number of these police agents was utterly insignificant, and they could have been easily overpowered, but even the most ardent monarchists when they found themselves face to face with the military, and called upon to risk some personal injury for the sake of their political opinions, yielded at once. It was not cowardice, for the Brazilians are not a cowardly people, but simply the feeling that it was not worth while to risk anything for a mere opinion. The priesthood, the whole effect of whose teachings for centuries has been to obliterate the inherent distinction between right and wrong, and to confuse the minds of the people on the fundamental principles of ethics, is without doubt chiefly responsible for this demoralization.

Conditions of Life: The superior wisdom of "The Fathers," and the necessity of accepting as final their ideas and judgments in all matters of faith and doctrine have been drilled into the people from their earliest infancy for many successive generations, until the habit of looking backward seems to have become ingrained into the Brazilian nature, leading them to hold on with an almost religious pertinacity to old-fashioned business methods, antiquated modes of transportation and farming (solid-wheeled oxcarts and packmules compete with railroads in some parts of the country, and not one farmer in a thousand has ever seen a plow), and the most unhygienic ways of living and eating. The unparalleled progress of the United States is, doubtless, largely owing to the fact that every man seeks to improve upon the methods of his father, and eagerly experiments with any proposed change which promises to be an improvement. The average Brazilian, however, regards any innovation with suspicion, simply because it is an innovation, and is very apt to receive suggested improvements with a smile of half-scornful superiority, and to say: "Your implements and methods are very good for you and your country, but the ways of our fathers, who have been working here for centuries, are doubtless best for us in this country." This difference of mental attitude is of itself enough largely to account for the difference between the two countries, and for it the Church of Rome is largely, if not wholly, responsible.

It is suggestive that even the roads through the country are only cared for as they have to do with the parish churches. Once a year, upon an appointed day, all landholders are required to present themselves at their respective parish churches carrying hoes, brush hooks, or axes. Then all start together for their homes, cleaning and repairing the roads as they go; dividing as they successively reach the turning leading to their houses, thus leaving a wide cleared road from each house to the parish church. These roads were formerly called sacramental roads, as, in order to incite to the prompt and faithful performance of this task, the priests used to refuse to carry the sacrament to the dying except over a well-prepared road of the regulation width. There are no road inspectors and no provision made for the care of crossroads, even tho leading to a railroad station. So all over the country there has been a constant effort to make everything center in the Church.

The doing things for show and effect is a prominent Brazilian characteristic. "Para Inglez ver," for the English to see, is an expression applied originally to parliamentary measures which it was known at the time would have a good effect upon outsiders, especially upon investors in that land whose ready money has done so much to develop the resources of this country; but it has passed into proverbial phrase to indicate whatever is done for show or effect. The tendency which this phrase characterizes, and of which the late emperor was thought to have been an illustrious example, is evident in all departments of the social, political, and business life of the Brazilian people. Their style of dressing and building, their business and professional methods, their school system and newspaper articles, public speeches and private entertainments, all reflect the soulless externality which is characteristic of their religious life.

Education: So-called religious instruction occupies the principal place in the public schools, hours being spent in learning by heart the prayers and liturgies of the Church in an unknown tongue, and another considerable part of the time in memorizing the Catechism, which, being learned parrot-like without explanation, is almost equally unintelligible to the pupils. As a result it is not at all unusual to find Brazilian children who have been at the public schools for two or three years, but can barely spell through a sentence, and are ignorant of the simplest rules of arithmetic. In the rural districts one often comes across children who, having learned out of books copied by the teachers, are quite familiar with handwriting, but cannot read print at all.

Following the system of rote teaching, which is the only one admissible in their religious instruction, the sole aim of the teacher, even in the higher schools, seems to be to store the memory; no attempt is made to develop the reasoning powers or to encourage original thought or investigation. The child's head is stuffed with lists of names, numbers and rules, without any attempt to explain principles or verify or apply them in practice. Mathematics are taught most superficially, while the generally received test of an educated person is the ability to speak a number of languages, like the last emperor. As a consequence, tho linguists are common, scientists are very few, indeed. About the only thing that is tolerably well taught is Latin, and that only because it is an essential part of the priestly education.

Under such circumstances it is not surprising that fully 84 per cent. of the population is returned as illiterate. Yet the land has been under the care of the Church for 250 years, and when William Penn made his treaty with the Indians the Archbishop of Brazil already had a splendid cathedral and all its appurtenances at Rio de Janeiro.

Early Attempts at Evangelization: It is a very deeply interesting fact that the very first effort of the Christian Church after the Reformation to engage in foreign missions was that of the church at Geneva to send the Gospel to the inhabitants of Brazil. Coligny, the great French Huguenot, and other friends of the truth conceived the idea of establishing a Protestant colony in South America as a place of refuge for their persecuted brethren.

In 1555 an expedition, consisting of three small vessels, under the command of one Villegagnon, a distinguished French naval officer, sailed from Havre de Grace to what is now the harbor of Rio de Janeiro, where they established themselves on an island, called to this day Villegagnon, in honor of the leader, and, as he afterward proved to be, treacherous destroyer of this expedition. Their joyous reception by the natives, who were at war with the Portuguese, and other circumstances seemed to warrant high hopes of success.

On the return of the vessels to Europe great interest was awakened for the establishment of the reformed religion in those remote parts; and the church at Geneva, under Calvin and his colleagues, sent two ministers and fourteen students to accompany the second expedition. However, soon after these new colonists reached their destination, the real and villainous character of Villegagnon revealed itself in a series of annoyances and persecutions against the faithful Huguenots, who, having gone thither with the hope of enjoying full liberty of conscience, found their condition worse than before. The ruin of the colony was soon consummated. Many of the colonists returned to Europe. Of those who remained, three were put to death by their infamous persecutor, and others fled to the Indians and Portuguese. Among the latter was one named John Boles, who is noted, even in the annals of the Jesuits, as a man of considerable learning, being well versed in both Greek and Hebrew. Escaping from Villegagnon, John Boles went to St. Vincente, near the present site of Santos, the earliest Portuguese settlement in that part of the country, where the Jesuits had a colony of Indians catechized according to their mode. According to the Jesuit chroniclers themselves, the Huguenot minister preached with such boldness, eloquence and erudition that he was likely to pervert great numbers of their adepts. Unable to withstand him by arguments, they caused him to be arrested, with several of his companions. John Boles was taken to Bahia, about a thousand miles distant, where he lay in prison eight years. When, in 1567, the Portuguese finally succeeded in expelling the French from that part of their dominions, the governor sent for the Huguenot prisoner and had him put to death on the present site of the city of Rio de Janeiro, in order, it was said, to terrify his countrymen, if any of them should be lurking in those parts.

The Dutch attempted to establish themselves at different points in the northern part of the country, from Bahia to Maranhão, during more or less of the second quarter of the 17th century. Godly pastors accompanied their expeditions and preached a pure Gospel in their settlements. But this can hardly be classed as missionary effort for the permanent dwellers of the land; and all trace of their labors seems to have passed away with the language and authority of the bold invaders, except the mention by Southey, in his *History of Brazil*, that they had prepared a catechism in the language of the Indians and other books of an evangelical character in Portuguese.

The ABS and the BFBS were the first societies to attempt in recent times the evangelization of the Brazilians. Several individuals went to Brazil as missionaries about the same time, but their aim was to benefit seamen and others of their own countrymen. Of such were Messrs. Spalding and Kidder, of the ME Church, who labored in Rio de Janeiro between 1836 and 1842. A missionary of the American and Foreign Christian Union followed these pioneers with the same purpose in view. The first evangelistic mission in Brazil conducted in the Portuguese language seems to have been that carried on from 1855 to 1876 at his own expense by Dr. Kalley, formerly of Madeira.

In 1859 the PN commenced its mission in Rio de Janeiro. There are now in Brazil 28 mission stations maintained by 13 different societies in America and Great Britain, and manned by about 60 missionaries of both sexes. The extent of this missionary effort is less striking when it is realized to be the only evangelistic effort made for fourteen million of people. For the spiritual wants of 140,000 Protestant foreign residents, twice this number of chaplains and pastors have been provided.

South America, Protestant Missions in, Reach (H. P.), and others, New York, 1900; *Brazil and the Brazilians*, Kidder (J. C. and D. P.), New York, 1896.

BREATH, Edward: Born in New York, January 22, 1808. Highly recommended as a Christian and "an accurate, neat, ingenious, and every way competent printer," he was appointed by the ABCFM, and sailed July 21, 1839, for Urmia, Persia. In 1847 he visited the United States, was married, and reembarked, 1849. He cut the matrices and cast for the mission beautiful fonts of Syriac type with a hand before unpractised in that art, but which made a rare and complete success. He thus saved thousands of dollars to the American Board. Through the press under his charge he issued more than 80,000 volumes, including several editions of the Scriptures in modern Syriac, thus giving to the people about 16,000,000 pages in a language never before printed. He died of cholera in 1861 at Seir, near Urmia, Persia.

BREKLUM MISSIONARY SOCIETY. See GERMANY; MISSIONARY SOCIETIES IN.

BRETHREN, Missions of the. See CHRISTIAN MISSIONS.

BRETHREN'S SOCIETY for the Furtherance of the Gospel among the Heathen. See MORAVIAN MISSIONS.

BRIDGETOWN: Capital of the island of Barbados, West Indies, on a large open roadstead, Carlisle Bay. Population (1891), 20,000, among whom are many white people. Station of the

Moravian Missions (1829), with 1 missionary and his wife, 29 native workers, men and women, 2 chapels, 3 Sunday schools, 5 village schools, and 605 professing Christians. Also station of the SDA (1890), with 4 missionaries and their wives, 9 native workers, 2 chapels, 10 Sunday schools, 1 village school, 1 book depot, and 605 professing Christians. Also station of the Salvation Army.

BRIDGMAN, Elijah Colman: Born at Belchertown, Mass., April 22, 1801, of Puritan ancestry. Was converted in a revival before he was twelve years of age. He graduated at Amherst College, 1826, and at Andover Theological Seminary, 1829. The ABCFM proposed to him while in the seminary to go to China as its missionary. He acceded, was ordained October 6, 1829, sailed on the 14th, and reached Canton, February 25, 1830.

In May, 1832, Mr. Bridgman was chosen editor of the *Chinese Repository* and continued to edit it for nearly twenty years. In 1839 the measures taken by the Chinese to suppress the opium traffic resulted in war with England, which interrupted the operations of the mission at Canton. In 1842 the war terminated, and by the treaty of Nanking five ports were opened, and Hongkong ceded to the English. Thither Mr. Bridgman was removed. About this time he prepared the *Chinese Chrestomathy*, a volume of 730 pages. In 1844 he was secretary of legation to Mr. Cushing, sent by the United States Government on a special mission to China, and of his services Mr. Cushing spoke in high terms. After the conclusion of this enterprise Dr. Bridgman's time was divided between the *Repository*, the revision of the Scriptures, preaching at the hospital, and the instruction of a Bible class. In 1847 he removed to Shanghai to aid in the revision of the Scriptures. Early in 1852, after an absence of twenty-three years, he visited the United States for his health. In 1854 through him a new mission was commenced in Shanghai, of which he was the senior member till his death in 1861.

Tho his great work was that of translation, he distributed tracts and religious books, and preached to individuals or companies in streets and villages wherever he could gather them. He was interested also in whatever could in any way promote the welfare of China, and was always ready to perform his part for that object. When the plenipotentiaries of the four great treaty powers—England, France, Russia and the United States—were conducting their negotiations which resulted in the Tientsin Treaty of 1858, he was consulted by them, and frequently translated official documents for them. In his thirty-two years in China he was more intimately connected with and known by the foreign community at Shanghai and Canton than any other missionary, and by all was highly esteemed.

BRINDABAN: A town situated on the Jumna River near Muttra, in the United Provinces, India; station of the ME, with 2 missionary women, one of them a physician, 29 native workers, 20 Sunday schools, 6 village schools, 1 high school, a Young People's Society and 590 professing Christians.

BRITISH AND FOREIGN BIBLE SOCIETY: About the middle of the 18th century, during the revival that spread over England, interest was aroused in the various means for the promotion of religious knowledge, both at home and abroad, and several societies were formed which made Bible distribution one part of their aim, or their sole object within restricted bounds. Of such were the Society for the Propagation of the Gospel in Wales, established about 1662; the Society for Promoting Christian knowledge, 1698; the Society for the Propagation of the Gospel in Foreign Parts, 1701; the Book Society for Promoting Christian Knowledge among the Poor (London), 1750; the Religious Tract Society (London), 1779; the Bible Society, 1780, restricted to labors among soldiers and seamen, and afterward called the Naval and Military Society; the Dublin Association, 1792, and the French Bible Society (London), 1792, for circulating the Bible among the Catholics of France. The French Revolution cutting off communication between the two countries, the funds were turned to the distribution of the Scriptures among "poor Catholics and others in the United Kingdom of Great Britain and Ireland." None of these societies contemplated *universal* distribution of the Scriptures, nor indeed contemplated or admitted the cooperation of the different parties and sections of evangelical Christendom.

The Rev. Thomas Charles, of Bala, Wales, aroused by the dearth of Bibles in that section, and the difficulty of securing the needed supply from existing organizations, visited London in 1802 and conferred with Rev. Jos. Hughes, William Wilberforce, Charles Grant and others. The result was a conference, on a general plan drawn up by Samuel J. Mills, on March 7, 1804, at the London Tavern. About three hundred persons, representing different denominations, were present. Granville Sharp was elected chairman, and the Rev. Mr. Owen (afterward clerical secretary), deeply stirred by the altogether novel spectacle of different denominations met in union to promote one glorious cause, moved the resolutions embodying the name and general form and constitution of the British and Foreign Bible Society. These were "adopted with unanimous demonstrations of cordiality and joy," and more than £700 was immediately subscribed. The committee appointed at this meeting afterward proceeded to adjust the machinery of the Society. Rev. Josiah Pratt, secretary of the CMS, to represent the Church of England, Rev. J. Hughes, the Dissenters, and Rev. Mr. Steinkopff (afterward replaced by Rev. J. Owen), foreign Christian Churches, were chosen secretaries. A prospectus was then prepared and widely distributed. Lord Teignmouth became the first president. Among the first vice-presidents were the bishops of London, Durham, and Exeter, and William Wilberforce.

The new society was heartily received. The Presbytery of Glasgow, the Synod of Glasgow and Ayr, and other ecclesiastical bodies directed contributions to be received for it from all the churches and chapels within the bounds. Wales, stimulated by Mr. Charles, of Bala, sent a contribution the first year of about $9,500, mostly from the poorer classes. Germany, Switzerland and other European countries hailed the society with delight. Nuremberg was the seat of its first foreign branch. It began its career with such general support as was a prophecy of its worldwide usefulness.

Organization. The conduct of the business of the Society is entrusted to a committee of 36 laymen, of whom six are foreigners, resident in London or vicinity, 15 are members of the Church of England, and 15 belong to other denominations of Christians. Thirty of these who shall have most frequently attended the meetings, are eligible for reelection. This committee appoints all officers except the treasurer. The president, vice-presidents and treasurer are members of the committee *ex officio*, as also the secretaries for the time being, no other person deriving any emolument from the Society having that privilege. Subscribers of various amounts are annual or life members or governors, and every clergyman of the Church of England and every Dissenting minister, who is a member, is entitled to attend and to vote at all meetings of the Committee.

The executive staff of the Society includes two secretaries, four superintendents of the editorial, literary, home and publishing departments, two assistant secretaries, fourteen district secretaries in England and Wales, six secretaries in India and South Africa, and twenty-four foreign agents in different parts of the world.

The first auxiliary was formed in 1809, and in ten years 629 auxiliaries had been formed in Great Britain. The Society now has over 7,900 auxiliaries, branches and associations, of which over 5,860 are in England and Wales. These meet their own expenditures, including in some cases colportage, etc., and remit the balance of their collections to the Society. The Society has also about 250 trade depots in the London metropolitan district, aside from those in other parts of the United Kingdom.

Development of Work: Immediately upon the organization of the Society steps were taken to obtain large supplies of the Welsh Scriptures, and subsequently the Irish, Gaelic, Manx, and, for the Channel islands, the French. Stereotype printing had just come into use, and the committee decided to countenance it, and ordered stereotype plates in several languages. The first New Testament printed expressly for the Society, brought out in September, 1805, was in English, and was printed from stereotype plates, the first instance of the use of that process in the printing of the Scriptures. Editions in Spanish and French were printed for the 30,000 prisoners of war at that time in the country, and other editions for resident foreigners, notably Germans.

In 1812 the demand for English Scriptures became so great that the two universities (Oxford and Cambridge) added to the number of their presses, and his Majesty's printers were induced to engage in the work as their patent permitted. It is from these three (the only authorized) sources that the supply of English Scriptures is obtained by the Society.

In connection with the abolition of slavery throughout the British colonies (August 1, 1833) a special fund of £16,249 5s. 9d. was raised amid great enthusiasm to put a copy of the New Testament into the hands of every freedman who could read or was the head of a family. This measure was ultimately accomplished, August 1, 1836, when 100,000 copies were thus disposed of. Other similar special exigencies have been met in the same liberal manner. From its earliest history the Society has had to meet considerable and at times bitter opposition. An element in the Established Church looked on its recognition of dissenters with disfavor, and tried to have it print the Prayer Book as well as the Bible; its willingness to assist continental societies that used the Apocrypha also raised much opposition, and occasioned the withdrawal of the Scotch Association and the subsequent organization of the National Bible Society of Scotland, altho in 1827 such assistance was forbidden. Later an attempt to impose a trinitarian test of membership failing, the Trinitarian Bible Society was formed, and the controversy over the word "baptize" resulted in the Bible Translation Society of the Baptists.

Of specific interest are the publishing of the first penny Testament in 1834 and of Scriptures in raised letters for the blind in 1837; the lowering of the price of Bibles in 1839 through the cessation of the monopoly of the King's printer in Scotland, the introduction of colportage into Great Britain in 1844, and the acceptance for circulation of the Revised Version of the Bible in 1901.

Immediately on the formation of the Society correspondence was commenced through a sub-committee with foreign lands, with a view to learn both the needs and the best methods of work in those lands. The first grant made was one of £100 to encourage the formation of a society in Nuremberg, in May, 1804. One of the earliest foreign correspondents was a Roman Catholic clergyman in Swabia, to whom 1,000 German New Testaments were granted for distribution. The first foreign edition of the Scriptures printed by the Society was John's Gospel (2,000 copies) in Mohawk and English.

Various grants were made to encourage the printing of new editions of the Scriptures and for the establishment of auxiliary societies on the Continent. In 1812 a Bible committee was formed in Paris. Auxiliaries were formed in Zurich (1812), St. Gall (1813), Wurtemberg (1813), Frankfort and other places (1812), Presburg in Hungary (1812). Leander Van Ess, a Catholic priest and professor in the University of Marburg, made a translation of the New Testament; £200 was granted him to enable him distribute 3,000 copies. The Berlin Auxiliary was formed in 1805 and soon printed 20,000 copies of the Scriptures in the Bohemian and Polish tongues. In 1807 means were taken to supply the need in Iceland, and in 1823 it was reported that there was not a family without the Scriptures. An auxiliary was founded in Copenhagen in 1814. In Russia an auxiliary for Finland was organized in 1812, with the approval of the Czar, Alexander I., and in 1813 one for Russia at St. Petersburg. Prince Galitzin became its first president, and members of the Russian Greek and the Armenian churches were present at the inauguration of the work. The Czar donated 25,000 roubles, and became an annual subscriber to the amount of 10,000. Auxiliaries were formed, various translations made, and a great impulse given to Bible distribution and study. Nearly one hundred editions in thirty languages were published, and hundreds of thousands of Scriptures distributed. Alexander's successor, Nicholas, suppressed the Society in 1826, but permitted the formation of a Protestant Society for supplying Protestants with the Bible. In 1809 an association was formed in Stockholm through which Lapland also was reached. In 1814 the Netherlands Bible Society was instituted at Amsterdam. It was found that, while the majority of the adherents of the Reformed Church had Bibles, the Lutherans generally were unprovided, and the Catholics had very few copies among them. Societies were rapidly multiplied to supply the need, and generous grants were made to them. Efforts made by the pope to check the work in Poland and Russia failed. Austria refused to permit the work in her territories, and the Hungarian Bible Society was suppressed; and yet many eminent Roman Catholics heartily assisted the Society in its work.

Up to 1826 it had been the aim of the Society to encourage foreign countries to institute societies of their own, on its principle of circulating the Scriptures without note or comment. This aim was remarkably successful. Holland, Germany, Poland, Russia, Switzerland, France, Hungary, Denmark, Sweden, Norway, Iceland were aroused in a remarkable degree to provide the people with the Bible. In the Lutheran and Reformed Churches the various Protestant translations were distributed, while among the Roman Catholics, versions of their own, but without note or comment, were adopted for distribution by the Society. On account of the position taken in regard to the Apocrypha, most of the continental societies withdrew, and latterly the British and Foreign Bible Society has carried forward its work in Europe by means of agencies under its own immediate control.

The Society completed one hundred years of arduous service March 6, 1904. That day, falling on Sunday, was observed in all Protestant countries as a day for setting forth in the pulpit the debt which the world owes to the Bible, and for commemorating the services of the Bible societies to mankind.

The growth of the Society's work is indicated by the following figures as to its issues and receipts: Up to March 31, 1808, its issues were 81,157 volumes, of which 63,113 were New Testaments. The next year showed 77,272 with 40,862 New Testaments and 35,910 Bibles. From that time the growth has been constant, until in 1902 the total issues were 5,067,421, including 939,706 Bibles, 1,364,116 New Testaments, 2,763,599 portions. The total issues up to March 31, 1902, were 175,038,965.

The income of the Society has grown from £691 10s. 2d. in its first year to £241,143 2s. 11d. in 1902.

Bible Women: The Society has of late years made a special feature of the employment of **Bible Women**, especially in the East, to reach the homes with reading and instruction. During 1901, 621 were thus employed in Asia, either by the Society direct or through its auxiliaries or the different missionary societies, and they reached over 35,000 women and taught 2,384 in India, Ceylon and Egypt to read.

Editorial Work: An idea of this branch of the Society's work is furnished by the statement that, during the year ending March 31, 1902, the Editorial Committee considered matters bearing on versions of Scripture in 151 languages and dialects, of which 33 belong to Europe, 55 to Asia, 43 to Africa, 6 to America and 14 to Oceania. Negotiations have been conducted with the owners of the Revised Version in English, with a view to issuing it in forms suited to schools and the cottages of the poor. Among items of special interest are a German Bible in Latin characters, a pocket Bible in Persian, a Revised Testament in Tibetan, a new whole Bible in the Ningpo dialect of China, plans for a Union version in Nyasa, etc.

Agencies: Of the 24 foreign agents of the Society seven are located in Europe, at Paris, Berlin, Florence, Madrid, St. Petersburg, Ekaterinburg and Constantinople; four are in Africa, at Alexandria, Algiers, Tangier and Sierra Leone; six are in Asia, at Bushire, Rangoon, Singapore, Shanghai, Seoul and Yokohama; one is at Manila, one in New Zealand; three are in South America, at Buenos Aires, Rio de Janeiro and Callao; one is at Belize, British Honduras, and one at Kingston, Jamaica. There are also five secretaries in India, at Madras, Bombay, Calcutta, Allahabad, and Lahore; and one at Cape Town in South Africa.

Agencies in Europe: The work of the Society in Europe is carried on by colportage, through Bible depots, and by grants to existing local organizations. In France there were in 1902, 43 colporteurs; in Belgium 8, Germany 26, Austria-Hungary 45, Italy 36, Spain 22, Portugal 10, Russia 72, Turkey and Greece 28. The last two include some work in Asia. New methods are adopted as needed, instanced by the use of a colportage motor-car and the appointment of women as colporteurs in France; work in the railway shops of Belgium, among the soldiers of Germany, the emigrants from Italy, and the convicts of Sicily. Everywhere the strongest opposition comes from the Roman Catholic priesthood, but the evangelical movement among the priests in France, the "away from Rome" impulse in Austria, the independent ambitions of Hungary, and the influx of new ideas into Italy and Spain, all affect the work of the Bible Society and are manifest in increased sales. How much is accomplished is indicated by the following figures of sales by colporteurs, not including those in depots or to other Bible societies: France 55,324, Belgium 7,391, Germany 97,892, Austria-Hungary 72,940, Italy 60,413, Spain 29,934, Portugal 6,062, Russia 217,212, Turkey and Greece 25,095. In some countries, notably Germany and Russia, there are also large sales in the depots; Germany 205,495, and Russia 244,952 copies.

The agent at Constantinople has care of the work of the Society in that city, in Western Asia Minor, chiefly near the coast; in the islands of the Egean, in Bulgaria north of the Balkans, in Albania and in Greece. By arrangement with the American and Scottish Bible societies duplication of labor is avoided. In recent years the chief difficulty has arisen from the opposition of the Greek Church to the circulation of the New Testament in modern Greek.

Egyptian Agency: This includes, besides Egypt and the Sudan, Syria, Palestine, Cyprus, Malta, Arabia and Abyssinia, with the East Central Africa sub-agency at Zanzibar. In Syria, Egypt, and a portion of the Sudan, the American Bible Society also works; elsewhere the British Society occupies the field alone; thus it covers the most important part of the Arabic speaking world. The headquarters are at Alexandria, and during 1901 fourteen colporteurs were employed, who sold 13,640 copies of the Scriptures. Almost an equal number were sold to various missionary organizations, and still more granted to missionaries, etc., so that the entire circulation was over 52,000 copies. Among the special features of the work are efforts to reach the sailors who pass through the Suez Canal and the pilgrims at Jerusalem; a cordial letter from King Menelek of Abyssinia; colportage on the Nile steamers and among the non-African population, Indian, Arab and European, of East Africa.

North Africa: The two agencies, one for Algeria, with Tunis and Tripoli, and one for Morocco, are among the most difficult fields of the Society; illustrating its principle of going into regions that are needy, irrespective of returns in the form of sales. With four colporteurs in Algeria selling 7,218 copies (1902) and three in Morocco selling 5,959 copies, it is easy to understand that the work has many perplexities. The French are scornful, the Mohammedans hostile, and, especially in Morocco, the national spirit is very bitter. The Society works in close relation with the North African Mission, the London Jews' Society and the Geneva Evangelical Society.

West Africa: This agency covers the territory from the Gambia to the Congo. The agent, who resides at Freetown, Sierra Leone, works chiefly through local auxiliaries and the missions of the CMS, the WMS and the Basel Missionary Society.

South Africa, including Cape Colony, Natal, Orange River Colony and the Transvaal, is under the general supervision of the South African Auxiliary (founded in 1840), whose secretary resides at Cape Town. The recent war closed a number of the depots, yet the work has gone on with considerable success, both among the English and the Dutch, as well as the natives, the sales and grants amounting, in 1902, to about 50,000. Madagascar and Mauritius are both provided with auxiliary societies, the sales being about 20,000 in Malagasi and 2,000 in Mauritius.

Persia and Turkish Arabia: The agent at Bushire, on the Persian Gulf, has charge of this section, including all but the part of Persia north of Teheran, which is occupied by the American Bible Society. The sales by 10 colporteurs were (1901) about 6,000 copies, while the total circulation was 15,548. The agency is in three divisions: 1. the provinces of the Persian Gulf, with Bushire as center; 2. South Central and Eastern Persia, with center at Julfa, near Ispahan, and sub-depots at Sultanabad, Yezd and Shiraz; 3. Turkish Arabia, with center at Baghdad, and including Kermanshah in Western Persia. A considerable portion of the work is among Armenians and Jews.

India: The Society's work here has from the first been organized under separate auxiliaries, six in number: Calcutta, Bombay, Madras, Bangalore, North India and Punjab. On the respective committees, the various missionary societies are largely represented and their committees fix prices and decide discounts to missions and other purchasers. The Society's colporteurs and depots always work in close harmony with these missions. The 138 colporteurs employed in 1901-2 sold 181,743 copies of the Scriptures, while the total circulation was 577,035, the highest figures reached in any year. One feature of the work is the employment of 406 native Bible women.

The three auxiliaries in charge of Bible work in Ceylon, at Colombo, Jaffna and Kandy, report 10 colporteurs, 9,847 copies sold and a total circulation of 43,216.

Burma is under a special agent located at Rangoon, who reports eight colporteurs and total sales of 15,179 copies.

Malaysia is divided into North and South, with headquarters at Manila and Singapore. In the Philippines the work is shared with the American Bible Society, the British Society reporting (1901) 35,638 copies sold, of which over 26,000 were in the Philippine dialects and the great majority were portions, those in Spanish and Chinese each amounting to about 3,600 copies. From Singapore the agent superintends work in the Straits Settlements and native states, Sumatra, Java, Borneo, Celebes, Moluccas, and lesser Dutch Islands, 28 colporteurs selling 43,395 copies, very nearly the entire circulation. Here Chinese takes the lead among the languages, next coming Malay, Javanese and Tamil.

China: This large agency, covering China proper, Manchuria, Mongolia, Sungaria and Tibet, is superintended by an agent resident at Shanghai, with 11 sub-agents in the different provinces. There are 15 principal depots and 8 others under the superintendence of missionaries. There were 153 native colporteurs at work during the year, and the sales were 382,036 copies, the total circulation being 431,446 against 604,462 in 1900 and 856,156 in 1899. A significant feature is the large number of complete Bibles called for, the largest in any one year of the agency. The decrease, due to the Boxer troubles, has been chiefly in the colportage, the sales from the depots not having materially lessened. The China agency also includes the work in Formosa, which has shown steady development, the circulation (1901) being 25,763 copies.

Korea has an agent resident at Seoul, who reports a circulation of 16,814 copies, against 38,006 in 1900, 46,121 in 1899 and 34,813 in 1898. This decrease is explained by the severe drought, which has raised prices, and the fact that in 1900 the native church members supplied themselves with the newly issued Testament.

Japan is worked by a joint committee representing the British, American and Scotch societies.

Bible work in Australia is conducted by 43 auxiliaries with 476 branches, and in New Zealand by 61 auxiliaries and branches, which not only care for their own fields, among the Maoris, sailors, etc., but contribute liberally to the parent society.

In Oceania the Society assists the various missionary societies with grants, but has no special organized work.

South America: In this continent are three agencies: the Argentine, including Argentina, Uruguay, Paraguay and Bolivia; Brazil, and a new one called the Republics of the Andes, including Colombia, Ecuador and Peru, the work of the Society in Chile being limited to assisting the Valparaiso Bible Society. In all, 16 colporteurs have sold 24,758 copies. This is somewhat of a falling off compared with the sales of previous years.

The five Republics of Costa Rica, Nicaragua, Salvador, Guatemala and Honduras are worked by an agent resident at Belize, British Honduras. Seven colporteurs in that region sold 9,135 copies, almost the entire circulation.

The West Indian Agency, including Dutch, French and British Guiana, the West Indian Islands and Bermudas, with its center at Kingston, Jamaica, has the credit of a larger proportion of Bibles sold (27,911 out of a total circulation of 53,090) than any other foreign agency of the Society. Some of the 83 auxiliaries and branches are supplied direct from London, so that the above does not represent the entire work done.

British North America is thoroughly organized with 12 auxiliaries and over 1,100 branch societies, the auxiliary for Upper Canada, with its headquarters at Toronto, being the largest and most influential of all those in British Colonies. It covers the entire territory from the Great Lakes to the Pacific Coast.

PERIODICALS: *The Bible Society Reporter,* London; *Bible Society Gleanings.*
History of the Bible Society (from 1804 to 1854), London 2 vols.

BRITISH EAST AFRICA: A large territory bordering on the east coast of Africa and extending into the heart of the continent, comprising the East African Protectorate proper, the Uganda Protectorate, and the Zanzibar Protectorate. The territory is bounded on the west by the Congo Free State and lies between the Sudan, Abyssinia and Italian Somaliland on the north and German East Africa on the south. The entire area of this part of the British territory in Africa is estimated to exceed 1,000,000 square miles.

The East African Protectorate proper includes the whole of the coast from the Umba to the Juba River, extending inland as far as Uganda and merging to northward into the Egyptian Sudan, with an area of about 350,000 square miles and a population of about 4,000,000. Arabs and Swahilis inhabit the coast territories, while farther inland are found tribes of Bantus, and in the northern part the Masai, Somalis and Gallas. The territory is governed by the Foreign Office through a Commissioner and a Consul General with their subordinates. The capital is Mombasa, a town of 27,000 inhabitants, situated on an island of the same name. A railway runs from Mombasa to Uganda at the Victoria Nyanza.

The missionary societies established in this region are the CMS, the United Methodist Free Churches, the Africa Inland Mission, the Scandinavian Alliance, the Leipzig Missionary Society and the Neukirchen Missionary Society. These societies occupy 17 stations altogether, the most of which are under the CMS.

Travel in the Coast Lands of British E. Africa, Fitzgerald (W. W. A.), London, 1898; *The Last of the Masai,* Hinde (S. L. and H.), London, 1901.

BRITISH SYRIAN MISSION SCHOOLS and Bible Work (1860): In the year 1860 the Druses rose against the Maronites and Greeks in Damascus and the region of the Lebanon and Anti-Lebanon, and fearful massacres resulted. The condition of the 20,000 widows and orphans who were left aroused the sympathy of Mrs. Bowen Thompson of England, who had spent many years in Syria as the wife of a physician, and was thoroughly acquainted with the country and its peoples.

She went to Beirut and opened an industrial refuge, where 200 women and children gathered the first week. Schools were established and a training institution opened in Beirut. Within a few years the work spread to other towns and villages in Syria, and schools were attended not only by the children of the Christian denominations, but by Jewesses, Muslims and Druses. Mrs. Bowen Thompson was soon joined by her sisters, Miss Lloyd, Mrs. Smith and Mr. and Mrs. Mott. With their aid and that of a small staff of native Bible women the work was well organized before Mrs. Thompson's death in 1869.

The schools of the mission extend from Damascus to Tyre. There is a night school of special benefit to Lebanon soldiers, day schools for boys, for girls, for the blind of both sexes, for Muslim girls and for Jewesses. In all, instruction is given in the Bible. Special classes are held for women, both on week days and on Sundays, and are largely attended.

In 1889 the corner-stone of a memorial school building was laid in Baalbec, and a medical work has been established in the same city. A quarterly paper, *Daughters of Syria,* is published in England in the interest of the schools.

There are 4 stations and 19 outstations, 21 English missionaries and 128 native workers, 51 day schools, 3,743 pupils and 3 dispensaries.

The organ of this Society is a quarterly paper, *Daughters of Syria.*

BROACH: Capital of the district of Broach, Bombay, India, situated on the Nerbada, 30 miles from its mouth. Population (1891), 40,168—Hindus, Muslims, Parsees. Language, Gujarathi. Station of the PCI (1887), with 2 missionaries and their wives, 2 missionary women, 9 native workers, men and women, 5 Sunday schools, 5 village schools, 1 orphanage and 21 church members.

BRODHEAD, Augustus: Born at Milford, Pa., May 13, 1831; graduated at Union College, 1855, and Princeton Theological Seminary, 1858; ordained May 4 same year; sailed for India, November 7, as a missionary of the PN, reaching Calcutta April 4, 1859. At Mainpurie and Fatehgarh he spent nearly twelve years. In 1872 he was transferred to Allahabad. Dr. Brodhead took a prominent part in the theological training school of the Synod of India, wrote and published valuable treatises in sacred and church history, edited the mission magazine published for the use of the native Christians, and assisted in preparing a hymn book for the church and Sunday school, for which he wrote and translated several hymns; took an active part in the North Indian Bible and Tract Societies, and the Christian Vernacular Education Society. A succession of severe attacks of illness compelled him to return home. Died at Bridgeton, N. J., August, 1887.

BROOKE, Graham Wilmot: Born at Aldershot, England, in 1866. He was preparing to enter the military academy at Woolwich when he became interested in the Mohammedans of North Africa and the seeming impossibility of informing them of the Gospel of Jesus Christ. He gradually reached a deliberate conclusion that it was his duty to try to reach the Mohammedans of the Sudan, who were then showing the fiercest fanaticism in connection with the outbreak of Mahdism in the region about Khartum, and to teach them how to walk in the light. He studied medicine at St. Thomas' Hospital and went as an independent missionary to Africa, but failed in every attempt to reach the Sudan. He then returned to England and was appointed the same year, December, 1889, as an honorary lay missionary of the CMS, in order to be, with the Rev. J. A. Robinson, joint leader of the new Sudan and Upper Niger mission. In May, 1890, the expedition went to Africa and by way of the Niger into the Western Sudan. He was principally at Lokoja. There he acquired the Hausa language and labored with energy in preaching, until he was smitten with fever and died at Lokoja, March 5, 1892, in the 26th year of his age.

Mr. Brooke was a hero in his calm, steadfast devotion to his mission. He felt called to preach in the Sudan, then one of the darkest regions of the earth. "But," as has been said of his determined attempt to obey the call of his Master, "the land was not easy of access. He tried to reach it by way of North Africa and failed. He tried to enter it by way of the Congo. Following the course of that great river, far into the interior, beyond where foot of missionary had yet trod, past large and populous towns unheard of by the civilized world, among nations whose atrocities equaled those of the South Sea cannibals, through untold risks and dangers, he pushed his way onward. But in vain. The Sudan was still barred to him. Finally he discovered that a door of entrance might be found by way of the Niger, and that he could best avail himself of it by joining the Church Missionary Society.

"How, arrayed in the native dress, which proved so commodious, he and the friends who with him started the Upper Niger Mission went about among the people of Lokoja and the country round, how quickly he obtained a mastery of the language, how he won favor among the Mohammedans as well as heathen, and found ready listeners for the Gospel story—all this has been told in detail in his journals and leaflets, and forms a most deeply interesting and instructive narrative. In spite of the many trials which came upon the mission, he was able to record at the end of 1891 that the Word of God had been fully preached over an area equal to that of Hertfordshire, Middlesex, Kent, Surrey, and Hants, and not merely preached, but understood."

Mr. Brooke, besides preaching, found time to translate several tracts into Hausa. But his life was much like that of David Brainerd, in that the remembrance of its high qualities is the chief legacy which he left to the Church. His was a case where "the highest mental and moral gifts, the prime of life with its vigor and its opportunities, were laid simply and wholly upon the altar of Christ, and this, not as a sacrifice, but as a matter of course."

BROUSA: Capital of the province of the same name, Asiatic Turkey, about 60 miles from Constantinople. Population, about 75,000, Mohammedans, Armenians, Greeks, etc. It is finely located at the base of the Bithynian Olympus. Has some mineral springs and is a health resort from Constantinople. It was the capital of the first Sultans of the Ottoman Empire, and the tombs built in their honor are well worthy of a visit.

Station of the ABCFM (1848), with 1 missionary and his wife, 1 missionary woman, 15 native workers, 12 chapels, 12 Sunday schools, 13 common schools, 2 high schools, 1 orphanage and 255 church members.

BROWN, Nathan: Born at New Ipswich, N. H., June 22, 1807; graduated at Williams College, 1827. While in college he composed the beautiful poem, *The Missionary's Call*, commencing, "My soul is not at rest." After studying theology in Newton Seminary he was ordained at Rutland, and embarked for Burma, December 22, 1832, under appointment by the Baptist Triennial Convention. Having spent two years in Burma, he was appointed by his brethren to commence with Mr. Cutter a new mission in Assam. After a four months' perilous journey through the Hugli, Ganges and Brahmaputra they reached Sadiya, about 45 miles N. E. of the present mission station of Dibrugarh. Here among savage tribes he began to learn the language without grammar or dictionary. He soon commenced the work of translation, tracts and books were distributed, schools were established and *zayats* built, where the Gospel was preached by the wayside. In 1839 Sadiya was attacked by the hill tribes, and many of the people and soldiery were massacred. Dr. Brown and his wife fled in a canoe in the darkness of the night with their two infant children, and at daybreak found protection in the stockade, still in possession of the British troops. Many natives of Sadiya having been killed or dispersed, the mission was removed to Jeypûr, and in 1841 to the densely populated district of Sibsagar. Here the missionaries had great success. Reenforcements arriving, new stations were established and churches organized. But Dr. Brown's great work was the translation of the Scriptures. In 1848 he completed the Assamese version of the New Testament. In 1855, with health greatly impaired by twenty-two years of toil and sufferings, he returned to his native land.

In view of the wonderful openings in Japan and the urgent calls for missionaries, Dr. Brown felt strongly drawn to that empire as a field for his personal labors, and in 1872, under appointment from the American Baptist Missionary Union, he set sail for Japan with his second wife, reaching Yokohama, February, 1873. Tho sixty-five years of age, he entered upon the study of the language with ardor, and in 1879 his translation of the New Testament in vernacular Japanese was printed. He strongly recommended the adoption of the Roman alphabet in place of the Chinese characters in writing the Japanese language, a reform which has since been zealously urged, not only by the missionaries, but by many Japanese. During his six years' residence in Japan Dr. Brown received 179 to his church at Yokohama, was permitted to welcome other laborers, and to see seven churches established containing between 300 and 400 members.

Dr. Brown was not only a translator of the Scriptures and a preacher, he was also the author and translator of hymns in the languages of Burma, Assam and Japan. His last work was the Japanese hymn-book. When no longer able to use the pen he dictated as he lay on his bed to his native preacher. He closed his useful and industrious life January 1, 1886, in the seventy-ninth year of his age.

Dr. Brown's published works are: Translation of the *New Testament* in Assamese; Portions of the *Old Testament* in Assamese and Shan; *Grammar of the Assamese Language*; *Catechism* in the Assamese and Shan Languages; *Arithmetic* in Burman and Assamese; *Hymns* in Burman and Assamese; comparative vocabulary of some fifty Indian languages and dialects, and the *Orunôdoi*, an illustrated monthly magazine.

BROWN, Samuel R.: Born at East Windsor, Conn., June 16, 1810; removed to Munson in early childhood; graduated at Yale College, 1832; sailed as a missionary of the ABCFM for China in 1838. His great work was education and translation. He it was who first induced Chinese youth to come to the United States for an education, and hundreds of young men from China— some from the highest families of the empire— found through him homes in towns and cities of the United States. On going to Japan in 1859 (under the RCA), he induced the government to send some of its princes to America for education, and he was active in securing Christian homes for them. His last services were in connection with the translation of the New Testament into Japanese, a labor of many years, in which he was associated with a committee from several denominations. This great work was just completed at the time of his death. He returned home in 1879 and died, June 20, 1880, in Munson, Mass.

BRUMANA: A village on Mount Lebanon,

Syria, a few miles east of Beirut. Station of the Friends' Foreign Mission Association (1873), with 4 missionaries and their wives, 4 missionary women (2 of them medical), 14 native workers men and women, 1 chapel, 3 Sunday schools, 2 village schools, 2 high schools, 1 dispensary, 1 hospital and 15 professing Christians. Brumana has been twice chosen as the place of meeting (the second in 1901) of an important interdenominational conference of missionaries and other Christian workers from all parts of the Levant.

BUA: A town on the island of Vanua Levu, Fiji Islands; station of the Australian Wesleyan Methodist Missionary Society, with 1 missionary, 207 native workers, 71 chapels, 92 Sunday schools, 102 village schools, and 2,135 professing Christians.

BUCARAMANGA: A city of 20,000 inhabitants in the district of Santander, Colombia, South America; station of the American Bible Society, with an agent and his wife and a book depot.

BUCHANAN: A village in Griqualand East, Cape Colony, S. Africa, situated about ten miles S. W. of Mount Frère; station of the UFS (1886), with 1 missionary and his wife, 31 native workers, 9 Sunday schools, 1 village school, and 702 church members.

BUCHANAN (Liberia). See GREAT BASSA.

BUCHAREST: Capital of the kingdom of Rumania; altho Oriental in external appearance, in other respects it is assuming more and more the aspect of a European city. Population (1890), 190,633. Mission station of the London Society for Propagating the Gospel among the Jews (1848), with 10 missionaries, 9 native workers, men and women, 1 chapel, 1 Sunday school, and 2 village schools. Also station of the PB (1899), with 2 missionaries, one with his wife, and 1 missionary woman.

BUDAON: A city S. W. of Bareilly, in the Rohilkhand district, United Provinces, India. Population, about 35,000. Station of the ME, with 4 missionaries and 38 native workers, men and women. It has 24 village schools, a high school, and 680 church members.

BUDDHISM: In discussing Buddhism it must be borne in mind that many systems known by tha name have appeared in different ages and in different lands. No other faith or philosophy has undergone so many and so great changes in the course of its development. The widely different opinions, therefore, which have been expressed as to its teachings, may each have found a degree of support in some particular phase or stage of the manifold system.

Another point to be settled is its relation to Hinduism. Was it a new and distinct system setting out in the first instance as a protest against the teachings of the Brahmans, or was it a later development in the mind of Gautama occurring after six years of ascetic life—a discovery or conclusion finally reached as he sat under the Bo tree? Professor Beall is undoubtedly correct in the opinion that Buddhism was an afterthought and not an original aim when Gautama left his palace. He broke with Brahmanism on its religious side; most of its philosophy he retained. He protested against the outrageous assumptions of the Brahmans, their intense sacerdotalism and imposture, their exaggerated doctrine of sacrifice, and their rigorous system of caste. He repudiated the absolute authority of the Vedas and the superstition, or ultra-religiousness, of the whole Brahmanical cult. He even flew to the opposite extreme of atheism, or, at least, a pronounced agnosticism.

Yet, at the same time, he cherished a sort of reverence for the high Brahmans or rishis. He tacitly maintained many of the speculations of the Upanishads. He cherished, with unabated ardor, the old Brahmanical theory that the connection of soul with matter is the source of all evil, and that self-mortification, through a series of transmigrations, can alone secure deliverance. Of the nature of the soul he held peculiar views, as will appear further on. These views have been more or less modified in succeeding ages.

A clear distinction must be made at the outset between the credible history of Gautama and the extravagant legends which sprang up in various lands long after his death. It has virtually been settled by the consensus of the best scholars that those accounts which are the oldest, which were authorized by the earliest councils, which have the concurrent testimony of both the Northern and the Southern literatures, and which are credible in themselves shall be accepted as the probable history of Gautama.

Briefly, the facts thus recognized are these: Gautama, otherwise known in his youth as Siddartha, was the son of Suddhodana, a rajah of the Aryan tribe of Sakyas, occupying a tract of country north by northwest of Benares.

He was born at Kapilavastu probably about 600 B. C., and was left motherless by the death of the Rani Maya Devi shortly after she had given him birth. The earliest accounts represent him as having been born by natural generation, and without the miraculous incidents of the later legends.

There are apparent evidences of a melancholy and more or less morbid turn of mind even in his youth, and of painstaking efforts on the part of his father to cheer his despondency by the allurements of a voluptuous Oriental court.

In spite of all this, satiety was an early result, and at the age of twenty-nine, and just after the birth of an only son and heir, he left his palace and his inheritance, and, like many other princes in various lands, he sought rest of soul in asceticism. The idea which has been so skilfully reproduced by Sir Edwin Arnold, that Gautama then and there set out to become a savior of men, has no foundation in fact. It is rendered impossible by the early traditions; he was simply fleeing from sorrow and distress, and seeking some way of peace.

Leaving his palace by night, attended by a faithful servant, he hastened to the open country, whence he sent back his horse, and exchanging garments with a peasant, he proceeded on foot to a forest retreat, where he entered upon a life of self-mortification.

Dissatisfied with his teachers, he himself became the head of a fraternity, and with five or six followers he sought even greater isolation and greater austerities for about six years.

He had at length fathomed the emptiness of the Brahmanical religion. He had given it a patient and even heroic trial, and had found it vanity. Self-mortification could go no further without absolute suicide. He was so weak from fasting that he fainted and fell to the ground. The crisis of his life had come. He abandoned his vain struggles and partook of needful food.

8

This step cost him the loss of all his influence; his disciples forsook him as an apostate and a failure; he was in extreme perplexity and distress. Should he return to his family and his inheritance, and appease his wounded pride by proclaiming that all religion was a sham? The temptation was strong, yet neither had his former possessions given him peace.

Very real and very great were his temptations. Fierce were his struggles with the world, on the one hand, and with conviction and pride on the other, as he sat alone under the shade of the Bo tree.

All candid men must acknowledge that the decision which Gautama reached, and the victory over self which he won, were sublime. Greater self-control has seldom if ever been attained by men, altho the power of the human will has sometimes found remarkable exemplifications.

John Foster, in his essay on *Decision of Character*, cites the case of a spendthrift who, after having exhausted a splendid fortune, had gone to the seashore with the purpose of destroying his life. But after a long period of reflection he sprang to his feet with an all absorbing resolve to retrieve his fortune, walked rapidly back to the city, engaged at once in the humblest occupations, and as a persistent miser actually accomplished his end.

With equal force of will, and in a far nobler cause, Gautama rose up from his reveries to become one of the most powerful leaders of mankind. He is supposed to have been at this time about thirty-five years of age. The passions of youth were not dead with him, worldly ambition may be supposed to have been still in force, but he chose the part of a missionary to his fellowmen, and there is no evidence that he ever swerved from his purpose. He had won a great victory over himself, and that fact constituted a secret of power.

He began at once the career which he had marked out. He sought, first of all, the disaffected disciples who had abandoned him, and who, doubtless, had proclaimed his fall. It is a strong evidence of the power of his own convictions that he speedily succeeded in winning them to his new standard.

It was just here that Buddhism began its career. It had still an ascetic element; it aimed to keep the body under for the sake of purity and power, but not as a matter of merit. In the place of idleness and repression for its own sake it substituted a life of beneficence.

Buddhism was a missionary religion from the outset; more aggressively so in that early age than in the later centuries, when it had lapsed into the monastic spirit of the original Brahmanism.

Gautama soon gathered a band of about sixty followers, whom, after five months of instruction, he sent out to proclaim the "Law." He himself preached continuously for forty-five years, and long before his death he was surrounded by a numerous order of mendicants, who received his word as law, and to whom he stood in the place of God. The gentleness of his bearing and the consistency of his life, as well as precepts, won men of high and of low degree with remarkable power.

During the more favorable seasons it was his custom to preach as an itinerant, wherever he found the most favorable openings, but in the hot and rainy months he gathered his mendicants about him in some shady grove or on a breezy mountain summit like the "Vulture's Peak." He died at the advanced age of fourscore years from an acute attack of indigestion.

The account given of his last hours in the *Great Decease* is full of pathos. He passed away like Socrates, in the full use of his faculties, and discoursing tenderly with his disciples to the end.

If now we turn from credible history to the later legends of the Buddha, we enter upon a story of the wildest extravagance.

The legends divide his life into three periods: (1) that of his preexistent states through several hundred transmigrations; (2) that of his earthly life before attaining Buddhaship; and (3) that of his ministry after he had become "enlightened." The preexistent states are set forth in the Jatakas or "birth stories" of Ceylon, which represent him as having been born 530 times after he became a Bodisat (a predestined Buddha).

As a specimen of his varied experience while becoming fitted for Buddhaship, we read that he was born 83 times as an ascetic, 58 as a monarch, 43 as a deva, 24 as a Brahman, 18 as an ape; as a deer 10, an elephant 6, a lion 10, and at least once each as a thief, a gambler, a frog, a hare, a snipe. He was also embodied in a tree. But as a Bodisat he could not be born in hell, nor as vermin, nor as a woman. He could descend no lower than a snipe.

The legends represent the Buddha as having "incarnated" for the purpose of bringing relief to a distressed world. He was miraculously conceived, entering his mother's side in the form of a white elephant. All nature manifested its joy on the occasion. The ocean bloomed with flowers, all beings from many worlds showed their wonder and sympathy. Many miracles were wrought even during his childhood, and every part of his career was filled with marvels.

At his temptation under the Bo tree Mara (Satan) came to him mounted on an elephant sixteen miles high and surrounded by an encircling army of demons eleven miles deep. Finding Buddha proof against blandishments, Mara hurled mountains of rocks against him and assailed him with fire and smoke and ashes and filth, all of which became as zephyrs upon his cheek or as presents of fragrant flowers. Last of all, Mara sent his three daughters to seduce Buddha.

In the Northern Buddhist literature, especially in the *Lalita Vistara* of Nepaul, many incidents of Buddha's childhood are given which show a remarkable coincidence with the life of Christ. It is claimed that his birth was heralded by angelic hosts, that an aged sage received him into his arms and blessed him, that he was taken to the temple for consecration, that a jealous ruler sought to destroy him, that he disputed with learned doctors; that he was baptized, tempted, transfigured, and translated. These seeming parallels will be noticed further on.

The Literatures of Buddhism: The teachings of Gautama were gathered up by his disciples in the form of belief aphorisms or sutras, and were orally transmitted for several generations before being committed to writing. They had various classifications, like the following: (1) *The Four Truths*, discovered while sitting under the Bo tree—viz.: the fact of sorrow, the cause of sorrow, the removal of sorrow, and the means by which this is to be done. The fourth was ramified into the eightfold path. (2) *The Middle Path*, as between the dominion of passion, on the one hand and the bootless extremes of asceticism on the other. (3) *The Ten Fetters*—viz.: (*a*) Delusion of Self; (*b*) Doubt; (*c*) Dependence on Rites; (*d*) Sensuality; (*e*) Hatred; (*f*) Love of Life on Earth; (*g*) Desire for Life in Heaven; (*h*) Pride; (*i*) Self-Righteousness; (*j*) Ignorance. (4) *The Ten Prohibitions*, sometimes called the Ten Commandments. One should not kill, should not steal, should not lie, nor get drunk, nor commit adultery. These five were for all men. Five others were for the religious orders. These should not violate certain strict rules relating to food, nor wear ornaments, nor use perfumes, nor sleep on a soft bed, nor indulge in amusements, nor possess silver and gold.

These prohibitions have often been compared with the Mosaic Decalog, but it will be observed that all the Godward precepts of the latter are wanting in the Buddhist code; even the parental relation is unnoticed, and the reference to the deeper principle of covetousness in the Hebrew Decalog is also wanting. Only the outward violation of the most obvious rules of common life is forbidden in the laity, and five frivolous injunctions are added for the religious order.

It is fair to say, however, that reverence for parents was inculcated in other sutras ascribed to the Buddha; that the restriction and abuse heaped upon woman by the laws of Manu were mitigated, and that, in general, benevolence toward all men and all living things was enjoined.

In the teachings of Gautama and his immediate disciples are found many precepts which compare favorably with those of the New Testament. They are, however, purely ethical, and can scarcely be said to have a religious import.

Of the collections of Buddhist literature there are two great divisions, known as the Little Vehicle (Hinayana) of Ceylon and other southern lands, and the Great Vehicle (Mahayana) of Nepal, Kashmir, and Tibet. China and Japan received translations from both, tho principally from the Great Vehicle of the North. The Pali text of the Little Vehicle was adopted by the council called by King Ashoka about 250 B. C., and was known as the Tripitaka (Three Baskets). This, as being the oldest and most authentic body of history and doctrine, is justly considered the Buddhist canon.

It is a strong point in favor of the authenticity of the Tripitaka, that it was borne into Ceylon by Mahinda, a son of Ashoka, soon after the council of Patna. He was received by Tissa, King of Ceylon, with great favor, and the faith, as it was preserved in his memory and that of his monks, was implicitly received in Ceylon. Mahinda soon after translated the Tripitaka from the Pali into the Sinhalese language, and from that time to the present day the two versions have corroborated each other.

Later teachings hold the same relation to the Tripitaka that the traditions and decrees of the Roman Catholic Church hold to the Canon of the New Testament.

The Mahayana, or Great Vehicle, consists of nine books, of which the two most important are the *Lalita Vistara* and the *Lotus of the True Law*. The former of these is a life of Gautama down to the time of his enlightenment. It was written partly in poetry and partly in prose, and evidently at different times. As above stated, it is in this poetic and exaggerated biography that those legends are chiefly found which resemble the life of Christ.

In the course of centuries important Buddhist works of greater or less merit appeared in the southern literature, mostly commentaries on the alleged teachings of the "Exalted One." Of these the most important are the *Dhammapada*, the *Sutta Nipata*, the *Great Decease*, etc. The *Dhammapada*, or "Path of Holiness," was written by Buddhagosha, an Indian monk, who went to Ceylon about 430.

The book is a sort of encyclopedia and commentary combined. It is a compend in Pali of all the commentaries which till his time had been preserved in Sinhalese only. The *Dhammapada* contains the best things of Buddhism, as the Bhagavad Gita sums up the choicest teachings of Hinduism. How far it represents the veritable words of Gautama and how far it embodies the sentiments of his followers can never be known, as it was written seven centuries after the adoption of the canon.

The Doctrines of Buddhism: These are (1) its peculiar conception of the soul; (2) its doctrine of Trishna and Upadana; (3) its theory of Karma; (4) the doctrine of Nirvana.

The soul is said to consist of five *skandas*. These in their interaction constitute what all others than Buddhists regard as the soul. They are (*a*) material properties, (*b*) the senses, (*c*) abstract ideas, (*d*) tendencies, (*e*) mental powers. The soul is the result of the combined action of these, as the flame of a candle proceeds from the combustion of its constituent elements. The flame is never the same for two consecutive moments. It seems to have a perpetuated identity, but that is only an illusion, and the same unreality pertains to the soul; it is only a succession of thoughts, emotions, and conscious experiences. We are not the same that we were an hour ago. In fact, there is no such thing as being, there is only a constant becoming. We are ever passing from one point to another throughout our life, and this is true of all beings and all things in the universe. How it is that the succession of experience is treasured up in memory is not made clear.

This is a most subtle doctrine, and it has many points of contact with various speculations of modern times. It has also a plausible side when viewed in the light of experience, but its gaps and inconsistencies are fatal, as must be seen when it is thoroughly examined.

Trishna is the second of these cardinal doctrines. Trishna is that inborn element of desire whose tendency is to lead men into evil. So far it is a misfortune, or a form of original sin. Whatever it may have of the nature of guilt hangs upon the issues of a previous life. Upadana is only a further stage in the same development. It is Trishna ripened into intense craving by our own choice and our own action. It then becomes incontrollable, and is clearly a matter of guilt. Now the momentum of this Upadana is such that it cannot be arrested by death. Like the demons of Gadara, it must again become incarnate, even tho it should enter the body of a brute.

Karma: This transitional something, this restless moral or immoral force which must work out its natural results somehow and somewhere, and that in embodied form, projects into future being a residuum which is known as Karma. Literally it means the "doing." It is a man's record, involving the consequences and liabilities of his acts. It is a score which must be settled.

A question naturally arises, How the record of a soul can survive when the soul itself has been "blown out?" The illustration of the candle does not quite meet the case. If the flame were something which, when blown out, immediately seized upon some other substance in which the work of combustion proceeded, it would come nearer to a parallel. One candle may light another before itself is extinguished, but it does not do it by an inherent necessity. But this flame of the soul, this Karma, must enter some other body of god, or man, or beast, or inanimate thing.

Again the question comes, How can responsibility be transferred from one to another? How can the heavy load of a man's sin be laid upon some newborn infant, while the departing sinner himself has no further concern in his evil Karma, but sinks into non-existence the moment his "conformations" are touched with dissolution? Buddhism acknowledges a mystery here; no real explanation can be given, and none seems to have been attempted by Buddhist writers. To be consistent, Gautama, in denying the existence of God and of the soul as an entity, should have taught the materialistic doctrine of annihilation. This, however, he could not do in the face of that deep-rooted idea of transmigration which had taken entire possession of the Hindu mind. He was compelled, therefore, to bridge a most illogical chasm as best he could. Karma without a soul to cling to is a something in the air. It alights like some winged seed upon a newborn set of *skandas* with its luckless boon of ill desert, and it involves the fatal inconsistency of investing with permanent character that which is itself impermanent.

But the question may be asked, Do we not admit a similar principle when we speak of a man's influence as something that survives him? We answer, "No." Influence is a simple radiation of impressions. A man may leave an influence which men are free to accept or not, but it is quite a different thing if he leaves upon a successor the moral liabilities of a bankrupt character. Gautama's own Karma, for example, ceased to exist upon his entering Nirvana; there was no rebirth, but his influence lives forever, and has extended to millions of his fellowmen.

The injustice involved in the doctrine of Karma is startling. The newborn soul that inherits its unsettled score has no memory or consciousness that connects it with himself; it is not heredity, it is not his father's character that invests him. This Karma may have crossed the ocean from the deathbed of some unknown man of another race. The doctrine is the more astonishing when we consider that no Supreme Being is recognized as claiming this retribution. There is no God; it is a vague law of eternal justice, a law without a lawgiver or a judge. There can therefore be no pardon, no commutation of sentence, no such thing as divine pity or help. The only way in which one can disentangle himself is by breaking the connection between spirit and matter which binds him with the shackles of conscious being.

The Doctrine of Nirvana: No doctrine of Buddhism has been so much in dispute as this. (1) It has been widely maintained that Nirvana means extinction. (2) Prof. T. W. Rhys Davids and others have held that it is the destruction of passion, malice, and delusion, and that it may be attained in this life—that Gautama reached Nirvana forty-five years before his death. They claim, however, that inasmuch as it cuts off Karma and rebirth, it involves extinction upon the dissolution of the body. (3) It is held by others that Nirvana is a return to the original and all-pervading Boddhi essence. This theory, which is really a concession to the Brahmanical doctrine of absorption into the infinite Brahm, has a wide following among modern Buddhists in China and Japan. It is a form of Buddhist pantheism.

As to the teachings of Gautama on this subject, Professor Max Müller, while admitting that the metaphysicians who followed the great teacher plainly taught that the entire personal entity of an *arahat* (an enlightened one) would become extinct upon the death of the body, yet reasons in his lecture on "Buddhistic Nihilism" that the Buddha himself could not have taught a doctrine so disheartening. At the same time he quotes the learned and judicial Bishop Bigandet as declaring, after years of study and observation in Burma, that such is the doctrine ascribed to the great teacher by his own disciples. Gautama himself is quoted as closing one of his sermons in these words: "Mendicants, that which binds the teacher to existence is cut off, but his body still remains. While his body shall remain he shall be seen by gods and men; but after the termination of life, upon the dissolution of the body, neither gods nor men shall see him."

Prof. Rhys Davids expresses the doctrine tersely when he says: "Utter death with no new life to follow is then a result of, but it is not, Nirvana."

Professor Oldenberg suggests with much plausibility that the Buddha was more reticent in regard to the doctrine of final extinction in the later periods of his life; that the depressing doctrine had been found a stumbling-block, and he came to assume an agnostic position on the question whether the ego should permanently survive.

The question, What is Nirvana? has been the object of a larger inquiry than its importance demands. Practically the millions of Buddhists are not concerned in the question. They find no attraction in either view. They desire neither extinction nor unconscious absorption into the Boddhi essence (or Brahm). What they anticipate is an improved transmigration, a better birth. The more devout may indulge the hope that their next life will be spent in one of the Buddhist heavens. Others may aspire to be men of high position and influence. A man of low tastes may forecast his next life in accordance with those tastes. The Buddhist holds even more strictly than the Christian that every man shall reap as he has sown, for in his view no interposing grace can change the result. It is wholly erroneous, then, to represent the system as presenting nothing more attractive to men than the prospect of extinction. However metaphysicians and Orientalists may settle the question of the last estate of those who become "enlightened," the multitudes care little for a goal which, according to Buddhist tradition, less than a dozen followers of Gautama have ever reached. "Tho laymen could attain Nirvana," says Professor Rhys Davids, "we are told of only one or two instances of their having done so; and, tho it was more possible for members of the Buddhist order of mendicants, we only hear after the time of Gautama of one or two who did so. No one now hears of such an occurrence." It is safe, therefore, to conclude that the hope of Nirvana has practically no influence on Buddhist minds. It lies at an infinite distance and is shadowy at best, while real existence lies between. That is the goal of hope and aspiration.

The Migrations of Buddhism: It is common to speak of Buddhism as a "missionary religion," and such it was in its earlier career. Gautama from the first and both by precept and example taught the duty of proclaiming the "Law." The fact that a son and a daughter of King Ashoka became missionaries in Ceylon must be accepted as evidence of the earnestness of the missionary spirit of their time. Other influences helped the movement, however. Ashoka made Buddhism the religion of the state, and, as we have seen, the political treaties formed between the Lamas of Tibet and the Chinese emperors extended the system even to Mongolia. In many instances Chinese travelers in India carried home with them the Buddhist system and became its advocates. But for several centuries real missionaries or volunteer teachers visited other lands for the promulgation of the Law. Buddhism was transmitted to Ceylon about 230 B. C., to Kashmir at the beginning of the Christian era, to China about 67, to Burma in the 5th century, to Japan in 552, and to Siam and Cambodia in the 7th century.

The Development of Northern Buddhism: In Ceylon, Burma and Siam there has been little change from the time-honored doctrine of the Pitakas, but in Nepal, Tibet, and among all branches of the Mongolian race there have been wide variations.

Closely connected with the legendary teachings which at length came to be associated with the history of Gautama was the theory that successive Buddhas have visited the world, and at intervals of five thousand years will continue to appear. When Gautama died, those who had learned to look upon him with a sort of worship felt the loss of a divine sympathy and help. The Buddha was dead, and according to his own teachings there was "nothing left of which it could be said I am." But the next Buddha was in course of preparation in some of the heavens, and perhaps could even now hear the voice of human prayer. Thus the Bodhisat "Maitreyeh" (future Buddha of kindness) came to be recognized even in Ceylon as a hopeful resource and a hearer of prayer.

But it was in the Northern Buddhism particularly that the evolution of a sort of semi-theism advanced from generation to generation.

Professor Rhys Davids maintains that the "keynote" of the Mahayana (Great Vehicle) was its change from the idea and aim of Arahatship, as taught in the south, to that of Bodisatship. In other words, a living Buddha to come was thought to be of more practical value to mankind than a dead Buddha of the past, however wise and saintly.

There was that felt demand of humanity, witnessed in all ages and races, for a divine helper. By the 4th century there were worshiped in Nepal two Bodisats named Manjusri and Avolokitesvara. The first was the personification of wisdom; the second represented power, and was the merciful protector of the world. These mythical personages were presented in the *Lotus of the True Law,* one of the nine books of the Great Vehicle. At a somewhat later period these two had become three, with a somewhat modified distribution of functions.

Vajrapani represented power; Manjusri, the personification of wisdom; while Avolokitesvara was the spirit of the Buddhas everywhere present in the church. This is wonderfully suggestive of a possible borrowing from the Christian Trinity, and the date of its development would render such a result possible.

Some time subsequent to the 7th century there were recognized five trinities—one for each of five world systems. In each trinity the first person was known as a *dhyana* or celestial Buddha; the second was the spirit of Buddhas in the church; and the third was the incarnate Buddha on earth. The trinity for our world consisted of the *dhyana* Amitaba, whom we shall notice farther on; Avolokitesvara, who also becomes important, and Gautama, who was our incarnate Buddha.

In the 10th century the Tibetans advanced a step further, and proclaimed the Supreme or *Adi-Buddha.* From him, the *One* and Absolute, all the Dhyana Buddhas emanated, while from them sprang the Bodisatwas, and from each Bodisatwa was evolved a kosmos or material world. Thus Buddhism had become essentially polytheistic.

Meanwhile the system had become exceedingly corrupt through a union with the Hindu doctrine of Saktism, or the worship of the female principle of Siva, and even in Tibet the hideous idols representing the gods and goddesses of Hinduism were everywhere present. By a subsequent reformation the Buddhism of Tibet was restored measurably to its original purity.

Lamaism or Lamism: The available functions of Avolokitesvara had rendered him exceedingly popular. To him all real supplications were offered. The chief abbot of Tibet, who was also temporal ruler, solidified and established his power by claiming to be an incarnation of this all-pervading Bodisat. At his death the indwelling one immediately became incarnate in some newly born infant who should succeed to the theocratic throne. To the great advantage of this supposed divinity was added an alliance with Kublai Khan and other Chinese emperors, by which, in exchange for political fealty to the Chinese Emperor, the Grand Lama of Tibet was constituted the high priest of Buddhism over China and Mongolia. Subsequently a disputed title to the Lamaship was settled by the inauguration of two Lamas, and for this purpose another indwelling Bodisat was found, viz.: Amitaba.

The Worship of Quan Yin: In China a different use was made of the ever available and popular Bodisat Avolokitesvara. He became impersonated in *Quan Yin,* the well-known goddess of mercy. That Quan Yin was regarded as a *female* finds its explanation in the influence of the Indian Saktism, which had not become quite extinct even in Tibet. Some of the abbesses in the Tibetan monasteries were regarded as incarnations of the wives of Siva. Quan Yin on the same principle was an impersonation of Avolokitesvara on the female side of his nature. Moreover, in this, as in some forms of historic Christianity, the notion that women's sympathy and compassion are most tender had, perhaps, some weight. In both China and Japan Quan Yin is one of the most popular, because the most merciful, of deities. She is represented as having attained Nirvana, but as having voluntarily submitted to rebirth in heaven that she might compassionate mankind.

The Buddhist Doctrine of Salvation by Faith: We have seen that the celestial or Dhyana Buddha of our world system was Amitaba. This mystical being has become in the Yodo and the Shin sects of Japan a complete savior. By the great merit which he has stored up through millions of ages he is able to save, vicariously and to the uttermost, all who in true faith call upon his name. By the Shin sect the doctrine is most fully developed. They claim that a single act of faith and trust in Amitaba will save the soul forever. There is a complete substitution or transfer of righteousness from the savior to the sinner. There is an abandonment of the notion of self-merit and self-help. Endless transmigration gives place to an immediate and lasting enjoyment of heaven beyond the setting sun. Asceticism is rejected as useless, and one's own merit is "as superfluous as furs in summer." Yet this faith is said to work by love, and good deeds are performed out of gratitude to Amitaba. It is very remarkable that Buddhism, beginning in sheer atheism, should finally have reached the very threshold of Christianity—*without the Christ.* There has never appeared a more clever and complete counterfeit. No other false system has ever paid so marked a tribute, tho involuntary, to the fundamental doctrines of Christianity.

The Present Buddhisms: We have seen how the system has been developed in different lands. In Ceylon and Burma it is still a mere ethical cult, while the religious aspirations of men are largely met by the worship of spirits. In Siam it is buttressed by an intimate relation to the government of the State. In India it has been virtually extinct since the 9th century. In Tibet, as has already been shown, it is a virtual theocrasy under the name of Lamism. In China there are thirteen Buddhist sects, but the system as a whole has become a constituent of the triangular system known as the *Sankaio,* or "The Three Religions," Confucianism, Taouism, and Buddhism. They are so united that each supplements the other. The Chinese Buddhism has borrowed from Confucianism its reverence for ancestors and for the State, and from Taouism its demigods and its geomantic superstitions. The Chinese are in turn Confucianists, Buddhists, or Taouists, as exigencies may arise.

The Buddhism of Mongolia has borrowed largely the Tibetan type, tho it has multiplied its Lamas almost indefinitely. Any distinguished Buddhist monk may come to be regarded as an incarnation of some holy Buddha, and through this open pathway of ambitious saintship, fraud and corruption have entered. The Mongolian Buddhism is of even a darker and more gloomy type than that of other lands.

The Buddhism of Japan has been greatly influenced by a union with Shintoism. It has embraced many of its popular superstitions, and as from Taouism in China, so from Shintoism in Japan it has adopted the national heroes and demigods and enshrined them in its temples. For a thousand years there was a mutual agreement that Shinto priests should solemnize all marriages and Buddhist priests officiate at all funerals. This relation was finally abolished by imperial edict.

The Alleged Coincidences between the Life of Gautama and that of Christ: We have already alluded to the incidents of Buddha's birth and early life, as set forth in the legends, particularly in the *Lalita Vistara* of Nepal. Great use has been made of these by the apologists of Buddhism. The inference which is generally drawn from them is that the Gospel narrative is largely borrowed from the earlier life of Gautama. Abundant refutations of this assumption have been presented by Eitel, Kuenen, Kellogg, Rhys Davids, and others.

1. "There is," says Rhys Davids, "no evidence whatever of any actual and direct communication of these ideas common to Buddhism and Christianity from the East to the West."

2. Many of the coincidences are merely accidental. The events in both cases are those which might naturally occur independently of any connection; such as the fact that both infants were welcomed with joy by friends as well as kindred, or that they were both consecrated in temples, or that both were tempted to turn aside from their great missions, or that both were credited with precocious wisdom.

3. The fact has already been shown that the *Lalita Vistara,* which gives most of these legends of Gautama's childhood, cannot be proved to have existed earlier than the 6th century. While there is no evidence of communication of the ideas common to Buddhism and Christianity from the East to the West, evidence is abundant that Christianity had been preached and had gained a foothold in India and Central Asia long before that date.

4. It is intrinsically improbable, not to say impossible, that a circle of disciples which embraced the mother and brethren of Jesus should have undertaken to palm off a false or borrowed history.

5. It is still more improbable that the disciples, whose whole aim was to show that Christ's advent was a fulfilment of Jewish prophecy and vitally connected with the Old Testament Church, should have clumsily copied a mass of heathen legends. Considering the Jewish horror of heathenism, no policy could have been more fatal.

6. The disciples of Christ taught a pure theism, in which supernatural elements appeared in an intense and special power. Would they base the story of one claiming to be the Son of God on the biography of a Gentile atheist?

7. Many of the coincidences are rather contrasts. Christ's preexistence was that of a Divine Being, Buddha's was merely a series of transmigrations. Christ had shared the equal glory of the Father; Buddha had been a soldier, a thief, an elephant, a tiger, a snipe, a frog; Christ's baptism was a religious rite, that of Gautama a bath in a river. Christ's miracles were sensible and useful, those of Buddha objectless, childish, grotesque.

The Alleged Humanity of Buddhism as Compared with Christianity: There has been great effort on the part of opposers of the Christian faith to exalt Buddhism as a superior system. It has been especially urged that the "Light of Asia" was the teacher of a gospel of peace, strangely contrasting with the belligerent doctrines and history of the Christian Church. In reply to this claim it should be said, in the outset, that in all comparisons between Asiatic faiths and those of Europe, differences of climate and race characteristics should be borne in mind. Between the soft and puny tribes of Southern

India or Ceylon and the Norsemen of the Baltic there are physical contrasts which no faith could wholly efface. But considering that Scandinavians, once the terrors of Europe, are now the most peaceful of men, we may point to the influences which Christianity has exerted upon them as among the highest triumphs of any religious faith. Moreover, northern races of Buddhists are by no means distinguished for a gentle and pacific spirit.

There is scarcely any country in which the life of a stranger is more imperiled than in Mongolia. The famous conqueror, Kublai Khan, was converted to Buddhism, but, as Ebrard has well shown, no change was wrought in his nature or his ambitious plans. The Japanese, tho Buddhists for thirteen centuries, have been a warlike race, and their temples are often crowded with the images of bloodthirsty heroes.

It is admitted that Gautama discountenanced the destruction of life, whether of man or of beast. Even insects were spared with punctilious care. But this was no new precept. Brahmans had long before taught the same, and the sect known as the Jains are most absurdly scrupulous of all. This sacredness of life is based on the doctrine of transmigration, which is common to all nations of Southern Asia. The meanest beast or reptile may be an incarnation of a human spirit. But the real humanities of Buddhism are infinitely inferior to those of Christianity. Ostentatious care of brutes is often seen side by side with utter disregard of human suffering. In Canton one may see a sacred asylum for swine, but he would look in vain for a home for the orphan or the blind. A missionary board in our day has been asked to provide some place in Bangkok for the insane, because such an asylum had never been imagined, so that all that could be done for a demented foreigner in that city was to lodge him like a criminal in jail.

The alleged instances of benevolence in the history of Gautama are chiefly found, not like those of Christ, in his earthly life, but in the brief stories of his former existences. Once as a hare he gave himself for a dinner to a hungry tigress. In another of his lives he gave his two children to a demon who desired to eat them, and as their blood streamed from the monster's mouth he simply said, "By the merit of this deed may rays of light emanate from me."

The attitude of Buddhism toward woman has been greatly emphasized in recent years by its special advocates in Christian lands. That it mitigated many of the wrongs which had been visited upon the female sex by the Brahmans will be conceded.

It was a great and important step when the Buddha, not on his own impulse, but by the persuasions of his kinsman and disciple, Ananda, admitted women to the privileges of the Samgha or holy order. The principle involved carried with it many social ameliorations. Yet the position of Gautama and the whole leaven of his influence in this respect was far below the standards of the New Testament. In the outset his example in forsaking his wife and child to become a recluse cannot be commended. Paul taught that a man might *remain* single for the sake of the kingdom, but to break away from the most sacred of obligations, and that stealthily and without consent, must be adjudged a crime. The baneful influence of this example, like that of Mohammed's immorality, has brought forth its evil fruit abundantly. In Burma any man desiring to be rid of his wife has only to enter a monastery and remain a year or even a month, after which he is free to leave his sanctities behind him and marry another wife.

Logically, Buddhism is opposed to all marriages, to all love for wife or children. The principle that human relationships are fraught with pain, and that to get rid of pain one must attain an equipoise which is tantamount to absolute indifference, would break up all society. This tendency was pointed out to Gautama, and he accordingly divided his followers into two classes, the monks and the laity. It was an illogical but necessary concession.

Buddhist monasticism rests upon a much more radical principle than that of the Roman and Greek churches. These, while maintaining that celibacy is conducive to the highest sanctity, nevertheless honor marriage, and make it a sacrament for the masses of men. Not so with Buddhism. It puts no honor upon the relation; it regards it as an evil. Many utterances are quoted from Buddha which cast reproach upon woman as woman.

Thus in the *Dhammikha Sutta*, "A wise man should avoid married life as if it were a burning pit of live coals." Again, "That which is named woman is sin." On another occasion Buddha said: "Any woman whatever, if she have a proper opportunity and can do it in secret, and if she be enticed thereto, will do that which is wrong, however ugly the paramour may be." No foul slander in the Laws of Manu can exceed this.

Two general precepts of Buddhism will suffice to show the discount which it puts upon woman. First, Gautama taught that, altho she could enter upon a holy life as a nun, she could not attain Nirvana without first being born as a man; and, second, it was held that, altho a Bodisat in his preexistent lives might be a wolf, a snipe, or a frog, he could never become a woman. Quite in accord with these ideas, the female sex has remained in general degradation in all Buddhist lands.

The fact that a low grade of morality exists in countries wholly under the influence of this system, that profligacy is unbridled in Mongolia, that thousands of children were sold for prostitution in Japan, that the vile custom of polyandry prevails unchecked in Tibet, will doubtless be set down to other causes by Buddhist apologists. But when we turn to the canonical books of the system and find passages so vile that the translators have not dared to translate them, no such excuses can be accepted. The Bishop of Colombo, in the *Nineteenth Century* of July, 1888, called attention to the fact that the translators and publishers of the Pitakas of Ceylon had omitted some portions which were absolutely vile. He did not complain that the omission had been made, but that no mention was made of the fact —that the English readers of the *Sacred Books of the East* were left to suppose that the culled and expurgated version of the Vinayana there given was a fair and honest representation of Buddhism as it really was and is. Professor Max Müller, in his introduction to the first volume of the *Sacred Books*, a volume relating to the Upanishads, admits that some things in Hindu literature were considered unfit for the English translation, but such notice is wanting in Professor Oldenberg's translation of the Pitakas, where especially such omissions should be explained, since Buddhism *par excellence* is paraded as a model of purity. Lest we may seem to do injustice to the Buddhist sacred canon of Ceylon, it should be said that the omitted passages are not positive recommendations of vice—quite the reverse; but the very prohibitions defile the mind.

The aim seems to have been to draw out the opinion of "The Blessed One" in regard to every vice and crime that the basest imagination could conceive of. Cases were stated, therefore, in which monks had fallen into every species of sin. The minutiæ, the sickening details, the prurient particularity of the recitals were such that the Bishop of Colombo concludes that the authors must have transcended the possibilities of actual sin, and in some instances drawn upon a depraved imagination in order to illustrate the wisdom of the Buddha.

Contrasts with Christianity: There is not space for even a brief allusion to the admixtures of Buddhism with lower forms of superstition which it has encountered and absorbed in many lands, such as the wide-spread spirit-worship, serpent-worship, and even fetishism. But a few of the many points of contrast between Buddhism and Christianity may be presented. We have admitted the probable sincerity of Gautama as a reformer and the great victory which he gained over his own evil propensities, also the general tone of benevolence which appeared in his teachings; but the system must be judged as a whole and in the broad perspective of its influence. It is thus that Christianity is judged.

1. Buddhism contrasts with Christianity in respect to God. The one, at least in its original form, is agnostic if not atheistic, and therefore derives no motives of action from any higher source than man himself or some blind law of moral cause and effect. The other makes God real, personal, and supreme—the source of all highest inspiration and help, the Author of every blessing present or future, the Arbiter of the human conscience, and the Rewarder of all who seek Him.

2. There is a marked contrast with respect to the soul. Buddhism recognizes no permanent entity or *ego*. There is only a transient interaction of physical properties and mental powers. At death only the Karma, or the good or evil desert remains. Christianity recognizes the soul as created in the image of God, as conscious and spiritual, a distinct and permanent being, destined to live hereafter, and capable of loving God and enjoying Him forever.

3. While Christianity represents sin as an offense against God and centers in Him the bond of all moral obligation, Buddhism sees only a personal inconvenience, an accumulation of consequences. The motive even in benevolent action is utterly selfish, as it aims at merit. Thus when the preexistent Buddha gave his children to be devoured by a demon, as stated above, he thought not of their suffering, or of his wrong toward them, but only of his own great merit. All laws of moral right and wrong seem distorted by such a conception.

4. Buddhism has no Savior. When Sir Edwin Arnold represents him as coming to save the world, he simply reads into Buddhism his own conceptions borrowed from the New Testament and his Christian training. Buddha relied wholly on himself and he taught all men to do the same. In later ages Buddhists in various lands have expressed a felt want of humanity by adopting various types of *quasi* theism, and have conceived of supernatural beings as divine helpers, but they have so far departed from real Buddhism. The term salvation is wholly out of place in such a system, while, on the other hand, Christianity is in its whole aim and its whole nature a system of divine redemption from sin and death.

5. Buddhism lays stress on self and self-interest. Its self-denials are for purely selfish ends and it cares nothing for the needs of mankind. In Christianity the ideal man denies himself for the good of the whole body of which he is a member, and subordinates self-will and self-interest to the welfare of mankind.

6. Buddhism has shown itself incapable of regenerating society. It was founded by one who had turned his back on all social life. It was very natural that the system should discount woman and the home, for its author was an ascetic, and the monastic spirit pervades all his teachings. Homelessness, mendicancy, suppression of all social and domestic instincts, destruction of love and desire, even the desire of future life, silence as of "a broken gong," and "solitude as of a rhinoceros"—these were the goal of the true Buddhist.

7. Buddhism is a system of pessimism, Christianity, a revelation of cheerful and immortal hope. Gautama aimed at "the death of deaths." Christ brought life and immortality to life.

The whole assumption upon which the "Great Renunciation" was made to rest is that the universe is out of order, that all life is a burden, that there is no benevolent creatorship, no kind providence, and no salvation. Whoever may have been responsible for such a world, it is one of universal misery and distress. Man and beast make common cause against it, and Buddha is the one great sympathizer. When he preached at Kapilavastu before his father's court the whole animal creation was there,

"Catching the opening of his lips to learn
That wisdom which hath made our Asia mild."

It appears to have been a grand indignation meeting of man and beast, the first and broadest of Communist gatherings, at which Buddha voiced the common protest against the order of nature, and pointed out the way of escape from the sad nexus of existence. All

"took the promise of his piteous speech,
So that their lives, prisoned in the shape of ape,
Tiger or deer, shagged bear, jackal or wolf,
Foul feeding kite, pearled dove or peacock gemmed,
Squat toad or speckled serpent, lizard, bat,
Yea, or fish fanning the river waves,
Launched meekly at the skirts of brotherhood,
With man who hath less innocence than these:
And in mute gladness knew their bondage broke
Whilst Buddha spoke these things before the king."

There was no mention of sin, but only of universal misfortune! As Sir Monier Williams remarks, the problem to which Christianity leads a man is: What shall I do to be saved? But that pressed upon men by Buddhism is: What shall I do to be extinguished?

In contrast with the deep shadows of a brooding and all-embracing pessimism like this, we need only to hint at that glow of hope and joy with which the Sun of Righteousness has flooded the world, the fatherly love and compassion with which the Old Testament and the New are replete, the divine plan of redemption, the great sacrifice, the superabounding grace, the brotherhood of man, and the eternal fellowship with God.

Special difficulties await the Christian missionary who attempts to convince educated Buddhists of the unique quality of the truths taught by Jesus Christ. He meets with men whose intellect is perverted by persistent violations of logic. It is easy for the mind trained by Buddhism to believe mutually exclusive propositions. Such a mind "feels no obstacle in believing that there is white blackness, slow swiftness, square roundness, or crooked uprightness." The real vitality occasionally seen in Buddhism is another difficulty which the missionary has to face. In Japan, the claim of championship of the highest morality and of love to the race is made by Buddhists with sharp arraignment of Christianity in these directions. In Ceylon the Buddhist clergy have adopted Christian methods of instruction of children in Sunday schools, of tracts and religious periodicals to control the minds of the masses, and of revivalist tours to stir their emotions.

What the missionary encounters in Buddhism is a religion founded upon a life, fortified by a literature, and witnessed to by the experience of multitudes. He must therefore study it profoundly, for this ancient system is not to be lightly regarded or quickly overthrown.

Davids (T. W. Rhys-), *Buddhism*, New York, 1896; Williams M.(Monier), *Buddhism in Its Connection with Brahmanism and Its Contrast with Christianity*, New York, 1889; Waddell, (L. A.) *Buddhism of Tibet*, London, 1894; Fielding (H.), *The Soul of a People*, London, 1898, (Buddhism in Burma;) *Missionary Review of the World*, vol. IX., pp. 253, 326, 416, 513, 582.

BUEA: A town in the mountain region of the German Colony of the Kamerun, of which it is the seat of the colonial government. Station of the Basel Missionary Society (1896) with 3 missionaries and their wives, 6 native workers, 4 outstations, 7 village schools and (1902) 91 communicants.

BUENOS AIRES: Capital of the Argentine Republic, on the estuary of the Rio de la Plata. The most important city in South America, it differs little in its character from American and European seaboard cities. Population (1895) 663,854.

Station of the ME (1836), with 2 missionaries and their wives, 1 missionary woman, 16 native workers, men and women, 5 chapels, 3 village schools, 1 high school, a printing house and 851 professing Christians. Station also of the SDA (1891), with 5 missionaries, 4 of them with their wives, 1 missionary woman, 8 native workers, 14 outstations and 386 professing Christians. Station also of the South America Missionary Society (1898), with 1 missionary and his wife, 11 native workers, men and women, 1 chapel, 2 village schools. Station also of the PB, with 1 missionary and his wife, 3 missionary women and 1 printing house. Station also of the Missionary Pence Association (1901), with 4 missionaries; also of the International Medical and Benevolent Association, with 1 missionary and his wife; also of the YMCA (1901), with 1 missionary and his wife; also of the BFBS, with 5 native workers and 1 book depot.

BUFF BAY: A town on the northern coast of Jamaica, West Indies; station of the CWBM, with 1 missionary and his wife, 2 chapels, 2 Sunday schools, 2 village schools, 4 young people's societies and 135 professing Christians. Also station of the Western Annual Conference of the Wesleyan Church in the West Indies, with 1 missionary.

BUGHI LANGUAGE: This belongs to the Malayan family and is spoken by above one million of the inhabitants of the island of Celebes. It is written with its own alphabet.

BUITENZORG: A station of the Dutch Missionary Society in Western Java, founded in 1869. It has 1 missionary, 5 native workers, and 165 communicants.

BUKALEBA: A settlement in the Usoga district of Uganda, Central Africa, situated near the N. extremity of the Victoria Nyanza; station of the CMS (1891), with 1 missionary and his wife, 57 native workers, men and women and 92 communicants.

BUKASA: A settlement on one of the Sese Islands in the Victoria Nyanza, Uganda, Central Africa; station of the CMS (1895), with 1 missionary and his wife, 143 native workers, men and women, 1 Sunday school, 3 village schools and 480 communicants.

BULANDSHAHR: A city in the United Provinces, India, situated S. E. of Delhi; a station of the ME, with 13 native workers, men and women, 7 chapels, 16 Sunday schools, 12 village schools, 2 young people's societies and 681 professing Christians. Also station of the ZBM, with 3 missionary women, 7 native women workers, 3 village schools and 155 Zenana pupils.

BULAWAYO: A town and railroad station in southern Rhodesia, Africa; station of the WMS, with 3 native workers, 2 chapels, 1 Sunday school, 1 village school and 145 professing Christians. Station also of the SPG (1893), with 3 missionaries, 1 native worker and 66 communicants. Station also of the SDA (1895), with 6 missionaries, 4 of them with their wives (1 a physician), 2 Sunday schools, 2 village schools, 1 orphanage, 1 dispensary. Also written Buluwayo.

BULGARIA: A country of the Balkan Peninsula, forming an autonomous principality under the suzerainty of the Sultan of Turkey. It is bounded on the north by Rumania, on the east by the Black Sea, on the south by European Turkey, and on the west by Servia. It is divided by the Balkan Mountains into two parts: Bulgaria proper on the north and South Bulgaria or Eastern Rumelia on the south of that range. Area of the whole, 38,080 square miles.

Except along the Balkan Mountains, which traverse the whole principality from east to west, the country is a vast plain. The climate is temperate. The plains are hot in summer, and along the Danube there is much malaria, but the highlands are healthy. The higher mountains have snow on their peaks the greater part of the year.

The census of 1900 gives a total population of 3,733,189.

The Bulgarians are descendants of the Slavs who inhabited the Balkan Peninsula in the 7th century. In the second half of the 9th century (860-64) Christianity was introduced in Bulgaria, and with it an alphabet was formed and the Scriptures were translated.

This was due to SS. Cyril and Methodius, who

are honored even to this day as patron saints by the Bulgarian Church.

The Bulgarians belong to the Greek (Orthodox) branch of the Christian Church. Their spiritual head is the Exarch, who resides in Constantinople and has the jurisdiction over the twelve bishoprics into which Bulgaria is divided. In 1893 the members of the (Orthodox) Greek Church numbered 2,606,786, the Mohammedans in the Principality numbered 643,258, the Jews, 28,307; the Roman Catholics, 22,617; the Armenians, 6,643; and the Protestants, 2,384. Of the Mohammedans about 200,000 are Bulgarians in race, language and customs and are known by the distinctive name of *Pomaks*.

The modern Bulgarian language has receded more than any other Slavic dialect from the ancient Slovenic or the ancient Bulgarian. While the latter belongs to the *synthetic* class of languages and is rich in cases and other grammatical forms, the modern Bulgarian has lost most of these forms and has become an *analytic* language, expressing the relations of cases by prepositions, as in English. The use of the article, which is placed after and not before the word, chiefly distinguishes it from the ancient language and from its cognate Slavic dialects.

Special missionary work for the Bulgarians was first organized by the ME in 1857, which has since conducted missionary operations in that part of Bulgaria lying N. of the Balkans (which was at that time a province of European Turkey). The field was organized into a Mission Conference in 1892. It now has as a working force 1 missionary and his wife, 2 unmarried women, and 11 ordained native preachers. Work is carried on in 12 places and the number of church members reported is 234. It also has a high school with 57 scholars.

The ABCFM about the same time commenced work for the Bulgarians on the S. of the Balkans. It now has in Bulgaria a working force of 18 missionaries, men and women, and 16 ordained native preachers. Its operations extend to 30 places, and the number of church members reported at 900. A collegiate institute, a theological school, a boarding and high school for girls and a publishing house are maintained at Samokov.

The BFBS and ABS have provided Bibles for this region and employ colporteurs for their dissemination.

BULGARIAN LANGUAGE: This language belongs to the Slavic branch of the Aryan family. It is spoken by more than four million people, chiefly found in Bulgaria and the adjoining districts of European Turkey. The alphabet used is substantially the same as the one invented by the bishop Cyril, in the 9th century, and now commonly called the Russian alphabet.

Old Bulgarian literature is written in the Slavic language and is not understood by the common people. A considerable modern literature in Bulgarian has sprung up since the Crimean War of 1853-56. To this growth of modern Bulgarian literature American missionaries have given a notable stimulus. The modern Bulgarian language, in fact, has been strongly and permanently affected by the translation of the Bible made by Dr. Riggs and Dr. Long and published by the Bible societies.

BULILIMA: A settlement in Bechuanaland, Africa, S. W. of Bulawayo; station of the LMS (1895), with 1 missionary, 1 native worker, 5 Sunday schools and 5 village schools.

BULL BAY: A town on the S. coast of Jamaica, W. I., about 12 miles E. of Kingston; station of the CWBM (1876), with 1 missionary and his wife, 4 chapels, 3 Sunday schools, 2 village schools, 2 young people's societies and 224 professing Christians.

BULLOM: A district of Sierra Leone, W. Africa, lying north of the Sierra Leone River; occupied by the CMS (1861) and now in charge of the Sierra Leone Church Missionary Society, with 10 native workers, men and women, 1 chapel 1 Sunday school, 6 village schools and 296 baptized Christians.

BULLOM LANGUAGE: The Bullom belongs to the negro group of African languages, and is spoken in the region of Sierra Leone, W. Africa, by a limited number of people. It has adopted some English words and is written with Roman letters.

BULONGOA: A settlement near the northern end of Lake Nyasa, in German East Africa; station of the Berlin Missionary Society (1895), with 1 missionary and 9 communicants.

BULRAMPUR. See BALRAMPUR.

BULUWAYO. See BULAWAYO.

BUMBULI: A settlement in German East Africa, situated in the Usambara country in the northeastern part of the Colony; station of the German Evangelical Society for Missions in East Africa (1899), with 3 missionaries (one having his wife), 1 chapel, and 1 village school.

BUNGABONDAR: A settlement in the Toba district of Sumatra, Dutch East Indies, situated near Sipirok; station of the Rhenish Missionary Society, with 1 missionary and his wife, 17 native workers, men and women, 1 Sunday school, 13 village schools and 921 communicants, the most of them converted Mohammedans.

BUNGU: A settlement in German East Africa, situated in the Usambara region about 50 miles N. W. of Vuga; station of the German East Africa Missionary Society (1901), with 1 missionary and his wife.

BURRISAL. See BARISAL.

BUONA VISTA. See GALLE.

BURDWAN. See BARDWAN.

BURHANPUR: A town in the Nimar district, Central Provinces, India; station of the ME, with 4 native workers, 3 Sunday schools, 1 village school, and 220 professing Christians.

BURGHERSDORP: A town in the northern part of Cape Colony, S. Africa; station of the South African Wesleyan Missionary Society, with 24 native workers, 2 chapels, 2 Sunday schools, 3 village schools and 164 professing Christians.

BURJA: A district in the Lohardaga section of Chota Nagpur, India; field of the Gossner Missionary Society, with 3 missionaries, 71 native workers, 38 chapels, 38 Sunday schools, 2 village schools, 1 high school, a book depot and 8,886 professing Christians. Also written Burju.

BURMA: Within the past seventy-five years the political map of Southeastern Asia, and especially that part of it lying between Tibet and Yunnan on the north and the Bay of Bengal on the south, eastern Bengal on the west and the Mekong River on the east, has been materially changed three times.

At present, and for missionary purposes,

Burma may be considered as composed of Upper and Lower Burma, Upper Burma comprising the late kingdom or empire of Burma, and Lower Burma all that portion of the country below the 20th degree of north latitude, as well as the Tenasserim provinces and the present mission stations in Arakan and Shan-land in the East, the whole now composing the most eastern portion of the British Indian Empire.

Burma is drained by three great rivers and their numerous affluents: the Irawadi, with a great and increasing commerce, about 1,400 miles in length from its sources in one or more of the great lakes in the lofty Himalayas, and navigable for 1,000 miles or more by large steamers; the Sitang, of inferior length, and having, at certain seasons of tide and southwest winds, a *bore* at its mouth, which renders the entrance very difficult; it bears on its bosom a constantly increasing commerce, steamers plying between Rangoon, Maulmain, Thayet-myo, and Taung-ngu; the Salwen, a long and navigable river, rising in the mountains of Yunnan, China, and pursuing a course almost parallel to that of the Irawadi. These rivers are separated in their upper courses by ranges of mountains varying from 4,000 to 6,000 feet in height, but as they approach the Bay of Bengal or the Gulf of Martaban these mountains subside into broad and fertile plains, and the rivers enter the bay or the gulf by many mouths, forming rich and extensive deltas, with a very rich soil, but often covered with a dense jungle which makes the climate sickly. The valleys of these rivers are of considerable breadth, and being well watered by their smaller affluents, are productive.

The beasts of prey are of great size and ferocity. The elephants of Burma attain a greater size than those of any other country in the world. The lion, tiger, leopard, of several species, and rhinoceros are all very destructive. The buffalo and the Brahmanee bull are trained, as are many of the elephants, as beasts of burden. Horses are few and are rarely used for draught purposes, the ox or buffalo taking their place. The rodent tribes exist in large numbers and are great pests, often destroying the rice crop in large districts. Pythons, boas, and other serpents, and especially venomous snakes, like the *cobra de capello*, are abundant. Lizards of all kinds are found everywhere. The birds are numerous and many of them beautiful. The insect tribes are annoying and many of them dangerous.

Burma has an area of 236,738 square miles (including Lower Burma, conquered in 1852, and Upper Burma, annexed on the overthrow of the tyrant Thebaw in 1885). Its population (1901) is 10,490,624.

There are said to be forty-two different races in Burma, but they are mainly divisible into four distinct peoples, of whom the first two are almost entirely Buddhist in religion. These are: 1. The Burmans, under which general name are included the Burmans proper, the ruling race, and the Arakanese. 2. The Talaings, or Peguans, once the lords of the country, but now greatly diminished in numbers. 3. The **Shans**, a generally nomadic race, but of different affinities, as Chinese, Siamese, and Burman Shans. Their national name is Tai. They occupy the eastern region of Burma, and extend into Northern Siam and Southwestern China. 4. The fourth race are the **Karens**, of whom there are more than thirty tribes, differing, in many respects, from each other in language, form, and habits, but all worshipers of Nats or demons. The Karens of Lower Burma readily received the Gospel, and those of them who were under Burmese rule bore courageously bitter and cruel persecution from the Burmans for its sake. The Sgau and Pwo tribes, which occupied Pegu and the Tenasserim provinces, have been largely converted to Christianity. The highland tribes of Central Burma, the Bghais, Pakus, Gecko, Toungthüs, and Red Karens, became converts at a later date.

Other tribes having few affinities with the Karens, yet, like them, worshiping demons from motives of fear, are found in Northern Burma and along the Arakan border, and are moving down the Irawadi into the vicinity of Mandalay and below, and toward Sandoway in Arakan. The largest and best known of these tribes are the Ch'ins and the Kach'ins. The latter are said to be the fiercest and most warlike tribe in Burma. No Burman soldier dares to set foot in one of their villages, which are always situated at the summit of high hills. They are supposed to be identical with the Singphos of Assam. Yet these rough and fierce men are yielding in considerable numbers to the power of the Gospel. It is worth noting here that in all Burman cities there is a considerable Chinese population engaged in trade, which they control.

Protestant Missions: The first attempt to plant a Protestant mission in Burma was made at Rangoon, in 1807, by Messrs. Chater and Mardon, English Baptists. Felix Carey, the eldest son of Dr. William Carey, of Serampur, joined them soon after, but Mr. Mardon left in a few months and Mr. Chater at the end of four years. The London Missionary Society sent two missionaries to Rangoon in 1808, but one died and the other removed in a year. Mr. Chater during his four years' stay translated Matthew's Gospel into Burmese, which was printed at Serampur. Mr. Carey remained till 1814, and then, having received an appointment and title from the Burmese emperor, he went to Ava to reside. There had been no attempt at missionary work except this translation of Matthew, and no Burman had heard that there was an eternal God. Mr. Carey's mission house was about two miles out of the city. Rangoon was at that time a miserable, dirty town of 8,000 or 10,000 inhabitants, with houses built of bamboo and teak planks and having thatched roofs. Its only importance lay in the fact that it was the capital of a rich and extensive province, governed by a viceroy, an official of the highest rank, who was a favorite of Bhodau Phra, the most bloodthirsty and brutal tyrant and the most bigoted Buddhist who had yet sat on the Burman throne. The viceroy at Rangoon was almost as brutal, but his chief wife was an amiable woman, well disposed toward foreigners, and possessing great influence over her husband.

On July 13, 1813, **Rev. Adoniram Judson** and wife arrived at Rangoon to open a Protestant mission there. He was a man who endured all things that he might find access to a people sunk in morasses of evil. It was not until 1819 that he was able to preach and teach religion in his *zayat* and receive inquirers there. June 27, 1819, he baptized the first Burman convert to Christianity, Moung Nau. In this year Bhodau Phra, the Burmese emperor, died, and was succeeded by his grandson, Phagyi-dau, a ruler equally arrogant, brutal and bloodthirsty with his grandfather, but with much less ability. His arrogance and tyranny brought on the first Burman War of 1825-26, and led to the cession to the East India Company of the Tenasserim provinces, Arakan, and Chittagong. In 1852, the second war with the English took place, and Rangoon, Pegu, and all Southern Burma became British territory. In 1853 Rangoon became again a station of the American Baptist Missionary Union, and from that time onward the Society has had great success in all parts of the land. Rangoon was also the first station (established 1859) of the Burma mission conducted by the SPG. The educational work of this Society has been of a high order and wide influence. The SPG is also laboring successfully among the Karens.

The ME Society has also carried on a mission in Burma since 1878, laboring especially for European colonists and Eurasians.

The WMS established a station at Mandalay in 1889, and is doing a remarkable educational work for women. It has also given attention to the lepers, maintaining an asylum which is not only a refuge but a portal to a new life to these wretched sufferers.

The YMCA and the YWCA have stations in Burma; so the Mission to Lepers, the Missionary Pence Association, the Leipzig Missionary Society; and the China Inland Mission has a single station at Bhamo, on the northern border.

It should be borne in mind that while many Burmese Buddhists have been converted, the simple, more approachable Hill tribes have furnished the larger part of the Christians now found in Burma.

Shans, Amongst the, Colquhon (A. R.), and Hallet (H. S.), London, 1885; *Bassein, Self-Support in,* Carpenter (C. H.), 1883; *Golden Chersonese,* Bishop (Mrs. I. B.), London, 1883; *With the Jungle Folk,* Cumming (E. D.), London, 1897.

BURMESE LANGUAGE: The Burmese, which is spoken throughout the Burmese Empire and Arakan, belongs to the Tibeto-Burman group of the non-Aryan languages of Asia. It is used by about six million people, and, being one of the aggressive languages, it is constantly increasing the area of its use. It is written with its own peculiar Burmese character.

BURNS, William C.: Born in the Parish of Dun, Scotland, April 1, 1815. Graduated at Aberdeen in 1834; studied theology at Glasgow, and after a period of successful labor in Ireland and among the French in Canada, was sent out by the E. P. Synod, in 1847, as its first missionary to China. On the voyage he began the study of Chinese with the only book found in London, Wiliiams' English and Chinese vocabulary, and a volume of Matthew's Gospel.

After spending a year or two at Hongkong and Canton, in 1851 he removed to Amoy, where and at Swatow he did a great work. Later he spent three years in Peking, and in 1867 he went to Newchwang to prepare the way for a mission in Manchuria. In a small room at an inn at that city, destitute of every comfort, he died on the 4th of April, 1868.

While Mr. Burns never interrupted his work of preaching, he accomplished important literary work. Of this we may mention a translation of the Pilgrim's Progress, and a collection of hymns in the Amoy dialect. With the aid of native preachers he put some of the hymns used at Amoy and Swatow into the spoken dialect of Fu-chau-fu. These he first printed in sheet form, and used them in street and chapel preaching, and then published them in book form.

Later he prepared a volume of fifty hymns in the Mandarin dialect, chiefly translations of home hymns, or hymns used in the south of China. Next he put in the dialect of Peking the *Pilgrim's Progress* complete in two volumes. Some copies were illustrated with wood-cuts. A translation of the Psalms from Hebrew was published in 1867.

BURNSHILL: A town northwest of King William's Town, Cape Colony, S. Africa. Station of the UFS, with 1 missionary and his wife, 2 missionary women, 29 native workers, 16 out-stations, 1 chapel, 16 village schools and 1,420 church members.

BUSI: A station of the CMS in Uganda, Central Africa, situated on the Victoria Nyanza, with 63 native workers, men and women, and 184 communicants.

BUSRAH. See BASRA.

BUTARITARI. See GILBERT ISLANDS.

BUTLER, William: Born in Dublin, Ireland, January 30, 1818. Died August 18, 1899. Soon after his conversion he entered the Hardwick Street Mission Seminary and Training School, in Dublin, and afterward Didsburg College, near Manchester, where he studied theology under the venerable Dr. Hannah. After preaching several years in the Irish Conference, he came to the United States, and labored for some time in the New England Conference. In the spring of 1855 he was deeply impressed by an article published by Dr. Durbin entitled "The Crisis," urging the needs of the India Mission on the heart of the Church, and in the following autumn he offered himself as missionary to this field. He was appointed superintendent of the mission, and he sailed with his wife and two children in April, 1856. The provinces of Bellary, the Deccan, Rajputana and others were brought to the attention of Mr. Butler as especially needy on his arrival in India; but after spending several weeks in Calcutta he went to the northwest to consider the opening in Oudh and Rohilkhand. These provinces, covering an area nearly as long as England and containing a population of 20,000,000 of unevangelized people, presented an attractive field to the heroic missionary; and in Oudh, in the very stronghold of the enemy, the Mission of the Methodist Church was established. The capital of Oudh, Lucknow, had three times the population of Boston; and this city was soon to be the storm center of the dreadful mutiny. Mr. Butler, with his family, settled at Bareilly, a city of 200,000 inhabitants; but soon his work was interrupted by the rumblings of the approaching outbreak. Within ten weeks of the establishment of his work, Mr. Butler was obliged to flee for his life; and ten months passed before it was possible for him to return to his station. Khan Bahadur, whó, during the mutiny, assumed the title of the Nawab of Rohilkhand, put a price on the head of each of the refugees, and, as a writer puts it, "Mr. Butler's being listed at five hundred rupees." The first meeting of Mr. Butler's mission was held at Bareilly, August 20, 1858. Three missionaries, one European helper and two natives answered the roll. Yet to this missionary was given the joy of living until he could see one hundred thousand of the people of India accepting Christ as Lord, brought into this new life through the agency of the Methodist Missions. Returning to the United States, Mr. Butler took charge of several churches in New England, and afterward he was called to the secretaryship of the American and Foreign Christian Union, an organization devoted to work in Papal lands. About this time Mr. Butler wrote *The Land of the Veda*, which had a large circulation.

Seventeen years after Mr. Butler was commissioned by his church to go to India to found a mission, he was called to perform a like service in Mexico. In 1873 he entered the Aztec land, and soon his influence was felt in the City of Mexico and throughout the surrounding country. President Diaz received him personally on several occasions, and the government of Mexico gave him full protection in laying the foundation of a mission that has prospered through the years. It was the pleasure of this venerable missionary, in 1883, to return to India, and after twenty-six years he gave thanks to God at Bareilly for the growth and power of the mission that was founded in the dark days of the mutiny. He spent his last days at Newton Centre, Mass.

Butler (Miss C.), *William Butler, the Founder of Two Missions*, Eaton & Mains, New York.

BUTTERWORTH: A town in the Transkei District of Cape Colony, S. Africa; station of the SPG (1883), with 1 missionary, 21 native workers, 21 outstations, and 760 professing Christians. Also station of the South African Wesleyan Missionary Society, with 1 missionary, 113 native workers (in the field of the station), 24 chapels, 14 Sunday schools, 24 village schools, 1 high school, 1 dispensary and 1,115 professing Christians.

BUXTON: A settlement in the Klondike region of the Yukon Territory, Canada; station of the CMS (1887), with 3 missionaries and their wives, 1 village school and 20 communicants.

BUYERS, William: Born in 1804, at Dundee, Scotland; studied at the Missionary College, Hoxton; sailed June 13, 1831, as a missionary of the LMS for India; was stationed at Benares from 1832 till 1840, when failure of health required his return to England. He died at Unchadek, near Allahabad, October 4, 1865. Mr. Buyers was an able missionary, and highly esteemed as a scholar and worker. His published *Letters on India* and *Recollections of Northern India* are very valuable.

BUZACOTT, Aaron: Born March 4, 1800, at South Molton, Devon, England; studied at Hoxton Academy; sailed as a missionary of the LMS, March 13, 1827, for the South Seas; stationed first at Tahiti, afterward at Raratonga. On May 30, 1836, he and Mrs. Buzacott accompanied a band of missionaries to Samoa, to aid them in their settlement, returning to Raratonga May, 1837. Mr. Buzacott was an accomplished linguist, and much of his time was spent, in conjunction with Messrs. Williams and Pitman, in translating the Scriptures into the language of Raratonga. He contributed also largely to the preparation of a native literature. In 1846 he sailed for England, and while there he, at the request of the Bible Society, revised and superintended the printing of the entire Raratongan Scriptures. In 1851 he returned with Mrs. Buzacott to Raratonga. In 1857 failure of health compelled him to retire from active service. Leaving Raratonga in November of that year, he went to Sydney, stopping on the way at Samoa. In July, 1860, he was appointed the agent of the Society in the Australian Colonies. He died at Sydney, September 20, 1864.

BWEMBA: A settlement on the Congo River, S. of Bolobo; station of the ABMU (1889), with 1 missionary and his wife, 18 native workers, 10 places of worship and 16 communicants.

BYINGTON, Theodore L.: Born at Johnsonsburg, N. J., March 15, 1831; graduated at Princeton College, 1849; spent four years in the study and practise of law; graduated at Union Theological Seminary, 1857; ordained at Bloomfield, N. J., June 4, 1858, and sailed as a missionary of the ABCFM for Turkey; commenced a station at Eski-zaghra, European Turkey, in 1859; returned to the United States in 1867 on account of ill health, and was released from his connection with the Board. He was reappointed as missionary of the Board in 1874 and stationed in Constantinople as editor of the Bulgarian family weekly, *Zornitsa*, and as member of the Mission Committee of Publication. Failing in health, he returned to the U. S. in 1885, and died in Philadelphia, June 18, 1888. He was a preacher of impressive earnestness and excelled as an extemporaneous speaker. His largest volume in Bulgarian was on the *Evidences of Christianity*, which has had a wide circulation. It is probable that the *Zornitsa* while edited by Dr. Byington contributed as much as any other instrumentality toward the development of those characteristics that have been so prominent among the Bulgarians in their long struggle for national independence.

C

CABACABURI: A settlement in British Guiana north of Queenstown; station of the SPG (1835), with 1 missionary, 2 outstations and 500 professing Christians.

CABRUANG. See TALAUT ISLANDS.

CACADU: A settlement about 20 miles N. E. of Queenstown, Cape Colony, S. Africa; station of the South Africa Baptist Missionary Society, with 2 women missionaries.

CACALOTENANGO: A town in Mexico, situated about 50 miles S. E. of Mexico City; station of the Mexican Mission Board, with 2 native workers, man and woman, 22 outstations, 1 chapel, 5 Sunday schools, 1 village school, a young people's society, and 175 evangelical Christians.

CACAUDROVE: A village in the northern part of the island of Vanua Levu, Fiji Islands; station of the Australian Wesleyan Methodist Missionary Society, with 1 missionary and his wife, 22 outstations, 90 chapels, 158 Sunday schools, 169 village schools, and 2,329 professing Christians.

CACHOEIRA: A town in the Province of Bahia,

Brazil, situated on the Paraguassir River, 45 miles W. of Bahia de Todos os Santos. Station of the PN (1873) formerly known as St. Felix from the fact that the missionaries lived in a place of that name on the opposite bank of the river. In 1903 the station had 1 missionary, 2 missionary women, 2 native workers, 5 outstations, 4 organized churches, 2 boarding schools, 2 day schools and 153 church members.

CACONDA. See KAKONDA.

CAFFRE. See KAFIR.

CAFRARIA: A part of the eastern section of Cape Colony, S. Africa. Also called Kafirland.

CAIRO: A city of Egypt, situated about nine miles south of the apex of the delta, where the Nile divides into the eastern, or Damietta, branch and the western, or Rosetta, branch. The city extends from the edge of the desert at the base of the Mokattam Hills on the east to the river on the west, and southward until it joins Old Cairo (Misr Atika) on the site of the ancient city Festat. This was the site of New Babylon, said to have been founded by the Babylonians after the conquest of Egypt by Cambyses, about 525 B. C. The new city, Cairo, was founded by Johar, the general of the Fatimite Caliph Mu'izz. It was called Misr el Kaḥira because it is said that at the precise time when the foundation of the walls was being laid, the planet Mars, which by the Arabs is called Kahir, crossed the meridian of the new city, and Mu'izz accordingly named it from this event. The city grew rapidly because of its position and the facility with which building material was found. It has become the largest city on the continent of Africa, and the second in the Turkish Empire, having a population of from 400,000 to 500,000.

Cairo was made the capital of Egypt in 973, and has continued to enjoy this preeminence during the many vicissitudes of 917 years.

From January 26, 1517, when the Ottoman Sultan Selim I. entered the city in triumph, until July 22, 1798, when, after the battle of the Pyramids, Napoleon I. entered the city, nothing of sufficient importance seems to have occurred to merit a place in history. And it was not until after Mehemet Ali was established as Viceroy of Egypt that the city began anew to enjoy prosperity. Ismail Pasha while Khedive made great and important improvements in and around the capital, such as extending the city so as to form the new part called for him Ismailiyeh, improving the Esbekiyeh public gardens, planting trees in and about the city, and uniting Cairo with the western bank of the river by a magnificent iron bridge. Since the British occupation of Egypt, in 1882, the city has been very much improved and many handsome buildings have been erected.

Among the objects of interest to the missionary, besides the Boulak Museum, is Jama-el-Azhar, which was changed from its original use as a mosque to a "university" by Caliph Aiz Billah on the suggestion of his vizier, Abu'l Farag Ya'kub, in the year 378 of the Hegira, and has become the most important Mohammedan institution of learning in the world.

There is nothing imposing in the appearance of the buildings, which have an old and dilapidated aspect. They occupy a large piece of ground, and consist of an open court with colonnades on the north and south sides, which are set apart for students from West Africa, East Africa, Syria, Lower Egypt, Upper Egypt, the Sudan, and other parts of the Mohammedan world. On the east of the court is the Liwanel Jama, or sanctuary, which covers an area of about 3,600 square yards, and has a low ceiling supported by 380 columns of granite and marble, but not uniformly arranged, as if they were not in their original places. Here the prayers are repeated and instruction given to groups of students who sit on mats before their teachers. This "university" has an enrolment of from 10,000 to 12,000 students, four-fifths of whom are from 12 to 18 years of age and who are taught by 321 Sheikhs or professors. The president is called Sheikh el Azhar, and receives a salary of about $500. The students spend from two to six years in the university, while some continue longer. No fees are paid by them, as all expenses are met from the endowments of the mosque, which are of great value.

The whole system of education consists of committing facts to memory, without exercises which train the mind to discern the truth and detect error, or lead to the forming of independent opinion. Mathematics and astronomy, which were studied by the ancient Egyptians, are not in the curriculum of this modern university of Islamism. And yet the professors and students are proud of their attainments, and look down with feelings akin to disdain upon the scientific and religious attainments of Western Christians. As a close observer has remarked, this education develops "a personality which is useless for any other occupation than that of teaching Arabic phonetics, grammar, and the Koran."

Missionary effort in Cairo is carried on by six Protestant societies. Of these the United Presbyterian Church of North America made it a center and station for their operations in 1854. This Society now (1902) has at that point and its dependencies 14 missionaries, men and women, 23 native workers, men and women, 4 Sunday schools, 5 high schools, 1 theological seminary, 1 book depot, and 690 Harim (Zenana) pupils. Cairo is a station also of the CMS (1882), with 12 missionaries, men and women, 13 native workers, men and women, 1 village school, 1 high school and 1 book depot. Also station of the Kaiserswerth Deaconesses (1884), with 8 deaconesses and a hospital. Also a station of the International Medical and Benevolent Association (1900), with 1 missionary and his wife. There are also two English societies working for the Jews in this city. It has not been possible to secure details of their work.

Whately (Miss M. L.), *Ragged Life in Egypt* (two series in one vol.), London, 1870; Poole (S. L.), *Cairo*, 3d. ed., London, 1897; Hartman (M.), *The Arabic Press of Egypt*, London, 1899; Charmes (G.), *Five Months in Cairo and Lower Egypt*, London, 1883; Duff-Gordon (Lady), *Letters from Egypt*, revised ed., London, 1902.

CAKAUDROVE. See CACAUDROVE.

CALA: A town in Cape Colony, S. Africa, situated about 40 miles N. W. of Clarkeburg. Station of the South African Wesleyan Methodist Missionary Society, with 72 native workers, 12 outstations, 15 chapels, 8 Sunday schools, 13 village schools, a Young People's Society and 740 professing Christians. Also station of the Episcopal Church in Scotland (1889), with 1 missionary, 3 missionary women, 10 native workers, 6 outstations, 6 chapels, 5 village schools, 1 high school, 380 professing Christians.

CALCUTTA: Capital of British India. It stands on the east bank of the Hugli River, one of the channels through which the Ganges reaches the Bay of Bengal, about 80 miles from the mouth of the river. The earliest mention of the name occurs in a revenue document of one of the Mogul emperors, in 1596, where Kalikata (Kali-Ghat, shrine of the goddess Kali) indicated a small Bengali village on the site of the modern metropolis. In 1686 the English merchants connected with the East India Company, owing to difficulties with the Mohammedan authorities, found it necessary to leave their settlement at Hugli and seek another site. Under Job Charnock, then the president of the little settlement or factory, they hit upon this site, Anglicizing the name into Calcutta. The growth of the place has continued almost unchecked to the present day; the hamlet on the eastern bank of the Hugli has thus, under the fostering care of English power, developed into one of the great political and commercial centers of the world. That portion of the city occupied by the English lies along the river front, and is adorned with palatial residences, imposing public buildings, churches of different denominations, and wealthy and well-stocked business houses. Back from the river, north and east of the English quarters, stretches the native part of the city, a mass of low, mean, and squalid huts, intersected by narrow and filthy streets, so that the saying has become current that Calcutta is a city of palaces in front and a city of pigstyes in the rear.

The population of Calcutta, with its suburbs, is (1901) 1,125,400. Nearly two-thirds of the population are Hindus and nearly one-third Mohammedans, and there is a sprinkling of Buddhists, Jains, Parsees, Jews, etc.

Calcutta has been in the control of the English from the moment that Job Charnock and his associates settled there in 1686 until the present time, with the exception of a few months in the year 1756. In June of that year the city was attacked by the Mussulman ruler, or Nawab, of Bengal—Suraj-ud Daula—one of the worst specimens ever known of that class of brutal despots which is popularly supposed to thrive in the Orient. It was at that time that the tragedy of the famous "Black Hole" of Calcutta was enacted. The wretched prisoners were thrust—146 in number—into a cell hardly 20 feet square, ventilated only by two small windows. In the morning only 23 persons were found alive. Calcutta was recaptured in January, 1757, by Admiral Watson and Lord (then Colonel) Clive. In the same year, at the battle of Plassey, the Nawab's army was defeated by a little force under Clive, and the question of English supremacy in Bengal and throughout India was virtually settled.

The history of missionary operations in Calcutta goes back to the year 1758, just after the rebuilding of Calcutta and the establishment in Bengal of English power. In that year Rev. Mr. Kiernander, a Danish missionary, whose successful labors south of Madras, at Cuddalore and vicinity, had been interrupted by hostilities between the English and French, arrived in Calcutta, seeking a field for his missionary activity. The Calcutta Government encouraged him. He started a school and gathered 200 pupils within a year. He preached to the natives, to the Portuguese, to the English soldiers. His baptisms at the end of the first year of work numbered 15; at the end of ten years there were 189 converts. Afterward he built a mission church chiefly at his own expense. Rev. M. A. Sherring's history of Protestant missions in India sums up his work by saying that "the seeds of Protestant missions in Northern India were first sown by him, and by him were the first fruits gathered in. He baptized hundreds of converts; he established important mission schools; he proclaimed the Gospel to the people, both European and native; he built a spacious church, and by these and other labors proved his earnestness and efficiency."

About the beginning of the last century the leading men in the employ of the East India Company, both at home and in India, became possessed with the idea that the promulgation of the Gospel in India might excite prejudice against the English rule and render the work of government more costly and more difficult. Under the influence of these fears the Government of India opposed to the utmost the landing of any missionaries within its borders. This opposition continued until Parliament renewed the charter of the East India Company in the year 1813, when a clause was inserted in the bill declaring that "it was the duty of this country to promote the introduction of useful knowledge and of religious and moral improvement in India." The same bill provided for an Indian bishopric, with an archdeacon for each of the three presidencies. It came into effect April 10, 1814.

It was during these years of opposition that **William Carey** undertook the establishment of a mission in India. It was with great difficulty that he was able to secure passage to Calcutta. Finally he reached there in 1793 on a Danish vessel. After encountering much hardship he was placed in charge of a factory at Malda, where he remained five years and where he was able to learn the Bengali language, translate the New Testament, and preach and teach among the natives, besides attending to his duties in connection with the factory of which he was in charge. Between 1797 and 1800 various desultory efforts were made by the Christian Knowledge Society to carry on the mission begun by Kiernander. Much help was given by Rev. D. Brown, Dr. Buchanan, and others, who were serving English residents as chaplains. In 1799 four more English missionaries arrived—this time in an American vesssel. They effected a landing in face of governmental opposition, but were obliged to retreat to Serampur, 15 miles up the river, which was then held by the Danish Government. The Danish governor was in sympathy with their work, and declined to give the missionaries up to the officials of the East India Company. Here Carey joined them, and thus was laid the foundation of the **Serampur** Baptist Mission. It was after this time that the earliest American missionaries reached Calcutta and encountered the same difficulties as their English brethren. At this time also came Henry Martyn as a chaplain in the East India Company's service.

With the granting of the new charter in 1813, the tone of the government changed. The missionary societies of England were waiting for the opening of the door to enter in. The Church Missionary Society came in 1815. The London Missionary Society had sent a missionary out in 1798, but he sought the interior. Their Calcutta Mission was begun in 1816. In 1837 their college was begun, now a large and successful institution. The earliest direct efforts in behalf of female education were attempted in 1821. A society for promoting female education was formed in

1824 and did efficient service. The Society for the Propagation of the Gospel began operations in 1820, taking charge in that year of Bishop's College, an institution for higher Christian education projected by Dr. Middleton, first bishop of Calcutta. The Established Church of Scotland in 1830 sent Dr. Duff to Calcutta. His energy and devotion gave an impetus to the missionary spirit in the home churches, was felt on all mission fields in India, and especially gave point and direction to educational efforts as a legitimate form of missionary work. He started a school which soon grew into a large college. In 1844, following the disruption in the Scotch Church, Dr. Duff and his associates threw in their lot with the Free Church and carried their work over into the hands of the new body. The old kirk, however, started a new mission in Calcutta, with a college of its own. In 1865 the CMS founded a college known as the Cathedral College.

Thus nearly every one of the great societies laboring in Calcutta came in time to have its institution or college for the higher education of native youth in the English language and under the influence of Christianity. The London Missionary Society early established a press, which since has passed into the hands of the Baptist Mission, and has done excellent service. The latter mission has also been fortunate in securing and wise in retaining the services of several learned and scholarly men who have devoted almost all their time to the translation of the Scriptures, and the revision and printing of successive editions. The duty of vernacular preaching both in the city itself and through the surrounding districts has been faithfully attended to, and among those who have been especially successful in this branch of work may be mentioned Lacroix, one of the ablest and most devoted of the London Society's laborers. The American Methodist Church began work in Calcutta in 1872 under the leadership of Rev. William Taylor, afterward missionary bishop of his church in Africa. The work of this mission has been largely among Europeans unreached by the labors of other churches, tho, as time has gone on, increasingly among natives also.

The publication of tracts and books in the varnacular languages is cared for by a tract society auxiliary to the Religious Tract Society of London, while an auxiliary of the British and Foreign Bible Society provides an ample supply of Bibles in the various languages used in the city and surrounding regions.

Calcutta is thus seen to be a center of no small amount of religious and intellectual activity. Under the influence of the several agencies above enumerated, it is natural that a strong and intelligent body of Bengali Christians should have grown up in Calcutta. The influence of the native Christian community of the metropolis has been, as was fitting, metropolitan in its character. Members of this community have been found in all ranks of life—among the lawyers, merchants, writers, editors, scholars, and preachers of the country. They have established and conducted with ability a newspaper printed in English, devoted especially to the needs of the native church of Bengal and of India, and in many ways have exerted an influence on the development of Christianity which has been widely felt.

Besides the missionary societies already named 11 others are carrying on enterprises in Calcutta or its suburbs: the WMS, the SDA, the Medical and Benevolent Association affiliated with the SDA, the local Bengali Mission, the Oxford Mission to Calcutta,the British and ForeignUnitarian Association, the YMCA, and, of the women's missionary societies, the Church of Scotland Woman's Missionary Association, the CEZMS, the Baptist Zenana Mission, the CWBM, and the YWCA.

The aggregate number of missionaries of all these societies in the city and suburbs is 184 men and women, with 586 native workers, men and women. The enterprises of these missions include, besides the colleges already mentioned, 86 Sunday schools, 130 common schools, 14 high schools, 5 orphanages, 3 theological schools, 2 training schools for women mission workers, 2 industrial schools and 1 hostel for native students. The BFBS maintains an agent in Calcutta and a book depot. There are 8 young people's societies, besides the YMCA and the YWCA. The professing Christians reported by these missions as connected with their churches form an aggregate of 2,783.

CALDWELL, Robert: Born May 7, 1814. Died August 28, 1891. The University of Glasgow conferred upon him the degree of LL.D. and the University of Durham the degree of D.D. He was missionary of the LMS from 1838-41, arriving in Madras, January 8, 1838. Joined the SPG and ordained deacon in Church of England, 1841, and priest in 1842, at Madras; consecrated Assistant Bishop of Madras March 11, 1877. Over forty years of Mr. Caldwell's missionary life was spent in Idaiyangudi, situated in the extreme south of Tinnevelli. In the early years of the 19th century the inhabitants of many villages in this district placed themselves under Christian instruction, and large numbers were received into the church by Gericke and Sattianadan; but Caldwell found only the wreck of these congregations, which soon felt his masterful influence. In less than three years he had formed 21 congregations and 9 schools; he received converts in 31 villages, and altogether 2,000 persons were brought under regular Christian instruction. A church building society was formed at Idaiyangudi in 1844, and so well was the duty of self-support impressed upon the congregations that in 1846 it was reported that the Idaiyangudi Christians "could be hardly surpassed in Christian liberality by the inhabitants of any country in similar worldly circumstances." During the years 1845-7 eleven churches and fourteen schools were built in the district; and at this time Mr. Caldwell reported the proportion of inhabitants of Tinnevelli which had embraced Christianity was larger than that of any other province in India. In many places entire villages renounced their idols and the movement in favor of Christianity extended from caste to caste and village to village. This description included the operations of the CMS and in 1850 the natives in Tinnevelli who, largely under the influence of the SPG and the CMS, led by Caldwell and his associates, had embraced the Christian religion, in number about forty thousand persons, forwarded an address to Queen Victoria expressing thanks to God for the blessings of his grace. As missionary Mr. Caldwell had to fulfil the various offices of pastor, doctor, magistrate, and general counselor. In 1875, when the Prince of Wales visited India, he was met by nearly 10,000 native Christians and an address was presented to him by Mr. Caldwell.

In 1880 Bishop Caldwell consecrated a church on which he had labored with his own hands from time to time for thirty-three years; in 1883 he removed his headquarters to Tuticorin, the chief seaport in Tinnevelli, and here during this year he confirmed 538 natives in one day; and in 1887 he celebrated the jubilee of his missionary career. In 1890 Bishop Caldwell, on the death of Bishop Sargent, assumed the entire episcopal oversight of Tinnevelli. He was the author of "Companion to the Holy Communion" and of several pamphlets.

CALHOUN, Simeon Howard: Born August 15, 1804, at Boston, Mass.; graduated at Williams College, 1829; studied theology with Dr. Griffin and Dr. Mark Hopkins; ordained in 1836; left the United States the following November for the Levant as an agent of the American Bible Society; received appointment as a missionary of the ABCFM in 1843; joined the Syrian mission in 1844 for the purpose of taking charge of the mission seminary at Abeih, on Mount Lebanon. To this he devoted his entire life. By him were trained most of the preachers and teachers now employed in the Syrian mission of the PN, besides several engaged by other societies in Syria, Palestine, and Egypt. He was also pastor of the church on Mount Lebanon. He was thoroughly versed in the Arabic and Turkish languages, and assisted Dr. Goodell in his first translations of the Bible into Turkish. He prepared and published text-books in philosophy, astronomy, and theology. He visited the United States in 1847, returning to Syria in 1849; again in 1866, returning the same year. He made his final visit to the United States in impaired health in 1875, but addressed the General Assembly on the subject of missions with great power. Tho he expressed the hope that he should rest on Mount Lebanon, he died in Buffalo, December 14, 1875. His wife and three children were with him. Dr. Calhoun's influence in Syria was great among all classes. Natives, whether Mohammedan or Christian, often went to him for counsel. While in college Dr. Calhoun was a sceptic and an opposer of religious enterprises. After his conversion, in 1831, and up to the end of his life, he was noted for the ardor and the simplicity of his piety. His delight in the Scriptures was exceptional. Hence he was powerful in explaining them to others.

CALICUT: A city on the coast of Malabar, S. India. Climate, temperate. Population (1901), 76,981. Hindus, Mohammedans, Parsees, Portuguese, French. Language, Malayalam, Tamil, Hindustani, etc. Religion, Hinduism, Islamism, Romanism.

Station of the Basel Missionary Society (1842), with 8 missionaries, 5 of whom are accompanied by their wives, 71 native workers, men and women, 6 outstations, 1 Sunday school, 8 village schools, 1 industrial school and 1,073 professing Christians. Also station of the Mission to Lepers in India and the East, with 1 home for the untainted children of lepers.

CALIOUB: A suburb of Cairo, Egypt; station of the Netherlands Society for the Extension of the Gospel in Egypt (1874), with 2 missionaries and their wives, 1 chapel, 1 Sunday school and 2 village schools.

CALLAO: A city of Peru, South America, which is an important seaport, although its population has latterly become reduced to 16,000.

Station of the ME, with 1 missionary and his wife, 11 native workers, men and women, 2 Sunday schools, 3 village schools, 1 high school and 180 professing evangelical Christians.

CALMUCKS. See MONGOLS.

CALVERT, James: Born January 3, 1813. Died March 8, 1892. The birthplace of Mr. Calvert was Pickering, York, England; and after his early education at Malton, he was apprenticed for seven years to a printer, bookbinder and stationer. After his appointment by the Wesleyan Missionary Society he was married in March, 1838, and Mr. and Mrs. Calvert embarked for Fiji, October of the same year, with John Hunt and T. J. Jagger as associates in their courageous work. During the following December they reached Lakemba, and six months later Mr. Calvert was in charge of a wide circuit, including thirteen towns, connected by no roads, besides twenty-four surrounding islands, some of which were over one hundred miles distant, with hardly a seaworthy canoe available by which to reach the savage inhabitants. He and Mrs. Calvert soon mastered the language, and they showed remarkable tact, perseverance and courage in their work among the Fijians. A printing press was sent out with this missionary party, and Mr. Calvert's thorough knowledge of printing and book-binding was now of great use to him. Soon a vocabulary and a grammar in the Lakemban dialect were ready for use. This press was moved from one island to another, and from it were issued thousands of helpful papers, while in 1847 a complete and well bound New Testament was ready for the natives. On the island of Oneata the work accomplished great good; a church and school were established, and, encouraged by the king of Nayau, many of the inhabitants renounced their heathen worship and embraced Christianity. Some of these endured persecution, exile, torture, and even death rather than compromise their principles. The conversion of the daughter of the king had great influence among the natives. Mr. Calvert did much toward the abolition of killing and eating human beings, and on April 30, 1854, the chief ordered that the death-drums be hereafter used to call the people together to worship the true God. In 1857, Thakombau, the king, after dismissing his many wives with all their wealth and influence, openly accepted Christ as his Savior. One of his last acts as king was to cede Fiji to the Queen of Great Britain, October, 1874. After seventeen years of labor in Fiji, Mr. Calvert returned to England, where, in 1856, he settled at Woodbridge, revising the Old Testament translation for the British and Foreign Bible Society; but the death of the ablest worker at Fiji caused him to return to his former post, where his power for good was greater than ever. In 1865 Mr. Calvert was again in England; October, 1872, he went to the South African diamond fields, where he did effective missionary work. Mr. Calvert attended the Jubilee of Christianity in Fiji in 1885. At this time there was not an avowed heathen in all Fiji. He found over 1,300 churches, 10 white missionaries, 65 native missionaries, over 1,000 head teachers, nearly 30,000 church members, over 42,000 pupils in nearly 2,000 schools, and 104,585 church attendants, out of a population of 116,000. Largely through his personal service he saw this people abolish heathen customs and accept the true God.

CAMBODIA: A kingdom of farther India, under the protectorate of France, and forming a part of French Indo-China. It lies southeast of Siam, and includes principally the valley and delta of the Cambodia River, one of the most fertile regions of southeastern Asia. Area, 37,400 square miles. Population, 1,103,000, chiefly composed of several indigenous races, with about 40,000 Malays and 250,000 Chinese and Annamities. The chief towns are Pnom-Penh, the capital, and Kampot, the only seaport.

The early history is obscure. Toward the close of the 17th century the Annamese set apart the southern portion for Chinese who had fled from their own homes for political reasons, and were a source of disturbance to the government. This became Cochin-China. In 1787 the king of Cochin-China was converted to Christianity through French missionaries. With the aid of France he then conquered Cambodia and Annam, combining all in the empire of Annam. He favored Christianity, and allowed the French missionaries many privileges. Under his successor, however, quarrels arose with France, which occupied Cochin-China and in 1863 established a protectorate over Cambodia. Roman Catholic Missions, only, operate in that region.

CAMPINAS: A city of Brazil, situated at an altitude of 2,300 feet, in the sugar growing district, 60 miles north of São Paulo. Population, 20,000. The climate is mild and semi-tropical.

Station of the PS (1869), with (1902) 1 missionary and his wife, 2 native workers, 3 outstations, 1 school and 57 church members. Station also of the SBC, with (1902) 1 missionary and his wife, 1 native worker, 1 theological class, and 27 church members.

CAMPOS: A town in the district of Rio de Janeiro, Brazil, about 150 miles northeast of the city. Station of the SBC (1890), with (1902) 1 missionary and his wife, 5 native workers, 10 outstations, 10 preaching places, and 702 professing evangelical Christians.

CANA: A settlement in Basutoland, about 10 miles from the boundary of the Orange River Colony; station of the Paris Association for Evangelical Missions (1873), with (1901) 1 missionary and his wife, 16 native workers, 9 outstations, 8 schools, and 723 communicants, with 366 candidates for admission.

CANADA; Baptist Missionary Societies of. See BAPTIST CONVENTIONS OF CANADA.

CANADA CONGREGATIONAL FOREIGN MISSIONARY SOCIETY: While the earlier efforts of the Congregational Churches of Canada were directed chiefly to home evangelization, a number of the stronger ones contributed to foreign missions through the LMS and the ABCFM, whose secretaries or agents appeared at the meetings of the Congregational Union, or preached by invitation in Montreal. Interest was also much excited in the foreign work by a visit, in 1870, of Rev. Dr. Mullens, Foreign Secretary of the LMS, and again, in 1874, when the first foreign missionaries, Rev. Charles Brooks and wife, went out, under the auspices of the ABCFM, to Constantinople. But it was not until 1881 that the claims of the heathen world upon the Canadian churches were sufficiently felt to lead to the organization of a separate Foreign Missionary Society. This society, while largely indebted to the ABCFM for advice in regard to the choice of its field, and working mainly through its channels, is yet entirely independent of the older society, holding its annual meeting at the same time and place as the Congregational Union of Ontario and Quebec, and being wholly subject to the control of its own board of directors. For the first three years it contributed through the ABCFM toward the support of the Canadian Foreign missionaries already in the field, viz., Rev. C. H. Brooks and wife, in Constantinople, the Rev. George Allchin, in Japan, and Miss Macallum, in Smyrna. But in 1884 Mr. W. T. Currie, a graduate of the Congregational College of Canada, having applied to the Society for appointment to foreign service, was accepted, and assigned, under advice of the ABCFM, to a new mission station in Bailunda, in West Central Africa, which was henceforth to be recognized as the Canadian Mission. Mr. Currie having been duly ordained and set apart to his work, sailed with his bride for Africa in June, 1886, but they had scarcely reached the station to which he had been appointed before she sickened and died. A memorial of her has since been erected in the form of a mission schoolhouse, known as the "Clara Wilkes Currie School," for which the necessary funds were collected by the Canadian Woman's Board. Mr. Currie afterward commenced a new station at Chisamba, and Mr. Wilberforce Lee, another alumnus of the same college as Mr. Currie, was ordained and sent out to assist him (1889). Others have since joined them and the station is recognized by the ABCFM as the special field of the Canadian Society.

There were (1902) 3 missionaries with their wives and 3 female missionaries, 9 in all. There are important schools, with an attendance of 274, more than a third of them girls; a hospital, with 4 buildings. The general evangelistic work is very prosperous.

In addition to this work in Africa a number of missionaries have gone from Canada to other fields: Turkey, China, India and Japan.

The Canada Congregational Woman's Board of Missions was organized June 10, 1886, in the house of the pastor of the church in Ottawa, Ont. Its beginnings were small, but in response to circulars sent out by the president, Mrs. Macallum, requesting the churches to form auxiliaries, several existing societies sent in their adhesion, and a number of auxiliaries and mission bands were organized. The lamented death of Mrs. Currie greatly quickened the general interest in the mission to which she had given her life, and nearly one thousand dollars were promptly contributed for the erection of the school to her memory before referred to. Almost every church has now its auxiliary or mission band, many of them having both.

CANADA; Methodist Church in. See METHODIST CHURCH IN CANADA.

CANADA; Presbyterian Church in. See PRESBYTERIAN CHURCH IN CANADA.

CANARESE LANGUAGE: Belongs to the Dravidian family of languages and is spoken by about 9,500,000 people in S. W. India. Its alphabet somewhat resembles the Tamil. It is also called Karnata.

CANDAWU. See TONGA ISLANDS.

CANDIA. See CRETE.

CANNANORE: A city on the coast of Malabar, S. W. India, situated about 50 miles northwest of Calicut. It is a military post and it is remarkable for the number of its mosques, two of which are of special fame. Station of the Basel Missionary Society (1841), with (1900) 10 missionaries, men and women, and 36 native workers. The work of the station covers evangelistic and educational work, and connected with it are 650 baptized Christians.

CANTON: Capital of Kwang-tung Province, China, on the north bank of the Pearl, or Canton, River, 90 miles from the sea. The Chinese name for the city is Kwang-chau-fu; the foreign name is supposed to be a corruption of Kwang-tung as pronounced by the early Portuguese visitors. It is also called Yeung-sheng, the "City of Rams," by the Chinese, in reference to a legend connected with its founding. The city proper is quadrilateral in shape, the side next to the river being a little less than two miles in length. It is surrounded by a wall of an average height of twenty-five feet, and from fifteen to twenty feet thick, in a good state of preservation, built of brick, with stone foundation. It is a universal custom in Chinese cities that the cardinal points of the compass determine the location of the four principal gates. In Canton these are found to be utterly insufficient for the needs of traffic, and there are eight other gates, some of them as large and important in fact, tho not in name. The city is divided into two parts, the old and the new. In the old city are the Tatar garrison, their parade-grounds, the residences and grounds of the Governor-General and Governor, the examination hall, with its rows of low cells for the competing students, and many fine temples and pagodas. Around the city proper are the suburbs, where the business of the city is carried on, especially on the west side, which is noted for its manufactures, its business, and its wonderful stores. Along the river front, junks and boats of every description and size find wharfage and landing places, and the vast carrying trade of the West and North rivers is conducted. The streets are narrow and closed by gates, which are shut at an early hour in the evening.

The stores are usually low buildings of a story in front and two behind, the whole front of the store being thrown open to the street. The only high buildings, with the exception of public buildings, are the fine eating houses and the pawn shops, which serve also as safe-deposit vaults. The streets are well paved with slabs of granite, beneath which is a sewer. As all the night soil is removed from the city to be used on the fields, this deficient drainage does not cause epidemics. In comparison with other cities of the East, Canton is clean. The houses are built of brick of a slate color, and the ground floor is of tiles. The water supply of the city is derived either from the river or the canals which pass through the city, or from wells, whose flow is affected by the tide, which filters through the sandy soil. Pure spring water can be obtained from the hills to the north of the city. The natives never drink water unboiled, and this custom has doubtless preserved the health of the people.

Not far from the walls of the city is the tomb of a so-called uncle of Mohammed, with a Mohammedan burying ground and place of worship. Opposite the city is the island of Honam, for a long time the residence of foreigners, when permission to live on the north shore was denied them.

The population is (1901) 850,000, its distinctive feature being that 300,000 people live in boats, rarely spending a night on shore. The river bank and the various canals are lined with boats of every variety and size, from the little skiff to the large ornamental hotel boat. These boats furnish to a great extent the means of communication. There are no horses used for that purpose, nor are the streets of the native city wide enough to permit the use of the cart of North China. The sedan chair is the only means of conveyance on land, and the facilities offered by the boats are largely utilized by the missionaries, whose residences, with few exceptions, are on the river front. Opposite the western suburbs, and separated from them by a canal, is a foreign settlement on ground made over a small island by surrounding it with a retaining wall, and filling in the space enclosed. Shamien, as it is called, is laid out in fine streets with overhanging trees, bordered by beautiful lawns, and covered with the fine residences of the European merchants. Shamien is one of the most beautiful European settlements in the East.

The people of Canton are the most highly civilized of China, and the luxury of the city is proverbial. The shrewdness and ability of the Cantonese as merchants has procured for them the nickname of the Yankees of China, and Canton men, or men from the Canton province, compose nearly the entire number of the immigrants to the various parts of the world where the Chinese are found.

The climate is more temperate than that of any other city in a like latitude. The heat in summer averages about 95°, and the minimum in winter is usually 42°. Ice rarely forms, and snow is almost never seen. April, May, and June are the rainy season; July, August, and September are the months for the southwest monsoons, which, with frequent thunder-showers, mitigate the heat. During the fall and winter the northern monsoon blows, and clear weather is continuous.

Canton, according to native annals, has existed four thousand years, and traces of its existence have been found 1200 B.C. Its first intercourse with foreigners was in the 16th century with the Portuguese, and since then the history of Canton has been the history of China, as many important events in modern Chinese history occurred at, or were connected with, this city.

The Protestant missionary enterprises at Canton are many and important. The LMS made the city one of its earliest stations by sending the Rev. Robert Morrison there in 1807. It was followed by the PN in 1844, the SBC in 1845, and the Berlin Missionary Society in 1867. The other societies now operating in the city are the WMS, the ABCFM, the UB Women's Missionary Association, and the Scandinavian American Free Mission. These societies have in Canton and suburbs an aggregate of 58 missionaries, men and women, 196 native workers, men and women, 84 preaching places, 24 Sunday schools, 52 village schools, 4 high schools, 5 theological or other special training schools, 1 hospital, 4 dispensaries, and 1 printing house. The total number of professing Christians at Canton connected with these missions is 4,727.

CAPE COAST CASTLE: A town and fort of the Gold Coast Colony, West Africa. Until 1664 it was a Portuguese military station. Population, 10,000. The town is regularly built in a well-wooded but poorly watered district, and has a damp, unhealthy climate. Station of the WMS, with 3 missionaries, 34 native workers, 4 common schools, and 1,240 professing Christians.

CAPE COLONY: A British possession comprising the extreme southern portion of Africa, extending northward to the boundaries of German Southwest Africa, the Bechuanaland Protectorate, the Orange River Colony, Basutoland, and Natal. It has an ocean coast line of about 1,400 miles, and an area with dependencies of 221,311 square miles. The population is (1891) 1,527,224. No census was taken in 1901, but the population is estimated at 2,433,000, the European population numbering 376,987 for the whole territory. The dependent provinces are East Griqualand, having 15,197 square miles; Tembuland, 7,594; Transkei, 2,552, and Walfisch Bay, 430.

A mountain range, in general parallel with the coast, dividing the drainage of the streams flowing into the Orange River from that of the coastal streams, is reached from the ocean, about 100 miles distant, by a series of terraces. North of the range the country slopes gradually toward the Orange River. About two-thirds of the colony consists of arid plains (called Karroos) presenting many depressions, containing rich soil, which only requires irrigation to make it productive.

Included in the south temperate zone, the climate presents many varieties, but in its general character is mild and very salubrious; epidemics seldom prevail. The rainfall is unequally distributed. The basin of the Lower Orange and Great Karroo plain and the Kalahari Desert receives occasional torrential downpours, but springs are rare. Wells are sunk and a system of irrigation resorted to. The flora is the richest in the world. Vineyards produce abundantly; cereals give a fair return. The forests are confined to the margins of the colony; one-third of the population is said to engage in stock breeding. There are about 10,000,000 sheep in the country. The wild animals have been largely driven north beyond the boundaries of the colony.

People: Malays were introduced by the Dutch as slaves, and are found chiefly in the seaports. The Griquas are half-castes, active, vigorous, enterprising and courageous, and superior to the aborigines in strength and stature, and number among them some of the best and some of the most desperate characters. Bushmen inhabit the western section of Cape Colony. They are remnants of the San races, are diminutive in stature, and have light, yellowish brown complexions, and are, perhaps, related to the Hottentots. They have made but little progress in civilization, and have no tribal organization. Scattered in various districts, they number, perhaps, 50,000 in South Africa. Hottentots, numerous in the western part of Cape Colony, amount to about 100,000. They resemble the Bushmen, except in stature and degree of culture. They occupy kraals, wear leather aprons and a sheepskin cloak. Tribal organization is preserved only among those beyond the boundaries of the European possessions.

By the census of 1891 there were in the Colony 732,047 Protestants, of whom 306,320 belonged to the Dutch Reformed communion, 139,058 to the Church of England, 37,102 were Presbyterian, 69,992 Independents, 106,132 Wesleyan, with Methodists, Lutherans, Moravians, Baptists and others. The Roman Catholics number 17,275, the Jews 3,000, Mohammedans 15,099. Pagan religions have still over 750,000 adherents. Government grants for the support of religious worship are being gradually withdrawn.

Cape Colony having so many European residents, the missionary enterprise there is carried on by the local churches, as well as by the missionary societies from abroad. Of these missionary societies the following carry on work in the colony: The Moravians, LMS, SPG, PB, Berlin Missionary Society, Rhenish Missionary Society, Hannover Missionary Society, International Medical Association, Mildmay Mission to the Jews, National Baptist Convention (U. S. A.), African Methodist Episcopal Church (U. S. A.), Episcopal Church of Scotland, Primitive Methodist Missionary Society and the Society of St. John. The whole number of places occupied as stations by these societies is 75.

Brown, *Guide to S. Africa*, London, 1899; Bryce, *Impressions of S. Africa*, London, 1899; Holub, *Seven Years in S. Africa*, London, 1881; Nicholson, *Fifty Years in S. Africa*, London, 1898; Wilmot, *Story of the Expansion of S. Africa*, London, 1897, and *History of Our Own Times in S. Africa*, London, 1893; Ellis (A. B.), *South African Sketches*, London, 1887; Edwards (J.), *Reminiscences of Early Life and Labors in South Africa*, London, 1886; *South African Year Book for* 1902-03, London, 1902.

CAPE MOUNT: A station of the American Protestant Episcopal Church in Liberia, West Africa (1877), with 5 missionaries, men and women, 1 native worker, 2 Sunday schools, and 8 communicants.

CAPE PALMAS: A district and town on the coast of Liberia, Africa. Seat of a missionary bishop of the PE, with schools and churches at Harper and Hoffman, on the Cape. Missionary circuit of the ME, with 7 missionaries, men and women, 12 native workers, 11 Sunday schools, 1 high school and 645 professing Christians.

CAPE PRINCE OF WALES: A settlement in the W. of Alaska, situated on Bering Strait; station of the American Missionary Association (1890), with 1 missionary and his wife, 2 native workers, man and woman, and 1 Sunday school.

CAPE TOWN: The capital of Cape Colony, S. Africa, situated at the foot of Table Mountain, on Table Bay. It was founded by the Dutch in 1651. It has a very fine harbor. The climate is moderate in temperature. Population (1891) 51,-250. Station of the Moravians (1887), the South African Wesleyan Methodist Missionary Society, the National Baptist Convention, the International Medical Missions and Benevolent Association, the Salvation Army, and the PB, with an aggregate of 10 missionaries, men and women, 57 native workers, men and women, 25 places of worship, 22 Sunday schools, 18 common schools, 1 orphanage, 1 hospital, 1 dispensary, 1 medical training class, 3 young people's societies, and 2,971 professing Christians. The BFBS also has an agency and a Bible depot here.

CAPE HAITIEN: A seaport in the northern part of the island of Haiti. It is the second town for size in the Republic, with a population of about 29,000. It has a good harbor hemmed in by hills. Station of the Jamaica Baptist Missionary Society (1875), with 1 missionary and his wife and 48 professing Christians. The Wesleyan Western Annual Conference of the West Indies also has a missionary here. Also called Cape Haytien, or Cape Hayti.

CARACAS: The capital of Venezuela, S. America, founded in 1567; situated at an altitude of 3,000 feet, 8 miles (or by railway 23 miles) from La Guayra, its seaport. Population, about 70,000. Climate agreeable and very healthful. Station of the PN (1897), with 1 missionary and his wife. Also station of the CA and of the PB.

CARAITES. See KARAITES.

CARAMANLIJA: The Turkish language as spoken by the Greeks of the interior of Asia Minor, who have lost the use of their own language. Retaining, however, the Greek in their church services, they have taught the Greek alphabet to their school children, have used it for writing Turkish, and have brought into that language Greek theological and ecclesiastical terms. The effect has been to produce a dialect which is named from the district of Caraman, where it has been most largely used. See **Turkish Language.**

CARDENAS: A seaport on the northern coast of Cuba, W. I., 25 miles E. of Matanzas, with an important trade in sugar. Population (1899), 21,940. Station of the PS (1899), with 7 missionaries, men and women, 1 school, and 45 professing Christians.

CAREY, William: Born Paulerspury, Northamptonshire, England, August 17, 1761. In his youth he worked with his father, who was a weaver, but at the age of sixteen he was apprenticed to a shoemaker at Hackleton, working at the trade for twelve years. At the age of eighteen he was led through the influence of a pious fellow-apprentice to the faith in Christ, became an earnest Christian, and a preacher of the Gospel. In 1786 he became pastor of the Baptist Church at Moulton, having previously preached at Paulerspury, his early home, and at Barton. His income being too small for the support of his family, he kept school by day, made or cobbled shoes by night, and preached on Sunday. At Moulton he was deeply impressed with the idea of a mission to the heathen, and frequently conversed with ministers on its practicability and importance, and of his willingness to engage in it. Andrew Fuller relates that once on entering Carey's shop he found hanging up against the wall a large map composed of several pieces of paper pasted together, on which Carey had drawn with a pen every known country, with memoranda of what he had read as to their population, religion, etc. At a very early age he had an intense desire for knowledge, eagerly "devouring books, especially of science, history, voyages," etc., and, notwithstanding his poverty, he learned Latin, Greek, Hebrew, Dutch, French, and acquired a good amount of general useful knowledge. But his heart was chiefly set on a mission to the heathen. From his ministerial brethren he received no sympathy. While at Moulton he wrote and published "An Inquiry into the Obligation of Christians to Use Means for the Conversion of the Heathen." In 1789 he became pastor of the church at Leicester. At a meeting of the Ministers' Association at Nottingham, May 31, 1792, he preached from "Enlarge the place of thy tent" (Isa. liv: 2, 3), laying down these two propositions: "Expect great things from God" and "Attempt great things for God." The discourse produced a great impression, and the result was, through the special cooperation of Fuller, Pearce, and the younger Ryland, the formation, at Kettering, October 2, 1792, of the Baptist Missionary Society. Carey's first wish was to work in Tahiti or Western Africa, but he offered to go wherever the Society might appoint him. India was selected for its first mission, and he was appointed with Mr. John Thomas, a surgeon, who had resided in Bengal, and been engaged in mission work. They embarked on an English vessel, but, on account of the objections made against missionaries by the East India Company, the commander of the ship was forbidden to take them, and they returned to land. After waiting a few weeks they sailed in a Danish vessel bound from Copenhagen to Serampur, and reached Calcutta November 11, 1793. Having sailed in a foreign vessel cleared at a foreign port, he landed unobserved. Believing it to be the duty of a missionary, after receiving some help at first, to support himself, Mr. Carey, soon after reaching India, relinquished his salary, and he and his family were reduced to serious straits. Leaving Calcutta, he walked fifteen miles in the sun, passing through salt rivers and a large marsh, to the Sunderbunds, a "tract scantily populated, and notorious for pestilence and wild beasts," intending to farm the land and instruct the people. Here he was found by Mr. Udney, of the Company's service, a pious man and a friend of missions, who offered him the superintendency of his indigo factory. As he would have not only a competent support for his family and time for study, but also a regular congregation of natives connected with the factory, he accepted the offer. The factory was at Mudnabatty, in the district of Malda, and this became the mission station. During the five years he spent there he translated the New Testament into Bengali, held daily religious services with the thousand workmen in the factory, itinerated regularly through the district, twenty miles square and containing 200 villages. His first convert was Ignatius Fernandez, of Portuguese descent, who built a church in 1797, and preached and labored as a missionary until his death, in 1829, when he left all his property to the mission. In 1799 the factory was closed in consequence of an inundation. While perplexed as to what he should do, Mr. Carey heard that four missionaries had arrived at Serampur, and that the Danish governor had proposed that they establish a mission there, promising him protection. They urged him to leave Malda. He assented, and removed to Serampur. In 1801 the Bengali translation of the New Testament was printed by Mr. Ward, and a copy presented to the Marquis of Wellesley, the governor-general, who expressed his great gratification at this result of missionary work. About this time Fort William College was established at Calcutta, and Mr. Carey was appointed by the Marquis professor of Sanskrit, Bengali, and Marâthi. This position he held for thirty years, and taught these languages. He wrote articles on the natural history and botany of India for the Asiatic Society, to which he was elected in 1805. The publication of the entire Bible in Bengali in five volumes was completed in 1809. That which gave Carey his fame was the translation of the Bible in whole or in part into twenty-four Indian languages or dialects. The Serampur press, under his direction, rendered the Bible accessible to more than three hundred millions of human beings. He prepared also numerous philological works, consisting of grammars and dictionaries in the Sanskrit, Marâthi, Bengali, Punjabi and Telugu dialects. His Sanskrit dictionary was destroyed by fire in the printing establishment. He contributed also several papers on grammar and East Indian matters to the *Journal of the Geographical Society*, in London. Carey had for years sought through Lord Wellesley the abolition of the suttee. In 1829 it was abolished, and the proclamation declaring it punishable as homicide was sent to Dr. Carey to be translated into Bengali. The order reached him as he was preparing for public worship on Sunday. Throwing off his black coat, he exclaimed: "If I delay an hour to translate and publish this, many a widow's life may be sacrificed." Resigning his pulpit to another, he completed with his pundit the translation by sunset.

Dr. Carey's work was now finished. After forty years of toil he passed away at the age of seventy-three, June 9, 1834. He was buried the next morning in the mission burying ground.

He, who was ridiculed and satirized by the witty Sydney Smith in the *Edinburgh Review* of 1808 as the "consecrated cobbler" and "maniac," accomplished a work for which he is held, and will be forever held, in high honor as the true friend and benefactor of India.

Smitto (G.), *Life of William Carey, Shoemaker and Missionary*, London, 1887; Culross (J.), *William Carey*, New York, 1882.

CARISBROOK: A station of the Moravians in Jamaica, West Indies (1895), situated in the parish of St. Elizabeth in a somewhat hilly and pleasant part of the island. The station has 13 native workers, men and women, 3 places of worship, 3 Sunday schools, and 151 communicants.

CARMEL: A station of the Moravian Missions (1887) in Western Alaska, near Fort Alexander. It now has 6 missionaries, men and women, 3 chapels, 1 common school, and 107 communicants.

CARNARVON: A town of 1,700 inhabitants in Cape Colony, S. Africa, situated in a mountainous district about 325 miles N. E. of Cape Town. It is occupied as a station by the Rhenish Missionary Society. The working force consists of 1 missionary and his wife and 3 native workers. These serve as instructors to a body of 666 baptized Christians in the town and neighboring regions. They also maintain a school.

CAROLINE ISLANDS: A group of islands in the Pacific, northeast of New Guinea and west of the Marshall and Gilbert groups. A few of them differ from the great majority of the islands of Micronesia in that they are of basaltic formation, while the rest are coral reefs. Kusaie and Ponapi have mountains two to three thousand feet high. Ruk is an immense lagoon 100 miles long, containing 10 large islands and many islets. Yap is also one of the high islands. The climate is perpetual summer, the thermometer ranging from 72° to 90°. On the coral islands the chief products are the coconut palm, often growing to a height of 80 feet, the breadfruit tree, the pandanus tree or screw pine, bearing a large bunch of juicy fruit, and an edible root called taro. On the high islands, especially Kusaie and Ponapi, there is a much larger range of products, including more than a dozen kinds of bananas. Various tropical fruits are introduced, and also some domestic animals, as pigs, chickens, and goats.

The inhabitants are of the brown Polynesian race, having straight hair. As no census has ever been taken, estimates of population vary greatly. Ponapi has a population of 5,000, the Mortlocks and Ruk about 14,000, Mokil and Pingelap about 1,250, Yap about 8,000 to 10,000.

The languages of different parts of the group are quite distinct but with affinities pointing to a common origin. They are not easily reduced to writing because of the shading of vowel sounds. This has been done, however, so that introduction of Christian ideas has meant resurrection to the language no less than new life to the people.

Spirits of ancestors and other spirits were worshiped, but no idols. The people were very superstitious, but had no conception of a Supreme God, and had no idea of sacrifice. Certain places regarded as the abode of spirits were not crossed. Some islands had priests, who in times of sickness and on special occasions practised their incantations, pretending to converse with the dead.

Missionary effort was begun on Ponapi and Kusaie in 1852 by the ABCFM. Twenty years later there were 250 church members on Ponapi and 226 on Kusaie. From the first a missionary spirit was cultivated in the converts, and when the evangelistic effort was to be pushed westward to other islands, native missionaries from Ponapi were the agents used, furnishing one of the most interesting chapters in missionary annals.

Political changes have hindered the progress of evangelization in these islands. Many of the islands have chiefs, whose authority is hereditary. On Ponapi there are several tribes, each having an independent king or chieftain. But in 1885 Spain laid claim to the whole group, as Germany had done to the Marshall Islands, and in the summer of 1886 took possession of Ponapi and later expelled the missionaries. In 1899 Germany purchased the Caroline Islands from Spain. In 1900 the missionaries returned to Ponapi. But these political changes have introduced to the people new types of white men, and the islanders have not been benefited by the acquaintance.

At present the force of workers consists of 24 missionaries, men and women (nine of them unmarried women), and 135 native workers of both sexes. The missionaries live upon Kusaie, Ruk and Ponapi, but their work takes in many other islands of this group. There are 57 outstations, with 99 schools, 2 printing houses, 2 dispensaries and 5,500 communicants in the various churches.

CARSHUNI. See SYRIAC.

CARTAGO: A town of 8-10,000 inhabitants, 13 miles E. of San José, Costa Rica, Central America. It was founded in 1553 and is situated in a fine valley at the base of Mt. Irazu, an active volcano. Station of the Jamaica Baptist Missionary Society (1901), with 1 missionary.

CARTHEN, Rev. Thomas H.: Was a Cornishman, born in 1856, and died in November, 1896. His boyhood was spent in the country of Durham, and when a very young man he entered the Christian ministry, pursuing a college course near his native place. In 1883 he united with the Free Methodist Church, and, after a brief stay at Oxford, he was appointed as missionary to Sierra Leone. After four consecutive years in a most unhealthy climate, he returned home in 1887; but soon after his return he learned of the great need of Christian work in East Africa, and without waiting for a formal appointment to this field, he entered it with characteristic zeal and enthusiasm. Here he labored for ten years.

He was a man of strong individuality, and while oftentimes acting independently of the Mission Board at home, he always commended himself by his faithful and untiring efforts. Seemingly in the midst of a useful career he closed his earthly labors in 1896.

CASABLANCA: A small seaport on the N. W. coast of Morocco, 56 miles S. W. of Rabat. Station of the NAM (1890), with a hospital in charge of 7 missionaries, men and women. The local name of the place is Dar al Beida.

CASHMIR. See KASHMIR.

CASHMIRI LANGUAGE. See KASHMIRI.

CASSA: An island off the coast of French Guinea, W. Africa; station of the Pongas Mission (1882), with 1 missionary and his wife, 2 native workers, man and woman, 2 chapels and 2 high schools.

CASSERGODE: A town on the coast of South Kanara, India, 28 miles south of Mangalore. Population, 6,400. Station of the Basel Missionary Society (1886), with (1902) 2 missionaries and their wives, 42 native workers, men and women, 103 communicants and 11 common schools with 727 pupils.

CASTLETON: A town in the island of Jamaica, W. I.; station of the CWBM, with 1 missionary and his wife, 1 common school, 1 Young People's Society and 430 baptized Christians.

CATHARINA SOPHIA: A village in Surinam, South America. Its climate is damp and rather unwholesome, the rainfall during the year averaging 79 inches. About the year 1849 the missionaries of the Moravian Church obtained permission to visit the plantations on the lower Saramacca. A work of itinerary was at once commenced, and the labors of the brethren were greatly blessed. The managers of the Catharina Sophia Plantation, which at that time belonged to the government, were kindly disposed toward the missionary and assisted him in every way. In 1855 the government offered to hand over to the Moravian Church authorities a chapel and a dwelling house for a missionary, which had been built of pitch-pine in Holland, and brought out to Surinam for the use of emigrants, most of whom had left the place. The offer was thankfully accepted, and the chapel was consecrated July 22, 1855. The congregation here consists of negroes, Chinese and East India coolies; there are now 1 missionary and his wife, 27 native workers, and 383 communicants.

CATORCE: A mining town in Mexico, situated at an altitude of 8,800 feet, 120 miles north of San Luis Potosi. Station of the AFFM (1898), with 1 missionary physician and his wife, 2 native women workers, 1 common school and 1 Young People's Society.

CATO RIDGE: A settlement in the northern part of Cape Colony, S. Africa; station of the South African Wesleyan Methodist Missionary Society, with 25 native workers, 6 places of worship, 2 common schools, 1 Young People's Society, and 385 baptized Christians. Also station of the Netherlands Missionary Society, with 2 missionary women and 1 common school.

CAUCASIA: A province of southeastern Russia, bounded on the north by the provinces of southern Russia and Astrakhan, on the east by the Caspian, on the south by Persia and Turkey, on the west by the Black Sea and the Sea of Azof. It is divided into two sections by the Caucasus range of mountains, that on the north being called Northern Caucasia, and that on the south Trans-Caucasia. Area, North Caucasia, 86,658; Trans-Caucasia, 95,799; total, 182,457 square miles. The population in 1897 was 9,723,523. It is composed of very heterogeneous elements. The languages found in the Caucasus are also numerous. The Russian government is making efforts to increase the use of the Russian language. Ararat Armenian and Azerbaijan Turkish are extensively used in the southern part of the region. As to religion many dissenters of the Russian (Greek) Church are found in Trans-Caucasia, which has been used as a place of exile for such. The Armenian Church has a large body of adherents there, and there is also a large Mohammedan population. There are small Protestant congregations at several points in the southern province.

Mission work has been attempted at various times in Trans-Caucasia by the Basel Missionary Society, the German Baptists and the missionaries of the ABCFM and PN, whose headquarters were in Persia and Turkey. Since the opening of railroads from Batum and Poti to Tiflis and the Caspian at Baku, missionaries have found that route most convenient for access to Persia. They have thus come in contact with a Nestorian colony at Tiflis, and the Armenians at Tiflis, Erivan, Schemachi, Shusha and Baku. The British and Foreign, and American Bible Societies have done a good deal of Bible work from Tiflis as a center. Protestant influence has been most powerful among the Armenians.

Bryce (J.), *Transcaucasia and Ararat*, London, and New York, 1878; Cunynghame (A. A. T.), *Eastern Caucasus*, London, 1872; Wolley (C. P.), *Savage Svanetia*, 2 vols., London, 1883.

CAVALLA: A settlement in the county of Cape Palmas, Liberia, W. Africa; station of the PE (1839). It was formerly the headquarters of the PE mission in the county. During the irruption of the heathen tribes (1887-1896) the station was broken up, the settlement devastated and the mission buildings destroyed. It is now (1901) occupied by 1 missionary and 3 native workers. There is 1 day school, 1 place of worship and 116 communicants.

CAWNPUR: A city in the United Provinces, India; entirely a British creation. It lies on the right bank of the Ganges, 130 miles above the junction of that stream with the Jumna. A body of English troops was stationed near this point something more than a hundred years ago, it being then on the frontier of the English territory. Around the camp, as its nucleus, a city sprang into being. It is now of great importance both as a railroad center and a manufacturing place; leather and cotton goods — especially the former — are produced here in large quantities. The chief historic interest centers about the memorial gardens, which occupy the site of the entrenchments within which a body of about 1,000 English (only 400 of whom were capable of bearing arms) took refuge from the native troops under Nana Sahib during the mutiny of 1857. The exact spot of the entrenchments is occupied by the memorial church; and the place of the well into which some 200 bodies were thrown, mostly women and children—the victims of Nana Sahib's massacre—is marked by a marble angel and a suitable inscription. Population (1901), 197,170, of whom about 125,000 are Hindus.

It is a station of the SPG (1839), with 22 missionaries, men and women, 46 native workers, men and women, 10 common schools, 2 high schools, 1 orphanage, 1 hospital and 2 hotels for students. Also station of the Woman's Union Missionary Society of America (1879), with 3 missionary women, 29 native women workers, 11 common schools, 1 orphanage, and 1 training school for women. Also station of the ME, with 4 missionaries, men and women, 29 native workers, men and women, 18 common schools, 2 high schools, and 430 professing Christians.

CAXIAS: A town in the province of Maranhão, Brazil; station of the PS (1896), with 1 missionary and his wife, 2 native workers, a dispensary and 37 church members.

CAYMAN BRAC: One of the Cayman Islands, off the N.W. coast of Jamaica, W. I. It has a large export trade in coconuts. Station of the Jamaica Baptist Missionary Society (1887), with 1 missionary and his wife, 5 places of regular worship, a Young People's Society, and 170 baptized Christians.

CEBU: A town on the island of the same name in the Philippine Islands, situated on the east coast, and having considerable commercial importance, being rated as the third port of the Philippines and a center of the hemp trade. It is well situated and destined to grow in the future. Population, 11,000. The people are of the Visayan stock and use a dialect peculiar to Cebu and Bohol. Station of the PN (1902), with 2 missionaries and their wives and 1 preaching place.

CEDARHALL: A station of the Moravian Missions, in the western part of the island of Antigua, W. I., established in 1822. At present (1900) under care of 1 missionary and his wife, with 14 native workers, men and women, 2 elementary schools, and 358 communicants.

CEDAR LAKE: A settlement in the territory of Saskatchewan, Dominion of Canada; station of the CMS, with 1 missionary, an elementary school and 34 communicants.

CEDRAL: A village near Catorce in the state of San Luis Potosi, Mexico; station of the American Friends Foreign Mission Association (1895). The working force is 1 missionary and his wife, 1 missionary woman and 3 native workers, with 1 chapel, 2 Sunday schools, a Young People's Society and 33 professing Christians.

CELEBES: An island of the Malay Archipelago, under the control of the Dutch, situated east of Borneo, and, like it, crossed by the equator. Area, 71,150 square miles. The interior is elevated and generally mountainous; the coast is low and exceedingly rugged in its outline. The island is well watered by small streams, and contains several lakes. The population is estimated at 1,500,000 They are true Malays for the most part, Mohammedans in religion, and speak the Bughi and Macassar languages, for which they have two different written characters. The Bughis are wild and savage in appearance, but of a quiet and peaceable disposition. The aborigines of North Celebes are classed with the savage Malays, altho the civilizing influence of the Dutch has greatly promoted their advancement. They make obedient servants, are gentle and industrious, and readily assume the manners and habits of civilized life. The island was probably discovered in 1525 by the Portuguese. The first intercourse with the Dutch was in 1607; they expelled the Portuguese in 1660, and since 1677 both the tribes have been subject to them, tho the Bughis, by far the most cultivated islanders of the archipelago, have frequently endeavored to throw off the yoke of their masters. Mission work in this island has been carried on by the Netherlands Missionary Society for some 70 years. The district of Minahasa, where the Dutch Government Mission of the 17th century had made some converts, has been entirely Christianized. There are about 150,000 Christians in the island, 35,000 of them being communicants. This whole district has now been given up by the missionary Society, its Christian institutions being supported by the Colonial State Church as a government charge.

Meyer (A. B.), *Die Minahasse auf Celebes*, Berlin, 1876; Wallace (A. R.), *The Malay Archipelago*, London, 1872, new ed., 1880.

CENTENARY: A station of the LMS (1897) in Rhodesia, Africa, about 90 miles west of Bulawayo, with (1901) 1 missionary, 2 native workers and 2 elementary schools.

CENTRAL AFRICA PROTECTORATE. See NYASALAND.

CENTRAL PROVINCES of India: This chief commissionership lies, as its name implies, at the very heart of India. Its limits of north latitude are 17° 50′ and 24° 27′; of east longitude, 76° and 85° 15′. Its greatest length is 600 miles, from east to west, while its longest north and south line measures 500 miles.

The population is chiefly (94 per cent.) rural. Only six towns have a population exceeding 20,000. The most interesting fact regarding the Central Provinces is that its hill and jungle regions, especially along the northern frontier, provided the refuge to which many of the aboriginal tribes resorted when too severely pressed upon by the later Aryan immigrants. These aboriginal tribes were largely of the Gond stock, and before the present political divisions came into existence a large part of what is now known as the Central Provinces was called, after the name of this great family of tribes, Gondwana. Yet of the entire population of the Central Provinces, these aborigines form but a comparatively small element, including both those who have embraced Hinduism as well as those still persisting in the old worship of their people; the last (1901) census enumerated only 1,744,556. Hindus number 9,745,579, Mohammedans 307,202 and Jains 48,183. It is worthy of note that while in this province Hindus, Mohammedans, Spirit Worshipers, Jains, and Buddhists all fell off in number in the decade 1891-1901, the Christians increased in the same time from 13,308 to 25,591, or 99 per cent.

The first mission was planted at Nagpur by the Free Church of Scotland in 1844. The country was then governed by a dynasty, and the native rajah claimed to have absolute authority over his subjects, which in his opinion involved the right to prevent the baptism of Christian converts. The supreme government of India was appealed to by the missionaries, and declined to interfere; but public opinion became so aroused that the Nagpur prince finally receded from his position. The Church Missionary Society began work at Jabalpur in 1854, and it has since occupied other stations. The German Evangelical Synod (US), the Swedish National Missionary Society, the FFMA, and the ME also have important work in this province. Altogether 12 Protestant missionary societies occupy 29 stations in the Central Provinces, with 142 missionaries, men and women. In 1856 a colporteur, in a journey of 200 miles, entered many large villages and saw but two schools, with hardly 40 pupils. In 1901 the schools conducted in connection with these mission stations alone number 116 of all grades.

CERRITOS: A village near Guadalcazar, in the State of San Luis Potosi, Mexico; station of the Associate Reformed Presbyterian Church of the South (1901), with 2 missionaries (one a physician), 1 missionary's wife, and a dispensary.

CESAREA. See KAISARIYEH.

CEYLON: The island of Ceylon lies between 5° 53' and 9° 51' north latitude, and 79° 41' and 81° 55' east longitude. It is somewhat smaller than Ireland, being 270 miles long and 140 wide, and containing 25,333 square miles.

The greater portion of the island consists of great plains, for the most part heavily wooded. They occupy the northern half of the island and reach south on each side of the mountains, completely encircling them with a plain of from 30 to 70 miles in width. At the extreme north lies a group of small coral built islands commonly called the peninsula of Jaffna, which have an importance as one of the centers of population and of mission work. The southern central part is occupied by a group of mountains rising to the height of over 8,000 feet. Adam's Peak, the most prominent of these, 7,352 feet high, has on its top a mark said by Hindus to be a footprint of Siva; by Buddhists, of Buddha; by Mohammedans, of Adam.

The Climate is very hot on the coast, but cooler in the mountain region. Owing to the surrounding sea, the temperature is extremely uniform, and the climate is not considered unhealthful for Europeans. The seasons are two—a wet and a dry, whose time is governed by the two monsoons. The northwest monsoon blows from October to May, the southwest from May to October. The rainfall in the north and south is small, but in the mountain region, especially on the southwest slopes, it is large.

Ceylon is an English crown colony, ruled by a governor, aided by executive and legislative councils. Most of the higher officials are English, but the natives who are fitted for it are admitted to office.

The Singhalese are said to have emigrated from Oude in 543 B. C. A kingdom was founded, records of which, as minute and as dry as the Saxon chronicles, were carefully kept. In 838 the Tamils, who had frequently invaded Ceylon, established a kingdom in Jaffna. In 1505 the Portuguese first visited Ceylon, and in 1518 acquired possessions in it. In 1658 their territory passed into the hands of the Dutch. The English gained possession of the island in 1796, and in 1815 the Kandian kingdom, the last vestige of native rule in Ceylon, fell into their hands.

The population of Ceylon (1901) is 3,576,990, divided as follows: Singhalese, 2,334,817; Tamils, 952,237; Moormen (Mohammedans, mostly descendants of old Arab traders), 224,719; Veddahs, 3,215; European descendants, 23,312; Europeans, 9,583. The great centers of population are the western coast, from Negombo southward to Point de Galle; certain portions of the mountain region, and the northern extremity, Jaffna.

The two principal races of the island, Singhalese and Tamil, differ widely from each other, not only in language and religion, but in vigor, intelligence, and personal characteristics. The Tamil is very industrious, and enterprising, so far as that word can be applied to any tropical race. Besides inhabiting exclusively the northern part of the island, the Tamils form the bulk of the laboring population in the cities, while the same race from South India supply the tea estates of Central Ceylon with almost their entire force of labor. The Tamils of the overcrowded peninsula of Jaffna push into other parts of the island in search of employment. Often they have a fair knowledge of English, and sometimes rise to honorable positions.

The Hinduism of the Tamils in Ceylon differs but little from Hinduism in South India. Like all the Dravidian races who have adopted the creed of Brahmanism, the Tamils retained much of their old worship of demons and nature. Devil trees and devil temples are common, and popular folklore consists largely of stories of the freaks of these demons. There is less of caste in North Ceylon than on the continent of India, tho even here it is the most difficult thing for Christianity to overcome. The Brahmans have here less influence than in India.

The Singhalese, occupying the southern and western parts of the island, are far less vigorous and energetic than the Tamils. Probably few races on the globe possessed of any degree of civilization have greater listlessness and indifference, greater torpidity of intellect and conscience, than the Singhalese. The religion of the Singhalese is Buddhism of the "Lesser Vehicle," and more akin to that of Siam and Burma than to that of Tibet and Eastern Asia. It has borrowed from its neighbor, Hinduism, so that temples to Hindu gods exist in some places by the side of temples to Buddha. The Singhalese have also, like their Tamil neighbors, retained the lower forms of superstition which Buddhism nominally displaced, so that demon-worship is still practised among them. In recent years the Buddhist clergy of Ceylon have shown considerable energy in moving the people to resist the progress of evangelization. They have made special meetings and polemic address a feature of their enterprise, aided in this by western enemies of the Gospel doctrine. They have also issued tracts and undertaken to teach the children religious dogma.

Ceylon has been mission ground for nearly 400 years, and has been the victim of some of the most remarkable experiments in Christianization that the world can anywhere show. Its missionary history may be divided into three epochs, corresponding to the governments which held it: the Portuguese, the Dutch, and the English.

Soon after the arrival of the Portuguese, Franciscan monks followed, and Colombo was made the seat of a bishopric. In 1544 St. Francis Xavier preached among the Tamil fishermen of Mannar, in the kingdom of Jaffna, and baptized between 500 and 600 of them.

Perhaps the chief means used by the Portuguese in Christianizing the Ceylonese is hinted at by the old historian, who says that many became Christians "for the sake of Portuguese gold." It is certain that baptism was made the gate to preferment, and was regarded by the people as a political rather than a religious ceremony. To this day Catholic processions, which have a suspicious resemblance to those of Hinduism, are perpetuated in Jaffna.

With the conquest of the Dutch the palmy days of Roman Catholicism ended. The priests were banished, Roman Catholic rites forbidden on pain of death, and the people were commanded to become Protestants. No unbaptized person was allowed to hold office or to own land, while Roman Catholics were placed under greater disabilities than Buddhists or Hindus. Soon converts to the Protestant Church were numbered by the hundred thousand. Again the Hindus of the north accepted the government religion with more readiness than the Buddhists of the south. But before long it was found that the converts were only Christians in name, and still held the beliefs and practised the rites of their old religions. Indeed, little was or could be done for their instruction. This state of things called forth the condemnation of the Classis of Amsterdam. Before the close of the Dutch period, the number of Christians had much diminished, and the ministers themselves plainly saw the uselessness of the course of compulsion taken by their government. No sooner had Dutch governors been driven from Ceylon than everywhere, except in a few large towns, the whole system collapsed, temples were rebuilt, and the people gladly laid aside the last remnants of "government Christianity."

After the occupation of Ceylon by the English the BMS was the first Protestant missionary society to enter that field (in 1812). Its work is mainly among the Singhalese. The WMS sent its first missionary to Ceylon in 1814, and it soon took up work in the north and the extreme south of the island in order to reach both Tamils and Singhalese. The ABCFM entered Ceylon, concentrating effort at Jaffna, when its missionary, Newell, was excluded from Bombay in 1813. The CMS mission for both Tamils and Singhalese was commenced in 1818 in Jaffna, in Kandy, and in Galle. The SPG took up work in Ceylon in 1838, laboring in connection with the Bishop of Colombo. In 1886 the Salvation Army established a mission in Ceylon, with "barracks" in most of the large towns. The YMCA and YWCA each have representatives in the island. The total number of Christians connected with the various missions is not far from 30,000. The total of Christians of all denominations shown by the census (1891) is 302,127.

Mission work has had peculiar difficulties to encounter in Ceylon. In addition to the abominations of Hinduism in the north, the fatalism of Buddhism in the south, and the torpidity of the tropics in both parts, there were the false impressions of nearly three centuries of "Government Christianity" to be rooted out before the seeds of a spiritual conception of Christianity could take root. This, however, has been done. While there is still much to be desired in the churches, there are many illustrations of pure, firm Christian life. Tho seldom obliged to leave their homes and villages, as often in India, the converts have endured tests not less strong, in the daily influence of those about them. That so many of the Christians have, under these adverse circumstances, held their profession unspotted, is a matter almost of wonder.

A good proportion of the churches support their own pastors and teachers. In Christian families there is a beautiful custom of taking a handful of rice from that to be prepared for each meal and setting it aside to be given to the Lord; and it is no uncommon thing for a man to pledge a month's salary for some special object in the church.

In comparison with either Hinduism or Buddhism, Christianity still appears very weak. But its growth cannot be counted by numbers alone. It is confessed, even by those opposed to Christianity, that the strength of the native religions is being sapped, and that the ultimate triumph of Christianity is only a matter of time.

Capper (J.), *Old Ceylon*, illus., London, 1878; *Ceylon Mission of the LMS*, London, 1879; Harvard (W. M.), *Narrative of the Establishment of the Wesleyan Mission in Ceylon*, London, 1823; Howland (W. W.), *Historical Sketch of the Ceylon Mission*, Boston, 1865; Leitch (M. & M.), *Seven Years in Ceylon*, New York, 1890; Rouse, *Missionary Pictures, Indian and Singhalese*, BMS, London.

CHAIBASA: Chief town of Singhbhum district, Bengal, India. Population (1891), 6,900, of whom 4,000 are Hindus and the most of the remainder are Mohammedans. A large fair attended by 20,000 visitors is held here annually at Christmas time. Station of the Gossner Missionary Society of Germany, with 1 missionary, 38 native workers, men and women, 2 common schools, 1 high school, and 3,412 baptized Christians.

CHAINPUR: A town in the Shahabad district of Bengal, India; situated about 120 miles S. W. of Patna, near the western border of the province. Station of the Gossner Missionary Society (Germany), with (1900) 2 missionaries, 34 native workers, 16 chapels, 2 elementary and 1 high school,1 book depot, and 3,360 baptized Christians.

CHAKA: A settlement on the W. side of Pemba I., off the eastern coast of German East Africa; station of the Anti-Slavery Committee of the Society of Friends (England), with 2 missionaries, 2 missionary women, 1 elementary school, 1 orphanage and a dispensary.

CHAKRADHARPUR: A town situated 20 miles N. W. of Chaibasa, in the Singhbhum district of Chota Nagpur, India. Station of the Gossner Missionary Society, with (1900) 1 missionary, 18 native workers, men and women, 9 chapels, 2 elementary schools and 1,100 baptized Christians.

CHALDAIC LANGUAGE: A dialect of the Modern Syriac.

CHALDEAN CHURCH: Name taken by those Nestorians of Mesopotamia who seceded from their own church in 1780 and accepted the supremacy of the Pope of Rome. This secession was led by the Nestorian Patriarch of Mosul, whose hereditary and official name was Mar Elias. The conditions on which these Nestorians submitted to Rome included the recognition of the orders of their clergy, and the privilege of using their ancient liturgy. The office of patriarch was continued under the title of Patriarch of Babylon, but it soon ceased to be hereditary in the family of Mar Elias. The liturgy has been gradually modified in some respects, and at present the Chaldean Church is quite fanatically opposed to many of those very peculiarities of the Nestorians for whose preservation their fathers stipulated. The number of Chaldeans hardly exceeds 75,000.

Laurie (T.), *Dr. Grant and the Mountain Nestorians*, New York.

CHA-LING-CHAU: Town in the eastern part of the Province of Hu-nan, China; station of the CIM (1898), with (1900) 1 missionary physician and a chapel.

CHALMERS, James: Born August 4, 1841. Died April 8, 1901. At the age of fourteen he entered a law office at Inverary, and it was about this time that his great interest in foreign missions was aroused by a letter from a missionary in the Fiji Islands. So powerful was the impression made upon him by this letter that, it is said, on his way home from the religious service he stopped in a lonely spot and, dropping on his knees, prayed that God might make him a missionary to the heathen. After his conversion he spent three years in study, during which time he was engaged in mission work, and then he was accepted as a candidate by the London Missionary Society, entering Cheshunt College when about twenty-one to prepare for the foreign field. Leaving Cheshunt at the end of his second year, he completed his training in the institution at Highgate conducted by the London Missionary Society. In January, 1866, he and his bride set sail for Raratonga, an island in the Cook group in the Southern Pacific. After a series of mishaps their ship became a total wreck on the reef at Savage Island (Niuè), and they finally arrived at Raratonga in the ship of the piratical Captain Hayes, one year and four months after leaving England. When Chalmers arrived at Raratonga he found that the natives had been raised from a condition of fierce savagery to a state of semi-civilization through the efforts of John Williams (1823) and Pitman and Buzacott; but immorality, especially drunkenness, still was rife. His time was largely occupied by his classes for the training of native teachers and by visiting the different stations on the island on preaching tours; but he considered his work at Raratonga as a course of preparation for missionary labors in New Guinea, where heathenism and savagery were rampant. In May, 1877, under the London Missionary Society, he and his wife sailed for their new field. Their first settlement was made at a point on the bay lying between South Cape and Suan. By his remarkable tact and personal magnetism, he soon disarmed the suspicions of the people; a house of worship was erected in a short time, and at the end of two years the work at Suan was sufficiently advanced to be left in the care of a teacher. His time was spent in constant journeys to new fields, and one of the most important of these trips was his visit to the natives of Motumotu, a district on the coast some distance west of Port Moresby, where the people were especially fierce and bloodthirsty. His numberless perils by land and sea he referred to simply as "the pepper and salt" which gave zest to his further and greater efforts. He and his associate, W. G. Lawes, worked well together. the one discovering and opening new fields, the other mastering and reducing to working form the language, and training teachers for the work on those fields. In 1882, after making a visit to his old station at Suan, Chalmers was able to write: "For over two years there have been no cannibal ovens, no feasts, no human flesh, no desire for skulls. Tribes that could not formerly meet, except to fight, now meet as friends and sit down side by side in the same house, worshiping the true God." In October, 1888, Southeastern New Guinea was formally annexed to the British Empire, and Chalmers and Lawes rendered valuable aid, through their knowledge of the country and people. After an absence of twenty years Chalmers returned to England, where his speeches aroused marked enthusiasm. In 1887 he visited Australia, and in 1890 he made a tour of the colonies. It was on a voyage to Samoa that Chalmers met Robert Louis Stevenson, the novelist, and a loving friendship was formed. In 1892 Chalmers was established at Saguane, at the mouth of Fly River; his field embraced the south coast of the island and the islands of Torres Straits as far as Murray Island. Sir William MacGregor, who for years held the position of Lieutenant-Governor of New Guinea, wrote these words: "Many teachers died of illness; several were killed by the people for whom they had come to work. In the history of the mission there loom out conspicuously the names of two great missionaries, the Rev. Dr. W. G. Lawes and the Rev. James Chalmers; the former typically a man of thought, the latter typically a man of action. Each of them has worked for and among the Papuans for over a score of years, and they still carry on work of the greatest importance." Since these words were penned Chalmers, the wonderful peacemaker of savage New Guinea, after living unscathed, tho many times condemned to death, has suffered martyrdom for Christ's sake. He and his young colleague, Oliver Fellowes Tompkins, were brutally murdered by a tribe of skull-hunters at Goaribari, on the Fly River.

Lovett (R.), *James Chalmers*, London and New York, 1902; Chalmers (J.), *Life and Work in New Guinea*.

CHAMA: A town in the Gold Coast Colony, W. Africa, about 50 miles west of Cape Coast Castle; station of the WMS, with (1901) one ordained native minister, 47 other native workers, men and women, 3 elementary schools, 23 preaching places, 3 Sunday schools, and 336 professing Christians.

CHAMARLAKOTA: A town in the Godavari district, Madras, India, situated 87 miles southwest of Vizagapatam. Population 13,400, of whom about 12,000 are Hindus. Station of the BOQ (1882), with 1 missionary and his wife, 3 native workers, men and women, 1 high school, a Y. M. C. A., and 44 church members. Also station of the ELGC, with 1 missionary and his wife.

CHAMBA: A town in the Punjab, India, at the foot of the Himalayas, 75 miles E. of Jammu. Population, 6,000, of whom 4,700 are Hindus and 1,200 Mohammedans.

Station of the Church of Scotland Foreign Mission Committee (1863), with 5 missionaries, men and women (of whom 3 are physicians), 11 native workers, 6 common schools, 1 dispensary, and 33 communicants. Also station of the CMS (1877), with 2 missionary women, 6 native workers, men and women, and 4 village schools.

CHAMBA LANGUAGE: Belongs to the Indic branch of the Aryan family of languages, and is a dialect of the Punjabi or Sikh. It is spoken in Chamba, a native state south of Kashmir, and is written with a modified form of the old Sanskrit alphabet.

CHAMBERLAIN, George W.: Born at Waterford, Penn., August 13, 1839; died July 31, 1902. Appointed in 1866 to the Brazil Mission of the Presbyterian Board (North). One of the most conspicuous figures of the Evangelistic work in South America, a great, good and heroic man whose work has been visibly blessed of God beyond what usually falls to the lot of those who serve Him in mission fields, a man to whom was revealed the secret of touching men's hearts.

Young Chamberlain first went to Brazil for his health. He had no idea of remaining, but was soon infected by Mr. Simonton's enthusiasm, and returned home to prepare for his life work there. He entered Union Seminary, but the course was interrupted by the death of Simonton, and he hastened to Brazil. Tho the junior member of the mission, Simonton's mantle fell naturally upon his shoulders. He gave himself to the work of winning Brazil for Christ with all the enthusiasm of an impetuous, ardent nature. Wife, children, friends, means, all the energy of his nature, were swept into the campaign.

The story of his life, when written, will make an inspiring book and will cover the essentials of the history of the Presbyterian Mission in Brazil. In Rio, São Paulo, Parana, Bahia, Sergipe and parts of Minas he is the best known of American missionaries, and the indelible evidences of his work are found all over this vast area. He may be justly called the builder of churches and the founder of schools.

Of great courage, matchless enthusiasm and tireless energy, he traversed the dangerous regions of the interior, on mule back, before the days of railways, and, tho repeatedly stoned, driven from the towns and threatened with death, he invariably returned and delivered the message, won hearts, and churches grew up in his wake. He was a peerless evangelist, pioneer and pathfinder.

CHAMBERLAIN, John: Sailed for India as a missionary of the English Baptist Missionary Society in May, 1802, reaching Serampur January 27, 1803. He had great aptitude for acquiring languages, and his progress in Bengali was so rapid that in a year he could speak it with an accuracy equal to that of any of the older missionaries. In January, 1804, he visited Saugur Island, where thousands were gathered at the annual religious festival. To these people he and his associates preached the Gospel and gave books and tracts. In the spring of this year he was stationed at Cutwa, 75 miles north of Calcutta. In reviewing his labors he says: "It is now five years since Providence fixed my lot here. Millions of the heathen have heard the glorious report, either from preaching or from the distribution of upward of a hundred thousand tracts and many hundreds of the Scriptures." In addition to this work he had a school of 40 pupils, for whose benefit he translated Dr. Watts' catechism and a few hymns. He also made several visits to Berhampur, a military station 45 miles from Calcutta, preaching the Gospel to the soldiers, among whom he gathered a church of 24 members. On account of his facility in acquiring languages, his knowledge of the original Scriptures, especially of Hebrew, and his zeal and experience in missionary work, he was sent in 1809 to Agra to establish a new mission. His health having failed, he sailed for England in 1827, but died on the passage.

Lewis (C. B.), *John Chamberlain,* Calcutta, 1876.

CHANDA: Chief town of the Chanda district, Nagpur division, Central Provinces, India. It is surrounded by charming scenery, but is subject to malarial fever in the autumn. A celebrated fair is held here in April. Population, 16,200, of which number 14,600 are Hindus. Station of the Episcopal Church in Scotland (1898), with 2 missionaries, 5 native workers, an orphanage, and a hospital.

CHANDAG: A village in the Kumaon district, United Provinces, India, situated among the lower spurs of the Himalayas not far from the boundaries of Kashmir. It has been the scene of the brave and effective work among lepers of Mary Reed, of the Methodist Episcopal (U. S.) Mission. A station of the Mission to Lepers in India and the East was opened here in 1883, and now has a chapel and a leper asylum.

CHANDAUSI: A city in the United Provinces, India, situated in the district of Moradabad, 40 miles W. of Bareilly. Population, 28,000, including 20,000 Hindus and 7,700 Mohammedans. Station of the ME (1881), with 16 native workers, 4 chapels, 16 Sunday schools, 16 elementary schools, a Young People's Society and 446 professing Christians.

CHANDBALI: A town in Orissa, Bengal, India, 9 miles from the sea and 60 miles N. E. of Cuttack. The climate tho hot is healthful, being tempered by sea breezes. The population is about 5,000, chiefly Hindus, with some Mohammedans. The Telugu language and the Bengali and Hindustani here come into rivalry with the Uriye. The General Convention of Free Baptists established a station here in 1888, and the present force of workers consists of 1 missionary and his wife, with 26 natives, men and women; 11 elementary schools are conducted in the town and its dependencies and a church of 25 members has been organized.

CHANDKURI: Station of the German Evangelical (Synod) Missionary Society (U. S.) in the Central Provinces, India, 25 miles S. W. of Bilaspur. The station has a force of 2 missionaries and their wives, with 24 native workers, men and women. There are 7 elementary schools, an orphanage, a dispensary, a book depot, 8 places of worship in the town and its vicintiy, and the number of baptized Christians is 520. The Mission to Lepers in India and the East also has a station here, opened in 1896, and maintains a chapel, leper asylum and a home for the untainted childern of lepers.

CHANDPUR: A town in the United Provinces, India, 37 miles east of Meerut. Population, 12,300, sixty per cent. being Mohammedans. Station of the New Zealand Baptist Missionary Society (1898), with 1 missionary physician and his wife, a missionary woman, 4 native workers, men and women, 1 elementary school and a hospital.

CHANG-CHAU-FU: A city in the province of Fo-kien, China, situated about 25 miles W. of Amoy, and possessing an important trade in silk and some iron works. Population, about 500,000. The LMS opened a station here in 1862, which is now occupied by 7 missionaries, men and women (one of them a physician), and 20 native workers, men and women. Connected with the station are a college, a hospital, 8 elementary schools, and a body of 351 professing Christians. The RCA also has a station here (1895), with 2 missionary women, 17 native workers, men and women, 3 elementary schools, a high school, and 14 places of worship in the city and surrounding regions. The number of professing Christians connected with the station is 312.

CHANGOMBE: One of the villages on the main

land near Mombasa, British East Africa. The CMS opened a station here in 1898, which has at present 4 missionaries, men and women, 7 native workers, men and women, 5 schools, a dispensary, and 16 communicants.

CHANG-KIA-KAU: A city lying 110 miles N. W. of Peking, China, and commonly called Kalgan. It lies at an altitude of 2,555 feet, and is an important depot of Russian trade. Population, 75,000. Station of the ABCFM (1865), with 5 missionaries, men and women, 13 native workers, 9 places of worship, 9 Sunday schools, 1 elementary school, 2 high schools, 1 hospital, 1 dispensary, a book depot and 236 church members.

CHANG-PU-HSIEN: A town in the province of Fo-kien, China, about 100 miles S. W. of Amoy; occupied as a station by the Presbyterian Church of England in 1874, and now having a force of 9 missionaries, men and women (of whom two are physicians), who carry on a hospital, a dispensary and a medical school.

CHANG-SHAN-HSIEN: A town in the province of Che-kiang, China, about 30 miles W. S. W. of Ku-chau-fu. Station of the CIM (1878), with a missionary and his wife, 1 missionary woman and 6 native workers, men and women. In the town and its neighborhood are 5 preaching places, and there are 41 professing Christians.

CHANG-SHU: 1. A village in the province of Kiang-si, China, situated near the Kan River, and occupied in 1895 as a station by the CIM. The present force is 1 missionary and his wife and 2 native workers. The number of baptized Christians is 10.
2. A town in the southern part of the province of Kiang-su, China. The MES occupied it as a station in 1890 and now have there 1 missionary and 2 native workers, with 3 preaching places and a book depot. The number of professing Christians is 112.

CHANG-TE-FU: A city in the northern part of the province of China, Honan; occupied in 1896 as a missionary station by the Presbyterian Church in Canada. The force now working there consists of 9 missionaries, men and women (of whom two are physicians), and 4 native workers. Besides a chapel, they maintain a hospital and dispensary. It is also a station of the Cumberland Presbyterian Missionary Board, with 5 missionaries, men and women, 1 native worker and a dispensary.

CHAO-CHAU-FU: A city of about 200,000 inhabitants in the province of Kwang-tung, China, situated about 20 miles north of Swatow. It is the prefectural city of an agricultural district, containing over ten million inhabitants; occupied as a mission central station by the Presbyterian Church of England in 1890. This mission now has there (1901) 2 missionaries (one a physician), 1 missionary's wife, 1 missionary woman, not married, 5 outstations, 1 hospital, 1 dispensary, 1 medical class. There is also a fine church building. The number of communicants reported from Chao-chau-fu jointly with Swatow is 2,140. Also a station of the ABMU (1894), with a missionary and his wife and 4 native workers, who have 3 places of worship in the district and 80 church members.

CHAO-CHENG: A town in the province of Shan-si, China, situated 30 miles N. N. E. of Ping-yang-fu. Station of the CIM (1901), with 2 missionaries.

CHAO-TUNG-FU: A city in the N. E. part of the province of Yunnan, China, which has important lead and silver mines. Population, about 50,000. Station of the Bible Christian Missionary Society (1888), with 4 missionaries, men and women, a native worker, an elementary school and a dispensary.

CHAO-YANG-HSIEN: A town in the northern part of China, beyond the great wall and near the western border of Manchuria, lying about 120 miles N. W. of New-chwang. It was occupied as a station by the LMS in 1887, and in 1902 was transferred to the PCI, the LMS having decided to withdraw from Mongolia. A school has been opened and the number of church members is 217.

CHARLOTTENBURG: A station of the Moravian Missions (1835) in Surinam, South America, and was the first plantation opened to the Moravians for the preaching of the Gospel, fifty years after the missionaries began their labors in Surinam. It lies on a curve of the river Commewyne, about 50 miles E. of Paramaribo. The banks of the stream are lined with fresh, green woods, among which here and there pretty hamlets may be seen. At present the missionary force consists of 1 missionary and his wife, with 12 native workers, men and women. There is a chapel and a school and the number of communicants is 255.

CHAU-KIA-KAU: A town in the province of Ho-nan, China, about 30 miles west of Chen-chau-fu. Station of the CIM (1884), with a force of 12 missionaries, men and women (one of whom is a physician), and 14 native workers, men and women. In the town and its neighborhood there are 9 preaching centers and 290 communicants.

CHAVAKACHERI: A town in the southern part of the Jaffna Peninsula, Ceylon, situated 11 miles E. of the town of Jaffna. Station of the ABCFM (1834), temporarily vacant and under care of missionaries at Udupitti. It has (1900) 69 native workers, men and women, 26 elementary schools and a dispensary. The number of church members is 285.

CHEFOO. See CHI-FU.

CHEMULPO: The most important of the treaty ports of Korea. The climate is temperate. It has about 2,000 foreign residents, most of whom are Japanese. Station of the ME, with 1 missionary and his wife, 5 native workers, 15 chapels, 2 elementary schools, 1 theological class, 10 Sunday schools and 1,081 professing Christians. Station also of the SPG (1890), with 2 missionaries, 1 native worker, 1 elementary school and 10 communicants.

CHENCHAUFU: A city and district headquarters in the eastern part of the province of Ho-nan, China. Station of the CIM (1895), with (1900) 1 missionary and his wife, 3 missionary women (of whom one is a physician), 2 native workers, 1 chapel and 23 professing Christians.

CHENGALPAT: Railway junction and chief town of the district of the same name; situated 35 miles S. W. of Madras, India. Population, 6,200, mostly Hindus. Station of the UFS, with 1 missionary and his wife, 1 missionary woman, 62 native workers, men and women, 20 elementary schools, 3 high schools, a YMCA and 125 church members. Also station of the Leipzig Missionary Society (1893), with 2 missionaries, 1 missionary's wife, 6 native workers, 4 chapels,

4 elementary schools and 357 professing Christians.

CHENG-KU-HSIEN: A town in the province of Shen-si, China; situated about 15 miles west by north of Han-chung. Station of the CIM, with (1899) 2 missionaries, one of them married, 7 native workers, 3 preaching places, 1 school, a dispensary and 87 professing Christians.

CHENG-TU-FU: Capital of the province of Sze-chwan, China. It is one of the finest cities in China, situated in the middle of a fertile and well-watered plain, surrounded by graceful hills. The people are reputed to be among the most polished in the empire. Population (1887) estimated at 800,000. Station of the CIM (1881), with 3 missionaries (two of them married), 9 native workers, men and women, 6 chapels, 3 elementary schools and 251 communicants. Also station of the Methodist Church of Canada (1891), with 5 missionaries (one a physician), 2 chapels, 1 elementary school, 1 high school, a hospital, a dispensary, a printing house, 2 book depots and 17 communicants. Also station of the Woman's Missionary Society of the Methodist Church in Canada (1893), with 8 missionary women (two of them physicians), 1 high school, 1 orphanage, a dispensary and a hospital. Also station of the ME, with 3 missionaries and their wives, 5 native workers, men and women, 2 chapels, 4 elementary schools, 1 high school and 64 professing Christians.

CHENG-YANG-KWAN: A town in the province of Ngan-hwei, China; station of the CIM (1887), with (1900) 3 missionaries, 2 native workers, and 1 chapel.

CHEN-KIANG-FU: A city in the province of Kiang-su, China; situated about 40 miles west of Nan-king on the right bank of the Yangtse River. Population (1901) 140,000. The place is a commercial center of importance. Its climate is damp, subject to sudden changes of temperature, but not unhealthful. Station of the ME, with (1901) 1 missionary and his wife, 4 missionary women (two of them medical), 2 native workers, 2 preaching places, 1 elementary and 1 high school and 79 professing Christians. Also station of the PS (1883), with (1901) 3 missionaries and their wives, 4 preaching places, 2 outstations. Also station of the CIM (1888), with 5 missionaries, men and women (two of them physicians), 1 native worker, 1 chapel, a hospital, and 11 communicants. Station also of the SBC, with (1902) 3 missionaries (one of them a physician), 2 wives of missionaries, 2 women missionaries, 3 native workers, 3 chapels, 3 schools and 35 church members. The National Bible Society of Scotland also has a station here under care of agent who supervises a depot and 25 native workers. In the missionary and commercial reports the name is written Chinkiang.

CHEN-YUEN-HSIEN: Town in the province of Kan-su, China, about 35 miles N. E. of Ping-liang-fu. Station of the CIM (1897), with (1900) 3 women missionaries, 3 native workers, 1 chapel, 1 high school and 1 refuge for opium eaters.

CHERIBON: A seaport on the north coast of Java, 125 miles east southeast of Batavia. It is the residence of a Dutch governor and a place of considerable trade. Population, 52,000, including about 600 Europeans. Station of the Netherlands Missionary Society (1865), with 1 missionary and 59 communicants.

CHERRA PUNJI: A village in the Khasia Hills, Assam, India, lying 25 miles S. W. of Shillong, at an altitude of 4,455 feet. The rainfall here is the heaviest known, the mean annual amount being 474 inches. The population is somewhat over 5,000. Station of the Welsh Calvinistic Methodist Missionary Society, with 1 missionary and his wife, 25 native workers, men and women, 16 elementary schools, 1 theological seminary, 22 preaching stations, 14 Sunday schools and 482 church members.

CHESTER, Rev. Edward, M.D.: Born in New York City, July 12, 1828; graduated from Union Theological Seminary in 1857 and entered upon his work in the Madura Mission, India, under the ABCFM in the spring of 1859. He spent nearly forty-two years on the foreign field, and in pursuing the duties of a faithful missionary of the Cross, his influence as an educator and a physician was deeply felt throughout the region of his labors. Altho before leaving America he prepared himself for medical practise in India, he spent a year at Madras, studying the forms of disease peculiar to the tropics, at the hospital, infirmaries and dispensaries of the presidency capital. When he was put in charge of the Madura hospital and dispensary, he completely transformed the methods of these institutions and the mission, and the patients increased from 3,100 to 51,000 annually. To these thousands the Gospel was daily preached, and a leaflet, which served also as a dispensary ticket, was given, containing the ten commandments, the Lord's Prayer and a brief statement of saving truth. Dr. Chester established the local missionary dispensary and medical service, and through his consecrated energy the district of Madura was better provided with a medical service for combating epidemics and common tropical diseases than any other district of South India. In addition to his extensive medical work, Dr. Chester, during all of these years, had charge of a mission district, with a large number of pastors, preachers, teachers and Bible women under his supervision, and also a number of schools and separate classes received his personal attention. He laid down his burden and entered into rest at Dindigul, March 26, 1892.

CHEUNG MAI: A city in the Laos country of Siam, 300 miles N. by W. of Bangkok. Charmingly situated among hills on the Mah Ping River. Population, 100,000. Station of the PN (1867), with (1901) 16 missionaries, men and women (one of them a physician), 4 native workers, 7 elementary schools, 2 high schools, 1 theological school, a hospital, 2 dispensaries, a printing house and 1,906 church members.

CHEUNG RAI: A city in the Laos country, Siam, about 100 miles N. E. of Cheung Mai. Station of the PN (1897), for some years known in the reports as Cheung Hai. The force occupying it (1901) consists of 2 missionaries (one of them a physician) and their wives, with 1 native worker. There are in this field 1 elementary school, 1 hospital, a dispensary, a Young People's Society and 312 church members. The field is nearly 200 miles long from north to south and nearly as wide from east to west. Within its limits are three organized churches.

CHHINDWARA: Chief town of a district in the Narbada division, Central Provinces, India. It is situated on a well-watered table land, 64 miles N. E. of Nagpur. The population is about

9,000, two-thirds of the people being Hindus. It was occupied as a station by the Swedish National Missionary Society in 1885. The present force there consists of 8 missionaries, men and women (one being a physician), and 16 native workers, men and women. The various enterprises of the station are 3 elementary schools, an orphanage, a dispensary and theological school, besides the usual preaching services. There are 83 professing Christians connected with the station. It is also a circuit of the ME, with 3 native workers and 97 professing Christians.

CHHUNG-JU: A town in Korea, 55 miles S. E. of Seoul; station of the PS (1896), with 7 missionaries, men and women (one a physician), 3 preaching places and 10 communicants.

CHIANG-CHIU. See CHANG-CHAU-FU.

CHIANG HOA: Town on the west coast of the island of Formosa, about 5 miles S. W. of Taichu. Station of the PCE (1889), with (1901) 2 missionaries (one a physician), 1 dispensary, 1 hospital and 23 preaching places (in district). The communicants connected with the central stations of Tainan and Chiang Hoa conjointly are 2,190. (The Chiang Hoa field is spoken of by the missionaries as the Taichu field very frequently).

CHICACOLE: A town in the district of Gangam, Madras, India; situated on the Navagalli River, 10 miles from the sea. Population (1891) 18,200, almost all Hindus. The BMP opened a station here in 1878, which now has 1 missionary and his wife, 2 women missionaries, 8 native workers, men and women, 1 high school, a hospital, a book depot and 45 church members. The name is also written Cicacole.

CHI-CHAU-FU: A city in the province of Ngan-hwei, China, situated on the right bank of the Yangtse River. Station of the CIM, with a missionary and his wife, 2 missionary women, 4 native workers, an elementary school and 21 professing Christians.

CHICHOLI: Town in the Narbada division, Central Provinces, India; station of the Episcopal Church in Scotland (1894), with (1900) 2 missionaries and their wives, 1 missionary woman, 4 native workers, an elementary school and 21 communicants.

CHI-CHOW. See KI-CHAU.

CHIENG-TOONG. See KENG-TUNG.

CHI-FU: A city and seaport in the province of Shan-tung, China. It is a commercial center for goods of foreign manufacture. The population is about 120,000. The climate is more agreeable to Europeans than that of any other open port in China, and the place is visited as a sanitarium by foreign residents in the south of the empire. It was occupied as a station by the PN in 1862, which now has a force there of 9 missionaries, men and women, 94 native workers, men and women (in the city and in 50 outstations). There are 39 preaching places, 40 elementary and 4 high schools, a dispensary, and 1,445 communicants. It is a station also of the SPG (1874), with 2 missionaries and 1 missionary's wife; also station of the CIM (1879), with 39 missionaries, men and women (one a physician), 4 native workers, 1 chapel, 5 schools, a hospital, a dispensary and 50 professing Christians.

CHIHUAHUA: Capital of the State of Chihuahua, Mexico; situated at the base of the Sierra Madre Mountains, 225 miles south of El Paso, Tex.; founded in 1706. The climate is dry, mild and healthful. It is a center for trade to neighboring gold and silver mines, and quite a number of citizens of the United States reside there. It was occupied as a station by the ABCFM in 1882, and the force now there is 1 missionary and his wife, 2 missionary women and 8 native workers, men and women. There are 2 elementary schools, a high school, a book depot, 17 outstations, 2 young people's societies, and 291 communicants. Station also of the Woman's Board of the MES (1890), with 3 missionary women.

CHIKALDA: A village in the district of Ellichpur, Berar, India; situated 43 miles N. W. of Amraoti, in the midst of beautiful scenery, at an altitude of 3,656 feet. Population about 5,000. Station of the Kurku India Hill Mission (1894), with (1901) 3 missionary women, 1 native worker, 1 orphanage, and 1 school, with industrial department.

CHIKBALLAPUR: Town in the Kolar district of Mysore, India, situated 36 miles N. E. of Bangalore. Population about 11,500. Station of the LMS (1892), with (1901) 2 missionaries, 15 native workers, men and women, 7 schools, and 30 church members.

CHIKORE: A settlement in the Melsetter district of Rhodesia, near the frontier of Portuguese, East Africa, and 170 miles W. by S. from Beira. Station of the ABCFM (1897), with (1901) 1 missionary physician and his wife, 2 native workers, 1 elementary school, 4 preaching places and 1 dispensary.

CHILAMBARAM: Town in South Arcot, Madras, India, situated 21 miles S. by W. of Cuddalore. Its temples to Siva are held in great reverence in S. India and Ceylon. Population, 18,600, of whom 17,000 are Hindus. Station of the Leipzig Missionary Society (1866), with (1900) 1 missionary and his wife, 15 native workers, 10 preaching places, 9 elementary and 1 high school, and 847 baptized Christians.

CHILDREN'S SPECIAL SERVICE MISSION (1868): The aim of this organization is to supplement the work of the Church, Sunday school, and home among children by its various publications, evangelistic services, and the Scripture Union, which was organized in 1879. Open air services are held, and by means of caravan and tent workers go from village to village, holding services and distributing Christian literature among the children. A Foreign Fund is used for the issue of such literature in 51 different languages, which is freely given to missionaries of all denominations, and grants are made to anyone visiting foreign countries who will make use of them. The Scripture Union Fund pays for itself through the contribution of one penny per annum from the members of the Union, and from the sale of its literature. Besides the publication of books, leaflets, etc., an illustrated penny monthly, *Our Own Magazine*, is issued, with a circulation of 120,000. *Our Boys' Magazine* is published, with special reference to school boys. The Scripture Union Fund supplies a Scripture Union Almanac and the monthly Letters, which are also translated into French, Dutch, Danish and Swedish, and issued in the Tamil monthly magazine. The greater part of the expenses for administration of the work of the mission is covered by the profits transferred to the General Fund, so that contributions are used directly for the work. Income (1902), General Fund, £5,205 16s; Foreign Fund, £799 2s ; Scripture Union Fund, £3,033 18s.

Headquarters, 13a Warwick Lane, Paternoster Row, London.

CHILE, Republic of: Lies on the western coast of the southern portion of South America, between the crest of the Andes and the ocean, from the Camarones River to Cape Horn. Its population is about 2,700,000, chiefly of Spanish descent, but including 50,000 Indians. The language is Spanish, and the religion of the state is Roman Catholic. Other religions are tolerated by law. The climate is that of the temperate zone, the temperature being modified, however, by the high mountains and by proximity to the sea.

While the Andes wall in Chile on the east, they are being pierced by a railroad which will soon open communication with the Argentine Republic.

Mission work is carried on by the Presbyterian Church (North), the ME, and the SAMS. The last-named Society is gaining a hold upon the Araucanian Indians.

CHILLAN: Capital of the province of Nuble, Chile; situated about 70 miles N. W. of Concepcion. Population (1901, estimated), 33,506. Station of the PN (1894), with (1901) 1 missionary and his wife, 1 native worker, 1 elementary school and 130 church members.

CHILPANCINGO: A town in the State of Guerrero, Mexico; situated about 65 miles N. E. of Acapulco, at an altitude of 4,800 feet. Station of the PN (1894), with (1901) 2 missionaries and their wives, 11 native workers, 3 schools, 8 outstations.

CHINA: By the name China is designated the possessions of the Chinese Empire in its widest sense, tho it is used more correctly and narrowly to name the eighteen provinces which constitute China proper. This immense country comprises one-third of Asia, one-tenth of the inhabitable globe, and is divided politically into China proper, Manchuria, Mongolia, Chinese Turkestan and Tibet.

The eighteen provinces, and usually one of the provinces of Manchuria (Sheng Ching) in addition, form that part of the empire which is distinctively known as China, and are inhabited by Chinese. The area of China is variously estimated from 1,348,870 to 2,000,000 square miles, since its western boundary is unsettled. Its greatest length in 1,474 miles and its breadth 1,355 miles. "It contains almost as much territory as is comprised in the states lying east of the Mississippi River, with the addition of Texas, Arkansas, Missouri, and Iowa."

Physical Features: In the northeast is a great plain, and the remainder of China is divided into three basins, separated by mountain ranges which run from east to west, and drained by three great rivers and their tributaries. In general, all that part of the country lying west of the meridian of 113° is mountainous; from that line down to the coast, south of the Yangtsekiang (kiang meaning river), is found hilly country alternating with the river valleys.

The Great Plain extends from the Great Wall north of Peking to the junction of the Yangtse River with the Poyang Lake, and is 700 miles in length. It has an average breadth of 200 miles north of latitude 35° north, and covers an area of 70,000 square miles; while in the parallel of the Yellow River it increases in breadth to 300 miles, until it reaches the Yangtse River, where it stretches 400 miles inland, covering 140,000 square miles in this southern portion, making a total of 210,000 square miles. This basin supports a population of 177,000,000, and is more densely populated than any other part of the world of equal size.

Rivers: Of the many rivers which flow from west to east across China the principal ones are the Hwang Ho (Yellow River), the Yangtse-kiang (Yangtsze River), and the Chu-kiang (Pearl River). The Yellow River is of very little use for navigation, owing to the great difference in its depth during summer and winter. On account of its habit of overflowing it has been justly called "China's sorrow." In a direct line its distance from source to mouth is 1,290 miles, but its numerous windings make its length double that distance.

The Yangtse River is deep and affords passage for ocean steamers for 200 miles from its mouth, and with the aid of modern engineering it would be possible for steam vessels to ascend 2,000 miles. Its basin is estimated at 548,000 square miles, and in the amount of water it discharges, the system of tributaries belonging to it, and the means of communication which it affords, it ranks with the great rivers of the world.

The Chu-kiang is formed at Canton by the union of the North, East, and West rivers, of which the latter is by far the largest. They drain the southwestern part of China, an area of 130,000 square miles, and, being intersected by numerous tributaries, form a perfect network of streams which afford the means of communication between the three southwestern provinces.

Lakes: There are few large lakes in China. Tung Ting Lake, in Hunan is the largest one. In Kiangsi is found the picturesque Poyang Lake, having important fisheries. There are smaller lakes in Chili, Shantung, and Yunnan, which support aquatic populations.

Provinces: In the division of the provinces made a hundred years ago, eighteen provinces were defined. The cities in the different provinces have a suffix added to the name, which denotes the rank of the city and the grade of the district of which it is the chief town. These suffixes are *fu*, *chau*, and *hsien*, and in general may be rendered "department," or prefecture, "primary district," and "secondary district," respectively.

Climate: The eighteen provinces occupy the same relative position on the continent of Asia as the United States occupy on the continent of North America, and the variations of temperature are similar. The average temperature of China is lower than that of any other country in the same latitude. The humidity, especially in the south, is relatively greater than countries in like latitudes, and, consequently, the heat is harder to bear. The excessive heat causes the prevalence of typhoons during July, August and September.

History: Chinese history may be divided into five periods: the Mythological, the Legendary, the Ancient, the Medieval, and the Modern. 1. The Mythological period comprises all the time antecedent to the accession of Fu Hsi, B.C. 2852, and native writers assign to it myriads of years. Pan Ku is described as having formed the world during this time. With chisel and mallet he cut out the earth; the sun, moon, and stars are his works; his head became mountains; his breath, wind and clouds; his voice, thunder; from various parts of his body came fields, rivers, and trees, and finally from the insects on his body came man. After this Chinese creator came a trinity of powers who ruled for thousands of years, and to them are ascribed many of the inventions of the ancient time. 2. The Legendary period ends with the accession of Yu in 2205. Eight monarchs in all reigned during this time, and the tales that are related of their prowess resemble the legends of other ancient nations. It was during this period, about the year 2200 B.C., that the Chinese settled around the bend of the Yellow River, and from this time on the records are more reliable, tho legendary in places. 3. Under the division of Ancient History may be included the dynasties commencing with the Hsia and ending with the Eastern Han, in 221, six in all. Of these six dynasties the most important and the longest recorded in history was that of Chau, which commenced with Wu Wang in 1122 B.C. and lasted till 255 B.C. China was then a loose aggregation of feudal states, and the power of the emperor was often merely nominal. The originator of the Chin dynasty, who gave the name to China by which it was known to the ancients, was the Napoleon of China. He divided his empire into thirty-six provinces, with governors over each. He also built the Great Wall, which stupendous work was completed in 204 B.C. after ten years of labor. If the wall made this emperor famous, his vanity made him infamous, for he wished to be considered the first emperor of the Chinese, and ordered the destruction of all books and records which antedated his reign, and slaughtered 500 of the *literati.* Many of the writings of Confucius and Mencius were thus destroyed, and many records were lost which might throw more light on the past. During the reign of the Emperor Ping (Peace) was born in Nazareth that King who came to bring peace to the world. The founder of the Han dynasty instituted the system of competitive examinations, and under his successors literature, commerce, arts, and good government flourished. 4. Under Medieval History may be placed the seventeen dynasties which ruled China after the overthrow of the Han family till the accession of the first monarch of the Ming dynasty, in 1368. During the first dynasty of this period the country was divided into three principalities, and the wars that ensued between the various princes gave rise to the Chinese historical novel, *The Three Kingdoms,* which portrays the conditions of society at that time. During the Eastern Chin dynasty, 323-419, Nanking was the capital, Buddhism was the chief religion, and the doctrines of Confucius were coming into universal favor. During the Tang dynasty, 618 to 908, China was the most civilized country on the face of the globe. It was the golden age of China, and to this day the natives in the south call themselves Tang-jen, men of Tang, for during that time they were civilized and amalgamated with the Chinese race. Arab travelers visited China during this period, and to them we owe much of the information possessed in regard to their civilization. During the reign of the Emperor Tai Tsung (627-40), the Nestorian missionaries presented themselves at court and were received with respect. The Yuen dynasty, 1280 to 1368, was a Mongol dynasty, inaugurated by the great Kublai Khan, whose exploits are related by Marco Polo. The expulsion of the Mongols and the restoration of native rule brings us to a period which is comparatively modern. 5. The last native dynasty was called Ming, or "bright," and lasted from 1368 to 1644, with sixteen monarchs in all. The Portuguese came to China in 1516, and the Jesuits gained an entrance in the country about 1580. The Manchus finally attacked the imperial forces, and, aided by native rebels in various parts of the empire, finally overthrew the dynasty, and Shun Chih took the throne in 1644, since which time the Ta Ch'ing, "great pure," dynasty has been in power, the Chinese submitting peacefully to its rule. The Manchu conquerors imposed their mode of wearing the hair in a queue upon the Chinese. Kang Hsi, who reigned sixty-one years from 1662, was one of the ablest rulers of China. He ordered a survey of the empire by the Romish missionaries, and superintended the publication of a great thesaurus, in addition to devoting himself with unwearying care to the solidifying of the country, the unifying of his people, and the encouragement of all that makes a nation happy and prosperous. His grandson, Chien Lung, reigned sixty years, which were characterized by the peace and prosperity of the country. Embassies from the Dutch, Russians, and English were received by him. The Emperor Tao Kuang, 1821-51, was a wise, able ruler. He waged bitter strife against the traffic in opium, and brought on the war with England and the consequent opening of his country to foreign intercourse. The Tai Ping rebellion broke out at his death and lasted the greater part of the life of his successor, Hien Fung. The minority reign of Tung Chih ended just as he was taking charge of the government, and he was succeeded by the present emperor, Kwang Hsü, who attained his majority in 1889. On September 22, 1898, however, an imperial edict transferred the direction of affairs to the Empress Dowager, who has since (1904) retained power. The following chronological table is taken from Williams' *Middle Kingdom,* and gives the accepted dates in Chinese history:

CHINESE CHRONOLOGY.

Dynasty.	Number of Sovereigns and Average Length of Reign.	Began	Duration.
		B. C.	
1. Hsia......	17; average, 26 years........	2205	439
2. Shang.....	28; " 23 "	1766	644
3. Chau......	34; " 25½ "	1122	867
4. Chin.......	2; one 37 yrs., the other 3 yrs	255	40
5. Han........	14; average, 16½ years.......	206	231
		A. D.	
6. East Han..	12; " 16½ "	25	196
7. After Han..	2; one 2 yrs. the other 41 yrs.	221	43
8. Chin.......	4; average 14¼ years........	265	57
9. East Chin..	11; " 9½ "	323	106
10. Sung......	8; " 7¼ "	420	58
11. Chi........	5; " 4⅔ "	479	23
12. Liang......	4; one 48 yrs; 3 together, 7 yrs	502	54
13. Chin.......	5; average, 6½ years.........	557	32
14. Sui........	3; one 16, one 12, one 2 yrs...	589	30
15. Tang......	20; average, 14⅓ years........	620	287
16. After Liang	2; one 8 years, one 7 years...	907	16
17. After Tang	4; average, 3¼ years.........	923	13
18. After Chin.	2; one 7 years, one 3 years...	936	10
19. After Han..	2; one 3 years..............	947	4
20. After Chau.	3; average, 3 years.........	951	9
21. Sung......	9; " 18½ "	960	167
22. South Sung	9; " 17 "	1127	153
23. Yuen......	9; " 9⅔ "	1280	88
24. Ming......	16; " 17 "	1368	276
25. Ching......	8 up to 1875; aver. 30 years..	1644	......

Opening of the Country to Foreigners: Until the early part of the last century China was practically closed to foreigners, for, tho the Portuguese had made trading voyages there, and tho the East India Company had sent out its ships to Canton, foreigners had no treaty rights until after the wars with Great Britain and France. The first war with Great Britain was what is called the opium war; it was precipitated by the seizure on the part of the Chinese Government of 20,000 chests of opium, which they claimed were being smuggled into the empire. The war commenced with the bombardment of Ting-hai on July 5, 1841, and continued till the ratification of the Nanking Treaty, on September 15, 1842. Canton, Amoy, Ting-hai, Shanghai, Ningpo and Chin-kiang were captured by British arms. Nanking was invested and would have been destroyed unless the Chinese had consented to pay the $3,000,000 demanded for its ransom. By this time the commissioners from the emperor were willing to sue for peace, and agreed to the terms of the famous Treaty of Nanking, including the opening of the five ports, Canton, Amoy, Fu-chau, Ningpo, and Shanghai, to British trade and residence. On October 8 of the following year a supplementary treaty was signed, which gave all foreigners the same rights at treaty ports as the British had been given. The United States sent Caleb Cushing as plenipotentiary to conclude a treaty of peace with China, and this treaty was signed at Wanghsia, a suburb of Macao, on July 3, 1844. At this time the Tai Ping rebellion broke out. Its leader, Hung, professed to be commissioned by God to accomplish the overthrow of the existing dynasty. He had been brought in contact with Christians, knew the principles of the Christian religion, assumed to be a Christian, and claimed to be led by visions and warnings from Heaven. However sincere he may have been in his convictions, he failed to comprehend the spiritual nature of Christianity. He began an insurrection in 1850 and finally captured Nanking, held in subjection five provinces, and threatened Peking. At this juncture Frederick Ward, an American, organized the "ever-victorious army," which under his leadership and the subsequent command of Colonel Gordon captured over fifty cities from the insurgents, and ended the rebellion in 1865, when the rebel pretender was taken prisoner and killed. The Manchu dynasty was once more supreme after fourteen years of war which shook the government to its foundations, devasted some of the fairest lands and cities of the empire, and caused the death of millions of its subjects.

The second war with Great Britain was brought on by the Chinese authorities at Canton boarding the lorcha "Arrow" and seizing some of the sailors. The war was ended by the treaties at Tientsin, in 1858, between China and the envoys of Russia, France, England, and America. "The toleration of Christianity, the residence of foreign ministers at Peking, and the freedom to travel through the land were avenues heretofore closed against the welfare and progress of China which the treaties opened, and through which she has made more real advances than ever before in her history." The Chinese did not observe the requirements of the treaty, and it was not until Peking had been occupied by the allied forces and the Summer Palace of the emperor destroyed that the treaties of Tientsin were finally ratified, October 24, 1860.

During the last forty years China has been a storm center; but out of all this disturbance there have arisen conditions that have encouraged new and better life for the whole empire. Mr. Burlingame's mission, which seemed to mark a new era in China's relations with the United States and with Europe, left Peking in 1867; but in 1871 a popular outbreak against foreigners occurred at Tientsin, resulting in a deplorable massacre. Altho the local authorities were exiled, and fifteen of the rioters were executed and a large indemnity was paid for the destruction of property and for the families of those who had perished, other similar uprisings were soon to follow. But these disturbances interrupted but slightly the determination of foreigners to influence more and more the destinies of the Middle Kingdom. The catastrophe of 1900 was foreshadowed by the troubles with Japan, the entanglements with Russia and Great Britain, and the seizure of Kiaochau, in Eastern Shantung, by the Germans. In recent years China has helplessly watched significant inroads made into her possessions; and her most strategic points, like Port Arthur and Wei-hai-wei, have been taken by Western nations. Germany has pressed her way into the province of Confucius and Mencius; Great Britain, not satisfied with the ownership of Hongkong, has extended her invasion to the adjacent mainland; France having secured a foothold, must possess more Chinese territory; Italy, by putting in her claim for San-mên Bay, shows plainly that she wants to be in the game; and China's next door neighbor, Japan, plans to shape the future of the empire. The young emperor was soon convinced either that his people would speedily lose all they possessed or else there would be a division of the country into spheres of influence. He imbibed the views of the reformer, K'ang Yü-wei; he read a large number of books prepared by missionaries, and actually began the study of the English language. Just at this time the Empress Dowager put forth her strong arm, and expressed, in no uncertain words, her strong mind. The Emperor's edicts of reform were mostly rescinded, and everything was turned in the other direction. The Boxer outbreak is familiar to all. "Starting as the work of secret sects, which have for centuries been a source of terror to the Empire, bands of men in the province of Shantung began to practise a rude sort of gymnastics, combined with an equally crude form of hypnotism, supposed to render the Boxers invulnerable." Hoping with such allies as these that she could drive out all foreigners, the Dowager Empress issued a secret edict against the foreigners, ending with this statement: "Let no one think of making peace, but let each strive to preserve from destruction or spoliation his ancestral home and graves from the ruthless hands of the invader."

It soon became apparent that the officials, sympathizing with the Dowager Empress, were opposed to the reform movement of the Emperor, the rise of German influence in Shantung, the constant discussion by foreign papers in Chinese ports of the division of the empire, and the Roman Catholic interference in the difficulties between the Boxers and native Christians. Altho the Boxers commenced their attack on the Roman Catholics, and followed it by persecution of native Protestant Christians, they soon announced that they intended to drive out all foreigners and foreign influence from the country. When they began to loot villages, burn churches, and destroy homes, the hoodlum element, with the prospect of gain, joined their ranks; and their influence over the superstitious and ignorant masses increased when it was announced that they possessed supernatural power. During the "Boxer Movement," 1899-1900, missionaries of the following societies suffered martyrdom:

CIM	58	Children,	20
Chris. and Miss. All.	21	"	15
ABCFM	13	"	5
BMS	13	"	3
PN	5	"	3
Scandinavian Alliance	5	"	..
Swedish (Mongolia)	3	"	1
SPG	3	"	2
BFBS	2	"	..
LMS	1	"	3
Sheo Yang Mission	11	"	..
	135		52

Men, 58; Women, 77.

British	71	Children,	28
Swedish	40	"	16
U. S. A.	24	"	8

To this list of missionary martyrs must be added the 16,000 native converts, very many of whom might have saved their lives and property by denying their Lord and renouncing their faith. The siege of Peking by the great Powers of the Occident and the events preceding and following this historic fact, seem to be blessings in disguise, and God is already making the wrath of man to praise Him. The following declaration, made by the Chinese Court after its defeat by the Western Powers, and relating to the establishment of a new Council of State, is not without significance:

"Where native methods come short, Western methods are to be used to supplement them. With a view to this the translations of foreign books are to be collected and compared, and our Ministers to Japan and other countries are to be called on for reports on the state and progress of those nations. For us the example of Japan is of special interest—not only as belonging to Asia, but for having in a short time risen to a place of power and influence." In his analysis of the Emperor's later Reform Edict, Sir Robert Hart's words are encouraging and suggestive: "The Empress Dowager has decided to push on reform, and, as a preliminary, sets aside such hampering distinctions as ancient and modern, native and foreign. Whatever is good for the State or for the people, no matter what its origin, is to be adopted; whatever is bad is to to be cast out, no matter what be its antiquity. Our national fault is that we have got into a rut, hard to get out of, and are fettered by red tape just as difficult to untie. Bookworms are too numerous, practical men too scarce; incompetent red-tapists grow fat on mere forms, and officials think that to pen a neat dispatch is to dispose of business. Old fossils are continued too long in office, and openings are blocked for men possessing the talents and qualifications the times require. One word accounts for the weakness of the Government—selfishness; and another for the decadence of the Empire—precedence. All this must be changed. Those who have studied Western methods have so far only mastered a smattering of language, something about manufactures, a little about armaments; but these are merely the skin and hair; they do not touch the secret of Western superiority. . . . . . . What must be insisted on as a principle is that self shall be nothing and public duty everything. We ourselves and the Empress Dowager have long cherished these ideas; and now the time has come to put them in force. Whether the State is to be safe or insecure, powerful or feeble, depends on this." The fact is apparent that, since the disasters of 1899 and 1900, the Emperor's anxiety for reform has greatly increased and we may hope that his interest in Christianity is sufficient to ensure great blessings for his country.

The events of recent years have not only strengthened the reform movement in China, but they have added to the influence of Protestant missions throughout the Empire. The heroic conduct of the missionaries during the appalling crises through which China has passed has awakened the admiration and elicited the sympathy of many of the people; the deep-felt need for a radical change in State methods and the recognition of the bitter fruit of ignorance and superstition, have given a wide extension to Western ideas of education; and the blood of the martyrs has already proven to be the seed of the Church. The four lines of Christian mission work—literary, educational, medical, and evangelistic—have taken upon themselves new life and power in China; new avenues for the introduction of the religion of Christ are opening; all civilized lands are recognizing, as never before, the practical utility of missions among this "the toughest-fibered, sturdiest, most vertebrate of the nations of the East;" the dark shadows of yesterday are giving place to the light, we may well hope, of a new day for China.

Government: The head of the government of China is the emperor. On ascending the throne the emperor takes a name or style by which his reign is known; the present emperor is called Kwang Hsü, "illustrious succession." He was born August 14, 1871, and began to reign in 1875. The theory of the government of China is the patriarchal; the emperor is the Son of Heaven and the father of his people. Beneath him the superior in age or rank has sway over the inferior *ad infinitum.* While the will of the Son of Heaven is supreme, and his power is said to be absolute, it is not unlimited, as one would think. He is bound by no constitution, no Magna Charta dictated by powerful barons limits his sway, but the accumulated force of centuries of tradition and law holds him to right and justice with an irresistible grasp. He must follow the behests of Heaven, or else the people will exercise the divine right of rebellion which they cling to, and which Confucius, and especially Mencius, defined with utmost boldness. When floods or famine, fire or pestilence come, the people look upon it as a judgment on the emperor, and he immediately offers sacrifices to heaven to appease its wrath. He is the high-priest of his people, and theoretically has their welfare at heart. Practically the people submit passively to his despotism, and rarely trouble themselves about the government in general, tho they may complain of the exactions of the local officers. Liberty is unknown. In the administration of the affairs of State the emperor is assisted by a Cabinet, a Council of State, and a number of boards. Under these boards are a multitude of office-holders. These officials are selected in accordance with the civil-service system, which is based upon literary merit, and is one of the institutions of China challenging the admiration of other nations. Theoretically, any one who does not belong to the proscribed classes may compete in the literary examinations for the various degrees, no matter how poor or ignoble he may be; practically, these honors are open only to those who have wealth, since many years of preliminary study are necessary. The great defect in the system is that the officers are not paid enough to live as their station requires, and corruption in bribe-taking and giving is widespread, while extortion is universal. Another great source of corruption is the selling of degrees and the favor shown to those who purchase them. In spite of this corruption and the abuses of power which can be seen, the officers of the government will compare favorably with those of other nations for talent and industry.

The Chinese People: The people of China have lived for so many centuries in their river basins, separated from the rest of the world, that their origin is shrouded in the mists of tradition and legends. About 2200 B.C. tribes from Central Asia came across the desert and settled around the bend of the Yellow River in what is now Shan-si. Where these settlers came from is still a matter of conjecture. A recent writer claims that they were emigrants from Babylonia. The presumptive proofs of this are in brief: Babylonia was a great agricultural country, and irrigation was everywhere to be seen; so in China; "The Middle Kingdom" was the name applied to Babylonia by its inhabitants, and that is the native appellation of China; the prehistoric period of China is divided by native writers into ten periods, and the same is attributed to Babylonia; the Babylonians were great astrologers; so are the Chinese, and the method of computing time is similar in the two nations. More direct proof is adduced by the researches of Mr. C. T. Ball, who has been able to lay down a series of phonetic laws by which he has converted into Accadian almost the entire Chinese dictionary. If this is the true origin of the Chinese people, it will explain what has hitherto been a mystery. Their language shows that at some time in the past they were a nomadic race, having their principal possessions in flocks and herds. This is also hinted at in their architecture; but as far back as records go, they are found to have been an agricultural race. The dwellers on the plains of Babylonia were descended from a parent stock who led a pastoral life in the mountainous country on the east. If, then, the Chinese are the descendants of the inhabitants of the plain, the references to a nomadic life in their language contain the remembrance of their earlier ancestors in the mountains.

In stature the majority of the Chinese are somewhat below the average height, especially the women; in the north of China the Manchu race is large and fine in appearance. They have black hair and eyes, yellow complexions, and obliquely-set eyes. The men are noticeable for an absence of beards, a thin mustache or a peaked goatee being the most hair that is seen on their faces. They have great endurance and are a strong, sturdy race, with unusual physical force. They possess the power of application to work of unvarying monotony for long hours at a time, without wearying or displaying that nervousness which is seen in European races; absence of nerves is one of their principal characteristics. They have a wonderful vitality, which seems to be unaffected by such lack of sanitary conditions as would be sure death to an American. Their skulls are thick, and they do not seem to be affected much by the burning heat of the sun. In spite of their custom of marrying early and their excesses in vice, they are very productive. The women mature rapidly, and are mothers at the early age of thirteen and fourteen. There are no special diseases to which they are predisposed, tho they are subject to consumption, skin diseases, and diseases of the eyes. They endure suffering so well, and recover so quickly from the shock and wounds of surgical operations, as to give credit to the theory that their nervous organization is not so highly developed or so sensitive as that of European races.

Qualities of the People: The Chinese are essentially an agricultural race. They are manual laborers, who possess industry, patience, and dogged determination in a great degree. While they are not aggressive, when aroused they are no mean foes, and when well officered, with men of daring and courage to lead the way, they will follow to the death with great stoicism. They work like automata, and excel in manufactures which require a fine tactile sense. They have no regard for truth for its own sake, and are noted for mendacity, deceit, and indirectness in all things. They are wonderfully polite, but this same politeness leads to a disregard of truth from the desire to avoid unpalatable facts, and is too often but an artificial veneer which conceals selfishness and conceit. They have great mental power, especially in memory, but are lacking in the imaginative and artistic temperaments. Logic and reasoning they are well skilled in, and they have a sense of humor which is of a quick kind. They are a slow, methodical, conservative, staid, phlegmatic people, and do not show much emotion; this is due as much to education as to nature, for they are taught to repress their feelings. They are more sullen than quick-tempered, more underhand than treacherous. They have great respect for learning, and reverence their superiors to the extreme, but are arrogant and conceited when learned themselves. When their anger is aroused they are more likely to vent it in words and imprecations than in blows, and street fights offend the ears oftener than they break the bones. In general, they are the finest of the Asiatic races, and their habits of domesticity, reverence of parents, submission to constituted authority, quiet industry, frugality, and temperance make them worthy of respect. In their manufactures they show a lack of inventive skill, but they possess a wonderful amount of imitativeness. Attention to detail and laborious minuteness is characteristic of their works of art. They show very little interest in the condition of any who are without their immediate circle of relations, but within that circle all that concerns the individual is discussed and commented upon by the many *ad nauseam*. They have little idea of privacy, and lack refinement in matters pertaining to man's physical nature and its needs and appetites. The laboring men are often (usually in the south) bare to the waist, but the women are modest in dress and behavior, keeping the entire body clothed, except among the poor peasantry, who labor in the field with the men.

Classes of Society: There is no caste in China, but there is a well-defined distinction between the classes—a distinction which is based on literary attainments and official position or on age. The old division of the people defined only four classes—the scholar, the farmer, the artisan, and the trader—and they ranked in the order named. The reverence which is paid to the scholar still exceeds that which is paid to the illiterate rich man. Filial duty is at the root of this division, for the scholar reflects credit on his parentage; the farmer is able to stay on his paternal acres and look after his family; the artisan is more often required to leave his home; and the necessities of a trading life impel the merchant to go to the city. Officials are distinguished from the common people by the dress which they are entitled to wear. The most noticeable feature of their dress is the button on the top of the hat. These buttons are of nine kinds, corresponding to the nine grades of rank. As the administration of the law is absolutely in the hands of the magistrates, we find no lawyers, in the Western acceptation of the term. The professions which sprang from the invention of steam, the use of electricity, and improved machinery have, until recent years, been wanting. The various religious sects have their priests, but these do not have the contact with the common people and the influence on their daily life that the clergy do in Christian countries; neither are they respected. There are now a goodly number of the editorial profession. Doctors there are, but the science of medicine is yet in its infancy. The superstitions of China do not permit dissection, and their knowledge of anatomy is vague and ridiculous. The body is thought to be a mass of flesh supported on the framework of the bones, without that intimate connection of the joints and tendons. The circulation of the blood is unknown, so far as its continuous course is concerned. The seat of the breath is supposed to be in the stomach, and that also is the seat of learning. Health and sickness depend on the preservation of the just proportions between the five elements—fire, earth, wood, metal, and water—or else they are due to the influence of evil spirits. There are no laws in regard to necessary qualifications for practising medicine, and most Chinese doctors are those who have much shrewd knowledge of human nature and some empirical knowledge of drugs. They use the vilest concoctions as medicine; some of the ingredients are scorpions, snakes, centipedes, lizards, chamois horn, bear's gall, and vegetable wax. Surgery is unknown; their superstitions prevent them from mutilating the human body, as such mutilation is supposed to endure throughout the future world. Acupuncture has been practised among them for centuries, and massage and blood letting by cupping or by leeches are well known to them. Within recent years the government has recognized the advantages to be gained from Western medicinal knowledge, and has encouraged the study of it so far as to employ Chinese graduates from medical schools taught by foreigners. The occupation of agriculture is considered an honorable occupation, tho a lowly one. Probably half the soil of China is owned by those who till it. To sum up, Chinese society acknowledges no aristocracy save that of brains, it is as homogeneous as possible, and is essentially democratic. Arrogance and conceit characterize the learned class, who think no knowledge of value except that in their classics, and no man wise except him who is well acquainted with their sages and books.

Status of Woman: The classical teachings in regard to woman are: 1. Woman is different from man as earth is from heaven. 2. Dualism in nature, consisting of the *yang* and the *yin* principle (the good and the bad, or the negative and the positive), is found here; woman is the *yin;* man is the *yang.* 3. Women are human beings, but they are of lower state than man, and can never attain to full equality with him. 4. Death and evils have their origin in the *yin* principle, but prosperity and life follow the subjection of the *yin* to the *yang;* therefore woman must be kept under the power of man, and must not be allowed any mind of her own. 5. The education of woman must aim at perfect submission, not at development or cultivation of the mind. 6. Woman has no happiness of her own; she must live and work for man. 7. As the mother of a son in the direct line of the family, she may escape from her degradation and become in a measure equal to her husband, but that only in affairs of the household and in the ancestral hall. 8. Her bondage does not end in this world, it is the same in the future world; she belongs to the same husband and is dependent for her happiness upon the sacrifices offered by her descendants. Such is the theory, but the condition of woman in China is not as miserable as it would be if the letter of the law were carried out. Woman is kept in subjection; she is practically immured, among the higher classes, with no education to engage her mind, no employment but household duties, fancy work, or gossip and gaming, and her one object in life is to be the mother of a son. As a wife she has more or less influence over her husband, but when she becomes a mother her influence over her children is great, and disobedience to her commands is one of the great sins. A son is not exempt from his mother's authority until her death, and then her spirit demands his reverence. Daughters are despised by the Chinese, since they pass entirely out of the family at marriage; the wedding fees must be met, and their labor and service are all rendered to the mother-in-law; whereas the son supports his parents, brings home a wife who is practically an upper servant to his mother, and, greatest fact of all, he can offer the sacrifices to the ancestral tablets insuring their future happiness. So little are girls esteemed that in some parts of China infanticide is not uncommon on account of poverty. The fact that the empire has been governed during the life of the present emperor by a woman is proof enough of the high position which woman can hold it China. The seclusion in which they are kept is not as absolute as in India, while it is a safeguard of their morals. That the women are not lacking in mental power, but only require opportunity to develop it, is shown by the rapid progress made in study by the pupils in the mission schools. As a rule the girls are not sent to school, tho noteworthy exceptions of literary women are recorded by Chinese writers. Among the poorer classes women work in the fields and do various kinds of manual labor along with the men; they are then on more of an equality with the men, and are not secluded from them.

Social Etiquette: Ceremonial observances in accordance with the strict laws of etiquette are reserved for formal or special occasions. The ordinary intercourse of the Chinese with each other is similar to that of other nations, with the exception of the difference due to the separation of the sexes. Introductions can be made by the parties themselves, one asking the other his "honorable surname," after which ensues a formal exchange of question and answer until the surname, age and condition, married or single, of each is brought out. Courtesy demands that refreshment be offered when calls are made, even tho it be but a cup of poor tea. Self-deprecation is characteristic of Chinese polite phrases, and exaggerated importance must be attached to all that concerns others.

Diet: When the seat of learning is assigned to the stomach, and an enlarged abdomen is the sign of a giant intellect, it may easily be understood that the Chinese are epicures. The poor live on rice or millet, with merely a relish of fish or pork; but the diet is more generous in direct proportion to the wealth of the person. Pork, poultry, and fish of all kinds abound. Fruit is found in abundance; no one with the money to procure it need famish for lack of palatable food. Dogs, cats, and rats, while occasionally, in some parts of China, figuring as table dishes, are by no means in ordinary use or regarded with universal favor. Wine-drinking occurs mainly at feasts, and drinking wine apart from eating is not a native custom. Their wine is a liquor distilled from rice, like weak brandy. It is an intoxicating drink, but it is used sparingly, and drunken men are rarely seen. Tobacco is used almost universally, and by the women as well as the men.

Dress: The men wear a tunic and trousers, and for special dress a long gown of bright colors, and short topped boots over the trousers. Their costume is rich and varied in color; and silks, satins, furs, and fine woolen goods are the materials used. The Chinese costume has been adopted by missionaries when it is of advantage to escape conspicuousness, and it is comparatively cheap and comfortable. The dress of the women differs little from that of the men. An embroidered skirt is worn over the trousers; the tunic is longer and the gown is absent. Bound feet, caused by the early compression of the feet with long strips of cloth, is a native institution; it is not countenanced by the reigning dynasty —the empress is a large-footed Manchu—but as a mark of social position it is hard to correct the custom, tho it is discouraged by the missionaries, and Christian sentiment is being educated against it. Within the past few years there has been a very strong effort made by the Chinese themselves to do away with foot-binding. Some of the strongest native writers have issued tracts against the custom, and societies, both those established by missionaries and by non-Christians, have done much to discourage the custom.

Religion: There is no one system of religion which is believed in by the Chinese to such an extent as to dignify it exclusively as *the* religion of the people. They are liberal in matters of belief so far as to share their worship among the three different systems of **Confucianism, Taouism,** and **Buddhism.** The proportion belonging to each is hard to estimate, for the prudent Chinese does in religious matters as a shrewd Yankee does in business ventures—takes a share in each—and if the three systems be regarded as the counterpart of the life insurance companies of the present day, the motive of the Chinaman in taking out a policy in each and paying the premium will be readily recognized. Whichever of these religious creeds he professes, the worship that most appeals to his heart is **Ancestor worship.**

At the same time the superstition which most strongly sways him is *Fung Shui*. This Chinese term signifies, "wind and water," and geomancy is its nearest English equivalent. It has influenced the science, religion, and customs of the Chinese to a large extent, and is responsible for a majority of their superstitions. The way in which their welfare is influenced is not always understood by themselves, and the laws which govern the so-called science are hard to define or detect. It was first systematized in the 12th century, and its influence has spread until it involves all the natural events and actions of life. It is founded upon the dual principle which pervades all nature, the male and female, the positive and the negative, the good and the bad. These must be kept in a state of equilibrium or else grave evil will result. The amount, position, and influence of each is determined by the geomancers, and houses must be built in accordance with *Fung Shui*, cities must be located, and especially must the graves be laid out in favorable positions, or the wrath of the dead will follow the living even as they return from the tomb. In obedience to its requirements, pagodas have been built to correct the proportion of high and low ground; streets are laid out crooked in deference to superstitions connected with it, and high buildings are few, unless of a public nature. As it now exists it is a gigantic system of extortion carried on by Buddhist and Taouist priests alike, who call to their help all of their small knowledge of sciences, and keep up the myriad delusions it gives rise to, that they may be employed to perform useless acts for useful fees. Every phenomenon of nature, simple as it is to those who are familiar with the sciences, has its effect on the ignorant Chinese, and the disturbance of the existing equipoise between the hills and valleys, and especially the encroachment upon the hill-side graves, form the chief obstacles to the building of railroad and telegraph lines in China—obstacles which cannot be thoroughly overcome until the light of science shall chase away the fogs of *Fung Shui*.

Mohammedanism: Early in the 7th and 8th centuries missionaries of Islamism came to Canton and Fu-chau along with the Arabian traders, who then made many voyages to China. Since that time disciples of the false prophet have been found in China, and in some districts late observers claim that they will eventually take the place of Buddhists and Taouists. They have preserved the belief in the one true God, and are known among the Chinese as the sect that will not eat pork. Their chief strength is in the northern provinces. In Peking they are estimated at 200,000. In Canton there is a plain tower said to have been erected by them during the Tang dynasty, and there is a mosque and the tomb of the maternal uncle of Mohammed not far from the wall of the city on the northeast. The stronghold of the religion is in Hang-chau-fu, and in some places its disciples form a third of the population, their entire number being estimated at 10,000,000 in the region north of the Yangtse alone.

Judaism: Jews have been found in China, but information in regard to them is scanty. They claim to have come to China during the Han dynasty. In the last three centuries they have lived solely in Kaifung, the capital of Honan. The Chinese name for them is Tiao-Chin-Chiao, "the sect that takes out the sinew." At present they do not number more than a few hundred persons, and are too poor to possess a synagog.

The attitude of government toward Christianity and Christian missions has been, in the past, simple indifference. The Chinese authorities simply tolerate the missionary. At the same time protection is given him. If it is denied, the refusal is due to the private whim of some subordinate official, in which he is not supported by the government. Damage to missionary property has been paid for when the matter has been brought to the attention of the high officials. It can easily happen that local feeling against the missionaries may be stirred up by violent men until the local authorities are unable to protect the foreigner, but such conduct is repudiated by the government, and the official is liable to punishment. When the treaties of 1858 were signed the rights of missionaries were defined. In the American treaty it was stipulated that "those who quietly profess and teach these doctrines shall not be harassed or persecuted on account of their faith. Any person, whether citizen of the United States or Chinese convert, who, according to these tenets, peaceably teaches and practises the principles of Christianity, shall in no case be interfered with or molested." The Russian, the British, and the French treaties contain similar stipulations.

Early Christian Missions in China: There is no doubt that Christian truths were taught in China at an early period of the Christian era. The first authentic account of early missionary effort is given in the tablet which was discovered in Hsi-ngan-fu in 1625. The Nestorian missionaries arrived in China as early as 505 A.D., and the date of the tablet is 781. From this time on till the travels of Marco Polo there is no doubt that the Nestorians had many converts; but from the time of the Yuen dynasty the records give no satisfactory account of their condition or fate.

The efforts of the Roman Catholic Church may be divided into epochs. The first epoch was in the 13th century, when John Corvino was sent to China in 1292, and was successful in establishing a mission, and from that time on till the expulsion of the Manchus, in 1368, many converts were made, and there were probably many Christian communities. The second period is one of 150 years, from the time when Matteo Ricci established himself in Shanking till the edict of expulsion by the Emperor Yung Ching, in 1736. Francis Xavier was one of the faithful men who strove to preach to the Chinese, but was detained by the governor of Malacca and died without reaching his field, tho he was buried on Chinese soil. Michael Ruggiero, of the Jesuits, finally arrived at Macao in 1580, where he was joined by Matteo Ricci, and the era of successful missions commenced. Twenty-one years later Ricci reached Peking and made a favorable impression on the court. From this time on Roman Catholicism was more or less successful in China. When the Manchus came in power the knowledge of astronomy which the fathers possessed brought them the favor of the court, and their labors were aided by noble and influential friends. Churches were built, new missions were established, and they numbered their converts by the thousands. At length the priests mingled with different parties in affairs of State, and the various political intrigues with which they were concerned led to an edict against them in 1665, and Schaal, their principal man, was disgraced and degraded from the high offices he held, and died soon after of grief. The accession of Kang Hsi brought them again in favor, and by their knowledge of astronomy and surveying they were given important positions, and favor and toleration were shown to their missionary efforts. During the latter part of the 17th century strife arose among the Jesuits and Dominicans in regard to the attitude of the Church toward the worship of Confucius, deceased ancestors, and the worship of heaven. Innocent X. issued a decree in 1645 in which this worship was declared to be idolatrous and not to be tolerated. As the Jesuits had held that it was merely political in its nature, they strove to have this decree vitiated, and in 1656 Alexander VII. approved their course and decided that the rites were civil in their nature, and could be tolerated by the missionaries. The emperor Kang Hsi was appealed to for a decision of the question, and in 1700 he answered to the effect that the worship of *tien*, heaven, was the worship of the true God, and that the other rites were merely civil. This answer was sent to the pope. Clement XI. finally reached a decision, and decreed that *tien* did not mean the true God, and that the rites were idolatrous, after which the emperor Kang Hsi refused to countenance such missionaries as did not follow the Jesuitical opinions and favor the retention of the sacrifices to ancestors and to Confucius. The first fifteen years of the 18th century were years in which Romish missions attained their greatest prosperity. There were 1,100 churches in Kiangnan and Kiangsi alone, and 100,000 converts were claimed. Soon after this time Kang Hsi began to see into the true nature of the propaganda, and his faith in the missionaries was lessened by their internal strife. In 1618 he banished all missionaries except those who would follow the teachings of Ricci. Yung Ching followed his father with a decree forbidding the propagation of the Tien Chu Chiao, as Roman Catholicism has been called ever since, and during the remainder of his life and that of Chien Lung, the Catholics were persecuted and lost much of the prestige which they enjoyed. Tho never entirely extinguished, their missions varied in success from that time till the treaties of 1858 brought toleration to them, as well as to all other sects.

Early Protestant Missions: The London Missionary Society very soon after its organization, in 1795, had its attention turned to China through the discovery in the British Museum of an ancient Chinese manuscript, but the East India Company, which had at Canton an important commercial center, was antagonistic to all missionary effort, and the Chinese themselves strongly objected to the coming of religious teachers, and it was only through the kindly interest of an American mercantile house, Olyphant & Company, of New York, that the LMS was at length, in 1806, enabled to send its first missionary to China. Robert Morrison sailed first to New York, thence to China, in an American sailing vessel, reaching Canton on September 7, 1807, and was for a time allowed to reside in the narrow space allotted to the factories of the East India Company outside the walls of Canton, but was soon obliged, with other English residents, to retire to Macao, which belonged to the Portuguese Government, and afforded a home to many of the early missionaries, and was one of the points of attack upon China, until China itself should be opened to the Gospel. Other places from which the missionaries found access to the strange people whom they wished to reach were Malacca, Batavia, Singapore, Borneo, and Bangkok, where there were great numbers of Chinese emigrants, and the LMS, the ABMU, the ABCFM, and other societies, established missions among them in anticipation of the time when the door of entrance to the empire should be opened.

The first associate of Morrison, William Milne, arrived in Canton, July, 1813, and in the following year sailed for the Indian Archipelago, taking with him a large number of New Testaments and tracts from Morrison's press. He proceeded to Java and thence to Malacca, returning afterward to Canton, but finding it difficult to prosecute missionary labor there returned to Malacca, where he remained until his death in 1822. William H. Medhurst, the third missionary sent by the LMS to China, was in 1822 sent to reenforce the mission to the Chinese at Batavia, in Java.

In 1829 the American Board of Commissioners for Foreign Missions sent to Canton its first missionary to China, the Rev. E. C. Bridgman. Mr. Bridgman was accompanied by the Rev. David Abeel, who had been sent out by the American Seamen's Friend Society, but who soon transferred his services to the ABCFM. They were received by Olyphant & Company, and a printing press was sent out for their use by the church in New York of which Mr. Olyphant was a member. In 1833 S. Wells Williams, then in his twentieth year, was sent out to take charge of it, and it remained at Canton until 1835, when it was removed to Macao, where Mr. Williams might have the benefit of the types of the East India Company's presses.

In 1834 Dr. Peter Parker joined the mission, and his medical skill added a new factor of the highest value in removing prejudice and in winning the hearts of the people. The Medical Missionary Society, formed at Canton by the joint efforts of the missionaries and the largehearted merchants residing in the city, was the result of Dr. Parker's success in starting medical work.

The American Baptist Missionary Union established its first missionary work for the Chinese at Bangkok in 1833, looking forward to the time when it should be able to enter China; and in 1838 the American Presbyterians began their first mission to the Chinese at Singapore. At all the various points, occupied in unremitting devotion to the study of the language, to the work of translation, and to the mission presses, the missionaries had accomplished a great work of preparation, when in 1842, at the close of the first opium war between England and China, five of the chief ports of China were opened to foreign residents, and the island of Hongkong was ceded to the British. At once taking advantage of the opening, the LMS appointed a conference at Hongkong of all its missionaries then resident at Macao, Malacca, Batavia, etc., and as a result the Anglo-Chinese College, founded by Dr. Morrison, was removed from Malacca, and the Society's printing establishment and medical work from Macao to Hongkong.

At the same time Mr. Abeel, of the ABCFM, and Rev. J. N. Boone, of the Protestant Episcopal Church, entered Amoy, and work for the Chinese on the mainland was fairly inaugurated.

From this time on the number of missionary societies laboring in China rapidly increased. The opening of nine additional ports by the treaties of Tientsin increased the opportunities, and the travels of Dr. Gützlaff aroused new interest, until nearly seventy societies are represented in that great empire.

Obstacles to Missions: 1. *Dislike of Foreigners:* The feeling is general that whatever is strange and different from the native is uncanny. For this reason the most common name for the foreigner is *fan kuei*, which is usually rendered "foreign devil," but it does not mean devil so much as it does something that is weird, strange, uncanny, and therefore to be feared. The missionary is an object of suspicion on account of his appearance, his actions, and his speech. If he wanders along the hillsides for recreation, he is supposed to be searching into the mineral wealth of the hills with eyes that can see through the rocks. If he picks a flower, it is to be used for medicine or as a charm. Everything that he does is susceptible of some wrong interpretation.—2. *The Conceit of the Literati.* It is a significant fact that at the utmost very few *Siu Tsai* (B.A.) and *Chu-jen* (M.A.) have been known to profess Christianity. The literati form the most difficult class to reach, and are the most bitter opponents of Christianity; for they are so puffed up with their knowledge, and so firmly convinced that whatever is Confucian and according to tradition is right, that they will not listen to or heed the religious teachings of the foreigner. The Mohammedans are also hard to reach.—3. *Superstitions.* When every little event of life is bound up in some way or other with their multiple superstitions, the teachings of the Gospel are choked by these thorns of error.—4. *Ancestor Worship.* By opposing the worship of parents, Christians are regarded as unfilial, and the doctrine which refuses the rites of worship to father and mother is viewed with dislike and scorn.—5. *Opium.* This is so serious an obstacle to the evangelization of the Chinese people that some detail is necessary to make its gravity apparent. Previous to the 18th century opium was used in China only in small quantities as a medicine. Till 1767 the trade with India was through the Portuguese, who imported annually about 200 chests, each weighing 140 lbs. Even as late as 1830 a large city like Hanchau had no opium-dens. Now it has 2,000. The rapid growth of the evil dates from 1773, when the East India Company entered on the business. In 1790, 4,054 chests were imported; in 1799, 5,000; in 1826, 9,969; in 1830, 16,800. In 1834 the East India Company closed its factory, but British officials continued the traffic, bringing 34,000 chests in 1836. After that, piculs of 133⅓ lbs. each were substituted for chests, and in 1850, 52,925 piculs were imported, the number steadily increasing to 75,308 in 1880; in 1887 it reached 96,746 piculs, thus growing from 12 tons in 1767 to 5,312 tons in 1887. The value of the opium imported into China in 1901 was $23,199,500.

Up to 1860 opium was smuggled into China. In 1780 (because they could not take it on shore) it was stored on two vessels anchored near Macao, and thence taken in charge by Chinese smugglers. The Abbé Raynal (Tract i., p. 424) writes in 1770: "The Chinese emperors have condemned to the flames every vessel that imports it." It was prohibited in 1796, 1799, 1809, 1820, 1836, and 1837, and always on moral grounds. In 1828 the severity of the laws almost destroyed the trade. In 1831 and 1834 England sent men-of-war to Canton and armed the lorchas of the smugglers. In 1830 strangling was the penalty for selling the drug, and an offender was thus executed at Macao in 1832, in the presence of a crowd of foreigners. Still Chinese prohibition did not prohibit.

A crisis came in 1839. The imperial commissioner, Lin, wrote to Queen Victoria, imploring her to put an end to the traffic, and in twenty days committed to the flames 20,283 chests of opium, thus destroying $10,000,000 worth of the drug, which was British property. This brought on the war of 1840, and at its close, besides ceding the island of Hongkong, China paid $12,000,000 for the expenses of the war, besides the price of the opium. But when Sir Henry Pottinger demanded the legalization of the trade, the Emperor is said to have replied: "True, I cannot prevent the introduction of the poison, but nothing will induce me to raise a revenue from the vice and misery of my people." It would seem as tho a Christian nation would have thanked God for such words from a heathen monarch, and rallied to his help. This refusal held until, in 1857, a smuggler bearing the British flag was fired on by the Chinese authorities at Canton, and its crew were held as prisoners. The refusal of the Chinese to make any reparation for an act which violated the treaty was punished by the bombardment of Canton. France joined with England in the enterprise of securing respect for solemn treaties. The allies continued their advance toward Peking. The Emperor was forced to grant new facilities to foreign commerce, besides paying $10,800,000 to England and $6,000,000 to France as indemnity. But the effect of the new treaty was to legalize the opium trade by teaching the Chinese that their bungling and technically illegal interference with it could but be punished. After 1860 the Chinese Government made few efforts to discourage the cultivation of the poppy; for, if opium must be used, they preferred not to enrich those who had so persistently fastened the plague upon the country. In the province of Sze-chuan, government interference with raising opium ceased in 1865. It was not long before the efforts of the government were directed toward securing the largest possible revenue from the opium trade.

An eminent British subject, Archdeacon Monle, of Shanghai, said in summing up the relations of Great Britain to the opium trade:"British authorities in India, well aware of the attitude of the Chinese Government, deliberately prepared and sent opium to China, with only two years intermission, for sixty years."

The terrible results upon the Chinese people of having opium placed within their reach quickly attracted attention. The Shanghai Conference of 1877 said emphatically: "We know that opium is a curse, both physically and morally, to the Chinese. We must appeal to the great heart of England, and when her heart beats warmly on this question this foul blot on her fair name will be wiped away."

Mr. Alexander Wylie, of the British and Foreign Bible Society, wrote about the same time: "Unless some means be found to check the practice, it bids fair to accomplish the utter destruction of that great empire."

Ten years later, Rev. J. Hudson Taylor wrote: "In China are tens of thousands of villages with small trace of Bible influence, but hardly a hamlet where the opium pipe does not reign. It does more harm in a week than all our missionaries are doing good in a year. The slave-trade was bad, the drink is bad, but the opium traffic is the sum of villainies. It debauches more families than drink, and it makes more slaves than the slave-trade." Such testimonies might be multiplied. The opium habit, encouraged by those members of a Christian nation who are interested in developing the revenues of India through poppy-culture, is a direct barrier to the progress of Christianity in China. How terribly true this is can be seen by noting the effects produced by the immense amount of opium consumed in China.

The opium-smoker can be detected in a crowd by his hollow eyes, sunken cheeks, emaciated frame, and sallow complexion. He needs three hours a day to inhale the drug, and then he cannot work more than two hours before he must repeat the dose. If he has not time for his rice and opium, he chooses the last. If he has not money enough for both, he buys only opium. If he has no money he pawns his clothes. If they are already pawned, he steals. He even sells his children into slavery, or his daughters to a life of shame, that his accursed appetite may be fed. Often wives are sold that the husband may have his opium. If he cannot get the drug, water flows from his eyes, his throat burns, his extremities are cold, and he dies in agony. One missionary reports that in three years he was called to attend thirty-six attempts at suicide caused by opium.

The opium habit has, furthermore, an indirect result in obstructing missions, because the Chinese who see its evil ascribe its prevalence to Christendom, holding all foreigners alike responsible for the defeat of the attempts of the authorities to break up the trade. An opium-smoker came to a missionary from a distant city to be cured of the habit. Soon he became so sick that the missionary feared he would die, and told him so. He thought it all over, and said, "Teacher, I take the responsibility: live or die, do for me what you can;" and, by the blessing of God, on the means employed the poor wretch was brought back from the very gates of death. A Chinese is apt to be very obtuse respecting vicious practises. But as to the evil and degrading tendency of the opium habit, he is of one mind with the missionary, who would quite as soon receive to the Church a burglar as an opium-smoker. The effect of this feeling upon the attitude of a considerable class of Chinese toward Christendom and its missionaries is illustrated by incidents like the following: A missionary in preaching happened to mention hell. "Yes," replied a respectable elderly man in the audience, "since you foreigners came, China has become hell."

The Protestant Missions now in China: We are indebted largely to Beach's *Geography and Atlas of Protestant Missions* for the information contained in the following summary statement concerning Protestant Missions in China:

The total number of Protestant missionaries laboring in China at the beginning of 1900 was 2,785. This number includes 610 ordained and

578 unordained men, 772 missionaries' wives and 825 other missionary women; and among these there are 162 male physicians and 79 women physicians. The number of native workers of both sexes was 6,388, and the roll of native evangelical Christians includes 112,808 names. The missionary organizations laboring in the Empire, including Bible societies and other organizations having foreign workers on the field, number sixty-seven. The seaboard provinces of China contain by far the largest number of Christians, tho missionaries are widely distributed over the eighteen provinces. The leading boards doing aggressive work in the provinces are: In Manchuria or Sheng-king the UFS, the PCI, and the Danish Missionary Society; in Chi-li, the ABCFM, the ME, the LMS and the SPG; in Shan-tung, the PN, the BMS, the German General Mission Society, the Berlin Mission Society, and the CIM; in Kiang-su, the PS, the CIM, the PN, the MES, and the German General Mission Society; in Che-kiang, the CIM, the CMS, the ABMU, and the PS; in Fo-kien, the CMS, the ME, the ABCFM and the Presbyterian Church of England; in Kwang-tung, the Basel Missionary Society, the Presbyterian Church of England, the Rhenish Missionary Society, the Berlin Missionary Society and the ABMU, the CMS, the SBC, and the PN; the Berlin Women's Society for China, the German Mission to the Chinese Blind, and the Kiel Mission to China; in Kwang-si, the CA, the WMS, and the CMS; in Yun-nan, the CIM; in Sze-chwan the CIM, the CMS, the ABMU, Friends' Foreign Missionary Association, the Barmen (Germany) China Alliance, and the Canadian Methodists; in Kan-su, the CIM, and the St. Chrischona Mission; in Shen-si, the CIM and the BMS; in Shan-si, the CIM, the BMS, and the ABCFM; in Mongolia, the LMS, the CA, and the Scandinavian Mission Alliance of North America; in Ho-nan, the CIM, and the CP; in Ngan-hwei, the CIM, the FCMS, the PE, and the St. Chrischona Mission; in Hu-pei, the LMS, the CIM, the WMS, the PE, and the Swedish Missionary Society; in Kiang-si, the CIM, the ME, the SBC, and the Barmen (German) China Alliance; in Hu-nan, the LMS, the CIM, the PN, the PE, and the CP; and in Kwei-chau, the CIM. The American, the British and Foreign Bible society, and the National Bible Society of Scotland, together with the Society for the Diffusion of Christian and General Knowledge among the Chinese, and the various tract societies, have exerted great influences for good in different parts of the Empire. At present, the forms of Christian work that are most effective among the Chinese are:

Medical Institutions: Many doors have been opened for effective Christian work by means of the practise of medicine among the natives. Dispensaries and hospitals are being established in many parts of the land, the number now existing (1900) being 259; and the 245 medical missionaries are recognized more and more as a power for righteousness in the whole field.

Educational Work: In the day schools hundreds of pupils are taught the rudiments of a Western education, and by means of the Bible, the truths of the Gospel are imparted to them. The pupils are brought into closer association with the missionaries in the boarding-schools; and, altho the numbers are comparatively few in these institutions, most effective results have been accomplished. There are 170 of the higher educational institutions in the missions in China. In our sense of the term, the highest education may not yet be imparted by the missionary universities, colleges and other such establishments, but practical education for Christian service through the station classes, and the faithful instruction that is being given in the theological schools serve an important purpose in intellectual uplifting of the people and in the better equipment of the native teachers and preachers.

Literature: The Chinese are preeminently a literary people, and much attention has appropriately been given to literature in Chinese missions. The preparation of educational works, the translation of the Bible, and the work on revised versions have been almost entirely the labors of missionaries; and through the mighty agency of the pen the coming of the Kingdom in the Middle Kingdom has been hastened.

Evangelism: Chapel services, street preaching, and house to house visitation at 653 stations and 2,476 outstations along the seacoast and through the inland provinces, have, as in apostolic times, proved to be divine means for the conversion of souls. The present outlook for the cause of Christ in China is most hopeful from every point of view. The testing season of 1899 and 1900 has not been without its blessing both to the missionary and the native Christian. The heroism displayed by Christ's servants; the calm martyrdom suffered by the missionary of the cross and the convert from heathendom; the object lessons of unexpected strength and Christlike forgiveness before the enemies of the cross; and the providential care shown many in dire distress—all these evidences of the divine grace have done much toward clearing the track for the chariot of our King. *China for Christ* should be the watchword for this generation. Amen.

Allen (R.), *Siege of the Pekin Legations*, London, 1901; Boulger (D. C.), *A Short History of China*, new ed., London, 1900; Chang (Chi T'ung), *China's Only Hope*, New York, 1900; Ching (Wen), *Chinese Crisis from Within*, London, 1901; Colquhon (A. R.), *China in Transformation*, London, 1898; ——, *Overland to China*, 1900; Gray (Ven. J. H.), *China (Laws, Manners, Customs)*, 2 vols., London, 1878; Gibson (J. C.), *Mission Problems and Mission Methods in S. China*, New York, 1901; Legge (J.), *Religions of China*, London, 1881; Martin (W. A. P.), *Cycle of Cathay*, New York, 1896; *Siege of Pekin*, ——, 1901; Oxenham (E. L.), *Historical Atlas of the Chinese Empire*, 2d ed., London, 1898; Smith (A. H.), *Chinese Characteristics*, New York, 1895; *Village Life in China*, New York, 1899; *China in Convulsion*, 2 vols., New York, 1901. Williams (S. W.), *The Middle Kingdom*, new ed. 2 vols., 1899; *Mission Review of the World*, Vols. XIII., XIV., XV., New York, 1900-1902.

CHINA; Christian Literature Society for. See CHRISTIAN LITERATURE SOCIETY FOR CHINA.

CHINA INLAND MISSION (1865): The founder of the China Inland Mission, the Rev. J. Hudson Taylor, went to China as a missionary in 1853, under the Chinese Evangelization Society. Conscientious difficulties soon afterward led to a friendly separation, and until 1860, when failing health compelled him to return to England, he worked independently. In 1862 Mr. and Mrs. Meadows went to take up the work he had laid down in the province of Che-kiang, followed in 1864 by four others.

In the meantime constant thought and prayer brought to Mr. Taylor the conviction that something ought to be done to reach the people of inland China; none of the existing societies seeming prepared to make the attempt. How to inaugurate such a work was a problem in itself. How to do it without diverting men and money from existing societies was another problem, for Mr.

Taylor determined that the new undertaking must "aid all and injure none." The result was the adoption of certain principles which rule the CIM: (1) It was foreseen that to meet the vast needs of inland China all the volunteers obtainable from every branch of the Christian Church would be required; nor was there felt any insuperable difficulty in working in the mission field with members of various denominations. The new work was therefore made interdenominational and international. (2) The workers have no guaranteed salary, but trust in the Lord whom they serve to supply their needs. (3) No personal solicitation or collection of funds is made or authorized by the mission, voluntary contributions alone being received.

Development: It is worth while here to note instances of the working of the third principle of the CIM. The needs of China were made known in a little book, *China's Spiritual Need and Claims,* as well as by public meetings, and volunteers were called for who should be willing to go to China with no guaranteed salary, in reliance on God to supply their needs in answer to prayer. Not long afterward the first missionary party was selected, and, as the time for their departure drew on, and the funds lacked, a daily prayer-meeting was commenced on February 6, 1866, to pray for from £1,500 to £2,000, as might be needful, to cover the cost of outfits, passages, etc. On March 21, that is after a month and six days, it was found that £1,974 5s. 11d. had been contributed in answer to daily prayer. Later on, a survey of the needs of the mission led its senior members, on November 25, 1881, to offer prayer for seventy new workers in the years 1882-3-4. In the years 1882-3-4, seventy-six new members reached the field of the CIM. The proportions, however, of men and women were not those that had been asked for. The Lord of the harvest reversed the proportions, sending only thirty men and more than forty women, thus anticipating the remarkable and unexpected developments of women's work, which will be noted further on.

It need scarcely be said that, together with the prayer for seventy, the necessary funds to send them out were also asked from God. Special prayers were asked for these funds on January 31, or February 1, 1882. On February 2, an anonymous donation of £3,000 was received at the offices of the mission in London for this very object. On September 1, 1884, the same donor sent £1,000 for the same fund. The contributions from the commencement up to May 25, 1876, amounted to £51,918 11s. 2d., a sum which had covered all the needs and left a small balance of general funds with which to commence the second decade, besides £3,700 specially contributed for work in new provinces. These funds were without solicitation, in answer to prayer.

In the second decade arrangements were made for the formation of a China Council of Senior missionaries to superintend the work in various provinces. The first session of this council (now meeting quarterly at Shanghai) took place in Ngan-king in November,1886, and one of the most important issues of that session was the appeal for a hundred new workers for the CIM to come out in the following year. Prayer was made for them. The £10,000 necessary to cover the expenses of this movement were also asked from God, with the particular request that this might be specially given in large sums, and in addition to the ordinary income of the mission. The annual volume of *China's Millions* for 1888 contained as its frontispiece the photos of the hundred who left England in 1887; and the report of the annual meeting held in London on May 29, 1888, records that the income of the year 1887 had been raised from £22,000 to £33,700, of which £10,000 had been received in eleven contributions, varying from £500 to £2,500 in amount. Once more, in 1890, the newly erected premises at Shanghai were occupied by the mission, the whole cost of site, building, furnishing and removing having been supplied for this purpose, in answer to prayer, without cost to the mission.

All the operations of the mission are in accordance with one general and comprehensive plan for the evangelization of the whole of China. In occupying a new province, the first station, if practicable, is opened in the capital. The next step is to open up stations in the chief prefectures, then in subordinate ones, leaving as a rule places less important to be occupied later on.

In carrying out the plan of the mission it was necessary to explore China anew, from the missionary standpoint, but in the meantime widespread, evangelistic and colportage work was done in nearly all the provinces, and also in parts of Manchuria, Mongolia, Siu-kiang, as far west as Kulja, Eastern Tibet and Upper Burma. Following this up stations were opened on the above mentioned plan in the capitals of the fifteen provinces, in which the CIM has work, as well as in subordinate cities. The report dated May 26, 1878, told of the missionary journeys of twenty pioneers, and contained a large map showing the routes each had taken, which covered an aggregate of 30,000 English miles.

One of the most noteworthy extensions of the second decade, and one fraught with far-reaching issues, was that of women's work in the interior of China. In January, 1876, when Miss Wilson, of Kendal, sailed at her own expense for China, there was only one unmarried CIM lady in the field, Miss E. Turner. A good many others followed Miss Wilson, and not only were stations opened for women's work in the interior of the nearer provinces, but within the short space of three years, from October, 1878 to December, 1881, women had been able to enter and settle in six of the inland provinces, besides bringing the Gospel to hundreds of women in Ho-nan and Hu-nan, where permanent residence was then unattainable. Only those who know the difficulties and trials of life in the heart of China and the dangers and hardships of long journeys in such a land can fully appreciate all that these facts mean; only those who have experienced continued loneliness, isolation and peril among the heathen, can know what those pioneer women endured; only those who, under such circumstances, have faced sickness, far from any medical aid, acute suffering, and even death itself, can understand what the sacrifice involved that was sealed by the first missionary graves in far-off Shen-si and Yun-nan

A far-reaching issue from the first session of the Mission Council at Shanghai was the formation of training homes for newly arrived missionaries, the preparation of a series of books to aid in the study of the Chinese language, and the drawing up of a course of study in six sections to be pursued until satisfactory examinations had been passed in each. Ngan-king was chosen as a suitable place for the Men's Training Home and Yang-chau in like manner was selected for the Women's Training Home.

The work whose development has thus been summarized has occupied nearly 40 years, for the embryo mission was organized in England in 1863, tho the first CIM party only reached Hanchau about the end of 1866. Each of the four decades has its own distinctive feature. In the first decade the mission struck its roots in China, and gained experience by opening and beginning to work stations in previously unoccupied districts of nearer provinces. The second decade was the one of widespread itineration and exploration of the more distant provinces, during which the first stations were opened in all the unoccupied provinces except Kwang-si. The third decade was marked by development and consolidation. Widespread itineration was exchanged for methodical visitation of small districts around established centers, in many of which churches were organized, and in others the fruit is beginning to appear. During the fourth decade the mission has gone through the severe test of the riotous outbreak against the undertaking.

Organization: During the first six years the home department of the CIM was administered by W. T. Berger, Esq., who became the first Honorary Home Director of the Mission. Failing health compelling him to lay down the work, in 1872 the London Council of the CIM was formed, and for two or three years two of its members acted as honorary secretaries, but the increasing needs of the work demanding additional help, a resident secretary was appointed, and further additions to the home staff have been made from time to time. This council meets weekly for the transaction of business. Auxiliaries have been formed in different countries as the work has grown, cooperating with the London Council in the selection and training of candidates and receiving the voluntary offerings for the mission. These funds are remitted to the treasurer in China and he supplies the needs of all those not otherwise supported, the funds being distributed pro rata.

In 1903 Mr. Hudson Taylor appointed Mr. D. E. Hoste, one of the Cambridge Seven, as General Director, thus relieving himself from the heavy duties of active leadership, while retaining the office of Consulting Director. Up to the year 1889, British candidates had been received and entertained by the General Secretary and his wife, but as the mission grew this was no longer possible. In that year an auxiliary council was formed in Scotland, to deal in an initial way with any Scotch candidates who were applying; a council of ladies was also formed in London and premises were taken as a home for lady candidates, to which two adjoining houses have since been added. Inglesby House, Newington Green, London, was acquired by the mission as a home for men candidates, and mission premises were erected in 1894 on a site behind this house.

Organization in the field: The direction of work in the field is not by a committee at home, but by a Missionary Director, assisted by a council of senior and experienced missionaries, who as superintendents of the work in the different provinces help and guide those who have less experience.

New workers on arrival in the field as probationers usually go to one of the training homes established by the mission. There, for about six months, they receive from European and native teachers careful instruction in the language, and are taught besides much that will be helpful to them as to the geography, government and etiquette of the country, the phases of religious thought, and the best method of communicating the Gospel to the people. Then they commonly proceed to some of the inland stations of the mission and continue their studies, assisting, as able, in the work, under the supervision of senior missionaries. A definite course of study is pursued, divided into six sections, and periodical examinations from time to time test the progress of the student. If his progress has been satisfactory, and there is promise of permanent and useful work, the probationer is accepted as a junior missionary at the end of two years, and assists one of the senior missionaries in his district. If at the end of five years he has done well, and has passed all his prescribed examinations, he becomes one of the senior missionaries, taking full responsibility for the work of a station, the district surrounding it, and such of the younger workers as are placed under his supervision. Over a number of these districts a superintendent is appointed; he has probably been in the country from ten to twenty years. The senior missionaries can be called together when necessary to act as a council and confer with the superintendent about the whole work of his provincial district. All the superintendents are members of the general council of the mission in China. From the extent of the country it is not possible for the whole number to meet together frequently, but a sufficient number of them are able to attend the quarterly meeting of the council to confer with the director and deputy director concerning matters that affect the whole work of the mission in China. The work of the mission being interdenominational, it is found helpful to cluster together workers whose views of church government sufficiently correspond to enable them to work happily together. When a number of natives have been converted, and the time comes to organize a church, the senior missionary who is responsible for the conduct of the work is perfectly free and unfettered, and will organize the church according to his own conscientious convictions. When a church has once been formed on any definite lines, those who afterward superintend the work do so on condition of carrying it on as it was commenced. Tho the mission embraces Episcopalians, Presbyterians, Congregationalists, Baptists, Methodists, and a few independent workers, all recognize each other as fellow-servants of the same Master, happily meet when occasion requires at the table of the Lord, and recognize each other's converts, however or by whomsoever admitted to the privilege of church fellowship, provided they are walking consistently before God and their fellow countrymen.

Missions: The Lammermuir party, consisting of Mr. Taylor, seventeen adults and four children, arrived in China in the fall of 1866, to find that, tho inland China was open for travel, it was not for residence. Efforts to obtain quarters in various cities and towns between Shanghai and Hanchau having failed, promises were finally secured in the latter city, and a fourth station was established in the province of Che-kiang; Ning-po, Shao-hsing and Fung-hwa having previously been occupied. During 1867, three more stations were opened in Che-kiang, and the first CIM station established in Kiang-su. Su-chau and Yang-chau were occupied in 1868 and additional stations gained in Che-kiang. In 1689 Ngan-king, the capital of the Ngan-hwei province, was occupied, and for many years the CIM was the only Protestant society in this field. The same year work was begun in Kiu-kiang, in the northern edge of Kiang-si, from which place over 100 towns and cities in the province of Kiang-si were reached by itinerations. No other province was entered till 1874, when Wu-chang, the capital of the Hu-pei province, was occupied with a view to entering the nine interior provinces, wholly untouched by Protestant missionaries. In 1875 a station was opened at Bhamo in Upper Burma, a site having been granted for this purpose by the King of Burma. The same year itinerating was begun in the province of Ho-nan, and about the same time a first visit was made to the antiforeign province of Hu-nan. By this time the CIM had 36 missionaries and 75 native helpers, occupying more than 50 stations and outstations; 28 churches were already formed, and there were baptized Christians and inquirers in many other places, altho the work had been largely pioneering. In 1876, the signing of the Chi-fu Convention enabled the CIM missionaries to visit remote provinces, and in this and the following year Shan-si, Shen-si, Kan-su, Sze-chwan and Kwei-chau were occupied and Kwang-si visited. During the next few years a more thorough survey was made of the parts of China unoccupied or less occupied by missionaries. Thus information essential to future work was gained, portions of the Scripture and tracts were distributed, and the Gospel was preached from the border of Korea to Ji-t'ang and Bat'ang in Eastern Tibet, and from Kan-su to Hai-nan. In 1897 extensive enlargements were made in the mission's schools at Chi-fu for the education of the children of missionaries and other foreign residents, and in 1898 a forward movement began, which was cut short by the Boxer uprising of 1900. In this terrible outbreak of fanaticism the CIM suffered heavier losses than any other society, fifty-eight missionaries and twenty-one children of missionaries having been put to death. In 1902 two more of its missionaries suffered martyrdom. The mission's policy of refusing indemnity for loss of life and property called forth one of the most remarkable government proclamations ever issued in China, and has done not a little to secure the good will of the officials and people.

Forces in the Field: There are now (1903) 509 stations and outstations in 18 provinces, 763 missionaries, men and women; 541 native workers, and 9,000 communicants in the field of the CIM.

Branches: Australian Council (1890), Melbourne; Finnish Auxiliary (1890), Helsingfors; Hamburg Branch (1898), Hamburg, Germany; North American Council (1888), Philadelphia; Norwegian Branch (1890), Christiania; St. Chrischona Branch (1895), Basel, Switzerland; Scottish Council (1889), Glasgow; Swedish Branch (1887), Stockholm.

Associate Missions: A number of independent organizations in various countries work in harmonious comradeship with the CIM, while not organically connected with it. These are: Finland: The Free Church Mission, Seutula, Dickursby; Germany: The China-Alliance Mission, Barmen, Germany; Norway: The Norwegian Mission in China, Christiania, Sweden; The Swedish Mission in China, Stockholm; United States of America: The Scandinavian Alliance Mission, Chicago.

Organ: *China's Millions*, monthly, London; *The Story of the China Inland Mission*, London.

CHI-NAN-FU. See TSI-NAN-FU.

CHINESE BLIND, Mission to the. See BLIND, MISSIONS TO.

CHINESE LANGUAGE: Belongs to the monosyllabic class of languages, and is considered by some to show affinity with the ancient Accadian of Babylonia. Whatever its origin, it is the oldest spoken language in existence, and, along with the Egyptian and cuneiform, the oldest written language. It is monosyllabic, without inflexion or agglutination; its nouns have no declensions, its verbs are not to be conjugated. A mythical personage, who is said to have flourished about the year 2700 B. C., is the reputed author of the characters. The earliest form of writing was similar to the Egyptian hieroglyphics, and in the main the structure of their characters is that of an ideogram. These characters are divided into six classes: 1. Imitative symbols; 2. Thought symbols; 3. Combined ideas; 4. Inverted significations; 5. Borrowed uses, and 6. Sound symbols, or phonetics. In general the characters are formed by the use of 214 radicals—some of these are simply strokes, but most of them are ideograms—combined with primitives, as they are called, which in reality are no older than the radicals, but denote simply the part of the character which is not a radical, or a combination of radicals. The number of characters given in Kanghi's Dictionary is 44,449, but the total of really different characters is much less, probably about 25,000, and for a good working knowledge of Chinese 10,000 will suffice. In the dictionaries the characters are found by looking up the radical; if there is more than one radical in the character the most prominent one is looked for first; then the number of strokes in the character, exclusive of the radical, is the guide to the place under its given radical where it may be found. The characters are the same throughout the eighteen provinces, and one who can write Chinese can be understood by that means anywhere. In writing the language six forms of characters are met with in common use, tho the fancy and art of the Chinese have devised many other forms, just as new type and fancy lettering are indulged in by printers and penmen in other countries. Of all these styles, the pattern style and the running style are the ones in most common use, and the foreign student may well be satisfied to master one—the pattern style. The Chinese language has no declensions, no conjugations, neither has it marks for the number and gender of nouns. This poverty of language is compensated for by the tones. The correct use of tones, and the ability to distinguish them when heard and to utter them correctly, is the hardest task in the acquirement of the language. Not only does the language become unintelligible when a wrong tone is used, but in Fu-chau, Amoy and Canton the misunderstanding may be very serious.

Grammar: As there are no case endings, position shows the case of the words. In general the subject stands first, then the verb; modifiers precede the word modified. Often the change of tone changes a noun to a verb. There are no articles; *a* man is spoken of as *one* man, and *that* takes the place of *the*. To form the plural of nouns a particle is added, as *wo*, "I;" *wo mun*, "we;" or the noun is duplicated, *yin*, man; *yin yin*, all men. Moods and tenses are denoted by position and by the use of particles. The relations of time are especially difficult to express in Chinese. The imperative, optative and potential moods are formed by the addition of the appropriate words. Pronouns are few and their use is avoided. In writing no distinction is made between a common and a proper noun, tho often one line drawn alongside the character denotes the name of a person, and two lines that of a place. Capitalization, which is exceptional, is produced by placing the character above the ordinary line level.

Dialects: There are in China numerous dialects, some of which are so different from the others and are spoken by so many people that they may well be termed languages. The principal dialects are:

1. The Mandarin or court language. Pekingese is the standard of this tongue, which is spoken with more or less local variation in the northeastern provinces. It is the Latin of China, as most learned men, and especially office-holders, are versed in it, and in all the provinces some are found who can converse in it.

2. The Cantonese. This is the standard for the province of Canton, tho there are several other dialects spoken in the Canton province. The Cantonese differs from the Pekingese in its idioms, in the multiplicity of its tones and in the number of consonantal endings.

3. The Amoy dialect differs still more from the Pekingese, and is also unintelligible to a Cantonese.

4. The Fu-chau dialect has much the same difficulties as the Amoy tongue, and is also different from the others. In addition to the principal dialects, there are variations of each and local patois in endless variety.

Book Language: A sharp distinction is drawn in Chinese between what is spoken and the same thoughts as written. The Chinese writer who would express himself in the every-day language of the people would be considered ignorant of the first principles of composition. We find, therefore, a book style, Wen-li, which is terse, concise, at times obscure, and so lofty in its expression that when read aloud to the uneducated man it is not understood. It is understood by the scholar, whether he be a native of Peking or Canton. There is also a modification of the Wen-li called the *Easy* Wen-li, which, as its name implies, is not so concise and is more intelligible than the strictly classical Wen-li. The fact that this written language is intelligible throughout the Empire binds the people together and is an efficient aid to the dissemination of Christianity, as books can be distributed, read, and understood where the distributer may be perfectly helpless, owing to the difference in the spoken language. In addition to the Wen-li, books have been translated into the different colloquial styles, and while they are sneered at by the *literati* as being fit only for women, they are read and understood by those who possess only a limited knowledge of characters and no great literary ability. In many instances attempts have been made by the missionaries to Romanize the various dialects, with such success as to receive the endorsement of the Missionary Conferences.

Methods of study: The degree of difficulty in mastering the Chinese language depends, as in all other languages, upon individual ability. To learn the spoken language the best way is to go right among the people; what seems jargon may not be understood, but the tones are impressed on the ear, while a vocabulary will be acquired at the same time. Unless his destination is definitely settled, it is practically useless for the missionary volunteer to commence the study of the language before reaching his field; but if the destination is known, some of the books in that particular dialect, which have the English and Chinese side by side, will be found of use for the general idea of the structure of the language and the idioms. In studying the written language the best way is to take up the study of the character separately, in order to recognize its form and to distinguish between those which differ in minute details. Writing Chinese is best learned by using the Chinese method of copying the characters, by writing on thin paper over a copy. Chinese is written in perpendicular columns from right to left.

Those who know the Chinese language best, while recognizing its deficiencies, can truthfully say with Dr. Morrison that "Chinese fine writing darts upon the mind with a vivid flash, a force, and a beauty of which alphabetical language is incapable."

CHINESE; Society for the Diffusion of Christian and General Knowledge among. See CHRISTIAN LITERATURE SOCIETY FOR CHINA.

CHING-CHOW-FU (Shantung). See TSIN-CHAU-FU.

CHIN-KIANG. See CHEN-KIANG-FU.

CHIOLE: A station of the Zambesi Industrial Mission, in Nyasaland, British Central Africa, situated about 100 miles N. W. of Blantyre. It has (1902) 2 missionaries, 1 missionary's wife, 1 woman missionary physician, 28 native workers, 10 elementary schools, 1 high school, with industrial department; 1 hospital, 1 dispensary and 169 communicants. By the use of native volunteers there is preaching in 40 neighboring villages every Sunday.

CHIPPEWAY LANGUAGE: Belongs to the central group of the N. American family of languages. It is spoken by Indians of Athabasca, Canada. It is written with syllabic characters.

CHISAMBA: A station of the ABCFM in Angola, W. Africa, situated about 50 miles N. E. of Bailunda, with (1902) 3 missionaries (one a physician) and their wives, 3 missionary women, 8 native workers, 6 elementary schools, 1 high school, 1 industrial school, 1 dispensary and 50 church members.

CHITTAPETTA: A town in the Godavari division, Madras, India, situated about 20 miles W. of Rajamahendri. Station of the PB, with 1 missionary and his wife and 2 missionary women.

CHITTAGONG: A town and seaport in Bengal, India, 212 miles east of Calcutta. It has considerable commercial importance. Climate, wet and unhealthy, diseases arising from impure water and imperfect drainage are very prevalent. Population (1891) 24,100, of whom nearly 75 per cent. are Mohammedans. Mission station of the BMS (1881), with 2 missionaries and their wives, 5 native workers, a school and 87 professing Christians.

CHITTUR: Capital of the district of North Arcot, Madras, India, 80 miles west of Madras City. Population, 5,809, Hindus, Muslims, Christians. Station of the RCA (1854), with 1 missionary and his wife, 43 native workers, 19 outstations, 18 elementary schools, 2 high schools, 21 Sunday schools, 6 young people's societies and 266 church members.

CHIVILCOY: A town in the Argentine Republic, South America; situated 109 miles W. of Buenos Aires. Population, about 11,000, of whom many are Italians. It is on a missionary circuit of the ME, with 1 native worker, 1 place of worship and 74 professing Christians.

CHOLCHOL: A town in the province of Arauco, Peru, situated about 100 miles south of the city of Arauco. Station of the South American Missionary Society (1895), with (1900) 1 missionary and his wife, a hospital and a dispensary.

CHOMBALA: A town in Malabar, W. India, situated about 25 miles N. W. of Calicut. Station of the Basel Missionary Society (1849), with (1902) 2 missionaries and their wives, 35 native workers, 6 outstations, 5 common schools, 1 high school and 219 Christians.

CHOTA-NAGPUR (little Nagpur): One of the four great districts which make up the province of **Bengal.** It lies west of Bengal Proper; Behar adjoins it on the north and Orissa on the southeast. Its western boundary is the native State of Rewa, and on the southwest it touches the Central Provinces. Its area is 26,963 square miles, and its population (1901) 4,900,429. Of these a little over 3,850,000 are reckoned as Hindus and about a quarter of a million as Mohammedans. Aboriginal tribes furnish nearly 800,000 of the population, but many of those included religiously under the term "Hindus" are connected by race with these tribes, the members of which are continually adopting more and more of Hindu practise, and merging by degrees into the body of Hinduism. The tribes belong principally to the Kol and Santal families, who had no education and no writing until Christian missions came among them.

Missionary work was commenced in Chota-Nagpur in 1845 by the German Gossner Missionary Society. Its task was to carry light to those Kols sunk in ignorance, to whom even Hinduism was somewhat of an advance beyond their ancient worship of demons. The mission enterprise had great success from the first. The SPG came into the field to take part in the work, and now the Christian movement seems to affect the people in mass, whole villages coming forward for instruction at once. The number of Christian Kols in Chota-Nagpur is about 80,000.

CHRISTIAN CHURCH; Mission Board of the: For many years the Christian denomination in the United States and Canada conducted its missionary operations under two separate organizations, as departments of the American Christian Convention, the ecclesiastical body of the denomination. The Foreign Mission Department was organized in 1886 and commenced work in Japan in 1887. More recently these separated bodies have been reorganized as one and incorporated under the above title.

The affairs of the Board are conducted by a Mission Board of nine (1903) members, elected quadrennially by the American Christian Convention and a Mission Council of five members, the Secretary of the Missionary Department of the Convention acting as President of the Board. There are also two Women's Boards, one for Home and one for Foreign Missions, both auxiliary to the Mission Board.

The foreign work of the Board is in Japan and Porto Rico (so considered by the Board). In Japan two stations are occupied, Tokio and Sendai, and there are 18 outstations. There are 7 missionaries, 10 native workers, 7 organized churches, with 382 church members and 795 Sunday school scholars. In Porto Rico the headquarters are at Ponce, with work at Salinas and 9 outstations; there are (1903) 4 missionaries, 1 native preacher, 1 organized church and 5 Sunday schools. The receipts for foreign work for the year closing October, 1902, were $10,329.40.

CHRISTIAN FAITH, Society for Advancing the: The Hon. Robert Boyle, distinguished for his learning and interest in the extension of Christianity, who was one of the governors of the "Corporation for the Propagation of the Gospel in New England" (1649), and a prominent director of the East India Company, not only contributed largely to various missionary enterprises, especially in the line of publications, but left a considerable sum in his will which formed the basis of a society organized after his death, in 1691, by his executors. This society, at first called the "Christian Faith Society," afterward the "Society for Advancing the Christian Faith," was designed for general charitable purposes, but the executors were directed to use the greater part for the "advancement of the Christian religion amongst infidels." The funds have been well invested and cared for and the grants have been of great value, many undertakings having been fostered which without this aid would never have succeeded. For many years grants were made to William and Mary College, in Virginia, for the education of Indian youth. Then attention was turned to the negro slaves in the West Indies and to Mauritius and other dependencies of the British Government.

CHRISTIAN AND MISSIONARY ALLIANCE:
I. History: In the summer of 1887 the Christian Alliance and the International Missionary Alliance were formed at Old Orchard, Me., "for the purpose of uniting in a purely fraternal alliance, members of evangelical churches who believe in the Lord Jesus as Savior, Sanctifier, Healer and coming Lord, and also of uniting their effort in the special aggressive work of world-wide evangelization."

The Christian Alliance was formed upon the special basis of this "Fourfold Gospel." It is not an ecclesiastical body, does not organize distinct churches, but aims at spreading abroad the truths on which it is based. Its chief methods of work are through local conventions and its printed publications. An important branch of its work at home is the formation of Rescue Missions.

The International Missionary Alliance had for its object "the immediate evangelization of the whole world by sending missionaries to unoccupied and neglected fields." The movement went on quietly and at the end of three years centers of work were established in India, Africa, China and Palestine. These two societies were united into the Christian and Missionary Alliance in 1897. "The Christian Alliance formed the sustaining constituency of the missionary work, and the Missionary Alliance was the natural outlet of the faith, love and activity of the Christian Alliance."

II. Organization: A central board of managers meets regularly for the transaction of business and has the oversight of the entire work. It consists of 24 members, elected triennially, one-third retiring every year.

The officers include a President, General Secretary, Superintendent of the Home Field, Superintendent of Missions, Treasurer, Financial Secretary and "various other executive officers." Auxiliaries and branches are formed under a strong State Committee, with a State or District Superintendent in charge of the field, while in each locality there are local branches under the care of a Committee and Superintendent as far as possible. The work is promoted by means of numerous conventions held in all parts of the country, the largest being at Old Orchard, Me.; Nyack, N. Y., and New York City. The work is sustained through voluntary contributions.

III. Institutional Work: The Gospel Tabernacle, New York City, is an independent church, incorporated by special charter under the laws of the State of New York, and intimately connected with the Alliance, organized in 1881. The New York Missionary Training Institute, founded in 1882, in connection with the Gospel Tabernacle, removed, in 1897, to South Nyack, N. Y. It is a coeducational school for the training of young men and women, who, with little or no education, consider themselves called of God to missionary work. Special attention is paid to the equipment of foreign missionaries and securing their adaptability to their various fields of labor.

The Beulah Park Summer School is maintained from June to September, the course of study being similar to that of the Nyack Institute.

The Berachah Home, established in 1884 for the purpose of offering a place of rest and instruction with reference to physical and spiritual life, with particular attention to divine healing, which is a principal tenet of the Christian Alliance, is now located at Nyack, N. Y., while the house in New York is continued as the "Alliance Home."

IV. Missions:

(1). *Palestine:* A station was established at Jerusalem in 1890 by Miss Lucy Dunn, who for a year carried on evangelistic work among the Jews. Reenforcements were sent out and Jaffa was occupied and the work extended to the Arab tribes near the town. In 1895, a mission was established at Safed in Galilee, chiefly for Mohammedans. In 1898 a training school was opened at Jaffa for the training of Bible women and teachers. Village work is carried on from Hebron as a center. There are (1902) 3 stations and 5 missionaries.

(2). *India:* There are four principal centers of work, with headquarters at Bombay. The oldest station is at Akola, in the Berar Province, where the CA took up the "Faith Mission" established in 1886 by the Rev. M. B. Fuller; there are now 8 stations and 25 workers; Khandesh has 4 stations and 8 workers; Gujerat, 5 stations and 20 workers.

The work consists of preaching services, evangelistic tours, and house to house visitation. Schools, orphanages and widows' homes have been established and churches organized.

There are (1902) 22 stations and 53 missionaries.

(3). *China:* The first station was opened at Wu-hu, in Central China, in 1890. Now there are 8 stations in and around Wu-hu, 1 at Wu-chang. In 1897 a station was established in Hunan and in 1899 Nan-ling-h'sien was occupied and a training school for women opened. Western China was occupied in 1896, and has 4 stations, one being within the borders of Tibet. In 1899 the Tibet station was destroyed by a mob, but was again opened. The Swedish China and Mongolia Mission was opened in 1893 at Kwei-h'wa as headquarters. This mission forms a chain of stations near the great Chinese wall from Kalgan in the east, several hundred miles westward in North China, and includes the Mongolian Mission, with headquarters at Kalgan City. The North China Mission has in Peking the strongest part of its work among women. Evangelistic work is carried on, and schools have been established.

At Tientsin work has been begun among the English-speaking Chinese, and a native church of young men has been organized; a missionary society has been formed, which supports native workers in all the provinces of China and in foreign lands. South China was entered in 1892, with Canton as headquarters. Two years later Macao was occupied. In 1895 the first opening was made in a humble village across the river from what is now Tung-tsun station. In 1896 Lo-ting was occupied, and the following year stations were organized at Wu-chow and Kwai-peng. In 1898 Nan-wing was occupied and a ladies' station opened at Tung-un. Village and girls' schools have been established and a training school opened.

There are (1902) 18 stations and 41 missionaries.

(4). *Africa; Sudan Mission:* There are 5 stations: Freetown, the capital of the British Colony of Sierra Leone; Magbele, in the same colony, 55 miles inland; Ro Bethel, in the same colony, 20 miles farther inland; Makomp, also in Sierra Leone, 125 miles inland, and Tubabudugo, 225 miles inland, among the Kuranko tribe on the N. E. border of the colony. The Kuranko people have been evangelized to a great extent from the last station and portions of the Scriptures have been translated into their language. Village and school work is carried on and a systematic itineracy established, which includes about 40 towns.

Congo: There are 4 principal stations and 3 outstations. Boma, the receiving and transport station, has many coast people, and services are held in English, while a school is established for their children. The other three stations are also on the lower Congo. School and station work is carried on by the natives under instruction, and evangelistic and medical work by the missionaries.

There are (1902) 11 stations and 39 missionaries.

(5). *South America:* The headquarters for the CA work are in Argentina, with its 4,000,000 people. Other stations are at Caracas, Venezuela, where native agents are employed in the outlying districts. Brazil has 1 station and 1 missionary; Chile, 2 stations and 4 missionaries; 2 stations are in Ecuador, where the Roman Catholic influence is very corrupt. In Bolivia, a single missionary is making evangelistic tours throughout the country. The principal work in all the Alliance missions is evangelistic. Books, papers and tracts are sold and distributed.

There are in South America (1903) 6 stations and 18 missionaries.

(6). *Japan:* Work was begun in a quiet manner about 1894. Since then the mission has had many vicissitudes, but is now reported as taking on new and more vigorous life. The headquarters are at Hiroshima. There are (1902) 4 stations and 3 missionaries.

(7). *The West India Islands:* Work has been begun in three of the West India Islands: in Jamaica (at Devon), in Haiti, and in San Domingo. An independent Alliance work has grown up in the city of San Juan, Porto Rico. Steps are now being taken by the CA toward work in the Philippine Islands.

The first publication of the Society was the *Gospel in All Lands.* Afterward the *Word, Work and World* was established, which was later merged into the present organ, the *Christian and Missionary Alliance Weekly.*

Another important publication is the *Alliance Colportage Library* of books setting forth the teachings of the Alliance, principally on Divine Healing and the Second Coming of Christ.

The Alliance has its own printing establishment at Nyack, N. Y.

CHRISTIAN LITERATURE SOCIETY FOR CHINA (Society for the Diffusion of Christian and General Knowledge among the Chinese, 1887): The founder of this Society was the Rev. Alexander Williamson, LL.D., of the United Presbyterian (Scotland) Mission, in China. He was a man of exceptional abilities, who went to China in the 50's and died in 1890.

In 1887 the Society was formally organized in Shanghai, by the missionaries, its object being the publication and circulation among the Chinese of "literature based on Christian principles." The Christian Literature Society for China was formed in Glasgow and Edinburgh in 1892, chiefly with the view of supporting this diffusion society. The two societies are thus practically one, and for convenience are generally spoken of as such. Its workers belong to all the leading missionary societies of England and America. Its editorial staff is composed of six men, representing the American M. E. (South), the English Wesleyan, Canadian Presbyterian, Church of England, General Evangelical German, and the English Baptist Missions. All these workers are devoting all or most of their time to the work of translating or preparing original work in the Chinese language. The chief magazine of the Society is *The Review of the Times.* It also publishes the *Chinese Missionary Review.*

The great reform movement of China in 1895-98 was largely due to the influence of the publications of this Society, which were read by the Emperor and the leading ministers and viceroys of the Emperor. It was largely through the influence of the General Secretary, the Rev. Timothy Richard, D.D., LL.D., that a college for Western learning was founded in the capital of Shan-si. In 1900, in consultation with the Educational Association of China, Dr. Richard drew up a general scheme of education for China, which was circulated in Chinese among the leading viceroys and governors. To the wisdom and ability of its secretary no little of the success of the Society is due.

In 1902, besides making free grants of smaller pamphlets to the value of $2,400 (Mexican) for distribution to the 100,000 students assembled periodically in the capitals of the maritime provinces of China, publications to the value of $62,685 (Mexican) were sold.

The members of the editorial staff are supported by the missionary societies which they represent.

CHRISTIAN LITERATURE SOCIETY FOR INDIA (formerly Christian Vernacular Education Society for India, 1858): The need of evangelical literature for the converts in the missions of India, Ceylon and Burma led to the formation of this Society in 1858. Its object is to train native teachers, instruct heathen children and publish Christian literature, the latter being its principal work.

The publications of the Society fall under two heads: school books and general Christian literature.

They have in the various languages 264 school books catalogd, some of which are so widely used that there is a steady demand for over 50,000 copies each, annually, the books being used in the schools of over forty missionary societies.

In supplying these school books the Society not only puts the thin edge of the Christian wedge into the secular schools of India, but receives from sale of the books a considerable profit which helps in the other branches of its work. For many years the Society has published annually, in the various languages of India, more books than all other societies put together. Since its foundation, the Society has issued in eighteen languages 2,601 publications averaging 131 pages, and of these, 26,417,000 copies have been circulated, and for some years the output has steadily increased.

In 1859 the Madras Auxiliary was organized, and no one man has had so much to do with the development of a Christian literature for all classes of people as its veteran secretary, John Murdoch, LL.D. In 1860 a second auxiliary was organized in Ceylon and a woman's auxiliary in 1896. There are (1901) 3 stations and 27 out-stations, 5 missionaries and 69 native helpers, 1 high school, with 89 students, 135 day schools, with 8,110 pupils.

CHRISTIAN MISSIONS, England (1827): The mission work of the denomination commonly known as Plymouth Brethren, but in its own preference called simply "The Brethren," was begun in 1827, the main object being "to spread the Gospel and build up churches." Missions have been established in Europe as well as in non-Christian mission fields as follows: (1903) *Europe:* Belgium, 2 stations and 4 missionaries; France, 3 stations and 5 missionaries; Austria, 1 station and 2 missionaries; Rumania, 1 station and 4 missionaries; Spain, 17 stations and 51 missionaries; Italy, 5 stations and 11 missionaries.

Asia: India (1836), 21 stations and 74 missionaries; Straits Settlements (1866) and Malay Peninsular (1900), 6 stations and 37 missionaries; Laos (1866), 1 station and 2 missionaries; Borneo, 1 station and 2 missionaries; China (1885), 14 stations and 55 missionaries; Japan (1888), 1 station and 2 missionaries.

Africa: Algeria, 4 stations and 10 missionaries; Morocco, 1 station and 2 missionaries; Central Africa (1881), 7 stations and 39 missionaries; South Africa, 2 stations and 4 missionaries.

America: Mexico (1890), 2 stations and 4 missionaries; British Guiana, 3 stations and 15 missionaries; West Indies, 4 stations and 10 missionaries; Guatemala, 1 station and 2 missionaries; Venezuela, 2 stations and 3 missionaries; Ecuador, 2 stations and 3 missionaries; Argentina, 4 stations and 16 missionaries; Chinese in U. S. A., 1 station and 2 missionaries.

One of the best known branches of the Christian Missions is the Garenganze Mission in Central Africa, which was established as an independent work by Mr. F. S. Arnot in 1881, and subsequently taken over by the Brethren.

Interested in Africa through the words of Livingstone when very young, a strong desire to go to Africa became a realization in 1881, when he sailed from London with Donald Graham. The latter remained at Natal because of failing health, but Mr. Arnot proceeded to Maritzburg.

After years of hard travel through the Zambesi and Barotse districts, finding locations suitable for Europeans, he established several stations. Other missionaries went out and an evangelistic work is thoroughly established in the region of the upper Zambesi. There are (1903) 5 mission stations from Bihé in Angola to Lake Mweru in the Congo Free State, with 15 missionaries.

Organ: *Missionary Visitor*, monthly.

CHRISTIANSBORG: A town in the Gold Coast Colony, W. Africa, 4 miles E. of Accra. The place was formerly a Dutch possession. In 1843 a Christian negro colony was transplanted thither from the West Indies. In 1850 the place was sold to the English, and that change gave occasion, in 1852, to some unfortunate disturbances. The climate is unhealthy. Station of the Basel Missionary Society (1858), with (1902) 12 missionaries, men and women; 22 native workers, men and women; 5 outstations, 3 Sunday schools, 5 elementary schools, 1 high school and 1,221 professing Christians.

CHRISTIANAGARAM: A village in Tinnevelli, S. India, situated about 25 miles S. of Tuticorin. Station of the SPG, with (1901) 31 native workers, 12 places of worship, 10 elementary schools and 1,448 baptized adult Christians.

CHRISTIANENBURG: A settlement in Natal, S. Africa, situated W. of Durban and about 9 miles S. of Botha's Hill station on the railway. Station of the Berlin Missionary Society (1854), with (1900) 3 missionaries, 21 native workers, 3 preaching places in the neighborhood and 456 baptized Christians.

CHRISTIAN VERNACULAR EDUCATION SOCIETY, for India. See CHRISTIAN LITERATURE SOCIETY FOR INDIA.

CHRISTIAN WOMAN'S BOARD OF MISSIONS (Disciples of Christ): Organized in 1874 in Indianapolis, where its headquarters have been located. Tho connected with the Church of the Disciples of Christ it is quite independent and unconnected with the **Foreign Christian Missionary Association.**

The first work of this Society was the revival of the mission in Jamaica, W. I., which had been practically abandoned. There are now connected with the Jamaica Association 21 churches, with 1,709 communicants and 480 day schools.

India: Work was begun at Bilaspur in 1885, in cooperation with the Foreign Christian Missionary Society; in 1886 a station was opened at Deoghur; at Bina in 1894; and Pendra, north of Bilaspur, was occupied in 1900. In the same year work was begun in the city of Calcutta.

Evangelistic, medical and educational work is carried on, zenanas are visited, lepers cared for and orphanages established. There are (1902) 5 stations and 10 outstations, 43 missionaries and assistant missionaries, 4 churches, with 287 communicants; 10 schools, 3 hospitals and dispensaries and 5 orphanages.

Mexico: A station was established at Monterey, Mexico, in 1897. The work is educational and evangelistic. Day and evening schools have been established and a church organized, with a Sunday school and Christian Endeavor Society. An eight-page weekly paper has been published and 30,000 copies circulated. Outstations have been established in the eastern and western sections of the city.

In *Porto Rico* the Bayamon school for girls was established in 1900 and a similar institution is being established for boys. The Board also carried on work throughout the United States.

Organ: *Missionary Tidings*, monthly, Indianapolis.

CHUANA LANGUAGE. See SECHUANA.

CHU-CHAU: A city in Ngan-hwei province, China, about 25 miles N. W. of Nanking. Station of the FCMS (1889), with (1900) 2 missionaries (one a physician) and their wives, 3 native workers, 1 common school, 1 training school for women workers, a dispensary, a book depot and 99 baptized Christians.

CHU-CHAU-FU: A town in the province of Che-kiang, China, 43 miles N. W. of Wenchow. Station of the CIM (1875), with (1900) 1 missionary and his wife, 1 missionary woman, 15 native workers, 1 school and 30 communicants.

CHU-CHI-HSIEN: A town in the province of Shen-si, China, situated about 35 miles west of Hsi-ngan-fu. Station of the CIM (1893), with (1900) 4 missionaries, one of them accompanied by his wife; 1 native worker, 1 preaching place, 1 high school, 1 opium victims' refuge.

CHUDDERGHAUT: A suburb of **Haidarabad**, the capital of the dominions of the Nizam.

CHU-KI-HSIEN: A town in the province of Che-kiang, China, lying about 80 miles W. of Ning-po. Station of the CMS (1894), of which the buildings and other property were destroyed by rioters in July, 1900. At last reports, up to the end of 1901 no missionary had gone there to reside. There were, however, remnants of the Christian community of about 250 (in the district) and these were regularly visited by missionaries and native pastors from other stations. Before the Boxer outbreak there were 6 missionaries, men and women, and 9 native workers here, with 8 schools in the town and district.

CHUNDICULLY: A station of the CMS in the Jaffna district, Ceylon (1818). It now has (1900) 2 missionaries, 1 missionary's wife, 1 unmarried missionary woman, 2 native workers, 1 chapel, 1 high school and a college.

CHUNG-KING-FU: A city and important river port in the province of Sze-chwan, China. It stands on a rocky promontory at the confluence of the Kialing and the Yangtse Rivers, 1,400 miles from the sea. A British commercial agent is located here and a customs service established. Population (1901), 300,000, or, with the suburbs, 700,000. Station of the CIM (1877), with (1900) 8 missionaries, men and women; 5 native workers, 2 schools and 34 communicants. Station also of the Friends' Foreign Missions Association (1890), with (1900) 2 missionaries (one a physician) and their wives, 3 missionary women, 10 native workers, men and women; 2 elementary and 1 high school and 1 dispensary. Station also of the LMS (1888), with (1900) 3 missionaries (one a physician), 2 missionaries' wives, 5 native workers, 5 elementary schools, an orphanage, a hospital and 72 church members. Also station of the ME, with 15 missionaries, men and women (three of whom are physicians); 20 native workers, men and women; 9 elementary and 2 high schools, 7 preaching places and 273 professing Christians. The National Bible Society of Scotland also has a book depot here, with an agent and his wife and 17 native workers.

CHUNG-PA: Town in the northern part of the province of Sze-chwan, China; station of the CMS (1894) which was broken up by the Boxer uprising. One of the missionaries returned to his station in 1901, but the reappearance of the Boxer effervescence in the province made missionary effort nearly impossible up to the beginning of 1903.

CHUNG-YANG-HSIEN: A town in the province of Hu-pei, China, situated about 70 miles S. W. of Wu-chang. Station of the WMS, with (1901) 2 missionaries, 4 native workers, 1 school, 1 chapel and 30 professing Christians.

CHUPRA: A town in the Nadiya district, Bengal, India, situated about 20 miles N. of Krishnagar. Station of the CMS (1845), with (1902) 1 missionary, 26 native workers, 1 place of worship, 1 school, 1 high school, an industrial enterprise for boys and 137 communicants.

CHURCH OF ENGLAND ZENANA MISSIONARY SOCIETY (1880): Upon the separation of the Zenana workers from the Indian Female Normal School and Instruction Society in 1880, the Church of England Zenana Missionary Society was formed to cooperate with the CMS, while retaining its independence of administration. It undertook the existing work in 17 stations with 31 missionaries in India. In 1883, in response to an urgent appeal from China and from the CMS, a missionary was sent to Fuchau, and in consequence of the liberal support given to the special fund for China, the Society has been able to occupy 13 stations in the Fo-kien Province. In 1889, through the efforts of Rev. and Mrs. J. Ireland Jones, late of Kandy, 2 stations were also established in Ceylon.

The Society has a "Home Workers' Band" of more than 800 women, who are kept in touch with the central workers by about 100 association secretaries and deputations from the home and foreign field. The "Daybreak Workers' Union" has a membership of about 150 bands, with a total membership of over 3,000 young people. The "Indian Widows' Union" is formed of British widows who unite with CEZ missionaries in work for Indian widows. Other women than widows are associate members.

Branches of the CEZ have been formed in Canada and Australia.

The missionaries of the Society are all women, but their work embraces every department of the mission service. They make evangelistic tours among the Hindu, Mohammedan, Singhalese and Chinese villages; they teach the women in the seclusion of their homes or the girls in school; they practise medicine and conduct hospitals and dispensaries; they train Christian women as assistant missionaries, Bible women, dispensers, nurses and teachers; they provide homes and classes for widows and destitute women in India and China; they provide orphanages for foundlings and famine orphans and give assistance to the deaf and dumb, the blind and the leper.

Missions (1903); 1. *North India* (1851): 19 stations, 41 missionaries, 250 native workers, 3 boarding and high schools, with 57 students, 75 other schools, with 3,139 pupils, 11,670 Zenana pupils, 1 orphanage, with 134 children, 1 hospital and 4 dispensaries

2. *South India* (1876): 16 stations, 42 missionaries, 318 native workers, 5 boarding and high schools, with 177 students, 58 other schools, with 3,017 pupils, 3,856 Zenana pupils, 3 orphanages, with 136 children, 1 hospital and 2 dispensaries.

3. *Punjab and Sindh* (1872): 24 stations, 69 missionaries, 144 native workers, 7 boarding and high schools, with 201 students, 51 elementary schools, with 2,353 pupils, 741 Zenana pupils, 5 orphanages, with 66 children, 9 hospitals and 22 dispensaries.

4. *Ceylon* (1889): 2 stations, 5 missionaries, 27 native workers, 1 boarding school, with 54 students, 15 other schools, with 461 pupils, and 1 dispensary.

5. *Travancore and Cochin* (1862): 7 stations, 11 missionaries, 92 native workers, 1 boarding school, with 299 students, 14 other schools, with 717 pupils, 21 Zenana pupils, 1 orphanage, with 44 children, 1 hospital and 2 dispensaries.

6. *China* (1884): 12 stations, 38 missionaries, 115 native workers, 12 boarding and high schools, with 360 students, 46 other schools, with 597 pupils, 45 Zenana pupils, 1 orphanage, with 41 children, 4 hospitals and 4 dispensaries.

7. *Singapore* (1900): 1 station, 3 missionaries, 2 native workers, 1 boarding school, with 70 students.

The organ of the Society is *India's Women and China's Daughters*, monthly, London. It also publishes in each quarter, *Daybreak*, for girl students, and *Little Torchbearers*, for children. For Medical work: Barnes (Irene H.), *Between Life and Death*, London, 1899; For work in India; Barnes (I. H.), *Behind the Parda*, London, 1899; Hull (E. C.), *Vignettes of Kashmer*, London, 1903.

CHURCH MISSIONARY SOCIETY for Africa and the East (1799): In the year 1786 twelve events occurred which led to an awakening of the missionary spirit in Great Britain. Of these twelve events, the principal were the three following: (a) Wilberforce dedicated himself to the abolition of the slave trade; (b) Granville Sharp planned to settle the liberated slaves at Sierra Leone, and (c) the Eclectic Society (founded in 1783 for mutual improvement by a few evangelical clergy and laymen of the Church of England), discussed foreign missions for the first time. In 1789 this Society again discussed foreign missions, but no marked advance was made. In 1791 Charles Simeon again brought the subject before the Eclectic Society. Only two or three out of the seventeen members present (presumably Simeon, Thomas Scott and Basil Woode) were favorable to a definite attempt at foreign missions, but long afterward Woode wrote across his notes of that meeting "this conversation proved the foundation of the Church Missionary Society"

In February, 1799, the matter was again brought before the Eclectic Society by the Rev. John Venn, who at this meeting laid down what afterward became essential and unchanging principles of the CMS:

"It is the right of Christian men who sympathize with one another to combine for a common object."

"Spiritual work must be done by spiritual men."

"The mission must be founded on the Church principle, but not the high-Church principle."

"If clergymen cannot be found, send laymen."

History: At this time the SPCK and the SPG were at the lowest point of energy and efficiency, and evangelicals were not allowed to cooperate with either; hence the necessity for a new missionary society. On the 12th of April, 1799, a public meeting was held at the Castle and Falcon in London, the same hotel in which, four years previously, the LMS was formed. Sixteen clergymen and nine laymen met in an "upper room," the Rev. John Venn in the chair. Resolutions were adopted, stating that "as the SPCK and SPG confined their labors to the British plantations in America and to the West Indies, there seems to be still wanting in the established Church a society for sending missionaries to the continent of Africa and other parts of the heathen world."

Therefore, "the persons present at this meeting do form a Society for that purpose;" and that "a deputation be sent to the Archbishop of Canterbury as Metropolitan, the Bishop of London as Diocesan and the Bishop of Durham as Chairman of the Missionary Committee of the SPCK, with a copy of the rules of the Society and a respectful letter."

At this time no name was given the Society, but six weeks later a second meeting was held which chose the name "The Society for Missions to Africa and the East." This name never came into practical use, and the present full name was not formally adopted until 1812.

In the meantime the deputation had difficulty in getting access to the Bishops, and not till July, 1800, was it able to make its report to the Society. The Archbishop was said to "appear favorably disposed, but cautious about committing himself."

During the early years of the CMS the bishops declined to ordain its candidates for service abroad, and it was obliged to look to Germany for its missionaries. The first missionaries, two Berlin students, were sent out in 1802, followed by others during the next few years.

Not until 1813, fourteen years after the foundation of the Society, did two bishops consent to ordain two of its candidates "for temporary work at home."

In 1819 an Act of Parliament gave the Archbishops of Canterbury and York and the Bishop of London power to ordain men for "His Majesty's Colonies and Foreign Possessions," under certain restrictions, and a technical objection which formed one of the early difficulties of the Society was thus entirely removed.

In 1841 two Archbishops and several Bishops joined the Society. In 1845 a proposition was made to unite the seven principal societies of the Church of England into a Church Union. The CMS committee deemed the action unwise, and it was therefore denounced in some quarters as "not a Church Society." Then the cry was raised that all missions should be worked "by the Church in the corporate capacity." This led to the famous defense of Henry Venn, known as the Appendix to the Thirty-ninth Report. The paper states that the CMS "may be regarded as an institution for discharging the temporal and lay offices necessary for the preaching of the Gospel among the heathen.

"The secretary of the CMS requests, by letter, the Bishop of London to ordain, in conformity with the provisions of the Act of Parliament, such persons as the Society is willing to support in some foreign station. The Bishop, by the imposition of hands, gives them authority to preach the Gospel, with a view to their foreign location. Hence, to call the acts of the CMS in selecting the station, paying the passage money, and agreeing to provide the salary—to call these acts a *sending forth* of preachers in an ecclesiastical sense is to confound names with things and to lose sight of all true Church principles."

In 1848 the Jubilee of the Society was observed and was marked by a special fund, amounting to £55,322, to be used in assisting disabled missionaries; in providing a boarding school for missionaries' children; to assist native churches in raising endowments, and for mission buildings.

In 1882 the subject of medical missions was brought under consideration and an auxiliary committee was appointed to prepare for an extension of work in this direction. The medical department of the CMS was fully organized in 1894, and its influence has been immeasurable in all missionary lands.

The direct employment of women missionaries by the Society began to be canvassed about 1882, altho long before single women had rendered it efficient service in educational work. The Women's Department of the Society was fully organized in 1895.

The centenary celebration of the CMS was held in 1899 after three years of preparation through the distribution of special missionary literature, the holding of special meetings, and united action in making the Society a subject for special prayer. The centenary celebration was a solemn, joyful and most impressive occasion in which the congregations throughout the immense field of the Society participated by special services.

The report of 1902 shows that the CMS has 1,276 missionaries, 8,290 native workers, 2,274 schools and educational institutions of all grades, with an attendance of 116,552 pupils. There are also 79,586 communicants in the aggregate on its church rolls.

The year 1841-1842 brought to the Society an alarming financial crisis, while opportunities for increase of work were greater than ever before. At this point the committee appealed to the country for help, on the distinct ground that they "looked for the Divine blessing upon the faithful, plain and full maintenance of the great principles of the truth as it is in Jesus, by all the agents and missionaries of the Society, without compromise and without reserve. It is the sustentation of that Scriptural, Protestant and Evangelical tone throughout all their ministrations, it is the upholding of the Bible and the Bible alone, as the foundation and rule of faith upon which the blessing of God has rested, does rest and ever will rest."

"Upon these principles the committee took their stand in a season of jeopardy, and made their appeal for special assistance." The result was that in May, 1843, they were able to report a larger income than up to that time had been received by any missionary society. Nearly all indebtedness was cleared off and a good beginning was made in the formation of a capital fund. At this time a finance committee of four bankers had been appointed to consider the situation, and they laid down the rule that, altho the Society is "called upon to occupy diligently with the talents committed to it, it is not to aim at occupying with more talents than God in His wisdom has been pleased to dispense." On receiving this enunciation from the finance committee the stand was taken by the general committee of the Society that the "talents" which God gives a missionary society are men, not money, and if He sends the men it is reasonable to believe that He will send the money for their support.

In 1853 this "Policy of Faith" of the CMS was clearly enunciated before a general meeting as follows: "The committee state in the presence of this vast meeting and before the Church at large, their willingness to accept any number of true missionaries who may appear to be called of God to the work. They will send out any number, trusting to the Lord of the harvest, Whose is the silver and the gold, to supply their treasury with the funds for this blessed and glorious undertaking."

In 1871-72 the low water mark was reached in the supply of candidates; a Day of Intercession was for the first time observed with reference to the situation on December 20, 1872, and a circular was issued, asking the constituency of the Society to pray for missionary candidates. Twelve months later, in May, 1874, at the end of the first complete financial year since this call to prayer for men went out, the Society was startled to learn that the receipts exceeded a quarter of a million. The ordinary income had advanced in one year £40,000!

In 1880 the finances again fell below par and a special joint committee of finance and estimates was appointed; their strong conviction was that "no religious society ought to run ahead of Divine Providence; that the Divine will is indicated by the amount of funds committed to the Society's administration, and, that while it is right to use every talent given to us, we are not responsible for talents not given to us."

This was the same position as that taken by the Special Finance Committee of 1841-42, which led the committee of the CMS to declare that God's will is indicated by the coming forward of men, not by money.

Following this declaration of a policy of retrenchment the report of 1881 showed a clear balance sheet, and men who had been kept at home were promptly sent out. But in 1887 the Estimates Committee warned the Society that the number of candidates was increasing more rapidly than the funds, and argued that expansion of the work should be limited by the funds at the Society's disposal. To this the Society answered that the candidates were unmistakably men sent by God, and it was reasonable to assume that He would provide the means to maintain them.

Ultimately it was determined to refuse no candidate merely on financial grounds. The Society thus unknowingly reverted to the policy of 1852-53. In 1893 the financial outlook was so serious that the President issued a letter headed "Ask the Lord and tell His people." It was proposed to abandon the "Policy of Faith," but on review of the seven years that the policy had been in operation it was found that the missionary staff had just doubled; the whole of their expenses had been paid, and in addition to all ordinary expenditure a mortgage of £20,000 on the Children's Home had been paid off. Thus the "Policy of Faith" enunciated in 1853, afterward forgotten; abandoned entirely in 1865, with the result of seven years' famine; partially acted upon in 1874-76, and dropped in 1877, with financial difficulties resulting; adopted as a new thing in 1887, and persevered in for seven years, had been honored of God beyond all anticipation. The resolution reaffirming the policy was carried *nem. con.* and at the annual meeting of 1902 the "Policy of Faith" was again reaffirmed.

Organization and Constitution: The Society is conducted by a Patron, always a member of the Royal Family; a Vice-Patron, the Archbishop of Canterbury; a President, who must be a layman; Vice-Presidents, usually clerical; a Committee and such officers as may be deemed necessary— all being members of the Church of England or Ireland. The general body of the Society includes members and governors who have made certain subscriptions to the funds of the Society or have rendered special service in its work. The Committee consists of 24 laymen and of the clergymen who have been for at least one year members of the Society. Of the 24 lay members, 18 are reappointed each year from the existing Committee, the rest being elected from the general body of the Society.

The official staff of the Society is more complete than that of any other missionary organization. Aside from two Honorary Clerical Secretaries there are 20 secretaries and assistant secretaries, divided among seven departments: Candidates, Foreign, Home organization, Editorial, Lay, Women's, and Medical. There are 19 Association Secretaries in England, 3 in Ireland and 2 in the Scottish Auxiliary, while 5 clergymen are employed in missionary meetings and special deputation work. Aside from these there is a large number of honorary district secretaries. The result is seen in the thoroughness with which the field is covered, the accuracy and completeness of the reports and the variety and attractiveness of the publications. The Society's annual report is *facile princeps* among reports, as are its monthly Church Missionary Intelligencer and Gleaner among other missionary periodicals. Similarly its income is larger than that of any other missionary society, in 1902 being, for the general purposes of the Society, £327,000 ($1,635,000).

A feature of the organization of the CMS is its use of auxiliary societies. These have been formed among those of all ages and stations in life. Prominent among these agencies for keeping the people informed and interested are the "Missionary Leaves Association," the Gleaners' Union and the Savers' Band. Of a similar nature are the Lay Workers' Union and the Younger Clergy Union. It has been the policy of the Society to form auxiliary committees in the colonies wherever the English community is strong enough to give practical aid to the work of the Society in its midst.

Development of Missions: With William Wilberforce as one of the charter members of the new society, and the prominence given the slave trade in Africa through his efforts and those of Granville Sharp, the attention of the CMS was at once directed to West Africa, the center of the slave trade, as a needy field, and especially in view of the fact that neither the Society for the Promotion of Christian Knowledge nor the SPG were working in that country. Its first missionaries were sent to the Susu tribe on the Rio Pongas in 1804, the mission headquarters afterward being at Sierra Leone. On the opening of India to missionary work in 1813, the United Provinces (formerly North West Provinces) Mission was begun at Agra by Abdul Masih, Henry Martyn's solitary convert from Mohammedanism, under the direction of Daniel Corrie, one of the famous "five chaplains" of India. The second mission of the Society was to the Maoris of New Zealand in 1814, at the invitation of Samuel Marsden, chaplain in New South Wales. The same year the South India Mission was opened at Madras by the first two clergymen of the Church of England to be sent as missionaries to India.

The Bengal Mission was established in 1816, and the same year work was begun in the Travancore and Cochin Native State, at the invitation of the British resident. In 1817 work was begun among the Singhalese and Tamils in Ceylon. The Western India Mission was inaugurated at Bombay in 1820. Two years later, in 1822, the North West Canada Missions were begun among the scattered Red Indian tribes. The treaty of Nanking in 1842 rendered China accessible, and in 1844 the Mid-China Mission was begun.

The following year the missions in Africa were extended and work was begun in East and West Equatorial Africa. In 1850 the Fo-kien Mission was established at Fu-chau.

In 1851, on invitation of Bishop Gobat, the Palestine Mission was opened,"beginning at Jerusalem." This year also the Punjab and Sindh Mission was begun, soon after the annexation of the province to British India. In 1856 Capt. Prevost, R. N., called the attention of the CMS to the Indians of British Columbia, and a young schoolmaster was sent to them. A mission was also begun the same year on the island of Mauritius. In 1862 work was extended to South China. In 1869 the first CMS missionary began work in Japan, and the Rev. R. Bruce of the CMS visited Persia and began a mission which was formally adopted by the Society in 1875. In 1876 the work in Africa was further extended and the Uganda Mission organized. In 1882 the Missions to Egypt and Turkish Arabia were begun, and in 1892 the West China Mission was started in the Province of Sze-chwan.

The Missions. I. *Africa.* (1) *Sierra Leone Mission* (1816): The first two missionaries of the CMS were sent in 1804 to the Susu tribes on the Rio Pongas. A few years later a station was opened at Yongro for the Bullom tribe, by Nylander, who labored for 19 years in Africa, dying at his post in 1825, never having returned home. In 1817, at the instigation of the slave dealers, the mission buildings were destroyed by fire, and opposition to their work became so formidable that the missionaries were compelled to take refuge in Sierra Leone, the depot for negroes rescued from slave ships by British cruisers. Here the missionaries remained. Great success attended their labors and in 1822 nearly 2,000 of the freed slaves were in the mission schools, and some hundreds had become sincere Christians. The work continued to prosper, but at great cost. Fifty-three missionaries and missionaries' wives died in this field between 1804 and 1824. This great mortality revealed the necessity for native agency, and in 1827 the Fourah Bay College was opened. Port Lokkoh in the Timne country was occupied from 1840 to 1850 and reoccupied in 1875. In 1840 the native Christians voluntarily established a Church Missionary Auxiliary, and undertook the support of the native schools in the various parishes. In 1852 the Bishopric of Sierra Leone was founded and ten years later the Sierra Leone Church was organized on an independent basis, and undertook the support of its own pastors, churches and schools, aided by a small grant from the CMS. In 1876 the Sierra Leone Church Missionary Society was founded and has since carried on the outlying missions established by the CMS in the Bullom and Quiah countries.

There are (1902) 21 stations and 22 outstations, 14 European missionaries and 167 native workers, 6,932 native communicants and 64 schools, with 4,830 pupils. More than 100 African clergymen have been ordained on the West Coast of Africa in connection with this and the Yoruba Mission. Several of them are government chaplains.

(2) *Western Equatorial Africa Mission* (1845): A large portion of the freed slaves gathered at Sierra Leone had been taken from the Yoruba country, a thousand miles to the eastward. About 1840 many of these natives, some of whom had become Christians, returned to their own people, and petitioned that a missionary be sent to them. In 1843 Mr. Henry Townsend paid a preliminary visit to Abeokuta and returned to Sierra Leone and to England with a favorable report. He and Mr. Gollmer with Samuel Crowther, a native of Yoruba and a liberated slave, reached Abeokuta in 1845, where they received a hearty welcome. Gradually the work extended to other towns and villages in the interior, and in 1857 Mr. Crowther accompanied a commercial expedition up the Niger River and laid the foundation of the Niger Mission by establishing stations at Onitsha, Gbebe and Idda.

In 1890 missionaries were sent out to locate at Lokoja, on the Upper Niger, and thence to try to reach the Mohammedan Hausa States. The climate proved fatal to the expedition, however. A subsequent attempt met with better success, and itinerations have been made in the direction of Sokoto and an effort has been made toward permanent work in the Hausa country.

There are (1902) 43 stations, 55 European missionaries and 202 native workers, 4,749 communicants and 80 schools, with 4,721 pupils.

(3) *Eastern Equatorial Africa Mission* (1844): The mission was begun by Dr. J. L. Krapf, who went to Mombasa after being expelled from Abyssinia. In 1846 he was joined by the Rev. John Rebman, who opened the station at Kisulutini and labored on the coast 29 years. Their remarkable journeys into the interior opened the way for subsequent geographical and missionary enterprises in East Africa. In 1874 the Rev. W. S. Price, formerly in charge of the asylum for rescued slaves at Nasik, Western India, was sent out; land was purchased for an industrial colony on the mainland near Mombasa; some 200 African Christians from among the freed slaves formed the nucleus of the colony and the new settlement was named Freretown, in honor of Sir Bartle Frere. To this place other rescued slaves were sent for care and training. Stations were opened in 1883 in the Taita country to the westward, and at Taveta under the shadow of the snow-capped Kilima Njaro, and in 1890 in the Jilore region, to northward of Mombasa, when in 1876 missionaries were sent by the Zanzibar route to establish the Uganda Mission. Intermediate stations were established at Mpwapwa in 1876, at Mamboia in 1879, and at Nassa, at the south end of the Victoria Nyanza, in 1888. For

these missions a new bishopric was established in 1884, the Rev. John Hannington being consecrated the first bishop. He was murdered by order of King Mwanga of Uganda in October, 1885.

There are (1902) 18 stations, 77 European missionaries and 91 native workers, 842 communicants and 49 schools, with 2,316 pupils.

(4) *Uganda Mission* (1876): In November, 1875, Stanley sent word to England that Mtesa, King of Uganda, would welcome missionaries. Shortly after this the CMS received two anonymous gifts of £5,000 each for work in Uganda, and in June, 1876, seven months later, the first missionaries for Uganda were at Zanzibar preparing for the march to the Victoria Nyanza, Rubaga, the capital of Uganda, was reached by two of the party, Lieut. Smith and Rev. C. T. Wilson, in June, 1877, who were warmly welcomed by Mtesa. Mr. T. O'Neill afterward joined them, but the temerity of this enterprise became evident in December, 1877, when Messrs. Smith and O'Neill were killed in a quarrel between a native chief and an Arab trader. Mr. Wilson was thus left alone in the middle of Africa. It was only after some months that he was joined by Mr. A. M. Mackay, who had been detained on the coast by illness for more than a year. In 1884 King Mtesa died, and Mwanga, his son, turned against the missionaries, and a period of danger and bloodshed followed the murder of Bishop Hannington and several native Christians. This many times threatened the existence of the mission, until finally in 1894 a British Protectorate was established over Uganda and within three or four years prosperity dawned for the State and for the mission. See **Uganda**.

There are (1902) 33 stations, 76 European missionaries and 2,435 native workers, 9,865 communicants, 5 schools, with 248 pupils and 12,117 others receiving instruction.

The more notable characteristic of this mission is the advance of the native Christians in intelligence and their acceptance of the duty of evangelizing neighboring regions. Busoga, Toro and Bunyoro have thus been opened to the missionaries.

(5) *Egypt* (resumed 1882): As far back as 1802 it was suggested to the CMS that it attempt the revival of evangelical religion in the Greek Church. In 1811 came a letter (which ultimately led to the Society's enterprises in the Mediterranean) from a Roman Catholic priest in Malta, Dr. Nandi, urging the needs of Mohammedans and Christians in the Levant and the duty of the CMS to relieve such needs.

In 1815 the Rev. William Jowett was sent to Malta "to survey the religious horizon," and begin work, followed soon afterward by Messrs. Connor and Hartley. In 1825 five men were sent to Egypt, among them Samuel Gobat. The work was carried on for more than 30 years, chiefly by J. R. T. Lieder, who died at Cairo in 1865. He and his brethren itinerated in the Nile Delta, into the Fayum and southward into Nubia. The missionaries could not work directly for Mohammedans and sought to stir up native Christians to life. The Coptic clergy were generally friendly, while those of the Greek Church were not. Schools were started and a boys' boarding school was established at Cairo, which in 1842 was changed into a theological seminary for Coptic clergy. The visible results of the work were small and no new recruits were sent out.

In 1862 the mission was dropped. In 1882 the British occupation of the Nile Valley took place. At once thank-offerings began to be sent to the CMS for an Egyptian Mission. This led to a decision to reopen the work in Egypt, this time among the Mohammedans. Dr. F. A. Klein of the Palestine Mission was sent to Cairo. Later on, medical work was begun at Cairo by Dr. Harpur. Cairo was regarded as a stepping stone to Khartum and the Sudan. But the timidity of the British Government respecting the effect of Christian missions in those regions has interfered with the execution of this design. The most urgent request of the CMS, presented in 1901, for permission to station missionaries at Khartum, received a courteous but firm refusal from the Secretary of State for Foreign Affairs, which concluded with the words: "It appears to me to be at present impossible to indicate any time when the restrictions now in force on the labors of missionaries in the Sudan could with safety be removed, but the matter will receive the most careful attention." Nevertheless, in 1903 British officials approved missionary labor for pagans in the S. districts of the Sudan, and permitted the CMS to open a school for Muslims in Khartum.

There are (1902) in Egypt, 4 stations of the CMS, 28 European missionaries, 25 native workers, 54 communicants and 4 schools, with 291 pupils.

II. *Palestine* (1851): When Samuel Gobat, for many years associated with the work of the CMS in the Levant, was appointed to the bishopric in Jerusalem, he appealed to the committee to begin work among the Jews. One result of this was the opening of the Palestine Mission by the Rev. F. A. Klein and Dr. Sandrecki, at Jerusalem.

The ultimate purpose of the Society in undertaking the work in this, as in their other Levant missions, was the evangelization of the Mohammedans. Several stations were successively occupied and other missionaries were added to the staff. In 1861, however, Jerusalem and Nazareth were the only stations in occupation, and for many years the work was on a reduced scale. Bishop Gobat had established mission stations at Nablus and Es Salt, besides 25 schools throughout the country. In 1873-5 this work was transferred to the care of the CMS and the occupation of other towns followed. In 1899 the CMS took over the work of the Female Education Society at Jerusalem and Shefamer.

There are now (1902) in the Palestine Mission 19 stations, 71 European missionaries and 127 native workers, 802 communicants and 59 schools with 3,609 pupils.

III. *Turkish Arabia* (1882): Baghdad was first occupied as an outpost of the Persia Mission, with the view of reaching Persian pilgrims who resort to famous Shii shrines near the city. The first missionaries were the Rev. T. R. Hodgson of the Indian Mission and Mr. Maimon, a converted Jew of Trieste. A good deal of their early work was among the Jews, the Persian pilgrims not being found very accessible. Medical work was begun in 1886 by Dr. Sutton. In 1898 the work was separated from the Persia Mission and continued as the "Turkish Arabia Mission." In 1900 Mosul was occupied by agreement with the PN, which had taken over that station from the ABCFM.

There are (1902) 2 stations, 7 European missionaries, 13 native workers, 61 communicants and 4 schools, with 148 pupils.

IV. *Persia* (1875): In 1869 the Rev. R. Bruce, of the CMS, visited Persia, when returning from England to India, and began work at Ispahan. In 1875 the Society formally adopted his work as one of its missions. In 1879 medical work was begun. Since that time doors have opened rapidly; the Babis have seemed friendly and the Muslims generally have been attracted through the medical services of the missionaries.

There are (1902) 5 stations, 35 European missionaries, 41 native workers, 100 communicants, and 6 schools, with 497 pupils.

V. *India* (1813): (1) *United* (formerly North West) *Provinces:* The Society's first agent in India was Abdul Masih, Henry Martyn's solitary convert from Mohammedanism, who was sent to Agra in 1813 under the direction of the chaplain of the forces at that station. In 1815 Meerut was occupied by a converted Brahman. In 1817 Daniel Corrie from Agra was appointed chaplain at Benares, and work was begun there.

By 1854, 4 other stations had been occupied. In 1857 occurred the terrible Sepoy rebellion, which concentrated intense interest upon India and incidentally upon its missions.

The CMS raised a special fund to replace buildings and apparatus destroyed and for a general expansion of the work. The most important event following the meeting was the occupation of Lucknow in 1858, immediately after its reconquest. Some years later a special work was begun among the Gonds (1879) and the Bhils (1880).

There are (1902) 27 stations, 131 European missionaries and 429 native workers, 2,146 communicants, 134 schools, with 10,359 pupils; native contributions, Rs. 7,742.

(2) *South India* (1814): The first two clergymen of the Church of England to go to India were sent to Madras by the CMS in 1814. A corresponding committee of the Society was organized to administer the work.

The Tinnevelli Mission was begun in 1820, at the request of the chaplain at Palamcotta. In 1838 the Madras Theological Seminary was established.

The Telugu Mission was begun in 1841 by Robert Noble, who established the famous English school at Masulipatam, and Henry Fox, who began a series of preaching tours which resulted in the foundation of an increasing Telugu native Church.

In 1870 work was begun among the Tamils and the people of the Nilgiri hills, with Utakamund as a center.

There are (1902) 82 stations, 62 European missionaries and 1,410 native workers, 18,223 communicants and 715 schools, with 23,764 pupils.

(3) *Bengal Mission* (1816): The CMS had an important part in the establishment of the Bishopric of Calcutta in 1814, and before missionaries were allowed in India a CMS Corresponding Committee was organized in Calcutta. When, in 1816, two CMS missionaries were sent out to open a station, the administration of the new work was placed under the care of this local committee.

The following year (1817) Burdwan was occupied and an effort was made to establish a National System of Education. Nadiya was occupied in 1831, and seven years later witnessed a remarkable revival, and in 1857 the mission to Santals was begun. In 1865 the Cathedral Mission College was established, but discontinued in 1880, the buildings being used for the CMS Divinity School for Bengal.

There are (1902) 28 stations, 71 European missionaries and 392 native workers, 2,806 communicants and 115 schools, with 4,432 scholars.

(4) *Travancore and Cochin* (1816): Work was begun in these semi-independent native states in 1816, at the request of the British resident, and continued for twenty years, largely in the hope of stimulating reform of the ancient Syrian Church of Malabar. Since 1837 the missionaries have worked independently of this church and with better results. In 1873 a remarkable revival occurred which resulted in the organization of a native church which continues steadily to grow.

There are (1902) 38 stations and 25 European missionaries, 612 native workers, 12,096 communicants and 265 schools, with 12,148 pupils.

(5) *Western India* (1820): In 1818 a Corresponding Committee of the CMS was formed in Bombay and two years later missionary work was formally inaugurated. In 1832 a new station was opened at Nasik, an important center of Brahman influence. At Bombay the Robert Money School, established in 1836, was handed over to the CMS. In 1854 the Rev. W. S. Price founded the agricultural and industrial settlement of Sharanpur, Nasik, which afterward became for a time a refuge for liberated African slaves.

Poona was occupied in 1882, and here there was established the CMS Divinity School for West India. Special efforts were made to reach the Mohammedans and Parsees.

There are (1902) 9 stations, 22 European missionaries, 182 native workers, 1,449 communicants and 59 schools, with 2,578 pupils.

(5) *Punjab and Sindh* (1850): As early as 1840 some English officers and civilians at Simla raised a fund for evangelistic work among the natives and applied to the CMS for a missionary. None being sent, they began an independent work at Kolgur in 1843 which was taken over by the Society in 1848. In 1850 it began the Sindh Mission at the commercial port of Karachi and the following year work was begun in the Punjab proper by establishing a station at Amritsar, the sacred city of the Sikhs, and extension became the order of the day, but the most important advance was made in 1855, when Peshawar, the military post on the Afghan frontier, was occupied. Lahore, the capital of the Punjab, became a station in 1867, and here the Divinity School was founded three years later.

There are in this mission (1902) 32 stations, 106 European missionaries, 180 native workers, 1,299 communicants and 42 schools, with 6,537 scholars.

VI. *Ceylon* (1817): Work was begun among both Singhalese and Tamils in 1815, the two races having distinct languages. Evangelistic, educational and pastoral work has been carried on, but the strongest influence of the mission has been exerted through the schools. During the first years the reports from the missionaries were almost uniformly depressing, while favorable impressions of its influence were given by the government officials. Two features of special interest in Ceylon are the Kandyan itineracy, begun in 1853, and the Tamil Coolie Mission, established in 1855.

Much indirect good came from a great Buddhist revival in 1862-4, and from that time both the Singhalese and Tamil Missions began to look more promising.

There are (1902) 22 stations, 53 European missionaries, 681 native workers, 3,525 communicants and 283 schools, with 17,914 pupils.

VII. *Mauritius* (1856): Early in 1854 Mauritius was visited by two CMS missionaries from Tinnevelli, who found a little band of Tamil coolie Christians from India, for whom Mr. A. Taylor of the Madras Auxiliary Bible Society was caring. The need of the field was reported to the CMS, and in 1856 it began work among the coolies. From the first there was much encouragement. An interesting development of the mission occurred in 1860, when the Government established an orphan asylum and industrial school, placing them in the care of the CMS missionaries. In 1875, in connection with Mauritius, work was begun in the Seychelles Islands, among the liberated African slaves, an industrial school settlement being established on the Capucin Mountain.

There are (1902) 10 stations, 10 European missionaries, 67 native workers, 365 communicants and 21 schools with 1,549 pupils.

VIII. *China* (1845): (1) *Mid China Mission:* After the treaty of 1842 a friend of the CMS, calling himself "less than the least," gave the Society £6,000, as the nucleus of a China fund. Two clergymen were at once sent out, with instructions to visit the treaty ports and Hongkong, and report upon the best place for locating the new mission. Shanghai and Ningpo were selected and occupied (1845-1848). In 1875 the Ningpo College was founded and has been a valuable agency in the work. The mission was gradually extended to Hang-chau and other places. In 1901, a Native Church Missionary Society was formed for further aggressive work.

There are (1902) 12 stations and 59 European missionaries, 105 native workers, 1,240 communicants and 51 schools, with 738 pupils.

(2) *Fo-kien* (1850): The city of Fu-chau was occupied in 1850, but for ten years the work was barren of results. In 1860 medical work was commenced and proved a helpful agency. In 1864-5 other large cities were occupied by native evangelists and rapid progress was made in spite of severe persecution. In August, 1895, occurred the terrible Ku-cheng massacre. Since then there has been marked advance. During the years 1900-1901 Boxer bands made trouble in various places.

There are (1902) 18 stations, 77 European missionaries, 415 native workers, 4,464 communicants and 185 schools, with 2,633 pupils.

(3) *South China* (1862): St. Paul's College in Hongkong had for some time been assisted by the CMS, but regular work was not begun until a mission was organized in 1862.

Several outstations were later established in the Kwang-tung Province, with Canton as a central station.

There are (1901) 6 stations, 38 European missionaries, 58 native workers, 360 communicants and 30 schools with 1,490 pupils.

(4) *West China* (1891): The most important CMS movement in China in recent years was the new mission in the western province of Sze-chwan begun by Rev. J. H. Horsburgh in 1891, who planned the work on very simple lines, the missionaries to "identify themselves as much as they could with the people, and spend as little money as possible." They went into the province after correspondence and an understanding with the CIM, whose missionaries already on the field welcomed and assisted them. They at once began to itinerate, this seeming the best method of work. By 1894 five cities were definitely occupied. In 1895 serious riots occurred in the province, but the CMS mission suffered small loss.

There were (in 1900) 10 stations, 41 European missionaries, 33 communicants and 1 school, with 15 pupils.

IX. *Japan* (1869): In 1867 the CMS received an anonymous gift of £4,000 for a mission in Japan. In 1868 came the revolution which restored the Mikado to the throne and in 1869 the first CMS missionary landed at Nagasaki. At first the work was carried on with difficulty, but in 1872 religious liberty was practically proclaimed and by 1875 four important centers were occupied. The new constitution proclaimed in 1889 gave increased religious liberty and made possible further extension of work.

There are (1901) 23 stations, 102 European missionaries, 156 native workers, 2,408 communicants and 15 schools with 559 pupils.

X. *New Zealand* (1814): The mission to the Maoris of New Zealand, the second of the Society's missions in order of time, was undertaken in 1814, when Samuel Marsden, with three laymen, sent out as pioneers, landed on the northern island. Other missionaries followed whose lives were entirely in the power of the ferocious cannibals, and were frequently in imminent danger. For eleven years no results whatever were seen. In 1825 the first conversion took place, and no other natives were baptized for five years. Then began the marvelous movement which resulted in almost the whole Maori nation being brought under Christian instruction and civilizing influences, and which led Bishop Selwyn, on his arrival in his new diocese in 1842, to write: "We see here a whole nation of pagans converted to the faith. . . . Where will you find more signal manifestations of the presence of the Spirit, or more living evidences of the kingdom of Christ?" In 1840 New Zealand was made a British colony, and immigration on a large scale ensued, introducing the vices as well as the benefits of civilization. The inevitable conflicts of race began and the continual disputes about the sale and possession of land led to prolonged and bitter wars, which shook the native church to its foundations and caused serious defections.

In 1883 a local CMS mission board was established to administer the Society's grants, which diminished annually and ceased in 1902.

There are (1902) 48 stations, 18 European missionaries, 346 native workers, 2,508 communicants and 7 schools with 295 pupils.

XI. *Northwest Canada* (1822): The work of the CMS among the Indian tribes scattered over what was formerly the Hudson Bay territory, was begun by the Rev. John West in 1822 at a little trading station on the Red River.

The first step in extending the mission was made in 1840, when a native teacher was sent to open a station at Deron. Now this district is the colonial province of Manitoba, and a large part of the CMS work has developed into the ministrations of the Church in the colony; one of its churches having even become the Cathedral of the Diocese of Rupert's Land.

The Ecclesiastical Province of Rupert's Land, the area of which probably exceeds that of the

Chinese Empire, is divided into eight dioceses, viz., Rupert's Land, Moosonee, Mackenzie River, Athabasca, Saskatchewan, Calgary, Qu'Appelle and Keewatin. In all these dioceses the Society's agents labor. The whole Bible and Prayer-book exist in Red River Cree, and considerable portions, with hymn-books, etc., in Moose Cree, Ojibbeway, Soto, Slave, Chipewyan and Tukudh.

A plan for the gradual withdrawal of the CMS financial aid to these dioceses, similar to that adopted in New Zealand, is to become effective as soon as practicable.

There are (1901) 60 stations, 73 missionaries, 37 native workers, 2,852 communicants and 76 schools with 2,300 pupils.

XII. *British Columbia* (1856): In 1856 Captain Prevost, R.N., drew the Society's attention to the savage state of the Tsimshean Indians on the coast of British Columbia, and a young schoolmaster, Mr. W. Duncan, was sent out. A great blessing was vouchsafed to his labors, and in 1862 the Christian settlement of Metlakahtla was founded. In 1881, Mr. Duncan, refusing to work on the lines of the Church of England, ceased to be a missionary of the Church Missionary Society. In 1887 he removed, with some hundreds of Indians, to a place 70 miles distant, within the territory of Alaska, renouncing allegiance to the Queen of England and coming under the protection of the United States, and the station at Metlakahtla was put in the charge of other missionaries sent out by the Society. Other missionary settlements are at Kincolith on the Naas River, among the Kitiksheans of the interior, the Hydahs of Queen Charlotte's Islands and the Kwa-gutl Indians of Fort Rupert, at all of which zealous work is being carried on.

There are (1901) 10 stations, 25 missionaries, 37 native workers, 407 communicants and 14 schools with 427 pupils.

The Church Missionary Society carried on missions at Antigua, Jamaica, Trinidad and at various points in British Guiana for many years with considerable success.

PERIODICALS: *Church Missionary Intelligencer* (Official organ of the CMS); *The Church Missionary Gleaner; Mercy and Truth* (Record of CMS medical work); *Awake* (For larger Sunday-school scholars); *The Round World* (for children). The above are all published monthly. Quarterly papers for the use of collectors, Annual *Almanack;* Annual Pocketbook and Diary, and Extracts from Annual Letters of Missionaries are also published. Stock (E.), *History of the Church Missionary Society,* 3 vols., London; Hole(C.), *Early History of the Church Missionary Society* (to 1814), London; *Church Missionary Atlas,* London.

CHURCH OF SCOTLAND; Foreign Missions of. See SCOTLAND, ESTABLISHED CHURCH OF.

CHURCH IN THE MISSION FIELD: When the missionary or evangelist has felt the joy of leading men to accept Jesus Christ, the fact comes to light that the converts have to be taught the necessity of growth as the well as the means of growth. Each individual has to be established in the faith, to be taught to recognize and resist temptation, the idea of which is new to him, and to be guided and encouraged as he tries to throw off old evil habits of thought and action. He cannot otherwise become an aggressive worker to win others to allegiance to Christ. Moreover, the new converts cannot stand alone. For their own growth they need mutual support, and to maintain their position in an unfriendly and often actively hostile community they need organization. Only through becoming members of an organic body can the converts take the place in the community and the nation where their influence will tell in support of the principles which they profess.

The church, then, must be established early in the mission field as a permanent institution for the work of Christ. It must be organized in all its different departments, placed on a firm foundation of faith, self-support, activity; be provided with the various means essential to its continued existence and growth. The Christian community is to be permeated with Christian ideas, its social life freed from its evil associations, brought into accordance with the spirit of the Gospel, its customs purified, its aims enlightened, its national life made to include a genuine and true patriotism. And so on in all the endless lines that open up before those who study what is involved in the establishment of the kingdom of God upon earth.

It is a mighty task, more perplexing even than the corresponding undertaking at home. And retrospect only makes its difficulties stand out more prominently. No one can travel in the Levant, over the roads where Paul led the way in Christian work, recall the story of those first centuries of growth, remember the subsequent centuries of stagnation and decay, and not wonder whether the story is to be repeated in the churches now gathering in every city and town, and almost in every village. Modern Christians are no more sincere or devoted than those of earlier ages; modern missionaries no more earnest or skilled than the apostles and fathers.

The question of the need of new church organization has come up with some sharpness in connection with work among the Oriental churches and in Papal lands. When missions were commenced in the Levant among the Armenians, Nestorians, Greeks, etc., there was no plan for a separate church organization. The old one, it was thought, was good enough, and it was far better to utilize that, introducing whatever of reform was necessary or practicable, but not severing historic associations, especially in view of the fact recognized by all, that the creeds of these old churches were essentially in accord with those of the more modern bodies. This, however, was found to be impracticable, and as a matter of fact Protestant church organizations have been formed wherever evangelical missionaries have gone.

The need to organize the Church on the mission field being admitted, the duty of doing this work falls upon the missionary. We expect the missionary to be fully occupied in winning converts. In actual fact, however, in every successful field, it speedily comes to pass that the greater part of the converts are won by the efforts and the explanations and the pure lives of the native Christians. This the native believers can do. But that which they cannot do for a long time is to bear the burden of culture and nourishing those whom they have been the means of winning to Christ. This duty falls upon the missionary.

The problem of the missionary is one of securing growth and permanency. The question he is constantly striving to solve is that of how to hold the vantage-ground gained, and make it the point of departure for new achievements. Here certain essentials must be kept in mind: 1. The development and growth of the individual church and community must be natural, not forced. The genius of the people must be studied, and that line of development found which will bring out the best that is in them. South Sea Islanders cannot be transformed into Europeans or Americans, and every effort so to transform them results in harm. At the same time they must be something different from what they have been. While it is doubtless true that the Asiatic must remain an Asiatic, it is also true that the Christian Asiatic must be as different from the heathen or Mohammedan Asiatic as the modern Englishman is from his Norman-Saxon progenitors. 2. The element of time is very essential. Occasionally a sudden transformation will come; but this is the exception rather than the rule, and he works best who is not disturbed if he has to admit that the growth of Christian character is a slow process. 3. The methods adopted must be primarily constructive, not destructive. Their object is to build up rather than to tear down. They do not attack systems, but seek to help individuals. It is not that Islam, Hinduism, Shintoism, or Fetishism is to be overthrown, but that individual Muslims, Hindus, Japanese, Africans, are to be guided and assisted into a higher life.

It is not only natural but inevitable that that organization should take the form to which the missionary himself has been accustomed; and thus it happens that the mission church, in most cases, seems to be an extension of the denominational differences of the home lands. It is, however, to be said that those differences are seldom if ever as sharply defined in foreign fields as at home; and, except in case of divisions resulting from unworthy rivalry, the members look upon them as formal rather than substantial. There are some cases where the form of church organization has been left almost entirely to the choice of the native community, with the result of an occasional departure from the denominational usage of the missionary. This is especially true of missions conducted by the Congregational Churches of England and the United States. As a rule, however, the polity preferred by the missionary has prevailed, not because he has felt tied to it, but because in it he can work to better advantage for the best growth of the Church.

More perplexing and difficult than any question of form is that of the material to be used in organizing the new church. Men who apply to be received are actuated by different motives, not necessarily from hypocrisy so much as from sheer inability to comprehend the insistence of Christianity upon moral purity. The duty of discovering who are sincerely and steadfastly taking the way that leads upward is a very weighty responsibility to be thrown upon a foreigner who has been but a few years among the people of the field.

In this connection the fixing of conditions upon which candidates may be admitted to baptism often seems difficult to the missionary. The time may arise in every field which has been known in many, where the tide turns in favor of Christianity and men come in crowds asking to be baptized. Sometimes the conversion of a leading man may bring a whole village in seeming sincerity to desire to be received into the Church. It is often argued that baptism cannot be refused to those who declare their faith in Jesus Christ. It is even urged that to take such applicants when they are in the mood to be received is the wisest course; since after they are committed to Christianity their instruction and development is facilitated. The fact that some of those received in this manner and in this expectation fall away and continue evil practises, bringing discredit upon the name of Christ because they have been classed as Christians by their neighbors, seems to be a conclusive reason for avoiding haste in receiving such candidates.

For the good of the Church it seems to be a duty to make careful choice, to be patient in giving instruction, and to be slow in coming to conclusions as to the principles of the new converts. Far better is it to watch such in order to be sure that the vitality of growth is in them. Intelligence, progress in education, intellectual championship of Christian doctrine may not be treated as grounds for admitting converts to the church. A living faith in Jesus Christ, which has kindled in the heart a sincere purpose to live in Him and for Him, must be the condition of admission, or the Church will be uncertain in its growth and too feeble to stand in the midst of the hostile powers of pagan lands. A reasonable certainty that the applicant has made the choice to turn from the low and self-seeking life to which he has been accustomed, with earnest desire to live for the higher things that belong to God's kingdom, must exist before the candidate can be safely acknowledged as a follower of Jesus Christ. At this point practical proof of faith, through the life and its trend, should outweigh the most glib proficiency in expression of doctrinal soundness. The Christian is to be a temple of the Holy Spirit, and if that great choice has not been made which opens a way for the Spirit to enter the heart as a dwelling, it is dangerous to hope that membership in the Church will serve as an incentive to an ultimate self-renunciation thus belittled at the outset.

Another perplexity which confronts a missionary who would organize a group of converts in a newly fruitful field, is the choice of those who are to be office bearers in the Church. Some may be prominent through education. But a convert highly educated in Confucius or the Vedas is not, necessarily, qualified to lead his fellows in spiritual growth. Others may be socially prominent through their possessions or position. But men who have had influence in the heathen community because of wealth or rank may not be the best men to carry responsibilities in the Church. The tendency of Asiatics to suffer themselves to be led by such will, perhaps, add to the difficulty of placing the most spiritual men in places where their influence will be widely felt. But happily the missionary, by careful study, can hope to reach a clear understanding of the ideas and motives of those who make up the material for the new church. Furthermore, the wise missionary will take counsel with the native evangelist who has had dealings with the people, and who understands the people as the missionary cannot hope to do. By such means selection of men must be made upon whom so much of the growth and the strength of the Church will depend.

The question of securing a right basis for church membership opens up the whole problem of discipline in the new churches. Peculiar perplexities are thrown about this part of the education of converts from non-Christian peoples by the difference between the missionary and his spiritual children in mere matters of ordinary civilization. In this matter missionaries are constantly forced to remind themselves that the ideal African convert, for instance, should not be a mere ape-like caricature of an English or American Christian. The real difficulties arising from the circumstances of the newly converted Christian are too great to leave room for the introduction of artificial ones. Such a man is surrounded by untoward influences which long experience alone will fit a foreigner to appreciate. Ties of family or clan have a strength which we cannot easily gauge; usages suspiciously like pagan usages appeal to the convert under the guise of patriotism or nationality; superstitious reverence for witchcraft is inbred; feudal subservience to the will of the chief or the lord of the manor in respect to observances and feasts is not easily thrown off; caste affects not only the vision but the conscience of the convert. The missionary teacher of the newly developing church needs direct guidance from on high if he is wisely to separate in his own mind those points of unaccustomed conduct which may be tolerated from those which must be attacked, while the influences which lead to them are resisted with flintlike immobility.

It should here be noted again that the missionary unaided cannot hope to train men by church discipline. He must work with, and as far as possible through, fellow workers born in that atmosphere, and, therefore, knowing the impulses and ideas of the people living in it.

The difficulties which surround the question of church discipline on the mission field cannot be better illustrated than by the case of those converts who have been brought up to polygamy. It is easy to declare that a polygamist may not be admitted to church-membership unless he first ceases to be such by putting away all but one wife. Yet some missionaries have been led to take the ground that each case must be judged by itself, lest a greater wrong be done in dismissing the wives under a fixed rule which takes no account of their rights and their feelings. In some cases one of the wives of an unbelieving and polygamous husband has become an humble and sincere believer in Jesus Christ. To admit her to the church will be to relax the fiber of the whole body in its stand against polygamy. To refuse her admission will be to deprive her of privileges and gracious influences which she has not forfeited by any act of her own. To insist on her leaving her husband as a condition of admission to the Church will be to smite her in her most tender human affections, as tho in punishment for having followed in ignorance the current of usage, without conscious and wilful wrongdoing. Such a situation is one that demands the highest wisdom in dealing with its complications.

The one principle that has to be followed in teaching the young churches to maintain discipline is to preach—and repeat—and root in the hearts of the Christians who make up the church-membership the fact that their witness for Christ is to be a positive witness, and that it cannot have this aggressive quality unless each member of the church is a living epistle, known and read of all men. As the members of the Church grow into understanding of the nature of Christian purity, and grasp withal the idea that a church whose repute among the heathen is marred by spots has no power to witness for Jesus Christ, they themselves will find solutions for many problems of discipline with which the missionary could not cope.

This sense of responsibility to witness for Christ has another bearing so self-evident that it need only be alluded to here. From the very beginning the members of the young church must be made to feel that duty to their Redeemer requires them to tell others how great things the Lord has done for them. It is easy for the missionary to delay this teaching through sense of the slender knowledge of the best of the new believers. But delay here is fatal. None are so ignorant, who have learned to try to follow Jesus Christ, that they have no light to give their neighbors. In pagan lands a glimmer of light is precious to those who live in darkness profound and eternal. Moreover, the convert who begins with regarding his Christian privileges as given him for his own happiness alone will find it hard ever to shake off that heresy. Without recognition of responsibility to take up the very work which Jesus Christ did when upon earth, the Church will lack the first elements of strength and stability. The members of the Church must gladly render others the loving service that reached them and awakened their desire for right living, or the Church will slowly die. The condition of life in the Church everywhere is that it must be constantly winning others to allegiance to its great Head.

The Church must not only learn from the very first to be exemplary in pure and honest living, and in eagerness to give to others the good which itself enjoys, but it must also learn from the first to give generously for the support of its own institutions that it may stand upon its own feet. This is no place to enter upon any discussion of the doctrine of "self-support" as it is technically called on the field. The principle is now universally admitted that the newly constituted church-members must be taught to give for the support of their own pastors and for other expenses of the church life. But missionaries often err in delaying to press this duty home upon the minds of converts at the very beginning. This is partly due to lack of understanding of the fact that the Church, which has learned to expect subsidy, will fall into confusion the moment the missionary and his subsidies are taken away. It is more often due to indolence. The missionary sees that the sums required are very small and feels that it is far easier to give them himself than to extract them from the pockets of people who seem, and who probably are, poverty-stricken. There should never be a day's delay in teaching the converts their duty to set aside, as the Lord has prospered them, funds for His uses.

The Church on pagan soil which has grown to the point of being what it can be among the forces of reform; able to stand without aid and incentive from foreign lands; to govern itself, to maintain itself, and to use with eager initiative every opportunity to advance the interests of the Kingdom, is thereafter the leaven hid in the mass, performing the part falling to it in its Master's plan. It has become a center whence Divine influences will radiate with beneficent results while life continues. And there is no earthly joy greater than that of the missionary in a land of thick darkness, who has served as an instrument in the hand of God to lead converts during their early essays at walking in the Way; to organize them into a church and to train them to fruitful activity in carrying on the work of Christ for the world. That missionary has had to efface himself, to cast himself upon his Leader for guidance in many a perplexing crisis; but he has had a share in a work of eternal duration, and whose pervasive influence none can measure. For such, a living church is the very body of Jesus Christ, precious in itself, and beyond price in its worth to the nation which is blessed by its presence.

CIENG BAU: A town in the province of Fokien, China, situated about 10 miles S. by E. of Kien-ning. Station of the CEZMS (1897), with (1902) 3 missionary women, 2 native women helpers, 1 elementary school, 1 high school and 8 converts brought in for baptism during the year.

CIUDAD DEL MAIZ: A town in the State of San Luis Potosi, Mexico, about 70 miles E. of the capital of the State. Station of the Associate Reformed Presbyterian Synod of the South, with 1 missionary and his wife, 1 missionary woman, 6 native workers, men and women, 2 places of worship, 2 elementary schools, 1 Sunday school, a Young People's Society and 54 church members

CITY MISSIONS: This term designates, in current usage, those agencies and methods of work through which the church ministers to the material and spiritual needs of the laboring classes and of the poor in the great towns and cities of Christian lands. It includes all efforts of Christian love for the ingathering and instruction of neglected children, the evangelization of the masses, the relief of the poor and wretched, or the rescue and reforming of the depraved and the vicious.

Great cities in all circumstances require work of this sort; its spirit and the model may be studied in the attitude held by our Savior toward Jerusalem. A large population inevitably includes a considerable proportion of poor people who need from their more prosperous neighbors the helping hand. The poor are compelled by the exigencies of their condition to inhabit the less desirable parts of the town. There is also certain to be a criminal or vicious element in every large town, for town life offers peculiar opportunities for escaping the restraints of public opinion, for evil companionship, and for vice and crime. It is therefore especially alluring to the profligate and the dishonest. Thus the vicious also tend to herd together; and since poverty promotes vice and vice begets poverty and crime, all three are frequently found together in regions which are by choice as far as possible from the churches and good and helpful influences. Such places unless subject to the patient and vigorous application of moral disinfectants become hotbeds and nurseries of every sort of evil.

But the amount and importance of the missionary effort which cities demand has been immeasurably increased by those social and industrial changes which modern times have brought to all civilized nations. The discovery of the steam-engine, its application to the industries, the development of machinery, with thousands of attendant discoveries and inventions, have together resulted in the transfer of a great share of the world's work from the rural districts to the towns, whither the world's workers have followed it. This immense development of manufactures and consequent increase of traffic caused cities in all civilized lands to grow with amazing rapidity throughout the 19th century, and especially during its latter years. It would be difficult to parallel in all history, in a city of the same size, the growth, for example, of Chicago, which in 1880 numbered 503,185 souls, in 1890, 1,098,576, and in 1900 had reached 1,698,575.

If the city churches had nothing more to do than to keep pace with the expanding population, their task would be one of no small magnitude; but other elements have entered into the problem which very seriously enhance these difficulties. The steady flow of the human stream into the great towns has crowded them to an oppressive and truly terrible degree. Such overcrowding has had a twofold evil effect upon the artisan; it has prodigiously increased his rent, plunging him into so much the deeper poverty; it has driven him into narrow, and more narrow quarters, until it has stripped him of every semblance of a home.

The census of 1880 reported one-third of the families in Glasgow as living in a single room, and another third as occupying but two rooms. Less than one family in ten in the Scottish metropolis enjoyed so many as four rooms for its home. Health and morality seem alike impossible to children brought up under such conditions. New York is even more straitly crowded than any of the old World cities, two-thirds of its people living twenty to each dwelling house, while London has but nine and is steadily increasing the space for housing the poor. Out of this overcrowding has sprung the tenement system, a system by which several families, usually not less than six or eight, sometimes as many as twenty-five, have been huddled together under a single roof, with common entries and halls, narrow rooms, and dark bedrooms. This plan of housing the working people is the one that generally prevails in American cities, altho there are some marked exceptions, like Philadelphia. Fully one-half of New York's population of 3,437,202 souls are at present living in her tenement-houses.

The ordinary city tenement offers to its unfortunate inhabitants the poorest conceivable apology for a home. Its atmosphere is both physically and morally unwholesome to a degree, and fairly poisonous, notwithstanding the efforts constantly made in London and New York to remedy these conditions. The saloon is at the corner, the drunkard reels up the common stairs; the shouts of countless rude, neglected children fill the air with shrill profanity; the discordant notes of the neighbors' quarrels and the wail of sickly babes pierce the thin partitions. There is no quiet day or night, no privacy, no chance for the development of healthy family life. From the midst of such environments the city missionary must glean his scanty harvest.

The problem of city evangelization is further complicated by the fact that in their growth the great towns have a tendency to remove those portions of society whose influence would naturally be conservative and helpful from those who most need their help. The dwellings of rich and poor are more and more widely separated from one another. The most flourishing and able churches are farthest away from the fields that most urgently require their aid. The suburban movement, like a great eddy, draws off into the beautiful park-like villages about the town great multitudes of the middle-class folk—the bone and sinew of the churches' strength.

In addition to these difficulties, religious effort in the cities of the United States meets with an even more serious obstacle in the complex and confusing mingling of nationalities in the population which it seeks to win. The immigrants constantly pouring into our land settle for the most part, or at least so far as the more ignorant and undesirable classes of them are concerned, in the towns. They and their children it is that people the tenements to-day. Seventy-six per cent. of the inhabitants of New York, seventy-seven per cent. of those of Chicago and Detroit, and nearly eighty-three per cent. of the people of Milwaukee are either foreign born or the children of foreign-born parents. Every nation of Europe and more than one Asiatic nation has its colonies, one or more, in our metropolis; but among the tenements, at least, there is no American quarter. Being of many races and speaking divers languages, having very few and meager conceptions of religion, and being opposed by habit to the fundamental ideas of the Protestant religious system, these denizens of the tenements have proven exceedingly difficult to reach, and have rarely been gathered in great numbers into the churches of our fathers. The latter have depended largely for their increase on converts from families of American stock; but such families bear only a small proportion to the population of most of the great cities. This explains the fact that while in the country at large more than one-fifth of the people are members of evangelical churches, in the great cities the proportion varies from one-tenth to one-twentieth. The reason also appears for the fact that while church-membership in the whole country has increased much faster than the population, in great cities it has fallen behind the population.

Notwithstanding these obstacles and difficulties, largely, perhaps, because of them, the work of city missions has been making wonderful advances in recent years. The broadening and deepening of public interest in its problems, and the increased amount of wealth and talent devoted to its aims, have marvelously enlarged the field and the scope of city missions.

The following are some of the most marked characteristics of the new development:

1. The aim of city missions has enlisted for its various forms of work, men and women of fine culture and large abilities in unparalleled numbers.

2. It is adopted as a rule that Christianity should minister to all the necessities of the helpless and ignorant and degraded, not only caring for their spiritual needs but for their physical and intellectual needs also, and to do this by personal contact of individual with individual.

3. It is seen that alms-giving is rarely a benefit or a remedy, and a scientific treatment is applied to poverty, pauperism, and crime.

4. The mission Sunday school is extended to include week-day meetings and classes for the general instruction of people of all ages, and the children of the tenements are given, as far as possible, a substitute for their lack of home-life, through societies, clubs, reading-rooms, evening classes, industrial instruction, and the like.

5. "People's churches" are substituted for mission chapels, and are equipped by the employment of pastors, missionaries, and other helpers; and the work is made more intensive and their influence more far reaching by establishing "parish houses," with reading-rooms, club-rooms, class-rooms, gymnasiums, etc.

6. A deepening interest is seen among religious people in the needs of the poor which cannot be met by a tract or gift of money.

7. There is a strong movement toward cooperation between denominations, and between congregations in any one denomination. This is manifested in three ways: first, by churches in prosperous communities combining to sustain and enlarge the work of the churches among the poor; second, by churches of different denominations uniting in schemes of general evangelization, including the canvass of the whole congested district of a city; and third, by the multiplication of strictly undenominational religious enterprises in the cities, which spring up independently of the initiative of the churches.

8. Christian literature is deemed a most effective means of influencing the people who are drawn into relations with the city missionary. The Bible societies do an effective work with cheap editions of the Scriptures or parts of Scripture, and the London Tract Society, the American Tract Society, and similar organizations provide attractive tracts and leaflets in all languages. These are not only granted freely for the use of city missionaries, but are very extensively circulated by the colporteurs of the societies themselves.

Every city of consequence in Great Britain, the United States and Canada, and many on the continent of Europe is the field of some sort of city mission work. With local variations the same problems are everywhere met, the same general method prevails, and the same tendencies are observable. The general plan adopted is first to minister to the immediate physical wants of the poor, then to help the unemployed to find work. Missionaries in the service of that church go from house to house, from room to room, learning needs, helping sufferers to seek and find relief, and preaching the Word; not one apartment is left unvisited, and weekly reports are made, at personal interviews with the pastor. Money is not given to the needy except in special cases, tickets being used upon which the orders are given. Provision is made for the care of orphans, for securing change of scene and rest for the exhausted and for convalescents, besides clubs, societies, meetings, and classes. Great vigor of life is a mark of the work in its efforts to give religious instruction, yet nothing is spasmodic, for the people are lifted by degrees. They are first touched by the missionary in their homes, are then persuaded to visit the mission chapels, and thus are lifted a step higher. By degrees they learn to enjoy the prayer-meetings and are finally brought into the regular services of the Lord's house. Under this system there is no hopeless class, however abandoned the people may have been.

As an illustration of the practical operation of the modern theory of city missions the following list is given of works for the poor and ignorant maintained by a single church in New York: Besides the regular religious services of the church, there are maintained services, in three different localities, in English and three foreign languages. The church also maintains a course of lectures for women and girls; a course of stereopticon lectures for men and women; a charitable bureau to aid the needy; an employment bureau; a loan association; a penny provident fund; a Chinese protection society to prevent imposition upon the Asiatics; a medical clinic, a surgical clinic, an eye and ear dispensary, a girls' club, with club-room, baths, mutual benefit fund, and regular classes in sewing, dressmaking, typewriting, stenography, etc.; a girls' club house, where members can reside temporarily when out of work, paying $3.50 or $4.50 per week for board; men's club, with reading rooms, billiards, gymnasium, baths, classes in gymnastics, bookkeeping, drawing and modeling; boys' club, with club-rooms, baths, military drill, and classes in typewriting, bookkeeping, drawing, etc. In a well managed club of this class the boys take a strong interest because they are made to feel at home, and come in contact with those Christian workers only, who understand and sympathize with their impulses and their needs.

Another of the religious agencies working among the congested districts of the cities is a class of interdenominational enterprises, of which the New York City Mission and Tract Society (1829) may be taken as a type.

The objects of this corporation are to promote morality and religion among the poor and destitute of the City of New York, by the diffusion of evangelical reading and the Sacred Scriptures, by the establishment of Sabbath schools, mission stations, and chapels for the preaching of the Gospel and for the ordinance of divine worship. The business affairs and the estate of the corporation are managed by a board of fifty directors, who are chosen from different religious denominations.

The Society has erected churchly buildings, has organized independent congregations on the principles of Christian union and cooperation, with the Apostles' Creed as the symbol of faith, and with a simple form of church government. The ministers in charge are regularly ordained by some one or other of the evangelical denominations, and associated with them for counsel and help are church officers chosen by the people. These missions are constituted on the basis of the Evangelical Alliance and their places of worship are called "churches for the people." Some of these edifices are large, spacious, elaborate in their accommodations and of architectural comeliness, combining beauty without and comfort within.

The methods adopted by the London City Mission are much the same as those which are pursued in other great cities for the relief and evangelization of the destitute and vicious classes. Each missionary visits once a month about 500 families, or 2,000 persons. Their work is to act as pioneers in places where the faithful pastor may in due time follow. They read the Scriptures, pray with and exhort the people, give them tracts, see that the children go to school, and that every family is possessed of a copy of the Word of God. While the Society's missionaries are forbidden to give money or to so deport themselves as to be looked upon as mere charity agents, they render most effective service in bringing relief to those whose destitution demands immediate attention; but their constant aim is, through Gospel instrumentalities, to reach and renovate the character, and thus transform the personal and family life. When this end is attained the family is at once found to be lifted permanently above the level of vice and want.

The field in London is so vast that it may be rightly termed unparalleled, imperial and national in its proportions.

In order to come into effective touch with this vast urban field, the Society divides and apportions its laborers to different districts, classes, and trades, and encourages the use of every means which experience has proved to be effective in reaching and rescuing the fallen.

The following constitute some of the departments of labor: House-to-house Visitation; Mission Halls; Open-air Work; Special Missions to Bakers, Day and Night Cabmen, Canal Boatmen, Chelsea Pensioners, Coachmen, Grooms and Hostlers, etc.; to the Docks, to Drovers in Islington, to the Factories, to the Fire Brigade, to the French, to the Germans, Italians, Spaniards, Asiatics, Africans, Jews, and Foreign Sailors; to Hospitals; to Navvies; to Omnibus and Tramcar Men, Railway Men; to Post-Office Employes, Telegraph Boys, City Police, Metropolitan Police, Public-houses, Common Lodging-houses and Coffee shops; to Hotels and Clubs; to Builders on Public Works; to Soldiers in London and Woolwich; to Theater Employes; to the Welsh; to Workhouses and Infirmaries; and to Gypsies.

The magnitude, severity, and difficulty of the work will more closely appear from the following citations, selected from among many which have been published in the past in connection with the Society's reports: "I have paid," says one missionary, "during the past year 5,694 visits and calls, in which I read the Scriptures 4,671 times, besides offering prayer. To the sick and dying I paid 556 visits. I have given away 10,665 religious tracts and periodicals, and 12 copies of the Scriptures; 32 persons were induced to attend public worship, of whom 9 became communicants; 23 families were induced to establish family prayer; 15 confirmed drunkards were led to abstain; 5 backsliders were restored; and 3 couples living together unwed were induced to marry."

One appointed to work in the "Angel Gardens" because he was young and strong, found the "Gardens" were filthy courts of tumble-down houses, whose population of several thousands (in a space of 280 by 160 yards) were vagrants and criminals, many of the houses being dens of thieves, robbers, and murderers. "I had not been many hours at work," he reports, "when I was accused of being a policeman in disguise. At once I was hounded out by a desperate, howling mob of thieves and outcasts. Upon my return home I was so cast down as to be able to gain relief only in tears and prayer. Very cautiously I went to work next day; but upon ascending a very steep, rickety staircase, a woman with hob-nail boots came on to the landing and declared, with bitter oaths, if I came a step higher she would kick my eyes out; so I retreated. Desperate efforts to gain a footing were continued for several months, and so hard was the conflict that I have sometimes stood at an entrance to the district in silent prayer for a quarter of an hour before I dared venture down. This perseverance, however, with the Word of the Living God, was effective, and constant, brutal opposition was overcome, tho for long years I was subjected to low abuse and occasional acts of violence. No Christian but myself dared venture into 'Angel Gardens,' and I was therefore called to visit the sick and dying at all hours of the day and night, and many a strange scene I witnessed. In full day I saw a gentleman, who had ventured down the place, surrounded, his coat taken off and run away with. One morning I saw two women dragging a 'slavey' into the yard by her hair. A few hours after, the child of thirteen was found beaten to death in the yard. At another time I saw two women fighting, when one who had fallen dragged the other down by the long hair of her head, then bit pieces out of her lips and cheeks and spat them out of her mouth. One Sunday, on going out early, I saw a woman on the ground with the blade of a knife sticking out of the chest-bone. She had robbed a sailor of all his money, and he had stabbed her. I also witnessed a murder when a Spaniard killed a girl named Norah with a dagger, and before I could prevent it, he blew half his head off with a pistol. After I had succeeded in opening a room for meetings, and a ragged-school in the center of my district, I was often stopped in the service by cries of murder and by fights.

"After many years of unceasing effort I gained entrance into many rooms, and into most of the dens. My care for the sick and the children disarmed opposition; then, in room after room, attention was secured by the reading of the Bible. Friendship on the part of many took the place of hostility, and I have been rescued from a band of roughs by a powerful and savage Irish woman, who on that very evening was arrested for robbery, and was transported for five years.

"The work went on; people listened; the ragged school was crowded, and the meetings were well attended; soul after soul was brought under conviction, and many were gathered into the fold of Christ. The neighborhood was opened up to the clergy and consecrated lay-workers; sanitary and other improvements were made; and so, through the entering in of the Gospel, the district changed its character to that of a far more respectable place."

Another class of these religious agencies may be encountered in some of the cities of Europe, where they have sprung from the kindly interest of a single individual, like the old Belleville mission in Paris. A lady named Miss De Broen, a worker in the Mildmay Mission, London, being in Paris, just after the outbreak of the Commune, visited Père la Chaise. Only the night before 500 communists had been shot there, and the long ditch into which they fell one by one became their common grave. A crowd of women and children surrounded the spot; their grief and despair were terrible to see; and Miss De Broen longed to do something for their relief. Every man engaged in the Commune was shot, transported, or had to flee the country. Thousands of women were thus left destitute and unable to obtain work. Even the priests and Sisters of Mercy shunned them. No one cared for them. Miss De Broen raised money by personal solicitation, engaged a room, and, passing to and fro in the streets of Belleville, which had been the center of the Commune, she spoke to the poor women, saying that she knew of their distress, and that if they would come to her room they would receive five pence for three hours of needlework ; at the same time she told them that her chief object was to tell them of the Lord Jesus. The kind invitation sounded strangely in their ears, the greater number hardly understood it, and the first time only three were present. Eight came to the next meeting, and from that time the numbers steadily increased. The ignorance of these poor women was surprising, and at first they were rough and sullen. Many had seen their own little ones pine in the cold and hunger of the siege; others had lost all—husbands, sons, and brothers—in the war and in those last awful days of the Commune; all had known the agony of lengthened starvation, buoyed by false hopes and cruel treachery. Goaded on by pangs of hunger, some had concealed weapons in their clothing, and had attacked the soldiers unawares; worse than this, in their frenzy, they had done. But after only a few months in the sewing-class a great change had come over the poor creatures; no fierceness and no sullenness now, but an earnest, even a softened, expression appeared on many a face. In addition to the sewing-classes and Gospel meetings at La Villette, night-schools were soon opened for the benefit of many men who had been imprisoned, at the time of the Commune, but who, no charge having been found against them, were liberated after a few weeks. They could not read or write, and were glad to be taught. The **McAll Mission** in France is another instance of similar work.

The **Salvation Army** has proved a most effective agency for mission work in cities. Its methods and style of presenting religious truth, and the language used by its members, arrest and secure attention. It has been called a mission "from the lower classes, by the lower classes, to the lower classes." Whether this characterization is just or not, its members never forget that a large part of the masses whom they would reach will not listen to those who have not warm sympathy of feeling for them, and that they can receive impressions and ideas through the simple, perhaps rough, but picturesque language, only, which the common people use. Besides its regular religious services in its own halls or "barracks," in almost every city, even to the ends of the earth, which permits the practise, it holds street meetings where they are most needed —near the resorts of the vicious. Its groups of "slum sisters" seek out the sick and needy, and comfort or otherwise help the despairing. It also maintains labor bureaus; various simple industries where the unemployed, however unskilled, can earn a living; lodging houses for men; inquiry bureaus; day nurseries for the small children of working women; shelter houses for homeless women; missions for the rescue of women who have gone astray, and homes for such to use as a means to reform, etc. The Volunteers of America do a similar work in several American cities, and have found a way to lay hands upon criminals in prison in order to lead them to honest ways upon their release. Whatever may be said, justly, in the way of criticism, the Salvation Army and its offshoots or imitators have certainly had great influence in stirring up the churches to an appreciation of the needs of the poor, and especially of the power of direct contact to win and elevate the outcast.

One of the earliest steps taken by Mr. Hogg, the boy-loving merchant of London, when he decided that street Arabs must be saved, was to become a shoe-black himself for six months, that he might know the boys, their needs, and their thoughts. As Dr. Josiah Strong has said, such persons "are in their own persons a revelation of God, and are demonstrating to us what has been demonstrated to every generation since Christ, that His love and sacrifice can be shown by the personal love and self-sacrifice of His followers to the most ignorant, hardened, and vicious, and that with saving power." This readiness to give self for others must underlie any successful city-mission work. Its instances are made conspicuous, not alone in work like that of the Salvation Army, but in the work of the Young Men's Christian Association and especially of the University Settlements in the great cities. It is through watching such methods that we see and realize that no poor and ignorant person is ever treated as Jesus would treat him when sent away with a mere gift of money.

The Boys' Club House, not connected with any church but exercising a strong uplift both moral and spiritual through bringing neglected boys into touch with those who have not been neglected, is an institution already developed into a power in many cities. New York has a number, of which the largest, with a membership counted by thousands, is the one built by Mr. Harriman at the corner of 10th Street and Avenue A. The type of this class of institutions can best perhaps be seen in the Polytechnic in London. This institution began when Mr. Quentin Hogg, at the age of 18, one evening in 1863 sat down under an archway in a London street, with a candle stuck in a bottle for light, to teach two street Arabs to read the Bible. It is now a vast enterprise equipped to win and develop and transform into useful and trusty men, the boys of the slums and the boys to whom poverty permits no respite for improvement. There are ten thousand members, and its graduates all over the world loyally help on its work. Such clubs are of priceless value, both in what they prevent and in what they secure.

While these religious agencies may be encountered in almost all cities in England, the United States and Germany, and while they are carried on by all denominations, including Roman Catholics and Hebrews; and while in Roman Catholic countries the various religious orders conduct city-mission work on very similar lines, such religious agencies are not by any means the only ones working for that general uplift of the poor which we have described as a part of the object of city missions.

So far as the purpose is concerned in beneficent care for their poor and their laborers, many municipalities do true city mission work by applying disinfectants to the hotbeds of vice and restoring home and family life destroyed by the congestion of cities. The work of Glasgow in reforming its tenement house districts would require a book itself, if the full and far-reaching results were to be made clear, of an intelligent and kindly interference of a city government. The introduction by law of decency, some measure of privacy, opportunity to enjoy light and air, and other inspiring improvements in the tenements, and the establishing of little parks and breathing grounds and play-grounds for the poor, tend to lift them out of depths to which the greed of landlord and employer has sunk them. This is true missionary work, altho cities do not commonly call their efforts in this direction by that name. Of the same class are a host of beneficent enterprises, found in greater or less degree in all cities, which do one part of the work of the city mission. An instance of such an instrumentality for improvement in the City of New York is the Charity Organization Society, founded in 1883, as a sort of link between the different charitable resources of the city, whether religious, denominational, or independent of church connection. It is entirely disassociated from questions of creed, politics, or nationality, and it does not administer alms from its own funds; but it advises, informs, and incites all who would aid in any way in bearing the burdens of the ignorant and helpless.

One of the benevolent independent bodies aiding the poor in New York is the Legal Aid Society, which comes to the aid of the poor in any case where deserving persons are unjustly treated by employer or landlord. Another is the Sanitary Reform Society, which sees to it that the requirements of the Board of Health as to tenement houses are obeyed. The number of the boys' clubs which are fostered on unsectarian lines is considerable in all the cities. Furthermore, besides the hospitals, there are diet kitchens for the sick poor, burial societies that provide for the needs of the dead, and many other enterprises aimed by kindly sympathy toward the help of those who need help. One of the most touching of such kindly undertakings is what is known as the Little Mothers' Aid Association, which has for its object the securing of needed rest for girls of from 10 to 14 years old, who have the care of younger brothers and sisters during working hours when the mother is away. It takes such girls to its Holiday House for a day's, or a week's rest and entertains them at Christmas or at Easter. Of the same class are the Fresh Air enterprises founded in every city, which aim to give summer outings and country life to mothers and children from the tenement house region. The money for the regular support of such agencies comes sometimes as thank-offerings, and often in large sums given unsolicited; but the means are never wanting.

As a result of all these evangelizing and humanizing instrumentalities there is less drunkenness, less pauperism, less crime, in the great cities today than ten years ago. The missionary spirit is abroad, and it is one of the modern miracles to see a city growing better while she is daily adding to her immensity.

Booth (C.), *Life and Labor in London*, 5 vols., London, 1903; *New York Charities Directory*, Charities Organization Society, New York; *Reports of the New York City Mission and Tract Society*; *Reports of the Brooklyn City Mission and Tract Society*; *Reports of the City Mission Society of Boston*; *Circulars of Information of the Armour Mission in Chicago*; *Reports of the Albany City Tract and Mission Society*; *Manual of the Union for Christian Work*, Providence, R. I.; *Yearbook* of the Cathedral Mission of the Good Samaritan, San Francisco; Hatton (G.), *St. Giles Christian Mission*, London, 1886; Dolling (R. R.), *Ten Years in a Portsmouth Slum*, London, 1896; Tollman (W. H.), *Industrial Betterment*, New York, 1900; Riis (J. A.), *How the Other Half Lives*, New York; Woods (R.A.) *Americans in Process*, Boston, 1903; Ufford (W. S.), *Fresh Air Charity in the United States*, New York, 1897; Am. Inst. of Social Service, *The Better New York*, New York, 1904; *City Missions*, Organ of the Foreigners' Mission, New York.

CIUDAD VICTORIA: Capital of the State of Tamaulipas, Mexico, situated about 125 miles N. W. of Tampico, at the foot of the Sierra Madre Mountains. Station of the PS (1880), with (1902) 1 missionary woman, 2 native workers, 6 outstations, 1 Sunday school, 1 elementary school and 31 church members. Station also of the American Friends' Foreign Mission Association (1887), with (1900) 1 missionary, 2 missionary women, 15 native workers, men and women, 8 outstations, 2 elementary schools, 1 high school, a printing house and book depot and 540 professing Christians.

CLANWILLIAM: Town in Cape Colony, South Africa, 140 miles N. by E. of Cape Town. Population, about 7,000. Climate, temperate and healthy. Station of the SPG (1898), with (1901) 1 missionary and 175 professing Christians.

CLARENDON: A town in the island of Jamaica, W. I., circuit of the United Methodist Free Churches (1858), with (1901) 1 missionary, 31 native workers, 4 places of worship, 4 Sunday schools, 3 day schools, and 236 professing Christians.

CLARK, Ephraim W.: Born Haverhill, N. H., April 25, 1799; graduated at Dartmouth College, 1824; Andover Theological Seminary, 1827; ordained at Brandon, Vt.; sailed as a missionary of the ABCFM, November 3, 1827, for the Sandwich Islands, reaching Honolulu, March, 1828. In 1852 he went with the first company of American and Hawaiian laborers to assist in commencing the mission in Micronesia. In this duty he represented the Hawaiian Missionary Society. In 1863, having been for fifteen years pastor of the large First Church at Honolulu, he resigned the pastorate, partly because of insufficient strength, but mainly that he might engage more fully in Bible revision. Having spent a year on that work at the islands, he was sent to New York in 1864 by the mission to superintend the printing of the Hawaiian Scriptures by the American Bible Society, reading proofs, preparing references, etc. This was followed by the translation and printing of the Tract Society's Bible Dictionary, and several other books and tracts. The last work completed was a hymn and tune book. He did not return to the islands. He died July 16, 1878, aged seventy-nine.

CLARK, Robert: Born 1825, at Harmston Vicarage, Lincolnshire. He took his degree as twenty-eighth wrangler at Trinity College, Cambridge, and was at once ordained to be his father's curate. In 1851 he offered himself to the CMS, and was sent to the Punjab Mission. He was one of the first two missionaries of the CMS to the Punjab, being stationed at Amritsar. In 1854 he was one of the first two CMS missionaries to Peshawar, and went there at a time when many believed that preaching the Gospel would be followed by assassination of the preacher. In most of the important stations in these provinces he did pioneer work. The most of his missionary life, however, centered at Amritsar. As secretary of the Punjab Bible and Religious Book Societies, he did much to provide and diffuse Christian vernacular literature. He was a good organizer, knowing how to make the most of men. In 1877 he organized the Punjab Native Church Council, and in the following year he established the Alexandra Christian Girls' School at Amritsar. After the publication of his Commentaries on the Gospel of St. Matthew, St. John, and the Acts of the Apostles, he received a Lambeth degree of Doctor of Divinity. Dr. Clark retained the office of Chairman of the Church Council for nearly ten years, the secretaryship of the CMS Mission till 1897, and the honorary secretaryship of the CEZ for a longer time. In 1900, the seventy-fifth year of his age and the forty-ninth of his missionary career, he entered his rest at Kasauli, in the Himalayas.

CLARKABAD: A Christian village in the district of Lahore, Punjab, India, situated about 45 miles S. W. of the city of Lahore. Station of the CMS (1869), with (1901) 2 women missionaries, 9 native workers, men and women, 1 chapel, 2 elementary schools, and 219 communicants. Also station of the CEZMS (1882), with (1902) 1 woman missionary, and 1 orphanage with an industrial department.

CLARKEBURY: A town in the northeastern part of Cape Colony, S. Africa, lying about 22 miles S. W. of Umtata. Station of the South Africa Wesleyan Methodist Missionary Society, with (1900) 1 missionary, 37 native workers, 9 preaching places, 8 Sunday schools, 2 high schools, 1 industrial school, and 600 professing Christians.

CLARKSON: Station of the Moravian Missions (1839) on the southern coast of Cape Colony, S. Africa. It is pleasantly situated on a mountain slope, about 80 miles W. of Port Elizabeth. The name of the settlement is that of a philanthropist who contributed largely toward the expense of the station's establishment. The present force at this station consists of 1 missionary and his wife, and 27 native workers, men and women, with 3 places of worship, 2 schools, and 214 communicants.

CLAY ASHLAND: A town of Liberia, West Africa, on the St. Paul's River, northeast of Monrovia. Station of the PE (1853), with (1901) 1 lay missionary and his wife, 2 native workers, 1 place of worship, 1 common school, and 25 communicants. Station also of the ME, with (1902) 1 native worker, 1 preaching place, and 81 professing Christians.

CLAYOQUOT: A settlement on the western shore of Vancouver Island, British Columbia; station of the Methodist Church in Canada (1899), with (1900) 1 missionary physician and his wife, 1 Sunday school, a dispensary, and 8 professing Christians.

CLYDESDALE: A town in Cape Colony, S. Africa (Griqualand East), situated 60 miles S. W. of Pietermaritzburg. Station of the SPG (1871), with (1900) 1 missionary, 18 native workers, 8 places of worship, 6 elementary schools, and 333 communicants.

COAN, Titus: Born at Killingworth, Conn., February 1, 1801; died at Hilo, Hawaii, December 1, 1882. In August, 1833, under the direction of the American Board, Coan sailed on a mission of exploration to Patagonia, and with Rev. Mr. Arms he was set ashore among the savages of Gregory Bay. For several months Coan and Arms lived among the ferocious nomads of the eastern coast of Patagonia; but the savages becoming suspicious of their motives, they escaped, returning to New London in May, 1834. Mr. and Mrs. Coan arrived at Honolulu, June 6, 1835, and the following month they reached Hilo. Upon his arrival Coan found that some leaven of the Gospel had already been cast into the lump of heathenism; missionaries had resided here for brief periods; schools had been established; one-fourth of the natives could read; and there was a church of thirty-six members. In three months' time he began to speak in the native tongue; and before the year closed he had made the circuit of the island by canoe and on foot, a trip of three hundred miles. He was incessant in his labors. He preached forty-three times in eight days, examined twenty schools and more than 1,200 pupils, conversed personally with multitudes, and ministered to many sick persons during a tour of thirty days through the island. On a tour made in the latter part of 1835, signs could be seen of the coming Pentecost. Multitudes gathered to hear the Word; and so eager were the people to hear the message of salvation that one morning he was constrained to preach three times before breakfast, which he took at ten o'clock. In 1837 the great revival commenced. Nearly the whole of the population of Hilo and Puna attended religious services; the sick and the lame were brought in litters and on the backs of men; and at any hour of the day or night a tap of the bell would gather thousands at the places for prayer and preaching. The great harvest years were 1838 and 1839. Seven or eight thousand natives had professed conversion; but very few had thus far been received into the Church. The utmost care was taken in selecting, examining, watching, and teaching the candidates. The first day of July, 1838, occurred the greatest accession to the Church; 1,705 took upon themselves the vows of God that afternoon; and 2,400 communicants sat down together at the table of the Lord. During the five years ending June, 1841, 7,557 were received into the Church at Hilo; and these composed about three-fourths of the adult population of the parish. To show the abiding result of this wonderful work of grace, about one in sixty came under discipline; the greater part of these were restored, and very few were finally cut off. Under the most careful training the people became more and more settled in faith and morals; and probably to-day the ratio of people in New England who cannot read and write is greater than among the Hawaiians in Hilo and Puna. In 1867 the old church was divided into seven local churches, six of them with native pastors. Mr. Coan's two books, *Adventures in Patagonia* and *Life in Hawaii*, are of great interest.

Coan (Mrs. L. B.) *Titus Coan*, Chicago, 1885.

COCANADA: A city in the Godavari district, Madras, India, situated 86 miles S. W. of Vizagapatam; navigable canals connect it with the Godavari River. Population (1891) 40,600, of whom 90 per cent. are Hindus. Station of the BOQ (1874), with (1902) 9 missionaries, men and women (two of them physicians), 19 native workers, men and women, 3 chapels, 25 Sunday schools, 9 elementary schools, 1 high school, 1 training class for Bible women, 1 industrial school, a dispensary, a printing-house and 234 communicants.

COCHIN: A native state on the W. coast of India, between the Western Ghats and the sea, and north of Travancore. It has an area of 1,362 square miles and a population (1901) of 812,025. The prevailing religion is Hinduism. There are, however, some groups of the ancient Syrian Christians of the Jacobite church still remaining in this region.

The CMS commenced mission work in Cochin in 1817, at first in association with the Syrian Church. Since 1847 it has worked separately, altho the reform party in the Syrian Church aid its ministers in evangelistic effort. The CMS has 2 stations in Cochin with which 143 Christians are connected and with 1,144 pupils in the mission schools.

COCHIN-CHINA: A province of French Indo-China, lying along the coast to the south and east of Cambodia. It has an area of about 22,000 miles and a population of (1901) 2,968,529. The population is composed chiefly of Annamites, Cambodians and Chinese, with a certain number of Malays, Indians and Europeans. The religion of the people is for the most part Buddhism, with a considerable number of demon-worshipers, a few Mohammedans and about 75,000 Roman Catholics. The chief production of the country is rice, of which large quantities are exported to China. A considerable portion of the trade of Cambodia reaches the sea through the ports of Cochin-China, of which Saigon and Cholen are the most important. Saigon until 1902 was capital of French Indo-China and the residence of the Governor-General, who now resides at Hanoi in Tonking. Protestant missions do not exist in Cochin-China, but the Roman Catholic missions are pressed with vigor and success.

Mouhot (A. H.), *Travels in the Central Parts of Indo-China*, 2 vols., London, 1864; Lagrilliere-Beauclere (E.), *A travers l'Indo-Chine*, Paris, 1900; Aymonier (E.), *Le Cambodge*, 2 vols., Paris, 1901.

COCHRAN, Joseph G.: Born in Springfield, N. Y., 1817; graduated Amherst College, 1842, and Union Theological Seminary, 1847; sailed the same year as a missionary of the ABCFM for the Nestorians. He took the place of Mr. Stoddard as principal of the male seminary at Seir, and with that school his life's work was identified. From 1851 till the death of Dr. Stoddard, in 1857, the two were associated in the conduct of the seminary. Mr. Cochran then became principal and continued such till 1865. During those seventeen years it is said that he did more than any other man to educate and equip teachers and preachers for the Nestorians and for Persia. When he took charge there was no congregation or Sabbath-school; before the close of his life several churches were organized and a presbytery formed, embracing twenty-five congregations. He was a voluminous author and translator in the Syriac. He prepared a very complete Bible Geography and History, and several school-books, as Algebra, Astronomy, Natural Philosophy, and later, a valuable work on Pastoral Theology and Homiletics. He died November 21, 1871, after an illness of thirty days.

CODACAL. See KODACAL.

COIMBATORE: Capital of the Coimbatore district, Madras, India, situated at an altitude of 1,348 feet in a hilly country, 84 miles S. E. of Calicut. The climate is cool and healthy, tho malaria infects the regions at the foot of the hills. Population (1901) 53,080. Station of the LMS (1830), with (1901) 6 missionaries, men and women, 103 native workers, men and women, 29 Sunday schools, 52 village schools, 1 high school, 1 home for boy and 1 for girl pupils and 279 church members. Also station of the Leipzig Missionary Society (1860), with (1900) 1 missionary and his wife, 1 missionary woman, 34 native workers, men and women, 10 chapels, 12 schools and 984 professing Christians. Station also of the SPG (1895), with (1901) 13 native workers, 1 chapel, 2 schools and 187 adult baptized Christians. The PB also has 1 missionary and his wife there.

COKE, Thomas, LL.D.: A clergyman of the Church of England and a graduate of Oxford. In 1776 he became the intimate friend of John Wesley, and entered heartily into his plans for the spread of the Gospel. He worked with Wesley for 15 years as superintendent of his work. In 1786 he set sail from England to begin a mission in Nova Scotia under the WMS. Returned to England to raise funds for the WMS mission in the West Indies. In the course of ten years Dr. Coke made four voyages for that mission, and also visited the United States at the formation of the Methodist Episcopal Church. He superintended the work on the West India Islands, and under his wise guidance the mission prospered exceedingly. He now turned his attention to Ceylon and India. He was so anxious to commence this mission for the WMS that he offered to defray all the expenses himself, amounting to £6,000, and to go with the missionaries. His friends tried to dissuade him from this long voyage, but he said, "If you will not let me go you will break my heart." He sailed from Spithead in company with six others. On the ship he was taken ill; a shock of paralysis followed, and he was found dead in his cabin. He was buried at sea June 1, 1814.

Etheridge (I. W.), *Thomas Coke*, London, 1860.

COLAR. See KOLAR.

COLESBERG: A town in Cape Colony, S. Africa, situated 57 miles north of Middelburg, on high land (4,400 feet). Population, 2,000. Station of the South African Wesleyan Methodist Missionary Society, with (1900) 22 native workers, 4 chapels, 5 schools and 260 professing Christians.

COLLEGAL: A town in the Coimbatore district, Madras, India, 34 miles E. S. E. of Mysore. Population (1891) 9,900, for the most part Hindus. Station of the PB, with (1900) 1 missionary and his wife, 4 missionary women and 1 orphanage. The name is also written Kollegal.

COLOMBO: Capital and chief seaport of the island of Ceylon; situated on a peninsula on the W. coast. It resembles a European town. Population (1901) 158,228, Tamil, Singhalese, Europeans and Eurasians. It is an important missionary center. The BMS established a station there in 1812, which now has 1 missionary and his wife, 1 missionary woman, 1 native worker and a high school. Also a station of the WMS, with 10 missionaries, men and women, 99 native workers, men and women, 7 outstations, 17 elementary schools, 2 high schools, 1 college and 552 communicants. Also a station of the CMS (1852), with 14 missionaries, men and women, 143 native workers, men and women, 67 elementary schools, 3 high schools and 608 communicants. Also a station of the SPG, with 1 missionary, 15 native workers, 1 elementary school, 1 high school and 1 college. The Christian Literature Society for India has a missionary and his wife there with 8 native workers, a printing-house and a book depot. The YMCA (1896) also has a missionary and his wife there; the YWCA has a woman missionary, and the Salvation Army a post, of which the statistics are not published.

COLOMBIA: A republic of South America, occupying the northwestern corner of the continent, adjoining the Isthmus of Panama, and bounded on the east by Venezuela and on the south by Ecuador. The whole of that section gained its independence from Spain in 1819, being officially constituted December 27, 1819, but soon split up into Venezuela, Ecuador and the Republic of New Granada. In November, 1903, the state of Panama drove out the Colombian officials and declared itself an independent republic.

The language is Spanish and the religion Roman Catholic, tho other religions are permitted so long as their exercise is "not contrary to Christian morals nor to the law."

The ABS has an agency at Bucamaranga and the PN has 3 mission stations with 18 workers, men and women, and 6 schools.

COLON: Town of 4,000 inhabitants in the Republic of Panama, situated on the N. side of the Isthmus of Panama. Station of the Wesleyan Methodist Western Conference of the West Indies. The working force in 1900 was 1 missionary.

COLONIAL AND CONTINENTAL MISSIONS: These are missions established by the different churches of England, Scotland and Ireland, primarily for work among the English residents of the colonies and on the continent of Europe, and secondarily, to assist various evangelical churches in Europe in their own home work. They carry on their work by sending out special missionaries, appointing chaplains, assisting in the erection of chapels, giving grants in aid to local churches and organizations, assisting in schools, providing for divine service at army and navy stations, etc. One of their most important lines of work is that of supplying services at the various resorts of summer and winter visitors on the continent of Europe. Almost every prominent resort of tourists has one or more chapels, where there is preaching on the Sabbath by a minister, who is on hand also through the week to render assistance such as a pastor can give in case of need. These stations are in some degree, sometimes entirely, supported by the gifts of those who attend. But it is the rule that some one of these societies is the actual supporter of the services, without which the Sabbath of the traveler would give no opportunity for congenial worship. Another line of work scarcely less important than the so-called regular foreign missionary work is that of supporting those evangelical churches that, under great discouragements and amid much opposition, in Belgium, France, Italy, Spain, Bohemia, and Moravia, are seeking to stem the tide of priestly domination and preach a pure Gospel. Many of them would be not only weakened, but crippled and even overpowered, but for the timely aid received by them from the Christians of Great Britain, largely through the medium of these societies.

Many of the foreign missionary societies carry on a colonial and continental work of the above description in connection with their work for heathen and Mohammedan lands. Among these are the Society for the Propagation of the Gospel, the South American Missionary Society, the Methodist and Baptist Societies.

COLUMBA: A settlement in the Transkei district, Cape Colony, S. Africa; situated about 18 miles S. E. of Butterworth. Station of the UFS (1878), with (1902) 1 missionary and his wife, 27 native workers, 18 schools, and 363 communicants.

COMBACONUM: The most sacred town in Madras, India; situated 22 miles N. E. of Tanjore in the most fertile part of the Cauvery River delta. Population (1901), 59,673, ninety-five per cent. of whom are Hindus. Station of the Leipzig Missionary Society (1856), with (1900) 1 missionary and his wife, 12 native workers, 10 chapels, 7 elementary schools, 1 high school, and 664 professing Christians.

COMBE. See PARAMARIBO, of which it is part, for joint statistics.

COMITY of Missions: Comity implies courtesy and kindly consideration and sympathy shown to others. The comity of nations is defined in the dictionaries as "that friendly and mutual courtesy under which various beneficial acts and recognitions, not obligatory, take place between nations." A certain self-restraint or even self-denial accompanying such kindly courtesy is suggested by this definition. Since Christians do not feel self-denial in doing kindly deeds for fellow Christians, we must modify the definition slightly in this place. Interdenominational comity of missionaries, or comity of missions, is that friendly and mutual courtesy under which various beneficial acts and recognitions take place between missionary societies or missionaries of different organizations because they are working for one purpose under the one Master and Lord, Jesus Christ.

In the presence of the principle of love to all men explained and enforced by Jesus Christ, there is hardly need to point out other reasons why missionaries struggling with a gigantic task in an unsympathetic multitude should be kindly and courteous to one another. Yet other elementary factors enter into the obligation to cultivate comity in the enterprise of missions. These are underlying truths such as God's unswerving purpose that His word shall be as the rain which waters the whole earth, making it to bud and bring forth, and give seed to the sower and bread to the eater. Because of that eternal purpose the work of disseminating knowledge of the Gospel is one and indivisible. Again, the effective agency in this work is God's word and not man's deductions from it. Hence the resulting fruitfulness of barren lands shall be to Jehovah—not to the men who are used as God's instruments in the work, but to Jehovah—for a name. Another of these elementary factors is the aim of missions. This aim is not to publish a human philosophy of the plan of salvation. It is to make Jesus Christ known to those who know Him not, in order that they may yield allegiance to Him and follow Him. In such a work all evangelical missions are united, becoming branches of a single, vast enterprise in which self-will of men must be subordinate to the King. This implies that the heresy must be resisted which would rate differences of interpretation and outward practise as a division of Christendom. Denominational differences cannot destroy unity of purpose and action unless the spirit of self-will has taken the place of the Spirit of Christ as the impelling power. Those who are *in Christ* are one body. The conclusion is irresistible that Warneck has struck a right note in urging upon all evangelical missionaries the point that when evangelical denominations are admitted to "possess such a measure of truth as is sufficient to show a sinner the way of salvation," believing that salvation is not by any church but by the Lord Jesus Christ, comity of missions is the logical consequence. All those who, in love to Jesus Christ, labor for the extension of His kingdom are fellow workmen in the one undertaking that is directed by the Divine purpose.

Comity of Missions, then, implies on the part of the missionary: 1. A truly affectionate sympathy for all others who seek to advance the Kingdom; 2. Readiness to aid such fellow workers in their problems and difficulties; and 3. Revulsion from any impulses to foster selfish aims at the expense of other Christian laborers. In other words, Comity of Missions is the application of the Golden Rule throughout interdenominational relations. It is the exhibition by missionary workers of those very principles of love for God and man which they seek to commend to the adoption of heathen and Mohammedans. A practical result of comity to the lonely worker in a heathen land is a mass of kindly sympathy, of experience, and of fraternal support from fellow workers of other names and nations; for those who are cut off by their calling from home influences it provides a spiritual environment; it places the resources of every mission at the service of all, and it so unites the missionary interests in any heathen land that they cannot be attacked with impunity nor disregarded with temerity. While a lack of comity produces distrust, anxiety, resentment over injuries, and waste of strength, the practise of comity brings to all missionaries in any land a quiet confidence, a mutual support in prayer, a mutual trust, and a courage strengthened by the sense that the great aim is being furthered by many instead of by few. The truth has been gradually receiving emphasis in the mission field that converts in Asia and Africa are not to be taught to copy the customs and dress and mannerisms of Europe and America. Little by little this rule will be extended until it also deprecates the teaching of the forms and customs of merely European or American types of Christianity. For the rule of missions requires subordination of personal preferences, of private interests, and of national or denominational rivalries to the general interests of the Kingdom of Jesus Christ. The demand of this great interest is similar in kind to current demands for the subordination of personal rivalries and interests in great business enterprises to the needs of economical administration and larger strength and business success. The time has come when lack of comity imperils the whole enterprise.

Dr. W. Newton Clark has said: "It is the work of foreign laborers in the East to bring into existence a native evangelizing force and a body of Christians that can permanently maintain Christianity in all the future." But when this delicate and important work is anywhere in progress, if another denomination appears in that place claiming a mission to preach some denominational peculiarity of observance, it not only throws despite on the whole teaching of the earlier missionaries in the field, but, by supplying the people with numerous foreign preachers, it tends to destroy the possibility of growth of infant churches into self-reliant and permanent aggressiveness for the Kingdom. To a layman, accustomed to consider the claims of courtesy in dealing with strangers and even with rivals, it may seem incredible that Christians engaged in this struggle for a new race type in the midst of hostile masses of people are not always able to suppress personal tastes for the sake of such a cause. But lack of the spirit of comity can sometimes be detected even in the periodicals which represent the missionary societies. These sometimes declare that a territory as large as New York State depends for light upon a single missionary. In actual fact a dozen missionaries are in the district besides the one referred to, but they are not within the circle of vision of the writer, because they belong to another denomination. Or in another of these magazines one may read the report of a missionary who accompanies his list of the year's additions to his church with the naive explanation that the number would have been more, had not all been won from the church of another denomination—"since it takes twice as much effort to convert one who is already a Christian as it does to convert a heathen." Such peculiarities of missionary literature suggest the direction of the selfish discourtesy and unkindness sometimes practised by missionaries toward those of another denomination. Many instances might be cited of the entrance of some narrow enthusiast into the mission field of another evangelical denomination to ply the church members with objections to some detail of the teaching by which they have been brought to Christ, and to present with feverish industry enticements to enter a different fold. Then some veteran missionary, aghast at such intrusion, writes home in humiliation, "Men whom I baptized in infancy thirty years ago, and whom I have lovingly nurtured into Christian manhood, are now being invited by these newcomers, who have neither called on me nor seen me, to canvass the question whether or not I am a minister of Christ." Moved by such a spirit of discourteous rivalry, the intruding missionary gathers up native workers who have been dismissed for cause, and church members who are under discipline, and lavishes upon them sympathy for the harshness with which they have been treated. The case has happened more than once that a rival enterprise, entering a field long cultivated, has taken up and trusted a native helper dismissed for grave misconduct. The act causes scandal in the older church and double scandal when the unrepentant sinner, thus encouraged to be bold, repeats his misconduct in his new position. Such intrusions work far-reaching harm to the general cause of the Kingdom. A clear-headed missionary, grieved in soul at the short-sightedness of those who can see no field so attractive as one which is already occupied, says: "China can never be Christianized on the principle of putting half a dozen denominations together in one town. It is too big and too hard-headed." This contempt of comity causes what the late Dr. A. C. Thompson called "evangelistic anarchy." It affects not unbelievers but Christians; it is an utterly needless waste of forces, and it imperils the welfare of the Church as a whole. This blind and heartless proceeding is an outrage which, by contrast, throws emphasis upon both the meaning and the beauty of comity of missions.

Happily, discourtesy is not the rule of evangelical denominations on the mission field. Brotherly love is the rule. To quote Dr. A. C. Thompson again: "In general, Christian brotherhood is nowhere so warmly felt as among laborers from different sections of the Church, toiling in the same great harvest-fields of heathendom." The veteran expert on mission theory and practise, Warneck, says: "The concord between missionaries of the different societies is greater than the discord; the esteem shown on all sides is stronger than the distrust, and respect for one another's bounds is more general than infraction of them."

When infringements of comity occur through inadvertence or insufficient information, kindly negotiations may often save the day; as, for instance, when a few years ago the Reformed Church in America had its Arcot field in India entered for a sectarian raid by another zealous denomination. The Society calmly explained to the intruder's superiors the effects of such intrusion, and these wise and Christian men at home promptly ordered the indiscreet agent to leave the Arcot field and to save his energies for enlightening the heathen.

From the beginning of modern missions attempts have been made to secure full practical application on the mission field of the principle of comity of missions. A favorite experiment has been to attempt delimitation of fields or spheres of influence. The natural feeling underlying such efforts led the Baptist (U. S.) Triennial Convention, as long ago as 1835, when contemplating an enlargement of their enterprise of foreign missions, to authorize the board of managers to establish new missions in every *unoccupied* field. The theory of territorial delimitation has generally suggested that in fields already occupied missionaries be instructed to keep out of the districts where others are laboring, and that in new fields missionary societies arrange among themselves bounds within which each will conduct operations. It is then assumed that priority of occupation must bar other denominations from entering territories so assigned. The action of Abraham and Lot in dividing Canaan is often urged as a model to be followed by missionary societies. Rev. Dr. Alexander Duff, on seeing the envious glances cast by some of his colleagues toward a prosperous field occupied by another society, said: "I would as soon leap into the Ganges as to think of going to Tinnevelli except as a brother to see the good work that is going on." A striking instance of a similar comity was seen a few years ago in the Island of Fernando Po. The island was once occupied by the Baptist Missionary Society (England), until it was expelled by the Spanish Government. After many years people in one part of the island asked the Primitive Methodists (England) to send missionaries for their instruction. People in another part of the island asked the Baptist Missionary Society to send missionaries. About the same time Bishop Crowther, of the CMS, hearing that there was now toleration in the island, went there with a view to opening missionary work. Residents in the island immediately begged the Bishop to send them preachers, and put into his hands $1,000 toward the expense of building a chapel. But when the Baptists, who had a claim of former occupancy, and the Bishop, who had a claim of present readiness, heard that missionaries of the Primitive Methodist Society were already on the way, they both withdrew; the $1,000 was given back to its donors, and when the Methodists arrived they found a clear field. Similar cases abound of territorial divisions and of spheres of influence respected by the different societies. Recent action respecting mission fields in Porto Rico and the Philippines, taken in conference together by the several American missionary societies, seems to show that this method of securing the fruit of comity is practical and effective. Dr. J. C. Gibson, of Swatow (in *Mission Problems and Mission Methods*), has published a diagram showing in a very telling way the waste of legitimate influence by the missionary enterprise through crowding centers of influence too closely together. Yet, notwithstanding all that can be said in favor of the plan of territorial lines which aim to secure observance of comity by keeping denominations apart, the result is often satisfactory. Where a missionary society is laboring among people of which some clans branch off into a region inhabited by people of another race and language, and already occupied by another society, it claims the right to follow up the people, disregarding merely territorial divisions. The passing of boundaries is conscientiously defended as necessary in cases like that of the Reformed Presbyterian missionaries to the Nusairiyeh in North Syria and Cilicia, of the missionaries of the Methodist Episcopal Church among low caste people of the Narbada Valley in India, and of missionaries to the Jews everywhere. Furthermore, with the increase of Anglican communities, both native and foreign, in India, the Church of England has decided (in 1900) that missionary agreements as to "spheres of influence" can no longer be observed. The Church of England must work under the usual principles of parish and diocese in territory which is part of the British Empire. Moreover, aside from these cases of objection to the theory of setting off districts and spheres of influence, the plan is not entirely effective in practise. The real end sought through such divisions of territory, besides avoidance of overlapping, and wastefulness, is relief from injury through disregard of the principle of comity. But those who will not regard the principle of comity will certainly not regard territorial limitations that exist on paper only.

A source of many violations of comity on the missionary field is discontent of native workers with the rules of the mission, and especially with those tending to develop self-support in the churches. It sometimes happens that such malcontents offer to transfer their service to missionaries of another denomination. It requires both coolness and common sense to refuse such applicants. And yet to accept them without close scrutiny will be unkind and unwise. In 1838 native workers of the Church Missionary Society in India, having been dismissed for cause, offered themselves, together with the field and its equipment, to the London Missionary Society. Of course the offer was refused. At a later period an able native minister in the employ of the ABCFM in Turkey became dissatisfied and appealed to the Church Missionary Society, offering to convey his whole congregation to the Anglican Church if a missionary could only be sent to teach them. The CMS refused to enter the field of the ABCFM, and after a time the party, which had vainly hoped to profit by sectarian feeling, returned to its former connection. Many attempts have been made to secure a general adoption by the missionary societies of rules looking to the erection of barriers which will prevent one denomination from becoming a house of refuge for church members under discipline in another, and salary from becoming a lodestone to draw men from their posts. The case has even arisen where enactments have been sought preventing adherents from applying uncomplimentary names to the adherents of another mission. As a means of settling such grievances, the establishment of "boards of conciliation" by the different missions has often been proposed. The proposal has never met with general favor. For all such troubles of the missionary a sincere adoption of the principle of comity would be a sufficient remedy, securing the same ends as a cumbersome board of conciliation.

Discussions of these various plans for securing mutual regard among missionaries and missionary societies have proved the value of regular conferences between missionaries of different denominations. Such conferences are a regular event in India, China, Japan, South Africa, etc., and similar conferences are established between the officers of missionary societies in Germany, Holland, Scandinavia, Great Britain, and the North American Continent. These **Interdenominational Conferences** have proved potent agencies for fostering comity of missions. It now seems that what territorial limitations and detailed rules as to the minutiae of missionary practice have so far failed to secure in the way of mutual confidence and consideration is in a fair way to be secured through acquaintance and face to face conferences. It is now clear that, when missionaries of different denominations become acquainted with each other, they see that the aim of all is the same, and the spirit of all, the spirit of the Master. One of the more recent results of this mutual fellowship between missions of different denominations is the discovery that various forms of cooperation between societies are possible, and also advantageous to all. An example of such cooperation may be seen in the Madras Christian College, founded long ago by the Free Church of Scotland, and now subsidized by the Church Missionary Society and the Wesleyan Missionary Society, and patronized by all societies, so that it has become the great representative of Christian higher education in South India. A similar representative institution at Peking, China, seems likely to be the ultimate result of the destruction of Methodist, Presbyterian and Congregationalist colleges there during the Boxer troubles of 1900. In Japan, in Mexico, and in other fields the presses of different denominations cooperate in producing literature that all can, and do, use in evangelistic work. In several countries the different branches of the Presbyterian Church have secured a degree of cooperation amounting to organic union between their missions. And in Japan the world has seen the thrilling spectacle of all evangelical Christian churches cooperating in repeated evangelistic campaigns through a union of Christian hearts and abilities which did not originate so much with the missionaries as with the native Christians who demanded and would have it. When a stage of development has been reached that makes such things possible, the history of discussions respecting practical applications of the comity of missions seems to be near its close.

There may be advantage, however, in summarizing, before leaving the subject, the points which seem to be now settled as to the practical applications of the principles of comity in the broad field of the missions of Protestant Christendom. There seems to be general agreement that:

1. Careless overlapping of mission forces and needless reduplications of apparatus and plant is not only a sin against comity but against the Lord of all missions, Whose resources are thus wasted.

2. All evangelical denominations have rights which must be respected on the mission field; and these rights are equal.

3. The presentation to pagans or Mohammedans of an impression of division in the Christian ranks must be avoided by all possible means. Hence (a) Every society will abstain from efforts to draw converts from other societies or to prove to the public its own superiority to other societies; (b) In choosing fields of action each society should select places where it will come in contact with persons not reached by other societies; (c)

Missionaries of different denominations should meet together, at stated times, wherever possible, for prayer and mutual encouragement and stimulus, and should hold general conferences for exchange of views on missionary problems at regular intervals.

4. Financial or other stringency has taught all that cooperation between evangelical missionary societies must be so extended as to make needless the reduplication of publishing houses, hospitals, and institutions for higher education.

5. For the better cultivation of interdenominational comity missionary candidates should receive instruction on the subject, and official organs of missionary societies should give the public, besides information respecting their own work, ample descriptions of important results gained by others.

Realization of the meaning and the basis of comity of missions carries the mind to a fuller grasp of the fact that in the many-sided missionary enterprises of the various denominations we have before us a movement resembling the march of the different columns of a great army, each independent and differently circumstanced, but all moving under the orders of one Chief, upon a single strategic point, with the certainty that at the critical moment all will be there, all ready for action, and all glad harmoniously to apply their whole power to the one object sought by the great Commander. It is the victorious march of the armies of Jesus Christ which we watch as we see this steady development of closer relations between its units, even while they are absorbed in the struggle with antichrist. Or, to adopt the figure and language of Rev. Canon Edmonds, of Exeter, "As we look at the work of missions we are watching the coming down from God, out of heaven, of the city of God." Let there be no trifling at such a supreme moment of history!

Report of the Centenary Missionary Conference, London, 1888; *Report of the Ecumenical Missionary Conference*, New York, 1900; *Conference of Foreign Missionary Boards of the United States and Canada*, New York, 1893–1903; *Report of a Conference of the Foreign Mission Boards of Great Britain and Ireland*, London, 1901.

COMMERCE AND MISSIONS: Commerce is the exchange of goods, commodities or other valuable property between different peoples. It is perfectly proper to give extension to the meaning of the word, so that it shall include the interchange of scientific and ethical and social ideas between nations, since this is an inseparable adjunct of that intercourse whose object is barter and trade. But in this article the relation to missions of commerce in its narrower meaning will be briefly discussed in order to suggest (1) What Missions owe to Commerce, (2) What Missions have suffered from Commerce, and (3) What Missions have done for Commerce.

(1) Missions owe to commerce the means of transportation and of communication. The earliest missionaries were enabled to reach India and China and Turkey and the coasts of Africa by those means of transportation which commerce had already provided. If the London Missionary Society sent its first missionaries to the South Seas in a vessel especially fitted out by the Society, it was still as a commercial venture that the "Duff" undertook the voyage, and it was through trade that its expenses were paid. In our own day missionaries use, as they would use the natural productions of the earth, the great steamships, the railroads, the telegraphs and the postal facilities which commerce has provided for its own uses. Merely to suggest these things is to show the greatness of the debt to the enterprise of commerce under which missions must ever lie in respect to the means of reaching the ends of the earth.

To commerce, again, missions are indebted for security of abode in many lands. Bitterly as the East India Company opposed the entrance of missionaries into the field of its operations, this purely commercial corporation finally became the protector of missionaries in India during many years. Not only in India, but in China, in Turkey and in Persia, missionaries have owed their safety and their opportunity of access to the people, to those laws and treaties which were designed to secure liberty and security for traders. Missionary enterprises in all of these countries have been carried forward with great freedom because missionaries had a right to claim and to enjoy the same privileges of safe-conduct which governments had secured for the benefit of merchants.

Again, commerce has served missions in the line of discovery and exploration of unknown regions and of acquaintance with unvisited races. There is no need to enter upon details of this part of the debt of missions to commerce. It was Captain Cook's report of his explorations which led the first missionaries to Tahiti. And it was Stanley's long determined struggle to solve the puzzles of Central Africa which prepared the way for other missionaries to follow in the footsteps of Livingstone, and finally to present a civilized Uganda and a peaceful Nyasaland to the merchants of the world.

(2) Nevertheless, commerce has often hampered and sometimes vehemently opposed the beneficent undertakings of missions. There is nothing contrary to any law of God or man in buying a commodity where it is abundant, in order to sell it at a profit where it is scarce and in demand. But no law, human or divine, can justify a commerce which takes advantage of the ignorant and defenseless or selects for its traffic articles that injure, degrade or destroy. The African slave trade was a notable example of such conscienceless commerce which long blocked the progress of missions on the western coast of Africa. Dr. Paton's indignant appeals against the infamies of the liquor traffic in Polynesia, supported by a long series of similar facts from other parts of the world, show how commerce has sometimes set itself to uproot the beginnings of moral training among child-like races who cannot discriminate between the benevolent missionary and the unprincipled trader. One shameful particular of this complaint against commerce may best be set forth in the form of incidents of actual history, which are, unhappily, typical of facts which may be duplicated in many places.

In October, 1825, Rev. W. Richards and family labored alone on Maui, one of the Hawaiian islands. The crew of the English whaler "Daniel," Captain Buckle, because the native women did not visit the ship as formerly, complained to the missionary. Mr. Richards tried to reason with them, but they replied with threats of burning his house and butchering his family. The missionary replied, "Come life, come death, we cannot undo the work of God." Next day the captain promised peace on condition that their demands were complied with. He himself kept a native woman on board, for whom he paid $160;

and when, the day after, the sailors came with a black flag, knives and pistols, and, like their predecessors in Sodom, pressed toward the missionary's door, the clubs of indignant natives drove the cowards away. Through night and day a guard was needed to protect the missionary from Christian sailors. Two years later the British consul at Honolulu, with this same Captain Buckle and several foreign merchants, demanded of King Kaahumanu that Mr. Richards be punished for writing an account of these things to the American Board!

On another occasion Lieutenant John Percival, of the U. S. schooner "Dolphin," took ground in Honolulu against the law that indorsed the seventh commandment, and on Sabbath, February 26, sent a detachment to the chief demanding its repeal. They were driven out after they had broken the windows, and only the prompt rally of natives saved the missionary and his family from violence, because an officer of the navy of the United States of America vowed that the law should be repealed.

History is full of wrongs inflicted by civilized traders in the name of commerce upon trustful and ignorant peoples. More than one missionary has been killed because simple islanders thought in that way to punish the traders who had stolen men from the islands of the Pacific in order to place them as laborers in plantations on the other side of the globe. More than one desolating war has been waged in Africa because the brutal voracity of commercial agents was discovered and resented by its victims. Only when men shall carry on commercial enterprises in non-Christian lands with that regard for right and honesty and justice to which they are forced to bow when at home will commerce help, not hinder, the kindly purpose of missions.

(3) As to that which missions have done for commerce, it constitutes a debt as easily overlooked as the debt which missions owe to commerce. The manner in which missionaries serve commercial development is first, by becoming intimately acquainted with the people of a backward race, through learning their language and living among them, and second, by cultivating higher tastes and aspirations among them. Missionaries go to an uncivilized land possessing an admirable climate and fertile soil, but the people are too slothful to do more than consume the fruits that Nature offers to their hands. No sooner has the Gospel entered the heart than those same men wake up to the possibilities of development, and the demand for the supply of new wants at once necessitates the supplies of commerce. This leads them not only to procure decent clothing, but also comfortable dwellings and convenient furniture in place of their unfurnished huts, for good clothing calls for clothes presses, and a corresponding advance in all directions. John Williams found that in the South Seas savages did not care for civilization until the Gospel woke them to a new life. European houses stood for years in Tahiti and no native thought of copying them. Missionaries wore civilized clothing, but no Tahitian women felt the need of a dress till the power of a new life led them to desire to dress like Christians.

Sir Bartle Frere, familiar with heathenism both in India and South Africa, says, "Civilization cannot precede Christianity. The only successful way of dealing with all races is to teach them the Gospel."

The pervasive civilizing influence of the teachings of Jesus Christ can best be seen by turning back to the beginnings of missionary effort in uncivilized lands.

Rev. J. C. Bryant wrote in 1849:

"Of fourteen young men who have left my employ within two years, one has since been converted, and of course clothes himself; the rest go naked as before, showing how impossible it is to civilize men without first converting them. Wash a pig and shut him up in a parlor, he may stay clean for a while, but as soon as free he will return to wallowing in the mire. To try to civilize heathen without converting them is to try to make lambs of swine by washing them and putting on them a fleece of wool."

Rev. L. Grout says that, with the Christian Zulus a level field is plowed by oxen, but among the heathen in the same tribe woman is both plow and ox, cart and horse. She is sold for oxen, which are never yoked, but only eaten by their lazy owners. On the other hand Christians buy plows and wagons, build houses and furnish them. In 1865, 500 American plows were sold in Natal with a growing demand for saddles and harnesses, clothes, books and maps, while the heathen were still marked by nakedness and misery. To-day American trade with South Africa is progressing by leaps and bounds.

English missionaries in Canada had skilled workmen to teach the Indians how to labor. But they would not work. They preferred their wigwams and skins, their raw flesh and filth, till inward transformation through the Gospel led them to work for the improvement of their outward condition. The same is true everywhere. Civilization does not reproduce itself. It must first be kindled, and can then be kept alive only by a power genuinely Christian.

The English *Journal of the Society of Arts* states that in Lagos, Western Africa, a native built himself an elegant house, furnished it in approved style, and yet with his family occupied a hovel adjoining it. Would he have done so if he had been converted?

Dr. J. L. Wilson says of Western Africa:

"Something more is needed to civilize heathen than specimens of civilized life. This would imply that ignorance alone hindered their improvement, whereas there inheres in heathenism an aversion to those activities which are essential to prosperity. We look in vain for any upward tendencies in pagans till their moral natures are quickened."

So in Turkey, while those who do not read the Bible live on in their gloomy and comfortless abodes, chairs and tables, books and book cases, Yankee clocks and glass windows, mark the homes of Bible-readers.

A missionary in that land wrote in 1880:

"The Oriental left to himself is entirely satisfied with the customs of his fathers; no contact with western civilization has ever roused him from his apathy, but when his heart is warmed into life by the Gospel, his mind wakes up, and he wants a clock, a book, a glass window, and a flour-mill. Almost every steamer from New York brings sewing machines, watches, tools, cabinet organs, or other appliances of Christian civilization, in response to native orders, that but for an open Bible would never have been sent; and now as you pick your way along the narrow streets, through the noisy crowd of men, camels, donkeys, and dogs, the click of a Yankee sewing-machine or the music of an American organ greet the ear like the voice of an old friend from home."

Rev. Mr. Harris of the London Missionary Society reports progress made in the Hervey Islands. Thirteen years before, when he began his work there, only copra (dried coconut) was exported. Now, besides that, lime-juice, coffee, fungus and oranges and cotton are regular articles of export. This enables the natives to purchase the products of other lands. All in Mangaia, both men and women, are clothed in European garments. Some wear watches, gold rings, lace, and embroidery. Nearly all have umbrellas

Sewing-machines abound. Cups and saucers, plates and dishes, lamps, knives and forks, and clocks are in nearly all the houses. The islands furnish a good market for European goods. These material benefits follow, they did not precede, the Gospel. An aged Mangaian said recently: "I owe to the Gospel all these beautiful clothes in which I stand upright;" but the uprightness of the man was more beautiful than his clothes.

The entire cost of the mission of the ABCFM to Hawaii up to 1869 was $1,220,000. But none can deny that this money used in civilizing the islands and opening them to intercourse with the world was well spent on seeing that in 1901 the imports of the Hawaiian Islands from the United States alone were valued at $21,780,000. Similar results of missions may be seen throughout Micronesia and Polynesia, for room has been made for commerce by taming and elevating the people through the Gospel.

Rev. Dr. F. F. Ellinwood writes of the relation of missions to commerce:

Three things have been found almost universally true: I. The Gospel has always elevated the character and established the power of our civilization in whatever lands its influence has reached. More than once it has been confessed that England could scarcely have retained her Indian possessions but for the conservative influence of those missions which restrained injustice while they promoted intelligence and loyalty.

II. The first contacts of commerce are for the most part evil. Whether adventurers precede or follow the missionary, they blight society. Whalers in the South Seas, convicts in Tasmania, slave traders in Congo, kidnappers in Melanesia, opium dealers in China, and liquor sellers among the Indians and in Africa—all have proved a curse.

There was a time in San Francisco when the courts were paralyzed, and true-hearted citizens felt driven to send to Hawaii for a missionary to come back and establish a church at home. Even saloon keepers joined in the call, alleging that without Christian institutions no man's life was safe.

III. Improvement generally follows. Christian homes are established, and the missionary is supported instead of opposed. Dark as Africa now is, civilization there fifty years hence will be full of life and light. But we should hasten to allow equal rights natural to the humblest native; and the proudest Caucasian might must not make right, but weaker nations should receive the same treatment as the strongest. Treaties should not be made merely for the convenience or profit of the great powers of Europe, and commerce should be so regulated by the golden rule of love as to bless and not curse the nations with whom we have to do.

Thus commerce reaps lasting benefits from the services of the missionary in changing the motives and elevating the aims of savages through instruction in the Gospel of Christ. Such a case as that of Henry Nanpei, the Christian Chief of Kusaie, in Micronesia, is a type, with the help which he gave to the perplexed German officials by his sane, statesmanlike influence over his people, when the foreigners came to take possession of the land. A case like that of Kekela, the native missionary to the Marquesas, is a type, again, of the help of missions to commerce in another direction. Peruvian "Coolie Pirates" had stolen many of the islanders to carry them into slavery. A chief whose son had been carried off vowed to kill and eat the first white man that fell into his hands. Mr. Whalon, first mate of an American whaler, was that man; and Kekela, a native missionary, ransomed him from the angry father with a new six-oared boat that he had just received from Boston. Abraham Lincoln heard of it, and sent him a valuable present. Kekela wrote in his reply: "As to this friendly deed of mine, its seed was brought from your own land by some of your own people who had received the love of God. It was planted in Hawaii, and I brought it here that these dark regions might receive the root of all which is good and true, and that is love. How shall I repay your great kindness? This is my only payment—that which I have received of the Lord—love."

To quote the words of the late Rev. Dr. R. S. Storrs of Brooklyn: "Missions always assist commerce. This is not the first work of missions, but it is a work which goes on with the propagation of the Gospel over all the earth. For commerce and the Gospel are in harmony in this, at least, that the aim of each is cosmical, is earth-embracing. There is no tribe so recent or so ancient, no tribe so remote or so degraded that the Gospel does not seek it, or that commerce will not reach out far for access to it. They go together. The home of commerce is on the liquid bands that separate and yet unite and encompass the continents; the horizon of commerce is the rim of the planet and nothing less; and so commerce and Christianity go together, Christianity helping commerce. Not that our missionaries go out for that purpose—they do not barter life for gold. But, wherever their errand is, and wherever their teaching is felt, there the way is opened for a widening commerce. Intensity of conviction carries them where the commercial agent gladly follows, but would not lead."

Report of Ec. Conference of 1900, v. I., p. 325 ff., New York, 1901. Storrs (R. S.) *Missionary Addresses of*, Boston, 1901.

CONCEPCION: Capital of the province of Concepcion, Chile, S. America. Station of the ME, with (1902) 13 missionaries, men and women, 7 native workers, 7 places of worship, 13 Sunday schools, 1 elementary school, 1 high school, 1 college for girls, 1 orphanage, a Young People's Society, and 417 professing Christians (in the district).

CONCORDIA: A town of the Argentine Republic, S. America, situated on the Uruguay River, in the Argentine Mesopotamia. Population, about 11,500. Station of the ME, with 1 missionary and his wife, 1 native worker, 1 elementary school, and 57 professing Christians.

CONCORDIA MINE: A settlement in the northeastern portion of Cape Colony, S. Africa, situated 7 miles N. E. of the Ookiep railway terminus. Station of the Rhenish Missionary Society, with (1900) 1 missionary and his wife, 3 native workers, 1 school, 1 Sunday school, and 232 baptized Christians.

CONFERENCES ON MISSIONS (Interdenominational): When the revival of missions commenced at the close of the last century, the great effort at home was to find enough of those interested in the work to justify making a beginning, and the great aim abroad was to find a field where missionaries could labor unmolested. The whole undertaking was then so novel that those engaged in it had not yet begun to know their ignorance. For to carry on the work of missions with success requires not merely a spirit of obedience to Christ, but some knowledge of the difficulties to be met and the best method of overcoming them, and only an actual advance could indicate the points on which they needed light. The missionaries found, moreover, that the more they advanced, the more questions multiplied. Even success only furnished new problems to be solved, that had not occurred to them before. For the solution of these they went, first of all, to the Lord Jesus, and then, as in apostolic times, when an unlooked-for emergency arose, "the apostles and elders were gathered together to consider the matter" (Acts xv. 6), so now in the constantly recurring inquiries, "How can we remove this evil, and secure that result?" each group of laborers felt the need of counsel from others who encountered similar obstacles. Hence missionary conferences came into existence naturally and unavoidably. From the first they were often interdenominational in character, and, therefore, precious examples of the **Comity of Missions**. Such missionary conferences are of two classes: 1st, Conferences of the missionary societies; and 2d, Conferences of missionaries of the various denominations.

1. *Conferences of the Missionary Societies:* The first union missionary conference between British or American societies was held in the United States May 4, 1854, the various missionary societies being moved by the presence of the celebrated Dr. Alexander Duff among them to propose such a convention in order to manifest the real unity of Christians, increase interest in the work, and secure a more intelligent cooperation in carrying it on. So 11 missionaries, 18 officers of missionary societies, and 150 persons in all, met in the chapel of Dr. Alexander's church in New York, and continued together a day and a half. They considered the comparative advantages of concentration and diffusion in missionary work on the field, and came to the conclusion that the best policy was to equip commanding centers thoroughly, and then operate from those centers by itinerating in the regions round about.

They expressed their satisfaction also that so little interference with each other had occurred among different societies, and recommended an agreement that as soon as an evangelical society had occupied any field, it should be left in undisturbed possession.

The next interdenominational missionary conference met that same year in London, October 12 and 13, and was somewhat limited in the range of its discussions, for unfortunately only a few secretaries of missionary societies were able to be present.

Next in order came the conference on missions at Liverpool, March 19 to 23, 1860, where twenty-five British societies were represented by their officers. Two missionaries from America were present, and nearly one hundred other members took part in the proceedings. Two sessions of three and a half hours each were held daily, preceded by a meeting for prayer in the morning, and followed by a soirée in the evening. The whole ended in a large public meeting in Philharmonic Hall. Two stenographers reported the discussions, and the whole proceedings were published in an octavo of 428 pages; of these the index alone fills 38.

Eighteen years passed away after the conference at Liverpool before another was held in England, in the large hall of Mildmay Park, on the north side of London, October 21 to 26, 1878. The conference at Liverpool represented only 25 British societies, but this one 37 in all—26 British, 6 American, and 5 from the continent of Europe. This one not only dealt more thoroughly with particular fields, but also viewed each in its relations to the whole world, noting what had been accomplished, and searching to see what might be brought to pass in the near future. In almost every case the leading speakers were men who had been on the ground, and could speak from personal observation. The conference closed with a general meeting in Exeter Hall, which seemed to gather into a focus the interest and energy that had been steadily increasing during all its ten sessions.

A similar conference was held in the same place in 1886, and these previous conventions rendered possible the Centenary Conference on Foreign Missions that met in London, June 9 to 19, 1888. During fifty years men had been asking for the results of the vast expenditures made for foreign missions. The Centenary Conference devoted fifty sessions to a searching scrutiny of every department of missionary work, and to the public record of the results. The great object was to encourage the churches to press forward in obedience to the last command of Christ by setting forth the experience of evangelical missions during one hundred years, and to confer on those numerous questions which the large expansion of the work had brought into the foreground. The Conference made no attempt to legislate for the churches, nor to stir up temporary excitement. The kingdom of truth advances by the spread of information concerning the principles of that kingdom and the facts connected with its progress in the past.

The great number of men and women that the Centenary Conference drew together from all parts of the world was a testimony to the advance that had taken place in the work. In 1860 about 129 met together; in 1878 about 158; and in 1888, 1,576—nearly ten times as many. In 1860 there is not one name of a woman in the entire list, and in 1878 only two appear, tho more than that number (five) took part in the proceedings; but in 1888 the names of 429 women appear on the roll—much more than the entire membership of previous conferences. In 1860 none were present from the United States. In 1878 one attended from the United States and one from Canada. In 1888, 183 names appear from the United States and 30 from Canada.

The number of missionary societies represented in the conference was 139; of these, 57 belonged to the United States, 9 to Canada, 18 to the continent of Europe, and 2 to the colonies, leaving 53 to the kingdom of Great Britain.

Many topics discussed at previous conferences were also discussed at this, but with much greater thoroughness: *e. g.*, Missionary Comity was the subject of two papers, and a prolonged discussion filled fifty-nine pages.

The Alliance of Reformed Churches holding the Presbyterian system at its meeting in Toronto in 1892, arranged to invite the officers or representatives of the foreign missionary boards of the United States and Canada to come together for conference in New York in 1893. Twenty-one missionary boards and committees, besides the ABS and the YMCA, sent representatives to the meeting held in response to this invitation. While the sessions were not private in any sense they were attended in the main by secretaries, and members, and missionaries of the various boards. The Conference sought a more complete mutual correspondence and a more thorough unity of action along all lines of missionary policy. Its deliberations were found so full of mutual advantage by the societies participating that a conference has assembled every year since under the name of the Interdenominational Conference of Foreign Missionary Boards and Societies in the United States and Canada. A similar conference between missionary societies in Great Britain and

Ireland has been held in London of late years with very satisfactory results.

On the initiative of the annual Conference of North American Foreign Missionary Boards, the "Ecumenical Missionary Conference" was convened at New York in April, 1900. It met in Carnegie Hall and continued in session during ten days. The late Hon. Benjamin Harrison, ex-President of the United States, presided, and representatives of more than 200 missionary societies were present from Canada and the United States, Great Britain, Germany, France, Switzerland, the Netherlands, Sweden, Norway, Finland, Asia, Africa and Australia. Upon the first day of assembly the President of the United States and the Governor of the State of New York made addresses of welcome to the Conference, and from the first day to the last public interest in the meetings was unabated. Meetings were held in neighboring churches for such as could not find admission to Carnegie Hall, and it is estimated that during the ten days nearly 200,000 persons attended the various sessions.

In greater degree than any of its predecessors the Ecumenical Conference was "a demonstration of the missionary character of Christianity. In that respect it was more truly a Christian council than some of the great ecclesiastical councils . . . and at the same time it demonstrated the essential unity of the evangelical churches." In this and in its diffusion of the matured fruits of experience among all engaged in the actual work of missions, this conference was epoch-making in its character.

Upon the continent of Europe the practise of holding conferences of the various missionary bodies has been thoroughly tried and its practical value is fully understood. Such conferences exist in Holland and in Scandinavia. A conference of German and German-Swiss missionary societies is held at Bremen once in four years which has had an important influence in fostering uniformity of mission policy and methods. The value to the societies and their work of a clear mutual understanding on such questions is so well understood that a periodical (*Allgemeine Missions Zeitschrift*) has been established for the express purpose of discussing mission methods and mission problems.

2. *Conferences of Missionaries* on the field which are interdenominational in character, commenced in a tentative way with the Calcutta Conference of 1855. They are now held at regular intervals in India, China, Japan, Mexico, various parts of Africa and South America, and in Syria. These conferences of workers in the field, dealing with practical problems which confront the missionary enterprise, are of immense value in working toward the establishment of what has been called a Science of Missions, while at the same time they have a strong influence in promoting harmonious relations between the various denominations and in showing to all the practical unity of all the evangelical bodies.

Proceedings of the Union Missionary Convention, New York, 1854; *Conference on Missions held in Liverpool*, 1860, London, 1860; *General Conference on Missions held at Mildmay Park*, 1878; London, 1879; *General Conference on Modern Missions, held at Mildmay Park*, 1886, London, 1886; *Centenary Conference on the Protestant Missions of the World*, London, 1888, 2 vols; *Annual Conference of the Foreign Missionary Boards in the United States and Canada*, New York, 1893-1904. *Ecumenical Missionary Conference*, New York, 1900, 2 vols.; *General Missionary Conference at Allahabad*, London, 1873; *General Conference of Protestant Missionaries at Calcutta*, Calcutta, 1855; *Decennial Missionary Conference*, Bombay, 1893, 2 vols.; *General Conference of the Protestant Missionaries of Japan*, Yokohama, 1883; *General Conference of the Protestant Foreign Missionaries in China*, Shanghai, 1878; Ditto (Conference of 1890), Shanghai, 1890; *Shang-tung Missionary Conference* (1893), Shanghai, 1894; Ditto (1898), Shanghai, 1899.

CONFUCIANISM: Confucius was one of a constellation of great names which appeared in the world's history about 500 B. C. (See **Taouism.**) Of these were his own countryman, Laotze; Gautama of India (See **Buddhism**), Pythagoras of Greece, and, in the opinion of Sir Monier Williams and some others, Zoroaster of Persia. They were all nearly contemporary with the Hebrew prophet Zechariah. To speak accurately, Confucius, or Kungfutze, was born, according to Chinese records, in the year 551 B. C. Laotze, tho contemporary, was born fifty years earlier. They both appeared in a degenerate age of Chinese history, and both aimed at what seemed almost hopeless reform. The ancient religion of China, which is still thought to be represented by the Temple of Heaven in Peking, had greatly declined, and a superstitious nature worship, with endless polytheistic manifestations, occupied the minds of the people. The various provinces now embraced in the one empire were more or less independent, and were often at war. Princes were corrupt and tyrannical, and their subjects were disheartened, reckless, and debased. Mencius, the commentator of Confucius, says of the times in which his great teacher arose: "The world had fallen into decay, and right principles were disregarded. Ministers murdered their princes and sons their fathers. Confucius was frightened at what he saw, and undertook the work of reform."

These environments and this one great aim will go far to explain the character and teachings of Confucius and the history of his life. It was no part of his purpose to establish a religion, and as such his system cannot be considered. He was a political reformer, and with that end in view he became a teacher of general ethics. The State was the supreme object of his effort, but to secure the highest welfare of the state the family must be considered, and all the minor relations of mankind. It has been common among ancient monarchs and lawgivers to regard the state, or rather its rulers, as of supreme importance, while its subjects were mere slaves, and little regard was had for the family. Confucius was wiser. He looked upon human society as a pyramid, and saw clearly that whatever entered into the lowest foundations concerned the whole structure. Both he and Laotze, even in that early age, taught that kings existed for the good of the people, and had no right to employ them merely as the means of furthering their own ambitious designs.

Confucianism emphasizes the worship of parents and ancestors, tho if strict definitions be observed, it might be difficult to draw any very clear distinction between the reverence to be paid to the dead and that which was due to those who were still living. In both cases reverence to parents, extending however many generations back, was supposed to prove a salutary influence in maintaining the perpetuity of the state and the welfare of society. The worship of trees, mountains, rivers, and countless other objects is a part of Taouism or of the old nature worship. Both Confucianism and Taouism honor heroes, tho their images are generally found only in the Taouist and the Buddhist temples.

The Life of Confucius: The incidents given of the life of Confucius are simple and have not, as in the case of Gautama, Mohammed, and even Laotze, been overlaid with absurd legends. The sage was the son of an old man, and was left fatherless at three years of age. At fifteen he evinced remarkable intellectual powers, and at twenty-two he was already instructing a class of disciples in the principles of government. At twenty-four he lost his mother, for whom he had a high regard. The conical tumulus which he raised over her grave is said to have been the pattern from which the circular grave-mounds of North China originated.

The earliest public recognition which Confucius received was his appointment, when he was about thirty years old, to the tutorship of two young princes of the Marquisate of Lu. At the dying request of their father they were taught political economy and the art of government. In accompanying his wards to the capital of the country, Confucius met Laotze. He is said to have sought instruction from the old sage, but he very soon found that there could be no agreement between them. Laotze was already suffering that keen disappointment which embittered his last days, and which Confucius himself at last experienced to some degree, and he received the young teacher with critical disdain. He considered him a noisy and pretentious reformer, all of whose roseate theories were yet to be tested. For himself, Laotze was too proud and self-sufficient to be a successful leader of men. He was utterly destitute of magnetism, and repelled where he should have striven to win. He was much more of a philosopher than Confucius, but was far less practical. He gloried in reticence, and thought that the zealous remonstrances of his rival against the public vices only advertised them.

On the other hand, Confucius confessed himself puzzled by the character of Laotze, and could only compare him to the incomprehensible ways of the dragon.

After two or three rather unsuccessful attempts as councilor of different provincial rulers, Confucius gave up political life, and devoted himself for fifteen years to teaching. He had been disgusted with the profligacy of those who had employed him, and despaired of the princes of his time. They all came short of a practical appreciation of his high standards of either private or political virtue.

As a teacher he met better success. He is said to have had not less than three thousand disciples—a fact which reflects great credit not only upon him, but upon the intellectual activity of his generation. Five hundred of these pupils became mandarins, and over seventy are said to have been distinguished scholars.

The last effort of Confucius as privy councilor was with the Marquis of Lu—supposably his former pupil. He was now fifty-two years old. For a time this prince by steady devotion to his public duties greatly prospered. He was becoming powerful, and to the neighboring princes formidable. The ruler of a rival province or chief city seeing this, sought to break the power of Confucius over him, and lead him into vice. A band of beautiful young dancing-girls were sent to him as a present, and with the desired effect. He soon became indifferent to the counsels of Confucius, and, giving himself up to pleasure, he crippled his power. The disappointed sage sought other similar engagements, but in vain. Many would gladly have employed him, but would not follow his high standards.

In the one great ambition of his life he met with constant disappointment, and his political career he considered a failure. But, altho not practically a statesman, he was one of the most successful political theorists that the world has known. Probably no other man ever stamped his ideas or his influence so deeply upon the institutions of his country as Confucius. No other has ever influenced so many millions of mankind, and contributed such marvelous stability and perpetuity to the government of a nation.

Confucius cannot be ranked among philosophers, strictly speaking. There was nothing speculative in his nature. He was a compiler of the ancient wisdom of his country, and he succeeded in putting it into such practical shape, and in urging it with so much sincerity and earnestness of purpose, as to enlist many disciples at the time, and to win at last universal honor and devotion. He was possessed of a sturdy honesty, and this he claimed from all men. His social system was a superstructure, on which he placed the state at the apex or head. His reasoning was as follows: The ancient princes, in order to govern their states, first regulated their families. To regulate their families they practised virtue in their own persons. In order to such virtue they cultivated right feelings. To have right feelings they cultivated right purposes. To this end they sought intelligence by studying the nature of things." This reminds one of the "eightfold path" of the Buddha, only that it is more logical, and is better adapted to all the wants of life. The "Five Relations" are those "between friend and friend, between brother and brother, husband and wife, father and son, ruler and subject." Such is the pyramid of Chinese sociology. Confucius, who in his lifetime could not hold permanently the position of privy-councilor to a petty prince of a province, has since his death ruled the empire for twenty-four centuries. The five relations had been recognized long before his time, but not in the same clear form and in the same practical application. Confucius so exaggerated the efficacy of his theories as to exclude God. The Emperor stands virtually in the place of Deity, and Chinese ancestors are the great cloud of witnesses from whom all celestial impulse is thought to descend upon men. And there are other exaggerations affecting social and domestic life. The father may be an unresisted tyrant over his child, and the older brother may exact a humiliating fealty from the younger. No social system can be entirely sound which subordinates woman to a position so inferior as that which Confucianism consigns her. Confucius himself, tho most reverent toward his mother, has been charged with indifference toward his wife. Compared with many other systems of the East, the ethics show a degree of respect to woman, but they fail of that symmetry and just proportion which the New Testament demands in all the relations of the household.

The Teachings of Confucius: From the age of sixty-six Confucius devoted his remaining years to the editing of books. He admitted that he was not an originator, but only a compiler and editor. Only one of his works, the *Chun tsew,* or "Spring and Autumn Annals," can be considered an original production.

His other works, the *Shoo King* or "Book of History," the *She King* or "Book of Odes," were only compilations or revisions. These, with the *Yih King* or "Book of Changes," had existed before his time, and in his revisions or abridgments they suffered at his hands. The *Shoo King*, especially, he cut down from about 3,000 paragraphs or verses, to less than 400. What might be considered the religious element in this work he almost entirely eliminated, reserving only those practical teachings which suited his theories of society and the government of the state.

Those remains of the Confucian ethics which are most highly valued by the Chinese are certain collections known as the *Lun Yu* or "Confucian Analects," the *Ta Hee* or "Great Learning," and the *Chung Yung* or "Doctrine of the Mean." The last two of these are supposed to have been edited by *Tsze-sze*, a grandson of the sage. They all claim to reproduce the teachings of Confucius, especially the "Analects."

The monopoly of Chinese wisdom was given to Confucius by a singular circumstance. About 220 B.C. the Emperor Che Hwang-te ordered all books to be burned, with the exception of the *Zoon Ti King* of Laotze. The execution of the order was very sweeping, but the works of Confucius were afterwards restored piecemeal, some from fragments, some from oral tradition; while the great body of literature from which he had made his compilations was almost entirely lost.

The wisdom of the ages, therefore, was represented almost exclusively by the works of Confucius. Mencius and others added comments, but the foundation was that received from the one great sage. Thus Confucianism became a monopoly, and was made canonical by the decrees of emperors and the common consent of the people. The national literature thus settled once for all was embodied in five classics, viz.: the *Yi King* or "Book of Changes," the *She King* or "Book of Poetry," the *Shoo King* or "Book of History," the *Le Ke* or "Book of Rites," and the *Chun-tsew* or "Spring and Autumn Annals." These were in whole or in part compiled by Confucius. There are besides what are known as "the Four Books," viz.: the "Great Learning," the "Doctrine of the Mean," the "Confucian Analects," and the "Works of Mencius." These books have for ages constituted the text-books in Chinese education; they are also the basis of the competitive examination for public office. That so narrow a field of study—one so destitute of science or general history, one which is in every respect so far behind the spirit and movement of the age—should be supposed to supply all knowledge requisite for the intelligent performance of all possible duties of statesmanship and diplomacy, is a marvel. Such a standard cannot be maintained for many generations longer.

When we consider the low and corrupt state in which Confucius found the religion of his country, we are not greatly surprised that he rejected that element from the fabric which he hoped to rear, and depended on social and political ethics merely. He was not an atheist, nor, in the strictest modern sense, was he an agnostic. According to the conclusions of Martin, Legge, Douglass, and Max Müller, he really believed in a supreme being, known as "Shangte," or the God of Heaven. He believed also in unseen spirits, and he taught his disciples to "respect the gods." He had, however, no moral sense of duty toward "the gods," nor the consciousness of any special dependence on them. "Treat them with respect," he said to his disciples, "but keep them at a distance," or rather, as Dr. Martin renders it, "keep out of their way."

The same author speaks of Confucianism as "the leading religion of the empire." Its objects of worship he divides into three classes—the powers of nature, ancestors, and heroes; and he adds: "Originally recognizing the existence of a supreme personal deity, it has degenerated into a pantheistic medley, and renders worship to an impersonal *anima mundi*, under the leading forms of visible nature. Besides the concrete universe, separate honors are paid to the sun, moon, and stars, mountains, rivers, and lakes." Tho Confucianism recognizes these objects, the system so far overlaps the pantheon of modern Taouism.

The teachings of Confucius must be acknowledged to have embodied many noble precepts. His political ethics were above the average of those practised by the most enlightened nations. The great end recommended to rulers was not their own gratification or glory, but the good of the people; and no teacher ever insisted more strenuously upon the duty of example. Princes were constantly reminded that public virtue could not be enforced in the face of royal vice and wickedness.

Reciprocity was one of Confucius' favorite expressions for social and political virtue. This, in the broad sense in which he employed the term, was nothing less than a practical application of the Golden Rule. Thus a father in exacting reverence from his son should be reverent toward the authority of the state, and he should render himself worthy of reverence by a proper regard to all his own relations and duties. The Prince in claiming loyalty from his ministers should fulfil all the conditions which might promote their fidelity.

Loyalty was another broad expression used by the sage. It included all duty, not only to a father or a prince, but to every interest of society. "Let the superior man," he said, "never fail reverently to order his conduct, and let him be respectful to others and observant of propriety; then all within the four seas will be his brethren."

Faithfulness was enjoined, as having, if possible, even a more sacred character than loyalty. "Hold faithfulness and sincerity as first principles," said the sage; "I do not see how a man is to get on without faithfulness." He maintained that while the subordinate must in all cases be faithful to his ruler, the latter must be equally faithful to his word and to his assumed character as the father of his people.

In the cultivation of social and political sincerity, Confucius taught that the very first step in the reform of a corrupt state was "The Rectification of Names." No vice or dishonesty should be allowed to take shelter under specious titles. All littleness or dishonor or incapacity should be exposed. Everything should be brought to par, and should be stamped accordingly. Men should be rated at their true value.

One great principle, which has doubtless had great influence in China, is known as the "Doctrine of the Mean." Confucianism assumes that many evils flow from extreme opinions. There is always another side, and the balanced truth generally lies between. Every virtue should be held in poise by some other. For a very early exemplar, a minister of the great Emperor Shun, when asked what are the nine virtues, replied: "Affability combined with dignity; mildness combined with firmness; bluntness combined with respectfulness; aptness for government combined with reverence; docility combined with boldness; straightforwardness combined with gentleness; easiness combined with discrimination; vigor combined with sincerity, and valor combined with righteousness."

It is but just to say that while reverence for sovereignty is so strongly enjoined, yet that reverence is coupled with discrimination. No history of any country deals more severely with the memory of unjust rulers than that of China, and in many instances tyrants have been overthrown.

It is perhaps due to the "Doctrine of the Mean" and to the conscious dignity of moderation, that the Chinese Government has often shown so much self-poise amid the exasperations of foreign diplomacy.

But the character and teachings of Confucius are far enough from perfect. It has already been shown that his ideal virtues were distorted to promote his theories of society. Reverence to parents was pushed to such extremes as to destroy that reciprocity which he made a test of highest character. The authority of the parent is not duly balanced by parental consideration, and the worst of tyrannies is often seen in the Chinese home. Practically, there is no such symmetry of the domestic virtues as that found in Paul's Epistles. Confucius was no model in respect to the rights of woman. He gave seven grounds of divorce, on some one of which he divorced his own wife. His code of morals, tho above the morality current in his age, was not high. He spoke slightingly of what he called the "small fidelity" which binds a husband to one wife, and he imposed a stricter virtue on the one sex than on the other. Polygamy was allowed in cases of barrenness, and was never a crime. The marital license allowed to the sovereign is of itself sufficient not only to ruin the royal line, but by the influence of high example to promote general immorality among the people.

Tho Confucius enjoined humility, he did not hesitate late in life to claim perfection. "At fifteen," he said, "my mind was bent on learning. At thirty, I stood firm; at forty, I had no doubts; at fifty I knew the decrees of heaven; at sixty, my ear was an obedient organ for the reception of truth; at seventy, I could follow what my heart desired without transgressing what was right." Unfortunately his character showed to the least advantage in his old age.

Professor Douglass, in speaking of the later political life of the sage, remarks: "It is impossible to study this portion of Confucius' career without feeling that a great change had come over his conduct. There was no longer that lofty love of truth and of virtue which had distinguished the commencement of his official life. Adversity instead of stiffening his back had made him pliable. He who had formerly refused money which he had not earned, was now willing to take pay for no other service than the presentation of courtier-like advice on occasions when Duke Ling desired to have his opinion in support of his own; and in defiance of his oft-repeated denunciation of rebels, he was now ready to go over to the court of a rebel chief in the hope possibly of being able through his means "to establish," as he said on another occasion, "an eastern Chow." His friend Tsze-loo expostulated with him upon his inconsistency, but he justified himself with a lame excuse.

Confucius evinced great weakness at the last, by being apparently more solicitous for his own good name than for the welfare of his country. When seized by a presentiment of death he said: "The course of my doctrine is run, and I am unknown." "Never does a superior man pass away without leaving a name behind him. But my principles make no progress, and I — how shall I be viewed in future ages?"

The Relation of Confucianism to the Ancient Worship of China: The sage had been peculiarly reticent in regard to a supreme deity and to the future life. "We do not know life," he said; "how can we know death?" Yet when his life-work was done he gathered his books, and, ascending a hill where the worship of Shangte was observed, he laid the books upon the altar, and then kneeling before them he gave thanks that he had been permitted to live to see their completion. There is a difference of opinion as to whether he believed in a supreme being, whom he saw fit to pass in silence for a purpose, or whether he was utterly agnostic. His teachings incline to general skepticism, but whatever may have been his personal views there is scarcely room for a difference on the question of whether a religious faith more or less monotheistic preceded Confucius. The best Chinese scholars agree so far. Real Chinese history can be traced no farther back than the reign of Yaou, 2356 B.C., and there we find clear and distinct traces of a worship of the supreme god Shangte. Yaou shared his throne with Shun, who succeeded him. Both have been looked upon in all succeeding ages as perfect models of sovereigns. Yaou was the King Alfred of China, who by his wise administration united all the warring states in one empire. He encouraged astronomical researches and all useful science. We are told that when he died the virtues of his colleague Shun "were heard on high," and he was therefore appointed to the throne.

One of his first acts after coming to full power was to sacrifice to Shangte, the supreme god. "Thereafter," we are told, "he sacrificed specially, but with the ordinary forms, to Shangte; sacrificed with purity and reverence to the Six Honored Ones, offered appropriate sacrifices to the hills and rivers, and extended his worship to the hosts of spirits." "This," says R. K. Douglass, Professor of Chinese in King's College, London, "is the first mention we have in Chinese history of religious worship, tho the expressions used ('but with the ordinary forms') plainly imply that the worship of Shangte at least had previously existed. It is to this supreme being that all the highest forms of worship have been offered in all ages. By his decrees kings were made and rulers executed judgment. . . . In all probability there was a time when the worship of Shangte was the expression of a pure monotheistic faith of the Chinese. By degrees, however, corruption crept in, and, tho Shangte always remained the supreme object of veneration, they saw no disloyalty to him in rendering homage to the powers of nature which they learned to personify, and to the spirits of their departed ancestors who were supposed to guard and watch over in a subordinate manner the welfare of their descendants."

Professor Legge of Oxford, in "The Religions of China," has illustrated this distinction by quoting the prayers of an emperor of the Ming dynasty, which were offered in the Temple of Heaven in the year 1538 A.D., in which he first invokes the spirits of the mountains and the hills, and asks their intercession with the supreme God, whose name he proposes slightly to change, that the change may be acceptable to Him. He then proceeds to pray directly to the God of heaven, whom he addresses as the creator and upholder and ruler of all things. These prayers show how, in spite of the teachings of Confucius, the old monotheism which he ignored still survived, and they show also what great truths underlie the worship offered in the Temple of Heaven in Peking.

In his prayer to the spirits he says: "Beforehand we inform you, all ye celestial and all ye terrestrial spirits, and will trouble you in our behalf, to exert your spiritual power and display your vigorous efficacy communicating our poor desire to Shangte, and praying him graciously to grant us his acceptance and regard, and to be pleased with the title which we shall reverently present."

"This prayer shows," says Professor Legge, "how there had grown up around the primitive monotheism of China the recognition and worship of a multitude of celestial and terrestrial spirits, and yet the monotheism remained." How differently does the Emperor proceed when, having thus invoked the interceding spirits, he approaches Shangte directly. He begins: "Of old, in the beginning, there was the great chaos, without form and dark. The five elements had not begun to revolve nor the sun and moon to shine. In the midst thereof there presented itself neither form nor sound. Thou, O spiritual Sovereign! camest forth in thy presidency, and first didst divide the grosser parts from the purer. Thou madest heaven; thou madest earth; thou madest man; all things got their being with their producing power." After stating the title which he proposes to give to Shangte, he adds: "Thou didst produce, O spirit! the sun and moon and five planets; and pure and beautiful was their light. The vault of heaven was spread out like a curtain, and the square earth supported all on it, and all creatures were happy. I thy servant presume reverently to thank thee." Farther on he says: "All living things are indebted to thy goodness, but who knows whence his blessings come to him? It is Thou alone, O Lord, who art the parent of all things."

The temple-worship of Shangte (for real personality is still recognized, tho the name be changed for Tien, heaven) has always been associated with the Confucian system. There is no evidence that it was ever suspended, even temporarily, after Confucius came; and here, in the prayers of the Ming emperor, two thousand years after his time, we find the old name Shangte reasserted.

No more impressive account has been given of this surviving monotheistic worship in Peking than the following from the pen of Dr. Wm. A. P. Martin, D.D.: "Within the gates of the southern division of the capital, and surrounded by a sacred grove so extensive that the silence of its deep shades is never broken by the noises of the busy world, stands the Temple of Heaven. It consists of a single tower, whose tiling of resplendent azure is intended to represent the form and color of the aerial vault. It contains no altar, and the solemn rites are not performed within the tower. But on a marble altar which stands before it a bullock is offered once a year as a burnt-sacrifice, while the master of the empire prostrates himself in adoration of the spirit of the universe. This is the high place of Chinese devotion, and the thoughtful visitor feels that he ought to tread the place with unsandaled feet. For no vulgar idolatry has entered here; this mountain top still stands above the waves of corruption, and on this solitary altar still rests a faint ray of the primæval faith. The tablet which represents the invisible deity is inscribed with the name of Shangte, the supreme Ruler; and as we contemplate the majesty of the empire prostrate before it while the smoke ascends from his burning sacrifice, our thoughts are irresistibly carried back to the time when the King of Salem officiated as 'Priest of the Most High God.'"

Professor Douglass charges Confucius with having promoted the spread of polytheism by attempting to suppress the knowledge of the supreme God. He substituted for *Shangte* (god), *Tien* (heaven); and that change has survived. But the people, feeling a need of something less vague, have fallen into the worship of countless other objects, and particularly the worship of ancestors. "But," says the professor, "in spite of the silence of Confucius on the subject of Shangte, his worship has been maintained, not perhaps in its original purity, but with works of reverence which place its object on the highest pinnacle of the Chinese Pantheon. At the present day the imperial worship of Shangte on the round hillock to the south of the city of Peking is surrounded with all the solemnity of which such an occasion is capable."

"There is no need," says Dr. Martin, "for extended argument to establish the fact that the early Chinese were by no means destitute of the knowledge of God. They did not, indeed, know him as the Creator (evidently the prayer of the Ming emperor recognized Him as such), but they recognized Him as supreme in providence, and without beginning or end. Whence came this conception? Was it the mature result of ages of speculation, or was it brought down from remote antiquity on the stream of patriarchal tradition? The latter, we think, is the only probable hypothesis."

There has been a long and earnest discussion among missionaries as to how far the identity of Shangte with the true God once made known to men may be traced. Certainly if there be a real succession many attributes have been lost and the conception in any Chinese mind is very dim. Yet is there not at least an important reminiscence, and may not the earnest missionary have the same grounds that Paul had for saying, "Whom ye ignorantly worship, declare I unto you"?

The missionary has to meet in the Confucian that self-centered temper and that inclination to evil which is familiar enough in Christian lands.

Men of the non-Christian races do not escape such irreligion by being without knowledge of Jesus Christ. What the missionary also has to meet among the followers of Confucius is an imperfect code of morals that he must make his ally wherever possible rather than his enemy. Confucianism does not perfectly repel influences from outside. The lesson of the Boxer outbreak of 1900 is that the people of China need a new moral energy, and that Christian missionaries are the ones to give them this energy, making full use, for the purpose, of their knowledge of the maxims and the aims of Confucius.

Douglass (R. K.), *Confucianism and Taouism*, London, 1893; Faber (E.), *The Mind of Mencius*, London, 1882; Jennings (W.), *Confucian Analects*, London, 1895; Legge (J.), *Texts of Confucianism* (Sacred Books of the East series), Oxford and New York; —— *Religions of China*, London, 1881.

CONGO FREE STATE: The exploration of the Congo by Stanley in 1876-77 opened a new door of entrance into the interior of Africa, and led to the establishment in 1884 of the Congo Free State. This is an independent state under the sovereignty of Leopold II., of Belgium. It lies between French Congo and the Egyptian Sudan on the north, and Rhodesia and Portuguese W. Africa on the south, reaching from the Atlantic Ocean, which it touches by only a narrow coast, to Lake Tanganyika and German E. Africa on the east. It is drained chiefly by the Congo and its tributaries. Its rich flora, vast forests and fertile soil make it a tropical garden of great agricultural possibilities, while its mineral wealth, mostly unknown, may be also of great importance. A commerce amounting annually to an exchange in imports and exports of about $16,000,000 has already been established (1903).

The lands of the Free State are divided into three classes: First, those in the actual occupation of the natives, who do not recognize private property in the soil, but hold their lands as long as they choose to cultivate them, but have no permanent title to them. The second class is composed of lands now occupied by foreigners, who hold by a government title. All these titles are registered, and there is no difficulty in the sale or transfer of these lands. The third class consists of lands as yet unoccupied. These to the extent of 25 acres can be occupied by a foreigner, if he comes to an understanding with the natives about them; but he cannot cut timber or open mines without a concession from the government.

The native population is difficult to estimate, more or less of it being nomadic, and but a small percentage sufficiently established in known localities to make calculation reliable. The estimates vary from fourteen millions to double that number. They are mostly of the Bantu race. There are some Azandes in the northeast and scattered tribes of pigmies in various sections. The religion is mostly a revolting fetishism, and cannibalism is not uncommon. Sorcerers and wizards are found everywhere, and exercise a predominant influence over the superstitious natives. Belief in evil spirits is universal and the religious ceremonies for the most part are grotesque and barbarous. Polygamy and slavery are an integral part of the social fabric and of family life. Many parts of the country remain unknown and in a condition of primitive wildness, while in some of the eastern districts the inhabitants are still terrified by the raids of Arab slave traders. At the same time there appears to be indisputable evidence that a terror of the Belgian officials is depopulating some districts as effectually as in former days did the terror of the Arab slave hunter.

Protestant missionary enterprises are carried on in the Congo Free State by the ABMU, the BMS, the FCMS, the RBMU, the PS, the PB, and the Swedish Missionary Society. These societies have established stations at 23 different places in the State.

According to official estimates there are 120 Protestant, and 180 Roman Catholic missionaries in the Congo Free State. Of the Roman Catholic missions there are four each under different organizations:

1. *The Mission du Saint Esprit*, at Banana and Boma. There are 4 priests and 2 lay brethren at these stations, and some small schools which give industrial training to the children.

2. *The Belgian Mission:* Established in 1888 at Kwa-mouth on the Upper Congo, with a second station projected at Luluaburg on the Lulua River, a branch of the Kasai, just on the southern boundary line of the Congo Free State.

3. *A New Mission at Bangola*, on the northern bank of the Upper Congo, about 125 miles above Equatorville. This is under the care of the Jesuits. The Catholic mission steamer, *Leo XIII.*, is plying on the Upper Congo.

4. *The Mission of the Pères d'Algérie* (Algerian priests), on Lake Tanganyika, in the southeastern part of the Free State. They have 2 stations, Kibanja on Burton Gulf, and Mpala at the mouth of the Lofuku, both on the lake. They are laboring among the Urua tribe, but do not report much success.

Bailey, *Travel and Adventures in the Congo Free State*, London, 1894; Bentley (Rev. W. H.), *Life on the Congo*, London, 1887; *Pioneering on the Congo*, London and New York, 1890; Burrows, *Land of the Pigmies*, London, 1889; Stanley (H. M.), *The Congo and the Founding of the Free State*, 2 vols., London, 1878; Guiness (Mrs. H. Grattan), *The New World of Central Africa*, London and New York.

CONGO, French. See FRENCH CONGO.

CONSTANTINE: Capital of a department of the same name in Algeria, N. Africa. It was the ancient Cirta, and stands on a detached rocky height, surrounded by ravines crossed by bridges. Its altitude above the sea is 2,165 feet and its population (1901), 41,138, of whom the overwhelming majority are Mohammedans. It is a station of the North African Mission (1886), with (1900) 6 missionaries, men and women, and a book depot.

CONSTANTINOPLE: Capital of the Turkish Empire, is located at the confluence of the Bosphorus and the Sea of Marmora and stands partly in Europe and partly in Asia. It is the natural center toward which converge the lines of interest, of trade, and population, of Southeastern Europe and Western Asia. Because it is partly in Europe and partly in Asia, it partakes of the character of both continents to such a degree that the natives of each find themselves at home in it. The beauty of its scenery is scarcely more marked than are the characteristics that make it a healthy residence at every season of the year, and a center whose influences make themselves felt in every portion of the empire. The value of its location has been much impaired by the restrictions upon trade of absurd custom-house regulations, and that jealousy of purely foreign investments that has characterized the Turkish Government. Produce that was formerly brought from the ports of the Black Sea and reshipped at the Golden Horn for Europe, now goes direct from Odessa, Varna, Poti and Trebizond.

Topographically the city is divided into three parts: 1. Stamboul, or the city proper, between the Marmora and the Golden Horn, occupying the site of the old city. 2. Galata and Pera, where are centered the European commercial interests. 3. The shores of the Bosphorus, the islands, and Marmora suburbs. The city stands on several hills, so that there is the best of natural drainage. The climate is, in general, mild through the whole year, the winter being tempered by south winds, while in the summer the prevailing winds are from the north. There is usually some snow, but it does not lie long, and there is rarely much ice. In the summer the thermometer very rarely rises above 90°. The chief drawback to residence is the heavy winds, which are hard for delicate throats and lungs to bear. The spring months, April, May and June, are the most favorable for visiting the city.

The buildings were formerly almost entirely frame houses, poorly put together, which burned like tinder when a conflagration was once started. Successive disasters of this kind have resulted in the use of brick and stone in a great degree, tho much that appears to be brick is really only stucco.

In its political relations Constantinople is the very key to the "Eastern Question," but, aside from this wider international importance, its political influence is a most important element in its national life.

It is the seat of all government for the empire. Every local official, from Adrianople to Bagdad, from Trebizond to Tepedelen, feels the influence that binds him to the capital, and this in more ways than the mere reference to responsible chiefs there. The sovereign keeps his eye not merely upon the pashas, but on every little village mudir; and no one, from the highest to the lowest, can tell when he may be called upon to account to headquarters for some act that it would be supposed was left entirely to his discretion. Hence if any disturbance occurs among the Kurdish Mountains, on the Persian border, it must be settled, not at the capital of the province (vilayet), but at Constantinople. The absolute centralization of the Turkish government in Constantinople is almost more marked than is that of Russia in St. Petersburg.

The same thing is true of the various hierarchical influences. The Armenian Patriarch resident in Constantinople is subordinate spiritually to the Catholicos at Etchmiadzine (in the Caucasus), but politically he is the head of the Armenian nation, and the supremacy of the Patriarchate is maintained in much the same way as is that of the Porte. So with the Greeks and other Christian communities.

So, again, Constantinople as the seat of the foreign embassies is the center for those foreign influences which permeate the empire to a degree almost inconceivable to any one not acquainted with the country.

Thus Constantinople is the center of all interests of the remotest sections of the empire.

The population of Constantinople is variously estimated at from 900,000 to 1,100,000 souls, of whom considerably more than half are Mohammedans. The Armenians and Greeks number perhaps 80,000 each, the Jews, 70,000, while the remainder comprise almost every race of Europe and Western Asia, for thousands of men come up from the villages of all Western Asia, spend a few years, and then having amassed a little money, return to their homes. The number of these it is impossible to estimate at all accurately. They make up by far the majority of the laboring class, the porters (hamals), boatmen, carpenters and even the petty tradesmen.

In former times each religious sect occupied a distinct quarter of the city. Stamboul had its Mohammedan, Armenian, Greek and Jewish quarters, while the Europeans were found chiefly in Pera, and social intercourse between those of different creeds was almost unknown. Of later years this has changed in a great degree; districts have encroached on each other until in some cases boundary-lines have been practically obliterated.

The languages are as varied as the races. The official court language is Turkish. Greek, Italian, English and German are almost essential to any one whose business relations are extensive, while the language of diplomacy, and the common language which every educated person of any race or nation is assumed to know, is the French. Armenian is used only among Armenians, who, however, all speak Turkish, while many of them write it. Besides these one hears a perfect jargon of sounds—Bulgarian, Russian, Arabic, Persian, Spanish, etc.—as he passes through the streets or stops in a restaurant or café.

4. *Mission Work:* The above statements will readily explain the importance that has always been attached to the occupation of Constantinople as a center for missionary operations. The British and Foreign Bible Society occupied it as a post in 1823 and has now (1902) an agency and a depot with 17 colporteurs and Bible women. The American Bible Society established an agency there in 1856, and now has an agent and a book depot and 10 colporteurs and Bible women. Both of these societies, together with the mission of the ABCFM, have publishing and editorial rooms, besides book storage depots and salesrooms in the Constantinople **Bible House.**

The ABCFM (1831) was the first Society to establish missionaries in the city. It now (1902) has there 17 missionaries, of whom 13 are women, and in the city and its 3 outstations in neighboring districts, 31 native workers, men and women, 13 preaching centers, 6 elementary schools, 1 publishing house and 390 church-members. The American College for Girls is also connected with this Society. **Robert College** (1860), an offshoot from this mission, is not in any way connected with it, but is under its own Board of Trustees in New York.

Missions to the Jews were the next to be established in Constantinople, beginning with that of the London Society for the Evangelization of the Jews (1835), followed by that of the Free Church of Scotland (1842) and the Established Church of Scotland. These Societies now (1900) have in the city, 11 missionaries, men and women (one a physician), 25 native workers, 3 preaching centers, 2 orphanages, 4 elementary schools, 1 high school and 1 dispensary.

The Kaiserswerth deaconesses also have a station here (1852) with a hospital and a kindergarten school, with 17 deaconesses in charge of these institutions.

Later enterprises are the FCMS (1879) and the Seventh Day Adventists' Mission (1887), which have both together 10 missionaries, men and women, and in the city and their 27 outstations in different parts of Asia Minor, 4 native workers, 6 preaching centers, 4 elementary schools and 462 professing Christians.

The political relations of the representatives of these various missionary bodies in a center of influence like Constantinople is a phase of missionary life which is found to be of no small difficulty, but of great importance. The missionaries themselves often have cases affecting their rights as citizens which must be carried to the embassy; and there are innumerable instances when their kind offices are sought in behalf of people who have been for one cause or another imprisoned or persecuted in every part of the empire. This work requires time, tact, patience, and an intimate knowledge of the country and its people, their laws and customs.

While there is much valuable missionary work done in Constantinople, its chief importance after all is as a strategic point. To withdraw or even weaken the force there would be to court disaster in the whole empire. If Constantinople can be held, the Levant will certainly be evangelized.

Amicis (E. de), *Constantinople*, New York, 1896; Grosvenor (E. A.), *Constantinople*, 2 vols., Boston, 1895; Dwight (H. O.), *Constantinople and Its Problems*, New York, 1901; Prime (E. D. G.), *Forty Years in the Turkish Empire*, New York, 1875.

CONSTERDINE, Rev. Charles: Born at Littleborough, Lancashire, September 15, 1869. From the time of his conversion at the age of fourteen he manifested the liveliest interest in Christian work, and in 1895 he was appointed by the Free Methodist Church, England, to Newton Abbott, in the Exeter Circuit, as pastor. As his heart was turned to the mission field, he soon offered his services to the Missionary Committee for East Africa, and, altho just before he sailed, the news reached him of the death of one with whom he hoped to be associated in his African work, which put new emphasis upon the malarial climate of British East Africa, he was heard to exclaim: "I am ready for a service of sacrifice." He first settled at Ribé, near Mombasa, British East Africa; but, soon after the Assembly of 1897, he became the colleague of Mr. Ormerod at Golbanti, farther inland, and it was there that he spent the remainder of his days. Soon after reaching the foreign field he impressed his associates by his intense zeal and enthusiasm; and his warm affection for the people among whom he lived and labored gained for him a remarkable influence with all classes. His self-forgetfulness led him to sacrifice himself, and, altho he was repeatedly urged to return to England for the restoration of his health, he would answer: "No, no; I have thought sometimes that I must return, but not now." On Thursday, January 23, 1902, a second attack of fever, followed by other and worse symptoms, brought his consecrated service to an end, and on the following Sunday evening he peacefully passed out of the shadows into the light.

COÑVA: A town in the western part of the island of Trinidad, W. I. Station of the PCC (1874), with (1900) 1 missionary and his wife, 1 missionary woman, 17 native workers, men and women, 2 preaching centers, 20 Sunday schools, 11 elementary schools and 100 church-members

CONVERTS IN MISSION FIELDS: The grace of God will do in India, in China, in Japan, in Africa, and unto the uttermost parts of the earth, what His grace will do in the United States.

In all mission fields large numbers of converts to Christianity prove their sincerity by their readiness to follow the light at any cost to themselves; and their stability is proved by the strong front which they oppose to temptations and persecutions, and only right leadership is needed to keep them in constant activity in spiritual affairs. In this article reference is made to instances in China, both as familiar to the writer and as particularly typical of the world-wide field.

In heathen countries the sincerity of a convert is subjected to severe testing at the outset. The demands of a Christian life bring the convert at once into antagonism with the social customs of his people. If he meets the demands he becomes a peculiar member of the family and of the community, and separation follows.

Separation, ridicule and ostracism are difficult to bear anywhere, possibly nowhere more difficult than in China. Nevertheless, all this the Chinese converts bear cheerfully; not only so, but they often, by their zeal, invite attention to the fact that they are Christians.

The writer once had under his supervision a newly organized church in China, which had met with much opposition from the community in which it was located. The chapels of Chinese Christians usually have, over the door, signs announcing that they are places of worship. The members of this church were advised to omit the sign and to proceed cautiously, seeking to quietly win over the community. Returning to the locality some months after our former visit, I found over the door of the little meeting place the usual sign, in large Chinese characters, "The Church of Jesus." The members said that they were acting within their legal rights in organizing the church and they wished to announce their place of worship for the help of all.

In countries where the Sabbath has not been known the sincerity of the native Christian is tested by the demand for Christian observance. It is a struggle for life in these crowded Oriental nations. The Christian must compete for a living with men who work seven days a week. All do not meet the test equally, but the church in mission fields affords numerous illustrations of loyalty to conviction and sincerity of purpose. Mr. Sun, a venerable man, was a cloth seller with his stand out on the great Hata Street, Peking. He became interested in the Bible, read it, pondered it, conversed about it with Christians, and was converted. His stand was well known, his patrons numerous. As a Christian he decided he must close his stand on Sunday. His patrons knew nothing about Sunday, and, finding every now and then when they came to make purchases that the stand was closed and the proprietor absent, began to transfer their patronage to others. This was a testing time for Mr. Sun, for a large family depended upon him. But he was loyal to his conviction, and held true until death, his influence being a power for good in the Peking community.

There are young men, trained in our mission colleges in Western science, mathematics and English, who are entering the Christian ministry and Christian educational work, at salaries not more than one-fifth the amount they could command in secular employment. The writer knows of a young man who graduated from college and was accepted by the Imperial Maritime Customs, and was to be assigned to a position that would have paved the way for a successful financial career. He wished to enter the customs service in order to help his father in the support of a large family. After accepting the position he spent a sleepless night in the conflict between desire and conviction, and the following morning reported that he must abandon his intention of a mercantile life, and give himself wholly to the work of the Church in saving others. To-day he is one of the most useful men in China. Every year graduates from mission colleges are manifesting the sincerity of their profession by turning aside from fine worldly positions to take up a life of toil, with small pay, for Christ's sake.

Stability: There may be sincerity of purpose, and yet purpose may fail under unusual strain. The cataclysm of 1900 in North China was calculated to test to the utmost the *stability* of the converts.

Hundreds died in the persecution who, by burning incense and bowing the knee to idols, might have saved their lives. In the London Mission a man named Fan, a gatekeeper, was called upon by the Boxers to recant. He refused. He was carried into an open lot, a hole was dug of a depth so that when he was dropped into it his head was below the level of the surface. The loose earth was filled in up to his knees and he was called upon to recant; he refused. Up to the waist; he refused. Up to the chin as he stood erect, and again he was called upon to recant and save his life. Once more he refused and the loose earth was filled up over his head, burying him alive.

A student, a young man twenty-one years of age, a senior in college, was caught by the Boxers and called upon to recant. He told them he could not. They discussed his case and agreed to compromise—to let him recant by proxy, one of their number burning incense and bowing the head in the young man's stead, and they offered if he would accept this substitute to let him go. Again he refused, saying, "If I did that, to say nothing of disobeying God, I could never go to Peking and look my teachers and classmates in the face again," and he began to exhort them. Angered by his refusal and his exhortations they cut off his lips, his arms, his legs, and he died, faithful to the end.

One young man, a preacher, whose father, mother, sister and brother were massacred by the Boxers, when asked by the magistrate what he wanted by way of indemnity, replied that he asked only that he might have the privilege of preaching the Gospel to those who had put his family to death. One of the leading British merchants of Tientsin, in a letter to the *Peking and Tientsin Times*, a secular paper published in Tientsin, called attention, shortly after the siege of Peking, to the fidelity and stability of the native Christians, which, he said, had come as a revelation to himself and to many of his friends of the business world.

Activity: Converts on the mission field often are earnestly active in attendance on public worship and in the performance of outward duties pertaining to their personal salvation, as they conceive it, while at the same time they are slow to apprehend their personal responsibility for the saving of their fellow-countrymen. This was the case with a certain preacher, who arose in a Methodist class meeting and announced that he had thought of visiting a distant village to tell the Gospel story to relatives there whom he had not seen since his conversion; "but," he added, "they will be so busy, all the time that I am there, trying to get money out of me that they will have no ears for the Gospel. Since they are bound to go to hell anyway, they can go to hell. I shall not visit them." Yet this man steadily preached the Gospel, and lived a life so exemplary that he was the trusted partner of the missionaries, and he finally gave his life for the Gospel's sake and now rests in a martyr's grave.

The training of native preachers, teachers, Bible women and colporteurs; and special work in the schools and in connection with evangelistic meetings, is developing an ever-widening and deepening sense of personal responsibility; and, year by year, an ever-increasing number of men and women are taking arduous posts, enduring hardship and persecution cheerfully, and exercising strong faith and offering prevailing prayers in behalf of their countrymen. Converts from Hawaii are the evangelists of Micronesia; converted Samoans have a noble record as pioneers in work for the savages of Polynesia and Melanesia; Fiji Christians are now devoting their lives to the evangelization of New Guinea; a converted Muslim from Turkey has been laboring among Mohammedans in Chinese Turkestan.

And the church members are more and more taking active part in the work of soul saving. They bring to the work a direct faith that is honored in inspiring results—as, for instance, when a group of church members united in prayer for the salvation of a girl sold into a haunt of vice and contaminated by five years' contact with the life there. Not knowing what to do, they prayed. They got the girl away from her vile keepers, and then did not know what to do with her; they prayed. A profligate young man, recently converted, said, "Let us begin the pure life together." They were married and from thenceforth went in and out among the church members, honored and happy. They were to the membership a revelation of the possibilities of faith, and their presence was, therefore, a blessing to the church, and those who had prayed in such perplexity spoke of the result with bated breath and reverently, as if feeling the Master near.

The Student Federation of the Young Men's Christian Association is enlarging the horizon of young men on mission fields and the ringing call of their motto, "The Evangelization of the World in this Generation," is awakening many young converts to splendid service.

In Peking the Christian young men have assumed responsibility for the street chapels, where they render effective service by their fervid testimony. They have also given themselves ungrudgingly to the distribution of Christian literature at the great examinations held in Peking, one of which, the Triennial Examination, calls together from ten to fifteen thousand students from all parts of the empire. This work calls for fortitude and forbearance and the efforts are not always well received. The Chinese have shown aggressiveness in mercantile life in stretching out to adjoining lands. We find them in Japan, the Philippines, the Straits Settlements, and in many other lands, and there is every reason to believe that when the Gospel is more widely diffused and has become more the dominant force in their lives, they will be equally aggressive in spiritual matters. They are essentially the dominant race of the East, and as goes China so goes the great Eastern world.

The mission fields are not yet producing men who are capable of independent leadership. The leaders must come from among those who are born to the perspective and wide horizon, the traditions and teachings of Christian lands.

Such leaders, with faith to hope all things and believe all things concerning the character and possibilities of the converts on mission fields, will find comrades there, talented and possessed of a singularly direct faith, quick to apprehend, apt at suggestion, skilful in affairs, who will follow anywhere, dare any danger, bear any hardship, stand true before the persecutor, and all sincere, steadfast and active in the service of the Great Captain to the last.

COOK ISLANDS. See HERVEY ISLANDS.

COOKE, Miss M. A.: In 1820 Miss Cooke was sent to India by the British and Foreign School Society, at the request of a local educational body at Calcutta, with a view of starting a school for Hindu girls. Female education had already been successfully begun at Serampur by Mrs. Marshman of the Baptist Mission; and Miss Cooke was to make an attempt in the East India Company's territory. After a few months the local body found itself without funds to continue, and Miss Cooke was transferred to the CMS. While she was still studying Bengali, and wondering in what way she might presently begin to work, an incident occurred which gave her an unexpected opening. On January 25, 1822, Miss Cooke visited one of the boys' schools in order to observe the pronunciation of the language. Because of her presence a number of the natives gathered round the school door; and in the crowd was a little girl, whom the native teacher drove away, telling Miss Cooke that the child had for three months been disturbing them by begging to be allowed to learn to read with the boys. Miss Cooke immediately determined to return next day and begin to teach her as well as she could. Next day she went again, accompanied by an Englishwoman who spoke the Bengali well; and they found fifteen girls assembled, with their mothers. This was the beginning of a work that has produced great results; and when Miss Cooke sent her first report to England, she could tell of fifteen schools and nearly four hundred girls in attendance. Miss Cooke suggested that girls' schools throughout England should be invited to contribute specially to this work; and the Calcutta Committee opened a special fund which speedily reached 3,000 rupees. Soon after this, Miss Cooke was married to Rev. Isaac Wilson of the CMS, but she continued her labors zealously both during her married life and long after she became a widow in 1828. In 1824 a Ladies' Female Education Society was founded at Calcutta which, with the assistance of a grant of £500 from the CMS, had established a Central School, with Mrs. Wilson at the head of it. In 1836 she was released from this Central School; and she was enabled to carry out the desire of her heart by establishing a female orphanage at Agarpara. In 1842 she herself united with the Plymouth Brethren; but she transferred her institution to the Society under which she had worked, and Agarpara became a CMS station. In the *Missionary Register* (1838), the Bishop wrote these words of Mrs. Wilson: "She is carrying on the greatest undertaking yet witnessed in India."

COOPER, Rev. David James: Born at Belfast, Ireland, in 1873; died at Fez, Morocco, October 17, 1902. After a short mercantile career, he was led to devote his life to missions; and in November, 1896, he was sent by the NAM to Tripoli, in Barbary, where he pursued his Arabic studies, and worked successfully in a medical mission. The lamentable death of Miss Herdman, of Fez, in the spring of 1899, made it necessary to find some one to take up the work; and it was evident that a man was needed who would combine sympathy, tact, good sense, and marked spirituality. Mr. Cooper was chosen for the work, and went to Morocco in the spring of 1900. He spent a short time at Tangier; and in the autumn of the same year he entered upon his work at Fez. The work was interesting, but for various reasons by no means easy. Mr. Cooper, by God's grace, succeeded beyond the expectations of his best friends; and not only did the work grow in solidity and strength, but some new Muslim converts were numbered among the Christians. Notwithstanding the fact that the country was rather disturbed on account of native dissatisfaction with the Sultan's progressive and European ideas, there seemed every prospect of a work of wide-spread usefulness and power. On October 16, 1900, Mr. Cooper wrote an interesting letter, giving an account of his journey up to Fez; and this letter reached the office of his mission board after his martyrdom. On October 17 he went on the streets with two of the colporteurs, and while he was standing near the principal mosque, a Mohammedan fanatic shot him in the back. Altho the best of medical care was given him, he died two hours after the fatal shot was fired. Within less than an hour after the death of Mr. Cooper, by order of the Sultan, his murderer was put to death; and the Sultan, after expressing his abhorrence of the crime, granted Mrs. Cooper £1,000 as an expression of his sympathy in her bereavement.

COORG: A small native state in Southern India, lying chiefly among the mountains of the Western Ghats. The name is derived from that of a fine, hardy race of mountaineers who once dominated the region, and whose descendants still form a noticeable element in the population. The dimensions of the territory are about 60 miles north and south, and 40 east and west. The population is 178,302, composed chiefly of Hindus. There are only about 27,000 left of the original tribes of the Coorgs. Mohammedans contribute only seven per cent. of the total. The chief town is Merkara, with a population of between eight and nine thousand. The Basel Evangelical Missionary Society has a mission in Coorg. The family of native chiefs who once ruled Coorg was deposed by the supreme government of India in 1834, and has since become extinct. The territory is directly under the supervision of the viceroy, and is administered by the British Resident at Mysore, who is also chief commissioner of Coorg.

COPAY: A station of the CMS in the Jaffna district of Ceylon, with (1901) 2 missionary women, native workers and a training school for teachers. The statistics are included under **Jaffna.**

COPIAPO: Capital of the Department of Atacama, Chile, situated on the Copiapo River, 50 miles from its seaport of Caldera, and at an altitude of 1,300 feet. It is the center of a mining district and has extensive silver refineries. The population (1900) is 9,301. Station of the PN (1870) with (1901) 1 missionary and his wife, 3 native workers, 1 chapel, 6 Sunday schools, 2 common schools, 4 chief outstations and 300 professing Christians.

COPTIC CHURCH: The relic of a once powerful and progressive Egyptian Christianity, dating from the 1st century. According to its traditions St. Mark was its founder and first Patriarch. Its ritual appears to be a close reproduction of early Christian originals. Its doctrine is of the Jacobite class, defending the Monophysite heresy, and its relations to all other Christian bodies have been bitterly exclusive.

The Coptic Church was a missionary and aggressive body up to the 4th century, carrying its missions into **Abyssinia** and beyond, almost to the equator. It is now sunk in ignorance, altho beginning to give some small signs of intellectual awakening through the influence upon the common people of American (U. P.) and English missionaries. Several priests and one bishop of this Church were educated in the CMS seminary, formerly conducted at Cairo.

The Coptic clergy consist of monks, deacons, priests, arch-priests, bishops and metropolitans; the whole hierarchy being under the direction of the Coptic Patriarch of Alexandria. The Patriarch has the right to appoint the metropolitan of Abyssinia, and even the privilege of issuing the religious authorization when occasion befalls for the coronation of a king of Abyssinia.

The prelates of the Church as well as the monks are required to observe celibacy, but on the other hand marriage is an absolute condition precedent to ordination of a priest.

Butcher (E. T.), *The Story of the Church of Egypt*, 2 vols., London, 1897.

COPTIC LANGUAGE: Belongs to the Hamitic family of languages. It was once the vernacular tongue of Egypt, but it was superseded by the Greek, more especially by the Arabic, and is now a merely literary language cultivated by Biblical scholars and a very few of the Coptic priests. There are three principal dialects in Coptic, viz., the *Memphitic*, *Sahidic* and *Bashmuric*. The Memphitic, found in the neighborhood of Memphis, is the least pure of the three; the Sahidic or Thebaic, found in Upper Egypt, is more purely Egyptian and the Bashmuric, found in the Delta, differs from the others chiefly by certain changes in the vowels and in some of the consonants. The Coptic alphabet is a slightly modified form of the Greek.

COPTS: A people of Egypt, numbering about 600,000 and supposed to be a survival from the Egyptians of the Pharaohs. The name Copt is a religious rather than an ethnic term, since it is applied to Christians only, while the Mohammedan Fellahin of Egypt are of the same stock and race.

The Copts are, however, far more intelligent and enterprising than their kinsmen who did not accept Christianity. Nevertheless when compared with other Oriental Christians, as Greeks and Armenians, or with Jews, they are seen to lack initiative. Wherever found the Copts are gentle and submissive to control; in lower Egypt and Tripoli they are clerks and traders, shrewd business men and able when under guidance. In upper Egypt they are more frequently industrious agriculturists.

American (UP) and English (CMS) Missions have done much toward stimulating the Copts into a new intellectual growth; and now the Copts have about 1,000 elementary schools which they seek to conduct somewhat upon Western principles. In these schools they now make it a point to teach the ancient **Coptic language.** About one-half of the males in the Coptic community can read and write. See also **Coptic Church.**

Lane (E. W.), *An Account of the Modern Egyptians*, 2 vols., London, 1871; Poole (S. Lane), *Cairo*, London, 1897; Fowler (M.), *Christian Egypt*, London, 1900.

COQUIMBO: A seaport town in the Department of the same name, Chile, S. America; situated on Coquimbo Bay, about 200 miles N. of Valparaiso. Population about 9,000. Station of the ME, with (1902) 2 native workers, 2 Sunday schools, and 69 professing Christians.

COREA. See KOREA.

CORDOVA: Capital of the province of Cordova, Argentina, S. America; situated near the center of the republic. It was formerly the ecclesiastical metropolis of South America. It has still somewhat of that character, having an important University, and a very influential part of the city being that in which the clergy and their nearest adherents reside. It is also an important commercial and railway center. Its population (1901) is about 50,000. Station of the SAEM, with 1 missionary and his wife and of the PB, with 2 missionaries and their wives. Name also written Cordoba.

COROZAL: A town in British Honduras, situated 62 miles N. of Belize. Population 5,000. Station of the WMS, with (1901) 1 missionary, 7 native workers, 5 preaching centers, 1 Sunday school, 1 common school and 45 professing Christians.

COSTA RICA: A republic of Central America. Area, 22,000 square miles. Population, 243,205, chiefly mestizoes, negroes and Indians. Language, Spanish. Religion, Roman Catholic. The capital is San José, in a beautiful valley in the central part of Costa Rica. Punta Arenas is the port of San José, situated on the Gulf of Nicoya, the best harbor and only port of entry on the Pacific coast. The main range of the Andes, entering Costa Rica from the southeast, traverses its entire territory, widening toward the northwest, and forming a table land, on which are situated the principal towns and centers of population. The rivers of Costa Rica, altho numerous, are of inconsiderable size, the San Juan, which serves as a boundary between it and Nicaragua, being the only one navigable for steamers. It has no lakes of any great importance, but numerous small ones at the foot of the mountain ranges. Costa Rica lies in a volcanic belt and is therefore subject to frequent earthquakes. The soil is very productive, and, tho less rich in minerals than some of the neighboring countries, it contains some rich gold-mines. The climate is mild and delightful in the uplands, hot on the plains, but everywhere healthful, except along the lagoons on the western coast.

Costa Rica has been a republic since 1821, and is governed under a constitution promulgated in 1859, but modified frequently since that date. Commerce is carried on with the United Kingdom, the United States and Germany. The exports are chiefly bananas, coffee and hides.

The BFBS has a Bible depot and an agent at San José and the Central America Mission Society has a mission station there also. The Jamaica Baptist Missionary Society and the West Indies Wesleyan Annual Conference have stations at Port Limon and Cartago.

COTTA. See KOTTA.

COTTAYAM. See KOTTAYAM.

COVENANTERS; Missions of the. See PRESBYTERIAN, REFORMED.

COWICHAN: A town on the eastern coast of Vancouver Island, British Columbia, situated on the Cowichan River. Population, about 1,500. Station of the MCC (1900), with 1 missionary and his wife, 1 Sunday school and 1 place of worship.

CRADOCK: Capital of a district in Cape Colony, S. Africa, situated on the railway, 56 miles S. E. of Middelburg, and at an altitude of 2,850 feet. Population, about 5,000. Circuit of the South Africa Wesleyan Methodist Missionary Society, with (1900) 6 native workers, 2 chapels, 12 outstations, 1 Sunday school, 1 elementary school, and 163 professing Christians.

CREE LANGUAGE: Belongs to the central group of the N. American family of languages. It is spoken by some 40,000 Indians found to the S. and W. of Hudson Bay. It is written with Roman letters and syllabic characters.

CREEK LANGUAGE: Belongs to the central group of the N. American family of languages. It is spoken by the Creek and Seminole Indians in the Indian Territory, and is written with Roman letters.

CREEKTOWN: A town in Southern Nigeria, W. Africa, situated on the Cross River 70 miles above its mouth. Climate, tropical. The population is composed mainly of the Ibo and Èwè tribes of negroes. Station of the UFS (1846), with (1902) 10 missionaries, men and women (one a physician), 5 native workers, 5 outstations, 5 schools, a hospital, dispensary, and 303 church-members.

CREIGHTON-GINSBURG, Rev. J. B.: When a young man at Kief, with several of his companions, he saved up money to go to London in order to learn more about a Jewish sect—Protestant Christians, who they heard rejected the Talmud and strictly adhered to the Bible. This project was prevented. For the next five years he continued preparing for the office of a rabbi. After his father's death he wandered about from city to city, conversing with learned Jews, in hopes of finding peace. On returning home, his prejudice against the Talmud and his appreciation of the Bible became known, and so, to avoid discussions he went into a Jewish house of learning, and for six weeks, he relates, "I never went to bed, never sat down, never uttered one word after the manner of the Pharisees. The only meals I partook were bread and water once a day, just to maintain strength; and the little sleep I enjoyed was standing, leaning on the desk with my head on my clenched fists; my time was employed in reading the Talmud and the Psalms, setting my heart to seek the Lord." This retirement satisfied the Jews, but his soul was not at rest. In the course of a long period of struggle, he got to know Dr. Biesenthal and Mr. Schwarz, both Hebrew Christian missionaries, who instructed him in the truth and gave him a New Testament in Hebrew, and a copy of "Old Paths." Other missionaries of the London Society for the Jews opened his eyes still further, but Mr. Goldberg was the final means of his being brought to the truth. After ten months' instruction, on May 16, 1847, he was baptized. In 1856 he became one of the Society's missionaries, laboring for thirty years at Mülhausen, Constantine, Algiers and Mogador. He finally was stationed at Constantinople, where for the next twelve years, until his death in 1898, he worked most faithfully, having won many Jews to know Christ as Savior.

CROATIA: A province of the Austro-Hungarian Monarchy, forming with Slavonia a part of the kingdom of Hungary. Area, 5,220 square miles. Population, 757,477, chiefly Croats, with a few Germans, Magyars, and Jews. Religion, Roman and Greek Catholic. Education, almost wholly neglected. Capital, Agram.

The only missionary work is that done by the colporteurs of the British and Foreign Bible Society. This work has increased during the last few years, with some evidences of encouragement.

CROATIAN LANGUAGE: Belongs to the Slavonic branch of the Aryan language family, and, like the Servian, is spoken throughout Servia, Bosnia, Herzegovina, Montenegro, Croatia, Slavonia, Dalmatia, etc. The difference between the Servian and Croatian is largely in the written character, the Croats writing their language with Roman letters.

CROATS: To the Servian branch of the Slavic race belong also the Croats, who inhabit Dalmatia, Slavonia, Croatia, and the western part of Bosnia, numbering hardly a million and a half of souls. The linguistic differences between the Servians and the Croats are insignificant; their chief distinction lies in their religious confession and in their alphabets. The Servians belong to the Eastern or Orthodox branch of the Christian Church, while the Croats are almost all Roman Catholics, and use the Latin alphabet in their literature. This distinction has led to a great deal of coolness and even hatred between the two peoples.

The Croats appeared on the Balkan Peninsula almost simultaneously with the Servians, and, like them, they received Christianity first from Rome, and then, in the second half of the ninth century, from Byzantium; but, unlike the Servians, they soon fell under the dominion of the Roman Church. Politically, the Croats remained independent till 1102 A. D., when they united themselves to Hungary and shared in the vicissitudes of Hungarian history. This union was a free and spontaneous union on the part of the Croats, and the Hungarian kings were styled kings of Croatia, Dalmatia, and Slavonia. The Croatians had a constitution of their own, and the country was ruled over by royal commissioners or *bans*. But in the present century the claims of the Hungarians to domineer over the Croats led to dissensions between the two nationalities, and to the bloody conflicts in 1848-50, since when the relations between them have been strained. The Dalmatian Croats, especially in the little republic of Ragusa, attained in the latter part of the 15th, the 16th, and 17th centuries a great literary development. A number of writers, especially poets, flourished in Ragusa, who were educated and trained under the influence of the Italian Renaissance, and who produced some very important poetical works. Other men who have gained a world-wide reputation, born in Ragusa, were the archeologist, Banduri, the mathematicians Boshcovitch, Ghetalditch, etc.

Aside from the work of the Bible societies in distributing the Scriptures, no regular missionary work has been opened among the Croats.

CROWSTAND: A station of the Presbyterian Church in Canada, opened in 1877 and situated on Swan River in the N. E. part of Assiniboia, Canada. It has 1 missionary, 3 women missionaries, a chapel, a school, and 30 church-members.

CREOLE: Name applied to people born in or near the West Indies of foreign, and especially of Spanish or French, ancestry. When applied to negroes the term means that they are born in the country, as distinguished from those imported from Africa. The European Creoles are generally tall but not proportionally robust. They are distinguished for the suppleness of their joints, which enables them to move with ease, agility, and grace. From the same cause they excel in penmanship, and in everything requiring flexibility of movement. The women are generally beautiful, and of fine figure. The Creole negroes present a marked distinction from those imported from Africa, being more slender, agile, and graceful, tho not less strong or capable of labor, with quicker perceptions and more volatile dispositions. The dialects which have sprung up in the W. I. and adjacent regions, formed by the corruption of Spanish, French, and English, are generally called Creole dialects.

CRETE, or CANDIA: An island in the Mediterranean Sea, belonging to Turkey. It is very irregular in form, about 160 miles long, and varying in breadth from 6 to 35 miles, with a total area of 3,326 square miles. Its population is (1900) 303,543. The predominating religion is that of the Greek Church (Orthodox). About ten per cent. of the population are Mohammedans and there are a few Jews in the island. The language is Greek (modern). The BFBS has an agent on the island, but there are no other Protestant missions there. Until the year 1899 Crete was a province of the Turkish Empire. At that date four European powers intervened to end a continuous state of insurrection and made the island an autonomous state under a high commissioner of the powers, altho nominally still subject to the suzerainty of the Sultan.

CRIM-TURKISH: A dialect of the Nogai Turkish language spoken by the Tartars of the Crimea. See **Turkish.**

CRITICISM OF MISSIONS: See OBJECTIONS TO THE MISSIONARY ENTERPRISE.

CROWTHER, Samuel Adjai: A native of the Yoruba Country; rescued from slavery in boyhood. Soon after he was taken from the hold of a Portuguese slaver to Sierra Leone he begged a half-penny to buy an alphabet card for himself; within six months he could read the New Testament; and after five years he was admitted the first on the roll of students of Fourah Bay College, of which a few months later he was a tutor. June 29, 1864, he was consecrated Missionary Bishop of the Niger Territory by the Archbishop of Canterbury, in Canterbury Cathedral; and in the same year the University of Oxford conferred on him the degree of Doctor of Divinity. He was the first native bishop; and in 1841 he accompanied the first Niger expedition. The Royal Geographical Society, in 1880, awarded him a gold watch for his travels and researches on the Niger. With the assistance of Rev. T. King, he translated part of the Bible and Book of Common Prayer into Yoruba; and his Yoruba Vocabulary and work on the Nupe and Ibo languages show his real ability. Bishop Crowther was eminently successful as a missionary; and, as one of his associates points out, in dealing with the masses of the people, with heathen chiefs and with the astute followers of Mohammed, his directness and transparent simplicity of purpose won their confidence and conciliated their blind bigotry of opposition. Even more marked than his tact and wisdom was Bishop Crowther's humility. His lowliness of mind seemed to increase with his exaltation in office and in the esteem of the Christian world. He died at Lagos, December 31st, 1891.

CUBA: The largest island of the West Indies, formerly ruled by Spain; is now under its own government. It contains an area of 45,872 square miles; a coast line of 2,000 miles; and has a population (1899) of about 1,575,000, of whom 500,000 are negroes and 15,000 are Chinese. The island is largely under Roman Catholic influences; not 50,000 of the population attend school; and only twenty-four per cent. of the adults have formed legitimate marriages. Previous to the American occupation Dr. Alberto J. Diaz, a converted Romanist, labored successfully under the auspices of the Southern Baptist Home Mission Board, amidst great difficulties; and during the last four years, in the new atmosphere of religious freedom, encouraging work has been maintained by a number of societies. The following societies are now engaged in missionary labors in the island: American Baptist Home Mission Society; American Bible Society; American Church Missionary Society; American Friends' Board of Foreign Missions; African Methodist Episcopal Society; Independent Baptist Missionary Movement; Methodist Episcopal Church (South) Board; Foreign Missions of the Presbyterian Church in the United States (Southern); Foreign Christian Missionary Society.

Fiske (A. K.), *History of the Islands of the West Indian Archipelago*, New York, 1899; Porter (R. P.), *Industrial Cuba*, New York, 1899; Rowan (A. S.) and Ramsey (M. M.), *The Island of Cuba*, London, 1898.

CUDDALORE: Capital of the district of South Arcot, Madras, India, situated on the sea coast, 65 miles N. of Negapatam. Climate, moderately healthy. Population (1901) 52,216, chiefly Hindus. A station of the Danish-Halle Mission was opened here in 1728, but was afterwards given up. The town is now occupied as a station by the SPG (1825), with (1901) 18 native workers, men and women, 6 places of worship, 13 outstations, 5 day schools, 2 boarding schools and 325 baptized Christians. Station also of the Leipzig Missionary Society (1856), with (1900) 1 missionary and his wife, 8 native workers, 3 outstations, 5 chapels, 2 elementary schools, 2 high schools and 413 baptized Christians.

CUDDAPAH: Capital of the district of the same name, Madras, India, 161 miles by rail from Madras city. Population (1891) 17,400, of whom 9,400 are Hindus and 7,600 are Mohammedans. The climate is one of the hottest in the district, unhealthy, malarious; mean temperature in summer 97° F. The town is badly built and squalid in appearance. Station of the LMS (1824), with (1901, Jamulamadugu included) 10 missionaries, men and women, 160 native workers, men and women, 190 outstations, 113 elementary schools and 1,182 church-members.

CULBERTSON, Michael Simpson: Born Chambersburg, Pa., January 18th, 1819; graduated at the Military Academy, West Point, 1839, standing high in character and scholarship; was Assistant Professor of Mathematics in the Academy 1839-40; served 1840-41, with the rank of lieutenant of artillery, at Rouse's Point during the Canada border disturbances. Resigning his commission in the army, he entered the Theological Seminary at Princeton, N. J., graduating in 1843. He was regarded by Dr. Hodge as "among the foremost members of the institution." He sailed for China in 1844 as a missionary of the Presbyterian Board; was stationed at Ningpo 1845-51, and at Shanghai, 1851-62. He visited the United States for his health in 1856. Dr. Culbertson's main work for several years was in connection with the translation of the Scriptures into Chinese. During his visit to this country he published a work entitled: *Darkness in the Flowery Kingdom; or, Religious Notions and Superstitions in North China.* He died of cholera at Shanghai, 1862.

CULEBRA: A town near Colon on the Isthmus of Panama, Station of the Jamaica Baptist Missionary Union (1900), with 1 missionary, 2 preaching centers and 2 Sunday schools.

CUMBERLAND PRESBYTERIAN Board of Missions and Church Erection (1852): As early as 1818 the Cumberland Presbyterian Church sent evangelists among the Chickasaw Indians, which resulted in a mission being established among them in 1820. In 1845 a board was organized for carrying on the Home Missionary work of the Church and in 1852 a similar organization was formed for the foreign work.

In 1857 the Rev. Edmund Weir was sent to Liberia, where he remained for ten years. Work in Turkey was undertaken in 1860, and the Rev. J. C. Armstrong was sent to Constantinople, but owing to troubles at home arising from the civil war, he was recalled.

In 1873 work was commenced on the island of Trinidad, and was continued for several years. The Board now carries on work as follows:

1. *China:* There is one station, Chan-te-fu, in the province of Hunan. Medical work has recently been begun in connection with this mission. There are 5 American missionaries.

2. *Japan:* There are 5 stations, Osaka, Wakayama, Tsu Ise, Tanabe and Shingu. There are 13 American missionaries, of whom two are physicians.

3. *Mexico:* There is 1 station, Aguascalientes, and 4 American missionaries. The mission gives increased promise of permanency. The 3 schools are doing well and an industrial department has been added to the boys' school.

The Woman's Board of Missions of the Cumberland Presbyterian Church was organized in 1880 for the purpose of cooperating with the general Board. Nine American missionaries are supported by it in Japan, 1 in China and 2 in Mexico. They are principally engaged in school work.

CUMBUM: A town in the Karnul district, Madras, South India. Population (1891) 5,700, of whom 3,000 are Hindus and 2,300 Mohammedans. The place is noteworthy for an irrigation reservoir of 15 square miles area, built as a precaution against famine. The place is very unhealthy from malaria, especially when the water is low in this reservoir. Station of the ABMU (1882), with (1901) 2 missionaries and their wives, 75 native workers, men and women, 30 places of regular preaching, 31 Sunday schools, 30 common schools, 2 boarding schools and 3,262 church-members.

CUNNINGHAM: A town in the Transkei region, Cape Colony, S. Africa, situated about 15 miles S. W. of Butterworth. Station of the UFS (1856), with (1902) 1 missionary and his wife, 45 native workers, men and women, 16 outstations, 16 schools and 1,546 church-members.

CUPANG: Capital of the western, Dutch part of the island of Timor, East Indies. The Netherlands Missionary Society maintained a station here from 1819 to 1858, and gathered in 860 baptized converts. After the work was passed over to the Dutch Government the number of Christians increased to 2,700; but, as Warneck has said, they seem to lack sufficient oversight and to be on a rather low level of moral and religious life.

CURITIBA: Capital of the state of Parana, Brazil, S. America; situated in a pleasant open plain, where Europeans have settled, many of them French. A railway connects it with the seaport of Paranagua, about 80 miles distant. Population about 6,000. Station of the PN (1885), with (1901) 1 missionary and his wife, 2 missionary women, 7 native workers, of whom 6 are women, 1 common and 1 high school and 1 Young People's Society.

CUTCH. See KATCHCH.

CUTCHI LANGUAGE: This is a dialect of the Sindhi; belongs to the Indic branch of the Aryan family of languages, and is spoken in the district of Cutch, W. India.

CUTTACK: Capital of the district of Cuttack, Orissa division, Bengal, India; situated in the delta of the Mahandai River at the head of its canal system. Population (1901) 51,364, of whom 75 per cent. are Hindus. Station of the BMS (1822), with 9 missionaries, men and women, 19 native workers, 6 outstations, 16 common schools, 1 high school, 1 theological seminary, 2 orphanages, a printing-house and 1,037 communicants. Also station of the Baptist Zenana Missionary Society (1891), with 4 missionary women, 11 native women workers, 6 schools and 100 Zenana pupils.

CUZCO: Capital of the Department of Cuzco, Peru, and formerly the capital of the empire of the Incas; situated at an altitude of 11,380 feet, 350 miles S. E. of Callao. Station of the RBMU (1897), with (1902) 2 missionaries and their wives.

CWENWENI: A settlement in the Transkei district, Cape Colony, S. Africa, situated about 15 miles S. W. of Umtata. Station of the South Africa Wesleyan Methodist Missionary Society, with (1900) 19 native workers, 8 outstations, 5 preaching centers, 3 schools, 4 Sunday schools and 290 professing Christians.

CYPRUS: An island, the third largest in the Mediterranean, 60 miles from the coast of Asia Minor and 41 miles from the coast of Syria. It is almost 150 miles long and 55 miles broad, with an area of 3,584 square miles. The greater part of the island is mountainous, a range 7,000 feet high running the whole length of the island.

Cyprus was placed under British control by a special treaty in 1878, altho it is still nominally Turkish territory. It is open to missionary operations because of the perfect security and religious liberty which British rule produces.

The population of the island (1901) is 237,022. Of these, 182,739 are members of the Greek (Orthodox) Church and 51,309 are Mohammedans. There are also a few Armenians and some Syrians of the Maronite Church. The prevailing language is Greek, but Turkish is much used in business and knowledge of English is increasing.

Mission work is carried on in Cyprus by the RP (U. S. A.), which has stationed at Larnaca a missionary and his wife and 1 native worker. A dispensary and primary school are conducted and 22 communicants have joined the mission church. The BFBS has a Bible depot at Larnaca.

CZECHS. See BOHEMIANS.

D

DACCA: A town in Bengal, India, situated on the "old Ganges," 150 miles northeast of Calcutta. Formerly capital of Bengal, and a most populous and brilliant city. It now retains none of its former elegance. Population (1901), 90,542, of whom about half are Hindus and a little more than half Mohammedans. Station of the BMS (1816), with (1900) 3 missionaries and their wives, 10 native workers, 3 outstations, 2 schools, and 74 church-members. Station also of the Baptist Zenana Mission (1870), with 3 missionary women, 8 native women helpers, 8 elementary schools and 50 Zenana pupils.

DAGHESTAN: Name applied to that part of Caucasia lying on the eastern slope of the Caucasus toward the Caspian Sea. Parts of the country are very mountainous, with deep valleys, numerous lakes, streams and glaciers. Western Daghestan is the chief abode of the Lesghians, a powerful tribe, chiefly Mohammedans. Farther north live Tatar tribes, all of them Mohammedans, more or less nomadic, living principally by the raising of cattle and horses. Most of them are peaceable Russian subjects. The few large towns, among them Derbent, the capital, are situated on the Caspian coast. There is no direct missionary work, tho the British and Foreign Bible Society has published the Gospel of Matthew in Kumuki.

DAHANA: A station of the Rhenish Missionary Society (1878) on the eastern coast of Nias, an island near the west coast of Sumatra, East Indies. It was partly on account of Mohammedan intrigues among the pagans of the place that the Dahana station was established. It now has (1900) 1 missionary and his wife, 3 native workers, 2 schools and 302 professing Christians.

DAHOMEY: Formerly an independent negro kingdom, now a colony of France, situated on the Gulf of Guinea, between Togoland on the west and Lagos and Nigeria on the east. In 1900 the boundaries were extended on the north to join the French military territories in the Western Sudan. It comprises about 60,000 square miles and has a population roughly estimated at 1,000,000, mostly negroes of the Ewè family. The climate is very unhealthful, the soil remarkably fertile. Kotonu, the best harbor on the coast, has been chosen as the terminus of a railway now being constructed to open up the interior. The chief coast town is Whydah, formerly a slave port, now exporting great quantities of palm oil. Abome, the capital, is 65 miles inland, and connected with Whydah by a road which continues to the Mahi country, 30 miles farther north. The religion of the natives is mostly the lowest grade of fetishism, and wholesale human sacrifices have been one of its characteristics.

The WMS has a station at Porto Novo, under charge of a French missionary and his wife, with some 20 outstations, at whose places of worship the average attendance is 2,200. The total of professing Christians is about 350 (1902).

Sketchley, *Dahomey as It Is*, London, 1874; Aspe-Fleurimont, *La Guinée Française*, Paris, 1900; Forbes (E. F.), *Dahomey and the Dahomeans*, London, 1851.

DAKA: Settlement in Rhodesia, S. Central Africa, lying N. W. of Bulawayo. Station of the National Baptist Convention (1900), with 1 missionary and 20 professing Christians.

DAKHANI LANGUAGE: This language belongs to the Indic branch of the Aryan family, being a dialect of the Hindu. It is used by the Mohammedans of Madras, is written in Arabic characters, and is sometimes called Southern Hindustani. It differs materially from the Urdu or Northern Hindustani.

DAKURA: A settlement in the northern part of the Mosquito coast, Nicaragua, Central America. Station of the Moravian Missions (1893), with 1 missionary and his wife, 16 native workers, men and women; 1 school, 1 Sunday school, 1 chapel and 107 professing Christians.

DALHOUSIE: A sanitary hill station for the Punjab established in a portion of the Gurdaspur district which is detached and lies within the native state of Chamba, on the borders of Kashmir. The station lies at an altitude of 7,700 feet and has a population of about 2,000. The CEZ has a sanitarium here, with 1 missionary woman in charge.

DALMATIA: One of the provinces of the Austrian Empire; it occupies a narrow strip along the eastern shore of the Adriatic, between Croatia on the north and Albania on the south. Herzegovina and Montenegro bound it on the east. With its adjacent islands it is the most southern crown-land of the Austrian Empire. Area, 4,940 square miles. The coast is steep and rocky, but numerous bays afford good harbors and ports. Spurs from the Dinaric Alps cross the interior, reaching an elevation of 6,000 feet in Mount

Orien, while on the north the Belebech Mountains rise to a height of 5,000 feet. The climate is warm and in general healthful. Most of the land is given up to pasture. The population (1900) is 593,784. With the exception of about 10 per cent., the people belong to the Morlacks of Dalmatians proper. The remainder are Italians, Albanians and Jews. Full liberty of faith and conscience is secured, and every religious body has the right of ordinary public worship or instruction. The majority of the population belong to the Roman Catholic and Greek Churches, but the Evangelical Lutheran, the Evangelical Brotherhood, the Gregorian Armenian and the Jewish churches are recognized by the state.

Dalmatians or Morlacks are a people belonging to the Servian race, and speak a dialect of Slavonic called the Illyric. Physically they are a fine race, tall, well-developed, with regular features and dark complexion. Those living on the coast are excellent seamen, noted for their daring and bravery. They were the chief strength of the military prowess of Venice during the Middle Ages. The Morlacks of the interior are lovers of liberty and independence, brave soldiers, who have withstood successfully the aggressions of the Turks. They are noted for hospitality, while at the same time they are deceitful, rapacious and addicted to drunkenness.

Mission work among the Dalmatians is confined entirely to the colportage of the British and Foreign Bible Society.

DAMASCUS: Capital of the Turkish province of Sham, Syria, about 60 miles from the Mediterranean. One of the oldest cities in the world, and especially honored by the Muslims, who call it *Sham-es-Shereef*, Damascus the Holy. The Arabs call it one of the four terrestrial paradises. The view of the city as one descends from the range of Lebanon is very beautiful, the surrounding gardens almost concealing the city itself, except as the minarets rise above the mass of houses. Inside, however, it is very like other interior Oriental cities, with narrow streets and miserable houses. The population, numbering about 225,000, are almost entirely Muslims, the Christians and the Jews being not only few in numbers, but weak in influence. At the time of the Druse massacre, in 1860, the Christian and Jewish population were driven from the city and numbers of them slain. Since then they have returned in some numbers, but the city is still the scene of much Muslim fanaticism.

Station of the Jewish Mission Committee of the Presbyterian Church in Ireland (1843), with (1900) 6 missionaries, men and women; 42 native workers, men and women; 11 outstations, 12 preaching places, 15 elementary schools, 4 high schools and 207 professing Christians. Station also of the British Syrian Mission Schools (1868), with 3 missionary women, 14 native women helpers, 3 outstations, 3 schools, 1 chapel and 1 Sunday school. Station also of the London Jews Society (1869), with 7 missionaries (one with his wife), 8 native workers, men and women; 1 chapel, 1 Sunday school, a book depot and 1 school. Station also of the Edinburgh Medical Missionary Society (1884), with 2 missionary physicians (one with his wife), 2 missionary women, 1 dispensary and 1 hospital.

DAMOH: A town in the Central Provinces, India; situated 55 miles N. W. of Jabalpur. The population is (1891) 11,800, of whom 9,000 are Hindus. Station of the FCMS (1894), with 11 missionaries, men and women (one of them medical); 12 native workers, men and women; 2 dispensaries, a hospital, 1 elementary school, 1 industrial school, a Young People's Society and 60 professing Christians.

DANG-SENG: A town in the Fo-kien province of China, lying about 50 miles south of Fu-chau. Station of the CEZ (1893), with (1901) 2 missionary women, 3 native women helpers and 2 boarding schools.

DANISH MISSIONS: To King Frederick IV. of Denmark belongs the honor of having initiated foreign missions in the Protestant, or Reformed, Church. As Crown Prince he manifested much interest in the condition of the colonies, which since 1620 had been part of the Danish Kingdom, and when he came to the throne, with the cordial assistance of the court chaplain, Dr. Lütkens, he arranged to send Bartholomew Ziegenbalg and Henrik Plütschau to India, where they founded, in 1705, the "Danish-Tamil," or "Danish Halle," Mission in Tranquebar. Until the death of Christian Frederick Schwartz, in 1798, this mission continued to receive partial support from the Danish Government, much of its material being furnished by the SPCK. The Royal College of Missions, founded in Copenhagen in 1714, did good work both for the Tamil Mission, that of Hans Egede in Greenland, and Von Westens Finmark Mission. Rationalistic influences, however, were strong and after the death of Schwartz interest declined. The English gained control of Hindustan, the missionaries received their support from the SPG, and in 1847 the church buildings and remaining interests were handed over to the Leipzig Society.

Meanwhile much work was done by Danish missionaries in the service of foreign societies, most of them among the Moravians. Ten were sent to Surinam, fourteen to Tranquebar, eleven to Labrador, of whom two had been in Greenland; seven to Danish West Indies, nine to English West Indies, one to North America, three to South Africa, one to the Mosquito coast, one to Australia. Altogether 53 Danish missionaries have been in the Moravian missions, among them the Greenland missionary, Jans Haven.

In 1843 the "Northern Schleswig Mission" was founded to help the Moravians in the Danish West Indies, altho later Southern Jylland was separated from Denmark. This Society still has its branches in Jylland, from which it received donations as late as 1888.

Danish Missionary Society (Danske Missionsselskab): Headquarters, Fredericia, Denmark. It is a general society of all the Danish Church people, and is conducted by a committee. Its own particular work is among the Tamils in India, but it works harmoniously with other missions. Its own missionaries are all ordained, and those who have been on mission ground for three years direct the affairs of the Society on the mission field. A yearly report must be sent to the home committee in Denmark. This Society has on its list Danish Greenland Mission, Danish Malay Mission, New Danish Tamil Mission, and Northern Santal Mission. It has also assisted the Loventhal Mission.

The mission movement in the beginning of the 19th century reached Denmark also, and inspired priest Bone Falck Ronne to found the "Danish Mission Society," June 17, 1821. Its motto was, "Be not fearful: only believe" (Mark 5: 15). This Society seemed to him a necessity, for the Mission College was not kind, and the strength of the free workers was very great. In 1823, on a journey to Fyen, Ronne had asked many of the priests to hang up boxes in the parsonage for free gifts to the mission. Bishop Plumb indicted him in the court of chancery, and Ronne was rebuked. The ministers had to take down their boxes, and Ronne was thankful for such slight punishment. The Danish Mission Society began to help the Greenland Mission by books, letters and donations, but the acts of the Mission College became more oppressive. They denied the mission in many ways, and would not allow the missionaries to write to any one else but the college about their work.

The Society supported for a little while from 1827 J. W. Cappellen, a Norwegian, in the Basel Missionary Institution, and in 1829 two men, P. P. Jäger and Andreas Riis, were sent out from Basel, and in 1832 arrived at Ussu, near Christiansborg, in what was then a Danish possession and is now the British Gold Coast Colony in W. Africa. Jäger soon died, but Riis worked for 13 years, first at Akra and later at Akropong, for four years the only missionary at this station. After the sale of the Danish possessions in Africa to England the work of the Society was somewhat feeble. Later, attempts were made to carry on work in Smyrna, Turkey, but without great success.

In June, 1860, at a meeting held in Nyburg, it was decided that the Danish Society should become the leader in all mission work in Denmark, and that Unions should be formed, and that the bishop issue a call to the ministers to interest themselves in the matter. Two years later a mission school was founded. In 1863 a delegate was sent from Germany to inquire if the Society would take the independent mission at Bethanien in South India, which Missionary Ochs had begun, after he had left the Leipzig Society on account of a difference between himself and the missionaries on the question of caste. Ochs was at that time in Europe, and came to Denmark, when the Danish Missionary Society promised to help him in India with gifts and workers.

This was the beginning of the New Danish Tamil Mission. In 1864 a large number of Danish missionary friends interested themselves in other mission work. A Greek-Danish Missionary Society was founded by Victor Block in 1863, with a plan to unite with the Greek (Orthodox) Church, and with this do a work among the Mohammedans, but the Danish Missionary Society would not consider it. In 1867 Pastor Block went to Athens, and the next year the mission was given up. In 1872 the first scholars of the Danish Missionary Society, Loventhal and H. Jensen, went to Vellur in India. They worked together till 1874, when Jensen went into the Danish Missionary Society's service, Loventhal carrying on an independent mission.

Greenland Mission: In May, 1721, Hans Egede, a minister of Vaagen, sailed for Greenland from Copenhagen. His interest in that country had been aroused by the report of the degradation of the people, brought by a brother-in-law, and he had for several years tried to arouse the Danish Church to do something. At last, with the help of 18,000 kroners subscribed by friends and 600 kroners of his own money, he started, accompanied by his wife and four children and a company of colonists. The enterprise met with great difficulties. It took him three years to acquire the language; the inhospitable climate was a heavy strain on his health; the support granted by King Frederick IV. was denied by Christian VI., tho afterward partially restored; an epidemic of small-pox swept through the community, leaving only three families out of 200; his wife died and the brave man was compelled to return to Denmark. Through his influence the king founded a seminary for the education of teachers and missionaries, and Egede was appointed superintendent. In 1740 he was made Missionary College director for all the work in Greenland, but was greatly distressed at the lack of care in choosing missionaries, resulting in injury to the work. The lack of concord between Egede and the Missionary College increasing, he retired to his own quiet home. He died in the merchant city, Stubbekjöbing, on November 15, 1758. His son, Paul Egede, succeeded him as director in the seminary.

The result of the work in succeeding years was that all Greenland became Christian, having the honor of being the earliest independent mission church resulting from the modern missionary movement. The Danish Missionary Society continues its interest in and superintendence of the work, having one missionary, with several native assistants, in their employ.

New Tamil Mission: After the caste difficulties with the Leipzig Society, Missionary Ochs visited Denmark, and made an agreement with the Danish Missionary Society for aid in the New Danish Tamil Mission. He then went to Pattambakam, and founded stations at Bethanien and Siloam, with a mission house and a school building, which was turned into a church. About 1882 they purchased some school property of the Baptists at Tiruvanammalai, and a few years later extended their work into Arcot, Ranipet and Sallesapet. There were (1900) 7 stations, 12 outstations, 20 missionaries, 18 native workers, 277 communicants, and 178 pupils in schools. For five years a mission was conducted among the Malays of India, at Assampur and neighboring villages, and another among the Red Karens at Pobja, Burma, but both were given up.

A mission has more recently been established in Manchuria (1896), and the reports in 1900 showed 4 stations, 1 outstation, 13 missionaries, 2 native workers, 26 communicants and 12 pupils in the schools. Special attention seems to be paid to medical missionary work, as there were 4 hospitals and dispensaries, with 1,000 patients.

The Danish Missionary Society also renders assistance to the organization known as the Indian Home Mission to the Santals.

Loventhal's Mission: Founded 1872 by Loventhal and H. Jensen (Copenhagen). The committee has nine members (all men of the Grundvigsk belief), with three head directors. The foundation of the Society is Baptism, its motto "Be born again," and it is a mission to the common people. The directors simply raise money, and do not give advice or instruction to the missionaries, who work independently. Loventhal and Jensen went out to India in 1872, and founded a station at Vellur. Loventhal's desire is to have converts retain their manners and customs as much as possible. He has no schools, and travels from place to place. He has 3 Hindu assistants, ordained by Jensen in 1880. His principal aim is to baptize the natives, whom he accepts if they seem honest in their desire to believe as the missionaries do. But one station, 2 missionaries and 3 native workers were reported in 1902.

The Utakamund Danish Evangelistic Mission: Known also as the *Emilies Minde* (memorial), or *Koefoed's Mission,* is a small organization for voluntary work in Madras, India. The missionaries receive no salaries.

DAPOLI: A town in the Ratnagri district, Bombay, India; situated a few miles from the sea and about 70 miles S. W. of Poona. Population a little over 5,000. It is one of the healthiest places in the Bombay Presidency. Station of the SPG (1878), with (1901) 1 missionary, 2 missionary women, 20 native workers, men and women; 1 place of worship, 4 day schools, 2 boarding schools and 20 baptized adult Christians.

DARAPURAM. See DHARAPURAM.

DARBHANGAH: Chief town of the district of the same name in Bengal, India; situated about 56 miles N. E. of Patna. Population (1901), 66,244. It was originally a purely Mohammedan city, but the Hindus now outnumber the Mohammedans almost in the ratio of 3 to 1. Station of the Zenana Bible and Medical Missionary Society, with (1903) 2 women missionaries, 3 native workers and 1 school. Also a circuit of the ME, with (1902) 4 native workers, 2 Sunday schools and 240 professing Christians.

DAR ES SALAAM: A seaport town of German East Africa, lying about 40 miles S. of the island of Zanzibar. Population, about 13,000, Arabs, Indians and Bantu negroes. The town gives access to the interior of the province by well-made roads, and a concession has been issued for a railway which is expected ultimately to be extended to the southern end of the Victoria Nyanza. Station of the Berlin Mission to East Africa (1887), with (1900) 2 missionaries (one with his wife), 1 native worker, 1 chapel, 1 school and 12 professing Christians.

DARFUR. See SUDAN.

DARJILING: A town in the district of the same name, Bengal, India, 360 miles from Calcutta by rail. It is a hill station (7,000 feet) and sanitarium, which is very popular. Population (1891), 14,100, of whom 8,600 are Hindus and 3,700 Buddhists. It is a place of many languages, Nepali and the Bhutia here meeting the Bengali and Hindi. The climate is good, but the rainfall is somewhat excessive. Station of the Church of Scotland Foreign Missions (1870), with 40 outstations, 5 missionaries, men and women; 73 native workers, men and women; 14 Sunday schools, 58 common schools, a dispensary and 306 professing Christians. Also station of the Church of Scotland Woman's Missionary Society (1886), with 4 missionary women, 9 native women helpers, 2 elementary schools, 1 high school, 1 industrial school and 38 Zenana pupils.

DARLING, David: Born 1790; sent by London Missionary Society to the South Seas in 1816. Stationed at Eimeo and Tahiti, making various missionary tours from Bunaania. In 1834 he went to Marquesas to commence a mission on those islands, returning the next year to Tahiti. He assisted in translating the Scriptures into the Marquesan language. Returning from a visit to England, 1852, he made his home in Tahiti till 1859, when he retired from active service and settled at Sydney, where he died December 6, 1867.

DARSI: A town in the Kistna district, Madras, India, situated about 25 miles N. W. of Ongole. Station of the ABMU (1894), but not occupied (1901), the work there being under care of the missionaries residing at Ongole and the statistics being summed with those of Ongole. The native Christian communicants at Darsi and its dependencies number about 3,250.

DASKA: A town in the district of Sialkot, Punjab, India, situated about 50 miles N. of Lahore. Population somewhat over 5,000. Station of the Church of Scotland Foreign Missions (1857), with (1900) 44 outstations, 1 missionary and his wife, 24 native workers, 1 chapel, 20 elementary schools, 1 high school, 1 theological seminary and 133 professing Christians.

DATAGANJ: Town in the Rohilkhand district of the United Provinces, situated about 20 miles S. W. of Budaun. Station of the ME, with (1901) 14 native workers, 16 Sunday schools, 2 common schools, a Young People's Society and 590 professing Christians.

DAVAO: A town and seaport on the island of Mindanao, P. I., situated on Davao Bay in the eastern part of the island and at the foot of the volcano of Apo. Station of the ABCFM (1902), with 1 missionary and his wife.

DAVID, Christian: Born in Moravia early in the 18th century, his father a Bohemian, his mother a German. He was a zealous Roman Catholic, but was converted to the Moravian views early in life and became a leader in the great Moravian emigration to Count Zinzendorf's estates. Of this, Zinzendorf writes: "Christian David was so intent on the Moravian emigration, that, when he was engaged in wainscoting the saloon of my house at Berthelsdorf in 1723, and had about finished his work, he left his tools, and set off, without hat, on a journey of nearly 200 miles, to Moravia, to lead back emigrants. He made eleven or twelve journeys in all, and, tho often in the most imminent danger from the officers of justice who rode in search of him, he was passed by or preserved from them in the most wonderful manner." The removal to Berthelsdorf began in 1722 with ten persons, and within seven years 300 others had joined the little company and built the town called Herrnhut. In 1733 Christian David accompanied the first Moravian missionaries to Greenland. After various journeys in the service of the church and another voyage to Greenland, he in 1748 accompanied the great missionary colony to Pennsylvania. In August, 1749, after revisiting Greenland, he made another visit to America, and assisted in building the chapel-house at Nazareth, Penn. He died at Herrnhut, 1750.

DAY, Samuel Stearns: Born Ontario, Canada, May 13, 1808; graduated Hamilton Literary and Theological Institute; sailed as a missionary of the ABMU to India, September 20, 1835. He was stationed first at Vizagapatam, then at Chicacole, and in 1837 at Madras. In Madras he spent three years preaching in Telugu and English, and organized an English church, of which he was the pastor. Having made several tours into the Telugu country, he fixed upon Nellore as the most suitable place for a mission, and in

1840 removed thither with his family. Mr. Day was the founder of the Telugu Mission. Amid many discouragements and obstacles he continued to labor, in firm faith that the Gospel would triumph in that heathen land. By reason of failing health he spent three years (1845-1848) in the United States and returned to Nellore. But in 1853 he was compelled to return to America and after years of physical suffering he died at Homer, N. Y., September 17, 1871.

DAYAK LANGUAGE: This language is found in the island of Borneo in two main dialects and belongs to the Malayan family. Missionaries of the Rhenish Missionary Society reduced the language to writing, using Roman letters, and have done some literary work in it. In German works on Borneo the name is spelled Dajak.

DEACONESSES: 1. *History:* Almost from the day of her birth the Christian Church had a two-fold ministry—the Ministry of the Word (*diakonia tou logou*), instituted by Christ Himself for the preaching of the Gospel and the administration of the sacraments (Matth. xxviii: 19, 20; Mark xvi: 15; John xx: 21), and the Ministry of Mercy (*diakonia he kathemeriné*) or the Diaconate (Acts 6: 1-6).

The latter was the direct outgrowth of the former. At first the apostles, like their Divine Master, combined both ministries in their own activity. But when the number of the disciples was multiplied, and the Grecians in the congregation at Jerusalem began to murmur against the Hebrews, because their widows were neglected in the daily ministration, the apostles, in order to secure such a systematic administration of the alms as their own growing duties of another kind made impossible, called the multitude of the disciples unto them and said: "It is not reason that we should leave the word of God, and serve tables. Wherefore, brethren, look ye out among you seven men of honest report, full of the Holy Ghost and wisdom, whom we may appoint over this business. But we will give ourselves continually to prayer and to the ministry of the word." The assembled believers did as they were commanded, chose seven men having the required qualifications, set them before the apostles, and these, "when they had prayed, laid their hands on them," *i. e.*, ordained them to this newly-created office of the Church.

To this ministry was committed the care of the poor and sick, under the supervision of the ministry of the Word. Tho Stephen preached (Acts vi: 8-10; vii: 1-53), and Philip both preached and baptized (Acts viii: 5, 38), the deacons were not primarily meant to be evangelists, but dispensers of charity and the more immediate overseers of the Church's temporal affairs. Thus they became the most direct and efficient "helps" of the ministry of the Word; and how beneficial this arrangement proved is evident from the further statement that the "word of God increased; and the number of disciples multiplied in Jerusalem greatly."

To this ministry of mercy women were also admitted at a very early date. The necessity for this evidently made itself felt almost at once, inasmuch as "the strict seclusion of the female sex in Greece and in some Oriental countries necessarily debarred them from the ministrations of men" (Dean Stanley). That women deacons were already found in the Apostolic Church is manifest from Rom. xvi: 1, 2. In this passage Paul speaks of one Phebe, "our sister, which is a servant (Gr. *diakonos*) of the church which is at Cenchrea." He indicates the character of her office and the nature of her work in the statement that she had been a succorer of many, and of himself also. For this very reason he commends her to the Christians at Rome, to whom she probably transmitted his letter, and admonishes them to "receive her in the Lord, as becometh saints," and to assist her in whatsoever business she had need of them. If, furthermore, the passage 1 Tim. iii: 11 refers, not to wives of the deacons, but to women deacons, as many able commentators contend, then the evidence is still more conclusive that the Female Diaconate was an established office in the Christian Church long before the close of the 1st century.

The office seems to have spread with the growth of the Church. At the beginning of the 2d century we find an undoubted reference to deaconesses in Asia Minor in the well-known letter of Pliny the Younger, Governor of Bithynia, to the Emperor Trajan. He writes: "In order to get at the truth of the matter (*i. e.*, concerning the life and customs of the Christians) I deemed it necessary to put to the rack two maids, who are called *ministrae*. But, beyond a most corrupt and boundless superstition, I could extort nothing from them."

The Female Diaconate reached its highest development in the 4th century, and in the Church of the East. At this time the references to it are frequent, and many women of noble birth are found in its ranks. Very complete information regarding it is contained in that body of ecclesiastical writings known as the "Apostolic Constitutions." This document enjoins that faithful and holy women be set apart as deaconesses, because the Church had need of them for many things; directs that they shall be inducted into their office by the bishop, with prayer and the imposition of hands, in the presence of the presbyters, deacons and deaconesses; and even prescribes the prayer to be used at the service of consecration. It also defines the duties of the deaconesses. They were to instruct the female catechumens; give the necessary external assistance at their baptism, visit and relieve the sick, the afflicted and the distressed of their own sex, minister to the confessors in prison, prepare the bodies of women for burial, serve as doorkeepers at the women's entrances to the churches, assign women their places at worship, facilitate communication between the bishop or presbyter and the female members of his congregation, and in general engage in all those helpful services from which heathen sentiment excluded the deacons.

After the 4th century the Female Diaconate began to decline. The causes of this are to be sought partly in changed conditions, but chiefly in the growing belief that God could be better served in a quiet, ascetic life than by a life of activity devoted to the good of others, and the consequent growth of monastic orders. The convent now became the retreat for pious unmarried women; and, by the 9th century in the Church of the West, and the 13th in the Church of the East, the Female Diaconate had practically disappeared. Only among the Waldenses and the Bohemian Brethren before the Reformation, and in some Mennonite congregations of Germany and Holland after the Reformation were traces of it left until its revival in the first half of the last century by the Rev. Theodore Fliedner, at Kaiserswerth-on-the-Rhine.

Fliedner became pastor of the small Protestant congregation at Kaiserswerth in 1822. On a collecting tour through Holland and England in behalf of his poverty-stricken church he became acquainted with numerous institutions of Christian mercy. These awakened in him the desire to undertake similar work himself. He began by making regular pastoral visits to the prisoners in the penitentiary at Düsseldorf. In 1826 he founded the Rhenish-Westphalian Prison Society, the first of the kind on the Continent. In September, 1833, the little summer house of the parsonage garden temporarily sheltered the first discharged female convict, and became the cradle of the Kaiserswerth institutions. Three years later he inaugurated the work with which his name will always be associated. Among the Mennonites of Holland he had found deaconesses. Others before him (Kloenne, von Stein, Amalia Sieveking and von der Recke-Volmarstein) had advocated the restoration of the ancient office, but had found no practical way of doing so. He himself had become persuaded that no one was by nature and grace so well fitted for the work of ministering love as a devout Christian woman, and to his mind the solution of the problem lay in establishing institutions for the special training of unmarried women in the various branches of charitable work, and in associating these in a close community. Accordingly, in the spring of 1836, with no money but with a large measure of faith, he bought the largest and finest house in Kaiserswerth, organized the Rhenish-Westphalian Deaconess Society, and on the 13th of October of the same year opened the Kaiserswerth Deaconess Motherhouse. Eight days later, Gertrude Reichardt, the daughter of a physician, became the first probationer. Now began a marvelous development. The number of sisters multiplied rapidly; one institution after the other was added at Kaiserswerth; outside "stations" were undertaken; Motherhouses were established at other places, and when Fliedner died in 1864 there were already 31 Motherhouses, with a total of 1,593 sisters engaged in 406 stations, the Kaiserswerth Motherhouse alone having 425 sisters working in four continents, on 111 stations.

In 1861 the Motherhouses organized on the Kaiserswerth model formed a Union or General Conference, which meets every three years at Kaiserswerth. In 1901 the number of houses belonging to the Union was 75, with 14,501 sisters in active service, and an annual income and outlay of $3,375,000. Forty-eight of these houses are in Germany, 7 in Holland, 7 in Russia, 4 in Switzerland, 2 in France, 2 in Austria-Hungary, 1 each in Denmark, Sweden and Norway, and 2 in the United States. One house in Germany, 2 in Holland and 1 in the United States have been received into the Union since 1901. Fifteen German houses have no connection with the Union.

The first effort to transplant the deaconess work to the United States was made in 1849, when, at the earnest request of the Rev. Dr. Passavant of the Lutheran Church, Fliedner himself brought over four deaconesses to become the nucleus of a Motherhouse at Pittsburg. For various reasons this first venture proved a failure. In 1884 another colony of German sisters was installed in the German Hospital, Philadelphia, where the work became firmly established in the splendid Mary J. Drexel Home and Philadelphia Motherhouse of Deaconesses, built, supported and endowed by Mr. John D. Lankenau (died 1901). In its organization, life and work this house of all American Deaconess houses most closely resembles the European type. Additional Lutheran Motherhouses are now (1903) found in Baltimore, Omaha, Milwaukee, Minneapolis, Chicago and Brooklyn. Since 1896 the American Lutheran houses have held four General Conferences of their own.

2. *The Motherhouse:* In the early Church the deaconess office was a congregational office. Those who were set apart to it were chosen from the congregation in which they were to serve, and beyond having the qualifications required by the apostles for the Diaconate in general (Acts vi: 3; 1 Tim. iii: 8-11), they received no special training for their work. This is not the case to-day. The deaconess of the present is prepared for her calling in an institution that makes this its special object, and to this institution, known as the Motherhouse, she remains permanently attached. By the Motherhouse she is assigned her field of labor, and from the Motherhouse she gets her support. Tho not an officebearer in the congregation in the sense of the early deaconess, she is nevertheless, by virtue of her consecration, and viewed from the side of her practical activity, as truly a servant of the Church in her sphere as the minister of the Word is in his. As the whole method of preparing and calling men for the ministry of the Word to-day differs in many particulars from that of the early Church, so, owing to totally changed conditions, the restoration of the Female Diaconate could take place only by adapting the method for doing so to these conditions. Hence the present institutional form of the work, which practical experience has so far shown to be not only the best, but the only possible form for securing abiding results; and in this particular only is an essential difference to be noted between the deaconess office of the early Church and the same calling to-day.

The internal management of the Motherhouse is committed to a Pastor and a Sister Superior. Candidates for admission must be between 18 and 36 (in some Motherhouses, 40) years of age, of unblemished Christian character, intelligent, unmarried and in good health. The impelling motive is beautifully expressed by Löhe, who puts these words into the mouth of the intending deaconess: "What is it my purpose to do? I will serve. Whom will I serve? The Lord Jesus in the persons of His suffering and needy brethren. What shall be my reward? I will serve neither for reward nor thanks, but out of a grateful and loving heart. My reward is that I am permitted to do so. And if I perish? 'If I perish, I perish,' said Esther, who knew not Him for Whom I would perish, but Who will not let me perish. And if I grow old in the service? Then my heart shall still flourish like the palmtree, and the Lord will satisfy me with grace and mercy. I go forth in peace and fear naught." The instruction, in which a so-called Training Sister (Probemeisterin) takes a prominent part, is of a kind designed to lead to the highest development of Christian character and practical ability. At the consecration which ends the period of probation the candidate makes no vows, but only promises faithfulness in her calling. She retains her evangelical liberty to relinquish it when once conscientiously convinced that she ought to do so, tho this does not often occur after one has been consecrated. Summarizing the advantages of the modern Motherhouse they may be stated as follows: It gives those who expect to devote their life to the work of Christian mercy in any of its forms a theoretical and practical training for it such as they could get in no other way, and at no other place; it affords the best possible opportunities for utilizing the special gifts of each one, and the gifts of all in common for the accomplishment of the largest measure of good; by the beauty of its worship, the frequency and variety of its services, the abundant preaching and teaching of the Word, the special pastoral care given each sister, and the healthful influence that comes from being closely associated with common aims in a common work, it is a most potent means for developing a strong Christian character and personal holiness; while, finally, it also serves as an outward protection and support by lifting the sister above the cares, frivolities and temptations of the world, providing for all her material necessities, sheltering her when disabled and offering her a quiet retreat in old age.

3. *Fields of Labor:* A deaconess of the Kaiserswerth type is not a female evangelist. Tho she embraces many an opportunity to speak the Word of instruction and comfort in private, and particularly in her work with the young has extraordinary advantages for religious teaching, she is nevertheless not called to the ministry of the Word, but, in accordance with Matth. v: 16, is rather to demonstrate the saving power of the Word by what she is and does. Nor is she only a nurse of the sick, tho thousands are thus engaged in hundreds of institutions. Besides the nursing of the sick, her work embraces the care of the aged and infirm, the insane, the feeble-minded and the epileptic; the care and instruction of children in Day Nurseries, Orphans' Homes and Little Children's Schools, and of girls in Industrial Schools, Servants' Training Schools and Girls' High Schools; the recovery of the fallen in reformatories, prisons and Magdalen asylums; the protection of the imperiled in working girls' homes and hospices; and above all, and as the crown of all, work among the poor, the sick, the bereaved, the ignorant and the needy of every kind in parishes, under the direct oversight of the pastor.

According to the statistics of the General Conference of 1901, a total of 98 deaconesses were then stationed in Asia, Africa and South America. In hospitals there were 14 at Alexandria, 9 at Cairo, 8 at Beirut, 8 at Jerusalem and 2 in the leper colony of Groot Chatillon, Surinam, South America; in orphans' homes 17 at Beirut, 11 at Smyrna, 10 at Jerusalem and 2 in the school and sanitarium at Areya on Mt. Lebanon; in parish work at Alexandria and Haifa 2; 15 were also employed in the hospital and 2 in the little children's school at Constantinople. On mission stations among the heathen there were 2 in Madagascar, 3 in Batavia, 2 in South Africa, 4 in West Africa and 4 in India.

4. *Other Types:* In the United States the deaconess cause has also struck roots in other Churches besides the Lutheran. In 1887-88 the work was taken up by the Methodist Episcopal Church, and in 1889, after various private efforts, the General Convention of the Protestant Episcopal Church adopted a canon authorizing the training and appointment of deaconesses. In the Methodist Church the work has had a remarkably rapid growth, extending not only into many parts of the United States, but also into Europe, Asia and Africa, with an enrollment in 1901 of almost 1,100 deaconesses; but in both Churches named the work differs materially from the Kaiserswerth type. The Methodist deaconess is to a great extent an evangelist, and neither in the Methodist nor in the Episcopal Church are the so-called "training schools" and "deaconess homes" real Motherhouses, possessing those distinctive features which European experience has shown to be essential for the healthy and permanent development of the Female Diaconate. Various institutions of a similar character, mostly interdenominational, and devoted almost exclusively to hospital work, conclude the list in the United States.

Schafer, *Die weibliche Diakonie*, 3 vols., Stuttgart (2d ed. 1887-1894); Wacker, *Der Diakonissenberuf*, Gütersloh, (1890), (Eng. trans. *The Deaconess Calling*, Mary J. Drexel Home, Phila., 1893); Wurster, *Die Lehre von der Inneren Mission*, Berlin, (1895); Uhlhorn, *Christian Charity in the Ancient Church*, New York, (1893); Jacobs, *The Female Diaconate of the New Testament*, Lutheran Church Review, January, 1892; Spaeth, *Phebe, the Deaconess*, Lutheran Church Review, July and October, 1885.

DEAN, Rev. William: For many years a missionary in Siam, under the ABMU. His work in that country began in 1835, and through his efforts the first Chinese church in Bangkok was organized two years afterward. On his return to America in 1845 he awakened great interest in his work by his addresses, and induced many to take a deeper interest in the cause of foreign missions. In 1864 he resumed his work at Bangkok, where he remained until 1884. He died at San Diego, August 13, 1895.

DEESA. See DISA.

DEHRA: A town in the Dehra Dun district, United Provinces, India. Prettily situated in a mountain valley more than 2,300 feet above the sea, 75 miles east of Ambala. Population (1891), 27,500, of whom 75 per cent. are Hindus and nearly 25 per cent. Mohammedans. Mission station of the PN (1853), with (1901) 5 missionaries, men and women (one of them a physician); 17 native workers, men and women; 1 common school, 2 high schools, and 101 professing Christians. Also station of the General Synod of the Reformed Presbyterian Church in North America, with 1 missionary, 5 native workers, men and women; 2 preaching places, 1 common school and special work for lepers.

DEINZERHÖHE: Station of the Neuen Dettelsau Missionary Society, situated on the E. coast of German New Guinea. The force is composed of 2 missionaries, who conduct a common school there.

DELAGOA BAY: A station of the WMS south of Lourenço Marques, Portuguese East Africa, situated on Delagoa Bay. In 1899 there were stationed here 1 missionary, 20 native workers, men and women; with 3 places of worship and 3 common schools. The South African war disarranged many of the missionary enterprises of these regions and revised reports have not yet (1903) been obtainable.

DELENA: A station of the LMS, on the S. coast of British New Guinea, about 50 miles N. W. of Port Moresby. The station was occupied in 1882 and is worked (1902) by 1 missionary and 16 native workers, with 17 elementary schools and 462 professing Chrisstians.

DELHI: A town of Punjab, India, 38 miles S. W. of Meerut. Noted for its wonderful old palaces and magnificent old buildings, in some respects the most beautiful and curious in the world. No city in India has finer thoroughfares than Delhi; most of its houses are of brick, well built and substantial. It is the easternmost of the great towns of the province, situated on a fertile plain on the right bank of the Jumna. It has great historical importance, having been the splendid capital of the Mogul (Turkish) emperor Shah Jihan, whose fine mosque, Jama Musjid, is a magnificent monument of the 17th century. Because Delhi was the former residence of the great Mogul, many Turks, Afghans, and Mongols have settled here, and life among the upper classes has a decidedly Mohammedan character. Delhi was besieged by the English during the mutiny of 1857. Its population (1901) is 208,575, two-fifths of whom are Mohammedans and nearly three-fifths Hindus. It is a station of the BMS (1818), with (1900) 8 missionaries, men and women; 24 native workers, men and women; 12 common schools, a theological class, a dispensary and 307 professing Christians.

Station also of the Baptist Zenana Mission (England 1868), with 8 missionary women, 20 native women workers, 6 common schools, 1 high school, a dispensary and 175 Zenana pupils. Station also of the SPG (1854), with (1902) 16 missionaries, men and women; 93 native workers, men and women; 10 places of worship, 19 common schools, 3 high schools and 873 professing Christians. Station also of the ME, with (1902) 11 native workers, men and women; 12 Sunday schools, a Young People's Society, and 999 professing Christians.

DEMERARA: A river and district in British Guiana (*q.v.*).

DEOBAND: A town in the Sahranpur district, United Provinces, India; situated 45 miles N. E. of Meerut. Population (1891), 19,300, of whom about 11,000 are Mohammedans and the most of the remainder are Hindus. Station of the ME, with (1902) 11 native workers, men and women; 1 place of worship, 10 Sunday schools, 1 Society for Young People, and 705 professing Christians. Also written Deobund.

DEOGARH: A town in the Santal Parganas, Bengal, India; situated 55 miles S. by W. of Bhagalpur. Population (1891) 8,300, chiefly Hindus. It contains 22 temples of Siva and is a famous center of pilgrimage. Station of the CWBM, with (1902) 7 missionary women, 2 of them physicians; 4 native workers, men and women; 3 preaching places, 2 schools, an orphanage, a dispensary, a leper home, and 130 professing Christians. Name also written Deoghur.

DEOLI: A town in Ajmere, India, 70 miles southeast of the town of Ajmere. Climate tropical. Population, 3,000, including Rajputs, low-caste Hindus and Minas. Station of the UFS (1871), with (1902) 1 missionary and his wife, 16 native workers, men and women; 3 common schools and 10 church members. The place has suffered severely from famine and the Christian community has been depleted by the removals of members to other places.

DEPOK: A village south of Batavia, Java, East Indies. It was Christianized in 1714, and was the seat of a Dutch Missionary Society (Nederl. Zending.) station from 1834 to 1852. In 1878 Schnurman having formed a Committee in Holland for its support opened a seminary here for training native workers for the whole archipelago. It has proved an efficient and valuable agency for bringing the different races of the islands into touch with each other and for cultivating closer relations between the various societies.

DERA GHAZI KHAN: A town in the Northwest Frontier Province, India; situated 45 miles west of Multan. Population (1891), 27,900, of whom 16,000 are Mohammedans and the larger part of the remainder are Hindus. Station of the CMS and the CEZ (1879 and 1893), with (1902) 4 missionaries, men and women (2 of them physicians); 3 native workers, 1 elementary school, 1 dispensary, 1 hospital and 44 professing Christians. It contains many mosques and a fine bazaar.

DERA ISMAIL KHAN: A town of the Northwest Frontier Province, India; situated on the W. bank of the Indus, 120 miles north of Multan. A well-planned town, with houses of modern construction, but very badly drained. Population (1891), 26,900, of whom 15,200 are Mohammedans, including many proud descendants of old tribal chiefs and other aristocrats. Station of the CMS and of the CEZ (1861 and 1884), with (1902) 5 missionaries, men and women (2 of them physicians); 9 native workers, men and women; 1 elementary and 1 high school, 2 dispensaries, 1 hospital and 57 professing Christians.

DERVISH: A Mohammedan Theosophist or Sufi; commonly a member of an order formed for the purpose of seeking mystical knowledge of God. Etymologically the word "dervish" means one who begs at a door, literally as a mendicant, or figuratively as a suppliant at the door of God's mercy. The latter meaning is the one which the older Dervish Orders insist upon. In Turkey popular contempt for the unattached, wandering, and begging Dervishes is expressed in a proverb which says, "The Christian's lazy man becomes a monk; the Mohammedan's, a Dervish" (*Kristianin tenbeli keshish olour, Mussulmaninki Dervish*). Yet comparatively few Dervishes are mendicants. It is customary to call Dervishes monks, but none of them are monks in any sense which implies vows of service in an order, celibacy or permanent residence in a monastery. Of themselves they prefer to say that they are "*Fakirs*," that is to say "poor" who desire to serve God. Therefore they have become followers of Sufism, or Theosophy (*Ehli Tesavvuf*).

The order of Dervishes is called a "Way" (*Tarikat*). It is a voluntary association, guarded in a few cases only by secret signs and passwords. The members are not bound to the Order by any promise of fidelity. Men often change from one Order to another, sometimes belong to two or more Orders at the same time, and lose no whit in regard of their fellows if they withdraw, even for the purpose of setting up a new and independent Order. The place of assembly of any Order, called a *Tekkè* or a *Zaviyè*, is built in some convenient place and endowed by legacies of the benevolent to serve for worship and other religious exercises according to the ritual of the Order. To this place all Mohammedans are permitted to resort for worship; there the special exercises of the Order are held, the public special exercises occurring once, twice, or three times in the week; there are the rooms or cells in which the Elder (*Sheikh*) resides with such of the members as have a vocation to do so. The place is not a monastery, however, and it may be on the same premises with the rooms where the wives of the Dervishes live. A *tekkè* of the *Bektashiyè* Dervishes commonly contains apartments for the wives, since they may be admitted to that order and are addressed as "Sister" by all the members.

What all the Orders of Dervishes have in common is, (a) the general doctrine of Sufism that man is capable of attaining to full knowledge of God, and to an ecstatic sense of union with God; (b) certain exercises of mind, of body, or of both, lead certainly to this knowledge of, and union with, God. These exercises constitute the "Way" to God (each Dervish order following its own method of attaining the common aim); (c) in order to follow the "Way" a perfect guide and absolute submission to his guidance is essential. This perfect guide is the founder of the order (called "*Pir*") and his successor (*Khalifa*), or the Elder (*Sheikh*), who has received grace from these to lead in the particular district where the Tekkè is established; (d) all those who seek God by any "Way" are brothers (*Ikhvan*); those yet learning are seekers or novices (*Murid*); those who are instructed and making progress in the way are "walkers" (*Salik*); and a *Salik* of long experience may be a "guide" (*Murshtd*) of novices and in due time perhaps a *Sheikh* of a separate chapter of the order; (e) the man who has many times repeated the ecstasy of the Divine Presence finally loses himself and becomes annihilated as to self-will, so that he is insensible to material things, is used by God as an instrument for carrying out His purposes, and thus can heal the sick or slay the strong by a breath, can read the thoughts of men, can know distant occurrences, and can transport himself through space. He is then a saint (*Veli*), of whom there are always some hundreds in the world.

The above tenets of Sufism are held by all Orders of Dervishes in common. The points of difference between the different Orders are, in the main, differences of method, but sometimes of interpretation or doctrine. The differences do not, however, as a rule, interfere with brotherly relations between the various Orders.

In theory the Dervish Orders derive their doctrine and the main points of their "Way" from Mohammed himself through the Caliphs Abu Bekr or Ali. This theory, however, is supported less by documentary evidence than by interpretations put upon detached sayings of the worthies of that ancient period, which are claimed to show belief in Sufism. Preferences chiefly as to minor points of their "Way" have led to a vast multiplication of Dervish Orders. But since each Elder or Sheikh at the head of any group of Dervishes must be able to prove himself possessed of the "grace" of God so that he is a trusty guide, each Order has a sort of a genealogical record of the line by which "grace" was received by its "*Pir*" or founder and by the successive generations of his followers. By study of these spiritual genealogies one may see that all the existing Orders are reducible to eight or ten which came into existence during the two hundred and fifty years next after the middle of the 12th century. These ten most ancient Orders are:

1. Kadiriyè (1150).
2. Rufai'iyè (1170); popularly called Howling Dervishes.
3. Mediniyè (1180).
4. Shaziliyè (1254).
5. Mevleviyè (1260); called Whirling Dervishes.
6. Bedaviyè (1260).
7. Nakshibendiyè (1300).
8. Saadiyè (1320).
9. Bektashiyè (1354).
10. Khalvetiyè (1390).

Excepting 7 and 9 in this list, which claim each an exclusive spiritual lineage, the above Orders all claim to have received "grace" through a certain saint named Juneid, who flourished in Baghdad in the 9th century; and excepting the Nakshibendiyè order (which carries its genealogy by way of Bokhara and Samarcand back to the Caliph Abu Bekr) all of them claim a spiritual descent from the Caliph Ali. Excepting the Mediniyè (No. 3), which is of strictly Arab (Moorish) origin, the Orders all sprang from great men of Persia or Central Asia.

The Kadiriyè, Rufai'iyè, Khalvetiyè, Mediniyè and Bedaviyè or their branches (Isaviyè, Dejaniyè Ekberiyè, Tayibiyè, etc.) are well known to all travelers in Egypt and North Africa as the men who howl, who cut themselves, who eat fire or lie on the ground for a horse to trample on them, etc. The fact should be kept in mind while watching such performances that these acts are deemed sure proof that the man who does them is insensible to material things because at that time self is annihilated and he is lost in God. This state, which has been called "auto-hypnosis," is the result of the religious exercises of the Order. The "devotees" (*Feda'is*), who made the Assassins famous in the Crusades, or those who run "amok" in Malaysia, or those who followed the pseudo-"Mahdi" stoically to death before the British squares in the Sudan, are other examples of the same condition.

The exercises by which this condition of divine ecstasy is produced differ in the different Orders, but the theory of all divides the exercises into three parts: (a) Worship and withdrawal of the thoughts from earthly things; (b) Concentration of the mind (on the Sheikh, then on the Pir or founder of the Order, and finally, by these easy stages, upon the Almighty himself; (c) Recitation (*Zikr*) of the phrase "There is no god but God" as the climax of a recapitulation of God's attributes continued until breathlessness. The *Zikr* is assisted by certain mechanical means: for instance, in the Kadiriyè and Rufai'iyè type, by swaying the body, stamping the feet, the whole congregation beating tambourines, etc., while the holy sentence is shouted in ceaseless repetition. In the Mevleviyè method, the *Zikr* is inaudible tho accompanied by plaintive music of reed flutes, while the devotees whirl like automatic tops. In the Nakshibendi "Way" the *Zikr* is also inaudible, while the tongue is doubled back upon the palate, the eyes are fixed upon the stomach, and the breath is retained as long as possible. In the Bektashiyè system it is alleged that spirituous liquors are imbibed after the assembly has gathered and before the *Zikr* commences. The use by several of the Orders of opium and hashish as an aid to religious fervor is a better attested evil.

The Dervish Orders are commonly at odds with the Mohammedan theologians because they exalt Ali almost as the Persian Shi'ites do, while all their wresting of texts and traditions and all their documentary evidence of spiritual descent from Arabs cannot make their belief and practice conform to Mohammedan orthodoxy. But the Mohammedanism of the Koran and the schools is essentially a religion of outward observances which keeps the eye of its follower fixed upon himself, his washings, etc. It has no idea that character can be developed in its followers, and certainly none of spiritual needs in man which God is .pleased to fill. The Dervish Orders promise Mohammedans a satisfaction for spiritual aspirations which otherwise would grieve their thirsting souls to the grave. It is but a little thing to men in such straits that the Dervishes have ransacked Persia and India for the dogmas with which they attract tens of thousands who are not satisfied with the teachings of Mohammed and who go from one Dervish Order to another, still ever groping after the true "Way of God" and the "perfect guide" who shall lead their souls to rest.

Altho the *Ulema*, or theologians, of Islam frown upon the Dervish Orders, the laity are their warm supporters. In Turkey many a minister of the Government has a Sheikh attached to his household to give him private instructions in the way, while the Sultan himself is said to be a member of the Shazili Order. The influence of the Sheikhs is tremendous. The rule requiring perfect submission to their will unites with the influence of an austere life and a prophet's vehemence in denouncing patent corruption to make people hope from the Sheikh effective leadership in reform. It was such promise of reform that gave power to the leader of the Kadiriyè and Khalvetiyè Dervishes of the Sudan when the whole land followed him as Mahdi until they had given him a power too great for his hands to wield. It is such promise of reform by return to God which gave to the plain, simple Sheikh of a group of Shazili Dervishes in Tripoli, less than forty years ago, the leadership of the Senoussiyè movement, which to-day is the most potent force in all North Africa, if not in Islam.

There is much in the teaching of the Dervishes which appears to be like a bridge between Islam and Christianity. The expressions of earnest desire to know God, of longing for annihilation of self and spiritual union with God and for escape from sin which are common in the mouths of Dervishes seem to be a ground on which every Christian may meet them. Closer study discourages this view by showing that the words are used in a special sense. "Desire for God" is desire for that feverish ecstasy produced by mechanical means, which the Sufis compare to drunkenness and which passes away leaving its victim morally what he was before. "Walking in the way to God," with escape from sin, does not imply loyal service, but suppression of responsibility for deeds done in the body. Union with God in the most of the Orders (the Nakshibendiyè and the Melamiyè; an obscure offshoot from the Khalvetyè Order are exceptions to this interpretation) does not mean fellowship, but absorption of the being, as a raindrop is absorbed in the ocean. With the Christian, union with God implies a higher type of manhood abounding in good works for others. With the Dervishes, it implies such a suppression of this world's intelligence that a naked idiot is the favorite type of its highest degree. Any analysis of Sufism reveals its subordination to Indian Pantheism and probably to the Gnostic delirium of early Christendom. The missionary must approach Dervishes as he would approach those known to be saturated with these Asiatic perversions of great truths, and who need to be taught the first elements of faith in God.
Brown (J. P.), *The Dervishes*, London, 1868; *D'Ohsson, Tableau de l'Empire Ottoman*, Paris; Lane (E.W.), *Modern Egyptians*, London.

DESTERRO. See FLORIANOPOLIS.

DEUTSCHE ORIENT MISSION. See GERMANY; MISSIONARY SOCIETIES IN.

DEVON: A CMS mission station in the Saskatchewan district, Canada. Station established in 1840, and about to be transferred to the Canadian Church. It now (1901) has 1 missionary and his wife, 3 native workers, 6 schools and 770 professing Christians.

DHAMPUR: A town in the district of Bijnaur, United Provinces, India. Population (1891), 6,700, of whom 4,000 are Hindus and the larger part of the remainder Muslims. Station circuit of the ME. Statistics included in **Bijnaur**.

DHAMTARI: A town in the Raipur district, Central Provinces, India; situated 160 miles E. by S. of Nagpur. Population (1891), 6,700, of whom 5,000 are Hindus. Station of the Mennonite Evangelizing and Benevolent Board (1899), with (1900) 5 missionaries, men and women (one of them a physician); 6 native workers, a hospital, an orphanage, an industrial school and 50 professing Christians.

DHANAURA: A town in the district of Moradabad, United Provinces, India, 35 miles E. of Meerut. Population, 5,300. Station circuit of the ME. Statistics included in Moradabad.

DHAR: A town and capital of the state of the same name in Central Provinces, India; situated 35 miles W. by S. of Indore. Population (1891) 18,400, of whom 75 per cent. are Hindus and about 20 per cent. Mohammedans. Station of the PCC (1895), with (1900) 4 missionaries, men and women (one a physician); 11 native workers, men and women; 1 preaching place, 3 elementary schools, 1 orphanage, 1 industrial school, 1 theological class, 1 hospital, 1 dispensary and 25 professing Christians.

DHARAPURAM: A town in Madras, India; situated 42 miles E. S. E. of Coimbatore; celebrated as a strategical center in the wars of the English with Tipoo Sahib and Hyder Ali. Population (1891), 7,700, of whom 5,900 are Hindus. Station of the WMS, with (1902) 1 missionary 10 native workers, men and women; 4 preaching places, 6 village schools, and 79 professing Christians.

DHARMSALA: Capital of a district in the Punjab, India; situated 95 miles N. W. of Simla at an altitude of 6,000 feet. It owes its name to an old Hindu *dharmsala*, or sanctuary. Population (1891), 6,200, ninety per cent. being Hindus. Station of the CMS. Statistics included in **Kangra.**

DHARWAR: A town of Bombay, India, capital of the district of the same name. It is situated 73 miles E. of Goa and is a railroad town and center of trade in produce, grain and cotton being extensively produced in the region. Population (1891), 32,800, of whom 23,900 are Hindus and 7,000 Muslims. Station of the Basel Missionary Society (1837), with (1902) 3 missionaries and their wives, 21 native workers, men and women; 3 elementary schools, 1 high school and 235 professing Christians.

DIADIA: A settlement in the Congo Free State; situated on the N. side of the Congo River, about 175 miles from its mouth. Station of the Swedish Missionary Society (1888), with 7 missionaries, men and women; 12 native workers, 1 preaching place, 1 high school, 1 orphan asylum, 1 dispensary and 394 professing Christians.

DIAMANTE: A town in the Argentine Republic, South America; situated on the Parana River, about 25 miles S. S. W. of Parana. Population about 2,000. Station of the SDA, with 2 missionaries and their wives. Statistics included under Buenos Aires.

DIAMOND HARBOR: A seaport in the district of the 24 Parganas, Bengal, India; situated at the head of the estuary of the Hugli, 30 miles S. S. W. of Calcutta. Population about 5,000. Station circuit of the ME, with (1902) 2 missionary women, 11 native workers, 5 Sunday schools, 5 common schools, 2 preaching places, 1 Young People's Society and 53 professing Christians.

DIARBEKIR: A city and capital of a province of the same name in North Mesopotamia, Turkey. It is the ancient Amida, called by the Turks *Kara* (Black) *Amida*, on account of the walls, which, being built of black basalt, have a peculiarly forbidding aspect. It is situated on the Tigris River. Being a center for trade, it has always been an important place. Population about 34,000, of whom about 20,100 are Mohammedans (Arabs, Turks, Kurds, etc.) and the remainder Christians of various sects. It was for many years a station of the ABCFM and was given up because of insalubrity as soon as the evangelical church was able to stand alone.

DIBBLE, Sheldon: Born at Skaneateles, N. Y., January 26, 1809; graduated at Hamilton College, 1825; Auburn Theological Seminary, 1830; ordained at Utica, October 6, 1830. Sailed the same year with the fourth company of missionaries sent by the ABCFM to the Hawaiian Islands. He translated part of the Old Testament, prepared eight text-books on grammar, natural history, and Scripture history in the Hawaiian language, and wrote a *History of the Sandwich Islands Mission* (New York, 1839) and a *History of the Sandwich Islands* (Lahainaluna, 1843). He died at Lahainaluna, June 22, 1845.

DIBRUGARH: Capital of the district of Lakhimpur, Assam, India; situated on the left bank of the Brahmaputra River, being the terminus of river trade by commerical steamers. Population (1891) 9,900, of whom 7,100 are Hindus and the remainder chiefly Muslims. Station of the ABMU (1896), with (1901) 2 missionaries (one with his wife), 2 native workers, 1 preaching place and 150 professing Christians.

DIG: A town in Rajputana, India, lying 25 miles N. W. of Bhartpur. It is built in marshy land and is surrounded by water during most of the year. Population (1891) 15,800. Station circuit of the ME, with (1902) 31 native workers, men and women; 1 preaching place, 10 Sunday schools and 520 professing Christians.

DIKELE LANGUAGE. See KELE.

DIKWELLA: A town on the southern coast of Ceylon, situated about 10 miles E. of Matura. Station of the WMS, with (1902) 1 missionary, 19 native workers, men and women; 3 preaching places in neighborhood, 6 Sunday schools, 6 elementary schools, and 18 professing Christians.

DINAPUR: A town in Bengal, India, situated on the left bank of the Ganges, 11 miles W. N. W. of Patna. Population (1891) 44,000, of whom 32,300 are Hindus and about 10,000 Mohammedans. Station of the BMS, with (1900) 1 missionary and his wife, 3 native workers and 2 elementary schools.

DINDIGAL: A town in Madras, India, 30 miles northwest of Madura. The name means "Rock of Dindu" and is taken from a remarkable wedge-shaped rock, 1,200 feet high, on which a fort has been constructed. The place was formerly of considerable importance. Population (1891), 20,000, of whom 14,600 are Hindus. Station of the ABCFM (1835), with (1901) 1 missionary woman, 71 native workers, men and women; 19 preaching places, 19 common schools, 12 Sunday schools, 3 high schools, 1 dispensary, 1 hospital and 607 professing Christians. Also station of the Leipzig Missionary Society (1890), with (1900) 1 missionary and his wife, 8 native workers, 4 preaching places, 1 common school, 1 high school, and 400 professing Christians.

DIP POINT: Station of the New Hebrides Mission on the island of Ambyrm. See New Hebrides.

DISA: A town in Baroda, West India, lying about 20 miles W. of Palanpur. Station of the Presbyterian Church of Ireland (1893), with (1900) 1 missionary and his wife, 7 native workers, 4 common schools, 1 orphanage and 14 professing Christians.

DISCIPLES OF CHRIST. See FOREIGN CHRISTIAN MISSIONARY SOCIETY, and CHRISTIAN WOMAN'S BOARD OF MISSIONS.

DIX COVE: A settlement in the Gold Coast Colony, situated on the coast about 60 miles W. S. W. from Cape Coast Castle. Station of the WMS, with (1902) 1 missionary, 54 native workers, men and women; 29 preaching places, 5 Sunday schools, 1 common school and 261 professing Christians.

DJANDJI MATOGU: A settlement in the island of Sumatra, Dutch East Indies, situated on the Toba Lake about 50 miles N. E. of Siboga. Station of the Rhenish Missionary Society, with (1900) 1 missionary and his wife, 2 native workers, 2 day schools and 40 professing Christians.

DJEMÂA SAHRIDJ: A village in Algeria, situated near the coast about 40 miles east of Algiers. Station of the North Africa Mission (1882), with (1902) 2 missionary women, 1 assistant missionary and his wife, 2 native workers, man and woman; 2 preaching places, 1 Sunday school, 1 blind school and 40 Christians.

DJOCJAKARTA. See JOKYAKARTA.

DOANE, Edward Topping: Born at Tompkinsville, Staten Island, N. Y., May 30, 1820; graduated at Illinois College, Jacksonville, Ill., 1848; Union Theological Seminary 1852; ordained 1854, and embarked June 4, the same year, as missionary of the ABCFM for Micronesia, arriving February 6, 1855. Tho circumstances made it necessary for him to be transferred temporarily to the Marshall Islands and to Japan, yet the people of Ponapi, where he was stationed, had his heart, and to them he returned and for them labored with unwearied gentleness and courage, and with cheering success. In 1887, when the Spanish forces occupied the island, Mr. Doane was seized, put in the hold of a vessel, and sent as a prisoner to the Philippine Islands. The natives were so roused by his unwarrantable act, that, being without Mr. Doane's influence to restrain them, they rose and took the life of the Governor. Through the efforts of Julius Voigt, the United States Consul at Manila, Mr. Doane was liberated by the Spanish Government, and was returned with apologies to his station. His influence throughout the islands was increased by what had happened. Tho his health declined, he clung to his work till the spring of 1890, when he was conveyed by the "Morning Star" to Honolulu, where in two weeks he quietly breathed his last, at the house of the Rev. Dr. Hyde, on the 15th of May. He had been 35 years a missionary.

DOBER, Leonard: The first missionary of the Moravians to the Danish West Indies. He was a potter by trade. His attention was called to this field through a conversation in 1731 with a servant of Count Zinzendorf, who stated that he had a sister in St. Thomas, W. I., and desired some one sent to instruct the slaves in Christianity. Whoever went to these poor people on the island of St. Thomas must become a laborer to work among them, and Leonard Dober offered himself to be sold as a slave, if necessary, in order to reach them. It was a year before anything was done. When it was determined by lot, in 1732, Dober was selected, and Nitschman, who was to go with him to St. Thomas and then return to Herrnhut. The Moravians at this time knew very little of missionary undertakings, and gave them only these instructions: "In all things follow the guidance of the Spirit of Christ." They set out for Copenhagen, with only their staves in their hands and only six dollars in their pockets. They were told at Copenhagen that it would be impossible to get a vessel to go to St. Thomas, but their stedfastness of purpose raised up some influential friends for them among the royal family, councilors of state, and her majesty's chaplains. They arrived in St. Thomas, December 13, 1732, and immediately found the servant's sister, who, with her companions, rejoiced to see them. For four months Dober and Nitschman worked happily together, when Nitschman had to return to Europe. Dober was left destitute, for there was no clay on the island suitable for the making of pottery. He was for a time tutor to the governor's son, but this interfered with his missionary work among the negroes, and he went to Tappus, a small village, where he lived in great poverty. In 1733 helpers came from England to take his place. Two months later Dober returned to Europe, to fill the office of superintending elder in the Moravian congregation at Herrnhut.

DOBRUDJA: The portion of the Balkan Peninsula on the right side of the Danube, extending from Silistria and Varna to the mouth of that river, offering the most accessible military route from the north to Constantinople. The country is flat, containing several large swamps and lakes on the coast. Some parts are very fertile, and produce good crops of grain; others are covered with grasses. The population is made up of Greeks, Bulgarians, Wallachs and Tatars. Under the treaty of Berlin (1878) this district was taken from Turkey and added to Rumania, of which it is now a part.

DOBU: A settlement on the northern end of Normandy Island, British New Guinea. Station of the Australian Wesleyan Methodist Church, with (1900) 2 missionaries and their wives, 2 missionary women, 37 native workers, 4 common schools, an orphanage, a dispensary and 6 baptized Christians.

DODANDUWA: A town in the southern part of Ceylon, situated on the coast about 20 miles N. W. of Galle. Station of the CMS, with (1902) 1 unordained missionary, 1 missionary woman, 1 native worker, 1 preaching place, and 2 industrial schools.

DOHAD: A town in the district of Panch Mahals, Bombay, India. Population (1891), 12,900, of whom 8,300 are Hindus and the remainder mostly Mohammedans. Station of the Presbyterian Church of Ireland (1891), with (1900) 1 missionary and his wife, 1 missionary woman, 7 native workers, men and women; 4 common schools, a dispensary and an orphanage.

DOHNAVUR: A district in Tinnevelli, India, giving name to a church circle of the South India Mission of the Church Missionary Society; founded in 1827 by a special gift of Count Dohna.

DOLAIB HILL: A settlement in the Fashoda district of the Sudan, situated on the Sobat 540 miles by river from Khartum. People of the neighborhood, pagans. Station of the UP (1902), with 2 missionaries and their wives, one of them a physician.

DOLE, Daniel: Born at Bloomfield (now Skowhegan), Maine, September 9, 1808; graduated at Bowdoin College, Maine, in 1836; Bangor Theological Seminary, 1839; sailed as a missionary of the ABCFM, November 14, 1840, for Honolulu. On his arrival he was appointed principal of the Punahon school, and when the school was incorporated as Oahu College he became the president, which position he held until 1855. He died at Koloa, Kauai, August 26, 1878.

DOLORES: A town in Argentina, situated about 150 miles S. E. of Buenos Aires. Station circuit of the ME, with (1902) 2 native workers, 3 preaching places and 67 professing Christians.

DOMASI: A mission station of the Church of Scotland in Nyasaland; situated about 40 miles N. by E. of Blantyre. The station was occupied in 1884, and has now (1900) 3 missionaries (2 of them with their wives), 2 unmarried missionary women, 33 native workers, men and women; a chapel, 12 common schools, 1 high school, 1 industrial school, 1 dispensary, 1 printing house, and 138 professing Christians.

DOMBURG: An important government plantation, lying on the western bank of the Surinam River, in Dutch Guiana, South America, about twelve miles above Paramaribo. At and near the village there is a population of about 1,200 persons connected with the Moravian Church, and many heathen in the surrounding districts. Station of the Moravian Missions (1891), with (1900) 1 missionary and his wife, 21 native workers, 1 preaching place and 341 communicants.

DONDO: A trading station in Angola, West Africa, situated on the Quanza River, 180 miles from its mouth, at the head of steamboat navigation. Population, 5,000. Station circuit of the ME, with (1902) 1 native worker and 50 professing Christians. In the cemetery are the remains of several missionaries who lost their lives in the attempt to become accustomed to its insalubrious climate.

DOREH: A settlement on the W. coast of the western extremity of New Guinea, Malaysia. Station of the Utrecht Missionary Society (1878) with (1902) 1 missionary and his wife, 2 native workers, 2 outstations, 2 common schools and 40 professing Christians.

DOTY, Elihu: Born 1812; graduated at Rutgers College 1835, and the Theological Seminary at New Brunswick, N. J., 1836; was ordained the same year as a missionary to the heathen. He was a member of the first mission sent by the Reformed Dutch Church and the ABCFM to Java, where he labored from 1836 to 1840, when he was transferred to Borneo and labored among the Dyaks. Thence he was removed to China in 1844. Mr. Doty was an excellent Chinese scholar and preacher; an indefatigable, courageous, self-denying laborer; a man of singular frankness; and was closely identified with the mission at Amoy from its origin until his death in 1865.

DOUGLAS: A town in Cape Colony, S. Africa, situated on the Orange River, about 60 miles S. W. of Kimberly. Population, about 1,500. Station of the Berlin Missionary Society (1894), with (1900) 1 missionary, 1 native worker, and 138 professing Christians.

DOUGLAS ISLAND: North of Admiralty Island, Alaska, and about 75 miles N. E. of Sitka. It is the site of the Treadwell Gold Mine. Station of the American Friends' Foreign Mission Board (1887), with (1902) 1 missionary and his wife, 2 missionary women, 1 native worker, and 1 outstation. Station also of the PE, with (1901) 1 missionary woman, 1 preaching place, supplied from Juneau, and 16 communicants.

DOUTHWAITE, A. W., M.D.: Dr. Douthwaite left for China in connection with the China Inland Mission, in 1874; and the first eight years of his life there were spent in the province of Che-kiang, at the stations of Shao-hsing-fu, Kü-chau-fu and Wen-chau-fu, successively. At Kü-chau-fu he formed a church of 90 members, and during his first year at Wen-chau-fu he treated 4,075 patients. At a time when the Mission was in great financial stress he was offered a government post at a handsome salary, but he resisted the temptation, and was faithful to his Christian work through years of severe trial. In 1882 he was obliged to recruit his health in the bracing air of Chi-fu. With this place his name is inseparably linked, and throughout the Shan-tung Province he won the confidence often of thousands of Chinese patients. In 1884, when Korea opened its doors, Dr. Douthwaite left Chi-fu and entered that land. Journeying into the interior, he preached the Gospel, circulated copies of the Word of God and healed the sick. After a most effective work in Korea, he returned to Chi-fu in 1886, where he labored, in spite of bereavements and severe illness, for twelve years. During that time his medical work grew so extensively that his Chinese patients numbered 20,000 annually; and in 1896 the out-patients numbered 23,700; in-patients, 216, and surgical operations, 856. Chinese, high and low, acknowledged the good results of his work, and from the official to the beggar all sought his aid. Yet, with all his skill and success, no one more readily recognized the very limited powers of a medical man and the absolute need of the hand of God in the healing of the sick. Decision and determination were strong features in his character, and enabled him to accomplish an amount of work which would have taxed the powers of younger and stronger men. The services of medical missionaries during the war with Japan were highly appreciated by the Chinese Government; and at the conclusion of the war, the emperor conferred on Dr. Douthwaite and ten other medical missionaries the Imperial Order of the Double Dragon (considered to be equivalent to the Order of the Bath in England). When Dr. Douthwaite was leaving Chi-fu the Chinese general came with a guard of honor and drew up in front of the hospital. After expressing to him the gratitude of the Chinese people for his services, they escorted him to the jetty. When his lifework was coming to a close, he said: "Had I a thousand lives instead of one, I would ask for no greater joy, no greater honor, than to be permitted to spend them all in the glorious work of winning China for Christ." He died on October 6, 1899.

DOWLAISHVARAM: A town in the Godavari district, Madras, India, 32 miles by the shortest canal from Cocanada, and 4 miles south of Rajahmundry. Population (1891), 10,500, mostly Hindus. When first built, the town was a place of much importance; at present it is a permanent station of the district engineering staff, and the government workshops here turn out much work for the Public Works Department. The town is connected with several points on the coast, by navigable canals. Mission station of the Evangelical Lutheran General Council, with (1901) 1 missionary and his wife, 21 native workers, men and women; a preaching place, 24 common schools, and 700 professing Christians. Station also of the PB.

DRIEFONTEIN: Station of the South African Methodist Missionary Society, situated in Natal, with (1900) 64 native workers, 4 preaching places, 5 common schools, and 1,048 professing Christians.

DRUSES: A peculiar race and sect living in North Syria, among the slopes of Mount Lebanon and Anti-Lebanon. There are also some settlements in the Hauran and a colony at Safed, Palestine. They are found as far north as Beirut, as far south as Tyre, and as far east as Damascus. About 120 towns and villages are occupied exclusively by them, and, together with the Maronites, they compose the population of over 200 more. They are estimated at 65,000. Deir-el-Kamar, about 15 miles southeast of Beirut, is their chief town.

The origin and ethnographical affinity of the Druses are by no means settled. The most credible theory is that they have sprung partly from the Cuthites, by whom the devastated cities of Samaria were repeopled under the rule of Esarhaddon; partly from the warlike Mardis, who were brought to Lebanon by Constantine IV. in the 7th century; and partly from the Arabs, with, perhaps, a little of the blood of the Crusaders mingled with their very mixed ancestry. Whatever their origin, their characteristics had become fixed at the close of the 10th century. They speak Arabic as correctly as the people of Mecca; they possess a knowledge of the Chinese Empire, with which their own traditions connect them; and they exhibit a refinement in conversation and manners, an appreciation of education, especially that of women, which is in striking contrast to the other Syrian races with which they are surrounded.

Hakim B'emrillah (the name is a title and means *Ruler by command of God*), Caliph of Egypt, who began to reign in 996, is the reputed author of their peculiar religion. Twenty-five years of tyranny wild and terrible leave little doubt of his insanity, under the influence of which he claimed to hold direct intercourse with the Deity, and proclaimed himself the incarnation of God.

His claims were made known in a mosque at Cairo by one Darazi, but they were received with such bitter hostility that Darazi fled to the mountains of Lebanon, where he taught the new faith, and the word Druse is supposed by some to be derived from this first apostle. Hamza, a Persian, and vizier of Hakim, is regarded as the real founder of the sect, for he formulated the creed and succeeded in gathering together a large body of adherents.

The Druses believe in one only God, who is without form or substance, incomprehensible, without attributes, and before whom man is dumb and blind. Ten times has this God revealed himself in human form, Hakim being the tenth and the last incarnation. A fixed number of human souls exist which can neither be added to nor subtracted from, and all who are living now have lived before, and will continue to live in other bodies until the end of the world. At the death of one man the soul occupies a new body, of noble or base quality, according to the deeds done in the life before. After myriads of reincarnations, when the soul has been purified from every stain, it will enter rest in God. The correspondence of this part of the Druse doctrine with Indian philosophy is noticeable and probably came to them through Persian Sufism. The Druses do not acknowledge the claims of any other religions, but they countenance an outward profession of any religion whenever it may be expedient, and unite with the Mohammedan in his prayers and washings with the same indifference with which they sprinkle holy water in the Maronite churches. This apparent apostasy is due to the fact that no converts are desired or permitted, and the faithful are enjoined to keep their religion sacred and concealed, if necessary. Seven commandments of Hamza take the place of the five great points of Islam. These are: 1st. Truth speaking (only between Druses); 2d. Combination for mutual defense; 3d. Renunciation of all other creeds; 4th. Social separation from all who are in error; 5th. Recognition of the unity of Hakim with God; 6th. Complete resignation to his will; 7th. Obedience to his orders. Druses do not pray, for prayer is impertinent interference with the Creator. There is none of the fatalism of Islam, however, for they recognize the freedom of the human will. Among themselves they divide men into two classes: 1st. Those who know the truth of religion, who are called *Akkals*, or intelligent; and 2d. Those who do not know, the *Jahils*, or ignorant. The Akkals, having attained knowledge of God, are holy and have no need of the observances of religion. On the other hand, the Jahils have need of ceremonial observances as a means of training. Polygamy is not permitted, but divorce is freely allowed.

About the year 1860 the jealousies long existing between Druses and Maronites were fanned into fierce flame by fanatical Mohammedans who thought to check the growing influence which the Roman Catholic Maronites acquired through the protection given them by France. Horrible massacres of Christians followed in which the Druses acted with the Mohammedan rabble as the enemies of all Christians, and which were met with terrible reprisals whenever the Maronites found opportunity. The result was a European intervention, with permanent exclusion of Turkish officials from the Lebanon, and the establishment of autonomous government for that district, with a Roman Catholic governor and mixed council, under a constitution drawn up by the European powers. Since that time the prosperity of the Lebanon has been in marked contrast to the surrounding territory, and Druses and Maronites live on perfect equality before the law, which is gradually extinguishing the ancient feuds and the habit of settling them by murderous attacks. The Druses are fine looking, brave, industrious and enterprising, and live in great part through agriculture.

Chasseaud (G. W.), *The Druses of the Lebanon*, London, 1854; Churchill (C.H.), *Mount Lebanon*, London, 1853; Wortabet (J.), *Researches into the Religions of Syria*, London, 1860; Carnarvon (Earl of), *Recollections of the Druses*, London, 1860; Guys (H.), *Theogonie des Druses*, Paris, 1863.

DUALLA LANGUAGE: Of the Bantu family. It is spoken by some of the tribes found in the Kameruns, W. Africa, and for missionary purposes has been reduced to writing in the Roman alphabet. Missionaries of the Baptist Missionary Society (BMS) and later of the Basel Missionary Society have done literary work in this language.

DUFF: A settlement in the Transkei region of Cape Colony, S. Africa, lying about 25 miles N. E. of Butterworth. Station of the UFS (1880), with (1902) 1 missionary, 18 native workers, men and women; 10 preaching places, 11 common schools, and 235 professing Christians.

DUFF, Alexander: Born April 26, 1806, in Perthshire, Scotland. He entered the university of St. Andrews at the age of fifteen, and studied under the celebrated Chalmers. The Church of Scotland having awakened to the duty of sending the Gospel to the heathen, Dr. Duff was appointed its first missionary, and at the age of 23 embarked, October, 1829, for India. During his voyage he was wrecked twice, first on a reef of rock while rounding the Cape of Good Hope, again on the coast of Ceylon, and barely escaped a third wreck near the mouths of the Ganges. In the first wreck he and his wife lost everything, including his library, plans of operation and many valuable manuscripts. He reached Calcutta after a voyage of eight months. One of the chief objects he had in view in going to India was the establishment of a collegiate institute which should confer the highest education on native youth. His school was to be conducted on two great principles: (a) the Christian Scriptures should be read in every class, be the entire foundation and pervading salt of the school; (b) since the vernaculars of India could not supply the medium for all the requisite instruction, the sciences of the West should be taught through the English language. This was against the opinion of the government, all learned Orientalists and the most experienced missionaries in Bengal. All these insisted that higher instruction ought to be given in Sanskrit. With the assistance of Rammohun Roy, who entered fully into Dr. Duff's views, the school was opened July 12, 1830, under a banian tree, with five young men, but was soon removed to a commodious building. The instruction was in English, and the Bible held a chief place. Before the end of the first week there were more than 300 applicants. Of these, 250 were received. At the end of the first year a public examination, attended by a large number of Europeans and natives of high rank, gave great satisfaction. The next year the number of applicants was more than trebled. In 1839 Dr. Duff wrote: "The five who entered the first day have since swollen to an average attendance of 800. The Governor-General, Lord Bentinck, considered the ablest and most enlightened Governor-General India has possessed, did homage to it by publicly proclaiming in the face of all India that it had produced unparalleled results." The number of pupils was soon increased to a thousand. Among the first converts were two from the educated and influential class. One was Babu Krishna Banerjea, a Brahman of high social position, editor of a newspaper, afterward a minister of the English Church, and a distinguished professor in Bishop's College, Calcutta. His influence on natives of all classes, especially the educated, has always been great. The other was Gopeenath Nundi, afterward a preacher in connection with the American Presbyterian Mission in the Northwest Provinces, who during the Sepoy mutiny, when threatened with death, nobly testified for Christ.

In 1834 Dr. Duff returned home in ill-health. On his recovery he made a tour through Scotland, and greatly increased the interest in the missionary cause by his thrilling appeals and the report of his successful work. The degree of doctor of divinity was at this time conferred upon him by the University of Aberdeen. He returned to India in 1839. At the disruption in the Church of Scotland in 1843 he cast in his lot with the Free Church, abandoning his beloved and prosperous institution, its valuable library and apparatus, and for twenty years conducted missionary work under that body. He built a new institution from the foundation, and equipped it as well as the old had been. The influence of his work continued to increase. Interesting conversions took place. In 1846, on the death of Dr. Chalmers, he was offered the office of principal and professor of theology in the Free Church College in Scotland, and, tho urged by Presbyteries, Synods and General Assembly to sacrifice his own predilections and accept, he declined, begging them to "allow him to retain, in the view of all men, the clearly marked and distinguishing character of a missionary to the heathen." In 1850 he again returned home to work for the missionary cause, and sought to arouse the Free Church to more earnest efforts in India. In 1851 he was elected moderator of the General Assembly. In 1854, under the auspices of Mr. George H. Stuart, he visited the United States, where, as also in Canada, he addressed thousands on the missionary work in India. The University of New York honored him with the degree of LL.D. Returning to India in 1857, he opened his school for high-caste girls in the house of a Brahman. At the first examination, attended by distinguished native gentlemen, who expressed great satisfaction, 62 were on the roll. In 1864, his health having utterly failed, he took a final leave of India. On leaving Calcutta he received from all classes of the community, native and European, heathen and Christian, emphatic testimony of the great value of his services rendered for nearly thirty-five years in India. During the fourteen years spent in Scotland he urged with great eloquence upon the churches their duty to give the Gospel to the millions of India. His correspondence was extensive, many letters being to native converts and Hindu students. He had the chief management of the foreign work of the Free Church. In 1873 he was again elected moderator of the Assembly. In 1867 he was appointed professor of evangelistic theology in the college of the Free Church, which office he held for eleven years. He died at Sidmouth, Devonshire, February 12, 1878, aged 72. He has been well described as "a man of dauntless will, consummate eloquence, impassioned piety, great self-reliance." His published works are: *New Era of the English Language and Literature* (1837); *Missions the Chief End of the Christian Church* (1839); *India and Indian Missions* (1839); *The Indian Rebellion, its Causes and Results* (1858). The *Calcutta Review* was mainly established by him.

Day (Lal Bahari), *Life of Alexander Duff*, London, 1878; Smith (G.), *Life of Alexander Duff*, London and New York, 1879 and 1881; Maratt, *Two Standard Bearers in the East*, London, 1882.

DUKE TOWN: A town in Lower Nigeria, W. Africa, situated on the left bank of the Old Calabar River, about 10 miles from the estuary. Population about 40,000. The climate is hot and unhealthy. Station of the UFS (1846), with (1902) 2 missionaries (one with his wife), 4 missionary women, 12 native workers, men and women; 1 high school, 1 industrial school, 1 dispensary, 1 hospital, 1 printing house and 394 professing Christians.

DULLES, John Welsh: Born Philadelphia, Pa., November 4, 1823; graduated at Yale College with high honor in 1844, and at Union Theological Seminary, New York, 1847; married Harriet Winslow, daughter of Rev. Dr. Miron Winslow; ordained October 2, 1848; sailed as a missionary of the ABCFM the same year for Madras. He was stationed at Rajapuram, having charge of the church and schools. In 1850 he made a tour with Rev. Henry Scudder with a view to establishing an outstation to the Madras mission, and on their advice Arcot was selected and afterward became the field of the Arcot mission. Mr. Dulles was well fitted by talents, education, acquisition of the language and genial manners for the missionary work. But his own ill-health and that of his wife compelled them to relinquish the field, and they returned in 1852. For three years after his return he served the American Sunday School Union. In 1856 he was appointed editorial secretary of the Publishing Committee of the Board of Publication in the New School branch of the Presbyterian Church. He was appointed to the same position in the reunited church in 1870, and, on the resignation of Dr. Schenck in 1885, was elected General Secretary of the Board. He wrote *Life in India* and *The Ride through Palestine*. Dr. Dulles died at his home in Philadelphia, April 13, 1887.

DUMAGUDIEM: A town in Madras, India, on the Godavari River, 115 miles N. by W. of Masulipatam. Population (1890), 5,000, chiefly Kois. Mission station of the CMS and CEZ, with (1902) 5 missionaries, men and women; 20 native workers, men and women; 1 preaching place, 15 elementary schools, 1 dispensary, 30 Zenana pupils and 830 professing Christians.

DUMAGUETE: A town in the southern part of the island of Negros, P. I. Beautifully situated in a fertile district. Population, 13,200. Station of the PN (1901), with (1902) 2 missionaries and their wives (one of them a physician), 1 high school, with industrial classes, and 1 dispensary.

DUMBOLE: A settlement in British Central Africa, S. of Lake Nyasa, about 80 miles N. W. of Blantyre. Station of the Zambesi Industrial Mission, with (1903) 1 missionary and his wife, 1 chapel, 4 common schools and 1 industrial school. Also written Domboli.

DUM DUM: Town in the district of the 24 Parganas, Bengal, India, 6 miles N. E. by E. of Ft. William, Calcutta. It is an important military station. Population (1891), 11,000, of whom 6,300 are Hindus and the remainder chiefly Muslims. Station of the WMS, with (1902) 1 missionary, 1 missionary woman, 8 native workers, men and women; 7 preaching places, 4 Sunday schools, 5 common schools and 44 professing Christians.

DUMISA. See UMZINTO.

DUMMAGUDEM. See DUMAGUDIEM.

DUNDEE: A town of Natal, 100 miles N. by W. of Pietermaritzburg. It has extensive coal fields. Population, 1,500. Station of the Swedish Church Mission (1895), with (1900) 5 missionaries, men and women; 8 native workers, 3 preaching places, 7 schools, 1 industrial school, 1 hospital, 1 printing house and 267 professing Christians.

DUNDEGAMA: Station of the SPG in the diocese of Colombo, Ceylon, with (1902) 1 missionary, 6 native workers, 2 places of worship, 1 common school, and 1,023 professing Christians.

DUNEDIN: A city and seaport of New Zealand; situated 60 miles S. S. W. of Oamaru, on the southwestern side of the bay running inland. It is the most important commercial city of New Zealand. First settled by members of the Free Church of Scotland in 1843. The discovery of gold near by changed the village into a city. Population (1891), 23,500, including suburbs. The Presbyterian Church of Otago has an enterprise here for heathen, with 1 missionary and his wife, 1 native worker, 1 common school and 8 professing Christians.

DURANGO: Capital of the State of Durango, Mexico; situated 195 miles N. W. of Zacatecas and near a remarkable hill of magnetic iron ore. Altitude, 6,320 feet. It was founded in 1551. Population (1889), 24,800. Station of the MES (1884), with 1 missionary and his wife, 2 missionary women, 1 native worker, 1 preaching place and 3 Sunday schools. Station also of the SBC, with (1902) 1 missionary and his wife, 3 native workers, 1 common school and 36 professing Christians.

DURBAN: Capital of Natal, South Africa, at the head of its harbor on Port Natal Bay, 45 miles east southeast of Pietermaritzburg. It contains several public buildings of importance, and has a large trade. Population, 17,900. Mission station of the ABCFM (1892), with (1901) 1 missionary and his wife, 34 native workers, men and women; 40 preaching places. Also station of the SPG (1872) among the 72,000 Indian coolies with (1902) 1 missionary and his wife, 5 native workers, men and women; 1 orphanage, 1 dispensary and 100 communicants. Also station of the National Baptist Convention (1900), with 2 missionaries, 1 missionary woman, 1 preaching place, 1 school, and 210 professing Christians. Also station of the South African General Mission (1895), with (1900) 1 missionary and his wife, 2 native workers, 2 preaching places, 1 theological class, and 70 professing Christians. Also station of the South African Wesleyan Methodist Mission, with (1900) 9 native workers, 6 preaching places, 1 common school, and 213 professing Christians.

DURU: A village in the Ranchi district of Chota Nagpur. Station of the SPG, with (1902) 7 native workers, 3 common schools, and 449 professing Christians.

DUTCH EAST INDIES: Name given to Asiatic territories and islands which are under the sovereignty of the Netherlands. The East India Company, created by the Dutch in 1602, conquered these islands and ruled them for nearly two centuries, but since 1798 the Company has ceased to exist, and the mother country rules the possessions, comprising Java, Madura, Sumatra, Rian-Lingga Archipelago, Banca, Borneo, Celebes, Moluccas, Timor Archipelago, Bali, Lombok, and New Guinea to 141 degrees east latitude, with a total area of 736,400 square miles and a population (1900) of about 36,000,000. The total number of Dutch or Dutch connections is 60,277, and the whole number of Europeans in the islands is 75,297. Of the remaining population 460,000 are Chinese, 24,000 Arabs, and 32,000,000 natives.

The pioneer missionaries to Dutch Borneo were from the American Board, who labored on the west coast from 1839 to 1849; but at present the Rhenish Society only is doing missionary work here, altho the British and Foreign Bible Society has done some temporary work. On five of the islands, lying between New Guinea on the east and Sumatra and Borneo on the west, we find the largest remnants of the earlier Dutch government evangelization; and here a number of missionary societies are doing successful work. The work in Sumatra was begun in 1820 by a Baptist missionary; and now representatives of five German and Dutch missionary societies are reaping a rich harvest. Miracles of grace have taken place in Java and Celebes as the result of the faithful labors of missionaries of six Dutch societies, the Neukirchener Mission and the agent of the British and Foreign Bible Society. Nearly 40,000 Mohammedans have accepted the Christian religion. In the whole Dutch East Indies, reports for 1897 show 502 government vernacular schools and 578 private vernacular schools, which give instruction to about 118,000 pupils. The whole number of Christians (native) reported in the census was 309,258. There were 133 Protestant and Roman Catholic missionaries in the islands in 1900.

Wallace (A. R.), *The Malay Archipelago*, London, 1869; Scidmore (Eliza), *Java, the Garden of the East*, New York, 1897; Schreiber (A.), *Besuch auf Sumatra*, 1877; and the same, *Zweiter Besuch auf Sumatra*, Barmen, 1882; Warneck (G.), *Nacht und Morgen auf Sumatra*, Barmen, 1872 and 1873; Bleeker (P.), *Reis door de Minahassa und den Molukshen Archipel*, Batavia, 1856; Warneck (G.), *History of Protestant Missions*, translated by Dr. Robson from the 7th German edition, New York, 1901.

DUTCH MISSIONARY SOCIETY. See NETHERLANDS MISSIONARY SOCIETIES.

DUTCH (SOUTH AFRICA) REFORMED MINISTERS' MISSION UNION. See SOUTH AFRICA DUTCH REFORMED CHURCH MISSION.

DWARAHAT: A town in the United Provinces, India, in the Kumaon district. Station of the ME, with (1902) 1 missionary and his wife and 148 professing Christians. Statistics included under Bareilly.

DWIGHT, Rev. H. G. O.: Son of Seth and Hannah Strong Dwight, born at Conway, Mass., November 22, 1803, but reared at Utica, N. Y. Graduated at Hamilton College, 1825, and at Andover Theological Seminary, 1828. Appointed missionary of the ABCFM. Sailed from Boston for Malta in 1830. With Rev. Eli Smith he explored parts of Asiatic Turkey, the Caucasus, and Persia, in a journey which occupied the year from May, 1830, to May, 1831. The whole journey was performed on horseback amid great perils, the two missionaries being compelled, for the sake of safety, to wear the Turkish robes and turban. These explorations led to the establishment of the ABCFM's missions among the Armenians of Turkey and the Nestorians of Persia. In 1832 Dr. Dwight was associated with Rev. William Goodell in the establishment of the station at Constantinople. He studied the Armenian language, and was on the most friendly terms with the Patriarch and leading men of the Armenian Church. In 1837 his wife and one of his sons died of the plague. In the autumn of the year 1861 he went to the United States to tell the churches of the wonderful changes of which he had seen the fruits. While engaged in this work he was killed by a railroad accident near Shaftesbury, Vt., January 25, 1862.

Dr. Dwight loved to preach, and to visit the people in their houses and shops in order to win them to spiritual life. He had an important part in introducing evangelical Christianity in Rodosto, Nicomedia and Adabazar, places which he used to visit repeatedly. He also gave much time to the preparation of books and tracts in Armenian, and, occasionally, to the editorial care of the weekly newspaper published by the mission in Armenian. He took a leading part in the publication of details of the persecution of evangelical Armenians by their own clergy, and was energetic in the steps taken to secure the intervention of the British government in behalf of religious liberty in Turkey.

Dr. Dwight had great executive ability, sound judgment, particularly in times of perplexity or danger, and an unfailing tact and courtesy in dealing with men.

The published works of Dr. Dwight are: *A Memoir of Mrs. E. B. Dwight; Christianity Revived in the East;* and a revised edition of the same, called *Christianity in Turkey,* published in London in 1854.

DYER, Samuel: Born January 20, 1804, at Greenwich, Eng.; educated at Gosport, and Missionary College, Hoxton; sailed, April 11, 1827, a missionary of LMS, for Malacca, but went to Penang, where he remained three years. In 1835 he removed permanently to Malacca. His most important achievement was the invention of movable metallic type for printing the Chinese Scriptures. He labored under every disadvantage, having only once seen the process of typefounding in England. He personally superintended all the work, and the type that he cast were remarkable for their beauty and finish. So great was the improvement over the old Chinese method of printing, that the Bible, formerly printed in half a dozen volumes, was reduced to one, and the New Testament to less than ninety pages. He also took an active part in the translation and revision of the Chinese Scriptures. He died at Macao in 1843.

E

EAST LONDON: A town and seaport in the southeast part of Cape Colony, S. Africa; situated at the mouth of the Buffalo River, 81 miles E. by N. of Grahamstown. Population, 6,900. Station of the SPG, with (1902) 1 native worker and 121 professing Christians; also station of the South Africa Wesleyan Methodist Mission, with 33 native workers, 6 preaching places, 6 Sunday schools, 6 common schools and 310 professing Christians.

EASTERN RUMELIA: An autonomous province formed (1878) by the Congress of Berlin. It lies between the Balkan and the Rhodope ranges of mountains, in European Turkey, with Philippopolis as its capital. In 1886 the people drove out the governor appointed by the Sultan, and it has since been treated as a part of the principality of Bulgaria. The ABCFM has a station at Philippopolis. The Friends (England) also have a medical mission there.

EBENEZER (Natal): A town in the southern part of Natal, S. Africa; situated 85 miles S. W. of Durban. Population, about 1,500. Station of the Free Methodists of America (1899), with branches at Itemba and Edwaleni, which are near by, with (1902) 4 missionaries, men and women; 4 native workers, men and women; 2 day schools, and 70 professing Christians. Station also of the Swedish Holiness Band (1893), with 1 missionary and his wife, 1 school and 140 professing Christians.

EBENEZER (Transvaal): A settlement in the Transvaal Colony, S. Africa, situated about 25 miles S. W. of Rustenberg. Station of the Hermannsburg Missionary Society (1872), with (1901) 1 missionary and his wife, 6 native workers, 1 preaching place, 7 day schools and 1,626 professing Christians. Station also of the Hannover Lutheran Free Church (1897), with 1 missionary and his wife, 1 native worker, 1 school, and 100 professing Christians.

EBENEZER (Bengal): A town in the Santa₁ Parganas, Bengal, India. Station of the Indian Home Mission to the Santals, with (1902) 4 missionaries, men and women; 32 native workers, men and women; 2 high schools, 1 printing house, and (in the whole field of Dijnapur and Ebenezer) 11,000 professing Christians.

EBENEZER WIMMERA: A station of the Moravian Mission in Victoria, Australia; established in 1859 and now (1900) having 1 missionary and his wife, 1 preaching place, 1 day school, and 11 professing Christians.

EBON. See MARSHALL ISLAND.

EBON LANGUAGE: One of the Micronesian family of languages, spoken by about 15,000 people in the Marshall Islands, and reduced to writing by missionaries, with use of the Roman letters.

EBUTE-META: A town at the mouth of the Ogun River, Gold Coast, West Africa, about 25 miles N. of Lagos. It has a congregation of the Lagos Native Pastorate Association, which was founded by fugitives from Abeokuta and is under the supervision of the CMS. It has (1902) 3 native workers, 2 schools, and 541 professing Christians.

ECUADOR: A South American republic, lying, as its name implies, on either side of the equator. It is bounded by Colombia on the north, on the east by Brazil, on the south by Peru, and on the west by the Pacific Ocean. Boundary disputes with Colombia and Peru, which are still unsettled, render it impossible to define its exact limits. Its area is about 116,000 square miles. Much of the land consists of lofty plateaus. Descending from the snow-capped mountains a temperate climate is met with, which then increases to tropical warmth as the plains are reached. The rainfall, especially at the head waters of the Amazon and its tributaries, is excessive. Earthquakes frequently occur, and there are at least 16 volcanoes. The population, estimated at 1,400,000, includes pure-blooded Indians (30 per cent.), mixed races (30 per cent.) and whites of Spanish descent. The religion of the republic is Roman Catholic. Primary education is gratuitous and obligatory. There is only one railway in course of construction, but there are 1,200 miles of telegraph lines. "The new régime inaugurated some years ago is firmer than ever, after crushing out armed revolution organized by priestcraft, introducing new reforms every year despite the revolutions, and setting forward prosperity in the country." Until within a few years, all Bibles were kept out of the republic, except Latin Bibles owned individually by the priests.

In 1900 the Department of Public Instruction established a series of Normal schools organized by a ME missionary and taught by Protestant teachers. Truly a brighter day is dawning in Ecuador.

EDEA: A settlement on the Edea, or Sanaga, River, Kamerun, W. Africa, situated at Edea Falls, 40 miles from the mouth of the river and at the head of navigation. Station of the Basel Missionary Society (1897), with (1903) 2 missionaries, 1 missionary's wife, 21 outstations, 20 native workers, 1 high school, 23 common schools, and 189 professing Christians.

EDENDALE: A town in Natal, S. Africa; situated about 12 miles S. of W. of Pietermaritzburg; station of the South African Wesleyan Missionary Society, with (1900) 50 native workers, 5 preaching centers, 5 common schools, a Young People's Society, and 700 professing Christians.

EDINA: A town in Liberia, W. Africa; situated at the mouth of the St. John's River near Buchanan. Circuit of the ME, with a small congregation and some few church members.

EDINBURGH MEDICAL MISSIONARY SOCIETY (1841): In 1841 the Rev. Peter Parker, M.D., of the ABCFM Mission in China, visited Edinburgh. Dr. Abercrombie was so interested by his accounts of medical missionary work that he invited a few friends to his home to hear Dr. Parker's story of his work and to consider the formation of an association in Edinburgh for the promotion of medical missions.

A public meeting was held on November 30, when the following resolution was adopted and the Society formed: "That this meeting, being deeply sensible of the beneficial results which may be expected to arise from the labors of Christian medical men cooperating with missionaries in various parts of the world, thus giving intelligent proofs of the nature and practical operation of the spirit of love, which, as the fruit of our holy religion, we desire to see diffused amongst all nations, resolve to promote this object and to follow the leadings of Providence, by encouraging in every possible way the settlement of Christian medical men in foreign countries, and that for this purpose a society be formed under the name of the 'Edinburgh Association for Sending Medical Aid to Foreign Countries.'" It was at the same time resolved that "the objects of the Association shall be to circulate information on the subject, to endeavor to originate and aid such kindred institutions as may be formed to prosecute the same work, and to render assistance at missionary stations to as many professional agents as the funds placed at its disposal will admit."

At the second annual meeting (November 28, 1843) it was resolved that the association should be designated "The Edinburgh Medical Missionary Society."

For the first year the income of the Society was only £114, and at the close of its first decade the annual income had never exceeded £300. Until 1851 the funds of the Society were mainly expended in diffusing medical missionary information.

Lectures on the subject of medical missions were delivered by several of the directors, and afterward were published and widely circulated; prizes were offered for the best essays on the subject, and every available opportunity taken to advocate the claims of this new organization. From time to time grants of money for the purchase of medicines and instruments were made to the few medical missionaries then at work in the foreign field.

The Main Point Mission Dispensary, the first home medical mission in Great Britain, was opened by Dr. Handyside in November, 1853. This became, in 1861, the Edinburgh Medical Missionary Society's Training Institution. Soon after the death of Prof. Miller, a memorial fund of above £2,000 was raised, and the house at 56 George Square, now known as the "Miller Memorial Medical Mission House," was purchased and made over to the Society as a residence for the superintendent and students. Medical Mission dispensaries were also opened in Glasgow, Aberdeen, Liverpool, London, etc., and are recognized as powerful auxiliaries to the work at home.

In 1877 the laying of the corner-stone of the Livingstone Memorial Medical Missionary Institution marked a new era in the history of the Society; the widespread efforts made to raise the funds for the erection of this building gave a great impulse to the cause of medical missions. Besides the work at home, the Society supports Medical Missions at Nazareth and Damascus, in Syria, and a training institution at Agra, India. For a time a Medical Mission was carried on at Niigata, in Japan, and the Society also helped to establish the Belleville Medical Mission in Paris. In addition to this regular work grants in aid are made to medical missionaries of all denominations the world over, for the purchase of instruments, medicines, etc. The Edinburgh Ladies' Auxiliary was organized in 1846 to assist the Medical Missionary Society in its work.

Missions, Agents and Students (1902): 1. Dispensary and Medical Mission College, Edinburgh; 2 physicians, 1 matron, 1 dispenser, 1 janitor, 21 men and 4 women students.

2. Nazareth Medical Mission; 1 physician, 2 native assistants, and 1 native nurse.

3. Damascus Medical Mission, called the Victoria Hospital; 1 medical missionary, 1 assistant, and 3 nurses.

4. Agra Medical Missionary Training Institution; superintendent and 21 native medical missionary students.

5. Hawthornbrae Convalescent Home, Duddingston; 239 patients during year.

The organ of the Society is a *Quarterly Paper*, published on the first of February, May, August and November at Edinburgh.

EDUCATION; Its Place in Missions: In the successful prosecution of foreign missions the need of education has come to be fully recognized. There may be differences of view as to its place and relative importance in the various fields, but there is general unanimity among missionaries as to its usefulness and desirability in all fields. All societies organized for general missionary work keep constantly in view as the great purpose of their existence the preaching of the Gospel. Educational, medical, literary and philanthropic work may conceivably be dispensed with; not so direct evangelistic endeavor for the conversion of the heathen. For this the disciples were commissioned by Christ; for this missionaries are commissioned.

But long experience, particularly in Oriental lands, proves that Christian education is not only a valuable adjunct or complement to evangelistic effort—it is itself a means of evangelism. *First*, it prepares the way for the Gospel by undermining the old systems, and showing (a) the falsity of much of the teachings of the heathen religions; (b) the groundlessness of their superstitions; (c) the immorality of many of their time-honored customs; and (d) the illogical and unphilosophical character of their explanations of the natural phenomena of the universe. Western science with its practical demonstrations effectually clears the opening mind of the fallacies and follies of Oriental wisdom, and prepares it for the reception of the fundamental truths of a faith which is not at war with science, philosophy, and reason. Thus, mental training and illumination may, and often does, prepare the way for the acceptance of the Christian faith.

Second, Christian education is indispensable to the highest type of Christianity. Men may have had saving faith in Christ while in a state of utter illiteracy and ignorance; but their influence as Christians will be narrow and their usefulness restricted. They must have training in the various branches of learning to fit them to be exponents and propagators of Christianity in the various spheres of life. The Christian native should be prepared to meet and overthrow the objections of the heathen native to the religion of Christ and to give an answer to every man that asks a reason for the hope that is in him. For those who enter the ministry, or take up certain kinds of Christian work, a thorough education is very desirable, and it is most convenient, economical and satisfactory to give all of these classes this higher education in colleges and universities in their own country. They could get it, of course, in the older and stronger institutions of the United States and Europe, but at much greater cost and under circumstances so different from those under which they must live and labor as Christian preachers among their own people, that the missionary society generally does not encourage candidates for the ministry to go to any Western land for their education.

Third, Christian education is necessary to fit men for business and professional positions in their own country. While the system of instruction provided by government in India, and latterly by government in Japan, and to some extent in China, is more or less Western in character, and is complete and thorough, it is purely secular, and aims to be impartial in its avoidance of religious topics. The churches of the United States believe that it is wise and necessary to have denominational institutions of higher education of equal grade with the best secular colleges and universities, that young men and young women may be under positive religious influences and teaching during the most impressive periods of their lives; and this reason has special weight in countries where heathen and antichristian religions prevail. Christian colleges in India, China, Japan, and other countries prepare men to take service under the government, and for professional and business pursuits. Most of them enter as heathen; many of them graduate as Christians. Their conversion is earnestly sought by members of the faculty, who never forget in their function as teachers their character as missionaries. It is due to these missionary colleges and universities that some of those high in the councils of government or distinguished in professional and business pursuits are Christians; while many others, who do not openly break with all old customs and ceremonies, carry with them a high respect for Christianity, and use every reasonable opportunity to advance the interests of the institutions in which they have been educated. Their attitude is in no case one of hostility, but of friendliness. The value of education of the Western type is so fully recognized in many Oriental countries by government that Christian institutions meet with little or no opposition from the constituted authorities. It is true that the schools and colleges in North China were destroyed in the Boxer movement of 1900, but simply because they stirred the hatred which the fanatical and superstitious rioters had for all things foreign. The potent influence of education in ameliorating the condition of women in the East is an element of vast importance in the working out of the great purpose of Christian missionary societies. There the woman, as among the Indians of the American continent and the savages of Africa and the South seas, is regarded as an inferior being, degraded, oppressed, abused, secluded, so that the finer qualities of the sex are in a state of suppression and she moves in a restricted sphere. Education not only enlightens the mind of her lord and master, so that he perceives her true place in the household and in society, but it tends to free woman herself from the chains of superstition and ignorance and reveals to her a nobler, sweeter and truer life, according to a larger and diviner plan than that to which she has been condemned by ancient idea, custom and usage. The educational institutions for girls are, therefore, quite as important in the working out of missionary purpose as are those for boys, and the growth in the number of these schools and the pupils attending them is one of the most significant signs of missionary progress. For it is clearly recognized by missionaries in the countries of the Orient that in the devotion of the women is the strength of the idolatrous religions. They cling tenaciously to the tenets and customs and ceremonies of the outworn faiths long after the men have become neglectful and indifferent; and it would be impossible to Christianize the masses without reaching the women. The women exercise large influence over the children, and indoctrinate the girls in particular in all the superstitions they themselves receive. The education of women is, therefore, a necessity in missionary enterprise.

Mission schools may be classified according to grade as collegiate, preparatory, elementary, kindergarten; according to nature of instruction given, as theological, biblical, medical or industrial. In grade the institutions range from kindergarten and elementary day schools to the boarding or high schools and seminaries and to the college and university.

Of the latter class Dr. Dennis, in his *Centennial Survey of Foreign Missions*, reports 94, of which nearly one-half, or 44, are in India, including Ceylon and Burma, 13 in China, 9 in Japan, 1 in Korea, 8 in Africa, and the rest (22) in Australia, Canada, Madagascar, Persia, Syria, Turkey, South America and the West Indies. In these 94 institutions there were, at the beginning of the century, 35,539 scholars, all males except 2,099. In India, where higher education appears to have been most fully developed, nearly 26,000 of the total number are to be found. There are fewer in China, strange to say (1,814), than in Africa or Turkey.

Of the boarding and higher schools and seminaries in which preparation is made for the college or university, there are 879, with nearly 86,000 pupils. Of these, 406 are in India, 166 in China, 85 in Africa, and 40 in Japan, including Formosa. In this class of schools the feminine sex has more adequate representatives than in the higher grade institutions, numbering 34,714, as against 49,612 male scholars. It is interesting to note that in China and Ceylon, Japan, Mexico, Oceania, Persia, Palestine, Syria, Turkey, South America, and the West Indies, girls predominate among the pupils. In India proper, the boy pupils outnumber the girls more than two to one; in Japan, the tables are turned and the girls are nearly three to one, while in Mexico the proportion is nearly ten to one.

Of theological or training schools, for preachers and Christian workers there are 375. India leads with 126, China comes next with 68, Africa, third with 59, Japan, fourth with 38. The rest are distributed over the other missionary countries of the world. In these institutions 11,765 persons are being trained, 8,284 males and 3,515 females, the latter predominating in number in Burma, Japan, Syria and Turkey.

Passing next to medical schools and schools for nurses we note that there are 67, with 651 pupils, of whom 230 are females. China takes the lead in the number of these institutions with 32, having 270 pupils, India coming second, with 191 pupils.

Of elementary or village schools there are 18,742, with 904,000 pupils, two-thirds being of the male sex. There are also 122 kindergartens, with 4,704 pupils.

It remains to note in this statistical survey, that there are 179 industrial training institutions and classes, in which 9,074 persons (of whom 2,352 are females) are being prepared for one or another branch of industrial life. Africa here takes the lead in the number of such institutions, tho not in the number of scholars. India has 51 institutions, with 4,305 pupils, while Africa has only 1,845 pupils.

The importance of industrial training in the Orient and in Africa and Oceania is more fully appreciated as Christian communities increase, as better methods of living are attained, and as converts are shut out of lines of work on account of their change of religion and customs. These schools are intended to prepare persons of both sexes for employment where skill is required and for which remuneration may be commanded. The Industrial Mission Aid Society of London seeks to secure opportunities for those so trained to engage in productive labor.

To summarize: Missionary societies have, in all, 20,458 educational institutions of all kinds, with 1,051,466 scholars, of whom 332,980, or about one-third, are females. The significance of these figures may easily be overlooked. Compared with the immense population of the fields in which these institutions are found, they appear almost infinitesimal. But they certainly bear a fair proportion to the number of Christian communities. The solidarity of the heathen and non-Christian populations, aggregating, perhaps, two-thirds of the grand total of the inhabitants of the world, is immense,—an overwhelming fact. After a century, more or less, of endeavor in Asia, all that can be claimed is that a beginning, a most encouraging beginning, has been made in Christian work, the extent of which cannot adequately be represented by mere numbers. The crumbling process is everywhere at work on heathen solidarity, and the attitude of the masses toward the old religions is by no means the same as it was a century or even a half century ago.

Moreover, the propaganda of education is a rapidly expanding propaganda. The oldest college in the mission field, that at Serampur, founded by Carey and called "The first Christian college in the East," dates back only to 1819. Of the 94 collegiate institutions reported at the close of the century, only twelve were founded before 1850. In the third quarter that number was increased to 25, while in the last quarter 57 were established. Thus, sixty per cent. of these institutions were organized in the last twenty-five years of the century, and of these, twenty fall within the last decade.

Still more notable is the recent origin of the institutions of the preparatory class. By far the greater number have come into existence in the last quarter of the century, particularly in the last decade. Of kindergartens in the mission fields there are none that go back of the ninth decade; most of them sprang up in the tenth. The growth of the educational institutions in mission fields in the ten years ending in 1900 is one of the most remarkable developments in the modern missionary movement. It is all the more remarkable when it is remembered that it is coincident with the multiplication of the hospitals, dispensaries, orphanages and other philanthropic agencies. It proves that those who are responsible for the shaping of missionary policy are convinced that education is an indispensable adjunct of evangelization.

The cost of the educational work of missionary societies is naturally a heavy charge upon their annual appropriations. The support of the missionaries who are charged with the responsibility of conducting it is provided usually in the annual budget, together with the wages of native leaders and others, with the items of rent, insurance, repairs, furniture, etc. Pupils may be expected to pay their board, and in certain classes of schools, fees for tuition, books, etc. Endowments are not numerous; but individuals in the home churches, classes in Sunday schools, young people's meetings and other organizations often assume the support of a girl or boy while in school. In India a government subsidy is given to schools of a certain grade on the basis of examinations conducted by representatives of the educational authorities of the State.

EFAT, or VATE. See NEW HEBRIDES.

EFATESE LANGUAGE: Belongs to the Melanesian family and is spoken with several dialects in the island of Efat in the New Hebrides. It was reduced to writing by Scotch Presbyterian missionaries and an effort has been made to combine dialects so as to provide the people with a single literary language. Roman letters are used in writing Efatese. It is also called Fate and Vate.

EFULEN: A settlement in Kamerun, W. Africa, situated east of the coast belt and 70 miles S. of E. of Great Batanga. Station of the PN (1893), with (1903) 2 missionaries (one a physician) and their wives, 3 native workers, 1 boarding school, 1 dispensary, 1 hospital and 150 professing Christians.

EGEDE, Hans: See DANISH MISSIONS.

EGEDESMINDE: An Eskimo settlement on the west coast of Greenland, situated on Disco Bay. Population about 1,200. Formerly a station of the Danish Missionary Society. The inhabitants being now professing Christians the place is under care of the Danish Church and is not considered as a missionary field.

EGYPT: Egypt proper extends from the Mediterranean on the north to Wady Halfa at the second cataract of the Nile on the south, and from the Suez Canal and the Red Sea on the east to an indefinite line of desert on the west. Politically it includes also a strip of Arabia on the east of the Suez Canal, Nubia, and an uncertain section of the Sudan. By far the greater part of this territory is practically uninhabited, so that of the officially reported 400,000 square miles, not more than 13,000 square miles contain a population of (1897) 9,734,405, giving a density of population three times as great as that of France, and even greater than that of Belgium and Saxony.

Of the population nearly 9,000,000 are Mohammedans and 25,000 are Jews. The Christians number 730,162. Of these, 608,000 are Copts, 53,500 belong to the Greek Church, 56,500 are Roman Catholics and the remainder are Armenians and Protestants, with a few unclassed individuals.

The language of Egypt is entirely Arabic. The Coptic, representing the old Egyptian hieroglyphs, has long been a dead language, existing only in the Scriptures and liturgies of the Coptic monasteries.

The climate of Egypt is in general very dry. Northerly winds prevail in summer and southerly winds in winter, so that there is a great uniformity in temperature, ranging in Cairo from 50° to 85°, the highest recorded being 116° Fahr. There is also very little rain—practically none at all in Upper Egypt—tho in Cairo there are some very heavy rainfalls; yet the rise of the Nile is accompanied with a great deal of moisture, so that, especially on the Red Sea coast, one seems to be in a vapor bath. The houses are built chiefly of sun-dried brick, except in the cities, where a porous stone is used.

The present ruler of Egypt, as a tributary province of Turkey, is Abbas Hilmi Pasha, who has the title of Khedive, or Prince. The administration is in the hands of native ministers subject to the ruling of the Khedive and the concurrence of the representative of Great Britain. The army of Egypt is commanded by a British general who holds an Egyptian commission and who employs a certain number of British officers in subordinate positions. There is also a force of about 5,000 British troops in Egypt, partly paid by that province and styled "The Army of Occupation."

The English control of Egypt (since 1883) altho advisory in form, is already revolutionizing the life of the common people by securing justice to a marked degree and gradually suppressing official corruption. The schools of all grades throughout the country are required to teach the English language besides the vernacular, and a date has been officially fixed after which English will be the language of all official transactions and correspondence.

Missionary work is carried on in Egypt by the United Presbyterian Church of the United States of America and the Church Missionary Society of England.

Of these two missions the former is much the more important. The latter has confined itself to work for Mohammedans, chiefly in connection with the schools established for Muslim children by Miss Whately, who died in 1889, leaving the schools under the general charge of the society. Missionary work among the Copts has never encountered so bitter opposition from the clergy as has been met in some other parts of the Levant. The government, too, has favored and valued the educational work of the missions. Under existing circumstances, government persecution of Mohammedans who incline to Christianity does not take place, and with the spread of knowledge of the English language and literature, an opportunity for evangelizing Mohammedans has been created which should be used to the full.

Besides the UP and the CMS, the BFBS, the Sudan Pioneer Mission (German), the Kaiserswerth Deaconesses, the (Dutch) Society for the Evangelization of Egypt, the North Africa Mission, the International Medical and Benevolent Association and the Egypt General Mission have stations in Eygpt. The WMS and the London Jews Society and four other societies have missions limited to the Jews in Alexandria, Cairo, Port Said and Suez. The whole number of Protestants in Egypt is returned as 11,894.

Penfield (F. C.), *Present Day Egypt*, new ed., New York, 1903; Poole (S. L.), *Social Life in Egypt*, London, 1884; ———, *Cairo*, 3d. ed., London and New York, 1897; Lane (E. W.), *An Account of the Modern Egyptians*, 2 vols., 5th ed., London, 1871; Fowler (M.), *Christian Egypt*, London, 1900; Watson (A.), *American Mission in Egypt*, Pittsburg, Pa., 1898.

EHLANZENI: A settlement near Greytown,

Natal, about 65 miles N. W. of Durban. Station of the Hermannsburg Missionary Society (1856), with (1902) 1 missionary and his wife, 11 native workers, 12 places of worship, 6 schools and 223 professing Christians.

EHLOMOHLOMO: A station of the Hermannsburg Missionary Society (1862) among the Zulus in the Vryheid district of Natal. The work has been very much interrupted by the Transvaal war and statistics later than 1901 are not at hand. There then were 1 missionary and his wife, 2 native workers, a chapel, a school and 175 professing Christians.

EKAMBA: Station of the Norwegian Missionary Society in Natal, S. Africa, about 40 miles east of Ladysmith.

EKOMBELA: A station of the Hermannsburg Missionary Society in the Vryheid district of Natal, situated about 5 miles N. E. of Luneburg. Founded in 1862. Has about 500 professing Christians in the center and outstations.

EKUHLENGENI: Station, at present (1902) without a missionary, of the Hermannsburg Missionary Society, in the Vryheid district of Natal; situated about 40 miles N. of E. from Vryheid. Has about 350 professing Christians.

EKULALENI: Station of the Church of Sweden Mission in Natal, S. Africa, situated among the Zulus north of the Tugela River. It was founded in 1888 and in 1900 had 5 missionaries, men and women, and about 75 professing Christians.

EHWENDENI: Station of the UFS in the Central Africa Protectorate, west of Lake Nyasa and among the Angoni tribes. It was founded in 1882 and now has (1902), together with Njuju and other outstations, 2 missionaries, one of them a physician, 50 schools with 144 teachers, 2 organized churches with 773 members, and 1 dispensary.

EL ARAISH: A seaport town in Morocco, 45 miles S. S. W. of Tangier. Station of the Gospel Missionary Union (1898), with 3 missionaries. Station also of the North Africa Mission (1899), with 2 missionary women and 1 dispensary.

ELAT: A town in the Kameruns, W. Africa, 75 miles E. of Efulen. Station of the PN (1896), with (1902) 5 missionaries, men and women (one a physician); an organized church, a school and a hospital.

ELEMA. See OROKOLO.

ELEUTHERA: One of the Bahama Islands, W. I., lying 200 miles E. of the coast of Florida, between Great Abaco on the N. W. and Cat Island on the S. E. Area, 132 square miles; population, 8,733. Station of the Wesleyan Methodist Missionary Society. At Governor's Harbor this Society has 1 male missionary, 22 native workers, 648 Christians in native Church, 4 church buildings, 4 Sunday schools, and at Rock Sound it has 2 male missionaries, 9 native workers, 2 outstations, 301 Christians in native churches, 4 church buildings, 4 Sunday schools. The SPG (1849) and the Baptist Society, entering the field later, have over 800 communicants and are doing excellent work.

EL FUERTE. See FUERTE.

ELIM (Cape Colony): A town in Cape Colony, S. Africa, situated in the Bredasdorp district, about 50 miles S. W. of Swellendam. Station of the Moravian Missions (1824), with (1900) 6 missionaries, men and women; 31 native workers, men and women; 2 preaching places, 2 schools and about 600 professing Christians.

ELIM (Natal): A settlement in the extreme south of the Alfred district, Natal, S. Africa. Station of the Hermannsburg Missionary Society (1870), with a missionary and his wife, a chapel and a school.

ELIM (Transvaal): A town in the Zoutspansberg district, Transvaal Colony, S. Africa, situated about 210 miles N. E. by N. of Pretoria. Station of the Romande (French Switzerland) Missionary Society (1879), with (1902) 10 missionaries, men and women (including physician and hospital nurses); 12 native workers, 14 schools, 1 hospital, and 184 baptized Christians.

ELIOT, John: Born, 1604, in Nasing, Essex County, England. He had eminently godly parents, "by whom," to use his own words, his first years were "seasoned with the fear of God, the Word, and prayer." He was educated at the University of Cambridge, in 1623, where he acquired a thorough knowledge of the original languages of Scripture, was well versed in the general course of liberal studies, had a partiality for philology, and was an acute grammarian. On leaving the university he became an usher in the grammar school of Rev. Thomas Hooker. To his connection with the latter he traces his conversion. Mr. Eliot resolved to devote himself to the ministry, and, being exposed to the tyranny of Laud on account of his non-conformity, followed Hooker to America, with sixty others, in the ship "Lyon," which reached Boston November 3, 1631. Some of his brethren who contemplated going to America exacted from him a promise that, if they came, he would be their pastor. On his arrival he supplied the place of Mr. Wilson, the pastor of the Boston church, then absent in England. In 1632 the brethren whom he had left came and settled in Roxbury. Mr. Eliot was installed as their pastor, continuing in that relation till his death, nearly sixty years. In 1639 he was appointed, with Welde and Mather, by the civil and ecclesiastical leaders of the colony to prepare a new version of the Psalms. This Psalter, issued in 1640, was the first book printed in America. It was entitled *The Psalms in Metre, faithfully translated for the Use, Edification, and Comfort of the Saints in public and private, especially in New England.* It was called *The Bay Psalm Book*, but afterward *The New England Version of the Psalms*. The book passed through twenty-one editions. Soon after Eliot was settled in Roxbury he became deeply interested in the Indians, and, the legislature having passed an act for the propagation of the Gospel among them, he resolved to learn their language that he might preach to them. Through a young Pequot, who had learned a little English and whom he had received into his family, he obtained some knowledge of their language. He soon became sufficiently familiar with its vocabulary and construction to translate the ten commandments, the Lord's Prayer, some texts of Scripture, and a few prayers. In October, 1646, he made his first visit, with three others, to their camp near the site of Brighton, on the border of Newton, and preached to them, assembled in the wigwam of Waban, their chief, the first sermon ever preached in North America in a native tongue. The service continued three hours, the Indians asking many questions. Two weeks after he made a second visit, when an old warrior asked with tears if it was not too late for him to come to God. In another fortnight he made a third visit, when a deep, serious interest was manifest, tho many Indians had been incited by the *powwows* against him. These men, who were conjurers or juggling priests, violently opposed him. At this third visit Waban was so impressed that he gathered his people at the evening campfire and talked to them about what they had heard. Desiring to civilize as well as Christianize the Indians, Eliot had those to whom he had preached gathered into a community on the site of their old camping ground. This was about five miles west of Boston, and to it, at the suggestion of the English, they gave the name Nonantum, signifying *rejoicing*. Eliot exerted great influence over them with rare tact and sagacity to encourage them to adopt the modes of civilized life. A simple civil administration was established, and in 1647 the General Court established a court, over which an English magistrate presided. With social and industrial improvements they were trained with the aid of some native helpers in religious duties. These Indians received the appellation of "praying Indians."

Another place for religious meetings and instruction was Neponset, within the limits of Dorchester, among a body of Indians whose chief was the first sachem to whom Eliot preached. A sachem at Concord now induced his people to petition for a tract near the English, that they also might be instructed. Their request was granted, a teacher was given them, and religious services were commenced. They adopted a code of rules regulating their civil and religious duties and their social comfort. In 1648 Mr. Eliot visited Pawtucket, 35 miles southward, where was a powerful chief. He and his two sons gave evidence of true conversion, and desired Mr. Eliot to live with and instruct them, offering him the choicest location. About this time came an earnest request from a chief living 60 miles from Roxbury, on the present site of Brookfield, that Mr. Eliot would come and teach his people. As the journey would take him through a region where his life would be in danger, a sachem through whose country he must pass came with twenty of his warriors to escort him. He set out on horseback. The exposure and fatigue severely taxed his strength. "I have not been dry," he states, "night or day from the third day of the week until the sixth, but so travel, and at night pull off my boots to wring my stockings, and on with them, and so continue. But God stepped in and helped." Not only did the sachems violently oppose him and persecute the praying Indians, but he had received no aid or cheer from others. His own countrymen even aspersed him. It was declared both "in Old and New England that the whole scheme was to make money, and that the conversion of the Indians was a fable." But despite the opposition of the sachems, the apathy of most of the English and the hostility of some, he pursued his work with heroic faith. In 1649 Christians in England were so stirred by the fame of his work that a society, entitled "The Society for the Propagation of the Gospel in New England," was formed and incorporated by Parliament. Collections were made throughout England and Wales, and liberal supplies were sent. This Society sent Eliot £50 per annum to supplement his salary of £60 at Roxbury. Eliot had long desired to have all his converts gathered in one settlement; the Indians favored the scheme, and the funds received from England made it practicable. A site was chosen on the Charles River, 18 miles from Boston, and a tract of 6,000 acres set apart and named Natick. All the praying Indians except one tribe were here gathered in 1650. The town was regularly laid out, a house lot assigned to each family, and a large building erected to serve for a church and school room. The governor and several others visited Natick, and were highly gratified. An Indian preached before the governor "with great devotion, gravity, decency, readiness, and affection," and a psalm lined by the Indian schoolmaster was sung "in one of our ordinary English tunes melodiously."

Mr. Eliot now began to train native preachers and teachers. The converts were formed into a church in 1660. His plan of gathering all the converts to the one mission at Natick failed, and thirteen other towns of praying Indians were formed. The industrial and educational work was pursued with success. The number of converts under his immediate care in 1674 was 1,100, the result of his thirty-eight years of labor; and scattered through Massachusetts, and on Nantucket and Martha's Vineyard, which he had visited, were 2,500 others, under the care of the Mayhews, Cotton, and Bourne, but whose conversion may be traced to the efforts and influence of Eliot. He lived to see twenty-four of the Indians preachers of the Gospel. In King Philip's War of 1675 the praying Indians suffered greatly. They were hated and hunted by the red men and cruelly treated by the whites. Mr. Eliot for protecting them was reviled and suspected by the English, but he remained their faithful friend.

A very important part of John Eliot's work was his translation of the Bible. The New Testament was, through the patronage of the English Society, issued in 1661, and the Old Testament two years later. Eliot's Indian Bible is the first Bible printed in America. It is the grandest monument of early American scholarship and evangelism. Of this work Edward Everett said: "The history of the Christian Church does not contain an example of resolute, untiring, successful labor superior." In 1631, 1,500 copies were printed, and 2,000 in 1685. He translated also Baxter's *Call to the Unconverted*, and various other treatises on practical religion. His original works were *A Catechism*, an *Indian Psalter*, a *Primer*, and the *Indian Grammar*. At the end of the latter he wrote: "Prayers and pains, through faith in Jesus Christ, will do anything." In English he published *The Communion of Churches*, *The Glorious Prospect of the Gospel among the Indians*, and other works. When, through age and infirmity, he was unable to preach or visit the Indians, he induced several families to send their negro servants to him once a week, that he might instruct them in Gospel truth. He died May 20, 1690, aged eighty-six.

Sparks' *American Biography*, Vol. V., Boston, 1836; Wilson (Dr.), *Life of John Eliot*, London, 1853; Calverly (R. B.), *Life of John Eliot*, London, 1881.

ELITUBENI. See Rainy.

EL KSAR. See Kasr el Kebir.

ELLICE ISLANDS: A group of small islands, S. E. of the Gilbert Islands. There are eight islands and small groups of islets, with an area of fourteen square miles and about 2,400 inhabitants. The LMS has worked this field with a number of native workers from Samoa, a missionary visiting them once or twice a year. This has not had entirely satisfactory results, and in 1901 a missionary was stationed at Beru, in the southern portion of the Gilbert Islands, who will give a closer supervision to the work in the Ellice group.

ELLICHPUR: A city in Berar, Central Provinces, India, situated 32 miles N. W. of Amraoti. It was once a great city. Population (1891), 26,600, of whom 19,000 are Hindus and about 7,000 Muslims. Station of the Kurku Inland Mission (1889), with 6 missionaries, men and women.

ELLIS, William: Born August 29, 1794, in London. Studied at Gosport and Homerton. Having offered himself at the age of twenty as a missionary to the LMS and been accepted, he spent a few months in acquiring a knowledge of printing and bookbinding; was ordained November 8, 1815, at Kensington, and sailed January 23, 1816, for the South Seas. He labored for a while at the islands of Eimeo and Huahine, setting up in Tahiti the first printing press in the South Sea Islands. He left Huahine for the Sandwich Islands, February 24, 1822, in company with Messrs. Tyerman and Bennet, the Society's deputation, reaching Hawaii March 21; visited Oahu in April, and, because of the affinity of the Tahitian and Hawaiian languages, was able to preach to the Hawaiians with facility in two months after his arrival. Being requested by the king and chiefs to join the mission in the islands, and the American missionaries cordially concurring in the request, he returned to Huahine, and removed his family to Oahu, February 5, 1823. Before two years had elapsed, illness of his wife compelled Mr. Ellis's return to England. During five years he served the LMS by addressing meetings in behalf of missions, and afterward, during nine years, he was Foreign Secretary of the Society. While filling that important office he wrote his great work on Madagascar, which is one of the classics of missionary literature. Ten years after he had resigned his office as Secretary, Mr. Ellis was again called to serve the LMS in 1853—this time by going to Madagascar in order to supervise the reopening of the LMS mission there. After several disappointments this was accomplished in 1862, and, his work being done, he returned to England in 1865, retaining connection with the LMS until his death, June 9, 1872.

Ellis (J. E.), *Life of William Ellis*, London, 1873.

ELLORE: A town of Madras, South India, in the Godavari district, 38 miles north of Masulipatam. Population (1891), 29,40, for the most part Hindus. Mission station of the CMS(1854) and of the CEZ (1881), with (1902) 4 missionaries, men and women; 103 native workers, men and women; 1 high school, 76 common schools (of which 65 are under the district church), 202 Zenana pupils, and 4,240 native professing Christians.

ELMINA: A town a few miles west of Cape Coast Castle in the Gold Coast Colony, W. Africa. Station of the WMS, where, in spite of many difficulties and much opposition, the church is in a healthy condition. It has (1903) 89 native workers, men and women; 40 outstations, 44 preaching places, 5 schools and 496 professing Christians.

ELUKOLWENIS: A town in Griqualand East, Cape Colony, S. Africa. Mission station of the Moravians (1875). It was at first dependent for instruction on the weekly visits made by the missionary stationed at Ezimcuka. It has now (1900) 16 native workers, men and women, and 210 professing Christians.

EMAKOSINI: A town in the Vryheid district of Natal, S. Africa; situated about 20 miles N. W. of Vryheid. Station of the WMS, with 1 missionary and 12 native workers of both sexes.

EMANGWENI: A settlement in Natal, South Africa, about 25 miles W. of Estcourt. Station of the Berlin Missionary Society (1863), where 1 missionary resides, with 5 native workers.

EMERSON, John S.: Born at Chester, N. H., December 28, 1800; graduated at Dartmouth College 1826; graduated at Andover Theological Seminary 1830; sailed as a missionary of the ABCFM for the Sandwich Islands November 26, 1831, reaching Honolulu, May 17, 1832. He was stationed at Wailua, on Oahu. There he spent the whole of his missionary life except four years, 1842-46, when he was professor at Lahainaluna Seminary. While there he published, with the assistance of Messrs. Alexander and Bishop, and S. M. Kamakan, an English-Hawaiian Dictionary, based upon Webster's Abridgment, a closely-printed volume of 184 pages, containing 16,000 words in English, with definitions in Hawaiian. He died in 1867.

EMFUNDISWENI: A settlement in the northeastern part of Cape Colony; situated about 30 miles S. of Kokstad. Station of the South Africa Wesleyan Methodist Missionary Society, with (1900) 1 missionary, 43 native workers, 18 outstations, 10 places of worship, 14 schools and about 500 professing Christians. The Woman's Association of the WMS also has a high school here.

EMGWALI: A town in Cape Colony, S. Africa; situated about 25 miles E. by N. from Stutterheim and not far from the Great Kei River. Station of the UFS (1857), with (1903) 1 missionary and his wife, 2 missionary women, 13 native workers, men and women; 10 outstations, 7 schools, and 438 communicants.

EMKINDINI: A settlement in Natal, situated in Zululand not far from the Umfolosi River. Occupied in 1900 as a station of the Zululand Missionary diocese.

EMLALAZI: A settlement in the Weenen district of Natal. Station of the Hermannsburg Missionary Society (1858), with (1901) 1 missionary, 5 native workers, 3 preaching places and 186 professing Christians.

EMMAUS (Natal): A settlement in the Upper Tugela region of Natal, situated about 30 miles N. of W. from Estcourt. Station of the Berlin Missionary Society (1847), with (1903) 2 missionaries, 13 native workers, 2 outstations, 8 preaching places and 365 professing Christians.

EMMAUS (Transvaal): A settlement in the Transvaal Colony, S. Africa, situated about 10 miles N. E. of Lichtenburg. Station of the Hermannsburg Missionary Society (1868), with (1901) 2 missionaries, 1 native worker, 2 preaching places and 1,150 professing Christians.

EMMAUS (West Indies): A station of the Moravian Missions in the northwestern part of the island of St. John, West Indies. It was established in 1782, and in 1900 had 1 missionary and his wife, and 8 native workers, men and women.

EMPANGWENI: A settlement in Natal, S. Africa, situated near Estcourt. Station of the Hermannsburg Missionary Society (1863), with (1902) 1 missionary and his wife, 11 native workers, 4 preaching places, 3 schools and a Christian community of 435.

EMTOMBENI: A settlement in Natal, S. Africa, situated on the Tugela River about 35 miles from its mouth and about 35 miles E. of Greytown. Station of the Hermannsburg Missionary Society (1897), with (1902) 1 missionary and 1 native worker.

EMUREMURA: A settlement in Southern Nigeria, W. Africa, situated on Cross River about 80 miles W. by N. of Duke Town. Station of the UFS (1889); at present (1903) unoccupied.

ENDWEDWE. See INDWEDWE.

ENFIELD: A town in the Island of Jamaica, West Indies, situated about 18 miles E. by N. of Kingston. Station of the United Methodist Free Churches (1891), with (1902) 1 missionary and 6 native workers.

ENGCHHUN. See YUNG-CHUN-CHAU.

ENGH, John: Born in Cudbrandsdalen, Norway, October 3, 1833. Died May 3, 1900. He began life as a carpenter in Christiania, but after his conversion he gave up his trade and spent five years at the Norwegian Mission Training School in Christiania. In 1865 he went to Zululand, and in the following year he entered upon his work in Madagascar. After remaining about a year in the capital, he went to North Betsileo and settled down in Betafo, where he did his life-work. He was the founder of the Norwegian Mission at this place. His health having failed, he returned home in 1886; but after a rest of two years he returned to his chosen field, where he labored, without interruption, for ten years. When he finally returned to his native land there were in his district more than 12,000 Christians, members of 76 local churches, and about 75 schools, besides the 1,200 or more baptized Christians who had been taken away by death. All this was largely fruit won through Engh's work. As he was the oldest of the missionaries he was called "Father Engh," and among Christians of all names and by many of the Christless he was greatly loved for his work's sake.

ENGLAND; Presbyterian Church of. See PRESBYTERIAN CHURCH OF ENGLAND.

ENGOTINI: A settlement in Cape Colony, S. Africa, situated about 30 miles S.W. from Queenstown. Station of the Moravians. It was founded in 1859 in a circle of twelve heathen Fingo "kraals," where the missionaries soon gained influence. The present force (1903) consists of 2 missionaries and 15 native workers, men and women.

ENON: A village in Cape Colony, S. Africa, 37 miles N. of Port Elizabeth. Population, about 1,500. Station of the Moravians, founded in 1818. The present force (1903) is 1 missionary and his wife, with 5 native workers and 200 communicants. The adherents have been diminished by the "Ethiopian Church" movement.

ENTAKAMO: Station of the Unsectarian Mission to the Zulu-Kaffirs, situated in Natal, S. Africa, on the Umzimkulu River, about 10 miles N. by W. of Stuart's Town.

ENTOMBE: A settlement in the Wakkerstroom district of the Transvaal Colony, S. Africa; station of the Hermannsburg Missionary Society (1861), which had about 400 professing Christians before the Transvaal war, but of which later details are not now (1903) available.

ENTUMENI: A settlement in the northeastern part of Natal, S. Africa, situated near Ft. Chater and about 10 miles S. W. from Eshowe. Station of the Schreuder Norwegian Mission, with (1900) 5 missionaries, men and women; a high school, a training class for women workers and 202 professing Christians.

ENYANISWENI: A settlement in the Transkei region of Cape Colony, S. Africa. Station of the South African Wesleyan Methodist Missionary Society, with (1900) 8 preaching places, 5 schools and 455 professing Christians.

ENYANYADU: A settlement in Natal; circuit of the South African Wesleyan Methodist Missionary Society, with (1900) 40 outstations and 850 professing Christians.

ENYEZANE: A settlement in the Kranzkop district of Natal, S. Africa. Station founded by the East Frisian Missionary Society in 1859 and at present carried on by the Hermannsburg Missionary Society, with (1902) 1 resident missionary.

ENZINCUKA: Settlement in Griqualand East, Cape Colony, S. Africa, situated about 15 miles N. W. from Mount Frere. Station of the Moravian Missions (1881), with (1902) 1 missionary and his wife, 2 preaching places, 2 schools and 340 professing Christians.

EPHRATA: A settlement in the Mosquito Reservation, Central America. Station of the Moravian Missions (1860), with (1903) 1 missionary and his wife.

EPI. See NEW HEBRIDES, API.

EPWORTH: A station of the WMS, near Salisbury, Rhodesia, Central Africa. There are about 500 people living here who are all nominally Christians. One missionary cares for the work and the native congregation in Salisbury.

ERAVUR: A town on the east coast of Ceylon, situated about 10 miles N. W. of Batticaloa. Station of the WMS, with (1903) 1 missionary and 22 native workers.

ERITREA: A colony of Italy in Egypt with autonomous administration. It lies on the Red Sea and is bounded landward by the Egyptian Sudan, Abyssinia and French Somaliland. The coast line is about 640 miles. The area is 99,500 square miles; population about 450,000, of whom about 2,000 are European. There is a military railway from Massaua to Maiatal, 23 miles, and 319 miles of telegraph line. The Swedish National Missionary Society has 5 stations in Eritrea, with 17 missionaries, men and women, and 135 communicant Christians.

ERMELO: A town in the Transvaal Colony, S. Africa, situated 63 miles S. W. of Barberton. Population, 2,000. Station of the Berlin Missionary Society (1899), but temporarily vacant in consequence of the late war.

ERODE: A town in the Coimbatore District, Madras, India, situated on the Cauvery River, 36 miles S. W. of Salem. Population (1891), 12,300, of whom over 10,000 are Hindus. Station of the Leipzig Missionary Society (1888), with (1903) 1 missionary and his wife, 10 native workers, men and women; 3 preaching places, 4 common schools, 1 high school, and 272 professing Christians. The Society lists give the name as Irod.

ERROMANGO. See NEW HEBRIDES.

ERUNGALUR. See IRUNGALUR.

ERZERUM: Capital of the province of the same name in Asiatic Turkey and an important fortress, situated 110 miles S. E. of Trebizond and a little south of the western branch of the Euphrates River. It is an important station of caravan trade between the Black Sea and Persia. Its altitude is 6,600 feet. Population about 39,000, of whom 26,500 are Mohammedans and the remainder Christians of different sects. Station of the ABCFM (1839), with (1902) 1 missionary and his wife (the wife being a physician), 2 missionary women, 35 native workers, men and women; 22 outstations, 16 preaching places, 28 common schools, 2 high schools and 350 evangelical Christian communicants. Many of the members of this church are emigrating in order to find security for life and property.

ERZINGAN: A city of Asiatic Turkey, 96 miles southwest of Erzerum. Situated on the Euphrates, in the midst of the mountains, it is an important military center and is noted for the energy of its people, both Turks and Armenians. An outstation of the ABCFM worked from Erzerum.

ESIDUMBINI: A settlement in Natal, S. Africa, about 35 miles N. E. of Durban. Station of the ABCFM (1849), with (1902) 1 missionary and his wife, 1 missionary woman and 10 native workers, men and women.

ESKIMO LANGUAGE: A branch of the North American family of languages which is found in the Arctic coast regions. It is spoken in varying dialects in the most northern inhabited regions of America, from Greenland to Alaska, and by a small section of the Arctic dwellers in Eastern Asia. It has been reduced to writing by missionaries by use of the Roman letters, and also in some cases by the invention of syllabary characters which better suit the nature of the language.

ES SALT: A town in Syria, lying east of the Jordan and 15 miles N. W. of Heshbon. Station of the CMS (1873), with 1 missionary and his wife, 7 native workers, men and women; 4 schools and 380 professing Christians.

ESPIRITU SANTO. See NEW HEBRIDES.

ESSEQUIBO: A settlement near the mouth of the Essequibo River, British Guiana, S. America, about 15 miles N. of Queenstown. Station of the Wesleyan Methodist Church of the West Indies (Eastern Conference), with 1 missionary and his wife, 5 preaching places, 3 schools and 360 professing Christians.

ESTABLISHED CHURCH OF SCOTLAND; Foreign Missions of. See SCOTLAND, ESTABLISHED CHURCH OF.

ESTACION CATORCE. See CATORCE.

ESTCOURT: A town in Natal, S. Africa, situated about 55 miles N. W. of Pietermaritzburg. Outstation of the SPG.

ESTRIDGE: A Moravian Mission Station on the northern coast of the island of St. Kitts, West Indies. The station was opened in 1845 and has 19 native workers, with 1 preaching place, 1 school and 450 professing Christians.

ETAH: A town and district in the United Provinces, India, situated 75 miles S. W. of Bareilly. Population (1891) 7,800, of whom 5,000 are Hindus and nearly 2,000 Mohammedans. Station of the ME, with (1903) 18 native workers, 1 preaching place, 24 Sunday schools and 1,340 professing Christians. Station also of the PN (1900), with (1903) 3 missionaries and their wives, 35 native workers, men and women; 25 outstations, 48 common schools, 1 high school, 1 evangelistic training class, 1 training class for women workers and 950 baptized Christians.

ETAWAH: A town in the United Provinces, India, on the Jumna River, 85 miles west by north of Cawnpore. It is a pleasant place, very picturesque, and contains several buildings of importance. It is regarded as the healthiest town on the plains of India. The population is (1891) 38,800, of whom 26,000 are Hindus and about 11,000 Mohammedans. Station of the PN (1863), with 1 missionary, 1 missionary woman and 11 native workers.

ETEMBENI (Natal). See ITEMBENI.

ETEMBENI (Cape Colony): A town in the eastern part of Cape Colony, situated about 15 miles W. by S. of King Williams Town. Station of the Berlin Missionary Society (1868), with (1903) 1 missionary, 4 native workers, and 258 professing Christians. Station also of the South African Wesleyan Methodist Mission, with (1900) 89 native workers, 38 schools and 1,520 professing Christians.

ETINAN: A settlement in the eastern part of the British Colony of South Nigeria, W. Africa, situated on the Kwo-Ibo (or Qua-Ibo) River, about 40 miles from its mouth. Station of the Qua-Iboe Mission (1898), with (1903) 1 missionary, 3 native workers and 2 outstations.

ETTAMANUR: A town in Travancore, S. India, situated about 30 miles to the eastward of Kottayam. An itinerary of the CMS, superintended from Tiruwella, with (1902) 18 native workers, men and women; 7 outstations, 9 schools and 1,165 professing Christians.

EURASIAN: A term employed to denote the offspring of European and Asiatic parentage, without regard to the proportion of the mixture. Such children are, in most cases, illegitimate, tho not necessarily so, and too often try to imitate the bearing of the European while living in subordinate positions like lower class Asiatics. Frequently they exhibit the worst moral characteristics of both races. Physically they are well formed, lithe, graceful, and often beautiful, and show great dexterity in all that requires deftness and delicacy of touch, such as is required in clerical work. They do not have strong constitutions and are particularly subject to pulmonary complaints. By reason of their parentage, the Eurasian girls are often neglected and sink in the social scale.

In recent years missions have found means of reaching numbers of Eurasians effectively in India and China, so as to help them make the most of whatever abilities their mixed blood has given them.

EVANGELICAL ALLIANCE, The: An association for the defense of religious liberty and promoting the unity of all believers in the essentials of Christianity and their cooperation for its progress. It sprang from the labors of some great exponents of the Christian faith in different lands toward the close of the first half of the 19th century. Notable among these were Thomas Chalmers of Scotland, John Angell James of England, George Fische of France, Merle D'Aubigné of Switzerland, and William Patton, Samuel H. Cox, Lyman Beecher, and others in the United States. In 1842 a meeting of the Congregational Union of England gave large consideration to the question of greater unity among the various denominations of Christendom. In that year also the Established Church of Scotland appointed a committee to report on the same matter. A celebrated letter, dated March, 1843, outlining such an organization, and asking that a meeting should be called in England to consider it, was written by Dr. William Patton, one of the founders of the Union Theological Seminary of New York, to John Angell James. The project made an important topic in the bicentenary of the Westminster Assembly held in Edinburgh, July, 1843. A conference of different denominations held in the Wesleyan Centenary Hall in February, 1845, also discussed the movement. John Henderson, a wealthy banker of Glasgow, collected, and in 1845 published, a volume entitled "Essays on Christian Union." A meeting preliminary to organization was held in Liverpool, October, 1845. At this meeting there assembled as many as two hundred ministers and laymen representing nearly twenty denominations.

A call was decided on for a great meeting to be held in the following year in London, and the provisional committee held its meeting in April, 1846. Several delegates were present from the United States. The meeting for organization assembled in the Freemasons' Hall in London, opening in August, 1846. Eight hundred delegates represented fifty denominations of Christians, and were in session fifteen days. It was in this meeting that John Angell James in an address gave to Dr. William Patton of New York the honor of first conceiving the idea of the alliance. A resolution was passed asking that branches of the Evangelical Alliance be formed in Great Britain and Ireland, United States, France, Belgium, French Switzerland and the Waldensian Valleys, North Germany, South Germany and German Switzerland, British North America and the West Indies, and additional branches from time to time.

Prominent among the subjects of discussion were sectarianism, infidelity, Popery, the Sabbath, and Christian education. There was great interest in this meeting among all the denominations and in the missionary centers of the world.

This organization has held a number of great ecumenical meetings, which have discussed the foremost questions of human thought and progress. Few religious conferences have engaged an interest so profound and widespread.

Branch national organizations have been formed in Scotland, Ireland, United States, Canada, New Brunswick, France, Switzerland, Germany, Holland, Denmark, Italy, Spain, Turkey, Greece, Syria, Egypt, South Africa, Japan, China, Persia, East Indies, West Indies, Palestine, Australia, New Zealand, Chile, and Mexico.

Besides the aid to the Christian faith throughout the world, the Evangelical Alliance has been most practically useful in averting and ameliorating persecutions and oppressions from time to time in various parts of the earth. By united action in the way of remonstrance and petition, and by creating a wholesome and strong public opinion, religious liberty has been promoted in many countries, especially in Spain, Italy, Austria, Sweden, Turkey, Russia, Japan, and Persia.

By emphasizing in statements of doctrine only essentials in which all are agreed, by collecting statistics which exhibit the religious condition and progress of the whole world, and by discovering the signs of the times in the discussion of advanced measures, these cooperating bodies have opened an ameliorating influence among widely differing churches, which results in better conformity of their denominational standards to the spirit of union and progress.

A few missionaries of different schools held a three days' meeting for prayer in Lodiana, India, in 1858, and the suggestion arose that a request be made to all the Christian world for an annual week of prayer. The Alliance soon published the call, and has ever since sent forth the program of topics to all Christendom, before the beginning of the year. Many are the revivals that have followed this annual call to prayer, now identified with the Alliance, which has for its motto "*Unum corpus sumus in Christo.*"

Headquarters: Alliance House, 7 Adam St., Strand, London, England.

The organ of the Society is *Evangelical Christendom*, monthly, London.

EVANGELICAL ASSOCIATION, Society of the: The Society was organized in 1839. For ten years its efforts were confined to New York and Canada, but in 1850 work was begun in Germany and later in Switzerland. The first distinctively foreign mission field was Japan, where a station was established in 1876. A new mission in China has long been contemplated.

There are (1903) 600 missionaries in the United States and Canada; 121 in Germany and Switzerland. In Japan there are 6 American missionaries and 24 workers, 1 station, 39 outstations, 906 church members.

The Woman's Missionary Society of the Evangelical Association was reorganized in 1892 and is auxiliary to the Missionary Society of the Evangelical Association. It includes 11 Conference Branch Societies and 153 auxiliaries. It aids in all departments of the work and supports 2 missionaries.

EVANGELICAL LUTHERAN CHURCH. See LUTHERAN CHURCH.

EVANSDALE: A settlement in the western part of Natal, S. Africa, situated about 10 miles S. W. of Dundee. Station of the South Africa Wesleyan Methodist Missionary Society.

EWÉ LANGUAGE: Belongs to the negro family and is spoken in Dahomey by an unknown number of people. It has been written with Roman letters. It has two known dialects, called Anlo and Popo.

EZINCUKA. See ENZINCUKA.

F

FAA: A parish in the extreme northwest of the island of Tahiti. Outstation of the Paris Evangelical Society, with 125 church members.

FAASALELEAGA: A settlement district on Savaii, Samoan Islands, Polynesia. Formerly occupied by the LMS as a station (1830); it is now (1902) the center of a Christian community of about 5,000, of whom 1,400 are church members. There are 90 native workers, 33 places of worship and 33 schools.

FAIRBANK, Samuel Bacon: Born in Stamford, Conn., December 14, 1822. He fitted for college at Monson, Mass., and in Jacksonville, Ill. Graduated from the Illinois College in 1842 and from Andover Theological Seminary in 1845. He went to India as a foreign missionary under the ABCFM in 1846, arriving at Bombay the same year. He was located at Ahmadnagar for four years, when he removed to Bombay and took charge of the mission press there. In 1857 he went to Vadala, in the Bombay Presidency, which was his headquarters until 1869. When Dr. Fairbank reached the usual limit of active service he decided to remain in India and devote his time to translation and literary work. Dr. Fairbank's language was the Marâthi, and in this language he did much for the literature of the Marâthi-speaking people, especially in the line of hymnology. He prepared the first book of musical notation for Western India. He was exceedingly fond of nature and a great student of the flora of India. Probably he did more than any man of this generation to teach the Indian farmers with whom he came in contact in his missionary work wiser methods of agriculture. This brought him personally into direct spiritual relations with many whom otherwise he could not have reached. In his own district he was chief spiritual authority for many Hindus as well as for Christians. He died of heat apoplexy on May 31, 1898, having served in India 52 years. In 1856 he married Mary Ballantine, daughter of a missionary to India. Six of their children became missionaries in India and Ceylon.

FAIRFIELD: A town in the southwestern mountainous part of Jamaica, West Indies. Station of the Moravian Missions (1823), with (1903) 1 missionary and his wife, 25 native workers, men and women, and 600 professing Christians.

FAIRFORD: A settlement in Manitoba, Canada, situated on the N. E. shore of Manitoba Lake. Station of the CMS, with (1902) 1 missionary, 4 native workers, 4 schools and 150 professing Christians. All the Indians in this place have learned to read and write English.

FAIRVIEW: A town in the southern part of Natal, S. Africa, situated on the sea coast about 12 miles N. E. of North Shepstone. Station of the Free Methodist Church General Missionary Board (1891), with (1903) 6 missionaries, men and women; 7 native workers, men and women; 2 schools, 1 industrial school and 100 professing Christians.

FAIZABAD: A town in the United Provinces, India, on the Gogra River, 78 miles east of Lucknow; a comparatively modern place, tho somewhat decayed in appearance. Population (1901) 75,085, Hindus, Muslims and Christians. Languages, Hindi and Urdu. A large military station. Station of the CMS (1862), with (1902) 12 native workers, men and women; 2 schools and 192 professing Christians. Formerly station of the Zenana Bible and Medical Mission, which withdrew in 1902, transferring its work to the CMS. Station also of the WMS (1876), with (1903) 2 missionaries, 2 missionary women, 58 native workers, men and women; 3 preaching places, 2 outstations, 8 common schools, 1 high school, 1 industrial school and orphanage and 173 professing Christians.

FAJARDO: A town on the eastern extremity of the island of Porto Rico. Station of the American Missionary Association, with 1 missionary and his wife.

FA-KU-MEN: A town in Manchuria, China, situated about 50 miles N. of Mukden. Station of the Presbyterian Church of Ireland (1899), with (1900) 1 missionary, 18 native workers, 6 outstations, 7 preaching places, 4 day schools, 1 boarding school and 225 professing Christians. Name also written Fa-ko-men.

FALASHA KARA: This language belongs to the Hamitic group of African languages, and is spoken by the Falasha Jews in the Kara district of Abyssinia. It is written with the Amharic characters.

FALASHA JEWS: These Jews live in Abyssinia, numbering about 200,000 souls. They occupy, according to Cust, the anomalous position of not being Semitic either in blood or in speech. Mission work among them was commenced in 1858 by the London Society for the Promotion of Christianity among the Jews, and since that time more than 1,500 of them have been baptized.

FALEALILI: A district on the southern shore of Upolu, the most beautiful of the Samoan Islands. Station of the LMS (1836), with (1902) 1 missionary, 58 native workers, 31 preaching places, 31 schools and 4,926 professing Christians, of whom 1,248 are church members.

FALLANGIA: A settlement town on the Lesser Ponga River, French Guinea, W. Africa. It was the starting point for the mission among the Susus by the West Indies Church Association, Barbados. The first white missionaries who visited those regions were killed by the slave-dealers, and in 1818 the mission was abandoned. The next who tried succumbed to the climate; but colored missionaries from Codrington College, Barbados, who arrived at Fallangia in 1855, had a fair success. The work is now carried on by the Pongas Mission in connection with the SPG.

FALLSCHER, Christian (of Germany): Forty-three years before his death on February 11, 1901, Christian Fallscher went to Jerusalem to work under the late Bishop Gobat. Six years later he was sent by him to Nablus, as a lay preacher, and there he remained for thirty-seven years, first in connection with Bishop Gobat and later with the CMS. Through his agency a church, schools, mission house and house for the mission ladies were built, and a year before his death a firman was obtained which enabled the CMS to build a large and handsome hospital. In 1891 medical work was opened in Nablus and ladies were sent to help in schools and hospital duties. He was loved and honored by Christian, Muslim and Jew, and by his patient endurance and unpretending piety his influence became potent and far-reaching. Notwithstanding his active evangelistic work among the people, he learned the difficult Arabic language, and by his perpetual intercourse with the natives he gained a clear insight into its idioms and intricacies. He was enabled, in a remarkable degree, by the grace of God, to identify himself with the people among whom he lived, and in many legitimate ways to follow their customs. He learned, in the Christian sense of the term, to lay aside much of his own personality and by coming into close sympathy with the people he was enabled to apprehend the Eastern point of view.

FAN-CHÊNG-HSIEN: A town in the province of Hu-pei, China, about 10 miles north of Hsiang-yang-fu. Station of the Hauges' Synod China Mission (1893), with (1900) 6 missionaries, men and women, of whom 2 are physicians; 8 native workers, men and women; 4 schools, 1 hospital, and 1 opium victims' refuge. Station also of the Swedish Evangelical Mission Covenant of America (1890), with (1900) 7 missionaries, men and women. Name also written Fan-cheng.

FANTI LANGUAGE: Belongs to the negro group of African languages, and is spoken by some of the tribes in the Gold Coast Colony, W. Africa, being a dialect of the Ashanti allied to the Otshi dialect. It was reduced to writing by missionaries of the WMS, who made use of the Roman letters. The beginnings of a literature have been created.

FARAVOHITRA: The favorite European quarter of Antananarivo, capital of Madagascar. It is situated at the northern extremity of the rocky ridge on which the city is built, and was bare and desolate in 1868, when the LMS chose it for a center of work. A memorial church was erected here in 1870 on the spot where in 1849 Christians were burned alive for refusing to give up Christ. The LMS has (1902) connected with Faravohitra and in the district 1 missionary and his wife, 256 native workers, 30 common schools and 4,412 professing Christians.

FARIDPUR (Bengal): Chief town of a district of the same name in Bengal, India, situated on one of the delta outlets of the Ganges about 120 miles N. E. of Calcutta. Central station of the Faridpur Mission (1867), with (1900) 5 missionaries, men and women, one a physician; 3 native workers, 6 schools and 1 hospital. Outstation of the SPG, with 250 professing Christians. Name also written Fureedpore.

FARIDPUR (United Provinces): A village 15 miles S. E. of Bareli, United Provinces, India. Population (1891), 6,400, of whom about 3,500 are Hindus and 2,500 Mohammedans. Circuit of the ME, with 20 native workers, men and women, and 306 professing Christians.

FARM AMSTERDAM. See AMSTERDAM FARM.

FARRINGIA: A settlement on the River Ponga in French Guinea. Station of the Pongas Mission.

FATÉ LANGUAGE. See EFATESE LANGUAGE.

FATEHGANJ WEST: A village in the United Provinces, India, situated 10 miles N. W. of Bareli. Circuit of the ME North India Mission, with 27 native workers, men and women; 1 preaching place, 8 day schools, and 725 professing Christians.

FATEHGARH (Punjab): A town situated about 15 miles N.E. of Batala, Punjab, India, occupied (1903) as an outstation of Batala by the CEZ.

FATEHGARH (United Provinces): A town in the United Provinces, India. Capital of the district of Farukhabad, adjoining the town of Farukhabad and situated 70 miles S. of Bareli. It was the scene of a massacre of about 200 Europeans during the mutiny of 1857. Population about 12,000. Station of the PN (1844), with (1903) 10 missionaries, men and women; 53 native workers, men and women; 6 outstations, 5 preaching places, 16 day schools, 4 boarding schools, 1 theological training class, 1 orphanage, 4 organized churches and about 400 professing Christians.

FATEHPUR: A town in the United Provinces, India, situated 70 miles N.W. of Allahabad. Population (1891), 20,000, of whom 10,000 are Hindus and 9,000 Mohammedans. Station of the PN (1853), with (1903) 5 missionaries, men and women; 9 native workers, men and women; 1 chapel, 2 schools and 2 outstations.

FAT-SHAN: A manufacturing town and river port on the Canton River, 9 miles W. S. W. of Canton, Kwangtung, China. A great part of the traffic on the three rivers which unite to form the Canton River passes through this place, and people from all parts of Kwangtung, Kwangsi and even Yunnan are met with. In former years the hatred of foreigners was great, and at any time preaching was likely to cause commotion and trouble. Population about 400,000. Station of the WMS, with (1903) 3 missionaries, of whom 2 are physicians; 7 native workers, 6 outstations, 3 preaching places, 1 day school, 1 hospital, and 115 professing Christians.

FAURESMITH: A town in the Orange River Colony, S. Africa, situated 65 miles S. S. E. of Kimberly; the Jagersfontein diamond fields are near this town. Population about 2,000. Station of the South African Wesleyan Methodist Missionary Society, with (1900) 23 native workers, 28 outstations, 3 preaching places, 2 day schools, and 414 professing Christians.

FAYUM: A large town of Central Egypt, in the oasis of that name. Population of town and oasis, 150,000. Mission district of the United Presbyterian Church of America.

FEN-CHAU-FU: A city in the province of Shan-si, China, situated on the plain, 60 miles S. W. of Tai-yuen-fu. Elevation, 3,000 feet. Temperate climate; lowest thermometer 50° F. A population of over a million is reached here, among whom are many Roman Catholics and a few Mohammedans, but the majority are followers of Confucius and Buddha. Station of the ABCFM (1887), which was broken up during the Boxer rising of 1900. Reopened in 1901, but the missionary has not yet (1903) taken up permanent residence there. There are (1903) 94 church members.

FENG-CHEN: A town in the province of Shan-si, China, situated 85 miles S. W. of Kalgan. It is a station of the CIM (1902), with 2 missionaries, 1 with his wife. It is also a station of the CA.

FENG-HSIANG-FU: A town in the western

part of the province of Shan-si, China. Station of the CIM (1898); broken up by the Boxer rising in 1900. Now occupied (1903) by 1 missionary and his wife and 1 foreign assistant. The name is also written Feng-siang.

FENG-HWA-HSIEN: A town in the province of Che-kiang, China, situated about 15 miles S. W. of Ningpo. Station of the CIM (1866), with (1903) 1 missionary and a number of professing Christians. The work suffered considerable disturbance during the Boxer rising of 1900. The name is also written Feng-hua.

FENG-HWANG-CHENG: A town in Manchuria, about 100 miles S. E. of Mukden. Station of the Danish Missionary Society (1899), with (1903) 2 missionaries, 1 missionary's wife, 1 dispensary, 3 professing Christians.

FENG-KANG: A town in the province of Kiang-si, China, situated about 25 miles E. by N. of Kan-chau-fu. Station of the CIM (1891), which was broken up at the time of the Boxer rising in 1900, and now (1903) is still vacant.

FENG-TSIANG. See FENG-HSIANG-FU.

FERGHANA: A territory of Asiatic Russia, formerly Khokand, one of the Khanates of Western Turkestan. It is enclosed by lofty mountains, and is for the most part well watered and fertile. The climate is severe in winter, and in the valleys is very hot in summer. It is noted for its fruits and its silk manufactures. The population is (1897) 1,560,000, composed of various tribes of Turks and Tatars. It was forced to accept a Russian protectorate in 1868 and was annexed to Russia in 1876. It is one of the regions where no Protestant missionary enterprise is allowed.

FERNANDO PO: An African island lying in the Gulf of Guinea, off the Kamerun coast, forming with the islands of Elobey, Annobon, Corisco, and other small islands, a colony of Spain. The area of all is 950 square miles; population 23,709, mainly Buwi negroes (of Bantu race). The island of Fernando Po is volcanic. Fernando Po has served at various times as a base of operations for missionaries wishing to enter Africa. The Primitive Methodist Missionary Society now has 4 stations there, with about 280 native Christians. The Spanish laws throw many restrictions about the missionary enterprise.

FEROZEPORE. See FIROZPUR.

FETISHISM: It is common for those who have a theory of evolution to support, extending to religions as well as to physical life, to assume that fetishism is invariably the lowest step in the ladder of man's ascent to higher religious conceptions; that, beginning with this simple alphabet, the race has gradually advanced through more and more complex and elaborate systems toward Christianity, which is the goal of the religions of the world. It is in one sense flattering to the Christian faith, but, in another, it is utterly subversive of some of its most fundamental doctrines.

It were better in approaching this subject to leave theories aside for a time, and to deal with simple facts.

What is fetishism as it is found still surviving among savage tribes in our time? What are the objects of worship to which we apply the name of Fetish?

It would take a volume to name and describe the Zulu's superstitions and give account of his religious views and practises. His superstitions are well nigh numberless. If a turkey-buzzard lights near a kraal, something will happen. For one of these birds to be caught in a snare is a bad omen. The man who kills one of them will die. If a cock crows in the early part of the night, some of the people or cattle will be sick or die. Feeding dogs on the beaks and claws of birds will make them fierce and swift for the chase. To wear the claws of birds or beasts or small horns of cattle about the neck will make a man courageous and give him prowess. Bits of bark, roots, or bones suspended from the neck will protect a man against poison, lightning, or the designs of an enemy. In the virtues and uses of charms, amulets, love potions, incantations, the African has great faith. Throughout Africa the curiously endowed objects known to us as fetishes are found to be of great variety, embracing amulets and charms worn about the neck, and consisting of tiger's teeth, serpent's fangs, stones washed into unusual forms, curious shells, bits of wood carved in fantastic fashion, etc. In Asia a passage from the Veda incased in a frame of transparent horn, or a potent verse of the Koran, or a line from the Avesta supposed to be powerful in driving away evil influences; in Africa a stone or rock of fantastic shape at the door of a hut, or a skull hung above its lintel; in America a totem raised on a scaffold by some Indian tribe—all these are virtually fetishes, since they are arbitrarily chosen objects to which is attached some supernatural power. As a rule they are not supposed to be divine in or of themselves, but rather to embody a divine influence of a mysterious and somewhat spiritual character.

The fundamental idea is that of an indwelling power that is concentrated and peculiar. This point may be illustrated by popular superstitions which still exist among civilized nations. The horseshoe has in itself no more efficacy than any other mass of iron, but in that particular form it is supposed to embody a lucky influence. Certain coins or rather sacred keepsakes, carried in the pockets or worn upon the person, are sometimes supposed to be attended by mysterious influences. No individual member of a group of thirteen persons embodies any baneful influence, but there are many in civilized countries who fear the vague fatality of that total number seated at a table. In fact the number of objects, incidents, relationships, etc., etc., to which is ascribed a sort of magic influence, by the people of all lands, is very great.

In North China and in various other countries certain uncanny animals, like the weasel, the fox, or the serpent, are supposed to be attended by baleful influence.

Wherever found, fetishism gives opportunity to the witch-doctor or the diviner. This again opens the door to the most terrible cruelty, through the "smelling out," and the appeal to trial by ordeal inevitably leading to sacrifice of human life and legalized butcheries, as in Dahomey or other **"ju-ju"** centers of West Africa. In its mildest form the appeal to the witch-doctor may still be seen among the Kaffirs and Zulus in South Africa. If one of the family, as the father, is taken sick, a deputation is sent with a cow or other present to the *inyanga*, or medical priest, to inquire what is the matter and what is to be done. The priest accepts the present and retires with the deputation to some nook near by, asks them to smite the earth with their rods, and so arouse the spirits, that he may hear what they have to say. After a long series of these performances the priest always comes out with a message from the divinities to the deputation that the sick man has neglected his religious duties; that it is a long time since he has slaughtered an animal in honor and for the benefit of his ancestral shades; that the best cow must now be offered, so the anger of the gods will be appeased, and the sick man get well. The messengers carry the word back, the sick man accepts it, prayers are offered, sins are confessed, the best cow is slaughtered, the blood and gall are sprinkled upon persons, houses, and premises, the beef is put away in a hut by itself for the night, and in the morning the people profess to believe that the divinities have been there, have tasted the meat, and are satisfied. The neighbors gather, the beef is roasted and consumed, and the hope is expressed that the sick man may recover soon. If so, all is well, and the doctor is extolled for his ability and skill in finding out the cause and cure of the sickness; if not, the doctor is denounced as a great humbug; he has got their cow, but they have got no good. And now they go with another cow to another *inyanga* and go through the same process, until finally the man does either recover or die.

How have these ideas gained currency among men? If when found among civilized peoples popular superstitious notions are empirical, if they are the result of slow growth and an imaginary experience, as they certainly are, we may assume that fetishism among savage tribes has had a similar development. Men have chosen their fetishes as they have come to place their confidence in certain remedies for bodily ailments. A certain medicine may have been selected by mere fancy at first, but if in repeated instances good results were supposed to follow, it gained currency. And so with the fetish. Indeed, many remedies are mere fetishes, and are given to drive away diseases which are supposed to be caused by evil spirits. Pharmacy and superstition go hand in hand among savage races, and are rarely separated. In both cases there is supposed to be a connection between the objects chosen and the mysterious power of unseen spirits.

So far from fetishism representing always the first stage of religious development, and that only, it proceeds side by side with higher forms of religion and intermingles with them. Many of its objects supposed to represent supernatural power have sprung up long after the higher faith was entertained.

Fetishism abounds in China, India, Burma, and Ceylon, in spite of the teachings of Confucius and Gautama. It has really more practical influence with the people than all the so-called book religions of the East. A distinguished civilian of Ceylon has declared that nine-tenths of the inhabitants of that country are really not Buddhists at all, but are the devotees of various superstitious fancies. The staple of the popular religion is devil-worship, or the fear of evil spirits. And the whole paraphernalia and ritual by which their evil influences are warded off belong to the category of fetishism.

The absurd and wide-spread superstition known in China as Fung Shui is practical fetishism; it is a supposed mysterious and supernatural something, which inheres in certain objects, resides in certain localities, or hovers over the abodes of the living or the dead. It is a system of geomancy, and is especially related to the graves of the departed.

It is estimated that in South America there are 7,000,000 of people who still adhere more or less openly to the fetishisms of their forefathers.

In almost all nations, that which is unusual—a river issuing from a cave, a tree growing in a peculiar shape, a rock which the waters have worn into grotesque forms, certain deformities of the human body—is supposed to be attended by weird and preternatural influence. And the functions of witch-doctors, jugglers, medicine-men, etc., are supposed to be directed to the proper management of these occult forces. The choice of lucky days or fortunate sites for buildings is supposed to belong to their province. Of the same class were the haruspices of the Romans, who inspected the entrails of animals or observed the flights of birds in order to direct aright the movements of armies or plan successful expeditions.

The theory of Comte that fetishism was the awestruck recognition of divine influence in all natural objects was incorrect; else why should particular objects be chosen, why one stone or tree or stream more than another? That which makes a fetish is the differential which distinguishes it from other objects and concentrates in it the divine and available power; this constitutes its value. It has been uniformly observed that one fetish differs from another in the degree of inherent efficacy. It may differ also from another in the different kind of utility which attends it, one accomplishing one good result, and another, another. Where the system becomes elaborate, each desirable object of attainment may have its fetish, by whose potency it is to be gained. One of these preternatural objects may avert a given disease, another secure victory over an enemy, another insure the birth of a son.

A little reflection will convince us that fetishism is one of the most wide-spread and permanent of all faiths, and that it coexists with every other. If we penetrate the lower strata of society we shall find it still existing in the most civilized countries. Among the colored population of our Southern States it prevails to a surprising extent. In spite of the white man's influence, and that of the Church and school, the "hoodoo" finds awe-stricken thousands to tremble before it. Fetishism is mixed up with the cure of diseases and the selection of times and seasons for entering upon any particular enterprise. It is at the foundation of the success of nostrums and quackeries, and manifold expedients supposed to be induced by the experience of others. Mankind everywhere find the forces of nature at their command, and the fact that these are little understood and always more or less involved in mystery, does not prevent constant experiment. In a sense and in a degree all are yet children groping their way amid occult forces, and those who are most enlightened by science and most exalted in religious privilege may well sympathize with benighted tribes who are left to their gropings merely. Considering their condition, it is not strange that in the silence of nature they are startled by the rustling leaf or by any exceptional phenomenon that arrests attention, and are only too ready with the help of fancy to clothe it with divine influence. It is not strange that when they hear the voice of the thunder, or the roar of the distant waterfall, or the soughing of the waves in some dark, mysterious cave of the rocky shore, they are awe-struck. To them there is no true enlightenment; there is nothing articulate or intelligible in the voices of nature which they hear, and they have learned no wisdom. Having no divine revelation, recognizing no Father above, and only bowed down with vague and mysterious fear, they are ready to accept any resource. And when some designing rain-doctor or juggler, witnessing their bewilderment and affliction, proffers his aid to relieve from drought or pestilence or famine, they must trust him; tho he has failed a hundred times they have no option. The totem on the scaffold, the amulets about their necks, are equally dumb and have often failed; but they have no other resource. Generation after generation they grope on amid failures; and such is the imperative necessity that man shall put his trust in something beyond the range of his own powers, that, altho fetishism has for ages proved barren as Sahara, yet it still exists and must exist till the knowledge of God, the Father of all, and Jesus Christ, the only Savior, shall be made known. Fetishism is something too serious to be regarded with ridicule. It is the most pathetic illustration of human ignorance and destitution. To one who knows that man is made in God's own image and destined to worship and enjoy Him forever, no spectacle can be more melancholy than to see him embracing with bootless and abortive faith a senseless amulet, a bleached bone, or a carved stick. As an appeal to missionary zeal, the fetishism of the world is pathetic and eloquent. It proclaims in strongest terms the desolation of a soul that was made to be a temple of the Holy Ghost, but is in fact worse than empty.

As to the manner in which the missionary should approach those who are under the thrall of fetishism we may quote from the remarks of Rev. Dr. George Robson, of the United Free Church of Scotland, at the Ecumenical Conference of 1900:

The more one learns of these fetish religions, the more is the conviction deepened that they are not wholly inventions of wickedness. . . . Behind all the deviltry and cruelty . . . and underneath customs and practises in themselves utterly to be reprobated, there are to be found relics of truth, survivals of purposes and aspirations that, however misdirected, were originally pure. To some, it may seem as if the proper attitude of Christianity (over against these degraded religions) is one of simple antagonism. . . . But this is not the manner of Christian science. . . . A true apologetic is here necessary for exhibiting the glory of Christianity as the final religion for all mankind; and to accomplish this in all directions is the function of the missionary enterprise. I venture to think that this department of missionary apologetic has been comparatively neglected, and that it is most desirable that it should receive immediate and systematic attention.

LITERATURE: Brinton (D. G.), *Religions of Primitive Peoples*, New York, 1897; Lyall (A.), *Natural Religion in 1885*, London, 1891; Schultze (F.), *Fetishism*, New York, India.

FEZ: A city in Morocco, situated at an altitude of 1,300 feet, 36 miles east by north of Mequinez. It is one of the three residences of the Sultan and is a very holy city, founded in 793. The tomb of its founder is a sanctuary for criminals of all kinds. It has a fine mosque. Station of the North Africa Mission (1888), with (1902) a missionary and his wife, 3 missionary women, 1 theological training class and a dispensary. It is also a station of the Gospel Mission Union (1894), with a missionary and his wife.

FIANARANTSOA: The capital of Betsileo, Madagascar, situated 190 miles S. of Antananarivo. Population about 10,000. It is the center of the work of the London Missionary Society in Betsileo province (1863), with (1902) 10 missionaries, men and women; 425 native workers, men and women; 46 Sunday schools, 138 day schools, 2 boarding schools, 1 dispensary, 1 hospital and 1,450 church members. Also station of the Paris Evangelical Mission Society, to which in 1897 the LMS transferred one of the three districts of the town. It has (1902) 7 missionaries, men and women; 30 schools, 1 theological training class, 1 high school and 600 communicants. Station also of the Norwegian Mission.

FIFE BAY: A settlement on the southern coast of the eastern part of British New Guinea. Station of the LMS (1896), with 1 missionary and his wife and 16 native workers.

FIHAONANA: A town in Imerina, Madagascar, situated about 30 miles N. W. of Antananarivo. Station of the Paris Evangelical Society, transferred from the LMS in 1897. It now (1902) has one missionary and his wife, 1 missionary woman, 45 native workers, 20 day schools, an orphanage and 450 professing Christians.

FIJI ISLANDS: A group of islands in the Pacific Ocean, lying about 1,000 miles north of New Zealand and 300 miles distant from the Samoan group on the northeast. In all there are more than 200 islands, of which about 80 are inhabited. Viti Levu, area 4,250 square miles, is the largest, and Vanua Levu, area 2,600, the next in size. Suva, the capital, is on the south coast of Viti Levu. Including Rotuma Island the total area of the group is about 8,045 square miles.

There is very little level country. The greater part of the islands consists of alternating hills and valleys, the peaks sometimes rising to the height of four or five thousand feet. The climate, tho warm and somewhat enervating to Europeans, is not unhealthy. The supply of water is abundant, as there are numerous streams. Tropical vegetation grows here in great abundance and luxuriance.

The aborigines, or Fijians proper, are classed midway between the Malay and the Papuan, or negro, type of races. The name Fiji was formerly synonymous with every cruelty and abomination that savages are capable of. Cannibalism was indulged in, sick and aged relations were killed, widows were not allowed to survive the death of their husbands, and slaves were slain to accompany their dead masters; yet hospitality and politeness characterized this savage race in a remarkable degree. The Fiji savages believed in a future existence, and in two classes of gods— one immortal (a large serpent was the chief god of this class), the other, the spirits of heroes and chiefs. The priest spoke the will of the gods who were not worshiped through idols. The women of the upper class enjoyed considerable freedom and wielded great influence.

There is one prevailing language, Melanesian in its character, with several dialects. It has a large vocabulary, is strong in its expression and flexible in its forms.

Fiji presents a wonderful illustration of the power of the Gospel to transform the lives of the most degraded and to turn an entire people to the worship and service of the living God.

The complete Old and New Testaments are in circulation in the islands; day schools and colleges are maintained, and 1,000 churches, with an attendance of 100,000, are changing the moral and social condition of the people.

In the Fiji Islands there are now (1901) 2,247 native preachers and 31,422 native church members, besides 10,107 candidates for membership. In Rotuma, a solitary island lying between Fiji and the Ellice Islands, but politically connected with Fiji, there are 35 native workers and 460 church members. These churches are the fruit of the labors of the WMS, but are no longer connected with that Society, being in ecclesiastical relations with the Wesleyan churches in Australia.

When first discovered Fiji had a population estimated at 200,000, but diseases imported by European colonists have caused great mortality. In 1901 the population numbered 117,870. Of these, 94,397 were Fijians, 21,026 were Indians and Polynesians and 2,447 Europeans. Of the non-European population 91,526 habitually attend the Wesleyan churches and 9,338 the churches of the Roman Catholic Mission.

Allen (W.), *Rotuma* (Australasian Association for Advancement of Science), Sydney, 1895; Williams (T.), & Calvert (J.), *Fiji and the Fijians*, London, 1858 and 1877; Cousins (G.), *Story of the South Seas*, London, 1894.

FIJIAN LANGUAGE: Belongs to the Melanesian family and is spoken by about 100,000 people in the Fiji Islands. It has several dialects considerably varying from each other. It was reduced to writing by missionaries of the WMS and is written with Roman letters.

FILE HILLS: A settlement in the eastern part of Assiniboia, Canada, situated about 60 miles N. E. of Regina. Station of the Presbyterian Church in Canada.

FINANCES OF MISSIONS: This is the application of modern and approved methods to the special and peculiar conditions surrounding the financial operations of Foreign Missions.

A successful system of accounting must take into consideration two facts: First, few missionaries are selected with a view to their knowledge of finances and accounting, and few sent to the field have any special adaptation to such work. Second, this work must be committed to those who have gone as missionaries with a far different purpose, and who are reluctant to allow anything to interfere with the primary object of their missionary life. It is at once apparent that a system of accounting must be sufficiently simple to be readily comprehended and so worked out in its details as to minimize the time required of the mission treasurer, both as to work on the books and on statements and correspondence necessarily involved. Sufficient analysis should be provided in the form of report to enable the home office to work out as far as possible the many items of detail necessary to a full comprehension of the work from the financial standpoint.

The missions organization in the past (and to a large extent the method is still in force) has had a treasurer for each mission and a treasurer for each station, the latter accounting to the former, who in turn accounted to the home treasurer. This has resulted in absorbing the time of a large number of missionaries with but measurably satisfactory results. Improved postal and banking facilities in even the countries most remote make it possible to eliminate the station treasurer, enabling one man, with a small amount of clerical help, to oversee the accounting of an entire mission or of several contiguous missions. Faithful and intelligent accounting is essential to the proper adjustment of the entire fabric of mission effort in its corelated departments. This can be best attained by sending to the field trained accountants whose entire time shall be given to the duties of mission treasurer and financial agent.

Estimates, Appropriations and Grants: These are the basis of all disbursements. The estimates are prepared on the field by the mission, and are intended to cover in detail the estimated expense of the coming fiscal year. The estimates should embrace the following items:

Cost of given work for the current year.
Estimated cost of the same work for the ensuing year.
Amount needed for additional or new work.
Estimate of field receipts from medical fees, tuition, subscriptions, press receipts, etc.

The estimates should closely follow the analysis of disbursements, and may be properly classified as follows:

CLASS I.—MISSIONARIES ON FIELD.
 Sub-Class A.—Salaries.
           B.—Children.
CLASS II.—MISSIONARIES NOT ON FIELD.
 Sub-Class A.—Home Allowance.
           B.—Children.
           C.—Wives (if in United States).
           D.—Freight.
           E.—Travel.
CLASS III.—NEW MISSIONARIES.
 Sub-Class A.—Outfit.
To be filled   B.—Travel.
  in   C.—Freight.
New York.   D.—Salary.
                 E.—Personal Teacher.
CLASS IV.—EVANGELISTIC.
 Sub-Class A.—Native Ministers.
           B.—Licentiates.
           C.—Bible Women.
           D.—Other Helpers.
           E.—Sunday Schools.
           F.—Itinerating.
           G.—Any other Work.
CLASS IV.—EDUCATION.
 Sub-Class A.—Boarding Schools.
           B.—Day Schools.
           C.—Colleges.
           D.—Theological Seminaries.
           E.—Other Schools or Work.
CLASS VI.—HOSPITALS AND DISPENSARIES.
 Sub-Class A.—Assistants (Foreign and Native).
           B.—Medicines, etc.
           C.—Expenses.
CLASS VII.—PROPERTY (IN USE).
 Sub-Class A.—Rent, including Missionaries' Houses.
           B.—Taxes.
           C.—Insurance.
           D.—Repairs.
           E.—Attendants.
           F.—Lights and Heating.
CLASS VIII.—PROPERTY (NEW).
 Sub-Class A.—Cost of Land.
           B.—Cost of Building.
           C.—Alterations and Additions.
           D.—Title Expenses.

CLASS IX.—MISSION AND STATION EXPENSES.
Sub-Class A.—Mission Meetings.
B.—Books, Printing, etc.
C.—Stationery, Postage, etc.
D.—Medical Allowance.
E.—Sanitariums.
F.—Personal Teachers.

CLASS X.—MISSION PRESS.

All estimates excepting those for Classes I., II., and III. are properly made in native currency, and this requires careful consideration by the home office of the probable course of exchange to ascertain the equivalent in American currency of the amount asked for in the estimates.

The next step is a calculation by the Finance Committee of the probable amount of income available for the ensuing year. This can never be determined to a certainty. It depends upon the degree of spiritual interest in the home church and the financial conditions prevailing. An average of receipts for a decade, provided the conditions mentioned are favorable, is a safe basis for estimate. The amount of probable receipts being determined, an allotment, based on the mission estimates, can be made, which allotment is termed "The Appropriations" (or Grants) for the ensuing year. When communicated to the missions, these are the authorization for the making of contracts and the planning of the work. They should not be changed during the year, save as larger receipts than expected warrant an increase where enlarged operations are demanded and justifiable.

Disbursements: The disbursements under appropriations or grants call for great care on the part of the mission treasurer. The accounts with each station should at the end of each month show whether any class of expenditure has exceeded the appropriation or grant. Some excess disbursements must be expected owing to unforeseen emergencies, but these are offset by a rule requiring a reversion to the general secretary of all savings. A voucher system should be used in connection with all disbursements. This is not only a safeguard to the treasurer, but facilitates a satisfactory audit. Mission field receipts cover receipts from all sources except the home treasurer. They include donations sent direct to workers on the field, fees from hospital patients and from personal services rendered by the medical missionary, and tuition and board in schools and colleges. Many institutions, owing to favorable conditions, are self-supporting, and unless so reported could be enlarged to a proportion unwise and unjust as related to other departments of the work. Disbursements under Class VIII. call for extreme care. The acquisition of new property and construction of new buildings should be limited to the real necessities of the work with a conservative outlook to future development. The difficulty of securing, in most cases, reliable estimates, the fluctuation in the prices of material and labor, make careful supervision on the part of the financial representative most essential. Periodical statements of the progress of building operations and the amount disbursed should be made to the home office. Charges and credits are largely multiplied because of the removal of the work from the base of supplies. The missionary and his family, in many instances, must be clothed, and, to a considerable extent, fed from America and Europe; schools and hospitals must be equipped with modern appliances and the dispensaries supplied with large supplies of drugs and medicines. To the original invoices must be added the cost of transportation, insurance, commission, etc. Shipments of this character contain goods for from ten to fifty different missionaries and institutions, and it is therefore necessary that the field treasurer should accurately apportion the various charges among those interested in the proportion of the cubic displacement.

A banking system is the natural outgrowth of a large and increasing foreign work. Direct and economical facilities for the transmission of funds are due the missionary and his friends. Certificates of credit can be purchased from the field treasurer, drawn on the home office for payments in Europe or America, and, on the other hand, friends in America can procure money orders payable on the field. By this method insurance premiums, payments for purchases and transmission of gifts can be facilitated. The method is simple, but calls for care and precision in accounting. The factor of exchange enters into all charges and credit, and is frequently a matter of some complication owing to the wide fluctuations of a depreciated paper currency in many of the countries, and the absence of banking facilities capable of furnishing reliable rates at the time needed. The average rate at which mission bills of exchange were sold during the previous month is a fair basis for adjustment in the succeeding month. Loss in exchange, resulting from the sale of bills of exchange for authorized work under the appropriations or grants, is properly chargeable to the home office unless an item has been included in the estimates for that purpose. Under certain exceptional conditions it may be desirable to make for some missions all appropriations or grants in gold. In 1902 the peso of one of the South American countries, which had been worth 25c. gold, fell to a value of 2½c. In this case, unless special relief had been extended, the saving in exchange to the home treasury would have resulted in disaster to the classes of work for which appropriations or grants had been made in local currency. The serious consequences of a worthless or fluctuating currency have become so apparent that many countries are considering the adoption of a currency on the gold basis, and when this becomes general a serious embarrassment in mission accounting will be overcome.

An item of no small importance is that of travel. The expenditure varies with the size of the mission board or society, the number of missionaries employed and the location of the missions and stations. This expenditure should be carefully safeguarded in order to avoid unnecessary cost whether from extravagance or inexperience. The home office should be a bureau of information and should require a careful accounting in detail of all expenditures, for its audit and approval.

Mission presses, colleges, schools, hospitals and dispensaries should be placed on a business basis, each keeping a full set of accounts. The annual balance sheet sent to the home office should show clearly all items of receipts and the sources from which derived. The disbursements should be classified, and separate schedules given covering the amount put into the plant, with a full inventory of materials or stock on hand at the close of the fiscal year. These statements are a safeguard against disproportionate expansion and the unnecessary accumulation of unsalable stock.

Outfit and freight allowances are properly limited to actual necessity, in each case a maximum limit being fixed as a precaution. Outfit lists should be carefully prepared and revised annually, and expenditures permitted only for such items as are recommended in the lists. Freight allowance is designated in measured tons, and necessitates careful measurement of all freight at the point of shipment, excess above the allowance being a personal charge. As prepayment of charges to destination is rarely possible, all charges should follow the freight to the field, such amount as covers the tonnage allowance being charged back to the home office.

Real Estate Property: The value of property held by the leading boards or societies amounts to many millions of dollars, and these values are constantly increasing. The amounts needed for the purchase of land, erection of buildings, improvements and extensions, are usually included in the annual appropriations or grants. The value or cost of property should be set up on the books of the home office so as to appear in the annual statement and balance sheet of the board or society. The showing of such a large amount of invested funds gives a credit in business transactions appreciated by the bankers of the world who purchase mission bills of exchange or drafts. Careful attention to this matter naturally leads to an intelligent investigation of land titles. The tenure of much mission property is still uncertain and insecure. There has been a great improvement in this regard during the past decade, and it is well to take advantage of the liberal tendency now shown by most governments in this particular.

Reports of Receipts and Expenditures: The success and efficiency of a system of accounting depends in the last analysis on the reports made to the home office. These should be sent quarterly, and at the close of the fiscal year. The value of quarterly reports lies in the opportunity to correct errors and explain disputed or misunderstood items before the preparation of the annual report. These reports should show the following items:

1st. Receipts, being debit items.
 Balance, Cash on hand first of year.
 Balance Bills of Exchange or Drafts on hand first of year.
 Bills of Exchange or Drafts received from Home Treasurer.
 Drafts made upon Home Treasurer.
 Charges by Home Treasurer (monthly statements).
 Certificates of Credit issued.
 Receipts on the field:
  Contributions.
  Rent.
  Interest.
  Sales.
  Medical Fees.
  Press Profits.
  School Receipts.
2d. Disbursements, being credit items.
 Disbursements under Appropriations or Grants, by stations.
 Property Disbursements.
 Outfits.
 Freight.
 Advances for travel.
 Money Orders from Home Office.
 Credits from Home Office.
 Receipts on the field used in current work as authorized.
 Balance of Cash on Hand.
 Balance Bills of Exchange or Drafts on Hand.

The reports must be accompanied by schedules giving in sufficient detail the items which in the quarterly or annual reports are given in totals. The annual report in every instance should bear the certificate of the mission auditing committee. With such reports in hand the home office can determine the balance of appropriations unexpended, the balance of cash or negotiable bills in the hands of the mission treasurers, and the sums needed to complete fully the work of the year. They also furnish a reliable basis for the compilation of an intelligent annual report for presentation to the home constituency of the board or society.

The annual report of a mission board or society is incomplete and unintelligible without the presentation of a balance sheet. This, if accompanied by sufficient explanatory schedules, will furnish a report that will be appreciated by the laymen of the churches and will create a degree of confidence in the management that is essential to the best success.

FINNISH MISSIONARY SOCIETY (1859) (*Name in Finnish, Suomen Lähetysseura*): Finland was the last northern land to become Christianized after a crusade of King Eric the Holy, of Sweden, under the Upsala Bishop Henrik, in 1157. Through Michael Agricola, Paul Junsten and other Finnish clergymen, the Lutheran doctrine was spread, and the whole Finnish people became Lutheran Protestants in the 16th century, but not till two centuries had elapsed was there any missionary interest. In 1742 a carpenter named Nyberg met with some Moravians at Copenhagen, and later went to Herrnhut and was sent out under the Moravian Church to Surinam, where he died. During 1820-1830 a religious movement spread over all Finland, and many clergymen, especially in Osterbotlen, wished to follow the example of the motherland, Sweden, which in 1835 founded its first missionary society. The most zealous of these was Jonas Lagus, who bought a house with the intention of opening a training school for missionaries, training being deemed an essential preliminary to good service. He asked permission of the government to found a missionary society, but all religious work not ordered in the ecclesiastical laws and manual was suspected and his request was refused. Later Lagus and other priests were summoned before the courts for placing collection boxes for missions before their doors. At this time Pastor Reinquist, of Sordavala, was also an earnest believer in missions, and was collecting funds, which he handed over to the Swedish Society. He also wrote books and pamphlets, which had much to do in keeping alive the missionary interest.

In 1857 it was proposed by the Bishops of Finland that a solemn feast should be held in commemoration of the introduction of Christianity 700 years before. Emperor Alexander II. approved, and ordered a jubilee on the eighteenth of June. All Finland was aroused and some young priests seized this propitious moment to propose the formation of a missionary society. A petition, signed by 200 persons of all classes, was presented to the Imperial Senate of Finland in 1858, and, after consultation with the Emperor Alexander II., the Senate gave its approval to the plan, and prescribed that the 16,000 Finnish marks ($3,200) given at the Jubilee feast should be turned over to the new society, and that in memory of this feast a collection for foreign missions should be taken on one Sunday in each year. Directors were chosen in Helsingfors for the new organization, and in memory of the first Christian preacher, Bishop Henrik, January 19, 1859, was chosen as the day of the first general meeting, and the name "Finnish Missionary Society" was formally adopted. During the first years of its existence the Society worked through the Leipzig Missionary Society, the Gossner Society, and the Hermannsburg Society of Pastor Harms; and it maintained a missionary from 1861 to 1867 in connection with the Gossner mission in Chota Nagpur, India.

In 1860 the first Finn presented himself to be trained for foreign work, and the first two scholars, Jurvelin and Malmström, were sent to Hermannsburg. In 1862 a missionary training school was opened at Helsingfors, and nine young men were chosen for a six years' course. The funds of the Society had reached the sum of 147,000 marks, and missions under Finnish management were seriously contemplated. That year Dr. Carl Hugo Hahn, a Rhenish missionary from South Africa, gave an account in Helsingfors of a journey he took to the Ovambo country and among the Hereros in what is now German Southwest Africa. The Finnish people became deeply interested, and after he had made a second journey, in 1863, sent 1,200 marks to Hahn's school for the education of native preachers among the Hereros. Two years later Hahn sent the Society his journal account of a tour to Ovamboland, and with it a strong appeal that they undertake work in that region. Accordingly an extra meeting of the members of the Society was held, and it was decided that in 1868 five of the mission scholars and three colonists should be sent to establish a mission in Ovamboland, arrangements being made with the Rhenish Society to divide the field. The Finnish missionaries remained for a time in the Rhenish Mission Institute in Barmen and at their stations among the Hereros that they might become accustomed to the climate and people, and study the language with Hahn in Otjimbingue.

Missions: Ovambo Mission. The Ovambo people inhabit the lands along the border between German Southwest Africa and the Portuguese Colony of Angola. The southern tribes of Ovambos belong to the German Colony, while the northern are under Portuguese jurisdiction. The first Europeans to visit the country were Mr. Galton from England and Mr. Andersen from Sweden, who traveled in this region in 1851. Several exploring tours were subsequently made among the Ovambos by Dr. Hahn of the Rhenish Society, and, in 1869, the first Finnish missionaries were sent out. At first they remained in Hereroland with Dr. Hahn, studying the Herero language, which is akin to the Ovambo, and learning from the veteran missionary the best methods of work. In 1870 they established a station at Omondonga, receiving a cordial welcome from king and people. Four of their number remained here to carry on the work, while the others pushed on; and by the following year five stations had been established among four Ovambo tribes. In 1872 the resident Portuguese stirred up the natives against the missionaries resident among the northern tribes, and during the succeeding years sickness and death decimated the working force, so that during 1878-1882 the Finnish Mission consisted of but three stations and four missionaries. The first convert of Ovamboland was a young girl whom one of the missionaries took to Finland, where she was baptized in 1876. Subsequently she returned to her native land and married a native evangelist. In 1880 four young men were converted and went to the Rhenish missionaries in Hereroland to be baptized, so as to escape the hostility of their own people. The first baptism in Ovambo territory was in 1883, when nine young men were received into the Church. It was noticeable that more converts were made in times of famine or sickness, when conjurers and sorcerers failed to provide remedies. In such times of trouble the people turned to the missionaries.

After the death of King Kambonda, in 1885, there were political disturbances which threatened to break up the work. His immediate successor was friendly to the missionaries, but unfortunately he lived but a short time, and at his death the tribes under his jurisdiction were divided into two rival factions, which were at war for many years. The king of one of these rival kingdoms, in which part of the mission stations were located, was friendly to the missionaries, and in 1888 the missionaries in the other section were compelled to flee, abandoning their stations. In 1889 an unsuccessful attempt was made to reopen one of the old stations; but sickness and death had so reduced the mission force that in 1890 there were but two workers in the field.

From 1890 to 1900 the tide turned in favor of the Christians. More missionaries were sent out to meet the demand of the natives for Christian teaching. The chiefs, one by one, ceased their opposition; old stations were reopened and new ones established. The people began to manifest great confidence in the missionaries. The German occupation of the southern part of the Ovambo territory has greatly improved the political situation among the tribes. In 1903 work was resumed among the Oukuambi and Ongandjera tribes. A printing press has been established; the New Testament and part of the Old Testament has been printed, as well as other Christian books and leaflets.

There are (1903) 5 stations, 15 outstations, 11 Finnish missionaries and 39 native helpers; 1,235 baptized Christians, of whom 455 are communicants, and 1,100 scholars in the various educational institutions.

2. *China* (1901): A station was established in 1901 in the northern part of the Province of Hunan, at the market town Chen-shu, a region previously untouched by the missionary. The Finnish missionaries who founded the station studied the language and peoples with the older missionaries at Hankow and Changteh. So far the Finnish Mission in China consists of this 1 station with (1903) 2 missionaries.

FIROZABAD: A town in the United Provinces, India, situated 20 miles E. of Agra. Population (1891), 15,300, of whom 9,500 are Hindus and 4,500 Mohammedans. Station circuit of the ME, with (1902) 8 native workers, men and women; 12 Sunday schools and 380 professing Christians.

FIROZPUR: A city in the Punjab, India, situated on the old high bank of the Sutlej River, 3½ miles from its present bed and 47 miles S. S. E. of Lahore. It is capital of a populous district, in which are hundreds of villages. The climate is regarded as exceptionally healthful. The population is (1891) 50,400,of whom 23,000 are Hindus and 22,000 Mohammedans. Station of the PN (1882), with (1903) 4 missionaries, men and women, one of them a physician; 2 dispensaries and 2 hospitals.

FISKE, Fidelia: Born at Shelburne, Mass., May 1, 1816; in 1831 was a pupil and then teacher at Mt. Holyoke Female Seminary with Miss Mary Lyon. She embarked March 1, 1843, for the Nestorian Mission of the ABCFM at Urmia,Persia, in company with Mr. and Mrs. Perkins and Mar Yohannan (returning to Persia). Miss Fiske's work was in the girls' school, and it was upon this school that she left the impress of her consecrated life. Not only the pupils but the women of the neighborhood learned to look to the school and to Miss Fiske for deep, spiritual instruction.

After laboring there 14 years impaired health compelled Miss Fiske to return to the United States in 1858.

She was usefully employed in the United States, giving addresses on missions and taking part in revival work at South Hadley. She died in Shelburne, Mass., July 26, 1864.

FLETCHERVILLE: A town in Griqualand East, Cape Colony, S. Africa. Station of the South African Wesleyan Methodist Missionary Society, with (1900) 23 native workers, 9 outstations, 4 preaching places, 7 day schools and about 300 professing Christians.

FLORIDA ISLAND. See SOLOMON ISLANDS.

FLORIDA ISLAND LANGUAGE: Belongs to the Melanesian family and is one of those purely local languages without affiliation to others which seem to be so numerous in the western Pacific. It is used by the people of Florida Island (see Solomon Is.) and has been reduced to writing by missionaries of the Melanesian Mission. Roman letters have been used for the purpose.

FLORIANOPOLIS: A town and capital of the Province of Santa Catherina, Brazil, South America; situated on the west side of the island of S. Catherina, 240 miles N. E. of Porto Alegre. Population (1890), 15,000, but rapidly increasing by immigration of Germans, Italians and Syrians. Station of the PN (1900), with (1901) 2 missionaries and their wives, 3 outstations, 1 Young People's Society and 35 professing Christians. Formerly called Desterro.

FOOCHOW. See FU-CHAU-FU (Fo-kien).

FOREIGN CHRISTIAN MISSIONARY SOCIETY (Disciples of Christ; 1875): As early as 1849 foreign mission work was carried on by the Disciples of Christ, but the missionary society was not formally organized until 1875. According to the constitution the society is composed of life directors, life members, annual members, and representatives of churches, Sunday schools, Sunday school classes and missionary associations. Its officers are a President, five Vice-Presidents, a Recording Secretary, a Corresponding Secretary and a Treasurer, elected annually. These officers constitute an executive committee, and, with the life directors, a board of managers.

The missions of the Society are as follows:

1. *Scandinavia:* The first intention of the new Society was to work only in distinctively heathen lands, but in 1876, a young Dane who had been converted in this country was, at his own request, sent to Denmark as a missionary. As he had opportunity he visited Norway and Sweden. From this beginning the work has grown till now there are (1903) 13 stations, 5 ordained missionaries and 11 churches, with 659 communicants.

2. *Turkey:* In 1879 a young Armenian convert in America was sent to Turkey at his own request, locating at Constantinople. In 1901 there were 17 stations and outstations, 4 missionaries and 23 native helpers, 18 churches, with 603 communicants. These results after twenty-one years of labor seemed to the Society "very meager and disappointing, and believing that Turkey as a foreign mission field is both limited and preoccupied," the executive committee recommended the Society to withdraw from the field as soon as practicable.

3. *India:* In 1882 work was begun in the Central Provinces of India with a station at Harda. In 1885 Bilaspur was occupied, Mungeli in 1887 and Damoh in 1895.

Evangelistic tours are made through the outlying districts and educational, industrial and medical work is carried on. Much time has been devoted to famine relief. A boys' orphanage has been established at Damoh, where the inmates are trained to be self-supporting; boy carpenters, weavers, shoe makers, farmers, blacksmiths, etc., are doing much work for the mission. A leper asylum is carried on, the finances coming from the Mission to Lepers in India and the East. There are (1901) 4 stations and 6 outstations, 22 American missionaries and 64 native workers, 5 churches, with 411 communicants, 9 day schools, 1 orphanage; total under instruction, 1,542; 4 hospitals and dispensaries; native contributions, $127.68.

3. *Japan:* A mission in Japan was established in 1883. The first station was in the district of Akita. The work is chiefly evangelistic, tho a beginning has been made in educational work.

There are (1901) 7 stations, 23 outstations, 13 American missionaries, 21 native workers, 13 churches, with 832 communicants, and 2 day schools.

4. *China:* Work was begun in China in 1884, and gradually extended until there are 5 principal stations where educational and medical work is carried on. Much evangelistic work is successfully done in the outlying districts. An important feature of the work is the distribution of Christian literature.

There are (1901) 5 stations and 11 outstations, 28 American missionaries and 51 trained Christian native helpers, 8 churches, with 576 communicants; 2 boarding schools, 5 theological classes, 7 day schools, 4 hospitals and dispensaries.

5. *Africa:* A station has been established at Bolengi, on the Congo. There are 7 missionaries (two of whom are physicians), and a very promising beginning has been made in medical, educational and industrial work, while evangelistic tours are made into the surrounding country.

6. *Philippine Islands:* In 1900 work was begun in the Philippines, special grants being made for this purpose, and a station was established at Manila.

In Cuba a station has been established at Havana, where preaching services are held in English and Spanish, and Sunday schools and day schools have been established.

7. *Hawaii:* In the Hawaiian Islands work has been begun at Honolulu, in a district peopled by Hawaiians, Portuguese, Chinese and Japanese.

The purpose is to work through the local church rather than build up a separate work. Two new missions have been begun; Sunday schools and day and evening schools established.

This Society also conducts missionary work in England and has missionaries in readiness to press into Tibet when the way shall be open.

ORGAN: *Missionary Intelligencer*, monthly Cincinnati, O.

FORMAN, Charles William: Died at Kassauli, India, August 27, 1894. Dr. Forman was a native of Kentucky, a graduate of Princeton Theological Seminary, and at the time of his appointment as a missionary a member of the Ebenezer Presbytery. He sailed for India, August 11, 1847, as a missionary of the American Presbyterian Board (N), while its mission work in that vast empire was still in its infancy. In 1846, at the close of the first Sikh war, the mission had crossed the Sutlej and planted a station at Jalandhar, within the Punjab. Soon after Dr. Forman's arrival in India, the annexation of the Punjab by the British Government, and the favor of the Board of Administration, which included the two Lawrences, Henry and John, opened the way for the occupation of Lahore, the capital of the new province, and the late Rev. John Newton and Mr. Forman were appointed to the station. It was in and from this center of influence that Dr. Forman did his missionary work. That work was varied as necessity or opportunity required. It consisted mainly, perhaps, in the organizing and superintending of a system of schools under mission control where the Word of God was habitually taught and from which thousands of young men have gone forth with at least an intellectual conviction as to the truth of Christianity, while it is believed that not a few have felt its regenerating power.

Dr. Forman was universally beloved. The devoutness of his spirit, the simplicity of his life, the strength of his character, the broadness of his views and sympathies, his indefatigable zeal, his grasp of the situation in India, and, above all, his interest in and affection for the native population of all classes won for him universal esteem. During the early part of his illness, when a rumor of his death was circulated, a notoriously antichristian newspaper published in Lahore devoted an editorial to the commendation of his life and work, stating that no foreigner had ever entered the Punjab who had done so much for the Punjab as "Padri Forman Sahib."

FORMOSA: An island lying between latitude 21° 53' 30" north and latitude 25' 33" north, about 90 miles from the mainland of China, from which it is separated by the Straits of Formosa. Its total length from north to south is 235 miles, and its greatest width is about 80 miles. Through the island from N. to S., but nearer the eastern than the western coast, runs a chain of mountains. The coasts are rocky and uninviting, with few good harbors. The climate is in general more salubrious than that of the opposite mainland.

The inhabitants are of three classes—the Japanese and the Chinese immigrants, the civilized aborigines, and the uncivilized ones. Some of the Chinese are from the Amoy district and some are Hakkas from Swatow. Those of the aborigines who have adopted in part the customs of the Chinese are called Pe-pa-hwan, while the untamed savages are called Che-hwan.

These aborigines are partly of the Malay stock, and are broken up into many tribes and clans. Physically they are of middle height, muscular and broad-chested, large eyes, round forehead, broad nose, and large mouth. Their language possesses no written characters, and there are many dialects. In the district of Posia alone, eight entirely different dialects have been recognized. The social condition of the natives is very low. The entire population of the island, according to the census of 1898, is 2,705,905.

The island of Formosa was known to the Chinese at an early date. In 1480 emigration to it was recorded. In 1624 the Dutch built a fort, Zealandia, at the place where now stands Taiwan, and their power was maintained for thirty-seven years. In 1682 the power of the Emperor Kang Hi was recognized, and Formosa formed a part of the Chinese Empire, tho outbreaks on the part of the aborigines were common until 1895, when it was ceded to Japan. The treaty of Tientsin, 1860, opened the island to European commerce, and Formosa tea is now found the world over.

With the cession of Formosa to Japan, the Japanese came to the island in large numbers. The officials show a sincere desire to maintain a righteous administration, and missionaries are now subject to the Japanese regulations.

The Presbyterians of Canada, under the consecrated labors of Mackay, accomplished much for the northern third of the island, and the Presbyterians of England have brought great blessings to the southwestern and central sections. Mr. Mackay, aided by a single foreign colleague and about 80 native assistants, gathered in his churches nearly 2,000 communicants, while his schools had in training 1,314 pupils, and Oxford College 43 students. An interesting feature of the situation is the presence of a number of evangelists sent by the Christian churches in Japan, and supported by them, to labor among Japanese in Formosa.

No missionary work has as yet been attempted among the wild savages of the eastern part of the island.

FORMOSAN LANGUAGE: The language of the aborigines of Formosa. It belongs to the Malayan family of languages. It was reduced to writing by a Dutch missionary in 1655, and has been written in Roman letters by English Presbyterian Missionaries.

FORSYTH, Nathaniel: The first missionary of the LMS to India. Of very few missionaries is so little known. In the last decade of the 17th century a certain landowner in Scotland named Holdane became fired with missionary zeal for the conversion of India, sold his magnificent estate, and proposed to devote his substance to this object, going himself and taking other workers with him. The British Government, however, could not tolerate any such schemes, and forbade the enterprise so persistently that the mission was abandoned. One of the party, Mr. Forsyth, then offered himself to the LMS, was accepted, and went out to India as a missionary but without salary, supporting himself from his own property. He landed at Calcutta in the latter part of 1798, while Carey was still in the despairs of his fruitless Indigo culture. He promptly learned that he would be expelled from India if he stayed in

Calcutta. So he quietly went 25 miles up the river to the Dutch settlement of Chinsurah. Quietly, perseveringly, conscientiously, he did his work, attracting no attention from the world, and even left for 14 years by his society absolutely unsupported. He was indefatigable in his efforts to do good, and he supported himself. So he was not heeded until he died, when in 1813 another missionary was sent to take up his work. Chinsurah, with Hugli, now is a flourishing mission center of the UFS, and the name of the pioneer evangelist of that field should not be forgotten.

FORT AIJAL: A military post among the Lushai Hills in Southern Assam, British India. Station of the Welsh Calvinistic Methodist Missionary Society, with (1900) 2 missionaries.

FORT ALEXANDER: A settlement in the eastern part of Manitoba, Canada; situated at the entrace of Winnipeg River into the lake of the same name, and 65 miles N. E. of Winnipeg. Station of the CMS (1864).

FORTALEZA: A seaport on the northeast coast of Brazil, situated on a cliff overlooking the small bay which serves as its harbor. It is the capital of the province of Ceara. Population (1890), 41,000. Station of the PS (1882), with (1902) 1 missionary and his wife, 2 native workers, 2 outstations, 1 preaching place, 1 day school, 1 organized self-supporting church with 156 members. Also called Ceara.

FORT CHIPPEWYAN: A military post and settlement on the N. side of Athabasca Lake, Athabasca, Canada. Station of the CMS (1867), with (1902) 1 missionary and his wife, and 1 native woman worker.

FORT CHURCHILL: A station of the Hudson Bay Company, situated in the territory of Kewatin, Canada, at the mouth of Churchill River, in a region whose mean annual temperature is 14.2°. Station of the CMS (1886), with (1902) 1 missionary and his wife, 1 native worker, 1 day school, and 798 professing Christians.

FORT DAUPHIN: A town on the S. E. coast of Madagascar, which has a somewhat important trade in india rubber. Station of the United Norwegian Lutheran Church of America, with (1900) 14 missionaries, men and women; 31 native workers, men and women; 16 outstations, 16 day schools, 3 high schools, and 100 professing Christians.

FORT GEORGE: Station of the Hudson Bay Company on the east side of James Bay, in the W. part of the Ungava peninsula, Labrador. Station of the CMS, with (1902) 1 missionary and his wife, 3 native workers, and 2 day schools.

FORT HAKA: A Government port among the Chin Hills in W. Burma, situated about 130 miles N. W. of Pakokku. Station of the ABMU (1899), with (1903) 3 missionaries, 1 a physician; 2 wives of missionaries, 4 native workers, and 2 schools.

FORT McLEOD: A town in Alberta, Canada, situated 92 miles S. by E. of Calgary, at an altitude of 2,400 feet. Station of the CMS (1880), with (1902) 1 missionary, 2 native workers, 2 schools and 80 professing Christians.

FORT MACPHERSON: A settlement in the northwest territory of Canada, situated on Peel River about 125 miles from its mouth in Mackenzie Bay. Station of the CMS, with (1902) 2 missionaries and their wives, 6 native workers, men and women; 1 day school, and 505 baptized Christians.

FORT NORMAN: A settlement in the northwest territory of Canada, situated on the Mackenzie River, at the junction of the Great Bear River and about 60 miles W. of Great Bear Lake. Station of the CMS (1871), with (1902) 1 missionary and his wife, 2 native workers, 1 school and 200 professing Christians; all the people having abandoned heathenism.

FORT PEDDIE. See PEDDIE.

FORT PITT: A settlement in the province of Saskatchewan, Canada, situated on the Saskatchewan River, about 90 miles N. W. of Battleford. Station of the CMS (1888), with (1902) 1 missionary and his wife (who is a physician), 1 school, a dispensary, and 253 professing Christians.

FORT SIMPSON (Canada): A settlement in the territory of Mackenzie, Canada, situated at the junction of the Liard and Mackenzie Rivers. Station of the CMS (1858), with (1902) 1 missionary and his wife.

FORT SIMPSON (British Columbia): A town at the N. end of the Tsimsian Peninsula, British Columbia, with a fine harbor. Station of the SPG, with 1 missionary.

FORT SMITH. See KEHURUKO.

FORT VERMILLION: A trading post in the territory of Athabasca, Canada, situated on the right bank of Peace River. Station of the CMS (1876), with (1902) 1 missionary and 142 professing Christians.

FORT YUKON: A military station in Alaska, situated on the Arctic Circle, at the mouth of the Porcupine, on the Yukon River. Station of the P. E., with 1 missionary and his wife and 500 baptized Christians (Indians and Eskimos).

FOTUNA. See NEW HEBRIDES.

FRANCKE, Aug. Herm.: The missionary movement of Pietism, which arose in Germany during the 18th century, produced remarkable results. Baron von Leibnitz, a philosopher of world-wide fame, came forward at this time as a vigorous advocate of missions; and in his work entitled *Novissima Sinica* and in the charter of the constitution of the Berlin Academy of Sciences, he embodied his views of the subject. The book of Leibnitz came into the hands of Francke, who addressed the author a letter in reference to it. That letter is not extant; but we have the interesting answer which Leibnitz wrote, which shows his genuine interest in the cause of missions. The missionary ideas of Leibnitz bore fruit in Francke and helped toward the first missionary activity of Protestant Germany. "Pietism united itself with missions, and this union alone enabled missions to live." Indeed, Lutheran Pietism was the spring and support of missions; and Francke was the real leader in the matter. Tho a pious layman, Baron von Weltz, in the 17th century tried to convince his fellow-Christians of their duty to send the Gospel to the heathen, it was not until the beginning of the 19th century, under the leadership of Zinzendorf, Francke and Spener, that a real impulse was given to this great cause; but within the space of thirty years, despite many difficulties, seven large missionary societies were founded. The pioneers of evangelical missions in India were sent out by Frederick IV. of Denmark. These were the pupils of Francke at Halle; and several of their successors were also Germans and Pietists.

Kramer (A.), *August Hermann Francke*, 2 vols., Halle, 1882.

FRANZFONTEIN: A settlement in German Southwest Africa, about 200 miles N. by W. from Walfish Bay. Station of the Rhenish Missionary Society among the Herero-speaking tribes, with (1903) 1 missionary and his wife, 9 native workers, men and women; 4 day schools, and 400 professing Christians.

FRAUENVEREIN für Christliche Bildung des weiblichen Geschlechts im Morgenlande. See GERMANY; MISSIONARY SOCIETIES IN.

FRAZER, Edward: A negro slave born in Barbados, W. I., 1798. He was taught to read and write by his mistress, joined a Methodist Church in 1819 and was appointed missionary of the WMS to Dominica in 1828, his master giving him manumission that he might accept the appointment.

FREE BAPTISTS; General Conference of (1833): The Foreign Missionary Society of the Freewill Baptists owed its organization to a correspondence between Elder John Russel, leader of the Freewill Baptists, and Revs. James Pegg and Amos Sutton, two of the earliest missionaries sent to India by the General Baptists of England. Their letters were published in the *Morning Star*, and resulted in the formation of the Society in "the old meeting house" at North Parsonsfield, Maine, in 1832, and in January the new organization was incorporated under the laws of the State. In 1835, after three years, the income of the Society amounted to $2,660; with this sum they sent their first four missionaries to India, Mr. and Mrs. Noyes and Mr. and Mrs. Phillips sailing from Boston in September of that year, arriving in Calcutta after a voyage of one hundred and thirty-six days. They at once proceeded to Cuttack, a station of the General Baptist Society of England, where they remained while acquiring the language. In January, 1837, they established a station at Sambalpur, in the hill district of Orissa, but the location proving unhealthful, it was abandoned the following year, and early in 1838 the General Baptists surrendered to them their work at Balasore, the northern district of Orissa. A station was established and the foundations of permanent missionary work were laid. From this beginning there has been steady growth. Much work is done among the Santals, and schools for them have been established throughout the jungles, taught by natives who have been trained in the mission schools. From 1848 to 1860 a school was sustained at Balasore for victims destined for human sacrifice who had been rescued by the British Government. In 1840 medical work was begun by Dr. Bachelor, who established a dispensary at Balasore. In 1862 this was transferred to Midnapur. That year a printing press was established, which has not only been self-supporting but of late years has contributed to other branches of the work. In 1865 Zenana work was begun. Schools have been established, orphanages opened, and Sunday schools and Christian Endeavor Societies organized. Book rooms are maintained, and special attention is paid to the circulation of Christian literature. From 1833 to 1892 the name Free Baptist Foreign Missionary Society was retained, but the latter year the title was changed to the General Conference of Free Baptists.

There are (1902) 14 principal stations and 31 missionaries, 12 churches with 861 communicants, 76 Sunday schools, with 3,463 scholars, 32 schools through all grades, with a grand total of 3,555 under instruction; total contributions 1,405 Rs.

The Free Baptist Woman's Missionary Society, organized in 1873, cooperates with the General Conference of Free Baptists. It has a separate organization, sends out and supports missionaries and teachers, especially for women and children, and establishes schools. The United Society of Free Baptist Young People, established in 1888, is auxiliary to the General Conference of Free Baptists.

Headquarters: Auburn, R.I.

FREE CHURCH OF SCOTLAND MISSIONS. See SCOTLAND; UNITED FREE CHURCH OF.

FREEMAN, John Edgar: Born in the City of New York, December 27, 1809; was apprenticed at the age of fifteen to a trade; in 1829 publicly professed his faith in Christ, and in the same year decided to study for the ministry; purchased the last year of his time for $80; graduated at Princeton College 1835, at Theological Seminary 1838; was ordained July 12, 1838, by Presbytery of Elizabethtown; sailed for India October 12 same year, as a missionary of Presbyterian Board of Foreign Missions; was stationed at Allahabad, having charge of orphan boys and girls until the death of Mrs. Freeman in 1849. In impaired health, he visited the United States April 28, 1850, with his two children. In 1851 he returned, with his second wife, and was stationed most of the time at Mainpuri for six years. In 1856 he removed to Fatehgarh. At the breaking out of the mutiny he attempted with others to reach Allahabad for safety, but was made a prisoner by the Sepoys and put to death at Cawnpur by order of the rebel chief, Nana Sahib, June 13, 1857.

FREE METHODIST CHURCH. General Missionary Society (1885): In the latter part of 1880 the Rev. E. F. Ward and his wife went out as foreign missionaries, partly at their own expense and in part supported by the Free Methodist Church, and were recognized as its missionaries. Their going was the immediate cause of the formation of the General Missionary Society, which was incorporated in June, 1885. The organization consists of a president, secretary and treasurer; a board of five directors, meeting each month for the transaction of business; a general board of sixteen members, advisory to the board of directors, composed of the four general superintendents, who are *ex officio* members; the general secretary and treasurer; seven members, representing the missionary districts of the church, elected by the General Conference, and three women, representing the Woman's General Foreign Missionary Society, and nominated by it, though elected by the General Conference.

The missions of the Society are as follows:

1. *Africa* (1885): The first missionaries of the Society sent to Africa, Mr. and Mrs. R. R. Shemeld, arrived at Durban in June, 1805, and went inland to Estcourt, where they opened a mission which was continued for some years and then abandoned. The same year Messrs. Agnew and Kelley with their wives began a mission at Inhambane, on the southeast coast. The location is unhealthful and the mission has suffered from sick-

16

ness and death. In 1890 the work was extended to Natal and in 1897 to Johannesburg.

There are (1903) 6 stations and 5 outstations, 15 American missionaries and 30 native helpers, 4 churches with 235 communicants, and 4 day schools.

2. *India* (1885): The first workers to be sent to India were Misses M. L. Rauf and Julia Zimmerman; other missionaries have been sent out from time to time. Schools and orphanages have been established, and churches and Sunday schools organized.

There are (1903) 2 stations and 1 outstation, 9 American missionaries and 13 native workers, 1 church with 80 communicants, 2 schools and 2 orphanages.

3. *Japan* (1895): Work was commenced by a young Japanese who had been educated in America. The special field has been the island of Awaji, tho some work has been done in Osaka, with the expectation of making it the headquarters of the mission.

There are (1903) 3 stations, 4 American missionaries and 6 native workers, and 2 churches with 51 communicants.

4. *Norway* (1892): Work was begun by three missionaries, but after a few years the mission was discontinued.

5. *San Domingo:* Work was begun here in 1893 and continued till 1899, when the field was abandoned.

Headquarters: 14-16 No. May St., Chicago, Ill.

FREETOWN: Capital of the British Colony of Sierra Leone, W. Africa. It is situated on the south side of the estuary of the Sierra Leone River. It is enclosed landward by encircling mountains. It has pure water and the climate is equable, but the town partly overlooks the marshes of Kroo Bay. It has a good harbor and is the greatest seaport in West Africa. The population is 34,500. The Europeans, half-castes, and immigrants occupy distinctive quarters of the town. The Church Missionary Society commenced its work in 1816, which is now conducted mainly in educational institutions, as a Sierra Leone native church has been organized. A college at Fourah Bay, two miles above Freetown, was built in 1840, and is the principal college in connection with the West African Mission. In 1876 it was reorganized and affiliated with Durham University. The native church withdrew finally from the CMS in 1889 so far as receiving aid from the parent society is concerned. It numbers (1902) 3,920 professing Christians. The CMS now (1902) has at Freetown 5 missionaries, men and women; 18 native workers, men and women (besides 16 in the native church); 752 professing Christians, and 4 schools. Freetown is also a station of the CA and the African Methodist Episcopal Church of the US, of which no statistics are issued. Station also of the WMS, with 9 missionaries and 66 native workers, men and women; also of the United Brethren (1854) with 7 missionaries, men and women, and 12 native workers; also of the United Methodist Free Church (1859), with 5 missionaries, men and women. These six societies maintain, besides the CMS College above named, 16 schools and (including the number given above) have connected with them about 11,000 professing Christians.

FRENCH CONGO: A colonial possession of France on the west coast of Africa, bounded on the north by the Kamerun and the Spanish colony of Cape San Juan, and on the east and south by the Congo River and the Congo Free State. The regions of Upper Ubangui, Bagirmi and Wadai, forming the northern section and reaching to Lake Chad and the Sudan, are recognized as a sphere of French influence. This recognition was published as a result of the failure of Marchand and the Fashoda expedition of 1898 to extend the French domination eastward to the Nile. An agreement was made by which the line between the French and English spheres of influence follows an irregular and unsurveyed boundary between the above-named districts and Darfur. The whole area is about 450,000 square miles, with a population estimated by the Statesman's Year Book at 8,000,000 to 15,000,000. The region, between the ocean and the Congo, and extending from 5° south latitude to 3° north latitude, consists of a series of terraces rising from the coast and skirted by chains of hills which vary from 1,000 to nearly 5,000 feet in height. It is well watered. The Kwilu has a total course of 360 miles, the Ogowè 720, and the Gabun is an estuary 40 miles long and 7 broad. There are two rainy seasons, September to December, and then, after an interval of fine weather, the rain sets in until May. During the hottest days in March and April the thermometer varies from 78° to 93° Fahr., and in the cool months of July and August 73° to 86° Fahr. The climate is insalubrious, both on account of its humidity and the poisonous exhalations from the morasses. The soil is sandy, and vegetation consequently not as rich as the abundance of moisture would lead one to expect.

The original inhabitants have been largely displaced by immigrants from the interior. The Mpongwe, of the Gabun, the remnant of a once powerful nation, are intelligent but frivolous. The Benga or Corisco are related to the Bakale, south of the Ogowè. These are now traders, packmen, etc. The Bangwe dwell between the upper and lower course of the Ogowè. The Fangs, who occupy most of the region east of the Gabun and north of the Ogowè, form two groups constantly at war with each other. They are light-complexioned, muscular and vigorous, the most energetic and industrious of all tribes of the region. They practise cannibalism in the inland districts. Among the Ashango forests and toward the Congo, the Abongo are shy and timid, of small stature, and dwell remote from the beaten tracks. The Balumbo, or Bavila, are largely runaway slaves from the Gabun and Congo factories who have found refuge in the inhospitable regions south of the Nyanga River. Of all varieties of the Bantu speech the Mpongwe is the most widely diffused in the coast lands. It was reduced to writing by American missionaries. A mission was established by the ABCFM in Gabun in 1842 and transferred to the PN in 1871. The Paris Evangelical Society has two stations on the Ogowè River and the BMS has a station at Wathen, farther south. Roman Catholic missions are of considerable importance. Wadai and the northern regions are still largely unexplored and are Mohammedan, chiefly following the great Sheikh es Senoussi in doctrine.

FRENCH, Thomas Valpy: Born in 1825, in Holy Trinity vicarage, Burton-on-Trent. Died at Mascat, May 14, 1891. Educated at Rugby School under Dr. Arnold, and at

University College, Oxford. B. A., 1846; 1848, Latin Essay; Fellow; M.A. 1849. In September, 1850, went to Agra, North India, as principal of proposed St. John's College. In 1854 he conducted with Pfander the famous public discussion with the Mullahs at Agra, which was the means of the conversion of Maulvie Imad-ud-din and Maulvie Safdar Ali. In 1862 he was appointed to the Derajat Mission. On December 20, 1877, he was consecrated in Westminster Abbey the first bishop of Lahore (jurisdiction, Punjab and Sindh) fourteenth bishop from the CMS ranks. Dr. French was always a pioneer. Four times he went to India to begin new agencies, and as a missionary his career may be divided thus: (1) as founder and principal of St. John's College, Agra, 1850-58; (2) as founder and leader of the Derajat Mission, 1861-63; (3) as founder and principal of the Lahore Divinity School, 1869-74. In all three enterprises he did most important service. Dr. French was a great missionary to Mohammedans, and through his influence not a few were brought to a knowledge of salvation by Christ. It was by the natives of India that French was called the "Seven-Tongued Man," because he could preach in the English, Urdu, Hindi, Punjabi, Persian, Pushtu and the Arabic. Besides this remarkable linguistic knowledge, he could use in teaching, if not in preaching, the Latin, Greek, Hebrew, Sanskrit and German languages. He was the author of a number of able works and published several volumes of sermons. In 1887 he resigned his see, and in the 40th year of his missionary service he went to Mascat to found a new mission that might, he hoped, reach the hearts of the people of neglected Arabia. But his worn body was not equal to the strain of that trying climate and at Mascat his labors came to an end.

Birks (H.), *Thomas Valpy French*, 2 vols., London, 1895.

FRENCH SWITZERLAND; Missions of. See SWITZERLAND.

FRERETOWN: A village in British East Africa situated 2 miles N. N. E. of Mombasa, on the eastern side of the inlet which separates Mombasa from the mainland. It is also known by the native name of Kisauni. Station of the CMS (1874), with (1902) 11 missionaries, men and women; 15 native workers, men and women; 1 day school, 1 high school, 1 theological class and 598 professing Christians.

FRIEDENSBERG: A station of the Moravians in the western part of the island of St. Croix, West Indies. It was begun in 1721, in order to reach the large number of slaves on the surrounding plantations. The mission house stands on a hill in the outskirts of Fredricksted. There are now at this station (1902) a missionary and his wife, with 12 native workers, men and women, and 432 professing Christians.

FRIEDENSFELD: A town on St. Croix Island, W. I., situated near the center of the island. It has the only country church in St. Croix, all the others being in the towns of Christiansted and Fredricksted, which are fifteen miles apart. Outstation of the Moravian Missions (1804), with (1900) 361 professing Christians.

FRIEDENSTHAL: Mission station of the Moravians (1754) in the island of St. Croix, W. I. It is situated on a hill to the west of the town of Christiansted, which, together with a great expanse of ocean, reaching as far as St. Jan and Tortota, is seen from the windows of the mission house. It is the scene of the labors of Frederick Martin, whose tomb is venerated to this day. At the station there are now (1900) 1 missionary and his wife, 18 native workers, men and women, and 435 professing Christians.

FRIENDLY ISLANDS. See TONGA ISLANDS.

FRIENDS' (AMERICAN) Board of Foreign Missions. See AMERICAN FRIENDS, ETC.

FRIENDS' FOREIGN MISSIONARY ASSOCIATION (England, 1865): The subject of foreign missions was brought before the central yearly meeting of the Society of Friends in England for the first time in 1835, at its meeting in London, and was seriously considered. From this time the matter was never lost to sight; in 1859 the interest was increased by George Richardson of Newcastle, who wrote to his fellow-members urging them to concerted effort for the salvation of the heathen. Stirred to action by this appeal, in 1861 an address was issued by the central governing body of the Society, calling on all its members to aid the cause of missions, and this action was emphasized by appeals from William Ellis, LMS missionary in Madagascar. This led, in 1865; to the formation of a provisional committee to promote the cause of missions among English Friends, the nucleus of the present Friends' Foreign Missionary Association. All annual subscribers are members of the association, which is governed by a board appointed annually by the meeting of members. This board appoints the treasurer and secretaries and has power to delegate any portion of its business to the care of committees from its members. Missionary work is carried on in India, Madagascar, Syria, China and Ceylon.

1. *India* (1866): The first missionary of the newly formed association was Rachel Metcalf, who went to India to assist Mrs. Leupolt of the CMS in an industrial school at Benares. In 1869 Elkanah and Irene Beard of America were sent out, and a separate station was opened, first at Benares, but removed to Jabalpur in 1870, where it remained till 1874. It was then permanently located at Hoshangabad, the center of a large district in the Narbada Valley, with a population of three or four millions, then unreached by Christianity. In 1881 the work was extended to Sohagpur. The next years were spent in laying the foundations of various lines of work. Evangelistic tours were made in the outlying districts; schools were opened, orphanages established for both girls and boys, an orphan industrial system started and Zenana and medical work begun. In 1890 two new stations were opened at Sioni Malwa, and Sihore in Bhopal. In 1892 industrial works were established at Rasulia, Hoshangabad, with funds contributed especially for this purpose; this work has been continued with only occasional aid from the FFMA. In 1893 the Itarsi station was opened and in 1898 Bankheri was occupied by the Society. There are (1903) 6 stations and 10 outstations, 34 missionaries, 42 native workers, 6 churches, with 379 members, 4 boarding and high schools, with 748 students, 24 other schools, with 1,203 pupils, 5 hospitals and dispensaries.

2. *Madagascar* (1867): In the same year (1866) that Rachel Metcalf went to India, two American Friends, Louis and Sarah Street, and James S. Sewall, of Hitchin, England, interested

in the mission work by the addresses of Dr. Ellis, offered themselves for service in Madagascar, where they arrived in 1867, just at that juncture when the adoption of the Christian religion by the queen had given an immense impulse to the existing missions. The Friends did not attempt to start a separate mission, but aided the educational department of the LMS mission in the suddenly increased demand for Christian instruction. As the work grew, however, it was necessary to divide the central province of Imerian into districts, and the care of the Ambohitantely church devolved upon the Friends. The area of the entire allotted mission district was 2,000 square miles, and when first taken in charge by J. S. Sewall, in 1868, contained 6 chapels, a number which was increased in 1872 to 62 congregations with 37 schools. At Antananarivo the Society established a boys' high school in the Ambohijatovo quarter, and one for girls in the Faravohitra quarter. In 1872 a printing office was started, which issues a monthly magazine for adults and one for children, and where the native boys are taught printing, lithography, map-making, etc. In 1880 the Society joined with the LMS in carrying on a hospital and medical mission at Analekely. In 1888 stations were opened at Arivonimamo and Mandridrano, in 1893 at Ambohimiadana and in 1899 at Amboniriana. In accordance with the regulations of the French government the teaching of carpentry and agriculture has been added to the curriculum of the boys' high school at Antananarivo, thus entitling it to substantial government grants. The schools in and about Antananarivo (Ambohijatovo, Faravohitra, etc.) are described in the FFMA reports under the French name of the capital, Tananarive. There are in Madagascar (1903) 5 stations, 23 missionaries, 830 native workers, 185 churches, with 2,482 members, 8 boarding and high schools, with 1,304 students, 180 other schools, with 11,254 pupils, 2 hospitals and dispensaries.

3. *Syria* (Commenced independently 1869, organized, 1874, under the name "Friends Syrian Mission;" transferred to the FFMA 1898): Meetings held by Eli and Sybil Jones in Syria and Palestine led to further missionary work. Three schools were established by them at Ramallah, Jaffa and Ramleh, and continued at their expense until 1874, when the Friends Syrian Mission Committee assumed their support. The following year a training home for boys and an industrial school were established near Brumana, in the Lebanon, and in 1881 a cottage hospital and a dispensary were opened and a girls' school established, mainly with funds raised by the New England Friends' Committee. The Ramallah mission has a school for boys, another for girls, a cottage hospital and a dispensary. In 1898 this mission was transferred to the New England Committee, in return for their share in the Brumana mission. In 1898 the entire work of the Friends Syrian Mission Committee was amalgamated with the FFMA. Schools have been established in the outlying villages; tuition was at first free, but in 1902 the principle of having the children pay a small fee was made general in all schools and was considered a success. Educational, industrial and medical work is carried on and many evangelistic tours are made; Bible women also make house to house visitations.

There are (1903) 1 station, 10 outstations, 13 missionaries, 47 native workers, 1 church, with 35 members, 2 boarding schools, with 109 students, 16 other schools, with 1,204 pupils, and 3 hospitals and dispensaries.

4. *China* (1886): The first station of the Society was opened at Han-chung by Robert J. and Mary J. Davidson. In 1890 Chung-king, Sze-chwan Province, was occupied, and in 1900 another station was opened by the Society Tung-chwan-fu in the same province. Schools for boys and for girls have been established; village schools, a Bible school for women and a school for training native helpers have been organized. Medical work is carried on at Tung-chwan and a vigorous evangelistic campaign is organized in each station. Street chapel preaching meets with success, and many tracts and copies of the Scriptures are sold and distributed.

There are (1903) 2 stations, 12 outstations, 18 missionaries, 24 native workers, 2 churches, with 36 members, 2 boarding schools, with 36 students, 4 other schools, with 169 pupils and 1 dispensary.

5. *Ceylon* (1896): Work is carried on in the district around Matale (Clodagh) in the hill country north of Kandy, and in the district around Mirigama, in the low country within forty miles from Colombo, the missionary in charge residing for the present in Colombo.

Work was begun at Matale in 1896 by Joseph and Frances J. Malcomson. Both the Sinhalese and Tamil languages are used.

In the Matale district itinerating evangelistic work is carried on, schools have been established for both boys and girls, and colportage work is carried on.

The Mirigama district is divided into two parts, each having a resident evangelist and one or two schools. So far the principal work is digging deep and laying foundations.

There are (1903) connected with these 2 stations, 13 outstations, 13 Sunday schools, with 266 in attendance, 15 schools, with 640 pupils.

Turkey (1881): Two Armenians who had become connected with the English Friends were sent to Constantinople by private benevolence in 1881 to open a medical mission. This enterprise has extended into educational, evangelistic and industrial efforts and is reported in the Friends' Magazine of Foreign Missions, altho not included in the list of missions of the FFMA.

Our Missions, monthly, London, contains letters from the various missions carried on by Friends.

FRIENDS SYRIAN MISSION. See FRIENDS FOREIGN MISSIONARY ASSOCIATION.

FRIENDSHIP: A station of the Wesleyan Eastern Annual Conference of the West Indies, near Georgetown, British Guiana, with (1900) 2 missionaries, 1 missionary's wife, 5 preaching places, 5 day schools and 814 professing Christians.

FU-CHAU-FU (Fo-kien): Capital of the province of Fo-kien, China, situated on the Min River, 34 miles from its mouth. It is a treaty port, opened after the British war of 1842. The location is healthful, begirt by hills four miles distant. The walled city is about three miles from the river, with its extensive suburbs extending to the river bank and beyond on the south side. A foreign settlement has been built up on Nantai Island in the river. The two banks of the river are connected by bridges and a large population is housed in boats upon the river. The city has an extensive trade in tea and produces many kinds of porcelain. The population is estimated at 650,000. Station of the ABCFM (1850), with

(1901) 18 missionaries, men and women, of whom three are physicians; 62 native workers, men and women; 11 preaching places, 31 day schools, 2 high schools, 1 college, 1 theological seminary, 1 training class for women workers, 1 kindergarten, 2 dispensaries and 1 hospital. Station also of the CMS (1850) and CEZ (1884), with (1903) 30 missionaries, men and women, of whom three are physicians; 90 native workers, men and women; 9 outstations, 6 preaching places, 40 day schools, 5 high schools, 1 industrial school, 1 woman's training class, 1 theological seminary, 2 dispensaries, 1 hospital and 1 school for lepers. Station also of the ME, with (1903) 29 missionaries, men and women, of whom three are physicians; 55 native workers, men and women; 10 outstations, 11 preaching places, 59 day schools, 2 high schools, 1 college, 1 theological seminary, 1 industrial school and 1 printing house. The aggregate number of professing Christians reported by these societies is (1903) 3,660. The name is also written Foo-chow and Fuh-chau.

FU-CHAU-FU (Kiang-si): A town in the province of Kiang-si, China, situated 128 miles S. by E. of Kiu-kiang. It has an important trade in native paper. Station of the German China Alliance Mission (1898). The name is also written Fu-cheo.

FU-CHEO. See Fu-chau-fu (Ki-ang-si).

FUERTE: A town in the province of Sinaloa, Mexico, situated about 170 miles S. W. of Chihuahua, on the Fuerte River. Population, about 3,000. Station of the ABCFM (1891). The name is also written El Fuerte.

FUH-DING. See Fu-ting.

FUH-NING. See Fu-ning-fu.

FU-KIANG-HSIEN: A town in the province of Kan-su, China, situated about 30 miles N. W. of Tsin-chau. Station of CIM (1899), which has not been reoccupied as a missionary residence since the Boxer outbreak, being now (1903) visited by missionaries at Tsin-chau.

FUKUOKA: The principal town in the northwestern part of the Island of Kiu-Shiu, Japan. It is a railway station and seaport 65 miles N. N. E. of Nagasaki, and is divided into two parts: the business quarter and port, called also Hakata, and the old feudal town, pervaded with the quiet and decorum of the olden time. The population is (1888) 53,800. Station of the CMS (1888), with (1902) 1 missionary, 2 missionary women, 5 native workers, men and women; 2 outstations and 249 professing Christians. Station also of the ME, with (1903) 2 missionaries, 2 women missionaries, 13 native workers, men and women; 8 outstations, 2 preaching places, 1 orphanage, and 404 professing Christians. Station also of the SBC (1893), with (1903) 2 missionaries and their wives and 2 outstations.

FUKUSHIMA: A town and railway station in the island of Hondo, Japan, situated 85 miles E. of Niigata. Station of PE, with supervision from Sendai.

FUKUYAMA: A town and railway station on the S. coast of Hondo, the main island of Japan, situated 112 miles W. by S. of Kobe. Population, about 15,000. Station of the CMS (1891).

FUK-WING: A city on the E. shore of the estuary of the Canton River, Kwang-tung, China. Mission station of the Rhenish Missionary Society.

FULLERTON, Robert Stewart: Born at Bloomington, O., November 23, 1821; graduated at Miami University, Ohio, and Alleghany Theological Seminary; ordained by Presbytery of Chillicothe, 1850; sailed the same year for India as a missionary of the Presbyterian board. He was stationed at Agra with his wife to commence and conduct two institutions, a male and a female school. He was relieved of the boys' school on the arrival of Rev. R. E. Williams. At this time he became pastor of the Presbyterian Church at Agra, which charge he continued to hold, and also that of the female school, till the mutiny in 1857 broke up both schools and mission. The girls' school, which had continued for five years, did much to elevate the tone of Christian feeling in the East Indian community, and the church had grown under his care. After the suppression of the mutiny he went to Fattehgarh to look after the scattered remains of the mission and prosecute the mission work. His labors at Agra, much to his regret, but necessarily, had been mainly in English. At Fattehgarh he gave himself with great diligence to the native language, and soon became a fluent and effective speaker. He recommenced, as soon as practicable, the Furrukhabad High School, and also cared for the native church in the city, besides spending much time preaching in the bazaars. Under all his labors his health at the end of three years gave way. He went to the Dehra station on the hills in 1864, laboring there faithfully till near the end of his life. A malignant disease attacked him, from which he died, after three months of great suffering, October 4, 1865.

FU-MUI: A town in the province of Kwangtung, China, situated about 15 miles S. E. of Hwei-chau-fu. Station of the Berlin Missionary Society (1885), with (1903) 1 missionary, 10 native workers, 10 outstations, 1 school, and 397 professing Christians.

FUNG-HWA-HSIEN. See Feng-hwa-hsien.

FU-NING-FU: A town on the E. coast of the province of Fo-kien, China, situated about 70 miles N. E. of Fu-chau. Station of the CMS (1882), with (1902) 8 missionaries, men and women, of whom 3 are physicians; 33 native workers, men and women; 10 outstations, 14 day schools, 1 high school, 1 training school for women workers, 1 hospital, and 2,041 professing Christians.

FUREEDPORE. See Faridpur.

FU-SAN: A treaty port on the S. E. coast of Korea, situated on the head of the Bay of Chosen; terminus of a railway to Seoul now (1903) in construction. Station of the PN (1891), with (1903) 6 missionaries, men and women, 1 of them a physician. Station also of the Woman's Missionary Union of the Presbyterian Church of Victoria (1891), with (1900) 5 missionaries, men and women. Station also of the SPG (for Japanese residents), with 1 missionary and 1 preaching place.

FUTSUKPHAI: A town in the province of Kwang-tung, China, situated about 75 miles east of Canton. Station of the Basel Missionary Society (1879), with (1902) 1 missionary, 10 native workers, men and women; 7 outstations, 4 day schools, and 470 professing Christians. Written by the Germans, Futschukpai.

FU-SHUN: A town in the province of Sze-chwan, China, situated on the To-kiang River, 30 miles N. W. of Lu-chau. Station of the CIM (1902), with 1 missionary.

FU-TSING-HSIEN: A town on the east coast of the province of Fo-kien, 25 miles south of Fu-chau. Station of the CMS, with (1902) 5 missionaries, men and women, one of whom is a physician; 56 native workers, men and women; 2 outstations, 19 day schools, 1 dispensary, and 5,828 professing Christians. Circuit station also of the ME, with (1903), 28 native workers, men and women; 11 places of worship, 18 schools, 1 high school, and 1,555 professing Christians. Also called Hok-chiang.

FUTUNA. See NEW HEBRIDES.

FUTUNAN LANGUAGE: Belongs to the Melanesian family, and is spoken by a few hundred people in the island of Futuna, New Hebrides. It was reduced to writing by missionaries of the New Hebrides Mission Society and is written with Roman letters.

FU-YIU-TSUN: A town in the province of Shen-si, China, situated about 32 miles N. E. of Hsi-ngan-fu. Station of the BZM (1898), closed (1903) since the Boxer outbreak of 1900.

FWAMBO. See KAWIMBE

G

GAGAEMALAE: A settlement on the island of Savaii, Samoan Islands. Station of the Australian Wesleyan Mission, with (1900) 15 native workers, 3 preaching places, 3 schools and 104 professing Christians.

GALELA: A settlement on the northeast coast of the island of Halmaheira, or Jilolo, in the Moluccas, Dutch East Indies. Station of the Utrecht Missionary Society (1866), with (1900) 1 missionary and his wife.

GALKISSE: A town in the outskirts of Colombo, Ceylon, East Indies. Station of the SPG (1846), with (1902) 12 native workers, men and women; 1 preaching place, 4 common schools and 251 baptized Christians.

GALLALAND: A country formerly of Abyssinia but now included, for the most part, within the bounds of Italian Somaliland, Africa.

The people, called Gallas, seem to form a connecting link between the negro and the Semitic races. They are intelligent, vigorous and warlike. Some of the northern Galla tribes have adopted Abyssinian Christianity. The Gallas found to the south and southwest of Abyssinia are believers in fetishism. Three dialects of the Galla language—the Shoa, the Ittu and the Bararetta—are known. All attempts made by missionaries to reach the Southern Galla tribes have failed through the fanaticism of the Arabs of Somaliland and the disturbed state of religion.

GALLE: A town and port on the southwestern coast of Ceylon, 66 miles S. by E. of Colombo, which has superseded it as a port of call for mail steamers from the Mediterranean to China, Australia, etc. A profusion of trees—palms, coconuts, bread-fruit—grow along the streets and the bluffs along the shore, and give a pleasing appearance to the settlement. Its name means "rock," and it is often spoken of as "Point de Galle." Population (1901), 37,000, composed of many races, including Singhalese, Hindus, Parsees, Arabs, Eurasians and Europeans. Station of the WMS (1814), with (1903) 1 missionary, 1 missionary woman, 101 native workers, men and women; 10 preaching places, 17 day schools, 2 high schools, 1 theological class, 1 industrial school, and 184 professing Christians. Station also of the SPG (1860), with (1903) 1 missionary, 12 native workers, men and women; a high school, an orphanage, and 167 professing Christians.

GA MATLALE. See MATALA.

GAMBIA: A British West African Colony of 69 square miles, at the mouth of the Gambia River. The population (1901) is 13,456, of whom 7,707 are Mohammedan, 5,340 Roman Catholic and Protestant Christians, and 2,209 pagans. Besides the colony proper, the banks of the Gambia constitute a British protectorate, the area of which is 4,500 square miles, and the population 76,948. The WMS has a missionary station at Bathurst, with about 1,000 church members.

GAMPOLA: A village in the central province of Ceylon, situated 11 miles S. by W. of Kandy, in a lovely valley. It was once the capital of the island. Station of the CEZ (1896), with (1903) 3 missionary women and 22 native women workers.

GANDA LANGUAGE. See UGANDAN LANGUAGE.

GANGIRU: A town in the United Provinces, India, situated 36 miles N. W. of Meerut and in the district of Muzaffarnagar. Population (1891) about 5,000. Circuit station of the ME, with 22 native workers, 16 Sunday schools, 9 day schools and 790 professing Christians.

GAN-K'ING. See NGAN-KING-FU.

GAN-REN. See NGAN-JEN-HSIEN.

GANSEE: A settlement in the Bush country of Dutch Guiana, S. America, situated on the upper portion of the River Surinam. Station of the Moravian Missions (1848), with (1902) 1 missionary and his wife.

GAN-SHUN. See NGAN-SHUN-FU.

GAN-TUNG. See NGAN-TUNG-HSIEN.

GARDINER, Captain Allen F.: Founder of the South American Missionary Society. He was born in England in 1794, and manifested even in childhood the spirit that controlled his later life. When found sleeping on the floor rather than in his bed, he gave as the reason that it was his intention when a man to travel all over the world, and therefore he wished to accustom himself to hardship. He began active service in the navy in 1810, when he was 16 years old, but resigned after the death of his wife in 1834, and wholly consecrated himself to his life-work: "to become the pioneer of a Christian mission to the most abandoned heathen."

He married a second time, and his family shared with him his trials and discomforts for a long time. Never discouraged, when he found the door closed on one side he turned another way. At one time he had joined the missionaries to South Africa, but the treachery of a Dutch trader forced them all to flee. Then he tried to secure an entrance to New Guinea. At last he settled upon South America as his mission-ground, went to the Falkland Islands as a point from which to reach Tierra del Fuego, and from that time on his life was one series of persevering effort and heroic endurance.

So anxious for the formation of the South American Missionary Society was Gardiner that in 1844 he guaranteed all expenses for three years and £100 a year thereafter. It was not until 1848 that he saw the mission undertaken, and in 1851 he and his companions in its pioneer effort died of starvation through failure of supplies.

Marsh (J. W.), and Stirling (W. H.), *The Story of Commander Allen Gardiner*, London, 1867; *Story of Mission Work in South America*, London, 1874; Young (R.), *From Cape Horn to Panama*, London, 1900.

GARENGANZE MISSION. See CHRISTIAN MISSIONS.

GARO LANGUAGE: Belongs to the Tibeto-Burman group of languages and is used by the Garo tribes, numbering some 25,000 souls, in the hill country S. of the Brahmaputra River in Assam. It is written with the Bengali characters.

GARRAWAY: A town and harbor on the W. coast of Liberia, W. Africa, situated N. W. of Cape Palmas. Station of the ME, with 1 missionary and 1 missionary woman. Also parish of the PE, with 1 missionary, 2 native workers, 1 day school and 50 communicants. Name written also Graway, with subdivisions Whole Graway and Half Graway.

GAUB: A station of the Rhenish Missionary Society in the northern part of German Southwest Africa, lying about 300 miles N. E. of Walfisch Bay.

GAUHATI: The largest town in Assam; situated on the Brahmaputra River, 45 miles N. by W. of Shillong. Climate unhealthful. Population (1891), 10,800, of whom 7,800 are Hindus and the remainder nearly all Muslims. Station of the ABMU (1843), with (1903) 8 missionaries, men and women; 21 native workers, men and women; 17 preaching places, 17 schools, 1 high school, and 778 church members.

GAYA: A town in Bengal, India, situated 58 miles S. by W. of Patna, among ridges running out of the Ganges valley, and in a region filled with traditions of early Buddhist history. Six miles S. of the town is Buddh Gaya, the dwelling place of the founder of Buddhism. There is shown a lineal descendant of the Pipul tree, under which he sat in meditation. The population of Gaya is (1901) 71,288, nearly three-fourths being Hindu and about one-fourth Muslim. Outstation of the BMS (1882) and station of the Baptist Zenana Mission (1890).

GAYAZA. See GYAZA.

GAZA: A town in Palestine, situated 26 miles N. W. of Beersheba, on the road leading to Egypt, between the Mediterranean and the desert, about three miles from the sea. It is built partly on the sides of the steep hill which was crowned by the ancient town and partly on the plain below. It is the seat of a Greek, and also of an Armenian, bishop. It is a station for the caravan traffic between Egypt and Syria, and has a population of 15,000, mainly Arabs. Station of the CMS (1878), with 5 missionaries, men and women, and a hospital.

GEDDIE, John: Born at Banff, Scotland, 1815; brought up and educated in Nova Scotia, whither his parents immigrated in his infancy. They were earnest Christians, strongly imbued with a missionary spirit, and at his birth dedicated him to be a missionary. He received his academical and theological education at Dalhousie College. There being then no organization in Nova Scotia to send him to a mission field, he was ordained in 1838, and settled as pastor of the churches of Cavendish and New London, in Prince Edward Island. Soon after his ordination he wrote a series of letters on foreign missions, addressed to the ministers and members of the Presbyterian Church of Nova Scotia, which were published in the provincial papers, and resulted in the commencement of a foreign mission by the Synod. The field selected was the South Seas, and Mr. Geddie, offering his services, was accepted as their first missionary. He had been settled seven years, and had a wife and three children. To prepare himself more fully for his work, he took lessons in printing, and obtained some instruction in medicine. He left for the South Seas in 1846 *via* Cape Horn, stopping at the Sandwich Islands and waiting two months for a vessel for Samoa. There he remained eight months waiting for the "John Williams" from England. At Honolulu and Samoa he obtained much valuable knowledge from seeing the working of the London and American Societies' missions. On the advice of the missionaries of Samoa he chose for his field Aneitium Island, New Hebrides, and Rev. Mr. Powell, one of the most experienced of their number, was appointed to assist in establishing the mission. Mr. and Mrs. Geddie had a hard and trying experience in dealing with a low and savage people. Hurricanes, diseases and deaths were attributed by the natives to the missionaries; the natives stole their property, threatened to burn their houses and take their lives. Mr. Geddie had, however, great aptitude for so treating the heathen as to gain their confidence, and in his efforts to dissuade them from the cruel custom of strangling widows his success was marvelous. Gradually several attended his instructions, and in two years forty-five assembled on the Sabbath to listen to his words and to worship God. Mr. Geddie had great readiness in acquiring the native language, and a remarkably retentive memory. He made early and extensive use of the press; was an excellent translator of the Scriptures; had great inventive power and was fertile in expedients: he could turn himself with facility to building a church, translating a Gospel, printing a primer, administering medicine, teaching a class, or preaching a sermon, traversing the island on foot, or sailing round it in his boat. In 1850 some of the chiefs and even sacred men joined him, of whom one, Waihit, supposed to have power over the sea, a man of fierce and cruel temper and much feared by the people, had his mind opened to the truth, and showed great eagerness to impart to others the truth he had himself discovered. Another chief of great authority in the district, and who joined the worshipers, was Nohoat. To prove his sincerity, which many doubted, he cut off his long hair, abandoned polygamy, and, tho sixty years old, attended the school every morning and the worship on the Sabbath. Official persons among the heathen, whose craft was in danger, and other parties, not native, whose proceedings were interfered with by the new teachers, combined in repeated attempts to rid themselves of the missionary. In 1851 his house, in which himself and family were sleeping, was set on fire at midnight. The excitement among the friendly natives over this dastardly act, tho held in check by the missionary, convinced the perpetrators that such opposition could be continued only at their peril. Subsequently, when the people of a heathen district planned to attack the people of a Christian village, the Christians from all parts of the island assembled to reason with the hostile people, and to persuade them to live in peace. These events rallied and strengthened the friends of Mr. Geddie, and from that day the Christian cause triumphed. In 1852 the first converts, 13 in number, were baptized, and a Christian church formed on Aneitium. In 1854 the whole population had abandoned heathenism. Mr. Geddie translated the Gospels of Matthew and John and most of the Epistles of Paul into the Aneitium language, and printed them himself.

His health being impaired he visited Nova Scotia in 1864, after 18 years' absence. He took with him the Book of Psalms, which he had translated, and had it published at Halifax. He was received at home with great enthusiasm. The Queen's University at Kingston conferred on him the degree of D.D., and the Synod honored him with the appointment of Moderator, which he declined. He returned to the island in 1866. In 1871 he went to Melbourne to carry part of the Old Testament through the press and was seized with paralysis, but recovered sufficiently to be removed to Geelong in Victoria, where he had left his wife and children. There he died, December 15, 1872.

GELEB: A settlement in Eritrea, Eastern Africa, situated about 70 miles N. W. of Massaua. Station of the Evangelical National Missionary Society of Sweden (1874), with 2 missionaries and their wives and 1 missionary woman.

GENADENDAL. See GNADENDAL.

GEOGRAPHY of the Expansion of Christendom: At the beginning of the geographical expansion of Christianity we can, on an ordinary atlas map, cover up all there was of Christendom in the world with the point of one finger; at the end of a century a whole hand will not suffice; at the end of three centuries the whole Roman Empire must be included; by the close of the 10th century all of Europe, including the Russias, has become Christian; while Persia, Syria, Africa and Spain are lost to Mohammedanism; the 15th century map shows losses in Asia Minor and the Balkan regions, gains on the Iberian peninsula, and displays a new hemisphere which brings the full extent of the missionary problem to the heart of Christendom. From that day the march was steadily forward, until at the close of the 19th century every section of the globe has been reached with more or less effect.

I. The Pentecostal Church: The geographical conditions which surrounded the infant church assembled in that upper room in Jerusalem make very manifest the small extent of the known world. As far as civilization was concerned, it was a Mediterranean world. A stretch of three thousand miles east and west, and of fifteen hundred miles north and south, contained it all. Britain was still unconquered. The warlike Parthian was the greatest organized enemy of Rome. This Scythian monarchy had learned some of the refinements of civilization from the downtrodden Persians, but was still essentially barbaric. India was known to navigators, and caravan routes were open through to China. Travelers occasionally brought in accounts of strange lands and peoples, but all about this confined area of *terra cognita* lay the great cloudland of *terra incognita*.

The immediate task before Christianity was the conquest of the center of civilization—the Roman Empire. The geographical characteristics of this Mediterranean civilization as related to the company of Christian believers in Jerusalem deserve notice. (1) It was an empire of cities. Christianity must needs handle centers of population, especially in the West. From four to five thousand cities must be reached. (2) The Mediterranean furnished easy access from city to city. It was covered with sails employed in a thrifty commerce. (3) Roman roads connected all parts of the empire, so that news was carried rapidly. Along these splendid highways trudged the messenger of the Gospel from city to city. (4) One hundred million people were thus by land and waterways compactly drawn together in a territory containing less than two million square miles. Geographically considered, no portion of the globe furnishes so interesting a field for religious conquest as the territory of the old Roman Empire.

Roman civilization spread itself outside its own regions by two methods—commercial and military—and Christianity must needs follow in the track of armies and merchants. The caravan routes all led into the common basin of the Mediterranean, from Central Africa through Sahara by several ways, down the Nile; from Yemen along the Red Sea; from the Persian Gulf through the Syrian desert; from Mesopotamia, the center of the trade of Central Asia, to which came the treasures from the Persian Susa, Hyrcania and Bactria, which in turn drew upon China through Statio Mercatorum, and from Hindustan and Farther India *via* Clisobra. Turning to the sea the routes are quite as numerous. The whole coast of southern Asia was familiar to the merchants, and regular routes by sea were open, finding their natural termini in the Persian Gulf and the Red Sea. Another thrifty line of commerce came pouring into the outlet of the Mediterranean from distant Britain, and daring navigators pushed along the coast of the North Sea and penetrated the Baltic lands in search of trade. That a little later Christianity should be found firmly planted in far-away places is not surprising. The door was open, and the disciples could easily go in.

Garrisons of Roman soldiers were stationed all along the borders of the empire. These military barracks soon became centers from which Christianity spread outside the civilized world, and these isolated spots along the Rhine, the Danube, the Euxine and the Euphrates became oases of the faith. When the armies pushed beyond the boundaries of the empire, Christianity was sure to go with them. Christian soldiers captured and enslaved by barbarians were the means of converting whole nations.

Another geographical condition of the greatest importance to Christianity was the wide extent of territory over which the Greek and Latin languages were spoken. At the opening of the Christian era Hellenistic Greek was the *lingua franca* of the Roman world. Greek colonies had been established all around the Mediterranean, and these had determined the language of commerce. Greek letters and arts had conquered Rome more effectually than the legions of the republic had overcome the peninsula of Hellas. The New Testament was composed in this universal language, and all through the early centuries Christian churches were Hellenistic. Later on the Latin tongue took the supremacy in the Western world, evidenced by the fact that it still remains the liturgical language of the majority of Christians.

More important, however, to the Christian Church than any of the conditions mentioned was the geographical distribution of the Hebrew race. Everywhere synagogs were the early preaching places of the apostles, and the majority of the Christians of the 1st century were of Jewish extraction. Christianity, as the fulfilment of the Old Testament religion, naturally turned to the believers in that revelation. Providentially, it seems, these seven millions of people, with their monotheism, their nobler conceptions of God and their purer ethics of life, had been scattered broadcast over the Roman world, and even beyond its boundaries. There were about four million Jews in Syria and Palestine at the opening of our era. One million lived in Mesopotamia and down the Tigris and Euphrates rivers. One million more were dwelling along the Nile and in the Delta, Alexandria having a large quarter entirely devoted to this people. A million more were estimated to have been distributed elsewhere about the Mediterranean. Paul and the other apostles found them everywhere. Most cities had a Jewish section. This race was especially numerous along the north coast of Africa, in Spain, up the Rhone and about Rome, the commercial center of the world. The Sibylline Oracle says that "every land and every sea" was filled with them. Strabo, writing of the century before our era, says that the Jewish people had already come into every city and that it was not easy to find a place in the world which had not received this race and was not occupied by them. We find them in Southern Arabia (Yemen), Ethiopia (Abyssinia), Armenia, Parthia, Iberia, Crimea, Hyrcania, and even China. Wherever there were Jews the door was open to the preachers of the Messiah.

With a Roman government to police the world, with highways and harbors facilitating journeys by land and sea, with a universal language at their command, and with Jewish people and prayer-houses distributed all over the empire, the apostles went forth to conquer. As the centuries went on we shall find the Christian churches most numerous and thriving where these conditions were most favorable.

II. *The Apostolic Church:* At the close of the 1st century a very inadequate presentation of the extent of the advance of the Christian Church is possible. The persecuted Church was more or less in hiding for three centuries, and the notices of geographical matters in Christian or heathen literature are only incidental. Legends and doubtful traditions have thrown a haze over the whole subject. By the time of the death of the apostle John there were Christian churches all over Syria, Asia Minor, Macedonia, Greece proper, the islands and Italy. There seems to be every probability that Paul may have carried out his desire to visit Spain between the two imprisonments at Rome. Peter was probably at Babylon and Mark in Egypt. Beyond this there is little certainty. The list of the converts on the day of Pentecost (Acts ii: 9-12) would lead us to infer that Christianity got a footing in Parthia, Media, Elam, Cappadocia, Pontus, Asia, Phrygia, Pamphylia, Egypt, Cyrene, Rome, Crete, Arabia "and in every nation under heaven" (Acts ii: 3). Ethiopia (of doubtful location) may have learned of Christ through the eunuch baptized by Philip. The apostle James familiarly addresses "the twelve tribes which are of the dispersion." Peter addresses the "sojourners of the dispersion in Pontus, Galatia, Cappadocia, Asia and Bithynia." He sends greetings from Babylon (Rome? in Egypt? or on the Euphrates?—probably the latter). The innumerable traditions about the apostles and early disciples must be dismissed as unreliable and misleading—such as that of Paul in Britain, Lazarus in Gaul, Thomas in India, Bartholomew in Parthia, Andrew in Russia, Thaddeus in Edessa, Philip in Scythia, Matthew in Ethiopia and Judas the Zealot in Arabia. Yet these men were certainly busy somewhere, preaching the Gospel and building up churches.

This is certain—Christianity found a lodgment during the 1st century from Spain to Babylon (3,000 miles) and from Rome to Alexandria. It had taken the whole Mediterranean as its field of work. In 30 A. D., at Jerusalem there were at most 500 Christians; 100 A. D. there were probably 500,000. A map of the Christian world at this date, containing only certainties, would not give a true impression of the geographical extent of Christianity. From the unexampled spread a little later, it may well be inferred that there was a large growth in these early times before the great persecutions. The map should show the routes Paul took on his missionary journeys and on his way to Rome. The cities of Ælia Capitolina (Jerusalem after 70 A. D.), Samaria, Joppa, Cæsarea, Ptolemais (Acre), Tyre, Sidon, Damascus, Salamis, Antioch, Tarsus, Derbe, Lystra, Iconium, Antiochia, Hierapolis, Colossæ, Philadelphia, Sardis, Thyatira, Pergamum, Ephesus, Smyrna, Philippi, Thessalonica, Beræa, Corinth, Cenchræa, and Rome should be plainly marked. The following cities and countries should be put down as probable: Babylon, Edessa, Arabia, Petræa, Alexandria, Cyrene, Ancyra (in Galatia), Perga, Troas, Athens, Rhodes, Crete, Mileta, Puteoli, Carthage and Southern Spain. It is possible that Dalmatia, Britain and the Rhone valley should be included. Clement of Rome (30 A. D.—102 A. D.), in his first epistle to the church at Corinth (§ 42), says there was "preaching everywhere in country and town."

The Apostolic Church was to all intents and purposes a Greek-speaking church. It was largely drawn from the Jewish element, altho Gentiles took more and more a prominent part. Christian prejudice against the Jew as a Jew had not yet arisen. The hopeful, buoyant tone of the apostolic letters indicates a growing success in the work. The churches do not seem to have been thoroughly organized as one church and consequently there were no internal geographical divisions.

III. The Ante-Nicene Church: The Church of the 2d and 3d centuries is under a denser cloud than that of the 1st. The absence of apostolic writings leaves us to rely upon the casual references of historians or other indications. The era of representative Church councils was just beginning. Justin Martyr (105-167), the still more reliable *Epistle to Diognetus* of the same century, Irenæus, bishop at Lyons, on the upper Rhone (130-202), and Tertullian, who wrote in the 2d and 3d centuries, unite in representing the Christians as a "great multitude," "a majority of every state," "dispersed even to the ends of the earth," and including "every sex, age and condition, and persons of every rank also." Among nations enumerated are the Gætulians (Moors), "all the limits of Spain," "the diverse nations of the Gauls," "the haunts of the Britons, inaccessible to the Romans, but conquered by Christ," the Sarmatians, Dacians, Germans and Scythians.

Church councils and martyrologies furnish some information concerning the spread of Christianity in this obscure period. Eight savage Roman persecutions of the Church took place before Christianity won for itself imperial recognition, and the universality of several shows how widely the faith had spread. The fact that the wisest Roman emperors ordered the severest persecutions, because they feared the spread of its secret religio-political cultus, as they considered it, is another indication of the numerical strength of the Christians. It is estimated that by the opening of the 4th century there were 10,000,000 Christians in the Roman empire, as contrasted with the 500,000 at the close of the 1st century. A conservative guess as to the number of churches at the close of this period places them at 1,000 Oriental and 800 Occidental, but the data are very unsatisfactory. Important Church councils were held at Carthage (254), Elvira (Spain, 305), Arles (Gaul, 314), Ancyra (Asia Minor, 314) and Nicæa (Asia Minor, 325). Contemporary documents give the names of the bishops or presbyters who were present, but not a third of the churches could have been represented. Martyrologies help out somewhat. The 525 cities where there were churches at the time Christianity was coming out from under persecution were distributed as follows: In Europe, 188 in all (Britain 3, German lands 3, Gaul 38, Spain 45, Italy 52, Southeastern Europe 37); in Asia 214 (Asia Minor 136, Northern Syria 36, Palestine 24, Arabia 18); in Africa 123 (Egypt and Lybia 28, North Africa 95). A map indicating this condition of things would be sprinkled all over with cities containing Christian churches. Multiply them by three or four and it becomes apparent why the secular mind of Constantine the Great led him to throw in his lot with the Christians. Besides York, Lincoln and London, represented at the Council of Arles (314), there were doubtless churches scattered all over the land as far north as the Roman wall. All along the Rhine and Danube frontier we see a string of Christian fortresses. Roman soldiers were the missionaries in this dangerous region. The Euxine was fringed all around with churches. Italy, Asia Minor, Syria, Egypt, North Africa, Southern Spain and the Rhone valley were thickly dotted with churches. Christianity is still strictly municipal, as might have been predicted.

IV. The Imperial Church (311-600): With Constantine's decree of amnesty to Christians (311) the Church entered upon a new era. Christianity became a state religion. The centers of civilization were won. Within the empire paganism was slowly going to pieces. Under Julian the Apostate it made one spasmodic effort to regain its ascendancy, and then gradually disappeared, or was absorbed by the Church or by some of the heretical sects. At the close of this period there were probably thirty or forty million Christians in the territory occupied by the empire when at its widest extension. Besides the heretical sects already mentioned, some of which did most of their work in this period (Arianism, Donatism and Manichæism) are to be noted the Nestorians at work in the far East early in the 5th century, the Monophysites in Syria and Egypt a little later, and a century after, the Monothelites.

Outside the empire, this propaganda, which had been going on for several centuries, now came to notice and was carried on more systematically. Armenia, the battle-field between Roman and Persian, was the first nation, as such, to embrace Christianity, early in the 4th century. The whole country seems to have received the new religion. Schools and churches were built and the Bible was translated. Since that time the **Armenian Church** has had continuous life.

During days of persecution Christianity made its way around the border of the Euxine, pushed into the interior of the Caucasus range and won over the Albanian and Iberian tribes. A most interesting mission of this period was to the Goths, various tribes of whom had been moving along the north shore of the Euxine and up the Danube. During their inroads they penetrated in the 3d century as far as Ephesus and Athens. A large number of Christian captives from Cappadocia were dragged northward across the Danube to the Dacian rendezvous of these rude northmen, and thus the first Gospel seeds were planted. Progress must have been made, for the Gothic bishop Theophilus was present at the council of Nicæa (325). The apostle of the Goths, however, came a little later in the person of Ulfilas, a son of Cappadocian captives. Beginning early in the 4th century (313), his work was spread over the century. He and his converts went through fiery persecutions (350 and 370), but the work of conversion seems to have gone on with increasing momentum. Both the East and West Goths were reached effectually, and through all their wanderings disseminated a more or less helpful Christian faith.

From the first Christianity had been pushing rapidly eastward. Mesopotamia must have had a large Christian population. Bishops came to Nicæa from as far east as Arbela and Nisibis. Persia had been reached at an early period. During the reign of Sapor II. (390-379) terrible persecutions indicate a large Christian population. When the Nestorians were driven from the Roman dominions, they commenced their missionary march eastward, making a first lodgment in Persia in the 5th century, at a time when Christianity was tolerated, and in the 6th and 7th centuries, sending missionaries southwestward into Arabia, to the southeast into India and Ceylon, and eastward to China; but it is impossible to know the extent of the spread of Christianity in these vast regions. The St. Thomas Christians in India and the Christians of the Syrian cult at Urmia in northwestern Persia are all that have remained faithful up to modern times.

Turning to Africa there was a most interesting expansion of Christianity in Abyssinia during this period. Under the Syrian missionary, Frumentius, this great upland of Africa seems to have received the Gospel. Axum, the capital, was first reached. The Bible was translated into Ethiopic, and long before the Mohammedan invasions the whole nation had become Christian. The king or Negus was in communication with the court of Constantinople, and at various times championed the cause of Christianity in Arabia. Nubia and the upper Nile were reached, but not as effectively as the mountainous regions of Abyssinia proper.

It is not certain when missionary work on the peninsula of Arabia began. Doubtless the deserts south and east of Syria furnished a refuge to Christians during times of Roman persecutions, and the much-frequented caravan routes gave easy access to all parts of the peninsula. Hermits betook themselves to the rocky fastnesses of Pella and the Sinaitic peninsula, and at an early date came in contact with Bedouin tribes. During the 4th century there were missionaries among the Himyarites in the extreme southwest of Arabia, and a traveling bishop followed the wandering tribes of the Syrian desert. A number of tribes were completely won over to Christianity—the Ghassanites, the inhabitants of Najran, part of the tribes of Tay and Kudaa, the Rabia, Taghlab, Bahra and Tunukh tribes, as well as the Arabs of Hira (Nestorian influence). There was also a terrible persecution of the Christians of Najran by the Jewish usurper, Dhu Nowas. By 600 Arabia was thickly sprinkled over with indications of Christianity.

Turning to the extreme northwest limit of the known world, we find the Christian faith in this period laying hold of an island that long before it learned of Christianity was called "The Sacred Island." We are told of the anger of Druids against Cormac, a prominent monarch in Hibernia or Scotia Major or Ireland about the middle of the 3d centruy, who turned from them "to the adoration of God." For many years Christianity seems to have quietly spread from individual to individual. It was not, however, until the 5th century that Christianity had any substantial following in Ireland. The career of Patrick, a native of Brittany in Gaul, as a missionary to Ireland began early in that century and lasted probably until very near its close. Through his exertions the faith seems to have spread in every direction and to have taken possession of the island, altho paganism still lurked about. The inroad of the pagan Picts from the north of Great Britain and the heathen Angles, Saxons and Danes from the east, during this century, drove the British Christians into the western mountains, and thousands of them must have flocked across the channel to Ireland. Thus reenforced, Patrick made the most substantial advance, so that at his death (492?) the whole island was Christian, altho the statement that he founded 365 churches in the island must be received as legendary.

Columba, or Columbkille (521-597), after a rather impetuous career on his native island, in 563, with twelve companions retired to Iona, off the Scottish coast, and established a monastery which became a beacon-light of the faith in northwestern Europe.

Britain proper was lost to Christianity, and the heathen Saxons and kindred tribes exterminated the faith except in Cornwall, Wales and Cambria. The Isle of Man seems to have been Christianized during this period. Clovis the Frank became a Christian after the Roman type and led his followers to accept the Gospel.

The German border was in constant turmoil owing to the ceaseless invasions from the north and east. The Gothic hordes that swept over the country had received a crude sort of Christianity, and so had the Vandals; but Attila the Hun was a heathen. Many of the Christian institutions founded in the 4th century were swept away. However, Valentinus preached the Gospel in the Tyrol (441), Paulinus was martyred at Ratisbon (470), Severus, bishop of Treves, was making efforts to spread the truth in Germany (435), and Severinus in Noricum and Pannonia (453). The Burgundians, the Franks and the Lombards were reached effectively, as well as the Alans and the Suevi. The Slavonians and Avars in Illyria and Mœsia received Christianity about 550.

Few, if any, Teutonic or Slavonic tribes were converted during this era before they entered the confines of Christendom. At the close of this period, however, all about the borders of Christendom there was a lacework of Christian missions. The only striking loss was southern Britain, which was soon to be won back.

V. *The Feudal Church* (600-1095): Great changes took place in the geography of Christendom during the feudal period, gains and losses balancing each other. The greatest organized enemy of Christianity, Islam, began its decimating work early in the 7th century. Arabia, Syria, Persia, Egypt, the north coast of Africa to the Atlantic, Spain and the Mediterranean islands were successively conquered. Christianity was wiped out in Arabia, Nubia and North Africa. Feeble churches remained in Persia, Egypt and Syria. In Spain Christianity still was vigorous. The mountainous regions of the peninsula were never wholly conquered, and even in the conquered portions Christianity flourished under the lenient reign of the Caliphate of Cordova. In the Asturias and Navarre the Christians were independent of Muslim rule. In Egypt and Nubia the monophysite Christians for the most part turned traitors, caring less for orthodoxy from Constantinople than fancied protection from Medina. Nestorianism was cut in two by the conquest of Persia and already began to decline, tho its work went on in the Far East. Timothy, Patriarch of Syria (778-820), sent missionaries to China and India. In 845 Christians were proscribed in China, altho they had been tolerated all through the 8th century. The Taurus range and the highlands of Armenia remained the frontier fortresses of the Eastern Church for many centuries, but as this period was closing, were being successfully penetrated by a new scourge from the East—the Turk.

All through Europe missionary work made substantial geographical gains. Pagan England was reclaimed and thoroughly Christianized. The heathen made a fierce struggle, but between the Irish Church on the north and west and Augustine and his zealous followers on the south, the victory of Christianity was inevitable, and

England with Ireland, Scotland and Wales, was thoroughly Christian at the close of the feudal period.

In the meanwhile the fervid missionary zeal of the Irish Church was at work on a larger arena. In the 7th century Ireland was called "the Isle of Saints," largely because of its numerous monastic establishments. Having won over the Picts and Scots to the faith, thousands of Irish monks looked longingly toward the heathen wilds of the Continent. Columbanus (born about 543), a disciple of Comghall, Abbot of Bangor, went from place to place, and finally settled among the Vosges Mountains, on the German frontier. St. Gallus, his disciple, gave name to an illustrious monastery and to a Swiss canton. Other Irish missionaries set the rather sluggish churches of the Continent examples of simplicity, piety and missionary zeal that electrified the whole of western Christendom. From Gaul went forth Amandus (died 681 or 684) and Eligius (died 659), from England, Willebrord (Clement) and Boniface (Winfrid), "the apostle of Germany." The Frisians were slowly won over from an unusually savage paganism. The last and overwhelming argument came from the sword of Pepin D'Heristal. Willebrord made a futile attempt to reach the Danes. A century later Ansgar (800-865) became the apostle of Denmark. About this time the sword of Charlemagne compelled the stubborn Saxons to cast away their idols and accept the Cross. Sweden was reached by Ansgar, but the real influence that brought Denmark, Sweden and Norway to Christianity came somewhat later from England. Siegfried, Trygvason and St. Olaf were the leaders. In 912 Rollo the Norman obtained Neustria and was baptized as Robert, Duke of Normandy.

While the Belgians, Normans, English, Frisians, Danes, Swedes, Norwegians, Saxons and other Teutonic tribes in Germany were being won over largely if not exclusively by the Irish, English and Gaelic missionaries, the Roman Church was fighting for life itself with marauders from the north and Saracens from the east and south. North Africa and Spain were entirely lost. Sicily, Sardinia and Corsica soon fell before the crescent. Later, as the flood-tide of Islam began to subside, the missionary efforts from Rome became more noticeable. The heathen Magyars crossed the Carpathian Mountains in the 9th century and settled on the Theiss and Danube. In 972 their leader, Geyza, married a Christian princess, Sarolta, daughter of the Transylvanian prince Giula, who had been converted during a stay at Constantinople. German missionaries pushed down into the country more and more. In 994 Adelbert of Prague baptized with the name of Stephen Goyza's son Voik, who was afterward famous as St. Stephen, the patron-saint of Hungary. Under his lead Hungary became thoroughly Christianized and has ever been a firm adherent to the Roman Church.

Turning to the Greek Church we find a more promising field for missionary zeal. The Bulgarians are first heard of as a race of Finnish or Tatar blood, living on the Volga. In the 7th century a portion of them moved southwest, crossed the Danube and spread over the country between that river and the Balkan Mountains. The Slavonic tribes occupying this region submitted to the newcomers, but in turn gave their language to their barbaric conquerers. The Bulgarians received Christianity during the 9th century. Cyril, the theologian, and Methodius, the painter, both natives of Salonica, were the apostles of this race. King Borogis was impressed by a painting representing the Judgment Day, and the conversion of the whole nation followed. After a sharp contest between the ecclesiastical powers at Rome and Constantinople, the Bulgarians received an archbishop from the Greek Church, and have ever since been loyal to that body. The Servians and Croats were reached by these same missionaries.

Christianity reached the Czechs of Bohemia and Moravia, also a Slavonic race, a little later in this same century (9th). Methodius spent the last years of his life in this work. The Czechs had already been reached by German missionaries, but not until the baptism of Barziway, the Duke of Bohemia, and his wife, and the arrival of Methodius, was much progress made. Even then there were several reactions. Under Boleslas II. Christian influence predominated and a bishopric was established at Prague (973). A century later all traces of paganism had vanished, and in 1092 the sacred forests were cut and the last heathen priests were banished.

The most important conquest of Christianity during this period was the conversion of the Russians at Kief. The traditions linking the Apostle Andrew to this country must be set aside entirely. During 955 Princess Olga visited Constantinople, and was so impressed with the Christian ceremonial that she was baptized and adopted the Christian faith. Returning to her northern home, her attempts to spread the faith were for a long while ineffective. When her grandson Vladimir came to the throne, missionaries from Muslims, Jews, Roman and Greek Christians urged upon him their respective religions. After some superficial investigation the decision was in favor of Greek Christianity, which brought with it the hand of the sister of the Byzantine emperor in marriage. In 988 Vladimir, his court, and all his subjects were baptized at one time in the river Dnieper at Kief. The story of the spread of Christianity throughout the vast European tracts owned by Russia to-day is obscure. The consequences of the conversion of Vladimir, however, are immeasurable.

Greek missionaries from Moravia reached another Slav race, the Poles, early in the 10th century. In 966, their ruler, who had married a Bohemian princess, was baptized, and a large number of his court and people followed him.

The gain of territory that must have astonished Christendom most during this period was far across the Northern Atlantic, in Iceland and Greenland. Iceland was visited in the latter part of the 8th century by Irish monks, and was settled a century later by Norwegian pagan emigrants. Through their mother country they became acquainted with the Gospel, and by the year 1000 Christianity was officially recognized as the religion of the settlement. Greenland was discovered in the 9th century and two small Christian settlements were established.

Christendom also made notable gains during this period through the checking of the Saracens at Constantinople by Leo III., the Isaurian, and at Tours by Charles Martel (752). Crete and Cyprus were soon won back by the Byzantine Empire. The Muslims were out of place in France, and soon were driven out of Narbonne, Arles and Nimes. In Spain Charles the Great pushed them back to the Ebro. In 1017 Sardinia was reclaimed from the Saracen, and, in 1050, Corsica.

Such was the geographical status of the feudal church. Altho it was a dark age, and Mohammedanism almost pressed out the life of the church, it must be considered on the whole an age of astonishing progress. The dark age was above all a missionary age. It prepared the soil for the more substantial harvests that were to be reaped in a later and happier era. Its gains were mainly superficial and so were its losses. Vital Christianity was not swept away by Islam.

VI. The Crusading Church (1095-1500): The geographical gain of Christendom during this period was almost altogether military in character. The appeal everywhere was to the sword. It was a desperate fight for life with Islam and paganism in Spain, Sicily, Palestine, Asia Minor, the Balkan peninsula, Russia and along the Baltic.

The Crusades did little or nothing for the expansion of Christendom. They may, however, have put a check upon the Seljuk Turk, which gave Europe a respite before the more serious onset of the Ottoman Turk.

The first crusade was proclaimed by Pope Urban II. at Clermont, 1095, and in 1290 Acre, the last Christian stronghold in Syria, fell, bringing the Crusades to an end. The Crusades broke the aggressiveness of the Seljuks, but the capture of Constantinople by the Crusaders weakened the Byzantine Empire so that it was powerless against the Ottoman Turks, who appeared on the scene of action during the middle of the 13th century. By 1299 they were firmly established on the borders of the already lessening Byzantine Empire, with Brusa as their capital. With the exception of Trebizond, Cilicia, the strip of land along the Bosphorus, and a few fragments, the Christian emperors of Constantinople had lost all their Asiatic possessions by 1340. The well-disciplined Ottoman army entered Europe 1354, and held Adrianople within seven years. Then followed a rapid advance to the Danube and down along the Hellenic peninsula. Servia and Wallachia from being dependent states soon became a part of the Sultan's dominions. A momentary check, caused by the victory of Tamerlane over Bajazet at Angora, 1402, gave Constantinople a brief respite; but in 1453 the last vestiges of the Eastern Roman Empire fell with the capital city. The movement of the Ottoman now was northward. The heroism of the Christian nations of Southeastern Europe, unaided to any valuable extent by Western Europe, was of no avail against the Muslim battalions, armed with the most approved weapons. The whole southern shore of the Euxine was gained. The remainder of the Greek mainland followed, with Albania and Bosnia. Eubœa fell and the other islands followed, the brave Knights of St. John holding on to Rhodes to the last. Early in the next period the Janizaries crossed the Danube, took Hungary, Transylvania, Podolia, and controlled the whole coast of the Black Sea. During the last part of the 17th century the tide turned and European Christendom has ever since slowly but surely been recovering its territory from the Muslims.

In the meanwhile another Mongol horde, pagan as to religion, had been penetrating Christendom further to the north. Genghis Khan, after spreading his rule through vast regions in Asia, moved westward north of the Caspian, invaded Russia, captured Moscow, Kief, burned Cracow and defeated the German armies under Henry the Pious at Wahlstatt (1241). Then the Mongols retired from Europe, leaving the "Golden Horde" on the lower Volga, which for two centuries kept Russia in turmoil. At length, late in the 15th century, Moscow and Novgorod and other dependent Russian states threw themselves against the several khanates into which the "Horde" had been broken up, and, under such leaders as Ivan the Great and Ivan III., succeeded in making the Tatars dependent. The long-drawn battle between Russian and Tatar (Turk) still goes on, and must to the end. The Nestorians seem to have been favored by the Tatars of this time, who accepted their missionaries. The mysterious Prester John was a Tatar prince converted in the 12th century. Late in this period another Mongol appears—Tamerlane—a descendant of Genghis Khan, but a Muslim who made himself master of the countries from China to the Mediterranean and from the Volga to Egypt. He defeated the "Golden Horde," and thus indirectly helped the Russian Christians, but in his bloody advances in Asia he made havoc with the Nestorian churches in the far East and Central Asia. Christianity was almost completely blotted out of those regions. A few colonies of Nestorians remained, which were visited by Roman Catholic missionaries in the 13th and 14th centuries. Tamerlane died in 1405.

Turning to the southwestern corner of Europe there were in this period substantial geographical gains for Christendom. As in Russia so in Spain, no outside forces were called in during the long, successful crusade. At the middle of the 14th century the Moors were hemmed up in the mountainous retreats of Granada. At length, through the joint efforts of the King of Aragon and the Queen of Castile, Ferdinand and Isabella, the last rampart was taken, and in 1492 Boabdil, the last Saracen ruler, sailed away to Africa.

Turning to the land of the Baltic, a most interesting gain to the territory of Christendom during this period, came through the valor of the Teutonic knights. In the 11th century some progress had been made among the Wends, a Slavonic people living on the Baltic between the Elbe and the Vistula. Gottschalk, their ruler, suffered martyrdom in 1066. Vicelin worked among them in the following century successfully, and the Wends slowly accepted Christianity. In 1155 Saint Eric, the Swedish king, undertook the conquest and conversion of Finland, across the Gulf of Bothnia. This crusade against heathenism went on for centuries with varied success, but the Christianity of Finland was superficial until after the Reformation. The Knights of the Sword, or Sword-bearers, conquered Lapland early in the 13th century, and Prussia was gained by the Teutonic Knights, or Knights of St. Mary, a little later. Lithuania and Pomerania were next won. Heathenism gave way to the Cross at nearly every point, and at last Russian Christianity was met more than half way by the militant faith from the west.

Enough has been said to justify the calling of this the crusading era of Christendom. Very little missionary work of the ordinary kind was done during these stirring centuries. In 1265 mendicant friars were sent among the Moguls by Innocent IV. In 1315 a disastrous attempt was made to convert Muslims in Africa. Franciscans in Northwestern Persia are said to have had several thousand adherents at the close of the 14th century. In 1344 the Canary Islands, off the Atlantic coast, became a fief of the Pope. The Madeiras (1418-20), the Azores (1432-57) and the northwest coast of Africa (1486-97) received missionaries. The Cape of Good Hope was reached, the way to the East Indies opened up, and a new world was discovered just at the close of this period and the whole geographical problem that faced the Christian Church began to be understood.

VII. The Colonizing Church (1500-1700): Great as had been the expansion of Christendom in each of the previous periods, that of the 16th and 17th centuries was unexampled. The Russian Church, after the defeat of the "Golden Horde," quickly spread all over the territory now occupied by European Russia. In 1580 Gen. Yermak crossed the Ural Mountains, and within eighty years the Pacific was reached and over 4,000,000 square miles were added to the territories of Christendom—the whole upper half of the largest continent in the world. Church and state went hand in hand. The zeal of the Church carried it over the straits to Japan, and across the arm of the sea to Alaska.

But the great expansion of Christendom took place across the Atlantic, largely under the banners of Spain, Portugal and France, and through the instrumentality of Dominicans, Franciscans, and Jesuits. The fervid imagination of the Church was set on fire by the great discoveries of this period. The chivalric spirit threw itself into the work of the discoverer and the missionary. By 1585 Mexico was conquered and brought nominally to Christianity, somewhat in the same way as the greater part of Europe had been. A little later Central America, Peru, Chile and the rest of South America, with the exception of the extreme southern peninsula, were dealt with in a similar fashion. Paraguay was a republic under the Jesuits as early as 1586. California, New Mexico and Florida were reached.

The earliest attempt of Protestants to do foreign missionary work was also colonial in quality. Under the patronage of Coligny a missionary colony was undertaken in Brazil in 1555, but the venture which, after all, was more political than religious in its character, soon collapsed through the treachery of the leader. In 1559 Gustavus Vasa began mission work in Lapland, and substantial progress was made. Another attempt at planting a missionary colony in America, made by Coligny under Ribaut in Florida, was unsuccessful, the colonists having been savagely butchered by the Spaniards in the so-called "last crusade." In the meantime the English colonies in North America brought substantial gains to the territories of Christendom. France pushed up the St. Lawrence and the Jesuit missionaries found their way to the great lakes. In the meantime actual missionary work was pushed vigorously in the East. The Franciscans were the vanguard. The bishopric of Goa was established in 1520. In 1528 the Capuchin order was founded. In 1540 the *Societas Jesu* was established at Rome. Francis Xavier went to India and Japan. Father Ricci was in China. In 1622 the Propaganda was organized at Rome. Great but ineffectual efforts were made to do missionary work in Africa, especially on the Congo and in Morocco. In 1688 the missionaries were expelled from Japan, and a terrible massacre of native Christians occurred. The Dutch followed upon the heels of the Portuguese in the East Indies. In 1602 the Dutch East India Company was chartered. Ceylon was taken (1636), as well as Java, Formosa, Amboyna, Sumatra, Celebes and other islands. The natives were forcibly Christianized.

The map of the globe by the year 1700 was fairly complete. The great discoveries had all been made. The Christian world was at last fully aware of the nature of the world-problem. Siberia, South America, Central America and Mexico, the West India Islands and the Atlantic seaboard in North America were the special additions to the territory of Christendom; in all fully 12,000,000 square miles.

VIII. The Church Evangelistic (1700-   ): It is not until we enter this period of the geographical expansion of Christendom that we find the Church pushing forward at all systematically to the conquest of the globe for Jesus Christ, and regaining the apostolic principle that such expansion only is gain as carries with it the hearts of the people of any territory newly occupied. The Propaganda was founded at Rome in 1622, but during the 18th and 19th centuries all the religious bodies of Western Christendom have one by one awakened to the duty of overcoming paganism and Mohammedanism. With experiments of the German pietists in the Danish mission in Tranquebar in 1705, and the organization of the little Moravian Church at Herrnhut in 1732, a new spirit appeared among Protestant Christians. A desire to obey the command of Jesus began to spread which was not alloyed by political aims or entanglements. Men in the different denominations began to feel for means of securing the extension of the kingdom in lands entirely closed to the influence of the Gospel. Among these prophets of a new era for the Protestant world, Carey stood almost alone in 1792, but his words carried conviction, and the great missionary societies sprang up one after another and sent out their messengers until the pagan world is covered with a network of the agencies of evangelization; the Gospel is being preached and printed in every great language and in numbers of lesser dialects; the children and youth of heathendom are having their minds molded in Christian schools and a new type of manhood, purer, kindlier and more spiritually-minded, is attracting the people to enquire whence it has come. A summary of progress and results during this period will be found in the article **Modern Missions**, and need not be repeated here.

As we look on the map and discover small parcels of pagan territory like Hawaii, Samoa, Fiji, New Zealand and other islands of the Pacific which have been entirely Christianized within a century, and as we see men who were heathen like the people of these islands, like those of Southern India, of Japan, of South Africa, of Uganda, who are seriously taking up the work of evangelization, it is clear that this period of the expansion of Christendom is to continue until the maps of the world show no point which has not heard and adopted in some sort the gracious laws of the King of Kings.

GEORGENHOLTZ: A settlement in the Transvaal Colony, S. Africa, situated in the Zoutpansberg region on the River Pafari. Station of the Berlin Missionary Society (1877), with 1 missionary and 5 native workers.

GEORGETOWN: Capital of British Guiana, South America, situated on the right bank of the Demerara River, near its mouth and where it is nearly one mile wide. It has a surprisingly large number of deaths from consumption every year, due, it is said, to overcrowding. The population is (1891) 53,200. The city was formerly called Stabroch. It was occupied as a mission station by the WMS in 1815 and since 1885 has been under control of the Eastern Annual Conference of the Wesleyans of the West Indies, with (1901) 6 missionaries, men and women; 6 outstations, 8 preaching places, 6 day schools and about 2,000 professing Christians. In 1903, by request of the Conference of the West Indies, the WMS decided to resume the charge of work in this field. Station also of the SPG (1855), of the Seventh Day Adventists (1887), of the PB, of the NBC (1892) and of the AME, the last named societies having together (1900) 18 missionaries, men and women; 28 native workers, men and women; and 880 communicants.

GEORGIAN LANGUAGE: Belongs to the Ural-Altaic family of languages and the Caucasus branch. It seems to stand aloof from other languages, showing affinity for them solely by the words which it has borrowed. It is written with characters peculiar to itself and with the further peculiarity of having two alphabets, one of which is known to the priests only and is used for sacred purposes, while the alphabet known to the people is considered too profane for use in the best literature.

GERLACHSTHAL. See SPRINGFONTEIN.

GERMAN EAST AFRICA: A German protectorate and sphere of influence, lying between Portuguese E. Africa and British Central Africa on the south and British E. Africa and Lake Victoria Nyanza on the north. It has a coast line on the Indian Ocean of about 620 miles, and extends west to Lake Tanganyika and the Congo Free State. The area is 383,079 square miles, the population (estimated) 6,750,000, mostly composed of Bantu negroes. The German E. African Company in 1888 acquired a fifty years' lease of the coast territory, and in 1890 the German Government bought the rights of the Sultan of Zanzibar, by whom the lease had been made, thus acquiring a protectorate over a territory larger by one-half than the entire German empire in Europe. A convention with England has fixed the boundaries between the protectorate and the British E. African territories. The seaboard (the Swahili coast) is a swampy and alluvial region, intersected by numerous streams. The climate is malarious, the rainfall abundant, and vegetation luxuriant. All the tropical plants and several European species flourish. Mountain ranges, toward which the coast region gently rises, separate this region from the plateaus which form the water-shed between the sources of the seaward rivers and of those of the Congo region. The regions west of Usagara and Nguru, consisting of waterless plains, have a dry climate and are largely sterile. The first of these plains separates the Usagara from the populous district of Ugogo. Beyond that district a second arid plain is crossed, and the water-shed, averaging from 4,000 to 5,000 feet above the level of the sea, is reached. Hence flows the Shimuyu River northward to the Victoria Nyanza, whence, emerging, it becomes the Nile. The Rufigi also rises here and flows eastward to the Indian Ocean, and streams which empty into Lake Tanganyika, and thence find their way to the Congo, have their birth here. A railway is open from Tanga to Mombo (82 miles). There are well-kept roads between the principal towns.

The principal inhabitants of the German Protectorate are:

1. The Swahili (or coast tribes), the people of the coast and island of Zanzibar. They are of Bantu stock, and, while intermingled with immigrants from all the neighboring regions, have a national unity supplied by their profession of the Mohammedan religion. The Arab element has enriched and extended their language, modified their usages, and developed their trading instincts.

The Swahili language is the general medium of intercourse with the tribes of the interior, and is spoken of as one of the 12 most important languages of the world, with reference to the vast area over which it is spoken. Besides the Bible and many religious treatises, it possesses already collections of proverbs, legends, poems, etc., and its literature is receiving constant accessions. The Arabic alphabet is being replaced by the Roman.

2. The Wasagara, inhabiting chiefly the Usagara highlands, which separate the coast regions from the interior plateaus, have, in some of their clans, become more or less civilized through intercourse with explorers, while other clans remain in unrelieved barbarism. Their language is widely extended. The pierced lower lobe of the ear, which sometimes hangs down so as to touch the shoulder, serves to hold tobacco-pouches, instruments, etc., and is a mark of freedom. Slaves are forbidden to pierce or ornament the ears.

3. The Wazaramo are coterminous with the Swahili tribes on the west. Contact with the coast people has had a civilizing influence upon some of the tribes, who wear the Arab dress and have discontinued many of the ferocious practises which still prevail among their kin in the remoter districts. They do not practise circumcision, tho in many respects under Mohammedan influence. Their possession of firearms renders them formidable slave-hunters.

There are 7 Protestant missionary societies operating in this region the German East Africa Mission, the Berlin, the Leipzig, and the Moravian societies and the Universities Mission and the CMS. The whole number of stations occupied is 36.

The Roman Catholic Missions have their headquarters at Bagamoyo.

GERMAN EVANGELICAL SYNOD of North America (1884): Previous to 1884, all the foreign missionary work of the Synod was done through European societies. Those interested in the work, however, felt that they should have work of their own, and a monthly periodical called *The Missionary* was issued to stir up the people with this end in view. Another element in the denomination, intimately connected with the Basel Society, the North German Society (of Barmen), etc., desiring that these societies should be supported, began the publication of the *Evangelical Friend of Missions*, to advocate their cause. Many members of the Synod deprecated this course, and a committee of nine was appointed to consider the advisability of the Synod's undertaking an independent foreign work and to report to a general meeting of the Synod in 1883.

Besides the above named missionary interests an independent, union mission society had been organized during the year 1865, in New Brunswick, N. J., by members of various churches and denominations, including Lutherans, German Presbyterians, Moravians, German and Dutch Reformed, and Evangelicals. The official name of the society was *German Evangelical Mission Society in the United States*. It sent the Rev. Oscar Lohr to India, in 1867, with instructions to choose his special field of labor according to God's leading. Through the pleadings of the Rev. Mr. Cooper of Nagpur, on behalf of the Chamars of Central India, he was induced to begin work among these people, the first station being established at Bisrampur, near Raipur. The work was placed on a firm material basis, inasmuch as Mr. Lohr was able to buy a large tract of land (1,926 acres), upon which he colonized his first converts. This tract is the site of Bisrampur station. By 1883 two outstations had been established at Ganeshpore and Raipur.

This union organization having found that it could not support the growing enterprise in India, proposed to the General Conference of the Synod that it undertake the care and support of this work. The offer was accepted and in 1884 the mission was transferred. At that date there were but two ordained missionaries in this field.

The two mission publications were merged into the *Deutscher Missionsfreund*, published monthly in German. The missionary work of the Synod is controlled by a Board of seven members, elected every four years by the General Conference. The increase in the interest of the churches at home has kept pace with the gradual expansion of the work in India, the direct contributions increasing from $8,000 in 1891 to nearly $21,000 in 1902. The only field of the Synod is India. There are (1903) 4 stations and 44 outstations, 15 American missionaries, 119 native workers, and 2,263 communicants. There are also primary schools and orphanages, and an asylum for lepers at Chandkuri, with financial assistance from the Mission to Lepers in India and the East.

GERMAN INNER MISSIONS: Inner missions embrace the whole work of loving faith in Christ as Rescuer, and seek by the Gospel and its applied truth in deeds of mercy "to renew, within and without, the condition of those multitudes in Christendom upon whom has fallen the power of manifold external and internal evils, which spring directly or indirectly from sin, so far as they are not reached by the usual Christian offices with the means necessary for their renewal."(Wichern). All evil of every kind, in every social form and every class of men, is to be overcome (1) by the fullest, freest spreading of the Gospel, (2) by careful, comprehensive Christian charity.

History: While the unified labor as well as the definition of Inner Missions did not begin before Johann Hinrich Wichern (born 1808, died 1881), its direct precursors in evangelization, apart from the indirect stimulus of the Reformation and Pietism, were the "Christenthums-Gesellschaft," founded by J. A. Urlsperger (Augsburg, 1780), a union of all living Christians to relieve the spiritual destitution of the masses, the Bible societies (the earliest: Nuremberg, 1804; Stuttgart, 1812; Berlin, 1814), the Tract societies (Wupperthal, 1814; Berlin, 1814; Hamburg, 1820), the Gustav Adolf Society, to aid evangelical Christians in Roman Catholic countries with churches and pastors (founded November 6, 1832 by Dr. Grossmann of Leipzig). In social works of mercy J. Fr. Oberlin (1740-1826), the uplifter of the Alsatian Steinthal; Freiherr v. Kottwitz (1757-1843), the provider of work for the poor in Berlin (1806); Johannes Falk (1768-1826), the founder of the orphans' home at Weimar; Christian H. Zeller (1779-1860), founder of the Institute of Mercy and for Teachers among the poor in Beuggen; Amalia Sieveking (1794-1859), "the Tabitha of Hamburg," are to be specially noted.

In 1833 Wichern founded a home for the rescue of depraved children in Horn, near Hamburg (*Das Rauhe Haus*), and developed a brotherhood. Independently, Theo. Fliedner (1836) universally renewed the female diaconate. In 1848, at the "Wittenberg Kirchentag" (diet), Wichern first aroused evangelical Germany to enthusiasm for the whole work of Inner Missions. In his "Denkschrift," *Die Innere Mission der Deutschen Evangelischen Kirche* (1849), Wichern outlined the whole program of Inner Missions. It was necessitated by special, epidemic conditions of sin, which could not be met by family, State and Church. Inner Missions, twin-sister to Foreign Missions, sought especially the baptized that had lapsed. But in charitable work they had a wider scope. With the Church there was to be free cooperation, the churchly offices were to be respected, the confessional limits were not to be disturbed, but each confession was to work separately in the common spirit of Christ's love. Of the State and its ecclesiastical administration only the right of free association was asked. A central board and district societies were to be organized. The spiritually dead were to be revived, the general social condition was to be raised by Christian methods to be determined by the special needs and the locality. Wichern's program gave the whole outline of Inner Missions and largely determined their development. They were at first opposed by confessional Lutheranism, especially by Petri in Hanover, as leading to wrong unionism, checking the activity of the ministerial office, and usurping the work of the church. But confessional Lutheranism agreed with the spirit of love begotten of faith, and in Wilhelm Loehe in Neuendettelsau, Bavaria (1808-1872), arose the promoter of Inner Missions in the strict Lutheran acceptation.

The union of all forces since 1848 caused such developments as the homes for laborers (Perthes in Bonn), Martha Homes for servants, the Christian foundling asylums, and the Christian care of idiots and epileptics (the largest epileptic home is in Bielefeld; Pastor Bodelschwingh). Systematic care of the poor was stimulated by Pastor Shunk in Erlangen, and by work in Elberfeld. Social cooperation in loan societies was promoted by F. W. Raffeisen in Flammersfeld, while G. Werner in Reutlingen sought by "brother-houses" to develop a Christian socialism. Since 1871 Inner Missions received scientific recognition, and are now taught in the universities. In practical work all lines of evangelistic and charitable endeavor have been begun, but of special importance are the Christian social work to oppose unchristian socialism (Court Preacher Stoecker of Berlin), and evangelization (Pastor Schrenk).

Purpose: The purpose of Inner Missions in the evangelistic branch is to bring the Gospel to the masses, and to care for souls whom the regular work of the state church does not reach. Indirectly and without criticizing or hindering the established church, Inner Missions spiritualize those who lack living faith. In diaconic work Inner Missions seek to perform the tasks of mercy which rest upon family, state and church, and which these forms of social organization ought normally to undertake and accomplish with their means, but which they cannot, or cannot yet accomplish because of accidental, historical reasons.

Workers: As its agents, Inner Missions employ ministers as itinerants, or superintendents of institutions or city missions, trained male workers like the brothers of the Rauhe Haus, or deacons, patterned after the service of the ancient church, and frequently deaconesses, who represent the ancient female ministry of mercy (See **Deaconesses**). But in addition many free laborers are required, and, by emphasis upon the spiritual priesthood of believers, all Christians are encouraged to help.

The Work: This includes (1) training of children in day nurseries, Christian kindergartens, Sunday schools, orphanages, or educational societies; (2) the protection and education of the young in industrial schools for girls, homes for servant girls, young women's and men's associations, homes for apprentices and for traveling workmen (Herbergen zur Heimat); (3) the care of the sick in asylums for deaf and dumb, blind, idiots, epileptics, insane, cripples, children's hospitals; by fresh-air work, and through nursing of the sick poor in their homes; (4) the protection of the endangered, as workmen wandering from place to place with their families, seamen, and emigrants; (5) the reclamation of the lost in refuges for neglected children, homes for Magdalens and inebriates, farm colonies for tramps, and religious work among prisoners; (6) efforts to suppress social evils through city missions, parish work, care of the poor, savings banks, loan societies, Christian socialistic endeavors; (7) evangelizing the people by free addresses, preaching, distribution of sermons, tracts, Bibles, and Christian literature, and by free libraries.

The Methods are determined with care and deliberation. Besides the individual workers there is a central advisory board, and there are district associations and conventions to discuss the problems. To obtain what is needed, societies are organized. The society (Gesellschaft) is largely a financial agency to secure regular contributions. Above it is the Association (Genossenschaft), which seeks to reach some social betterment by common aid. It occurs in the form of building associations, workmen's associations, beneficial organizations, but all on a Christian basis. The highest associative form is the fellowship meeting (Gemeinschaft). This demands religious maturity of its members, who unite for prayer and edification in the unity of the Holy Spirit. The danger is spiritual pride, but when humility is retained the fellowship is the salt of the whole work. In addition to these forms of free association the modern Institution is needed for the helpers as well as those helped. While the Institution is not considered the finality, it is employed as the available means for training deacons, deaconesses, for aiding the sick and destitute and for saving the depraved. While societies and institutions appear to hinder family life, and demand sacrifice of the workers, yet the aim is to reestablish the home for others. The family altar is sought to be reerected in homes; the lost, wherever possible, are restored to their homes; masters and workmen, mistresses and servants are brought together in common bonds. As Inner Missions attempt to uphold the family, so they also aid the state. By doing work which is the state's, by opening up the popular understanding of real needs, they induce the state finally to a larger and better care of the poor, the socially neglected, and the criminal. Better legislation is fostered, and the public conscience aroused. The Church is the goal of all this work. Many workers are pastors, and the spiritual work is directed into churchly channels. The state church and its governmental administration will not allow the incorporation of Inner Missions in the church, because they would lose their vitality, become official and fail in interesting and finding support from the common people. But whenever occasion permits, and when the work can be carried on successfully by the organized state church, it is transferred. Still the principle of free association is maintained as the most effective stimulus.

The *efficiency* of Inner Missions is best seen in their development of all works of mercy. Almost every field has been occupied. The evangelistic work has constantly grown. The general religious life is sober, constant rather than intermittent, sensational, emotional. Southern Germany, especially Wurtemberg, has a larger element of feeling in its religion. The fruitfulness of consistent life is not, however, larger. Least effective have been the endeavors to meet socialistic ideas by Christian counterorganizations on the basis of a Christian socialism. The ideals of Christian socialism are either too advanced for the present ethical standard, or unjustly depreciate true individual ownership and right. The response has, therefore, been comparatively small.

Schaefer (Theo.), *Leitfaden der Inneren Mission;* Wurster (P.), *Die Lehre von der Inneren Mission;* Stevenson (W. F.), *Praying and Working;* Paton (J. B.), *The Inner Mission;* Williams, *Religious Life in Germany;* Wenner (G. U.), *The Inner Mission of Germany* (Evang. Alliance, 1893); Henderson (Chas. R.), *The German Inner Mission* (American Journal of Sociology, March, May, July, 1896).

GERMAN SOUTHWEST AFRICA: A German dependency on the west African coast which it borders for a distance of 930 miles from the boundaries of Angola on the north to Cape Colony on the south. The territory reaches to the east as far as the 20th parallel and is bounded east by the British territory of Bechuanaland. It includes Damaraland and Namaqualand. The area is estimated at 326,117 square miles and the population at 250,000, of whom 4,674 are Europeans, in great part Germans.

The cliffs stretch with greater or less regularity parallel to the coast, and at an average distance inland of about 120 miles. From the coast to this ridge the land is terraced. The land west of this ridge passes through deep depressions off into the Kalahari Desert and the Kubango basin. The rainfall is very slight, and much of the coast is a sandy waste, tho on the uplands much pasturage is afforded, and in the northern districts are vast fertile plains. Rich copper ores have been found in many of the plateaus. The population is very sparse, especially in the south, where droughts and famines have well-nigh depopulated the country. Hottentots occupy about three-fourths of the land, and constitute about one-fifth of the population. To the north are the Bantu tribes, Hereros and Ovambos, described as robust, intelligent, and industrious, but still in the pastoral stage. The Rhenish Missionary Society and the Finnish Missionary Society have established themselves in this country. Missionaries have great influence among the people. Their work commenced in 1842, and they have 25 stations in the territory.

GERMANY; Missionary Societies in: The actual names of many of the German Missionary societies being unfamiliar to English readers, search for them in their alphabetical place might prove fruitless. It has seemed best, therefore, to group them in this place, with mere reference to this article in their alphabetical order. The work of the Basel Society, territorially distinct from societies established within the German Empire, and that of the Moravian Brethren, which has an international quality, will be found described in the alphabetical place of each. As to the order in which the societies are named in this article, the alphabetical, rather than the chronological, order has seemed to offer advantages to our readers; altho the year book of the General Missionary Conference of Saxony, to which we are much indebted, follows the other order of arrangement.

BAPTIST MISSIONARY SOCIETY (*German*): This Society has relations with the BMS, but carries on independent work in the Kameruns. Its offices are in Berlin, and in 1902 it had in the Kameruns 5 stations, 14 missionaries, men and women; 40 native workers, 47 schools, and 2,170 professing Christians.

PERIODICAL: *Unsere Heidenmission*, monthly, Berlin.

BERLIN MISSIONARY SOCIETY (*Gesellschaft zur Beförderung der Evangelischen Missionen unter den Heiden. Often mentioned in German reports by the name "Berlin I."*): The originator of the missionary movement in Berlin was "Father" Jänicke (1748-1827), a man of honest, tho often rude, earnestness, who was an almost solitary witness to the Gospel in a time of little faith. He founded in Berlin in the year 1800 a school for training missionaries which rendered noble service to the cause of foreign missions during more than 25 years.

It was interest aroused in missions by the work of Jänicke's school which, in 1823, led ten men, including Neander, Tholuck, von Gerlach, Lecoq, and others, to issue "An Appeal for Charitable Contributions in Aid of Evangelical Missions." They next presented to King Frederick William III. the status for a society, which received his approval, and the organization of the Berlin Missionary Society was completed in 1824. An effort was made, but unsuccessfully, to unite this with Jänicke's school. Nevertheless, a few years after Jänicke's death the school was discontinued, and the royal grant was transferred to the Berlin Missionary Society. For a time the income was divided by the Society chiefly between Moravian and Basel mission work, but in 1830 a training institute on the same general basis as Jänicke's was started, and in 1834 the Society sent out its own missionaries.

Organization and Home Department: The management of the Society is in the hands of a self-perpetuating committee, about 18 in number. The greater part of the funds come from auxiliary unions, of which there are over 300 in the different states of Germany, and which have been combined in provincial leagues. The training institute is the chief feature of the Home Department. Applicants must have a good common school education; be, as a rule, 20 to 25 years of age; have fixed Christian character and some maturity of Christian experience; have a good knowledge of the Bible; show good mental ability, especially in the acquiring of languages. A probationary year in Berlin is required and then comes the course of five years. The studies include the classics, English, Hebrew and German, exegesis, church history, history of missions, theology, etc. Special emphasis is laid on the devotional study of the Bible.

An important factor in all the German societies is their relation to the confessions, liturgy, and ecclesiastical order of the Lutheran Church. The Basel Society is very broad and liberal in its relations. In laying down the principles for the Berlin Society, the following clause was inserted: "The fraternal cooperation of evangelical Christians of all confessions, who have preached the Word according to the Scriptures, without human additions and without strife over unessential differences of opinion, has won for Christendom much fruitful territory among the heathen peoples."

This principle has been in spirit the ruling one in the work from the first, but not without incidents that have been sometimes embarrassing to the work. There was the more variation because the circumstances were novel, and new paths had to be marked out. The union position in the statutes in 1824 could not be carried out to the letter; in 1833 the first missionaries that were sent out were directed to model churches after the Lutheran plan, for the great majority of the supporters were of the confession. In the years following it was repeatedly declared that the symbolic books of the Lutheran Church were the basis of instruction in the seminary next to the Scriptures. The ministerial rescript of 1842, which regulated the examination and ordination of the students by the Consistory, directed that the Augsburg Confession should be the basis. The instructions given to the missionaries in 1859, and again the revised rules of 1882, require of them that their belief and teaching shall be that of the "canonical books of the Old and New Testaments, according to the Augsburg (unchanged) Confession and the Luther Catechism." These directions are not regarded as being in conflict with the principles of the statutes, but were occasioned by the necessity of the case. Instruction, church organization, preaching, must, if they are to go beyond the first principles, be in accordance with some one of the great religious systems. In practise the disputed points can be kept in the background, and the spirit of the liberal principle that was laid down can be the ruling one.

In 1850 and 1851, while, on the one hand, the mission was taking on a more confessional character, there was a movement on the part of a minority of the committee for a broader platform. The majority, however, were against such abandonment of Lutheran organizations; the crisis was reached when one of the inspectors attempted to introduce ultra-Lutheran ideas into the seminary. This was intolerable to some of the students and committee; the withdrawal of the inspector upon his lapse to the Separated Lutheran party restored peace to the Society.

An important element in the general policy of the Society is the aim, constantly kept in view, to make the stations self-supporting, and that not only through the beneficence of the converts, but by profitable enterprises within the limits of the stations.

The usual method of establishing a station is to acquire by purchase or by cession a property which may not simply serve for a lot on which to erect the buildings of the mission proper, but will be large enough to furnish dwellings for the native converts who are to constitute the parish. The community thus gradually grows in numbers by settlement upon mission land; church and dwelling-house are erected; a school is established and, perhaps, a store, a mill, or whatever enterprises are fitting, one aim in it all being to engage the natives in some civilizing employment. If the size of the station warrants it, a catechist comes to the aid of the missionary; native helpers are employed; outstations are opened up, and other preaching places in addition. These in turn are made independent of the original one as their growth or prospects warrant. In localities where there are German immigrants as well as natives, the work among the latter often begins as a branch of the activity of the former in their own church.

Missions: I. *Africa,* (1) *Orange River Colony:* The first missionaries of the Berlin Society went, in 1834, to open work among the Bechuanas of South Africa. They were unsuccessful and three of the five men first sent out founded a station called Bethanie in Orange River Colony. Other stations founded in that mission were, Peniel, (1845), Adamshoop (1867), Kimberly, Bloemfontein (1875), and Beaconsfield (1885). The opening of the diamond mines brought into the field a mass of the worst elements, and a controversy with the British Government as to the legal ownership of the land occupied by the station had a depressing influence on the work. Of late the situation has improved and the mission reports: (1903) 8 stations, 65 outstations, 15 missionaries, 125 native helpers, 3,254 communicants, 1,084 pupils.

(2). *Kaffraria:* In 1837 work was begun at Bethel, but without much apparent success for some years, largely due to the disturbed political condition. Other stations are Petersburg (1857), Emdizeni (1864), Etembeni (1868). There are reported (1903) 5 stations, 9 outstations, 7 missionaries, 26 native helpers, 500 communicants, 366 pupils.

(3). *Cape Colony:* Work in this section was commenced at Zoar (1838) in connection with the South African Missionary Society, and conducted with varying fortunes until 1867, when the entire work was assumed by the Berlin Society. The principal stations are Amalienstein (1856), Riversdale (1868), Herbertsdale (1872), Mosselberg (1879), Laingsberg (1883). There are reported (1903) 7 stations, 31 outstations, 20 missionaries, 89 native helpers, 2,712 communicants, 1,100 pupils.

(4). *Natal:* Emmaus was occupied in 1847; other stations are Christianenberg (1848), Stendal (1860), Emangweni (1863), Hoffenthal and Königsberg (1868). There are reported (1903) 6 stations, 38 outstations, 10 missionaries, 72 native helpers, 1,345 communicants, 390 pupils.

(5). *Transvaal:* In 1848 the Society decided to discontinue work that it had undertaken in the East Indies, and after some years it enlarged its work in Africa, occupying the Transvaal, with a mission which has become the largest and most prosperous one under its care.

The first station was Gerlachshoop (1860), afterward destroyed in the tribal wars. So also Khatilolo (1861) had to be abandoned for some years. Botshabelo (1865) grew rapidly even through the English and Boer troubles, a printing establishment and training school being established there. Other stations in South Transvaal are Pretoria (1866), Wallmansthal and Neuhalle (1869), Potchefstrom (1872, formerly under care of the WMS), Heidelberg (1875), Wogenthin (1876), Arkona (1877), Lobethal (1877), Mossegu (1880) and Johannesburg. In the South Transvaal Mission are reported (1903) 13 stations, 112 outstations, 17 missionaries, 191 native helpers, 6,000 communicants, 1,683 pupils, and in the North Transvaal 16 stations, 167 outstations, 19 missionaries, 198 native helpers, 2,850 communicants, 1,700 pupils.

(6). *German East Africa:* With the partition of Africa and the adoption of European spheres of influence the different German missionary societies undertook to care for the German sections. As early as 1891 the Berlin Society occupied Wangemannshöh, near the upper end of Lake Nyasa, and it extended its operations in that vicinity, establishing stations at Manow (1892), Muakereri and Ikombe (1893), and Bulongoa in 1895. Two years later, with the formal delimitation of boundaries, there was a great advance, and in 1897 6 stations were established—Kidugala, Ilembule, Lupembe, Mbejela, Mufindi and Muhanga, this last being the farthest north. There are reported (1903) 14 stations, 29 outstations, 25 missionaries, 20 native helpers, 115 communicants, 300 pupils.

II. *China:* In 1846 Gützlaff, who had been in China nearly twenty years, most of the time as an independent worker, appealed to the Rhenish and Basel societies for assistance, and four years later by a personal visit aroused much interest. Various unions were formed, but eventually consolidated into two, at Stettin and Berlin. The three organizations worked on with varying success until the prosperity of the Berlin mission in South Africa made it seem feasible for it to undertake a wider work, and in 1882 it took over the work in Canton, arranging boundaries with the Basel Society, and since then it has been prosperous. Most of its work is in the vicinity of Canton, but 2 stations, Syn-yin (1893) and Tschichin (1898), are some distance to the north. There are reported (1903) 11 stations, 88 outstations, 28 missionaries, 140 native helpers, 1,418 communicants and 500 pupils.

In sending out its statistics the Society reports a class of native Christians in almost every instance very nearly double the number of communicants.

The periodical publications of the Society are: *Berliner Missionsverichte,* monthly; *Missionsfreund,* monthly; *Kleiner Sammler,* quarterly; *Kleiner Missionsfreund* (for Sunday schools), monthly; *Hosianna* (for children), monthly. All these are published in Berlin.

BERLIN WOMAN'S MISSIONARY SOCIETY FOR CHINA (*Berliner Frauen-Missionsverein für China*): This Society, organized in 1850, largely under the influence of Gützlaff, has for its special purpose the care of Chinese girls who have lost or been separated from their parents, and their training into Christian workers. Its sole enterprise is the Bethesda orphanage at Hongkong, where 3 missionaries have 118 girls under their care.

PERIODICAL, for members: *Mitteilungen des Berliner Frauenvereins, etc.,* quarterly.

BLIND OF THE FEMALE SEX IN CHINA; GERMAN MISSION TO THE: This Society has its headquarters at Hildesheim. Its work has been limited to the single station of Tsao-kwong, near Hongkong, where it carries on a school for blind Chinese girls and where it has 2 women missionaries and 6 native workers, 16 pupils in the school, and 20 converts. It has now (1903) opened another school for the blind, in Kow-long, the territory on the mainland facing the island of Hongkong, which has been placed under the protectorate of Great Britain.

PERIODICAL: *Tsaukwong*, quarterly, Berlin.

BREKLUM MISSIONARY SOCIETY (*Schleswig-Holsteinische Evangelisch-Lutherische Missionsgesellschaft in Breklum*): Among the churches uniting in the North German Missionary Society were a number in the province of Holstein. After some years one of the pastors, Jensen, who for a few years had edited a paper in which mission work was a special feature, was urgent that the churches of that section should have their own society. He did not at first receive much support, but went forward on his own account and in 1876 bought the ground for a mission institute, later securing the endorsement of about fifty churches. A board of twelve directors, clergymen and laymen in equal numbers, was appointed, the Lutheran Church Confessions adopted, and the institute was dedicated the next spring at Breklum. The first missionaries were sent out from the institute in the winter of 1882; two went in the service of the Netherlands Missionary Society, and two under the auspices of the new organization. The field to be occupied was suggested by a missionary of another society—viz., the kingdom of Bastar, in the Central Provinces of India. The difficulties in this inland region, however, were very great, and after some delay the missionaries removed to the Vizagapatam district and formed a station at Sahir. The work was fairly inaugurated in 1885, and since then it has developed until there are (1903) 7 stations, 51 outstations, 23 missionaries, 70 native helpers, 3,741 baptized Christians, 1,088 pupils.

PERIODICALS: *Schleswig-Holsteinisches Missionsblatt*, monthly; *Sontagsblatt für's Haus*, weekly; *Frauen-Missionsblatt*, monthly; *Der Kleine Missionsherold*, monthly; (in Danish) *Vort Missionsblad*, monthly, Breklum.

CHINA INLAND MISSION, German Branches: (1.) *China Alliance Mission, Barmen:* This Society, organized in 1884, has 7 stations in the provinces of Che-kiang and Kiang-si, China. In 1902 it had in the field 13 missionaries, men and women; 19 native workers, 3 schools and 73 professing Christians.

ORGAN: *Der China-Bote*, monthly, Barmen.

(2.) *German Branch, Liebenzell in Würtemberg:* It was organized at Hamburg in 1899, and has 3 stations in the provinces of Kiang-su, Hunan, and Shan-si, China. It has (1902) 7 missionaries, men and women; 1 native worker, and 2 schools.

ORGAN, *China's Millionen*, monthly.

DEUTSCHE ORIENT MISSION: This organization grew out of sympathy for the needs of destitute Armenian survivors from the Turkish massacres of 1895-96. It is under the general direction of Dr. Lepsius, its founder, and devotes itself chiefly to school and orphanage work wherever Armenian refugees are found in Bulgaria, Persia, and Turkey.

PERIODICAL: *Der Christliche Orient*, monthly, Berlin.

EVANGELICAL MISSIONARY SOCIETY FOR GERMAN EAST AFRICA (*Evangelische Missionsgesellschaft für Deutsche Ostafrika;* Berlin III): This Society, organized in 1886 by Pastor Diestelkamp, carries on an extensive work on and near the coast of German East Africa. There are two centers, Dar-es-Salaam, just south of Zanzibar, and Tanga, near the border of British East Africa, opposite the Island of Pemba. The confessional question appears to have occasioned some temporary difficulty, but to have been settled on a broad, liberal basis.

In the southern section there are (1902) 3 stations, and in the northern 6 stations occupied in the following order: Dar-es-Salaam 1887, Tanga 1890, Hobenfriedeberg 1891, Kisserawe 1892, Bethel (Neubethel) 1893, Manerumango 1895, Vuga 1895, Bumbuli 1899, Bungu 1903. There are reported (1902) 28 missionaries, 26 native workers, 642 native Christians, 889 pupils in schools.

PERIODICALS: *Nachrichten aus der Ostafrikanischen Mission*, monthly; *Kindergade*, monthly, Berlin.

GENERAL EVANGELICAL PROTESTANT MISSIONARY SOCIETY (*Allgemeine Evangelisch-Protestantische Missionsverein*): Under influences from Switzerland this Society was organized at Berlin in 1884, to represent the more liberal theological views in the Lutheran and Reformed churches. Its aim is to labor particularly among the upper classes, in the more civilized countries, and it lays special stress upon literary work and scientific instruction. It has (1902) 2 stations in Japan (Tokio and Kioto) and 2 in China (Shanghai and Kiao-chau). Altogether in both countries it has 8 missionaries, 140 baptized Christians, with 180 pupils in its schools.

The Society publishes two monthly magazines: *Zeitschrift für Missionsstunde und Religionswissenschaft;* and *Missionsblatt des allg. ev.-prot. Missionsverein.*

GOSSNER MISSIONARY SOCIETY (*Gossnersche Missionsgesellschaft, Berlin* II): Johannes Evangelista Gossner (1773-1858) was baptized and educated in the Roman Catholic Church, and held a small benefice at Munich. He came early under the influence of Martin Boos, and gradually his evangelical tendencies became so apparent that in 1817 he lost his benefice. But he did not publicly embrace Protestantism until 1826. From 1829 to 1846, when he retired as pastor emeritus, he had charge of the Bethlehem Church in Berlin.

The missionary zeal which gave his life its peculiar character of grandeur may have been awakened by Martin Boos, who, tho he never left the Church of Rome, was himself a kind of evangelical missionary, and for that reason was violently chased from place to place by the Jesuits. But otherwise it was a spontaneous outgrowth of his own nature, and he received his specific impulse toward the preaching of the Gospel to the heathen from his intimate connection with Spittler, one of the founders of the Basel Mission Society and a representative of the Pietist circles in Germany, and from the Moravian Brethren, who for a whole century had been the sole representatives of the missionary idea in German civilization. He became, in 1831, one of the directors of the Berlin Missionary Society, but in 1836 withdrew because he could not bring his ideas of what a Christian missionary should be into harmony with the Society's ideas of how a Christian mission should be worked. He had his eyes fixed upon the Apostle—a man driven onward by the fire of his faith and throwing all his cares on God, while the Society had adopted the English model of a mission—a thoroughly organized institution, supported but also governed by the Christian community that established it. Gossner felt perfectly certain that he was not wrong, but it was a long time before he came to understand that the Society was not wrong either. He seems to have given up in despair, and felt very much perplexed when, some months later, eight young men, artisans, who could and would support themselves wherever they went in the world, came to him and asked to be instructed and prepared so as to be sent out by some mission society, or to go out on their own account to preach the Gospel to the heathen. However, "this comes from the Lord," he said to himself, and undertook the task. After about six months' preparation these young men went, under the leadership of the Scotchman, Dr. Lang, to South Australia, and in the meantime new pupils had been received.

Then came difficulties with the ecclesiastical authorities and the government, but in 1842 the Society received royal sanction. This, however, made no essential change in methods, the missionaries being transferred to other societies or left to their own conduct. Such a system could not continue, and Gossner was forced at last to accept an organization on a broader foundation.

In 1844 a number of Gossner's pupils had their attention directed to the Kols of Chota Nagpur, in India. The race was degraded and it was five years before a single convert was baptized. Then came such overwhelming success that the question was not about a more or less slow progress by single converts, but about the conversion of a whole people. "We will have them all," exclaimed Gossner in his enthusiasm; "every one of them." But it was evident that in its then organization—a loose association of individual efforts—the mission was not able to manage the affair. When the missionaries fell out with each other, Gossner had no other means of setting them right than telling them: "If you don't agree, I shall stop praying for you." Then two great calamities befell the undertaking—the Sepoy rebellion and the death of Gossner. At first the rebellion actually threatened to extinguish the mission. The missionaries fled to Calcutta; their houses, schools, and churches were demolished, and the native members of the congregation were exposed to harsh persecution. When this news reached Berlin, Gossner made an offer to transfer the whole institution to the English Church Missionary Society, in order to secure its continuation. For some reason the Society gave no immediate answer, and in the meantime the national feeling in Germany became thoroughly roused and sorely hurt by the idea that this undertaking, German in its origin and so promising of success, should be left to others to be carried through. Suddenly Gossner took a decision without waiting for the answer from the English Society, and, shortly before he died, he transferred the mission and all his personal property to a Curatorium. From his accounts it appeared that in twenty-one years he had received from others 300,000 marks, which he had spent on his mission, besides paying out of his own pocket 33,000 marks. He left personal property worth 150,000 marks, which he wished to have invested as a permanent fund. The total number of missionaries he had sent out was 141.

After the rebellion restitution for property destroyed by the rebels was made, but proved a bone of contention, resulting in the secession of a considerable number of the older missionaries, teachers, and helpers, with about 7,000 members, who petitioned the SPG to take charge of their interests, which it did. The original Society has, nevertheless, held in its way in Chota Nagpur, and reports (1902) 23 stations, 283 outstations, 46 missionaries, 360 native helpers, 51,557 baptized Christians and 4,978 pupils.

PERIODICALS: *Die Biene aus der Missionsfelde*, monthly; *Die Kinderbiene*, monthly, Berlin.

HERMANNSBURG MISSIONARY SOCIETY (*Evangelisch-Lutherische Missionsanstalt zu Hermannsburg*): Louis Harms (1808-1865) was the son of a pastor at Hermannsburg, Hannover, and was ordained in 1844 assistant to his father, whom he ultimately succeeded. Always deeply interested in foreign missions, he became a director in the North German Missionary Society, and was offered a position as teacher in its institute, but declined. On the removal of that Society to Bremen, he was urged to form a society more distinctly Lutheran in its character which should provide a means for utilizing the missionary zeal of his church, and this he did as soon as he became full pastor of the church. From the first it was supported by the peasants, without special canvassing for funds, and the men chosen to go out as missionaries were from peasant homes.

Good public-school training was the only educational qualification required for admission to the institute that was at once established. The course was at first four years, later lengthened to six. In this school not only books were taught, but also farming, carpentering, and the like; for one prominent feature of the proposed mission was that colonization should be united with evangelization. Christianity and the arts of Christian civilization should be introduced together. Moreover, the mission station should be largely self-supporting, in order that the home contributions might be devoted chiefly to defraying the expenses of sending out men. Music was emphasized from the first, as is also the case on the field. Practical homiletical training was gained by the pupils by holding mission meetings in the neighborhood.

In 1853, the first men—eight missionaries and as many colonists—were ready to enter on the work, and they were late in that year sent out on the "Candace," one of the mission ships that play so important and romantic a part in the history of missions. A printing establishment was founded in 1856-7, and in the latter year the mission was chartered. It was to remain a private affair, yet to be under direction of the Hannover Consistory, in so far as that ordination was to be by this body; a report was to be made to it annually, and the right of inspection to be yielded to it. An advisory committee of ten to twelve persons was established, to which the property of the mission was transferred. In 1860 a second Mission House was erected, the two alternating in receiving pupils for the whole course. The Institute, drawing at first only from the immediate neighborhood, is now so widely and favorably known that it is patronized from all parts of Northern Germany. Louis Harms was succeeded in the Director's office by his brother, Theodore Harms, during whose term of office there was a schism in the Hannover Church. This resulted in the formation of the "Free Church in Hannover," under the lead of Harms. Popular interest in the mission, however, was so great that after Harms' death an arrangement was made for cooperation, each church being represented on the Board.

Of special interest is the policy of the Society, carrying out that of its founder. This was to Christianize the land into which his laborers should go; not simply to convert certain heathen, and attend to their spiritual welfare, but to infuse into heathendom the leaven of Christianity, that should influence the whole land, and that thoroughly. This was his reason for sending out colonists; this led him to be satisfied with slow advance if only his object was reached in the territory already occupied; this led him also to counsel the establishment of a central station from which the new ones should be supported and supplied—a veritable swarming process. There was in his scheme not a little touch of old apostolical fervor: for example, among the settlers upon a station there should be perfect community of property; each was to work for the common good, and all acquisition was to be applied to mission purposes. The ordained missionaries, tho not working for material prosperity, were none the less employed in mission work; and, on the other hand, the colonists were to be regarded as of equal rank with the clergy, tho their chief work was to supply the physical needs of the community. There has been from the first a most intense Lutheran spirit in the Society. Harms would have all the ordinances of that church introduced on the mission ground; liturgy and church government, as well as creed, should be identical with the home church. The stations should have a complete organization, ecclesiastical and also political, tho it has been found necessary to modify the forms of the churches, to adapt them to the peculiar needs of mission communities.

In all these respects the influence of the founder has maintained itself, and yet many changes have been introduced in the course of the years in the details of practical management. The stations were never quite self-supporting. Community of property has been abandoned; it was found impractical, for it was but natural that the farmers attached to the mission disliked to be entirely destitute of property, while those not attached to the station were making provision for their families. So long as the colony remained composed of unmarried men (and none others were sent) life in common could be maintained; but so soon as their brides were sent to them from home it was found impossible to maintain the custom. Separate homes must be established. Moreover, there was friction continually arising between the ordained missionaries and the colonists as to the division of the work; the latter demanding more assistance from the former than they were inclined to give, the former asserting their superiority in unpleasant ways: so the colonist feature of the work was discontinued in 1869. Quite early in the history of the Society superintendents were appointed over the various sections of the field.

Missions; 1. *Africa:* The first colony was directed to the Galla territory in East Africa, but met with such difficulties that the settlement was made, not there but in Natal. From this the Zulu mission was developed, with stations at Hermannsburg, Ehlanzeni, and various points on the Tugela River. This mission had some hard experiences.

After waiting in vain for fruit of their hard labor, the experiment was tried of requiring all natives who were cultivating mission land to send their children to school, or pay rent, or vacate; the first they would not, the second they could not, and the third they did do, until, the experiment thus proving unsuccessful, they were allowed to come back. Another more successful scheme was the establishment here of a seminary for training native helpers. Pupils came from the whole field, and their presence and example finally secured the interest of the natives. More encouraging is the work of the Bechuana Mission. As early as 1857 a call came from a Bechuana king, supported by a letter from the Dutch authorities, for the undertaking of work in West Transvaal; the mission was therefore started, tho quite foreign to the original plan. Moreover, it was with hesitation that the missionaries turned in that direction, as for many reasons it did not promise well. It is now, however, one of the Society's most promising and fruitful fields of labor. The colonization scheme was never employed in this mission. Beginning in 1858, gradually a network of stations was formed over the whole western half of the Transvaal Colony, and extended also into the British Bechuanaland on the west. This extreme western section had been occupied by English missionaries, but they had retired before the Dutch Boers; later the Hermannsburg Mission gave up the field to the LMS. There were reported (1900) 46 stations, 103 outstations, 45 missionaries, 396 native workers, 25,400 communicants, about 40,000 baptized Christians and 6,058 pupils.

2. *India:* In 1866 an appeal came to the Society for work among the Telugus of India, and men were at once sent out who established a central station at Naidupett. The work has increased but slowly, and there were reported (1900) 9 stations, 13 outstations, 12 missionaries, 91 native workers, 1,693 communicants, 870 pupils.

Other enterprises commenced have been subsequently abandoned. One to New Zealand was given up, and one to Australia was handed over to the Evangelical Lutheran Immanuel Synod of Australia. A work was also begun in Persia, which, however, has not been developed.

PERIODICALS: *Hermannsburger Missionsblatt,* fortnightly; *Missionsblatt für unsere liebe Jugend;* Hermannsburg, Hannover.

JERUSALEM UNION IN BERLIN (*Jerusalems-Verein zu Berlin*): Founded by Court-preacher Strauss in 1852. In aid of German evangelical institutions in the Orient, in the vicinity of Jerusalem, this Society supports schools, hospitals, and hospices, for the "inner and outer mission" among the native inhabitants of that region, and among Germans resident there. The conduct of its affairs is in the hands of a committee of at least 16, who elect their own successors.

The Union has, from the first, enjoyed royal support, and for long years was under the special protection of Empress Auguste. Since the present Emperor's visit to the Levant, in 1897, it has received special support and encouragement.

The chief activity of the Union is in Jerusalem, tho here it has a less distinctively mission character than in other stations. Here the funds are supplied to support in part various German institutions which have a mainly national character. It contributes to the salary of the pastor of the German church, who makes quarterly visits to the Germans in Haifa and Jaffa, and to that of the assistant preacher, who is also teacher in the German school. As early as 1867 a collection was made in Germany for church building in Jerusalem; in 1869 the Prussian crown came into possession of the Murestan, the site of the old convent Santa Maria Magna; the locality was excavated and now a fine church has been erected there. In connection with the parish is a Men's Union, and lately a Youths' Union has been established.

Other places occupied are Bethlehem, Betjala, Hebron, Haifa, Jaffa, and, latest, Bet Sahur. There are 2 orphanages, for Syrians and Armenians, an educational institution (Talitha Kumi) for girls, a hospital under the care of the Kaiserswerth deaconesses, a leper asylum, etc. There were (1902) 430 pupils in the 8 schools.

KIEL MISSION TO CHINA: This Society was formed in 1897, with headquarters in Kiel but with its responsible head in the field. In 1902 it had 3 stations in China, in the district near Pakhoi, with 6 missionaries, men and women; 3 native workers, 1 school, and 33 professing Christians.

ORGAN: *Er Kommt*, fortnightly, Kiel.

LUTHERAN FREE CHURCH OF HANNOVER, MISSIONARY SOCIETY OF: This Society has its headquarters in Hermannsburg. It is a branch of the Hermannsburg Missionary Society, and carries on missions in Natal and Transvaal in S. Africa. In 1902 it had in the field 9 missionaries, 41 native workers, 17 schools, and 4,050 professing Christians at 8 stations.

PERIODICAL: *Missionsblatt der Hannover'schen ev.-luth. Freikirche*, monthly, Hermannsburg.

LEIPZIG EVANGELICAL LUTHERAN MISSION SOCIETY (*Evangelisch-Lutherische Mission zu Leipzig*): As early as 1819 there was in Dresden a missionary association closely affiliated with and working through the Basel Society. With the development of the confessional question and the desire to emphasize distinctively Lutheran creed and organization, the individualistic methods of Basel were not altogether satisfactory, and in 1832 the Dresden association established its own mission school, which in 1836 developed into a complete missionary seminary, and in the latter year it also constituted itself an independent mission society, which was removed to Leipzig in 1846.

In 1844 Dr. Karl Graul became president of the Society and director of its seminary. He traveled extensively in the East and came to conclusions which resulted in the complete dissolution of the connection between the Leipzig and the Basel societies. The Basel Society, in accordance with all pietistic missionary labor, aimed simply at individual conversions. Dr. Graul, on the contrary, looked for a national conversion, and he consequently demanded more from the missionaries he sent out, namely, an intimate acquaintance with the whole state of civilization,—religious, scientific, literary, political, and social—among the people to whom they were sent. He also wished to make the Leipzig Society the center of the entire missionary activity of the Lutheran Church, and he gave its labor a strictly Lutheran character, which imposed upon the laborers a certain reserve toward their colaborers of other denominations.

Missions. 1. *India:* As was natural, the attention of the Society was turned to India, and some of its missionaries commenced work among the Tamils in 1840. This gave good occasion for the transfer to them of the interests and property of the old Danish-Tamil Mission (itself conducted on high-church Lutheran principles), when Tranquebar was ceded to England in 1845. Two years later the transfer was complete, and the Leipzig Society entered into the inheritance of Ziegenbalg and Schwartz.

The caste question at one time threatened to endanger the success of the work, as the policy of the Society in regard to it was rather too lenient. That, however, was overcome, and the growth and strength of the mission is indicated by the following figures (1902): 40 stations, 769 outstations, 41 missionaries, 743 native workers, 19,178 communicants, 9,407 pupils.

2. *Africa:* In 1892 the Leipzig Society joined the number of German organizations working in Africa, and took charge of a mission in British East Africa, which had been founded by a Bavarian Society. This mission, called the Mahamba Mission, has (1902) 3 stations, Jumpa (near Mombasa), Ikutha (near Mt. Kenia), and Mulalngo, with 9 missionaries.

A little later the Society began a distinct mission in the vicinity of Mt. Kilima Njaro, in German territory, known as the Majagga Mission. This reports 6 stations, and 16 missionaries.

The Women's Aid Society of the Leipzig Evangelical Lutheran Mission (*Frauen-Hilfs Vereine der Evangelische-Lutherishen Mission zu Leipzig*) is auxiliary to the Society, with special reference to its work for women in India.

PERIODICALS: *Evangelisch-Lutherische Missionsblatt*, fortnightly; *Die kleine Missionsglocke* (for children), monthly, Leipzig.

NEUENDETTELSAU MISSIONARY SOCIETY (*Gesellschaft für Innere und Aussere Mission im Sinne der Lutherische Kirche*): This Society was organized first, in 1849, with special reference to work among Lutherans in America, and, to some extent, among the Indians. Later, in 1885, in connection with the Immanuel Synod of Australia, it commenced work among the natives, and the same year celebrated the occupation of Kaiser Wilhelmsland (New Guinea) by sending missionaries there. It reports (1902) 7 stations, 15 missionaries, 30 communicants, 90 pupils.

PERIODICAL: *Freimund's kirchliches und politisches Wochenblatt*, weekly (with supplement relating to work in North America, Australia, and New Guinea).

NEUKIRCHEN MISSIONARY INSTITUTE (*Neukirchener Missionsanstalt*): This Society was founded in 1882 by Pastor Doll of Neukirchen, partly to carry out a vow made during a severe illness, and partly to provide for Germany an institution representing the standpoint of the China Inland and similar faith missions. It has, however, come to be conducted on the same general principles as the other societies.

The fields of labor are Java and British East Africa. There are reported (1902), in Java, 7 stations in the two districts of Samarang and Rembang, 9 missionaries, 46 native helpers, 565 baptized adults, 562 pupils. The classes reached are Mohammedans, Javanese, Chinese and some Arabs.

In Africa the work among the Mohammedans, along the Tana River, has not proved successful, but one baptized adult being reported at Lamu after 14 years of effort. Among the Swahili there has been better success. There are (1902) 4 stations, 8 missionaries, 142 baptized adults, 171 pupils.

PERIODICALS: *Der Missions und Heidenbote*, monthly, with supplement; *Jugendmissionsblatt*, monthly; *Die Ührenleserin auf dem Missionsfelde*, bi-monthly, Neukirchen.

NORTH GERMAN MISSIONARY SOCIETY (*Norddeutsche Missionsgesellschaft*): As early as 1802 there was formed in East Frisia, in response to influences from the Moravian and the London Missionary Societies, a "Mission Society of the Mustard Seed," for the purpose of collecting funds in aid of missions. Other similar unions were formed throughout North Germany, the most important being one in Bremen in 1819. The collections were sent to Jänicke in Berlin and to Basel, and two men presenting themselves for service aroused great interest. Other unions were organized at Lübeck (1820) and Hamburg (1823), but no movement toward affiliation was made until 1834. In 1836 seven unions, Bremen, Stade, Hamburg, Lauenburg, Ritzebuttel, Lehe, and Bremerhaven, organized the North German Missionary Society, with headquarters at Hamburg, where in 1837 a Missionary Institute was established.

From the beginning there were in these unions numbers of both the Lutheran and the Reformed bodies, and this resulted both in difficulties on the field and divided counsel at home. Gradually, as the discussion grew sharper, several of the more distinctively Lutheran unions withdrew; the headquarters were removed to Bremen, and the Society gradually became largely Reformed, tho the union feature never disappeared, and there are Lutheran as well as Reformed members on its committee.

Missions: The first movement of the Society was toward New Zealand, where work was commenced in 1842 but not developed, tho one of the two missionaries remained for some time and continued to receive help. The next year men were sent to the Telugus in India, but that work was handed over to the American Lutherans, and the Society concentrated its efforts on the west coast of Africa, just east of the Gold Coast Colony. Among the principal stations are Accra, Anyako, Keta, etc. The terrible climate has been a heavy drawback, but the Society has persevered and reported (1902) 5 stations, 37 outstations, 27 missionaries, 74 native workers, 2,908 communicants and 1,487 pupils.

PERIODICAL: *Monatsblatt der Nordd. Miss.-Gesellschaft,* monthly, Bremen.

RHENISH MISSIONARY SOCIETY (*Rheinische Missions-Gesellschaft in Barmen*): A small missionary union of twelve laymen was formed in 1799 in Elberfeld. As it grew in numbers it inaugurated the Bergische Bible Society and the Tract Society of Wupperthal. In 1819 a similar union was formed at Barmen, which worked in connection with the Basel Missionary Institute but organized its own school in 1825. Three years later these two, joined by unions at Cologne and Wesel, formed the Rhenish Missionary Society, with headquarters at Barmen. The first missionaries went to South Africa and landed at Cape Colony in October, 1829. In that region 40 missionaries under the direction of the Moravian Brethren, the London Missionary Society, the Wesleyans, and the Scotch Free Church were already at work at 30 stations among the Hottentots, Kafirs, Negroes, Bastards, etc. Therefore the Rhenish missionaries hesitated where to go. Finally, in the beginning of 1830, they founded their first station at Wupperthal, and in 1832 they built and consecrated their first church at Unterbarmen.

In 1834 the Society found that they had more missionaries ready for work than could be employed in Africa, and, moved by what they had heard from the American missionary, Abeel, and the LMS missionary, Medhurst, they decided to open a new field in Borneo, to which they afterward added two other islands in the Dutch colonies of the East Indies, Sumatra in 1862, and Nias in 1865. In 1846 they also began a Chinese mission, and in 1887 inaugurated work in Kaiser Wilhelmsland, in New Guinea. In its general character the Rhenish Society has followed the main lines of the Basel Missionary Society, and carries the cordial support of both Lutherans and Reformed. It met with financial difficulties in 1881, which compelled the transference of parts of its Chinese mission to the Basel and Berlin societies, but it soon regained lost ground and continued to enlarge its work.

Missions. 1. *Africa:* There are three missions in Africa: Cape Colony, Namaqua-Herero, and Ovambo. The Cape Colony mission covers the region in the vicinity of Cape Town, altho one station, Carnavon, is in the center of the colony, and three others, Steinkopf, Concordia, and Komaggas, are in the northwest part of the colony. The work is among the Hottentots, Negroes, half-breeds, etc. The schools are crowded and the industrial and commercial elements of the work are well developed. There are (1902) 10 stations 14 missionaries, 136 native helpers, 6,547 communicants, 2,547 pupils.

The Namaqua and Herero mission is in German West Africa, and covers the entire territory occupied by the Namaqua Hottentots and the Herero Negroes. There are (1902) 24 stations, 35 outstations, 35 missionaries, 123 native helpers, 5,303 communicants, 2,405 pupils.

The Ovambo Mission is on the border of German West Africa and the Portuguese district of Angola. The youngest of the missions, it has 3 stations, 5 missionaries, 2 native workers, 35 communicants, 130 pupils.

2. *Dutch East Indies:* The work of the Rhenish Society in Borneo was commenced in 1842 among the Dyaks of the southeastern portion of the island. The first efforts met with little success, no convert being baptized in eight years. They adopted two measures, both of which miscarried: *i.e.,* the ransoming of "pandelings," or slaves, for debt, and compulsory attendance at their schools. The Dyak is either very poor or very rich: one has not a rice-seed to eat, and another has a gold crown so heavy that he cannot bear it. Then the poor man borrows of the rich, but the rate of interest is so outrageous that a very small debt will in a very short time make a man a "pandeling." He likes, of course, to be ransomed, but that ransom cannot make him a Christian. By the agency of the Dutch government the Dyak children were driven to the mission school, but that was not the true entrance to Christianity either. In 1859 the whole fabric suddenly tumbled down. The Dyaks rose in rebellion, seven missionaries were killed, the rest fled to Bandjermasin, the seat of the government, and all the stations were burnt down. In reality, the rebellion was raised against the Dutch government, but the missionaries were the sufferers, and they were not able to resume work until 1866. From that time, however, the work has progressed steadily and surely. There are reported (1902) 8 stations, 16 outstations, 11 missionaries, 42 native workers, 1,085 communicants, 688 pupils.

A mission in Sumatra was organized in 1862, and has rapidly developed into the most important field of the Rhenish Society. Circumstances were propitious. The climate is much better than that of Borneo, as most of the stations are situated at an altitude of 2,000 feet or more. The country is well filled up, and the Battas, the Malayan tribe among which the mission works, are possessed of some civilization. They have themselves reduced their language to writing, and they like to read. Dutch missionaries have long ago mastered the language for all scientific and literary purposes, and the whole Bible is translated into Batta. Very fortunate also it was that the Rhenish missionaries early came in contact with the Battas. Hence the sensitiveness shown elsewhere concerning missions to Islam was not allowed free play. When the Mohammedans of Sumatra petitioned the king of the Netherlands for the expulsion of the Christian missionaries, the request was refused.

There are reported (1902) 32 stations, 205 outstations, 60 missionaries, 1,152 native workers; 22,524 communicants, 10,902 pupils.

A mission in Nias was commenced in 1865. It reports (1902) 12 stations, 12 outstations, 20 missionaries, 77 native workers, 3,904 communicants, 820 pupils.

The youngest mission of the group, in the island of Mentawei, south of Nias, was organized in 1901, and reported in 1902 1 station, 2 missionaries, 1 native worker, 7 communicants, 10 pupils.

3. *China:* Since 1846 the Rhenish Society has had a mission in Hongkong and vicinity, and 1 station, Tai-ping, in the southwestern part of the Kwang-si province. The report shows (1902) 6 stations, 10 outstations, 14 missionaries, 29 native helpers, 883 communicants, 296 pupils.

4. *New Guinea:* Soon after the formation of the Colony of Kaiser Wilhelmsland the Rhenish Society felt the responsibility for mission work among the Papuans and in 1887 opened a station at Bogadjim. There are (1902) 4 stations, 7 missionaries, 128 pupils.

PERIODICALS: *Missionsblatt Barmen*, monthly; *Der Kleine Missionsfreund*, monthly, Barmen.

SUDAN PIONEER MISSION: A society formed in 1900, with headquarters at Eisenach. In 1902 it had in the field 1 missionary and 1 woman missionary, 3 native workers, and 2 schools, with 150 scholars, all at Assouan, in upper Egypt.

ORGAN: *Der Sudan-Pionier*, monthly.

WOMEN'S SOCIETY FOR CHRISTIAN EDUCATION OF THE FEMALE SEX IN EASTERN COUNTRIES (*Frauen verein für Christliche Bildung des Weiblichen Geschlechts im Morgenlande*): This Society, organized in 1842, is known also as the "Berlin Woman's Missionary Association" and the "Woman's Oriental Union." Its chief work is the sending out of teachers and deaconesses to various fields, chiefly India, who work in connection with other societies. Many of these teachers are under the CMS. The Society has for its own chief work a foundling asylum at Sikandra, North West Provinces. In 1900 and 1901 two women were sent to China. The principal of the Talitha Kumi orphanage of the Jerusalem Union was sent out by this Society.

Missionsblatt des Frauenvereins, etc., monthly, Berlin.

The German Foreign Missionary Societies have united in forming an "Executive Committee" (*Ausschuss der deutschen Evangelischen Missionsgesellschafter*), which has advisory functions when called upon by the societies to discuss questions that affect the whole missionary interest, and which represents the united societies in all relations with the Government. This Executive Committee is composed of five members elected annually, and meets, whenever necessary, at the call of the secretary. The secretary for the year 1903-04 is Rev. A. Merenski, D.D., of the Berlin Missionary Society.

GERTRUDSBERG: A settlement in the extreme north of the Transvaal Colony, S. Africa. situated in the Zoutspansberg district, on the slopes toward the Limpopo River, and among the Bawemba tribes. Station of the Berlin Missionary Society (1899).

GHAZIABAD: A town and railway junction in the United Provinces of India, situated 15 miles E. N. E. of Delhi, in the district of Meerut. Population (1891), 10,000, of whom about 6,000 are Hindus and about half that number Muslims. Circuit station of the ME, with (1900) 12 native workers, men and women; 8 day schools, and 1,000 professing Christians. Station also of the CMS (1894), with (1903) 2 missionary women and a dispensary.

GHAZIPUR: A city in the United Provinces, India, situated 40 miles E. N. E. of Benares, on the lowlands bordering the Ganges. The district of Ghazipur is one of the hottest and dampest in this part of India. The city has a monument to Lord Cornwallis, who died there in 1806. It is the center of the government opium monopoly and manufactory. Population (1891), 45,000, of whom about two-thirds are Hindus and one-third Muslims. Station of the Gossner (German) Mission, and of the Zenana Bible and Medical Mission.

GHEG LANGUAGE. See ALBANIAN.

GIATWANGAK: A settlement in British Columbia, situated on the Skeena River, about 120 miles from Metlakahtla. Station of the CMS (1882), with a constituency both among the Indians and among Chinese employed in salmon canning works.

GIBARA. See JIBARA.

GIBEON: A station of the Rhenish Missionary Society in German Southwest Africa, situated about 190 miles N. E. of Angra Pequena. It has (1903) 1 missionary and his wife, 3 native workers, one a woman; 1 day school, and 383 professing Christians. The people among whom this station is established are Namaquas in the main.

GIFU: A town and railway station on the main island of Japan, situated 75 miles E. N. E. of Kioto. It is the capital of the prefecture of the same name, and has a population (1898) of about 31,000. Station of the CMS (1890), with (1903) 4 missionaries, men and women, and 7 native workers, men and women. Two interesting features of the work here are the home for ex-convicts and the school for the blind.

GIKUKI: A settlement in Portuguese East Africa, situated on a high bluff overlooking Inhambane Bay. Station of the ME (1884), with (1903) 1 missionary and his wife, 9 native workers, men and women, a printing house and a high school.

GILBERT ISLANDS: A cluster of coral islands in Micronesia, lying on both sides of the equator. Population estimated at 32,500. The climate is equable, and tho warm is not oppressive. The inhabitants resemble the Malays. Before the advent of missionaries they were fond of war and prone to suicide; kind to their children, hospitable, generous, and more considerate of women than is usual among savages. They ate human flesh occasionally, but were not habitual cannibals. These islands are now under Britain, and missionary work at the beginning of the 20th century is under the Hawaiian Evangelical Association (in cooperation with the ABCFM), greatly aided by the new conditions which foreign control supplies. The training school for the Gilbert Islands is at Kusaie (Caroline Is.), where one of the missionaries resides. Literary work for the islands occupies another missionary residing at Honolulu, H. I. A third missionary spends his time in touring from island to island in a vessel chartered for the purpose. One missionary and his wife (Hawaiians) reside on the island of Maiana. On the islands of Marakei, Aranaka, Kuria, and Nonouti the additions to the Church (in 1901) numbered 80. The southernmost islands of this group have been under care of the LMS and are virtually Christianized.

GILBERT LANGUAGE: Belongs to the Micronesian family of languages and is spoken by the people of the Gilbert Islands. It was reduced to writing by missionaries of the ABCFM with the use of Roman letters.

GILL, William: Born January 14, 1813, at Totness, England; sailed April 11, 1838, as a missionary of the LMS for Raratonga; stationed at Arorangi in that island. In 1842, in the absence of Mr. Buzacott from Raratonga, he took charge also of his station and of the institution at Avarua. Between 1843 and 1846 he visited the other islands of the Hervey group, spending six months in Mangaia and the New Hebrides, New Caledonia, and the Loyalty Islands, returning by way of Samoa to Raratonga. In addition to his evangelistic and pastoral work he revised the Raratonga version of the Scriptures, and wrote several books in that language. His wife devoted herself to the elevation of the native women. In 1853 he went to England and did not return to the mission field. Before his connection with the Society ceased he printed the second edition of the Raratongan Bible, besides other books in that language. In October, 1856, he was settled as pastor at Woolwich, and died at Blackheath in 1878.

GILLESPIE: A settlement in Griqualand East, Cape Colony, S. Africa, situated near Mt. Ayliff. Station of the UFS (1889), with (1903) 1 missionary and his wife, 15 native workers, men and women; 12 outstations, 1 day school, and 600 baptized Christians.

GILMOUR, James: Born near Glasgow, June 12, 1843. Died in Mongolia, May 21, 1891. With his master's degree won at Glasgow he entered Cheshunt College, near London, where he took a two years' theological course. On February 22, 1870, he sailed from Liverpool as a missionary of the LMS, and on May 18 he reached the Chinese capital, which was to be the headquarters of his future work, so far away over the Great Wall on the Mongolian highlands. He arrived in China at the critical time when an anti-foreign storm was on the eve of breaking out at Tien-tsin; but the young missionary, within three months after his arrival, started up through the famous South Pass, toward the frontier city of Kalgan. The Mongolian field stands as a buffer state between Siberia and China proper, with an area more than one-third as large as the United States. Much of Gilmour's missionary life was spent among the agricultural Mongols; and singlehanded he addressed himself to the work of introducing the Gospel among 2,000,000 of the most superstitious and exclusive persons in all the East. Between the years 1818 and 1841, the missionaries Stallybrass and Swan had labored at Selingsk and Onagen Dome, with several assistants; and they left, besides the graves of some of their number, a Buriat-Mongol translation of the Bible and several earnest converts. Save for a few copies of the Scriptures found here and there, preserved carefully by a few native Christians, Gilmour found little to build upon; but this itinerant evangelist for years was untiring in his journeys, living usually with the nomadic tribes in their tents, and witnessing for Jesus as they gathered about him in the fields or along the mountain sides. As a lay physician, Gilmour was greatly aided in securing the confidence of the Mongols; and at his street-tent dispensary in towns, nearly 300 miles northeast of Peking, he blessed the bodies and souls of hundreds of this rude people. After 1886 he made Chao-yang his headquarters. Mrs. Gilmour was a genuine helpmeet to her husband, and her educational work among the women and children was far-reaching in its influence. Besides his work far from the cities, Gilmour labored also at Peking, Tien-tsin and Shantung; but on the Mongolian plains he loved most to witness for his Master.

Gilmour (J.), *Among the Mongols*, 1884; Lovett (R.), *Gilmour of Mongolia*, London, 1892.

GISBORNE: A town and port of entry in New Zealand, situated on Poverty Bay, on the E. coast of the North Island, 85 miles N. E. of Napier. Population, about 3,000. Station of the CMS, with (1903) 2 missionaries, one missionary's wife, 85 native workers, men and women; 11 outstations, 2 village schools, 1 theological training institute and 4,000 baptized Christians.

GIZ LANGUAGE: Giz is another name for the ancient Ethiopic language of Abyssinia, now found in books only and replaced by the Amharic in ordinary use. It is written with the same letters as Amharic except that it lacks one or two letters added to the latter language under influence of the Arabic.

GLEASON, Anson: Born at Manchester, Conn., May 2, 1797. In 1822 he became an assistant missionary of the ABCFM, and in January, 1823, started for the Choctaw country. He traveled the long journey on horseback. After eight years of service among the Indians, the health of his family obliged him in 1831 to return north. He then came into connection with the Mohicans settled near Norwich, Conn., and a church having been formed, he was ordained as its pastor. For a time he was district secretary of the ABCFM in Vermont and New Hampshire; for ten years he labored among the Seneca Indians near Buffalo, and he afterward became a city missionary, serving with unabated interest until his death, in Brooklyn, N. Y., February 24, 1885.

GLENDALE: A settlement in Natal, S. Africa, situated on the Umvoti River, 35 miles N. of Durban. Station of the South African Missionary Society.

GLEN HAVEN: A town in the eastern part of Jamaica, W. I., situated in Portland, about 7 miles S. W. of Buff Bay. Station of the AFFM (1881).

GLENTHORN: A settlement in Cape Colony, S. Africa, situated near Linton in the district of Bedford. Station of the UFS (1840), with (1903) 1 missionary and his wife and 2 native workers.

GNADENDAL: The oldest mission settlement of the Moravians in South Africa. It was founded in 1737 by George Schmidt. On his expulsion from the colony the work was suspended for nearly fifty years; it was then, in 1792, renewed, an old convert of Schmidt's being discovered still residing there, and carefully preserving a Dutch Testament he had given her. The settlement is situated in the district of Caledon, 65 miles E. of Cape Town, near the junction of a rocky glen called Barian's Kloof with the valley of the Sonderend, down which it extends nearly a mile and a half. The name means "Valley of Grace," and was chosen, it is said, by one of the old Dutch Governors, who was moved by sight of the work of the mission. It has now (1901) 14 missionaries, men and women; 87 native workers, men and women; 4 preaching places, 4 day schools, 1 theological seminary (founded 1838) and 740 communicants.

GOALPARA: A town in Assam, British India, situated on the left bank of the Brahmaputra, 70 miles W. of Gauhati. It is a very malarious situation, as unhealthful for natives as for Europeans. The civil officials live on a hill 250 feet above the plain. Population (1891), about 5,500, of whom 3,500 are Hindus. Station of the ABMU (1867), with access to the Garos and Rabbhas.

GOBAT, Samuel: Born at Crémine, Berne, Switzerland, January 26, 1799. At the age of nineteen, having an earnest desire to be a missionary, he entered the Basel Missionary Institution, previously perfecting himself in the German language. In 1823 he was sent to Paris to study Arabic at the Missionary Institution. He studied also Amharic and Ethiopic. At the end of a year, on recommendation of the directors of the Basel Institution, he was accepted as a missionary candidate by the CMS, and resided some months in the CMS College in Islington, devoting himself chiefly to Oriental study. Appointed in 1826 to commence a mission in Abyssinia, he returned to the continent, received Lutheran ordination, and sailed for Egypt in September of that year. He spent three months at Jerusalem in 1827 in making acquaintance with the Abyssinians at the monastery in that city, and from 1830 to 1833 he traveled extensively in Abyssinia proclaiming the Gospel to priests and people. His health having failed, he left for home at the close of 1836, and was associated in 1839-42 with the Society's missionaries at Malta, in superintending the translation of the Bible into Arabic, and taking charge of the printing press. He was appointed vice-president of the Malta Protestant College in 1845, and the same year, visiting England, was ordained deacon in the Church of England. After the bishopric of the Anglican Church at Jerusalem became vacant by the death of Bishop Alexander, Mr. Gobat was nominated as his successor by the King of Prussia (Frederick William IV.), and consecrated at Lambeth July 5, 1846. His work in Jerusalem left a permanent mark on the country, being notable for piety, vigor, tact, and good judgment. He died in Jerusalem May 11, 1879. He wrote *A Journal of Three Years in Abyssinia* (London, 1847).

GOCHAS. See GOKHAS.

GODDA: A town in the Santal Parganas, Bengal, India, situated W. of the Rajmahal Hills, about 140 miles S. E. of Bhagalpur. Station of the CMS, with (1903) 1 missionary and his wife, 232 native workers, one of them a woman; 7 outstations, 18 day schools, 1 boarding school, 1 dispensary, and 432 baptized Christians.

GODHRA: A town in the Bombay Presidency, India; situated in the Panch Mahals district, about 40 miles N. E. of Baroda. The town is almost entirely surrounded by jungle. Population (1891), 14,700, of whom 7,500 are Mohammedans and the most of the remainder Hindus. Station of the ME, with (1902) 1 missionary and his wife, 45 native workers, 1 orphanage, and 522 professing Christians.

GOEDE HOOP. See GOOD HOPE.

GOED FORTUIN: A settlement in British Guiana, S. America, situated on the Demerara River, about 12 miles S. by W. of Georgetown. Station of the West Indies Wesleyan East Conference, with (1901) 1 missionary and his wife, 5 outstations, 5 preaching places, 4 day schools, and 391 professing Christians. This, with other work of the W. I. Wesleyan Conferences, was transferred back to the WMS in 1903.

GOEDERWACHT: A settlement in Cape Colony, S. Africa, situated about 35 miles west of Piquetberg and about 90 miles N. by W. of Cape Town. The place was originally a Hottentot settlement founded by a planter who bequeathed the land to his faithful slaves. The name, meaning "well guarded," refers to the nature of the site, which is a deep glen in a spur of the Piquetberg, overlooking St. Helena Bay. Station of the Moravian Missions (1845), with (1900) 2 missionaries and their wives, 25 native workers, men and women; 1 chapel, 1 day school, and 200 professing Christians.

GOGO (Gogha): A town in Kathiawar, Bombay Presidency, India; situated in the district of Ahmadabad, on the W. side of the Gulf of Cambay, 45 miles W. of Broach. The climate is temperate and healthful. The natives are considered the best sailors in India. Population (1891), 6,600, of whom 3,200 are Hindus and the most part of the remainder Muslims. Gujarati is the language of the district, but a dialect peculiar to the Muslims is also used and known as Musulmani. Station of the Presbyterian Church in Ireland (1843), with 1 missionary and his wife and 2 native workers.

GOGO LANGUAGE: Belongs to the Bantu family, and is spoken by about 100,000 people living in the central part of German East Africa, west of Mpwapwa. It was reduced to writing by missionaries of the CMS and is another case of the use of Roman letters by illiterate tribes.

GOKHAS: A station of the Rhenish Missionary Society in the eastern part of German Southwest Africa, situated among the Namaquas, about 300 miles S. E. of Walfisch Bay and 260 miles N. E. of Angra Pequena. It has (1903) 1 missionary and his wife, 3 native workers, 1 day school, and 383 baptized Christians. The name is written by the Society, according to German rules, Gochas.

GOLAGHAT: A village in Assam, situated 88

miles S. W. of Dibrugarh, in the district of Sibsagar. Population, about 5,000. Station of the ABMU (1898), with (1903) 1 missionary and his wife, 17 native workers, men and women; 14 preaching places and outstations, 2 day schools, 1 high school, and 900 professing Christians.

GOLBANTI: A village in British East Africa, situated on the Tana River, 116 miles north by east of Mombasa. It is also spoken of sometimes by the name Borabini. Station of the United Methodist Free Churches (England) (1885), the mission being directed especially to the Gallas, tho reaching to some extent the Pokomo also. It has (1903) 1 missionary and 3 native workers. It is preparing for industrial instruction of the people, and owns an estate of four miles frontage on the Tana River and two and a half miles depth.

GOLD COAST: A British colony on the Gulf of Guinea, having a coast line of about 360 miles. The protectorate that embraces Ashanti and Adumassi is included with the colony proper under the general designation of Gold Coast. The colony proper has about 42,000 square miles, the whole territory about 72,500 square miles. The population is estimated at 1,500,000 negroes, chiefly of the Akkra and Tschi (or Otji) tribes.

In the Upper Volta basin and interior highlands the aborigines have held their ground as separate groups. But the distinctions of language, customs, and physical characteristics are rapidly disappearing. The aborigines are called Potoso, that is, "barbarians," by the Ashanti conquerors. Their language is the Gwany, Nta, and allied idioms, which, tho unintelligible to the Ashanti peoples, yet belong to the same family of languages as the Otji or Ga. The Otji peoples include the Ashantis, Dankiras, Wassaws, Akims, Assins, and Fantis, and are the ruling race. They are well developed physically, and, perhaps, owe some of their characteristics to Berber and Arab blood. They are farmers, artisans, merchants, stock breeders, fishermen, according to their surroundings. The missionaries use for their translation of the Bible, prayer-book, hymns, etc., the Akwapem dialect. The incredible cruelty and carnage of Ashanti power, with human sacrifices and slaughter, have largely been stopped by the British annexation. A railway has been opened from Sekondi on the coast to Kumasi.

The WMS and the Basel, and the North German Missionary Society occupy 22 stations in this colony.

Macdonald, *The Gold Coast, Past and Present*, London, 1898; Reindorf, *History of the Gold Coast and Ashanti*, Basel, 1895.

GOLOVIN BAY: A settlement on the W. coast of Alaska, situated at the head of Golovin Bay and about 40 miles N. E. of Cape Nome. Station of the Swedish Evangelical Mission Covenant of America (1892), with 2 missionaries and 2 missionary women.

GOND LANGUAGE: Belongs to the Dravidian family, and is spoken by 1,500,000 people inhabiting the Central Provinces, India. It is related to both Tamil and Telugu. It has no alphabet peculiar to itself, but attempts have been made to introduce the Hindi (*nagari*) characters among the northern Gonds and the Telugu characters among those bordering on the Telugu country.

GONDA: A town and capital of a district in the United Provinces, India; situated 69 miles E. by N. of Lucknow. The name means a "safe fold," and is due to the origin of the settlement, which was built about a cattle fold in the center of a dense jungle. Population (1891), 17,400, of whom 11,600 are Hindus and the remainder chiefly Mohammedans. Station of the ME, with (1902) 2 missionary women, 110 native workers, men and women; 5 preaching places, 62 Sunday schools, 12 day schools, 1 orphanage, and 1,130 professing Christians.

GONDIA: A village in the Central Provinces, India; situated on the railway about 50 miles E. by N. of Nagpur. Station of the Pentecost Bands of the World (1899), with 3 missionaries, one a man, and an industrial school.

GONDS: A non-Aryan race of Central India, numbering some 2,000,000 and forming the largest remnant of the Dravidian aborigines, so called, who were pushed back by the later Aryan immigration into the mountainous, ill-watered, jungle covered region known as Gondwana (the land of the Gonds), which is some 400x300 miles in extent and lies between 18° 40' and 23° 40' Lat. and 78° to 82° Long., mostly within the Central Provinces, Bastar and Berar. The Gonds are thinly scattered over this region, sharing the more accessible plains with the Hindus. The Rajputs of Malwa early intermarried with the Gonds, forming the Raj-Gonds, who have retained the physical peculiarities, but have laid aside the rough habits of the Gonds and taken on some elements of Hindu civilization. The wild Gonds form the mass of the population of Bastar, whose ruler is a Gond. In the north of this state they are called Muriyas (forest people); southward about the Godavari and Prauhita valleys dwell a branch known as Kois (hill people), while those who live higher up in the hills are known as Gu-te-koi (high-hill people). The Khonds, another branch, are found in Orissa east of Gondwana. The long-continued independence of the Gonds as a race has been due to the arid, inaccessible character of their country, but their race unity is now broken, as time goes on they are approaching more nearly to the language, customs and religion of their Hindu neighbors. The Gonds are short in stature, have dark, nearly black skin, small deep-set eyes, thick lips, thin beards and long black hair, and are strong and hardy. They are of good disposition, comparatively honest and truthful, grateful for kindness and hospitality. A rag about the loins and strings of beads are the chief articles of dress, and, in the N. W. of Bastar, the women content themselves with abbreviated aprons of leafy twigs. The sexes are intellectually and socially on an equality; women are freely wooed and marry usually after they are sixteen. A village is a straggling line of cultivated enclosures with a hut in each. They are in demand as mineworkers. The language of these tribes is called *Gondi*. The northern Gonds speak also a corrupt Hindi, and the southern, including the Kois, use Telugu. The religion of the Gonds, allied to the Bhuta cult common to the uncultured people of South India, consists of the worship of nature and of the spirits of the dead, involving human sacrifice until its suppression by the British, when images of the horse and food were substituted as offerings. In religious ceremonies the rudest symbols are employed, the representation of their chief deities, Pharsa-Pen, Loha-Pen and Bhera-Pen, being a hatchet, a nail and a chain.

The priests exercise large power. The more advanced Gonds have borrowed from the religion of the Hindus, worshiping Siva and Kali especially, and the Raj-Gonds have developed a system of caste which is foreign to Gond tradition.

The Free Church of Scotland began in 1845 a mission to the Gonds, under Rev. S. S. Hislop, who took into the employ of the mission the remaining members of an earlier German effort. The United Free Church of Scotland Mission, with headquarters at Nagpur, tho no longer distinctly a mission to the Gonds, now carries on this work for this people. The "Bhalagat Mission" to the Gonds, begun in 1894, had, in 1902, some half dozen European agents, who labored among the wild Gonds in the forests, with a center at Behir. The Swedish Evangelical National Society has undertaken work for the Gonds in Chindwara and the Methodist Episcopal Church (U. S.) at Sironcha. But the chief mission to this people is that of the Church Missionary Society, which established in 1854 a station at Jabalpur, in part as a basis for a Gond mission, with which, however, the pressure of other work seriously interfered. Upon the initiative of two earnest Christian workers stationed in that region, Col. Colton and Capt. Haig, the mission to the Kois was begun in 1860, the first fruit of which has, however, been more among other races than among the Kois. As a result of the Conference on non-Aryan Missions in 1877 a Gond Mission was established at Mandla, to which stations at Marpha and Patpara have been added. Five hundred converts were enrolled by the CMS in 1900, but many of them were not Gonds, the low caste Hindus proving more accessible and progressive. Thus, while the Gonds during a long period have been regarded as a field of singular promise, missions to them are still in the day of small things. Gondwana was the most sorely stricken region in India during the famine of recent years and the missionaries exemplified the Gospel by extensive relief work.

Imperial Gazetteer of India (Article Gonds); *History of the Church Missionary Society:* King (W. R.), *Aboriginal Tribes of the Nilgiri Hills*, London, 1870; Watson (J. F.) and Kay (J. W.), *Races and Tribes of Hindustan*, 4 vols., London, 1868-70.

GOOD, Adolphus Clemens: Born December 19, 1856, near Dayton, Pa. When but a lad he made public confession of his faith in the Presbyterian Church. He received his preparatory training in Glade Run Academy from 1873 to 1876; was graduated from Washington and Jefferson College in 1879 and from the Western Theological Seminary in 1882. His degree of Ph.D. was given by Washington and Jefferson College in 1890. In June, 1882, he was ordained by the Presbytery of Kittanning as an evangelist, preparatory to sailing for Africa, having been previously appointed a missionary by the Presbyterian Board of Foreign Missions (N.). He chose the Dark Continent as his field of labor mainly because it was a hard field and because few at that time were found willing to enter it. He sailed for Africa September 18, 1882, and on his arrival was assigned to Baraka station, near the mouth of the Gaboon River. Being a man of fine linguistic ability, he soon mastered the Mpongwe language and ten months after landing preached his first sermon in the native tongue.

It was his chief delight to itinerate along the river, carrying the Gospel to those sitting in darkness. In this work he was greatly blessed. For several years there was an almost continuous outpouring of the spirit, and hundreds of converts from heathenism were baptized. Largely through his own instrumentality the one church existing in 1884 multiplied to four before his final removal from that field in 1893. During his last year or two on the Ogowe, when burdened with the care of the widely scattered churches, he also revised the entire New Testament in Mpongwe and the Hymn Book then in use, adding quite a number of hymns to the latter. During this period and also later Dr. Good made some valuable contributions to natural history by sending many choice specimens to the Western University of Pennsylvania.

Dr. Good made three distinct journeys into the unexplored interior, with no companions save native carriers. Altho he made light of the discomfort encountered and of the danger to which he was exposed, no one can read his unvarnished narrative of travel without being impressed with the heroic spirit of the man. He marched day after day along the beds and on the edge of streams, sometimes through mud a foot deep, his clothing constantly soaked with the dense foliage kept wet by frequent tropical showers. But these were small matters in his estimation compared with the joy of being able to open a pathway for the Gospel to the savage tribes of the interior. The joy increased as the range of his vision widened and he found the Bule people to belong to the great Fang family, and to be widespread and quite accessible.

He was pushing exploration and translation with all his might, with the intention of joining his family in America the next spring; intending while here to prosecute his literary work and see through the press the Gospels and possibly other parts of the Scriptures, when his life closed in 1893.

GOODELL, William: Born in 1792, at Templeton, Mass. Graduated at Dartmouth College and Andover Theological Seminary. Appointed as missionary of the ABCFM, he sailed December 9, 1822, for Beirut, where, after a few months spent at Malta, he arrived November 16, 1823, expecting to proceed to Jerusalem, but the disturbed state of the country in consequence of the Greek revolution prevented. At Beirut he aided in establishing a mission and pursued the study of the Turkish and Arabic languages. War raging between Greece and Turkey, and persecution from the ecclesiastics prevailing, his work was interrupted, and, consular protection being withdrawn, he was often in great peril. In 1828 he went with his family for a time for safety to Malta. There he issued the New Testament which he had translated into Armeno-Turkish. In 1831 he was transferred to Constantinople to take part in establishing the new mission to the Armenians. His time here was chiefly occupied in translating the Old Testament into Armeno-Turkish. He was full of genial humor, simple, courageous and of deep spirituality; among his associates and the natives of Turkey his influence was weighty. His great work, the translation of the Bible into Armeno-Turkish, was completed in 1841; but so anxious was he to secure perfect accuracy that it underwent repeated revisions, and the final one was not finished till 1863, four years before his death. On the day that he finished it he wrote to Dr. John Adams, his teacher at Andover: "Thus have I been permitted by the goodness of God to dig a well in this distant land, at which millions may drink, or, as good

Brother Temple would say, to throw wide open the twelve gates of the New Jerusalem to this immense population."

In 1851 he visited his native land, where he remained two years. In 1853 he returned to Constantinople, where he labored with enthusiasm and success till 1865, when, on account of failing health, he requested a release from the Board, after forty-three years of missionary work. He died in 1867, aged 75, at the residence of his son in Philadelphia.

GOOD HOPE: A settlement in the northern part of the Transvaal Colony, S. Africa, situated in the Zoutspansberg district, about 60 miles E. of Blauberg. Station of the WMS, with (1903) 1 missionary, 105 native workers, men and women; 22 outstations, 48 preaching places, 20 Sunday schools, 4 day schools and 783 professing Christians. Station also of the Hannover Evangelical Lutheran Free Church, with (1900) 2 missionaries, 2 native workers, 6 outstations, 2 schools and 287 professing Christians. The form given to the name by the German Society is Goede Hoop.

GOOTY: A town in Madras, India, 50 miles east of Bellary. The place is celebrated in history for its very strong fort, captured by the British in 1799 from Mysore. The climate of Gooty is dry and hot. Population (1891) 6,600, of whom 4,400 are Hindus, who speak Telugu. Station of the LMS, opened at Nandyal in 1855 and transferred to Gooty in 1881. It now (1902) has 4 missionaries, 69 native workers, men and women; 56 outstations, 51 Sunday schools, 51 day schools, 1 theological school, 1 woman's training school and 5,000 professed Christian adherents.

GOPALGANJ: A village in Bengal, India, situated in the Faridpur district, about 40 miles S. of Faridpur and on one of the streams of the Ganges Delta. Station of the Bengal Evangelistic Mission (1894), with (1901) 21 native workers, 5 preaching places, 9 day schools, 1 boarding school, 1 industrial school, 1 dispensary and work among lepers.

GORAKHPUR: A city in the United Provinces, India, situated on the Rapti River, 100 miles N. by E. of Benares, at an altitude of 256 feet. Population (1901) 64,000, of whom 41,000 are Hindus and 22,000 Muslims. Station of the CMS (1823), with 7 missionaries, men and women; 37 native workers, men and women; 14 day schools, 1 boarding school and orphanage, 1 college and 1,042 professing Christians. Station also of the Zenana Bible and Medical Mission, with 3 women missionaries and 18 native women workers.

GORDON, Andrew: Born in Putnam, N. Y., September 17, 1828; graduated at Franklin College, O., 1850; studied theology at Canonsburg, Pa., 1853; appointed by synod missionary to Sialkot, North India; sailed September 28, 1854. Dr. Gordon was the founder of this mission of the United Presbyterian Church. He was a devoted and useful laborer with pen and tongue. He returned to the United States in 1865 greatly debilitated, but having gained sufficient strength to warrant active labor again, he reembarked in 1875 and was stationed at Gurdaspur, Northern India. He returned home the second time because of illness of members of his family, and looked forward confidently and eagerly to a return to his work in India. After a long and painful illness he died in Philadelphia, August 13, 1887. Dr. Gordon was preparing a version of the Psalms in the Urdu language when he returned. He published a valuable work, *Our India Mission* (1886).

GORDON, Marquis Lafayette, M.D.: Born in Waynesburg, Pa., July 18, 1843. Graduated from Waynesburg College in 1868 and from Andover Theological Seminary in 1871 and from Long Island College Hospital, Brooklyn, N. Y., in 1872. He also studied in the College of Physicians and Surgeons, in New York, from which he received the degree of M.D. While securing his education he spent three years in the army during the Civil War. He entered Japan as a missionary of the ABCFM in 1872 and was stationed at Osaka. He early became identified with the work of the Doshisha at Kioto and was soon recognized as one of the ablest and most efficient of the missionaries of any Board in Japan. Altho Dr. Gordon had qualified as a physician, after reaching the field he was convinced that he could work successfully in but one profession. He chose the ministry of the Word, gave up the practise of medicine, and devoted himself entirely to evangelistic and educational work. Through his marked ability, his affection for the people and his great tact, as well as the spiritual power of his life, he won a strong position for himself in the affection and the confidence of the people. This position he held to the time of his death. In 1893 he published the volume, *An American Missionary in Japan.* At the time of his death, in Auburndale, Mass., on the 4th of November, 1900, he had in press his second volume, *Thirty Eventful Years in Japan.* These two books contain a comprehensive history of the work and methods of the American Board in that empire. Dr. Gordon was married to Miss Agnes Helen Donald at Andover, Mass., in 1852. Two daughters of his are now in Japan.

GORDON MEMORIAL: A station of the United Free Church of Scotland, in Natal, S. Africa. See UMSINGA.

GOSHEN: A settlement in Cape Colony, S. Africa, situated about 7 miles N. by W. of Cathcart. Station of the Moravian Missions (1892), with (1901) 2 missionaries and their wives, 13 native workers, men and women; 1 chapel and 1 school.

GOSPEL IN FOREIGN PARTS; Society for the Propagation of. See SOCIETY FOR THE PROPAGATION OF THE GOSPEL.

GOSSNER MISSIONARY SOCIETY. See GERMANY; MISSIONARY SOCIETIES IN.

GOVERNMENTS; Relation of Missionaries to: This is a matter of great perplexity, difficulty and importance. The missionary is in one sense a man without a country. In another sense he is a man of many countries. He does not renounce his nationality or citizenship. As Paul at times fell back on his high position as a Jew and Pharisee, so the missionary must often assert his privileges of birth and country. At the same time he is a resident of foreign lands and inevitably related to foreign governments, on his own account, as an individual; in behalf of the property and other local interests acquired by his mission, and in behalf of converts and adherents, who rely on him for advice and sympathy as to enjoying justice and protection in secular things. As Paul appeared now before Ananias, the high-priest; now before Felix and Festus, Roman governors; now before Agrippa, and finally appealed to Cæsar, so the missionary may find himself tossed between different, often conflicting, sources of authority, seeking to reach some supreme Cæsar, often finding only Herods and Pilates who will make friendship over his defeat.

The relation which he sustains to the government of the country where he works may have to be one of virtual defiance. Ever since the Apostles met the prohibition of their persecutors by saying, "We ought to obey God rather than men," and rejoiced "that they were counted worthy to suffer dishonor for His name," the first preachers of the Gospel have encountered in most non-Christian countries the hostility of the powers that be. From Stephen to Bishop Hannington they have found hostile peoples and rulers arrayed against them, and yet have persisted in gentle defiance of threat and command and force. The first Protestant work in Japan was in quiet disregard of hostile laws, proclamations and penalties. And for years before, Catholic priests had been at work sustaining suppressed Christianity, "sleeping," as one of them expressed it, "by day, working by night." Long have they also done the same in Korea, where, at last, our own missionaries entered for the understood purpose of establishing a prohibited religion. Their position at Seoul, the capital, afforded for some years a most interesting instance of the curious intermingling of possible relations with different governments. As foreigners at an open port they were under the diplomatic protection of their home governments. As court physicians, heads of hospitals, asylums, schools, etc., they were under the protection of the Korean government, received distinct appointment as Korean officials of a certain rank, and had a kind of private policemen assigned them for protection and service. In private they were also recognized as missionaries. Yet in all this public capacity, mission labor was prohibited; in any capacity it was liable to be stopped at any moment. The situation was full of complications both for the judgment and the conscience. But Christianity has taken root in Korea; it has made progress more rapidly than in Japan at the start and it has won for itself a place in the land.

In Japan one restriction long remained which involved the question of the true relation of the missionaries to the Japanese government. Outside of the open ports, passports were required and could be had for travel only for purposes of health and science. It was often a question among missionaries whether such traveling passports ought to be used for evangelistic purposes.

The first missions to India were in defiance, not so much of heathen as of Christian government. The history of the East India Company's friendship with heathenism and hostility to Christian effort is one of disgrace, happily relieved, however, by noble exceptions, and steadily improved by the pressure of the better sentiment of England until, with the assumption of rule by the British government in 1857, the present policy of friendly neutrality was adopted. At the time, however, there was often nothing for the deported or prohibited missionaries to do but seek some other country, like Burma, or cast themselves on the help of a friendly government like that of Denmark at Serampur, or wait in quiet and disguise for reluctantly extorted permission to go on with work.

In Turkey the Christian laborer stands under the protection of his own government, with explicit recognition of his character as a missionary. Yet so far as his work touches Mohammedanism, he is engaged in an endeavor to lead persons to violate by a change of religion the most stringent provisions of the law of the land. This change only the most persistent pressure on the part of Christian governments has induced the Turkish government to relieve, in theory, from punishment by death. Practically it is still bitterly opposed and severely punished. The relation of a missionary to a government thus compelled against its will is of necessity strained. He must have constant dealings with lower and higher officials who on the most flimsy pretext, or with no pretext at all, seek to close his schools and chapels, stop his printing press and silence his native preachers, while the unthinking multitude are stirred up to riot against Protestants, and wildest excesses are committed, until the claims of humanity force the powers at Constantinople to interfere. The censorship of the press exercised in Turkey and especially directed against the missionaries is in many cases only more ignorant than it is severe. To keep in communication with hostile officials, to endure oppressive edicts while contending for equitable treatment promised by treaty or by law, to press important cases on the attention of the American consul or minister—these are among the great embarrassments and hardships of a missionary's life, not only in Turkey, but in China, Korea and possibly to some extent in Japan.

To specify one further question that is full of embarrassment to the missionary: When a missionary is hampered by the unwillingness of local officials to give him rights secured by law, how far may he follow usages that prevail in Turkey or in China and secure his civil rights by payments which will induce the official to do his duty instead of evading it? Backshish is expected and demanded in Turkey and Persia. Yet its influence is demoralizing. How far shall the missionary seem to sanction the prevailing corruption? How far must he resist it? This most practical question repeatedly recurs. The missionary's difficulties are more subtly perplexing in case he enters into anything like an alliance with any government. But these difficulties are not peculiar to the foreign field. They must be dealt with as they are dealt with at home. For every such alliance is in effect a union of Church and state. The failings of Roman Catholic missions in this respect, whether in North and South America, in Japan, China, India, or other countries, are too well known to be told. They form a most instructive part of the history of missions. France and Germany to-day are eager to offer such alliance to missionaries. France, in particular, has sought to advance its diplomatic and colonial interest through claiming to be the protector of all the missions of the Roman Propaganda. It has long sought to gain political power in China by posing as the patron of all Roman Catholic missionaries of whatever nationality. It has regarded and treated both Catholic and Protestant missionaries as its own emissaries in pushing its colonial schemes. The Legion of Honor medal has been recently conferred upon M

Casalis, an old French Protestant missionary, for "extending the influence of France in Basutoland," in the sphere of British influence in South Africa.

Germany, too, has the colonial fever, and the interest in missions has been increased all over the land because it is believed that, even if missionaries are not successful as Christianizers of heathendom, they can be used wisely as Germanizers of certain parts of it. As a veteran missionary friend in Germany puts it: "The opinion of the German African Society with regard to missionary societies is that they are not unselfish attempts to spread the Gospel, but merely handmaids to colonial politics—a cow to give milk to the mother-country."

This alliance with the government on missionary ground gives rise to a new set of hostile relations. France wants only French, Germany only German, missionaries. The language and sentiments of each country must be exclusively taught in the colonies of that country. Missionaries of other nationalities must be excluded, for they neither could nor would enter into such alliances for political and national schemes.

The missionary may be often tempted to assume an attitude of critic or mentor to half civilized officials of the land where he is preaching the Gospel. For a large class of questions is added to those which perplex the missionary when he is appealed to by native Christians to secure government aid or interference in behalf of them and their interests. The expectation and hope of such aid and protection from the missionary is one of the motives most damaging to the sincerity of new converts. It harms the missionary, too, by filling his time and thoughts with civil matters, lawsuits, appeals, etc.

For instance, in Travancore, the question of the caste privileges of Christians comes up. They are said to be low caste, which would shut them off from much. They claim to be no caste. One typical case decides many. The privileges of entire communities are at stake; the courts must decide, the missionaries must make up, present, and push the case. That may keep them in the courts for years. Anywhere in India the right of Christians to use the village well or fountain may be denied. But the government has declared the wells free to all. The missionary is impelled by kindly compassion to bring such a case before the collector.

In China and in Turkey or Persia officials are not strict observers of the laws. When they oppress the Christians the influence of the missionary is incessantly invoked to help his adherents. Natural sympathy for those in distress and the desire to see fair play have made some men allow most of their time for years to be consumed by such lawsuits, whose result, of whatever sort, was sure to be harmful to their spiritual work.

Another such connection with the local government often appears to work for good. From their superior education and ability missionaries are often appointed to some official position. Dr. Verbeck was for some time a state official of Japan. President Martin, of Peking, at the head of the Imperial College, was appointed by the government of China. Dr. Allen and Mrs. Bunker were the court physicians of the King and Queen of Korea. Dr. McKenzie at Tien-tsin was closely related to the Viceroy Li Hung Chang. Others have served for a time as diplomatic agents of the home government, like S. Wells Williams or Dr. Whitney, of Tokio. The appointment of such men to such positions often prepares the way for the Gospel and commends it to strangers.

Yet as a rule, contrasting the high calling of a simple missionary with any other position, one might say of some who turn aside from the mission to official work what Dr. Carey wrote regretfully of his son: "Felix has shrunk to an ambassador."

The general rule of the Church Missionary Society, as published among its regulations, is as follows: "Every missionary is strictly charged to abstain from interfering in the political affairs of the country or place in which he may be laboring;" "Never assume a position of hostility to the ruling powers;" "Stand aloof from all questions of political leadership and political partisanship;" "Tribute to whom tribute is due, custom to whom custom, fear to whom fear, honor to whom honor."

It is not strange, when one sees what a snare is spread in all dealings with magistrates and civil authorities, that many of those who are most consecrated and experienced should decide that the only safe plan for missionaries is that of silent abstention in all such matters. The best they can ask from any government is to be let alone, and regarded with friendly neutrality. The best they can do for the mission is to lean on no arm of flesh, invoke no aid of consul or magistrate, but rely on God and what He may do for His servants. They are not the foes of any people, they should not be the political engines of any government, nor should they make any government their engine.

Another complication of this question is the attitude toward missionaries sometimes adopted by ill-informed officials of the home governments. Such officials sometimes regard missionaries as pestiferous lunatics whose object in life is to get themselves into trouble with a view to disturbing the peace of officials abroad who are charged with the protection of their wandering fellow-countrymen. The ignorance which fosters such opinions may be gauged by perusal of the article in this book on **The International Service of Missions.** We cannot better close the discussion of these delicate problems than by the following suggestions prepared for this work by the veteran missionary and student of missions, Rev. James S. Dennis, D.D., which foreshadow, perhaps, opinions to be set forth in the third volume of his *Christian Missions and Social Progress:*

"We shall not undertake to call in question the fact that under exceptional circumstances, under the pressure of misunderstandings, or as the outcome of religious fanaticism, the entrance of Christianity into non-Christian lands has been unwelcome, and awakened more or less opposition. This is natural, perhaps inevitable, and historical precedents would lead us to expect it. It seems to be incidental to the propagation of Christianity, and yet so long as the missionary teacher is within recognized and acknowledged treaty rights, and does not transgress international agreements, he is not called upon to refrain from pursuing his calling by fear of diplomatic difficulties. So long also as his appeal is only to the reason and free moral nature of man, without attempting to exact an unwilling adherence by any expedient which forces the conscience, he is strictly within the bounds of that universal exercise of moral freedom which belongs to man as man. It is not in fairness or justice within the sovereign rights of any government, despotic or liberal, to exercise lordship over the conscience in the realm of religious freedom. That would be to usurp a power which belongs to God alone and which He has never delegated to human rulers. As a religious teacher of God's truth and God's law of righteous living, using only the moral instrumentalities of appeal and persuasion, the Christian missionary has the right of way the world over. Within his proper limitations he is unimpeachable as a moral force among men. The highest authority which mankind is called upon to acknowledge has commissioned him to discharge a duty which is *sui generis* in history. He may be hindered, opposed, persecuted and martyred, but his credentials are authoritative, and cannot be destroyed. He may be silenced temporarily, or banished for a time, but his opportunity is certain to come, and he is bound to avail himself of it.

"It becomes him under these exceptional conditions to discharge his duty with meekness, patience and tact, to exemplify in his own character and conduct the wisdom, gentleness and sincerity of the religion he teaches, and to seek only moral victory by legitimate spiritual means. Where the missionary service is rendered in this spirit it is rarely, if ever, offensive, and any possibility of disturbing goodwill is reduced to a minimum. In fact, the charge which has sometimes been made indiscriminately that missions are the cause of international alienation has been greatly exaggerated. There has been much misunderstanding on this point, and some considerable misrepresentation. The conspicuous illustration, of course, has been China, and on the basis of a false induction, a sweeping and railing accusation has been made against missions in general as a cause of trouble among the nations. While it is no doubt true that the political assumptions of Roman Catholic missions in China are offensive to the Chinese officials, yet it can be safely said that Christianity as exemplified in Protestant missions, exercising its simple and legitimate function as a teacher in the sphere of morals and religion, is guiltless in the matter of political meddling. In reference to the Boxer disturbance of 1900 in China, and other similar outbreaks which preceded it, it is sufficiently clear that the aversion of the Chinese to foreigners, and especially their resentment at foreign encroachments upon official prerogative, territorial integrity and native industries, are adequate explanations of the uprising, which has aimed at the foreigner of whatever class as an intruder, but chiefly in his official and commercial character rather than at the missionary as a religious teacher. In fact, the missionary, all things considered, has made it safer and more possible than it would otherwise have been for all foreigners to reside in China. Numerous friendly acts and proclamations by high officials of the empire, since the convulsions of 1900, have indicated a specially kindly feeling to missionaries. The Missionary Peace Commission of 1901 in Shansi is a remarkable evidence of the respect and consideration shown to missionaries by many Chinese officials since the troubles of 1900. The recent opening of Hunan province by the missionaries of the London Society has reclaimed in a measure an immense section of China to foreign residence, which will be a boon both to missions and commerce.

"At the Seventh Annual Conference of Foreign Mission Boards of the United States and Canada, held in New York City January, 1899, a report was presented embodying the results of a careful canvass of mission fields throughout the world as to the attitude of civil governments toward Christian missions and missionaries wherever they had been established. The report revealed the fact that almost the world over the attitude of local governments was friendly and helpful, with few signs of friction and opposition. In view of the many regrettable incidents in the contact of Western nations with Eastern peoples, and the objectionable personal example and conduct of many foreigners residing in the East, the outcome above indicated is especially significant and speaks much for the respect accredited to missions and their representatives."

GOVERNOR'S HARBOR: A station of the WMS in Eleuthera Island, Bahamas, with (1903) 1 missionary, 24 native workers, 4 preaching places, 1 day school, and 593 professing Christians.

GOVINDPUR: A village in Chota Nagpur, India, situated about 25 miles S. W. of Ranchi. Station of the Gossner Missionary Society, with (1900) 2 missionaries, 76 native workers, men and women; 37 preaching places, 2 day schools, 1 boarding school, 1 dispensary, and 8,722 professing Christians.

GRAAF REINET: A town in Cape Colony, S. Africa, situated in the district of the same name, 58 miles S. W. by S. of Middleburg, on a small plain nearly enclosed on one side by mountains, and on the other by a bend of the Sunday River. It is one of the oldest towns in the colony and is celebrated for its sulphur springs. Station of the SPG (St. James Parish), with (1900) 1 missionary and 1 native worker.

GRACEBAY: A mission station of the Moravians (1797) on the island of Antigua, West Indies, 6 miles west of Gracehill.

GRACEFIELD: A town on the northern coast of Antigua, West Indies. It is pleasantly situated close to the sea, the cool seabreeze making it one of the healthiest places on the island. Station of the Moravian Missions (1840), with (1900) 9 native workers and 134 communicants.

GRACEHILL: A town in Antigua, W. I., 8 miles E. S. E. of St. Johns. Station of the Moravian Missions (1774), with (1900) 1 missionary and his wife, 17 native workers, 2 schools, and 466 professing Christians.

GRAHAM'S HALL: A little village in British Guiana, situated on the Industry Plantation, 10 miles east of Georgetown. The population is composed chiefly of negroes from the Barbados and some East Indian coolies. Station and center of the Moravian Mission in Guiana (1878), with (1900) 35 native workers, 2 schools, and 395 professing Christians.

GRAHAMSTOWN: A town in Cape Colony, S. Africa, situated in the district of Albany, 55 miles W. S. W. of King William's Town on the railway to Kimberly and at an altitude of 1,800 feet. It is the most important city of the first plateau, with extensive woolen manufactures. It is the seat of an Anglican and a Roman Catholic Bishop. Station of the SPG (1861), with a missionary and a theological school. Station also of the South African Wesleyan Missionary Society, with (1900) 48 native workers,

18

4 preaching places, 3 day schools, and 492 professing Christians.

GRAN CHACO. See ARGENTINE REPUBLIC and SOUTH AMERICAN MISSIONARY SOCIETY.

GRAND CAYMAN: One of the Cayman Islands, West Indies, 176 miles northwest from the west end of Jamaica. The island is 17 miles long and 4 to 7 miles broad. Climate, tropical; population, 4,500, composed of English mulattoes and pure negroes; language, English; religion, Protestant. The United Free Church of Scotland has (1902) 2 stations on Grand Cayman, with 2 missionaries and 8 native workers, and 534 church members.

GRANT, Asahel, M.D.: Born at Marshall, N. Y., August 17, 1807; died April 24, 1844. Graduated in medicine at Pittsfield, Mass. Practised medicine at Baintrim, Pa., until the death of his wife. Appointed medical missionary of the ABCFM among the **Nestorians** in 1834. Arrived at Urmia, Persia, November 20, 1835. The medical skill of **Dr.** Grant was at once called into active exercise. Altho the ignorance and superstitions of the people hampered his efforts, he soon acquired great influence. Patients came from distant regions—from Mesopotamia or from the Caucasus; haughty Mohammedan mollahs kissed the hem of his garments; in his life in the wild mountain regions he was more than once indebted for his safety to recognition by some patient who had seen him in Urmia.

Dr. Grant's thrilling adventures among the Nestorians of the mountains made his name famous. His work there was broken up by the massacres of 1843. Two years later he died. His influence as a physician opened the way for his successors and his personal attractiveness won him friends who long mourned his early death.

GRASSMAN, Andrew: Born February 23, 1704, at Senftleben, Moravia; called "to the clearer light of the Gospel" through **Christian David** in 1725. Persecuted in Moravia, he, with others who sympathized with him, removed in 1728, under the leadership of Christian David, to Count Zinzendorf's estate at Berthelsdorf, afterward called Herrnhut. From 1731 till 1737, he, with some Moravian companions, traveled, learning successively the Swedish, Finnish and Russian languages, supporting themselves at their respective trades, and making known the Gospel, as opportunities offered, in parts of Germany, Sweden and Lapland. His attempt in 1738 to reach the Samoyedes in the Russian Empire led to his arrest and imprisonment for six months, followed by his expulsion from the country.

Mr. Grassman subsequently labored as a missionary in Greenland. He was made Bishop of the Moravian Church in 1756. He died March 25, 1783.

GREAT ABACO ISLAND: One of the northernmost islands of the Bahamas, with a population of 3,300. Circuit of the WMS, with (1903) 23 native workers, men and women; 7 preaching places, 5 Sunday schools and 450 professing Christians.

GREAT BASSA: A town and seaport in Liberia, W. Africa. Station of the PE (1853), with 4 native workers.

GREAT BATANGA: A settlement and district in the Kamerun Colony, W. Africa, situated S. of the Lokunje River in the S. W. part of the colony and 170 miles N. of the Gabun. In climate, the district is one of the healthiest and most agreeable on the coast, and German and English traders resort there. Station of the PN (1885), with (1903) 10 missionaries, men and women, one of whom is a physician; 15 native workers, men and women; 10 outstations, 10 day schools, 2 boarding schools (closed temporarily), 1 dispensary and 800 professing Christians.

GREAT SANGI ISLANDS. See SANGI ISLANDS.

GREBO LANGUAGE: Belongs to the negro class of African languages and is used in the regions inland from Liberia. It was reduced to writing by missionaries of the PE, and is written with Roman letters.

GRECO-TURKISH LANGUAGE: The Turkish language as written with Greek letters by Greeks of Asiatic Turkey.

GREECE: The Hellenic Kingdom embraces a territory of about 25,000 square miles, and has a population of (1896) 2,433,806, Greeks and Albanians. Scotland has the same extent of territory and almost twice as many people. As for wealth and natural resources, Greece is proverbially the poorest country in Europe.

Agriculture occupies the attention of the majority (seven-eighths) of the inhabitants. Only seven cities can boast of more than 10,000 people. Fifteen cities (from Athens, 114,355, to Missolonghi, 6,324) contain only 250,000 inhabitants, or about one-ninth of the whole population of Greece. Nearly ten per cent. are shepherds; as many are seafarers. There are 100,000 Albanians scattered about the kingdom. They began migrating southward over four hundred years ago, at the time of the Turkish conquest. These people, who still speak their unwritten language, have become largely Hellenized, yet are easily distinguished from the Greeks proper. They are found mainly in Attica, about Thebes, on the Isthmus of Corinth, throughout ancient Argolis, in the southern district of Euboea, and in a few neighboring islands.

The war of the revolution (1821-9) left Greece in a deplorable state. The Protocol of London declared her a kingdom under the protectorate of England, France and Russia. Prince Otto of Bavaria ascended the throne January 25, 1833. King George, son of the King of Denmark, succeeded King Otto in 1863. Under both these reigns the kingdom has seen slow but steady advancement. Under the present constitution (adopted October 29, 1864) the whole legislative power is vested in a single chamber of representatives, called the *Boulé*, and the executive power is in the hands of the king and his responsible ministry. The fact that only a fraction (2 millions out of 8 millions) of the Greek-speaking people in the Levant are included in the present kingdom of Greece keeps the ambitious little country continually in a restive condition, and the great powers have frequently been obliged forcibly to compel the Greeks to keep the peace. This restriction is received with bad grace by the people. An extension of the territory of the kingdom to the north (1881) only whetted its appetite for more. The island of Crete has been in a chronic state of unrest and now looks toward annexation to Greece at no distant day.

Athens has been the capital of "the Kingdom

of the Hellenes" since 1830, and has grown from a squalid Turkish village, clinging to the northern slope of the Acropolis, to a large, clean and beautiful city, with its palace and gardens, its fine hotels and boulevards, its cathedral and university, its art museums and its public schools. To the scholar and student of modern life it is one of the most interesting cities in the world. The city is a busy hive of educational institutions. The English Church and the Protestant Evangelical Greek Church are to the east of the Acropolis, near the ruins of the temple of Jupiter Olympus. The British and American schools for research in Greece are on the southern slope of Mount Lycabettus.

The *Boulé* meets November 1 (old style) every year, and the city thereafter presents a brilliant scene, in which the royal retinue, the deputies, the foreign ambassadors, the military classes, the church hierarchy, the throng of students from the whole Greek world, together with foreigners from every clime, make the modern city vie with its ancient self in picturesqueness and interest.

The inhabitants of the kingdom are mostly adherents of the **Greek Orthodox** Church.

The most encouraging thing about modern Greece is its splendid system of schools. There has never been a time when Greece has been absolutely destitute of educational facilities. Even during that long period of abject oppression under Turkish rule—which lasted from the opening of the 16th century until the war of independence, 1821-29—the rudiments of an education had been taught by the clergy of the Greek Orthodox Church. Even during the revolution schools were covertly carried on. When the country came out of this baptism of blood the national mind was roused as only a great struggle for freedom can rouse it, and efforts were immediately put forth to put its schools on a solid foundation. It was necessarily a most difficult undertaking. The country was bankrupt. At that critical hour in the nation's life the influence of English, French and American sympathizers was a large factor in starting the whole long and interesting development of educational affairs in Greece. American influence was felt especially in two directions—the study of the Bible in all Greek public schools, and the education of the girls of Greece. Two more fundamental results *could* not have been attained, and from all appearances these *would* not have been attained but for American impetus. Since 1863 educational affairs have moved on faster than ever. Teaching has become a regular profession, and the old age of teachers is provided for by a judicious pension system, regulated by the term of service. More than half the teachers in the elementary schools are women—a remarkable fact when we consider that through the centuries of Turkish oppression the education of woman was almost entirely neglected. One of the most interesting institutions in Athens is the "Arsakeion," a girls' school, named from its founder, M. Arsakes, a wealthy merchant, originally from Epirus. It was the result of the American idea fostered by Dr. and Mrs. Hill. To-day it is by far the finest girls' school in Greece. The institution is graded carefully up from the kindergarten to the normal department, taking a girl from the age of four or five up to eighteen or twenty. It is a custom for far-away villages to select their brightest girls, collect money for their expenses, and send them to the Arsakeion, that they may have efficient teachers for their village girls. Since its start this school has scattered more than 2,500 graduates over Greece and Greek-speaking lands, and most of them teach.

The list of private benevolences for educational purposes might be indefinitely increased. In proportion to her size, population, and wealth, the little Hellenic kingdom surpasses even openhanded America in this point.

Mission Work: When the struggle for independence called the attention of the civilized world to Greece, Christian work was begun in the land by various churches of America. The CMS had already sent missionaries in 1815, their operations being mainly confined to the Ionian Islands.

The PE sent out Rev. J. J. Robertson in 1828 to see whether Greece presented an encouraging field for the efforts of this Church.

This mission was reenforced in 1830 by the arrival of Rev. Dr. and Mrs. **Hill**. They went first to the island Tenos, where they spent six months; then removed to Athens, the scene of their long and successful educational work, carried on in the spirit of the instructions given, with a careful avoidance of anything that might look like a wish to proselyte from the Greek Church.

In 1828 Rev. **Jonas King** of the ABCFM, whose previous sojourn in Jerusalem and Smyrna had given him an opportunity to acquire some knowledge of the modern Greek, and also awakened a deep interest in their spiritual condition, was chosen by a committee of ladies in New York to take charge of supplies for the physical wants of the impoverished Greeks. His knowledge of the language enabled him at once to do something to meet their still deeper spiritual wants, and he was permitted to remain, supported by these ladies, till 1831, when the American Board decided to enter Greece as a mission field, and Mr. King was transferred to its service and removed from Tenos, where he, too, like Dr. Hill, had begun his work, to Athens, where he established schools of a high grade for boys, held preaching services, and also devoted much time to the preparation of religious literature, for which he was particularly fitted by his great and varied attainments as a Christian scholar. In 1834 Dr. and Mrs. **Elias Riggs** opened a school at Argos, and were subsequently joined by Mr. Benjamin. This station was given up in 1837, Mr. Riggs going to Smyrna.

About this time (1837) the Rev. S. Houston and Rev. G. W. Leyburn of Virginia, also in connection with the American Board, went to Areopolis, in Laconia, in response to an earnest invitation of Pietro Bey Mavromihalis. They soon had two schools for boys in successful operation, in one of which the Rev. M. D. Kalopothakes, now so long associated with evangelistic work for his countrymen, received his earliest religious impressions.

The Baptists also began a mission under Mr. Buel and Mr. Arnold.

A printing establishment had been founded by the ABCFM at Malta, where publications in the various languages of the East were printed. Very soon there was a much greater demand for those in Greek than in any other language. In 1830 the Rev. Mr. Temple, who was in charge of this department of the work, reported that the previous year the press had been employed wholly on modern Greek, to the amount of 4,670,000 pages, chiefly schoolbooks. The demand for books was such that they rarely accumulated on the shelves.

Those were years of hope for all who were looking for the renovation of the Greek Church, both clergy and people seeming gratefully to appreciate the advantages extended to the community. But soon a change came. The missionary enterprise began to be regarded with suspicion through the gross misrepresentations of the Greek press, both as to the motives and practises of foreigners. There is every reason to believe that this was brought about by outside intrigues, working through individuals here who found it for their interest to appear very zealous for the "faith of the fathers."

Through the same influence a change in the constitution was effected, restricting the full religious liberty which was granted by the first constitution to toleration of recognized religions, but forbidding proselytism. The American Board withdrew all its representatives except Dr. King, who was unwilling to go. The Baptist missionaries also returned after a time to America.

In 1890-1900 a new movement appeared for the better instruction of the clergy and for the circulation of the Scriptures in the vernacular, the ancient Greek being unintelligible to the common people. This movement had the support and sanction of the Metropolitan of Athens and promised permanent and valuable results. But now, as at the beginning of the independence of Greece, a conservative and ignorant party aroused the people against the movement to translate the Bible into modern Greek. There were riots in Athens, and in the end the clamor was only appeased by the stoppage of Bible work and the expulsion from office of the Metropolitan and the Prime Minister supposed to be responsible.

After the Americans withdrew, about 1863, the native element became prominent. Dr. Kalopothakes, Rev. G. Constantine and Rev. D. Sakellarios worked for some years together under the American and Foreign Christian Union. Later there were distinct organizations. The Baptists were represented by Mr. Sakellarios. The Congregationalists sustained Mr. Constantine, who, besides preaching, did much valuable work through the press.

The organization known distinctively as the Greek Evangelical Church was under the care of the Southern Presbyterian Church during the thirteen years previous to 1886.

At the close of 1885 the Evangelical Native Church withdrew its connection with the Southern Presbyterian Church and became independent.

Since that time there has been no "mission work," so called, in Greece, except the primary school for poor children founded by the late Mrs. Hill, sustained by the Protestant Episcopal Church of the United States.

There is a school for the better classes—in a certain sense a continuation of Mrs. Hill's work—on the same premises—under the efficient direction of her niece, Miss Masson.

The Rev. Mr. Sakellarios, too, continued until his death independently the work he formerly carried on under the Baptist Missionary Union of the United States. So also with the work of the native Greek Evangelical Church with which Dr. Kalopothakes is connected. This work, even when under the mission, differed to a considerable extent from other missions in the fact that it was inaugurated and carried on for many years through native instrumentalities, so that the native element had a training from the first calculated to develop the capacity of the church for active forms of service and for responsibility, and through this an inclination to independence of action which was bound speedily to lead to self-support.

The Greek Evangelical Church is Presbyterian in doctrine and form of government. A local synod has been organized called the "Synod of the Free Evangelical Church in Greece." It has under its care the Bible work of the British and Foreign Bible Society. The colporteurs employed are all Christians who are able to do an important evangelistic work in connection with their sales of the Scriptures. The Εφημερίς τῶν Παιδῶν, a monthly paper for children edited by Dr. Kalopothakes, is now in its twenty-fourth year and has an annual circulation of about 7,000 copies. The *Star of the East*, the weekly paper, was discontinued at the close of 1885.

Through the kindly assistance of the Religious Tract Society of London thousands of tracts are printed and circulated yearly. The work of the American Bible Society was for more than 25 years under Dr. Kalopothakes' care, and on its withdrawal from Greece in 1886, the agency of the British and Foreign Bible Society being entrusted to him, the same assistance to the work and moral support comes through it.

Tuckerman (C. K.), *The Greeks of To-day*, London and New York, 1873; Bent (J. T.), *Modern Life and Thought amongst the Greeks*, London, 1891; Guerber (H. A.), *The Story of the Greeks*, London, 1898.

GREEK CHURCH: Several names and titles are used by writers who mention this church: *e. g.*, The Greek Orthodox Church, The Eastern Church, The Orthodox Imperial Church, The Greek Catholic Church and The Orthodox Eastern Church of Christ. The name and title preferred by the Greeks themselves and claimed by them as the most correct is "The Holy Catholic and Apostolic Orthodox Church of the East," (Ἡ Ἁγία Καθολικὴ καὶ Ἀποστολικὴ Ὀρθόδοξος Ἐκκλησία τῆς Ἀνατολῆς).

Adherents: It claims as its adherents those who accept and abide by the decisions of the first seven ecumenical councils, viz.: Nice, 1st, 325, and 7th, 787; Constantinople 2d, 381, 5th, 553, 6th, 680; Ephesus 3d, 431; Chalcedon 4th, 451. It represents the state religion of Greece, Russia, Bulgaria, Servia and Rumania, and of the larger part of the Greek and Slavic people in Turkey and other parts of the world. Its numerical strength is estimated at a little less than 100,000,000 souls. These, in round numbers, are distributed as follows: In Greece, 2,400,000; in Turkey, 5,000,000; in other parts of Asia, 4,000,000; in Africa, 3,000,000; America, 50,000; Bulgaria, 2,000,000; Servia, 2,000,000; Montenegro, 290,000; Rumania, 4,800,000; Austria-Hungary, 3,100,000; Russia, 73,300,000.

History: The claim of the Greeks, that this is the oldest Christian Church, is founded on the facts (a) that they are the heirs of the original Greek Empire of Byzantium or Constantinople; (b) that they still use in their worship the Greek of the Apostles and the liturgy of the early Fathers; (c) that the Greek Fathers were in the majority at the first seven ecumenical councils (of the 318 Bishops at the first council 310 were from the East), the decisions made and the doctrines established being largely colored by Greek philosophy and Greek thought, and finally (d) that their church history begins in the Passion week, or "The Great Week," of our Lord's life. The Syrian Church claims the precedence because (Acts xi: 26) "The disciples were called Christians first at Antioch." But the Greeks point to John xii: 20, 23: "There were certain Greeks among them, that came up to worship," and to the Master's words: "The hour is come that the Son of man should be glorified."

It is fair to state that the Armenian Church makes the claim (which the Greeks dispute) that these so-called Greeks were Armenians sent from their King Abgar and that under the preaching of the Apostles Thaddæus and Bartholomew they were the first to accept Christianity as a nation. Greek tradition tells us that the earthquake at the time of the Crucifixion was felt in Athens and that Dionysius the Areopagite exclaimed: "Either God suffers or the universe is being destroyed," and that thus he and certain others were prepared for the preaching of Paul.

The political and organic history of the Greek Church begins with the conversion of Constantine, 312 A. D. This was followed by the cessation of persecution and the establishment of Christianity as the state religion. A more perfect organization was secured by the council of Nicea in 325. In this year also was begun the Cathedral Church of St. Sophia, and the founding of the first Christian city, "New Rome," or Constantinople, dedicated "To the service of Christ" May 11, 330. The natural jealousy of Rome, the former imperial city, and the rivalry springing up between the two cities, created parties not only in political but in religious life as well.

The Bishop of Rome was not ready to yield precedence to the Bishop of Constantinople, or even to acknowledge the latter's equality with himself. Decisions of various councils in regard to this matter were acceptable to neither party. (The Council of Constantinople in 381 declared that the Bishop of New Rome should be inferior only to that of Old Rome.) Seventy years later, the equality of the two was decreed at Chalcedon.

In the latter part of the 6th century the Patriarch of Constantinople claimed precedence over all Christian Churches, but in 606 the Emperor Phocas gave this honor to Boniface of Rome. Minor differences in customs and in forms of theological statement were enlarged as the centuries moved on. There were endless controversies as to methods and times of fasting, the administration of the Sacraments and the procession of the Holy Spirit. While the Latins declared that the Holy Ghost proceeds from Father and the Son, the Greeks claimed that the procession was from Father alone. Pope Leo III., at the Council of Aix-la-Chapelle in 809, approved of the expression "*Filioque*" (and from the Son) and soon after, in order to give greater authority, the canons of the great Council of Constantinople were falsified by the interpolation of the disputed clause. This was deemed by the Easterns the great sin of the Western Church and has never been forgiven.

As the Greek Empire decreased in power and renown, the power of the Papacy became more deeply rooted, and when the Pope of Rome, aiming at universal supremacy, began to interfere indirectly with the affairs of the East, and Michael Cerularius, Patriarch of Constantinople, protested, papal legates visited Constantinople and on the 16th day of June, 1054, repairing to the great church of St. Sophia, they there in the name of the Pope excommunicated the Patriarch and all his adherents. "After pronouncing this dread anathema, they placed their sentence on the High Altar of the Church, and shaking the dust off their feet they left the city."

The separate histories of the Eastern and Western Churches may properly begin at this date—June 16, 1054.

The great missionary work of the Greek church began in 861, when the brothers Cyril and Methodius went from Thessalonica to Bulgaria. The Slavic alphabet and literature, and the Bible in the vernacular, are the result of their work. Thus the way was opened for the evangelization and instruction of the Servians and Rumanians, and in due time of the Russians also. The conversion of the Russians, following the visit to St. Sophia of the envoys sent by Vladimir; the baptism of Czar and people in the Dnieper at Kief; the building there of the first Christian Church and the marriage of Anne, sister of the Emperor Basil, to Vladimir the Czar took place in 988. Kief remained the metropolitan city until its destruction by the Mongols in 1240, when the see was removed to Vladimir and afterward transferred to Moscow.

Church Government: The government of the Greek Church is Episcopal, with orders of Patriarch, Bishops, Priests, Deacons, Sub-deacons, etc. In the Turkish Empire it is divided into four metropolitan sees—Constantinople, Alexandria, Antioch and Jerusalem. Each of these is presided over by a Patriarch. All have equal rights, but special honor is conceded to the Patriarch of Constantinople. The latter presides over the "Grand Synod," which is made up of the Bishops of the surrounding provinces. It is theirs to elect or rather nominate the Patriarchs. The full election waits upon the approval and confirmation of His Majesty the Sultan. He recognizes the Patriarch of Constantinople as the responsible head of the Church and the medium of communication between the sovereign and the Greek people.

In Greece the supreme authority of the Church is the Synod at Athens, which consists of five clerical and two lay members. Their former dependence upon the Patriarch of Constantinople ceased in 1833, tho a few external rites and honors (the preparation of the anointing oil, etc.) are still reserved to that prelate. For six centuries the Russian Church was dependent on the Patriarchate of Constantinople and was governed by Metropolitans, some of them Greeks sent directly from the Patriarch, others Russians elevated to the office. Even up to the middle of the 17th century the Patriarch or Primate of Moscow had to have his appointment confirmed by the Patriarch of Constantinople. Peter the Great in 1712 curtailed the authority of the Primate of Moscow and substituted that of the "Holy Synod," over which the influence of the Czar is supreme. Thus the Czar became head of the Church as well as of the state in Russia. Without the presence of the procurator of the Czar the "Holy Synod" can hold no meetings nor are their decisions valid without his consent. In Rumania the government of the Church rests with two Archbishops, the first of them styled the Primate of Rumania, the second the Archbishop of Moldavia. There are, besides, six Bishops of the national Church. In Servia, the Church is governed by the Synod of Bishops, all the ecclesiastical officials being under the control of the Minister of Education and Public Worship. The Greek Church of Bulgaria was dependent upon the Patriarch of Constantinople until April, 1870, when the various Bulgarian sees were united under one chief bishop known as the Bulgarian Exarch.

Church Buildings and Services: The Eastern hierarchy resembles the Jewish type, and the Eastern church building is a reminder of the Jewish temple. It has three divisions: (1) The Holy Place; (2) The Body of the Church, and (3) the Narthex or Porch. Above the latter is the latticed apartment for the women. The narthex was originally set apart for catechumens or for penitents under discipline and the body of the church for the congregation. The Holy Place, separated by the screen of wood or marble covered with pictures, is for the priests and their attendants and for preparation of the bread and wine upon the "Holy Table." The church building must invariably stand east and west. The entrance is always at the west, so that the worshipers may face the east. The schoolboy who (not in a Sunday school but in the ordinary primary school) is taught the mystical meaning of all parts of the church building, and of each portion of the priest's dress, tells us that "the worshiper thus turns his back upon the deeds of darkness and his face toward the Sun of Righteousness who is to arise with healing in His wings."

The Greek Church lays stress on its acceptance of the first seven ecumenical Councils, and on its doctrine that the Sacraments of the New Testament are seven, the Jewish symbol for completeness. The seven sacraments are: Baptism, The Lord's Supper, Chrism, Confession, Ordination, Marriage, and the Anointing of the Sick. She believes in baptismal regeneration and at baptism receives each child into full church membership. She uses candles and incense in worship; she rejects images, but adores pictures. The worshiper himself kisses the picture of the saint and lights a candle before the shrine. Such pictures are found not only in the churches, but in the homes of the people, in hotels and in ships at sea. Baptism is by three-fold immersion. Leavened bread is used in the Communion, and the laity partake of the cup also. She allows her priests to be married before ordination, but never after. Celibacy is limited to Bishops and monks. The clergy are not allowed to shave or to have the hair cut after entering sacred orders.

The liturgy of St. Chrysostom (an abridgment of that of St. Basil) is used each Lord's day. Instrumental music is not allowed. The music is by a double choir of boys and men. Preaching has not been common excepting in Lent, but it is becoming more frequent in certain localities. After the exaltation of the Host, and the sacred procession about the church, the people are invited to the Communion at each service, but this invitation is rarely accepted, excepting after the three longer fasts of the Church, viz.: at Christmas, Easter, and the Fast of the Sleep of the Virgin, in August.

In addition to the three longer fasts every Wednesday and Friday are fasting days, and there are other special fasts, in all over 200 days during the year. In fasting the rule is to abstain from all animal food, including eggs, milk, butter and cheese. On certain special days fish is allowed.

The Greek calendar still follows the old style, and was during the 19th century 12 days, and since 1900 (which in the Orient was regarded as Leap Year), 13 days behind the new style introduced by Gregory XIII.

Schaff (P.), *History of the Creeds of Christendom*, New York; Ricault (P.), *The Present State of the Greek and Armenian Churches*, London, 1679; Neale, *History of the Holy Eastern Church*, London, 1848; Neale, *Paraclete of Antioch*, London, 1873; Palmer (W.), *Dissertations Relating to the Oriental or Eastern Catholic Communion*, London, 1853; Clark (E. L.), *The Races of European Turkey*, New York, 1878; Grosvenor (E. A.), *Constantinople*, Boston, 1895; Dwight (H. O.), *Constantinople and Its Problems*, New York, 1900; *The Churches of Christendom* (St. Giles Lectures), Edinburgh, 1884; Stanley, *History of the Eastern Church*, London and New York, 1884; Hore (Canon), *Eighteen Centuries of the Orthodox Greek Church*, London, 1899; Tozier, *Church in the Eastern Empire*, London, 1888; *Reply of the Holy Catholic and Apostolic Church of the East to the Encyclical of Pope Leo XIII. on reunion*, Constantinople, 1895 (Published in Greek and English).

GREEN, Samuel H.: Born Worcester, Mass., October 10, 1822; practised medicine for a while in Worcester; sailed for Ceylon as a medical missionary of the ABCFM April 20, 1847; returned home on account of ill health in 1873. He continued the preparation of medical works in the Tamil language. Several standard volumes were prepared by him, covering in all between three and four thousand pages, and are used as text-books in India. Dr. Green's name stands a household word among the people of the island to whose interest he devoted his life. He died at Worcester, May 28, 1884.

GREENBAY: A settlement on the island of Antigua, W. I., near St. John's. After the emancipation of the slaves in Antigua, the idle, the vicious and immoral gathered here and made the place notorious for vile deeds of every description. The Moravians in 1848 opened a preaching place, with such success that in a short time the character of the people changed completely. At present (1901) there are 14 native workers, men and women, with 2 preaching places, 1 school and 413 communicants.

GREENLAND: An extensive region, including 46,740 square miles, belonging to Denmark, lying northeast of North America, from which and its outlying islands it is separated by Davis' Strait and Baffin's Bay. Cape Farewell, its southern extremity, is a point on a small island from which the east coast extends northeast toward Cape Brewster, where it takes a more northerly course, and stretches toward the Pole to an unknown distance. The southern part of this coast is rugged and barren, with cliffs and precipices visible far out at sea. The climate is very healthful, the temperature varying according to the distance from the Pole. Fogs are prevalent most of the year, and but little rain falls. The population, except about 300 Danes, consists entirely of Eskimos who live by hunting and fishing, and number 11,895 (1901). A few live on the east coast, where is the only mission station to heathen Eskimos. All the villages and settlements are on the west side, upon the lowlands along the fiords. Greenland is divided for administrative purposes into two inspectorates, North and South Greenland, each subdivided into seven districts, having a director who is assisted by a parliament chosen from the principal men. The crown of Denmark has a monopoly of the trade, which is carried on under the direction of the Greenland Trading Company. After years of discouraging efforts on the part of missionaries, all the natives have been converted to Christianity. The religious instruction of the people is in the hands of the Church of Denmark. In 1900 the Moravians, who had several stations in Greenland, withdrew, considering their work was done. The Eskimos have given up their nomadic habits and enjoy the benefits of civilization, while they are afflicted with fewer of its vices than are the Indians who have come into contact with the white man elsewhere. Liquor is prohibited in all the settlements.

GREENVILLE: A town in Liberia, W. Africa, situated on the Sinoe River near its mouth, and included in Sinoe in missionary reports. Station of the PE (1853), with (1901) 5 native workers and 57 communicants. Also station of ME, with (1902) 1 missionary and his wife, 15 native workers, 10 outstations, 8 preaching places, 1 industrial school, and 462 professing Christians.

GRIFFITHS, Davis: Born December 20, 1792, at Glanmeilwch, Carmarthenshire, Wales; educated at Wrexham and Gosport; sailed as missionary of the LMS for Madagascar, October 25, 1820. He made the first translation of the whole Bible into the Malagasy language, assisted by Mr. David Jones. In 1834 his connection with the Society was dissolved, and he returned to England. Returning afterward to Madagascar, he settled at Antananarivo for purposes of trade, but made great efforts to assist the persecuted Christians. Returning to England in 1842, he became pastor at Welsh Hay. He published *History of Madagascar* in Welsh, revised the Malagasy version of the Bible, and prepared numerous works in the Malagasy language. He died at Machynlleth, March 21, 1863.

GROOT CHATILLON: A settlement in Dutch Guiana, S. America; situated on the Surinam River, about 12 miles S. of Paramaribo. Station of the Moravian Missions, with 4 missionaries, men and women; 1 native worker, 2 preaching places, 1 school and a leper asylum known as "Bethesda."

GROOT SANGIR ISLANDS. See SANGIR ISLANDS.

GUADALAJARA: A town in Mexico, the second in importance of the republic, and capital of the State of Jalisco; situated on the Santiago River 120 miles S. S. W. of Zacatecas, and at an altitude of 5,000 feet. It was founded in 1542, and has many churches and convents, a university, a mint, and an academy of painting. Population (1900), 101,208. Station of the ABCFM (1882), with (1902) 6 missionaries, men and women; 4 native workers, 5 outstations, 1 girls' boarding school, 1 theological seminary and training school. Station also of the International Medical Association (Seventh Day Advent), with 3 missionaries, 1 dispensary, and 1 hospital. Station also of the MES (1884), with (1901) 5 missionaries, men and women, and 1 native worker.

GUADALCANAR ISLAND. See SOLOMON ISLANDS.

GUAM, or GUAHAN: An island of the Ladrone or Marianne group, in the Pacific Ocean, N. of the Caroline Islands. It is the largest island in the group and was ceded to the United States by Spain in 1898. It is about 32 miles long, contains about 200 square miles, and is surrounded by coral reefs. It is thickly wooded, well watered, and fertile in soil. The population (1903) is estimated at about 9,000, two-thirds of the whole number living in Agania, the capital. They are mostly immigrants from the Philippines. Spanish is the official language and Roman Catholicism the religion. The first Christian mission on the island was established by Luis Sanoitores, a Jesuit, in 1668. The ABCFM established a mission in Guam in 1900. It now has a station at La Punta, near Agania, with 1 missionary and his wife, 1 day school, 1 boarding and industrial school, and 61 professing Christians, of whom 30 are communicants.

GUANAJAY: A town in the island of Cuba, W. I., situated about 22 miles S. W. of Havana. Population, 9,500. Mission station of the MES.

GUANAJUATO: A town in Central Mexico, 160 miles northwest of Mexico City. A pleasant city, built on both sides of a narrow defile in the mountains at an altitude of 6,500 feet. It lies in a rich mining district, and has a population (1900) of 41,486. Station of the ME, with (1902) 1 missionary and his wife, 2 women missionaries, 11 native workers, men and women; 2 preaching places, 2 day schools, 1 dispensary, 1 hospital, and 314 professing evangelical Christians.

GUANTANAMO: A town in Cuba, W. I., situated 40 miles east of Santiago, in a very productive region of sugar estates. Population, about 24,000. Station of the American Baptist Home Missionary Society (1899), with 1 missionary and his wife.

GUARANI LANGUAGE: Belongs to the South American family of languages, and is spoken by the native population (mixed blood) of Paraguay. It is written with Roman letters.

GUATEMALA: A republic of Central America, bounded on the north by Yucatan, east by British Honduras, the Bay of Honduras, and the republics of Honduras and San Salvador; south by the Pacific, and west by the Mexican State of Chiapas. Its greatest length, from northeast to southwest, is 325 miles, its greatest breadth about 300 miles; area, about 48,800 square miles. Climate, excessively hot in the low, and cool in the high, regions, is generally healthful. The soil is exceedingly fertile, but poorly cultivated. Population (1900),1,647,300; about sixty per cent. are pure Indians, very few descendants of Europeans, and the rest mestizos, a mixture of Spanish and Indian blood. The Indians live mostly by themselves, and the civil authorities immediately governing them are chosen from their own race. Indolence and licentiousness are the besetting vices of all the people. Language, Spanish; religion, Roman Catholic, but all other creeds have liberty of worship. The government is republican; the legislative power is vested in a congress, and the executive is a president, assisted by three ministers, elected for four years. The capital is Guatemala, by far the finest city in Central America, situated in a picturesque plateau in the southwest part of the republic. The missionary societies operating in Guatemala are the PN, with 2 stations, and the Central American Mission, with 1 station. The ABS also has an agency at Guatemala city.

Brigham (T.), *Guatemala*, New York and London, 1887; Sapper (K.), *Mittelamerikanische Reisen und Studien*, Braunschweig, 1902; *Missionary Review of the World*, Vol. XIV., p. 168, New York, 1901.

GUATEMALA LA NUEVA: Capital of Guatemala, Central America, situated at an altitude of 4,850 feet in the southern part of the country, 50 miles from the Pacific and 150 from the Bay of Honduras. The climate is very healthful. Population (1898), 74,000, of whom five-sixths are of European origin. The houses are rather low and squalid looking, being constructed with a view to escaping damage from earthquakes. Station of the PN (1882), with 1 missionary and his wife. Station also of the Central America Mission (1899), with 6 missionaries, men and women. Agency of the American Bible Society.

GUAYAQUIL: A seaport in Ecuador, S. America; capital of the province of Guayas, situated on the right bank of the Guayas River, 35 miles above its mouth, and 165 miles S. W. by S. of Quito. Population, 51,000, of whom about 5,000 are foreigners, the most of the remainder Indians and half-breeds. Station of the Gospel Missionary Union (1896) and of the PB.

GUAYMAS: A seaport of Mexico, situated on the Gulf of California, 275 miles W. of Chihuahua. It is connected by railroad with the United States railroad system. Population, about 7,000. Station of the MES, with 1 missionary and his wife and 1 native worker.

GUBBI: A town in Mysore, India, situated 50 miles N. W. of Bangalore. Population, 4,000. Station of the WMS, with (1903) 1 missionary and 66 native workers.

GUDUR: A town in the district of Nellore, Madras, India, situated 24 miles S. W. of the town of Nellore. Population, about 5,000. Station of the Hermannsburg Mission, with (1902) 1 missionary and his wife, 10 native workers, men and women; 1 preaching place, 3 outstations, 4 schools and 296 professing Christians.

GUIANA: An extensive territory on the northeast coast of South America, bounded on the north by the Atlantic, on the east and south by Brazil, and on the west by Brazil and Venezuela. The country slopes from the south, where the mountains reach an altitude of 7,000 feet, to the lowlands of the north. Six large rivers, whose general trend is north, drain the country. In the lowlands the hot climate is tempered by the easterly breezes, which blow all the year. Terrific thunderstorms often occur, and at times earthquake shocks may be felt. The fertility of the soil is unsurpassed in South America.

The three Guianas are the only European colonies on the Continent, and combined they are not larger than Wyoming and Colorado.

1. *British Guiana,* formally ceded to Great Britain in 1814, is the largest of the three colonies, and includes the settlements of Demerara, Essequibo, and Berbice, named from the three rivers. It extends from 9° to 1° north latitude, and from 57° to 52° north longitude, including an area of 109,000 square miles. The government is administered by a governor, assisted by a court of policy. There are over 150,000 acres under cultivation, half of which is devoted to the raising of sugar. Population (1891), 278,477, composed of negroes, mulattoes, East Indians, and Chinese. For many years Chinese immigrants were brought to work on the sugar plantations, but about 1870 all organized importation was discontinued, and there are now only about 4,000 Chinese in the colony. Of East Indians there are 115,463. There are 159 schools which receive government grants, with 21,384 pupils. Georgetown is the capital and principal city.

Mission work in British Guiana is carried on by the Moravian Brethren, the National Baptist Convention, the LMS, the SPG, the SDA, and the PB.

2. *French Guiana (Cayenne)* was acquired by France in 1626, and includes an area of 46,850 square miles. It is by far the hottest of the three colonies, is poorly cultivated, and its trade is very insignificant. Cayenne is the capital and largest city. This is the only country in South America untouched by Protestant missions. Its total population is about 35,000.

3. *Dutch Guiana (Surinam)* is separated from French Guiana on the east by the river Marowijne, and on the west from British Guiana by the river Corantyn. It was first acquired by the Netherlands in 1667 in exchange for New Netherlands in N. America, and was finally surrendered to its possession by the peace of Paris, 1815. The area is 46,060 square miles, much of it consisting of flat and swampy land, while the high mountains are found toward the south. The population is (1900) 68,968, exclusive of the negroes living in the forests, engaged principally in agriculture. Sugar is the principal product. Paramaribo is the capital. The government is in the hands of a governor and the council, who are nominated by the queen. Entire liberty is accorded to the members of all religious confessions, and in 1902 there were the following connections: Reformed and Lutheran church members, 9,584; Moravian Brethren, 28,027; Roman Catholics, 12,771; Jews, 1,100; Hindus, 11,158; Mohammedans, 3,918. Mission work in Surinam is carried on by the Moravian Brethren (1735).

GUINEA: Name formerly applied to much of the western coast of Africa south of the Gambia River. It is now commonly applied to Portuguese Guinea lying adjacent to Senegambia, and to French Guinea south of the former and north of Sierra Leone.

Portuguese Guinea: A colony of Portugal, is on the coast, entirely surrounded on the land sides by French territory. It has an area of only 4,440 square miles, and a population of 820,000 (estimated). It includes the Bissagos Islands off the coast. The chief port is Bissao, or Bissau.

French Guinea: A colony of France on the western coast of Africa, detached from the colony of Senegal in 1890, and organized as a colony in 1893. It has an area of about 95,000 square miles, and an estimated population of 2,200,000. It extends from Portuguese Guinea on the north to Sierra Leone and Liberia on the south, and is bounded on the east by the French dependencies behind Senegal and the Ivory Coast. The coast is low and unhealthful.

GUJARAT: A region in Bombay, India. The name does not refer to any political division of the Bombay Presidency, but rather to the area within which the Gujarati language is the ordinary vernacular of the Hindu inhabitants. This region is composed in part of districts belonging to the Bombay Presidency, and in part of the territories of many different native states. It lies along the shore of the Indian Ocean, at its northeastern angle, and between the coast and the Western Ghats, which stretch along about 30 miles from the sea, north and south. On the south it reaches to latitude 20° north, some 70 miles north of Bombay; its most northern point, where it touches Rajputana, is in latitude 24°

45'. It includes the peninsula of Kathiawar, Kachchh, the native states of Baroda, Cambay, those of Mahi Kantha, Rewa Kantha, and Palanpur, and several other inferior chieftainships. It also includes five districts of the Bombay Presidency, which contain together a population of 3,000,000. The total area, including feudatory states, is 70,038 square miles, and the total population about 10,000,000. The city of Surat is one of the oldest missionary stations in India; it was occupied by missionaries of the London Missionary Society as early as 1815. In 1846 the mission was transferred to the Irish Presbyterians, who now have 10 stations in that district. The ME and the CA have latterly established stations in this region also.

Jeffrey (Rev. R.), *Fifty Years' Work in Kathiawar and Gujarat*, London.

GUJARATI LANGUAGE: Belongs to the Indic branch of the Aryan family of languages, and is spoken by some 9,000,000 people in the northern part of the province of Bombay, India. It is near of kin to the Hindi, and is written with the Devanagari letters, or with its own peculiar letters derived from Devanagari.

GUJRANWALA: A town in the Punjab, India, 40 miles north of Lahore, in a dead level plain which lacks natural drainage. Climate, cool, with frost in winter, extremely hot in summer. Population (1891), 26,800, of whom 14,000 are Mohammedans and 9,000 Hindus. It is the birthplace of Runjit Singh, the organizer of Sikh nationality. Station of the UP (1863), with (1903) 8 missionaries, men and women; 25 native workers, men and women; 21 day schools, 3 boarding schools, 1 orphanage and industrial school, and about 500 professed Christians. Station also of the PS, which, in 1902, voted to withdraw from the place, but the local presbytery has not agreed to this course.

GUJRAT: A town in the Punjab, North India, between the rivers Chenab and Jhelum, 70 miles north of Lahore. Climate, unusually changeable, subject to very severe extremes of temperature. The place has abundant water and good sanitation. It is noted for its brassware and inlaid metal work. Population (1891), 18,100, of whom 12,700 are Mohammedans. Station of the Church of Scotland Foreign Mission Committee (1865) and of the Church of Scotland Woman's Association for Foreign Missions (1877), with a hospital, dispensary, orphanage, and 17 missionaries, men and women.

GULBARGA. See KULBARGA.

GULEDGUDD: A town in the Bombay Presidency, India, situated 53 miles south of Bijapur. Population, 15,500, of whom 13,600 are Hindus. Station of the Basel Missionary Society (1851), with (1903) 4 missionaries, 1 missionary's wife, 21 native workers, men and women; 4 outstations, 6 day schools, and 668 professed Christians.

GULICK, Luther Halsey, M. D.: Born June 10, 1828; died April 8, 1891. His parents were missionaries in Hawaii when the subject of this sketch was born, and his boyhood days were spent at Koloa, with a year at school in Honolulu. Then came the trip to the United States, the country chosen by his parents for better educational advantages. In 1847 he entered the New York College of Physicians and Surgeons, and each Sunday found him engaged in city mission work. In 1851 the Hawaiian Missionary Society was formed as auxiliary to the American Board; and Mr. Gulick learned that a mission to one of the Micronesian Islands had been projected, and that the Hawaiian Island Mission was to act upon it the following May. He immediately offered himself to the American Board, and the intervening months were spent in hospital practise in New York City, in further study of Greek and Hebrew, and in attendance upon lectures. On October 29, 1851, Dr. Gulick was married to Miss Louisa Lewis, and on November 18 they sailed from Boston to the islands of Micronesia. On their way out they spent several days at Hawaii, and on September 6, 1852, they reached the island of Ponape, the largest of forty-eight islands which form the Caroline group, and the one by which all Micronesia had been judged. Dr. Gulick's labors were multiform. He was at once physician, carpenter, student, cook, shoemaker, dressmaker, and preacher. In 1854 he was stricken with smallpox, an epidemic of which raged through half the year. As soon as he recovered he journeyed, preached and translated for his prostrate people as never before; and they, with renewed zeal, began their reading, writing, and Bible work. A year later Dr. Gulick helped to build the schoolhouse, chapel and hospital; and, in 1857, came their first crude printing press. In October, 1860, after nine years of continuous service, Dr. Gulick left Micronesia for Honolulu, and from there he visited the United States. In 1863 he was again in Hawaii, having accepted the position of Secretary of the Board of the Hawaiian Evangelical Association. In 1870 his labors at Hawaii ended. After twenty-five years of work for the American Board he received a call from the American Bible Society, and Japan and China were offered to him as a field of labor. In 1880 he began a new era of Bible work in Japan; he founded the Bible house at Yokohama—in his estimation one of the great successes of his life. In 1881 the large field of China was assigned to him; and from a circulation of 74,800 volumes of the Bible in 1878, the number grew to 252,875 in 1887. On the plain gray granite monument that marks the grave of Luther Halsey Gulick at Springfield, Mass., are these words: "For forty years a foreign missionary."

GULICK, Peter J.: Born at Freehold, N. J., March 12, 1797; graduated at Princeton College 1825, and at Princeton Theological Seminary 1827; sailed November 3, the same year, a missionary of the ABCFM, with the second reenforcement for the Sandwich Islands. He was stationed first at Waimea; then Koloa, on Molokai, till 1847; then at Waialua, Oahu, till 1857, when he removed to Honolulu. In 1874, after forty-seven years of service, he went with his wife and daughter to reside with his son, O. H. Gulick, in Japan. He died in Kobe, December 8, 1877. Six of his children became missionaries of the American Board.

GUMLA: A village in Chota Nagpur, India, situated about 35 miles south by west of Lohardaga. Station of the Gossner Missionary Society, with (1903) 2 missionaries, 20 native workers, men and women; 13 preaching places, 7 Sunday schools, 2 day schools, and 1,911 professed Christians.

GUMPUR: A town in the Madras Presidency, India, situated 50 miles N. of Chicacole in the District of Vizagapatam. Station of the Breklum Missionary Society (1900), with 1 missionary and his wife and 1 native worker.

GUNDERT, Herman: Born in Stuttgart, 1814. Died in 1893. He joined the Basel Mission in Malabar, India, in 1839, and for twenty-four years he exerted a wide and potent influence in India and other lands. Dr. Gundert was a man of great learning, and his pen was a blessing to the cause of missions. He was the author of many Malayalam books; his dictionaries did much toward the development of the language and dialects of the people among whom he labored, and his Bible translations were painstaking and scholarly. His failing health necessitated his return home, where he became editorial secretary and principal of the "Calwer Verlagsverein."

GUNNAUR: A town in the district of Budaon, United Provinces, India, situated about 3 miles from the left bank of the Ganges. Population (1891) 5,500, of whom 3,200 are Mohammedans. Circuit station of the ME, with (1901) 500 professing Christians.

GUNONG SITOLI: A town on the E. coast of the island of Nias, Dutch East Indies, W. of Sumatra. Station of the Rhenish Missionary Society, with (1903) 2 missionaries, 1 missionary's wife, 13 native workers, men and women; 2 outstations, 4 day schools, and 853 professing Christians.

GUNTUR: A municipality and district in the Presidency of Madras, India, situated in the region of the Kistna, about 20 miles W. of the river, in a region that is quite healthful but rather difficult of access. Population (1891) 23,400, of whom 17,300 are Hindus. Station of the ELGS, with (1902) 18 missionaries, men and women; 62 native workers, men and women; 22 preaching places, 42 Sunday schools, 32 day schools, 1 college, 1 orphanage, 1 hospital and dispensary, and 4,848 professing Christians.

GURDASPUR: A town in the Punjab, North India, 44 miles northeast of Amritsar. Unimportant except as a trading center for the produce of the neighboring villages. In appearance and sanitary arrangements it is fairly good. Climate, cool and pleasant. Population (1891) 6,000, of whom 3,000 are Hindus and 2,600 Mohammedans. Station of the UP (1872), with (1903) 1 missionary and his wife, 3 women missionaries, 12 native workers, men and women; 39 outstations, and 16 village schools.

GURZALLA: A town in the Madras Presidency, India, situated on the Kistna River, about 85 miles S. E. of Haidarabad. Station of the ABMU (1895), with 1 missionary and his wife, 23 native workers, men and women; 8 outstations, 4 preaching places, 12 day schools, 1 boarding school, and 5,000 professing Christians, of whom 1,800 are baptized adults.

GUTU'S: A settlement in Rhodesia, Central Africa, situated about 175 miles E. N. E. of Bulawayo. Station of the Berlin Missionary Society (1892), with (1903) 3 missionaries, 1 missionary's wife, 1 native worker, 13 outstations, 12 preaching places, and 150 professing Christians.

GUTZLAFF, Karl Friedrich August: Born at Pyritz, in Pomerania, July 8, 1803. He early showed great zeal in study, and expressed a strong desire to be a missionary, but, his parents being too poor to educate him, he was apprenticed to a saddler at Stettin. At the age of eighteen he made known his wishes for a missionary life in a sonnet which he addressed to the King of Prussia, which led to his being admitted to the Pädagogium at Halle, and afterward to the mission institute of Jänicke in Berlin. On leaving the school he visited England, and meeting Dr. Morrison, the Chinese missionary and scholar, his mind turned strongly to China as his ultimate field of labor. In 1826, under the auspices of the Netherlands Missionary Society, he sailed for Batavia, where, by close study and intercourse with Chinese residents, he made great proficiency in the Chinese language. In 1828 he severed his connection with the Netherlands Society, and resolved to go on his own account to China. Between 1831 and 1834 he made three voyages along the coast of China, Siam, Korea, and the Lu-chu islands. In these he went at first in the disguise of a Chinaman, afterward as an interpreter, surgeon, and chaplain on the British ship "Lord Amherst." On the death of Dr. Morrison, in 1834, he was appointed interpreter and secretary to the British ambassador, and finally superintendent of trade, which office he held till his death. During the opium war and the negotiation of the treaty of peace at Nanking, May 29, 1842, he rendered valuable service to the British by his knowledge of the language and customs of the people.

His medical skill and great learning won the respect and confidence of the people. An attempt made by him and others, in 1844, to spread Christianity by means of native agents proved premature and unsuccessful. But his indefatigable personal efforts for the cause of religion and Christian civilization in China deserve to be held in grateful remembrance by the Church. He made a translation of the New Testament into Siamese, and was associated with Medhurst in translating the Bible into Chinese (Wenli). He also, aided by shipwrecked Japanese sailors, translated the Gospel of John into Japanese in 1838. In 1849 he visited England, Germany, and other countries in Europe, and by his addresses gave a new impulse to missionary effort in China. He returned to China in 1851, and died at Victoria, Hongkong, August 9 of the same year.

GWAMBA LANGUAGE: Belongs to the Bantu family of African languages. The term is used by a subtribe in the Transvaal. Better acquaintance with them has revealed the fact that the name is merely a local name for the Tonga language.

GWELO: A town in Rhodesia, Central Africa, situated about 100 miles N. E. of Buluwayo, among the Matabili. Station of the SPG (1895).

GYAZA: A settlement in Uganda, Central Africa, situated about 15 miles N. of Mengo. Station of the CMS (1895), with (1903) 1 missionary and his wife, 119 native workers, men and women; 1 preaching place, 3 day schools, and 2,437 professing Christians. The name is also written Gayaza.

H

HAI-CHENG-HSIEN: A town in the province of Liao-tung, Manchuria, China, situated about 32 miles E. by N. of Newchwang. It was the scene of a defeat of the Chinese army by the Japanese in the war of 1894. Station of the UFS (1876), with (1903) a missionary and his wife, 25 native workers, 8 outstations, 5 day schools, and 865 professing Christians.

HAIDARABAD: Capital of the native state of the same name in S. Central India, situated on the Musi River, a tributary of the Kistna, amid wild and picturesque scenery. Towering above all other buildings is the splendid pile of the British Residency. The city was founded in 1589, and its population, numbering (1901) 448,466, is the most varied in India, as well as the most turbulent in appearance. The inhabitants are, for the most part, Mohammedans, making Haidarabad the largest Mohammedan city in India and second in the world of Islam to Constantinople alone. It is a station of the CMS (1901), with (1902) 1 missionary, 5 native workers, and 30 professing Christians. Station also of the WMS, with (1903) 3 missionaries, 60 native workers, men and women; 4 preaching places, 11 day schools, and 193 professing Christians. Station also of the ME, with (1902) 1 missionary and his wife, 3 women missionaries, 19 native workers, men and women; 8 day schools, an orphanage, and 28 professing Christians. The YWCA also has a representative there.

HAIDARABAD: A city in Sind, India. The city is a naturally and artificially fortified town, formerly the capital of Sind. It stands on a low limestone ridge E. of the Indus, and is noted for its silks and its manufactures of fine work in the precious metals. Population (1891) 54,600, of whom 32,000 are Hindus and the remainder nearly all Mohammedans. Station of the CMS (1856) and the CEZ (1885), with 1 missionary and his wife, 3 women missionaries, 22 native workers, of whom 8 are women; 10 day schools, and 1 boarding school. There are also 356 pupils in the zenanas.

HAIDARABAD: One of the largest and most important of the so-called feudatory states of India, governed by a native prince. The ruler is called the Nizam, who is a Mohammedan, the descendant of the "Nizam-ul-Mulk," or viceroy of the Deccan, who ruled the country as viceroy of the Mogul emperors of Delhi nearly two centuries ago, but in the decadence of the Delhi power rebelled and set up as an independent prince. A British resident is maintained at the Nizam's court. This state is often called "the Nizam's Dominions." Among the people it is popularly spoken of as "the Mogalai,"—in allusion to the Mogul origin of its rulers. It lies in the center of the great tableland which occupies almost all of India south of the Vindhya Mountains. The area of the state is about 80,000 square miles. The population (1901) is 11,141-142. Of this number about 10 per cent. are Mohammedans, and as the ruling dynasty is Mohammedan, persons of that faith occupy not only the principal positions of trust and authority but also pervade the lower ranks of both civil and military employment. The state lies just where several language areas meet; accordingly there is a great diversity of dialect within its borders. Marâthi is spoken by the Hindu population of the west and northwest; Kanarese by the Hindus of the southwest; Telugu by those of the eastern districts; Hindustani by the Mohammedans throughout, tho Persian is the court language; and the aboriginal tribes (Gonds, etc.) have, as elsewhere, each its own tongue. The habit of carrying weapons is quite universal among Mohammedans throughout the state; to some extent Hindus also adopt it. It is not unusual to see, in some village bazaar, a man with a long matchlock musket over his shoulder, a curved sword in his hand, two or three daggers and knives of different patterns stuck into his girdle, and a shield of ancient pattern hanging down his back. The presence everywhere of these walking arsenals, together with the violent and bitter fanaticism of the average Mohammedan, and the feeling prevailing in the minds of the Muslim inhabitants of the Haidarabad State that it is a territory sacred to their faith and power, often renders missionary work there difficult, not to say dangerous; no Christian preacher has ever been actually assailed, tho sometimes threats of violence are made. While it was considered unsafe, some years since, for strangers to enter Haidarabad City without protection, this is not the case at present. In other parts of the territory life and property are usually safe. Education in the Nizam's state is rather backward, and the general condition of the country, as shown by its roads, postal system, and other appliances of civilization, attests the inefficiency and carelessness of Oriental rule. Yet the constant example of the British Government is not lost upon the leading men in the Haidarabad State, and the government is striving, not altogether without success, to pattern its operations after the model thus set before it. Three lines of railway pass through the territory, and thus the capital city is brought into direct communication with outside civilization. The WMS, the SPG, the ME, and the ABMU are the missionary societies chiefly engaged in the territory of Haidarabad. The whole number of missionaries in the 19 stations is 54, both men and women. They carry on 136 schools of all grades, and the number of communicants connected with these stations is about 5,500. The whole number of Christians reported from the Nizam's territory by the census of 1901 is 22,996. On the whole, altho this Mohammedan area in the midst of territories under the control of an enlightened Christian nation, is still to a degree benighted, yet rays of light are beginning to dawn over it, and civilizing influences are slowly penetrating it from all sides.

HAIFA: Also called Caiffa; it is the Scaminium of St. Jerome, a seaport in Syria, situated at the foot of Mt. Carmel, 9 miles S. S. E. of Acre. It is the terminus of a railway from Damascus to the coast through the Hauran. There is a German colony and a colony of Russian Jews at this place. Population about 3,000. Station of the Jerusalem Verein (1891), with (1903) 1 missionary and his wife, 1 deaconess, 1 place of worship, and 1 village school. Station also of the Jerusalem and the East Mission Fund; outstation of the CMS, the statistics being included in Acre (or

Acca); also outstation of the London Jews Society, statistics being included with Safed.

HAIG, General F. T.: Born in 1827. Died in 1901. General Haig, though not a missionary, for many years was an active Christian worker in India, and later in relation to the North Africa Mission. In 1883 he visited Algeria, and when the mission was reorganized later in the year he consented to join the Council of the Society. He was a most active member of it, and several times visited the mission field, and also by his pen and his voice stirred up interest at home. After he retired from the army his thought was largely given to mission subjects; and his wide experience made him a most valuable adviser on almost every missionary topic, while his self-denying generosity forwarded the good work. It was largely as a result of his journeyings, and at his suggestion, that the North Africa Mission Society began work in northern Arabia and Egypt, and it was through a letter of his that the Hon. Ion Keith Falconer went out to Aden, and the CMS sent Dr. Harpur to the Arabian coast of the Red Sea. His work in Upper Godavari, Calcutta, Arabia, Egypt and other parts of Africa was attended always by the most heroic consecration, and one who knew him well said of him: "Of all the men I have met I never knew one who seemed more thoroughly true-hearted and devoted in the service of Christ." In 1885 he published a pamphlet on the spiritual needs of Arabia, and wrote a number of articles urging the evangelization of that long-neglected land.

HAI-LUNG-CHENG-TING: Town in Manchuria, situated about 130 miles N. E. of Mukden. Station of the UFS (1897), with (1903) 1 missionary and his wife, 4 native workers, 5 outstations, 4 day schools, 1 dispensary, and 735 professed Christians.

HAINAN: An island lying off the coast of Kwangtung, China, between lat. 20° 8l′ N. and lat. 17° 52′ N. It has a total length of 150 miles from north to south, and a width of 100 miles from east to west. It is separated from the peninsula of Liuchau by the Strait of Hainan, which is twenty miles wide.

On account of its insular position the climate is more moderate than that of the mainland; 97° F. is the extreme of heat even during the heated term. Its inhabitants are estimated at a million and a half, and consist of three different elements—Chinese immigrants, partially civilized aborigines, and the rude savages. The Chinese language used in the island is a dialect which has been called the Hainanese and resembles the Fo-kien dialect. It is understood even by the aborigines. Many other Chinese dialects are also found, among which Mandarin, Hakka, and Cantonese are the most prominent. Among the aborigines numerous dialects are found which seem to be allied to those of the Shan tribes of Burma. The people are disposed to be friendly to foreigners. The island is a political part of Kwangtung province, and the obstacles to missionary work arise from the officials more than from the common people. The aborigines differ from the Chinese in having higher cheek-bones; they are of a copper color, and their eyes are not oblique. The capital is Kiung-chau, on the Limu River, four miles from its mouth. It is a well-built city of 100,000 inhabitants. Hoi-hau, at the mouth of the river, is the port. All the thirteen district towns lie on the coast, and the interior of the island is given up mainly to the aborigines.

Missions: In 1630 the Roman Catholics commenced a mission at Kiung-chau. All that remains of their work now is the cemetery of the missionaries and a few hundred descendants of the early converts. Protestant missionary work began in 1881 with the medical and missionary labors of Mr. Jeremiassen, an independent self-supporting missionary. In 1883 Rev. B. C. Henry, of the Presbyterian Board Mission (U. S.) at Canton, made a visit to the island. In 1884 a preaching place to the Hakkas was opened at Nodoa, a Hakka settlement. In 1886 the PN sent two missionaries who made Kiung-chau the center of their work. During the last decade the Gospel has been preached in nearly every part of the island, several chapels have been built, hospitals have been opened, schools have been established, and largely through medical missions many have been won to Christ.

HAINANESE LANGUAGE: Belongs to the Tai group of the Indo-China family of languages, being spoken by the inhabitants of the island of Hainan, South China. The Roman letters have been used in writing it for missionary purposes by missionaries of the PN.

HAI-TAN. See HE-TAN ISLAND.

HAITI, or HAYTI: An island of the West Indies, next in size to Cuba, and lying between Cuba on the west and Porto Rico on the east. It is mountainous, with the ranges running from east to west throughout the island. The soil is exceedingly fertile, and mineral wealth is supposed to be considerable. About two-thirds of the island is occupied by the Republic of Santo Domingo. The western part, comprising a little more than one-third of the whole area, belongs to the Republic of Haiti. The island was discovered by Columbus in 1492 and entered by Spaniards in 1493. The western part was occupied by French buccaneers in 1632 and annexed by France in 1697. A century later the slaves revolted against the French and after bloody wars proclaimed their independence in 1801. The eastern or Spanish part of the island was conquered by the Haitians in 1822-23, but revolted in 1843-44, becoming the Dominican Republic. The western part of the island was ruled by emperors for some years and finally adopted the republican form of government. The area of the whole island is 28,250 square miles.

HAITI, or HAYTI, Republic of: An independent territory in the western part of the island of Haiti. The republic is of the French type and has suffered from numerous revolutions and wars. The people are largely blacks (some 10,000 of whom are immigrants from the United States) and a very few whites. The population of the republic was about 950,000 in 1887; a church census in 1901 claims that it is now 1,294,400. The language is a dialect of French, and the religion is Roman Catholic, altho the voodooism of the Africans is extensively mingled with the Christianity of the common people.

Protestant missions were begun in Haiti by the WMS in 1816. They received a fresh impulse in connection with the emigration of negroes from the United States, in 1824. Many of these were Methodists and others were Baptists. Several preachers were among these American negroes, and a Methodist Conference organized among them in connection with the African Methodist Church of the United States continues to this day. The Baptists also have several churches in Haiti which were established in consequence of this emigration. The American Baptists maintained missionaries in three or four places for several years, but gave up the field to the BMS, and, at present, the Jamaica Baptist Missionary Union aids some smaller Baptist congregations, the general work being under charge of the Haitian Baptist Union, composed of the pastors of churches which have no financial aid from abroad.

Colored Episcopalians from the United States having emigrated to Haiti in 1861, the field was taken up by the PE, and there are now six regular congregations, superintended by a Bishop, and with a theological seminary for training a native ministry. The field is very needy, since the people of the country districts are ignorant and rather to be classed as fetish worshipers than as Christians.

Justin (J.), *Etude sur les institutions Haitiennes*, Paris, 1894; St. John (Sir Spenser), *Haiti, or the Black Republic*, London, 1889; *Missionary Review of the World*, Vol. VIII., p. 179. See also number for September, 1903, Saint Remi, *Vie de Toussaint L'Ouverture*, Paris, 1850.

HAJIN: A town in Asiatic Turkey, about 30 miles north of Adana, in the heart of the Taurus Mountains. The population is almost entirely Armenian. Station of the ABCFM (1880), with (1902) 1 missionary and his wife, 3 women missionaries, 38 native workers, men and women; 7 outstations, 4 preaching places, 2 village schools, 2 high schools, an orphanage, a Young Woman's Christian Association, and 615 church members.

HAKA. See FORT HAKA.

HAKKA: A distinct race found in the Canton province, China, near Canton and Swatow. They are of a lower social rank than the Pun-ti or native Chinese, and speak a different dialect. They are also found in the island of Hainan.

HAKKA LANGUAGE: A dialect spoken by a peculiar race or tribe who inhabit the mountains of Kwangtung province in China. It is written with the Chinese characters. Missionaries of the Basel Society have had some success in introducing the Roman letters as a more convenient means of writing it.

HAKODATE: A seaport on the southern extremity of the island of Yezo, Japan. The town is built along the base of a rocky headland, and is not unlike Gibraltar in its situation. A landlocked bay affords ample shelter and anchorage for the largest vessels. The governor of Yezo resides at Hakodate, where there are a government hospital and medical college. The streets are clean and well kept. Population (1890) 55,700. Station of the CMS (1874), with (1903) 3 missionaries and their wives, 3 women missionaries, 23 native workers, men and women; 4 outstations, 5 preaching places, 5 day schools, 1 boarding school, 1 theological class, 1 industrial school, 1 hospital, and 675 professing Christians. Station also of the ME, with (1902) 2 missionaries and their wives, 5 women missionaries, 41 native workers, men and women; 9 outstations, 15 preaching places, 2 day schools, 1 high school, and 749 professing Christians.

HALL, Gordon: Born at Tolland, Mass., April 8, 1784; graduated at Williams College 1809 with the highest honors of his class; studied theology with Dr. Porter (afterward professor at Andover); was licensed to preach, but, declining several invitations to settle, his heart being set on going to the heathen, he entered Andover Seminary in 1810. Here he was associated with Mills, Richards, and a few other kindred spirits, who prayed and conferred in reference to personal labor among the heathen. After studying medicine he was ordained at the same time with Judson and others, and sailed February 18, 1812, as a missionary of the ABCFM for India, reaching Calcutta August 8. Peremptorily required by the East India Company to leave its territories, and unsuccessful in his attempts to obtain permission to establish a mission, he presented to the governor of Bombay an earnest appeal, which brought him official permission to remain. In Bombay he labored thirteen years, visiting the temples and bazaars with the Gospel message, discussing with the Brahmans and translating the Bible. Having completed the translation of the New Testament into the Marâthi, he left Bombay for a preaching tour on the continent. At Nasik, a hundred miles distant, he found multitudes dying of cholera, and ministered to the sick till his medicines were exhausted. He then started to return to Bombay. At Durlidhapur, spreading his mat in the veranda of a heathen temple, he lay down to sleep. Rising at four o'clock in the morning to resume his journey, he was violently seized with cholera, and, after eight hours of great suffering, breathed his last at the age of forty-two, March 20, 1826. The lads who were with him buried him shrouded in his blanket, without a coffin. A stone with an inscription in English and Marâthi marks the place of his interment. "No missionary in Western India," says one, "has ever been more respected among the Brahmans and higher classes for his discussions and pulpit discourses." His tract, *The Conversion of the World, or the Claims of Six Hundred Millions*, which he prepared in connection with Mr. Newell, was widely circulated in America and England and produced a profound impression.

HALL, William Nelthorpe: Born in Sheffield, Yorkshire, England, April 19, 1829. In 1849 he was called to the regular ministry, having already been a lay preacher. But his health failed, and he went into business. In 1859, the Methodist New Connexion having decided to commence a mission in China, Mr. Hall offered to go, and in the autumn of 1859 he sailed with the Rev. J. Innocent as a missionary of the Methodist New Connexion. On their arrival in China they remained for a brief period in Shanghai. Mr. Hall was anxiously desirous of settling at Su-chau-fu, which was then in all its glory. He visited the place, then made it the center of his operations, while Mr. Innocent went to Tien-tsin, which had just been opened by treaty. The Taeping rebels devastated Su-chau, and prevented the establishment of a mission there, and Mr. Hall went to Tien-tsin and united with Mr. Innocent in laying the foundations of a very prosperous mission. During the Tien-tsin massacre of 1870 the Protestant chapels, eight in number, were ruined and the members dispersed, many of them being beaten and some of them killed. Mr. Hall remained in the city during the awful outbreak, cheering the faint-hearted and seeking to rescue those who were in danger. The storm exhausted itself, quiet was restored, compensation was demanded and to some extent made, and the work of the mission was resumed. But it took a long time to retrieve the losses incurred.

In 1873 he returned home on furlough, and devoted his whole time to obtaining money to support an institution for the training of native preachers. He obtained £3,200, and then returned to China and built the Training College at Tien-tsin.

Mr. Hall was pursuing his manifold works with intense enthusiasm, when in the spring of 1878, already weakened by his labors, he was smitten by typhus fever. He died May 21, aged 49 years. He was a man of vigorous and cultured intellect, copious eloquence, and undying energy. He had an iron will and dauntless courage. His one purpose found expression in words which were constantly on his lips—"China for Christ."

HAMADA: A town in Japan on the west coast of Honshiu, 200 miles N. E. by N. of Nagasaki. Station of the CMS (1895), with 2 women missionaries and 3 native workers.

HAMADAN: A city in Persia, supposed site of the ancient Ecbatana; situated at the E. base of Mt. Elvend, 185 miles W. S. W. of Teheran. Altitude, 6,000 feet. A trade center for caravans between Baghdad and Teheran. Population, 50,000. Station of the PN (1880), with (1903) 8 missionaries, men and women (one a physician); 25 native workers, men and women; 5 outstations, 4 day schools, 2 high schools, and 186 professed evangelical Christians.

HAMLIN, Cyrus: Born near Waterford, Me., January 5, 1811; died at Lexington, Mass., August 8, 1900. Left an orphan in his infancy, Cyrus Hamlin was brought up in poverty by a mother who wrung a living from a little farm representing all her property. He was not a promising child, and when old enough was set to learn the jeweler's trade with a relative. A taste for books revealed itself while he was at this work, and led to his decision to earn a college education and become a minister. The carrying out of this decision in spite of utter lack of means revealed an initiative, resourcefulness, self-abnegation, and consecration to Jesus Christ which marked his whole career. Having graduated at Bowdoin College in 1834, and then at Bangor Theological Seminary, he sailed for Turkey in December, 1838, as a missionary of the ABCFM. He there acquired a literary knowledge of the Armenian and a colloquial knowledge of Turkish and modern Greek, and was entrusted, in 1839, with the opening of a boarding school for the training of preachers and teachers for the service of the mission. Several of Dr. Hamlin's high qualities immediately came to light in the energy and ingenuity by which he overcame obstacles put in his way by Mohammedan, Armenian, and Roman Catholic bigotry. The school was an experiment; its equipment was largely created by Dr. Hamlin, for in becoming its principal he had undertaken in the mission councils to build up a theological seminary at Bebek out of nothing. The school was a success; the men whom it trained for the ministry are remembered among the most sturdy pillars of the mission enterprise in Turkey, and other men who were there taught the nobility of honest toil by Dr. Hamlin in his stove factory, last factory, flour mill, bakery, or laundry, have been among the most successful and most honored laymen of the Evangelical Churches of the Ottoman Empire. The various industries just named were not carried on as a part of the work of a theological seminary. The last three enterprises came into being in connection with the Bebek Seminary, but with the purpose of providing means of livelihood for those destitute Evangelical Armenians who had been ruined by the boycott pronounced against them as a part of the major excommunication hurled at "free thinkers" by their ecclesiastical chiefs. There is rarely to be found in the history of missions a more picturesque spectacle than that of Dr. Hamlin during the Crimean War (1854-56), observing the wounded English soldiers landed on the quays of Constantinople; abandoning his school duties in order to verify and remedy the facts; berating English officers of every grade for the red tape that made possible a criminal neglect of suffering soldiers; finally taking contracts to supply the hospitals and depot camps with eatable bread and thoroughly cleaned linen, and then executing the contracts with brilliant and beneficent efficiency by turning to the work all his energies and those of all of his students and teachers, and of scores of poor creatures who had been left without work because of their faith. And there is hardly a more impressive figure of self-forgetfulness among the many devoted missionaries of the world than that of Dr. Hamlin, after having carried this enterprise through by his own wonderful and unaided abilities, taking the $25,000 which fell to him as his legitimate profit, and covering it all into the missionary treasury to be used in aiding the little native communities to build chapels and churches. The whole episode of his services to the English army was magnificent as an achievement and thrilling as revealing the man. But the incipient theological seminary became almost obliterated under the weight of the flour mill and bakery. While the question was under discussion of improving the efficiency of the seminary for training the native agency needed by the mission, Dr. Hamlin resigned his connection with the ABCFM at the invitation of Christopher Robert, of New York, in order to establish Robert College at Constantinople. The first class of this college was received in 1863. The enormous difficulties in regard to site, authorization, and construction of the college buildings were overcome by the same indomitable energy, resource, and pluck which made Dr. Hamlin inimitable, and the structure on the Bosphorus hills, which is the enduring monument to his memory, was opened in the summer of 1871. In 1873 Dr. Hamlin returned to the United States and his connection with Robert College ceased. He excelled in works of preparation and in dealing with initial difficulties. Others could endure better than he the steady drudgery of organizing and developing the College in order to carry it satisfactorily forward into the place assigned to it in the preconceived plan.

Dr. Hamlin was professor of dogmatic theology at Bangor Seminary from 1877 to 1880, and president of Middlebury College in Vermont from 1880 to 1885, and after his retirement to Lexington, Mass., was much sought after for lectures and information for newspaper articles.

He was a most spiritually-minded man and of very deep feelings. A little quick in temper, and sometimes disposed, in a land of turbulence like Turkey, to take the law into his own hands when a hopelessly irreconcilable element needed to be removed, he was extraordinarily ready to make amends, in a tender, whole-souled way that did really make amends, for any injustice done in haste. No American missionary, without exception, ever gained such hold upon the hearts of the evangelical native community in Turkey, nor is regarded by them as having accomplished so much, as Dr. Hamlin for the spiritual and moral renovation of that land of darkness.

My Life and Times (autobiography), Boston, 1894; *Missionary Review of the World*, Vol. XIII., p. 7888; Vol. XV., p. 31.

HANAMAKONDA: A town in the native state of Haidarabad, India; 86 miles northeast of the capital. Climate, tropical; population, 8,000. Station of the ABMU (1879), with (1903) 1 missionary and his wife, 2 women missionaries, 27 native workers, men and women; 18 outstations, 14 day schools, 1 hospital, and 513 church members.

HAN-CHENG-HSIEN: A town in the province of Shen-si, situated on the Hoang-Ho River, 120 miles N. E. of Hsi-ngan-fu. Station of the CIM (1897), with (1903) 1 missionary and his wife and 3 women missionaries.

HAN-CHUNG-FU: A town in the province of Shen-si, China, situated on the Han River, 225 miles N. E. of Cheng-tu-fu, at an altitude of 2,000 feet. It is a center for trade with Sze-chwan. Station of the CIM (1879), with (1903) 2 missionaries and their wives.

HANG-CHAU-FU: A city in the province of Che-kiang, China, situated at the southern terminus of the Grand Canal, and at the head of Hang-chau Bay, 110 miles southwest of Shanghai. Its beauty of location is celebrated in a popular Chinese proverb, and, with the beautiful western lake, in which are fairylike islands, and around which stand villas and monuments, with its extensive circuit of twelve miles, its well-paved, clean streets and numerous public buildings, it well deserves the name of an earthly paradise. It is a great center of Chinese commerce and learning. Marco Polo celebrated its beauty under the name of Kinsai, and in a northeast corner of the city is the Nestorian Church of which he speaks. The population is estimated at 800,000. Station of the PN (1859), the CMS (1864), the CIM (1866), the PS (1867), and the ABMU (1899). These societies together report (1903) 41 missionaries, men and women; 85 native workers, men and women; 26 outstations, 25 places of worship, 5 high schools, 18 village schools, and 1,500 professed Christians. The PN has a college here and a school for training women for evangelistic work; the ABMU has a printing house, and the CMS has 2 hospitals and dispensaries, a refuge for opium victims, and some special work for lepers. Besides these special features of the missionary enterprise, the Mission to Lepers in India and the East has two houses for the children of lepers. In reports the name is written Hangchow.

HANDS, John: Born December 5, 1780, at Roade, Northamptonshire; studied at Gosport; sailed May 5, 1809, as a missionary of the LMS, for India. He was first stationed at Bellary. In 1829 he visited England, and returned to India in 1831. He translated the whole Bible into Kanarese, and superintended its printing. He was subsequently appointed agent of the Society in Ireland, arriving in Dublin January 24, 1843, where he died June 30, 1864, aged eighty-four.

HAN-KAU: A city in the province of Hu-pei, China, situated on the north side of the Yangtse River, at its junction with the Han, about 450 miles west of Shanghai. It is the largest commercial center of Middle China, was opened to foreign trade in 1858, and is connected with Shanghai by regular steamships. The British settlement is on the river front in the eastern portion of the city, where foreign houses and roadways are built. The native city is surrounded by a wall eighteen feet high and four miles in circumference. It contains a population estimated at 300,000. Wu-chang, the capital of the province, is on the southern bank of the Yangtse, opposite Han-kau, and the two are often spoken of together with Han-yang, which faces Han-kau on the other side of the Han River, as one city. The population of the three cities together is about 1,200,000. Station of the LMS (1861), the PE (1868), the WMS, the CIM (1889), the American Norwegian Lutheran Church (1891), and the United Evangelical Church (1900). These societies together have (1903) 35 missionaries, men and women; 72 native workers, men and women; 32 outstations, 11 places of worship, 19 day schools, 2 boarding schools, 5 dispensaries, and 5 hospitals. The WMS has special work among the blind, and the LMS has a theological school and a training school for women evangelistic workers. The National Bible Society of Scotland has here a printing house under charge of two agents (with their wives), and 27 native workers. Name also written Hankow.

HANKEY: A village in Cape Colony, S. Africa, situated in the Humansdorp division, 45 miles W. of Port Elizabeth. Population, about 1,600. This settlement was established by the LMS in 1828 as a refuge for freedmen, upon land which the Society had purchased. After some years the quality of the negro population began to deteriorate, and in 1875 the LMS ceased to provide for their care and spiritual nurture. In 1900 it took up this work again and established a school there for the higher education of the children of colored Christians throughout the colony. It now (1903) has 2 missionaries and their wives, 18 native workers, 3 day schools, 1 boarding school, and about 1,600 professing Christians, of whom 370 are church members.

HANNINGTON, James: Born at Hurstpierpoint, England, September 3, 1847. Love of nature, of fun, and of adventure was phenomenal with Hannington. He shrank from no risk which promised a view or a specimen. Averse to study, he left school at the age of fifteen, and was put in his father's counting-room at Brighton. To whatever suited his tastes or habits he applied himself with untiring perseverance, never to be outdone, and never to be foiled. As captain of a battery and as commander of a steam yacht he early displayed ability in the control of men, and resource under exigencies. But he was as disinclined to business as to study. In boyhood the love of his mother was the sheet-anchor of his life. He not only never neglected the externals of religion, but was never wholly satisfied with a life apart from God. About the age of twenty-one he decided to prepare for the ministry of the Church of England, and to that end, in October, 1868, entered St. Mary's Hall, Oxford. He soon established an ascendancy over his fellow-students, which he maintained without a rival through his university course, and this influence was often beneficial, but it cannot be said that he was studious, except in the line of his pursuit as a naturalist. He was ordained a deacon in 1874, and took charge of a small parish in Devonshire. There he experienced a new conversion, and in 1875 a conversation on missions with two ladies led him to study that subject thoroughly. Three years later the cruel death of Messrs. Smith and O'Neil, two missionaries on the shores of the Victoria Nyanza, in Africa, greatly moved him. Believing that he had certain elements of character as well as experiences of life that fitted him for pioneer mission work, and obtaining the consent of his wife, who could not accompany him, he offered himself to the CMS for the African field for five years. The offer was accepted, and he was entrusted with the leadership of a party of six to reenforce the Central African Mission at Rubaga. An appeal from him in the *London Times* for subscriptions to enable him to take a boat to navigate the lake was successful. He sailed with his party May 17, 1882, for Zanzibar. On the voyage he studied Swahili, the language spoken by the natives on the coast, and the knowledge so obtained was very useful to him. The party set out for Uganda by the "old route," via Mamboia, Myui and Msalala, thence by boat across Victoria Nyanza to Rubaga. He soon had severe attacks of African fever, dysentery and rheumatic fever. His health being greatly shattered, it was decided that he must return to England. In January, 1883, he started for Zanzibar, and embarking there, reached England June 10. After his health was restored he was consecrated Bishop of Equatorial Africa, and in January, 1885, returned again to the Dark Continent. On reaching Freretown, which he intended to make his home, he began the visitation of every prominent mission station within 250 miles of the coast. To reach the important station at Taita, on the mountain Ndara, 2,500 feet above the plain, he had to traverse swamps and 200 miles of difficult and dangerous desert. He had frequently formulated in his mind the idea of opening up a new route to Uganda, through a shorter, more elevated and healthier region than the one which had shattered his constitution two years earlier, and early in 1885, after careful consultation, he started with 200 porters from Mombasa. The party reached Kwa Sundu, near the Victoria Nyanza, after many adventures. Bishop Hannington pushed forward with a part of his men to Uganda. On November 8 word was brought to those left at Kwa Sundu that the bishop and his party had been killed. Four only of the fifty escaped to bring the sad news and to tell the manner of his death. The encroachments of the various foreign powers on African soil had naturally awakened suspicion of whites, including missionaries. There was a strong prejudice in Uganda against the approach of foreigners from the north. When Mr. Thomson penetrated to Usoga two years before, his arrival occasioned new alarm and suspicion. A report of the highhanded proceedings of the Germans in Zanzibar added fuel to the flame, and the chiefs at once counseled killing all the missionaries, "who," they said, "were only the forerunners of invasion." At this critical time the arrival of Bishop Hannington at the north side of the lake was announced, and the council decided that he should be put to death. Mwanga was at first unwilling, and suggested that he should be sent back. The thought of booty decided the point. The bishop was enticed from his men by a band led by an Arab. He was dragged with great violence over the ground, and forced into a filthy hut, and, after eight days, led forth to be killed. His men were speared to death. He was shot with his own rifle October 29, 1885. He died without fear, and said to the soldiers appointed to kill him: "Go, tell Mwanga that I die for the Baganda, and that I have purchased the road to Uganda with my life."

His last words to his friends in England, scribbled by the light of some camp-fire, were: "If this is the last chapter of my earthly history, then the next will be the first page of the heavenly—no blots and smudges, no incoherence, but sweet converse in the presence of the Lamb."

Dawson (C. L.), *James Hannington*, London and New York, 1888.

HANNOVER; Missionary Society of the Lutheran Free Church of. See GERMANY; MISSIONARY SOCIETIES OF.

HAN-YANG: A town in the Hupei province, China, situated at the confluence of the Han and Yangtse Rivers, opposite Han-kau. It has iron and steel works of some importance. Population about 400,000. Station of the WMS, with (1903) 1 missionary, 2 women missionaries, 10 native workers, men and women; 1 outstation, 2 preaching places, 1 day school, 1 boarding school, 1 dispensary, and 138 professed Christians. Station also of the ABMU (1893), with (1903) 6 missionaries, men and women; 10 native workers (one a woman), 8 preaching places, 2 day schools and 531 professing Christians.

HAPPY GROVE: A village 7 miles N. W. of Kingston, Jamaica, W. I. Station of the AFFM, with 3 women missionaries.

HARBOUR ISLAND: An island lying at the N. end of Eleuthera Island, Bahamas, W. I. Station of the WMS, with (1903) 2 missionaries, 141 native workers, men and women; 8 preaching places, 7 Sunday schools and 802 professing Christians.

HARDA: A town in the Central Provinces, India, 48 miles southwest of Hoshangabad. Population (1891) 13,600, of whom 10,000 are Hindus. Station of the FCMS (1882), with (1901) 8 missionaries, men and women; 21 native workers, men and women; 4 outstations, 2 places of worship, 3 day schools, 2 dispensaries, 1 hospital, 1 orphanage, 1 theological class and 1 leper asylum. Name also written Hurda.

HARMSHOPE: A settlement in Bechuanaland, S. Africa, situated 70 miles N. of Mafeking and close to the Transvaal frontier. Station of the Hermannsburg Missionary Society (known in 1865 reports as Patu Letschopa, given its present name in 1876). It now has about 1,400 professing Christians under charge of 1 native preacher and 4 helpers.

HARPER: A settlement at Cape Palmas, Liberia, W. Africa. Station of the PE (1836), with (1901) 10 native workers, men and women; 2 places of worship, 1 orphanage and girls' school and 400 professing Christians, of whom 260 are communicants.

HARPUR: A town in the United Provinces, India, situated 23 miles S. by E. of Meerut. Population (1891) 15,000, of whom 8,500 are Hindus and 6,000 Muslims. Station circuit of the ME, with (1902) 23 native workers, men and women; 2 preaching places, 11 day schools and 1,300 professing Christians.

HARPUT (*Armenian Kharpert—Rock castle*):

A town in Asiatic Turkey, situated near the Murad Su branch of the Euphrates, about 60 miles N. W. by N. of Diarbekir. It stands at an altitude of 4,100 feet on a hill that overlooks a most fertile plain. The population of the town is about 12,000, chiefly Mohammedans, but with a certain number of Armenians and a few Syrian Christians. At Mezerè, a small village 3 miles distant, is the residence of the Governor-General of the province of Mamuret-ul-Aziz (commonly called the province of Harput). The Armenian part of the town and the villages of the plain were devastated in November, 1895, and thousands of the Armenian inhabitants massacred after the authorities had first induced the villagers to give up, as a token of loyalty, what guns they possessed. At the time of the massacre artillery was turned upon the Armenian quarter of the town, and eight of the buildings of the American Mission were looted and destroyed. Station of the ABCFM (1855), with (1902) 13 missionaries, men and women; 119 native workers, men and women; 40 outstations, 38 preaching places, 58 village schools, 5 high schools with industrial department and 1,450 evangelical Christians. The most important feature of this station is the Euphrates College, which offers higher education to the people of a wide expanse of country in the heart of Asiatic Turkey. The college has a department for girls, which is wholly separate from the department for young men, altho under the same administration. In 1901 there were in all departments, from kindergarten up, 1,057 students, of whom 476 were girls, and 100 boys and girls were in the four college classes. The buildings burned in 1895 have been rebuilt. The indemnity paid by the Turkish Government was not, however, enough to cover the cost.

HARRISMITH: A town in the Orange River Colony, S. Africa, situated 127 N. W. of Pietermaritzburg. Population about 2,000. Circuit of the South African Wesleyan Methodist Mission, with (1900) 60 native workers and 586 professing Christians.

HASBEIYA: A town in Syria, Asiatic Turkey, situated 22 miles E. S. E. of Sidon, in a deep glen on the ridge of Mt. Hermon. It has asphalt pits in its neighborhood. Population about 5,500. Station of the British Syrian Schools Committee (1866), with (1900) 2 women missionaries, 6 native women helpers, and 7 day schools in the place and neighboring villages.

HASKELL LECTURESHIP for India. See BARROWS LECTURESHIP.

HASSAN: A town in Mysore, India, situated 63 miles W. by N. of the City of Mysore. Population about 6,000. Station of the WMS, with (1903) 1 missionary, 54 native workers, men and women; 6 places of worship, 13 day schools, 1 orphanage, and 169 professing Christians.

HASTINGS, Eurotas Parmelee: Born at Clinton, N. Y., April 17, 1821; graduated at Hamilton College 1842, and Union Theological Seminary 1846; ordained at Clinton, October 6, 1846; embarked for Ceylon, November 18, the same year, as missionary of the ABCFM. On his arrival he was appointed by the mission as an instructor in the Batticotta Seminary, where he remained five years. On a brief visit to the United States, he married. In 1853 he reembarked for Ceylon and resumed his connection with the seminary until it was closed two years later by the deputation from the Board; he was then stationed for two years at Chavakachcheri, and then for twelve years at Manepy. In 1870 he again visited the United States, and engaged with Mr. Sanders in collecting funds for a college in Jaffna. Returning, he was appointed in 1872 president of the college. After occupying the presidency of the college for seventeen years, he retired in 1889, on account of increasing physical infirmities, and removed to the Manepy station, of which he took charge. He died July 31, 1890, after an illness of two or three days.

Altho Dr. Hastings devoted himself largely to educational work, this did not prevent his preaching. He had the active superintendence of several churches while ostensibly burdened with the care of Jaffna College.

HASTINGS: A village in Sierra Leone, situated about 12 miles S. E. of Freetown. Station of the WMS, with (1903) 33 native workers, men and women; 4 preaching places, 2 day schools, and 319 professing Christians. Station also of the Sierra Leone native church in cooperation with the CMS, with (1903) 6 native workers, men and women; 2 preaching places, 2 day schools, and 613 professing Christians.

HATHRAS: A town of the United Provinces, India, situated in the district of Aligarh, about 22 miles S. of that city. Population (1891) 39,200, of whom 33,700 are Hindus and about 5,000 Muslims. Station circuit of the ME, with (1902) 21 native workers, men and women; 11 day schools, and about 800 professing Christians.

HA TSCHEWASE: A tribal settlement in the Transvaal Colony, S. Africa, situated in the Zoutpansberg District, about 15 miles W. of Georgenholtz. Station of the Berlin Missionary Society (1872), with (1903) 1 missionary, 15 native workers, men and women; 9 outstations, and 233 professing Christians.

HATTON: A village in Ceylon, situated 25 miles S. W. of Kandy and just north of Adam's Peak. Station of the WMS.

HAUSA LANGUAGE: Belongs to the negro group of African languages. It is the medium of intercommunication between the inhabitants of extensive districts in the Niger region in West Africa. It is customary to speak of "the Hausa people," "Hausa land," "Hausa language," etc. Since CMS missionaries went to live in that country, however, it has become apparent that these terms exist outside of Africa only. Hausa means "the language," and the name is applied to the language of the Habes race, which has spread until it is spoken by a number of different tribes within and without the Fulani Kingdom. Some of these tribes are Mohammedans in religion and some are still heathen. The language has been printed with Roman letters by missionaries of the CMS.

HAVANA: Capital of Cuba, situated in the western part of the island and on the N. coast. It has a beautiful harbor. Population, 225,000. Station of the American Church Missionary Society (1876), the AFFM (1899), the FCMS (1899), the MES, and the African Methodist Episcopel Church. These societies have 12 missionaries, men and women, and 11 native workers. The ABS also has a depot in the city in charge of an agent.

HAWAIIAN EVANGELICAL ASSOCIATION

(1823): Less than five years from the landing of the first missionaries on Oahu of the Hawaiian Islands, a "General Meeting" of the missionary fathers was convened. This was held annually for thirty-one consecutive years, from 1823-1854, with but seven exceptions. At the first meeting the object of the gathering was stated:

"We, the undersigned, ministers and missionaries of the Lord Jesus Christ in the Sandwich Islands, being set for the defense of the truth and the enlightening of the Gentiles, agree to unite in an association for mutual improvement and mutual aid in laying the foundation, maintaining the order, and building up the house of the Lord in these islands of the sea." In 1854 this General Meeting became the Hawaiian Evangelical Association; three years before, in 1851, the Hawaiian Missionary Society of the fathers had been formed, for the purpose of cooperating with the American Board in its new missions in the island world; this was continued till 1863, when the Hawaiian Evangelical Association was remodeled by being opened to representatives of the native churches, and the Board of the Hawaiian Evangelical Association, commonly known as the Hawaiian Board, was formed. The Association consists of "all ordained clergymen, both native and foreign, of the Congregational and Presbyterian orders on the various islands of Hawaii, and of Micronesia and the Marquesas Islands, together with such laymen as may be elected from time to time by a two-thirds vote, and lay delegates appointed annually by the local island associations; six from Hawaii, four from Maui and Molokai, four from Oahu, and three from Kauai and Niihau." This Association appoints the members of the Hawaiian Board, of whom twenty-two are white men and eleven are natives. It is the duty of this Board to perform any agency requested of it by the Prudential Committee (American Board), in respect to former missionaries of the ABCFM at these islands; and the education of their children at the islands, and to take charge of home missions on the Hawaiian Islands, the education of a native ministry, and of females who may become teachers and pastors' wives; of the preparation, publication, and circulation of useful books and tracts, and also of foreign missions, so far as the conduct of them from these islands shall be found practicable and expedient, and shall take charge of and disburse funds contributed for these objects. The home mission work of the Hawaiian Board consists of evangelistic and educational work among the native Hawaiians, and the English-speaking population, and among Chinese, Japanese, Portuguese, and Gilbert Islanders resident in the islands. Total expenditure for home missions, $31,801.12, as follows: home missions $7,068.07, Japanese missions $5,005.20, Chinese mission $9,641.50, Portuguese mission $5,371.35, North Pacific Missionary Institute $2,435, Kohala Girls' School $2,280.

The foreign work of the Hawaiian Board began in 1852, when three Hawaiian families went with the American Board missionaries to establish the Micronesian Mission. A year later a chief from one of the Marquesas Islands landed at Lahaina, and asked that missionaries be sent to his islands. Two Hawaiian pastors volunteered to respond to the call, and one of them still remains there. Since the beginning of its foreign work, the Hawaiian Board has sent more than thirty Hawaiian families to the Micronesian and Marquesas Islands, and the native church has given, upon a conservative estimate, not less than $112,000 to this work

Total expenditures for foreign missions (1901): Salaries $911.10, publications $177.31, fund $73.70; grand total $1,162.01. Publications (190; chiefly hymn books and Bibles), $1,931.37. Receipts for all purposes (1901) $435.71, invested funds $146,619, property $102,800.

The organ of the Society is *The Friend*, monthly, Honolulu, H. T.

HAWAII, or SANDWICH ISLANDS: A group lying in the middle of the Pacific Ocean, in latitude 19° to 22° north, and longitude 155° to 160° west, about 2,000 miles from San Francisco, and constituting a territory of the United States. The islands were discovered by Captain Cook in 1778, and were named by him the Sandwich Islands, but they have always been called Hawaii by the natives themselves. The principal islands and their respective areas are: Hawaii, 4,850 square miles; Maui, 750 square miles; Oahu, 700 square miles; Kauai, 780 square miles; Molokai, 170 square miles; Lanai, 170 square miles; Niihau, 110 square miles, and Kahulawe, about 40 square miles.

Almost the entire surface of Hawaii is composed of the slopes of four volcanic mountains. Mauna Loa, 13,600 feet high, is one of the few active volcanoes. Mauna Kea, on the opposite north side of the island, is 13,805 feet in height and is the highest peak in the Pacific Ocean. This island is of historical interest as being the place where Captain Cook was killed, and a monument is erected at Kealakeakua Bay. Maui has also mountains of volcanic origin, with fertile valleys lying between. Kahulawe, together with Lehua, is a large sheep pasture. Molokai is formed by a backbone ridge, with lateral spurs enclosing ravines. A leper settlement is the only object of interest found on this island. Oahu is noted for the beauty of its scenery. Peaks, cliffs, ravines, cascades, and tropical vegetation unite to please the eye. It is traversed from southeast to northwest by two parallel ranges of hills. By some volcanic upheaval a bay of the sea has been converted into a plain some twenty-five feet above the level of the ocean, and this is the site of Honolulu, the capital of the territory. Kauai, like the rest of the islands, is mountainous, but has many valleys which are very fertile, and the north side of the island is the choicest land for growing sugar in the whole group. Niihau has a dry, fertile soil, and is used for pasturing sheep.

The climate of nearly all the islands is noted for its healthfulness, for, tho warm, it is equable, and there is very little variation in temperature between the winter and summer. Clear skies and regular land and sea breezes combine to render the islands one of the most delightful habitations in the world. The rainfall is quite excessive, especially on the windward side of the larger islands.

The natives of the Hawaiian Islands belong to the Malay race, as modified in the Polynesian type. Physically, they are among the finest races in the Pacific, and they have shown considerable intellectual capacity. Previous to the introduction of Christianity they were not much superior in moral character to any of the other savages in the Pacific. Polygamy, infanticide, and polyandry all prevailed. The idolatry of the Kanakas, as the natives are called, was barbarous and bloodthirsty, for human sacrifices were frequently offered during the sickness of a chief, at the dedication of a temple, or at the inception of a war. On the other hand, the natives are even-tempered, light-hearted, and a pleasure-loving race. When the islands were discovered the natives were estimated at 400,000, but they seem to be dying out, for the census of 1900 gives only about 30,000 natives, and it is feared that in the course of a few years the total extinction of the race will ensue. The remainder of the population consists of 7,835 half-castes, 28,533 white foreigners and people of foreign descent, 58,500 Japanese, and 25,742 Chinese. There are restrictions on Chinese immigration. The language is a branch of the Malao-Polynesian, and can be understood by New Zealanders. It is a soft, liquid, vocalic tongue, containing only five consonants, k, l, m, n, p, an aspirated h, five vowels, and a vocalic w.

The former scanty costume of the inhabitants has now given place to modern European dress, tho the women still cling to the holoka, a loose white or colored garment with long sleeves.

Leprosy is prevalent, and the government has established a settlement on Molokai, where sufferers from this disease are isolated.

Religion: Since the spontaneous movement of 1819-20, when idols and temples were destroyed by the natives, the Gospel has been preached until the whole nation is now practically Christian. The American missionaries arrived in 1820, and, in addition to accomplishing the conversion of the islanders to the Christian religion, they taught them to read and write, reducing their language for the first time to a written form. All forms of religion are tolerated. Roman Catholics, Anglicans, and Congregationalists are the principal denominations. Schools are established all over the island.

Mission Work: The history of the mission work of the ABCFM in Hawaii relates one of the most significant triumphs of the Gospel. Its work in the islands has all been passed over to the Hawaiian Evangelical Association. The SPG has carried on work among the Chinese in the islands, but upon the annexation of Hawaii to the United States their work was transferred to the PE. According to the census of 1896 there were 26,363 Roman Catholics (largely Portuguese) in the islands, 23,779 Protestants of all denominations, 4,886 Mormons, 44,306 Buddhists, and 10,192 not described.

Alexander (W. D.), *A Brief History of the Hawaiian People,* New York, 1892; Whitney (C.), *Hawaiian America,* New York, 1899; Bingham (H.), *Residence of Twenty-one Years in the Sandwich Islands,* Hartford, 1847; Brain (B. M.), *Transformation of Hawaii,* New York, 1899; Staley (T. N.), *Five Years' Church Work in Hawaii,* London, 1868.

HAY RIVER: A trading post in the Mackenzie Territory, Dominion of Canada, situated on the Great Slave Lake at the mouth of Hay River. Station of the CMS.

HAZARIBAGH: A town in Bengal, India, capital of the district of Hazaribagh. It stands on a high plateau at an altitude of 2,000 feet, and is picturesquely situated among conical hills about 60 miles S. S. E. of Gaya. Population (1891), 16,700, of whom 12,100 are Hindus. Station of the Gossner Missionary Society (Berlin II.), with (1903) 1 missionary and his wife, 7 native workers, 2 preaching places, 1 village school, and 141 professing Christians.

HEBRON (Labrador): A village in a sterile and forbidding region on the E. coast of Labrador. Population, 2,000. Station of the Moravian Missions (1880), with (1900) 3 missionaries and their wives.

HEBRON (Natal): Station of the Hermannsburg Missionary Society (1882), situated in the E. part of Natal, near the Tugela River, and about 60 miles from Pietermaritzburg. It has (1902) 1 missionary and 6 native workers.

HEBRON (Palestine): A town in Palestine, Asiatic Turkey, situated in a long, narrow valley about 20 miles S. W. of Jerusalem, at an altitude of about 2,200 feet. It has an important relic of antiquity in its "sanctuary" built over a cave traditionally known as the Cave of Machpelah. Station of the CA. Outstation of the Jerusalem Verein of Berlin. The town is known lccally by the title given to Abraham, *El Khalil:* the Friend (of God).

HEBRON (Transvaal): Station of the Hermannsburg Missionary Society (1872; opened at Matlare in 1866), with (1902) 2 missionaries, 1 missionary's wife, 5 native workers, 4 preaching places. There were before the war 1,044 professing Christians here, but the present situation has not been reported by the Society. Hebron is situated in the Transvaal Colony about 18 miles N. W. of Pretoria.

HEERENDYK: A substation of the Moravian Missions in Dutch Guiana, S. America. It is one of a number of plantations situated on the northern banks of the Comewyne, where a large number of converts were gathered by the traveling missionary. In 1856 a piece of land was purchased, a church and mission house erected, and a regular congregation formed. It now has 26 native workers and about 250 professing Christians.

HEIDELBERG: A town in the Transvaal Colony, S. Africa, situated about 25 miles S. E. of Johannesburg. Station of the WMS, with (1903) 1 missionary, 25 native workers, 10 outstations, 6 places of worship, 5 Sunday schools, 1 day school and 530 professing Christians. Station also of the Berlin Missionary Society (1875), with (1903, as far as can be learned since the war) 19 native workers (the missionary in charge being in Germany), 15 outstations, 1 day school, and 828 professing Christians.

HENG-CHAU: A town in the province of Hu-nan, China, situated on the Hsiang River, 50 miles S. of Hsiang-tan. Station of the PN (1902), with 2 missionaries and 1 dispensary. The name is sometimes spelled Heng-chow.

HENZADA (Henthada): An important and growing town in Lower Burma, British India, situated on the Irawadi River, 100 miles northwest of Rangoon. It is the center of a large rice trade. Population, 19,800, of whom 15,000 are Buddhists. Station of the ABMU (1853), which has two distinct fields of labor—the Karens and the Burmese. It now (1903) has 7 missionaries, men and women; 172 native workers, men and women; 89 outstations, 81 preaching places, 63 day schools, 3 boarding schools, 53 Sunday schools, 74 organized churches, and about 10,000 Christian adherents, of whom 3,693 are church members.

HERBERTSDALE: A village in Cape Colony, S. Africa, situated about 40 miles N. W. of Mossel Bay, with (1903) 1 missionary, 1 woman missionary, 10 native workers, men and women; 2 outstations and 662 professed Christians, of whom 167 are communicants.

HERMANNSBURG: A settlement in Natal, situated in the Umvoti division, about 15 miles E. of Greytown. Station of the Hermannsburg Missionary Society (1854), with (1902) 1 missionary and his wife, 10 native workers, men and women; 2 outstations, 2 preaching places, 2 day schools and 625 professing Christians.

HERMANNSBURG MISSIONARY SOCIETY. See GERMANY; MISSIONARY SOCIETIES IN.

HERMON: A village in Basutoland, S. Africa, situated near the W. frontier, about 5 miles E. of Wepener. Station of the Paris Evangelical Society, with (1902) 1 missionary and his wife, 22 native workers, 8 outstations, 9 preaching places, 9 day schools and 1,639 professing Christians, of whom 954 are church members.

HERMOSILLO: A town in Mexico, capital of the State of Sonora, situated on the Sonora River, 110 miles north of Guaymas. Population 7,100. Station of the ABCFM (1886), with (1902) 1 missionary and his wife, 3 native workers and 21 outstations.

HERSCHEL: A village in Cape Colony, S. Africa, situated in the angle between Basutoland and the Orange River, 22 miles E. by N. of Aliwal North. Station of the SPG (St. Michael's parish), with (1902) 1 missionary and 1,660 professing Christians.

HERVEY, or COOK, ISLANDS: A small group in the Pacific, between 18° and 22° south latitude, and 157° and 170° west longitude. The population consists mainly of emigrants from Tahiti and Samoa, and numbers about 12,000. In 1889, at the invitation of the chiefs and people, a British protectorate was proclaimed, and in 1901 the islands were annexed to New Zealand and a British resident stationed at Rarotonga to control enactments. Owing to the efforts and careful work of the London Missionary Society, whose missionaries commenced evangelizing these islands in 1823, the majority of the inhabitants are now Christians, and take high rank among the converts in Polynesia. The principal islands are the following: *Rarotonga*, 20 miles in circumference, with about 2,000 inhabitants. It was occupied by the LMS in 1823, and there are now (1901) on the island 2 missionaries and 1 missionary woman, 5 native workers, 5 Sunday schools, 6 common schools and 524 communicants. *Mangaia*, with 1,540 inhabitants, was occupied by the LMS in 1823. There are now there 1 missionary, 78 native workers, men and women; 3 Sunday schools, 5 common schools and 562 communicants. *Aitutaki*, 12 miles in circumference, has 1,170 inhabitants. It became a mission station in 1821. There are now there 1 missionary, 3 native workers, 3 Sunday schools, 5 common schools and 282 communicants. *Atiu* or *Vatiu* has 920 inhabitants. It was entered in 1823 by the LMS and there are there and in surrounding islets 7 native workers and 690 communicants.

HE-TAN ISLAND: An island belonging to China and lying off the coast of the province of Fo-kien. The CMS has mission work in Tang-tau in the N. E. part of the island.

HIAI-CHAU. See KIAI-CHAU.

HIAO-I. See HSIAO-YI-HSIEN.

HIAO KIAN. See HSIAO-KAN-HSIEN.

HIAU KAN. See HSIAO-KAN-HSIEN.

HILL, John Henry: Born 1791; graduated at Columbia College, New York; for several years was engaged in commercial pursuits; pursued a theological course at the seminary, Alexandria, Va., and was ordained deacon and presbyter by Bishop Meade in Norfolk, 1830. He and Dr. Robertson were appointed by the American Episcopal Missionary Society as missionaries to Greece. They sailed October, 1830, landing on the island of Tenos, where they remained six months, and then removed to Athens. In 1832 Mrs. Hill, aided by her sister, Miss Mulligan, opened a female school in their own house, with the Bible as a text-book. From the first the school was crowded and within two years more than 300 children were daily instructed in a stone building erected for it. Three generations of Greek women have there received a Christian education. Other schools for boys and girls were soon established. The schools of the missionary were the models for the municipal and national schools afterward established, and furnished teachers for them. The normal school, too, was placed in charge of graduates from the Hill institution. Once a week Mr. Hill met the boys of all the schools for the study of the Septuagint, which they translated into modern Greek and which he then explained. On Sunday the scholars were taught the Gospel for the day, or the Bible in course containing the history of Christ's life. Four years later he wrote: "When we think of our humble origin from a dark, dirty, vaulted cellar of an old Venetian tower, our progress thence to an old Turkish house and two miserable chambers, and gradually to our own residence, and the filling up first of one room and then of another, and now look at our large and commodious schoolhouse, the largest in Athens, completely filled from top to bottom with industrious children, numbering nearly six hundred, we are astonished."

In 1845 Mr. Hill was appointed chaplain to the British Legation, and for many years officiated as such in the English Chapel of St. Paul at Athens. The appointment was unsolicited by him, and "it was justly due to him for his gratuitous services to the English residents for twelve years past." In 1869, in view of his advanced years and that of his wife, he handed in his resignation to the Board. The committee resolved to "provide for his comfortable support in Athens, the city of his adoption and life's work, until his death."

In token of the appreciation by the nation of his educational work, Dr. Hill received from the Minister of Education an official document, dated June 18, 1881, in which occurs the following paragraph: "Upon the fiftieth anniversary of your school, which was the beginning of the more systematic education of the young women of Hellas, I take pleasure in transmitting herewith the congratulations of his Majesty."

While Dr. Hill's main work was the education of the young, he performed other useful labors. In connection with Dr. Robertson and others of the mission he translated valuable English textbooks, secular and religious, into modern Greek. By his preaching, teaching and personal intercourse he communicated much Christian truth to the clergy. He died at Athens July 1, 1882, aged ninety. The Greek Government gave him a public funeral.

HILL, Joseph Sidney: Born 1852. Died 1894. Native of Barnach, Swindon; educated at Islington C. M. College. On October 14, 1876, he went to Leke, Lagos, W. Africa, and in September, 1878, was stationed at Wairoa, New Zealand Mission, where his connection with the CMS closed in 1882. In 1883 he became chaplain of H. M. Prison, Auckland; in 1892 was appointed Commissary of the Archbishop of Canterbury and Director of Niger Mission, and in the same year was made Bishop-Designate of the Niger. In 1893 Durham University conferred on him the Hon. D.D. Degree, and in the summer of this year he was consecrated in St. Paul's Cathedral second Bishop of the Niger, now named "Western Equatorial Africa," with two native Assistant Bishops. Both Bishop and Mrs. Hill died at Lagos of fever, January 5, 1894. Bishop Hill combined the highest standard of spirituality with a singularly forbearing spirit, and his influence left a lasting impression on the Niger.

HINDERER, David: Of Schorndorf, in the Kingdom of Württemberg. Missionary in Lagos, Western Africa, under the CMS. He was a graduate of the Basel Missionary Training school. After a short time of preparation at Abeokuta he was directed to go forward into the further interior and try to reach the Mohammedan Hausa people. This he did not succeed in doing; but on May 20, 1851, he was the first white man to enter the great town of Ibadan, the name of which was ever afterward associated with his own. In the following year he visited England and married Anna Martin, whose missionary life was as heroic and successful as her husband's. During twenty-eight years of labor in Western Africa, Mr. Hinderer did much pioneer work; and in 1874-5, when he paid his last visit to his old field, he opened up new work to the east of Lagos, leading in 1876 to the occupation of Ode Ondo by Charles Phillips, afterward bishop. Mr. Hinderer died in 1890, and in 1898 a new church was completed at Ibadan as a memorial to David and Anna Hinderer.

Mr. Hinderer's literary work was in the Yoruba language, and included a translation of the book of Isaiah, of the Pilgrim's Progress, and of some hymns. He also revised Bishop Crowther's translation of the Bible.

HINDI LANGUAGE: The language of the Hindus in distinction from that of the Mohammedans of India. It is based upon the ancient Sanskrit, and is called by the literary class Prakrit in contrast to the purer Sanskrit of literature. It is written like Sanskrit, with the Devanagari letters. Traders and in general the lower class of natives often write (and print) the Hindi in an imperfect imitation of the Devanagari, which is called Kaithi. The Hindi language is the vernacular of more than fifty millions of people in the north of India, and possesses an extensive literature aside from the ancient Sanskrit literature.

HINDUISM: In order to gain a clear understanding of the religious systems of India it is important to observe a distinction in names. Brahmanism and Hinduism are not interchangeable. Brahmanism properly denotes an earlier stage of development in the faith of the Hindus; Hinduism denotes that more complete and composite system which embraced all previous stages, and, like a spreading banian-tree, covered all the superstitions and philosophies which had been known to the Indo-Aryan race. If we go back to the earliest teachings of the Vedas and attempt to characterize the faith disclosed in those ancient hymns, we may properly call it Aryanism or Vedism. It is a simple and well-nigh monotheistic nature worship, largely imported by the Indo-Aryan conquerors from the original cradle of the Aryan race in the high tablelands of Central Asia. Nature, under the more frequent name of Varuna or Purusha, is worshiped as the source and the upholder of all things, and is invested with moral attributes and a moral government of the world. Some of the hymns to Varuna seem truly devout. At that early period we find no well-defined polytheism, though there is a tendency toward it in the disposition to address separate powers of nature,—the sun, the sky, the dawn, the rain, fire, etc.,—as embodying the one deity who is supreme.

There is no trace of idolatry or the worship of images and symbols; there is no developed pantheism, no system of caste, no doctrine of transmigration, no widow-burning, nor authorized infanticide. The dead were buried in that early period instead of being burned, and the oppression of woman was comparatively mild. There was no hint of divine incarnations, and no Trimurti or Hindu Trinity.

The next development may be called Brahmanism. It was a galling and oppressive system of sacerdotalism, instituted and enforced by the Brahman or priestly caste. It was well developed by about 800 years B.C., and it bore undisputed dominion for 300 years. It made use of such portions of the Vedas as supported, or seemed to support, its assumptions; and by comment and interpretation, and additions to the sacred hymns, it produced what were known as the Brahmanas. These were based upon such allusions in the Vedas as were supposed to relate to forms and acts of worship, and they became, under the Brahman's hands, complete rituals. They dealt with every question and every interest which concerned the Brahman caste. They traced its divine origin, set forth its superiority and its relative rights. They assigned bounds and limitations to the three subordinate classes, viz.: the *Kshatreya* or soldier caste, the *Vaisya* or farmer caste, and the lowly *Sudra* or the menial caste. These distinctions were fixed immovably. Barriers were raised which might not be passed, and disabilities were laid upon the lower orders from which there was no escape. Marriage, social relations, industries, and vocations, military service, rights of property, laws of inheritance—every interest of human life was subordinated to the dominion of caste.

The privileges and exemptions of the Brahmans involved an intolerable oppression of every other caste. The life of a Brahman was inviolable even by kings.

In connection with this caste system the most absurd and burdensome system of sacrifice sprang up. It has been common for the races of mankind to observe the custom of offering sacrifices to deity. They have generally been expiatory; often they were offerings expressive of gratitude, or they were free gifts made in the hope of securing favor and the bestowment of some desirable boon. In Vedic times there were significant traces of vicarious sacrifice—even of a divine and altogether voluntary sacrifice made by deity for the benefit of others. One is reminded of the Great Sacrifice made once for all, as set forth in the New Testament; and it has been claimed by eminent Oriental scholars that these Vedic references denote strange traditional reminiscences of a prediction once made to man of the "Lamb slain from the foundation of the world."

But under the teachings of the Brahmana period the doctrine of sacrifice became a monstrosity. It was a system of bargaining between earth and heaven. A sort of tariff of values was fixed, which the gods could not disregard. If one were rich enough in sacrificial gifts he might bankrupt the gods by hopeless obligations. It was claimed that the sacrifice of a hundred horses might demand the throne of India. Sometimes even demons placed the gods in their power and wrought anarchy in the universe by the abundance of their sacrifices. Of course the explanation of these extravagances is found in the fact that the Brahman or priestly caste derived an immense revenue from their bloody offerings. In a real sense they ate what the gods were supposed to eat in a spiritual sense, and in all the endless ritual of worship they were handsomely paid for their services. Not only for the living but for the dead were sacrifices demanded. Not even the Church of Rome in the palmy days of Tetzel and Leo X. derived such revenues from the doctrines of Purgatory and Indulgences as accrued to the Brahmanical priesthood of India. The land was deluged with sacrificial blood, the people groaned under the awful burden, and the day of reckoning drew near.

About 500 B.C. the more intellectual classes of India became restive; schools of philosophy sprang up; men were led to consider the great mysteries of life, and, if possible, to solve the problems of human destiny. They were no longer content to be mere ignorant slaves under a galling sacerdotalism. Men rose up and threw off the system of sacrifice or greatly weakened its power. At the same time Buddhism arose with its protest not only against caste and sacrifice, but against the whole system of superstition which the Brahmans had created. Tired of the extreme religiousness of Brahmanism, it went to the opposite extreme of rejecting all religion. Gautama became atheistic. For six years he had tried ascetic Brahmanism and found it barren and illusive. He therefore taught a system of ethics and of self-reliance and self-righteousness, as a substitute for the national religion.

The development of Buddhism and the Darsanas or Six Schools of Philosophy had been preceded by the Upanishads—a system of speculative teachings partly drawn from, and partly reared upon, the philosophic portions of the Vedas, as the Brahmanas had been built up from their scattered references to ritual. These Upanishads were the earliest sources of Hindu philosophy, and from them the weapons were first drawn which crippled the power of the Brahmans.

But over against this movement was a desperate effort of the Brahmans to resist its rationalistic influence. Its results are seen in the so-called Dharma Sastras or Code of Manu. It is not definitely known in what precise order these conflicting movements of the great minds of India proceeded. Strict chronology is the one thing wanting in all Hindu literature; it has well been said that the historic instinct is wholly unknown to the Hindu mind. But it is supposed that the dangerous philosophic tendencies of the times specially stimulated the Brahmans to guard and buttress their assumptions by those laws which, tho produced by different authors and in different periods, are thrown together in the massive compilation ascribed to Manu.

A brief account of these various elements in Hindu literature will set forth their relations more clearly. The Vedas, classified under the various divisions of *Mantras* or Hymns, *Brahmanas* or Rules of Ritual, and *Upanishads* or Vedic Philosophy, are known as *Sruti* or Direct Revelations. Those subsequent works now to be considered are called *Smriti* or unreveled teachings of eminent sages.

The *Darsanas* or Six Philosophic Schools were all in agreement on certain points, such as the eternity of matter past and future; the eternity of soul—both the infinite and the individuated soul; the necessary connection of soul with matter in order to enable it to act (even the infinite soul is unconscious until it evolves the universe which is its body); the attendant evil of all such connection with matter, however necessary; the need of transmigration in order to throw off by long discipline the evil consequences of such connection; and that pessimistic doctrine which makes it the great end of human existence to get rid of itself by being absorbed into deity.

In their separate and distinctive characters the Six Schools were these:

(1) The *Nyaya*, founded by the Brahman Gotama, and which maintained that all the evils of life result from false knowledge or misapprehension, and that the remedy is to be found in acquiring right methods of investigation and reflection. It proposed an elaborate classification of knowledge, and framed a syllogism more elaborate than that of Aristotle. It was really a system of salvation by logic.

(2) The *Vaiseshika*, founded by Kanada, was an advance upon the Nyaya, tho in the same direction. Both were analytical. The latter applied logical and analytical processes to all the facts of nature and of life. It claimed to solve the mystery of creation on an atomic theory like that of Lucretius and the extreme evolutionists of our day.

Like some more modern evolutionists, divided as to the existence of a first and moving Cause, the adherents of these two systems resolved themselves into two classes: the Agnostic or Atheistic school; and those, especially of a later day, who recognized the being of Isvara (God).

(3) Another important school was the *Sankhya*, founded by Kapila. This was synthetic rather than analytic. It ascribed the origin of the visible world to an active principle, regarded as the pre-existing substance (*hypostasis*), the subatomic entity, the "rootless root" of all things. In order to the energizing or activity of this universal source of being it must come into contact or cooperation with soul. It is active, but not intelligent. Soul is intelligent, but inactive and helpless. Each supplements the other. The existing substance called Prakriti constantly clothes the souls which it meets with bodies, and invests them with life; and so the teeming universe is produced.

This dualism of Prakriti and soul was illustrated among philosophers by the relation of the two sexes, and with the low and unphilosophic classes this led to the notion of the male and female principles in the gods, and to the endless corruptions which have been developed in India along these lines.

(4) A fourth system of philosophy was the *Yoga* by Pantaljali. In one view this was rather a ritual than a philosophy, since it related wholly to the observances of the ascetic life, and gave endless rules therefor. But in prescribing methods for ridding the soul of the corrupting influence of matter, it dealt with subtle metaphysics and finely elaborated processes of logical analysis, and often evinced a marvelous philosophic acumen.

(5) A fifth school was the *Maimansa* by Jaimini. It was a reaction against the rationalism of the Nyaya and the Sankhya, and aimed to exalt the word and testimony of the Veda even to the place of God. In its root-principle it was a system of book-worship. It made the Veda self-existent and eternal; even the sound of its spoken words was eternal, and had always been audible. In its details it was an elaborate ritual for the right reading and interpretation of the sacred hymns. A false syllabic quantity in reading, or an inspiration where there should have been an expiration of the breath, was a heinous if not an unpardonable sin. The Veda was a fetish in the fullest sense.

(6) The sixth school was the *Vedanta*, founded by Vyasa. This was out-and-out pantheism—a fuller development of it than has appeared in the Upanishads. "Brahman (neuter noun for the Self-existent) is this very universe, and he has no second." From him, in him, and for him all things exist. The visible world and even our consciousness are only phenomenal and illusory, as when in his evening walk one thinks he sees a snake and makes it very real, while in fact it is only a rope lying across his path. The Vedanta school has molded the intellectual classes of India through all subsequent ages. Whatever superstitions have grown out of the Sankhya, and whatever extravangces may have attended the asceticism of the Yoga, the men of thought have been Vedantists, and are to this day. In the famous Sanskrit schools of Benares this is the prevailing philosophy. And it is that which chiefly gives to Indian thought its strong hold upon the non-Christian and naturalistic minds of all lands.

The Laws of Manu: There is some evidence that the Laws of Manu preceded the full development of the Schools of Philosophy, tho they bear internal evidence of having followed the Upanishads. They do not allude to Buddhism by name, tho certain references to "Atheists" are supposed by some to refer to the followers of Gautama. The supposition is not necessary, as there were other Atheists besides Buddhists. Manu makes no reference to the *Trimurti*—Brahma, Vishnu, and Siva—nor to the doctrine of Bakti (faith) in relation to Krishna. Both that and the doctrine of Saktism (the worship of the female energy) were of later date. Manu was severe in his humiliation of woman; yet her position in his time was not so hedged or so degrading as in later days. Widow-burning is not alluded to in his code, tho in the time of Alexander's conquest it had been introduced, and from 327 B.C. (or earlier) to 1829 its terrible cruelties were perpetuated by the sanction and even instigation of the priesthood.

Sir Monier Williams has classified the contents of the Code under six heads: (1) Its religious teachings, embracing doctrines of Vedic revelation, duties of Brahmans, the rites of Sraddha or offerings to dead ancestors, etc. (2) Its philosophy. This is supposed to have been antagonistic to the national tendencies of the times, and yet, so far as was consistent with its pronounced Brahmanical theories, it was itself philosophical. Some of the principles subsequently evolved by the schools it had already presented. Its unique account of creation, found in Book 1st, represents many subordinate portions of the creative work as having been deputed to eminent Manus. Its fatalism is uncompromising and complete. It is also pessimistic, and finds the usual Oriental explanation of life's mysteries in the doctrine of transmigration. (3) Its social regulations. Whatever relates to caste distinctions is here set forth. Also the duties and privileges of Brahmans, the regulation of trades and vocations of the respective classes, the rites of marriage, and the duties of the householder, etc. (4) Its penal laws and rules of government. Aside from their intense and absurd partiality toward the Brahmans, these laws were in the main just and wise. The system of taxation discriminated in favor of the poorer classes. The duties of a king were carefully prescribed, and that on just principles. He should hold court for the administration of justice, accompanied by counselors. The laws of property, covering transfer, deposit, entail, and the rates of interest, were strict and just. Even laws on bottomry were prescribed. In criminal law the principle of the *lex talionis* was applied generally and rigorously. (5) Laws of penance. (6) Its doctrine of future recompenses by transmigration. This occupies an important place. It was one element of great power in the laws of Manu that their penalties reached beyond the grave and involved man's future estate.

Two or three points presented in the Code of Manu claim special attention. (1) Its peculiar theory of creation. A seed is said to have appeared upon the expanse of waters, which became a golden egg. From this egg the Infinite himself, after the elapse of a year, emerged, and became the progenitor of the world. From this First Cause, which is indiscernible and eternal, was produced that male "Parusha," who is known in the world as Brahma. He divided himself in halves, which became heaven and earth. From himself also he drew forth the mind, and from the mind that ego which has the power of self-consciousness; also the soul and the five senses. By joining particles of the last six with particles of himself he created the living bodies of all beings. He also created the gods, who are endowed with action.

(2) The fatalism of Manu's theology. "In the beginning he (Brahma) assigned names, actions, and conditions to all beings. . . In order to distinguish actions he separated merit from demerit. To whatever course of action the Lord first appointed each kind of being, that it has spontaneously adopted in each successive creation (transmigration). Whatever he (Brahma) assigned to each at its first creation,—noxiousness or harmlessness, gentleness or ferocity, virtue, or sin, truth or falsehood,—that clings to it."—(Manu, Book I., 6-13.)

(3) The singular place assigned to austerities. Dividing his own body, the Lord became half female. With that female he produced Viraj. Viraj, having performed austerities, produced Manu. Thus Manu, speaking to the sages, says: "But know me, O most holy of the twice-born, to be the Creator of this whole world, whom Viraj himself produced, having performed austerities. Then I, desiring to produce created beings, performed very great austerities, and thereby called into existence ten great sages, lords of created beings. They created seven other Manus, possessing great brilliancy, gods and classes (ranks) of gods, and great sages of measureless power. Then many other creations are named. Thus was the whole creation produced by those high-minded ones by means of austerities, and at my command."

(4) Woman's sad estate. Tho Manu is exonerated from even a mention of the Suttee, which became a custom before Alexander's invasion, yet there is little doubt that the influence of his Code, by a logical process, led on to it. Ramabai quotes many passages from the Vedic literature which bespeak kindness and honor for woman, but she adds many strong contrasts from the Code of Manu. In strict accordance with the fatalism above named, we read in Book 9, 17, that "when creating them, Manu allotted to women a love of their bed, of their seat, and of ornament, impure desires, wrath, dishonesty, malice, and bad conduct." Manu made woman, and yet Manu has pronounced upon her the most blighting curse.

(5) Transmigration. To the great sages, Bhrigu sprung from Manu, answered thus: "Hear the decision concerning this whole connection with actions: Actions, which spring from the mind, from speech, and from the body, produce either good or bad results. By action are caused the various conditions of men: the highest, the middling, and the lowest. Know that the mind is the instigator, here below, even to that action which is connected with the body, and which is of three kinds, has three locations, and falls under ten heads. (These are given.) A man obtains the result of a good or an evil mental act in his mind, that of a verbal act in his speech, that of a bodily act in his body. In consequence of many sinful acts committed with his body, a man becomes in the next birth something inanimate; in consequence of sins committed by speech, a bird or a beast; and in consequence of sins of the mind, he is born in low caste." The above is a verbatim statement (Manu, Book XII.) of the threefold principle of all transmigration.

The Fully Developed Hindu System: Without dwelling longer on this remarkable code, probably the most widely influential that was ever promulgated, we notice briefly the irruption of Buddhism into the Hindu system, and its influence upon it. Springing up about 450 to 500 B.C., it gained such power within two centuries that it became the state religion of India—not that it supplanted Brahamanism; it merely dominated it. The immense system of sacrifices it effectually crippled, and it rebuked some of the most extravagant assumptions of the priests.

It produced a more humane spirit toward man and beast, and exemplified a higher code of ethics. To some extent it alleviated the condition of woman. Above all, it resisted the extreme rigors of caste, tho its theories of human equality and mutual right were forced to compromise with a system which it could not wholly overthrow. By its more sympathetic character it so won the people that after Buddha's death the Brahmans as a stroke of policy included him among Vishnu's incarnations. Meanwhile both systems largely influenced each other. Brahmanism embodied so much of Buddhism as served its purpose, while it strongly opposed the influence of the Sangha or Buddhist order. Thus it gradually superseded and finally persecuted the rival system, and drove it from India. Nevertheless, Buddhism bore with it to other lands many fundamental principles borrowed from the Brahmans. Meanwhile Brahmanism had captured the two popular epic poems which celebrated the military exploits of the heroes Rama and Krishna, and turned them to its purpose by interweaving with them many doctrinal and mythological elements. The popularity of these heroes, both of whom belonged to the soldier caste, had excited the jealousy of the Brahmans; yet they could not resist the tide; they must utilize it. They therefore raised Rama and Krishna to the rank of deity, and so brought them within the same lines of pedigree with themselves. Meanwhile they had gradually developed the doctrine of the Trimurti or Trinity, of Brahma the Creator, Vishnu the Preserver, and Siva the Destroyer and Renovator. Vishnu was the most popular as the preserver and sympathizer, and it was a natural and easy device to make all the alleged deliverers of Hindu tradition incarnations of Vishnu. Buddha was finally added as the ninth avatar, and prophecy predicted a tenth, who shall yet come as a spiritual deliverer to establish a kingdom of righteousness.

Thus, by an accretion of whatever was desired of Vedism, Brahmanism, Buddhism, and philosophy, was developed the all-embracing system which we may call *Hinduism*. Its distinction from the earlier sacerdotal system known as Brahmanism will readily be seen.

It not only embraced the systems above named, but it also borrowed many popular superstitions from the Dravidians, Kols, Santals, and other previous invaders whom the conquering Aryans found in the country. The system has been compared to some old building which through a long period has been patched and repaired and enlarged by additions till nearly every original aspect has disappeared, and the result is an entire hamlet rather than a simple structure. Certain elements of Mohammedanism have been incorporated into Hinduism since the Mogul invasion, and some writers claim to have found traces of an influence borrowed from the so-called Syrian Christians who migrated to Malabar in the early centuries of the Christian era. In any case, it is certain that in our own time, Hinduism is borrowing largely from Christianity and the ethics and humanities of our Christian civilization. Under British rule, and in contact with the educational influence of missionary and government education, it has thrown off some of its most debasing customs, and under the title of Revived Aryanism is now proclaiming Christian ethics on what claims to be Vedic authority.

As already intimated, it is in the great Epics, the Ramayana and the Mahabharata, that the Trimurti with their incarnations are developed in the most popular form. They are ancient as heroic poems; they are of later date as Brahmanized religious treatises. Probably they were molded into their present form somewhere between the fourth and the second century before our era, tho parts were added later.

The Bhagavad Gita: The eclectic poem known as the Bhagavad Gita was embedded in the encyclopedic mass of the Mahabharata probably as late as the first or second century of Our Lord. The interpretation given by the great commentator Sankaracharya bears a much later date.

The original author evidently gathered what he regarded as the pure honey from all flowers of Hindu literature. It is certainly a remarkable production, and seems to present many parallels to the New Testament, till one discovers that its mystical pantheistic meanings are often the very opposite of Christian truth, and that the similarities are only in phrases.

Very much has been made of the alleged resemblances of certain passages in the Bhagavad Gita and selected texts from the New Testament. Translators who have proceeded with this theory in view, and especially those who have desired to discredit the Christian Scriptures as a probable plagiarism upon the Hindu poem, which claims to be of an earlier date, have read into their translation many phrases and many conceptions borrowed from Christianity, and of which a Hindu translator would never have dreamed. Large numbers of alleged parallels have been pointed out, most of which are fanciful and strained, while others seem plausible till we take into account the different ideas which the same language would convey to Hindu and to Christian minds respectively. "Union with God," which to a Christian means fellowship, would to a Hindu pantheist signify displacement of the human ego by the divine. In the one case it would imply loyalty, in the other the removal of all personal responsibility. The words "sin," "righteousness," "savior," "salvation," "heaven," find no corresponding terms in Sanskrit which convey our meaning, and the use of these and similar terms in translating Hindu literature is wholly misleading.

The hero of the Mahabharata is Arjuna, a cousin of Krishna, but in the Bhagavad Gita Arjuna is eclipsed. Indeed, he becomes a humble suppliant, while Krishna, a hero of the old border wars of the Punjab, a brave, large-hearted, but dissolute leader, is made divine—nay, the Supreme: He is the One only existing God. He is Vishnu, not the Vishnu of the Trimurti, but the sole, self-existing and all-governing One.

It should be said that under the strong influence of a surviving monotheistic feeling the last two representatives of the Trimurti became each supreme in the worship of his respective followers, and to this day the worshipers of Vishnu and of Siva are distinct sects. Krishna was a further development of Vishnu worship.

In the later Puranas, dating not earlier than the 6th century A.D., the mythology of Vishnu, Krishna, and others runs wild, and, as has been shown by the late Dr. Wilson, of Bombay, the character given to those deities in the Vishnu Purana will scarcely bear the light.

In alluding to the pantheistic meaning of the Bhagavad Gita, we have touched the secret spring of that rare subtlety which the missionary so often encounters in the Hindu mind, and which enables it to parry all attempts to find a lodgment for the saving truth of the Gospel.

Rev. Ram Chandra Bose has said that the first challenge which an agnostic foreigner in India presents to the missionary is the alleged parallels of the Bhagavad Gita to the New Testament, and generally with the assertion that the former, as being the older, must be the source of the latter. The most extravagant laudations are heaped upon its ethics and its philosophy. The Bhavagad Gita is supposed to have been written by some unknown author about the beginning of the 2d century A.D., and it was thenceforth embodied in the epic poem Mahabharata. It attempted to reconcile the conflicting schools of philosophy, and to gather into one dramatic production all the loftiest sentiments found in previous literature. Its alleged resemblances to the New Testament are largely due to the Christian conceptions which have been read into it by modern translators, and by the use of words which would convey to Hindus and Christians respectively entirely different meanings.

Subtle Influence of the System: The practical influence of Hinduism on individual life and character presents a marked contrast with that of Christianity. The life of the high-caste Brahman is intensely religious; no other system is so exacting as his, and yet his wearisome service is abortive, and even belittling. The code of Brahmanism never deals with general principles in the regulation of conduct, as does the Gospel. It inculcates no such great central motives and sources of action as faith and love. Instead of prescribing, as Christ did, the comprehensive law of love to God in supreme degree, and love to our neighbor as to ourselves, it makes endless petty exactions. "Unlike Christianity, which is all spirit and life," says Dr. Duff, "Hinduism is all letter and death."

The Infinite, Brahm, left no thinking or judging to be done by man in the sphere of religious duty, but revealed from heaven every act and observance, every posture and motion of the hand or turn of the eye, connected with worship. A devoted Brahman must in the morning clean his teeth with the twig of a particular tree, uttering at the time a prescribed prayer; and he must be specially careful in throwing away the twig. He must bathe in a particular kind of water, and if it be an inferior stream or fountain, he must pray the Ganges "to be included in this small quantity of water," by what Roman Catholics would call a "real presence." He must also sip the water, sprinkling it in prescribed directions, and offering certain prayers. Another of his morning duties is to salute the sun, which must be done with a lock of his hair tied in a particular way on the top of his head, while a large tuft of casa grass is held in his left hand, and three spires of a different grass in his right hand. He must also be sure to sip water, and with his wet hands touch his head, eyes, ears, nose, shoulders, breast, and feet. Should he happen to sneeze or spit, he may not sip water till he has first touched his right ear. In the Ganges, especially amid the crowds at Benares, or at the great Melas or bathing festivals, this sipping goes on, however filthy the water may have become by the constant treading of the multitudes.

The whole life of a Brahman, if he be supposed to follow his ritual, is a slavish round of petty observances—sippings, and rinsings of the mouth; changes of attitudes and of apparel; drawings of lines on the ground, and smearings with clay, or meal, or cow-dung; kindlings of fires to expel evil spirits; shiftings of sacred threads or hallowed dishes; compoundings of herbs, and rice, and fruit; wreathings of flowers, and repetitions of endless prayers, and texts of the Vedas, and sacred names.

We have given only a small portion of the daily routine, to say nothing of the greater acts of worship rendered to particular gods in the temples. All acts of life are according to program. In marrying, a Brahman must select a girl with neither too much nor too little hair, and it must not be red. She should not be deformed nor talkative, nor afflicted with an unlucky name.

This holy man must be a close student of the Vedas, but should never read them with a sour stomach, nor with his limbs crossed, nor with his feet on a bench. He must not read in a cow-pasture, nor in any place of offensive odors. He must close his book if a dog has barked or a jackal howled or an ass has brayed. He must never cut his own hair, nor bite his nails, nor step upon hair or ashes. He must not look at his wife when eating or sneezing or yawning. He must not stand under the same tree with idiots or washermen. He must never run when it rains, nor spit in a stream of water, nor step over the tether of a calf, nor ride after oxen with imperfect horns or ragged tails.

Reforms and changes: There have been many attempts to reform or to supplant Hinduism, and all except that of Christianity have failed. The impression made by Buddhism was altogether the most profound, and came nearest to permanent success. But, as we have seen, after centuries of contact and rivalry it failed. Tho its aggressive missionary work, which Hinduism did not attempt to emulate, extended into many lands, where it still prevails, yet on the same field, and in what seems to have been a fair trial of strength, Buddhism finally succumbed to its older and more subtle rival. Hinduism had the advantage of an appeal to the supernatural, toward which the hearts of men naturally incline. Moreover, it recognized the being of God and the real entity of the human soul. Doubtless, also, it found substantial aid in the entrenchments of caste, and in the power of venerable custom. Each system was greatly influenced by the other, but the mastery remained with the Brahmans. Even in far-distant lands Buddhism has always recognized, however inconsistently, the power of Hinduism. The twelve Buddhistic sects of Japan, as we find them. in our day, have one thing in common—it may almost be said only one, viz., that in all their temples the images of the gods of Hinduism are invariably found. Protesting as it does against polytheism and idolatry, and virtually atheistic as it is, at least in its old orthodox teachings, Buddhism yet clings to Hindu polytheism with all its dumb idols.

Nearly a thousand years ago Mohammedanism swept into India with all the power and prestige of a conquering race, and a fanatical and everywhere victorious faith. Raised to the seats of arbitrary power, and strong in the clear and consistent monotheism, which it had borrowed from the Old Testament Scriptures, it might have been expected to supplant Hindu idolatry as it had overcome other faiths in many lands. Yet, after more than eight centuries of opportunity and power, it left Hinduism still triumphant; and the forty millions of Mohammedans, less than a fifth of the total population, still give evidence of having received from the old Brahmanical cult quite as much as they imparted.

Sikhism was another attempt at the reform of Hinduism. Nanak, its founder, in his disgust with the pravailing idolatry, hoped to effect a compromise between Hinduism and Islam. Upon the monotheism of the latter a superstructure of the best teachings of the Vedas was to be reared, and an ideal faith thus secured. But Sikhism has also failed to make any serious impression on Hinduism. For a time it won military and political supremacy in the Punjab, but it is little more than the worship of a book; it knows nothing of the true God; the essence of Hindu idolatry still remains.

The influence of the Somajes of our own time upon the heterogeneous, changeful, and yet ever vital Hinduism has not been slight. The **Brahmo Somajes** of Mohun Roy and Chunder Sen were indeed disappointing in their results, yet they promoted the disintegration of the old system, and did much to bring discredit upon the foul corruptions of modern Hinduism. Like Mohammedanism and Sikhism, they urged a return from polytheism to the simple monotheistic worship of Vedic times, and they opposed the injustice and cruelty so long visited upon woman. Chunder Sen exalted the Messiah of the Christians as the chief of all the world's prophets and teachers, but his system has declined.

The most imposing of all these monotheistic movements at the present time is the **Arya Somaj**. So far as the Arya Somaj or any other form of revived Aryanism hopes to regenerate India, it is doomed to disappointment. It cannot long utilize the forces of Christian ethics and Christian civilization under Vedic labels. The fraud will be discovered. The world cannot be convinced that this modern creed is real Hinduism, and the reaction will be proportionate to the illusion. On the other hand, when the real teachings of the Veda come to be known, as they are sure to be, the emptiness of the old cisterns will fully appear. Prof. Max Müller in one of his many lectures has dwelt upon the disappointment and dismay with which intelligent Hindus have observed the disclosures which modern scholarship has made of the sterility of the Vedic literature, and he ascribes to this cause the virtual collapse of the earlier Somajes.

In reply to the confident assumptions of the leading Aryas, Rev. Martin Clark, D.D., of Amritsar, has also exposed the rotten foundation on which they build, by publishing some literal and damaging Vedic translations.

The Contrasts of Hinduism and Christianity: Hinduism has some elements in common with Christianity which it is well to recognize. It is theistic; it is a religion, as distinguished from the agnostic ethical systems of the world. Hinduism recognizes a direct divine revelation which it regards with profound reverence, and through all its variations and corruptions it has inculcated in the minds of the Indian races a deeply religious feeling. It has been claimed that the Hindus are the most thoroughly religious people in the world. Like Christianity, Hinduism appeals to man's intellectual nature; it is inwrought with profound philosophy; it has its trinity, its incarnations, and its predictions of a Messiah who shall restore the truth and establish righteousness.

But, compared with Christianity, the contrasts of Hinduism are far greater than its resemblances. *First*, as to the nature of God. There is an infinite distance between the cold and unconscious Brahm, slumbering age after age, without thought or emotion, or any moral attribute, and the God of Israel, Whose power and wisdom and goodness, Whose mercy and truth and tender compassion, are so constantly set forth in the Scriptures. The latter compares Himself to a father who cares for his children, and who has redeemed the world by an infinite sacrifice. *Second*, there is a striking contrast in the comparative estimates which Hinduism and Christianity place upon the human soul. Unlike Buddhism, Hinduism does recognize the existence of a real soul, but it is only a temporary emanation, like the moon's reflection in the water. It resembles its source as does the moon's image, but coldly and in a most unsatisfactory sense; there is no capacity for fellowship, and the end is absorption. On the other hand, Christianity teaches us that we are created in God's image, but not that we are His image. We are separate, tho dependent; and if reunited to Him through Christ, we shall dwell in His presence forever. *Third*, the two systems are in strong contrast in the comparative encouragement and hope which they hold out for the future. The doctrine of transmigration casts a gloom over all conscious being; it presents an outlook so depressing as to make life a burden, and the acme of all possible attainment is individual extinction; Christianity promises an immediate transfer to a life of unalloyed blessedness, and an endless growth of all the noblest human powers and capacities. Hinduism finds the explanation of life's mysteries and inscrutable trials in the theory of sins committed in a previous existence; Christianity recognizes the same trials, but mitigates them, with the hope of solutions to be found in a future life of compensating joy. The one turns to that which is past, unchangeable, and hopeless, and finds only sullen despair; the other finds encouragement in immortal hope. *Fourth*, Hinduism has no Savior and no salvation. It is, therefore, not a religion in the highest sense, for by the very derivation of the word, religion is the reuniting of the soul to God; it implies the ruin of sin, but provides a rescue from it. That is unworthy of the name which presents no omnipotent arm stretched forth to save. Hinduism provides nothing above the low level of unaided human struggle and merit, and there is no divine helper, no sacrifice, no mediator, no regenerating spirit. It has no glad tidings to proclaim, no comfort in sorrow, no victory over the sting of death, no resurrection unto life.

There are a thousand other peculiar principles in Hinduism whose subtle influence is felt in society and in the State, and to which the faith and influence of the Gospel present the very strongest contrasts.

Christianity has raised woman to a position of respect and honor, and made her influence felt as something sacred and potential in the family, in all society, in the State. Hinduism has brought her down, even from the place which she held among the primitive Aryans, to ever-increasing degradation; it has made her life a burden and a curse.

The following impassioned prayer, quoted by Ramabai from the lips of a high-caste woman who had spent her life from childhood as a "child widow," reveals the anguish which falls to the lot of woman under the Hindu social and religious system:

"O Father of the world, hast Thou not created us? Or has perchance some other God made us! Dost Thou only care for men? Hast Thou no thought for us women? Why hast Thou created us male and female? O Almighty One, hast Thou not power to make us other than we are, that we too may have some part in the comforts of life? The cry of the oppressed is heard even in the world; then canst Thou look upon our victim hosts, and shut Thy doors of justice? O God Almighty and unapproachable, think upon Thy mercy, which is a vast sea, and remember us. O Lord, save us, for we cannot bear our hard lot."

In its broad influence, Christianity has raised the once savage tribes of Europe to the highest degree of culture, and made them leaders in civilization, and rulers of the world. Hinduism has so weakened and humbled the once conquering Aryans that they have long been an easy prey to every invading race. Christianity shows in its sacred books a manifest progress from lower to higher moral standards; from the letter to the spirit; from the former sins that were winked at to the perfect example of Christ; from the narrow exclusiveness of Judaism to the broad and all-embracing spirit of the Gospel; from prophecy to fulfilment; from types and shadows to the full light of redemption. The sacred books of Hinduism have degenerated from the lofty aspirations of the Vedic nature-worship to the vileness of Saktism and the Linga, from the noble praises of Varuna to the low sensuality of the Tantras, from Vedic conceptions of the creation sublime as the opening of John's Gospel, to the myths of the divine turtle and the boar, or the amorous escapades of the supreme and "adorable Krishna."

Christianity breaks down all barriers which divide and alienate mankind, and establishes a universal brotherhood in Christ; Hinduism has raised the most insurmountable barriers, and developed the most inexorable social tyranny ever inflicted on the human race. Christianity enjoins a higher and purer ethic than it has ever found in the natural moral standards of any people; it aims at perfection; it treats the least infraction as a violation of the whole law; it regards even corrupt thoughts as sins; it bids us be holy even as He is holy in Whose sight the heavens are unclean; Hinduism, on the contrary, is below the ethical standards of respectable Hindu society. The better classes are compelled to apologize for it by asserting that that which is immoral and debasing in men may be sinless in the gods. The offenses of Krishna and Arjuna would not be condoned in mortals; the vile orgies of the "lefthanded worshipers" of Siva would not be tolerated but for their religious character. The murders committed by the thugs in honor of Kali were winked at only because a goddess demanded them.

It is the peculiar distinction of India that it has been the theater of nearly all the great religions. Brahmanism, Buddhism, and Mohammedanism have all made trial of their social and political power, and have failed. Last of all came Christianity. The systems which preceded it had had centuries of opportunity, and yet Christianity has done more for the elevation of Indian society in the last fifty years than they had accomplished in all the ages of their dominion. Neither Buddhism nor Mohammedanism had made any serious impression upon caste; neither had been able to mitigate the wrongs which Brahmanism had heaped upon woman— Mohammedanism had rather increased them. The horrors of the Satti (Suttee) and the murder of female infants, those bitterest fruits of priestly tyranny, were left unchecked till the British Government, inspired by missionary influence and a general Christian sentiment, branded them as infamous, and made them crimes.

The sentiment even of the better classes of natives in India is now greatly changed by these influences, and the conventional morality is rising above the teachings of the national religion. Widow-burning and infanticide belong almost wholly to the past. Child-marriage is coming into disrepute; and caste, tho not destroyed, is crippled, and its preposterous assumptions are falling before the march of social progress.

Perhaps the very highest tribute which Hinduism has paid to Christianity is seen in the fact, already noticed, that the modern Arya Somaj has borrowed its ethics and some of its religious doctrines, and is promulgating them upon Vedic authority. It has renounced those corruptions of Hinduism which can no longer bear the light, together with such social customs as caste, child-marriage, child-widowhood, and the general oppression of woman. It denounces the incarnations of Vishnu as mere inventions, and, therefore, cuts up by the roots the whole Krishna cult, with its divine assumptions. It abhors polytheism, and not only proclaims the supremacy of one only true God, self-existent, the Creator and Upholder of all things, but it maintains that such was the teaching of the Vedas, and that when various names were used, they all referred only and always to One and the Same.

Müller (F. Max), *Sacred Books of the East*, Vols. I. and XV., Vols. X. and XXXII.; Bühler (G.), ditto, Vols. II., XIV. and XXV.; *Bhagadavita*, ditto, Vol. VIII., London, 1875; Bose (Ram Chundra), *Hindu Philosophy*, Funk & Wagnalls, New York, 1884; Macdonald (K.S.), *The Vedic Religion*, London, 1881; Williams (Monier), *Brahmanism and Hinduism*, London, 4th ed., 1891, and *Hinduism*, London, 1890; Wilkins (W. J.), *Hindu Mythology*, Calcutta, 1882; Slater (T. E.), *The Higher Hinduism in Relation to Christianity*, London, 1903; *Hindu Sacred Books*, 3 vols., Cnristian Literature Society, Madras, 1903;

HINDUSTANI LANGUAGE. See URDU.

HING-AN. See HSING-NGAN-FU.

HING-I. See HSING-I-FU.

HING-HUA. See HSING-HWA-FU.

HING-PING-HSIEN: A town in the province of Shen-si, China, situated about 30 miles W. of Hsi-ngan-fu. Station of the CIM (1893).

HINNEN. See HSING-NING-HSIEN.

HIRAMPUR: A town in the Santal Parganas, Bengal, India, situated about 20 miles S. of Barhawa. Pastorate of the CMS, with (1903) 8 native workers, 5 preaching places, 3 day schools, and 256 professed Christians.

HIROSAKI: A town in the main island of Japan, situated about 15 miles S. W. by S. of Aomori. Population, 29,100. Station of the ME, with (1902) 6 missionaries, men and women; 12 native workers, men and women; 1 day school, 1 boarding school for girls, 1 kindergarten, and 218 professed Christians. Station also of the PE (1876), with (1902) a missionary and his wife and 1 woman missionary.

HIROSHIMA: A town in Japan, situated 155 miles W. by S. of Kobe. It is noted for its great temple of Miyajima. Population (1898), 122,306. Station of the MES (1886), the PN (1887), the CA (1891), and the CMS (1896). These societies report at this place 14 missionaries, men and women; 24 native workers, men and women; 19 outstations, 10 preaching places, 1 high school, 1 day school, and about 550 professed Christians.

HISLOP, Stephen: Born in Scotland; studied at the Universities of Glasgow and Edinburgh, and the New College. In 1844 Major-General Hill, stationed at Jalna, in the Nizam's territory, presented to the Free Church of Scotland the sum of £2,500 for the founding of a new mission. Mr. Hislop, who had distinguished himself as an accomplished scholar, was secured for the mission. He began his work in February, 1845, at Kamptee, ten miles from Nagpur city, cordially welcomed by Captain Hill and other British officers, who handed over to him a school which they had established, and otherwise greatly encouraged him. He was assisted by three German artisans. In 1846 he removed to the city of Nagpur, containing a large Mahratta population, and opened, with thirty scholars, a school in the vicinity of the Rajah's palace. The school soon took a high position as a missionary institution and for many years sent forth annually between 250 and 300 pupils. It is called the Hislop Missionary College. The Central Provinces being ruled by a heathen government, and the people having no desire for education, his position was a trying one. His life was often in peril. In 1853, in connection with caste prejudices and the baptism of several natives, a serious riot occurred, and an attack was made on the mission house, which, but for his heroic defense by the native Christians, would have resulted in the death of the missionary. The next year he was attacked by a fanatical Mohammedan mob, but rescued by the aid of an old pupil and some Sepoys. He was conveyed to the mission house in an apparently dying state, ten deep gashes appearing on his head, and his body greatly bruised. In 1857, having received information privately from a Mohammedan of a combined plot of the up-country Sepoys and the Mussulmans of the city to massacre all the Europeans on a given day, he informed the authorities, so that the design was frustrated, and the Madras and Bombay Presidencies were thus saved from the rebellion. This devoted missionary met with an early and tragic death. On September 4, 1863, he rode into a river in the night and was drowned.

HISSAR: A town in the Punjab, India, situated 98 miles W. N. W. of Delhi. Population (1891), 16,900, of whom 10,000 are Hindus. Station of the SPG, with 2 women missionaries.

HISTORY OF MISSIONS: The true history of missions is far more than the mere record of the extension of Christianity. It includes the development of the mission idea within the Church as well as its outward application in the conduct of mission enterprise. It covers, too, the development of method and organization. The present complicated machinery of missions, which seems to many so cumbrous and so unlike the simple evangelization of the apostolic days, or even of the earlier missions of the present era, is really but a growth. Each new wheel or band or cog in the mechanism has been added not to meet a theoretical conception, but an actual need, and no history can be complete that does not touch at least upon this element in mission progress. The history of missions has to do also with the effect of missions upon the world apart from the results usually tabulated. Aggressive Islam, reviving Hinduism, Buddhism, Shintoism, each must be dealt with in reckoning up the sum total of results of mission effort. It is evident that so wide a reach is impracticable within the limits of this work, which must be content with the more common, if narrower, conception of a record of the extension of Christianity through the agency of missionary enterprise, merely indicating some of these other topics as suggestive for further reading and study.

To facilitate this, the general topic is treated under five titles: Geography of the Extension of Christendom, summarizing the article in the first edition on the Historical Geography of Missions, and giving a bird's-eye view of the extension of Christianity over the world in the different periods; Apostolic and Early Christian Missions, giving a survey of the general character and methods of the first six centuries; Medieval Missions, describing the movements and influences that made Europe Christian, and covering the period up to the Reformation; Roman Catholic Missions, from the Reformation to the present day, and Modern Protestant Missions, covering the same period. These different articles, of necessity, somewhat overlap, but no more than seems essential to the accurate conception of each subject, and the four periods are so distinct that separate treatment is inevitable.

HO: A station of the North German Missionary Society (1859) in Togoland, W. Africa, situated near the western border of the colony, about 60 miles N. by W. of the mouth of the Volta River. It has (1903) 8 missionaries, men and women; 31 native workers, men and women; 18 outstations, 21 day schools, and 1,568 professed Christians.

HOACHANAS: A settlement in German Southwest Africa, situated among the Namaqua tribes about 230 miles E. S. E. of Walfisch Bay. Station of the Rhenish Missionary Society, with (1903) 1 missionary and his wife, 2 native workers, 1 day school, and 286 professed Christians.

HOBSON, Benjamin: Born January 2, 1816, at Welford, Eng.; studied medicine in London; sailed July 28, 1839, as a medical missionary of the LMS for China, reaching Macao December 18. There he was occupied with his medical work till the beginning of 1843, when he removed to Hongkong, and, on June 1, opened a hospital. In 1859, his health having failed, he returned to England, and, being unable to resume work in China, he retired after a while from the service of the Society. Besides his labors in Chinese hospitals, he wrote and translated into Chinese treatises on anatomy, surgery, medicine, midwifery, and natural philosophy, which have had a very wide circulation. He died at Forest Hill, near London, February 16, 1873.

HO-CHAU: A town in the province of Shan-si, China, situated about 100 miles S. S. W. of Tai-yuen-fu. Station of the CIM (1886), with 2 women missionaries, 6 native workers, men and women. The work of reorganization after the disasters of the Boxer outbreak has hardly (1903) proceeded to the point of definite information of the state of the church members at this place.

HOFFENTHAL: A settlement in Natal, S. Africa, about 40 miles W. S. W. of Colenso. Station of the Berlin Missionary Society (1868), with (1903) 2 missionaries, 10 native workers, 6 outstations, 1 day school, and 257 professed Christians.

HOFFENTHAL, or HOPEDALE: A settlement on the east coast of Labrador. Station of the Moravian Missions (1782), with (1900) 6 missionaries, men and women; 10 native workers, 1 day school, 1 dispensary, 1 hospital, and 70 church members.

HOFFMAN: A settlement in Liberia, situated at Cape Palmas and near Harper. Station of the PE (1856), with (1902) 1 missionary, 2 native workers, 6 outstations, 2 day schools, and 144 professed Christians.

HOH-CHAU. See Ho-Chau.

HOHENFRIEDEBERG: A settlement in German East Africa, situated in the Usambara region about 70 miles N. W. of Tanga. Station of the German East Africa Mission, with theological and industrial schools and a leper asylum.

HOISINGTON, Henry R.: Born at Vergennes, Vt., August 23, 1801; learned the printer's trade in 1815 in Buffalo, and pursued it in Utica and New York. He fitted for college under Dr. Armstrong at Bloomfield Academy; graduated at Williams College in 1828, and Auburn Theological Seminary in 1831; ordained and settled in Aurora, N. Y., the same year; sailed as a missionary of the ABCFM for Ceylon in 1833. In 1834 he was sent with Mr. Todd to the city of Madura to establish a new mission. In 1836 Mr. Hoisington returned to Jaffna, and was placed at the head of the seminary. On account of ill-health he visited the United States in 1842, and returned to Jaffna in 1843, but continued ill-health compelled him to give up his lifework as a missionary in 1849. Mr. Hoisington possessed a vigorous and acute mind, and his work as instructor of Tamil youth led him to study profoundly Hindu science, metaphysics and theology, and in the department of higher Tamil literature he had, perhaps, no superior in Southern India. After his return home he wrote for the American Oriental Society a syllabus of the Siva Gnana Pothum, a Tamil translation of an old Sanskrit Agama, which treats of deity, soul, and matter; also an English translation of the same work, with an introduction and notes. He published also in the *Bibliotheca Sacra* an essay on the tenets of philosophical Hinduism. He died at Centre Brook, Conn., May 16, 1858.

HO-KAU: A town in the province of Kiang-si, China, situated in the N. W. part of the province about 135 miles S. E. of Kiu-kiang. Station of the CIM (1878), with 3 women missionaries.

HOK-CHIANG. See Fu-tsing-hsien.

HO-KEO. See Ho-Kau.

HOK-SU-HA: A town in the province of Kwang-tung, China, situated in the hill country, about 135 miles N. E. of Canton. Station of the Basel Missionary Society (1886), with (1903) 2 missionaries and their wives, 18 native workers, 16 outstations, 11 day schools and 429 professed Christians. Name also written Hokschuha.

HO-LIN-KOH-RI: A village in the province of Shan-si, China, situated in the N. part of the province, about 28 miles W. N. W. of So-ping-fu. Station of the CA.

HOME MISSIONS in the United States: The

United States is one of the greatest mission fields of the world. Ever since the days when the discovery of the New World and the condition of the savage Indians stirred up the Christians of the Old World to send missionaries, the history of Christian effort in the United States has been one of continual and almost unabated zeal and earnestness. The work has gone through the various stages of evangelistic and pastoral agencies in the older and more settled districts of the country, but there are always new regions to be cared for and new people to evangelize.

The urgency, diversity, and magnitude of the work of Christian missions in the United States can best be understood by looking at the different elements which compose the population, and the influences which affect the efforts of the church.

1. *Work for the Native Population:* Under this head we can consider the term "native" as including that part of the people who are native born or who have been located in the country for a period long enough to be naturalized: the Indians, the negroes, as well as the native Americans. This work will be shown in the detailed account of the various Home Missionary societies, which follows. The general facts in regard to this element of the population may be dwelt upon but briefly.

The development of the great territories in the West, and the consequent migration of the inhabitants of the older and more settled states, has caused the growth of mission work, and the division of Christian work into two heads, pastoral and evangelistic. Pastoral work is carried on in the settled states; in the large cities it is combined with the work of City Missions in order that the poor and the rich may have an equal chance to hear and profit by the teachings of the Gospel. But, as has been well said, man is kept in the right path as much from fear of the censure of the surrounding community as by the desire and purpose to do right for right's sake; and when the adventurous ones leave the well-ordered communities to go where they will be pioneers of civilization, they, too, often forget to take their religion with them; amid the freedom and license of the new life the ungodly become more so, while the nominal Christian soon loses even the name. Then the evangelistic methods of the Church must be brought to bear upon these migratory multitudes, and the parent churches send out missionaries to look after the stray sheep, as well as to claim those who have belonged to no fold. The rapidity with which the Western states are increasing in population is phenomenal. How great a proportion of this increase is due to migration, and how much is properly referred to the arrival of emigrants from other countries, cannot be determined without more data than have yet been furnished by the Census Bureau; but the lessening rate of increase in many of the older states, such as Ohio, Indiana, Iowa, Missouri, and Illinois, is distinctly traced to the migration of the people. Hence a great proportion of the rapidly increasing population of the Western territories and states is made up of those who have severed family, social and religious ties by moving into the new districts. Must these ties be left with no new objects around which to cling, until they shrivel up and respond but slowly to any stimulus? Or shall the Church keep pace with the world and supply new church ties as soon as the old ones are severed; new places of worship, ere the habit of church-going ceases to exist; new influences for good before the careless or seared conscience fails to respond? These questions indicate the nature of home mission work in so far as it concerns what might be called the peculiar objects of the Church's care—her own wandering sons and daughters.

2. *Work for the Immigrants:* Attracted by visions of wealth, justice, and liberty of action; driven out from their home-lands by poverty, increase of population, tyranny and misrule; aided by cheapness of travel and the short time required for the journey, the emigrants of European countries have poured in upon the United States in a steady stream. This influx of foreigners is regarded as the greatest of dangers to the civil and religious life of the country. The time is past when the immigrant was hailed with joy. There is now no great urgency for his labor. His morals, his socialistic, anarchistic tendencies, his conception of liberty as license, his inability to appreciate the honor and responsibility which go with the right of franchise—all these make the average European emigrant one of the most objectionable of strangers. The results of this immigration are seen distinctly upon the statistics of crime. Many of these immigrants come from Christian communities, but they are influenced in the same way as the native American is when he changes his home; but by far the greater number belong to the bilge-water of the various ships of state in the old countries. The absorption and Americanization of such immigrants is a herculean task thrown upon the State and the Church. The State is devising means to escape the conflict which is imminent by stopping the inroads; but with strange lack of the sense of proportion, the immigration of a few thousand Chinese has been prohibited, while hundreds of thousands of immigrants are yearly coming to our shores from Southern and Eastern Europe. The Church has the greater task, for many of these immigrants come from countries where they have had little religious instruction; and in addition to the difficulties which arise from the nature of the case—the known character of the people, the isolation of their life—there are added other factors which complicate still further the problem. These are, as ably set forth in Strong's *Our Country*, Romanism, intemperance, Mormonism, wealth, and the collection of people in cities. Mormonism has officially abolished polygamy, but even if this were other than a purely formal and nominal abolition, it is still the foe to the best interests of the individual and the state; of the papacy, this is not the place to speak; intemperance is so well recognized as an enemy to the Church and the Commonwealth that it needs no words of description; city life and its dangers are seen on all sides; and the influence of the inordinate desire for wealth is keenly felt by all.

This, in brief outline, is the condition of affairs which makes the field of the Home Missionary societies one of paramount importance by reason of the enormous extent of territory, the number of the people, the interests at stake, and the conviction that the future of this nation will depend upon the success with which the Church fulfils the obligations thus imposed upon her.

Home missions is the name given to the work of the church for those in our own country, whether it be among aborigines, immigrants, or frontier settlers; and every denomination is actively engaged in this work, whether or not it is made a separate department, and classified and reported separately from the general work of the church. The ways are many, but the end is the same, and the means adopted substantially agree.

We give here a sketch of the work of some of the older and larger bodies laboring in the Home Mission field in the United States.

Baptist: The American Baptist Home Missionary Society was organized April 27, 1832, in New York City, where it still has its general offices. Its object is "to promote the preaching of the Gospel in North America." Until its organization, missionary work in the new settlements of the West had been prosecuted to a limited extent by some of the Baptist Conventions of the older States, and especially by the Baptist Missionary Society of Massachusetts, organized in 1802. This Society took the initiative in the formation of the General Society. Rev. John M. Peck, who for many years had rendered remarkable service as a missionary in the Mississippi Valley, and Rev. Jonathan Going, of Massachusetts, who was sent out to confer with him, were foremost spirits in the new movement. Dr. Going became its first Corresponding Secretary, serving for five years; then, in succession, Rev. Luther Crawford, two years; Benjamin Hill, D.D., twenty-two years, from 1840 to 1862; Jay S. Backus, D.D., twelve years, 1862-74; James B. Simmons, D.D., seven years, 1867-1874; E. E. Taylor, D.D., five years, 1869-1874, the work being divided among them during the period of their contemporaneous service; Nathan Bishop, LL.D., two years, 1874-76; S. S. Cutting, D.D., three years, 1876-79; H. L. Morehouse, D.D., fourteen years, 1879-93; T. J. Morgan, LL.D., nine years, until his death in 1902, when Dr. Morehouse, who had been Field Secretary for this period, was recalled to the general secretaryship, and E. E. Chivers, D.D., was appointed Field Secretary.

Until 1845 its constituency included Baptists of the whole country, numbering then about 385,000, fully half of whom were in the South. Then came the disruption over the question of slavery and the withdrawal of Southern Baptists to form an organization of their own.

The West was the chief field of the Society's operations—Detroit, Chicago, and many other important points were occupied. Exploring and pioneer missionaries traversed whole states and territories by most primitive methods. In 1845 its first missionaries went overland to Oregon, and in 1849 via the Isthmus to California. With the expansion of civilization in the West, as precious metals were discovered, railroads constructed and lands opened to settlement, its pioneer missionaries were quickly on the new fields. The first year of its history its force of laborers was fifty; in 1854, one hundred and seventy-five. For the thirty years ending 1862 its receipts were $795,259. In that period 1,242 churches were organized and 27,911 persons baptized. After the war the Western work assumed greater proportions and has continued to make heavy demands upon the Society. In many states and territories nearly all the churches have had the Society's fostering care. Of its entire missionary force in 1903 (aggregating 1,310), 881 were in the Western states and territories. Its missionary expenditures there have been about $4,000,000.

A Church Edifice department of the Society was contemplated in 1854 and a little was done during subsequent years. In 1869 it was definitely organized, and by 1875 about $275,000 had been secured as a loan fund to aid churches in erecting houses of worship. By 1879, chiefly in the West, 333 churches were thus aided. In 1881 the Gift Fund was established, and as large contributions were secured for it, the Society by 1885 was aiding over 100 churches annually in gifts and loans, and within twenty-two years had helped in the erection of 1,866 church edifices, chiefly in the way of gifts. Its permanent Church Edifice Loan Fund is $150,000 and the Permanent Gift Fund, the income only to be used, $158,000.

The Society's work for the Freedmen, began in 1862, expanded into a large educational department, in addition to the distinctively missionary efforts put forth in their behalf. The total expenditures for these purposes have been about $4,000,000. It aids wholly or in part twenty-nine schools, twelve of which are higher and seventeen secondary institutions; tho much secondary work is also done in the higher institutions. Most are coeducational; two are for young women only, viz., Hartshorn College, Richmond, and Spelman Seminary, Atlanta, the latter probably the largest and best-equipped school of its kind in the world. There is a high-grade theological school as a department of Virginia Union University, Richmond; while in all the other higher schools considerable attention is given to the training of students for the ministry, of whom between 400 and 500 are in attendance yearly. The Leonard Medical School, a department of Shaw University, Raleigh, has a thorough four years course and a strong corps of instructors, about 120 being enrolled last year. Special attention is given at several points to normal training for teachers, and there are well-equipped industrial departments at several schools. The total enrollment for 1902-3 was 6,947. It is estimated that the total enrollment from the first is quite 80,000. A pronounced religious and missionary spirit dominates all these institutions, which have powerfully affected for good not only the two million negro Baptists of the land but multitudes besides. The valuation of these school properties is approximately $1,500,000. The Society's annual expenditures for these purposes is about $150,000. Endowments are greatly needed, the total funds of this character being only $288,132. Many capable negro teachers, a number as heads of schools, are in the force of instructors.

Among the foreign populations the Society in 1903 had 282 missionaries laboring among fifteen nationalities from Europe and two from the Orient, the total number of nationalities or peoples among which it labors being twenty-one. The work begun in 1846 among the Germans has grown to large proportions, the membership in the German Baptist Churches of the United States being over 24,000. Similarly the work begun among the Swedes in 1848, also among the Danes and Norwegians about the same time, has enlarged until now the Scandinavian Baptists here number over 27,000. Missions to the French Canadians, chiefly in New England, since 1870 have resulted in the acquisition of at least 3,500 converts from Romanism. In recent years missions have been undertaken with good results among the Bohemians, Poles, Italians, Portuguese, Finns, Hungarians and Russians. The enormous immigration of recent years has afforded a great opportunity for the evangelization of multitudes ignorant of the essential truths of the Gospel.

To the Chinese, after ineffectual attempts to secure a suitable laborer sooner, the Society appointed a missionary at San Francisco in 1870. There were many hindrances to this enterprise during the anti-Chinese agitation on the Pacific coast. The chief missions now are in San Francisco, Portland, Seattle, Spokane, Butte, Chicago and New York City. There is a flourishing mission to the Japanese in Seattle.

The North American Indians have been included in the Home Mission Society's field since 1865, when the Indian missions of the Missionary Union were transferred to it. Continuously since then have missions been maintained among them. For many years work was limited mostly to the five civilized tribes, among whom very gratifying progress has been made. Within the last decade missions have been established among the "blanket Indians," with truly remarkable results among the Kiowas. The Society's missions embrace twelve Indian tribes, among whom there are over 4,000 members of Baptist churches. There are two excellent schools for the Indians, at Tahlequah and near Muscogee, Indian Territory. The missionary and teaching force among them in 1903 was twenty-nine.

The Spanish-speaking peoples of this continent and adjacent islands are part of the Society's field. The first evangelical preacher to go to Mexico was a Baptist minister, Rev. James Hickey, in 1862, which led to the organization of a Baptist Church at Monterey in 1864. During the troublous period of the war and the unsettled state of affairs in Mexico, until the overthrow of the Maximilian Empire, missionary work there was difficult. In 1870 the Society appointed its first missionary and has gradually extended and strengthened its work in that Repubic until now there are ten churches, several having good church properties, and about 600 members. The Society's printing press at the City of Mexico issues a bi-monthly paper edited by Rev. W. M. Sloan, who also has prepared and published a Spanish concordance of the Bible.

Hardly had the smoke of war with Spain cleared away before the Society took steps to occupy Cuba and Porto Rico. By an amicable arrangement with the Home Mission Board of the Southern Baptist Convention, the Society has the two eastern provinces of Cuba and all of Porto Rico as its field. In January, 1899, missionaries were appointed to both these islands, where the work has been wonderfully prosperous. There are now 22 Baptist Churches, with over 1,000 members and about 2,000 enrolled in Sunday schools, while several valuable church properties have been secured and other edifices are in process of erection at a cost of quite $50,000.

City mission work in cooperation with City Mission Societies was taken up in 1896 and the Society is now prosecuting missions in this manner in six of the chief cities of the land. In 1903, in response to the expressed will of the denomination, the Society undertook the organization of a general evangelistic effort in cooperation with other Baptist missionary organizations, with promise of excellent results.

During its entire history of seventy-one years the Society has issued 28,117 commissions, and its laborers have reported 5,730 churches organized, 179,107 persons baptized and nearly as many others added by letter to mission churches. Its receipts for all purposes have been about $13,500,000; its permanent invested funds of all kinds are $876,000, besides $516,000 annuity funds. Its receipts for 1903 were $621,387.32. For all this vast and varied work of three great departments, Missionary, Church Edifice and Educational, covering every state and territory, Alaska, some Canadian Provinces, Mexico, Cuba and Porto Rico, there is one Board of Managers, one Corresponding Secretary, and one Treasurer, with necessary assistants, the cost of administration being only about six per cent. of its receipts.

Congregational: When the American Home Missionary Society was organized, in 1826, several local organizations for home missionary work were in operation, some of which originated in the last century. The Society for Propagating the Gospel among the Indians and others in North America was founded in 1787; the Missionary Society of Connecticut, and the Berkshire and Columbia Missionary Society, in 1798; the Massachusetts Missionary Society in 1799. Others of a later origin existed in the other New England States and in New York. Some of them confined their operations within their own geographical limits. Others sent missionaries to the destitute in the new settlements of Northern New England, and the remoter wilderness, even to the banks of the Mississippi. But as these societies acted independently of each other, some sections were over-supplied with laborers and others were left in utter destitution. Moreover, the laborers sometimes came into competition and conflict with each other, and the funds contributed for their support were worse than wasted. It was evident that a more comprehensive and effective system must be devised to supply the destitute portions of the country with Gospel ministrations; but no direct steps were taken toward the solution of this problem till 1825, when plans were formed which resulted in the organization of the American Home Missionary Society.

The United Domestic Missionary Society, undenominational in its principles and spirit, was formed in 1822. At an important meeting, composed of eminent New England ministers, held in Boston January 11, 1826, a resolution was adopted recommending that the United Domestic Missionary Society of New York become the American Domestic Missionary Society. The Executive Committee of the UDMS cordially responded to the overture from the Boston meeting and issued a circular to friends of Home Missions in all parts of the United States, inviting them to meet in New York to form an American Home Missionary Society. One hundred and twenty-six individuals, representing thirteen States and four denominations, responded to this invitation, and met in New York (Brick Church) on May 10, 1826. On May 12, the United Domestic Missionary Society, in responding to the proposition made by the convention meeting in the Brick Church, adopted the following resolution:

"*Resolved*, That the recommendation of the convention be adopted, and the UDMS now become the American Home Missionary Society, under the constitution recommended by the convention."

Officers were at once elected and the work begun.

Its Constituency: Of the churches cooperating, the Associate Reformed shared but little either in its labors or benefactions. The Reformed

Dutch churches withdrew when their own Board was organized in 1832. The New School Presbyterian churches continued to cooperate until 1861, when the General Assembly instituted its Presbyterian Committee on Home Missions. Thus the AHMS, without any change either in its constitution or principles of action, became the organ of Congregational churches only. On the 1st of October, 1893, by permission of the Supreme Court of the State of New York, the corporate name of the Society was changed to "The Congregational Home Missionary Society" and it has ever since been known as such.

Its object was "to assist congregations that are unable to support the Gospel to the destitute within the United States." It was to supply the destitute everywhere, but especially those in the new settlements on the northern, western and southern frontiers, with the privileges of the Gospel through the ministry of the Word and the Church of God.

Its method has been to supplant the former plan of mere missionary tours, pursued by the Domestic Missionary Societies, by providing permanent churches and a permanent ministry, entering into partnership with each church in sustaining its minister, stipulating that it shall bear its full share of the burden, an annually increasing share, until the church shall become self-supporting. The stimulating effect of this system is seen in the fact that, during the last ten years, about forty churches have been annually brought to self-support; and the average annual expenditure for a year of missionary labor has been $300.

Through the *Woman's Department* no inconsiderable portion of revenue has been obtained. The estimated value of gifts sent in "missionary boxes" during the last twenty years has exceeded $50,000 annually.

Its Foreign Department: When the Society was organized, our population was being increased by only 10,000 immigrants annually. In view of the peril to our country involved in this vast increase of foreign immigration, the Society in 1883 entered upon a more distinct systematic effort in behalf of this class of our population. In these twenty years the work has made rapid progress, and the number of missionaries who have preached in foreign languages during the last year (1903) is 230, including German, Scandinavian, Bohemian, Polish, French, Mexican, Italian, Spanish, Finnish, Danish, Armenian, Greek and Welsh.

Summary: Of the 5,650 Congregational churches in the United States, more than four-fifths of the whole were planted, and many more have been fostered, by the Congregational Home Missionary Society and its auxiliaries. Since its organization in 1826, 507,072 members have been added to churches under its care.

In 1902-3, 1,907 home missionaries were employed, 4,946 hopeful conversions were reported, 8,250 members were received into home missionary churches, 2,573 churches and stations were regularly supplied with the Gospel, 57 churches reached self-support, 95 new churches were organized, 72 houses of worship were built, 102 parsonages were erected, 141,269 Sunday school scholars were cared for, 159 Sunday schools were organized, 60 young men connected with home missionary churches were preparing for the ministry, 230 home missionaries were laboring among the Germans, Welsh, French, Swedes, Norwegians, Danes, Bohemians, Spanish, Indians and Mexicans. Total expenditures in 47 States and Territories, $569,734.47. The work of church erection is carried on by a distinct organization, the Congregational Church Building Society.

Lutheran: The Lutherans have been actively engaged in missionary work in Alaska and among the American Indians and negroes. As early as 1840 a house of worship was erected at Sitka, the capital of Alaska, and the membership at one time numbered 150. Ethokin, one of the governors, was a native of Finland and a Lutheran, and when he entered upon the duties of his office he brought with him a Lutheran minister. This work came very near dying out. The Swedish Missionary Union, composed of members from the Waldstroemian party, have been sending missionaries to Alaska since 1886, and the Swedish Lutherans of America have lately become greatly interested in Alaska as a mission field. The entire work of the early Indian missionaries had only a temporary existence, and altho the Lutherans did faithful work among the red men, for years they found that congregations were organized and schools were planted only to be disbanded and broken up in course of time. The onward march of immigration into the territory of the Indian and its fruits of immorality and unjust treatment made the Indian suspicious of the white man's dealings. In 1845, Vraemer, afterward professor in Concordia College, Springfield, Ill., began work among the Chippewa Indians by establishing a school for children, and largely through this agency he became acquainted with the language, and was enabled to speak to large assemblies of Indians. The work grew, and Baierlein was sent out from Germany. Baierlein traveled about, visiting one tribe after another, and he established a station about sixty miles from Frankenmuth, built a log house for living and school purposes, which proved to be a center of good. Miessler, sent out by the Leipzig Society, came to assist Baierlein. In his study of the language, Baierlein's reader and spelling book in the Chippewa language was of great service. The mission was eventually transferred to the Missouri Synod. The general uprising of the Indians in defense of their rights put an end to the station in Minnesota under the faithful supervision of the missionary Cloeter. The American Norwegians are carrying on a successful work among the Indians in the neighborhood of Wittenberg, Wis., where, in 1885, they erected a schoolhouse, and under the care of Rev. Mr. Morstad the work has prospered. The United Synods of Wisconsin, Minnesota and Michigan are conducting mission work among the Apache Indians, and a missionary plant has been established near San Carlos, Arizona. The Synods have recently appropriated a considerable sum of money to be used in the erection of houses for missionaries.

The Lutherans are also doing excellent missionary work among the American negroes.

Methodist Episcopal: The origin of Domestic Missions in the Methodist Episcopal Church was in 1812. Bishop Asbury about this date began soliciting funds for the support of ministers upon missionary circuits. This was the period of vigorous, aggressive work in the then Far West and in the New England States. In 1819 the Missionary Society of the Methodist Episcopal Church was formed, the organization growing out of a revival among the Wyandot Indians. In the Preachers' Meeting of New York, held April 5, 1819, in the Forsyth Street Church, it was "*Resolved*, That it is expedient for this meeting to form a missionary and Bible Society of the Methodist Episcopal Church in America." Article XIII, of the Constitution provided that the Society should be established "wherever the Book Concern may be located," and the General Conference was authorized to insert articles into the Constitution for such purpose, and to make the book-agents treasurers, and also to provide for the appropriation of funds within the object specified.

The plan of procedure was to organize auxiliaries in all the principal cities. The first auxiliary formed was the Female Missionary Society of New York, about ninety days after the parent Society was instituted, one of the earliest missionary organizations of women in the land. The General Conference in Baltimore, May, 1820, adopted the report of a committee on organization, and gave the Society and the missionary cause a great and effectual impulse. The existence of the Society really dates from this General Conference of 1820. In the autumn of 1820 the Society actively began its operations, sending Rev. Ebenezer Brown of the New York Conference to labor among the French people of Louisiana.

Present Scope: The Domestic Missions, as to languages used, may be classified as English-speaking and non-English-speaking, the latter including work among the Bohemians, Chinese, Finns, French, Germans, Indians (14 tribes), Italians, Japanese, Portuguese, Scandinavians, and Welsh. The field embraces the Arizona, Atlantic, Black Hills, Gulf, Kalispell, Nevada, New Mexico English, New Mexico Spanish, North Montana, North Pacific German, Pacific Japanese, Porto Rico, Utah and Wyoming Missions, together with those administered by Annual Conferences. All Domestic Missions are administered under the direction of the presiding bishops, who (except for Missions outside of Annual Conferences) draw upon the Missionary Society for grants-in-aid not to exceed in amount sums fixed yearly in advance by the "General Missionary Committee," a representative body acting under the authority of the General Conference of the Methodist Episcopal Church. Disbursements for Domestic Missions in 1902 amounted to $482,811. Appropriations for 1903 amounted to $495,297.

Work for *Bohemians* is carried on in five Annual Conferences, the Upper Iowa Conference alone conducting Bohemian missions in three of its districts. There are four missions in Chicago, besides those in Baltimore and Cleveland, and the Coke Mission of the Pittsburg Conference.

The ME Church has missions for *Chinese* in several cities of California, with headquarters at San Francisco, besides the work carried on in New York, Boston, and Portland, Ore. Seven missionaries and 6 local preachers are engaged in this work.

For *Finns* the ME Church conducts special work in California, Michigan and Minnesota.

There are thriving Methodist societies of *French*-speaking people in Worcester and Lowell, Mass., and in Dover and Manchester, N. H. In addition to these the French Church in Chicago reports 37 members and probationers, and the French Mission in Crowley, La., reports 120 members and probationers.

From the time of the conversion of William Nast, in 1835, the ME Church has labored among *German*-speaking people. There are nine regular Annual Conferences and the North Pacific German Mission Conference, with a combined membership of 62,480. In charge of this membership is a corps of 541 pastors, 266 of whom receive financial aid from the Methodist Missionary Society.

Indians: Twenty-one Methodist Episcopal missionaries and 22 local preachers are reaching about 12,000 Indians. At present there are Indian missions within the bounds of 13 Conferences, of which missions 17 are in Michigan, 5 in New York State, 9 on the Pacific Coast, 1 in Minnesota and 1 in Wisconsin. The tribes reached are these: Ukiah, California Digger, Onondaga, Oneida, Chippewa, Seneca, Tonawanda, Ottawa, Paintes, Washoe, Black Feet, St. Regis, Klamath and Nooksack.

The ME Church has missions among *Italians* in Boston, Buffalo, Chicago, Cincinnati, New Orleans, New York, Philadelphia, and Providence, besides those in smaller towns.

The Pacific *Japanese* Mission Conference of the ME Church covers the work in Hawaii and the Pacific Coast. There are 14 stations, with 18 missionaries, 6 local preachers and a membership of 1,100.

There are 20 *Negro* Conferences in the ME Church, with a membership of 278,000, cared for by 1,420 pastors, 806 of whom receive financial aid from the Missionary Society. Those charges which are helped by funds of the Missionary Society are almost all in the Southern states.

Work among *Portuguese* is confined to the New England and New England Southern Conferences. There are missions in East Cambridge and New Bedford, Mass., and in Providence, R. I.

In 1845 the work of the ME Church among the *Scandinavians* was begun by Olaf G. Hedstrom, a member of the New York Conference. Since that time work has grown to such an extent that there are 4 Annual Conferences among the Swedes and 2 Norwegian and Danish Conferences, besides the work carried on under the administration of 7 English-speaking Conferences. Of the 218 Methodist pastors laboring among Scandinavians, 212 are supported in part by the Missionary Society.

Spanish: This work includes the efforts put forth in the New Mexico Spanish and Porto Rico Mission Conferences. In the New Mexico Spanish Mission Conference there are 46 stations and circuits, 34 of which have church buildings. There were 2,704 members and probationers in 1902. The work in Porto Rico was begun by Dr. C. W. Drees, formerly in the South America Mission. He arrived in San Juan March 25, 1900. There are already 19 stations on the island, with 17 missionaries, 14 native workers and 888 members and probationers.

Besides the work among the classes mentioned above, the Methodist Episcopal Church contributes, through its Missionary Society, to the support of 520 pastors among white people of the Southern States, many of whom are working among the illiterate thousands in the mountains of Tennessee, Kentucky, the Virginias and the Carolinas; to the support of 1,758 churches among other white people in the United States, to the Deaf-Mute Missions of Baltimore and of Chicago, to the Mission among the Hebrews of Boston and other cities and to the City Mission enterprises of Brooklyn, New York, Jersey City, Hoboken, Newark, Paterson, Philadelphia, Pittsburg, Detroit, St. Louis, Kansas City, and St. Paul, Minn.

In addition to the work above set forth, the other benevolent societies of the Methodist Episcopal Church, such as the Board of Church Extension, the Sunday School Union and Tract Society, the Board of Education, the Freedmen's Aid and Southern Education Society, and especially the Woman's Home Missionary Society, which is auxiliary to the parent board, expend large sums on work having a distinct home missionary outcome.

Methodist Episcopal Church, South: By the law of the General Conference of the Church each annual conference is authorized to organize a Board of Missions auxiliary to the General Board. Said Conference Board appoints its own officers, regulates its own affairs, and has control over the missions it may establish within its bounds and of the funds raised for their support, provided it is responsible for the maintenance of such missions, and provided it secures the consent of the Bishop presiding over the conference. These Conference Boards of Missions have work in all the cities of the South, in factory towns and centers, among mining populations, and in remote rural districts. The number of home missionaries supported in part or in whole for 1902 was 1,270, and the amount raised by the several conference boards for this purpose was $188,259.

The General Board makes some appropriation annually to the work in the Western fields. No greater moral heroism has been displayed in any field than by many of those men who have gone to the firing line at the call of the Church. In view of the peculiar conditions and of the tremendous drift of population unreached by any church, in many cases lying along the watershed east and west of the Rocky Mountains, appropriations are made to a number of smaller conferences and assistance given to those who are entrenching Christianity at strategic points. In addition to this the General Board at its last annual meeting in St. Louis, Mo., face to face with the rapid growth of urban and factory population, authorized the adoption of a plan of city missions which looks not only to the strengthening of Christian forces in our cities, but to the training as well of those who are to become leaders in evangelistic work.

The Woman's Home Mission Society of the Methodist Episcopal Church, South, was established in 1886. The returns for the year 1902-3 are as follows: Members, 14,414; teachers and missionaries, 58; day and night schools, 11; pupils, 1,324; parsonages helped, 112; value of supplies distributed, $14,309, and total collections, $87,685.

The work of the Society includes aid in building parsonages, both through the local and connectional organizations, the distribution of supplies for orphanages, missionaries, mission schools and Rescue Homes, the maintenance of schools, of which there are three in Florida for Cuban children, two for the children of mountaineers in Kentucky and in North Carolina, one on the Pacific Coast for Chinese and Japanese, a Rescue Home and Training School, an annex to Paine College, Augusta, Ga., for the industrial training of negro girls and a school for Indians at Anadarko, Indian Territory. A mission has also been maintained among the miners of West Virginia. The Society also is interested in the Scarritt Bible and Training School in Kansas City, Mo., where five deaconesses have been trained and consecrated for work among the needy. These cooperate with the pastors of churches and with the sixteen missionaries and twelve City Mission Boards which have been formed. No missionary organization in the church has made greater progress and managed its affairs more wisely than this Society.

While the General Board of Missions appropriates funds to the German and Indian Mission Conferences they fall in the same class with those in the remote West as domestic or home missions. The German work began over fifty years ago among the immigrants who were coming into New Orleans. Later the mission extended into Texas and in 1890 became the German Mission Conference. The results of this work have been most encouraging. The membership of 11,440 contributes annually for missions one dollar per capita and from eight to ten dollars for other purposes. A Joint Commission of representatives of the other Texas Conferences, with one from the German Conference, has done much to inspire and bind these German Methodists into closer union with the whole Church.

The earliest missionary work of the Church was in behalf of the Negroes and Indians. The former have been set apart into the Colored Methodist Episcopal Church, with an independent organization and presided over by bishops of their own race and selection. The Indians are still the wards of the Church, but the rapid influx of the white population into Oklahoma and the Indian Territory has steadily driven them in upon themselves until the work has become narrowed down to a limited area where fullbloods and "blanket" Indians are preached to by a few of their own men and by white preachers of the Indian Mission Conference through interpreters. The policy which has been pursued in the Indian Mission work has not been as wise nor as effective as that adopted in the foreign field. The membership has become so thoroughly intermingled with that of the white population that it is impossible to give correct statistics.

Presbyterian: About the time of the founding of the first Presbytery (1700-1705), the ministers of the early church followed the colonists wherever they went, and the Gospel was preached along the Atlantic coast, up to the foot of the Alleghanies and beyond, not only to English but to all settlers of whatever tongue or faith. Missions to the Negroes and the Indians were established. Records of the first synod show that continual demands were made upon Princeton College in its earliest days for means to support missionaries and open missions in destitute places. An interesting item is the fact that the first recorded grant of missionary money was made to the First Presbyterian Church of New York City.

At the first meeting of the General Assembly, which was organized in 1789, it was resolved to send forth missionaries to the frontiers to organize churches and attend in general to the religious and educational needs of the people.

In 1802 the work had grown to such dimensions that the first regularly constituted Board was formed under the name of the Standing Committee of Missions. Nominations of missionaries were made by it and presented to the General Assembly for Confirmation.

After the War of 1812 the Committee felt

unable to cope with the increased needs and opportunities of the work, and the General Assembly in 1816 organized a larger and more comprehensive body to take up the work, called "The Board of Missions." Its power was such as to enable it to conduct the missions and decide all questions as to the appointment of missionaries and the payment of salaries without waiting for the approval of the Assembly; it was further empowered to organize branch societies, and the Church was urged to cooperate in such organizations.

Other churches felt the need of evangelizing the masses seeking homes in what was then the West, and in 1826 the American Home Missionary Association was formed. In its directorship were many Presbyterians, and Presbyterian Churches contributed to its support and benefited by its aid.

When the division took place in the Presbyterian Church in 1839, the Board of Missions remained in connection with the Old School branch, and in 1857 underwent a change in name, being called "The Trustees of the Board of Domestic Missions of the General Assembly of the Presbyterian Church in the U. S. A.;" the New School threw in its allegiance for a time with the AHMS (see above), but gradually separated from it. The first step in departure was the organization in 1855 of the Church Extension Committee, which carefully disclaimed all intention of interfering with the work or support of the AHMS; but the differences grew, until finally in 1861 the New School Presbyterian Church withdrew entirely from the AHMS, organized a Presbyterian Committee of Home Missions, which superseded the Church Extension Committee and which conducted the home mission work of that branch of the Church, until finally in 1870 the glorious reunion of the two Assemblies took place, and the two bodies, the Presbyterian Committee of Home Missions and the Board of Domestic Mission, were merged into one Board. At the time of reunion the New School committee had the names of 530 missionaries on its roll and the Old School Board 613. The new Board was incorporated in New York in 1872.

Organization: The members of the Board are appointed by the General Assembly, and number 10 ministers and 11 laymen; one of the ministers is the president of the Board. In addition there are a secretary, two assistant secretaries, a treasurer and a superintendent of school work. The Board reports annually to the General Assembly, to which it is responsible for its actions, tho it has absolute jurisdiction in the interim between the meetings of the General Assembly, but appeal can be had to the General Assembly. Its administrative offices are at 156 Fifth Avenue, New York City.

The work of the Board is two-fold: that of the missionary pastors and the missionary teachers. The latter is committed to the Woman's Board and is outlined more fully below. The former resolves itself into two forms: (1) The salary raised on the field is supplemented by the Board. (This is the case in most of the churches in the States, the few exceptions being limited to some work among Indians or some other unusual fields.) (2) The Board sometimes assumes the entire salary of the minister, as in certain fields in Alaska, in Porto Rico, or in other practically unformed localities. In every such instance strong effort is put forth to secure from the people part of the pastor's salary as speedily as possible.

The Woman's Board, organized in 1878 as the Woman's Executive Committee, and known as the Woman's Board since 1897, cooperates with the Board of Home Missions, undertaking no work without its approval. Its officers are: president, corresponding secretary, young people's secretary, editor, recording secretary, treasurer and corresponding secretary Freedmen's department.

The work of the Woman's Board is: (1) To raise money for the support of the educational work under the care of the Board of Home Missions—namely, teachers' salaries, school buildings and equipment—and for general home mission purposes. Mission schools are located in Alaska, Porto Rico and Cuba and, in the States, among the Indians, Mexicans, Mormons, mountaineers of the South, and foreigners.

As an adjunct to the Board of Home Missions and the Woman's Board, vitally connected with them both, stands the *Young People's Department*, which has for its special care the enlistment of the young people's societies in home mission work, the assignment of synodical "specials" and the gathering and disseminating of information concerning the mission fields.

Self-supporting Synods: In 1886 the Synod of New Jersey assumed charge of the home mission field within its own bounds. Other Eastern Synods have since taken the same action till in 1903 the Board is relieved, wholly or in part, of the work in New York, New Jersey, Pennsylvania, Baltimore, Kentucky, Ohio, Indiana, Illinois, Michigan, Wisconsin and Iowa.

Results: The whole work of the Board for the century closing with 1900 may be briefly summarized as follows:

First Standing Committee on Home Missions appointed, 1802; Board of Home Missions organized, 1816; Number of commissions issued since that time, each representing one year's work, 74,063; Whole amount expended in this work from the beginning, $23,000,000; Number of missionaries in 1900, 1,371; Number of missionaries aided by self-supporting Synods in 1900, 754; Whole number of missionaries in 1900, 2,125; Whole number, including teachers in mission schools, 2,373.

Protestant Episcopal: Early in the 19th century home missionary work was undertaken to a limited extent under the auspices of voluntary societies in the Dioceses of New York and Pennsylvania. These efforts, however, tho they accomplished much good at the time, were not steadily sustained or adequately supported, and did not reach beyond the western borders of the States named. It was not until 1835, the year in which the principle was accepted that the Church itself is the divinely constituted missionary society, that aggressive mission work at home was undertaken on any extended scale in the name of the whole Church. In that year the Rev. Dr. Jackson Kemper was elected the first missionary bishop and was sent to the West, with a jurisdiction covering the territory now comprised in the states of Indiana, Missouri, Kansas, Nebraska, Iowa, Minnesota and Wisconsin. In truly apostolic spirit Bishop Kemper devoted himself to the religious welfare of the people in what was then the Far West. When he began his work he found a few small and scattered congregations, still fewer clergy and but a few communicants. In the section over which he once exercised supervision there are to-day (1903) 13 dioceses, 16 bishops, 586 other clergy and 69,000 communicants. This is but one instance, tho perhaps the most striking, of the rapid growth of the Protestant Episcopal Church in the Far West during the last half of the 19th century.

The work of the Protestant Episcopal Church is organized on the principle that every foot of territory over which the flag of the nation waves, whether on the North American Continent or elsewhere, shall be under the supervision of a bishop. These areas of supervision in sections of the country where the Church is strongest are known as dioceses, and support their own bishops. In other parts of the country where the population is still comparatively scattered and the Church less strong, these areas of episcopal supervision are known as missionary districts, and the support of the bishops is provided by the Domestic and Foreign Missionary Society. The dioceses are being steadily divided and subdivided and number at the present time 60, with 68 bishops. The missionary districts on the continent number 18, with 17 bishops. There are also the extracontinental districts of Porto Rico, Honolulu and the Philippines, each with its own bishop.

Broadly speaking, there are three different kinds of home mission work: (1) That carried on by the Church as a whole, under the general supervision of the Board of Managers of the Domestic and Foreign Missionary Society, and known as "Domestic Missions." (2) That carried on by each diocese under the direction of its bishop and the local board of missions, and known as "Diocesan Missions." (3) That carried on, generally under diocesan supervision, among the poor and the foreign-speaking populations of nearly all the large cities, and known as "City Missions." It is only of the home mission work carried on by the Church as a whole, that this paper is supposed to treat. This general work naturally follows four lines:

(I) *Among White People:* Missions among the white people are maintained in all of the missionary districts, and at the present time in some 33 of the dioceses, whose local resources are not sufficient to do all the aggressive work that should be done in establishing the Church in new centers. This work varies widely in extent and in character. Aid is given for the maintenance of missionary work in an old State like Maine, as well as in the newer commonwealths of the Middle and Far West. It may be carried on in a New England college town, in the midst of a Western farming community, or among the mining camps of the mountain States. In all cases the aim is to build up strong self-supporting congregations which may in turn give aid to other places. In some places elementary schools are maintained, as among the mountaineers of North Carolina and Kentucky. Again, aid is given to boarding schools of high grade, and in a number of localities excellent work is being done through Church hospitals. The value and success of this home mission work are seen in the fact that in a number of dioceses and districts where this aid is given the baptisms and confirmations form a much larger percentage of the Church population than is the case in many of the older and stronger dioceses.

(II) *Among the Negroes:* The Church's work among the Negroes is done in twenty-four dioceses, first, by providing opportunities for worship through mission churches and chapels in many country districts as well as in the larger cities of the South; secondly, through 90 day schools and 3 general industrial schools, in which latter training is given the boys and young men in various trades, and the girls and young women in domestic economy; and thirdly, through 3 hospitals exclusively for colored people. One hundred clergy are at present working successfully among the colored people, many of them Negroes themselves. There are at present 22,000 baptized members and about 8,500 communicants connected with the Negro congregations.

(III) *Among the Indians:* The Church has been exceedingly successful in its missions among the Indians, particularly in the Northwest. Great pioneer missionaries like the Right Rev. Henry B. Whipple, D.D., sometime Bishop of Minnesota, and the Right Rev. William Hobart Hare, D.D., the present Bishop of South Dakota, with great devotion have carried the Church to these aboriginal Americans and have demonstrated how thoroughly adapted it is to meet their moral and spiritual aspirations. The strongest Indian missions are found in Minnesota and South Dakota, but the work is also carried on in 12 other dioceses and districts. At the present time there are in the Episcopal Church between 15,000 and 18,000 baptized Indian Christians, of whom about 6,000 are communicants. The Indian clergy number about 30, and services are conducted by scores of other Indians, as catechists and lay helpers.

(IV) *Among Foreign-speaking People:* Among foreigners comparatively little has been done by the Church as a whole, missionary work in this direction being generally left in the hands of the local diocesan and parochial authorities. One general missionary is maintained among the Swedish congregation of the East, and aid is given to a number of smaller congregations in the Central West and Northwest. Aid is also given in the maintenance of the mission and home for Japanese in San Francisco. In some localities thorough work is being done among Chinese by the parishes.

Four domestic missionary districts present conditions differing so greatly from what is usually known as home mission work that a few words may be said about them individually.

1. *Alaska:* Nothing was done by this Church in Alaska, beyond a preliminary investigation, until 1886, when the Rev. Octavius Parker was appointed to begin work wherever he might find it practicable among the Indians along the Yukon River, the Presbyterians already having excellent missions in the southeastern section. The work thus begun has been gradually extended along the whole length of the river, and as the white population increased missions were established in the centers occupied by them. At the present time the Church in Alaska is ministering to white people, Indians and Eskimos. Day schools and boarding schools are maintained at a number of Indian stations and four mission hospitals are now rendering valuable service. The development of the Alaska missions is due chiefly to the heroic work of Bishop Rowe and pioneer helpers like the Rev. John W. Chapman, the Rev. Jules L. Prevost and Dr. John B. Driggs.

2. *Porto Rico:* Prior to the war with Spain there existed at Ponce a congregation connected with the English diocese of Antigua. When Porto Rico became American territory this was transferred to the Protestant Episcopal Church in the United States. Services were also begun in 1898 in San Juan by an Episcopal army chaplain. The work has been continued by the appointment of regular missionaries under the leadership of the Right Rev. James H. Van Buren, S.T.D., who was consecrated Bishop in 1902. Stations are now maintained at San Juan, Ponce, Puerta de Tierra and in Porto Mula, on the island of Viequez. The Bishop plans to open missions in other points as rapidly as the equipment can be provided.

3. *Hawaiian Islands:* Here again missionary work had been undertaken by the Church of England prior to the annexation of the islands to the United States. The Right Rev. Henry B. Restarick, D.D., who was consecrated bishop in 1902, found that work was already being carried on among the Hawaiian and English-speaking people in Honolulu and vicinity, as well as among the Chinese of the city. Two good boarding schools, Iolani College for boys and St. Andrew's Priory School for girls, established under the English mission, have been greatly strengthened. The work has also been extended to all of the larger islands. It is carried on not only in the towns, but in some instances among the large plantation communities. The work among the Chinese has been increased by additional Sunday schools, night schools and settlement work, besides personal visits to the homes of well-to-do families. Similar work is about to be commenced among the large Japanese population, upon the arrival of a native clergyman from the Protestant Episcopal Mission of Japan.

4. *Philippine Islands:* The first work of the Church in these islands was undertaken by army chaplains in 1898. The beginning thus made has been steadily followed up by the appointment of a number of missionaries, including 5 clergymen, 1 physician, 3 nurses, 2 parish workers and 1 kindergartner, under the leadership of the Right Rev. Charles H. Brent, D.D., who reached his jurisdiction in 1902. Manila has been made a strong center, and work has been begun upon the erection of the cathedral church and parish house. Medical, settlement and kindergarten work is also carried on, and one missionary has been assigned exclusively for work among the large Chinese population. Outside of Manila stations have been opened at Iloilo to the south and at Baguio and Bontoc in the north. The latter points are centers of a region peopled chiefly by the Igorrote tribes, among whom no other Christian work has yet been attempted.

The home missionary staff of the Protestant Episcopal Church includes 20 bishops, 790 other clergymen, 160 laymen and 225 women.

The annual receipts of the Domestic and Foreign Missionary Society for home work are about $600,000. In addition to this amount it is estimated that $350,000 is given annually through various diocesan channels for home mission work in the several dioceses.

In the sixty-eight years since the Church began aggressive home missionary work she has grown rapidly both in extent and influence. In 1835 there were 15 bishops, 763 other clergy and 36,500 communicants. In 1903 there were 88 bishops, 5,000 other clergy and 760,000 communicants.

Reformed (Dutch): Until the independence of the American Reformed Churches in 1772, they were themselves missionary ground. At the close of the Revolution the list shows 85 churches, 32 ministers serving 53 of these churches, and 2 licentiates.

In 1786 the General Synod took the first action on the subject of church extension, and appointed a committee to devise some plan for sending the Gospel to destitute localities. They reported to the next Synod, and recommended that voluntary collections be taken up in all the congregations to aid in the extension of the church. This was the first effort made. The moneys collected were to be transferred through the Classes to the Synod.

The subject of church extension is found inserted as an item in the regular business of each Classis as early as 1790. A Classis at this time would collect from $50 to $100 annually. At the close of the century all the Classes were forwarding money (most of the churches contributing), except the Classis of Kingston, for the cause of church extension.

The Synod of 1800 formally appointed the Classis of Albany to take charge of all the missionary operations in the northern States.

1806-1822. The Synod now appointed a committee of ministers and elders, with plenary powers, to whom should be confided all her missionary operations. They were located in Albany till 1819, when they were directed to locate in New York. They were known as the "Standing Committee of Missions for the Reformed Dutch Church in America."

The committee began their operations on the old plan—short tours by settled pastors; but such efforts proved unsatisfactory. Settled ministers were wanted.

With the transfer of the committee to New York the mission to the Canadian churches was abandoned. Some of the Classes now began to retain their money for their own missionary necessities. At the suggestion of Rev. Paschal N. Strong a number of individuals, in January, 1822, organized themselves into a society, to be known as "The Missionary Society of the Reformed Dutch Church." This act was made known to the Synod, and the matter was referred to the Committee on Missions. The birth of the society was hailed with joy. Its board of managers was made Synod's Committee on Missions, and the churches were exhorted to form auxiliary societies.

1822-1832. The policy of the new Society was to employ as many of the graduates of the Theological Seminary at New Brunswick, N. J., as were willing to undertake mission work, to have auxiliary societies in every congregation, and to take up collections at the monthly concerts for prayer. During the ten years of its existence the Society collected more than $30,000, aiding about 100 churches or stations and 130 missionaries. It also started, in 1826, the *Magazine of the Reformed Dutch Church*, which, four years later, was transformed into the *Christian Intelligencer*. In 1833 the Missionary Society became auxiliary to the Board, and for nine years the Board depended on Classical agents. In 1837 the first church of the denomination was formed in the then Far West at Fairview, Ill. In 1841 there were enough churches to organize the Classes of Illinois and Michigan, and ten years later the Classis of Holland. Later the name of the Board was changed from the "Board of Missions" to the "Board of Domestic Missions of General Synod." In 1849 the Board was reorganized, and in 1866 was incorporated under the name of The Board of Domestic Missions of the Reformed Protestant Dutch Church. In 1870 the corporate name was changed to the present title, viz.: The Board of Domestic Missions of the Reformed Church in America. Its administrative offices are at the Reformed Church Building, 25 East 23d Street, New York City.

In 1854 the plan of a Church Building Fund was adopted, the object being to raise funds to aid feeble churches by loans to erect houses of worship and parsonages. In 1882 the Women's Executive Committee was organized as an auxiliary to the Board. Beginning with the specific work of raising money for the erection of parsonages, they have extended their efforts, till now, besides furnishing many mission churches, providing comforts for pastors' families and Christmas boxes for Sunday schools, they wholly support missions and schools among the Indians in Oklahoma and the mountain whites in Kentucky. In the year ending April 30, 1903, they collected $36,357 for their work. The original charter of the Board restricted its work to "aiding weak and founding new churches of the denomination." In 1900 the charter was amended so as "to allow its missionaries to engage in evangelistic work which may not immediately eventuate in the founding of new churches." In the year ending April 30, 1903, the Board had under its care 245 churches and missions located in twenty States and Oklahoma Territory, and helped to support 175 missionary pastors, besides student missionaries. In that year the Board received and expended $98,965.

Southern Baptist Convention: In response to a call made for the purpose, by the Virginia Baptist Foreign Mission Society, the Southern Baptist Convention was organized in Augusta, Ga., in 1845.

The object of the movement was declared in the first paragraph of the Constitution adopted, which stated it to be "for the purpose of carrying into effect the benevolent intentions of our constituents by organizing a plan of eliciting, combining and directing the energies of the whole denomination in one sacred effort to the propagation of the Gospel."

The Convention created two boards, one for Foreign Missions located at Richmond, Va., the other for Home Missions located at Marion, Ala., where it remained until 1882, when it was removed to Atlanta, Ga.

The Home Mission Board has been, and is still, the special agency for carrying forward the purposes of the Southern Baptist Convention as expressed above. Its work, therefore, has been largely along the line of discovery, development, and combining.

The policy of the Board from the date of its organization has been that of cooperation. Under instructions from the Convention it has sought to form auxiliary relationship with State Conventions, District Associations and Missionary organizations. Its field of labor has, during these years, become more clearly defined and may be described as follows: Maryland, Kentucky, Indian Territory, Oklahoma, and all the States south of these, together with the four Western Provinces in the island of Cuba, the Board having relinquished its work in the two Eastern Provinces of Cuba in favor of the Home Mission Society of New York.

The work of the Board has naturally become divided into the following distinct departments: Frontier Missions, which includes a portion of Arkansas, Texas, Oklahoma and Indian Territory; The Mountain Regions, embracing a large area of territory extending from West Virginia through Virginia, the Carolinas, Tennessee, Kentucky and Georgia into Alabama; Work in the Cities, such as New Orleans, Memphis, St. Louis, Baltimore, etc. The imperative needs of this feature of the work are being pressed upon the Board with renewed emphasis, work among the foreign population rapidly becoming one of the most important features of the work of the Board; Cuba, in which gratifying progress has been made and which is exceedingly promising for the future. The other department of the Board's work is that of Work among the Negroes, to which more special attention is likely to be directed in the immediate future than ever before. The spiritual welfare of the negro, however, has been a matter of concern to Southern Baptists ever since Africans were imported to this country. During the antebellum days they were baptized and received into fellowship of the white churches. Since their separation and organization into churches of their own race, the Board has constantly aided them in the proper formation of church government, as well as in moral and theological training.

The first annual report of the Board showed the appointment during that year of six missionaries, one in Virginia, one in Florida, one in Alabama, one in Louisiana and two in Texas. The work accomplished by the Board has constantly increased until its last Annual Report shows the following summary of work:

Missionaries, 671; weeks of labor, 24,355; churches and stations, 3,133; sermons and addresses, 85,335; prayer meetings, 12,232; religious visits, 163,587; baptisms, 8,969; received by letter, 9,716; total additions, 18,690; churches constituted, 127; houses of worship built and improved, 280; Sunday schools organized, 494; Bibles and Testaments distributed, 17,903; tracts distributed (pages), 3,044,888.

Since its organization the Board has had under annual appointment an aggregate of 10,190 missionaries. They have reported 222,505 additions to churches, and 3,504 churches constituted. The Board has been instrumental in establishing something over 17 per cent. of all the white Baptist Churches within the bounds of the Southern Baptist Convention. It has aided weak churches in their early struggles in the capital city of every State, save one, including the capital of the nation, as well as nine-tenths of all points of importance in the Southern States.

The constituency of the Home Mission Board consists of 1,737,466 white Baptists, organized into 19,919 churches. In the same territory the number of negro Baptists is estimated to be 1,927,089.

HONAN-FU: A town in the province of Honan, situated in the N. W. part of the province about 20 miles S. of the Hoang-ho. Station of the CIM (1902), with 2 missionaries.

HONDURAS: A republic of Central America, lying between the Caribbean Sea on the east, the Pacific Ocean and San Salvador on the west, and separating Nicaragua from Guatemala. It became part of the Central American Confederation in 1822, but asserted its independence in 1838, and is now governed by a president elected by popular vote for four years. It has almost the exact area of Mississippi, with a population of (1900) 587,500, the majority of whom are aboriginal Indians and Mestizos, with 5,000 descendants of the early Spanish settlers, and 5,000 negroes. In general, the country is mountainous, the Cordilleras crossing it from north to south. There are many rivers, most of them flowing east. On the highlands the climate is pleasant and equable, but along the Caribbean coast it is hot and malarious. The soil is extremely fertile, and luxuriant, tropical vegetation is found along the coast. Roman Catholicism is the religion of the country. The coming in of North Americans and other foreigners is introducing good roads and improved methods of living, so that a better future is before the republic. When the President of Honduras visited the Bay Islands in 1900 he invited the Protestant workers to come into the interior, and the invitation is being accepted.

HONDURAS, British: A crown colony on the Caribbean Sea south of Yucatan, east of Guatemala, and 660 miles west from Jamaica. It has an area of 7,562 square miles and a population of 27,542. The capital is Belize, with 5,800 inhabitants. Mission field of the WMS, the SPG, and the Jamaica Baptist Missionary Society. Over 2,000 members are gathered in 35 organizations, 2,500 pupils are taught in 20 day schools and many more in Sunday schools, and 12 missionaries are doing valiant service throughout the colony.

HONGKONG: An island at the mouth of the Canton River, off the southeast coast of China, about 40 miles E. of Macao and 90 miles S. of Canton. It is a British possession, having been ceded by the treaty of Nan-king (1842). It is a rocky, mountainous island, nine miles long and from two to six broad, and comprises an area of 29 square miles. Previous to the occupation of the island by the British, it was the home of a few fishermen, who oftentimes changed their occupation to that of piracy when opportunity offered. Now it is one of the most important British possessions in the East. Victoria, the capital and main city, is on the northern shore of the island, by the side of a safe and ample harbor. Fine streets and terraces cut in the side of the mountains, laid out with the best of engineering skill, and, beautified with trees and tropical plants, have changed the entire appearance of this rocky island. Other settlements in the colony are Aberdeen, on the south side of the island, and Kowloon, a strip of land on the peninsula of that name, which was ceded to the British in 1861, and increased to an area of 376 square miles by a lease of adjacent territory under the treaty of 1898. The healthfulness of the colony is as good as any in a like latitude. Oppressive heat and humidity last from May to October, but during the four winter months the bracing, cool atmosphere makes residence there delightful. Hongkong is a port of call for the lines of mail steamers from Europe, America, and Australia. Daily steamers run between Victoria and Canton and Macao, while numerous lines ply between Victoria and the coast ports of China. The population (1901) is 283,905, of whom 6,000 are white of all nationalities (only one-third English), and 233,263 Chinese. The government supervises 178 schools, attended by 7,700 pupils. In these schools English is taught. Mission work in Hongkong is identified with the early history of the various missionary societies who work in China. The societies at present laboring here are the LMS (1843), the Basel Society (1852), the CMS (1862), the ABCFM (1883), the WMS, the SDA, the Rhenish Society (1847), the Berlin Ladies' Society, and the German Mission to Chinese Blind. Together, these Societies have (1903) 40 missionaries in Hongkong, men and women; 122 native workers, men and women; 24 outstations, 18 preaching places, 4 boarding schools, 50 day schools, 1 orphanage, 1 blind asylum, and 2,500 professed Christian adherents. The BFBS has an agent here, and the YMCA has made it a regular station since 1899, with a man and his wife to foster the extension of the YMCA.

HONOLULU: The seat of government and principal seaport of the Hawaiin Islands, situated on the southeastern coast of Oahu, is a fine commercial city. Its mild and equable climate ranges from 67° in January to 83° in August, making the annual mean 75°, with a variation in either direction of only 7°. It is a port of call for the steamers plying between San Francisco and Australia, and occasionally for the steamers between San Francisco and Hongkong, while it is the terminus of a line of steamers running semi-weekly to San Francisco. The inhabitants number 39,305, among whom are a great many Japanese, Chinese, half-breeds, and natives of various islands of the Pacific. The P. E. Church has a bishop at Honolulu. There is also a Roman Catholic bishop. Mission work is carried on by the Hawaiian Evangelical Association, and by other denominational agencies. The ABCFM (1819) was first in the field, and the Hawaiian Evangelical Association has taken up its work. The ME, the FCMS, the PE (taking over the work of the SPG), the SDA, and the Peniel Society all have enterprises in Honolulu, largely among the Japanese, the Chinese, and other immigrants, many of whom are Portuguese and Roman Catholics.

HONWAR: A town in the Bombay Presidency, India, situated about 18 miles W. S. W. of Bijapur. Station of the Basel Missionary Society (1845), with (1903) 1 missionary and his wife and 9 native workers. The name is written Honor in the Basel Society's publications.

HO-NYEN: A village in the province of Kwang-tung, China, situated in the highland district not far from Ho-su-van. Station of the Basel Missionary Society (1901), with (1903) 2 missionaries, 1 missionary's wife, 23 native workers, men and women; 17 outstations, 8 day schools, 2 boarding schools, and 626 professed Christians.

HOOCHOW. See Hu-chau-fu.

HOOGHLY. See Hugli.

HOPE FOUNTAIN: A settlement in Rhodesia, South Central Africa, situated about 7 miles S. W of Buluwayo. Station of the LMS (1860), with (1903) 2 missionaries, 1 missionary's wife, 3 native workers, 3 day schools, 1 industrial institute, and 900 professed Christian adherents, of whom 15 are church members.

HOPE VALLEY: A settlement in the N. part of Queensland, Australia, situated on the seacoast near Cookstown. Station of the Neuendettelsan Missionary Society (1886), with (1900) 6 missionaries, men and women.

HORDEN, John: Born in 1828; died in 1893. In 1851 left England to work as a lay missionary in an extremely remote corner of Rupert's Land, but soon afterward he was appointed by the CMS as missionary to Moose Fort, Northwestern Canada. In 1852 Bishop Anderson visited Moose and Mr. Horden was ordained deacon and priest the same year. When the diocese of Rupert's Land was divided in 1872, he was chosen Bishop of Moosonee, a diocese coextensive with the shores of Hudson Bay, and running from 300 to 500 miles inland, and as far north as human beings exist. Owing to the difficulties of locomotion his episcopal duties were confined entirely to the south of the bay until 1879, when, in visiting the northern portion of his diocese, he had to descend south for several hundred miles, then go west by the Canadian Pacific Railway, through three dioceses, then take a northerly direction through Rupert's Land, and finally veer round to northeast to reach York Factory. This journey required the greater part of the summer; and during the winter his time was fully occupied in day school work, visiting, personal interviews with all classes of the community, in learning the vernacular and in giving instructions respecting the verbal construction of the language. In February, 1880, he took the journey by sled to Churchill, when the thermometer averaged 37° below zero, and he remained there until April, working among the people at the post and among the Chipewyans and Eskimos. In the summer of this year, amid the greatest difficulties, he visited the outstations of York Factory. These visits were very successful and hundreds turned from heathenism and accepted Christianity. When death came to him at Moose, January 12, 1893, he was engaged in revising his own translations and Dr. Mason's Cree Bible, after forty-two years' service as missionary and bishop. His literary works consist of Bible translations, prayer book, hymn book, Gospel history into the Cree languages, several translations into the Saulto, Eskimo and Ojibbeway languages, and other minor translations.

HOSCHUWAN. See HO-SU-WAN.

HOSHANGABAD: A town in the Central Provinces, India, situated on the left bank of the Narbada River, 40 miles S. S. E. of Bhopal. It is on the high road to Bombay, having an excellent trade. Population (1891), 13,500, of whom 9,910 are Hindus and the larger part of the remainder are Mohammedans. Station of the FFMA (1874), with 9 missionaries, men and women; 8 day schools, 1 boarding school, 1 industrial school, and 1 dispensary.

HOSHIARPUR: A town in a district of the same name in the Punjab, India, situated 45 miles N. of Ludhiana. Population, about 20,000. Station of the PN (1867); at present (1903) not occupied by missionaries. It is in charge of a native worker with his wife and 1 native woman worker who is a physician. There is an orphanage, with industrial department, a hospital, and 1,206 professed Christians, of whom 774 are communicants.

HOSTEL: Some of the missionary societies apply this name to boarding houses for students established at a missionary station in connection with or near a high school or college which attracts young men from a distance. Hostels are sometimes established for Christian students in order to strengthen them against influences to which they are exposed while living at a distance from their Christian homes. Others are opened for non-Christian students, and such become a most effective method of evangelization in view of the influences which they bring to bear on heathen or Mohammedan students who, during their education, are removed from the anti-Christian pressure surrounding them in their homes. The SPG missionaries in Delhi, India, for this reason regard such a hostel as the heart of their Christian work in that city.

Hostels are being established by some missions in places where they have no higher educational institutions, and with the direct purpose of bringing non-Christian students at secular colleges under moral and Christian influence.

HO-SU-WAN: A town in the province of Kwang-tung, China, situated in the highlands near the headwaters of a branch of the Tung River, about 40 miles N. E. of Hwei-chau-fu. Station of the Basel Missionary Society (1885), with (1903) 1 missionary and his wife, 7 native workers, 4 outstations, 2 day schools, 1 boarding school, and 346 professed Christians. Name written by the Society, Hoschuwan.

HO-TSIN-HSIEN: A town in the province of Shan-si, China; situated in the S. about 32 miles W. of Kiang-chau, and a little above the confluence of the Fen-ho and Hoang-ho. Station of the CIM (1893), with (1903) 1 missionary and his wife.

HOTTENTOT-BUSHMAN RACE: When the southern angle of Africa was first visited by Diaz and De Gama four centuries since, as when it began to be colonized also by Europeans in 1652, it was found to be occupied by a somewhat peculiar aboriginal race, which soon came to be known as the Hottentots. Out of this parent stock have come several affiliated groups known as Bushmen, Namaquas, Korannas, and Griquas. The Hottentots called themselves originally *Khoi-Khoi*, "Men of Men." Prichard regarded their present name as a corruption of Houteniqua, the name of an extinct tribe. But those who know the language, finding in it no roots of such a word, prefer the opinion advanced by T. Hahn, a scholar who knew the language as his mother tongue, having been born and bred among them as the son of a missionary, that the Dutch gave them this name, Hottentot, because of the curious sounds, especially in the clicks, in which their language abounds, as if they stammered and stuttered. Indeed, in Low German, the word Hottentot, or Hüttentüt, is found, meaning, it is said, a "quack." More than two centuries since, they were represented by the traveler, Dapper, as "speaking with clicks like Calicut hens." These clicks, of which there are several kinds, as labial, palatal, dental, or lateral, seem to have had their origin in the onomatopoetic principle, in the Hottentot tongue, and from this to have been taken over and adopted into some of the neighboring languages, especially into Kaffir and Zulu. The Hottentot abounds also in harsh consonants and aspirated gutturals, which, with the clicks, are hard for a foreigner to acquire. The eminent comparative philologist, Dr. Bleek, who had the best of means for forming a correct opinion, calls the Hottentot a suffix-pronominal, sex-denoting language, and classes it with the Hamitic of North Africa. According to T. Hahn, it is strictly monosyllabic, and every root ends in a vowel. It uses suffixes and postpositions, has three grammatical genders and three numbers, four clicks and three tones. It has an extensive oral literature of songs and animal stories, is highly developed, and anything but the mere jargon which the early Dutch settlers fancied it to be.

Grout, in his *Zulu-Land*, says: "The geographical position of the Hottentot, from the time he was first known to the European, situated as he was at the southern extreme of the African continent, and flanked from sea to sea on his north or inland side by a broad belt of people of a very different language and appearance, would seem to indicate that any search for his pedigree and ancestry, provided the present be not his original home, must be made in regions far removed in respect to both time and place. Happily, within the last few years, a careful study of his language and a comparison of this with the old Egyptian and Coptic tongue have given a clew to his ancient abode. If we may credit some of the most learned and acute philologists of the present day, and those who have had the best opportunities for studying the Hottentot and Bushman, together with other African dialects, this Gariepine tongue of the southern extreme belongs to the same family as the old Egyptian and Coptic, the Berber, and Ethiopic, in the farthest north of the continent; and what is also highly interesting and important, this southern branch of the family is found to surpass all the rest in the integrity with which it has preserved the more essential characteristics of the original stock.

"Admitting the correctness of these views, we can have no doubt as to the early ancestry of the Hottentot and Bushman class, including the Koranna and Namaqua, and that their origin is the same as that of the nations of northern Africa, the old Egyptian, and kindred tribes, including, perhaps, the Libyan or Berber and the Guanches."

The likeness of the Hottentot, in many respects, to the old Egyptian family would indicate that the former was once a part of the latter. It follows, then, that these extreme southern tribes were once sundered by some dividing wedge from the extreme northern, and by this new incoming power or alien race, of a very different language, were driven on southward from age to age, till they finally reached their present abode in the southern angle of the continent, from which they could be driven no farther. The linguistic argument is supported by the fact that the appearance, manners, customs of the Hottentots, differ in many respects essentially from those of the Bantu race on their northern border, and yet afford good ground for classing them with the old Egyptian and other North African nations. Some of the learned at the Cape of Good Hope have found pictures and impressions among the antiquities of Egypt so like the Hottentot as to make it certain, as they think, that the original of these representatives must have been people of this race. Then again, the Hottentots of South Africa, in days of old, as the early travelers in that region and their own traditions tell us, were wont to worship the moon—the like to which, the historian tells us, was found among the northern nations of Africa in their sidereal worship. And yet we find no trace of this worship among their neighbors of the Bantu race. The gods of the Zulus are regarded as having their home beneath and never above. The northern nations of olden times, like the Hottentots from time immemorial, made use of the bow and arrow, while the Zulu and his neighbors of the Bantu race use the spear, short sword, and war club. And yet it is in looking at the more permanent and marked feature of the Hottentot, his language, and its likeness to that of the old Egyptian, that we find the strongest proof that he is related to the men of North Africa.

With facts like these before us, it is easy to believe this stock, originally one, was, at an early age, split and separated into the two parts we now find, one in the extreme north and another in the extreme south of the continent, by the incoming of the sundering wedge of another race, as the Bantu, from the northeast. Eruptions from that quarter, in those early ages, were not uncommon, as we know from the incoming of the Israelites and of the Shepherd Kings. As the families in the northeast grew and multiplied, it was but natural that some of them should press to the south and west, as from the Euphrates into Egypt. Finding Egypt already filled by a previous family, some of which had, doubtless, begun to move on up the Nile, southward, it was easy for the new race to split the old, and push a part before it, each advancing up the Nile and onward to the south, like one wave after another, till finally that in the lead was crowded into the extreme south and flanked by the other on its northern border, the former now called the Hottentot, the latter the Bantu race, each of them continuing to keep up its distinctive aboriginal traits in a remarkable manner.

In personal appearance the Hottentot is short in stature, of a yellowish brown in color, like a faded leaf, with high cheek bones, chestnut eyes, nose flat, hair twisted into clusters. When first mentioned by the Portuguese, Hottentots are described as pastoral in their pursuits, rich in cattle, scant in dress, living in huts, and remarkable for the excellence of their morals. But almost everything in respect to their freedom, mode of life, and morals was greatly changed, often for the worse, by the coming in of the white man. Subsequently, by the introduction of a better rule and much missionary work in their behalf, the condition of many of them was greatly improved. Some of the tribes have been civilized, and many of the people become good citizens, intelligent, steady, and industrious, and not a few are brought to embrace the Gospel. Many are in the employ of the Dutch farmers; but their tribal home, so far as they have any, is on the Orange River, from the Atlantic eastward half across the continent.

Out of this original Hottentot stock, at an early date, came a large branch, the *San* tribe, now called the Bushmen. This name is an Anglicized form of the Dutch Bosjes-men. Indeed, some speak of the original stock as opening out into two branches, the *Khoikhoi* and the *San*, the former being, primarily, given to the pastoral mode of life, the latter to hunting. For this wandering, hunting, predatory kind of life the Bushmen of to-day have the same love as their ancestors, the *San*, had when first seen centuries ago by Europeans. Their habitat is here and there among the wild regions of the Orange, in the bush, among the rocks and ravines of the hills, or secluded recesses of the mountains, on the outskirts of other tribes. They build no houses, have neither flocks, herds nor tents. They are very diminutive in stature, of a dark yellow color, their hair like wool twisted together in small tufts. They have no nationality, and it would seem that their religion consists chiefly in a few superstitious notions concerning evil demons. In their unsettled, wandering condition it has been difficult to carry on mission work among them, tho some have been induced to join stations among other tribes, being in this way brought to a knowledge of the Gospel. They speak essentially the same language as the Hottentots, and yet the points of difference are many. In one respect they are an enigma, that is, in the "signs they have given of intelligence and artistic skill; for," as Dr. Cust says, "they have exhibited a wonderful power of graphic illustration. The rocks of Cape Colony and the Drakenberg have everywhere examples of *San* drawing, figures of men, women and children, animals characteristically sketched, and as a proof that the art is not extinct, figures of their enemies, the Boers, appear unmistakably. Rings, crosses, and other signs have given rise to the speculation, quite unsupported, that they may represent some form of indigenous writing, but the facts, such as they are, must not be stretched beyond what they actually evidence, and this is sufficiently noteworthy."

Another tribe of Hottentots, the *Namaquas*, living as nomads near the Atlantic along the Orange River, the *Great Namaquas* on the north side and the *Little Namaquas* on the south, speak essentially the same language, have the same complexion, kind of eyes and hair, as the Bushmen and other Hottentots, and yet are tall, well-proportioned, and under the training of missionaries have come to be somewhat enterprising and industrious. Many of them have been educated and led to embrace the Christian faith. Not unlike to these are the *Korannas* and the Hottentot tribes who live along the Orange, to the east of the *Namaquas*. Going still farther east, to a region near to where the Vaal and Modder enter the Orange, we come to where the noted *Griqua* tribes began to be gathered and consolidated with others a century since. Being a mixed race, many of them the offspring of colonists and Hottentot women, they speak two languages, the Hottentot and the Dutch, tho the latter is fast supplanting the former. Their well-watered valley, a little north of the Orange, had an attraction for others, and soon became the abode of free blacks and Hottentot refugees from the Cape Colony; and soon they were joined by two companies of mixed bands from Little Namaqualand, in the lead of Adam Kok and his sons, all of mixed blood. Neighboring clans of *Korannas* and Bushmen became a part of the settlement. A mission station was formed among them at Klaarwater, and Messrs. Anderson and Kramer began to teach them the Gospel, how to read, to cultivate the soil, and build houses more substantial than mat huts. Their history for all these generations, like that of other Hottentot and Bushmen tribes, has been remarkably diversified—in many respects sad, and full of wrongs. Many of them, profiting by the teachings of the missionaries, as the years have gone by, have become intelligent, industrious, Christian men, while others have continued to prefer the savage life.

A negro race on the west coast, north of the Orange, having been subjugated by the *Namaquas* and called *Damara*, or "conquered," tho adopting the language of their conquerors, do not really belong to the Hottentot race. Those of the *Damara* who speak the Hottentot are called the *Hill Damara*, to distinguish them from the *Herero*, who are of the Bantu race, and called *Cattle Damara*.

For all these tribes much good mission work has been done. Through the patient endurance of many trials, in face of much opposition from those who should have been helpers together with them, the missionaries laboring to raise these benighted, persecuted tribes to a better plane of life have seen their labors greatly blessed, have seen great secular, social, civil good brought to them, and souls, not a few, fitted for immortality.

Merriman, *Passages of Missionary Life*, London, 1853; Moffat (R.), *Missionary Labors and Scenes in South Africa*, London, 1842; Fritsch (G.), *Die Eingeborenen Sud-Afrikas*, Breslau, 1873; Ridsdale, *Scenes and Adventures in Great Namaqualand*, London, 1883; Wendland, *Bethanien in Namaland*, Berlin, 1885.

HOWLAND, William Ware: Born in West Brookfield, Mass., on the 28th of February, 1817. His father was the fifth generation from John Howland, who was one of the first band of Pilgrims who sailed in the *Mayflower*. Mr. Howland graduated from Amherst College in 1841, and from Union Theological Seminary in New York in 1845. He reached Jaffna, Ceylon, early in 1846 as a missionary of the ABCFM, and was located at Batticotta, where he assisted in teaching a select class in the seminary for young men, but he gave most of his time to preaching in the vernacular and in village work. In 1868 he moved to Tillipally, and for ten years had charge of the vernacular training and theological institution. After the death of "Father Spaulding" in 1873, Mr. Howland became the senior missionary in the American Mission in Ceylon. He also succeeded to the title "Father," and even to-day, among both missionaries and natives, Christian and Hindu, he is reverently known as "Father Howland." For fifteen years he was located at Oodooville and had charge of the station where he died August 26, 1892, after nearly half a century of life and labor among the Tamils of Jaffna, making only one visit to the homeland during the period. Mr. Howland married Miss Susan Reed in 1846, herself a trained educator. Four of their children entered missionary service under the American Board. Dr. Howland was preeminently an evangelist and preacher of the Gospel of Jesus Christ.

HOWRAH: A large town and important railway center on the Hugli River, Bengal, India, opposite Calcutta, of which it is practically a suburb. Population (1901), 157,594, about three-fourths of the people being Hindus and one-fifth Muslims. Station of the BMS (1821) and BZM (1881), with (1903), together, 2 missionaries and their wives, 1 woman missionary, 10 native workers, men and women; 6 day schools, and 215 professed Christian adherents, of whom 60 are church members. Station also of the SPG (1821), with (1903) 14 native workers, 2 outstations, 3 places of worship, 3 day schools, and 299 baptized Christians, of whom 148 are communicants. Station also of the CEZ (1891), with 4 women missionaries, 14 native women workers, and 4 day schools.

HSIANG-CHENG-HSIEN: A town in the province of Ho-nan, China, situated about 20 miles W. by S. of Hsu-chau. Station of the CIM (1892), with (1903) 1 missionary and his wife. Name written by the Society, Siang-cheng.

HSIANG-TAN-HSIEN: A town in the province of Hu-nan, China, situated on the left bank of the Siang River, 210 miles S. S. W. of Han-kau. It is a mart for drugs and medicines for the whole of China. Population, 1,000,000. Station of the PN (1900), with (1903) 8 missionaries, men and women (two of them physicians); 2 native workers, 1 preaching place, 1 day school, 1 dispensary, and 1 hospital.

HSIAO-KAN-HSIEN: A city and railway station in the province of Hu-pei, China, situated about 40 miles N. W. of Han-kau, in a very densely populated district. Station of the LMS (1880), with (1903) 3 missionaries, one of them a physician; 2 wives of missionaries, 27 native workers, men and women; 22 outstations, 5 day schools and 1 hospital. The number of Christians is included in the 5,000 reported in Hankau statistics. There is also a mission to lepers aided by the Society for Lepers in India and the East. Name written by the Society, Hiau Kan.

HSIAO-MEI: A town in the province of Che-kiang, China, situated in the S. of the province, about 70 miles W. of Wen-chau-fu. Station of the CIM (1896); not occupied in 1903.

HSIAO-YI-HSIEN: A town in the province of Shan-si, China, situated about 60 miles S. W. of Tai-yuen-fu. Station of the CIM (1887); not occupied (1903) since the Boxer rising of 1900, when two missionaries were killed here. Name written by the Society, Hiao-i.

HSI-AN-FU. See HSI-NGAN-FU.

HSI-CHAU: A town in the province of Shan-si, China, situated about 115 miles S. W. of Tai-yuen-fu. Station of the CIM (1885), with (1903) 1 missionary and his wife. Name written by the Society, Si-chau.

HSIEN-YU-HSIEN: A town in the province of Fo-kien, China, situated about 25 miles W. S. W. of Hsing-hwa. Station of the CMS and the CEZ, with (1903) together 1 missionary and his wife, 3 women missionaries, 28 native workers, men and women; 18 day schools, 1 boarding school, and 638 professed Christians. Station also of the ME, with (1903) 2 women missionaries, 64 native workers, men and women; 4 outstations, 37 preaching places, 1 village school, 1 women's training class, and 1,005 professed Christians. Name written by the Societies, Sing-iu.

HSI-HSIANG-HSIEN: A town in the province of Shen-si, China, situated about 30 miles S. E. of Han-chung-fu. Station of the CIM (1895), with (1903) 2 women missionaries and a day school. Name written by the Society, Si-hsiang.

HSIN-AN-HSIEN: A town in the province of Ho-nan, China, situated about 20 miles W. of Ho-nan-fu. Station of the CIM (1899), with (1903) 1 missionary and his wife and 1 woman missionary. Name written by the Society, Sin-an-hsien.

HSIN-CHANG-HSIEN: A town in the province of Che-kiang, China, situated about 20 miles E. of Hu-chau. Station of the PS (1892), with (1902) 2 missionaries, one with his wife; 1 woman missionary, 4 native workers (one a woman), 1 boarding school, and 100 professed Christians. Name written by the Society, Sinchang.

HSIN-CHANG-HSIEN: A town in the province of Che-kiang, China, situated 45 miles S. W. of Ning-po. Station of the CIM (1870), with (1903) 1 missionary and his wife. Name written by the Society, Sin-chang.

HSIN-CHAU: A town in the province of Shan-si, China, situated in the central part of the province, about 45 miles N. N. W. of Tai-yuen-fu. Station of the BMS (1885), with (1903) 1 missionary and his wife, 5 native workers, and 6 outstations. Station also of the BZM, not yet (1903) reoccupied since the Boxer outbreaks. Name also written Hsin-chow.

HSIN-CHENG: A town in the province of Ho-nan, China, situated 40 miles S. of Chang-te. Station of the Presbyterian Church in Canada (1892), but since 1900 an outstation of Wu-hwei.

HSIN CHOW. See HSIN-CHAU.

HSIN-FENG-HSIEN: A town in the province of Kiang-si, China, situated about 40 miles S. by W. of Kan-chau. Station of the CIM (1899), with (1903) 2 missionaries. Name written by the Society, Sin-feng.

HSI-NGAN-FU: A town in the province of Shen-si, China, situated in a vast wheat field, S. W. of the confluence of the Wei-ho and King-ho Rivers, and at the convergence of many natural trade routes. It was founded in the 12th century, B. C., and for 2,000 years was the capital of Eastern China. Its environs are rich in antiquities. One of the most important relics preserved in this city is the tablet setting forth the relations of Nestorian missionaries of the 8th century to the Chinese government. The place is probably the same as the Thinai of Ptolemy, and it is called Changan by Marco Polo. The town stands at an altitude of 1,500 feet, surrounded by high walls which enclose considerable pieces of cultivated land. The streets are straight and clean. Population, about 500,000. Station of the CIM (1893), with (1903) 4 missionaries and 2 wives of missionaries, who are engaged in giving an impulse to the work checked by the Boxer movement. Station also of the BMS (1894), who have now (1903) no missionary actually in the city. Station also of the Swedish Alliance Mission, and agency of the BFBS. Name also written Singan.

HSING-HWA-FU: A town in the province of Fo-kien, China, situated on the coast 50 miles S. W. by S. of Fu-chau. It is built at the foot of hills looking out over a fertile plain and over the Hing-hwa Bay. An important literary center; it has an examination hall seating 3,000 students. Station of the ME (1864), with (1903)

1 missionary, 3 women missionaries, 119 native workers, 6 outstations, 48 places of worship, 34 Sunday schools, 3 day schools, 2 boarding schools, special work among lepers, 1 printing house, 1 industrial school, and 1,769 professing Christians. Station also of the CMS (1894), with 3 missionaries (one wife of a missionary), 2 women missionaries, 13 native workers, 9 day schools, 1 boarding school, 1 theological class, 1 dispensary, 1 hospital, and 661 professed Christians.

HSING-I-FU: A town in the province of Kweichau, China, situated 140 miles S. S. W. of Nganshun-fu. Station of the CIM (1891), with (1903) 1 missionary and his wife. Name written by the Society, Hing-i.

HSING-MIN-TING: A town in Manchuria, China, situated 30 miles E. N. E. of Mukden, on the Sia-ho River. Station of the PCI (1899), with (1901) 1 missionary, 21 native workers, 15 places of worship, 2 day schools, and 300 church members. Name written by the Society, Hsin-min-tun.

HSING-NGAN-FU: A town in the S. of the province of Shen-si, China. Station of the CIM (1898), with (1903) 3 missionaries and their wives. Name written by the Society, Hing-an.

HSING-NING-HSIEN: A town in the province of Kwang-tung, China, situated about 78 miles N. W. of Swatow. Station of the Basel Missionary Society (1887), of which the headquarters have now (1903) been removed to Pyang-tong, with 2 missionaries, 1 missionary's wife, 6 native workers, 5 outstations, and 429 professed Christians. Name written by the Society, Hin-nen.

HSI-NING-FU: A town in the province of Kan-su, China, situated on the Hsi-ho River, 35 miles E. of Lake Kukunor, in a fertile and populous district. It is a center for caravan trade with Lhassa, Tibet. Altitude, 7,500 feet. Population, 60,000. Station of the CIM (1885), not now (1903) occupied. Name written Si-ning by the Society.

HSIN-MIN-TUN. See HSING-MIN-TING.

HSIN-TIEN-TSZE: A town in the province of Sze-chwan, China, situated about 20 miles N. of Pao-ning-fu. Station of the CIM (1892), with (1903) 2 women missionaries. Name written Sin-tien-tsi by the Society.

HSIN-TU: A village in the province of Szechwan, China, situated about 12 miles N. N. E. of Cheng-tu-fu. Station of the CMS (1894), with (1903) 3 missionaries, two of them with their wives. Work was very much broken up in 1902 by the renewal of Boxer disturbances. Name also written, Sin-tu.

HSIN-YANG-CHAU: A town in the southern part of the province of Ho-nan, China, situated 110 miles N. N. W. of Han-kau. Station of the American Norwegian China Mission. Name written by the Society, Sin Yong.

HSIPAW: A city in Burma, situated 90 miles N. W. of Mandalay. Station of the ABMU (1890), with (1903) 1 missionary (a physician) and his wife, 8 native workers, men and women; 1 hospital, 2 dispensaries, and 1 boarding school.

HSIU-YEN: A town in Manchuria, China, situated about 100 miles S. E. of Mukden. Station of the Danish Mission Society (1898), with (1903) 1 missionary in charge.

HSÜ-CHAU: A town in the province of Sze-chwan, China, situated on the Yangtse River, about 125 miles W. S. W. of Chung-king-fu. Station of the CIM (1888), with (1903) 1 missionary and his wife, who are preparing new premises in a different quarter of the city from that formerly occupied. Station also of the ABMU (1889), with (1903) 6 missionaries, men and women; 5 native workers, men and women; 29 places of regular worship, 2 day schools and 70 church members. Name written Sui-chau by the missionaries.

HSÜEN-HWA-FU: A town in Chi-li, China, situated on the Yang River, 85 miles N. W. of Peking. Station of the CIM (1902), with 1 missionary and his wife. It is also a station of the CA.

HSÜEN-LANG-KAU: A town in the province of Sze-chwan, China, situated 38 miles N. N. W. of Cheng-tu-fu. Station of the CMS (1902), with 2 women missionaries.

HSU-CHAU-FU: A town in the province of Kiang-su, China, situated 160 miles N. W. of Nanking. Population, about 120,000. Station of the PS (1897), with 7 missionaries, men and women, two of whom are physicians; 2 native workers, 4 preaching places, and 1 dispensary. Name written by the Society, Hsuchou-fu and Chuchow-fu.

HUACHO: A town and seaport of Peru, South America; situated about 78 miles N. W. of Lima, with which it is connected by railway. Station of the PB, with 1 missionary and a printing house.

HUAHINE: An island of the Society group in the South Pacific Ocean, lying 120 miles N. W. of Tahiti. The surface is mountainous and the soil fertile. Population, 2,000. Mission field of the Paris Evangelical Missionary Society, with 576 church members.

HUBLI: A town in the Presidency of Bombay, India, 13 miles S. E. of Dharwar, on the main road from Poona to Hariwar. The center of the cotton trade of the Marathi country. Population (1901), 60,214, of whom about two-thirds are Hindus. Station of the Basel Missionary Society (1839), with (1903) 3 missionaries, 2 wives of missionaries, 16 native workers, men and women; 2 outstations, 3 day schools, and 472 professed Christians. Outstation also of SPG, with (1902) 2 native workers, 1 place of worship, 1 day school, and 116 professing Christians. The YWCA has a missionary here and a young women's society.

HUME, Robert Wilson: Born at Stamford, Conn., November 9, 1809; graduated at Union College, 1833, taking high rank as a scholar in a large class; studied theology at Andover and Princeton; attended medical lectures; ordained in 1839, and sailed April 1, the same year, as a missionary of the ABCFM for Bombay. He was stationed for fifteen years at Bombay, spending a part of the cool months making tours. For some years he was secretary of the *Bombay Temperance Union*, and editor of its journal, called the *Temperance Repository*, which attained a high place for ability and usefulness. For ten years he was secretary of the Bombay Tract and Book Society. It was through his influence that, instead of gratuitous distributions, as had formerly been the custom, colporteurs were employed, who went into all the districts of Western India, and sold hundreds of thousands of these publications. One of the Bombay journals, referring to this

Society, says: "The rapid advance the Society has made of late years has been due mainly to Mr. Hume's prudent and energetic management." Soon after his arrival in India, a monthly magazine in the native language was commenced by the Marâthi missions with a view to diffusing correct religious knowledge. The magazine was called *Dnyanodaya*, and Mr. Hume was the editor for ten years. It was the only Christian journal in any native language in Western India. His labors were highly appreciated. In 1854 he was taken very ill, and the physicians decided that his life could be saved only by his going to a colder climate. He proceeded in an English vessel to Cape Town, but he died November 26, in sight of the coast of Africa, a week before the arrival of the ship at Cape Town.

HUMPHREY, William John: Educated at Queens College and Ridley Hall, Cambridge; B.A. in 1884; M.A., 1888; *ad eundem*, Durham, 1893. On July 17, 1888, he was accepted as a missionary by the CMS; in September, 1890, entered Sierra Leone Mission as principal of Fourah Bay College, Sierra Leone; in 1890 also in charge of the work at Cline Town, and after this date, altho his health was failing, he was incessant in his labors. In April, 1898, the brief message, "Humphrey killed," reached England from Sierra Leone. Early in this year the imposition of a "hut tax" by the British Government upon the natives of Sierra Leone caused discontent and revolt among the Temnes and other tribes. The insurgent chiefs had several encounters with the British troops and covered the country between Port Lokkoh and the mission stations at Makomp and Ro-Gbere. On March 12, 1898, Humphrey, who had been sent to Grand Canary for his health, returned to Sierra Leone, and immediately, as secretary of the mission, hurried to Port Lokkoh to look after the interests of the missionaries and their fellow-workers. This first journey was made in safety, but on a second occasion, as he, accompanied by two porters, was passing through the Kassi country for Ro-Gbere, he was murdered by an insurgent.

HUNT, Phineas R.: Born at Arlington, Vt., January 30, 1816. From his conversion in early life he was an active and zealous Christian. He went to India in 1839 as a missionary printer of the ABCFM, and was stationed at Madras. His warm-hearted, Christian efforts among the English-speaking population, native and foreign, and his generous sympathy endeared him to a wide circle of friends. He had the charge of the mission press in Madras, and was also treasurer of the mission, in both of which departments he discharged his duties with great fidelity. He greatly improved the style of Tamil printing. The Tamil Bible and the dictionary of Dr. Winslow, both printed by him, are monuments of his skill and painstaking efforts.

On the discontinuance of the Madras mission he went to Peking in 1868, a veteran of twenty-nine years' service in a foreign field, to fill a similar post. His labors were invaluable to the mission. He established the first printing office in Peking in which the foreign press and metallic movable type were used. He died May 29, 1878.

HU-CHAU-FU: A town in the province of Che-kiang, China, situated on the Tai-hu Lake, 90 miles W. S. W. of Shanghai. The climate of the surrounding plains is malarious. Population, about 70,000. Station of the ABMU (1888), with 2 missionaries (one a physician) and their wives, 10 native workers, men and women; 9 outstations, 2 day schools and 241 professed Christians, of whom 40 are communicants. Station also of the MES (1900), with 1 missionary and his wife, 6 native workers, 5 outstations, 4 preaching places, 1 dispensary, and 158 professed Christians. Name also written Hoochow.

HUEI-KING: A town in the province of Ho-nan, China, situated 110 miles S. W. of Chung-tu-fu. Station of the PCC (1902), with 1 missionary and 1 native worker. Name is sometimes spelled Hwai-king and Hwei Ch'ing.

HUGLI: A town in Bengal, India, capital of a district of the same name. It is situated on the right bank of the Hugli River, 25 miles N. of Calcutta. It is said to have been founded by the Portuguese in 1537, and the adjoining town of Chinsurah was a Dutch town. The population, with Chinsurah (1891), is 33,100. Station of the LMS in 1798 and transferred to the UFS (1849), with (1903) 3 missionaries, 1 wife of a missionary, 2 women missionaries, 124 native workers, 50 day schools, 3 boarding schools, and, including Kalna also, 330 communicants. Station also of the Chinsurah and Hugli Zenana Mission (1875), with 1 woman missionary, 10 native women workers, 5 day schools, and 100 Zenana pupils.

HUMENE: A settlement on the east coast of the island of Nias (near Sumatra), Dutch East Indies. Station of the Rhenish Missionary Society, with (1903) 1 missionary, 20 native workers, men and women; 3 outstations, 4 day schools, and 1,458 professed Christians.

HUNG-TUNG-HSIEN: A town in the province of Shan-si, China, situated on the Pei-ho River about 15 miles N. by E. of Ping-yang-fu. Station of the CIM (1886), not yet (1903) reoccupied as a missionary residence since the Boxer rising of 1900. Name written Hong-tong in reports of the Society.

HUN-YÜEN-CHAU: A town in the province of Shan-si, China, situated north of the great wall, in the E. part of the province. Station of the CIM (1898), vacant (1903) since the Boxer outbreak of 1900, when the missionaries were killed.

HURDA. See HARDA.

HURRICANE HILLS: A settlement in Assiniboia, Dominion of Canada, situated 30 miles S. E. of Regina. Station of the Presbyterian Church in Canada, opened in 1897 as an Indian Reserve, where are about 200 souls, all pagans.

HUTA BARAT: A village in the island of Sumatra, Dutch East Indies, situated between Siboga and Toba Lake, about 3 miles from Pea Raja. Station of the Rhenish Missionary Society among the Battaks, with (1903) 1 missionary, 62 native workers, men and women; 10 outstations, 11 day schools, and 3,676 professed Christians, of whom 1,731 are communicants.

HWAI-KING. See HUEI-KING.

HWAI-NGAN-FU: A town in the province of Kiang-su, China, situated on the Grand Canal, 100 miles N. E. of Nanking. Population, about 150,000. Station of the PS (1895), at present (1903) unoccupied.

HWAI-YÜEN: A town in the province of Ngan-hwei, China, situated at the confluence of the Hwai and Ko rivers, on a low site which is flooded every three or four years. The river is an artery of commerce for the provinces of Ngan-hwei and Ho-nan. Population 20,000. Station of the PN (1902), with 4 missionaries (2 with their wives), 1 woman missionary, 2 native workers, 1 hospital, and 1 dispensary.

HWANG-HSIEN: A town in the province of Shantung, China, situated about 50 miles N. W. of Chifu. Station of the SBC, with (1900) 7 missionaries, men and women, 1 of whom is a physician.

HWANG-YEN-HSIEN: A town in the province of Che-kiang, China, situated about 75 miles S. of Ning-po. Station of the CIM (1896), with (1903) 1 missionary and his wife, 2 women missionaries, 13 native workers, 12 outstations, and 1,019 professed Christians.

HWEI-CHAU-FU: A town in the province of Ngan-hwei, China, situated 97 miles W. by S. of Hang-chau. Station of the CIM (1884), with (1903) 1 missionary and his wife, 6 native workers and 4 outstations.

HWEN-YUEN. See HUN-YUEN-CHAU.

HWO-LU-HSIEN: A town in the province of Chi-li, China, situated 218 miles S. W. of Peking. It is an important commercial center, lying at the foot of a pass over the Shan-si Mountains, by which the road leads to Tai-yuen-fu. Station of the CIM (1887), with (1903) 1 missionary and his wife and 1 woman missionary.

HWUY-CHAU. See HWEI-CHAU-FU.

HWUY-LUH. See HWO-LU-HSIEN.

HYDE, Rev. Charles McEwen: Born in New York, June 8, 1832. Died at Honolulu, October 13, 1890. Educated at Williams College and Union and Princeton Seminaries. He was ordained at Brimfield, Mass., in 1862, and was pastor there and in Haverhill until 1876. On May 31, 1877, he arrived at Honolulu. Soon after his arrival in the foreign field he took a prominent part in the mission work among the Hawaiians, and as a preacher, a teacher, and an organizer his influence was felt. He reorganized the theological school at the North Pacific Missionary Institute, and until his death he was a leader, especially in educational matters, on this important field. He labored effectively among the Chinese, Japanese, and Portuguese, as well as among the Hawaiians.

HYDERABAD. See HAIDARABAD.
HYDRABAD. See HAIDARABAD.

I

IAIAN LANGUAGE: A language of the Melanesian group, which is peculiar to Uvea, the most northerly of the Loyalty Islands.

IARINDRANO: A district in the province of Betsileo, Madagascar, lying south of Fianarautsoa. Mission field of the LMS (1864), with (1903) 1 missionary and his wife, 320 native workers, men and women; 24 Sabbath schools, 79 day schools, and 2,744 professed Christians, of whom 918 are communicants.

IBADAN: A walled city in the Yoruba country, W. Africa, situated 83 miles N. N. E. of Lagos, with which it is connected by railway. Population, about 120,000. Station of the CMS (1852), with (1903) 1 missionary, 2 women missionaries, 11 native workers, men and women; 4 day schools and 984 professed Christians, of whom 351 are communicants. Mohammedans are gathering many converts in the country. Yet a few Mohammedans are converted to Christianity each year. Circuit station also of the WMS.

IBANSH: A town in the Congo Free State, Africa, situated about 45 miles N. by E. of Luebo, at an altitude of about 1,000 feet. It is an important center of trade for the Bakuba tribe. Station of the PS (1897), with (1903) 2 missionaries, 1 with his wife; 10 native workers, men and women; 2 outstations, 2 places of worship, 1 day school, and 600 professed Christians, of whom 197 are communicants. Name also written Ibanj and Ibange.

IBO LANGUAGE: Belongs to the negro group of African languages and is spoken by an unknown number of tribesmen found in the Calabar region, between the Niger and Cross rivers in W. Africa. It has been reduced to writing by missionaries of the CMS, Roman letters being used for the purpose. Some beginnings of a literature have appeared.

IBUNO: A settlement in Southern Nigeria, W. Africa, situated on the Kwa Ibo River not far from the coast. Station of the Qua Iboe Mission (1887), with (1903) 1 missionary, 5 native workers, 3 schools, 1 dispensary, 1 printing house, 1 industrial farm, and 525 professed Christians. The mission has also a steam launch for river touring.

IBWIJILI: A settlement in German East Africa in the Chigogo district, not far from Mpapwa. Station of the CMS (1901), with (1903) 1 missionary and his wife, 3 native workers, 1 day school, 1 dispensary, and 20 professed Christians.

ICELAND: A large island in the North Atlantic Ocean, subject to the Danish crown, 160 miles northeast of Greenland and 600 miles west of Norway. Area, including adjacent islands, 39,758 square miles, of which 16,243 are habitable. Iceland is of volcanic origin, and therefore all its mountains are volcanoes. It is remarkable for its numerous geysers and intermittent hot springs. The climate is colder than when it was first settled, since great masses of ice yearly drift from Greenland to its shores and remain for months encircling the island in a compact mass. The Gulf stream makes the southern portion warmer and more rainy than the northern. Population (1901), 78,470, who are descendants of the first Norwegian settlers, speaking the purest Norse. The men are tall, fair-complexioned and blue-eyed, with frames hardened by frequent exposure to rough weather. Tho perhaps inclined to idleness and intemperance, they are strictly upright, truthful, generous, and hospitable. The women are industrious and chaste. Religious faith and the domestic virtues are traditional in every household. Education is universal, and it is hard to find an adult who is unable to read and write. Their church is exclusively Lutheran, but lately three missionary stations have been established by the Roman Catholics. Foreigners have the same rights of residence, holding property, etc., as natives.

I-CHANG-FU: An important inland town and treaty port in the province of Hu-pei, China, situated on the left bank of the Yangtse River, 165 miles W. of Hankow (363 miles by river). Lying at the outlet of the river after it has come 350 miles through mountain passes and rocky ravines, the town is exposed to considerable risk from floods, and in 1870 many houses were washed away. It stands at the head of steam navigation on the Yangtse, but access to it is so hampered by rocks that its value for foreign trade is slight. Altitude, 500 feet. Population, 33,000. Station of the Church of Scotland Foreign Missions and Woman's Committee (1878), with (1900) 10 missionaries, men and women; 14 native workers, men and women; 6 day schools, 1 hospital, and 206 professing Christians. Station also of the PE (1889), with 4 native workers. Station also of the CIM (1895), with (1903) 1 missionary and his wife. Station also of the Swedish Missionary Society (1894), with a dispensary and a day school.

I-CHAU-FU: A town in the province of Shantung, China, situated 220 miles N. by W. of Nanking. Station of the PN (1891), with (1903) 11 missionaries, men and women (2 of them physicians); 5 day schools, 2 dispensaries, 2 hospitals, 1 medical class, and 364 church members. Name written by the Society Ichow.

I-CHENG: A town in the province of Shan-si, China, situated 32 miles S. E. of Ping-yang-fu. Station of the CIM (1902), with 1 missionary and his wife.

IDAIYANGUDI: A town and district in Madras, India, situated on the seacoast in the extreme south of Tinnevelli, about 40 miles S. W. of Tuticorin. The inhabitants are chiefly of the Shanar or Palmyra rearing caste, and poorer and more ignorant than those farther north. The majority of the people became Christians early in the 19th century, but afterward, through neglect, were suffered to relapse into evil ways and heathenism. Station of the SPG (1825), with (1903) 43 native workers, men and women; 24 places of worship, 12 day schools, 2 high schools, and 3,082 professed Christians, of whom 791 are communicants.

IDUTYWA: A district or reserve in Cape Colony, S. Africa, situated in the Transkei region, some 70 miles N. of East London. Station of the SPG (1893), and the Episcopal Church in Scotland (1896), with (1903) 1 missionary, 31 native workers, 17 outstations, 12 places of worship, 17 day schools, and 2,800 professed Christians, of whom 763 are communicants.

IGATPURI: A town in the Bombay Presidency, India, situated in the district of Nasik, 72 miles N. E. of Bombay. Population (1891) 7,500, of whom 4,800 are Hindus. Station of the ME, with (1903) 1 missionary and his wife, 5 native workers, 1 preaching place, 4 Sunday schools, 1 day school, and 277 professed Christians.

IH-YANG. See I-YANG-HSIEN.

IJEBU ODE: A town in the Yoruba country, W. Africa, situated 35 miles N. E. by E. of Lagos. Population, about 30,000. Station of the CMS native Church, with (including Ijebu Igbo, 1903) 19 native workers, 7 day schools, and 3,768 professed Christians, of whom 623 are communicants. Station also of the WMS, with (1903) 1 missionary, 34 native workers, men and women; 35 places of worship, 6 day schools, and 407 professed Christians. Name also written Jebu Ode, Ijebu, and Ode.

IKOKO: A settlement in the Congo Free State, 320 miles N. E. of Stanley Pool. Station of the ABMU (1894), with (1903) 2 missionaries, 1 missionary's wife, 3 women missionaries, and 5 native workers.

IKONETA: A settlement in Southern Nigeria, situated on the Cross River, near Creek Town. Station of the UFS (1856), but now (1903) operated as an outstation of Ikorofiong. Name written by the Society Ikunetu.

IKOROFIONG: A town in the Old Calabar region of W. Africa (now called Southern Nigeria) situated on the right bank of the Cross River, about 12 miles N. W. of Creek Town. Station of the UFS (1858), with (1903) 2 missionaries, one with his wife; 1 woman missionary, 14 native workers, 5 outstations, 11 day schools and 88 professed Christians.

IKWEZI LAMACHI: A settlement in Alfred County, Natal, South Africa, near Harding. Station (1877) of the Young Men's Foreign Missionary Society of Birmingham, England (YMCA), with 1 missionary and his wife, 14 native workers, 9 outstations, 6 day schools and 2 industrial schools.

ILALANGINA: A mission district in Madagascar, situated in the Betsileo province and near Fianarantsoa, extending to the N. E. from that place. Occupied by the LMS in 1870. It now (1903) has 1 missionary and his wife, 180 native workers, men and women; 20 Sabbath schools, 60 day schools and 1,670 professed Christians, of whom 480 are communicants.

ILESHA: A town in the Yoruba country, near the border of Nigeria, W. Africa, situated about 155 miles N. E. by E. of Lagos. Population about 40,000. Station of the CMS native Church, with (1903) 8 native workers, 3 preaching places, 3 day schools and 845 professed Christians, of whom 132 are communicants. Name also written Ilesa. The WMS also has a native worker here, with a growing congregation.

ILOILO: A town and seaport in the Philippine Islands, situated on the E. coast of the island of Panay. It is, next to Manila, the chief port of the islands. Its largest export is sugar. Population about 11,000. Station of the PN (1900), with (1903) 2 missionaries and their wives (one a physician), 6 native workers, 3 outstations, 1 hospital and dispensary.

IMAD-UD-DIN, Rev. Maulvi, D.D.: Born at Paniput, North India, in 1822. Died at Amritsar, August 28, 1900. He was a Mohammedan Maulvi, and a lineal descendant of the famous Mohammedan saint, Qutub Jamal, who was a descendant of the ancient royal house of Persia. Imad-ud-din was educated at the Government College at Agra; was converted to Christianity as a result of a discussion in public between missionaries and Muslim doctors; received into the Church at Amritsar, April, 1866, and became the native preacher at Amritsar. He was appointed Examining Chaplain to the Bishop of Calcutta for Hindustani candidates, and afterward he was Chaplain to the Bishop of Lahore. In 1884 the degree of Doctor of Divinity was conferred on him by the Archbishop of Canterbury, and his pen produced the following works: *Hidáyat-ul-Muslimin*; *Haqiqi 'arfan*, being 12 tracts on the Christian Religion; *A Short Commentary on the Book of Revelation*; *A Popular Life of Mahomet*; *A Tract on the Resurrection*; *A Commentary on St. Matthew's Gospel*, and a number of other able works.

As a young man Imad-ud-din was full of Muslim bigotry and fanaticism, and he was arrayed against Dr. Pfander and Mr. French in their famous discussions with Mohammedans at Agra. It was a wonderful time. The mutiny had yet to come, and hoary Islam had yet to he humbled, politically as well as spiritually. The old confronted the new, and who could foresee that three out of the four leading opponents of Christianity would one day bow the knee to the Christ they then despised? The fourth, Maulvi Rahmat Ullah, a close friend of Dr. Imad-ud-din's, fled to Mecca after the mutiny and there died. The history of Imad-ud-din's struggles before he accepted Christianity is one of thrilling interest. Learned in all that Islam had to teach and soul-hungry for something higher, he turned to that esoteric philosophy, which as the Vedanta, and as Sufism, the Transcendentalism of the East, purports to offer to the longing soul the peaceful vision of God and communion with Him. For many months be obeyed its precepts and sounded its lowest depths, and finally, worn in body and wretched in soul, he was brought under the influence of Rev. Robert Clark in the Mission Church at Amritsar, where he surrendered to the call of Christ, and from that time throughout his long and eventful life he never wavered in his loyalty to his divine Master. This distinguished convert from Islam to Christianity was a remarkable preacher of the Gospel; but he was a more remarkable writer of Christian truth. A long series of volumes, dealing with every type and phase of Mohammedan controversy, came in rapid succession from his pen, and his books have found their way to all Mohammedan lands, and their effect has been felt in places as far apart as Java and Montenegro. He had the joy of seeing his aged father and younger brother enter into the Christian life.

IMPOLWENI: A settlement in Natal, S. Africa, situated 12 miles N. N. W. of Pietermaritzburg. Station of the UFS (1872), with (1903) 1 missionary and his wife, 5 native workers, 2 outstations, 6 day schools and 381 professed Christians.

IMPUR: A village in Assam, British India, situated in the Naga hills, near the Burman frontier. Station of the ABMU (1876), with (1903) 3 missionaries and their wives, 15 native workers, men and women; 8 preaching places, 9 day schools, 1 boarding school and 467 professed Christians.

IMVANI: A settlement in Cape Colony, S. Africa, situated in the Queenstown district, about 20 miles S. E. of Queenstown. Station of the Episcopal Church in Scotland (1854), with (1900) 2 missionaries, 1 woman missionary, 47 native workers, 10 outstations, 12 schools and 620 professed Christians.

INANDA (Lindley): A settlement in Natal, S. Africa, situated about 15 miles N. by W. of Durban. Station of the ABCFM (1847), with (1903) 1 missionary, 2 women missionaries, 24 native workers, men and women; 7 day schools and 1 boarding school for girls, with industrial department.

INDIA: A region of Asia between the Himalaya Mountains on the north, the Arabian (or Indian) Ocean on the west and southwest, and the Bay of Bengal on the east. Its extreme northern point is in latitude 35°; on the south it stretches to within 8° of the Equator. North and south its greatest length is about 1,900 miles; east and west —from the mouth of the Indus to the head of the Bay of Bengal—the distance is about as great. Yet the shape of the land is not four-sided, but triangular; its northern parts are the broadest; toward the south it narrows gradually to a point at Cape Comorin. Politically, Assam and Burma, on the east, tho peopled by races bearing slight affinities with those of India proper, and Baluchistan, on the west, are comprised in the Anglo-Indian empire. The area of the whole vast territory is nearly one and a half million square miles, and the population (according to the census of 1901, the last taken, which will be the basis of reference throughout this article) more than 294,000,000. Three well-marked areas, each characterized by its peculiarities of physical structure, divide India proper between them. These are: 1. The Himalayan strip, lying along its northern frontier, and forming on that side a wall of protection and demarcation from the rest of Asia. Much of the Himalayan territory, however, is outside of the political limits of India. 2. The great valley of the Ganges, of which the Himalayan area forms the northern slope. 3. That part of India bounded on the north by the valley just mentioned, on the southwest by the Indian Ocean, on the east by the Bay of Bengal. This is for the most part a tableland, of which the western edge, buttressed by a mountain range (the Western Ghats) rising in some cases to 4,000, 5,000 and even 8,000 feet above sea-level, is about 2,000 feet above the sea, and slopes gradually eastward toward the Bay of Bengal. India presents to our observation not a united and coherent nationality pervaded by the oneness of a national life, but merely a vast number of peoples, differing in language, in religion, often in race, and held together by the strong and external pressure of British might. Physically also, tho India can hardly be called a continent, yet it is certainly the epitome of a continent on a very large scale. Vast mountain chains and mighty rivers, arid deserts and fertile valleys, wild jungles, forests of tropic density, broad alluvial deltas, and plains rolling in gentle undulations over wide areas of surface, are all found within its limits. Its climate embraces the Arctic cold of the Himalayas, with their perpetual snows and their glaciers, which feed fertilizing and navigable rivers, hot desert winds, deluging rains, atmospheres now like a vapor-bath and now like a blast from a furnace, bracing breezes from the sea, and the parching heat of unclouded suns falling upon treeless plains.

This vast and various territory is for the most

part under the rule of the British crown and Parliament. In many scattered portions of Indian territory the original power of native rulers is still acknowledged; these states sometimes cover large tracts of country, with their millions of inhabitants, and sometimes embrace but a single town, with its dependent villages, or a bit of mountain jungle where the authority of some half-savage aboriginal chief is owned by the handful of his tribe. But even these native states are under the "protection" and watchful care of the paramount English power; the authority of their ostensibly independent native rulers is circumscribed within definite limits at the dictation of that power, while its actual exercise is carefully superintended, with more or less minuteness of detail, by English officials appointed for that purpose.

Political Divisions: Such a diverse territory can be best described in the present work by treating of its separate political divisions in their proper alphabetical order under separate headings. With the exception of the native states, all of which come more or less directly under the supervision of the paramount power through a class of officials known as "residents," all of India is governed, in the name of the British sovereign, by a Viceroy, or Governor-General, assisted by a Council, whose seat is at Calcutta. For purposes of administration the country is divided into eight great "provinces," each under the control of a governor, lieutenant-governor or commissioner, according to rank of the province.

These provinces are: Madras, Bombay, Bengal, United Provinces of Agra and Oudh, Punjab, Burma, Assam, Central Provinces. In addition to these provinces there are four "minor charges," each under a Chief Commissioner. These are Coorg, Ajmere-Merwara, British Baluchistan and the Andaman Islands. The Northwest Frontier Province, with seat of administration at Peshawar, is administered by a military officer whose title is Agent to the Governor-General.

Population: The people of India, with whom in their religious relationships our interest, now principally lies, are divided by race, by caste, by language, and by religion into many different classes. The broadest division is that by religion. The census of 1901 shows the distribution of the population according to religion (including the native feudatory states) to be as follows: Of the 294,233,345 souls comprised in the total population of the Indian Empire, 207,146,422 are classed as Hindus; 62,458,061 as Mohammedans; 9,476,750 are Buddhists; 8,584,349 are spirit-worshipers (chiefly the aboriginal tribes); 2,923,241 are Christians; 2,195,268 are Sikhs; 1,334,148 are Jains; 94,190 Parsis; 18,228 Jews; and 2,686 are of other shades of belief or disbelief.

The division of the people into castes obtains only among the Hindus. The ancient fourfold division is well understood by every one who has ever heard of India. The Brahmans or priests occupy the highest place; the second caste is that of the Kshattriyas, or soldiers; merchants, or Vaisyas, form the third; while the fourth, including the vast body of the people, is that of the laborers, or Sudras. In modern times, however, this simple division has become exceedingly complicated. The Brahmans still maintain their preeminence as the first and highest caste, altho within the limits of Brahmanism there are many subdivisions, between some of which intermarriage is not allowed. The great mass of agriculturists also still acknowledge themselves as members of the fourth or Sudra caste. But, instead of finding between the castes of first and fourth rank distinctly marked gradations indicating the limits of the second and third, we find a great multitude of castes, partly formed of what may be regarded as the fragments of the old soldier and merchant castes, partly the result of intermarriages between men of higher grade and women of lower (the offspring of such marriages occupying a social position midway between that of their parents), and partly due to the inevitable complication of social relations, as the process of social evolution went on. Among this mass of caste names the old titles still exist of Kshattriyas and Vaisyas. The Rajputs of Northwestern India are descendants of the old second or soldier caste; the merchants (in many places known as *Wanis* or *Banyas*) may usually be regarded as belonging to the old third or merchant caste, tho its subdivisions are exceedingly numerous. Thus, while the old nomenclature still exists with reference to the Brahmans and the Sudras, it has been for the most part superseded with reference to the soldiers and the merchants, owing to the divisions of these old castes, and the origin of new, as the development of Hindu society progressed. In addition to the castes already mentioned, the followers of every species of trade and handicraft form a caste by themselves. Thus there is the caste of goldsmiths, of tailors, of carpenters, of blacksmiths, of weavers, of shoemakers and leather workers, of potters, etc. Some of these castes occupy a position above the Sudras; some, especially the shoemakers and potters, below them. Below all these respectable castes of Hinduism are ranged the great body of the outcaste population, who are not allowed to live within the village limits, who are sometimes debarred even from entering the street in which Brahmans reside, who must not draw water from the wells or streams used by those of higher rank, and whose very touch, sometimes even whose mere shadow, is pollution. Yet they often perform important services in the social life of an Indian village. These outcastes are often spoken of collectively as *Pariahs*—which is the term used to designate them in Tamil—tho all the Indian vernaculars possess words by which individuals of this description are locally denominated. The origin of the caste system is lost in the dimness of remotest antiquity. It is probable that it originated in some such way as this: The Aryans, who entered India from the Northwest some fifteen centuries before the Christian era, found the land as they advanced already in the possession of a previous population. This population, the Aryans with their stronger character, higher civilization and more cultivated language (the Sanskrit), in process of time overcame. Gradually diversity of function within their own body gave rise to a corresponding diversity of social position, or caste; the priests, the soldiers and the merchants segregated themselves into their own distinct classes, the distinct existence of which as such was ensured by the custom that the son should follow the calling of his father. The former inhabitants of the land seem for the most part to have accepted the religion, and to some degree—tho in an inferior form and with many corruptions—the language of their Aryan conquerors, and to have been relegated by the latter to the lowest position in the social scale, that of laborers or agriculturists. Thus the three higher castes were of Aryan origin, while the fourth or Sudra caste, between which and the three that range above it there is a much wider gap than between any two of the higher themselves, was composed of the great body of the previous population. It is probable that the outcaste bodies (Pariahs, Mahars, Mangs, Dheds, etc.) represent early aboriginal tribes, brought into some dergee of union with the new social organism arising after the Aryan invasion, but too low to become actually incorporated in it, as members in good repute, as those composing the fourth Hindu caste were. Probably the tribes still existing apart and usually spoken of as aboriginal tribes (Santals, Gonds, etc.) are descended from aboriginal bodies who refused to yield to the Aryan invaders, or to accept the low position to which their brethren—the progenitors of the outcastes of to-day—were consigned.

Languages: It is exceedingly probable that the tribes which were thus overrun by the Aryans had themselves overrun, in previous ages, still other and inferior races who held the soil before them. Repeated invasions and conquests must have marked the earliest history of India, as they have its later developments; and these repeated processes of invasion have left their evidences in the strata of tribes and races which to-day make up the complex population of Hindustan. Not only can the diversity of caste be in part accounted for in this way, but also the great diversity of language which characterizes India. It is stated by philologists that within the limits of both Hither and Farther India (meaning by the last term that peninsula which includes Burma and Siam, of which only a part is politically connected with the Anglo-Indian empire) three hundred distinct languages and dialects are in actual use at the present time. The variety of the aboriginal tribes already so many times alluded to, of which each one has usually its own distinct form of speech, accounts in large measure for the great number. The principal languages of India, each of which is spoken by millions, and which have all received more or less literary cultivation and development, are much fewer in number.

The Indian languages can be conveniently distributed into several groups, according to their affinities. The first division consists of the most important tongues used in northern and western India. These are: The Bengali, spoken in the province of Bengal by about 37,000,000 of people. It is subject to several dialectic variations, especially upon the borders of its territory, where it comes in contact with other languages, by the intermingling of which in the speech of the people the purity of all is corrupted. About half of those using the language are Mohammedans; their form of the language is known as Mohammedan Bengali and forms another dialect of the language. On the northeast of Bengal, in the Brahmaputra valley, about 2,000,000 of people use the Assamese, which is most probably a language allied to the Bengali. Southwest, in the province of Orissa, the Uriya tongue is used by some 8,000,000 of people. The Hindi language, occupying an immense tract northwest of Bengal, covering the Northwest Provinces, and overlapping on every side into the surrounding regions, is the most widely used tongue of all of the modern languages of India. The number of those to whom it is vernacular is estimated at 80,000,000. More than half of these, however, use the Hindustani or Urdu, which is the dialect formed by the Mohammedan conquerors of India, with many Arabic and Persian words and written with Arabic instead of Hindu letters. Other dialectic variations are numerous. The Bengali, the Uriya, the Assamese, the Hindi, the Sindhi, the Gujarathi and the Marâthi, with their many dialects, are sister-tongues of the Aryan family, tho incorporating into their substance many elements of grammar, of idiom, and of vocables from the non-Aryan languages with which the spoken Sanskrit of a former period gradually became corrupted. Of these Aryan vernaculars only three — the Bengali, the Hindi, and the Marâthi—have received any high degree of cultivation, or possess any important literature. It is possible that the other languages of this group may ere long disappear; but these three are widely prevalent and cultivated tongues, which seem destined to permanence.

The Hindu population of South India presents us with a second great family of languages, much farther removed than those of the north and west from the Sanskrit, and owing to it smaller—tho important—obligations. These languages are usually spoken of as the Dravidian group. The term "Dravire" or "Dravida" is found in Sanskrit literature as applied to the part of the Indian peninsula where the chief languages of the group are now spoken. The most important of them all is the Tamil, covering the area from a few miles north of the Madras to the extreme south of the eastern side of the peninsula, and running more than half the distance across the peninsula toward the Indian Ocean. North of the Tamil area, on the east side of Lower India, lies the Telugu country, along the Bay of Bengal, and up into Central India, until it meets the Uriya language along its northeastern edge and the Marâthi along its northwestern. West of the Tamil and Telugu areas lies that of Kanarese, which also meets the Marâthi on the northwest. The Malayalim stretches along the western coast of India from Cape Comorin northward nearly 300 miles. The Tamil, the Telugu (sometimes from its abundance of vowel and liquid sounds called the Indian Italian), the Kanarese, and the Malayalim are all cultivated languages, possessing a literature and a distinctive alphabetical character. The Tamil is by far the most important and richest of them all, and is used by the largest number of people—nearly 15,000,000 in all. Tamil is also used extensively in Northern Ceylon, and by many emigrants to Burma, the Straits Settlements, Mauritius and the West Indies.

Besides the cultivated language of the Dravidian group just described, languages of the same family are used by some of the jungle tribes of India, as the Gonds and Khonds, the people of Chota Nagpur and of the Nilgiri Hills and some others. The total number of persons using Dravidian forms of speech must be more than 60,000,000.

Religions: Regarding the religious condition of

the people, it will be sufficient to refer the reader to the several articles in this work in which the different religions practised in India are treated in detail; with the remark that for the most part the people cling to those religions with the tenacity—often an unthinking tenacity—which is to be expected of those who have been educated from their earliest years to believe that adherence to the customs of one's ancestry, and to the religious rites practised by one's forefathers, is the first and highest law of life. In them the intense conservatism of all Oriental nations is thus reenforced by religious sanctions, and is exalted to the position of religious obligation. Hinduism has been interwoven with the developing life of the Hindu people for a period of more than thirty centuries; it has presided over the formation of their philosophies, their social customs, their intellectual habits and their literature; and it lies at the very basis of their lives in all possible relations to a degree which is hardly paralleled elsewhere. These facts account for the extreme difficulty and slowness of Christian progress among the Hindus. The Mohammedans in India do not derive their religion from ages so remote as the Hindus, and on this account their momentum along the line of present religious development might be supposed to be less, yet they show fully as much determination in upholding their peculiar tenets as the Hindus do in upholding theirs; they are characterized by the same intense conviction that they are God's chosen people, commissioned to take and purge the earth, which has made Mohammedan armies so often victorious in battles, which renders them individually impervious to argument and reason, and even leads them to deeds of private, personal violence in support of their faith.

Civilization: The people of India have their own civilization developed gradually through long ages of progress, different from that of the West, yet wonderful to contemplate, and in many respects admirable The main resource of the people being agriculture, the process of tilling the soil and making it yield its wealth have been carefully studied; and tho their implements are clumsy and their methods those of a bygone age, to which they still cling with that tenacious conservatism which they show in everything, yet the results of their efforts are by no means contemptible. They have especially constructed immense tanks and reservoirs for storing water and complicated sluiceways and canals for distributing it in the dry season over their fields, which in size and utility are remarkable. These are found chiefly in Central and South India. The English Government has done much to extend facilities for irrigation by the construction of costly systems of canals, fed by the rivers, whose waters are diverted into them by finely constructed dams. Such works exist in all parts of India, and the canals are sometimes of sufficient size to be available for purposes of navigation. Their manufactures—tho entirely by hand—especially of certain textile fabrics, such as muslins and silks, as also of jewelry and brass ware, have long been famous in the markets of the world. In the development of social and political life they have wrought out a system of efficient communal government in their villages which has been the subject of careful study by European lawyers and historians. Its object, in a word, was to make each village self-supporting and independent, furnishing it, within its own walls and by means of its own organism, with farmers, artisans and day-laborers, in sufficient number, variety and proportion to provide every article of ordinary use—both clothing and implements of every sort—which the village could need; while the public affairs of every village were regulated, and all disputes between villages settled, by the headmen and elders of the village, to whom long usage had relegated those duties. In literature the Indian civilization has given to the world the Sanskrit language—one of the most copious and highly polished tongues with which scholars have ever become familiar; poetry and philosophy have been especially cultivated; to some degree also mathematical and astronomical science. In geography but little has been done, in history nothing; in fact the historic sense seems to be largely wanting in the Indian mind. Their achievements in art are confined chiefly to the department of architecture; in painting they have done nothing; in sculpture they have merely succeeded in fashioning images of their gods and heroes of a character hardly rising above the level of caricature, and sometimes falling to that of absolute hideousness; sometimes the sculptures of a cave temple (for instance that of Elephanta in Bombay harbor) will be found to possess a considerable degree of dignity and artistic excellence. But such exceptions to the general character of grotesqueness are not frequent. Numerous temples—some cut from the solid rock; some built of stone with neither mortar nor cement; some whose towers arise to imposing heights, like those of Southern India; some merely stone-built shrines, a simple cube with a pyramidal roof; some built last year, and others in various stages of decay attesting their foundation centuries ago; some covered with rudely fashioned images of gods and of animals esteemed sacred, oftentimes in various obscene attitudes; and some wholly plain, and with no attempt at ornament—are the sole creations of their architectural skill. In music the Indians have perfected a system of their own, with notation, time, and intervals different from those of Western music, wholly destitute of harmony, yet not without a certain plaintive beauty in its melodies. Their singing is apt to be rather nasal, and their instrumental music seems to a European nothing but a discordant clamor of drums and screeching of shrill wind-instruments; but some of the stringed instruments in use among them are more pleasing in tone. For a long time the associations of Hindu music, being almost wholly those of the Hindu temple, and the Hindu festival were considered insuperable objections to its use among Christians. But of late years, in more than one part of the great Indian mission field, native poets have arisen, who have composed Christian hymns in the meters of Hindu prosody and have adapted them to such Hindu melodies as seemed best fitted for the purpose. In many churches of Indian Christians these hymns and tunes are now used with most excellent effect.

Preachers and street evangelists in the bazars and villages find many of these native tunes with Christian words most useful in gaining the ear of the people for the proclamation of Christian truth. This conversion of Indian poetry and song to the uses of Indian Christianity was a decided step of progress in the work of naturalizing Christianity among a people the essential genius of whose mind seemed in some respects ill adapted to receive it.

It is difficult to describe in a few words the intellectual condition of the Indian people. In some respects, and among certain classes, an intellectual cultivation has existed for centuries whose twofold result is seen to-day, in a keenness of mind and a faculty of profound speculative thought which is remarkable, in the philosophical treatises, the commentaries upon them, the hymns and the poems which compose the body of Hindu classic literature. On the other hand, the people as a rule are unable to read, and are content to live on, generation after generation, with no intellectual progress, content if they get rice or other grain enough to keep them from starvation, and careless of mental or spiritual sustenance. It is among the Brahmans that the intellectual cultivation of India has reached its fullest result. They have been not only the priests, the religious leaders of the people, but also the creators of its intellectual, philosophical and literary development, and the depositaries of its intellectual wealth. With the exception of an occasional lyric poet arising from among the lower orders of the people, whose homely verses in the vernacular of his own district would often obtain an immense currency and exert a vast influence, especially over the class from which the poet himself had sprung, nearly all the thinkers, students, and authors of India have been Brahmans. The elaborate grammar of the Sanskrit language is due to their assiduous cultivation; Indian theology, philosophy, poetry, and science have been developed almost wholly by them. The Brahman intellect is keen, acute, subtle, and speculative; but their logic is apt to be fallacious and their argumentation specious rather than profound and thorough. The education of the merchant class consists of but little else than reading, writing, and such practical operations of arithmetic as will make ready and correct accountants. The royal and soldier castes have been apt to affect a lofty contempt for all literary accomplishments, as things fit only for Brahmans; and have paid the penalty of their folly in many a case by being compelled to employ Brahman secretaries, prime ministers, and financiers, who, little by little, would absorb the real power of the throne, while its nominal occupant was busy with his elephants, his horses and soldiers, or else sunken in ignoble debauchery. The great masses of the people are not to-day, and never have been, able even to read their own vernacular; thus they have become on the one hand the dupes of a crafty priesthood and on the other the prey of cunning money-lenders on whose advances of cash they are forced to depend, but whose wiles and tricks they are too ignorant to detect. Such education as the children of Hindu families enjoyed before the establishment of missionary and government schools was imparted by Brahman schoolmasters, who were wont to collect the boys wanting instruction (girls were never taught) and to teach them to repeat by rote verses from the Sanskrit poets, to read and write their own vernacular, and to perform operations in simple arithmetic. Brahman youths who wished for a thorough training in the sacred language, religion, and philosophy would attach themselves to some noted scholar and would be by him put through an elaborate course of instruction, extending to many years. In this way large numbers of young Brahmans would sometimes be found attending upon the instructions of such a learned man, or *guru*, composing thus a sort of college. But such a course of instruction would be confined, in its subjects, to the Sanskrit language, the practise of the Hindu religion, including familiarity with the sacred books, or *Vedas*, and to skill in Hindu philosophy; while its recipients would not extend beyond the ranks of the Brahman caste. Merchants did not need such training, soldiers did not care for it, and the Sudras were deemed unworthy of it.

Morals: The moral condition of the people should be described as one of apathy or even deadness rather than as one of violent and malignant opposition to virtue. Their lives are destitute of stimulus and incentive. Their religion furnishes no motive for the present and incites no aspiration for the future. The thought of bettering their own condition, or of doing aught to benefit another's, is foreign to their minds. The Oriental doctrine of fate is ever present to quench all upward endeavor. It is their destiny to be what and as they are; and who are they to contend with destiny? The chief faults of the people are lack of truthfulness —which, especially among traders, merchants and money-lenders, develops rapidly and deeply into manifold forms of cheating and fraud— and licentiousness. Yet caste rules constitute some safeguard for the virtue of their women, for a female of good caste detected in immorality is apt to be promptly dealt with and expelled by the caste authorities. Intemperance is not usually a vice of the Hindu people, tho in recent years the introduction of cheap foreign liquors, often miserable adulterations, and the course of the government in licensing drinking-places, has stimulated the use of intoxicating liquors among all classes. The disposition of the people is mild, and crimes of violence are no more common among them than among the people of other races. The ranks of the professional thieves and bandits are largely recruited from certain of the wild jungle tribes, who have been robbers from time immemorial.

Modern History: The Aryans, entering India some twenty centuries before Christ, gradually extended themselves—first through the valley of the Ganges, then into Southern India. They have left behind them no written history. But Hindu princes of various families founded dynasties and ruled over realms of greater or less extent, until they were in turn reduced to submission by the Mohammedans. These fierce and relentless conquerors entered India through the same northwestern door as those who had preceded them. The year 1000 may be taken as marking approximately their first appearance in Hindustan. Mahmoud, King of Ghazni, a city in Afghanistan, was the first Mohammedan leader to undertake the conquest of India. He made twelve expeditions into the country—the first a few years before the approximate date above given. Mohammedan power slowly grew; one dynasty after another continued the work of invasion, until first the Punjab, then the Ganges valley, and at last all of India was reduced to Muslim sway, tho the country was never long at peace. Rebellions were constantly keeping the land in turmoil, headed sometimes by an ambitious Mohammedan upstart, sometimes by a Hindu whose limbs were galled by the chains of Muslim rule. In the middle of the 17th century a Mahratta chieftain named Sivaji consolidated into a formidable power the strength of the Mahratta race and made great inroads upon the power of the Mohammedans. He overran all India, carried desolation wherever he went, and dynasties of Mahratta houses were established both in North and South India. But their power was broken at the battle of Pannipat, near Delhi, in 1761, when they contended unsuccessfully against an army led by Ahmed Shah of Afghanistan.

The English came to India very early in the 17th century, first as merchants in a small and humble way. Their mercantile operations were conducted by the East India Company, whose original charter was signed by Queen Elizabeth, near the close of her reign. Little by little their power and the scope of their influence extended itself. Establishments, or "presidencies," defended by forts and armies, under the command of this company of merchants, were placed at Madras, at Calcutta, at Bombay. From these points the authority of the Company silently but steadily grew. When the Mahratta power fell in 1761, the English were already strong enough to step into the first place of power in Hindustan; in fact, the question of English supremacy in Bengal, and by consequence in India, had been settled at the battle of Plassey, near Calcutta, in 1757, when Clive defeated the troops of Suraj-ud-Daula, the Mohammedan ruler of Bengal. From these small beginnings and along a path providentially prepared for them by the fall of the Mahrattas, the only native race capable of offering an effectual resistance, the East India Company proceeded to its manifest destiny of absorbing and ruling—not as merchants, but as conquerors and princes—the whole of India. When the great mutiny of 1857 burst upon India —a movement fomented among the native troops in the employ of the Company, and used by certain dispossessed heirs of old Indian princes in the hope of destroying the English supremacy, and regaining the lost control of their own land— English power for a moment trembled; but the result of the mutiny was merely the transfer of the supreme power in India from the hands of the East India Company to the direct control of the British crown and Parliament.

More and more have the English rulers of India realized that they have a duty and mission to perform in that land. They have governed the country with a stern and rigorous justice, with a benevolent and paternal despotism. If they have not always been conciliatory toward the natives, and have failed largely in winning the love of the subject races, they have always been respected for their justice and integrity, and their rule has been prized for the good order, the peace, the prosperity, which they have given to the country. They have encouraged and fostered education; they have established post-offices, post-roads, railroads, telegraphs; they have developed agriculture, manufactures, and commerce; they have provided hospitals and medical treatment for the diseased, and have fed the multitudes in time of famine.

Missionary work in India is carried on under the strong protection of a government, which, while wholly neutral in religious matters, undertakes to assure to every one religious liberty, and to protect all in the exercise of it.

Christianity in India: While we may regard the tradition that the Apostle Thomas introduced Christianity in India during the 1st century as unauthentic, we know that a representative of the Christian College at Alexandria found Christians on the Malabar coast before the close of the 2d century who were in possession of the Hebrew Gospel of St. Matthew, and we learn that a Bishop of India was present at the Council of Nicæa in A. D. 325. In the 6th century Syrian missionaries of the Nestorian faith propagated the Gospel in India, and Christian churches still existed on the Malabar coast and in Ceylon. From the time of Marco Polo's visit to India, in the 13th century, when he reported seeing Christians at many points where he touched, until the dawn of the 19th century, when the era of modern missions began, nearly every century witnessed earnest work by Roman Catholic missionaries in India; but in the 18th century Christianity had comparatively few consistent followers in the land.

The King of Denmark began the work of evangelical missions in India. Bartholomew Ziegenbalg and Henry Plütschau, Germans from Halle, who were sent out by Frederick IV. of Denmark, reached Tranquebar, a Danish possession, in 1706; and they may be regarded as the pioneers of the great missionary host that wrought so faithfully during the following century for the redemption of this great land.

The details of the modern missionary history of India must be sought under the titles treating of the several districts, races and missionary societies in this land; but here we may appropriately refer to the following interesting facts: As to the societies doing Christian work in India, America furnishes 35; England, 34; the Continent, nine, and the international societies and missions from other lands number 15. We are impressed by the words of Sir William Hunter in his work, *The Indian Empire:* "Between 1851 and 1890 the number of mission stations increased three-fold, while the number of native Protestant Christians has multiplied more than five-fold, the number of communicants nearly fifteen-fold and the number of churches or congregations sixteen-fold. This was largely due to the extended employment of native agency in the work. The native ordained pastors increased from 21 in 1851 to 797 in 1890, and the native lay preachers from 493 to 3,491."

The *Statesman's Year-book* gives the following facts concerning education in India: Number of educational institutions, March 31, 1901, 147,344, of which 62,039 are private and unaided; scholars under instruction, 4,417,422; number of colleges for men, 175, with 21,615 students; women's colleges, 11, with 205 students; students matriculated in the 5 universities in 1900, 7,528. The numerical increase of the evangelical forces in India during the last decade of the 19th century should inspire gratitude and kindle hope.

Year	Foreign Missionaries	Native Christians	Communicants	Pupils
1890	857	559,651	182,722	279,716
1900	3,836	591,310	376,617	342,114

We may hope for far greater blessings than these to come to India during the opening decade of this century of our Lord; but if the percentage of increase is equal to that of last decade the year 1910 will witness a Protestant community of more than one million and a quarter in this great empire.

Dubois (Abbé J. A.), *Hindu Manners, Customs and Ceremonies*, London, 1817–1899; Fuller (Mrs. M. B.), *Wrongs of Indian Womanhood*, 1900; Hunter (Sir W. W.), *The Indian Empire*, London, 1892; Ditto, *The India of the Queen, and other Essays*, London and New York, 1903; Modak (S.), *Directory of Protestant Indian Christians*, 2 vols., Calcutta, 1900; Sherring (M. A.), *History of Protestant Missions in India* (1706–1881), London, 1884; Tisdall, (W. St. Clair), *India: Its History, Darkness and Dawn*, London, 1901; Townsend (M.), *Asia and Europe*, London, 1901; Hough (Jas.), *History of Christianity in India from the Commencement of the Christian Era*, 5 vols., London, 1849–60; Irving (B. A.), *Theory and Practice of Caste*, London, 1853; Jones (J. P.), *India's Problem: Krishna or Christ*, New York, 1903.

INDIAN HOME MISSION to the Santhals (1867); This Missionary Society is not indigenous in India and its title may mislead some. It should therefore be noted at once that the Society is to be reckoned among Danish Missionary Societies. It was founded in 1867 by the Rev. H. P. Boerresen of Copenhagen and the Rev. L. O. Skrefsrud. The last named missionary, who is a Norwegian, was sent out under the Gossner Society in 1863, and Mr. Boerresen went out the following year with the intention of joining him in the Gossner Society's station in Purulia, Chota Nagpur. Not finding the situation such as they had expected, they, before long, withdrew and began an independent work among the Santals, their design being to set up a "Home" which should be a center of all those influences which flow from the home. The first three Santals to be converted were baptized in 1869, one of whom was afterward ordained. Schools were established and the pupils brought to the Middle-vernacular standard, while also receiving manual training after the custom of the people. In 1880 a colony was started in Assam for Christian Santal emigrants, the soil being more fertile than in Bengal; in 1890 the mission purchased a tea garden near the colony for its benefit. The Ebenezer Missionary Society supports a work at Dinajpur, fifty miles distant, in the care of native helpers. A mission press has been established at Ebenezer, from which a monthly paper, *The Friend of the Santhal*, is issued, and school books, hymn-books, the catechism and other Christian literature have been printed. The Gospels have for some time been in circulation, and the whole Bible is now being printed at the expense of the British Bible Society.

In 1902 there were 10,600 baptized Santals connected with this mission. There are 5 stations, 15 outstations, 5 missionaries, 46 native helpers, 9 day schools, with 375 pupils. The support of the mission comes partly from its tea plantations (in 1902 the tea culture brought in 30,000 rupees), and in the main from collections made in Scandinavia (42,000 rupees), the United States (14,500 rupees), Great Britain (2,000 rupees), and India (500 rupees). Committees exist to collect funds in England, in Scotland, Denmark, Sweden, Norway, and the United States.

INDO-PORTUGUESE: A dialect of Portuguese found among the descendents of the ancient Portuguese settlers in Ceylon and other places in the Indian seas.

INDORE: A town and capital of a district in the native State of Haidarabad, India, situated 93 miles N. by W. of the city of Haidarabad. Station of the WMS, with (1903) 1 missionary and 7 native workers, men and women. Name written by the Society Indur.

INDORE: The capital of the native state of Indore, and Residency of the Governor General's Agent for Central India. It is situated 107 miles W. S. W. of Bhopal, in a healthful region, at an altitude of 1,786 feet. Population (1891) 83,000, of whom 60,000 are Hindus, 18,000 Mohammedans, and 2,500 Jains. Station of the PCC (1877), with (1903) 10 missionaries, men and women, 2 of whom are physicians; 2 dispensaries, 1 hospital, 1 orphanage, 1 widows' home, and 1 college affiliated to Calcutta University.

INDRAMAYU: A town and seaport on the north coast of Java, Dutch East Indies, situated at the cape of the same name, about 108 miles E. of Batavia. Station of the Netherlands Missionary Union (1864), with (1900) 1 missionary. Name written by the Society, Indramajoe.

INDUSTRIAL MISSIONS AID SOCIETY: This Society was established in London in 1897 by Mr. W. H. Fry, and marks a wider effort in industrial missions. The Society proposes to develop the industrial element in missionary operations by associating, where practicable, agriculture and other industries with the work of Foreign Missions, financially separate, but linked in close fellowship. The Society began by opening factories at Ahmednagar for the manufacture of rugs, metal work, etc., thus giving employment to those trained in the mission orphanages and schools and to other Christians. It plans to do for missions generally such a work as the Basel Industrial Committee is doing for the adherents of the Basel Missions. It has sent out to India a skilled operator, whose business it is to study Indian products and the world's markets that he may advise wisely regarding the articles to be produced by industrial schools and plants, and be able to market the output to advantage.

An organization having a similar purpose and called the *Foreign Missions Industrial Association* has been organized by Mr. Fry in New York. It was incorporated early in 1904, and has in connection with it a Ladies Auxiliary Committee.

INDUSTRIAL TRAINING IN MISSIONS: Industrial education and training institutions have a growing place in missions because they are found to supply economic and moral deficiencies and necessities of converts, and to be an effective instrumentality for the Christian regeneration of heathen communities. These economic necessities of the convert are due, for one thing, to his isolation. By allying himself with the new religion, he cuts himself off from his family, his tribal relations and rights, his interest in common land, cattle, implements, and cooperative business enterprises; he loses caste; he is precluded from all low and immoral occupations, from parasitic dependence upon a rich or high-caste master, and from the priesthood and all the occupations associated with idols, superstitions and heathenworship. Because of the ill-will of his former coreligionists, he is usually at a disadvantage in legitimate lines of trade, and oftentimes is shut out from them entirely. The mission accompanies, in many cases indeed opens the way for, the overwhelming competition of Western trade. So the missionary finds the convert in a poverty deeper and more hopeless than that of his heathen neighbors, and cannot escape a sense of responsibility for his condition. Not only so, but new wants and necessities are the speedy fruitage of the Gospel. Decent clothing instead of a loin cloth, decent housing instead of herding in a one-room hovel, care for health through sanitation and medical treatment, education for the children, a Bible, and at least a few books, a church and minister are now essential to him as a man and a Christian. He may be unable to meet the expense of the old grade of living; much more is he helpless before that of the new ideals, which the missionary has inspired. Either the essentials of decent life must be supplied him as a gift, to the sapping of his manhood, and to the increasing burden of missionary treasuries, or the way must be opened for him to earn that wherewith he may pay for them himself; and, more than this, he ought to be earning something for the extension of the kingdom among his own people. The embarrassment is greater still in the case of the thousands of orphans whom Christian charity has compelled the missionaries to shelter during famine, persecution, or other disasters, and whom they cannot turn out again to die. How shall they be supported, and what shall they do when it is time for them to leave the orphanage? In the first stage of missions, when converts are few, the most of them may be utilized as servants or helpers of the missionary and as Christian workers; but all are not fitted for such service; false hopes are engendered by the system, and as the Christian community grows larger, the proportion that can be thus provided for becomes smaller. The demand for clerks, teachers and the like is very limited in most missionary lands, and in India the multiplication of over-educated non-producers is the cause of serious alarm to the authorities. Under such conditions restlessness and discontent are a natural result. Industrial helplessness is settling down upon the Christians of India.

Educational Value of Manual Training: The solution to which the working missionary early tho reluctantly came, was that industrial education and work must be provided; and the theory of missions has been adjusting itself more slowly to a like conclusion. This conclusion would have seemed to impose an intolerable burden, had it not been soon discovered that not only economic, but also moral and spiritual, needs are met by industrial training, in which a new and effective instrumentality is provided for redemptive work. Manual training is now generally recognized by educators as having an important educational value, fostering interest in work, power of initiative and sustained effort and constructive ability, and, in general, effective manhood and womanhood. Industrial education, as developed at Hampton, Tuskegee, and other schools, has proved the most promising agency in the uplifting of the negro and Indian. The mind of the barbarous and degraded heathen is dull and sluggish, encased in the conceit of ignorance and indifferent to high things. But a better way to make a board, a box or a blanket interests the dullest, while the wonders of the workshop, with its powerful engine and its ingenious tools, are as stirring as a miracle, convincing him of his ignorance, breaking down his prejudices and making him willing to hear upon other subjects the man who can do such marvels and teach others to do them.

Industrial training dignifies manual labor, which is generally despised by the inferior races and by those educated in a purely literary course. Furthermore, it discourages the dependent pauper spirit, and encourages self-respect and self-reliance by enabling the pupil to make at least a partial return for the expense of his education; it is wholesome, checking physical vice; and it affords a test of character by which lazy, inefficient pupils may be detected and the motives of those who ask for help be discovered. Once more, the native agents, ministers, and teachers, upon whom ultimate evangelization depends, need such training to fit them for efficient leadership, which calls, not for visionary, bookish individuals, but for self-reliant, practical men, frugal themselves, and able to earn part of their own support if need be, and to economically build and administer church or school. Industrial training more often than not is vital to the accomplishment of the ultimate object of missions, for a self-supporting, self-governing native church possessed of initiative to propagate itself cannot be formed until the members are able to support themselves. The problem of providing a native ministry in most fields is not more that of finding devoted preachers and pastors than it is of developing thrifty layman to support them. Nor does the time given to manual labor hinder general education. Government examinations in India and South Africa show that pupils in schools with industrial courses are on a level in literary attainments with their competitors from purely literary schools, the time given to work being compensated for by the greater alertness and application of the industrial pupil. The same testimony comes from the schools for the American negro.

The Growth of Industrial Training in Missions: Under the impulse of such motives manual industry has always had some place in the history of missions. Our Lord and His apostles honored labor and were mindful of the physical and material welfare of their followers. The early missionaries to the now Christian countries of Europe were pioneers of industry as well as of religion, introducing the ideal of peaceful toil in settled homes as an offset to the wild life of adventure and rapine, which was the ideal of early barbarism. The Moravians from the first sent out artisans as well as teachers, and the continental societies were generally in advance of the British and American in Industrial mission work. Carey supposed that missionaries could support themselves, and so set an example to their converts; a larger proportion of the earliest missionaries of the London Missionary Society also were artisans. Missionaries have been ahead of educationalists at home in their appreciation of the value of manual training, household industries being a usual feature of the earliest girls' boarding schools. Cyrus Hamlin, with his bakery and his stove and rat-trap factory, was a generation in advance. Lovedale in Africa had been doing its work for the negro some twenty years before Hampton was founded by Gen. Armstrong, himself the son of a Hawaiian missionary.

Much of the industrial work of missions has been begun without aid from the boards at home, the cost incurred being met by special contributions from individual philanthropists convinced by missionaries who saw the need of this form of effort. Up to the year 1880 but 29 industrial schools and classes were reported in the whole field of foreign missions. By 1890 there were 55. In his "Centennial Survey" (statistics to

1900) Dr. Dennis reports 179 industrial institutions and classes with 9,074 pupils, of whom 6,622 were males and 2,452 females. Of these schools 63 with 1,845 pupils were in Africa, and 62 with 5,288 pupils in India and Ceylon. Since 1900 the number of such industrial enterprises has grown more rapidly, Husband's Protestant Mission Directory for 1902 enumerating 97 missionary institutions in India and Ceylon in which trades were taught.

Nature of the Existing Industrial Enterprises: These may be loosely classified as follows: (1) Schools with industrial features whose chief object is discipline and self-help. An increasing number of orphanages and boarding schools are of this sort. At the Ecumenical Conference of 1900, Miss Barnes described such a school in India, in which the girls cultivate the cotton, spin the cloth, make their clothes, tend garden, cook, keep house, and take care of the clothing, food and health of the younger children, at the same time heading the schools of the district at the Government examinations. The Ramabai schools and orphanages at Poona and Mukti are of this class. The girl graduates of such schools are in demand as wives and are a power in domestic and social regeneration. (2) Schools where trades are taught, aiming not only at a disciplinary education, but to fit the pupil for a definite life work. They require a larger equipment and expenditure. Of these, the UFS institution at Lovedale, S. Africa, is one of the oldest and most useful. Normal and theological, as well as industrial, courses are maintained, but all the students are given careful instruction in ordinary school studies and in religion, and all are required to do some kind of manual work as a discipline and contribution to self-support. Its enrollment includes pupils from almost all the South African peoples, as well as Dutch and English, and from all denominations, the unsectarian character of the instruction being carefully guarded. The school receives support from the missionary funds and from government grants. A full course is given in printing, book-binding, blacksmithing, wagon-making, basketry, carpentry, farming, telegraphy, and domestic science. At least eighty per cent. of the 2,000 who have received its training have led useful lives; very few have reverted to their former conditions, and the majority have proved strong, energetic Christians. A large proportion of the present pupils are children of the Christian negroes whom Lovedale taught a generation ago. Blythswood Institution, also in S. Africa, is an offshoot, and Livingstonia, in Nyasaland, owes much to its assistance. Another typical trade school is the Lutheran Industrial Mission at Muhlenburg, Liberia (1840), where, among other occupations, farming and coffee-raising are made a specialty, the exports of coffee providing the school with its working capital. Graduates have cleared a group of plantations about it, and established settlements, schools, and churches in other parts of Liberia. The PN school at Sidon, Syria, the LMS school at Malua, Samoa, which is self-supporting, the ABCFM Industrial School at Tillipally, Ceylon, also self-supporting, the CEZ industrial classes in spinning and embroidery, more than self-supporting, and the Petit School of Industrial Arts, Ahmednagar, India, named after its Parsi benefactor (under the ABCFM), and giving extended courses in wood work, metal work and weaving, are further examples. The trades taught in schools of this class include carpentry and cabinet-making, blacksmithing and metal work, printing and bookbinding, weaving, tailoring, shoe-making, masonry, and embroidery. The largest number of such institutions are in India, with Africa second, and they have been an important agency in planting Christian civilization in the South Sea Islands and the New Hebrides, and agricultural schools especially have done much for the aborigines of North America.

(3) The Industrial community, in which industrial establishments where Christians may find temporary or permanent employment are added to trade schools, is a further development. The classical example is found in the Basel Society's Industrial Missions, with factories at Calicut, Cannore, Codacal in Malabar, and Palghat in Madras. The Basel Society missionaries began, as far back as 1842, various experiments to meet the necessities of their destitute converts, and the Home Committee took up the problem. A circular issued in 1854 by its Industrial Commission defined its object as two-fold: first, to lessen and, as far as possible, to remove the social difficulties which the institution of caste opposes to the missions in their endeavors to establish new congregations, and second, what may perhaps be called a mission in itself, not by preaching, but if possible by power of example, by Christianity in its practical, every day life, a mission by the exemplification of Christian diligence, honesty, and respectability. Later the whole control of the industrial enterprises was transferred to the Basel Industrial Committee, whose only connection with the Committee of the Basel Missionary Society is that some members are common to both, and the two committees work in close cooperation. The funds for the industries have been sufficiently supplied by donations, upon which the donors receive five per cent. interest, and the remaining profits are devoted to the extension of the industries, to charities, and to contributions to the Basel Mission. An improved native product, "Basel Mission cloths" (including the Khaki cloth now adopted for military uniforms), and roofing tiles of a novel pattern have been the most notable products of the Basel enterprise in India. Large numbers of converts are employed in these works, but a considerable proportion now work independently as carpenters, bookbinders, and weavers, having been assisted by the mission in making a start for themselves. They are even employed in the establishments of rival firms which copy the Basel tiles and Basel cloth. By the last report of the Basel Industrial Missions, after paying 5 per cent. on the capital invested and various donations to funds for the support of invalids, widows, and orphans, $57,780 was turned over to the Evangelistic work of the Basel Society. Tho many difficulties have beset the progress of the work and reasons for discouragement are not wanting, the supporters of the mission are convinced that it has done a great good and is on the right lines. A similar mission has been maintained by the Basel Society in the Gold Coast Colony, Africa, with gratifying results ethically and financially. Another example that will repay study is Frere Town, Mombasa, East Africa, established by the CMS as a refuge for freed slaves, in whose well-ordered settlements the freed slaves of 1885 were received, cared for, fed,

clothed, and taught by the freed slaves of 1875, now baptized Christians and leading a life of quiet industry. On the other side of the world, old Metlakahtla, of the CMS, and New Metlakahtla, established independently by William Duncan, are illustrations at once of the difficulties and benefits of industrial communities. The most extensive industrial mission undertakings yet attempted are in Central Africa. In 1875 the Free Church of Scotland, at an initial expense of $50,000, sent out for the founding of Livingstonia Mission, on Lake Nyasa, a company under the guidance of Lieut. Young, consisting of Dr. Laws and another minister, a carpenter, blacksmith, engineer, agriculturist, and seaman, who first established civilization at Cape McClear and then at Bandawe, where the wilderness has been transformed into a cultivated field, and idle, war-loving savages into an industrious Christian community. Those trained in the mission establishment engage in trade and farming in the vicinity of the mission, and many others are scattered widely over Central Africa in useful employment. The Established Church of Scotland has developed a like community at Blantyre. The Universities' Mission and the Nyasa Industrial Mission are working with success in similar lines. Newer industrial enterprises in missions are the Industrial Evangelistic Mission of Northern India, founded in 1902 by Rev. and Mrs. J. C. Lawson of Philibit, with Mr. C. W. Cotton as the Secretary of the London Committee, and the Scottish Mission Industries' Company, a purely business enterprise in relations with the UFS similar to those held by the Basel Industrial Committee to the Basel Missionary Society.

Some principles of the successful conduct of industrial missions have become established:

(1) *The Object:* The kingdom of God as the end of industrial, as of all other forms of missions, must ever be kept in view. Not physical comfort of converts, not civilization, not economy in missions, but the making of Christian men and Christian communities is the goal. In the Basel Mission the greatest care is taken to develop manhood; wages are only paid for value received, charity being administered from a fund. Malua made it a rule not to sell any of the products of the school farm, as this was found to cultivate commercialism in the pupils. "The harmonious training of the head, hand and heart is the key to the redemption of Africa," says Dr. Day of Muhlenberg.

(2) *Adaptation:* Equal need does not exist for industrial missions in all fields. Where there is a well-developed industrial system, as in China and Japan, there may be no need of them, except as a means of self-help and discipline, or the need may be small compared with that in the fields where the people are of inferior race and where Mohammedan or Hindu supremacy denies industrial opportunity to the Christian. There must be adaption of the industrial experiment to the varying conditions of each community; to the genius and capacities of the people; to the materials at their disposal; to the market available for the goods produced, and to the openings for the practise of various trades. The mission fields are strewn with the wrecks of industrial enterprises and their machinery, resulting from the blind imitation of useful institutions elsewhere. That the convert may overcome the prejudice against him as a Christian, have permanent employment, maintain his self-respect and bring honor to the cause, he must be trained to be a better workman than his heathen competitor and the Christian workshop must turn out the better goods. The same reasons advise the giving of a more expensive training in trades which promise a reasonably sure and adequate return rather than of short, cheap courses in easier trades which can never yield enough to meet the Christian's enlarged necessities. It has been found unwise to attempt the production of articles in competition with Western manufacture, unless protected against these by distance or other cause. Either a new article or an improved article for home consumption or native products of fine quality suitable for export have proved most remunerative. It should be added that those who labor for the submerged classes in great cities, for the American negro and Indian, for the African and the islander, and those who are interested industrially in India, where land-owning and agriculture are beset with peculiar difficulties, alike place growing emphasis upon the soil as furnishing the most wholesome, permanent, and promising employment for those whom they seek to benefit.

(3) *Equipment and Superintendence:* Efficient superintendence and liberal capital and equipment are essential. The employment of native artisans as instructors has proved a failure, and in few cases have ordained missionaries been found competent as instructors or superintendents of industrial work. The successful superintendent is a trained artisan with sufficient breadth and culture to enable him to study the conditions and adapt the work. He will be the better for knowing something of a variety of trades. He might well be apt to teach, but one thing he must be—an honest Christian, who puts the kingdom of God before all else as the purpose of his mission. Such a man should be placed on an equality with other missionaries, and experience has proved him worthy of it.

Industrial education is expensive at home and cannot be otherwise in the mission field. Necessity for trained superintendents and for apparatus makes it difficult to begin in a small way, but the most successful industrial enterprises have started cautiously and felt their way to their larger work. Usually the successful industrial institution is the outcome of a single devoted life with genius for organization and leadership. Hamlin and Bebek with its mill and bakery; Amstrong and Hampton, Washington and Tuskegee, Stewart and Lovedale, Laws and Livingstonia, Duncan and Metlakahtla, Ramabai and Poona—such linking of names might be continued indefinitely to illustrate the point. Having granted that industrial training is a necessity in most mission fields, the discovery of the godly man of genius to plan and organize is a first condition of success.

Mildmay Conference Foreign Missions, London, 1878, pp. 68–76; *Centenary Conference on Foreign Missions*, London, 1888, pp. 402–406; *Ecumenical Missionary Conference*, New York, 1900, Vol. II., pp. 147–167; *History of the Church Missionary Society*, Vol. III.; *Report of the Conference of Foreign Missionary Societies of Great Britain and Ireland*, 1902, p. 77; *Missionary Review of the World*, XI., p. 550; XII., 500; XVI., 686, 689, 758, 788; XVII., 13 ; Noble (F. P.), *Redemption of Africa*, pp. 562–578; 1899; Jack (J. W.), *Daybreak in Livingstonia*, London, 1900; Young (R.), *African Wastes Reclaimed*, London, 1902; Stewart (J.), *Dawn in the Dark Continent*, New York, 1903.

INDWEDWE: A town in Natal, S. Africa, situated about 28 miles E. of Pietermaritzburg.

Station of the South Africa Wesleyan Methodist Church, with 29 native workers, 20 outstations, 2 schools, and 265 professed Christians. Name written by the Society, Endwedwe.

ING-CHUNG: A city and district in the province of Fo-kien, China. The district begins 125 miles southwest of Fuchau and extends 100 miles in a northwest direction. Its mountains are high, its hill roads are long, its villages sparse, and the workers few. Station circuit of the ME, with (1903) 1 missionary and his wife, 2 women missionaries, 26 native workers, 10 preaching places, 3 day schools, 13 Sunday schools, and 403 professed Christians.

INGHOK. See YUNG-FU-HSIEN.

INGLE, James Addison: Missionary bishop of Han-kau, China; born in Frederick, Md., March 11, 1866; died in Han-kau, December 7, 1903. After his graduation from the University of Virginia in 1888 he studied for the ministry of the Protestant Episcopal Church at the Virginia Seminary in Alexandria. In 1891 he received an appointment as missionary of the PE to China and was assigned to the charge of the important station at Han-kau in the province of Hu-pei. For ten years he worked here with great success and in 1902 was consecrated first bishop of Han-kau. During his episcopate of less than two years he greatly strengthened the work of his Church in Central China. He gave special attention to the training of native clergy, catechists, and teachers, and through them, as well as through his staff of American clergy, was enabled to carry on a widely extended and very successful evangelistic work. He also greatly developed the boarding and day schools of his district and enlarged the service of the mission hospital.

INHAMBANE: A village and seaport in Portuguese East Africa, situated on the E. side of the bay of the same name, and about 230 miles N. E. of Lorenço Marques. Station of the SPG (1895), with 3 missionaries. Also outstation of the Free Methodist (American, 1885), with a day school. The original native pronunciation of the name is Inyambane, the name Inhambane being the Portuguese spelling of the African name.

INNER MISSIONS. See GERMAN INNER MISSIONS.

INTELLECTUAL UPLIFT BY MISSIONS: A few preliminary postulates must stand at the outset of even a brief discussion of this topic. Thus it is freely granted that in all mission lands other factors coming from without besides Christianity exert an intellectual influence upon the people; and it is often difficult to differentiate between the work done by missionaries and that accomplished by the Christian civilization which enters with them, or precedes their coming. Again, it is evident that thus far Protestant missions, which are alone being considered here, have been numerically but a small factor in the life of most non-Christian nations. Thus, in China, in 1900, there were some 140,000 Chinese to every Protestant missionary residing there, and the native Protestant counted only as one to about 400 of his countrymen. A third postulate has to do with the grades of society affected. As will be shown, the intellectual influence of missions varies largely with the original status of the people to whom missionaries are sent. Finally, it should be remembered that the very aim of missions differs from that of commerce or political conquest in that Christianity has as its sole object the salvation and uplifting of the community. The very nature of the system thus necessitates the elevation rather than the degradation of society. For the present purpose a threefold classification of mission lands will suffice to show the varied intellectual effects of missions upon non-Christian peoples.

I. The lower races, many of them savage, and the rest barbarous, have naturally been most extensively influenced on the intellectual side through missionary effort.

1. The very presence of the missionary and his belongings constitute an intellectual quickening. Before his ship reaches the land, if it happens to be an unvisited island of the South Seas, its appearance suggests that he came from heaven and was borne on the wings of the wind to these shores, and this gives rise to questionings. In more advanced countries, as soon as he lands, he is an object of intellectual curiosity. He brings with him the garb and furnishings of the Occident, many of them being new to the natives. In countries where there is no native press, gossip supplies its place, and hence the story of his possessions and their uses spreads through large regions and is everywhere the subject of remark and wonder.

2. His study of the language is a new impulse to discussion and thought. He asks questions concerning their native tongue which never occurred to them. Other queries are raised by him which tax the knowledge of the wisest of savage peoples.

3. In those races where there is no written language, an unspeakable impulse to intellectual development is imparted through the introduction of the alphabet. In some 100 languages this wonder-working process has been wrought through the missionary; and from the New Hebrides, where the "talking chip" with its speaking characters aroused wonder, to the heart of Africa, where the introduction of alphabetical writing was regarded as little short of miracle, there is a remarkable impulse given to thought through the introduction of writing. A little later, when the same missionary produces the first printed literature of a tribe or a nation, this intellectual influence is widened and strengthened. In this latter process, especially among the nations where there is already a rude form of written speech, the language is greatly enriched by new ideas and the more systematic use of an already existing tongue.

4. A concomitant of the two processes just mentioned is the enlistment from among the people of a body of the best educated men obtainable as evangelists and teachers. When mental culture becomes indigenous, it raises men to a position of intellectual predominance and awakens desires in the minds of multitudes of others. Even those who have never studied an hour feel the contagion of this transformation of a few.

5. Education is especially necessary to the program of missions among the lower races. In many cases it is the very first work of the sort ever attempted. So simple a matter as the use of a picture to enable the missionary to explain what is being taught those who are studying, raises the onlookers far above their former position of mental sluggishness. Thus, on one of the great African lakes, when this process was first employed, it took much time for the older ones

to see a picture and only gradually were the dog, ox, etc., made out. While education in these countries is usually elementary, it is for that very reason more widely pervasive than in cultured countries, since among the lowest races the only possibility for education is found in the mission school. Tho religious instruction is the main aim, the elements of science are taught; and thus the rude philosophy of nature races, which has as its explanation the so-called superstitions of animism, fetishism, etc., is gradually displaced, and true knowledge for the first time shines upon the people.

6. The Bible, or those portions of it which are usually translated at an early stage of the enterprise, aside from its religious value is, likewise, a very strong intellectual stimulus to the masses. Its varied contents, its practical doctrines affecting the daily life, and the portion of the earth which forms its background, are a help to breadth of view and a step toward international unity. Just as all western countries have the Bible as a common heritage, and as its institutions have insensibly influenced them, thus bringing them together, so as an intellectual bond the Bible first unites savage or uncivilized tribes to a higher civilization.

7. The Christian books which are numerously prepared act upon the few as a strong motive to leaven others. Teaching the alphabet and simple reading is the key to religious truth, and thousands gain possession of the key who do not enter into the religious treasures which it was the primary purpose to open to them. They have, nevertheless, come to a position of intellectual enlightenment which would not have been brought to them from commercial or anti-religious sources.

8. In these countries of lower development it frequently happens that the missionary is the pioneer and abettor of commerce and trade. Elements of material culture are thus indirectly the fruitage of his efforts, and there can be no large development in this direction which is not at the same time a stimulus to the intellect. While it is true that there are dangers in this direction such as are seen in the cultured countries of the old world, they do not so greatly affect peoples just emerging from the savage or barbarous state.

9. The stimulating intellectual forces above named are broadly scattered in this class of races. Comparatively few such races have an intensive work done among them, but the very fact that the missionary found them without a developed mind has made his presence a more marked factor in the national or tribal life.

II. The cultured races of the old world are, on the one hand, less open to the intellectual influence of missions than the races just named, while at the same time they furnish better material for development. Here, therefore, the work is more intensive than extensive in its character, considering the amount done by a single missionary.

1. The missionary brings not merely a new religion to these peoples, but also new theories of life which constitute the basis of enlarged intellectuality. The discussion between a missionary and a Brahman in India, or between representatives of Christianity and Buddhism in Japan, quickens the thought of hundreds of onlookers who carry away with them the main arguments of the disputants. These are in turn talked over by new groups of interested listeners. Moreover, a prominent theory which the missionary is likely to defend is that of the necessity for knowledge on the part of every believer of the new religion. This gives the first impulse to the education of women, and implants or strengthens the desire to learn in many from lower walks in life.

2. A new science brought to such nations and empires frequently occasions a revolution in prevailing theories. China's literati have been astounded, tho not outwardly manifesting interest, at the rational explanation of an eclipse or the arguments adduced to prove the rotundity of the earth. One remembers what a revolution it caused in the minds of those boys who constituted Dr. Duff's first school in India, when he gave them their first lesson in English based upon the unimportant word O-X. Upon those simplest letters of the English alphabet he hung truths which burst in a moment the bonds of ignorance. Superstition must always abound until a true philosophy of the external world is made known to a people, and the simpler explanations of its phenomena often fly with great rapidity from lip to lip.

3. Missionaries have also carried into this class of countries new means of intercommunication. Tho their languages had hitherto been committed to writing and a considerable literature may have existed, the missionaries introduce ready impartation of ideas through the publication of periodical literature and interesting tracts and books. Thus the Christian Literature Society of India, through its present and earlier organization, has stimulated Hindus to similarly impart information. Almost the sole influence in the earlier history of missions in China, India and Japan, leading to the rapid development of native periodical literature, came from the work of missions.

4. Such literary efforts, however, cannot long be carried on without the production of a reformed language. Just as the New Testament in the early Christian Church enriched the classical Greek, and as the literary efforts of Dante affected Italy, and Luther's translation of the German Bible enriched that tongue, so to-day China is coming into the possession of a form of the Mandarin which is hardly conceivable, had there been no missionaries in that country. The same is true in all lands of this class, since before the coming of the missionary there has been an aristocracy of letters which selfishly kept to itself a monopoly of learning, with the result that the language was far above the comprehension of the ordinary people.

5. The more rational method of teaching, and the scientific material brought to these nations through the schools established, have been an impetus toward intellectual life. Turkey and Egypt owe to missionaries the stimulus which compelled them in self-defense to establish schools in great numbers. While in India the government has aided native schools, it has done it largely through missionaries, both by encouraging them to enter the work and by its grants-in-aid. It is to be remembered also that in such an empire as Japan the educational system owes more to a missionary, Dr. Verbeck, and to Joseph Neesima, a native apostle of Christian education, than to almost any other source, tho Mr. Fukuzawa advocated it, in private life, and in later years the Government assumed the guidance and expense of educational reform.

6. Only through missions have the lowly and despised classes in the community been touched intellectually through education. In Mohammedan countries, as well as in great empires like India and China, women and girls have not hitherto been considered as fit subjects for intellectual culture. The Christian school aims to reach these strategic factors in society quite as much as it does to educate boys and men; so that in India to-day and in Mohammedan countries the educated women and girls are the product almost wholly of missionary schools.

III. Tho there is a question in the minds of many authorities on missions about the wisdom of conducting Protestant missionary work in nominally Christian lands, most of them Papal countries, missions do exist among such peoples. Here the intellectual contribution of missions is naturally less marked than in the two classes previously named.

1. The representative of Protestantism who comes in contact with a perverted or less developed form of Christianity must naturally spend much of his time in discussion. He must give a *raison d'être* for his presentation of Protestantism. His opponents are often keenly intellectual, and even where they are not well educated they strongly present the claims of their ancestral faith. Listeners are keenly alert and their thought processes are quickened as never before by the arguments adduced.

2. The stimulus coming to the native press through the publication of Protestant literature in those countries is helpful to all. Even in the shadow of the Vatican, where the Scriptures are now being published, in periodicals and in the vernacular, at a low rate and under Papal sanction, it is hardly probable that it would have been done were it not for the strong Methodist work carried on in the Holy City. In South America and Mexico it has been especially true that Protestantism has imparted a wide stimulus to the thought of the people.

3. Mission schools in Papal lands have been an unexpected help to education, particularly in Latin America. The work done in São Paolo, Brazil, has influenced education in that extensive republic, and in less degree other institutions in South America, Mexico, Austria and Spain have been an intellectual blessing to the people. Probably nothing in the latter country has been so helpful as an object lesson as the Institute for Girls under the charge of the late Mrs. Alice Gordon Gulick.

4. Protestant efforts in these lands have developed a native leadership of wide influence. Diaz in Cuba is an illustration of many who in Latin America and in the Philippines have come to a position, not only of religious influence, but of intellectual power.

IV. A few illustrations of the positions above taken will indicate the extent to which tribes and nations are indebted to the intellectual uplift of missions.

1. A few instances are adduced of communities which have been most thoroughly leavened by the Gospel and its accompanying intellectual life. The Hawaiian Islands, now a part of the United States, are both intellectually and spiritually the product of the American Board's work. Schools were quite as much emphasized as in New England, and they became the foundation of present-day Hawaiian society and the stepping-stones to her present political position. The Fiji Islands, which in the childhood of many now living were without missionaries and the abodes of cannibal cruelty, are not only the banner country of the world in the matter of church-going, but in 1901 the Wesleyans alone had 1,473 schools, accommodating 28,491 scholars. At that time the entire population of the colony was only 117,870, so that about one-fourth of the entire number of inhabitants were studying in the schools of one Protestant missionary society. The Karens in Burma are another illustration of a despised race, hardly deemed worthy of an education, who, through the efforts of the American Baptist Missionary Union, were brought to an intellectual and spiritual condition which is most remarkable, the Karen schools of the Union having in 1901 some 13,049 scholars. Uganda, too, in the very heart of Africa, owes its marvelous intellectual progress of the past few years to the educational work accomplished by the Church Missionary Society. An even stronger illustration is derivable from the history of missions in Madagascar, where, until recent times, the representatives of the London Missionary Society have been almost the sole educators of the entire people.

2. Figures may give a better view than the above illustrations of what is actually being accomplished in intellectual lines through Protestant missions. Beach's *Geography and Atlas of Protestant Missions*, the statistics of which are mainly those of 1900, gives the number of educational institutions conducted by Protestant missions as 24,728, in which there were 1,127,853 pupils or students. This included instruction in a variety of educational institutions, from the kindergartens to the full-fledged universities. Dr. Dennis's *Centennial Survey of Foreign Missions*, which gives the condition at the end of 1899, states that the entire Bible had been translated by missionaries into 99 languages or dialects, while the entire New Testament had been rendered into 121 additional tongues. Portions of the Bible had been translated into 236 other tongues, making the total number of missionary versions of a part or all of the Bible, 456. There were, according to the same authority, 159 mission publishing houses and printing presses, with an output for the year reported of 381,166,106 pages. This included 379 periodicals published by the missionaries, which were general or religious in character. One can imagine the intellectual as well as the spiritual value of such a record as the above. It does not suggest, however, the intellectual stimulus imparted, which can best be realized by a comparison of sections of the same country or tribe, which have been reached by missions, with other portions not so touched. In Burma, the Karens, who are intellectually below the Burmans, have been so benefited by the mental and religious instruction received that they now outstrip in many respects their naturally stronger neighbors. The same is, to a less degree, true of certain low castes in Northern India, who, through teaching, have become the peers of those several degrees higher in the social scale. In China, the late viceroy, Li Hung-chang, applied to a Christian educational institution for all its graduates, promising to permit them to observe Sunday, tho living in a Sabbathless land. These men are from the lower ranks in life, who were desired merely because of their intellectual attainments, and were thus preferred to native scholars possessing

high degrees. Christianity has in mission countries been especially a quickener of thought, so that the traditions of ages or generations are replaced with the science of the West, and lives have been changed to correspond with this new light.

INTERNATIONAL MEDICAL MISSIONARY AND BENEVOLENT ASSOCIATION (Battle Creek, Mich., 1893): While this Association is denominationally connected with the Seventh Day Adventists, its work is not sectarian. The object for which it was formed was to "erect and manage homes for orphan children and for friendless aged persons; hospitals and sanitariums for the sick poor and others; to establish dispensaries and medical missions at home and abroad; to provide visiting nurses; to educate missionary physicians and nurses; to provide for the needy poor, and to promulgate the principles of health and temperance."

Fields: *India* (1897) : 2 stations, 1 outstation, 10 missionaries, 1 hospital. *Africa* (1896) : 4 stations and 2 outstations, 13 missionaries, 3 hospitals and dispensaries. *Australasia* (1896): 10 stations and 9 outstations, 19 missionaries, 10 hospitals and dispensaries. *Oceania* (1893): 4 stations, 8 missionaries, 4 hospitals and dispensaries. *Hawaiian Islands—West Indies* (1895): 1 station, 1 missionary; (1896): 4 missionaries, 1 hospital and 1 dispensary. *Guiana* (1895): 3 stations, 4 missionaries. *Mexico* (1894) : 2 stations and 1 outstation, 15 missionaries, 2 hospitals and dispensaries. *Europe* (1900): 1 station, 2 missionaries.

INTERNATIONAL MEDICAL MISSIONARY SOCIETY (New York, 1881): In the spring of 1881 a meeting was held at the house of Dr. T. A. Sabine, New York City, to consider the formation of an organization similar to the Edinburgh Medical Missionary Association. Six persons were present: the Rev. Wm. M. Taylor, D.D., three physicians, one lawyer, and a business man. Geo. D. Kowkoutt, M. D., explained the character, scope and aim of the proposed work, and it was at once decided to organize a society to aid and train candidates, of either sex, for service as medical missionaries under any evangelical missionary society. The society thus organized has since then served all sections of the Christian Church under a strictly interdenominational constitution.

Besides the original undertaking of the Society, the generosity of an individual has enabled it to establish a "Place of Rest" for missionaries and other Christian workers, together with a summer training school for missionary candidates. The seat of the Society and its home for medical students is in New York, but the Place of Rest and summer school are on the property belonging to the Society at Goshen, Mass., a summer resort 1,500 feet above sea level.

The aid given to medical students who are preparing for missionary service is based upon the plan of aiding for last bills only, after the student and his family or friends have done what they can for his support.

Since the organization of the Society nearly 150 medical students whom it has aided have been sent to the foreign field by various missionary societies, and its former students are now laboring in Syria, Persia, India, Ceylon, Burma, China and the New Hebrides.

INTERNATIONAL MISSIONARY UNION (1884): The founder of this unique organization was the Rev. J. T. Gracey, D.D., of Rochester, N. Y. After assisting at a series of missionary meetings at the campground at Niagara Falls, Ont., where he had stipulated that all the speakers should be missionaries, he conceived the idea of an organization of missionaries of all denominations the world over, who should come together once a year to talk over the varied phases of their work, compare notes, and profit by one another's successes or failures. The project was laid before an assembly of missionaries who were on furlough, and met with an enthusiastic response. A simple constitution was drawn up, and the title, "International Missionary Union," was given to the new organization. Foreign missionaries of both sexes, of any evangelical denomination, are eligible for membership, whether on the active or retired list, as well as all missionaries under appointment. The sole condition of membership is that the missionary must be in good standing with his Board.

The entire dues of the members consist of an initial fee of fifty cents; there are no yearly dues.

In 1896 the Union had grown so rapidly that it became necessary to organize more fully, and the constitution was revised. Its officers consist of a president, vice-president, secretary, treasurer, and librarian, with a board of control and an executive committee appointed to act as occasion may require.

For several years the annual meetings of the Union were held at different places, but in 1890 Dr. Henry Foster, of the Clifton Springs Sanitarium, Clifton Springs, N. Y., suggested that thereafter all the annual meetings of the Association should be held at that place, offering free entertainment to all members of the Union during the week of the annual session. This generous offer was accepted, and the following year Dr. Foster erected a beautiful and commodious tabernacle on the sanitarium grounds for the use of the Union so long as it should hold its meetings at Clifton Springs.

With an initial membership of forty, the Union now has over 1,200 members. In 1902 many young men and women under appointment to the foreign missions' field were present. Consequently, special classes were held for them, and opportunities arranged for them to confer with experienced missionaries from the fields to which they were going. This proved so valuable that it is now to be made a permanent feature of the annual meetings of the Union. These annual meetings are held for one week, beginning the first Wednesday in June. The Union has no income; a collection is taken on the one Sunday of the year when it is in session, to defray the expense of the publication of the annual report, the *International Missionary Index*, and of notices, etc.

INTERNATIONAL SERVICE OF MISSIONS: Missions were not established to promote diplomatic amenities or aid backward nations in assuming international functions. They have, nevertheless, accomplished much incidentally in these directions by forging connecting links of contact and intercourse, cultivating good will, solving difficulties, giving friendly advice, facilitating acquaintance with Western administrative systems, mediating between foreign diplomacy and native misunderstandings, encouraging that status of mutual confidence which promotes peaceful relationships, and often ministering as the almoners of international philanthropy in times of calamity and distress. If these statements are well founded, missions are proving themselves to be among those evolutionary forces which work for the kindly recognition of mutual obligations among the nations of mankind.

Illustrations of this can be discovered not only in modern times, but in the history of missions during earlier centuries. It is the missionary, quite as much as the political or commercial motive, which seems to assert itself in many of those initial ventures which have led on to the exploration of an unknown world, and the making and molding of new nations. The apostolic age of the Church was international in the expansiveness of its evangelistic aims, and in the scope of its missionary activities. Subsequent centuries bear witness to the outreaching touch of Christianity, bringing nation into contact with nation. The Nestorians pushed boldly into China as early as the 7th century, and into India probably at a date still earlier, following Pantaenus, who had preceded them in the latter part of the 2d century. Ulfilas was a messenger to the Goths in the 4th century, as were Cyril and Methodius to the Slavs in the 9th. In Central and Northern Europe, including the British Isles, we can trace the entrance of Columba, Augustine, Columbanus, Gallus, Eligius, Boniface, Willibrord, Ansgar, and many others equally zealous tho less conspicuous in the annals of those formative centuries. Hans Egede linked Denmark with Greenland in the 18th century. The Moravian missionaries followed, and from that time Herrnhut became an active factor in the international contact of the world. Labrador was reached by Jens Haven in 1764; Francis Xavier linked Portugal with India in the 16th century; Heurnius was a connecting bond between Holland and the Dutch East Indies in the 17th century; and in the 18th century Ziegenbalg, Plutschau, and Schwartz brought Denmark into spiritual relations with India. These were all international messengers upon an errand of peace, good will, and friendship.

The maritime discoveries of the 15th century were undertaken, among other motives, with a definite and pronounced missionary purpose. That ponderous work entitled *The Jesuit Relations and Allied Documents* reveals to us immense and prolonged contributions of Roman Catholic missionaries toward the establishment of international intercourse between France and America for nearly two hundred years. The footsteps of those indefatigable missionary pioneers can be traced during the 17th century along the St. Lawrence, and on both sides of the Great Lakes, on into the Far West. They deflect southward into Maine, into Illinois, and even as far as Louisiana, and penetrate northward toward the inhospitable, icy wilderness of Hudson Bay. The British colonial establishments in North America, moreover, were missionary in spirit to an extent which makes them almost the forerunners of the foreign missionary societies of a later age. Their charters usually had a strong missionary clause, and their noblest men were Christian pioneers as well as statesmen. They sought not only religious liberty and opportunity for themselves, but they were in many conspicuous instances intent upon the dissemination of the Gospel among the aborigines. In the first Charter of Virginia, given by James I., in April, 1606, it was stipulated that "the Word and service of God be preached, planted, and used as well in said colonies, as also as much as might be among the savages bordering among them." In a letter to Sir Walter Raleigh, referring to the project of the Virginia colony, Hakluyt writes expressing his pleasure in Raleigh's plans, because "you meane to sende some such good Churchmen thither (to Virginia) as may truly say with the Apostles to the Sauvages, wee seeke not yours but you." Bradford declared the propagation of the Gospel of the Kingdom of Christ as one of the great hopes of his pilgrimage. Winthrop confessed to the same motive, and in his journal are numerous references to his desires for the conversion of the aborigines. The Charter of Massachusetts Colony emphasizes the missionary motive as one of the inspirations which prompted its establishment. Macdonald's *Select Charters and Other Documents Illustrative of American History*, 1606-1755 (Pages 2, 3, 16, 25, 42, 126, and 184), gives the text of some of these chartered asseverations of missionary aims in our early colonial history.

Those mighty ties of spiritual interest which now link India with all Christendom are the outcome of missions. In their own sphere of moral and religious influence missionaries have cooperated with English statesmen, and rendered a service of value both to Great Britain and to India. The strange and unwarranted attitude of the old East India Company toward missionary effort has long ago changed, and the value of missions to British interests in India is now freely recognized. Since the days of the mutiny it has become more and more apparent that a native Christian community is a valuable ally of English rule, and, so far as its influence goes, a moral guarantee of fidelity and good will. The sailing of Captain James Wilson and thirty-six missionaries in the *Duff*, which was owned and sent out by the London Missionary Society in 1796, opened the South Pacific to those largesses of light and civilization which missionary effort has sent there during the past century. The west coast of Africa first felt the touch of Christian sympathy and helpfulness when Peter Greig, the Scotch missionary, went there in 1797. The cooperation of the Church Missionary Society, the Wesleyan Missionary Society, and the United Presbyterian Missions of Scotland, has contributed in no small measure to the opening up of the vast regions of the Niger Basin, and has been a factor in furthering the present political supremacy of Great Britain throughout Nigeria. The marvelous story of African colonization during the 19th century is indissolubly linked with missionary devotion and achievement. Such names as Vanderkemp, Philip, Krapf, Rebmann, Moffat, John Mackenzie, Livingstone, and Bishop Mackenzie of the Zambesi, as well as many others later in the century, certify to the truth of this statement. We may almost reckon the Uganda Protectorate as virtually the outcome of missions, with that colossal achievement of a railway from Mombasa to the Victoria Nyanza as a necessary result. Khama's country, and the whole of British Central Africa, including the upper waters of the Zambesi, where the French Mission labors among the Barotsi, serve the same purpose of illustrating an international value in missionary enterprise.

Turning to China, we find Morrison and Gutzlaff, the former in the double capacity of missionary and interpreter for the East India Company, serving in international affairs before its formal opening to the foreigner. The Rev. E. C. Bridgman and Dr. Peter Parker were associated with the Hon. Caleb Cushing in negotiating the first treaty which the United States made with China, in 1844. Both these men were masters of the Chinese language, familiar with the customs of the country, and acceptable media of communication. The aid which they rendered was extremely useful. Mr. Cushing declared that "they were invaluable as advisers." It was in the early British negotiations that Morrison and Gutzlaff rendered a similar service. The former was associated with Lord Amherst in 1816, being for some years interpreter and secretary to the British Ambassador, and Gutzlaff was his successor in the same position. When the Treaty of Nanking was made, the latter participated in the negotiations and rendered important aid. It would thus appear that the initial word of friendly diplomatic intercourse between China and two great governments of the West was spoken through the medium of missionary secretaries and interpreters.

A few years later, in 1858, when the notable Treaties of Tientsin between the four governments of the United States, Great Britain, France, and Russia were drawn up with China, in the case of the United States treaty two American missionaries whose services in the negotiations were of historic importance and value were associated with the Hon. W. B. Reed, the minister who represented the United States on that occasion. Dr. S. Wells Williams and Dr. W. A P. Martin, both missionary scholars and diplomatists, took an active part in the preliminary conference, and in fixing the provisions of the document, as well as securing its acceptance. It was due to Dr. Williams that the memorable Toleration Clause, afterward included substantially in the British treaty, was inserted. Thus, to American missionaries is due the credit of securing a treaty incorporating the policy of a tolerant recognition of Christianity on the part of the Chinese Government. Dr. Williams was given to understand at the time that no Toleration Clause would have been inserted in the British treaty had it been left out in the American. This concession had not been before included in formal treaties, altho the French Minister, in 1844, had secured from the Emperor, Tao-kwang, an imperial rescript revoking persecuting orders, and proclaiming an edict of toleration. This, however, was practically a dead letter, and would have been of little value so far as any permanent international policy was concerned. It should be remarked, also; that the British missionaries at Ning-po and Shanghai had addressed Lord Elgin on the subject of toleration before the British treaty was drawn up, but, judging from his reply, the appeal was of little avail. The treaty concession of Tientsin may, therefore, be called the Magna Charta of religious freedom in China. Dr. Williams, and in a measure Dr. Martin also, were its sponsors, and thus to American missionaries belongs the high honor of establishing the principle of religious freedom in a permanent historical setting, before the view of "almost the two halves of the human race." Dr. Williams was subsequently appointed to the office of Secretary and Interpreter of the United States Legation in China, and served in this capacity—chiefly at Peking—until his resignation in 1876. It was he who secured official quarters for the United States ambassadors in Peking, and his efficient executive discharge of his duties was an important service during those early years of ministerial residence at the Chinese capital. He was, on many occasions, left in charge of the legation as acting ambassador.

Another Presbyterian missionary, the Rev. D. B. McCartee, M.D., had a long and useful career in diplomatic positions both in China and Japan. He accompanied Flag Officer Stribling, of the American Navy, on an expedition to treat with the rebels at Nanking at the time of the Taiping troubles, and through his personal influence with the Chinese leaders he was largely instrumental in securing a "sealed guarantee of protection for all Americans against violence from the rebels, and for all natives in the employ or care of American citizens." In connection with his services in the Mixed Court in Shanghai, in 1872, he was appointed on a special mission to Japan to treat for the return of three hundred Chinese coolies who had been driven on the Peruvian vessel, *Maria Luz*, by a typhoon into the harbor of Yokohama. The Chinese authorities presented him with a gold medal and a complimentary letter in recognition of the successful issue of the mission. He subsequently became professor of law and of natural science at the University of Tokio, and from that time his services, for a period of some twenty-eight years, were given to Japan. He was instrumental in establishing a Chinese embassy in Japan, and became himself its foreign secretary and adviser. At the time of General Grant's visit to Japan, when the General was asked to arbitrate the respective claims of China and Japan to the possession of the Lu Chu Islands, Dr. McCartee, who was thoroughly acquainted with the historical facts and their diplomatic bearing, placed such information before General Grant that he was able to give the matter his attention.

In those memorable negotiations which signalized the entrance of modern Japan into the comity of nations, at the time of Commodore Perry's expedition, we find Dr. S. Wells Williams accompanying, at the special request of the Commodore, both the first and second expeditions, in 1853 and 1854. He took an active and influential part in the negotiations, and it was at his suggestion that the "most favored nation clause" was introduced into the Japanese treaty, the first compact of Japan with Western nations. His serious and vivid appreciation of the historic significance of his diplomatic services appears in private letters and extracts from his journal. He writes of the scene in the Bay of Yeddo: "It was the meeting of the East and the West, the circling of the world's intercourse, the beginning of American interference in Asia, the putting the key in the door of Japanese seclusion." Speaking of the presence of the American ships, he writes: "Behind them and through them lie God's purpose of making known the Gospel to all nations, and bringing its messages and responsibilities to this people, which has had only a sad travesty of the truth as it is in Christ Jesus. I have a full conviction that the seclusion policy of the nations of Eastern Asia is not according to God's plan of mercy to these peoples." Surely this missionary-diplomatist, with his faith and foresight, was an instrument chosen of God to participate in those momentous events which inaugurated the opening of both China and Japan to an era of modern progress destined to be the most wonderful in their history. The memorial monument to Commodore Perry erected in 1901 on the shores of Japan was an appropriate and graceful tribute, but the services of Dr. Williams most assuredly deserve also a grateful commemoration on the part of Christendom. The services of several distinguished missionaries in Japan have been of international import. Dr. Guido F. Verbeck and Dr. S. R. Brown were especially useful and helpful to the Japanese during the critical period of the reorganization of their national life, since the introduction of those monumental changes which have characterized the *Meiji* era of modern times. Dr. Verbeck suggested the plan of the now historic embassy sent by the Japanese Government to America and Europe in 1871, and the project was finally executed, in large part under his advice and cooperation. Its results proved to be of decisive influence in permanently establishing the friendly relations of Japan with the nations of Christendom, and was a factor of practical moment in securing that religious toleration which has distinguished the Empire of Japan in the modern history of the East. It is a matter of further interest that the recent revision of Japanese treaties, which has established a basis of equality with Western nations since July, 1899, has been both favored and facilitated by resident missionaries out of a sense of justice and fairness to Japan. By manifestoes, resolutions, and public meetings, as well as by private influence, they have made it known that they regarded the aspirations of Japan in this matter with sympathy and favor.

The diplomatic relations of the United States with Korea have been also facilitated by the services of Dr. Horace N. Allen, who was the first American missionary to arrive in Korea. He went there in 1844, and was soon appointed physician to the Court. He subsequently, in 1887, accompanied the first Korean Embassy to Washington as its secretary, returning to Seoul in 1890 as secretary of the United States Legation. In 1897 he was appointed United States Minister to Korea, a position which he still (1904) occupies.

Not only have the treaty relations of Christian nations with the great Asiatic governments of China and Japan been facilitated by missionary cooperation, but diplomatic negotiations with smaller tribes and kingdoms—especially in Oceania—have received aid from the same source. Missionaries have often prepared the way for the establishment of such international ties by initial intercourse and friendly residence, thus becoming pioneer media of information and contact. A capital illustration of this is New Guinea, where Chalmers and Lawes, and other missionaries of the London Society, became the forerunners of the present British protectorate. The services they rendered in anticipation of the British occupation of Southern New Guinea, in 1884, have been cordially acknowledged by Sir James E. Erskine and Sir Cyprian Bridge, both high officers in the British Navy. In the same way missionary labors in New Zealand brought Maori hearts into touch with Christianity and civilization to an extent which no doubt greatly facilitated its peaceful political attachment to the British Empire. The earliest mission was especially successful among the Ngapuhi tribe, and it was the chiefs of this important and powerful clan who, in February, 1840, at Waitangi Falls, were the first signers of the treaty accepting British supremacy. Nearly two-thirds of the entire Maori population had professed Christianity in 1859. Marsden, as early as 1814, and Selwyn, later, were all unconsciously pioneer empire-builders in New Zealand. The peaceful, and even cordial, ceding of Fiji to Great Britain by its chiefs and people, in 1874, followed long years of successful missionary toil by the English Wesleyans, resulting in a marvelous preoccupation of native hearts throughout the islands by the Gospel which the Wesleyans brought. A British protectorate was established over the Tonga group by peaceful negotiations in 1900, but years before that English missionaries had labored there in friendly contact with that proud and vigorous race. The Samoan Islands, now portioned out between Germany and the United States, were annexed to Christianity half a century or more before their political destiny was determined. The Cook, or Hervey, Islands were Christianized and civilized by the London Missionary Society over a generation before the British protectorate was established, in 1888. As early as 1864 the natives petitioned Great Britain for annexation, but a protectorate only was instituted in 1888, which at the request, again repeated, of the native chiefs was changed to annexation to New Zealand in 1900. Thus a reclaimed race was made ready by missions for relations of peaceful diplomacy with a great nation of Christendom. The Santa Cruz group —now a part of the British Empire—was the scene of the martyrdom of Young and Nobbs, in 1864, and of John Coleridge Patteson, in 1871. Thousands of hearts throughout Christendom have read the story with tender interest, and some day no doubt a fitting memorial of Patteson will commemorate under the British flag that pathetic incident which, as Gladstone said of Patteson himself, was a "pledge of nobler destinies."

The virtual preemption of the New Hebrides, as destined in all probability to have their political future linked with the British Empire, may be regarded as the outcome of a missionary occupation which has been sealed by martyrdom, and crowned by the uplifting transformation of savage tribes into aspirants for political order and moral civilization. In 1820 two English missionaries—Ward and Burton—endeavored to secure a foothold in Sumatra among the fierce Battaks, but were unable to do so. In 1832 two American missionaries—Munson and Lyman—made another attempt, but were martyred by cannibals. Thirty years later a third endeavor, on the part of the Rhenish Society, was successful, and a region in North Sumatra, previously wholly inaccessible to the white man, was opened by a peaceful missionary occupation. From that martyr seed has sprung a Christian population of some fifty thousand native Battaks now living in a state of peace and good order which promises a developed civilization. The Dutch Government in the East Indies is surely a debtor for this missionary achievement.

Hawaii, now United States territory, was largely molded and fashioned for her destiny by missionary pioneers whose labors have assumed an importance which may fairly be regarded as of international interest. During the whole of the 19th century, while by the irresistible growth of economic and political ties, and the manifest trend of history, it belonged *in posse* to the United States, missionary toil was fitting it for the consummation when it would become so *in esse*. Ex-Secretary of State the Hon. John W. Foster, in his admirable volume, *American Diplomacy in the Orient* (page 108), places a high estimate upon the beneficial effects, social and political, of American missions in Hawaii. There are other groups whose political destiny is now linked with European nations—the Gilbert Islands, with Great Britain, and the Marshall and Caroline, with Germany—which have long been under the careful training of missionary teachers from America. Whatever opinion may be held of the political wisdom of the occupation of the Philippines by the United States, there is no valid reason to doubt that beneficent results are most assuredly to follow in those islands from this foreign occupation. The recognition of missionary obligation on the part of American Christianity is, moreover, a strenuous and clearly manifest result, which, let us hope, will be fruitful in moral good and social betterment to the people of the islands.

Not only in connection with diplomacy, but in times of war and public calamity, the services of missionaries have been of benefit. During the mutinies and uprisings in Uganda they served in defense of life and property. At the siege of Peking the conspicuous and brilliant services of missionaries in defense of the Legations during the perilous summer of 1900 were universally acknowledged. The successful issue was due in no small measure to the skilful and heroic participation of missionaries in that victorious defense. Not only were the lives of the ambassadors saved, but consequences were averted which might have precipitated unparalleled calamities. There is a manifest international value, moreover, attaching to the efforts of missionaries in the sphere of philanthropy. In times of famine, earthquake, epidemics, and great disasters, sympathy and help are given, and charitable funds administered. That international scourge and scandal of the slave trade has been checked and all but abolished largely through the helpful cooperation of missionaries. In the promotion and establishment of peace among the nations there is also an undoubted value to the service and influence of missionaries. They neither strive nor cry, nor is their voice heard in the streets, nor have they the power of diplomats or rulers to determine issues, but they, nevertheless, do a quiet and often effective and unique service of counsel, conciliation and restraint. The work that they do in promoting good government is, moreover, in the interests of peace. Mission converts are men of peace, not the advocates of massacre and disorder. They are inclined to friendliness and forbearance rather than to treachery and violence, and in the face of some very appreciable Oriental perils they may at times safeguard, as hardly any other agency can do, both the lives and property of foreigners. The Moravians in their work in Dutch Guiana, during the latter half of the 18th century, and until the middle of the 19th, achieved a victory over the Bush Negroes which was a boon to the Dutch Government. The work of early missionaries in South Africa was an influential factor in solving native problems and promoting their peaceful solution. In times of disorder and massacre in the Turkish Empire they have acted as mediators, pacificators, and saviors of lives and property, as in Mount Lebanon during the troubles of 1860, in Bulgaria in 1876-77, and Asiatic Turkey in 1895-96.

The exposition and accentuation of the principles of international law have also been a feature of missionary service. Verbeck did important preliminary work in this direction in Japan, and Martin in China. When the latter went to reside in Peking in 1863 he carried with him a translation into Chinese of Wheaton's *Elements of International Law*. This was welcomed by the Chinese Foreign Office as a timely guide amid the perplexities arising out of the new international compacts into which they had just entered. Dr. Martin supplemented the above translation by Chinese versions of Woolsey, Bluntschli, and Hall, on international relations. Chalmers taught the very alphabet of the law of nations to the natives of New Guinea, and in 1899 Secretary Wardlaw Thompson, of the London Missionary Society, reported the curious fact that Mr. Abel, one of their missionaries in New Guinea, was instructing the people, and especially the school children, "to repeat a brief statement of the British laws which has been prepared for the benefit of all the inhabitants of British New Guinea. These simple rules of conduct are learned as the commandments are learned, and thus law and order are associated with religion." It is certainly a novel feature of education and of religious worship to associate the commandments, the creed, and the laws of the land, in an all-round summary of human duty. Here seems to be an admirable hint for the reformer and the earnest advocate of higher standards of citizenship.

The immensely effective and beneficial influence of Christianity in evolving throughout Christendom that remarkable code of national chivalry—voluntary in its sovereignty and sacred in its dignity—which we have come to designate as international law, has been perpetuated and extended among Asiatic and other foreign peoples largely by the initiative of missionary teachers and statesmen. They have sought to introduce the humane provisions of the code in times of war, and they have secured also, among many savage tribes, the practical recognition of another of its requirements—the safety of shipwrecked mariners. On the other hand, missionaries have not been unmoved spectators of infractions or dubious applications of the international code by Western powers in their contact with Oriental nations. The missionary protest in the face of some notable lapses in these respects, especially in China, has been vigorous and uncompromising. On the subject of opium the missionary body is a unit, and this is substantially true of their opposition to the territorial dismemberment of the Chinese Empire.

It would thus appear that the messenger of the Gospel in mission lands has long been assigned an international rôle—not, to be sure, in any formal or official capacity, but as contributing incidentally, and sometimes unconsciously, to the sum total of good-will and friendship among the nations. Missionaries have borne their part in promoting kind feeling between widely separated races, and in breaking down barriers between distant and alien peoples; they have also struck the note of brotherhood—stirring on the one hand generous impulses, and on the other awakening gratitude. They have facilitated diplomatic relations, and aided in establishing peaceful and mutually beneficial ties between the nations. This remarkable service, it may be noted, has been coincident with monumental changes in world-politics and with ethnic intercourse brought about by discovery, colonization, and commercial enterprise. Missionary expansion has thus given a certain impetus, as well as kindly tone, to that interchange of intellectual, spiritual, and material commodities which has become the unique glory of our age, and is leading on as much as any other single influence to the goal of universal peace and unity. Imperialism—the irrepressible note of the age—is given an ethical significance, and directed toward a sublime ideal, by this international leaven of missions. Paul's conception of the relationship of superior to inferior races has hardly been taken seriously among the nations. That great missionary-apostle and statesman regarded himself as "debtor" even to the barbarians—an aspect of inter-racial obligation which has been to a surprising extent a negligible consideration in the diplomatic intercourse of the nations. The spirit of missions, however, like a voice crying in the wilderness of international selfishness, has sought diligently to promote kindly consideration, good will, and fair dealing, and has endeavored faithfully to exemplify them in its own sphere.

INYATI: A settlement in Rhodesia, South Central Africa, situated among Matabele tribes, about 47 miles N. E. of Buluwayo. Station of the LMS (1860), with (1903) 1 missionary, 4 native workers, 4 day schools, and 639 professed Christians, of whom 60 are communicants.

IPOLI: A village on the Malay Peninsula, situated on the Kintah River in the state or district of Perak. The climate is healthful. Station of the ME, with (1903) 2 missionaries, 1 missionary's wife, 11 native workers, men and women; 3 outstations, 2 day schools, 2 boarding schools, and 287 professed Christians. The work in this place is chiefly among the Chinese, but it also reaches the Hindu coolies, and, what is of considerable importance in such a mission field, it reaches the English and English-speaking foreigners, whose example counts for so much with the natives. The BFBS furnishes the ME funds for employing a colporteur and 2 Bible women in this district.

IPOLELA: A village in Natal, S. Africa, situated 46 miles W. by S. of Pietermaritzburg. Station of the SPG (1874), with (1903) 1 missionary and 460 professed Christians, of whom 220 are communicants.

IQUIQUE: A seaport town in Chile, S. America, situated on the west coast. It is an export center for the nitrate trade. Water is very scarce in the neighborhood. Population (1895), 33,031, and January, 1902 (estimated), 42,498. Station of the ME, with (1903) 4 missionaries and their wives, 2 outstations, 3 Sabbath schools, 1 boarding school, 1 Seamen's Bethel, and 342 professed Christians. Station also of the SDA.

IRELAND; Presbyterian Church in. See PRESBYTERIAN CHURCH.

IRELAND, William B.: Born near Oswesty, Shropshire, England, December 21, 1821; graduated at Illinois College 1845, Andover Theological Seminary 1848; ordained the September following; sailed as a missionary of the ABCFM for Africa, October 14, 1848, being stationed at Infumi in Natal. In 1855 he was appointed by the mission to take charge of the boys' seminary at Amanzimtote, and for seventeen years he devoted his heart and strength to its welfare. But his impaired health prevented his bearing the burden of so responsible a work. He occupied a large place in the mission, and in the affections of the Zulus and of all who knew him. He died in Boston, October 12, 1888.

IROD. See ERODE.

IRUNGALUR: A town in the Presidency of Madras, India, situated to the N. of the Coleroon branch of the Cavary River and about 12 miles N. of Trichinopoli. It was a stronghold of the Jesuits, who came there in the 18th century, and had influence enough to prevent Schwartz, the early Halle missionary, from being allowed to preach there. In 1830 some 16 neglected congregations of the descendants of the early converts of the Jesuits put themselves under the care of an SPG missionary. The place has been occupied by the SPG since that time, with (1903) 62 native workers, men and women; 17 places of worship, 15 day schools, 1 girls' boarding school, and 1,294 professed Christians, of whom 647 are communicants.

IRWIN HILL: A village on the northern side of the island of Jamaica, West Indies, pleasantly situated on a slight ridge about 4 miles from Montego Bay. Mission station of the Moravians (1828), at present in charge of native workers.

ISABEL ISLAND LANGUAGE. See BOGUTU.

ISFAHAN. See ISPAHAN.

ISHI-HSIEN: Town in the S. of the province of Shansi, China, situated about 20 miles N. W. of Ki-ai-chau. Station of the CIM (1891), with 6 missionaries, men and women, who are (1903) reorganizing the work broken up by the Boxer uprising.

ISMID. See NICOMEDIA.

ISOAVINA: A town and district in Madagascar, situated about 11 miles E. of Antananarivo. Station of the LMS (1867), with (1903) 1 missionary and his wife, 104 native workers, men and women; 32 day schools, and 4,157 professed Christians, of whom 1,319 are communicants.

ISOTRY: A ward in the city of Antananarivo, Madagascar, and a missionary district connected with the church in that ward, under the LMS. It now has 11 native workers, 20 day schools, and 488 professing Christians, of whom 238 are communicants.

ISPAHAN: A city of Persia, 226 miles south of Teheran, on the Zenderud River. It was formerly capital of the Empire and a great center of trade, especially with Baghdad. It has never recovered from the Afghan invasion of 1722. Like many Oriental cities, large sections of it are deserted, the people finding it cheaper and easier to remove than to rebuild. The population, estimated at 80,000, is mostly Persian, tho there are about 13,000 Jews and some Kurds. Connected with the city by bridges across the river is the suburb of Julfa, which is the real center of missionary work for Ispahan. Ispahan is the residence of the Anglican bishop, and CMS missionaries from Julfa keep up a dispensary also. Station also of the London Jews Society (1847), with (1902) 1 missionary, 5 native workers, 2 day schools, 1 industrial school.

ITARSI: A town and railway junction in the Central Provinces, India, situated in the district of Hoshangabad, about 10 miles S. of the town of that name. Station of the FFMA (1893), with (1901) 1 missionary and his wife, 1 dispensary, and 2 day schools.

ITEMBENI: A settlement in Natal, S. Africa, situated on the Mooi River, about 15 miles N. W. of Greytown. Station of the Hermannsburg Missionary Society (1856), with (1900) 1 missionary and his wife.

IVORY COAST: A French colony on the Gulf of Guinea, West Africa, lying between Liberia and the Gold Coast Colony, and joining on the north the French Military Territories and Senegambia. It has an area of about 116,000 square miles, and a population estimated at 2,000,000. The colony has vast valuable forests and gold mines of unknown riches. The capital is Bingerville (formerly called Adjame). The principal rivers are the Tanwé, Kindjabo, and Akba, the last said to be 240 miles in length, affording splendid access to the interior. The origin of the inland peoples is not definitely known. The trading tribes about Ebne Lagoon are called by the English nickname "Jack-Jack;" west of the Lahu are the Avekvoms, commonly called Qua-Quas; while farther west are the Kroomen. The coast tribes are mild and trustworthy.

The only Protestant mission in this territory consists of 3 settlements, which fall within the field of the PE mission in Liberia.

I-YANG-HSIEN: A town in the province of Kiang-si, China, about 180 miles S. E. of Kiukiang. Station of the CIM (1890), with (1902) 4 women missionaries. Name given as Ih-yang in CIM publications.

J

JABALPUR: A town in the Central Provinces, India, 160 miles northeast of Nagpur. It stands at an altitude of 1,460 feet, in a rocky basin, surrounded by a series of lakes which are shaded by fine trees and bordered by rocky crags. Its streets are wide and regularly laid out. It is perhaps the most important railway center in all India. Population (1891), 84,500, of whom 60,900 are Hindus and 19,400 Mohammedans. Station of the CMS (1854), and CEZ (1875), with, together (1900), 4 missionaries, 3 with their wives; 4 women missionaries, 39 native workers, men and women; 3 outstations, 19 elementary schools, 1 boarding school, 137 professed Christians, and 387 Zenana pupils. Station also of the ME, with (1900) 2 missionaries and their wives, 2 women missionaries, 46 native workers, 4 outstations, 5 day schools, and 389 professed Christians. Station also of the WMS, with (1900) 2 missionaries, 17 native workers, men and women; 4 day schools, and an orphanage.

JACKSON, Bishop William Walrond: Born in Barbados, January 9, 1811. Died at Ealing, November 25, 1895. Missionary of the SPG. Educated at the best school in Barbados; one of the first candidates confirmed by the first Bishop of Barbados; licensed as catechist at the age of seventeen, and entered as the first student of Codrington College, where, after winning a scholarship, he became the Senior Theological Scholar. From the beginning of his ministry (ordained deacon in 1834 and priest in 1835) he was in charge of important parishes in Barbardos, Trinidad, and St. Vincent. In Trinidad he roughed it through the forests, visiting small stations; and in St. Vincent his chief work was among the Caribs and Negroes. He was a member of the Governor's Council in Antigua; exerted a strong influence in legislation, and some of the laws that he had enacted were beneficial especially to the poor man and laborer. On his departure from the diocese in 1879, people of all classes and creeds, in the fourteen islands under his episcopal supervision, gave him a valuable testimonial of their loving esteem.

JACOBITE: A name given to the Monophysite churches of the East, especially the Syrians residing in Northern Syria, Southern Asia Minor, and Mesopotamia. Their principal headquarters are at Mosul, Diarbekir, Maadan, and Aleppo. They have also a bishop at Jerusalem. Other important centers are Oorfa, Mardin, Jazireh, and a district of Jebel Tour, east of Diarbekir. They have found it difficult in many places to cope with the aggressive influences of the Roman Catholics, who have sent large numbers of monks to establish themselves especially in Mesopotamia, in the cities of Mardin and Mosul, and, having enticed many of the priests, have succeeded also in forcing the congregations to follow them by refusing any of the sacraments except as they adopted the Roman Catholic faith.

Protestant mission work among the Jacobites has been somewhat successful, especially as carried on from Mardin, Diarbekir, and Mosul. The relations between the Jacobite leaders and the American missionaries have been quite cordial, and the constant effort to come into pleasant relations with them has been productive of good results. The larger part of the Protestant communities of Mardin, Jebel Tour, and the villages about Diarbekir are made up from the Jacobite communities.

JAESCHKE, Heinrich August: Born in Herrnhut, Saxony, May 17, 1817. He was descended from a family of those Moravian exiles who found refuge and freedom on the estates of Count Zinzendorf at the settlement of Herrnhut. After two years' study in the theological seminary at Gnadenfeld he was appointed, in 1837, a teacher in the boys' academy in Christiansfeld, where the Danish language chiefly was used. He acquired the language so rapidly that in a short time he was able to compose and preach in Danish. Five years later he was appointed a professor in the Niesky Pædegogium, where he instructed in ancient and modern languages. He here began the study of Arabic, Persian, and Sanskrit. He was a proficient in Greek. He became acquainted also with Hungarian, Bohemian, Polish, and

Swedish. His diary was kept in seven languages. In 1856 he joined Messrs. Pagell and Heyde in mission work at Kailang, a village in the province of Lahoul, on the borders of Tibet, intending as soon as the way was open to enter with them and labor among the Chinese Mongols. Having acquired the language he compiled a German-Tibetan, and some years later an English-Tibetan, Lexicon, both of which are considered standard authorities. The British Government published the English-Tibetan Lexicon for the use of English officers in Kashmir. He also wrote and translated several books and tracts for the converts, for pupils in schools, and for distribution among the people. He prepared also a small Tibetan grammar in the English language for the use of missionaries and others. He now began the translation of the Bible, but after ten years of almost incessant labor his health failed, and he was obliged to return to Europe. There, in great weakness, he continued the work, and completed the translation of the New Testament, which was published by the British and Foreign Bible Society. He left materials which were used by Mr. Redslob in the translation of the Old Testament. He died at Herrnhut, September 24, 1883.

JAFFA: A town in Syria, lying 33 miles N. W. of Jerusalem, of which it is the seaport and with which it is connected by railroad. It is regarded as an important center for missionary work, because all pilgrims and visitors to Jerusalem, whether Christians, Jews, or Muslims, naturally land at Jaffa. There are fourteen colonies of Jews from abroad in the immediate neighborhood of the town, making with those in the town itself a body of some 6,500 Jews. The population of Jaffa is about 16,000. It is a station of the Tabeetha Mission Schools (1863), of the CMS (1876), of the Jaffa Medical Mission (1878), of the London Society for the Promotion of Christianity among the Jews (1882), of the Jerusalem Union (Berlin), and of the Christian and Missionary Alliance. Together these societies have at Jaffa 20 missionaries and 29 native workers, men and women, with 12 day schools, 1 boarding school, 1 industrial school, 1 hospital, and 2 dispensaries.

JAFFNA: A town in Ceylon, situated on the S. coast of the island or peninsula of Jaffna, 116 miles N. W. of Trincomalee. It is the district town, and has the administrative buildings, a college, and a public library. The fort is the most perfect little military work in Ceylon—a pentagon built of blocks of white coral. Traces of the Dutch occupancy of the town can still be seen, and not a few of the churches date back to the time of the Portuguese. The industry of the Tamil inhabitants has changed the sandy soil to a fertile district, with luxuriant tropical vegetation. Its trade is mainly in tobacco and Palmyra timber. Population (1891), 43,000. Station of the WMS, with (1903) 3 missionaries, 2 women missionaries, 67 native workers, men and women; 6 outstations, 21 day schools, 2 boarding schools, 1 college, and 455 professed Christians. The Society uses the name Pettah to designate its station here.

JAGATAI TURKISH LANGUAGE. See TURKISH LANGUAGE.

JAGDALI DIALECT. See MULTANI.

JAGERS FONTEIN: A village in the Orange River Colony, South Africa, situated 67 miles S. W. of Bloemfontein. Population, 4,000. Station of the SPG, with 1 missionary, and of the South African Wesleyan Methodist Missionary Society, with 23 native workers, 23 outstations, and 340 professed Christians.

JAINS: A religious sect in India, who are found in Upper Hindustan, in the provinces of Mewar and Marwar, along the Ganges, and in Calcutta. They are also found in some other parts of India, especially along the Malabar coast. They are considered heterodox by the Hindus, and in their belief they adhere to some of the tenets of Buddhism and to some of the teachings of the Brahmans. Like the Buddhists, they deny the origin and authority of the Vedas, and they worship some of the same saints. Like the Brahmans, they recognize the distinctions of caste, and worship some of the deities of the Hindu pantheon, tho they reject all the rites which cause the sacrifice of animal life. They believe in final emancipation, when the vital spirit is released from the bonds of action, and they define the size of such souls, their home, their qualities, their length of life, and all that pertains to them. The Jains are divided into two orders—the priest and the layman. The former leads a life of abstinence and general self-denial. He carefully avoids the destruction of animal life, even covering his mouth to avoid inadvertently swallowing insects. The layman is supposed to practise the virtues of liberality, gentleness, piety, and penance. He also carefully strains the water which he drinks, and covers all liquids lest an insect may be drowned therein. There are other differences among them which govern their dress and decorations. They worship a number of deified saints, called Jina, to whom they ascribe attributes of the most extravagant character. Two of these are now the principal objects of worship. The origin of the sect is lost in obscurity, but it probably was subsequent to the rise of the Buddhist religion.

JAIPUR: A town in Chota Nagpur, India, situated 8 miles W. of Purulia. Outstation of the SPG (1869), with (1902) 11 native workers and 831 professed Christians, of whom 399 are communicants. Name also written Jaypur.

JAIPUR: A town in the Madras Presidency, India, situated in the district of Vizagapatam, 95 miles N. W. of the town of that name, at an altitude of 2,000 feet. Population (1891), 5,000. Station of the Breklum Missionary Society (1887), with (1903) 1 missionary and his wife, 7 native workers, men and women, and 750 professed Christians, of whom 239 are communicants. Name written by the Society, Jeypur.

JAIPUR: A city in Rajputana, India, the capital of a native state of the same name, situated at an altitude of 1,438 feet, about 80 miles E. N. E. of Ajmere. It stands in a small plain which seems to have been the bed of a lake. The city was founded in 1728 by Jai Singh II., and its streets are regular and wide. It is the chief commercial center of Rajputana. Population (1891), 159,000. Station of the UFS (1866), with (1903) 2 missionaries, 1 with his wife; 3 women missionaries, 39 native workers, men and women; 11 elementary schools and 1 dispensary. Name also written Jeypore.

JALA: A town in Chota Nagpur, India, situated about 50 miles N. W. of Purulia. Station of the Gossner Missionary Society, with (1900) 1 missionary, 8 native workers, and 1 elementary school.

JALALPUR: A town in the Bombay Presidency, India, situated 18 miles S. by W. of Surat. Station of the German Baptist Brethren Church.

JALALPUR: A town in the Punjab, India, situated about 20 miles N. of Wazirabad. Station of the Church of Scotland Foreign Missions' Committee (1899), with 2 missionaries, 5 native workers, and 1 dispensary and hospital.

JALANDHAR: A town in the Punjab, India, situated 47 miles E. S. E. of Amritsar. Population (1901), 67,735, of whom 39,000 are Mohammedans and 23,000 Hindus. Station of the PN (1846), with (1903) 1 missionary and his wife, 2 women missionaries, 41 native workers, 6 day schools, and 1 boarding school. Name written by the Society, Jullundur.

JALAPA: A town in the State of Vera Cruz, Mexico, situated 56 miles W. N. W. of Vera Cruz City, at an altitude of 4,300 feet. Jalap grows wild in the vicinity and takes its name in medicine from the town. Population about 18,000. Station of the PN (1897), with (1903) 1 missionary and his wife, 4 native workers, 1 day school and 755 professed evangelical Christians.

JALAPUR. See JALALPUR.

JALESWAR: A town in Orissa, Bengal, India, situated 24 miles N. E. of Balasore. Station of the Free Baptist Missionary Society (1885), with (1900) 1 missionary and his wife and 11 native workers, men and women. Name also written Jellasore.

JALNA: A town in Haidarabad, India, situated 36 miles E. by S. of Aurungabad, in arid land but surrounded with fruit gardens which are famous. Altitude, 1,632 feet. Population, 6,300. Station of the UFS (1862), with (1903) 2 missionaries, one with his wife; 2 women missionaries, 51 native workers, men and women; 13 outstations, 12 elementary schools, 1 boarding school 1 dispensary, 1 hospital and 268 communicants.

JALPAIGURI: A town in Bengal, India, situated about 50 miles S. E. by S. of Darjiling, at an altitude of 270 feet. Population (1891) 9,700, of whom 5,700 are Hindus. Station of the BMS (1888), with (1903) 1 missionary and his wife and 6 native workers.

JAMALPUR: A town in Bengal, India, situated in Behar, 32 miles W. of Bhagalpur. Population (1891) 18,000, of whom 14,000 are Hindus. Station of the CEZ (1894), with (1903) 3 women missionaries and 13 native women workers.

JAMMALAMADUGU: A town in the Presidency of Madras, India, situated in the district of Cuddapah, 102 miles E. by S. of Bellary. Population (1891) 6,000, of whom 4,200 are Hindus. Station of the LMS (1891), with (1903) 2 missionaries, 3 women missionaries, a dispensary and a hospital. The church statistics are included in those of Cuddapah.

JAMMU: A town in Kashmir, India, situated about 80 miles N. of Amritsar. It was formerly the capital of an independent Rajput kingdom, and possesses a citadel and a number of extensive ruins. The place has been rated as very unhealthful on account of its bad water supply. This, however, has been remedied. Population (1891) 34,800. Occupied as an outstation by the SPG in 1892.

JANDIALA: A town in the Punjab, India, situated 55 miles S. E. by E. of Amritsar in the Jalandhar district. Population about 7,000. Station of the CMS and CEZ (1881), with (1903) 3 women missionaries, 11 native workers, men and women; 12 elementary schools, a hospital, 95 Zenana pupils and 55 professed Christians.

JANGAON: A town and railroad station in the native state of Haidarabad, India, situated about 48 miles N. E. of Secunderabad. Station of the ABMU (1901), with (1903) 1 missionary and his wife.

JANICKE, "Father": Born of Bohemian parents in Berlin in 1748; died in 1827. He was a weaver by trade, but having conceived an ardent desire to possess a university education, he turned all his energies upon this, and with many interruptions he succeeded, after enduring great privations, in fitting himself to enter Leipzig University, whence he graduated in due course, and in 1779 became pastor of a Bohemian Church in Berlin.

Early in life he was much under Moravian influences, and his own brother was a missionary in India. Hence missions in every form were close to his heart. He was a very earnest man, and had the not uncommon trait of earnest men in a brusque manner that aroused violent opposition among some whose offices in the Church ought to have ensured him their sympathy.

It was a layman, von Schnirding, who suggested to Janicke the idea of founding a training school for missionaries in Berlin. This school, whose influence had a large place in the founding of the Berlin Missionary Society, was opened in 1800. In 1805 Father Janicke founded a Bible Society, which developed into the Prussian Central Bible Society. In 1811 he founded a Tract Society which has become renowned.

Is was characteristic of this great-hearted man that when he opened his Training School for Missionaries, he made its needs his own. He had in the school seven scholars, for whose expenses he depended upon von Schnirding. That gentleman suddenly lost his property and the enterprise seemed to be doomed. But Janicke, with only 47 thalers in hand, decided to carry on the school. In spite of all obstacles and of much opposition he succeeded, and in 1820 he had the gratification of receiving the sanction of the King of Prussia to the enterprise. This gave the school a secure basis. Up to the time of his death in 1827 Janicke had trained for the foreign field eighty missionaries, some of whom became men of high renown in the annals of the English and Dutch societies which sent them out to different parts of the world.

JANVIER, Levi: Born at Pittsgrove, N. J., April 25, 1816; graduated at Princeton College 1835, Theological Seminary 1838; ordained December 31, 1840; sailed in 1841 as a missionary of the PN for India; was stationed at Fatehgarh, Ludhiana, Ambala and Sabathu. He was much occupied in the translation of the Scriptures, and was connected with the press from the beginning to the close of his work. After he had mastered the Punjabi language, he, with his cousin, Dr. Newton, of the same mission, commenced the preparation of a dictionary of that language. It was completed and published at the mission press in 1854, a quarto of 438 pages, in the Gurmukhi character. Dr. Janvier possessed great energy of character, and was full of zeal for the salvation of the heathen. He met his death March 24, 1864, at a *mela* in Anandpur, where he was engaged in preaching and distributing tracts. In the evening he was met by a fanatic Sikh, and felled to the ground with a club. He lingered insensible till morning, when he died.

JAO-CHAU-FU: A town in the province of Kiang-si, China, 60 miles S. E. of Kiu-kiang. Station of the CIM, with (1903) 1 missionary and his wife and 2 native workers. Name written by the Society, Rao-chau.

JAPAN: The archipelago and empire of Dai Nippon (great dayspring), called "Japan" by foreigners, consists of a chain of islands bordering the Continent of Asia between Russia at Kamchatka and the Chinese coast opposite Formosa and the Pescadores. It is set in a quadrilateral nearly 9,000 miles wide and 2,000 miles long. The most northern island is Araito (latitude 50° 56′), the most southern Formosa (latitude 21° 42′), the most eastern Shimushiu (longitude east 156° 32′), the most western Yonaku (longitude east 122° 45′). Of the great quadrilateral thus drawn about Japan's extremities, the total land area is but 150,000 square miles; the remaining 17,840,000 square miles being ocean water which surrounds nearly 4,000 islands having 43,000 miles of coast line. The largest island is Hondo or Hon-shiu, that is, main island, or main country, and on unrevised maps is called Niphon, which is the Dutch spelling of the name of the whole empire, the native common name being Nippon, or Nihon. Hondo, Kiu-shiu, Shikoku and Yezo, or Hokkaido, are the four largest islands. The lesser groups of islands, besides Riu Kiu and Chishima, are Awaji, Tsu-shima, Goto, Iki, Oki, Sado, Shichijima, Ogasawara (Bonin), etc. All the outlying islands from Tsu-shima to Sado are on the western side of Hondo, which is, in general, destitute of harbors; while the eastern front is well indented and contains numerous places suitable for anchorage and commerce. The general shape of the main group of islands is that of an archer's bow recurved at each end, the cord or string bisecting the Sea of Japan, the arrowrest being at Tokio, the capital, which is thus almost exactly at the center of the empire.

Physical Features: Geologically, Japan is part of the chain of volcanoes stretching from Kamchatka into China, the islands being the tops of otherwise submerged mountain plateaus of granite and old schists and clay slates on which late and active volcanoes have superimposed their peaks, and the islets being the fragments of the great lines of upheaval, once long causeways but now broken into fragments and fantastic shapes by ages of wave-action. The geographical division of the empire into nine dō (circuits or roads) is made in general accordance with the physical features of the country, especially the great lines of mountains and islands. The whole surface of the country consists of mountains and valleys, large plains and great rivers being nearly unknown, while lakes, except Biwa and Inawashiro, are few and small. The scenery is rarely wild and imposing, tho in general beautiful, and in many places exceedingly lovely. Most of the mountains are rounded and forest-covered.

Only about ten per cent. of the total area is cultivated, which, however, is nearly all that is available, since the arable land is almost wholly in the valleys and river plains. Surrounded on every side by the ocean, fish food is cheap, abundant and nourishing. In the tertiary age the Japanese islands were united to the continents of Asia and America, after which began the great upheavals which have both separated and made mountainous this island-chain. Not only is the climate of Japan quite similar to that of the United States between the lower Mississippi and the Atlantic Ocean in the amount and distribution of rain and the variations of temperature, but the flora of these two portions of the world are closely related both in general character and the large number of plants common to each. Extending through twenty-seven degrees of latitude, there is great difference in climate in various places and at different altitudes. The monsoon winds and the Kuro Shiwo (black stream) are the chief regulating factors. The western coasts, under the influence of the cold-water currents from the north, have lower temperatures, more fog, rain, snow and ice than the eastern sides of the country, which, being nearer the gulf stream, are warmer and more free from snow and ice. The average temperature from April to October is 68° F., from June to September 74°. In many parts of Yezo the winter lasts from November to May, but the cold rarely drops to 28°. The rainy time of the year is between March and November, the wettest month being September and the driest January. The rainfall, tho in some years reaching 145 inches, in Tokio had an average during 1876-1888 of 58.33 inches. Taken all in all, it may be said that there are as many working days in the year as in the Carolinas of the United States.

The greatest plagues of Japan are typhoons and earthquakes (to which one writer adds rats), and the phenomena of these are studied, as well as those of wind, temperature and moisture. Vessels are warned of coming typhoons from nearly fifty stations. From a study of the climatology of Japan it is evident that the conditions of the air, wind, temperature and moisture are very much like those of adjacent countries, except that the extremes of summer heat and winter cold and dryness reached on the neighboring continent are hardly known in Japan. The frequency of earthquakes seems to be compensated for in the comparative rarity of thunderstorms and danger from lightning. Japan may be safely called one of the healthful countries of the north temperate zone, and ordinary precautions as to choice of building-sites and habits of life will secure the same possibilities of health as in the same latitude in Europe or America. The months liable to the dreaded typhoons are, in a decreasing order of severity, September, August, October, and July. Four or five typhoons pass over Japan annually, of which Tokio receives about one. Occasionally a typhoon comes as early as April. The native houses, admirable for summer use, are not usually habitable by Europeans in winter. The numerous mountain resorts, and the easy accessibility of Yezo, where the climate is cooler, furnish Japan with sanitariums for rest, recuperation, or prolonged vacation.

The peculiarities of the climate of Japan are reflected in its vegetation. During eight months of the year plant life is active, during four almost at a standstill, the herbage in early summer and autumn being at its best. Evergreens are the characteristic features of the landscape. Nearly all types of vegetation, temperate, arctic and tropical, prevail, and the Mediterranean, Pacific and north European coasts will be recalled by travelers. These types meet, especially in central Japan, where, at the higher elevations, the birch and the beech are still common, while the bamboo and the camphor-laurel flourish in the milder lowlands.

Japan is the land of the monkey and the giant salamander. Except the ass, sheep and goat, most of the common domestic animals exist here. The chief mammals are the monkey, bat, bear, badger, marten, dog, wolf, fox, squirrel, rat, hare, wild boar, stag, antelope. About 400 species of fish have been catalogd, with 1,200 species of mollusca, the seas being amazingly rich in life of every form able to exist in salt water.

Population: In round numbers, the population of Dai Nippon in 1899 was 44,000,000.

Except the Ainus, in Yezo, the people are now a homogeneous race, made up of several stocks. The chief peculiarities in physical appearance, language and customs are found in Lu Chu and other outlying islands. The language spoken in the capital, Tokio, is now the standard, and using this a good speaker can be understood easily all over the empire, as the variations in dialect, tho numerous, are comparatively slight, and are vastly less than in China. In comparison with China, India, Siam or indeed with any Asian country, Japan is politically more of a unit, and her people the most homogeneous of any Asiatic nation. The Kuazoku, or nobility, includes the members of the imperial family, those persons of the old-landed nobility formerly called daimio (great name) and others who for talent or illustrious services have been ennobled by patent. The Shizoku or gentry include the former samurai (servants of the emperor) whose ancestors served the feudal lords as retainers, or who have in various ways risen to social rank, and who, altogether, under the old order constituted the military and literati of the empire. The Heimin, or common people, were formerly divided into several distinct classes, beneath which were the eta, outcasts, and hi-nin (not human); but all the people—farmers, artisans, merchants, etc.—are now equal before the law, and subject to the same political and social forces and liabilities. The agricultural people comprise one-half of the population, after which in order come traders and artisans.

In physical stature the Japanese are an undersized people, the average height of the men being 5.5 feet, and that of the women 4.5 feet. Further, the native is not proportionately developed. The inveterate habit, continued for ages, of sitting on their knees without chairs, the hams resting on the heels or ankles, has resulted in a curious malformation, or, rather, lack of growth, by which the upper part of the body is disproportionately longer than the lower. The Japanese do not smoke opium or bind the feet of their women, but the use of tobacco in the form of smoke is almost universal; and the custom of "drinking" or filling the lungs with the volatilized tobacco-vapor may be one of the causes of the common lung diseases and flat breasts of the men. The most common fatal diseases of the Japanese are, in their order, those of the nervous, digestive and respiratory organs, tho skin disorders are frightfully common, and epidemics are not rare.

In mental traits the Japanese are bright, quick, perceptive and in general clever, maturing in intellect probably earlier than the European, and from fifteen to forty years of age being peer, probably, to any people in the world, tho it appears that arrested mental development and decay come earlier than with the Germanic races. In universal courtesy and politeness, the Japanese people have probably no peers, the kindly greetings and gentle manners being common to all grades of society, even the language (between equals, only) being infused with the eminently Christian idea of each esteeming the other better than himself.

Government: The government is that of a monarchy, the chief ruler, the Mikado, being hereditary emperor, who is assisted by a senate, a privy council, and a cabinet of ministers, each of whom has charge of a department. For administrative purposes the empire is divided into 46 *ken* or prefectures, the three large municipalities, Tokio, Osaka, and Kioto, being organized as *fu* or imperial cities. These *ken* consist, as a rule, of two of the old geographical divisions of *kuni* or provinces united, there being in the empire 85 provinces, 805 kori or districts, 12,185 cities and towns, and 58,456 villages. The sub-prefectures number 566, and the towns and cities having mayors number 11,377. The smaller villages are under the care of a *nanushi* or head-man, and the entire populace is arranged into responsible groups of five households—a system which enables the government to keep the most minute oversight of all subjects of the Mikado. For further details of the government, the reader is referred to the constitution of Japan, proclaimed February 11, 1889. This being the culminating point of Japanese history, since it has led to the suppression, by consent of the Western nations, of the extraterritoriality clauses of the treaties, we now turn to a survey of the origin of the people and to the condensed story of the religious and political development of the nation, which, by adopting such a constitution, solemnly declared its purpose to change its political system from an Asiatic despotism to a modern representative government.

Political History: The true history of Japan is now in process of construction out of the materials obtained by a critical study of geology and cognate physical sciences, languages, the native legends, poetry and mythology, and a comparison of Chinese, Korean, and Japanese historical records. The most ancient literature extant is not older than the 8th century, and the early writers draw no clear line of demarcation between myth and history. Hence there is little to be depended on until the 4th century.

At the dawn of history, the archipelago is found populated. The conquerors from the Asian highlands, who, by way of Korea, landed in Kiushiu and by gradual conquest northward established themselves in central Hondo near Lake Biwa, at Nara and Kioto, found on their arrival inhabitants who were hunters and fishermen. To these the conquerors were a superior race of men, and they parceled out the land among themselves, compelling the aborigines to be their serfs. To this day, at least two types of countenance are easily distinguishable, and the characteristics of a mixed race appear in the people. The round, flat, "pudding face" of the lower classes and the more oval countenance of the aristocrats, with its more delicate features and profile, are in noticeable contrast, being, according to some writers, types of the Ainu and the invading Yamatu, respectively. Others argue that Japan was peopled by two different streams of immigration from Korea, which supplied these types; and that, as neither recorded history, nor tradition, nor mythology shows any traces of migration from the southward, we are to look upon the Koreans as the nearest congeners of the Japanese. Tho historically the Ainus occupied the soil of Hondo, it is claimed by some able writers that the Japanese and Ainus are as distinct in race as the whites and Indians in North America.

From about the year 400, when calendars, writing, and Chinese appliances of civilization were introduced, Japanese history becomes clear. Ancestor-worship was the religion of the invaders, and out of their method of deifying their famous patriarchs and heroes grew up the Kami-no-Michi, or, in later Chinese phrase, Shinto (*theos-logos*), the way or doctrine of the gods, which is a compound of the worship of nature and of deified human beings. This is a cardinal feature of the Japanese system. The Mikado rules over Japan by divine right from all eternity, and the divine origin and right of the ruler is the central doctrine of Shinto as the national religion. Upon this religion the fabric of government was built. What a blended religious and political system might have developed into we have no means of knowing, but immediately upon the importation of foreign influences from China, the germs were planted for mighty growths in politics, social, religious, and intellectual life, which were profoundly to affect and notably modify the nation and its development. From the 6th to the 12th century the history of Japan includes on its political side the abolition of the rude feudalism of the conquerors, and the gradual centralization of the government in Kioto, with the adoption of codes of law, boards or ministries, the division of the empire into provinces, governed by officers sent out by, and directly responsible to, the central government, and the gradual unification of the whole body of tribes and outlying portions of the population into one homogeneous people. Such a result was not accomplished without much military energy, and many bloody victories of the disciplined imperial troops over the brave but poorly armed mountaineers and distant tribes. A far-reaching effect on society was the gradual separation of the military from the agricultural class, the physically strong and intellectually gifted becoming permanent soldiers, continually in camp and clothed constantly in armor and helmet. Such a body or bodies of men on the distant frontiers were far more likely to know, respect, believe in, obey, and follow their favorite commander than to heed the mandates of the distant and shadowy court at Kioto. The foundations of a new feudal system were thus laid. Out of the military class, or *buké*, has been evolved the samurai, the soldier-scholar, the most picturesque and interesting figure in the national history. From this class, which now constitutes over one-twentieth of the populace, have arisen nearly all the great warriors, statesmen, scholars, reformers, Christian thinkers, and philanthropists of modern times, while the man of the agricultural class is still the typical ultra-conservative. The *buké* or Samurai were the military, the *kugé* or civil court nobles and officers were the civil, servants of the Mikado, who was in theory the owner of all the land.

The further growth of government in Japan can best be viewed from the standpoint of the relation of religion to its development. We therefore turn to the subject of the religions of the Empire.

Religions: In religion the Ainus are fetish-worshipers, and the superstitions of fetishism, shamanism, the worship of the reproductive powers of nature, and the veneration of ancestors are ingrained in the people of the Nippon archipelago. These primitive beliefs underlie the other national religions, Shinto and Buddhism; the former being the possibly indigenous cult based on ancestor-worship and the deification of heroes, and the latter having been imported from India by way of China and Korea, with remarkable development and variations on Japanese soil. Shinto is the state religion, as has been noted already.

Buddhism: In the formation of the total product of evolution in Japan Buddhism has been a most potent factor. Introduced in 552 A.D. from Korea, with its elaborate systems of ethics, ritual, dogma, and scriptures, it soon completely overshadowed the bald and impoverished cult of Shinto. Its complete victory was heralded when Kōbō, the reputed inventor of the Japanese syllabary, the profound scholar of mighty intellect, who had visited China and mastered the Sanskrit, proclaimed in the beginning of the 9th century his scheme of reconstruction and of reconciliation, by which the older and indigenous faith was swallowed by the foreign religion. This man, the Philo and Euhemerus of Japan, declared, after revelation from the gods, that all the Shinto deities were avatars or incarnations of Buddha. He therefore baptized them with Buddhist names, and in place of the Shinto festivals appointed others to be celebrated according to the Buddhist liturgies. Having already obtained a foothold in the palace, and by its influence turned the emperors into cloistered monks and empresses into nuns—thus dealing a blow at Shinto in its vitals, and by weakening government prepared the way for the decay of the imperial authority and the supremacy of the military classes—the victory of Kōbō's system was easy. Further, the Buddhist monks were explorers, road-makers, bridge-builders, improvers of diet and living, chaplains of the army, almost the only scholars and learned men apart from the court, the benefactors of the people, the exponents of civilization, and the foster-fathers of art, of literature, and of material development. From the 6th to the 12th century is the missionary era of Japanese Buddhism, after which for two centuries the development of doctrine followed, in which emerged those new and startling forms of the faith of Sakamuni which have made Japan the land of dreadful heresies to the coreligionists of Siam and China. In Shin-shiu, or "reformed" Buddhism, we see the circle of development complete, and the beginning and the end meeting in what seems a caricature of Christianity. Of the six great sects in Japan, one originated in India, one in China, and four in Japan, viz., the Shin-gon, Jō-dō, Shin, and Nichiren. These sects of purely native origin are mainly developments of the pantheistic principle initiated by Kōbō and reenforced by local and patriotic considerations. The common people, tho not ignorant of the Confucian ethics, have been instructed almost wholly in Buddhism; while the gentry, or samurai, hostile or indifferent to Buddhism, have been nursed in the virtues as well as in the vices of feudalism,— the Chinese system fitting admirably into the needs of a society framed on the feudal basis. Now that the feudal system has been abolished, the samurai, in a sense not so true of the common people, is left without a religion,—a sect which may explain why most of the Christian converts thus far made, as well as the agnostics, skeptics, and indifferents, are samurai, while the mass of the people are still Buddhist.

Roman Christianity: It will thus be seen that the religion of Japan is Buddhism, and that when in 1549, ten years after its first sight by a European, Roman Christianity reached Japan in the person of its pioneer and then ablest exponent, Francis Xavier, the only serious obstacle to propaganda and conversion was the cultus imported originally from India. Shinto was out of sight, and buried in mythology, and the first missionary efforts were aided rather than hindered by the contemporary political condition of Japan, which was that of civil war, during which Novunaga humbled the pride and mightily diminished the power of the Buddhists by his military persecution of them. At Kagoshima, in Satsuma, Xavier made one hunderd converts in a year, and labored for short periods at Hirado, and Yamaguchi, in Nagato, having also fruitlessly visited Kioto. Leaving Torres and Fernandez, his fellow-missionaries, Xavier left for China, dying on his way thither, at Sancian. In 1553 reenforcements arrived, and tho driven out of Yamaguchi by civil outbreaks, the Portuguese friars assembled at Bungo, Vilela, visiting also Kioto and Sakai and gaining converts. Some years of prosperity followed, and in 1583 a mission was dispatched to the Papal See, headed by three Japanese noblemen.

The Pagan Reaction: When, however, in 1587 the Taiko Hidéyoshi succeeded to power and subdued the southern daimiōs and provinces, in which were most of the Christian converts of rank, including the famous generals Kuroda and Konishi, he issued an edict ordering the foreign missionaries to Hirado, in order to send them out of the country. He hoped they would depart peacefully, and not compel him to deport them by force. They, however, finding that the edict was not pushed by force, scattered again, and finding asylum in the provinces of the daimiōs professing Christianity, began propagating the faith more vigorously than ever, even in Kioto, despite the official ban. Further, all the missionaries thus far engaged in Japan were Jesuits; but in 1590, in the train of the Spanish envoy from the Philippine Islands, four Franciscans arrived, who, despite the protests of the Jesuits, who laid before them the Papal bulls excluding all but Jesuits from Japan, and, still more, despite their solemn promise to Hidéyoshi not to preach their doctrines, went vigorously to work at the propaganda. Hidéyoshi, now at leisure, thoroughly alarmed at what he considered the treacherous disobedience of the Portuguese friars, and at the growing Christian party, which threatened not only his own future but that of the empire, determined to root up the foreign faith, and to do this he laid two plans.

In the first place, he declared war against Korea, and sent armies of invasion thither, in which were many Christian officers and soldiers, among them Generals Konishi and Kuroda. No sooner were the leaders of the Christians immersed in war duties in a foreign land than Hidéyoshi, the next year, 1593, seized nine missionaries, six Franciscans and three Jesuits, in Osaka and Kioto, and sent them to Nagasaki, where they were publicly burned to death. For the next few years the open propaganda was less active, tho work was secretly carried on and converts multiplied. The Jesuit friars established a printing press, and, using type from Europe, published a number of interesting works, some of which had already circulated in manuscript. After Hidéyoshi's death the whole country was excited by civil troubles between the adherents of Iyéyasu and of Hidéyori, the son of Hidéyoshi, but missionary work went on until the Christians numbered over a million and a half. While Iyéyasu was busy in subduing his enemies, he ignored Christianity, an example which the lesser political lights followed; but on gaining the victory over the southern army, in which were many of the Christian leaders, at the battle of Sékigahara in October, 1600, he, like Hidéyoshi, threw off the mask and issued a decree of expulsion of the foreigners. Busy, however, with reorganizing the empire from his seat of government in the distant east at Yedo and Fuchiu (Shidzuoka), Iyéyasu could not, or did not, press his policy of expulsion, and large numbers of Spanish and Portuguese priests continued to secure entrance into Japan. In 1608, by the Papal bull, priests of all orders were allowed to reside in Japan. In 1610 the Dutch, and in 1613 the English, secured a foothold at Hirado. At this time there were two hundred missionaries, with "two million converts;" but the strength was apparently in numbers only, for without leaders or men of influence in the state its weakness was made apparent when in Kiushiu, between 1600 and 1614, the daimiōs changed, adopted, or annihilated popular Christianity at their pleasure, using it simply as the tool of their ambition. Whatever may have been the motive, in 1614, of the sudden and fiercely energetic action of Iyéyasu in issuing that decree, which was at once executed with blood and iron,—the inherent Japanese jealousy of foreign influence, the pressure of the Buddhist priesthood, the intrigues of the Protestant, Dutch and English, or his own despotic purpose to secure peace, and even national independence, by isolating Japan from all the world,—it is certain that his purpose succeeded. From Sendai to Satsuma the Christians were compelled to renounce their faith, and, failing to do so, were imprisoned, exiled, tortured, or beheaded, while the foreign *religieux* were deported. Thousands of natives fled to China and Formosa, or, outwardly recanting, kept alive their faith even until their teachers from Europe returned in 1858. By compelling the owners of seaworthy vessels to burn them and pronouncing the death sentence alike upon the Christian and the returned Japanese castaway, the ruling powers in Japan now kept their country insulated from the world. The Dutch merchants on their little island in front of Nagasaki were the sole exceptions to these rigid laws of exclusion. During two and one-half centuries the Dutch and the Japanese lived in harmony. Moreover, the intercourse of the Japanese with the little Dutch colony was a fertile source of intellectual stimulus and culture to the Japanese mind, and prepared the way for that easy acceptance of foreign ideas which has so surprised the world since the diplomatic victory of Commodore Perry.

Indeed, it will be found on examination of the antecedents of nearly every reformer and leader in the modern progress of Japan, that his first enlightenment, or motive to renovation of mind, came from his own or his father's contact with the Dutch or Dutch learning. Further, abundant facts coming to the light in these days, when New Japan is so busily engaged in building the monuments of the martyrs she once imprisoned and beheaded, show beyond doubt that the beginnings of modern Protestant, tho unorganized, Christianity in Japan were prior to the coming of the missionaries, and sprang from the Dutch. Some of the sons and grandsons of these inquirers or martyrs are now pastors of Christian churches, and this wide area of propædeutics for modern civilization and Christianity gives strongest hope of its reality and permanence in the hearts of the people. Other disconnected events belong to the story of the revival of ideas of progress in Japan.

With the opening of the Pacific to American commerce and the development of the fur trade and whale-fishery, the number of rescues of Japanese waifs became every year increasingly numerous. To return these involuntary exiles to the land they loved was dictated by humanity. One notable attempt of this class was that made by the owners of the ship "Morrison," who, in 1837, shipped by their vessel to Japan seven Japanese, with Dr. S. Wells Williams and Dr. Gutzlaff as interpreters. The ship was fired on at Uraga, July 30, in Yedo Bay, and also repulsed at Kagoshima, in Satsuma. From these waifs Messrs. Gutzlaff and Williams in China learned the language, and translated into it portions of the Bible. In the gradual evolution of a complete version of the Holy Scriptures in Japanese, this work of Gutzlaff and Williams, and that of the natives who translated from Dutch Bibles obtained at Déshima, with that of Bettelheim, a missionary supported in the Lu Chu Islands by a British Naval Society from 1846 to 1854, may be considered historical links. The settlement of California and the discovery of gold there again called the attention of the American Government to Japan. By a coincidence that suggests the hand of Providence, the present Emperor of Japan was born November 3, 1852, on the very day that Perry was ready to sail into Yedo Bay. The success of this naval diplomatist is matter of history, but the treaties signed by the Shogun, or military commander-in-chief, offended the nation. A condition of anarchy followed which was full of hostility to foreigners. This was regarded by the Western nations as wanton disregard of treaties, which was chastised by the combined fleets. Shortly after the Japanese had thus felt the power of the West a reaction took place in favor of learning the secret of this power. The popular ferment was accompanied by a determination to suppress the military form of government which had opened the doors to the West. A short civil war, in the winter of 1867-68, disposed of the Shogun and his adherents, and the Mikado or actual Emperor was restored to his rightful supremacy. Several serious revolts tested the stability of the new political order. The most serious of these began early in 1877 and continued during seven months. Since that time the progress of Japan has been rapid and, one may say, marvelous.

With this revival of national feeling and patriotism, the importance became enhanced of relations between Japan and Korea, over which country China and Japan exercised a joint-protectorate. The wide difference between Japanese and Chinese theories, as to progress and as to the reforms which Korea needed to adopt for its own best interests, led to friction and finally to war in 1894-95. After the Chinese troops had been expelled from Korea, and her naval arm broken, a peace was signed by which the fortress of Port Arthur and its immediate territory were ceded to Japan. At that moment, however, Russia unexpectedly came forward with a "recommendation" that Japan restore Port Arthur to China. The reason alleged was that the occupation of that fortress by a foreign power would be a menace to the independence of both China and Korea. Germany and France supported Russia in this view, and Japan was forced to yield the fortress which had been taken by hard fighting.

Such forcible interference was enough in itself to cause immediate attention by Japan to the problem of increasing her military and naval equipment. When, three years later, Russia, by arrangement with China, occupied the fortress which she had forced Japan to evacuate, it became certain that sooner or later the Mikado would cross swords with the great Czar. The clash of policies came in the autumn of 1903, and the cause of dissension was the question of securing the independence of China and Korea, threatened by the somewhat equivocal attitude of the Russian authorities in Manchuria. Not having received what she considered satisfactory pledges on this point, Japan, on the 6th of February, 1904, broke off diplomatic relations with Russia, and resorted to arms as the champion of the rights of China and Korea, but with a zest which showed that the Port Arthur episode of 1895 had not been forgotten. One feature of the case which should be born in mind is that in 1902 the British Government entered into an engagement with Japan to support her at any time when the integrity of either China or Korea might be about to be destroyed by any hostile coalition. This agreement between the Asiatic and the European island empires contains as much of danger to the peace of Europe as it does of consolation to Japan in undertaking war against Russia.

Missions in Japan since the Reforms: The Roman Catholics. On the opening of Japan, missionaries of Greek, Roman, and Reformed Christianity at once entered the empire, the Roman Catholics to discover their brethren and continue the old methods of propaganda, and the Russians or Greek (Orthodox) and the Protestant missionaries to break new ground. As early as 1846 the Pope had nominated a bishop and several missionaries, who in the Lu Chu islands awaited the opening of the country. At Urakami and other places near Nagasaki there were found, in 1865, thousands of people who possessed some prayers and books, with many of the old sacramental words of Latin origin, and practised some of the minor rites of the faith, besides abstaining from acts significant to Buddhist, and especially

Shinto worshipers. Until toleration became the fact, which was even before it became the law, in 1872, many of these people were imprisoned, exiled, and otherwise persecuted, as indeed were occasionally even the converts of Protestant missionaries. Many interesting relics and survivals of Roman Christianity of the 17th century have been discovered by the priests, and here and there small bodies of descendants of former believers have been more easily converted because of the sentiment of historic continuity. In the thirty-one years of their revived work, making diligent use of the methods peculiar to Roman Catholic missionary operations, they have again established themselves widely over the empire, but especially in Kiushiu. The missionaries are mostly French, and their zeal and consecration are worthy of praise.

The Greek Church: The missionaries of the Church of Russia began operations at Hakodaté in 1870, and have steadily continued their labors. A large native ministry has been trained, the Bible has been read, used, and taught, and in the freedom allowed their converts the Russian priests are much like the Protestants. Among the most magnificent buildings in the capital of Japan are those of the Russian Church, the indefatigable head being the archimandrite Nicolai, who is assisted by three other Russian clergy, and having about 1,700 baptized converts and 25,000 adherents. In a recent informal conference of native Christian workers without reference to the branches of the Church universal, the Greek Church was well represented. In some parts of Japan where these churches have been planted they have not held their own, the weak converts lapsing into heathenism and the earnest Bible-readers passing into Protestant churches.

Protestant Missions: The gates of Japan were first opened to the world through the influence of Americans, and the first Protestant missionaries to enter the country were Americans. The Protestant Episcopal, the Presbyterian, and the (Dutch) Reformed Churches in the United States sent out missionaries—Williams, Hepburn, and Verbeck—who settled in 1859 at Nagasaki and Yokohama. These missionaries at first obtained the right of residence only as teachers of English in Japanese schools; and when Goble, of the American Baptists, came to Japan in 1860, and Ensor, of the CMS, in 1869, and Greene, Gulick, and Davis, of the American Board, in 1871, they were allowed at first to work as teachers rather than as preachers of the Gospel. This "silent sowing" continued until 1873, when the old edict against Christianity was repealed; and after this date many missionary societies, from America, England, Scotland, and Germany, entered the promising field. The revolution in 1868 left Japan in a state of unrest; and during the next fifteen years, as a witness of the events narrates, the condition of affairs is almost without parallel. "Missionary schools were crowded with the sons and daughters of high and low. A missionary was called to lay the foundation of a national university, and to be a general adviser of the government. Statesmen, men of wealth, governors, and lower officials became the patrons of Christian schools and sometimes opened their houses for religious services. From all quarters came requests to hold meetings in school-houses and theaters; audiences numbering several hundreds, sometimes 1,000 or 1,500, were readily got together, and they would listen to a succession of speakers through four or five hours, or even longer. We have seen the power of God to-day was a frequent ejaculation. Witnesses of those scenes will never forget them. In every three years the Church was doubled. These years of the appropriation and more or less thorough assimilation of the best of Western thought and life were the most momentous in the nation's history. This period more than all others was creative of the New Japan." Indeed, until 1889 Japanese missions grew steadily in power; but from that time until now the work has been marked by lessening progress, pause, and even retrogression. From 1884 until 1889 the number of adult evangelical Christians rose from 5,000 to 29,000; but in 1899 it was only about 41,800. In 1888 the number of adult baptisms for the year reached 7,700; but in 1892 it was only 3,700, and now it scarcely keeps up to this number. As Warneck says: "The rapid advance was occasioned far less by a universal hunger and thirst after righteousness, than by the cooperation of a number of factors unconnected with religion, which wrought a change of mind in favor of Christianity as an educational and cultural force, particularly among wide circles of the educated classes. The disestablishment of the native religions of the state, the new legislature, which paved the way for Christianity, and the recommendation of it on grounds of politics and culture produced an atmosphere favorable for missions, in which the plenteously scattered seed of the Gospel was shone on as by the sun." The reaction that followed lasted until nearly the close of the last century; but the period of opposition seems to have reached its culmination. Since the revision of the treaties, in 1899, and the attitude of Japan in the Chinese Boxer uprising of 1900, a change for the better is apparent, and the forces that make for righteousness are moving forward. The latest statistics available give the following data for 1900: Missionaries 757, stations 157 (including many where more than one society labor, so that the number is too large by about fifty); organized churches 443, of which 95 are self-supporting; church members 42,451, native ministers 321, unordained preachers and helpers 558, Bible women 224. There are 16 boys' boarding schools, with 2,270 pupils, 45 girls' boarding schools with 3,361 pupils, 85 day schools with 6,086 pupils, 949 Sunday schools, with 36,310 pupils, 16 theological schools with 120 students, 13 schools for Bible women with 175 students, 6 hospitals and 8 dispensaries, at which 2,121 patients had been treated during the year. Of the societies at work in Japan, there are thirty-one from America and Canada, seven from Great Britain, one from the Continent, and these are enforced by the work of the Salvation Army, the Hephzibah Faith Mission and four local societies.

Christian literature in the vernacular is one of the most powerful forces in the evangelization of Japan. From 1895 to 1899 the Tract Society issued 2,460,000 tracts, and the religious press has been busy in this line of work.

The Bible in Japanese: A veteran missionary ascribes one-half of all the results of Christian missions in Japan to the work of the Bible societies. Of these, the American, the British and Foreign, and the National Bible Society of Scotland have agencies in Japan, and have diligently prosecuted the work of publication and distribution, besides making generous contributions for the expenses of translation. The work of giving the Bible to this nation was begun, as said above, by Rev. Karl Gutzlaff and Dr. S. Wells Williams, and vigorously pressed forward by Rev. J. Goble, S. R. Brown, D.D., and Dr. J. C. Hepburn on the opening of the country by treaty. In 1872 all the Protestant missionaries were invited to meet in Yokohama to form a Translation Committee, which in June, 1874, began its sittings, and on the 3d of November, 1879, finished its work of translation and revision of the New Testament. In April, 1880, the complete New Testament was in the hands of the native Christians. A few months previously Rev. Nathan Brown, D.D., published a version of the New Testament in which the words relating to baptism were translated, and not, as in the union version, transliterated, from the Greek. Plans for translating the Old Testament were not made until 1876, nor perfected until 1882. On the 3d of February, 1888, at a large meeting held in Tokio, the completion of the entire Bible in Japanese was celebrated. Besides many missionaries there were in hearty and able cooperation with the committee the native scholars, Matsuyama, Takahashi, Iyémura, Ibuka, and others. These brethren have enabled their foreign teachers to present to the Japanese people a version at once scholarly, idiomatic, readable, rhythmic, and destined in all probability to be the standard for generations to come. In the language of this union version of the Holy Scriptures special prominence is given to the native element, as against the Chinese-Japanese so fashionable during the last half-century or more.

Since January, 1890, the total sales and gifts of Bibles have been 29,156; New Testaments 116,371 and portions 749,455, making a total of 944,000. One Bible seller sold (largely portions) during the last four months of 1899, 22,298 volumes. While in 1883 there were only four religious journals, in 1894 there were forty, and in 1900 there were ninety-five reported, of which four were weekly newspapers and seventy were monthly.

Tokio, the capital, is largely the distributing center of the Gospel in Japan; and here twenty per cent. of all the workers are located, and institutional Christianity has a plant established at this commercial emporium valued at 1,200,000 yen, or about $600,000.

A notable meeting of the Evangelical Alliance of Japan was held at Osaka in April, 1900, and it was decided to enter upon special evangelistic work throughout the Empire at the beginning of the new century. The General Conference of Missionaries, which met at Tokio in October, 1900, appointed a committee of ten to cooperate with the Committee of the Alliance in furthering this special work for Japan's evangelization. These efforts have been attended by blessed results. From May 12 to June 30, 1901, meetings were held in fifty-two churches in Tokio alone, attended by more than 100,000, and resulting in 5,307 converts or inquirers. Japanese students have been deeply affected by this evangelistic movement; and in October, 1901, during the meetings held by Mr. John R. Mott, over four hundred, within three days, decided to become disciples of Jesus Christ. Many are praying, working and hoping for the redemption of Japan during the first generation of the 20th century; and this blessed result depends upon the faith and works of the people of God.

Griffis (W. E.), *Japan in History, Folklore, and Art*, New York, 1892; *The Mikado's Empire*, New York, 1896; ——*Verbeck of Japan*, New York, 1899; Gulick (S, L.), *Evolution of the Japanese*, New York, 1903; *The Ainu of Japan*, London, 1892; Bishop (Isabella Bird), *Unbeaten Tracks in Japan*, 3d ed., New York, 1883; Gordon (M.L.), *American Missionary in Japan*, Boston, 1892; Thorpe (P), *History of Japan*, London, 1885; Peery (R. B.), *The Gist of Japan*, New York, 1901.

JARKEND. See YARKAND.

JARO: A suburb of Iloilo, in the S. E. of the island of Panay, Philippine Islands. Station of the ABMU (1900), with 1 missionary and 1 native worker.

JATKI LANGUAGE. See MULTANI.

JAUNPUR: A town in the United Provinces, India, situated on the Gumti River, 37 miles N. W. by N. of Benares. It was formerly the capital of a large Muslim kingdom. It has many fine buildings, and is celebrated for its manufactures of perfumes. Population (1891), 42,000, of whom 26,000 are Hindus and 16,000 Mohammedans. Station of the Zenana Bible and Medical Mission, with (1900) 3 women missionaries, 10 women native workers, 6 day schools and a dispensary.

JAVA: An island of the Indian Archipelago, situated in latitude 5° 2' to 8° 50' south, and longitude 105° 12' to 114° 39' east, is one of the richest colonial possessions of the Netherlands, and in respect to its population, its natural beauty, the mildness of its climate, and the industry of its people, is the most important of all the islands of the archipelago. The area of the island is 50,260 square miles. Its greatest length is from east to west, 666 miles, with a breadth varying from 56 to 136 miles. With Madura included in the official Java, its area is 50,554 square miles. The mountain range which forms the central ridge is of volcanic nature, and there are still many active volcanoes. The highest is Semeru, 12,238 feet. The climate of Java, with the exception of some marshy districts in the northern plains, is healthful and very salubrious. The heat is not intense, but the long continuance of it proves trying to European constitutions, which at first are not affected by it. In the interior tablelands the climate is colder and more bracing.

Java is under the government of the Netherlands. The East India Company, created by the Dutch in 1602, gradually conquered the Dutch East Indies, and when the Company was dissolved in 1798 the mother country took over the control of all its Dutch possessions, and since 1830 the Netherlands has been undisturbed in its supremacy. The island is divided into residencies, each governed by a resident, who, with his assistants, exercises almost absolute control by means of a vast hierarchy of native officials. There are 22 of these residencies, including Madura. The population is very dense, numbering in 1900 28,745,698. Of these, over 50,000 are Europeans, 225,500 Chinese, 15,000 Arabs, and the remainder natives. The natives belong to the Malay race, and are divided into the Javanese proper, the Sundanese, and the Madurese. The Malay type is best retained in the Sundanese, while the Javanese are the most civilized. In early times a warlike, ferocious spirit must have characterized the Javanese, but now they are peaceable, docile, sober and industrious. Under Dutch rule the condition of the people has been most prosperous, and is improving rapidly under their wise and judicious administration.

Religion: Nominally the natives are Mohammedans, since the Hindu dynasty was overthrown in the 15th century by the Mohammedans; in former times they were Buddhists and Brahmans, as Hindu civilization was introduced early in the Christian era. The result has been that fragments from all these religious systems are interwoven with their original spirit-worship, and the latter has absorbed the foreign element and still remains the dominant faith of the people.

Language: Javanese is the prevailing speech, and is found in two distinct styles—the court speech and the plain talk among the people.

The three principal towns of Java are Batavia (115,887), Samarang (89,286), and Surabaya (146,944).

Mission work is carried on by the Netherlands Missionary Society in East Java, where the Dutch Baptist Society has also one station. The Netherlands Missionary Union has stations in West Java. Besides these there are the following societies: The Protestant Church in Netherlands East Indies, Java Comité, Mennonite Missionary Society, Ermelo Missionary Society, Christian Reformed Church, and the Dutch Missionary Society. The Netherlands Missionary Union has at this date (1902) 13 missionaries employed on the island, and a church membership of 25,000. The chief station of all missions on the island is Modjowarno, but in connection with this center of missionary activity there are a number of churches, a seminary for native preachers, several schools and a hospital. The Christian community under the care of these missionaries outnumber 4,000.

JAVA COMITÉ. See NETHERLANDS; MISSIONARY SOCIETIES OF THE.

JAVANESE LANGUAGE: Belongs to the Malayan family and is spoken by about 13,000,000 people in the island of Java. It has been used for literary purposes by missionaries of Dutch societies, and sometimes written with Roman letters. It is more often written with the Javanese characters, however, and sometimes with Arabic letters.

JAYPUR. See JAIPUR.

JEHLAM: A town in the Punjab, India, on the north bank of Jehlam River. Climate, hot; healthful in winter. Population (1891), 12,900, of whom 7,400 are Mohammedans and 4,300 Hindus. Station of the UP (1875), with 2 missionaries and their wives, 4 women missionaries, 3 day schools, a medical class, and a dispensary. Name also written Jhelum.

JELLASORE. See JALESWAR.

JERICHO: A settlement in the Transvaal Colony, S. Africa; situated 28 miles N. N. W. of Pretoria. Station of the Hermannsburg Missionary Society (1880), with (1900) 1 missionary and his wife, 1 native worker, and 1 day school.

JERUSALEM: From the time of the Crusades Jerusalem has been a special point for missionary work. Each of the different branches of the Christian Church, European and Oriental, have had their representatives there. The strongest element has been and still is the Greek, the Greek Patriarch receiving the support and encouragement of the Russian Government. Next in strength come, perhaps, the Armenians, who have a large convent and church. The Latins have not been very strong until recent times. The conflicts between these different branches of the Church have been such as to excite the derision and contempt of the Muslims, who have been compelled to guard the holy places by sentries in order to prevent Christians from destroying each other in the places that they affect to reverence. Jerusalem has also been, naturally, a gathering place of the Jews, and numerous efforts have been put forth, like the present Zionist movement, to establish this race in their ancient capital. It has seemed, however, as if the very presence of the Holy Place acted upon them so as to destroy all sense of religion, and the Jews of Jerusalem have been notoriously the worst specimens of their race. Of late years, however, with the efforts of such men as Sir Moses Montefiore, and those who with him have sought to establish Jewish colonies, not in Jerusalem itself, but in the country, somewhat of a change has taken place. Modern Jerusalem is the capital of a detached district of Asiatic Turkey, the governor reporting directly to Constantinople. A large, new city has grown up outside of the walls. The population is estimated at about 40,000. Station of the London Society for Promoting Christianity among the Jews (1823), with (1903) 38 missionaries, men and women; 29 native workers, 3 day schools, 1 industrial school, 2 dispensaries, 1 hospital, and a printing house. Station also of the CMS (1851), with (1903) 17 women missionaries, 1 elementary school and 1 hospital. Station also of the Berlin Jerusalem Union, and of the Christian and Missionary Alliance, and of several independent missionary enterprises. When the ABCFM sent its first missionaries to the Levant in 1810, they were expected to establish themselves at Jerusalem and thence go forth to other parts of Turkey. This was quickly found to be impracticable, and from that day to this there has been no disposition on the part of either of the American societies working in Turkey to enter a place already occupied by many missionaries. All the branches of the Eastern Church have patriarchs or bishops at Jerusalem. It is an important ecclesiastical center of the Roman Catholic Church, and the Church of England also maintains a bishop there.

JERUSALEM UNION (in Berlin). See GERMANY; MISSIONARY SOCIETIES IN.

JEWETT, Fayette: Born at Newbury, Vt., August 15, 1824; graduated at Vermont University 1848; studied medicine and practised at Nashua, N. H. In September, 1852, he decided to devote himself to the foreign mission work, and being accepted by the ABCFM, sailed for Turkey March 14, 1853. He was first stationed at Tocat, then at Sivas, and in 1858 at Yozgat, these changes being required by the necessities of the work and the missionary families. He was a pioneer in medical work in these places. He was ordained as an evangelist at Constantinople May 28, 1857. In 1860 he returned to the United States to seek relief from a peculiar and distressing affection, and on the return journey he died at Liverpool, June 18.

JEWETT, Rev. Lyman: Born in Waterford, Me., March 9, 1813; graduated from Brown University in 1843 and took a course of study at Newton Theological Institution. He was appointed a missionary of the ABMU in 1847.

He began his labors at Madras, afterward removing to Nellore; but in the closing years of his missionary service he returned to Madras, there closing a period of thirty-eight years of consecrated, wise and successful work in the foreign field. He was notable for a rare combination of true humility and great self-reliance. For years he was the only missionary on the Telugu field, and it was largely due to his self-sacrifice and firmness of purpose that the field was not abandoned by the Baptists of America. He lived to see the fruitage of his early toil. He died at Fitchburg, Mass., January 7, 1897.

JEWS, The: *Locality and Religious State:* In the time of Christ, Jewish communities had spread through all the countries bordering on the Mediterranean, and only a small part of Israel was still living in Palestine. This part was still further reduced, if not completely destroyed, by Titus in 70, Hadrian in 135 and Heraclius in 628, and not until the 19th century did Palestine once more become the abode of a large Jewish population. As civilization advanced toward the north, Jews became domiciled also in Central Europe. In the middle ages they were chiefly settled in Spain and Germany. But persecution drove many Spanish Jews to the other Mediterranean countries, especially to Italy, Asia Minor and Palestine; and for the same reason many German Jews moved toward the East, into the Polish empire, at that time reaching from the Baltic to the Black Sea. Still earlier some emigrations had taken place to Arabia, Persia, India and China; but as those sporadic settlements — with which must also be reckoned the Fallashas of Abyssinia, who had adopted Judaism—maintained no regular communications with the main bulk of the people, they actually lost the knowledge of their own religion, and the revival which lately has taken place among them is due to the exertions of the Jews in Europe. The Jews also took part in the European colonization of America, going mostly to the northern part of that continent, less frequently to the southern and central; and recently both Australia and South Africa have received some smaller and less important Jewish colonies. The table below, based on the Jewish Year Book for 1902, gives a general view of the distribution of the Jewish race, it being remembered, however, that, as is stated below, such tables are estimates impossible of verification:

EUROPE:
Germany	581,519	
Austria-Hungary	1,868,222	
Russia	5,186,000	
Turkey in Europe	132,737	
Rumania	269,015	
Servia	5,012	
Italy	38,000	
Switzerland	12,551	
Greece	5,792	
Denmark	4,080	
Sweden-Norway	3,402	
Great Britain-Ireland	230,356	
Holland	103,988	
Belgium	4,000	
Spain	402	
France	80,000	
		8,525,076

ASIA:
Turkey in Asia	246,511	
Turkestan	14,000	
Persia	35,000	
China	1,501	
		297,012

AFRICA:
Egypt	15,000	
Tunis	45,000	
Tripoli	8,000	
Algeria	57,132	
Morocco	150,000	
Abyssinia	120,000	
		395,132

AMERICA:
United States	1,136,240	
Central and S. America	14,780	
		1,151,020

Total..10,368,240

These ten and one-half million Jews are, as the table shows, very unequally distributed over the earth, and it seems apparent that the missionary activity developed among them should stand in some proportion to the density and strength of each single settlement. Thus, as long as there are countries which have only one missionary for every 50,000 Jews, new mission stations should not be established in countries which have a much smaller Jewish element in their population. Nor should the activity ever be concentrated to such a degree as is the case in Palestine, where there is a missionary for every one thousand Jews.

The medieval division of the Jews into Sephardim or Spaniards, Aschkenasim or Germans, and Moghrabim or North Africans, has lost to some extent its significance. Other distinctions have become more prominent than that of descent. Nevertheless in some connections it is still instructive.

Sephardim communities, numbering in all hardly more than 400,000 members, are found in Italy, Greece, Turkey and sporadically also in France, Holland and England. The Aschkenasim, who form the principal mass of the Jewish people and number over five millions, have their chief seat in Germany, Austria-Hungary and Russia, but make also the larger part of the Jewish population in France, Italy, England and Palestine. The North American Jews are almost without exception Aschkenasim. The Moghrabim, numbering about 160,000, live in North Africa and Palestine.

On account of their common German descent all the Aschkenasim used originally the German language, in an old and somewhat mutilated dialect, strongly mixed up with Hebrew words, and in Poland and Russia also with Slavic words. This language was by the Jews themselves called simply "Jewish," but by others either Judæo-German, or, by a mistake, "Judæo-Polish." In Germany it has now nearly disappeared. There, as in Hungary, England, France and America, it has, at least among the educated Jews, been wholly superseded by the language of the land. In Russia, Poland and Galicia, however, and among the numerous emigrants thence to England, North America and Palestine, "Jewish" is still the common speech, and a missionary among them must understand it. The Sephardim in the Orient have also retained their Spanish dialect. The Moghrabim generally speak the Arabic dialect common in the land in which they live.

All three classes of Jews—that is, so far as their members can be designated as belonging to the old faith—follow the rabbinical law such as it has been laid down in the Talmud, and afterward codified in the Mischna, Thora and Schulchan Aruch. Their form of worship has a common basis, fixed in Babylonia between the 6th and 9th centuries. Through different additions and changes in the different countries, there developed from this common basis quite a number of different rituals, but most of these have afterward given way either to that of the Aschkenasim or to that of the Sephardim.

In religious belief, however, there are, as above indicated, Jews of the old faith and Jews of the new faith. When toward the close of the 18th century the Jews began in great numbers to take part in the development of modern civilization, those concerned in the movement could not fail to recognize that the rabbinical law contains much which is superstitious and inhumane; that the divine service needed a reorganization, especially by the introduction of sermons in the language of the land; that the youth ought to have a fuller instruction in the Bible and the elements of doctrine and ethics; and, acting on this conviction, the natural result was that there arose a distinction between the Jews living in central and western Europe, or in the United States, and the Jews settled in, or coming from, eastern Europe. The latter retained Judaism in its old medieval form; the former entered upon a development demanded by the times.

Among the Jews of the new faith there must further be made a distinction between the orthodox party and the party of the reform. The orthodox follow the rabbinical law, tho purged from its extravagances; use Hebrew in their own worship, tho with occasional sermons in the language of the land; and expect, through confidence in the promises of the Prophets, that all Israel shall some day return home to Palestine. The reformers reject the rabbinical law, use partially or wholly the language of the land in their divine service, and consider themselves genuine citizens of the state to which they belong. But most of them have given up confidence in the infinite development of the moral and religious truths contained in the law and the Prophets, and many of them have lost all religious conviction, and become absorbed in mere materialism.

In the 18th century there also developed two larger groups among the Jews of the old faith, namely, the Peruschim or Mithnagdim and the Chasidim. The Peruschim are followers of the Talmud, the Chasidim of a later form of the mysticism of Theosophy. This must not be understood, however, as if the Peruschim stood in no relation to the Kabbala, for the Kabbala has so thoroughly permeated medieval Judaism that it has left traces of itself on every leaf of it. Nor are the Chasidim in opposition to the Talmud; they only wish to keep the study of it within certain limits, in favor of prayer and contemplation. Characteristic of them is their reverence for holy men who through prayer and contemplation are said to have come into closer relations with God, and thereby to be able to give infallible counsel and to confer heavenly blessings on their adherents.

Violent controversies take place between the Peruschim and the Chasidim, between the orthodox and the reformers, between those of the old faith and those of the new faith; one party accuses the other of having dealings with Gentiles (Christians) and the other turns off the accusation by scoffing at the superstitions of its antagonists. But they all agree in the profession of belief in one single God, with whose very essence the idea of a trinity is as incongruous as that of an incarnation, and in the conviction that Israel is specially selected to represent this faith among the nations of the earth. Thus, while the monotheism of the Old Testament is directed against polytheism, the monotheism—or rather, unitarianism—of modern Judaism is a protest against Christianity. No one of the four parties is any nearer to Christianity than the other three. The orthodox are prevented from accepting the Gospel by their strict but superficial legality, the reformers by their loose religious sense, the Peruschim by their hair-splitting subtlety—the result of their Talmudic studies—and the Chasidim by their blind fanaticism.

Missions among them: The mission among the Jews is as old as the Christian Church, and the Church can never fully do justice to the last words of the Savior without preaching the Gospel unto the Jews. Altho the cross was a stumbling block to them, yet the first Christian community consisted entirely of Jews.

Commencing with the family of Jesus, Himself, we have Mary, Joseph, with the at first unbelieving brothers, but afterward all united with one accord in prayer and supplication (Acts i: 14); James and Joseph and Simon and Judas (Matt. xiii: 55); further, Mary, the wife of Cleopas (John xix: 25), and, then, the greater number who were converted by the miracles of Christ on His travels (John viii: 20; x: 42). We must not omit Mary Magdalene (Luke viii: 2), Joanna, the wife of Chuza, Herod's steward (Luke viii: 3; xxiv: 10), Susanna (Luke viii: 3), Salome, the mother of the apostles John and James (Matt. xx: 20); Mary and Martha, the sisters of Lazarus of Bethany (John xi), and Mary, the converted sinner.

In the higher ranks we find Nicodemus, Jairus, one of the rulers of the synagog (Mark v: 22); the nobleman at Capernaum with his whole house (John iv: 46); Zacchæus, the chief among the publicans (Luke xix: 2); Joseph of Arimathæa, an honorable counselor (Mark xv: 43; Luke xxiii: 50). To these are to be added the multitudes who were healed by Christ's miracles, and who therefore believed in Him—such as blind Bartimæus (Mark x: 46); the disciples of John, who were by him directed to the Lamb of God; the twelve apostles, with Matthias (Acts i: 25); the seventy disciples, who were appointed and sent forth after the twelve (Luke x:). According to 1 Cor. xv: 6, Christ was, after His resurrection, seen of above five hundred brethren at once. When Matthias was numbered with the eleven apostles, there were about one hundred and twenty members of the congregation called together. By the preaching of Peter at the Pentecost three thousand souls were added (Acts II.). By the preaching and bold confession of Peter and John the number was increased to about five thousand, when it is said believers were the more added to the Lord, multitudes both of men and women (Acts v: 14), and the number of the disciples multiplied in Jerusalem greatly, and a great company of the priests were obedient to the faith (Acts vi: 7). At his last sojourn in Jerusalem Paul finds there "many thousands of Jews," or rather "tens of thousands" (Acts xxi: 20), which believed, altho the greatest portion of the congregation, after the murder of Stephen, were all scattered abroad by the great persecution, as far as Phenice, Cyprus and Antioch (Acts viii: 1; xi: 19).

The assistants of the apostles, who left Jerusalem in order to preach the Gospel were: first, Saul, the Benjaminite; then Joseph Barsabas, surnamed Justus (Acts i: 23); Joses Barnabas, the Levite of Cyprus (iv: 36); Ananias, the disciple at Damascus (ix: 10); John Mark the Levite, evangelist, son of Mary (xii: 2; xv: 37); Timothy, son of the Christian Jewess, Eunice (xvi: 1); Aquila, with his wife Priscilla (xviii: 2); Apollos of Alexandria (xviii: 24); Zenas, the lawyer who preached the Gospel in Crete (Titus III: 13); Rufus and Alexander, the sons of Simon the Cyrenian (Mark xv: 21; Rom. xvi: 13).

Besides John, certain of the number of Jewish believers were prophets of the New Covenant; thus the daughters of Philip the evangelist (Acts xxi: 9); Judas and Silas (xv: 32); Agabus (xi: 28); Simon, Niger and Lucius of Cyrene and Manaen (Acts xiii: 1).

It is stated that the inhabitants of Saron and Lydda turned to the Lord; one of them was Eneas (Acts ix: 33). At Joppa many believed in the Lord on account of Tabitha being raised from the dead by Peter (Acts ix:). At Cesarea Paul found many believers, among whom were Philip the evangelist (already mentioned) with his four daughters, and Mñason, an old disciple (xxi: 16).

Beyond the boundaries of Palestine we find Christians in Antioch (Acts xiii: 43), and a great multitude of believers at Iconium (xv: 1). We may mention Jason, Aristarchus and Secundus at Thessalonica (xvii: 6; xx: 4); Sopater, of the flourishing congregation at Berea (xx: 4); Gaius of Derbe (Rom. xvi: 23); Tyrannus, who kept a school at Ephesus; Justus and Crispus and Sosthenes, chief rulers of the synagog at Corinth (Acts xviii: 7, 8, 17; 1 Cor. i: 1), and the numerous believing Jews at Philippi and Rome (Acts xxviii: 24).

The first nucleus of the seven apocalyptic churches consisted also of Israelites. Peter wrote the first epistle in the midst of a Jewish-Christian Church at Babylon, and addressed it to the strangers scattered throughout Pontus, Galatia, Cappadocia, Asia and Bithynia. James also wrote his epistle "to the twelve tribes which are scattered abroad," and this proves that in the most remote countries there were believing Israelites.

It is but natural to assume that these believing Israelites were the means of spreading, if not the Gospels as such, yet the sayings of Jesus. Thus these sayings found their way into the Talmud, a fact overlooked by modern Jewish apologists who claim the priority of the Talmud to the New Testament, and make the latter the copy of the former.

According to Eusebius, up to the reign of the Emperor Hadrian (120) there were fifteen Jewish-Christian bishops at Jerusalem. Among the teachers of the ancient church who were of Jewish origin we may mention *Hegesippus* (150-180); *Ariston of Pella*, and especially *Epiphanius*, Bishop of Constantia, who also tells (*Haeres.* xxx) of the conversion of the Jewish patriarch Hillel, a descendant of the famous Gamaliel.

Without dwelling on the manner in which the Christian Church developed itself, which, on the one hand gave cause to the Jews for complaining of the great zeal of the Church in converting them, and on the other hand, to the Church for complaining of the great obstinacy of the Jews, we will glance at some of the most famous converts prior to the Reformation, who were especially animated to spread the Gospel among their former coreligionists. But be it remembered that these converts were only samples of a whole list of witnesses to the power of the truth—single ears selected out of a multitude of sheaves gathered into the garner of God.

Commencing with *Spain* we find in the latter part of the 7th century *Julian Pomerius*,[1] archbishop of Toledo (died 690), author of a work against the errors of Judaism concerning the coming of the Messiah, entitled: *De sexta aetatis comprobatione contra Judaeos.*

Between 1066 and 1108 flourished *Pedro Alfonso*, formerly Rabbi Moses of Huesca in Aragon, physician to King Alfonso VI., and author of an apologetical work against the Jews.

A contemporary of Pedro Alfonso was *Samuel*, by birth an African, but baptized in Toledo in 1085. He returned to Morocco, where he held a public discussion with a learned Arab on the truth of Christianity. Of other converts we mention *John de Valladolid;* also *John de Podico* of the 14th century; Joseph Hallorki, called after his baptism *Hieronymus de Sancta Fide*, of the 15th century, famous as Talmudist and physician.

But the greatest of all were *Paulus of Burgos*, and *De Santa Maria*, formerly Rabbi Solomon Levi of Burgos, and baptized with his four sons in 1390. He studied theology after his baptism and received from the University of Paris the degree of Doctor of Divinity. He was appointed Archdeacon of Burgos, and subsequently Bishop of Carthagena and lastly Bishop of Burgos, where also he died August 25, 1440. Of his four sons, Don Alfonso, who for many years was archdeacon of Compostella, succeeded his father in the bishopric of Burgos. He took his seat at the Council of Basel in 1431, as a representative of Castile, and was treated with high honor on account of his great talents and distinguished excellence.

Without increasing the number, suffice it to say that even the Jewish historian Graetz, by no means a friend of the Church, still less of converts, must admit: "By the conversion of learned and educated men, physicians, authors, poets, Judaism was deprived of many talents; some of them were possessed of a zeal for conversion, as if they were born Dominicans." (*Geschichte* viii: 83.)

In *France* we hear, besides, of *Nicolas de Lyra*, professor of theology (1300-1340), who was of Jewish descent; of *Philipp D'Aquin* (died 1650), professor of Hebrew at Paris; *Louis Compiegne de Veil* and his brother *Charles*; *Pierre Vignoles* (died 1640), for fifty years professor at the College of Paris.

In *Italy* the Jews had to listen, since the time of Gregory XIII., once a week to a sermon, and many a one was thus led to Christ. Paul III. founded in 1550 a special institute for the conversion of the Jews. The 16th century is especially rich in Jewish converts, of whom we mention the following: *Andreas de Monte, Jechiel Pisaurensis*, philosopher and physician, and his contemporary, *Paul Eustachius de Nola*, Hebrew teacher of Thomas Aldrobrandin, brother of Pope Clement

---

[1] For more particulars the reader is referred to my articles on this and other converts in McClintock and Strong's *Theolog. Cyclop.* including vol. xi., xii. forming the supplement volumes.

VIII.; *Sixtus Senensis*, author of the *Bibliotheca Sancta* (Venice, 1566); *Alessandro di Francesco*, friend of Clement VIII. and Bishop of Forti; *Fabianus Fioghi*, professor of Hebrew at the college of the Neophites at Rome; *Emmanuel Tremellius*, one of the most celebrated men of his time (said to have been converted by Marco Antonio Flaminio), who died in 1580; *Paulus Canossa;* also *Paulus Paradisus*, professor of Hebrew (died 1543); *Felix Pratensis* (died at Rome, 1539), editor of the First Rabbinic Hebrew Bible; *Raphael Aquilino, John Baptista Elianus*, and others too numerous to be mentioned.

In *England* the Jews had their vicissitudes. Yet in spite of the manifold troubles special care was taken of those who embraced Christianity. Special buildings, converts' houses, were created, in which the Gospel was not only preached to the Jews, but the converts were educated there, and many a dignitary in the State and Church proceeded from these houses. We shall again speak of England in the sequel.

In *Germany* the Jews had to undergo many sufferings. The inroads of the Tatars, the Crusades, more especially the Black Death, were causes for persecutions. Compulsory baptisms were the only means of escaping the fiercest persecutions, and it was in vain that some popes, and teachers like Bernard of Clairvaux, protested against such compulsory measures. Yet there were not wanting such among the Jews who could not resist the workings of the divine grace, and who of their own conviction joined the Church. This we see especially in the case of Herman of Cappenberg, who after his baptism entered in 1123 the order of the Premonstratensians and became abbot of Cappenberg in Westphalia. He, too, protested against compulsory measures, but in vain. In the 19th session of the Council at Basel in 1434 it was enacted that the bishops everywhere should see that the Jews were instructed in the Christian religion. The worldly powers showed a better disposition toward the Jews by protecting them, altho this protection was bought at a great price. Yet, after all, shortly before the Reformation, a better spirit seemed to prevail in Germany, which had the good effect that many a Jew was brought to the truth as it is in Christ, without compulsion.

In our rapid survey we have come down to the Reformation period, with which a brighter morning came, tho, on the whole, the Reformation, whether in its early days or in later times, with all its great teachers and numerous adherents, effected little or no change in the disposition of the Christians toward the Jews. Luther appeared well disposed toward them in the beginning of his career as a reformer. But afterward he spoke very differently of the Jews, either from indignation at some theologians of Wittenberg, whom he looked upon as infused with the leaven of rabbinism, or from disappointment because the Reformation, by which he had promised a favorable influence over the minds of the Jews and their conversion to the Gospel, found no more favor or assistance than Romanism with this entirely singular nation.

Yet after all it cannot be denied that the influence which the Reformation exerted, especially by the more careful study of the Bible and its translation, had a salutary effect on the people in general and on the clergy especially. In speech and in writing, the preachers and teachers endeavored to impress upon the Jewish mind the truth as it is in Christ, and in this respect they were assisted by the writings of such Jewish Christians as *Paul Staffelsteiner*, professor of Hebrew at Heidelberg; *John Harzuge*, who in 1540 published his translation of the New Testament in rabbinical type; *Christian Gerson* and *Georg Philip Lichtenstein*, both ministers of the Gospel; *Victor von Carben*, a priest at Cologne; *Paul Weidner*, and others of the Roman Catholic Church.

A new impulse was given to the missions among the Jews in the 17th century, especially by the efforts of Esdras Edzard, of Hamburg. He had studied at different universities and had especially devoted himself to the study of rabbinic literature. Buxtorf, in Basel, and the Jewish rabbi of his native place, Cohen de Lara, were his teachers in Talmudic literature. In 1656 he took his degree as licentiate of theology at Rostock without entering upon the academical career. Being a man of means, he lived as a private man at Hamburg, devoting his knowledge and time to the conversion of the Jews, and he succeeded in bringing a great many Jews to Christ. He not only preached the Gospel, but also helped those in a practical manner who had joined the Church, and founded a sinking fund, the interest of which was to be devoted to missions among the Jews. From all parts of Europe scholars flocked to Hamburg to hear from him how to converse with Jews and how to refute their arguments. After his death, in 1708, Edzard's sons continued the work of their father, and the sinking fund, founded in 1667, is now under the administration of the Hamburg Senate, still serving the original purpose. The good seed sown by Edzard bore its fruit in due season, and in many places houses were built for the temporal relief of Jewish converts.

Outside of Germany, the Christians of *Holland* showed an especial interest for the conversion of the Jews, to whom, toward the end of the 16th century, permission had been granted to settle again in Holland. The Synod, held at Dort in 1619, at Utrecht in 1670, and at Delft and Leyden in 1676 and 1678, passed resolutions concerning the spiritual welfare of the Jews. Men like *Hugo Grotius, Labbadie, Isaac Vossius, John Hoornbeck*, the two *Spanhems, Coccejus, Episcopius, Hulsius, Witsius, Serarius*, and others, wrote with a view of convincing the Jews, and many a Jew was received into the Church.

The Jews, formerly banished from *England*, were again allowed to settle there under Charles II. We have already spoken of the early missionary work among the Jews in England. Suffice it to say that after the resettlement of the Jews the work of converting them was continued. Of the literary productions of this period we only mention Bishop Kidder's *A demonstration of the Messiah, in which the truth of the Christian religion is defended, especially against the Jews*, London, 1684-1700, and translated also into German by F. E. Rambach, Rostock, 1751. Another missionary work was Leslie's *A short and easy method with the Jews*, London (1698, and after).

But we return again to Germany, where with the 18th century a new era commenced for the Mission among the Jews.

The first quarter of the 18th century was a period of great religious excitement in Germany, owing to the indefatigable labors of Spener and A. H. Francke (especially by the "collegia pietatis" of the former), which quickly spread far and wide, among high and low, poor and rich. The Bible, which had been entirely neglected and forgotten, was taken in hand and read again; and how extreme the desuetude into which the word of God had fallen may be gathered from the fact that Spener had to procure a special order from the Elector for the practical explanation of some part of the Bible at the universities. A fruit of this new life in the Church (for it was a complete regeneration) was the foundation of the University of Halle. Bible and missionary societies were also called into existence. Nor were God's ancient people forgotten. An interest for the Jews was evinced to a degree exceeding anything known in former periods of the Church. It seems as if rulers, magistrates, professors, the clergy had been alike animated with zeal for the conversion of Israel, for we find that Reineccius, in one of his works, published 1713, says: "The general topic of conversation and discussion of the present day is about the conversion of the Jews." This new-born zeal for the Jewish cause was so great that we are told that many Christians learned to read Jewish-German in order to make themselves better acquainted with Jewish books and more efficient for conversation with Jews. Professor Callenberg lectured on that language and had an auditory of 150 persons.

The Rev. John Müller of Gotha, who very often came in contact with traveling Jews, and took a lively interest in them, wrote a tract for the Jews, entitled *The Light of Eventide*, in dialogical form, which was intended to prepare the Jewish mind for the reception of Jesus Christ the Messiah, and through the extraordinary exertions of Dr. Frommann, a physician and Jewish convert, it was published in Jewish-German for wider circulation among the Jews. This tract produced the greatest sensation. For soon it was not only reprinted and translated into Hebrew, but also a German (1736), Dutch (1735), Italian(1732),French (1748) and an English translation was published, the latter by the Society for Promoting Christian Knowledge, in the year 1734, and it is still used for missionary purposes. Even Roman Catholic priests took an interest in its circulation and sent subscriptions for promoting it to Prof. Callenberg. This tract is the more remarkable because it became in part the foundation-stone for the well-known *Callenberg Institution*, or *Institutum Judaicum*, established in 1728, the object of which was the conversion of the Jews, and also of Mohammedans. This institution, however, was closed in 1792. But the interest in behalf of the Jews was not confined to Germany alone; it also spread beyond the Continent, for the well-known Jewish missionary, *Stephen Schultz*, tells us in his *Leitungen des Höchsten* (iv: 74), that when he visited England in 1749, he was told that there were many laymen in London zealous for the conversion of the Jews.

Next to Spener we must mention the early efforts made by the Moravian Brethren. It was in the year 1738 that Leonhard Dober, who had established the first mission among the negroes in the West Indies, felt an earnest desire to labor for the conversion of the Jews. For this purpose he repaired to Amsterdam and hired a lodging in the so-called Juden-Dork. In 1739 Samuel Lieberkühn succeeded Dober in Amsterdam, who devoted himself entirely to the service of the Jews. On account of his knowledge of Hebrew and his love of Israel, the Jews called him "Rabbi." For thirty years Lieberkühn labored among the Jews with great success.

The Callenberg Institute, as we have seen, was closed in the year 1792, but in the providence of God soon another way was to be opened for the mission among the Jews. It was only a few years after the first great thunderclap of the French Revolution, when three German students, in whose hearts God had begun a work of grace, were assembled together for mutual consultation and direction, in a room in the metropolis of Northern Germany. They were pondering in their minds what they should do, and whither they should go, that they might be successfully employed in the cause of missions. Berlin, their native metropolis, was at that time the stronghold of rationalism, the center of religious infidelity; and evangelical religion, or pietism, was above all things hated and almost universally spoken against. Where, therefore, were the three German students to go? Pastor Jänicke and some few other pious Christians in Berlin, who had established a seminary where six or seven students were trained for missionary enterprise, were often in the greatest straits for want of funds. Their cause met with little sympathy and they were almost in despair, when one day help came in time of need from another great metropolis, with a demand for three missionaries to occupy an important missionary post among the heathen tribes of Africa. This was in the autumn of 1801. Our three students went to London in order to enter the service of the London Missionary Society, and one of these was a Christian Israelite, C. F. Frey by name, who died in 1853 in America, a member of the Baptist denomination. During his stay in London it was put into his heart to visit his brethren after the flesh. He found them in a state of total darkness and bondage worse than that of their fathers in Egypt. He spoke to them of Christ and His salvation. He engaged a few Christian friends to feel a concern for their spiritual welfare. He made known to the directors of the London Missionary Society his earnest desire to be permitted to preach the Gospel to his own brethren. This application was favorably considered by the directors; they acceded to his request, and some three years having been consumed in the needful preliminary preparation, we find him, in 1805, commencing in earnest missionary work under the auspices of the London Missionary Society. It was soon, however discovered that the work required distinctive and peculiar machinery. Accordingly, after the brief existence of a few years, in 1808 a separate society, which contemplated Jews exclusively as its object, the present London Society for Promoting Christianity among the Jews, was founded in the beginning of 1809. The main promoter of this Society was the nobleman Lewis Way. It was in the year 1808 that Lewis Way, while riding with a friend of his in Devonshire, passed a park where some very fine trees attracted their attention. His friend told him that the owner of this park in her last will forbade the cutting down of these trees until "the Jews would again have come to Jerusalem." These words so deeply impressed themselves on the mind of Lewis Way that he never forgot them. From that day he devoted his large fortune as well as his talents to the conversion of the Jews. At the first the newly constituted society was composed both of churchmen and dissenters. In 1815, by an amicable arrangement, the dissenting members retired from its management, and its liabilities having been discharged by Way's munificent donation of £10,000, it entered on the present phase of its existence as a Church of England Society on the 11th of March, 1815. In the year 1814 the Duke of Kent, the father of the late Queen Victoria of England, laid the foundation-stone of the Episcopal Chapel in Palestine Place, in which up to this day divine service is held in different languages. This Society, which was so small at the beginning, has not only its own printing establishment of Hebrew Bibles, tracts, etc., but also its stations in Europe, Asia and Africa, occupying 52 stations, with a staff of about 200 laborers, of whom nearly 100 are Christian Israelites. It has recently also opened a station at Montreal, Canada. We have reached that period in the history of the mission among the Jews from which time on mission work is carried on systematically. In speaking of the missionary societies we must commence with England, as the motherland of the present Protestant Jewish mission.

I. *Great Britain:* 1. *England:* The London Society for Promoting Christianity among the Jews, founded in 1809, has over 50 stations, with 200 missionaries. It employs nearly 100 Christian Israelites, and has its stations in Europe, Asia, Africa and Canada. The Society has different institutions, as homes for inquiring Jews, homes for converts, homes for learning a trade, schools, hospitals, churches and colleges. The "Operative Institution," founded in 1831, has admitted about 1,000 persons, of whom more than 100 have entered the missionary service. The Wanderers' Home has received during the forty-five years of its existence over 2,500 Jews, most of whom were baptized. The Society records over 5,000 Jewish baptisms; the church record of Zion's Church, at Jerusalem, the oldest evangelical church in the East, shows nearly 600 Jewish baptisms. The annual income of the Society amounted March 31, 1903, to over £48,000. It receives an annual contribution from the Emperor of Germany and from India, Sierra Leone, Australia and Canada.

The British Society for the Propagation of the Gospel among the Jews, founded in 1842. It has 34 missionary workers in 18 stations in England, Germany, Austria, Russia, Turkey and Italy. It has schools, medical missions and homes for aged converts. Whereas the London Society distributes the Hebrew New Testament of Delitzseh, the British Society distributes the Salkinson-Ginsburg version, both Christian Israelites.

The Presbyterian Church of England, founded in 1860, has 8 missionary workers in London, Aleppo, Corfu, and a medical mission at Morocco.

The London City Mission (Jewish branch) employs 8 Hebrew Christians as missionaries to Jews and other foreigners.

The Parochial Missions to the Jews at Home and Abroad, founded in 1876, has 10 missionary workers in London, Manchester, Liverpool and Bombay.

The Mildmay Mission to the Jews, founded in London in 1876 by the Rev. John Wilkinson, has 67 missionary workers in London, Odessa, Minsk, Warsaw, Wilna and Lublin. The New Testament in Hebrew and Yiddish is distributed everywhere, and thousands of Jews in every part of the world are thus supplied with the word of God.

The Barbican Mission to the Jews, founded 1879; *The Hebrew Christian Testimony to Israel,* founded in 1894; *The Kilburn Mission to the Jews,* founded in 1896; *The Jerusalem and the East Mission Funds; The East London Fund for the Jews; The Wild Olive Mission; The East End Mission to the Jews; The Brook Lane Mission; The Hebrew-Christian Mission to Israel; The Christian Chief Corner-Stone Mission to the Jews; The Prayer Union for Israel,* and other small independent societies in London, Liverpool, and other English cities, are all concerned about Israel.

II. *Scotland: The Jewish Mission of the Church of Scotland,* founded in 1840, employs 40 workers in Smyrna, Salonica, Alexandria, Constantinople and Beirut, and has 10 schools.

The United Free Church of Scotland Mission to the Jews, founded in 1843, employs 80 workers in Edinburgh, Breslau, Budapest, Constantinople, Safed, and Tiberias, and has 8 schools.

The Scottish Home Mission to Jews, in Glasgow; *The Jewish Medical Mission,* in Edinburgh; *The Bonar Memorial Mission,* in Glasgow, and some small local societies all do good work.

III. *Ireland: The Jewish Mission of the Presbyterian Church in Ireland,* founded in 1841, has 20 workers in Hamburg, Altona and Damascus. The work in Hamburg is flourishing.

The Church of Ireland Jews' Society, founded in 1889, carries on work in Cork, Dublin and Belfast.

IV. *Germany:* Besides the Esdras Edzard Fund, mentioned already, we have:

The Society for Promoting Christianity among the Jews, in Berlin, founded in 1822. It has its stations in Berlin, Vienna and Stanislau.

The Central Organization of Evangelical Lutheran Missions among Israel, founded in 1871, in Leipzig, is supported by the Jewish missionary societies in Saxony, Bavaria, Wurtemberg and Hannover.

The West German Association in Cologne, founded in 1842, carries on its work in Cologne, Frankfort and Strasburg.

The Instituta Judaica, one at Leipzig, the other at Berlin, help to prepare theological students for the work among the Jews by making the students acquainted with Rabbinic and Jewish literature.

V. *Switzerland: The Society of the Friends of Israel,* in Basel, has a station at Strasburg and Prague.

VI. *France: The French Society for the Evangelization of Israel* employs 4 workers in Paris, Oran and Algiers.

VII. *The Netherlands: The Netherlands Society for Israel,* founded in 1861, has 2 missionaries at Amsterdam.

VIII. *Norway, Sweden and Denmark: The Central Committee for Jewish Missions,* in Christiania, works in Braila and Galatz.

The Evangelical National Society, in Stockholm, employs a missionary in Hamburg.

The Society for Missions to Israel, in Stockholm, has 9 workers in Sweden, Hungary and Russia.

The Swedish Missionary Union has 2 missionaries in Algiers.

The Society for Missions to Israel, in Copenhagen, supports a missionary in Stanislau.

IX. *Russia:* Missionary work is carried on by Pastor Faltin, of Kischinew.

X. *Africa, Asia and Australia:* In Africa we have the *Alexandria Jewish Mission;* in Asia we have small local societies in Bombay, Calcutta, Hebron, Jerusalem, whereas 4 missionary societies are working in Australia.

XI. *America:* There are some 30 American societies, denominational and undenominational or interdenominational. As missionary work is also carried on by individuals, it is very difficult to give correct lists.

Of the denominational societies we mention:
1. *The Church Society for Promoting Christianity among the Jews,* founded at New York in 1842. Its stations are in New York and Philadelphia.
2. *The Board of Foreign Missions of the Presbyterian Church,* founded in 1871, has been carrying on work among the Jews in Persia and Syria.
3. *The Reformed Presbyterian Mission to the Jews,* founded in 1894 at Philadelphia.
4. *Messiah Mission of Chicago,* founded in 1896 by Rev. Chalmers, continued since 1899 as *Mission of the Women's Association of the United Presbyterian Church of North America.*

The Lutheran Church is represented by
5. The Norwegian *Zionsforeningen for Israelsmissionen blandt Norske Lutheraneren i Amerika,* founded in 1878 at Minneapolis. It has stations in New York, Minsk and Odessa.
6. *Jewish Mission of the Evangelical Lutheran Synod of Missions, Ohio and other States,* founded in New York, 1885.
7. *Jewish Mission of the Joint Synod of Ohio,* founded 1892.
8. *Mission of the German Lutheran Synod in Chicago,* founded in 1894.
9. The Methodists founded in 1892 the *New York City Extension and Missionary Society.*
10. The Baptists founded in 1887 the *Missionary Society of the Seventh-Day Baptists.* Besides these missions, there are a number of independent workers and societies, which makes it impossible to give very accurate and complete statistics. Nevertheless, the work goes on everywhere. A German missionary has stated that during the 19th century about 300,000 Jews joined the Church; this number, if based upon records, is undoubtedly a conservative minimum, since it is very difficult to get access to the church records of the Roman Catholic and Greek Churches. Prof. Heman, in the third edition of the *Protestant Encyklopädie,* now edited by Prof. Hauck, of Leipzig, estimates that among the more than 10,000,000 Jews of the globe, more than 50 societies with about 500 workers do missionary work. According to the tables of the Rev. L. Meyer (see Appendix) this is a very low estimate.

The Rev. A. E. Thomson, in his book, "*A Century of Jewish Missions,*" gives the following numbers:

America	has 47	stations, with	80	missionaries.
Great Britain	" 120	"	" 481	"
Europe	" 29	"	" 40	"
Africa	" 2	"	" 2	"
Asia	" 13	"	" 43	"
Australia	" 2	"	" 2	"
Total	213		608	

A very interesting table is given by Prof. Heman, son of the late H. W. D. Heman, an excellent Hebrew Christian, and for several years the director of the home for Jewish converts at Basel. He says:

Great Britain,	with	200,000 Jews,	has	124 workers.
France,	"	77,000 "	"	5 "
Germany,	"	568,000 Jews,	has	24 workers.
Austria-Hungary,	"	1,860,000 "	"	17 "
Belgium,	"	3,000 "	"	— "
Denmark,	"	4,000 "	"	— "
Greece,	"	5,800 "	"	— "
Holland,	"	97,000 "	"	2 "
Italy,	"	50,000 "	"	3 "
Portugal,	"	300 "	"	— "
Rumania	"	300,000 "	"	11 "
Russia,	"	4,500,000 "	"	10 "
Servia,	"	4,700 "	"	— "
Bulgaria,	"	31,000 "	"	1 "
Spain,	"	2,500 "	"	— "
Sweden,	"	3,400 "	"	8 "
Switzerland,	"	12,500 "	"	1 "
Turkey,	"	120,000 "	"	21 "
Turkey in Asia,	"	150,000 "	"	103 "
Persia,	"	30,000 "	"	10 "
Asiatic Russia,	"	40,000 "	"	— "
Turkistan and Afghanistan,	"	14,000 "	"	— "
India and China,	"	19,000 "	"	5 "
Egypt,	"	25,000 "	"	12 "
Abyssinia,	"	50,000 "	"	7 "
Tripolis,	"	58,000 "	"	— "
Tunis,	"	60,000 "	"	12 "
Algiers and Sahara,	"	48,000 "	"	2 "
Morocco,	"	100,000 "	"	2 "
Transvaal,	"	12,000 "	"	— "
Cape Colony,	"	1,500 "	"	— "
United States,	"	1,000,000 "	"	150 "
Canada,	"	5,000 "	"	— "
The Antilles,	"	3,000 "	"	— "
South America,	"	12,000 "	"	— "
Australia,	"	17,000 "	"	2 "

It is impossible to give an accurate estimate of the Jewish population of the world.

Prof. Dalman, in his *Handbook of Jewish Missions,* published in 1893, sets the total down as 11,404,250. In *Israel, My Glory,* published in 1892, Rev. John Wilkinson makes an independent estimate, the total of which is 9,706,500. The American Jewish Year-Book for 1901-1902 puts the number down at 10,766,749. A comparison of the figures with those of the Statesman's Year-Book for 1903 shows great differences. At the Zionist Congress, in London, in August, 1900, it was stated that "according to the latest statistics we muster about 12,000,000." From all it may safely be stated that the population is, perhaps, between 11,000,000 and 12,000,000. But whatever the number, Judaism is not a unit. It is divided and split up in parties. The great mass is indifferent and this indifference is especially seen in the number of mixed marriages. A Jewish writer in a pamphlet published in 1900 tells us that during the years 1891-1896, 2,087 mixed marriages took place in Prussia, and 985 in Berlin alone. In New South Wales, we glean from another source, as many as 361 mixed marriages took place, whereas 1,562 Jews married within their own religion. Many Jews belong outwardly to Judaism, but their children are brought up as Christians. The rich and influential Jews have no interest whatever in Judaism, and "Zionism" is to the ones a stumbling block, to others, foolishness. What the Jews need is the Gospel as the only power which can burst the chains in which their consciences lie stricken, and fill their unsteady hearts with that peace which passeth understanding.

The Jews like to say that there are no converts really convinced of the truth of Christianity; that they were all bought, somehow or other, etc. It would be a waste of time and of paper and ink to refute these assertions. It were a very easy matter to mention a host of professors, ministers, teachers and others, who were blessed with earthly means, and yet became followers of Christ. If names count, we could fill page after page with names of Jewish converts who distinguished themselves in every sphere of life.

We could mention bishops, translators of the Bible, physicians, statesmen, church historians, etc. That they thus became famous was not because they happened to be born within the pale of Judaism, but because Christianity gave their lives a new direction. Modern Jews, with whom not religion, but the race, is all, are prone to call these followers of Christ "apostates" and "renegades," but this arrogant and insulting nomenclature will neither disgrace the Jewish converts nor hinder others from joining the army of apostates. We know that there are different views concerning the mission among the Jews. There are many well-meaning Christians who think that the Jews should be left alone. But the command of the Lord is still valid, and it is the duty of the Church to be obedient to that command, leaving the result of the work to Him Who commanded it.

JEYPUR. See JAIPUR.

JHALOD: A town in the Bombay Presidency, India, situated in the district of Panch Mahals. Population (1891) 6,000, of whom 5,000 are Hindus. Station of the Presbyterian Church in Ireland (1895), with (1900) 1 missionary and his wife, 9 native workers, 5 day schools and an orphanage.

JHANG BAR: A district in the Punjab, India, lying along the Chenab River and about 100 miles west of Lahore. Station circuit of the CMS (1899), with (1903) 1 missionary, 13 native workers, 1 day school and 4,699 professed Christians, of whom 176 are communicants. The field covers some 5,000 square miles and the Christians are scattered in 130 congregations, separated sometimes by considerable distances.

JHANSI: A town in the Central Provinces, India, 65 miles south of Gwalior. A walled town, strongly fortified; surrounded by fine groves. It is a military post and a railway center. Climate, intensely hot. Altitude, 855 feet. Population (1891), 52,000, of whom 35,400 are Hindus and 8,100 are Mohammedans. Station of the PN (1886), with (1903) 1 missionary and his wife, 2 women missionaries, 4 native workers, men and women, and 4 elementary schools. Station also of the WMS, with (1903) 1 missionary, 7 native workers and 4 outstations. Station also of the Woman's Union Missionary Society (1898), with 2 women missionaries, 3 native women workers, 1 dispensary and 1 hospital. The YWCA also has 2 women agents here and a Young Woman's Christian Association.

JHELUM. See JEHLAM.

JIAGANJ: A town in Bengal, India, situated in the district of Murshidabad, on the Bhagarathi River, about 14 miles N. of Berhampur. Population, with Azringanj, on the other side of the river, is 13,500. Station of the LMS (1892), with (1903) 1 missionary and his wife, 2 women missionaries, of whom one is a physician; 7 native workers, men and women; 4 day schools and a hospital.

JIBARA: A town and seaport in the Island of Cuba, W. I., situated 70 miles N. N. W. of Santiago. Population 26,300. Station of the AFFM, with 1 missionary and his wife, 2 women missionaries and 1 day school. Name also written Gibara.

JIKAU: A town in the Congo Free State, Central Africa, situated on the Maringa River, 600 miles from Stanley Pool. Station of the Regions Beyond Missionary Union (1889), with (1900) 4 missionaries, 2 with their wives; 2 women missionaries, 2 native workers, 1 day school and a dispensary.

JILORE: A settlement in British East Africa, among the Giriama tribes, and situated in the valley of the Savaki River, about 75 miles N. of Mombasa. Station of the CMS (1890), with (1903) 1 missionary, 15 native workers, men and women; 13 outstations, 2 day schools and 161 professed Christians, of whom 50 are communicants.

JIMBA. See JUMBA.

JODHPUR: A town in Rajputana, India, capital of the native state of Jodhpur (also called Marwar). It is situated 98 miles W. of Ajmere. The town was built in 1549 and is surrounded by a strong wall six miles in circuit, with seventy gates. The Maharaja's palace stands on the crest of a hill overlooking the town several hundred feet below. Population (1901) 60,437, of whom more than three-fourths are Hindus. Station of the UFS (1885), with (1903) 1 missionary and his wife, 1 woman missionary, 3 native workers, a dispensary and a hospital. Name also written Jodpur.

JOHANNESBURG: A town in the Transvaal Colony, S. Africa, situated 30 miles S. by W. of Pretoria, at an altitude of 5,600 feet, in the Witwatersrand gold fields. The climate is pleasant and healthful. The European population exceeds 40,000, and the whole population is (1896) 105,000. Station of the WMS, with (1903) 12 missionaries, 278 native workers, men and women; 99 preaching places, 9 elementary schools, 1 boarding school and 3,029 professed Christians. Station also of the Berlin Missionary Society (1887), with (1900) 1 missionary, 11 native workers, 7 outstations, and 395 professed Christians. Also of the ABCFM (1893), with 1 missionary and his wife and 1 woman missionary. Also station of the South Africa Baptist Missionary Society, with 1 missionary.

JOHNSON, Albert Osborne: Born at Cadiz, O., June 22, 1833; graduated at Jefferson College, 1852; Western Theological Seminary, 1855; ordained by Presbytery of Ohio in June and sailed July 17, same year, for India, as a missionary of the PN. He was stationed at Fatehgarh. At the commencement of the Sepoy mutiny he with others attempted to reach Allahabad, a British station, but was made prisoner and put to death at Cawnpur by order of the rebel chief Nana Sahib, June 13, 1857.

JOKEA: A settlement in British New Guinea, situated on the S. coast of the island, about 90 miles N. W. of Port Moresby. Station of the LMS (1894), with (1903) 1 missionary and 2 native workers.

JOKYOKARTA: A town in Java, Dutch East Indies, situated 55 miles south of Samarang. It is the capital of the Dutch residency. Population 59,000. Station of the Reformed Church of the Netherlands (1895), with (1900) 2 missionaries (one of them a physician) and their wives, 2 native workers, 2 outstations and 1 dispensary. Name written by the Society, Djokjokarta.

JOLOF LANGUAGE: One of the Negro group of African languages. It is spoken by a considerable number of tribesmen inhabiting the region bordering on the Gambia River in West Africa. It has been reduced to writing by missionaries, with use of the Roman alphabet. It is also called Wolof.

JROD. See ERODE.

JUDÆO-GERMAN, JUDÆO-SPANISH, etc., language: These and similar compounds are used to designate the form, when written with Hebrew letters, of the German, Polish, Spanish, etc., languages used by Jews to whom these languages (or some dialect of them) have become vernacular.

JUDD, Gerrit Parmelee: Born at Paris, N. Y., April 23, 1903; studied medicine with his father at Paris, and at the Medical College, Fairfield, N. Y.; sailed as a medical missionary of the American Board for the Sandwich Islands, reaching Honolulu March 31, 1828. In 1840 he accompanied Captain Wilkes in his exploring expedition through the islands. After fourteen years' faithful missionary work his connection with the mission ceased, and in 1842 he became recorder and interpreter to the Government of Kamehameha III. When Lord George Paulet took possession of the islands in 1843, Dr. Judd was appointed one of the joint commission to represent the king. When the government was restored to Kamehameha July 31, 1843, he was invited by the king to organize a ministry, which he did, and this was the first Hawaiian cabinet. In 1844 he became minister of finance, which office he held till 1853. He extricated the government from its financial embarrassments and in many ways was eminently serviceable to the nation. He died at Honolulu, January 12, 1873.

JUDSON, Adoniram: Born at Malden, Mass., August 9, 1788; graduated at Brown University, first in his class, 1807. After graduating he taught school for a year, and published *Elements of English Grammar* and *Young Ladies' Arithmetic*. In 1808 he entered Andover Theological Seminary, not as a candidate for the ministry or a professor of religion, but as a person deeply in earnest on the subject, and desirous of arriving at the truth. In the seminary that year he was converted. The reading of Buchanan's *Star in the East* and his association with Mills, Richards and Hall, who had arrived at Andover from Williams College, led him to resolve to become a missionary to the heathen. The ABCFM having been formed in 1810, and its funds not being sufficient to justify the appointment of the six young men who wished to go on a foreign mission, Mr. Judson was sent to England to secure the cooperation of the London Missionary Society in the support of a mission in the East. On the voyage the English ship was captured by the French and he was thrown into prison at Bayonne. Released, he proceeded to England. Unsuccessful in the immediate object of his journey, he was, on his return, appointed by the American Board as a missionary to India or Burma, and, embarking February 19, 1812, reached Calcutta June 17. Having changed his views with regard to baptism, he severed his connection with the Board. Being forbidden to remain in the East India Company's territories, he went, with his wife, to Mauritius. Here he remained four months, laboring among the English sailors of the garrison, and then sailed for Madras. Fearing to remain in the Company's territory he embarked for Rangun, Burma, which he reached July, 1813. He and his wife took up their residence in the house of Mr. Felix Carey, who was then absent, and who afterward resigned his mission in their favor. After six years' labor, the first convert, Moung Nau, was baptized. From 1824 to 1826, during the war of England with Burma, Mr. and Mrs. Judson endured terrible hardships. Suspected of being a spy, he was arrested in his house by an officer, accompanied by an executioner, who seized him, threw him on the floor, bound him fast with cords and dragged him away from his wife. He was thrown into the death-prison, and for seventeen months confined in the loathsome jails of Ava and Oung-pen-la, being bound during this period with three and, during two months, with five pairs of fetters. His sufferings from fever, heat, hunger, and the cruelty of his keepers were excruciating. Mrs. Judson also suffered, tho not imprisoned. By her persistent entreaties and large presents, and finally by the demand of General Campbell, he was, at the end of two years, released. In 1826 the headquarters of the mission were transferred to Amherst. But he was soon called to Ava to act as interpreter in the negotiation of a new treaty between the English and the Burmese. In his absence his wife died. In 1829 he joined the Boardmans at Maulmain, which became the chief seat of the Baptist missions in Burma. Desiring to carry the Gospel to Central Burma, Mr. Judson in 1830 made long tours in the interior, and spent three months in futile efforts to establish a mission in the ancient city of Prome. Before returning to Maulmain he spent a year in Rangun. At a great festival here he was applied to by thousands for tracts. In 1831-32 Mr. Judson made three tours among the Karens, and with encouraging success. In 1834 he was married to Mrs. Sarah H. Boardman. During that year he completed the translation of the Bible into Burmese, which he had commenced seventeen years before in Rangun. In 1838 he says there were above a thousand converts from heathenism formed into churches. In 1839, threatened with pulmonary disease, he took a short voyage, returning to Maulmain in two months with health somewhat improved. In 1842 he commenced, at the urgent request of the Board, the preparation of a Burman dictionary. In 1845 he embarked for America for his own health and that of his wife, accompanied by two Burman assistants to help him in his work on the dictionary. Mrs. Judson died at St. Helena. He reached Boston October 15. Too weak for public speaking, he addressed crowded assemblies through an interpreter. Having again married, he returned to Burma in 1846, and soon resumed work at Rangun on the dictionary. But the intolerance of the Burmese Government and the sickness of the missionaries caused him to leave Rangun and return to Maulmain, which reached September 5, 1847. Here he worked steadily at the dictionary, which he was compelled to leave unfinished, for his health had so utterly failed that in 1850 he set out for a long sea-voyage as the only hope of saving his life. He died April 12, 1850, scarcely three days out of sight of the mountains of Burma, and his body was committed to the deep. Dr. Judson was a man of vigorous intellect and fervent piety, a close student, and very thorough in his work. He was well known throughout India. The Crown Prince of Siam invited him to visit Siam at his expense. The English authorities profoundly respected him, and the native converts greatly revered and loved him. Numerous converts, a corps of trained native assistants, the translation of the Bible and other valuable books into Burmese, and a large Burman and English dictionary nearly completed are some of the direct fruits of his thirty-seven years of missionary service.

JUDSON, Ann Hasseltine: Born at Bradford, Mass., December 22, 1789; taught for several years after leaving Bradford Academy; married Dr. Judson and embarked with him for Burma February 19, 1812, and in July, 1813, reached Rangun. Her health having failed in a year and a half, she sailed for Madras January, 1815, returning after an absence of three months with health much improved. Several thousands of Siamese being in Rangun, she studied that language, and with the assistance of her teacher translated into it the Burman Catechism, a tract, and the Gospel of Matthew. She also translated a celebrated Siamese work into English. She had frequent meetings with the women. In 1820 she became seriously ill, and was taken by Dr. Judson to Calcutta, partly for a voyage and partly to procure medical assistance. She returned with health improved, but soon was again prostrated, and August 21, 1821, embarked for America by the way of England, reaching home in September, 1822. While there a history of the Burman mission, begun by her in London, was published in England. With health partially restored she returned to Burma with Mr. and Mrs. Wade, reaching Rangun December 5, 1823, and with Dr. Judson removed to Ava. There she soon had a school of native girls. But on the breaking out of war with England she was called to share in his sufferings. While he was fettered in the death prison, she was guarded in her own house by ten ruffianly men, deprived of her furniture and most of her personal effects. Being released the third day, she sought in various ways the comfort and release of her husband. "She followed him from prison to prison, ministering to his wants, trying to soften the hearts of his keepers, to mitigate his sufferings, interceding with government officials or with members of the royal family. For a year and a half she thus exerted herself, walking miles in feeble health, in the darkness of the night or under a noonday sun, much of the time with a babe in her arms." After a treaty of peace was concluded, Dr. and Mrs. Judson were again at Rangun March 21, 1826, having been absent two years and three months. The English having made the new town of Amherst their capital, Dr. and Mrs. Judson established the mission there. During his absence at Ava as interpreter for the English and Burmans, Mrs. Judson built a small bamboo dwelling-house and two schoolhouses, in one of which she gathered ten children; in the other she herself assembled the few native converts for worship on the Sabbath. In the midst of these toils she was attacked with fever, and, after sixteen days' illness, died, October 24, 1826, in the 37th year of her age. She was a woman of mental endowments, earnest piety, self-sacrificing devotion, great perseverance, unaffected dignity and refinement.

JUDSON, Emily Chubbuck: Born at Eaton, N. Y., August 22, 1817; taught at Utica; married Dr. Judson, and in 1847 sailed with him for Burma. A popular writer, she wrote, under the pseudonym of "Fanny Forester," articles of prose and poetry for various magazines. She wrote also several Sunday school books. While in Rangun she wrote the memoir of Mrs. Sarah B. Judson, and in Maulmain composed several of her best poems. After her husband's death she returned home in 1851 with health much impaired, and devoted herself to the care of her children and aged parents, and to literary pursuits. She gave much time to the preparation of the papers for President Wayland's Memoirs of Dr. Judson. She died at Hamilton, N. Y., June 1, 1854.

JUDSON, Sarah Hall (Boardman): Born at Alstead, N. H., November 4, 1803; married Rev. George Dana Boardman and embarked July 16, 1825, for Burma, but was detained in Calcutta by the war till 1827. After Mr. Boardman's death she determined, tho urged by friends in America to return, to remain in Tavoy, and for three years of her widowhood she continued her husband's work, proclaiming Christ to Karen inquirers, conducting schools and making long tours, often in drenching rains, "through wild mountain passes, over swollen streams and deceitful marshes, among the craggy rocks and tangled shrubs of the jungle." In April, 1834, she was married to Dr. Judson. She was familiar with the Burmese language, having acquired unusual fluency and power in conversation and prayer, and writing it with accuracy. She conducted weekly prayer-meetings with the female church-members and another for the study of the Bible. She translated into Burmese the first part of *Pilgrim's Progress*, several tracts, twenty of the best hymns used in the *Chapel Hymn-book*, four volumes of *Scripture Questions for Sunday schools* and a series of Sunday cards, each containing a short hymn. She learned also the language of the Peguans, and superintended the translation of the New Testament and the principal Burmese tracts into that language. Her health having failed, she left for home with Dr. Judson April 26, 1845. She died on shipboard in the harbor of St. Helena, September 1, 1845 and was buried on the island, having spent twenty-one years in mission work.

JUIZ DE FORA: A town in Brazil, S. America, situated on the Parahiba River, 85 miles N. of Rio de Janeiro, at an altitude of 2,300 feet. Population (with the district) 15,000. Station of the MES (1884), with (1900) 3 missionaries and their wives, 3 women missionaries, 3 native workers, 2 outstations, 8 Sunday schools, 2 day schools, 1 boarding school, 1 theological training school and 328 professed evangelical Christians. Also called Parahibuna.

JU-JU, The Long: This was a fetish jealously guarded by the Aro tribe at a point not far from Cross River in Southern Nigeria. The Aro tribe has long been celebrated for slave-hunting, cannibalism, guardianship of this important shrine, and determined refusal to recognize the British rule or to permit foreigners in their land. In the heart of their country the Long Ju-ju was shrouded in mystery. Fierce and bloodthirsty guards surrounded the place, in a circle of villages where all had to settle who wished to consult the Ju-ju. Such visitors after some delay were taken in batches, blindfolded, and led to the terrible place which no man of West Africa mentions without a shudder. Few who trusted themselves to the guards of the Long Ju-ju ever returned. Those who did return were worn and prematurely aged, stripped of all possessions and unwilling to speak of what they had seen.

A case reached the ears of the British Government where 800 wretches from Nigeria, who had been charged by their tribes with various crimes, had sought to prove their innocence by the weary pilgrimage involved in an appeal to the arbitrament of the Long Ju-ju. A miserable remnant of 136 feeble and broken creatures was all that ever returned, and since the Aro country is in British territory, credit for the horrors of the great fetish was laid at the door of the English.

After much evidence that the place was a center of infernal rites and beastly cannibalism, the British Government demanded that the Aros suppress these practises. The demand having been insolently refused, a force was sent into the country in 1901 which broke the power of the Aros and captured the Long Ju-ju shrine.

The place of the shrine was a narrow pit-like crater seventy feet deep and 200 feet long, surrounded by dense brush. In the bottom of the crater was a singular, rent rock from which poured forth two large streams of water. This curious double stream pouring from rents in the solid sock, was the Long Ju-ju. It was shut in by a roof of human skulls and veiled by a curtain of cloth and matting. In front of the double water source were two altars foul with blood and covered with votive offerings and the recently stripped skulls of men. The water of the great double spring flowed away in a stream of some depth, and in the water were fish. There were numbers of fish—strange, yellow-eyed creatures, tame through confidence that abundance of blood and offal from human sacrifices would continue to fatten them as of old. All the approaches to this awful place were bordered by piles of human skulls.

It was the last stronghold of the infernal cult of fetishism which insists on human flesh for its sacrament. But one thing could be done with a place of such infamy and influence, and the English commander had the place blown up with dynamite.

JULFA: A town in Persia, lying on the Zende Rud, opposite Ispahan, with which it is connected by bridges as a suburb. It is peopled largely by Armenians, the descendants of captives brought by Shah Abbas from the Caucasus. Station of the CMS (1875), with 14 missionaries, men and women (including hospital nurses); 32 native workers, men and women; a printing house, 3 day schools, 2 hospitals and dispensaries and 245 professed Christians. Great extension has been given to medical work here, which has offered special channels of access to Mohammedans. There is also a sub-agency of the BFBS, with branch depots at Yezd, Shiraz and Sultanabad.

JULLUNDUR. See JALANDHAR.

JUMBA: A settlement in British East Africa, situated about 20 miles N. W. of Mombasa. Station of the Leipzig Missionary Society (1886), with (1900) 4 missionaries, one with his wife. Name also written Jimba.

JUNGO: A settlement in Uganda, Central Africa, situated on the northern shores of the Victoria Nyanza, about 32 miles S. W. of Mengo. Station of the CMS (1895), with (1903) 109 native workers, men and women; 1 preaching place, 1 day school and 2,320 professed Christians, of whom 423 are communicants.

JU-NING-FU: A town in the province of Ho-nan, China, situated in the E. part of the province, about 100 miles east of Nan-yang. Station of the American Norwegian Church Mission Society (1899), with (1900) 1 missionary and his wife and 1 native worker. Name written by the Society Running Fu.

JUNNAR: A town in the Bombay Presidency, India, situated about 50 miles N. of Poona. Station of the CMS (1843), with (1903) 1 missionary and his wife.

K

KABAKADA: A settlement on the island of New Britain, or Neu Pommern, in the Bismarck archipelago, Western Pacific Ocean. It is situated at the northern extremity of the island, and is a station of the Australian Wesleyan Methodist Mission Society, with (1900) 1 missionary, 65 native workers, 4 outstations, 21 places of worship, 23 day schools, 1 theological training school and 331 professed Christians.

KABANIROE: A town on the western coast of Sumba Island, Dutch East Indies. Station of the Reformed Church of the Netherlands (1892), with 1 missionary and his wife, 2 native workers and 281 professed Christians.

KABAROLE: A settlement in the Toro district of Uganda, Africa, situated 170 miles W. of Mengo. Station of the CMS (1899), with (1903) 4 missionaries, two with their wives; 2 women missionaries, 30 native workers, 1 village school, 1 female helpers' training class, 1 dispensary, 1 hospital and 2,209 professed Christians, of whom 645 are communicants. The Butiti Church statistics are included with these.

KABOEROEANG ISLAND: The same as Kabruang in the Talaut Islands, Dutch East Indies.

KABYLE LANGUAGE: Belongs to the Hamitic family of African languages and is spoken by various tribes found in Algeria and Tunis. It is written with Arabic letters. It is also sometimes called the Kabail language, Kabail being the plural of Kabyle.

KACHABARI: A village in Lohardaga, district of Chota Nagpur, Bengal, India, situated 20 miles southeast of Lohardaga. A station of the SPG, with 9 native workers, 1 chapel, 3 day schools and 311 professed Christians.

KACHCH: A native state situated in the Bombay Presidency, India, between Kathiawar and Sindh. Its southwestern border rests upon the

Indian Ocean. Its habitable area is about 6,500 square miles, and its population (1901) 487,374. North and east of the state, covering an area of nearly 9,000 square miles (making the total area within the limits of Kachch over 15,000 square miles), stretches a salt desert, uninhabitable, untillable, and often in the rainy season impassable, known as the "Rann of Kachch." It is believed to be the bed of what was once an arm of the sea, but which has been raised above its original level and cut off from the ocean. During the rainy season it is often inundated, partly by the waves of the sea, driven against it by strong southerly winds, and partly by the rainfall from the adjacent region draining into it. During the dry season its surface is often encrusted and glittering with salt. The surface of Kachch as a whole is described as treeless, rocky and barren. It is cut by ranges of hills, rising at the highest point to an altitude of 1,450 feet above the sea. There is a fair proportion of good soil, tho grain figures among the articles imported. Kachch is especially noted for its beautiful embroideries and for its manufactures of silverware. The population is about three-fifths Hindu and a little more than one-fifth Mohammedan; the Jains number about 67,000. The roads are poor, and during the rainy months the country is nearly impassable. Missionary operations have been undertaken by the Kurku Inland Mission at one point (1897), where is now a beginning of a Christian community.

KACHHWA: A town in the United Provinces, India, situated about 20 miles W. of Benares. Station of the LMS (1897), with (1903) 2 missionaries and their wives, 1 hospital and 1 dispensary.

KADDAVELLY: A town in the N. W. part of Ceylon, India, situated about 40 miles S. of Jaffna. Station of the WMS, with 44 native workers, 7 outstations, 8 Sunday schools, 8 day schools and 76 professed Christians.

KADING. See KIATING.

KADIRI: A town in the district of Cuddapah, Madras, India, 88 miles N. N. E. of Bangalore. Population (1891) 6,000, of whom 4,000 are Hindus. Station of the LMS (1890), with (1903) 1 missionary and his wife, 20 native workers, men and women; 11 outstations, 11 Sabbath schools, 10 day schools and 293 professed Christians.

KAFIR LANGUAGE: Belongs to the Bantu family of African languages and is spoken in the Transkei district of Cape Colony, South Africa. It has been reduced to writing by missionaries of the WMS, the Roman alphabet slightly modified being used.

KAFIRLAND: A region in the eastern part of Cape Colony, South Africa, lying between the rivers Kei and Umzimkulu, once occupied by the Kafirs. It was also sometimes called Cafraria. It is now known by the names of the different districts into which it has been divided: Transkei, Tembuland and Griqualand East. The great attractions of the country, it being at once the most salubrious, fertile and picturesque region of South Africa, have helped to overcome the difficulties and dangers of colonization, and there is now a continuous zone of European settlements throughout the region.

KAFIRS: The Xosa, or Kafirs, are a tribe of Bantu blood found in the eastern part of Cape Colony. Their account of themselves is that they came gradually down from the northeast, some two or three hundred years ago, and settled in districts lying between the Kei and the Umzimkulu, out of which they crowded the weaker Hottentot and Bushman tribes. The name Kafir, which in Arabic signifies infidel, or those who do not hold the Muslim faith, was first applied by Arabs to the heathen tribes with which as traders they came in contact, along the East Coast of Africa, which would seem to give sanction to the above historic saying. And then, too, in the Kafir's practice of polygamy and the rite of circumcision, and especially in his proud bearing and martial spirit, in his somewhat Arabian features, and in his hue, not generally so dark as that of the pure negro, many see proof of his having been for a time associated with the Arab race.

KAGOSHIMA: A town in Kiushiu, Japan, situated on a bay on the S. E. coast, opposite the volcanic island of Satawa Shima, and about 88 miles S. S. E. of Nagasaki. One of the most ancient cities of Japan. It has a large number of pottery factories. Population 50,000. Station of the RCA (1893), with (1903) 1 missionary and his wife, 1 woman missionary, 5 native workers, 5 outstations, 1 chapel, 3 Sunday schools and 75 professed Christians. Station also of the CMS (1895), with (1903) 1 missionary and his wife, 1 woman missionary, 3 native workers, 1 outstation, 2 Sunday schools and 104 professed Christians, of whom 34 are communicants. Station also of the ME, with (1900) 2 women missionaries, 1 native worker, 1 chapel, 3 Sunday schools and 47 professed Christians.

KAI-FÊNG-FU: The capital of the province of Ho-nan, China, situated 110 miles E. of Ho-nan-fu and about 9 miles from the right bank of the Hoang Ho. It was the capital of the empire from 1280 to 1405 under the name of Tung King. It possesses the only Jewish colony in China, with an entire population of 100,000 people. Station of the CIM (1902), with 4 missionaries and 1 dispensary.

KAI-HSIEN: A town in Sze-chwan, China, situated 55 miles W. by N. of Kwei-chau-fu. Station of the CIM (1902), with 1 missionary and 4 outstations.

KAILANG: A village in the Punjab, India, situated in the Lahoul region, 45 miles northeast of Dharmsala. Station of the Moravian Mission (1856), with (1900) 3 missionaries and their wives, 4 native workers, 10 day schools, 1 industrial school. Name sometimes spelled Kyelang.

KAIRWAN: A city in Tunis, N. Africa, situated in the center of a vast plain 31 miles W. S. W. of Susa. It was founded in 670. For two centuries it was the capital of successive Arabian dynasties. It has fine mosques, of which the largest is 460 feet square. Population about 10,000. Station of the North African Mission (1897), with (1900) 1 missionary and his wife, 2 women missionaries, and a dispensary.

KAISARIYEH: A city in Asiatic Turkey, situated in the province of Angora and about 200 miles S. by W. of the City of Angora. It lies in a fertile plain at an altitude of 3,585 feet, near the foot of Mt. Argeas (*Erjish*). It was in ancient times capital of Cappadocia, and is now the seat of an Armenian bishop. The climate is dry, pleasant and healthful, with a tendency to extremes of heat and cold, however, owing to the altitude of the plain. Population, 72,000, of whom 45,000 are Mohammedans, 14,500 Greeks, 9,000 Armenians, and about 2,000 Evangelicals. The Christian part of the population furnish many enterprising business men who find their way into foremost places in Constantinople, Smyrna, Adana, etc., and have even made their mark in mercantile circles in London, Manchester and New York. Evangelistic work was begun in Cesarea in 1823 by Mr. B. Barker, Agent of the BFBS. The Scriptures which he distributed here were as seed falling into good ground. Later the persecution of Protestant Armenians in Constantinople had for one of its incidents the exile to Cesarea in 1839 of a preacher, Hohannes der Sahagian, and of other Evangelicals in 1845. These all preached the Gospel wherever they were, with the result that a number of the people of the city, in 1849, sent to the ABCFM missionaries at Aintab an earnest request for a preacher. In 1854 the ABCFM sent Rev. W. A. Farnsworth and Rev. J. N. Ball to occupy the city as a permanent station. It now (1903) has 3 missionaries and their wives, 6 women missionaries, 74 native workers, men and women; 35 outstations, 25 places of worship, 31 day schools, 2 boarding schools, 1 hospital, 1 dispensary, and 1,088 evangelical Christian communicants. The place is commonly called Cesarea by English-speaking people, the name Kaisariyeh being the Turkish corruption of this.

KAI-YUEN: A town in Manchuria, Chinese Empire, situated in the province of Liao-tung, 68 miles N. N. E. of Mukden. Population, 35,000. Station of the UFS (1896), with (1903) 1 missionary and his wife, 1 woman missionary, 17 native workers, 4 outstations, 18 Sunday schools, 1 hospital, 1 dispensary, and 838 professed Christians.

KAKONDA: A town in Portuguese West Africa, situated 140 miles S. E. by E. of Benguela in the district of that name. Altitude 5,500 feet. Station of the FCMS (1900), with 1 missionary and his wife.

KALAHASTI: A town in the north Arcot district, Madras, India, 60 miles N. N. W. of Madras, on the Suvarnamukhi River. Population, 11,800. The town has large bazars, and is a place for pilgrimage, as it contains one of the most famous temples of Siva. Station of the Hermannsburg Missionary Society (1873), with (1902) 1 missionary and his wife, 6 native workers, 2 outstations, 3 day schools, and 198 professed Christians, of whom 104 are communicants.

KALASAPAD: A town in the district of Nellore, Madras, India, situated about 62 miles northwest of Nellore. A station of the SPG (1861), with (1903) 1 missionary, 60 native workers, 3 chapels, 53 day schools, 2 boarding schools, and 4,732 professed Christians, of whom 1,477 are communicants. Name sometimes spelled Kalsapad.

KALGAN. See CHANG-KIA-KAU.

KALIBASI: A settlement in Natal, S. Africa, 33 miles N. N. E. of Ladysmith. Station of the UFS (1897), with (1903) 1 missionary and his wife, 14 native workers, 14 outstations, 10 day schools, and 427 professed Christians.

KALIMPONG: A town in Bengal, India, situated on the borders of Bhutan and Sikkim, about 15 miles E. by N. of Darjiling, at an altitude of 5,000 feet. It is a strange meeting place of races and religions. The town has about 13,000 inhabitants, who are Nepalis, Lepches, Bhutias, and other hillmen, besides plainmen of various classes. In religion there way be seen Buddhists, Hindus, Spirit-worshipers, Mohammedans, and Christians, and all contrive to carry on traffic in spite of divergences of language and creed. Station of the Church of Scotland Foreign Missions' Committee (1873), and the C. of S. Woman's Missions Committee (1899), with, together (1900), 3 missionaries and their wives, 4 women missionaries, 12 native workers, men and women, and 1 dispensary. Another name of this place is Dalingkot.

KALITJERET: A town in the island of Java, Dutch East Indies, situated 30 miles S. W. of Samarang. Station of the Neukirchen Missionary Society (1885), with 2 missionaries, 11 native workers, 10 outstations, and 2 schools.

KALKA: A village in the Punjab, India, 23 miles S. W. of Simla. Altitude, 2,000 feet. Population, about 5,000. Station of the BMS (1888), with (1903) 3 missionaries, 1 missionary's wife, 15 native workers, men and women; 5 outstations, and 9 day schools.

KALKHAS LANGUAGE: A Mongolian dialect used in Chinese Mongolia. The alphabet is nearly the same as that of the Manchu.

KALLAKURCHI: A town in the Presidency of Madras, India, situated 58 miles W. of Cuddalore. Station of the Danish Missionary Society (1894), with 2 missionaries and 2 native workers. The station is called by the Society, Bethesda.

KALLAR: A village in the E. part of North Ceylon, India, situated about 20 miles S. E. of Batticaloa. A station of the WMS (1903), with 24 native workers, 12 outstations, 13 chapels, 12 Sunday schools, 12 day schools, and 121 professed Christians.

KALMUCKS. See MONGOLS.

KALMUNAI: A town on the E. coast of Ceylon, India, situated about 26 miles S. E. of Batticaloa. Station of the WMS with (1903) 2 missionaries, 1 woman missionary, 35 native workers, 6 outstations, 7 chapels, 7 Sunday schools, and 178 professed Christians.

KALNA: A town in the district of Bardwan, Bengal, India, on the right bank of the Bhagirathi River, 42 miles N. of Calcutta. Population (1891) 9,700, of whom about 8,500 are Hindus. Medical station of the UFS, with (1903) 2 missionary physicians, 4 native workers and 4 dispensaries. The church statistics are included in those given at Hugli.

KALUTTURAI: A town in the western part of Ceylon, situated about 27 miles south by east of Colombo. Population, 11,000. A station of the SPG, with (1903) 40 native workers, 3 chapels, 8 day schools and 189 professed Christians. The WMS also has a station at this place, with (1903) 2 missionaries, 35 native workers, 8 outstations, 8 chapels, 8 Sunday schools, 12 day schools and 169 professed Christians, of whom 126 are communicants. Name is also sometimes spelled Kalutara.

KAMAMET: A town in Haidarabad, India, situated 100 miles N. W. of Masulipatam. It is a station of the CMS (1888), with (1903) 1 missionary and his wife, 42 native workers, 1 chapel, 8 village schools and 1,464 professed Christians, of whom 348 are communicants. Station also of the CEZ (1889), with (1903) 2 women missionaries, 28 native workers, 7 village schools and 1 dispensary. The name is sometimes spelled Khammamet and Khummamett.

KAMBIA: A town in Sierra Leone, W. Africa, situated near the frontier of French Guinea and about 25 miles from the sea. Station of the Pongas Mission (1897), with 1 missionary and his wife.

KAMBOLE: A settlement in British East Africa, situated about 25 miles S. W. of the southern end of Lake Tanganyika. Station of the LMS (1894), with (1903) 2 missionaries and their wives, 6 native workers, 9 schools and 1 dispensary.

KAMERUN: A German protectorate in Western Africa, lying between Nigeria on the northwest and the French Congo on the east, extending to Lake Chad on the north, and having the Bight of Biafra for its western boundary, with a coast line of 199 miles. Its area is 191,130 square miles, with a population estimated at 3,500,000. The coast mountains over against the island of Fernando Po rise at one point to a peak of 14,000 feet, surpassed on the African continent only by Kenia, Kilima-Njaro, Simen (in Abyssinia) and the lately explored Ruwenzori. Its lower portions are covered with a luxuriant vegetation of palms, acacias, fig-trees, kokas, plantains and other trees and shrubs. At a height of 7,000 feet are found ferns, grasses and heather. Springs are rare, none being found above 9,100 feet. The summit is bare, except for a few trailing plants sheltered in the hollows. The surrounding country is well watered by small lakes and rivers, with their confluents and deltas. But little of the region has been explored or brought under the influence of its European masters. In the summer rainy season (May to August) the rainfall is very heavy, and the season of the winter rains is characterized by squalls, tornados and dense vapors. The chief station and seat of government is Buea, beautifully situated on the mountain.

Kameruns is a name applied collectively to a dozen populous villages on the east side of the Kamerun estuary.

The chief inhabitants are of Bantu origin and speech. These include the lively, intelligent and daring but very superstitious Bakwiri, between the coast and the mountains; the industrious and equally superstitious Bakundu of the northern slopes; the communistic Balonga and trading Abo east of the Bakundu; the tom-tom beating and well-known Dualla of the Kamerun estuary; farther south the savage Bakoko and the Batanga, who are the most skilful boat-builders in Africa, and the Fangs, who are pressing to the coast from the interior.

In the northern portion of the territory the population is composed almost entirely of the Sudanese negroes.

The first missionary operations in this region were undertaken by the BMS in 1858, when its missionaries were driven from Fernando Po by Spanish bigotry. At that time the missionaries found danger from the savages on the mainland less than that of the Europeans who ruled the island. They transferred their work to the Basel Missionary Society in 1886, two years after the German Protectorate was announced. The PN (1885) and the German Baptists (1891) also have stations. There are altogether in Kamerun 16 stations where missionaries reside, with 115 schools of various grades and about 2,500 native communicant Christians.

KAMPTI: A town in the Central Provinces, India, 8 miles N. E. of Nagpur, and just below the confluence of the Kanhan with the Pench and Kolar Rivers. It has considerable trade in timber and grain. Population (1891), 43,000, of whom 28,500 are Hindus and 11,500 are Mohammedans. Station of the ME, with (1900) 1 missionary and his wife, 14 native workers, men and women; 5 day schools, an orphanage and 83 professed Christians.

KAMUNDONGA: A town in Angola, W. Africa, 245 miles E. of Benguela. Station of the ABCFM (1886), with (1901) 2 missionaries and their wives, 2 women missionaries, 7 native workers, 1 industrial school, 1 theological training class, 1 hospital, 1 dispensary and a printing house,

KANA: A settlement in the Transvaal Colony, S. Africa, 52 miles E. by N. of Pretoria. Station of the Hermannsburg Missionary Society (1867), with (1900) 2 missionaries, 1 missionary's wife, 9 native workers, 5 outstations, 5 day schools and 1,467 professed Christians.

KANAUJ: A town in the United Provinces, India, situated in the district of Farukhabad, 49 miles N. W. of Cawnpur, on the right bank of the Kali Nadi, formerly bed of the Ganges. The change in the bed of the river ruined the town. Anciently it was a city of importance, capital of a great Aryan kingdom. It was the scene of several battles of the Turkish conquerors of India. Population (1891) 17,600, of whom 10,000 are Hindus. Station circuit of the ME, with (1903) 14 native workers, 14 Sunday schools, 5 day schools and 89 professed Christians.

KANAZAWA: A town in Japan, situated on the W. coast of the main island of Hondo, 125 miles N. N. E. of Kioto. It is celebrated for its manufactures of fans, pottery, and bronze ware overlaid with gold and silver. Population 96,600. Station of the PN (1879), the PE and the Methodist Church in Canada (1891). Taken together these missions have (1900) 4 missionaries, 3 wives of missionaries, 6 women missionaries, 7 native workers, men and women; 3 outstations, 3 day schools, 1 boarding school, 1 orphanage, 3 industrial schools, 5 places of worship and 3 Sabbath schools.

KAN-CHAU-FU: A town in the province of Kiang-si, China, situated on the Kia-kiang, 213 miles N. N. E. of Canton. It has somewhat important manufactures of Chinese ink and varnish. Station of the CIM (1899), with (1903) 5 missionaries, two of whom are accompanied by their wives.

KANDUKUR: A town in the Madras Presidency, India, 58 miles N. of Nellore. Population (1891) 7,600, of whom 6,000 are Hindus. Station of the ABMU (1893), with (1903) 1 missionary and his wife, 9 native workers, 21 outstations, 2 places of worship, 1 day school and 783 professed Christians.

KANDY: A town situated near the center of the island of Ceylon, built on the margin of an artificial lake 1,734 feet above the sea, 58 miles N. E. by E. of Colombo. It was formerly the capital of a kingdom called by that name, and contains the tombs of the Kandian kings, together with many handsome temples. Population (1891) 20,400. It is the headquarters for mission work and instruction in the central part of Ceylon. Station of the CMS (1818) and CEZ (1889), with together (1903) 4 missionaries, three with their wives; 6 women missionaries, 279 native workers, men and women; 120 day schools, 1 boarding school, 1 college (Trinity College), and 5,050 professed Christians, of whom 1,788 are communicants. Station also of the WMS, with (1903) 1 missionary, 1 woman missionary, 48 native workers, men and women; 9 outstations, 9 places of worship, 11 Sunday schools, 12 day schools, 1 boarding school, 1 industrial school for girls and 223 professed Christians. Outstation also of the BMS (1844), with a self-supporting church under a native pastor.

KANG-HWA: A town situated on the west coast of Korea, about 30 miles northwest of Chemulpo. A station of the SPG (1893), with (1902) 4 missionaries, 6 native workers, 4 chapels, 1 high school and 24 Christians. Name sometimes spelled Kang Hoa.

KANG-PUI: A town in the province of Kwangtung, China, 45 miles east of Canton. Station of the Rhenish Missionary Society, with (1903) 1 missionary and his wife, 4 native workers, 4 outstations, 5 day schools and 239 professed Christians, of whom 163 are communicants.

KANGRA: A town in Punjab, India, situated 90 miles E. N. E. of Amritsar. It was formerly called Nagarkot. Population, 5,200, of whom 4,000 are Hindus. It is a station of the CMS (1854), with (1903) 1 missionary and his wife, 12 native workers, 1 chapel, 1 dispensary, 3 village schools, 1 industrial school, and 99 professed Christians, of whom 44 are communicants. The church statistics of Dharmsala are included in the above.

KANGUNDO: A settlement in British E. Africa, in the Kikuyu region, about 15 miles from the Ft. Smith station of the Uganda Railway. Station of the Africa Inland Mission (1896), with 3 missionaries, 2 of them with their wives.

KANIGIRI: A town in the Madras Presidency, India, 74 miles N. N. W. of Nellore. Station of the ABMU (1892), with (1903) 1 missionary and his wife, 91 native workers, 70 outstations, 31 Sunday schools, 62 day schools, and 8,877 professed Christians, of whom 3,641 are communicants.

KANNANUR. See CANNANORE.

KANO: A town in North Central Africa, situated west of Lake Chad and about 320 miles N. N. W. of Lokoja on the Niger. It lies in the territory of the British Niger Protectorate, commonly called Northern Nigeria. It is one of the most important commercial centers in Africa, having been known as an emporium for ivory, ostrich feathers and gum arabic as early as the 10th century. Up to the present time the ordinary currency used in trade has consisted of slaves. Kano is often spoken of as an important town of the "Hausas," but there is no people called locally by that name, Hausa being the name of a language widely used in trade by different people who are not by any means a coherent nation, altho the most of the Hausa-speaking peoples are dominated by Fulani Mohammedans, who rule the land in various independent states, of one of which Kano is the capital. In 1903 the British troops, to punish the Mohammedan Emir for the murder of a British official, attacked and captured Kano and deposed the Emir. This breaking of the Fulani yoke caused great rejoicing among the pagan majority of the population, whom the Fulani Mohammedans have long used as serfs. Kano has a population estimated at 200,000. The CMS will establish a station here at an early day.

KANYA: A settlement in Rhodesia, South Central Africa, situated about 60 miles N. N. W. of Mafeking. It is the chief town of the Bangwaletsi tribe and residence of the chief, Bathoen. Station of the LMS (1871), with (1903) 1 missionary and his wife, 40 native workers, men and women; 3 schools, and 2,400 professed Christians, of whom 642 are communicants. Name written by the Society, Kanye.

KAO-YU-CHAU: Town in the province of Kiang-su, China, situated on the Grand Canal, 40 miles N. of Chen-kiang-fu. It is the "Cayu" of Marco Polo. Station of the CIM (1888), with (1903) 1 missionary women, 3 native workers, 1 day school, and 1 boarding school. Name written by the Society, Kao-yiu.

KAPASDANGA: A village in the district of Nadiya, Bengal, India, situated 20 miles N. E. of Krishnagar. Station of the CEZ (1885), with (1903) 2 women missionaries, 3 native workers, 1 village school, and 1 female helpers' training class. The central station has now been transferred to Ratnapur. The CMS has here (1903) 8 native workers, 750 Christians, 1 chapel, and 4 day schools. The work is now in charge of the local district church council.

KARACHI: A town and the capital of Sind, India, situated 90 miles W. S. W. of Haidarabad on a small bay W. of the Indus. It carries on an important export trade in wheat. Population (1891) of 98,200, of whom 51,400 are Muslims and 42,000 are Hindus. Station of the CMS (1850), with (1903) 1 missionary and his wife, 4 native workers, 1 chapel, 3 day schools, and 99 professed Christians, of whom 53 are communicants. Station also of the CEZ (1880), with (1903) 3 women missionaries, 18 native workers, 7 village schools. Station also of the ME, with 1 missionary and his wife, 14 native workers, 1 chapel, 3 Sunday schools, 2 village schools, and 292 professed Christians, of whom 40 are communicants.

KARAITES: A Jewish sect, existing in Russia (chiefly in the Crimea), Austria (Galicia), Turkey, and other countries of the East, are distinguished by a strict adherence to the Biblical books, and the rejection, except as exegetical aids, of all oral traditions and Talmudical interpretations. They themselves trace their origin to the time of Shalmanesar, and since he carried the ten tribes of Israel to the north, they hold they must worship with their faces to the south. Karaite historians are now, however, greatly divided on the subject of this origin. The Karaites have produced a valuable literature, not only on Biblical interpretations, dogmatics, and other religious topics, but also on philosophy and mathematics, written partly in Hebrew or Arabic, partly in a curious dialect of Turkish, which is a peculiar idiom of their own, in a region bordering on the Black Sea, and partly in the languages of the several countries which they inhabit. Their literature is, however, very little known to the Occidental world. Several of their principal writings have been published at Eupatoria, in the Crimea. The name is also written Caraites.

KARAITIC TARTAR TURKISH. See TURKISH LANGUAGE.

KARAKAL: A town in South Kanara, Madras, India, 30 miles N. E. of Mangalore. Station of the Basel Missionary Society (1872), with (1903) 2 missionaries, 1 with his wife; 13 native workers, 4 outstations, 5 elementary schools, and 188 professed Christians. The name as written by the Society is Karkala.

KARASS LANGUAGE: Name improperly given to the Nogai dialect of Turkish.

KARATA: A settlement in Nicaragua, Central America, in the Mosquito Reservation, about 140 miles north of Bluefields. Station of the Moravian Mission (1880), with (1900) 1 missionary and wife, 6 native workers, men and women; 1 chapel, and 1 day school.

KARELIAN LANGUAGE: A dialect of the Finnish which is spoken in the district of Tver in Russia. It is written with the Russian alphabet.

KARENS: The Karens include several related tribes, scattered over various portions of Lower Burma, and extending into Northern Siam. All told they number probably not far from one million. Evidence seems to indicate that their ancestors came into Burma from western China. Indeed they bear a considerable resemblance to the alien people of western China to-day, called by the Chinese *Ya-yin* or "wild people." The language of the Karens is of the monosyllabic class and Tibeto-Burman family. It was unwritten until the coming of the missionaries, who adapted the Burmese alphabet to its use. Its various dialects so far resemble each other that missionary work is carried on mainly through the use of two, the Sgau and the Pwo dialects. Dr. Mason has grouped the various Karen tribes concisely under three sub-divisions, viz., the Sgaus, Pwos, and Bghais. With the Sgaus proper he included the Pakus, Maunephghas, and the small tribe of the We-was; while the Mopghas are classed with the Pwos. The total number of Pwos and of Sgaus has been given as 310,000 and 260,000, respectively. Both these tribes are scattered widely over lower Burma, between the eastern and western Yoma mountain ranges, over the deltas of the Irrawaddy and the Salwen, and on the extreme south of the province of Tenasserim. The Sgaus and allied tribes extend as far north as Prome and Taung-ngu, the Pakus being found in the southern portion of the Taung-ngu district, while the Maunephghas are east from Shwegyin. The Pwos are possessed of rather stronger natural traits, and stand rather higher in the scale of civilization than the Sgaus. Being more Burmanized, however, they are less accessible to the Gospel, and the transforming power of Christian education is seen chiefly among the Sgaus. These tribes are somewhat low in stature, with olive complexion, and dark hair and eyes and gentle manner; attractive faces are common. In the plains the so-called villages are simply small groups of houses, usually from six to twenty, in the rice fields, a village of fifty houses being unusual. The people are chiefly agriculturists, those of the plains industriously raising rice in large quantities.

The Bghais, including several minor tribes, as the Geckhos, Padaungs and others, inhabit the mountains N. E. of Taung-ngu. They are fierce and warlike, and, except where modified by Christianity, locate their villages on elevations difficult of accesss. Each village consists of a single house, through which runs a long hall, with rooms opening off either side. The Red Karens, classed by Dr. Mason with the Bghais, receive their name from the color of their dress. They occupy a territory N. E. of Taung-ngu, separate from other tribes, and are the most warlike of the Karens, never having been conquered by the Burmese.

The Karens are notably simple-minded, and except for the wilder hill-tribes, are lovers of peace, and possess a character that is a curious mixture of timidity and courage. Timid and retiring ordinarily, on occasions, as during the Anglo-Burman wars, they have risen to notable heights of courage, showing complete indifference to death. Nevertheless, the Red Karens aside, their natural quietness of disposition, together with the smallness of their numbers, kept them in subjection to the Burmese, prior to the British occupation of lower Burma. With a certain stoicism under misfortune, they unite a good deal of natural, tho undemonstrative, kindliness. They are both obstinate and tractable, it being a common saying that a Karen can be led anywhere, but driven nowhere. Petty lying is universal, treachery rare. Much inferior to the Burmese in personal cleanliness, they are also much less immoral. Their extreme clannishness is perhaps an outcome of their long oppression under the rule of other races. The Karens of the plains, however, have largely adopted the Burmese mode of dress, while the use of the Burmese language is rapidly on the increase, especially among the Pwo-Karens. When instructed they develop a decided taste for music, excelling in singing. Under education, their mental processes are slow, but persistent and fruitful. The original *nat*, or spirit-worship, prevalent among the Karens, has been less modified among the Bghais than in any of the others. God has but little active concern in the world at present, and nothing is to be feared either from him or from good spirits. The Karens in general, therefore, give little thought to either, but concentrate their effort upon misleading, or placating, a personal devil, in whom they believe, and the innumerable *nats* or evil spirits which swarm on every hand, in mountains, streams, trees, and in almost every natural object. Idolatry is found only among those Karens, chiefly Pwos, who have adopted Buddhism.

The remarkable body of precepts and traditions handed down from the Karen elders has often arrested attention, and has led some to infer a Jewish origin for this people, many of the precepts possessing much beauty and moral elevation. A few condensed extracts from the traditions are here given:

"Anciently God commanded, but Satan appeared deceiving unto death.
The dragon beguiled the woman and Tha-nai.
A white fruit took the great dragon,
And gave to the daughter and son of God.
They kept not all the law of God; were deceived—deceived unto death."

The story of the creation of woman from the rib of the first man, and of the forbidden fruit, the woman first transgressing, then persuading her husband, closely resembles the Scripture narrative.

Sense of estrangement from God, and an almost Messianic hope mingle in the following:

"God formerly loved the Karen nation above all others, but because of their transgression he cursed them.
God departed with our younger brother, the white foreigner.
When God departed, the Karens became slaves to the Burmans."

In the midst of their suffering they remembered the ancient sayings of the Elders:

"That God would yet save them, that a Karen king would yet appear.
When he arrives there will be but one monarch, Everything will be happy;
And even lions and leopards will lose their savageness"

Missionary work among these people has been much helped by the traditions of which these lines are samples:

"Our ancestors said, that when our younger brothers come back,
The white foreigners, (in ships from the west), Who were able to keep company with God, the Karens will be happy.
Hence the Karens longed for those who were to come by water."

KARIB, or **KARIF**: The aboriginal inhabitants of Dutch Guiana, South America.

KARIKAL: A town on the Coromandel coast, India, and a French possession, situated 13 miles N. of Negapatam. It has an important rice trade. Population (1891) 70,500. Station of the Leipzig Missionary Society (1895), with 3 native workers and 130 professed Christians.

KARIMGANJ: A town in Assam, 28 miles E. of Sylhet. Station of the Welsh Calvinistic Methodist Missionary Society, with (1900) 1 missionary and his wife, 1 woman missionary, an elementary school and a dispensary.

KARIMNAGAR: A town in the native state of Haidarabad, India, situated about 85 miles N. E. of Haidarabad. A station of the WMS, with 1 missionary, 45 native workers, 19 chapels, 28 Sunday schools, 23 day schools and 1,495 professed Christians, of whom 373 are communicants.

KARKALA. See KARAKAL.

KARKLOOF: A village in Natal, S. Africa, situated in the Weenen district, 10 miles N. E. of Weenen. Station of the Maritzburg Missionary Association, with 1 missionary and 480 professed Christians.

KARNAL: A town in the Punjab, India, situated 50 miles south by east of Ambala. The city is of great antiquity. Population (1891) 22,000, of whom 17,000 are Hindus. A station of the SPG (1862), with 2 missionaries, 1 missionary woman, 10 native workers, 4 day schools, and 22 professed Christians. Name sometimes spelled Karnaul.

KARNUL: A town in the Madras Presidency, India, situated in the district of the same name on a rocky point at the junction of the Hindri and Tangabhadra Rivers. It is the center of a large Telugu population. Climate on the whole malarious. Population (1891) 24,400, of whom 12,000 are Muslims and 10,000 Hindus. Station of the ABMU (1870), with (1903) 1 missionary and his wife, 41 native workers, men and women; 20 outstations, 10 day schools, 2 boarding schools and 1,036 communicants. Station also of the SPG, with (1902) 1 missionary, 51 native workers, men and women; 20 day schools and 2 boarding schools. Name written by the societies Kurnool.

KARONGA: A post of the African Lake Corporation in Nyasaland, Africa, situated on the west shore of Lake Nyasa at the eastern terminus of the Stevenson Road. Station of the UFS, with (1903) 1 missionary and his wife, 59 native workers, 24 outstations and 27 elementary schools.

KARRACHI. See KARACHI.

KARS: A strongly fortified city of Turkey in Asia, historically important, and taken by Russia from Turkey in the war of 1877-78. Its population (12,000) is largely Armenian, and it was successfully worked as an outstation of Erzerum (ABCFM) up to 1879. After the city became Russian territory the Evangelical Armenian Church was officially recognized and protected by the government, but the missionaries were not allowed to visit it. The permanency and vitality of the missionary church at this place has been tested by this experience and it has not failed under the test.

KARSHUN LANGUAGE. See SYRIAC.

KARSIUNG: A town in Bengal, India, situated 12 miles S. W. of Darjiling. Station of the Church of Scotland Woman's Missionary Committee (1896), with 2 women missionaries and 2 native women workers.

KARUNKODDATIVE: A town on the east coast of Ceylon, India, situated 38 miles S. S. W. of Batticaloa. A station of the WMS, with 1 missionary, 9 native workers, 2 outstations, 1 chapel, 4 Sunday schools, 4 day schools and 59 Christians.

KARUR: A town in the district of Coimbatore, Madras, India, situated about 44 miles west north west of Trichinopoli. It is the capital of the ancient kingdom of Chera, taken by the English in 1801. Population 11,000, nearly all of whom are Hindus. Station of the WMS, with (1903) 4 missionaries, 38 native workers, 4 outstations, 5 chapels, 8 Sunday schools, 13 day schools, 1 high school, 1 industrial school, 1 orphanage and 219 professed Christians, of whom 130 are communicants.

KASERGOD. See CASSERGODE.

KASHGAR: A city in Chinese Turkestan, the most western city of the Chinese Empire, and capital of the province of Sin-kiang. It stands at an altitude of 4,000 feet, at the confluence of several routes of travel, in a rich oasis. Population 50,000. Station of the Swedish Missionary Union (1894), with (1900) 3 missionaries and their wives, 2 native workers, a day school and a dispensary.

KASHING. See KIA-HSING-FU.

KASHMIR. See SRINAGAR.

KASHMIR: A native state in India, lying among the great mountains of the Himalaya range north of the Punjab. Tibet touches it on the east, and after passing the great Karakorum range on the north, one enters soon the territories of Kashgar, wholly outside the limits of India. The country is for the most part an elevated valley, over 5,000 feet above the sea, surrounded by lofty mountains. Total area, nearly

81,000 square miles, with a population of 2,543,952. The ruler is known as the Maharaja of Kash-Cashmir, and, like the other native rulers of India, he is in political subordination to the British Government. The predominant religion is Mohammedanism, Hinduism being the religion of about one-third of the people. About one per cent. of the population are Buddhists. Missions have been conducted there with the utmost difficulty until within very recent times on account of the hostility of the native government (the Maharaja is a devout and intense Hindu) and also because the regulation debarring Europeans from permanent residence in the valley compelled the missionaries to break off their labors with the close of the season and leave the country entirely for a large part of each year. In 1854 and again in 1862 explorations and tours were made through Kashmir by missionaries of the CMS stationed in the Punjab, who made an unsuccessful attempt to establish a permanent mission in 1864. In 1865 Dr. Elmslie, a Scotch medical missionary in the service of that Society, reached Srinagar, and in spite of all obstacles had made a promising beginning, when his labors were terminated by his death, in 1872. The Society, however, has been able to carry on the mission since, and it has been of great benefit to the people, especially during the famine of 1880 and the distress following the great earthquake in 1884, and the cholera epidemics which sweep through the land almost periodically. The CMS now has two mission stations in Kashmir.

KASHMIRI LANGUAGE: Belongs to the Indic branch of the Aryan family of languages. It is spoken in Kashmir and is written with Arabic letters slightly modified for the purpose.

KASUR: A town in the Punjab, India, situated 32 miles S. by E. of Lahore. Population (1891) 20,300, of whom 15,400 are Muslims. Station of the Zenana Bible and Medical Mission, with (1900) 4 women missionaries.

KATANA: A village on the west coast of Ceylon, situated about 25 miles north of Colombo. Station of the WMS (1903), with 1 missionary, 12 native workers, 3 outstations, 5 chapels, 5 Sunday schools, 5 day schools and 80 professed Christians, of whom 61 are communicants.

KATCHCHI LANGUAGE: Belongs to the Indic branch of the Aryan family, being a dialect of Sindhi, strongly affected by the Gujarati. The alphabet used is the Hindi, with some slight modifications.

KATHIAWAR: A peninsula, nearly square in shape, which forms the western part of Gujarat (q. v.).

KATNI: A town in the Central Provinces, India, situated 50 miles N.E. of Jabalpur. Station of the CEZ (1897), with (1903) 1 woman missionary, 13 native workers, 1 outstation and 2 village schools. The CMS also has a station here, with (1903) 1 missionary and his wife and 1 outstation.

KAU: A settlement in the island of Halmaheira, Moluccas, Dutch East Indies, situated on Kau Bay in the east central part of the island. Station of the Utrecht Missionary Society (1898).

KAVALI: A town in the Presidency of Madras, India, situated in the district of Nellore, 33 miles N. of Nellore City. Population (1891) 5,000. Station of the ABMU (1893), with (1903) 1 missionary and his wife, 2 women missionaries, 34 native workers, men and women; 20 outstations, 3 places of worship, 4 day schools, 1 boarding school, 1 dispensary and 1,200 professed Christians, of whom 331 are communicants.

KAWATARIA: A station of the Australian Wesleyan Methodist Missionary Society on the Trobriand Islands, lying off the E. shore of British New Guinea, South Pacific Ocean. It now (1900) has 1 missionary and his wife, 2 women missionaries, 5 native workers, 2 outstations, 4 places of worship, 3 day schools and a theological training class.

KAWIMBE: A village in Nyasaland, Central Africa, situated at an altitude of 5,300 feet, about 21 miles E. S. E. of the southern end of Lake Tanganyika. Station of the LMS (1887), with (1903) 3 missionaries, 1 missionary's wife, 6 native workers, 13 schools and 1 industrial school.

KAYIN, or **KAYINTOCHAU.** See KIA-YING-CHAU.

KAZAK, or **KAZAN TURKI LANGUAGE.** See TURKISH LANGUAGE.

KEBOEMEN: A town in the island of Java, Dutch East Indies, situated about 75 miles S. W. of Samarang. Station of the Reformed Church of the Netherlands (1900).

KEDIRI: A town in the island of Java, Dutch East Indies, situated in a lovely valley 60 miles S. W. of Surabaya. Population 16,000. Station of the Netherlands Missionary Society (1849), with (1900) 1 missionary and his wife, 26 native workers, 15 outstations, 11 day schools and 1 industrial school.

KEDOENG PENDJALIN: A town on the northern coast of Java, Dutch East Indies, about 45 miles N. E. of Samarang. Station of the Netherlands Mennonite Board of Missions (1865).

KEETMANNSHOOP: A station of the Rhenish Missionary Society in German Southwest Africa, situated 180 miles E. of Angra Pequena, among the Namaquas. It has now (1903) 2 missionaries, 1 missionary's wife, 4 native workers, 1 day school and 1,329 professed Christians, of whom 546 are communicants.

KEGALLA: A town in Ceylon, situated 20 miles W. of Kandy. Station of the CMS (1880), with (1903) 1 missionary, 2 women missionaries, 3 native workers, 7 outstations, 1 village school and 1 high school. Name is sometimes spelled Kegalle.

KEHURUKO: A station in the Kikuyu district of British East Africa, situated near Ft. Smith, on the Uganda Railway, about 300 miles N. W. of Mombasa. Station of the CMS (1883), with (1903) 1 missionary, 1 woman missionary, 1 native worker, 1 day school and 6 Christians. The place is sometimes spoken of as Kikuyu.

KEITH-FALCONER, Ion: Born in Edinburgh, Scotland, in 1856. Died at Sheikh-Othman, Aden, Arabia, May 11, 1887. Born of a noble lineage, surrounded by the most attractive social advantages, blessed by a strong body and vigorous mind, he, early in life, dedicated all of his powers to the service of his Lord. While pursuing his brilliant career at Cambridge, the missionary spirit burned in him, and before leaving his native land for the foreign field he entered upon varied forms of Christian service. He became the leader of a band of Christian students who, in an old theater, near Cambridge, carried on ragged school work and Gospel evangelism, and in after years he joined Mr. Charrington in his Tower Hamlets Mission in the East End of London. After he passed his last examination at Cambridge, in 1880, he commenced the study of Arabic, including the Koran, and afterward, in order that he might acquire the colloquial language and learn the temper of the Arabic mind in following the Mohammedan faith, he went to the Nile, and to Assiout, residing, for several months, with the well-known missionary, Dr. H. W. Hogg. In the autumn of 1885 he went to Aden "to prospect," and as a result he determined to locate at Sheikh-Othman, within the territory but 10 miles from the town of Aden. While visiting Scotland in 1886 he laid his plans for a large work in Southern Arabia. He decided to establish a school, a medical mission and a depot for the distribution of the Scriptures. He was willing to put himself under a Scottish Foreign Mission Board with the understanding that he was himself to pay all costs of the mission. In the winter of 1886 he laid the foundation of his mission premises and work, and soon the impress of his consecrated life was felt among the Muslims. But the Aden fever proved a fatal foe, and in May, 1887, the "Martyr of Aden entered God's Eden." The Keith-Falconer Mission to Arabia has not died; it is carried on by the United Free Church of Scotland, and since its founder was buried new impulse has been given to the attempt to carry Christianity to the land of Ishmael.

KELE LANGUAGE: Of the Bantu family. It is spoken by tribes found in the Gabun district of the coast region of French Congo, W. Africa. Missionaries of the PN have made literary use of it, writing it with Roman letters. Also called Dikele.

KELLOGG, Samuel H.: Dr. Kellogg went out to India, as a missionary of the American Presbyterian Board (N), in 1864, sailing from Boston on December 20. He had been graduated from Princeton College in 1861, and from the Princeton Theological Seminary in 1864. In 1876 Mrs. Kellogg died, and he was obliged to return home on account of his inability to arrange otherwise for his four motherless little children, all of them under ten years of age. Early in 1877 he became pastor of the Third Presbyterian Church of Pittsburg, and in September of the same year succeeded Dr. A. A. Hodge in the Western Theological Seminary. On May 20, 1886, he became pastor of the St. James Square Presbyterian Church of Toronto, Canada, where he exerted a great influence until his resignation in September, 1892, when he returned to India to accept the appointment of the North India and British and Foreign Bible societies as one of a committee of three to translate the Old Testament Scriptures into Hindi.

Dr. Kellogg was a man of great mental power and notable scholarship. In 1891-92 he was Stone Lecturer in Princeton Theological Seminary; and besides the section of Leviticus in the Expositor's Bible Series, a book on the *Jews in History and Prophecy*, and his last book on *Comparative Religion*, he had written a great deal, both in the way of books and articles. In his death, by accident, May 3, 1899, the mission cause suffered a profound loss.

KEMENDINE: A village in Burma, British India, situated 4 miles north by west of Rangun, with a population of 5,000. Station of the SPG, with (1902) 1 missionary, 35 native workers, 3 day schools, 2 high schools, and 1,090 professed Christians, of whom 183 are communicants.

KENDAL: A village on the N. coast of Java, Dutch East Indies, about 10 miles N. N. W. of Samarang. Station of the Neukirchen Missionary Society (1894).

KENG TUNG: A town in Burma, British India, situated in the Laos or Shan states, about 240 miles E. by S. of Mandalay and 150 miles N. N. W. of Chieng Mai, in Siam. Station of the ABMU (1901), with (1903) 1 missionary and his wife and 3 native workers. Name locally pronounced Chieng Toong.

KENT: A town in Sierra Leone, Africa, situated on Cape Shilling 25 miles S. of Freetown. The church there has charge of religious work in the Banana Islands. Station of the CMS (1819), with (1903) 16 native workers, 6 outstations, 1 chapel, 1 Sunday school, 7 village schools, and 958 professed Christians, of whom 347 are communicants. The work, however, is carried on by the local church.

KEPPEL ISLAND: An island about 22 miles in circumference lying in the South Atlantic near West Falkland Island and a little to the N. of it. The South American Missionary Society occupied this island in 1855 in order to make of it a base for missionary operations in Tierra del Fuego. At the first they did not permit any natives to land upon the island, but after buildings had been erected an industrial and training school was opened with the purpose of preparing the Tierra del Fuego children for usefulness among their own people. The island is not at present retained on the Society's list of stations.

KERAK: A town in Syria, Turkey (Kir of Moab), formerly the capital of Moab. It has a citadel founded in 1131. The town was captured during the crusades, and is now the seat of the bishop. Population, 8,000, of whom 6,000 are Muslims. This town is the last on the road from Damascus to Mecca where Christians may live. It may be seen from Jerusalem, 50 miles away, since it stands on the mountains of Moab. It is rapidly growing in importance by reason of the Pilgrim Railroad now being built to Mecca. The Turkish Government hampers the mission there considerably, with especial vigilance against the entrance of Western ideas. Station of the CMS (1894), with (1903) 1 missionary and his wife, 1 native worker, 1 dispensary. The statistics are included under Es Salt.

KERBELA: A town in Mesopotamia, Asiatic Turkey, situated about 100 miles S. W. of Baghdad. It is famous for the tombs of Hassau and Hussein, the murdered sons of the Caliph Ali. Since these two men are regarded by the Shi'ite Muslims as martyrs, the place of their burial is sacred. To the Shi'ites Kerbela is quite as important a place of pilgrimage as Mecca.

KEREPUNU: A settlement on the southern coast of British New Guinea, situated about 70 miles S. E. of Port Moresby. Station of the LMS (1877), with (1903) 1 missionary and his wife, 35 native workers, men and women; 21 schools, and 1,400 professed Christians, of whom 644 are communicants.

KERMAN: A town in the province of Kerman, Persia, situated 225 miles N. by E. of Bender Abbas. It stands on a plain surrounded by mountains, just at the confluence of several trade routes. It is a great trading emporium and has many lofty and well-built bazars. Altitude, 5,680 feet. Population, 40,000. Station of the CMS (1897), with (1903) 1 missionary and his wife, 3 women missionaries, 1 native worker, 1 village school, 1 dispensary, and 7 professed Christians. The name is sometimes spelled Kirman.

KERR, John G., M.D.: Died at Canton, China, August 10, 1901. Dr. Kerr was born in Ohio in 1828, and was appointed by the PN a medical missionary to China in 1853; he remained on the field until 1876, when he came home to educate his children. He remained in the United States until 1878, during which time he was engaged in missionary work among the Chinese in California. He returned to his work at Canton in 1878, and with the exception of the usual furloughs in the United States, he labored with wonderful fidelity and success until his death, completing a service of over forty-four years.

During this period he published twelve works, of thirty-two volumes, in Chinese, on medicine and surgery, besides contributing to many other lines of Chinese literature. His great work was in the Canton Hospital, which he built up from a daily dispensary. During the last few years he was deeply interested in providing a refuge for the insane, and at the time of his death had a building accommodating fifty patients.

It is impossible in a brief sketch to give more than a glimpse of the life work of Dr. Kerr. He has gone to his reward, but his works will remain as monuments to his memory.

KETA: A town in the Gold Coast Colony, W. Africa, situated 150 miles E. of Christiansborg. Station of the North German Missionary Society (1853), with (1903) 3 missionaries, 1 with his wife; 3 missionary women, 17 native workers, men and women; 7 outstations, 9 day schools, 1 boarding school, 1 woman's training school, and 710 professed Christians.

KETI: A settlement in the western part of Madras, India, situated in the Nilgiri Hills, about 25 miles N. W. of Coimbatore. Station of the Basel Missionary Society (1846), with (1903) 3 missionaries and their wives, 47 native workers, men and women; 26 elementary schools, 24 elementary schools, 1 normal school for teachers, 1 theological training class, and 473 professed Christians.

KHADSAWPHRA. See Mao-phlang.

KHAIRAGARH: A town in the Central Provinces, India, about 48 miles W. N. W. of Raipur. Station of the Pentecost Bands of the World (1901), with 1 missionary and his wife and 1 woman missionary.

KHAMLA: A town in the Central Provinces, India, situated near Bithron, about 40 miles W. S. W. of Bhopal. Station of the Kurku Indian Mission (1889), with (1903) 1 missionary.

KHAMMAMETT: A town in the native state of Haidarabad, India, situated about 115 miles E. of the city of Haidarabad. Station of the CMS (1888) and CEZ (1889), with (together, 1903) 1 missionary and his wife, 2 women missionaries, 50 native workers, men and women; 10 village schools, 1 hospital, 1 dispensary, and 1,464 professed Christians, of whom 348 are communicants.

KHANDALA: A town in the Bombay Presidency, India, well known as a sanitarium, situated about 41 miles N. W. of Poona. Station of the Poona Indian Village Mission, with 3 missionary women and a dispensary.

KHANDWA: A town in the Central Provinces, India, headquarters of the district of Nimar, and situated 70 miles S. S. E. of Indore. The climate of Nimar district is, on the whole, good, tho the jungle parts inhabited by the hill tribes are extremely malarious. Population (1891) 15,500, of whom 10,000 are Hindus and 4,500 Muslims. It was once a famous seat of the Jain worship. Station of the ME, with (1903) 1 missionary and his wife, 1 woman missionary, 23 native workers, men and women; 18 Sunday schools, 2 day schools, 1 orphanage, and 689 professed Christians, of whom 70 are communicants.

KHARAR: A town in the Punjab, India, 27 miles N. by W. of Ambala. Population, 5,000. Station of the BMS (1890), with (1903) 1 missionary and his wife, 33 native workers, men and women; 16 outstations, 5 Sunday schools, 16 day schools, 1 boarding school and 530 professed Christians, of whom 281 are communicants.

KHARMATAR: A town in Bengal, India, 12 miles S. S. E. of Madhapur. Station of the PB, with 1 missionary and his wife and an orphanage. Name written by the missionaries, Karmatar.

KHARTUM: A town on the left bank of the Blue Nile, close to its confluence with the White Nile, founded by Mohammed Ali Pasha, Viceroy of Egypt, in 1823. It stands at an altitude of 1,273 feet, and has been a center of considerable commerce. For many years it was the capital of the Egyptian Sudan, and was the scene of the tragic death of General Gordon when it was captured by the Mahdi's troops in 1885. It was recaptured by the Anglo-Egyptian forces under General Kitchener, September 4, 1898, and was then found to be in a ruined condition. It has since been recovering its lost prosperity. Population (estimated) 25,000. Station of the UP (1900), with 2 missionaries, 1 a physician. Station also of CMS (1902), with 1 missionary and 1 day school.

KHASI HILLS: A range of mountains forming with the Jaintia Hills the border between Assam and Bengal. These mountains are inhabited by various hill-tribes,—the Garos, the Khasis, the Jaintias, Nagas, etc.,—who were very degraded, without books or a written language, and engaged mainly in hunting, and at times in robbery. In 1834 the British Government made a treaty with the kings of Khasi, providing for the establishment of a military post at Cherra and the construction of a road to Assam. In 1840 the Welsh Calvinistic Methodist Missionary Society sent out their first missionary to the hills, where now, in the seven districts, flourishing churches have been formed, with a membership of over 3,000; and within the day schools and Sunday schools about 10,000 pupils are gathered.

KHASIAN LANGUAGE: Belongs to the aboriginal and non-Aryan languages of Assam. It was written in the Bengali character by Dr. Carey in 1827. Late missionaries, and especially those of the Welsh Calvinistic Society, have adapted the Roman letters to its uses, and have taken steps toward the beginnings of a Khasian literature.

KHATITOLO: A village in Chota Nagpur, Bengal, India, situated 60 miles S. W. of Lohardaga. Station of the Gossner Missionary Society, with (1903) 2 missionaries, 72 native workers, 33 places of worship, a day school, a boarding school, and 14,357 professed Christians. Name written by the Society, Khutitoli.

KHED: A town in the Bombay Presidency, India, situated 22 miles N. of Poona. Station of the Poona Indian Village Mission, with 4 women missionaries and a dispensary. Name written by the Society, Khed-Shiwapur.

KHERWARA: A town in Bombay, India, situated 90 miles N. E. of Ahmadabad, in the Bhil country of Rajputana. Station of the CMS (1880), with (1903) 1 missionaries, 2 of them with their wives; 2 women missionaries, 15 native workers, 11 village schools, 1 dispensary, 1 orphanage, and 169 professed Christians. These statistics include Bilaria and Lusaria.

KHOKAND: A territory in Western Turkestan, annexed by Russia in 1876, and now called Ferghana.

KHORAI. See KURAI.

KHUDAWANDPUR: A station of the Kurku Indian Mission (1900), in the outskirts of Ellichpur, in the Central Provinces, India. It consists of the station buildings connected with an orphanage and a flourishing industrial enterprise for the instruction and support of the orphans. The name, which means City of God, was given to it by the missionaries.

KHULNA: A town in Bengal, India, 78 miles east-northeast of Calcutta. It is a place of considerable importance, with a thriving trade, as all the boat traffic for Calcutta from the E. and N. E. passes by this point. Population (1891) 8,700, of whom 5,000 are Hindus and nearly 3,000 Mohammedans. Station of the BMS (1860), with (1903) 2 missionaries and their wives, 37 native workers, men and women; 15 outstations, 23 day schools, 1 boarding school, 1 dispensary, and 1,039 professed Christians, of whom 339 are communicants.

KHUMMAMETT. See KAMAMET.

KHURJA: A town in the United Provinces, India, situated in the district of Bulandshahr, 50 miles S. by E. of Delhi. It is quite a center of trade and has a population (1891) of 26,300, of whom 14,800 are Hindus and 11,000 Mohammedans. Station circuit of the ME, with (1903) 12 native workers, 4 places of worship, 35 Sunday schools, 5 day schools, and 1,056 professed Christians, of whom 490 are communicants.

KHUTITOLI. See KHATITOLO.

KIA-DING. See KIATING.

KIA-HSING-FU: A town in the province of Che-kiang, China, situated on the Grand Canal, midway between Soo-chow and Hang-kau. Built in 897. It is an important commercial center, celebrated for its rice, tiles, and brass-work. Station of the PS (1895), with (1903) 3 missionaries and their wives, 1 woman missionary, 5 native workers, men and women; 2 places of worship, 3 day schools, 1 boarding school, and 1 dispensary.

KIAI-CHAU: A town in the province of Shan-si, China, 215 miles S. W. of Tai-yuen-fu. Station of the CIM (1895), with (1903) 1 missionary and his wife, 2 women missionaries, 4 native workers, and 1 boarding school. Name written by the Society, Hiai-chau.

KIAI-HIU. See KIE-HIU-HSIEN.

KIANG-CHAU: A town in the province of Shan-si, China, situated on the Fen River 165 miles S. W. of Tai-yuen-fu. Station of the CIM (1898), vacant as yet (1903) since the massacre of missionaries during the Boxer troubles.

KIANG-TSIN: A town in the province of Szechwan, China, situated 28 miles S. W. of Chungking-fu. Station of the CIM (1902), with 1 missionary and his wife.

KIANG-YIN-HSIEN: A town in the province of Kiang-su, China, situated on the south bank of the Yangtse River, 85 miles from Wu-sung. Population, about 200,000. Station of the PS (1895), with (1903) 2 missionaries and their wives, 1 native worker, 4 outstations, and 4 places of worship.

KIATING: A town in the province of Kiang-su, China, 28 miles N. W. of Shanghai. Station of the PE (1882) and of the MES. Name also written Kading and Kia-ding.

KIA-TING-FU: A town in the province of Szechwan, China, situated 82 miles S. of Cheng-tu on the right bank of the Min River, at the confluence of the Tung-ho and Ya-ho. It is a center of the silk-weaving industry in that province. Population, about 25,000. Station of the CIM (1888), with 1 missionary and his wife, 2 women missionaries, 4 native workers, 1 day school and 1 dispensary. Station also of the Methodist Church in Canada (1892), with (1900) 2 women missionaries, 1 day school, 1 dispensary, and 1 hospital. Station also of the ABMU (1894), with (1903) 2 missionaries and their wives, 6 native workers, 10 outstations, and 11 places of worship. Name written by the Societies, Kia-ting.

KIA-YING-CHAU: A town in the province of Kwang-tung, China, among the Hakka people; situated on the Min River 68 miles N. N. W. of Swatow. Population, about 30,000. Station of the Basel Missionary Society (1883), with (1903) 3 missionaries (one with his wife), 7 native workers, men and women; 4 outstations, 1 boarding school and 357 professed Christians, of whom 261 are communicants. Station also of the ABMU (1890), with (1903) 2 missionaries with their wives, 8 native workers, men and women; 4 outstations, 3 places of worship, 3 day schools, and 455 professed Christians, of whom 105 are communicants. The name is written by the Societies Kayintschu and Kayin.

KIBOKOLA: A town in Angola, W. Africa, 280 miles N. E. of San Paolo de Loanda. Station of the BMS (1899), with (1903) 3 missionaries and 2 wives of missionaries.

KIBUNZI: A settlement in the Congo Free State, W. Africa, situated near the right bank of the Congo River, about 20 miles N. of Bansa Manteka. Station of the Swedish Missionary Society (1887), with 1 missionary woman, 12 native workers, 15 outstations, 1 boarding school, 1 orphanage, 1 dispensary, and 385 professed Christians.

KI-CHAU: A district in the province of Chi-li, China, lying about 200 miles S. W. of Tien-tsin.

Station field of the LMS (1888), with (1903) 4 missionaries and their wives (the missionary residence being at Hsiao-chang), 17 native workers, men and women; 33 outstations, 2 dispensaries, 1 hospital, and 950 professed Christians, of whom 704 are communicants. Name of district written by the Society, Chi-chow.

KI-CHAU: A town in the province of Shan-si, China, about 50 miles west of Ping-yang-fu. Station of the CIM (1891), with (1903) 1 missionary and his wife, 1 woman missionary, and 1 native worker. Name written by the Society, Kih-chau.

KICHELWE: A settlement in German East Africa, about 12 miles E. S. E. of Dar es Salaam. Station of the Universities' Mission (1893), with (1900) 1 native worker, 2 native women workers, 2 day schools, and 160 professed Christians.

KIDUGALA: A settlement in German East Africa, about 40 miles N. E. from the north end of Lake Nyasa. Station of the Berlin Missionary Society (1898), with (1903) 2 missionaries.

KIE-HIU-HSIEN: A town in the province of Shan-si, China, situated 60 miles S. W. of Tai-yuen-fu. Station of the CIM (1891), with (1903) 1 missionary and his wife, 2 women missionaries, and 1 native worker. Name written by the Society, Kiai-hiu.

KIE-YANG-HSIEN: A town in the province of Kwang-tung, China, 25 miles N. W. of Swatow. Station of the ABMU (1896), with (1903) 1 missionary and his wife, 2 women missionaries, 22 native workers, men and women; 26 outstations, 14 places of worship, 7 day schools, and 2,600 professed Christians, of whom 639 are communicants. The name is written by the Society Kit-yang.

KIEL MISSION TO CHINA. See GERMANY; MISSIONARY SOCIETIES IN.

KIEN-CHANG-HSIEN: A town in the province of Kiang-si, China, 42 miles S. W. of Kiu-kiang. Station of the German China Alliance (1898), with 2 missionaries and a native worker. Station also of the PB.

KIEN-CHAU: A town in the province of Shen-si, China, situated about 40 miles N. W. of Hsi-ngan-fu. Station of the CIM (1894), with (1903) 1 missionary and his wife and 1 woman missionary.

KIEN-NING-FU: A town in the province of Fo-kien, China, situated 90 miles N. W. by N. of Fu-chau. Station of the CEZ, with (1903) 5 women missionaries, 1 native worker, and 1 hospital. The CMS also has a station there (1874), with (1903) 4 missionaries, 2 of them with their wives; 11 native workers, 1 chapel, 1 boarding school, 2 dispensaries, 1 hospital, 1 institute for lepers, and 260 professed Christians, of whom 98 are communicants. This Society writes the name Kien-Ning.

KIEN-PING-HSIEN: A town in the province of Ngan-hwei, China, 65 miles S. S. E. of Nanking. Station of the CIM (1894), with (1903) 1 missionary and his wife, 2 women missionaries, and 1 native worker. Name written by the Society, Kien-p'ing.

KIEN-YANG: A town in the province of Shen-si, China, 95 miles W. N.W. of Hsi-ngan-fu. Station of the CIM (1897), with (1903) 1 woman missionary.

KIEN-YANG-HSIEN: A town in the province of Fo-kien, China, situated 118 miles N. W. of Fu-chau. A station of the CMS (1891), with 3 women missionaries. Name is sometimes written Kien-yang.

KIFWA: A settlement in the Congo Free State, Africa, situated about 60 miles E. S. E. of Stanley Pool. Station of the ABMU (1890), with (1903) 2 missionaries (one with his wife), 35 native workers, 39 outstations, 4 places of worship, 39 day schools and 492 professed Christians.

KIH-CHAU. See KI-CHAU.

KIH-YAN. See KI-NGAN-FU.

KIKUYU. See KEHURUKO.

KILIMANI: One of the settlements on the Island of Zanzibar, situated S. of the town of that name. Station of the UM (1893), with 4 missionary women, 2 native workers, a day school and a boarding school.

KIMBERLY: A town in Cape Colony, S. Africa, situated in Griqualand West, 647 miles by railway N. W. of Cape Town. It is capital of the Kimberly District, and stands at an altitude of 4,000 feet in the midst of the great diamond fields not far from the W. border of the Orange River Colony. It is lighted by electric lights and is furnished by aqueduct with good water. Station of the Berlin Missionary Society (1875), with (1903) 1 missionary, 2 missionary women, 8 native workers, 5 outstations, and 939 professed Christians, of whom 370 are communicants. Station also of the SPG (1881), with 1 missionary; also of the South African Wesleyan Methodist Society, with (1900) 41 native workers, 12 outstations, 9 places of worship, 5 day schools and 476 professed Christians.

KI-MBUNDU LANGUAGE. See MBUNDU.

KINCAID, Eugenio: Born at Wethersfield, Conn., 1797, graduated at Hamilton Literary and Theological Institution 1822, in the same class with Rev. Jonathan Wade. Appointed a missionary of the Baptist Triennial Convention for Burma; sailed May 24, 1830. On his arrival in Burma he preached to the English congregation at Maulmain, but soon entered upon work among the natives. Bold, ardent, brave, he determined to establish a mission at the capital, and in 1833 he went to Ava. There he baptized his first converts. In 1837 he undertook to reach Assam by crossing the mountains between Burma and that country, but was forced to turn back, and having been repeatedly taken prisoner and robbed, he reached Ava in extreme destitution, after a journey of thirteen days. After a short residence in Arakan he was obliged to leave Burma and the missionary service on account of ill-health. In 1850 he returned to Burma under the ABMU and won the confidence of the king, who showed him much favor. After his return to Burma the same year, he labored principally at Prome until 1863, when he took his final departure from the mission field. He was an energetic missionary, especially noted for his long journeys into unexplored regions of heathen territory. He died at Girard, Kan., April 3, 1883.

KIN-CHAU-FU: A town in Manchuria, China, situated about 75 miles W. N. W. of Niu-chwang. Station of the Presbyterian Church in Ireland (1891), with (1900) 2 missionaries and their wives, 2 missionary women, 27 native workers, men and women; 10 outstations, 11 places of worship, 7 day schools, 1 theological training class, 2 dispensaries, 2 hospitals and 180 professed Christians.

KINCOLITH: A settlement in Alaska on the W. side of Portland Canal. Station of the CMS (1866), with (1903) 1 missionary and his wife, 2 native workers, 1 Sunday school, 2 village schools, 255 professed Christians, of whom 75 are communicants.

KING, Jonas: Born July 29, 1792, at Hawley, Mass. His father was a farmer noted for his love of the Scriptures and rigid adherence to their teachings. Under his instruction Jonas read the Bible through once between the ages of four and six, and then once yearly until the age of sixteen. His conversion occurred at the age of fifteen. Without funds or aid he determined on an education, learned the English grammar while hoeing corn, read the twelve books of the Æneid of Virgil in fifty-eight days, and the New Testament in Greek in six weeks. He graduated at Williams College 1816, and Andover Seminary 1819. While in Andover his mind was strongly drawn toward foreign mission work, especially in the East, and he desired to go to Europe to study Arabic, and then enter whatever field of labor should be open—perhaps among the Arabians or Persians. He decided to go to Paris to study with the celebrated De Sacy. On the eve of embarkation he was appointed professor of Oriental languages in Amherst College. Advised to accept the appointment, and the trustees approving his plan to study abroad, he sailed for Paris August 18, 1821. While engaged in this study he received a pressing invitation from Pliny Fisk—Mr. Parsons having died—to join him in mission work in the Holy Land. Having served during three years in Syria and Egypt, he left Beirut for America in 1827, going overland to Smyrna, where he spent several months in the study of modern Greek. After his return home he was invited by a ladies' committee in New York to go to Greece to distribute aid to the people suffering from Turkish oppression. He resigned his professorship at Amherst, declined a similar appointment at Yale, and went to Greece, reaching Poros July 28, 1828. He visited many important places, everywhere preaching, establishing schools, and relieving want. In 1829 he married a Greek lady of influence, who proved an efficient helper in the mission work. In 1830 the mission was transferred to the American Board. Having previously visited Athens, and arranged to reside there after the Turks had vacated the place in 1831, it became his permanent home. Here he built a school house, in which he had service in Greek every Sabbath till 1860. The establishment of schools was a prominent object with Dr. King, and he made it a condition that in them the Scriptures should be studied. At the "Evangelical Gymnasium," which he established, he gave religious instruction several times a week to about seventy pupils varying in age from ten to thirty-five years. He also formed a theological class composed of Greeks and Italians, to whom he gave regular and frequent instruction. Some of these have occupied important positions as teachers or in the employment of government. But the hierarchy became alarmed at the influence of his preaching, his schools, and his persistent circulation of the Scriptures. At the instigation of the Greek Synod he was brought before the Areopagus, the highest court in Athens, charged with reviling the "mother of God" and the "holy images." He was not, however, tried. After many threats against his life, in 1852 he was again arrested, put on trial for blasphemy and condemned to imprisonment and expulsion from the country. This sentence was quashed through the influence of the United States Government.

Dr. King was never free from petty persecution until he died, May 22, 1869, in his seventy-seventh year. He was a thorough linguist, having studied eleven languages, and speaking fluently five. His original works in Arabic, Greek and French were ten in number, some of them being widely read, and translated into other tongues. He revised and carried through the press eleven others. He distributed 400,000 copies of Scripture portions, religious tracts, and school books in Greece and Turkey, besides what he scattered during his travels in other parts of Europe and in Palestine, Syria and Egypt. He left his impress on the Greek nation. To him preeminently is it owing that the Scriptures since 1831 have been so extensively used in the schools, and that in Greece the Word of God is not bound.

KI-NGAN-FU: A town in the province of Kiang-si, China, situated about 160 miles S. W. of Nan-chung-fu, on the left bank of the Kan River. Station of the CIM (1891), with (1903) 1 missionary and his wife, 1 native worker and 1 opium refuge. Name written by the Society, Kian-fu.

KING-CHAU: A town in Kan-su, China, situated on the King River, about 45 miles E. S. E. of Ping-hang-fu. Station of the CIM (1895), with (1903) 1 missionary and his wife and 1 native worker.

KINGSBURY, Cyrus: Born at Alstead, N. H., November 22, 1786; graduated at Brown University 1812; Andover Theological Seminary 1815; ordained as a missionary of the ABCFM to the Choctaws and went to the Cherokee country in 1816, commencing a station at Brainerd. In June, 1818, he left Brainerd with Mr. and Mrs. Williams, to commence the mission among the Choctaws. They traveled in a wagon four hundred miles through the wilderness, to the place afterward called Eliot. In May, 1820, a new station called Mayhew was established, and in November Mr. and Mrs. Kingsbury made it their permanent home. Mr. Kingsbury continued in the Choctaw Mission, laboring with zeal and success until the ABCFM withdrew in 1859, and then continuing in the same field in connection with the Presbyterian and Southern Presbyterian Boards till his death, June 27, 1870. His period of missionary service was fifty-four years.

KING-TSE-KWAN: A town in the province of Ho-nan, China, situated on the Tan River, about 95 miles W. of She-ki-chen. It is a frontier station, with a custom-house. Population about 10,000. Station of the CIM (1896), with (1903) 1 missionary and his wife and 1 native worker.

KING WILLIAM'S TOWN: A town in Cape Colony, S. Africa, situated 29 miles W. N. W. of East London, at an altitude of 1,300 feet. It has been an important center of trade for the Kafirs. Population, 7,200. Station of the SPG, with (1902) 1 native worker and 280 professed Christians. Station also of the South African Wesleyan Methodist Mission, with (1900) 39 native workers, 6 outstations, 10 places of worship, 6 day schools and 383 professed Christians.

Station also of the National Baptist Convention (1900), with 1 missionary, 2 native workers and 25 professed Christians.

KIN-HWA-FU: A town in Che-kiang, China, 75 miles S. S. W. of Hang-chau. Climate, tropical, 25°—95°. Population, 50,000. Natives outwardly very prosperous; morally low. Station of the CIM (1875), now (1903) vacant. Station also of the ABMU (1883), with (1903) 2 missionaries (one with his wife), 3 women missionaries, 8 native workers, 5 outstations, 3 places of worship and 354 professed Christians, of whom 159 are communicants.

KINKEL: A town in Chota Nagpur, Bengal, India, 58 miles S. S. W. of Lohardaga. Station of the Gossner Missionary Society, with (1903) 2 missionaries, one having a wife; 58 native workers, men and women; 21 places of worship, 2 schools and 7,258 professed Christians, of whom 1,348 are communicants.

KINKENGE: A settlement in the Congo Free State, 10 miles W. of Bansa Manteke. Station of the Swedish Missionary Society (1897), with (1900) 3 missionaries, two of them with their wives; 1 boarding school and 1 dispensary.

KINWHA. See KIN-HWA-FU.

KIOTO: An important city of Japan, situated in the southwestern part of Hondo, the main island, and 329 miles by railway S. W. of Tokio, 5 miles from the S. end of Lake Biwa, with which it is connected by a navigable canal. It was founded in 723, and until 1868 was the capital of Japan. With its schools, hospitals, lunatic asylum, prisons, dispensary, almshouses, fountains, public parks and gardens, exquisitely beautiful cemeteries, and streets of almost painful cleanliness, Kioto is the best arranged and best managed city in Japan. It is noted for its manufactures of crape, bronze goods, and porcelain. For a long time foreigners were jealously excluded from this sacred city.

The town and the vicinity are crowded with objects of interest. The Mikado's palace covers 26 acres, and is a collection of very fine buildings. Among other objects of interest are the temple of 33,333 images of the Goddess of Mercy, and the bust of Buddha, 58 feet high. The climate is temperate. Population (1898) is 353,139. Station of the ABCFM (1875), with (1902) 5 missionaries (three with their wives), 2 women missionaries, 15 native workers, 29 outstations, 18 Sabbath schools, 1 boarding school, 1 theological class, 1 training class for women nurses, 1 hospital, and an important college known as the Doshisha. Station also of the MES (1898), with 1 missionary and his wife. Also station of the PE, with 4 missionaries (one with his wife), 2 women missionaries, a day school and a boarding school. Station also of the UB (1900), with 1 missionary and his wife. Also station of the PN (1890), with (1903) 1 missionary and his wife and 1 woman missionary. Also station of the German General Evangelical Missionary Society (1900), with 1 missionary and his wife. The YMCA has also established an agency there (1901).

KIRCHDORF: A village in Natal, S. Africa, near New Hanover. Station of the Lutheran Free Church of Hannover (1892), with (1903) 1 missionary, 1 native worker, 1 day school, and 200 professing Christians.

KIRGHIZ TURKI LANGUAGE. See TURKISH LANGUAGE.

KIRIN: A city in Manchuria, China, capital of the province of Kirin, situated 225 miles N. E. of Mukden, in a charming region encircled by hills on the north and by the Sungari River on the south. It stands at the head of navigation on this river, and many junks are built here. Population, 200,000. Station of the Presbyterian Church in Ireland (1894), with (1900) 2 missionaries, 1 with his wife; 22 native workers, 10 outstations, 11 places of worship, 8 day schools, 1 theological training class, a dispensary, a hospital, and 115 church members. The BFBS has an agency here with a Bible depot.

KIRMAN. See KERMAN.

KIRWINA. See KAWATARIA.

KISAUNI, or Frere Town: A village in British East Africa situated on the E. side of the inlet bordering Mombasa on the E., and 2 miles N. N. E. of Mombasa. Station of the CMS (1874), with (1903) 5 missionaries, four of them with their wives; 4 women missionaries, 15 native workers, 1 chapel, 2 boarding schools, 1 theological class, 1 orphanage, 565 professed Christians, of whom 208 are communicants.

KISMAYU: A settlement in the northern part of British East Africa, situated on the coast near the mouth of the Juba River. Station of the Evangelical Swedish National Missionary Society (1897).

KISSARAWE: A town in German East Africa, situated 30 miles S. W. of Dar es Salaam. Station of the German East Africa Missionary Society (1892), with (1903) 4 missionaries, 1 with his wife; 8 native workers, 7 outstations, 3 places of worship, 7 day schools, 1 industrial school, 1 theological training class, and 197 professed Christians.

KISSY: A town on the coast of Sierra Leone, Africa, situated 3 miles S. E. of Freetown, with a population of 2,000. Station of the CMS (1816), with (1903) 8 native workers, 4 day schools, and 1,714 professed Christians, of whom 1,094 are communicants. The congregation of this station is now under the care of the native church.

KITKATLA: A settlement 20 miles S. by W. of Port Errington, British Columbia. Station of the CMS (1903), with 1 missionary and his wife, 2 native workers, 1 Sunday school, 1 village school, 241 professed Christians, of whom 59 are communicants.

KIT YANG. See KIE-YANG-HSIEN.

KIU-CHAU. See KU-CHAU-FU.

KIU-KIANG-FU: A city in Kiang-si, China, on the south bank of the Yangtse, not far from the outlet of Lake Po-yang, and 135 miles by river S. E. of Han-kau. It was formerly the great center of the tea traffic. The climate is fairly good, hot in the summer, but bracing and cold in the winter. Opened to foreign trade in 1861. Population, about 35,000. Station of the ME, with (1903) 2 missionaries and their wives, 6 women missionaries, 19 native workers, men and women; 5 outstations, 5 day schools, 2 boarding schools, a college, a dispensary, a hospital, and 781 professed Christians. Station also of the CIM (1889), which serves as a center for the business transactions of the missionaries in the province, with (1903) 2 missionaries and their wives and 1 native worker. Station also of the PB; outstation of the PE, with 1 native worker and a sanitarium for the missionaries of the Society. Name also written Ku-kiang.

KIUNGANI: A suburb of the town of Zanzibar on the E. coast of the island. Station of the Universities Mission (1870), with (1900) 6 missionaries, 1 missionary woman, 23 native workers, 1 day school, 1 boarding school and 1 dispensary.

KIUNG-CHAU: A town in the province of Sze-chwan, China, situated 40 miles S. W. of Cheng-tu-fu. Station of the CIM (1901), with 2 missionaries, one with his wife.

KIUNG-CHAU-FU: A town on the island of Hainan, China, 250 miles southwest of Hongkong. Population, about 200,000. Station of the PN (1885), with (1900) 5 missionaries, 3 wives of missionaries, 2 women missionaries, 5 native workers, men and women; a dispensary, and a hospital. Name written by the Society, Kiung Chow.

KIUNKANI LANGUAGE: A dialect of the Marâthi, which belongs to the Indic branch of the Aryan family of languages. It is spoken by about 1,000,000 people of the Bombay Presidency living in the region between the Western Ghats of India and the shore of the Arabian Sea. It is written with the Marâthi or Modhi characters.

KLEIN POPO. See LITTLE POPO.

KLEINSCHMIDT, J. C.: One of the first missionaries of the Moravian Church to Greenland. He went to Lichtenau, about 40 miles from the Danish colony, Juliannehaapt, in 1777. After Kleinschmidt had worked in Greenland nineteen years he visited Europe, and after his return he completed the translation of the New Testament in June, 1821. All the missionaries joined in revising it, and it was sent to the British and Foreign Bible Society.

KLERKSDORP: A town in the Transvaal, Africa, situated about 123 miles southwest by west of Pretoria, and 7 miles north of the Vaal River. It is the oldest town in the Transvaal and the center of a small gold field. Population, 1,500. Station of the WMS, with (1903) 1 missionary, 40 native workers, 34 outstations, 3 chapels, 9 Sunday schools, 2 day schools, and 887 professed Christians, of whom 562 are communicants.

KLIPDAM: A village in the Transvaal Colony, S. Africa, situated 25 miles N. W. of Pietersburg. Station of the National Baptist Convention, with (1900) 2 missionaries and 1 missionary woman. Outstation also of the Berlin Missionary Society, its statistics being included in Kreuzburg, two miles distant.

KNIGHT, Joseph: Born at Stroud, Gloucestershire, England; educated by Rev. Dr. Williams at Stroud; ordained deacon September 21, 1817, and priest, 1818, by Bishop of Gloucestershire; embarked as a missionary of the CMS December 15, 1817, for Jaffna, North Ceylon; was stationed at Nellore. He was probably unsurpassed, if not unequaled, by any in India in his critical knowledge of the Tamil language. He was engaged for several years in preparing a Tamil and English dictionary and had made great progress in it when failure of health required him to leave for England in 1838. On his return in 1840 he died at Colombo, October 11, having been twenty-three years in the service.

KOBE: A city on the main island of Japan, 22 miles west of Osaka, on a small bay adjoining Hiogo Bay. It was opened to foreign commerce in 1878 at the same time as Hiogo, but owing to more favorable harbor conditions it has attracted foreign commerce more than Hiogo, and has grown so as to form with Hiogo one large city. The vicinity is beautiful and interesting. The climate is pleasant and healthful. Population of Kobe and Hiogo together, 104,000. Station of the ABCFM (1869), SPG (1876), ABMU (1881), MES (1886), PS (1890), with (1902) all together and including outstations, 13 missionaries, 10 wives of missionaries, 17 women missionaries, 92 native workers, men and women; 22 places of worship, 41 Sabbath schools, 6 day schools, 5 boarding schools, 1 theological school, 1 training school for women workers, 1 dispensary, and 1,300 professed Christians. Special features of the missionary equipment here are the fine college for girls (ABCFM) and the vessel for missionary touring of the Inland Sea (ABMU).

KOCHANNES: A town of Eastern Turkey, near the border of Persia, in the most inaccessible part of the mountains of Kurdistan. The seat of the Patriarch of the Nestorians. Missionaries of the ABCFM and the PN have frequently visited the place, but the only attempt to establish a station there was in 1882, when Mr. Wahl, sent out by the Archbishop of Canterbury, endeavored to set up a printing press and establish a school. There are now (1900) 2 missionaries of the Archbishop's mission there.

KOCHI: A town on the southeast coast of Shikoku, Japan, situated at the head of a beautiful bay. Population, about 40,000. Station of the PS (1885), with (1903) 1 missionary and wife, 1 woman missionary, 3 native workers, 27 outstations, 8 Sunday schools, and 1,750 professed Christians, of whom 750 are communicants.

KODAKAL: A town in Madras, India, situated in the region formerly known as Malabar, 32 miles S. E. of Calicut. Station of the Basel Missionary Society (1857), with (1903) 4 missionaries, two with their wives; 37 native workers, men and women; 7 outstations, 8 day schools, and 1,387 professed Christians, 649 of whom are communicants.

KODAIKANAL SCHOOL FOR MISSIONARY CHILDREN: A school at a summer resort in the Madras Presidency, India, established in 1902 by the concerted action of missionaries of the ABCFM and the RCA and benevolent friends in the United States. The site is at a mountain village, 50 miles N. W. of Madura, at an altitude of 7,000 feet, where the air is bracing and unaffected by the intense heat of the plains. The buildings belong to the ABCFM, and the school is under the management of a joint committee of the two missions interested. It designs to furnish instruction for missionaries' children between the ages of ten and fifteen years. While the school has been established for the children of members of the Madura mission and the Arcot Mission, children of other missionaries will be admitted.

Long experience has shown that white children cannot safely live in the hot plains of tropical India after they are nine or ten years old. This fact and the lack of suitable schools for American children in outlying districts have led to those separations of children in tender years from their parents which are among the most wearing griefs of missionaries in that land. But it has now been shown that young children can safely stay at Kodaikanal during ten months of the year. By the simple expedient of establishing a suitable school on that height, the missionaries can have their children near them some years longer than has been possible hitherto.

KODUR: A town in the Madras Presidency, India, situated 85 miles N. W. of Madras. Station of the Hermannsburg Missionary Society (1883), with (1903) 1 missionary and his wife and 10 native workers.

KOELLE, Sigismund Wilhelm: Born at Kleebroun, Württemberg, in 1822; died in 1902. He was educated at Basel Seminary and C. M. College, at Islington, and, with marked success, he studied Arabic under Prof. Ewald at Tübingen, which university conferred on him its Ph.D. degree. He was first sent by the CMS to Sierra Leone in 1847, and there he taught Hebrew to the Fourah Bay College students, with the result of enabling several negroes to read the Old Testament in the original. During his five years on the west coast he collected the materials for his great work, *Polyglotta Africana*, in which one hundred African languages and dialects are compared. This book was submitted to the French Institute, and Koelle was given the Volney prize. In 1855-59 he was attached to the Egypt and Palestine Missions, and in 1862 he joined Dr. Pfander at Constantinople in the mission started by the Society after the Crimean War. He held this position for twenty years, receiving many Mohammedan inquirers who came to him by night, and who were generally, after a time, caught by the Turkish police and disappeared. In 1880 Dr. Koelle's name was brought prominently into public notice. He and a distinguished Muslim Ulema named Ahmed Tewfik, who was assisting him linguistically, were arrested in the street by order of the minister of police. Koelle was soon released, but the Ulema was sentenced to death. The outrage produced great excitement in England, and it was only after an ultimatum had been sent to the Porte and the British fleet was ordered to the Dardanelles that the Sultan yielded and reprieved Ahmed Tewfik, who afterward embraced Christianity.

Koelle was one of the greatest linguists on the CM Society's roll of missionaries. He was the author of *Syllabic System of Writing amongst the Vei Tribe*, *Grammar and Vocabulary of Vei Language*, *Grammar of Kanuri or Bornu Language*, *Bornu Literature and Vocabulary*, *Polyglotta Africana*, *Kanuri Proverbs*, *Food for Reflection*, *Life of Christ*, *Prophecies Concerning Christ*, *The Death of Christ* (in English and Turkish), Translation of Book of Common Prayer into Turkish, and *Mohammed and Mohammedanism*. The last named work is a very severe analysis of the character of Mohammed as described by Muslim writers. It is too merciless for general acceptance, but is an admirable corrective when taken with the many works which err upon the side of unrestricted praise of the man of Mecca. For this work alone Dr. Koelle merits remembrance.

KOENIGSBERG: A settlement in Natal, Africa, 10 miles S. W. of Newcastle, and station of the Berlin Missionary Society (1868), with (1903) 2 missionaries, 12 native workers, men and women; 7 outstations and places of worship, and 510 professed Christians, of whom 213 are communicants.

KOFU: A town in Japan, situated on Hondo, the main island, 70 miles W. of Tokio. Station of the Methodist Church in Canada (1876), and of the Women's Society of that Church (1889), with (1900) 3 missionary women, 8 native workers, men and women; 15 outstations, 6 places of worship, 1 day school, 1 boarding school, 1 training class for women workers, and 360 professed Christians.

KOHIMA: A frontier post in the Naga hills, Assam, India, and the headquarters of the British Government supervising the hill tribes. It is at an elevation of 5,000 feet, and has a healthful climate. Population, 4,000; language, Angami Naga. Station of the ABMU (1879), with (1903) 1 missionary and his wife and 3 native workers.

KOI LANGUAGE: A dialect of the Gond, one of the Dravidian languages of Central India, and spoken by about 100,000 people. It has been reduced to writing by natives under the direction of the CMS, and is written with Roman letters.

KOIMBATUR. See COIMBATORE.

KOIS. See GONDS.

KOKSTAD: A town in Cape Colony, Africa, lying in Griqualand East, 65 miles W. of Shepstone. Station of the Church of Scotland (1878), with (1900) 2 missionaries, 6 native workers, 3 outstations, 4 places of worship, 1 day school and 396 professed Christians.

KOKURA: A town on Kiushiu Island, Japan, fronting on the Inland Sea, and situated 100 miles N. E. by N. of Nagasaki. Population, 14,000. Station of the SBC (1892), with 1 missionary and his wife, 2 native workers, 2 outstations, 1 Sunday school and 64 professed Christians. Station also of the CMS (1898), with 1 missionary and his wife, 2 women missionaries, 6 native workers, 3 outstations, 1 chapel, and 242 professed Christians, of whom 119 are communicants.

KOLAR: A town in the native state of Mysore, India, situated 39 miles E. by N. of Bangalore. Population, 11,000. Station of the ME, with (1903) 1 missionary and his wife, 8 women missionaries, 37 native workers, men and women; 5 preaching places, 6 day schools, and an orphanage with industrial department.

KOLHAPUR: Capital of the native state of that name, Bombay, India, situated about 97 miles W. of Bijapur, opposite a gap in the Sahyadri Hills. It is a picturesque town, and quite a flourishing trading-place. The people, who are mainly high-caste Hindus, together with the aborigines and low-caste, speak the Marâthi and Hindustani languages. There are Buddhist remains of the 3d century B.C. in the vicinity. Population (1891), 45,800. Station of the PN (1853). The work was commenced by Mr. Wilder, as an independent enterprise, and was taken over by the PN in 1870; the station has now 2 missionaries and their wives, 3 women missionaries, 13 native workers, 4 outstations, 5 day schools, and 1 boarding school. Station also of the SPG (1870), with (1900) 2 missionaries, 1 woman missionary, 17 native workers, 2 day schools, and 2 boarding schools. The place is locally called Karvir.

KOLLEGAL. See COLLEGAL.

KOLLUPITIYA: A village in Ceylon, situated 3 miles southwest of Colombo. Station of the WMS, with 26 native workers, 4 outstations, 4 chapels, 6 Sunday schools and 118 professed Christians. The name is sometimes spelled Kolluputiya.

KOLO: A settlement in Basutoland, S. Africa, 10 miles N. W. of Morija, and a station of the Paris Evangelical Mission Society, with (1903) 11 native workers, men and women; 3 outstations, 4 day schools and 533 professing Christians.

KOLOGWE. See KOROGWE.

KOLS: Name of a collection of aboriginal tribes mainly occupying the mountain districts and plateaus of the Chota Nagpur division of western Bengal, India, and found to a smaller extent in Orissa and in some districts of the Central Provinces. Chota Nagpur is of about the area of England. Kol is a generic word for the whole group of tribes included linguistically within the word Kolarian, but it is usually applied to three principal tribes, the Mundah Kols, of the Lohardaga District; the Larka ("fighting") Kols or Hos, mostly of Lingbhum; and the Brumij Kols of Manbhum, one part of whom, however, have been assimilated to the Mundahs, and the other to the Hindus. Another tribe, the Oraons, scattered over Chota Nagpur, tho not really such, are classed with Mundah Kols, as they live in amity and have many customs and most beliefs in common. But the Oraons will not intermarry with the Kols, to whom they regard themselves as superior. The census of 1891 gave Mundahs 362,000, Hos and Kols 393,000, Oraons 482,000, out of a population of 4,628,000 in Chota Nagpur, the majority of whom belong to diverse aboriginal tribes. The bulk of the Kol people live in little mud-hut villages, less than five per cent. of the population of Chota Nagpur dwelling in towns. They follow the chase, do a very little in agriculture, engage somewhat in mining and washing for gold and many go to Calcutta and Assam to labor. Both sexes of the Hos are clothed with a loin cloth, and the women adorn themselves with a profusion of beads and earings. They eat anything, including carrion. The Mundahs especially are ugly people, with thin, flat faces, high cheek bones and tawny skin. Monogamy is the rule, women being married not earlier than the 14th year. Dancing in connection with worship is a national institution, and is the occasion of licentiousness and drunkenness. Cheerfulness is a marked characteristic, and in truthfulness and honesty the Kols compare favorably with the Hindus. The Kol language is a dialect of the Gond, and unwritten except as the missionaries have elaborated it.

The Kols are filled with superstitious fears and worship evil spirits. Belief in witchcraft is common and witches are severely treated. The Hos have the sun, moon and stars for their chief deities. The Mundahs use no idols. Sinbhongu, the sun, is to them the supreme being, the beneficial creator and preserver, to whom they sacrifice fowls, goats and buffalos, but they recognize secondary deities, mostly malevolent. Some of the richer Mundahs worship Kali.

To this rude, degraded people, four disciples of Pastor Gossner of Berlin went in 1845, and established themselves at Ranchi. The first convert was baptized in 1850, after which the expansion of the work was most remarkable, 700 baptisms taking place in the next seven years. The Sepoy rebellion temporarily interrupted the work, and during a dissension between the older missionaries and the Society in Berlin, after Gossner's death, the Society for the Propagation of the Gospel received a party of the missionaries and 7,000 of the converts and occupied the Gossner territory in active rivalry, which has since given way to a tolerable *modus vivendi*. At Ranchi the Gossner Mission has a beautiful, large church, hospital, schools, a divinity college and a large body of workers; Burju and Govindpur are also important centers, and there are many outstations and a well-developed church in rapid growth. Among the Oraons a Christian movement has embraced the whole population of many villages. According to Warneck (1901) 68,000 Christians, including candidates, belong to this mission. The following year 4,000 baptisms were reported. A branch mission to the Kols who have emigrated to Assam has been established.

The SPG, beginning in 1869 with the Gossner defection, has worked mostly in the Ranchi district, with some stations in the Hazaribagh district to the north and Lingbhum to the south. Schools of all grades are maintained. In 1901 the mission enrolled 16,261 Christians, scattered in some 500 villages.

The progress of the Protestant missions, especially the SPG, has been hampered by the violent prosecution of a Jesuit counter mission, which at one time baptized within a few days 10,000 heathens without preparation, and boasted of 90,000 Catholic Kols. Catholic sources in 1901 reduced this number to 33,155, including 5,436 catechumens, and little is now heard of the Kol mission of which they formerly boasted so greatly. That so primitive and degraded a race should have been so lifted in half a century is one of the marvels of missions, and the promise of the future is bright.

Imperial Gazetteer of India, article Kols; *Two Hundred Years of the SPG*, London, 1902.

KOMAGGAS: A station of the Rhenish Missionary Society among the Nama or Namaqua people; situated in the N. W. part of Cape Colony, S. Africa, 60 miles S. E. of Port Nolloth. The station was founded by Mr. Schmelen, of the LMS, in 1824 and was transferred to the Rhenish Society in 1840. It now (1903) has 1 missionary and his wife, 6 native workers, 1 school, and 498 professed Christians, of whom 271 are communicants.

KONAKRY: A station of the Pongas Mission in French Guinea, W. Africa, situated on a small island off the coast. It was occupied by the mission in 1899, and has (1901) 1 missionary and his wife, 1 native worker and 2 places of worship.

KONDOWI. See LIVINGSTONIA.

KÖNIGSBERG. See KOENIGSBERG.

KONKORDIA. See CONCORDIA MINE.

KORAPAT: A town in the Presidency of Madras, India; situated in the District of Vizagapatam, 18 miles N. W. of Salur. Station of the Breklum Missionary Society (1884), with (1903) 2 missionaries (1 with his wife), 7 native workers, 10 outstations, 2 day schools, 8 places of worship, and 1,925 professed Christians.

KOREA: The kingdom of Korea, properly called Cho-sen (Morning Calm), comprises the peninsula lying between Japan and the mainland of China, together with a multitude of adjacent islands. It is washed by the Yellow Sea on the west and the Japan Sea on the east; on the north it is bounded by Chinese and Russian territory. Its surface is rugged and mountainous, being divided into two watersheds by an irregular range of mountains running from north to south near the eastern coast. The country is well watered, the largest rivers falling into the Yellow Sea. Considering the mountainous character of the country it is exceedingly productive. All kinds of cereals are produced, from wheat in the northern part to rice in the more temperate southern provinces. The pine and fir grow almost side by side with the bamboo. The mineral wealth of Korea is very great; large deposits of gold, silver, and coal have been found; but the mineral resources have not yet been fairly tested. A few mining concessions have been granted to foreigners during recent years.

Government: Korea is an absolute monarchy of the paternal type. There is a written constitution which serves as a guide, in a loose way, to the administration of government, but this does not include anything like representation of the people in Government Councils. While the country is nominally independent, its position between China and Japan makes it liable to attack from either; and it has many times been a vassal state of either or both. It has also suffered several times as the battle-field on which China and Japan have settled their differences. In 1876 Japan invaded Korea and forced the king to sign a treaty opening certain ports to foreign commerce, and accepting in principle certain reforms of internal administration held to be essentials of development to the country. The United States had vainly attempted in 1870 to open negotiations with Korea, even going so far as to attack and capture a number of fortified ports in order to punish officials who fired upon the ships bearing the embassy. But the actual opening of diplomatic and commercial intercourse between Korea and the Western nations was secured by Japan. In 1894 China undertook to encourage Korea in resisting reform, and to resume the protectorate which she had formally renounced. Japan declared war, drove the Chinese armies from the country, and having thoroughly broken the military power of China, dictated a peace by which the independence of Korea was secured. In 1897 the king assumed the title of Emperor, the privileges of the aristocracy were abolished, and important reforms were introduced, among others the adoption of English and German principles of law and justice. A strong reaction against these radical changes did not fail to show itself; and Russia, which had acquired railway interests in neighboring regions in Manchuria, in 1900, began to take advantage of these reactionary tendencies to become a rival of Japan for the privilege of serving as tutor to the Emperor. The steady, onward march of Russian influence, interfering in Korean affairs at innumerable points, has been a potent factor in deciding Japan to take arms against such encroachments. The war opened in February, 1904, between Russia and Japan, whatever it decides, must trample down Korean territory once more and seriously retard the civilization and development of the country, that strangers may settle their differences with least inconvenience to themselves.

People: The population of Korea is probably about 12,000,000, altho the lack of a proper census renders an exact estimate impossible. This population is distributed unevenly over the eight provinces composing the kingdom, the most thickly settled portions being the southern and western provinces. The people of Korea are of undoubted Mongolian origin. Successive tribes sweeping down from the north and overrunning the country, together with large numbers of Chinese who from time to time found in Korea an asylum from the oppression of their native land, have produced a conglomerate mass, of whose origin it is impossible to say more. The affinities of the people are Japanese rather than Chinese. But there is not much affection for the Japanese among the common people.

Language: The language of the Koreans is distinct from that of their neighbors in its grammatical construction and idioms, but it has borrowed from the Chinese a large number of words, just as English has borrowed largely from the Latin. The Chinese character is used in all official and literary writing, and in fact in all writing on the part of the better class of people. The Korean language was reduced to writing about three hundred years ago. It has an alphabet whose simplicity, flexibility, and comprehensiveness compare favorably with those of any other known alphabet. It is as unlike the inflexible syllabary of Japan as it is unlike the unwieldy ideograms of China. The Korean written language is used only by the lower classes, who form, however, the vast majority of the population.

Religion: The religious history of Korea may be divided into five periods or movements. The first includes the early centuries of the kingdom, and terminates about 350 A.D. Of the religious history up to that time little is known. It is probable that there was no one form of religion prevalent throughout the different tribes and clans living in the land, but that each had its own religious observances and rites. But during the 4th century a general consolidation of the different parts of the country took place, and at the same time Buddhist missionaries appeared and taught their faith. It flourished, and in the space of a few centuries we find Korea a Buddhist nation, with numerous monasteries filled with people from every station in life. In the course of time the teachings of Confucius began to have their influence upon the people and gradually supplanted the religion of Buddha, and for many centuries past Confucianism has been holding sway over the masses of the people. Buddhism still exists, but is confined exclusively to a few monasteries, whose inmates are looked down upon by the people at large.

Near the close of the 18th century some of the members attached to the Korean Embassy to Peking came in contact with Roman Catholic missionaries and brought back that faith to Korea. It took root almost immediately and spread with great rapidity. But the history of Roman Catholicism in Korea is one of persecutions from the very beginning of the 19th century. In 1864 the last king of the Yi dynasty died—a king under whom the Romanists were not only tolerated, but even allowed to obtain a great deal of influence in the affairs of the kingdom. The reins of government fell into the hands of a regent who was intensely opposed to foreigners, and to the Romanists in particular. Soon after he took the lead of affairs Bishop Berneux and eight of his associates were seized and put to death, and an inquisition was instituted which bade fair to exterminate Christianity from the land. It is not known how many native converts there were at that time, but there must have been not less than 60,000. Of these, 10,000 were put to death. In some localities whole communities and villages were put to the sword. The effects of this persecution were very widespread and permanent, and it is probable that the power of the Romanists has never rallied from the stroke it then received. The horrors of that time implanted in the whole people a dread of foreign religions which is as great a drawback to Protestant as to Romanist mission work.

There is now a strong force of Roman Catholic missionaries in Korea. One of the greatest benefits that they have conferred upon the cause is the compiling and publishing of a complete lexicon and grammar of the Korean language.

Protestant Missions: The first Protestant mission work for Korea was done by the Rev. John Ross of the United Presbyterian Church of Scotland. About 1875 he came in contact with Koreans near the border between Korea and China. He took up the Korean language, and, altho never having set foot upon Korean soil, he translated the whole of the New Testament into Korean and sent it across the border, together with large numbers of Chinese Bibles. He thus became the means of beginning a work of great importance in Northern Korea. When Protestant missionaries came to Korea later they found whole communities in the north professing Protestant Christianity, studying the Bible among themselves, and only waiting for some one to come and teach them. The treaty between Korea and the United States was signed in 1882; and then for the first time the eyes of the civilized world were turned upon Korea. The first movement made toward putting men in the field was the appointment by the American Presbyterian Board of Dr. J. W. Heron, M.D., as medical missionary to Korea in the spring of 1884. His coming was delayed, and in the summer of the same year Rev. R. S. McClay of the Japan Methodist Conference was sent to look over the ground and report on the advisability of sending missionaries. Before his favorable report was acted upon, Dr. H. N. Allen, M.D., of China, was transferred from that field to Korea, and he, arriving with his family in the autumn of 1884, became the first resident Protestant missionary. Meanwhile the report of Dr. McClay had been acted upon, and the Missionary Society of the Methodist Episcopal Church of America had appointed to the field Dr. Wm. B. Scranton and Rev. H. G. Appenzeller, and the Woman's Foreign Missionary Society of the Methodist Episcopal Church appointed Mrs. M. F. Scranton. In November of the same year the Presbyterian Board appointed Rev. H. G. Underwood. In December of 1884, before any of these appointees had arrived in Korea, occurred the riot in Seoul, during which Prince Min Yong Ik was severely wounded. The skilful and successful treatment of the case by Dr. Allen produced such a favorable impression that a general government hospital was founded by his majesty, and Dr. Allen was placed at its head. In this way a great impetus was given to the good feeling that had already begun to make itself manifest on the part of Koreans toward foreigners. In the spring of 1885 Rev. H. G. Underwood, who had been spending some months in Japan studying the Korean language, arrived in Korea. For a time the object of his coming was kept from the Korean officials through fear that the interests of the missionary work might be endangered; but that fear proved to be groundless, and soon it became generally known that he had come, and that the object of his coming was something besides medical work. The Methodist Mission was opened the same year.

The first Korean was baptized in the autumn of 1886, and from the first the work took on a most encouraging aspect. Large numbers of inquiries came in from distant parts of the country, and it was not long before a little native church was organized. Korea is to-day thrown wide open to the Christian religion; the Emperor is the open friend of Protestant missionaries, and while recently destroying thirty heathen temples in and about Seoul, and officially deploring the money annually squandered upon the worship of idols, he allows Christian churches, schools and hospitals to be scattered throughout the land. Christian literature in the vernacular and several mission periodicals are disseminating the truth; a Bible society, which sold 70,000 copies of the Scriptures in 1900, has been formed; and of the 70,000 Catholics and Protestants, 40,000 have been gathered in during the last decade. One of the Korean leaders recently remarked: "The only hope of the country is in the churches. There is no moral character in Korea. It is being created in the churches. To convert and educate the common people is the only hope of the land."

Bishop (Isabella Bird), *Korea and Her Neighbors,* London and New York; Gifford (D. L.), *Everyday Life in Korea;* Gale (J. S.), *Korean Sketches;* also, *The Vanguard,* New York, 1904.

KOROGWE: A town in German East Africa, situated on the Pangani River, in the Usambara region, 55 miles by railway from Tanga. Station of the Universities Mission (1892), with (1900) 2 missionaries, 7 native workers, 3 outstations, 4 day schools, and a boarding school.

KŌSHI, Rev. Kōshi: Born in February, 1825. Died in November, 1898. A Syrian Christian, who, after his education at Kottayam College, became, under the CMS, a catechist, translator and lay reader, being finally ordained. During his useful career he was stationed at Kottayam, Trichur, and other places, and was appointed one of the examining Chaplains to the Bishop of Madras. In 1885 he was made Archdeacon of Mavelicara, and in 1891 the degree of Doctor of Divinity was conferred on him by the Archbishop of Canterbury in recognition of his labors as a translator and litterateur. In his early days he was taught the Malayalam language, and afterward, under the ablest teachers, he studied to make himself proficient in this and other tongues. When quite a young man he was offered the post of Head Interpreter to the Travancore Government, a lucrative and honorable post, but he chose the poorer and more honorable work of the mission. As pastor, as archdeacon, and as vice-chairman of the Church Council, he exercised great influence and did much to develop the spiritual and intellectual life of the native church; but his great work was associated with the Malayalam Bible Revision. He was regarded as one of the best Malayalam scholars in Travancore, and he was, for the most of the time, the only native delegate on the Revision Committee. What the late Mr. Baker, Senior, was to the Malayalam CMS Mission, from a missionary point of view, Archdeacon Koshi was from the native—a valuable link with the past—and one regrets that he has left no history of the mission written from his actual knowledge. He spoke to one of his associates of the early days when portions of the Old Testament were first received at his home on the Rani River. The Syrian Christians would assemble round a lamp in the house of one who happened to possess a copy of the valuable document, and listen while chapter after chapter was read until the night grew into the morning; and then he lived to see the work develop into an orderly diocese with all the congregations ministered by pastors of their own race, and supported, in great part, by native contributions; and himself as archdeacon, and vice-chairman under the Bishop, of a church Council embracing twelve pastorates and more than 15,000 Christians. He was the Chief Reviser on the Prayer-book Committee; and it was especially for this work that the Archbishop of Canterbury conferred on him the degree of D.D., on the recommendation of Bishop Speechly. Among his other works may be mentioned his translation into Malayalam of the Pilgrim's Progress, *James' Anxious Inquirer, Doddridges' Rise and Progress, The Holy War, Pulleli Kunju,* and his many articles in a periodical called *The Treasury of Knowledge,* which he conducted for seven years.

KOTA. See KOTAH.

KOTAGERI: A town in the Presidency of Madras, India, situated in the Nilgiri district, about 27 miles E. of Utakamand. Station of the Basel Missionary Society (1867), with (1903) 1 missionary and his wife, 15 native workers, men and women; 8 outstations, 6 day schools, and 314 professed Christians.

KOTAH: A town in Rajputana, India; situated 120 miles S. of Jaipur, on the Chambal River. Population (1891) 38,600. Station of the UFS (1889), at present (1903) carried on by 18 native workers, men and women.

KOTA-KOTA: A village in the British Nyasaland Protectorate, Central Africa, situated on the W. shore of Lake Nyasa. It is celebrated for its fine crops of rice, and was formerly an important center of Arab commercial operations in the interior. Station of the Universities' Mission (1894), with (1902) 1 missionary, 2 missionary women, 5 native workers, 6 schools, a dispensary and 378 professed Christians, of whom 92 are communicants.

KOTGARH: A village in the Native Hill States, Punjab, India, situated 20 miles E. of Simla. A station of the CMS, with 3 missionaries and their wives, 6 native workers, 1 chapel, 2 village schools and 58 professed Christians, of whom 28 are communicants. Name sometimes spelled Kotgur.

KOTPAD: A town in the Presidency of Madras, India, situated in the Vizagapatam district, about 120 miles N. W. of the town of that name. Station of the Breklum Missionary Society (1885), with (1903) 3 missionaries (one with his wife), 1 woman missionary, 23 native workers, men and women; 8 outstations, 3 day schools, 1 orphanage, 1 theological training class, 1 dispensary and 3,207 professed Christians, of whom 1,657 are baptized. Name also written Kotapad.

KOTGUR. See KOTGARH.

KO-THA-BYU: The first convert to Christianity from the Karens, a people among whom the labors of the Baptist missionaries in Burma have met with remarkable success. He was a robber and murderer in early life, and was the slave of a Buddhist Burman at Rangun, when he was redeemed and became a servant in the family of Adoniram Judson. He was converted after some time and was baptized by Rev. George Dana Boardman at Tavoy on May 16, 1828. He very soon began to manifest a wonderful zeal and power in winning his own people to Christ, and was constantly bringing them to the missionaries for conversation and instruction. He traveled to remote portions of the country preaching the Gospel. More than one thousand persons, it is estimated, were converted as a result of his labors. He was not highly educated and his preaching was not sought by the more intelligent Christian Karens, yet he had a power second to none of his race over a congregation of untaught Karens. He died in 1840 in Arakan, whither he had gone with the missionaries Abbott and Kincaid to provide a place of refuge for the persecuted Karens of Burma. He was certainly one of the most remarkable native evangelists that Burma has produced.

KOTTA: A town in Ceylon, India, situated about 6 miles S. E. of Colombo. A station of the CMS (1882), with (1903) 1 missionary and his wife, 1 woman missionary, 96 native workers, 48 village schools, 3 high schools and 1,375 professed Christians, of whom 315 are communicants. Name sometimes spelled Cotta.

KOTTAYAM: A town in the province of Travancore, Madras, India, situated 32 miles S. E. by E. of Cochin, with a population (1881) of 11,300. A station of the CEZ (1871), with (1903) 10 native workers and 2 day schools. Station also of the CMS (1882), with (1903) 4 missionaries (three of them with their wives), 2 women missionaries, 49 native workers, 1 printing press, 5 village schools, 1 high school, 1 theological school and 1 college. There are also in the Native Church Council of the district 172 native workers, 90 village schools and 20,645 professed Christians, of whom 5,194 are communicants. Name sometimes spelled Cottayam.

KOTZEBUE: A station of the AFFM on the N. shore of Kotzebue Sound, an inlet of Bering's Strait, on the W. coast of Alaska. The station was established in 1897 and has a missionary and his wife and 1 woman missionary.

KRAPF, John Ludwig: Born in Württemberg, 1810; educated in the Basel Mission House; sent by the Church Missionary Society to join the Abyssinian Mission begun by Gobat in 1830, and conducted by Isenberg and Blumhardt. Two or three months after his arrival they were all expelled, through the hostile influence of two French Romish priests, who persuaded the Prince of Tigré that they themselves were more in accord with Abyssinian Christianity than the

Protestants. Having been invited by the King of Shoa to visit his country, Dr. Krapf left Suez with Mr. Isenberg, January 27, 1839, with the hope of entering Abyssinia by way of Zeila, and after many difficulties reached in May the kingdom of Shoa, lying south of Abyssinia, and in its widest sense including the whole of the Ethiopian highlands. The king received them favorably and promised his protection. Isenberg went in November to England to prepare for the press Amharic works, while Dr. Krapf remained, studying the Galla language and laboring among the Abyssinians. In 1840 he accompanied the king on an expedition to the Gallas, a brave, vigorous, and daring nation, inhabiting a vast extent of territory stretching southward nearly to Mombasa, and numbering from six to eight millions. The slave-trade was carried on by them. In a second visit he noted three places where a Galla mission might be established and had many opportunities of proclaiming the Gospel message. The population of Shoa is to a large extent nominally Christian, similar to the Coptic Church in Egypt, but the Gallas were heathen. The committee were so impressed with the providential openings, both in Abyssinia and among the heathen Galla tribes, that they resolved to form the Abyssinians into a new mission, to be called the East Africa Mission. In 1841 the people of Shoa expressed great desire for the Word of God. Dr. Krapf spent three years among them, but in 1842 he was again excluded through Romish influence. He greatly desired to reach the Galla tribes. He translated the Gospels into their language. To devise a plan to reach them from the Indian Ocean he sailed down the coast in 1843, and visited Aden. Having received the approval of the committee, he sailed with his wife for the Zanzibar coast, landing January 3, 1844, at Mombasa, which, after visiting Zanzibar, he selected as the site of his mission. Here he and his wife were prostrated by fever, and in two months she and their infant child died. He now devoted himself with zeal to the work of the mission, especially to the study of the languages of that region. He made excursions among the Wanika and Wakamba tribes, preaching and surveying the ground with reference to future operations. He found the natives extremely degraded, intemperate, and in the habit even of selling their children to obtain the means of indulgence. He applied himself to the work of translation, and in three years after the founding of the mission had translated Acts, Romans, Galatians, Peter, 1 John into the Swahili language, and had completed a dictionary of 10,000 words of the Swahili, Wanika and Wakamba languages. Repeated attacks of fever had greatly impaired his constitution. Yet he continued his missionary tours, gathering valuable information concerning the interior tribes and preaching the Gospel, which the natives who heard it would repeat to others.

In 1846 he was joined by John Rebmann, and together they established the mission station at Kisulutini in the Rabai district, fifteen miles inland. They were both laid aside for some weeks with fever, and before they had fully recovered their strength they set out for the new mission. They found the place more salubrious than Mombasa, but the people were deeply sunk in ignorance, superstition and sensuality.

Continuing their explorations in the interior, they found wonderful openings, and came in sight of the Galla country, so long the object of Dr. Krapf's desire. Dr. Krapf visited Usambara and Ukamba, and sailed down the coast as far as Cape Delgado. In 1849 he proceeded to Ukambani, 300 miles to the northwest, to visit the Wakamba tribes, numbering about 70,000 people. He went again the next year with the view, as instructed by the committee, of founding a mission among the Wakamba on the heights of Yata. But the plan failed. In this journey he sighted Mount Kenia. On the journey he was repeatedly in the greatest extremity from hunger and thirst, wild beasts and savage robbers. He continued the study of the language and the translation of the Scriptures. He came to the conclusion that from the Galla boundary to the Cape of Good Hope there is one family of languages, which he calls the Swahili stock, which stock, he thinks, judging from specimens he had received of West African languages, commences on the southern bank of the Gabun River. The missionaries in their tours obtained much geographical information. In 1850 Dr. Krapf visited England and Germany and on his return explored the interior, penetrating to Ukamba, but was forced to return by extraordinary sufferings, perils and enmity of the tribes. In later years he established and directed the remarkable "Pilgrim Mission," in connection with the St. Chrischona Institute, which was to begin the "chain of missions" from the north instead of from the east. Twelve stations were planned, embracing Egypt, Nubia and Abyssinia. He afterward visited Usambara and was well received by King Kmeri, who desired him to establish a mission on a mountain thirty miles distant, offering him his protection. In 1855 he returned to Europe, and tho he went again twice to Africa on temporary missions, the great work of his later years was linguistic, in his quiet home at Kornthal in Württemberg, preparing dictionaries of several languages and translating the Scriptures into the East African tongues. He was found dead at his home, on his knees in the attitude of prayer, November 26, 1881, and on the 30th his body was buried in the presence of 3,000 people, assembled from all parts of the country.

Claus (Von W.) *Johann Ludwig Krapf*, Basel, 1882.

KREUZBURG: A settlement in the Transvaal, S. Africa, situated about 22 miles N. E. of Pietersburg. Station of the Berlin Missionary Society (1899), with (1903) 1 missionary, 28 native workers, men and women; 11 outstations, and 799 professed Christians.

KRISHNAGAR: A town in the district of Nadiya, Bengal, India, situated 55 miles N. of Calcutta. It has a population of (1891) 25,500, of whom 17,500 are Hindus. Station of the CMS (1831), with (1903) 2 missionaries and their wives, 21 native workers, 1 place of worship, 1 chapel, 4 day schools, 3 boarding schools and 320 professed Christians, of whom 119 are communicants. The CEZ also has a station there (1871), with (1903) 7 women missionaries, 21 native workers, 1 high school, 2 dispensaries, 1 hospital, and 39 Zenana pupils.

KRISHNAGIRI: A town in Madras, India, situated in the district of Salem, 53 miles S. E. of Bangalore. Population (1891), 9,700, of whom about 7,000 are Hindus. Station of the German Evangelical Lutheran Synod, of Missouri, Ohio and other States. The station was opened in 1895, and it has (1900) 2 missionaries (one with his wife) and 3 native workers.

KROONSTAD: A town in Cape Colony, S. Africa, situated in the district of the same name, of which it is the capital, 96 miles S. S. W. of Johannesburg. Population, 2,000. Station of the South African Wesleyan Methodist Missionary Society, with 63 native workers, 37 outstations, 3 day schools, and 951 professed Christians.

KRÜGERSDORP: A settlement in the Transvaal, Africa, situated 18 miles northwest of Johannesburg. A station of the Berlin Missionary Society (1899), with (1903) 1 missionary, 5 native workers, 5 outstations and 78 Christians. Station of the WMS (1903), with 1 missionary, 10 native workers, 11 outstations, 11 places of worship, 1 Sunday school, 1 day school, and 261 professed Christians, of whom 173 are communicants.

KUALA LUMPUR. See KWALA LUMPUR.

KUANGCHI. See KWANG-CHI-HSIEN.

KU-CHAU-FU: A city in Che-kiang, China, on the left bank of the Yangtse River, 106 miles S. W. of Hang-chau. It is a large and prosperous place, and considered one of the keys to the empire. Station of the CIM (1872), but as yet (1903) vacant since the Boxer troubles of 1900. Name written by the Society, Kiu-chau.

KU-CHENG. See KU-TIEN-HSIEN.

KUCHING, or **SARAWAK:** A town in British Borneo, Malaysia, capital of the district of Sarawak; situated at the head of navigation of the Sarawak River, 18 miles from its mouth. Population, 25,000. A station of the SPG (1848), with (1903) 2 missionaries, 11 native workers, 4 outstations, 4 places of worship, 2 high schools, and 689 Christians.

KUDAT: A station in British North Borneo, Malaysia, situated on an inlet running west from Marudu Bay. A station of the SPG (1889), with (1902) 5 native workers, 2 places of worship, 2 day schools, and 584 professed Christians, of whom 285 are communicants.

KU-DE: A town in the province of Fo-kien, China, situated 58 miles N. W. of Fu-chau. Station circuit of the ME, with (1903) 45 native workers, men and women; 15 places of worship, 20 Sabbath schools, 10 day schools, and 890 professed Christians, of whom 516 are communicants.

KUDELUR. See CUDDALORE.

KU-DING: A town in the province of Chekiang, China, situated 50 miles north by west of Hang-chau. A station of the PS (1895), with (1903) 1 missionary and wife, 4 native workers, 3 outstations, 4 places of worship, 3 Sunday schools, 2 day schools, and 218 professed Christians, of whom 100 are communicants.

KUEI-LIN. See KWEI-LIN-FU.

KUENENG: A station of the Paris Evangelical Missionary Society in Basutoland, S. Africa, situated in the northern part of the territory, with (1902) 10 native workers, 3 day schools, 5 outstations, and 563 professed Christians, of whom 336 are communicants.

KU-HSIEN: A town in the province of Szechwan, China, situated 48 miles E. N. E. of Shun-king-fu. Station of the CIM (1898), with (1903) 1 missionary and his wife and 1 woman missionary. Name written by the Society, Ku-hien.

KUH-TSI-ING. See KU-TSING-FU.

K'UH-WU. See KU-WU-HSIEN.

KULBARGA: A town in the native state of Haidarabad, India; situated on an undulating plain in the district of the same name, of which it is the chief town, and 75 miles E. N. E. of Bijapur. It was the capital city of a powerful dynasty from 1347 to 1432, and its chief mosque is a copy of that in Cordova, Spain. Its fine palaces, however, are mostly allowed to decay uncared for. Population, 29,000. Station of the ME, with (1903) 1 missionary, 6 native workers, and an orphanage.

KULESA: A station of the Scandinavian Alliance (U. S.) in British East Africa, situated 30 miles N. W. of Witu.

KULLUKO: A village in Eritrea, East Africa, situated on the frontier of Abyssinia, about 135 miles W. S. W. of Massaua. Station of the Evangelical National Missionary Society of Sweden (1867), with (1900) 2 missionaries, 1 of them accompanied by his wife.

KUMAGAI: A town on the Hondo, or main island of Japan, situated about 50 miles N. N. W. of Tokio. Station of the PE.

KUMAMOTO: A town on the island of Kiushiu, Japan, situated about 50 miles E. by N. of Nagasaki. It is the most populous city in the island and is the center of a large rice trade. It has a celebrated fortress built of enormous stones. Malaria prevails in the region. Population, 47,600. Station of the CMS (1888), with (1903) 2 missionaries (one with his wife), 4 native workers, 1 place of worship, 2 Sunday schools, and 234 professed Christians, of whom 109 are communicants. The ELUS also has a station there (1898), with 1 missionary and his wife. Also station of the SBC, with (1903) 1 missionary and his wife, 1 native worker, 1 Sunday school, and 15 professed Christians. Station also of the ME, with (1903) 2 missionaries, 4 native workers, 1 outstation, 1 place of worship, 4 Sunday schools and 160 professed Christians.

KUMASE. See KUMASSI.

KUMASSI: A town situated 104 miles north by west of Cape Coast Castle, in the Gold Coast Colony, Western Africa. A station of the Basel Missionary Society (1896), with (1903) 2 missionaries and their wives, 5 native workers, 3 outstations, 4 day schools and 80 professed Christians. Station of the WMS also, with (1903) 1 missionary, 8 native workers, 35 outstations, 35 places of worship, 4 Sunday schools, 4 day schools, and 55 professed Christians. Name sometimes spelled Kumase.

KUMBAKONAM. See COMBACONUM.

KUMUKI DIALECT. See TURKISH LANGUAGE.

KUNDAKUR. See KANDUKUR.

KUNDI: A village in the eastern part of the native state of Rewa, Central India, near the Chota Nagpur frontier. A station of the WMS, with (1903) 1 missionary, 13 native workers, 7 places of worship, 7 Sunday schools, 7 day schools, and 444 professed Christians, of whom 57 are communicants.

KUNNANKULAM: A town in the native state

of Cochin, India, situated about 28 miles S. W. of Coimbatore. A station of the CMS (1854), with (1903) 35 native workers, 4 outstations, 7 day schools, and 97 professed Christians.

KUNSAN: A village and seaport of Korea, situated on the western coast, about 150 miles south of Chemulpo and near the mouth of the Chang-po River. Station of the PS (1896), with (1903) 3 missionaries, two of them with their wives; 1 missionary woman, 3 outstations, 1 day school and 1 dispensary.

KUNSO: A settlement in Sierra Leone, W. Africa, situated 120 miles N. E. of Freetown. Station of the Wesleyan Methodist Connexion of America (1890), with (1900) 2 missionaries and their wives, 1 missionary woman, 5 native women workers, 1 place of worship and 1 printing house.

KURAI: A town in the Central Provinces, India, situated in the district of Sagar, 78 miles N. E. of Bhopal. Population (1891) 6,300, of whom 4,700 are Hindus. Station of the Evangelical National Missionary Society of Sweden (1900), with 1 missionary and his wife. The name is written by the Society Khurai.

KURDS: To say that the Kurds are the Carduchi mentioned with painful reminiscences by Xenophon, does not answer the question of their origin. Nor can one define their relations by saying that they are the people of Kurdistan. No definite territory called by that name exists, and the Kurds, wherever found, live as detached groups in the midst of other races. They abound in the regions extending from the Russian border at Erivan on the north to the fig-producing hills of the Sinjar in Upper Mesopotamia and the flower-gardens of Shiraz on the south, and from the plains of Urmia and Ispahan on the east to the Tigris, the Euphrates at Samosata, the Taurus at Marash, and the Anti-Taurus in Cappadocia and Pontus on the west. The districts where they are most numerous include the Turkish provinces of Erzerum, Van, Hekkiari, Mosul (eastern portion), Bitlis, Diarbekir and Mamuriet el Aziz (Harpoot, eastern portion), and in Persia the western portion of Azerbaijan, Ardilan and Luristan. The mass of the Kurds dwell to this day within these limits, that is to say, near the western end of that mountainous highland which forms a raised causeway from the east to the west of Asia.

Any map will reveal within these limits mountain chains running in all directions. The central portion of the region is west of Lake Urmia and east of Tigris. About the size of Palestine in its palmiest days, the part best beloved by the Kurds is a perfect sea of mountains, with mountain peaks that vie with one another in their efforts to pierce the regions of the upper air, and rise from 10,000 feet to 15,000 feet above the level of the sea.

The antiquity of the region as the abode of man is attested by the absence of forests.

Out from this system flow the Araxes and the Halys on the north, the one to the Caspian and the other to the Black Sea; and to the south, the Euphrates, and the Tigris, with its tributaries, into the Persian Gulf.

Such endless combinations of mountains and valleys, lakes and gorges, rivers and plateaus, snow-clad peaks and grassy plains, render the scenery beautiful, grand, weird, and wild by turns.

The region described above was inhabited, in the times of the Assyrian Empire, by a warrior race named "Gutu," *i. e.*, warrior. The Assyrians called them Gardu and Kardu; the Greeks later called them Kardokas (*Kardakes*). They were Scythians or Turanians. After the subjugation of Assyria the Gardu were absorbed by a still more energetic race (the southern Kurmanj), who claim to be lineal descendants of Madai, the son of Japheth, and of the same stock as the Medians. The Kurds also claim that one of the tribes of the "Gutu" remaining in its early habitat produced Nebuchadnezzar and in the Babylonian Empire became imbued with Semitic qualities of blood. From this stock sprang the Guran tribes of southern Kurdistan. In a similar manner emigrations of Lurs from Persia and of Wends from Afghanistan brought in Aryan blood, so that the eastern Kurds have distinctly Aryan qualities. These various traditions of the Kurds conform to the truth in one particular, namely, that the Kurds of to-day are of mixed Aryan, Semitic and Turanian stock. But to seek to identify the various strains of blood or their source is useless in a land where the people have clung to their rocky heights while they have been trampled into many forms during fifteen centuries by conquering hosts coming from south and north and east and west.

The Kurds to-day are found in three great groups, the Kurmanj, the Guran and the Lur. The Lur are found in Persia, and the two first named groups in both Turkey and Persia. The language of each group is a separate dialect, and many of the tribes of each family have also their own dialect.

For various reasons exactness in statements of the numbers of the Kurds is simply impossible; the following tabulation gives only approximate estimates:

Kurmanj	Northern—Turkey		2,000,000
	Southern—	Turkey	150,000
		Persia	200,000
Guran	Turkish Provinces		200,000
	Persian "		150,000
Wend and Lur	Turkish "		110,000
	Persian "		90,000
	Afghanistan (southwest portion)		500,000
		Total,	3,400,000

As to mode of life the Kurds are of three classes: (*a*) Those who are purely pastoral are nomadic (called *Göchers*) and oscillate between the mountains and the plains, occupying the former in summer and the latter in winter. (*b*) Those partly pastoral and partly agricultural occupy fixed abodes in winter, but in summer dwell in tents among pastures not remote from their harvest fields. (*c*) Those purely agricultural remain throughout the year in fixed abodes. Some Kurds also have taken up trades and live in cities as merchants and mechanics. Generally speaking, one-half, perhaps more, of the Kurds belong to class *a*, while the remainder are distributed between classes *b* and *c* in the proportion of 2 to 1.

The Kurds of these three classes are of two distinct types—the northern and the southern. The northern Kurd is bold, but not courageous, hospitable but full of theft and treachery, loud-voiced and brutal, lazy and ignorant, fond of intrigue, feudatory. He is thriftless and likewise shiftless in regard to his person, dress and manners. He has black eyes and hair, is of fine physique and athletic, is temperate and of sturdier morals than his Turkish ruler. As a rule he is monogamous, and treats his wife more after the manner of Europeans than of the Turk. He is intellectually dull, and dogged in his commercial dealings; ready to owe and acknowledge a debt, but slow to cancel it. The southern Kurd who has learned to dwell in a fixed abode is not less athletic, but of finer grain, more polite in his bearing, more quiet in his manners, and more careful of his person and dress than the northern type or the southern nomad Kurds. He has a more intellectual cast of features, and is brighter looking. The organization of the southern Kurds is more compact than that of the northern tribes, and there is among them the quiet consciousness of power. They obey Abdul Hamid more as Caliph than as Sultan. A considerable number of the southern Kurds have been educated in Arabic and Persian literature, and such are to be found in high office under the Turkish Government. In general, Kurds are the untamed highlanders of Turkey and Persia—fond of freedom, but lawless in their use of it, thereby occasioning great uneasiness to both those powers. Clannishness and tribal feuds are powerful preventives of their racial homogeneity and political power.

All Kurds are Muslims. They are about equally divided between the *Sunni* and the *Shi'i* denominations. The *Shi'i* Kurds are the Lur and Wend tribes of Persia and Afghanistan, the Kurmanj of Bohtan, Sert, and Bitlis, and the Gurans of the Dersim Mountains in Turkey. All Kurds are bigoted and are fanatically attached to their Sheikhs, if not to their religion. Comparatively few of them have an intelligent grasp of Islam, which indeed is a foreign religion in a foreign tongue.

Missionary work among the Kurds does not exist, because neither Turkey nor Persia would tolerate organized work in their behalf; and their contact with the evangelistic efforts of the Eastern Turkey and West Persia missions for the nominal Christians residing in their midst is of the slightest.

The evangelical churches of Turkey support a "Kurdish Mission," which is conducted from Harpoot; but it is for Kurdish-speaking Armenians, and not for the Kurds. In connection with this work a translation of the New Testament and also a small hymn-book have been published in Kurmanj Kurdish.

Some effort for Kurdish-speaking Syrians is now prosecuted by the Mardin station of the ABCFM. It would seem the intention of Providence to use these evangelized Kurdish-speaking Christians as an entering wedge for work among the Muslim Kurds when "all things are ready" for such a movement. The Persian Mission of the PN and that of the CMS are also making efforts to reach this neglected people in many unobtrusive ways.

As a rule those who have come into close acquaintance with Kurds have acquired a profound respect for their sturdy and admirable qualities of heart, their mental abilities and their capacity for religious and political development. Not a few believe that through their progress in culture may be found a solution of the Eastern question.

KURDISH LANGUAGE: Belongs to the Iranic branch of the Aryan family of languages. Its immediate relations seem to be still unsettled, altho there is reason to connect it with the Pehlevi. It is found in two distinct dialects—the Kurmanj and the Gurani, which are Western Kurdish, and the Lur and Wend, which are Eastern. These two groups are broken into many smaller dialects to the formation of which there seems to be no limit, such as is found in the existence of a literary class. Nothing in Kurdish has ever been printed except by strangers. The Kurds have a vast collection of materials for a literature, but they have not even an alphabet as yet, making use of the Arabic alphabet for correspondence, etc. Certain Armenians who speak Kurdish use the Armenian alphabet, and missionaries have printed some books for their use in Kurdish written with Armenian letters.

KURNOOL. See KARNUL.

KURSEONG. See KARSIUNG.

KURUMAN: A town and district in the Bechuana country in the northern part of Cape Colony, S. Africa; situated 100 miles N. W. of Barkly West and 90 miles S. W. of Vryburg. Station of the LMS (1818), with (1903) 1 missionary and his wife, 13 native workers, 14 schools, and 666 communicants.

KUSAIE: The easternmost of the Caroline Islands, North Pacific Ocean. It is used by the ABCFM as a center for work among the Micronesian islands. It is also called Strong Island and Ualan.

KUSAIE LANGUAGE: Belongs to the Micronesian family. It was reduced to writing by missionaries of the ABCFM working among the people of Kusaie, one of the Caroline Islands. They have done a certain amount of literary work in this language, writing it with Roman letters.

KUSHIRO: A town and the capital of the Kushiro province in Hokkaido, Japan, situated on the S. E. coast of the island, about 205 miles E. N. E. of Hakodate. Its exports are sulphur and coal. Station of the CMS (1889), with (1903) 1 woman missionary, 8 native workers, 2 outstations, 1 place of worship, 3 Sunday schools, 3 day schools, and 321 professed Christians, of whom 128 are communicants.

KUSHTIA: A town in the Nadiya District of Bengal, India, situated on the right bank of the Ganges, about 60 miles E. S. E. of Murshidabad. Population, 11,200, of whom 6,000 are Muslims and 5,000 Hindus. Station of the CMS (1901), with (1903) 1 missionary, 4 native workers and 26 professed Christians.

KU-TIEN-HSIEN: A town in the province of Fo-kien, China, situated about 50 miles N. N. W. of Fuchau. Station of the CMS (1887), with (1903) 1 missionary and his wife, 60 native workers, 2 outstations, 1 place of worship, 28 day schools, 1,780 professed Christians, of whom 682 are communicants. Station also of the CEZ (1889), with (1903) 3 women missionaries, 2 native workers, 1 boarding school. Station also of the ME with (1903), 2 missionaries and their wives, 2 women missionaries, 44 native workers, 6 outstations, 10 places of worship, 10 Sunday schools, 14 young people's societies, 9 day schools, 1 hospital, 1 dispensary, and 939 professed Christians, of whom 521 are communicants. Station of the Mission to Lepers in

India and the East (1892), with 1 place of worship and 1 leper asylum. Name sometimes written Kucheng.

KU-TSING-FU: A town in the province of Yun-nan, China, situated 68 miles E. N. E. of Yun-nan-fu. Station of the CIM (1889), with (1903) 2 missionaries and their wives, 3 women missionaries, and 1 native worker. Name written by the Society, Kuh-tsing.

KU-WU-HSIEN: A town in the province of Shan-si, China, situated 30 miles S. of Ping-yang-fu. Station of the CIM (1885), with (1903) 1 missionary and his wife, 1 woman missionary, 6 native workers, 3 outstations, 2 schools, 1 dispensary and 1 opium refuge. Name written by the Society, Kuh-wu.

KU-YÜ-SHU: A town in Manchuria, China, situated about 62 miles N. N. E. of Kirin. Station of the Presbyterian Church in Ireland (1899), with 1 missionary, 21 native workers, 4 schools, and 170 communicants (1900).

KWAGUTL LANGUAGE: Belongs to the Pacific Coast branch of the North American family of languages, being spoken by Indians of Vancouver Island. It has been reduced to writing by missionaries of the CMS, the Roman alphabet being used for the purpose.

KWALA KAPUAS: A station of the Rhenish Missionary Society, in Southeastern Borneo, Dutch East Indies, 30 miles N. by W. of Banjermassin. The station was opened in 1866 and now (1903) has 1 missionary and his wife, 7 native workers, 15 Sunday schools, 6 day schools, and 568 professed Christians, of whom 303 are communicants.

KWALA LUMPUR: A town in the district of Selangsor, Malay Peninsula; situated near the head of the Klang River. It is the capital of the British protectorate, and is destined to grow in importance as time passes. Station of the ME, with (1903) 1 missionary and his wife, 3 native workers, 2 Sunday schools, 1 day school, and 205 professed Christians.

KWAMAGWAZA: A town in Natal, Africa; situated in the district of Eshowe, 9 miles N. W. of the town of that name. Station of the Zululand Diocese of the Church of England (1886), with (1900) 1 missionary, 4 women missionaries, and 2 native women workers.

KWAMERA: A mission station of the New Hebrides Missionary Society, on the southern part of the Island of Tanna, New Hebrides. It was established in 1858 and has (1900) 1 missionary and his wife and 2 native workers.

KWAMERA LANGUAGE: A dialect of the Measisi spoken in the Island of Tanna, New Hebrides.

KWAN-CHAU: A town in the province of Ho-nan, China, situated 70 miles S. E. of Ju-ning-fu. Station of the CIM (1899), with (1903) 1 missionary.

KWAN-CHENG-TSZ: A town in Manchuria, China, situated in the district of Kirin, 62 miles W. of that city. It has a considerable trade in indigo and opium. Population, 70,000. Station of the Presbyterian Church in Ireland (1891), with (1900) 4 missionaries (three with their wives), 25 native workers, men and women; 10 outstations, 11 places of worship, 1 day school, 1 theological seminary, 1 dispensary, 1 hospital and 120 church members.

KWANG-CHI-HSIEN: A town 75 miles southeast of Wu-chang in the province of Hu-pei, China. Station of the WMS (1903), with 1 missionary, 7 native workers, 5 chapels, 3 Sunday schools, 2 day schools, and 140 professed Christians.

KWANG-FENG-HSIEN: A town in the province of Kiang-si, China, situated 138 miles E. N. E. of Nan-chang-fu. Station of the CIM (1889), with (1903) 4 women missionaries, 5 native workers, men and women, and 3 outstations.

KWANG-HSIN-FU: A town in the province of Kiang-si, China; situated on the Kin River, 150 miles N. W. of Wen-chau and 135 miles E. of Nan-chang-fu. Station of the CIM (1902), with 2 women missionaries. Name is sometimes spelled Kwang-sin-fu.

KWANG-NING-HSIEN: A town in Manchuria, Chinese Empire; situated in the province of Liao-tung, about 45 miles N. N. W. of New-chwang. Station of the Presbyterian Church in Ireland (1895), with (1900) 2 missionaries (1 with his wife), 27 native workers, men and women; 24 outstations, 16 places of worship, 4 day schools, 1 theological training class, 1 dispensary, 1 hospital, and 300 church members. Name written by the Society, Kwangning.

KWANG-TÊ-CHAU: A town in the province of Ngan-hwei, China; situated 138 miles E. N. E. of Nang-king-fu. Station of the CIM (1890), with (1903) 1 missionary and his wife. Name written by the Society, Kwang-teh.

KWANG-YUEN-HSIEN: A town in the province of Sze-chwan, China; situated about 124 miles N. E. of Cheng-tu-fu. Station of the CIM (1889), with (1903) 2 women missionaries. Name written by the Society, Kwang-yuen.

KWAN-HSIEN: A town in the province of Sze-chwan; situated on the Min River at the northwestern edge of the Cheng-tu plain and about 70 miles N. W. of the city of Cheng-tu-fu. Station of the CIM (1889), with (1903) 1 missionary and his wife and 2 native workers.

KWATO: A town at the S. E. extremity of British New Guinea. Station of the LMS (1891), with (1903) 1 missionary and his wife, 11 native workers, 15 schools, and 214 communicants.

KWEI-HWA-CHENG-TING: A town in the province of Shen-si, China; situated at an altitude of 3,600 feet in the N. W. part of the province, 50 miles N. W. of So-ping-fu and about 250 miles W. N. W. of Peking. The town is divided by gardens and public squares into two sections, the traders occupying one section and the military and the religious bodies occupying the other. It stands at the confluence of trade routes to the Kokonor region and Eastern Turkestan, being the southeastern terminus of a route across the desert of Gobi. Population, about 200,000. Station of the Christian and Missionary Alliance.

KWEI-K'I. See KWEI-TSI-HSIEN.

KWEI-LIN-FU: A town in the province of Kwang-si, China; situated at the headwaters of the Kwei River, 230 miles N. W. of Canton. Station of the CMS (1899), with (1903) 2 missionaries (1 with his wife) and 1 dispensary. The CA also has a station at this place. The name is sometimes written Kwei Lin.

KWEI-TSI-HSIEN: A town in the province of Kiang-si, China; situated about 90 miles E. S. E.

of Nan-chang-fu. Station of the CIM (1878), with (1903) 8 missionary women, 11 native workers, men and women; 8 outstations, 9 places of worship, 2 day schools, 1 boarding school and 246 professed Christians. Name written by the Society, Kweiki.

KWEI-YANG-FU: A town in the province of Kwei-chau, of which it is the capital; situated 310 miles S. W. of Chang-te in Hunan, at the sources of important affluents of the Yangtse River. It has considerable commercial importance. Station of the CIM (1877), with (1903) 4 missionaries, 2 wives of missionaries, 2 missionary women, and 5 native workers.

KYELANG. See KAILANG.

KYOTO. See KIOTO.

L

LABRADOR: The easternmost portion of British America, on the Atlantic coast, comprising the region draining into the Atlantic bounded northeast and east by Hudson Strait and the Atlantic Ocean, southeast by the Strait of Belle Isle, and west by Ungava and Quebec. It is a dependency of Newfoundland and its area is about 120,000 square miles. The population is estimated (1901) at 3,947. The climate is very cold. The coasts are rugged and forbidding. Vegetation is scanty, because of cold, and only stunted trees, shrubs, and lichens grow well there. The people are chiefly Eskimos, with some descendants of early French adventurers. Their occupations are fishing in the summer, hunting and trapping in the winter. The important settlements are scattered along the shore of the Strait of Belle Isle, and on the ocean coast to Cape Webeck, just north of Hamilton Inlet.

The Moravians are the foremost Christian workers in Labrador.

Their stations are, from S. to N., the following: Rigolet (1901), Makkovik (1896), Hopedale (1782), Nain (1771), Okak (1776), Hebron (1830) and Ramah (1871).

The Labrador Medical Mission is also in the field. Dr. Grenfell, of the Medical Mission, in his hospital yacht, steams from point to point, healing the sick among the Eskimos and preaching the Gospel.

The CMS, through Mr. Peck, has accomplished good results in Labrador.

Grenfell (W. T.), *The Vikings of Today*, 1895.

LABUAN ISLAND: A small island off the N. W. coast of Borneo and about 6 miles distant. It belongs to the British North Borneo Company, is flat, well-wooded and has extensive coal mines, and produces sago flour in large quantities. It has an area of 30 square miles and a population of 6,000. Station of the SPG (1889), with (1903) 1 missionary, 4 native workers, 14 outstations, 2 places of worship, 1 day school and 114 professed Christians, of whom 46 are communicants.

LA CAROLINA: A village in the S. part of the State of Maranhão, Brazil, S. America, near the Tocantins River. Station of the South American Evangelical Mission, with 2 missionaries, one with his wife.

LACCADIVE ISLANDS: A group of 14 islands, only 9 of which are inhabited, lying in the Indian Ocean, about 200 miles off the west coast of Madras, India. Population (1891), 14,473, called Moplas. They are of mixed Hindu and Arab descent, and in religion are Mohammedan. The Malayalam language is spoken, but Arabic characters are used in writing. Coconuts are the principal agricultural product, and coir forms the principal article of trade. Its manufacture is carried on mainly by the women. The northern portion of the islands is attached to the collectorate of South Kanara, and the remainder to Malabar district, for administrative purposes.

LACROIX, Alphonse Francois: Born May 10, 1799, at Lignieres, Switzerland; studied at Bakel, near Rotterdam; ordained August 11, 1820, as a minister of the Dutch Reformed Church; sailed for India, October 1, 1820, as a missionary of the Netherlands Missionary Society; was stationed at Chinsurah in the Dutch Territory. On the decision of the Netherlands Society to give up its missions in India Mr. Lacroix in 1827 became a missionary of the LMS, two years later removing to Calcutta, the scene of his life work. He was one of the most eloquent and effective vernacular preachers in India. He could always secure a large audience by the charm of his manner and voice, by a felicitous use of idiomatic Bengali, and by the beautiful imagery in which he clothed his ideas. He conducted through the press a new edition of the Gospels of Matthew, Luke and John in Bengali for the Calcutta Bible Society, and, in conjunction with Dr. Duff, superintended the printing of Isaiah in the same language. He also conducted a theological class. After an eminent mission service in Bengal of nearly forty years, he died July 8, 1859, having just completed the sixtieth year of his age.

Mullens (J.), *Life of A. F. Lacroix*, London, 1862.

LAC SEUL: Station of the CMS in Keewatin, Canada, with (1903) 1 woman missionary, 2 native workers, 2 outstations, 4 day schools and 530 professed Christians, of whom 75 are communicants.

LADISMITH: A village in Cape Colony, Africa, situated 65 miles N. E. of Swellendam. Station of the Berlin Mission Society (1856), with (1903) 1 missionary, 12 native workers, 6 outstations, 2 day schools and 624 professed Christians, of whom 288 are communicants.

LADRONE ISLANDS: A group of about 20 islands in the North Pacific Ocean. The islands are of volcanic formation, mountainous, well watered and well wooded. Magellan discovered these islands in 1521, and named them Ladrones, from the thievish disposition of the inhabitants; they were afterward called the Lazarus Islands; and in 1667, when the Jesuits settled there, they were renamed Marianne, or Mariana, in honor of the Spanish queen. The islands formerly belonged to Spain. In 1898 Guam, the largest of the group, was ceded to the United States. The next year (1899) the remaining islands were ceded by Spain to Germany. The present inhabitants of the islands are immigrants or the descendants of immigrants from the Philippines. Guam has an area of about 200 miles and a population of 9,000. Of these, two-thirds live in Agaña, the capital. The ABCFM has a station here (1901). Spanish has been the language of the islands, but English is making progress in Guam.

LADYSMITH: A village in the Klip River district of Natal, Africa, situated 80 miles N. N. W. of Pietermaritzburg. Population, about 300 people. Station of the Maritzburg Missionary Association (1856), with 1 woman missionary. Station also of the South African Wesleyan Methodist Mission Society, with 77 native workers, 22 outstations, 14 chapels, 2 Sunday schools, 1 society for young people, 5 day schools and 1,228 professed Christians.

LAGOS: A town in Lagos Colony, West Africa, situated 48 miles S. of Abeokuta, on an island in a lagoon at the mouth of the Ogun. It is accessible to vessels of considerable size, and has water communication far into the interior. Since 1861 a British possession; often called the "African Liverpool," on account of its enormous exports of palm-oil. It is now the capital of the district. The name is Portuguese; the native name is Ago, or Eko. Population (1901), 41,847, of whom 10,636 are reported as Christians (233 Europeans) and 22,080 Mohammedans; only 9,000 of the townspeople are reported as pagan. The city is connected with Abeokuta and Ibadan by a railway (122 miles). Station of the CMS (1852), with (1903) 4 missionaries, one with his wife; 3 women missionaries, 36 native workers, 8 day schools, 2 boarding schools, 1,930 professed Christians, of whom 932 are communicants. It is also the field of the native church in connection with the CMS. Station of the NBC (1878), with (1900) 10 missionaries, 5 women missionaries, 4 native workers, 11 outstations, 19 chapels, 10 Sunday schools, 10 day schools, 1 theological class and 1,600 professed Christians. Station also of the SBC (1853), with 1 outstation, 1 chapel, 1 Sunday school, 1 day school and 1 theological class. The work is, however, in charge of the Native Baptist Church. Station of the WMS, with (1903) 1 missionary and his wife, 53 native workers, 17 chapels, 6 Sunday schools, 6 day schools and 1,736 professed Christians, 678 of whom are communicants.

LAGOS: A British Colony and Protectorate on the Gulf of Guinea, West Africa, between Dahomey and Southern Nigeria, and northward within undefined boundaries to the French possessions on the Middle Niger The colony proper comprises Lagos Island and about 140 miles of coast, containing altogether 3,460 square miles; the protectorate extends inland, with 25,450 square miles. The estimated population of all (1901) is 1,500,000.

Missions were commenced in this territory by Christianized negroes removing from Sierra Leone to Abeokuta about 1840. Their representations led to the establishment by the CMS of stations at Badagry (1845), Abeokuta (1846), Lagos (1852) and Ibadan (1852). The CMS has since occupied three other stations. The WMS, the SBC and the National Baptist Convention also have missionaries at some of these same stations, and altogether there are 89 missionary schools and about 7,500 native communicants.

LAGUBOTI: A village on the S. shore of Toba Lake, Sumatra. Station of the Rhenish Missionary Society, with (1903) 2 missionaries, one with his wife; 12 native workers, 13 outstations, 10 Sunday schools, 11 day schools and 3,245 professed Christians, of whom 870 are communicants.

LAHAGU: A village in the central part of the island of Nias, Dutch E. Indies, situated about 20 miles S. W. of Gunong Sitoli. Station of the Rhenish Missionary Society, with (1903) 1 missionary and his wife, 1 day school, 1 Sunday school and 208 professed Christians, of whom 124 are communicants.

LAHORE: A town in Punjab, India; situated on the left bank of the Ravi River, 32 miles W. of Amritsar. Has several fine mosques and a number of Hindu temples. The surrounding country is covered with vast ruins, attesting the ancient magnificence of the city. Population (1901), 202,964, Muslims, Hindus and Sikhs. Punjabi and Urdu are the most prevalent languages, but Pashti and Kashmiri are also spoken. Mission station of the CMS (1867), with (1903) 3 missionaries, 2 with their wives; 1 woman missionary, 2 native workers, 1 place of worship, 2 day schools, 1 theological class, 1 hostel, and 317 professed Christians, of whom 130 are communicants. Station also of the ME, with (1903) 1 missionary and his wife, 12 native workers, 2 chapels, 5 Sunday schools, and 620 professed Christians, of whom 60 are communicants. Station also of the PN (1849), with (1903) 6 missionaries and their wives, 3 women missionaries, 15 native workers, 10 outstations, 5 places of worship, 5 Sunday schools, 8 day schools, 2 boarding schools, 1 college, 1 dispensary, and 215 professed Christians. The YMCA (1899) and the YWCA both have agents here with branches of their respective associations. Station also of the ZBM, with (1903) 11 women missionaries, 12 native workers, 2 boarding schools, and 240 Zenana pupils.

LAHUSA: A village on the S. coast of the island of Nias, Dutch E. Indies; situated about 35 miles S. of Gunong Sitoli. Station of the Rhenish Missionary Society, with (1903) 2 missionaries, 1 with his wife; 6 native workers, 2 outstations, 1 Sunday school, 2 day schools, and 311 professed Christians, of whom 202 are communicants.

LAI-AN. See LAI-NGAN-HSIEN.

LAI-NGAN-HSIEN: A town in the province of Ngan-hwei, China; situated about 20 miles N. by E. of Chu-chau. Station of the CIM (1899). Name also written Lai-an.

LAINGSBURG: A village in the District of Prince Albert, Cape Colony, Africa; situated on the railroad to Kimberly, 213 miles from Cape Town. Population, 1,500. Station of the Berlin Missionary Society (1884), with (1903) 1 missionary, 11 native workers, 15 outstations, 2 day schools, and 880 professed Christians, of whom 284 are communicants.

LAITLYNKOT: A village in Assam, India; situated 10 miles S. by W. of Shillong. Station of the Welsh Calvinistic Methodist Missionary Society, with (1903) 1 missionary and his wife, 24 native workers, 14 outstations, 15 places of worship, 10 Sunday schools, 13 day schools, 1 dispensary, and 346 professed Christians, of whom 99 are communicants.

LAKAWN: A town on the Me Wang, Siam; situated 65 miles S. E. of Chieng Mai. Population is composed very largely of Laos. Station of the PN (1885), with 5 missionaries, 4 with their wives; 1 missionary woman, 4 native workers, 3 outstations, 1 chapel, 4 Sunday schools, 2 boarding schools, 1 hospital and 209 professed Christians. Name also written Lakon.

LAKEMBA ISLANDS: A group of small islands east of the Fiji Islands, to which they politically belong. It is occupied by the Australian Wesleyan Missionary Society, with (1900) 2 missionaries, 251 native workers, 11 outstations, 72 places of worship, 72 Sunday schools, 73 day schools, and 2,469 professed Christians. Name written by the Society Lakeba.

LAKHIMPUR: A village is Assam, India; situated 55 miles W. S. W. of Dibrugarh. Population, 5,000. Station of the ABMU (1893), with (1903) 2 missionaries and their wives, 19 native workers, 7 outstations, 4 chapels, 1 Sunday school, 5 village schools, 1 boarding school, 1 dispensary, and 392 professed Christians.

LALITPUR: A town in the District of Lalitpur, United Provinces, India; situated 110 miles S. by E. of Gwalior. Population 11,300, 8,700 of whom are Hindus and 1,600 Muslims. Station of the Reformed Episcopal Foreign Mission Society (1888), with (1900) 2 missionaries,1 with his wife; 2 women missionaries, 17 native workers, 5 outstations, 1 place of worship, 5 Sunday schools, 2 young people's societies, 5 day schools, 2 industrial training schools, 1 dispensary, 1 medical class, 1 orphanage, and 131 Christians.

LAMBARÉNE: A settlement on the Ogowe River, French Congo, Africa; situated about 150 miles from its mouth. The PN opened a mission station in 1867, but transferred it to the Paris Evangelical Society in 1895. It now (1903) has 4 missionaries, 3 with their wives; 1 woman missionary, 5 outstations, 1 chapel, 1 Sunday school, 2 day schools, and 1 dispensary.

LAMU: A town and the capital of the District of Tanaland, British East Africa; situated on the east side of Lamu Island. The island is 7 miles long and separated from the land by a narrow channel. It lies off the coast about 150 miles N. W. of Mombasa. The town is a port of call for English and German steamers, and is connected with Mombasa by telegraph. It has a population of 5,000 people, and is a mission station of the Neukirchen Mission Society (1889), with (1901) 3 missionaries and their wives and 1 boarding school.

LAN-CHAU: A town in the Province of Chi-li, China, about halfway between Tien-tsin and Shan-hai-kwan. Station of the ME (1884). Altho the mission work was broken up and the missionaries driven out in the Boxer troubles, it is now being reorganized and carried on with (1903) 16 native workers, 6 outstations, and 744 Christians.

LAN-CHAU-FU: The capital of the province of Kan-su, China; situated on the right bank of the Hwang-ho in a narrow valley which the town fills, 450 miles W. N. W. of Hsi-ngan-fu. It has important manufactures of coarse woolen goods. Altitude, 5,000 feet. Population, 250,000, of whom many are Mohammedans. Station of the CIM (1885), with (1903) 6 missionaries, 2 with their wives; 1 woman missionary, 1 chapel, and 1 dispensary.

LANDAUR: A village and sanitarium in the District of Dehra Dun, United Provinces, India; situated 77 miles E. of Ambala. Altitude, 7,459 feet. Population (1891), 2,000. Station of the PN (1874), with (1903) 1 missionary and his wife, 1 woman missionary, and 1 boarding school. Station of the ZBM, with (1903) 2 women missionaries, 2 native workers, and 81 Zenana pupils. The name is sometimes spelled Landour. The place is also called Woodstock.

LANG-CHAU: A town in the province of Shen-si, China, situated 115 miles W. N. W. of Hsi-ngan-fu. Station of the CIM (1893), with (1903) 1 missionary and his wife, 1 woman missionary and 1 chapel.

LANGUAGES; Missions and the Unwritten: Christianity had its origin in the midst of the highest civilization of the times. It was not born in some obscure corner of the earth. It found its way at once into the imperial centers of the mightiest empire of the ancient world. It expressed itself at the outset in the supremest language the human race has ever invented. The oracles out of which it sprung had already been translated into this tongue, and the new oracles of the New Covenant were given in the same speech.

It is a significant fact that cannot be too often commented upon that Christianity at once conquered the best and possessed it for the New Kingdom. It speedily also began to invade the other living languages of power and influence— the Syriac, which reached out eastward to the Euphrates and beyond, and the Latin, which was the speech of the civilization of the West. This could not take place without affecting the very life and forms of these languages, changing their vocabulary, enriching their content.

It would be interesting to trace the influence of Christianity—aggressive, conquering, missionary Christianity—on these languages, already the vehicle of polished thought. Without doubt the very language of Greece, in which the New Testament was first given form, received a new imprint from these holy writings.

So too the Scriptures, translated into the Vulgate, the common speech of the Latin peoples, had their modifying influences on the language of the Cæsars. Except, however, in adding elevation of thought and in the gift of spiritual ideals it is doubtful whether Christianity really added anything to these already classic languages. When we come to another class of languages another set of facts are to be considered. Christianity, ever restless and moving outward from its early centers, came in contact in the West with peoples that had already developed incipient literatures. They had created their alphabets and begun their progress. The new light of the Spirit, however, proved a mighty leaven, and as we trace these origins of literature we find, as in our earliest forms of English literature, the presence of the creative power of the Christian story. Even later in their development it is the power of the Bible translated by the missionary church into their tongue that fixes it as in England and in Germany, or the power of a missionary soul that lifted it to its loftiest possibilities, as Dante, the tongue of Italy.

But this is not enough for Christianity. It is not satisfied to vivify existing literature, and give a mighty uplift to those in the weakness of their infancy—it has created the very forms of literature and has made languages.

The language of Russia and Bulgaria, and Servia, all the languages however modified that take their origin from the old Slavic of the early centuries, owe their very letters, their alphabet, to missionaries from Constantinople: Cyril and Methodius, who in the 9th century went to the South Slavic peoples and gave their language form in the quaint characters that abide to this day. This work of missionaries in the 9th century is being carried forward by missionaries in the 20th century. A missionary in Central Africa has just reduced the Kairondo language to writing and begun the translation of the Gospel into this speech. In the year 1903 the complete New Testament translated by the Rev. E. H. Richards was issued in Sheetswa, the speech of millions of people on the east coast of Africa who had no written language until the advent of the missionary. What is true of these African tribes is also true of the many peoples living in the scattered islands of Micronesia. In 1856 the Rev. Hiram Bingham, the son of one of the first missionaries to the Sandwich Islands, left the United States on the Morning Star. He arrived in Apaiang in November, 1857. He spent the first eighteen months after his arrival in acquiring the language and putting it in writing. In February, 1859, he commenced the translation of the New Testament, which was not completed until 1873, and the Old Testament twenty years later. The whole story is a fascinating one. In the translation nearly 400 foreign words had to be introduced for which there were no equivalents in the new tongue.

The language of Ponape, one of the Caroline Islands, was also reduced to writing by missionaries. Matthew and John were translated in 1859. This translation was made by the Rev. Dr. Gulick, who had the help of a runaway Portuguese who had been on the island, and who had acquired the language and had been converted by reading the Portuguese New Testament given him by a missionary, so that from this incident we see how the Divine Word reproduces itself by giving shape to languages which had no written form until the missionary influence came in contact with it.

In the Marshall Islands the missionaries reduced the language to writing in order to translate into the language the Holy Scriptures. The New Testament was finally given to these people in 1885.

What was true of the Gilbert Islands and the Ponape and the Marshall Islands was also true of Kusaie and the Mortlock and Ruk languages. Another interesting group of languages which has been reduced to form by missionary effort is that of the Indians of North America. It is true that the Cherokee language owes its alphabet to a newspaper enterprise,—a certain educated Cherokee, Geo. Guess, purposing to introduce the "talking leaf" to his people. The missionaries, however, much to his disgust, made use of his work for circulating the Scriptures, and the first actual printing in type from the letters originated by the newspaper enterprise was the Book of Genesis, translated by the Rev. S. A. Worcester, D.D., and published in 1827.

The work of the Moravians among the Delawares and of the American Board missionaries among the Dakotas and among the Choctaws, all had to do with the shaping and forming of these languages. So much was it realized that this missionary work had been an important aid in the civilizing of the tribes that in 1887 the Dakota Indians appealed from the decision of the United States abolishing the use of the vernacular in their schools on the ground that the Vernacular Bible had been a great and effective agency in their civilization.

Not only has missionary effort, especially in connection with the translation of the Scriptures, been a creative power giving shape and form to many unwritten languages, of which the above incidents are simply occasional examples, and giving an elevation and dignity to those that already had been reduced to writing, but in many instances the work of the missionaries has been the only influence that has given permanence to these languages. In some cases the only memorial of these languages that exists is the product of the labor of the missionary.

LAN-KI-HSIEN: A town in the province of Che-kiang, China, situated 75 miles S. W. of Hang-chau. It is an important commercial center. Population, 200,000. Station of the CIM (1894), with (1903) 3 women missionaries, 5 native workers, and 1 chapel. Name is sometimes written Lan-k'i.

LAN-TIEN-HSIEN: A town in the province of Shen-si, China, situated 28 miles S. E. of Hsingan-fu. Station of the CIM (1895), with (1903) 1 missionary and his wife, 1 native worker, 1 chapel, 1 Sunday school, and 1 day school. The name is sometimes written Lan-t'ien.

LAO-HO-KAU: A town and river port on the Han River, in the province of Hu-pei, China, situated 200 miles N.W. of Han-kau. Station of the CIM (1887), with (1903) 2 missionaries and their wives, 9 native workers, 1 outstation, 2 places of worship, 1 Sunday school, 1 day school, and 44 Christians. Station also of the Norwegian Lutheran China Mission (1894), with (1900) 3 missionaries, 2 with their wives; 4 women missionaries, 1 day school, and 1 boarding school. Station also of the PB, with 1 missionary and his wife and 2 women missionaries. Name spelled by the Society Lao-ho-k'ou and Lao-ho-keo.

LAO-LING. See Le-ling-hsien.

LAOS: The name Laos is the French method of writing the name Lao, given by the Siamese to a people of the Shan stock, often called Eastern Shans, and found in North Siam and in the French territories of Indo-China. The word has become naturalized in English through the adoption of the French spelling by writers in English. The northern limits of the Laos tribes have not yet been fixed, but they are said to form the majority of the population as far north as the southern part of the Chinese province of Yun-nan. The hill tribes of the Chinese island of Hai-nan also speak a dialect which can be understood by the Laos of Siam. The general theory of the Shan race is that they lived in China before the Chinese appeared, were crowded into the hills first, and so gained their name Shan (mountain), and were next crowded gradually southward, those who took the western river valleys becoming the Shans of Eastern Burma, and those who followed the eastern valleys becoming the Siamese and Cambodians, the later comers becoming known to the world by the name Lao, applied to them by the Siamese. They call themselves "Tai," which means the free.

The number of these people is variously estimated at from five to ten millions. Estimate in any case is little better than a guess, since the northern regions of their domains have not been fully explored. Various hill tribes inhabiting the same regions as the Laos are often confounded with them because those of them who write use the Laos written characters. But they are not of Laos blood and their languages are entirely distinct from the Laos dialects. Of these hill tribes several are found in Siamese territory, such as the Musu, the Kamu, the Meo, the Yao, and Lwa. The first two of these hill tribes have been reached to some extent by missionaries. They are worshipers of ancestors or of spirits, and some of them are notable exceptions to the rule of laziness which governs the Laos. They also show considerable mechanical aptitude in a rude way.

In stature the Laos are rather short, averaging about five and a half feet in height. In complexion they are rather tawny, with brown eyes but black hair. In bearing they are manly, and they have considerable pride of race. The peasants are attached in feudal style to some lord, but with considerable liberty to change their relations to a lord less severe. For this reason, perhaps, the feudal lords are somewhat restrained in exacting labors from their retainers. Slavery exists to some extent among the Laos. Slaves are handed down by inheritance, or purchased, or captured in war. In their slavery, too, there is some amelioration in the fact that the slaves are often allowed to live by themselves, merely answering when called upon for service for a few days or a week at a time.

The Laos treat women as equals, and upon marriage it is quite common for the husband to leave his father and mother and join the family of his wife. They are hospitable to strangers, rather inclined to laziness, and passionately fond of gambling. A curious custom in reference to the disposition of their dead, is that the body of a deceased friend is embalmed and kept at the house for weeks and perhaps months, as is done in some parts of China, and the final disposition of the body is by cremation.

Mission work among the Laos of Siam was commenced by Messrs. McGilvary and Wilson of the American Presbyterian Board (N.) in 1867. After a careful exploration of the country, they selected Cheung Mai as the first station, and from the first marked success met them. The Laos mission of the PN is now in a very flourishing condition.

Curtis (Lillian J.), *The Laos of North Siam* Philadelphia, Westminster Press, 1903: *Missionary Review of the World*, Vol. X., 214; XII., 268, 332, 337; XIV., 355, 358; XV., 349, Funk & Wagnalls, New York; Picanon (E.), *Le Laos Francais*, Paris, 1900.

LA PAZ: A town in Bolivia, South America, and capital of the Republic. It has an altitude of 12,300 feet and a population of about 57,000. Station of the Baptist Society of Ontario and Quebec (1899), with (1903) 2 missionaries and their wives and 1 native worker.

LAPLAND: The country where the Lapps live; has no longer a distinct political or geographical existence, but is territory which is included in the dominions of Norway and Sweden and Russia. The region belonging to Norway and Sweden lies in the northern and northeastern part of the Scandinavian peninsula, and includes the provinces of Norrland and Finmark in Norway, and North and South Bothnia in Sweden. Russian Lapland lies in the northwestern districts of the empire, and is included in the grand duchy of Finland. In Norway the area of Lapp territory covers nearly 26,500 square miles, with 5,000 true Lapps; in Sweden, 50,600 square miles, 4,000 Lapps; in Russia, 11,300 square miles, 8,800 Lapps. In addition to the natives, Finns, Swedes, Norwegians and Russians are found in large numbers.

For the greater part of the year the climate is severely cold, tho that of the coast regions is tempered by the Gulf Stream. During July and August the sun never sets for several weeks in the northern districts, and the heat is great. Forests of birch, pine, fir, and alder abound, but large tracts of country are utterly barren.

The Lapps or Laplanders belong to the same branch of the human race as the Finns and Esthonians, and physically are undersized, with straight black hair, somewhat yellow skin, low foreheads, small eyes, and beardless chins.

Tho somewhat despised by their Norwegian neighbors, they have good mental powers and are manually dexterous. Honesty, a strong affection for their native land, and great religious depth and constancy characterize their best men.

The Swedish Church embraces, nominally, about the whole of the population of the country; but a large portion of the people, partly because of indifference and partly because of the distance from the churches, seldom participate in religious services. With an area of nearly 116,000 square kilometers, and with a population of 60,000, only seventeen churches hold services every Sunday.

LA PLATA: A town in Argentina, South America, situated 30 miles E. S. E. of Buenos Aires, and capital of the province of Buenos Aires. Population, 65,000. Station of the ME, with (1903) 3 native workers, 1 place of worship, 2 Sunday schools, and 123 professed Christians, of whom 53 are communicants.

LARACHE. See EL ARAISH.

LARAISH. See EL ARAISH.

LARANGEIRAS: A town in the State of Sergipe, Brazil, 19 miles W. N. W. of Aracaju; situated at the head of steam navigation on the Cotindiba River. Population, 3,000. Occupied as a station by the PN in 1884, and left in care of native workers in 1901, the missionary removing to Estancia.

LARES. A town in Porto Rico, West Indies, situated 50 miles W. S. W. of San Juan, with a population of 17,100. Station of the American Missionary Association, with (1901) 1 missionary and his wife, 2 women missionaries, 1 Sunday school, and 1 day school.

LARNACA: A town on the S. coast of Cyprus, situated 23 miles S. E. of Nicosia. It is the chief commercial port of the island and has many ruins of antiquity. It is the ancient Cilium. It is occupied by the RP (1891), with (1901) 2 missionaries and their wives, 3 native workers, 1 place of worship, 2 Sunday schools, 1 day school, 1 dispensary and 22 professed Christians.

LAS FLORES: A town in Argentina, South America, situated 165 miles S. W. of Buenos

Aires. Station of the RBMU, with (1901) 1 missionary and his wife and 1 Sunday school.

LATAKIA: A town and seaport of Syria; situated 75 miles W. of Tripoli. It has the remains of the ancient Roman city of Laodicea *ad Mare*. It is the chief town of the Nusariyeh region. Population, 12,000. Station of the RP (1859), with (1901) 3 missionaries and their wives, 3 women missionaries, 14 native workers, 4 outstations, 1 place of worship, 2 Sunday schools, 1 society for young people, 1 book-room, 4 day schools, 2 boarding schools, 1 dispensary, 1 hospital, and 196 professed Christians.

LAVRAS: A town in Minas Geraes, Brazil, South America, situated in the mountain district, 200 miles N. N. E. of Santos. Climate is healthful and dry. Altitude, 2,900 feet. Population, 4,000. Station of the PS (1892), with (1903) 1 missionary and his wife, 3 women missionaries, 4 native workers, 13 outstations, 3 places of worship, 1 Sunday school, 1 boarding school, 1 printing press, and 110 Christians.

LEALUYI. See LIALUI.

LEBAK: A village of Java, situated 50 miles S. W. of Batavia. Station of the Netherlands Mission Society (1894), with (1901) 1 missionary, 2 native workers, 1 outstation and 1 hospital.

LEBANON: A semi-autonomous province in Syria comprising the range of mountains of the same name, with an area of 2,500 square miles. It was given a constitution by the Turkish Government, under pressure from the great powers of Europe, who intervened to stop the massacres of 1860. The Governor of the Lebanon is not removable by the Sultan, nor can any but a Christian be appointed to the post. In consequence of these arrangements it is far more prosperous and progressive than any neighboring districts of Turkey.

LEGGE, James: Born at Huntly, Aberdeenshire, Scotland, in 1815; graduated at King's College and University, 1835. After studying at Highbury Theological College, London, he was appointed in 1839, by the LMS, a missionary to China, and reached Malacca in December of the same year. In 1840 he took charge of the Anglo-Chinese college, founded by Dr. Morrison and Dr. Milne. In 1843 the Society decided to change the college into a theological seminary for the training of native ministers for China, selected Hongkong for the seat of the institution, and appointed Mr. Legge as its president. He did some of his best work in this school, altho he finally left it because he was not satisfied with the result of his work as a teacher. Some of the best and most useful native workers in the mission were trained by Mr. Legge. In 1867 he visited England, and while there was presented by the government of the colony with a service of plate "in acknowledgment of the many valuable services freely and gratuitously rendered." A number of the Chinese inhabitants presented him with a costly and beautiful silver tablet, made after the Chinese fashion. In 1870 he received from the University of Aberdeen the degree of Doctor of Laws. In this year he returned to Hongkong. In 1876 he was elected professor of Chinese languages and literature at Oxford University. Dr. Legge took a prominent part in 1847 in the discussion concerning the proper rendering in Chinese of the words God and Spirit, and published a volume in 1852 under the title of "*The Notions of the Chinese concerning God and Spirits.*" The work of preaching to the Chinese was that which Dr. Legge loved best. But the work which has made him renowned over all the earth is the edition which he brought out of the Chinese classics, with the Chinese text, a translation in English, notes critical and exegetical, and copious prolegomena. For these and translations of other important Chinese works, he received, on occasion of its first award, in 1875, the Julien prize from the Academie des Belles Lettres et Inscriptions of the Institute of France.

Missionary Review of the World, Vcl. XI., 284.

LEH: The capital of the Ladakh province, Kashmir, India, situated about 5 miles from the Indus River and 160 miles east of Srinagar. It is a commercial center for trade between Punjab and Tibet on one hand and Chinese Turkestan on the other. It is also a market for Turkestan shawl wool. Altitude, 11,530 feet. Population, about 4,000. Station of the Moravian Missions (1885), with (1903) 3 missionaries and their wives, 1 woman missionary, 1 outstation, 2 places of worship, 2 Sunday schools, 3 day schools, 1 printing press, 1 dispensary, 1 hospital, and 17 professed Christians.

LEIDENBURG. See LYDENBURG.

LEIPZIG EVANGELICAL MISSIONARY SOCIETY. See GERMANY; MISSIONARY SOCIETIES IN.

LE-LING-HSIEN: A town in the N. of the province of Shan-tung, China, situated 68 miles N. by E. of Tsi-nan-fu. Station of the Methodist New Connexion Missionary Society, with 3 missionaries and their wives, 57 native workers, 159 outstations, 160 places of worship, 30 Sunday schools, 1 book room, 28 day schools, 2 boarding schools, 1 female helpers' training class, 1 hospital, 1 medical class and 1,883 Christians. The name is sometimes written Lao Ling.

LENAKEL: A village in New Hebrides, Oceania, situated on the W. coast of Tanna Island.

LEON: A town in the state of Guanajuato, Mexico, situated 31 miles W. by N. of Guanajuato. There are considerable manufactures in this town. Altitude, 5,000 feet. Population, 50,000. Station of the ME, with (1903) 1 missionary and his wife, 1 Sunday school, 1 place of worship, and 61 professed Christians, of whom 11 are communicants. Station also of the SBC (1896), with (1903) 1 missionary and his wife, 1 native worker and 1 Sunday school.

LEOPOLDVILLE: A town in the Congo Free State, Africa, capital of the Stanley Pool District, situated on the left bank of the Congo River at the outlet of Stanley Pool. It is the most important trading post in the Congo Free State and is used as a business center for the missionaries in the Congo region. The climate is good and the water supply excellent. Station of the RBMU (1899), with 1 missionary and his wife.

LEPCHA LANGUAGE: A dialect spoken in Sikkim, north of Darjiling and on the southern border of Tibet. It belongs to the Tibeto-Burman linguistic group, and is written with the Pahari alphabet.

LEPERS; Special labor for: Previous to the year 1860 but little effort had been made to ameliorate the condition of the lepers, or to take the Gospel to them in their isolation. As early as 1812 Dr. Carey of Serampur, India, witnessed the burning of a leper and was so impressed by the helplessness of these outcasts that he established a hospital for them in Calcutta, probably the first in all India. In 1818 the Colonial Government of South Africa, fearing the spread of leprosy, erected a hospital at Hemel en Aarde, and four years later a larger hospital was erected, and the Governor requested the Moravian Church, already working among the Hottentots, to send missionaries to manage the institution and look after the spiritual as well as the material welfare of its inmates. In 1846 the establishment was removed to Robben Island, and was continued in the care of the Moravians till 1867, when the English Government appointed a chaplain of the Church of England, and the Moravians withdrew.

As early as 1840 provision for lepers was made at Almora, India, through the efforts of a government official, and in 1849 the work was turned over to the LMS. In 1855 an asylum for lepers was established at Ambala, Punjab, by missionaries of the PN, again aided and largely supported by a government official. But, with the exception of the one asylum in South Africa and the two institutions in India, practically nothing was done for lepers during the years previous to 1860. During the next thirty years Christians were slowly but surely awakening to a sense of the pressing need of these neglected classes, especially in India, where leprosy is so prevalent. Asylums were established at Chamba, Rawal Pindi, Sabathu and Tarn Taran, in the Punjab; at Agra, Allahabad, Almora, Banda and Chandag, near Pitthoragarh in the N. W. (United) Provinces; at Purulia in Bengal, at Ujjain in Central India and at Aleppie, Mangalur and Neyoor, in the south of Hindustan. The CMS established a leper settlement on the Zanzibar coast in Africa and the Norwegian Missionary society began work for lepers at two stations in Madagascar. In Jerusalem the Moravians established an asylum and home for lepers.

While the various existing missionary organizations were directly or indirectly working for lepers, the expansion of the work during this period is largely due to the formation of the society called the "Mission to Lepers in India and the East," by Mr. Wellesley C. Bailey, who, while a missionary of the American Presbyterian Church in the Punjab, as early as 1869 became much impressed with the condition of the lepers at the Ambala asylum of that mission. In 1874 he visited Great Britain and succeeded in forming a society for developing this special work. While as an organization it is independent, it cooperates with the various societies engaged in the work.

Work especially directed to lepers has greatly expanded since 1890. At that date organized effort for lepers did not exist in China, Japan, Burma and many other countries, and there were but twenty institutions for lepers in all the mission fields together. Since 1890, sixty-two asylums and homes for these afflicted people have been established, more than three times as many as in all previous years. Twenty-two prominent missionary societies are receiving aid in their work from the Mission to Lepers, which now has fifty-five stations in India, Burma and Ceylon, ten in China, two in Japan, and thirty asylums or hospitals in these countries owned by the Mission to Lepers itself, altho other societies cooperate in the service rendered the inmates.

In addition to these, fourteen institutions for lepers, owned by various societies, are partly supported by the Mission to Lepers. Fourteen homes for the untainted children of lepers have been established. Missionary work is also carried on in the asylums established by the British Government in several important cities of India, and in institutions supported by private benevolence which are found in various parts of India. Perhaps the best known among the workers for lepers in India is Miss Mary Reed, of the American ME Mission, who contracted the disease while working in India, and has lived among the lepers at Chandag, with no other associates than the afflicted natives, since 1890.

The first institution for lepers in Burma was opened in 1891 at Mandalay. At Singapore, a government leper colony is regularly visited by a missionary. At Lakawn, among the Laos people, the native Christians support twenty leper families. At Pak-hoi, in South China, in 1891 the CMS founded one of the finest institutions for lepers in the foreign field, and has since opened work for them at Hang-chau-fu, Fuchau-fu, Kien-ning-fu, Lo-ngwong and Ku-tien-hsien. In 1895 the first leper asylum in Central China was established by the LMS. The American ME Mission has a work for lepers at Hsing-hwa-fu, and the Protestant Episcopal Church, U. S. A., has begun work at Ngan-king, on the Yangtse River. Work for the lepers of Japan was begun by the American Presbyterians in 1894 in a suburb of Tokio, and the CMS has a hospital at Kumamoto.

In Africa, besides the colony on Robben Island, the Moravian missionaries work among the lepers within the bounds of their mission north of Lake Nyasa. In the Transvaal, the Hermannsburg Mission has a work at Mosetta. The government asylum at Emjanjana, in Kaffraria, is visited by a missionary of the Scottish Episcopal Church. Another leper colony is cared for near the town of Zanzibar. In Madagascar the LMS began work for lepers in 1895, about four miles from Fianarantsoa. Manakavaly, the leper village near Isoavina built by the LMS, has been taken over by the Paris Evangelical Missionary Society.

The Norwegian Missionary Society has a station for lepers at Antsirabe, and another at Fianarantsoa. The United Norwegian Lutheran Church of America also has a leper home and asylum in Madagascar. The French Roman Catholics have two hospitals for lepers in the island and also work for them at Port of Spain, Trinidad, and at Mandalay.

In Hawaii a leper settlement was established by the Government at Molokai, in which work is carried on by the Hawaiian Evangelical Association and the Roman Catholics. This leper colony was the scene of the labors of Father Damien, who established the Roman Catholic Mission there in 1873, contracted the disease, and died at his post in 1889.

In the New Hebrides a leper colony has been established by the Melanesian Mission in one of the Banks Islands, and the LMS began work in 1897 among the lepers of Belep Islands.

The first work for the lepers of Persia was begun by the American Presbyterians at Tabriz in 1894. In 1896 the Moravian Missionary Society established an asylum at Surinam, in South America. Summary (1901)—Africa: 6 asylums and settlements, with 840 inmates. Burma: 2 asylums, with 162 inmates; 1 home for untainted children, with 6 inmates. Ceylon: 1 asylum, with 271 inmates. China: 11 asylums and settlements, with 636 inmates; 1 home for untainted children, with 5 inmates. India: 47 asylums and settlements, with 3,302 inmates; 12 homes for untainted children, with 222 inmates. Japan: 2 asylums, with 43 inmates. Madagascar: 4 asylums and settlements, with 377 inmates. Malaysia: 2 asylums and settlements, with 25 inmates. Oceania: 3 asylums and settlements, with 1,120 inmates. Palestine: 1 asylum, with 35 inmates; 1 home for children, with 35 inmates. Persia: 1 settlement, with 150 inmates. South America: 1 asylum, with 13 inmates.

Totals: 71 asylums in 12 different fields; 6,528 inmates; 15 homes for untainted children, with 268 inmates.

Missionary Review of the World, Vol. V, 136; Vol. VI, 434; Vol. VIII, 358; Vol. IX, 376; Vol. X, 345; Vol. XI, 330; Vol. XII, 683; Vol. XIV, 537, Funk & Wagnalls, New York.

LERIBE: A village in Leribe district, in the north of Basutoland, Africa. Station of the Paris Evangelical Society (1859), with (1903) 1 missionary and his wife, 20 native workers, 12 outstations, 1 place of worship, 1 Sunday school, 13 day schools and 1,137 professed Christians, of whom 752 are communicants.

LES CAYES. See AUX CAYES.

LEVUKA: A town on the island of Ovalau, former capital of the Fiji Islands, Oceania, situated on the E. coast and surrounded by hills. Station of the Australian Wesleyan Missionary Society, with (1900) 1 missionary, 87 native workers, 56 places of worship, 103 Sunday schools, 123 day schools and 1,091 Christians. The SPG also has a station there, with 1 missionary.

LIALUI: A village in the Barotsi valley, Rhodesia, Africa, situated on a low hill, 15 miles E. of the Zambesi River, with which it is connected by a canal constructed by the Barotsi chief Lewanika. Station of the Paris Evangelical Society (1892), with (1903) 2 missionaries, 2 women missionaries and 1 day school. The name is sometimes spelled Lealuyi.

LIANG-CHAU-FU: A town in the province of Kan-su, China, situated in a fertile plain, 180 miles from Lan-chau. The plain is often flooded by the Shwan-tai River. Altitude, 5,000 feet. Population, 20,000. Station of the CIM (1888), with (1903) 3 missionaries, 2 with their wives, and one woman missionary.

LIANG-SHAN: A town in the province of Sze-chwan, China, situated in the S. W. near the boundary of Yunnan, at the foot of the mountains of the same name. It is important for its deposits of a salt of lead used in the manufacture of porcelain ware. It is a station of the CMS (1902), with 1 woman missionary.

LIAO-YANG-CHAU: A town in the province of Liao-tung, Manchuria, China, situated 40 miles S. S. W. of Mukden. It is a mission station of the UFS (1882), with (1903) 4 missionaries, 2 with their wives; 4 women missionaries, 37 native workers, 16 outstations, 13 Sunday schools, 5 day schools, 1 dispensary, 1 hospital, and 650 professed Christians.

LIBERIA: A republic on the coast of Western Africa, including 500 miles along the coast, with an average breadth of 100 miles, and an area of about 35,000 square miles. It lies between Sierra Leone on the west and the Ivory Coast on the east, and is bounded on the north by French Guinea. A colony of negroes from America was planted here in 1816 by an American colonization society, with the object of giving the negro a chance for self-improvement. An unfortunate selection of locality caused the failure of the attempt, as the climate was fatal. A treaty made with the native princes in 1821 secured a more healthful locality. The land was portioned out; settlements sprang up, and were named Monrovia, the capital; Caldwell, Edina; new lands were acquired; neighboring chiefs were received into the colony, and hostile chiefs were conquered, until, in 1847, Liberia was declared an independent government, with a president, senate and house of representatives. A property qualification restricts the right of suffrage, and, for the time, whites are not allowed citizenship. Great Britain and other European powers recognized the republic. The original plan of the colony has not been fully carried out, since it draws its people more from the surrounding districts and native tribes than from the emancipated negroes in North America. In 1880 the kingdom of Medina, a rich and populous country, was annexed.

The people are estimated at 2,000,000, of whom 60,000 speak the English language. Sugar is the principal product of agriculture, tho farming of all kinds is conducted with results in crops of cocoa, coffee, cotton, and rice. Trade is in gold-dust, ivory, palm-oil, coffee, and other products, but is badly managed and languishes.

The inhabitants are the seafaring Kroos, between Cape Palmas and the Sinu River; the Bassas, the Barlins, south of the St. Paul; the Mandingan Veis, agriculturists; the fierce Golas, dwelling along the western affluents of the St. Paul; the war-like Pussis and Bussis; and, in the uplands of the interior, the powerful Mandingans. The Protestant faith prevails along the coast. The PE, the ME, the ELGS, and the African Methodist Episcopal Church all have missions in Liberia.

Stockwell (G. S.), *The Republic of Liberia*, New York, 1868; Blyden (E. W.), *A Chapter in the History of Liberia*, Freetown, 1892.

LIEN-CHAU-FU: A town in the N. part of the province of Kwang-tung, China, situated about 130 miles N. W. of Canton. Station of the PN (1891), with (1903) 3 missionaries, 2 with their wives; 1 woman missionary, 7 native workers, 3 outstations, 4 places of worship, 3 Sunday schools 6 day schools, 1 boarding school, 1 dispensary, 1 hospital, and 207 professed Christians. The name is sometimes spelled Lien Chow.

LIFU: The largest of the Loyalty Islands, Oceania. Station of the LMS (1843), with (1903) 1 missionary and his wife, 216 native workers, 28 Sunday schools, 1 boarding school, and 3,855 professed Christians, of whom 2,027 are communicants.

LIJDENBURG. See LYDENBURG.

LIKHOÉLÉ: A village in Basutoland, Africa, situated about 18 miles S. E. of Hermon. Station of the Paris Evangelical Missionary Society (1886), with (1903) 1 missionary and his wife, 23 native workers, 7 outstations, 1 chapel, 1 Sunday school, 8 day schools, and 1,362 professed Christians, of whom 813 are communicants.

LIKOMA ISLAND: An island 5 miles long in Lake Nyasa, Africa. It is the headquarters of the UM, with 5 missionaries, 4 women missionaries, 7 native workers, 3 outstations, 1 chapel, 5 day schools, 2 boarding schools, 1 theological class, 1 dispensary, 1 hospital, 1 printing press, and 555 professed Christians, of whom 415 are communicants.

LI-LONG: A town in the province of Kwangtung, China, about 75 miles S. E. of Canton, on Mirs Bay. Station of the Basel Missionary Society (1852), with (1903) 3 missionaries, 2 with their wives; 9 native workers; 3 outstations, 1 theological class, 1 boarding school, and 397 professed Christians, of whom 229 are communicants.

LIMA: The capital of Peru, South America, situated in a valley 6 miles from Callao. It was founded in 1535 by Pizarro as the capital of the vice-royalty, and is the most handsome city in South America, with important buildings and large manufactures of glass and gold laces. Its climate is pleasant, but not healthful, owing in part to bad sanitation. There is little or no rain, but dews and fogs are abundant in winter. It has an altitude of 565 feet, and a population of (1891) 103,000 people. Station of the ME (1891), with (1900) 1 missionary and his wife and 1 woman missionary.

LIMAO: A settlement in Bechuanaland, Rhodesia, Africa, situated about 10 miles W. of the railroad station of Ramoutsa. Station of the Hermannsburg Missionary Society (1864), with (1903) 1 missionary and his wife, 2 native workers, 1 outstation, 1 chapel, and 2 day schools.

LIMON: A town and seaport on the E. coast of Costa Rica, Central America, situated about 80 miles E. of San Jose. Station of the Jamaica Baptist Mission Society (1888), with (1901) 4 missionaries, 3 with their wives; 7 outstations, 7 chapels, 6 Sunday schools, and 367 Christians. These statistics include Ebenezer or Porvenir. The West Indies Wesleyan Methodist Conference has there (1901) 1 missionary and his wife, 22 native workers, 5 outstations, 6 places of worship, 1 Sunday school, 1 Young People's Society, 1 day school, 1 temperance society, and 281 Christians. Name is also written Port Limon.

LINARES: A town in Nuevo Leon, Mexico, situated 90 miles S. of Monterey. Population, 10,000. Station of the PS (1887), with 1 missionary and his wife, 1 native worker, and 2 day schools.

LIN-CHING. See LIN-TSING-CHAU.

LINDLEY, Daniel: Born August 24, 1801, in Washington County, Penn.; graduated at Ohio University and Union Theological Seminary, Va., in 1829. He preached three years in Charlotte, N. C., and, in 1834, was appointed missionary to Africa by the ABCFM. The disturbed state of the country made Mr. Lindley's first few years in Africa exceedingly dangerous and wearing. At length, in 1839, he established himself at Durban (then called Port Natal), and labored among the Zulus for thirty-five years. He not only preached to them the Gospel of Christ, but, tho not a mechanic, he showed the native Christians who wished to improve their modes of life how to make brick, build houses, construct implements and furniture. He often defended the people with his rifle from the attacks of wild beasts, and in sickness ministered to them. In 1846 five commissioners were appointed by the Colonial Government to allot lands to the natives and to encourage them to industry. Mr. Lindley was one of these commissioners. He was always greatly honored and loved by the Zulus. The Dutch Boers used to say: "If there be a human name that warms the heart of a Natal Teck Boer, it is the ever-to-be-remembered name of Daniel Lindley." He returned home in ill-health in 1874, and died at Morristown, N. J., September 3, 1880.

LIN-KIANG-FU: A town in the province of Kiang-si, China, situated 195 miles S. S. E. of Han-kau. Station of the CIM (1898), with (1903) 1 missionary and 1 chapel.

LINOKANA: A village in the Marico District of the Transvaal, Africa, situated 15 miles N.W. of Zeerust. Station of the Hermannsburg Missionary Society (1859), with 1 missionary and his wife, 1 native worker, 2 outstations, 1 place of worship, 2 day schools and 1,113 professed Christians.

LIN-TSING-CHAU: A town in Shan-tung, China, situated on the W. border of the province, on the Wei-ho River, about 75 miles W. of Tsi-nan-fu. Station of the ABMU. Altho the mission work was broken up by the Boxer outbreak it is now (1902) being reorganized and carried on with 2 missionaries, 1 with his wife; 10 native workers, 5 outstations, 5 places of worship, 5 Sunday schools, 1 day school, and 60 Christians. The name is sometimes spelled Lin-ching.

LIQUOR TRAFFIC AND MISSIONS: It is an axiom in physics that without the application of force water will not rise higher than its source. In the light of this truth a glance at the use of ardent spirits in some Christian lands may show us what to expect in their commerce with heathen tribes. Belgium is a fair specimen of a papal country, and there 70,000,000 litres—a litre = 2.113 pints—are consumed annually. Every year her 6,000,000 of population spend eight times as much for liquor as for public instruction, and the amount that is drunk continually increases. The net revenue from the excise in Great Britain in 1902 was £31,597,962, all but £674,468 of it from the manufacture and sale of liquor.

Such figures prepare us for dark pages in the records of commerce with heathen, and we are not disappointed; the reality even exceeds the expectation. In 1887, 180,000 gallons were imported from Christian lands into Sierra Leone alone, and into the neighboring district of Lagos 1,231,302 gallons were sent annually. Rev. W. Allan states that the Niger Company imported 220,000 gallons in two years, and 500,000 gallons went with him in the ship Caliban from Liverpool. The Hon. and Rev. James Johnson, a native member of the government, who has labored there for eighteen years, states that packages of gin and rum were found everywhere. Large steamers loaded with liquor lay at anchor; warehouses were crammed with the article to the very doors; canoes were heavily laden with it; streets and lanes, highways and byways, the river banks, and even the bush, were littered with demijohns. The very soil of Abeokuta seemed composed of broken bottles; and at Afarjupa, forty miles inland, the seats in the church were empty gin-boxes. The traders at Bonny complain that cotton goods remain on the shelf, and the only demand is for rum and gin, which is sold for four and even threepence per bottle. Such prices seem fabulously cheap, but the following incident may explain its cheapness: A gorilla from the Gaboon River died on board a steamer, and to preserve the body it was placed in a cask of this trade rum; but when it was opened at Liverpool, the hair and skin were found burned off as by vitriol, and the flesh in a state of horrible putrefaction. And this is the kind of liquor sold to be drunk by the natives! In 1885 more than 10,000,000 gallons of such liquor was sent to Western Africa. Of this flood of ruin England furnished 311,384 gallons, Germany 7,823,042, Netherlands 1,096,146, the United States 737,650, Portugal 91,525, and France, of alcohol, 405,944. Germany here enjoys a preeminence that is by no means to be envied. The motive for such intense activity in evil is found in the enormous profits of this trade, amounting in some cases to 700 per cent., and to those greedy for filthy lucre 700 per cent. profit is a tremendous motive.

These lists of figures are full of mourning, lamentation, and woe, for while among us some can use intoxicating drinks for a long period with rare self-control, it is not so with savage races. They seem to lack the power to resist, and give themselves up at once and without reserve to the destroyer. The one thing they seek is to get drunk, to feel the thrill of intoxication; and soon property, health, and life itself are engulfed in the abyss. The red men of our own land are sad examples of this tendency; and tho in bondage, the lack of money and the strong hand of the master intent on his own gains held back the black man from this swift decline, in Africa his tendencies are uncontrolled. Missionaries give some very sad glimpses of the work of ruin, but neither pen nor pencil can do it justice.

Rev. H. Waller, F.R.G.S., does not confine himself to vague generalities, but sets the concrete ruin before our eyes when he testifies to seeing hundreds of young women lying beastly drunk round the wagons of the rumsellers. If there were women, there were also men, and here we have all the elements for a very pandemonium of abominations; and if any think Mr. Waller's experience exceptional, that comfort is wrenched away from us when Dr. Clarke uses precisely the same words concerning young women in South Africa, only where Mr. Waller says hundreds Dr. Clarke says thousands. What hope is there for a people in such a vortex of destruction? It corroborates this testimony of two witnesses in different fields when Mr. Moir, of the African Lakes Trading Company, says: "I have seen boys and girls of fifteen years of age getting their wages in rum,"—and such rum as has already been described. Rev. H. G. Guinness describes it as "infamously bad gin, scarcely fit to make paint with."

It may be said this is the testimony of missionaries; yes, and in it they are unanimous. Christ-like love for men neither disqualifies to see nor to describe the truth; but we are not confined to missionary testimony. Sir Richard Burton states: "It is my sincere belief that if the slave trade were revived with all its horrors and Africa could get rid of the white man with his powder and rum, she would be a gainer by the exchange." This is strong testimony from one who had himself seen the state of things which he thus describes. One of these rum-sellers, without intending it or perhaps even being aware of his damaging concessions, has turned State's evidence. Mr. Betts, a leading merchant of Sierra Leone, tells thus his story: "The liquor traffic destroys body and soul. It is a greater evil than the slave trade. I am myself a large dealer in spirits. I have on the road now thousands of gallons of rum, and several thousand demijohns of gin. I am by no means insensible to the evil this traffic does to these lands and to commerce itself. And I regret it much. They have become slaves to the white man's rum. Rum and gin is their incessant cry."

The Rev. J. Johnson, already quoted, styles this "a criminal trade," and calls upon his people to protest with all their might against this deadly traffic of Europe with Africa. Let the guilt of ruining our land for gain be the guilt of strangers only, if they persist in their un-Christian course, and all good people in Christian lands say Amen. Again he says: "There has been no peace in Africa for centuries, but this drink traffic makes it worse. Negroes have survived the evils of the slave trade, cruel as they were, but they cannot withstand the terrible evils of the drink. If they go on, the extinction of the negro is simply a question of time."

Malike, King of Nupé, wrote thus to Bishop Crowther: "Liquor has ruined our country. It has made our people insane. I favor all trade, except in liquor. We implore Crowther, the great Christian minister, to beg the great Priests (the Church Missionary Society Committee) to beseech the Queen of England to keep liquor out of this land. Let him help us in this for God's sake. He must not let our country be destroyed."

This evil is not confined to Western Africa, nor is the native opposition to it limited to that region. The Sultan of Zanzibar has forbidden the traffic, but he has no power to control Europeans, who are the leaders in this wrong, and so his own people are becoming demoralized in spite of all his efforts.

The natives of the diamond-fields in South Africa implored the Cape parliament to have the saloons removed from among them, but their petition was refused. The market for British spirits could not be interfered with, whatever misery it brought to the natives.

Mr. W. S. Caine, M.P., while traveling in Egypt, found more than 400 saloons in Cairo with English names and English placards, setting forth the excellence of their wares, and heard an Egyptian speaker denounce in a large meeting the foreigners who introduced the traffic into his country.

Rev. W. Allan conversed with some of the owners of two lines of steamships to Western Africa, and they not only did not deny his statements, but informed him that the whole of their cargoes which they took out from Hamburg and Rotterdam consisted of nothing but rum and gin. He had heard this on the coast, and now it was confirmed at headquarters. The Secretary of the Hamburg Chamber of Commerce, in reply to a letter from Rev. Mr. Lang of the Church Missionary Society, says: "Merchants here interested in the African trade are of the opinion that measures for limiting this traffic (in liquors) are injurious to the development of trade with those countries, and that the importation of liquors as carried on at present has no injurious effect upon the natives." We can understand the first part of this, but how to reconcile the closing sentence with truth, in the light of the testimony of Mr. Betts, through whose hands a part of these same liquors passed in Africa, is beyond our power.

Khama, the Bechuana chief, voices the sentiments of the Africans themselves when he says: "I fear Lo Bengula less than I fear brandy. I fought with Lo Bengula, and drove him back, and he never came again, and God, who helped me then, would help me again. Lo Bengula never gives me a sleepless night, but to fight against drink is to fight against demons and not men. I dread the white man's drink more than all the assegais of the Matabele, which kill men's bodies, and it is quickly over, but drink puts devils into men and destroys both their souls and bodies forever; its wounds never heal." And for this reason he forbade European drinkers to live in his land.

So far our view has been confined to Africa, but the deadly fruits of this traffic are not peculiar to Africa. India also suffers, and that, too, at the hands of Christian England. The government sells the monopoly of distilling and selling liquor in its several districts, and the purchaser urges his sales regardless of consequences to the natives, and in spite of the remonstrances of the better classes, so that, tho the people were almost entirely total abstainers before the British rule began, the land is becoming demoralized. Even the converted natives suffer with the rest. This must exert a fearful power to hinder the Christianization of India.

Mr. W. S. Caine, M.P., gives some striking instances of this policy of the government. The collector at Darjeeling compelled a tea-planter, ignorant of the law, to open a saloon on his farm, and at Burrisal the collector tried to compel a zeminder to reopen a saloon which he had closed on his estate. The native refused, and defeated the collector when the case came into court. Still there remains the unspeakable shame of an English official in heathen India using his authority to compel a native to reopen the saloon which his sense of duty had led him to close. Mr. Caine quotes the following from Mr. Westland, a member of the vice-regal council: "We look hopefully for an increase in the excise system in Northern India." In other words, he hopes that the revenue will be increased by increasing drunkenness among the people. In connection with this it should be added that the revenue from native spirits was then increasing at the rate of ten per cent. annually.

The *Bombay Guardian* states that the result of this govermental stimulating of the sale of liquor in order to increase its revenue is that the number of consumers has doubled in ten years. We might trace the same influences operating in other heathen lands, but it would only be repeating the same things with a change of name. Africa has been selected, because that continent at present bears the brunt of this attack on the welfare of heathen nations. India has been referred to, because there a Christian nation has a glorious opportunity to bless the population which the Providence of God has entrusted to its care; but in other lands we would only see the same causes operating only under circumstances less favorable to success, tho, alas! heathen countries can raise few barriers against national ruin which Christian nations cannot trample down when so disposed.

Missionary Review of the World, Vol. I, 595; Vol. II, 412; Vol. IX, 506, Funk & Wagnalls, New York.

LITERATURE in the Mission Field: The methods by which the missionary may deliver his message and make his power felt have been classified under three heads: First, the words of his mouth uttered in the hearing of all; second, his life lived in the sight of all; and third, his written words, which persist after his voice has been silenced forever. This inventory of the messenger's means of expression holds good in all departments of missionary effort. Whether the missionary is man or woman, whether preacher, house-to-house visitor, school teacher, physician, or hospital nurse, the means of reaching the hearts of men, there to prepare the way of the Lord; the means ever accepted by the Holy Spirit as opening doors for His peculiar work, are these three. Each of the great departments of missionary activity common in schemes of missions depends upon use of these three means of influencing men for that soul-winning effectiveness which alone can justify its presence among the apparatus of aggressive activity. Each of them would be one-sided and uncertain in exhibiting to men the perfections of Jesus Christ, did it not command all three of these means of missionary expression. The place, then, of the written word of truth, that is to say of literature, in the apparatus of missions, is at the very foundation, as one of the three means of witness for Christ upon which the enduring effectiveness of the whole enterprise depends.

With respect to importance a sharp distinction must be drawn between the Bible and its subsidiary literature. Yet with respect to place in evangelistic effort, all writings which help the understanding of God's love for man and of man's need of his Savior, which bind together faith and practise, or which illuminate the steady onward march of the Kingdom, are means of expression. From these the missionary selects, according to the need of the moment, the one that will carry his message beyond the range of his voice and penetrate where he cannot go. This is true whether such writings are his own words or those of the Bible itself. A point to be regretted in the past and avoided in the future is that the home churches and some missionary societies have tended, because of the supreme importance of the Bible, to think the place of literature in the scheme of missions filled so soon as the Bible has been issued in the language of any field. Thus the provision of a full literary equipment for the missionary has often been left to the independent action, for which apology has sometimes been offered, of a weary and overloaded missionary suddenly brought face to face with the fact that without such an equipment he is a cripple. Missionaries now know that on the field the primer, the text-card, the lesson-paper, the exposition and comment and illustration are as inseparable from the Sacred Book as the candle which illumines its pages in thick darkness or the lens which brings its writings within the range of defective eyesight.

This coordination of the Bible and other Christian literature, as to place in the equipment of missions, appears clearly in the practise of the pioneers. Ziegenbalg, when making for the whole Church of Christ his tentative essays in the science of missions in South India, wrote home, in

1708, as one of his first discoveries, "Great progress in Christianity cannot be expected until the people possess the Word of God in their own tongue." So Ziegenbalg straightway fell to work—upon translating the Bible? No; before he began his translation of the New Testament he prepared a Tamil primer and grammar and dictionary. For such work no funds had been provided, and the missionary had much ado to collect the money, part from merchants in India and part from European scientists who could appreciate such an addition to their apparatus for linguistic study. Henry Nott of Tahiti, plain, uneducated mechanic as he was, became the one mighty man in that first band of English missionaries to the South Seas, because he alone saw the place which literature must take at the very foundation of all stages of missionary success. His message reached a whole nation because it was written, and it began with a tract-primer. Dr. Elias Riggs of Turkey was preeminently a Bible translator. Yet among his earliest, as well as his most important, works were primers and catechisms and hymns. As lately as twenty-five years ago missionaries in China unitedly pled for general Christian literature to be allowed a place by the side of the Bible, urging the Bible Societies to permit colporteurs to distribute tracts and religious books as well as the Bible, and repeatedly begging that the Bible be printed with notes needed to open the Scriptures to the comprehension of the ignorant and non-Christian reader. It was no mere burst of rhetoric which led some of the missionaries in Turkey, on issuing a primer, to print on the cover as its appropriate title: *Key to the Bible*. To be properly equipped for work, every missionary must have within reach a printing press which can issue those essential works which Bible Societies cannot provide.

To the preacher the importance of such literature appears as soon as he begins to preach. Men of dull minds have listened to the preacher's words, but drift away from the congregation with hardly one complete idea of what it is all about. If such a one can be overtaken by a tract which repeats and explains words but half understood, in many cases that tract becomes the pivot on which turns that man's future relation to the missionary's Master. When a number of persons have become interested in the message and have taken up the reading of the Bible, a thousand questions are at once suggested to each one. Alone, the missionary would be unable to attend to new cases because of the multitude of these questions. He is himself multiplied, so to speak, if he has booklets to give to inquirers. The same situation exists in the work of the medical missionary. One of his greatest needs is an invention for multiplying his means of expression to the people, who throng the dispensary or lie through long days in the hospital. Such an invention is found in the text-cards, leaflets and books, which speak while the overworked staff are attending to the bodily ailments of others. The same is true of the woman evangelist. A woman visits people in their houses. She leaves a little book here, a tract there, a picture card in another place. The heathen who has had his curiosity excited by one of those little printed works becomes instantly but unwittingly a worker for Christ by showing it to some friend and discussing with him its strange message of peace and good will. A child in the street or the Sunday school receives a leaflet or an illustrated paper. He is certain to carry it to his parents and to explain it as far as he has heard. With lip and printed sheet together the child becomes a messenger of the Cross to a fortress garrisoned by superstition against any direct approach of the missionary. In Uganda this office of literature in evangelization used to be fully understood. The phrase by which a besotted heathen rejected the invitation of the Gospel used to be: "No, I do not wish to become a reader." To read was to commit oneself to respect the message of the missionary. Hence, to be a "reader" used to be the earliest mark of a follower of Jesus. It is safe to say that it is because of the free use of the press in that field that the Uganda church is now a type of the power of the Gospel, for, within one single generation from ferocious savagery, it is taking its little books and evangelizing all adjoining regions.

In the Arctic regions of our own continent, the Eskimos of Blacklead Island in Cumberland Sound have realized, perhaps quite as clearly as we, the effect of the printing press in multiplying preachers, for after having grasped the fact that thought can be conveyed through written words they said, "Letters are as good as men, because they, too, can speak."

The fundamental importance of literature to the educational work of missions is particularly hard to be realized in lands where books seem to grow of themselves like the fruit in an apple orchard. In Christian lands the chief task seems to be to teach children to read books. In non-Christian countries the task of the missionary is to teach the children to read and also to make the reading sheets and the primers and many others of the books used in the school; for there books for the young either do not exist or they are as much to be shunned and dreaded as the heathen practises which they inculcate.

Let us look beyond the region of school books, however. After the people have been taught to read, what are they going to read? Those who leave the schools in the early part of the course, where their work has been largely that of the memory, ought to have books which it is worth while to remember. Those who have stayed at school long enough to gain some training in the comparison of facts, need to have books which contain facts. But on the mission field, if literature exists, it is saturated with superstition, vice and the foolish science of the Dark Ages. If it does not exist, to those who leave school at twelve or fourteen years of age the world is almost a blank so far as stimulus to further growth is concerned. Men in Christian lands rely upon the library to be high school, college and university to the half-educated part of the community and even to act as an auxiliary force for the mental, moral and spiritual nurture of the families of the educated. But on the mission field there are no libraries for the common people, and books that will foster development can come from mission presses only, until the growth of the Christian community shall have made native Christian publishing houses possible.

Such a situation compels us at this point to face the question of the completeness of our plans for forwarding the enterprise of missions. Let us not belittle the great work that has been done for the production of books by the various societies directly or indirectly missionary in aim. The total number of missionary printing houses found in strictly non-Christian lands is 122. These are distributed as follows:

Angola, W. Africa	2
Arabia	1
Basutoland	2
Cape Colony, Africa	3
British East Africa	3
China	22
Congo Free State	5
Eritrea, Africa	1
German East Africa	2
India and Ceylon	45
Japan and Formosa	3
Korea	2
Liberia, W. Africa	2
Madagascar	4
Nigeria, W. Africa	3
Nyasaland, Central Africa	3
Oceania	8
Persia	2
Portuguese East Africa	1
Siam	2
Singapore	1
Turkey (including Syria and Bulgaria)	4
Uganda	1

The power for good of these printing establishments is incalculable. It is well, however, to note in passing that they do not fill the need, first, for lack of proper equipment, not more than thirty of them being on a scale that would entitle them to the name of printing house in civilized lands; second, because a number of them were opened in a period when the necessity for cooperation in such matters was not understood, and some of the best equipped offices crowd each other while populous regions are without means of publication; thus of the 22 mission presses in China 14 are concentrated in four provinces; of the 45 printing establishments in India seven are in the United Provinces, and the four presses in Madagascar are all in one city. In the third place, the inability of these 122 presses to meet the need of the non-Christian field is because of the vast number of different languages which have to be dealt with. Missionaries are at work in somewhat over 300 languages, and altho some thirty of the missionary printing establishments are on a scale that permits printing in several languages, one cannot pretend that these can meet the needs of the vast field of the world.

As matters are at present, the lonely worker in the mission field, weighed down by the knowledge that multitudes are not reached by his voice, longing to use the press as a means by which a few can sway the thoughts of masses of men, is eating out his heart in helplessness because the necessary means of expression are grudgingly supplied. The case offers special justification for the proposal of a witty friend of missions for the formation of a Society for the Prevention of Cruelty to Missionaries.

Some desirable things which ought to be done to improve the literary department of the missionary enterprise are: (1) For missionary societies to select and set apart qualified missionaries, men and women, for literary work. (2) To increase the number and especially to improve the quality of the periodicals published in native languages by missionaries on the fields. These periodicals have considerable influence in non-Christian lands. There are now about three hundred such periodical publications, varying in importance from the Sunday school lesson-paper, and the children's illustrated paper, to the family weekly newspaper and the monthly magazine. Improvement in the quality of these periodicals is of very great importance for the increase of their influence. (3) Plans should be made in a large way for the development of a permanent Christian literature in all non-Christian lands. For this purpose discussion of the needs and the possibilities of the literary department should be a permanent feature in the programs of interdenominational conferences of missionary societies or of missionaries. Much can be accomplished by a wise cooperation between existing presses.

The task of providing books for masses of people is not so stupendous as it appears, since one powerful and good book in a land where a living literature does not exist is equal in point of influence to a hundred good books in the lands where each competes with multitudes of others for a hearing. The most sanguine optimist cannot, however, claim that provision has been made enabling mission presses to publish works for the nurture of communities already evangelized and seeking growth. The expenditure of great sums for the maintenance of schools and colleges is an accepted feature of the scheme of missions. But many a missionary revolts against teaching people to read when he must drop them, as they leave the school house door, into the morasses of doubt and corruption gladly made ready for them by non-Christian and anti-Christian writers.

Another unsupplied need which springs to light in this connection is the need to train and bring forward native writers to be the spokesmen of the native Christian element in each nation. Such writers cannot be developed in non-Christian lands until the missions have funds for encouraging their efforts and fostering the creation of an indigenous Christian literature. Until the missions receive a mandate from the homeland to engage seriously in literary work in non-Christian lands, Christendom will look in vain for Eastern scholars to appear who can stand forth as champions of Christ against the men in the guise of Eastern sages who already wait by the doors of our churches to rehash for us at home ideas and arguments furnished to the men of the East by Western rationalists.

Another point of serious gravity in this situation is that Christiantiy should take a commanding position in the revival of literature, already begun in Japan and rapidly approaching in India, China and the Mohammedan countries. One century ago representatives of Western nations in all heathen lands confronted despotic rulers, whose bearing toward Christians and Christendom was the arrogance of unassailable might. Before the end of the century the sceptre of world-sovereignty passed to Christendom, and now every non-Christian ruler throughout the world is dependent upon the tolerance of Christian nations for the privilege of maintaining a semblance of power. To the Christian there is solemn meaning in this change of the centers of domination. But has this change not been used by the Almighty to bring the educated Hindu and Chinese and Japanese and Turk and Persian under compulsion to examine its causes? Never before have missionaries in those lands stood upon the vantage ground of rank as representatives of the world's progress. If they are given means to publish, then by virtue of intellectual and moral superiority they can hold that position of influence while they clearly set forth the causes which have lifted Christian peoples to supremacy. If supplied with funds in time, missionaries in all these lands can take leadership in the approaching revival of literature, injecting into the thought of many lands a strong Christian element with all that this means of gain to the people in justness of vision and elevation of national ideals. At such a time, as Edwin Greaves of Benares has said, "what we need is not writers of Christian books, but Christian writers of books."

It is true that as at present supported by the missionary societies cannot assume the expense of book publication to the extent demanded by the requirements of the growing opportunity during years which must elapse before the people of the various fields can fully sustain the Christian publishing enterprise. But some solution of the problem of providing literature essential to the full success of missionary effort should be diligently and strenuously sought by all bodies to which belong the discussion and improvement of missionary methods. Some steps should be taken of common accord, also, to bring before the almoners of great wealth at home the fact that in non-Christian lands books do not grow, but for some time to come must be painfully provided by the beneficence of those who appreciate their permanent and penetrating and vitalizing power.

LITITZ: A mission station in the S. part of the island of Jamaica, West Indies, situated about 7 miles W. N. W. of New Broughton. Station of the Moravian Mission Society (1839), with (1900) 1 missionary and his wife, 41 native workers, 1 outstation, 2 places of worship, 2 Sunday schools, 2 day schools, and 602 professed Christians.

LITTLE-POPO: A village of Togoland, Africa, situated 10 miles E. of Porto Seguro. It has a strong Roman Catholic mission. Station of the WMS, with (1903) 1 missionary, 14 native workers, 11 outstations, 11 places of worship, 7 Sunday schools, 6 day schools, and 367 professed Christians, of whom 238 are communicants. The German official name is Klein Popo.

LIU-HO-HSIEN: A town in the W. part of the province of Kiang-su, China, situated about 20 miles N. of Nan-king. Station of the AFFM (1898), with (1901) 1 missionary and his wife, 1 woman missionary, 4 native workers, and 1 Sunday school. Name is sometimes written Luhhoh.

LIU-NGAN-CHAU: A town in the province of Ngan-hwei, China, situated 48 miles W. of Lu-chau. Station of the CIM (1890), with (1903) 1 missionary and his wife. The name is sometimes written Luh-gan.

LIVERPOOL (Africa). See LUKOLELA.

LIVINGSTONE, David: Born in Blantyre, Scotland, March 19, 1813. Died May 1, 1873. His parents were religious, and he was early impressed with the noble life of Jesus spent in healing the body and instructing the ignorant. At ten, part of his first week's wages as "piecer boy" at a loom bought a Latin grammar. His evening hours, often from 8 o'clock till midnight, were spent in the study of Latin, Greek, botany, and geology. At nineteen he resolved to be a medical missionary. By "plain living" and "high thinking," working as a spinner in the summer and studying in Glasgow in the winter, meanwhile "picking up as much of carpentry and other useful trades as possible," he prepared himself for his future life. After his acceptance as a missionary by the LMS in 1838, he studied theology, medicine, and science for two years in London, took his medical degree in the Faculty of Physicians and Surgeons in Glasgow, sailed December 8, 1840, for Cape Town; thence proceeded to Kuruman, the station of Moffat and Hamilton. For two years he traversed the Bechuana country, visiting the Bakwains and other tribes. In 1843 he selected Mabotsa for a mission station. Here a lion crushed his arm, and nearly put an end to his life. A fearful drought compelled Livingstone to seek a more favored region, and the whole tribe followed him to Kolobeng. While there he visited the Boers. They regarded with hostility any who treated as men the natives, whom they looked upon as "black property," and resisted every attempt to found a mission near their settlements. The river at Kolobeng, which had yielded him water for irrigation, gradually failed, and in the fourth year disappeared. Livingstone had heard of "a great lake," surrounded by a manly tribe, ruled by Sebituane, a powerful chief, friendly to strangers. There he hoped to find a place for future labors. Accompanied by Oswell and Murray, English travelers, he crossed the Kalihari Desert, and on August 1, 1849, he sighted Lake Ngami, but failed to reach Sebituane through the jealousy of a chief who refused to transport him across the Zouga River. A second attempt failed owing to the illness of his children. A third, with his family and Sechéle, was successful. In June, 1851, Livingstone reached the Zambesi River at Sesheke in E. longitude 25°. This was an important geographical discovery, as it had been supposed to rise much further east. His family having suffered greatly from illness, he decided to send them to England for two years, himself explore the country in search of a healthful center for mission work, also to trace the Zambesi to its source and to the coast. On May 23, 1853, he reached Linyanti, on the Chobe, capital of the Makololo, was cordially received by Seketu, Sebituane's son and successor, and remained for some months, "preaching the Gospel and healing diseases." He proceeded, November 11, tracing the course of the Zambesi and its affluent, the Leeba, to its source in Lake Dilolo. On this hazardous expedition he took twenty-seven men provided by Seketu, partly in the hope of opening up a trade-route between their own country and the coast. They suffered from extreme hunger and thirst, fever and dysentery, attacks of wild beasts, robbers, and hostile tribes. Proceeding from Lake Dilolo, he arrived, May 31, 1854, at St. Paul de Loanda, capital of Angola, on the west coast.

In great physical prostration and mental depression by disease, hunger and care, he was kindly received by the British Commissioner. The Portuguese merchants and officials also were most hospitable and courteous. From this place he sent his astronomical observations to Maclear, royal astronomer at the Cape, and an account of his journey to the Royal Geographical Society of England, which awarded him its highest honor, the gold medal. Maclear, speaking of the number and accuracy of his astronomical and geographical observations, says: "You could go to any point across the entire continent, along Livingstone's track, and feel certain of your position."

After recuperating, Livingstone began his journey across the continent of Africa. In November, 1855, he discovered the famous Victoria Falls of the Zambesi. He arrived March 2, 1856, in an emaciated condition, at Tete, the most western outpost of the Portuguese East African colony. He reached Quilimane, on the Indian Ocean, May 20, four years from the last departure from Cape Town, having traversed the continent from ocean to ocean and traveled on foot over 11,000 miles. He then embarked for England, December 12, 1856. He was received with great honor by the London Missionary Society, the Royal Geographical Society, the universities of Cambridge and Oxford, and by all classes of society. At Glasgow, Edinburgh, Dublin, Oxford and Cambridge his addresses were heard with great interest by learned and unlearned, old and young. While at home he published his *Missionary Travels and Researches in South Africa*. In his travels the atrocities of the internal slave-traffic had so revealed themselves to him, and the obstacles it presented to mission-work in Central Africa had so impressed him, that the question of its suppression became "the uppermost idea in his mind." Hitherto his explorations had aimed solely at opening fields for mission work; thenceforth they sought to open up the country to legitimate and productive commerce as a means of superseding the destructive and inhuman traffic in flesh and blood. His motive appears in these words: "The opening of the new central country is a matter for congratulation only so far as it opens up a prospect for the elevation of the inhabitants. I view the geographical exploration as the beginning of the missionary enterprise. I include in the latter term everything in the way of effort for the amelioration of our race."

Having severed his connection with the LMS, he returned in 1858, appointed British consul for Eastern Africa and the districts of the interior, and also leader of an expedition for exploring Eastern and Central Africa. He was accompanied by his brother Charles, Dr. John Kirk, and others. At Cape Town he was accorded a reception by the people and authorities of the Colony, the Governor presenting him with 800 guineas in a silver casket, as a testimonial to the value of his services. Most of the year was spent by the party in exploring the Shiré River and making the discovery of Lake Shirwa, April 18, and Lake Nyasa, September 16, 1859. Around the latter the missionary found the slave-trade rampant, "desolating the country and paralyzing all effort." Returning to Tete in 1860, he fulfilled his pledge made three years before to his Makololo friends by taking them to their homes at Linyanti. In 1861, accompanied by his brother and Dr. Kirk, he made another trip to Lake Nyasa, and remained, exploring for several weeks. His wife, whom he had welcomed only three months before, died April 27, 1862, at Shapunga, on the Zambesi.

The Universities' Mission to Central Africa, proposed by Livingstone in 1857, was established in 1859, Archdeacon MacKenzie of Natal consecrated bishop for the mission in 1861, and the mission was settled at Magomero. In July, 1862, the bishop died from exposure and fatigue.

In the new iron steamer, the "Lady Nyasa," the explorers steamed up the Shirè; but before it could be carried over the cataracts his brother and Dr. Kirk were obliged by sickness to return home. He resolved to continue the explorations alone. An order from home recalling the expedition, he set sail for Zanzibar in 1864 in the "Lady Nyasa." Needing funds and desiring to sell the vessel built with the avails of his book, he manned the little craft with nine natives and four Europeans, himself navigating her to Bombay, which he reached after an adventurous voyage of a month. Thence he embarked for England. He published *The Zambesi and Its Tributaries*. When urged by Sir Roderick Murchison to relinquish the missionary work and attend only to discovery, he wrote: "I would not consent to go simply as a geographer, but as a missionary, and to do geography by the way." In this spirit he accepted the commission of the Geographical Society to ascertain "the watershed of South Central Africa," to "determine whether the ultimate sources of the Nile" were "among the hills or lakes" south of the point where Speke and Grant saw that river flowing from the Victoria Nyanza, and also to "settle the relation of the Nyasa with the Tanganyika." He had also the appointment of British consul in Central Africa, but without pay. From Zanzibar he reached the continent March 24, proceeded up the Rovuma River as far as he could, and August 8 reached Lake Nyasa, a well-watered, fertile region, but largely depopulated by slave-hunters, the tokens of whose barbarities lay all along their march. Thence, baffled by inundations, hostile slave-dealers, treacherous attendants, want of supplies, and severe sickness, he proceeded northward toward Tanganyika, which he sighted April, 1867. Two of the men who deserted took with them his medicine-chest, and he was without means to control the attacks of fever and dysentery which prostrated him. When sufficiently recovered he passed westward, and in November discovered Lake Mœro, and July 28, 1868, Lake Bangueolo, or Bemba, 150 miles long, 75 wide. "Constant wettings and wadings" prostrated him, and for the first time in nearly thirty years he was carried on the march. Returning to the Tanganyika, he reached Ujiji March, 1869. On July 12 he started westward, and September 21 reached Banbarré, a town in Manyuema. He struggled forward, accompanied by three faithfuls, Susi, Chuma, and Gardner, but was driven back to Banbarré by sickness. Disabled for three months by ulcers on the feet, and further delayed by the treachery of natives sent from Zanzibar with supplies, and by slave-hunters, it was only by indomitable persistence that he reached the town of Nyangwe, an Arab settlement, the western limit of his explorations of the Lualaba. He had now traced the great river which, rising as the Chambeze in the uplands between Nyasa and Tanganyika, traverses a chain of lakes, issuing successively from Bangueolo as the Luapala, from Mœro as the Luvwa, from Kamolondo as the Lualaba, and had also suggested what later investigations proved true, that it enters the Atlantic Ocean as the Congo. He had ascertained also that the Tanganyika does not belong to the same drainage system as the Nyasa.

Racked by disease and tortured in spirit by the horrors perpetrated by the slave-hunters, he was forced back by his affrighted attendants from

Nyangwe, "a ruckle of bones," as he said, to Ujiji, 600 miles, which he reached October 23, only to find that the rascal who had charge of his stores had stolen and used them all. While Livingstone was making this journey under compulsion to Ujiji from the western extremity of his explorations, Henry M. Stanley, the traveling correspondent of the *New York Herald*, sent from America by Mr. James Gordon Bennett to find and relieve him, was urging his way from the east coast in search of him, and reached Ujiji five days later than Livingstone. Not in vain had the missionary in his extremity recorded: "I commit myself to the Almighty Disposer of events." He and Stanley together visited the north end of the lake, and settled in the negative the long disputed question whether the Tanganyika was connected with either the Victoria Nyanza or the Albert Nyanza. At the end of the year 1871 they journeyed together to Unyamyembe, where Stanley had left stores brought for Livingstone. Here they parted March 15, 1872, Stanley bearing with him the precious journal of six years, which "contained a wealth of information about countries and peoples hitherto unexplored and unknown," and Livingstone, with renewed health and spirits, ready to pursue his work on the arrival of reliable men from Stanley. He started, August 25, 1872, to make another exploration of the Chambeze system. To Mr. Moffat he writes: "I set out on this journey with a strong presentiment that I shall never finish it." He was most of the time wading through "sponges" and wet with torrents of rain. Dysentery in aggravated form renewed its exhausting attacks, and his constitution could no longer withstand it. He had to be carried in a litter, by turns suffering excruciating pain and for hours insensible or fainting from loss of blood. Still he would at times ask regarding distant hills, or of the rivers crossed, whence they came and whither they flowed. Approaching Ilala, on the south shore of Lake Bangueolo, men were sent in advance to build a hut for him, and he was laid upon his bed of sticks and grass. Next morning Chief Chitambo called, but he was too ill to talk. At about 1 A.M., May 1, he asked Susi for his medicine-chest. Selecting the calomel and asking for water, he added: "All right, you may go out now." Before dawn the boy, who slept within the hut to be ready at his call, found him kneeling by the bed, his head buried in his hands upon the pillow. The spirit had departed. His faithful men, after embalming the body as well as they could, wrapped it in calico and bark, and carried it, with all his papers, instruments, etc., a year's journey, to Zanzibar. On April 15, 1874, accompanied by Susi and Chuma, it arrived in England, and was deposited in Westminster Abbey, the arm which had been crushed by the lion being a means of his identification. His journals kept during these last seven years' explorations were published in 1874 under the title of *The Last Journals of David Livingstone in Central Africa.* (2 vols.)

Personal Life of David Livingstone, London, 1880; Blaikie (W. G.), *David Livingstone,* London and New York, 1881; Noel (R.), *Livingstone in Africa,* London, 1895.

LIVINGSTONIA: A settlement in Nyasaland, British Central Africa. Station of the UFS (1875), with (1903) 12 missionaries, 3 with their wives; 3 women missionaries, 32 native workers, 1 chapel, and 87 professed Christians. The station was originally opened at the S. end of the Lake, was abandoned in 1883 for Bandawe on the W. shore, and later removed to Kondowi, nearly 100 miles N. of Bandawe.

LOANZA: A settlement on the W. shore of Lake Mweri, in the southern part of Congo Free State, Africa. Station of the PB (1900), with 2 missionaries and 2 missionary women. The name is sometimes written Luanza.

LOBETHAL: A settlement in Kamerun, Africa, situated about 20 miles W. S. W. of Edea Falls. Station of the Basel Mission Society (1892), with (1903) 3 missionaries, 1 with his wife; 17 native workers, 21 outstations, 21 day schools, 1 boarding school and 962 professed Christians, of whom 824 are communicants.

LOBETHAL: A town in the Transvaal, East South Africa, northwest of Leydensburg. Station of the Berlin Mission Society (1877), with (1903) 1 missionary, 14 native workers, 8 outstations, and 634 professed Christians, of whom 345 are communicants.

LOEWENTHAL, Isidor: Born in Posen, Prussian Poland, 1829, of Jewish parents; died at Peshawur in 1864. At an early age he showed great aptitude for language and philology. In 1851 he became a Christian, and in 1852 entered the Theological Seminary at Princeton, taking high rank in philology and writing important articles for the *Biblical Repertory.* He was tutor in Princeton College in 1855; ordained by the Presbytery of New York as an evangelist, and sailed in 1856 as a missionary of the Presbyterian Board for Northern India. He acquired a knowledge of Persian, Arabic, Kashmiri, Hindustani, and the Pushto, the language of the Afghans. He could speak Persian fluently. He completed a translation of the New Testament into the Pushto, which is now in circulation among the Afghans. He was shot one evening in 1864 in his own garden by his watchman, a Sikh, who alleged that he mistook Dr. Loewenthal for a robber. He had nearly completed a dictionary of the Pushto language, and left a collection of Pushto works in manuscript.

LOFTCHA: A town in Bulgaria, 20 miles south of Plevna, 80 miles northeast of Sofia. Climate, foggy, damp. Population, 7,020. Station of the ME (1857), with (1903) 4 women missionaries, 19 native workers, 3 outstations, 4 chapels, 6 Sunday schools, 1 boarding school, and 189 professed Christians, of whom 60 are communicants.

LOHARA: A village in the Central Provinces of India, situated near the E. border of Rewa, and about 65 miles N. by W. of Bilaspur. It is a mission station of the PB (1900), with 3 missionaries, 2 with their wives; 1 woman missionary, 2 native workers, 1 Sunday school, 1 industrial school, and 1 orphanage.

LOHARDAGA: A town in the Chota Nagpur district of Bengal, India, situated 155 miles S. by W. of Patna. Population, 7,100. Station of the Gossner Mission Society, with (1903) 2 missionaries, 1 with his wife; 55 native workers, 27 places of worship, 19 Sunday schools, and 4,137 professed Christians, of whom 2,029 are communicants. There is also a leper asylum, a home for incurables, 1 orphanage, and 1 dispensary. The Mission to Lepers in India has 1 chapel and 1 home for untainted children of lepers. The name is also written Lohardugga.

LOIKAW: A village in Burma, British India, situated about 100 miles N. E. of Taung-ngu. The people are Karens. Station of the ABMU (1899), with (1903) 2 missionaries and their wives, 26 native workers, 19 outstations, 20 chapels, 14 day schools, 1 boarding school, 1 dispensary and 3,468 professed Christians, of whom 132 are communicants.

LOKOJA: A town in the district of Gando, Nigeria, W. Africa, situated on the right bank of the Niger, above the confluence with the Benue. It was occupied by the British in 1865, and a strong force of troops is kept there now. The climate is less unhealthful than at the mouth of the Niger. The CMS has a mission station there (1865), with (1903) 2 missionaries, 1 with his wife; 2 native workers, 1 outstation, 1 chapel, 1 day school, and 179 professed Christians, of whom 27 are communicants.

LO-KONG: A village in the highlands of the province of Kwang-tung, China, situated near Hsin-ning-hsien. Station of the Basel Mission (1901), with (1903) 2 missionaries, 7 native workers, 2 day schools, and 287 professed Christians.

LOLODORF: A village in the Ngumba district of the Kamerun, Africa, and German official headquarters, situated 90 miles N. E. of Great Batanga. It is on the Government road to the interior and is a station of the PN (1897), with 2 missionaries and their wives, 1 place of worship, 1 boarding school, and 1 dispensary.

LOLOMBOLI: A settlement about 5 miles from Strombu, on the S. W. coast of the island of Nias, Dutch E. Indies. Station of the Rhenish Missionary Society, with (1903) 1 missionary and his wife, 1 native worker, 1 day school, and 62 professed Christians, of whom 36 are communicants.

LOLOWUA: A settlement in the center of the Island of Nias, Dutch E. Indies. Station of the Rhenish Missionary Society, with (1903) 1 missionary and his wife, 6 native workers, 1 outstation, 1 Sunday school, 2 day schools, and 584 professed Christians, of whom 366 are communicants.

LOMAS DE ZAMORA: A town in Argentina, South America, situated near Buenos Aires. Station of the ME, with 2 missionaries and their wives, 2 native workers, 2 chapels, 2 Sunday schools, and 260 professed Christians, of whom 66 are communicants.

LOMBOK: An island of the Dutch East Indies, lying between Bali and Sumbawa, to the eastward of Java. Its inhabitants are Malays and Mohammedans, and no regular missionary work is now carried on among them.

LOME: A village on the coast of Togoland, Africa, situated near the W. frontier of the colony. Station of the North German Mission Society (1896), with (1903) 2 missionaries, 1 with his wife; 8 native workers, 2 outstations, 4 day schools, 1 kindergarten, and 216 professed Christians, of whom 104 are communicants.

LONAND: A village in the Poona District of Bombay, India, situated about 40 miles S. E. of Poona. Station of the Poona and Indian Village Mission, with (1901) 2 missionaries, 1 day school, 1 Sunday school, 1 theological class, and 1 dispensary.

LONDE: A village in the Congo Free State, N. E. from Matadi; station of the Swedish Mission Society (1892), with 2 missionaries, 1 with his wife; 2 native workers, 2 outstations, 1 place of worship, 1 Sunday school, 1 boarding school, 1 temperance society, 1 printing press, 1 dispensary, and 64 professed Christians.

LONDON MISSIONARY SOCIETY (1795): During the latter part of the 18th century the preaching of George Whitefield and others brought to the Christian Church a realization of its larger responsibilities, and some people dropped their watchword of "England for Christ" for the larger one of "the world for Christ," and thus the great modern missionary movement had its genesis. An additional impetus was given by Carey's Essay in 1792, and his sermon on attempting and expecting great things from God, which led to the formation of the Baptist Missionary Society. These bore fruit beyond the bounds of his own denomination, and associations of the Independent churches began to consider the question of missionary duty. Ministers belonging to several denominations united in 1793 in founding The *Evangelical Magazine*, for the purpose of arousing the Christian public from its prevailing torpor, and exciting a more clear and serious consideration of its obligations to use means for advancing the Redeemer's kingdom. The principal editor of the new publication was an Episcopal clergyman, the Rev. John Eyre, of Homerton; the Rev. Matthew Wilks, famous as the minister of Whitefield's Tabernacle, was also connected with the movement, and both men were afterward prominent in founding the Missionary Society.

Another clergyman of the Establishment whose writings aroused interest in missions was the Rev. Melville Horne, at one time chaplain to the colony of Sierra Leone, a quality which gave practical weight to his words. His views on what ought to be done found instant response in Dr. Haweis' declaration that "only by a general union of all denominations can a broad basis be laid for missions." Dr. Haweis caused an offer of £500 to be inserted in the *Evangelical Magazine* for the equipment of the first missionaries. The Rev. Dr. D. Bogue, of Gosport, pointed out through the same publication that the Independents alone were doing nothing in the line of foreign missions, and urged not only the equipment of missionaries, but also their appropriate mental and spiritual training in a seminary established for this distinct purpose. The result of this appeal was a meeting held November 4, 1794, at Baker's Tavern. The ministers who attended it were of various connections and denominations, but "glowing and harmonious" in their missionary zeal. These ministers sent out, in January, 1795, a circular to various persons in which it was proposed that a meeting should be held in London the ensuing summer for the purpose of organizing a missionary society. On the 15th of January a number of ministers convened in the city of London, and appointed a committee to ascertain the sentiments of ministers throughout the country in regard to the great plan under consideration. Accordingly, a circular letter addressed to ministers was drawn up acquainting them with the plan and object of the proposed Society; they were requested to make the matter known to their congregations, and to send delegates to the convention, which was appointed for the 22d, 23d, and 24th days of September.

On the evening preceding the meeting a consultation of ministers was held. Interesting letters from ministers and "private Christians" were read, and an address delivered by the Rev. Dr. Haweis of Aldwinkle. Dr. Rowland Hill closed the meeting with prayer, and the assembly broke up with feelings of delight, "which the highest gratification of sensuality, avarice, ambition, or party zeal could never have inspired." The following day, September 21, a large congregation assembled at Spa Fields Chapel. Dr. Haweis preached an animating sermon from Mark xvi: 15, 16, and after the meeting a large number of ministers and laymen adjourned to the "Castle and Falcon," Aldersgate Street, and formed "The Missionary Society." In the evening a sermon was preached by the Rev. G. Burder, and on the three following days successive meetings were held in different parts of the city. The cause of missions was pleaded with solemnity and earnestness, and the Christian world seemed to awake as from a dream, wondering that it could have slept so long while the heathen were waiting for the Gospel of Jesus Christ. For the first time Christians of all denominations, forgetting their party prejudices and partialities, assembled in the same place, sang the same hymns, united in the same prayers, and felt themselves one in Christ. This unanimity of spirit, which time has only served to strengthen, is found embodied in the constitution of the Society, which has remained unchanged.

Constitution and Organization: "The Missionary Society" was largely assisted, in its early years, by Presbyterians and Episcopalians, but is now supported mainly by the Independent or Congregationalists, the other denominations directing their gifts in large measure to the societies since formed in their own communions. But the fundamental principle of the Society remains the same as at the outset, namely: "That its design is not to send Presbyterianism, Independency, Episcopacy, or any other form of church order and government (about which there may be difference of opinion among serious persons), but the glorious Gospel of the blessed God, to the heathen, and that it shall be left (as it ought to be left) to the minds of the persons whom God may call into the fellowship of His Son from among them, to assume for themselves such form of church government as to them shall appear most agreeable to the Word of God."

The sole object of the Society is to spread the knowledge of Christ among heathen and other unenlightened nations.

The condition of membership in the Society is an annual payment of one guinea.

A general meeting of members is held annually in London during the month of May, for the purpose of appointing a treasurer, secretaries, and directors; to receive reports and to audit accounts; and to deliberate on any measures which may promote the object of the Society. All matters proposed are determined by a majority vote of the members present.

The management of the Society is in the hands of a Board of Directors, annually chosen out of the members of the Society, not more than one-third of whom reside in or near London. The directors are empowered to collect and receive all moneys contributed to the Society, and to expend the same in its behalf; to select and manage mission stations; to appoint, send forth, and fittingly maintain missionaries; to make, alter, and amend by-laws for the general conduct of business, and otherwise to carry out in a suitable manner the object of the Society.

The directors appoint the salaries of the secretaries, but themselves transact the business of the Society without emolument.

For greater facility and expedition in the conduct of business the directors are empowered to subdivide into committees, but no proceedings of committees are valid until ratified by the board.

It is interesting to note that the experience gained by this Society in bringing into existence and successfully carrying on an undenominational organization for missionary work led to the foundation, on the same catholic basis, of the Religious Tract Society, and the British and Foreign Bible Society. As the years passed many local missionary societies were formed in different cities, and their existence made it necessary that this "Missionary Society" have a more definite name. It soon, therefore, became known as the London Missionary Society.

The constituency of the Society being largely Congregational, the plan was adopted in 1889 of electing the majority of the directors from that denomination. In 1891 two crowded and earnest meetings for conference and prayer were held, with reference to deficiency of means and consequently of men. The directors decided to go forward, enlarge the existing missions, and attempt to add one hundred new missionaries to the working staff before the LMS centenary in 1895. An appeal for men and money was sent out, and the response was instantaneous, and a forward movement began by which the debt was paid, the work and workers increased, and a large balance remained in the treasury. Nevertheless, in 1894 the Society again faced a crisis and a large deficit. The centenary fund was now opened, and somewhat relieved the situation; nevertheless, the directors felt it necessary to issue a statement declining further offers of service until the finances improved.

The centennial of the Society was celebrated by a meeting in the Mansion House, on November 3, 1894, and on January 15, 1895, the meeting at the Castle and Falcon Inn was also commemorated. Both gatherings were attended by large and most enthusiastic audiences.

In 1902 the directors summoned a large and representative committee to consider the financial situation, which had again become grave in view of the increasing pressure from the field for expansion. This committee, after carefully discussing the situation, decided that it is not desirable that any policy of withdrawal should be seriously contemplated. At the same time, recognizing that the Society had got so far in advance of its supporters that its position was critical, the directors resolved that "the Board give to the constituency of the Society the assurance that during the next five years they will not increase the average expenditure of 1901-2, unless additional contributions are provided, and then only to the extent of such additional contributions."

Development of Foreign Work: Soon after the formation of the Society, its members were called upon to decide in what part of the world its work should begin. Like Carey, Dr. Haweis had become much interested in the South Sea Islanders from Captain Cook's "Narrative of his Voyages in the Pacific Ocean," and in an address delivered at Surrey Chapel drew such a picture of these "dark places of the earth" that intense interest was excited, and the directors decided to establish a mission at Tahiti.

At the same time attention was especially called to Africa, where the Baptist Missionary Society had during the previous year made an attempt to establish a mission. The London Missionary Society joined with the Glasgow and Scottish Missionary societies in 1796 in sending an expedition to Sierra Leone. This, however, not proving a success, and the recent conquest of Cape Colony directing public notice to South Africa, in December, 1796, Dr. Vanderkemp and his associates set sail for Cape Town. In 1798 a missionary was sent to Calcutta, where he was not allowed to stay, and there was no definite mission organized in India until 1804, when Messrs. Ringeltaube, Crane and Des Granges were stationed at Vizagapatam and Travancore, and Mr. Voss at Colombo, Ceylon. It was not until 1816 that the North India Mission was definitely inaugurated. In 1800 the Rev. William Moseley, an Independent minister at Long Buckby, Northamptonshire, published a valuable "Memoir on the Importance and Practicability of Translating and Publishing the Holy Scriptures in the Chinese Language." He had discovered in the British Museum a manuscript containing a Harmony of the Four Gospels, the Acts of the Apostles, the Epistles of Paul, and the first chapter of the Hebrews in Chinese. It was a folio volume, and was lettered by mistake "Evangelica Quatuor Sinice." On a blank leaf, at the beginning of the volume, is the following note: "This transcript was made at Canton in 1737 and 1738, by order of Mr. Hodgson, who says it has been collated with care and found very correct. Given by him to Sir Hans Sloane, Bart., in 1739." It was this Memoir by Mr. Moseley which first turned the attention of the friends of missions to China, and in 1804 the Rev. Robert Morrison was engaged by the LMS to study the Chinese language. In January, 1807, he sailed from England for Canton, with a particular view to the translation of the Holy Scriptures into Chinese, inaugurating thus the work of Protestant missions in China proper.

At the same time (1807) an urgent call from a West Indies planter gave the impulse for the founding of a mission in British Guiana, which afterward extended to Jamaica. Then followed the mission to Mauritius (1814) consequent on the occupation of that island by the British Government; and in 1818 was commenced in Madagascar a work that has been one of the marvels of the Christian church.

The Levant was not without its interest for England, and in 1816 a missionary of the LMS was stationed at Malta with a view to work in Greece. A few years later the Ionian Islands were occupied. This effort, however, was not continued, and the missionaries entered other departments of labor, one of them becoming an efficient agent of the British and Foreign Bible Society.

1818 saw the commencement of a mission to Siberia and Tatary, afterward closed by Russian edict in 1840, and of one to Malacca and the Dutch East Indies, since given over to the Netherlands Society.

Then followed a long period during which existing work was strengthened. The first new mission was really the resuscitation of an old one, when in 1869 the mission to Mongolia was established to reach Tatary from the east. In 1879 the LMS responded again to the call from the Dark Continent, and established a mission in Central Africa, taking as its district Lake Tanganyika. This closed the long story of effort with which the Society has sought to girdle the earth. Single ventures there have been, besides, such as one to Buenos Aires and another to Prince Edward's Island, but they did not result in permanent work, and are of interest chiefly as indicating the breadth of view of the founders and promoters of the Society, who were resolved that if possible no nation should remain without the Gospel. The fields upon which the Society has concentrated effort are in Polynesia and the South Pacific, India, Africa, China, and Madagascar.

The Missions: 1. *Polynesia* (1796): A. *Tahiti, Samoa, etc.*: The Society purchased the full-rigged ship "Duff," of a little less than 300 tons burden, to convey its first expedition to the South Seas. Great public interest was felt in the enterprise, and important contributions of stores, furnishings and equipment were sent in by merchants and others, while high officials of government showed in many ways their good will. Captain James Wilson, a man bred to the sea and matured by hardship and by dangers of battle in America and the East Indies, offered his services gratuitously to command the ship. On the morning of August 10, 1796, the "Duff" hoisted the mission flag—three white doves with olive branches on a purple field—and sailed from London, having a crew of twenty men, and carrying a mission band of four ministers, one surgeon, and twenty-five artisans. The voyage proved prosperous, and after 208 days the "Duff" anchored safely in Matavai Bay, Tahiti. The missionaries were welcomed and protected by the notoriously savage and barbarous king, Pomare, and his wife, Idia, who never withdrew their friendly aid. A large bamboo house was placed at their disposal, and seventeen out of the thirty missionaries were soon settled in this dwelling. Everything seemed to favor them, yet one may well imagine the solemnity of the moment when they realized their position of isolation as the "Duff" sailed away to the Friendly, or Tonga, Islands.

The "Duff" arrived at Tongatabu, one of the so-called Friendly Islands, twelve hundred miles west of Tahiti, in April, 1797, where nine unmarried missionaries were landed. Captain Wilson then took one missionary to Santa Christina, one of the Marquesas Islands, and after leaving him there revisited Tahiti, and sailed for England by way of China.

The story of the missionaries thus left at Tongatabu is of two and a half years of horror. The island was overrun by released convicts from Australia, who incited the savages to attack the missionaries and steal their property. One of the laymen belonging to the mission deserted his comrades and joined the natives. War breaking out among the islanders, one band chased five of the missionaries, and on capturing them stripped them of all their property, even to the clothing which they had on. Another band of savages attacked the other three missionaries and dashed out their brains. The five survivors buried the bodies of the three martyrs and contrived to live, tho in unspeakable wretchedness, until they attracted the attention of a passing vessel and were rescued from the island. This ended the first mission to the Friendly Islands.

The missionary who single-handed had undertaken the establishment of a mission at Santa Christina was more kindly treated, but by a curious accident he was carried away from the island in an American vessel to which he had gone for a visit, but which was driven to sea by a gale. The Americans landed him on another island of the group. But after working there some months, he took an opportunity of returning to England to plead with the Society to give him associates in the work.

Meanwhile an attempt had been made to strengthen the Polynesian Mission by sending out the "Duff" a second time, in December, 1798, with thirty more missionaries. But the ship was captured by a French frigate off the coast of South America and taken with all her belongings as a lawful prize of war. The missionaries after being carried about the ocean for some weeks were finally put ashore at Lisbon.

The party of missionaries landed at Tahiti at the first seemed to have promise of great prosperity. Two Swedish sailors, long resident in Tahiti, acted as their interpreters and helped them learn the language, while the chiefs were won to favor the mission by the skill of the artisans. The missionaries encountered their first serious trouble when a merchant ship came to the island and several of her crew deserted. The missionaries tried to secure the runaways, but natives interfered to prevent this and knocked the missionaries about pretty roughly. The affair was not serious, but eleven of the missionaries, panic-stricken, fled to Australia; only one of them with his wife (Mr. and Mrs. Henry) afterward returning. Of the little group of seven men and one woman (Mrs. Eyre) who remained at Tahiti, one fell away and left the work, another lost his health and went back to England, and a third separated himself from his associates, married a native wife, and was murdered not long afterward. Including the two who returned from the flight to Australia, but five men and two women now remained of the band of missionaries landed by the "Duff" at Tahiti in 1797. They were reenforced in 1801 by the arrival of nine new missionaries, and a more hopeful spirit prevailed, especially as Henry Nott and Mr. Jefferson had now so far mastered the language that they could preach in it, and, having reduced the language to writing, began making books, from which the children were taught to read. But the spirit of war seems to have possessed the whole world. Piracy made the long voyage from England uncertain and dangerous, and five years passed before either stores or letters reached the missionaries from England. Meanwhile their clothes dropped to pieces; their shoes wore out and they were left barefoot; their tea, sugar, and other household comforts were exhausted. They seemed to be abandoned by their home friends, as well as by the Society which sent them out.

Some things, however, had been accomplished. It was a great thing to have acquired the language and to have reduced it to writing. But they had not won a single soul to acceptance of the Gospel, and they were in constant difficulties through wars between different parties of natives. King Pomare protected them as best he could, and so did his son (also called Pomare), after the death of the old king. But what made the vicious young king their friend was interest in their ability to write his language. He wished to learn to write, but did not care to hear the Gospel. His power, moreover, was not supreme, and in 1808 he notified the missionaries that they were no longer safe under his protection. All but four single men of the missionary band now fled from Tahiti to Australia, and in the next year the rebel tribes destroyed the mission house, melted the type belonging to the printing press into bullets, and drove the four remaining missionaries from the island. Twelve years of hardship for the sake of these people had resulted in this! Two of the four missionaries now went to Australia. The other two, Messrs. Nott and Hayward, chose to remain, and took refuge in the islands of Huahine and Eimeo (now called Moorea). There Mr. Nott devoted himself to translating the Bible, which he was certain that the people would sometime accept.

The Society in London began to discuss abandoning so unprofitable a field. Some earnest friends of continuance of the mission appointed a day of prayer for the conversion of King Pomare and the triumph of Christianity. This was in July, 1812, and at the very same time King Pomare came to the missionaries at Eimeo, asking to be baptized. The king's conversion was the turning point. Altho, naturally, the missionaries insisted that they must delay his baptism until he had received more instruction, he was, from that time, a changed man. Eight of the missionaries who had fled to Australia came back to Eimeo on his invitation, and the next year, two of the missionaries having ventured again to Tahiti, found, to their surprise, two Christians there. These men had remembered the teachings of the missionaries, and together had tried regularly to worship God as the missionaries had done. By the time that Rev. John Williams and William Ellis arrived at Eimeo in 1817, a church of native believers had been formed, the islands of Huahine, Raiatea, and Tahiti had destroyed their idols, not without fierce opposition from the priests, and peace, prosperity and progress had begun to rule. So long as the people were heathen they cared not to better their material condition. But as soon as they accepted the Gospel, they began to build houses and to learn useful arts. King Pomare built a great church at Tahiti, in which he was at last baptized. Little more than a score of years after the first missionaries reached the island grateful native Christians of the Society Islands sent a contribution to the LMS amounting to £1,700.

Mr. Williams now settled at Raiatea, and began that splendid career of evangelization among neighboring islands which gave him the title of the Apostle to Polynesia. Going out by boat to the next islands; sending out native workers, who were of like devotion with himself; building, without tools or lumber, a little ship, that he might go the further, Mr. Williams and his native co-workers evangelized the Hervey or Cook Islands, Samoa, began a work on Fiji Islands, and finally in the midst of the blessed work of building up and extending the kingdom, when he would enter the New Hebrides, 1,500 miles from his Samoan home, with the Gospel, he was killed by the cannibal inhabitants of Erromanga, November 20, 1839. In twenty-two years of arduous service he had visited and opened a great number of islands of the South Pacific to the Gospel. He also had infused his own devoted spirit into the converted islanders in such a degree that they were unfailing in responding to calls for volunteers for dangerous and seemingly impossible service. At his death a wail went up from all parts of the broad Pacific, "Oh my father! my father! Williamu!"

The devoted service rendered by the native workers sent out from the stations of the LMS, in preparing the way for the occupancy of the New Hebrides by the Nova Scotia Presbyterians and the present New Hebrides Mission, has already been described elsewhere. The same heroic devotion of converts to Christ opened the way for missionary occupancy of New Caledonia (1841), the Loyalty Islands (1841), the Tokelau Islands (1858), Niuè or Savage Island (1830-1859), Ellice Islands (1865), and Gilbert Islands (1870).

The progress of the mission in Polynesia has been injuriously affected, as elsewhere, by the coming in of European traders, bringing with them liquors and arms, which it is their determination to induce the natives to buy, as well as vicious practises quickly credited to Christianity by the islanders. But its most serious calamity fell upon it when the French Government in 1838-41 used force at Tahiti to make the islanders receive Roman Catholic missionaries, and in 1841 took possession of the islands. A similar attack by the French Government was made upon the mission of the LMS in Lifu (Loyalty Islands) in 1873. A French man-of-war entered the harbor and ordered the missionaries to cease teaching the people in the native language, for which French must be substituted. When the missionaries questioned the authority for such orders, the French marines destroyed the mission buildings and the native houses near them. The indignation caused in England by these proceedings led the French Government to modify its plans, and the work of the missionaries was resumed and carried on under restrictions. The suspicion and dislike shown toward the English missionaries led to the transfer of the work in the Society Islands and in Mare (Loyalty Islands) to the Paris Evangelical Society, which now has charge of the field of laborious efforts of the LMS during eighty-nine years. In the Loyalty Islands something like liberty has been granted to the workers, and chapels have been erected and schools opened, with students eager for work. The French resident at Lifu is a Protestant, in full sympathy with the mission. Native workers from the Loyalty Islands are carrying on missionary enterprises among the savages of New Caledonia, where the result of the French occupation prevents English missionaries from establishing themselves.

During all these years since John Williams built the first missionary ship of the LMS the work in the island world has been done in a substantial vessel, which, happily, bears his name. The first missionary vessel, the "John Williams," was built by the children, and for twenty years sailed the Southern Seas. In 1864 she was wrecked, and the following year a second vessel was launched, only to go on the rocks at Niuè twelve months later. In 1868 the third "John Williams" was built, and for a quarter of a century carried on the work. But a steamer was needed, owing to the vast area to be covered, and in 1893 the fourth "John Williams" was sent out.

Training institutions were established at Raratonga in 1839, and the Malua Institution of Samoa in 1845, where the native teachers, evangelists and pastors receive efficient training for their work.

B. *New Guinea:* In 1870 the LMS Directors sent Rev. S. Macfarlane of Lifu as a pioneer to New Guinea. At the May meeting of the Loyalty Islands Mission eight native helpers were consecrated for the work. In May, 1871, Messrs. Macfarlane and Murray, with the native helpers and their families, sailed for the new field of labor, landing on July 1 at Darnley Island, where the chiefs consented to try a teacher for a year. Native teachers were placed on other islands in Torres Straits and near the coast of New Guinea, Mr. Murray taking temporary supervision of the new work and making his headquarters at Cape York, in Australia. In 1875 three English missionaries began work in New Guinea itself, and several Raratongan teachers were added to the native staff.

An institution for training Papuan preachers was opened at Murray Island, and, later, a similar institution was established at Port Moresby, where in 1881 the first church was formed and the first three Papuan converts in New Guinea were baptized. Since then other stations have been occupied by missionaries of the LMS, and native workers are laboring in several places on the southwestern coast of British New Guinea. The whole New Testament has also been translated into the language most widely used. On April 8, 1901, Rev. James Chalmers and Rev. Oliver Tomkins, with a native chief and several native youths, started out to explore the Aird River, one of the streams that are like roads promising to lead into the interior of the island from the northwest part of the Gulf of Papua. Near Goaribari Island, at the mouth of the river, they were attacked, killed, and eaten by cannibals. This terrible event made an impression upon Christians at home as profound as that produced by the murder of John Williams sixty years before. Plans were immediately made for reaching the men, who did this thing, with that Gospel of love which can change their savage nature. These plans are still under consideration and will certainly be carried out unless means fail. There are now 13 missionaries in the New Guinea Mission (10 with their wives), 114 native workers, 6 schools, and 1,500 professed Christians, of whom 813 are communicants.

In Polynesia, as a whole, including New Guinea, the LMS reports (1903) 57 English missionaries, men and women, and (including wives) 840 native helpers, 49,920 professed Christians, of whom 18,605 are communicants; 272 schools, and 11,854 pupils. Native contributions, £5,162.

2. *Africa.* A. *South Africa:* Cape Colony in South Africa was a settlement of the Dutch East India Company, commenced in 1652. The Dutch settlers drove back the Hottentots, making slaves of a large part of those whom they did not destroy. Dr. Vanderkemp was the first missionary of the LMS, sent to Africa in 1789. He made a strong effort to establish a mission among the Kaffirs in eastern South Africa, but after some years was obliged to retire for safety to Graaf Reinet, where, meanwhile, other missionaries of the Society had settled. As soon as the mission at this place began to be successful the Dutch colonists raised an outcry that it was sheltering Hottentot robbers and murderers; they even went so far as to try to kill Dr. Vanderkemp for his friendship to the Negroes. The English Governor of Cape Town then advised him, in 1820, to establish his Hottentots upon a piece of land which the Government gave him near Algoa

Bay (Port Elizabeth). Almost immediately after this the country passed again into the hands of Holland, and the Dutch Governor, on hearing complaints that he harbored robbers and murderers, persuaded Dr. Vanderkemp to give up his settlement and remove to another place less favorable, which, however, was called Bethelsdorp. This experience was a sample of what Dr. Vanderkemp had to encounter during his whole missionary life. He was champion of the rights of the Hottentots against grasping and conscienceless white settlers, and, at his death, after thirteen years of work of this nature, he had fairly won the hearts of many Hottentots and Kaffirs and so had prepared the way for those who were to follow him.

Messrs. Kicherer and Kramer were sent out by the LMS at the same time as Dr. Vanderkemp, and they went to the western part of South Africa, attempting to reach the Bushmen. While Hottentots and Griquas became Christians, the Bushmen would not listen to the missionaries, and Kicherer having resigned in 1806 in order to become pastor of a local (Dutch) church, the mission was abandoned. This mission first brought the Bechuanas to the knowledge of the Christian world. Another effort to reach the Bushmen was made at Colesberg in 1814, and with some success. This excited the enmity of the white settlers, and the missionaries were ordered by the Government to abandon this outpost and retire within the limits of the Cape Colony, where the work of the Society was steadily growing.

Messrs. A. and C. Albrecht were sent by the LMS in 1806 to work in Namaqualand, north of the Orange River. The region was infested by the outlaws led by Africaner. This chief was a Hottentot slave, who, driven by a mad desire to be revenged for punishment inflicted upon him by his master in Cape Colony, had fled to the wilderness; a price was set upon his head, and he was the terror of the whole country. The missionaries settled at Warmbad, about one hundred miles west of Africaner's place of abode. The outlaw was friendly to the missionaries at first, but some other settlers at Warmbad having made an expedition against him, he became furious, and the missionaries were compelled to flee before his anger.

The next attempt in this direction was by Rev. Dr. Moffat, who, in 1817, established himself in the village where Africaner lived. It was but a short time before this terrible chief became a Christian, was baptized, and went with Dr. Moffat to Cape Town to express his willingness to live at peace with the colonists. This visit in 1818 was almost the first convincing evidence offered to officials and colonists of the advantage of missions. Messrs. Ander and Crane, two other missionaries of the Society, founded a station in Griquatown in 1820. This place is about one hundred miles west of the diamond fields of Kimberly, in Griqualand West. Their labors among the people were crowned with success, but after a few years the Governor of Cape Town, having sent a demand that the missionaries should send the best of their young men to serve in the army, the people became suspicious and hostile. This caused a withdrawal of the missionaries and the work was practically broken up.

To this place Mr. Moffat went in 1820, and reorganized the work. After seeing the enterprise in good hands he moved on to the Kuruman River, some distance to the northwest, where a LMS missionary named Hamilton had been working among the Bushmen tribes since 1819. The station took the name of Kuruman, which it holds to this day. The station center was moved about eight miles to a better piece of land in 1832. For several years the people seemed heedless, and terrible wars kept both missionaries and people in a restless condition. Mr. Moffat was not satisfied with his progress in the language, and, leaving his wife in his house, he went in 1827 to live among the natives in order to acquire their language for the sake of translating the Bible. Not only did he learn the language, but he also learned the ways of the people, found his way to their hearts, and in 1829 the baptism of six converts took place. Dr. Moffat then prepared the way for mission stations farther north, in what is now Rhodesia. In 1838, having finished the translation of the Bible into Bechuana, he carried it to London for publication, and there his influence was a factor in the decision of Livingstone to offer his services to the LMS, in 1840, to go to Africa. Meanwhile, other stations of the Society were opened in the eastern part of Cape Colony, among them one in 1813 at Theopolis, near Algoa Bay and on the border of Kaffirland, which was a very successful station until the Kaffirs undertook to destroy it as being an outpost of the whites. The Hottentots resented this attack and drove the Kaffirs out of the colony. The Government praised the Hottentots for their work, and then rewarded them by taking away their land for the use of white settlers. Another station was opened on the Caledon River, afterward being transferred to the Paris Evangelical Society. Another station was opened at Pacaltdorp, about halfway between Cape Town and the site where Port Elizabeth now is. This station gave place to Hankey in 1822, founded as a refuge for freed slaves. After having been abandoned by the society in 1875, Hankey was reoccupied in 1891 as a place for training the children of converts from the northern tribes of Cape Colony and Bechuanaland.

The extension of the Society's work to the northward was prepared by Dr. Livingstone. He settled in the first instance, in 1843, in Bechuanaland (now the northern part of Cape Colony). In 1846 he went northward to visit the chief, Sechele, who became a Christian and had great influence in forwarding the acceptance of Christianity among his people. In 1849 Dr. Livingstone moved still farther north and discovered Lake Ngami. This led the way for an advance of the missionary forces into what is now called Rhodesia. But this advance was not accomplished without serious losses. The mission was broken up for a time by the Boers, who in 1853 attacked the natives among whom Livingstone was working, and robbed the station, ordering the missionaries out of the land. After Livingstone's resignation a party of LMS missionaries set forth from Kaffirland in 1859 to go to the Makololo tribes in the direction of Lake Ngami, a distance of about one thousand miles. Within a week after their arrival at their destination several were taken sick, and one by one the whole party died, with the exception of one man, who returned to Kaffirland alone. About the same time a party of missionaries led by Moffat were sent to Matabililand (Rhodesia) to begin work in that region, establishing stations at Inyati and Hope Fountain. One of the most marked results of this mission is the development of such a Christian chief as Khama, whose influence for good throughout South Central Africa has been marked.

B. *Central Africa:* Three years after the death of Livingstone, in 1873, means for opening a mission in Central Africa came to the Society from Mr. Arthington of Leeds, who gave the Society $25,000 to purchase a site for a mission station on Lake Tanganyika. The missionaries set out from Zanzibar to go to Lake Tanganyika in June, 1877, but before thay had marched much more than one hundred miles, two-thirds of the oxen had died, and it was impossible to proceed. After enormous difficulties they succeeded in getting porters to carry their stores, and after a journey of fourteen months they reached Ujiji, on Lake Tanganyika, but not without great difficulties. One of the missionaries gave up the task as too hard. Another was sent to explain the situation to the Society in England, three died within a few weeks after reaching Ujiji; fever attacked others, two of whom died, and by the middle of the year 1882 one missionary only remained alive at the lake. But this was not all. Dr. Mullens, Secretary of the LMS, on learning of the unexpected difficulties, arranged to go to the spot and study how to overcome them, and in 1879, before he had covered one-half the journey from Zanzibar to the lake, he was taken sick and died by the roadside. In fact, all that could be pointed to as a result of four years' struggle and expenditure at this point was that God had been merciful in preserving the lives of some of the laborers. New workers reached Ujiji in 1883, and a steamer was sent out (in pieces) for use on the lake. It was put together and began to render its valuable service in 1886. Since that time the growth and prosperity of the mission has been uninterrupted, excepting in 1889, when a war broke out between the Germans and Arabs, causing the murder of one missionary, who happened to be on the road at the time, and cutting off all communication between the Society and the mission during the next two years. The work now goes on with success and a promise of permanency. As to the results of the work of the LMS in Africa the Society began early to urge the native churches in Cape Colony to prepare for independent existence. The Congregational Union of South Africa was formed and the churches slowly became connected with it, so that in 1883 these churches ceased to appear in the reports of the Society. Hankey alone remains of the LMS stations in the coast regions of Cape Colony. It is quite impossible to tell exactly the number of Christians resulting from the efforts of the Society, but when the census of Cape Colony was taken, in 1891, seventy thousand of the native population gave in their names as Congregationalists, the greater part of whom may be regarded as the fruit of the labors of the LMS missionaries, from Vanderkemp down.

The Society now has in Bechuanaland 8 stations, in Matabililand 5 stations, and in the lake region 4 stations. At these stations there are 50 missionaries, including missionaries' wives; 155 native workers, 15,763 professing Christians, of whom 4,041 are communicants; 57 Sunday schools, with 3,747 scholars; 89 village schools, with 6,611 scholars, and the contributions of the natives, together with the fees paid to the mission schools, amounted in 1902 to £1,669.

3. *North India* (1798): The first missionary of the LMS in India was Mr. Nathaniel Forsyth, who reached Calcutta in 1798, and who, not being allowed to establish himself there, labored for fourteen years in the Dutch settlement of Chinsurah, a few miles north of that city. In 1809 Mr. May was sent out to aid in carrying on the work. He was enthusiastic in education of the children, and by 1812 he had succeeded in establishing thirty schools, obtaining from the Government grants in aid of their support. These efforts at Chinsurah, continued through thirty years, were the foundations of the splendid work now carried on by the UFS in that district, the station having been transferred to the Free Church of Scotland in 1849. Two missionaries of the LMS were sent in 1816 to work among both English and natives in Calcutta. A fund was locally raised and the Union Chapel was built in 1821, which has been a center of Christian influence ever since. Five schools for girls were opened the same year. This marks the beginning of work for women in India. A Miss Piffard of Calcutta voluntarily undertook the supervision of these schools, and, what is more, has defrayed their expenses. The work in the city and vicinity is now actively pressed in twenty-one separate centers, and has become very important in influence and extension.

A chapel was opened on the road to Bhowanipur, a southern suburb of Calcutta, in 1820. Mr. Lacroix in 1827 took charge of the work in the villages south of the city, and in 1837 took up his place of residence at Bhowanipur. He there opened a boarding school for boys, and the following year a girls' boarding school and an English school for native children. That English school afterward was developed into the present Bhowanipur Institution. When pupils were converted in 1843, the natives, panic-stricken, withdrew their children. But the desire for English education outweighed the fear of Christianity, and in 1845 branch schools had to be established, to relieve the pressure on the main institution; these were located at Behala and Ballygunge. The present noble Institution building was completed in 1845, at a cost of nearly £7,000. When conversions continued among the pupils, the parents tried to force their grown children to hold to Hinduism, and in some cases they sued the missionaries for abduction. These proceedings were resisted in the courts, and the result was that verdicts were given for liberty of conscience. The native church building was built in 1867 and paid for by the people. Bhowanipur is now the chief site of the LMS work in the city of Calcutta.

Surat, on the western side of the peninsula of Hindustan, was occupied by the LMS in 1816. Messrs. Fyvie and Skinner translated the Bible into Gujarati, and Mr. Skinner went to Bombay and learned printing in order to carry on a printing house. The enormous mass of publications issued from that printing house made Surat a center for Christian literature second to Carey and Ward's Serampore only. After thirty years of vigorous activity the mission there was transferred in 1847 to the Irish Presbyterian Church, which now carries it on. Benares was occupied for the LMS by Rev. M. T. Adam in 1819, who gave much of his time to translation and other literary work, and the station has been the center of much effective influence up to this time.

A station was opened at Almora by Rev. J. H.

Budden and wife in 1850, and from the beginning school work prospered. Two orphanages have been established there, but the most striking feature of the mission has been the Lepers' Asylum. Recently the work of the station has been extended to Bhot, in the extreme north of the district, where a school, a dispensary, and Zenana work have been established on the very frontier of Tibet. The years that immediately followed the Mutiny marked the beginning of Zenana work in North India by Mrs. Joseph Mullens, who was a pioneer in that work, if not the very first to grasp the idea of its possibilities in missions.

The work thus begun has spread among all classes of the people, Hindu, Mohammedan, and European, and includes medical, evangelistic, and educational work, the latter being particularly strong.

There are now in the North India section of the LMS Indian missions, 9 stations, 58 missionaries, men and women, including wives of missionaries; 242 native workers, 2,996 professed Christians, of whom 798 are communicants; 63 Sunday schools with 2,292 scholars, 104 other schools with 5,753 pupils.

4. *South India* (1805): Messrs. Cran and Des Granges of the LMS established a station at Vizagapatam in 1805. They began work among the English as well as the native population; translated the Gospels into Telugu, and established schools. A later missionary here, John Hay, laid the Church in India under incalculable obligation by his notable literary labors. But tho the station is still occupied the results have not reached great proportions. Mr. and Mrs. Loveless began work in Madras in 1805. This beginning has been followed up in the city in Blacktown and the suburb of Vepery, and in the district, where are twelve outstations. Mr. Hands established a station at Bellary in 1810, and by 1812 he had translated the first three Gospels into Kanarese. He could not get permission to print them until 1819. By that time he had the whole Bible ready. His labors were the beginning of a strong and blessed work here. Work was begun at Belgaum in Bombay Presidency in 1820. It has been slowly extending, but the Society has decided to give it up to some society having other stations in that region. In the same year missionaries went southward to Bangalore to open a station. No real foothold was gained, however, until 1827. Mr. Reeves then took up the work and the success of the station has been steady and important. Ten years later Mr. Benjamin Rice began work at Bangalore, and for twenty years was at the head of the Kanarese Seminary for training native workers. In 1857 the English Institution was opened for education of Hindus and Mohammedans. A theological class was conducted in connection with it, and the work continues quietly to progress to the present time. Cuddapah was occupied as a station of the LMS by Mr. Hands in 1822. Little fruit appeared from his work until 1851. Then suddenly whole villages renounced heathenism and desired baptism. A new station was established at Nandyal in 1855, which was continued till 1881, when the missionary force was transferred to Gooty, thus bringing the stations of the LMS at Bellary, Gooty, and Cuddapah into line with Belgaum on the west and Madras on the east, and forming a belt across India from sea to sea. At Gooty, because of its central position, a training institution for teachers and catechists has been opened.

South of the Nilgiri Hills and north of Travancore are three stations of Salem, Tripatur, and Coimbatore. The work continues to gain in the outlying districts year by year, tho interrupted in 1901 at Tripatur by plague and other diseases, accompanied by famine of both food and water. School houses have been built, teachers supplied, and the missionaries as well as the native evangelists make long tours from village to village. Medical work is successfully carried on, with a well equipped hospital at Jammalamadugu. There are (1903) 14 stations and 382 outstations, 78 English missionaries, including wives and unmarried women; 691 native workers, 27,886 professed Christians, of whom 2,796 are communicants, and 356 schools with 14,534 pupils. The school fees paid by the pupils in 1902 amounted to £3,300 and other native contributions to the Society were £296.

5. *Travancore* (1806): Among the missionaries of the LMS who went out to India in 1804 was Mr. Ringeltaube. While his colleagues went to Vizagapatam he returned to Travancore. He had previously had experience in work in India under the Society for the Promotion of Christian Knowledge. He studied Tamil for a time at Tranquebar. In 1806 he undertook to begin his mission in the native State of Travancore. He was not permitted to reside in Trivandrum, and therefore began the Travancore mission from Palamcotta, a CMS station in Tinnevelli. The first foothold in Travancore was gained at Meiladi, sixty miles distant, where forty people were soon baptized and the first chapel was built, and by the end of 1812 Ringeltaube reported 677 communicants. In 1815 he broke down from overwork, and was succeeded by Mr. Mead in 1818. The quality of Ringeltaube's work was such that, tho left to themselves during three years, the native preachers and their churches were in vigorous life when the new missionaries came. Mead and Knill opened a station at Nagarcoil and the Word grew mightily and prevailed. In 1822 the number of Christian adherents was found to be 5,000. The field was then divided, the eastern part being worked from Nagarcoil, and a new station being opened at Neyoor as a center for the western district.

Quilon, in the north of Travancore, had been occupied in 1821, but the enterprise was not successful; another attempt was made in 1827, with some success in educational work. The first church was formed in 1837. Trivandrum was at last made a missionary station in the same year. The progress of Christianity has been steady and remarkable in Travancore. There was a sharp outburst of persecution in 1827-30, renewed in 1858 and 1859. The ostensible cause of the persecution was the course of Christian women in covering the upper part of the person as soon as their awakened sensibilities made them feel the indecency of going without covering. On the other hand, Hindu caste rules required that the women of the caste to which these belonged must wear nothing above the waist. It is characteristic of the debasing effect of Hinduism that even educated men saw no weak point in their demand that Christian women should not wear the shoulder cloth. This was made the ground for a great destruction of Christian property and a vast amount of brutality toward Christians. At last the Travancore Government ordered that the Christian women be permitted to cover themselves provided their shoulder cloths were made of "coarse material." The persecution served to spread knowledge of the Gospel, and great extension has resulted.

There are in Travancore (1903) 7 stations, 344 outstations, 27 missionaries, men and women; 916 native helpers, 75,065 professed Christians, of whom 8,688 are communicants; 380 schools with 16,323 pupils, local contributions amounting to £1,948

6. *China* (1807): The pioneer missionary of the LMS and of Protestant Christendom to China was Robert Morrison. Having met a young Chinaman in London he had studied the language with him, and had made considerable progress both in speaking and in writing. Landing at Canton on the 7th of September, 1807, he was at once beset with difficulties; Chinamen were forbidden to teach the language to foreigners under penalty of death; no one could remain in China except for trade, and the Roman Catholics, already there, stood ready to stir up the authorities against him. Amid untold deprivations, amid obstacles and with great physical suffering, Morrison waited on God for his opportunity. In 1809 relief came; he was engaged by the East India Company as Chinese translator, with a salary of £500 a year. In this capacity he could go about freely with a recognized standing while in no way diverted from his real purpose in coming to the country. In 1812 his grammar of Chinese was finished and printed; then tracts, a catechism, the Acts, and the Gospel of Luke. An edict was then issued declaring the penalty for such publications to be death; but Morrison paid no heed, and at the end of 1813 the whole New Testament was printed. Mr. and Mrs. Milne joined Morrison and his wife at Macao in 1813, and five days later they were ordered to leave within eight days. They went to Canton, where the Morrisons followed them.

The next question was to find a secure place for a mission station. Mr. Milne spent the next few months in exploring Java and the Malay Peninsula, finally deciding to establish himself at Malacca. Morrison now formulated a scheme for establishing at Malacca an Anglo-Chinese college. He himself contributed £1,000 to the institution. Buildings were erected and students came; printing presses were set up, and a flourishing work began. In consequence of the outbreak of war with England, nothing could be done in China; but on the conclusion of peace in 1842 the LMS missionaries to the Chinese at Batavia, Penang, Malacca, etc., decided to close their work at these scattered outposts, and to establish themselves at the newly opened ports of China. The Anglo-Chinese College at Malacca was removed to Hongkong, to serve as a training institution for native workers. Dr. Hobson removed to Hongkong and opened a hospital. Mr. Medhurst and Dr. Lockhart established themselves in Shanghai. In 1844 Messrs. Stronach and Young opened a station in Amoy. The work progressed slowly during ten years, and then came a change. In the year 1854, seventy-seven converts were baptized. Outstations were rapidly established in the outlying districts, and new centers were established in the large towns. The church rose to a sense of its duty and became earnestly evangelistic. The one church grew to eleven, nine of them self-supporting, and the work was extended to a center of vice at Pholam, up the North River. In 1851 the Tai-ping rebellion checked missionary enterprise. In 1859 and 1860 Griffith John went two hundred and fifty miles up the Yangtse River to the headquarters of the Tai-ping leader, at Nan-king, where he succeeded in getting a writ of toleration for missionaries to work in the districts where the insurgents were in power. He then pushed on into the interior and established stations at Han-kau, Wu-chang, and Han-yang, the three cities facing each other at the junction of the Han and Yangtse Rivers. About the same time Messrs. Edkins and Lee began work in Tientsin, and Mr. Lockhart, after twenty years' service in Shanghai, volunteered to open a station in Peking. It was in 1879 that the power of the medical mission was illustrated in Dr. Mackenzie's help to the sick wife of Li Hung Chang, which won the friendship of that statesman, which continued until Dr. Mackenzie's death. The work at Tientsin progressed steadily until the riots of 1870, when eight chapels were burned, and heavy losses affected the church, the native Christians of most profound convictions only coming through the fire of persecution unscathed.

During the Boxer movements of 1900 the LMS in North China suffered with the others, one missionary, the Rev. J. Stonehouse, losing his life. In Peking the East City Church lost more than one-half of its numbers, and two chapels in Tientsin were left in ruins. But since the outbreak was suppressed, there has been a general advance.

There are in the China mission of the LMS (1903) 19 stations and 208 outstations, 112 English missionaries, men and women (including wives); 326 native workers, 17,782 professed Christians, of whom 9,983 are communicants; 113 schools with 2,904 pupils, 13 hospitals and dispensaries, native contributions to the general work, £159, and as fees to the schools, £857, making a total sum from the people of £1,016.

Mongolia: In 1819 the LMS commenced a mission to the Buriat Mongols of southern Siberia. Messrs. Stallybrass, Swan, and Yuille were the missionaries sent out for this work, and they established themselves at Selenginsk, near the Chinese frontier, a little to eastward of the southern end of Lake Baikal. Russian territory was chosen rather than Chinese for this enterprise, because of the liberal views of the Czar Alexander I., then on the Russian throne. The Czar not only gave the mission a grant of land, but a considerable sum of money for erecting buildings. Messrs. Stallybrass and Swan translated into Mongolian and printed the Old Testament and the Gospels. They had a printing house, schools, and regular services in Mongolian, and were rejoiced by several converts, among them two Buriat nobles, who were Buddhists before conversion. In 1838 the Society reported satisfactory progress in the girls' school at Khodon, while at Onagen Mr. Swan was training ten Buriat youths "whose chief desire" was "to impart to their countrymen the blessings they so much prize." But after the Czar Alexander's death in 1825, his brother Nicholas I. came to the throne and made a point of destroying every vestige of the religious liberty which Alexander had favored. The various evangelical missionary enterprises established in Russia under patronage of the late Czar were one by one suppressed. The turn of this hopeful mission of the LMS came in 1841. The missionaries were curtly informed that their work must stop and they must leave the country "because the mission did not coincide with the form of Christianity established in the Russian Empire." Twenty-two years' accumulation of material was sacrificed, but we may not believe that the results of that long period of self-sacrificing labor were utterly lost.

After a lapse of nearly thirty years, the new relations established with China made it possible to resume efforts among Mongols from the Chinese side of the frontier. The LMS in 1870 assigned Rev. James Gilmour to this work. Mr. Gilmour, in the latter part of that year, set forth from Peking, crossed the desert of Gobi, and visited the former stations near Selenginsk, finding the graves of the dead from the missionary families the sole relic of the enterprise.

The people whom Mr. Gilmour was to reach were nomads and, therefore, not easily taught, and they were Buddhists, and therefore not easily made to feel lacks in character or mental equipment. During twenty years Mr. Gilmour had for his sole object in life the evangelization of these people. He made his headquarters at Peking, to which he returned for a part of each year. But his long marches over the Mongolian plains, his life in Mongol families, and his earnest efforts to conquer Mongol suspicions, were the essentials of a missionary activity for the most part meeting with but slight return from this shy and undemonstrative people. It was not until 1884 that the first Mongolian was baptized. The eastern part of Mongolia, where the people led a more settled life, was the field of operations after that year, and in 1887 Chao-yang was occupied as a permanent center of work. Gilmour died in 1891. Others took up his work, but the effort to reach the Mongolians has practically failed. The missionaries in Eastern Mongolia succeeded in collecting a Christian church of about two hundred members, chiefly from the Chinese population. In 1901 the LMS transferred this mission to the Irish Presbyterian Church, which has extensive missions in Manchuria, and withdrew its missionaries to other stations in China.

7. *British Guiana* (1808): A Dutch planter named Post, living on the banks of the Demerara River, sent an urgent appeal to the LMS in 1807 for some one to instruct his negroes in Christian conduct. In response to this appeal the Rev. John Wray was sent to Guiana the following year. A church and a house for the missionary were built, chiefly by contributions from the planter and his friends, and a very encouraging work was begun among the negroes at Le Resouvenir estate. The next year Mr. Post gave a house in Georgetown to be used as a school, and Rev. John Davies was sent out to take charge of it. These proceedings excited alarm among the planters, who knew enough about Christianity to know that it is dangerous to give a man Christ's teachings if freedom is not also given him. The history of the mission during the next twenty-five years is one of struggle for the right to teach negro slaves against the will of slave-owners and Government officials. There is little in missionary literature more inspiring by way of record of fortitude and devotion than the story of this struggle, in which the missionaries Davies and Smith sacrificed health and life against the greed that made it a crime for a negro slave to know the love of God. The result was to build up a strong body of negro Christians in Guiana, and later among the emancipated slaves of Jamaica. The Congregational churches of Jamaica and Guiana have long been independent, and the LMS now maintains but one missionary in the West Indies. He is stationed in Guiana, and his main duty is to superintend the training of candidates for the ministry.

8. *Madagascar* (1818): The history of the development of this field of the LMS is so fully described in the article on **Madagascar** that its repetition in this place is needless. The Society now has in that field (1903) 17 principal stations, 57 missionaries, men and women, including missionaries' wives; 3,323 native workers, 72,000 professed Christians, of whom 24,716 are communicants; 630 schools with 31,770 scholars; 1 hospital and dispensary, and local contributions amounted to £5,822 in 1902.

The organs of the society are: *The Chronicle*, a monthly magazine established in 1813, and for young people; *News From Afar*, monthly, established in 1845, under the name of *The Juvenile Missionary Magazine*. For fuller information about the Society the following may be consulted: Lovett (J.), *History of the London Missionary Society*, 2 Vols., London, 1900; Horne (S.C.), *The Story of the L. M. S.*, London, 1894 (a good summary).

LONGHEU: A town in the province of Kwang-tung, China, situated 8 miles N. E. of Li-long. Station of the Basel Mission Society (1882), with (1903) 1 missionary and his wife, 8 native workers, 4 outstations, 1 boarding school, and 602 professed Christians, of whom 365 are communicants.

LO-NGWONG: A town in the province of Fo-kien, China, situated on the coast about 30 miles N. E. of Fu-chau. Station of the CMS (1889), with (1903) 31 native workers, 12 day schools, and 1,021 professed Christians, of whom 318 are communicants. Station also of the CEZ (1893), with (1903) 3 women missionaries, 3 native workers, 6 day schools, 2 boarding schools, 1 dispensary and 1 hospital. Station also of the Mission to Lepers in India and the East (1891), with 1 chapel and a home for untainted children of lepers.

LOOMIS, Augustus W.: Died at San Francisco, Cal., July 26, 1891. He first went as a missionary of the Presbyterian Board (N.) to China in 1844, and was there until 1850. In 1852 he began mission work among the Creek Indians, and was with them about a year. In 1859 he was called to take charge of the Chinese work in California, in which department of Christian missions he spent the remainder of his life. Dr. Loomis published several important works in connection with Chinese missions, and his whole work has been of the highest value. He was a man of great intellectual attainments, and his Board will find it difficult to supply his place in their missionary force.

LOURENCO MARQUES: A town in Portuguese E. Africa, situated on the coast in the N. W. of Delagoa Bay, founded as a trading post of the Portuguese in 1544. Station of the MR (1889), with (1903) 2 missionaries and their wives, 3 women missionaries, 10 native workers, 8 outstations, 9 places of worship, 9 Sunday schools, 1 book room, 21 day schools, and 1,508 professed Christians, of whom 624 are communicants. Station of the SPG (1894), with 1 missionary, 1 woman missionary, 7 outstations, and 475 professed Christians, of whom 101 are communicants.

LOVEDALE: A town in Cape Colony, Africa, 700 miles northeast of Cape Town, near Alice. It is the site of a missionary institution, which is of absorbing interest, since its methods of work when it was commenced were novel, and have been proved to be successful—the Lovedale Mission. In 1841 Rev. William Govan opened here a missionary institute, and the place was called Lovedale, after Dr. Love, the first secretary of the Glasgow Missionary Society. The aims of the institution were these: 1st. To take young men of intellectual and spiritual qualifications and educate them to be preachers. 2d. To train young men and women as teachers for native mission schools. 3d. Industrial education in various arts, such as wagon-building, blacksmithing, printing, bookbinding, telegraphy and agricultural work of various kinds, was carefully to be given to the natives in order that they might be industrious and useful citizens. 4th. To give an education of a general character to all whose course in life had not yet been definitely determined. The two departments, industrial and educational, are carried on in two buildings, one for the males and the other for the females. Each department has its own special aim, but the grand purpose of each and both is to Christianize, not merely to civilize; and the conversion of the individual is the great aim and the desired end of all the work that is conducted. The solution of the problem how to develop Christian character and energy amid the existing conditions surrounding barbarous and indolent races is fraught with many difficulties; and in order to Christianize successfully, it has been proved of great assistance to civilize at the same time. The principles which govern the management of the Lovedale Institution are: (1) It is non-sectarian and undenominational. The United Free Church of Scotland supports it financially, but all denominations in the country have been represented in it at one time or another. At Lovedale among the pupils all colors and nearly all tribes in South Africa and Rhodesia are represented. No influence is brought to bear upon the students to join the Free Church of Scotland in preference to the church with which they are connected. Even in the theological course those who are trained as agents for other bodies are not weakened in their denominational ties. (2) Broad Christianity does not mean lax Christianity. Instruction in the Bible and in practical religion is the first work of the day in all the classes. Morning and evening worship is held in the dining-halls. At noon every Wednesday a prayer meeting is held, and each workman drops his tools and takes part in the meeting, altho it involves a pecuniary loss by reason of the time taken from the week's work. (3) Self-support is the theory. In the trades departments especially this principle is carried out.

In addition to these general principles other lesser ones are: The education is practical; habits of industry and activity are urged and encouraged, and promotion in the classes depends first upon the moral character, then upon the intelligence and activity.

The curriculum in the educational departments includes three courses, each of which occupies three years. These are: The elementary school, the literary course and the theological course. The subjects studied are those usually taught in like institutions. In regard to the teaching of Latin and Greek to theological students, there has been some discussion, but the tendency now is to drop these studies from the course as not being essential to the equipment of the native pastor. The training of native teachers for elementary native schools is second in importance. Teachers who hold certificates from the educational department have a higher status, and can secure good salaries. A general education is given to all, and men in all the walks of life receive as much education as may be necessary or expedient for them to undertake. In the industrial department various arts are taught. The native apprentices, after a trial of three or six months, are indentured for five or six years, if satisfactory. In the evening they are given a part of the studies of their general education. In addition to their board and lodging they receive pay at rates varying from two to five dollars a month, of which a small part is retained each month in trust for them, and is paid to them at the end of their apprenticeship. No one is allowed to be idle. Those who are not apprentices or engaged in other work are employed in manual labor about the fields and gardens. There is a farm of 2,800 acres connected with the institution. So attractive is the education provided at this institution that many Europeans have availed themselves of its advantages, and mingle freely with the natives in the classes. The resources of the institution are native fees, government grants, and the produce of the farm and gardens. The receipts from the two first sources in 1902 amounted to £7,175, or $34,725. The government grants amounted to £2,200, or a little less than $11,000. It is a mission station of the UFS (1841), with (1903) 19 missionaries, four with their wives; 6 women missionaries, 16 native workers, 5 outstations, 2 places of worship, 4 day schools, 1 boarding school, 1 theological class, 1 hospital, 1 dispensary, 1 printing press, 1 Young Men's Christian Association and 475 professed Christians.

Young (R.). *African Wastes Reclaimed*, London, 1902; *Report of Mildmay Conference on For. Missions*, ⸀p. 68-76, London, 1878; *Report of Centenary Conference on Missions*, pp. 402-406, London, 1888.

LOWRIE, Reuben Post: Born at Butler, Pa., November 24, 1827; graduated University of New York, 1846; was tutor there in 1849, attending also a course of lectures at Union Theological Seminary; finished his theological course at Princeton; was principal of an academy at Wyoming, Pa., 1849-51; was a missionary a few months among the Choctaw Indians. He was ordained 1853, appointed to China as a missionary of the PN and sailed April 22, 1854. He was stationed at Shanghai 1854-60. He made rapid progress in the acquisition of the language, and within a year was able to conduct public exercises in Chinese. He also devoted much time to the completion of a dictionary of the *Four Books*, commenced by his brother Walter. He translated also the *Shorter Catechism* and a catechism on the O. T. history. When, enfeebled by constant work and the enervating climate, he was advised to visit his native land, he replied that he would not leave China "until he had looked death in the face." He had nearly finished a commentary on the Gospel of Matthew, when he died at Shanghai of chronic diarrhea, April 26, 1860.

LOWRIE, Walter Macon: Born at Butler, Pa., February 18, 1819; graduated at Jefferson College 1837, with the first honor; decided while in college to be a missionary to the heathen; graduated at Princeton Theological Seminary 1840; ordained November 9, 1841; sailed January, 1842, for China as a missionary of the PN. In August, 1846, he published several essays in the *Chinese Repository* on the proper Chinese words to be used in translating the name of God into Chinese. His views agreed with those of Drs. Boone and Bridgman, but differed from those of Medhurst and others. He commenced also the preparation of a dictionary of the *Four Books*, and decided to include also the *Five Classics*. These books contain the body of the Chinese language. This work, he thought, would require two or three years without interfering with more direct and important missionary labors. His plan would include biographical and historical notices of China from B. C. 2100 to B. C. 300, in a large quarto volume. But he did not live to complete the work. In 1847 he was appointed one of the delegation for the revision of the Chinese translations of the Bible. While attending the meeting of the revision committee at Shanghai he received a message requesting his immediate return to Ningpo. On the 19th of August while on this journey they were attacked by pirates armed with swords and spears. One of the boatmen who was near him states that while the pirates were maiming the sailors and ransacking the boat, Lowrie sat at the bow reading his pocket Bible, and as they were in the act of seizing him, he turned himself partly round and threw his Bible on the deck. Three men seized him and threw him into the sea. The Bible was a copy of Bagster's 12mo. edition in Hebrew, Greek and English, the same copy he had preserved with great difficulty in the shipwreck of the "Harmony." The death of Mr. Lowrie was a great loss to the missionary cause, since his natural and acquired preparation for important literary work in the Chinese language was of the first order.

LOYALTY ISLANDS: A group in the South Pacific, consisting of Uvea, Lifu and Marè, besides some smaller islands. Lifu, the largest, is about 50 miles long and 25 broad, and contains a population of about 6,000. The island is of coral formation, and the thin layer of soil is productive of vegetables and fruit. Marè has about 6,000 people. Uvea is a circle of 20 islets enclosing a lagoon 20 miles wide, and has 2,500 inhabitants. The islanders belong to the Melanesian race, and each island has its own tongue. Christianity was early introduced into the islands by natives from Raratonga and Samoa. In 1841 the LMS sent its first missionaries to this field. The French Government instituted a commandant in the islands in 1864, considering it a dependency of New Caledonia. Under French rule the English missionaries were interfered with, but an understanding has been reached which permits freedom of worship. The work in the island of Marè was transferred by the LMS to the Paris Evangelical Society in 1891. There are (1902) two mission stations on the island, Ro and Netche, with 1 ordained missionary and 2 preaching places. The LMS has retained control of the work in Uvea (1856) and Lifu (1843), having (1902) 1 missionary on the last named island, and on both islands together 182 native workers and 2,300 church members.

LUANZA. See LOANZA.

LU-CHAU: A town in the province of Szechwan, China, situated on the left bank of the Yangtse River at the confluence of the To River, about 146 miles S. E. of Cheng-tu. It is an important salt market. Population 100,000 (estimate). Station of the CIM (1890), with (1903) 2 missionaries, one with his wife; 2 women missionaries, 3 native workers, 1 chapel, 1 Sunday school and 1 day school.

LU-CHAU-FU: A town in China, situated near Chaohu Lake, about 85 miles N. by E. of Nganking-fu. Station of the FCMS (1894), with (1900) 2 missionaries, one with his wife; 1 native worker, 1 place of worship, 1 society for young people, 1 book room, 1 day school, 1 dispensary, 1 hospital and 19 professed Christians. The Society spells the name Lu-cheo-fu.

LU-CHENG-HSIEN: A town in the province of Shan-si, China, situated about 15 miles N. E. of Lu-ngan-fu. Station of the CIM (1889), with (1903) 3 women missionaries, 3 native workers, 1 outstation, 2 places of worship, 1 Sunday school, 1 boarding school and 2 refuges for opium victims. The name is sometimes written Lu-ch'eng.

LUCHU ISLANDS: A chain of 37 islands in the North Pacific, between Japan and Formosa. Their surface is very rugged and the soil variable, but the islands abound in grass and trees, and are very picturesque and beautiful. The climate is hot, but the heat is never excessive, tho there are frequent injurious droughts and typhoons. Population, 170,000, consisting of two races, the Japanese and the Lu Chuans proper. These races are of the same stock and greatly resemble each other, tho the Lu Chuans are more effeminate and less intelligent, and, unlike most other Mongolian tribes, wear a full black beard. Their book learning and religion are for the most part Chinese, and the higher classes are well educated. Their principal occupation is agriculture, but the mode of cultivation is primitive, the implements are rude, and the soil is generally tilled by hand. The land all belongs to the government, which lets it to large tenants, who sublet it to small farmers. The government is administered in the name of a king, and is in the hands of an aristocracy consisting (as in China) of the literary class, who appear to live in idleness, while the poor are greatly oppressed. About 400 years ago the principal island was divided into three kingdoms, which were subsequently united, and became subject first to China and then to Japan. The CMS, the ABMU, the ME, and the BFBS carry on work on these islands largely through Japanese Christians, who work under their direction. Most of the New Testament has been translated into the Luchu dialect. The islands are also called Riu-kiu.

Missionary Review of the World, Vol. XII., p. 522, Funk & Wagnalls, New York, 1899.

LUCKNOW: A city in the United Provinces, India, on the Gunti River, 42 miles from Cawnpur and 199 miles from Benares. It is the capital of a district, and formerly of Oudh. Viewed from a distance, Lucknow presents a picture of unusual magnificence and architectural splendor, which fades on nearer view into the ordinary aspect of an Oriental town. Nevertheless, it is one of the most important cities in India, and many of its streets are broader and finer than in most Indian towns, and the sanitary condition of the city is constantly being improved. It has a celebrated school of Mohammedan theology, manufactures silver and gold work and embroidery, and has extensive railway workshops. During the mutiny of 1857 it was besieged by the rebels for six months, when the garrison was saved by Sir Colin Campbell. Altitude, 369 feet. Population (1901), 264,000, of whom 146,000 are Hindus and 99,000 are Mohammedans. Station of the CMS (1857), with (1903) 4 missionaries, 3 with their wives; 14 native workers, 1 outstation, 5 village schools, 2 boarding schools, 1 dispensary, and 473 professed Christians, of whom 174 are communicants. Station also of the ME, with 6 missionaries, 1 with his wife; 9 women missionaries, 16 native workers, 2 chapels, 37 Sunday schools, 1 printing press, 17 day schools, 1 boarding school, and 2 colleges, 432 professed Christians and a deaconess' home. Station also of the WMS, with (1903) 1 missionary, 27 native workers, 4 chapels, 14 Sunday schools, 7 day schools, and 98 Christians. Station also of the ZBM, with (1903) 11 women missionaries, 27 native workers, 3 day schools, 1 dispensary, and 1 hospital.

LUDD: A town in Palestine, situated about 1½ miles S. E. of Jaffa, on the caravan road from Damascus to Egypt. It is the Lydda of the New Testament. St. George is said to have been born and buried here. Station of the CMS (1876), with (1903) 1 native worker, 1 day school. Name is spelled by this society Lydd. The Jaffa Medical Mission has (1898) 2 women missionaries, 1 native worker, 1 Sunday school, 1 dispensary. This Society spells the name Lydda.

LUDHIANA: A town in the Ludhiana District of the Punjab, India, situated about 3 miles S. of Sutlej River, and 73 miles S. E. by E. of Amritsar. Altitude, 812 feet. Population (1891), 46,300, of whom 30,300 are Muslims and 13,900 Hindus. Station of the PN (1834), with (1903) 4 missionaries and their wives, 6 missionary women, 54 native workers, 9 outstations, 9 places of worship, 40 Sunday schools, 4 day schools, 2 boarding schools, 1 industrial school, 1 printing press, and 320 professed Christians. Society spells the name Lodiana. Mission station of the North India School of Medicine for Christian Women (1895), with (1901) 10 women missionaries, 6 native workers, 1 Sunday school, 1 Young Woman's Christian Association, 1 female helpers' training class, 5 dispensaries, 2 hospitals, 1 medical class, 1 lepers' asylum.

LUEBO: A settlement in the Congo Free State, Africa, situated on the left bank of the Lulua River at its confluence with the Luebo River. Altitude, 1,350 feet. The climate is much better than in the lower lands. Station of the PS (1891), with 4 missionaries, 1 with his wife; 2 women missionaries, 10 native workers, 3 chapels, 1 Sunday school, 1 printing press, 1 day school, 1 dispensary, and 1,000 professed Christians, of whom 657 are communicants.

LUFILUFI: A settlement in Samoa, Oceania, east of Apia on Upolu Island. Station of the Australian Wesleyan Mission, with (1900) 2 missionaries, 101 native workers, 8 outstations, 20 places of worship, 29 Sunday schools, 29 day schools, 1 theological class, and 556 professed Christians.

LU-GAN. See LU-NGAN-FU and LIU-NGAN-CHAU.

LU-GANDA: The Bantu term for the language spoken by the Wa-Ganda; the term might be rendered into English as Ugandan, q. v.

LUH HOH. See LIU-HO-HSIEN.

LUKANOR ISLAND. See MORTLOCK ISLANDS.

LUK-HANG: A town in the province of Kwang-tung, China, situated about 28 miles N. by W. of Canton. Station of the Berlin Mission Society (1897), with (1903) 3 missionaries, 29 native workers, 19 outstations, 2 day schools, and 769 professed Christians, of whom 549 are communicants.

LUKOLELA: A settlement in the Congo Free State, Africa, situated on the left bank of the Congo River, surrounded by dense forests. Station of the BMS (1884), with (1903) 1 missionary and his wife, 1 native worker, 1 outstation, 1 day school. The station is also known under the name of Liverpool.

LUKUNGA: A town in the Congo Free State, Africa, on the Congo River, about midway between the mouth and Stanley Pool. Station of the ABMU (1882), with (1903) 2 missionaries and their wives, 22 native workers, 19 outstations, 1,022 professed Christians, of whom 511 are communicants; 10 chapels, 1 Sunday school, 19 day schools, 1 boarding school, and 1 dispensary.

LULANGA: A settlement in Congo Free State, Africa, situated at the confluence of the Lulanga River with the Congo, about 50 miles N. of Equatorville. Station of the RBMU (1889), with 5 missionaries, 2 women missionaries, 1 native worker, 1 place of worship, 1 Sunday school, 1 day school, 1 dispensary. Society spells the name Lolanga.

LULL, Raymund: Born in 1235. Died in 1315. From Zwemer's biography of this first and, perhaps, greatest missionary to Mohammedans, we gather the following facts: Raymund Lull lived during a most eventful epoch. Five years after his birth the rise of the Ottoman Turks occurred, and before he was twenty Louis IX. had failed in his crusade, and the Inquisition had begun in Spain to torture Jews and heretics. As he was growing into manhood, the beneficial effects of the Crusades were being felt; physical science was struggling into feeble life; discoveries of distant lands were being made; the University of Oxford was founded, and the world, as Lull knew it, was the world of medieval legend and classic lore. The Mohammedan world was, with all Europe, in a state of ferment, and Raymund Lull was raised up to prove what the Crusades might have done if they had fought for the cross with the weapons of the Prince of Peace. Lull was a member of a distinguished Catalonian family, and when the island of Majorca was taken from the Saracens by James I., King of Aragon, Lull's father was rewarded with large estates in the conquered territory, for his distinguished services. A succession of twenty proud sovereigns reigned from the year 1035 to 1516, and at such a court, probably in the capital town of Zaragoza (Saragossa), Lull spent several years of his life. He was a court poet, and a skilled musician. Gifted with rare mental accomplishments, the heir to large wealth, he was a gay knight at the banquets of James II., before he became a scholastic philosopher and an ardent missionary. It was at Palma, when thirty-two years old, that he made his decision to forsake all and become a preacher of righteousness. His conversion reminds one of the experience of Saul on his way to Damascus, and of St. Augustine under the fig tree at Milan. He sold all his property, gave the money to the poor, and reserved only a scanty allowance for his wife and children. He determined to attack Islam with the weapons of Christian truth; and assuming the coarse garb of a mendicant, he made pilgrimages to various churches in the island, praying for grace and assistance in the work of his life. In the 13th century, Islam, the mistress of philosophy and science, had political influence and prestige; and against this mighty power this knight of Christ was to lead an attack with the weapons of love and learning, instead of the Crusaders' weapons of force and fanaticism. He entered upon a thorough course of study, mastered the Arabic language, spent much time in spiritual meditation, and at about the age of forty he entered upon the most useful part of his life, as author and missionary. His *Ars Major* was completed in 1275, and under the patronage of the King of Majorca this first book of his *Method* was published. Soon after the publication of this work, he persuaded James II. to found and endow a monastery in Majorca, where Franciscan monks should be instructed in the Arabic language, and trained to become able disputants among the Muslims. In 1276 such a monastery was opened, and thirteen monks began to study Lull's method and imbibe his spirit. Lull now longed for a new Pentecost, and for world-wide missions. Fired with apostolic zeal, he went to Rome and Paris; and, altho in his fifty-sixth year, he determined to set out alone and single-handed and preach Christ in North Africa. On arriving at Tunis he invited the Muslim literati to a conference. He announced that he had studied the arguments on both sides of the question, and was willing to submit the evidences for Christianity and for Islam to a fair comparison. The challenge was willingly accepted, and after a long, fruitless discussion Lull advanced the following propositions, which strike the two weak points of Mohammedan monotheism: "Lack of love in the being of Allah, and lack of harmony in his attributes." Some accepted the truth and others became fanatical. Lull was cast into a dungeon by order of the Sultan, and, at this time, narrowly escaped death. After bitter persecutions he returned to Europe; but he made other missionary journeys, and in 1307 he was again on the shores of North Africa, fifteen years after his banishment. Altho he was now sixty-six years of age, despite the conditions of travel in the Middle Ages we find him visiting Cyprus, Syria, and penetrating into Armenia, striving to reclaim the various Oriental sects to the orthodox faith. In 1307 he set sail again for North Africa, and at Bugia, in a public place, he stood up boldly and proclaimed, in the Arabic language, that Christianity was the only true faith; and once again violent hands were laid upon him. He was flung into a dungeon, and for six months remained a close prisoner, befriended only by some merchants of Genoa and Spain, who took pity on the aged missionary of the cross. He was banished again from Africa, with threats that his life would be taken if he ever returned, but with unabated love and zeal he went there again in 1314. For over ten months this veteran of the cross dwelt in hiding, talking and praying with his converts, and trying to influence those who were still in darkness. Weary of seclusion, he, at length, came forth into the open market and presented himself to the people as the man whom they had expelled, and who desired still to preach Christ to them. He seemed to court martyrdom. He was seized and dragged out of the town, and by the command, or at least the connivance, of the king, he was stoned to death. Lull's life-work was three-fold: he devised a philosophical or educational system for persuading non-Christians of the truth of Christianity, he established missionary colleges, and he himself went and preached to the Muslims, sealing his witness of Christ with his blood. There exists no complete catalog of his books, but he wrote on nearly every known subject, and in the first published edition of his works (1721) two hundred and eighty titles are given.

Neander (I. A. W), *Church History*, Vol. IV.; Maclear, *History of Christian Missions in the Middle Ages*, London, 1863; Zwemer (S. M.), *Raymund Lull*, New York, Funk & Wagnals, 1902.

LUMBAN NA BOLAN: A settlement in the Toba Lake region of Sumatra. Station of the Rhenish Missionary Society, with (1903) 1 missionary and his wife, 1 native worker, 1 Sunday school and 1 day school.

LUNDU: A settlement in Sarawak, Borneo, situated on Datu Bay, about 40 miles W. of Kuching. Station of the SPG (1853), with (1903) 1 missionary, 3 native workers, 2 places of worship, 2 day schools and 60 Christians.

LU-NGAN-FU: A town in the province of Shan-si, China, situated in the S. E. of the province, about 100 miles N. N. E. of Ho-nan-fu. Station of the CIM (1889), with 2 missionaries, 3 native workers, 1 chapel, 1 Sunday school and 35 professed Christians. Name is sometimes spelled Lu-gan.

LUNG-CHAU. See LANG-CHAU.

LUNG-TSUEN-HSIEN: A town in the province of Che-kiang, China, situated about 95 miles W. of Wen-chau. Mission station of the CIM (1894), with (1903) 1 missionary and his wife, 4 native workers, 1 chapel and 1 Sunday school. The name is sometimes spelled Lung-ch'uen.

LUPEMBE: The name of a tribe found 100 miles E. of the north end of Lake Nyasa in German East Africa, among whom the Berlin Mission Society carry on work (1899), with (1903) 3 missionaries, 4 native workers, 2 outstations, 1 day school and 11 professed Christians.

LUTHERAN FOREIGN MISSIONARY SOCIETIES in the United States: The early Lutheran Church in the United States was predominantly German, tho with some Scandinavian and Dutch elements, and was chiefly confined to Pennsylvania. The lack of a regular ministry and the heavy strain on a few pastors resulted in an earnest appeal to Europe for help. Francke, at Halle, was much interested, and at his request Heinrich Melchior Muhlenberg, who had been intending to go as a missionary to India, came to Philadelphia in 1742. While chiefly absorbed in the organization of the Church (which gave him the title of Patriarch Muhlenberg) he kept missionary work among the Indians at home as well that in foreign lands constantly in mind.

The first direct interest in foreign missions appears to have been aroused by the work of the Rev. C. T. E. Rhenius, a German Lutheran missionary of the CMS in India. In 1821 the General Synod at its first meeting resolved to form a missionary institute, and some aid was sent to the work of Rhenius in India. Contributions were also made to the ABCFM, then a distinctively undenominational organization. In 1833 the General Synod urged the subject upon the district synods, and in 1835 the Central Missionary Society was organized at Mechanicsburg, Pa., followed in 1837 by the German Foreign Missionary Society in the U. S. A. It was hoped that all would unite in this, but the German Reformed Church and several Lutheran churches held aloof. Soon the name was changed to The Foreign Missionary Society of the Evangelical Lutheran Church in the U. S. A. From this time until 1869 the greater part of the Lutheran churches contributed through this organization, but in that year the General Council organized its own board of missions and since then other Lutheran bodies have followed this example.

At first it was a question whether to begin work among the Indians in the United States or in India, but after some deliberation it was decided to commence operations in Southern India, in connection with the ABCFM, and the Rev. C. F. Heyer was appointed as missionary to that country in 1840. A year later, fearing complications from this proposed connection, he resigned and was appointed to the same field by the Synod of Pennsylvania, which had formed a separate missionary organization in 1836. He sailed from Boston October 14, 1841, and arrived in India the following spring. In June and July an exploring tour was made with a view of selecting a field for permanent residence and work. On July 31, 1842, he reached Guntur, where he commenced the work assigned him.

At the next meeting of the Foreign Missionary Society, held in May, 1843, the proposed union with the American Board was given up, and arrangements made with the missionary society of the Pennsylvania Synod to send out another missionary to cooperate with Rev. Heyer. Rev. Walter Gunn received the appointment, and he and his wife reached Guntur June 18, 1844. They labored faithfully until July 5, 1851, when Mr. Gunn died. Mrs. Gunn soon after returned to the United States.

Meanwhile a new station had been opened in Palnad in 1849, and in 1851 the North German Missionary Society transferred the station at Rajamahendri, begun in 1845, to the American Lutheran Society, with two missionaries. Other missionaries were sent from America to reenforce the mission, but were soon obliged to return home. In 1857 Mr. Heyer, after 14 years of service, also returned to America. In 1861 a fourth station was opened at Samulcotta, and Rev. Mr. Long, who went out in 1858, was placed in charge of it and remained there until 1865, when he was obliged to go to Europe to recover his health, and the Rev. Mr. Unangst was left with entire charge of the four stations—Guntur, Palnad, Rajamahendri and Samulcotta. It being utterly impossible for him to give proper attention to all, a proposition was made to transfer the Rajamahendri station to the Church Missionary Society.

Mr. Heyer was in Germany when he heard of this, but hastened at once to the United States and presented to the Synod of Pennsylvania an earnest protest. Negotiations with the General Synod made it evident that they would be glad to have the field remain in Lutheran hands, and the CMS was entirely willing to be relieved of additional burdens. Overtures were made to the General Council, and at its meeting in Chicago, November, 1869, it formally accepted the responsibilities. During the same year the General Synod effected a reorganization of its work under a new name.

General Synod of the Evangelical Lutheran Church in the U. S. A.: Headquarters of the Board of Foreign Missions, 1005 West Lanvale St., Baltimore, Md.

The General Synod has worked through its own Board of Foreign Missions since the arrangement with the General Council in 1869.

1. *India:* That arrangement left under the care of the Foreign Missionary Society of the General Synod the Guntur and Palnad stations, embracing a territory about one hundred miles in length by sixty miles in width, with a population of about 1,000,000 souls, chiefly Telugus, among whom practically nothing had been done at that time. Rev. E. Unangst remained the only missionary on this field until 1871, when he was obliged to take his family to America. Remaining there only one year to recruit, he returned to India in 1872 without his family, accompanied by the Rev. J. H. Harpster. Since then the mission has been reenforced at various times, and a large force of native laborers has been raised up in the different departments of work.

At the close of 1902 there were 27 missionaries (including wives), 6 Eurasian assistants, 220 native evangelistic workers, including pastors, catechists, Bible women, etc., and 286 teachers. The number of stations has increased to 7, while 449 congregations assembled regularly and the villages reached number 618. The buildings were 7 churches, 157 prayer and school houses, 11 mission bungalows, 1 hospital, 1 college and 1 printing house. The communicant membership was 8,386, and there were 9,163 inquirers and 35,525 under direct Christian influence, the baptisms in a single year numbering 2,551. The Sunday school work has grown until there are 269 schools, with 465 teachers and 15,965 scholars.

Closely associated with this is the medical and Zenana work carried on by 5 missionary women, with 4 assistants and 52 teachers. Of these, 9 are specially engaged in the home work, visiting 115 homes and instructing 150 Zenana pupils. In the hospital there are 650 patients, while the dispensary patients were 15,759.

In common with other successful missions in India, considerable attention is paid to education. The policy of the mission is to educate the children as far as the primary grade, when they are sent to the branch schools at Guntur, where are the college under the presidency of the Rev. L. B. Wolf, D.D., a boarding and training school for boys, etc. The report for 1902 shows in the college 7 Christian, 21 Hindu and 4 Mohammedan teachers, 73 Christian, 552 Hindu and 50 Mohammedan pupils, a total of 675. The year showed an increase of 87 in attendance and an income amounting to 88 per cent. of total expenses aside from the missionary's salary. The total number of elementary schools is 232, with 286 teachers and 6,700 pupils, of whom 3,151 were Christians and 3,549 non-Christians; 4,404 boys and 2,296 girls.

2. *Africa:* In 1859, through the long-continued efforts of Rev. Morris Officer, a mission to Africa was decided upon, and Mr. Officer was appointed to superintend its establishment, and, with the Rev. Henry Heigerd, arrived in Liberia April 5. The location selected, and still occupied by the mission, is a high bluff on St. Paul's River, about thirty miles above Monrovia. A grant of one hundred acres of land was secured from the Liberian Government for a mission farm, and a reserve of two hundred acres more for future settlers about the mission. Suitable buildings were erected, and a short time afterward 40 children were secured from a large number of recaptured slaves that had been landed at Monrovia. These children were bound to the mission by the government, were then named after well-known women in the church at home, and thus the Muhlenberg Mission was begun, and the foundation laid of the Christian settlement which has since grown up around the mission. A native Christian church, organized in 1861, is self-sustaining, and there are two other churches and five outstations. The pastor was one of the slave children with whom the mission was started and a corps of native workers has been developed. The industrial department has always been one of the special features of this mission, and its coffee plantation was long relied upon to meet many of the current expenses. Difficulties in marketing the coffee emphasized the mercantile side so much that there was a general feeling that the distinctively missionary element was being crowded out, and of late the coffee farm occupies a minor place in the view of the missionaries. Meanwhile, educational and general evangelistic work is being pushed very vigorously, both in Liberia itself and in the surrounding districts, from which come appeals for teachers and preachers.

A Woman's Home and Foreign Missionary Society of the General Synod of the Evangelical Lutheran Church in the United States was organized in 1879 and carries on work in India, Liberia and the United States, employing 12 foreign missionaries. It publishes a children's missionary paper, tracts and programs for missionary meetings. It has 20 synodical and 584 auxiliary societies, with about 20,000 members. Its headquarters are in Baltimore, Md.

A number of Lutheran bodies which have no separate missionary organizations contribute through the General Synod.

General Council of the Evangelical Lutheran Church in North America: Headquarters of the Board of Foreign Missions, 1522 Arch St., Philadelphia, Pa.

1. *India:* The foreign mission work of the General Council was commenced in 1869, when the stations of the North German Missionary Society at Rajamahendri and Samulcotta, Southern India, were transferred to its care by the General Synod. The work is now in charge of the Foreign Mission Committee of the General Council, and comprises the districts of Rajamahendri, Dowlaishwaram, Samulcotta, Tallapudi, Velpur, Jagurupad and Bhimawaram.

There are (1903) 6 missionaries, assisted by 3 native pastors and 140 evangelists, catechists and teachers. The whole number of mission workers employed is 157, of whom 5 are Zenana Sisters, 2 devoting their whole time to dispensary and hospital work. Special attention is paid to educational work and there are over 4,000 pupils in the various schools established in 120 villages, those of higher grade being at Rajamahendri and Peddapur. The extent of the evangelistic work is indicated by the number of baptized Christians (adults and children), given as 6,159, in the 210 villages where preaching is conducted.

2. *Porto Rico:* In the summer of 1899 the Board undertook mission work in Porto Rico. Mr. S. G. Swensson of the Augustana Seminary had gathered a small congregation in San Juan, including several from the Danish Church at St. Thomas, and his work was taken up by the Rev. H. F. Richards and wife, who have carried it on since, now with the assistance of a woman teacher. There is (1903) a Spanish congregation, in addition to the English one, and a flourishing Sunday school; and the reports of success are encouraging. The Board made a proposition to the Home Board to take up the work as more distinctly within its province, but that Board declined for lack of funds.

Organ of the Society: *Missionsbote,* monthly.

A Woman's Home and Foreign Missionary Society has been formed in connection with the General Council of the Evangelical Lutheran Church in North America, with its headquarters at 33d and Diamond Sts., Philadelphia, Pa.

United Synod of the Evangelical Lutheran Church in the South: Headquarters of the Board of Missions and Church Extension, 376 Spring St., Atlanta, Ga.

This society was organized in 1886, but did not commence distinct foreign work until 1892, when a missionary, the Rev. J. A. B. Scherer, was sent to Saga in Japan. There are now (1903) three ordained missionaries, one of them being Rev. R. B. Peery, Ph.D., author of *The Gist of Japan,* etc. There are also 3 native evangelists at work in Saga and Kumamoto and the 3 Sunday schools are prosperous. The number of church members reported is 77 and there are about 150 in the Christian community.

Several synods combine in this work, as also three organizations conducted by women.

LUXOR: A village on the left bank of the Nile, situated 2 miles S. of Karnak, on the site of ancient Thebes, and having magnificent ruins of temples in a rock-bound valley. The name is from the Arabic El Kusr (The Palaces). Station of the UP (1875), with 1 missionary and his wife, 1 woman missionary, 11 native workers, 5 outstations, 1 Sunday school, 1 boarding school, 3 day schools and a boat on the Nile for missionary tours.

LYALLPUR: A growing city in the Jhang district of India, situated about 100 miles W. S. W. of Lahore. Station of the Reformed Presbyterian General Synod, with (1900) 1 missionary, 2 native workers, 1 outstation, 63 professed Christians, 1 place of worship and 1 Sunday school. Society spells the name Lyalpur. Station of the UP (1869), with (1903) 1 missionary and wife, 4 women missionaries, 36 outstations, 4 Sunday schools, 4 day schools and 110 professed Christians.

LYDD, or **LYDDA.** See LUDD.

LYDENBURG: A town in Eastern Transvaal, Africa, south of the Limpopo River, northeast of Pretoria. Population, 2,000. Station of the Berlin Mission Society (1866), with (1903) 1 missionary, 19 native workers, 9 outstations and 1,921 professed Christians, of whom 992 are communicants. Name also written Leidensburg and Lÿdensburg.

LYMAN, Henry: Born 1810, in Massachusetts; graduated at Amherst College 1829, Andover Seminary 1832; studied medicine and sailed with Rev. Samuel Munson, 1833, under the ABCFM, with instructions to explore the Indian Archipelago. Landing at Batavia, April, 1834, they visited Padang in Sumatra and the Butu group of islands, spending there a month, and collecting much valuable information. Thence they went back to Sumatra, intending if practicable to visit the Battas of the interior. They were advised, on account of dangers, not to attempt it. But as others had visited the interior with safety they ventured to proceed, and June 23 set out on foot with a few native assistants, among them an interpreter. After five days' journey they came to Sacca, a region where war was raging between the villagers, and they were soon surrounded by two hundred armed men, and Mr. Lyman was shot and Mr. Munson pierced with a spear. A terrible punishment was inflicted on the murderers. The people of the neighboring villages having learned that the strangers were good men, who had come to benefit the Batta people, leagued together, burnt the village of Sacca, killing many of the inhabitants, and destroyed their gardens and fields. The death of these men produced a deep sensation throughout the Christian world. Mr. Lyman was the author of *Condition of Females in Pagan Countries*.

Lyman (Miss), *The Martyr of Sumatra*, New York, 1856; Thompson (W.), *Samuel Munson and Henry Lyman*, New York, 1839.

M

MABUMBU: A village on the highlands E. of the Zambesi valley, Africa, situated 13 miles E. by N. of Lialuyi. Station of the Paris Evangelical Mission Society (1899), with (1903) 1 missionary, 1 native worker, 1 day school.

MACAŌ: A town on an island of the same name in Canton River, China, situated 38 miles W. by S. of Hongkong. It is divided into two parts—Chinese and Portuguese. It was here that Camoens composed much of his *Lusiad* in 1559. The town was rented to the Portuguese in 1856, but the treaty was revoked in 1868, and the Portuguese now hold Macao with two adjacent islands as a colonial possession. Population (1896), 78,627, of whom 74,568 are Chinese. Mission station of the CA. The Canton College (PN) is temporarily established at Macaō.

MACASSAR LANGUAGE: A Malayan dialect, spoken in the island of Celebes, Dutch East Indies. It is written with characters special to the dialect. The full form of the name is Maugkasar.

MACEDONIA: Name given by foreigners to the Turkish provinces of Kosovo, Monastir, and Salonica, in the main coincident with a part of the ancient Macedonia. Mission work is carried on there by the ABCFM, the Church of Scotland missions to the Jews, and the BFBS.

MACEDONIAN-ROUMANIAN LANGUAGE: A dialect of the Roumanian, which is spoken by Wallachs settled in European Turkey. When written, the Slavic (Cyrillian) letters in their modern form, or modified Roman letters, are used.

MACFARLAN: A town of Cape Colony, Africa, situated 12 miles N. by E. of Alice. Station of the UFS, with (1903) 16 native workers, 6 outstations, 1 place of worship, 7 day schools, and 564 professed Christians.

MACKAY, Alexander M.: Born at Rhynie, Aberdeenshire, Scotland, October 13, 1849; a son of a minister of the Free Church. At three years of age he read the New Testament; at seven, Milton's *Paradise Lost*, Gibbon's *Decline and Fall of the Roman Empire*, and Robertson's *History of the Discovery of America*. His father taught him geography, astronomy, and geometry, stopping in their walks to demonstrate a proposition of Euclid, or illustrate the motions of the heavenly bodies, or trace the course of a newly discovered river of the Dark Continent with his cane in the sand. He listened with interest to letters and conversations of men of science, as Hugh Miller, Sir Roderick Murchison, and others, who were sometimes visitors at the manse, sometimes in correspondence with his father. He chose engineering as his profession, and for some time he was draughtsman and designer to a large engineering establishment in Berlin. In 1875, in response to an appeal from the CMS for a practical business man to go to Mombasa, he offered himself, but another person had been secured. Later in the year an offer of a highly lucrative secular position was made him, but he declined it, that he might be ready, when the Lord should permit him, to go to the heathen. Early the next year he was appointed by the CMS to go to the Victoria Nyanza, reaching Zanzibar May 29, 1876. In November, on the march through Ugogo, he was taken very ill, and was sent back by Dr. Smith, but recovered before reaching the coast. Instructed by the secretary not to return before the close of the rainy season, he constructed 230 miles of road to Mpwapwa. In November, 1878, he reached Uganda. Alluding to the kind treatment he had received from the natives, he says: "Wherever I find myself in Stanley's track, I find his treatment of the natives has invariably been such as to win from them the highest respect for the face of a white man." Mr. Mackay had acquired a knowledge of the Swahili language, and was able immediately to print portions of the Scriptures (cutting the type himself), and to read and explain them to the king and his people. King Mtesa showed much interest in the truth.

In 1884 the native church consisted of 86 members. But in that year King Mtesa died, being succeeded by his son Mwanga, who proved to be weak and vacillating, lending himself now to the Mohammedan and now to the Roman Catholic party, persecuting the evangelicals, and often threatening Mr. Mackay with expulsion. But Mr. Mackay held his ground, and was allowed for a time to continue his work, his skill as an engineer and mechanic, of which the king often availed himself, helping to secure his favor. In 1886 the persecution broke out again, many under great tortures exhibiting a Christian fortitude and heroism unsurpassed in apostolic times. In 1887 the Arabs succeeded in persuading Mwanga to expel Mr. Mackay. Having locked the mission premises, he embarked July 20 for the southern end of the lake, making his abode at Usambiro. Here he remained for three years, translating and printing the Scriptures, teaching the Christian refugees from Uganda, instructing the natives of the district, as far as he could, with an imperfect knowledge of their language, and working at house-building, brick-making, and the construction of a steam-launch with which to navigate the lake. He was attacked with malarial fever, and died February 8, 1890. Mr. Mackay utilized the knowledge of both classical and modern languages in reducing the vernacular of Uganda to writing. He was a born leader of men, as gentle as he was brave. He was no mere industrial and civilizing missionary, and took a leading part in the evangelistic work of the mission.

MACKENZIE, J. Kenneth, M.D.: A medical missionary of the LMS; was first appointed to Hankau; he took charge of the mission hospital there till 1878, when in the autumn he was transferred to Tientsin. A dispensary was opened in the Viceroy Li Hung Chang's theater, with a female department, and large subscriptions were made by the Viceroy and other high officers toward the building of a hospital. In 1881 the hospital, on the premises of the London Mission, was opened by the Viceroy, and plans were adopted for a medical school, to which the students formerly sent to the United States of America by the government were sent to be trained as doctors, and a thorough organization of a medical staff for the Chinese army and navy was in course of formation. Amid his arduous duties Dr. Mackenzie found time to pursue evangelistic work, both among the poor patients and those "in Cæsar's household," for the favor of the Viceroy secured him access to many of the high officials. The work at Tientsin grew and enlarged, so that in his last report, 1887, he gave the number in attendance at the dispensary as 13,799, in-patients in the hospital 591, and 9 medical students. He was called suddenly away from his work by death, April 1, 1888.

MACLEAG: A settlement on Lake Alexandrina, S. E. of Adelaide, South Australia; it was founded in 1858 by the Scotchman, Taplin, who translated parts of the Bible into Narrinyeri, wrote a grammar of the tongue, and made a careful study of 22 native dialects.

MACLEAR: A town of Cape Colony, South Africa, situated in Griqualand East. Station of the Episcopal Church in Scotland (1896), and SPG, with (1900) 1 missionary, 5 native workers, 3 outstations, 3 chapels, 3 day schools, and 116 Christians.

MACUATA: A settlement on the S. side of Vanua Levu, Fiji Islands, situated near Cacaudrove. Station of the Australian Wesleyan Mission, with (1900) 1 missionary and his wife.

MADAGASCAR: An island in the Indian Ocean nearly parallel with the eastern coast of South Africa, from which it is separated by the Mozambique Channel, which varies in width from 220 to 540 miles. Its northernmost point is in 11° 57' 30" south latitude, and the southernmost is in 25° 38' 55" south latitude. Its breadth is at the widest point over 7° of longitude. Its extreme length is 975 miles, and its breadth varies from 250 to 350 miles. Its area is about 230,000 English square miles. It is the third largest island in the world, ranking only below Borneo and New Guinea.

Madagascar has a coast-line of over 2,000 miles, and on the northwestern, northern, and northeastern coasts there are many good and some excellent harbors; but south of latitude 19° there are very few roadsteads where a vessel can ride in safety, either on the east or west coast. The island is of volcanic origin, and has many extinct volcanoes and some which, if not now active, have been so within the historic period. Its general structure includes three or four ranges of mountains, not parallel, but extending from north to south, with many spurs; these are in the central portions of the island, tho nearer to the east than the west coast. Some of the ranges extend nearly to the northern limit of the island, and others to the southern coast. This mountainous region constitutes the finest portion of the island. Immediately below this region is a forest region varying in latitude from 1,800 to 4,000 feet, and in breadth from 30 to 50 miles. From the forest belt to the coast extends the alluvial region, flat, low, and marshy, and from 20 to 30 miles wide on the east coast, but from 40 to 60 on the west coast. It is sickly and hot, the decaying vegetation producing fevers and miasmatic diseases.

The climate is temperate and healthful in the highland provinces, the temperature rarely above 85° F. or below 40° F., except in the mountains, where it sinks to 32° at night perhaps once or twice in a year. In the forest belt, less healthful and more moist, and at times hot; in the more open timber the climate is delightful. In the littoral region the heat is intense, and the Malagasy fever prevails, and very often proves fatal to those who are not fully acclimated.

Natural History and Products: Madagascar is remarkable in its zoology. There are no great beasts of prey. The lemur takes the place of the various families of monkeys; there are several species of ant-eaters, two or three civet cats, the aye-aye, an animal found nowhere else, and there are several rodents. Reptiles are numerous, but, except the crocodile and three or four species of pythons, are generally harmless. Birds are numerous, and many of them of beautiful plumage. About two-thirds of the birds are peculiar to the island.

The fish are plentiful, and many of them of edible species. Most of the domestic animals have been introduced, and cattle and sheep are raised and exported in great numbers. Wild dogs are so numerous as to be a pest.

The flora of Madagascar is abundant, and about 700 out of 3,000 species are peculiar to the island. Many of them are of exquisite beauty. It is a paradise for the orchids, more and more beautiful species being found here than in all other countries. The forests abound in peculiar and valuable timber.

Ethnology and Tribal Divisions: The origin of the Malagasy and their race affinities with the other Oriental nations have led to great controversies among the most eminent ethnologists. It is generally agreed that the original inhabitants of the island were from some of the African races, and most probably Zulus or Kaffirs. Tho dark, they seem to have been negritos rather than negroes. A small remnant of them were still living in 1843, and it is believed that a few are yet to be found in the southwest.

In regard to the present inhabitants of the island, known as the Malagasy, these facts are settled: They all speak the same language, the dialects differing no more than the Yorkshire and Lancashire do in England; and this language is of very close kindred with the Malay. There is a marked difference in color, features, and hair among the different tribes: some are of fine stature and physique, but very dark, with curly or frizzly black hair; their features are more Polynesian than negro; others are of lighter complexion, with straight or very slightly curled hair, generally of good height, and well formed. The Hovas, who have been the ruling tribe, are generally somewhat below the middle stature, of a light-olive complexion, frequently fairer than the Spaniards, Portuguese, or Italians. Their hair is black, but soft, fine, and straight or curling; their eyes are hazel, their figures erect and, tho small, well proportioned; the hands and feet small, and their gait and movements agile, free, and graceful.

The theory of their origin which is best supported seems to be that these tribes are of Malayan or Malayo-Polynesian stock; that they came to the island at different times, crowding the aboriginal inhabitants before them, and in the case of the Betsileo tribes south of Imerina, perhaps, intermarrying with them.

In 1810 the principal tribes of Madagascar were: 1. The Sakalava, divided into the northern and southern tribes, occupying the western coast and including many smaller clans; their members were estimated at 1,500,000. 2. The Betsimisaraka, with several clans, and including the Betanimena, occupying the east coast, about 1,500,000 more. 3. The Sihanaka and Tankarana, northeast provinces; about 500,000. 4. The Bara and Tanala and some smaller tribes, in the southeast, 500,000. 5. Imerina, the land of the Hovas, then about 600,000; and 6. The Betsileo, 1,200,000. The last two were the highland provinces.

Social and Religious Conditions: Tho discovered in medieval times, no effort was made by Europeans to explore or colonize Madagascar till 1506, when the Portuguese, after some exploration in 1540, undertook to enslave and Christianize its inhabitants. They made repeated efforts to this end in the next hundred years, landing small colonies and establishing trading-posts, whence they sold the people who came under their power as slaves. These natives were Sakalavas, who did not choose to be the prey of European slave-dealers, and massacred the Portuguese colonists and priests in 1548, 1585, 1600, and 1615. The English and Dutch made several attempts to plant colonies at various points on the coast of the island between 1595 and 1640. Both nations were at that time engaged in the slave trade.

In 1642 the French undertook to colonize Madagascar, and within the next 170 years they had organized several great companies or societies, and planted many colonies, in which Lazarist and Jesuit priests were always conspicuous; but owing to their maintenance of the slave-trade, and their treacherous dealings with the natives, four or five of these colonies were attacked and massacred. The last of these societies was obliged, in 1686, to surrender its charter and its whole property to Louis XIV., King of France, who claimed, but never exercised, authority over it. For the next thirty or thirty-five years the northern part of the island was the most formidable rendezvous of pirates who infested the Indian Ocean. They treated the natives well, and several of the tribes were on friendly terms with them; but their rendezvous was finally broken up in 1723. It was not until 1754 that another attempt was made by the French to plant a colony in Madagascar, and this was broken up by a massacre; and during the war between France and England, in the year 1811, the only two remaining trading-posts, Tamatave and Foule Point, with a mere handful of men in each, were surrendered to the English, as the sole possessions of France in Madagascar.

In all these 170 years of French occupancy there is no mention of more than one Malagasy convert. He had been taken to France and educated, and was killed by his own countrymen with some French priests murdered in 1663. The social condition of these tribes at the beginning of the 19th century was deplorable. They were in continuous war with each other, taking captives to sell as slaves to any foreign merchant who was willing to buy. In fact, the staples of Madagascan trade being slaves and rum, the state of morals was as low as it could be.

The religious system of the Malagasy exercised no influence on their moral natures, and indeed made no pretense of doing so. It was simply supposed to confer upon them temporal benefits; why or for what service on their part does not appear. Their religious system was not as artificial or philosophical as that of many heathen nations. They believed in a supreme being who ruled over all; they also had an idea of subordinate deities, who ruled over certain places, persons, or interests. They also paid a sort of homage to their deceased ancestors, but reared no temples or statues to them. There being no idol temples, there were few idolatrous processions, no priestly class in rich robes and exerting almost regal power.

In the place of priests were "medicine men," who were masters of divination, and who professed to discover crime by the ordeal of administering poison to the suspected one. As to religious worship in public, on certain great feasts, such as the new year, the curious fetishes which served for idols were brought out and during five days were carried about in procession. Meantime all law was in abeyance and the most horrible licentiousness prevailed.

The government of the various tribes was by chiefs. It was not necessarily hereditary, tho confined to the class of nobles (Andriana), and was as often, perhaps, in the female as in the male line, and there was much intrigue, and sometimes bloodshed, before the ruler was selected. Once on the throne, however, the chief's government was an absolute despotism, sometimes "tempered by assassination." There was no written language in any of the tribes; the decrees of the sovereign were promulgated by heralds. The government was feudal in its character; the chief and the nobles held the tribe in bondage; they owned all the land, and the people as well; if either the ruler or the nobles required any work done, the clansmen were called out and required to perform the service, providing themselves with food and clothing for the time required. This forced service was called *fanompoana*, and it existed in a modified form until some time after Madagascar became a French colony.

For the most part, during the 17th and 18th centuries, the Sakalavas, who were divided into two great tribes—the Northern and Southern Sakalavas—seem to have been in the ascendancy. The Hovas and Betsileos were at this time unknown to the outside world. Neither the Portuguese, the French, the Dutch, nor the English had ever heard of them except in terms of contempt. They were the dogs, the slaves of the Sakalavas. But in 1785 an *Andrian*, or chief, of the Hovas, called Impoinimerina (the desire of Imerina), succeeded in uniting the divided clans of the province of Imerina under his own authority, and by his superior abilities and diplomacy gained to his cause several of the smaller adjacent tribes; but while he proceeded to subdue most of the forest tribes, he was yet compelled to pay tribute to the Sakalava of the western coast. Between 1808 and 1810 he died, and his son, trained in part by Arab teachers, and not over 17 years of age, was proclaimed as Radama, King of the Hovas.

Radama was a very remarkable man. It was his purpose from the day he ascended the throne to throw off the Sakalava yoke and make himself king of Madagascar. To carry out this purpose he negotiated a treaty with the English Governor of Mauritius, Sir Robert Farquhar, by which in return for a promise to suppress the export of slaves from Madagascar, the king was to receive yearly from the British Government money, arms, ammunition, etc., etc. This treaty was ratified after much difficulty October 11, 1820. Meanwhile, early in 1818, without waiting for the final ratification of the treaty, the LMS sent two missionaries, Rev. S. Bevan and D. Jones, with their families, as their first missionaries to Madagascar. Messrs. Bevan and Jones landed at Tamatave August 18, leaving their families in Mauritius. They were kindly received by some of the chiefs, and collected together a number of children, whom they taught, and made some studies in the language. Two months later they brought their families to Andovoranto, on the coast, where a station was established. But soon all were attacked with the deadly Madagascar fever, and before two months had passed Mr. Jones was the sole survivor of the two families. Mr. Jones was obliged to go to Mauritius to recuperate, and did not return to Madagascar until October 4, 1820. King Radama welcomed him cordially, and gave the fullest permission for English Protestant missionaries to settle at his capital. The LMS, awake to their great opportunity, sent forward their missionaries, teachers, and artisans as rapidly as practicable, and very soon the mission work was actively prosecuted in all directions. The first work, of course, was the acquisition of the language and its reduction to writing. The missionary teachers were preparing books in the Malagasy language; the artisans were teaching the people carpentry, weaving, tanning, and blacksmith work; and a printing-press having been sent out, and fonts of Malagasy type cast in England, they were soon printing school-books and portions of the Scriptures, and instructing the young and teachable Malagasy boys in the art of printing. No missionaries ever worked harder, and none had more evident manifestations of the divine blessing on their labors. Necessarily, the schools held a prominent position in their work for the first few years. Nearly 100 schools were established in the capital and its vicinity, and between 4,000 and 5,000 pupils of both sexes passed through them before 1828, having received the elements of a good education. The instruction in the arts and trades was also making great progress. A church was organized from the English residents in the capital, and tho small in numbers, it was very active in Christian work, and those who understood the Malagasy tongue were encouraged to gather the young Hovas for religious instruction and singing. Two congregations of natives for Christian worship were formed in Antananarivo, and very fully attended; others were formed in villages around the capital. In January, 1828, the Gospel of St. Luke in Malagasy was put to press, and other portions of the Scriptures were printed as rapidly as they could be properly prepared.

It was at this time, when the missionaries were beginning to feel encouraged at the great success which seemed to be within their grasp, that King Radama died, on the 27th of July, 1828. Radama was not a Christian, and his death, at the early age of thirty-six, was undoubtedly due to his excesses. But he had many good traits: he was patriotic, manly, and truthful; he was far-sighted; ambition led him to desire the improvement and elevation of his people, and without any convictions of the necessity of personal religion, he was persuaded that Christianity would be better for his people than heathenism. The loss of such a ruler, at such a time, seemed the severest blow which could be inflicted upon this infant mission. Radama had selected his nephew as his successor, if he left no son; but one of his twelve wives contrived to secure the throne, which she ascended as Ranavalona I. Her first official act was the putting to death of all the near relatives of the late king, and all the officers who had been most attached to him. Some of these were speared, but others of the highest rank, and among them the mother and sister of Radama, and the husband of the latter, were starved to death. No one was left alive who could contest her claim to the throne. The British resident, Mr. Lyall, was ordered to leave the country at a few hours' notice, and his family were subjected to gross insults. The missionaries and their followers were naturally alarmed at these indications of a coming storm of persecution.

In 1829-1831 the queen was engaged in war with the French, whom she defeated. The revolution in France prevented a renewal of the invasion, and the queen turned her armies upon the coast tribes, ravaging their lands and slaughtering the inhabitants during three years. During this period she found little time to persecute the Christians, among whom she believed there were very few natives; while she hated the missionaries, she was disposed for a time to allow them to improve the condition of the people. Accordingly, at the end of six months after Radama's death, the missionaries were permitted to resume their labors, and the schools, the translation of the Scriptures and other books and their printing went forward rapidly; the New Testament translation was completed, and soon after, by the aid of the British and Foreign Bible Society, its printing was commenced. Through the children in the schools, and those who had gone out from them, these portions of the Scriptures were widely circulated; and when in 1832 all the boys above thirteen years of age in the schools were drafted into the army, large quantities of these and other good books were widely circulated. In 1833 not less than 15,000 copies of parts of the Scriptures were finished, and upward of 6,000 of them were sent out.

Meantime there were many converts. On the 29th of May Mr. Griffiths baptized twenty, and the first native church was formed. In the course of a few months there were several churches with nearly 2,000 members. Then the queen withdrew the permission to baptize converts, forbade the use of wine at communion, and those of her officials who had been baptized were put into inferior positions. Before 1833 the attempt was made to divest the education given in the schools of any religious character. In July, 1834, the queen forbade any native except those in the government service to learn to read or write. This and other proclamations indicated that the whole force of the queen's displeasure was to be visited on the native Christians; and a few who had manifested some friendship for the Christians (tho not one of those who had received baptism) began to withdraw from them, and associate with the heathen portions of the community.

Ratsimanisa, who had been the commander-in-chief of the army, and about this time became prime minister to the queen, was the chief persecutor, and prompted her to greater cruelties than even her brutal nature demanded. It was clear to him that if Christianity was not arrested the idolatry of the country would be overturned, and the customs of their ancestors forgotten; and in January, 1835, at his instigation, a formal accusation was made against the Christians, before the chief judges of the Hovas, and the following charges were preferred: 1st. They despise the idols; 2d. They are always praying; 3d. They will not swear, but merely affirm; 4th. Their women are chaste; 5th. They are of one mind with regard to their religion; 6th. They observe the Sabbath as a sacred day. It seems that their enemies could allege nothing against them, "except it were concerning the law of their God."

Five of the missionaries were now ordered to leave the island on the ground that their permits of residence had expired. On the 26th of February, 1835, several officers, headed by Ratsimanisa, entered the chapel at Ambatonakanga in the capital and read a letter from the queen addressed to the missionaries, forbidding religious worship, the rite of baptism, and the assembling of a society, to her subjects. The Europeans were permitted to follow their own customs and religious practises, but they could not be allowed to teach them to the subjects of Ranavalona. They would be allowed to teach such arts and sciences as would be beneficial to her subjects, but nothing beyond these.

A great mass meeting, or *kabary*, of all the people was now called for March 1. There was firing of cannon and musketry, and the soldiers surrounded the multitude to inspire them with terror, and then the principal judge addressed the *kabary*, delivering a long message from the queen, calling upon all who had been baptized, all who had worshiped and kept the Sabbath, or had entered into a Christian society, to come forward and accuse themselves, and confess such crimes, under pain of death. Ratsimanisa repeated the substance of the queen's royal message, and some of the head men replied to it with servility. Others seemed reluctant to make reply, when Rainiharo, one of the queen's chief officers, and for twenty-five years a prime minister, the bitterest of persecutors, said that unless the guilty came forward within a month to accuse themselves, the officers and judges would cut off their heads. The queen reduced the time for confession to a week. About two thousand confessed, and on the 9th of March, 1835, she pronounced sentence on them. Some hundreds of Christian officers were degraded and about 1,600 persons not in government service were fined, while any Malagasy seen in company with a missionary was ordered to be put in chains. All portions of the Scriptures and other religious books were ordered to be given up, under the severest penalties; but many were concealed, and gave comfort to the persecuted ones in after years. All religious meetings were prohibited, and spies commissioned to hunt the Christians and their forbidden books.

Altho in June and August, 1835, Messrs. Cameron, Freeman, Chick, and Kitching left Madagascar by order of the queen, Rev. Messrs. D. Johns and E. Baker remained to give what comfort and help they could to the little band of faithful disciples. They also determined to complete the translation and printing of the entire Scriptures and of the *Pilgrim's Progress*. Their Malagasy printers and compositors had been compelled to leave them, but they toiled on till they had completed both books, and printed an edition of about one thousand copies, which were soon absorbed by the Christians, who concealed them, as far as possible, from the government spies. Probably the larger part were eventually confiscated, but a considerable number came to light after Ranavalona's death. Being again ordered to leave the island, Messrs. Johns and Baker departed in July, 1836, but not till they had bid the converts an affectionate farewell, preaching at great risk in the old chapel at Ambatonakanga from the text, "Lord, save us; we perish." They retreated to Mauritius, but Mr. Johns, at least, visited the island more than once, and in 1840 penetrated to the capital, where he found to his sorrow that many of the disciples had been called to suffer martyrdom, while nine at the time of his visit were put to death at Ambohipotsy. Mr. Johns made great efforts to secure the escape of some of the Christian fugitives to Mauritius. A few did escape, but the strict watch kept up by the queen rendered it almost impossible for them to evade her spies. In 1843 Mr. Johns again visited the

French island of Nosi-Bè, near the northwestern coast of Madagascar, but succumbed to the fever, and died a martyr to his zeal for the rescue of the Malagasy converts.

Greatly to the astonishment of Queen Ranavalona, her plan for extinguishing Christianity in Madagascar signally failed. She had closed the schools; prohibited all religious meetings; sent away all the missionaries; confiscated all the Scriptures and religious books she could find; degraded, fined, and whipped the Christians, and threatened them with severer punishments; and yet their number was increasing every day. She determined upon severer measures, for she had sworn a solemn oath to root out Christianity if she had to put every Christian to death.

Early in 1836 Rafaravavy, a woman of high rank, was accused of Christianity, and was condemned to death; but the queen, being alarmed by a great fire in the capital, spared her life, but fined her heavily. The avowed executions for professing Christianity did not begin until August, 1837, when a prayer-meeting was discovered and broken up. The storm of persecution now increased in violence, and a large number of Christians were condemned to death. There were many hundreds of these sufferers for Christ's sake, but none of them turned back to the vile life of the heathen; and, what was especially astonishing to the queen, there were scores of adherents to the new faith for every one whom she put to death. The persecution raged fiercely in 1839, 1840, 1841, and 1842.

The years from 1843 to 1848 were marked by a decided lull in the persecution. The queen was in difficulties with both England and France, and her attention was diverted from the Christians by the incidents of the war. In this lull of the persecuting spirit the Gospel made great progress. The queen's son, Rakoto (afterward Radama II.), took a great interest in the Christians, and it is said professed conversion; Prince Ramonja, his cousin, was already an active Christian, and had suffered for the faith, and, among others of noble rank, the son of Rainiharo, the prime minister of the queen, and the most violent persecutor among the Hovas, had joined the Christians. The native preachers preached and baptized almost openly in the suburbs of the capital, and very many were added to the churches. Another fiery baptism came in the early months of 1849. Some of the Christians were hurled over the cliffs; some were burned at the stake—many were crucified.

Every possible indignity was inflicted upon those who were condemned to death. These executions were continued till hundreds had perished. In addition to those who endured the extreme penalty of death by these various modes of destruction, a far larger number suffered in other ways, and in very many cases their sufferings terminated in death or helplessness. Thirty-seven preachers, with their wives and families, were consigned to a life of irredeemable slavery. Altogether, in the early spring of 1849 probably more than 2,000 were thus punished and tortured as Christians or friends of Christianity. This cruel persecution went on for years. Numbers fled to the mountains, or hid themselves in the depths of the neighboring forests, eking out a scanty subsistence, until want and exposure put an end to their lives. Others constructed hiding-places in their own houses, in their rice-pits, and on their own farms, and were there tended and supplied with food by their relatives for years, reappearing long after they had been accounted dead. All the testimony, both heathen and Christian, shows that not only was there no recantation among these converts to Christianity, many of whom were illiterate and but recently brought to Christ, but that they bore the gross indignities and the cruel and terrible deaths to which they were subjected with quiet heroism and unfaltering trust in God. "Let us go and see how these Christians behave: they are said not to be afraid to die," were the words of some of the principal officers of the royal household. The same officers said afterward: "We were near, and saw all that took place. The Christians were not afraid, and did not recant."

Their fortitude and courage produced a deep impression on the minds of the people. Many said: "This is the finger of God; there must be something divine in this belief;" and they were led to become Christians notwithstanding the peril to which it exposed them.

This persecution continued with great fury till 1852, when the death of Rainiharo, the prime minister; the influence of the young prince, which was exerted in favor of Christianity; and of his cousin Ramonja, who was an active Christian—were instrumental in producing greater toleration.

During this period of comparative quiet, **Rev. William Ellis,** Foreign Secretary of the London Missionary Society, made three visits to Madagascar, in the hope of bringing comfort to the suffering, faithful disciples in Imerina, in 1853, 1854, and 1856. In these visits he was able to cheer and comfort many of the Christians, to distribute many copies of the Malagasy New Testament, and in his third visit to make the acquaintance of the young Prince Rakoto (later Radama II.). He was also presented to the queen, who treated him courteously, but coldly. Three months after his last visit, on the 3d of July, 1857, the last great persecution commenced. On that day the population of the capital were driven from their homes by the soldiers to a great National Assembly. The queen announced her determination to stamp out Christianity. All suspected persons were imprisoned, and daily meetings were held in the city and its neighborhood to denounce the Christians. It was believed that this was the most fatal of all the persecutions. A large number were sentenced to the tangena ordeal, by which many died, and many more were put in chains and reduced to slavery. This persecution was maintained for nearly three years. But on the 15th of August, 1861, the queen died. She had reigned thirty-three years, and twenty-five of those years had been marked by vain efforts to root out Christianity from the island. The result had been that those who were persecuted "went everywhere, preaching the Word." Christian life had attained a depth, power, and reality which would have been impossible in a time of ease and prosperity. Several thousands had been put to death in various ways. Yet the little company of believing men and women, left as sheep without a shepherd in 1836, had multiplied at least twenty-fold in 1861.

On the 18th of August in that year, Prince Rakoto, the son of Ranavalona I., succeeded his mother with the title of Radama II. "The sun did not set on the day on which Radama II. became King of Madagascar," says Mr. Ellis, "before he had proclaimed equal protection to all its inhabitants, and declared that every man was free to worship God according to the dictates of his own conscience, without fear or danger."

Within a month after the queen's decease eleven houses were opened for the worship of God in the capital and great numbers in the adjacent country, and churches were being erected everywhere, and filled Sabbath after Sabbath with rejoicing worshipers. Within a very few years memorial churches were erected on the chief places of martyrdom. Thus, Antananarivo became famous alike for its churches and palaces.

Radama II. invited the missionaries of the LMS, and especially his friend, Rev. William Ellis, to return. Mr. Ellis reached the capital in June, 1862, and was followed by three ordained ministers, a medical missionary, a teacher and a printer, who were all soon busy resuming the work laid down in 1836. Christianity had triumphed. The 2,000 adherents to the Christian cause, who then braved the rage of the persecuting queen, had become a host of 40,000, only about one-fifth of them baptized believers, but all witnesses for Christ, and ready to suffer and die for Him. Back of these were more than 100,000 who, tho not believers, had rejected idols and were ready to embrace Christianity.

Radama II. was a man of fair abilities and of a kindly and amiable disposition. He had, in the later years of his mother's life, been very heartily in sympathy with the Christians, and had boldly defended them, sometimes at the peril of his own life. He had never united with any of the churches, nor did he profess to be a Christian after he came to the throne. But he cordially invited religious teachers to come to the country, and extended the invitation to foreign traders, at the same time abolishing all export and import duties. The immediate result of this was that the cheap, vile rum of the Mauritius was poured into the island in immense quantities, and the great trade in bullocks and other commodities was paid for in this horrible stuff. The king now became intimate with a Frenchman named Lambert, who led him into intemperance and other vices. While intoxicated the king signed contracts conceding to Lambert over one-third of the arable land of Madagascar, the privilege of working all its mines, and of bringing in as many Jesuits as he wished. The king also surrounded himself with dissolute young men who controlled appointments and really governed the realm. The devotion of the king to these boon companions led to a revolution, and Radama II. was strangled, being succeeded by the queen, Rabado.

In all her relations with the missionaries and Christians, the queen, who took the name of Rasoherina, was a good and just ruler, and during her reign the churches prospered, and the mission work went on. She died April 1, 1868. On the 2d of April, 1868, Ramoma, a niece or cousin of the late queen, was proclaimed Queen of Madagascar under the title of Ranavalona II. The prime minister, Rainilaiarivony, a man of extraordinary ability, was not, probably, at that time a Christian, tho he had been for years a student of the Scriptures. One after another changes were now made, and it soon became understood that Madagascar was to be a Christian kingdom, and that Ranavalona II. was to be the first Christian queen of the island. On the 3d of September, 1868, the first public occasion when the sovereign formally appeared before the people took place. It was celebrated with great pomp and ceremony, and prayers were offered by one of the native pastors. On the 19th of February, 1869, the queen, following the example of former queens, was married to the prime minister, Rainilaiarivony. Two days later, after a very careful and thorough examination, the queen and prime minister were baptized and received into the palace church by Audriambelo, one of the most eloquent and devoted of the native pastors. It was the custom with each sovereign of Madagascar to erect at the beginning of the reign some stately building, usually a palace, in the royal enclosure. Queen Ranavalona II. commenced the erection of a stone church in the palace enclosure in July, 1869.

The idol-keepers and the idol-worshipers of Imerina saw that the power would soon pass out of their hands, and they were enraged. The principal idol-keepers came to the palace and demanded that the queen should return to the worship of her ancestors. The language used was treasonable, and after a hasty consultation it was decided to burn the idols of the Royal Palace. This was done on the 8th of September, 1869, in the presence of many witnesses. The people followed the example of the queen, tho with many apprehensions of evil and disaster, and the greater part of the idols were destroyed.

In a few days requests came from all parts of the island: "You have destroyed our gods, and we know not how to worship according to the new religion; send us teachers." So many requests of this sort came to the prime minister that he called the missionaries together, and after deliberation 126 teachers were sent out, all selected by the missionaries of the LMS.

Thus was the final blow struck which insured the supremacy of Christianity in the island of Madagascar. Fifty years before they were in the darkest depths of heathenism; forty years before there was not a native Christian among the millions of the Malagasy; now there were probably 50,000 communicants, 150,000 adherents, many thousand scholars in the schools, and a population of at least 1,500,000 asking for Christian instruction. Outside of Imerina, the Sakalava, the Bara, the Betanimena, the Betsimisaraka, and many of the smaller tribes— that is to say, at least two-thirds of the whole population—were still savages and idolators of the worst sort, liars, thieves, bloodthirsty, and lustful; they persisted in making raids for plunder and slaves, until the queen's firm and gentle management made them ashamed. Even of her own Hova and Betsileo people, nearly 2,500,000 in number, only about 150,000 were nominally Christians; and the rest, tho their idols were burned, were liable to lapse into idolatry again if they had a determined leader.

The queen, as soon as possible, sent missionaries and teachers among these tribes who were in darkness. Above all her other acts of patriotism were those relating to slavery. She, by severe edicts, prohibited the importation or sale of any slaves in Madagascar; and, finding these edicts evaded, she ordered that every Mozambique slave should be set free, and be at liberty to return to Africa or remain on the island. As there were about 150,000 of these, the cost of this liberation was borne by her husband and herself from their own private fortunes. They had previously emancipated all their own personal slaves. This heavy sacrifice was made for the good of her country, and to please God.

It was now settled that Madagascar would henceforth be a Christian country, ruled by a most devoted Christian. This is not the place to go into details of the later history of Madagascar, or of the attacks made upon it by France. What seemed at first an incredibly absurd pretension, presented under the ill-grounded influence of Lambert and his Jesuit friends, finally became a stringent and formal demand, supported by the military force of a great nation. Queen Ranavalona II. died in July, 1883, in the midst of preparations to resist, by a patriotic uprising, the ultimatum which she deemed baseless, unreasonable, and outrageous. Her successor, Queen Ranavalona III., was an educated and active Christian. She carried on the war during two years, and then, defeated at all points, in 1885 she accepted the protectorate of France over her country. In 1896 this protectorate became annexation to the French colonial establishment, and in February, 1897, the queen was deposed by the French Governor and the Malagasy nationality ceased to be.

Tho France is not now a professedly Roman Catholic state, yet in its intercourse with foreign nations in Asia and Africa, and in the administrations of its colonies, it is represented by officials who seem inclined to place their whole power at the disposal of the Jesuits and other Roman Catholic missionaries. Consequently, there was a period of five or six years when it seemed as if the evangelical church and school buildings in Madagascar would be transferred like captured property to the Roman Catholic Church, their pastors and teachers treated as public enemies, and their English instructors expelled. "This (French) occupation," says Professor Warneck, "gave the Jesuits, who since the end of the fifties had been forcing their way into the country, the opportunity they desired of turning the hatred felt by the fanatical French colonial politicians toward the British to account, in order to procure, by skilful intrigue, the systematic oppression of the evangelical missions. Under the watchword, 'French is equivalent to Catholic,' the religious liberty which was proclaimed with so much display of rhetoric has been set at defiance. Evangelical Christians and native pastors have been suspected as rebels, imprisoned and put to death; many evangelical churches and chapels have been confiscated, and by the violent introduction of French * * * many evangelical schools have been ruined, not to speak of the numerous conversions wrought by violence and cunning among the terrorized people." But there is light in the dark cloud. The Paris Missionary Society has come heroically to the rescue during these trying times; the Anglicans, the Quakers, and the Norwegians have suffered comparatively little from the violent counter-mission of the Jesuits; and a change for the better has taken place in the educational work. At the Ecumenical Conference of 1900, Mr. Cousins uttered these encouraging and significant words: "So far from lessening the number of workers in the various Protestant missions, the troubles of recent years have brought new workers into the field." At this writing there are nearly 200 Protestant European missionaries at work in Madagascar—a much larger number than ever before; and the societies working on the island, with their stations, are as follows: Friends' Foreign Mission Association, 5 stations; London Missionary Society, 12 stations; Paris Evangelical Mission Society, 14 stations; Society for the Propagation of the Gospel, 21 stations; Norwegian Missionary Society, 23 stations, and the Lutherans have 8 stations.

Ellis (W.), *History of Madagascar*, 2 vols., London, 1838; the same, *The Martyr Church*, London, 1869, Boston, 1870; the same, *Madagascar Revisited*. London, 1867; Shaw (G. A.), *Madagascar of To-day*, London, 1886; Sibree (Jas.), *Madagascar before the Conquest*, London, 1896; Keller (C.), *Madagascar, Mauritius and other African Islands*, London, 1900; Cousins (W. E.), *Madagascar of To-day*, London, 1895; *Missionary Review of the World*, Vol. IX, pp. 9, 422; Vol. XI, 67, 148, 225, 272; Vol. XV, 436, Funk & Wagnalls, New York.

MADANAPALLI: A town in the District of Cuddapah, India, situated 45 miles N. by W. of Chittur, with a population of 6,500. Mission station of the RCA (1865), with (1903) 1 missionary and wife, 71 native workers, 14 outstations, 12 chapels, 15 Sunday schools, 3 young people's societies, 13 day schools, 3 boarding schools, 1 dispensary, and 581 professed Christians, of whom 170 are communicants.

MADARIPUR: A town and river mart in the district of Faridpur, India, situated at the confluence of the Arial Khan and Kumar Rivers, 40 miles S. W. of Dacca. Population, 13,800, of whom 9,100 are Hindus and 4,700 Muslims. Mission station of the BMS (1886), with (1903) 2 missionaries and their wives, 43 native workers, 17 outstations, 23 day schools, 29 Sunday schools, 4 young people's societies and 3,394 professed Christians, of whom 1,071 are communicants.

MADIUN: A town of about 18,000 inhabitants in Java, Dutch East Indies, situated 80 miles W. S. W. of Surabaya. Mission station of the Netherlands Mission Society (1854), with (1900) 1 missionary and wife, 3 native workers, 1 outstation, and 1 day school. The Society spells the name Madioen.

MADRAS: Capital of the Madras presidency, and the third city in size and importance in all India, being outranked only by Bombay and Calcutta. It is situated on the east coast of the peninsula of India. Population (1901) 509,346. The first settlement was begun in 1639, when a grant of land was obtained by Mr. Francis Day, a servant of the East India Company, from the Hindu prince who possessed jurisdiction in that region. A factory or mercantile establishment of the Company and slight fortifications were at once erected, and the city has grown steadily from that beginning. The origin of the name is uncertain. The word "Madressa" signifies a Mohammedan school, and some scholars consider the name of the city to have been derived from that word. In 1653 Madras was made the seat of the local government or presidency of the East India Company's territory in South India. In 1746, during the time when the French power in South India threatened to eclipse the English, it was taken by the French commander La Bourdonnais, but was restored two years later by the treaty of Aix-la-Chapelle. Within a century of the first settlement Madras had become the largest city in South India. Its growth since then has been less than that of Calcutta or Bombay, for its natural advantages are far less than those enjoyed by its sister cities. It has no natural harbor; vessels are obliged to lie off at a distance of a mile, more or less, from the shore, and for many years freight and passengers were transported between the shore and the ships in surfboats, for the skilful management of which, through the surf which breaks unceasingly on the beach, the boatmen of Madras are famed. In 1862 a pier was constructed, which extends out 300 yards into the sea; and more recently still the construction was undertaken of an artificial harbor, consisting of two parallel breakwaters curving toward each other at the outer end. The city is by no means compact, but stretches along the shore of the Bay of Bengal for more than 9 miles, and its territory extends 3 miles inland. Of the population more than three-fourths are Hindus. The Mohammedans number only one-eighth; Christians nearly as many. Tamil is spoken by more than half of the entire population; Telugu by a litle less than a quarter.

Danish missionaries had been operating at Tranquebar and other points south of Madras for a number of years early in the 18th century before any form of Christian work was attempted in Madras itself. In the year 1716, with the help of the English chaplain at Madras, they commenced a Christian school, which, however, languished and soon ceased altogether. In 1726 Schultze, one of the missionaries at Tranquebar, made a journey to Madras, began the school work again, and laid the foundations of the first Protestant mission in the capital of South India. A few years afterward the Society for the Propagation of Christian Knowledge, of England, undertook its support, Schultze continuing in charge of it. The missionary labored hard, preaching, teaching, translating and writing. Results were not slow in appearing. In the one year 1729 Schultze baptized 140 persons; by the end of 1736 the converts numbered 415. The mission was encouraged by the Madras Government. Other missionaries arrived from Europe, and the work went on apace. In 1746 the capture of the city by the French was the occasion of much distress to the mission; its work was interrupted, its buildings destroyed, and its church used by the French conquerors as a magazine. In 1748, when the city was returned to the English, the missionaries and Christians who had fled during the troubles came back, and operations were resumed—still under the fostering care of the government. By the end of the 18th century some 4,000 persons had been received into the Christian church. With all this apparent success it may be doubted if the real achievements were very great. These numerical results were not carried over into the present century; on the other hand, when the first converts died off there seemed to be no vital Christianity behind them as a basis for further progress. With all their devotion and industry the earlier missionaries did not use the best methods of labor.

With the beginning of the 19th century began the new era of missionary work in Madras and throughout all India. Of the great missionary societies which were formed near the year 1800 the London Missionary Society was first on the ground at Madras in 1805. Their collegiate institution was begun in 1852, and has had a most successful and useful career. The CMS began work in 1814. From the first this mission paid much attention to education, as well as to preaching, and schools for both sexes were carried on with vigor. The CEZ began its work for women in 1876. The WMS came in 1816. About the year 1826—just 100 years after its establishment by Schultze—the original mission of the Christian Knowledge Society was transferred to the care of the SPG. The ABCFM entered the field in 1836, but withdrew in 1864 in order to concentrate its strength more effectively elsewhere. The Leipzig Society entered Madras in 1848. The Established Church of Scotland began a mission in 1837, and devoted its energies, as in Calcutta and Bombay, especially to the higher education, through the medium of the English language. The fervid eloquence of Dr. Duff of Calcutta during his first visit home is said to have been the exciting cause of the beginning of the Madras work. The Scotch institution was begun in 1837 with 59 pupils, but had 277 on its rolls before the end of the following year. After the disruption of the Scotch Church the Madras missionaries sided with the Free Church and their work is now carried on by the UFS. In 1843 another mission of a similar character was begun by the Old Kirk, and in 1893 the Church of Scotland Woman's Committee took up work there. The Strict Baptists have a small mission in Madras, begun in 1866, and the Danish Lutherans another dating from 1878. The Christian Literature Society for India has here its central station, tho its schools for the training of teachers are in other parts of India. There is also a mission especially for lepers, over 400 of whom were reported in the census of 1881. The usual missionary agencies are reenforced by the Bible and Tract Societies and by the Society for the Propagation of Christian Knowledge—the venerable organization which so long supported the mission started by Schultze, but which now works wholly through the press. The ME, under the lead of Rev. Wm. Taylor, began work in 1872, at first directing its efforts especially to unevangelized Europeans and Eurasians, tho not neglecting persons of other races who might be brought under its influence. The ABMU commenced its operations in 1878. The YMCA and the YWCA also have flourishing centers in the city. The Salvation Army has a strong post here.

Besides the mission chapels, the city is well provided with Protestant churches for the accommodation of Europeans, and with Roman Catholic churches for persons of all nationalities who adhere to that form of Christianity. The usual institutions of a philanthropic or literary character which spring up everywhere in the path of enlightened and liberal government, such as hospitals, libraries and the like, are not wanting in Madras. Education is in a fair state of progress. Taking all of the societies together the Protestant missionary enterprise in Madras and its suburbs now (1903) has 104 missionaries, men and women; 766 native workers, men and women; 36 places of worship, 135 day schools, 18 boarding schools and higher educational institutions, 2 printing houses and 8,551 professed Christians, including baptized children and 4,508 communicants.

MADRAS PRESIDENCY: One of the general divisions into which British India is divided. It is ruled by a governor and council appointed by the crown under the governor-general and viceroy of India. This presidency covers the southern portion of the Indian peninsula—with the exception of the territory still under native princes. Its eastern boundary is the Bay of Bengal, its western the Indian Ocean. But the territory of the presidency extends along the coast of the former for some 1,200 miles, while its western shore line, along the Indian Ocean, extends only 540 miles. On the north and northwest it joins (proceeding from east to west) Orissa, a part of the Bengal presidency; then the Central Provinces; then the dominions of the Nizam at Haidarabad, and finally, as its boundary line nears the Indian Ocean, the presidency of Bombay. Near the center of this irregular triangular territory is the great native state of Mysore, including five smaller native states which are closely related to the Madras Government, and directly subordinated to it. The total area of the presidency is 149,092 square miles, and the population (1901) 42,400,000. The presidency may be divided, as to its physical aspects, into three well-marked areas. Along the eastern coast, between the range of hills known as the Eastern Ghats and the sea, is a broad strip of low country. A similar, tho narrower and more diversified, strip of land extends along the western coast, between the Western Ghats and the Indian Ocean. The interior consists of a tableland, supported on its western edge by the Western Ghats and sloping down gradually toward the Bay of Bengal on the east, its boundary on that side being the eastern range just alluded to. Much of the high interior is occupied by the native state of Mysore. The mountains rise to greater heights as they go south; the highest peaks of Southern India are those of the Nilgiri and Anumalai groups, several of which are between eight and nine thousand feet high.

The population is chiefly Hindu. 37,026,471 Hindus, 2,732,931 Mohammedans and 1,934,480 Christians, with 673,905 Animists or spirit-worshippers, make up the list of religions in the census of 1901, whose adherents exceed 30,000.

The Hindus of this presidency, and some of the so-called aboriginal tribes also, belong to the Dravidian family, of which the strongest subdivision is that now known as the Tamil. People of this race appear, in prehistoric times, to have occupied the Gangetic valley, and to have been pushed south by the invading Aryans as they moved down the valley and spread over the peninsula.

The language of the Dravidians still persists in the various languages of South India. Of these the Tamil is the most important and is spoken by over 12,000,000 in the presidency; the Telugu is used by almost as large a number; the Kanarese is spoken by about 1,300,000; the Tulu is preserved only by a remnant of the people among the mountains in the west of the presidency and is doomed doubtless to disappear as a spoken language. The Coorg and the Malayalam (2,400,000) also belong to this stock. The languages of the aboriginal tribes above mentioned are also Dravidian. The original religion of the Dravidians, before the coming of the Aryans, was probably some form of demon-worship, such as the jungle tribes still preserve.

A word must be said as to the connection of the English with the presidency. Calicut and Cannanore on the west coast were occupied by the East India Company as places of trade in 1616. The Company had been preceded first by the Portuguese, and as their power waned, by the Dutch. But finally the former concentrated themselves at Goa, and the Dutch withdrew. On the east coast, Masulipatam, north of Madras, was occupied by the English traders in 1611. The first English settlement on the site of Madras City was in 1639 (see Madras City). The French occupied Pondicherri, south of Madras, in 1672. It was not until the middle of the 18th century, when the English and French powers were in armed rivalry in Europe, that the thought of a possible rivalry for supremacy in India began to be realized. In 1746 Madras was overpowered and captured by the French commander La Bourdonnais, but restored to the English two years later, at the peace of Aix-la-Chapelle. But the country was occupied with weak and tottering dynasties of native princes. In their contests among themselves, the English would befriend one princeling and the French another. The strife between the Oriental principals could not fail to extend itself to the European powers by which they were respectively seconded; and for half a century the fate of South India hung undecided between the French and English. Dupleix undertook to unite the native powers into one combination under French protection, but his plans were defeated by the military skill first of Lord Clive, afterward of Sir Eyre Coote. Haidar Ali, and his son Tippu Sultan, the only members of a Mohammedan dynasty which erected itself on the ruins of a Hindu principality in Mysore, withstood the progress of English power with a fierceness which at one time threatened to stop it altogether. But in 1799 Tippu Sultan died in the breach at his capital, Seringapatam, the English entered the fort in triumph, and military opposition, from whatever quarter, to the English power in South India was at an end. Since then the English Government has had hardly any use for its Madras army, save for police purposes.

To the historian of Indian Christianity the Madras Presidency is the most interesting portion of India. Tradition says that the Apostle Thomas preached the Gospel here, and Mount St. Thome, near Madras, is his traditional burial place. Pantanus found Christians in India in the 2d century. A branch of the Syrian Church settled on the west coast, near Cape Comorin, centuries ago, and this "Syrian Church of Malabar" preserves its ancient liturgies, and still acknowledges subjection to the patriarch of Antioch. Here also Xavier preached and baptized in the 16th century, and the Jesuit missionaries of Madura in the 17th. And here was the beginning of the Protestant missionary movement in India, by the hands of two young Danish missionaries (Bartholomew **Ziegenbalg** and Henry Plutschau), in 1705. Tranquebar (on the coast south of Madras) was the first station occupied. The Society for Promoting Christian Knowledge in a few years assumed support of the mission. But it was long before a distinctively English mission was founded. **Schultze** came in 1719, and in 1726 began the first really successful mission in Madras City. Kiernander came in 1740; but in 1746, when the French were besieging Cuddalore, where he was stationed, and rendering his operations there impossible, he removed to Calcutta, and became the father of Protestant missions in the Bengal presidency. In 1750 Christian Frederic **Schwartz** landed in South India, and until his death in 1798 labored uninterruptedly for the good of the people and the progress of the cause of Christ. No better or greater name adorns the history of Protestant missions in India than his.

By the labors of these great and good men and their associates congregations were gathered, schools established and churches founded at Tranquebar, Madras, Trichinopoli, Tanjore and other places. Converts were baptized by the hundred and the thousand. Yet with all their excellences of character, their ability, their piety and their zeal, these men did not plant a self-sustaining, manly and vigorous Christianity. Their churches exist, but with diminished numbers and enfeebled strength. The churches gathered by them have in many cases been surpassed by those more recently organized, not alone in numbers, but in aggressive character and influence. For about a hundred years the work begun by the missionaries of the 18th century was subsidized by the SPCK, which to a large extent furnished the funds, while the missionaries themselves came from Denmark and Germany. Early in the 19th century this Society transferred the missions to the SPG, and in due time the *personnel* of the mission staff came to be recruited wholly from the English Church, even as the money came from the same source.

The introductory labors of the missionaries of the 18th century were followed by work on a larger scale, more systematically and energetically pursued during the 19th century. We record here the principal agencies operating in this more recent era. The London Missionary Society leads the way. Two missionaries of this Society occupied Vizagapatam, on the east coast, far north of Madras, in 1805, during a period when the Indian Government, taught by the directors of the East India Company at home, was bitterly opposed to the entrance of missionaries in India. The missionaries at Vizagapatam, however, were not molested, and when in 1814 Parliament, in the new charter granted that year to the company, inserted a clause favoring missionary operations, and the opposition of the government ceased in consequence, the LMS was all ready to establish a station in Madras City. Bellary, northwest of Madras, near the boundary line now separating the presidency from that of Bombay, had been occupied in 1810, and Coimbatore was occupied in 1830. The Church Missionary Society entered Madras City in 1815, and took over the Palamcotta station (in the Tinnevelli district) from the Danish missionaries, who had planted it in 1785, in 1817. In the same year the SPG began work at Cuddalore, and assumed, during the years 1820-29, charge, from the Society for Propagating Christian Knowledge, of most of the old Danish missions. The Wesleyan Missionary Society appeared upon the scene at Madras in 1816, and at Trichinopoli two years later. The Basel Evangelical Missionary Society began its work, which since has spread over all the western portion of the presidency, and into many of the Kanarese districts of the Bombay presidency, in 1834. The English Baptist Missionary Society planted a station in the Ganjam district, the most northerly of those bordering on the Bay of Bengal, in 1837. The American Board of Commissioners for Foreign Missions, whose mission among the Tamil-speaking people of Jaffna, in North Ceylon, had been begun soon after 1820, colonized thence, first to Madura in 1834 and to Madras in 1836; Arcot was occupied by this Society in 1855, but its work there was a year or two afterward transferred to the Dutch Reformed Church (as it was then called) of the United States, by which church it has since been maintained with much vigor. The Church of Scotland came to Madras in 1837, and since the Disruption in 1843 two Scotch missions have worked there side by side, and to some extent also in the interior. The American Baptist Missionary Union began its work—now of large proportions and of extraordinary success—in Nellore and other parts of the Telugu portion of the presidency, in 1840. The Leipzig Lutherans came in 1841 to Tranquebar and adjacent stations, where the Lutherans of the preceding century had labored with such assiduity. There are also small German missions elsewhere in the presidency—that of the Hermannsburg Lutherans at Nellore (1865), of the American German Lutherans in the Krishna district (1842), and an independent tho successful German mission in the Godavari Delta, which dates from 1838.

The chief successes of this army of Christian laborers have been won in the Tinnevelli district, where the Christian churches and communities are very numerous, and where the native Christians are numbered by thousands. In the Telugu districts, also under the charge of the American Baptists, there have been ingatherings of surprising vastness and power; the American missionaries in the Arcot and Madura districts have also been very successful. Probably in no other part of India has Christianity taken so firm a hold.

MADSCHAME. See MAJAM.

MADURA: A city (and district, the city being the capital of the district) in the Madras presidency, India, situated on the S. bank of the Vaigal River, about 275 miles south-southwest from Madras. The population of the city is (1901) 105,984, of whom 94,000 are Hindus. The language of the Hindus is Tamil, tho with the progress of education the rising generation of natives is more and more familiar with English. Madura has long been a most important place. It was the seat of an ancient dynasty of Hindu kings (the Pandyan), whose history stretches back into prehistoric times, and is adorned with the usual wealth of myth and legend. As the Mohammedan power stretched south in the 15th and 16th centuries this Hindu kingdom was overthrown, tho no Mohammedan dynasty took its place; but on the ruins of the old state rose another Hindu dynasty—that of the Nayaks—which culminated in the 17th century, when most of the architectural works at Madura, which still attest the power and wealth of this line of princes, were completed. During the political chaos of the next century the Nayak kingdom in its turn crumbled. Mahratta and Mohammedan armies successively overran the region, until at last the British came, and in 1801 Madura passed into their possession. The religious history of the place chiefly concerns us now. It contains one of the most famous Hindu temples—that of the goddess Minakshi—in India. The temple enclosure is 847 feet long and 744 feet broad, and contains, besides the shrines of the goddess and of the god Siva, a vast collection of buildings—halls, bazars, etc.—occupied by the priests and temple attendants. The conspicuous features of the temple are the great towers, 9 in number, which rise above its outer walls, in one case reaching to the height of 152 feet.

The Christian history of Madura is of much interest. The famous Roman Catholic missionary Francis Xavier gathered a little church here in the 16th century. In 1606 a Jesuit mission was begun here by Robert de Nobilis, who lived as an ascetic, was renowned for his sanctity and learning, and his complete mastery of the Tamil language. Following him were men of like spirit, notably John de Britto, who suffered martyrdom in 1693, and Beschi, who prepared the first Tamil grammar, and whose writings are regarded as models of pure Tamil style. The native converts in the region about Madura were estimated at a million or more, won largely by the great concessions to Hinduism which the missionaries made. The number of Catholic Christians now in the district has greatly dwindled, hardly 70,000 being returned in the census of 1881.

The history of Protestant effort begins in 1834, when the place was occupied by Messrs. Todd and Hoisington, connected with the ABCFM mission in Jaffna, Ceylon, which had been founded in 1816. The work of the American missionaries has been carried on vigorously and successfully ever since. In process of time they occupied most of the important towns in the district round Madura as mission stations, established schools of different grades, gathered congregations of Christian adherents and founded churches, composed of such as gave credible evidence of piety. They have labored as preachers on their tours and in the churches, as teachers in their schools, as writers, and editors through the medium of the press, as physicians through their labors in hospitals and dispensaries. This Society now (1902) has at Madura 2 missionaries and their wives, 3 women missionaries, 140 native workers, men and women; 18 outstations, 14 preaching places, 13 day schools, 3 high-grade boarding schools, 2 hospitals, 2 dispensaries and 700 professed Christians. It is a station also of the Leipzig Missionary Society (1874), with (1903) 2 missionaries, one with his wife; 1 woman missionary, 22 native workers, men and women; 14 outstations, 10 places of worship, 5 day schools, 1 boarding school and 727 professed Christians, of whom 697 are communicants. The SPG also has a native evangelist here.

MADURANTAKAM: A town in Madras, India, situated about 50 miles S. by W. of Madras. Station of the WMS, with (1903) 1 missionary, 46 native workers, 10 outstations, 13 chapels, 21 day schools, 14 Sunday schools, 1 theological class, and 174 professed Christians, of whom 108 are communicants.

MAEBASHI. See MAYEBASHI.

MAFEKING: A town on the railway to Buluwayo, near the Transvaal boundary, and about 800 miles N. E. of Cape Town. Station of the WMS, with (1903) 2 missionaries, 118 native workers, 23 outstations, 155 chapels, 23 Sunday schools, 8 day schools, and 1,513 professed Christians, of whom 1,223 are communicants.

MAFUBE: A settlement in Griqualand East, S. Africa, situated about 90 miles N. W. of Shepstone. Station of the Paris Evangelical Mission (1884), with (1903) 1 missionary and wife, 22 native workers, 9 outstations, 1 Sunday school, 8 day schools, and 1,000 professed Christians, of whom 637 are communicants.

MAGDALA: A village on the Mosquito Coast, Nicaragua, Central America, situated 15 miles N. by E. of Bluefields. Station of the Moravian Missions (1855), with (1901) 1 missionary and his wife, 7 native workers, 1 outstation, 1 Sunday school, 1 chapel, and 87 professed Christians.

MAGOMERO: A settlement in British Central Africa, situated in the Shirè region, about 25 miles N. E. of Blantyre. In 1861 Bishop Mackenzie, leader of the Universities Mission, on his way up the Zambesi met a gang of slaves. He liberated them, settled them at Magomero, and began their education. The insecurity of the region at that time made a change necessary in the locality where such waifs were to be taught, and in 1864 the whole colony was removed to Mbweni, on the island of Zanzibar.

MAGOYE: A settlement in German East Africa, situated in the district north of the N. end of Lake Nyasa, a little to the N. of Bulongoa, on high land free from malaria. Station of the Berlin Missionary Society (1900), with (1903) 1 missionary, 1 native worker, 2 outstations, 1 day school, and 28 professed Christians.

MAHABELASHWAR: A town in Bombay Presidency, India, situated on a long ridge 4,500 feet high, and 70 miles S. E. of Bombay. Station of the Poona and Indian Village Mission, with (1900) 7 missionaries, one with his wife; 2 women missionaries, and a rest home.

MAHAICA: A settlement in British Guiana, South America, situated on the Mahaica River, 40 miles S. of Better Hope. Station of the West Indies Wesleyan Eastern Annual Conference, with 1 missionary and his wife, 4 outstations, 5 chapels, 5 Sunday schools, 6 young people's societies, 3 young men's Christian associations, 5 day schools, 1 temperance society, and 422 professed Christians.

MAHANORO: A town on the E. coast of Madagascar, situated about 90 miles S. E. of Antananarivo. Station of the SPG (1884), with (1902) 1 missionary, 1 woman missionary, 1 native worker, 1 day school, and 629 professed Christians, of whom 124 are communicants. Society spells the name Mahonoro.

MAHASOARIVO: A suburb of Antananarivo containing the normal school (for Imerina) of the Paris Mission. Station of the Paris Evangelical Society (1899), with 1 missionary and wife, 1 missionary woman, 3 native workers, and 1 hospital. Society spells the name Mahazoarivo.

MAHE ISLAND. See SEYCHELLES ISLAND.

MAHERESA: A village in Madagascar, 125 miles W. of Fianantsaroa. Station of the Paris Evangelical Mission Society (1898), with (1903) 3 missionaries, two of them with their wives; 102 native workers, 37 outstations, 7 Sunday schools, 3 societies for young people, 2 young men's Christian associations, 2 young women's associations, 37 day schools, 2 boarding schools, 1 industrial school, 1 dispensary, 2 orphanages, 1 theological class, and 850 professed Christians. Society spells the name Mahereza.

MAHITSY: A village and district in Imerina, Madagascar, lying to the N. W. of Antananarivo, on the Majunga road about 15 miles from the city. Station of the LMS (1902), with 1 missionary and his wife.

MAHOBA: A town in the United Provinces, India, situated 87 miles S. S. W. of Cawnpur on the railway between Banda and Allahabad. Population, 8,500. Station of the CWBM (1895), with (1903) 1 missionary and his wife, 6 women missionaries, 3 native workers, 1 chapel, 2 Sunday schools, 1 day school, 1 kindergarten, 1 dispensary, 1 orphanage, 91 professed Christians.

MAHONORO. See MAHANORO.

MAHOW. See MHOW.

MAIANA. See GILBERT ISLANDS.

MAIDZURU: A town in Hondo, Japan, situated near the coast about 40 miles N. of Kobe. Station of the PE (1895), with (1903) 1 missionary, 1 native worker, 4 chapels, 4 outstations, and 25 professed Christians.

MAIJAM: A town in Bengal, India, situated about 30 miles N. by W. of Raniganj. Station of the PB, with (1900) 1 missionary and wife and 1 orphanage. Society spells the name Mihijam.

MAI-MAI-KAI: A town in Manchuria, China, situated 120 miles N. N. E. of Mukden. Station of the UFS (1898). The work has not been fully reorganized since the Boxer disturbance, but is carried on (1903) with 14 native workers, 6 outstations, 2 places of worship, 5 Sunday schools, and 377 professed Christians.

MAIMANSINGH: A town of Bengal, India, situated by Nasirabad, 74 miles N. of Dacca; capital of the District of Maimansingh. Population, 11,600, of whom 6,500 are Hindus. Station of the Victoria Baptist Foreign Mission Society (1885), with 1 missionary and wife, 3 women missionaries, 6 native workers, 2 places of worship, 2 Sunday schools, 2 young people's societies, 2 day schools, 1 orphanage, and 23 professed Christians. Society spells the name Mymensingh.

MAIN: A village in the Transkei District of Cape Colony, Africa, situated 78 miles N. of East London. Station of the UFS (1876), with 1 missionary and his wife, 26 native workers, 12 outstations, 1 place of worship, 11 day schools, and 573 professed Christians.

MAINPURI: A town in the United Provinces of India, situated 40 miles W. of Fatehgarh; capital of the District of Mainpuri. The town is in two sections, one of which is called Mukhamganj. Population, 18,600, of whom 13,800 are Hindus and 4,000 Muslims. Station of the PN (1843), with (1903) 2 missionaries and their wives, 11 native workers, 2 outstations, 1 place of worship, 14 Sunday schools, 5 day schools, 1 boarding school, and 220 professed Christians, of whom 44 are communicants. Society spells the name Mainpurie.

MAIRANG: Village in Assam, India, situated in the Khasia Hills, near **Mao-phlang**, with which its mission statistics are included.

MAJAM: A village in German East Africa, situated in the Wajaga region on the slopes of Mt. Kilima Njaro, 190 miles N. W. from the seaport of Tanga. Station of the Leipzig Mission Society (1893), with (1903) 1 missionary and his wife, 7 chapels, 4 day schools, 1 high school, and 40 professed Christians, of whom 19 are communicants. Society writes the name Madschame.

MAJAWERAM. See MAYAVARAM.

MAKAPAANSPOORT: A village in the Transvaal, South Africa, situated in the Waterberg district, at the foot of the Sefakaolo Mountain. Station of the Berlin Missionary Society (1865), with (1903) 1 missionary, 13 native workers, 10 outstations, 1 day school, and 487 professed Christians, of whom 247 are communicants. The chief, Lekalekale, when the missionaries first took up their residence at the station, prohibited his tribe, on pain of death, from intercourse with them, and what success the station has had has been won in the face of great obstacles.

MAKAPAN-STADT: A village in the Transvaal, Africa, situated on the Aapies River, in the Waterberg district, about 32 miles N. of Pretoria. Station of the WMS, with 1 missionary, 9 native workers, 14 outstations, 24 places of worship, 14 Sunday schools, 9 day schools and 1,771 professed Christians, of whom 1,497 are communicants.

MAKERE: A settlement in British East Africa, situated on the Tana River, about 60 miles N. of Golbanti. Station of the Neukirchen Mission Institute (1898), with 2 missionaries, one with his wife, and 1 day school.

MAKOTOPONG. See KREUZBURG.

MAKOULANE: A settlement in Portuguese East Africa, situated in the extreme S. W. of the colony, about 60 miles S. W. of Lourenço Marques. Station of the Romande (French Switzerland) Missionary Society, with (1903) 1 missionary and his wife, 2 native workers, 3 outstations, 4 places of worship, 4 Sunday schools, 4 day schools and 28 professed Christians.

MAKOWE: A settlement in Zululand, South Africa, about midway between Durban and Lourenço Marques. Station of the South Africa General Mission (1896), with 1 missionary and his wife, 1 woman missionary, 1 native worker, 1 chapel, 1 Sunday school and 1 day school.

MALA: A station of the New Hebrides Mission Society at the southern end of Espiritu Santo Island.

MALA: The island usually called Malayta, in the Solomon group, Melanesia.

MALABAR, Syrian Church of: Travancore and its sister kingdom, Cochin, which adjoins it on the north, are famous as the home of an exceedingly ancient branch of the Christian Church, usually known as the "Syrian Church of Malabar," Malabar being the name applied for many centuries to the strip of coast embracing the kingdoms named and the British district just north of them. The origin of this church is doubtful. The traditions current among the people go back to the preaching of Thomas, in the middle of the 1st century; but scholars suppose that a small colony from Antioch (Syria) may have landed here in the 4th century. The church is Syrian in doctrine and ritual, maintaining the Nestorian type of Christology, and is subject to the Patriarch of Antioch, tho the Romanists have tried hard to subject it to the Pope, and did succeed, in 1599, in detaching some 80,000 members from the patriarch, and in thus forming a Romo-Syrian community, which is still allowed, however, to retain the Syrian ritual and language. The remainder of the Roman Catholic population represents chiefly the results of Francis Xavier's missionary activity in the 16th century. The existence of this ancient Syrian Church attracted the attention of Rev. Dr. Buchanan (then chaplain to the East India Company at Tinnevelli), and at his urgent suggestion the Church Missionary Society, in 1816, sent missionaries to labor among its members. At first the Syrian priests cooperated with them, but in 1838 signs of hostility appeared, which culminated in the Syrian *Metran* (or Metropolitan) dissolving all connection with the English missionaries. Since then the Church Mission has devoted its attention to the people at large, with the most gratifying results, drawing their converts from the old church in part, but very largely from Hindus, and especially from certain low castes. Gradually there has arisen in the Syrian Church a reform party which is in close relations with the CMS missionaries and appears to be gaining influence for the awakening of the long slumbering Malabar church.

Missionary Review of the World, Vol. IX, p. 750; Funk & Wagnalls, New York, 1896.

MALACCA: A portion of the Straits Settlements of Great Britain, lying along the western coast of the Malay peninsula between Singapore and Penang; consists of a strip of territory about 42 miles in length and from 8 to 24½ miles in breadth. Its surface is hilly, but not mountainous, and it is drained by five navigable rivers, making the soil alluvial and rich. The climate is equable and healthful. In 1901 the population numbered 95,487, of whom 73,833 were Asiatics, 74 Europeans or Americans and 1,498 of mixed blood. There is no mission station in Malacca.

MALAGASI LANGUAGE: A language of the more civilized peoples of Madagascar. It is of the Malayan family and was reduced to writing by missionaries, being written with Roman letters.

MALAN: A village in the Transkei district of Cape Colony, South Africa, situated 13 miles N. E. of Butterworth. Station of the UFS (1875), with (1903) 1 missionary and his wife, 14 native workers, 15 outstations, 20 Sunday schools and 655 professed Christians.

MALANG: A village in the Loanda district, Angola, Africa, situated about 250 miles W. from San Paolo de Loanda, on the line of the railway from that place. Station of the ME (1885), with (1903) 4 missionaries, two of them with their wives; 3 women missionaries, 1 place of worship and 6 professed Christians.

MALAYALAM LANGUAGE: One of the Dravidian family of Indian languages, spoken by the people of Malabar and Travancore in the southwest part of the peninsula of Hindustan. It is the vernacular of about three millions of people and is written with characters peculiar to itself. It is also called Malayalim.

MALAYAN LANGUAGES: A family of languages, of great simplicity of structure and of sounds, used by the natives of the Malay peninsula, of Madagascar, of the islands of the Dutch East Indies, the Philippines, Polynesia and New Zealand. The tribes in the interior of the larger of these islands have languages generally classed as of independent stock, and the same seems to be true of the people of the Melanesian Islands, altho they are often classed as Malayan. Australians have an entirely distinct language. In the case of those islands which we have named, the Malay characteristics are clearly evident, altho the various dialects are numerous. The Malay language proper is the *lingua franca* of the East Indian Archipelago. Its most cultured dialect is that of the towns of Sumatra and Java. Its phonetic elements are simple, the grammatical structure is regular and its vocabulary, especially in nautical terms, is very copious. It has the five vowels, *a, e, i, o, u*, short and long, with one diphthong. The consonants are *b, d, g, h, j, k, l, m, n, ñ. p, r, s, t, w, y, ng, ch*. Malay is a dissyllabic language, with the accent as a rule on the penultimate, except where that syllable is open and short. Derived words are formed by prefixes, affixes, infixes and reduplication. Much skill is displayed in the idiomatic use of the hundred or more derivative forms. There are no inflectional forms to distinguish number, gender or case. Number is denoted only when absolutely necessary by the use of the adjectives *sagāla*, all, and *bāñak*, many, or by *sa* or *satu*, one, with a classifier. As in the Chinese language, classifiers are numerous, such as *orang*, used in speaking of persons; *kĕping*, piece, for flat things. Gender is distinguished by the use of auxiliary words. Case is indicated by position. Verbs have no person, number, mood, or tense. Long sentences are avoided, and in a sentence first comes the subject, then the verb, followed by the object, and qualifying words follow the words they qualify.

The Arabic alphabet is used for writing Malay, having been introduced at the time of the Mohammedan conquest. A great number of Arabic words have also been introduced into the vocabulary.

The literature of the Malays consists mainly of proverbs, and love poems of four lines. Their religious literature is remarkable mainly for its independence, and the fact that it does not show the influence of Islam.

The great branches of the Malayan language are the Polynesian, found in the islands of the South Pacific, the Hawaiian, the Malagasi and perhaps the Fijian, found in the Fiji Islands. As said above, the evidence of a Malayan origin for the language of Fiji and the multitudinous dialects of Melanesia is not conclusive.

The earliest recorded use of a Malayan language for evangelistic writings was in 1662, when Brouwers, one of the Dutch Church ministers in Java, began a translation of the Bible, using Roman letters in writing it. Roman letters have become established as the alphabet for writing the Malagasi and the Polynesian Malayan languages. But in the Malaysian Islands the Arabic letters having become naturalized long before the date above named, the use of Roman letters in writing Malay has not widely found favor.

MALAYS: 1. In its strictest sense this name is given to the inhabitants of the Malay peninsula, Penang and Sumatra, who belong to the Mongol race, modified by the mixture of other blood. In physical appearance they are of somewhat short stature; brown complexion—not so light as the Chinese or so dusky as the Hindu; have straight, black, coarse hair; no beard; large mouth; flat nose; large, dark eyes; somewhat thick lips; small hands and feet, with thin, weak legs. In temperament the Malays are thoroughly Asiatic—taciturn, undemonstrative, cunning, treacherous, and at times cruel. Their passions are easily aroused, and under specially exciting circumstances, such as love, jealousy or religious fervor, they reach a height of frenzy during which they run "amuck," assailing violently all whom they meet.

We find three principal classes: the *Orang benua*, "men of the soil," or hill-tribes; the *Orang laut*, "men of the sea," who are the daring, skilful, adventurous seafaring men of the Indian Archipelago, and the *Orang Malyeru*, or Malays proper, the civilized class, who exhibit more of refinement and are courteous and kind to their families and friends. The Malay sailors were the formidable pirates who formerly menaced commerce and were the dread scourge of the Indian seas. Their deeds of cruelty, treachery and cunning, aided by their daring, brave, audacious seamanship, are still the theme of stories of adventure. Even at the present time few ship captains care to have a crew composed entirely of Malays, tho they form the largest part of the sailors on the Indian and Chinese coasts.

Mohammedanism was embraced by the Malays in the 13th and 14th centuries, the fierce, uncompromising, aggressive spirit of that religion finding quick response in their natural temperament.

2. In a wider sense the term is applied to the races inhabiting the Indian Archipelago and the islands of the Pacific, embracing an area 13,000 by 5,000 miles, from Easter Island to Madagascar and from New Zealand to the Hawaiian Islands. This wide dispersion of the race has been the subject of much study and theory, but the causes of it, and proof as to the fact, are not within the limits of this article. A classification of this wider definition is as follows: (1) Malay. (2) Malay Javanese: the inhabitants of the Ladrones, Formosa, Philippine Islands, the Dutch East Indies and Madagascar. (3) Melanesia, Fiji Islands, which, by the way, is not always admitted. (4) Polynesian: The Hawaiians, Marquesas Islanders, Tahitians, Raratongans, Samoans, Tongans, Maoris. To these Wallace adds the Papuans, who are the farthest removed from the Malays, yet whom he considers to be of the same stock. They represent the extreme difference in type, due to the mingling of other races with the Malays, and have frizzly hair, are tall and black, bearded and hairy-bodied. The mental characteristics of the Papuan are also different from the Malay type, and they are impetuous and noisy. Between the two extremes every gradation is found, varying with the preponderance of either the Malay or Papuan type. In some of the provinces of China, in Formosa and Hainan, the aborigines, who seem to have affinity with the Shans and Laos, are also allied to the Malays. Mohammedanism does not accompany the Malays in their dispersion, and low forms of superstition, of fetishism and of demonolatry take its place. Christianity has made considerable headway, not only in Madagascar and Polynesia, but in the Malay Archipelago and even among Mohammedan Malays.

MALAYTA ISLAND: One of the Solomon Island group in Melanesia, lying S. E. of Isabel Island. It has an area of 2,395 square miles. Station of the Melanesia Mission. Society spells the name Mala.

MALEGAON: A town in Bombay Presidency, India, situated in the District of Nasik, on the Gurna River, 64 miles N. W. of Aurangabad. Altitude, 1,460 feet. Population, 15,500, of whom 9,800 are Muslims and 5,600 Hindus. Station of the CMS (1848), with (1903) 1 missionary and wife, 43 native workers, 2 outstations, 16 day schools, 1 dispensary, and 619 professed Christians, of whom 172 are communicants. Society spells the name Malegam.

MALITZI: A village in the Transvaal, South Africa, situated 16 miles N. W. of Pietersburg. Station of the Berlin Missionary Society (1877), with (1903) 1 missionary, 9 native workers, 6 outstations, 2 day schools, and 232 professed Christians, of whom 114 are communicants. Society spells the name Moletsche.

MALIYI: A settlement in the Shirè Highlands, British Central Africa, situated about 13 miles N. W. of Blantyre. Station of the Zambesi Industrial Mission, with 1 missionary and his wife, 3 outstations, 1 place of worship, 4 Sunday schools, 4 day schools, 1 industrial farm, and 10 professed Christians. Society spells the name Maliya.

MALLICOLLO ISLAND. See NEW HEBRIDES.

MALNA: A settlement in Upolu, Samoa, and station of the LMS.

MALO: Station in southern part of Espiritu Santo Island in the New Hebrides. See MALA.

MALOKONG: A village in the Transvaal, South Africa, situated about 35 miles W. by N. of Pietersburg. Station of the Berlin Missionary Society (1867), with (1903) 1 missionary, 11 native workers, 15 outstations, 1 day school, and 281 professed Christians, of whom 186 are communicants.

MALTA: An island in the Mediterranean, south of Italy; a British crown colony, and an important naval station. Area, 95 square miles. Population, 188,141 (English, 2,138; foreigners, 1,097, the remainder natives). Language, a patois of Arabic. Religion, Roman Catholic, the old laws of the island for the defense of that church being maintained by the British Government.

Malta was for many years the most important missionary station in the Mediterranean, and was occupied by all the missionary societies seeking to work in the Levant. The mission press of the ABCFM was established here prior to its removal to Smyrna, and it was here that Wm. Goodell and his associates studied the Turkish and Armenian before establishing themselves at Smyrna, Constantinople, and Beirut. It is now occupied as a preaching station by several of the Colonial Societies of England and Scotland, especially the Scotch Free Church. Representatives of other societies visit the island, and the Bible has been published in Maltese with some acceptance.

MALVALLI: A town in Mysore, India, situated about 30 miles W. N. W. of Mysore City. Station of the PB, with 2 missionaries and their wives, 1 woman missionary, and 1 orphan asylum.

MAMBA: A village in German East Africa, situated on the slopes of Mt. Kilima Njaro, in the Wajaga District, about 10 miles N. by W. of Taveta. Station of the Leipzig Mission Society (1894), with (1903) 3 missionaries, 4 places of worship, 2 day schools, 1 boarding school, and 65 professed Christians.

MAMBOIA: A town in German East Africa, situated in the Usagara Hills, about 130 miles W. by N. of Bagamoyo. Station of the CMS (1879), with (1903) 1 missionary, 2 women missionaries,

3 native workers, 4 outstations, 4 places of worship, 7 day schools, 1 dispensary, and 64 professed Christians, 22 of whom are communicants.

MAMRE: A village in the Malmesbury District of Cape Colony, Africa, situated 28 miles N. of Cape Town, with a population of 1,500. Station of the Moravian Missions (1808), with 3 missionaries and their wives, 36 native workers, 1 place of worship, 2 day schools, and 511 professed Christians.

MANAGUA: Capital of Nicaragua, Central America, situated 157 miles S. S. E. of Tegucigalpa, on Managua Lake, and connected by rail with Granada on Lake Nicaragua. Station of the Central America Mission, with 2 missionaries and their wives and 1 woman missionary.

MANAKAVALY: A village of lepers, in Madagascar, situated 3 miles N. of the LMS station of Isoavina, 12 miles E. of Antananarivo. It was built some ten years ago on the initiative of Rev. Mr. Peake (LMS), and its preacher and inhabitants are all lepers, maintained by the French Government, cared for by the deaconesses of the Paris Missionary Society, but aided in church and school work by the LMS. The Paris Evangelical Society has there 2 women missionaries, 4 native workers, and 1 leper asylum, belonging to the French Government. There is also a home for untainted children of lepers. The LMS has 1 native worker and 1 place of worship, with 200 professed Christians, all lepers.

MANAMADURA: A town in Madras, India, situated 30 miles S. E. of Madura. Station of the ABCFM (1864), with (1903) 2 missionaries and their wives, 36 native workers, 36 outstations, 14 places of worship, 4 Sunday schools, 6 day schools, 2 boarding schools, 1 industrial school, and 153 professed Christians.

MANAMBONDRO: A village on the E. coast of Madagascar, situated about 116 miles N. of Ft. Dauphin. Station of the Norwegian Missionary Society.

MANANJARY: A town in Madagascar, situated at the mouth of Mananjary River, on the E. coast. Station of the SPG, with (1903) 2 missionaries, 1 native worker, and 796 professed Christians. Society spells the name Mananjara.

MANANTENINA: A settlement on the E. coast of Madagascar, situated about 62 miles N. E. of Ft. Dauphin. Station of the Lutheran Free Church Mission Society (1895), with 1 missionary and wife, 10 native workers, 7 outstations, and 1 place of worship.

MANASOA: A village in Madagascar, situated about 63 miles E. of St. Augustine's Bay. Station of the Lutheran Free Church Mission Society (1901), with 1 missionary and wife, 4 native workers, 4 outstations, and 1 place of worship.

MANCHU LANGUAGE: The language of Manchuria, Chinese Empire, and the court language of the present Imperial dynasty of China. It belongs to the Tungusian branch of the Ural-Altaic family, and on the whole is the best-known of the Tungusian tongues. It follows the rule of all Tatar languages in observing the requirements of harmony in the vowels of words, insisting on the division of vowels into "hard" and "soft" classes. Naturally, it has received and adopted a certain number of Chinese words. It is written with an alphabet peculiar to itself, which, however, can be traced to the letters of the Syriac alphabet.

MANCHURIA: One of the divisions of the Chinese Empire lying north of China proper, between latitude 42° and 53° north. In accordance with the treaty of 1860 between Russia and China, nearly one-half of the former territory was given over to Russia, and the present limits are the Amoor on the north, the Usuri and Sunga-cha on the east, Korea on the south, from which it is separated by the Shan-Alin range, and on the west the Khingan Mountains, the Sira-Muren River, and the district of Upper Sungari separate it from the desert of Gobi. Its area is about 363,000 square miles. The population of Manchuria is estimated by the Chinese as 8,500,000. Physically, the country is divided into the mountain ranges on the north and east, among which lie numerous fertile valleys, and the plain which stretches south from Mukden to the Gulf of Liao-tung. The climate varies from 90° F. in the summer to 10° below zero in the winter. During four months of the year the rivers are frozen up; a short spring is followed by the heat of summer, and a few weeks of autumn usher in the snow and ice of the winter. Manchuria is gradually losing its native language and system of education under the influence of the Chinese. Until Russia's interference in 1900 the native Manchus had been used to reenforce Manchu garrisons in China, while a tide of Chinese had been pouring in. Russia has changed all this. The native Manchus are a finer race physically, mentally, and morally than the Chinese; they are of larger frame, lighter color, and have greater intellectual capacity. Mission work in this part of China is carried on by the Presbyterian Church of Ireland, and the UFS in the western and central districts, and the Danish Missionary Society in the coast regions of the south. Since the strategic points from Harbin to Port Arthur are mission stations, the military necessities of the Russian war with Japan have (1904) interrupted missionary work in what has hitherto seemed to be one of the most promising fields for Christian missions.

Ross (J.), *The Manchus*, London, 1880; James (H. E. M.), *The Long White Mountain*, London, 1888; Colquhon (A. R.), *The "Overland" to China*, London, 1900; Hozie (A.), *Manchuria*, London, 1901; Williams (S. Wells), *The Middle Kingdom* (Chinese Empire), 2 vols., new ed., New York, 1899; Williamson (A), *Journeys in North China, Manchuria and Eastern Mongolia*, 2 vols., London, 1870.

MANDAILUNG LANGUAGE: A dialect of the Batta (or Batak), spoken in Sumatra.

MANDINGO LANGUAGE: An African language belonging to the Negro group, and spoken by rather a large body of people found in French Guinea, West Africa, south of the Gambia River. It has been reduced to writing by missionaries, Roman letters being used for the purpose.

MANDALAY: A town in Upper Burma, British India, situated 386 miles by rail N. of Rangoon in a plain 2 miles from the Irawadi River. Part of the city is walled and is now a British military post, called Fort Dufferin. There are large manufactures of silk goods. Population, 168,300, of whom 147,000 are Buddhists and 13,700 Hindus. Station of the ABMU (1886), with (1903) 4 missionaries, three with their wives; 2 woman missionaries, 46 native workers, 279 professed Christians, 2 places of worship, 6 Sunday schools, 1 day school, and 2 boarding schools. Station also of the Mission to Lepers in India and the East (1890), with 1 place of worship and 1 home for untainted children of lepers. Station also of the Missionary

Pence Association (1892), with 1 missionary and his wife, 1 native worker, 1 outstation, 1 place of worship, 2 Sunday schools, and 40 professed Christians. Also station of the SPG (1868), with (1903) 1 missionary, 16 native workers, 1 day school, 1 place of worship, 1 boarding school, and 283 professed Christians, of whom 160 are communicants. Station also of the WMS, with 3 missionaries, 1 woman missionary, 21 native workers, 8 outstations, 6 Sunday schools, 7 day schools, 1 boarding school, 1 temperance society, and 166 professed Christians, of whom 137 are communicants.

MANDARI LANGUAGE: One of the non-Aryan languages of India; also called the Kol, and spoken by the Kolarian aborigines of Chota Nagpur in Bengal. It has been reduced to writing by missionaries with use of the Roman letters.

MANDOMAI: A village in the island of Borneo, situated 35 miles N. W. of Banjermassin. Station of the Rhenish Missionary Society, with (1903) 1 missionary and wife, 1 woman missionary, 10 native workers, 5 outstations, 1 Sunday school, 6 day schools, and 449 professed Christians, of whom 288 are communicants.

MANDRIDRANO: A town in Madagascar, situated 50 miles S. W. of Antananarivo. Station of the FFMA (1888), with (1901) 1 missionary and wife, 1 woman missionary, 80 native workers, 40 outstations, 250 professed Christians, 40 places of worship, 40 Sunday schools, 1 Young People's Society, and 1 dispensary.

MANEPY: A village in Ceylon, situated 5 miles N. W. of Jaffna. Station of the ABCFM (1831), with (1902) 1 missionary and his wife, 41 native workers, 4 outstations, 12 day schools, and 308 professed Christians.

MANGAIA. See HERVEY ISLANDS.

MANGALORE: A town and seaport in Madras, India, and capital of the District of South Kanara, situated on the W. coast of Hindustan, at the mouth of Netravati River, 127 miles N. N. W. of Calicut. Much of the coffee grown in Coorg is exported here. Population (1891), 41,000, of whom 23,000 are Hindus, 10,000 are Christians, and 7,600 are Muslims. Station of the Basel Mission Society (1834), with (1903) 15 missionaries and their wives, 3 women missionaries, 77 native workers, 6 outstations, 1 Sunday school, 18 day schools, 1 kindergarten, 1 theological class, 1 boarding school, and 2,799 professed Christians, of whom 1,687 are communicants. Station also of the Mission to Lepers in India (1891), with 1 leper asylum. The Societies spell the name Mangalur.

MANGAMBA: A village in Kamerun, Africa, situated about 10 miles N. of Bonaberi. Station of the Basel Missionary Society (1889), with (1903) 3 missionaries and their wives, 29 native workers, 38 outstations, 29 day schools, 1 boarding school, and 442 professed Christians.

MANGARI: A village in the United Provinces, India, situated near Babatpur Station on the railway, 14 miles N. W. of Benares. Station of the LMS (1874), with (1903) 1 missionary and wife, 28 native workers, 7 Sunday schools, 1 Young People's Society, 9 day schools, and 19 professed Christians.

MANILA: The principal city and capital of the Philippine Islands, situated on the S. W. coast of Luzon Island, at the head of Manila Bay. It has important suburbs on the N. bank of Pasig River. It was taken by the Spaniards in 1571, and by the U. S. in May, 1898. It has extensive commerce in sugar, hemp, tobacco, rice and dyestuffs. It has been many times visited by earthquakes, and is subject to typhoons. The climate is hot, damp and unhealthful. Population, 300,000. Station of the ABS (1899), with 1 agent. Also of the BFBS, with 1 agent and 1 bookroom. Also station of the ME, with 3 missionaries and their wives, 3 women missionaries, 5 places of worship, 4 Sunday schools, and 1,489 professed Christians, of whom 597 are communicants. Also station of the PE, with 4 missionaries. Also station of the Peniel Mission Society, with 2 women missionaries. Station also of the PN (1899), with 3 missionaries, one with his wife; 6 native workers, 1 place of worship, 1 Sunday school, 3 day schools, 1 dispensary, and 360 professed Christians. Station also of the United Brethren Women's Association (1901), with 2 missionaries. The YMCA (1900) also has a representative here and a Young Men's Christian Association.

MANISA: A town in Asiatic Turkey, about 50 miles east of Smyrna; the ancient Magnesia. It is still an important city. Population about 40,000, Muslims, Greeks and Armenians. For many years it was a station of the ABCFM, used as the missionary residence, on account of the heat of Smyrna. It is now (1903) an outstation of Smyrna, which is again the missionary center for the field.

MANKAR: A town and railway station in Bengal, India, situated in the District of Bankura, 32 miles N. W. of Burdwan. Station of the CEZ (1895), with (1903) 2 women missionaries, 6 native workers, 1 day school, and 1 dispensary.

MANNARGUDI: A town of Madras, India, situated 24 miles E. S. E. of Tanjore. Population (1891), 20,400, of whom 19,300 are Hindus. Station of the Leipzig Missionary Society (1897), with (1903) 10 native workers and 5 day schools. Church statistics are included in Sidambaram. Station of the WMS, with (1903) 3 missionaries, 73 native workers, 4 outstations, 7 places of worship, 12 Sunday schools, 12 day schools, and 201 professed Christians, of whom 133 are communicants.

MANNING'S HILL: A village in Jamaica, W. I., situated about 7 miles N. W. of Kingston. Station of the CWBM, with 1 missionary, 133 professed Christians, 1 place of worship, 1 Sunday school, 1 day school, and 1 Young People's Society.

MANONA: An islet of the Samoan Islands, situated 2 miles from the W. end of Upolu. It forms a natural fortress with the adjacent isle of Apolima, and has had great importance in local history. Station of the Australian Wesleyan Methodist Society, with 9 native workers, 2 places of worship, 3 Sunday schools, 3 day schools, and 67 professed Christians. Society spells the name Manono.

MANOW: A village in German East Africa, situated about 20 miles N. W. of the N. end of Lake Nyasa. Station of the Berlin Missionary Society (1892), with 1 missionary, 2 native workers, and 37 professed Christians.

MANSINAM: A village of New Guinea Malaysia, situated on the W. shore of Geelvink Bay, near its mouth. Station of the Utrecht Mission Society (1864), with (1901) 1 missionary and his wife, 2 native workers, 1 day school, and 56 professed Christians.

MANSURA: A town in lower Egypt, situated on the right bank of the Damietta arm of the Nile, about 28 miles N. E. by E. of Tanta. It is an important commercial town and has a population of 26,900. Station of the UP (1866), with (1903) 2 missionaries, 1 woman missionary, and 2 boarding schools. Society spells the name Monsurah.

MANUANE: A village in the Transvaal, South Africa, situated in the Marico District, about 27 miles N. W. of Zeerust. Station of the Hermannsburg Mission Society (1882), with (1901) 1 missionary and his wife, 6 native workers, 1 place of worship, 1 day school, and 1,392 professed Christians.

MANZANILLO: A town and seaport in Cuba, West Indies, situated on the E. side of a large bay on the S. coast, 85 miles W. by N. of Santiago. Population, 34,000. Station of the American Baptist Home Missionary Society (1899), with (1901) 1 missionary, 2 Sunday schools, and 42 professed Christians.

MAO-PHLANG: A village in the Khasia Hills, Assam, India, situated about 18 miles S. W. of Shillong and 60 miles N. W. of Karimganj. Station of the Welsh Calvinistic Methodist Mission, with (1903) 1 missionary and wife, 51 native workers, 114 outstations, 54 places of worship, 87 Sunday schools, 102 day schools, and 2,794 professed Christians, of whom 1,084 are communicants. Society spells the name Mawphlang.

MAORI LANGUAGE: The language of the aborigines of New Zealand. It belongs to the Polynesian branch of the Malayan family, and is written with Roman letters.

MAORIS: The aboriginal inhabitants of New Zealand, who belong to the Malay family of mankind. They claim to have migrated to New Zealand 500 years ago from "Hawaiki," which is supposed to be either Hawaii or Savaii of the Samoan Islands. They are a fine race, of average stature, with olive-brown skins, and their heads exhibit a high order of intellectual development. They are beardless, as a rule, but that is due in part to the custom of plucking out the beard with shells. Most of the race have long black hair, but some have reddish hair, and in others it is frizzly. Large eyes, thick lips, and large, irregular teeth are characteristic. The women are smaller than the men, and, generally, inferior to them. Tattooing was a universal practise previous to the introduction of Christianity. The custom of *taboo*, which has given a word in universal use among English-speaking people, was practised by the priests to make any person or thing sacred and inviolable. Such regard was paid to the sanctity of the taboo that even in war time tabooed persons or things were not harmed. Cannibalism was practised by the heathen Maoris, but has disappeared, together with infanticide, slavery, and polygamy, under the enlightening influences of Christianity.

The Maoris, like most races in tropical climates, marry young, but they are not a very prolific race. The people are very fond of music and songs.

MAPHOUTSING. See BETHESDA (BASUTOLAND).

MAPLES, Chauncy: Second Bishop of Likoma, Africa. Born February 17, 1852. Died 1895. Sailed for Zanzibar in March, 1876; and in July, 1877, he left Zanzibar for Masasi, where, for some years, he was to labor. About a year after Maples' arrival, a new station was founded at Newala, nearer the River Rovuma, where a number of native Christians from Zanzibar were settled; and from these two stations the missionary work gradually extended. From Newala, accompanied by a fellow-missionary and ten Masasi men as porters, he took a journey south from the Rovuma River into the unexplored country lying between it and the Mozambique, a tract which was an almost uninterrupted blank on the maps of those days and which he was the first European to penetrate. On the 12th of July they reached the goal of their journey, after a walk of three hundred and sixty miles in three weeks. On the 29th of July they arrived at the port of Luli, and thence they sailed northward by dhow and started northwest from Kisanga for another three weeks' walk, which brought them to Masasi, after they had accomplished over nine hundred miles of difficult country in sixty-eight days. In the latter part of 1886 Mr. Maples was appointed Archdeacon of Nyasa, and in the Autumn of 1887 he left Likoma to visit the wild Gwangwara bands on the mainland. Among these "thieves, robbers, and murderers," as he called them, he labored heroically, and never lost faith that "God's grace is able to turn these savage hordes into the children of Christ's Church." He was consecrated Bishop of Likoma in St. Paul's Cathedral in 1895, and without delay he set out again for Africa, where, nearly twenty years before, he entered upon his missionary career. When he reached Fort Johnston, at the junction of Lake Nyasa with the Shiré River, he found a little sailing boat belonging to the mission, and, not waiting for the German steamer, he decided to go by the boat to Likoma at once, by way of Kota-kota, on the west shore, where he was to leave his fellow-worker, Mr. Williams. During a violent storm the vessel sank, and both Bishop Maples and Mr. Williams were drowned. Bishop Maples had a special facility for acquiring languages, and in the first four years of his sojourn in Africa he mastered Swahili and Yao, and enough Makua to begin the translation of the New Testament.

MAPOON: A settlement on the W. side of Cape York Peninsula, Australia. Station of the Federate Churches of Australia, with (1900) 2 missionaries, 1 with his wife; 1 woman missionary, 1 Sunday school, 2 day schools. Station also of the Moravian Missions (1891), with (1900) 1 missionary and his wife, 1 woman missionary, 1 place of worship, 1 Sunday school, 1 day school, and 8 professed Christians.

MAPUTA: A settlement in Portuguese East Africa, situated on the River Maputa, about 25 miles from its mouth in Delagoa Bay. The territory between Maputa and the Bay is called one of the most pestilential districts of Africa. Station of the South African General Mission (1898), with 1 missionary, 1 native worker, 3 outstations, 1 place of worship, 1 Sunday school, 1 day school, 1 dispensary, and 3 professed Christians.

MARAKEI. See GILBERT ISLANDS.

MARAKESH: A town in Morocco, N. Africa, situated about 120 miles E. of Mogador, the southern capital of the Empire. Station of the South Morocco Mission (1891), with 3 missionaries, 2 with their wives; 3 women missionaries, 1 day school, 1 dispensary, and 1 hospital. The place is also called Morocco by Europeans.

MARANHÃO. See SAO LUIZ DE MARANHÃO.

MARAPJANE. See NEU HALLE.

MARASH: A town in the Province of Aleppo, Asiatic Turkey, situated about 80 miles N. of Aleppo. Station of the ABCFM (1854), with (1902) 2 missionaries, 1 with his wife; 3 women missionaries, 65 native workers, 15 outstations, 13 places of worship, 17 Sunday schools, 39 day schools, 1 boarding school, 1 theological class, 1 college, 2 orphanages, and 1,582 professed Christians. Site of the Asia Minor Apostolic Institute (1895), with 1 native worker, 1 Sunday school, 1 day school, 1 boarding school, and 1 orphanage.

MARATHI LANGUAGE: One of the Indic branches of the Aryan family, spoken by a large part of the population of the Bombay Presidency. It is a language of culture, and is written with the Devanagari characters slightly modified. In trade and common life a special set of characters is used called the Modhi character. The modified Devanagari character used in writing Marathi is called Balbodh. Missionaries have attempted to introduce the Roman letters for writing this language, but without great success.

MARBURG: A village near the E. coast of Natal, South Africa, situated 70 miles S. W. by W. of Durban. Station of the Hermannsburg Mission (1867), with (1902) 1 missionary and wife, 2 native workers, 1 day school, 2 places of worship, and 128 professed Christians.

MARDIN: A town in the N. of Mesopotamia, Asiatic Turkey, situated about 50 miles S. of Diarbekir, with a population of 15,000. Station of the ABCFM (1858), with (1902) 2 missionaries and wives, 1 woman missionary, 43 native workers, 18 outstations, 20 places of worship, 12 Sunday schools, 21 day schools, 1 boarding school, 1 hospital, and 346 professed Christians. The seminary furnishes evangelists and teachers to the CMS and the RCA in Arabia.

MARKAPUR: A town in Madras, India, about 18 miles N. E. of Cumbum. Station of the ABMU (1895), with (1903) 1 missionary and his wife, 23 native workers, 26 outstations, 7 places of worship, 9 Sunday schools, 10 day schools, and 4,060 professed Christians, of whom 2,700 are communicants.

MARIANNE ISLANDS. See LADRONE ISLANDS.

MARONITES: The Maronites of Syria take their name from John Maron, their political leader and first patriarch, who died in 701. During the 6th and 7th centuries of our era the Monophysite controversy was raging throughout the Eastern church. Armenia, Syria, and Egypt, frontier lands of the Byzantine Empire, were deeply infected by the heresy. The Emperor Heraclius (610-640) was anxious to reunite the church that he might the more effectually ward off the Saracen invasion from Arabia, which threatened to despoil the empire of its southeastern provinces. With the help of Sergius, Patriarch of Constantinople, a Syrian, he arranged a compromise doctrine which he hoped would put a stop to the rancorous theological dispute. The statement proposed was that, whatever might be said as to Christ having one (divine) or two (human and divine) natures, all ought to agree that He has but one will (divine, and therefore sinless). Honorius, Bishop of Rome, assented to this proposition, and many of the Monophysites agreed to accept it. But no imperial decree could stop the quarrel; and after a long controversy (during which the Saracens conquered Syria, Egypt, and all North Africa) the case was decided against the Monothelites (*monos*, one, *thelo*, to will), and Bishop Honorius (afterward called "Pope") was declared heretical.

Among many who accepted the Monothelite heresy were Christians of Syria who fled to the mountains before the Saracen invader. John Maron was their leader. High up on the shoulders of Lebanon and Anti-Lebanon these vigorous people managed for five hunderd years to maintain their independence in the face of Byzantine Greek and Saracen. Defended by tremendous ravines and snowy mountain passes, they were never seriously in danger. The long contest developed manly qualities and industry. They spoke Syriac, and used it in all their services. A sort of feudal system developed itself. The government was theocratic, the head of the state being styled "The Patriarch of Antioch and all the East." The episcopal dioceses were Aleppo, Ba'albek, Jebeil, Tripoli, Ehden, Damascus, Beirut, Tyre, and Cyprus. Village *sheikhs* were elected, as were all the officers, secular and religious.

The Crusaders brought to light this interesting people, so long cut off from Christendom. William of Tyre and Jacob de Nitry have left us accounts of the Maronites, who leagued themselves with the Crusaders, and in 1182 opened communications with the papal hierarchy. They gradually dropped their heretical tendencies, adopted the Arabic language as their vernacular, and in 1445, at the Council of Florence, were taken entirely under the wing of the Roman Church. They were allowed to retain their Syriac liturgy, the celebration of the communion in both kinds, the marriage of the lower clergy, their own fast-days, and their own saints. In 1596 the decrees of Trent were accepted by them; transubstantiation, prayers for the Pope, and other novelties were introduced. A special college was established at Rome (Collegium Maronitarum) for investigations by Maronite scholars, which gave to the world the learned Assemani. Schools for the clergy and printing presses were established in Syria. A papal legate was sent to Beirut, and to-day the Maronites are submissive followers in the Latin Church.

There are about 250,000 of this sect scattered all over the Lebanon range and the Anti-Lebanon. They are massed somewhat in the northern districts of Lebanon (Kesrawan and Bsherreh), and have complete control of local affairs. They are found as far south as Mt. Hermon, in the heart of the **Druse** country. The hostility of Druse and Maronite, fostered by the Turks through policy, culminated in the massacre of 1860, in which thousands of the Maronites were butchered. European intervention compelled the Sultan to organize the semi-autonomous province of the **Lebanon**, which is under protection of the great powers of Europe. The stronghold of the Maronites in the North Lebanon region is high up on the mountains, with surpassing views over the Mediterranean to the west. It is a bit of the Middle Ages left over. The priests have complete control, and the people are frugal and industrious. They are illiterate for the most part, and only recently began to favor schools as having other value than as a means of keeping their people from Protestant influences. The rough mountain sides are terraced, and every available bit of soil utilized. The raising of cattle, silk-culture and weaving, vineyards, grain, maize, and potatoes (Irish) occupy the attention of the people. Hundreds of monasteries are scattered over the mountains, the most notable one being the monastery of Kennôbin, which is romantically situated in the gorge of the Kadisha River, and is the summer home of the Maronite Patriarch. At the head of this profound ravine is the famous group of 400 ancient cedars, which are carefully guarded as sacred. Some of them are 40 feet in circumference and over 100 feet high.

When the American missionaries entered Syria, in 1823, the Roman Catholic authorities became alarmed, and have put forth every effort to hold the Maronites to allegiance to the Pope. In the early days of this rivalry a young Maronite, Asaad Shidiak, who had adopted the evangelical faith, was imprisoned in the Kennôbin monastery, where he died from rigorous treatment. He has been called "The Martyr of Lebanon." The Jesuits and Lazarists now have in hand the task of holding the Maronites to the Latin faith. A fine school for boys is found at Antura, conducted by the Lazarites, not far from Bkurkeh, the winter home of the Patriarch. The Jesuit College at Beirut is an imposing institution, with a fine library and a very complete scientific apparatus. The Jesuits were forced to issue an Arabic Bible in order to compete successfully with the Protestants, and it is interesting to note that they made the translation from the original Greek and Hebrew Scriptures.

At the time of the massacre of 1860 the Protestant missionaries had the privilege of caring for thousands of Maronite orphans and other fugitives in Sidon and Beirut. But as yet the northern portions of the Lebanon range have been impervious to Protestant influence. Rev. Isaac Bird, in the early days of the mission, was driven from the region, and missionaries have made no attempt since then permanently to reside in the Kesrawan and in Bsherreh. Missionaries occasionally have summered in the mountains above Tripoli, and the prejudice against them is gradually subsiding. An incidental benefit of Mr. Bird's attempt is that the potatoes which Mr. Bird left behind in his garden have spread all over the mountains, and form a staple of agriculture along with maize. Other societies besides the Presbyterian Board are reaching the Maronites. The Free Church of Scotland has occupied the Metu region just south of Kesrawan for some years. The English schools for girls, established after 1860, and which are scattered over the mountains to the south, are doing very efficient work. The mission of the Irish Presbyterian Church in Damascus is reaching the Maronites in that region. In spite of the great care of the Roman Catholics, education is transforming the whole sect, and evangelical truth is more and more winning its way among them.

Churchill (C. H.), *Ten Years' Residence in Mt. Lebanon*, 4 vols., 2d ed., London, 1862 (the 4th vol. refers to Druses and Maronites).

MARPHA: A village in the Central Provinces, India, situated in the Gondwana District, 20 miles N. N. W. of Mandla. Station of the CMS (1892), with (1903) 4 missionaries and 1 woman missionary. Further statistics included in Mandla.

MARQUESAS ISLANDS: A group of islands belonging to France in the South Pacific, northwest of the Society Islands. Area, 480 square miles. Population, 5,000. During the last forty years, mission work in these islands has been repeatedly begun and abandoned, and the natives have been made to suffer greatly by this. They have also been injured by the evil influence coming among them from godless foreigners.

The Paris Evangelical Society now occupies Atuona and Puamau, with (1902) 1 missionary and 1 native pastor. The Hawaiian Evangelical Association also has 2 stations in the islands, at Atuona and Hakehatau.

MARSHALL ISLANDS: Two chains of lagoon islands, in Micronesia, called Ratack (13) and Ralick (11); comprise an area of 1,400 square miles, with an estimated population of 10,000. A missionary of the ABCFM is located at Kusaie, in the **Caroline Islands**, and the work among the various islands is carried on by native preachers and teachers under his supervision. Ebon and Jalut and nine other islands have schools and preaching stations. The whole group contains 11 churches, 8 pastors, and 15 preachers. The German occupation of the islands has not improved the morals of the natives.

MARSHMAN, Joshua: Born April 20, 1768, in Westbury-Leigh, Wiltshire, England. When young he showed a great passion for reading. His parents being poor, his school education was defective, and he followed the occupation of a weaver till 1794. Removing then to Bristol, he taught a small school, and at the same time became a student in Bristol Academy, where he studied Latin, Greek, Hebrew and Syriac. Having decided to be a missionary to the heathen, he offered himself to the BMS, and in 1799 was sent, with three others, to join Dr. Carey in his mission north of Bengal. As the East India Company prohibited missions in its territories, they were advised not to undertake to land at Calcutta, but to go direct to the Danish settlement of Serampur. They reached Serampur October 13, 1799, and were cordially received by the governor, Colonel Bie. Carey soon joined them. Dr. Marshman, finding the support granted by the Society insufficient, with the aid of his wife opened two boarding schools for European children and a school for natives. The income from these schools rendered the mission nearly independent of support from the Society. The Society disapproved of the course followed, and altho Dr. Marshman went to England to make explanations, the Serampur mission was separated from the BMS for some years. This disturbance of pleasant relations, the death of his associate, Mr. Ward, and family afflictions prostrated him, and he died December 5, 1837. Dr. Marshman studied Bengali, Sanskrit and Chinese. He translated into Chinese the Book of Genesis, the Gospels, and the Epistles of Paul to the Romans and Corinthians. In 1811 he published *A Dissertation on the Characters and Sounds of the Chinese Language; The Works of Confucius*, containing the Original Text, with a Translation; *Clavis Sinica*: Elements of Chinese Grammar, with a Preliminary Dissertation on the Characters and

Colloquial Mediums of the Chinese. He was associated with Dr. Carey in preparing a Sanskrit grammar and Bengali-English dictionary, and published an abridgment of the latter. Raja Rammohun Roy having assailed the miracles of Christ in a work entitled *The Precepts of Jesus the Guide to Peace*, Dr. Marshman replied in a series of articles in the *Friend of India*, afterward published in a volume entitled *A Defence of the Deity and Atonement of Jesus Christ*. To this Rammohun Roy replied. The degree of D.D. was conferred on Mr. Marshman by Brown University in 1811.

MARSOVAN: A town in the western part of the Province of Sivas, Asiatic Turkey, situated about 130 miles N. W. of Sivas, and 60 miles S. W. of Samsun, its port. Station of the ABCFM (1852), with (1902) 4 missionaries and their wives, 4 women missionaries, 51 native workers, 17 outstations, 12 places of worship, 32 Sunday schools, 18 day schools, 1 boarding school, 1 theological class, 1 industrial institute, 1 dispensary and 1 hospital, and 661 professed Christians. The educational center of the Western Turkey Mission. Anatolia College, a flourishing institution whose buildings make the mission premises conspicuous through all the surrounding district, is the only establishment of its high grade to be found within a radius of 250 miles.

MARTYN, Rev. Henry: Born at Truro, Cornwall, February 18, 1781; attended the grammar school of Dr. Carden in his native town; entered St. John's College, Cambridge, 1797; received in 1801 the highest academical honor of "senior wrangler," and also the prize for the greatest proficiency in mathematics. In 1802 he was chosen fellow of his college, and took the first prize for the best Latin composition. He was twice elected public-examiner. It was his intention to devote himself to the bar, but the sudden death of his father and the faithful preaching and counsels of Mr. Simeon, the university preacher, led to his conversion and dedication to the ministry. In 1802 a remark of Mr. Simeon on the good accomplished in India by a single missionary—William Carey—and a subsequent perusal of the *Life of* David Brainerd, led him to devote himself to the work of a Christian missionary. He was ordained deacon October 22, 1803, then priest, and served as curate of Mr. Simeon. But his heart was still set on work in heathen lands, and he designed to offer himself to the Church Missionary Society. Financial disaster made it necessary for him to take a position which would give him the means of supporting his sister, and he accepted a chaplaincy under the East India Company. In October, 1806, he went to his station, Dinapur. On the boat he studied Sanskrit, Persian, and Arabic, and translated the Parables. At Dinapur and Cawnpur most of his work in India was done in the space of four and a half months. He not only labored among the soldiers and English residents as chaplain, but preached to the natives in their vernacular, established schools, and spent much time in the work of translation. He studied Sanskrit, soon became fluent in Hindustani, and had religious discussions daily with the *munshis* and pundits. In February, 1807, he finished the translation of the Book of Common Prayer in Hindustani, and, soon after, a Commentary on the Parables. In March, 1808, he completed a version of the New Testament in Hindustani, which was pronounced by competent judges to be idiomatic, and intelligible by the natives.

In April, 1809, he was removed to Cawnpur, 628 miles from Calcutta. He went in a palankeen in the hottest season. In his journey of 400 miles from Chunar, the intense heat nearly proved fatal to him. On his arrival he fainted away. There being no church building at Cawnpur, he preached to a thousand soldiers, drawn up in a hollow square in the open air, with the heat so great that many were overpowered, tho the service was held before sunrise. At the end of this year he made his first attempt to preach to the heathen in his own compound, "amidst groans, hissings, curses, blasphemies, and threatenings," but he pursued his work among the hundreds who crowded around him, comforting himself with the thought that if he should never see a native convert, God "might design by his patience and continuance to encourage other missionaries." He now translated the New Testament into Hindi and the Gospels into Judæo-Persic. Having perfected himself in the Persian, he prepared, by the advice of friends, with the assistance of the *munshi* Sabat, a version of the New Testament in that language. His health being seriously impaired, the doctors ordered him to take a sea voyage; and his version not being sufficiently idiomatic, he decided to go to Persia and correct it with the aid of learned natives, and also revise the Arabic version, which was nearly finished. After preaching in the new church, whose erection he had accomplished, he left Cawnpur October 1, 1810. Delayed at Calcutta a month, he left, January 7, 1811, for Bombay, and after a five months' journey reached Shiraz June 9, 1811, where, with the help of learned natives, he revised his Persian and Arabic translations of the New Testament. He made also a version of the Psalms from the Hebrew into Persian. He held frequent discussions with the mollahs and sufis, many of whom were greatly impressed. "Henry Martyn," said a Persian mollah, "was never beaten in argument; he was a good man, a man of God." To counteract the effect of these discussions and of his translation of the New Testament into Persian, the preceptor of all the mollahs wrote an Arabic defense of Mohammedanism, to which Martyn replied in Persian. He had also a public discussion with a professor of Mohammedan law, and another with Mirza Ibrahim, in a court of the palace of one of the Persian princes in the presence of a large body of mollahs. Having ordered two splendid copies of his manuscript of the Persian New Testament to be prepared, one for the Shah of Persia, the other for Prince Abbas Mirza, his son, he left Shiraz for the Shah's camp to present them. The Shah refused to receive them without a letter from the British ambassador, and he proceeded to Tabriz to obtain one from Sir Gore Ousley. On this journey he suffered much from fever, but after arriving at Tabriz he was tenderly cared for by the ambassador and his lady. Being too ill to make the presentation to the Shah, Sir Gore kindly performed this service, and received from his majesty a letter of acknowledgment, with appreciative mention of the excellence of the translation. After a temporary recovery, he found it necessary to seek a change of climate. On September 12, 1812, he left Tabriz on horseback, with two Armenian servants, for England via Constantinople, 1,300 miles distant. Tho the plague was raging at Tokat, he was compelled to stop there from utter prostration, and, after a week's illness, died, October 16, 1812, in the thirty-second year of his age, among strangers, with no friendly hand to care for his wants. His body rests in the Armenian cemetery. A monument was erected over the grave in 1813 by Mr. Claudius James Rich, the accomplished British resident at Baghdad, with an inscription in Latin. The East India Company had another constructed, bearing on its four sides an inscription in English, Armenian, Turkish, and Persian. The monument stands in the Armenian cemetery.

He published *Sermons Preached in Calcutta and Elsewhere* (1812); *Controversial Tracts on Christianity and Mohammedanism* (1824); *Journals and Letters* (1837). The great work of Martyn's life was the translation of the Bible. His versions of the New Testament in Hindustani and Persian, spoken by many millions of people, are enduring monuments not only to his scholarship, but to his Christian zeal.

Bell (C. D.), *Henry Martyn*, London and New York, 1880: Wilberforce (G.), *Henry Martyn, His Journals and Letters*, 2 Vols., London, 1837; Sargent (J.), *Life of Henry Martyn*, London, 1819 and 1867.

MASASI: A village in the fertile Rovuma region of German East Africa. Station of the UM (1877), with (1903) 3 missionaries, 18 native workers, 12 outstations, 1 place of worship, 13 day schools, 1 boarding school, and 1,129 professed Christians, of whom 942 are communicants.

MASCAT: Town and capital of Oman, Arabia, situated on the south coast of the Gulf of Oman, on a bay closed in front by a small island, and bordered E. and W. by high rocks with fortifications. It is an important commercial center in trade between Persia, Arabia, and India. The climate is very hot and malarious. Population, 40,000, mostly Arabs. Station of the RCA (1893), with 1 missionary, 1 native worker, and 1 boarding school. Society spells the name Muscat.

MASERU: A village in Basutoland, Africa, situated on Caledon River about 100 miles N. N. E. of Aliwal North. Station of the Paris Evangelical Society, with (1902) 10 native workers, 2 outstations, 1 place of worship, 1 Sunday school, 3 day schools, and 555 professed Christians, of whom 351 are communicants. Society spells the name Maserou. Also station of the SPG, with 1 missionary.

MASITSI: A village in the S. part of Basutoland, Africa, situated near the Orange River, 63 miles N. N. E. of Aliwal North. Station of the Paris Evangelical Mission Society (1886), with (1903) 1 missionary and his wife, 31 native workers, 11 outstations, 1 place of worship, 1 Sunday school, 13 day schools, 1 industrial school, and 1,660 professed Christians, of whom 1,106 are communicants. Society spells the name Massitissi. Station of the SPG (1887), with 1 missionary. Society spells the name Masiti.

MASON, Rev. Francis: Born York, England, April 2, 1799. Died at Rangoon March 3, 1874. He was appointed by the American Baptist Missionary Convention as a missionary December 17, 1829, ordained May 23, 1830, and sailed May 26 for Burma. After spending a short time at Maulmain he was stationed, January, 1831, at Tavoy. The province contained fifty Burmese villages. He was met at the wharf by Mr. Boardman. He accompanied Mr. Boardman on his last tour among the Karens, and witnessed his triumphant death. Entering upon the work in his new field, he labored earnestly among the Karens, visiting them in their jungle homes, preaching, organizing churches, establishing schools. The rainy season was occupied in translating the Scriptures, and instructing in the theological seminary established for training Karen preachers.

Mr. Mason was not only a preacher among the Karens; he was also a man of science and a linguist. He translated the Bible into the two principal dialects of the Karen, the Sgau and Pwo. He also translated Matthew, Genesis, and Psalms into the Bghai, another dialect. He wrote and printed a grammar of the first two for the use of missionaries. Wishing to give the pupils of his theological school some scientific knowledge, he wrote an original treatise on *Trigonometry, with its Applications to Land Measuring, etc.* This was printed in Sgau and Burmese, and the government paid for an edition in Bghai Karen. At the request of English residents at Maulmain he prepared and had printed a work on the natural productions of the country, entitled *Tennasserim; or, Notes on the Fauna, Flora, Minerals, and Nations of British Burma and Pegu*, of which *The Friend of India* says: "It is one of the most valuable works of the kind which has ever appeared in this country, not only for the complete originality of its information, but also for the talent exhibited in collecting and arranging it." His motive in investigating these subjects was the more accurate translation of the Scriptures, having observed that incorrect renderings of words used to designate natural objects often made the sense obscure or absurd. He studied medicine after reaching Burma, and wrote a small work on *Materia Medica and Pathology*, in three languages. His greatest literary work was a *Pali Grammar with Chrestomathy and Vocabulary*, which was received by scholars with great favor. In 1842 he started a Karen periodical, the first native paper published east of the Ganges, and the next year a similar monthly in Burmese at Maulmain. The Karens had no books but many traditions, among which were many remarkable Scripture traditions, all of which Mr. Mason collected. Those relating to Scripture were published in an appendix to his *Life of Ko-Thah-Byu*. In 1846 he yielded to the advice of the mission to return for rest to America. On arriving in Calcutta with health improved, he concluded to return to Burma and work on the translation of the Old Testament, stopping at Maulmain in order to have the advice of the missionaries there. The translation was finished in 1853, and, returning to Tavoy, he had the entire Bible printed. In appreciation of his marked literary and Biblical attainments the degree of D.D. was conferred upon him in 1853 by Brown University. After the printing of the Karen Bible he took his final departure from Tavoy for England and America. On reaching Maulmain with health improved, he decided to visit Taung-ngu, the ancient capital, and begin a new mission. He started, with Mrs. Mason, in a canoe, and found the people, who had never heard the Gospel message, wonderfully eager listeners. Dr. Mason continued to labor until utter exhaustion compelled him to leave. He returned to Taung-ngu in 1857. There, living next to the printing office, he learned the printer's trade after he was sixty years old. In 1874 he set out for Calcutta to see one of his works through the press, but was attacked with fever at Rangoon and died after 46 years of missionary labor.

Besides the works mentioned, he published a memoir of his second wife, Mrs. Helen M. Mason, *Life of Ko-Thah-byu, the Karen Apostle*, a collection of Karen hymns, and *The Story of a Workingman's Life*, an autobiography.

MASSAUA: A town and seaport, capital of Eritrea, Africa, on a coral island in the Red Sea, 200 yards from the mainland. It is connected with the mainland by an embankment, which also carries an aqueduct. It is the chief trading exchange for Abyssinia. Its climate is unhealthful, dysentery and fever being prevalent. Its population is 20,000 and is very mixed. It has a strong Roman Catholic mission.

MASULIPATAM: A city and seaport in Madras, India, situated in the District of Kistna, 143 miles N. E. by N. of Nellore. Population, 38,800, of whom 33,500 are Hindus. The name means Fishtown and its port is called Mashlibandar(Fishport). This gives the official name to the town, which is Bandar. Station of the CEZ (1875), with (1903) 6 women missionaries, 53 native workers, 10 day schools, 1 boarding school, 1 industrial school, 1 orphanage, and 1,072 Zenana pupils. Station of the CMS (1841), with (1903) 5 missionaries, four of them with their wives; 77 native workers, 1 outstation, 1 place of worship, 1 young men's Christian association, 43 day schools, 2 boarding schools, 1 college, and 4,675 professed Christians, of whom 867 are communicants.

MATADI: A trading post in the Congo Free State, Africa, on the left bank of the Congo, opposite Vivi, just below the lowest falls. It is the starting point of the Congo Railroad. Station of the BMS (1898), with (1903) 1 missionary and his wife, 1 native worker, and 1 day school. Station of the RBMU (1889) for forwarding stores to other stations.

MATAIEA: A village on the S. side of Tahiti Island. Station of the Paris Evangelical Mission Society (1886), with (1902) 1 missionary and wife, 1 place of worship, 1 Sunday school and 135 professed Christians.

MATALA: A village in the Transvaal, South Africa, situated about 22 miles N. W. of Pietersburg. Station of the Berlin Missionary Society (1865), with (1903) 1 missionary, 12 native workers, 4 outstations, 1 day school and 304 professed Christians, of whom 116 are communicants. Society writes the name Ga Matlale, the meaning being "At (chief) Matlale's."

MATALE: A town in the central province of Ceylon, situated 12 miles N. of Kandy. Population, 5,000. Station of the BMS (1837), with (1903) 1 missionary, 5 native workers, 5 outstations and 2 day schools. Station of the FFMA (1896), with (1901) 2 missionaries, one with his wife; 17 native workers, 4 outstations, 7 places of worship, 6 Sunday schools, 8 day schools and 1 dispensary.

MATAMOROS: A town in the state of Tamaulipas, Mexico, situated on the Rio Grande del Norte, 185 miles E. by N. of Monterey. Population, 13,000. Station of the AFFM (1871), with (1900) 1 missionary and wife, 2 women missionaries, 5 native workers, 1 place of worship, 1 Sunday school, 1 day school, 1 boarding school, 1 temperance society and 100 professed Christians. Station of the PS (1874), with (1903) 1 woman missionary, 1 native worker, 13 outstations, 1 Sunday school, 1 day school, 1 boarding school and 30 professed Christians.

MATANZAS: A town and seaport on the N. coast of Cuba, situated 48 miles E. of Havana. It has a large trade in sugar. Its climate is malarious. Population, 27,000. Near by are some very fine stalactite caves. Station of the American Church Missionary Society (1883), with (1900) 2 missionaries, one with his wife; 4 women missionaries, 7 native workers, 1 place of worship, 1 Sunday school, 1 day school, 1 industrial class, 1 orphanage. Station of the MES, with (1902) 1 missionary, 2 women missionaries, 1 native worker and 1 day school.

MATARA: A town on the S. coast of Ceylon, situated 24 miles E. S. E. of Galle. Population, 8,600. Station of the SPG (1841), with (1903) 1 missionary, 38 native workers, 6 outstations, 3 places of worship, 7 day schools, 1 boarding school and 280 professed Christians, of whom 110 are communicants. Station of the WMS, with (1903) 2 missionaries, 2 women missionaries, 53 native workers, 7 outstations, 2 places of worship, 13 Sunday schools, 15 day schools, 2 boarding schools and 109 professed Christians.

MATATIELA, or **MATATIELE:** A settlement in Cape Colony, South Africa, situated in Griqualand East, 110 miles W. S. W. of Pietermaritzburg. Station of the ECS (1878), with (1900) 3 missionaries, 18 native workers, 7 outstations, 9 places of worship, 7 day schools and 372 professed Christians.

MATAUTU: A settlement in Savaii, **Samoa.** Station of the LMS.

MATEHUALA: A village in the state of San Luis Potosi, Mexico, situated 22 miles W. S. W. of Catorce. Station of the AFFM (1889), with (1900) 1 missionary and wife, 3 native workers, 1 place of worship, 1 Sunday school, 1 Young People's Society, 1 printing press, 1 day school, 1 temperance society and 30 professed Christians.

MATHER, Robert Cotton: Born November 8, 1808, at New Windsor, Manchester, England; educated at Edinburgh, Glasgow, and Hamerton College; sailed July 9, 1833, for India, as a missionary of the LMS. He was stationed at Benares for four years, and then removed with his family to Mirzapur, founding a new station. In 1844 he went to England for his health. Returning in 1846, he continued his work in and around Mirzapur, and prepared Christian vernacular literature. He again visited England in 1857, where he resided during three years, at the request of the North India and the British and Foreign Bible Societies, engaged in making a revision, with marginal references, of the whole Bible in Urdu. This was carried through the press, and the New Testament in English and Urdu was reprinted. He reembarked for India November 20, 1860, with Mrs. Mather. In 1862 he received the degree of LL.D. from the University of Glasgow. In 1869 he left Mirzapur for Almora, seeking to benefit his health. He aided in mission work while carrying on his literary work, completing a new edition of the entire Bible in Urdu printed in Roman letters. He commenced work on an edition in Urdu printed in Arabic characters with references. He returned to Mirzapur in 1870. In 1873 he left India on his final return to England. At the request of the Religious Tract Societies of North India and London, he undertook to prepare and carry through the press a Hindustani version of the New Testament portion of the Tract Society's Annotated Paragraph Bible. This was completed in two years. He then undertook the preparation of a similar version of the Old Testament portion of the same work. Unable to resume foreign missionary work, he thus continued in England to work for India with his pen. He died at Finchley, near London, April 21, 1877.

MATOUTOUENE: A settlement in Portuguese East Africa, situated about 40 miles S. by W. of Lourenço Marques. Station of the Swiss Romande Mission (1902), with (1903) 1 missionary and his wife, 7 native workers, 15 day schools, 10 outstations, and 353 professed Christians, of whom 46 are communicants.

MATSUMOTO: A town in Hondo, Japan, situated 135 miles S. W. of Niigata. Population, 21,000. Station of the Church of England in Canada (1894), with (1901) 1 missionary and his wife, 1 woman missionary, 4 native workers, 1 outstation, 1 female helpers' training class and 19 professed Christians. Also station of the Methodist Church in Canada (1900), with 1 native worker, 1 place of worship, 1 Sunday school and 5 professed Christians.

MATSUYAMA: A town and seaport on the N. W. coast of Shikoku, Japan, situated 115 miles W. S. W. of Kobe. Population, 24,600. Station of the ABCFM (1876), with (1903) 1 missionary and his wife, 2 women missionaries, 10 native workers, 5 outstations, 3 places of worship, 6 Sunday schools, 1 boarding school and a hostel for girls. Station also of the MES (1888), with (1900) 1 missionary and wife, 2 native workers, 3 outstations, 2 places of worship, 4 Sunday schools, 2 young people's societies, 1 Young Men's Christian Association and 63 professed Christians. Station also of the PE, with (1903) 1 native worker, 1 place of worship, 1 Sunday school and 14 professed Christians.

MATSUYE: A town on the W. coast of the main island, Japan, situated about 70 miles N. W. of Okayama. Station of the CMS (1891), with 1 missionary, 4 native workers, 2 outstations, 1 place of worship, 1 day school and 307 professed Christians, of whom 174 are communicants.

MATTOON, Rev. Stephen: Born at Champion, N. Y., U. S. A., May 5, 1816; graduated at Union College 1842, at Princeton Theological Seminary 1846; sailed for Siam as a missionary of the Presbyterian Board July 20, 1846, reaching Bangkok March 22, 1847. Bitterly opposed at first, he soon won the confidence of the people, and carried forward the missionary work with great success. He was the first to translate the Gospels into the Siamese tongue, and his last great work before returning home was the revision of the entire New Testament in that language. He was a leader in all the enterprises connected with the mission, and his prudent counsel was sought and his advice accepted by all. He resided and labored mainly in Bangkok, and was pastor of the First Presbyterian Church in that city from 1860 to 1866. In the latter year, on account of the failure of Mrs. Mattoon's health, he returned home. He was in the pastorate and in educational work in the United States, never neglecting the opportunity to preach until he died in 1889.

MAUBIN: A town in the district of Thongwa, Burma, British India, situated 32 miles W. of Rangoon. Population, 5,300, mostly Karens, and of whom 4,500 are Buddhists. Station of the ABMU (1879), with (1903) 1 missionary and his wife, 1 woman missionary, 27 native workers, 17 places of worship, 4 Sunday schools, 6 day schools, 1 boarding school and 879 professed Christians.

MAUI: One of the Hawaiian Islands, between Hawaii and Oahu. The inhabitants, 12,109 in number, are all nominally Christians. Station of the Hawaiian Evangelical Society.

MAULMAIN: A town and seaport on the left bank of the Salwin River, Burma, British India. Low hills run north and south through the town with European quarters on the west and native on the east of the hills. Population (1901) 58,446, of whom 27,000 are Buddhists and 13,500 are Hindus. Station of the ABMU (1827), with (1903) 4 missionaries and their wives, 8 women missionaries, 125 native workers, 38 outstations, 37 places of worship, 4 boarding schools, 1 dispensary and 1 hospital, 43 Sunday schools, 42 day schools and 5,300 professed Christians, of whom 2,542 are communicants. Station of the SPG (1859), with 1 missionary, 1 woman missionary, 27 native workers, 2 day schools, 2 boarding schools and 109 professed Christians. The name is also written Moulmein.

MAULVI BAZAAR. See MULVI BAZAR.

MAURITIUS: An island lying in the Indian Ocean, 500 miles east of Madagascar. Area, 708 square miles. Together with its dependencies, the Seychelles group, Rodriguez and Diego Garcia (total area, 172 square miles), it forms a colony of Great Britain. Climate tropical, and very malarious and unhealthful on the coast. Population in 1901 was nearly 376,000; of this number 251,550 are Indians, and the remainder are Africans, mixed races, and whites. The Chinese number 3,935. The people are divided in their religious belief as follows: Hindus, 206,000; Roman Catholics, 113,000; Mohammedans, 41,000, and Protestants, 6,644. State aid is granted to both Roman Catholic and Protestant churches. English, French, and the languages of the different races represented are spoken there. The island was originally a French colony, and a stronghold of pirates in the Indian Ocean. In 1810 the English took possession of it, and in 1834 the 90,000 negro slaves were emancipated. The island is one of the foremost sugar-producing places of the globe, and the emancipation of the slaves necessitated the importation of labor from China and India, with the resulting conglomerate population. Education is conducted partly in government and partly in state-aided schools. There is also a Royal College. Missionary work was commenced here in 1814 by the LMS. After the Society gave up the mission in 1832 Mr. Le Brun, their missionary, returned to the island and took the pastoral care of the people, and the church of 50 members. When persecution in

Madagascar (1836) drove out both Christians and missionaries, one of the latter, Mr. Johns, went to Mauritius, and continued to labor among the Malagasy. A plot of land was procured, and a congregation of Malagasy refugees was gathered together in 1845, after Mr. Johns' death, and theological instruction was given to young men from Madagascar, to prepare them for work, as soon as the persecution ceased. In the meantime Mr. Le Brun continued his labors among the natives, and in 1850 there were 173 church-members at the stations of Port Louis and Moka. The SPG and the CMS are practically confining their efforts to the immigrants from India, who are engaged in work on the sugar plantations. These form two-thirds of the population. The language difficulty is a very serious one. A missionary writes that a class of thirty received instruction in five languages—the English, French, Creole, Tamil, and Hindi. Even in this difficult field harvests have been gathered, and the CMS has received over 5,000 in the course of its work.

MAURITIUS-CREOLE LANGUAGE: A dialect of the French which has become the medium of business in Mauritius and is the society language of the Creoles of the island.

MAVELIKARA: A town in the native state of Travancore, India, situated 25 miles N. of Quillon. Station of the CEZ (1893), with (1903) 2 women missionaries, 8 native workers, 1 young women's Christian association. Station also of the CMS (1839), now under charge of the local Church Council, with 143 native workers, 78 day schools, and 12,245 professed Christians, of whom 3,706 are communicants.

MAWLAI: A village in Assam, India, situated in the Khasi Hills, 8 miles S. W. of Shillong. Station of the WCM, with (1903) 1 missionary and his wife, 9 native workers, 8 outstations, 6 places of worship, 6 Sunday schools, and 659 professed Christians.

MAWPHLANG. See MAO-PHLANG.

MAYA LANGUAGE: A South American language, spoken by about half a million Indians of Yucatan. It has been reduced to writing with use of the Roman letters.

MAYAVARAM: A town in Madras, India, situated in the district of Tanjore, 28 miles N. N. W. of Negapatam. Population (1891), 23,800, of whom 22,000 are Hindus. Station of the Leipzig Missionary Society (1845), with (1903) 1 missionary and his wife, 39 native workers, 14 outstations, 9 places of worship, 12 day schools, 1 boarding school, and 1,370 professed Christians. Society spells the name Majaweram.

MAYEBASHI: A town in Japan, situated 70 miles N. W. of Tokio, having an important silk trade, Mayebashi silk being among the best of raw silks. Population, 20,000. Station of the ABCFM (1894), with (1902) 1 missionary and his wife, 2 women missionaries, 11 outstations, 4 places of worship, 9 Sunday schools, 1 boarding school, and 1 orphanage. Station of the PE (1888), with 1 missionary, 1 woman missionary, 1 native worker, 2 places of worship, and 46 professed Christians. The name is also written Maebashi.

MAYHEW, Experience: Born Martha's Vineyard, Mass., 1673. Died in 1758. He was the oldest son of Rev. John Mayhew, and great-grandson of Gov. Thomas Mayhew. In 1694, at the age of twenty-one, he began to preach to the Indians, having the oversight of six congregations, which continued until his death, a period of sixty-four years. He learned the Indian language in his infancy, and having afterward thoroughly mastered it, he was employed by the Commissioners to make a new version of the Psalms and the Gospel of John. This was accomplished in 1709, in parallel columns of English and Indian. He was offered the degree of Master of Arts by Cambridge University, which he declined; but it was conferred at the public commencement July 3, 1723. He published in 1727 *Indian Converts*, comprising the lives of 30 Indian preachers and 80 other converts; also a volume entitled *Grace Defended*.

MAYOMBO: A settlement in British East Africa, situated 8 miles from the Uganda Railway station for Kikuyu, about 150 miles S. E. of the railway terminus at the Victoria Uganda, and 338 miles N. W. from Mombasa. It is in a fine forest district at an altitude of 6,300 feet, and has a bracing and healthy climate. Station of the CMS (1901), with 2 missionaries and 1 missionary's wife. The station at Fort Smith has been removed to this place.

MAZAGAN: A town and seaport on the W. coast of Morocco, in a fertile district, which gives it commercial importance. The climate is not unhealthy. Station of the South Morocco Mission Society (1891), with (1900) 2 missionaries, one with his wife, and 1 dispensary.

MAZATLAN: A town on the W. coast of Mexico, situated 100 miles S. W. by W. of Durango. It is a trade center for the mining district of Sinaloa. The climate is healthy from November to May, but hot, wet, and unhealthy the rest of the year. Population, 20,000. Station of the MES (1890), with (1903) 1 missionary and wife, 1 native worker, 1 outstation, 1 Sunday school.

MAZERAS: A settlement in British East Africa, 15 miles W. by S. of Mombasa. Station of the United Methodist Free Church (1893), with (1903) 1 missionary, 3 native workers, 2 outstations, 2 places of worship, 2 day schools, 2 Sunday schools, and 163 professed Christians.

MAZIZINI: A village on the W. side of Zanzibar Island; a suburb of the town of Zanzibar. Station of the UM (1889), with (1900) 2 missionaries, 6 native workers, 1 place of worship, 1 day school, 1 boarding school, 1 theological class, and 10 professed Christians.

MBEYELA'S: A settlement, in Africa, of a chief whose tribe is found about 75 miles E. N. E. of the north end of Lake Tanganyika and 9 miles S. of Mpangile. Station of the Berlin Missionary Society (1899), with 1 missionary and 19 professed Christians.

MBUNDU LANGUAGE: An important African language belonging to the Bantu family, and spoken in Angola, Portuguese West Africa, and as a trading language over a wide region to the eastward. There are two principal dialects, the Ki-Mbundu and the U-Mbundu; indeed, some consider these as separate languages, whose differences are radical and permanent. It is to be hoped, however, that they will follow the general laws of language under civilized environment, and tend to become one. The Ki-Mbundu was reduced to writing by Roman Catholic missionaries in 1642, and grammars and dictionaries of it in Portuguese have long existed. The Methodist missionaries (U. S.) have done good work in studying its peculiarities and establishing a Christian literature in it. In Bihè the ABCFM missionaries are doing the same kind of work in the U-Mbundu branch.

MBWENI: A village on the W. side of Zanzibar Island, a little S. of Zanzibar town. Station of the UM (1874), with (1903) 2 missionaries, 6 women missionaries, 15 native workers, 1 outstation, 2 places of worship, 3 day schools, 1 boarding school, 1 industrial school, 1 dispensary, and 456 professed Christians, of whom 268 are communicants.

McALL MISSION: Known in France as the *Mission Populaire Evangélique*. Headquarters, 36 rue Godet de Mauroy, Madeleine, Paris. Founded in 1872 by the Rev. Robert W. McAll, then a pastor in Hadleigh, England, in response to the remark of a Parisian workingman to the effect that the people of France would have nothing to do with "an imposed religion of forms and ceremonies," but were "ready to hear" if any one would teach them "a religion of freedom and earnestness." These words, spoken August 18, 1871, moved Mr. and Mrs. McAll, after taking counsel with eminent Parisian pastors, to devote themselves to the evangelization of the working people of France. The requisite permission was obtained from the police commissioner, and on January 17, 1872, the mission was opened in Belleville, the communistic quarter of Paris. Its opportuneness at once became evident. Calls for new stations came from many quarters, and volunteer service was freely offered, especially by French pastors and laymen. It was several years before any salaried worker was added to the staff, and Dr. and Mrs. McAll never received any stipend from the Mission.

By 1888 the number of mission halls was twenty-two in Paris and its environs, and 108 in provincial towns and cities, including Corsica, Tunis, and Algiers, with 20,000 sittings and an aggregate attendance of 1,555,600. The number of mission halls has since been gradually reduced by nearly one-third, altho the number of persons reached is greatly increased. The smaller number of mission halls is in part due to financial necessity, but mainly to development in the activities of the French Protestant churches, many of which have taken over one or more of the mission halls. Thus the McAll Mission is becoming more and more a pioneering agency and feeder to the churches. Its halls, however, are still centers of a great variety of activities: Sunday and Thursday Bible schools, mothers' meetings, Christian endeavor, temperance work, dispensaries, lending libraries, domestic visitation, and an extensive circulation of tracts and of the Scriptures. But all these works are tributary to the evangelistic purpose of the mission, evangelistic meetings being held in every hall at least twice, and in many, seven times a week. The teachings are purely evangelistic, no criticism or comment upon other forms of teaching or worship being allowed. No effort is made to win converts from the church of Rome, and many who are unquestionably converted remain in its communion. The majority of converts, however, are from free thinking and atheistic ranks—that immense multitude that have shaken off allegiance to Roman Catholicism.

Except in one or two cases of extreme urgency the Mission invests no money in buildings and founds no churches. Its halls are hired shops, and converts are sent to unite with some neighboring church, with whose pastor they are well acquainted through his regular work in the mission hall. It has often occurred that the majority of new members of a church in any given year are from the nearest mission hall.

The expenses of the Mission (which average less than $1,000 annually per hall) are met by voluntary contributions from Great Britain, Ireland, Protestant Europe, the United States, Canada, the descendants of the Huguenots in South Africa, and, in ever increasing amount, from the Protestants of France. The American McAll Mission Association, founded in 1883 to collect funds for the Mission, has 67 auxiliaries and provides more than a third of its income.

An important work was carried on in the three exposition years, 1878, 1889, 1900, by the Mission, in cooperation with the British and Foreign Bible Society and the Religious Tract Societies of London and Paris. Halls were opened near the exposition gates, with unceasing services, opportunities for religious conversation, and an enormous distribution of tracts and Scripture portions. In 1890 a citizen of New York provided 10,000 copies of the "Marked New Testament" in French, which were put to judicious use. Many remarkable conversions were due to this work in the exposition.

About 1885-1888, a missionary vessel having been lent to the Mission by Mr. Henry Cook, of the English Seaman's Mission, an important work was carried on in the seaboard towns of Brittany and Normandy, and up the Seine to Paris, resulting in the founding of several important stations. The chief advantage of the method was that the vessel, being commissioned and equipped to hold meetings, encountered no delay in obtaining local permits or suitable halls for the purpose. This suggested a similar mission along the inland water-ways of France. Two chapel boats, expressly designed for the work, now carry the Gospel along these "silent highways." **"Le Bon Messager"** was commissioned in 1890, and **"La Bonne Nouvelle"** (mainly the gift of an American woman) in 1902. This pioneer work has been singularly fruitful. Municipal and communal authorities almost invariably, and parish priests not unfrequently, show hearty sympathy. The people come in crowds, making necessary two and often three successive services evening after evening. An increasing number of permanent works follow the boats, established by French Home Mission Societies or by resident Protestants.

In January, 1892, the Mission celebrated its twentieth anniversary, and Dr. McAll's seventieth birthday, with many tributes of honor and gratitude. In these the French Government joined by conferring upon Dr. McAll the cross of the Legion of Honor. On May 11, 1893, worn out with excessive care and labor, Dr. McAll went to his reward, being buried with military honors in the cemetery of Père La Chaise. He had already called to the Honorary Presidency a prominent business man of Paris, M. Louis Sautter, and to the active direction of the work the Rev. C. E. Greig, trained in the Mission under his own eyes. Since then the success of the Mission has been unabated, its importance increasingly recognized by French Protestants. The most important events of recent date (1903), besides the growing success of the boat work, are a remarkable awakening in nineteen mountain villages in the south of France, due to itinerating work from Grasse as a center, and a still more notable revival in Corsica, where, after many years of persecution of McAll missionaries, the people of Aullène have abandoned the Church of Rome, provided funds to build a church and asked the Government to send them a Protestant pastor.

McALL, Rev. Robert Whitaker: The founder of the McAll Mission, Paris, began his ministry in 1848 at Sunderland, and had successive pastorates in Leicester, Birmingham, Manchester, and Hadleigh. Mr. McAll was known as a keen student of natural history, being an accomplished botanist, and becoming a Fellow of the Linnean Society. The three subjects, architecture, botany, and geography, were specially interesting to him, and he turned them all to good account in his pastoral work, and later on in his mission work in France.

In the summer of 1871 Mr. and Mrs. McAll crossed the Channel for the first time for a short visit to France. Taking with them a supply of French tracts, they made a point of distributing them wherever they went, and on the last evening of their stay in Paris, August 17, 1871, they found their way to the populous quarter of Belleville, where the people had so terribly suffered during the Commune, and began to give away their tracts among the crowds of working people that were thronging the streets.

While Mrs. McAll was giving the tracts around, inside of a café on the Boulevard de Belleville, Mr. McAll was accosted by an intelligent workingman, who could speak a little English, and who came forward saying to him, "Are you not a Christian minister, sir? I have something to tell you. Throughout this whole district, containing tens of thousands of workmen, we cannot accept an imposed religion. But if anyone would come to teach us religion of another kind, a religion of freedom and reality, many of us are ready for it."

Could it be that this was a call from God for them to go over and try the experiment and take the Gospel to the people of Paris? After much thought and prayer, and after consulting friends at home and in France, especially Pastor Georges Fisch and Pastor Theodore Monod, the important decision was made, and in October Mr. McAll resigned the pastorate of the church at Hadleigh, and December found him in Paris, with a small sum in hand for current expenses, and his slender patrimony on which to subsist.

On the 18th of January, 1872, the first "McAll Mission Hall" was opened on the rue Julian Lacroix, Belleville, the first of a long list. Friends rallied round him, and Pastors Fisch, Monod, Bersier, de Pressensé, Appia, Vallette, Recolin, Dhombres, Hollard, and many others were his warmest supporters. The importance of the work accomplished, from a purely philanthropic point of view, was recognized by two societies conferring medals on the founder, the "Société Nationale d'Encouragement au Bien," and the "Société Libre d'Instruction and d'Education Populaire." The government of the Republic made Mr. McAll a knight of the Legion of Honor in July, 1892.

In 1892 Dr. McAll's health failed, and he resolved to go to England for a change, but after a winter of severe suffering he returned to Paris, where, in his 72d year, on Ascension Day, the 5th of May, 1893, he peacefully passed away.

McMULLIN, Robert: Born at Philadelphia, Pa., November 30, 1832; graduated at the University of Pennsylvania 1850, and at Princeton Theological Seminary 1854; ordained July 27, 1856, and sailed for India September 11, the same year, as a missionary of the PN. He was stationed at Fategarh. A few months before his capture by the Sepoy rebels he wrote: "We are trying to be calm and trustful, but this cloud is fearfully dark. No matter whether our lives be prosperous or adverse, God has some gracious purpose, which will sooner or later be made manifest." When the mutiny broke out he, with other missionaries, endeavored to reach Allahabad, a British station, but was made prisoner, and put to death at Cawnpur by order of the rebel chief, Nana Sahib, June 13, 1857.

MEDAK: A town in the native state of Haidarabad, India, situated on a branch of the Manjira River, 48 miles N. by W. of Haidarabad. Population, 7,000. Station of the WMS, with (1903) 1 missionary, 4 women missionaries, 14 outstations, 137 native workers, 10 places of worship, 27 Sunday schools, 27 day schools, 1 boarding school, 1 dispensary, 1 orphanage, 1 hospital, 1 industrial school and 1,532 professed Christians, of whom 724 are communicants.

MEDELLIN: A town and the capital of the state of Antioquia, Colombia, situated at the foot of Mt. Santa Elena on the Porce River, 150 miles N. W. of Bogota. It is a mining center and the supply depot for large regions. It was founded in 1675 and is next to the city of Bogota in importance. It has railroad connections with Magdalena River at Porto Berrico. Altitude, 5,000 feet. Population, 18,000. Station of the PN (1889), with (1903) 1 missionary and his wife, 1 woman missionary, 1 Sunday school, 1 day school and 23 professed Christians,

MEDHURST, Walter Henry: Born at London, England, 1796; learned the trade of a printer; was educated for the ministry, and, having decided to be a missionary to the heathen, was appointed by the LMS, and sailed as its missionary in 1816 for Malacca. He was ordained there in 1819. In 1822 he was established at Batavia, in Java, remaining there eight years, during which time, and for several years afterward, he performed missionary work in Borneo and on the coasts of China. Having spent two years in England, he was stationed at Shanghai after the conclusion of the war in 1843. There he remained till his final return to England in 1856. This was the earliest Protestant mission in that city. The printing press owned by the LMS, which had to this time been worked at Batavia, was now removed to Shanghai, and was under the charge of Mr. Medhurst. The University of New York conferred on Mr. Medhurst in 1843 the degree of D.D. In 1847 delegates from several missions convened in Shanghai for the revision of the Chinese versions of the Sacred Scriptures. After the completion of the New Testament Messrs. Medhurst, Milne and Stronach, by instruction of the directors, withdrew from the general committee, and prosecuted the work of revision of the Old Testament. This was completed in 1853. The result of this revision was virtually a new version of the Bible, very correct in idiom and true to the meaning of the original.

Dr. Medhurst left Shanghai in 1856 in impaired

health for England, and died two days after reaching London, January 24, 1857. A remarkable linguist, he was a proficient in Malay, well versed in the Chinese, Japanese, Javanese and other Eastern languages, besides Dutch and French, in all of which he wrote.

MEDICAL MISSIONS: "The history of Medical Missions is the justification of Medical Missions."

One of the oldest Buddhist writings recognizes the close connection between body and soul, and that the doctor should also be a missionary. We find the following expression: "No physician is worthy of waiting on the sick unless he has five qualifications for his office: 1. The skill to prescribe the proper remedy; 2. The judgment to order the proper diet; 3. The motive must be life and not greed; 4. He must be content and willing to do the most repulsive office for the sake of those whom he is waiting upon; and 5. He must be both able and willing to teach, to incite, and to gladden the hearts of those whom he is attending by religious discourse."

In view of the fact that healing was made so prominent in the Apostolic Church, we cannot but wonder at the extent to which, in the ages after the apostles, it dropped out of the Church's work.

The Roman Catholics of the 16th and 17th centuries used medicine largely as an aid to mission work. It is to them chiefly that we owe the use of cinchona, which has rendered mission work possible in fever-stricken lands; as well as ipecacuanha and many other remedies which we probably should not have known so soon had it not been for their labors.

America has been the foremost nation in this cause. Her sons, and later her daughters, have been among the earliest to enter the field. The first medical missionary to leave the United States was Dr. John Scudder, who, with his wife, sailed in 1819 from New York for India, where he labored until his death in 1855. In 1849 there were just forty medical missionaries in the world—26 from America, 12 from Great Britain, 1 from France, and 1 from Turkey or Arabia, at Jaffa. It was not until 1879 that the value of this agency for reaching the outcast and depraved in our large cities was realized sufficiently to lead to action. In this particular Great Britain has taken the lead, forming a large number of separate medical missions.

In 1876 Dr. William H. Thomson, with the desire of aiding medical missionary students, succeeded in establishing seven scholarships at the University of the City of New York, U. S. A. In April, 1879, Mr. E. F. Baldwin opened in Philadelphia the first organized medical mission in America, which was followed in 1881 by the International Medical Mission Society in New York City.

The power of medical missions is now universally recognized.

In all the heathen world the practise of medicine in marked by the densest superstition and characterized by the most extreme cruelties.

Even the Chinese have no doctors worthy of the name; they have absolutely no reliable knowledge of anatomy, physiology, chemistry, physics, surgery, or of obstetrical practise, and their "doctors" often do more harm than good. The sick are often left to die in the streets and not even a drink of water is given to the wounded after a battle, who, if unable to drag themselves away, are abandoned to perish. In India charms and incantations are a common resort, the sick are dosed with putrid Ganges water, and patients are suffocated with charcoal-fires.

The Arab resorts with the greatest confidence to the most ridiculous, severe, or disgusting remedies. A slip of paper, containing certain written words, is swallowed with avidity; a man in the last stages of consumption takes a prescription directing him to feed, for a fortnight, upon the raw liver of a male camel, and fresh liver not being attainable, he continues the use of this diet in a putrid state until he dies; while the Arab's most common remedy for all diseases is the "kei," or the burning of the skin, entirely around the seat of pain, with a red-hot iron.

To every missionary a knowledge of medicine is of essential importance, for he may find himself removed many days' journey from a physician, even, as has happened repeatedly, 250 to 800 miles. Let missionaries possess medical education, to enable them (1) to look after their own health; (2) to relieve the physical suffering around them; (3) to obtain ready entrance for the Gospel; and (4) to enable them to support themselves as far as possible. At Melange, in Africa, 400 miles from the coast, Mr. Heli Chatelain, a few days after his arrival, was offered by a trader a home in his house and $1,200 a year to look after his family alone, and he was assured that others in the town would increase the sum to $5,000 per annum if he would consent to remain.

Advantages and Benefits: The benefits of medical missions may be well nigh placed beyond computation in value. "It will not strike you with surprise," said Dr. J. L. Maxwell of Formosa, "when I tell you that again and again the lives of valued missionaries in China have escaped destruction at the hands of evil and fanatic mobs just because they were providentially recognized to be the associates of the mission doctor at this or that missionary hospital. During the Afghan war the tribe of the Wazaris destroyed the town of Tank, and even the government hospital, but spared the mission hospital of the Church Missionary Society, because of their esteem and affection for the medical missionary. In the Chinese village of Na-than, 100 miles to the north of Swatow, a most remarkable work has been carried on without the agency of a resident missionary. It is the dwelling-place of a leper who, after having visited the hospital at Swatow, where he was converted, returned to his home and gathered about him a congregation of men and women whom he instructed in the Word and in the worship of the living God. In South Formosa I could point to four different congregations which lie far removed from each other, and at a distance from the mission headquarters, each of which sprang from men who had received their first religious impressions in the mission hospital, and these congregations have established flourishing schools."

We may sum up these benefits as follows:

1. Medical missionaries, as far as possible, become self-supporting, and go out on an unsectarian basis.

2. This plan does not conflict with the work of the regular mission boards, but, on the con-

trary, its purpose is to supplement their efforts and pioneer where they may follow.

3. Where a dispensary has been located a church has soon been formed.

4. Medical mission work destroys caste. In the waiting-room in India may be seen, day after day, sitting side by side, the Brahman, Sudra and Shanar, the Pulayar and Pariah, the devil-worshiper, the worshiper of Siva, the Mohammedan, the Roman Catholic, and Protestant; men, women, of all castes and creeds, while waiting their turn to be examined, listening attentively to the reading of God's Word, and the preaching of the Gospel, thousands of whom, otherwise, would never have an opportunity of hearing the tidings of salvation.

5. Medical mission work secures protection and provision. Dr. Summers, with thirty-six carriers, penetrated Africa 1,500 miles in a direct line, securing from his grateful patients all the means and material which they needed upon the long and difficult tour, and during his whole career of three and a half years he did not receive one dollar from the Home Society.

6. Medical missions are far-reaching in their results. As many as 1,200 to 1,400 towns and villages have been represented in a single year among the in-patients of one hospital, who, returning to their homes, carry with them some of the truth received.

7. Medical mission work is lessening the antiforeign feeling, is diminishing the power of superstition which connects disease with evil spirits, and is giving constant proof of the unselfish character of the Christian religion.

8. "One thing is perfectly certain," said Dr. Post of Syria, "namely, that medical mission work never fails. Other work may fail, but this affording of relief for physical suffering goes on the debit side of Christianity in all cases, and opens the way for other work to follow."

As it is impracticable to notice in detail the growing work of medical missions in foreign lands, it may be well to give some account of the service performed by these missions on one or two fields, thus illustrating the power and possibilities of this factor in Foreign Missions.

The published reports of 1902 show that China has the largest number of medical missionaries, missionary hospitals and dispensaries. In that land there were, in 1901, 128 hospitals, 245 dispensaries, which during the year treated 1,674,571 patients; and more than 150 foreign physicians were in this service. In 1895 the men doctors were fourteen per cent. of all the missionaries, the women doctors were four per cent., and for each doctor there were more than 4,000,000 of the population of China. The need of medical missions in this vast field is appalling. The Chinese doctors are quacks of the worst type; their medicines are mostly decoctions of herbs, mixed with certain vile substances; their *materia medica* is, perhaps, the worst on earth; their ignorance of the simplest principles of physiology is marvelous; and the "medicine man" is deceitful and unscrupulous in playing upon the credulity and superstition of these people. While nearly all diseases are common in this thickly settled country, smallpox is the most common. Vaccination was discovered during the last decade of the 18th century; and, soon after its discovery, Dr. Alexander Pearson, surgeon to the East India Company, introduced it into China. It has been said of him that he "opened China to the Gospel at the point of the lancet." But Dr. Peter Parker is known as the first medical missionary of China, and, commencing his work under the American Board in 1835 in Canton, he brought physical blessings to at least 53,000 patients by his own hands, and many hundreds of thousands have been blessed indirectly by him. Dr. Parker said: "I have no hesitation in expressing it as my solemn conviction that, as yet, no medium of bringing the people under the sound of the Gospel and within the influence of other means of grace can compare with the facilities afforded by medical missionary operations." Dr. Parker's hospital at Canton still continues to exert a wide influence throughout Southern China, and until 1899 it was under the care of Dr. J. G. Kerr. It belongs to the Canton Medical Missionary Society, and, while the largest hospital work in China is at Swatow (English Presbyterian), this Canton hospital comes first in importance, for it is the first institution which combined the alleviation of human suffering and the extension of Christianity, and was, indeed, the pioneer of modern medical missions. In this hospital, during 1898, more than 26,000 patients were treated, and over 1,000 operations took place. By Dr. Kerr and under his supervision some 700,000 patients have been treated, and about 48,000 operations performed; and in addition to this active practise, he published thirty-two books on surgery and medicine. The writer of these words concluded, after visiting the foreign mission fields in 1895 and 1896, that no institution in China was accomplishing more good than the hospital at Canton.

It was largely through the influence of a physician that India was opened to English trade. As far back as 1636 Dr. Gabriel Boughton, an Englishman, while practising at the court of the Great Mogul, cured a princess who was badly burned, and, as his only reward, requested that his countrymen might have the privilege of trade with India. The Danes established a medical missionary work at Tranquebar and Madras in 1730-32. Through the skill of Dr. Thomas, who went out with Carey as a medical missionary, Krishna Pal was cured of serious hurt, was converted and was the first Hindu baptized. The first woman medical missionary from any land was Dr. Clara A. Swain, sent by the American Methodists to Bareilly, India; and they also began the first medical class for women at Naini Tal in 1869. In 1900 there were 111 missionary hospitals and 255 dispensaries in India. The native practises are barbarous; the death rate in British-India is almost twice that of the United States; cholera and small-pox are more or less prevalent among all classes of the natives; the millions of demon-worshipers retard by their ignorance and superstition the work of the physician; and it is estimated that of the 67,000,000 of the people who have but little of British superintendence, hardly two per cent. of them live within twenty-five miles of a European doctor. At Neyoor, under the London Missionary Society, is the largest medical mission in the world. In 1901 there was here a hospital with fifteen dispensaries, and eighteen native medical evangelists; and in 1899 there were 109,029 cases treated. In describing the opening of a new dispensary at Sangli, a writer says: "The patients began to arrive at daybreak, continuing to come till ten o'clock, the hour for dispensing. A native Christian assistant was secured as interpreter and medical helper. He, aided by other native preachers, taught and preached to the people, while they gathered and waited for treatment. Scripture texts were pasted on their medicine bottles, and tracts distributed."

In all foreign lands medical missions are becoming more popular and more powerful. It is an interesting question whether any missionary should be sent out without some knowledge, at least, of the healing art. The Christian physician is honored and welcomed always and anywhere in foreign fields; national and religious prejudices vanish before him, and in one year he can do what it would take another missionary many years to accomplish. It is stated that Dr. Asahel Grant had twenty times more intercourse with the Mohammedans of Persia than the missionary who was sent out expressly to labor among them. Many who are studying thoughtfully the great problem of the evangelization of the nations agree that the consecrated medical missionary and the well-equipped hospital are most important elements of success in the foreign field.

"God had only one son and He gave Him to be a medical missionary," exclaimed Dr. Livingstone; and we recall the impressive fact that this Great Physician sent forth His first disciples to heal as well as to preach. Only a few hundred Christian physicians has America sent forth to the billion of suffering people across the seas; but we predict that the first decade of this century will witness a great awakening on this important question.

Statistics of Hospitals, Dispensaries and Patients treated annually. From *Survey of Foreign Missions*, by Rev. James S. Dennis, D.D.:

Location.	No. of Hospitals.	No. of Dispensaries.	Total Individual Patients.	Total No. of Treatments.
Africa	43	107	139,283	486,459
Alaska	3	4		
Arabia	1	4	7,380	27,525
Burma	7	9	22,620	13,122
Canada & Labrador	10	11	5,176	10,865
Ceylon	4	10	9,324	15,911
China	128	245	685,047	1,674,571
Formosa	3	3	4,948	17,524
India	111	255	842,600	2,453,020
Japan	8	17	35,195	68,845
Korea	8	15	28,968	74,224
Madagascar	3	9	19,349	40,277
Malaysia	3	7	8,380	47,943
Mexico	2	5	6,338	7,221
Oceania	2	2		2,885
Palestine	11	21	72,881	184,156
Persia	6	13	38,646	120,577
Siam and Laos	7	11	14,644	25,986
South America	3	5	2,794	4,041
Syria	6	17	27,685	62,877
Turkey	10	13	37,778	88,076
	379	783	2,009,036	5,426,105
Estimate for 45 hospitals and 113 dispensaries not reporting			338,744	1,016,322
Totals	379	783	2,347,780	6,442,427

Ecumenical Missionary Conference Report, Vol. II., pp. 188-239, New York, 1900; *Missionary Review of the World*, for Theory of Medical Missions, Vol. III., 354, VIII., 666, XII., 770; for Historical Notes, VII., 281; IX., 657; for Instances of Influence, III., 919; in Ceylon, XII., 641, 738; India, XI. 362; in Korea, V., 58; XI., 668; XII., 296; XIV., 688, 690; in Mexico, XII., 535, 773; XV., 416; in Persia, XI., 662; in Siam, XII., 778; XV., 349; in Syria, VI., 641; IX., 910; in Uganda, XV., 407; for Statistics, Dennis (J. S.), *Centenary Survey of Foreign Missions*, pp. 192-211, 222-224, 271, New York, 1902; for General Discussion and Surveys, Williamson (J. R.), *The Healing of the Nations*, New York, 1899: Wanle s (W. J.), *The Medical Mission*, New York, 1901; Penrose (V. F.), *Opportunities in the Path of the Great Physician*, Westminster Press, Philadelphia, 1902.

MEDIEVAL MISSIONS: From the 5th century to the Reformation, the history of missions is practically confined to the movements in Europe which resulted in making that continent Christian. The Eastern Church, except the comparatively minor work of the Nestorians, and the vague rule of the Tatar Prester John, settled down into the sleep from which even the shock of Islam could not arouse it. Altho Russia became Christian during this period, that was hardly a conversion—rather a political transition. The Western Church, too, did very little as a Church. The record of the middle and dark ages in missionary activity is the record of the devotion, ambition and unflagging patience and energy of a comparatively small company of earnest workers. The personal element dominated and the story is almost entirely a series of biographies.

The conversion of Ireland in the 4th century was the real foundation of Medieval Missions. To Ireland, much more certainly than to Rome, the Christianization of England, Scotland and Germany was due.

South Britain, under the Romans, shared in the general Christianity of the Empire; but when the heathen English came over from northern Germany and Jutland, they, in their slow, stubbornly contested advance, swept the land as clean of its civilization and historical remembrances as of its religion. The still unconquered Britons, retreating into the Welsh mountains, with difficulty maintained there a Christianity which the conquering English utterly despised. And when, in 597, the Benedictine abbot Augustine, and his companions sent by Pope Gregory the Great, persuaded the men of Kent to accept the Gospel, which from Kent spread among the West, East and Middle Saxons, the Middle and Northern English remained but little affected. The real Christianization of Northumbria came from Ireland. Columba, a youth of the royal blood of Ulster, having, as a penance for a civil war kindled through his fiery Celtic temper, been required to exile himself to Caledonia, and to spend the rest of his life in laboring for the conversion of the Picts, founded the famous monastery of Iona in the Hebrides, from which he and his disciples poured out with irresistible zeal and with complete success over the lands of the Northern Picts, the Southern Picts being already largely Christian. They were aided by the fact that western Caledonia was largely occupied by Christian Scots of Irish extraction. The Scottish kings, succeeding through intermarriage to to the Pictish throne, gave the name of Scotia to the whole land, and withdrew it from Ireland, which was the original Scotia. From Iona came the humble and zealous bishop, Aidan, to Northumbria, where he labored with great success. But the full Christianization of the country was accomplished through his disciple Cuthbert. Of simple habits, dauntless courage, strong sense, ready wit, tenderness of heart, deep devotion, and of a missionary zeal inflamed by the example of his Irish masters, he became the Apostle of the North. The Mercians likewise gave up the old gods with one consent, and England was now Christian from the Firth to the Channel, being bounded by the Christian Scots on the north and the Christian Welsh on the west, which latter, however, in their implacable animosity against their conquerors, had refused to take the slightest share in the work of conversion.

In all this Rome had comparatively little share, so far as direct influence was concerned, and yet her merits in the conversion of England are not small: (1) she initiated evangelization after the earlier Christianity was almost extinct; (2) she mainly converted the Saxons, as distinguished from the Anglians; (3) she introduced the Gospel among the Anglians; (4) she undertook and carried through, with general consent of the English, that to which the Irish were everywhere utterly incompetent, namely, the organization and practical conduct of the English Church, which she thus held in unity with the general body of Christendom, and preserved it from erratic developments and from final disintegration and anarchy, such as befell the Irish Church, and finally induced even her to submit herself to the organizing skill of Rome.

The Irish Church was, during the early Middle Ages, equally zealous and equally effective in the work of conversion on the Continent. She was, indeed, the great Missionary Church of this era. The reception of the Gospel in Ireland, altho it did nothing to control the intertribal anarchy and to remove the moral rudeness of the people generally, evoked unbounded enthusiasm in thousands of elect spirits, who gathered around their abbots in multitudes of monasteries, surrounded by pious families, and gave themselves up to an extravagant asceticism, but also to noble intellectual pursuits, and a deep study of the Scriptures. While Irish piety had a very imperfect control over the passions of anger and wrath; was deficient in that moral dignity which was congenial to Roman, and still more to the higher English piety; on the other hand, it was ethereal, full of tender and delicate sentiment and pervaded with the glow of a fiery enthusiasm, which, finding insurmountable obstacles at home in an anarchy which it knew not how to reduce into order, poured itself in an irresistible flood upon Western and Middle Europe. The Irish at this time were incomparably superior to the Romans in point of knowledge, while the Irish temperament and the Irish mind had an extraordinary power of communicating its convictions. The Irish monks, caring little for the secular clergy, allowed them to marry. They honored an abbot vastly more than a bishop. But they themselves, in their unsparing asceticism, presented to the wretched Continental populations of that era, succeeding the fearful devastations of barbarian conquest, the impressive spectacle of men living, by their own free will, a more wretched life than the wretched peasants, and yet making not the least account of this destitution of earthly comforts. They were listened to with profoundest reverence, and contributed mightily to the fuller Christianization of their fellow-Celts (of the Cymric branch), the rural populations of Gaul, and to the rooting of the Gospel in Switzerland and in various parts of Germany, especially the south.

The great Irish missionary on the Continent was Columban (not to be confounded with the earlier Columba, of Iona), who established his monastery in 590 among the Vosges Mountains in Eastern Gaul. His rule was severe but practical, combining ascetic self-discipline, manual labor in various forms and study, especially of the Scriptures. He laid great stress on the inward state, and subordinated all observances to this. But his courageous opposition to the wickedness of Queen Brunehild caused his expulsion from Frankish Gaul into what is now Switzerland. His enemies, however, following him up, expelled him after three years from his missionary labors here also. He withdrew into Italy, where he died in 613, in the monastery which he had founded at Bobbio, near Pavia.

He left behind, however (detained by sickness, like St. Paul, among the Galatians), a beloved pupil, a young Irishman of good family, named Gallus. Gallus sought out a retreat in the deep woods of Eastern Switzerland, where he founded the monastery famous for so many centuries as St. Gall, the nucleus of the present canton of that name. It became a great center of population, civilization, learning and Christianity for Eastern Switzerland, the Tyrol and Southern Germany. Somewhat later came the Irish Fridolin, laboring in Alsace, Switzerland and Suabia, and the Irish Thrudpert (whom the Germans call St. Hubert), laboring in the Black Forest. The Irish Cilian, after 650, labored in West Thuringia, toward the middle of Germany. And these are only shining examples of an endless succession of missionary monks that poured out for two or three centuries from Ireland into Gaul, Switzerland, Southern and Middle Germany. Before Boniface began his labors, about 720, Southern Germany seems to have been mainly, and Middle Germany largely, Christianized. The Saxons, who filled the great northern plain of Germany, gave not the slightest heed to the Gospel, the acceptance of which they regarded as the mark of subjection to their rivals, the Catholic Franks.

From of old, along the Rhine and the Danube, and even farther in the heart of Germany, there had been Christian congregations. And tho these had been ravaged and trodden down in the tumultuous movements of the migration of the nations which overthrew the Roman Empire, they still offered a good many points of attachment for the Irish missionaries. The most illustrious of these were, on the Danube, Severinus, whom some held to be a North African and some a Syrian, and, near the Rhine, Eligius, of an old Christian family of the Franks, originally a goldsmith, afterward a bishop. Both these men distinguished themselves by boundless compassion and works of mercy, sometimes redeeming captives, sometimes interceding successfully for the wretched people with their barbarian conquerors, and thus laying foundations the traces of which still subsisted when the Irish missionaries subsequently began their labors. Eligius, indeed, was later than the earliest of these missionaries.

There was, however, the same difficulty with Irish missionary work on the Continent that there had been in England, namely, a want of unity and of organizing power. In Ireland itself, beyond a general deference paid to the abbey and bishopric of Armagh, there was no ecclesiastical unity. The priests had no defined parishes, the bishops no defined dioceses. The abbots were the real ecclesiastical rulers, but every abbot only of his own monastic sept. And this confusion and jarring individualism was reflected in the Irish work abroad. Ireland, moreover, having been for a long while cut off by the wall of English heathenism from the rest of Western Europe, had diverged in various particulars, not so much of doctrine (for both parties stood on the foundation of the great councils, including the Council of Orange) as of ecclesiastical usage in discipline, worship and polity, points which necessarily occasioned a perpetual friction. Especially was it intolerable that while the Romans had adopted a corrected Easter cycle, the Irish still adhered to the earlier, unreformed cycle. Thus, before Oswiu of Northumbria had wisely decided to accept the Roman discipline, the Northumbrian kings had sometimes been holding the Easter rejoicings while their Kentish or Saxon queens were still in the sadness of the Passion-week.

Germany, therefore, compelled like England to commit her Christian future either to the erratic uncertainty of Irish impulse or to the steady, tho certainly much harder, hand of Roman discipline, decided, and doubtless on the whole decided wisely, for the latter. Many free influences and simpler Christian apprehensions were, it is true, compelled to give way for a time. But in reality the Irish national spirit was as distinctly alien from Germany as the Roman. And, except in some casual particulars, the spiritual depth and evangelical freedom of the future Protestantism were no more anticipated in Celtic than in Latin Christianity. Protestantism was, as to its human source, an entirely original creation of the Teutonic genius, which first really apprehended the full significance of the apostolate of Paul. That Rome prevailed, and Ireland gave way, in the final settlement of the German Church, cannot, therefore, be regarded on the whole otherwise than as a providential good. The more we learn of the Middle Ages, the more fully we become aware that there were never absent from them seething forces of spiritual and social anarchy, which Rome could hardly control, and which Ireland, herself anarchical, could not have controlled at all. There were, moreover, still latent in the Saxons of Northern Germany, and yet more terribly in the brooding cloud of Scandinavian piracy that was one day to burst forth over Europe, aggressive forces of heathenism, which could not have been withstood by any fabric less firm than that great organism owning Rome as its center, which finally extended to the very Orkneys, and at last took in Ireland herself, and grappled with the most formidable enemy by incorporating the Scandinavian North. Neander, regretfully as he recounts the ultimate prevalence of Rome, acknowledges that the rude nations needed a rigorous discipline of centuries before they would be ripe for spiritual and national independence.

The conference at York, in the year 664, before King Oswiu, between Bishop Colman, of the Irish use, and the Presbyter Wilfrid, of the Roman use, decided the Northumbrians and Mercians to join with the Saxons and Jutes of Southern England in accepting Rome, rather than Iona, as their future spiritual metropolis. It decided no less the ecclesiastical destiny of Germany. For it was an Englishman that was finally to bring Germany into conformity with Rome, and away from conformity with Ireland.

Winfrid, as he was properly called, was born in Kirton, Devonshire, in the year 680. His father, a man of wealth, destined him for some secular profession, but, humbled by a reverse of fortune, yielded at length to his son's ardent desire for a monastic life. In this Winfrid developed the same qualities of fervent piety, deep disinterestedness, unquailing courage, practical skill, monkish narrowness of mind, and intolerant orthodoxy which distinguished him subsequently when acting, under the name of Boniface, as the papally invested missionary archbishop of Germany. As a Saxon he had, of course, an affinity of race with the Germans, which doubtless came into play in his long contest with the Irish missionaries of the Continent. To him the Roman discipline and the Roman supremacy were of the very essence of the Gospel. He was incapable of making the slightest concession to the Irish monks, altho they had converted so much of Germany, for in his eyes the Irish hardly deserved to be called Christians at all, and he suffered grievous troubles of conscience that he could not altogether avoid an intercourse of social civility with them.

He began his missionary labors in 715, among the Frisians of the German coast. His elder countryman, Willibrord, after twelve years of study in Ireland, had begun a mission in Friesland, aided by various other Englishmen. Willibrord, altho of Irish education, yet, as an Englishman, conformed to the Roman discipline and visited Rome to solicit the papal sanction on his new mission. He was there ordained by the pope himself bishop of Utrecht, where he died after thirty years of not ineffective work. Winfrid first went to Friesland during one of the many intervals of adversity in the mission. He afterward, however, returned and labored for three years under Willibrord with encouraging results. Declining the aged bishop's offer to consecrate him as his successor, he journeyed to Thuringia, in Middle Germany, where he baptized two princesses and in various visits admitted at least 100,000 persons to the Church. In Hesse, his boldness in felling the sacred oak of Donar (whom the Scandinavians called Thor) so appalled the heathen that large numbers forsook the worship of gods who seemed unable to defend their own honor. He had already twice visited Rome, and at his second visit, in 723, had been ordained regionary bishop by the pope, with what we might call a roving commission, taking an oath of obedience and conformity to the Apostolic See, which became the keynote of his whole subsequent policy. Turning away from his nearest German kinsmen, the Saxons (who were, indeed, at this time wholly insensible to Christianity), he spent most of the rest of his life in incessant, sincere, intolerant and finally successful efforts to bring Middle and Southern Germany under the Roman obedience. His double controversy with Virgil, the learned Irish abbot, subsequently bishop of Salzburg, was, it is true, unsuccessful. Rome, tho a great admirer of her servant Boniface, decided both points against him, not without some gentle quizzing of his hyperbolical orthodoxy. But Virgil was willing to come under the new system, and after his death was impartially canonized by the Apostolic See.

In 738 Boniface visited Rome a third time, and received the fullest legatine powers, as archbishop of Germany. He held numerous synods, supported at length by Pepin, who, having been authorized by Pope Zachary to set aside the outworn Merovingian line and to assume the royal dignity for himself, was then, in the pope's name, anointed by Boniface, and thus stood committed to the closest union with Rome. Henceforth Boniface had good assurance of complete success in his effort to transform the German Christianity from the Irish to the Roman type. His veneration for Rome, however, had in it nothing of the slavishness of modern Ultramontanism. He did not apprehend the pope as Universal Bishop, but as the court of highest instance in a graduated scale of episcopal preeminence. He himself meant to establish the German primacy at Cologne, but, being disappointed in this by an intrigue, fixed it, less suitably, at Mentz. He also founded the renowned Benedictine abbey of Fulda, which for 1,000 years was the Monte Cassino of Germany. In all his organizing plans and administrative acts, his unsympathetic, heresy-hunting, Romanizing orthodoxy was accompanied by a large forecast of cool statesmanship, which in him decidedly prevailed over enthusiasm. Not even his most admiring disciples, says Neander, ascribed to him a single miracle. It is the judgment of one who has given much attention to his course that the deepest instinct of his heart was, after all, not that of the ecclesiastical administrator, but of the monastic missionary. To this his early life agrees, and much of his middle life, and, above all, his end. For in 755, abandoning his great see of Mentz, he set out for his early mission field of Friesland, and there, having fixed a day on which many of his baptized converts should return to him for confirmation, was, on that very day, surprised by a heathen band, and, in his seventy-fifth year, with many of his companions, joyfully received the crown of martyrdom.

It may be disputed, in view of the earlier successes of Ireland, whether we have a right to call him the apostle of Germany. Nor can we be blind to his deep defects, or at least to his narrow limitations. Yet after all abatements he stands forth as one of the great characters of Christian, of German and English, and of missionary history.

Germany was now two-thirds Christian. Its full Christianization, in the abandonment of heathenism by the mighty Saxon race of the northern plain, was accomplished, not by the missionary, but by the crowned soldier, Charles the Great. His spiritual adviser, the English abbot Alcuin, bitterly remonstrated against his unevangelical employment of force, and against his imposition of the tithe. But Charlemagne persisted, being convinced that his empire could never have peace until the Saxons were brought into the national and spiritual communion of his great realm. And tho they were thus compelled into the Church, yet, so soon as the national pride of their adherence to paganism had been broken, they rapidly assimilated Christianity, and soon became perhaps the most stanchly Christian of all the German tribes. And when the fulness of the time had come, at the Reformation, for the complete emancipation of the Gospel, it was in Northern Germany that the adult Christianity of Protestantism found its home. Luther himself, it is true, tho called a Saxon, was only such by that curious territorial lapse which had transferred the ancient name from its proper seat, and made it the designation of a Middle German race.

The conversion of Northern Germany laid the basis for the Christianization of the three Scandinavian realms. The Apostle of Scandinavia, St. Ansgar, is a character of peculiar beauty. He was a native of the Frankish kingdom, having been born in the diocese of Amiens, A. D. 801. The delicacy of his imagination, and the sweet courtesy of his character, make it probable that he was a Roman rather than a German Frank; in other words, that he was a Frenchman proper. He early became a monk in the neighboring Corbie, under the abbot Adalhard and the learned teacher, Paschasius Radbert. But when Charles the Great (Charlemagne), having forcibly converted the Saxons, wished to instruct them in their new religion, and removed a colony of monks from Corbie to the Weser, calling the daughter-abbey Corvey, Ansgar was one of the colonists. He had early been sensible of a vocation to the missionary life, and his whole life showed that he "was not disobedient to the heavenly vision." The pious and statesmanlike Ebbo, archbishop of Rheims, having gained over to Christianity King Harold of Denmark, on a visit to the Emperor Lewis, deputed Ansgar to accompany the king on his return to his fierce heathen subjects, a journey then so much dreaded that Ansgar could only find a single monk, Authbert, to go with him, who, soon dying, left him alone. After two years of residence, and some initial successes, he and King Harold were both expelled. But now better prospects began to open in Sweden. Seeds of Christianity had already begun to germinate there. Ansgar, therefore, during some two years' residence found much encouragement. His favorable report, on his return from Sweden, induced the Emperor Lewis to establish the archbishopric of Bremen-Hamburg as the basis of the Northern mission, and to dispatch Ansgar to Rome, where he received episcopal consecration and was invested with the archiepiscopal pallium. During many years, from the basis of his metropolitan see, with a flexible patience that knew no discouragement, that availed itself of every opportunity, and recovered itself after every shock of heathen aggression, such as once laid his own diocese waste, Ansgar steadily pursued his great purpose. He was aided by suffragan bishops in Denmark and Sweden, whom he supported as occasion required by personal visits. At last, the heathen having already become accustomed by many instances of deliverance after invoking the name of Christ, to regard Him as a mighty deity, Ansgar visited the national assembly of Gothland, in the south of the peninsula, and that of Sweden proper, in the middle, and obtained from each a decree that the preaching and acceptance of the Gospel should be freely permitted. Ansgar, having made arrangements for the more effective prosecution of the missions, returned to Bremen. There were many subsequent vicissitudes, especially in Denmark, for the Gospel seemed to cohere more intimately with the nature of the milder and perhaps more thoughtful Swedes, who, moreover, are of a deeply devotional turn. But the foundations laid by Ansgar remained. Danish conquest in England, moreover, reacted for the evangelization of Denmark, especially through the influence of the mighty Canute. The process of conversion was slow but steady. By the year 1100 it is doubtful whether any traces of avowed heathenism remained in either Denmark or Sweden.

After more than thirty-four years of labor for the salvation of the heathen nations of the north, when past the age of sixty-four he was attacked by a severe fit of sickness, from which he died.

His character seems to have the effectiveness of Boniface without his hardness, and the zeal of the Irish missionaries without the wrathful impatience adhering to some of them—a most winning embodiment, certainly, of missionary excellence.

The Christianization of the Mongolian Finns resulted in part from the conquest of Finland by St. Eric, the first Swedish king of that name, but still more from the evangelical labors of St. Henry, the first bishop of Abo. St. Henry's Day is still a conspicuous festival of the Lutheran Church of Finland.

The introduction of Norway within the Christian pale resembles in its earlier stage a chapter of Muslim and, in its later stage, of Buddhist, propagandism more than any chapter of genuinely Christian missionary effort. It seems to have had very little root in the religious instincts of the people, altho genuine Christian influences are by no means absent. But the kings who finally subdued the whole of Norway under them, and rooted out the power of the petty local monarchs, being convinced that effective government could only rest on the foundation of a wider and richer civilization, and that this could only be supported by Christianity, really forced Christianity on their subjects at the point of the sword. And when these were once baptized, the Roman missionaries unfolded the utmost magnificence of their ritual—here again like the Buddhist missionaries in Japan. And as the Norsemen, says Herder, had the profoundest faith in the efficacy of magical rites and regarded the Roman ceremonies as merely a more exalted and a purer kind of magic, they finally surrendered themselves to the new worship without any further thought of resistance. But the fact that so few Norwegian kings or heroes have cared to be buried in the metropolitan cathedral of Trondhjem, is noted by Mr. Froude as signifying that they had little heart in their professed Christianity until the Reformation gave them a form of it which they could really believe. Lutheran Norway is now a genuinely and zealously Christian country. But the religious development of Sweden, both under Latin and under Lutheran Christianity, has been (as is natural, in view of its much greater population) a far richer and more conspicuous one. In the 14th century St. Brigitta, the widowed Swedish princess, may be regarded as "the bright consummate flower" of the Scandinavian race, showing, it is said, almost equal vigor of the practical, the poetical and the prophetic instinct, and, under the veil of an extravagant devotion to the Virgin, revealing many deep evangelical perceptions, true harbingers of the Reformation. And altho her ashes rest in Rome, and her name stands in the Roman calendar, yet her prediction is on record that "the throne of the pope shall yet be cast into the abyss."

By this time Germany, France, Great Britain, Denmark, Sweden and Norway were all included within the pale of Latin, and Russia within that of Greek, Christianity. Poland and Bohemia and the other Slavonian countries were thus morally certain, sooner or later, to yield to the irresistible influence of what was becoming the religion alike of Southern and of Northern Europe. Moravia and Bohemia, indeed, the two principal Slavonic countries of Middle Europe, rather antedated than followed the conversion of Scandinavia. By an unusual providence, they were Christianized by two Greek missionaries, Cyril and his brother Methodius. These had already been active among the Bulgarians, who also received missionaries from the pope, but after some wavering settled down under the patriarchal rule of Constantinople. Cyril and Methodius then labored among the Mongolian Chazars, in the Crimea, with a good deal of success. They then came up into Central Europe, among the Moravians, not far from the year 850, and therefore while Ansgar was still laboring in the north. German missionaries sent out by the Archbishop of Salzburg had already effected a good many conversions. But their foolish obstinacy in adhering to the Latin liturgy was in the way. Methodius (for Cyril soon became a monk in Rome), with his more flexible Greek character, boldly introduced the Slavonian tongue into worship. The German bishops murmured; but the pope, who had already consecrated Methodius Archbishop of Moravia, stood forth as his defender. Bohemia, then dependent on Moravia, was Christianized from it. The Germans still wrangled with Methodius over his independent jurisdiction and over his Slavonic liturgy, so that at last he went to Rome, and seems to have followed his brother Cyril into retirement. But the Christianizing impulse had now become so strong among the Slavonians that, by somewhat obscure stages, the whole Slavonic race from Bohemia to the Adriatic is found to be Christian. It is interesting to note that, after long interruption, the use of the Slavonic liturgy has lately been conceded again, by Pope Leo XIII., to the Slavonic Illyrians.

The propagation of Christianity among the Slavonic Wends, between Bohemia and the Baltic, is a confused history of genuine missionary successes, of armed proselytism by over-zealous princes, and of violent and persecuting heathen reactions. Yet ultimately Christianity prevailed here also, by an historical necessity. Poland, like its great Slavonian sister and rival, Russia, was Christianized mainly from above, not far from the year 1000. But while Russia took Constantinople for her spiritual capital, Poland, as might have been expected from her rivalry, chose Rome. The Teutonic order of military monks had much to do with the suppression of paganism along the Baltic.

The Magyars, of Mongolian race, who wrought fearful devastations in Germany in the earlier Middle Ages, but were finally shut up to their new kingdom of Hungary, of which they still form the dominant race, were found after this check not altogether inaccessible to German missionaries. St. Adalbert, Archbishop of Prague, who afterward died a missionary martyr among the Slavonic Prussians (near Poland), spent some time in Hungary. Prince Geisa and his wife were baptized, but remained about as much pagan as before. Their son Stephen, however, (St. Stephen) was a thorough and zealous Christian. He married a German princess, received the rank of king from the Christian Emperor Otto, and succeeded in impressing on the kingdom of Hungary that deep character of medieval yet kindly Catholicism which it still retains. Protestantism is there powerful, and honorably considered; but nowhere in Europe does the ecclesiastical magnificence of the Middle Ages remain so little disturbed. The Archbishop of Gran, the Primate of Hungary, is the only primate of actual jurisdiction in the Latin Church. And at a coronation the lines of splendid horsemen wearing the insignia of mitred abbots show that in Hungary the illustrious Benedictine order still retains its ancient preeminence. The Hungarian Christianity, which glories in the monarch's title of Apostolical King, has been the anvil that has worn out the Muslim hammer of the kindred Turks. But this Mongolian Christianity has shown its zeal rather in the field of war than of spiritual achievement, in which the Mongolian race has seldom been preeminent.

The latest surrender of a whole European nation to the profession of Christianity took place in 1384, when Ladislaus Jagiello, Grand Duke of the then very extensive and powerful principality of Lithuania, obtained the hand of Hedwig, Queen of Poland, and went over, with all his people, from paganism to the Church.

Such were the missions, proselytizing crusades, and proselytizing compacts of Catholic Europe, Eastern and Western, between the year 500 and the year 1500. The principles of the Gospel seem to have been most thoroughly carried out in the Christianization of England, Scotland, Switzerland, Southern and Middle Germany and Sweden, and to have been the farthest departed from in the cases of Northern Germany and Norway, the former of which, however, became soon, and the latter ultimately, sincerely and zealously Christian. Not even the Gospel, accepted in this wholesale way as a national creed, could avoid large complications with uncivilized rudeness, with violence, and with selfish policy. The Reformation brought in that sifting process which is every day becoming more rapid. Yet there is great occasion to thank God that over so large a proportion of medieval Europe so great a number of humble and self-devoted men of God secured the genuine conversion of so many individuals and nations to the Gospel of Christ.

While these movements were winning Northern Europe for Christianity, on the south there arose the conflict with Islam. The crusades were scarcely missions, and yet there was a distinctly missionary spirit in the desire to overcome Islam by Christianity as well as to rescue the Holy Sepulchre. So, too, the monastic orders which arose in this period, Augustinian, Carthusian, Cistercian, Carmelite, Franciscan, Dominican and others, while specially organized for the development of a devotional type of piety, had a direct relation to the centralization of the Church, and were not devoid of the missionary idea, as became manifest when they came to their full fruitage in the succeeding period. Francis of Assisi, when he forced his way to the presence of the Sultan of Egypt and preached Christianity in his court, was but the predecessor of Xavier and his associates. There was, however, one missionary of this type who has won a high place among the laborers for the spiritual extension of the faith. The story of Raymund Lull is like a romance of modern missions. Turning from the scientific studies in which he won great renown, he applied himself to the task of overcoming Islam. In this work he sought the aid of the king of Majorca, of the pope, of the Council of Vienne, of England. Every effort to arouse the Church having failed, he went himself once and again to Cyprus, Asiatic Turkey and Tunis, where at last his life was a sacrifice to his zeal.

In considering the character of this period it becomes apparent that it is but the development of the close of its predecessor. The Church as a whole had no interest whatever in the extension of Christianity. A comparatively small number of individuals, by superb devotion, saved Europe and laid the foundations of the development in the centuries that followed, in the educational institutions to which Germany and England owe their preeminence, in political and intellectual as well as spiritual life. It was the missionaries of the Middle Ages to whom the modern European owes much of the best life that he enjoys. In the degree that Southern Europe failed to share their influence, it fell below their standard.

So far as methods were concerned, there was little of what may be called popular influence through these missions. The missionaries sought the leaders, relying upon them to bring with them their people. Even in their educational enterprises it was to the possible leaders that they gave attention. The era of the common people had not yet come.

So, too, the motive was inadequate. It was very largely the Church, its aggrandizement, its victory. Even with Raymund Lull, the great ambition was not so much the salvation of Muslims as the defeat of Islam. It remained for the Reformation to find for the individual soul his proper place in the scheme of a world's salvation.

Maclear (G. F.), *Christian Missions During the Middle Ages*, London, 1863; (———), *Apostles of Mediæval Europe*, New York, 1869; Smith (T.), *Mediæval Missions*, Edinburgh, 1880; Kingsmill (J. J.), *Missions and Missionaries, Apostolic, Jesuit and Protestant*. London, 1854; Barnes (L. C.), *Two Thousand Years of Missions before Carey*, New York, 1901; Zwemer (S. M.), *Raymund Lull*, New York, 1902.

MEDINGEN: A village in the Zoutspansberg District of Transvaal, Africa. Station of the Berlin Missionary Society (1881), with 1 missionary, 19 native workers, 8 outstations, 6 day schools, and 1,121 professed Christians, of whom 619 are communicants.

MEERUT: A town in the Punjab, India, capital of the district of Meerut, situated 39 miles N. E. of Delhi. It is the headquarters of a British military division, with extensive camps. The mutiny of 1857 began here. Altitude, 737 feet. Population (1891), 73,600, about evenly divided between Muslims and Hindus. Station of the CMS (1815), with (1903) 2 missionaries and their wives, 2 women missionaries, 58 native workers, 7 outstations, 1 place of worship, 17 day schools, 2 boarding schools, and 1,401 professed Christians, of whom 116 are communicants. Station also of the ME, with (1903) 1 missionary and his wife, 2 women missionaries, 36 native workers, 38 Sunday schools, 1 college, 10 day schools, 1 boarding school, and 1,275 professed Christians, of whom 480 are communicants. Station also of the RPS, with 2 native workers, 1 outstation, 1 college, 1 Sunday school, and 55 professed Christians.

MEESTER CORNELIS: A village in the island of Java, situated 10 miles S. E. of Batavia. Station of the Netherlands Missionary Society (1886), with (1903) 1 missionary, 5 native workers, 3 outstations, 3 day schools, and 258 professed Christians, of whom 142 are communicants.

MEIGS, Benjamin Clark: Born at Bethlehem, Conn., August 9, 1789; graduated, 1809; spent two years and a half at Andover Theological Seminary. While there he determined to devote himself to a missionary life. He was ordained June 21, 1815, and sailed October 23 following as one of the original founders of the ABCFM in Jaffna, Ceylon. There he labored forty years. Failure of health in 1858 compelled him to relinquish the mission work. He died in New York City, May 12, 1862, aged sixty-three.

MEIKTILA: A growing town, military and railroad station in Burma, British India, situated 80 miles S. by W. of Mandalay. Population, 7,200 (1902). Station of the ABMU (1890), with (1903) 1 missionary, 3 native workers, 1 place of worship, 1 Sunday school, 1 day school, 1 outstation, and 14 professed Christians.

MELANESIA: The name given to that part of the islands of the Western Pacific Ocean which lie south of the Equator and between the Fiji Islands on the east and New Guinea on the west. The people are a branch of the Papuan race, and much darker than the true Polynesians. They are also more savage and have less advancement in such simple arts as have been naturally developed among the Pacific islanders. The language of the various groups of islands is one, with great variation into dialects in the different groups. The islands are mostly of volcanic origin, but rest on a coral foundation, and are sometimes surrounded with coral reefs. The principal groups included in this division are the Bismarck archipelago, **Solomon Islands,** the Louisiade archipelago, and the **New Hebrides.** New Caledonia, New Guinea, and the Fiji Islands are ethnologically connected with the same division of Oceania.

Mission work was begun in the New Hebrides by the visit of the Rev. John Williams of the LMS to Erromanga in 1839 at the expense of the United Presbyterian Church of Scotland. John Williams was killed by the islanders, and the effort to evangelize the islands was continued by the LMS through native workers from Samoa, until 1848. In that year the Rev. John Geddie, sent out by the Presbyterian Synod of Nova Scotia, established himself on Aneitium, and after terrible hardships succeeded in his work, so that over his grave is written "When he came to the island in 1848, there was not a single Christian; when he left in 1872, there was not a single heathen."

From that beginning the work has spread through more than 20 islands. It is now carried on by a society composed of a sort of federation of Presbyterian bodies, known as The New Hebrides Mission. The organization now has 50 missionaries in the islands. The total of professed Christian adherents is about 17,000.

The northern part of the New Hebrides and the Solomon and **Santa Cruz Islands** are occupied by the Melanesian Mission, founded by Bishop Selwyn in 1849, and made fruitful by the blood of martyrs. This mission has its headquarters, and a fine training school for native workers, at Norfolk Island, and has gradually extended its work through the northern islands of Melanesia, until it now has about 25 missionaries and a very large force of native workers, with about 15,000 professed adherents.

The **Loyalty Islands** were entered by the LMS in 1841. Since 1891 the Paris Evangelical Mission Society has taken over the work on the island of Maré, in deference to the susceptibilities of the French officials. The LMS has found it possible to begin evangelistic work through native workers in New Caledonia, from which its missionaries are excluded by the French Government. The whole number of professed Christian adherents under the LMS and the Paris Society in this group is about 10,000, and the aggregate native Christian population of Melanesia is probably over 40,000. What this means, as a testimony to the power of the Gospel, can be realized by those only who know the condition from which these converts have risen.

MELANESIAN MISSION: Headquarters, Norfolk Island.

The diocese of the first Anglican bishop of New Zealand embraced a large number of the islands of the South Pacific, and a suggestion was made to Bishop Selwyn, on his consecration in 1841, that he should establish an Island Mission apart from that of New Zealand. He took up the idea with the thought of making these island regions a missionary field that would call out missionary spirit in the colonies. From 1847 to 1849 Bishop Selwyn made several voyages to neighboring regions. From year to year, as his acquaintance with the seas and the people increased, he extended his voyages toward the north, and most of the islands between New Zealand and the Santa Cruz group were visited, and little by little the confidence of chiefs and leading men was gained. Thus, the islands of Melanesia were opened to missionary effort, and at a meeting of the bishops of Australasia, held in Sydney in 1850, this part of the island world was adopted by them as the mission work of their churches.

By contributions from Australia, the " Border Maid," a schooner of 100 tons, was furnished for the mission; and in 1851 Dr. Tyrrell, the Bishop of Newcastle, New South Wales, who had been Bishop Selwyn's comrade in the Cambridge University boat, accompanied him on a voyage, seeing for himself the admirable way in which Bishop Selwyn dealt with the savages.

In 1855 the Rev. **John Coleridge Patteson** joined the mission at his own charges, in 1861 was consecrated Bishop of Melanesia and was joined by Rev. R. H. Codrington, of Oxford. The chief sphere of Bishop Patteson's labors was in the Northern New Hebrides, the Banks, and Solomon groups. Between the latter are the Santa Cruz and Swallow Isles, where he eagerly sought openings; and it was in the Swallow group that he, with Rev. J. Atkin and a native teacher, was murdered in 1871. Dr. Codrington, while declining the bishopric, continued the mission, which now owes more than can be said to his labors in every field of the work, but especially to his management of the school at Norfolk Island and to his unwearied researches into the philology of the island languages and his application of them to the practical work of translations. In 1873, Rev. J. R. Selwyn, a son of the pioneer bishop, and Rev. John Still volunteered for the work, and the former was, in 1877, consecrated Bishop of Melanesia. The present field of the Melanesian Mission embraces groups of islands from the northern part of the New Hebrides to the Solomon Islands.

From the earliest days of the mission the Bishop of New Zealand hoped to work these islands by means of native teachers and a native ministry. To use his own phrase, "The white corks were only to float the black net." To carry out this purpose, the islands are divided into districts, each headed by a white clergyman or member of the staff, and from these districts boys are brought every year to Norfolk Island, where they are trained. The school work breaks up in April, when the island voyages begin, and is not taken up again till they are over, in November. These winter voyages are the most arduous part of the work connected with the mission, and are prosecuted under circumstances of continual hardship and danger over seven months of the year and 18,000 miles of sea; but without them and the mission vessel, the "Southern Cross," the mission could not be maintained.

The income of the mission is derived from subscriptions from England, Australia and New Zealand, and from an endowment fund, a large portion of which was bequeathed by Bishop Patteson, and which produces about £1,500 a year. In New Zealand the mission is adopted as a work of the Church, and collections are made for it in every parish. In Australia the help is less definite, and comes largely from Sunday schools, which support scholars at the mission.

Mission fields: 1. *New Hebrides:* As the Presbyterian New Hebrides Mission increased in strength and enlarged its borders among these islands, the Melanesian Mission confined its labors to the most northern islands, while extending its efforts toward Santa Cruz and the Solomon Islands. Its present stations in the New Hebrides are on Maewo, or Arorae, Opa or Lepeis Isle, and Arahga or Pentecost Island. All were visited by Bougainville, who took possession of them in the name of the King of France, and by Cook. All had a bad reputation, but the reception accorded to Bishops Selwyn and Patteson was, in the main, friendly, and where there was opposition or apparent enmity, it could be traced to treachery or abuse by Europeans.

2. The group of islands, discovered by Mendana in 1568, and called by him the *Solomon Isles*, because he supposed them to be the source of King Solomon's "gold, ivory, apes, peacocks," lie about 200 miles to the northwest of the New Hebrides group. They were first visited by Bishop Selwyn and Mr. Patteson in 1857, and from that time until his death, in 1871, Bishop Patteson put forth every effort for them, with the result that stations and schools are now established upon most of the islands of the group. At Isabel, the most northerly of the Solomon Isles, there are three schools, and Christianity has gained a great hold on the people. Other islands upon which many schools and churches have been established are San Christobal, Ulawa, and Malayta.

3. *The Banks Islands*, lying to the north of the New Hebrides, have been the most successful field. Mota is a Christian island, under the charge of a native pastor, as are also Mohlav and Ra. Schools well attended and well taught fairly encircle the islands, so that the people almost everywhere have an opportunity of attending one or other of them within reasonable distance. The Santa Cruz Islands have for three centuries borne a tragic relation to European life. Mendana in 1595, Capt. Carteret's expedition in 1797, La Perouse in 1788, and D'Entrecastreaux in 1798 all suffered at the hands of the islanders, and it was near them, while planning for them, that Bishop Patteson was murdered in 1871. Rev. J. Alkin and a native teacher, and later Commodore Goodenough, also died by their hostile arrows. Still a hold has been secured even there.

The report of the Mission shows, in 1900, 28 missionaries, about 400 native workers, 14 stations, 1,700 communicants, about 170 day schools with 15,000 pupils, 2 higher schools with 280 pupils.

MELOLO: A settlement on the E. coast of Sumba Island, Dutch East Indies. Station of the Netherlands Reformed Church (1880), with 1 missionary and wife, 1 native worker, 1 outstation, 402 professed Christians.

MELSETTER: A town and county seat in S. E. Rhodesia, Africa, situated 25 miles N. by W. of Mt. Silinda, and 150 miles W. by S. of Beira. Station of the ABCFM (1902), with 1 woman missionary and 1 day school.

MELUR: A village in Madras, India, situated 20 miles N. E. of Madura. Station of the ABCFM (1857) with 1 missionary and wife, 13 native workers, 10 outstations, 8 places of worship, 10 Sunday schools, 8 day schools, 1 boarding school, 1 Young Men's Christian Association, and 119 professed Christians.

MEMIKAN: A village west of Urmia, Persia, on the border of Turkey. At various times missionaries from Urmia have been stationed there for work among the mountain Nestorians, but the work is usually conducted by the native church and pastor.

MENADO: A town in Minahassa, the northeastern peninsula of Celebes, Dutch East Indies, noted as a great coffee emporium. From 1830 to 1874 it was the chief seat of the Netherlands Missionary Society, which worked with great success among the heathen Alifures. Difficulties arising from the different languages spoken by the Alifures were overcome by the introduction of the Malayan language in church and school, and in the peninsula there are now 147,000 Christian Alifures as the result of this mission. Lack of money compelled the missionaries to enter the service of the state church in 1870, and the Society supports a printing house and a few schools only, the support of pastors, as well as their appointment, resting with the Colonial Government. The Batavia Committee for the evangelization of the Sangir and Talaut islands use Menado as a supply station for their mission.

MENDI LANGUAGE: An African language of the Negro, as distinguished from the Bantu group. It is spoken by a small part of the population of Sierra Leone in West Africa, and has been reduced to writing by missionaries with use of Roman letters.

MENDOZA: A town in Argentina, South America, capital of the state of Mendoza, situated 95 miles S. of San Juan and 620 miles W. by N. of Buenos Aires. Its altitude is 2,559 feet. Its climate is dry and temperate. All its finest buildings were destroyed by earthquake in 1881. Population of 18,000. Station of the ME, with (1903) 1 missionary and wife, 1 place of worship, 1 Sunday school, and 73 professed Christians, of whom 72 are communicants.

MENGNANAPURAM: A town in Madras, India, situated in Tinnevelli about 25 miles S. of Tuticorin. Station of the CMS, with (1903) 2 women missionaries, 1 Sunday school, 2 boarding schools, and 23 native workers. The church is entirely self-supporting and independent, and its statistics are no longer given by the Society.

MENGO: A village in Uganda, Africa, capital of the native kingdom, which is a province of the British Uganda. It is situated to the N. of Lake Victoria Nyanza. Station of the CMS (1887), with (1903) 8 missionaries, 3 of them with their wives; 5 women missionaries, 223 native workers, 1 Sunday school, 1 theological class, 1 female helpers' training class, 1 industrial school, 1 dispensary, 1 hospital, 1 medical class, and 12,058 professed Christians, of whom 3,310 are communicants.

MEQUINEZ: A town in Morocco, situated 36 miles W. by S. of Fez. It stands on the side of a high mountain in a fertile valley, and is the summer residence of the Sultan. Altitude, 1,755 feet. Population, 30,000. Station of the Gospel Mission Union (1895), with (1901) 1 missionary and his wife. Station of the PB, with (1901) 1 missionary and his wife.

MERCEDES: A town in Argentina, South America, situated 60 miles W. by N. of Buenos Aires. Population, 9,500. Station of the ME, with (1903) 2 missionaries and their wives, 8 native workers, 3 places of worship, 2 Sunday schools, 1 day school, 1 theological school, and 164 professed Christians, of whom 100 are communicants.

MERGAREDJA: A town on the N. coast of Java, Dutch East Indies, situated about 140 miles W. by N. of Surabaya. Station of the Netherlands Mennonite Mission Society (1849), with (1903) 3 missionaries (two of them with their wives), 12 native workers, 4 outstations, 3 places of worship, 4 day schools, 1 boarding school, 1 dispensary, and 194 professed Christians.

MERIAM, William B.: Born Princeton, Mass., U. S. A., September 15, 1830; graduated at Harvard University, 1855; Andover Theological Seminary, 1858; ordained November 29 of that year; sailed as a missionary of the ABCFM January 17, 1859, for Turkey. After spending a few months at Adrianople in studying Turkish, he went with Mr. Clark to the new station of Philippopolis, where he remained till his death. Returning from Constantinople with his wife in July, 1862, he was met by five mounted brigands, who shot him as he was alighting from his horse. His death was almost instantaneous.

MERKARA: A town in the native State of Coorg, India, of which it is the capital; situated 64 miles E. S. E. of Mangalore. Altitude, 3,605 feet. The climate is very damp. Population, 7,000, of whom 5,000 are Hindus. Station of the Basel Mission Society (1870), with (1903) 3 missionaries (two of them with their wives), 6 native workers, 4 outstations, 1 day school, and 156 professed Christians, of whom 90 are communicants.

MERSINE: A town and seaport in the province of Adana, Asiatic Turkey, situated 36 miles by rail S. E. of the city of Adana. Population, 9,000, of whom 5,000 are Muslims and 3,500 Christians. Station of the RP (1883), with 1 missionary and wife, 2 women missionaries, 11 native workers, 3 outstations, 1 place of worship, 2 Sunday schools, 3 day schools, 2 boarding schools, 1 dispensary, and 72 professed Christians. Outstation also of the ABCFM. Statistics included in Adana.

MESOPOTAMIA: Originally the country "between the rivers," *i. e.*, the Tigris and the Euphrates. It is not now a political division, and the term is used differently by different writers, but in general it may be said to include the whole plain of the valley of the Tigris from Mardin in the north to Bagdad, or even Bassora, on the south, and from the Euphrates on the west to the Zagros Mountains of the Persian border on the east. The land is extraordinarily fertile, and even now, if properly cultivated, would yield a wonderful increase. The population is chiefly Mohammedans and Christians of the **Jacobite** and **Chaldean** sects. Nomad **Kurds**, living on the mountains, come into the plains for their winter pasturage.

METHODIST CHURCH IN CANADA; Missionary Society of the: The Missionary Society of the Methodist Church was organized 1824. At that time, in addition to work among the white settlers, some efforts were being made to reach the scattered bands of Indians in Ontario with the Gospel message, and it was with a view of extending the work that the Society was formed. There are now six departments: Home, Indian, French, Chinese and Japanese in British Columbia, and Foreign. The home work (called Domestic Missions) embraces all the dependent fields of the Church among the English-speaking people throughout the Dominion, in Newfoundland, and Bermuda. These fields are 450 in number, with 350 missionaries, 69 assistants and 34,826 communicants.

The Indian missions are in Ontario, the Northwest, and British Columbia. They are 68 in number, with 39 missionaries, 14 native assistants, 15 teachers, and 7 interpreters, or a total missionary force of 75. The number of communicants is 5,505.

The results of mission work among the Indians have been of the most encouraging kind. Whole tribes have been reclaimed from barbarism and superstition, and many of them walk worthy of their high calling as followers of the Lamb. A significant illustration of the value of these missions is found in the fact that not one member or adherent of the Methodist Church among the Indians, nor, so far as is known, of any Protestant mission, was implicated in the revolt that occurred a number of years ago.

The French missions are entirely in the province of Quebec. They are 6 in number, with 6 missionaries, 6 teachers, and several colporteurs.

The Foreign work of the Society is in Japan and China. The former was begun in 1873, the latter in 1891.

The work in Japan is in the districts of Tokio, Shizuoka, Tamanashi, Kanazawa and Nagano. There are 27 stations, 44 missionaries, 1 assistant, and 1 teacher. The number of communicants is 2,750. The Japan mission of this Society has been an earnest advocate of a union of Methodist Missions in Japan, corresponding to that of the Presbyterian and Reformed churches. The mission in China is located in the province of Szechwan, two stations being occupied, Chentu and Kiating. While there was temporary suspension during the Boxer troubles, there was little actual loss, and the hospitals in the two places were not disturbed. The Press of the mission has also done excellent work. The ten missionaries (men) are devotedly laboring in the two stations, but the Society does not see fit to publish statistics of their work and its results. By careful searching of the reports one may gather, however, that there are 2 hospitals, a printing establishment, some Sunday schools, and at least 60 or 70 professed Christians.

ORGAN: *The Missionary Outlook*, monthly.

METHODIST EPISCOPAL CHURCH IN U. S.; Missionary Society of the (1819): The conversion of a colored man by the name of Stewart, and his subsequent work among the Indians, profoundly stirred the Methodist Episcopal Church, and was the first impulse toward the formation of a missionary society for the whole Church. Local organizations had previously existed in Philadelphia, Boston, and possibly other places, when at a meeting of the preachers of the Methodist Episcopal Church in New York City, held in 1818, the Rev. Laban Clark proposed the organization of a Bible and Missionary Society in the church of which they were members. The subject having been fully discussed, the formation of such a society was resolved upon, and Messrs. Clark, Nathan Bangs, and Freeborn Garrettson were appointed a committee to draft a constitution, which was approved by the Preachers' Meeting, and subsequently submitted to a public meeting of the members of the church and friends of the missionary cause convened by the Preachers' Meeting, and held in the Forsyth-street Church, on the evening of April 5, 1819. As organized, the Society had the double character of a Bible and Missionary Society. This met with some opposition, and the new organization had but a precarious existence for the first year. In May, 1820, at the meeting of the General Conference, the Society was heartily endorsed, and the constitution was amended so as to make it a purely missionary society.

Until 1844 the Society represented all the churches of the denomination. In that year, however, a division was made, and the Methodist Episcopal Church (South) was formed, and established its own Missionary Society. The Missionary Society of the Methodist Episcopal Church (in the U. S.) is really the Church itself acting through its various forms of organization.

The General Conference for the prosecution of its missionary work appoints two bodies, one a Board of Managers, and the other a General Missionary Committee.

The Missionary Committee is composed of the bishops, as *ex officio* members, one representative from each of fourteen districts, and the secretaries and treasurers; also fourteen members of the Board of Managers.

The Board of Managers is composed of the bishops as *ex officio* members, thirty-two laymen, and thirty-two traveling ministers of the church elected by the General Conference.

The General Conference meets once in four years, the General Missionary Committee once every year, and the Board of Managers monthly, or oftener, as may be required. Honorary managers and patrons, by virtue of donations, have the right of attending the meetings of the Board of Managers, but do not vote. The appropriation of money and the selection of fields rests entirely with the General Missionary Committee, except that the Board of Managers may provide for any unforeseen emergency that may arise in any of the missions, and meet any demands to an amount not exceeding $25,000. Wherever a foreign mission is organized into a conference it receives notice of appropriations directly from the General Missionary Committee. Wherever missions are not thus organized as a conference, they receive their information of appropriations through the Board of Managers. For those missions that are organized as a conference, the Board of Managers acts simply as the executive body of the Missionary Committee. All funds, however, for all missions pass through the hands of the Board of Managers, who account to the General Missionary Committee, and that body to the General Conference.

Each mission, whether it be organized as a conference or not, is divided into districts, over which certain ministers are appointed by the bishop as presiding elders, who superintend the work of that district and are in a sense sub-diocesan bishops.

In 1839 the Board of Managers, to celebrate the centenary of the Methodist Society in London, collected a fund for a mission house, and the first building in New York City was dedicated in January, 1848. At the centenary of American Methodism in 1866, and the Missionary Jubilee in 1869, the fund was greatly increased, a new building secured, and in 1887 the present building on Fifth avenue and 20th street, New York, was erected, the Society owning one-third, free of encumbrance.

Development of Work: The first field entered by the Society was Africa, in 1833. Three years later came the opening of the missions in South America (1836), followed by China (1847), India (1856), Bulgaria (1857), Japan (1872), Mexico (1873), Korea (1885), Malaysia (1885). During the same period work was undertaken in a number of European countries, Germany (1849), Norway (1853), Sweden (1854), Switzerland (1856), Denmark (1857), Italy (1871), Finland (1884).

The Missions. I. *Africa;* (1) *Liberia:* In 1824 the General Conference decided as soon as the funds permitted to send missionaries to the colony established by the American Colonization Society in Africa. In 1831 the Rev. Melville Cox was appointed to Liberia, his support being guaranteed by the Young Men's Missionary Society. He sailed in 1832 and reached Sierra Leone in 1833, welcomed cordially by the Wesleyan Missionaries and also by the Governor. Soon after reaching Liberia he succumbed to the fever; but others followed; the next year a more healthy location was found, and by 1836 the different Methodist churches were recognized as the Liberia Annual Conference. Three years later the Conference seminary was opened, and the work extended to several outstations. Industrial work was encouraged from the very start. In 1851 there was reorganization, both of the Conference and the seminary, and from 1857, for 20 years, no white missionary was sent out.

To meet the difficulty of ordination, Francis Burns was elected bishop and ordained in the U. S. in 1859. He pressed for extension of the work into the interior, as did his successor. In 1876 the visit of a deputation, including Bishop Haven and Dr. J. T. Gracey, resulted in the appointment of Rev. Joel Osgood to press the interior work. The obstacles, however, were such that little was accomplished, and at the opening of 1884 there were no foreign missionaries or well qualified teachers on the field. The school buildings were dilapidated, ministers unordained, and the conference in need of superintendence.

In May, 1884, Bishop William Taylor was elected Missionary Bishop of all Africa. Bishop Taylor arrived at Monrovia in January, 1885, and, having general jurisdiction, was able to harmonize the different enterprises while carrying on his own work, already begun in Angola. He made extensive journeys with special view to the development of his scheme of self-supporting missions, and by the end of 1888 there were stations along the banks of the Cavally River for 100 miles. The scheme of self-supporting missions proved impracticable, however, and as soon as this became evident, it was given up.

As now organized the Liberia Conference embraces the western coast of Africa north of the equator, and is divided into three districts: Cape Palmas and Sinoe, Monrovia and Bassa, and the St. Paul River District. In Monrovia there is a strong self-supporting church, and the Methodist College of West Africa is located here. The mission press is established in the capital, from which is issued *The New Africa*, a thirty-two-page monthly, and Sunday-school literature, tracts, and other publications. There are (1903) 52 stations, 25 American missionaries, 62 native helpers, 2,798 church members, 2 high schools, with 295 students, and 25 other schools with 431 pupils.

(2) *West Central Africa:* On the 20th of March, 1885, a company of missionaries, which numbered more than forty, counting women and children, arrived at St. Paul de Loanda, the capital of the Portuguese colony of Angola, under the care of Bishop Taylor. Their objective point was the Tushalange country, some twelve hundred miles inland. It was decided to proceed slowly, by founding a chain of stations, beginning with St. Paul de Loanda. Here a site was purchased, and a building erected for church, school, and residence. Other stations occupied were Ndondo, 200 miles distant, at the head of steamboat navigation on the Congo River; N'hangue, 51 miles over the mountains; Pungo Ndongo, 39 miles farther on, and Malange, 60 miles beyond. In 1886 a new plan was adopted by the bishop, who decided to attempt to reach the Tushalange country by way of the Congo and the Kassai, going by the latter river to the interior. He secured a small steamer, but it being found impracticable at the time to obtain portage around the falls, the steamer was used on the Lower Congo. To reach the Congo District from Malange, the last station in Angola, involved a march of a thousand miles to Lualuaburg. Other stations occupied are Kimpoko, at Stanley Pool; Isangila, on the Lower Congo; Vivi, Natombi, Kabinda and Massubi.

With the retirement and death of Bishop Taylor and the appointment of Bishop Hartzell in 1896, a change was made in the principle of support, and the burden of gaining a living in a savage country was lifted from the missionaries. The other burden of building has been materially lightened, also, by regular appropriations and special gifts for this purpose.

In 1900 the Congo Conference was divided. The West Central Africa Mission Conference lies on the west, from St. Paul de Loanda about 350 miles inland; with it are included the Madeira Islands. Organized in 1902 it reports 11 stations or circuits, 22 American missionaries, 25 native workers, 87 church members, 14 day schools, with 205 pupils.

(3) *East Central Africa:* This Mission Conference includes the stations in East Africa south of the equator, and was formally organized by Bishop Hartzell in November, 1901, at Umtali, Rhodesia. There are two principal centers of work in Portuguese East Africa, one at Inhambane and another at Beira. At Umtali a third center has developed, with work among the white population. Here is a self-supporting academy with five departments. An industrial mission is proving helpful in the work. There are (1902) 7 stations or circuits, 14 American missionaries, 15 native workers, 62 church members, 1 high school with 95 students, and 1 day school with 75 pupils.

II. *South America* (1836): The Rev. Fountain E. Pitts sailed July, 1835, to South America with the view of examining fields, and the establishment of missions at Rio de Janeiro and Buenos Aires, where the American and English residents had especially encouraged the work. At Rio de Janeiro Mr. Pitts formed a small society of religious people, with a promise that a pastor should be sent at no distant day. Rev. Justin Spaulding, by appointment, went to Rio, sailing in March, 1836, and Rev. John Dempster, appointed to Buenos Aires, sailed in October.

There were indications of an improvement in the general conditions. A large English-speaking population welcomed the missionaries; the Bible could be distributed, and the American, and British and Foreign Bible Societies supplied Spanish and Portuguese Bibles and Testaments, the people eagerly receiving a book which, until recently, had been interdicted.

Mr. Spaulding was joined by Rev. Daniel P. Kidder and R. M. McMurdy, who entered upon extensive itinerations, preaching and scattering Bibles and tracts. In Rio the work grew, a Sunday-school was begun, and larger accommodations were needed. The hostility of the Roman priests was awakened, and the missionaries subjected to every possible annoyance and hindrance. But these efforts were short-lived and served to advertise the mission. The missionaries claimed their rights under the toleration act of the constitution. So eager were the people for the Scriptures that it was at first feared there was a general plan to secure copies to destroy them, but it was found that nearly every copy was appropriately used. Work for seamen and tours through the country showed good results, but through financial embarrassment the Board abandoned Brazil at the close of 1841, and the work was discontinued until 1880, when the Society again entered the field, occupying Para and later Maranhao, Pernambuco, Bahia and Rio de Janeiro. The Rev. (afterward Bishop) William Taylor endeavored to inaugurate self-supporting stations, but with no great success. Still, the work advanced and the Brazil Conference was organized in 1889.

In 1836 Mr. Pitts took up the work in Buenos Aires, which the Presbyterians had left, and was joined by the Rev. John Dempster. They could only secure permission from the governor to preach to the foreign population, and this restriction lasted till 1852. Meanwhile, work had begun in Montevideo, and was prospering when political disturbances caused orders to be issued to discontinue the mission. An earnest protest from the foreign residents and a pledge of financial help resulted in the withdrawal of the order, and there followed a most interesting period when all religious restrictions were removed, and the work took a new start at Montevideo and extended to Esperanza, Rosario, and Cordova. In 1880 the General Committee changed the name of the mission in the Rio Plata region to

"Southeast South American Mission." The name "Western South America" was used on their lists for the stations established by William Taylor in Peru, at Callao, Lima, Mollendo, Arica, and Tacna, Iquique, Pabellon de Rico, and Huanillas; in Bolivia at Antofagasta, and in Chile, at Calendra Copiapo, Coquimbo, Valparaiso, Talcahuana and Concepcion. The stations in the basin of the Amazon and adjacent regions at Para, Pernambuco, and Manaos; and at Colon on the Isthmus of Panama, were known as the "Northeastern South America." The name "South America Mission" was, however, restored two years later. Missionaries made exploring tours over an immense territory extending 300 miles up the Parana River and from the Uruguay River to the sea, and in 1882 Bishop Foster passed along the coasts of the continent studying the work at Buenos Aires, Montevideo, and Rosario, in its far-reaching relation to the southeastern part of the continent. With the withdrawal of Bishop Taylor from the supervision of the self-supporting stations established by him, in 1884, they passed under the control of the "Transit Building Fund Society of Bishop Taylor's Self-supporting Missions."

In 1893 the Transit and Building Fund Society offered their entire property in Chile to the Missionary Society, on condition that the work be still conducted on the self-supporting basis. The offer was accepted and these stations passed into the care of the Society. The same year, after full discussion had taken place, all the stations of the Society in South America were organized into an annual conference. This event marked the close of the first period in the history of Methodism in South America. The newly organized conference comprised six districts and its work extended to eight of the ten nations of the continent. In 1897 the conference was divided into the South America Conference, including the republics of Argentina, Uruguay, Paraguay, Brazil, and Bolivia east of the Andes; and the Western South America Mission Conference, including the countries of South America bordering on the Pacific Ocean. This conference has two divisions: the Peru Mission, including Peru, Bolivia, and Ecuador, and the Chile Mission, including the Republic of Chile.

The South America Conference has (1902) 26 stations or circuits, 29 American missionaries, and 139 native workers, 3,713 church members, 5 high schools with 387 pupils, and 14 day schools with 1,182 pupils.

The Western South America Conference has 18 stations or circuits, 43 American workers, 21 native helpers, 1,848 members, and 32 day schools with 2,839 pupils.

III. *China* (1847): As early as 1835 the Missionary Lyceum of the Wesleyan University at Middletown, Conn., warmly advocated a mission to the Chinese Empire, and $1,450 was raised as the beginning of a fund for such a mission. The matter was held in abeyance, however, until 1846. In that year at the annual meeting of the Society Dr. W. C. Palmer proposed to be one of thirty to give $100 a year for ten years to support a mission in China. The General Committee accepted, and the following year Rev. M. C. White and Rev. J. D. Collins were appointed to China, reaching Macao in August. The missionaries proceeded to Fu-chau, where the missionaries of the ABCFM welcomed them and opened to them a house which had been rented for one of their own missionaries. Thus, Methodism was at last planted in China. Schools were opened the next year and a church erected in 1855. The foreign population joined in the movement, and by 1858 the entire organization of a Methodist Episcopal Church was completed, with its class meetings, quarterly meetings, and collections.

The work of the mission in 1859 began to extend westward. This year the To-cheng appointment, about fifteen miles northwest of Fuchau, began with a class of thirteen members; this year, also, native workers were licensed and employed. In February more reenforcements joined the mission, notable among whom were the Rev. and Mrs. Stephen L. Baldwin. In November a school for girls was established on a broader and more permanent basis than had theretofore been attempted. Other places were entered, among them Kiu-kiang (1867), Peking (1869), Tientsin (1874). In 1881 the Anglo-Chinese College at Fuchau was organized, followed a few years later by the printing press, with its publication, the *Fohkien Christian Advocate;* medical work at Fuchau (1892), and a theological school at Hing-hwa, which had been made a station in 1885. In 1901 a Home Missionary Society was organized.

(1.) *The Fuchau Conference* is divided into eight districts. There are (1902) 45 American missionaries, 261 native workers, 10,572 church members, 1 theological school, 9 high schools, 133 day schools, 2,916 scholars.

(2.) *The Hing-hwa Mission Conference* (1896): This includes the prefectures of Hing-hwa and Ing-chung, in Fo-kien Province, and continued a part of the Fuchau mission till 1896, when it was organized as a separate conference. The theological school, boys' and girls' boarding schools, and graded schools are well attended. The Hing-hwa Conference is divided into five districts, with 12 Amercian missionaries, 268 native workers, 3,823 church members, and 8 day schools with 125 scholars.

(3.) *Central China Mission* (1869): Missionaries connected with the Fuchau Mission began work in Central China in 1867, and two years later it was set apart as a separate mission. In 1870 Mr. Hart at Kiu-kiang was reenforced; others followed, circuits were organized, including Hwang-mei, Nan-kang, and Shin-chang; the Fowler Institute, at Kiu-kiang, was opened (1881); Wu-hu, Nan-king, Chin-kiang, and Nan-chang were occupied. In 1891 the anti-foreign riots caused some disturbance, but resulted in the work being established on a firmer basis than ever before. The special feature of 1892 was the opening of a press building on the Kiu-kiang Institute premises, and the mission closed the first quarter of a century of its history in 1893 with large encouragement.

The mission suffered in common with others in the Boxer movement of 1900, and this was followed by floods in the Yangtse Valley. The central station of the Central China Mission is now (1902) Nan-king. There are 30 stations or circuits, 38 American missionaries, and 54 native helpers, 1,420 church members, 4 high schools with 299 students, 26 day schools with 412 pupils.

(4.) *North China Mission* (1869): This Conference includes the Provinces of Shan-tung and Ho-nan, and all China north of them. Work was begun by missionaries from Fuchun in 1869. The riots in Tientsin (1871) did not hinder as much as was feared, and in 1877 the work in both cities was well organized, and extended both north and south. The famine of 1878, followed by pestilence, opened many doors, and the illness of the wife of Li Hung Chang led to the firm establishment of medical work at Tientsin, and the opening of the Isabella Fisher Hospital for Women in 1881. Then followed Peking University (1885), at first known as Wiley Institute, and a dispensary at Tsun-hwa, the beginning of the hospital. Intermediate schools were established at Peking, Tientsin, Tsun-hwa, Tai-an, and Lan-chau, and day schools were formed wherever possible. In spite of floods and famines the work progressed. Yet appropriations were cut down until in 1902 they were twenty-five per cent. less than ten years before. The Boxer movement paralyzed the work, tho fortunately no missionaries of the society lost their lives, and the work has been taken up again with renewed energy. The report (1902) shows 6 districts, 49 stations, 28 American missionaries, 91 native helpers, 2,784 members, 1 college, 7 high schools, and 19 day schools, with 801 pupils in all.

(5.) *West China Mission* (1881): This is confined almost wholly to the Sze-chwan Province. When the General Committee met in 1880 they appropriated $5,000 to inaugurate this work, contingent on a like amount being given. This was pledged by the Rev. John J. Goucher, D.D., of Baltimore. The Rev. L. U. Wheeler, D.D., accompanied by the Rev. Spenser Lewis, arrived in Chung-king in December, 1882. There was no difficulty in organizing schools for boys, while numerous applicants appeared for entrance to a prospective girls' school. Public preaching was commenced in February, 1883; in October of the same year a girls' school was opened, and a similiar one for boys in 1884. In consequence of an anti-foreign riot, which destroyed the buildings in 1885, the mission was discontinued for a year, but in 1887 the Rev. Olin Cady recommenced the work, which increased rapidly. In 1890 Chen-tu was occupied, and tho cholera was followed by the political disturbances culminating in the Boxer movement, the growth was phenomenal.

There are (1902) 11 circuits or stations, 25 American missionaries, 56 native workers, 1,252 church members, and 17 day schools with 396 pupils.

IV. *India* (1856): As early as 1852 the General Committee resolved that "a fund be created and placed at the discretion of the Board and bishops for commencing a mission in India," and $7,500 were appropriated for this purpose. It was not, however, till 1856 that the work was begun, the Rev. William Butler arriving at Calcutta with his family in September. After careful investigation, Mr. Butler located in the Northwest Provinces, with the Rohilkhand and Oudh as his particular field. The territory which comprised the mission field of the M. E. Church extended from the Himalayas on the north, on the west and south to the Ganges, to a point between Cawnpur and Benares, and on the east to the boundaries of Oudh. To man this district Mr. Butler asked for eight men for Lucknow, four for Bareilly and Moradabad, respectively, three for Faizabad, and two for Shahjehanpur, Budaon, and Pilibhit each. Religious services were at once opened at Bareilly, but before much could be accomplished the Sepoy rebellion broke out, and the work was interrupted. The headquarters at Bareilly were destroyed, and when the work was resumed in 1858 Naini Tal and Lucknow were visited and became the basis of operations. Services were held in English and Hindustani, a school for boys was started in the Naini Tal Bazar and another for girls in the mission house. In January, 1859, work was begun in Moradabad, and the following month Bareilly was again occupied. In July of that year the first convert was baptized. Reenforcements were sent out, who proceeded at once to Lucknow, where a general gathering of the missionaries took place. Among the newcomers were Revs. James M. Thoburn, J. W. Waugh, E. W. Parker, J. R. Downey, and their wives. It was decided to occupy Shahjehanpur and Bijnaur. In 1860 a printing office was established at Bareilly and publication was begun—the foundation of the Book Concern at Lucknow, to which city it was removed in 1866. Schools and orphanages for both boys and girls were established, and during the next decade the work was carried on from nine centers, manned by native preachers, from which it spread to the surrounding villages. The Rev. J. T. Gracey and wife began work at Sitapur in 1861, a region not formally occupied by any missionary society. In 1869 some land lying on the edge of Oudh was purchased for a Christian settlement, and by 1875 the little village had reached a period of insured success. The necessity of trained native preachers had long been felt, and in 1872 a gift of $20,000 was received for the endowment of a theological seminary at Bareilly. In January, 1873, the India Mission Conference became an Annual Conference, and in 1877 the Northwest Province east of the Ganges and the province of Oudh were organized into the

1. *North India Conference:* This includes the districts of Bareilly-Kumaon, Bijnaur, Garhwal, Gonda, Hardoi, Moradabad, Oudh (with Lucknow), Pilibhit and Sambhal. Reid Christian College at Lucknow, with 479 students; the publishing house at the same place, which sent out in one year 74,600,000 pages; the Isabella Thoburn College and High School, deaconess' home, and the theological seminary at Bareilly are indications of the attention paid to education and mental as well as spiritual training. The report (1902) shows 54 missionaries, 1,379 native workers, 30,884 church members, 451 schools with 11,053 pupils.

2. *Northwest India:* This includes the districts of Ajmere, Aligarh, Allahabad, Cawnpur, Kasganj, Meerut, Muttra, and the Punjab. It was in this conference that the great evangelistic movement (1888-1893) brought into the Church such great numbers of the sweeper caste—a movement which has steadily progressed. At present the special outlook is toward the Punjab, and northward into Central Asia. The report (1902) shows 38 missionaries, 1,054 native morkers, 40,804 communicants, 448 schools with 10,692 pupils.

3. *South India:* This conference includes the districts of Godavari, Haidarabad, Madras, and Raichur. It was originally a part of the Bombay, Bengal, and Madras Mission and was organized in 1876. The work commenced with the visit to India of William Taylor in 1870, which resulted, in connection with the labors of other missionaries, in a remarkable revival through the following years. Among the special features of the mission work are the Anglo-vernacular Girls' Boarding School at Haidarabad, and the pub-

lishing house at Madras. Zenana work under the special care of the Woman's Foreign Missionary Society has had good fruit. The report (1902) shows 37 missionaries, 218 native workers, and 2,206 members.

4. *Bombay:* This Conference, including the districts of Bombay and Gujarat, and the Central Provinces, was set apart from the Bombay and Bengal Conference in 1891. Then, as in South India, the work received its impulse from the visit of Mr. Taylor in 1870, and enjoyed much support from the Rev. George Bowen. As the work progressed the extent of territory covered and the exigencies of superintendence compelled the division, so that what was at first one general conference of South India became three conferences. The special features of the work in the Bombay district are: the publishing house at Bombay, seamen's rests at Bombay and Kimari, a Mission Institute at Nariad, medical work at Poona, and general educational work. The report (1902) shows 43 missionaries, 459 native workers, 12,576 members, 240 schools, with 7,456 pupils.

5. *Bengal:* This Conference, including the districts of Calcutta, Calcutta Bengali, Asansol and Tirhoot, was set off from the South India Conference and organized in 1888. At first it included Burma and the Straits Settlements, but these were afterward separately organized. A special feature of the mission is the Methodist weekly paper, the *Indian Witness*, which ranks as the foremost religious paper in India. A training school for girls, orphanages, a seamen's rest, boarding and day schools, as well as general educational and evangelistic work, make up the record of missionary effort. The report (1902) shows 27 missionaries, 121 native workers, 2,339 members, 45 schools, with 2,916 pupils.

6. *Burma:* This Conference, organized in 1901, to include the Burma district of the Bengal-Burma Conference, carries on its work chiefly in Rangoon, tho there are missionaries in Pegu and Thandaung. In Rangoon the work is among the Burmese, English, Tamils, and Telugus. An English girls' high school and an industrial training school at Thandaung are doing good work. The report (1902) shows 13 missionaries, 38 native workers, 583 members, 5 schools, with 184 pupils.

V. *Bulgaria:* In 1854 Rev. Elias Riggs, of the ABCFM at Constantinople, wrote a letter to the Society, urging it to take up work in Bulgaria, since there was an opportunity which his own Society felt unable to use. Accordingly in 1857 Rev. Albert L. Long and Rev. Wesley Prettiman, M.D., were sent out and opened stations at Varna and Shumla. Subsequently Tirnova and Tultcha were occupied, work in the latter city reaching the Molokans, a body of Russian dissenters. The work met with both success and discouragement, and in 1864 Dr. Long removed to Constantinople and commenced the publication of a weekly paper, the *Zornitza*, which afterward passed into the hands of the ABCFM, and exerted a great influence among the people. In 1871 Dr. Long joined the staff of professors in Robert College, where he remained until his death, always interested in and identifying himself with work for evangelizing and elevating Bulgarians. For a time the difficulties were so great and success apparently so little that (1871-1873) the mission was practically suspended. In 1873, however, it was taken up again and extended so as to include all the section north of the Balkans. Several Bulgarians, educated in the U. S., were added to the missionary force, and prospects were brighter, when the Russo-Turkish war, following on the Bulgarian massacres, darkened the sky. The establishment of the principality of Bulgaria brought a measure of religious liberty, but worked adversely, in that the Bulgarians looked upon those who left the Bulgarian Church as traitors to the nation. Still the work has continued, and in 1892 a mission conference was organized. Several times since then there has been question of discontinuing the mission, but the Society has held on, and in 1902 reports 4 missionaries, 42 native workers, 314 members, 2 schools, with 25 pupils. Especially encouraging is the girls' school at Loftcha.

VI. *Japan:* The heavy demands made by other missions delayed the General Conference in entering on work in Japan, but in 1873 a party, including Messrs. R. S. Maclay, John C. Davison, Julius Soper, and M. C. Harris, arrived in Yokohama. They were followed by others and in August the mission was organized in Yokohama. The stations at first occupied were Yokohama, Tokio, Hakodate, Matsumai and Nagasaki. From the first there were most cordial relations with other missions, especially with that of the Canada Methodist Church, and arrangements were made to cooperate so far as possible. This has developed until plans are maturing for a union of all the Methodist missions in Japan. In 1882 a fine girls' school was opened at Nagasaki, and in 1886 the Philander Smith Bible Institute was completed at Yokohama. In 1884 the Mission was organized as a conference, and in 1898 divided into two, the Japan and South Japan conferences.

1. *The Japan Conference* includes the districts of Tokio, Yokohama, Hakodate, Hirosaki, Nagoya, Sendai, Sapporo, and Shinano. The mission has shared in the various experiences attending the work in Japan—the advance, the period of depression, and the more recent forward movement. The report (1902) shows 47 missionaries, 236 native workers, 5,272 communicants, 11 schools, with 1,427 pupils. The total enrollment in the Bible Institute (Aoyama Gakuin) was 259. The press work shows 9,357,800 pages printed during the year, including 19,114 volumes, 242,000 tracts, 363,000 S. S. periodicals.

2. *The South Japan Conference* includes the districts of Fukuoka and Nagasaki. The naval station at Sasebo and the government works at Mitsu Bishi furnish peculiar opportunities for work among sailors and laborers, and the Chingei Seminary at Nagasaki is a finely equipped school. The report (1902) shows 20 missionaries, 31 native workers, and 1,289 communicants.

VII. *Mexico:* In 1873 the General Conference sent Dr. William Butler, who had served in India and as secretary of the American and Foreign Christian Union, to Mexico. In company with Bishop Haven he visited Vera Cruz, Puebla and Mexico City, and finally located in the capital, securing a site originally occupied by a palace of the Aztec sovereign Montezuma, and later by a Roman Catholic monastery, which had been seized by the Mexican Government. Dr. Butler was joined by others, some of whom, knowing Spanish, were able to begin work immediately.

The success attending their efforts aroused the bitter opposition of the Roman Catholic priests, resulting in several outbreaks, the murder of Mr. Stephens of the ABCFM, and of a number of Mexican Protestants, and the destruction of several of the Methodist buildings. Still the work prospered and was extended so that in 1884 the mission was organized as a conference. The report (1902) shows 5 districts: Central (Mexico City), Oaxaca, Orizaba, Hidalgo, and Mountain. Among the special features are the Methodist Institute and the publishing house at Mexico, the medical work and the schools. The press issued over 5,000,000 pages of Christian literature. There are 31 missionaries, 185 native workers, 5,592 members, 58 schools, with 3,553 pupils.

VIII. *Korea:* In 1883, the year after the treaty between Korea and the U. S. was made, Dr. John F. Goucher offered to the Missionary Society $2,000 for the purpose of starting a mission in Korea, and $3,000 toward the purchase of a site. The Missionary Committee accepted it, made an additional appropriation, and in 1884, Dr. R. S. Maclay, who had already been identified with pioneer work in China and Japan, arrived at Chemulpo, secured a favorable reception from the King, and, with Dr. W. B. Scranton and Rev. H. G. Appenzeller, commenced the work at Seoul. Dr. Scranton's medical skill proved most advantageous, and Mr. Appenzeller secured some pupils for his school, which soon received official recognition. Later, the work was extended to Wonsan, Pyeng-yang and Kongju. Wonsan, however, was afterward handed over to the M. E. Church South. Medical work is still confined to Pyeng-yang, but urgent need is felt of extending it to other stations. In educational matters there is cordial cooperation with the M. E. Ch. South, as there is hearty sympathy in other lines of work. The success attained by the mission is seen in the figures of the report (1902), 26 missionaries, 26 native workers, 5,855 communicants.

IX. *Malaysia:* The Malaysia Mission had its origin in appeals that went from Singapore to Dr. J. M. Thoburn at Calcutta in 1879. He made special inquiries and a few years later (1884) Bishop Hurst, at a meeting of the South India Conference, made such representations resulting from a visit to Singapore, that the Rev. W. F. Oldham was appointed to commence work in that city. He reached his station in the spring of 1885 and soon acquired such influence among the Chinese that they contributed liberally to schools and a church. Work was also established among the Tamil coolies. In 1889 the mission was organized which developed into the Malaysia Mission Conference in 1893, and the Malaysia Annual Conference in 1902. In the Malay Peninsula the chief places occupied are Singapore and Penang, but to these was added the work in the Philippine Islands, commenced in 1899. Services are conducted in English, Malay, Tamil and Chinese, and the school facilities for all classes are good. At Singapore there is also a mission press.

In the Philippines work has been undertaken at Manila, Malolos, San Fernando and Gerona. There is a small but complete publishing plant and the *Philippine Christian Advocate* has commenced publication. The report (1902) shows 28 missionaries, 72 native workers, 3,403 communicants, and 8 schools, with 1,166 pupils.

X. *European Missions:* The work of the Society in the Protestant lands of Europe had its origin in the conversion in America of some who had come from Europe as emigrants, and who desired to return and give to their own people the new conception of spiritual life that had come to them. Thus the work in Norway and Sweden was begun by Olof Gustaf Hedstrom in 1845, and that in Germany by Rev. Ludwig S. Jacoby, who landed at Bremen in 1849. From these, missionary effort has extended over the whole of Northern Europe. The Society employs no American missionaries, but gives some assistance to the native churches. The report (1902) shows in North Germany 63 ordained and 39 unordained preachers, 6,690 communicants; in South Germany, 75 ordained and 151 unordained preachers, 10,412 communicants; Switzerland, 47 ordained, 5 unordained preachers, 8,803 communicants; Norway, 41 ordained, 68 unordained preachers, 5,894 communicants; Sweden 93 ordained and 30 unordained preachers, 17,077 communicants; Denmark, 19 ordained, 21 unordained preachers, 3,465 communicants; Finland, and St. Petersburg, 13 unordained preachers, 1,012 communicants. In Sweden are reported a considerable number of other helpers, including teachers.

In 1832 Dr. Charles Elliott commenced to press upon the Methodist churches the feasibility of a mission in Italy. For some years his plan was scarcely treated seriously, but in 1850 it was taken up with some earnestness. It required, however, 20 years more of consideration before the mission was fairly inaugurated, and in 1871 Dr. Leroy M. Vernon arrived in Genoa. After a careful survey of the field he recommended Rome for the headquarters of the mission, with other stations at Naples and Genoa. Then followed an earnest protest from Father Gavazzi, of the Free Italian Church, against the introduction of Methodism into Italy, but in 1872 it was decided to proceed, but to make Bologna the headquarters. Subsequently Rome was again chosen, and has been the center of work ever since. In 1874 an exceptionally fine site for a church was offered for sale and promptly purchased, and St. Paul's M. E. Church was erected and consecrated on Christmas Day, 1875. In 1881, the Italy Annual Conference was organized, and the work steadily progressed, not a few representatives of prominent families joining the churches. In the Rome district is included work in Northern Italy and Switzerland. The report (1903) shows 10 missionaries, 40 Italian workers, 2,716 communicants, and 11 schools.

Woman's Foreign Missionary Society of the Methodist Episcopal Church: About ninety days after the organization of the Miss. Soc. of the M. E. Church (July, 1819), a woman's auxiliary was formed, in New York City. It was not very active, however, and by 1855 had largely been crowded out by other organizations. Meanwhile (1847) a ladies' China Missionary Society had been formed in Baltimore, but on the organization of the Women's Union Missionary Society in New York in 1860, a number of Methodist women joined in that Society. There arose, however, a feeling that there should be a church society, and in 1869 the present organization was completed. The conduct of the Society is in the hands of an Executive Committee, which meets regularly, but really has no headquarters, except an office at 150

Fifth ave., New York City, where literature is distributed. The secretary is Mrs. J. T. Gracey of Rochester. The funds, receipts, and appropriations are kept entirely distinct from those of the Missionary Society, and the missionaries are listed separately. Thus, while there is complete and cordial cooperation, the two societies are distinct. According to the report (1902) the woman's society has 204 missionaries and 964 native workers. These are chiefly in China, Japan and India; very few in Africa. They are included in the statistics given above under each conference. The total appropriations for the year were $431,111, while the total for Foreign Missions by the Missionary Society was $683,942. It appears, thus, that the WFMS represents about two-fifths of the foreign mission work of the church

The work of the young people for missions has, in the M. E. Church, been very fully developed under the Epworth League organization. Mission study classes have been organized at home with a view to training up a force of missionary workers as well as givers. On the field, too, this organization has been most effective.

ORGAN: *World Wide Missions*, monthly; Reid (J. M.), *Missions and Missionary Society of the Methodist Episcopal Church*, 3 vols., New York, 1895.

METHODIST EPISCOPAL CHURCH, SOUTH (U. S. A.); Board of Missions: At the first General Conference of the Methodist Episcopal Church, South, held in 1846, a Home and Foreign Missionary Society was organized. Its operations were committed to a Board of Managers, who, in conjunction with the Bishops, determined the fields that were to be occupied, selected the missionaries, and apportioned the amount to be collected among the annual conferences. The home and the foreign fields were under the management of the same board.

In 1866 the General Conference placed the work of the Missionary Society under two boards, one having charge of the foreign and one of the home field. In 1870 the missions of the church were again placed under one board, and in 1874 the Constitution was again changed, bringing the work in foreign lands under the Board of Missions and the work in the home field under the Annual Conference Boards of Missions.

The General Board has charge of the foreign missions and all others not provided for by the Annual Conferences. It consists of a president, vice-president, two secretaries, and twenty-five managers. The bishops and treasurers are *ex officio* members of the board. The Board meets annually to determine what fields shall be occupied, and the number of persons to be employed in each; to estimate the amount that may be necessary for its missions; and to divide the same among the annual conferences.

The first work of the Board was among the colored people and Indians of the United States, and then it launched out into a larger field, opening work in the Chinese Empire.

1. *China:* The offer made by Charles Taylor, of the South Carolina Conference, in 1843, to go to China as a missionary, was the origin of the action of the first General Conference held in Petersburg, Va., in May, 1846, when it was decided to commence a mission to China. Mr. Taylor was appointed, studied medicine, and in April, 1848, with his colleague, Mr. Benjamin Jenkins, sailed for China with their families. Shanghai was selected as the best location for the mission. On arriving at Hongkong, after a four months' voyage, the illness of Mrs. Jenkins prevented her from going any further, and Dr. Taylor began work in Shanghai in September alone. Nine months later Mr. Jenkins and his wife arrived, and as soon as a sufficient knowledge of the language had been acquired the two missionaries opened a chapel for preaching, attracting many who came in those days through mere curiosity. Few Christian books were published in Chinese at that time and the work was largely that of talking to the people by the wayside and preaching to them in front of temples and as they were gathered in street chapels; but as the language was acquired more perfectly, converts were made and a nucleus of a church was formed. The first convert was providentially a man from the upper middle class—Liew Sien Sang. His name has been familiar to Southern Methodists ever since. He was an eloquent and useful native preacher whose vigorous mind, quick apprehension, ready and fluent utterance and noble piety made him universally beloved and heeded.

The mission was strengthened in 1852 by the arrival of Rev. W. G. E. Cunnyngham and his wife; but the work and the climate began to tell on the pioneers, and Drs. Taylor and Jenkins, with their families, were soon obliged to return home. The Tai-ping rebellion was in progress, and in that year Shanghai was captured and remained in the hands of the insurgents for eighteen months. Little work could be done. Fire and the ravages of the contending armies arrested evangelistic work; misfortunes culminated in the burning of the only chapel and the two mission houses.

The mission was reenforced in 1854 by three married missionaries, Revs. D. C. Kelley, J. W. Lambuth, and J. L. Belton; but the war continued, and the constant nervous strain and unsanitary conditions brought on sickness, and the withdrawal of two missionaries. Despite difficulties, however, inquiries increased, and several were received into the church.

In 1859 two more missionaries were sent out, and others followed later, but several were compelled to withdraw. In 1869 the record of the mission during the twenty-one years of its existence showed that eight missionaries with their families had been sent out; death had removed one missionary and two missionaries' wives; one had withdrawn from the work, four had returned to the United States, and two were left in the field, Messrs. Allen and Lambuth. About sixty natives had been baptized, and among the converts were two native preachers of great gifts and usefulness. In 1870 three stations had been occupied—Shanghai, Soochow, and Nantziang, of which Shanghai remained the principal station, having substantial mission houses and two chapels. Faithful work was beginning to have its effect and the mission was becoming strong and aggressive. The full significance of this work appears in the fact that for ten years, or from 1860 until 1870, the missionaries were not supported by their Board—the Civil War in the United States having destroyed the resources of the South. Messrs. Lambuth, Allen and Wood sustained themselves as best they could, the last named missionary returning home during the decade, having lost his wife.

J. W. Lambuth, ably seconded by his wife, in

addition to efforts at self-support by interpreting and teaching, bent his energies to the strengthening of the native church. Native helpers and Bible women were trained and put to work, itinerating tours were made into the surrounding country, a church was gathered together at each of the three stations, boarding and day schools were opened and the work grew in importance. Dr. Lambuth's boat became a familiar object within a radius of fifty miles around Shanghai. On the streets, in the temples, or in the little rented chapels of Tsing-pu, Nantziang, Kia-ting, and many other places, he could be seen, the center of a wondering crowd. His life was as powerful as his words, and to him was due largely the credit of laying the foundations for the extensive evangelistic work which now reaches far into the interior of the province.

An early and urgent need of the mission, and in fact of the entire missionary movement in China, was men capable of producing an acceptable and effective literature. China is a nation of students. He who seeks to catch and hold the attention of her literati must conform to their high standard of style and clothe his arguments with the skill of a master. Cut off from home supplies, Dr. Young J. Allen, while maintaining himself and family by teaching and translating in the Kiang-Nan arsenal, was constantly thrown in contact with that bright and more advanced class of Chinese officials who had been entrusted with the management of the difficult problem of intercourse with foreign nations. Finding Dr. Allen a man of wide and varied information they sought his counsel and gave him their confidence. He conceived the idea of a periodical that should give the Chinese in their own language the salient facts of a Western religion, philosophy, science, and politics, and such general information as should, in a measure, prepare them for the constantly increasing contact with Western civilization. From this grew the *Wan Kwok Kong-Pao* (World's Magazine). It immediately became popular, and it now circulates over the Straits Settlements, Japan, Korea, and the Pacific Coast, as well as throughout China. In addition, a number of volumes have come from Dr. Allen's pen. His *History of the Chinese-Japanese War* received the acknowledgment of three emperors. Kang-yu-wei, chief adviser of the Emperor of China in the reforms of 1898, and the leading Chinese patriot, while a refugee from the Empress Dowager, said, "I owe my conversion to reform, and my knowledge of reform, to two missionaries—Rev. Timothy Richard and Dr. Young J. Allen."

The pressing demand for trained native preachers was more and more making itself felt in the mission. Moreover, the children of the converts were growing up and the missionaries were face to face with the necessity of providing for them the means of a Christian education. In the autumn of 1875 Dr. A. P. Parker, now President of the Anglo-Chinese College in Shanghai, joined the mission. He was appointed to Soochow, a newly opened station, and placed in charge of a few boys who had already been gathered by J. W. Lambuth into a school in Shanghai.

Soochow, the second station of the mission, was one of the most important and one of the most difficult fields of the Empire. The large number of Confucian scholars, literary chancellors, viceroys, and other high officials that have gone forth from its walls have won it first rank as a literary center. Under the conditions of life which prevailed there, and with the deep-seated prejudice encountered among the literati, it was necessary that the preaching of the Gospel should have associated with it some phase of Christian work which should incarnate the spirit and ministry of Christ. It was with this purpose that the Board of Missions decided to open medical work under Dr. Walter R. Lambuth in 1882, having associated with him Dr. W. H. Park, who successfully carried on the medical mission after his colleague was appointed to Japan in 1886.

During 1878 the Woman's Foreign Missionary Society entered the field, sending out Miss Lochie Rankin as its first missionary. At a later date a hospital was opened in Soochow under its auspices. Slowly a foothold has been gained and prejudice overcome. No agency in the mission has been of more value than the work of the women, especially in the educational and medical departments.

The work of the M. E. Church, South, owing to its location in Central China, suffered little from the storm of 1900. The cloud in the north growing out of the Boxer movement threatened destruction, but it passed over, and renewed impetus seems to have come upon the work. One remarkable fact is worthy of note: While the Legations were besieged in Peking the Chinese friends of the medical and educational work in Soochow—and among them were some of the highest officials—were paying their subscriptions pledged for the establishment of the Soochow University under the able presidency of Dr. D. L. Anderson.

The statistics of the mission for 1902 are as follows: Missionaries, including their wives, 35; missionary women, 17; native preachers, 15; Bible women, 66; communicants, 1,944; Sunday schools, 34; scholars, 1,809; Epworth Leagues, 22; members, 725; organized churches, 52; boarding schools, 8; pupils, 476; day schools, 41; pupils, 1,170; hospitals, 3; patients treated, 23,700; total value of mission property, $231,409.

2. *Mexico:* The work of the M. E. Church, South, in Mexico is conducted in three sections:

(1) Central Mexican Mission Conference: The conversion of an educated Mexican soldier, Alejo Hernandez, was the providential beginning of the work in Mexico. Bishop Marvin, in 1871, appointed Hernandez to the territory bordering on the Rio Grande River between Laredo and its mouth. He was reappointed to the same field for 1872. Bishop Keener visited the City of Mexico in 1873, purchased property, organized a mission, and sent Hernandez to this new field. Later the Bishop appointed Rev. Joel T. Daves, of the Louisiana Conference, Superintendent of the mission. In 1879 the work had extended from the City of Mexico to the cities of Leon, Cuernavaca, Cuautla, Toluca and Orizaba. Guadalajara was included in 1883, and the work was carried well down the western coast.

(2) Mexican Border Conference: This mission was also the outcome of the work of Hernandez in the valley of the Rio Grande. In 1874 there were two stations, the one at Brownsville, Texas, and the other in Rio Grande City. Two schools were opened in 1882 under the charge of missionaries of the Woman's Board, one at Concepcion and the other at Laredo. The latter has become as large an educational plant as is found in any

mission. Including its day school feeders, there were last year over one thousand children under instruction. By 1883 the evangelistic work had extended two hundred miles south into Mexico, and of the twenty-three places occupied nine were in Texas, four were on both sides of the Rio Grande, and ten were on the south of it. In 1886 the mission was formed into an Annual Conference.

(3) *Northwest Mexican Mission Conference:* This was organized in 1890 and extends as far north as Phœnix, Arizona, reaches down the Gulf of California below Mazatlan, and on to the east from El Paso, until it touches the Mexican Border Conference. It also includes the important cities of Chihuahua, Torreon, and Durango. In the first and the last cities the Woman's Board has two flourishing schools. The missionaries engaged in this field have had the difficulty of vast distances to travel, the inveterate prejudice of Roman Catholics to encounter, and the climatic influences of life in high altitude. But they have wrought well, as the following statistics will indicate: Missionaries, including wives, 36; missionary women, 21; native traveling preachers, 45; communicants, 5,807; Sunday schools, 113; scholars, 3,921; Epworth Leagues, 42; members, 1,462; organized churches, 149; boarding and day schools, 14; pupils, 1,020; Bible women, 19; hospitals, 1; patients treated, 1,417; total collections, $5,871. In addition to the foregoing, special mention should be made of the hospital work in Monterey under Dr. U. H. Nixon, and the Instituto Laurens, supported by the "Rosebuds" of Virginia.

(3) *Brazil:* In 1875 the Board of Missions constituted Rev. J. E. Newman, for some years a resident in Brazil, its first missionary, and early in the following year Rev. J. J. Ransom joined him. The province of São Paulo was first occupied, but in 1877 work was begun in Rio de Janeiro. In 1881 two missionaries went out under the Woman's Board, and in 1887 an annual conference was organized, under the Presidency of Bishop John C. Granbery.

The Brazil Mission is perhaps the most aggressive and successful one of the church. Notwithstanding its great area, its small force of trained workers, and meager appropriations, very great results have been secured. In the extension of circuits, in creating and circulating Christian literature, in placing the educational work upon a secure basis, and in unceasing labors to reach the people with the Gospel, no body of men and women have accomplished more than these workers in Brazil.

The statistics for 1902 show that this mission has the largest increase in membership, the largest collections on the field, and more self-supporting churches than any other mission of the church. The new building for Granbery College at Juiz de Fora is approaching completion and when thoroughly equipped will prove an invaluable auxiliary. Already it has gained an enviable position in the state. Missionaries, including their wives, 29; missionary women, 16; native traveling preachers, 19; communicants, 3,895; Sunday schools, 74; scholars, 2,555; Epworth Leagues, 12; members, 548; organized churches, 55; churches self-supporting, 7; boarding and day schools, 12; pupils, 358; Bible women, 9; total collections, $8,382.00.

4. *Japan:* In 1886 Bishop H. M. McTyeire, then in charge of the China Mission, appointed J. W. Lambuth, W. R. Lambuth, and O. A. Dukes, who were engaged in missionary work in China, to open a mission in Japan. On the 25th of July Dr. J. W. Lambuth and wife and Dr. Dukes landed in Kobe and found a field of most inviting character around the great Inland Sea open to their efforts. Joined later on by Dr. W. R. Lambuth, the inauguration meeting of the Japan Mission was held on the 17th of September, 1886, just thirty-two years after the landing of the senior Lambuth in Shanghai, China. At the close of the first year six members of the church were reported, including one Chinese and one Japanese.

Dr. W. B. Palmore, of St. Louis, visited Japan about this time, and pledged $100 annually for a supply of sound religious literature. Out of this gift grew the Palmore Institute, which, by influencing young men through the teaching of English and the Bible, has been one of the most helpful feeders of the church. A Sunday school of twenty scholars was opened; a weekly collection for a church building was started. The wives of the three missionaries entered fully into the work, and sixty women of good families were soon gathered for Bible reading and study. The whole length of the Inland Sea was repeatedly visited. Circuits were mapped out and addresses delivered in many towns from which appeals had come for instruction. Incessant activity characterized the early years of this mission and tested the strength and resources of the missionaries to the utmost. During the first year of their work a converted Japanese pilot, by the name of T. Sunamoto, offered his services. He had just returned from San Francisco with his heart yearning to bring his own people to a knowledge of Chirst. Proceeding to his native city of Hiroshima, a Buddhist stronghold and the military center of western Japan, he urged the missionaries to cooperate with him and was the means of planting the Gospel along the northern shore of the Inland Sea in the very towns and cities where, years before, he had piloted rice junks in from the sea and then spent nights in revelry and dissipation. With his help, and that of two or three others of similar zeal, the church in Japan sprang quickly into a position where the open doors offered opportunity far exceeding the power to occupy.

The Girls' school in Hiroshima is the largest Christian school for girls in the Empire, and commands an enviable reputation among all classes. Every department is filled to overflowing and applicants are constantly turned away, while the Lambuth Bible and Training School in Kobe is doing an equally important work in training Bible women and others for Christian service. The Kwansei Gakuin at Kobe, under the presidency of Rev. Y. Yoshioka, and the leadership of Dr. S. H. Wainwright, has collegiate and Biblical departments which are doing advanced work. The ideals held up in this institution for young men, both as regards religious and intellectual culture, are of the highest, and already the college has sent out men into the ministry and into professional life, who are contributing their influence to the upbuilding of a Christian empire. It takes a foremost place among the educational institutions in the country. The statistics for 1902 are as follows: Missionaries, including their wives, 39; native traveling preachers, 14; **communicants,**

855; Sunday schools, 43; scholars, 2,040; Epworth Leagues, 2; members, 89; organized churches, 15; boarding and day schools, 10; pupils, 1,321; total collection, $1,429.

5. *Korea:* At the urgent request of the Vice-Minister of Education, Hon. T. H. Yun, at one time a student of Emory College and of Vanderbilt University, Bishop E. R. Hendrix and Dr. C. F. Reid visited Korea in October, 1895. The providential indications were so plain that the Bishop decided to open a mission, and appointed Dr. Reid Superintendent and pioneer missionary. The latter moved from Shanghai, China, in August, 1896. A large section of country stretching from Seoul to Songdo was entirely unoccupied by the mission forces previously in the field, and work was begun at Koyang and at Songdo, a city of 65,000 inhabitants. A line of stations was also opened between these points, and the mission was reenforced.

The Woman's Board, in the autumn of 1897, transferred to Korea from China Mrs. J. P. Campbell, who was afterward joined by other ladies. Mrs. Campbell has specific charge of the Carolina Institute in Seoul, a flourishing boarding school for girls. The work so auspiciously begun in Koyang and Songdo has spread not only to neighboring villages but to Wonsan on the east coast. The spirit of self-support and self-propagation characterizes the native converts, and, if continued, will develop a successful and aggressive church.

The latest statistics show: Missionaries, including their wives, 12; helpers, 25; communicants, 454; Sunday schools, 15; scholars, 519; schools, 6; pupils, 82, and Bible women, 10.

6. *Cuba:* Some work had been done on the island prior to the war with Spain, but immediately after the close of the war it was necessary to reorganize the mission, which was reduced to a small congregation in Havana, holding occasional meetings in a private house. Under the administration of Bishop Candler, stations were established one after another in the cities of Santiago, Cienfuegos, Santa Clara, Matanzas, and Havana. The work was affiliated with that already being carried on in Tampa and Key West, where large numbers of Cubans were settled in colonies, but in 1898 the work on the island was brought under the General Board of Missions, while that on the mainland was attached to the Florida Conference. Cuba has offered a wide and fruitful field for intelligent effort. The failure of Roman Catholicism morally and intellectually to uplift the people has prepared the way for a presentation of the truth backed by the personal character of the Protestant missionaries. So convincing has this appeal been that many thoughtful Cubans have accepted the Gospel with joy and thanksgiving. It is the lifting of a long night of superstition and hopelessness and is a prophecy of daybreak everywhere.

The statistics for 1902 are: Missionaries, including their wives, 28; native traveling preachers, 22; communicants, 751; Sunday schools, 16; scholars, 718; Epworth Leagues, 6; members, 185; organized churches, 12; schools, 6; pupils, 424; collections, $3,530.

Summary: Thirty years ago the Board of Missions of the M. E. Church, South, occupied but one foreign field, China, and had in that field only two missionaries and their wives, 4 native workers, men and women, and about 30 church members.

In its six foreign fields, China, Japan, Korea, Mexico, Brazil, and Cuba, it has now, including 66 of the Woman's Board, 241 missionaries, 95 native traveling preachers, 104 Bible women, 12,906 church members, 295 Sunday schools, with 11,570 scholars; 84 Epworth Leagues, with 3,009 members; 312 organized churches, of which 17 are entirely self-supporting; 101 boarding and day schools, with 4,482 pupils; 8 hospitals and dispensaries, which have treated 27,342 patients, and $21,716 has been collected in the field for all purposes.

The receipts of the General Board from all sources were $366,180, and of the Woman's Board, $112,458, making the total receipts of both Boards $478,638.

ORGANS: *Review of Missions, Women's Missionary Advocate.*

METHODIST NEW CONNEXION MISSIONARY SOCIETY: The Methodist New Connexion, the earliest offshoot from the stem of the parent Wesleyan body in 1797, took its first steps in missionary enterprise in 1824. Attention was first directed to Ireland, and in 1826 a mission was established in Belfast and contiguous towns.

In 1835 Canada was suggested as a sphere for missionary operations, and in 1837 the Rev. John Addyman went as the first agent of the Connexion to the Dominion. The mission expanded until in 1875 it united with the other Methodist bodies in Canada, and became the Methodist Church of that country. When the union took place the Mission comprised 396 churches, 7,661 church members, 167 Sunday schools, and 9,259 scholars.

In 1859 a long-cherished wish of the Connexion was realized by the formation of a mission to the heathen. China was selected as the field of labor, and Revs. John Innocent and William N. Hall were the first agents of the Society sent there. They worked at Shanghai for a time, and eventually settled in Tientsin.

In 1862 a mission to Australia was commenced and churches were raised in Adelaide and Melbourne. In 1887, these churches not having developed resources to make them independent, and the energies of the Society being demanded by the increasing claims of the Chinese work, they were given up. The church in Adelaide united with the Bible Christians, and that in Melbourne with the Wesleyans.

The Society is managed by a committee, consisting of a president, a treasurer, and a secretary, with 16 ministers and 16 laymen, appointed annually by the Conference.

The mission in China has three circuits. The first and earliest, in Tientsin, has a fine establishment in the British compound, consisting of a college for the training of young men for the native ministry, also a female college for the education and training of native girls and women for Christian work. There are two chapels in the city where daily preaching of the Word is carried on, and the English Church, in which united services are held, stands on ground owned by the Society. In addition to these, there are a chapel and native church in Taku, and the same in Hsing-chi, a city to the west of Tientsin. This society was the first to enter this great city, but it has been joined since by the agents of several other societies.

The second circuit, in the Shantung Province, resulted from the visit to the mission of a farmer from the village of Chu-chia-tsai, 140 miles south of Tientsin. Under the influence of a marvelous dream he had traveled to the great city to listen to the foreign teachers of religion. He became an earnest believer in Jesus, and went to his home carrying with him Bibles, hymn-books, and other Christian publications. He invited his neighbors to his house, announcing to them his conversion and reading to them the Bible. A great awakening took place in the village, which spread by degrees over the district, with the result that a pressing appeal was sent to Tientsin for a missionary to come down and take charge of the great work.

In recent years a third sphere of labor has been occupied in the neighborhood of Kai-ping, north of Tientsin. Near this city extensive mines are worked by a syndicate of Chinese mandarins, who applied to the Society for a medical missionary, offering to afford facilities for the teaching of Christian doctrine among the workmen. An extensive circuit is worked round the neighborhood of the Tang-san collieries, extending to Yung-ping-fu, an ancient and important city near the old wall.

The mission suffered heavily at the time of the Boxer outbreak. Aside from the one chapel in the compound at Tientsin, there was not a single property left in the Tientsin circuit in which the Christians could gather for worship, while in the Shantung and Kai-ping circuits the situation was about the same. In Tientsin the Provisional Government granted the mission the use of a Buddhist temple, and afterward of a military Yamen in the heart of the city. In Tang-shan the mission suffered not a little inconvenience at the hands of the German troops who occupied the premises, and seemed indisposed to vacate until appeal was made to Count von Waldersee. The question of indemnity proved a difficult one, but was in a fair way of settlement, and the outlook for this Society, as for others, was most encouraging. The faithfulness of the native workers, and the devotion of the great majority of the Christians, was an indication of the substantial character of the work done, and an earnest of future success.

The mission reports emphasize the necessity of more attention to education than has been given in past years, as also to medical work. The statistics of members and probationers are also spoken of as probably within the truth, in view of the number who have not yet had the courage to return to their homes. There were reported in 1902, for the three circuits, 8 missionaries, 93 native helpers (with Sunday school workers a total of 102), 100 churches, 211 chapels and preaching places, 3,479 members and probationers. The school returns were incomplete on account of reorganization.

Headquarters of the Society: 23 Farringdon Ave., London. E. C., England.

METHODIST PROTESTANT CHURCH; Board of Foreign Missions of the: For many years the missionary interest of this denomination was directed to assisting the work of other churches. Some of the funds collected went into the treasury of the Woman's Union Missionary Society of New York and were applied to the support of Miss L. M. Guthrie in Japan. Miss Guthrie, on a subsequent visit to America, went to Pittsburg, Pa., and met some of the ladies who had become interested in her work. The result was the formation of the Woman's Foreign Missionary Society of the Methodist Protestant Church, in 1879. Three years later the General Conference organized the Board of Foreign Missions, and the two societies have continued to work together.

The interest first aroused in regard to Japan made it natural to establish the mission there, and Yokohama was occupied. Subsequently, Nagoya and Shizuoka were also made stations, and the work was fully organized.

The report for 1902 shows 19 charges, served by 15 pastors, 4 foreign and 11 native; 8 churches, 619 members. The Nagoya Anglo-Japanese College reports 90 students, more than half of whom are Christian, while none can be called anti-Christian. At the meeting of the Conference in 1902 action was taken accepting the basis of union proposed for the Methodist missions in Japan.

The Woman's Foreign Missionary Society has 5 missionaries in Japan, engaged chiefly in educational work. The school at Yokohama numbers 70 and there is a kindergarten with about 40. Sewing circles, mothers' meetings, YPSCE and other organizations are developed in good degree. The Society has also established work in Hu-nan, China, at Chang-te, and has 2 missionaries working in alliance with the mission of the Cumberland Presbyterians.

The headquarters of the Society are in Pittsburg, Pa.

METHODS OF MISSIONARY WORK: Methods adopted in missionary work may be considered as, 1st, Evangelistic; 2d, Pastoral. The first has primary reference to the conversion of men, the second to their development into a likeness to Christ.

To use the language of a secretary of the CMS, we have: "1. The preaching of the Gospel to the unconverted; 2. The building up of the native church as it is pictured to us in the concluding chapter of St. John's Gospel, where Christ's servants are represented in figure, first as fishers casting the Gospel net, and then as shepherds feeding and tending the flock. Education is a part of each. For the heathen and the Mohammedan it is undertaken solely as a means of evangelization. For the Christian population, whether elementary for the children, or professional for the future pastor or teacher or evangelist, it is a department of pastoral work. So, too, publication is a department of each. Medical work is primarily evangelistic; its benefit to converts is rather incidental."

I. We now mention first methods that are common to both evangelistic and pastoral work, not undertaking to be exhaustive in the statement of them, but rather to indicate the lines along which the missionary works.

1. *Personal Conversation:* The prime element in all missionary work is the personal. Men are drawn to men. Just as it was Christ's personality that drew men to Him, so it is largely the personality of the missionary that draws men to him, and through him to the Savior. This has been most markedly shown in the lives of the great leaders, Henry Martyn, Judson, Livingstone, Goodell, Hannington and others. Indeed, almost all who have had success in missionary work have found their greatest power in the close, intimate relation of personal conversation, personal contact, where the needy soul felt the touch of the full soul, drew strength from it, and was satisfied; where the hard soul felt the power of the

magnetic soul, and despite itself was drawn away into a higher life; where the cold, indifferent soul felt the heat of a soul on fire with the love of God, and expanded into a nature purer far than it had dreamed of.

It is no easy thing for an Occidental to come in contact with Oriental ideas, prejudices and habits, and to exert such influences as shall bring about change without doing harm. It is easier to repel than attract, to harden than to soften, especially in public. Men are swayed by the power of the mass of their fellow-men. A single soul in a multitude may be overwhelmed; in private conversation it may be developed.

Thus the fundamental method of missionary work in every land is intercourse with persons. Not only is this true of the inception of any work, but also of its continuance. It is just as important and universal to-day as when mission work was commenced. It is employed by every different agency, foreign and native, missionary, pastor, catechist; especially by Zenana workers, and almost exclusively by Bible readers; it is adapted to every class, and is almost the only means of reaching some.

In the pastoral division of missionary work the element of personal influence is, if anything, stronger than in the evangelistic—certainly so far as the missionary himself is concerned; and it is here that personal genius makes itself felt most markedly. It not infrequently happens that to a passing traveler the missionary appears to be doing little missionary work. He seldom preaches; he may not be an educator or a translator. Hour after hour and day after day he is in his study, or among the people, talking, talking, talking. Could the observer hear and understand the conversation, he would marvel at the range of topics, covering every department of human life and every phase of religious doctrine. Shall tithes be given? How shall a church be organized? What is a Christian's duty toward an unjust, tyrannical government? The following, jotted down in a few moments by a missionary, will give an idea of the keenness of the questioners: "Why has Christian civilization not accomplished in America what you preachers claim that it is fitted to accomplish?" "Why are your Indians so bitter against you, and repressible only by force?" "If friends pray for us on earth, why should their hearts be dried up and their mouths be stopped when they go to heaven?" "Can a man be a believer who has not been an infidel? Must he not first challenge, then establish, then believe?"

Any missionary can give instance after instance where he has had to call up every line of study that he has ever pursued, to meet the difficulties that occur to the minds of those he seeks to help. But not only does he have to meet personal queries. The missionary must be a statesman. Church quarrels occur on mission ground as well as in Christian lands, and it is often owing chiefly to the missionaries' personal power that they are overcome. Conflicts with persecuting relatives furnish some of the most difficult cases. But instances need not be repeated to show that personal influence of one who is full of the Holy Spirit is the effective instrumentality in modern as in ancient missions.

2. *Public Preaching:* This is the development of personal conversation—is, in fact, personal conversation on a somewhat extended scale. It is not oratorical, but conversational; not instructive, so much as hortatory. And it is universal. Not a few have the idea that preaching is taking a secondary place in the importance of modern mission work. In the large cities, schools, colleges, Bible houses, printing presses, are often more prominent than the preaching places, and many a traveler passes through and reports that mission work, which is primarily concerned with saving souls, has become a means of diffusing education and civilization—all good in its way, but a departure from fundamental ideas. Thus a Christian man visited the city of Constantinople, saw Robert College, the Bible House, the American College for Girls, the school and dispensary of the Scotch Free Church Mission, etc., and said he was glad to see such good work being done, but was sorry to see so little preaching! The missionary said: "Come with me on Sunday." Then he took him from one end of the city to another, and in Stamboul, Scutari, Galata, Hasskeuy, showed him gathering after gathering, where preaching to audiences numbering from 75 to 300 was going on in Turkish, Armenian, Greek, Spanish and English. The traveler went away, satisfied that missions had not made a new departure in that line. The same thing is true of every mission station in the world. Comparatively few of the missionary societies report the number of preaching places, partly for the reason that accurate statistics are almost impossible, partly because there is such a wide divergence of usage. If we take the term preaching place to mean a place where divine service is held regularly, whether conducted by a pastor, preacher, evangelist or catechist, the number will considerably exceed the number of stations and outstations. For there are a large number of places where preaching services are held with regularity in connection with evangelistic tours, and in many sections of India and China there is not a little of public street preaching. The fact, too, that there are fully 4,000 to 5,000 ordained preachers, and a very much larger number of unordained evangelists, catechists, etc., whose chief work is preaching, shows that preaching is relied upon as a chief means of bringing the knowledge of the Gospel within the reach of men.

Passing to the pastoral division, we find the preaching assuming more the character of that in our home churches. It is less conversational, more rhetorical; less hortatory, more educational. Its range of topics widens, and it touches upon every and all the various needs of society and the nation, as well as of individuals. Yet always and everywhere, it is intensely personal; the man is never lost sight of in the community.

3. *Sunday Schools:* These need no special description. They are carried on in much the same way as in home lands, exert much the same influence, and hold much the same general position, both in their evangelistic and pastoral use. An idea of the universality of their use is gained in the fact that in the reports of many societies they are not classified apart from the churches and attendance, the rule being that wherever there are services there is a Sunday school, with not far from the same average attendance. The fact that they do not appear in most of the reports is by no means an indication that they are not widely used as an evangelizing agency. The chief hindrance lies in the lack of competent teachers, but that is constantly

diminishing in force. According to Rev. Dr. Dennis' *Centennial Survey* the number of Sunday schools connected with the Protestant foreign mission enterprise throughout the world is 25,889, and the number of attendants 1,227,594.

4. *Education:* In the earlier stages of missionary enterprise this form of work was not regarded as a method of evangelization and was often held to be inconsistent with the strictly evangelistic aim of the missionary enterprise. Later it became readily recognized as an essential. Converts implied churches; churches needed pastors, and the contrast between pastor and missionary must not be so great that the people should not be willing to look to the former as their leader. Education as a direct means of evangelization, as has been shown in the article on **Education,** has come to hold a more and more prominent place in the minds and plans of missionaries.

1st. It is an essential to the reading and understanding of the Bible, and upon the knowledge of the Bible conversion must depend in a great degree. Illiteracy in mission lands involves not merely ignorance of letters, but of words, as expressive of ideas. The child in a primary school who has learned to read has a better understanding of Bible truth than his parents.

2d. It corrects false ideas, thus opening the mind to receive the truth. In many cases it is almost an absolute prerequisite to such appreciation of truth as must precede conversion.

3d. It secures a positive religious influence upon the individual, whether child or adult, by which the old prejudices may be softened and new ambitions and hopes aroused. This is one of the most important elements in the influence of education as an evangelizing agency.

Looking now at education as it is actually conducted, it is so similar to that in Christian lands as to scarcely need description. The concomitants of rooms, seats, floor, walls, windows, etc., are often different; but the text books are much the same, the methods are very similar. The kindergarten has not been confined to the Occident, but helps the Orient as well, and every form of modern advance in style of instruction is adapted to the needs of Arabs, Hindus, Japanese and Kafirs.

Grading is conducted on much the same principle as in other lands. Small villages have little more than the primary school, where children (and sometimes grown people) learn to read and write, and get some idea of the great realm of knowledge that opens before them. The larger towns and the cities have every grade up to the high school. Boarding schools are established for those who, having passed the lower grades in village schools, are anxious for higher education, or may be fitted for work as teachers. Colleges, too, with courses of study comparable with those of England and America, are found everywhere. In the same general line is the movement for **Industrial education.**

It is, however, in the nurture of the Christian community that the value of education in missions is seen in its fullest degree. Without undertaking to give a detailed statement of the extent to which higher education is carried by the different societies, it is sufficient to say that it has been developed in direct proportion to the appreciation of this second part of missionary work. When it became evident that the only salvation for the convert himself lay in his opportunity and ability to grow, and that this opportunity could not and would not be given or the ability developed unless the society lent a helping hand, then the high schools and colleges sprang up on every side. The tendency now is, also, to make these higher schools more nearly self-supporting.

We now note some of the advantages gained through the higher educational institutions in missions. 1. The furnishing of an educated ministry, which not only takes the place of the missionary, leaving him free for the work of superintendence, but enables the churches to be placed upon a more substantial basis of development for aggressive work. 2. The supply of support to the ministry in the form of an educated laity, able to hold its own in matters of faith, resist any undue desire for ministerial authority and exert influence in the community at large. 3. Solution of questions of social customs by bringing the community in contact with the best results of social development in other lands. This has its dangers as well as its advantages, yet it is a positive necessity. Customs of social life a people must have. If heathen ones are discarded, something must be provided to take their place. It is chiefly through the higher education that the best Christian social usages reach the people of non-Christian lands. 4. The establishment of womanhood in proper relations in the home, the church and the community. The occasion for the development of the American College for Girls at Constantinople was the feeling expressed by parents of the wealthier classes, that they wanted a Christian education for their daughters, which should fit them, not only for teaching, but for presiding in their homes. Any one who would accurately judge the value of the work of the institution should follow those young ladies, not only to the village life of Asia Minor and Bulgaria, but to the more pretentious homes of the cities. 5. Proving intelligibly to the great mass of the indifferent in mission lands, that the Gospel takes in the whole man and develops the best that there is in him. In these days of the telegraph and easy communication, Christianity is judged by its ability to develop as well as to impart. Islam and Buddhism are losing their hold upon men largely by reason of their failure in this very regard, and Christianity is being watched most closely to see whether it meets the need.

5. *Publication:* As an evangelizing agency the preparation and dissemination of Christian literature have always held a foremost place. The place of the publication work in the mission scheme has been sufficiently discussed in the articles **Bible Distribution** and **Literary Work in Missions.** For evangelistic work, tracts, leaflets, helps to Bible study, hold a first place next to the Bible itself. The weekly papers and other periodicals also have a high value. They have more of secular matter, but are always not merely evangelical, but evangelistic in tone and reach multitudes who hold aloof from direct missionary influences.

In pastoral work, missionary publications include theological and other text books and general literature. There is not as much of this as there ought to be, chiefly because, in the great strain upon the time and strength of missionaries, only that is done which at the moment is most essential. As, however, higher education provides mature minds among the natives, this want is being supplied more fully.

II. Turning now to those missionary methods which are distinctively evangelistic or pastoral, we notice, as belonging to the former class:

Attention to physical and social needs, including especially medical work. The relief of physical suffering, the supplying of social wants, is a department of missionary work where, except in the single item of medical work, classification is impossible. Acting upon the general principle that the state of the body affects most vitally the condition of the mind, missionaries in every land have adopted the various means now used so freely and successfully in the large cities of Europe and America. "The gospel of a clean shirt," or even of any shirt at all, has proved in many cases a most powerful one in lands where social customs were of the lowest. But, even in communities where that particular form of evangelization was not called for, there has almost invariably been need of more or less attention to these wants, in order to secure entrance to, and appreciation of, divine truth.

In the earlier history of missions, far more than now, persecution took a form that left the convert without even the means of subsistence. An excommunication that forbade the baker to sell him bread, meant more than trial; it meant starvation to the man who was bold enough to accept the new faith. In such circumstances the missionary was compelled to meet the emergency in such way as he best could. Of recent times that has not been so true; but the need has come in the form of widespread distress from deluge, famine and pestilence. India, Turkey, Persia, and notably China, have repeatedly furnished instances where the supplying of material food has prepared the way for the reception of the spiritual, and hunger, cold and nakedness have unbarred many a door hitherto held tight closed by prejudice and hostility.

Undoubtedly there is danger in this, and none are so quick to recognize it as the missionaries. How to give help without pauperizing, how to avoid the appearance of a bribe to accept Christianity, has required the most careful judgment.

Medical missions have come to the front as a direct means of evangelization with a rapidity that makes one wonder why the Church was so slow to recognize their value and power. Their general character is noted in the article on **Medical Missions**; here we have simply to mention the various ways in which they effect their work.

1. The most important end that they meet is the alleviation of physical pain, so that the soul can comprehend the force of the divine message. No one who has been in mission lands can have failed to see instance after instance where preacher and teacher have failed, but the doctor has succeeded, primarily by removing the obstacles inherent in a diseased body, and by the positive attraction of gratitude for the kindness rendered.

2. The medical missionary is often a pioneer, securing entrance and acceptance where a preacher or teacher would be immediately rejected. This is especially true in such countries as China, where the prejudice against foreign influence is so strong as to yield to almost nothing else. Another notable example is found in the history of missions in Korea.

3. The physician is often able to exert an indirect influence in favor of evangelical work by winning the favor of influential men. Notable instances of this have occurred in the Mohammedan lands.

The distinctively pastoral methods of mission work are chiefly connected with organization and superintendence, and have been treated in the article on the **Church in the Mission Field**.

The culture of converts, so that their insensible influence shall become a power, is worth emphasizing in this connection. The daily life of the convert is an instrument of evangelization of which missionaries should never lose sight.

Family life has always received the attention on the mission field which has only recently been given to it in Christian countries as a direct agency for proving the truth of the claim of the Gospel to renew mankind, and for arresting the attention of those who have not heard of Jesus Christ. This is true in almost every land, but is especially marked in purely heathen countries. The relations and mutual duties of husbands and wives, parents and children, form not only the theme of much earnest thought on the part of the missionary, but of much careful council. To raise the wife from the position of a slave to that of an associate; to develop in the husband and father the sense of responsibility for something more than the supply of the physical needs of those dependent upon him; to educate the children to a genuine reverence rather than the obedience of fear; to give the home character as a center of pure and godly life—these are some of the problems which can only be solved by recognizing that the fostering of a right family life is a true agency of pastoral work for the community at large.

Social life, or the relations of families with each other, may, perhaps, be considered as one of the problems rather than a method of missionary influence. It is, however, gaining increased inportance from the latter point of view in the eyes of those who are watching the development of Protestant Christianity in foreign lands. A man leaves his old faith and accepts the new one. He cannot, however, break away entirely from his old associations, which may include those dependent upon him—certainly those to whom he has duties. He meets them daily in home, in business, in the social circle; is bound together with them in many ways. He cannot if he would isolate himself from them. It is the old question of the times of the Apostles, and creates as much perplexity now as then. To meet it wisely, and place the settlement on a firm, enduring basis, requires that the missionary make a specialty of its study in all its bearings, and be able, not merely to show where the old is wrong or weak, but to present something that shall commend itself to all as clearly preferable. That this is being done increasingly is evident to all who watch carefully the discussions of missionary methods.

Community and national life are but the development of the social. There are fields, however, where they involve questions of greater perplexity. Wherever Church and State are united, and political privileges depend upon ceremonial observances, such questions arise. In some cases practically new states have been formed, with their entire paraphernalia of offices and officers. When this has not been the case, still the new Christian community has invariably had a distinct if not a corporate existence, which has come to be recognized as having an important influence in rendering the position of the Church complete and permanent. Here the missionary meets the questions of submission to unjust laws and the demands of unchristian governments. Each case cannot be settled merely upon its own merits: the foundations of a Christian's relation to the "powers that be" must be thoroughly thought out and clearly stated. Most marked instances of the influence of missionaries in this have been given in the article on the **International Service of Missions**.

The Christian state, not so much as an accomplished fact, but as an ideal, is a most practical and important element in the methods by which Christianity is to be ultimately established.

Many things will occur to those intimately acquainted with the methods of missionary work which might have been mentioned. If, however, the impression shall have been given that Christian propaganda should be no mere haphazard carrying out of a vague, altho noble, impulse, but a calm, determined, well-considered effort on the part of the churches through their representatives to establish Christian faith, worship and life on a permanent and natural foundation in every section of the globe, the chief end of the writer will have been attained.

METLAKAHTLA: A village on the W. coast of British Columbia, occupied by Christianized Tsimsian Indians. Station of the CMS (1856), with 1 missionary and wife, 4 women missionaries, 4 native workers, 2 day schools, 1 boarding school, 1 hospital, 1 dispensary and 244 professed Christians, of whom 47 are communicants.

MEXICO: Capital of the republic of Mexico. It is beautifully situated on a plateau 7,500 feet above the level of the sea, in the Tenochtitlan valley, not far from lake Tezcuco. In the midst of lofty mountains, the climate is temperate and healthy. The older parts of the city, however, being on marshy ground, are subject to malaria. The streets are well paved, broad, and well lighted, and raised paved roads, called *paseos*, which lead out into the country, and are shaded on either side by fine trees, add much to the natural beauties of the place. The Roman Catholic religion is the state religion, but other religions are tolerated. In addition to the many churches, monasteries, convents, and other religious or benevolent institutions are plentiful. Schools and colleges, theaters and the buildings for the government offices give the city an attractive appearance.

This city was founded by Cortez in 1522 and stands on the site of a sacred Aztec high place. Population (1900), 344,721. Protestant missionary work was begun in the city by the PE in 1870, its aim being care for the spiritual needs of Protestant residents quite as much as for the native Mexicans. The PN followed in 1872, the ME and MES in 1873, the Baptist Home Missionary Society in 1883 and the SDA in 1894. These societies together have now (1903) in the city 35 missionaries, men and women; 161 native workers, men and women; 16 places of worship, 21 elementary schools, 7 higher or special training schools, 1 hospital and dispensary, 3 printing houses and 2,172 professed evangelical Christians.

MEXICO: In form Mexico is shaped like a cornucopia, whose mouth opens toward the United States. It anticipated the United States as a European colony by about a century. Yet eighty years ago it was glad to copy our national institutions, and from that time to this, in spite of the restrictions of papal bigotry, it has continued to receive some of its choicest blessings from this country—at the same time, as must be confessed, yielding up some of its most valuable territories by the arbitrament of war.

Mexico, as it now stands, is a country with nearly 6,000 miles of coastline, more than two-thirds of which are on the Pacific and the great Gulf of California. It has no navigable rivers. The east coast is peculiarly lacking in good harbors. It is, moreover, low-lying, and as a rule insalubrious. Mexico can boast but few islands, and those are insignificant in character or extent. The mountain ranges, which seem to form a sort of vertebral column throughout this hemisphere from Alaska to Patagonia, are prominent in Mexico, tho cut off from the South American chain by the low-lying Isthmus of Darien. The high tableland intervening between the eastern and western branches of this great mountain range constitutes an admirable highway for railroad development and for international traffic—a fact which did not escape the eye of the great explorer and philosopher Humboldt. There is a vast portion of land in the country that can never become arable, but for this deficiency there are partial compensations: first, in the prevalence of mineral resources, and, second, in the fact that the coast is everywhere easily reached. With the establishment of artificial harbors and breakwaters, access can be found for maritime commerce, both on the Pacific and on the Gulf of Mexico. Yet the whole situation indicates that the chief commerce of the country must be carried on with the United States.

In the northern portions of the republic there are great barren expanses, which, tho sufficiently level for tillage, are so lacking in fertility as to promise but a slender reward to agriculture. Farther south, and along the east coast, however, there is an affluence of fertility; and altho the climate is often unhealthful, the fruitfulness of the country is such as to supply a large population, if need be, and a lucrative commerce. In Michoacan and other still more southern States there are extensive forests of all the most valuable timber-trees.

The country is in many places volcanic, and from an elevated position in the City of Mexico one can behold several greater or smaller cones which are manifestly of volcanic origin, and near them extended plains of flinty lava. About the middle of the last century the mountain known as Jorullo, in the State of Michoacan, was thrown up about 1,600 feet above the plain by volcanic action.

The mines of Mexico, especially those of silver, have long been regarded as the richest in the world. It is said that for two or three centuries Mexico has produced at least one-half of the entire yield of silver possessed by mankind. From 1537 to 1880 the total yield of this metal is said to have been nearly three thousand millions. The yield of gold in the same time has been nearly one thousand millions of dollars.

The entire area of the country is 763,804 square miles. The population (in 1900) is nearly 14,000,000, of whom 19 per cent. are of pure or nearly pure white blood, 43 per cent. of mixed race, and 38 per cent. of Indian race.

In speaking of the Indian population, an able writer has justly said: "A wide difference exists between the Indians of the United States and British America and the so-called Indians of Mexico. They are a different race. The Mexican Indians are docile and industrious; they engage in agriculture, in mining, and in such rude arts as are practised in countries which do not enjoy the advantages of modern transportation. In all the wars in which Mexico has been engaged the Indians have constituted largely the rank and file of her armies. They are now enfranchised citizens under the laws of their country, and to the extent to which they are taxed they enjoy equal political rights with those of the Spanish race. While the Indians and the inhabitants of mixed blood comprise the menial class, yet from the ranks of the aborigines have sprung men of mark—men who have risen to distinction in science, in arts, in letters, in educational employments, in the church, in military life, and in the conduct of state affairs."

The Ancient Inhabitants: The Toltecs, who preceded the Aztecs in the valley of Mexico, are supposed to have migrated from the north. Like other Indian races on the Western Hemisphere, they probably passed over the narrow channel known as Bering's Straits from northern Asia, and were attracted southward by more friendly climates and more abundant supplies of food. Ebrard has given good reasons for supposing that other migrations also occurred—perhaps in some instances by accident—from Japan across the Pacific, and from Europe and Africa across the Atlantic. The Aztec civilization and that of the Mayas of Yucatan have many things in common with Eastern cults, and particularly with the hieroglyphic inscriptions of ancient Egypt.

The Toltec's were in some respects more highly civilized than the Aztecs, who finally conquered them. Their strength lay in the arts of peace, as that of the Aztecs was developed by war. The terrible system of bloody sacrifice was established in connection with the warlike spirit of the Aztec conquerors. The Tezcucans, who entered into a triple league with the Aholcuans and the Aztecs, and were finally betrayed and conquered by the latter, presented the highest perfection of the ancient Mexican civilization. One of their kings was one of the grandest figures in history.

The Aztecs were characteristically a warlike race; and, like the Lombards in the Roman Empire, they took on the culture of the vanquished peoples. Like the Venetians, who, when driven by northern barbarians into the Adriatic, built upon the very lagoons and marshes a mighty dominion—more invincible because built upon the marshes—so the Aztecs, harassed at first by other tribes, took refuge upon a small island in the shallow lake of Tezcuco. This, gradually enlarged by driven piles and the dredging of their canals, became the impregnable stronghold from which they at length dictated terms to all their neighbors, till they had built up a great empire, extending from sea to sea.

No chapter of history is more pathetic than that which describes the invasion of this empire by Cortez and his followers in the early part of the 16th century. The combination of prowess and treachery, and the heartless cruelty inflicted in the alleged service of the Cross, have left an indelible blot upon the Christian name, and the Aztecs, in spite of their bloody religion, have the sympathy of mankind.

The three centuries which followed the conquest are historically a barren waste.

The Dawn of Political Liberty: This condition of arrested development continued until the spirit of liberty and independence was awakened in a comparatively recent period. It seems wonderful that Napoleon I. should have been the man to strike at last the keynote of liberty among all Spaniards on both hemispheres; but so it was. There had been in all the colonies a sort of chivalric loyalty to the sovereigns of Castile, however severe their oppression. But when in 1808 Napoleon sent his armies into Spain and dethroned Ferdinand VII., placing the scepter in the hands of a Bonaparte, the spell of loyalty was forever broken. In 1810 the standard of independence was raised, a patriotic priest leading the movement. By the year 1821 the independence of Mexico and several other Spanish-American States had been won, and by the year 1828 all the Spanish colonies on the Western Hemisphere had become free republics. But the work of reform was as yet only partial—religious liberty had not been achieved. We come now to another series of providences in relation to Mexico, and those, too, which have to do with our own history.

In the year 1835 Santa Anna, then President of Mexico, brought about a *coup d'état*, by which the governments of the different States were abolished, and all the power was concentrated in the central government under his dictatorship.

Yucatan on the south and Texas on the north at once rebelled, and so grave was the Texan rebellion that Santa Anna himself was compelled to take the field. His armies attacked and dispersed the Texan Legislature, and prisoners of war whom they captured were mercilessly shot by his orders, thus rendering the reconciliation of the people of Texas forever impossible.

At the battle of San Jacinto, Santa Anna was vanquished and taken prisoner by General Houston, and for nine years Texas maintained her independence. In 1846 Texas applied for admission to our union and was admitted, and Mexico thereupon declared war upon the United States. The oppressive acts of the Mexican dictator were considered a first-rate pretext. And, besides, the fashion of our English cousins in making conquered nations pay the expense of conquering them was also thought to be the right thing to do; and so we concluded to defend Texas all the way from the Gulf of Mexico to the Pacific.

General Taylor appeared on the battlefields of Matamoras and Monterey. General Scott marched triumphantly from Vera Cruz to Mexico city. General Kearney was heard from in Arizona, and Fremont in California.

The Advent of Religious Freedom: Up to the year 1867 there was no religious liberty in Mexico. It is true that the Liberal party had in 1857 drafted a constitution demanding liberty of faith, abolishing conventual establishments, and confiscating church properties in mortmain; but they were not able to enforce them.

As Napoleon I. had unconsciously promoted

the political independence of all the Spanish-American states a half-century before, so Napoleon III. became the unconscious cause of the later movement for religious freedom and political consolidation. He also attempted the dispensing of crowns and scepters. The War of the Rebellion in the United States had furnished the opportunity. A Swiss banker had an exaggerated financial claim against the Mexican Government, which by the adoption of the banker as a citizen of France furnished the emperor with a pretext. England and Spain also had claims, and an alliance was formed for an armed intervention.

In 1862 the united fleets appeared at Vera Cruz with their contingents of men. But England and Spain soon withdrew from the enterprise. The French army under Generals Forey and Bazaine fought their way over the Cordilleras to the capital, where they established a provisional government known as the "Regency of the Empire." This virtually French Assembly submitted the choice of a ruler to the patronizing French emperor, who was politic enough to give the crown of Mexico to the house of Austria. The Archduke Maximilian accepted and, with his young and accomplished wife, prepared for a changed destiny. On the 10th of April, 1864, amid all the pomp of royalty, this ill-starred couple left their charming abode and embarked for Mexico. They arrived in May at Vera Cruz. Their journey to Mexico City was one series of ovations from the clerical party. Having proceeded first of all to the great cathedral to celebrate mass, they were escorted to the old vice-regal palace, amid the ringing of bells and the rejoicing of the Reactionists that the republic was dead, and an empire was once more established.

But General Sherman was already on his march to the sea; and within four months General Grant received a sword presentation at Appomattox which attracted the attention of France, and of all the courts of Europe. From that day everything went wrong with the French power in Mexico. It was patent to all men that the empire would prove a failure; and the French people especially were vexed at the stupendous blunder of their ambitious and meddling emperor.

Meanwhile, Maximilian and Carlotta had both sincerely endeavored to conciliate the people—he by special franchises, she by indefatigable charities.

But in July, 1866, matters had assumed so grave an aspect that the young empress, then only twenty-six years of age, set out with a few attendants to visit the court of France and remonstrate with Napoleon against the withdrawal of his support.

The spring of 1867 brought the beginning of the end. Maximilian's chief forces, with himself among them, were at Queretaro under siege. In an attempt to escape he was betrayed by one of his generals, placed under arrest, tried by a military tribunal, and, with Generals Miramon and Mexia, was sentenced to be shot. Meanwhile the republic which for ten years had existed, we might almost say in the person of a single man—Benito Juarez—returned from its exile and took the place of the mushroom empire.

With the establishment of the republic under Juarez in 1867 that religious liberty which had been proclaimed in 1857 was fully realized, and, notwithstanding the efforts and the bitter persecutions of the Roman Catholic clergy, it has been maintained till the present time.

The Record of the Papacy in Mexico: Even by the judgment of candid Roman Catholics, the religion of Mexico from the very beginning of the Spanish conquest has been a mixture of Christianity and heathenism, the latter often predominating. For centuries no religion except that of the Roman Catholic Church was known in Mexico. When the republic was established in 1823, and thence onward to the proclamation of religious liberty in 1857, an express provision in the constitution declared that the Roman Catholic faith was the religion of the state, and that no other could be tolerated.

One-third of the real property of the republic came at length into the possession of the hierarchy. Conventual establishments for either sex were greatly multiplied. Mexico City might almost have been said to be a city of convents at the time when religious liberty was established. The people, wearied with the long dominion of an unscrupulous hierarchy, and remembering that the church had been implicated in all the measures designed to overthrow the popular liberty, carried reform to an opposite extreme of intolerance. It confiscated a large portion of the church property, silenced the clangor of convent-bells, which the public patience had so long endured, ordered the long robes and shovel-hats and other insignia of the priesthood and other sacred orders to be laid aside when appearing upon the public streets, and suppressed all public processions and various childish pageants. The Jesuits were banished from the country, as they had been at various times from so many nations of Europe. It is difficult for any who desire to be entirely candid to decide whether the papacy, as it existed in Mexico fifty years ago, was on the whole a blessing or a curse.

It can hardly be doubted that altho the Virgin Mary was almost made to take the place of Deity, yet enough of Christ was communicated to many souls to save them from sin and death. Yet the influence of the priesthood was declared by many who were residents in the country to be positively corrupting to the public morals. The licentiousness of their lives was scarcely disguised, and their exactions for the performance of the marriage ceremony were so oppressive that to a large extent the masses dispensed with the sacred rite altogether, and, with the poor, concubinage became the rule. The Bible was strictly kept from the people, or if found in their possession was burned as a poisonous and pestilent thing. In the desecration of the Sabbath the priesthood, by example, at least, might be said to take the lead. The perfunctory ceremonies of the morning mass once over, they were among the promptest and most enthusiastic at the bull-fights. Gambling was a favorite pastime within the monasteries, and that excessive wine-drinking took the place of vigils and of fasting was too plainly indicated by the rotund figures and sodden faces of the padres whenever they appeared in public.

This easy-going life was not inconsistent with the most fiery zeal for dogma, and the bitterness that could persecute even unto death.

The priesthood of Mexico was in touch with the priesthood of Spain in the palmy days of the Inquisition. This institution was established in Mexico by Philip II., and the spirit of the infamous Torquemada did not fail to stamp itself upon the new continent, as upon the old.

When the Northern Methodist Mission purchased a confiscated monastery in Puebla in 1872, and proceeded to adapt it to their missionary uses, they found in the substructure skeletons of Christian martyrs who had been walled into their cells to perish from the sight and memory of men. Juarez was from the first in favor of the more enlightened influence of Protestantism, and every president since 1867 has exerted his influence for freedom of opinion. Among those of liberal sentiments there have been two classes—some undoubtedly mere freethinkers, who cared for no religious faith, but were staunch supporters of freedom. Others, even tho Catholics, have advocated liberty of thought, and welcomed Protestantism, not only because such freedom is the dictate of wise government, but because they believe that the disintegration of the one dominant mass of the papacy is more favorable to national liberty. Of this class was General Esquibedo, who in 1879 was heard to express his satisfaction at the introduction of Protestantism, because he believed that its influence, even its rivalries, would prove a benefit to the Mexican Catholic Church, and make it more like the Catholic Church in the United States.

The Present Status of the Republic: A great advance in industrial and commercial resources has been made since the more complete establishment of the republican government in 1867, at the close of the Maximilian empire. The cause of public education has also greatly advanced since the separation of Church and State. It certainly is not creditable to the Roman Catholic Church, which for more than three centuries had held dominion over the country, that the breaking of its dominion was the signal for a great advance in the education of the people. In the year 1857 the University of Mexico was abolished, and was replaced by special schools of law, medicine, letters, agriculture, mines, science and a military college.

The country has so long been exempt from serious political disturbances that the confidence of capitalists has been fully established, and the wealth which springs up with stable government has of itself become a strong conservative factor, and a new warrant for future prosperity.

The capitalists of the country cannot afford the luxury of the old-time pronunciamento, and they are now a more influential class than the impecunious adventurers who follow political revolution as a profession.

The Catholic party have not ceased to reecho the old cry of "patriotism" as a means of opposition to Protestant missions and all American influence, but the most enlightened statesmen have learned long ere this that Protestantism is a better friend to Mexico than the papacy. Nothing is more foreign to the purpose of Protestant missions than to promote annexation to the United States. The more free thought and general enlightenment of the people are promoted, the better are they prepared to maintain their independence. Such a result is the desire and hope of all Protestant missionaries for Mexico.

The Era of Protestant Missions: For the beginning of the Protestant movement we must go back to a period anterior to the proclamation of religious liberty. The seed-sowing of the truth followed immediately the rude plowshare of the so-called Mexican war. The Bible was borne into the country by General Scott's army. This divine talisman, that had wrought such marvels in the civil and religious institutions of the Northern republic, was a stranger on Mexican soil. It was as novel as a falling meteor from another planet. The simple truths of the Gospel were received by the people with a sort of hunger.

The American Bible Society had from an early period cherished a deep interest in Mexico, but almost nothing could then be done for the spread of the truth. But after the Mexican war direct effort was made to introduce the Word of God.

Rev. Mr. Thompson was employed as a Bible agent in Brownsville, Tex., in 1860. Bible distribution was carried on in connection with the missionary work of Miss Melinda Rankin in Brownsville, in 1854. In 1866 she established a school in Monterey, Mexico. As an example of the way in which this word found its way and began to work like leaven, we may cite Ville de Cos, a mining community in the State of Zacatecas.

An "ecclesia" like those of New Testament times was formed in a private house where people met to read the Word of God in secret. The proclamation of liberty of thought in 1857 gave them courage, and the little company grew in numbers and in knowledge. Sending to Monterey for a clergyman, they received the rite of baptism, and organized themselves into a church.

They appointed one of their own number to conduct services and administer the sacraments. They were instructed and variously assisted from time to time by Dr. G. W. Provost, an American physician of Zacatecas. By the year 1872 they had erected a church, and the number of communicants had risen to over a hundred. In 1861, Rev. James Hickey, a Baptist minister residing in Texas, being adverse to slavery and unwilling to be drawn into the impending conflict, crossed the Rio Grande to Matamoras, where he acquired some knowledge of Spanish, and began to preach to the Mexicans. From there he went to Monterey in November, 1862, where, in January, 1864, the first Baptist church was organized, which to-day is one of the strongest evangelical bodies in Mexico. He died in 1866. For about three years the work was maintained by the little body of believers until 1869, when the American Baptist Home Missionary Society appointed a missionary to that field. Since that time the Society has prosecuted its work successfully in the republic, as stated in the article on **Home Missions**.

Another example of the leaven of Bible-distribution was found years later in Zitacuaro, in the State of Michoacan. A Presbyterian native preacher, Rev. Mr. Forcada, on commencing missionary work at that point in 1877, learned that a Bible depository had been opened there by a Mexican six years before, and that four hundred Bibles and many religious tracts had been sold. Thus the way had been prepared for an unexpected welcome to the missionary, and a most gratifying success. At present, within a radius of forty miles, there are sixteen congregations of Protestant Christians.

Undenominational Missionary Work: Through the influence of Miss Rankin at Monterey, the attention of Rev. Henry A. Riley was called to Mexico as a promising missionary field, and in 1869 he proceeded to the capital, where he found the harvest ripe beyond his expectations. He began his labors under the auspices of the American and Foreign Christian Union, and he succeeded in purchasing at a low price a valuable confiscated church property. Meanwhile an important movement had already begun in the City of Mexico, where a few prominent priests openly avowed their renunciation of the Roman Catholic dogmas and corruptions.

The first was Francisco Aguilas, a man of great fervor and eloquence. Alarmed at his boldness and success, a fellow-priest, Manuel Aguas, set out to prepare himself to refute the teachings of Aguilas, who had already been joined and encouraged by Mr. Riley. While Aguas pursued his investigations in search of arguments, he himself became a convert, and a most successful preacher of the Gospel. Unfortunately for the cause which they had espoused, both of these eloquent men died after a brief career. The converts who were gathered by Father Aguas were organized into a church based upon the doctrines and order of American Episcopacy, and known as the Church of Jesus.

The Protestant influences that have been introduced into Mexico have come largely from North America, and the following societies have accomplished most effective results: The Northern and Southern Presbyterian Boards; the Associate Reformed (South); the Cumberland Presbyterian; the Northern and Southern Methodist Boards; the American Baptist Home Mission Society; Independent Baptists of the South; the Foreign Mission Board of the Southern Baptist Convention; the Protestant Episcopal Board; the American Board (Congregational); the Christian Woman's Board of Missions; the Friends' Work; the American Bible Society; the Seventh Day Adventists and their medical work; and the Woman's Christian Temperance Union. The Plymouth Brethren of Great Britain, and the Junta Misionera, of Mexico, are also engaged in active service for the redemption of Mexico.

Bancroft (H. H.) *Resources and Development of Mexico*, San Francisco, 1894; Butler (W.), *Mexico in Transition*, New York, 1892; Hale (S.), *Mercedes*, Louisville, 1895; Johnson (H.M.), *About Mexico*, Philadelphia, 1887; Lummis (C.F.), *Awakening of a Nation*, New York, 1898; Rankin (M.), *Twenty Years Among the Mexicans*, Cincinnati, 1875.

MEYER, Philip Lewis Henry: Born at Neuwied-on-the-Rhine, Germany, November 13, 1826, of earnest Christian parents. Died at Marburg, Germany, August 2, 1876. At his confirmation in 1840 the love of Christ mightily took possession of his heart. Successively a cabinet maker, a school teacher, a student of medicine, he was thus variously qualified for mission service, and received a call to South Africa in 1854. He reached Cape Town November 3 of the same year. He found the mission station at Shiloh and Goshen in ashes by a recent Kafir war, and commenced rebuilding at once, studying the Kafir language, teaching the natives handicraft, and inculcating Gospel truths. In 1859 he founded a new station, not far from Shiloh, in a plain watered by the River Engoti, and called it Engotine. In 1869 he received an invitation to teach a Kafir tribe 240 miles from Engotine. War having scattered the tribe, Mr. Meyer and his family were left alone. But he followed the Kafirs to preach to them in their mountain fastnesses. After peace was restored the people began to come to the station to hear the Gospel, and soon church and school were built and a church was organized. Mr. Meyer was permitted to found one more mission, but his health failed, and he was obliged to return to Europe.

MHOW: A town in Central India, situated 13 miles S. W. by S. of Indore. There is a military post 1 mile distant. Population, 31,800, of whom three-fourths are Hindus. Station of the PCC (1877), with (1903) 2 women missionaries, 37 native workers, 3 outstations, 1 place of worship, 3 Sunday schools, 4 day schools, 1 industrial school, 1 dispensary, 1 orphanage, and 43 professed Christians. Station also of the WMS, with (1903) 1 missionary, 5 outstations, 1 place of worship, and 35 professed Christians. Name also written Mahow.

MICRONESIA: Certain groups of small islands in the Pacific Ocean mostly north of the equator, and between the meridians of 130° and 160°. This part of the Oceania includes the Gilbert (Kingsmill), Marshall (Mulgrave, the Radack and Ralick chains), and Caroline Islands, the Marianas (or Ladrones), and Bonin Island, and many other small atolls and groups. With few exceptions the islands are low atolls of coral formation. The groups vary in extent—from the single islet half a mile long to the extensive archipelago enclosed by a coral reef 200 miles or more in circumference. The depth of the island-studded lagoon thus enclosed varies from 5 to 100 fathoms. Some islands are accessible to the largest ships, having good channels through breaks in the reef, and furnishing commodious harbors, while some have channels which cannot be entered with the prevailing winds, and others are entirely enclosed by reefs and have no anchorage. Ocean currents, with frequent calms, render navigation very uncertain and often dangerous. The area of land in any of these atolls is insignificant compared with the size of the lagoon or the extent of the supporting reef. The land, ranging in elevation from 5 to 20 feet above high-water mark, is composed of coral rocks and sand washed up by the waves, and forms a series of islets resting at varying distances from one another upon the reef. At high tide the waves roll over the reef at a depth of 4 to 10 feet and between the islets into the lagoon, while at ebb tide the reef is bare, and furnishes a connecting pathway from islet to islet, except where it is broken by a channel. The average area of land in the atolls is probably from 5 to 10 square miles.

The high islands are of volcanic origin, have the physical peculiarities of the atolls, only that the lagoon is replaced by elevated land.

The people resemble the brown Polynesian race, but they are evidently of mixed blood; and their language is not the true Polynesian, but distinct and split up into separate languages in the different groups. They are simple in construction, easily acquired, yet quite difficult to reduce to writing because of the shading of sounds, and also on account of the presence of close consonants at the end of words. Five of these languages have been reduced to writing. Portions of the Bible, hymn-books, and various school-books have been printed. Some of the dialects are very expressive, and tho not having extended vocabularies, are rendered flexible by the use of pronominal suffixes, verbal directives, and terminations to indicate place and to express comparison. Degraded in past usage, the introduction of Christian ideas means resurrection to the language no less than life to the people.

The religion of the islanders used to be not greatly unlike modern spiritism, and their social usages imposed no family ties. Polygamy was tolerated among the chiefs, but not very extensively practised. Children belonged to brothers and sisters of the parents as much as to the mothers.

The people wore little, if any, clothing, tho the habits of different groups show great variety. In the Gilbert Islands men had no covering of any kind; the women wore a fringed skirt 10 or 12 inches long, the children being nude. In the Marshall Islands men wore a fringe skirt 25 to 30 inches long, and the women two mats, about a yard square each, belted about the waist. Upon the Caroline Islands some covering was used. The dwelling-houses were mere shelters of simple construction, tho the council-houses were large.

The forms of government varied, but were all founded on the idea of the aggrandizement of the chief rather than the good of the subject. Human life was slightly regarded, and even petty chiefs sent many a victim to the executioner.

Missionary work was begun on Ponape and Kusaie (Caroline group) in 1852 by three American missionaries (L. H. Gulick, A. A. Sturges, and B. G. Snow) with their wives. They were accompanied by two Hawaiian missionary helpers with their wives. The first five years were discouraging. Many times the enterprise seemed ready to fail. Opposition of foreigners (self-exiled and more degraded than the natives), small-pox on Ponape, insurrection on Kusaie, disastrous results of contact with the whaling fleets, and the dense paganism of the natives themselves had all to be overcome by the faith of earnest men. The year 1857 saw Apaiang (Gilbert Islands) and Ebon (Marshall Islands) occupied.

During the next five years (1857 to 1862) the harvest began. During the last twenty years there has been a constant increase of both hearers and converts.

The changes which have been wrought through the efforts of the missionaries are truly wonderful. The transforming power of the Word of God has never been more manifest than in this field. There has been a marked development of stability in the character of the natives. Formerly they were dishonest and untruthful. There was a belief among them that the Great Spirit used deceitful means for the accomplishment of His plans or for maintaining His authority, and the people accordingly cultivated deceit. Ships were often pillaged and the crews murdered. But the Gospel has in many islands effected a complete revolution. Social ideas have been changed. The family has been built up, and the ceremony of marriage is becoming more and more common. The practise of family-worship has done much to purify and crystallize social ideas, and a strong sentiment of his duty to guard the household and defend his family from the lust of even the chiefs is rising in the mind of the head of the household.

Better dwellings, greater personal cleanliness and tidiness have also followed the moral reformation. Intellectual progress is quite marked. The schools are well attended. Native teachers have done very efficient work. The mother-tongue has become the vehicle of blessing. From the first a missionary spirit has been cultivated, and the young convert has been taught to keep in view the prospect of becoming a teacher of the new doctrine on his own island, or, if need be, on other islands. When the work was to be pushed westward from Ponape it was done by native missionaries, furnishing one of the most interesting chapters in the annals of missionary work. Going forth to a people of diverse tongue, these men and women prepared themselves for the work, and soon gathered in large numbers of converts.

The American Board has training schools at Kusaie and at Ruk. There are 51 churches, with over 6,000 communicants. The LMS has a flourishing work in the southern islands of the Gilbert group.

MIDDLEDRIFT: A settlement in the Transvaal, S. Africa, situated on the S. side of Limpopo River, about 130 miles N. by E. of Pietersburg. Station of the NBC (1897), with (1900) 1 missionary and his wife, 5 native workers, 9 outstations, 4 places of worship, 9 Sunday schools, 3 day schools, 1 temperance society, and 340 professed Christians.

MIDNAPUR: A town in Bengal, India, situated 65 miles W. by S. of Calcutta, with which it is connected by canal. It is the center of a silk and indigo industry and has a population (1891) of 32,500, of whom 24,700 are Hindus and 6,800 Muslims. Station of the Free Baptist Missionary Society (1863), with (1903) 2 missionaries and their wives, 3 women missionaries, 54 native workers, 6 outstations, 1 place of worship, 6 Sunday schools, 2 boarding schools, 16 day schools, 1 theological class, 1 dispensary, and 213 professed Christians, of whom 125 are communicants. The Society spells the name Midnapore.

MIDONGY: A village in Madagascar, situated 70 miles N. W. of Fianarantsoa. Station of the Norwegian Mission Society (1894).

MIEN-CHAU: A town in the Province of Szechwan, China, situated on the Fu-kiang, 62 miles N. E. by N. of Chengtu-fu. Population, 70,000. Station of the CMS (1894), with (1903) 6 missionaries, 2 with their wives; 2 women missionaries, 1 native worker, 1 place of worship, 1 dispensary, 1 day school, and 8 professed Christians. A general reorganization after the Boxer outbreak is now under way. The Society spells the name Mien-Cheo.

MIEN-CHU-HSIEN: A town in the Province of Sze-chwan, China, situated 45 miles N. of Cheng-tu-fu. Population, 50,000. Station of the CMS (1894), with (1902) 2 missionaries, 1 with his wife; 1 woman missionary, and 5 Christians. The Society spells the name Mien-Chuh.

MIHIJAM. See Maijam.

MILDMAY INSTITUTIONS AND MISSIONS: The Mildmay Conferences were inaugurated in 1856 by the Rev. William Pennefather, Vicar of St. Jude's, Mildmay Park, at Bermet. The chief purpose, to persuade members of various Christian Churches openly to acknowledge their spiritual union in Christ, seemed to many fraught with danger of an actual exhibition of disunion and confusion. In fact, they were so successful that in 1869 the corner-stone of a large Conference Hall was laid at Mildmay, and the institution became a center of union for Christians of all denominations, and has facilitated the prosecution of a variety of evangelistic and missionary enterprises.

The Conference Hall is used not merely for the annual conferences, but for weekly evangelistic services, and there are special rooms for Bible classes, mothers' meetings, tea meetings, etc. Closely connected with it are a deaconess house, a training home for lady workers for home and foreign missionary work, called "The Willows," a nurses' house, Memorial Cottage Hospital and orphanage, while a mission hospital at Bethnal Green, and a convalescent home at Ossulston are under the same management. Special interest attaches to the Pennefather Memorial Home for Mildmay workers who are disabled by sickness or age, and to the mulberry tree in a corner of the Park, under which it has been the custom to gather afternoon meetings during the conferences.

The three departments especially connected with foreign mission work are the Bible class for men in Conference Hall, which has sent out a large number of workers, ordained and lay; the Deaconess House, and the Willows Training School. The Bible class is represented in the Church of England, Free Church pastorates, on the foreign fields in China, India, Persia, South America, and Africa, and in work for the Jews. The Deaconess House is the administrative headquarters for the three branches of its work: medical, home and foreign missions. The graduates are found in every part of city work as well as on the foreign field, including some of the most difficult sections, as Arabia, Kashmir and Central Africa. For the most part Mildmay workers go in connection with the regular missionary societies, and in the training institute there is a special class in preparation for the CMS. The organization is more closely in charge of work among the Jews, particularly in London and Eastern Europe, and the Jaffa Medical Mission and Hospital is closely affiliated with it. The City Mission work includes rescue work, house-to-house visitation by the deaconesses, and any phase of benevolent effort that seems important.

The whole organization is under the care of a board of trustees and council, including representatives of the Church of England and the Free Churches.

MILLER: A village in Cape Colony, S. Africa, situated in the Transkei district, 35 miles S. E. of Clarkebury. Station of the UFS (1887), with (1903) 2 missionaries and their wives, 8 native workers, 8 outstations, 2 places of worship, 1 Sunday school, 4 day schools, 1 dispensary, and 37 professed Christians.

MILLS, Samuel John: Born at Torringford, Conn., April 21, 1783, the son of a minister. He entered Williams College in 1806 and graduated in 1809. After entering college he was accustomed to meet with a few students in a grove for prayer and religious conference, and on a memorable afternoon, when driven by a thunderstorm to continue their conference under a haystack, he first suggested the idea of personal responsibility for sending the Gospel to the benighted portions of the earth. The young men later formed a society, whose object was stated to be "to effect in the persons of its members a mission to the heathen." In 1810 Mills entered Andover Theological Seminary, where he found Hall, Newell, Judson, and Nott deeply interested in the same subject, and he proposed that they unite in an appeal to the General Association of Massachusetts, soon to meet at Bradford. This memorial led to the formation of the American Board. Mills, after his graduation, was active in organizing Bible and other benevolent societies in different parts of the United States, and was sent to Africa by the American Colonization Society to choose a site for a colony of negroes from America. There he contracted a fever from which he died on shipboard June 16, 1818.

Tho not permitted to engage personally in a foreign mission he accomplished much for the conversion of the world. From the mind of Mills arose plans for the American Board of Commissioners for Foreign Missions, the American Bible Society, the United Foreign Missionary Society, and the African School under the care of the Synod of New York and New Jersey, beside impetus given to Domestic Missions, to the Colonization Society, and to the general cause of benevolence in both hemispheres.

Bridgman (E. C.), *Samuel John Mills*, New York, 1864.

MILNE, William: Born in Aberdeenshire, Scotland, in 1785. His fixed purpose to engage in missionary work was formed in 1805, at the age of twenty. After this he spent five years in securing a support for his mother and sisters. His early opportunities for education were meager. Entering the missionary college at Gosport, he went through the regular course of study, under the direction of the Rev. David Bogue. He was ordained in July, 1812; received his appointment to China, under the LMS, arriving at Macao July 4, 1813, where he was welcomed by Dr. Morrison. China being closed against missionaries, and the Portuguese, who controlled the neighboring islands and points on the mainland, being hostile, he was ordered in ten days to leave Macao.

Leaving Mrs. Milne with Mrs. Morrison, he went to Canton, almost the only place in China where he could live in safety. Here he remained six months, engaged in the study of the language. The next eight months he spent in a tour through the East Indian Archipelago, distributing among Chinese residents copies of the New Testament and other books. After rejoining Dr. Morrison at Canton, Milne was sent to open a mission to the Chinese in Malacca, arriving at Penang in 1815. He opened a free school and gave much time to planning for an Anglo-Chinese College at Malacca, which he opened in 1820, the idea and much of the early support coming from Dr. Robert Morrison of Canton. His main work from 1815 to the close of his life was the preparation of religious literature. He aided Morrison in the work of translating the Bible into Chinese, the Books of Deuteronomy and onward to Job being translated by him. He prepared a Commentary on the Epistle to the Ephesians, an "Essay on the Soul," in two volumes, and fifteen tracts, all acceptable to the Chinese. He had great skill and readiness in the use of the language, and in addition to his literary labors performed much evangelistic work. His first convert, Leang-Afa, whom he baptized, was the first ordained Chinese evangelist, remained in the service of the LMS for many years, and was the teacher from whom the leader of the Taiping rebellion derived his respect for Christianity. Dr. Milne's health failing, he took a sea voyage, but returned weaker, and died in 1822, at the early age of thirty-seven, and when but ten years in the missionary work.

Besides the works mentioned, he published *Retrospect of the Protestant Mission in China*. Philip (R.), *William Milne*, New York, 1840.

MILLPORT HARBOR: A settlement in British New Guinea, situated on the S. coast, about 80 miles W. of Kwato. It is a lovely situation on a hill with a bay on each side. Station of the LMS (1896), with 1 missionary.

MING-CHIANG. See MIN-TSING-HSIEN.

MINGRELIA: A district of Asiatic Russia, in the Caucasus, lying between Tiflis and the Black Sea. Area, 2,600 square miles. Surface generally mountainous, sloping toward the south. Climate warm and damp; fevers are prevalent; soil exceedingly fertile, and vegetation rapid. The mountains are covered with magnificent forests, and much good land lies waste. The district is without external improvement, and has a savage and deserted appearance. Population, 240,000, most of whom belong to the Georgian race, but are generally inferior in appearance to the mountaineers of the Caucasus. The dominant religion is that of the Greek Church. Mingrelia corresponds with ancient Colchis. It was long a part of the kingdom of Georgia, was afterward independent under a long line of native princes, and became subject to Russia in 1804, but its prince remained nominally sovereign till 1867, when he sold all his rights to the emperor of Russia for 1,000,000 roubles.

There is no distinctive mission work carried on among the Mingrelians, tho colporteurs of the British and Foreign Bible Society go through the country occasionally.

MIN-TSING-HSIEN: A village in the province of Fo-kien, China, situated on the Min River 28 miles N. W. of Fu-chau. Station of the ME, with (1903) 3 women missionaries, 25 native workers, 7 outstations, 19 places of worship, 17 Sunday schools, 14 day schools, 1 boarding school, and 1,457 professed Christians, of whom 784 are communicants. The Society spells the name Ming-chiang.

MIRAJ: A town in Bombay, India, situated 70 miles W. of Bijapur and 32 miles E. N. E. of Kolhapur, near Kistna River. Population (1891) 26,100. Station of the PN (1892), with (1903) 5 missionaries, four of them with their wives; 2 women missionaries, 7 native workers, 1 place of worship, 2 Sunday schools, 3 day schools, 2 boarding schools, 1 dispensary, 1 hospital, 1 medical class, 1 orphanage, and 37 professed Christians. The Mission to Lepers in India and the East supports a leper asylum here, in connection with the Presbyterian Mission.

MIRAT. See MEERUT.

MIRZAPUR: A town in the United Provinces, India, situated on the right bank of the Ganges, 30 miles W. S. W. of Benares. Population (1901) 79,862, of whom five-sixths are Hindus. Station of the LMS (1837), with (1903) 2 missionaries, 1 with his wife; 2 women missionaries, 16 native workers, 1 outstation, 6 Sunday schools, 9 day schools, 1 boarding school, 1 orphanage, and 137 professed Christians, of whom 46 are communicants.

MITO: A town in Japan, situated 65 miles N. E. by N. of Tokio. Has a large fish export trade. Population, 19,600. Station of the ABMU (1899), with (1903) 1 missionary and wife, 1 woman missionary, 5 native workers, 5 outstations, 3 places of worship, 5 Sunday schools, and 93 professed Christians. Station also of the AFFM (1888), with 1 missionary and wife, 2 native workers, 1 Sunday school, 1 industrial school, and 30 professed Christians. Station also of the PE (1901), with (1903) 1 missionary, 1 native worker, 2 places of worship, 1 day school, and 1 hospital.

MITSIDI: A settlement in the Shirè district of British Central Africa, situated 30 miles W. by N. of Blantyre. Station and plantation of the Zambesi Industrial Mission (1900), with 5 missionaries, two of them with their wives; 1 woman missionary, 1 outstation, 1 place of worship, 2 Sunday schools, 2 day schools, 1 industrial farm, 1 dispensary, 1 hospital, and 30 professed Christians.

MITYANI: A village in Uganda, Africa, situated in the district of Singo, 40 miles W. of Mengo. Station of the CMS (1893), with 2 missionaries, one with his wife; 76 native workers, 1 printing press, 1 theological class, 1 dispensary, and 2,380 professed Christians, of whom 598 are communicants. Society spells the name Mityana.

MIYAZAKI: A town in Kiushiu, Japan, situated near the E. coast, about 100 miles E. S. E. of Nagasaki. Population, 5,000. Station of the ABCFM (1894), with (1902) 1 missionary, 1 woman missionary, 8 native workers, 25 outstations, 3 places of worship, 7 Sunday schools, 1 Young People's Society, and 1 orphanage.

MJOZI: A settlement in Pondoland, Cape Colony, S. Africa, situated near Mount Ayliff and about 45 miles S. E. of Kokstadt. Station of the South Africa Baptist Mission Society, with 1 missionary and his wife, 1 outstation, 1 place of worship, and 3 professed Christians.

MKUNAZINI: A village on the W. coast of the Island of Zanzibar, Africa, and one of the suburbs of Zanzibar town. The UM has its headquarters here. Statistics given under Zanzibar.

MLANJE: A village in British Central Africa, situated on a range of hills 25 miles S. of Lake Shirwa. Altitude, 8,000 feet. Station of the CSFM (1887), with (1900) 2 missionaries, one with his wife; 7 native workers, 3 outstations, 1 place of worship, 1 Sunday school, 4 day schools, 1 boarding school, 1 industrial school, and 19 professed Christians.

MLENGANA: A parish in the W. of Pondoland, Cape Colony, Africa. Station of the Episcopal Church of Scotland (1892), with (1902) 2 missionaries, 5 native workers, 5 outstations, 5 day schools, 1 place of worship, and 307 professed Christians, of whom 112 are communicants. The Society calls the parish St. Barnabas.

MODERN PROTESTANT MISSIONS: For two centuries after the Reformation there was practically no missionary activity in the Protestant churches. Erasmus taught the duty of world-wide evangelization, but as something for the future rather than the present. Luther seemed careless of everything but the preparation of his own community for the "last days," and the settlement of the violent controversies that were the inevitable attendant upon the sudden enfranchisement of individual opinion. There were, however, a number of enterprises, individual or political: the Calvin-Coligny colonies in Brazil and Florida (1555-64), more political than religious in character, and all failures; a mission to Lapland (1559) under the auspices of Gustavus Vasa; an effort by the Dutch to introduce Christianity among the natives of Java (1619), following the establishment of a college for the training of missionaries at Leyden (1612), and extending to the Dutch colonies in India and Brazil; the early efforts for the Indians of North America by Eliot, the Mayhews and others, resulting in the granting by the Long Parliament of the first charter to a missionary society "for the promoting and propagating the Gospel of Jesus Christ in New England," a society still in existence under the name, "The New England Company."

With the middle of the 17th century commenced a new movement, inaugurated, not by the clergy, but by the laity, and including some prominent jurists of Lubeck. One, Peter Heiling, reached his field, Abyssinia. In 1664 an Austrian baron, Von Welz, issued an earnest appeal for the conversion of the heathen, to which Ursinus of Ratisbon responded that Greeks were responsible for the Turks; the Danes and Swedes for the Greenlanders and the Lapps, and that it was absurd, even wicked, to cast the pearls of the Gospel before the dogs of cannibals.

Two years before this, however, Spener had been made pastor at Frankfort, and with his friend, Francke, led the German Pietists in giving a distinctly missionary character to the new University of Halle, while in 1700 the philosopher Leibnitz urged upon the Berlin Academy the duty of propagating "the true faith and Christian virtue among the remote and unconverted nations," especially China. The first action under the new impulse was the founding of the Danish Tamil Mission by King Friederich IV., of Denmark, in response to the representations by Court Chaplain Dr. Lütkens, and the sending of Ziegenbalg and Plütschau to Tranquebar in 1705 (see Danish Missions).

The Danish, gave rise to the Moravian movement. Count Zinzendorf, who had given the persecuted Bohemian Unitas Fratrum a home on his estate at Berthelsdorf, visited Copenhagen in 1731, and saw and heard of Foreign Missions. The result was that, in 1732, two Moravians went to St. Thomas, W. I., in 1733, two more to Greenland, and within four years other Moravian missionaries went to Dutch Guiana, to South Africa, to the Indians of Pennsylvania and Georgia. This last enterprise became the link connecting with Germany still another chain of missionary endeavor.

In 1729 the Oxford Club, of which the Wesleys were prominent members, was founded, and six years later the two brothers went with General Oglethorpe to Georgia, and came in contact with a Moravian missionary. This led to a visit by John Wesley to Herrnhut in 1738, and to acquaintance with Zinzendorf and Francke, whose influence in Methodism has been great. It was not, however, till some time later that the distinctively missionary feature of the movement became apparent.

During this period, with the exception, in a degree, of the Moravians, the dominant idea was the colonial. England, Holland and Denmark had reached out to enlarge their commercial relations. The needs of the colonists were uppermost in the thought of the home churches, and the conversion of natives in the colonies seems to have been considered more from the political than from the spiritual standpoint. Under the influence, however, of the revival spirit which spread through England and the United States, and which brought to the front the Wesleys, Whitefield, Wilberforce, the Countess of Huntington, Henry Venn, Thomas Scott, Philip Doddridge, John Watts, Hannah More, Jonathan Edwards, the Tennents, and a host of others, a sterner sense developed of Christian duty toward a world lying in sin. In 1746 a prayer concert was continued during seven weeks, in which Jonathan Edwards had a share. But no practical application of this new conception was made to the work of missions until Carey's famous "Inquiry," and his two sermons, "Expect Great Things from God," and "Attempt Great Things for God," in 1792. From these resulted the Baptist Missionary Society, which inaugurated the era of aggressive Protestant missions.

From this time on development of the missionary idea was rapid and multiform. Chronological statement becomes confusing, and the topical presentation of progress on the whole gives a clearer view. Three divisions stand out prominently: 1. The development of the missionary idea in the church; 2. The occupation of the field; 3. The results achieved.

1. *Development of the Missionary Idea:* It is an interesting fact that the first influence of the missionary spirit has always been to subordinate differences of creed or polity. The entire evangelical element in England felt the power of the initiative of the Baptists, and three years later a number of representatives from the Independent (Congregational), Wesleyan, Presbyterian and Episcopal bodies met and organized "The Missionary Society," now known as The London Missionary Society. That afterward they separated was due to no lack of sympathy with each other, but to the simple fact that they felt they could accomplish more for the great work by developing their own particular fields. Thus, in 1799, the Evangelical churchmen formed the Church Missionary Society, in 1814 the Wesleyans established their own organization, and later the Presbyterians did the same. But the influence of these societies was by no means confined to their own circles. Two Church of England organizations, the Society for Promoting Christian Knowledge, founded as early as 1698, and the Society for the Propagation of the Gospel (1701), which had hitherto confined their attention almost entirely to the home and colonial needs, broadened their outlook and their efforts, and became, in their own spheres, distinctively missionary societies. So, also, the General Baptists (Arminian or Free Will) followed the lead of their Particular (Calvinistic) Brethren, and in 1816 established their own society. The other Methodist societies did not come into existence until later, with the exception of the Bible Christians' organization, which dates from 1821.

Parallel with this movement in England was a similar one in Scotland. There, too, as early as 1709, a society for Promoting Christian Knowledge had been formed, which established a board of correspondents in New York in 1741, and assisted in supporting workers among the Indians, among them David Brainerd. Following on the organization of the Missionary Society in London, similar societies were formed in Edinburgh and Glasgow, from which later grew the great enterprises of the Established, Free, and United Churches.

It was characteristic of the broad view of the leaders in the evangelical and missionary movement that great emphasis was laid from the beginning on the necessity for the fullest of information and the best direction of thought and study. Besides the two Societies for Promoting Christian knowledge already mentioned, there were formed (1793) the Religious Book and Tract Society of Scotland, (1799) the Religious Tract Society in London, (1804) the British and Foreign Bible Society, followed by similar organizations in Scotland, afterward united in the National Bible Society of Scotland.

In America, up to the time of Carey, the evangelistic thoughts and action of the churches had been directed almost entirely to the Indians, tho before the Revolution application was made from New England to the Presbyterian Synod of New York for assistance in sending missionaries to Africa. The sailing of Carey and the formation of the LMS aroused great interest, and a number of societies were formed in New York and New England, in 1796-97, primarily for work among the Indians, but in some cases with special mention of the needs of foreign lands. Several magazines were founded and funds were raised to assist the enterprises started in England. The foundation of Andover Seminary (1806) had special reference to the preparation of preachers for mission work. As in England, individual enterprise had a great influence, and the munificent gifts of Robert Ralston and others, of Philadelphia, helped to arouse the interest of the churches.

The special initiative for active work was furnished by three students in Williams College, Samuel J. Mills, Gordon Hall, and James Richards. At the famous haystack prayer meeting in 1806, they pledged themselves to the work, and on entering Andover Seminary in 1809, pressed the matter upon public attention so earnestly that the General Association of Congregational Churches, at a meeting in Bradford, Mass., considered the question of a society. As a result, in June of that year the American Board of Commissioners for Foreign Missions was organized. As in the case of the LMS, different denominations, chiefly Presbyterian and Reformed, united with the Congregationalists. The Baptists continued to send their gifts to Serampore, until the news of the change of views on the part of Judson and Rice aroused them to the opportunity for a work of their own, and the American Baptist Missionary Union was formed in 1814. The Methodists established their work in 1819, and the American Bible Society (1816) was followed or attended by various tract societies united in The American Tract Society in 1823.

On the continent of Europe, the influence of the movement in England was felt at once both in Holland and in Germany. In Holland the sending out of Van der Kemp by the LMS occasioned the organization (1797) of the Netherlands Missionary Society, at first as an auxiliary to the English work, but later independent in its labors. In Germany the missionary interest in Halle had practically died out; a new movement at Basel, in Switzerland, however, took its place. As early as 1780 a society had been formed for the development of evangelical life, and its members were in close touch with the movements in England. This resulted in 1815 in the establishment of the Basel Missionary Institute. In Berlin, too, a similar movement was inaugurated by Pastor Jänicke, in 1800, and as a result the Berlin Missionary Society (1824) was organized.

The Foreign Missionary enterprise inaugurated by Carey, and undertaken in the United States, Holland and Germany, passed through a period of severe trial. Early years of such enterprises are years of seed-sowing rather than of reaping, and the new organizations had all they could do to hold their own. After a period, however, there seemed to come a new impulse to the work. One after another of the churches that had been content to act the part of assistants assumed the position of principals. Thus, in England, the Welsh Calvinistic Methodists (1840), the Presbyterians (1847), Primitive Methodists (1842), United Methodist Free Churches (1857), Methodist New Connexion (1859), and Friends (1866), established their own work; while in the Church of England, the South American Missionary Society (1844), Universities Mission to Central Africa (1858), led the impulse toward special work which developed in a number of minor societies. In 1865 the China Inland Mission marked almost an epoch in missionary enthusiasm, and in 1872 was formed the East London Institute, since reorganized with some others as the Regions Beyond Missionary Union.

In the United States a similar impulse was felt. The Episcopalians (1835), Presbyterians (1837), Lutherans (1838), led the way, and other branches of the Church followed, until scarcely any, even of the smaller denominations, are without a regular missionary organization.

The same development occurred in Europe; and Germany, Holland, Denmark, Norway, Sweden, Switzerland and France joined the ranks of Christian missions. (See articles on these countries for details.)

It is to be noted, however, that the activity of the Church was by no means confined to what may be called its regular organizations. Innumerable associate movements were started. There were missions to the Jews, missions for seamen, missions in aid of special branches of work or fields of labor, medical missions, missions to lepers, to the blind, for recovered slaves, a Turkish Mission Aid Society, an Association in Aid of Moravian Missions, organizations for the conduct of schools, orphanages, asylums of one kind and another. The mere catalogue of the societies of one name or another in England, the United States and Europe, more or less closely connected with mission work, would outrun the limits of this article.

Three movements, however, have been so prominent and so extended as to call for special attention: 1. Work for women by women; 2. Work for young people by young people; 3. Work independent of the regular organizations, based upon a belief or feeling that there was too much of machinery in them.

1. *Women's Work for Women:* The first distinctively woman's society was formed in 1825, in England, for promoting education in the West Indies. Nine years later, in response to an earnest appeal by the Rev. David Abeel, an American missionary in China, the Society for Promoting Female Education in the East was established. The next step was the organization of societies in connection with those already representing the different churches, and there are also independent societies, either for specific departments of work, or for denominations, but affiliated, rather than organically connected, with the various general church societies. In the United States women were directly interested in the

work of the Boards, and it was not until 1861 that the Woman's Union Missionary Society was organized, representing six denominations. In 1868 the Congregational Woman's Board connected with the ABCFM was formed, and since then the movement has spread until there is scarcely a denomination that has not some form of organization in which the women of the church combine either for independent work or for assistance to the Board of their own denomination.

In Germany, the famous Kaiserswerth Deaconess Society was organized for local and home work in 1836, but did not commence foreign work until 1851. A woman's society for Christian Female Education in Eastern countries, in Berlin, dates back to 1842, and a similar society for work in China to 1850, but this covers the list of special organizations of this kind. France and Sweden report women's organizations, but in the other countries of Continental Europe this department of missionary activity has not as yet been developed.

2. *Young People's Work:* The earlier organizations of young people, including in the term students, clerks, etc., were for the most part distinctly local in character. An exception was found in the different societies of inquiry, and similar organizations in the seminaries and colleges of the United States, which resulted from the one started in Williams College in 1806, and transferred to Andover Seminary. These all had special reference to the study of missions, and the claims of the foreign field. The first YMCA was established in America in 1854, following that in London (1844), and almost immediately there developed the idea of confederation. A central committee (1854) brought together the first world's conference (1855). The central committee later became the International Committee, which has grown into one of the largest and most efficient organizations for Christian work in the world. The college department (1877) prepared the way for an Interseminary Missionary Alliance (1880), and the Student Volunteer Movement (1886), which has developed a world-wide influence for serious study of the needs of non-Christian peoples and for bringing forward recruits for the missionary service in all denominations. The more distinctively young people's societies, as the United Society of Christian Endeavor (1881), Epworth League (1889), Baptist Young People's Union (1891), and others have had an important share in the growth of missionary interest in the different denominations, through missionary meetings, mission study classes, and their affiliation with similar societies in the mission field.

3. *Faith Missions:* Under this popular, yet incomplete and in some respects misleading, title are often grouped a number of societies and enterprises, more or less loosely organized, which have found their occasion in a feeling that the mechanism of missionary organization is in danger of dwarfing, if not quenching, the spiritual element in the conduct of missionary work. The regular salaries paid or allowances given to the missionaries, the detailed control of action on the field by committees at home, the paraphernalia of executive offices and officers, have seemed to some inconsistent with the apostolic type of missionary labor. With many, too, the doctrine of the second coming of Christ has fostered a conception of the missionary enterprise as chiefly heraldic in character. Such a conception tends to tell the Gospel to as widely extended an audience as possible. This has been most manifest in the **China Inland Mission,** the **Christian and Missionary Alliance,** the **Regions Beyond Missionary Union,** and the **Gossner Missionary Society.** As the work of societies of this class becomes effective, however, the necessity for nurture of the spiritual life of converts tends to lead it to assume the form of the older and more complete organizations.

II. *Occupation of Mission Lands:* The record of missionary enterprise in the different countries of the world will be found in the articles on those countries and the societies. Here it is necessary only to give a bird's-eye view of the movement.

Previous to the arrival of Carey in India (1793) the only countries occupied by missionary effort had been: South India by Ziegenbalg (1705), Greenland (1721), South Africa (1737), Surinam (1738), and Labrador (1752), by the Moravians, aside from the work among the North American Indians; and in no case was the occupation, except, perhaps, that by the Danish-Tamil mission, on any extensive scale. With the formation of the LMS, however, a new system was inaugurated, and both in the South Seas (1797) and South Africa (1798) missionary occupation meant more aggressive work.

With the opening of the 19th century the CMS entered W. Africa (1804), and the LMS South India the same year, adding its Chinese missions in 1807. Then commenced a marvelous growth. In rapid succession, West Africa, Burma, the East Indies, New Zealand, Syria, Ceylon, Madagascar, the Hawaiian Islands, Egypt, Greece, Siam, Persia, Abyssinia, Asia Minor, South America, Malaysia, the New Hebrides, Assam, Central America, Melanesia, Bulgaria, Japan, Formosa, were occupied, while reenforcements poured into India, China, Africa. With the last half of the century there seemed to come a new impulse. Not merely the regular missionary societies, but others less distinctively foreign and evangelistic in character, joined in the movement, until, by the close of the century, the world field was fairly well occupied, as will be evident from the tables in the appendix.

America: The mission fields of the northern continent include: Alaska: 11 societies, 118 missionaries, 53 stations and outstations. Canada and Labrador (Indians and Eskimos): 11 societies, 329 missionaries, 202 stations. United States (among the Indians): 17 societies, 233 missionaries, 293 stations. Mexico: 21 societies, 210 missionaries, 532 stations. Central America: 11 societies, 102 missionaries, 105 stations. West Indies: 36 societies, 444 missionaries, 814 stations. South America: 36 societies, 672 missionaries, 575 stations.

The Pacific Islands: Oceania: 15 societies, 338 missionaries, 2,120 stations. New Zealand, Australia (aborigines), New Guinea: 14 societies, 135 missionaries, 202 stations. Malaysia: 26 societies, 305 missionaries, 659 stations.

Asia: Japan: 47 societies, 772 missionaries, 1,100 stations. Korea: 11 societies, 141 missionaries, 380 stations. China: 68 societies, 2,775 missionaries, 3,129 stations. Siam, Laos, Straits Settlements, etc.: 9 societies, 164 missionaries, 69 stations. Burma: 11 societies, 202 missionaries, 586 stations. Ceylon: 11 societies, 229 missionaries, 459 stations. India: 93 societies, 3,836 missionaries, 6,624 stations. Persia: 6

societies, 85 missionaries, 93 stations. Turkey: 31 societies, 637 missionaries, 648 stations.

Africa: (The figures are for the whole continent): 95 societies, 3,051 missionaries, 6,838 stations.

Europe: Roman Catholic countries: 27 societies, 274 missionaries, 480 stations.

A somewhat detailed chronological table of the extension of modern missions will be found in Appendix II.

In this extension, in the earlier history, availability and popular interest seem to have governed in the selection of fields, rather than any definite and well considered plan. The wall built around India by the East India Company and the impenetrability of China compelled the societies to look elsewhere, while the reports of navigators brought the conditions in the Pacific islands and along the African coast so vividly before Christians as to rivet attention upon their needs. As soon, however, as the barriers were down, even partially, there was a general rush for the countries that loomed so large in the public eye. The result was inevitably a congestion of missionary effort in certain localities, especially the centers, while large sections remained unoccupied. This has often been commented upon adversely as indicating a desire to reap where the harvest was easiest, and where the brunt of the battle had already been met by others, and the conduct of the Moravians, whose special aim seems to have been to go where nobody else wanted to go, regardless of any possible results, has been commended. Undoubtedly some harm resulted. Different ecclesiastical systems, different nationalities, have never yet been able to work side by side without some unpleasing rivalry. It may, however, be doubted whether on the whole more good than evil did not result. Monopoly may be as unfortunate in mission enterprise as in the commercial world, and the most conscientious conduct of an enterprise is not without stimulus from the proximity of another aggressive agency. This is no excuse for the lack of comity (merely another term for courtesy); it is but a recognition of the fact that the individualism of Protestantism has been a factor in the extension of missions, with its advantageous as well as disadvantageous results. Now that there are few new fields to enter, and, it may be hoped, no new societies are to be formed to enter them, the time seems to have come for a careful coordination of the existing forces of the Church of Jesus Christ.

Results: In a sense this entire volume is the record of the results achieved during a century of missionary activity. It remains here only to indicate the lines in which these results have been secured.

At Home: There is a very general idea that the churches organized on the foreign field and the number of members represent all, or nearly all, the results of missionary effort. In truth, results are manifest fully as clearly in the communities that send the missionaries as in those to which they go: indirectly, in their contributions to science, commerce, and the general life of the nations; directly, in their influence upon the Church, both in its activities, in its spiritual life, and in confirming its faith in the unique power of the Gospel of Jesus Christ. Indirect results of missions are suggested in the articles **Commerce** and Missions, **Science** and Missions, and **International Service of Missions.**

Important as are these indirect results, they are far less significant than those manifest in the life of the churches.

Of those, perhaps, the most prominent is the **organization** of mission work. (See also articles on Finances, on Study classes, etc.) There is to-day no more thoroughly organized enterprise in the world than the work of foreign missions, and not a year passes but some detail is perfected in the effort to bring not merely every church, but every member, and even every attendant, into touch with the work that links America and Europe to every part of the world. To some, these boards, committees, officers, branches, and cradle rolls, periodicals, study classes, campaigns, systematic and proportionate giving, cent-a-day mite societies, and so on, savor of too much machinery, yet not a single factor but has come into existence because of some evident need. It was a comparatively simple matter for the Baptist ministers to hand over to William Carey their £13 2s. 6d. It is a very different thing to gather from thousands of churches and hundreds of thousands of individual givers millions of dollars, and to send them in all sorts of currencies by every conceivable means to the farthest corner of the world, and to have record of the use made of every cent. Yet this is but one of the many departments of the home organization.

Turning to other departments of church life, it is noticeable that everywhere the work at home has grown in proportion to the work abroad. Home missions, in their various phases, are the result of foreign missions. This is, of course, a general statement, to which exception may be taken in details, but it remains unquestionably true that the foreign missionary work of the Church has led the way, and marked the path for its activities in very nearly every direction.

Other results are manifest in the number of books, not to speak of periodicals, leaflets, etc., published each year, that have a direct relation to missions, either descriptive of them, or suggested by them, all of which indicate what a hold missions have upon the public interest. The early tract societies were organized to supply, through benevolence, those books which the ordinary publisher could not afford to print. To-day the most enterprising publishers are glad to get good books on missions, or by missionaries, on various questions of international importance. Through this and through travel, largely under the lead of missions, the Church has come into a sane and wholesome relation and sympathy with the people it seeks to reach with the Gospel. The word "heathen" is fast following the word "barbarian" into oblivion, not because the sin and evils of heathenism are any less real, but because the individual heathen is coming to be looked upon as a man and not as little more than a beast. (See International Service of Missions.)

Even more marked, however, have been the results of the foreign mission enterprise upon the character and life of the Church at home. The individual Christian has been inspired and lifted into a higher spiritual life by the influence of those who have gone as their representatives to the foreign field. Brainerd, Carey, Judson, Livingstone, Moffat, Selwyn, Paton, Goodell, Hannington, among the pioneers, and even in recent years, the noble army of martyrs in China have been a power for individual consecration. The development of such leaders as Henry

Venn, Rufus Anderson, and others, has been no small service to the cause of Christian work. To foreign missions, too, is very largely due expansion in the benevolences of the Church. It is not merely that they practically originated organized systematic giving for work outside the bounds of the local community, but they still lead the way in broadened sympathies that seek to mitigate the horrors of famine and pestilence in the Antipodes.

The one line of growth, however, which is more distinctively the result of foreign missions than any other in this field, is that which abates the rigors of rivalry between different branches of the Church, promoting harmonious and cooperative action. Differences in church organization and government, and even differences in creed, inevitably diminish in importance in the foreign field before the tremendous problem of making men feel the need of Christ and learn the beauty of truth, purity, and love. For close contact with sincere, unselfish workers breeds mutual respect and fellowship, and walls of partition cannot remain barriers when mutual helpfulness has opened breaches in them. Not that missionaries have been or are disloyal to their own, but they recognize the essentials of unity in Christ. (See **Comity**.)

In fact, wherever we look in the life and activity of the Church, we find the work of foreign missions in its various departments always identified with progress and growth, until the whole Church is becoming what the Moravian Church has been from its inception—an organization for Christian missions, using the term in its broadest sense, to denote the whole enterprise of building up the kingdom of God at home and abroad.

Abroad: The most common representation of the results of mission effort in foreign lands is in the form of tables of statistics. These statistics are found in detail in reports of societies, and an abstract of their essentials will be found in the appendix to this work. Their most important meaning, however, is not always visible to a casual reader.

As at home, so abroad, mission work is thoroughly organized. The mission organization is not a mere aggregation of missionaries and converts—it is a mechanism, sufficiently closely reticulated to give it efficiency, and yet so elastic as to give it unlimited power of adaptation. In this mechanism is now seen a most important result of years of labor. The native church is becoming less a mere company of converts, led by the missionary; more a responsible agency for aggressive work and a center for an independent community, a national life which shall be Christian. (See **Church on the Mission Field**.) Another result is that with this broader conception of the purpose and function of missions has come in foreign lands, as at home, the adoption of varying methods, with this significant difference: that, whereas in Christian lands very much of the general training for citizenship is secular, in mission fields it is, for the most part, distinctly Christian. The schools, industrial enterprises, hospitals, asylums, etc., are not merely for the purpose of mental and physical development and the relief of suffering, but for all these as assisting men toward Christian life, and forwarding the establishment of the kingdom of God. These different departments of labor are described in detail in other articles, **Medical Missions, Education, Literature** in the mission field, work for the **Blind**, for **Lepers**, and **Relief Work** in times of calamity. It is significant of the far-reaching and statesmanlike views of the pioneers of missions that scarcely a feature of modern evangelistic work in the foreign field escaped their notice or failed of their approval. The various phases of work have simply been improved and developed into their proper relations to the general science of missions. They are not to be viewed separately. All are but parts of the whole: the wheels, cogs, arms, pulleys, bands of a vast mechanism, which is a result of missions, and which is increasing in power and effectiveness every year.

The efficiency of these various departments of missionary work becomes apparent to the most casual observer on observing any of their lines of influence upon the peoples outside of the Christian community in the mission field. It is not too much to say that the existing educational movement in China, Africa, the Pacific islands, Turkey, India and Japan was initiated and is fostered by Christian missions. The establishment of mission schools has been in some cases the first glimmer gained by the people of such a thing as culture and growth. In other cases where education was known in theory but neglected in practise, the opening of mission schools has compelled the non-Protestant communities to establish schools of their own rather than let their children be taught by strangers. Even where, as in India, Japan and elsewhere, governments have placed education on a secular basis, the original impulse, and not a little of the subsequent direction, has been provided by missionaries. It is impossible to measure the results in this direction of the labors of Verbeck of Japan, Miller of India, Hamlin of Turkey, or Stewart of South Africa.

It is another inestimable result of missions that to-day scarcely a people in the wide world has not either in its own vernacular or in some kindred dialect a portion, at least, of the Bible. The Bible has led the way for other Christian literature, and books, papers and leaflets have been scattered broadly where Christian teachers could not go. To do such a work, missionaries have reduced to written and grammatical form the illiterate tongues, and have mastered the languages whose literatures have classical antiquity. If it be true that mission schools have trained the leaders, it is no less true that mission literature has helped to train those whom they have led, and without whom their leadership would have been vain. (See **Intellectual Uplift**.) As in education, so in intellectual life outside of the schools. Islam, Buddhism, Hinduism have been stirred to their depths and compelled to meet treatise with treatise. The intellectual seething of modern times in Asia is to be traced directly to the influence of Christian missions.

Another result of missions is their general influence for genuine spiritual life in the surrounding communities. Church rolls and community lists do not include all those who are truly Christians. Especially is this true in lands like the Levant, South America, Mexico and Spain. The original purpose there was not so much to organize a Protestant church, as to assist those in the Oriental and Roman Catholic Churches to a more spiritual life. This first plan proved impracticable, owing chiefly to the hierarchies, who resisted the growth of individual and independent thought. But in all these lands, and in each church, there has been, in consequence of the missions, a growth in spiritual life which gives good hope for the future. In the Oriental churches of the Levant there is found to-day much genuine Christian preaching, teaching and living. The same thing is true, in some degree, in countries where Protestant missions have been established among Roman Catholics. Not merely do many laymen of the Roman Church, but many in the priesthood, accept the essence of evangelical teaching, and are grateful for the influence it has exerted for a higher spiritual life; but they remain in their own communion, that they may use their best endeavors to spread the same truth there. The same thing is undoubtedly true, tho in a less degree, in non-Christian communities. There are not a few Muslims, Hindus, Buddhists and others who at heart accept the Christian faith and seek to live its life, but for one reason or another do not make public profession. It is not well to judge such too harshly, as lacking in courage. It is difficult for us to realize what it means, not merely to themselves, but to those they love and who are dependent upon them, to break openly with a faith inherited from ancestors extending back to the earliest periods of history.

The existence of such intellectually convinced men in the ranks of Hinduism and Mohammedanism recalls to mind the vast numbers of others who have partly adopted Christian ideas. In Hinduism the Brahmo Somaj, the Arya Somaj and other groups who are trying to adapt Christian ideas to their conceptions of what their own religion ought to teach, or who have adopted the doctrine of one only God and are seeking to make their ancient religious writings support the teachings of monotheism, point to another result of missions. In Mohammedanism the doctrines of the Babis and of the liberal Muslim party in India, which proposes to modify Mohammedan worship, ritual, fasts, etc., so as to "agree with the requirements of modern civilization," point to the same result. The long years of missionary effort have brought us at last to some of the identical fruits of Christian teaching which preceded the downfall of heathenism in the Roman Empire. There the heathen philosophers tried to adapt doctrines which they learned from Christians to their own uses, claiming that their own religion had always taught love and purity and spiritual life. They did not know that thus they destroyed their own religion. The crowning result of the teaching of the Gospel must ever be the undermining of the ancient and pagan beliefs. This crowning result of Christian missions is beginning to appear in India, and, perhaps, in some parts of China.

To pursue inquiry into the results of missions through the social, industrial and political life of the world would unmanageably lengthen this article. The elevation of woman, the suppression of cannibalism, human sacrifices, and cruelties like the suttee of India; the loosening of the chains of caste; the breaking of the bands of ecclesiasticism, and the opening up of new opportunities through the light that is newly dawning in Asia, Africa, and the Pacific Islands, are changes in which missions have had an important part, since Carey landed in Calcutta, Van der Kemp in Africa, and that first company in the South Seas. Other influences have had their share; missionaries have not held a monopoly in the general uplift of peoples long submerged that characterizes the opening of the 20th century. It is, however, unquestionable that in most cases missions furnished the initial impulse, and they have always been in the forefront of every advance.

Dennis (J. S.), *Christian Missions and Social Progress*, Vols. I. and II. (Vol. III. in preparation), New York, 1897, 1899; (——), *Centennial Survey of Foreign Missions*, New York, 1902; Beach (H. P.), *Geography and Atlas of Foreign Missions*, New York, 1903; Warneck (G.), *History of Protestant Foreign Missions*, translated by G. Robson from 7th German edition, Edinburgh and New York, 1901.

MODIMOLLE: Native name of the point at which the Berlin Missionary Society established its station of **Waterberg**, in Transvaal, South Africa.

MODJO-WARNO: A town in the island of Java, Malaysia, situated about 25 miles S. W. of Surabaya. Station of the Netherlands Mission Society (1848), with (1903) 5 missionaries, 3 of them with their wives; 15 native workers, 10 outstations, 10 day schools, 1 industrial school, 1 hospital, 1 medical class and 1,411 professed Christians.

MOEARA SIPONGI: A village in Sumatra, Dutch East Indies, situated in the mountains, 115 miles N. by W. of Padang. Station of the Netherlands Mennonite Mission Society (1891), with (1903) 1 missionary and his wife, 2 native workers, 1 place of worship, 1 day school and 30 professed Christians.

MOFFAT, Robert: Born at Ormiston, East Lothian, Scotland, December 21, 1795, of humble parentage. Died at Leigh, near Tunbridge Wells, August 9, 1883. His mother had carefully trained him in the Bible, and told him much of the early Moravian Brethren. Having resolved to be a missionary, he offered himself at the age of nineteen to the LMS, was accepted, and after spending some time in special study, sailed from England for South Africa October 31, 1816, and arrived at Cape Town in 1817. His request to proceed inland being refused by the governor of Natal, he remained several months at the Cape, studying in the meantime the Dutch language, then much in use among Europeans in South Africa. At length Moffat was allowed to set out for Namaqualand, in the Orange River country, and especially for the district controlled by Africaner, a chief who had been outlawed for barbarous crimes, so that his name was a terror to all the region. But he had become a convert to Christianity. The farmers did not believe the reported conversion, and predicted Moffat's destruction. After incredible perils and difficulties he reached a mission station called Warm Baths, where the native Christian teacher and the people insisted on his remaining. But a party of Africaner's men appeared and carried him on to the kraal of Africaner, beyond the Orange River. He arrived January 26, 1818, and was cordially received by the chief, who ordered some women to build a house for the missionary. In this hut he remained six months, maintaining regular day schools and preaching services; exposed to the sun, rain, dogs, snakes and cattle; doing his own sewing and cooking; often having nothing to cook and consoling himself with his violin and the Scotch Psalms. Africaner was a regular attendant, and proved himself to be a true Christian, very docile, a firm friend and efficient helper of the mission. In 1819 Moffat visited the Cape for the double purpose of getting supplies and introducing Africaner to the governor. The governor received Africaner with great kindness, and expressed his pleasure at seeing one who had been the "scourge of the country and the terror of the border colonists." He was also much struck with this result of missionary enterprise. The colonists, too, were much astonished at Africaner's mild demeanor and his knowledge of the Scriptures. In 1821 Moffat, having married, commenced a mission at Kuruman, where for many years he labored, preaching, teaching, without seeing the people converted. In 1829 he visited the Matabele tribes living south of the Zambesi. About 1830 he completed a translation of Luke, and printed it at Cape Town, himself learning the printer's art and taking back with him to Kuruman a press and its equipment. After this the mission greatly prospered. He made frequent excursions into the interior to visit other tribes, where, amid great perils and strange adventures, he made known the Gospel, and prepared the way for other laborers. By 1838 the entire New Testament was translated, and in 1857 he completed singlehanded the translation of the whole Bible into Bechuana, which was printed at his press in Kuruman. The first church was formed in 1829, at Kuruman. In 1870, enfeebled by age and work, Mr. Moffat returned to England. Mrs. Moffat, who for more than a half century had been a sharer of his labors and trials, died in 1871. In 1872 Moffat received from the University of Edinburgh the degree of doctor of divinity, and a testimonial of about £6,000. When he entered upon his work Moffat found the people murderous savages. When he died he left them with a written language of their own and able to appreciate and cultivate the habits of civilized life. It was his genial humor, his heroic faith and his strong will that enabled Moffat to overcome every danger and every difficulty.

Walters (W.), *Robert Moffat* London, and New York, 1882; Moffat (J. S.), *Robert and Mary Moffat*, London and New York, 1885.

MOGADORE: A town and seaport on the W. coast of Morocco, situated 128 miles W. by S. of Morocco City (Marakesh), on a rocky promontory surrounded by sandhills. It is in three sections, like most Moroccan towns, each enclosed by walls, one being the city proper, another the fortified official residence quarter, and the third the Jews' quarter. It was founded in 1760 and has the export trade of a large district. Population, 19,000, of whom 8,000 are Jews and 10,000 Muslims. Station of the London Society for Promoting Christianity among the Jews (1875), with (1901) 2 missionaries, one with his wife, and 1 native worker. Station of the Southern Morocco Mission Society (1899), with (1901) 1 missionary and his wife, 1 woman missionary and 1 dispensary.

MOHALLES HOEK: A settlement in Basutoland, S. Africa, situated in Kornet Spruit district, not far from the Orange River. Station of the SPG, with 1 missionary and 300 professed Christians.

MOHAMMEDANISM: *I. The Problem:* Islam is the greatest organized opponent of Christianity. Geographically it has an unbroken field from the Philippine Islands in the Pacific to Sierra Leone on the Atlantic, and from the snows of Siberia to the equator. It has been successful with every race type—Semitic, Aryan, Turanian. It has won to its banners polytheists, pantheists, Jews and Christians. It has steadily grown in war and peace for over a thousand years, and to-day controls the religious life of two hundred million human beings. It has a common religious language (Arabic), which is rich and expressive, and which is the medium of a literature of wide range and enduring power. It is the language of commerce throughout two-thirds of the continent of Africa, and is preparing the way for the extension of a Muslim civilization. There is a simplicity of practise in Islam which easily adapts itself to its environment wherever it has gone. Altho politically Mohammedanism has always tended toward despotism, there is running through it all a democratic spirit which recognizes the brotherhood of man, and which places all believers on a common level. Its doctrinal code is lofty and pure as contrasted with all extra-Biblical religions, being based on the Biblical standards. The ethical theory, too, is often put into practise with quite as much success as is found in many degraded forms of Judaism and Christianity. It develops strong individuality, and yet binds the faithful together as few religions have been able to do as effectively. In the earliest days Islam was a political as well as a religious unit. As a type of the ancient life which fashioned the nation into an engine for conquest, Islam was a success for centuries; but under the new conditions, when nations are being more and more fashioned on the industrial principle, it can never succeed politically. Muslim powers are steadily weakening as civilization advances. In the endeavor to imitate the vitality of the progressing nations, Muslim rulers invariably impoverish their lands to the last degree and make industrial progress impossible. Muslims flourish best under Christian rule or under a controlling Christian influence. Syria under the Sultan is growing poorer every day, while Egypt under English guidance is growing richer.

But while the political power of Islam is weakening, and as far as civilization is concerned may be counted as dead, the last few years have witnessed a great religious revival in the Muslim world, especially in Turkey, India and Africa. Steamship lines make Mecca more accessible, and religious zeal, fanned to a white heat at the pilgrim festivals, is winning adherents to the party that cries out for union in Islam. Loss of political power seems to permit unity of religious life to the Mohammedan world, the like of which has not been witnessed since the Ommeiads from Damascus ruled an unbroken territory from the Indus to the Atlantic. Islam is throwing itself with all its combined forces upon the inferior races of Asia, Australasia and Africa, and is winning them to its faith. It is its last opportunity.

Mohammed, by accepting Jesus as the promised Messiah of the Old Testament, seems to have allied himself with Christianity rather than with Judaism. He professed to give all credit to the Old and New Testament Scriptures, and his rejection of the crude tri-theistic Christianity about him merely indicates the natural vitality of his religious instinct. Nevertheless, he was chiefly moved by Judaistic influences, and every religious reformer in Islam urges to-day "return to the faith of Abraham." The minutiæ of detailed ceremonial in Islam were unquestionably the result of Jewish influences. Probably the same is true of the idea of making Muslims a chosen people, and of the further idea of the relation of conqueror to conquered as the ideal relation between God's chosen people and all other nations. The Jewish expectancy of a Messiah in the last days made it reasonable that Mohammed should claim to be the successor of Jesus who failed, and to prove by his triumphs that he himself was the prophet foretold from the beginning. In short, the genius of Mohammed coined the precious and other metals at his hand and put his own image and superscription upon the mixed resultant.

In 627 A. D. Mohammed sent from Medina the following letter to Heraclius, Emperor at Constantinople. It was his first strictly foreign missionary effort:

In the name of God the Compassionate, the Merciful. Mohammed, who is the servant of God, and is His apostle, to Hergal, the Qaisar of Rum; peace be on whoever has gone on the straight road. After this I say, verily, I call you to Islam [submission to God]. Embrace Islam, and God will reward you twofold. If you turn away from the offer of Islam, then on you be the sins of your people. O people of the Book, come toward a creed which is fit both for us and for you. It is this—to worship none but God, not to associate any with God, and not to call any others God. Therefore, O ye people of the Book, if ye refuse, beware! But we are Moslems, and our religion is Islam.

[SEAL]   MOHAMMED, The Apostle of God.

This letter reveals the thought in the mind of any Muslim sovereign to-day as he looks over into the Christian lands of wealth and power. It is not unlike the letter sent by the Mahdi of Khartum to Emin Pasha. It is a thought of peace—an offer of peace—on condition of submission to, or adoption of, Islam, but this kindly thought is coupled with a grim suggestion to beware of Islam's sword, which those understand who have felt its edge.

Happily in this day none but the isolated fanatics of Africa are ignorant enough to imagine it expedient to indulge in such language toward Christian governments.

Mohammed's admissions respecting Jesus as the "Word of God" and in regard to the Scriptures in the hands of the Jews and Christians form the open door for the Christian apologist. Our task is to prove to these 200,000,000 votaries of Islam that we do "worship none but God," and that we do not "associate any with God" nor "call others God." It was a misconception from the first (natural enough when we consider the phase of Christianity presented to Mohammed), and it is a misconception emphasized by a thousand years of contact with half idolatrous Christian sects in a state of decadence. The problem before the Christian Church is to take away this misconception, to present the Gospel in its simplicity and to lead this great unitarian disaffection back to the truth. The doctrine of the Trinity is vitally involved, and the Arian controversy must be fought all over again.

Recent controversy over the usefulness and power of Islam has called attention away from the true issue. Muslims can never be won over to Christianity by a series of wholesale maledictions, nor by a weak yielding of the vital facts of a true faith. The truths contained in the Korân should be readily acknowledged, since they are derived from the Bible; but it must be understood by way of caution that truths may be so connected that the result may be a great falsehood. Good bricks may be used in putting together useless structures. Islam has happily been characterized as a broken "cistern"—so badly broken that it must be all torn down, and many new bricks added before it may hold water; but it is a cistern still. There cannot be a question but that Mohammed and his early followers looked upon the Abyssinian Christians as their religious neighbors and kinsmen. From the first that peculiar relationship has been admitted, also, on the Christian side. Dean Stanley calls special attention to this when he says: "Springing out of the same Oriental soil and climate, if not out of the bosom of the Oriental church itself, in part under its influence, in part by way of reaction against it, Mohammedanism must be regarded as an eccentric heretical form of Eastern Christianity. This, in fact, was the ancient mode of regarding Mohammed. He was considered not in the light of the founder of a new religion, but rather as one of the chief heresiarchs of the church." Döllinger agrees with this, and says: "Islam must be considered at bottom a Christian heresy, the bastard offspring of a Christian father and a Jewish mother, and is indeed more closely allied to Christianity than Manichæism, which is reckoned a Christian sect." Ewald calls it "the last and most powerful offshoot of Gnosticism." John of Damascus, who did his work early in the 8th century, at the very seat of the Ommeiad dynasty, did not consider Islam a new religion, but only a Christian heresy. The same was true of Samonas of Gaza, Bartholomew of Edessa, Peter, Abbot of Clugny, Thomas Aquinas, Savonarola, and most of the medieval writers. Radulfus de Columna, who wrote about 1300 A. D., says: "The tyranny of Heraclius provoked a revolt of the Eastern nations. They could not be reduced, because the Greeks at the same time began to disobey the Roman Pontiff, receding, like Jeroboam, from the true faith. Others among these schismatics (apparently with the view of strengthening their political revolt) carried their heresy further, and founded Mohammedanism." The very errors in this statement are instructive. Dante consigned Mohammed to the company of **heresiarchs** in the "Inferno." Turning to the early Protestant confessions, we find similar statements that regard Mohammedanism as a mere offshoot from the Church. The Augsburg Confession condemns as heresies Manichæism, Valentinianism, Arianism, Eunomianism, Mohammedanism, "and all similar to these." The second Helvetic confession condemns Jews, Mohammedans, and all those heresies teaching that the Son and the Spirit are not God.

Doubtless there has been a tendency to carry this idea of the identity between Islam and Christianity too far, and we are in a reactionary period just now. But without a certain sympathy and an open acknowledgment of the truth in Mohammedanism, the missionary can never hope to win Muslims. When once the principles of higher criticism are understood in the Mohammedan world, Mohammed's admissions as to the inspiration of the original Christian Scriptures will be used with effect, for we have manuscripts of the New Testament older by several centuries than the rise of Islam. His admission of the miraculous birth of Jesus, of His miraculous power, of His deathlessness, and that He will be the Judge at the last great day, will also play an important part in the controversy. Already a Muslim writer in India has seen this and has declared that Christianity cannot be overthrown until the deathlessness of Jesus is exploded.

The great difficulty is that Islam erects barriers against sympathy of feeling among its adherents by making belief in Mohammed a condition absolute of the brotherhood of man. For its permanent object it holds up the supplanting of Judaism and Christianity; justifying the most extreme views on this point by claiming divine appointment and obligation to extirpate all other religions, if need be by force, that it may be alone in the world. In its view fanaticism is an essential quality of devotion to God. When it can have its own way, not only is it death for a Muslim to accept Christianity, but for a Christian to present to a Muslim proofs of the true nature of the Korân. It is death for a Christian even to set foot on the sacred soil of Mecca.

It is into the vast field, thus fortified, that the Christian Church is sent by its Master. The problem confronted is as various as the sects and nationalities in the Muslim world. Patient labor, instruction in fundamental questions of philosophy and religion, the cultivation of an historic sense, the example of pure lives and a Christlike self-denial must at last open to the striving of the spirit these hearts of flint.

II. *Pre-Islamic Arabia:* Arabia, cut off from the rest of the world by deserts and seas, unconquered by Assyrian, Babylonian, Persian, Egyptian, Greek, or Roman, was the last place to which a prophet would have looked for the rise of such a phenomenon as Islam. It was not always thus isolated, for the latest research gives evidence of a very ancient civilization, which was the connecting link between Egypt and Babylonia in the earliest periods. But up to the time of Mohammed the Arabs had remained free. The peninsula, together with adjacent regions inhabited by Arabs, covered about 800,000 square miles, or an area as large as the United States east of the Mississippi. Throughout the early centuries its inhabitants probably averaged from 9,000,000 to 10,000,000 people, divided up into tribes, some of which were nomadic, while the large majority were settled. The southern portion of the peninsula was well cultivated, and furnished many valuable articles of commerce. The tribes were for the most part independent, or were loosely bound by confederacies. There was no nation of Arabs until the genius of Mohammed welded together the heterogeneous mass and gave Arabia a distinct mission, which harmonized with a latent pride and love of conquest.

In the earliest days commerce seems to have been a predominant occupation in Arabia. The caravan trade furnished occupation to a large proportion of the inhabitants. At that era commerce was almost entirely confined to the land. The influence of Rome, and the development of a merchant marine under government protection and patronage, and the disturbed condition of the Persian frontier, broke up the monopoly of the Arabs, and many tribes were compelled to betake themselves to a nomad life. We have traditions of great emigrations from the more crowded south northward, which occurred before the historic period, which removals were doubtless caused by the interruption of the caravan trade.

The story of Arabia until the period of Mohammed is confused. Putting aside conjecture, which has taken great license with the mysterious peninsula, we learn of a number of kingdoms which wielded considerable power. The Himyarites in the southwest formed the most prominent political combination in Arabia. Their king, Abd Kelâl, who reigned about 275, is said to have been converted to Christianity by a Syrian stranger, and was murdered by his subjects. His son, Marthad, was famous for his religious toleration. He is reported to have said: "I reign over men's bodies, not over their opinions. I exact from my subjects obedience to my government; as to their religious doctrine, the judge of that is the great Creator." Constantius, the Byzantine emperor, about the middle of the 4th century sent an embassy to the Himyarites, wishing to strengthen his alliance with them and to attract them to Christianity. Two hundred Cappadocian horses of the purest breed were sent as a present, and Bishop Theophilus undertook the mission work. Churches were built at the capital, Tzafar, at Aden, and one on the Persian Gulf. Arabian historians make no mention of this mission. A little later the Himyarites began to decline, and became a sort of dependency of Abyssinia, a Christian kingdom across the Red Sea. Between 490 and 525 Dhu Nowas, in the district of Najran, took the reins of power in his hands. He was a recent convert to Judaism, and persecuted Christians bitterly in that region. They were offered Judaism or death, and twenty thousand are said to have perished. One intended victim, Tholaban, escaped to Hira, and, holding up a half burnt copy of the Gospel, invoked, in the name of outraged Christendom, retribution. Justin I. sent a message to the Abyssinian monarch, asking him to inflict punishment on the usurper. Dhu Nowas was defeated and the Najran became an Abyssinian dependency. A zealous Christian, Abraha, had become Abyssinian viceroy somewhat later in Yemen. Bishop Gregentius was sent by the Patriarch of Alexandria to assist in pushing the interests of Christianity. A cathedral was built at Sana, and an attempt made to make it the Mecca of the peninsula. The Meccans were displeased, and killed one of the Christian missionaries. A Koreishite from Mecca defiled the cathedral at Sana, whereupon Abraha set out on an expedition, about 570, to destroy the Kaaba. His army was destroyed, and the episode has come down in Mohammedan story as the affair of "The Elephant." Mohammed was born a few months after. By the aid of the Persians the Abyssinians were finally expelled in 603, and Southern Arabia became thereafter loosely dependent upon that eastern rival of the Byzantine empire, until it was absorbed, in 634, by Muslim conquest.

Along the Persian frontier was another considerable political power—the kingdom of Hira, founded in the 2d century of our era, and having political autonomy until the spread of Islam. It looked to Persia for help in its various wars, and tended more and more toward a dependent condition. Along the Syrian border, and more or less under Byzantine influence, was the kingdom of the Ghassanides, which early came under the influence of the Western civilization. Christianity had a strong following in this region from the first, and the whole kingdom was under Christian influence. The kingdom of the Kindis, in Central Arabia, was another political unit, but much weaker than the other three. At Mecca we find the powerful Koreish tribe, which had control of the Kaaba, the religious center of native Arabian religion.

The religion of Pre-Islamic Arabia may be called heathen, with constant tendencies in the nobler minds toward a conception of one supreme God. Mohammed speaks of the era before him as "the times of ignorance," which he came to do away with. At the Kaaba there were said to have been three hundred and sixty-five images of the gods, who were looked upon as the children of Allah, the creator of all. Idols were found in every house, and formed an important article of manufacture. Religion was a sort of barter, which the individual carried on with the gods or goddesses whose aid he desired or whose vengeance he wished to avert. Festivals and pilgrimages, punctiliously attended to, made up a large part of religious life and worship. There was a considerable stir of literary life, and renowned poets contested at the annual fairs for preeminence. The successful poems were displayed on the walls of the Kaaba. These poems, some of which have come down to us, show the lowest grade of morals. Drunkenness, gambling, gross love intrigues, vengeance, theft, the loosest possible family ties, the degrading of woman to a mere animal existence—all these traits, common throughout Arabia, make plain the utter inadequacy of the prevailing faith to elevate the life. Add to this the widespread tendency toward atheism and indifference.

Such a state could not last long. Serious minds turned in every direction for help. There arose an ascetic fraternity who called themselves Hanifs (penitents). They sought to go back to the simple faith of Abraham, whom they styled the first Hanif. They proclaimed themselves as seekers after truth, and adopted the life which had been set before them for centuries by Christian hermits, whose rigid vigils had impressed the Oriental mind. Among these Hanifs were Obeidullah, own cousin of Mohammed; Waraqah and Othman, cousins of Khadijah, all three of whom found their way to Christianity. Zaid ibn Amr, an aged Hanif, was seen leaning against the Kaaba, and sadly stretching his hands upward, and praying: "O God, if I knew what form of worship is most pleasing to Thee, so would I serve Thee; but I know it not." Mohammed was touched when this was reported to him, and said: "I will pray for him; in the resurrection he, too, will be a community." It cannot be said that these Hanifs were Jews or Christians, yet they could not have arisen without these two religions as forerunners. They anticipated the central idea contained in the word "Islam" (resignation), and their conception of God was summed up in the word "Judgment." We shall see later how Mohammed became a Hanif, and gave shape, proportion and continuity to a half faith which was floating about Mecca and Medina (Yathrib), and how he originated a church polity in closest union with a political organization, the combination of which was destined to make him the moral ruler over more human beings than have ever been controlled by any other man.

The whole question of Christianity in Arabia is very obscure. Christians fled for refuge from the Roman persecutions to the fastnesses of the Syrian desert in the early days of Christianity. Paul himself spent three years among Arabs, whether on the Sinaitic peninsula or along the border of the desert south of Damascus. A local church council at Bostra shows a large growth of Christianity east of the Jordan before the close of the 3d century. The Ghassanides were first reached, and bishops were appointed to follow the wandering tribes in their migrations. The faith penetrated the desert south and east along caravan routes, and we may be sure that by the middle of the 3d century Christianity was well known in many parts of Arabia. We have seen how the Himyarites were reached in the succeeding century. Hira and Kufa, along the Persian frontier, about the same time, learned of Christianity through Nestorian missionaries. A king of Hira was converted in the 6th century. Other tribes, such as the Beni Taghlib of Mesopotamia, the Beni Haris of Najran, the Beni Tay, and various tribes about Medina (Yathrib), became nominally Christian. Ali Saad sneeringly said: "The Beni Taghlib are not Christians; they have borrowed from Christianity only the custom of drinking wine." In the first wars between the Persians and the rising Muslim power the Christian Arabs of the northeastern frontier joined the Persians. But in spite of this spread of Christian knowledge throughout the peninsula, it did not seem to take any vital hold. It was swept away at the first onset of Islam. The nomad life in the desert was not conducive to Christianity.

The legends of the Talmudic traditions found there congenial soil and won high honor as inspired Scripture, so that hostile Judaism to some extent neutralized the efforts of Christianity. Furthermore, the form of Christianity which penetrated Arabia was most inferior. Northern Arabia was a battle ground between Persian and Byzantine. But in the peninsula itself the apocryphal gospels were held as of equal value with the real gospels. The doctrine of the trinity was travestied by a crude tri-theism, in which the three persons of the Godhead were God the Father, God the Son, and the "Virgin Mary."

Jacobite and Nestorian influences predominated. It is doubtful whether the Bible or any portions were put into the vernacular. The haughty nature of the Arabs could with difficulty accept the humble and forgiving spirit of the Gospel. The Abyssinians, altho making up a powerful Christian kingdom, were of negro blood, and hence uninfluential. "In fine," says Muir in summing up this subject, "viewed thus in a religious aspect the surface of Arabia had been now and then gently rippled by the feeble efforts of Christianity; the sterner influence of Judaism had been occasionally visible in a deeper and more troubled current; but the tide of indigenous idolatry and of Ishmaelite superstition, setting from every quarter with an unbroken and unebbing surge toward the Kaaba, gave ample evidence that the faith and worship of Mecca held the Arab mind in a thraldom rigorous and undisputed. Yet, even amongst a people thus enthralled, there existed elements which a master mind, seeking the regeneration of Arabia, might work upon. Christianity was well known; living examples of it were amongst the native tribes; the New Testament was respected, if not reverenced, as a book that claimed to be divine; in most quarters it was easily accessible, and some of its facts and doctrines were admitted without dispute. The tenets of Judaism were even more notorious, and its legends, if not its sacred writings, were familiar throughout the peninsula. The worship of Mecca was founded upon patriarchal traditions believed to be common both to Christianity and Judaism. Here, then, was a ground on which the spiritual fulcrum might be planted; here was a wide field, already conceded by the inquirer, at least in close connection with the truth, inviting scrutiny and improvement. . . . The material for a great change was here. But it required to be wrought, and Mohammed was the workman."

Jews had made their homes in the Arabian peninsula in the earliest times. From the days of Solomon the Red Sea was the avenue of a thrifty commerce, and Hebrews had probably located at the trading ports. Later the conquests of Palestine by Assyrians, Babylonians, Persians, Egyptians, Greeks and Romans had sent waves of Jewish immigration into the desert. The fall of Jerusalem and the rebellion of Bar Cochab had driven thousands of Jews in the footsteps of their brethren. A number of native Arab tribes embraced Judaism, and in the time of Mohammed we find this people scattered all over the peninsula, in small, compact colonies. There were a large number of colonies near Medina, and from their teachers Mohammed drew much of the material found in the Korân. At first he hoped to win them to Islam, and contemplated making Jerusalem the Kibla. Their obduracy changed his temper, and in the conflicts that ensued thousands of Jews were butchered, and most of the others submitted to Islam. Communities of Jews are still to be found in Southern Arabia who have clung to their faith all these centuries.

III. The Life of Mohammed: Into this world of conflicting dogmas Mohammed was born in the year 570, at Mecca. This city, situated on the caravan route between Yemen and Syria, had for centuries been famous for the Kaaba, which contained the sacred Black Stone and formed the religious center of the Arabian peninsula. The leading tribe had for years been the Koreish, and Mohammed sprang from the Beni Hashim, a noble tho somewhat waning branch of this tribe. His father's name was Abdallah. Returning from a mercantile trip to Syria, Abdallah was taken sick at Medina, and died some months before the birth of Mohammed. His mother, Amina, according to the prevailing custom, put the infant out to nurse with Halîma, a woman of the Beni Sâd, one of the Bedawin tribes, where he remained four or five years, acquiring the free manners and the pure tongue of the nomads. His Bedawin nurse was more than once alarmed by epileptic symptoms in her charge, and at the age of about five years he was given back to the keeping of Amina. The following year, while traveling toward Medina with her boy, Amina died, and the orphaned Mohammed was taken up by his uncle, Abu Tâlib, who became his faithful guardian. At the age of twelve years Mohammed accompanied his uncle on a mercantile trip to Syria, when he first came in contact with the rites and symbols of Oriental Christianity. As a youth he lived for the most part quietly, keeping the flocks of Abu Tâlib, and at the age of twenty-five, his uncle being poor, he entered the service of a rich widow named Khadîja. He was sent by her on a trading journey to Syria, and superintended the caravan. Khadîja was delighted with her agent's service, and tho almost double his age, soon became his wife. She bore him four daughters and two sons. Both sons died. The youngest daughter, Fatima, married Ali, and thus became the ancestress of all the Muslim nobility.

When approaching his fortieth year Mohammed began to retire from his family for the purpose of meditation. The gross idolatry of Arabia oppressed his mind. He was aroused but not satisfied by his slight knowledge of Judaism and Christianity. For days at a time he would continue in a lonely cave on Mount Hira. Ecstatic reveries accompanied his meditations, and he finally came to believe himself called to be the reformer of his people. After a period of silence known as the *fatrah*, these revelations continued with more or less frequency till the end of his life.

Khadîja was his first convert. The first three years of his preaching resulted in the conversion of some forty of his relatives and friends, among whom were Ali, Zeid, Abu Bekr, and Othman. His teaching against idolatry developed fierce opposition, in which Mohammed was safe under the protection of Abu Tâlib, but others suffered persecution, and in 615 eleven men fled to Abyssinia. In 620 Abu Tâlib and Khadîja died. Mohammed afterward married other wives, nine of whom survived him. Proceeding to Tâif, he was unsuccessful in his appeal to the people there, but returned strengthened by a dream of a journey to heaven. In 621 his cause was greatly advanced by the addition of twelve pilgrims from Medina, and the following year the band was increased to seventy, who were pledged to receive and defend the prophet in Medina. His brightest hopes now centered about the northern city. Abandoning Mecca, he and 150 followers in little bands fled to Medina. This date marks the era of the Hégira (migration), 622.

At Medina Mohammed built a mosque, instituted rites of worship, and declared war against unbelievers. The Jews rejecting his claims, he became their bitter foe. In 623 the battle of Bedr resulted in a signal victory for the Muslims over the Meccans. A year later he was defeated by the Koreish at Ohod, and Medina was unsuccessfully besieged by 4,000 Meccans. About this time the Beni Koreitza, the last of the Jewish tribes in the neighborhood, surrendered to the power of Mohammed, and over 600 men were beheaded by his order. In the sixth year of the Hégira, Mohammed, with 1,500 followers, made a pilgrimage to Mecca, but was refused admittance. A truce was signed at Hodeibia, near the city, suspending hostilities for ten years, and granting permission for a pilgrimage the following year. Discontent was allayed among the Muslim converts by an expedition against the Jews of Khaiber, yielding rich booty.

His plans now widened, and the same year he sent written demands to the Persian king, Chosroes II., Emperor Heraclius, the Governor of Egypt, the Abyssinian king, and several Arab tribes.

Chosroes tore up the letter and Muta killed the envoy. To revenge this insult Mohammed fought what proved to be a losing battle at Muta, on the Syrian border, where his friend Zeid was killed.

A breach of the truce at this time by the Koreish gave grounds for attack, and Mohammed at the head of 10,000 men entered Mecca in triumph in 630.

In the course of that year Tâif submitted, and this ended opposition in the peninsula. In 632 Mohammed with his wives and 40,000 adherents performed the "Farewell Pilgrimage" to Mecca. The rites of this pilgrimage are still scrupulously followed. Three months later Mohammed fell sick and died in the house of his favorite wife,

Ayesha, after having liberated his slaves and distributed alms to the poor. He was buried in the room where he died, which is now included within the Great Mosque.

The person of Mohammed was attractive. Tho little above the ordinary height, his presence was stately and commanding. His expression was always pensive and contemplative. His eyes and hair were black, and a beard reached to his breast. His gait was quick, and is said to have resembled a man descending a hill.

As to his character, up to the end of his life in Mecca his sincerity cannot be doubted, and his conduct seems beyond reproach. He believed himself to be the divinely appointed messenger for the overturning of idolatry, and he suffered for years the taunts of a nation with apparently no ulterior motive but the reformation of his people. Secular history can furnish no more striking example of moral courage than Mohammed bearing patiently the scorn and insults of the Koreish. From the beginning of life in Medina temporal power and the acquisition of wealth and glory mingled with the Prophet's motives. Cruelty, greed, and gross licentiousness were justified by special "revelations." His conduct during the last ten years of his life seems to bear out this estimate of his character, "that he was delivered over to the judicial blindness of a self-deceived heart."

IV. *The Korân:* Like Christianity, Islam centers about a book. This book is the Korân ("reading" or "that which is to be read"). The Korân is the foundation of Islam. The orthodox believe that the original text exists from all eternity, or at least was the earliest creation and is inscribed in the highest heaven upon the "well-guarded Tablet." By a process of "sending down," one piece after another was communicated to the Prophet, who in turn proclaimed them to his immediate circle of followers, and so to the world. The angel charged with conveying these portions is generally called "Gabriel," who dictated the words directly to Mohammed. This being the origin and nature of the Korân, all Muslims hold to its absolute verbal inspiration, and regard it as the rule of faith and practise, from which there can be no appeal.

The Korân as given to the Muslim world is in Arabic, a volume slightly smaller than the New Testament. It is divided into 114 chapters or *suras,* of very unequal length. This collection constitutes the Revelation proclaimed by Mohammed as received during the last twenty-three years of his life. The *suras* are not spoken of by number, but by a title peculiar to each, derived from its contents or some special quality. The heading of each *sura,* indicating whether it was revealed at Mecca or Medina, is the work of commentators, and forms no part of the inspired text. Every *sura* is in turn divided into verses, tho these subdivisions are not numbered in manuscript copies.

The 114 chapters are arranged seemingly in a most artless manner, without regard to chronology or doctrine, the only order discernible being that the longest are placed first, with the notable exception of Sura I., called the *Fâtiha*. So far as is known, Mohammed himself never wrote anything down, and if he was acquainted with the arts of reading and writing (which some have disputed), it seems that he found it more convenient to employ an amanuensis whenever he had anything to commit to writing. At the time of his death the revelations existed only in scattered fragments, on bits of stone, leather and flat bones. The great repository of truth was in the minds of his followers. With the marvelous tenacity of the Arab memory, large numbers of Muslims at the time of their Prophet's death could repeat the principal suras, and soon after some are mentioned who could recite the whole without an error. With Mohammed's death the canon was closed, but up to this time no attempt had been made to systematically arrange or even to collect the contents. In the second year after this event a vast number of the best reciters of the Korân were slain at the battle of Yemâna, and Omar became convinced that the divine revelation ought to be put on a less precarious footing. The attention of Abu Bekr being called to the matter, he speedily appointed Zeid, the chief amanuensis of the Prophet, to make the collection.

Zeid worked diligently, and brought together the fragments of the Korân from every quarter, gathering them from palm-leaves, stone tablets, the bones of sheep and camels, from bits of leather, "but most of all from the breasts of men." The tablets of the Arab memory were at that time the reliable source of much of the revelation. The manuscript thus formed remained during the caliphate of Omar the standard text.

As transcripts of this original were made variety crept in, and in the caliphate of Othman, some time a little later than 33 A.H., Zeid was appointed to make a recension of his former text. With a committee of three Koreish to act as final judges in disputed cases, the new collection was made in the pure Meccan dialect, which Mohammed himself used. The former copies were called in and burned, and the recension of Othman has remained down to the present day unaltered. All the facts warrant us in supposing that the Korân as now existing contains the very words as delivered by the Prophet. Various readings are practically unknown.

One source of the Korân's power is its sonorously musical diction. Another is the simplicity of its doctrine. The unity of God, Judgment, and Islam (that is, submission to His will) are the fundamental teachings. The whole substance of the religion is comprehended under two propositions, which are sometimes spoken of as the Mohammedan "Confession of Faith," viz.: "There is no God but God, and Mohammed is His Prophet." The former sweeps away idolatry, and the latter at once lends divine authority to every precept of Mohammed. The portion of confession pertaining to faith embraces six branches: Belief in God; in His angels; in His scriptures; in His prophets; in the resurrection and the day of judgment; in God's absolute decree, and predestination of both good and evil. In practise five things are necessary: (1) Confession of Faith, (2) Worship, (3) Alms-giving, (4) The Fast and (5) a Pilgrimage to Mecca.

Salvation, according to the Korân, is by free grace and is not a thing to be won by merit. But the gracious gift from God depends upon Confession of Faith. Whoever confesses belief in God and His Prophet will be finally saved from hell altho his sins may be punished there. On the other hand, tho a man confess belief in the One God, if he does not declare belief in Mohammed as the Prophet of God he cannot be accepted by God. The believer is bound also to do good works, that is to say, to observe the ordinances with strict fidelity. Large portions of the Korân deal with the narratives of the Jewish and Christian Scriptures, showing that Mohammed had come in contact with the corrupt forms of these religions then in Arabia. The Old Testament characters, especially the Patriarchs and Prophets, and Our Lord Himself, are regarded with the greatest reverence. The narratives given in the Korân are drawn from the Talmudic traditions, which Mohammed perhaps supposed to be the O. T. Scripture, and from the Christian apochryphal Gospels. It is often said that the Korân is the most widely-read book in existence. In one sense this is true, since the mere reading of the book, without understanding, is commonly held to exert a magical influence for good. But it should be remembered that the Korân is not understood by readers outside of Arabia (even where Arabic is vernacular), excepting in the limited circle of well educated men.

V. *The Hadith, or Traditions:* The Korân prescribes an ethical code which is obligatory on Muslims, since all regard it as the only revelation of the Divine will. But along with the Korân, Mohammedans receive well-authenticated sayings of the Prophet as authoritative comments on religious, ethical and ceremonial subjects. These traditions are in fact considered as inspired sayings, handed down by men liable to error. They inform us not only what Mohammed said and did, but what he allowed others to say and do unrebuked. Mohammed was much afraid that he would be misreported, and commanded his adherents as follows: "Convey to other persons none of my words except those ye know of a surety. Verily he who represents my words wrongly shall find a place for himself in the fire." How poorly this injunction was followed is evident from the fact that Abu Daud received only 4,800 traditions out of 500,000. Thus it appears why there is such a diversity of opinion among Mohammedans. Various canons of criticism have been laid down by learned Muslims by which these traditions may be sifted—such as the integrity of the persons transmitting the saying, the number of links in the chain of narrators, the style of composition, etc. The first attempts to collect these traditions were made in the 8th century. The work of Imam Malik is held in the greatest esteem. The six standard collections (out of 1,465 in all) are by (1) Mohammed Ismail al Bukhari, A.H. 256; (2) Muslim ibnu'l Hajjaj, A.H. 261; (3) Abu 'Isa Mohammed-at-Tirmizi, A.H. 279; (4) Abu Da'ud as-Sajistani, A.H. 275; (5) Abu 'Abdi'r-Rahman an Nasa'i, A.H. 303; and (6) Abu 'Abdi 'llah Mohammed Ibn Majah, A.H. 273.

All the Muslim sects receive the traditions altho disagreeing as to their number and their content. The following are a few characteristic sayings of Mohammed:

"I am no more than a man, but when I enjoin anything respecting religion, receive it, and when I order anything about the affairs of the world, then I am nothing more than a man."—"I have left you two things, and you will not stray as long as you hold them fast. The one is the book of God, and the other is the example (Sunna) of his prophet."—"Some of my injunctions abrogate others."—"My sayings do not abrogate the Word of God, but the Word of God can abrogate my sayings."

The following is a specimen of the way a tradition was handed down in the collection of at-Tirmizi:

"Abu Kuraib said to us that Ibrahim ibn Yusuf ibn Abi Ishaq said to us from his father, from abu Ishaq, from Tulata ibn Musarif, that he said, I have heard from Abdu'r-Rahman ibn Ausaja that he said I have from Bara ibn 'Azib that he said I have heard that the prophet said, 'Whoever shall give in charity a milch-cow, or silver, or a leathern bottle of water it shall be equal to the freeing of a slave.'"

VI. *Muslim Worship:* The forms of worship have so much importance in Islam, both as a means of acquiring merit before God and as shaping the religious ideas of the Muslim, that it may be well to illustrate what this worship is. Five times every day every Mohammedan man or woman must recite the prescribed litany in Arabic in a specified manner. Each of the five services or exercises consists of a certain number of "rounds" or repetitions of the litany; one service differing from the other in the number of "rounds" rather than in variety of the words used. The example here given is the service of morning worship, either in the congregation at mosque or alone in the house. We condense the directions from one of the books of instruction in use among the Sunnite Mohammedans:

The morning worship consists of four rounds (*rakat*), two of which are obligatory and two are of usage (following the custom of Mohammed).

The worshipper, having performed ablution, stands facing in the direction of Mecca.

1. He must declare his purpose (inaudibly), saying, I purpose to perform the first obligatory (or usage) round of morning worship.

2. He then lifts both hands, palm to the front, until the thumbs touch the lobes of the ears; then he says, "God is most great!"

3. Folding the hands across the stomach, the right hand over and clasping the left, he says, "Glory to God! Praised and blessed be Thy name, O Most High, and there is no other God but Thee! I take refuge in God from Satan the bestoned! In the name of God the Merciful and the Compassionate! Praise God the Lord of all creatures, etc. (the first chapter of the Koran); "God is one God, the Eternal; He begetteth not, neither is He begotten, and there is none like unto Him."

4. The worshipper now bows, saying "God is most great!" and, placing his hands upon his knees, taking care to keep the line of his head and back straight.

5. Remaining in that position he says: "Praise God the Lord, the Great One," three times. (If he is able to say it five or seven times the merit is greater.)

6. Saying "May God attend unto his praise," the worshipper regains the upright position.

7. He now drops upon his knees, sitting upon his heels, and then, saying, "God is most great!" he touches his forehead to the ground; one hand being on each side of his head, palm downward upon the ground.

8. In this prostrate position the worshipper says three times, "Glory to the Lord on High!"

9. Saying "God is most great!" he recovers position on his knees.

10. Saying "God is most great," he touches his forehead to the ground again.

11. In this prostrate position he repeats three times, "Glory to the Lord on High!"

12. Saying, "God is most great!" the worshipper now recovers position upon his knees again.

This completes one round of worship, and the worshiper rises to his feet and begins the second round, which consists of a repetition of the first.

After the four rounds are completed, and indeed at the end of every service, no matter of how many rounds, the worshiper, standing, repeats, "Glory to God," thirty-three times, and "Praise be to God," thirty-three times, and, "God is most great," thirty-three times. He may then, if he chooses, abandon the Arabic language, and in his own tongue, as best he knows how, he may ask of God anything that his heart desires.

Whatever the service is (whether morning, noon, mid-afternoon, sunset, or evening) must be definitely expressed at the beginning, as well as whether the round is to be obligatory or of usage. If the worshiper does not do this, his worship is defective. Whatever is prescribed for any particular posture or any particular "round" of worship must be exactly said. If too much or too little is said, the worship is defective. In such cases the "round" must be done over from the beginning, or a special form for the correction of defects must be gone through.

It is hardly necessary to remark that these rules of worship go for much in that severance of religion from morals which one sometimes notices in Mohammedans. The effect of fixing the litany in the Arabic language, which is not understood by a vast number of Muslims, and of having the services of worship consist of a greater or less number of repetitions of the sentences above recorded, is to settle in the worshiper's mind the idea that religion is an outward form. The result of making the acceptableness of worship turn upon precision in posture and in utterance, is to turn the thought during worship upon self instead of upon God; while the doctrine that the greatness of merit is measured by the number of perfect repetitions of these sentences, gives to the worshiper who can repeat them glibly a greater self-complacency than is found among the adherents of any other religion.

VII.—Islam and the Bible: Mohammedans profess to regard the Old and New Testament Scriptures, as well as the Korân, as the revealed Word of God. Mohammed and his immediate followers seem to have considered the Korân as being in perfect harmony with the Bible. When the antagonism between the two was pointed out somewhat later, the learned Muslim doctors claimed that the current Scriptures had been corrupted since Mohammed's time. They claimed that the Korân was in perfect accord with the original Scriptures to which their prophet had access. The existence of texts of the New Testament older than Mohammed's time has seriously weakened that argument. When once Mohammedans are compelled to admit the genuineness and antiquity of these manuscripts, they will be compelled to show reason for the discrepancies.

The Korân gives a large part of the Old Testament history in a garbled and legendary form as tho from hearsay. Adam, created out of earth, the "chosen one of God," was the first man. Eve, his wife, was created by God from a rib of Adam's left side. Iblees (Satan) tempted them; they fell and were cast out of Paradise. The story of Abel and Cain is embellished with rabbinical additions. Noah, "the Prophet of God," is a prominent person in the Korân, and the narrative of the flood is told with many amusing details. Abraham, "the Friend of God," is mentioned very freely, together with Ishmael and Isaac. The story of the conversion of Abraham is of a high order. "When the night overshadowed him he saw a star and he said, This is my Lord. But when it set he said, I like not those that set. And when he saw the moon rising he said, This is my Lord; but when it set he said, Verily, if my Lord direct me not I shall assuredly be of the erring people. And when he saw the sun rising, he said, This is my Lord. This is greater. But when it set he said, O my people, I am clear of the objects which ye associate with God. Verily I turn my face unto Him who hath created the heavens and the earth; following the right religion I am not of the polytheists." The story of his sojourn in Babylonia is given elaborately. His journey to Palestine, his dealings with corrupt Lot, the half-miraculous birth of Isaac, the destruction of the cities of the plain, the attempted sacrifice of Isaac, together with apocryphal incidents, are tediously set forth. Abraham gives direction to his children as to Islam, the true religion, and is accounted the first "Hanif," the founder of the Muslim faith in its present form. The stories of Isaac, Ishmael, Joseph, the life and bondage of the Hebrews in Egypt, Moses and the wanderings in the desert, Joshua (slightly mentioned), Samuel, Saul, David, Solomon, Job, Elijah, Elisha, Isaiah, Jonah, Ezra, are given in a prolix fashion. Turning to the New Testament we find mention of Zacharias, with John the Baptist, his son, and Gabriel. There is no evidence in the Korân that Mohammed ever saw a copy of the New Testament, but he constantly mentions it as the "Injil which was given to Jesus." The Korân says (lvii. 27): "We caused our Apostles to follow in their (*i.e.*, Noah's and Abraham's) footsteps, and We caused Jesus the son of Mary to follow them, and We gave him the Injil, and We put into the hearts of those who followed him kindness and compassion, but as to the monastic life, they invented it themselves." Again (iii. 2): "He has sent thee a book (Korân) confirming what was sent before it, and has revealed the Law and the Gospel before, for the guidance of men." (See also vii. 156; iii. 43; iii. 58; xlviii. 29; ix. 112; v. 50, 51, 70, 72, and 110; xix. 31.)

Very full statements are made concerning Jesus Christ. He is called Jesus ('Isa), Jesus the Son of Mary, the Messiah, the Word of God, the Word of Truth, a Spirit from God, the Messenger of God, the Servant of God, the Prophet of God and illustrious in this world and the next. Mohammed taught that Jesus was miraculously born of the "Virgin" Mary (Sura iii. 37-43; xix. 16-21), who was the sister of Aaron. The infant vindicated the chastity of its mother miraculously by speaking in its cradle (xix. 22-34; xxiii. 52). Jesus performed miracles in his youth (Apocryphal Gospels) and in his maturity (iii. 43-46; v. 112-115). He was commissioned as a Prophet of God to confirm the Law and reveal the Gospel (lvii. 26, 27; v. 50, 51; ii. 81, 254; lxi. 6; vi. 85; iv. 157; iii. 44). The Korân affirms that Jesus did not die, but ascended to heaven miraculously, and another victim was, unknowingly to the Roman soldiers, substituted for Jesus on the cross (iii. 47-50; iv. 155, 156). After he left the earth his disciples disputed as to whether he was a prophet, like Moses or Isaiah, or a part of the Godhead, making up the Trinity as "The Father, the Mother, and the Son." (xix. 35, 36; iii. 51; 52; xliii. 57-65; ix. 30; iii. 72, 73; v. 19; v. 76-79; iv. 169; v. 116, 117). The Traditions teach that Jesus will come a second time, and that he will be the Judge at the last great day, and that even Mohammed will be judged by him. It is claimed that he predicted one that should come after him who should carry out his mission, and Muslim theologians affirm that Mohammed was that person. Mohammed himself calls himself "Ahmad" (Sura lxi. 6), "The Praised," to adapt his name to the title used by Christ which Muslims claim had been perverted from "Paraclitos" to "Paracletos," because the former, meaning "the Praised," clearly designated Mohammed ("The Praised").

Sir William Muir says: "After a careful and repeated examination of the whole Korân I have been able to discover no grounds for believing that Mohammed himself ever expressed the smallest doubt at any period of his life in regard either to the authority or the genuineness of the Old and New Testaments as extant at his time. He was profuse in his assurances that his system entirely corresponded with both, and that he had been foretold by former prophets; and as perverted Jews and Christians were at hand to confirm his words, and as the Bible was little known among the generality of his followers, those assurances were implicitly believed."

VII. Mohammedan Conquests: At the time of Mohammed's death (June 8, 632, in the 11th year of the Muslim era) the whole of the Arabian peninsula had embraced Islam, with the exception of a few southern tribes which preferred Moseylema, the "false prophet" of the Nejd. The few hours that succeeded the death of Mohammed were critical ones for Islam. Ali, the nephew and son-in-law of the prophet, a young man, and Abu Bekr, the old, stanch follower of Mohammed, and the father of Ayesha, the prophet's favorite wife, were the natural candidates for the leadership. Abu Bekr was at last proclaimed caliph (*Khalifa*, successor) and the wisdom of the election was made plain by the vitality which characterized his reign of two years. The rebellious tribes of Arabia were subdued, the government was thoroughly organized and centralized, and the long career of victory was begun. Under Khaled the armies crossed the Syrian frontier, occupied Bosrah, overran the Hauran, defeated the Byzantine army on the plains of Eznadin, and invested Damascus. After a seventy days' siege this capital of Southern Syria fell August 3, 634 (13 A.H.). Sweeping eastward and northward, Khaled defeated a second Byzantine army at Yamook. In the meanwhile Omar succeeded to the caliphate, August 22, 634. Jerusalem was conquered, and all Syria was in the hands of Muslims. In the meantime an army was pushing across the Persian frontier. At the battle of Kadisiya the initial failure of the Arabs was retrieved, Ctesiphon and Susa fell, Mesopotamia was gained, and on the field of Mahavend (641) the Sassanid dynasty of Persia received a death blow. The whole of Persia, Khorasan, Kerman, Mekran, Seistan, and Balkh were conquered and assimilated. The century had not passed before the Oxus was the eastern boundary of the caliph's empire.

In 641 Amr invaded Egypt, which fell with hardly a struggle, the Monophysite Christians throwing in their lot with the Arabs as against the Orthodox Byzantines. Othman succeeded to the caliphate in 644. The armies steadily pushed westward. Libya, Tripoli, Tunis, Algeria, and Morocco fell successively. A Christian civilization made a firm stand at Carthage, but in the battle of Utica (698) the power of African Christianity was broken, and Musa rode to his saddle-girths into the Atlantic, and with raised sword took possession of the regions beyond in the name of God.

Othman had been assassinated in 656, and Ali, Mohammed's nephew, was at last raised to the caliphate. A rebellion was put down at the battle of the Camel, fought at Basra, November, 656. The murder of Othman aroused the Koreishite faction. Mo'awiya of this tribe, the Syrian governor, did not recognize Ali as caliph, and Ali saw it was a hopeless task to subdue him. The strength of Ali was in Kufa. The Syrians gained the battle of Siffin by fastening copies of the Korân to their lances (657). Disaffection arose among the caliph's forces, and he was murdered in January, 661, becoming a martyr in the eyes of a large part of the Muslim world, and occasioning that great split in the faith which has ever since divided *Shi'i* (Ali's faction) from *Sunni* (traditionists). Mo'awiya was proclaimed caliph by his soldiers. Muslim Persia proclaimed Hassan, a son of Ali, as caliph; but on being defeated in battle, Hassan retired from the struggle. Hussein, another son of Ali, was not so tractable. The Syrian caliph showed great statesmanship in the management of his empire, which was expanding in every direction. Armenia, Cyprus, Cos, and Crete were conquered, and even Constantinople was invested. Mo'awiya died at Damascus, which he made the capital of the Ommeiad dynasty, of which he was the founder, 680, and was succeeded by his son, Yezid I. This voluptuous caliph ordered the prefect of Medina to strike off the head of Hussein, a son of Ali, if he would not yield. Hussein fled toward Kufa with all his family. The Ommeiad army met him in the plain of Kerbela, near Kufa, and surrounded his little company. Hussein declared himself ready to renounce all pretension to the caliphate, but on October 9, 680 (9th of Moharram, A.H. 61), on his refusal to surrender his person to the enemy, he and all his followers were cut to pieces. The Shi'ites observe the 10th of Moharram as a day of public mourning. The news of this bloody ending of the son of Ali spread consternation far and wide. Revolts were with difficulty put down. Ali, son of Hussein, wisely refused to put himself at the head of the opposition. Medina was plundered, and Mecca was in a state of siege, when news came of the death of the caliph at Damascus (November 11, 683). Mo'awiya II., Merwan I., Abd al Melik, al Walid, and the other caliphs in the Ommeiad dynasty saw Islam extend in every direction. Tarik crossed the strait, ever after called from him Jebel Tarik (Gibraltar), into Spain in 711; Roderick, the last of the Visigothic kings, lost his crown and life in the battle of Xeres; Malaga, Granada, Cordova, Seville, Toledo, Saragossa, Barcelona, and the whole Spanish peninsula, except a few mountain retreats, were rapidly conquered. In 731 Abder-Rahman crossed the Pyrenees and swept up as far as Tours, where his host was defeated by Charles Martel in 732.

In the meanwhile the Ommeiad dynasty at Damascus began to decline. Ibrahim, great-grandson of Abbas, the uncle of the Prophet, of the house of Hashem, put himself at the head of a revolt, which under his son, Abd Allah Abu-Abbas, the "Blood-shedder," was successful. The Ommeiad dynasty gave place to the Abbassides, and the newly built city of Baghdad became the capital of Islam.

The year 750 was the turning-point in Muslim history. There were still further conquests to be made in Central Asia, India, and Central Africa, but the unity of the Muslim world was broken forever. The Abbassides controlled affairs in the east, but the Ommeiads held on in Spain. In 755 Abder-Rahman founded the caliphate of Cordova, which ran a brilliant career until 1013, when Muslim power in Spain was broken up into various factions. Christians were treated with great leniency, universities were established, libraries collected, literature, science, and art fostered, and from these centers went forth light which hastened the dawning of modern civilization. The "Mozarabes" ("Arabs by adoption") were Christians living under this mild rule, who were the instruments of this wide diffusion of Arab learning throughout Europe.

The Saracens did not long remain in France. In 760 Pepin the Short drove them over the Pyrenees. Charles the Great (Charlemagne) drove them back in Spain beyond the Ebro. By the year 1030 the kingdom of Leon was well established. Navarre, Aragon, Castile, and Portugal were gathering headway. Sardinia in 1017 was reclaimed from the Arabs, and Corsica in 1050. The Balearic Islands were won by Aragon. By the middle of the 14th century the Saracens had nothing left in Spain but the little mountainous kingdom of Granada. In 1492 the combined forces of Castile and Aragon, under the lead of Ferdinand the Catholic, extinguished this last faint glimmer of Muslim rule in Southwestern Europe, at the close of a crusade lasting eight centuries.

With the downfall of the Ommeiad dynasty at Damascus Arabia lost political power in the Muslim world. The Abbassides at Baghdad were non-Arab in tendency. The subtle skepticism of Persia brought a looseness and indifference in sharp contrast with the strict and fanatical Arab type. Founded in 750, this dynasty existed until 1258. For a hundred years it ran a brilliant career. Baghdad was the resort of learned men from every region. Greek letters and philosophy were cultivated. Haroun er-Rashid (768-809) gathered at his court an assemblage of the wisest and wittiest minds in his empire. Arabic literature expanded under his patronage. He sent an embassy to the court of Charles the Great, and gathered information from every quarter. But the first century of Abbasside rule was followed by four centuries of decay. The Karmathian revolt in Arabia greatly weakened the central organization. Turkish mercenaries at Baghdad, called in as a body-guard of the caliph, acquired more and more power, and the last caliphs were mere puppets in their hands. Province after province was dismembered. In 1258 Hulagu, grandson of Genghis Khan, overthrew Baghdad and extinguished the Abbasside rule.

In 909 the Fatimite dynasty was founded in Egypt by Obeidallah, a supposed descendant of Ali and Fatima. Cairo was founded and made the capital. The story of the rule of the extravagant Sufi mysticism there is revolting in the extreme. Saladin put an end to this dynasty in 1171.

In the meantime Islam had been pushing steadily eastward. Large bodies of Turks and Tatars were converted. The Seljuk Turks appeared as an independent body of marauders as early as 1035, conquered Persia and pushed south and west to the Mediterranean. They then set up a powerful kingdom in Central Asia Minor, threatening destruction to the Byzantine empire. Their abuse and murder or enslavement of Christian pilgrims to the holy places about Jerusalem excited the Crusades, which held the attention of Europe from 1095 to 1291, and which resulted in checking the power of the Seljuk Turk, but left Syria a prey to discord. A little later the Ottoman Turk appeared, and by 1300 had a firm position on the border of the Byzantine empire. After absorbing the Seljukian domains and all the Greek territory in Asia, the Ottoman armies entered Europe in 1354; Constantinople fell a century later (1453), and the whole Balkan peninsula was under the crescent. The armies of the sultans pressed northward into Poland and westward as far as Vienna, their footing in Europe not becoming precarious until well on into the 18th century.

Islam obtained a firm foothold in India as early as 1000. An attempt to conquer Sindh in the 8th century had failed. It was not until the Turk adopted Mohammedanism that Islam made headway. Seventeen invasions and twenty-five years of fighting under the leadership of Mahmud of Ghazni (1001-1030) had reduced only the western portions of the Punjab. Bengal was conquered in 1203. By 1306, as a result of the barbarous conquests of three centuries, there was a powerful Mohammedan rule in Northern India. The story of Islam in India is one of constant revolts, or uninterrupted invasions and steady aggrandizement. There were a large number of independent Mohammedan states when the "Mogul" dynasty (1526-1761) made its appearance. Babar, the Turk, (1482-1530), having gathered headway on the Afghan side of the Indian passes, pushed through in 1526 and conquered right and left, until at his death his empire stretched from the river Amu in Central Asia to the delta of the Ganges. This vast power began to decline as early as 1707. Independent Muslim kingdoms were detached from the main body. The Mahrattas grew in power until they were able to break the "Mogul" Empire into pieces. The English East India Company was already at work in India, backed by the British army. The first governor, Lord Clive, took the helm in 1758. The Company grew until nothing less than a great military power could properly care for the immense territory and the millions under its control. Since 1858 the Mohammedans of India have been directly under English rule.

The spread of Islam in China, Australasia and Central Africa cannot here be traced in detail. Having conquered the Mediterranean coast of Africa in the year 698, Mohammedanism pushed up the Nile valley and across the Sahara. Abyssinia alone has been able to withstand the Muslim onset, and remains like an island in a sea of Islam. The native terminology of the geography of all Northern Africa as far south as the equator is Arabic. Misr (Egypt), Sahara, Sudan, Bahr el Abyad (White Nile), Bahr el Asrak (Blue Nile), Bahr el Ghasel, are specimen names. The Arabic has penetrated south beyond the Zambesi River, as is shown in "Kafir" (Caffre), which means infidel or unbeliever. In Zanzibar and throughout Central Africa the Swahili dialect of the Arabic is the language of commerce. Islam has spread in Africa by three agencies—the sword, commerce, and the missionary, but wherever it has gone the principle of action has been the same—to ruin whatever it cannot rule.

IX. *The Extent of Islam To-day:* It is impossible to estimate accurately the numerical strength of the Mohammedan world. For many years it was reckoned at 160,000,000, but the latest investigation pushes it up nearly to 200,000,000. The following table is drawn from the most recent data:

Rumania	44,000
Bulgaria	600,000
Servia	14,500
Bosnia and Herzegovina	548,500
Montenegro	14,000
Greece	24,000
Turkey in Europe	2,500,000
Turkey in Asia	16,000,000
Russia	14,000,000
Persia	9,000,000
Afghanistan	4,000,000
India	62,500,000
Ceylon	250,000
Baluchistan	770,000
China	30,000,000
Malaysia	13,200,000
Egypt	9,000,000
Zanzibar	100,000
Morocco	8,000,000
Tripoli	1,800,000
Tunis	1,000,000
Algeria	4,000,000
Egyptian Sudan	3,500,000
Sierra Leone and Nigeria (British)	7,600,000
French Sahara, etc	8,375,000
Nyasaland	500,000
E. African Protectorate	500,000
Uganda	800,000
German E. Africa	750,000
Somaliland	1,100,000
Kamerun	2,000,000
Cape of Good Hope, detached groups of islands, America, etc., etc.,	60,000
	193,550,000

Let us examine more in detail the various countries. Rumania, Servia, Montenegro, and Greece have nearly rid themselves of the Turks. Those who remain are scattered about as land-owners and merchants. It is said that they are moving toward Asia Minor slowly, and before long will not be an appreciable part of the population. In Bosnia, Herzegovina, and Bulgaria, over a million Muslims still remain. Turkey in Europe has two million Mohammedans, scattered from the Adriatic to the Bosphorus. These are more stationary, altho there is a constant movement toward Asia, as European civilization more and more gives equal civil rights to unbelievers in the Balkan peninsula. It should be remembered, however, that by far the greater number of the Muslims of European Turkey, etc., are not Turks, but natives of the land who accepted Islam. What course they will take is by no means certain.

Mohammedanism in European Russia is largely confined to Southern and Eastern Russia—territory which for centuries has been occupied by "Tatars," etc., who are neither more nor less than Turks of near kin to the Ottomans. There are said to be 20,000 muftis, mollahs, and other teachers in European Russia. A majority of the population of the Transcaucasus district are Muslims, as might have been expected. As Russia has pushed down toward the Persian and Afghanistan borders she has taken in more and more tribes of Mohammedans. Professor Arminius Vambéry, an intelligent tho not unprejudiced witness, in writing of these Muslim portions of the Russian Empire, has said:

In the cities of Central Asia, where Islam has taken much firmer root than in the Caucasus or the other parts of the Mohammedan world, there can be no probability of the old and knotty trunk of religious education being soon shaken. On the whole, Islam stands everywhere firmly on its feet, nor can Christianity succeed in weakening it. Indeed, when subjected to Christian rule, it seems to become stronger and more stubborn, and to gain in expansive force. This we see in India, where, in spite of the zeal of the Christian missionaries and the millions spent in their support, the conversions to Islam become daily more frequent. We see this, too, in Russia, where statistics prove that the number of mosques has considerably increased in the course of this century, and that the heathen among the Ural-Altaic people are more easily converted by the mollah than by the pope. . . . Bokhara will still long continue to boast of being the brightest spot in Islam, and her colleges will not soon lose their attraction for the studious youth among the Muslims of Inner Asia.

The British Empire is the greatest Mohammedan power in the world, in that it rules over more followers of the Prophet than does any other one sovereignty. The statistics for India are elaborately worked out. The figures given in the table are those for 1901. It is often said that Mohammedanism is making rapid growth. But the census does not bear out this theory. In speaking of the growth of Islam in India, Sir William Hunter says: "Islam is progressing in India neither more quickly nor more slowly than the rest of the population. If you take a hasty view of India and add up totals, you will find that Islam now has a great many more followers than it had ten years ago. But you will find that the whole population has increased." This statement had reference to 1881. The increase of Mohammedans in India during the decade 1891-1901 has been a little less than 9 per cent., which is also about the rate of increase of the population of India as a whole.

The extent of Islam in China must remain conjectural for many years, but it is probable that 30,000,000 of Muslims is a conservative estimate for China.

The wide spread of Mohammedanism in Malaysia is becoming more and more evident. It is spreading among the whole Malay race, and assumes a peculiar type. It established itself in the Malay Peninsula, in the 14th century, and crossed into Sumatra, Java, and adjacent islands in the 15th century, thus anticipating the Portuguese by only a few years. There are large numbers of Malay Muslims on the Malay Peninsula, in the native states, and under the English flag. Sumatra has a population of whom 70 per cent. are strict Mohammedans. Java before 1478 was Hindu in religion. In that year Islam overthrew the chief Hindu principality of Majapahit, and the conversion of the whole island to Mohammedanism followed within the century. The Celebes, with a population of over 800,000, is largely Mohammedan in religion. Islam had just been introduced when the Portuguese landed in 1525. It spread in a hundred years over all the districts it now occupies. The south peninsula is divided into nine native Muslim states, which form a kind of Bugís confederacy. They are in alliance with the Dutch. North of this is a smaller Mandar confederacy of states, only partly Mohammedan. There are Muslims also along the north coast of Celebes, altho we have a Christian majority in the Minahassa peninsula. Concerning Islam in the Dutch possessions, the Rev. Dr. Schreiber of the Rhenish Missionary Society says:

Wherever Mohammedans and heathen are in contact Islam is winning ground, sometimes slowly, sometimes more speedily. . . . Only a small portion of the whole population remains still heathen, and those only small and insignificant tribes scatt.red in the forests of Sumatra and Borneo. There are some strong and unmistakable signs of the increasing vigor of Islam in Dutch India. According to the official statements there is a steady increase in the number of pilgrims to Mecca. . . . Those Mohammedan sects whose well known hostile and aggressive tendencies make them so dangerous are more and more supplanting the more placable-spirited folks, formerly so common among the Mohammedans of Dutch India, especially of Java. Another hardly less ominous sign is the astonishing growth of Mohammedan schools. In 1882 there were in Java 10,913 of those schools, numbering 164,667 pupils; in 1885 we are told there were 16,760 schools, with not less than 225,148 pupils; thus, within three years, an increase of not less than 55 per cent. Even in the residency of Tapanoeli in Sumatra, where the whole of Mohammedanism is of comparatively recent date, we find 210 such schools and 2,479 pupils.

Turning eastward from the Dutch possessions, we find Mohammedanism constantly pushing forward. The large islands of Butu and Muna are inhabited by Muslim Malays. The coast villages of Buru, west of Ceram, are inhabited by semi-civilized Mohammedans. In Ceram we have villages nominally Mohammedan. In Amboyna, Banda, Goram, Manowolke, Ka, Mysol and Sumbawa there are considerable numbers of Muslims. Bali and Lombok are the only islands in the Malay Archipelago which maintain their old Hindu religion. The Sulu Archipelago, belonging to the Philippine Islands, comprises 150 islands, inhabited by Mohammedans of the Malay race, speaking a peculiar language, which they write with the Arabic character. Taking all these facts into consideration, the figures set down in the table for Islam in Malaysia may be too small.

Turning to Africa, we find ourselves in still greater difficulty. The data for Egypt, Zanzibar, Algeria, Tunis, and Tripoli are correct enough. For the interior we are obliged to use the guesses of officers engaged in pressing forward the interests of the various European governments. The figures in the table are no more than estimates. It should be said, however, that the more the Niger region is explored the more clear does it become that we have been overestimating the number of Mohammedans among the tribes, many of whom are Mohammedan subjects, but have not even been invited to accept the Mohammedan religion. Crossing the Atlantic to South America, we find the Protestant missionaries asking for Arabic Bibles to use with Muslims who have immigrated for purposes of trade.

X. *Sects in Islam:* It is related that Mohammed said: "Verily it will happen to my people as it did to the children of Israel. The children of Israel were divided into seventy-two sects, and my people will be divided into seventy-three. Every one of these will go to hell except one sect." If the number was put too low for the Christian sects (probably confused with the Jews), the corresponding number is far too low for the Muslim world, and the bitterness of feeling indicated by the traditional utterance of the prophet holds true to-day in the fanatical world of Islam. Sheikh Abdu'l-Kadir says there are 150 sects in Islam; but there are infinite shades between them which make them practically innumerable. The two grand divisions of the Muslim world are *Sunnites* and *Shi'ites.* Upon the death of Mo'awiya (A. H. 60), Yezid obtained the position of Imam or caliph without the form of election, and hence arose the great schism, which is as strong to-day as ever, between the *Sunni* and the Shi'i Muslims; the *Sunni*, being close observers of the traditions as to the example of Mohammed, and the *Shi'i* considering many of the traditions too uncertain to be binding. The *Sunni* Muslims account Abu Bekr, Omar and Othman as legitimate caliphs. The *Sunni* embrace by far the larger part of the Muslim world, and this article is written rather from their standpoint. They are divided into four parties or sects: (1) Hanafiyē, in Turkey, Central Asia, and Northern India; (2) Shafiyē, in Southern India and Egypt; (3) Malakiyē in Morocco and North Africa, and (4) Hambaliyē in Eastern Arabia and Eastern Africa. These four divergencies of practise, however, are not considered as forming any break in the unity of Islam, since they have discussed and agreed that the divergence is permissible.

The division between *Sunni* and *Shi'i* is of a different nature, involving a bitterness that is quite unappeasable, since the *Shi'i* reject the first three caliphs and exalt Ali, the nephew and son-in-law of the prophet, as the only legitimate caliph, and as nearly the equal of Mohammed in the sanctity of his calling. The peculiarities of the *Shi'i* Muslims must, however, be discussed in a separate article.

Other sects of Islam are the **Dervish** orders, who have introduced into Islam everywhere foreign elements from India, Greece, and Persia under the name of **Sufism** (*Tesawwuf* or Theosophy); and the Babis of Persia, who have carried to an extreme some of the Sufi doctrines, and used them to exalt the doctrine of the *Mahdi.*

In Arabia we find the Wahhabis, founded in 1691, by Mohammed, son of Abdu'l Wahhab. This sect grew out of the Hambaliya sect. Its founder was the Luther of Mohammedanism, calling Muslims back to the original scriptures of Islam. He proposed to do away with saint-worship, which permeated the Muslim world. The Wahhabis call themselves "unitarians," and claim that any man who can read the Korân and sacred traditions can judge for himself in matters of doctrine. They forbid prayers to any prophet, wali, pir, or saint. They hold that at the judgment-day Mohammed will obtain permission of God to intercede for his people. They forbid the illumination of shrines, or prayers, and ceremonies in or about them, not excepting Mohammed's shrine. Women must not visit graves, because they weep so violently. This sect has always been fanatical. The sword was appealed to. Abdu'l Aziz, the leader after 1765, pushed his conquest to the limits of Arabia. He was assassinated in 1803. His son Sa'ud carried the victorious banner beyond the peninsula, and threatened the Turkish empire. Mecca was conquered in 1803. All sorts of ornaments and pipes were burned. Tobacco was prohibited on pain of death. Sa'ud sent commands to Mohammedan sovereigns in every direction that pilgrims to Mecca must conform to these puritan regulations. Missionaries were sent out. Disturbances were occasioned in Northern India. A little later, Mohammed Ali of Egypt sent a strong force into Arabia under Ibrahim Pasha. The Wahhabis were thoroughly subdued, and Mecca released from the strict rule of this Protestant phase of Islam. The sect since that day has made little if any progress, altho its tenets have found adherents among the Dervishes of the Sudan.

In India some call Sikhism a sect of Mohammedanism. This is hardly correct, altho it is a mixture of Hindu and Mohammedan ideas, and has its chief strongholds in the Punjab. There are, however, in India several new sects of Mohammedans which claim to be seeking to improve the religion by adapting it to modern requirements, like the Aligarh movement. In Africa the great Senoussiyè movement is in fact a new sect in Islam. To what it may grow is not as yet clear, but it represents force, and fanaticism, and such appeal to the consciences of Mohammedans that it has swept through the Barbary states with tremendous vigor of popularity.

XI. The effect of Missions on Islam: Such being the state of the Muslim world, what success has up to this time attended the efforts of the Christian Church to win Mohammedans? We must believe that God has some beneficent aim in view even when He allows Islam to arise and spread from the Pacific to the Atlantic. Could we fully understand, we should probably see some underlying scheme of Providence which is being worked out before our eyes, even tho the conversion of idolaters and fetish-worshipers to Islam seems to fill them with a perennial satisfaction in themselves which resists Christianity far more successfully than does heathendom itself. Mohammedanism has undoubtedly some elevating influence upon the heathen it wins. It develops a strong individuality, it theoretically and most frequently practically frees from drunkenness, cannibalism, and other degrading heathen practises. It elevates womanhood and the family to a certain degree. It gives a regular order of life, and has introduced letters to some extent wherever it has gone. It leaves the people stranded at its own low level, and its use of the sword to bring them to that level recalls to some the method by which Christianity made its largest territorial conquests in Germany, Spain, South and Central America, Siberia, etc. The answer to this suggestion is that such conquests were never universally approved in the Christian Church, nor were they continued century after century, nor with the widespread and wilful devastation of territory that has been a usual accompaniment of Mohammedan propaganda. We have only to look at the English government reports from the Hausa and Fulani regions in Nigeria to discover that so lately as 1902 the Mohammedan advance, in that part of Africa, loudly proclaimed as most peaceful, is accompanied by the spectacle of armies sweeping through a peaceful land to carry off herds of slaves for the uses of the Mohammedan territory, and to force the survivors into submission and tribute-paying. Because of this contrast in methods the fact is startling that, altho Christian missions have been in contact with Islam for so many years, so little real progress has been made in winning individual Mohammedans to Christ. The task has appeared so formidable, even in lands like India, under Christian control, that no great missionary society has been organized with the special object of reaching them, altho we have several societies for the conversion of the Jews, who number at most eight millions as contrasted with two hundred million Muslims. The number of Mohammedans who have been won to Christ is comparatively very small. In the Turkish empire the government uses its whole power to prevent Muslims from embracing Christianity. Nevertheless, some have done so and have proved their sincerity by useful and unspotted lives. A few in Africa have become Christians, but a larger number of nominal converts to Christianity have fallen away to Islam. In Persia, Mohammedanism seems to be disintegrating through internal forces. That country stands midway in the Mohammedan world. Over a hundred conflicting Muslim sects are found among the seven or eight millions of Aryan race dwelling between the Caspian Sea and the Persian Gulf. Persia is a strategic point in Islam. If it could be won to Christ, Asiatic Islam would be cut in two. The naturally speculative Persian mind is open to new influences, and a few Persian Mohammedans have become Christians. In India, converts from Islam have been more numerous, and in some cases men of great weight in the community have been converted and have become preachers of Christ, with power. But the most interesting successes have been achieved in the Dutch East Indies, where some 40,000 Muslims have become Christians, nearly half of that number in Java alone.

It should be noted, however, that in all Mohammedan lands thousands of copies of Scriptures are sold to Muslims every year, and it is rare that the sale is due to mere curiosity. Nevertheless, it is impossible to avoid the conviction that the Christian Church is dealing with Islam incidentally. The best that can be said is that up to this time it has been laying foundations, and perhaps this is all that could have been done, for the obstacles are very great.

XII. Obstacles and the means used to overcome them: (1) The Mohammedan religion contains truth that has come from God. The heart which desires to find God recognizes this truth, and clings to the error that goes with it with all the power of a faith that is hungry to be fed. (2) The Mohammedan is taught that God's decree has made him one of the elect from the foundation of the world. If he can cherish the thought of fighting against such a decree of the Most High, his pride in being one of the chosen people holds him back from listening to Christians who are not given this high favor by God.

(3) In every Mohammedan land the law makes belief in Islam with fidelity to it a condition of civil rights, of liberty, and even of life. The man who turns from Islam after once having believed in it is an outlaw, dead in the eye of the law, and without a right that any one is bound to respect.

(4) Access to Mohammedans is obstructed because the Korân forbids intimate relations between Mohammedans and Christians. In Muslim lands the government will prevent social relations with Christians by police interference; and in lands where the police cannot be used for this purpose those of a man's own household, as well as the whole Muslim community, will intervene to prevent the formation of any such intimate relation of friendship as would imply opportunity for quiet conversation in private.

(5) The Mohammedan religion as a whole allies itself with the natural and less noble impulses of man. Its essence is an outward

form; it has a glittering theory of lofty ethical aims, and at the same time it regards God as too merciful to insist on putting these noble theories in practise. Adhesion to Islam solves for a man the problem of yielding to selfish and sensual impulses and at the same time retaining the favor of God as a model of religious devotion.

As to that which has been done toward overcoming these obstacles: In the first place the Christian Scriptures have been put into the sacred language of the Korân, and into all the other languages vernacular to any considerable masses of Mohammedans. The Bible thoroughly circulated in Mohammedan regions is far more effective than an army of missionaries sent forth without the Book ready to hand. The second great agency for reaching Mohammedans with Christian truth is the long array of Christian colleges and schools of less importance, which are now scattered over the larger part of the Mohammedan world. Without considering the permanent effect of ideas implanted in the minds of the young, we must give such educational institutions credit for a power of polemic that is gauged by the difference of level between the science of the time of Mohammed and that of this century. Mohammedanism is hopelessly entangled with the science of the 7th century. A third agency for reaching Mohammedans is the establishment of Christian homes, and to some extent bodies of truly Christian people, where Mohammedans are forced to see them and to draw comparisons and conclusions. Of the whole number of Mohammedan converts to Christianity it is probable that nine-tenths have been convinced by the powerful example of some native Christian neighbor.

Without attempting to exhaust the catalog of agencies in use in reaching Mohammedans, we will mention lastly Protestantism or evangelical Christianity as the only phase of Christianity likely to be successful in this great work. Pictures and images used in the service of the Greek Orthodox, Roman Catholic, Coptic, Nestorian, Abyssinian, and other decayed forms of Christianity are utterly revolting to followers of Mohammed, and churches using these can never hope to make headway among Mohammedans. The simple Gospel simply proclaimed must be the effective weapon.

On the whole, there is everything to urge the Western Christian Church to move forward upon this its greatest organized enemy. In the near future the battle must be squarely joined. Civilization is slowly but surely opening the way. Before long all political opposition to the propagation of Christianity in Muslim lands will be over. The followers of Christ never had a more serious undertaking on hand when looked at from the theological, social, ethical, or political standpoint. It calls for the keenest minds and the most consecrated hearts. We must undertake the task at whatever cost. *"Deus vult."*

Hughes (T. P.), *Dictionary of Islam*, London, 1885; Wherry (E. M.), *Commentary on the Koran* (with the text), London, 1882; Smith (R. B.), *Mohammed and Mohammedanism*, New York, 1889; Koelle (S. W.), *Mohammed and Mohammedanism*, London, 1889. (This book and that of R. B. Smith are both excellent; but they are diametrically opposed to each other. Neither should be read without reading the other.) Dwight (H. O.), *Constantinople and Its Problems*, New York, 1901; Burton (R. F.), *A Pilgrimage to Medina and Mecca*, London, (n. e.), 1880 (admirable for its translations of Muslim prayers and liturgy); Geiger (A.), *Judaism and Islam*, London (Society for the Promotion of Christian Knowledge); Tisdall (W. St. C.), *The Sources of Islam* (translated by Sir W. Muir), Edinburgh, T. & T. Clark; Zwemer (S.), *Arabia, the Cradle of Islam*, New York, 1900; Sell (Canon E.), *Historical Development of the Quran*, London (CMS); *Essays on Islam*, London, Simpkin, Marshall & Co.; *Missionary Review of the World*, Vol. IX., p. 758 (worship); Vol. X., p. 225, 422 (in Persia); XI., 721; Malaysia, 359; XII., p. 277 (in China); 764 (a Muslim's view); Vol. XIV., p. 130; XV., p. 732 (Africa); *Islam and Christianity* (American Tract Society), New York, 1902; Chatelier, *L'Islam dans l'Afrique Occidental*, Paris; Jessup (H. H.), *Kamil*, Philadelphia (Pres. Board of Pub.), 1899; Tisdall (W. St. Clair), *Manual of Mohammedan Objections*, London (SPCK).

MOHULPAHARI: A village in Bengal, India, situated in the Santal Parganas, about 135 miles N. W. of Calcutta. Station of the Indian Home Mission to the Santals, with (1901) 1 missionary and 2 native workers.

MOI-LIN: A village in China, situated 85 miles W. N. W. of Swatow. Station of the Basel Missionary Society (1889), with (1903) 2 missionaries and their wives, 17 native workers, 8 outstations, 7 day schools, and 583 professed Christians, of whom 437 are communicants. The Society spells the name Moilim.

MO-KAN-SHAN: A town in the E. part of the province of Che-kiang, China, not far from Wen-chau. Station of the CIM (1900), with 1 missionary and his wife.

MOKNEA: A village in Algeria, Africa, about 50 miles S. E. of Algiers. Station of the Committee of the Mayor Mission (1883), with 1 missionary and his wife, 1 day school, and 1 Sunday school.

MOK-PO: A town and treaty port in the S. W. part of Korea on the Krumsan River, about 8 miles from the mouth. Station of the PS (1898), with (1903) 3 missionaries, two of them with their wives; 1 woman missionary, 2 native workers, 1 place of worship, 1 Sunday school, 1 day school, 1 outstation, 1 dispensary, and 33 professed Christians.

MOLETSCHE. See MALITZI.

MOLOPOLOLE: A village in the N. E. of British Bechuanaland, Africa. It is the chief town of the Bakwena tribe and residence of Chief Sebele, who is a Christian. Altitude, 4,020 feet. Climate, temperate. Station of the LMS (1866), with (1903), 1 missionary and his wife, 1 woman missionary, 10 native workers, 4 Sunday schools, 3 day schools, and 800 professed Christians.

MOLOTE: A village in the Transvaal, Africa, situated 22 miles S. W. of Johannesburg. Station of the Hermannsburg Missionary Society (1895), with (1901) 1 missionary and his wife, 4 native workers, 4 outstations, 1 place of worship, 4 day schools, and 688 professed Christians.

MOLUCCA ISLANDS (*also called Spice Islands*): A group of islands scattered over the sea from Celebes on the east to Papua on the west, and lying S. E. of the Philippines. Area, 42,946 square miles. The number of these islands is said to be several hundreds. Many of them are small and uninhabited. The large islands are Ceram, Jilolo or Halmaheira, and Buru. Nearly all are mountainous. The climate is hot, but not excessively so. Population is about 430,000 natives and 2,600 Europeans. The native population consists of two races, the Malays and the Papuans. The Malay is the common language, and the Arabic character is employed in writing it. Mohammedanism is the prevailing religion, but some few profess Christianity. The laws are chiefly founded on the precepts of the Koran. The chief power is in the hands of the Dutch. Missionary work was carried on until 1865 by the Netherlands Missionary Society. The 45,000 Christians in Ceram, Amboina, Banda, and other islands are now treated as part of the established Church of Holland, and the Government appoints and supports their pastors. The Government also supports a theological school which was founded in 1835. The Utrecht Missionary Society has stations on the islands of Halmaheira (Jilolo) and Buru, with about 1,700 professing Christians.

Pfluger (A.), *Smaragdinseln der Sudsee*, Bonn, 1901; Lith (Dr. P. A. van der), *Encyclopedie van Nederl.-Indie*, Leiden, 1895.

MOMBASA: A town and seaport, and capital of British East Africa, situated on the N. side of a small island, 3 miles long and 2 miles from the mainland. The island is mentioned as early as 1331 and was visited by Vasco da Gama in 1497. It was occupied by the Portuguese in 1529. It has a considerable trade in ivory, gums, and produce. Population, 15,000. Station of the CMS (1844), with (1903) 4 missionaries, 2 of them with their wives; 5 women missionaries, 7 native workers, 3 outstations, 137 professed Christians, 1 place of worship, 3 day schools, 1 dispensary, and 1 hospital.

MONASTIR: A town in Turkey in Europe, situated near the ruins of ancient Heraklia, 87 miles W. N. W. of Salonica. It is capital of the province of the same name and railway terminus. The name is derived by the Turks from a neighboring monastery. The Bulgarians call the place Bitoli and it is sometimes mentioned by English writers as Bitolia. Altitude 1,700 feet. Population, 50,000, of whom 20,000 are Muslims and 30,000 Christians of various creeds, and Jews. Station of the ABCFM (1873), with (1903) 1 missionary and his wife, 2 women missionaries, 9 native workers, 3 outstations, 3 places of worship, 3 Sunday schools, 3 day schools, 1 boarding school, and 79 professed Christians.

MONE. See MONGNAI.

MONGHYR: A town in Bengal, India, situated on the S. bank of the Ganges, 34 miles W. N. W. of Bhagalpur. In has manufactures of firearms and iron articles. Population (1891), 57,000, of whom 44,000 are Hindus and 12,000 are Muslims. Station of the BMS (1816), with (1903) 2 missionaries, 1 with his wife; 5 native workers, 1 outstation, 4 Sunday schools, 6 day schools, and 185 professed Christians, of whom 25 are communicants. Station also of the BZM (1870), with (1903) 2 women missionaries, 6 native workers, 1 Sunday school, 5 day schools.

MONGNAI: A town in Burma, British India, situated 175 miles S. E. of Mandalay. It is the chief town of the Shan States. Station of the ABMU (1892), with (1903) 2 missionaries with their wives, 1 woman missionary, 9 native workers, 1 outstation, 3 places of worship, 1 Sunday school, 1 day school, 1 dispensary, 1 hospital, and 60 professed Christians. The name is also written Mone.

MONGOLS: A term given to a large branch of the human family which has been designated Turanian by ethnologists. It comprises, in its proper limitations, the tribes of Buriats, Bashkirs, and Kalmucks, and, more widely, the Chinese, Indo-Chinese, Tibetans, Burmese, Siamese, Japanese, Eskimos, Samoieds, Finns, Lapps, Turks, and Magyars. In very ancient times they formed the Median Empire in Chaldea, tho they are the characteristic nomadic people. Another offshoot settled in the plains of China at a remote period. To the Greeks the Mongols were known as Scythians, to the Romans as Huns. Under Genghis Khan, in the 13th century, they overran and conquered the greater part of Asia, and Russia and Hungary in Europe. It should be noted, however, that the Turks weighed for much in this irruption of Genghiz. The Mongols proper are divided into three branches: the East Mongols, the West Mongols, and the Buriats. Of the East Mongols the Khalkas inhabit the region north of the Gobi, the Shara Mongols are found south of the Gobi along the Great Wall, and the Shairagut are found in Tangut and North Tibet. The West Mongols are found in Kokonor, Kansuh, on the eastern slope of the Thianshan Mountains, and many of them under the name of Kalmucks are under the rule of Russia. The Buriats are in the Russian province of Irkutsk, around Lake Baikal.

The original Mongols are thus described by Dr. Latham: "Face broad and flat; the cheekbones stand out laterally and the nasal bones are depressed. The eyes are oblique; the distance between them is great, and the carunculæ are concealed. The iris is dark, the cornea yellow. The eyebrows form a low and imperfect arch, black and scanty. The complexion is tawny, the stature low. The ears are large, standing out from the head; the lips thick and fleshy, forehead low and flat, and the hair lank and thin." In the more civilized nations of Mongol origin these original characteristics have been modified. In the western Turks, for example, one seeks Mongol features in vain.

MONGOLIA: The land of the Mongols is a vast part of the empire of China, lying in the interior of Asia, comprising 1,300,000 square miles of territory between latitude 37° and 54° north and longitude 85° and 125° east. On the north it is bounded by Siberia, on the east by Manchuria, on the south by China proper, and on the west by East Turkestan and Jungaria. Its population is estimated at 2,500,000, one-fifth of whom are Chinese. A high plateau, 3,000 feet above sea-level, occupies the greater part of the region. In the center is the Desert of Gobi, where sand and stones, dust in summer and snow in winter, render habitation unbearable. The northern part is occupied by ranges of mountains forming part of the Altai chain. On its slopes rise the Selenga, the Kerlow, and Onon, which form the Amoor. In the south are rich meadowlands, which afford food for cattle. Chinese have introduced agriculture to some extent. Mountain ranges are again found on the west. On the east is a strip of fertile land. On the southeast of the desert of Gobi is the mountain range of Alashan, which reaches in some places the height of 15,000 feet above the sea. Along its hills pasture-land is found. The climate is in general cold, subject to sudden changes, and in summer intolerably hot. With the exception of the work of the early representatives of the LMS, who labored in the north, the southern portion of Mongolia has been practically the only field occupied by Protestant missionaries. The ABCFM is the most prominent force on the field.

Gilmour (J.), *Among the Mongols*. New York, 1883: *More About the Mongols*, New York, 1893.

MONGOLIAN LANGUAGES: A family of languages of a low order of development spoken by various peoples and tribes in the northern parts of Asia, and deemed by many sufficiently described by the term Turanian languages. They certainly have the Turanian peculiarity of never obscuring the root, of vowel euphony, and of making words by agglutination. But on the other hand, their structure is so rudimentary that this test hardly applies unless the term Turanian is taken in the wide sense of non-Aryan. The language of the people of Chinese Mongolia, of the Khalkas of the Gobi desert, that of Manchuria to some extent, and that of the Buriats of Siberia, and the Kalmucks of Eastern Russia, is all Mongolian in character. Recent investigations seem to point to a closer relation between the Mongol and Turkish languages than has been commonly known; but the subject is not clearly defined, and it is safer to rate the Mongolian and Turkish languages as distinct until the relation certainly existing between them has been more accurately defined. In general literature great confusion has been produced by the use of the term Mongol for any of the languages spoken by nomads in Siberia and Mongolia. There is a literary Mongolian which is written with characters peculiar to itself, of which the Manchu characters are the most fully developed form. These Mongolian characters are placed in perpendicular lines, under the powerful Chinese influence. But nevertheless they are a monument which has endured more than a thousand years to the Christian missionary spirit, being based on the Syriac alphabet taught by ancient Nestorian missionaries to these wanderers of northeastern Asia.

MONKULLO: A settlement on the mainland N. of Massaua, Eritrea, Africa. Station of the Swedish National Evangelical Mission Society (1877), with (1900) 1 missionary, 1 native worker, 1 outstation, 1 place of worship, 1 day school, and 4 professed Christians.

MONROVIA: A town, capital of Liberia, Africa, situated on the Mesurado River near the coast. Population, 4,000. Station of the African Methodist Episcopal Mission Society. Station also of the ME (1833), with (1903) 6 missionaries, 4 of them with their wives; 1 woman missionary, 21 native workers, 12 outstations, 13 Sunday schools, 1 printing house, 1 boarding school, 1 college, and 1,357 professed Christians. Station also of the PE (1853), with (1903) 4 native workers, 2 outstations, 3 places of worship, 2 Sunday schools, 1 day school, 1 boarding school, and 178 professed Christians.

MONSEMBE: A settlement in the Congo Free State, Africa, situated about 100 miles N. by E. of Equatorville on the Congo River. Station of the BMS (1891), with (1903) 4 missionaries, 3 of them with their wives; 12 native workers, 1 outstation, 14 professed Christians, 2 day schools and 1 dispensary. Society spells the name Monsembi.

MONSURAH. See MANSURA.

MONTEGO BAY: A village in Jamaica, West Indies, situated on the N. coast, 18 miles W. of Falmouth. Station of the West Indies Wesleyan Methodist Mission Conference, with (1903) 1 missionary.

MONTEMORELOS: A town in the State of Nueva Leon, Mexico, situated 52 miles S. E. of Monterey. Population, 10,000. Station of the American Baptist Home Missionary Society, with (1900) 1 missionary and his wife, 1 chapel, 2 Sunday schools, 1 day school, and 83 professed Christians. Station of the PS (1900), with (1903) 1 woman missionary and 1 native worker.

MONTENEGRO: An independent principality in the W. of the Balkan Peninsula. It is bordered on the east, south, and southeast by Turkey, on the north by Herzegovina. A narrow strip of Austrian territory separates it from the Adriatic on the west, excepting a seaboard of 28 miles in length on the Adriatic. The entire area is estimated at 3,630 square miles, with an extreme length of 100 miles and a width of 80. The population is estimated at 236,000.

The government is a limited monarchy, according to the constitution dating from 1852. The prince holds the executive authority, and practically the will of the prince is law.

The religion of the kingdom is that of the Greek Church, under the direct influence of the prince, who appoints the bishops. Nominally, Church and State are independent, but virtually not so. The number of adherents is 222,000; the Mohammedans number 10,000 and the Roman Catholics 4,000. Elementary education is compulsory and free, the government supporting the schools. In 1901, 4,000 male and 500 female pupils attended 96 elementary schools.

The Montenegrins are Slavs of the Servian stock, and have many noble characteristics. A dialect of the Servo-Illyrian Slavonic is the language spoken. Agriculture is the leading occupation of the people, and live-stock of all kinds are reared. There are no missionary societies at work in Montenegro.

MONTEREY: A town, the capital of the State of Nueva Leon, Mexico, situated 240 miles N. E. by N. of Zacatecas, on the San Juan River. It is surrounded by mountains and is the center of a silver mining district. It was founded in 1596. Altitude, 1,600 feet. Population, 50,000. Station of the American Baptist Home Missionary Society, with 3 women missionaries, 4 native workers, 3 outstations, 1 day school, 5 Sunday schools, and 215 professed Christians. Station also of the CWBM (1897), with (1903) 1 missionary and his wife, 2 women missionaries, 1 outstation, 15 professed Christians, 1 day school. Station also of the MES (1883), with (1903) 3 missionaries and their wives, 2 native workers, 6 outstations, 1 place of worship, 8 Sunday schools, 1 day school, 1 theological class, 1 hospital, 1 dispensary.

MONTEVIDEO: A seaport and the capital of Uruguay, South America, situated on the N. side of the Plata River, 120 miles E. by S. of Buenos Aires. One of the handsomest cities in South America, built on the seaward side of the bay, with good light system, broad streets, and good water. Exports live-stock, hides, and preserved meats. It was founded in 1726. Its climate is healthy and agreeable. Population (1892), 238,000, including many Italians, Spaniards, and French. Station of the ME, with (1903) 1 missionary and his wife, 2 women missionaries, 19 native workers, 3 outstations, 912 professed Christians, 5 places of worship, 14 Sunday schools, 1 day school, and 2 boarding schools. Also station of the Salvation Army.

MONTGOMERY: A town on the N. W. part of

Tobago Island, West Indies. Station of the Moravian Society (1827), with (1900) 1 missionary and his wife, 30 native workers, 1 place of worship, 3 Sunday schools, 4 day schools, and 610 professed Christians.

MONTGOMERY, Giles Foster: Born at Walden, Vermont, U. S. A., November 8, 1835; graduated at Middlebury College 1860; Lane Theological Seminary 1863; sailed as a missionary of the ABCFM, and reached Aintab, Turkey, December 23, 1863. He was sent to open a station at Marash. Three times he was driven away with fierce violence by the Armenians, and in 1895 he was almost killed. He was a good business man, a powerful preacher and unusually successful in influencing men. After fifteen years of labor at Marash he left it for Adana, two strong, self-supporting evangelical churches having been formed from the very men who had once sought his life in their blind outburst of furious bigotry. At Adana Mr. Montgomery's high qualities again made themselves felt in healing a breach in the church and stirring up the church members to Christian work. In 1887 a terrible famine threatened to decimate the population of Adana and the region round about. Mr. Montgomery appealed for aid to to Europe and America and devoted himself to its distribution, largely by means of relief works where those able to work could earn their bread. The tremendous strain of this work in the hot season was too much for him, and after a period of illness he died December 4, 1888. He had literally given up his life for the people of Adana, and all sects and denominations mourned by his grave.

MONTSERRAT: One of the Leeward Islands, West Indies, 10,083 inhabitants. Mission station of the Baptist Missionary Society (England); 3 missionaries, 2 native teachers, and 67 church members.

MONYWA: A town in Burma, on the left bank of the Chindwin River, 53 miles W. by N. of Mandalay. Population, 6,300. Station of the WMS, with (1903) 1 missionary, 21 native workers, 3 outstations, 1 place of worship, 2 Sunday schools, 6 day schools, and 37 professed Christians, of whom 28 are communicants.

MOOSE FACTORY: A post of the Hudson Bay Company, in Ontario, Canada, situated on the W. side of an estuary of the Moose River, Hudson Bay. It is the seat of the Bishopric of Moosonee. Station of the CMS (1851), with (1903) 1 missionary and his wife, 7 native workers, 3 outstations, 1 day school, and 350 professed Christians, of whom 35 are communicants.

MOOSEHIDE: A settlement in the Yukon Territory of Canada, close to Dawson City, in the Klondyke region. Station of the CMS (1897), with (1903) 1 missionary and his wife, 1 place of worship, 1 day school, and 81 professed Christians.

MORADABAD: A town in the United Provinces of India, and capital of the Moradabad District, situated 50 miles N. W. of Bareilly, on a ridge on the right bank of the Ramganga River. It has manufactures of fine metal work. Population (1901), 75,000, of whom 39,000 are Muslims and 31,000 are Hindus. Station of the ME, with (1903) 3 missionaries with their wives, 3 women missionaries, 294 native workers, 21 chapels, 178 Sunday schools, 105 day schools, 2 boarding schools, and 14,866 professed Christians, of whom 6,031 are communicants.

MORAR: A town in the State of Gwalior, Central India, situated on the Morar River, in an alluvial plain, 34 miles E. of Gwalior. Population (1891), 24,500, of whom 18,000 are Hindus. Station of the PN (1874), with (1903) 1 missionary and his wife and 1 native worker.

MORAVIAN HILL: A station of the Moravians in Cape Town, Cape Colony, South Africa, established in order to watch over the spiritual welfare of native Christians attracted to the city by hope of employment.

MORAVIAN MISSIONS (Missions of The Unitas Fratrum, or the Unity of Brethren, 1732): In 1722 Augustine and Jacob Neisser and their families, descendants of John Huss, followed Christian David to Saxony, where they founded the town of Herrnhut on the estate of Count Zinzendorf, who had offered them an asylum. Other descendants of the Brethren emigrated from Bohemia and Moravia, and joined them at Herrnhut. Count Zinzendorf became the leading Bishop of the resuscitated Moravian Church, and gradually came to devote his means as well as his time to the spread of the kingdom of Christ through the agency of the Brethren. He established on the continent of Europe, in Great Britain and in America exclusively Moravian settlements, from which the "world" was shut out, and in which was fostered the highest form of spiritual life. At the same time members of the Moravian body undertook extensive missions in heathen lands, established many schools for young people not of their communion, and began the so-called "Diaspora" Missions among members of the State churches of Europe. The exclusive system still continues in Germany in a modified form; in England, also, there are a few Moravian settlements, but the last vestige of it in America disappeared in 1856. The following year at a general synod held at Herrnhut, the constitution of the *Unitas Fratrum* was remodeled, the new development being completed at the General Synod of 1899. The Moravian Church now consists of four provinces, the German, the British, and the American, North and South, which are united as one body in regard to doctrine, ritual, discipline, and the work of foreign missions. Each province of the Moravian Church has a synod as its legislative body, composed of ministers and laymen, and an executive board elected by and responsible to it. The executive boards of the four provinces form the Directing Board of the Brethren's Unity. A General Synod, composed of elected delegates from the several provinces, and certain *ex officio* members, meets every ten years. In this synod the missions are also represented. It supervises the life, doctrines and activities of the entire Moravian Church, which forms one organic ecclesiastical body throughout the world. A Mission Board, composed of five members, three of whom are chosen from the German, British and American divisions of the Church, is elected by the General Synod, and is responsible to that body for its administration. This Mission Board appoints and directs missionaries and superintendents and has full charge of the finances. Subordinate officers are the treasurer of missions, at Herrnhut, Saxony; the secretaries of missions, in London, and America, and the various agents of missions in Germany, England and America, all of whom are appointed by the central body.

Associated with this Mission Board is the Financial Committee of the Missions, composed of four business men elected by the General Synod, one of whom is the Manager of the Financial Office of the Missions. All important financial measures, investments, etc., must go before this Committee before final action is taken by the Mission Board, which must be guided by them.

Finally, the General Synod, constituted of representatives of the entire Church and acting by commission of all its provinces, institutes a searching inquiry into the financial management and the entire administration of the affairs of the missions. It formulates and amends the regulations, determining the relations of the missionaries to the Board; reviews and revises the constitutions of the several mission provinces, determines the principles governing salaries, furloughs, retirements, pensions, and the education of missionaries' children, and indicates the general spirit in which the mission work shall be conducted. In the last resort, the missions stand directly under control of the General Synod, and therefore also of the entire Moravian Church, which may really be looked upon as an ecclesiastical missionary society. There are also several auxiliary organizations: *e. g.*, The Brethren's Society for the Furtherance of the Gospel, founded in 1741, in London, and constituted wholly of members of the Moravian Church, the British Provincial Elders being *ex officio* directors, provides for the current expenses of the mission in Labrador, in part by trade. The Society of the United Brethren for Propagating the Gospel among the Heathen was reorganized at Bethlehem, Pennsylvania, in 1787, the original association having been founded at Lancaster, Pennsylvania, in 1745. Chartered in 1788, its directors are the trustees of a fund bequeathed by Godfrey Haga of Philadelphia in 1825. The Provincial Elders of the American Moravian Church, North, are *ex officio* directors, and this society, with the aid of the American congregations, has assumed the financial support of the mission in Alaska, besides being specially obligated to aid the missions among the Indians of North America. The Brethren's Missionary Society of Zeist was established in 1793, and devotes its energies especially to the support of the enterprise in Surinam. The London Association in Aid of the Missions of the United Brethren occupies the unique position of a missionary evangelical alliance which devotes its entire income to the support of Moravian Missions. Established in 1817 by friends who sympathized with the Church in its embarrassment caused by losses sustained during the Napoleonic wars, it consists exclusively of members of other churches than the Moravian. During the decade preceding the General Synod of 1899, this association contributed $475,000. The Missionary Union of North Schleswig, founded in 1843, has rendered aid especially to missions in Danish colonies. Besides these, there are a number of Women's, Young Men's, and Juvenile societies, generally local in their membership.

Of these, two exercise administrative powers in accordance with agreements with the Mission Board, the Society for the Furtherance of the Gospel in London having charge of the Labrador work, and the Society for Propagating the Gospel in Bethlehem having charge of the Alaskan and Indian missions in North America.

Development of Mission Work: A memorable day of prayer and conference was held at Herrnhut on Ferbuary 10, 1728, when Zinzendorf and his brethren discussed the possibility of a forward movement. Distant lands were to be won for Christ—Turkey and Africa, Greenland and Lapland. "But it is impossible to find a way thither," it was objected. "The Lord can and will give grace and strength for this," was the reply of Zinzendorf. On the following morning twenty-six unmarried men came together, and solemnly declared themselves ready to go, at the call of the Lord. The missionary purpose was there, and already the Lord was preparing to use it. In July of the same year Zinzendorf returned from a visit to Copenhagen, accompanied by a negro from the West Indies, who described the great need of the slaves in the Islands to such purpose that two young men, Messrs. Dober and Leopold, offered to go to them as missionaries. At the same time the needs of assistance for the work of Hans Egede, a Danish Lutheran missionary in Greenland, were made known by two Eskimos, and two other young men, Messrs. Stach and Boehnisch, offered to go to his relief.

But Zinzendorf deemed it best to delay their departure that their fitness for these undertakings might be thoroughly tested. In August, 1832, Dober set out on foot from Herrnhut, accompanied by David Nitschman. With two ducats and three thaler as their capital they made the journey of several thousand miles to Copenhagen, whence they sailed on October 8, 1732, arriving at St. Thomas on December 13 of the same year. On April 10, 1732, Matthew and Christian Stach, cousins, and Christian David sailed from Copenhagen for Greenland, where they were warmly welcomed by Egede. About a mile distant from his colony they established their mission, which they called New Herrnhut. The following year the new mission was reenforced by the arrival of Frederick Boehnisch and John Beck.

Coincident with the preparation of the mission in Greenland, the attention of Zinzendorf and the Brethren had been called to the Laps, but their missionaries on setting out learned that a Danish mission had been begun among this people in Norway. Accordingly Andrew Grasmann, Daniel Schneider, and John Nitschman, Jr., spent the winter of 1734 in Stockholm, and in the spring went to Tornea, and thence inland, but finding the people under the nominal supervision of the State Church, they at once withdrew.

That same year arrangements were made with the Dutch Surinam Company by which the Brethren were allowed to settle in Surinam, and Messrs. Piesch, Berwig and Larish left Herrnhut March 7, 1735, their primary purpose being a preliminary tour with a view to a later settlement. This led to the founding of a mission which was placed on a permanent basis in 1745. During the years 1735 and 1738 work was begun among the Indians and negroes in the American colonies, a work directly linked with the founding of the Moravian Church in America. The call to the next undertaking came in 1736, for missionaries to work among the Hottentots in Cape Colony. As soon as the call reached Herrnhut, George Schmidt volunteered to go. Within a week he started for Holland to study Dutch before sailing.

He left for Cape Town on March 17, arriving on the 9th of July, 1737, and settled among the Hottentots on the Zondereind River, about 10 miles west of what is now Genadendal.

In 1737-38 Messrs. Grasmann, Schneider and Miksch attempted work among the Samoyedes and other heathen tribes on the Russian shores of the Arctic Ocean, but were arrested as Swedish spies, and after an imprisonment in solitary confinement were sent back to Germany with word that their services were not needed.

In 1739 Abraham Richter learned of the need of the slaves in Algeria, and was sent to them by the Church, arriving in Algiers in 1740, but in less than six months he died of the plague. At this time prospective missions in Ethiopia, on the Madras coast of India, in China, in Persia, in Canstantinople, and in Wallachia were discussed. A severe check was received when Russia's welcome to Lange, Hirschel and Kund, on their way to Mongolia and China, took the form of imprisonment. In 1747, almost coincident with the removal of their fetters, Messrs. Hocker and Rüffer went as missionaries to the Guebres in Eastern Persia, but found it impossible to penetrate beyond Ispahan; they learned, however, that most of the Guebres had been massacred or exiled, and so started on their return journey. Rüffer died on the way, but Hocker reached the home church in 1750, and, undeterred by what he had encountered, in 1752 he returned to Egypt with the intention of proceeding to the Copts of Abyssinia, but political disturbances prevented his going beyond Cairo. He made another effort in 1758, taking passage with one associate on an Arab vessel on the Red Sea. Wrecked on the Island of Hassani, the missionaries lost all their valuable medical supplies, and again the enterprise failed. Eight years later Hocker again sought Egypt, accompanied by Messrs. Danke and Antes. It was impossible to proceed to Abyssinia, but Danke pushed on to the Coptic settlement at Behnesa in Egypt, where he died in 1772. In 1782 Hocker also died, and the absolute inhibition of labor among the Mohammedans finally caused the abandonment of the enterprise.

In 1754 two members of the Church in England asked for missionaries to instruct their slaves on the Island of Jamaica, and, with two companions, Z. G. Caries volunteered for this service, leaving for the new field in October of that year. This year, 1754, distinctively termed "the colonial year" by the Moravian writers, was of significance also for the mission in Surinam, which had already had a beginning in the tour of exploration twenty years previous.

In 1760 Messrs. Volker and Butler, with eleven artisans, inaugurated the Moravian Tranquebar Mission, with the approval of the Danish Government. They purchased a tract of land in the vicinity of the town, and named the little settlement Brüdergarten. Scarcely had the little mission in Greenland begun to approach success than the Brethren turned their attention to Labrador, urged by the men working in the former country. The proposition was not approved by Zinzendorf, but in 1752 merchants who were members of the London congregation fitted out a ship for trade and colonization on the coast of Labrador, and in July of the same year the first four pioneer missionaries reached their destination, naming the bay in which they landed Nisbet's Haven, in honor of James Nisbet, an active promoter of the enterprise. Owing to the treachery of the natives, however, the mission was abandoned, and it was not until 1770 that it was finally established on a permanent basis.

In 1768, six Brethren were sent to establish a mission on the Nicobar Islands, more colonists joining them the following year, but owing to the mortality the colonial project was abandoned. In 1777 the work was extended to Serampur in Bengal, by invitation of the Danish Company, and seven years later a new station was opened at Patna. The whole mission proved so discouraging that in 1786 the Unity Elders' Conference sent a deputation to investigate its prospects, with the result that the mission at Patna was at once given up, the Nicobar Islands and Serampur were abandoned in 1788-1791, and four years later, in 1795, the Conference decided to withdraw entirely from the East Indies. A visit of two of the members of this deputation to Cape Town in 1787 led to the renewal of the mission in Cape Colony, which had been abandoned fifty years before, and in 1792 Messrs. Marsveld, Schwinn and Kuhnel were sent out to reestablish the station of Baviaans Kloof, now called Genadendal. In 1818 a new mission was established four hundred miles east of Cape Town, on the White River, for work among the Kaffirs, and in 1828 the first station in Kaffraria proper was established.

In 1847 Messrs. Pfeiffer and Reinke were sent on an exploring tour to the Mosquito coast of Central America, and reported so favorably that a mission was established in 1849, at Bluefields. In 1850 the pioneer Moravian missionaries arrived in Australia, and a station was opened in the Lake Boga District.

From almost the beginning of its missionary operations the Moravian Church, under the leadership of Count Zinzendorf, had looked toward Mongolia and the Chinese Empire, and on the suggestion of Dr. Gutzlaff it was decided to attempt an entrance from the west. In 1853 the pioneers reached the CMS station of Kotgarh, in the Punjab, and from that place as a base, in 1856, land was purchased near Kailang, in the valley of the Bhagar, in Lahul, where the headquarters of the Himalayan Mission to Tibet was established.

In 1865 a leper asylum was established at Jerusalem, by a German lady, and in 1867 the Moravians undertook its supervision. In 1878 the emigration of West Indian negroes to British Guiana, South America, led to the establishment of a mission in that colony. In 1885 a mission was permanently established in Western Alaska for the aborigines of the American continent. In 1887 the Moravian Church received an unexpected legacy, and about the same time an appeal from Mackay of Uganda for a Moravian Mission in Central Africa resulted, in 1891, in the sending out of four missionaries, who began work in the Konde Highlands of German East Africa, northwest of Lake Nyasa. In 1896 the Moravian Church took over the Urambo Mission of the LMS, thus becoming responsible for the evangelization of the western half of German East Africa, south of Lake Victoria Nyanza, and extending to Lake Tanganyika.

In 1900, in accordance with the desire of the Danish Government, the Moravian stations in Greenland were transferred to the care of the Danish Church, since the people being Christianized, actual missionary work there was a thing of the past.

The Missions: 1. *West Indies* (1732): The first two missionaries of the Moravian Church, Messrs. Dober and Nitschman, landed in St. Thomas, West Indies, December 13, 1732, after a long and perilous voyage from Copenhagen. For the first four months Nitschman supported his companion and himself by carpentering, but in April he returned to Europe, and Dober was in great straits, as he was obliged to labor for his support while attempting to work among the slaves. While on the one hand a letter from Anthony, the West Indian whom Zinzendorf had met in Copenhagen, had given him a ready welcome among the blacks, on the other hand he met with great opposition from the planters. In June, 1734, Tobias Leopold and seventeen others arrived, some of whom were to take up the work he had commenced, while others were to go to St. Croix to begin a second station on the estates of Count Pless, at his request. By the end of the following January eight of their number had died. In February eleven persons were sent to their aid, but the mortality continued, and by December 1, 1736, the last survivor from St. Croix returned to St. Thomas. The bitter opposition of the planters was increased, when in 1837, with the assistance of a friendly planter, an estate was purchased for the mission known as Posaunenberg, later New Herrnhut. In 1739 Count Zinzendorf visited the mission, and his personal representations, with petitions from influential friends, on his return home, practically secured religious liberty from the Danish crown. In 1740 the St. Croix Mission was reopened and the following year the work was extended to St. John Nisky, in St. Thomas, Friedensthal in St. Croix, and Bethany. In February of 1854 a station was opened in Jamaica at the request of Messrs. Foster and Barham, two wealthy planters, who gave a plot of ground for the new mission, which was called Carmel. Mr. Caries and his two companions, pioneers, were reenforced by other workers, and outposts were established at Bogue, Island, and Mesopotamia, three other plantations. In 1756 the missionaries on St. Thomas commissioned Samuel Isles to investigate Antigua as a prospective mission field. He was well received by the governor and planters, and his first convert was baptized the following year.

In 1765 Messrs. Wood and Rittmansberger were sent to open a mission in Barbados. Within a month of their landing at Bridgetown, Rittmansberger died of fever, and Wood, after struggling on alone for a year, abandoned the enterprise. The next year another missionary was sent out, only to die within a week of landing. In 1767 the work was undertaken by Mr. Brookshaw, who succeeded in enduring the climate and laying the foundation of the mission. Everywhere the negroes were ready to listen, and the work progressed rapidly in spite of some opposition on the part of the whites.

Tidings of the happy results of the mission in Antigua reached the neighboring island of St. Kitts, and the planters desired missionaries to teach their slaves. At the request of Mr. Gardiner, Messrs. Gottwalt and Birkby were sent to St. Kitts in 1777, and were kindly welcomed. In 1782 the gift of land on the island of St. John made possible the founding of a second station, which was called Emmaus.

The missionary work of the Moravians at Tobago dates from 1787, when Mr. and Mrs. Montgomery, after a visit to a planter named Hamilton, reported an open field, and commenced work in 1790. The work was interrupted by a fierce outbreak of soldiers and people against the Government and by a disastrous hurricane a month or two later. Before the end of the year Mrs. Montgomery died, and soon after Mr. Montgomery returned to Barbados, only to die. For eight years no attempt was made to reopen the mission, chiefly on account of uncertain political conditions.

During the ensuing years the Moravian Mission in the West Indies was intimately connected with the movement for the abolition of slavery. In May, 1792, the Danish King fixed a date for the slave trade to cease in the Danish possessions. At the same time repeated requests came from land owners on St. Thomas to the Unity Elders' Conference that the Brethren should assume the religious and civil education of the children of slaves. The work was greatly hindered by droughts followed by sickness; and the mission premises at St. Thomas and St. John were devastated by a tornado in 1793. But in spite of these adverse circumstances the work everywhere prospered. In 1801 St. Thomas surrendered to the British and the other Danish Islands speedily did likewise. During the next years new stations were occupied and a widening of educational activities characterized the work. On the Danish Islands, on December 24, 1830, the work of the Brethren was put on an equal footing with that of the State Church. At the close of 1834, after a little more than a hundred years of labor, the missions on the Danish Islands numbered 10,321 members; St. Thomas 1,998, St. Croix 6,682, St. John 1,641. That same year, by an act of Parliament, slavery was prohibited throughout the British colonies. The connection of the missions with trade for the support of the work was gradually dropped. A system of education was established by the Government, and in 1839 Governor-General Van Scholten, at the instance of the King of Denmark, visited Herrnhut and laid before the authorities of the church his plan for elementary schools, proposing that a beginning be made at St. Croix, and that the mission supply the teachers, while the Government erect the buildings and aid financially. In 1841 the first school was opened on Great Princess Plantation; others were established on the island of St. John, and in 1847 the system was extended to St. Thomas. The same year a normal school was established in Antigua, a similar one being already in operation at Fairfield, Jamaica. In 1854 a training institution for women teachers was established at St. Johns, in Antigua. In 1856 the ordination of John Buckley as a deacon at St. Johns marked an important step in West Indian development, for with him began the line of Moravian ministers of African blood.

In 1863 a General Conference was convened at St. Thomas, when self-support, a native agency, local management, and education were discussed. Jamaica fell into line except for the outlay for buildings and the traveling expenses of missionaries. The Danish Islands, with St. Kitts and Tobago, were to have a gradually decreasing grant for a decade, in the hope that in the interval local resources might attain a sufficient development. Antigua and Barbados were unable at once to make the change.

But such happy anticipations were interrupted. Cholera, yellow fever and a hurricane compelled the missionaries to turn their houses into hospitals. In spite of these reverses, however, the work went steadily on, and in 1869 steps were taken for the gradual emergence of the West Indian congregations from the status of missions, so that they might be made a fourth federated province of the Brethren's Unity. Earthquakes and tornados of repeated occurrence involved losses from which it has taken years to recover. One important measure was the founding of a theological seminary at Fairfield, in Jamaica, in 1876. In 1879 a conference of ministers and delegates met at Nisky, St. Thomas, to take steps preparatory to carrying out the legislation of the General Synod, and which should prepare the way for provincial autonomy. At this time it was decided to divide the work into two provinces. General mission conferences were appointed in both missionary provinces for every five years, at which time three executive members were to be chosen. In each case the election of these executive members must be approved by the Board of Missions. At this time a second theological seminary was opened in St. Thomas.

In 1884 the church in Jamaica was recognized as a body corporate, title to the mission property being vested in the Provincial Conference of the island together with the President of the British Provincial Elders' Conference and the Mission Secretary in London. This year the one hundred and fiftieth anniversary of Moravian missions in the Eastern islands was commemorated by the erection of a memorial church at St. Thomas. In 1899 the two provinces were granted practical independence with certain restrictions. A fixed annual grant, normally of $3,500, was to be allowed each province for ten years, together with certain specific donations. The cost of maintaining one theological seminary on the islands, and the expenses of the foreign Brethren then in the field, were to be borne by the Mission Board. Foreign missionaries thereafter appointed were to receive one-half their expenses from the Board and the other half from the province. Since then Jamaica has averaged contributions amounting to $41,184, and has drawn from the general treasury $2,534; the Eastern division averaged $40,109 each year, and required aid amounting to $3,552. There are (1903) 45 stations and 23 outstations, 86 European and American missionaries, 813 native helpers, 40,107 church members, 108 day schools with 23,368 pupils, 3 other schools with 34 students.

2. *Dutch Guiana* (1735): Arrangements having been made with the Dutch Surinam Company for the Brethren to settle in that country, a preliminary tour was made in 1735 by Messrs. Piesch, Berwig and Larisch. Arrawak, Warrau, and other Indian tribes, free Bush negroes, and negro slaves made up the bulk of the population, while the country was as unprepossessing as its inhabitants. After the exploring party returned in 1738 Messrs. Daehne and Gültner were sent out by invitation of a planter on the Berbice River. They established Pilgerhut, about one hundred miles inland; the following year work was begun at Paramaribo, but such was the hostility that the missionaries removed to a small plantation on the Cottica, where they remained till 1745, when this was also given up and the working force returned to Pilgerhut, where in 1748 the first convert was baptized. In 1754 the good will of the authorities at Paramaribo was secured, and permission was given for the founding of mission colonies. In 1756 Sharon on the Saramacca, and Ephraim on the Corentyne, were successfully established for work among the Indians. Repeated wars, the nomadic tendency of the tribes and their proneness to intoxication caused the work to progress but slowly. In 1761 and 1763 the Bush negroes rose in rebellion and threatened the extinction of the Indian missions. In 1766 work was begun among these Bush negroes. Slowly a congregation was gathered, and in 1773 a settlement was formed at Bambey, in the interior. In 1776 the first convert was won at Paramaribo, and in 1778 the first church was built. In 1785 the Government offered the mission a tract of land, and Sommelsdyk was established. In 1793 permanency was given to the mission by the formation in Zeist, Holland, of the *Zendinggenootschap der Broedergemeente*, for the special support of the Brethren's work in the Dutch Colonies. The same year the mission at Hope, on the Corentyne, was removed to a more fertile spot on Aulibissi Creek; industrial work was vigorously inaugurated, and before long a mission boat was regularly used to carry produce to Berbice. In 1806 Hope suffered from a disastrous fire, and later the indifference of the Indians led the missionaries to turn to the slaves on the plantations. The opposition of the planters closed two stations. But new estates began to be thrown open—by 1826 six, thirteen during the following year, and ninety within a decade. In 1828 the Dutch Society for the Promotion of Christian Knowledge among the Negroes of Surinam was founded. The spiritual care of prisoners and slaves in the forts of New Amsterdam, at Paramaribo, and the suburb of Combe was transferred to the Brethren. The mission made marvelously rapid strides. Station was added to station—Worsteling Jacobs in 1838, Salem in 1840, Beekhuizen in 1843, Rust-en-Werk in 1844. Liliendal became an independent station with the consecration of its church in 1848; Annaszorg was made a center for work among the plantations on the Warappa and Mattapica creeks in 1853. In 1855 Catharina Sophia on the Saramacca; Heerendyk in 1856. The first attempt to train negro lads for teachers was made in 1844, and in 1851 a normal school was successfully established at Beekhuizen. In 1856 the Government placed in the care of the Brethren the non-Catholic inmates of the leper hospital at Batavia. Then followed Beersheba, Waterloo and Clevia. In 1861 John King was baptized at Paramaribo, and returned to Maripostoon to do evangelistic work among his own people, and from this beginning he made long evangelistic tours in all parts of Surinam. In 1863 the slaves of Surinam were emancipated, each ex-slave being required to declare himself either a Jew or a Christian to obtain the royal favor.

Education now became a marked feature of the Moravian missions; in 1866 the normal school was transferred to the capital, and supplied well qualified teachers. In 1875 a primary school was also established in the capital. In 1882 Rust-en-Vrede was established, and Wanika in 1886. At this period the "native helpers" began a movement for a higher standard of discipline, and in 1893 the colonial government materially aided the mission by altering the laws which had impeded true marriages of the negroes. The work spread among the Bush negroes of the interior, tho it was impossible for a white man to permanently endure the climate. In 1891 the first Chinese helper was appointed for work among the immigrant Asiatic heathen; in 1897 a missionary and two deaconesses were appointed to work among the Protestants in the leper hospital at Groot Chatillon.

In June, 1902, the first native pastor was ordained, and in November of the same year the foundation-stone of the training institution for native workers was laid at Paramaribo. There are (1903) 18 stations and 25 outstations, 93 European and American missionaries, and 364 native helpers, 29,200 church members, 27 day schools with 2,896 pupils, 1 training school with 6 students.

4. *South Africa* (1737): The first Moravian missionary, George Schmidt, arrived in Cape Town in July, 1737, and located among the Hottentots on the Zondereind River; but the following year the mission was transferred to Baviaanskloof (Genadendal), where in 1742 the first convert was baptized. The following year Schmidt was summoned to Holland to report as to the validity of his proceedings, and was not allowed to return. In 1748 John Martin Schwälber volunteered to take up the work at his own expense, and remained at Baviaans-kloof till 1756, when he died during an epidemic. In 1789 Bishop Reichel visited Cape Colony, and advised that another attempt be made. Accordingly in 1792 two men were sent out, and the Government donated the place where Schmidt had labored for the new mission premises. In March a school was commenced, and industrial work was begun. But the Boers saw with alarm the improvement of the people under the instruction of the Moravians, and even the friendly inspector yielded to the opposition. The Moravians must withdraw to the Bush country. In 1794 no native was allowed to settle at Baviaanskloof without written permission from a Boer. Then a paper was circulated demanding the expulsion of the missionaries and the enslavement of the Hottentots and Bushmen. A climax was reached in 1795 when the British fleet took possession of Cape Colony, and the missionaries were assured protection. Then the mission grew apace. In 1800, after the restoration of the Colony to Holland, the name of the station was changed to Genadendal, at the suggestion of the Dutch governor, who was impressed by the improved condition of negro converts. In 1808, two years after the Colony had again become a British possession, a new station was established at Groenenkloof (Mamre), forty miles north of Cape Town. In 1815 a third center was established at Enon, as a basis of work among the Kaffirs, but owing to the violence of the latter the place was abandoned in 1819. In 1823 the Government hospital for lepers at Hemel-en-Aarde came under the care of the Moravians; the following year Elim was established about forty miles southeast of Genadendal. In 1828 Shiloh in Kaffraria was occupied, and early the next year the first converts were baptized. In 1834 slavery was abolished, and a remarkable revival occurred at Genadendal. In 1838 the corner-stone for a training school for Hottentots was laid, and opened the following year with nine students. In 1839 the work was extended to some fugitive Kaffirs at Zitzikamma, where in 1840 a great awakening took place. Extension became the order of the day, and in 1845 a missionary society was organized at Genadendal; in spite of frequent wars and famine new stations were established. In 1858 the work was extended to the Piquetberg range, near St. Helena Bay, eighty miles north of Cape Town, in the valley of Goedverwacht, but the uncertain tenure of the land decided the purchase of the neighboring farm of Wittewater as the center of operations. During the next years the printing press came to the front. Missionary periodicals and other literature were published.

The gradual advance into Kaffraria gave special importance to a conference of missionaries engaged in the eastern group of stations, held at Shiloh in 1863, a first step in the direction of a separation into a distinct missionary province. In 1867 the Moravian missionaries withdrew from the oversight of the leper hospital, which had been removed to Robben Island, and it passed into the care of the Anglican Church.

In accordance with the resolution of the synod in 1869, the South African Mission was divided into the Eastern and Western Provinces. In the Western Province special attention was paid to the normal school at Genadendal. Mamre, distinguished as the point of extension in the Western Province through its sub-station, Johanneskerk or Pella, enjoyed a deepening of its religious life, and a revival at Elim in 1876 gave promise of a bright future. The churches at Enon and Clarkson were enlarged and new schools established at Mamre and Elim, without drawing on the mission treasury.

In the Eastern Province the extension of labor among the "red" Kaffirs called forth all energy. In independent Kaffraria, Baziya formed a vantage point for the extension of the work. In 1870 a mission was established among the Hlubis at Emtumasi. By August, 1873, there were thirteen converts; outstations were soon required. The following year, by the request of a chief, Entwanazana was founded on the Umtana River. But now perplexities thickened. The mission was refused a grant of land at Emtumasi. Moreover, the natives persisted in regarding the work of the missionaries from a tribal standpoint. Then came a Kaffir uprising against the British rule. But in the meantime the older stations in the Eastern Province were taking a more distinctively Christian character.

In 1887 a theological department was added to the normal school at Genadendal. The Kaffir mission, embracing the three older posts in the Colony proper, Shiloh, Goshen and Engotini, with the two widely separated groups in Tembuland and East Griqualand, experienced fluctuations, tho on the whole expansion prevailed. In both provinces of the South Africa field difficulties arose in relation to the title to the stations and mission property. Negotiations began with a view to secure a permanent decision in the Colonial Parliament, and in 1888 seemed favorable to the mission. Both Provinces advanced steadily toward self-support. In 1896 a training school for native teachers was established at Muenyane, in the Eastern Province. A theological seminary was also established in Kaffraria. In 1902 the mission Board was directed by the General Synod to make appropriations for the Western Province only in case of extraordinary need. The great work of the missionaries is firmly to establish the congregations and make them self-supporting. There are (1903) 22 stations and 26 outstations, 86 European and American missionaries, with 483 native helpers, 16,645 church members, 54 day schools with 3,867 pupils, 2 training schools with 30 students.

5. *Labrador* (1770): In the fall of 1751 Messrs. Stach and Drachart, of the Moravian Mission in Greenland, urged a similar mission in Labrador, and suggested that trade be combined with evangelization. Zinzendorf did not favor the proposition, but members of the London congregation took it up, and in 1752 fitted out a ship for trade and possible colonization on the coast of Labrador, James Nisbet promoting the scheme. Erhardt and other Brethren took passage in her, and on July 31 reached their destination, which they called Nisbet's Haven. Here four prospective missionaries landed and prepared to build a house, calling it Hopedale, while Erhardt sailed northward, but with his companions was murdered by the natives, and the captain of the schooner persuaded the Brethren at Hopedale to abandon their enterprise. In 1764 a second attempt was made by Jens Haven, and the following year, accompanied by Drachart, they made a tour of exploration, going some distance into the interior. In the autumn of 1767 turmoil in Labrador itself hastened the founding of the mission, and in May, 1769, an order of Privy Council with royal approval sanctioned the undertaking and granted to the resuscitated Society for the Furtherance of the Gospel, which had been founded in London in 1741 by Spangenberg, one hundred thousand acres of land on the coast of Labrador. In March, 1770, a small brig, the "Jersey Packet," was purchased, and on May 5 of the same year the missionary party sailed for Labrador, arriving the 10th of August, and locating about 180 miles north of Hopedale. Friendly relations with the natives were soon established and the new station was called Nain. In 1773 the founding of two additional stations was sanctioned by the Unity Elders' Conference. The following year a tour of exploration was made northward, which resulted in the occupation of Okkak, 150 miles north of Nain, in 1775. In 1782 Hopedale was reestablished. At first the outlook was most discouraging, owing to the influence of European traders, but in 1804 an awakening began and by 1818 six hundred people were gathered around the mission stations. During 1836-1837 a famine raged at Nain, Okkak, and the newly organized station of Hebron, and the missionaries strained every nerve to help their people. During the next twenty years occasional tours were made and preaching services held in various parts of Labrador, but the main efforts of the missionaries were spent in strengthening the existing missions. In 1864 the station of Zoar was founded, to the south of Nain. In 1865 an orphanage was established at Okkak. Two years later another attempt was made to explore the country, and attempts were made to establish stations at Saeglek, Nachwak and Nullatatok Bay, but in each case the Hudson Bay Company interfered and the missionaries withdrew. In 1871 a second and successful attempt was made at Nullatatok Bay, the new station being called Ramah. From the beginning the Labrador mission had carried on trade with the natives in connection with the regular missionary work, but the difficulties inevitable to a mingling of the two led to a complete separation between the spiritual and temporal administration in 1866, and this separation was continued till 1876, when a partial return to the old basis was made, but the perplexities it entailed seriously handicapped the missions. In 1893 Zoar was abandoned, and in 1896 Makkovik was founded, south of Hopedale, and arrangements were made for another station at Rigolette, still further south. There are (1903) 6 stations, 38 European and American missionaries, 38 native helpers, 1,273 church members and 6 day schools with 242 pupils.

6. *Mosquito Coast* (1847): At the request of Prince Schönberg-Waldenberg the Moravian Church commissioned Messrs. Pfeiffer and Reinke of the Jamaica Mission to make a tour of exploration in Central America. Proceeding via Greytown they reached Bluefields in May, 1847. The "king" urged them to establish a mission, offering land for it in Bluefields. The Germans desired stated services in their language and the British Consul promised hearty cooperation. The new mission was inaugurated in March, 1849, and in 1853 the first convert was baptized. In 1855 a new station was established at Pearl Key lagoon, called Magdala, and two years later a church was built at Rama Key. In 1858 the work was greatly helped by the gift of a small schooner from friends at Zeist. Two years later Ephrata was founded at Waunta Hallorn. In addition to this new undertaking, Joppa was established in Corn Island among the negro population. In 1864 Bethania, at Tasbapauni, was made an independent station. The following year a terrific hurricane devasted the Mosquito coast; everywhere the missions suffered, but deep sympathy led to larger gifts from the homeland, and the missionaries were enabled, to some extent, to rebuild and start afresh. In 1871 it became necessary to abandon Joppa, on Corn Island, chiefly because of the lack of men. In 1875 a gift was received for the establishing of Karata, on the Wawa River, and another outstation was established at Kukallaya, some distance inland. In 1876 the missions again suffered from the violence of a hurricane, Bluefields, Rama, Magdala and Bethany suffering severely. In May, 1881, an awakening began in Magdala, which spread to all the surrounding villages, as well as to the other stations of the mission. Indians, Negroes, Creoles and Spaniards were alike aroused; several hundred heathen asked for instruction and baptism; chapels were erected in buildings not regularly occupied, and three outstations were added. In 1888 the translation of the New Testament into the Mosquito-Indian tongue was completed and printed at the expense of the Herrnhut Bible Society. The year 1894 was critical in the extreme for the Mosquito Mission, when the Reserve was wholly incorporated into the Nicaragua Republic. Business was unsettled, the regulations altered, and the expenses of the mission materially increased. Nevertheless, there was a steady advance, the number of stations and outstations being increased by five, and the membership by nearly two thousand.

There are (1903) 16 stations and 11 outstations, 34 European and American missionaries, 99 native helpers, 5,433 church members, and 9 day schools with 319 pupils.

7. *Australia* (1849): The aborigines of Australia claimed the attention of the church in the years following the synod of 1848. In Herrnhut, Niesky and other German congregations, Australian associations had been formed, looking

toward a future mission. Messrs. Täger and Spieseke were sent out as pioneers, arriving in Melbourne February 25, 1850, where they were cordially welcomed by the Lieutenant-Governor. To his influence mainly was due the favorable negotiations for land, and the establishment of the missionaries in their new home in the "Mallee" or scrub.

Permanent work was begun in October, 1851, on a reserve in the Lake Boga District. In 1856 the missionary superintendent abandoned the field, without consulting the authorities at home, being in poor health and tried by the rush of gold diggers into the district and the resulting difficulties. The Conference condemned this hasty action, and two years later the Moravian missionaries were again in the field, and decided to locate in the Wimmera District, near Antwerp, a station belonging to Mr. Ellerman, who gave land for the new mission and aided in every possible manner. The new site was called Ebenezer. In 1860 the first convert was baptized, and from that time the progress was rapid. This success led the Presbyterian Assembly of Australia to offer to supply funds for another station, if the Moravians would undertake the work. On a reserve near Lake Wellington, and on the banks of the Avon, the new post was founded in 1863, and called Ramahyuk. Here the first convert was baptized in 1866. A vigorous school soon came into existence. A third station was attempted near Cooper's Creek, in the wilderness, 800 miles north of Ebenezer, in 1866, and at Yorke's Peninsula, about 100 miles west of Adelaide, but after varying success both stations were abandoned. At Ebenezer and Ramahyuk industrial work proved a help to the mission. In 1876 an orphanage was established at Ramahyuk, in charge of native Christians.

There are (1903) 4 stations, 12 European and American missionaries, 106 church members, 3 day schools with 172 pupils.

8. *West Himalaya* (1853): When on a visit to Herrnhut, in 1850, Dr. Gutzlaff, of China, persuaded the Moravians to try and enter the Chinese Empire from the west. Messrs. Pagell and Heyde were selected for the new undertaking, arriving in Calcutta in November, 1863; their first destination was Kotgarh, where some time was spent in linguistic study under a Tibetan lama. In April, 1855, they made an investigating tour; at Leh, in Ladak, they were most unwelcome, nor was the prospect brighter in Chinese territory. The following winter was spent in Kotgarh, and the first station was founded among the Tibetan-speaking Buddhists of Lahul, as near as possible to the frontier of Chinese Tibet. Land was secured in 1856 in the valley of Bhagar, sixty miles from the border, near Kailang. Before winter the mission house was completed—a solitary outpost of Christianity amid the Western Himalayas, over against the fortress of the Dalai Lama. Early in 1857 the future leader of the new mission, **Mr. H. A. Jaeschke**, arrived, and a new stage of work began. In 1859 a printing press was established, and Jaeschke began to distribute broadcast his translation of the Harmony of the Gospels. In 1865 a second station was established at Poo, in Kunawar, nearer to the border which they wished to cross. That year the first convert was baptized. Meantime, an unexpected opening came. Smallpox was making fearful ravages in Chinese Tibet. In their extremity the people of Tso-tso sent to Pagell to stay the scourge by vaccination; but, his work being accomplished, he was forced to return to Poo, where a second convert was baptized in 1868. At Kailang also a few others were added to the little church, and indifferent tolerance on the part of the natives changed to bitter hostility. In 1872 an ex-lama from Lhassa was baptized, and in 1876 the conversion of a Mohammedan teacher in the school at Kailang was followed by the conversion of five of his pupils. Mission tours were frequently made, and large numbers of tracts and parts of the New Testament were distributed.

In hope against hope the mission was continued. In 1886 a station was established in Leh, the capital of Ladak, an important town near the western border of Tibet, permission being granted when a medical missionary was sent to care for the hospital and dispensary in the city. Two years later, in 1888, a church was dedicated. In the meantime the entire New Testament had been printed in Tibetan, and the Old Testament was well under way. During the closing years of the century occasional gleams of hope were manifest; new outposts were established at Chot and Gui, near Kailang, and at Scheh, near Leh. In the schools some few of the senior students were taking theological studies, the work of the native assistants holding hope for the future.

There are (1903) 6 stations and 1 outstation, 22 European and American missionaries, 9 native helpers, 110 church members, 10 day schools with 266 pupils, 1 training school.

9. *British Guiana* (1878): The migration of West Indians to Demerara caused an extension of the work to this South American colony. The proprietor of the Bel Air estate offered to provide the salaries of a missionary and an assistant who should teach school, for five years. The offer was accepted, and in November of 1878 work was begun at Cummings Lodge. The following year, Mr. Quintin Hogg, the proprietor, asked that a missionary be sent to the Reliance Plantation, near the Essequibo, and Mr. Pilgrim was sent to open the work in April, 1879. In 1882 a further extension followed, when fifty-seven people who had left the Congregational Church at Beterverwachtung asked to be taken into the Brethren's Church, and regarded as constituting an outstation of Graham's Hall. Both these stations grew rapidly in numbers, while Reliance was abandoned, the work not proving successful. At the end of 1884 the proprietor gave notice that he would be unable as largely to sustain the work in Demerara as heretofore. In 1896 a new beginning was made at Georgetown and an attempt was made to work among the coolies and Chinese, who were pressing into the colony. In 1902 land was purchased and a church and parsonage erected in the Queenstown ward of the City of Georgetown.

There are (1903) 2 stations and 1 outstation, 29 native missionaries, 912 church members, 2 day schools with 203 pupils.

10. *German East Africa* (1890): This mission originated in the receipt of a large legacy, and an appeal from Mackay of Uganda, conjointly with Bishop Parker of Equatorial Africa. The directors of the East Africa Colonial Company in Berlin promised cooperation. Accordingly, in the spring of 1890, Messrs. Meyer, Richard, Martin, and Häfner set out for the country north of Lake Nyasa. Martin's grave paved the way for the advance at Kararamuka, but Rungwa

was founded among the Konde people in August. Rutenganio and Ipiana were established in 1894, and Utengula, among the Safuas and Sangos, in 1895.

There are (1903) 10 stations and 1 outstation, 41 European and American missionaries, 63 native helpers, 9 day schools with 562 pupils.

11. *Southern California* (1890): The destitute condition of the mission Indians, former protegés of the Roman Catholics, appealed to the Woman's National Indian Association, who applied to the Moravian Church, and Mr. Weinland was sent to open work among them. He established at Potrero the "Ramona Mission," and in 1896 Martinez, in the desert, was occupied. Other stations have since been established at Rincon and La Jolla, and an outstation at Yuma, in Arizona.

12. *Alaska* (1885): At the annual meeting of the Society for Propagating the Gospel Among the Heathen, held at Bethlehem, Pa., in 1883, an appeal came from Dr. Sheldon Jackson that the Moravians establish a mission among the Indians and Eskimos in Alaska. Messrs. Weinland and Hortmann were commissioned to make an exploring tour, arriving in Unalaska in May, 1884, and thence proceeded across Bering Sea to the mouth of the Nushagak. Passing on to the Kuskokvim, they traveled up this river beyond Kolmakovsky. On returning to Bethlehem they recommended that a mission be established on the Kuskokvim River, about eighty miles from its mouth. In the spring of 1885 the pioneer band, consisting of Messrs. Weinland and Kilbuck and their wives, and Hans Torgersen, a carpenter, were en route to Bethel, as the new station was to be named. On June 19 they reached the Kuskokvim, but before their goods had all reached the mission Torgersen was drowned, and the two young and inexperienced couples were left alone to face the rigors of an Arctic winter; but they persevered and by October 10 had their house built and ready for habitation. In the summer of 1886 a second station was founded on the Nushagak River, near Fort Alexander, and named Carmel. During the ensuing two winters the stations were beset with hardships on every hand. But dawn was at hand. During Passion Week, 1888, the Moravians, in common with the Brethren throughout the world, held daily services. An awakening resulted, and in September the first converts, eight Eskimos, were baptized. The same year Mr. Weber was sent to the assistance of Mr. Kilbuck, Mr. Weinland having been compelled to retire because of ill health. On the arrival of Weber, Kilbuck started for Carmel, to consult with the missionaries about the work, but after an absence of seventy-three days he returned home, more dead than alive, suffering from the extreme cold. During his absence his wife became seriously ill from overwork, and it seemed as tho she must give up the work. Both stations needed reenforcements, and a call was sent out for volunteers. Fully nineteen persons responded. In 1889 Mr. Schoechert was sent to Carmel, and Miss Delterer to Mrs. Kilbuck's assistance at Bethel, while Mrs. Bachman, with her youngest son, went to the latter station for a year. By 1899 the membership numbered 987. Ougavigamute was founded, eighty miles up the Kuskokvim from Bethel. The latter station had 6 outstations, Carmel 3, and Ougavigamute 2, while more than 20 natives rendered efficient service.

There are (1903) 3 stations, 18 European and American missionaries, 11 native helpers, 596 church members, 2 day schools with 51 pupils.

MORELIA: A town and the capital of the state of Michoacan, Mexico, situated 125 miles W. N. W. of Mexico City in a valley surrounded by high mountains. It has a fine aqueduct dating from 1788. Altitude, 6,400. Population, 30,000. It was formerly called Valladolid. Station of the SBC (1894), with (1903) 1 missionary and his wife, 6 native workers, 5 outstations, 2 places of worship, 2 Sunday schools and 112 professed Christians.

MORGENZON: A village in the Transvaal, South Africa, situated in Rustemburg district, 68 miles N. W. of Johannesburg. Station of the Hermannsburg Missionary Society (1876), with (1902) 2 missionaries with their wives, 1 boarding school. Society spells the name Morgensonne.

MORIAH: A town on the N. coast of Tobago, West Indies, in the eastern part of the island. Station of the Moravian Society (1842), with (1901) 1 missionary and his wife, 26 native workers, 1 place of worship, 2 Sunday schools, 2 day schools, and 522 professed Christians.

MORIJA: A village in Basutoland, South Africa, situated 83 miles N. N. E. of Aliwal North. Station of the Paris Evangelical Mission Society (1833), with (1903) 4 missionaries with their wives, 38 native workers, 17 outstations, 1 place of worship, 1 Sunday school, 16 day schools, 1 printing press, 1 college, and 2,029 professed Christians, of whom 1,379 are communicants.

MORIOKA: A town on the main island of Japan, situated 85 miles E. by S. of Aomori. Population, 23,000. Station of the RCA (1887), with (1903) 1 missionary and his wife, 1 native worker, 2 outstations, 1 place of worship, 1 Sunday school, and 79 professed Christians. Also station of the ME, with 1 native worker.

MORLEY: A railroad station in Alberta district, Canada, on the C. P. R. R., 882 miles W. of Winnipeg. Station of the Methodist Church in Canada (1873), with (1901) 1 missionary and his wife, 2 outstations, 1 place of worship, 1 boarding school and 302 professed Christians.

MOROCCO: A Mohammedan empire in the N. W. of Africa, bounded north and west by the Mediterranean and Atlantic, and east by a conventional line separating it from Algeria. It extends southward into the desert to a greater or less extent, according to the activity and power of the reigning Sultan. Its area can only be estimated and is probably for the most time as much as 220,000 square miles; the population, also very indeterminate from year to year, is perhaps 6,000,000. It consists of three states, subject to the Sultan-Sheriff: the kingdoms of Fez, in the north, Morocco in the southwest, and the oásis of Tafilet, besides several semi-independent tribal territories of the desert. The Atlas (Deren) range, from 4,000 to 13,000 feet, traverses the country from northeast to southwest. For the rest, the surface is occupied by rolling steppes diversified by mountain spurs, and merging into the lowlands of the Sahara and the Atlantic shores. The rainfall is greater than that of the other Mauritanian states, as also the number and size of the rivers, none of which, however, is capable of floating any but very light crafts. The flora is that of Southern Europe, most resembling that of Spain. The same may be said of the animals, except the lion, the panther, and the ostrich, not yet extinct in Morocco. The climate is mild, equable and very salubrious. The government is an Oriental despotism, cruel and barbarous, and the country is infested by lawless bands. There are no proper means of transportation in the interior, which is largely unknown to Europeans; agriculture is of the most primitive kind, and the rich resources of the country remain undeveloped. In Tangier there are about 5,000 Europeans and other Christian residents, engaged in trade for the most part, and, outside of Tangier, not 1,000 can be found in all of the rest of the empire.

The Berbers, original inhabitants of the country, form two-thirds of the population, and are divided into several groups, as the Kabyles of the north, the Shellahas of the southern slopes of the Upper Atlas range, the Haratins of the south. The Shellaha language is that most extensively spoken. Arabic is also largely diffused, especially in the north. The Arabs are called Moors in the towns, where they form the majority of the population. The Jews, still calling themselves "exiles from Castile," number over 100,000. They speak Spanish and to some extent Arabic. The negro population, pure and half-caste, are constantly recruited by the slave trade with the Sudan. Mohammedanism is the religion of the empire. Morocco ranks next to Arabia in the Muslim mind as an orthodox and noble country; and the Sultan-Sheriff is to the Western Mohammedans what the Turkish Sultan is to those of the East. There is great and conscientious intolerance toward all who are not of the state religion, and travel in the interior of the land is impossible for this reason.

Missions in Morocco have been addressed to the Jews in the main. The North Africa Mission, the Gospel Missionary Union, the Southern Morocco Mission, and the PB, however, are endeavoring to reach the Berbers and other classes of the population. Medical work is here found an especially effective means of access to the people. Nevertheless, little has been accomplished beyond what one missionary calls "gathering up the stones" preparatory to seeding the ground.

Amicis (E. de), *Morocco and its People* (translation), London, 1879; Hay (Si- J. D.), *Morocco and the Moors*, London, 1896; Grove (Lady), *Seventy-one Days Campaigning in Morocco*, London, 1902; Canal (J.), *Géographie Générale de Maroc* Paris, 1902.

MORRISON, John Hunter: Born in Wallkill Township, New York, June 29, 1806; graduated at Princeton College 1834, and Theological Seminary 1837; sailed for India as a missionary of the PN in 1838. He was stationed at Allahabad, Agra, and other places. He was characterized by great earnestness and boldness in the presentation of truth. On account of his fearlessness in dealing with men in that fanatical region, he was in mission circles styled "the lion of the Punjab." Yet no one was more affable than he, more genial in personal intercourse. Dr. Morrison's name should be cherished, since it was he who, after the Sepoy mutiny in 1857, proposed to the Lodiana Mission to call upon all Christians to observe an annual week of prayer for the conversion of the world. That one thought of this missionary in India has done more toward breaking down denominational reserve among Christians than any other influence in the 19th century. He died of cholera at Dehra Dun, September 16, 1881, aged seventy-six, and in the forty-fourth year of mission work.

MORRISON, Robert: Born at Morpeth, Northumberland, England, January 15, 1782, of humble Scotch parentage. He was an apprentice learning to make lasts and he studied while at work. At the age of fifteen he joined the Scotch Church. As early as 1801 he began the study of Latin, Hebrew and theology with the minister of Newcastle, and after fourteen months' study entered the Independent Theological Academy at Hoxton, to prepare for the ministry. Soon after his admission he decided to become a missionary to the heathen. In May, 1804, he was appointed the first missionary of the LMS to China, and he thus became the founder of Protestant missions in China. Entering the Mission College at Gosport, he spent two years not only in special preparatory studies, but also in acquiring Chinese. He sailed for China January 31, 1807, but the Chinese being hostile to the English on account of the opium difficulties, he was obliged to go via New York instead of going direct from London. Reaching Canton September 7, he adopted the Chinese dress, diet, and habits, but soon resumed his usual mode of life. An edict being issued about this time by the Chinese Government prohibiting the printing of religious books and the preaching of the Gospel, Mr. Morrison set himself at once to study the language and translate the Bible. His health having suffered from incessant study and too rigid economy, he left Canton for Macao, where he remained a year in consequence of political troubles which made residence in Canton unsafe. In 1809 he was offered the position of translator to the East India Company's factory at Canton. This at last secured for him a permanent residence in China, ready access to some of the people, and time for the translation of the Scriptures and preparation of his Chinese dictionary. He held this office to the day of his death—twenty-five years. To the end he had the confidence of the East India Company, and they advanced large sums at different times for the publication of his various works. Tho much occupied with office work, he found time for Bible translation and the preparation of religious books. In 1810 a revised and amended version of the Acts of the Apostles, based on his copy of the manuscript in the British Museum, was printed—the first portion of the Scriptures in Chinese printed by any Protestant missionary. In 1812 the Gospel of Luke was printed. Early in 1814 the whole of the New Testament was ready, and the East India Company furnished a press and materials, also a printer, to superintend its printing. In this year, seven years after his arrival in China, he baptized Tsai-A-Ko, the first Chinese convert to Protestant Christianity, a sincere believer, who continued stedfast in his faith till his death in 1818. In 1815 a Chinese grammar of 300 quarto pages, prepared in 1805, was printed at the Serampur press. In 1817 he published *A View of China for Philological Purposes*. In this year the University of Glasgow conferred upon him the degree of doctor of divinity. In 1818 the translation of the entire Bible was completed, in part with the aid of Dr. Milne, and was printed in

1821. This version is said to be too literal, and not idiomatic. But it was the first attempt, and the difficulties were enormous. He was convinced of the necessity of a thorough revision, and hoped to be able to revise the work. The Old Testament formed 21 volumes 12mo. His most laborious literary work was the Chinese dictionary, published in 1821 by the East India Company at an expense of £15,000. Neither the value and importance of this work nor its stupendous difficulty in that stage of the missionary enterprise can be overstated. In 1824, for the purpose of recruiting his health and awakening an interest in the mission, he visited England, where he spent two years. Everywhere he was received with distinction by civil and religious bodies. He had an audience with George IV., to whom he presented a copy of the Sacred Scriptures in Chinese. In 1826 he returned to China. Tho not vigorous, he continued his public labors for nine years more, devoting himself more than ever to the missionary work, preaching, translating and distributing printed works among the Chinese. He conducted religious services on the Sabbath, both in English and Chinese. In 1832 he writes: "I have been 25 years in China, and am now beginning to see the work prosper. By the press we have been able to scatter knowledge far and wide." He accompanied Lord Napier to Canton as interpreter in negotiating a treaty with the Chinese Government, and died there August 1, 1834. Among the good works of his life was his work with Dr. Milne in founding the Anglo-Chinese College at Malacca (now at Hongkong). For the buildings of this college he subscribed £1,000 and for its maintenance £100 each year.

Besides the works mentioned, he published *Horæ Sinicæ*, being translations from the popular literature of the Chinese, and *Chinese Miscellany*.

MORSI: A town in Berar, India, situated 31 miles N. E. by N. of Amraoti. Population, 7,000, of whom 5,700 are Hindus. Station of the Kurku Indian Hill Mission (1895), with (1902) 1 missionary and his wife.

MORTLOCK ISLANDS: A group of Micronesian coral islands included in the Carolines. They have been partly Christianized and the work there is under the supervision of the ABCFM station at Ruk, and the workers are in the main supported by the Hawaiian Evangelical Association. The largest island in the Mortlock group is Lukanor, where there are about 900 Christians. The Bible was translated into the Mortlock language in 1884 by missionaries of the ABCFM.

MOSCHI: A village in German East Africa, situated in Majagga region on the S. slopes of Mt. Kilima Njaro. Station of the Leipzig Mission Society (1896), with (1903) 4 missionaries, one with his wife; 4 places of worship, 1 boarding school, 2 day schools, 1 printing press, and 59 professed Christians.

MOSETLA: A village in the Transvaal, South Africa, situated in the Buschveld about 30 miles N. of Pretoria. Station of the Hermannsburg Mission Society (1867), with (1901) 1 missionary, 2 native workers, 4 outstations, 2 places of worship, 3 day schools, and 758 professed Christians.

MOSSEL BAY: A town and district capital in Cape Colony, South Africa, situated on Mossel Bay, about 225 miles E. of Cape Town. Population, 15,000. Station of the Berlin Missionary Society (1879), with (1903) 1 missionary, 1 woman missionary, 11 native workers, 1 outstation, and 684 professed Christians.

MOSUL: A town in Mesopotamia, Asiatic Turkey, capital of the province of Mosul, situated on the right bank of the Tigris River, 220 miles N. W. of Baghdad. The site of ancient Nineveh lies on the opposite side of the river. The climate is hot and trying to Europeans. Population, 61,000. It was occupied as a station first by the ABCFM, then transferred to the PN, and by it transferred to the CMS, who now have (1903) 1 missionary and his wife, 2 women missionaries, 6 native workers, 3 day schools, 1 dispensary, and 76 professed Christians, of whom 26 are communicants.

MOSQUITIA, or MOSQUITO COAST: A department of Nicaragua, Central America, bordering on the Caribbean Sea, and inhabited by Mosquitos, a mixed race with both African and Indian blood. For a long time it was known as the Mosquito Reservation, under the protectorate of Great Britain. It was ceded to Nicaragua in 1860, but maintains the native form of government under supervision of that country. Population about 15,000. Missionary operations are carried on by the Moravians at 14 stations.

MOTIHARI: A town in Bengal, India, capital of the Champaran district of Behar, situated on Buri Gandah River about 48 miles N. W. of Muzaffarpur. Population, 8,000, Hindus and Muslims. Station of the RBMU (1901), with (1903) 2 missionaries and their wives.

MOTIVE OF THE MISSIONARY ENTERPRISE: That the motives which prompt to missionary effort are powerful is evident. No weak motives would lead thousands of earnest men and women to spend their lives among uncongenial people, far from the associations and the opportunities of home and country, nor would weak motives induce the Christians of Europe and America to give millions of dollars annually for the maintenance of the missionary enterprise. In fact, various motives are involved. Some operate upon one class of minds and some upon another, and all of them do not appeal with equal force to the same person. For convenience, they may be divided into two main classes, primary and secondary, tho this classification is arbitrary, and tho there may be differences of opinion as to the class to which certain motives properly belong. Something depends upon the viewpoint.

1. The following motives, which are influential with many Christian people, may be classed as secondary:

(a) *The philanthropic motive:* This is stirred by the consciousness of human brotherhood, and the natural desire to relieve the appalling suffering and ignorance which prevail throughout the heathen world. Christ is the Great Physician, now as of old. As we see the prevalence of disease and misery, the untended ulcers, the sightless eyes to which the surgeon's skill could bring light, the pain-racked limbs pierced with hot needles to kill the alleged demon which causes the sufferings, and the fevered bodies which are made ten times worse by the superstitious and bungling methods of treatment, our sympathies are profoundly moved, and we freely give and labor that such agony may be alleviated. Medical missions, with their hospitals and dispensaries, strongly appeal to this motive, as do also educational missions, with their teaching of the principles of better living. The Gospel itself is sometimes preached and supported from this motive, for it is plain that the sufferings of men are diminished, and the dignity and the worth of life increased, by the application of the principles of Christianity to human society.

(b) *The intellectual motive:* Missionaries have vastly increased the world's store of useful knowledge. They have opened to view hitherto vaguely known lands. They have probably done more than any other class of men to extend knowledge of the earth's surface and its inhabitants. Geography and ethnology, entomology and zoology, botany and kindred sciences, gratefully enroll the names of missionaries among their most successful explorers, and many thoughtful men appreciate this and give their sympathy to the cause which the missionaries represent.

(c) *The commercial motive:* Some business men frankly assign this as the reason for their gifts. The missionary in the typical heathen land is the representative of a higher civilization. His teaching and his manner of living incidentally, but none the less really, create wants and introduce goods. He lights his house with a lamp and straightway thousands of the natives become dissatisfied with a bit of rag burning in a dish of vegetable oil. So foreign lamps are being used by millions of Chinese, Japanese, Siamese, and East Indians. The missionary marks time with a clock, and German, English, and American firms suddenly find a new and apparently limitless market for their products. He rides a bicycle on his country tours, and the result is that to-day the bicycle is as common in the cities and many of the villages of Siam and Japan as it is in the United States. His wife makes her own and her children's dresses on a sewing machine, and ten thousand curious Chinese, Japanese, and Laos are not satisfied till they have sewing machines. And so the missionary opens new markets and extends trade. He has been one of the most effective agents of modern commerce, not because he intended to be, not because he reaped any personal profit from the goods which he introduced, but because of the inevitable tendencies which were set in motion by the residence of an enlightened family among unenlightened people. And this appeals to some minds as a motive of missionary interest. It begets hundreds of addresses on the reflex influence of foreign missions, and it undoubtedly secures some support for the cause from those who might not be responsive to the other arguments.

(d) *The civilizing motive:* This is closely allied to the preceding motives. In the ways that have been indicated, and in others that might be specified, the missionary is "the advance agent of civilization." As the product of centuries of Christian civilization, with all its customs and ideals, he appears in a rude village in Africa. He opposes slavery, polygamy, cannibalism, and infanticide. He teaches the boys to be honest, sober and thrifty, the girls to be pure, intelligent and industrious. He induces the natives to cover their nakedness, to build houses, to till the soil. He inculcates and exemplifies the social and civic virtues. His own home and his treatment of his wife and daughters are an object lesson in a community which had always treated woman as a slave. The inertia of long-established heathenism is hard to overcome, but slowly it yields to the new power, and the beginning of civilized society gradually appears. Volumes might be filled with the testimonies of statesmen, travelers, military and naval officers to the value of missionary work from this viewpoint. Ask almost any public man to speak at a great missionary meeting, and he will probably respond with an address in which he enlarges upon this aspect of missionary effort. The British officials in India have been outspoken in their praise of the civilizing influence of missionaries in that country. Darwin's testimony to the usefulness of missionary work in the South Seas is another classic illustration, and hundreds of others might be cited.

Dr. James S. Dennis has collected a vast mass of facts bearing on this subject in his noble volumes on *Christian Missions and Social Progress,* and the cumulative power of this class of evidence is doubtless a large factor in the growing respect for missions in the public mind.

(e) *The historical motive:* With many people of the utilitarian type, this argument from results is the most decisive. They want to see that their money accomplishes something, to know that their investment is yielding some tangible return. They eagerly scan missionary reports to ascertain how many converts have been made, how many pupils are being taught, how many patients have been treated. To tell them of successes achieved is the surest method of inducing them to increase their gifts. Mission Boards often find it difficult to sustain interest in apparently unproductive fields, but comparatively easy to arouse enthusiasm for fields in which converts are quickly made. The churches are eager and even impatient for results. Fortunately, in many lands results have been achieved on such a magnificent scale as to satisfy this demand. But in other lands, not less important, weary years have had to be spent in preparing the soil and sowing the seed, and hard-working missionaries have been half disheartened by the insistent popular demand for accounts of baptisms before the harvest time has fairly come.

There is, apparently, a growing disposition to exalt this whole class of motives. The basis of missionary appeal has noticeably changed within the last generation. Our humanitarian, commercial, and practical age is more impressed by the physical and temporal, the actual and the utilitarian. The idea of saving men for the present world appeals more strongly than the idea of saving them for the next world, and missionary sermons and addresses give large emphasis to these motives. We need not and should not undervalue them. They are real. It is legitimate and Christian to seek the temporal welfare of our fellow-men, to alleviate their distresses, to exalt woman and to purify society. It is, moreover, true and to the credit of the missionary enterprise that it widens the area of the world's useful knowledge, introduces the conveniences and necessities of Christian civilization, and promotes wealth and power; while it is certainly reasonable that those who give should desire to see some results from their gifts and be encouraged and incited to renewed diligence by the inspiring record of achievement. But these motives are, nevertheless, distinctly secondary. They are effects of the missionary enterprise rather than causes of it, and the true Christian would still be obliged to give and pray and work for the evangelization of the world, even if not one of these motives existed.

What, then, are the primary motives of the missionary enterprise? The following may be briefly enumerated.

(a) *The soul's experience in Christ:* In proportion as this is genuine and deep will we desire to communicate it to others. The man who feels that Christ is precious to his own heart and that He has brought strength and blessing into his own life, is immediately conscious of an impulse to give these joys to those who do not have them. Expansion is a law of the spiritual life. The inherent tendency of Christianity is to propagate itself. A living organism must grow or die. The church that is not missionary will become atrophied. All virile faith prompts its possessor to seek others. That was an exquisite touch of regenerated nature and one beautifully illustrative of the promptings of a normal Christian experience which led Andrew, after he rose from Jesus' feet, "to find first his own brother, Simon, and say unto him,' We have found the Messiah.'"

No external authority, however commanding, can take the place of this internal motive. It led Paul to exclaim: " Woe is me if I preach not the Gospel." It made him plead "with tears" that men would turn to God; to become "all things to all men; that he might by all means save some;" to speed from city to city, the burden of his preaching evermore, "We pray you in Christ's stead, be ye reconciled to God." Because this is one of the primary motives of missions, the cause chiefly depends, humanly speaking, upon the piety of the Church. Other motives may and often do help for longer or shorter periods. But the real and permanent dependence must be upon a spiritual experience with Christ so rich and joyous that it makes missionary effort the natural and necessary expression of its life.

(b) *The world's evident need of Christ:* The fact that the heathen are morally and spiritually debased is not, indeed, of itself sufficient to beget an overmastering and enduring desire to help them. But the fact that they need Christ, and that we have Christ, does beget such a desire in a rightly constituted mind. If we have any knowledge which is essential to the welfare of our fellow-man, we are under solemn obligation to convey that knowledge to him. It makes no difference who that man is, or where he lives, or whether he is conscious of his need, or how much inconvenience or expense we may incur in reaching him. If we can help him, we must get to him. That is an essential part of the foreign missionary impulse. We have the revelation of God that is potential of a civilization which benefits man, an education that fits him for higher usefulness, a scientific knowledge that enlarges his powers, a medical skill that alleviates his sufferings, and above all, a relation to Jesus Christ that not only lends new dignity to this earthly life, but which saves his soul and prepares him for eternal companionship with God. "Neither is there salvation in any other." Therefore, we must convey this Gospel to the world. Christ has commanded us to go, but we should have had to go anyway. The missionary impulse in the breast of every true disciple would have stirred him to spontaneous action. Christ simply voiced the highest and holiest dictates of the human heart when He summoned His followers to missionary activity and zeal. We do not hear so much as our fathers heard of the motive of salvation of the heathen. That consideration appears to be gradually drifting into the background. Our age prefers to dwell upon the blessings of faith rather than upon the consequences of unbelief. And yet, if we believe that Christ is our life, it is difficult to avoid the conclusion that without Christ is death. Various statements and figures are used in the New Testament to express the condition of those who know not Christ, but whether they are interpreted literally or figuratively, their fundamental meaning is as plain as it is awful. Jesus came "to save," and salvation is from something. Nothing is gained but much is lost by ignoring facts, and the appalling fact that men are lost without Christ is a motive of the first magnitude for trying to save them.

(c) *The command of Christ:* "Go ye into all the world and preach the Gospel to every creature." If this were the only motive, foreign missionary work would be a mechanical performance of stern duty, the missionary merely an obedient soldier. But taken in connection with the preceding motives, it adds to them the impressive sanctions of divine authority. For Christ's word is not a request. It is not a suggestion. It leaves nothing to our choice. It is an order, comprehensive, unequivocal, ending all argument, silencing all cavil—a clear, peremptory, categorical imperative "Go." Such a command dispels all possible uncertainty, removes any misgiving, and, for those who need it, reduces the question of missionary effort to one of simple obedience to our Lord and King.

These are and ever must remain the supreme motives of the missionary enterprise. They have inherent and independent force. Whether men are civilized or not, whether they trade with us or not, whether present results are few or many, the Christian Church must continue its missionary work. The results of a hundred years of missionary effort are most encouraging, but if they were not, it would make little difference. The man who knows that he is working with God, for God, and in obedience to God, is not controlled by worldly ideas of success. He is content to leave results with God, knowing that His Word will not return unto Him void. After Judson had been toiling for years in Burma without making a single convert, some one wrote to him asking what the prospects were, and he flashed back, "As bright as the promises of God!" When ten years of labor in Bechuana had failed to accomplish any visible result, Mrs. Greaves, of Sheffield, wrote to Mary Moffat asking what she needed, and that heroic woman answered: "Send us a communion service." Temporary defeat has no power over the true missionary. With Lincoln, when taunted with the defeat of his plans, he exclaims, "Defeat! if it were not one but one hundred defeats, I should still pursue the same unchanging course." To his own generation, Christ's life was a failure. So was Paul's, and Peter's, and Stephen's. But later generations saw the rich fruitage. Like them, the true missionary toils from motives which are independent of present appearances. If Jehovah is the only true God, the whole world ought to be told about Him. If Jesus Christ is our salvation, He can be the salvation of others, and it is our imperative duty to carry or send the good news to them. There may be questions as to method, but no objection lies against the foreign missionary enterprise which does not lie with equal force against the fundamental truths of the Christian religion.

The foreign mission cause is at some disadvantage as compared with the other enterprises in which the church is engaged in that it cannot make so strong an appeal to patriotism or self-interest. The foreign missionary impulse is really the Christ impulse. It is prompted by no selfish motive. It summons us to toil and sacrifice for races which are beyond our sight and touch, and for which we naturally feel but little concern, especially as they ordinarily cling to their old faiths and sometimes resent our well-meant efforts. In these circumstances, foreign missions can effectively appeal only to those motives of spiritual experience and unselfish love and glad obedience which prompted Christ to seek a lost race. Indeed, the Master plainly declared to His disciples: "As the Father hath sent me into the world, so send I you into the world." But to these motives it does appeal as the wretchedness and guilt of old appealed to the heart of infinite love. The missionary advocate makes a grave mistake when he bases his appeal solely on financial needs. The fact that an enterprise wants money is not a sufficient reason why it should receive it, nor is the begging argument apt to secure anything deeper than the beggar's temporary dole. Our appeal should be based on those high motives which center in our relation to the Savior's love and presence and command. Paul said, "We preach not ourselves, but Christ Jesus the Lord; and ourselves your servants for Jesus' sake." "For Jesus sake!" That is the spring of all holy living, of all noble endeavor, of all large achievement. "For Jesus' sake!" the missionary goes into distant lands. "For Jesus' sake" he toils and prays for the salvation of his fellow-men. And "for Jesus' sake" Christians at home ought to sustain those who go. The searching and tender words of Christ to Peter comprehend the whole matter,"Lovest thou me?" then "feed my sheep."

MOUKDEN. See MUKDEN.

MOULMEIN. See MAULMAIN.

MOUNT ARTHUR: A town in Cape Colony, South Africa, situated in the Glen Grey District, about ten miles N. E. of Lady Frere. Station of the South Africa Wesleyan Methodists, with (1900) 103 native workers, 46 outstations, 1,012 professed Christians, 25 places of worship, 25 Sunday schools.

MOUNT AYLIFF: A settlement in Cape Colony, South Africa, situated in Griqualand East, 105 miles S. W. of Pietermaritzburg. Station of the Episcopal Church in Scotland (1888), with (1903) 1 missionary, 1 native worker, 2 outstations, 2 places of worship, 2 day schools, and 29 professed Christians.

MOUNT FRERE: A settlement in Cape Colony, South Africa, situated in Griqualand East, 125 miles S. W. of Pietermaritzburg. It is also called Mbonda. Station of the Episcopal Church in Scotland (1890), with (1903) 1 missionary, 17 native workers, 12 outstations, 8 places of worship, 8 day schools, and 598 professed Christians. Station also of the UFS (1894), with (1903) 1 missionary and his wife, 29 native workers, 24 outstations, 1 place of worship, 8 Sunday schools, 11 day schools, and 760 professed Christians.

MOUNT SILINDA: A settlement on the eastern edge of Matabililand, Rhodesia, South Central Africa, situated in Melsetter district, about 150 miles W. S. W. of the Portuguese seaport of Beira. Station of the ABCFM (1893), with (1903) 3 missionaries with their wives, 2 native workers, 4 outstations, 1 day school, 1 Sunday school, 1 boarding school, 40 professed Christians, and 1 dispensary. It has also an industrial enterprise with 27,000 acres of land.

MOUNT TABOR: A settlement in Zululand, Natal, South Africa, situated on the St. Lucia River, at the entrance to St. Lucia Lake. Station of the South Africa General Mission (1899), with (1900) 2 missionaries, one with his wife; 3 women missionaries, 1 native worker, 1 place of worship, 1 Sunday school, 1 day school, and 2 professed Christians.

MOYAMBA: A village in Sierra Leone, W. Africa, situated in the Mendi country, about 25 miles S. E. of Rotifunk, on the railway from Freetown to Bo. Station of the UB, with (1901) 1 missionary and his wife, 1 woman missionary, 2 native workers, 1 place of worship, 1 Sunday school, 1 day school, and 1 Young People's society.

MOZAMBIQUE: Formerly capital of Portuguese West Africa. It is situated on a small coral island in latitude 15° 2′ south, and was the original fortress of the Portuguese. It has three strong forts. Since the abolition of the slave-trade its export trade, principally with India, is of little importance. Population about 6,000, of whom about 300 are Europeans and as many more Arabs. Education and religion are under the control of the Roman Catholics, and are at a very low ebb.

MOZAFARPUR. See MUZAFFARPUR.

MPANGILE: A station of the Berlin Mission Society in German East Africa, situated about 35 miles E. by N. from the northern extremity of Lake Nyasa. Statistics given under Mbeyela's.

MPAPWA: A settlement in German East Africa, situated in the Usagara region, about 52 miles W. by S. of Mamboia. Station of the CMS (1878), with (1903) 2 missionaries, one with his wife; 10 native workers, 8 day schools, 1 dispensary, and 219 professed Christians, of whom 66 are communicants. Society has spelled the name Mpwapwa, but, at the request of the local officials, in 1904 adopted the spelling Mpapua.

MPHOME: A town in North Transvaal, Africa, south of Limpopo River. A station of the Berlin Mission Society (1878), with (1903) 1 missionary, 34 native workers, 15 outstations, 3 day schools, 1,801 professed Christians, of whom 1,180 are communicants.

MPONDA'S: A village in British Central Africa, situated in Nyasaland at the issue of the Shire River, from Lake Nyasa. The climate is healthy. Station of the UM (1896), with (1900) 4 missionaries, two of them with their wives; 2 native workers, 2 outstations, 2 places of worship, 2 day schools, 1 boarding school, and 27 professed Christians.

MPONGWE LANGUAGE: An African language belonging to the great Bantu family, and spoken by a limited number of people in the coast regions of the French Congo. It has been reduced to writing by missionaries with use of the Roman letters.

MPUTOLI: A village in Cape Colony, South

Africa, situated in the Transkei district on the Indwe River, 28 miles S. E. of Queenstown. Station of the South African Baptist Mission Society, with 1 missionary and his wife and 1 woman missionary. Name sometimes written Mputola.

MPWAPWA. See MPAPWA.

MSALABANI: Station of the UM in German East Africa, situated in the Usambara region, about 30 miles W. S. W. of Tanga. It was established in 1875 and has been called Magila. The name Magila having now been applied to the whole district, the station has been renamed Msalabani, which means "at the Cross." It now (1903) has 4 missionaries, 12 elementary and 2 higher schools, and 1,071 professed Christians.

MUAKERERI: A settlement in German East Africa, in the Konde District, N. of Lake Nyasa, about 25 miles N. W. of the northern end of the lake. Station of the Berlin Missionary Society (1893), with (1903) 1 missionary, 4 native workers, 1 day school, and 49 professed Christians, of whom 26 are communicants. Name sometimes written Muakaleli.

MUANG NAN: A town in Siam in the Laos district, situated on the Me Nan, about 125 miles E. of Cheung Mai. Station of the PN (1894), with (1903) 3 missionaries and their wives, 3 native workers, 1 Sunday school, 1 dispensary, 1 day school, and 57 professed Christians. Name sometimes written Nan.

MUANG PRAA: A town in Siam, in the Laos district, situated on the Me Yonz, about 65 miles S. E. of Lakawn. Station of the PN (1893), with (1903) 1 missionary and his wife, 2 native workers, 16 outstations, 2 places of worship, 2 Sunday schools, 1 day school, 1 boarding school, 1 dispensary, 1 hospital, and 220 professed Christians, of whom 120 are communicants. Name sometimes written Pre.

MUDEN: A village in Natal, South Africa, situated in the Weenen district on the Mooi River, about 12 miles N. W. of Greytown. Station of the Hermannsburg Missionary Society (1859), with (1903) 2 missionaries, one with his wife; 9 native workers, 3 places of worship, 3 day schools, 2 outstations, and 593 professed Christians, of whom 178 are communicants.

MUFINDI: A settlement in German East Africa, in the Heheland district, situated on the Ngololo River, about 120 miles N. E. of the northern end of Lake Nyasa and about 420 miles S. W. of Dar es Selam on the shore of the Indian Ocean. Station of the Berlin Mission Society (1899), with (1903) 2 missionaries, one with his wife, and 15 professed Christians. The station will be removed soon to a more populous district.

MUHANGA: A settlement in German East Africa, situated on the Lukosse River, about 50 miles N. E. of Mufindi. Station of the Berlin Mission Society (1899), with (1903) 1 missionary and 4 outstations.

MUHLENBERG: A settlement in Liberia, West Africa, situated on the St. Paul's River, about 46 miles N. E. of Monrovia. Station of the ELGS (1860), with (1903) 5 missionaries, two of them with their wives; 2 women missionaries, 6 outstations, 6 day schools, 2 boarding schools, 1 dispensary, 1 industrial school, and 110 professed Christians.

MUKDEN: A town, the capital of Manchuria, China, situated in the province of Liao-tung, on the Hun-ho, 110 miles N. E. of New-chwang. It was the former residence of the present reigning dynasty of China, dating from 1625. The streets are broad and straight. Population, 250,000. Station of the UFS (1875), with (1903) 5 missionaries, three of them with their wives; 2 women missionaries, 29 native workers, 17 outstations, 1 place of worship, 10 Sunday schools, 11 day schools, 1 female training institute, 1 dispensary, and 1,540 professed Christians. Station also of the Presbyterian Church in Ireland (1889), with (1901) 1 missionary and his wife, 2 women missionaries, 9 native workers, 4 outstations, 6 chapels, 1 Sunday school, 2 day schools, 1 theological college, and 79 professed Christians. Work in the college is supported conjointly with the UFS. Societies spell the name Moukden. The BFBS has an agent at this place.

MUKIMVIKA: A village in Angola, Africa, situated on the left bank of the Congo River at its mouth. Station of the ABMU (1882), with (1903) 3 missionaries, one with his wife; 2 native workers, 1 place of worship, 1 Sunday school, 1 day school, 1 hospital, and 1 dispensary.

MUKIMBUNGU: A settlement in Congo Free State, Africa, situated on the right bank of the Congo River. Station of the Swedish National Evangelical Miss. Association (1882), with (1901) 3 missionaries, one with his wife; 2 women missionaries, 17 native workers, 15 outstations, 1 place of worship, 1 Sunday school, 1 boarding school, 1 college, 1 dispensary, and 392 professed Christians.

MULANGO: A settlement in British East Africa, not far from Mt. Kenia. Station of the Leipzig Mission Society (1899), with (1903) 2 missionaries, one with his wife; 9 outstations, 1 place of worship, 1 day school.

MULKI: A town in Madras, India, situated in the district of South Kanara on the W. coast, 13 miles N. by W. of Mangalore. Population, 5,000. Station of the Berlin Mission Society (1845), with (1903) 2 missionaries and their wives, 27 native workers, 6 outstations, 7 day schools, 1 boarding school, and 800 professed Christians, of whom 436 are communicants.

MULLENS, Joseph: Born in London, England, 1820; entered Coward College, 1837; graduated, 1841, at the London University; ordained, 1843, and embarked the same year for Calcutta as a missionary of the LMS. In 1865, after visiting the missions in India and Ceylon, he sailed for England to be assistant secretary with Dr. Tidman. On Dr. Tidman's death he became foreign secretary of the LMS. In 1870 he visited the United States as delegate of the London Society to the American Board. In 1873 and 1874 he visited Madagascar in the interest of the missionary work. In 1875 Dr. Mullens accompanied several missionaries to assist in the organization of a mission on Lake Tanganyika, Central Africa. But at Mpwapwa he was overcome by exposure and fatigue and died of peritonitis July 10. The degree of doctor of divinity was conferred upon him in 1851 by Williams College, Mass., and in 1868 by the University of Edinburgh. He published *Twelve Months in Madagascar*, *A Brief Review of Ten Years' Missionary Labor in India between 1852 and 1863*, *London and Calcutta Compared in their Heathenism, Privileges and Prospects*.

MULTAN: A city in the Punjab, India, situated

190 miles S. W. by W. of Lahore, about 7 miles from Chenab River. The commercial center of the region. It has silk, cotton and carpet manufactures. A very ancient town existing at the time of Alexander the Great. Altitude, 420 feet. Climate warm and rainfall light. Population (1901), 87,394, of whom 43,000 are Muslims and 34,000 are Hindus. Station of the CMS (1856), with (1903) 2 missionaries, 4 women missionaries, 9 native workers, 1 place of worship, 1 day school, 1 boarding school, and 115 professed Christians, of whom 37 are communicants.

MULTANI LANGUAGE: An Aryan language of the Indic branch, used by the people of Multan and Dernar, of Muzaffergarh, and of the state of Bhawalpur. It is also spoken by the Khetran tribe in the territory behind the Suleimani Mountains. Altogether about two and a half millions of the people of Northwestern India speak Multani. They themselves call it Jagdalli or Jatki, the name Multani being given to it by neighboring peoples. The language is allied to the Punjabi and to the Sindhi. The Arabic character is used in writing it.

MULVI BAZAAR: A village in Assam, India, situated in Sylhet district, about 30 miles S. W. of Sylhet. Station of the WCM, with (1903) 1 missionary and his wife, 15 native workers, 1 boarding school, and 15 professed Christians. Name sometimes written Maulvi Bazaar.

MUNGELI: A town in the Central Provinces, India, situated 135 miles S. E. by E. of Bilaspur. Population, 5,000. Station of the FCMS (1887), with (1901) 1 missionary and his wife, 10 native workers, 1 outstation, 10 Sunday schools, 1 place of worship, 1 female training school, 1 dispensary, 1 hospital, 1 medical class, 1 lepers' institute, and 90 professed Christians. Station also of the Mission to Lepers in India and the East (1897), with 1 place of worship and 1 lepers' home for untainted children of lepers.

MUNSON, Samuel: Born at New Sharon, Me., March 23, 1804; graduated at Bowdoin College 1829, Andover Theological Seminary 1832; ordained October 10; sailed June 10, 1833, as a missionary of the ABCFM, with Rev. Henry Lyman, under instructions to explore the East Indian Archipelago, and reached Batavia September 30. In April, 1834, they undertook to visit the Batta country in Sumatra, and were both killed. For an account of their expedition and death, see the article on Mr. **Henry Lyman.**

MURHU: A village in Bengal, India, situated in Chota Nagpur, 30 miles S. by W. of Ranchi. Station of the SPG, with (1903) 22 native workers, 1 place of worship, 6 day schools, 1 boarding school, and 2,071 professed Christians, of whom 1,028 are communicants.

MURRAYTOWN: A village in Sierra Leone, Africa, situated about 5 miles W. of Freetown. Station of the UMFC (1891), with (1901) 1 missionary and his wife, 12 native workers, 1 outstation, 2 places of worship, 2 Sunday schools, and 311 professed Christians.

MUSCAT. See MASCAT.

MUSH: A city of Eastern Turkey, 83 miles southeast of Erzroom, in a large plain, one of the most populous of the whole section. The population is Kurdish and Armenian. The Kurds are very fierce, and treat the Christians most oppressively. The district of Sasun, notorious as the scene of horrible massacres of Armenians in 1893, and again in 1904, lies S. W. of Mush in the same administrative division. The name is also written Moosh and Moush.

MUSIC AND MISSIONS: Missions touch music at two points: 1. The missionary as a man of culture studies the poetry and songs of the people among whom he labors. 2. After a mission has become successful the newly formed churches are helped in their worship, especially in the department of Praise, and this demands a thorough knowledge of the foundation principles of music.

As to the study of the music of savages by missionaries we may cite some examples. Rev. A. L. Riggs has made a very interesting study of Dakota music, publishing specimens of songs of love and war, songs of sacred mysteries and social songs. They are extremely simple, and abound with the repetitions so natural to untutored minds. A widow's lament expresses the deepest heartweariness and despair.

Their music is also very simple. It consists of melody alone, with rude accompaniment, mainly for marking time. The men sing, while the women sound one single falsetto note *ai, ai, ai,* keeping time with drums. They do not appreciate harmony. The minor key is their favorite, tho the major key occurs in their war songs. Their instruments are the drum, rattle, and pipe. The drum is more than a foot in diameter, and from three to ten inches deep. The rattle is made of segments of deer hoops tied to a tapering rod of wood. The conjurer uses a gourd shell with a few pebbles inside. The usual pipe is a sumac flageolet, nineteen inches long, with a diameter of five-eighths of an inch. A peculiar partition forms the whistle. Six notes are burnt on the upper side, and a brass thimble forms the mouthpiece. The pitch is A Prime, changed to G Prime by a seventh hole. Sometimes the pipe is made of the long wing or thigh-bone of a crane or swan. Dakota music is rude, but its power is measured by the adaptation of its wild melody to savage life in the wilderness, where in the misty moonlight the night air bears the plaintive sounds, with the hollow bass of the drum-beat, along the waste, full of possible warwhoops, and where each bush may hide an enemy.

Dr. S. Wells Williams has given in his *Middle Kingdom* a graphic description of Chinese music and musical instruments. However small their attainments in both theory and practise, no nation gives to music a higher place. Confucius taught that it was essential to good government, harmonizing the different ranks in society, and causing them all to move on in unison. The Chinese have sought to develop instrumental rather than vocal music.

The names of the notes, ascending regularly from the first line of the staff to the third space above it, are as follows: first line, *ho;* first space, *sz;* then *i, chang, ché, kung, fan, liu, wu;* first space above, *i,* then *chang, ché, kung, fan,* the last being on the third space above.

The real tone cannot be represented by our staff. The second octave is denoted by affixing the sign *jin,* a man, to the simple notes. No chromatic scale exists—at least no instrument is made to express flat and sharp notes.

There are two kinds of music in China—the northern and the southern. The octave in the former seems to have had only six notes, while the eight-tone scale prevails in more cultivated circles. Music is written for only a few instruments, and the notation good for one is useless for another, because marks meaning to push, fillip, hook, etc., are added to denote the mode of playing; indeed, the combinations are so complicated that the Chinese usually play by ear. All music is in common time; no triple measures are used. Of harmony and counterpoint they know nothing. Marks to regulate the expression are unknown, nor are tunes set to any key.

No description can do justice to their vocal music, and few can imitate it. Some notes seem to issue from the larynx and nose; tongue, teeth, and lips having little to do with them. Singing is usually in a falsetto key, somewhere between a squeal and a scream, and yet it is plaintive and soft, and not without a certain sweetness.

Chinese musical literature is voluminous. A work on beating the drum dates from A. D. 860, and contains a list of 129 symphonies. Among 12 instruments described in the chrestomathy are 17 drums of various sizes, then gongs, cymbals, tambourines, and musical vases in considerable variety. Stringed instruments are not so numerous. They have nothing that resembles the lyre. The *kin* or scholar's lute is deemed the finest. *Easy Lessons* for this lute is a work in two volumes, explains 109 terms, and has 29 pictures of the position of the hand in playing. The instrument itself is ancient, and is named *kin*, "to prohibit," because it restrains evil passions. It is a board, four feet long and eighteen inches wide, convex above and flat below, where two holes open into hollows. Seven strings of silk pass over a bridge through the board at the wide end, and are fastened by nuts beneath. They are fastened to two pegs at the smaller end. The sounding-board is divided by thirteen studs, so placed that the strings are divided into halves, thirds, quarters, fifths, sixths, and eighths, but no sevenths. The seven strings enclose the compass of a ninth, or two-fifths, the middle one being treated like A on the violin, and the outer ones tuned to one-fifth from that. The interval is treated like our octave in the violin, for the compass of the *kin* is made up of fifths. Each of the outer strings is tuned a fourth from the alternate string within the system, so that there is a major tone and interval tone less than a minor third, and a major tone in the fifth. The Chinese leave the interval entire and skip the half tone, while we divide it into two unequal parts; so the mood of the music of the *kin* is different from our instruments, and for that reason none of these can do justice to Chinese airs. There are other instruments like the *kin*, one with 30 and another with 13 strings. Some resemble the guitar, lute, and spinet, with strings of silk or wire, but never of catgut. The *pipa*, a balloon-shaped guitar, has four strings, is three feet long, with twelve frets to guide the player. The strings are tuned to the intervals of a fourth, a major tone, and a fourth, so that the outer strings are octaves to each other. The *san hien*, or three-stringed guitar, resembles a rebeck in shape, but the head and neck are three feet in length. The strings are tuned as fourths to each other, and their sound is low and dull. The *yueh kin*, or full-moon guitar, has four strings in pairs that are unisons with each other, with an interval of a fifth between the pairs. It is struck briskly, and used for lively tunes.

The two-stringed fiddle is merely a bamboo split stuck into a bamboo cylinder, with two strings fastened on pegs at one end of the stick and passing over a bridge on the cylinder to the other end. They are tuned at intervals of a fifth. As the bow passes between the two strings much care is needed in playing not to scrape the wrong string. The harsh grating of this wretched machine is very popular among the natives. The *ti kin* (crowing lute) has a coconut shell for its body, and is even more dissonant than the last. The *yang kin* is an embryo piano, consisting of brass wires of different lengths, tuned at proper intervals, and fastened on a sounding board. The sounds are very attenuated. The *sang*, in like manner, is an embryo organ, a cone-shaped box, with a mouthpiece to blow in, and thirteen reeds of different lengths, inserted in the top, the valves of some opening upward and others downward. They are provided with holes also that may be opened or closed by the player. It is very ancient. Some think it the organ invented by Jubal (Gen. iv: 21). The Chinese think it more curious than useful.

Their wind instruments are numerous. The *hwang tih* (flute) is twice the length of our pipe, made of bamboo, and pierced with ten holes. The two near the end are not used. The mouth hole is one-third of the way from the top. The *shu tih* (clarionet) takes the lead in musical performances. It has seven holes, but no keys. Its tones are shrill and deafening, and therefore popular. A street musician fits a flageolet, or small clarionet, to his nose, slings a small drum under one shoulder, hangs a frame of four cymbals on his breast, and with a couple of monkeys sallies forth, a peripatetic choir and orchestra.

The stem of the horn is retractible, like a trombone. There are other varieties, however.

The *lo* (gong) is the standard type of Chinese music. A crashing harangue of rapid blows on this, with a rattling accompaniment of drums, and a crackling symphony of shrillness from clarionet and cymbal, is their *beau ideal* of music. They have heard good Portuguese music for ages, but have never adopted either an instrument or a tune.

A Chinese band makes the European think of Hogarth's "Enraged Musician." Each performer seems to have his own tune, and bent on drowning the noise of all the rest; yet they keep good time, only no two of them are tuned on the same key.

The Rev. Dr. Eli Smith, of the American Syria Mission, found that hymns composed in Arabic measures could seldom be sung in our tunes, and our musicians were puzzled by the intervals in Arab music. On the other hand, Arabs could not repeat our scale. A treatise on Arab music by Michael Mishakah of Damascus explained the difficulty; and from that, with Rosegarten's edition of Ispahany's *Book of Odes*, and Faraby on *Ancient Arab Music*, Dr. Smith wrote a valuable paper which was published in the *Journal of the American Oriental Society*. The principles are quite near to those of Persian and Turkish music also. He says that sounds are naturally divided into groups of seven, rising one above the other, each the response to the one below, and the bass of the one above. The group is called an octave, *diwan*, and the octaves are composed of tones, *burj*, pl. *buruj*. The first is called *yegâh*, then *ösheiran*, *ârak*, *rest*, *dugâh*, *sigâh*, and *jehârgâh*. This is the first octave. The second is *nawa*, *huseiny*, *auj*, *mâhûr*, *muhaiyar*, *buzrek*, and *mahûrân*. The last is the response to *jehârgâh*.

The first of the third octave is *remel tûty*, the response to *nawa*. The next octave is the response to the response of *nawa*, and so on *ad infinitum*. So in the first series below *yegâh* they say the base to *jehârgâh*, to *sigâh*, and so through the list, then the base to the base of *jehârgâh*, etc. The intervals between these notes are unequal. They are divided into two classes, one containing four quarters and the other three. The former are from *yegâh* to *öshieran*, from *rest* to *dûgâh*, and from *jehârgâh* to *nawa*. The latter from *öshieran* to *arak*, from *arak* to *rest*, from *dûgâh to sigâh*, and from *sigâh* to *jehârgâh*. The first class then has three intervals with twelve quarters, and the second four intervals with twelve quarters. The modern Greeks divide the intervals into seconds, and make three classes. One class, corresponding to the first of the Arabs, divides the interval into twelve seconds; the second class divides it into nine seconds, and is from *dûgâh* to *sigâh*, and from *huseiny* to *auj*. The third class, from *sigâh* to *jehârgâh*, and from *auj* to *mahur*, has seven seconds to the interval. So their octave contains seven intervals and sixty-eight seconds. The Arab and Greek scales coincide only at four out of the sixty-eight seconds.

This is the substance of only four of the thirty pages of the paper. Chapter II. describes Arab melodies now in use, and Chapter III. is devoted to musical rhythm, and Chapter IV. to musical instruments, describing stringed instruments like *el ud* (literally the wood, whence our word "lute") the Arab guitar, the *kemenjeh*, or Arab fiddle, with a coconut shell for its body, like the Chinese *ti kin*; the *tambur*, a kind of mandolin, and the *kanûn*, corresponding to the *yang kin* of the Chinese orchestra, only, it would seem, a better instrument. Then of wind instruments, the *nay* or flute, *kerift, mizmar, sunnây, urghan* (organ, see Chinese *sang*), and *jenah*.

In India, music was formerly much more scientific than at present. There idolatry has degraded music, and the martial music of the country has changed with its government. Its religion now has little to do with music, except in connection with the dancing girls of the temples. Operas are unknown, and theatrical music is of a low order. Marriages furnish the chief occasions for musical display. There are many kinds of musical instruments, as drums, trumpets, horns, cymbals, hautboys, and violins, but the performers have little skill and less taste. The wedding orchestra varies from six to twenty performers. Singing is an accomplishment of women of doubtful morality, who are much employed for this purpose by the wealthy.

Christianity is changing all this, not generally, it is true, but gradually and permanently, for the native convert must give vent to his new joy in songs of praise, and they do this not only in the church, but also in their families and when alone. Even before conversion, music does much to prepare the way.

A favorite and most successful mode of introducing the Gospel in western India is the *kirttan*, *i. e.*, solo singing by native evangelists with orchestral accompaniment. In September, 1880, Rev. Mr. Bruce of Satara visited Wai with his kirttan choir. The people crowded to hear, especially as the leader had been a Muslim. Hundreds stood outside of the building in the rain, and listened for the first time to the way of salvation through a Redeemer. The whole city was moved, and Christ was the great topic of conversation for many days.

Rev. H. Ballantine, called the Dr. Watts of the Mahratta Mission, prepared a hymnal for the churches, and another for the children, which met with great acceptance among the people.

Rev. E. Webb was an enthusiast in his researches into the laws of Tamil poetry. It is extremely elaborate in its rhythmical construction. In 1853 he published a Tamil hymn-book, containing hymns in our meter, children's hymns, and chants with music, but the largest part of the volume was made up of hymns in native meters. Many copies were taken at once by the English missions in Tanjore and Tinnevelli, and singing was introduced in congregations of the American missions in places where it had been unknown before. An edition of 2,000 copies was soon exhausted, and a new one was issued in 1858. Tho the people hear listlessly the most important truth in prose, they give eager attention to the same truth when versified and sung. In October, 1860, Mr. Webb gave an account of Tamil versification to the American Oriental Society, defining the two kinds of syllables, then the feet and the stanzas in which they were combined. Tho the natives could see no measure in our verses, or melody in our music, yet hymns written in their own meters, and set to their own melodies, are extremely popular. He read some of them in Tamil with elaborate rhyme assonance and alliteration. He described also the music of the Hindus, known all over India under the same Sanskrit titles, and indicated its relation to our own scale. Ancient India excelled Greece in her cultivation of music; and tho no new tunes have appeared for centuries, those of the best periods still exist, and for these the hymns were composed.

Tho in other missions there may not have been the same zeal for native music, yet in them all, as soon as men receive "the light of the knowledge of the glory of God in the face of Jesus Christ," they feel impelled to praise the name of the Lord, and missionaries are glad to assist the effort to praise as soon as the spirit of praise appears.

It is interesting to look over the record of the beginnings of work on this line in the various missions. In Turkey, tho at that time they had few hymns ready for use, yet they could not wait to prepare more, but in 1850 issued an Armenian hymn-book of only 55 pages. This was followed in 1853 by one in Armeno-Turkish, *i. e.*, Turkish in Armenian letters, of 112 pages, and the next year saw an Armenian *Hymn and Tune Book* of 300 pages, so rapidly grew their hymnology. That same year (1854) the Greek hymn-book appeared, of 100 pages, tho 16 pages of hymns had been printed as early as 1833. All these were 16mo, but in 1855 appeared a work on church music, in Armenian, of 44 pages, 8vo. Then in the same language a hymn and tune book for children was published in 1860, 40 pages 8vo. This was followed by 24 8vo pages of additional hymns and music in 1863. It seemed as tho good men kept on composing hymns, and, as fast as they did so, the churches could not wait, but had them printed for use at once. Next year (1864) appeared a hymn-book of 104 16mo pages in Arabo-Turkish, *i. e.*, Turkish in Arabic type. The following year four hymns were printed on one 8vo sheet, and in 1866 a supplement to the Armeno-Turkish hymn-book, of 88 pages 16mo, made its appearance. Next came an Armenian Sunday-school hymn-book of 134 16mo pages, followed next year by a Sunday-school hymn and tune book in the same language, of 128 8vo pages. The year 1869 saw a volume of Armenian hymns and prayers of 192 pages 16mo. The same year welcomed a Greco-Turkish hymn-book of 264 16mo pages, and a second edition came out ten years later. In 1869 the Armenian hymn-book had grown to 426 pages, and four years later a fresh edition contained 430 pages. This was followed by a supplement of 56 8vo pages to the Armenian hymn and tune book in 1877, and as tho that was not enough, an appendix of 16 pages more was issued the same year. Such a list of publications indicates an abounding spiritual life that makes what would otherwise be the driest of statistics an occasion of great joy to all who love the prosperity of Zion. In Bulgarian, three pages of hymns and tunes were printed in 1861, the year following a hymn-book of 24 12mo pages, and in 1865 a hymn and tune book of 64 8vo pages. The hymn-book in 1872 had grown to 154 16mo pages. In Syria, while the mission was still under the care of the American Board, 200 pages of versified Psalms were printed about 1868. The same year gave 200 pages of children's hymns to the Sunday schools, and before the mission passed into the hands of the Presbyterians a hymn-book appeared, first of 300 pages, and after that of 500. About 1874 a hymn and tune book was printed, containing an introduction teaching how to read our musical notation. This was afterward printed separately, 30 pages 8vo. Since then hymns have been prepared to suit the Arab tunes, and are now published with the tunes. A curious feature of these hymns and tune books is that the music has to be reversed to suit the Arabic system of writing from right to left. In 1882 the Psalms in verse were printed for the use of the United and Reformed Missions, hymns alone, 400 18mo pages; with tunes, 500 12mo pages; and with tonic Sol Fa notation, 600 12mo pages. In 1885 a new 8vo hymn and tune book, containing 327 hymns and 280 tunes, was prepared by Rev. Samuel Jessup and Rev. George Ford, and a second edition was called for in 1889. A hymn-book without tunes appeared in 1885, of 418 pages 18mo. This advanced to a second edition in 1887, and a third in 1889, showing a very encouraging demand for such a work.

In the Persian Mission the hymn-books have gone through several editions. The last, issued in 1886, has about 300 hymns, mostly translations, but adapted to the expression of Christian feeling in Persia, and also to the wants of the young in their Oriental homes.

Music has been taught by the missionaries. The popular tunes are those used in congregations in the United States. The chants of the ancient Syriac and ancient Armenian are used in religious worship, and are very popular. The words, of course, are in the vernacular, and so the congregation can join. They are used especially in chanting the Psalms, and also some other portions of the Scripture, such as are found in books for responsive reading at home.

MUSKOKI LANGUAGE. See CREEK.

MUSSOOREE: A town and sanitarium in the United Provinces, India, situated in the district of Dehra Dun, 78 miles E. of Ambala, and 7 miles N. E. by N. of Dehra, forming practically one station with Landaur. Population (1891), 5,100. Station of the CMS (1894), with (1903) 2 missionaries, one with his wife; 1 native worker, 1 place of worship, 1 day school, and 81 professed Christians. Station also of the ME, with (1903) 1 missionary and his wife, 10 native workers, 2 places of worship, 2 Sunday schools, 1 theological class, and 282 professed Christians, of whom 126 are communicants. Societies write the name Mussourie.

MUTTRA: A town in the United Provinces, India, situated on the right bank of the Jumna River, 23 miles N. N. E. of Bhartpur. This place was mentioned by Ptolemy as Modoura of the gods. Population (1901), 60,042, of whom 48,000 are Hindus and 10,500 are Muslims. Station of the BMS (1893), with (1903) 1 missionary and his wife, 10 native workers, 1 outstation, 3 Sunday schools, 2 day schools, and 35 professed Christians, of whom 18 are communicants. Station also of the CMS (1878), with (1903) 1 missionary, 2 women missionaries, 20 native workers, 1 place of worship, 2 day schools, and 64 professed Christians, of whom 30 are communicants. Station also of the ME, with (1903) 1 missionary and wife, 2 women missionaries, 44 nativ workers, 4 places of worship, 2 Sunday schools, 8 day schools and 731 professed Christians, of whom 454 are communicants.

MUTUNGO: A village of Uganda, Africa, situated near Mengo, Uganda. Station of the CMS (1902), with 2 missionaries and 1 industrial institute.

MUTYALAPAD: A town in Madras, situated 30 miles N. E. of Jamulamadugu, on a branch of the Penner River. Station of the SPG (1855), with (1902) 1 missionary, 80 native workers, 43 places of worship, 33 day schools, and 2,893 professed Christians, of whom 951 are communicants.

MUZAFFARNAGAR: A town of Muzaffarnagar district, United Provinces, India, situated 30 miles N. of Meerut. Population, 18,200, Hindus, Mohammedans, Jains, and a few Christians. Climate formerly very unhealthy and malarious, but lately, owing to modern sanitary improvements, it has been made much more salubrious. Station of the ME, with (1903) 28 native workers, 1 place of worship, 4 day schools, 16 Sunday schools, and 1,656 professed Christians, of whom 319 are communicants. Station of the Reformed Presbyterian Church of Scotland, with (1901) 1 missionary, 3 native workers, 2 outstations, 1 place of worship, 1 Sunday school, 1 lepers' asylum, and 195 professed Christians.

MUZAFFARPUR: A town in Bengal, India, 35 miles north-northeast of Patna. Population, 49,000, of whom 35,000 are Hindus. It is well built and clean, with good schools, temples, court-houses, and other public buildings. Has a large trade. Station of the Gossner Mission Society, with (1903) 1 missionary, 1 native worker, 1 Sunday school, 1 day school, 1 orphanage, and 90 professed Christians. Society spells the name Muzafferpur. Station also of the ME, with (1903) 16 native workers, 3 places of worship, 7 Sunday schools, 2 day schools and 328 professed Christians, of whom 238 are communicants.

MVENYANE: A settlement in Cape Colony, South Africa, situated in Griqualand East, 23 miles W. of Kokstadt. Station of the Moravian Missions (1888), with (1903) 3 missionaries, two of them with their wives, 18 native workers, 1 place of worship, 1 Sunday school, 3 day schools, 1 theological class, and 102 professed Christians.

MVUMI: A settlement in German East Africa, situated in the Chigogo District, about 26 miles W. by N. of Mpapwa. Station of the CMS (1883), with (1903) 1 missionary and his wife, 1 native worker, 2 outstations, 5 day schools, and 2 professed Christians.

MWENA: A settlement in the Congo Free State, Africa, situated near the headwaters of the Cualaha, about 25 miles S. W. of Lake Mwena. Station of the PB, with 2 missionaries, one with his wife.

MWENZO: A settlement in British Central Africa, situated on the Stevenson Road, about 100 miles W. by N. of Karonga, on the W. shore of Lake Nyasa. Station of the UFS, with (1903) 1 missionary and his wife, 2 native workers, 4 outstations, 5 day schools, 1 dispensary, and 14 professed Christians.

MYINGYAN: A town in Burma, British India, situated on the left bank of the Irawadi River, 60 miles N. W. of Meiktila, with which it is connected by railroad. Population, 19,000, of whom 17,000 are Buddhists. Station of the ABMU (1887), with (1903) 2 missionaries and their wives, 8 native workers, 1 Sunday school, 1 day school, 1 dispensary, 1 hospital, and 27 professed Christians.

MYITKYINA: A town in Burma, British India, situated in the Kachin region at the extremity of the railway, 75 miles N. by E. of Bhamo. Station of the ABMU (1894), with (1903) 1 missionary with his wife, 5 native workers, 2 outstations, 2 places of worship, 1 Sunday school, 1 boarding school, 1 day school, and 150 professed Christians, of whom 50 are communicants.

MYMENSINGH. See MAIMANSING.

MYNPURI. See MAINPURI.

MYSORE: A large and important native state in South India. Its territory is entirely surrounded by the British dominions belonging to the presidency of Madras. It lies at the point where the ranges of the Western and Eastern Ghats come together, and most of its territory is on the elevated plateau lying between these ranges. Its limits of north latitude are 11° 40' and 15°, and of east longitude 74° 40' and 78° 30'. The area is 29,444 square miles, and the population, 5,539,399, according to the census of 1901. Its surface is much broken by rocky hills and ravines; the drainage of the country is almost wholly to the east; in the northwest one river falls in a fine cascade over the precipitous wall of the Western Ghats, and seeks the Indian Ocean. Otherwise the streams all reach the Bay of Bengal through the Tungabhadra on the north, the Kaveri on the south, and several smaller rivers between these two more important streams. These rivers, like almost all those of India, while useless for navigation, support large systems of artificial irrigation. Mysore was included in the territories ruled from time immemorial by old prehistoric Hindu dynasties of South India, whose existence can dimly be traced in the uncertain light of early Indian times. The last of these dynasties was overthrown by the Mohammedans in 1565. As the latter in turn began to lose their power a Hindu chief seized the fort of Seringapatam in 1610, and became the founder of the present Mysore principality. The Hindu rulers were displaced by Mohammedans under Haider Ali in the latter part of the 18th century. But after the English finally defeated his son, Tippu Sahib, in 1799, they replaced the old Hindu family on the throne of Mysore.

Of the entire population the Hindus amount to nearly 95 per cent., Mohammedans to a little less than 5 per cent. The total number of Christians is given as 34,402. Of these, 28,600 are native converts. About one-fourth of the Christians are Protestants, the others Roman Catholics. The language almost universally used is Kanarese. The cultivation of the Kanarese is greatly indebted to the missionaries; grammars and dictionaries, a translation of the Bible and the beginnings of a worthy native literature are due to missionary labor.

The first Protestant mission in Mysore was that of the Society for the Propagation of the Gospel, established at Bangalore in 1817. In 1820 the London Missionary Society planted a station at the same city. The Hindu government seems to have been unfriendly to the work of the missionaries, and opportunities for preaching in Kanarese—the vernacular of the people—were at first greatly curtailed by this fact. The first few years of the mission were not prosperous, but since its earlier difficulties have been overcome, it has had a career of much success. The Wesleyans also entered Mysore, planting their principal station in the city of that name; shortly after the London Society entered Bangalore. Both these missions have now many stations throughout the state.

MYSORE: A town, capital of the native state of Mysore, India, situated 10 miles S. W. of Seringapatam. In 1542 a fort was built here. Population (1901), 68,111. Station of the CEZ (1892), now temporarily vacant. Station also of the WMS, with (1903) 4 missionaries, three of them with their wives; 11 native workers, 8 outstations, 12 places of worship, 7 Sunday schools, 27 day schools, 2 boarding schools, 1 theological class, and 270 professed Christians, of whom 211 are communicants.

N

NAAS. See NASS.

NABLUS: A town in Palestine, Turkey, situated in a verdant vale, 30 miles N. of Jerusalem and between Mt. Ebal and Gerizim. It stands on the site of Shechem of the Old, and Sychar of the New Testament Scripture. Population, 16,000. Station of the CMS (1876), with (1903) 1 missionary and his wife, 2 women missionaries, 12 native workers, 4 outstations, 1 hospital, and 328 professed Christians, of whom 153 are communicants. Some write the name Nabulus. Station also of the BMS (1888), with (1903) 1 missionary and his wife, 8 native workers, 4 outstations, 1 day school, and 129 professed Christians.

NADIAD. See NARIAD.

NAGANO: A town in Hondo, Japan, situated 94 miles S. W. by S. of Niigata. It has a great Buddhist temple, which stands in much the same relation to the town as the temple of Diana did to Ephesus, since the prosperity of the place depends upon the number of pilgrims to the shrine. Population (1898), 31,319. Station of the Church of England in Canada (1892), with (1901) 3 missionaries, 1 with his wife; 1 woman missionary, 10 native workers, 6 outstations, 50 professed Christians, 1 place of worship, 1 dispensary, 1 hospital. Station also of Canada Methodist Missionary Society (1891), with (1901) 3 native workers, 4 outstations, 5 places of worship, 3 Sunday schools, and 63 professed Christians. Station also of the RCA (1894), with (1903) 1 missionary and his wife, 3 native workers, 2 outstations, 1 place of worship, 4 Sunday schools, and 80 professed Christians.

NAGARKOIL: A Christian village in Travancore, India, situated 40 miles S. S. W. of Tinnevelli and about 1 mile from Kotar. Station of the LMS (1809), with (1903) 3 missionaries and their wives, 2 women missionaries, 163 native workers, 77 outstations, 1 printing house, 89 day schools, 1 boarding school, 1 college, 1 orphanage, 11,833 professed Christians, of whom 2,055 are communicants. Post of the Salvation Army also. The name is also written Nagercoil.

NAGASAKI: A town on the island of Kiu-shiu, Japan, the principal seaport of the western coast. It is picturesquely situated at the head of a small inlet four miles long and a mile wide. It has thus one of the finest harbors in the world. The surrounding hills, 1,500 feet high, and the numerous small islands with which the harbor is dotted add greatly to its beauty. The city is laid out with great regularity, in rectangles. A stream of water flows through it. There is a foreign concession separated from the main city by an arm of the bay. For more than 200 years this was the only port where foreigners were allowed to land. A hospital was established here in 1861—the oldest now in Japan, and there is a fine government school, in which hundreds of young Japanese are instructed in European languages and sciences. The city is noted for its temples and the magnificence of its festivals. It is also an important coaling station. The climate is salubrious, and the city is a pleasant one in which to live. Population (1898) 107,422. Station of the CMS (1869), with (1903) 1 missionary and his wife, 3 women missionaries, 3 native workers, 1 outstation, 1 place of worship, 1 Sunday school, 1 boarding school, and 163 professed Christians. Station also of the ME (1869), with (1903) 2 missionaries and their wives, 4 women missionaries, 12 native workers, 3 outstations, 2 places of worship, 2 Sunday schools, 2 boarding schools, 1 theological class, and 570 professed Christians, of whom 366 are communicants. Station also of the RCA (1859), with (1903) 2 missionaries, 2 women missionaries, 18 native workers, 3 outstations, and 125 professed Christians, 1 place of worship, 3 Sunday schools, 2 boarding schools, and 1 college. Station also of the SBC (1896), with (1903) 1 missionary and his wife, 1 native worker, 2 cutstations, 1 Sunday school, and 12 professed Christians.

NAGERCOIL. See NAGARKOIL.

NAGOYA: A city on the main island of Japan, situated on the railroad midway between Tokio and Kioto. It is in the midst of a broad, fertile plain, surrounded by thriving towns and villages, and is connected with Gifu by an almost continuous street of 20 miles. Population (1898), 244,145. It is the central point of the Nagoya district, and its importance as a base of operations is fully recognized. Such a strategic position for missions was early availed of by the Reformed (Dutch) Church (U. S. A.), but there is no representative of that mission there at present. Station of the PS (1887), with (1903) 2 missionaries and their wives, 2 women missionaries, 13 native workers, 28 places of worship, 11 Sunday schools, 1 boarding school, and 800 professed Christians, of whom 375 are communicants. Station also of the Methodist Protestant Church (1885), with (1903) 2 missionaries with their wives, 2 women missionaries, 8 native workers, 9 outstations, 1 place of worship, 12 Sunday schools, 1 theological school, and 60 professed Christians. Station of the CMS (1896), with (1903) 1 missionary and his wife, 2 women missionaries, 6 native workers, 2 outstations, 1 place of worship, 1 Sunday school, 2 day schools, and 1 kindergarten. Station also of the ME, with 3 women missionaries, 22 native workers, 7 outstations, 7 places of worship, 11 Sunday schools, 1 boarding school, and 516 professed Christians, of whom 338 are communicants.

NAGPUR: City in Central Provinces, India, 42 miles east-northeast of Bombay. It is a large city, but not a very fine one, altho there are many relics of its former greatness still to be seen, and the handsome tanks and gardens outside the city and the pretty scenery give the place a very attractive appearance. Climate, healthy. Population (1901), 127,734, of whom 99,000 are Hindus and 21,000 Muslims. Station of the UFS (1845), with (1903) 4 missionaries, 3 of them with their wives; 50 native workers, 5 outstations, 1 place of worship, 10 day schools, 2 higher institutions, 1 orphanage, and 240 professed Christians. Name also written Nagpore.

NAHORUOP: A village in Sumatra, Dutch East Indies, to which has been removed the Rhenish Mission station of Sigompulon. It lies in the Batang Toru Valley, about 20 miles E. N. E. of Siboga. Station of the Rhenish Mission Society, with (1903) 1 missionary and his wife, 47 native workers, 7 outstations, 7 Sunday schools, 9 day schools, and 2,990 professed Christians, of whom 1,403 are communicants.

NAIDUPET: A town in Madras, India, situated on the Suvarnamukhi River, about 15 miles S. of Gudur. Station of the Hermannsburg Mission Society (1867), with (1903) 3 missionaries, 2 of them with their wives; 21 native workers, 9 outstations, 1 place of worship, 10 day schools, 1 theological school, 1 industrial school, and 950 professed Christians. Some write the name Nayudupeta.

NAIHATI: A municipality in Bengal, India, situated on the Hugli River, about 25 miles N.

of Calcutta. Population (1891), 29,700, of whom 24,800 are Hindus. Station of the CEZ (1891), with (1903) 1 woman missionary, 11 native workers, and 4 day schools.

NAIN: A town in Labrador, situated on the E. coast. Has a good harbor. Station of the Moravian Missions (1771), being the first place occupied by them in Labrador. It now (1901) has 4 missionaries with their wives, 16 native workers, men and women; 1 day school, 1 place of worship, and 110 communicant Christians.

NAINGOLAN: A settlement in Sumatra, Dutch East Indies, Malaysia, situated on the S. coast of Toba Island in Toba Lake. Station of the Rhenish Mission Society, with (1903) 1 missionary and his wife, 2 native workers, 2 day schools, 1 outstation, 1 Sunday school, and 43 professed Christians.

NAINI TAL: A town in Kumaon district, United Provinces, India, picturesquely situated on the banks of a lovely little lake which nestles among the spurs of the Himalayas. Favorite sanitarium and summer resort of Europeans from the plains. Altitude, 6,400 feet. Population (1891), 7,900, chiefly Hindus. Station of the ME, with 3 missionaries and their wives, 11 native workers, 1 place of worship, 2 Sunday schools, 3 day schools, 2 boarding schools, 1 society for young people, 1 Young Women's Christian Association, and 119 professed Christians.

NAKANONYI: A village in Uganda, Central Africa, situated 30 miles N. E. of Mengo. Station of the CMS (1895), with (1903) 1 missionary, 103 native workers, 1 day school, and 2,890 professed Christians, of whom 1,068 are communicants.

NAKAWN: A village in the Malay Peninsula, Siam, situated near the E. coast about 500 miles S. of Bangkok. Population, 10,000. Station of the PN (1900), with (1903) 2 missionaries, 1 with his wife; 3 native workers, 2 outstations, 93 professed Christians, 1 place of worship, 1 dispensary, and 1 day school.

NAKKO: A small group of islands belonging to Nias Island, Malaysia, W. of Sumatra, Dutch East Indies. Station of the Rhenish Mission, with 1 missionary and his wife and 300 professed Christians, of whom 62 are communicants.

NALGONDA: A town in the native State of Haidarabad, India, situated 57 miles E. S. E. of Haidarabad City. Station of the ABMU (1890), with (1903) 1 missionary and his wife, 1 woman missionary, 34 native workers, 20 outstations, 1 place of worship, 6 Sunday schools, 4 day schools, 1 boarding school, 1 hospital, and 964 professed Christians.

NAMAHACHA: A sanitarium and settlement in Portuguese E. Africa, situated in the Lebombo Mountains and serving for the missionaries occupying stations near the coast, as at Inhambane, etc. Station of the SPG, with 4 missionaries, 3 of them with their wives; 1 native worker, 1 boarding school, 1 day school, and 50 professed Christians, of whom 12 are communicants.

NAMAQUA LANGUAGE: A very difficult language of the African family and the Hottentot group, spoken in the German Southwestern Africa, north of the Orange River. The difficulty of the language is largely due to its containing four curious smacking sounds which Europeans do not readily understand or imitate. The language has been reduced to writing by German missionaries with use of the Roman letters. Many call this language the Nama, rather than the Namaqua language.

NAMKHAM: A town in Burma, British India, situated among the Shans, 56 miles E. S. E. of Bhamo. Altitude 2,630 feet. Station of the ABMU (1893), with (1903) 2 missionaries, 1 with his wife; 15 native workers, 3 outstations, 3 places of worship, 2 Sunday schools, 1 day school, 1 boarding school, 2 dispensaries, 1 hospital, and 160 professed Christians, of whom 62 are communicants.

NAN. See MUANGNAN.

NAN-CHANG-FU: A town in the Province of Kiangsi, China, on the right bank of the Kiakiang, 173 miles S. E. by S. of Han-kau, the emporium of the porcelain manufacture E. of Lake Poyang. Station of the CIM (1898), with (1903) 1 missionary and his wife and 1 place of worship. Station also of the ME, with 2 missionaries and their wives, 9 native workers, 6 outstations, 6 day schools, 7 Sunday schools, 26 places of worship, and 1,316 professed Christians. Station also of the PB.

NANDGAON: A town in the Central Provinces of India, situated in the native state of the same name, of which it is the capital, and 42 miles W. by S. of Raipur. Station of the Pentecost Bands of the World (1898), with (1900) 3 missionaries, 2 of them with their wives; 2 women missionaries, 2 native workers, 1 place of worship, 1 Sunday school, 1 book-room, 1 industrial school, 1 orphanage. Society writes the name Raj Nandgaon.

NANDIAL: A prosperous town in Madras, India, situated in the district of Kurnool, 108 miles E. by N. of Bellary. Population, 10,700; Hindus, 5,000; Muslims, 3,500. Station of the SPG (1854), with (1903) 3 missionaries, 110 native workers, 11 places of worship, 1 boarding school, 1 theological school, and 2,251 professed Christians, of whom 544 are communicants. Some write the name Nandyal.

NANG-WA: A town in Fo-kien, China, situated 20 miles N. E. of Yen-ping-fu. Station of the CEZ (1891), with (1903) 2 women missionaries, 2 native workers, and 1 day school.

NAN-KANG-FU: A town in the Province of Kiang-si, China, situated 12 miles S. by W. of Kiu-kiang. Station of the CIM (1887), with (1903) 1 missionary and his wife and 1 native worker. Some write the name Nan-k'ang.

NANKING: The "southern capital" of China; so called from its having been the seat of government during the Ming dynasty (1368-1644). It is situated in the Province of Kiang-su, on the south bank of the Yangtse, which makes a right angle, and borders the city on the north and west, 223 miles west of Shanghai, and almost midway between Canton and Peking. It formerly possessed one of the finest walls known, 20 miles in circuit, 70 feet high, 30 feet wide, and pierced with 13 gates. The interior of the city has much unoccupied ground. The famous Porcelain Tower, built by the Emperor Yung Loh (1403-28), was an object of the wonder and admiration of Europeans, until it was destroyed by the Tai-ping rebels during their occupancy of the city in 1853-6, at which time most of the public buildings were ruthlessly destroyed. It was formerly a literary center, and was noted also for its industries. Cotton cloth, called nankeen, from the name of the city; satin, crêpe, and pottery were all manufactured. An arsenal is located at Nanking under European superintendence, where firearms and vessels of war are manufactured. Sir Henry Pottinger signed here the famous Nanking treaty in 1842.

Not far from the city are the tombs of the emperors of the Ming dynasty, with an avenue leading to them guarded by gigantic stone figures of men and animals.

By a treaty made with France in 1858, this port was thrown open, but practically no commerce is carried on with foreigners. The climate is warm and dry, and not unhealthy. Population (1901), 225,000. The importance of the city as a center for educational work has been appreciated by the Methodist Episcopal Church, who have established here a university with an endowment of $200,000. The Disciples of Christ are also about to erect a college. The medical work in connection with the Methodist Episcopal Hospital, said to be the largest in China, is most important. The missionary societies at work in Nanking and vicinity are the following: The American Adventists, AFFM (1890), FCMS (1887), ME (1867), and PN (1876). These societies now (1903) have 46 missionaries, men and women; 57 native workers, 12 places of worship, 16 day schools, 16 higher institutions, 3 hospitals and dispensaries, 1 printing house, and 711 professed Christians. The YMCA has a representative here.

NAN-PU-HSIEN: A town in the Province of Sze-chwan, China, situated on the river, about 12 miles S. by E. of Pao-ning-fu. Station of the CIM (1902), with 2 women missionaries and 1 place of worship.

NANUOYA: A village in the Central Provinces of Ceylon, situated about 26 miles S. of Kandy. Station of the CMS Tamil Coolie Mission, with (1903) 1 missionary, 87 native workers, 44 day schools, and 1,140 professed Christians.

NANZELA: A settlement in Northwest Rhodesia, Africa, situated in Barotseland, about 60 miles E. S. E. of Ndala and 160 miles N. of Victoria Falls. Station of the Primitive Methodist Missionary Society, with (1903) 1 missionary and his wife, 2 native workers, 1 outstation, 1 Sunday school, 1 dispensary, 1 day school, and 14 professed Christians.

NAORANGPUR: A town in Madras, India, situated on the Indravati River, about 18 miles N. E. of Kotpad. Station of the Breklum Missionary Society (1889), with (1903) 3 missionaries, 1 with his wife; 5 native workers, 3 outstations, 1 place of worship, 1 Sunday school, 2 day schools, 1 orphanage, and 728 professed Christians, of whom 428 are communicants. Name also written Nowrangapur.

NARIAD: A town in Bombay, India, situated in the District of Kaira, 30 miles N. E. by N. of Cambay. It is the center of an extensive trade in tobacco. Population (1891), 29,000. Station of the ME, with (1903) 1 missionary and his wife, 103 native workers, 33 Sunday schools, 92 day schools, and 5,809 professed Christians. Some write the name Nadiad

NARAINGANJ: A town in Bengal, India, situated on the Lachmia River, 10 miles S. S. E. of Dacca. Population, 17,700, of whom 9,700 are Hindus and 7,000 Muslims. Station of the BMS (1898), with (1903) 1 missionary and his wife, 5 native workers, and 18 professed Christians. Society writes the name Narayangunge.

NARASARAOPET: A town in Madras, India, situated in the Kistna District, about 230 miles north of the City of Madras. Station of the ABMU (1883), with (1903) 2 missionaries, 1 with his wife; 41 native workers, 121 outstations, 12 places of worship, 30 Sunday schools, 17 day schools, 1 boarding school, 1 dispensary, 1 hospital, and 4,936 professed Christians. Station of the ELGS also. Name is also written Nursaravapetta.

NAROWAL: Town in the Punjab, India, situated in the District of Sialkot, 35 miles N. of Amritsar. It is famous for its leather-work. Population, 5,000. Station of the CEZ (1885), with (1903) 2 women missionaries, 9 native workers, 1 boarding school, 2 day schools, 1 dispensary, 1 hospital. Station also of the CMS (1859), with (1903) 1 missionary and his wife, 14 native workers, 1 place of worship, 1 day school, 2 boarding schools, and 1,366 professed Christians, of whom 50 are communicants.

NARRINYERI LANGUAGE: A language of the Papuan group, which is found among the surviving aborigines of South Australia. It has been reduced to writing with use of the Roman letters.

NARSAPUR: A town in Madras, India, in the District of Godavari, on the right bank of the river Godavari, 39 miles E. by N. of Masulipatam. Population, 7,500, of whom 6,600 are Hindus. Station of the PB, with (1900) 4 missionaries, 1 with his wife, and 5 women missionaries.

NARSINGHPUR: A town in the Central Provinces, India, situated in the District of N., of which it is the capital, 50 miles W. S. W. of Jabalpur. It is an important trade center for the Narbada Valley. Population, 10,200 (Hindus, 7,600). Station of the ME, with (1903) 1 missionary, 22 native workers, 1 place of worship, 22 Sunday schools, 1 day school, and 253 professed Christians.

NASA: A village in German East Africa, situated on the east coast of Lake Victoria Nyanza, near its S. extremity. Station of the CMS (1888), with (1903) 2 missionaries, 1 of them with his wife; 6 native workers, 1 place of worship, 4 day schools, and 78 professed Christians, of whom 36 are communicants.

NASARAPUR: A town in Bombay, India, situated in the native State of Bhor, S. W. of Poona. Station of the Poona Indian Village Mission, with (1900) 12 missionaries, 5 women missionaries, 1 native worker, 1 Sunday school, 1 industrial school, 1 dispensary, 1 hospital, 2 orphanages.

NASIK: An important town in Bombay, India, situated on the Godavari River, 89 miles N. W. of Ahmadnagar. It is a famous resort of Hindu pilgrims, and has considerable manufactures of metal wares. Population, 21,700. The Christian village of Sharanpur is one of its outskirts. Station of the CMS (1832), with (1903) 1 missionary and his wife, 38 native workers, 1 place of worship, 13 day schools, 1 boarding school, 1 industrial school, 2 orphanages, 1 widows' home, and 519 professed Christians, of whom 190 are communicants. Station also of the ZBM, with (1903) 3 women missionaries, 18 native workers, 1 outstation, 6 day schools.

NASIRABAD: A town and cantonment in Ajmere, India, situated about 18 miles from the town of Ajmere, on a bleak, open plain, which slopes eastward from the Aravalli Hills. Station of the UFS (1861), with (1903) 2 missionaries, 1 with his wife; 3 women missionaries, 1 outstation, 69 native workers, 7 Sunday schools, 10 day schools, 2 high schools, 1 dispensary, 1 hospital, 1 orphanage, and 99 professed Christians.

NASS: A settlement in British Columbia, situated at the mouth of the Nass River, 50 miles N. E. of Port Simpson. Station of the MCC (1877), with (1903) 1 missionary and his wife, 1 Sunday school, and 96 professed Christians. Society calls the station Naas River.

NASSAU: The capital of the Bahama Islands, West Indies, situated on the N. coast of the island of New Providence. Population, 11,000. Station of the WMS, with (1903) 3 missionaries, 11 native workers, 3 outstations, 6 places of worship, 7 Sunday schools, 6 day schools, and 814 professed Christians, of whom 749 are communicants.

NATAL: A crown colony of Great Britain in South Africa. It has an area of 42,000 square miles, now including the Province of Zululand, annexed in 1897, and about 7,000 square miles taken from the Transvaal and annexed in 1903. The population, including the annexed areas (1901), is 985,000, that of Natal, including Zululand, being 925,118. The colony lies to the south of the Transvaal and Portuguese E. Africa, has a coast line on the Indian Ocean of about 350 miles, and is bounded south and west by Basutoland and the Griqualand dependencies of Cape Colony. Utrecht and Vryheid, taken from the Transvaal, carry the northern boundary to the Pongola River.

The Drackenberg Mountains, from 9,000 to 10,000 feet high, separate it from Basutoland and the Orange River Colony. Pietermaritzburg, one of the most delightful cities in Africa, is the capital. Durban, the only port, is 1,000 miles from Cape Town. The climate is delightful and invigorating. The temperature ranges from 56° to 82° Fahrenheit. The coast region is semi-tropical, and produces the sugar-cane, pineapple, banana, and coffee. Wool, corn, and sugar are the staple products. In the northern districts magnificent coal deposits are found. All the European cereals are cultivated. Hippopotami, monkeys, baboons, and crocodiles are to be seen. Antelopes abound. There are many poisonous snakes. The population consists of whites (English, Dutch, and Germans), Zulus, and Asiatic coolies.

The crown is represented by a governor and legislative council of 12 members, including one for Zululand. There are (1901) 626 miles of railway, including a main line from Durban, which connects with the lines to Johannesburg and Pretoria.

Natal may be called civilized, tho there are sections where the old heathenism may still be seen. The WMS, the UFS, Wesleyan Mission, the Free Church of Scotland, the Norwegian and the Berlin Missionary societies, the Hermannsburg Society, the SPG, the ABCFM, and the Roman Catholic Missions are each and all doing a good work in Natal. The ABCFM Mission began in 1835, and was the first among the Zulus, who were then a savage people, with a language as yet unwritten and unknown. The above named societies have 23 stations in Natal, with about 15,000 children in their schools.

Brooks (H.), *Natal* (descriptive), London, 1887; Ingram (J. F.), *Natalia* (historical), London, 1897; Robinson (Sir J.), *A Lifetime in South Africa*, London, 1900; Russell (R.), *Natal*, 6th edition, London, 1900; Tyler (J.), *Forty Years in Zululand*, Boston, 1881.

NATAL: A town and seaport on the E. coast of Brazil, capital of the State of Rio Grande do Norte, 160 miles N. of Pernambuco. The harbor has a water area of 2 square miles. Population, 6,000. Station of the PS (1895), with (1903) 1 missionary and his wife, 225 professed Christians, 1 Sunday school, 1 day school, 4 places of worship.

NATIVE AGENCY: The Native Agency in mission work is considered in this article in contrast with the Foreign Agency necessary to the beginnings of the Gospel in heathen lands. The complete evangelization of any country by foreign agency alone is historically unknown and, humanly speaking, impossible. When the Apostle Paul went on his mission from Asia to Europe his method was not to carry with him a sufficient force of Asiatic missionaries to supply all the points he desired to reach with Gospel preaching. He went to the strategic centers, where, after he had gathered bands of converts, he organized churches over which he placed native pastors and teachers, and from which were ultimately sent out native evangelists. When the Church is once planted in any country these native workers are the proper agents for its propagation, because they only possess the identity of speech and modes of thought which are necessary to bring them into touch with the people, in such a way as fits them to become channels for the communication of spiritual light and power.

The term Native Agency in its widest sense means the Native Church. The aim of missions in every land is to establish churches that will be so filled with the life-giving spirit of God that it will be impossible for them to be anything else than *agencies*. Such was the Apostolic Church, and such have usually been first churches established in new mission fields. But the more of this aggressive spirit the churches have, the more they will need various kinds of leaders to direct it. The term Native Agency in the technical sense is usually applied to these native leaders.

The first form of native agency employed by the foreign missionary is always that of a *personal teacher* or *interpreter;* but inasmuch as the function of such native helpers is purely mechanical, the simple mention of them is sufficient for the purposes of this article. The forms of agency specially to be considered are those included in the term *Native Ministry*, in its two branches of evangelists and pastors. Among the ascension gifts of Christ prominent mention is made of these two. Therefore, wherever Christ gives to missionary labor the material for a church we may expect to find included in it the material for evangelists and pastors.

1. *Evangelists:* Every foreign missionary, whether preacher, teacher, doctor, translator or writer of books, is essentially an evangelist, the success of whose work depends upon his ability to multiply himself by the native evangelists he finds, trains, and guides.

In the earlier stages of mission work all native

agents employed by missionaries are naturally called "native helpers." This descriptive term has persisted in missionary literature beyond the point where it is properly descriptive of the actual situation. In the later stages of mission work the native agency becomes the main force, and the missionary becomes the "helper." The timely recognition of this change in the relative position of the workers will always greatly contribute to the harmonious and successful prosecution of their cooperative work.

With reference to finding evangelists, it may be said that, being given of Christ, the missionary can always find as many of them as Christ wishes him to have at any given time. This implies, however, that he seek the kind of evangelists that Christ wants, and in the way that Christ would approve. To this end it is essential always to keep in mind the real character of the end in view, which is the planting and extension of the kingdom of God on earth. The mode of propagating the kingdom must depend on the nature of it, and the evangelist's qualifications must be those that fit him for that specific work. If the end in view were the propagation of Western civilization or Western ideas of government, a certain character of native agency would of course be required for that purpose. In China, for instance, such a man as was the late Li Hung Chang, not converted, but thoroughly Westernized, would make the best possible evangelist. But the kingdom of God is "not of this world," altho its mission is to save the world; to send out ameliorating and regenerating forces into every department of the world's life. But to do this effectively it must be kept and given to the world as the pure, spiritual and divine thing that it is. This view of the nature of the kingdom gives us our first suggestion as to the necessary qualifications of the native evangelist. He must be, first of all, a child of the kingdom, a man spiritually alive, called out of the world, and yet, because of the Christ spirit in him, loving the world somewhat as Christ did, and ready, as He was, to live and die for its salvation. He should, of course, be a man properly taught, for otherwise he cannot be a teacher of others. "If the blind lead the blind, both will fall into the ditch." He should have the gift of utterance necessary in all teachers to the imparting of the knowledge they possess. He should be a man of strong personality and force of character. Men who, before their conversion, by reason of possessing this quality are natural leaders in their communities, are sure to be, after their conversion, the most efficient ones in leading men to Christ.

Social position and literary culture will be conducive to the evangelist's power and usefulness, provided they are not associated, as is too often the case in Oriental lands, with intellectual pride, lack of sympathy with the common people, and aversion to work. The literati of China are as a class disqualified by these weaknesses for making successful evangelists, even when they are converted to Christianity; for it usually requires not only regeneration but quite a long period of progressive sanctification also to eradicate these traits, characteristic of their class, from their characters. The evangelists drawn from the Samurai class in Japan were very effective in reaching those of the same social grade to which they belonged. But for the evangelization of the common people in Japan there is now a felt need for a supplementary body of evangelists, drawn from the masses, so as to be in full sympathy with them, and so as to be free from the class spirit, and trained to hard work. The next great step of progress in evangelizing Japan will probably be made when a supply of this kind of evangelists has been provided. It is probably for these reasons that of the original twelve chosen by Christ at least ten were previously laboring men. On the other hand, the great evangelist in every country is likely to be a man who, like the Apostle Paul, adds to high social position, literary character and intellectual quality, a natural enthusiasm which pharisaic formalism could not kill in him as it did in the common run of Scribes and Pharisees. So it is that altho "not many wise men after the flesh, not many mighty, not many noble are called" to this work, the few of this kind who are called are the ones who make the greatest and most successful leaders in the propagation of the Gospel.

Owing to the seclusion of women in the Orient it is necessary to send out women as missionaries, who need native female help for the prosecution of their work. These female native workers are usually called **Bible Women**. They are evangelists for the heathen women who could not otherwise be reached with the Gospel. They need the same qualifications, in a large degree, as are needed by the male evangelists. Their work differs from that of the male evangelists in that is it done almost exclusively in the home, and by the wayside, rather than in public assemblies.

2. *Native Pastors:* The Native Church is organized by the ordination in it of one or more Native Pastors. The qualifications of native pastors are given in the Scriptures with a minuteness and detail that seem to indicate Christ's estimate of the great importance of not getting the wrong men into that office. It is to be remembered that these qualifications were laid down at a time when the churches to be supplied with pastors were in their youth. The presence in most of them of Jews of the Dispersion, who had had training in the Old Testament Scriptures, made it easier to find men possessing these qualifications than is now the case in young churches organized in heathen lands of the present day. A very important question is: What modification should be made in the requirements for ordination to the pastoral office in our modern mission churches because of the scarcity of those who can fulfil them even in a tolerable degree? Some great and wise missionaries think that great allowance should be made for the condition prevailing in any given place, and that the church should be organized as soon as possible with the best material for pastors to be found in it. Others hold that it is better to ordain no natives to the office of pastor until they have the men that are fitted for it, even tho they have to wait for the second generation of Christians to obtain them. This article is perhaps not the proper place for the discussion of this question. It does not admit of question that so soon as properly qualified men for native pastors can be found, the church should be organized and placed under their pastoral care. It must be well, also, under any circumstances, to remember the Scriptural admonition to lay hands on no man suddenly for responsible office in the church. It will always be true that novices clothed with authority are in danger of being lifted up with

pride and thereby falling into the condemnation of the devil.

3. *Training:* The training of native pastors, evangelists and other helpers is one of the things of chief importance in the work of the foreign missionary. When the institution of the Christian home has been long enough established in any field to furnish the native supply of Timothys and Tituses, the problem of their training becomes practically the same as that of our home ministry. Mission schools should be established at an early stage of the work and their development made to keep pace with the development of the native church, so that when the time comes that the native church has need of them, the regularly organized Christian College and Theological Seminary may be on hand to do their necessary work. In the earlier stages of the work the missionary home should be made a center around which young men and young women may be gathered for Bible study. Much effective use has been made of summer schools and institutes, where those who have had previous training with the missionary have the benefit of lectures and other forms of oral instruction. An essential feature of any good method of training will always be that which gives emphasis to the missionary's personal influence. Jesus ordained the twelve, first, "that they should be with him," and then, "that he might send them forth to preach." Hence the supreme importance of the missionary himself being the right man rightly trained for his work; for the men he trains are likely to be spiritually the reproduction of himself. As he is or is not, so will the native ministry he trains be or not be, sound in the faith, mighty in the Scriptures, humble, meek, emptied of self and full of the power of the spirit of Christ.

Missionary Review of the World, Vol. XI., 265, 288; *World-Wide Evangelization* (Student Volunteer Movement), pp. 43, 435, 485, 542.

NATIVE STATES: The collective term applied to those portions of India which are not under the direct control of the British Government, being still ruled by native princes and chiefs. These states are scattered over the whole of India. Some of them are large and important districts, covering thousands of square miles, with millions of inhabitants, with military and civil departments of administration, with mints, postal establishments, educational systems, courts, and all the machinery of modern government; some of them are hardly large enough to be noted upon an ordinary map, and consist simply of a village or so with a handful of inhabitants, under the control of some petty descendant of the chief of an aboriginal clan. Between these two extremes the native states range themselves in all degrees of importance. They vary greatly with reference to their populations. Some of them consist almost wholly of Hindus, under a Hindu prince. In others, the ruling family will be Mussulman, tho the population will consist of persons of all the races usually found in the districts of Hindustan. Others again are made up almost wholly of aboriginal tribes, still owning the headship of the hereditary chieftain. The manner in which it has come about that, in the midst of territory under the authority of the British Government, these islands of native rule should be left, may be briefly and generally explained as follows: The English acquired territory in India little by little. As they were brought into contact and relations with the native chiefs and princes, conflicts more or less bitter were natural. The result of these conflicts often was that the territory of the native prince passed wholly into the hands of the British. Some of these wars were waged by the English in self-defense; some of them, it is to be feared, had less of justification. Sometimes the territories of a prince joining English districts would be so ill-governed and mismanaged that this fact, of itself, became a ground for annexation. Nevertheless, among the native rulers with whom the British power has been brought in contact, there have been those whose authority over hereditary domains there was no valid reason for disturbing. Some such reigning families have been allied by treaty to the growing British power for a century or two, and have always been faithful friends and allies. Some princes and chiefs have been confirmed in their possessions simply because in the absence of glaring reasons their removal would provoke hostility inconvenient to face. Thus it has happened that while, as the result of conquest, almost all India has now passed under British rule, many purely native governments still continue in enjoyment of their ancient power. The control exercised over the native states varies in different cases, but all are bound by treaty to the "paramount power," which undertakes to guarantee to them protection against foreign enemies. No one of them is permitted to enter into relations with any other power or with each other, save through the English Government, or to maintain military establishments above a specified limit. In order to protect the populations of these states from misgovernment, as well as to insure a due degree of subjection to the paramount power, they are all closely supervised by the British Government, acting through a class of officials designated to that duty. These officials are known as "residents," or "political agents," or "political superintendents." A resident is one appointed to reside permanently at the court of a native prince, and to be the medium of communication and influence between the prince and the paramount power. Political agents and superintendents usually have supervision over groups of smaller states not large and important enough to require each the services of a resident. There are many such groups of inferior states or chieftainships connected with all the provinces and commissionerships. The political superintendent will often be the nearest British magistrate, who discharges the duties of supervision in connection with the general duties of his official station in British territory. Under the supervision of these officers the internal affairs of the several states are usually left to be managed by their own princes. Continuous and incorrigible incompetence will generally result in the deposition of a prince by the English Government; in this case the government of his state will often be administered by the English until his successor, if a minor, be of age; or some successor will be at once placed upon the throne.

The most important native states—some of which have been made the subject of separate treatment in this work—are Kashmir, in the far north; Baroda, in the northern part of the Bombay Presidency; the dominions of Holkar and of Sindia, in Central India; of the Nizam of Haidarabad, in the Central Deccan; of Mysore, in the Madras Presidency, and of Travancore and Cochin, at the extreme south of the peninsula.

In some of these states missionary operations are carried on successfully. This is notably the case with Travancore and Cochin; also with Mysore. In others the degree of independent action which the chieftain or prince is suffered to exercise, united with the fact that these princes are usually Hindus or Mohammedans who consider themselves set, as it were, for the defense of their respective faiths, is sufficient to prevent any large and effective evangelistic agencies. Of late years, however, the more important native states have become more and more tolerant. Often some of the smaller states will be found the most backward, the most difficult to enter, and the most impervious to all new influences of enlightenment.

NAVULOA: Settlement in the Fiji Islands, Polynesia, situated on the S. E. coast of the island of Viti Levu. Station of the Australian Wesleyan Mission, with (1900) 1 missionary, 297 native workers, 2 outstations, 32 places of worship, 41 Sunday schools, 68 day schools, and 1,256 professed Christians.

NAYUDUPETA. See NAIDUPET.

NAZARETH: Town in Palestine, 65 miles north of Jerusalem, with a history linked with that of the Christian Church from the time of Jesus Christ. It is beautifully situated in a valley surrounded by hills on all sides. The houses are mostly well built of stone. The population has a more prosperous appearance than in most parts of the country, and the women of Nazareth are famous for their beauty. Population, 7,000, the Roman Catholic element being influential. Station of the CMS (1852), with (1903) 1 missionary and his wife, 6 women missionaries, 27 native workers, 17 day schools, 1 outstation, and 434 professed Christians, of whom 161 are communicants. Station also of the Edinburgh Medical Mission Society (1861), with (1903) 1 missionary and his wife, 3 native workers, and 1 dispensary. The Turkish name of the town in Nasira.

NAZARETH: A town in Madras, India, situated in Tinnevelli, about 25 miles S. by E. of Palamkotta. Station of the SPG (1826), with (1903) 1 missionary, 91 native workers, 39 places of worship, 19 day schools, 8 boarding schools, 1 theological school, and 6,615 professed Christians, of whom 2,424 are communicants.

NAZARETH: A town in Natal, Africa, situated in the valley of the Tugela River, about 90 miles N. by W. of Durban. Station of the Hermannsburg Missionary Society (1879), with (1901) 2 missionaries, 1 of them with his wife; 3 native workers, 1 outstation, 2 places of worship, 1 day school, and 178 professed Christians.

NDEJE: A settlement in Uganda, Central Africa, situated in the Bulemezi District, 20 miles N. W. of Gyaza and 32 miles N. N. W. of Mengo. Station of the CMS (1895), with (1903) 1 missionary and his wife, 2 women missionaries, 517 native workers, 2 day schools, 1 dispensary, 1 theological class, and 4,457 professed Christians, of whom 1,448 are communicants.

NEEMUCH. See NIMACH.

NEESIMA, Joseph Hardy: Born in Japan, February, 1844—ten years before Commodore Perry's fleet awaited in the Bay of Yeddo the opening of Japan to the world. At five years of age he was taken to the Shinto temple to give thanks for his life. When in his teens, having never seen a Christian nor heard of the Gospel, Neesima had some conviction of His presence Who is not far from any one, and of the vanity of idols. When he met in a Chinese book the words, "In the beginning God created the heaven and the earth," he said: "this is the God for whom I am looking;" "this is the true God," and secretly determined to know more of that God, even if he left all to find him. These words from the Bible as he understood were brought by an American, and to America he must go. To leave his country was unlawful, and punishable with death. But this he risked, concealed himself among some produce in a boat, and reached Shanghai and ultimately America, working his way as a sailor. The owner of the vessel in which he sailed was the late Hon. Alpheus Hardy of Boston, who, on his reaching America, received him into his family, and provided for his education, giving him nine years in Phillips Academy, Amherst College, and Andover Theological Seminary. The elevation of his countrymen became his absorbing purpose.

While in his course of study, the Japanese Embassy that visited this country and Europe in 1871, to observe the condition of education in Western countries, summoned Mr. Neesima to act as its interpreter. He replied that he was an outlaw from his country, and was subject to no ruler save the King of Kings. He thereupon received formal pardon for leaving his country. He visited with the embassy the principal colleges and universities of the United States, Canada, and Europe. Not only was he thus brought into close and friendly relations with Japanese officials of high character and position and of enlarged views, but his wish to devote his life to the Christian education of his countrymen was greatly strengthened. He was appointed a corresponding member of the Japanese Mission of the ABCFM and was ordained in 1874 in Mount Vernon Church, Boston. In response to his modest but moving plea at the meeting of the American Board in Rutland, nearly $4,000 were pledged for the school which he proposed to establish in Japan. After ten years' absence, he arrived in his native land, in November, 1874, "cherishing," as he says, "in my bosom this one great purpose, *i.e.*, the founding of an institution in which the Christian principles of faith in God, love of truth, and benevolence toward one's fellow-men" should "train up not only men of science and learning, but men of conscientiousness and sincerity."

In November, 1875, he opened the **Doshisha College** at Osaka. A remarkable revival occurred in the Doshisha in 1884, during which the strain upon his health was such as obliged him to leave the country for a while. He revisited the United States in 1885. On returning to Japan in 1886, he formed a plan for the enlargement of the Doshisha, so that it might have the rank of a university. Not in any wise concealing his purpose to make it a Christian institution, he yet appealed for aid to the non-Christian statesmen and influential men of Japan. He so won their confidence that he secured contributions from those in high social and official positions amounting to nearly $60,000, and also the gift of $100,000 from an American gentlemen for the same purpose. In 1889 he received from Amherst College the degree of Doctor of Laws.

In the fall of 1889 he was in Tokio working to interest leading men at the capital and secure funds for his enlarged plans. He took a severe cold, and, renewing his efforts too soon, was prostrated. His wife and other friends were summoned, and pastors, teachers, and students flocked from east and west to catch some farewell word. Maps were brought at his request to his bedside, and eagerly, almost with dying breath, he pointed out places which ought at once to be filled by the Christian teacher. He passed away January 23, 1890. All classes united to attend his funeral. The governor, the chief justice for the district, and many other officials were present. The students from one government school and one private school were in the procession. One banner from Tokio was inscribed with one of Mr. Neesima's own sentences: "Free education and self-governing churches: if these go together, the country will stand for all generations." Another was inscribed: "From the Buddhists of Osaka."

NEGAPATAM: A town in Madras, India, chief port of the Negapatam District, situated 49 miles E. by S. of Tanjore, on the Bay of Bengal. It was one of the earliest Portuguese settlements on the Coromandel coast. Population (1901) 57,190, of whom 39,000 are Hindus and 14,000 Muslims. Station of the Leipzig Mission Society (1864), with (1903) 1 missionary and his wife, 16 native workers, 21 outstations, 2 places of worship, 5 day schools, 1 boarding school, and 419 professed Christians. Station also of the SPG (1825), with (1903) 8 native workers, 1 place of worship, 3 day schools, and 447 professed Christians, of whom 233 are communicants. Station also of the WMS, with (1903) 3 missionaries, 109 native workers, 9 outstations, 11 places of worship, 11 Sunday schools, 25 day schools, and 205 professed Christians, of whom 171 are communicants.

NEGOMBO: A town on the west coast of Ceylon, 20 miles north of Colombo. Population, 19,400. Station of the WMS, with (1903) 2 missionaries, 71 native workers, 8 outstations, 25 places of worship, 20 Sunday schools, 22 day schools, and 902 professed Christians, of whom 631 are communicants.

NEGRO RACE: Much ignorance and confusion attend the use of the word Negro, and there is much trouble in properly classifying the race. In its widest sense the term is applied to those sections of the human race who have black, or distinctly dark, skins as opposed to those who have yellow or brown complexions. In this somewhat ill-defined use it designates the inhabitants (1) of Africa south of the Sahara, (2) of the peninsula of India south of the Indo-Gangetic plains, (3) of Malaysia and the greater part of Australasia. In this wide dispersion the peculiar characteristics of the pure Negro have been modified by contact with the Mongol on one side and the Caucasian on the other.

In a more restricted sense, the Negro race includes two classes: the true Negro of African type, and the Papuan, or Melanesian, type.

I. African Negro: While it is true that all Negroes of this class are Africans, it is not true that all Africans are Negroes, and the two terms should not be used synonymously. The geographical distribution of the true Negro race includes all of the west coast lying along the Niger, the Senegal, and Gambia rivers, and the country between them, together with parts of the Sudan. This area is thus a thin belt of territory along the center of Africa, not all of which is inhabited solely by Negroes, and which forms but a very small part of the whole continent. Here and there, scattered through other sections, especially to the south, occasional tribes of true Negroes may be met, but the limits above given are in the main correct. The home of the race in its purity is in the district between the Volta and Niger, the Kong Mountains and the coast, where are found remains of the Negro kingdoms of Benin, Dahomey, and Yoruba, while just west of the Volta is Ashanti. Different tribes are found throughout this whole territory, such as the Jolofs and Mandingoes in Senegambia, the Susu on the Rio Pongas, the Temne, inland from Lagos, the Ibo on the Lower Niger, the Hausa-speaking tribes north of the Niger confluence, besides the tribes about Lake Tchad and in the parts about Darfur.

It is the generally accepted opinion that the Negroes were the aborigines, or, at least, the first settlers, in the region they occupy. If, as seems plausible, they belong to some branch of the Hamitic family, the indications are that they were among the first to come from Asia into Africa. The Bantu race followed, crowding the Negro to the south and west, and pushing the Hottentot Bushmen ahead until the three divisions of the African races occupied their respective localities as now defined. Within these limits, however, the Negroes have been subject to much unrest and change. The slave trade dimished their numbers, and in later years the return of the descendants of former slaves has perhaps modified in a slight degree their racial characteristics.

Racial Characteristics: The true Negro is marked by an unusual length of arm; projecting jaws; small brain; black eye; flat, short nose; thick, red, protruding lips; thick skull; short woolly hair; weak legs, prehensile great toe, and projecting heel; black or brown skin, thick and velvety, with a strong odor.

In their native home the race is regarded as naturally inferior in mental development to many of the races of the world. The possibilities of development are affirmed and denied by writers of equal weight. In the aboriginal state the Negro is a mere savage. His nature is sunny and childlike. Inordinately susceptible to flattery, he can easily be influenced. While rendered cruel by the lust for gold, he is naturally gentle. He appreciates the beautiful, and is fond of songs and mirth. The victim of gross superstition, he retains belief in a supreme being. He is indolent, slothful and improvident. If his animal wants are satisfied, he is content. He knows how to conceal his real feelings, and can be an enigma hard to solve if he so chooses.

He responds quickly to kindness, and will prove his gratitude by great devotion. Morally, his standard is very low. Polygamy is practised, but marriage ties are almost unknown. The women are the slaves of the men. Cannibalism is sometimes indulged in, and human sacrifices have been offered to the fetish objects of their worship, some of which are most hideous. Some of the tribes have a great degree of skill in the arts and manufactures. Buildings, metal-work, clothes of skins,—all show a degree of civilization which is proof of the capabilities of the race. Mungo Park found Sego, the capital of Bambasa, a city of 30,000 people, with two-story houses, containing mosques in every quarter, with ferries over the Niger for men and beasts. To sum up, in the words of Dr. Cust: "Many great races in ancient times have had their day of greatness, exhausted the power that was in them, and have been completely broken up, trodden down, or utterly effaced by younger and more powerful races. But this cannot be said of the Negro race: they are not broken, fewer in number, or poorer in resources; tho pressed upon from without, they have proved to be the only race suitable to the climate. Their soil is wonderfully fertile, their minerals abundant, their power of reproduction exceeding calculation. We know now from the instances of men who have had the advantages of culture that they are not deficient in intelligence, probity, and even genius, yet they have left absolutely not a monument to tell of the material greatness of any particular tribe, or of any ancient civilization, as in Central America and Asia; not a written or sculptured document; they have but a scant store of proverbs and traditions."

Language: The zone occupied by the Negro presents a greater diversity of tongues than is to be found elsewhere in the world, except perhaps in parts of America, in Melanesia, or Caucasia. In the Cust-Müller classification of African languages the Negro is one of six divisions, and in it are included four sub-classes, such as the Atlantic, Niger, Central, and Nile; in the entire group 195 languages are recognized and 49 dialects. They belong to the agglutinating type, and are often characterized by intricacy of structure and delicate alliterativeness. The Grebo language on the coast of northern Guinea is monosyllabic, and is spoken with great rapidity. The Mandingo language, spoken in Senegal and Gambia, is a smooth tongue, with a predominance of vowels, and a remarkable minuteness in defining the time of an action.

II. *Papuan Negro:* The name Papua is a Malay term meaning "frizzled," and points at once to the mark which distinguishes the frizzly-haired Negro from the straight-haired Malay. The purest type of the Papuan is found on the western part of the island of New Guinea or Papua, but the influence of the race is felt throughout the whole of Melanesia and parts of Polynesia, where they mingle and amalgamate with the Malay or Mongoloid race. In the words of Mr. Wallace: "The Papuans are well-made, have regular features, intelligent black eyes, small, white teeth, curly hair, thick lips, and large mouth; the nose is sharp but flat beneath, the nostrils large, and the skin dark brown." The Polynesians are considered by some ethnologists as differing in no fundamental particular from the Papuans, while others class them with the Malay, as an intermediate type between the Malay and the Negro.

In their temperament and customs the Papuans show many traits similar to those of the African Negro. Their belief in sorcery, their superstitions in regard to bits of wood and stone as causes of disease, their easy-going, listless life, light-hearted and boisterous moods, all point to similarity of origin. In their architecture, rude as it is, they follow the Malay fashion of building on piles. They show a great degree of skill in agriculture. The men build the houses, hunt, and fish, leaving the heavier work to be done by the women. The latter are more modest than the rest of the Polynesian races. The Papuan languages form a class by themselves, differing widely from the Malayo-Polynesian languages, and split into dialects by so small an obstacle to intercourse as a brook.

III. *Mixed Races:* The slave-trade has scattered the Negro race throughout the globe. In most countries of the eastern hemisphere the Negro is lost in the general population; and altho a trace of black blood is seen in Morocco, in Arabia, Malabar, and Ceylon, and in the various races lying between India and New Guinea, where the Papuan type is met with, they have left no distinctive mark, and no statistics are available to indicate the number of Negroes, or the proportion of the population which they form.

The degree of intermingling which has gone on in the western hemisphere has given rise to many mixed races, with more or less of Negro blood in them. The terms Creole, Quadroon, Octoroon, or Mulatto are well known and generally understood, but there are other less common terms, such as: *Mestizo*, half-breed, of either white and Negro, or Indian and Negro; *Creole*, in addition to the common meaning of one born in Spanish America, of European parents, is also applied in Peru to the children of Mestizoes; *Zambo*, half-breed, but usually the issue of Negro and Indian, or Negro and Mulatto; *Zambo Preto*, progeny of Negro father and Zambo mother. In the South American countries these terms are multiplied until almost every shade of mixture has its appropriate term.

Tho the slave-trade is carried on in a few places still, yet practically slavery is extinct, and the many Negroes who are in the countries to which they have been taken as slaves are now freedmen.

The American Negro: 1. *In the United States.*—From the time of the first arrival of Negroes as slaves in the colony of Virginia in 1619 till the Emancipation Act in 1865, Negro slavery has been identified with and has greatly influenced the history of the nation. The final solution of the great question of slavery left the country with a greater question confronting it, which is called the Negro Question. During the first half of the last century the number of Negroes brought to the United States was from 60,000 to 70,000 annually, and the number multiplied, until in 1900 the Negro or colored element numbered 8,840,000, or $11\frac{1}{2}$ per cent. of the whole population. Comparatively few of this number are of unmixed blood, while many retain but a trace of Negro origin, and are in their mental and physical characteristics almost entirely Caucasian. In the Southern States, the purer type of Negro is found, and they exhibit the characteristics already described. A jovial, light-hearted race, fond of a laugh, living only in the present, contented with mere animal pleasures, full of superstition which in some has taken the form of religious fervor, not strict in their ideas as to the rights of property, possessing a low order of cunning rather than intelligence, full of moral sentiment and lofty emotions, but prone to immoral actions and low crimes; fearing the Voodoo woman with her fetishes, and yet shouting amen in Christian services with much unction—the Negro, as modified by his environment in the United States, presents a mixture of good and evil, of childlike simplicity and cunning secretiveness, of deep feeling and weak character, of hopelessness and of possibility, which may well stagger the faith and try the patience of those who are trying to educate and Christianize him. Notable instances of full-blooded Negroes there are who have shown an intelligence, a strength of mind and executive ability, a stedfast faith and upright life, equal to that of the Caucasian; and these instances, when viewed in connection with their as yet meager opportunities, may fairly be placed in comparison with the great majority which seem to give weight to the opinion that the Negro is mentally and morally inferior to, and can never be on an equality with, the white race which surrounds him.

It has been suggested that the Negro is not so much immoral as non-moral, for there seems to be such a lack of the perception of right and wrong that a Negro will stop on his way to or from a prayer-meeting, at which he takes a fervid part, to lift a chicken from a neighbor's hen-roost. The Rev. Dr. Tucker, at the American Church Congress in 1883, brought out this side of the American Negro character when he spoke of Negro missionaries who were earnest and successful, unconscious of hypocrisy, but who were guilty of lives of the grossest immorality, were addicted to lying and thieving, and yet were respected and heeded by their flocks.

The Negro question is looked at in two distinct ways, not only by the politician but by the Christian, and the difference is due mainly to presence or absence of perspective. By those who live away from the daily contact with the Negro, who look at him idealized, as a man entitled to the rights of men, to all the privileges of citizenship, and to all the yearning love which a fallen image of God should excite in the Christian heart, the practical difficulties in the way of civilizing, Christianizing, and elevating the Negro to the lauded plane of equality are oftentimes overlooked, and theory takes the place of practise, sentiment of common-sense, and faith and hope overpower "works." To those who live among the Negroes, who daily see the deficiencies in their character, in their capabilities, in their morals, there is an absence of perspective, and they take the other extreme view: that little can be done for them, that liberty and equality should for some time, at least, be mere words without practical meaning. This is not only true of upright and honorable men who are not distinctively Christian, but men who are anxious to save the souls of the Negroes are just as averse as their political neighbors to contact with Negroes on terms of equality, or to recognition of their political rights. Among the men who are ready to keep the Negro from the polls, by violence if necessary, are men who are active in Christian work. Between these two widely divergent views of the Negro there is, without doubt, as in all things, a middle ground, and to that mean the opinion of wise men is turning; but as yet it cannot be clearly defined, nor is the question yet solved.

While the political part of the Negro question is taxing the thought of the statesmen, the Church is doing her part to aid in the solution. In addition to the missionary work of the different churches, and that of the American Missionary Association, there is a large and flourishing church among the Negroes themselves. The African Methodist Episcopal Church was organized in 1816, and in 1880 it had a total membership of over 400,000, and supported a missionary society which was organized in 1844 as the Parent Home and Foreign Missionary Society. In 1888 nearly 300 missionaries were engaged in the home work of the church, tho it has been only within the last ten years that any successful mission has been established in foreign lands. In addition to their own church, the Negroes form fifteen conferences of the Methodist Episcopal Church (South). Of the Baptists, a large proportion in the Southern States are Negroes, and many of the ministers have been men of great power and of great zeal in religious life. There is also a considerable number of Negroes in the Episcopal Church, and a certain number are Roman Catholics.

2. *In Mexico:* It is difficult to calculate the number of Negroes in Mexico, for there the mixture is so blended that Negro ancestry is hard to trace. Of the population (1900), 13,500,000, the Negro element is put at 60,000. But by the constitution of 1824 all distinctions of race were abolished, and they are virtually amalgamated with the rest of the people. About 43 per cent. of the people are of mixed race, Negroes, Indians, and other races.

3. *Central America:* The number of the colored or Negro population in Central America has been estimated at 50,000. In this section of the country intermingling with the Indians and other races is very great, and there is little social distinction between them.

4. *South America:* Brazil was the last country in America to abolish slavery. In 1850 the slaves were estimated at 2,500,000; in 1887 the slaves were given on the official returns as numbering 723,419, and by a law passed in 1888 slavery was abolished. The Negroes are found principally in the provinces of Pernambuco, Bahia, Rio de Janeiro, and Minas, and according to the census of 1890 numbered 2,097,426, besides those of mixed blood. In the other countries of South America the Negroes are so mixed with the other races (as in Peru), or form so small an element in the population, that no definite statement as to their numbers can be attempted.

5. *West Indies:* The number of Negroes in the West Indies is about 3,000,000. Slavery was abolished in the British West Indies in 1834, in the French possessions in 1848, and in Cuba in 1886.

The vitality of the race is surprising and is unaltered by their location, except when they leave the tropics or sub-tropics. The farther north they go, the greater the mortality, and their stability as a race, in constitution and numbers, depends upon the restriction of their habitation to the warm climates.

NELLORE: A town in Ceylon, situated about 30 miles S. E. of Jaffna. Station of the CMS, with (1903) 1 missionary and his wife, 1 native worker, 1 place of worship and 1 boarding school. Church statistics are included in Jaffna.

NELLORE: The capital of a district of the same name, Madras, India; stands on the Tenner River, 96 miles N. by W. of Madras. Has important irrigation works on the river. Population (1891), 29,300, of whom 22,600 are Hindus. Station of the ABMU (1840), with (1903) 3 missionaries, 2 of them with their wives; 5 women missionaries, 35 native workers, 2 outstations, 3 places of worship, 5 Sunday schools, 5 day schools, 3 boarding schools, 1 dispensary, 1 hospital, and 2,500 professed Christians, of whom 843 are communicants.

NELSON HOUSE: A trading post in the Dominion of Canada, situated in Keewatin Territory, about 450 miles N. N. W. of Winnipeg. Station of the MCC (1871), with (1903) 1 missionary and his wife, 2 outstations, and 93 professed Christians.

NEMURO: A town in Japan, situated on the E. extremity of Hokkaido. Station of the ABMU (1887), with (1903) 1 woman missionary, 4 native workers, 5 outstations, 1 place of worship, 2 Sunday schools, and 86 professed Christians.

NEPAL: An independent kingdom lying along the southern slopes of the Himalayas, in North India, and tho there are treaty stipulations between its government and that of British India, it is outside of the immediate circle of British influence. To the north its territory extends up the sides of the Himalayan range until it meets that of Tibet, along an unsurveyed and indefinite frontier. Its southern boundary is usually about 30 miles from the foot of the Himalayas. On the west a small stream separates it from the sub-Himalayan British province of Kumaon; and its eastern limit is the small mountain state of Sikkim, north of Calcutta. Its greatest length northwest and southeast is 512 miles; its breadth varies from 70 to 150 miles. The total area has been computed at about 54,000 square miles. No census of population has ever been taken. The Nepalese estimate is about 5,500,000; the soberer, and probably more correct, opinion of Anglo-Indian officials places the population at 4,000,000. There are many aboriginal tribes in Nepal, most of whom seem to be of Tatar origin. But the regnant tribe is that of the Gurkhas, who are descended from the Rajputs of Northwestern India, and who migrated in the 12th century from the original home of their people during the early ascendancy of one of the invading Mussulman dynasties. Most of these aboriginal tribes are Buddhists, but Buddhism is gradually disappearing before the stronger Hinduism of the ruling race. Rice is the staple food of the people. The highest known mountain in the world,—Mt. Everest, 29,002 feet high,—as well as many Himalayan peaks inferior only to that, lie within the limits of Nepalese territory. Since the subjugation of the country by the Gurkha dynasty, several bloody revolutions, marked by the true Oriental features of assassination and usurpation, have occurred. The last was in 1885, when the prime minister and two other prominent men were murdered by the head of a rival faction. The murderer at once made himself prime minister. Violent as the revolution was, it was considered a probable step toward much-needed reforms within the kingdom. Nepal has never been open to the entrance of Europeans, tho the Indian Government has usually maintained a resident there. No missionary stations have yet been permitted. The capital is Khatmandu. Population supposed to be about 50,000.

NEPALESE LANGUAGE: An Aryan language spoken in the kingdom of Nepal, north of India, and written with the Nagari characters. The extent to which it is in use has not yet been learned.

NESTORIAN CHURCH: The name is derived from that of Nestorius, who was patriarch of Constantinople for three years previous to his excommunication by the Council of Ephesus, A.D. 431; but the Nestorians repudiate the name, and call themselves the Church of the East. Their separation from the great body of Eastern Christians was due mainly to political and national forces. Christianity spread eastward very early. The Syriac-speaking Christians of the great Mesopotamian plains, with a smaller number of Persian and Arab Christians, were the subjects of the Parthian, and then the Sassanian kingdom. Syriac was the ecclesiastical language of all. The persecuting zeal of the Persian kings was increased by the feeling that their Christian subjects were secret allies of the Roman enemy. The school of Edessa, the theological center of these Christians, was closely associated with that of Antioch; and Theodore of Mopsuestia, the true father of Nestorian theology, was revered. Hence, it was natural for the Persian Christians to espouse the cause of Nestorius against Cyril, of Antioch against Alexandria, and at the same time to gain greater security by dissociating themselves from the Christians of the Roman Empire, in repudiating the creed of Ephesus, and erecting the See of Seleucia into a patriarchate. On their part, the emperors hastened the schism by persecution. In 489 the Persian school was expelled from Edessa, in Roman territory, and established beyond the Persian border at Nisibis. The great organizer of the Nestorian Church was Barsumas, Bishop of Nisibis. A similar cooperation of political and theological forces led, in the next century, to the organization of the other Syrian National Church, the Jacobite. The centers of Nestorian population were about Nisibis, Mosul, and Seleucia, and in Khuzistan, in Southern Persia, while considerable bodies were found in Khurasan, Armenia, and Arabia.

The technical expression of the Nestorian Christology is "two natures, two hypostases (Syriac *qnuma*), and one person (Syriac *parsopa*)." The terms are difficult of definition, but *qnuma* is defined in the theological treatises as including the generic attributes, that part of the *nature* possessed by each individual, while *parsopa* includes those that are individual. Thus, it is said that Peter, Paul, and John are separate *qnumas* with respect to common qualities, and separate *parsopas* with respect to differing qualities. It is argued that *nature* implies such individualization and is incomplete without it. They conceived of the Incarnation as an indwelling, the union of the divine person with an individual human personality and not with human nature. A corollary is the denial to the Virgin Mary of the title *Theotokos*, mother of God.

Practically, this Christology served as a badge of separation, and had little effect otherwise. In other regards, the Nestorian Church differed from other Oriental churches by way of arrested development. Its liturgy is briefer, and less explicit in some doctrines, but it contains the invocation of the saints and prayers for the dead. The cross is revered, but neither pictures nor images are used. The real presence, and the sacerdotal character of the clergy are taught, but not transubstantiation or confession to priests. The parish clergy marry, but monasticism was a powerful institution, and the bishops were chosen from the monks. For several centuries the episcopal succession, contrary to the church canons, has become dynastic, usually passing from uncle to nephew. The patriarchal seat was first Seleucia, then Baghdad, later Mosul, and finally Kochanes, in the heart of the Zagros Mountains.

The history of this church is checkered and obscure. The bloody persecutions of Christians by the Sassanian kings were previous to the rise of Nestorianism, but the Nestorians were harassed by some of the Sassanian kings, and were outlawed by the Roman emperors. Islam at first was mild by contrast, and the Arab conquest was welcomed. The Church extended more widely than ever, and Nestorians, especially as physicians and secretaries, were in high favor in the Caliph's court, while their bankers and artisans amassed wealth. They were the translators of Greek literature, and the transmitters of philosophy to the Arabs. The toleration extended was limited and in the end worse than persecution. The Christians were subject to special taxes, and held an inferior status before the law. The Caliph exercised the right of investiture of the patriarchs, and thus the highest office became the prize of bribery and was secularized. Along with this went a tacit acceptance of the prohibition of proselyting Mohammedans. The missionary spirit was deadened but not extinguished, and found vent in work for non-Mohammedans. Christianity had entered India before the rise of Islam, and bishops were still appointed to that country. During the 8th Christian century active propaganda was carried on among the pagan tribes on the borders of the Caspian, and about 630 A.D. Nestorian monks entered China. Christian cemeteries, medieval travelers, and Syriac historians testify to the existence for several centuries (about 800-1300) of large bodies of Turkish and Mongol Christians in Central Asia, and in Northwest China, especially along the northern bend of the Yellow River. When the Mongol hordes overran Western Asia, not a few Christians were numbered in their ranks and some were high in office. It seemed as if the opportunity for Christian triumph had come, but in reality its downfall was near. The large Christian population had been decimated by the anarchy, famine, pestilence, and war that had cursed Western Asia; and finally the Nestorian Church was well nigh exterminated in the terrible Mongol forays ending with the massacres of Tamerlane. Since A.D. 1400 its history is only that of a few shattered dioceses of the mighty line that once spanned Asia.

At present the number of Nestorians, including those who have seceded to other Christian churches, is little more than one hundred thousand. They live in three distinct regions, the plains of ancient Assyria, the rugged valleys of the Zagros Mountains in Turkey, west of Lake Urmia, and the plains in Persia, between the mountains and the lake. The large majority are engaged in agricultural or pastoral pursuits. Those in the mountains, like the Kurds among whom they live, have maintained a precarious independence, but the Sultan is steadily subjecting them to taxation, without, however, maintaining peace and security in those wild regions. Those in the plains of the Tigris, and a few elsewhere, are Roman Catholic. The majority of those in Persia are enrolled as members of the Greek Church. A smaller but very influential body, mainly in Persia, are Protestant. Probably less than half of the whole number still acknowledge the authority of the Nestorian patriarch.

The part of Persia in which the Nestorians live is closely united to Russia in an industrial way. The rapid development of Transcaucasia has given work to thousands of Nestorians, while many more have gone farther into Russia. Almost every adult male has at some time spent several years in Russia. This fact has given a sense of Russia's power and a conviction of its future supremacy, while the absence from home has had a disintegrating religious and moral effect. The increasing misgovernment of Persia has made the people long for a change, a temper induced also by the various missionary operations. All these influences prepared for the Russian Mission of 1898, that received in Urmia an extraordinary welcome. Without any religious persuasion almost all the adherents of the Nestorian Church in the region of Urmia renounced its teachings and professed their acceptance of the Orthodox faith. Subsequent events disappointed the political aims of the new converts, but it is safe to count the mass of them as permanent additions to the Russian Church. Time must reveal the future of this ancient church, but the political predominance of Russia makes very probable the absorption of most of the Nestorians, in Turkey as well as in Persia, into the Russian Church. The old church has not the strength to stand. The only body that seems to have the promise of a separate destiny is the small but vigorous body of Protestant Nestorians.

Badger (G. P.), *Nestorians and Their Ritual*, London, 1852; *Missionary Review of the World* (Nestorians and the Russian Church), Vol. XII., p. 745.

NETHERLANDS MISSIONARY SOCIETIES: The first missionary work by the Dutch was connected with their colonial extension, and dates back as far as the beginning of the 17th century, when the Dutch East India Company was formed (1602). This commercial society was bound by its charter to care for the church interests of the colonists, and also to endeavor to teach the heathen. There were no special missionaries, but the colonial clergy were relied upon for work, and in order to the provision of the right class of men, there was organized at Leyden (1622) a seminary for the training of candidates. The seminary was not long continued, and, tho some earnest and faithful workers were sent out, for the most part the colonial clergy were very perfunctory in the performance of their work. Some fairly good work appears to have been done in the way of Bible translation and education of native clergy, but work for natives, for the most part, was very superficial. This was due partly to the short service of the preachers, partly to their small number, and chiefly to lack of interest on the part of the Government. The influence of the Roman Catholic Missions, e. g., in the Moluccas, was disadvantageous. Baptisms were made by wholesale, and on such easy terms that at the close of the 17th century it was reported that there were 300,000 Christians in Ceylon, 100,000 in Java, and 40,000 in Amboina. The West India Company, formed in 1621, made some attempts in the same line in Brazil, tho with no practical result, but laid the foundation for the Dutch Church in the American Colonies.

During the 18th century all these undertakings gradually fell into decay, and at the revival of missionary interest in the last decade of the century, there was almost no missionary spirit in the churches of Holland. An appeal from the LMS soon after its organization stirred the hearts of some clergymen and laymen and resulted in the formation of the *Netherlands Missionary Society* in 1797. For some time they worked through the LMS, but later established missions of their own. For half a century this remained the only Dutch society, but beginning with 1847 a number of societies were formed by those who felt unable to accept the somewhat rationalistic and formal management of the old society. These included: *The Mennonite Union* (1847), *The Christian Reformed Missionary Society* (1854), the *Java Comité* (1855), the *Ermelo Association* (1856), *Netherlands Mission Union* (1858), *Utrecht Mission Union* (1859). Of these, the Christian Reformed Missionary Society and the Netherlands Reformed Mission united in 1892 to form the Mission of the Reformed Churches in the Netherlands. There is also a society auxiliary to the Moravian Missions (formed in 1793), and there are several aid societies.

1. **Netherlands Missionary Society, 1797**: (*Nederlandsch Zendelinggenootschap*): The oldest of the Dutch societies owes its origin to the influence of Dr. Van der Kemp, who went to South Africa in the service of the LMS. It represents chiefly the Established Church, tho from the beginning it has had relations with the Reformed Church, and the General Synod has no immediate control over its conduct.

The first missionaries of the Society under its own direction, Vos, Erhardt, and Palm, were sent to Ceylon, but they were unable to accomplish very much in that field, owing perhaps to the hostility of the Dutch Consistory of the island. In 1812 three missionaries, Kam, Supper, and Bruckner, were sent to Java. Mr. Kam established himself at Amboina, in the Molucca Islands, Mr. Bruckner at Samarang, and Mr. Supper at Batavia. Two years later, Holland, having regained its independence from France, the Society reorganized the seminary, and sent out five missionaries to work with Mr. Kam. These established themselves at Celebes, Ceram, Ternati, Banda, and Timor, and found abundant opportunities for labor. In 1833 Mr. Kam, who had endured much exposure in his efforts to travel from island to island, and had been often employed, even by the government, as a peace-maker among the tribes, died from the effects of overwork. In 1826 the same Society sent out Mr. **Gutzlaff** to China. A mission was also established at the Dutch colony of Surinam in Guiana, and Alphonse F. **Lacroix** was sent to the Dutch territory in India. When in 1825 the Dutch settlements on the continent of India were ceded to the British Government, their four missionaries connected themselves with the different English societies, thinking it better not to render their time and labor and knowledge of the languages of the people of no avail. The fields at present (1901) occupied are Java, Celebes, Sumatra, and Savu, near Timor. In 1900 it had 24 missionaries, 62 native helpers in 11 stations and 49 outstations, 1,722 communicants, 42 schools with 2,707 pupils, 1 physician, and 1 hospital, with 4,000 patients.

2. **Mennonite Missionary Union,** 1847 (*Doopsgezinde Vereeniging*): The Anabaptists of Holland had worked through the BMS of England, but in 1847 formed their own organization as above, and commenced work in Java and Sumatra. The report (1900) shows 11 missionaries, 26 native workers, occupying 4 stations and 8 outstations, with 458 communicants, 9 schools, with 366 pupils, 1 hospital treating 2,280 patients.

3. **Java Committee** (1855), (*Java Comité te Amsterdam*): The first of the societies organized in protest against the Netherlands Society in 1855. It carries on work in Java, and has (1900) 6 missionaries, 11 native workers in 6 stations and 8 outstations; 500 communicants, 8 schools, 225 pupils.

4. **Mission of the Reformed Churches in the Netherlands,** 1892 (*Zending van de Gereformeerde Kerken in Nederland*): The Dutch Reformed Missionary Society was founded at Amsterdam in 1859 by the Rev. Dr. Schwartz, missionary of the Free Church of Scotland to the Jews in that city. The original intention was to form a society for the propagation of the Gospel among the Jews living among the heathen and Mohammedans in the Dutch (Indian) colonies, and through them to reach the heathen and Mohammedans. The government, however, out of deference to the Jews in Holland, refused to recognize the proposed society, and it was resolved to commence work among the heathen and Mohammedans in the island of Java. Additional cause for this resolve lay in dissatisfaction with the old Netherlands Missionary Society, on account of its rationalism. Already there had been formed the "Utrecht Mission Society" and the "Netherlands Mission Union," neither of which, however, tho founded on orthodox principles, accepted the confession of the Dutch Reformed churches, and the new Society was therefore formed to act in conformity with the recognized standards of these churches, in general following the Presbyterian polity. In 1892 this Society united with the Christian Reformed Union, under the title as above. The work is in Java, and the report (1900) shows 16 missionaries, 12 native workers, 6 stations, 9 outstations, and 718 communicants.

5. **Netherlands Mission Union,** 1858 (*Nederlandsche Zendingsvereeniging*): This Society, organized in 1858, began its work in Western Java among the Sundanese. It had (1900) 11 missionaries, 32 native helpers, 9 stations and 19 outstations, 871 communicants, 24 schools with 851 pupils.

The Utrecht Missionary Society, 1859 (*Utrechtsche Zendingsvereeniging*: It employs (1900) 14 missionaries, 41 native workers in 7 stations and 43 outstations, with 246 communicants, 41 schools with 1,070 pupils.

The Committee for the Mission to the Sangir and Talaut Islands (1886): This Committee collects aid for various needs of the work of the 13 missionaries and 210 native workers. Their salaries are assumed by the Dutch Government. The number of communicants reported in the islands is 10,459, a very much larger number than is shown by any other Dutch Society working in that region. There are also 26 schools with 4,184 pupils.

NEU BETHEL. See BETHEL, GERMAN EAST AFRICA.

NEUEN DETTELSAU MISSIONARY SOCIETY. See GERMANY; MISSIONARY SOCIETIES IN.

NEUENKIRCHEN: A station of the Hermannsburg Missionary Society in Natal, South Africa, situated in the Tugela valley. It has (1901) 1 missionary and his wife, 3 native workers, 2 places of worship, 1 day school, and 58 professed Christians, of whom 37 are communicants.

NEU HALLE: A village in the Transvaal, South Africa, situated about 80 miles N. E. of Pretoria. Station of the Berlin Missionary Society (1873), with (1903) 1 missionary, 13 native workers, 4 outstations, and 1,008 professed Christians. The village was formerly called Marapjane in the Society reports.

NEU HANNOVER. See NEW HANOVER.

NEUKIRCHEN MISSIONARY INSTITUTE. See GERMANY; MISSIONARY SOCIETIES IN.

NEW AMSTERDAM: A town in British Guiana on the right bank of the Berbice River, near its mouth, 63 miles S. E. of Georgetown, with which it is connected by railway. Station of the Moravian Missions, with (1900) 1 missionary and his wife, 19 native workers, 3 outstations, 4 places of worship, 2 day schools, and 293 professed Christians. Station also of the SDA, with 2 missionaries, 1 physician; church statistics in Georgetown. Station also of the SPG, with 1 missionary, 2 native workers, 1 day school, and 130 professed Christians. Station of the West Indies Wesleyan Methodist Conference, with 1 missionary and his wife, 5 outstations, 4 places of worship, 5 Sunday schools, 5 day schools, and 409 professed Christians.

NEW CALEDONIA: An island in Melanesia which, together with its dependency, the Loyalty Islands, is a French colony, lying about 720 miles northeast of Australia, in latitude 20°-22° 30′ south and longitude 164°-167° east. It is 200 miles long, 30 broad, with an area of 6,000 square miles, and a population (1901) of 51,000: 29,000 natives, the remainder colonists, soldiers, and convicts. The natives resemble the Papuans. The Roman Catholics have established missions at various points on the island, but so far little Protestant work has been undertaken beyond that which Christian natives of the Loyalty Islands are able to do. It was occupied by the French in 1853, and has been a penal settlement since 1872.

NEW CARMEL: A village in Jamaica, W. I., situated in the W. part of the island, S. E. of Savanna la Mar. Station of the Moravian Missions (1827), with (1901) 1 missionary and his wife, 28 native workers, 1 outstation, 1 place of worship, 2 Sunday schools, 1 Society for Young People, and 688 professed Christians.

NEWCHWANG: One of the treaty ports of China, in the Manchurian province, Shing-king; situated on a branch of the Liao-ho, 35 miles from the Gulf of Liao-tung, in a vast alluvial plain, extending seaward. The real port is Ying-tze, farther down the river, to which the name of Newchwang is also applied. The port is closed by ice for four or five months in the year. The product of pulse and beans is the principal export. Population about 50,000. Station of the Presbyterian Church in Ireland (1869), with (1901) 1 missionary and his wife, 21 native workers, 8 outstations, 10 places of worship, 1 theological class, and 110 professed Christians. Station also of the SPG (1892), with a chaplain for English residents.

NEWELL, Samuel: Born at Durham, Me., U. S. A., July 24, 1784; graduated at Harvard College and Andover Seminary. He was one of that band of young students whose devotion and earnest entreaty to the ministers of Massachusetts called the American Board into existence. He married Harriet Atwood, and sailed February 19, 1812, as a missionary of the American Board for Calcutta. Forbidden by the East India Company to remain in its territory, he sailed with his wife for Mauritius to establish a mission for that island and Madagascar. Mrs. Newell died soon after their arrival, and Mr. Newell went to Ceylon, the opening there for a mission being favorable; but in January, 1814, he joined his former fellow-students and his associates under the ABCFM, Hall and Nott, at Bombay. Seven years later a terrible epidemic of cholera swept through the country. Mr. Newell devoted himself to the sick until he himself took the disease from the natives and died May 30, 1821. His grave is in the English cemetery at Bombay.

NEW ENGLAND COMPANY: Headquarters, 1 Hatton Garden, London, E. C., England. In the early part of the 17th century the English colonists of New England, headed by the renowned John Eliot, "the Apostle to the North American Red Men," began the work among the Indians which laid the foundations for the New England Company. The accounts of the work among the Red Men, circulated throughout London in writings called "tracts," aroused so much interest in the great city that the needs of the Indians were brought before Parliament, and on July 27, 1649, an act was passed with this title: "A Corporation for the Promoting and Propagating the Gospel of Jesus Christ in New England." In this act was recognized the necessity of work among the Indians for the purposes of evangelization and civilization, and provision was made for the expenditure involved in the furtherance of such work. The ordinance enacted that there should be a corporation in England consisting of a president, treasurer, and fourteen assistants, and invested the corporation with power to acquire lands, goods, and money.

History: Soon after the action of Parliament and the appointment of the members of the Corporation, a general subscription was directed by Cromwell, the Lord Protector, and nearly £12,000 was raised for the purposes of the corporation. Commissioners and a treasurer were appointed in New England, and work was carried on by itinerant missionaries and school-teachers, chiefly near Boston. On the restoration of Charles II., in 1660, the corporation created by the Long Parliament became defunct, but through the efforts of the Hon. Robert Boyle a charter was granted by the king. This charter was completed in 1662. By it the company was limited to forty-five members; the first forty-five named; the object defined; the name decided as "The Company for Propagation of the Gospel in New England and the parts adjacent in America;" the duties and powers of the officers defined; and, in fact, the complete constitution was made and adopted. In 1899 a supplemental charter was granted by Queen Victoria, authorizing the expenditure of the whole of the company's funds in any part of British North America.

The work progressed in the New England

states until the outbreak of the War of American Independence, when the company was obliged to cease its labors there. The field was, therefore, transferred to New Brunswick, but after a fair attempt was found unprofitable, and was removed to Ontario, where since 1822 the work has been permanently maintained. Between the years 1823 and 1840 large sums were contributed toward aiding the missions in the West Indies, but the increase of the work in North America of late years has necessitated the withdrawal of funds from that quarter, and all have been devoted to the missions of the company.

Present Work: The funds of the company are derived from three sources, the original charter fund and two legacies. The money coming from two of these sources may be used only for work among the American Indians and work in American dependencies of the British crown, while that from the third may be used for spreading the Gospel in any British colonies. The work carried on now by the company is evangelistic and educational among the Indian tribes of British North America. The company's stations at the present time are:

1. The Grand River Indian Reserves, among the Mohawks, Oneidas, Onondagas, Cayugas, Senecas, and Tuscaroras, settled on the banks of the Grand River between Brantford and Lake Erie.

2. Mohawk Institution, Brantford, Ont., an industrial boarding school for Indian children of both sexes.

3. St. George's School, near Lytton, British Columbia, an industrial boarding school for Indian boys.

NEW GUINEA. See PAPUA.

NEW HANOVER: A town in Natal, South Africa, situated in the N. Hanover district, 22 miles N. N. W. of Pietermaritzburg. Station of the Hermannsburg Missionary Society (1862), with (1900) 1 missionary and his wife, 3 native workers, 2 outstations, 1 place of worship, 3 day schools, and 227 professed Christians.

NEW HEBRIDES ISLANDS: A group included in Melanesia, Pacific Ocean, lying between latitude 21° and 15° south, and longitude 171° and 166° east, about 1,000 miles north of New Zealand. They were discovered and described by Cook in 1773. There are about 30 islands of volcanic origin, mountainous, with wooded ridges and fertile valleys, nearly all of them inhabited. Coconut and other magnificent trees grow in profusion, and the soil, like that of most volcanic islands, is very fertile, and fruits and vegetables are raised in abundance. The population numbers perhaps 80,000, and belongs in general to the Papuan race. The general type is rather ugly, below the middle height, fairer than the typical Papuan, with low, receding foreheads, broad faces, and flat noses. Bracelets, earrings, and noserings made out of shells very often used to be their only clothing, tho oil and red clay were smeared over the body in some of the islands. The characteristics and habits of the people differ greatly in the various islands, several islands having become Christianized, while on some of the other islands cannibalism is still possible. The languages of the islands are about twenty in number, and sometimes two or three are used on the same island, so that the missionaries laboring at opposite sides of the islands are unable to use each other's books for their respective congregations. These languages are alike in grammatical construction, and belong to the Melanesian family. Many of them have been reduced to writing by the missionaries.

The history of these islands furnishes many illustrations of the short-sightedness of the theory that savage tribes ought to be given civilization "through commercial intercourse" rather than through religion. It also offers abundant proof of the power of the Gospel of Jesus Christ to change and elevate the most degraded races, and to develop stable and noble character in converts from heathenism.

Traders were the first Europeans to deal with the inhabitants of the most of the islands. The aim, of course, of these men was the benefit of the trader, not of the people whom commercial intercourse was to civilize and elevate. Just at this point—of aim, and interest, and motive—is where the expectation breaks down that savages will be civilized through commerce. Religion only controls beneficently the dealings of men with those who are ignorant and unsuspicious of the powers which civilization confers. The articles of barter of the European traders were largely weapons and liquors, both of which fed the flames of war among the tribes. But these early agents of "civilization" used fraud and deceit; they seized, by force, what they could not get by free consent; they even carried off men's wives, and later they kidnapped men to sell as plantation laborers, wherever there might be a market for sturdy muscle of chief or peón; and their brutality and ungovernable passions drove the islanders to frenzy. If the savages were cruel and treacherous, the traders made them more savage and treacherous and cruel, while the loathsome diseases these strangers introduced decimated the population of the teeming islands, and made it certain to all that white men can cause disease and death. Thus the New Hebrides became one of the most dangerous and discouraging of mission fields.

Beginning at the southern end of the group the following are the more important of the islands: *Aneitium* is a very picturesque, and even imposing, island, with a climate in general good, and not unhealthful to those who understand how to avoid the malaria of the lowlands. It was visited in the first quarter of the 19th century by European traders seeking sandalwood. In 1841 the LMS sent native converts from Samoa there to teach the people. They had to flee for their lives, and, returning later, were always in jeopardy. They were followed in 1848 by the Rev. John Geddie, sent out by the Presbyterians of Nova Scotia, and he, after long and perilous efforts, won a hearing. The inhabitants are all Christians now, and it is a station of the New Hebrides Mission, with a missionary physician and his wife and about 50 native workers occupied in different parts of this and neighboring islands. *Tanna* contains an active volcano which shines in cloud by day, and in fire by night—"the lighthouse of the South Pacific, lit by the finger of God." This island was occupied in 1839 by native teachers from Samoa, sent by the LMS. Two missionaries of the LMS barely escaped from it with their lives in 1848, and the story of savagery and hostility was repeated during ten years. At last a permanent missionary settlement was effected in 1868. There are now 3 missionaries of the New Hebrides Mission at Tanna, with several native workers, a printing house, and about 30 communicants. At *Fotuna*, the first missionaries were Samoan converts, sent by the LMS in 1841. They were at once killed and eaten by the inhabitants. In 1851 a convert from Aneitium was sent there who succeeded in gaining the hearts of some of the people. It is still treated as an outstation of Aneitium, and the people have made progress in adopting Christian principles of life. *Aniwa*, like the other islands, is of volcanic formation, but it is only 300 leet in height, and is girt about by a reef of coral upon which the surf is ever breaking. The LMS sent Samoan teachers there in 1840, one of whom was killed. Other teachers were sent from Aneitium, but little progress was made until Rev. J. G. Paton arrived there in 1866. This was the island of scanty water supply, where the back of heathenism was broken by the tact of the missionary in digging a well which supplied the people with water. It is now a station of the New Hebrides Mission, with 1 missionary and his wife, 1 missionary woman, 5 schools, and 80 church members. *Erromango* was visited by Rev. John Williams, of the LMS, in 1839. He chanced to go toward a place where the natives were holding a feast. Traders had seized the food from such feasts in years gone by, and the natives, supposing that Mr. Williams and his companions were about to do the same, killed him in self-defense. The LMS sent native converts from Samoa there in 1840, but they were driven away. Others were sent in 1852, some converts were made, taken away, and educated by the LMS and sent back to teach their own people; and in 1857 the Rev. G. Gordon and his wife were sent there by the Nova Scotia Presbyterians. They were both murdered. Mr. Gordon's brother went out to take up the martyr's work, and he, too, was murdered. The same year the New Hebrides Mission sent another missionary and his wife to Erromanga, and this temerity has been justified, for in 1900 there were 330 church members in the island under charge of a missionary and his wife, and 16 native workers. *Efate*, or *Vate*, is a beautiful island about thirty miles long, described by the earliest missionaries as teeming with a population of noble aspect and gentle manners. The traders, with their oppression and their brutal crimes, had driven these people to fury, and the first missionary teachers, sent by the LMS in 1839, were killed and eaten. More Samoan teachers went there in 1845, and the New Hebrides Mission sent a missionary there in 1865. It now has about 250 church members. *Nguna* was first entered by the native teachers of the LMS in 1845. The people now are all Christians, and there are 800 church members. *Api* was another of the islands on which the LMS stationed teachers who were converts from other islands. Missionaries of the New Hebrides Mission settled there in 1882. It now has 480 church members. *Ambrym* is a small island in the central part of the group, with an active volcano. It was occupied as a station by the New Hebrides Mission in 1892, after having been visited by native missionary teachers. It is now a center of work for several neighboring islands, with a hospital and a strong missionary force. *Mallicolo* is one of the larger islands, being about sixty miles long. It is inhabited by cannibals still. It has 3 missionaries of the New Hebrides Mission. *Espiritu Santo* is seventy miles long,

and is the largest of the New Hebrides. It was discovered by the Spaniard Fernandez de Quiros in 1606. He supposed it to be a great continent, bestowed upon it the pious and cumbersome name *Tierra Australis del Espiritu Santo*, and sailed away to announce his discovery. The name is commonly reduced in practise to Santo, or at most to E. Santo. Cannibals are still found on this island also. The New Hebrides Mission has established there several flourishing stations and an industrial school. The northern part of the New Hebrides, with the Banks Islands and the Torres Islands, is the field of the Melanesian Mission, begun by Bishop Selwyn of New Zealand in 1859. This has been a very successful mission. In Mota the inhabitants are all Christians, and in Merelava and Motalava there are strong Christian churches with some hundreds of members.

Taking the New Hebrides as a whole, probably few mission fields have so brought into prominence the splendid courage and devotion of both missionaries and native workers, and the depth and permanence of the change produced in a barbarous and heathen people by acceptance of the leadership of Jesus Christ.

Armstrong (E. S.), *History of the Melanesian Mission*, New York, 1900; Paton (J. G.), *Autobiography*, London, 2 vols., 1897; Codrington (R. H.), *Melanesians; Studies in Anthropology, etc.*, London, 1891; Inglis (J.), *In the New Hebrides*, London, 1886; Paton (Mrs. M. W.), *Letters and Sketches from the New Hebrides*, London, 1883; Montgomery (H. H.), *Light of Melanesia*, London, 1896.

NEW HEBRIDES MISSION: This is a synodical union of missionaries of several different Presbyterian Boards carrying on mission work in the New Hebrides Islands. The eight churches supporting this mission are the Presbyterian Church in Canada (formed by the union in 1876 of the various branches of Scotch Presbyterians in Canada); the United Free Church of Scotland, and the Presbyterian Churches of Victoria, New Zealand, Otago, Tasmania, South Australia, and New South Wales. The Established Church of Scotland also renders support in connection with the Church in Canada.

The representatives of these various branches of the Presbyterian Church have formed themselves into one Synod, called the "New Hebrides Mission Synod," which meets annually, and is the supreme authority in the mission in all general matters, each missionary being under the Synod in a general way, while personally responsible only to the church by which he is supported.

The first missionary was the Rev. John Geddie, sent out in 1848 by the Secession Church in Nova Scotia. He was joined later by the Rev. John Inglis of the Reformed Presbyterian Church of Scotland, originally appointed to the Maoris of New Zealand, and followed in 1857 by Rev. John G. Paton and Rev. Josiah Copeland. Then one by one the other churches came into the union, some sending workers, some contributing to the general support of the mission. The field of the mission is found in the islands of the **New Hebrides**, excepting those farthest to the north, which fall within the field of the Melanesian Mission.

NEW NICKERIE. See NICKERIE.

NEW ROTTERDAM. The same as **Nickerie**.

NEWTON, Rev. C. C.: Missionary of the Southern Baptist Missionary Convention to the Yorubas, Africa. Born 1844, died July 20, 1894.

His body was buried in the ocean about 240 miles from Lagos. He was a laborious, deeply pious, and successful missionary. His wife preceded him to her heavenly home only by a few months. Both died from exposure to the terrible African climate. These two have a special claim to remembrance by the church to which they belonged, in that they helped greatly in the reestablishment of Southern Baptist Missions in Africa after the interruption caused by the Civil War in America.

NEWTON, John: Born about 1811; appointed missionary to India, 1835; died Muree, India, July 21, 1891.

Dr. Newton went to India as a missionary of the PN in 1835, arriving at Calcutta in June of that year, accompanied by Rev. James Wilson and his wife. Setting out from Calcutta in a native boat on the Ganges they began their long journey of 1,200 miles to their chosen field at Ludhiana.

His labors were most various. Always foremost with him was the direct preaching of the Word, and that hand-to-hand effort by conversation with individuals which he felt to be one of the missionary's most effective methods. He was a powerful and attractive preacher, both in English and in the vernaculars.

Dr. Newton took with him when he first went to India an old-fashioned wooden printing press, which he set up in a little house secured for that purpose, and thus laid the foundation for that publishing establishment which, during the next fifty years, was destined to issue about two hundred and sixty-seven million pages in ten different languages. In this literary work, Dr. Newton throughout his missionary career was eminent. The Punjabi language is indebted to him for the foundation of its religious literature. Besides the translation of the New Testament into Punjabi and numerous tracts in that language, his literary labors, with those of his associate, Rev. L. Janvier, included a Punjabi grammar and dictionary, a commentary on Ephesians in Urdu, and important tracts in both Urdu and Hindi.

From the Ludhiana Mission, of which Dr. Newton was then the senior missionary, was issued in 1858 that call to the observance of the week of prayer, which has since become so widespread and so fixed a custom throughout the Christian world.

NEW ZEALAND: The colony of New Zealand consists of three islands, viz., North, Middle, and South, or Stewart's Island, together with certain small islets. The North Island is 44,000 square miles, the Middle Island 55,000, and Stewart's Island 1,000 square miles. Thus the area of the three islands in round numbers is about 100,000 square miles. The principal islands are separated by Cook's Straits, and Foveaux Straits separate Stewart's from Middle Island. The entire length of the colony is 1,100 miles, and resembles Italy in form, while in size it is somewhat less than Great Britain and Ireland. In the North Island the mountains occupy one-tenth of the surface, and vary from 1,500 to 6,000 feet in height. There are a few loftier volcanic mountains, as Tongariro (6,500 feet), which is occasionally active; Ruaperhui (9,100 feet) and Mount Egmont are extinct volcanoes above the snow-line. In the Middle Island Mount Cook rises to about 13,000 feet in height. New Zealand is situated in the South Pacific Ocean, 1,200 miles south of the Australian continent, and about 8,000 miles from San Francisco. The entire group lies between 34° and 48° S. latitude and 166° and 179° E. longitude.

The climate is unquestionably one of the finest in the world. The mean annual temperature of the different seasons for the whole colony is, in spring 55°, in summer 63°, in autumn 57°, and in winter 48°. In future it will become the favorite resort of persons seeking health from all parts of the world, possessing, as it does, within a limited area, the most charming scenery and most desirable climate. The death rate is only 10.29 per 1,000.

The natives (called Maoris) are of Malay origin, and superior to other inhabitants of the Pacific intellectually and physically. The Maori is the average size of a European, viz., 5 ft. 6 in., but not so well developed. Mentally the natives are capable of very considerable development, and may hereafter fulfil Lord Macaulay's prediction of them.

The government is administered by a Governor appointed by the crown, and a Ministry, a Legislative Council nominated by the crown, and a House of Representatives elected by the people. The population is about 800,000; of these, 40,000 are Maoris.

New Zealand was first discovered by Tasman in 1642, and surveyed by Captain Cook in 1770. Thereafter it was frequently visited by whalers, and Maoris from New Zealand were frequently taken to Australia. It was to this circumstance that the beginning of missionary work in New Zealand is due. The apostle to the Maoris is the Rev. Samuel Marsden, of the Church of England, who was chaplain of the penal settlement at Port Jackson in Australia. He was struck by the superiority of the Maoris whom he saw, and in 1807 he persuaded the CMS to undertake a mission in New Zealand. Matters did not move quickly, and it was not until 1814 that Marsden set out with three lay missionaries in a brig that he had bought for the purpose. He had with him several Maoris, with whom he had become acquainted; two of them chiefs. He landed his party at the home of one of these men, and on Christmas Day, 1814, inaugurated the mission by an open-air service, the first Christian service ever held in New Zealand; one of the Maoris translating to the people what Mr. Marsden said in his sermon.

The work went on in a marvelous manner until, the European settlers in the islands having greatly increased in numbers, Bishop Selwyn was consecrated as Bishop of New Zealand in 1841. He was amazed at what he found. Everywhere he found the natives eager for instruction, meeting for daily prayers, keeping Sunday, learning to read the portions of Scripture that had been translated into their language. "In short," he wrote home, "I seem to see a nation born in a day." But not long after this war broke out in the islands, largely due to indignation at land-grabbing by English settlers; the "Hau-hau" superstition invaded the churches, and within twenty years the whole missionary enterprise seemed doomed, through the rapid diminution of numbers of the natives.

Meanwhile, the Church of England was consolidating and increasing its forces among the European settlers. It sought from the beginning to make the adjacent islands of the Pacific the field of its own efforts at evangelization, and has nobly fulfilled its duty. It was Bishop Selwyn who began that work in the New Hebrides which is now the Melanesian Mission, and as early as 1855 the martyr Bishop Patteson was appointed over the islands, which now form a diocese of New Zealand, while New Zealand itself is hardly to be called a foreign mission field.

The WMS was the first society to follow in the footsteps of the CMS. It sent its first missionaries to New Zealand in 1822. But disaster followed the effort. In five years no impression had been made; the mission station at Kaeo, in what is now the district of Auckland, was destroyed by hostile Maoris, and the missionaries, barely escaping with their lives, retired to Australia early in 1827. But they returned and opened a new station in New Zealand the same year. After five years more of seemingly fruitless work light began to appear, and in 1834 eighty-one converts were baptized in one day. In 1855, when the Australian Wesleyan Conference was formed and took the control of the mission, there were 16 circuits or stations, 500 European and 2,500 Maori members, 2,500 European and 7,500 Maori adherents, 40 churches or other places of worship for Europeans, and nearly 200 for Maoris. Then the same experience befell the Wesleyans that for a time seemed to overwhelm the Church of England missions. War and the revival of superstitions paralyzed growth. The Maoris shot Whiteley in 1869, a missionary who had given his life to their welfare. The whole enterprise seemed to be coming to an end. But, as in the case of the Church of England, so in the case of the Wesleyans: the European Wesleyan churches of New Zealand grew and prospered; in 1784 the Wesleyan Conference of New Zealand was formed and the local church has since then done its share in the work of evangelizing the remains of the Maori people.

New Zealand as a Christian country has also its Presbyterian Church organization. The Presbyterian missions to the Maoris began in 1841. While the Presbyterians of New Zealand have done their share of the local work of evangelization, their special field has been the New Hebrides mission, well known to the world through the thrilling descriptions of the saintly Paton.

The Congregationalists also have local churches in New Zealand and give their funds for missionary work to the LMS, with which they cooperate. The Baptists came late into the field, but they have a vigorous missionary organization and besides work for the Maoris they maintain missionaries of their own in India.

Work of missions for the Maoris is thus seen to be a work of the churches in a Christian land, aided also by volunteers like the Salvation Army, who have come into the islands and attracted the attention of the Maoris in their own way. New Zealand is no longer an outpost of evangelization, but a new center whence the blessed influences go forth.

Meanwhile contact with the great outside world has brought to the natives a variety of adverse influences. One notable example of this is a comparatively recent invasion of Mormons, who, it is reported, have won 3,000 native converts. Those who have carefully studied the subject speak of the Maoris' future as not promising. Christianity has striven to elevate the natives; but so-called civilization, introducing alongside the Gospel message many forms of vice, has done much to degrade and destroy.

Page (J.), *Among the Maoris*, New York, 1894; Shortland (E.), *Maori Religion and Mythology*, London, 1882; Williams (W.), *Christianity among the New Zealanders*, London, 1866. See also *Missionary Review of the World*, Vol. XV., p. 326.

NEYOOR: A town in Travancore, India, 22 miles N. of Cape Comorin. Station of the LMS (1828), with (1903) 3 missionaries and their wives, 2 women missionaries, 229 native workers, 71 outstations, 59 day schools, 61 Sunday schools, 1 boarding school, 7 dispensaries, 8 hospitals, 1 leper asylum and 13,259 professed Christians, of whom 1,699 are communicants. Station also of Mission to Lepers (1887), with (1903) a home for untainted children of lepers.

NGANDA: A settlement in the French Congo Territory, Africa, not far from the Congo River. Station of the Swedish Missionary Society (1890), with (1901) 3 missionaries, 2 of them with their wives; 2 women missionaries, 15 native workers, 15 outstations, 1 place of worship, 1 Sunday school, 1 boarding school, 1 dispensary, 1 industrial school, and 248 professed Christians.

NGAN-HSIEN: A village in the Province of Sze-chwan, China, situated 25 miles N. W. of Mien-chau. Station of the CMS (1894), with (1903) 2 missionaries and their wives, 1 woman missionary, and 8 professed Christians. The name is also written An-hsien.

NGAN-JEN-HSIEN: A town in the Province of Kiang-si, China, situated 45 miles N. E. of Fu-chau-fu. Station of the CIM (1889), with (1903) 3 women missionaries, 4 native workers, 3 outstations, 4 places of worship, 1 Sunday school, 1 day school, and 66 professed Christians. Some write the name Gan-ren.

NGAN-KING-FU: A town in the province of Ngan-hwei, China, on the left bank of the Yangtszekiang, 100 miles S. W. by W. of Wu-hu. Station of the CIM (1869), with (1903) 2 missionaries, 1 with his wife; 3 outstations, 1 Sunday school, 1 day school. Station also of the PE (1894), with 3 missionaries, 4 native workers, 1 place of worship, 2 day schools, 1 dispensary, and 69 professed Christians, of whom 26 are communicants. Some write the name An-k'ing.

NGAN-LU-FU: A town in the province of Hu-pei, China, situated on the left bank of the Han-kiang, 65 miles N. E. of I-chang. Population, 50,000. Station of the WMS, with (1903) 1 missionary, 7 native workers, 1 outstation, 5 places of worship, 1 Sunday school, 2 day schools, and 154 professed Christians, of whom 74 are communicants.

NGAN-SHUN-FU: A town in the province of Kwei-chau, China, situated 30 miles S. W. of Kwei-yang-fu. Station of the CIM (1888), with (1903) 2 missionaries, 1 of them with his wife; 4 native workers, 2 outstations, 3 places of worship, 1 Sunday school, 1 day school, and 63 professed Christians. Some write the name Gan-shun.

NGAN-TUNG-HSIEN: A town in the province of Kiang-su, China, situated at the head of the estuary of the old course of the Hoang-ho, and about 23 miles N. E. of Hwai-ngan-fu. Station of the CIM (1893), with (1903) 3 women missionaries and 1 native worker. Some write the name An-tung.

NGAO: A German mission station in British

East Africa, on the Tana River, about 12 miles N. by W. of Golbanti. Station of the Neukirchen Mission Institute (1887), with (1903) 2 missionaries and their wives, 2 outstations, 1 place of worship, 1 Sunday school, 3 day schools.

NGAZI. See VUGA.

NGOGWE: A village in Uganda, Africa, situated in South Kyagwe region, N. of the Victoria Nyanza and about 26 miles E. by S. of Mengo. Station of the CMS (1893), with (1903) 1 missionary and his wife, 2 women missionaries, 235 native workers, 4 day schools, 1 dispensary, and 3,795 professed Christians, of whom 1,453 are communicants.

NGOMBE: A town in the Congo Free State, West Africa, situated about 60 miles S. W. of Leopoldville and about 6 miles from the left bank of the Congo River. Station of the BMS (1884), with (1903) 5 missionaries, 3 of them with their wives; 1 woman missionary, 166 native workers, 6 outstations, 4 places of worship, 467 professed Christians, 1 day school, 1 dispensary, and 2 hospitals. Wathen is the name given to the place by Europeans.

NGU-CHENG: A village in Fo-kien Province, China, situated 22 miles S. W. of Fu-chau-fu. Station of the ME, with (1903) 3 women missionaries, 24 native workers, 2 outstations, 5 places of worship, 19 Sunday schools, 2 boarding schools, 11 day schools, and 2,192 professed Christians.

NGUNA: An island in the **New Hebrides** group. Station of the New Hebrides Mission Society, with (1900) 2 missionaries, 1 with his wife; 32 native workers, 1 Sunday school, 1 day school, 1 dispensary, and 820 professed Christians.

NIAMKOLO: A settlement in British Central Africa, situated at the S. end of Lake Tanganyika. Station of the LMS (1889), with (1903) 2 missionaries and their wives, 14 native workers, 31 professed Christians, 1 Sunday school, 4 day schools, 1 dispensary, 1 industrial school.

NIAS: An island lying to the west of Sumatra, in latitude 1° north. Area, 2,523 square miles. The Rhenish Missionary Society has 10 stations on the island. The population is estimated at 250,000. They are a lively, active people, fond of dancing and of cutting off heads; and they are pagans who have so far resisted the invitations of Mohammedan missionaries. These islanders are in race allied to the Battaks of Sumatra, but their language is a dialect peculiar to the locality. The number of Christians in the island (1900) is 4,300, with some 2,000 more who are candidates for baptism.

NICARAGUA: A republic of Central America, bounded north by Honduras, east by the Caribbean Sea, south by Costa Rica, and west by the Pacific Ocean. Area, about 49,500 square miles. The principal mountains are in a range from 10 to 20 miles back of the west coast, and running parallel to it, sometimes rising in high volcanic cones, sometimes subsiding into low plains or places of slight elevation; it seems to have been the principal line of volcanic action, and Nicaragua is marked by some very high volcanoes. The Coco River, which rises in the Segovia Mountains, is the longest in Central America, its course being about 350 miles. The San Juan River, 120 miles in length, is the only outlet of the beautiful lakes Managua and Nicaragua, and plays an important part in the plan for an interoceanic canal by the Nicaraguan route. Climate, except in the very highest portions, is essentially tropical; the northeast part is very damp; rainfall is moderate. The soil is very rich, particularly on the Pacific slope, where all tropical fruits and plants thrive abundantly. Population is about 500,000, consisting of aborigines, mulattoes, negroes, and mixed races. The full-blooded Indians, who are civilized, are a sober and industrious race, but the half-breeds are lazy, vicious, and ignorant. The executive power is in the hands of a President, elected for four years. The legislature has but one house. Education is at a low ebb. The state religion is Roman Catholic, and other religions are not publicly tolerated. The chief industry is cattle-raising. The capital, Managua, has 30,000 inhabitants.

Mission work in Nicaragua is carried on by the Moravians on the Mosquito Coast. In 1890 permission was given the Moravians by the Nicaraguan Government to follow their converts into the interior, from which the missionaries have been jealously excluded.

NICKERIE: A village in Dutch Guiana, South America, situated on the estuary of the Corentyne River. Station of the Moravian Mission (1888), with (1901) 1 missionary and his wife, 9 native workers, 1 place of worship, 2 Sunday schools, 1 day school, and 113 communicant Christians.

NICOBAR ISLANDS: A small group of islands attached to British India, lying in the Bay of Bengal, northeast of Sumatra, and south of the Andaman Islands. There are 8 large islands and 12 small ones. Great Nicobar is 30 miles long and from 12 to 15 miles wide. The islands are well wooded and fertile. Coconuts are raised in great abundance. The inhabitants, numbering (1901) 6,310, are of the Malay race, and speak a form of the Malay language. They have been known to history for at least 1,500 years. The Nicobar swallow is the builder of the edible birds' nests, so highly prized by the Chinese, and these nests are the principal exports, together with bêche-de-mer, tortoise-shell, and ambergris.

Mission work is carried on in these islands chiefly by the Danish Mission Society.

NICOMEDIA: A town and seaport in Asiatic Turkey, situated 53 miles E. S. E. from Constantinople, at the head of the gulf of the same name. It was the ancient capital of Bithynia, being built by Nicomedes I. in 264 B.C., and during the Roman Empire it was frequently used as an imperial residence. Under Turkish rule it decreased very much in importance, but has grown again since the extension of the railway from Constantinople to the interior of Asia Minor. It has a Turkish navy yard. Population about 15,000. Station of the ABCFM (1847), but now (1903) an outstation with 6 native workers, 2 places of worship, 4 Sunday schools, 2 day schools, and 258 professed Christians. The Turkish name of the place is Ismid.

NIEN-HANG-LI: A town in Kwangtung, China, situated about 90 miles N. E. of Swatow. Station of the Basel Missionary Society (1866), with (1903) 3 missionaries, one of them with his wife; 18 native workers, 3 outstations, 9 day schools, and 893 professed Christians, of whom 489 are communicants.

NIGERIA: A British possession and sphere of

influence in W. Africa. It comprises Northern Nigeria, Southern Nigeria, and **Lagos**. Its southern limit is on the Gulf of Guinea and it extends northward to Lake Chad and the French Sahara. On the east it is bounded by Kamerun, and on the west by Dahomey and the French military territories. The whole area is about 400,000 square miles, with an estimated population of 25,000,000, almost wholly native tribes. Much of this territory was formerly administered by the Royal Niger Company, but in 1900 that company turned all its rights over to the crown. The revenues are collected by the coast ports of Lagos and Southern Nigeria, and apportioned to the provinces by the colonial secretary.

Northern Nigeria, divided into 8 administrative provinces, has an area of about 320,000 square miles. The region to the northward is especially subject to the raids of slave traders. In 1900 the country was ravaged as far south as Jebba and Bida. An expedition was made against the raiders, and as a result of these disturbances the emirs of Bida and Kontagora were deposed, and new rulers acceptable to the natives were appointed. A decree was issued making all children born after April 1, 1901, free, forbidding the removal of domestic slaves for the purpose of sale, and applying the penalties for slave dealing to the entire protectorate.

The Arab Berbers constitute a portion of the inhabitants, and many of the natives are nomadic. The Fulani race has ruled the land, with headquarters at Sokoto. It is the great Mohammedan power in all this region. It has openly or secretly opposed the British efforts to break up the slave trade. In 1902 and 1903 punitive expeditions under British officers have done much to bring the Fulani Mohammedans to terms. The Hausa language is the one in general use among the tribes north of the Benue river. Missionary stations are established at Gierko (1903) north of the Benue, and in the regions near the confluence of the Niger and the Benue rivers, in the southern part of the territory.

Southern Nigeria, with an area of 48,000 square miles, with seat of government at Old Calabar, in the Oil River region on the Gulf of Guinea, is inhabited by the Jakri, the Idzos, the Ibos, and other tribes, some of which are more or less cannibalistic. Cannibalism is, however, being gradually stamped out. Missionary enterprise is active in the territory. The CMS is the society occupying the most points in Nigeria. The UFS has a strong mission in the Oil River region, and the Primitive Methodists have missionaries on the coast. About 20 points are occupied, all but one being in S. Nigeria.

Bacon (R. H.), *The City of Blood*, London, 1897; Bindloss (H.), *In the Niger Country*, London, 1899; Goldie (H.), *Old Calabar and Its Mission*, 1890.

NIIGATA: A seaport and the place of greatest commercial importance on the west coast of the main island of Japan; situated on a low strip of land at the mouth of the Shinano River, 137 miles N. N. W. of Tokio. The city is neatly laid out, the streets leveled, paved with gravel, well drained, cleaned, and lighted with coal-oil obtained in the neighborhood. Many streets have a canal in the center. It has a flourishing inland trade, and contains private and national banks, a government hospital, and a school of foreign languages. Climate extreme both in summer and winter. Population (1898), 53,856. Station of the ABCFM (1883), with (1902) 2 missionaries with their wives, 1 woman missionary, 1 native worker, 13 outstations, 5 places of worship, 8 Sunday schools, and 100 professed Christians.

NIKA LANGUAGE (*Ki-nika*): Belongs to the Bantu family and is spoken by some tribes in the vicinity of Ribe, British East Africa. It has been reduced to writing by missionaries of the CMS, and missionaries of the United Free Methodists (of Britain) have also made literary use of it. It has been written with Roman letters.

NIMACH: A town of Central India, situated in Gwalior state, 134 miles N. W. by N. of Indore. Altitude, 1,613 feet. Population (1891), 6,300, of whom 3,800 are Hindus and 1,300 are Mohammedans. Station of the PCC (1884), with (1903) 4 missionaries, two of them with their wives; 15 native workers, 2 outstations, 1 place of worship, 3 Sunday schools, 7 day schools, 2 dispensaries, 1 hospital, 1 orphanage, and 27 professed Christians. Society writes the name Neemuch.

NIMBE: A village in West Africa, situated about 25 miles from the mouth of Brass River in the Delta of the Niger. Station of the CMS (1868), with (1903) 1 missionary and his wife, 4 native workers, 1 place of worship, 2 day schools, 1 boarding school, 1 industrial school, 1 dispensary, and 595 professed Christians, of whom 59 are communicants. These statistics include also Brass Tuwon, at the mouth of the river. Society writes the name Brass Nembe.

NIMPANI: A town in the Central Provinces of India, situated in the Narbada division, 18 miles S. of Hoshangabad. Station of the Swedish Evangelical National Society (1886), with (1902) 2 missionaries and their wives, 4 native workers, 2 outstations, 1 place of worship, 1 day school, and 115 professed Christians, of whom 61 are communicants.

NING-HAI-CHAU: A town in the province of Shantung, China, situated on the coast 18 miles E. of Chi-fu. Station of the CIM (1896), with (1903) 1 missionary and his wife, 1 woman missionary, 3 native workers, 1 place of worship, 2 day schools, 1 dispensary, and 32 professed Christians.

NING-HAI-HSIEN: A town in the province of Che-kiang, China, situated 35 miles S. S. W. of Ning-po-fu. Station of the CIM (1868), with (1903) 1 missionary and his wife, 1 woman missionary, 6 native workers, 1 outstation, 2 places of worship, 1 day school, and 57 professed Christians.

NING-KWO-FU: A prefectural city in the province of Nganhwei, China, 92 miles northwest of Hang-chau. Station of the CIM (1874), with (1903) 2 missionaries and their wives, 1 woman missionary, 7 native workers, 1 Sunday school, 1 day school, and 131 professed Christians, of whom 88 are communicants.

NING-PO-FU: One of the five treaty ports of China opened to foreigners by the treaty of 1842. Situated in the province of Che-kiang, east of the mountains, in a plain on the left bank of the Ningpo River, 16 miles from its mouth. The old wall surrounding it, 25 feet high and 16 feet broad, is in a good state of preservation. There are the usual gates of all Chinese walled cities, north, east, south and west, and two others, besides two passages for boats, in the 5 miles circuit. The principal striking buildings are the large ice-houses, the pagoda, 160 feet high, and the Drum-tower, built earlier than the 15th century. Temples and monasteries are numerous and very handsome. The houses are mostly built of brick, and are usually of but one story. The city suffered from the ravages of the insurgents during the Taiping rebellion, when it was occupied for six months (1864). It has a library of 50,000 volumes.

The foreign trade of Ningpo is quite considerable. Silks, cottons, and white-wood carvings are the principal products. It was occupied by the English forces on the 12th of October, 1841, after the fort at the mouth of the river Chinhai was successfully stormed.

The climate of Ningpo is variable: the usual range of temperature is from 20°-100° F. The rainfall is excessive, and foreigners are subject to malaria. Population (1901), 225,000.

The following missionary societies carry on various enterprises in the city and adjacent region: The ABMU (1843), CMS (1848), PN (1854), CIM (1859), and the UMFC (1864). These societies, together, now have (1903) 45 missionaries, men and women; 175 native workers, 32 day schools, 7 boarding schools or higher educational institutions, 7 hospitals and dispensaries, and 4,801 professed Christians.

NING-TE-HSIEN: A town in the province of Fo-kien, China, situated on the coast about 45 miles N. E. of Fu-chau. Station of the CMS (1896), with (1903) 5 women missionaries, 51 native workers, 2 outstations, 12 day schools, 1 boarding school, and 1,243 professed Christians. Society writes the name Ning-Taik.

NISBET, Henry: Born September 2, 1818, at Laurieston, Glasgow, Scotland; studied at Glasgow University, Relief Divinity Hall, Paisley, and Cheshunt College; sailed August 11, 1840, as a missionary of the LMS to Tanna, one of the New Hebrides Islands. The natives were so hostile that he went to Upolu, Samoan Islands, where he settled at Fasitoonta, and had the charge of ten villages. He spent much time in visiting the outstations, and was one of the missionaries who accompanied the Nova Scotia brethren to select their station in the New Hebrides, on the island of Aneitium. He was one of the revisers of the Samoan Bible.

Later he had charge of the Mission Seminary and of the Press at Malua. During his residence at Malua he prepared for the students many lectures, sermons, notes of Scripture, etc., which were subsequently published in England under his supervision. He spent some eight years longer in the mission field in various departments of usefulness, and died at Malua May 9, 1876. He received the degree of LL.D. from the University of Glasgow.

NISKY: A town on south coast of St. Thomas Island, West Indies, one and one-half miles from St. Thomas town. Station of the Moravian Missions (1753), with (1900) 1 missionary, 4 native workers, 1 place of worship, 2 day schools, and 249 communicant Christians.

NIU-CHWANG. See NEW-CHWANG.

NIUE or SAVAGE ISLAND: An island lying between the Hervey and Samoan Isles, and administratively connected with the former. Climate hot; temperature 75°-98° Fahr. Population, 4,726 stationary and 363 away in ships, etc. Race, light copper-colored Malays, Polynesians. Language, a combination of Tonganese and Samoan. Missionary work was commenced here in 1849 by the LMS. Out of a population of 4,850 about 4,000 are Christians, 1,650 of them members of the church. The natives of this place have lately maintained a certain number of evangelists in New Guinea, who come home at intervals to tell of the blessing of God on their work.

NKALA: A settlement in northwest Rhodesia, Central Africa, situated in Barotsiland about 125 miles E. of Lealui. Station of the Primitive Methodist Missionary Society, with (1903) 1 missionary and his wife, 1 native worker, 2 places of worship, 1 Sunday school, and 4 professed Christians.

NOAKHALI: A town in Bengal, India, situated in the Noakhali district, 180 miles E. of Calcutta. Population, 5,500, of whom 2,800 are Hindus and 2,600 are Mohammedans. Station of the Queensland Australian Baptist Mission Society (1889), with (1901) 2 missionaries, 1 woman missionary, 9 native workers, 1 outstation, 1 day school, and 10 professed Christians.

NODOA: A town on the island of Hai-nan, Chinese Empire, situated about 90 miles S. W. of Hoi-hau. It lies in a wide plain almost entirely surrounded by mountains, and has very pleasing environs. The people are of several distinct races, many of them being Hak-kas from the province of Kwang-tung. The different dialects found here constitute a serious obstacle to missionary work. Station of the PN (1892), with (1903) 9 missionaries, 1 woman missionary, 6 native workers, 2 outstations, 2 places of worship, 1 Sunday school, 1 day school, 2 boarding schools, 1 hospital, 3 dispensaries, 1 printing house, and 84 communicant Christians.

NOGUGU: A settlement on Espiritu Santo Island, **New Hebrides.** Station of the New Hebrides Mission Society, with (1900) 1 missionary and his wife, 8 day schools, and 24 professed Christians.

NONGSAWLIA. See CHERRA PUNJI.

NONGOMA: A settlement in Zululand, Natal, Africa, situated about 12 miles N. E. of Bethel. Station of the Zululand Missionary Diocese (1892), with 1 missionary and his wife, 5 native workers, 3 outstations, 2 day schools, and 1 dispensary.

NORFOLK ISLAND: An island situated in the Pacific Ocean, between New Zealand and New Caledonia, about 1,200 miles E. N. E. of Sydney; a dependency of New South Wales. Population, 800. Headquarters of the Melanesia diocese and of the Melanesia Mission. The training school for all the native workers for the Solomon Islands, Banks Islands, and the northern New Hebrides is at Norfolk Island. The other inhabitants of the island are descendants of the "Bounty" mutineers from Pitcairn Island. The SPG maintains a chaplain at Norfolk Island for their benefit. The Melanesia Mission has (1900) 3 missionaries, 1 with his wife; 1 theological class, 1 printing house, and a steamer.

NORTH AFRICA MISSION: With the fall of the French Empire and the establishment in its place of the French Republic, religious liberty was granted not only to France, but also to Algeria, which was subdued by her in 1830. Thus was North Africa opened for the introduction of the Gospel. Mr. George Pearce, who visited Algeria in 1876, revisited it in 1880, and returning to England aroused considerable interest in the Kabyles, or the Berber tribes inhabiting the mountains a little to the east of the city of Algiers. A mission to these interesting people was started. Mr. Grattan Guiness, who paid a brief visit to Algeria, and Mr. Edward Glenny, who had independently been making investigations as to the condition of Morocco and Algeria, united in forming a committee for its management. In November of 1881 Mr. Pearce, accompanied by Mr. Glenny, returned to Algeria, taking with him two young brethren to work under Mr. Pearce's direction. They settled at Djemmâa Sahrij, but met with so much difficulty through the suspicion and opposition of the French local administrator, that one of the young men, a Syrian, retired from the work, and the other returned in the summer of 1882 to Europe to seek a fellow-laborer with a French diploma who might be more favorably received by the local authorities. After encountering many difficulties, which threatened again and again to destroy the whole work, the mission was reorganized in 1883. Several other friends joined in forming a council, and a fresh band of workers was taken out by Mr. Glenny, who then proceeded to Tangier, the council having determined to widen its sphere to the other aboriginal or Berber races of North Africa. Since then it has step by step extended its work, establishing stations in various places in Morocco, Algeria, Tunis, and Tripoli, and a branch mission to the Bedouins in Northern Arabia. It now no longer confines itself to the Berbers, but seeks to evangelize among all the Muslims, and is hoping to do definite work also among Europeans and Jews. There are seven fields into which the work is divided, which, tho they are small, are each worked under distinct direct control from London.

The character of the mission is like that of the Young Men's and Young Woman's Christian Associations, evangelical, and embraces members of all denominations who are sound in their views on fundamental truths. The missionaries seek, by itinerant and localized work, to sell or distribute the Scriptures far and wide; and by conversation in the houses, streets, shops and markets, in town and country, to teach Christian doctrine, encouraging to profession of faith and baptism.

Educational work is not a prominent feature in this mission, but is subordinate to evangelistic work. Medical aid has been found most useful in removing prejudices. A hospital and dispensary are established at Tangier and a dispensary at Fez, but in Algeria much difficulty has been experienced through the law forbidding the practise of medicine without a French diploma.

The Mission in Algeria has stations at Djemmâa Sahrij, with two missionary women; Shershell, two women; Constantine, 7 missionaries; Algiers, 7 missionaries. Total in Algeria, 18, of whom 5 are men. In Morocco: Tangier, 10 missionaries; Fez, 5 missionaries; Tetuan, 4 missionaries; Casablanca, 5 missionaries; El Araish, 2 missionaries. Total, 26 missionaries, of whom 6 are men. Tunis: Tunis, 9 missionaries; Susa, 9 missionaries; Kairwan, 4 missionaries; Bizerta, 2 missionaries. Total, 24, of whom 5 are men. Tripoli: Tripoli, 6 missionaries (2 men); Egypt: Alexandria, 4 missonaries; Shebin-el-Kom, 7 missionaries. Total, 11 missionaries, of whom 4 are men. This great preponderance of women indicates the general type of work, viz., house to house visiting, with some instruction of children and women. It is much like the Zenana work in India.

NORTH AMERICAN INDIANS: The name Indian as applied to the aborigines of America perpetuates the mistaken supposition of Columbus that he had landed upon the eastern shores of India. While the use of this misnomer has continued, the people are now generally designated as American Indians or Red Indians, to distinguish them from the inhabitants of India.

Origin: Archeological investigations are bringing to light evidence that man was on this continent during glacial times, but whether he existed here at as early a period as in Europe, is an unsettled question. Nor is it yet determined whether the natives are autochthons or came hither from Europe or Asia. There is reason to believe that during the past ages there had been intercourse between the two continents by way of the islands of the Atlantic, on the one side, and those of the Pacific on the other, but there is no proof that this intercourse left here any dominant influence, or was potent in bringing about the civilizations developed on the uplands of Peru, or in the valleys and plateaux of Central America and Mexico. Whatever had been achieved in North or in South America was the work of the same race that was here discovered by Columbus.

Culture: The aborigines of America suffered a serious drawback because of the absence, upon this Western continent, of animals capable of domestication. The llama had been tamed, but its habitat was limited, nor could it serve man as did the sheep, ox, and horse of the eastern continent. These latter animals had given stability to man's food supply, and, by supplementing his strength in work, had secured to him both time and energy for the exercise of his thought upon the devising of means for his individual and social advancement. The native of America was without such animal assistants. He had to hunt and fish and depend upon his unaided efforts for whatever he possessed. His development of the maize from a tropical plant of slender capacity to a productive staple, capable of being grown over a wide geographic range, a range which even our race has not been able to greatly extend, was a remarkable agricultural achievement, requiring time, careful observation, and persistent labor. He had mastered the art of irrigation, which was extensively used in the semi-arid regions, and hundreds of miles of ditches can to-day be traced upon the abandoned plains of the Southwest. Fruits and vegetables were cultivated for food; cotton was grown and woven into cloth; wool from the buffalo and mountain sheep was spun for clothing; different vegetable fibers and the inner bark of trees were woven into articles of use; dyes were manufactured and employed for ornamentation; the carving of stone, wood, and bone; pottery-making, basketry, and the making of implements and weapons were among the widespread industries of the peoples. Skill in workmanship and beauty of design were particularly noteworthy in the native baskets and vases. Village life was the rule. Habitations were of stone, adobe, wood and tanned skins. The legends and folk-tales recounted about the fireside were dramatic in character and contained wise and witty sayings, while the myths and rituals connected with the ceremonies were replete with lofty symbolism and touched with poetic fervor. Song accompanied all religious and social gatherings, as well as the daily avocations of the people; they pled for the lover, inspirited the warrior, and sped the departed to the spirit land. That the culture of the tribes was unequal was, in part, owing to their varying environments and to the isolation and enmities caused by the great diversity of languages upon the continent. Altho some languages have disappeared within the last two hundred years, there are to-day within the limits of the United States about forty linguistic stocks, each of which contains several languages and dialects.

Organization: The political organization of the people was tribal. Most of the tribes were composed of a number of clans, but in all, the kinship group was fundamental, and to it the rights of the individual were subordinate. The ruling power was vested in a council of chiefs and leaders, but the duty of enforcing the traditional rules or laws devolved upon the chiefs. Marriage was generally exogamous, that is, a man or woman could not marry within his or her kinship group or clan, and in a large number of the tribes descent was traced through the mother only. In many instances the tribal structure was elaborate in its details, and among all of the tribes the religious ideas and symbols of the people were closely interwoven with their political organization.

Religion: Among peoples so diverse as to language, avocations, and general culture, it is almost impossible to generalize their religious beliefs and practises. Broadly speaking, all regarded the vital and formulative force of the universe as akin to that peculiar quality or power of which man is conscious within himself as directing his own acts—as willing a course to bring about certain results—in a word, as a deified will power. This mysterious, invisible, animating force manifested itself in all forms, each of which it had endowed with some special gift or capacity. The stars, sun, moon, winds, thunder, the earth, water, and all living creatures, were manifestations of this power and served as intermediaries through which man could seek help of the mysterious one. The priestly class—men "whose minds were open to the teaching of the gods"—had charge of the rites by which these intermediaries could be addressed. Fasting, prayer, acts of purification, and occasionally sacrifice, were observed in all religious ceremonies. While the underlying thoughts of the native religion were high and reverent in character, the overlying rites were sometimes distorted by practises arising from the abuse of priestly privilege. The belief in a future life was universal, and the character of a man's life here was considered as affecting his life hereafter. Truthfulness, honesty, justice, and hospitality were persistently inculcated by priests, chiefs, and leaders.

Missionary work in the 17th and 18th centuries: Protestant missionary work began soon after the founding of the colonies. In 1621 the "East India School" was organized and endowed at Charles City, Va. The uprising in the following year would have been far more disastrous to the settlers had not the Christian and friendly Indians both warned and protected the colonists. This unfortunate event checked all systematic missionary efforts by this colony until near the close of the century, when, in 1691, a legacy from the Hon. Robert Boyle was used to form the Brasserton school, "that the Christian faith may be propagated amongst the western Indians." This school was connected with the newly chartered college of William and Mary.

In New England the natives were early instructed in the Christian religion, but no mission work exclusively Indian was undertaken until John Eliot, in eastern Massachusetts, and Thomas Mayhew, in Martha's Vineyard, began their labors. In 1641 Thomas Mayhew obtained a grant of Martha's Vineyard and the neighboring islands, and became both patentee and governor. His son, Thomas Mayhew, Jr., was minister to the settlers and extended his work to the Indians living thereabouts, who numbered several thousands. He mastered the native language, and soon had a successful mission. The first convert, Hiacoomes, placed himself under Mr. Mayhew's instruction, and later became a teacher and afterward a preacher to his own people. In January, 1651, the first school in New England for the instruction of Indians was established by Mr. Mayhew. In October, 1652, the first native church was organized, with 282 members; the covenant was prepared by Mr. Mayhew in the Indian language. In 1657, when on his way to England to solicit aid for his work, Mr. Mayhew was lost at sea. His father, the governor, altho seventy years old, began at once the study of the native language, and carried on the mission, preaching at least once a week at some of the plantations, "walking sometimes twenty miles through the woods to the Indians," and continued these labors until his death, in his ninety-third year. His grandson, John, became associated in the work and continued in it until his death in 1688, when his son Experience took up the task and continued to preach to the Indians for thirty-two years. In 1709 he translated the Psalms, and later the Gospel of John. In 1670 the first Indian church with a native pastor was organized, the adult Christians on the island numbering about three thousand.

John Eliot was born in Essex, England, 1604. He came to New England in 1631, and the next year was settled over the First Church at Roxbury, and continued in this charge until his death in 1690. Soon after his arrival he began the study of the native tongue and taught all the Indians who visited him from two catechisms he had framed in their language. In 1647 the General Court set apart a tract of land at Nonantum, on the borders of the present towns of Newton and Watertown, for the use of the Indians. As John Eliot's mission work progressed, he gathered the Christian Indians into towns, which became known as "Praying Indian Towns." He established schools, taught the natives various industries, and organized a form of government similar to that proposed by Jethro to the Israelites. The first of these towns was located at Natick in 1651 and six other towns were soon after established. Between 1670 and 1673 seven more towns were organized, and in 1674 these towns contained one thousand one hundred and fifty church members. In 1675 King Philip's war broke out. The first warning came from the Christian Indians who, in the face of fearful hardships, rendered invaluable service to the colonists. The story of the grievous wrongs done these faithful friends can be read in Mr. Daniel Gookin's narrative, "An Historical Account of the Doings and Sufferings of the Christian Indians of New England, in the years 1675, 1676, and 1677, impartially drawn, by one well acquainted with that affair." In 1658 John Eliot completed the translation of the Book of Psalms, which, together with the catechism, was printed at Cambridge the same year. No copy is extant. In 1661 the New Testament was printed and two years later the entire Bible. This was the first Bible ever printed on the America continent. A new edition was called for and printed in 1680.

In 1734 the Rev. John Sargent, of Yale College, opened a school among the Housatonnuchs, and in two years had a church with fifty-two members, which later increased to two hundred and fifty. In 1751 the Rev. Jonathan Edwards took a double charge at Stockbridge, of both whites and Indians. When a child he had picked up the language of the natives, and this knowledge proved of service to him in his work among the Indians in western Massachusetts.

When, in 1657, John Eliot attended a council held at Hartford, Conn., he preached to the Podunks, but they utterly refused to receive a missionary, because the English having "taken their lands sought to make them servants." Rev. James Fitch, pastor of the church at Norwich, Conn., being acquainted with the language of the Mohegans, succeeded in establishing a church among these Indians, with some forty members.

The Moravians began work at Sharon, western Connecticut, in 1742. In the following year Rev. Eleazer Wheelock, of Lebanon, Conn., took into his family a young Mohegan, Samson Occum, as a pupil. The rapid advance made by this Indian youth in English, Latin, Greek, and Hebrew enabled him to become a teacher at New London, Conn., in 1748, and to be ordained to the ministry in 1756. Mr. Wheelock's success with Samson Occum led to the establishment, by the aid of Mr. Joshua Moor, of the Moor Indian school at New Lebanon. In 1765 the Rev. Samson Occum went to England to raise funds for this school, and succeeded in securing some ten thousand pounds from friends of the cause in England and Scotland. On his return, Dr. Wheelock removed the school from New Lebanon, Conn., to Hanover, New Hampshire, where, after a time, it became merged in Dartmouth College. A number of notable Indians were trained under Dr. Wheelock, who became teachers, missionaries and leaders among their people.

Four chiefs of the Iroquois of New York visited England in 1708 to ask Queen Anne that missionaries be sent to instruct their people. Their request was granted, and a school was opened in Albany among the Mohawks, and a portion of the Scriptures translated into their language. The mission prospered, and in 1743 Rev. Mr. Andrews reported that but a few remained unbaptized in the tribe. Altho the war of 1744-48 interfered with the work, still just before the Revolution, the Rev. John Stuart reported that the Indians were cultivating their lands, learning trades and were "as regular and virtuous in their conduct as the white people."

The Rev. Samuel Kirkland, a pupil of Dr. Wheelock's school, and later of Princeton, began a mission among the Oneidas of New York in 1760. He led the people forward in agriculture and in Christian living. Through the influence of Mr. Kirkland the Oneidas remained neutral during the Revolutionary War or were friendly to the Colonists. In 1793 the Hamilton Oneida Academy was founded for the higher education of the white and Indian youth. This academy afterward developed into Hamilton College.

The headquarters of the Moravian Church in America was established at Bethlehem, Penn., in 1740. From this center various missionary enterprises were undertaken among the Delaware tribes with wonderful results. The native villages and others which grew up around the missions became prosperous and orderly, and the inhabitants Christian in their belief and in their mode of living. The history of the Moravian missions in Pennsylvania and Ohio is a dark page in our annals, and presents a fearful record of suffering, heroism, and martyrdom on the part of these friendly Christain Indians. (Heckewelder's *Narrative of the Missions Among the Delaware and Mohegan Indians.* Schweinitz: *Life of David Zeisberger.* Loskiel: *History of the Mission to the Indians.*)

In Georgia the Moravian Church started a mission on the Savannah river, but difficulties between the Spaniards and the English resulted in the breaking up of the school, and the return of the missionaries to Bethlehem, Penn. No further work was undertaken until the 19th century.

While few if any of the mission stations established during the 17th or 18th centuries remain at the present day, this fact does not indicate failure of the Christianizing work of the missionaries, but is due to the great changes that have rapidly followed the displacing of the native population by the white race in the settlement of the country. The unselfish labors of the early missionaries were not lost; they have borne double fruit, as, on the one hand, in the improved condition of the descendants of those Indian tribes who were the subject of so much care and solicitude, and, on the other hand, they tended to foster in the white race the growth of a broader view of human relations, and a philanthropy that has since found practical expression in beneficent laws and generous government acts toward the natives of this country.

Governmental Relations: Among the problems that confronted the leaders of the American Revolution, none was more pressing than that of the Indian. On June 17, 1775, the Continental Congress appointed a Committee on Indian Affairs, with Gen. Schuyler as chairman. At the suggestion of this committee, Congress divided the colonies into three departments, northern, middle, and southern, and appointed commissioners to superintend each department. By this plan the tribes were to be brought directly in contact with accredited officials within their own territory, and efforts made to reduce to a minimum the dangers of Indian hostility to the colonies. Care was also exercised to institute measures looking to the betterment of the natives. The first direct connection between the general government and mission work occurred April 10, 1776, when the Continental Congress directed the commissioners of the Middle Department to employ a minister, a schoolmaster, and a blacksmith for the Delaware Indians. In September of the same year, as a means of conciliating the friendship of the Canadian Indians, Congress directed that $500 be paid to Dr. Wheelock, president of Dartmouth College, to maintain the Indian youth under his tuition. On July 31, 1781, Congress authorized the payment of one hundred and thirty-seven pounds, "currency of New Jersey, in specie, for the support and tuition of three Indian boys of the Delaware nation, now at Princeton College."

By Article IX of the "Articles of Confederation," "the United States in Congress assembled" were charged with the sole and exclusive right and power of managing all affairs with the Indians. In 1784 "the Secretary of the War Office" was directed to cooperate with the commissioners when making treaties. Two years later the Indian "departments" were reduced to two, the Ohio River being the dividing line, and a superintendent placed over each and made subject to the Secretary of War. After the adoption of the Constitution, and the creation of a War Department, August 7, 1789, the Indians continued to be under the charge of the Secretary of War. By the Act of March 3, 1849, the Department of the Interior was created. The Bureau of Indian affairs was transferred to this Department, and the Indians passed from military to civil control. (*Indian Education and Civilization.* A. C. Fletcher. Senate Ex. Doc. No. 95. 48th Congress 2d Session.)

Indian Land Tenure: In the proclamation of George III., dated October 7, 1763, four principles of government in Indian affairs were laid down which have ever since been in force: 1st. The recognition of the Indian's right of occupancy. 2d. The right of the Government to expel white intruders on Indian lands. 3d. The sole right to purchase Indian lands vested in the Government, and, 4th, The right to regulate trade and license traders.

In 1783 the "Congress of the Confederation" issued a proclamation forbidding private purchase or gift of lands from Indians, or any settlements to be made upon unceded Indian territory.

Upon the adoption of the Constitution in 1789 the right of eminent domain was vested in the United States. (Article IV.) The relation of the Government's right of eminent domain to the Indian's right of occupancy was fully set forth by the Supreme Court in the decision rendered by Chief Justice Marshall in the case of Johnson *v.* McIntosh:

"On the discovery of this immense continent, the great nations of Europe . . . were all in pursuit of the same object. It was necessary, in order to avoid conflicting settlements, and consequent war with each other, to establish a principle which all should acknowledge as the law by which the right of acquisition, which they all asserted, should be regulated as between themselves. This principle was, that discovery gave title to the Government by whose subjects, or by whose authority, it was made, against all other European governments, which title might be consummated by possession.

"In the establishment of these relations the rights of the original inhabitants were in no instance entirely disregarded, but were necessarily to a considerable extent impaired. They were admitted to be the rightful occupants of the soil, with a legal, as well as a just, claim to retain possession of it, and to use it according to their own discretion; but their rights to complete sovereignty, as independent nations, were necessarily diminished, and their power to dispose of the soil at their own will, to whomever they pleased, was denied by the original fundamental principle that discovery gave exclusive title to those who made it. . . . However extravagant the pretension of converting the discovery of an inhabited country into conquest may appear, if the principle has been asserted in the first instance and afterward sustained, if a country has been acquired and held under it, if property of the great mass of the community originates in it, it becomes the law of the land, and cannot be questioned. So, too, with respect to the concomitant principle that the Indian inhabitants are to be considered merely as occupants, to be protected, indeed, while in peace, in the possession of their lands, but to be deemed incapable of transferring the absolute title to others. However this restriction may be opposed to natural right and to the usages of civilized nations, yet, if it be indispensable to that system under which the country has been settled, and be adapted to the actual condition of the two people, it may, perhaps, be supported by reason, and certainly cannot be rejected by courts of justice."

In the early years of the Government the treaties with the Indians often defined a boundary line between the "Indian country" and the United States. At first this extended from the lower of the Great Lakes to Florida, and beyond this line the United States claimed no control, so that the citizen who ventured to pass over into the Indian country could claim no protection from the Government. Gradually trading and military posts were established, and the land adjoining them secured from the Indians; then roadways between these stations were obtained, until finally the Indians were hedged in by their cessions, and were restricted to defined tracts known as "reservations." These were established either by treaty or by order of the President.

The reservations held by treaty, Act of Congress, patent, or acknowledged Spanish grants, number about 110, and cannot be alienated except by consent of Congress. They are located in Arizona, California, Colorado, Idaho, Indian Territory, Iowa, Kansas, Michigan, Minnesota, Montana, Nebraska, New Mexico, New York, North Carolina, North Dakota, Oklahoma, Oregon, South Dakota, Washington, Wisconsin and Wyoming.

At the request of the Indian Department, the President is authorized to set apart public lands as Indian reservations. (The Public Domain, 1883, p. 243.) There are between sixty and seventy "Executive Order" reservations. This class can be restored to the public domain by the President without an Act of Congress.

Three hundred and seventy treaties have been made with Indian tribes. The first was with the Delaware, September 7, 1778, and the last with the Nez Percé, August, 1868. The Act of March 3, 1871, prohibited the making of any future treaty with Indians; since then "agreements" have been made with the tribes, subject to the approval of Congress. The first of these "agreements" was with bands of the Sioux, September 20, 1871; the last, with the Choctaw and Chickasaw, March 21, 1902. (Report of Com'r Ind. Affs., 1903.)

All these treaties and agreements had reference to land. The payments to the tribes for the cessions made were sometimes cash, but generally in the form of annuities. The bulk of these annuities were in clothing, food, etc., with perhaps a small payment of money. This form was more acceptable to the white merchants than to the Indians, and the interests of trade have predominated in determining the kind of payment that should be given the Indian for his lands.

The land within a reservation was regarded as belonging to the tribe, and not subject to individual ownership. This condition tended to perpetuate tribal relations and to retard the progress of the people along the lines of the civilization of the white race. As early as the middle of the last century, a number of treaties made at that time contained provisions for the allotment of individual holdings to Indians, but this policy did not become general until the passage of the Severalty Act of February 8, 1887. The provisions of this act are applicable to lands that are agricultural and grazing, but not to lands that are fitted only for grazing, or which require irrigation. This law gives 80 acres of agricultural land to each member of the tribe, regardless of sex or age. Where the land is classed as grazing, the amount is doubled.

Section 5 states: "That upon the approval of the allotments provided for in this act by the Secretary of the Interior, he shall cause patents to issue therefor in the name of the allottees, which patents shall be of the legal effect, and declare that the United States does and will hold the land thus allotted, for the period of twenty-five years, in trust for the sole use and benefit of the Indian to whom such allotment shall have been made, or, in case of his decease, of his heirs according to the laws of the State or Territory where such land is located, and that at the expiration of said period the United States will convey the same by patent to said Indian, or his heirs, as aforesaid, in fee, discharged of said trust and free of all charge and encumbrance whatsoever; *Provided,* That the President of the United States may, in any case in his discretion, extend the period."

Under this act a number of reservations have been allotted to the tribes living thereon, and the remainder of the lands purchased by the Government and thrown open to white settlement. The work of allotment is still going on, and the time is not far distant when the Indians' tenure of land will have ceased to be merely the right of occupancy, and will be the same as that of white land-holders.

Population: According to the report of the Commissioner of Indian Affairs for 1903, the Indians within the limits of the United States, exclusive of Alaska, number 258,665. These people are sparsely scattered within the States or Territories in which their reservations lie, with the exception of the Indian Territory, where their numbers and location are such as may enable these tribes to become a political power.

Citizenship: Section 6 of the Severalty Act of 1887 provides as follows: "That upon the completion of said allotments and the patenting of the lands to said allottees, each and every member of the respective bands or tribes of Indians to whom allotments have been made shall have the benefit of and be subject to the laws, both civil and criminal, of the State or Territory in which they may reside; and no Territory shall pass or enforce any law denying any such Indian within its jurisdiction the equal protection of the law. And every Indian born within the territorial limits of the United States, to whom allotments shall have been made under the provisions of this act, or under any law or treaty, and every Indian born within the territorial limits of the United States, who has voluntarily taken up, within said limits, his residence separate and apart from any tribe of Indians therein, and has adopted the habits of civilized life, is hereby declared to be a citizen of the United States, and is entitled to all the rights, privileges, and immunities of such citizens, whether such Indian has been or not, by birth or otherwise, a member of any tribe of Indians within the territorial limits of the United States, without in any manner impairing or otherwise affecting the rights of any such Indian to tribal or other property."

About 41 per cent. of the Indian population are now citizens of the United States, by virtue of the Act of 1887. This percentage will be largely increased in the near future when the "Five Civilized Tribes" of Indian Territory have relinquished their separate form of government, while the number is constantly increasing as allotments are made.

Self-support: Self-support is becoming more and more the rule and dependence upon the Government the exception. When the rapidity with which enforced changes have come upon the tribes in regard to their food supply are considered, together with the bewilderment and difficulties which attend the extinction of old customs and habits, the progress that has been made is a credit to the race, and promises well for the future of the Indian.

Education: One of the earliest authentic expressions from the United States Government, in reference to Indian education, occurs in the instructions given to Brig.-Gen. Rufus Putnam, who, in May, 1792, was sent to negotiate with the late hostile Indians near Lake Erie:

"That the United States are desirous of imparting to all the Indian tribes the blessings of civilization, as the only means of perpetuating them on the earth. That we are willing to be at the expense of teaching them to read and write, to plow and sow, in order to raise their own bread and meat, with certainty, as the white people do." (Amer. State Papers, Ind. Affs., Vol. 1, p. 235.)

The first treaty provision was made December 2, 1794, with the Oneida, Tuscarora, and Stockbridge Indians, who had been faithful to the colonists.

The first general appropriation for Indian education was made March 3, 1819, for $10,000. The policy to be pursued is indicated in the following extract from the circular issued September 3, 1819:

" . . . The plan of education, in addition to reading, writing, and arithmetic, should, in the instruction of boys, extend to the practical knowledge of the mode of agriculture, and of such of the mechanical arts as are suited to the condition of the Indians; and in that of the girls, to spining, weaving, and sewing. It is also indispensable that the establishment (of schools) should be fixed within the limits of those Indian nations who border our settlements. Such associations or individuals who are already actually engaged in educating the Indians, and who may desire to cooperate with the Government, will report to the Department of war." (Amer. State Papers, Ind. Affs., Vol. II., p. 201.)

In 1825 there were 38 schools under the charge of various missionary organizations. Toward their support the Government contributed that year $13,620.41, and the Indians gave from their annuities and by their treaty provisions, $11,750. (*Ibid.*, pp. 587, 669.)

In 1848, 16 manual labor schools and 87 boarding and other schools were in operation. The following year the Indian Commissioner reported that "nearly the whole of the large amount

35

required for the support and maintenance of the schools now in operation is furnished by the Indians themselves out of their national funds." And he urged that the annual appropriation of $10,000, made in accordance with the Act of 1819, be raised to $50,000.

In 1865 the Secretary of the Interior recommended:

"That Congress provide a civilization and educational fund, to be disbursed in such mode as to secure the cooperation and assistance of benevolent organizations."

By a treaty made with the Osage Indians, September 29, 1865, Article 2 provided that the proceeds from the sales of certain ceded lands should, under the direction of the Secretary of the Interior, be applied to the education and civilization of Indian tribes residing within the limits of the United States. This fund amounted to $770,179.42, and was exhausted by 1882.

Up to 1873 Indian schools had been maintained either wholly by missionary funds or jointly with the aid of the Government, except of those schools supported entirely from tribal funds and under the charge of United States teachers. At this time Government day schools were established, and later boarding schools, the number increasing with each year. During the last decade of the past century all Government financial support to mission schools ceased, and at the present time most of the Indian schools are under the classified service of the Government. Where mission schools exist, they are entirely independent of the Government and supported by missionary organizations.

During the year 1903 the Government maintained 26 boarding schools off the reservations. These are large industrial and manual training schools located in the midst of thrifty communities, and their capacities range from 90 to 1,000 pupils. A valuable adjunct to these schools is the "Outing System." This "System" was instituted and has reached its highest development in connection with the Training School at Carlisle, Pa.

"This system consists in placing Indian boys and girls . . . out in the families of surrounding farmers, the boys for general farm work, and the girls for various household duties. . . . They usually attend public schools and are paid a stipulated sum for their labor, thus learning the value of labor in dollars and cents, and the resultant benefits of thrift." (Rep. Ind. Com'r, 1903.)

The average attendance at these schools for 1903 was 7,793; 91 boarding schools were in operation on the different reservations, with an average attendance of 11,209; 140 day schools were in operation on the reservations, and their average attendance was 4,497.

These figures do not include Indians attending the public schools in different parts of the country, or those pursuing higher branches in various institutions and colleges, or under missionary training.

The appropriation made for Indian education by Congress for the year ending June 30, 1904, was 3,522,950 dollars. This sum does not include the full amount expended upon Indian schools by the Government, for there are several schools on reservations which are either wholly or in large part maintained by tribal funds.

As a result of education, Indians are to-day to be found in all avocations—as farmers, mechanics, laborers, clerks, merchants; in the professions, as clergymen, physicians, lawyers, teachers; as authors and artists, and also in the army and navy of the United States.

While the favored have advanced and are well on their upward course, the transition period is still pressing heavily upon a large proportion of the people. Their faith in the ancient ideas of their fathers is shaken or gone, while faith in the new is not yet established. The old tribal laws and restraints no longer exist; old avocations are closed; old social honors and pleasures have disappeared; the people thus bereft and distraught stand to-day in greater need of the wise missionary than ever before. While his work is difficult and more onerous than in the past, it is more hopeful and less isolated; its problems have become akin to those which confront his fellow-workers in our cities and rural districts, and demand a similar treatment.

GENERAL INFORMATION: Bancroft (H. H.), *The Native Races of the Pacific Coast*, New York, 1874–76, 5 vols.; James (G. W.), *The Indians of the Painted Desert*, Boston, 1903; Fletcher (Miss A. C.), *Indian Education and Civilization*, Washington, 1888 (Special report of Bureau of Education; also in Senate, Ex. Doc. No. 95, Forty-eighth Congress, Second Session); Hailman (W. N.), *The Education of the Indian*, Albany, 1900 (in monographs on Education in the United States, Vol. II.); Walker (F. R.), *Indian Citizenship*, New York, 1878; *Indian Rights Association Reports*, Philadelphia, 1889–1903; *Commissioner of Indian Affairs Reports (U. S.)*, Canada: *Superintendent of Department of Indian Affairs' Reports*, Ottawa, 1885–1901.

MISSIONS: Bartlett (S. C.), *Missions of the ABCFM among the North American Indians*, Boston, 1876; Campbell (Charles), *Historical Sketch of Early Missions among the Indians of Maryland*, Baltimore, 1846; Eastman (Mrs. M. H.), *Dacotah*, New York, 1849; Eells (Myron), *History of Indian Missions on the Pacific Coast*, Philadelphia, 1882; Everhard (P.), *History of Indian Baptist Missions in North America*, Boston, 1831; Finley (J. B.), *History of the (ME) Wyandot Mission at Upper Sandusky, Ohio*, Cincinnati, 1840; Garret (J. B.), *Historical Sketches of Missions among the North American Indians*, Philadelphia, 1881; Goode (W. H.), *Outposts of Zion*, Cincinnati, 1863; Gookin (D.), *Historical Account of the Doings and Sufferings of the Christian Indians of New England in 1675–1677*; Heckewelder (J. G. E.), *Narrative of the Moravian Missions among the Delaware and Mohegan Indians*, Philadelphia, 1882; Jones (Peter), *History of the Ojibway Indians*, London, 1861; Kip (W. I.), *Historical Scenes from the Old Jesuit Missions*, New York, 1875; Loskiel (——), *History of the Moravian Mission to the Indians*; Riggs (S. R.), *Mary and I: Forty Years among the Sioux*, Chicago, 1880; Romer (H.), *Die Indianer und ihr Freund D. Ziesberger*, Gutersloh, Germany, 1890; Whipple (Rt. Rev. Bishop), *Lights and Shadows of a Long Episcopate*, New York, 1899.

NORTH GERMAN MISSIONARY SOCIETY. See GERMANY; MISSIONARY SOCIETIES IN.

NORTH LAKHIMPUR. See LAKHIMPUR (North).

NORTH AND SOUTH SHEPSTONE: Towns in Natal, South Africa, situated on opposite sides of the Umzimkulu River at its mouth. Station of the Swedish Holiness Band (1889), with (1900) 2 missionaries and their wives. Station also of the PB, with (1900) 1 missionary and his wife. Societies write the name Port Shepstone.

NORWEGIAN MISSIONS: The missionary activity of the Norwegian people began with Hans Egede. But as Norway at that time was united to Denmark, and as Egede was supported and controlled by the royal government in Copenhagen, he has been identified with Danish Missions. Entirely national both in origin and operation are the three Norwegian Mission societies now at work—the Norwegian Mission to the Finns, the Norwegian Mission Society, and the Mission of the Norwegian Church by Schreuder.

The Norwegian Mission to the Finns: Headquarters, Stavanger, Norway. On February 28, 1888, Bishop Skaar of Tromsö, to whose diocese the Finns who occupy the northern part of Norway mostly belong, sent out an appeal to the Norwegian people that missionaries or itinerant preachers who could speak the Finnish language should be sent out among them. This appeal was promptly taken up, and by means of a yearly subscription of about 4,000 crowns it has already been possible to set two Finnish-speaking Norwegian preachers to work among them.

The Norwegian Mission Society (*Det Norske Missions Selskab*): Headquarters, Stavanger, Norway. In the third decade of the 19th century, after Norway had become an independent state by the separation from Denmark in 1814, there were formed all over the country, but more especially among the followers of the great revivalist, Hans Nilsen Hauge, a number of minor mission associations, the first and the largest among which was that of Stavanger, 1826. These associations sent their money and their missionaries, if any they had, to Basel. The Stavanger Association, however, placed its first missionary, Hans Christian Knudsen, in the service of the Rhenish Mission Society. In 1827 the "Norsk Missionsblad" was founded, and in 1845 followed "Norsk Missionstidende," which still is the organ of the mission to the heathen. Then, in 1841, Jon Hougvaldstad, a small tradesman from Stavanger, but a personal friend of Hauge, and seventy-one years of age, went to Germany to investigate mission societies and missionary schools; and the result of his journey was, that August 8, 1842, all the minor associations in Western Norway consolidated into one society. In 1843 they were joined by all the minor associations of Eastern Norway, and thus was formed the Norwegian Mission Society. This movement was carried on almost exclusively by laymen, while the Norwegian Church, in its official position as a state institution, assumed a very cool and reserved attitude toward it—a circumstance which later proved of importance for the formation of the Mission of the Norwegian Church by Schreuder.

The Norwegian Mission Society is thoroughly democratic in its organization. The minor associations, numbering 900, besides 2,300 women's societies, still exist, and have retained a considerable proportion of autonomy. They form eight circles, each circle holding a conference two years in succession, in June and July, and the third year the General Assembly meets. The central administration, consisting of the director of the Mission School, a secretary and eight members elected by the Conferences, has its seat in Stavanger.

The society receives some annual support from the Norwegian churches in the United States, and owns a fund of 200,000 kroners, a donation from Mr. P. von Möller, at Helingsborg, Sweden, from which it pensions old and worn-out missionaries, or missionaries' widows and children; but its missionaries are not allowed to marry without the permission of the Central Board. It maintains a mission-school at Stavanger, founded in 1843, closed in 1847, but reopened in 1858, and also owns a mission steamer, presented to it by special subscription, and usually stationed at Madagascar.

The denominational character of the Society is strictly Lutheran. According to its laws its missionaries must receive ordination from a bishop of the Lutheran State Church, and a license from the king, which is valid only for a certain field.

The Society is engaged in two different fields: (1) Zululand and (2) Madagascar.

(1) The Zulu Mission was begun in 1844 by Schreuder. To the Norwegians, as to other missionaries, Zululand proved a very hard, but after the first hindrances were overcome, a very promising field. The first station was founded at Umpumulo, in 1850, and in 1858 the first convert, a Zulu girl, was baptized at Umpumulo. When Bishop Schreuder in 1876 transferred his services to the Mission of the Norwegian Church, he carried with him a part of the field already under cultivation; but the Society continued its labor with great energy and considerable success. In 1900 there were reported 27 missionaries (including wives), 41 native workers, 15 stations and 73 outstations, 1,016 communicants and 2,060 adherents, 32 day schools with 714 scholars, and 1 of higher grade with 182 pupils.

(2) The Madagascar Mission was begun in 1866, and soon assumed large proportions, including not only the Hovas in the inland, with a station in the capital, Antananarivo, but also, since 1874, the Sakalavas, on the western coast, and since 1888 some points on the southern coast never before visited by Europeans. In 1900 there were reported 88 missionaries (including wives), 1,795 native workers, 23 stations and 839 outstations, 34,649 communicants and 51,371 adherents, 950 day schools and 4 of higher grade, with 57,475 scholars, 3 physicians, and 2 hospitals.

The Norwegian Church Mission by Schreuder (*Den Norske Kirkes Mission ved Schreuder*): Headquarters, Christiania, Norway. Hans Palludan Smith Schreuder, born at Sogndal, Norway, June 18, 1817; died at Untumjambili, Natal, Africa, January 27, 1882, consecrated bishop of the Cathedral of Bergen 1866, was the father of the Norwegian Mission. His "A Few Words to the Church of Norway," 1842, had a great effect throughout the whole country. He started the Zulu Mission under tremendous difficulties, and it is indebted for its success to his powerful personality. During the war between the English and the Zulus most of the English and German mission stations were disturbed or fully destroyed. But Entumeni was not touched, owing to the deep respect of King Cetewayo for Schreuder. The Madagascar Mission he also directed and superintended at its beginning. Nevertheless, altho he served the Norwegian Mission Society for thirty years, it was always his wish to be the missionary of the Church of Norway, of the official state institution, and not the missionary of any private association. Accordingly, in 1873 he separated from the Society and a committee was formed, with Bishop Tandberg at its head, and representing the Church of Norway. Bishop Schreuder took Entumeni with him, and shortly a new station was founded at Untunjambili in Natal, where a church was built and consecrated in 1881. After his death the mission was continued by his pupils, among whom are several natives, under the direction of the above mentioned committee, which has its seat in Christiania. In 1900 there were reported 13 missionaries, 8 native workers, 3 stations, 323 communicants, 665 adherents, 3 schools with 180 scholars.

In addition to these there are several minor societies: The Norwegian Committees, in aid of the Indian Home Mission to the Santals; the Bethany China Mission in Trondhjem, assisting the China Inland Mission, and the Norwegian Lutheran China Mission Association. These are closely allied to the State Church, but there are several that have sprung from the spirit manifest in the China Inland Mission and Christian and Missionary Alliance, such as the Norwegian Board of Missions, organized in 1889 as the Free East Africa Mission, which carries on work in China as well as Africa; the Norwegian China Mission, in alliance with the CIM, and the Missionary Union of the Norwegian YWCA, also in alliance with the CIM. There is also a Committee for the Norwegian Medical Mission in Madagascar, and the student movement has had great influence and accomplished much for the general interest in missions.

NOTT, Henry: Born in 1774; sailed in 1796 under the LMS for the South Seas. He was not an ordained missionary, but a plain, godly bricklayer, sent out to instruct the islanders in the trade of which he was master. On arrival he was stationed at Tahiti. He at once showed superior traits of character. When a panic seized the missionaries, and eleven of their number abandoned the island, Nott was a leader of those who insisted on enduring yet longer. When it was important to explore the island Nott was one of the two who made that dangerous missionary tour. When preaching to the natives at last began, after five years of study, Nott was one of the two men who had mastered the language. And when in 1809 a rebellion broke out against King Pomarè, and the mission houses were burned, the types from the printing office melted into bullets, and twelve years of heroic effort seemed to have ended in utter failure, it was Nott who remained alone at Eimeo, while all his associates, excepting Hayward, at the neighboring island of Huahine, fled to Australia. It was the admission of the Society, and of Mr. Nott's associates, that this bricklayer was the salvation of that mission. It was he who saw, as others did not, that little could be done by preaching unless the people read the Bible in their own tongue. He worked twenty-seven years upon the preparation for the work and upon the work itself, sending home in the meantime for books to enable him to learn Hebrew and Greek. When the translation was complete he broke down in health, carried his manuscript to England in 1836 that he might give it a final revision, induced the BFBS to publish the book, and in 1838 loaded 3,000 of the new Bibles on a ship and sped away to his beloved island home. The great work of his life was done. He died at Tahiti, May 2, 1844.

NOWGONG: A town in Assam, British India, situated in the district of Nowgong, 56 miles E. by N. of Gauhati. Population, 5,000. Station of the ABMU (1841), with (1903) 1 missionary and his wife, 2 women missionaries, 21 native workers, 7 outstations, 5 places of worship, 5 Sunday schools, 13 day schools, 1 boarding school, and 417 professed Christians, of whom 281 are communicants.

NOWGONG: A town in Central India, situated in the Bundalkhand region, 15 miles N. W. of Chatarpur. Population, 10,000, of whom 6,700 are Hindus. Station of the AFFM (1896), with (1901) 3 women missionaries, 4 native workers, 1 outstation, 3 Sunday schools, 2 day schools.

NOWRANGAPUR. See NAORANGPUR.

NSABA: A settlement in the Gold Coast Colony, West Africa, situated 45 miles N. E. of Cape Coast Castle. Station of the Basel Missionary Society (1891), with (1903) 3 missionaries, 2 of them with their wives; 28 native workers, 51 outstations, 17 day schools, and 1,582 professed Christians, of whom 724 are communicants.

NTONDA: A plantation of 1,000 acres in Angoniland, British Central Africa, situated south of Lake Nyasa, about 100 miles N. N. W. of Blantyre. Station of the Zambesi Industrial Mission, with (1902) 2 missionaries, 1 with his wife; 6 outstations, 1 place of worship, 9 Sunday schools, 9 day schools, 1 boarding school, 1 industrial farm, and 150 professed Christians.

NUBA LANGUAGE: A language spoken in the Sudan, Dongola and surrounding regions of Africa, belonging to the Nuba-Fulah group of African tongues, and written with Arabic characters. Missionaries have tried without success in this language to substitute Roman for Arabic letters in the favor of the people. The language is used by about a million people and has great vitality.

NUBA-FULAH RACE: A very considerable number of tribes, some in Egyptian Sudan, and some over against them on the west coast of North Central Africa, are found to differ so much, both linguistically and ethnographically, from the several races into which the Africans have been heretofore divided, that some of the ablest recent writers on these subjects, such as F. Müller and Dr. R. N. Cust, have added a new class or group, with two sub-groups, which they call Nuba and Fulah. This twofold race, Nuba-Fulah, is evidently very ancient—doubtless aboriginal in the lower basin of the Nile, which still continues to be the headquarters of the Nuba portion of the general group. It finally came to have its headquarters in the lower basin of the Senegal, and there came to be known as the Filatah, Fuladu, Pulah, or Fulah people, being so called because they were of a light brown, and thus in strong contrast with the Negroes of a purer black around them. The present scattered or fragmentary condition of the Nuba-Fulah race, a portion of it being found on the east of Victoria Nyanza, as the Kwafi and Masai, other portions on the sources of each of the two Niles, and yet other portions in different parts of the Sudan, all the way from Darfur to the Senegal, or in groups here and there among the mid-African tribes, all goes to support the idea that the original Nuba-Fulah race was broken and scattered, as already indicated, by the divisive and propelling force of another powerful race, like the **Bantu**, at an early age of African history.

One important branch of the Nuba stock still has its home in the original abode of the race—the basin of the Nile from the first to the second cataract. The earliest account we have of them represents them as a powerful, superior race, of good features, not so dark on the northern border as farther south, and quite distinct from both the Egyptian and the Negro. They were once Christians, but now, like all their neighbors, profess the Muslim faith, and speak, some the Arabic, and some their own vernacular language.

Some live as nomads in tents, and some as a settled, industrious, thriving people, in well-built houses. There is also a tribe or group of tribes, evidently related to the Nuba family in both blood and language, in Kordofan and Darfur. They differ from the Negroes around them, believe in Islam, and speak, some of them, what is called the Koldagi dialect, some of them the Tumale, and some the Konjara. Other tribes of this class, as the Kwafi and Masai, who call themselves Loikob, and designate their language as the Enguduk, are found on or near the equator. The Kwafi have the Victoria Nyanza on their west and the Masai on their south. Both tribes, differing materially, as they do, from the Hamitic race on the north, and from the **Bantu** on other sides, are counted as belonging to the Nuba-Fulah group. They are represented as the most savage of all East African tribes. Still another group of tribes, such as the Berta and Kamail, belonging to the Nuba-Fulah race, has its home on the Blue Nile, north of the Gallas and west of Abyssinia. In this race are included also the Nyam-Nyam, together with the Golo and the Monbutto on the sources of the White Nile and the Shary.

Turning now and going westward between the 10° and 15° of north latitude, we come upon several families of the sub-Fulah group, scattered here and there all along from Darfur through the Hausa and Mandingo countries, till we come to where they abound in Bundu, Futa Jalo, and Futa Toro, south of Lower Senegal, where "they dominate," says Dr. Cust, "as Mohammedan foreign conquerors. They have placed their foot firmly down in the land of the Wolof, and the people of the coast have come under their influence as far as the river Nunez. They are numerous and powerful in Mandingoland and in the kingdom of Massina, south of Timbuktu. The kingdom of Sokoto and Gando is their creation, including the whole of the Hausa-speaking territory. Far to the east we find them in Bornu, Mandara Logon, Baghirmi, Wadai, and even in Darfur. Their tendency to expand is not on the wane, and they have made a powerful impression on the Negro population; from the union of the two races a mixed population has sprung up called Torodo, Jhalonki, Toucouleur, and other names." It is unnecessary here to detail their history or speculate on their origin. Their movement has been comparatively of late date, by force of arms, and coupled with the spread of the Mohammedan religion. They are spoken of by a recent writer as "an interesting Mohammedan people of the Western Sudan in Africa, remarkable for their enterprise, intelligence, and religious zeal. They are a race, and not a nation; have many tribes, several shades of color and varieties of form, probably from the fact that they have blended with various subject races. They cultivate Mohammedan learning with much enthusiasm. Their history is quite obscure. Sokoto is their principal state, but they are the predominant people of many countries in the Sudan."

Very little mission work of a Protestant Christian character has been as yet done or even attempted for any part of this race; but the eyes of not a few are on the great region they occupy, with high purpose and hope of reaching them soon.

NUEVO LAREDO: A town in Mexico, situated on the right bank of the Rio Grande, opposite Laredo, Texas. Station of the American Baptist Home Missionary Society, with (1900) 1 missionary and his wife, 2 orphanages, 1 place of worship, 1 Sunday school, and 28 professed Christians.

NUKUALOFA: A settlement on Tongatabu, Tonga Islands. Station of the SDA and of the Medical Mission Society of the same church, with (1900) 3 missionaries, 2 of them with their wives; 1 place of worship, 1 Sunday school, 1 dispensary, and 10 professed Christians.

NUMPANI. See NIMPANI.

NUPE LANGUAGE: A language belonging to the Negro group, and spoken in the country W. of Lokoja, Nigeria, W. Africa. It has an uncertain constituency, but appears to be of considerable vitality. Missionaries have written the language with Roman letters.

NURSARAVAPETTA. See NARASARAOPET.

NUSAIRIYEH: The origin of the Nusairiyeh people seems lost in the obscurity of antiquity. In asking one of their chiefs concerning their origin the most he could say was that it was very ancient. Another says that they descended from the Persians; others from the Philistines or from the tribes that Joshua drove out of Palestine. They have dwelt for hundreds of years in the mountains of northern Syria, and the regions along the Mediterranean coast as far as the plains of Cilicia. It is probable that the ethnologists and historians have taken little or no notice of them because of their political insignificance and low state of civilization. However, their religious practises sustain the theory that they are descended from some of the ancient heathen tribes of Palestine. At present they are a mixed race, as are the most of the races bordering on the Mediterranean, owing, in this case no doubt, to the Crusades, when many thousands of Europeans were lost and became mingled with the inhabitants of the country. This circumstance probably accounts for the existence of so many blonde complexions among these swarthy tribesmen. They receive their name from Nusair, who, with his son Abu Shai, was a renowned leader and teacher among them some centuries ago. They inhabit Northern Syria and Cilicia, and number about three hundred thousand souls.

As to their religion, they are a branch of the Shi'ites, who separated under the leadership of Nusair; and their religious system was brought to perfection by one of his descendants named Khusaib. Nevertheless, while claiming to be followers of Mohammed, in private they are practically pagans. They reject the caliphate of Abu Bekr and his successors down to Abd ul Hamid, the present Sultan-Caliph, and claim that the succession belonged of right to Ali. Tradition says that Abu Bekr compassed the death of his rival, Ali, by strategy, the circumstances being that Ali was praying in a mosque, and Abu Bekr, learning of it, sent two of his retainers to simulate a deadly quarrel outside the mosque, knowing that Ali, hearing the disturbance, would rush out to separate the combatants. The men would resent this interference, and would fall upon Ali and kill him. The result was as anticipated, and the deadly feud was begun which continues to this day.

This branch of the followers of Ali devised a religion of their own, and, being in the minority and fearing persecution, they bound themselves by the most horrid oaths to keep it secret. None are initiated into its mysteries under 18 years of age. The applicant for initiation to the secrets of the Nusairiyeh religion must bring twelve men as security, and these must be vouched for by two others. Such is their distrust of mankind, however, that the situation is not secure even after this, and the candidate is required to swear by the sun, moon, and stars that he will never reveal the mysteries about to be made known to him, and that if he violates his promise, he will accept the penalty of having his head, hands, and feet cut off; the same penalty being his due if he fails to complete the course of study now begun. For this reason the Nusairiyeh are extremely reticent on the subject of their religion. To reveal it is an unpardonable sin. Some years ago one of their number, a certain Suleiman Effendi of Adana, made some revelations respecting their mysteries, in a book which he published in Arabic, and which has been used in preparing this article. After the publication of the book, Suleiman Effendi suddenly disappeared and was never heard of again. Doubtless he suffered the penalty. Women are not taught religion, excepting a single prayer, which is supposed to have effect in promoting purity. In fact, women are held to have a different origin from men. When mankind sinned, Ali created the devils out of men's sins. The sins of the devils were then used as the material from which womankind was created.

The Nusairiyeh system of religious belief recalls to mind some of the Gnostic sects, being a conglomeration of almost all religions, ancient and modern, false and true. They have introduced the beliefs and the ceremonies of the Jews, the Greeks, the Egyptians, and Phenicians, the Mohammedans, and the heathen in general. They worship the Caliph, Ali Ibn Abu Talib, the prophet Mohammed, and Suleiman the Persian. They consider Ali the Father, Mohammed the Son, and Suleiman the Holy Spirit, but they pay their chief adoration to Ali, ascribing to him the divine nature and attributes, and also creative power, and the devout worshiper is represented as supplicating "his Lord, Ali Ibn Abu Talib, with a reverent heart and an humble spirit, to deliver him from his wickedness." They teach that Ali created Mohammed, and that Mohammed created Suleiman, and that Suleimen created five great angels, and that the angels created the universe, and that each angel is entrusted with the management of some particular part thereof, viz.: One has charge of thunder, lightning and earthquakes; another of the heavenly bodies; another, of the winds, and receives the spirits of men at death; another has charge of the health and sickness of human beings, and another furnishes souls for the bodies of men at birth. Fatima, daughter of Mohammed, and wife of Ali, is given a place very much like that assigned by Roman Catholics to the Virgin Mary. They consider that the moon is Ali's throne, and that the man in the moon is Ali with a veil over his form, but in the hereafter the veil will be removed and all true believers will see him as he is. Hence they worship the moon. They believe that the sun is Mohammed, and pay divine honors to it. They worship fire, the wind, the waves of the sea—anything that manifests power—the shades of ancestors, and even living men of influence and renown. These last they consider to be possessed of the spirits of the prophets, it may be of Ali himself. They believe in the transmigration of souls, teaching that Muslim religious teachers after death will enter the bodies of asses. The teachers of Christians will enter the bodies of swine, and those of the Jews, the bodies of apes. Wicked Nusairiyeh are destined to enter the bodies of clean beasts. Those who are part evil and part good enter the bodies of those who belong to sects other than the Nusairiyeh, while all good Nusairiyeh enter the bodies of Nusairiyeh, each one according to his grade and station. If one of another belief should unite with them, they claim that in past generations he was of them, but for some sin he was compelled to enter a strange sect and remain a stated time as a punishment, when he was allowed to transmigrate to his own religion. Should one of the Nusairiyeh apostatize they declare that his mother committed adultery with one of the sect with which he has united, and that he has returned to his source.

The chief moral duty of the Nusairiyeh is to make a perpetual effort for the good of their religion. This sacred effort is divided into two parts. The first part is to revile and curse Abu Bekr, Omar, Othman, the first three caliphs, and utter imprecations against all who believe that any of the prophets, or Ali, were born of women, had bodies, excepting in an illusory sense, or ate or drank, or married as other men do. The second part of this sacred effort consists in keeping their religion secret from the world. This supreme effort to preserve secrecy respecting their religious belief has cultivated deceit among the Nusairiyeh to an astonishing development. They will not acknowledge that they believe in Ali. They will rather deny the belief with an oath, because admission of it would be to reveal a part of their religion. For this reason, too, this people easily distance all competitors in hypocrisy. They always accommodate themselves to their surroundings, provided they are not able to overcome them. For example, should one enter a mosque with a Muslim he performs the prostrations and genuflexions like his companion; but instead of praying as does the Muslim, he inwardly curses Abu Bekr and all his successors, and likewise him who bows at his side. Their theory in such a case is that the Nusairiyeh religion is the body, while all other religions are clothing to be worn and thrown aside at pleasure; and it matters not what a man wears; it does not injure him; and he who does not dissemble thus lacks good sense, for no sensible person will walk through the streets naked. The Nusairiyeh are revengeful, and practise blood atonement in righting wrongs among themselves. They are thievish, and consider stealing, especially from infidels, a virtue. Nevertheless they are cowardly and will not attempt either revenge or theft unless assured of personal safety. In social relations they are semi-barbarous, and there are many feuds among them, tribe against tribe. They often have bloody encounters, and leave the bodies of the slain to the hyenas and jackals. Their morality is low. All classes practise polygamy. Social purity is disregarded among the upper classes—as when one chief becomes the guest of another of like rank the host sends a wife to share the room of his guest.

This abomination is not practised among the common people. Politically they are under the absolute sway of the Turk, and are therefore much oppressed. A wall of dense prejudice met the pioneer missionaries at the outset; but as the continued dropping of water will wear away the adamantine rock, so persistent effort, personal contact, uniform kindness, and patient forbearance for Christ's sake wore away the prejudices of the people, and if the mission were blotted out of existence to-day it would be considered a public calamity. By aiding the destitute, by healing the sick, by sympathizing with the sorrowing, a way was made for the Gospel of peace, and, notwithstanding the dogged, determined, persistent opposition of the authorities, in closing the schools and otherwise hindering the work, the mission has enjoyed encouraging success. Converts to Christianity have been won. But such converts have been cruelly maltreated by the Turkish Government. Some were imprisoned and others drafted into the army, the authorities thus hoping to destroy the germs of Christianity that had taken root among the Nusairiyeh; and in this they were aided and abetted by the chiefs of the people themselves, who began to fear the consequences. One of the converts, David Makhloof, was very sorely tried. He was in the army during the Turco-Russian War. His Bible was taken from him. He was flogged and imprisoned in a dungeon with the design of forcing him to deny Christ; but with all the fortitude of the early Christian martyrs, he stood firm, holding fast to the profession of his faith without wavering. He was wonderfully preserved, having several horses shot under him while in action. He was in the siege of Plevna, but was providentially spared to return to his family, and he is now a burning and shining light in his own native mountains. Were it not that the Turkish authorities place every possible obstacle in the way of the education and enlightenment of these people, the rising generation would soon be brought under the power of the Gospel.

NYASALAND: This territory, also called the Central African Protectorate, lies along the west and south shores of Lake Nyasa, with a spur extending southward toward the Zambesi, and is bounded on the west by Northeast Rhodesia. The area is 42,217 square miles; the population about 900,000, of whom about 450 are Europeans. Lake Nyasa is about 360 miles long, varying from 14 to 60 wide, and covers an area of 12,000 square miles. It, like the Tanganyika, is a deep fissure in the earth's surface. Furious gales sweep over it, rendering care in navigation necessary. It is drained by the Shirè River, which sweeps over the Murchison Falls, where navigation from the lake is arrested. By means of the channel afforded by the Chindé River, navigation between Murchison Falls and the ocean is uninterrupted. The lake is nearly surrounded by mountains. The densest population is found at Karonga, on the northwestern shore of the lake. This region is unhealthful in the rainy season, during which the missionaries resort to Mombera, in the upper part of the valley. Kota Kota, on the west coast, 120 miles from the southern extremity, is the main center of trade, and was a great market for slaves. Kiswahili is the dominant tongue. Ninety miles south of Lake Nyasa, in the Shirè upland, is Blantyre, founded in 1876 by Scotch missionaries, and named after Livingstone's birthplace. It has a population of 6,000. Its elevation above the sea level is 3,400 feet. A telegraph line runs through the territory, and steamers ply on the lake. The traveled roads are kept in good condition between the principal towns.

The Church of Scotland, the English Universities Mission, the Zambesi Industrial Mission, and the National Baptist Convention all carry on missionary enterprises in Nyasaland. Altogether there are (1901) 101 missionaries and 304 native workers, men and women, established at 17 stations, with 161 schools and about 2,000 church members.

Caddock (Helen), *A White Woman in Central Africa*, London, 1900; Johnston (Sir H.), *British Central Africa*, London, 1897; Rankin, *The Zambesi Basin and Nyasaland*, London, 1893.

NYENHANGLI. See NIEN-HANG-LI.

NYLANDER, J. C.: Born in Germany; appointed missionary of the CMS to Sierra Leone in 1806. Here Mr. Nylander became chaplain of the colony till about 1816, when he went to Yongroo Pomah, opposite Free Town, and seven miles from it, where he commenced a mission among the Bulloms. He labored among this superstitious people with unremitting zeal, teaching and preaching. He translated into the Bullom language the four Gospels, the Epistles of St. John, morning and evening prayers of the Church of England, hymns, and elementary books. The mission was abandoned on account of the slave-trade, but Mr. Nylander transferred his flourishing school to Sierra Leone, taking his scholars with him. He died in 1825.

O

OBJECTIONS AND CRITICISMS: If the Church has always contained and contains to-day people who are in no sympathy with missions, it is natural that there should be objections to, and criticisms of missions in as well as outside the Church.

Much of the criticism is due to the failure to apprehend what Christianity is. Men who do not believe in Christ as their Savior, and who have no personal understanding or experience of His religion, cannot be expected to sympathize with the effort to spread it over the world, unless they do so on merely ethical or philanthropic grounds. And within the Church merely nominal Christians who for one reason or another accept the form, while ignorant of the power of Christianity, are not likely to value highly an effort to extend what has no vital meaning to themselves to the people of other lands.

Beside the criticisms resting on these fundamental differences of view, there is, of course, a mass of unintelligent objection springing from ignorance or utter misconception of the facts of the work, of the operations of the human mind, or of the course of history. The common criticism of the immense extravagance of the missionary propaganda illustrates the first. Travelers are constantly expressing amazement at the vast sums expended on foreign missions, and the good that this could do at home. The total amount spent by all nations annually would not pay the naval expenditures of Japan for one year, or the cost of maintaining the German army for two months. A different type of ignorance is illustrated in criticisms like General Chaffee's, to the effect that he did not meet in Peking "a single intelligent Chinaman who expressed a desire to embrace the Christian religion," as tho this were a fact that had any bearing on the matter at all except a sorrowful reflex implication. A great mass of current criticism rests on such sheer ignorance of the idea of the propagation of religion or the facts in the case of Christianity, as when a Hindu writes in an American magazine: "Notwithstanding their (the missionaries') great efforts, not a single true Aryan has been converted in these three or four hundred years." Such critics must choose between the alternatives of falsehood and ignorance.

But criticism of missions cannot be dismissed by attributing the great bulk of it to absence or lukewarmness of Christian faith on one hand, or to ignorance or malice on the other. The supporters of missions cannot neglect objections which spring from these sources. Such objections may be classified in four groups:

I. Criticism of the missionary idea or principle.
II. Criticism of the methods of missions.
III. Criticism of the agents of missions.
IV. Criticism of the results of missions.

I. *Criticism of the Missionary Idea:* 1. It is objected that Christianity is not the only true religion, that the other religions of the world are good enough for the people professing them, that Christianity can only claim to be one of the world's religions, and not necessarily the best for all, and that there is salvation in other names than Christ's. Of course, this involves eliminating or interpreting away the words of Christ, "I am the way, the truth and the life. No man cometh unto the Father but by Me." "No man knoweth the Son but the Father, and no man knoweth the Father save the Son, and he to whomsoever the Son willeth to reveal Him;" and the words of Peter, "Neither is there any other name under heaven, that is given among men, wherein we must be saved."

It is replied to-day that the truth of these words is not denied, but that it is the Christian God and the essential Christ who are found in the non-Christian religions. But this is to raise a simple question of fact: "Do the non-Christian religions produce the fruits of Christianity?" In reply, and as covering the entire question of comparative religion, it may be said: (1) There are good things in the non-Christian religions, but (a) these are concealed and overlaid, (b) they are held in distortion, unbalanced by necessary counter truths, as the Muslim idea of the divine sovereignty, and the Hindu idea of immanent deity, and (c) the good of all these religions is found in Christianity also, there rightly related and perfectly fulfilled. (2) There is good in Christianity which is not found in any other religion, as indicated in the modern larceny of Christian doctrine and moral ideals by all other religions—Hinduism, for instance, having undergone, under missionary influence, a complete transformation. (3) Each of the non-Christian religions is full of evils from which Christianity is free. (4) The worst evils of heathen lands are the products of or are sanctioned by the non-Christian religions. All the evils of Christian lands are under the ban of the Christian religion. (5) The best virtues of heathen people are, in the main, their racial qualities, unaffected by their religion. The best virtues of Christian peoples are the direct product of Christianity. (6) Christianity is the only purely moral religion. It alone identifies religion and ethics, demanding that personal religion be expressed in personal ethical behavior. In all other religions, ceremonial behavior will suffice. (7) The sacred Book of Christianity is different from other sacred books, not in degree, but in kind. (8) The non-Christian religions grow worse and worse. The chasm between their best ideal and the actual reality widens constantly, save as they borrow from Christianity. Christianity alone has the power of self-renovation. (9) Christianity is the only religion of progress, and it alone can live with the spirit of progress, because it alone is the truth. (10) The non-Christian religions at their best are the imperfect aspirations of men toward God. Christianity is the self-revelation of God to man. They are religions, not of one, but of different classes. Christianity is exclusive and unique. All others stand together. As Mr. Griffith John says:

> The offer of Christ to sinful men wherever they can be found is not the offer of an alternative religion to them in the sense in which Hinduism and Taoism and Confucianism are religions. It is the offer to men of the secret of life, of something that will enable them to realize their true selves, and become men in the true and full sense of the word. We do our Master little honor when we place Him among a group of teachers competing for the acceptance of men. He is not one of the many founders of religions. He is the Source and Fountain of all, in so far as they have caught a prophetic glimpse of His truth, and anticipated something of His spirit, and given a scattered hint here and there of His secret. He is the truth, the type, the saving grace of which they faintly and vaguely dreamed; the desire of all nations, the crown and essence of humanity; the Savior of the world, who, by the loftiness of His teaching, the beauty of His character, the sufficiency of His atoning sacrifice, is able to save to the uttermost all who will come to Him and trust in Him.

2. It is contended that all religions are but elements in the evolutionary process, that Christianity itself is a development, and the one suited to our Western minds; while the non-Christian religions are the religious influences developed in the growth of these peoples as best suited to them. Even if this were true, it is true also that since these other nations develop, as they are fast developing, into a life which adopts the principles of Western civilization, the evolutionary theory itself would allow for a religious development also, and the acceptance of a religious opinion and life conformable to the new stage of progress. As Mr. Griffith John again has remarked:

> The nations called Christian are everywhere pressing hard upon all other nations. Western civilization in all directions is disintegrating both the customs of savage nations and the more stable civilization of the East, and it is everywhere being shown that in this general break-up of old and effete orders there is an imminent peril. For where our civilization penetrates without our religion it is invariably disastrous in its effects. It never fails to destroy the confidence of subject races in their own creeds and customs without furnishing anything in place of their sanctions and

restraints. The result is everywhere to be seen in the way in which heathen nations neglect our virtues and emulate our vices. The advice sometimes given to the missionary, therefore, to leave the people to whom he ministers to their simpler faith, is beside the mark. These faiths are inevitably going; soon they will be gone; and the question presses: What then? If history proves anything, it proves that a nation without a faith is a doomed nation; that it cannot hold together; that it inevitably decays and dies. From this point of view alone, then, there is a tremendous responsibility laid upon us. The impact of our civilization is breaking up the fabric and undermining the foundations of the ethnic religions. Without religion of some sort, nations must perish. Therefore, we must see to it that we give something in the place of what we take away, and that something must be the Christian faith or it will be nothing.

But more than this is to be said. As Mr. Gulick has shown in *The Evolution of Japan*, it is the Christian convictions, however veiled, which are the really powerful forces in working the transformation of the backward nations. In the development of mankind, the religious force is indispensable. The evolutionary hope makes a demand for Christian missions.

3. Some deny this and would have missions, as a disturbing factor, eliminated from the forces which the West is wielding upon the East. But (1) this is to misunderstand entirely the character and source of Western civilization, which derives its power and virtue from the altruistic stream, as Mr. Kidd calls it, which poured into humanity from the life and cross of Christ. (2) It is to surrender the heathen world to the purely material, selfish, and often shamefully iniquitous side of our Western life. Commerce and diplomacy have done an immense and salutary work in the non-Christian world, but there is room for the protest of an "Uncommercial Traveler" against the idea that secular civilization is to redeem the world:

I, too, have spent some eight years away from the United States, during which time I have seen this flaunted foreign commerce vying with native merchants in corrupting the custom house officials; seen fabricated liquors fraudulently sold; seen cheap goods with false American trademarks; seen the ignorant Indians debauched by bad rum, in order to swindle them in trade; seen hostile savages supplied with firearms. I have seen chafing boxes to polish off traces of gold dust from foreign gold coin before it is put in circulation; placer gold dust mixed with copper to increase the weight; in fact, many kinds of deceit practised, but little that is elevating or good done by foreign merchants. It is a well known fact that large firms in England are engaged in the manufacture of idols, which are sent out to the heathen."

There is no unfairness in stating clearly that the character of Western commercial and political intercourse with the non-Christian world has been no unmixed blessing. Mr. Fukuzawa contended that as to Japan, it would have resulted in rupture had it not been for the missionaries. And (3) to demand the elimination of missions is to admit as to the worst we possess a principle denied as to the best. How can any one justify a position which results in freedom to sell rum to the world, but in refusal of liberty to give the Ten Commandments and the Sermon on the Mount, and the Story of the Resurrection?

4. It is objected that the newer theological teachings of the love of God for all mankind, with their consequence in universalism, render unnecessary a difficult and unappreciated effort to preach Christianity everywhere. But what makes it difficult? Such a character in the non-Christian peoples as indicates their need of the very message they do not welcome. How could General Chaffee's intelligent Chinese be expected to desire Christianity, when (1) they do not understand what it is, (2) when from the conduct of nominally Christian nations they suppose it to be something quite different from its real character, and (3) when they had just been engaged in gratifying that spirit of murder against which the Christian spirit is perpetual protest? The difficulties in the way of missions reveal the world's need of them. Any "new theology" would be a poor substitute for the old which was deterred from doing its duty by difficulties to which a more antiquated doctrine refused to surrender. For just in proportion as any body of men believe themselves to be possessed of the best doctrine of God, they will be eager to spread it over the world. No amount of talk about a loving God will persuade the world that those who speak believe in such a God unless they show a proportionate eagerness to make Him known to all mankind. Missions have much to fear from insincerity, but nothing from the love of God. It was that that produced them. "For God so loved the world." "For His Name's sake, they went forth."

5. It is said that the heathen will not be lost without the Gospel; that God would condemn no man for ignorance of Christ. No one has ever contended that men would be lost for not accepting a Savior of whom they have never heard. Men are lost because sin destroys. Their condition is not a matter of eschatological speculation. They are lost, not as heathen, but as sinners, just as enlightened people in Christian lands who have rejected Christ. There is no space here to deal with the question of the future fate of the heathen. Future destiny is only a consequence of present faith and character, and regarding this enough has been said. Some who are perplexed here, however, may well read the words of Mr. R. E. Welsh in his recent book, *The Challenge to Christian Missions:*

The heathen today are B. C. What operated B. C. in God's treatment of the Jews operates proportionately in Asia and ev.ry continent and island which is not yet Anno Domini. That the Jews had fuller light and clearer symbols of the Unseen is beside the point here. God's method or principle is the same for all alike, when dealing with different races all of them B. C. The grace which was at least within reach of the humble hearted Jew has always been and now is within reach of the Gentile in proportion as there is similar response to appeals of the Spirit.

"Our conception of salvation itself has been changing at the very time when our theory of the heathen has been changing, and the one comes in aptly to interpret or correct the other. The enlightenment which has been enlarging our sympathies has, in the same process, been deepening our insight into the true nature of salvation. Here enters the principle, that salvation is salvation from sin, not from destinies. The real and urgent question is not a matter of destinies at all, one way or the other. It is one of present moral condition and character. It is not what we are coming to, but what we are becoming, that matters. Destinies, good or bad, while momentous enough, hang entirely on the character which constitutes their quality. The actual problem is, not the man's future, but the man. Look at pagan peoples with the most godlike eye, and there is enough in their condition to appall our hearts, if we can see beneath the surface of their natural content. However large the mercy of heaven, they most palpably stand in dire need of being morally saved from sin's degradation, and spiritually enlightened and enfranchised as the sons of God."

6. It is argued that the need at home is so great that it should first be met. But (1) who is responsible for this long continuance of a great

need at home? Phillips Brooks' reply is unanswerable: "'There are heathen enough at home; let us convert them first, before we go to China.' That plea we all know; and I think it sounds more cheap every year. What can be more shameful than to make the imperfection of our Christianity at home an excuse for not doing our work abroad? It pleads for exemption and indulgence on the ground of its own neglect and sin. It is like a murderer of his father asking the judge to have pity on his orphanhood." (2) The acceptance of this plea nineteen hundred years ago would have condemned Europe to perpetual heathenism. The agreement proposed here is tantamount to an abolition of missions. There will always be need at home. The tares will be in the wheat until the harvest. (3) The only way to meet the need at home is to increase the spirit which sends missionaries abroad to the heathen.

7. The simple fact is that the missionary spirit is the Christian spirit; that the possession of good is an obligation for its transmission. The best spirit of the modern world is now permeated with this conception, and we must either give up our Christianity as of no use even to ourselves, or share it with the world. We are debtors. We must also be ready to pay.

II. *Criticisms of the Methods of Missions:* It is impossible to sympathize with criticisms of the missionary idea. That is the essence of Christianity—even of common honesty and courtesy, and fair and kindly dealing among men. To deny this is to display some radical lack of character, and an utter failure to appreciate the finer side of life, and the nature of the Christian religion. But criticism of the methods of missions is a different matter. So long as a man is earnestly supporting missions, he may be allowed liberty to criticise methods he disapproves. But the man who is doing nothing for missions at all, who has no genuine sympathy with the idea, has no right to rest his disapproval of missions on the methods pursued.

No one is more anxious than the missionaries to discover the best methods, or more ready, accordingly, to listen to sincere criticism. Canon Isaac Taylor justified his assault upon missions in the *Fortnightly Review* in 1888 by the words of Bishop Steere, "Let me say that all missionaries owe a debt of gratitude to those who call attention to the mistakes and failures of missions;" and Canon Taylor said, in closing, that Mackay of Uganda had encouraged him to make his criticism public.

1. A common criticism is that the cost of administration is extravagant, that "it costs a dollar to send a dollar." There never was any ground for this criticism, nor is there any. In the absence of any even partial justification, its origin and continuance can only be called malicious. The cost of administration of the great foreign mission agencies ranges from 4 to 10 per cent. The higher amount is due largely to the cost of collection, publication, deputation work, and other measures for arousing interest. Roughly, it is accurate to say that the cost of sending a dollar to foreign missions is the price of a foreign postage stamp.

2. It is said that the business methods of missions are inefficient. It is not possible to make any better answer than to say that every missionary society will welcome examination at this point. Mr. John Wanamaker, as successful a business man as America has produced, recently examined the Presbyterian work in India, and on returning expressed this judgment:

"I went out and about, simply as an individual, saying: 'I will see for myself exactly what this business of foreign missions is, and whether it is worth while or not!' . . . By personal contact with the work and workers, I convinced myself that the work of missionaries—clergymen, teachers, doctors and Christian helpers—was healthy, eminently practicable and well administered. In its business administration, it is quite as economically done as any business firm could establish and support business extensions permanently and successfully in lands far distant from home, climate and custom requiring different modes of living. No private business man, in my judgment, can administer from the United States, properties and finances in India more effectively for less, as a rule, than the Board is administering them at this time.

3. The missionaries are accused of living on too expensive a scale, instead of imitating the lives of the fakirs or dervishes or holy men of the non-Christian lands. Mr. Wanamaker reported his judgment on this point also:

It is an unjust aspersion on the Church and its heroic men and women for any fair person to say that, because the customs of the country oblige missionaries, if they are to maintain influence with the people, to employ servants and live in houses common to hot climates, such as are used by other private families, therefore they live in luxury, idleness or extravagance. While I saw homes of Christian workers in large cities, bought from thirty to fifty years ago, for small sums, now worth much more than they cost—which is to the credit of the wisdom of the fathers and brethren of the Missionary Board—I failed to find any extravagant buildings in use by missionaries or others in the services of the Board. As to the servants, they board themselves, coming in the morning and going off at night, for the pay of ten to twelve rupees a month, which, on an average, is $3.63 a month for house servants. It is impossible to find anywhere in the world simpler and more consistent home living than at the homes and tables of the mission houses.

4. The idea that by adopting the ascetic ideal and living as the natives do, the missionary would increase his influence is often advanced by those who are under precisely as much obligation to pursue this course as may rest on the missionary. The conception that the ascetic method will be more fruitful than the general method has often been tested. George Bowen gave it a fair trial in Bombay. His life was one of great value and of large influence, but not more so than the lives of scores of other missionaries who never followed his plan, and who were far more successful in winning converts and in establishing self-supporting churches. There is room for the ascetic ideal, but it is not the only ideal.

5. A great many criticisms on the methods of missions are mutually contradictory. One urges that the native churches should be sooner trusted and left to themselves. General Armstrong complained that this was done too soon in Hawaii. One urges that educational and medical work should be diminished, and the direct preaching of the Gospel absorb all the time and strength of the missionaries. The newspapers, the diplomats and the wandering publicists see in those forms of work the only really valuable part of the missionary enterprise. One complains that the missionaries are timid and cautious. Others that they are reckless and aggressive, and should be confined to fixed stations. One regards the attitude of solicitude for native customs as wicked; others think that even polygamy and ancestor-worship should be tolerated. And so opinions vary on a hundred points and correct one another.

6. Criticism, both just and unjust, has been directed at the confusion of missions with politics. The Boxer uprising brought the subject forcibly before the world. While there were

other and far more responsible causes for the outbreak than any connected with missions, the interference of Chinese Christians under cover of missionary, and ultimaltely consular, protection, and to some degree the interference of missionaries themselves in Chinese law courts, did help to increase the anti-foreign feeling of the people, and to confuse in their minds the missionary propaganda with the political movement of the West upon China. Whatever errors individual missionaries may have made at this point, the body of Protestant missionaries has not offended the burden of guilt resting on the Roman Catholics.

The whole discussion has been profitable as defining more clearly the spiritual character of the missionary enterprise and also as illustrating how easily missions are criticised for adopting, however slightly, the principles of those who praise the benevolence of the movement but deprecate its religious character. If missions are valuable and justifiable, as the critics allege, solely because of their philanthropic spirit, interference in behalf of the wronged in law suits would be eminently proper.

III. Criticism of the Agents of Missions: Some such critics are foolish extremists. Mr. Sydney Brooks represented this class during the discussion of the relation of missionaries to the Boxer uprising. He declared that the missionaries in China were "not well educated," were untactful, careless of local prejudice, spoke a "bastard Chinese," were guilty of "blundering provocation," and ignorant of the philosophy they are "intent on overthrowing, or the language which must be their chief weapon," bigoted and sectarian, and many of them "enthusiastic girls, who scamper up and down the country." Such criticism, of course, answers itself. It is enough to ask the critics the names of the missionaries they know. This judgment rests on no personal knowledge, but on the gossip and talk of steamer saloons or clubs in the ports, whose resentment is often due to the fact that their spirit and conduct are condemned by the standard which the missionary sets up. Where the common criticism of the missionary does not spring from such a source, it is due in large measure to a total want of sympathy with the mission idea, and to a want of appreciation of the Christian faith.

Other critics are more cautious than Mr. Brooks. Mr. Henry Norman says:

So far as education goes, both men and women among the Protestant missionaries are often quite unfitted to teach at home, where there would be little danger of misunderstanding; in their present sphere of work they are often not too hardly described by the phrase which has been applied to them, 'ignorant declaimers in bad Chinese.' . . . I am well aware, of course, that to some missionaries the world is deeply indebted for its knowledge of the Chinese language and literature; and that among the Protestant missionaries of the present day there are some men of the highest character and devotion, upon whose careers no criticism can be passed. These, however, are a small minority.

The profound scholars are, of course, a minority, but the statement that the men of highest character and devotion, upon whose careers no criticism can be passed, are also a minority, is a simple untruth due to the writer's ignorance of the men of whom he is writing, to the difference of standard prevailing between him and them, as illustrated in his interest in what the missionaries have always ignored or deplored (*e. g.*, the Yoshiwara in Tokio), and finally to his readiness to accept his judgments at second-hand from men as ignorant as himself. In any large body like the missionary body there will be men of all grades. But in general it is true to say of them that they love and understand their people; that they know men about them and can talk with them more freely than any other foreigner, Mr. Yen, of Shanghai, even asserting that the average missionary is a more fluent and accurate speaker of Chinese than the Chinese themselves; that missionaries as a class are the ablest and most highly respected foreigners in Asia, and that without their correcting influence the nauseous immorality of many commercial centers in Asia would be viler than it is. It is not the element of most intelligence and character in these cities and at home which attacks the missionaries. Of missionaries in the Orient generally, the Hon. John W. Foster declares that "up to the middle of the last century the Christian missionaries were an absolute necessity to diplomatic intercourse." Of S. Wells Williams, most prominent in this diplomatic service, U. S. Minister Reed declared: "He is the most learned man in his varied information I have ever met. . . . He is the most habitually religious man I have ever seen." And on a visit to India in 1894, the Rev. Francis Tiffany, a distinguished minister of the Unitarian Church, bore the testimony:

To the missionaries, decried and sneered at on every hand, are due the inception and first practical illustration of every reform in education, in medicine, in the revelation of the idea of common humanity, in the elevation of the condition of woman, afterward taken up by the Government. It seems, however, to be the correct thing for the ordinary tourist to speak with unutterable contempt of missionaries, and then, to avoid being prejudiced in any way, carefully to refrain from ever going within ten miles of them and their work. The thing to be taken for granted is that they are narrow-minded bigots, with nothing they care to import into India but hell fire. To all this, I want to enter my emphatic and indignant protest. Such of them as I have fallen in with, I have found the most earnest and broadminded men and women anywhere to be encountered—the men and women best acquainted with Indian thought, customs and inward life, and who are doing the most toward the elevation of the rational and moral character of the nation. It has brought tears to my eyes to inspect such an educational establishment for girls and young women as that of Miss Thoburn, in Lucknow, and to see what new heavens and new earth she is opening up to them. The consecration of spirit with which these young women are dedicating themselves to the work of getting ready to lift out of the gulf of ignorance and superstition their sister women of India was one of the most moving sights I ever beheld.

Missionaries might be better and abler men and women than they are. That could be said of any body of men and women in the world. But none wish this for themselves more ardently than the missionaries; and, speaking in careful comparison, it may be maintained that the missionaries of the Christian Church have been and are the best body of men and women who have ever given their lives to a great cause.

IV. Criticism of the Results of Missions: It is said that foreign missionaries have accomplished nothing, or that they have accomplished nothing justifying the great expense in money and life, or that they have accomplished too much and done more harm than good.

1. *"They have accomplished nothing":* This was naturally a much more common criticism some years ago than to-day. At first, the work had to produce its results. Now that it has produced them, it is possible only for ignorance to deny them. For a time all professed converts were "rice Christians," but now there are too many millions who get no rice, and there have been too many martyrs. As that severe but intelligent critic, Mr. Michie, says, "It is a very gratifying fact, which cannot be gainsaid, that Christians of the truest type—men ready to burn as

martyrs, which is easy, and who lead 'helpful and honest' lives, which is as hard as the ascent from Avernus, crown the labors of missionaries, and have done so from the beginning." The mass of testimony to the beneficent religious, moral, and social influence of missions has become too great to deny any longer. Dr. Dennis' great argument, in *Christian Missions and Social Progress*, is unanswerable. It would be easy to enlarge this evidence. Two testimonies must suffice:

"It is they" (the missionaries), says Sir H. H. Johnston, "who in many cases have first taught the natives carpentry, joinery, masonry, tailoring, cobbling, engineering, bookkeeping, printing, and European cookery; to say nothing of reading, writing, arithmetic, and a smattering of general knowledge. Almost invariably, it has been to missionaries that the natives of interior Africa have owed their first acquaintance with a printing-press, the turning-lathe, the mangle, the flat-iron, the sawmill, and the brick mould. Industrial teaching is coming more and more in favor, and immediate results in British Central Africa have been most encouraging. Instead of importing painters, carpenters, store clerks, cooks, telegraphists, gardeners, natural history collectors from England or India, we are gradually becoming able to obtain them amongst the natives of the country, who are trained in the missionaries' schools, and who have been given simple, wholesome local education, have not had their heads turned, and are not above their station in life."

"Whatever you may be told to the contrary," said Sir Bartle Frere, former Governor of Bombay, "the teaching of Christianity among 160,000,000 of civilized, industrious Hindus and Mohammedans in India is effecting changes, moral, social, and political, which for extent and rapidity of effect are far more extraordinary than anything that you or your fathers have witnessed in modern Europe."

If any other testimony to the efficacy of missions is needed than this evidence of their general influence, and the undeniable fact of the independent and self-supporting Christian churches which have been built up, it can be found in the absolute transformation in Hinduism and Buddhism produced by the influence of Christian missions. The history of the Brahmo Somaj is an illustration. Fifty years ago, men who wanted to come as far as this toward Christianity had to break with Hinduism. Now the Vedanta movement within Hinduism allows men who want to hold Christian opinions and still live Hindu lives to remain in their old faith. Outside of the limits of their converts, missions are transforming the world. Other forces are working with them, but none with more power.

2. *"They have accomplished nothing justifying the expense"*: That depends on the critic's standard of value. The Congo River railway in Africa is 225 miles long. It cost 4,000 lives. The cause of missions has cost but a fraction of this. Is that railroad more valuable than the results summarized in Dr. Dennis' great volumes? The armies of Europe cost per annum $1,046,354,848. All the Protestant churches combined give per annum $19,598,823 to foreign missions. Which expenditure accomplishes most for the world? The annual cost of the government of India is $360,000,000 (1901-1902). The annual cost of missions in India is an insignificant fraction of this. Which is the more beneficent expenditure? Let Sir W. Mackworth Young, K.C.S.I., late Lieutenant-Governor of the Punjab, answer:

As a business man, speaking to business men, I am prepared to say that the work which has been done by missionary agency in India exceeds in importance all that has been done (and much has been done) by the British Government in India since its commencement. Let me take the Province which I know best. I ask myself what has been the most potent influence which has been working among the people since annexation fifty-four years ago, and to that question I feel that there is but one answer—Christianity, as set forth in the lives and teaching of Christian missionaries. I do not underestimate the forces which have been brought to bear on the races in the Punjab by our beneficent rule, by British judgment and enlightenment; but I am convinced that the effect on native character produced by the self denying labors of missionaries is far greater. The Punjab bears on its historical roll the names of many Christian statesmen who have honored God by their lives and endeared themselves to the people by their faithful work; but I venture to say that if they could speak to us from the great unseen, there is not one of them who would not proclaim that the work done by men like French, Clark, Newton and Forman, who went in and out among the people for a whole generation or more, and who preached by their lives the nobility of self-sacrifice, and the lesson of love to God and man, is a higher and nobler work, and more far-reaching in its consequences.

3. *"They have done more harm than good"*: This is the current form of criticism. The critics used to call missionaries inoffensive and their work futile. Now they have swung over to the opposite extreme. The missionaries are pestilentially active and effective, and are turning the world upside down. "For my own part," says Mr. Norman, "I am convinced that if the subscribers to Chinese missions could only see for themselves the minute results of good and the considerable results of harm that their money produces, they would find in the vast opportunities for reformatory work at home a more attractive field for their charity. At any rate, in considering the future of China the missionary influence cannot be counted upon for any good." The omission of a bill of particulars is often a convenient oversight for critics. "The minute results of good" is a judgment which time will reveal in its true ludicrousness. What are "the considerable results of harm"? Mr. Sydney Brooks took up this tale. He held that the influence of the missionary is subversive, and that his propaganda will have revolutionary effects. In a sense this is not true. The missionary's work is not destructive. It follows the lines of national character and qualification. Christianity has adapted itself to more peoples, and more diverse peoples, than any other religion, and it is compatible with any orderly and righteous government, of whatsoever form. It does not attack the Chinese political system or social life. Yet, in a sense, the charge is true. Christianity is a power of upheaval and renovation. It turns the world upside down. It begets wrath against injustice, eagerness for liberty, impatience with ignorance and sloth, and passion for progress. It has done this in China. It will continue to do this in China, whether in war or in peace; whether with the sympathy of the Christian nations or with petty criticism and futile opposition of newspaper publicists. That is its mission in the world.

A larger and nobler and truer view of the influence of missions was expressed in the speech of President McKinley at the Ecumenical Conference in New York City in 1900:

I am glad of the opportunity to offer without stint my tribute of praise and respect to the missionary effort, which has wrought such wonderful triumphs for civilization. The story of the Christian Missions is one of thrilling interest and marvelous results. The services and the sacrifices of missionaries for their fellow men constitute one of the most glorious pages of the world's history. The missionary, of whatever church or ecclesiastical body, who devotes his life to the service of the Master and of men, carrying the torch of truth and enlightenment, deserves the gratitude, the support, and the homage of mankind. The noble, self-effacing, willing ministers of peace and goodwill should be classed with the world's heroes. . . . They count their labor no sacrifice. "Away with the world in such a view and with such a thought," says David Livingstone "it is emphatically no sacrifice; say, rather, it is a privilege." They furnish us examples of forbearance, fortitude, of patience and unyielding purpose, and of spirit which triumphs, not by the force of might, but by the persuasive majesty of right. . . . Who can estimate their value to the progress of nations? Their contribution to the onward and upward march of humanity is beyond all calculation. They have inculcated industry and taught the various trades. They have promoted concord and amity, and brought nations and races closer together. They have made men better. They have increased the regard for home; have strengthened the sacred ties of family; have made the community well ordered, and their work has been a potent influence in the development of law and the establishment of government.

But all this is secondary. The supreme aim of missions is the religious aim, but the success with which the movement is realizing that aim is evidenced by the affluence of its secondary beneficent results. And the end of all will be that Kingdom of God on earth—the Kingdom which is righteousness and peace, and toward whose establishment the missionary movement is in this age an indispensable agency, capable of improvement and expansion, but not capable of omission or abridgment.

OCHILONDA: A village in Angola, W. Africa, situated in the Bihè region, about 25 miles S. W. of Chisamba. Station of the PB, with 4 missionaries, 3 of them with their wives, and 1 woman missionary.

ODUMASI: A town in the Gold Coast Colony, W. Africa, situated 6 miles from the right bank of the Volta River, and about 20 miles N. W. of Akropong. Station of the Basel Mission Society, (1859), with (1903) 6 missionaries, 3 of them with their wives; 22 native workers, 9 outstations, 1 Sunday school, 9 day schools, 1 kindergarten, and 683 professed Christians, of whom 288 are communicants. Some write the name Odumase.

OETA RIMBAROE: A village in Sumatra, situated about 47 miles S. E. of Siboga. Station of the Java Committee, with 1 missionary and his wife and 1 day school.

OGBOMOSHO: A town in West Africa, 145 miles N. E. by N. of Lagos. Climate tropical, tho not oppressively hot; unhealthy, but better than on the coast. Population, 60,000. Religions, idolatry and fetishism. There are many gods, but few carved idols; certain trees, nuts, shells, rocks, etc., used as symbols. Social condition very low, but improving. Polygamy and domestic slavery common. Station of the CMS (1893), with (1903) 1 native worker, 1 day school, and 86 professed Christians. Station also of the SBC (1856), with (1903) 2 missionaries and their wives, 2 native workers, 2 outstations, 2 places of worship, 2 Sunday schools, 2 day schools, 1 theological class, 1 dispensary, and 152 professed Christians, of whom 121 are communicants. Some write the name Ogbomoso; also Ogbomoshaw.

OHNEBERG, George: A missionary of the Moravians to St. Croix, West Indies. He was one of the first of the United Brethren who succeeded in establishing himself on this island. He went from the island of St. Thomas to St. Croix in April, 1751. The Christian negroes welcomed him with open arms, for since the mission was suspended in 1742 they had received only occasional visits from the missionaries at St. Thomas. He was hardly settled there before both himself and the Christian slaves had to endure many persecutions from the pagans by whom they were surrounded. The huts of the negroes were set on fire, and sometimes entirely destroyed. Mr. Ohneberg's house was burned, but his furniture was saved by the efforts of the Christian negroes. When these pagan people found they could do nothing to unsettle Mr. Ohneberg, and that he went on with his work, they gave up their persecution and left him in peace. An estate of four acres was soon purchased by the Brethren, where they built a church and dwelling-house, and named the place "Friedensthal." The work increased more and more till the little church at Friedensthal could not contain the hearers, and service for nearly twelve months was held in the open air. As many as a hundred negroes were annually baptized into the church.

OITA: A town and seaport on Kiushiu Island, Japan, 105 miles E. by N. of Nagasaki. Silk yarn is produced in large quantities. This town was visited by the Portuguese adventurer, Mendez Pinto, in 1543 and by the Jesuit missionary St. Francis Xavier about 1550. Population, 15,200. Station of the CMS (1894), with (1903) 1 missionary and his wife, 4 native workers, 2 outstations, 1 place of worship, 2 Sunday schools, and 51 professed Christians, of whom 25 are communicants. Station also of the MES (1886), with (1903) 1 missionary and his wife, 2 native workers, 1 outstation, 1 place of worship, 2 Sunday schools, and 28 professed Christians.

OJI: A village in the suburbs of Tokio, Japan, now containing paper and cotton mills, but still a favorite holiday resort on account of its picturesque scenery and especially in certain seasons when flowering trees are in bloom. Population, 3,000. Station of the Christian Church Mission Board (1889), with (1903) 1 missionary and his wife, 1 woman missionary, 2 native workers, 5 outstations, 1 place of worship, 3 Sunday schools, and 65 professed Christians. Station also of the PE (1899), with (1903) 1 native worker.

OKAHANDYA: A mission station of German Southwest Africa, 90 miles E. N. E. of Swakopmund. Station of the Rhenish Mission Society, with (1903) 2 missionaries and their wives, 11 native workers, 3 outstations, 4 day schools, and 1,150 professed Christians, of whom 497 are communicants. Some write the name Okahandja.

OKAK. See OKKAK.

OKAT: A settlement in the Oil River region of South Nigeria, Africa, situated near Kwa Ibo River, 25 miles from its mouth. Station of the Qua Ibo Mission (1893), with (1903) 1 missionary and his wife, 1 woman missionary, 2 native workers, 6 outstations, 1 place of worship, 1 Sunday school, 5 day schools, 1 theological school, 1 dispensary, and 43 professed Christians.

OKAYAMA: A town in South Japan, 100 miles west of Kobe, on the highway thence to Hiroshima, 5 miles from Inland Sea. Climate mild, humid. Population (1898), 85,025. Station of the ABCFM (1879), with (1903) 1 missionary and his wife, 2 women missionaries, 6 native workers, 18 outstations, 6 places of worship, 12 Sunday schools, 1 industrial school, 1 orphanage. Station also of the SPG (1897), with (1903) 1 missionary, 4 native workers, 1 place of worship, and 47 professed Christians, of whom 25 are communicants. Station also of the Salvation Army. The Okayama Orphanage is an independent enterprise of value, founded by Mr. Ishii and placed under a board of trustees, composed partly of missionaries.

OKAZAKI: A town in Hondo Island, Japan, situated 85 miles E. of Kioto. Population,

13,200. Station of the PS (1890), with (1903) 1 missionary and his wife, 4 native workers, 5 outstations, 1 Sunday school, and 80 professed Christians.

OKAZEVA: A village in German Southwest Africa, situated about 180 miles E. by N. of Swakopmund. Station of the Rhenish Mission Society, with 1 missionary, 3 native workers, 1 day school, and 49 professed Christians, of whom 9 are communicants.

OKKAK: A settlement in Labrador, situated on the E. coast, 80 miles N. W. of Nain. Station of the Moravian Mission Society (1776), with (1900) 3 missionaries and their wives, 20 native workers, 1 day school, 1 place of worship, and 156 professed Christians.

OKOMBAHE: A mission station of the Rhenish Mission Society, in German Southwest Africa, about 120 miles N. N. E. of Swakopmund, with (1903) 1 missionary and his wife, 8 native workers, 2 outstations, 3 day schools, and 568 professed Christians, of whom 166 are communicants.

OLD CAIRO: A mission station of the CMS (1899), and a suburb of Cairo, Egypt, with (1903) 1 missionary and his wife, 2 women missionaries, 5 native workers, 2 day schools, 1 dispensary, 1 hospital, and 60 professed Christians, of whom 34 are communicants.

OLUKONDA: A settlement in the N. part of German Southwest Africa, in the territory of the Ambo tribes. Station of the Finnish Missionary Society (1871), with (1900) 3 missionaries, 2 of them with their wives; 1 woman missionary, 9 native workers, 4 outstations, 1 place of worship, 1 kindergarten, and 142 professed Christians.

OMARURU: A village in German Southwest Africa, situated in Damaraland, about 135 miles N. E. of Swakopmund. Station of the Rhenish Mission Society, with (1903) 1 missionary and his wife, 7 native workers, 3 outstations, 5 day schools, and 595 professed Christians, of whom 150 are communicants.

OMBURU: A village in German Southwest Africa, situated in Damaraland, about 150 miles N. E. of Swakopmund. Station of the Rhenish Mission Society (1903), with 1 missionary, 4 native workers, 3 outstations, 4 day schools, and 149 professed Christians, of whom 54 are communicants.

OMBOLATA: A settlement on Nias Island, situated on the E. coast about 5 miles S. of Gunong Sitoli. Station of the Rhenish Mission Society, with (1903) 1 missionary and his wife, 6 native workers, 3 outstations, 1 Sunday school, 5 day schools, and 1,411 professed Christians, of whom 390 are communicants.

OMUPANDA: A village in German Southwest Africa, situated in the Ambo region, near the frontier of Angola, and about 30 miles N. of Olukonda. Station of the Rhenish Mission Society, with 2 missionaries, 1 of them with his wife, 1 native worker, 1 day school, and 102 professed Christians, of whom 28 are communicants.

ONDANGUA: A settlement in the N. part of German Southwest Africa, in the Ambo tribe territory, situated about 25 miles N. W. of Olukonda. Station of the Finnish Mission Society (1890), with (1900) 1 missionary and his wife, 1 woman missionary, 5 native workers, 3 outstations, 1 place of worship, and 54 professed Christians.

ONDJIVA: A village in German Southwest Africa, situated in the territory of the Ambe tribe, on the border of Angola, and about 40 miles N. of Olukonda. Station of the Rhenish Mission Society, with (1903) 1 missionary and his wife, 1 woman missionary, 1 native worker, 1 day school, and 33 professed Christians.

ONGOLE: A town of 9,000 inhabitants in the Nellore district, east coast of Madras, India, half-way between Nellore and Masulipatam. Missionary work was begun in the Nellore district in 1842. From 8 members in 1867 the Christian community increased to 3,269 in 1877. Then the famine came. Idols were prayed to, but in vain. The missionaries came to the rescue, and with the aid of English relief money a canal was built, which will prevent the recurrence of any similar famine. The grateful Ongolites then came in large numbers to listen to the preaching of their benefactors. Station of the ABMU (1866), with (1903) 4 missionaries and their wives, 3 women missionaries, 144 native workers, 40 Sunday schools, 6 boarding schools, 1 orphanage, 1 college, 1 industrial class, and 19,421 professed Christians.

ONICHA: A village and mission station in South Nigeria, W. Africa, on the left bank of the Niger opposite Asaba. Station of the CMS (1857), with (1903) 2 missionaries, 6 women missionaries, 3 native workers, 4 outstations, 1 place of worship, 2 day schools, 1 boarding school, 1 industrial school, 1 hospital, and 427 professed Christians, of whom 125 are communicants. Some write the name Onitsha.

ONIIPA. See ONYIPA.

ONITSHA. See ONICHA.

ONOMICHI: A town in Japan, situated in Hiroshima district, 135 miles W. by S. of Kobe; a prosperous town on the Inland Sea, noted for its manufacture of ornamental mats. Population, 18,700. Station of the MES.

ONYIPA: A settlement in the N. part of German Southwest Africa, situated in the territory of the Ambo tribe, about 30 miles N. of Olukonda. Station of the Finnish Mission Society (1874), with (1900) 2 missionaries and their wives, 2 women missionaries, 7 native workers, 2 outstations, 1 place of worship, 1 printing house, and 101 professed Christians. Some write the name Oniipa.

OODOOVILLE: A town in Jaffna, North Ceylon, forming a suburb of Manepy. Hot, but healthy. Population, 2,354. Station of the ABCFM (1831), with (1903) 2 women missionaries, 34 native workers, 4 outstations, 10 day schools, 2 boarding schools, and 486 communicant Christians.

OOTACAMUND. See UTAKAMAND.

OPOTIKI: A post town in New Zealand, situated on the North Island, 110 miles N. by E. of Napier. Population, 1,500. Station of the CMS, with (1903) 1 missionary and his wife, 16 native workers, and 1,500 professed Christians, of whom 102 are communicants.

ORAN: A seaport of Algeria, Africa, situated 70 miles N. E. by N. of Tlemsen. It was in Spanish hands from 1509 to 1708 and from 1732 to 1792, and was occupied by France in 1831.

At 6 or 7 miles S. is the Great Salt Lake of Oran, 27 miles long and 3 to 6 miles wide. Population (1901), 87,801. Station of the Algiers Spanish Mission, with (1900) 2 missionaries and their wives and 1 woman missionary. Also station of the French Society for Evangelizing the Jews, with 1 missionary.

ORANGE RIVER COLONY: A territory of South Africa, formerly the Orange Free State. It was annexed to Great Britain May 24, 1900, as a consequence of the Boer War. There is a governor over the Transvaal, and the Orange River Colony is governed by a lieutenant-governor under him. The colony has an area of 48,326 square miles. The population (1900) was 207,503, of whom 129,787 were natives. It is believed that the white population has been reduced in consequence of the war. The colony lies between the Transvaal on the north and Basutoland and Cape Colony on the south, extending east and west from Natal to Bechuanaland. The arable area is small, pasturage for grazing furnishing much of its resources.

Since the British accession English has become the official language and must be taught in all schools. The principal religious bodies are the Dutch Reformed Church, with (1890) 68,940 adherents, the Wesleyans with 753, the Church of England with 1,353. There are also Lutherans, Roman Catholics, and a few Jews. The natives are of the Basuto and Bechuana branches of the Bantu race, nearly allied to the Kafirs. The Berlin Missionary Society has 4 stations in this colony, the SPG 2, and the South African Wesleyan Missionary Society has 8 stations, with a considerable body of native adherents.

ORGANIZATION OF MISSIONARY WORK: The purpose of this article is to furnish a statement of the different forms of organization used in mission work, and the agencies of administration, employed both at home and on the foreign field.

1. *At Home:* Into the question of the degree of organization needed, it is not necessary to enter here. It is sufficient to say that the present forms have been the direct outgrowth of the pressing needs of the situation. 1. Missionaries in foreign lands must be supported (the instances of self-support being so few and so exceptional as to be practically ruled out of the question), and money must be raised and forwarded to them. 2. It is not every man or woman who, however willing, can advantageously work in foreign lands; there must be some means for selecting those who are best qualified. 3. In the conduct of foreign work two things are essential: first, that expenditures be proportioned to receipts; second, that different sections of the great work shall not assume relatively undue importance. It thus becomes necessary that there be some central authority to keep, so far as practicable, an even hand over the whole enterprise. 4. Those who give for the support of missions have a natural and righteous desire to know what is accomplished by them, and there must be the means of collecting and imparting information. 5. As mission work in most instances involves the holding of property, there must be some form of corporation, having a recognized existence before the law.

The necessity of meeting these demands has resulted in the formation of missionary societies or boards, so organized as to provide for these varied departments. These societies or boards may, for convenience' sake, be classified into groups.

I. Societies which are engaged directly in general foreign missionary work by sending out missionaries, and which are not confined by their constitutions to any particular phase of that work or to any special country. They are either interdenominational, *i.e.*, drawing their support from different churches, or represent some one of the different denominations.

II. Woman's Boards, organized by women, with special reference to work among women, and either independent, *i.e.*, sending out their own missionaries, or acting in connection with some general society.

III. Societies which are limited by their constitutions to specific branches of work or to distinct territories. These include: (*a*) Aid societies, which merely collect funds to assist other societies, especially from people who are interested in their work, but are not naturally included in their constituency. (*b*) Bible and tract societies, which engage directly in foreign work by the employment of colporteurs and distributing agents. (*c*) Medical missionary societies, whose object is to train and furnish physicians, men or women, who shall enter the foreign work, either independently or in connection with some general society.

IV. Individual efforts and miscellaneous organizations. We are concerned in this article chiefly with the general statement of the organization and its agencies of administration.

V. *Organized Missionary Societies or Boards:* These may be classed under three general heads: 1. Those directly controlled by some ecclesiastical organization. 2. Those ecclesiastically connected with some denomination, but not controlled by it. 3. Those independent of any ecclesiastical connection.

1. Those directly controlled by some ecclesiastical organization include the Presbyterian Boards; the Missionary Society of the Methodist Episcopal Church, U. S. A.; the Domestic and Foreign Missionary Society of the Protestant Episcopal Church in the United States; the Missionary Society of the Moravian Church; and most of the Lutheran Boards of America and Europe. In them the society or board is a committee appointed by and responsible to the general governing body of the church or denomination. These are: the General Assemblies of the various Presbyterian Churches; the General Conference of the Methodist Episcopal Church; the General Convention of the Protestant Episcopal Church in the United States; and the General Synod of the Moravian Church. Whenever there are so-called members, directors, etc., the term is merely honorary, indicating that such persons have by virtue of certain grants of money been allowed certain privileges, *e.g.*, of receiving regularly the Society's publications, or attending certain regular meetings. They do not indicate any right to vote upon any action of the Society or Board. Officials are required to belong to the denomination, and missionaries must have received ordination from authorities recognized by the Church. In case of difference between the missions and the board there is an appeal to the General Assembly, etc.

2 Those ecclesiastically connected with some denomination, but not directly controlled by

it, comprise such societies as the Church Missionary Society, the Society for the Propagation of the Gospel, and various Baptist, Methodist, and Wesleyan Societies of England, the United States, and Canada. In these the societies or boards are composed of members of the denomination which they represent, either by virtue of grants of money or by appointment to represent certain churches. Their officials and missionaries are members of the denomination, and are required to conform to its customs and discipline. So far as the direction of the affairs of the society or mission is concerned, the authority of the board itself is final—there is no appeal.

(3.) Those independent of ecclesiastical relations include the American Board of Commissioners for Foreign Missions, the London Missionary Society, the Paris Evangelical Society, the Basel and Berlin Missionary societies, the Bible societies, and most of the special societies. Here, however, we find again two classes: (1) Those which are general in their membership, and (2) those that are self-perpetuating, or close corporations.

The first class includes the London Missionary Society, the Bible Societies, and most of the special societies. In them the membership is absolutely unlimited in number, and any person can become a member by acceding to certain conditions. He then has the right to vote in the annual or general meetings of the Society when the special committees or boards are elected.

The second class includes the ABCFM, the Paris Evangelical Society, and the Basel and the Berlin, and other German independent societies. In them the membership is restricted in number, and the right to vote at any meeting of the society is confined to the actual members of the society, who alone have the right to elect other members.

In neither class is there any restriction of denominational connections or of special ordination and discipline, tho, as a matter of fact, both the ABCFM and the London Missionary Society have become Congregational societies. The decision of the general society in every case is final—there is no appeal.

VI. *Faith Missions:* These in general are mission enterprises, in which the missionaries go to the foreign field without the assurance of any definite or continued support from the home land. They usually claim to put forth no efforts to secure such support, beyond the offering of prayer to God. In some cases they seek to support themselves by some occupation on the ground; but as a rule they give themselves entirely to their work, relying solely upon whatever gifts may come to them from friends at home, or may be given by travelers and others who visit them. For the most part such missions are carried on by individuals, but occasionally they have a more or less elaborate organization. The most prominent instance of the last named type is the **China Inland Mission.** There is no formal organization, but a committee or council receives and forwards funds, publishes reports, and renders accounts. The same thing is practically done by individual friends for all the smaller Faith Missions. Public appeals are seldom made, as in the case of the organized societies, and the missionaries are absolutely independent (in most cases) of any ecclesiastical direction, tho they are always connected with some religious body.

The agencies employed by the organized societies for the administration of the undertaking in its different departments, viz., collection and forwarding of funds, selection of missionaries, direction of the foreign work, furnishing reports, and holding of property, are, 1. A committee; 2. Executive officers.

1. *The Committee:* In the case of the societies of the first class enumerated above, viz., those directly under the control of an ecclesiastical organization, the committee and the board are identical. In other classes they are generally appointed by the general society, tho in some cases, as in the American Baptist Missionary Union, the society appoints a Board of Managers, which in its turn appoints an Executive Committee. However appointed or however named, —Board of Managers, Executive Committee, Prudential Committee, Advisory Committee, etc.—its duties are to conduct the affairs of the society under the general direction of the society or the church. All matters pertaining to the particular policy or active operations both at home and abroad are discussed and decided in its meetings, and it is rarely the case that an appeal is taken to the general society or church, or, if taken, sustained. In fact, these committees are, for all practical purposes, the societies, the latter doing, as a rule, little more than mark out general lines of policy. Each committee appoints sub-committees for the special departments. These vary greatly in their form, according to the differing customs of each society.

2. *The Executive Officers:* These are the secretaries, treasurers, agents, etc. Scarcely any two societies apportion their duties in the same way, but those duties are so familiar that they need no special mention. They are never voting members of the committee, but merely executive officers. The definition of a few of the terms in general use among such of the societies as make a distinction between the different officers will suffice.

A *foreign* secretary has charge of the correspondence with the missions, presents to the committee all questions relating to the conduct or interests of the foreign work, and the estimates for the missions. A *home* secretary has general charge of the home department, with special reference to the raising of funds, and the relations of the committee or board to the churches. In some cases all applications for appointment to the foreign field pass through his hands; in other cases they go to the foreign secretaries. An *editorial* secretary has general charge of the publications of the society, edits the periodicals and the annual reports, and superintends, when he does not prepare, the various leaflets, tracts, etc., by which the knowledge of the society's operations is disseminated. A *field* secretary is one whose special work it is to visit the churches, attend meetings of ministers, and arrange plans for public presentations of the needs of the society. This work of visiting is shared by all the secretaries, according to their time and ability. In some cases there is a *recording* secretary, as a permanent official, whose special duty it is to keep the record of all the transactions of the committee. In other cases that work is divided up among the other secretaries. Some societies also employ *district* secretaries, who have special charge of certain sections of country, gather the subscriptions, arrange for visits and addresses, and report to the committee, generally through the home or the recording secretary. The *treasurer* has charge of all moneys and accounts. He receives all remittances, makes all payments, keeps all accounts, and receives and disburses the appropriations after the estimates have been passed upon in committee. He furnishes to the monthly periodicals full statements of moneys received, and his accounts are submitted to auditors for careful examination. In some instances the office of treasurer is honorary, the regular work being conducted by an assistant treasurer or a financial secretary. Usually there is also a general or business agent, who has charge of the publishing department, and the purchase and forwarding of outfits, supplies, etc., for missionaries.

The term *honorary* secretary, etc., is applied in British societies to persons who serve without receiving any remuneration.

The executive officers are the only persons connected with the society who receive salaries. Members of committees or of boards invariably serve gratuitously.

In the case of some of the smaller societies, where the duties are not numerous or heavy, they are performed, commonly without salary, by some minister or layman, but in all the large societies, where the duties require time, salaries are paid.

The work of administration of a missionary society commonly comprises:

1. *The Collection and Application of Funds:* The income of a missionary society includes: (*a*) donations, collections, subscriptions, whether by individuals, churches, Sunday schools, auxiliaries, bands, etc. These are sent either direct to the treasurer or through some local or church organization, and are, as a rule, applied to the general work of the board.

(*b*) Legacies. These are usually payable in full by the executors of a will, but are in some instances subject to conditions of annuity or application to some specific purpose.

(*c*) The income of invested funds. In some cases these funds have been dedicated to special objects by their donors; *e.g.*, the payment of the salaries of the executive officers, or the support of certain departments of mission work. It has become increasingly the custom for the large societies to own the premises where their offices are located. The original erection or purchase of these has been, in almost every case, from moneys contributed for that special purpose, and entirely apart from the ordinary donations to the missionary work of the society.

The remittance of money to the field is generally through some well-known banking-house of New York or London which has commercial dealings with the country where the mission is located, and is in the form of bills of exchange or letters of credit such as are issued to travelers.

2. *The Selection of Missionaries:* This is one of the most difficult duties that devolves on a mission board. The peculiar elements that enter into foreign life, the strain of changed climate, food, habits of life, the new language, the necessity of intimate relations with associates, the demands of sudden emergencies, etc., all enter into the consideration. Then, again, the strange misconceptions as to nature of the missionary work, the idea that personal consecration is the only quality needed, often cause great perplexity to the officers of the board. The subject of the **qualifications necessary** for missionaries has been treated elsewhere. It will be sufficient here to indicate the course pursued in their selection and appointment.

This course varies greatly in different societies, and even in the same society there is no iron-clad rule. There are, however, certain points common to all. The most important of these are: 1. Examination on doctrinal beliefs and ecclesiastical relations. In certain denominations this amounts to no more than the ascertaining of the antecedent action of church authorities (Episcopal or Presbyterial ordination is accepted as final), and in all it is in the great majority of cases more formal than minute, with a view to securing that the missionary shall be in substantial harmony with those whose representative he is, and with those who are to be his associates. 2. Physical examination. This is with a view to secure those only whose physical health is such that there is a reasonable probability that they will be able to endure the strain of life in a foreign land, and not be obliged to return home after all the expense incidental to their being sent out is incurred. 3. The general circumstances and fitness of the candidate. Are there relatives who may be compelled to look to him for support? Is there ability to acquire with comparative ease a foreign and difficult language; such a temperament as will make it easy to cooperate with others; the faculty of adapting oneself to circumstances, etc.? These examinations are conducted with great courtesy, kindness, frankness, and thoroughness, as is instanced by the small number of failures on the foreign field, and the few examples of those who have felt aggrieved by the refusal of the board to grant an appointment.

The examinations being satisfactory, the appointment is given, and preparations are made for the departure. In the case of an increasing number of societies, especially in England and Germany, there comes then a period of special training and preparation with a view to fitting the missionary for his work. In America the whole question of the preparation of missionary candidates is still under discussion. (See **Training**.)

3. *The Conduct of the Foreign Work:* The Missionary Society, as indicated in the article on **Methods of Work**, is: (1) A great evangelistic agency, employing hundreds of men and women whose chief duty is to preach the Gospel. (2) A bureau of education supplying every grade of instruction to thousands who would otherwise be absolutely ignorant. (3) A publishing society with different departments of translation, editing, publication, and distribution. (4) A building society for the erection of churches, colleges, hospitals, etc. (5) A charitable society for the assistance of the suffering poor, the diseased, the widowed and orphaned. All these various departments that in Europe and America are divided among a dozen different organizations are combined in the foreign work of every great missionary society.

As a rule, the decision in regard to the detailed conduct of the missions is committed to the missionaries on the field. Questions, however, are constantly arising which can only be decided by the home authority. Such are: 1. The question of expenses to be incurred in different departments, and the accounting for payments made. 2. The beginning of new work. 3. Relations between different missions and different societies in the same field. 4. General questions of policy. These are all perplexing questions, and questions in regard to which there is much division of opinion even among those best informed on the field. Perhaps the most difficult one is the first, which is more fully treated in the article **Finances of Missions.** To enter into detail more fully is beyond the limits of this article. Enough has already been said to show that the men who meet weekly or oftener to consider and decide such complicated questions are no less earnest and consecrated in their labor than those who go to the foreign field.

4. *Reporting to the Churches:* This is becoming more and more an important branch of the home work of the societies. There is a marked difference between societies in this particular. Some societies publish very full reports, like the CMS (which has the services of skilled editors and contributors), and some very meager. Some most carefully arrange and index everything; others give interesting general statements, but are not explicit in details.

5. *The Holding and Securing of Real Estate:* This has great importance in the prosecution of missionary work. The laws relating to the holding of property are very different in different lands; but whatever be the form of title, the actual ownership rests with the committee at home.

II. *On the Foreign Field:* Turning now to the organization of mission work abroad and the administrative agencies employed, we find that the organization is: 1st, Territorial; 2d, Ecclesiastical. The agencies are: 1. Missionaries; 2. Native Pastors or local Ecclesiastical Bodies.

A. *Organization:* 1st. *Territorial organization.* 1. Missions; 2. Stations; 3. Outstations or substations.

Missions: The word "mission" is used in a great variety of senses, denoting sometimes a single undertaking; but, as found in the majority of the reports of the missionary societies, it indicates an organized (or simply associated) body of missionaries occupying a certain territory, *e. g.*, the North Africa, the Mid-China, the Japan Mission. It includes a number of stations, with their outstations and fields, and its extent is usually regulated by the ease of communication between the different parts. In the usage of the Methodist Episcopal Churches of the United States the mission, upon the formation of a regular local ecclesiastical organization, becomes a conference. The Wesleyan Methodists of England limit the use of the word so that it is practically synonymous with district, having (*e.g.*) four missions in the island of Ceylon. The Society for the Propagation of the Gospel uses the term in the most restricted sense, combining its individual missions in dioceses. The CMS passes over parts of the supervisory work of the mission to qualified local bodies, and reports such work in a separate category.

Speaking now of missions in the general sense, as organizations or associations of missionaries occupying a certain territory or working for a special race, we find them, in the majority of cases, including the Baptist, Congregational, Presbyterian, Methodist, and most of the Episcopal societies, having a more or less complete form of organization. They have regular meetings, conferences, or councils annually or semi-annually, with permanent officers, treasurer, secretary, or presiding elder. Action affecting the mission as a whole is transacted in these meetings, and transmitted to the home department through the appropriate office. Thus the estimates arranged at the annual meeting are transmitted by the secretary of the mission to the foreign secretary of the board; the appropriations made by the board return to the treasurer of the mission, who keeps all the accounts.

Stations: This word also has varied meanings. Usually it denotes some city or large town occupied by one or more missionaries, from which the work extends to the surrounding territory. Sometimes it includes the whole field worked from that place as a center, but the restricted use is the more common, and is that usually adopted in this Encyclopedia. In the stations, too, there is, as a rule, some organization, especially when there are a number of missionaries, an extended field, and many departments.

Outstations or Sub-stations: These are places—sometimes an important city, more often a town or village—where mission work is carried on by native workers alone. Usually there is a church or congregation ministered to by native preachers, and the schools are under native teachers. It is seldom the case that an outstation is the residence of a missionary. In the usage of the Methodist and some Baptist boards, however, there is really no distinction between stations and outstations, except as the most important centers of work are called principal stations and the remainder stations; the missionaries frequently reside at the different stations in turn. They also use the term circuit in the foreign field as at home, to indicate what other societies mean by station field.

2. *Ecclesiastical Organization:* This varies greatly with the different societies, is governed by the rules of the denominations at home, and follows the lines of the three classes mentioned above. Wherever the missionary societies are organically connected with the church, the missions, whether as Presbyterian Synods, Conferences, etc., are organic parts of the church. They are thus entitled to representation in the governing body of the church, and as a matter of fact are usually so represented.

In the second class, where the relation of the board to the church is not organic, the missionaries are under the ecclesiastical discipline of the church or churches at home, by the laws of the Society. In the third class individual missionaries are free to arrange their own ecclesiastical relations, entirely independent of the board.

With regard to the native churches, there is a wide difference of custom. As a rule they follow the lead of the missionaries, tho, except in the Episcopal Churches, there is no law governing them; and there is a large liberty left by almost all the societies to their representatives in the field in regard to the details of formal organization.

B. *Administration:*

1. *Foreign Missionaries* are the first of the administrative agencies. These are ordained—lay, female, and medical.

The great majority of foreign missionaries are, and except in special instances always have been, ministers regularly ordained according to the laws of the churches to which they belonged.

Specific instances in the history of the early missions of the London Missionary Society and the Moravians of the sending out of entirely or comparatively uneducated parsons, to encounter the perplexities, trials, and hardships of missionary life, made it all the more evident that the rule must be that a man to be a successful foreign missionary must be a man of education and special training. This was for many years synonymous with preparation for the ministry, and probably it was due as much to this as to the special work of preaching that it became so decided a rule that all missionaries should be ordained preachers. There were instances where laymen went out as printers, but that was considered exceptional, and in some instances they afterward received ordination. Another element in the case was the fact that the people of many foreign lands could not understand how a man who was not a "priest" could administer spiritual help and counsel, and they were somewhat unwilling to apply to any one whose ministerial status was not of the highest. As, however, missionary work has developed its different departments, as education in the home lands has become more general and in foreign lands more exacting, as medical work opened up, as the general work has extended to include publication, treasury work, etc., the lay element in mission service became more prominent.

At the present time, in all the organized societies, lay missionaries are employed chiefly as business agents, printers, instructors in the higher schools and colleges, and in medical work. It is increasingly the custom to put a layman in charge of the treasury, the accounts, and the publication work of the different missions. In medical work it is becoming increasingly evident that a physician who is to excel in his profession cannot also be a theologian, and in his practise he finds less and less need of it; indeed, it is in many cases a positive hindrance to be known as a preacher or priest.

Women missionaries take an increasingly important position, both in numbers and in work done. Whether as wives or as single women, they have done and are doing some of the best work, both pioneer and constructive, that is found. They are not always mentioned separately in the tables of statistics, except in the reports of the European societies.

(a) *Location:* It has been the custom in most countries to send and locate two or more missionaries and their families together. The reasons for this are so obvious that they only need to be mentioned: Mutual consultation in cases of perplexity, sympathy in trial, support in anxiety, social relief from the strain of work, division of labor. In much the same way as it has been found to be wise for missionaries, as a rule, to be married, so it is wise for families to be associated. When female missionaries, whether as teachers or Zenana workers, are sent out, they also, as a rule, go "two and two" together, and establish a home of their own, or else join with the families of the stations. Thus a mission station almost invariably forms a social circle of educated, refined Christian people, whose individual labors are scarcely more important than their combined power as a Christian community. Since the increase in numbers and importance of lay workers, there has risen a "community" method of life which is somewhat peculiar. Without being in any sense monastic, it seeks to reap the advantage of association. This is primarily economy, both of funds and of men. Under the community method a number of lay workers can be supported for the same sum that it costs to maintain a single missionary family. Another advantage lies in the possibility it offers of utilizing agencies that otherwise would hardly be available. The China Inland Mission and the Salvation Army have largely adopted it and other societies are considering it.

(b) *Manner of Life:* It is the universal custom in foreign missions to provide for the missionaries, so that their manner of life shall differ as little as possible from their home life. The limitations of surrounding customs, etc., are of course considered, and great expense is avoided; but so far as it is practicable it is the policy of the societies to enable their missionaries to have such comforts as a family in moderate circumstances is accustomed to have at home. These are: a substantial, healthy, dwelling comfortably furnished; clothing and food adapted to the climate and their habits of life; service sufficient to enable them to give their whole time to the mission work, so much of adornment of the home as shall make it home-like. It is primarily a question of economy. To send a man or a man and wife to Africa, India, or Japan, and compel them to live as the natives do, would, in the immense majority of cases, doom them to early death, or at least to permanent disability. It pays for a mission board to keep its missionaries in good health. But there is an additional reason. With rare exceptions, a missionary has influence in proportion as he preserves his own individuality. In pioneer work it may be wise to conform to the customs of the land, and sink the foreigner in the native; but after his position is once established, the rule is that his own national and racial individuality should assert itself. This is matter of experience, as well as of theory; and notwithstanding the constant reappearance of the other idea, it has a stronger hold to-day than ever before.

(c) *Method of Support:* This is usually by a fixed allowance, arranged either by or in consultation with the missionaries themselves, and graded according to circumstances of location or of family. The basis is an adequate support from year to year for the missionary and his family, without accumulating property.

(d) *Vacations:* It is the custom in most if not all missionary societies to allow the missionaries to return to the homeland once in a certain number of years. This, too, is the result of experience, and is found to be economy in the long run. It is needful for the missionaries: first, for rest from the unintermitting strains of missionary life; second, for recuperation by contact with vigorous life, and for the purpose of retaining a sympathetic relation with the churches; third, for the care of children and arrangements for their education.

2. *Native Workers:* These constitute naturally the great body of the working force. Not only is it impossible, but it is undesirable, for the missionary to undertake to do all the work of his field. His chief aim, next to the conversion of individual souls, is the establishment of the Christian Church on its own distinct basis, with all its different departments. As soon as there are converts they are utilized as workers, each with some responsible share in the work of the missionary,—at first as Bible-readers; then

as catechists, teachers, preachers; and at last as pastors, in full charge of the general work of an organized body of believers. The missionary is the organizer and superintendent, and thus, in a degree, director; yet those who in a sense work under him still work with him, and follow him as leader, rather than obey him as master. It has been the custom of many missionary societies to keep the missionary and native force entirely distinct. This has been due not to any lack of appreciation of the value of native work, or to any desire to exalt the missionary, but rather to the feeling that it was not advantageous from the point of view of the best development of the native churches to a position of independence of all missionary direction and assistance. In those societies where the work is but the extension of the home church this becomes less noticeable, and in them it is frequently the case that native clergy are placed on the same official basis as the missionary. A marked instance of the success of this is the great work done by Bishop Crowther of the Church Missionary Society in Africa. In every case there is the fullest mutual consultation not only in regard to plans, but estimates; and it is very seldom a step is taken by the missions without the full concurrence of the native workers.

The question of their support is one of varying difficulty in different fields. At first it is usually assumed by the mission, but as the churches grow they are urged to take the entire support of their preachers and teachers, and also of those who do the aggressive work. In some missions the custom is adopted of requiring that a certain proportion of the pastor's salary be met by the people before they can have a distinct organization. There is, however, no rule, different arrangements being made according to circumstances of time, place, and condition of the people. In the older-established communities in many cases the entire running expenses of preaching and teaching are met by the native churches, the mission only assuming the support of those engaged in distinctively mission work, *e.g.*, Bible, book, and tract translation, colportage, etc. Even this work is in some cases assumed by native organizations, such as the Bulgarian Evangelical Alliance, the Church Councils of Travancore, under the auspices of the Church Missionary Society, etc. In some countries, notably in Japan, the churches commence their life with a good degree of self-support, and such an organization as the United Church of Christ in Japan is a wonderful power for good, by reason of its development of native workers, identified with the native church.

Innumerable questions come up in this connection with regard to the amount of education to be given, the salaries to be paid, etc., which can only have a mention here, with the simple statement that whatever rules are adopted by different societies working in different fields, they all have one specific end in view—the training up, as rapidly as possible, but not too hastily, of a body of workers native to the land and in perfect sympathy with their churches, so that in due time the foreign element may retire and take up other work, confident that the church thus left dependent upon itself will grow stronger rather than weaker, until it becomes able to itself cope with the problems of Christ's kingdom in its own land. (SEE **Native Agency**.)

The classification of native workers is not essentially different from that of Christian workers in America or Europe. Pastors, preachers, evangelists, catechists, colporteurs, Bible-readers, teachers, are essentially the same, and have similar duties and relations wherever they are found.

ORISSA: One of the subdivisions of the lieutenant-governorship of Bengal, India. It constitutes the southwestern part of Bengal. The area is 9,841 square miles, and the population (1901), 4,343,150. Several tributary states lie adjacent to the territory now described, and are under the political supervision of the Orissa officials. The area of these is 15,187 square miles, and the population about a million and a half, largely consisting of aboriginal tribes. This native district occupies the northwestern part of the territory, a hilly region, with a sparse population. British Orissa consists largely of fertile alluvial plains formed out of the deltas of three large rivers—the Mahanadi on the south, the Baitarani on the north, and the Brahmani between them. The people are almost exclusively agriculturists; rice is the staple food. Over 95 per cent. of them are Hindus and only 2¼ per cent Mohammedans. The number of aborigines in British Orissa is over 130,000, most of them being included among the Hindus; only about 7,000 still practise their ancient aboriginal religion. Of the million and a half in the tributary states a fraction less than 75 per cent. are Hindus, and a fraction less than 25 per cent. are aborigines, many of whom have professed Hinduism tho still holding to many of the customs of spirit-worship. The most important of these aboriginal tribes are the Kandhs, the Savars, the **Gonds**, the Bhumijs, the Bhuiyas, and the Pans; there are also some Kols and Santals, who are more numerous elsewhere. Some of the larger tribes also spread beyond the borders of Orissa into adjacent districts of the Central Provinces or the Madras Presidency. A few Mohammedans, Buddhists, and Christians make up the rest of the population. The aborigines—it need hardly be said—for the most part cling to the hills, while the Hindus inhabit the valleys lying between. It was among the Kandhs that the practise of semi-annual human sacrifices to their earth-god prevailed, until the entrance of the British authority in 1835 put a stop to it. Kidnaping for sacrifice—for the victims were usually obtained by raids among the quiet inhabitants of the valleys—was then made a capital offense; and the Kandh priests were induced to substitute buffalos for human beings in their sacrificial rites. The Kandhs are finely developed and intelligent specimens of humanity, possessing capabilities which it may be confidently believed will before long be fully brought out by Christian education. The language of Orissa among the Hindus is the Uriya, an Aryan dialect closely related to the Bengali; sometimes it has been classed simply as a dialect of that tongue, but the latest scholars regard it as distinct. Among the aboriginal tribes different languages prevail; those of the Kandhs and the Gonds belong to the Dravidian family of South India. The Kols, Santals, and Bhumijs speak languages of the Kolarian family. Many dialects are in use by as many distinct tribes inhabiting Orissa and other regions.

Brahmanical records in the Great Temple of Jagannath profess to trace the chronology of the earliest Hindu kings of Orissa to the year 1807

B. C. Little reliance can be put upon these dates, but this much they make clear, that for many centuries before Christ Orissa was governed by Hindu rulers. Doubtless it was under these kings that the Kols, Gonds, Santals, and Kandhs were pushed back from the plains to the mountains. Then from about 500 B. C. to the Christian era is the period of Buddhist development and dominion. Buddhist caves, dug out during this period, probably (tho some assign a date as low as 1000) still exist at Raninur. Then followed the period of the Yavana invasions, tho just who the Yavanas were is not fully settled. They came, however, from some northern quarter. They were at last expelled, and Orissa was governed by two successive Hindu dynasties from the 5th century of our era until well on into the 16th. The worship of Jagannath, which, according to tradition, had long been practised in Orissa, was restored, after the Buddhist and Yavana eras, by one of these dynasties, and the present Great Temple at Puri built by the other, in the 12th century. During the 16th century the Mohammedans came, and Orissa became a part of the Mogul Empire of Delhi. In the 18th century, when the Mogul power faded before the rising Marathas, the latter ruled for a time over this province. From them it was taken by the English in 1803.

The Hindus of Orissa are excessively religious. Temples and shrines abound. But the chief one, and one of the most famous in all India, is the one sacred to Jagannath ("Lord of the World," one of the titles of Vishnu), at Puri. To this temple 300,000 pilgrims have been known to come in one year. The great Car Festival alone sometimes draws to it as many as a third of that number. The government has done all in its power to prevent the outbreak and spread of disease among these crowds, and to enable the pilgrims to reach home safely. With Western people the general idea of this great festival is associated with that of the self-immolation of devotees under the wheels of Jagannath's car as it is dragged from the temple to the "Summerhouse" of the god, a mile away. The descriptions of these religious suicides have been exaggerated. The cult of Jagannath is opposed to the sacrifice of life, tho probably some devotees in moments of religious frenzy have caused themselves thus to be destroyed. But self-immolation during recent years may be said to be almost wholly unknown. The long traditional connection of Jagannath with Orissa helps to make his worship popular within the province itself; the popularity of it beyond the limits of Orissa is maintained, and within the province is still further helped by the fact that he is represented as a god of the people, without reference to caste or sect; he is the "Lord of the World." In short, the religious peculiarities of Orissa are of the utmost interest; the Jagannath worship involves some of the noblest as well as some of the most corrupting features of Hinduism; and its historic development is associated with the memory of some of the noblest souls in all the annals of Hindustan.

Owing to the exposed situation of Orissa it suffers occasionally from inunda'ions from the sea. Vast tidal waves, impelled by the tremendous cyclones which sweep at times over the Bay of Bengal, accompanied often by heavy falls of rain which aggravate the disaster by swelling the rivers, will devastate several hundred square miles of low-lying territory, and cause enormous destruction of life and property.

The Baptist missionaries at Serampore undertook, previous to the year 1820, evangelistic work in Orissa, but they withdrew in favor of the General Baptist Society (formed in England in 1816), which began work in this province in 1822. Cuttack, the chief city, was first occupied, and later Puri, the seat of Jagannath's temple and worship. The BMS now carries on work in these and three other stations. The American Free Baptist Missionary Society entered the northern part of Orissa in 1835, and now (1900) has seven stations in that part of Bengal. The two Baptist societies, together, have in Orissa about 8,000 professed Christian adherents, including church members.

ORIZABA: A town in Mexico, situated in the state of Vera Cruz, 78 miles E. by S. of Puebla. Altitude, 4,200 feet. Population (1900), 31,512. Station of the ME, with (1903) 1 woman missionary, 19 native workers, 358 professed Christians, of whom 233 are communicants; 9 places of worship, 9 Sunday schools, and 7 day schools. Station of the PB, with (1900) 3 missionaries and their wives and 1 printing house.

OROKOLO: A settlement in the Elema district of British New Guinea. Station of the LMS (1893), with 1 missionary and 8 native workers.

ORURO: A town in Bolivia, capital of the district of Oruro; formerly capital of the republic; situated 155 miles by rail S. S. E. of La Paz. It is the center of a tin and silver mining district. Population, 8,500. Altitude, 12,117 feet. Station of the BOQ (1898), with (1903) 2 missionaries, one with his wife; 1 woman missionary, and 1 day school. The first Protestant church in Bolivia was organized here in 1902.

OSAKA: One of the large cities of Japan, situated on the main island, 25 miles southwest of Kioto. It is one of the three imperial cities; is well built and clean, and is the center of large tea districts. A government college and academy are located here. The climate is mild. Population (1898), 821,235. Its importance as a center of influence has been fully recognized by the missionary societies, of which eight are represented in the city. Station of the ABCFM (1872), with (1903) 2 missionaries, 3 women missionaries, 3 native workers, 10 outstations, 14 places of worship, 20 Sunday schools, 1 boarding school, 1 dispensary, and 1 printing house. Station also of the CMS (1874), with (1903) 5 missionaries, four of them with their wives; 6 women missionaries, 17 native workers, 4 places of worship, 3 day schools, 2 boarding schools, and 745 professed Christians, of whom 305 are communicants. Station also of the Cumberland Presbyterians (1880), with (1903) 2 missionaries with their wives, 2 women missionaries, 16 native workers, 2 outstations, 14 places of worship, 4 Sunday schools, 1 boarding school, and 214 professed Christians. Station also of the PN (1881), with (1903) 1 missionary and his wife, 2 women missionaries, 9 native workers, 2 outstations, 3 places of worship, 1 day school, 1 boarding school, 1 kindergarten. Station also of the MES (1890); with (1903) 1 missionary and his wife, 3 native workers, 2 outstations, 3 places of worship, 4 Sunday schools, and 121 professed Christians. Station also of the ABMU (1892), with (1903) 2 missionaries and their wives, 2 women missionaries, 3 native workers, 10 outstations, 14 places of worship, 20 Sunday schools, and 1 printing house. Station also of the FCMS (1899), with (1902) 1 missionary and his wife, 1 woman missionary, 6 native workers, 1 outstation, 1 place of worship, 2 Sunday schools, 2 day schools, 1 kindergarten, and 43 professed Christians. Station also of the PE, with (1903) 3 native workers, 3 places of worship, 2 Sunday schools, 2 day schools, and 230 professed Christians.

OSBORN: A station of the South Africa Wesleyan Methodist Mission Society, situated in Griqualand East, Cape Colony, about 8 miles S. E. of Mount Frere. It has (1900) 1 missionary, 68 native workers, 13 places of worship, 11 Sunday school, 14 day schools, 1 industrial school, and 942 professed Christians.

OSCARSBERG: A settlement in Natal, Africa, situated 42 miles E. by N. of Ladysmith. Station of the Church of Sweden Mission (1878), with (1900) 2 missionaries, one with his wife; 2 women missionaries, 7 native workers, 6 outstations, 2 places of worship, 3 day schools, and 140 professed Christians.

OSGOOD, Dauphin William: Born at Nelson, N. H., November 5, 1845; studied medicine at Brunswick, Me., and Lowell, Mass., graduating at the University of New York in 1869; sailed as a medical missionary of the ABCFM for Fuchau, China, December, 1869. He soon mastered the intricacies of the Chinese language, acquiring a knowledge of both the Mandarin and local dialects. One of his earliest efforts was the establishment of the Fuchau Medical Missionary Hospital. During the ten years of its existence medical aid was given gratuitously to 51,838 patients among the poorer classes. He established also in connection with the mission an asylum for the victims of opium, and in two years 1,500 patients received treatment, a large number of whom were cured. He was frequently called as a consulting physician by his medical confrères.

Every hour he could spare from the active duties of his profession for the last four years of his life was devoted to the translation into Chinese of a standard work on anatomy. The finishing touches were put to it only on the day before his death. The work has been published in five volumes, illustrated by numerous plates. It is the first of its kind in the Chinese language, and has been much used in China.

He died at the sanitarium near Fuchau August 17, 1880.

OSHIMA: A town in Japan, situated on Kiushiu Island, about 10 miles E. of Nagasaki. Station of the Scandinavian Alliance Mission, with (1900) 1 woman missionary.

OSMANLI TURKISH: The Western dialect of the Turkish language as distinguished from the Eastern. It is used in Turkey, and the Eastern dialects, of which the Jagatai is the type, are used by Turks of the main stock in Central Asia. The term Osmanli Turkish is needlessly used by some also to distinguish the Turkish language when written with the Arabic letters from the same written with other letters. See **Turkish Language.**

OSSETIAN LANGUAGE: The language of some of the tribes inhabiting the Caucasus region of the Russian Empire. It belongs to the Iranic group of the Aryan family of languages. It has no alphabet of its own, but has been written with Georgian and also with Russian (Cyrillian) letters. There are three recognized dialects, and probably more than three.

OSTYAK LANGUAGE: The language of a people found in Western Siberia in the provinces of Tomsk, adjoining the Altai Mountains, and Tobolsk, lying E. of the Ural range. It belongs to the Finnic or Ugrian branch of the Ural-Altaic family of languages and has been written with Russian (Cyrillian) letters.

OTAKI DISTRICT: A post in New Zealand, on the W. coast of North Island, about 45 miles N. N. E. of Wellington. Population, 1,500. Here the CMS has (1903) 1 missionary, 14 native workers, 1 day school and 1,297 professed Christians, of whom 235 are communicants.

OTJIHAENENA. See OTYIHAENENA.

OTJIMBINGUE. See OTYIMBINGUE.

OTJOSAZU. See OTYOSAZU.

OTJOZONDJUPA. See OTYONDYUPA.

OTYIHAENENA: A village in German Southwest Africa, situated in the Herero country, about 230 miles E. by N. of Swakopmund. Station of the Rhenish Missionary Society, with (1903) 2 missionaries and their wives, 12 native workers, 6 outstations, 6 day schools and 481 professed Christians, of whom 113 are communicants. Some write the name Otjihaenena.

OTYIMBINGUE: A mission station of the Rhenish Missionary Society in German Southwest Africa, situated on the railway about 110 miles E. N. E. of Swakopmund, with (1903) 1 missionary and his wife, 6 native workers, 1 outstation, 1 day school, 1 Sunday school and 764 professed Christians, of whom 476 are communicants. Some write the name Otjimbingue.

OTYONDYUPA: A settlement in German Southwest Africa, situated in the Herero district, about 230 miles N. E. of Swakopmund. Station of the Rhenish Missionary Society, with (1903) 1 missionary and his wife, 7 native workers, 6 outstations, 7 day schools, and 319 professed Christians, of whom 131 are communicants. Some write the name Otjozondjupa.

OTYOSAZU: A village in German Southwest Africa, situated in the territory of the Herero tribes, about 180 miles E. by N. of Swakopmund. Station of the Rhenish Missionary Society, with (1903) 2 missionaries, one with his wife; 9 native workers, 3 outstations, 4 day schools, and 537 professed Christians, of whom 168 are communicants. The Society writes the name Otjosazu.

OUDH: Formerly an independent native kingdom, annexed by England in 1856. Now a part of the **United Provinces.**

OUGAVIGAMUTE: A settlement in the S. W. part of Alaska, situated on the Kuskokvim River, about 125 miles from its mouth. Station of the Moravian Mission (1892), with (1901) 1 missionary and his wife, 2 outstations, 1 place of worship, 1 Sunday school, and 60 professed Christians. The name is sometimes written Ugavigamiut.

OURO PRETO: A town and railway station of Brazil, capital of the state of Minas Geraes, situated 180 miles N. by W. of Rio de Janeiro. The city is overlooked by the double peaked Itacolumi. It owes its origin to gold deposits discovered in 1698. Population, 20,000. Station of the "Help for Brazil" Mission.

OWEN, Joseph: Born at Bedford, New York,

June 14, 1814; graduated at Princeton College, 1835, and theological seminary 1839; ordained as an evangelist by the Presbytery of Westchester October 2, 1839; sailed as a missionary of the PN for India, August 5, 1840. Most of his life was spent at Allahabad (1840-68). His labors, like those of most missionaries in India, were various —preaching, teaching, translating, and revising former translations of the Scriptures, and preparing commentaries on different books of the Bible. He was president of the Allahabad Missionary College, and professor in the Allahabad Theological Seminary. After 28 years of continuous labor he left in ill health for America via Scotland, intending, after spending a few days in Edinburgh, to visit his native land, and then return to India, but died in Edinburgh December 4, 1870. He took high rank as a scholar. When he left India he had just completed a second revision and edition of the Old Testament in Hindi and a commentary on Isaiah in Hindustani for the American Tract Society. He wrote a new translation of the Psalms in Hindustani and several commentaries in the same language.

OXFORD MISSION TO CALCUTTA: Headquarters, Calcutta, India. The mission was founded in 1880 in answer to an appeal from the Bishop of Calcutta to the University of Oxford to "send out men to work among the natives of that city who have received or are receiving the advantages of the system of education provided by the English Government." The form selected for the mission was that which was suggested by the late Bishop Douglas of Bombay —that of a "missionary brotherhood." It was decided, therefore, that the Oxford Mission should form a community under a superior, altho its members would not be bound by any vows for life, but would be allowed to withdraw at pleasure. The rules of the community were tested by two years' work in Calcutta, after which the bishop incorporated the first members of "The Oxford Brotherhood of the Epiphany."

The mission consists of 8 ordained and 2 unordained members, all Oxford University men, who carry on work in Calcutta and Patna, in three lines: 1. Interviews with the natives, lectures, and discussions. 2. The conduct of a school for native Christian boys. 3. The editing of a weekly paper called *The Epiphany*, in which free discussion of all religious questions is carried on between members of the mission and inquirers. The brotherhood also undertakes special work in India, for which funds are provided by the SPG. There is also a Ladies' Association, organized in 1887, in aid of the Oxford Mission.

OYO: A town in West Africa, situated 180 miles N. N. E. of Lagos, in the Yoruba country. Population about 50,000. Station of the CMS, with (1903) 2 missionaries, one of them with his wife; 3 women missionaries, 3 native workers, 2 day schools, 1 theological class, and 142 professed Christians, of whom 50 are communicants. Station also of the SBC, with (1903) 2 missionaries and their wives, 4 native workers, 2 places of worship, 1 Sunday school, 1 day school, and 43 professed Christians. Station also of the WMS, with (1903) 10 native workers, 6 Sunday schools, 5 day schools, and 176 professed Christians, of whom 150 are communicants. Some write the name Awyaw.

P

PABALLONG: A town in Cape Colony, Africa, situated in Griqualand East, near the border of Basutoland, and about 15 miles S. of Matatiela. Station of the Paris Evangelical Missionary Society (1876), with (1902) 1 missionary and his wife, 12 native workers, 7 outstations, 1 place of worship, 1 Sunday school, 5 day schools, and 365 professed Christians.

PABNA: A town in Bengal, India, situated 75 miles W. N. W. of Dacca. It has a large indigo factory. Population, 16,500, of whom 6,400 are Hindus and 9,000 Mohammedans. Station of the Furreedpore Mission (1890), with (1901) 2 missionaries, one with his wife; 2 women missionaries, 7 native workers, 4 day schools, and 1 place of worship.

PA-CHAU: A town in the province of Sze-chwan, China, situated 150 miles N. by E. of Chung-king-fu. Station of the CIM (1887), with (1903) 1 missionary and his wife, 3 women missionaries, 2 native workers, 1 place of worship, 1 day school, 1 Sunday school, and 47 professed Christians.

PACHUCA: A mining town in the State of Hidalgo, Mexico, about 56 miles N. E. by N. of Mexico City. Silver mines were worked here before the Spanish conquest, and silver has been extracted almost continuously ever since. The mines of Pachuca and the neighboring Real del Monte produce one-sixth of the aggregate silver mined in the year in the whole country. Station of the ME, with (1903) 1 missionary and his wife, 2 women missionaries, 30 native workers, 5 outstations, 8 places of worship, 9 Sunday schools, 9 day schools, 1 boarding school, and 1,494 professed Christians, of whom 508 are communicants.

PADANG: A town in Sumatra, Dutch East Indies, situated on the W. coast. Station of the Rhenish Mission Society, with (1903) 1 missionary and his wife and 64 professed Christians, of whom 59 are communicants. Station also of the Seventh Day Adventists (1900), with (1900) 1 missionary and his wife and 1 boarding school.

PAGODA ANCHORAGE: A seaport in the province of Fo-kien, China, situated on the S. side of the mouth of the estuary of the Min River, about 18 miles E. of Fu-chau. Station of the ABCFM (1890), with (1903) 3 missionaries and their wives, 60 native workers, 30 outstations, 30 places of worship, 30 Sunday schools, 26 day schools, 3 boarding schools, 1 dispensary, 1 hospital, and 501 professed Christians.

PAHANDUT: A village in Southern Borneo, Dutch East Indies, situated about 95 miles N. W. of Banjermassin. Station of the Rhenish Mission Society, with (1903) 1 missionary and his wife, 3 native workers, 2 outstations, 1 day school, and 75 professed Christians, of whom 34 are communicants.

PAHARI. See SANTALS.

PAKHOI: A town at the head of the Gulf of Tonkin, Kwan-tung, China; is a treaty port, with a population of 25,000. Station of the CMS (1886), with (1903) 3 missionaries and their wives, 4 women missionaries, 12 native workers, 2 day schools, 2 boarding schools, 1 dispensary, 1 hospital, 1 lepers' asylum, and 173 professed Christians, of whom 72 are communicants.

PAKOKKU: A town in Upper Burma, India, capital of the district of Pakokku, on the right bank of the Irawadi, 20 miles N. E. of Pagan. Population, 20,000, of whom 18,400 are Buddhists. Station of the WMS, with (1903) 1 missionary, 19 native workers, 7 outstations, 7 Sunday schools, 6 day schools, and 60 professed Christians, of whom 51 are communicants.

PAKAUR: A town and railway station in Bengal, India, situated in the E. of the Santal Parganas, about 160 miles N. N. W. of Calcutta. Station of the ME, with (1903) 1 missionary and his wife, 18 native workers, 1 place of worship, 6 Sunday schools, 5 day schools, and 279 professed Christians, of whom 79 are communicants. Some write the name Pakur.

PAKUR. See PAKAUR.

PALABALA: A village in the Congo Free State, West Africa, 110 miles from the mouth of the Congo River, and a few miles from the left bank of the Congo River, near Matadi. Station of the ABMU (1878), with (1903) 3 missionaries, 2 of them with their wives; 12 native workers, 7 outstations, 3 places of worship, 7 day schools, and 800 professed Christians, of whom 324 are communicants.

PALAKONDA: A town of Madras, India, situated 70 miles N. N. E. of Vizagapatam. Population, 10,400, of whom 10,100 are Hindus. Station of the Canada Baptist Convention of the Maritime Provinces (1892), with (1900) 1 missionary and 3 native workers.

PALAMKOTTA: A town in Madras, India, situated about 5 miles E. of Tinnevelli. Population, 5,000. Station of the CMS (1820), with (1903) 7 missionaries, 5 of them with their wives; 6 women missionaries, 4 boarding schools, 1 theological class, 1 college, 462 day schools, 861 native workers, and 54,970 professed Christians, of whom 13,439 are communicants (including the district of Tinnevelli Church Council). Station of the CEZ (1881), with (1903) 5 women missionaries, 66 native workers, 3 day schools, 1 boarding school, 1 industrial school, 1 dispensary, and 1,139 Zenana pupils. Some write the name Palamcotta.

PALNI. See PALNI.

PALAPYE See ROWE.

PALESTINE. See SYRIA.

PALGHÁT: A town in the Malabar district, Madras, 30 miles south-southwest of Coimbatore, 68 miles east of Calicut, in a famous pass of the Western Ghats. Has a large trade and active manufactures. Population, 39,500, of whom 33,000 are Hindus. Station of the Basel Missionary Society (1858), with (1903) 3 missionaries, 2 of them with their wives; 27 native workers, 5 outstations, 1 Sunday school, 5 day schools, and 443 professed Christians, of whom 248 are communicants.

PALI LANGUAGE: One of the Indic group of the Aryan family of languages. It is the language of Buddhistic sacred literature in Ceylon and Farther India, and is written with various local characters. It is classed as an old colloquial Prakrit, as contrasted with the literary or Sanskrit, but it is not now colloquial in the lands where it is cultivated in literature.

PALIPI: A village in the Toba Lake region of Sumatra, Dutch East Indies. Station of the Rhenish Missionary Society, with (1903) 1 missionary and his wife, 1 native worker, 1 Sunday school, 1 day school, and 7 professed Christians.

PALKONDA. See PALAKONDA.

PALLAM. A town of Travancore, India, situated about 4 miles S. W. of Kottayam. Station of the CMS (1845), with (1903) 1 missionary and his wife, 43 native workers, 11 day schools, 1 boarding school, and, in the district including Kottayam, 188 native workers, 90 day schools, and 20,645 professed Christians, of whom 5,194 are communicants.

PALMANER: Town in North Arcot, Madras, India, near the summit of the Magli Pass, 2,247 feet above the sea and 115 miles W. of Madras. A healthy station, 10° cooler than the rest of the district. Population, 1,931. There is a busy trade. Station of the RCA (1857), with (1903) 1 missionary and his wife, 1 woman missionary, 16 native workers, 1 place of worship, 4 Sunday schools, 2 day schools, 1 theological class, and 145 professed Christians, of whom 61 are communicants.

PALMIETFONTEIN: A settlement in the Klipplaat region of Cape Colony, S. Africa, situated about 54 miles S. W. of Graaff Reinet. Station of the Hannover Lutheran Free Church Mission Society (1896), with (1901) 1 missionary and his wife, 4 native workers, 4 outstations, 5 places of worship, 5 day schools, and 1,500 professed Christians.

PALMUR: A town in the native state of Haidarabad, India, situated about 63 miles S. W. of the city of Haidarabad. Climate healthy but hot. Station of the ABMU (1885), with (1903) 1 missionary and his wife, 29 native workers, 5 outstations, 10 places of worship, 14 Sunday schools, 10 day schools, 1 boarding school, 1 dispensary, 1 hospital, and 851 communicant Christians.

PALNI: A municipality in Madras, India, situated about 28 miles W. N. W. of Dindigal. Population, 16,900, of whom 15,000 are Hindus. Station of the ABCFM (1862), with (1903) 1 missionary and his wife, 34 native workers, 12 outstations, 10 places of worship, 11 Sunday schools, 9 day schools, 1 boarding school, and 169 professed Christians. Some write the name Palani.

PALWAL: A municipality in the Punjab, India, in the district of Gurgaon, 33 miles S. by E. of Delhi. It is of great antiquity, and is said to have been restored by Vikramaditya in 57 B. C. Population, 11,200, of whom 7,400 are Hindus and 3,700 are Mohammedans. Station of the BZM (1891), with (1903) 6 women missionaries, 7 native workers, 4 Sunday schools, 2 day schools, 1 industrial school, 1 dispensary, 1 hospital, and 84 Zenana pupils. Station also of the BMS

(1895), with (1903) 2 missionaries and their wives, 8 native workers, 3 outstations, 6 Sunday schools, 3 day schools, 3 dispensaries, and 120 professed Christians, of whom 59 are communicants.

PANADURE: A village in the Western Province of Ceylon, India, situated on the W. coast about 15 miles S. of Colombo. Station of the WMS, with (1903) 1 missionary, 20 native workers, 7 places of worship, 5 Sunday schools, 5 day schools, and 145 professed Christians, of whom 126 are communicants.

PANAIETI: An island of the D'Entrecasteaux group in Malaysia, lying about 40 miles S. E. of the extreme eastern point of New Guinea. Station of the Australian Wesleyan Methodist Mission, with (1901) 1 missionary, 5 native workers, 6 places of worship, 5 Sunday schools, 5 day schools, and 47 professed Christians.

PANCHGANJ: A town in Bombay, India, situated 22 miles N. N. W. of Satara. Station of the ZBM, with (1903) 4 women missionaries, 7 native workers, 1 outstation, 1 boarding school. Some write the name Panchgani.

PANGASINAN LANGUAGE: One of the languages belonging to the Malayan linguistic group and spoken by about 1,000,000 of the inhabitants of Luzon, P. I. It is written with Roman letters, having been reduced to writing by the Spanish friars.

PANGALOAN: A village in Sumatra, on the Batang Toru River, 23 miles E. by N. of Siboga. Station of the Rhenish Mission Society, with (1903) 1 missionary and his wife, 1 woman missionary, 84 native workers, 6 outstations, 1 Sunday school, 8 day schools, and 3,700 professed Christians, of whom 1,665 are communicants.

PANGHAREPAN: A town on the island of Java, near the head of Wynkoop's Bay, on the W. coast and about 50 miles S. of Batavia. Station of the Netherlands Missionary Society (1872), with (1901) 2 missionaries, 7 native workers, 1 outstation, and 166 professed Christians.

PANGARIBUAN: A village in Sumatra, Dutch East Indies, situated 32 miles N. E. of Siboga. Station of the Rhenish Mission Society, with (1903) 1 missionary and his wife, 41 native workers, 8 outstations, 7 Sunday schools, 12 day schools, and 1,623 professed Christians, of whom 748 are communicants.

PANG-CHUANG: A town in Shan-tung, China, 53 miles from Tsi-nan-fu, 125 miles south-southwest of Tientsin and 6 miles southeast of Grand Canal. Natives poor, low, crowded for room in which to live. Station of the ABCFM (1879), with (1903) 2 missionaries and their wives, 2 women missionaries, 39 native workers, 24 outstations, 24 places of worship, 24 Sunday schools, 8 day schools, 2 boarding schools, 1 dispensary, 1 hospital, and 734 professed Christians.

PANGKOH: A village of South Borneo, Dutch East Indies, Malaysia, situated 32 miles W. N. W. of Banjermassin. Station of the Rhenish Mission Society, with (1903) 1 missionary and his wife, 7 native workers, 3 outstations, 3 day schools, 1 Sunday school, and 271 professed Christians, of whom 121 are communicants.

PANGKUMU: A village in Mallicollo, New Hebrides, situated S. of Aulua. Station of the New Hebrides Missionary Society, with (1900) 1 missionary, 12 native workers, 1 outstation, 9 day schools, 1 boarding school, and 37 professed Christians.

PANGOMBUSAN: A village in Sumatra, Dutch East Indies, situated at the S. E. extremity of Toba Lake. Station of the Rhenish Mission Society, with (1903) 1 missionary and his wife, 29 native workers, 3 outstations, 1 Sunday school, 4 day schools, and 206 professed Christians, of whom 126 are communicants.

PANHALA KODOLI: A town in Bombay, India, situated 12 miles N. by E. of Kolhapur. Station of the PN (1877), with (1903) 3 women missionaries, 11 native workers, 6 outstations, 6 Sunday schools, 7 day schools, 1 dispensary, and 164 professed Christians.

PANSURNAPITU: A settlement in Sumatra, Dutch E. Indies, situated in the Silindung Valley, about 24 miles N. E. of Siboga. Station of the Rhenish Missionary Society, with (1903) 1 missionary and his wife, 47 native workers, 2 outstations, 4 Sunday schools, 4 day schools, and 2,588 professed Christians, of whom 1,257 are communicants.

PANTA: A station of the Netherlands Bible Society, in the Island of Celebes, Dutch East Indies, situated near Posso Lake. A missionary and his wife are stationed here for Bible translation work.

PAO-KING-FU: A town in the province of Hu-nan, China, 250 miles S. of I-chang. It is a small but very busy place. The missionary was driven out by a mob in 1902, but later allowed to return. Station of the CIM, with 1 missionary. It is a center for German associates of the CIM.

PAO-NING-FU: A town in the province of Szechwan, China, situated 145 miles N. N. W. of Chung-king. It is the center of a large silk-producing district. Station of the CIM (1886), with (1903) 6 missionaries, 2 of them with their wives; 6 women missionaries, 6 native workers, 4 outstations, 5 places of worship, 1 day school, 1 Sunday school, 1 boarding school, 1 hospital, 1 dispensary, and 162 professed Christians.

PAO-TING-FU: A town in China, in the province of Pe-chi-li, about 80 miles S. W. by S. of Peking. At this point the missionaries of the ABCFM, PN, and CIM were all killed by the Chinese during the Boxer movement in 1900. Station of the ABCFM (1873), with (1903) 3 missionaries and their wives, 2 women missionaries, 8 native workers, 9 outstations, 9 places of worship, 9 Sunday schools, 3 day schools, 2 boarding schools, 2 dispensaries, 1 hospital, and 234 communicant Christians. Station of the PN (1893), with (1903) 5 missionaries, 4 of them with their wives; 2 women missionaries, 3 outstations, 1 place of worship, 1 Sunday school, 2 day schools, 2 dispensaries, 1 hospital, and 150 communicant Christians.

PAO-TEO (Mongolia). See PAO-TU.

PAO-TU: A town in Mongolia, China, situated near the Hwang-ho River, about 335 miles W. of Peking. Station of the Scandinavian Alliance of N. A., with (1901) 2 missionaries and 1 woman missionary. Some write the name Pao-teo.

PAPEETE: A town in Tahiti, on the N. W. coast of the island in the small bay at the mouth of the River Papeete, of charming aspect. All the houses are surrounded by gardens. It is in regular communication with France by New Caledonia, with New Zealand, and San Francisco.

Station of the Paris Evangelical Missionary Society (1863), with (1903) 4 missionaries and their wives, 6 women missionaries, 4 native workers, 2 outstations, 2 places of worship, 2 Sunday schools, 2 day schools, 1 boarding school, and 293 professed Christians. Station also of the Seventh Day Adventists (1891), with (1901) 5 missionaries, 2 of them with their wives; 1 native worker, 3 outstations, 2 places of worship, 5 Sunday schools, 1 printing house, and 80 professed Christians.

PAPETOAI: A town on the N. coast of Eimeo Island, in the Society group. Station of the Paris Evangelical Mission Society (1867), with (1903) 1 missionary and his wife, 1 place of worship, 1 Sunday school, and 100 professed Christians.

PAPUA, or **NEW GUINEA:** Is the largest island on the globe, except Australia and Greenland. It is very irregular in its outline, but extends for about 1,300 miles between latitude 0° 30′ to 10° 40′ south, and longitude 131° to 150° 30′ east, and contains an estimated area of 312,329 square miles. It has not been fully explored and surveyed. In general it is a mountainous country in the northern part, while the southern coasts are low and wooded. Vegetation is very luxuriant; tropical fruit trees are found in abundance, while the woods of the interior produce fine timber trees. In the cultivated portions sugar-cane, tobacco, and rice are raised. The climate is healthful, tho great changes in temperature occur during a very short time. The inhabitants, so far as they have been classified, are kin to the negro race, tho there are several varieties of Polynesians represented. In number they are estimated at 800,000. Of their language the only knowledge we have is gained from the researches of the missionaries, who collected a vocabulary. This seems to show that the Papuan languages belong to a separate class from the Malayo-Polynesian languages. The three great powers exercise authority over the country as follows: British New Guinea, 29 per cent. of the territory, the S. E. quarter of the island; German New Guinea, 23 per cent., its territory north of that of Great Britain, and Dutch New Guinea, constituting 48 per cent., the western half of the island. The missionary first entered the Dutch portion of the island, but the communicants in the Dutch churches are few in number. The London Missionary Society next sent missionaries from the Loyalty Islands into British New Guinea, and ever since this Society has accomplished the largest results in New Guinea and has had the strongest force. Australian Anglicans opened a mission on the northeast shore in 1891. In German New Guinea two German Societies are laboring.

PARAGUAY: A republic in South America, situated between 22° and 27° 35′ south latitude, and 54° 35′ and 61° 40′ west longitude, southwest of Brazil and northeast of the Argentine Republic. Area, 91,970 square miles. The country in general consists of a series of plateaus with wooded slopes and grassy plains. The climate is very fine, tho at times the heat is excessive. The mean temperature for winter is 71°, and for summer 81°.

According to the Constitution of November, 1870, the government consists of a president, a Congress of two Houses, a Senate, and a House of Deputies. The senators and deputies are elected directly by the people, and the president holds office for four years.

The population (1899) is 530,103, besides 100,000 partly civilized Indians. There are twice as many females as males. The prevailing language is Spanish, but large numbers speak the Guarani; the mixture of Indian blood is stronger in Paraguay than in other states.

The principal cities are Asuncion (45,000), the capital, rapidly growing in population and importance; Concepcion (15,000), San Pedro (8,000). One-third of the inhabitants live in the central districts, containing the capital; one-third in the districts of Villa Rica and Cuasapa, and the remainder in the cultivated portion of the country. Agriculture and the raising of cattle are the principal occupations of the people, and Italian, Spanish, and German colonists are developing its resources in both these directions. Railway, telegraph and telephone lines are in operation. The Roman Catholic is the established religion of the state, but other religions are tolerated. Education is free and compulsory. The Protestant Societies located in Paraguay are the South American Missionary Society and the Missionary Society of the Methodist Episcopal Church of the United States. The republic is open to Gospel influences, and the prospect of Christian missions is bright.

PARAMARIBO: Chief town of Surinam, South America, situated near the mouth of the Surinam River. Population, 31,000. In the year 1835 the first Moravian missionaries landed in Surinam. The object was at first to commence a mission in Berbice, making Paramaribo the headquarters. Here a company of five Brethren worked at their trades in order to support themselves and the mission in Berbice. Their attention was soon directed to the negroes in Paramaribo. At first they had to face a good deal of opposition, but they gradually overcame ill-grounded prejudice, and were permitted to purchase a piece of land in the town. For a considerable time their missionary work continued very limited, but gradually it expanded, and Paramaribo became endowed with a vigorous negro Christian church, which has five separate places of worship in the city, the branches being Rusten Vrede, Wanica, Combe, and Saron. The Moravian Mission Society has here (1903) 21 missionaries, 19 women missionaries, 5 places of worship, 4 Sunday schools, 3 day schools, 1 kindergarten, and 3,098 professed Christians. Station also of the SDA (1887), with 1 missionary, 3 native workers, and 10 professed Christians. The auxiliary International Medical and Benevolent Association also maintains (1901) 1 missionary here.

PARANTIJ: A town in Bombay, India, situated 31 miles N. N. E. of Ahmadabad. Population, 8,800, of whom 5,800 are Hindus. Station of the Presbyterian Church of Ireland (1897), with (1901) 2 missionaries, 9 native workers, 1 place of worship, 2 Sunday schools, 2 day schools, 1 orphanage, and 15 professed Christians.

PAREYCHALEY: A district in Travancore, India, situated between Neyoor and Trivandrum. It is the meeting-place of the Tamil and Malayalam languages. Population of the district, 130,000. It gives name to a station of the LMS (1845), with (1903) 1 missionary and his wife, 175 native workers, 85 outstations, 85 Sunday schools, 67 day schools, and 22,060 professed Christians, of whom 2,083 are communicants.

PARGARUTAN: A village in Sumatra, Dutch East Indies, situated about 50 miles S. E. of Siboga. Station of the Java Committee, with (1901) 1 missionary and his wife and 1 day school. Some write the name Pargaroetan.

PARIS EVANGELICAL MISSION SOCIETY: The Paris Society for Evangelical Missions among non-Christian Nations (*Societié des Missions evangéliques chez les Peubles non-Chrétiens, établié à Paris*) was formed in November, 1822, as a result of the general religious revival in Western Europe. Before this time several missionary committees had been organized in Alsace, in Southern France, and in Paris, which now joined the Paris Society as auxiliary associations. Among the founders of the Society were some of the most prominent of the French Protestants. Its first president was Admiral Count Verhnël, and Jean and Frederick Monod, Baron A. de Staël, and other celebrated men were on this first committee. Its first general assembly was held in 1824, and in the same year an institution for training future missionaries was established at Paris.

Until 1840 the work of the Society went steadily forward; from this time its funds began to diminish, and after the Revolution of 1848 the want of money forced the Society to close the training institute. Of the 82 pupils who had joined it, 34 were laboring as missionaries in heathen countries, 17 as pastors in France, and 6 as teachers; the mission work in Basutoland, South Africa, was still carried on in spite of difficulties.

One of the Society's first missionaries, the Rev. E. Casalis, returned to France in 1849. His missionary addresses, delivered in churches all over the country, were crowned with most remarkable success, and a new love for missions seemed to spring up everywhere. The yearly income soon amounted to 180,000 francs. In 1856 the Training Institute was reopened, with M. Casalis at its head, and new spheres of labor were soon added to that in South Africa. Missionaries were sent to China (1859) and to Senegambia (1862). The colonial policy of the French Government being hostile to non-French organizations in the colonies, the Society was called on to take up work that had already been started by others. Thus in 1863 it took over the work of the LMS in Tahiti, and later that of the American Presbyterians (in part) in the Gabun region. In 1885 additional work was undertaken among the Kabyles or Berber tribes living in North Africa, and in 1886 a long-hoped for mission was begun on the Upper Zambesi. In 1889 mission work was begun in the French territories on the Ogowe and Congo Rivers. Until 1887 the training-school, being dependent on hired rooms, had migrated from one end of Paris to the other; in that year a mission-house admirably adapted to its purpose was erected at 102 Boulevard Arago. In 1896, as a result of the French conquest of Madagascar, application was made to the Society to take up at least a portion of the work there. Altho the task seemed herculean it was met courageously and successfully, with the result that the other societies laboring in Madagascar were also placed on a better foundation.

The Paris Society is undenominational. Its management is in the hands of a council composed of a president, two vice-presidents, two secretaries, two auditors, a treasurer, and twelve assessors. This council makes its own laws, and also the regulations to be followed by auxiliary committees formed outside of Paris. The services of the council are rendered gratuitously. A general assembly of the whole membership of the Society is held annually.

The present (1903) fields of the Society are: 1. Basutoland (Lessonto); 2. Senegal; 3. Tahiti, Loyalty Islands; 4. Zambesi; 5. French Congo; 6. Madagascar.

1. *Basuto Mission:* The first three missionaries of the Society, Messrs. Bisseux, Lemne, and Rolland, went, in 1829, to South Africa and settled in Wellington and at Kuruman, in Bechuanaland. The work, however, progressed but slowly, and these enterprises were handed over to the LMS and the German Berlin Society, and the Paris Society concentrated its efforts in a mission in Basutoland, commenced in 1833 at Morija. There were reported (1902) 17 missionaries, 8 teachers, 367 native workers, 22 stations and outstations, 12,676 church members, 176 schools, 11,626 pupils. The mission suffered from the Transvaal war, but has since been rallying strength.

2. *Senegal:* In 1862 the Society commenced work on the West Coast of Africa, in the French colony of Senegal. For a number of years St. Louis was the only station occupied, but in 1886 work was inaugurated at Kerbala, 80 miles inland, up the Senegal River. The climate has been very difficult to endure, but the work, especially among the children of freed slaves, encouraging.

3. *Tahiti and French Polynesia:* The occupation of Tahiti by the French in 1845 was followed by a request from the LMS to the Paris Society to send missionaries to that field. This was done, and in 1865 the entire work was handed over to it by the English. So thoroughly Christianized are the islands that they belong to the home rather than the foreign field. It has, however, been extended to Raiatea (1893), Atieana, in the Marquesas group (1899), and to the Loyalty Islands, Maré (1891-1900). The number of European missionaries is small (12, including 6 teachers), but there are 35 native pastors and 4,451 church members in 37 parishes. In the Loyalty Islands there is an interesting temperance movement.

4. *Zambesi:* In 1877 Mr. and Mrs. François Coillard, who for many years had labored among the Basutos in South Africa, endeavored to open among the Banyai tribes, north of the Limpopo River, a mission field for the native churches of Basutoland. They were made prisoners by the king of the Matabele, and their project failed. Subsequently they traveled to the Upper Zambesi, and found the tribes there had been conquered by the Basutos, and spoke the language of their conquerors. This language being familiar to Mr. and Mrs. Coillard, and their interest in these Zambesian tribes being aroused, they decided to give up home and work in Basutoland, and to open a mission where the people were unspeakably degraded, and where no missionary had ever penetrated. In 1880-81 they visited Europe to plead for this part of Africa. As a result the Evangelical Mission to the Zambesi was founded. A committee was appointed in England and Scotland to receive funds for its support.

In 1885, after a very difficult journey of more than 1,000 miles from Basutoland, Sesheke, on the Upper Zambesi, the residence of 15 chiefs, was reached. Here the missionaries took up their abode, and in the midst of many hardships a station was opened. In 1886 Mr. Coillard left Sesheke and undertook the first wagon journey ever made to the Barotsi valley, a distance of 500 miles. After a most toilsome journey of two months he succeeded in reaching Sefula. He returned to Sesheke, for Mrs. C., who, in the face of great perils, went with him to Sefula, where a station was opened.

Subsequently the mission was assumed by the Paris Society and has become one of its most interesting fields, as well as one calling for great effort. The climate has proved very severe, 9 missionaries dying in three years (1899-1901). Of late, however, the work has been more successful, and there were reported (1904) 17 missionaries (11 ordained), occupying 7 stations. The Society's reports are not clear upon the details of work in this field.

5. *French Congo:* In 1887 the American Presbyterian Board of Missions asked from the Paris Missionary Society some French teachers to help in their school work on the Gabun and Ogowe Rivers, the French Government having forbidden the instruction of the natives in any language but French. Accordingly three teachers and one industrial assistant were sent out in 1888. In 1889 two young ordained missionaries were sent to the Ogowe River to visit the American stations.

From this developed a work in the French Congo which now includes four stations: Talagouga (1892), Lambarene (1893), Ngoma (1898), Samkita (1900). In this field the Society is making an experiment with industrial training, following the lead of the Basel Mission. The schools are successful. The force of 18 European workers includes 10 missionaries, 3 female teachers, 4 artisans, and 1 assistant.

6. *Madagascar:* Seldom in the history of missions has a society met such a crisis as faced the Paris Evangelical Society in Madagascar. With the occupation of the island by the French forces it seemed that the power of the Jesuits would crush out all evangelical work. Under the plea that all foreign influence was hostile, and therefore should be eliminated, they sought to outlaw the churches founded by the LMS, the Norwegian Society, and the Friends. The only remedy was in securing French evangelical workers, and an earnest appeal was made. Offers of redistribution of field and work, on the most advantageous terms, were made, and altho it seemed as tho its existing work was all that the Society could carry, it took up work in this field courageously. The result has been most happy. The French churches have become interested in their new field; the old Societies have been enabled to continue their work, and the French Government has come to recognize the value of their services to the general interests of the community. In 1902 the President of the Society, with his wife, went to the island for a two years' residence, so as to become more thoroughly acquainted with the needs of the work and the methods to be employed. The stations occupied are: Antananarivo (1896); Ambatomanga, Ambobibeloma, Tsiafahy, Fihaonana, and Fianarantsoa (all in 1897); Anosibe, Maheresa, and Ambositra (1898); Mahasoarivo (1899); Ambatolampy (1900). The force includes 33 Europeans, 1 French pastor, 8 missionaries, 9 school directors, 5 male and 7 female teachers, 2 deaconesses, 1 assistant missionary. An idea of the nature of the educational work in which the Society is rendering invaluable assistance to the government is found in the seven districts of Imerina, including the capital. There are 275 schools, with 344 native teachers and 16,000 pupils. The thoroughness of the drill is manifested in the proportion of successful candidates in the official examinations. At Antananarivo the rates were: Paris Society, 78 per cent.; LMS, 64 per cent.; official schools, 65.5 per cent.; Roman Catholic, 58 per cent. At Fianarantsoa the rates were: Official schools, 96 per cent.; Paris Society, 90 per cent.; Norwegian Society, 72 per cent.; Roman Catholic, 69 per cent.

More than once it seemed as if the limit of ability of the French Evangelical churches was reached, but the churches have always responded to renewed appeals, and the other missions have not suffered.

PARLIAMENT OF RELIGION: A gathering of adherents of the various religions throughout the world, which met at Chicago from September 11 to 27, 1893, during the Columbian Exposition, and in one of its buildings. Such an Exposition would bring men together from different parts of the world and would afford an opportunity for telling all nations what place religion holds in the world, and what it has done. In this way it seemed to be possible to have at the World's Fair what might even be called an Exhibit of the World's Religions.

The leading mind occupied in organizing this great Parliament was that of Rev. John H. Barrows, D.D., pastor of one of the churches in Chicago. The aims of the Parliament as they presented themselves to his mind may be stated as follows: 1. To bring together representatives of all historic religions; 2. To show what and how many truths all religions teach in common. 3. To foster sentiments of brotherhood. 4. To set forth accurately the essentials of each religion. 5. To open up the fundamental facts on which rests the acceptance of Theism, and so to unite all religions in opposing materialism. 6. To bring together full statements, from different parts of the world, of the effect of the different religions upon the great problems of life. 7. To ask what light each religion affords to other religions. 8. To acquire accurate information of the present conditions of each one of these religions. 9. To learn what light each of the various religions has to offer upon current social and moral problems of the world. 10. To aid in bringing nations into a more friendly fellowship with each other.

The plan of holding such a Parliament was violently opposed in many quarters. The Holy Synod of Russia put its ban upon it; and so did the Sultan of Turkey, forbidding Mohammedans under his influence from attending it. The Archbishop of Canterbury also used his influence against it. Official representatives were present at the Parliament from the Roman Catholic Church of America; from China; from the Buddhists of South India, from the Brahma Somaj, and one or two similar groups in India. But altho aside from these, no official representatives of the various religions appeared at the Parliament, eminent individuals were there belonging to all leading religions, except Islam. This last religion was represented by some rather heretically liberal adherents, and by an American who professed faith in Mohammed, but was not admitted by the organs of the Caliph to be qualified to speak for that faith.

The sessions of the Parliament were marked by the most cordial feeling on the part of the Christians present, altho it sometimes appeared that foreign attacks upon Christianity put a heavy strain upon the patience of the audience. Once only in the whole seventeen days of the Parliament was there any unseemly conduct on the part of the assembly. This was when Mr. Mohammed Webb undertook to justify polygamy, his voice being drowned in a storm of cries and hisses. The Parliament, in short, thoroughly satisfied the expectations of its promoters; and when at its close a fine choir sang the "Hallelujah Chorus," in circumstances in which it had never been sung before, to the excited minds of many it seemed like a prophecy of the triumph of Christianity over all who now hesitate to accept it.

The Parliament undoubtedly did a good work in showing what of truth there is in some of the Oriental faiths which are so little known among the masses of people in the Western lands. It probably served a good purpose also in leading the various Christian denominations to realize once more how near they are to each other. It did not, however, draw from the representatives of non-Christian religions the cordial goodwill which had been hoped for.

One curious result of the gathering was to convince many thinking men in Eastern countries that the Parliament betokened a lack of faith in Christianity among Christians who attended the meetings. Another somewhat unexpected result was to introduce to American audiences eloquent philosophers, like Swami Vivakananda, who did not fail to make the utmost possible use of the opportunities which the Parliament suggested and left to them as a sequel to its meetings. On the whole, one is inclined to judge that, so far as Orientals are concerned, the alluring scheme of holding such a Parliament of Religions was somewhat in advance of their present stage of development.

Barrows, (J. H.), *The Parliament of Religions*, 2 vols., Chicago, 1893.

PARKER, H. P.: Died March 26, 1888, at the Victoria Nyanza. As Secretary of the CMS mission at Calcutta he accomplished great good; but he left this important post, at the suggestion of the Society, and entered upon work at Mandla, among the Gonds. Among this people, in the midst of the most trying difficulties, he labored faithfully and effectively until he was called to be the second bishop of Eastern Equatorial Africa. His six years' service as the Society's secretary at Calcutta, and his experience in the jungles of Central India, prepared him for his new position. He landed at Frere Town on November 27, 1886, and for six months, like his predecessor, Bishop Hannington, he gave all his energies to the East Africa Missions proper, setting things in order at Frere Town and Rabai, and visiting Wray at Taita, Fitch in Chagga, and the native teachers at other outlying stations. In June, 1887, he, accompanied by Mr. Blackburn, started for the interior, and, taking an entirely new route, they went direct from Rabai to Mamboia; thence, passing westward, they reached the south end of Nyanza, by the way of Mpapwa and Uyui, where they found Mackay in the Msalala district. Here the first Missionary Conference was held in the interior; and, largely through the advice of Parker, wise conclusions were reached in the Society's future policy toward the savage natives. Bishop Parker urged the importance of women missionaries for East Africa, and in April 5, 1887, a committee of the Society took the initiative in this important matter.

PARKER, Peter: Born at Framingham, Mass., June 18, 1804. He graduated at Yale College in 1831, spent two years in Yale Divinity School, and took a course of medical study, receiving the degree of M.D. in 1834. He was appointed medical missionary to China by the ABCFM, was ordained at Philadelphia May 26, 1834, and sailed the next month for Canton. He opened a hospital at Canton for diseases of the eye, which contributed greatly to disarm prejudice, and furnished opportunities for making known religious truth. In 1836 his eye infirmary had received 1,912 patients at a cost of $1,200, all of which was given by resident foreigners. In this hospital he was forced to receive patients suffering from other than eye diseases, and became famous for wonderful surgical cures. He, using the influence thus gained to secure a hearing, preached to his hospital patients regularly. He also educated Chinese young men in the practise of medicine, one of whom became an expert surgeon. The outbreak of war with the English in 1840 making it necessary to close the dispensary, Dr. Parker visited the United States. In 1842 he returned to Canton. In 1844, with the hope thereby of aiding the missionary work, he accepted the appointment of Secretary and Interpreter to the United States Legation to China, and his connection with the American Board was soon after dissolved, tho he did not cease missionary work, and his labors in the hospital continued till he resigned his secretaryship on his return to America in 1855. He often acted during these years as chargé d'affaires *ad interim*. Soon after his return he was appointed United States Commissioner to China, with plenipotentiary powers for the revision of the treaty of 1844. This service being completed in two years, he returned to America with health impaired, owing to the effects of a sunstroke. He resided in Washington, and in 1868 was elected Regent of the Smithsonian Institution. He died in Washington, January 10, 1888, aged 83. He published *A Statement respecting Hospitals in China*, and an account of his visit to Lu-Chu Islands and Japan.

PARLA-KIMEDI: A municipality of Madras, India, situated 75 miles S. W. by W. of Ganjam. Population, 16,400, of whom 15,900 are Hindus. Station of the Canada Baptist Convention of the Maritime Provinces (1892), with (1903) 1 missionary and his wife, 6 native workers, 1 outstation, 1 place of worship, 2 Sunday schools, 95 professed Christians.

PARPAREAN: A village in Sumatra, Dutch East Indies, situated in the Toba Lake region, near the S. E. extremity of the lake. Station of the Rhenish Missionary Society, with (1903) 1 missionary and his wife, 15 native workers, 2 outstations, 3 day schools, and 485 professed Christians, of whom 200 are communicants.

PARRAL: A town in Northern Mexico, 200 miles east-southeast of Chihuahua. Climate even, healthy. Population, 6,000. Station of the ABCFM (1884), with (1903) 1 woman missionary, 3 native workers, 10 outstations, 3 places of worship, 7 Sunday schools, 3 day schools, 1 boarding school, and 277 professed Christians.

PARSEES: A people in India, numbering less than 100,000, resident mostly in Bombay, which, because of its romantic history, unique religion, commercial enterprise and fine character, is of an interest and importance beyond the expectation excited by its numbers. The Parsees, *i.e.*, "Persians," are descendants of the Zoroastrians who flourished in Persia until the 7th century, when the sword of the Mohammedans well nigh exterminated them, less than 10,000 of the sect, now called Guebres, surviving to-day in Persia. But a portion of the Zoroastrians escaped to India, where they settled in Gujarat as agriculturists until Muslim conquest in India again dislodged them and drove them southward. They reached Bombay between 1650-1700, about the time that this island city was ceded to the English by Portugal. The contact with Europeans, and especially with the English, caused a wonderful transformation, awakening in this hitherto agricultural people a genius for business which has brought them immense wealth and prestige. They early became and have continued to be the chief factors in the English trading houses in Bombay, and successful as traders, shopkeepers, and contractors on their own account. Up to the middle of the 19th century, when the development of the great steamship companies changed conditions, practically the whole of the trade of Bombay and China passed through their hands. Much of the latter was in their own ships, and the business was transacted through their own houses in London and the East. They also established themselves as dealers in European goods in the larger and in many of the smaller cities of India. A long succession of master builders in the government shipyards in Bombay have been Parsees; some have achieved success as army and railway contractors, Jamshedji Dorabji, tho without rudimentary, and much less engineering schooling, being the builder of large sections of the great India Peninsula Railway, and of other public works to the extent of a million sterling; some have established in Bombay extensive cotton and silk mills, while others became bankers; and the *Times of India*, one of the leading English papers in India, owes its origin to Parsee enterprise. In recent decades they have entered the learned professions and held prominent positions in the Bombay government.

Existing as a community by themselves in the midst of the composite mass of the Indian population, separated from others by their peculiar religion and customs, and with their own social organism, the Parsees are everywhere well-to-do, intelligent, and thrifty. The average degree of wealth is probably higher among them than among any other class in India. A Parsee beggar is never seen; the Parsee community always attends to the wants of its own poor, and suffers no members of its race to become a public burden. Their dress, dwellings, table appointments and social usages are a Hindu-European combination, in which the latter element tends to increase. Their ladies, handsomely dressed, with faces unveiled, are seen driving in well-appointed carriages and at public functions. Family life among them is generally happy. Formerly child marriages were a Parsee custom, but have now been abandoned, largely through growing appreciation of education for boys and girls.

Zeal for education is a notable characteristic of the Parsees. Up to the time of their contact with the English, education in their common speech, Gujarati, was rare. A smattering of English was at first acquired for business use, but the educational movement dates from the early part of the 19th century, when Parsees chiefly took advantage of the English schools opened by Eurasians. The Bombay Native Educational Society, founded in 1820 under the patronage of Governor Mountstuart Elphinstone, was the open door to higher education for the Parsees especially. Upon the retirement of this most eminent governor of Bombay, the Parsees took a leading part in commemorating his services by raising an endowment for the Elphinstone Institute for the teaching of the higher branches of European sciences and literature, and to this institution the little Parsee community has always supplied the majority of the students and in later years occupants for important chairs. They have also been quick to take advantage of the opportunities offered by the Jesuit, and the Scotch Presbyterian Missionary schools and colleges, and by the English and vernacular schools, established by the government and by private individuals.

But they have not been merely recipients of educational favors. In 1842, upon the knighting of one of their eminent men by the Queen, the Parsees celebrated the event by forming the Sir Jamshedji Jijibhoi Translation Fund, to be used in the translation of useful books into the Gujarati language, and the knight and his lady responded to the compliment by founding the Sir Jamshedji Jijibhoi Parsee Benevolent Institution, with an endowment providing a revenue of not less than 40,000 rupees per annum, devoted to the support of schools and maintenance of poor and aged Parsees. This and other endowments have provided a complete system of schools, which furnishes an English education for practically the whole rising generation of Parsees, and many, continuing their studies in the technical schools of Bombay and in Europe, have attained distinction as teachers and professional men. The Parsee Girls' School Association has made generous provisions for female education. Gifts for education have been a part of a larger benevolence, for the Parsees have not only been eminent as money-makers, but as money-givers as well, and they have set a good example to Western donors in making it their habit to give during their lifetime, rather than by legacy. Bombay is so dotted with roads, bridges, wells and fountains, hospitals, asylums, and colleges given by them that the city itself may be said to be their monument. At the time of his death in 1859, Sir Jamshedji Jijibhoi bore the palm in the history of philanthropy, having given more than $1,500,-000 to public charities, and he by no means stands alone as a princely Parsee giver. Their philanthropy has extended beyond their own people, and city, and country, as is evidenced in their assumption of the heavy tax imposed by Persia upon their fellow-Zoroastrians, the Guebres, and by their gifts to various funds in England and to the Sanitary Commission during the Civil War in the U. S. The Zoroastrian or Parsee religion is a monotheism, recognizing but one God, Ahura Mazda, or Ormuzd, the Creator, Ruler, and Preserver of the universe, without form and invisible, and to him all praise is to be given for all the good in this world and for all the blessings we enjoy. Under him are two spirits, Spento Mainyush (the creator spirit), and Angro Mainyush (the destructive spirit), through whose agency and interaction he is the cause of all causes in the universe. The Parsee creed also includes belief in guardian spirits or angels, in immortality, in the resurrection of the body, and in rewards and punishments. The Zend Avesta (the Zoroastrian Scripture), written in the Bactrian branch of the Iranian language, is free from immorality and cruelty, both in its characterization of deity and its directions for worship. It counsels resistance to all the activities of the evil spirit, and predicts the final triumph of good over evil.

Parsee temples are small, simple buildings, and contain no idols or other sacred objects except the ever-burning fire. The priesthood is hereditary. Worship consists in reading the Zend Avesta, adoring the sacred fire as the fittest symbol of Ahura Mazda, to whom, and the good spirits, prayer is offered, sprinkling with consecrated water, partaking in common of bread and wine, and offering up the juice of the Homa plant, which is done not only in the temples but in the houses twice a day. Magiism has influenced the development of the religious system, and astrology is practised in connection with all important events of life. The Parsees are frequently called fire-worshipers, but they resent this appellation, and claim that they use fire as the best symbol through which to worship deity, just as the Roman Catholics claim to use images, with probably a similar measure of truth. Reverence for the four elements, earth, air, fire, and water, is a part of their faith and has induced that peculiar method of disposing of the dead which is their most commonly known peculiarity. According to their belief, a dead body, the result of the working of the powers of evil, is unclean, and must not be allowed to contaminate by its presence any of the elements; it can neither be buried nor burnt nor thrown into the water, for in that way one of the elements would be defiled. It is therefore exposed in a circular structure without a roof, round the interior of which runs a shelf slightly sloping toward an opening at the center. After being deposited in this place the vultures make swift work with it, and the bones, stripped of flesh, are afterward swept down through the central aperture into a cavity below. These structures are called "towers of silence," and by their use the elements are saved from contamination and sanitation is maintained.

The study of the Parsee faith and people invites the judgment "not far from the kingdom of God." Their outward life and demeanor is always respectable and decorous. It is to be feared that their religion exerts but small influence over them, and that it has deteriorated to the level of a merely perfunctory formalism. Practically they are materialists—or at least secularists, given up to the enjoyment of the good things of this world and satisfied with the practise of the ordinary secular virtues. And their success in securing riches and station has induced a pride that makes them little accessible to the Gospel. The Parsee community was greatly stirred and made formal protest to the government when in 1839 two Parsee youths, who afterward served long as Christian ministers, were converted through the teaching of Dr. Wilson. Tho this resentment quickly subsided, and gave place to marked affection for that distinguished missionary, few Parsees have been converted since; and because the other inhabitants of Bombay present a so much more promising field, little missionary work has been done among them. But their close and intelligent contact with the people and literature of Christendom has already modified their belief. With their readiness to profit by the adoption of foreign usages in other departments of life, the hope is not groundless that they may yet, like their Magi of old, be drawn to Christ and prove a power in establishing His kingdom in the East.

Dosabhai Franji Karaka's *History of the Parsis*, 2 vols.

PARSONS, Justin Wright: Born at Westhampton, Mass., U. S. A., April 26, 1824; graduated at Williams College 1848; sailed April 24, 1850, as a missionary of the ABCFM, for Turkey. He was stationed at Nicomedia and Bardezag. For thirty years he labored with unflagging zeal, never so well contented as when upon tours among the hills and valleys of the district he traversed so often, that he might preach Christ to the villagers, who learned to love him and heed his teachings. Brave enough and cool enough to lead an army, he carried with him no weapon save the gospel of peace, and with this he had successfully disarmed, through a long series of years, all the opposition he met. He was on a missionary tour with Dudukian, a native Christian, when one evening in August, 1880, they camped for the night on the mountain side. During the night some nomad Turks chanced that way and shot the sleeping missionary and his companion for the sake of plundering their meager traveling kit. The outpouring of the whole population at the funeral bore witness to the power which the man's simple, devoted life had among the people.

PARSONS, Levi: Born at Goshen, Mass.; July 18, 1792; graduated at Middlebury College 1814; sailed November 3, 1819, with Pliny Fisk for Smyrna as a missionary of the ABCFM. After spending some months in Smyrna and at the Greek College on the island of Scio in order to learn the modern Greek, Mr. Parsons with Mr. Fisk made a tour of exploration through the region of the "Seven Churches of Asia." This was an experience of considerable danger at that time as well as of great interest. Leaving Mr. Fisk at Smyrna, Mr. Parsons went to Jerusalem in January, 1821, to prepare for its permanent occupation. He was the first Protestant missionary ever resident in Jerusalem with the intention of making it his field of labor. He had letters to prominent Greek ecclesiastics there and was cordially welcomed. But the outbreak of the Greek Revolution placed the Greeks of Syria in jeopardy of their lives, and Mr. Parsons was compelled to return to Smyrna, where in fact the danger from Turkish fanaticism was still greater. After Mr. Parsons and Mr. Fisk met again, the two went together to Egypt, hoping to reach Jerusalem safely from the south. But Mr. Parsons sickened and died at Alexandria February 10, 1822, a victim to his zeal to perform his duties as a pioneer in that strange undertaking to carry the Gospel to the people living heedless in the land where it was first proclaimed.

PARUR: A town in Madras, British India, situated in the district of S. Arcot, about 32 miles S. W. of Madurantakam. Population, 5,000. Station of the PB, with (1900) 1 missionary and his wife.

PARVATIPUR: A town in Madras, India, situated 75 miles N. of Vizagapatam. Population, 10,100, of whom 9,900 are Hindus. Station of the Berlin Missionary Society (1889), with (1903) 1 missionary and his wife, 19 native workers, 2 outstations, 1 place of worship, 1 Sunday school, 3 day schools, 1 theological class, 1 dispensary, and 67 professed Christians.

PASHTU LANGUAGE: The language of some 5,000,000 people inhabiting Afghanistan and adjacent territory. It is also called the Afghan language, or Afghani. It belongs to the Iranian group of Aryan languages, and is written with Arabic letters modified by adding dots, as in Persian, and in a few cases in a fashion peculiar to Pashtu.

PASUMALAI: A town in Madras, India, 3 miles southwest of Madras City, on the railway to Tuticorin. Climate healthy; average annual temperature, 85° F.; rainfall, 35 inches. Station of the ABCFM (1845), with (1903) 2 missionaries, one with his wife; 36 native workers, 7 outstations, 1 place of worship, 9 Sunday schools, 6 day schools, 2 boarding schools, 1 theological school, 1 printing house, 1 industrial school, 1 dispensary, and 215 professed Christians.

PASPUR: A town in the Punjab, India, situated in the district of Sialkot, 47 miles N. by W. of Amritsar. Population, 9,200, of whom 2,400 are Hindus and 6,400 Mohammedans. Station of the UP (1876), with (1900) 1 woman missionary, 8 Sunday schools, 5 day schools, and 74 communicant Christians.

PATERSON: A town in Cape Colony, South Africa, situated in the Transkei region, about 18 miles W. by N. of Blythwood. Station of the UFS (1868), with (1903) 1 missionary and his wife, 25 native workers, 14 outstations, 2 places of worship, 5 Sunday schools, 11 day schools, and 1,408 professed Christians

PATHANKOT: A municipality of the Punjab, India, situated in the district of Gurdaspur, about 68 miles N. E. of Amritsar, the nearest railway station to Kangra and Dalhousie, a sanitary hill station. Population, 5,000. Station of the UP (1880), with (1900) 1 missionary and his wife, 1 woman missionary, 4 outstations, 1 day school, and 1 Sunady school.

PATIALA: An ancient town in the Punjab, India, about 24 miles W. by S. of Ambala. Population, 5,000. Station of the ME, with (1903) 15 native workers, 2 places of worship, 28 Sunday schools, 11 day schools, and 474 professed Christians, of whom 35 are communicants. Station also of the Reformed Presbyterian General Synod of the United States, with (1901) 1 woman missionary, 5 native workers, 4 outstations, 60 professed Christians, 2 places of worship, 1 day school, and 1 dispensary.

PATNA: A city in Bengal, India, on the Ganges, 320 miles northwest of Calcutta. The town is extensive, but its streets are narrow and crooked, and its houses irregularly built, of many materials. It is on the East Indian R. R., and is the center of the opium trade. Climate said to be unhealthy, but the natives are strong in physique and give no evidence of this. Population (1901) 134,785. Station of the BMS (1888), with (1903) 2 missionaries and their wives, 3 native workers, 1 Sunday school, and 1 day school. Station also of the ZBM, with 7 women missionaries, 7 native workers, 1 day school, 1 dispensary, 1 hospital, and 150 Zenana pupils.

PATPARA: A town in the Central Provinces of India, situated in the district of Mandla, 42 miles S. E. of Jabalpur. Station of the CMS (1887), with (1903) 2 missionaries and their wives, 1 place of worship, 6 day schools, 1 hospital, 1 orphanage, and 576 professed Christians, of whom 103 are communicants (including Marpha). Station also of the MLI (1895), with (1903) 1 leper asylum

PATTERSON, Alexander: A native of Leith, Scotland; sent out by the Scottish Missionary Society to explore Tatary in 1802, accompanied by Henry Brunton. On arriving at St. Petersburg he met so many discouragements that he felt inclined to turn back, when he unexpectedly found a friend in the lord of the emperor's bedchamber, M. Novassilgoff. Passports were given him, and full liberty granted to travel through the empire, and select any place as a residence agreeable to him. The government also gave them a large grant of land, and permission to keep under their care and instruction any Tatar youths they might ransom from slavery until they were twenty-three years of age.

They chose a Mohammedan village called Karass, in the Nogai Steppe, as the place for the commencement of their mission. Both the missionaries studied the Turkish language. As soon as they began circulating some tracts they had written in the language great interest was excited, and discussions arose as to the merits of Christ and Mohammed, and many persons of rank became interested in the teachings of the Gospel.

In 1805 Mr. Patterson had the joy of seeing several of the ransomed youths embrace Christianity and be baptized. They also went with him on his journeys, acting as interpreters. In 1810 the mission was making such progress among the people that the Mohammedan priests became alarmed, and aroused the bitterest opposition. The Mohammedan tribes south of Karass were so zealous that they threatened to kill all who bore the Christian name. The Mohammedan schools were crowded with scholars, who were taught to read that they might defend the faith.

In 1813 the missionaries were obliged to move to the fortified town Georghievisk, about 30 miles from Karass, on account of the constant irruptions of hostile Turks. While here the translation and binding of the New Testament were finished. In 1814 the missionaries again went back to Karass. In 1816 Mr. Patterson took with him one of the ransomed slaves and made a tour through the Crimea, distributing tracts and Turkish Testaments. The journey almost cost him his life, but he felt amply repaid in the reception he met from all classes of people.

PATTESON, John Coleridge: The missionary bishop and martyr of Melanesia, born London, England, April 2, 1827. His father was Sir John Patteson, a distinguished English judge, and his mother a niece of Samuel Taylor Coleridge, the poet. He was educated at Ottery St. Mary, Devonshire, 1835-37; at Eton, 1838; Baliol College, Oxford, graduating B.A., 1845. In 1849 he obtained a scholarship in Merton College. Through his schooldays he took high rank as a linguist. In 1852 he became a Fellow of Merton College. In 1853 he was curate of Alfington, and in 1854 was ordained. In 1855, March 29, he sailed with Bishop Selwyn to the Melanesian Islands, in the South Pacific. During the voyage he acquired the Maori language. For five years he was assistant to the bishop in conducting a training school for native assistants. In 1861 he was made bishop of the Melanesian Islands. He now reduced to writing several of the island languages, which before this had never been written. He also prepared grammars of these languages and translated parts of the New Testament into the Lifu language. His headquarters after being appointed bishop were at Motu, in the Northern New Hebrides, from which he made frequent excursions and voyages to the other islands of his diocese in the mission ship "The Southern Cross," exerting himself in various ways for the good of the people. When the missionary ship, as it cruised among the islands, approached Nakapu Island, some of the islanders, mistaking it for a craft which had kidnaped some of the islanders, determined to avenge themselves. The bishop, unsuspicious, lowered his boat, and went to meet them coming in their canoes. According to their custom, they asked him to get into one of their boats, which he did, and was taken to the shore. He was never seen alive again. Immediate search was made, and his body found, pierced with five wounds. In early life he was a leader in all athletic sports. The same elastic strength of body and skill in manipulation fitted him to be preacher, teacher, navigator, friend, and exemplar in the useful arts to the Melanesian tribes.

PAUL, Samuel: Born in 1843. Died in 1900. A native Christian of India. Educated at Palamcotta Preparandi Institution. Appointed by the CMS catechist at Ootacamund, and in 1874 he was ordained pastor of the Tamil local mission at the same place. He was the first to organize this mission, and after his faithful service at Ootacamund he was transferred to the Northern Pastorate, in the city of Madras, where he accomplished much for the development of the congregation at Black Town. Subsequently Sachiapuram, in the Tinnevelli district, was his headquarters, and he was appointed vice-chairman of the native church council in Tinnevelli, and chairman of two important church circles. Mr. Paul did a good work for Tamil Christian literature. He prepared for publication a large number of important works—original and translations—which have been widely read by Tamil Christians. The following works from his pen are worthy of special mention: Edited (in Tamil) *History of the Church of England; History of the Book of Common Prayer; Geography of the Madras; "Zillah;" Geography of the Nilgherries*, and several translations from the Madras Tract Society and the Christian Vernacular Education Society. Chiefly for his literary work he was honored by the Government with the title of "Rao Sahib" ("Rao" is a Hindu title for a chief or prince). Mr. Paul left a deep impression for good upon his native land.

PAURI: A town in the United Provinces, India, situated in the district of Garhwal about 25 miles N. N. W. of Dwarahat. Station of the ME, with (1903) 1 missionary and his wife, 1 woman missionary, 60 native workers, 7 places of worship, 12 day schools, 2 boarding schools, 1 orphanage, 35 Sunday schools, and 521 professed Christians, of whom 218 are communicants.

PAYNE, John: Born in 1814; appointed in 1836 by the Protestant Episcopal Missionary Society in the United States as missionary to Africa, and sailed May, 1837, reaching Cape Palmas, Liberia, on the 4th of July following. He was consecrated missionary bishop July 11, 1851. During thirty-four years he was a faithful and laborious worker, both as a missionary and bishop, in one of the most unhealthy portions of the globe, until the strain of it left him a mere wreck of a man. He resigned his office in 1871, and died at Oak Grove, Westmoreland Co., Va., October 23, 1874, aged 60.

PEA RADJA: A settlement in Sumatra, Dutch E. Indies, situated in the Silindung Valley, about 25 miles N. E. of Siboga. It is the central point of the Rhenish mission in the Silindung region, with (1903) 3 missionaries and their wives, 4 women missionaries, 90 native workers, 8 outstations, 8 Sunday schools, 11 day schools, 1 dispensary, 1 hospital, and 8,046 professed Christians, of whom 3,701 are communicants.

PEDDAPUR: A town of Madras, India, in the district of Godavari, 87 miles W. S. W. of Vizagapatam. Population, 13,700, of whom 13,000 are Hindus. Station of the BOQ (1891), with 1 missionary and his wife, 1 woman missionary, 24 native workers, 7 outstations, 7 places of worship, 11 Sunday schools, 8 day schools, 7 places of worship, and 320 professed Christians. Some write the name Peddapuram.

PEDDIE: A town in Cape Colony, Africa, situated 25 miles S. W. of King William's Town. Station of the SPG, with 1 missionary and 236 professed Christians. Station also of the South Africa Wesleyan Methodists, with 1 missionary, 43 native workers, 20 outstations, 6 places of worship, 6 Sunday schools, 4 day schools, and 391 professed Christians. Station also of the Women's Society of the same church, with 1 woman missionary and 1 boarding school. Some use the name Fort Peddie.

PEDI LANGUAGE: One of the Bantu family of African languages, spoken by a number, not yet known, of tribes inhabiting, for the most part, the Transvaal Colony in South Africa. It has been reduced to writing by missionaries, and for this purpose the Roman alphabet has been used.

PEGU: A town in Burma, British India; the former capital of the kingdom of Pegu, 40 miles northeast of Rangoon, on the railroad to Mandalay. The inhabitants are largely Talaings or Peguans. Station of the ABMU (1887), with (1903) 2 women missionaries, 13 native workers, 6 outstations, 5 places of worship, 2 Sunday schools, 3 day schools, and 275 professed Christians. Station also of the ME, with (1903) 1 missionary and his wife, 6 native workers, 5 Sunday schools, 1 day school, and 157 professed Christians, of whom 39 are communicants.

PEI-KAN: A town in the province of Kiang-si, China, situated 56 miles E. of Nan-chang-fu. Station of the CIM (1893), with (1903) 2 women missionaries, 3 native workers, 2 outstations, 4 places of worship, and 25 professed Christians. Some write the name Peh-kan.

PEKING: Capital of the Chinese Empire, situated on a plain about 12 miles southwest of the Pei-ho, in latitude 39° 54' 36" north, longitude 116° 27' east. Its name means Northern Capital, in opposition to Nanking, which was the capital for a time. It became the seat of government under Kublai Khan in 1264, and has continued to be the capital ever since, except during the years when the emperors held their court at Nanking. The city is divided into two parts, each surrounded by a wall. The inner or Manchu city, where are the palace, government buildings, and barracks, is surrounded by a wall of an average height of 50 feet and a circumference of 14 miles. Adjoining this at the south is the outer or Chinese city, whose wall is one of the finest in the world, being 10 miles in circuit, 30 feet high, 15 feet broad at the top and 30 feet at the ground, pierced with 16 gates, each one surmounted with a many-storied tower 100 feet high, with embrasures for cannon. Within both walls is enclosed about 26 square miles, and the great size of Peking, with the numerous public buildings, the palaces, pagodas, temples, broad avenues, lofty gates and massive wall, has challenged the wonder of all visitors since the stories of Marco Polo gave him an unjust reputation as a second Munchausen. Within the Manchu city a smaller enclosure, of three miles in circuit, surrounds the "Forbidden City," containing the palaces of the emperor and his consort. The age of the city is not definitely known. It has been built and rebuilt many times, and now is not at the zenith of its magnificence, which it attained at the time of the Emperor Kanghi. It is the best specimen of a purely Asiatic city now existing. The population is of a most varied character. Chinese predominate, but Manchus are numerous, and Kalmucks, Tatars, Koreans, Russians, and representatives of almost every country of Central Asia are found in the crowds that throng its streets, and add to the picturesqueness of its appearance by the motley and diversified colors of their dress. The number of inhabitants has been variously estimated from 1,000,000 to 3,000,000—the mean between these two estimates is probably correct. By reason of the lack of tall spires or buildings, the view from a distance is not imposing, the only prominent buildings being the Clock Tower, where a water clock measures the time, and the Bell Tower, whose ancient bell (cast in 1406), the largest suspended bell in the world (120,000 lbs. weight), tolls forth the watches of the night. Of the many noteworthy buildings, none is of such interest to the missionary as the altars where the emperor offers worship to Heaven and to the Earth. (See **Confucianism**.) The Altar to Heaven stands to the left of the south gate, within the Chinese city; the Altar to Earth is without the walls, to the north of the Manchu city. Separated only by a wall from the Altar to Heaven is the "Altar of Prayer for Grain," often wrongly called the Temple of Heaven, which was one of the most beautiful buildings of the East. Its triple, dome-shaped roofs towered 100 feet high, and were covered with blue porcelain tiles. Its base was a triple terraced altar of white marble. Large teakwood pillars arranged in circular rows supported its roofs, and it was enclosed with windows, shaded with blinds of blue-glass rods. The destruction of this temple by fire in the fall of 1889 was regarded by the Chinese as a visitation of the wrath of Heaven upon the emperor himself. Not only is worship paid to Heaven, but the temples of almost every form of religious belief are found here. Islam is represented by the mosque outside of the southwestern angle of the Imperial city, in the midst of a number of Mohammedans who came from Turkestan over a hundred years ago. Not far from the mosque, to the southwest, is an old Portuguese church, and inside of the Manchu city, west of the Forbidden City, is the Roman Catholic cathedral. The Greek Church and various Protestant churches also have their respective houses of worship, besides Buddhism and the pantheon of Chinese gods or deified heroes.

In the limited space of this article no more than a mere mention can be made of the Sacrificial Hall to Confucius; the monument to the lama who died, some say was murdered, at Peking; the examination hall, and the parks and artificial lakes with which successive emperors have beautified the city. The ruins of the Summer Palace, which was destroyed by the allied French and English forces during the occupation of the city in 1860, lie to the northwest of the city, about 7 miles away. Here small hills with intervening vales had been beautified with pleasure-houses and bowers in the best of Chinese style, and in the various buildings were collected the treasures of many dynasties and monarchs; a rich booty they proved to the wanton pillage of the soldiers. Following the Boxer outbreak and the memorable siege of the British Legation, the troops which saved the beleaguered foreigners in August, 1900, similarly looted the palaces of the Forbidden City. The incidents of the weeks of foreign occupation of Peking will not readily be forgotten by any Chinese.

The streets of Peking are in general wide and spacious. The center is sometimes paved and is somewhat higher than at the sides. In summer the dust from the unpaved portion, and in winter the mud, make them intensely disagreeable to the passer-by. The aspect of the city entirely differs from that of the other Chinese cities, where commerce brings a distinctive European element and settlement. The climate is healthy, but subject to extremes of heat and cold, and the dryness for ten months of the year is hard to bear. Peking Mandarin, as the language of the capital is called, is the standard language of the empire.

Missionary work is carried on in Peking by the following Societies: LMS (1861), PN (1863), SPG (1863), ABCFM (1864), ME (1869), CA, and the Mission to Chinese Blind. These societies together have (1903) 57 missionaries, men and women; 48 native workers, 24 places of worship, 22 schools, 9 dispensaries or hospitals, 2 printing houses, and 1,473 professed Christians. Besides these societies the YMCA has a local secretary here and the National Bible Society of Scotland maintains an agent, with 8 native workers.

PELLA: A town in the Transvaal, South Africa, in the district of Rustenberg, and about 100 miles W. by N. of Pretoria. Population, 3,000. Station of the Hermannsburg Missionary Society (1868), with (1901) 1 missionary and his wife, 2 native workers, 1 outstation, 2 places of worship, 1 day school, and 728 professed Christians.

PELOTAS: A town and seaport of Brazil, South America, situated in the State of Rio Grande do Sul, at the S. W. of Lake Patos. Population, 33,000. Station of the American Church Missionary Society (1892), with (1901) 1 missionary and his wife, 1 outstation, 2 places of worship, 1 Young People's Society, and 93 professed Christians.

PEMBA ISLAND: An island off the E. coast of Africa, 30 miles N. of Zanzibar, and belonging to the British protectorate of Zanzibar. It produces excellent timber and plentiful supplies for shipping. Population, 10,000. Station of the Universities Mission to Central Africa (1898), with (1903) 1 missionary and his wife, 1 woman missionary, 3 native workers, 1 outstation, 1 place of worship, 2 day schools, 1 boarding school, 1 dispensary, and 41 professed Christians, of whom 24 are communicants.

PENANG, or PRINCE OF WALES ISLAND: An island lying at the north entrance of the Straits of Malacca, and one of the Straits Settlements belonging to England. It contains 106 square miles, reaches an altitude, in the hilly district, of 2,922 feet, and has a rich, fertile soil, where tropical fruits and spices are cultivated. The climate is healthy, and rain falls every month in the year. Georgetown, the capital, is at the northeastern end of the island. Population, including Province Wellesley and the Dindings (1901), 248,207, of whom 140,102 are Chinese, Malays, and other Asiatics. The Europeans and Americans number 1,160. Station of the ME, with (1903) 2 missionaries, one with his wife; 4 women missionaries, 8 native workers, 1 outstation, 4 places of worship, 10 Sunday schools, 4 day schools, 2 boarding schools, and 242 professed Christians, of whom 132 are communicants. Station also of the PB, with 5 missionaries, four of them with their wives, and 4 women missionaries. Station also of the SPG (1871), with (1903) 5 native workers, 2 places of worship, 2 day schools, and 143 professed Christians, of whom 25 are communicants. The BFBS has an agent residing here.

PENDRA ROAD: A railroad station in the Central Provinces of India, situated about 60 miles N. N. W. of Bilaspur. Station of the CWBM (1901), with 1 missionary and his wife.

PERAK: A protected British state in the Malay Peninsula, lying S. of Siamese Kedah and Province of Wellesley, and N. of Selangor. In Perak is a station of the PB, with 2 missionaries and their wives and 1 woman missionary. There is a station also of the SPG, with (1903) 1 missionary, 1 native worker, 2 places of worship, and 45 professed Christians.

PERIAKULAM: A municipality in Madras, India, situated 44 miles W. N. W. of Madura. Population, 16,400, of whom 14,000 are Hindus. Station of the ABCFM (1856), with (1903) 1 missionary and his wife, 52 native workers, 42 outstations, 34 places of worship, 29 Sunday schools, 23 day schools, and 996 professed Christians.

PERIE: A village in Cape Colony, South Africa, situated 15 miles N. W. of King William's Town, in a well-timbered region. Station of the UFS, with 1 missionary and his wife, 23 native workers, 9 outstations, 1 place of worship, 9 day schools, and 737 professed Christians. Some write the name Pirie.

PERKINS, Justin: Born at West Springfield, Mass., March 12, 1805; graduated at Amherst College, 1829; studied theology at Andover; embarked September 21, 1833, as a missionary of the ABCFM, and one of the founders of the Nestorian Mission at Urmia, Persia. Schools established by Dr. Perkins and Dr. Grant are now flourishing seminaries. Dr. Perkins translated the Scriptures and several religious books into Syriac. He visited the United States in 1842, accompanied by the Nestorian bishop, Mar Yohannan, whose presence and addresses awakened a deep interest in the mission. Returning to Persia in 1843, he labored successfully at his post, and ably defended Protestantism against misrepresentation and persecution. In 1869 impaired health compelled him to relinquish the work, in which he had been engaged for thirty-six years. He died at Chicopee, Mass., in the same year.

PERNAMBUCO: A city and seaport on the N. E. coast of Brazil, S. America, situated at the mouth of the Beberibe and Capeberibe. It is the greatest sugar mart in the country. The business houses of the city are chiefly built on a low, sandy peninsula called Recife, and the city is often spoken of as "Recife" for this reason. The central part of the city stands on the island of S. Antonio, while the finer residential districts are at Bōa Vista, on the mainland. Formerly the city was very dirty and suffered from a lack of water. This has now been changed to a great extent, as prosperity has brought wealth and attracted Europeans as residents. The population (1890) is 111,555, composed of very mixed elements. Station of the PS (1873), with (1903) 1 missionary and his wife, 5 native workers, 2 places of worship, 1 theological class, 1 dispensary, 18 outstations, and 576 professed Christians. Station also of the SBC (1889), with (1903) 2 missionaries and their wives, 12 native workers, 34 outstations, 2 places of worship, 5 day schools, 2 Sunday schools, and 569 professed Christians. Station also of the Help for Brazil Society.

PERSIA: The modern kingdom of Persia, called by the natives *Iran*, occupies, roughly speaking, that part of Western Asia lying between the Caspian Sea on the north and the Persian Gulf on the south, Afghanistan and Baluchistan on the east and Turkey on the west. Its exact boundaries have not as yet been definitely located, but starting from Mount Ararat at the northwest, the river Aras forms the greater part of its boundary line between that part of Russia lying west of the Caspian Sea, tho there is a small strip of country extending south of the river Aras along the Caspian Sea which does not belong to Persia. East of the Caspian, Russian Turkestan bounds it on the north, tho the exact limits of Persian territory have not been accurately settled, Russian authorities claiming more than is allowed by other European powers. On the east the boundary lines between Afghanistan and Baluchistan have been determined by British commissioners at different times, altho some parts of it are still disputed. Its southern and southwestern boundary is the coast-line of the Arabian Sea and the Persian Gulf. Its western boundary from Mount Ararat in a general southwesterly direction to the Persian Gulf is the disputed Perso-Turkish frontier, for the settlement of which a mixed commission, appointed in 1843, labored for 25 years, with the result that the disputed territory has been defined rather than the exact boundaries delimited.

Persia extends for about 700 miles from north to south, and 900 miles from east to west, and includes an area estimated at 628,000 square miles. The greater part of this region is an elevated plateau, almost a perfect tableland in the center and on the east, but cut up by mountain chains on the north, the west, and the south. More than three-fourths of its entire surface is desert land, but many of the valleys between the high mountain ranges are wonderfully fertile and exceedingly beautiful. Rare flowers, luscious fruits, valuable timber, and mountain brooks and torrents make the land a scene of picturesque beauty which is celebrated in history and song, and indissolubly connected with the ideas of Persia. With such a diversity of physical characteristics there is of necessity a diversity of climate. On the plateau the climate is temperate; at Ispahan summer and winter are equally mild, and regular seasons follow each other. At the north and the northwest severe winters are experienced, while the inhabitants of the desert region in the center and on the east of it are scorched in summer and frozen in winter. Along the Caspian Sea the summer heat is intense, while the winters are mild, and heavy and frequent rainfalls make the low country marshy and unhealthy. In the southern provinces, tho the heat in autumn is excessive, winter and spring are delightful; and summer, tho hot, is not unpleasant, since the atmosphere of Persia in general is remarkable for its dryness and purity.

The population of Persia is about 9,000,000. The majority are engaged mainly in agriculture, and the best wheat in the world, together with other cereals, is raised, and cotton, sugar, rice, and tobacco are produced in the southern provinces. The wandering tribes dwell in tents, and move about with their flocks and herds as the seasons succeed each other, spending the spring and summer on the mountain slopes and the winter on the plains. The two principal races are the Turks and the Persians. There are also Arabs, Kurds, Leks, and Baluchis.

The principal cities of Persia, with their population, are: Teheran, 250,000; Tabriz, 185,000; Ispahan and Meshed, each with 80,000; Kerman and Yezd, each with 60,000. It is estimated that 8,000,000 of the population belong to the Shiah faith, 750,000 are Sunnis, 10,500 Parsees, 20,000 Jews, 53,000 Armenians, and 30,000 Nestorians.

The government of Persia is similar to that of Turkey. It is a kingdom whose king is called the Shah. He is the absolute ruler and the master of the lives and goods of all his subjects; but tho his power is absolute, he must not act contrary to the accepted doctrines of the Mohammedan religion as laid down by the prophet and interpreted by the highpriesthood. The laws are based on the precepts of the Koran, and the Shah is regarded as vicegerent of the prophet. A ministry, divided into several departments, after the European fashion, assists him in the executive department of the government. A governor-general is appointed over each one of the 27 provinces, who is directly responsible to the central government. The nomad tribes are ruled over by their chiefs, who are responsible to the governors.

The only instruction of the bulk of the population is from the teachings of the Koran, but there are a great number of so-called colleges supported by public funds, where students are instructed not only in religion, and Persian and Arabic literature, but also in scientific knowledge.

History: It is not the province of this article to give any sketch of the history of the country of Persia, but the following dates of the principal epochs in its history may be of service. From the earliest records, dating back to about 2,000 B.C., the first rulers of Persia were the Medes, who conquered Babylonia and established a Medo-Persian empire, which lasted, under the rule of famous kings—Cyrus, Cambyses, Darius, Xerxes, and Artaxerxes—until the conquest by Alexander the Great, 331 B.C., when the Greek and Parthian Empire was established, which ended about the middle of the 2d century. The Sassanian Empire, from the beginning of the 3d century lasted until about the end of the 7th, when the period of Arabian domination commenced, and gradually grew in extent and influence. Mohammedanism completely captured the life and permeated the thought of the people to the very core. Persia was at times a province, and the center of the Arabian Empire, under successive rulers of Arab, Turk, or Mongol origin. The sway of the Timurides and Turkomans lasted from 1405 to 1499. From 1499 to 1736 the Sufi or Sufawi dynasty ruled the country. Its founder was Ismail Sufi. With the accession of Nadir Shah, 1736, the last native Persian dynasty passed away. At the death of Nadir Shah in 1747 a period of anarchy, followed by short reigns of various despots, ensued, until in 1794 Agha Mohammed ascended the throne—the first of the reigning dynasty of the Kajars. The present Shah, Muzaffar-ed-din, succeeded his father in 1896.

Missions in Persia: When the religion of Christ was accepted by Constantine (312) it was stigmatized by the rival empire of the East as the religion of the Romans. Religious zeal and national feeling united against it, and bitter persecutions continued in Persia for a century after they had ceased in the Roman Empire. The sufferings of Christians under Shapûr II., the Sassanian, were as terrible as any experienced under Diocletian.

In the face of these obstacles it is clear that the Christian faith had a harder mission field in Asia than in Europe. The 3d century saw Christian missions there advancing generally in peace. The 4th century was full of conflict and persecution, with an open door and many adversaries. The pious and zealous monks of Egypt and Syria were the leading missionaries, and their labors are still attested by the many churches that bear their names in Mesopotamia and among the Nestorians. The Armenians were largely converted, and the Georgians. In this century also strong heretical sects took shape, that have left relics to the present day.

In the 5th century the bitter controversies within the church resulted in the separation of the Eastern Christians from the West. The Nestorian controversy at the Council of Ephesus (431) resulted in a schism which was carried thence to Edessa, and thence to Persia. The separation of the main body of Christians under the Persian rule was completed in a council held at Seleucia 499. There were political reasons for this separation as well as theological. It gave satisfaction to the Persian Government to have its Christian subjects break their connection entirely with the Romans, and thus it gave rest from persecution. In the 6th and 7th centuries there was much missionary activity by the Persian Church.

Under the Caliphs: 641-1258. The dominant religion of Persia from the primeval days had been the faith of Zoroaster. Christianity failed to overthrow it. To this mighty religion, which once seemed likely to supersede all others and be proclaimed in the edicts of the great king over Europe as well as Asia, the fatal blow came suddenly, and from a quarter least expected. The Persian Emperor received a letter one day from "the camel-driver of Mecca," bidding him abjure the faith of his ancestors and confess that "there is no God but God, and Mohammed is the prophet of God." The indignant monarch tore the letter to pieces, and drove the camel-drivers who brought it from his presence. But before ten years had passed the Arab hordes had driven the Persian from his throne. Persia, defeated in two decisive battles, reluctantly gave up the contest. The whole system fell with a crash, and the only remnants left to perpetuate its rites are some 5,000 souls in Yezd, a city of Persia, and 100,000 Parsees in Bombay.

The faith of Mohammed from that day to this has ruled in Persia. The Persian is the only Aryan race that accepted Islam.

Under the Mogul Tartars: 1258-1430. The Moguls arose in Chinese Tartary. The last of the race of Christian kings—Christian in name, doubtless, more than in reality—was slain by Genghis Khan about 1202. Genghis had a Christian wife, the daughter of this king, and he was tolerant toward the Christian faith. In fact, the Mogul conquerors were without much religion, and friendly toward all. The wave of carnage and conquest swept westward and covered Persia, and overwhelmed the Caliph of Bagdad in 1258. This change was for a time favorable to the Christians, as the rulers openly declared themselves Christians, or were partial to Christianity. The patriarch of the Nestorians was chosen from people of the same speech and race as the conquerors—a native of Western China. He ruled the church through a stormy period of seven reigns of Mogul kings; had the joy of baptizing some of them, and of indulging for a time the hope that they would form such an alliance with the Christians of Europe against the Muslims as would render all Asia, across to China, a highway for the Christian faith. But the period of such hope was brief, and soon ended in threatened ruin. The Christian faith was thrown back upon its last defenses, and became a hunted and despised faith, with only a remnant of adherents clinging with a death grip to their churches and worship.

The Period of Greatest Depression: 1400-1830. Persia was torn by factions and wars for a century. As France rejected the Reformation and reaped her reward in anarchy and blood, so Persia suffered on a larger scale. The Christian Church was lost—a buried and apparently lifeless seed only remaining—and the Christian name became a by-word.

The Sufi or Sufawi kings (1499-1736) ruled over large populations of Armenians and Georgians, Nestorians, and Jacobites in what is now Russian and Turkish territory. Meanwhile the Reformation came to Europe, and the revival of the spirit of propagandism in the Romish Church. Toward the close of the 16th century occurred some events bearing on Persian missions, especially during the reign of Shah Abbas the Great (1582-1627), the contemporary of Queen Elizabeth. One was diplomatic intercourse between England and Persia. The first attempt was a failure, for in 1561 Anthony Jenkinson arrived in Persia with letters from Queen Elizabeth for Tamasp Shah. At their interview the Shah's first question was, "Are you a Muslim or an infidel?" He replied that he was not a Muslim nor was he an infidel. But the Shah expressed his dissatisfaction, and the Englishman retired, and every step of his was immediately sprinkled with sand and swept to remove the defilement of his contact with the royal court. But in 1598 Sir Anthony and Robert Shirley had better success, for they arrived in Persia with a numerous retinue, and for many years were intimately associated with Shah Abbas, and laid the foundation of English influence in the East.

Following upon the Sufawi kings was an Afghan invasion of Persia, lasting through seven years of massacre and misrule. Then arose Nadir Shah, who extended the Persian frontier far eastward and westward, and pillaged India. A generation of anarchy and civil war followed until the rise of the present line of kings, called the *Kajar* line, from the ancestral tribe from which they spring. Since the opening of the 19th century these kings have ruled, and an era of comparative peace has come. For twelve centuries Mohammedanism, in one form or another, has controlled the government, and molded the laws and morals and destinies of the millions of Persia.

Modern Christian Missions: Manifestly the ancient and medieval missions in Persia have failed to Christianize the nation. The way for modern Protestant missions began to open with the opening of the 19th century. The Persian language, through the Mogul emperors and the conquests of Nadir Shah, became the polite language of a large part of India, and the *lingua franca* of all Western Asia. The East India Company required their officials to study the Persian, until the time of Lord Macaulay, when English became the official language. Persia also from its position has an importance as a political power that was courted by Napoleon, by Russia, and by England. Thus it came to pass that splendid embassies were sent to Persia early in the century, and English influence most of all controlled affairs for several decades. Henry Martyn was a chaplain in India, and there acquired the Persian language. He came to Persia in 1811 to complete and improve the Persian translation of the New Testament. No one can read his memoir covering the eleven months that he spent in Shiraz and not marvel at his boldness in confessing Christ and his deliverance from the bigoted Mollahs. But both his witness and his book were rejected with scorn. The devoted missionary left the country without knowing of a single convert. Nevertheless his translation of the New Testament and the Psalms was the lasting fruit of his labors. He wrote on completing it this prayer: "Now may the Spirit who gave the word, and called me, I trust, to be an interpreter of it, graciously and powerfully apply it to the hearts of sinners, even to gathering an elect people from the long-estranged Persians." Many wonderful facts in later years show that this prayer is being answered.

The next laborer was the Rev. C. G. Pfander, of the Basel Missionary Society. He visited Persia in 1829, and at intervals for a few years sojourned there, passing part of his time in Shusha, Georgia, where his brethren from Germany then had a flourishing mission. This learned and devoted man came near sealing his testimony with his blood at Kermanshah, in Western Persia, but was preserved for protracted labors. He died at Constantinople in 1869. His great work for Persia is "The Balance of Truth," a book comparing Christianity and Mohammedanism. This work and several other treatises on the controversy with Islam were published in India, and are doing a great deal secretly in Persia to direct the thousands whose faith in their religion is shaken. The same works, perhaps unwisely published in Turkey before Dr. Pfander's death, led to severe persecution, and to a strict suppression of all books aimed at the system of Islam. But the books still live, and have their work to do, for they are exhaustive and unanswerable.

After several such sporadic missionary ventures in Persia, Dr. Joseph Wolf, about 1827, visited Persia. He was a converted Jew, a great traveler, and a voluminous writer. To this latter fact was due the decision of the ABCFM to send men in 1830 to examine the condition of the Nestorian Church, described by Dr. Wolf. As a result the ABCFM determined to establish a mission to the Nestorians. Rev. Justin Perkins and his wife embarked in the fall of 1833. They reached Tabriz about a year later, and in the summer of 1835 were joined by Dr. and Mrs. Grant. This little company of two missionaries and their wives arrived at Oroomiah formally to occupy the place as a station in November, 1835. Meanwhile the ABCFM in 1834 sent out the Rev. J. L. Merrick, who had specially prepared himself to explore the Mohammedan field of Persia and Central Asia. He continued a missionary till 1843. He traveled extensively in company with Mr. Haas, and both came near losing their lives in an encounter with the Mollahs in Ispahan. Mr. Merrick's labors resulted only in teaching some Persian youths the English language and science, and in translating the Shi'ite traditional Life of Mohammed. It became evident that Providence had not yet opened the way to labor directly for the Mohammedans.

The roll of this mission counts fifty-two missionaries, men and women, sent out previous to 1871. Time would fail to tell of all these. The pioneers, Messrs. Perkins and Grant, were enthusiastic and apostolic men. One of them, Dr. Grant, finished his career in 1845. Thousands in America and England became familiar with his work through his letters and his book on the *Mountain Nestorians*, and his *Memoir*, written by a colleague in the mountain work, Dr. Laurie. His grave is by the shores of the Tigris, while the account of his labors has passed into the annals of the Church's heroes.

Justin Perkins, D.D., was spared to labor for more than thirty-six years, dying on the last day of 1869. His eminent services were seen in pioneer work, and in making known the Nestorians. In his later days he was a real patriarch, with all the venerable bearing and deep piety of the best fathers of old.

The force of missionaries was steadily increased from time to time by the arrival of other men. The work of the ABCFM was almost entirely for the Nestorians, numbering about 100,000 souls, partly in Persia and partly in Kurdistan, under Turkish rule. The preparatory work was followed by a remarkable ingathering, and then came years of organizing and training.

The work accomplished was to establish an enterprise with all the appliances and parts of an aggressive reformation in this old church, a thousand miles east of Constantinople, in the heart of Islam—the press, the training-schools for young men and young women, a band of over fifty native pastors and evangelists, an aggregate of over eighty schools and congregations. The results were great in themselves, and greater in their bearing upon the future.

The Presbyterian Board, 1871 to this day: By the union of the two great branches of the Presbyterian Church in 1870, the New School body ceased its support of the ABCFM, and claimed a portion of the mission as its heritage. "The Mission to the Nestorians" was transferred to the care of the Presbyterian Board in 1871. The work has since been widely extended into Eastern Persia and to reach Armenians, Kurds, and to some extent Persian Mohammedans. On the other hand, the work among the Nestorians has been profoundly affected by the entrance of Russian missionaries, who have won a large proportion of the Nestorian Church to rejoin the Eastern Church from which their fathers seceded fifteen hundred years ago.

A notable event was the celebration of the jubilee of this work in 1885, followed by prevailing revivals in many of the congregations. The hope of the work is in the gift of the Holy Spirit in its convincing and renewing power.

The Archbishop's Mission to the Nestorians (the word Archbishop referring to the Archbishop of Canterbury, in England) is another enterprise of a missionary character. No time need here be spent upon it, however, since it has been sufficiently described in another place.

The Mission of the CMS: In 1869 the Rev. R. Bruce, of the CMS, on his way back to India visited Persia. He found the Muslims of Ispahan so friendly, and the Armenians so anxious to learn of the Christianity of the West, that he delayed to leave. His stay was prolonged year after year; Dr. Bruce opened schools and found his hands full of work that he had not expected to take up. Finally in 1875 the CMS decided to assume these enterprises and prosecute the work so incidentally begun. Three other stations have been occupied, and medical missions and Zenana missions have been undertaken. Moreover, God has given His blessing to this new enterprise in Persia.

The following societies are now at work in Persia: The Presbyterian Board, North; the Archbishop's Mission to the Assyrian Christians; the London Society for Promoting Christianity amongst the Jews; the Church Missionary Society, and the Bible societies. Educational work has received prominence from the beginning of modern missions in Persia, and the work of medical missionaries has been highly appreciated by the Persians. The great need of Persia was suggested by Lord Curzon in 1892: "Those philosophers are right who argue that moral must precede material and internal reform in Persia. It is useless to graft new shoots on to a stem whose sap is exhausted or poisoned. We may give Persia roads and railroads; we may work her mines and exploit her resources; we may drill her army and clothe her artisans; but we shall not have brought her within the pale of civilized nations until we have got at the core of the people, and given a new and a radical twist to the national character and institutions." This need can only be met by divine message, borne to Persia by the missionary of the cross.

Barrett (J.), *Persia, the Land of the Imams*, New York, 1888; Benjamin (S. G. W.), *Persia and the Persians*, London and New York, 1887; Bird (Isabella), *Journeys in Persia and Kurdistan*, 2 vols., London, 1893; Curzon (G.), *The Persian Question*, 2 vols., London, 1892; Watson (R. G.), *A History of Persia* (1800–1858), London, 1873; Landor (H. S.), *Across Coveted Lands*, 2 vols., London, 1902.

PERSIAN LANGUAGE: The Persian is one of the Indo-Germanic family of Aryan languages, of sufficient importance in itself to be sometimes called the Western Aryan. It is called *Irani* in Persian and in the West of Asia it is known as *Farsi*. This latter name is identical with the well-known name Parsee or Parsi, the people of Western Asia often using "f" where their eastern neighbors use "p." The ancient sources of the Persian as it exists to-day are the Zend, which is very near to the Sanskrit; the Ancient Persian, of which few literary remains exist, some of these being found in the book of Daniel, but which is still near to the Sanskrit in many particulars, and the Pehlevi, or Sassanian of the first seven centuries of our era. The latter has a considerable number of Chaldèe words, and differs materially from the Zend in having few inflections and terminations in comparison with the older language. A later dialect of the Pehlevi shows a distinct purpose to avoid the use of other than true Persian words and to return to the Ancient Persian forms. The modern Persian is very simple in its grammar. In fact, it is often said to have no grammar worth disturbing oneself about. It has no gender of noun, adjective or pronoun, except by use of a special word to show sex. Its case declensions are few, its plural is regularly formed in every case, one of the two pluralizing terminations being used for animate and the other for inanimate objects. In the verb great use is made of auxiliary combinations. At the same time, and perhaps because of this, the language has a wonderful fulness and flexibility. No other Asiatic language compares with the Persian in elegance and in the sonorous sweetness of its tones.

Persian is widely cultivated throughout Asia for its literary qualities and its literature. Whether in the East or the West, in India or in Turkey, the educated man must as a matter of course know Persian. At the same time, since the Mohammedan era it has lost much of its purity through adoption of numbers of Arabic words which are not always naturalized—that is, are not always subjected to Persian rules of inflection and construction. In the earlier periods of Persian writing the cuneiform characters were used as well as letters derived perhaps from the Syriac. At present the Arabic alphabet is universally used for writing Persian. Additional dots supplied to Arabic letters furnish the sounds which Arabs do not use, and the Persian taste gives an angle to the letters which neither Arabs nor Turks permit, but aside from these peculiarities the Arabic letters are unchanged. The Persian has been used to some small degree for missionary purposes. Its territorial expansion suggests the wisdom of making greater use of it for Christian publications. Such use cannot avail, however, unless the writer is a master of Persian in every sense.

PERU: A republic of South America, which lies between the Pacific Ocean on the west and Brazil and Bolivia on the east, Ecuador on the north, and Chile on the south. It contains three distinctive physical divisions—the coast region, the region of the Andes, and the tropical forests within the valley of the Amazon. Its area is 695,733 square miles, divided into eighteen departments and two provinces (Cholos and Zambos). Every variety of climate is found in Peru, on account of the difference in elevation in various parts. The population in 1876, when the last census was taken, was 2,660,881. The Geographical Society made an estimate of the population in 1896, which showed the total number of inhabitants as 4,600,000, besides an unknown number of uncivilized Indians. In the census of 1876 the population was composed of whites, 13 per cent.; negroes, 1 per cent.; Indians, 58 per cent.; 26 per cent. mixed blood, and 2 per cent. Asiatics. The chief cities are Lima, the capital (100,000), Callao (16,000), Arequipa (35,000), and Cuzco (20,000). The total working length of railways (1902) is 1,035 miles, with about 45 miles in construction. There is also a steamboat service on Lake Titicaca. Roads are poor and few. The constitution, proclaimed in 1856 and revised 1860, provides that a president and a congress of two houses shall be elected every four years. The constitution prohibits the public exercise of any other religion than the Roman Catholic, tho in reality there is a certain amount of tolerance, since Anglican churches and Jewish synagogues are found in Callao and Lima. Education is compulsory, and is free in the municipal public schools.

The American Bible Society through its colporteurs prosecutes the only Protestant work so far in Peru, by distributing the Bible translated into Spanish. The principal agent of the Bible Society is an Italian minister, who has been holding church services in Callao, where he gathered a congregation of over a hundred, to whom he preached in Spanish. His success in making converts roused the opposition of the priests, who viewed with unconcern the services in English, but saw that preaching in Spanish was likely to prove a potent means of enlightening the people, and on the 25th of June, 1890, Mr. Penzotti, the minister, was arrested and put in prison, charged with violating the law. He having been acquitted, his persecutors appealed, and finally carried the case to the Supreme Court. They thus obtained an interpretation of the law in favor of Mr. Penzotti, and general religious liberty, altho they had hoped for something quite different. Again, in 1895, the Roman Catholic clergy tried to prevent Bible circulation, and the result was a decree from the Government under which the circulation of the Bible is freely allowed. The constitution prohibits the public exercise of any religion but Roman Catholicism. But in fact there is a certain amount of tolerance, and the ME, the RBMU and the Independent Baptist Missionary movement have 5 stations, with both chapels and schools, in Peru.

Markham (C. R.), *Peru*, London, 1880; Adams (W. H. D.), *The Land of the Incas*, London and Boston, 1883 and 1885; Squier (E. G.), *Peru*, New York, 1877.

PESHAWAR: A town and British military post in the Northwestern Frontier Province of India, and capital of a district of the same name which was formerly a part of Afghanistan. It is situated about 88 miles W. N. W. of the great British fortress of Rawal Pindi, and 18 miles from the east entrance to the celebrated Khaibar Pass on the road to Cabul. Under British rule the prosperity of the town is reviving and the appearance of the suburbs is much improved. The town itself has small architectural pretensions, the houses being generally built of mud bricks, held together by a frame of wood. Except the main thoroughfares the streets are narrow and crooked. Sanitary arrangements are good, and water plenty. The fruit gardens of the environs are a favorite pleasure-ground of the people. Altitude, 1,180 feet. Population (1901) 95,147, of whom 70,000 are Mohammedans, 17,500 Hindus, and 5,500 Sikhs. Station of the CEZ (1882), with (1903) 5 women missionaries, 12 native workers, 3 day schools, 1 boarding school, 2 dispensaries, 1 hospital, and 15 Zenana pupils. Station also of the CMS (1885), with (1903) 4 missionaries, two of them with their wives; 4 native workers, 2 outstations, 2 day schools, 1 boarding school, 1 dispensary, 1 hospital, and 94 professed Christians, of whom 35 are communicants. Station also of the WMS, with (1903) 1 missionary, 3 native workers, 4 places of worship, 1 Sunday school, and 57 professed Christians.

PETCHABUREE: A town in Siam, on the west side of the Gulf of Siam, 85 miles southwest of Bangkok, with which it is connected by railroad. Has 10,000 inhabitants. Station of the PN (1861), with (1903) 3 missionaries and their wives, 1 woman missionary, 5 native workers, 2 outstations, 1 place of worship, 1 Sunday school, 1 day school, 2 boarding schools, 1 dispensary, 1 hospital, and 97 professed Christians.

PETERSBURG: A town in Cape Colony, South Africa, 6 miles S. S. W. of King William's Town. Station of the Berlin Missionary Society (1856), with (1903) 2 missionaries, 1 woman missionary, 9 native workers, and 478 professed Christians, of whom 128 are communicants (including Emdigeni in these statistics).

PETROPOLIS: A German colony in Brazil, South America, 28 miles N. of Rio de Janeiro. It is the summer residence of the rich inhabitants of the city. Station of the MES (1895), with (1903) 3 women missionaries, 49 native workers, 2 outstations, 1 place of worship, 1 Sunday school, 3 kindergartens, and 106 professed Christians.

PFANDER, Karl Gottlieb: Born, 1803; died, 1865. Prepared for his missionary work at the Training Institution, Basel, from 1820 to 1825. Pfander, who had a gift for languages, was destined by the Basel Committee for Asia, and particularly for the translation of the Bible into Asiatic languages. He was first sent with Zaremba, the former Russian count, also a graduate of the Basel Institute, to the Armenians living in the vicinity of Shusha, in the region near the Caspian Sea, which is now known as the Russian province of Transcaucasia. He and his associates were, soon after their arrival, in danger of death by starvation, for the Prince of Persia besieged Shusha for forty days, in 1826. The Shusha Mission was intended to be a work among the Mohammedan population, but its influence was felt among many Eastern Christians. Pfander, only 22 years old, had now to learn three languages: Turkish, Armenian, and Persian. The Turkish had not been provided with grammar and vocabulary till the missionaries used it. The Persian was necessary, that he might be able to cope with learned Muslims. Pfander also studied the tone of the Mohammedan thought, by frequently conversing with the people, and studying their books, especially the Koran. The greatness of the problem of attracting, reaching, and saving the Mohammedans grew upon him. He was impressed by the facts that here was a people who acknowledged God as their Master and Owner, but who took Mohammed as their example; that they covered a large proportion of the world's surface; that for a thousand years they had waged a bitter combat against Christianity; that they had great difficulty in receiving the truths of the Gospel; that their religious books contained many sparks of truth, and that the problem was complicated by the Mohammedans being divided into sects, which had been engaged in deadly combat with each other. He wrote a little book for distribution among them, and it was blessed mightily by God. In 1829 he decided to go to Baghdad to learn Arabic, and when the dangers of such a journey were brought to his attention, he wrote: "I have no care for my life; it will be preserved as long as it is needed for the service of the Almighty." He left Baghdad after heroic work, to visit Persia, and in 1831 we find him in Ispahan. His book, written in German, had been, with the help of the natives, translated in Armenian, Turkish, and Persian, and one of his objects in the present journey was to make the Persian edition more correct. He joined a caravan, wore native dress, and on his journey he spoke to Tatars and Kurds of the Christian religion, and distributed tracts and Persian New Testaments. He favorably impressed Catholic and Armenian Christians, and the Syrian archbishop asked for and received a number of Syrian and Arabic New Testaments. His visits proved a great blessing to Syrian Christians, and he greatly strengthened them by his words, both spoken and written, in their purpose to honor God. In the town of Kirmanshah he had a struggle with fanatical Mullahs. He knew the danger of declaring publicly truths that opposed the prevailing thought of Mohammedanism; but, putting his trust in God, he answered boldly all of their questions and preached unto them Christ. The enraged Mullahs held a council at night, and it was announced next day in the mosques that his books must be destroyed, and that he must be killed. A rumor that some of his books were bound in pigskin greatly disturbed the peace of these followers of Mohammed. He visited the Prince of Kirmanshah, and was protected from further persecution. On his way to Ispahan he distributed the Scriptures, preached the Word, and had the joy of seeing souls saved by the grace of God. From Shusha he visited and labored in the neighboring towns of Shamakhi and Baku, and for eight years, having been a pilgrim in missionary work among many peoples, he visited Europe, where he spent a year. In 1835 he and his companions were bidden by the Russian Government to cease at once and forever from all missionary work in the country, and from March to September, Pfander and Kreiss were engaged in a journey of exploration through Asia Minor to Constantinople. Soon afterward they both received appointments under the CMS, started for India by the way of Persia and the Persian Gulf, and after thirteen months they reached Calcutta. He spoke of the years from 1837 to 1841 as a waiting time, but he was engaged during this period in studying the Hindustani, in familiarizing himself with the customs and religions of India, and in making a revised edition of his remarkable book, *The Balance of Truth*. Before leaving Shusha he wrote three books, which treated of sin, salvation, the divinity of Christ, the Trinity, and the inspiration of the Scriptures. These were designed to remove stumbling blocks from the way of the Mohammedans—and, in India, they proved to be a power for good. Until the Mutiny broke out in 1857 he worked in Agra and

Peshawar, and during this terrible uprising he showed the firmest faith and the highest courage. The Mutiny over, he visited Europe, and in 1858 he was sent to Constantinople, accompanied by Dr. Koelle. Here, as elsewhere, his tongue and pen were mighty forces in the proclamation of the truth. This gifted missionary, able writer, and great linguist left a permanent impression upon each of the peoples among whom he labored, while his books struck Mohammedanism in its weakest point, and still exercise a powerful influence in India, in Persia, and in Turkey and Egypt.

PHALANE: A settlement in the Transvaal, South Africa, situated about 46 miles N. W. of Pretoria. Station of the Hermannsburg Missionary Society (1867), with (1901) 1 missionary and his wife, 4 native workers, 1 outstation, 2 day schools, and 651 professed Christians.

PHALAPYE. See SEROWE.

PHILIP, John: Born in England; studied at Hoxton Academy; was appointed as a deputation with Rev. John Campbell to visit the stations of the LMS in South Africa; sailed December 10, 1818, reaching Cape Town February 26, 1819. Accompanied by Mr. Moffat and Mr. Evans, the deputation visited the stations within the colony, but were prevented by the Kafir war from proceeding beyond. Mr. Philip returned to Cape Town. In 1820 he received from Princeton College, New Jersey, U. S. A., the degree of Doctor of Divinity. The Deputation having completed their work, Dr. Philip was appointed superintendent of the Society's missions in South Africa. He was also pastor of an English congregation at Cape Town. In 1826 he visited England by invitation of the directors, his place as superintendent being supplied by Rev. R. Miles. He earnestly championed the rights of the Hottentots as against greedy and unprincipled settlers, and secured certain regulations which ameliorated their civil status. On his return to South Africa he was sued for libel and made to pay a fine of £1,200. Dr. Philip died at Hankey, South Africa, August 27, 1851. His *Researches in South Africa* were published in 2 vols. in London, 1828.

PHILIPPOPOLIS: A city in Eastern Rumelia, Bulgaria. It is the most important city of the southern province. Population (1900), 42,849. The city stands upon and between three isolated syenitic rocks (the highest 695 feet) on the right bank of the Maritsa, 97 miles N. N. W. of Adrianople. It was founded 340 B.C. by Philip II. of Macedon. Station of the ABCFM (1859), with (1903) 2 missionaries and their wives, 27 native workers, 17 outstations, 12 places of worship, 17 Sunday schools, 8 day schools, 1 printing house, and 472 professed Christians.

PHILLIPS, Jeremiah: Born at Plainfield, N. Y., January 5, 1812; attended Madison (now Colgate) University, but did not complete his course of study, the Committee of the Missionary Society desiring that he should accompany Dr. Sutton on his return to India. He was ordained at Plainfield, and embarked for Calcutta in company with Dr. E. Noyes, September 22, 1835, under the Free Baptist Missionary Society. His field of labor was Orissa, a region of country hitherto wholly untouched by missionary effort, which was occupied in 1836. Balasor was first occupied in 1840 and a boarding school opened, with six native children. The same year Mr. Phillips commenced a new station at Jaleswar with some of the Balasor boarding scholars and native converts. He was the first to discover the Santals, a race of aborigines previously unknown to missionaries. He reduced their wild language to writing, prepared and published a grammar and dictionary, and established schools among them—for the first time in their existence, so far as known. As a result of his correspondence and published articles in the papers of India and America, seven missions have been established, and are successfully working among them. He translated the Gospels and other portions of the Bible into their language, and also prepared schoolbooks. The degree of doctor of divinity was conferred upon him by Bates College, Maine. The India Government officially thanked Dr. Phillips for his great work among the Santals. He died at Hillsdale, Mich., December 9, 1879, having served 43 years in India.

PHILIPPINE ISLANDS: A group of islands lying in the Western Pacific Ocean, and extending almost due N. and S. from Formosa to Borneo and the Moluccas, through 16° of latitude and 9° of longitude. The group contains nearly 2,000 islands, some of which are mere islets. The largest islands are Luzon, with a population of 3,500,000; Panay, 735,000; Negros, 391,777; Cebu, 504,000; Samar, 200,753; Leyte, 270,491; Mindoro, 200,000; Palawan, 70,000, and Mindanao, 600,000. The whole area of the group is estimated at 122,000 square miles, and the population is about 8,000,000. The climate of the islands is varied, according to position and altitude. In general it may be described as hot, tempered somewhat by ocean breezes, but very moist and more than ordinarily trying to American residents. One of our people going to the islands in perfect health and remaining two or three years without taking regular change of air in the mountains, will find his general health seriously affected. Vegetation is luxurious and on the whole offers the people an easy support.

The majority of the inhabitants are of the Malay stock, now very much mixed. There are about 25,000 Europeans in the islands, about 100,000 Chinese, in whose hands are the principal industries, and a considerable number, not yet ascertained, of wild tribes, some of whom seem to be Negrito dwarfs. The languages of the people are numerous. Spanish has been the official language and is used by educated Filipinos, but has not at all displaced the native languages in the households of the people. It will now be quickly replaced by English. The chief of the forty or fifty native languages spoken in the islands are the Tagalog, the Pampangan, the Pangasinan, the Visayan, in two main dialects, the Cugnan and the Zambales, besides the Moro dialects of the south, which have taken up a certain number of Arabic words.

The Philippines were discovered and conquered by the Spaniards in the 16th century. Having received a certain amount of advantage from Spanish control and tutelage during 350 years, and having been ceded to the United States by the treaty of peace signed December 10, 1898, they wait to see whether the American influence will be more beneficent and stimulating than the Spanish. With the exception of the southern portion of Mindanao and the Sulu archipelago, inhabited by Mohammedan Malays, whom the Spaniards called *Moros* (Mohammedans or Moors), the islands are under civil government, with practical autonomy in the municipalities, and with 39 provinces, each under a governor elected by the people through their municipal councilors. The law-making power rests with a commission at Manila under a Governor appointed and supervised by the President of the United States.

The religion of the Philippines, excepting that of the Mohammedan Sulu archipelago and parts of Mindanao, is overwhelmingly Roman Catholic, altho in the mountain districts of the larger islands paganism in the form of ancestor-worship and spirit-worship also exists. The Roman Catholic Church has divided the islands into nearly 900 parishes, of which some 600 have been administered by foreign friars of the Augustinian, Dominican and Franciscan orders. These friars have had not only the religious, but in actual fact, the civil, control of the islands, and have used their power for the advantage of their orders rather than of the people. They have acquired ownership, for instance, of more than 400,000 acres of choice land in the islands, besides holding title to a great number of churches and other public buildings. Through various causes needless to enumerate this body of foreign friars, that is to say the Roman Catholic establishment, has alienated the affections of the mass of the Filipinos, and as soon as the Spanish power in the islands was broken all of the friars were forcibly expelled from their parishes, saving their lives by taking refuge in Manila or even in foreign lands. The people have said: "Our people have had 300 years of friars' religion, and now we want a better one." This does not, however, imply a revolt from Roman Catholicism, for most of the people know of no other form of religion. In some provinces the Roman Catholic clergy still sharply control public sentiment, but in others there is a tendency to form a national Roman Catholic Church, which has been commenced by certain of the native clergy who have thrown off allegiance to the Pope of Rome. The whole situation of Roman Catholicism in the islands is one which causes the gravest inquietude among the august prelates at Rome, the change which withdraws national support from that church and establishes schools outside of the control of the bishops, being one to which European Roman Catholics cannot readily adapt themselves.

In the meantime the condition of the common people in the Philippines who are Christians in name has attracted the sympathetic attention of the Protestant missionary societies of the United States. While there are exceptions among the educated classes, the characteristic qualities of the common Roman Catholic Christian Filipino (that is to say, of the mass of the people) are the following: There is a strange lack of either religious or political fraternity between them, a mere dialect separating neighbors as widely as the ocean. Like all Asiatics, they look upon representatives of Western civilization with an instinctive dislike and suspicion, and they hardly know the meaning of lofty ambitions or aspirations. They are immoral, have a rooted conviction that all foreign clergy are immoral, and they allow nothing in the religious teaching of foreigners to restrain them from being idle, dissipated, deceitful, vacillating and essentially worthless. The two interests capable of thoroughly engaging their attention are, first, cock-fighting (with gambling), and, second, gorgeous church processions. It is clear that no great future awaits such a people unless through a more profound understanding of the Gospel of Jesus Christ.

The Presbyterian Board of Foreign Missions in the United States (North) was the first Protestant society to establish a mission in the Philippines. It first proposed to the great denominational societies a conference for such arrangements as to comity and territorial limitations as will prevent any impression of rivalry between the denominations. This has resulted in the formation of "The Evangelical Union of the Philippine Islands," each denomination adding in brackets its distinctive name. Comity being settled upon, the PN established Mr. Rogers its first missionary in Manila in April, 1899. It now has 4 other stations on the islands of Panay (1900), Negros (1901) and Cebu (1902), with 10 organized churches, several schools, one of them industrial; 2 hospitals and about 500 communicants. The CA has sent out missionaries temporarily working with the PN. The Methodist Episcopal Church in the United States, after Methodist laymen had commenced holding meetings in Manila in 1899 (before the Presbyterian mission was opened), organized a mission station there in May, 1900, taking for its field the northern section of the island of Luzon. It now has work in 27 places, with three central stations, besides its station in Manila. It has about 4,000 professing Christians under its care, 1,000 of them being communicants. The American Baptist Missionary Union opened its first station in 1900 on the island of Panay, and its second in 1901 on the island of Negros. It now has 3 organized churches, 5 places of worship and about 400 communicants. It has given much attention to printing and circulating the Scriptures and general evangelistic literature. The Protestant Episcopal Church has a strong station at Manila (1902), where the missionary bishop resides, and another in the highlands of Benguet (Luzon), with especial reference to the untamed *Igorrotes* who live there and have never known Christianity except as the religion of the men who have guns and kill people. The United Brethren in Christ have also a mission station in Manila (1902) and another in the Ilocano speaking provinces (1901) in the N. W. coast of Luzon. The ABCFM has a station (1902) in the island of Mindanao. All of these missions are working with the hope of benefiting the people. It is not their aim to waste time in fighting the Roman Catholic Church. The B and FBS and the ABS also have agencies in the islands and are pressing forward Bible translation and have circulated about 80,000 copies per annum of the Gospels and other portions already printed.

El Archipelago Filipino, 2 vols. and atlas, Washington, D. C., 1900; *Report of the Philippine Commission*, 4 vols., Washington, D. C., 1900–1901; Foreman (J.), *The Philippine Islands*, 2d ed., London and New York, 1899; Worcester (D. C.), *The Philippine Islands and Their People*, New York, 1898; Sawyer (F. H.), *The Inhabitants of the Philippine Islands*, London, 1900. In the *Missionary Review of the World* are some valuable articles on the Philippines: Ethnology, Vol. XI., p. 821; Vol. XV., p. 536; Religion, Vol. XI., pp. 517, 520; XIV. (with a survey of mission prospects), pp. 510, 586; Vol. XV., p. 678.

PHOKWANE: A railway station in S. Bechuanaland, Africa, situated about 70 miles N. of Kimberly. Station of the SPG, with (1903) 1 missionary and 905 professed Christians. Some write the name Phokoane.

PHYENG-YANG: A town in Korea, about 80 miles W. by S. of Wonsan, beautifully situated on the right or N. bank of the Taedong, 50 miles from the sea. The river on which it stands is navigable by vessels of moderate draught to within 15 miles of the city. It is the center of a large silk industry. The Japanese defeated the Chinese at this place in September, 1894. Population, 20,000. Station of the ME, with (1903) 4 missionaries, three of them with their wives; 3 women missionaries, 11 native workers, 17 outstations, 18 places of worship, 2 Sunday schools, 1 day school, 1 dispensary, 1 hospital, and 2,079 professed Christians, of whom 269 are communicants. Station also of the PN (1893), with (1903) 8 missionaries, seven of them with their wives; 2 women missionaries, 51 native workers, 185 outstations, 136 places of worship, 40 day schools, 1 boarding school, 1 dispensary, 1 hospital, and 4,358 professed Christians, of whom 2,926 are communicants. The name is also written Pyeng-yang.

PIETERMARITZBURG: Capital of Natal, Africa, situated in a fertile plain, 2,000 feet above the sea, surrounded by a circle of hills, and 40 miles N. W. of Durban. It has an excellent climate, especially curative of pulmonary complaints, and the rich vegetation of its gardens and surrounding woods makes it one of the most delightful cities of Africa. Its population, numbering (1901) 30,000, is most cosmopolitan in character, consisting of Zulus, Kafirs, Europeans, Hindus, Chinese and Arabs. Station of the Swedish Holiness Union (1893), with (1901) 1 missionary and his wife, 1 woman missionary, and 1 day school. Station also of the Mission Association for the diocese of Natal (1868), with (1901) 1 missionary, 2 women missionaries, 2 native workers, 1 theological class, 1 industrial school, and 215 professed Christians. Station also of the UFS, with (1903) 2 missionaries and their wives, 2 outstations, 1 place of worship, 4 day schools, and 701 professed Christians. Station also of the South Africa Wesleyan Methodists, with (1900) 56 native workers, 14 outstations, 14 places of worship, 2 Sunday schools, 9 day schools, and 978 professed Christians.

PIETERSBURG: A town in the Transvaal, South Africa, Zoutpansberg division, about 140 miles N. N. E. of Pretoria. Population, 1,500. Station of the Berlin Missionary Society (1896), with (1903) 1 missionary, 10 native workers, 4 outstations, and 304 professed Christians, of whom 134 are communicants. Station of the SPG, with (1903) 1 missionary.

PILGRIM MISSION at St. Chrischona. See St. Chrischona.

PILKINGTON, George Lawrence: Born in Ireland, 1865. Died in Africa, 1898. Educated at Cambridge, and for a short time he was Assistant Master at Harrow and Bedford Schools. Sailed January 23, 1890, under the CMS to join the Uganda, Africa, Mission.

On March 9, less than three months after his arrival, he had already, with the help of Henry Wright Duta, translated almost half of the Acts of the Apostles, induced the natives to translate Old Testament stories from Swahili, and begun to compile a Luganda grammar. He had completed the grammar and vocabulary, finished the Acts, and translated about twenty hymns by the end of May in the same year. Of the books of the New Testament, all but I. and II. Corinthians, Hebrews, James, I. and II. Peter were translated by January, 1892. The Gospels had been translated previously. The New Testament was finished, sent home, and printed by the Bible Society by Christmas, 1893. The Old Testament, of which he translated all but some of the minor prophets, was completed in 1896.

Nor was Mr. Pilkington a translator only. The letters of that period show that he took his full share in teaching with the rest, and in all the events of that troublous time. The prominent position he took very early is shown by the fact that when, on December 27, 1891, only a year after Mr. Pilkington's arrival in Uganda, Mwanga, in one of his many changes, announced his intention of becoming a Protestant, it was to Mr. Pilkington that the chiefs first took the news.

Early in the year 1898, while he was engaged in aiding as interpreter the British officers sent to restore order, he was struck down by the Sudanese mutineers. Mr. Pilkington's translations make a long list, and one which, for a young man of thirty-three, is amazing. In the forefront of them all, he completed the translation of the whole Bible into Luganda, in itself an enduring monument. He also revised and in part translated the Prayer Book, translated a hymn-book, catechism, and Bible stories; wrote a small work, *Anonyalaba* ("He that seeketh findeth"), in Luganda; compiled a Luganda grammar, a Luganda-English and English-Luganda vocabulary, and other smaller works. While at home he wrote, aided by Mr. Baskerville, a pamphlet called *The Gospel in Uganda* and made designs for *Central Africa for Christ*.

Harford-Battersby (C.F)., *Pilkington of Uganda*, London and New York, 1899.

PING-LIANG-FU: A town in the province of Kan-su, China, situated in the eastern part of the province, 145 miles E. by S. of Lan-chau-fu, and a short distance E. of the Liu-pan pass over the mountains. This is the center for the Scandinavian Alliance Associates of the CIM (1895), with (1903) 1 missionary and his wife, 1 woman missionary, 2 native workers, 1 place of worship, and 1 Sunday school. Some write the name P'ing-liang.

PING-TU-CHAU: A town in Shan-tung, China, situated about 95 miles S. W. of Chi-fu. Station of the SBC, with (1903) 1 missionary and his wife, 1 woman missionary, 5 native workers, 4 outstations, 10 places of worship, 3 Sunday schools, 7 day schools, 1 boarding school, 1 dispensary, and 354 professed Christians. Some write the name Ping-tu.

PING-YANG-FU: A town in the province of Shan-si, China, situated on the right bank of the Fen-ho, 380 miles S. W. of Peking, 105 miles N. W. by N. of Ho-nan-fu. This is one of the holiest towns of the empire, and one of the oldest in the world. It is also one of the places which felt the full force of the Boxer fury against foreigners. After peace was restored, the people for some time held aloof from all Europeans. Station of the CIM (1879), with (1903) 2 missionaries, one of them with his wife; 2 women missionaries, 2 native workers, 1 place of worship, 1 Sunday school, and 89 professed Christians.

PING-YANG-HSIEN: A town in the province of Che-kiang, China, situated near the coast in the

S. part of the province, and 28 miles S. W. of Wen-chau. Station of the CIM (1874), with (1903) 2 missionaries, one of them with his wife; 27 native workers, 24 outstations, 25 places of worship, 2 day schools, 2 boarding schools, and 475 professed Christians. Some write the name Bing-yae.

PING-YAO-HSIEN: A town in the province of Shan-si, China, situated about 37 miles S. by W. of Tai-yuen-fu. Station of the CIM (1888). The work at this station has been disorganized by the Boxer attacks. It has (1903) 4 missionaries, two of them with their wives; 9 native workers, and 7 outstations.

PIRACICABA: A town in Brazil, South America, 86 miles N. W. of São Paulo, on the river Piracicaba. Population, 5,000. Station of the MES (1877), with (1903) 1 missionary and his wife, 2 women missionaries, 1 native worker, 2 outstations, 2 places of worship, 2 Sunday schools, 1 theological class, and 358 professed Christians.

PIRIE. See PERIE.

PIROZPUR: A village of Bengal, India, situated in the district of Bakarganj, 100 miles E. of Calcutta. Population, 12,200, of whom 8,100 are Hindus and 4,100 are Mohammedans. Station of the BMS (1890), with (1903) 1 missionary and his wife, 18 native workers, 5 outstations, 8 day schools, 8 Sunday schools, and 304 professed Christians, of whom 113 are communicants. The name is also written Pirojpur.

PITHORAGARH: A village and military post in the United Provinces, India, situated near the Nepal frontier, 32 miles E. of Almora. Station of the ME, with (1903) 1 woman missionary, 48 native workers, 4 places of worship, 15 Sunday schools, 1 boarding school, and 391 professed Christians.

PITSANULOKE: A town in Siam, situated east of the Po River, about 227 miles N. of Bangkok. Station of the PN (1889), with (1903) 2 missionaries and their wives, 4 native workers, 1 Sunday school, 1 boarding school, and 1 dispensary.

PITZ, Deaconess Charlotte: Born November 19, 1819, at Gemund, in Eifel, Germany. Died July 27, 1903, at Jerusalem. She was a veteran in the German Evangelical work in the East, having labored for a half-century in the Kaiserswerth Deaconess' enterprise at Jerusalem. She began her labors in 1853, supervising a school in which she taught thirty hours weekly. Her work of teaching had many interruptions. During the Mohammedan uprising against Christians in 1860, she was in great danger and had to have an underground refuge made for the 25 children in her school. When the smallpox raged she nursed the sick until she was seized by the disease. When famine followed the locust plague, she visited Germany and Holland, and secured money to feed the sufferers.

Notwithstanding such difficulties, the work progressed and consequently her duties increased. The commodious new building just outside of Jerusalem, called "Talitha Kumi," was planned and successfully supplied with money by her, and in January, 1868, it was dedicated to the work of educating girls to be teachers in the Holy Land. In connection with it was a children's school, and a Swedish school for boys and girls was opened, and all were placed under Sister Charlotte's supervision. In 1894 a hospital building was dedicated and given over to her charge. There men, women, and children of all nationalities and religions receive treatment. In 1902 there were 666 Syrians and 112 other patients in the hospital, cared for by the eight nurses, who belonged to the Kaiserswerth order of deaconesses.

Sister Charlotte's work was recognized in Germany as well as in Jerusalem. The Crown Prince of Prussia (later Emperor Frederick of Germany) visited Jerusalem in 1869, and took pains to go to Talitha Kumi and express to Sister Charlotte his pleasure with the work. The Emperor William II. having visited Jerusalem in 1898 for the dedication of the new German Evangelical Church of the Redeemer, also took pains to go to Talitha Kumi and the hospital to see the work of the deaconesses. Great honor was shown Sister Charlotte on March 25, 1903, when the members of the German colony in Jerusalem met to express their appreciation of her work, and as a token of this appreciation they gave her the duty of laying the cornerstone of a new school building. She was presented with a Bible from the Empress of Germany, and addresses were made in behalf of Germany in the name of the colony in Jerusalem, and of the children for whom she had worked.

PLAISANCE: A town near the center of the Island of Mauritius, about 45 miles S. E. of Port Louis. Station of the CMS, with (1902) 2 missionaries, 1 with his wife; 23 native workers, 1 orphanage, and 392 professed Christians, of whom 50 are communicants.

PLYMOUTH BRETHREN; Missions of the. See CHRISTIAN MISSIONS.

PNIEL: A village of Cape Colony, South Africa, situated in Griqualand West, about 5 miles N. W. of Kimberly on the left bank of the Vaal River. Station of the Berlin Missionary Society (1845), with (1903) 2 missionaries, 1 woman missionary, 27 native workers, 3 outstations, and 1,964 professed Christians, of whom 1,692 are communicants.

PODILI: A town in Madras, India, situated 27 miles W. by N. of Ongole. Station of the ABMU (1894), with (1903) 1 missionary and his wife, 116 native workers, 44 day schools, 1 Sunday school, 6 places of worship, and 8,088 professed Christians, of whom 3,288 are communicants.

POELO TELLO: A settlement in the Butu Islands, Dutch East Indies, situated S. E. of Nias Island and W. of Sumatra. Station of the Netherlands Lutheran Missionary Society, with 1 missionary and his wife and 1 day school.

POERBOLINGGO: A town in Java, Dutch East Indies, situated in the central part of the island, about 75 miles S. W. of Samarang. Station of the Neukirchen Missionary Society, with 2 missionaries, 1 of them with his wife; 5 native workers, 5 outstations, and 1 day school.

POERWOREDJO: A town in Java, Dutch East Indies, situated in the S. part of the island, about 60 miles S. S. W. of Samarang. Station of the Reformed Church of the Netherlands (1878), with (1903) 2 missionaries and their wives, 3 native workers, 3 outstations, 3 day schools, and 1 theological class.

POINT BARROW: A settlement in Alaska, situated on the coast of the Arctic Ocean and on the most northerly point of U. S. territory. Station of the Presbyterian Home Missionary Society (1890), with 1 missionary, 1 woman missionary, 1 chapel, 1 Sunday school, 1 day school, and 30 professed Christians.

POINT PEDRO: A town in Ceylon, India, situated in the Northern Province on the N. coast of Jaffna, about 114 miles N. W. by N. of Tricomali. Station of the WMS, with (1903) 1 missionary, 1 missionary woman, 126 native workers, 20 outstations, 25 Sunday schools, 29 day schools, 22 places of worship, 1 boarding school, and 204 professed Christians, of whom 97 are communicants.

POLADPUR: A town in Bombay, India, situated in the Kolaba district, about 30 miles S. of Bombay. Station of the Mission to Lepers (1894), with 1 home for untainted children of lepers.

POLES: The Poles form the most numerous branch of the Western Slavs. They number about 10,000,000, distributed by the division of Poland in Russia, Prussia, and Austria. They are all Catholics, except 500,000 Protestants, and they use the Latin alphabet, modified so as to express the sounds peculiar to their language. Their language belongs to the western branch of Slavic languages, and is divided into four or five dialects, which, however, are not very different from each other. The Polish language has been influenced more than any other Slavic language by the Latin (which in olden time was the literary and church language of Poland), the German and the French. Its distinctive characteristics are the nasal expression or *rhinesmus* of *a* and *b*, peculiar to the ancient Bulgarian or ancient Slovenic, but which has disappeared from common use now among the Slavs, and that it always accents the penultimate syllable of words. The Polish language bears quite a close resemblance to the language of the Bohemians and the Lansatian Serbs.

The history of the ancient settlements of the Poles is uncertain. Their history becomes more trustworthy with the introduction of Christianity among them, which took place in 965 or 966. It is deemed probable that the doctrines of the Eastern Church were taught among them in the time of Sts. Cyril and Methodius, the Slavic apostles, long before this date, but were soon supplanted by Latin Christianity. If so, the Eastern form has been so thoroughly extirpated that it has left no traces in Polish literature. Along with the introduction of Latin Christianity through German preachers, the Latin language acquired a firm footing in Poland, and was the language of the learned and higher classes, as well as of the courts. Luther's reformation penetrated into Poland, where it found zealous and ardent defenders and followers; but, in spite of all the earnestness with which it was defended, it was overcome by the Roman Catholic reaction. The political history of Poland is too long to be treated in detail here. We can characterize it in a few words by saying that it was full of political vicissitudes, of glorious deeds, and of internal instability. The *shlahta*, or nobility, had the upper hand, while the common people had very little share in the government. The jealousies and the arrogance of the nobles was always a hindrance to regular administration, and on more than one occasion the king's authority was set at naught. So the internal condition of Poland grew worse and worse, internal dissensions and strifes tended to weaken the government, and Poland fell a prey to more powerful neighbors, who resolved upon her partition, and thus put an end to her independent political existence.

POLFONTEIN: Village in the Transvaal, South Africa, situated about 20 miles E. S. E. of Mafeking. Station of the Hermannsburg Missionary Society (1877), with (1903) 1 missionary and his wife, 1 native worker, 3 outstations, 3 places of worship, 3 day schools, and 540 professed Christians.

POLONIA: A village in Transvaal, South Africa, situated 20 miles W. by N. of Pretoria. Station of the Hermannsburg Missionary Society (1883), with (1900) 1 missionary and his wife, 2 native workers, 2 outstations, 1 place of worship, 1 day school, and 389 professed Christians.

PONAPI. See CAROLINE ISLANDS.

PO-NA-SANG: A station of the ABCFM (1849), in the suburbs of Fu-chau-fu, *q. v.* for statistics.

PONCE: A station of the American Baptist Home Mission Society (1899) in Porto Rico, West Indies, with (1900) 2 missionaries and their wives, 1 woman missionary, 1 native worker, 2 outstations, 2 Sunday schools, and 80 professed Christians. Station also of the Christian Church (1901), with 2 missionaries, 1 of them with his wife. Station also of the PB, with 1 missionary and his wife. Station also of the Peniel Missionary Society, with 2 women missionaries and 1 outstation. Station also of the UB, with (1903) 3 missionaries and their wives, 1 day school, 1 dispensary, 8 places of worship, 1 printing house and 73 professed Christians.

POO: A town in Kunawar, on the border of Punjab, India, toward Tibet, situated on the Sutlej River, about 100 miles N. E. of Simla. Station of the Moravian Mission Society (1865), with (1903) 1 missionary and his wife, 1 native worker, 1 outstation, 2 places of worship, 2 Sunday schools, 2 day schools, and 13 professed Christians. The aim of the enterprise is to convey knowledge of Christianity into Tibet by means of Tibetans who come to these border regions for trade. So far, low caste people, almost to be regarded as slaves, are the only ones who have been converted here.

POONA: Capital of a district of the same name in Bombay, India. Situated in a plain, on the Moota River, 119 miles by railway southeast of Bombay. It was formerly the capital of the Mahratta power. The seven quarters of the city are named after the days of the week. Its climate is very pleasant and salubrious, making it a favorite place of resort during the rainy season. Population (1901) 153,320, including the garrison in the cantonment about two miles northeast of the city. Marathi, Gujarati, and Hindustani are the languages of the various races included in its mixed population. Station of the UFS (1831), with (1903) 2 missionaries, 3 women missionaries, 27 native workers, 2 outstations, 1 place of worship, 5 day schools, 1 boarding school, 1 orphanage, 1 printing house, and 186 professed Christians. Station also of the Church of Scotland Women's Board (1841), with (1900) 12 women missionaries, 38 native workers, 8 day schools, 1 boarding school, 1 dispensary, 1 hospital and 1 orphanage. Station also of the CMS (1882), with (1903) 2 missionaries, 23 native workers, 1 outstation, 9 day schools, 1 theological class, and 398 professed

Christians, of whom 174 are communicants. Station of the Ramabai Association, with a home for widows which is called Sharada Sadan. Station also of the ME, with (1903) 2 missionaries, one with his wife; 2 women missionaries, 38 native workers, 3 outstations, 5 places of worship, 9 Sunday schools, 17 day schools, 2 boarding schools, and 2 orphanages. Station also of the Poona Indian Village Mission, with 3 missionaries, 3 women missionaries, 1 place of worship, 1 printing house, 1 dispensary. Station also of the WMS, with (1903) 1 missionary, 2 native workers, 2 outstations, 1 place of worship, 1 Sunday school, and 35 professed Christians. Station also of the ZBM, with (1903) 27 native workers, 5 day schools, 1 boarding school, and 1 orphanage. Station also of the Salvation Army.

POOR, Daniel: Born at Danvers, Mass., June 27, 1789; graduated at Dartmouth College, 1811; studied theology at Andover Seminary; ordained and appointed missionary to Ceylon by the ABCFM, embarking October 23, 1815, with the first party of missionaries sent to that field by the Board. He was stationed as Tillipally until 1823; then appointed to charge of Batticotta seminary for boys; transferred temporarily to the Madura mission in 1836; returned to Tillipally, 1841; visited the United States 1848-1851; on his return to Ceylon was stationed at Manepy until his death by cholera in 1855, after 39 years of mission service and in the sixty-sixth year of his age. He received the degree of D.D. from Dartmouth College in 1835.

Dr. Poor was one of the founders of the ABCFM mission in Ceylon and left the impress of his strong personality upon its policy, as well as upon the Madura mission. He was in advance of his age in appreciating the place of higher education in the scheme of missions. Consequently he had to defend his views more than once or twice. He opened a school at Tillipally shortly after his arrival, and the seminary for boys at Batticotta, to which all the other mission boarding schools should be feeders, was largely the child of his mind as well as the convincing proof of the soundness of his theories of education. In the Madura mission also he was largely responsible for the establishment of some 35 schools in the first five years of its existence.

He excelled all his associates in the use of the Tamil language, in which he preached his first sermon one year after his arrival in Ceylon. His familiarity with the language and his knowledge of Hindu literature, his clear mind, his self-command and quickness of repartee, coupled with a rare courteousness in debate, enabled him to meet the arguments and expose the sophistries of learned Hindu opponents with telling effect.

During Dr. Poor's visit to the United States in 1848-49 he was much in demand among the churches for addresses on missions, and the powerful addresses which he gave were cherished memories with many who heard him.

POPO LANGUAGE: A dialect of the Ewe, used as a vernacular by tribesmen in Dahomey and Togoland, living between Lagos and the Volta River.

PORAYAR. A suburb of Tranquebar, Madras, India, situated in the district of Tanjore, 21 miles N. of Negapatam, and 5 miles N. W. of Karikal. Population, 14,500, of whom 11,000 are Hindus. Station of the Leipzig Mission Society (1842), with (1903) 2 missionaries and their wives, 21 native workers, 7 outstations, 8 places of worship, 25 day schools, 4 boarding schools, 1 industrial school, and 2,003 professed Christians, of whom 921 are communicants. The name is also written Poreiar.

POREIAR. See PORAYAR.

PORT ARTHUR: A town and military port in Manchuria, China, situated on the N. side of the Strait of Chi-li. It was leased to Russia in 1898 by the Chinese Government. Connected with the trans-Siberian railway by a branch line through Manchuria, which is to become the main line. Station of the Danish Mission Society (1896), with (1903) 1 missionary and his wife, 1 woman missionary, 2 native workers, 1 outstation, 1 place of worship, 1 day school, 1 dispensary, and 33 professed Christians.

PORT ELIZABETH: A maritime town of Cape Colony, Africa, situated in the district of Port Elizabeth, 125 miles S. W. by W. of King William's Town, with an open but safe harbor on Algoa Bay, in which vessels load from and discharge into lighters and steam tugs plying between two jetties. Population, 23,000. This was the earliest landing place of missionaries destined to the Zulu country. Station of the Moravian Missions (1898), with (1903) 1 missionary and his wife, 5 native workers, 22 professed Christians, and 1 place of worship. Station also of the SPG, with 1 native worker and 200 professed Christians. Station also of the South African Wesleyan Methodists, with 56 native workers, 14 outstations, 5 places of worship, 5 Sunday schools, 2 day schools, and 509 professed Christians.

PORT LIMON. See LIMON.

PORT LOKKO: A town in Sierra Leone, west coast of Africa, 35 miles E. N. E. of Freetown. Climate tropical. Station of the CMS (1875), with (1903) 1 missionary, 7 native workers, 2 outstations, 1 place of worship, 1 Sunday school, 1 day school, and 35 professed Christians.

PORT LOUIS: Capital of Mauritius, situated on the northwest coast of the island, at the head of a bay. It is open on one side to the sea and enclosed on the other three by picturesque mountains. Of late years its prosperity has declined, fevers having become so prevalent that many have deserted it for other parts of the island. This has enabled the Chinese to get possession of the greater part of the town. Population (1901), with suburbs, 52,740. Station of the SPG (1856), with (1903) 2 missionaries, 2 native workers, and 365 professed Christians, of whom 125 are communicants. Station also of the CMS, with (1903) 1 native worker and 353 professed Christians, of whom 25 are communicants.

PORT MORESBY: A station on the southern coast of New Guinea, under English authority. It was founded in 1873 by the LMS and has a college in which natives from Tahiti, Rarotonga, Samoa, etc., are educated, and from which 17 stations are provided with teachers. There are (1903) 1 missionary and his wife and 14 native workers.

PORTO ALEGRE: A town and seaport in Brazil, South America, situated in the state of Rio Grande do Sul, of which it is the capital. It is the chief commercial port in S. Brazil. Population, 52,421. Station of the American Church Missionary Society (1890), with (1901) 1 missionary and his wife, 1 woman missionary, 2 native workers, 1 outstation, 3 places of worship,

2 Sunday schools, and 133 professed Christians. Station also of the MES (1890), with (1903) 1 missionary and his wife, 4 native workers, 6 outstations, 4 Sunday schools, and 60 professed Christians. Station also of the SDA, with 1 missionary and his wife.

PORTO NOVO: A town in Dahomey, West Africa, under French authority, situated about 50 miles E. of Whydah. Station of the WMS, with (1903) 1 missionary, 44 native workers, 12 outstations, 31 places of worship, 9 Sunday schools, 7 day schools, and 417 professed Christians, of whom 25 are communicants.

PORTO RICO: An island of the West Indies, lying east of Haiti. It contains an area of 3,550 square miles and a population (1899) of 953,243, of whom over 350,000 are negroes or of negro blood. It is described as "the healthiest of all the Antilles." Slavery was abolished by the National Assembly on March 23, 1873. The principal towns, with their population, are: San Juan, 32,000; Ponce, 28,000; San Germain, 38,000.

Porto Rico became United States territory by the treaty with Spain December 11, 1898. The adjacent islands of the Virgin group are also possessed by the United States and contain about 6,000 inhabitants.

PORT SAID: A town and seaport in Egypt, situated at the entrance to the Suez Canal, about 160 miles E. of Alexandria. Station of the Peniel Mission Society, with 3 women missionaries, 1 native worker, 1 day school. The BFBS also maintains an agent here, with a Bible depot and a colporteur.

PORT SHEPSTONE. See NORTH AND SOUTH SHEPSTONE.

PORT SIMPSON: A town and seaport in British Columbia, N. A., situated on the S. side of the entrance to Portland Channel. Station of the MCC (1874), with (1903) 2 missionaries, one of them with his wife; 6 women missionaries, 1 place of worship, 1 Sunday school, 1 boarding school, 1 dispensary, 1 hospital, 1 industrial school, and 404 professed Christians.

PORT OF SPAIN: Capital of Trinidad and Tobago, West Indies. It is one of the handsomest towns of the West Indies, with a good harbor and an active trade. Temperature, 70°-93° Fahrenheit. Population, 34,000, English, English and French creoles, Indian coolies, Chinese, Spaniards, and Portuguese. Each race speaks its own language, and the creole dialects of French, Spanish or English. Social condition, tho far from good, is better than in most of the West Indies. Station of the UFS (1836), with (1903) 1 missionary and his wife, 1 outstation, 1 place of worship, and 250 professed Christians. Station also of the Moravian Missions, with (1903) 1 missionary and his wife, 22 native workers, 2 outstations, 3 places of worship, 4 Sunday schools, 2 day schools, and 234 professed Christians. Station also of the SDA (1893), with (1900) 2 missionaries, one of them with his wife; 16 native workers, 7 outstations, 1 place of worship, 5 Sunday schools, 1 day school, and 220 professed Christians; the auxiliary International Medical and Benevolent Association also has here 1 woman missionary. Station also of the African Methodist Episcopal Church, with 1 native worker.

PORTUGUESE EAST AFRICA: A colony of Portugal, lying along the east coast of Africa for a distance of nearly 1,000 miles, extending from the Rovuma River and the borders of German East Africa on the north to Amatongaland on the south, and reaching back to Lake Nyasa, Matabililand, and the Transvaal on the west. The total area is about 297,750 square miles; the population about 1,500,000. It comprises three districts: Mozambique, Zambesia, and Lourenço Marques, to which, however, must be added the district of Inhambane, formed when the administrative concession to the Inhambane Company failed in 1889, and the Gaza region, which constitutes a military district. Two trading companies, the Nyasa and the Mozambique Companies, administer certain regions under a royal charter that confers sovereign powers. Mozambique, Beira, Inhambane, and Lourenço Marques are the most important towns. The Delagoa Bay railway, touching the coast at Lourenço Marques, has a length in the colony of 57 miles, and extends to Pretoria. The Beira railway extends in the colony 222 miles, and is continued in British territory to Bulawayo. Telegraphs, with a mileage of 1,850 miles, connect the principal towns and communicate with the British systems. The country far from the coast and from navigable rivers is still largely unexplored by white men. The climate is subject to sudden changes, but the mean annual temperature is high, and, with moderate care, danger to health is avoided. The whole region is intersected by numerous rivers, and is very fertile, but the tsetse fly is, in some districts, very destructive. Valuable timbers are found in the forests. The mineral resources (gold, copper, iron and coal) are of exceptional importance. The Chindé River, 45 miles south of Quaqua, is a mouth of the Zambesi, and furnishes a channel three fathoms deep and 500 yards wide, with good anchorage. An ordinary steamer can thus pass directly into the river. Formerly goods, after several days' journey up the Quaqua, had to be carried eight miles over a swampy depression to the Zambesi, where they were transferred to the small Zambesi steamers. The Tongas (a name applied in a collective sense to the tribes originally inhabiting the southern part of this territory, are a peaceful and industrious people. Their language has been reduced to writing, and a hymn-book and the whole New Testament have been translated. The Zulu language is spoken by a great majority of the people. There are two other extensively spoken languages—the Isisena, spoken from the Sabi to the Buzi, the Isinhlwenga south of the Sabi. North of the Buzi the Sena language is spoken by a people who only occasionally use the Zulu. Roman Catholic Missions have long existed in the colony, and of Protestant Missionary Societies the SPG, the Free Methodists of America, and the Swiss Romande Mission have stations in the southern coast regions.

Monteiro (Rose), *Delagoa Bay, Its Natives and Natural History*, London, 1891; Worsfield (W. B.), *Portuguese Nyassaland*, London, 1899.

PORVENIR. See LIMON.

POTOANE: A village in Transvaal, South Africa, situated on the Aapies River, 32 miles N. by E. of Pretoria. Station of the Hermannsburg Missionary Society (1871), with (1901) 1 missionary, 1 native worker, 1 place of worship, 1 day school, and 169 professed Christians.

POTRIBO: A village in Dutch Guiana, South America, situated in the Connewyne district, about 30 miles E. by S. of Paramaribo. Station of the Moravian Society (1896), with (1903) 1 missionary and his wife, 22 native workers, 1 place of worship, and 129 professed Christians.

POTCHEFSTROOM: A town in the Transvaal, South Africa, 90 miles southwest of Pretoria. Population, 2,000. Station of the SPG (1864), with (1903) 1 missionary. Station also of the Berlin Missionary Society (1872), with (1903) 1 missionary, 13 native workers, 4 outstations, and 1,298 professed Christians, of whom 343 are communicants. Station also of the WMS, with 1 missionary, 81 native workers, 38 outstations, 22 places of worship, 22 Sunday schools, 8 day schools, and 1,582 professed Christians, of whom 380 are communicants.

POWERS, Philander O.: Born at Phillipston, Mass., August 19, 1805; graduated at Amherst College, 1830, and Andover Theological Seminary, 1834; sailed November 10 the same year as missionary of the ABCFM, arriving at Smyrna January 12, 1835; released from the service of the Board, 1862; reappointed in 1866; he was stationed at Broosa, Trebizond, Sivas, Antioch, Kessab, Urfa, and Marash. His self-sacrificing spirit appeared in his readiness to leave one missionary field for another, never allowing the comforts of home to interfere with or keep him from his work at a distance. He had a fine taste for music. This talent, together with his skill in versification, made him an excellent hymnologist. Many of the best hymns in the Turkish are from his pen. He died October 2, 1872, at Kessab, an outstation of Antioch, in the house he had built, and the funeral services were held in the large and pleasant chapel, the erection of which he had superintended. His remains rest at the foot of Mount Cassius.

PRASLIN. See SEYCHELLE ISLANDS.

PRATT, Andrew T.: Born at Black Rock, near Buffalo, N. Y., February 22, 1826; graduated at Yale College, 1847; studied one year at Union Theological Seminary, New York, and two in New Haven; pursued medical studies at the New York College of Physicians and Surgeons; ordained August 6, 1852; sailed December 22 the same year as a missionary of the ABCFM in Turkey. His first station was Aintab, but he removed to Aleppo in 1856 and to Marash in 1859. In 1868 he was transferred to the Western Turkey Mission, and removed to Constantinople, there to be engaged, especially with Dr. Riggs, in the work of revising the Turkish Scriptures, in the hope of securing a uniform version for both Christian and Muslim readers. He died December 5, 1872. His grammar of the Turkish, partly a translation of a Turkish work and partly his own, is proof of his proficiency as a Turkish scholar. In fact, he was a distinguished scholar, with extensive general information. He was fond of music and had a poetic taste. He was, therefore, an excellent hymnologist, and wrote original hymns in Turkish, as well as translating others from the English. He was a good physician, and trained several native Armenians as physicians, who became useful in the medical profession.

PRESBYTERIAN CHURCH IN CANADA; Home and Foreign Missions of: In June, 1875, the four Presbyterian churches of Canada—two were in the Maritime Provinces and two in the Western Provinces—met in Montreal and constituted the "General Assembly of the Presbyterian Church in Canada," to take up and prosecute the home and foreign missionary operations of the several churches. Already, in 1848, the Nova Scotia church had sent Rev. John Geddie to commence work in the **New Hebrides.** For many years this New Hebrides work absorbed the interest of the church, but in 1869 another Nova Scotian, Rev. John Morton, commenced work in the island of Trinidad, and three years later George Leslie Mackay, of Toronto, went to North Formosa. About the same time some Canadian women had gone as missionaries to India, and when the organization was completed these four missions were in operation. Work in China was commenced in 1887, Demerara 1896, Korea 1898. As early as 1866 special efforts were made for the North American Indians, and in 1891 the needs of the Chinese in Canada were recognized.

1. *New Hebrides:* After the efforts of the LMS in the New Hebrides, and the martyrdom of John Williams at Eromanga, work in these islands was confined chiefly to occasional visits by the LMS missionary ship until 1848, when the Nova Scotia Presbyterian Church sent Rev. John Geddie to settle at Aneityum. The Secession and Reformed Presbyterians churches of Scotland had, for a long time, a deep interest in that field, and sent Rev. John Inglis and Rev. John G. Paton to take up the work. The Canadian Presbyterians have been from the beginning a strong element in the **New Hebrides Mission Synod,** made up of representatives of eight Presbyterian churches. In the apportionment of mission work, between the Eastern and Western divisions of the Presbyterian Church, these islands, very naturally, fell to the Eastern division. As its share of the work it reports (1903) on the three islands of Santo, Efate, and Eromanga 6 missionaries, and 3 churches with 400 members.

2. *Trinidad and Demerara:* In 1869 the Rev. John Morton, a minister of the Presbyterian Church of Nova Scotia, who, having visited Trinidad for the benefit of his health, noticed the deplorable condition of the imported laboring people, and on his return home offered his services to go and establish a mission for their benefit. In 1871 he was joined by the Rev. Kenneth J. Grant, who is now at San Fernando, a considerable town on the island, and from time to time the mission has been reenforced and in 1896 was extended to include Demerara. This also is under the care of the Eastern division, and reports in the two fields 18 missionaries, 72 native workers, 9 churches with 917 communicants. Special attention is paid to education, and there are 59 schools with 5,095 pupils.

3. *Formosa:* The Mission in Northern Formosa has been one of the Church's most successful enterprises. It was commenced in 1872 by Rev. George Leslie Mackay, a native of Oxford County, Ontario. In 1875 he was joined by Rev. J. B. Fraser, M.D., and subsequently by Rev. Kenneth F. Junor, now of New York. At present the Rev. John Jamieson, of Ontario, is associated with Dr. Mackay. Dr. Mackay married a Christian Chinese lady, who was very helpful to him in gaining the attention of the women and in superintending the girls' school. His efforts to train a native agency and his custom of taking with him on his journeys his class of young men proved most effective, and, while he had most able associates, the success of the work, both among the Chinese and the Pepohoan, was largely due to him.

The 4 missionaries (1903) and 57 native workers had the care of 27 churches and 61 outstations, with 2,037 communicants. Oxford College, at Tamsui, had over 50 students.

4. *Central India:* Previous to the union of 1875, two of the Canadian Churches had broken ground in India by sending thither female missionaries who were associated with a mission of the Presbyterian Church of the United States. In 1875 Rev. James Fraser Campbell, of Nova Scotia, was sent to Madras. About the same time, the Rev. James Douglas, of Ontario, was sent to Indore, Central India, situated about four hundred miles west by north from Bombay. From that beginning the work has developed until (1903) 7 stations are occupied by 47 missionaries and 88 native workers. There are 7 churches with 418 communicants, and in the 12 schools of all grades are 1,152 scholars. Medical work and work among the Bhils, and for the famine children, have received special attention. In 4 hospitals over 20,000 patients are treated.

5. *China:* This mission was begun in 1888, by the appointment of the Rev. Jonathan Goforth and Rev. Donald MacGillivray, graduates of Knox College, Toronto, the Rev. James Smith, M.D., of Queen's College, Kingston, and Mr. William McClure, M.D., who was ordained as an elder and designated as a medical missionary to this field. The year following three students of the Presbyterian College, Montreal, were ordained and set apart as missionaries to Ho-nan, viz., Messrs. Murdoch Mackenzie, John Macdougall, and John H. MacVicar, a son of the principal of the college. The General Assembly of 1889 authorized the formation of a Presbytery in Ho-nan, which was accordingly constituted on the 5th of December in that year. This is, perhaps, the first instance of a Presbytery being formed before its constituent members had even reached the field of their prospective labors. This unique Presbytery held its first meeting, not in Ho-nan, but in the adjoining province of Shan-tung, and then and there fixed upon desirable points in Ho-nan at which to commence missionary operations.

Subsequently Dr. MacGillivray removed to Shanghai to take part in the work of the Society for the Diffusion of Christian and General Knowledge. In 1902, with a view to utilizing the wish of Chinese converted in Canada for work among their own people, a mission was started in Macao. The report (1903) shows in China 32 missionaries, with 12 native workers. There are 200 communicants, and in the 2 hospitals 2,150 patients were treated.

6. *Home Work:* Missions to the Chinese are carried on in Montreal and Toronto, and British Columbia, and to the Indians in the Northwest, Manitoba, Saskatchewan, Assiniboia. There are 12 missionaries in the former, and 61 in the latter work, reporting 50 and 375 communicants. In the Indian work some attention is paid to schools, there being 16 with 370 pupils, the great majority being in boarding schools. The woman's work of the Church is carried on by two Women's Foreign Missionary Societies, with headquarters at Toronto and Halifax, representing the Eastern and Western divisions of the Missionary Enterprise.

PRESBYTERIAN CHURCH OF ENGLAND, Foreign Missions: The Presbyterian Church of England, virtually founded in 1570, was the legal form of doctrine in 1641. After the time of Cromwell it gradually became the mere representative of the divided Presbyterian Church in Scotland, till 1776, when the congregations (in England) of the Free and United Presbyterian Churches united and formed the Presbyterian Church of England.

The Missionary Society was organized in 1847, and its first work was to send a missionary, Rev. Wm. C. Burns, to China. In 1865 it commenced work in Formosa, in 1875 in Singapore, and three years later in India. As the Scotch churches have aided in the conduct of the China Mission, so, in 1902, it was resolved that the English churches should have a share in the Livingstonia Mission in Africa.

1. *China:* For the first four years after Mr. Burns' arrival in China, he worked at Hongkong, Canton, and the neighborhood, but in 1851 he visited Amoy on business, and was so much impressed with the needs of this city, and the opening it gave for missionary effort, that he transferred his work there, and made it the first center of the organized labor of the Presbyterian Church of England. As the work grew, the Society sent out, in 1853, the Rev. James Johnson to join Mr. Burns; but in 1855 he was obliged to return home, and his place was filled by the Rev. Carstairs Douglas, who, with the Rev. David Sandeman, was sent out by the Scottish branch of the mission.

The work has since developed, until it is now carried on in three districts: Amoy, including the stations of Amoy, Yung-chun (Engchhun); Tsuen-chau (Chinchew), and Changpu; Swatow, including Swatow, Chao-chau-fu, and Sua-bue; Hakkaland, including Wu-king-fu and San-ho (Samho).

By an arrangement with the American Reformed Church, the native churches in the Amoy district are united in one presbytery, and the theological college represents both boards. The founding of an Anglo-Chinese College in 1898 indicates the interest felt in education, while the fact that the 9 medical missionaries, with 8 native assistants in the three districts, have treated over 20,000 patients, shows the attention paid to medical work. The report (1903) shows 16 ordained missionaries in the three districts (11 married), 9 medical missionaries (7 married), 4 missionary teachers (3 married), 25 missionaries of the Women's Association (including 3 physicians). There are 180 congregations, including 29 native pastorates, and 5,666 communicants. The Mission suffered from the general disturbance in the Boxer rebellion, but has also shared in the renewed interest manifest since.

2. *Formosa:* This Mission was commenced in 1865. By arrangement with the Canadian Presbyterian Board, that mission occupies the parts of the island north of a line a little above the 24th parallel of latitude, while the English Board cares for the southern section. This is divided into 6 districts with 79 congregations, of which 34 have trained preachers, 2,325 adult members, and 10,620 candidates preparing for baptism. There are 5 ordained missionaries (3 married), 3 medical missionaries (2 married), 1 missionary teacher (married), 3 missionaries of the Women's Association. The college at Taerian, with 53 students, and the pressroom are influential agencies. Since the Japanese occupation of the island the work of the Mission has been made easier. The Japanese officials have manifested interest in the work, and the restric-

tions in regard to opium have been helpful. The Mission in the Pescadores Islands is carried on by the native church, at its own expense, tho under the general supervision of the Mission.

3. *Singapore:* Work among the Chinese who came to the Straits Settlements was commenced in 1875, but the first ordained missionary went out in 1881. The work has since developed among the Babas, and there are now under the supervision of the one ordained missionary (married) 12 congregations, including 2 pastorates, with 7 native preachers, 240 communicants.

4. *India:* Work in Rampur Bealia, in Bengal, was begun by the Rev. D. Morrison in 1878, and has (1903) 1 ordained and 2 medical missionaries (1 married). The chief work is medical, nearly 8,000 patients having been treated.

The Women's Missionary Association, organized in 1878, cooperates with the Foreign Mission Committee of the Church, and there is also a Students' Missionary Society, of the Presbyterian Church of England, organized in 1878 for general assistance in the work.

ORGAN: *Monthly Messenger;* of the Women's Association: *Our Sisters in Other Lands.*

PRESBYTERIAN CHURCH OF IRELAND, Foreign Missions: Headquarters, 12 May Street, Belfast, Ireland. In 1840 the "Synod of Ulster" and the "Secession Synod" became united under the name of the "General Assembly of the Presbyterian Church in Ireland." Led by Dr. Duff's eloquence and a missionary survey which Dr. John Wilson, of Bombay (both of the Free Church of Scotland), had made of the states of Kathiawar, they chose India for their first field and sent out as their first missionaries the Revs. A. Kerr and J. Glasgow. These men had not offered themselves for the service, but had been chosen and called upon by the Assembly's Committee to undertake it. As this mode of obtaining missionaries was deemed by them preferable to the ordinary practise of receiving voluntary offers of service, they recorded it, "that it may serve to be a precedent in all time to come."

The missionaries proceeded to Kathiawar in Gujarat, and located in Rajkot, one of the principal towns. As reenforcements arrived other places were occupied, including Gogo (1844), Surat (1846), Borsad (1860), Ahmadabad (1861), Anand (1877), Broach (1887). In 1900 there were 43 missionaries, 251 native workers in 13 stations and 18 outstations, 674 communicants, 120 schools with 6,929 pupils. The medical department is carried on by 5 physicians, of whom four are women.

China: The work of the Irish Presbyterian Church in China was begun in 1879 in the province of Manchuria, North China. Their earliest station was New-chwang, from which, as a center, itinerating journeys were made over all the province to the far north. The work is carried on in close proximity to and fraternal cooperation with the UFS mission in the same regions. There were, in 1900, 28 missionaries, 195 native workers, occupying 9 stations, and 93 outstations, 1,589 communicants, 33 schools with 375 pupils, 6 physicians (one a woman), 5 hospitals and dispensaries with 12,761 patients.

The Assembly has Jewish missions in Syria and in Germany; Colonial missions in Canada, Australia, and New Zealand, and Continental work in various parts of Europe.

The Women's Association for Foreign Missions to Women in the East, headquarters 119 University Street, Belfast, Ireland, was organized in 1874 and carries on the women's work in connection with the Foreign Mission Board of the Presbyterian Church in Ireland.

PRESBYTERIAN CHURCH (North), U. S. A., Board of Foreign Missions: Foreign Missions were undertaken by the Presbyterian Church in the United States at a very early date. The "Society for Propagating Christian Knowledge," formed in Scotland in 1709, established in 1841 a "Board of Correspondents" in New York, by whom the Rev. Azariah Horton, a member of the Presbytery of New York, was appointed to labor as a missionary among the Indians on Long Island. The second foreign missionary of the Presbyterian Church was David Brainerd, who was ordained by the Presbytery of New York, then meeting at Newark, N. J., June 12, 1744. In 1763 the Synod of New York ordered a collection to be made in all its churches for the support of the Indian missions, and in 1766 sent the Rev. Chas. Bealty and the Rev. George Duffield upon a mission to the Indians on the Muskingum River in Ohio. In 1796 was formed the "New York Missionary Society," independent of any presbyterial supervision, altho it consisted principally of members of the Presbyterian Church. In 1797 the "Northern Missionary Society," like its predecessor an independent body and composed in part of Presbyterians, was instituted, and both prosecuted missions to the Indian tribes for several years. In the year 1800, however, the General Assembly of the Presbyterian Church took up the work of foreign missions in a systematic manner. In 1802 the General Assembly's Standing Committee on Missions addressed a circular to all the Presbyteries under its care, urging collections for the support of missions, and making inquiries for suitable men to be employed. In 1803 the Rev. Gideon Blackburn established a mission among the Cherokee Indians in Georgia. After eight years' labor Mr. Blackburn's health failed, the General Assembly was not able to fill his place and the Rev. Mr. Kingsbury, acting under the American Board, established himself in the Cherokee country and built up a flourishing mission. From 1805 to 1818 the General Assembly carried on work among the Indians in various directions, and with some degree of success; but in 1818, a new society, consisting of the Presbyterian, Reformed Dutch, and Associate Reformed Churches, was formed, called the "United Foreign Missionary Society," whose object was "to spread the Gospel among the Indians of North America, the inhabitants of Mexico and South America, and other portions of the heathen and anti-Christian world," and until 1826 all the existing missionary interests of the Presbyterian Church were merged in this society. In 1826, when the Society had under its care nine missions, with a force of 60 missionaries, the whole work was transferred to the ABCFM, and the "United Foreign Missionary Society" ceased its operations.

Many Presbyterians desiring to prosecute foreign missions through the Church of their preference, the Synod of Pittsburgh, which from its organization in 1802 had shown great missionary zeal, formed in 1831 the "Western Foreign Missionary Society," intended not for that synod alone, but for all others which might wish to unite with it.

Operations were at once commenced, and the

Society, organized for the purpose of "conveying the Gospel to whatever parts of the heathen and anti-Christian world the providence of God might enable it to extend its evangelical exertions," succeeded in planting missions among the American Indians, in India and Africa, and was contemplating work in China, when in June, 1837, a Board of Foreign Missions was established by the General Assembly, to which the work of the Society was surrendered. At this point (in 1838) the Presbyterian Church was divided, and the "Old School" Assembly carried on its work through the "Board of Foreign Missions," while the General Assembly of the "New School" continued to prosecute its missions by its "Committee on Foreign Missions" through the ABCFM. Upon the reunion of the Old and New School Assemblies in 1870, the Persian, Syrian, Gabun and several Indian missions were transferred from the American Board, and since that period all the missions of the Presbyterian Church, with the exception of those carried on by the Southern churches, have been prosecuted through the "Board of Missions of the Presbyterian Church."

The Board of Foreign Missions is simply a Permanent Committee of the General Assembly. The members, 21 in number, are appointed by the General Assembly, which possesses exclusively the general authority, supervision and control of the work of the missions, the Board being but a form of its executive agency. From 1838 to 1870 the Board was composed of 120 members, from whom an Executive Committee was appointed of persons residing in or near New York City, the Board's headquarters. At the reunion, the membership was reduced to fifteen, and the Executive Committee was dispensed with, and in 1900 the amended charter provided for the present number.

Development of Work: On its organization in 1837, the Board found one Presbyterian mission already established in India, where the Rev. John C. Lowrie and the Rev. William Ross had commenced work in Ludhiana in 1833. The next fall (1837) two missionaries were commissioned to open work for the Chinese, with headquarters at Singapore. One of these, the Rev. R. W. Orr, spent a month in Bangkok, and sent home an urgent plea for a mission to Siam, which was accordingly commenced in 1840, tho by the failure of health of the missionary in 1844, work was not fully established until 1847. In 1856 work in South America was fairly inaugurated at Bogota, Colombia. Three years later the open door of Japan was entered and in 1860 the mission to Brazil was established. The next decade witnessed no new enterprise, but in 1870 on the reunion of the Old and the New School branches, three missions started by the American Board:—Syria (1819), Persia (1833), and Gabun (1842)—were transferred by that society to the Presbyterian Board. In this selection of the fields, regard was had to the special interest of the Presbyterian members of the ABCFM, as well as to the desire to extend the interest of the Church as much as possible. In 1872 the mission in Mexico was started, and in 1873 the work commenced by the American and Foreign Christian Union in Chili was taken over. Guatemala was occupied in 1882; in 1884 the Korean mission was started, in 1897 Caracas in Venezuela received a missionary, and in 1899 the Board entered with vigor upon the new opportunities presented by the Philippine Islands. The work among the North American Indians undertaken at different times and in different localities has been discontinued, passed over to local presbyteries, or to the Board of Home Missions of the Presbyterian Church in the U. S. A.

Statement of Missions. *I. India:* The first missionaries of the Western Foreign Missionary Society, the Rev. John C. Lowrie and the Rev. Wm. Reed, reached Calcutta in November, 1833, and decided to locate in Ludhiana, then a frontier town of the Northwest Provinces. Mr. Reed's health failing, Mr. Lowrie was left alone, but he was soon reenforced and other places were occupied until, when the work was transferred to the Assembly's Board in 1837, there were four stations, Ludhiana, Allahabad, Saharanpur, and Sabathu. The nature of the foundation work is indicated by the establishment of a mission press and the appointment of a practical printer as early as 1838. The Anglo-Vernacular High School here was the first started in North India.

(1.) *Punjab Mission:* From the first attention was specially directed to the Punjab, and in 1846, after the first Sikh war, Jullundur was occupied, followed in 1848 by Ambala. Then came the second Sikh war, and almost on the heels of the British forces Messrs. John Newton and C. W. Forman entered Lahore (1849), and commenced the work with which they were identified for nearly half a century, and one of the fruits of which is the Forman Christian College, with a larger number of students than any college, government or missionary, north of Calcutta. Other stations have since been added: Dehra (1853), with a fine Christian girls' boarding school; Hoshyarpore (1867), where the work is entirely under the control of native workers; Mussoorie (1847), a fine sanitarium in Landour, chiefly known through the Woodstock School, originally established for the children of missionaries, but later developed into a college; Ferozepore (1882) and Kasur. This mission, originally called by the name of its first station, Ludhiana, is now known as the Punjab mission. Its medical and leper work, as well as its educational and general evangelistic work, has been pressed forward, and from the first it has had the hearty endorsement of the British officials, from Lord Lawrence and Sir Herbert Edwardes to Lord Curzon. It reports (1903) 38 outstations, 65 missionaries, 227 native workers, 20 organized churches, 2,109 communicants, 50 schools, 4,878 pupils, 4 hospitals, and 8 dispensaries, with 41,847 patients.

(2.) *Furrukhabad, or United Provinces Mission:* This was started in 1836, by the Rev. James McEwen, who while on his way to Ludhiana remained for a time at Allahabad to superintend the replacing of some lost parts of a printing press. This remains the chief station of the mission, well provided with educational institutions, a blind asylum, a leper asylum, as well as a printing press. Other stations are: Mainpuri (1843); Fategarh, with its native city, Furrukhabad (1844), notable as the only station where missionaries lost their lives in the mutiny of 1857; Fatehpur (1853); Etawah (1863); Morar, the capital of Gwalior, and the only station in a native state (1874); Jhansi (1886); Etah (1900) and Cawnpore (1901). Aside from Allahabad and Furrukhabad, the work of this mission is more distinctively evangelistic. The report

(1903) shows 20 outstations, 174 native workers, 10 churches, 646 communicants, 89 schools, 1,779 pupils, 1 hospital, and 3 dispensaries, with 35,951 patients.

(3.) *Western India Mission:* This mission, lying in the Deccan, south of Bombay, was started in 1853 under the auspices of the ABCFM, by the Rev. Royal G. Wilder, who located at Kolhapur. Subsequently on the refusal of the ABCFM to approve some of Mr. Wilder's educational plans, he started an independent mission, which in 1870, at the time of the reunion, was accepted by the Presbyterian Board. Other stations are: Ratnagiri (1873), the only station in British territory; Kodoli (1877); Sangli (1884); Miraj (1892); Vengurle (1900). The work of the mission is largely in the villages, and it has done much for the sufferers from famine. There is an industrial school with 42 famine lads at Vengurle, and the Brownie Orphanage, with 600 children, at Kodoli, as well as a hospital and leper asylum at Miraj. The report (1903) shows 12 outstations, 41 missionaries, 68 native workers, 7 churches, 1,180 communicants, 34 schools, 1,554 scholars, 2 hospitals, and 4 dispensaries, with 31,095 patients.

The special phases of work carried on through all the India missions are: the Zenana work, Christian literature, including Bible translation, commentaries, periodic literature, etc., medical and asylum work, educational work, higher and lower, work among the outcasts, and especially the development of a native church.

II. *China:* Three months after its organization, in December, 1837, the Presbyterian Board sent two missionaries, Revs. J. A. Mitchell and R. W. Orr, to commence work for the Chinese at Singapore. Mr. Mitchell died soon after reaching Singapore, and Mr. Orr was compelled by failure of health to return home. Mr. McBride, sent out in 1840, returned for the same reason in 1843. In the same year Dr. J. C. Hepburn and Mr. Walter Lowrie were sent out. They transferred the mission from Singapore to Amoy, reenforcements were sent to them, and a most important agency, the mission press, was established. A special appeal for funds was made by the Board, and as a result a large force of workers was sent to strengthen the mission, and Macao, Amoy and Ningpo were occupied as stations. Amoy was afterward dropped, Canton took the place of Macao as a headquarters and Ningpo became the first station of the Central China mission.

(1.) *Central China:* This mission includes Ningpo (1844), Shanghai (1850), Hangchau (1859), Suchau (1871), Nanking (1876) and Hwai-Yuen (1901).

Ningpo, one of the five ports opened in 1842, was entered in 1844 by Dr. McCartee. A few months later he was joined by a large force of missionaries, among them the Rev. W. M. Lowrie, who was in 1847 killed by pirates. The first convert was baptized in 1845, and a church was organized later in the same year. The girls' boarding school dates from 1846, the industrial school for women from 1861, and the Presbyterial Academy, for the sons of native Christians, and almost wholly supported by the tuition fees and the native churches, from 1881. The boys' boarding school, organized early in the mission, was removed to Hangchau in 1877.

Shanghai, also one of the five ports, was occupied by Messrs. Culbertson and Wight in 1850. While other lines of work are efficiently prosecuted, the great work of this station is the Mission Press, one of the most powerful agencies in the Chinese Empire. It has furnished fonts of type for other Chinese and European presses, has done work for the Bible and Tract Societies, published a number of periodicals, and not only meets all expenses but turns in several thousand dollars a year into the mission treasury.

Hangchau, visited by Dr. Nevius (1859), but not occupied as a place of residence until 1865, has a fine college for boys with about 85 students and a new boarding school for girls. Suchau (1871) has always been the seat of special hostility to foreigners, but the Tooker Hospital has done much to disarm this feeling. Other stations are Nanking (1876) and Hwai-yuen (1901). The report (1903) shows 37 outstations, 62 missionaries, 121 native workers, 20 churches, 1,841 communicants, 25 schools, with 961 pupils, 1 hospital and 3 dispensaries, with 3,712 patients.

(2.) *Canton Mission:* This was started at Macao, but Canton was occupied in 1845, and this was for more than thirty years the only station. In 1879 a chapel was leased at Lienchau, and in 1886 Yeung-kong was made a center of work. Kong-hau in the Hakka country was long visited by the missionaries and a church was organized in 1890, but it was subsequently deemed advisable to withdraw the missionaries and leave it under the care of a native pastor. The work in Canton has been successful, a number of churches having been organized, both in the city and the immediate vicinity. This is the seat of the Canton Christian College, founded by Rev. A. P. Happer, D.D., now under a separate Board of Trustees, but cooperating with the mission. It was at Canton also that Dr. Peter Parker in 1835 gave the first impulse to distinctive medical missions, and there is now a fine hospital owned by the Medical Missionary Society in China, tho the physicians are supplied by the Presbyterian Board. Other departments of educational, philanthropic and evangelistic work are carried on. The report of the mission (1903) shows 60 outstations, 31 missionaries, 117 native workers, 20 churches, with 3,854 members, 32 schools, with 892 pupils, 3 hospitals and 5 dispensaries, with 41,847 patients.

(3.) *Hai-nan Mission:* Mission work in the island of Hai-nan was begun in 1881 by Mr. C. C. Jeremiassen as an independent enterprise, but was taken up by the Canton Mission in 1885 and organized as a separate mission in 1893. There are three stations: Kuing Chow and Nodoa, both occupied in 1885 and Kachek (1902). The work is largely among the Loi tribe, aboriginal inhabitants, and offering some special attractions to missionary effort. But many Hakkas from the mainland are also included in this field. The report (1903) shows 5 outstations, 21 missionaries, 23 native workers, 131 communicants, 5 schools, with 152 scholars, 1 printing press, 2 hospitals and 3 dispensaries, with 14,932 patients.

(4.) *Hunan Mission:* The Canton Mission for many years looked toward the province of Hunan as one offering a fine field for work, but it was not until 1900 that the Rev. W. H. Lingle, Dr. H. W. Boyd and Dr. Leila M. Doolittle were authorized to open a station at Siang-tau. Then came the Boxer uprising and they were obliged to withdraw. They have since returned and a new station has been opened at Heng-chau (1902). The work, still (1903) in its infancy, reports 10 missionaries, 2 native workers, 6 communicants, 1 school, with 12 pupils.

(5.) *Peking Mission:* Work in Peking was begun in 1863 by Rev. W. A. P. Martin, who withdrew from the mission in 1869 to take the presidency of the Imperial Lung-wen College, but has always been identified with the mission. As in the case of Canton, the work for many years was confined to the city of Peking, and was developed successfully there. In 1893 a new station was opened at Pao-ting-fu. The Peking mission suffered severely during the Boxer rebellion. The company of missionaries at Paoting-fu were massacred, including Dr. Taylor, Mr. and Mrs. Simcox and three children, and Dr. and Mrs. Hodge. The buildings in both stations were destroyed. Since the subsidence of the troubles the work has been resumed with energy and the report (1903) shows both stations occupied, 4 outstations, 29 missionaries, 211 communicants. Both school and medical work have suffered and are not yet fully reorganized.

(6.) *East Shantung Mission,* including the stations of Teng-chau, Chi-fu and Tsing-tau.

(7.) *West Shantung Mission,* including the stations of Chi-nan-fu, Wei-hsien, I-chow-fu and Chining-chow.

For many years these two were included in one Shantung mission, afterward divided for convenience of administration.

The province of Shantung, the home of Confucius, Laotze and other Chinese sages, was first visited by the Rev. J. L. Nevius, who opened the station of Teng-chau in 1861 and that of Chi-fu in 1862. The next place entered was Chi-nan-fu (1872), followed by Wei-hsien (1882), I-chow-fu (1891), Chining-fu (1892) and Tsing-tau (1898). Severe famines in 1877 and 1889 occasioned the organization of relief work, which, under the general supervision of Dr. Nevius, who had become by extensive itineration personally known and respected all over the province, enabled the missionaries to gain a strong hold upon the people. Dr. Nevius made a thorough study of methods of mission work with special reference to the development of the native church, and in this respect he and his associates were most successful. Educational and medical work also were pushed, and the Teng-chau College is one of the best in China. The entire work was disorganized by the Boxer uprising, and churches and hospitals were destroyed, tho the college was uninjured. Thousands of native Christians lost their lives, but, largely through the skill and energy of Mr. Cornwell, the U. S. Consul at Chi-fu, the entire missionary force escaped in safety to Chi-fu. Since then the work has gradually resumed its former conditions and the report (1903) shows for the East Shantung mission 71 outstations, 30 missionaries, 117 native workers, 46 churches, with 2,038 communicants, 48 schools with 770 pupils, 1 hospital and 2 dispensaries, with 8,519 patients. The figures for the West Shantung Mission are not complete, but as given show 158 outstations, 31 missionaries, 168 native workers, 15 churches with 3,952 communicants, 51 schools with 565 pupils, 3 hospitals and 4 dispensaries with 28,124 patients.

III. *Siam and Laos.* (1.) *Siam Mission:* The Rev. R. W. Orr on his way to Singapore in 1838 spent a month in Bangkok and sent back an urgent plea for a missionary to work among the Chinese. Rev. W. P. Buell arrived in 1840, but left in 1844 on account of ill health, and it was not until 1847 that Rev. Stephen Mattoon and Rev. S. R. House, M.D., were permanently established there. For four years they were obliged to work very quietly because of the bitter hostility of the king, but the accession to the throne in 1851 of Prince Somdet Phra, who had been under the instruction of Rev. Jesse Caswell, of the ABCFM, made a great change. From that time the mission work has had the cordial support of the government and repeatedly missionaries have been placed in positions of honor and influence. Special attention has been given to medical and educational work and the preparation of Christian literature, but also to touring, and a mission schooner, the *Kalamazoo,* is well known all along the coast. It was difficult, however, to secure results and it was not until 1859 that the first Siamese convert was baptized. Among the most important schools is one for girls, which numbers among its pupils a great many from the upper classes.

Other stations are: Petchaburee, occupied in 1861, Rajaburee (1889), Pitsanuloke (1889), Nakawn (1900). In all the stations there has been much earnest labor, with comparatively small visible results. The enervating climate, to which so many workers have succumbed, the mobile, unretentive character of the people, whose unthinking acquiescence is more discouraging than opposition, are obstacles to be overcome only by great faith and endurance. In no mission of the Board has the effort to secure self-support among the native churches met with so much opposition. In Petchaburee, the boarding schools were closed and many individuals who had been employed or assisted by the Mission withdrew when obliged to depend upon themselves. The recent revival of interest in Buddhism does not seem as yet to have affected the work greatly. The presence of some strong self-supporting churches is a pledge of future success. The report (1903) shows 7 outstations, 29 missionaries, 25 native workers, 9 churches with 439 members, 6 schools with 437 pupils, a printing press, 3 hospitals, and 4 dispensaries with 7,035 patients

(2.) *Laos Mission:* The missionaries in Siam were led to consider the claims of the Laos tribes who occupy the hill country in the north of Siam, by encountering a settlement of Laos refugees near Petchaburee. In 1864 a deputation visited Chieng Mai and three years later Rev. Daniel McGilvary and Rev. Jonathan Wilson opened a permanent station there. Success was more rapid than among the Siamese and there were several converts within a few months. Then followed bitter persecution and the work was checked, but received a new impulse until 1878, when in consequence of the bitter opposition of the people to Christian marriage without the usual ceremonies of devil-worship, appeal was made to the king of Siam, which resulted in a proclamation of religious liberty to the Laos. From that time the work progressed rapidly. The general policy of the Mission, based on the experience of other missions, has been from the beginning to throw the responsibility of maintaining the work on the people themselves, with the result that the evangelistic work is now virtually supported by Laos Christians, including a foreign mission to the Ka Mu tribe across the Me-kong in French territory. There has also been a comprehensive scheme of education, a mission press established and the medical work has been one of the most effective agencies in disarming opposition and reaching the people. Other stations occupied are Lakawn (1885), Muang Pré (1893), Nan (1894), Chieng Rai (1897). Lampun was occupied in 1891, but on account of its proximity to Chieng Mai it was united to that station.

The Mission is anxiously looking forward to work among the other Laos tribes, particularly those in French territory, but is hampered by the objections of the French Government. The report (1903) shows 23 outstations, 40 missionaries, 28 native workers, 16 churches with 2,706 communicants, 17 schools with 300 pupils, 4 hospitals and 4 dispensaries with 7,632 patients.

IV. South America: The first mission work of the Presbyterian Church in South America was undertaken in Buenos Aires in 1827, but was soon abandoned; another attempt in 1853 was also without permanent results. In 1856 a missionary was sent to Colombia, reaching Bogota in June. The next step was to Rio de Janeiro in 1860. In 1873 work which had been established in Chile in 1850 by the American and Foreign Christian Union was assumed by the Presbyterian Board, and that again was followed in 1897 by the opening of a station in Caracas, Venezuela. The work in Brazil developed so that a division seemed best into Central and Southern Brazil Missions.

(1.) *Colombia:* The early years of this mission from its commencement in 1856 were times of great difficulty on account of opposition of the Roman Catholic Church. The revolution in 1860, however, threw the government into the hands of the Liberals; the Jesuits were banished; monastic orders restricted, and mission work received a new impulse. The mission has never had the success apparent in some of the Asiatic fields. Not only is there bitter opposition on the part of ecclesiastics, but the intelligent classes are largely indifferent or skeptical; the poorer people very ignorant. Bogota was the only station for a number of years, then in 1888 Barranquilla was occupied, followed by Medellin in 1889. The report (1903) shows 16 missionaries, 11 native workers, 3 churches, 181 communicants, 4 schools, 220 pupils.

(2.) *Southern Brazil Mission:* The first missionary to Rio de Janeiro, Rev. A. G. Simonton, was peculiarly qualified for pioneer work in such a country, and to his wisdom and scholarly qualities is largely due the success of the work. Three years later the city of São Paulo was occupied, and made the center of the educational and publishing work, which have been two of the most important departments of the mission. In 1886, Horace M. Lane, M.D., was put in special superintendency of the educational work, and under his lead Mackenzie College has been developed into a most influential institution. Other stations at present occupied are Curytiba (1885), Novo Friburgo (1891), Florianopolis (1898). Work has also been done in Rio Claro and in Brotas. The strongest churches are those in São Paulo, which grew up under the care of Dr. G. W. Chamberlain. But all through the mission there has been excellent evangelistic work done. The report (1903) shows 40 outstations, 13 missionaries, 4 native workers, 29 churches, 3,107 communicants, 26 schools, 762 pupils. (Some of these figures are incomplete.)

(3) *Central Brazil Mission:* This field includes the states of Bahia, Sergipe and parts of others. The stations are: Bahia (1871), Cachoeira (1873), Sergipe (1886), Villa Nova da Rainha (1900). Work in this section has presented unusual difficulties, yielding less fruit than any other of the mission fields in Brazil, owing partly to the population, principally made up of blacks and their descendants, and partly to the power of the ecclesiastical element. The hope is to extend the work into the interior provinces, inhabited exclusively by Indians, some independent tribes, others semi-civilized and varying greatly in character. Appropriations were made in 1899 for this work, but Mr. George Witte, who was assigned to it, and an associate, were both smitten by fever, and it was for the time being postponed. The report (1903) shows 39 outstations, 13 missionaries, 4 native workers, 7 organized churches, with 467 communicants, 11 schools with 400 pupils.

In 1888 the missions of the Northern and Southern Presbyterian churches were united in the Synod of Brazil, which meets every three years and is entirely independent of the General Assemblies in the United States. The Synod has a vigorous Home Mission Society, and supports the theological seminary at São Paulo. At its triennial meeting in 1900 a membership of 7,000 communicants was reported, a gain of ten per cent. in the three years. In view of the excellent work of this Synod, the American societies are reaching out toward the distant regions as yet unevangelized.

(4) *Chile:* The first American missionary in Valparaiso was the Rev. D. Trumbull, representing the Seamen's Friends Society, and the American and Christian Foreign Union. He labored chiefly for the English-speaking people; but others came to enter upon Spanish work. A Spanish paper was established, and a school and orphanage conducted. The Presbyterians took charge of it in July, 1873. Other stations are: Santiago, occupied first in 1861; Constitucion (1885), Concepcion (1880), Chillan (1892), Talca (1896), Copiapo (1888). Aside from the educational, publication and general evangelistic work, much has been done in the outlying sections, and in the mining regions. The work in Chile has shared in the change that has come over so many of the South American states in the control of Liberals, and in 1888 the mission received a special charter. The report for 1903 shows 34 outstations, 12 missionaries, 29 native workers, 10 churches, 522 members, 4 schools, 560 pupils.

(5) *Japan:* While the Christian Church was watching the opening of Japan, the Presbyterian Board requested Dr. McCartee, a missionary in China, to visit that country and make inquiries preparatory to mission work. He was, however, unable to reach Japan, and as the treaty opening the ports of Yokohama and Nagasaki was to take effect in July, 1859, in the previous April, the Board commissioned Dr. J. C. Hepburn and wife, formerly of China, to enter the country. They reached Japan early in October and settled at Kanagawa, a few miles from Tokio. The Buddhist temple was obtained as a residence, the idols were removed, and the people were found to be civil and friendly. There was, however, constant surveillance, and aggressive work was scarcely possible. Meanwhile, there was opportunity for studying the language, and Dr. Hepburn devoted himself to it, laying the foundation for

a translation of the Scriptures and a Japanese-English Dictionary, the first edition of which was published in 1867.

In 1862 the station was moved to Yokohama, and a dispensary and hospital were opened. Other missionaries arrived, and gradually the field of work enlarged. In February, 1869, three converts were baptized. During this decade, also, occurred the political revolution which changed the entire policy of Japan toward the outer world, and which brought into prominence as leaders several young men who had come under the influence of Dr. Hepburn, and Dr. Verbeck, of the Reformed Church in America, and others.

In January of 1872 a week of prayer was observed by all of the missionaries and English-speaking residents of all denominations in Yokohama, and the result was a great manifestation of spiritual life. Two years later there were still more marks of divine favor. Churches were organized, and the Presbyterian and Reformed Missions worked together in cordial sympathy. In 1876 a movement was initiated by these two missions, together with that of the United Presbyterian Church of Scotland, which resulted in the organization of the United Church of Christ in Japan, an independent self-governing Japanese Church, in which the missionaries were only advisory members. An effort, in 1889, to unite the Congregational churches with this body failed, and soon after the term "United" was dropped from the title.

In 1877 a Union Theological School was organized, and a Union College in 1883. In 1886 these were united, and with the special department then organized became the *Meiji Gakuin,* "College of the Era of Enlightened Principles."

The unprecedented advance of these years was followed by a reaction of intense prejudice against foreigners and foreign teaching, which again was largely overcome by the bearing of the Christians during the war with Japan, and has been more recently followed by a renewed increase of interest.

(1) *Eastern Japan Mission:* The work commenced at Yokohama has resulted in two self-supporting churches. But the headquarters of the mission were changed in 1869 to Tokio, the capital, where the first church was organized in 1873. The mission work includes open-air evangelistic work, a Training School for Bible Women, a Girls' Boarding School, and a Training School for Nurses. Other lines of work connected with this mission include the work in Hokkaido and the Kurile Islands. The headquarters of this section are at Sapporo (1887), but several other places are occupied. In one, Otaru, the work began as a Sunday school for the fishermen's children. There is now a church and an excellent school, with two kindergartens and three Sunday schools. The report in 1903 shows 24 outstations, 31 missionaries, 59 native workers, 8 schools with 882 pupils.

(2.) *Western Japan:* The first station occupied on the Western coast was Kanagawa, by Rev. T. W. Winn, in 1879. At that time, so far as known, there was not a single Christian living in those provinces. To-day every important city has its groups of Christians, and a number of vigorous churches. The next station to be occupied was Osaka (1881), followed by Hiroshima (1887), Kioto (1890), Yamaguchi (1891), Fukui (1891), Matsuyama (1901). In all of these places the mission work includes evangelistic and educational departments, and Hiroshima is peculiarly attractive for its opportunities for work among the soldiers and sailors. Educational work at Kioto is especially interesting, while from Yamaguchi efforts are being made to reach the neighboring island of Kiushiu. The report for 1903 shows in Western Japan, 29 outstations, 30 missionaries, 77 native workers, 8 schools, 463 pupils. The church statistics for both missions are 36 churches, 5,825 communicants.

VI. Africa. (1.) *Liberia:* Presbyterian work in Liberia was commenced in 1833 by Rev. J. B. Pinney, especially for the aborigines, and stations were established along the Kroo coast near Cape Palmas. The climate proved so fatal that the experiment was tried of sending colored ministers, but it was found that these were not exempt from fever, and lacked the ability to organize and superintend. Other white men were sent out, including Rev. D. A. Wilson, and among the colored men Rev. E. W. Blyden, and several new stations were occupied. In 1857 there came a great encouragement through a revival. As the Methodists, Lutheran, and Protestant Episcopal churches have successful work in that region, the Presbyterian Board in 1894 decided to withdraw, and by 1899 had transferred all its interest to the Presbytery of West Africa, including 15 churches with about 400 members.

(2.) *West Africa:* In 1842 the ABCFM occupied the station of Baraka in the Gabun district, sending out Rev. J. L. Wilson, Rev. Benjamin Griswold, Rev. Albert Bushnell, and Rev. William Walker. Eight years later the Presbyterian Board established a station on the island of Corisco, sending out Rev. J. L. Mackey, Rev. C. De Heer, and Rev. Ibia J'Ikenge. On the union of the old and new school branches, in 1870, the mission of the ABCFM was transferred to the Presbyterian Board, and the two missions became known as the Gabun and Corisco Mission. Subsequently, on the extension of the work into the interior among the Fang tribe, the name was changed to the West Africa Mission.

The work of the American Board was extended to several stations, and there was good success among the Dikele people, but the occupation of the coast by the French brought special restrictions, and the unhealthy climate and the hostility of the people combined to reduce the work so that there remained but the one station at Baraka at the time of the transfer. Similarly the work in Corisco suffered from the Spanish Government (which forbade the teaching of any religion except the Roman Catholic), the unhealthy climate and the tribal quarrels, and there, too, the four stations were reduced to one, tho the native church is a strong one.

In 1865 the Rev. George Paull founded Mbade station on the Benito River, north of Corisco, and on his death, after thirteen months, the work was taken up by Rev. R. H. Nassau, the patriarch of the West Africa Mission. The next field to be occupied was on the Ogowe River, south of Corisco; and Mr. Nassau opened a station at Belambila (1874), which was later (1876) removed to Kangwe. In pursuance of a plan to form a line of stations to the Congo, Talaguga was occupied in 1882 and three years later Rev. A. C. Good entered upon his work. Several churches were organized and the mission was progressing favorably when the interference of the French

Government, forbidding any language but French in the schools, and hampering the evangelistic work, became so serious that the Board decided in 1892 to transfer its work to the Paris Evangelical Mission Society.

Then came the development on the North. Batanga, at first an outstation of Benito, was made a regular station in 1889, and to this station was transferred the work which had been commenced on the Ogowe River. Under the German Government work has been less difficult, and Dr. Good's explorations and the long experience and faithful service of several of the missionaries who have been identified with the mission from its beginning are bearing fruit. Baraka and Benito still remain as centers of work, but the extension of the mission from Batanga includes Efulen (1893), Elat (1895), MacLean Memorial Station, Lolodorf (1897). This last station is the result of a report by Dr. A. C. Good of a visit to the dwarfs. Miss Margaret MacLean, of Glasgow, Scotland, had become interested in these people through Stanley's letters, and offered to support a mission among them, under the auspices of the Board. The work is extremely difficult because of the climate, the diversity of languages, and the timidity of the little people.

The report (1903) shows 58 outstations, 34 missionaries, 49 native workers, 13 churches with 1,716 communicants, 22 schools with 984 pupils, 2 hospitals, and 2 dispensaries with 1,900 patients.

VII. Syria: Mission work in Syria was commenced under the ABCFM, by Pliny Fisk and Levi Parsons, who went to Jerusalem in 1821, but were unable to stay there. In 1823 Messrs. Bird and Goodell arrived at Beirut, and except for a time when (1828-1830) they withdrew to Malta on account of political disturbances, this has been the center of mission work. The other stations occupied were Abeih (1843), Tripoli (1848), Sidon (1851). After the transfer of this mission from the ABCFM to the Presbyterian Board (1870) an extension of work into the Lebanon was planned and the station of Zahleh opened in 1872.

From the very first special attention has been paid to education and publication. Messrs. Bird and Goodell brought with them a printing press and immediately commenced translation and publication. Dr. Eli Smith commenced a translation of the Arabic Bible, completed by Dr. C. V. A. Van Dyck, which is one of the finest in existence. Schools were established in Beirut in 1824, including one for girls. From these have grown seminaries in Beirut, Sidon, and Tripoli, while the **Syrian Protestant College** at Beirut is one of the finest educational institutions in mission lands. Not organically connected with the mission, it has always, nevertheless, been in closest sympathy with evangelistic work. Medical work under the lead of Drs. Van Dyck and Post has from the first had a prominent place. The medical department of the college has furnished physicians for the entire Arabic-speaking sections of Western Asia and Northern Africa.

Evangelistic work has been always rendered difficult by the peculiar situation of the country, the rivalry of the different communities, the hostility of the Government and of the Roman Catholics, especially the Jesuits, who have taken advantage of French influence in Syria to hinder, so far as possible, the work of Protestant missions. The churches have suffered also from emigration.

Still there has been good progress and the advance in the number of communicants from 294 in 1870 to 2,542 shows good results. The report for 1903 shows 106 outstations, 38 missionaries, 207 native workers, 29 churches, 2,542 communicants, 108 schools, 5,982 pupils, 1 hospital, and 1 dispensary with 5,622 patients, while the press issued 23,395,410 pages.

In this last item appears a hint of what is, after all, the greatest work of the Syria Mission. As a center from which the whole Arabic-speaking world may be reached, the fruits of labor here are found all over Asia and Africa, and in the East Indies. In scarcely any other mission in the world do the actual, immediate returns, as given in statistical tables, give so meager a view of the real results.

VIII. Persia: The first American missions to Persia grew out of a visit of Messrs. Eli Smith and H. G. O. Dwight of the ABCFM in 1829. On their representations that Society determined to establish a mission in Persia for the Nestorians, and appointed Justin Perkins the first missionary. He sailed in 1833 and reached Tabriz a year later. In 1835 he was joined by Dr. Asahel Grant, and a station was established at Urmia, in November, 1835. One of the most intelligent of the Nestorian bishops, Mar Yohanan, gave Mr. Perkins instruction in the language. A school was opened very soon, and other helpers were added after a few years, among them, in 1843, Fidelia Fiske, who came to take charge of the Girls' School. For some years there was considerable discouragement, but then came a revival, and for twelve years it continued, the number of converts being very large. At first the effort was to reform the old Church, but a separation became absolutely essential, and in 1862 the first Conference was held, and a confession of faith adopted, as also rules, discipline, etc. In 1870 this mission was transferred from the ABCFM to the Presbyterian Board, and then commenced a policy of extension. Teheran was occupied in 1872, Tabriz in 1873, Hamadan in 1880. Distance between the stations and the diversity of language occasioned the division into two missions, a Western and an Eastern, Urmia and Tabriz constituting the former, and Teheran and Hamadan the latter.

(1.) *Western Persia Mission:* The work in Urmia is chiefly among the Nestorians of that city, the surrounding plains and in the Kurdish Mountains. It is the seat of a college, originally established at Mt. Seir, and for which David Tappan Stoddard did much; more lately removed to a fine location in the plain near the city. This college has exercised a great influence throughout the entire section. Fiske Seminary also has become well known throughout that whole region. The missionary press established here has been successful, and the work of Bible translation and the preparation of Christian literature commenced by Dr. Perkins, and more lately carried on by Dr. Benjamin Labaree, has been very effective. Medical work has always been prominent. Originally started by Dr. Grant, and carried to a high success with a hospital and a training school by Dr. Cochran, it has been one of the most effective agencies employed. More than once the medical men of the mission have been its protectors in times of stress. The greater number of churches connected with the Nestorian work are in the plain, but there are quite a number through the mountains, extending across the Turkish border into Mesopotamia. For a time the work among the Syrians of Mosul was taken over by the Presbyterian Board from the ABCFM, but was afterward transferred to the CMS on account of the great distance, the difficulty of access, etc. The work in Tabriz, as also in the outstation of Salmas, is largely among the Armenians. Work for the Muslims has been carried on with some success, altho the number of converts is not great. The mission has felt the hostile influence of Russian officials, as Russian political power has developed in North Persia; also the unfortunate effect of the number of independent workers, who have won support from Plymouth Brethren, German Lutherans, and others.

The report (1903) shows 117 outstations, 28 missionaries, 178 native workers, 21 churches with 2,653 communicants, 99 schools with 2,279 pupils, 3 hospitals and 2 dispensaries with 26,312 patients.

(2.) *Eastern Persia Mission:* The city of Teheran was occupied in 1872 by the Rev. Jas. Bassett, after an extended tour, including Tabriz, Teheran, and Hamadan. Educational and medical work has been carried on successfully, and the recognition of the physicians by the Government has been one element in securing a considerable attendance of Mohammedans in the school for boys. From Teheran tours are made to Kazvin and Resht (on the Caspian) and occasionally to Meshed, one of the Muslim holy cities. Hamadan was first visited by colporteurs from Urmia in 1869, made an outstation of Teheran in 1872, and a station in 1880. The work in both Teheran and Hamadan is chiefly among the Armenians; but at Hamadan there is a Jewish church. The report (1903) shows 5 outstations, 24 missionaries, 44 native workers, 4 churches, 244 communicants, 6 schools, 513 pupils, 1 hospital and 4 dispensaries with 8,393 patients.

IX. Mexico: In 1872 the General Assembly voted to open work in Mexico, and in September of the same year Messrs. Thomson, Phillips, and Pitkin, with their wives, went to Mexico City. There they found a large body of Mexican believers of anti-prelatical convictions, gathered in nine independent congregations, largely the result of the work of Miss Rankin, Mr. Riley and others. Most of these joined one or another of the different missions that entered the country and furnished the nucleus for their work. The next year Zacatecas and San Luis Potosi were occupied, then Saltillo (1884), Zitacuaro (1893), Chilpancingo (1894), Jalapa (1897). The work in Saltillo is the immediate successor of Miss Rankin's work at Monterey. The story of the mission contains many incidents of great heroism, in bitter persecution, especially in Guerrero and Zitacuaro. Educational and publication work has had a prominent place, and the press at Mexico City has been a most effective evangelistic agency. For a time there were two missions, Northern and Southern. In 1884 these were united, and the native churches have been organized in three presbyteries, Zacatecas, Mexico City and the Gulf. The Mexican Home Mission Board, organized in 1890 by the Presbytery of the City of Mexico, supports two evangelists in Guerrero and Mexico.

The report (1903) shows 146 outstations, 23 missionaries, 81 native workers, 45 churches, 3,902 communicants, 29 schools, 638 pupils.

X. Guatemala: Work was commenced in Guatemala in 1882 in response to special appeals for Protestant teaching and the assurance by President Barrios of sympathy and full freedom of action. The first work of the Rev. John C. Hill was the organization of a church for the Europeans and Americans. This has since become independent. A little later work in Spanish was commenced, Rev. E. M. Haymaker, formerly of Mexico, assisting greatly in the undertaking. School work has also been established. While no other station than that at Guatemala City has been opened much good has been done by tours and in outstations among them Quezeltango and San Augustin. Everywhere there is the greatest opportunity. There is absolute religious liberty, and even many loyal Roman Catholics welcome Protestant missions as an agent for the purification of their church. The report (1903) shows 2 native workers, 2 churches with 85 communicants, 1 school with 38 pupils. The climate has proved difficult, and the missionaries who have built up the work were compelled to return, their places to be filled soon by others.

XI. Korea: The first mission work in Korea was by Messrs. Ross and McIntyre, of the Scotch United Presbyterian Mission in Manchuria. A number of conversions resulted, and it was evident that a good basis for mission enterprise existed. In 1880 a Korean of high rank, representing the Government in Japan, became a Christian and begged earnestly for missionaries for his country. In response to this appeal, the Presbyterian Board, in 1884, appointed Dr. H. N. Allen, then a medical missionary in China, to go to Korea. He was appointed physician to the United States Legation at Seoul, and thus was assured safety and favorable reception. His influence soon became very great, and he was received as physician to the royal household and placed in charge of the Government hospital. Some months later Dr. Heron and Rev. H. G. Underwood joined the mission. For several years the work was chiefly medical and literary. The first convert was baptized in 1886, and the first church organized in 1887. After 1890 the advance was marvelously rapid. In the "Presbyterian Council" including the two Presbyterian Missions from the United States, the one from Canada, and the Woman's Union of Victoria, the number of catechumens and adherents was over 22,000 in 1903. The opportunities for direct preaching have so absorbed the energies of all that schools have been less prominent than in some other missions, yet there is a well-established system of education. Medical work has developed so that there are three hospitals at Seoul, Fusan and Phieng-yang, all powerful evangelistic agencies. In addition to the work at Seoul, other stations have been opened at Fusan (1891), Phieng-yang (1893), Taiku (1898), and Syen-chun (1901).

At the time of the terrible cholera epidemic in 1895, the missionaries of all the Boards turned their attention to hospital work, and were able not merely to save many lives, but to overcome much of the hostility to mission work. The work among the women has from the beginning had phenomenal success, and the general indications for permanent church life are most satisfactory.

The report in 1903 shows 340 outstations, 64 missionaries, 140 native workers, 3 organized churches (312 incompletely organized churches), 5,481 communicants, 66 schools, 1,082 pupils, 2 hospitals and 5 dispensaries, with 2,824 patients.

The printing press at Seoul has done most excellent work, issuing over 400,000 pages.

XII. The Philippine Islands: Immediately after the Philippine Islands passed into the hands of the United States the Presbyterian Board took up the question of sending missionaries there. The Rev. J. B. Rodgers, who had already had experience in Spanish work, was sent to Manila in 1899. Iloilo, on the Island of Panay, was occupied in 1900; Dumaguete, on the Island of Negros, in 1901; and Cebu, on the Island of Cebu, in 1902. As was natural, there was at first a marked interest in the work; then followed somewhat of a reaction, but the later reports show that the congregations are developing steadily in numbers and in earnestness. The very general belief in the unbounded wealth of the United States makes it a little difficult to secure self-support in the native churches, but the progress is encouraging and the opportunity, as one of the missionaries expressed it, is "for all there is in a man." Especially attractive is the field among the young men. Efforts were made to arrange some apportionment among the different missionary societies, but not with the greatest success. The work done in India and in Japan by preachers from this country led to a visit by Dr. George F. Pentecost to the Philippines in 1902, the results of which are most gratifying, not merely among the natives, but in the American community. The hostility or lack of interest on the part of American officials, of which something has been made, has been more apparent than real, in consequence of the peculiar religious situation.

The report of 1903 shows 28 outstations, 15 missionaries, 32 native workers, 10 churches, 469 members, 2 schools with 234 pupils, 2 hospitals, 635 patients.

The foreign mission work of the women of the Presbyterian Church (North) is carried on through seven societies, all auxiliary to the Board of Foreign Missions of the Presbyterian Church in the U. S. A. These are:

1. *Woman's Foreign Missionary Society of the Presbyterian Church:* Headquarters, 501 Witherspoon Building, Walnut Street, Philadelphia, Pa.; organized 1870.

2. *Woman's Board of Foreign Missions of the Presbyterian Church, New York:* Headquarters, 156 Fifth Avenue, New York City; organized 1870.

3. *Woman's Presbyterian Board of Foreign Missions of the Northwest:* Headquarters, 40 Randolph Street, Chicago, Ill.; organized 1870.

4. *Woman's Presbyterian Foreign Missionary Society of Northern New York:* Headquarters, Auburn, N. Y.; organized 1872.

5. *Woman's Occidental Board of Foreign Missions of the Presbyterian Church:* Headquarters, 708 Powell Street, San Francisco, Cal.; organized 1873.

6. *Woman's Presbyterian Board of Foreign Missions of the Southwest:* Headquarters, 4,020 Westminster Place, St. Louis, Mo.; organized 1877.

7. *Woman's North Pacific Presbyterian Board of Missions:* Headquarters, 741 Hoyt Street, Portland, Ore.; organized 1888.

Reference should be made to the exceptionally complete arrangement of the library connected with the Board's office in New York City, and to the organization of mission study classes. In both departments the Board has the advantage of the free-will service of two gentlemen of means. The literature department also is specially well developed.

ORGAN: *The Assembly Herald, Woman's Work for Woman.* History: Howard (W. H.), *Origin of the Board of Foreign Missions of the Presbyterian Church,* New York, 1872; Speer (R. E.), *Presbyterian Foreign Missions,* Philadelphia, 1901.

PRESBYTERIAN CHURCHES OF SCOTLAND; Missions of. See SCOTLAND.

PRESBYTERIAN CHURCH IN THE UNITED STATES (South); Executive Committee of Foreign Missions of the: The history of the missionary work of the Presbyterian Church of the southern portion of the United States runs parallel with that of the northern portion up to the year 1861. At that time, in consequence of the civil war, the synods of the Southern States united in the formation of a separate body, known as the General Assembly of the "Presbyterian Church in the Confederate States of America," which title, subsequent to the war, was changed to the "Presbyterian Church in the United States."

Immediately on the organization of the Southern Assembly, at Augusta, Ga., in December, 1861, a committee was chosen to conduct the work of foreign missions, with the Rev. J. Leighton Wilson, D.D., as Secretary, and the Rev. James Woodrow, D.D., Treasurer. Dr. Wilson had labored nearly twenty years as a missionary in Africa, but for some time previous to the outbreak of the war had been connected with the Foreign Mission Office of the Presbyterian Church in New York. Dr. Woodrow was a professor in the theological seminary at Columbia, South Carolina. The Committee was located at Columbia. The first efforts of the committee were directed to the Choctaws, the Chickasaws, and other tribes of the Indian Territory. During the continuance of the war more than a dozen faithful laborers were sustained in this field, among them Drs. Kingsbury and Byington. A number of Presbyterian missionaries, natives of the Southern States, were laboring in foreign lands, and invitations were extended to these, who had originally been sent out by the Presbyterian Board in New York, to become the representatives of the Southern Church in their respective fields. Some of these labored in Africa, others in China, Japan, and Siam. As the outcome of these negotiations, the Rev. Elias B. Inslee of Hang-chau, China, entered into a correspondence with the committee, which resulted in the establishment of its first mission in foreign lands. This, however, was not until the close of the war. Mr. Inslee, who was a member of the Synod of Mississippi, returned to the United States in 1866, was formally appointed, and sailed for his field in China in June, 1867. In August of the same year the committee appointed Miss Christine Ronzone, a missionary under its care, to Italy. In 1868 the Rev. G. Nash Morton was sent to Brazil.

Missions were established in Mexico and Greece in 1874, in Japan in 1875, and in the Congo Free State in 1890. In 1889 the Indian Mission was transferred to the Home Mission Committee.

Statement of Missions: I. China: (1.) *Mid-China:* The first station of the mission was Hang-chau, to which Rev. Mr. Inslee returned in 1867, and where he was joined the following year by several associates, including Rev. M. H. Houston. Others are Su-chau (1872), Hsin-chang (Sinchang) (1892), Kiang-yin (1895), Kia-hsing (1895). In common with other missions this one suffered interruptions during the Boxer uprising, but less loss than those in the north. During their enforced absence from the interior stations the missionaries improved the opportunity to study and work among the sailors and soldiers at Shanghai. Since their return the various departments of work, including the girls' boarding school at Hang-chau, other schools at the different stations, and the medical work have been resumed with success.

(2.) *North Kiangsu:* This mission includes the stations of Chin-kiang (1883), Su-tsin (Suchien) (1894), Tsing-kiang-pu (1887), Hwaingan-fu (Whai-an-fu) (1897), and Hen-chau-fu (1897). Here also the missionaries were obliged to withdraw during the Boxer troubles, but native workers remained, and except for a few weeks, services were continued. Since the reopening of active work this mission has shared with others the increased interest on the part of the natives and the larger opportunities for each department of work.

The report (1902) shows for the Mid-China Mission 24 outstations, 42 missionaries, 36 native workers, 7 churches with 448 communicants, 10 schools with 204 pupils. North Kiang-su Mission, 6 outstations, 26 missionaries, 10 native workers, 1 church with 95 communicants, 1 school with 12 pupils.

II. Brazil: (1.) *Southern Brazil:* This includes the stations of Campinas (1869), Lavras (1892), Araguary (1895), São Paulo (1895), São João del Rei (1895). As in so many cases, the early history of the mission was one of patient labor in the face of great difficulties, but of late there has been considerable improvement. The organization of the Synod of Brazil, by the cordial cooperation of the Northern and Southern Presbyterian Churches in the U. S., has been a distinct advantage, and the single theological institution at São Paulo for both boards has been very helpful. The development of Mackenzie College also has made possible a concentration of educational work. The 16 missionaries, besides their care of schools and press work, superintend 60 outstations, and report 1,316 communicants.

(2.) *Northern Brazil:* The work in this mission was commenced in 1873 at Recife (Pernambuco). In 1882 Fortaleza or Ceara was occupied, followed by Maranhão (1885), Parahyba (1894), Natal (1895), Caxias (1896). An indication of the difficulties encountered is found in the statement in the report for 1902 that even at Pernambuco it is still rare for services to be conducted in the chapel without stones being thrown at the building. The prevalence of gambling and intemperance makes work very difficult and the general poverty of the people hampers the sale of Bibles and other books. There are (1902) 14 missionaries, 18 native workers, 17 outstations, 10 organized churches, 1,114 communicants, 3 schools with 127 pupils.

III. Mexico: The work in Mexico was commenced in 1874 at Brownsville, Texas, and the city of Matamoros, just across the Rio Grande River. It has since been extended to include Victoria (1880), Linares (1887), and Montemorelos. The 5 missionaries and 11 native helpers care for the work in 53 outstations, with 10 organized churches and 602 communicants. As the country is sparsely populated there is a large amount of traveling necessitated. As in Brazil, the churches connected with the two Presbyterian Boards (North and South) in Mexico united in 1901 in the Synod of the Presbyterian Church in Mexico. The movement has had the cordial support of the Board and the churches have already felt the advantage from the union.

IV. Cuba: In response to an earnest appeal from Protestant Christians in Havana, the Executive Committee sent Mr. Graybill of the Mexico Mission to Cuba in the summer of 1890. This visit resulted in the organization of two Presbyterian churches, one in Havana and one in Santa Clara, a town in the interior of the island. Mr. Graybill also licensed and ordained to the work of the Gospel ministry Sr. Evaristo Collazo of Havana.

The disturbed condition of the country seems to have interfered with the continuance of the work, but at the close of the Spanish War in 1899 the Board took up the field again and placed a missionary, Rev. J. G. Hall, at Cardenas. Work has also been undertaken at Caibarien and Remedias. The report (1902) shows 7 missionaries, 2 native workers, 1 organized church, 63 communicants. Attention is paid to education, and in one instance the missionary gained access to a large private school, with free permission for Bible instruction in return for lessons in English.

V. Japan: The first station founded in Japan by this Board was Kochi (1885). Then followed Nagoya (1887), Tokushima (1889), Kobe and Okazaki (1890), Takamatsu (1893) and Susaki (1898). There are also 80 outstations, and the missionary force of 28, with 35 native helpers, reports (1902) 4 organized churches, with 1,458 communicants. These churches are identified with the Church of Christ in Japan. The strength of the mission is given to evangelistic work, and the 20th century forward movement under the auspices of the Japan Evangelical Alliance has had manifest good results in uniting the churches, giving them greater courage and success, and emphasizing before the community the essential unity of the Japanese Churches.

VI. Africa: For many years the Southern Presbyterian Church had cherished a desire to plant a mission in Africa. During the latter part of his life, the Rev. Dr. J. Leighton Wilson, the father of the mission work of his Church, and who had himself labored nearly twenty years in Africa, earnestly laid this matter before the General Assembly; but various obstacles prevented the accomplishment of his heart's desire until he had passed to his rest. In the mind of the Southern Church there was an abiding conviction that because of the large negro population within her own bounds she was specially called of Providence to undertake this work. Accordingly, at the meeting of the General Assembly in 1889, the Executive Committee of Foreign Missions was directed to take steps looking to the opening of the long-contemplated mission in the "Dark Continent." Early in 1890 the Rev. Samuel N. Lapsley (white), of the Synod of Alabama, and the Rev. W. H. Sheppard (colored), of Atlanta, Ga., were commissioned and sent forth with instructions to found a new mission in the Congo Free State. The appointment of Mr. Sheppard (who had already proved to be a most valuable worker) was of special interest, since he was the first fruits of a long-cherished desire on the part of many in the Southern Church to see some of this race bearing the Gospel to the land of their forefathers. He was also the first fruits, in this direction, of the Theological Seminary in Tuscaloosa, Alabama, which had been established some years before by the Southern Presbyterian Church exclusively for the purpose of training a colored ministry. Proceeding first to England, and then to Brussels in Belgium, they received every encouragement and assistance in preparation for their work. King Leopold himself granted Mr. Lapsley a personal interview, in which he expressed the deepest interest in his mission. They have gone as pioneers, with instructions that their station be sufficiently separated from other missions to give it the character of a thoroughly independent work. They were instructed to seek a locality as healthy as possible, on some highlands removed from the coast, and yet not too distant from the basis of supplies. Luebo, near the southwestern border of the Congo State, and the junction of the Luebo and Lubua rivers, was selected and has been the headquarters of the mission. In 1897 Ibanzi, a short distance from Luebo and a point of convergence for the trade of a large section of territory, was occupied. The missionaries are enthusiastic over the outlook, hoping for results as remarkable as those manifest in Uganda, as the tribes already reached seem peculiarly accessible to the Gospel. The report (1902) shows 9 missionaries, 20 native helpers, 8 outstations, 854 communicants, 226 pupils in the 2 schools. A noticeable fact is the addition of 382 members in a single year.

VII. Korea: The first work of the Board in Korea was in 1892, but the present location was not made until 1896, when the station of Chung-ju was opened, followed by Kunsan (1896) and Mokpo (1898), all on or near the west coast south of Seoul. There are (1902) 18 missionaries, and special attention is paid to medical work, one of the physicians from the Woman's Board reporting 1,250 visits from women patients at Chung-ju. There are 3 churches with 124 members, and one of the most interesting features is the employment of a native evangelist by a few of the native Christians.

In 1874 work was commenced among the Greeks at Athens, extending afterward to Bolo and Salonica. Later it was confined to the last city and finally, under pressure of need elsewhere, was passed over to the care of the ABCFM. Women's work in connection with this Board is represented by individual church societies and Presbyterial unions.

ORGAN: *The Missionary*, monthly.

PRESBYTERIANS OF WALES; Missions of. See WELSH CALVINISTIC METHODISTS' FOREIGN MISSIONS.

PRETORIA: Capital of the Transvaal Colony, S. Africa, situated about 280 miles W. by N. of Lourenço Marques. White population about 10,000. Station of the Berlin Evangelical Missionary Society (1866), with (1903) 1 missionary, 17 native workers, 6 outstations, and 2,628 professed Christians, of whom 1,232 are communicants. Station also of the SPG (1870), with (1903) 3 missionaries. Station also of the Swiss Romande Mission (1897), with (1903) 2 missionaries, one of them with his wife; 1 woman missionary, 1 place of worship, 1 printing house, 2 day schools, and 36 professed Christians. Station also of the WMS, with (1903) 5 missionaries, 25 native workers, 5 outstations, 7 Sunday schools, 3 day schools, 1 theological class, and 680 professed Christians, of whom 412 are communicants. Station also of the African Methodist Episcopal Missionary Society.

PRIMITIVE METHODIST MISSIONARY SOCIETY: Publishing House, 48 Aldersgate St., E. C., London. The Primitive Methodists are a body which arose in England in 1810. Finding themselves gaining strength, they organized in 1843-44 a foreign missionary society, adopting Canada, New Zealand, and Australia as their fields of labor. These fields were afterward transferred to Methodist bodies in those countries, and the Society, aside from its home department, carries on foreign work in West Africa (Fernando Po), South Africa (Cape Colony), and Central Africa (Upper Zambesi). The work in Fernando Po was commenced in 1870, in response to an appeal by a sea captain and carpenter who visited Santa Isabel and found a small community gathered by an English Baptist missionary who had been driven away by the Spaniards. Spanish law having changed, the Missionary Committee of the Primitive Methodist Connexion sent two missionaries, Revs. R. W. Burnett and H. Roe, with their wives, to open a station at Santa Isabel. They met with a hearty welcome. In 1871 Rev. D. T. Maylott joined them, and an attempt was made to open a new station along the west coast. The plan met with some difficulties, but in 1873 George's (or San Carlos) Bay was occupied.

Associated with Mr. Maylott in this mission was the Rev. W. N. Barleycorn, one of the first converts of Santa Isabel, and his work among the Bubis was very successful, the first convert of the west mission being baptized in 1874. Since then several new missionaries have been sent out, and stations have been opened at Banni, Bottlenose, Idua, Jamestown, Urua Eye, and Ikot Nteka, and schools have been established in a number of towns. There are 5 missionaries and 4 native teachers.

In 1869 an appeal for help came to the Missionary Committee from Aliwal North, a town and district in Cape Colony, bordering on the Orange River, and in 1870 Rev. H. Buckenham sailed for Cape Colony and settled in Aliwal North. He was joined later by others, and the work grew, extending across the river into Orange Free State. The war disturbed it greatly, but since the return of peace the natives are returning to their homes, and the work of the Mission has been resumed. Aside from the two missionaries a native pastor, the Rev. John Msikinya, a graduate of the **Lovedale** Institution, is associated in the work at Aliwal. A training-school for native youths has been opened, which it is the purpose of the Mission to make, as far as possible, self-sustaining.

It had long been a wish of the Missionary Committee to send a missionary party to the Upper Zambesi, but owing to the expense of pioneer work in such a difficult region, they had not been able to collect funds sufficient for the purpose.

In April, 1889, however, the Rev. H. Buckenham (formerly at Aliwal North) and Mrs. Buckenham, with Rev. A. Baldwin and Mr. J. Ward, sailed for Africa and opened the way for the establishment of four stations: Nkala, Nanzela, Moomba, and Walker's Drift, besides several outstations. It is still largely pioneer work, even in the work of reducing the language of the Sajobas to form. Schools are successful and medical work has brought many within reach of the preaching.

There were in the three missions in Africa, in 1900, 39 missionaries (including wives), 10 stations and 11 outstations, 1,463 communicants, and 2,600 adherents. A Woman's Foreign Missionary Society, organized in 1897, is auxiliary to the general society.

PRINCE ALBERT: The chief settlement of the district of Saskatchewan, Canada, on the North Saskatchewan River, about 35 miles above its confluence with the southern branch. Station of the Canada Presbyterian Church (1866), with (1903) 1 woman missionary, 1 Sunday school, and 1 day school. Station also of the CMS (1879), with (1903) 1 missionary, 2 native workers, 3 outstations, 3 day schools, 1 college, and 426 professed Christians, of whom 167 are communicants.

PROME: A city in the district of Pegu, Burma, India, on the Irawadi, 166 miles north-northwest of Rangoon. Climate temperate, healthy. Population, 30,000, of whom 27,000 are Buddhists. Station of the ABMU (1854), with (1903) 1 missionary and his wife, 15 native workers, 3 outstations, 3 places of worship, 4 Sunday schools, 6 day schools, and 273 professed Christians, of whom 192 are communicants. Station also of the SPG (1871), with (1903) 1 missionary, 1 native worker, and 57 professed Christians, of whom 24 are communicants.

PROTESTANT COMMUNITY: In Turkey the system of civil administration requires each tribe or race, or other division of the people to have a chief to whom the Turkish officials can look for its proper control. From the time of the conquest of Constantinople the religious heads of the various sects found in the Turkish empire have been recognized as political chiefs of their respective flocks, with certain official rights and privileges. In 1843-47 the prelates of the Armenian Church withdrew from their friendly attitude toward the American missionaries and excommunicated and boycotted those who adopted the idea of independent study of the Bible, using their position as political chiefs to turn the Turkish police force upon the work of extirpating the "heresy."

To secure the Evangelical Armenians against such persecution, the British Ambassador at Constantinople obtained from the Sublime Porte recognition of the "Protestant Community" as a separate political body, having a civil head (called in Turkish *Vekil*, or representative), and liberty of conscience in matters of religion for all who might place themselves under protection of the new political organization. In 1850 an imperial edict confirmed these arrangements, placing the Protestant community upon the same political footing as the Greek Church or the Armenian Church.

This community now numbers about 100,000 souls, adherents of the various evangelical denominations in different parts of the empire. All of these "Protestants," or evangelicals, look to their civil head, or *Vekil*, to represent them and their civil and political interests at the palace of the Sultan, and to inform them of their sovereign's wishes or commands.

Anderson (R.), *Missions to the Oriental Churches*, Boston, 1870; Dwight (H. G. O.), *Christianity Revived in the East*, New York, 1850.

PROTESTANT EPISCOPAL CHURCH IN THE UNITED STATES OF AMERICA: 1. Domestic and Foreign Missionary Society. 2. American Church Missionary Society. The American Protestant Episcopal Church, being, in its early history, a mission itself, generations passed before it felt strong enough to found missions on a large scale, either within or without its own borders. In the beginning of the 19th century interest in missionary work became manifest in the American Church, one of the prime movers in the cause being Bishop Griswold, who in correspondence with the Secretary of the Church Missionary Society suggested that an American clergyman be sent out by that Society into the foreign field. The English society, however, (1817) urged the formation of an American Board and offered pecuniary aid. This advice was acted upon, and the Domestic and Foreign Missionary Society was instituted in 1820, the Rev. J. R. Andros being the first of the American clergy to offer himself for the foreign field.

I. *Domestic and Foreign Missionary Society:* Altho organized in 1820 as a society it was not until 1835 that it assumed its present character and became but another name for the Church herself. Previous to that time the administration of the Society's work had been committed to a Board of Directors, who through its Executive Committee had made several attempts to found missions in heathen lands, but had only succeeded so far as to appoint a lay teacher in Africa and two clergymen to China. They had, however, sent two clergymen to Greece in 1830. In 1835 a change was made in organization, which provided that the Society should be considered as "comprehending all persons who are members of this Church." This action placing general mission work immediately under the direction of the Church, was hailed with enthusiasm, the newly awakened interest being particularly manifested in the marked increase in the contributions.

The Board of Missions meets triennially and is composed of both Houses of the General Convention and the Board of Managers. The Missionary Council meets annually, except in convention years, and is composed of all the bishops, the Board of Managers, such other clergymen and laymen as the convention may select, and one presbyter and one layman from each diocese or missionary district, to be chosen by its convention or convocation. The Board of Managers, elected by General Convention, consists of 16 bishops, 15 clergymen and 15 laymen. The other bishops, and the Secretary and Treasurer of the Domestic and Foreign Mission Society, and of the Board of Managers, are members *ex officio*, but have no vote.

The first foreign field chosen by the Society immediately on its organization was Africa, but it was not until 1830 that work was actually begun in Monrovia, where the American Colonization Society had founded a colony of free colored people.

In 1830 Greece was chosen as a field where general Christian intelligence and education were sorely needed, and Athens was decided upon as the most favorable point for location.

In 1834 the Society voted to make China a field for missionary labor, and in 1835 Rev. F. R. Hanson and the Rev. H. R. Lockwood were accepted as laborers for that field.

In 1859 Rev. Messrs. C. M. Williams and J. Liggins, the first Protestant missionaries to Japan, were sent there by the Society of the Protestant Episcopal Church of America. In 1865 a mission commenced by a clergyman four years before in Haiti was transferred to the Society of the Protestant Episcopal Church, and became one of their fields of active labor.

Africa: The mission work in Africa is confined to the Republic of Liberia. Mr. and Mrs. J. M. Thompson (colored), residing at Monrovia, were appointed as missionary teachers in 1835, and in 1836 Rev. Thomas S. Savage, M.D., the first foreign missionary, landed at Cape Palmas. During the early years of the mission frequent difficulties occurred between the colonists and the native "bushmen," and the missionaries and mission property were often in danger. In 1843 troubles arose which compelled the missionaries at Cape Palmas to abandon the town and take refuge on a U. S. ship, and the school at Cavalla, an outstation, had to be closed. The next year found the work going on quietly, but in 1845 the disturbances again threatened the mission; still in spite of the political troubles there were substantial proofs of the progress of the mission. In 1849 the corner-stone was laid of the first Episcopal church edifice of Liberia, and in 1850 Rev John Payne was appointed Missionary Bishop of Cape Palmas and the parts adjacent. The work gradually extended its borders from this time, with the exception of the years of financial trouble at home during the Civil War, when, owing to the reduced support, the mission was obliged to discontinue work at some of the stations and curtail it at others. The principal native tribes reached by the mission are the Grebos in the northern, the Bassas in the central, and the Veys in the southern section of the country.

For administrative purposes the mission is divided into four districts: Cape Palmas, Sinoe, Bassa, and Montserrado, Monrovia being the sea town. The report (1903) shows 18 clergymen, 69 catechists and teachers, 88 places where services are held, 1,767 communicants (1,137 native and 630 Liberians), 38 day schools, 18 boarding schools, 1,490 pupils (including 1,169 natives).

Greece: The work in Greece was begun at Athens in 1830 by the Rev. J. J. Robertson and the Rev. J. H. Hill. The principle on which the mission was established was that of not attempting to make proselytes, or to withdraw the people from their own Church, but simply to spread Scriptural truth among them in the expectation that this would lead eventually to the reformation of the Church by the Greeks themselves. The work was begun by establishing schools, and a printing-press set up at Athens, which last, however, was given up. In 1837 a station was begun on the island of Crete, but was occupied only a few years. In 1839 the Rev. Dr. Robertson removed to Constantinople with a view to working specially among the Greeks, but the object of the Mission was afterward extended to the other Eastern Churches. The mission in Greece has been wholly educational, and after the death of Mr. Hill the Society ceased to consider it a part of its field.

China: The China Mission dates from the landing at Canton of the Rev. Messrs. Hanson and Lockwood in 1835. They proceeded, however, to Java, to labor there, at Batavia, among the Chinese. The third missionary, the Rev. W. J. Boone, M.D., reached Batavia in 1837. In February, 1840, he really began work on Chinese soil by the opening of a station at Amoy. Four years later he was consecrated as the first bishop of the Anglican communion in China. In 1845 the mission moved from Amoy to Shanghai, and in 1846 Mr. Kong Chai Wong, afterward a clergyman, was baptized, the first convert, on Easter Day. In 1868 stations were opened in Wu-chang, capital of the province of Hu-pei, and in Han-kau. The work is now divided into two districts, Shanghai and Han-kau. The former includes, as stations, Kia-ting (Kia-ding) (1882), Shanghai City and Tsing-pu (1902). The latter, besides Han-kau and Wu-chang, Shasi and Ichang (1886), Han-chiuan (1892), and Wu-hu (1891), Kin-kiang (1901) and Ngan-king.

Aside from the evangelistic work which is pushed energetically, St. John's College, at Shanghai, one of the best in China, and hospitals at Shanghai, Wu-chang and Ngan-king are kept up to a high grade of efficiency.

The missionary staff includes (1903) 3 bishops (one, the venerable Dr. Schereschewsky, residing in Japan), 34 Presbyters (19 foreign, 15 Chinese), 13 deacons (2 foreign), 8 physicians (foreign), 21 missionary teachers (foreign), 25 wives of missionaries, and 157 other native workers.

There are 56 places of preaching, 1,449 communicants, 45 day schools, and 9 boarding schools, with about 1,500 pupils. English services are also conducted at several places.

Japan: This mission was established in 1859 by the Rev. Messrs. C. M. Williams and J. Liggins, who were the first Protestant missionaries to settle in the empire. The first baptism was reported in 1866. Until 1874 the Mission was under the jurisdiction of the Bishop of China, but in that year, owing to the increased extent of both fields, it was decided to separate them into two dioceses. Rev. C. M. Williams, then Bishop of China, was appointed Bishop of Japan, and a new bishop set over China. With the growth of the work Japan was divided into two dioceses: Tokio and Kioto. The former includes the stations of Tokio (1873), Matsuyama, Takasaki, Mayebashi (1888), Fukushima (1893), Sendai (1894), Hirosaki (1897), besides a number of subordinate stations. The diocese of Kioto includes Kioto (1889), Nara (1887), Osaka (1875), Kanazawa (1897), and a number of subordinate stations.

Holy Trinity Cathedral, at Tokio, has a full series of services in Japanese and in English, and a church house is arranged for near the Imperial University, as a center for work among students. There also are Trinity, Divinity, and Catechetical School, St. Paul's College, and St. Margaret's School, all rapidly growing. The medical department includes St. Luke's Hospital, Tokio, and St. Barnabas Hospital, Osaka.

The missionary staff includes (1903) 3 bishops (one, Bishop Williams, retired), 34 Presbyters (14 Japanese), 9 deacons (7 Japanese), 2 physicians, 39 other foreign workers, including wives of missionaries, 138 other native workers. There are 74 places of preaching, 2,033 Japanese communicants, 19 schools, with 1,357 scholars.

Haiti: The Board's connection with Haiti dates from 1865, when the financial responsibility for the work at Port-au-Prince, carried on by Rev. J. Theodore Holly, was transferred by the American Church Missionary Society. It was conducted from that time until 1874 as a mission, when the church in Haiti was recognized under certain conditions by the General Convention and Dr. Holly consecrated as its first bishop. The work has been constantly hindered by fire, war, pestilence, and famine; yet, considering the very limited resources at any time at the command of the bishop, the work has been exceedingly successful. By action of the House of Bishops, taken in 1883, the church in Haiti was reorganized as an independent church, but, nevertheless, regular assistance is given by the Society to it as a Church in communion with the Protestant Episcopal Church.

Aside from the Bishop, 12 clergymen are enrolled as missionaries; there are 22 places of preaching, 537 French-speaking and 41 English communicants, 9 day schools with 185 pupils. There is also some work among the Spanish-speaking people of Santo Domingo.

Mexico: The work of the Society in Mexico is carried on both among Spanish-speaking and English-speaking people. Assisting the Church's representatives are 10 presbyters and 7 deacons, all Mexicans, who minister to 871 communicants. There are also several schools.

The Philippines: In the fall of 1901 the Board of Missions commissioned Bishop Brent to take charge of work in the Philippines, and he arrived at Manila in May, 1902. Already two clergymen were at work there and a lay worker. One of these was assigned to English services and the other took up Spanish work. Later a missionary was appointed to labor among the Chinese population, who had come from Amoy. For the present the plan appears to be to press the work among the American colony, while making careful investigation as to the possibilities among the native tribes.

The Woman's Auxiliary to the Board of Missions, headquarters Church Missions House, 4th Av. and 22d St., New York City, was organized in 1871, and has been a most efficient factor in the work of the Church in all its departments.

II. American Church Missionary Society: While there was no formal agreement it had been generally understood that the Foreign work of the Church should be left in the hands of what was known as the Low Church party, while missionary work in the U. S. was committed to the High Church element. In 1850 a local society was formed in Philadelphia for the purpose of collecting and distributing funds for the work of the Episcopal Church in the West, on what were known as strictly evangelical lines. Then came a demand for a general society of the same character, and after several preliminary meetings, such a society was organized at New York City in May, 1860, for the conduct of mission work on a purely voluntary and independent basis. Various efforts were made to effect some arrangement between the two societies, and in 1877 an agreement was reached by which the American Church Missionary Society retains its charter and organization, but is recognized as an auxiliary to the Domestic and Foreign Missionary Society. It agrees not to send missionaries to China, Japan, or Africa, while the Domestic and Foreign Society promises to send to those countries, with the approval of the Bishop, in each case, any missionaries possessing the qualifications required by its rules, who shall be nominated, and whose support shall be provided by the American Church Missionary Society. In regard to Domestic Missions, an agreement for mutual appointment and approval of missionaries has been made.

The foreign work of the Society is in Brazil. There are 8 clergy, including the bishop, 7 churches or chapels, 488 communicants. The headquarters of the mission are at Port Alegre, and among other places occupied are Pelotas, Jaguerdo, and Rio Grande.

The Society has also taken up work in Cuba, where it occupies Havana and Matanzas with 5 clergy, who report 256 communicants, 3 schools with 250 scholars, and 1 orphanage with 58 inmates.

ORGAN of the Domestic and Foreign Missionary Society: *The Spirit of Missions,* monthly.

PROVINCE WELLESLEY: A strip of territory on the west coast of the Malay peninsula, opposite **Penang,** 45 miles in length, with an average width of about 8 miles, including a total area of 270 square miles. It forms part of the British Colony of Straits Settlements. Station of the SPG (1879), with (1903) 1 missionary, 8 native workers, 2 places of worship, 5 day schools, 2 boarding schools, and 260 professed Christians, of whom 75 are communicants.

PUBNA. See PABNA.

PUDUKATTAI: A town in Madras, India, 28 miles southeast of Trichinopoly; is unusually clean, airy, well built; small, but having a fine mosque, a palace, and several temples. Population, 15,384, Hindus, Muslims, Christians. Station of the Leipzig Missionary Society (1849), with (1903) 2 missionaries and their wives, 24 native workers, 7 places of worship, 5 day schools, 3 boarding schools, and 256 professed Christians, of whom 153 are communicants. Station also of the SPG, with (1903) 28 native workers, 16 places of worship, 9 day schools, 2 boarding schools, and 1,591 professed Christians, of whom 621 are communicants. Some write the name Pudukotei.

PUEBLA: A city in Mexico, 76 miles east-southeast of Mexico City. The sacred city of Mexico, containing many religious and charitable institutions. Population (1900), 93,521. Station of the ME (1881), with (1903) 1 missionary and his wife, 1 native worker, 6 outstations, 6 Sunday schools, and 105 professed Christians. Station also of the ME, with (1903) 2 missionaries, 1 of them with his wife; 3 women missionaries, 26 native workers, 1 place of worship, 2 Sunday schools, 3 day schools, 2 boarding schools, 1 theological class, and 414 professed Christians, of whom 193 are communicants.

PUNGO NDONGO: A town in Portuguese W. Africa, a few miles to the N. of the Kwanza, and 180 miles E. S. E. of S. Paolo de Loanda. It is the chief entrepot of trade with the interior and a Portuguese military post. It is one of the ancient cities of Angola, and a health resort. It is beautifully situated in the midst of masses of conglomerate rocks. Station of the ME, with (1903) 1 missionary and his wife, 1 outstation, 1 place of worship, 1 Sunday school, 1 day school, and 14 professed Christians. Some write the name Pungo Andongo.

PUNJAB: One of the great provinces of British India; its highest northern point is in latitude 35°, its most southern, 27° 39'. Its limits of east longitude are 69° 35' and 78° 35'. The area of that portion of it under British administration is 97,209 square miles; population, 20,330,000. But there are 34 native states whose territory is intermingled with that of the British possessions—all of which are under the political supervision of the Punjab Government, tho each has its own native chief (see article Native States, where these relations are explained more at length), and the area of these swells the total area of the Punjab to 133,741 square miles, and its aggregate population to 21,000,000. The Punjab is governed by a lieutenant-governor, under the general supervision of the governor-general and viceroy of India. It contains one-fifth of the Mohammedan population, but only one twentieth of the Hindu. The name means "Five Waters," and is derived from the fact that its territory is intersected by five great Himalayan rivers; these are the Sutlej, the Beas, the Ravi, the Chenab, and the Jhelum. The Indus River, into which these all flow, and which runs near the western (political) boundary, and the Jumna, which forms a part of the eastern (political) boundary, describe a course outside the territory to which the name was originally given; but that name has recently been made to cover the entire province placed under the administration of the local government. On the north and west the Punjab meets the N. W. Frontier Province.

The history of the Punjab is of exceeding variety and interest. So extensive and so various is it, that it must here be left almost wholly untouched. Suffice it to say that here was the original Indian home of the Aryans; here the Vedic rites were first practised, and here probably the Vedas written; here Hinduism began its development; and hence did the Hindu race, as it swelled to larger size and power, emerge for the conquest first of the great Gangetic valley, and then of all the Deccan and Southern India. The beginning of this Hindu history cannot be later than 1500 B.C., and may be earlier. Here also the Mohammedan power in India first took root. Lahore was the first Mohammedan capital; after a time Delhi was occupied as their imperial city, and later still Agra, by a few of the Mogul emperors in the 16th and 17th centuries.

The city of Delhi, which indeed lies outside of the natural area of the Punjab, tho now within its political area, stands on the site of Indraprastha, a prehistoric Hindu capital, the foundation of which is said to go back to the 15th century B.C. It was in 1849 that the Punjab was finally made a part of the English dominions.

Classifying the people by religions, nearly 60 per cent. are Mohammedans; about 40 per cent. Hindus; nearly 7 per cent Sikhs. In round numbers, there are 11,000,000 Mohammedans, 8,000,000 Hindus, and 1,500,000 Sikhs. There are nearly 38,000 Jains, and over 40,000 Christians, of whom less than 5,000 were natives. The preponderance of Mohammedans is explained partly by the fact of early and long Mohammedan possession of the Punjab by rulers of that faith (as just described), and partly by its propinquity to the Mohammedan countries on the northwest, whence immigration is so easily accomplished.

The people of the Punjab are largely agriculturists. A sixth of the population of British Punjab is thus returned. The commercial and artisan classes number nearly 1,500,000. The rainfall is slight; in some parts of the province artificial irrigation is resorted to with good results. The rivers swell with the melting of the mountain snows, and when they subside leave well-watered strips of alluvial land enriched with the fresh deposits of each season. Education is in a tolerably forward state. It is stimulated somewhat by the existence of the Punjab University, which dates only from 1882, with which a number of colleges are affiliated. The language of the Hindus is Punjabi—allied to Hindi. Hindustani and Persian are used by the Mohammedans. The Afghans speak Pashtu.

Missionary work in this province began in 1834. The American Presbyterians were first on the ground, and their earliest station was at Ludhiana, where, besides the usual work of preaching, schools were at once begun, and a printing-press established, from which have since issued multitudes of books and tracts, including Biblical translations. Many other places have since been occupied. The Church Missionary Society occupied Amritsar in 1851. In 1870 that Society began a theological school at Lahore for training native preachers, which was the first school of the sort in India, it is said, to include Hebrew and New Testament Greek in the curriculum of study for native Christian students. The United Presbyterians of America have a mission in the Punjab, in Sialkot, and adjoining districts. The Church of Scotland has a station at Chamba. Several leper asylums have been founded in connection with one and another of these missions, but these are now managed by the "Mission Lepers in India."

The Moravians, true to their instincts of selecting the most difficult, laborious, and apparently unpromising fields, started a mission in 1855 at Kailang, far up among the Himalayas, tho in British territory, among the Tibetan mountaineers. Their work has involved severe hardship and unusual self-denial, but it has not been without its direct results. Circumstances have impelled the Punjab missionaries to labor among Mohammedans probably to a greater extent than has been attempted elsewhere in India. More than half the population being Mohammedans, opportunities have been constantly presented for meeting them, which it has not seemed right to disregard, altho there has not been hope of great success. Several of the missionaries of the Punjab have studied the religion of Mohammed profoundly, and have published scholarly works in elucidation of it, while not neglecting the preparation of other works designed to commend Christianity directly to the Muslims themselves. Their labors have resulted in the conversion of many Mohammedans, some of whom have become able and fearless preachers of the Gospel.

PUNJABI LANGUAGE: A language spoken by Sikhs and others in the Punjab, India. The number using this language is estimated at over 20,000,000. The language belongs to the Indic group of the Aryan family, but it has much profited by borrowing from Arabic as well as Persian. It is written with characters called Gurmukhi and derived from the Sanskrit Devanagari.

PURDIE, Rev. Samuel Alexander: Born in the

State of New York March 5, 1843. Died in San Salvador, Central America, August 6, 1897. In 1871 he entered upon his work in Mexico, being the first foreign missionary sent out by the American Friends. Locating at first in the city of Matamoros in the state of Tamaulipas, he gathered a church of believers, opened a boys' and girls' school, established a printing and publishing house, and founded a monthly paper, *El Ramo de Olivo*, which continues to be published, and is now in its thirty-first volume. This paper has a large circulation, and it has gained entrance into nearly all Spanish-speaking countries and islands, carrying the Gospel where the living messenger has not come. Primarily to supply the schools he compiled and printed school-books, inserting in them passages from the Bible and extracts from Christian books. He translated and printed a number of religious books and tracts. His influence was felt not only through the printing press. He traveled throughout the entire state of Tamaulipas, preaching in cities, towns, and ranches. He had the joy of seeing seven of his converts become faithful ministers of the Gospel. He established six regular churches and many preaching places, all of which he visited annually, and some of them more frequently. Into these churches he received more than six hundred by baptism. In 1887, because of the decline of Matamoros as a business center and the removal of the capital of the state to C. Victoria, he removed to this city, and hereafter his headquarters were there. In 1897, while visiting San Salvador, Central America, he died of tetanus, induced by a slight injury to his hand, received while binding a book which he had just translated and printed.

PURI: The chief town of the district of the same name in Orissa, India; is situated on the coast, covers an area of 1,871 acres, and is a city of lodging-houses. Its ordinary population in 1891, 28,800, is almost entirely Hindu, but during the great festivals of Jagannath, which are held here, there are 100,000 pilgrims added to the ordinary residents. Station of the BMS, (1825), with (1903) 1 missionary and his wife, 11 native workers, 3 outstations, 3 Sunday schools, 4 day schools, and 645 professed Christians, of whom 300 are communicants.

PURNEAH. See PURNIAH.

PURNIAH: A town in Bengal, India, and capital of the district of Purniah, 50 miles N. E. by N. of Bhagalpur. It has a large jute trade. It is subject to severe epidemics of fever. Population (1891) 14,600, of whom 9,600 are Hindus and 4,800 are Mohammedans. Station of the BMS (1899), with (1903) 1 missionary and his wife and 2 native workers. Some write the name Purneah.

PURULIA: Capital of the Manbhum district, Chota Nagpur, Bengal, India. Population, 5,695. It has good public buildings, a hospital, and considerable trade. An important center for mission work among the Kols. Station of the Gossner Missionary Society, with 4 missionaries, 37 native workers, 7 places of worship, 5 Sunday schools, 1 boarding school, 1 home for untainted children of lepers, and 1,673 professed Christians, of whom 870 are communicants. Station of the Mission to Lepers (1887), aiding the leper work carried on by the Gossner Society.

PUTIKI: A town and port of North Island, New Zealand, situated 79 miles S. E. of New Plymouth, on the Wanganui River, crossed by an iron bridge 600 feet long. It is the principal port on the W. coast and has sawmills, woodenware factories, foundries, flour mills, etc. Near the town is a Maori college for the education of native youths. Population, 5,000. Station of the CMS, with (1903) 1 missionary and his wife, 16 native workers, 1 day school, and 320 professed Christians. The district appears in report sometimes as Wanganui.

PYENG-YANG. See PHYENG-YANG.

Q

QUALIFICATIONS OF THE MISSIONARY: In Missions, as in all human enterprises, the man is the central factor. "One Paul did more for the spread of the Gospel than the ten Apostles." That is true and but expresses in the concrete the supreme importance of the selection of men. Livingstone wrote: "The sort of men wanted for missionaries are men of education, standing, enterprise, zeal, and piety. It is a mistake to suppose that any one, so long as he is pious, will do for this office. Pioneers in everything should be the ablest, best qualified men, not those of small ability and education. This especially applies to the first teachers of truth in regions which may never before have been blessed with the name and Gospel of Jesus Christ." Qualifications are more important than numbers. "Missionaries must be weighed and not counted." He who is to represent Christ and the Church before heathenism, should be Christ-loving and Christlike, should have a passion for the salvation of souls, and should not hesitate to give up luxury and life as his Master did, in order that the world may come to a knowledge of the Gospel that saves. The conversion of men, the spiritual vitality of converts, the interest and enthusiasm of the Home Church will depend upon the quality of the Church's representatives in the foreign field. At no point are carefulness and discrimination more important than at the selection of candidates, for if a high standard be not maintained, defeat and disappointment are inevitable.

The qualifications that should be expected in a missionary do not differ essentially from those expected in any other true minister of the Gospel of Christ in any land. These qualifications have been so amply illustrated in the lives of eminent and successful missionaries, and so frequently portrayed in manuals and addresses, as to be familiar to all who are acquainted with mission literature. In the Pastoral Epistles, especially, but elsewhere in the New Testament as well, such prominence is given to these qualifications, and they are delineated with so much detail as

39

clearly to indicate their importance to the future church. The following are some of the characteristics specified as essential to ministerial usefulness: 1. A bishop must be *anepiléptos* (I. Tim. iii: 2) or *anegklétos* (Titus i : 7), both of which are translated "blameless." These terms mean, that his character should have nothing upon which an enemy can take hold, or against which he can hurl an accusation. 2. He must be "apt to teach," capable, by natural gifts and scholarly attainments, of imparting instruction to others. 3. He must be "sober," having a calm, well-balanced, judicial judgment, that can view a subject from every standpoint and reach deliberate and wise conclusions. 4. "No Striker," a man who will not, under the impulse of passion, be provoked to strike back; who, when reviled, reviles not again. The experience of missions justifies attaching much importance to this feature of character. 5. "Temperate," having such a control of all powers of body and mind as can utilize them to the best advantage, resulting in that mental poise, that self-reliance which is the anticipation of victory. 6. "Vigilant," having eyes and ears open to see and hear, and turn everything to good account. 7. "Zealous," fervent in spirit—that enthusiasm that can concentrate on one thing—under the constraint of love. 8. An affectionate disposition (I. Thess. ii: 7-12) which wins affection in return and secures sympathy for the message he has to give. Such references as these to missionary character are scattered throughout the New Testament, and their careful study and classification will repay any candidate for this sacred calling.

Instead of more minute inquiry in that direction, however, it may prove even more profitable to gaze upon the features of the Master Himself, who was the great missionary and is the model for all missionaries. Certain salient characteristics of His life may be regarded as essential and fundamental, and, indeed, inclusive of all others that fill in a complete equipment.

1. Jesus Christ was called to the work. He was sent of the Father. "As the Father sent me, even so send I you." How that call is to be recognized and distinguished is one of the perplexities of many an earnest life, and an exceedingly important problem. With the call of God assured, to fall back upon, courage will not fail in the darkest hour, but without that certainty, there will often be misgivings lest after all there may have been a mistake. How can the mind of the Master be known in this matter? To Paul the call received on the way to Damascus was unmistakable. Anskar had his visions and commissions. Voices came to him out of the ineffable light, "Go hence and return to me with the martyr's crown." "Fear not; I am he that blotteth out thy transgressions." Francis of Assisi heard a voice amid the silence of the Umbrian hills, "My temple is falling into ruins, restore it." In the strength of that inspiration he not only became a missionary, but sent forth an army of missionaries, who counted it a privilege to lay down their lives for Christ's sake. Some men, prominent in history, who were epoch-makers, have had such calls, but ordinarily men must reach their conclusions by processes less impressive. No two are cast in precisely the same mold, and each will be directed by heart and intellect, according to his own temperament. The weighing of such considerations as health, education, domestic claims, relative needs of home and foreign fields, may seem commonplace in comparison with visions and supernatural voices, yet they are the basis of ordinary human action, and through them the will of God is, for us, made known. The man whose heart is right with God, who wishes to present himself a living sacrifice and uses his intelligence calmly and unselfishly, will reach a decision as unmistakably from God as was the call of St. Patrick or Isaiah. The chief danger lies in the deceitfulness of the unwilling heart. Jesus Christ came not to do His own will. He had the single eye and saw clearly His commission and work.

2. The Holy Spirit was given to Him without measure. All His faculties were formed and developed in the Holy Ghost. His study of the Holy Scriptures and all His utterances were in the illumination and energy of the Spirit. When he entered upon His public ministry there was a special anointing, the Spirit descended as a dove and rested upon him. He was led of the Spirit into the wilderness to be tempted of the devil, and in the power of the Spirit He returned into Galilee. His miracles were performed in the Spirit, and His last crowning act—His sacrifice upon the cross—was done in the Spirit. "Who through the eternal Spirit offered Himself without spot to God." That was the ideal life. In the truest and fullest sense the Spirit-filled life was His.

Does the question arise whether such a life is possible for His disciples? Let that question be answered by another. Did he not take upon Him our nature, and if so, are not both subject to the same law?

In order to fulfil the purpose of His life the fulness of the Spirit was necessary, as the light of the sun is necessary to the perfection of the flower. It is so with us. "Not by might nor by power, but by my spirit," is the condition of spiritual life, and of spiritual service. No combination of natural qualities, however distinguished, will compensate for the lack of this gift. Hence we are commanded to be filled with the Spirit. "He giveth the Holy Spirit to them that ask Him." Altho our natures may have been starved and stunted, and have become irresponsive on account of sin, yet to the humble seeker great possibilities are in store. Let it be declared with all solemnity and emphasis, that the missionary without this gift, and without a sense of its supreme importance, had better abandon his profession. His ministry will prove a disappointment and a waste.

3. Jesus Christ was mighty in the Scriptures. In childhood that became apparent. He breathed the atmosphere of the Prophets. In the brief record of His earthly life preserved to us, so many quotations are found as to indicate familiarity with every part of the Old Testament, to which He constantly referred as the Scriptures that cannot be broken. Such familiarity, needless to say, was not mere effort of memory, but a profound appreciation of the value and relations of truth, the result of habitual meditation. They were more precious than gold or silver, and His meditation all the day. To Him the Scriptures were divine in origin, and the final appeal, "What saith the Scriptures?" "Search the Scriptures;" "The Scriptures cannot be broken." "That the Scriptures might be fulfilled." He staked His all upon their integrity, and instilled the same confidence into the minds of His disciples. They, too, quoted freely in their epistles, and the addresses of Peter at Pentecost, and of Stephen

before the Council were but rehearsals of the Old Testament story. The Scriptures are the sword of the Spirit, the weapon used by the Apostles and by the Church in all the ages. There is no other weapon. The success of any Gospel ministry must depend upon the ability to use the revealed truth of God. The missionary should accept it as axiomatic that his mind must be steeped in the truth, that his whole nature must be charged with a sense of the glory of the Message, and the magnitude of the interests at stake. It ought not to be necessary to say, and yet men need to be reminded that this does not consist simply in a knowledge of theological books, nor even in an acquaintance with the mechanism of the books of the Bible, all of which may be very important in their way. It is an experience of the heart and life, so that, like the Apostles, he must speak it out. "We cannot but speak the things we have seen and heard."

4. Jesus Christ emptied Himself. He made Himself of no reputation, and took upon Him the form of a servant. By right His place was in the glory, where from eternity He dwelt with the Father. Yet He surrendered His place and on earth had nowhere to lay His head.

He might have delivered essays that would have become the literary classics of all the ages, but He emptied Himself of the right to speak and became an echo of the Father. "He that sent me is true, and I speak to the world those things which I heard of Him." By nature He was the brightness of the Father's glory, and yet that glory was laid aside, and He became obedient unto death. He who knew that all things were given into His hands, and that He was come from God and went to God, girded Himself with a towel and washed the disciples' feet. He who could have commanded twelve legions of angels, allowed Himself to be bound and buffeted and scourged. He emptied Himself of His power. What an emptying that was, that He might in due time be exalted! He became the perfect High Priest through suffering, and now is seated at the right hand of God, a Prince and a Savior.

This is hard doctrine. Who can receive it? The old nature dies hard. Yet it is the parting of the ways. The missionary who will take up his cross and follow Christ in this respect will share with Him the victory, while the other way leads to failure and defeat. Among the supposed sayings of Jesus, found in Egypt, is this sentence: "Unless ye fast from the world ye shall not find the Kingdom of Heaven." Whether the saying is authentic or not its testimony is true. Love not the world, neither the things of the world; set your affections upon the things that are above where Christ sitteth.

The missionary life is exposed to peculiar temptations in this respect. He labors among a people intellectually and morally beneath him. He naturally shrinks from the closest identification with such people and craves the companionship of better society. It is a great temptation, but where not resisted, an impossible gulf is fixed between him and success. He must empty Himself that he may be filled. He must humble Himself that He may be exalted. He must become all things to all men that He may save some. Jesus made His *soul* an offering for sin; He went down to the depths that He might lift men up to God. The great Apostle strove in all things to be an approved minister of God, in much patience, in afflictions, in necessities, in distresses. He endured hardness and cultivated the graces of humility and Christian charity that the ministry might not be blamed, and that the Kingdom of God might come. He emptied Himself before receiving the crown of righteousness that fadeth not away.

5. Jesus Christ had faith in the future. He had no misgivings as to the ultimate triumph of the Kingdom. His hopes were built upon the eternal promises that could not fail. He saw in vision Satan fall from heaven, and the judgment of this world, altho the work had only begun. The fulness of the Spirit clarified His vision and enabled Him to see the end from the beginning. The golden age of the prophets of old would dawn in due time, and He could leave the times and the seasons in His Father's hands. In such a frame He could never yield to despondency and despair.

Missionaries are disposed to, and many of them are afflicted with, despondency, and their conditions are often extremely discouraging. They are few in number, and seem so helpless among so many. After years of toil the harvest does not appear. Sometimes encouragements seem to be at hand, when suddenly they vanish as the early dew. Converts are disappointing, and public sentiment is against them. They are the objects of unkindly criticism, and sometimes of hostile attack. Climatic and physical conditions are depressing, and health is not buoyant. It is natural that under the strain body and mind should lose elasticity and hopes should die. Yet when that happens strength and usefulness are impaired. It should not be so, and will not be so if their lives are anchored in the unchangeableness of the living and true God. The missionary is but a small part of a mighty movement, and his contribution will not be lost. His works will follow him. Other men may reap what he has sown, but they will rejoice together. It is a winning conflict in which the Church is engaged, and the joy of ultimate victory should thrill and inspire every missionary with ever-increasing energy and hopefulness.

6. Jesus Christ had power in prayer. Prevailing prayer is a central law of His kingdom. Indeed, if in anything He might seem to be chargeable with rash and extravagant statement, it is in this connection. "If ye abide in me, and my words abide in you, ye shall ask what ye will, and it shall be done unto you" (John xv: 7). "Whatsoever ye desire, when ye pray, believe that ye receive them and ye shall have them" (Mark xi: 24). This is surely giving men an unlimited privilege of drawing upon infinite resources, yet it is the plane on which He himself moved. At the grave of Lazarus He said to the Father, "I know that thou hearest me always." In that confidence His requests were made known. He lived in this as in all other respects up to the standard of His teaching. He understood the secret, and without it, even He would have failed in His mission. He so taught His disciples. As Andrew Murray quaintly says, He did not teach His disciples to preach but taught them to pray. Is it not true that they who can preach well are more in number than they who can pray well? The greater the gift the greater the sacrifice necessary to acquire it. Never will the largest results be reached until the Church has a ministry at home and abroad that has been divinely taught how to pray. Some men stand out prominently in history who had, and because

they had, learned this art. The Acts of the Apostles are punctuated with prayer. It is from the "Prayer Watch" that the remarkable record of the Moravian Church sprang. Louis Harms and Gossner and Fliedner and Brainerd and Müller and Hudson Taylor are admonitions as well as encouragements to the Church to take advantage of this power, which she is invited to exercise. The extent of the field, the vastness of the work to be done and the inadequacy of the forces at work, ought to impress every thoughtful man and woman with that absolute dependence of the Church upon the help that comes from above. If men are to be born into new life, it must be done through the creative power of the author of life. He hears and answers prayer; therefore, pray without ceasing.

7. One more qualification must be mentioned, as the most important of all. Jesus Christ acted under the constraint of love. It was love that impelled the Father to give His Son. And it was love that constrained the Son to give His life a ransom for many. Even as His Father loved Him, so did He love sinful men. That is the one motive that will abide. There are many other considerations, such as the civilizing power of the Gospel, the moral and spiritual condition of the heathen, commercial and political advantage, the success of Missions—all of which have weight, but will not make and sustain missionaries, nor will they make a missionary church.

When Peter the Hermit aroused Europe to attempt the rescue of the Holy Land from the hand of the infidel, his battle cry was, "It is the will of God." "It is the will of Christ" is our battle cry. The constraint of the love of Christ is alone strong enough to maintain this conflict.

Dr. Griffith John says that he often thought of Paul and the Yang-tsze together. The great river in its way to the sea encounters many obstacles and flows in varied channels. Now it dashes against the rocks like a mad thing and then rushes through a narrow gorge at a wild race speed. It then emerges into a wider and more even channel, and flows quietly, calmly, and majestically, but it flows on continuously and irresistibly. Try to turn it back, and you will find it impossible. Ask it to stop, and it will tell you it cannot. Ask why, and it will tell you, "Almighty law has taken possession of me and I cannot help myself. The law of gravity constraineth me." So with Paul, a mighty law, the law of love, took hold of him and he could not stop. "The love of Christ constraineth me."

The same writer quotes the advice given to a novice by a senior missionary in China. "Try as fast as possible to learn to love the Chinese for Christ's sake, for you will find it very difficult to love them for their own sake."

The heathen are His and He loves them and for His sake even the most unlovely can become the object of our affection. A heart overflowing with much love will not find it hard to associate with the downcast and fallen, and will quickly elicit a response. Love is the world's need and hope.

In conclusion, let it be said there is work for all; and missionary training should vary with the class of men and the work they are expected to do, yet the qualifications specified above should be common to all. Certain attainments in scholarship may be beyond the reach of some who, nevertheless, would be useful in the foreign field, but all can acquire and none will be useful without the Christ-like spirit.

There are many points of a physical, intellectual, and practical nature that deserve mention, and will claim the attention of earnest candidates, but need not here be detailed. On the other hand, there are points that deserve notice in order that they may be avoided, which, tho in themselves apparently trivial, have been stumblingblocks, and have brought disaster into many a mission. Good men have sometimes come under the influence of peculiar views as to questions of economy, or salary, or prophecy, that have impaired, if not wrecked, their usefulness. Better judgment might still have entertained these views, while not offensively obtruding them upon others, and thus the loss of influence would have been avoided. A loving, prayerful spirit will ever be on the alert lest the enemy gain an advantage. "Lo, I am with you always" is the guarantee of wisdom and guidance in every time of need. The missionary above all men needs to realize the apostle's prayer: "To be strengthened with might by His spirit in the inner man, that Christ may dwell in your hearts by faith, that ye, being rooted and grounded in love, may be able to comprehend with all saints what is the breadth and length and depth and height, and to know the love of Christ which passeth knowledge, that ye might be filled with all the fulness of God."

Somerville (Andrew), *Lectures on Missions and Evangelization*, Student Volunteer Movement; *Call, Qualifications and Preparation of Missionary Candidates*, New York, 1901; *Ecumenical Conference on Foreign Missions*, Vol. I., pp. 301-324, New York, 1900.

QUDSHANIS. See KOCHANES.

QUEENSTOWN: A town in British Guiana, South America, situated on the W. bank of the estuary of the Essequibo River. Station of the PB, with 1 missionary and his wife and 1 woman missionary.

QUEPE: A river in Chile, South America, which gives the name to the Agricultural and Industrial station of the SAMS at Maquehue Reserve, situated about 30 miles S. E. of Cholchol, and 10 miles S. of Temuco. The people reached by this mission are Mapuche Indians. The station has (1903) 2 missionaries, 1 native worker, 2 day schools, 1 dispensary, 1 hospital, and 1 industrial school.

QUESSUA: A settlement in Angola, West Africa, situated about 185 miles E. by S. of S. Paolo de Loanda. Station of the ME, with (1900) 2 missionaries and their wives, 1 boarding school, 2 Sunday schools, 4 native workers, and 44 professed Christians, of whom 25 are communicants.

QUETTA: A town in Baluchistan, India, situated about 190 miles N.W. of Shikarpur, in the Northwest Frontier Province, India, with which it is connected by railway. Station of the CMS (1886), with 4 missionaries, three of them with their wives, 8 native workers, 1 place of worship, 1 hospital, and 42 professed Christians. Station of the CEZ (1895), with (1903) 2 women missionaries, 10 native workers, 3 day schools, 1 boarding school, 1 hospital, and 50 Zenana pupils.

QUEZALTENANGO: A town in Guatemala, Central America, situated about 125 miles N. W. of Guatemala city, nearly destroyed by an earthquake in 1902, and it is not now a missionary residence. Station of the PN (1898), with 1 missionary and his wife and 1 outstation.

QUICHUA LANGUAGE: A South American language spoken by various tribes of Indians in the western and northwestern part of the continent. The name is applied by the Indians of Peru to any mountaineers, and at the time of the Spanish conquest the dominant race in Peru being Quichua Indians, the Jesuit missionaries gave the name to the Indian language. Quichua is still spoken in parts of Peru distant from the coast. It is found also with variant dialects among the Indians of Ecuador, Colombia, and, perhaps, in Bolivia and Argentina. It is written with Roman letters.

QUIHONGOA: A town in Angola, West Africa, situated about 160 miles S. E. of S. Paolo de Loanda. Station of the ME, with (1903) 3 missionaries, one of them with his wife; 1 place of worship, 1 Sunday school, 1 printing house, 1 industrial school, and 150 professed Christians.

QUILON: An ancient town and seaport in Travancore, South India, situated on the Malabar coast, 40 miles N. of Trivandrum. It had a trade with China as early as 851. Portuguese established a trading post here in 1503, which was afterward seized by the Dutch. Population, 35,000. Station of the CMS (1821), with (1903) 1 missionary and his wife, 78 native workers, 20 outstations, 24 Sunday schools, 1 boarding school, 44 day schools, and 2,515 professed Christians, of whom 472 are communicants.

R

RABAI: A town in British East Africa, situated about 10 miles N. W. of Mombasa, on the mainland. Station of the CMS (1846), with 1 missionary and his wife, 2 women missionaries, 15 native workers, 1 place of worship, 2 day schools, 1 boarding school, 1 dispensary, and 839 professed Christians, of whom 399 are communicants.

RAGHAVAPURAM: A village in Madras, India, situated between the Kistna and Godavari Rivers, about 60 miles E. by S. of Kamamet. Station of the CMS (1872), with (1900) 1 missionary and his wife, 16 native workers, 1 place of worship, 15 day schools, and 2,608 professed Christians, of whom 461 are communicants.

RAIATEA: One of the Society Islands in the South Pacific, situated N. W. of Tahiti. It played an important part in the early history of the LMS mission to Tahiti, having yielded almost the first encouragement in the depressing period of early effort. Station of the Paris Evangelical Mission Society, with 2 missionaries, 4 native workers, 4 places of worship, 1 day school, 1 printing press, and 646 professed Christians at four different villages on the island.

RAINY: A settlement in W. Pondoland, Cape Colony, South Africa, situated 40 miles N. W. of Port St. Johns. Station of the UFS (1897), with (1903) 1 missionary and his wife, 21 native workers, 15 outstations, 1 place of worship, 12 day schools, and 183 professed Christians. Some use the old name Elitubeni.

RAIPUR: A town in the Central Provinces, India, situated in Chatisgarh division, about 150 miles W. by S. of Sambalpur. Population, 24,948. Station of the German Evangelical Synod of N. A. (1880), with (1903) 2 missionaries and their wives, 36 native workers, 16 outstations, 11 places of worship, 1 Sunday school, 8 day schools, 1 boarding school, 1 dispensary, 1 orphanage, and 910 professed Christians. Station also of the ME, with (1903) 1 missionary and his wife, 22 native workers, 1 outstation, 2 places of worship, 5 Sunday schools, 4 day schools, 2 orphanages, 1 industrial school and 524 professed Christians, of whom 88 are communicants.

RAJAMAHENDRI: A historic town in Madras, India, on the left bank of the Godavari River, 32 miles W. by N. of Cocanada. Population, 24,555. The surrounding country is rich and the people are prosperous. Station of the General Council, Evangelical Lutheran Church in N. A. (1869), with (1903) 2 missionaries, one of them with his wife; 2 women missionaries, 1 place of worship, 1 Sunday school, 1 printing house, 2 boarding schools, 1 industrial class, 1 dispensary, 1 hospital, and 139 native workers. Some write the name Rajahmundry.

RAJGANJPUR: A town in Chota Nagpur, India, situated in the Ganjpur state on the Bengal and Nagpur Railway, about 78 miles S. W. of Chaibasa. Station of the Gossner Mission Society, with (1903) 1 missionary, 39 native workers, 2 day schools, 31 Sunday schools, and 9,192 professed Christians, of whom 194 are communicants.

RAJ NANDGAON. See NANDGAON.

RAJPUTANA: A vast territory in the northwest of India, which derives its name from the Rajput clans who inhabit it. The word "Rajput" means "son of a king," and the Rajputs trace their origin from the princely families among the original Aryan invaders of India. Some of these clans have had their abodes here from time immemorial. The exact boundaries of Rajputana it is difficult to give. In a general way it may be said to lie between Sindh on the west, the Punjab on the northwest, the United Provinces on the northeast and the Mahratta states of the Gaikwar, Sindhia, and Holkar on the south. Its limits of north latitude are 23° and 30°, and of east longitude 69° 30', and 78° 15'. Its area is supposed to be about 127,541 square miles, containing a population (1901) of 9,723,301 people. The population is prevailingly Hindu, only about 10 per cent. being Mohammedan and about half as many Jains. Those of other faiths furnish a mere sprinkling in the total mass. There are many wild jungle tribes—especially Bhils, of which any exact enumeration is well nigh impossible; the Bhils, however, are supposed to number nearly 200,000, included mostly among the Hindus, whose religion they follow.

Much of the territory of Rajputana, especially in the western part, is mere desert. The southeastern portion is more fertile. The chief city is Jaipur, capital of the native state of the same name. Population (1901), 160,000. Missionary work in Rajputana is chiefly that of the United Free Church of Scotland, and dates from 1860. The principal stations are Jaipur, Ajmere, Nasirabad, Deoli, Beawar, Todgarh, Udaipur, Alwar, and Jodhpur. Much attention has been given to medical work, and the diligence of the missionaries in relieving distress during famine has given them a firm hold upon the hearts of the people. There is a mission press at Ajmere. Education is making fair progress, tho female education is neglected. The Rajputs, who have given their name to the country, and who constitute its aristocracy, furnish only about half a million of the population.

RAKAI: A town in Uganda, Central Africa, situated in the province of Koki, on the west of Lake Victoria Nyanza and 105 miles S. W. of Mengo. Station of the CMS (1895), with (1903) 2 women missionaries, 35 native workers, 1 day school, and 631 professed Christians, of whom 200 are communicants.

RALUANA: A settlement at the E. end of the Island of New Britain (now called Neu Pommern) E. of New Guinea. Station of the Australian Wesleyan Methodist Mission Society, with (1901) 1 missionary, 83 native workers, 4 outstations, 29 places of worship, 29 Sunday schools, 29 day schools, 1 theological class, and 502 professed Christians.

RAMA CAY: An island on the Mosquito Coast, Nicaragua, situated about 15 miles S. of Bluefields. The name comes from the Rama Indians, who inhabit the island. Station of the Moravian Missions (1858), with (1901) 1 missionary and his wife, 5 native workers, 1 place of worship, 1 day school, 1 Sunday school, and 244 professed Christians.

RAMACHANDRAPURAM: A town in Madras, India, situated in the Godavari district, 18 miles S. W. of Cocanada. Station of the BOQ (1892), with (1902) 1 missionary and his wife, 1 woman missionary, 27 native workers, 15 outstations, 12 places of worship, 12 day schools, 2 boarding schools, 28 Sunday schools, and 463 professed Christians, and 1 leper home. Station of the Mission to Lepers (1899); this Society aids the asylum above-mentioned.

RAMAINANDRO: A town in Imerina, Madagascar, situated about 55 miles S. W. of Antananarivo. The mission there was sacked and destroyed by rebels in 1895. Station of the SPG (1882), with (1900) 1 missionary, 3 native workers, and 402 professed Christians.

RAMALIANE: A village in the Transvaal, South Africa, situated in Lichtenburg district, 45 miles N. W. of Klerksdorp. Station of the Hermannsburg Missionary Society (1872), with (1902) 1 missionary and his wife, 6 native workers, 3 outstations, 5 places of worship, 6 day schools, and 1,470 professed Christians.

RAMALLAH: A village in Palestine, Turkish Empire, situated about 5 miles N. of Jerusalem. Station of the AFFM (1869), with (1900) 2 missionaries and their wives, 22 native workers, 7 outstations, 1 place of worship, 4 Sunday schools, 4 day schools, 2 boarding schools, 1 dispensary, and 34 professed Christians. Station also of the CMS (1877), with (1903) 1 missionary and his wife, 2 women missionaries, 2 outstations, 1 day school, and 1 dispensary. Church statistics of the station are included in Jerusalem statistics of CMS.

RAMIAPATAM: A town on the Bay of Bengal, India, about 43 miles N. of Nellore. Climate not unhealthy, but generally debilitating. Mission station of the ABMU (1869), with (1903) 3 missionaries and their wives, 1 woman missionary, 20 native workers, 5 outstations, 2 places of worship, 4 Sunday schools, 5 day schools, 2 boarding schools, 1 theological class, and 2,000 professed Christians, of whom 727 are communicants. The name is also written Ramapatam.

RAMNAD: A town in Madras, India, situated about 65 miles S. E. of Madura, near the line of islands stretching toward Ceylon, which are known as "Adam's Bridge." Of this "bridge" the princes of Ramnad used to be the guardians. Station of the SPG (1825), with (1903) 1 missionary, 24 native workers, 3 places of worship, 6 day schools, 3 boarding schools, 1 industrial school, and 665 professed Christians, of whom 217 are communicants.

RAMPART CITY: A settlement in Alaska, within the Arctic circle, situated on Porcupine River at the frontier of British Columbia. Station of the PE, with (1903) 1 missionary, 1 native worker, 1 place of worship, 1 hospital, and 25 professed Christians.

RANCHI: A town in Chota Nagpur, Bengal, India, capital of Lohardaga division. Population, 13,000. Station of the Gossner Missionary Society, with (1903) 7 women missionaries, 93 native workers, 38 places of worship, 27 Sunday schools, 8 day schools, 2 boarding schools, 1 theological class, 1 dispensary, 1 hospital, and 8,200 professed Christians, of whom 4,446 are communicants. Station also of the SPG, with (1903) 3 missionaries and their wives, 2 women missionaries, 178 native workers, 1 place of worship, 5 day schools, 2 boarding schools, and 13,867 professed Christians, of whom 6,209 are communicants. These statistics include the district with the town.

RANGOON: The capital of Burma, British India, situated on the left bank of the Rangoon River, 26 miles from the sea. It was annexed by Great Britain after the war of 1852. Large sums of money have been expended in improving the city, and the European quarter contains many fine buildings, tho the native town is not much improved. Buddhism has here its stronghold, and the city is noted for the number and splendor of its temples and shrines. The most magnificent and venerated one is the Shoay Dagon, or Golden Dagon *dagoba*, said to be 2,300 years old. It is heavily decorated with gold, and is the receptacle of relics of the last four Buddhas, including eight hairs of Gautama.

Much internal and foreign commerce is carried on in Rangoon, as it has communication by rail and by water with the upper provinces. An English newspaper is published here. Population (1901), 234,881. Station of the ABMU (1813), with (1903) 19 missionaries and their wives, 13 women missionaries, 332 native workers, 29 outstations, 150 places of worship, 67 Sunday schools, 75 day schools, 3 boarding schools, 2 theological classes, 1 printing house, and 9,196 professed Christians. Station also of the SPG (1864), with (1903) 3 missionaries and their wives, 62 native workers, 6 day schools, 4 boarding schools, and 3,750 professed Christians. Station also of the Leipzig Missionary Society (1878), with 13 native workers, 7 outstations, 1 place of worship, 1 day school, 2 boarding schools, and

325 professed Christians, of whom 272 are communicants. Station also of the ME, with (1903) 2 missionaries and their wives, 4 women missionaries, 40 native workers, 5 Sunday schools, 3 day schools, 2 boarding schools, and 490 professed Christians, of whom 218 are communicants. The YMCA has 1 missionary and 1 Young Men's Christian Association here, and the YWCA has 2 women missionaries and 1 Young Woman's Christian Association. The BFBS also has an agent here, with 3 native Bible workers.

RANIGANJ: A town in Bengal, India, situated on the railway 55 miles N. W. of Burdwan. Population, 19,578. Station of the Mission to Lepers (1891), which aids the leper work of the WMS. Station of the WMS, with (1903) 2 missionaries, 14 native workers, 5 outstations, 9 places of worship, 6 Sunday schools, 7 day schools, 1 orphanage, 1 lepers' asylum, and 262 professed Christians, of whom 241 are communicants.

RANIPET: A town in Madras, India, situated in the N. Arcot district, 65 miles W. of Madras City. Station of the RCA (1856), with (1903) 1 missionary and his wife, 2 women missionaries, 81 native workers, 35 outstations, 30 places of worship, 24 Sunday schools, 1 boarding school, 1 hospital, 1 dispensary, and 1,565 professed Christians, of whom 406 are communicants. Some write the name Ranipettai.

RAO-CHAU. See JAO-CHAU-FU.

RAROTONGA. See HERVEY ISLANDS.

RAROTONGAN LANGUAGE: One of the Polynesian languages, and one of several spoken in the Hervey or Cook's Islands. It is the dialect found in those islands, selected by the missionaries for printing, and has been reduced to writing in Roman letters.

RATNAGIRI: A town in Bombay, India, and capital of the district of Ratnagiri, situated 82 miles N. W. of Kolhapur. Population, 12,616. Station of the PN (1873), with (1903) 1 missionary and his wife, 8 women missionaries, 10 native workers, 3 outstations, 2 places of worship, 5 Sunday schools, 1 boarding school, 1 orphanage, 1 leper asylum, and 63 communicant Christians. Station of the ZBM, with (1903) 5 women missionaries, 2 native workers, and 1 day school.

RATNAPUR: A village in Bengal, India, situated in the Nadiya district, 62 miles N. N. W. of Calcutta. Station of the CEZ (1894), with (1903) 7 women missionaries, 10 native workers, 3 outstations, and 1 hospital. Station also of the CMS, with (1903) 12 native workers, 1 place of worship, 4 day schools, and 804 professed Christians, of whom 111 are communicants.

RAWAL PINDI: A town and military post in Punjab, India, situated about 88 miles E. S. E. of Peshawar. Because of its broad, straight, handsome streets, and its excellent drainage and sanitary arrangements, it is said to present a cleaner appearance than any other town in Northern India. Trees have been freely planted, and give the place a very pleasing appearance. Bishop Milman was buried here. Population (1901), 87,688. Altitude, 1,652 feet. The place is now fortified in a very elaborate manner. Station of the UP (1856), with (1901) 3 missionaries with their wives, 3 women missionaries, 20 outstations, 1 Sunday school, 1 college, 1 hospital, 1 orphanage. Station also of the WMS, with (1903) 1 missionary, 2 native workers, 6 outstations, 1 Sunday school, 6 places of worship, and 83 professed Christians.

REBMANN, John: Born in Germany; was appointed, in 1846, by the CMS, to the East African Mission. On his arrival at Mombasa arrangements were made by him and Dr. Krapf for commencing a mission among the Wa-Nikas, and Kisulutini (Rabai), fifteen miles inland, was selected for the station. The people gave their consent for a mission, assuring the missionaries of their friendship and protection. They found the place more healthful than Mombasa, but the people exceedingly ignorant, superstitious, intemperate, sensual, and cruel. They now began the journeys in the interior which led to the remarkable Central African discoveries. They brought to light a new country highly favorable for missionary labor, and three groups of mountains, from 4,000 to 5,000 feet high, enclosing the Taita country. In 1847 Mr. Rebmann made a new journey to Kadiaro in the Taita country, and in 1848 he explored the country beyond the Taita, called Jagga or Chagga, 300 miles inland, the Switzerland of East Africa, traveling on foot for seven days in a thorny jungle infested by wild beasts. On May 11 he discovered the magnificent mountain, Kilima Njaro. Rebmann and Krapf, tho giving much time to exploration, were above all missionaries. Their grand aim was the spreading of the Kingdom of God. Yet their regular work led to great results for science. Their remarkable journeys into the interior were the basis for many years of both missionary and scientific enterprises in East Africa. In 1856 Rebmann, being alone at Rabai, was driven from the place by an incursion of the Masai, who destroyed the station and dispersed the Wa-Nika people. Retiring to Zanzibar, he continued his linguistic studies for two years, and then, returning to his old station, resumed his labors. Until 1875 he was there alone. He finally became blind. When the mission was reenforced in 1875, he returned home. An attempt to restore his sight was unsuccessful. He took up his abode near Dr. Krapf in Konthal, and died October 4, 1876, after a missionary service of twenty-nine years. Rebmann translated Luke's Gospel into Ki-Swahili, and compiled also Ki-Nika and Ki-Nyasa dictionaries of great value. After discovering the two snow-capped mountains, Kilima Njaro and Kenia, a map was prepared from native information, showing a great inland sea two months' journey from the coast, which led to the journeys of Burton, Speke, and Grant, and later influenced the travels of Livingstone, and the expeditions of Stanley and Cameron.

RECIFE. See PERNAMBUCO.

REEVE, William: Born in England, 1794; studied at Gosport; sailed April 22, 1816, as a missionary of the LMS to India; stationed first at Bellary. In January, 1821, accompanying Mrs. Reeve to Madras, on her way to England for health, he remained in Madras, occupied in the revision of the Kanarese version of the Old Testament. He returned in October to Bellary, leaving again for Madras in January, 1824, to arrange for printing his Kanarese and English dictionary. The same year he sailed for England; reembarked for India in 1827, and was stationed at Bangalore. In 1831 he went to Madras to superintend the printing of his Kanarese and English dictionary, which, being completed, he returned to Bangalore. In 1834, on account of ill-health, he left with his family for England. He died at Bristol February 14, 1850.

REFORMED (Dutch) CHURCH IN AMERICA, Board of Foreign Missions: As early as 1643 missionary work was carried on by ministers of this body among the Mohawk Indians, and the interest grew with the years. In 1816 the Church united with the Presbyterian and Associate Reformed Churches in forming the United Missionary Society, which sent missionaries to the Indians, until 1826, when it was merged in the ABCFM. In 1832 the General Synod elected "The Board of Foreign Missions of the Reformed Protestant Dutch Church," which, tho operating through the American Board, was allowed to conduct its missions according to the ecclesiastical polity of the Church. It continued its connection with the American Board until 1857, when an amicable separation took place, due to no dissatisfaction, but to a growing conviction that more would be accomplished if the two Boards acted independently. In the same year the American Board transferred to this Board the mission at Amoy, in China, and the Arcot Mission in India, with the individual missionaries composing them. The contributions, which were in 1857 but $10,076, rose the next year to $25,034; and have since gone on increasing, till in 1902-3 they reached the sum of $158,895.

Constitution and Organization: The Board of Foreign Missions of the Reformed Church in America consists of 27 members, ministers and laymen, of whom at least one-half shall be ministers, chosen by the General Synod, and regularly incorporated under the laws of the State of New York. Its members are chosen for three years, and are divided into three classes, so that one-third of the membership is elected each year.

In addition to the regularly constituted Board, each Classis nominates from its own members a missionary agent, subject to the approval of the General Synod, for the purpose of advancing the interests of foreign missions within the bounds of the Classis. These agents are, by act of General Synod, authorized to attend any or all meetings of the Board, and to participate in its proceedings. This agency serves a very useful purpose as a medium of communication between the Board and the churches, and in developing and fostering a greater interest in missions throughout the churches.

In 1875 "The Woman's Board of Foreign Missions of the Reformed Church in America" was organized. In 1880 it assumed the support of the work of the Church Board for women and children in all its mission fields, including the maintenance of several seminaries for girls in China, India, and Japan. Its contributions have steadily increased, and have usually been more than sufficient for the purpose named. In 1875 it received $2,891; in 1903, $50,911, and in the twenty-eight years of its existence, $631,691.

Development of Foreign Work: The foreign missions of the Reformed Church have been six in number, of which five are now maintained. The earliest mission was established on the island of Borneo in 1836. Four missionaries, with their wives and an unmarried woman, sailed for Borneo in that year. Two stations were established at Sambas and Pontianak, with schools and preaching services in three languages. The first missionaries were joined at different times by five others, and part of the force began work among the Chinese colonies in Borneo. In 1844 two of the missionaries, Messrs. Pohlman and Doty, were transferred to the more promising field of Amoy; others were obliged, from ill-health, to return home, and the mission was abandoned.

China: The Mission of the Reformed Church in Amoy was the first in that field. It was commenced by Rev. David Abeel, in 1842, when Amoy, at the close of the opium war, became an open port, and was reenforced in 1844 by Messrs. Pohlman and Doty, who had been laboring among the Chinese colonists in Borneo. The district occupied by it is about 60 miles square, and has a population of 3,000,000. In this district are four stations and forty-three outstations and preaching places. There are at present in the mission 6 ordained missionaries and one unordained, and 16 women (eleven unmarried). The first church was organized with eleven members in 1851, and there are now (1903) in the field 12 churches, of which all are practically self-supporting, with a total of 1,389 communicants. The contributions from these churches during the year amounted to $7,051 Mexican.

Medical and educational work is carried on. During the year 1889 a hospital was built in the station of Sio-ke. Connected with the hospital force is a native helper, and to all who come for treatment and medicine the Gospel is preached. In 1898, Hope Hospital and the Netherlands Women's Hospital were opened at Amoy, the latter built and supported by friends in the Netherlands, but conducted by the Mission. The educational work of the Mission is represented by 13 day schools with 298 scholars, a Bible school where native women are fitted to become Bible women, 3 seminaries, one male and two female, and a union theological seminary, which is carried on by the American Reformed and English Presbyterian Missions conjointly.

India: The Arcot Mission was organized in 1853 by Revs. Henry M., William W., and Joseph Scudder, three sons of Rev. John Scudder, M.D., one of the pioneers of American missions among the Tamils. The Mission occupies chiefly the Arcot districts of the Madras Presidency, with an area of 8,333 square miles, and a population of about 2,400,000, nearly equally divided between Tamils and Telugus. The people are divided into three general classes or castes, and the intense caste feeling forms one of the great difficulties of the mission work. The Brahmans, altho but 4 per cent. of the population, are by far the most influential section. The Sudras form 75 per cent. of the population and are virtually the people. They are, like the Brahmans, tenacious caste-holders. The Pariahs, or outcastes, form 20 per cent. of the population, and are in a most pitiable condition, being little more than slaves. Much of the success of mission effort has been among this class.

The mission has 8 stations and 163 outstations. These outstations are placed under the care of native pastors and catechists, who also preach in the surrounding villages. The catechists are unordained helpers, but perform the same labors as a pastor, with the exception of administering the offices of the Church. There are now on the field 9 ordained missionaries, 3 of whom are physicians, and 1 unordained, together with 16 women (6 unmarried). The number of churches is 20, and of communicants, 2,511, of which number 105 were received last year. There are in the Mission 8 boarding schools (4 male and 4 female), 18 caste girls' schools, and 171 day schools.

There is also at Palmanér a theological seminary, opened March, 1888, for which a special endowment fund of about $50,000 was raised by Rev. Jacob Chamberlain, D.D., while in the United States in 1887. The Mission has also a hospital and dispensary at Ranipet, near Arcot, and the Mary Tabor Schell Hospital for Women, at Vellore. At Vellore is also the Elizabeth R. Voorhees College, with more than 1,000 students.

A mission to Japan was begun in 1859, when Rev. G. F. Verbeck and Rev. S. R. Brown, with Dr. D. B. Simmons, sailed for that Empire. Mr. Verbeck went to Nagasaki, and Dr. Brown to Kanagawa, and later to Yokohama. In 1889 the Mission was divided into the North Japan Mission, having its center at Tokio-Yokohama, and the South Japan Mission, with its headquarters at Nagasaki.

The *North Japan Mission* has a force of 20 missionaries, six ordained men and one unordained; seven married and six unmarried women. It occupies five principal stations: Yokohama, Tokio, Nagano, Morioka, and Aomori, with 24 outstations and preaching-places. Many churches have been gathered and organized, with thousands of communicants, which have no longer any formal connection with the Mission, and of which no report can be made. The churches or congregations at present directly under its care are two, with 498 communicants, whose contributions, in 1901, amounted to $1,059. Its principal institutions are the Ferris Seminary at Yokohama, a boarding school for girls, with 96 pupils, and the Meiji Gakuin at Tokio, the support and conduct of which it shares with the Board of Foreign Missions of the Presbyterian Church. This institution has an academical department with 168 students and a theological department with 12.

The *South Japan Mission* has its field in the large southern island of Kiushiu. Eleven missionaries are connected with it, five ordained men, two married and four unmarried women. It occupies four stations: Nagasaki, Saga, Kagoshima, and Kumamoto. It has 4 churches under its care, with 339 communicants, whose contributions amounted to $990. At Nagasaki are located the Steele College for boys and young men, having 100 students, and the Sturges Seminary for girls, with 54 students.

The *Arabian Mission* was established as an independent and undenominational Mission in 1889 for special work among Mohammedans. It was adopted by the Reformed Church in 1894. Its stations, on the west coast of the Persian Gulf, are three: Busrah, Bahrein, and Muscat, with two outstations at Amara and Nasariyeh. In all the territory occupied by it there is no other mission. It has access to a population estimated at 1,600,-000. Its missionaries are 13, seven men, of whom two are physicians and one unordained; four married women, of whom two are physicians, and two unmarried. During the year 1902 were sold 4,059 Bibles, Testaments, and Scripture portions, in seventeen different languages; 3,362 were sold to Mohammedans. The Mason Memorial Hospital at Bahrein, for which a donation of $6,000 was received in 1901, was completed in 1902, and promises to be an efficient aid in the work of the Mission.

It was doubtless the original intention of the Reformed Church, as expressed in the constitution of its Board of Foreign Missions, that Classes or ecclesiastical bodies similar to those in the United States, and having organic relation to the Synod, should be organized at as early a date as possible in each of its mission fields. This purpose has been carried out only in the Arcot Mission in India. The Classis of Arcot was organized in 1854. The attempt to secure a similar organization at Amoy was made in 1857. It was met, however, with earnest remonstrance by the members of the mission, who were closely associated in sympathies and labors with the missionaries of the English Presbyterian Church. Their view finally prevailed, and the missionaries of both churches, together with their native pastors and elders, now form a single ecclesiastical body.

In 1876 the union of the missionaries of the Reformed Church in Japan with those of the United Presbyterian Church of Scotland and the Presbyterian Church (North) of the United States in the "Council of United Missions," and the formation of the "United Church of Christ in Japan," embracing the churches organized under these missions, was approved by the Synod.

In 1886 the General Synod formally approved the stand taken by its Board of Foreign Missions "on the important subjects of Union and Cooperation in Foreign Missions, etc.," and "permitted and advised" the Classis of Arcot "to initiate such measures as shall tend to bind together the churches of the Presbyterian polity in India." In September, 1902, the "Synod of the South Indian United Church" was constituted, by the union of the Classis of Arcot, with the Madras Presbytery of the United Free Church of Scotland.

The Reformed Church, therefore, occupies advanced ground in relation to the principle of cooperation in mission work, and the establishment in each mission field of a national, self-governing, self-supporting, and self-propagating church, "that shall grow from its own root."

ORGAN: *The Mission Field*, monthly; *The Mission Gleaner* (Woman's Board), monthly; *Neglected Arabia* (Arabian Mission), quarterly.

REFORMED (German) CHURCH IN THE UNITED STATES; Foreign Missions of the: The Board of Commissioners for Foreign Missions of the Reformed Church in the United States was organized on September 29, 1838, at Lancaster, Pa. The suggestion came from the Home Missionary Society, and met with a most cordial response.

From 1840 to 1865 the Board had no foreign missionary of its own, but was a regular contributor to the ABCFM toward the support of Rev. Benjamin Schneider, D.D., missionary in Turkey.

Beginning with 1860, the Synod became dissatisfied with this method, and in 1865 it decided to establish its own mission, applying its funds to the support of the India Mission, and to the work among the Winnebago Indians in Wisconsin. In the year 1873 the Board was reorganized, and laid the foundation for its present flourishing mission in Japan.

The first missionaries, the Rev. A. D. Gring and his wife, settled in Yokohama in 1879, but it was thought best to remove to Tokio, and there, in May, 1884, he organized the first church. Other fields of labor in Japan have been Fukushima, Sendai, North and South Miyagi, Yamagata and Akita. The report (1901) shows 19 missionaries in charge of about 50 places, where work is conducted in the different fields, assisted by 10 ordained ministers and 25 evangelists. The church membership was 2,142, and there were 40 schools, with 130 teachers and 1,420 pupils. The Mission suffered a serious loss in the burning of the girls' school building at Sendai, but the result has been enlargement rather than retrenchment. The Industrial Home at Sendai is another important feature in the work.

In 1899 the Board commenced work in China, sending out Rev. Mr. Hoy and, later, Rev. Frederick Cromer to Yo-chow, in the province of Hu-nan. A medical missionary and his wife, also a physician, have been more recently appointed.

Auxiliary to the Foreign Mission Board is the Woman's Missionary Society, General Synod of the Reformed Church in the U. S., with headquarters at Tiffin, Ohio.

REFORMED PRESBYTERIAN (Covenanter) CHURCH IN NORTH AMERICA; Foreign Missions of the: At a meeting of the Synod of the Reformed Presbyterian Church in North America held in 1818, a committee was appointed to inquire into the expediency of establishing a foreign mission. Nothing was accomplished then, however, and it was not until 1841 that the question was seriously studied, and plans for foreign work proposed. In 1843 a committee was chosen to select a field for cultivation, and the island of St. Thomas, in the West Indies, was chosen. In 1864 this spot was abandoned in favor of Haiti, and a mission commenced in 1847, which, however, was discontinued in 1849;

At a meeting of Synod, held in 1856, interest in missions was revived, and it was resolved to recommence foreign work. Syria was chosen as the field of operations. The Rev. R. J. Dodds and Joseph Beattie were chosen missionaries, and with their families sailed for Syria in October, 1856. After spending some time in Damascus and Zahleh, Latakia, on the Mediterranean, was selected in October, 1859, where the mission was permanently established.

In 1867, the United Presbyterian Church of Scotland having abandoned its mission to Aleppo, Dr. R. J. Dodds took charge of it until his death in 1870. The work was extended to Suedieh on the River Orontes in 1875, to Tarsus, in Cilicia, in 1882, and later to Mersine. The Latakia Mission has also undertaken work on the island of Cyprus. Within recent years a Chinese mission has been in progress in Oakland, Cal., and Indian missions have been established at several points in the United States, and more recently a station has been opened at Te-tsing-chau (Tak-hing-chau), in the western part of the province of Kwang-tung, China.

The work in Syria has been chiefly among the **Nusairiyeh,** who, while nominally Muslims, are really a pagan people. They are the lineal descendants in race and religion of the Canaanites who fled before Joshua, and are as yet almost absolutely inaccessible to any Christian influence. Holding to their ancient faith with a pertinacity that is wonderful, yet compelled by a relentless oppression to cover their belief under the forms of a hated religion, they have developed a power of deceit and dissimulation probably not equalled in the history of any race. They have repelled, in their gloomy isolation, all Christian workers, except the sturdy Scotch Covenanters, who, with persistency not less dogged than their own, but with a faith which lays hold on the power of the highest, have commenced their attack

The missionary force consists (1900) of 20 missionaries, 48 native workers, in 4 stations and 9 outstations, with 310 communicants, and 730 pupils in 14 schools. In China there are (1903) 8 missionaries (2 physicians). The work is yet in its infancy.

REGIONS BEYOND MISSIONARY UNION (*Formerly known as the East London Institute for Home and Foreign Missions*): In 1873 the Rev. H. Grattan Guinness, D.D., a Baptist minister in London, organized the East London Institute for Home and Foreign Missions, for the special purpose of training for missionary service those anxious to enter it, but unable to do so for lack of means. An old-fashioned house on Stepney Green was secured, and during the first year 32 students were received. A second house was taken, and as the needs increased a third was added, as also a wing to the original building, known as "Harley House." From the beginning the enterprise has been strictly undenominational, its property vested in a board of trustees representing different Christian bodies, and has had the cordial support and counsel of such men as Rev. F. B. Meyer, G. E. Morgan, Esq., of *The Christian*; George Hanson, D.D., R. Wright Hay, and others. More than eleven hundred men and women have had a longer or shorter training in this institute, and have gone to the foreign field in connection with about forty missionary societies, or as independent, self-sustaining missionaries. They have represented various nationalities: English, Scotch, Irish, and American, French, German, Italian, Spanish, Swedish, Danish, Russian, Bulgarian, Syrian, Egyptian, Kaffir, Negro, Hindu, Parsee, Kurd, and Hebrew. They have gone into all parts of the world: to China, India, Syria, Armenia, Egypt; to France, Spain, Portugal, Italy; to the east and west coasts of Africa, Natal and Cape Colony; to Prince Edward's Island, Cape Breton, Canada, and the Western States of America; to the West Indies, Brazil, and the Argentine Republic; Australia and New Zealand.

In addition to this foreign work, a large home-mission work is carried on in the East London district of Bromley, where students and deaconesses receive practical training in evangelistic and medical mission work, and a large amount of helpful influence is brought to bear upon the neglected masses of the great city.

For some years the attention of Dr. and Mrs. Guinness was confined to the institute, but with the opening up of the Congo there arose an earnest desire to send the Gospel into the interior far beyond the points upon the coast then occupied. Rev. A. Tilly, of Cardiff, one of the directors of the BMS, turned to Dr. Guinness and invited the cooperation of the institute in an attempt to send a few evangelists right into the interior. Messrs. Cory, of Cardiff, and Irwine, of Liverpool, promised assistance, and upon the publication of Stanley's letters, in the fall of 1877, it was decided to attempt an entrance into Africa by the new route, the friends above named forming themselves into a committee for the conduct of the enterprise, to which was given the title, The Livingstone Inland Mission. The Mission was to be evangelical, but undenominational, and it was hoped at first that it might be made self-supporting; but this idea was soon relinquished by the committee. Funds to start with having been contributed chiefly by the committee, volunteers were furnished by the Institute. Mr. Tilly acted as Secretary for the first three years, but in 1880 the work had so increased as to require more time than he could spare from his pastoral duties, and Dr. and Mrs. Guinness were asked to undertake the sole responsibility of the Mission and its support as a branch of the East London Institute, the committee to resign all share in its management, and act only as an advisory council. Dr. and Mrs. Guinness assented to this plan, and the Mission was thus conducted for several years.

In 1883 the ABMU turned its attention to the Congo, and overtures were made to it by the Institute to take up the work, which was already well established, and leave the English organization free to go to the "regions beyond." The policy of the ABMU was one of concentration and radiation from a center, while the idea upon which the Livingstone Inland Mission was organized was a chain of stations to reach far into the interior. The Union felt that the Livingstone Mission, with its extreme stations, 800 miles apart, would give them room enough and to spare for several years to come, and they were unwilling to extend operations beyond the equator. The directors of the Institute, on the other hand, were constantly asking what of the region beyond, with its tens of millions of people yet to be evangelized? And at length, in 1888, they resolved to take up the African work again, extending it farther up the Congo and along the tributary rivers. Thus the Congo Balolo Mission was formed to be in perfect harmony with, but independent of, the ABMU.

The Swedish missionaries, when the mission passed under American management, formed a separate society and continued work on the north bank of the cataract of the Congo, one of their number, Nils Westlind, translating the entire New Testament into the dialect used there.

In 1886 Dr. Harry Guinness became associated with his father and mother in the work of the Institute, and in 1891 sailed for the Congo to study the conditions and possibilities of missionary service in Central Africa. Subsequently he turned his attention to Central and South America. Gradually the scope of the Society's work enlarged until in 1899 it assumed the name of "The Regions Beyond Missionary Union," by which it is now known; the central thought being to reach lands beyond those already within the sphere of missionary labor. Dr. Guinness visited Panama, Ecuador, Peru, Bolivia, and Chile, crossed the Andes and descended the Amazon. The result was the establishment of mission work at Cuzco, in Peru, and in Argentina. The last field occupied by the Union is in India, where it commenced work in 1899 in Behar, one of the darkest and most needy sections of the empire.

Livingstone Inland Mission: The pioneer of this mission, Mr. Henry Craven, with a Danish sailor, who was quickly recalled as unworthy, reached Banana, at the mouth of the Congo, in February, 1878. A passage in a trading vessel was secured to Boma, 70 miles up the river, and by canoe to Yellala Falls, 30 miles farther. After the usual African experience a landing stage was built at Matadi, at the end of the lower river navigation, and a station formed at Pala Vala, 15 miles inland on a plateau 1,600 feet above the sea, where the population were, in the main, friendly. Two associates joined the mission in the summer, and seven more by the end of the year, and a station was formed at Bansa Manteka. The question of transportation became a most difficult one. The natives were unreliable, the *Kroo-men* from Sierra Leone expensive. A well-equipped party from England arrived in 1880 to find that several of the company that preceded them had died; but they pressed on toward Stanley Pool. In 1881 the little steam-launch "Livingstone" was sent out with another band of volunteers. The vicissitudes of the work, the sickness of so many, and the loss by death of five, led to doubts as to the wisdom of continuing the attempt. The experience of other societies, however, encouraged them, and new stations were formed until, when in 1884 the mission was transferred to the ABMU, seven stations were in working order: Mukimocka, Palabala, Bansa Manteka, Mukimbunga, Lukunga, Leopoldville, and Equatorville. The "Henry Reed" was afloat on the Upper Congo, and twenty missionaries, four of them married, formed the working staff of the mission.

Since the foundation of the work nearly fifty had volunteered for it and had been sent out. A few proved unfit and were recalled, some were broken in health, and eleven had given up their lives on the Congo.

Congo Balolo Mission: Until early in the 19th century, the dwellers on the southern bank of the Upper Congo were peaceful members of the Bantu race. At that time a great nation came traveling westward, and took possession of the left bank of the stream, turning out the former occupants and bringing in a new language, customs and people. The powerful invaders were significantly called Balolo, Ironpeople, or *the strong tribe.* The country which the invaders conquered, and have since kept and dwelt in, is nearly five times as large as England, and fills the horseshoe bend of the Congo—extending from the Lomami in the east to Lakes Mantumba and Leopold on the west, and from Lopori on the north to the headwaters of the Bosira and Jaupa on the south.

In 1888 Mr. John McKittrick, of the Livingstone Mission, returned to England on furlough from the advanced outpost of the mission, Equator Station, with an intense interest in the Balolo, and also a living specimen of the race, a Balolo boy named Bompole. The result of this apparently accidental visit was the organization of the Balolo mission. When the pioneer party for the new field was ready to sail a farewell meeting was held at Exeter Hall, in March, 1889. Many speeches were made—one at least unexpected and unpremeditated. It was spoken by Bompole's dark lips, and in his high, shrill voice. Hundreds of listeners in the great hall were hushed into silence to hear the few and ignorant words framed into broken sentences, for Bompole's vocabulary was very limited, and of grammar he knew nothing. The little lad said his people "wanted Gospel," and then asked, "Isn't it a shame—shame to keep Gospel to yourself? Not meant for English only! Isn't it a shame? My people wanting gospel! Isn't it—isn't it a shame?" Was ever the cause of foreign missions more forcibly put? The mission band sailed from England on the 18th of April, 1889, and reached its destination on the Lulonga River in the middle of August—four months only to accomplish what ten years before could not have been done at all! How different the experience of this party from that of the pioneers of the Livingstone Mission! The hearty cooperation of the missionaries already in the field not only facilitated the journey, but also averted the danger from exposure and inexperience to which the earlier workers in so many cases had succumbed. No fatal illness occurred on the journey, and the missionaries have since their arrival continued in good health. Early in 1890 the second party arrived, and with them the Mission's own steam-launch, the "Pioneer," which had been built in London, and was to be reconstructed as the "Henry Reed" had been, at Stanley Pool. This was followed in 1902 by the "Livingstone," a much finer boat than its predecessor. Of the 96 missionaries who, in the thirteen years, 1889-1902, entered the service of this mission, 30 have died, 35 remain on the mission staff, 6 are in the home work, 8 have joined other missions, 9 broke down in health and retired, and 8 proved unsatisfactory. The results in the field have not been as apparent as in some other sections, notably the cataract region, where the ABMU and the Swedes are working; but later reports show spiritual awakening, and there are classes of enquirers numbering 100. In the schools there are about 1,500 children, and to these the missionaries look for the best fruit.

Argentina and Peru: The work of the Regions Beyond Missionary Union in South America was the result of the visit to that continent of Dr. Harry Guinness, after his visit to Africa. There seems to have been no definite enterprise, as in the case of the Congo-Balolo Mission, but a number of those who had graduated at Harley House went out independently, and afterward were gathered into two missions in Argentina and Peru, tho without any very complete organization. In Argentina, work, partly evangelistic, partly educational, is carried on at Buenos Aires, Las Flores, Coronel Suarey, and Tres Arroyos, in each case under the care of a missionary and his wife, with the assistance of native evangelists and teachers. The schools are on the pay system and the income contributes materially toward the expense of the mission work, the RBMU meeting deficiencies. In Buenos Aires a group of nurses has been established, especially for maternity work, and access being thus gained to families, a wider influence is secured. Throughout the whole of Argentina the hearts of the people are becoming more open to spiritual instruction. School work may not be profitable from a pecuniary point of view, but is of great value for its effect upon the parents, as well as the children.

In Peru the work was commenced in 1893 by two men, Messrs. Jarrett and Peters, who secured an entrance into Cuzco despite the most bitter opposition. The clergy daily preached against them in all the churches, the people passed them with averted glance, and every door was closed at their approach. Their assassination was advocated by some, and at last they were compelled to leave (1895). Another attempt the next year was unsuccessful, but in 1897 they established themselves. Opening a British art-store as the reason for their residence, and supporting themselves partly by the sale of photographs, they succeeded in gaining the confidence of the people until after six years they were welcomed in every part of the city, and were free to speak the Gospel message wherever they chose. Two of the missionaries, Mr. Newell and Mr. Peters, were even invited to give instruction in athletics and drawing in the Government schools. In February, 1903, the first evangelical church in the interior of Peru was organized by Mr. Jarrett at Cuzco. Mr. Peters has been made a citizen of Cuzco and been elected a member of the municipality—a striking illustration of the change that is taking place in more than one South American community.

REHOBOTH: A town in German Southwest Africa, situated in the Herero country, about 170 miles E. S. E. of Swakopmund. It is celebrated for its hot springs. Station of the Rhenish Mission Society, with (1903) 2 missionaries, one of them with his wife; 6 native workers, 1 Sunday school, 2 day schools, and 1,209 professed Christians, of whom 484 are communicants.

RELIEF WORK OF MISSIONS in Public Calamities: In the limits prescribed, it will be impossible to give any history or statistics of missionary relief work. This article will treat only the necessity, principles and wider results of such effect.

I. Necessity: The object of Christian Missions is to extend the spirit and teaching of Christ. He taught by act as much as by word. He went about doing good. When John the Baptist, in prison, sent for proofs of Jesus' Messiahship, he was referred to the acts of mercy which the Christ was doing. Jesus said that He would recognize His followers at the day of judgment by their treatment of the hungry, naked, sick and homeless. Works of mercy, considered meritorious even under Mohammedan and heathen systems, are of the essence of Christianity. It is the wiser and deeper, tho often unconscious, working of the spirit of Jesus that has differentiated Christendom, through sentiments, institutions and laws for the care of the orphan, the blind, the deaf and dumb, the sick, insane, and poor, and for the humane treatment of even the lower animals. No one who is callous to suffering or slack in its relief is a fit representative of civilization, still less a worthy herald of the Good News. The necessity, therefore, of missionaries engaging in relief work in times of great public calamity does not admit of argument. They are under even greater obligation to such service than are ministers and churches in the homeland. For the missionary is often the only one on the ground with knowledge, ability and character enough to cope with the situation. The wealth and sympathy of Christendom would have been powerless to ameliorate the sufferings of the survivors of the Armenian massacres but for the American missionaries who stood at their posts during those awful years, and with wisdom, courage and fidelity acted as the almoners of $2,000,000 of relief funds from Europe and America. Referring to this service, at the time when all the powers of Europe have failed to fulfil their treaty obligations to protect the Christian subjects of Turkey, Sir Philip Currie, British Ambassador at Constantinople, declared: "The American Mission, through its missionaries, furnishes the only oasis in the great desert of calamity that marks this land." Another ground of the necessity for missionaries doing relief work is revealed in the modest remark of Mr. W. W. Peet of Constantinople, Treasurer of the Turkish Missions of the American Board. He says: "One good result of the relief work at least was that it made life endurable for our missionaries during those awful years. I tell you we could not have lived there if we had not been engaged in that sort of work." It may, therefore, be concluded that there is on the part of missionaries, officers of boards, and the Christian public, a firm and glad acceptance of the proposition that philanthropy is always a legitimate feature of missions, and that in seasons of acute and wide-spread distress, through famine, flood or earthquake, through pestilence or war, relief work may rightly, for the time, absorb the strength of an individual or even of a whole mission, to the apparent detriment of the regular literary, educational or even evangelistic forms of service.

II. Principles Governing Mission Relief. 1. *Fidelity:* It goes without saying that funds placed in the hands of missionaries for relief should be not only sacredly guarded, but also applied in accordance with the exact wishes of the donors. It is a great tribute to the integrity of missionaries the world over that, so far as the writer's knowledge goes, no questions are raised as to their fidelity in handling the vast sums of money that from time to time are thrust into their hands. This is the more striking in view of the fact that relief work is with them a self-imposed task, that they are almost invariably people with no support except a small living salary paid them for other less arduous services, and that they are under no bonds, nor any supervision in the management of the trust committed to them. Because of the confidence reposed in them, and as a justification of its continuance, missionaries should always, from the outset of any relief effort, keep exact accounts of all moneys received and expended, and render these accounts, duly audited, to the boards, committees, periodicals, or individuals through whom the funds have been transmitted. Many such reports are remarkable for detail and accuracy, especially when we consider the many and pressing cares resting on those who prepared them.

2. *Selection of Beneficiaries:* The first and, in general, the principal consideration should be that of need. In questions of life or death no tests of race or creed should hold. Help should be given the starving Kurd or Armenian, and to the plague-stricken Christian or Hindu or Chinaman on the same principle that the Father "maketh his sun rise on the evil and the good." Such impartiality is especially imperative where relief funds have been raised by appeals to the general public on purely humanitarian grounds, to which people of all classes have responded. The missionary should resist any temptation to use funds so given in such a way as to directly favor the institutions or the spiritual results which he may have at heart. He must be content to scatter the bread on the waters with impartial hand. In so doing he will discharge his plain duty and may in the end find that he has given to blind and prejudiced hearts the most impelling proof of the truth of his message. I would not modify the above principle in spite of a conviction, based on an experience of several years in raising popular funds for sufferers by the Armenian massacres and by the famines of India, that at least nine-tenths of the moneys contributed, even through purely secular committees, came from Protestant people of a positively religious character. Jews and Catholics maintain splendid charities of their own, but do not, as far as I have been able to ascertain, contribute largely to general relief funds of the above character. But while trying to do good to all men, the missionary and his constituency at home will also, naturally, make special provision for "them who are of the household of faith"; and after the crisis of a calamity is over, and the relief problem ceases to be that of saving life, the missionary will be freer to continue the relief on more limited lines, both as to its nature and recipients. Popular funds will then dwindle, and the money that continues to come will be from people who are in full sympathy with the aims of the mission and who will approve of orphanages, industrial schools, etc., which shade into the regular work of the missionary.

3. *Methods of Relief:* In order to know who are most in need, some sifting process is necessary. This may be done either by actually going to the homes of the people, finding out their exact circumstances, and giving them money and provisions, or, on the other hand, by providing remunerative labor under such conditions that only those most in need will apply for it. The latter method has much in its favor. In the first place, it will save much time and expense. Secondly, by a process of natural selection it will eliminate impostors. Thirdly, it avoids pauperizing, an evil second only to the calamity itself. Fourthly, it can make relief funds go further by being used over and over. For instance, raw cotton or wool spun into thread by one set of poor people can be woven into cloth by another, made up into garments by a third, and finally sold at reduced prices or given to the absolutely helpless. Fifthly, the relief work may be so planned as, in a measure, to forestall such disasters in the future. This end may be attained by setting the people to work digging wells, reservoirs and canals, to insure a better water supply; or making roads for better transportation; or by erecting buildings for orphanages and hospitals; or by teaching new and improved arts and trades, by which the people can earn more and not be so largely dependent on agriculture for a living. The large and excellent results that have often been achieved by missionaries with such efforts is a splendid proof of their administrative ability and practical wisdom. The first method of seeking out the needy in their homes must also often be followed. For there are some too ignorant, others too young or feeble to come of themselves, and there are others prohibited by social station, caste, or sex from public and promiscuous labor. It is just these classes, often most destitute and beyond the scope of government aid, for whom wise and sympathetic special provision should be made by the missionary.

4. *Spirit:* But the fidelity, impartiality and wisdom emphasized above need to be exercised in a spirit as sympathetic as it is wise, and as patient as it is masterful, if the work is to bear spiritual as well as material fruits. Even in the conduct of well-organized charities and asylums in Christian lands it is necessary to guard against a hard, sordid, and demoralizing tendency among the employes. The poor, faint, and distracted victims of disaster will appreciate what is done for them all the more if done in a gentle and kind way.

III. Wider Results of Missionary Relief Work.
1. *On the Missionary:* The first and most apparent result may be the exhaustion and possible breakdown of some of the missionaries under the great strain, physical, mental, and moral. This should be foreseen by the Boards and needed rest provided at the earliest moment,

with a complete change of scene if possible. Barring a breakdown, the missionary will find himself better equipped than ever. The closer intimacy with the people should give him a better understanding of their conditions of life, sentiments, and moral qualities. Missionaries have frequently developed greater efficiency through the calling out of latent faculties under the stress of enlarged responsibility. The need of thoroughly practical and common-sense methods is brought out by these crises, and the lessons they teach should be fruitful in correcting defects of the missionary system. Industrial schools and manual training, now widely maintained with enthusiasm and success, are in many cases the direct outgrowth of relief work. The product of these schools cannot fail to be a more manly and competent type of convert, who will help to solve the problem of self-support.

2. *On the Native Christians:* There is every reason to believe that the above influences affecting the missionary for good are felt also by the native Christians. A despiritualization of the churches in connection with the relief work has been reported in some cases. This may be true to some degree, especially when, as in Armenia, the relief work necessitated by the massacres was not only so great as very seriously to interfere with the regular work of the churches and schools, but also had to be continued so long as to lose something of the sacred tenderness felt by all at the outset. Jealousies sometimes arise among church members over the selection of distributers of relief, and the handling of large sums of money proves a temptation to some, as it does in every land. Another unfortunate result is said to be an impression that the missionaries have unlimited means at their command, and hence that they should be less urgent about native contributions.

3. *Evangelistic Results:* The effect on the unevangelized is generally reported to be highly beneficial. This is the case in proportion as the people understand that missionary relief funds are not supplied by any government treasury, but are free gifts from the people of Christian lands, made and dispersed without any proselytizing, but in the spirit of loving service personified by Christ. So conducted, relief work will not encourage "rice Christians." That no money sticks to the fingers of the missionaries is an object lesson not lost in lands where official corruption is the rule.

4. *Reflex Influence:* The effect on the constituencies of the boards is helpful, first, by stimulating sympathy and overcoming the selfishness which is chiefly responsible for the niggardly gifts of many to missions. There is abundant evidence that relief funds are not disadvantageous to the treasuries of the boards. The gifts of regular contributers are not lessened by these special appeals, while many whose first gift is for relief become interested in the missionaries and the support of their regular work. Secondly, these crises are of great educational value through the popular interest aroused in the conditions of life and characteristics of races who are the objects of missionary effort. Thirdly, the dark background of a great calamity often serves to show, in strong relief, if only for a moment, the noble and truly great personality of missionaries who by the nature of their calling must labor in spheres so remote and humble as to escape the recognition they richly deserve.

The effect on the general public is also most salutary, resulting as it does in the exercise and consequent strengthening of the noblest sentiments. Every relief effort is a practical assertion of the brotherhood of man. There is no doubt that relief from one or many lands to another in distress is productive of international good feeling and hastens the day when the nations shall not learn war any more.

"We hate those whom we have injured," said a philosopher of heathen Rome. It is equally true that we love those whom we have befriended. Every wisely conducted relief effort may therefore be encouraged both as a cause and an effect of the coming of the Kingdom.

Ecumenical Missionary Conference *Report*, Vol. 2, pp. 230-250, New York, 1901.

RELIGIOUS TRACT SOCIETY (1799): During the outbreak of missionary enthusiasm that marked the close of the 18th century, a group of practical Christian men, among whom were Rowland Hill and the Rev. G. Burder, met at St. Paul's churchyard and founded a society for the dissemination of Christian literature, which became known as the Religious Tract Society. From the beginning it has been unsectarian in principle, always selecting its committee from churchmen and nonconformists equally. It works through its agents and colporteurs, and by means of special grants to missionary and tract societies throughout the world.

It was not till 1818 that the Society made its first grant for foreign work, to aid the French Protestants, which led to the founding of the Paris Tract Society (1820), and of the Toulouse Book Society (1835). In the beginning of its work most of the foreign publications were prepared at the central office in London, but at an early date the greater part of the work for France was transferred to Paris and Toulouse, while the decision as to what should be published still rested with the London committee.

Assisted by the missionaries of the various evangelical denominations, the Society has printed books and tracts in 250 languages, dialects, and characters; the circulation of this literature being carried on as far as possible without the expense of agents. The sale of publications has been made to cover all expenses of manufacture, and the whole amount of contributions has been applied to the circulation of publications. The Society aids the various organizations engaged in philanthropic and missionary work in the home field, and makes grants to parochial, congregational, and individual workers throughout the country, and especially to Sunday and day school libraries. Work is done also in connection with hospitals, infirmaries, and other institutions, and for soldiers, sailors, fishermen, hop-pickers and navvies.

Depots are maintained by the Society upon the Continent of Europe, at Lisbon, Madrid, Budapest, Vienna, Gratz, and Warsaw. Publication work at large centers, such as Paris, Toulouse, Baden-Baden, Florence, Rome, Berlin, and Constantinople, has been aided by liberal grants. In the mission fields of the world, where the help given takes the form of large grants of money, printing paper and of publications, wherever possible, such grants are made only to auxiliary book and tract societies, under the control of committees representing the evangelical denominations. Where there is no such organization, the Society aids individual workers.

In France the Society makes grants in aid of the Dépôt Central, the Paris Tract Society, the McAll Mission and smaller grants to individual Christian workers. The Geneva Evangelical Society of Switzerland and the Belgian Evangelical Society of Belgium both receive small grants. In Italy the depot at Rome and the Italian Evangelical Publication Society, Florence, have received annual grants. Since 1870 the work of the Society in Spain has been carried on from Madrid as a center, with subdepots at Barcelona, Saragossa, Seville, and Gibraltar. In 1902 those at Saragossa and Seville were closed. Colporteurs are employed to visit the villages with Bibles and Christian literature. In Portugal a depot is maintained at Lisbon, and a subdepot at Oporto, but in 1902 it was decided to discontinue the latter. Colporteurs are employed, and the publications of the Society are scattered through the country. At St. Miguel (Azores), and S. Vicente (Capo Verde), depots are maintained without expense to the Society.

In Germany grants are made to the German Evangelical Book and Tract Society; the Baden Christian Colportage Union, the Society for the Free Distribution of Holy Scriptures and Religious Tracts, Dresden, and several individuals are aided in Christian work. In 1902 the committee of the Society became convinced that the time had come to place upon the Protestants of Germany the task of carrying on their evangelical work, and decided to reduce the annual grants to German organizations. Individual grants are made to Christian workers in Holland and Denmark, chiefly for distribution among sailors. In Sweden the Society has made an annual subsidy to the National Evangelical Society of Sweden, one of the most active centers of religious publications in Europe, but in 1903 it was decided to discontinue this grant. In Norway the Society has assisted the Christiania Home Mission. In Russia every opportunity for disseminating Christian literature has been seized, and the committee are ever on the lookout for new openings. A depot is maintained in Poland at Warsaw, and grants are made to individual workers; assistance has also been given the Bible-Bag Mission of Finland. In Greece the only regular work of the Society for some time has been tract publication work under the superintendence of Dr. Kalopothakes, of Athens. In Austria work is carried on in Vienna in conjunction with the British and Foreign Bible Society, and at Gratz and Budapest. Subdepots were for many years established at Lemberg, Trieste, Bucharest, and Belgrade, but were discontinued in 1902. Aid has been given an active evangelical pastor in Prague, Bohemia. For over 35 years the Society has had a depot in Hungary, but not until 1902 was it granted a legal existence by the government, and able to work openly without hindrance.

In Turkey the Society has made grants to the publication work in Constantinople under the American Board, to the Mission Institute in Samokov, Bulgaria, and to individual missionaries in Turkey in Asia, especially at Aintab and Marash. Since 1871 the Society has sustained an important publication work through the American Press at Beirut in Syria, and special grants have been made to individual workers in Syria and Palestine.

Since 1813 the Society has made grants for the preparation of a vernacular Christian literature in India, and many large auxiliary tract societies have been formed in various parts of the empire, all of which have been aided by the Society. Perhaps the most important of these organizations is the Christian Literature Society for India, which cooperates with the RTS. The Calcutta Book and Tract Society has been aided annually since 1831. The North India Christian Tract and Book Society, Allahabad, has received grants of money and printing paper. The Bombay Book and Tract Society, founded in 1827, has received yearly grants from the Society since its formation. The Gujarat Tract and Book Society and the Orissa Tract Society receive annual grants of printing paper. The Madras Religious Tract and Book Society, the oldest existing organization of this kind in India, has received grants since its formation in 1818. Other societies in India receiving regular aids of money or printing paper from the RTS are the Bangalore Tract and Book Society, the Malayalam Religious Tract Society, the South Travancore Tract Society, the Ceylon Christian Literature and Religious Tract Society, while grants of stock have been made to the depots in Burma, at Rangoon, Maulmain, and Mandalay. Publications connected with the various missions in India have been aided and grants have been made to individuals working in the empire. The Decennial Conference of Indian Missionaries convened at Madras in 1902 sent to the Society an acknowledgment of the services it had rendered in India: "Without the books, tracts, and leaflets published with the aid of this and kindred societies, mission workers would be seriously crippled."

In China the Society cooperates with the Society for the Diffusion of Christian and General Knowledge among the Chinese, and works through the various auxiliary organizations of the empire. The Chinese Tract Society of Shanghai receives grants in aid of the vernacular publication work, and in 1899, with the support and encouragement of the London Committee of the RTS, published an annotated Bible for the Chinese—one of the greatest works ever undertaken by the missionary body in China." For twenty-six years the Central China Religious Tract Society has been at work, with centers at Hankow, Wuchang and Hanyang. It is managed by a committee representing four nationalities and six missions, but its mainstay has been the RTS, of London, yearly grants having been made for its work ever since its formation. Annual grants are made to the Hongkong Religious Tract Society, and to the Bible, Book, and Tract Depot in that city; to the Religious Tract Society of Canton, Amoy, and West China; to the North China Tract Society, and the Manchurian Tract Society. Special grants have been made for the colportage work of the National Bible Society of Scotland, the China Inland Mission, and individual missionaries of other denominations in China. In Japan the Society makes large grants to the Japan Book and Tract Society, located in Osaka, and made a special grant in 1903 to be expended on Christian literature for the visitors of the Osaka exhibition.

Few organizations have such a far-reaching scope as the Religious Tract Society. Besides its work in the larger countries of Europe and Asia, it makes grants to workers in the Straits Settlements, in Persia, in North Africa, Algiers and Tunis; Eastern and Central Africa, through the CMS workers. In South Africa the Port Elizabeth Railway Mission is supplied with literature at reduced rates, the South African Auxiliary of the Bible Society received grants of tracts for hospital use; books were granted at half price for the Dutch Girls' Home, at Cape Town, and for Sunday school libraries in six or more denominations, as well as grants of pictures, tracts, etc., for individual workers. In West Africa grants of books, tracts, pictures, electrotypes, etc., have been made to missionaries of various creeds and nationalities. In Madagascar a grant of paper aids the LMS Mission Press; tracts and pictures have been sent to Mauritius, and a single grant has been made to a worker on Ascension Island in the South Pacific. In Canada grants are made in aid of the Montreal Auxiliary Religious Tract Society, the Bible Society Auxiliary of Quebec and to individual workers. In Nova Scotia the British American Book and Tract Society of Halifax receives annual grants of tracts and favorable terms on books for Sunday school libraries, and for colportage work on the coasts of Newfoundland and Labrador. Special grants have been made to individual workers in Newfoundland. A single grant of tracts was made in British Columbia, and to the American Seaman's Friend Society, at New York, applied for by the Secretary.

In Mexico the United Tract Committee of Mexico City received aid for Spanish tract printing, and workers have been aided in British and Spanish Honduras and in Costa Rica. In South America at British Guiana, Brazil, Argentine Republic, Chile, and Colombia, to individual workers. In the West Indies grants of books for colportage work have been made, for Sunday school and day school libraries, and tracts for general distribution at Jamaica, Antigua, Bahamas, and Bermudas. In Australia the same grants have been made to New South Wales, Victoria, South Australia, Western Australia, and Tasmania. In New Zealand grants have been made of publications at reduced rates to the Scripture Gift Association of Auckland; the New Zealand Bible Tract and Book Society at Dunedin and Woodville for use in the Bush country.

The LMS Mission Press of New Guinea receives grants of printing paper. In Samoa a like grant is made. In Fiji the Wesleyan Missionary Society has been aided with literature, and in Tahiti a missionary of the Paris Evangelical Society has received grants of French and English publications.

During 1903 the total circulation from the Home Depot, including books, tracts, periodicals, cards, and miscellaneous issues, was 29,481,210, of which 14,034,350 were tracts. The total issues from the foreign depots have been estimated at 20,000,000, making about 49,481,210 issues for the year, a grand total of 3,540,196,440 since the formation of the Society. The receipts of the Society from all missionary sources amounted to £19,501 to the General Fund, and £1,474 to the Centenary Fund. Grants of money, paper, electrotypes, books, tracts, and other publications in Great Britain and Ireland, £11,175; similar foreign grants, £7,084; a total of £18,259.

REWA: A settlement in the Fiji Islands, situated on the E. coast of Viti Levu. Station of the Australian Wesleyan Methodist Missionary Society, with (1900) 1 missionary, 620 native workers, 23 outstations, 220 places of worship, 480 Sunday schools, 527 day schools, 1 theological class, and 6,729 professed Christians.

RHEA, Samuel Audley: Born at Blountville, Tenn., January 23, 1827; graduated at Knoxville University, 1847; Union Theological Seminary, New York, 1850; ordained February 2, 1851; sailed as a missionary of the ABCFM March 4, same year, for the Nestorian Mission. In 1851 Mr. Rhea went to the new station at Gawar, among the mountain Nestorians. His health broke down under the strain of that lonely and arduous life, and he was obliged to visit the United States for recuperation in 1859. After his return in 1860 he was stationed at Urmia. He was well versed in Hebrew and Syriac; spoke the modern Syriac with great accuracy and fluency; was able to preach in Azerbaijan Turkish with acceptance to the Armenians and others. While at Tabriz he pursued investigations in the Eastern Turkish, with the view of translating the Scriptures into that tongue, having already rendered in it the Sermon on the Mount. While in Kurdistan he studied Kurdish, and wrote a valuable synopsis of the grammar. He was treasurer of the mission, and its business agent in general. He also had the charge of evangelistic work in fifteen villages, some of them very large. His travels among the wilds of Kurdistan were often protracted and perilous. In 1865 he fell ill as a result of exposure while touring. The next day he appeared convalescent, and started to return to Urmia, but died at the wayside village of Ali Shah, September 2, 1865.

RHEES, Rev. Henry Holcombe: Appointed a missionary of the ABMU July 15, 1878, and went immediately to Tokio, Japan, where he built the first American Baptist Mission house in Japan. In 1882 he moved to Kobe, where the remainder of his missionary life was passed. He visited America in 1889 and 1891, and the latter year he received the degree of Doctor of Divinity from Shurtleff College, Alton, Ill. The writer of these words met him at Kobe in the year 1895, and was deeply impressed by his intelligent views on the mission work in Japan, his indefatigable spirit, and his self-sacrificing service for his Master. For years he was the senior missionary of the Baptist Mission in Japan; and the influence of this consecrated servant of God in all departments of the work was potent and permanent. He fell in sleep at Kobe, May 10, 1899.

RHENIUS, Charles Theophilus Ewald: Born November 5, 1790, at the fortress of Gaudens, West Prussia. He was led to become a missionary by reading the writings of the Moravians. He sailed for India as a missionary of the CMS, February 22, reaching Madras July 4, 1814. He soon proceeded to Tranquebar, his appointed station. At the end of five months he was sent to Madras to found a new mission, being the first to labor there under the CMS. During the five years of his residence in Madras he was constantly employed preaching the Gospel in public meetings, conversing with individuals, holding discussions with Brahmans or other learned men, studying the Tamil and Telugu, and making frequent tours to various cities and temples. It was then decided by the committee that Mr. Rhenius should establish a mission in Tinnevelli district, and in June, 1820, he removed to Palamcotta, the chief city of the district. Mr. Hough, the English chaplain, having left Palamcotta in 1821, Mr. Rhenius held an English service on the Sabbath for English residents until the arrival of another chaplain. In 1822 a seminary was established for the education of youth, which has furnished catechists and schoolmasters for the mission. A distinguishing feature of this mission, largely due to Mr. Rhenius, was the formation and settlement of Christian villages. In order to withdraw the converts from the influence of heathenism, pieces of land were purchased, those who forsook idolatry were located on them, and formed into a Christian congregation. A catechist was appointed, a school established, and a small chapel erected. But when, in 1826 and the following years, the Christian villages had increased in number, to relieve the missionary of the burden of their management an association of natives was formed called "The Native Philanthropic Society," having for its object the settling of native Christians in villages, the building of schoolhouses, the acquisition of grounds, etc., for these purposes, and the rendering of other assistance to the native Christians in their external affairs. In 1832 an unhappy controversy arose between Mr. Rhenius and the CMS on the subject of the form of ordination to be used for native ministers. This led to his dismissal from the service of the Society, and his continuance in the same field as an independent missionary, often at variance with his former missionary associates. He continued this independent mission work until June 5, 1836, when he died of a stroke of apoplexy.

Mr. Rhenius was one of the greatest missionaries working in India in the first half of the 19th century. He had extraordinary power over those natives who came under his personal influence. The happy union of cheerful piety and masculine energy with a bodily constitution capable of great and sustained exertion rarely appears in the missionary field. In addition to this, Mr. Rhenius was an accomplished scholar and a master of the Tamil language. To him it was given to revise and improve Fabricius' version of the Tamil Scriptures. The New Testament was printed in 1828, but the Old Testament was left unfinished at his death. Differences of opinion as to the principles of translation led him to publish in 1826 a valuable essay of 60 pages on the *Principles of Translating the Holy Scriptures*. He also prepared in Tamil a *Harmony of the Gospels*, which remains in general use. Other works in Tamil were *The Essence of the True Veda*, *A Summary of Divinity*, and a very useful *Tamil Grammar*.

RHENISH MISSIONARY SOCIETY. See GERMANY; MISSIONARY SOCIETIES IN.

RHODESIA: A British territory and sphere of influence in South Central Africa, comprising the region lying to the north and west of the Transvaal Colony and Bechuanaland, bounded on the east by Portuguese East Africa, on the north by the Congo Free State and on the west by German Southwest Africa. Total area is estimated to be about 600,000 square miles. It is divided by the Zambesi River into Northern and Southern Rhodesia.

Northern Rhodesia was first opened by David Livingstone. It is divided into Northeastern Rhodesia and Northwestern Rhodesia, both provinces being administered by the British South African Company, the defense of the territory being assumed by the British Central African Protectorate. Northeastern Rhodesia has about 120,000 square miles, and a population of about 339,000. It comprises the region lying between Lake Nyasa and Lake Mwera, with its affluent, the River Luapula, and extends from Lake Tanganyika nearly to the Zambesi.

Northwestern Rhodesia, or Barotseland, with an indefinite area, somewhat larger than Northeastern Rhodesia, extends from the Congo Free State southward to the German territory and the Zambesi, and is bounded east and west respectively by Northeastern Rhodesia and Portuguese West Africa.

Southern Rhodesia, with an area of 144,000 square miles and a population of about 500,000, embraces the territory from the Zambesi to the Transvaal and Bechuanaland, extending westward from Portuguese East Africa to the German territories. It includes Matabililand and Mashonaland. It is especially in the line of the British immigration and mining movements of Central and South Africa, and is fast being explored and exploited. In Matabililand about 15,000,000 acres of land, and in Mashonaland about 12,000,000 acres, have been surveyed. Townships to the number of 12 have been organized. In 1901 there were about 11,000 Europeans in the territory. Lines of railway, built and projected, connect the chief centers with Cape Colony. There are about 3,000 miles of telegraph. The territory has deposits of gold. The vast tableland of the north and northeast has an elevation of about 5,000 feet, and is well watered, with a rich soil and fine climate. The Matabili, so called from an immense shield behind which they were "hidden" in war, were originally a band of Zulu warriors, whose ranks were recruited from the lands they conquered. They are very fierce, daring, and proud. The Makalaka and Mashona were the former masters of the land. The former were nearly exterminated, the latter form the substratum of the northern population, and are very industrious. The Banyai are distinguished by their physical strength, light complexion, cleanly habits, and by the respect paid to women. In 1896 there was a native revolt in Matabililand, immediately followed by a similar disturbance in Mashonaland. Both these were thoroughly quelled.

The Missionary societies operating in Rhodesia are the LMS with 8 stations, the SPG with 7 stations, the Paris Society in the N. W., the ME and the ABCFM, in the extreme east, besides the WMS, the PB, the SDA, and the Berlin Society.

Brown (W. H.), *On the South African Frontier*, London, 1897; Greswell (W. P.), *Geography of Africa South of the Zambesi*, London, 1893; Hensman (H.), *History of Rhodesia*, London, 1900; Lenard (A. G.), *How We Made Rhodesia*, London, 1896; Powell (R. S. S. Baden-), *The Matabele Campaign*, London, 1901; Du Toit (S. J.), *Rhodesia, Past and Present*, London, 1897.

RIBÈ: A settlement in British East Africa, situated near the coast about 15 miles N. of Mombasa. It stands on a high tableland, with a fine view over the ocean. Station of the United Free Methodist Churches (1861). The estate belonging to the UMFC Mission is about 750 acres. There are (1903) 2 missionaries, 8 native workers, 2 outstations, 5 places of worship, 2 day schools, 5 Sunday schools, and 359 professed Christians.

RIBEIRAO PRETO: A town in Brazil, South America, situated in the State of São Paulo on the railway, about 200 miles N. by W. of São Paulo city. Station of the MES (1895), with (1903) 2 missionaries and their wives, 2 women missionaries, 2 native workers, 3 outstations, 2 places of worship, 3 Sunday schools, 2 boarding schools, and 550 professed Christians.

RICHARDS, William: Born at Plainfield, Mass., U. S. A., August 22, 1792; graduated at Williams College 1819, Andover Theological Seminary 1822; sailed November 29 same year as a missionary of the ABCFM for the Sandwich Islands, accompanied by four natives educated in the United States. He was stationed at Lahaina, on Maui. In 1837 he visited his native land with his wife and six children, arriving in May and returning in November. In 1838 the king and chiefs requested him to become their teacher in the science of government and laws, and also their chaplain and interpreter in their intercourse with foreigners. The code of laws adopted by the nobles and people was translated into Hawaiian by Mr. Richards, occupying 228 pages. From 1842 to 1845 he was absent on a mission to secure the acknowledgment of the independence of the islands by Great Britain, France, and the United States. After this recognition by foreign powers, he was sent as ambassador to England and other courts. On his return in 1845 he was appointed minister of public instruction, which office he held till his death, November 7, 1847. His influence with the king and government was very great.

RICHMOND: A settlement on one of the small islands of the Fiji group, S. of Viti Levu Island. Station of the Australian Wesleyan Missionary Society, with (1900) 1 missionary, 228 native workers, 11 outstations, 76 places of worship, 150 Sunday schools, 150 day schools, and 2,331 professed Christians.

RIETFONTEIN: A settlement in Bechuanaland, Cape Colony, South Africa, situated on the frontier of German Southwest Africa, about 320 miles E. of Angra Pequena. Station of the Rhenish Missionary Society, with (1903) 1 missionary, 2 native workers, 1 day school, and 420 professed Christians, of whom 168 are communicants.

RIFIAN LANGUAGE: The tribes inhabiting the Rif Mountains in the northern part of Morocco use this language, which belongs to the Hamitic group of the African languages. It is probably to be classed as a Berber dialect, altho often spoken of as a distinct language. So far as it is written the Arabic alphabet has been used for the purpose.

RIGGS, Elias: Born at New Providence, N. J., November 19, 1810. Died at Constantinople, Turkey, January 17, 1901. During his early years he showed decided linguistic talent, and while at college he applied himself especially to the mastery of Hebrew, Syriac, Arabic, Chaldean and modern Greek, and produced an Arabic grammar and Chaldean manual. While he was completing his last year at Andover Theological Seminary he was invited by the American Board to join its mission in Greece, and on September 20, 1832, he was ordained. With Mrs. Riggs, on October 30, 1832, he sailed from Boston, and three months afterward joined Rev. Jonas King at Athens. For six years he labored at Argos, largely along educational lines, in Greece; and in 1844, because of governmental restrictions, he was transferred to Smyrna, Turkey, where he continued his work among the Greeks in that city. In 1844 he was assigned to the Armenian branch of the mission; and the greater part of his time from 1845 to 1852 was engaged in the work of translating the Scriptures into Armenian. In 1853 he was transferred to Constantinople, and for three years he was in charge of the Greek department and instructor in theology in the Bebek Training School. He visited the United States in 1856, and after filling the position of instructor of Hebrew at Union Theological Seminary, he was offered a professorship in that institution. Upon his return to Constantinople he began the translation of the Bible into Bulgarian, another language he had mastered, and the complete edition of this work was issued in 1871. In 1873 the American and British and Foreign Bible societies appointed a committee to revise the Turkish translation of the Bible, so as to make it acceptable both to the mass of the people and to the educated. The members of the committee were Dr. W. G. Schauffler, Rev. George F. Herrick, Rev. Robert Weakley, and Dr. Riggs. In 1878 the work, which has become the standard, was issued in both Arabic and Armenian characters. Besides his more important translations, Dr. Riggs wrote numerous tracts, school-books, and devotional books; and he produced during his long missionary life, either as translations or originals, no less than four hundred and seventy-eight hymns in the Bulgarian language alone. To give an idea of the linguistic attainments of Dr. Riggs, it may be stated that he had a working knowledge of twenty languages, and was a master of twelve. There are four nations reading the Word of God as he translated it for them; and as Dr. Herrick says: "The homes, the schools, the churches, where Dr. Riggs' translations of the Word of Life are read, and where the hymns he has translated are sung, are numbered by the tens of thousands, and extend from the Adriatic to the Persian Gulf, from the snows of the Caucasus to the burning sands of Arabia."

RIGGS, Stephen R.: Born Steubenville, Ohio, U. S. A., March 25, 1812; graduated at Jefferson College; studied theology at Alleghany Seminary; ordained April 6, 1837; went at once, with Mrs. Riggs, under appointment of the ABCFM to the mission among the Dakotas. Here he labored with great zeal and success in missionary and literary work at various places till the Sioux outbreak of 1862, when, barely escaping with his life, he fled to St. Paul, returning soon as chaplain of the military forces sent to suppress the outbreak. After a long and painful illness he died, August 24, 1883, aged 71, having spent over 45 years in active and successful work among the Indians. Dr. Riggs reduced the Dakota language to a written form, organizing and adapting it to religious expression, and translated into it nearly the entire Bible. He prepared also a Dakota dictionary of more than 16,000 words, which was published by the Smithsonian Institution. Upward of 50 volumes, religious and literary, partly translated, partly original, were prepared by him for the use of the Dakotas in their language. He lived to see ten churches organized and efficient, under native pastors. Of his eight children, five entered the missionary field, four among the Indians and one in China.

RIO DE JANEIRO: The capital of Brazil and the most important commercial city of South America. It is situated on one of the finest harbors of the world, 75 miles west of Cape Frio. The bay is land-locked and is entered from the south. It extends inland 17 miles, with a greatest breadth of 12 miles, and is said to be the most spacious and secure bay in the world. The city itself, like Rome, is built on seven hills, and the houses, with their white walls and red roofs, clustering in the valley or extending along the sides of the green slopes, present a most picturesque appearance as one approaches from the sea. The old part of the town lies nearest the bay, while the elegantly built new town is situated on the west of it. Here are fine streets, handsome public buildings, hospitals, asylums, over fifty chapels and churches, and many convents and nunneries. A national college, academy of medicine, theological seminary, and a national library meet the literary and educational wants of the people. A splendid aqueduct conveys pure spring-water from a mountain three miles southwest of the city. The climate is tropical, ranging from 54° in August to 97° in December. The annual rainfall is about 60 inches, one-fifth of the whole amount falling in February. The commerce of Rio de Janeiro is great and steadily increasing. As Brazil is the greatest coffee-producing country in the world, Rio is the largest coffee-exporting city. The population consists largely of Portuguese, with a mixture of negro blood, and is estimated (1900) at 750,000. Station of the MES (1878), with (1903) 3 missionaries, 1 of them with his wife; 2 women missionaries, 2 native workers, 2 outstations, 1 place of worship, 4 Sunday schools, 1 printing house, and 345 professed Christians. Station also of the SBC (1884), with (1903) 1 missionary and his wife, 4 native workers, 3 outstations, 1 place of worship, 1 printing house, and 233 professed Christians. Station also of the SDA (1891), with (1900) 5 missionaries, 4 of them with their wives; 1 woman missionary, 6 native workers, 25 outstations, and 697 professed Christians, 18 Sunday schools, 5 day schools. The YMCA (1892) and the ABS (1876) each has an agent here and the BFBS has an agent and 13 native Bible workers.

RIO DE ORO: A possession of Spain on the Atlantic coast of northwest Africa, extending from Morocco to Cape Blanco in Senegambia, and inland to the Sahara. It is governed by a sub-governor under the governor of the Canary Islands. The area is about 243,000 square miles; population about 100,000. In case of the future sale of the territory the right of preemption has been given to France. The inhabitants are Moors, Berbers, and negroes, chiefly Mohammedan. No missionary enterprises have been undertaken in this territory.

RIO MUNI: A territory of Spain, on the Gulf of Guinea, having Kamerun on the north and the French Congo on the east and south. Area 9,000 square miles. Population about 300. There is one missionary station of the PN in this territory, situated on the Benito River near its mouth.

RIO VERDE: A village in Mexico, situated in the state of San Luis Potosi, on the Rio Verde. Station of the Associate Reformed Presbyterian Synod of the South (1895), with (1900) 1 missionary and his wife, 1 native worker, 1 outstation, 2 places of worship, 1 Sunday school, 1 day school, 1 orphanage, and 23 professed Christians.

RIU KIU ISLANDS. See LU-CHU ISLANDS.

RIVERSDALE: A town in Cape Colony, South Africa, 150 miles E. of Cape Town, and 50 miles W. of Mossel Bay, on the railway thence to Cape Town. Station of the Berlin Evangelical Missionary Society (1868), with (1903) 2 missionaries, 3 women missionaries, 22 native workers, 8 outstations, 4 day schools, and 1,417 professed Christians, of whom 512 are communicants.

ROATAN ISLAND: An island in the Bay of Honduras, Central America, about 30 miles long. Population, 3,000. Station of the WMS, with (1903) 1 missionary, 38 native workers, 4 outstations, 22 places of worship, 11 day schools, 16 Sunday schools, and 737 professed Christians, of whom 575 are communicants. The name is also written Ruatan.

ROBBINS, Elijah: Born at Thompson, Conn., March 12, 1828; graduated at Yale College 1856, and East Windsor Theological Seminary 1859; ordained August 3; sailed as a missionary of the ABCFM September 29 of the same year for the Zulu Mission, where he labored for nearly thirty years. He was stationed first at Umzumbi, but the latter portion of his life was spent in connection with the Mission Training School at Amanzimtote. He died there June 30, 1889. This seminary for training Zulu men for the mission is in a great measure the fruit of Mr. Robbins' zeal and perseverance. The quality of the native laborers in the field testifies to the thoroughness of their teacher.

ROBERT COLLEGE, Constantinople: Robert College is an outgrowth of American missions in Turkey. It was founded in 1863 by Christopher R. Robert, a merchant of New York, in connection with Rev. Cyrus Hamlin, D.D., who became its first president. The aim was to establish at Constantinople something as nearly as possible like a first-class New England college, thoroughly Christian, but not sectarian, and open to young men of all the nationalities and religions of the East, with the English language as the common ground upon which all could meet. The College was opened in an old mission building at Bebek, with four students, all English or Americans. It was transferred in 1871 to its present location on a commanding eminence on the Bosphorus, six miles from Constantinople, where it owns some fifteen acres of land, secured to it by an imperial charter. It now has three large stone buildings, one of which is used for classrooms and dormitories, a second for scientific instruction and public assemblies, and a third for the preparatory department. Besides these a gymnasium is now (1903) in process of erection, and other buildings are projected. The College also owns a president's house and two professors' houses.

Incorporated under the laws of the State of New York, it is governed by a Board of Trustees, residing in or near the City of New York, who have charge of its funds and appoint its president, professors and tutors. Local affairs are administered by the president and faculty, by whom also all other teachers are appointed. Its endowment fund is now about $250,000, and the value of its real estate at Constantinople is estimated at about the same amount. Of this total sum Mr. Robert contributed somewhat more than $400,000. Its board of instruction consists of 36 persons, of whom 15 are Americans. The students now number over 300 annually, representing from 12 to 15 nationalities, chiefly

Armenian, Bulgarian, Greek and Turkish. The number of languages which must be taught in the College is eleven, and more or less instruction is given in half a dozen more. The common language of the College, however, is English, in which all public exercises are conducted and in which all the students after the third preparatory year become proficient.

There are two departments in the College, the preparatory, with a three years' course, and the collegiate, with five classes. The collegiate course is modeled on that of the smaller American colleges, affording to the students a certain amount of choice between classical and scientific or commercial studies, and leading up to the degree of A. B. or B.S. About 20 students now graduate each year. The aim of the College is, however, to give to those who are unable to take the full course a thorough general education in accordance with American ideas and Christian principles. As the majority of them expect to become business men a course has recently been organized which, while retaining the more important liberal studies, includes a number of commercial subjects, but omits Latin and the more advanced mathematics. Arrangements have also been made for more thorough instruction in the physical sciences. In the appointment of instructors great care is exercised to obtain men who are in cordial sympathy with the Christian purpose by which the founders of the College were animated. While there is no interference with the religious beliefs of the students, it is the earnest effort of the faculty to develop in them a manly, Christian character. All are required to be present at morning prayers, and all boarders at the Sunday services. They also meet regularly for the study of the Bible, and the different nationalities have their separate YMCAs, while there is one general association whose exercises are conducted in English. It is its moral, quite as much as its intellectual, tone which has given the College such wide renown throughout the East and which attracts to it Mohammedans and Jews, as well as members of the Greek and Armenian churches. It has not only sent out many Christian men, but has exerted an important influence upon these churches, as well as upon the political and social development of the countries from which its students come and to which they return.

About 2,500 young men have spent an average of three years in the College, and it has graduated in all 414, who have become preachers, teachers, government officials, judges, editors, lawyers, physicians, army officers, civil engineers, and business men in all parts of the world. Some 80 of them now fill official positions in Bulgaria.

Since the resignation of Dr. Hamlin in 1877, Rev. George Washburn, D.D., LL.D., who had previously been connected with the College for eight years, has been its president. Its success has been in large measure due to his eminent ability and his thorough knowledge of oriental character and life. In September, 1903, having reached the age of seventy years, he resigned the office, and, on his nomination, Rev. C. Frank Gates, D.D., LL.D., formerly president of Euphrates College at Harpoot, was chosen to succeed him. Dr. Washburn continues to give instruction as before, and it is hoped that the College may long have the benefit of his wisdom and his large experience.

The officers of the Board of Trustees are: President, John S. Kennedy; Secretary, Rev. Edward B. Coe, D.D.; Treasurer, Frederick A. Booth.

ROBINSON, Rev. John Alfred: Born in 1859 at Keynsham vicarage, Somerset. Died, 1891, at Lokoja. Educated at Liverpool College, and at Christ College, Cambridge, where he took the Carus University Greek Testament Prize. He received his B.A. degree in 1881, and his M.A. degree in 1884. During 1882-84 he was curate of the parish church at Trowbridge, and from 1884-1887 he was House Master of Neuenheim College, Heidelberg. In 1886, September 13, he was accepted as a missionary under the CMS; on February 5, 1887, he was appointed Secretary of the Niger Mission; and in 1889 he was transferred at his own desire to the new Sudan and Upper Niger Mission. He devoted much of his time to the study of the Hausa language, and left contributions on the subject, with a translation of St. Matthew's Gospel. At the time of his death, he was writing a new Hausa grammar and preparing a revision of Dr. Schön's dictionary. His researches into the dialectic differences of the Hausa language have brought to light much that is quite new, and the results of his studies have been a great aid to other missionaries. In a short while he, by his charm of manner, gained a great influence over the natives, and, as one said, he might have been a Hausa born, so perfectly was he at his ease among them. His was a brief but brilliant career as a missionary of the Cross.

ROCK SOUND: A settlement on the E. of Eleuthera Island in the Bahamas, lying 50 miles E. of Nassau. Station of the WMS, with (1903) 4 native workers, 4 Sunday schools, 1 place of worship, and 192 professed Christians.

RO GBERE: A village in Sierra Leone Colony, situated about 45 miles E. N. E. of Port Lokkoh. Station of the CMS (1896), with (1903) 1 missionary and his wife, 4 native workers, and 2 outstations.

ROMAN CATHOLIC MISSIONS: Under this head are included those missions which have been undertaken since the Reformation by Roman Catholics as distinct from Protestants.

While it is probably true, in a considerable degree, that the Roman Catholic missions among the heathen were undertaken to make good the losses of Rome from the great Protestant defection, the prime motive was the sudden enlargement of opportunity offered by the Spanish and Portuguese discoveries. From the very first the Spanish Church and the Spanish State were zealous to convert the newly discovered natives, and to protect them against the rapacious adventurers who poured out from the Iberian peninsula, and both efforts were unremitting and slowly effective, tho not until great multitudes had been swept away.

Rome has never claimed the right to compel unbelievers to receive baptism. Thomas Aquinas distinctly disavows this right for the Church, and even in Spain the bishops at various times rebuked the zeal of the princes for forcible proselytism. But as the rebukes of Alcuin did not deter Charles the Great from his policy of forcing Christianity upon the Saxons, so those of the Spanish bishops were often equally ineffective to prevent the forcible proselytizing of Jews and Moors. In the south, as in the north, religious unity was esteemed by the rulers the only certain foundation of civil unity, and the

State did not allow itself to be deterred by the inconsistency of forcible proselytism with the Gospel, from applying it where it was likely to avail. And the Roman Church, which maintains her own right to compel the baptized to remain, thereby broke the force of her protest against compelling the unbaptized to enter. Latin Christianity, indeed, being so predominantly an institute, cannot possibly be quite so sincerely disinclined to the ruder forms of conquest as Protestant Christianity, which emphasizes the necessity of inward appropriation of the Gospel.

Spanish America: Here there appears to have been but little forcible proselytism. The conquerors, indeed, prohibited the pagan worship on the ground that the worship of the true God, as practised by Christians or Jews, has alone a right to demand toleration of a Christian government, but the actual incorporation of the American natives into the Christian Church was essentially the work of persuasion. The conquered Indians, indeed, except where they retreated as untamable tribes into the Andes or the Sierras, had little reluctance to accept the forms of the conquering religion. A French priest, however, declares that the Mexicans are Catholics, but are not Christians, as Southey says of the common people of England before the Wesleys, who had gone through two religions, but were not yet evangelized.

The first Mexican missionaries were Franciscans. They are charged with having afterward, at least in Northern Mexico, become hard slave-holders, who brought back their runaway Indians with the lasso. But it does not appear that any shadow rests on the names of the early missionaries. They came first in 1522 from Ghent. One of them, as Kalkar relates, Pedro de Musa, a simple lay-brother, who devoted fifty years of unwearied activity to the spiritual and temporal interests of his Indians, reports in 1529 to his Provincial that in six years they had incorporated 200,000 souls with the Church of Christ; in eight years the Archbishop of Mexico is said to have been metropolitan of a million Christians. This splendid see was refused by Musa, and also by the Emperor Charles the Fifth's near relative, Pedro of Ghent, likewise a simple lay-brother. He writes to his imperial kinsman: "Because the people possess a peculiar skilfulness, I can truly say that there are among them good copyists, preachers, and singers, who might well be cantors in Your Majesty's chapel. In a school and chapel built here there are every day 600 boys instructed. A hospital has been put up near our cloister, which is a great comfort, and a means of conversion." "Most heartily, and in the true evangelical temper, he raised his voice to plead against all oppression of the natives." The Mexican Indians, however, unlike the West Indian and the Peruvian, were treated mildly, or at least with comparative mildness, except in the mountain mines.

In 1526 appeared the first Dominicans, who henceforth furnished most of the bishops. Then came Augustinians, Antony de Roa being the most distinguished. In 1572 came Jesuits, who went into New Mexico, where they have always remained the chief influence. By their skilful kindness they allured the natives from the cliffs and cañons, and established them in villages.

The Inquisition was soon transplanted and raged fearfully. The Indians, however, were not so much exposed to it as the whites, partly from their simplicity, partly from the contempt in which their intellect was held as hardly capable of heresy (tho sometimes of pagan practises), and partly from repeated royal edicts of exemption, lest haciendas and mines should be deprived of their peons. The devotion of the natives to the sacrament of penance was most edifying, confession of sin being a main element of the Aztec religion. On the other hand, it is said that up to the 19th century few of them were thought mentally competent to be admitted to the communion, altho a rite analogous to this was also found in their old religion. Mexico, converted, became, in her turn, a basis of missions, particularly to the Philippines and Ladrones.

The Indians of the West Indies, a gentle and pleasing race, but of singular vileness of morals, who turned their memorial visits to the tombs into veritable orgies of lewdness, met the first wave of Spanish adventure, fierce, cruel, and rapacious, as yet unchecked by the slower steps of civil justice or religious benevolence, and were almost at once swept away.

Peru was conquered in 1533, and after twenty years of disturbances was brought to tranquility in 1555 by the viceroy Mendoza, who took care to provide the natives with priests of good conduct. The Indians passed easily from the mild paganism of sun-worship into a nominal and formal Catholicism. Throughout Spanish and Portuguese America little pains seems to have been taken to build up an intelligent Christianity, adapted to deeply influence the heart and life, altho now and then a preacher of enlightened and energetic apprehensions of evangelical truth exerted a marked influence.

The famous Jesuit mission of Paraguay was established in 1586, after the intolerable tyranny of the Spaniards had long rendered fruitless all the attempts of the Franciscans and some lesser orders to secure the conversion of the Indians. The Jesuits, judging that the Spaniards needed reconverting first, turned their efforts toward their reformation, with so good effect that before long the Indians, believing, at length, that there must be something in a religion which could change the conduct of the whites, began to return to Christianity, or to seek baptism for the first time. The Jesuits were indefatigable. There was no tropical wilderness too intricate or wide-stretching for them to traverse, no water too wide for them to cross in their hollow logs, no rock or cave too dangerous for them to climb or enter, no Indian tribe too dull or refractory for them to undertake. Their only weapons were the Word of God and the language of love. The Jesuit, like a Christian Orpheus, would often go up and down the rivers drawing the savages to him by the force of music and sacred songs.

The missionaries, apparently becoming convinced that the reformation among the Spaniards, tho sufficient to set the good work of Indian conversion in motion, was neither extensive nor deep enough to make them, on the whole, desirable neighbors for their converts, obtained from the King of Spain the right to govern their 200,000 or 300,000 neophytes with entirely independent authority. Under their mild control the Guaranis enjoyed a hundred and sixty years of simple happiness until the Jesuits were expelled in 1767. The withdrawal of personal and minute supervision and leadership, as in other Roman Catholic Missions, resulted here in the loss of all that had been gained, and the Indians relapsed into their idolatry and savagery.

North America: In 1526 Pamphilus de Narvaez, a Spanish explorer, set out to conquer Florida. Accompanied by a number of Franciscan monks, he landed at Pensacola Bay April 16, 1528. Disheartened by the exposure, suffering, and toil of a few months, they turned back, and on reaching the coast built frail boats, in which they attempted to reach Mexico. They reached land, only to perish later on from starvation, sickness, or at the hands of the natives. Little is known of the work of these missionaries beyond the fact that no regular organized mission was established.

In 1545 a Dominican Father, Louis Cancer de Barbastro, with three associates, proceeded to the coast of Florida, where he and two of his associates were murdered, and the mission came to naught. Another mission to Florida was attempted by a number of Dominicans, but, like the preceding efforts, ended in suffering and death for the missionaries. From 1566 to 1570 some French Jesuits sustained a mission near the present site of St. Augustine. The first successful mission to Indians in territories now belonging to the United States was planted at St. Augustine in 1573 by the Spanish Franciscans. This mission continued until 1763, and had during this time over six hundred converts.

In 1539 Father Mark, a Spanish monk, attempted to reach the Zuni Indians, but succeeded only in planting a large cross on the hill which commanded the Zuni city of Cibola. Of the missionaries who went out with De Soto's expedition, every one perished before the remnant of the company reached the coast. In 1597 Franciscan monks made a successful attempt to establish a permanent mission in New Mexico. Thirty years later this mission reported over eight thousand converts to Christianity. So rapid had been the progress among these missions that large numbers of the Indians could read and write before the Puritans had begun missionary work in New England.

The first religious body to do missionary work among the Indians of Canada and of the West was the French Jesuits. In all the early French exploration the missionary idea was as prominent as that of the extension of territory.

Cartier's commission authorized him to explore "in order the better to do what was pleasing to God, our Creator and Redeemer." De Monts was also required to have the Indians "instructed, invited, and impelled to a knowledge of God, and the light of faith and Christianity."

In 1608 De Monts planted his first settlement at the mouth of the St. Croix, on Bonn Island. A short time later this mission was transferred to the Nova Scotia shore, where it received the name of Port Royal. This was the first foothold of France and the Catholic Church in the North.

In 1611 two Jesuit missionaries began work among the Micmacs of Nova Scotia, removing a little later to Deer Island, near the mouth of the St. Croix River, in order that they might work among the Indians known to the French as the Abenaquis, or Abnakis, and to the English as the Tarantuns. These Indians were one of the most powerful of the Algonquin tribes, occupying a greater part of what is now known as the State of Maine. They were settled in villages, and passed most of their time in hunting and fishing. This first mission among them was shortly attacked and destroyed by the English under Argal. A little later (1619) the Recollects, or Reformed Franciscans, also opened a mission in Acadia, but made their principal station on the St. John's River. They continued their efforts until 1624, but no authentic account of their work remains. The real work for the Abnakis of Maine began in 1642, when some of them were rescued from captivity by missionaries at Sillery, near Quebec. The captives were sent back to their homes on the Kennebec in 1646, Father Gabriel Druilletes accompanying them as far as Norridgewock, the chief settlement of the Abnakis. Thirty-eight years this devoted man spent in the effort to Christianize the Abnakis and other Indian tribes, traveling great distances and enduring every fatigue and every danger. As Father Druilletes traveled to the North and West as well as to the South, the Abnakis took up the habit of going to Quebec to see him. Many of them settled at Sillery, which station was moved in 1683 to the south side of the St. Lawrence, at the Chaudiere Falls. It was not until 1688, seven years after the death of Father Druilletes, that two other missionaries were sent to Norridgewock. Before the end of the century most of the Abnakis had become Christians, and at this time the Indians of the Jesuit missions of Maine were equal in piety and devotion to the priests of the seminary at Quebec. The wars between the French and English now disturbed the progress of the Mission; the country was devastated; missionaries lost their lives, and after the English finally occupied Quebec in 1763 the Mission was abandoned. In the War of the Revolution the Abnakis sided with the Americans. After the close of the war a petition was sent to Bishop Carroll, of the Society of Jesus in Maryland, asking for a missionary, and in 1784 one was sent from France, who for ten years lived at Oldtown and ministered to the Abnakis.

The nation known to the French by the name of Hurons and to the English as Wyandots occupied, when the French settled Quebec, a strip of land to the south of Georgian Bay, about 75 miles long by 25 wide. They numbered about 30,000, living in 18 large, well-built, and strongly defended towns. One of the Recollects who came out in 1615 made a visit to their towns, and on his return Father Le Caron began labors among them. In 1623 Father Viel took his place, but was killed by the Indians two years later. In 1626 Father Brebeuf began his long and faithful service among them. War with England resulted in his being sent out of the country by the victors. On the restoration of peace he returned (in 1633), and eighteen years after the first missionaries entered the Huron country he began to find converts. In 1649, however, the Iroquois devastated the Huron country, murdered Father Brebeuf and his companion with horrible tortures and put an end to the Mission by scattering the Hurons in every direction. Fragments of the tribe moved to the vicinity of Quebec, and were gradually absorbed in the population. Others moved westward to Green Bay, finally settling at Detroit in 1702. The last Jesuit missionary among them died in 1781. The last remnant of the Hurons ultimately removed to the Indian Territory.

In 1641 two French Jesuits, Father Charles Raymbaut and Father Isaac Jorgues, were sent to visit the Chippewas on the Great Lakes. Only a short visit was made at this time, the intention being to return soon and establish a mission. The death of Raymbaut prevented this. Fifteen years later, a flotilla of Ottawas appeared upon the St.

Lawrence, seeking a French alliance and asking for French missionaries. Two missionaries started back with the expedition, but were captured by the Iroquois. Father René Menard, altho then an aged man, in August, 1860, renewed the attempt, setting up his little cabin one hundred miles west of Sault Ste. Marie, near Keweenaw. The following summer he was either murdered by hostile Indians or died of exposure. In 1665 Father Claude Allouez went to take up the Mission left vacant by the death of Menard. After two years of labor on the shores of Lake Superior, Allouez returned to Quebec, staying there only two days, and returned, taking with him Father Louis Nicholas as an assistant. During that fall and winter they received into the faith eighty converts. In the spring of 1668 the celebrated Father Marquette left Quebec, in company with Father Le Boesme, to join the Ottawa mission. In 1669 Father Claudius Dablon was appointed Superior of these missions, and Allouez proceeded to Green Bay, where he spent the winter and spring in ministering to the needs of the Sac and Fox, the Pottawatamies, and the Winnebagoes. Later, in the early summer, he went to the Monominees, and then to the Winnebagoes. In 1670 two new missionaries were sent to the Ottawa tribes on the islands and shores of Lake Huron, and Sault Ste. Marie. In the meantime, Marquette had opened communication with the Sioux, but war prevented work in that direction. In 1671 Marquette established the mission of St. Ignatius at Michilimackinac. The Jesuit mission work in the Northwest came to a close in 1781. It had been the fond hope of the Jesuit fathers for many years to extend their work to the Dakota or Sioux tribes. In 1680, while Father Hennepin was ascending the Mississippi on a voyage of exploration, he was captured by a band of roving Sioux, and for several months remained a captive among them, acquiring something of their language, but accomplished little as a missionary. Other attempts were made later, but the Jesuits never succeeded in planting a mission among this people. Following these efforts of the missionaries for half a century, the Indians of the Northwest were engaged in war, and ultimately not only the missions, but many of the results of their work, were obliterated.

The early history of the French Jesuits who went out from Montreal and Quebec to work among the Iroquois is one of terrible suffering, bloodshed, and death; and yet, after all this, a foothold for mission work was finally obtained among this warlike people. In 1669 Father Reffeix began, on a tract of land opposite Montreal, a mission for the Iroquois. The mission was named St. Francis Xavier des Près. In 1647 the village contained representatives not only of the five Iroqouis tribes, but also of the Hurons, Mohicans, Eries, Abnakis, and others. A form of government was adopted, and laws were passed excluding from the colony those who would not give up idolatrous practises, drunkenness, and the changing of wives. Missionaries were constantly engaged in instructing the people in religious and secular things. In 1676 the Mission, now numbering over two hundred, found that it had grown beyond the capability of the land to support, and emigrated to Portage River, where a new start was made. In 1679 an Iroquois boys' school was begun, and in 1680 a school for girls. These schools rapidly progressed, both boys and girls learning to speak, read, and write English. The breaking out of border troubles and the establishment of the line giving to the English all territory south of the lakes, including New York, gradually but surely broke up the French missions to the Iroquois.

Between 1717 and 1833 twenty Franciscan missionaries labored among the Indians of Texas. In 1769 Father Junipero Serra, a Franciscan monk, founded a mission at San Diego, California. Many of his associates died during the first months of hardship. A mission at Monterey was founded in 1770 by the same missionaries. Other missions were established, occupying the entire coast line from San Francisco to San Diego. Into these were gathered over twenty thousand Indians, who led regular and industrious lives. It is said of the Indians of California that they are devoted to Roman Catholicism with all their hearts, their highest feelings and ideals being bound up with its teachings.

The heroism, both natural and regenerate; the humbleness and unswervingness of devotion to the most dreary and unfruitful field of labor, the patience and sweetness of temper of the heroes of the Roman Church, who explored and sought to reclaim these vast and pathless wilds, form one of the noblest chapters of its history. Almost or quite all the original missionaries died as martyrs, commonly under atrocious torments, which they always foresaw, but from which they never shrank. The heroic Brebeuf, before his martyrdom, which he suffered conjointly with Père Lallemont, had baptized 7,000 Hurons. Even the most friendly historians, however, lament the measure in which the Jesuits accommodated themselves, never to Indian fierceness or immorality, but too often to the grossness of Indian superstition. But such writers also condemn the blind hatred with which the English followed them up in the inhospitable regions in which they bore every hardship for the love of God and men.

India: The first Christians from Europe to enter Hindustan were the Portuguese, who landed, under the lead of Vasco da Gama, in 1498, at Calicut, on the southwest coast. The dissensions of the many independent states opened the way for their conquests, of which, in 1510, Goa became the capital. Here a bishopric was established, which was then raised into an archbishopric, still existent, whose incumbent bears the title of Patriarch of the East. His metropolitan authority formerly extended from Southern Africa to China. Neither Archbishop nor Inquisition, however, could accomplish much amid the flood of sheer ungodliness which poured in from Europe. The reputed wealth of India brought an innumerable company of adventurers, whose unrestrained profligacy moved the indignation and incurred the indignant rebukes of the Hindus themselves. Meanwhile the uncertain endeavors of Diego de Borba and of Miguel Vaz, vicar-general of Goa, to extend the Gospel accomplished little. They established a school in Goa, it is true, for the Christian training of young people from India, China, and Abyssinia, which did good service for many years, but there was lacking anything like a fixed plan of work. At last the right men appeared in the Jesuits.

May 6, 1542, the illustrious Francis Xavier landed in Goa. Of the high nobility of Spain, distinguished for learning and for eloquence, he had, in Paris, been brought over by his fellow-Spaniard and fellow-Basque, Ignatius Loyola, from visions of earthly glory to a burning zeal for the cause of Christ and of Rome, which in his mind were so absolutely one that there is no reason to suppose that even the shadow of a suspicion of any possible divergence between them ever fell upon the simple loyalty of his mind. Of Jesuit astuteness and accommodation to a worldly standard, as they afterward developed themselves both abroad and at home, there does not appear to have been a trace in Xavier. Sunny frankness was the essence of his character. Himself one of the original Jesuits, he followed the wise temperance of its policy, and neither affected nor shunned privations and austerities. For the most part, however, he trod the way of hardship. He watched through the night with the sick; visited the prisons; trod half-shod the glowing sands of the Indian coast to care for the spiritual and the temporal wants of the oppressed pearl-fishers; met their savage oppressors with dauntless courage, with only the cross in his hand, and, in the might of the spirit, by the simple power of his rebuke, inspired them with such terror that they fled. No wonder that, himself, as it were, a visible Christ, he soon counted so many thousands of converts from among the heathen that his voice often failed for weariness, and his arms sank exhausted in the act of baptizing. He had, indeed, in these rapid and myriad conversions to submit to the necessity of leaving the greater part of his neophytes very ignorant of Christianity, altho he took care to have the catechism translated into Tamil, and to supply the new congregations with priests as fast as possible, leaving them meanwhile in the care of his most trusty laymen. It does not appear, however, that Xavier, whose labors were spread over so wide a field, both in India and Japan, laid the foundations of any very thorough instruction of his converts. He might have done more had he stayed longer, but the elder missionaries of the Roman Catholic Church in India were generally indifferent to popular instruction, while the modern missionaries have become convinced that they can only break up heathen superstition by a more thorough education, and are now behind none in their zeal for it.

The results of these early labors in India were scarcely satisfactory, even to the friends of the Jesuits, and the enormous difficulties presented by Mohammedanism, at that time the imperial tho not the prevailing creed of India, and the immovable prejudices of Brahmanical caste, finally led the Jesuits into a system of accommodation which met for a while with a brilliant outward success, but in the end showed its hollowness by its collapse.

A Jesuit, Robert de Nobili, of one of the most illustrious families of Tuscany, and who, therefore, had all the aristocratic habitudes which fitted him to play his new part to perfection, gave himself out for a Brahman of the West allied to princes (the last assumption being the truth); perfected himself in Sanskrit, Telugu, and Tamil; performed the usual Brahmanical ceremonies; suffered only men of high caste to approach him, and received these seated on a throne; produced a Sanskrit book which he declared to be a recovered fifth Veda, and produced the sworn attestation of his fellow-Jesuits that this audacious forgery had been received by them from the god Brahma, as containing a mysterious wisdom which alone could give life. The result of this unscrupulous falsehood and accommodation to the ways of heathenism was that in three years he had gained over seventy leading Brahmans, who accepted the Christian doctrine of God, creation, immortality, atonement, and the general teachings of Christian morality, and abandoned their idols, but who retained all the haughtiness of caste, and were permitted to sign themselves with the sacred ashes, interpreted, of course, as having only a social significance. That they were allowed to baptize their children by the old heathen names does not signify so much, as in the early Church no one scrupled to use such names as Phœbe, Demetrius, Diotrephes, Apollo, Hermes, and the like.

The accommodations of De Nobili and his followers did not disguise from the Brahmans at large that the sages of Rome proposed to them a fundamentally new religion. Angry oppositions arose, but before long 30,000 converts had been gathered. Separate churches were built for the higher and lower castes, the latter being rigorously forbidden to join with the former in their worship, while the pariahs, or outcastes, were forbidden even to approach the priests. Even the last sacraments were administered to them at the end of a staff, so that the administrator might not be defiled.

One of Robert de Nobili's chief associates was Juan de Brito, son of the viceroy of Brazil. He brought great numbers to the faith in the kingdom of Marava, and died a martyr in 1693. Another associate, Veschi, was equally able, learned, successful, and heroic, and barely escaped martyrdom. He lived to become a mortal antagonist of the more enlightened Danish missionaries, dying in 1747.

The accommodations of Robert de Nobili and the Jesuits to heathenism could not fail to arouse great scandal at home. The rumor even spread that De Nobili had apostatized. His kinsman, the great Cardinal Bellarmine, himself a Jesuit, tho better informed than to suppose this, expressed his grief over such principles of proceeding, saying: "The Gospel needs no such false coloring; that Brahmans are not converted is of much less account than that Christians should not preach the Gospel with joyful openness. The preaching of Christ crucified was once to the Jews a scandal, and to the Greeks foolishness; but St. Paul did not therefore cease to preach Christ, and him crucified. I will not," he continues, "argue as to individual points, but cannot refrain from declaring that the imitation of Brahmanical haughtiness is sadly at variance with the humility of our Lord Jesus Christ, and that the observance of their usages has something exceedingly dangerous to the faith." Unhappily the pressure of his order brought this great and good man at length to something very much like a retraction of these sound and evangelical principles.

The other orders were naturally scandalized over the Jesuit policy. While, as yet, it was represented at Rome that nothing was intended beyond an allowance of certain harmless national usages, Gregory XV., in 1623, had issued a bull not unfavorable to the Jesuits. But these took occasion, thereby, it is said, to push their compliances farther and farther, until at last, in 1703, the Pope sent Cardinal Tournon to India, where, after thorough investigation, he suggested the decree by which, in 1710, Clement XI. rigorously forbade all accommodations whatever to heathen usages.

The Jesuits, however, paid scarcely the least attention to the decree, and soon obtained from a later Pope, Clement XII., a virtual revocation. But Father Norbert, of the Capuchins, came to Rome, and there opened the matter with so much insight and unreservedness that Benedict XIV., in the bull *Omnium sollicitudinum*, of October 7, 1744, condemned and forbade the Jesuit practises in the most peremptory terms. Nevertheless, in India the order founded for the vindication of the Papacy became its antagonist, mocked at and scorned the other orders, engaged in mercantile and other secular undertakings, until these things also did their part in hastening its fall.

These conversions around Goa, proceeding from Robert de Nobili as a center, are to be distinguished from those in the more southern parts of the peninsula, and among the humbler classes, who did not provoke so much disingenuousness. No such stain, happily, rests on the memory of Xavier. He had his share of Spanish imperiousness, but nothing of De Nobili's Italian craftiness. The result of the collapse of Jesuit missions in India was, that more than half a century passed during which the Roman Catholic Christians of India were almost wholly abandoned to themselves. Nevertheless, when Catholic missions were resumed over a million converts, it has been claimed, were found to have remained stedfast to the great truths of creation and incarnate redemption, tho, of course, their minds had become greatly obscured as to all secondary Christian doctrine, and overspread with many heathenish superstitions. These numbers, however, must be too large, as the official statements of the Church make the number of Roman Catholic Christians (1901) to be only 1,214,415. About 100,000 of these Roman Catholics are proselytes from the Syrian Church of India, not from heathenism. There are also 534,000 so-called Goa Christians—Catholics who have fallen out of communion with Rome during the long disputes between Portugal and the Pope over the right of nomination to the Indian bishoprics, and over the prerogatives of the Archbishopric of Goa.

There are (1901) 7 archbishoprics, 18 bishoprics and 4 prefectures, 602 stations, 3,708 churches and chapels, 809 European missionaries, 349 native priests, 2,089 schools, and 191 orphanages. The Madura diocese comes first with 206,000; then follow Colombo, 198,120; Pondicherry, 133,-770; Quilon, 87,000; Kumbakonam, 85,000; Mangalore, 83,690, etc.

Farther India: Roman Catholic missions were established in Ava and Pegu (Burma) in 1722, in Cochin China, 1659; in Malacca, 1557; in Siam, 1662; Tonkin, 1627. These have developed into (1901) 1 diocese and 15 vicariates, with 948,820 members, 512 missionaries, 527 native priests, 858 churches, 2,787 chapels, 2,342 schools, and 250 charitable institutions.

Africa: The Roman Catholic Mission in the kingdom of Congo, near the mouth of the great river, began as early as 1491. A vast number of negroes were baptized, so that, as with Xavier, the missionaries could hardly hold up their hands for weariness. Père Labat puts the number of the baptized at 100,000! Of preliminary instruction there had been none; an enemy at hand moved the missionaries to enroll as many as possible of those who might soon fall in battle in the ranks of the regenerate. The people had followed the example of their king and queen. Soon, however, the scene changed. "The mysteries of the faith," says one of the Dominican Fathers, "were something of which they were very willing to hear. But when we began to preach the moral virtues to them—that was another matter." A persecution even unto death, and headed by the newly baptized king, broke out. But the crown prince Alphonso, soon coming to the throne, displayed a stedfast zeal for Christianity. He even became, tho not a priest, yet a zealous preacher. It appears, however, that he did not demand that his subjects should forsake their polygamy, but did demand, on pain of death, that they should forsake their idolatry. That rude mixture of superstition, Gospel and force, which is characteristic of Catholic medievalism, was shown here in its perfection.

Portugal, with the profound selfishness which distinguishes all her early dealings abroad, took advantage of this new influence in Congo to secure enormous supplies of slaves. Dependent as they were on Portuguese protection, the priests made faint opposition to this iniquity, and even became accomplices in it. Soon they declined in zeal, and the princes and the people in interest; "the shepherds became plunderers;" it is said they quarreled with their bishop, and went back to Portugal with great substance. Yet baptisms went on, and soon Congo was proclaimed "wholly Catholic!" The court relapsed into the deepest dissoluteness, which remained proof against the efforts of the few Jesuits who came to Congo about 1550, altho these did a good deal, temporarily, for religion and education among the people. But after 150 years, Christianity is little more than a shadow. This closes the first period of the Congo Mission.

The second period opens in 1640, when the Capuchin friars arrived, and set about counteracting the heresy of the Dutch, with the help of persecution. They, however, fell into the evil ways of their predecessors in many respects, and neither they nor the Benedictines were able to accomplish anything. In 1816 an English explorer, Captain Tuckey, found "no trace of Catholicism, except some crucifixes and relics, strangely intermingled with the amulets and fetishes of the country. A single man claiming to be a priest, with some sort of a certificate, announced himself as having a wife and five concubines."

Within the last quarter of a century, however, the Roman Catholic Church has done much to redeem the errors and failures of the past. Missions have been established in all parts of the continent, and the report for 1901 shows 53 provinces (mostly vicariates apostolic, and prefectures), with 481,782 members, 1,084 churches and chapels, 1,172 priests, 1,783 schools, and 287 charitable institutions. The largest communities are: Madagascar, 67,500; Egypt, 56,180; Victoria Nyanza (Uganda), 39,586; Benin, 16,400; the five Congo provinces, 15,081, etc. In this work the White Fathers of Algeria, under the lead of Father Lavigerie, have been the most important factor. While there has been frequent clashing between them and the Protestant missionaries, due to political ambition, there has been much noble work done. In Madagascar especially is the record of Roman Catholic work too nearly of kin to the type that caused the failure of the earlier missions.

China: In 1294 the Pope sent the Franciscan John de Monte Corvino to Peking, of which Rome afterward appointed him archbishop. He was a genuine missionary, spared no pains in giving the people the Word of God in their own language, and in encouraging the education of the children, as well as training up missionaries from among the people themselves. He translated the New Testament and the Psalms into the Mongol language, and had these translations copied in the most beautiful style, and made use of them in preaching. . . . He had, during his residence in this place, baptized from five to six thousand; and he believed that, had it not been for the many plots laid against him by the Nestorians, he would have succeeded in baptizing above thirty thousand. Finally, however, the reassertion of Chinese independence, under the Ming dynasty, and the overthrow of the friendly Mongols, drew after it the destruction of Christianity, of which every trace seems to have disappeared.

In 1517, Europeans, in the persons of the Portuguese, reentered China—this time by way of the sea. In 1556, for services rendered against the pirates, who have always been so formidable on the waterways of China, the Portuguese received the islands of Sancian (Chang-chwen) and Macao. It was on Sancian that, in 1552, Francis Xavier closed his heroic and consecrated life. "Rock, rock, when wilt thou open?" expressed the spirit of his last sighs, tho the words were those of an earlier missionary, in front of the frowning seclusion of the great heathen empire.

The first Roman Catholic missionary who came to China in this second era was the Provincial of India, Nuñes Barreto, S.J., who, traveling to Japan in 1555, twice spent a short time at Canton. Neither he nor his immediate Jesuit, Franciscan, and Spanish successors, however, were permitted to remain long. At last, in 1582-3, the Jesuit Michael Roger, after some five or six fruitless visits to China, obtained, with Paes and Matthias Ricci, who was afterward so notable in China, leave to remain, and many privileges from the viceroy of Canton. The first public baptism was given in 1584. In 1586 there were 40 Christians, but then persecution broke out. After the Jesuits had adopted the dress of the mandarins they were less annoyed. In 1598 Ricci, already in high repute for his scientific attainments, and now the head of the independent Chinese mission, was received in Peking, and established himself permanently there in 1601, dying in 1610. He is accused of having carried the conformity to Chinese usages to such a length as to have dispensed himself from his vow of celibacy, and to have married a Chinese woman, who bore him two sons. But the animosity of the other orders toward the Jesuits had become so great that we are not to be too sure of the justice of any particular accusation against these. This animosity, which seems to have been strongest in the Dominicans, had various grounds. Jesuitism had an alertness and flexibility that reached attainments in literature and science, and drew public favor to them, and showed a wise consideration of circumstances which was in marked contrast to Dominican practise. Thus, when the Dominicans asked the Jesuits how soon they intended to introduce the discipline of fasting for their converts, the latter replied: "Not until Providence relieves them from the continual fasts imposed by their poverty." In the great question of accommodation, the controversy turned especially upon the custom of ancestor-worship. The Jesuits argued—and the emperor, in a public edict, confirmed their position—that this, in China, is only a civil and social act, implying nothing in the nature of religious homage. The Pope, however, and the Protestant missionaries, after full investigation of the opposing arguments, have decided that the Dominicans and the other protesting orders were right and the Jesuits wrong.

In 1617 the Jesuits had about 13,000 converts; in 1650 about 150,000; in 1664, 257,000. The Franciscans and Dominicans together had hardly more than 10,000. The conversions went on increasing until toward the end of the century, when the papal decisions against the accommodations allowed by the Jesuits, and the bitterness with which the other orders and the papal legates enforced them, led to violent persecutions. One of the legates, Cardinal Tournon, was sent to Macao, and died in prison there. Some even say that the Jesuits poisoned him. Many Christians were martyred; much greater numbers fell away, partly under the terror of death, and partly under the exasperation of national feeling. Compromises were for awhile admitted by the representatives of the Pope, which somewhat stayed the desolation. But Rome at last, in 1742, in the pontificate of Benedict XIV., issued a peremptory and irrevocable decision, forbidding every accommodation that could be interpreted as a concession to paganism. Then the persecutions broke out more violently than ever, and the Christian faith was almost rooted out. This stand of the Pope, however, seems to have been taken with such haughtiness, such a contempt of the imperial representations, and such a determination to carry through the right position by overbearing will, that the emperor, the mandarins, and the people gathered the deep impression that if they would become Christians they must cease to be Chinese.

At various times the devoted Roman Catholic missionaries in China underwent various persecutions—banishment, imprisonment, scourging, and even death. The first actual martyr was the Jesuit Francis Martiñez, murdered in 1606. The Dominican Francis de Capillas was beheaded in 1648. In 1665 five Christian mandarins were beheaded. The regent who commanded this was, however, soon after punished by the young emperor with death. During the exasperation caused by the decree of Benedict XIV., the Dominicans, Peter Sanz, Serrano, Royo, Alcober Diaz, and the catechist, Ko (Sanz being a bishop), and the Jesuits, Anthemis and Henriquez, suffered death in 1747.

Only obscure accounts are accessible as to the subsequent resuscitation of Roman Catholic missions in China. There were still hundreds of families in which Christianity had become hereditary, and there have doubtless been many conversions in this century. In 1805 there was a cruel persecution; also in 1816 and in 1820. In these later persecutions three or four priests suffered death, one of them being Vicar Apostolic and Bishop *in partibus*.

As in Africa, so in China the last few years have seen a great advance. Roman Catholic missions now cover the entire empire, and report (1901) 720,540 members, 4,126 churches and chapels, 904 missionaries, 471 native priests, and 3,584 schools.

In the Boxer outbreak the Roman Catholics

suffered with the Protestants and maintained the early record of faithfulness. To what degree the political ambitions of the leaders have been responsible for the troubles it is difficult to say, but something of the same spirit that ruled and ruined formerly appears to have been manifest.

Japan: Japan had scarcely opened to Europeans when St. Francis Xavier, with some companions, hastened thither to plant the standard of the Cross. For a long while the preaching of the missionaries was undisturbed, and in less than 40 years there were more than 200,000 Japanese Christians, with 250 churches. Even three Daimios were baptized. At last, however, the Shogun Taiko, or Taikosama, gradually became jealous of the missionaries, suspecting them of being agents of Portugal, and, after the temporary union of the two Iberian crowns, agents of Spain for reducing Japan to dependence.

Taiko began to persecute the Christians about 1582. The stedfast chastity of Christian maidens is said to have been one of the causes which inflamed the wrath of the imperial voluptuary. The inconsiderate zeal of some Franciscans, also, who persisted in public preaching after the Jesuits had discontinued it, is said to have increased his displeasure. On the 5th of February, 1597, 6 Franciscans, 3 Jesuits, and 17 other Christians were crucified. With the sound of psalms these heroes and followers of Christ breathed out their souls. From 1598 till 1611, under a new Shogun, there was a respite. But then a fearful revolution of sentiment in the Shogun's mind brought him and his three successors to that persevering and concentrated cruelty toward the Christians which finally rooted out their religion. The guilt of this is laid by the Catholics on the Dutch, who revenged the cruelties of Spain toward them by stirring up the slumbering jealousies of the government toward Spain and Portugal, and toward the Jesuits, until its rage was so great that all common forms of torment being too little for the wrath of the rulers, they exhausted their ingenuity in devising new tortures.

It has well been said that the Roman amphitheaters never witnessed, in men, women, or children, more resolute heroism of martyrdom. Here again, for a good while, the blood of the martyrs was the seed of the Church. From Taikosama's death in 1598 to 1614 the Jesuits baptized 100,000 converts, and for many years afterward they baptized several thousand yearly. Some apostasies took place, but in general all the Christians—princes, nobles, men, women, and children—went joyfully to their doom. "Children endured the most terrible deaths, without giving a sign of suffering." When any were conducted to the crown of martyrdom so greatly desired, they would be accompanied by many thousand Christians, who followed in triumphal procession, praying, praising, and bearing lighted tapers in their hands. But persecution raged incessantly, and finally outstripped the increase of the Church. At last, in desperation, 37,000 Christians seized the fortified place Simbara, since known as the Mount of Martyrs, and there, after a long defense, were at length slain almost to the last man. Then were published the edicts forbidding "the God of the Christians, on pain of death, to reenter Japan." Then, too, was introduced the requirement, maintained till within a few years, that all the subjects of the realm should, once a year, trample on the crucifix.

When Japan was reopened by the Americans it was discovered that there were hundreds of concealed Roman Catholics in one province. A number of martyrdoms have taken place even since then, but are now, of course, discontinued. In the absence of Bibles, which unhappily, Rome, as usual, had neglected to provide, these secret Christians had even forgotten the baptismal formula, and used to baptize their children "in the name of the Holy Jerusalem!" A Jesuit missionary being asked whether such a formula would be valid, replied: "No, the Church must have her rules. But God is very much kinder than the Church."

The present number of Roman Catholic Christians in Japan (1901) is 53,400, and there are 115 missionaries, 32 native priests, 28 schools, and 20 charitable institutions.

In Korea there are reported (1901) 32,200 members, 39 missionaries, 9 native priests, 60 schools, 5 charities; in Java, 49,800 members, 50 missionaries, 29 schools; in the Pacific Islands, New Zealand, etc., 219,210 members, 742 churches and chapels, 421 missionaries, and 479 schools.

In Persia, Turkey, and the Balkan States, the work of Roman Catholic missions is confined to the different branches of the Eastern Church. They have been somewhat successful among the Jacobites by methods which are too distinctly political, but elsewhere they have not won over many. It is difficult, indeed impossible, to give statistics, as the figures in the "Missiones Catholicæ" for those countries include the Roman Catholic communities of Armenians, Maronites, etc.

Missionary Organization of the Roman Catholic Church: Rome divides the whole world into two great sections, *terra catholica* and *terra missionis*. Within the former her missionary organization has, properly and ordinarily, no application; within the latter it controls all ecclesiastical persons and processes whatever, archbishops and bishops themselves being subject to it.

Terra catholica (perhaps more properly *terræ catholicæ*) is definable as including all those countries whose governments lend the support of the secular arm for the coercion of all baptized persons, whether Catholics, heretics, or simple schismatics, into obedience to the Holy Roman Church; that is, to the Roman Bishopric, which claims a maternal superiority to all other churches, that is, bishoprics, and claims the right to instruct them, and by inference to govern them. All schismatics or heretics, therefore, within the limits of any bishopric, may (it is held by the prevailing opinion) be lawfully compelled to yield obedience to their Catholic bishop, and in him to the Supreme Bishopric of Rome, which possesses throughout the Church both an ordinary and an appellate authority. The latter is chiefly in use, but the former may at any time be exercised. Wherever, then, the civil government, being apprised by the Holy Office of the Inquisition (a commission of Cardinals, of which the Pope himself is the Prefect) that heresy or schism is prevailing within its jurisdiction, lends its authority to crush it, there, and there only, is *terra catholica*. All the rest of the world—Christian, Muslim, and heathen—is *terra missionis*.

Thus in Europe, Great Britain, Holland, Norway, Sweden, Denmark, Germany, the Balkan States and Greece are mission lands; in America, Canada, the United States, British and Dutch

Guiana and Patagonia; all of Africa, except Algiers and Tunis, and all Asia and Oceania.

The great political changes of the past half century and the great interest in the United States, as well as the loss of the temporal power of the papacy, have raised a question as to the continuance of this system which has manifest disadvantages as well as advantages. No decision has, however, been reached, and as there is still a noticeable distinction between the two regions, the popular and even legal presumption commonly recognizing Roman Catholicism as the predominant religion of the Catholic countries, Rome still thinks it prudent to maintain the distinction *dissimulando*.

Rome has no different agencies for proselytism of Christians, and for conversion of unbelievers. Any country which does not, through its government, give effect to its spiritual subjection to her, is indiscriminately included in the *terra missionis*. Even the Eastern Churches, altho their ordinations are acknowledged, and altho the prevailing Roman theory concedes to them spiritual jurisdiction, are, nevertheless, subject to the activity of the Propaganda, which, however, does not appear in fact to extend its operations among them except so far as they are in Muslim or pagan countries.

Rome, however, makes very important distinctions, within the *terra missionis*, between *infideles, schismatici*, and *heretici*. The first term includes all who have never embraced the faith. For the conversion of these, it is held, the only lawful means is persuasion, as they have never been subject to the jurisdiction of the church. *Heretics*, being baptized, are subject to her jurisdiction. For the restoration of these the lawful means are persuasion and coercion, the former being preferable. *Schismatics*, who are orthodox, but disobedient to Rome, may likewise, as occasion serves, be either persuaded or coerced into returning. Perhaps the only simple *schismatics* are the members of the Greek Church, which is not impeached by Rome of heresy, tho she impeaches Rome of heresy, and sometimes speaks dubiously of her orders, and even of her baptism. The Greek and even the Monophysite and Nestorian bishops appear to be often recognized by Rome as the legitimate bishops of their sees, and the few Greek bishops, at least, who chose to admit the papal supremacy were received without difficulty to an equal suffrage in the Vatican Council. But in the Levant, if Rome spies an advantage, she is very apt to forget her concessions, and to thrust in her own nominees where she cannot secure the submission of the actual incumbents. Reordination, however, of the Eastern clergy she does not permit, even where, as in Abyssinia, the rites are extraordinarily irregular and defective. The succession, she says, is unquestioned, and the sacramental intention is sound, and sufficiently expressed.

In the Protestant world, however, she is not embarrassed by any question of orders or of jurisdiction. Only as to the Anglican communion is there with her even a pause of thought as to the former, and since the accession of Elizabeth she has always treated the Anglican orders as null, maintaining that the probabilities against their valid transmission are so overwhelming as to leave her under no obligations to pursue remote considerations and abstract possibilities. And as to jurisdiction, she declares even the Old Catholics of Holland, Germany, and Switzerland to be void of this, altho she acknowledges the validity of their episcopal succession.

Protestants, therefore, are held to be destitute of all the ordinary means of grace except the sacraments of Baptism and Matrimony. She pursues her missions among them almost as if they were heathen. She does not, however, as often supposed, designate Protestant countries as *partes infidelium*. *Infideles*, as noted above, is the technical term of Rome and of Trent for all human beings who are neither baptized nor catechumens. Its application to cover heretics is casual, and seldom, if ever, official. *Partes infidelium* are those Mohammedan regions whose ancient Christian cities now give a titular dignity to some three hundred Roman Catholic bishops who have no actual dioceses. As they are largely employed in Protestant countries, their former style of "bishops *in partibus*" was often mistaken as referring to the place of their residence, and not, as it did refer, to the location of their nominal sees. To obviate this not unnatural misunderstanding, the present Pope has courteously directed that they shall henceforth be known as *episcopi titulares*.

All ecclesiastical activity of the Roman Catholic Church within the *terra missionis*, whether of proselytism, conversion, or ordinary administration, is subject to the control of the *Congregatio de Propaganda Fide*. This great and powerful congregation (the term Roman congregation signifying a committee of or commission of cardinals)—subject, of course, to the Pope's intervention at any point—exercises papal authority over all Roman Catholics throughout the Protestant, Oriental, Muslim, and pagan world. It was instituted by Pope Gregory XV. in the year 1622. This Pope was the first pupil of the Jesuits who had ascended the chair, and, therefore, was naturally interested in missions. The *Congregatio de Propaganda Fide*, familiarly called The Propaganda, has permanent authority of administration within regions yet extra-Christian, and within Christian regions until they become again *terræ catholicæ*. It has, of course, its seat at Rome, is composed of a varying number of cardinals, some being non-resident correspondents, having a Prefect, a Secretary, and Prothonotary, on whom the practical business mainly devolves. There are also consulters and a large force of officials. It also maintains a training college for pupils from almost every nation under heaven. There are also in Rome various national colleges and monastic training houses for missionaries. Yet the whole number of pupils appears to be small compared with those that are trained for the priesthood in Protestant countries and other missionary jurisdictions.

Where the Roman Catholics in a country, being few, have never been organized into a diocese, or where the bishoprics have fallen under Mohammedan or heretical control, there the Pope, as having ordinary jurisdiction throughout the Church, is sole diocesan. The first stage of organization is the appointment of a priest as papal representative, with the title of Prefect Apostolic. He has almost unbounded authority (under the Propaganda), being empowered to station priests at discretion within his prefecture, and to grant dispensations almost *ad libitum* from every ecclesiastical precept not included in the *jus divinum*, from which last, of course, the Pope himself cannot dispense. If the mission flourishes, and there is a call for a superintendent, with power to ordain to the priesthood, the Prefecture Apostolic becomes a Vicariate Apostolic. The distinction does not appear to be a hard-and-fast one, as there are occasionally Vicars Apostolic that are simply priests, who have to send elsewhere for new clergymen.

Almost all, however, are bishops *in partibus*, or, as they are now called, titular bishops. Both prefects and vicars are movable at pleasure.

If the Church has won or recovered such a following (especially in Protestant countries) as to warrant it, the Pope proceeds to organize a regular hierarchy of diocesan bishops, usually arranged in metropolitan provinces, each under the presidency of an archbishop, who, besides his ordinary diocesan authority, has a certain right of determining appeals from his suffragan bishops, and always presides in the Provincial Council, whose decrees, when ratified by the Pope, have binding force.

The diocesan bishops of England and America are not, like mere vicars apostolic, removable *ad nutum*, but are understood to enjoy fixity of tenure, like those of Catholic lands. The cardinal's rank enjoyed by the present Archbishop of Baltimore greatly increases his influence, but adds nothing to his episcopal or metropolitan authority. As cardinal he has no jurisdiction outside the city of Rome; and as belonging to a missionary jurisdiction, he, and all other American bishops, are still controlled by the Propaganda, due regard, of course, being had to the more developed character of their sees. The bishops enjoy the same powers as vicars apostolic, of dispensing from ordinary canonical restrictions. These powers, granted from Rome for terms of five years, are known as the Quinquennial Faculties.

Previous to the institution of the Propaganda missions were pursued in a somewhat disconnected way. Each order sent out its missionaries for itself, who rendered account of their activity only to their own provincials and generals, these latter, doubtless, frequently communicating with the Holy See, and obtaining from it such suggestions, exemptions, consecrations, pecuniary subventions, and other aids as it might be inclined to grant and they to receive. But since 1622 the control of all missions among heretics, schismatics, and pagans has lain in the hands of the Propaganda. Yet the bonds of connection within each monastic order are so strict, the authority of its superiors so unbounded, its policy and spirit, and even its doctrinal tenor, so specific, and the character attributed to each of the elder orders so sacred, that the comparatively new Congregatio de Propaganda Fide has, doubtless, to accommodate itself largely to this distinctness of action. In what way, and how far, the missionary operations of the orders, especially the Jesuits, have been actually subordinated to the Propaganda is not clear. It must suffice us to know that every missionary—Jesuit, Benedictine, Franciscan, Dominican, of whatever order or of the secular priesthood—is subject to the supreme and universal episcopate of the Pope as ordinarily exercised through the Propaganda.

The orders, notably the Dominicans and Capuchins over against the Jesuits, have carried on their mission, especially in India and China, with far more bitterness of controversy against each other than has prevailed between Protestant denominations the most widely remote. The Jesuits, indeed, long seemed disposed, both among pagans and Protestants, almost to claim a monopoly of conversions, and if any one of another order, especially among the heretics, was guilty of a success, their animosity would sometimes go to great lengths. These internecine wars came near to ruining Roman Catholic missions in the Far East, but since the suppression and restoration of the society, which has now an almost uncontested right of control in the Church, and which, in its turn, has doubtless learned wisdom by its tribulations, these dissensions no longer appear. The Jesuits, doubtless, take whatever fields of activity they wish, and leave the rest to others. There appear to be among the missionaries but few secular priests; that is, priests who, like the ordinary parish clergy, are subject only to the general authority of the Church, and not to that of any monastic order. The native clergy from among the heathen are probably for the most part seculars.

The Propaganda has been richly endowed, but has lost many of its resources, especially since the loss of the temporal power of the Pope, and its present (1901) income, about $135,000, is barely sufficient to support its personnel, college, university, and printing establishment. Roman Catholic missionaries on the field are expected, so far as possible, to secure their support among the people they are evangelizing, but where this is impracticable, they are provided for through charitable associations founded for this purpose. Of these there are several, the most important being The Society for the Propagation of the Faith, with headquarters at Lyons, France. There are also: The Association of the Holy Childhood; the Association of Oriental Schools in France; the Society of St. Francis Xavier in Aix-la-Chapelle; The Association of St. Peter Claver, in Salzburg; The Leopoldsverein, in Austria; The Ludwigsmissionsverein, in Bavaria. These all, however, as well as some others, are limited in aim or nationality, the only one which can, in truth, be called a general missionary society being the one at Lyons, and this deserves special mention.

The Society for the Propagation of the Faith: In 1815 Bishop Dubourg, of New Orleans, during a visit to France, interested in his work a widow, Mrs. Petit, and suggested the founding of a charitable association to aid in supplying the spiritual needs of Louisiana, fixing the contribution of members at twenty-five cents a year. The suggestion was enforced by earnest appeals for aid from missionaries in the East, and an effort was made, by the Seminary for Foreign Missions of Paris, to revive a union for prayer, which had been disbanded by the French Revolution. The benevolence of Christians in Lyons, in 1820, was thus turned to several separate objects. Two years later a visit to Lyons of the Vicar-General of Louisiana excited special interest in that field of labor. It then became clear to those interested in missions that if an aid society would be permanently successful it must undertake to aid all needy Roman Catholic missions, and so combine all interests. On this basis those engaged in helping one and another mission enterprise united, and the "Work (*œuvre* or *opus*) for the Propagation of the Faith" was organized at Lyons, May 3, 1822. This name is commonly translated into English as "Society for the Propagation of the Faith," and so produces in the minds of Protestant readers confusion with the great "Congregatio de Propaganda Fide" at Rome. But the duties of the Lyons "Society for the Propagation of the Faith" have relation to the financing, not to the establishment or control of missionary enterprises, nor to the choice of missionaries.

The Lyons Society has branches in various parts of France and of the world. The seat of the American "Society for the Propagation of the Faith" is at Baltimore, Md. The trustees of the American branch are the Archbishops of Baltimore, Cincinnati, Philadelphia, and St. Paul, and four other clergymen. Members of the Society are called "Associates" in the work. The conditions of membership are two: (1) The recitation daily, for the assistance of Roman Catholic Missionaries, of one *Our Father* and one *Hail Mary*, with this invocation: *St. Francis Xavier, pray for us;* (2) the giving of at least five cents monthly, or sixty cents a year, in alms for the missions. The usual method of collecting these funds is one that Protestant missionary societies might well consider and adapt to their purposes. The associates are formed into bands of ten, one of whom is authorized to act as promoter, with the double duty of collecting the offerings of the band for the local or central representative of the Society, and the no less important duty of circulating among the members of the band the periodical *Annals of the Propagation of the Faith*. Promoters are provided with membership certificates to be given new members, and with cards on which to record collections. The efficiency of the system and, in fact, the success of the whole work, rests upon the faithful diligence of the promoters. The Society has fixed a day in May and another in December as a time of special prayer and thanksgiving. Various popes have granted benefit of indulgences to associates in this work, and missionaries offer prayers and say masses for the associates. In the merits and prayers of the missionaries, and in masses said by them, both living and dead associates share.

The Society has two councils, chiefly laymen, at Lyons and Paris, respectively, and these, for ordinary purposes, divide the entire field of mission work, but act on common consent in the distribution of funds. No funds are invested, and at the beginning of each year the entire receipts of the Society for the previous year are distributed.

In 1822 the Society, through its central body at Lyons, collected about $4,000, of which one-third was sent to the Eastern missions and two-thirds to Louisiana and Kentucky. Other dioceses also were aided, and up to 1900 the Society had expended nearly $6,000,000 in missionary work in the United States. In 1827 gifts were sent to Africa and the Hawaiian Islands, and to-day it aids more than 300 dioceses, vicariates, and prefectures in all parts of the world. Its total distribution, from 1822-1900, was $65,690,017. Of this sum $1,120,420 went to the Society from the United States during the same period.

A list (see **Appendix**) of Religious Orders and Societies engaged in Roman Catholic mission work shows 56 such organizations. In addition to the clergy, there are more than 30 orders of Brothers and 125 orders of Sisters working as auxiliaries, in addition to the lay-brothers, catechists, and other native helpers.

Annals of the Propagation of the Faith, bi-monthly, Lyons, France, in French and in many other languages. American edition published at Baltimore, Md.; *Missiones Catholicæ*, Rome, 1901; *Actes des Apôtres Modernes*, Paris, 1852, 4 vols.; Bigot (J.), *Relation de la Mission Abnaquise*, Paris, 1858; Daurignac (J. M. S.), *History of the Society of Jesus*, translated by J. Clements, Cincinnati, 1865, 2 vols.; Montroud (M. de), *Les Missions Catholiques dans tous les Parties du Monde*, Paris, 1869.

ROMANDE MISSION. See SWITZERLAND (FRENCH).

ROODEPOORT: A settlement in the Transvaal, S. Africa, situated in the Potchefstroom district. Station of the Hannover Lutheran Free Church Mission, with (1903) 1 missionary and 5 outstations.

ROSARIO: A city of the Argentine Republic, South America, situated in the province of Santa Fé, on the right bank of the Paraná, 170 miles N. W. of Buenos Aires. Population (1901), 112,461. It is the second commercial city of the republic, is well laid out, with neatly-paved, gas-lighted streets, traversed by cars. It stands on a cliff, 80 feet above the river. The climate is temperate and healthful. Station of the ME, with (1903) 2 missionaries and their wives, 17 native workers, 7 outstations, 7 places of worship, 10 Sunday schools, 4 day schools, and 454 professed Christians, of whom 293 are communicants. Station also of the South American Missionary Society, with (1903) 3 missionaries, 1 of them with his wife; 15 women missionaries, 1 native worker, 1 place of worship, 1 day school, 2 boarding schools; the work of this Society extending into the suburban town of Alberdi.

ROSE, Rev. A. T., D.D.: Appointed missionary among the Burmans by the ABMU in 1851, and at the time of his death in 1896 he was one of the oldest missionaries on the staff of this Society. Most of his missionary life was spent at Rangoon; and, besides his influence as a faithful missionary, to him is largely due the development of the Burman Bible Training School, which became the Burman department of the Theological Seminary at Insein. Dr. Rose possessed a strong personality, was a powerful preacher, was especially gifted in opening up new work, and especially wise in his assistance to new missionaries, and in educational matters he showed marked ability. He passed from his earthly labors at Rangoon, July 5, 1896.

ROSE BELLE: A village in the island of Mauritius, situated about 150 miles S. E. of Port Louis, with which it is connected by railway. Station of the CMS (1856), with (1903) 1 missionary, 3 women missionaries, 1 orphanage, 2 day schools, and 162 professed Christians, of whom 45 are communicants.

ROSS: A settlement in Cape Colony, South Africa, situated in Tembuland in Mganduli District, about 25 miles E. of Clarkesbury. Station of the UFS, with (1903) 1 missionary and his wife, 25 native workers, 17 outstations, 14 day schools, and 364 professed Christians.

ROTUMA: An island about 300 miles N. N. W. of the Fiji Islands, to which colony it was annexed in 1880. It is 16 miles long and 4 or 5 miles wide, of volcanic origin and inhabited by about 2,500 people, who export a considerable quantity of copra. Mission work was commenced there in 1841 by the WMS missionaries stationed at the Fiji Islands. The people are now Christians, with 21 places of worship, 37 schools and 460 church members, and 35 native workers in connection with the Australasian Wesleyan Methodist Missionary Society.

ROTUMAN LANGUAGE: A language spoken in the island of Rotuma, which lies north of the Fiji Islands. Is belongs to the Melanesian type of languages and has been reduced to writing by missionaries with the use of the Roman letters.

ROUMANIA: A kingdom formed in 1878 from the united principalities, Wallachia and Moldavia. Its independence from Turkey was proclaimed by its people in 1877, and was confirmed by the congress of Berlin in 1878. Its area is estimated at 48,307 square miles. On the northeast it is separated from Russia by the River Pruth and the Kilia mouth of the Danube, which latter river forms its southern boundary west of Silistria. The Transylvanian Alps and the Carpathian Mountains form its western and northwestern boundaries. That portion which lies between the Danube and the Black Sea is called the Dobrudja, and differs greatly from the rest of the kingdom. The climate has great extremes of temperature; in winter the cold northeast winds are very trying, while in the summer the southwest wind is scorching in its intense heat. The rainfall is not abundant. Agriculture is the principal occupation of the people, tho not a few cattle and sheep are raised. The government is a constitutional monarchy, and the king is assisted by a senate of 120 members and a chamber of deputies of 183 members, all of whom must be Roumanians by birth or naturalization. The population of Roumania is of very mixed origin, including (1899) 6,000,000 Roumanians, 269,000 Jews, 250,000 Gypsies, 200,000 Bulgarians, 70,000 Germans, 60,000 Magyars, 7,000 Armenians, 4,000 French, 2,000 English, besides 5,000 Italians, Turks, Poles, and Tatars. The population of the Dobrudja is estimated at 175,000, and contains a larger Russian element than the other part of Roumania. The Orthodox Greek Church is the ruling church, but Roman Catholics, Protestants, Armenians, Lipovani (Russian heretics), Jews and Mohammedans are also found. Education is supposed to be compulsory, but there are very few schools, so that only about three per cent. of the population are able to avail themselves of the free instruction. The principal cities, with their population, are Bucharest, the capital, 282,000, and Jassy, 78,000.

Mission work in Roumania is carried on only by the colporteurs of the BFBS. The entire Bible has been translated into the Roumanian language, besides the Psalms and Isaiah into Polish for the Jews.

ROUMANIAN LANGUAGE: Belongs to the Græco-Latin branch of the Aryan family. It is spoken in Roumania, and is written with Roman letters, somewhat modified to suit peculiarities of pronunciation. In some respects it is closely allied to Latin. Wallachs from Roumania who have settled in Macedonia speak a dialect known as Macedonian Rouman, which is also a written language.

ROUMELIA: Name applied by some European writers to European Turkey in distinction from *Anatolia*, or Asiatic Turkey. The name is derived from the usual Turkish appellation of European Turkey: *Rum-ili*, which means "the Roman People" (or territory). Eastern Roumelia is a name sometimes applied to the southern part of the principality of Bulgaria.

RUATAN. See ROATAN ISLAND.

RUK, or **HOGULU, ISLAND.** See CAROLINE ISLANDS.

RUNGWA: A settlement in German Central Africa, situated about 35 miles N. W. of the N. extremity of Lake Nyasa, high up on the mountain slopes. The chief station of the Moravians among the Konde tribe is in this district (1891), with (1903) 4 missionaries, 2 of them with their wives; 1 place of worship, 1 day school, 1 boarding school, 1 industrial school, and 27 professed Christians.

RUNING-FU. See JU-NING-FU.

RURKI: A town in the United Provinces, India, 22 miles east of Saharanpur. It is a modern manufacturing town, and has the most important Engineering College in India. Altitude, 887 feet. The place is rather malarious. Population, 17,400; Hindus 10,200; Mohammedans 5,600. Station of the SPG (1861), with (1903) 3 missionaries, 1 of them with his wife; 2 women missionaries, 19 native workers, 3 places of worship, 3 day schools, 1 boarding school, and 112 professed Christians. Also station of the Mission to Lepers (1886), with an institute for lepers. Station of the ME, with (1903) 1 missionary and his wife, 57 native workers, 3 places of worship, 40 Sunday schools, 26 day schools, and 2,187 professed Christians, of whom 826 are communicants. Also station of the Scottish Reformed Presbyterian Church, with (1900) 1 missionary and his wife, 6 native workers, 3 outstations, 2 places of worship, 2 day schools, and 2 orphanages. Some write the name Roorkee.

RUSSIA; Empire of: A vast dominion, next to Great Britain the largest in the world, which includes eastern Europe, the whole northern part of Asia, and a considerable portion of Central Asia. It occupies fully one-sixth of the land surface of the earth, but is peculiar among the great empires of the world in possessing no colonies detached at any distance from the main mass of its territory. Its area is 860,282 square miles and its population (1897) about 128,932,173.

The purpose of this work does not require an extended topographical description of the Russian Empire. In population Russia comprises a greater variety of races than any other European state. While the Slavonic stock predominates in European Russia, the Finnish race is strong in the north and east, extending southward throughout the length of the Ural Mountains; many Turkish tribes are found in the valley of the Volga and in Russian Asia; other tribes of Tatar origin are found in the Crimea and the regions bordering the Caspian; Circassians, Georgians, Kurds, and Armenians people the Caucasus and Trans-Caucassia, while Mongols, differing but little from the Tibetan type, roam over vast spaces of territory north and east of the Central Asian provinces.

The government which holds this vast collection of races together is an unlimited monarchy. The Emperor or Czar of Russia is the supreme head of the church and of the legislative, executive, and judicial systems, as well as of the military and naval forces of the empire. The Holy Synod, composed of men selected by the Czar from among the higher clergy of the Russian Church, has control of the interests of religion throughout the empire, a procurator, or minister representing the Czar in its deliberations, and reporting its views to the Emperor for assent or otherwise. A council of state, whose members are chosen by the Czar, controls in a similar manner the political affairs of the State, a Secretary of State reporting to the Czar its plans and receiving his orders. There is nothing exactly corresponding to a cabinet of ministers, as the term is understood in other European countries. The minister in charge of a department of affairs prepares all plans for its administration independently of other ministers, and submits them to the Czar for his supreme permission. It often happens that two departments, for lack of joint responsibility, may pursue different and inconsistent, and even opposing, lines of policy. As to legislation, the Czar's approval must precede any elaboration of new laws; and after the council has discussed it, the Czar's decree alone makes a new law binding. This decree approving a new law may effectively issue even tho the council has disapproved it. At the will of the Czar the ordinary procedure of justice may be suspended and a criminal may be punished by "administrative process," which is resorted to especially in political cases. Notwithstanding this unlimited autocracy, a surprising degree of self-government is permitted the different village communes and tribal organizations. The tendency increases, however, to centralize authority by taking away or restricting such local privileges, and also by supplanting languages that have been recognized as a part of local privileges. The Poles, the Jews, the Finns and the Armenians have all suffered intensely from the determined effort of the Russian Government to extinguish their separate speech, and separate historical traditions, if not their separate religious belief and guaranteed liberties.

The religion of Russia is that of the Greek (Eastern) Church. All existing religions, however, are tolerated, and refusal to profess the State religion does not disqualify one for office or full enjoyment of civil rights. No one who refuses to accept the State religion is called a Christian. From the missionary point of view, Russia is noteworthy as the one government bearing the Christian name which permits in its territories no religious liberty in the sense of freedom of conscience. No Russian subject may leave the sect in which he was born, excepting that being born outside of the Russian Church he may join that church, that is to say, he may become a "Christian." Any missionary propaganda except that of the Russian Church is strictly forbidden; and any attempt by dissenters to teach religion to members of the Russian Church is a misdemeanor punished most severely. Through such laws Protestant missionary operations in Russian territory are made impossible, and the heathen and Mohammedan populations of Asiatic Russia are walled in against the Gospel, unless the Russian Church gives it to them. It often does, but not very effectively. At the same time the Russian Government permits and sometimes aids the circulation of the Scriptures in certain prescribed versions.

Mission work has been attempted at different times in different parts of this empire by the Basel and Moravian Missions, the London Missionary Society, the Scotch Church, etc., but it has never been of long duration, owing to the repressive action of the Russian Government. The American and British and Foreign Bible Societies have accomplished a good deal in the form of Bible distribution.

Russians: The Russians are the most numerous Slavic nation, numbering over 65,000,000. They are divided into three chief branches: Great Russians, Little Russians, and White Russians. The Ruthenians or Red Russians, living in Austria, are also classed as a branch of the Russians. The distinctions between these various branches are rather linguistic than national. While the great mass of the Russians belong to the Eastern Church, 3,108,000 are *Uniats* (members of the Eastern, who have united with the Roman Church), 500,000 Catholics, and the number of dissenters (*Raskolniks*) is variously estimated from 3,000,000 to 11,000,000 and even 15,000,000.

The Orthodox Russians use the Slavonic language in their church services; so also do the *Uniats* and the Dissenters, while the Roman Catholic Russians use the Latin liturgy. In their literature all the Russians use the alphabet invented by Cyril, the "Apostle to the Slavs." The Russian language belongs to the southeastern branch of Slavic languages, and is related to the Bulgarian and the Servian. It is divided into three dialects: the Great-Russian, the Little-Russian, and the White-Russian. The first of these dialects forms the Russian literary language of the present day; the Little-Russian may be considered as a distinct language, tho related to the Great-Russian, while the White-Russian occupies a middle place between Great-Russian and Little-Russian, and contains elements of both these and of the Polish language. The language of the Ruthenians in Austria is Little-Russian.

The origin of the Russians has been traced back to a group of Slavic tribes who inhabited the country around Kieff. They lived in separate communities, and were united into one government when Rurik, with his Varangian companions, came to rule over them. During the reign of Prince Vladimir (972-1015) Christianity was introduced into Russia from Byzantium, and with it the productions of Byzantine literature found their way into the country. Owing to the very close proximity then existing between the Bulgarian and Russian languages, the Russians copied also several of the productions of the ancient Bulgarian literature. The most ancient monument of this literature is "Ostromirov's Gospel," of 1053. In 1224 the Mongols invaded Russia and ruled over her for more than two centuries; and altho their rule did not denationalize the people, it left its imprint upon the civil administration of the country, upon the social condition of the people, and upon their language. The Mongol dominion retarded the onward progress of Russia, and it was only in the reign of Peter the Great (1689-1725) that Russia began its emancipation from its semi-Asiatic, semi-barbaric condition, and became fit to take rank among the European powers.

The reforms of Peter the Great could not be executed without producing discontent in the land. Before his reign the Patriarch Nikon, one of the greatest men on the patriarchal throne in Russia, roused the indignation of the people by attempting to revise the Bible and the liturgical books, and to purge them from the errors that had crept into them through the ignorance of the transcribers. Nikon was denounced as a heretic, his corrections were deemed sacrilegious, and a great many people refused to accept the revised books, and seceded from the Church. These were and are still called Dissenters (*Raskolniks*), and altho the points on which they originally disagreed with the Church were puerile, they have clung and do still cling to their notions with an astonishing pertinacity. In their eyes the present Russian Church is not a true Church, the Czar is an antichrist, and they only are the true Christians, because they hold to the old faith. The Russian Dissent has given rise to a great many sects, some of which profess the wildest vagaries. Nikon's revision of the church books is the one used now in the Russian, Bulgarian, and Servian churches, and its language, modified according to the Russian orthography, is known as the Church-Slavonic.

The Russian Church was governed originally by archbishops or metropolitans, ordained by the Greek Patriarch of Constantinople, and several of them were Greeks. But after the capture of Constantinople in 1453 the metropolitans began to be consecrated by a council of bishops, and in 1589 the chief metropolitan was raised to the rank and dignity of a Patriarch. The Patriarchate lasted till the time of Peter the Great, who, in order to curb the opposition of the clergy to his reforms, abolished it and replaced it by a Synod, whose head was to be the Czar. This is the present system by which the Russian Church is governed. But tho the Czar is the real president of the Synod, he never takes any part in its deliberations, but is represented by a substitute, usually a layman, who bears the title of *ober-prokuror*. The Synod can do nothing without the sanction of the *prokuror;* in fact he is the Synod. The Czar's prerogatives, however, are limited to the administration of the Church; his authority does not extend to matters purely spiritual, and he cannot interfere with the dogmas of the Church. The constitution of the Synod, and of the Russian Church in general, is such that it places the clergy under the authority and supervision of the government and makes it subservient to the interests of "the powers that be." The capture of the Nestorians of Persia by the Russian missionaries has been mentioned in the article on the Nestorian Church. Politically and religiously Russia is aggressive.

In recent years Russia has opened more than 300 schools in Syrian communities, and about $300,000 is spent every year on these. Russia's activity in Manchuria and in other parts of the East is attracting world-wide attention; and it cannot be denied that she is playing an intelligent diplomatic game, of which the prize is the control of all Asia.

Wallace (Mackenzie), *Russia*, 2 vols., London and New York, 1877; Hare (A. J. C.), *Studies in Russia*, London, 18 5; Kropotkin (P.), *Memoirs of a Revolutionist*, 2 vols., London, 1899; Pobyedonastseff (K. P.), *Reflections of a Russian Statesman*, London (Translation), 1898; Palmer (F. E. H.), *Russian Life in Town and Country*, London, 1901; Norman (H.), *All the Russias*, London, 1902.

RUSTENBURG: A town and district in the Transvaal, South Africa, situated 52 miles W. of Pretoria. Station of the Hermannsburg Missionary Society (1864), with (1901) 1 missionary and his wife, 2 native workers, 4 outstations, 3 places of worship, 2 day schools, and 1,032 professed Christians. Also station of the SPG (1874), with (1903) 1 missionary.

RUST EN VERDE: A part of Paramaribo, Dutch Guiana. The Moravian Missions have a congregation here, of which the statistics are included under Paramaribo.

RUTENGANIO: A settlement in German East Africa, situated about 35 miles N. W. of the N. end of Lake Nyasa. Station of the Moravian Missions (1894), with (1903) 4 missionaries, 3 of them with their wives; 1 place of worship, and 18 professed Christians. The mission has also established a coffee plantation in order to teach the people to support themselves so soon as means of transportation give access to markets.

S

SABÆANS or MANDÆANS: An ancient people of whom remnants are found in the lower Euphrates and Tigris regions of Mesopotamia. There is a group of people calling themselves Sabæans in the Hauran, Syria, but Chwolsen says they have no real relation to the Mesopotamian Sabæans. As to the Sabæans of Mesopotamia, they are also called Nasoreans, Zabians, and Christians of St. John. Some of their peculiarities have been expressed in theories formed as to the origin of their name. Gesenius derives the name Sabæan from *Tsaboth* (Heavenly Hosts), because they worship stars; Nöldeke and others derive the name from the Syriac *Subba* (wash, baptize), because they practise baptism with diligence. They seem to be entirely distinct from Jews, Christians, and Mohammedans. They are isolated from other races, not marrying outside of their own body. They are quiet and industrious people, occupied in raising cattle, and some follow trades like boat-building; some of them, too, are good silversmiths. In physical appearance they are tall, well made, with good features and fine black beards; the women go about unveiled and seem to be taller and rather more masculine than Mohammedan women. On feast days they all dress in white. Their language, which is known in Europe as Mandaitic, is a dialect of Syriac written with characters peculiar to itself. Priests only read and write the language and they refuse absolutely to teach it to strangers. Some Mandaitic manuscripts exist in European libraries which, however, are no more ancient than the 16th century. The Sabæans of lower Mesopotamia were numerous when Mohammedanism came into being in the 7th century, and under the Abasside Caliphs they had some four hundred places of worship in the regions about Baghdad. The Koran mentions the Sabæans along with Christians and Jews, as people who have a divinely inspired book. They themselves have a tradition that they are descended from the Egyptians of Pharaoh's host lost in the Red Sea. Sabæans are mentioned in the Bible, but none of the three people there called by this name can be certainly connected with those in Mesopotamia. During the brief era of literary and scientific activity among the Mohammedans of Baghdad, many of the philosophers and astronomers patronized by the Caliphs were really Sabæans, according to Chwolsen; it having been the practise of the Caliphs to bring together learned men from outside of the Mohammedan fold. The Sabæans have a sacred book which they hold in high veneration. The main points of their belief in regard to God are that all things proceeded from Chaos or "the Great Abyss." With Chaos was the "Spirit of Glory," or the King of Light; he called into being the *Hayye kadima*, "the primal life," who is the supreme God in Sabæan theology. From him proceeded Yushamin, Jehovah, and Manda Hayye, "the Messenger of Life." It is from the latter that they derive the name Mandæans, and he holds the place in their theology of mediator between man and his Creator, but is generally believed to have been carnate in Abel, Seth and other Biblical characters down to John the Baptist. The Sabæans also believe in a host of demi-gods or demons in the under-world, which has numerous hells and vestibules and guardians, and from which spring the evil of the world and the various powers that control the sins of men. The polar star is regarded as the central sun of the sky, and when the people meet for prayer they always face the north star. They do not have fixed places of worship, but construct low houses of hurdles for each occasion. As to their relations with other religions, they declare that all the prophets named in the Bible were false prophets, including Jesus Christ. They have deep reverence for Abel and Seth, and they hold that Abel was incarnate in John the Baptist, and that he baptized Jesus by mistake. They hold that Mohammed was a false prophet. As to religious rites, they observe Sunday as a feast-day and perform the rite of baptism every Sunday, primarily, somewhat as the Mohammedans do, with the idea of preparing for worship. These Sunday baptisms are by immersion. They have several religious feasts during the year, the chief one lasting five days, when all of them are baptized, by sprinkling, three times a day. Their most important service has been described as held at midnight, when every one on arriving at the appointed place goes into the hurdle hut provided for the purpose, bathes in water and puts on white clothes before joining the circle of worshipers. The sacred book lies open on the altar, the priest takes one of two pigeons, holds it up to the north star and sets it free, while reciting a prayer of adoration of the "Living one." Then while the assistant reads from the book, the High Priest takes fresh baked cakes, and, cutting the throat of the other pigeon, drops four drops of blood on each cake arranged in the form of a cross; he then puts a cake into the mouth of each worshiper, saying, "Be marked with the sign of the Living one." The pigeon is then buried with ceremony behind the altar. This curious people appears to be dying out. It is estimated that there are between four and five thousand living near Amara, Sukes-shiukh, Basra, and Mohammera.

Missionary Review of the World, Vol. IX., p. 736; Nöldeke, *Mandaische Grammatik*, Halle, 1875; Prideaux, *Sketch of Sabean Grammar* (in Trans. Soc. Bib. Arch., Vol. V); Ainsworth, *Euphrates Expedition* in Encyclopedia Britannica; Brandot (W.), *Mandaische Schriften*, 1895; Chwolsen, *Die Ssabier und der Ssabismus*, St. Petersburg, 1856.

SACHIAPURAM: A village in Tinnevelli, Madras, India, situated N. by W. of Tinnevelli town. Station of the CEZMS (1881), with (1903) 2 women missionaries, 37 native workers, 11 day schools, and 481 Zenana pupils. The place is called North Tinnevelli by the Society.

SAFED: A town, formerly of considerable note, on a hill overlooking the western coast of the Lake of Tiberias, Asiatic Turkey, 65 miles west of Damascus. Station of the London Jews Society (1843), with (1903) 1 missionary and his wife, 1 day school, 1 dispensary and 1 hospital. Station also of the UFS Jewish Mission Committee (1889), with 1 missionary and his wife, 2 women missionaries, 10 native workers, 3 day schools, and 1 dispensary. Also station of the CA.

SAFFI: A town and seaport of Morocco, situated on the W. coast, about 70 miles N. E. of Mogador. Population, 9,000. Station of the Southern Morocco Mission (1892), with (1903) 1 missionary and his wife and 1 dispensary.

SAGA: A town on the island of Kiushiu, Japan, situated 45 miles N. E. of Nagasaki. Population, 25,000. Station of the Evangelical Lutheran Church in the South (1893), with 3 missionaries and their wives. Also station of the RCA (1895), with 1 missionary and his wife, 9 native workers, 1 place of worship, 1 Sunday school, 12 outstations, and 150 professed Christians.

SAHARANPUR: A town in the United Provinces, India, situated in the Meerut division, 130 miles S. E. of Ludhiana. A large town, rather substantially built, and steadily improving in appearance and increasing in importance. Owing to its low, moist situation it was very unhealthful, but modern sanitary improvements have somewhat remedied this evil. Station of the PN (1836), with (1903) 2 missionaries and their wives, 1 woman missionary, 13 native workers, 3 outstations, 2 places of worship, 6 day schools, 1 boarding school, 1 theological class, 1 industrial school, 1 dispensary, 2 leper institutes, 1 orphanage, and 101 communicant Christians. Some write the name Saharanpore.

SAINT ANN: A town and seaport in Jamaica, West Indies, situated in the central part on the N. coast of the island. Station of the UMFC (1838), with (1903) 1 missionary, 40 native workers, 5 places of worship, 3 Sunday schools, 3 day schools, and 358 professed Christians, of whom 281 are communicants. The name is sometimes written Saint Ann's.

SAINT AUGUSTIN: A village in Madagascar, situated on the S. W. coast, 15 miles S. by E. of Tullear. Station of the United Norwegian Church in America, (1900) 5 missionaries, 1 of them with his wife; 3 women missionaries, 20 native workers, 18 outstations, 18 day schools, 1 boarding school, and 100 professed Christians.

SAINT CHRISCHONA PILGRIM MISSION (*Pilger Mission von St. Chrischona bei Basel*): This Society, organized first (1840) by Pastor Spittler of St. Chrischona, as a mission school, developed about 1860, a well-known and rather ambitious project for missions in Abyssinia, one feature of which was the "Apostelstrasse" (Road of the Apostles), consisting of a series of stations which were to connect Jerusalem and Abyssinia. The selection included Alexandria, Cairo, Assuan, Khartum, and Metammeh. Only two, however, Cairo and Alexandria, were occupied, and the severity of conditions in Abyssinia and the

Sudan led to the giving up of the work. The institute continued, but sent its graduates to other societies and interested itself more especially in evangelistic work. Since 1895, however, it has resumed foreign work as a recognized branch of the China Inland Mission. It occupies (1902) 4 stations, with 5 missionaries, and reports statistics through the CIM.

SAINT CUTHBERT'S: See TSOLO.

SAINT CROIX: One of the West Indies. It has been a Danish possession since 1716. It has an area of 74 square miles and an estimated population of 18,000. The inhabitants are mostly free negroes, and are engaged in the raising of sugarcane and the manufacture of rum. The Moravian Brethren commenced their mission to the Danish West Indies at this island in 1754, and now have stations at Friedensthal, Friedensberg, and Friedensfeld. The Danish Lutheran Church has also quite a membership here.

SAINT EUSTACHE: One of the Dutch West Indies, and forms part of the colony of Curaçao. It contains a population of 3,000 in its area of 7 square miles. Mission station of Wesleyan Methodist West Indian Conference.

SAINT HELENA: An island belonging to Great Britain in the Atlantic Ocean, 1,200 miles west of Africa and 2,000 miles east of South America. Area, 47 square miles. Population, 5,000, negroes and half-breeds. Mission field of the SPG: 3 stations, St. Paul's, Jamestown, Longwood, with 450 communicants. There are also 1 Roman Catholic and 2 Baptist chapels.

SAINT JAN, or **SAINT JOHN:** One of the Dutch possessions in the West Indies; has an area of 21 square miles and a population of about 1,000, among whom the Moravian Brethren commenced work in 1754, with stations at Bethany and Emmaus (see St. Thomas). Mission field of the Danish Missionary Society.

SAINT JOHN'S: The chief town on the island of Antigua, West Indies, situated on the W. coast. It is the seat of government for the British colony of the Leeward Islands. Population, 10,000, chiefly pure negroes and mulattoes. A station of the Moravian Brethren, opened in 1756 by a missionary from the Danish Islands, who was moved by the miserable spiritual condition of the negro population in Antigua to come to their assistance. He accomplished much, and his work is now (1903) being carried on by 3 missionaries and their wives, 1 woman missionary, 31 native workers, 2 outstations, 3 places of worship, 3 Sunday schools, 2 day schools, 1 theological school, and 887 communicant Christians.

SAINT KITT'S, or **SAINT CHRISTOPHER:** One of the Leeward Group of the British West Indies. Its greatest length is 23 miles, and it contains an area of 65 square miles, with a population of 45,000. The island is of volcanic origin, the scenery is rich and beautiful, and the soil is fertile and well watered. Basseterre, with a population of 7,000, is the capital. Mission field of the Moravian Brethren, with stations at Bethesda, Basseterre, Bethel, and Eastbridge. The Wesleyan Methodists have been for years active on this field.

SAINT LUCIA: One of the Windward Islands, British West Indies, has an area of 122 square miles, with a population about 50,000, principally negroes and half-breeds. Chief town, Castries. Little success in the Protestant Mission on this island. A number of schools have been established, with many pupils in attendance.

SAINT MARY'S ISLAND: A large island off the coast of Gambia, West Africa, at the mouth of the Gambia River, east of Cape St. Mary. The principal city on the island is Bathurst. Mission station of the Wesleyan Missionary Society, with a force of 6 missionaries, 40 native helpers, 6 chapels, and 5 schools containing about 1,000 pupils.

SAINT PETER'S (Indian Settlement): A village in Canada, situated on the S. end of Lake Winnipeg, apout 40 miles N. E. of Winnipeg. Station of the CMS, with (1903) 1 missionary and his wife, 17 native workers, 1,135 professed Christians, of whom 355 are communicants; 6 day schools, and 1 Sunday school.

SAINT PAUL DE LOANDA: Capital of the province of Loanda, in the Portuguese Colony of Angola, on the west coast of Africa. It is situated on a beautiful landlocked harbor, sixty miles by sea north of the mouth of the Quanza. Its population, estimated at about 20,000, consists of a few hundred Portuguese, and the rest are negroes.

SAINT THOMAS: A town on the island of St. T., West Indies. It is picturesquely situated on three hills on the south coast, overlooking a fine harbor. For many years it was the terminus of several steamship lines, a depot for the surrounding islands, and a port of call for vessels of all nations; but the laying of West India telegraph cable greatly changed these conditions, and its commercial importance is rapidly declining. It is the residence of the Danish governor. The inhabitants are largely negroes. In 1843 the Moravian Brethren, who had hitherto confined their labors to the sugar plantations, found it necessary to provide instruction for the many converts who had come to the town to live, and a place of worship was procured near the center of the town, where a school and preaching services were held. In 1882 a fine new building was completed, and was a memorial church of the 150th anniversary of the beginning of Moravian Missions. The Danish Government provided schools and churches for the people at a very early date in their occupancy of the island. The Moravian Mission now (1903) has there 1 missionary and his wife, 14 native workers, 1 place of worship, 1 Sunday school, 1 day school, and 421 communicant Christians. The town is also known as Charlotte Amalie.

SAINT THOMAS: One of the West India Islands belonging to Denmark (1716); has an area of 23 square miles and a population of 14,389, mostly negroes. Sugar, and rum are the products. Mission field of the Moravian Brethren (1732), with stations at New Herrnhut, Nisky, and St. Thomas.

SAINT THOMAS' MOUNT: A town in Madras, India, situated in Chengelpat district, 7 miles S. W. of the Government House in Madras. It is also a military station. On the summit of the Mount is a Portuguese Church, on the spot where in 1547 the "Mount Cross" was found. Population, 13,000, of whom 9,600 are Hindus. Station of the WMS, with (1903) 56 native workers, 12 outstations, 3 places of worship, 19 Sunday schools, 20 day schools, and 292 professed Christians.

SAINT VINCENT: One of the Windward Islands, West Indies; is a British colonial possession (1763), under an administrator and colonial secretary. Its area is 122 square miles. Population (1888), 46,872, mainly negroes and half-breeds. Kingston is the capital; population, 5,393. Mission field of the WMS and SPG.

SAKANJIMBA: A settlement in Portuguese West Africa (Angola), situated in Benguella about 35 miles N. E. of Bailundu. Station of the ABCFM (1893), with 1 missionary and his wife, 1 woman missionary, 5 native workers, 4 outstations, 2 day schools, 1 dispensary, 1 kindergarten.

SALATIGA: A town and district in Java, Dutch East Indies, situated in the central part of the island, about 35 miles S. by E. of Samarang. Station of the Neukirchen Mission Institute (1893), with (1903) 1 missionary and his wife. Church statistics are included under Samarang.

SALEM: A town in Madras, India, situated in the Salem district, 110 miles W. by S. of Cuddalore. Population (1901), 70,621, nine-tenths of whom are Hindus. The manufactures of Salem are carpets and cutlery, the last-named being famous. Station of the LMS (1827), with (1903) 4 missionaries, three of them with their wives; 2 women missionaries, 71 native workers, 14 outstations, 7 Sunday schools, 18 day schools, 1 boarding school, 1 theological class, and 711 professed Christians, of whom 321 are communicants. Also station of the SPG (1875), with (1903) 1 native worker, 1 place of worship, and 205 professed Christians, of whom 90 are communicants.

SALEM: A settlement in Dutch Guiana, South America, situated on the seacoast, about 90 miles W. of Paramaribo. Station of the Moravian Missions (1840), with (1903) 1 missionary and his wife, 25 native workers, 2 outstations, 3 places of worship, 3 Sunday schools, and 346 professed Christians.

SALMAS: A district in Persia, north of Lake Urmia, half way between Tabriz and Urmia and near the eastern boundary of Turkey. (It is spoken of as a city, tho there is really no city of that name.) Climate unusually pleasant and equable. Population, 35,000, Armenians, Muslims, Nestorians, Jews, and Kurds, each speaking its own language, and generally Turkish also. Station of the PN for work among the **Nestorians**.

SA-LONG: A village in the Province of Fo-kien, China, situated about 55 miles N. by W. of Fuchau-fu. Station of the CEZ (1893), with (1903) 3 women missionaries, 3 native workers, 1 dispensary.

SALONICA: A city and seaport in European Turkey, at the northeastern extremity of the Gulf of Salonica, which is an inlet from the Greek Archipelago. S. is the leading city of Macedonia, having commercial importance. Population, 105,000: Greeks, Bulgarians, Wallachians, Turks and Spanish Jews. Station of the ABCFM (1894), with (1903) 2 missionaries, 1 of them with his wife; 26 native workers, 22 outstations, 12 places of worship, 10 day schools, 23 Sunday schools, and 490 professed Christians. Also station of the Church of Scotland Jewish Committee, with 1 missionary and his wife and 1 day school.

SALT. See Es SALT.

SALTILLO: A city in Mexico, capital of the frontier state of Coahuila, 60 miles W. of Monterey. Climate, mild, temperate, and healthful. Population (1901), 23,996, mixed Spanish and Indian, speaking Spanish and Indian dialects. Station of the SBC (1880), with (1903) 1 missionary and his wife, 5 native workers, 7 outstations, 5 places of worship, 5 Sunday schools, 2 day schools, and 482 communicant Christians. Also station of the PN (1884), with 2 missionaries and their wives, 2 women missionaries, 18 native workers, 6 Sunday schools, 6 day schools, 1 boarding school, and 436 communicants. Station also of the MES (1887), with (1903) 3 women missionaries and 1 native worker.

SALUR: A town in Madras, situated in the Vizagapatam district, about 50 miles N. W. of Chicacole. Population, 10,633. Station of the Breklum Missionary Society (1884), with 2 missionaries, 1 of them with his wife; 2 women missionaries, 24 native workers, 5 outstations, 1 place of worship, 1 Sunday school, 4 day schools, 1 dispensary, and 326 professed Christians, of whom 313 are communicants.

SALVADOR: A republic of Central America, bordering on the Pacific coast for 160 miles from the mouth of the Rio de la Paz to the mouth of the Goascoran, in the Gulf of Fonseca. Its inland boundaries are Guatemala on the west and Honduras on the north and east. It is the smallest of the Central American republics, having an area less than New Jersey. Except along the coast, where there are low alluvial plains, the country consists of a high plateau, 2,000 feet above the sea, with many volcanic mountains. The volcanic forces are still at work, as shown by the frequent earthquakes.

Since 1853, when the union with Honduras and Nicaragua was dissolved, the government is that of a republic, with a president elected for four years by suffrage of all citizens, and a congress of 70 deputies. The population is nine times as dense as the average of the other Central American countries. The bulk of the inhabitants are of aboriginal or mixed races; only 12,000 are whites, or descendants of Europeans. The natives are engaged principally in agriculture, tho there is much mineral wealth as yet undeveloped. The climate is mild and pleasant. Roman Catholicism is the state religion, but there is tolerance of other religions. Education, which is under the care of the government, is carried on in free schools, attendance upon which is obligatory. Railway, telegraph and telephone lines are being built, and the resources of the country are being developed. The ABS is doing effective work in Salvador.

SAMARANG: A commercial center of great importance in Java, Dutch East Indies, situated on the N. coast of the island about 150 miles E. by S. of Batavia. Population (1900), 89,286, of whom 4,800 are Europeans, 12,372 are Chinese, 1,688 Arabs and other Orientals, and 70,426 are native Javanese. Station of the Neukirchen Missionary Institute, with (1903) 9 missionaries, men and women; 46 native workers, 46 places of worship, 11 day schools and 925 professing Christians.

SAMHOPA. See SAN-HO.

SAMKITA: A village in the French Congo, West Africa, situated on the Ogowe River, about

15 miles N. of Lambarene. Station of the Paris Evangelical Missionary Society, with (1903) 2 missionaries, 11 outstations, 1 place of worship, 1 boarding school, and 1 dispensary.

SAMOA: A group of islands in the South Pacific Ocean, 14 in number. The western islands belong to Germany, and those east of the 174th meridian to the United States of America. The people are of the finest Polynesians to be found in the Pacific. The men are above the average height, with straight, well-rounded limbs and erect bearing. The women are slight, symmetrical and graceful in all of their movements. The people are all nominally Christians—Protestants and Roman Catholics, with a few Mormons. Nearly all the population over seven years of age can read and write. In short, the islands offer one of the illustrations of the wonderful fruits of missionary enterprise.

German Samoa: The chief islands of German Samoa are Upolu, Manono, Apolima, and Savaii. There are some smaller islets. All of these islands are mountainous, very fertile and quite populous.

Upolu is the second in size of the islands, with a population (1901) of 18,341. Apia, the seat of government, is a seaport of this island, with a German Imperial Governor, supported by a native high chief and council. The LMS began its missions in Upolu in 1836 and now (1903) has stations at Apia (3 missionaries, 38 native workers, 38 schools, 1 industrial school, and 5,119 professed Christians); Malua (3 missionaries, 9 native workers, 10 schools, 1 boarding school and training institution, 1 printing house, and 2,133 professed Christians); Aana (1 missionary, 41 native workers, 21 schools, and 4,700 professed Christians), and Falealili (1 missionary, 55 native workers, 31 schools, and 4,700 professed Christians).

Savaii: Lying west of Upolu, has an area of 660 square miles and a population (1901) of 13,201. It was occupied by the LMS in 1830, which now has in the island stations at Faasoleleaga (1 missionary, 49 native workers, 33 schools, and 4,949 professed Christians), and Matautu (1 missionary, 32 native workers, 30 schools and 3,145 professed Christians).

Manono and *Apolima* are smaller islands, with a population, together, of barely 1,000.

American Samoa: This consists of the islands of Tutuila, Manua, and some smaller islets. The whole taken together is officially known as the Tutuila naval station. *Tutuila* is high and mountainous, of volcanic origin, thickly populated, and very fertile. The bay of Pago Pago is the coaling station which made the place desirable to the United States. The area of Tutuila is 54 square miles, and the population about 4,000. *Manua* is a smaller island, with about 2,000 inhabitants. The LMS has (1903) on Tutuila 3 missionaries, and on Tutuila and Manua together 38 native workers, 42 schools, and 5,366 professed Christians.

SAMOKOV: A town in Bulgaria, European Turkey, situated on a mountain plateau about 35 miles S. by E. of Sofia. Climate healthful. Station of the ABCFM (1867), with (1903) 4 missionaries, 3 of them with their wives; 4 women missionaries, 25 native workers, 9 outstations, 9 places of worship, 9 Sunday schools, 1 day school, 2 boarding schools, 1 theological class, 1 college, 1 kindergarten, 1 industrial department, and 300 professed Christians.

SAMSOUN: A city on the Black Sea, Asiatic Turkey, 500 miles E. of Constantinople. Population, Turkish, Greek, and Armenian. It is the port through which passes the greater part of the trade between Constantinople and northern and eastern Asia Minor. A carriage road has been built connecting it with the principal cities in Eastern Turkey, except Erzerum, and the missionaries for those cities as a rule land at Samsoun. It is very malarious, and continued residence has been impracticable for the missionaries. There is a thriving native church connected with the Marsovan station.

SAMULCOTTA. See CHAMARLAKOTA.

SANDOWAY: A very ancient town in Arakan, Burma, on the Sandoway River, 15 miles from its mouth. Climate, except in the town itself, unhealthful, owing to mangrove swamps. Before the Pegu province of Burma was taken by the English, Sandoway was the headquarters of the Bassein Karen Mission, and thousands were baptized there. Population about 2,000. Station of the ABMU (1888), with (1903) 1 missionary and his wife, 2 women missionaries, 42 native workers, 19 outstations, 18 Sunday schools, 6 day schools, 1 boarding school, and 460 communicant Christians.

SANDY LAKE: A settlement in Northwest Canada, situated in the territory of Saskatchewan, about 50 miles N. W. of Prince Albert. It is also called Asisipi. Station of the CMS (1875), with (1903) 1 missionary, 1 native worker, 2 day schools, and 260 professed Christians, of whom 86 are communicants.

SAN FERNANDO: A town in Trinidad, West Indies, on the W. coast, about 25 miles S. by E. of Port of Spain. Station of the UFS (1850), with (1903) 1 missionary and his wife, 1 native worker, 1 outstation, 2 Sunday schools, and 218 professed Christians, of whom 80 are communicants. Also station of the PCC (1870), with (1900) 2 missionaries and their wives, 1 woman missionary, 13 native workers, 2 outstations, 23 Sunday schools, 17 day schools, 1 boarding school, 1 theological class, 1 college, and 218 professed Christians. Station also of the AME, with 1 native worker.

SANG-HIA-CHUANG: A town in Shen-si, China, situated about 55 miles W. of Hsi-ngan-fu. Station of the CIM (1894), with (1903) 1 woman missionary, 3 native workers, 1 place of worship, 1 Sunday school, and 2 professed Christians. Some write the name Sang-kia-chuang.

SANGI or **SANGIR Islands:** A group of islands in the Dutch East Indies, lying between Celebes and Mindanao. The area of the group is about 350 miles, and the population about 45,000. The largest of the islands is called Great Sangir. Its characteristic feature is the volcano of Gunong Abu, to which belongs a terrible history of destruction. This island is also the center of evangelistic effort now supervised by the "Sangir and Talaut Islands Committee," whose seat is in Batavia. Other stations of this committee's mission are in the islands of Siauw and Tagulandang. Taking the Sangir group and the neighboring Talaut islands together, the number of professed Christian adherents found there (1901) is about 44,000.

SANG-YONG: A village in Fo-kien, China, situated about 55 miles N. of Fu-chau-fu. Station of the CEZ (1894), with (1903) 3 women missionaries, 5 native workers, 1 day school, and 1 boarding school.

SAN-HO: A town in the province of Kwangtung, China, situated about 20 miles N. of Swatow. Station of the PCE (1895), with (1903) 3 missionaries, two of them with their wives; 1 place of worship, and 1 dispensary. Some write the name Samhopa.

SAN JUAN: A town in the island of Porto Rico, of which it is the capital; situated on the N. coast of the island. Climate warm, but healthful. Population, 32,048. Station of the Am. Baptist Home Miss. Society (1899), with (1903) 2 missionaries, one of them with his wife; 1 woman missionary, 2 native workers, 2 outstations, 1 place of worship, 2 Sunday schools, and 96 professed Christians. Also station of the ELGC (1899), with (1903) 1 missionary and his wife, 1 woman missionary, 1 outstation, 1 place of worship, 2 Sunday schools, and 40 professed Christians. Station also of the ME (1900), with 4 missionaries, three of them with their wives; 1 woman missionary, 1 outstation, 1 day school, 1 boarding school. Station also of the PE, with 1 missionary. Station also of the Presbyterian Home Miss. Soc. (U. S.), with (1903) 3 missionaries, two of them with their wives, and 1 outstation. Station of the CA. The ABS also has an agency here.

SAN LUIS POTOSI: A town in Central Mexico, situated in the state of the same name, of which it is capital, and about 200 miles W. of Tampico. Climate, semi-tropical; elevation, 6,000 feet. It is an important mining center. Population (1900), 61,019. Station of the PN (1873), with (1903) 1 missionary and his wife, 5 native workers, 8 outstations, 3 day schools, 17 Sunday schools, and 392 communicant Christians. Also station of the MES (1883), with (1901) 1 missionary and his wife, 2 women missionaries, 1 native worker, 1 place of worship, 1 dispensary, 1 hospital.

SAN-SHUI-HSIEN: A town in Shen-si, China, situated 70 miles N. W. of Hsi-ngan-fu. Station of the CIM (1897), with (1903) 3 missionaries, one of them with his wife; 2 native workers, 1 place of worship, 1 day school, 1 Sunday school.

SANTA CRUZ ISLANDS: A group in Melanesia, lying southeast of the Solomon Islands and north of the New Hebrides, between longitude 165° and 170° east, and latitude 8° and 12° south. Santa Cruz is the largest island. The Melanesian Mission has labored in these islands since 1870, and now (1900) has 2 male missionaries, 1 female missionary, 16 native workers, 11 in native churches, 5 day schools. It will be remembered that Bishop Patteson was murdered on one of these islands in 1871. The Melanesian Mission lost 4 of its agents (1 missionary and 3 teachers, murdered by the natives) before it was able to effect a lodgment in this group.

SANTA MARIA: A town in Brazil, in the state of Rio Grande do Sul, about 180 miles W. of Porto Alegre. Station of the American Church Missionary Society (1900), with (1901) 2 missionaries, one of them with his wife; 1 native worker, 1 place of worship, 2 Sunday schools, and 5 professed Christians.

SANTALIA: A name sometimes applied to that portion of Bengal, India, which is inhabited by Santals, who speak a distinct language called Santali. It is in the main coincident with the district known as the Santal Parganas. It is the field of a number of the principal missionary societies, both European and American.

SANTALS: A people of British India, a remnant of the pre-Hindu Kolarian population, and numbering (census of 1901) 1,470,000 in Bengal, and 23,000 in Assam. Santalia, or the land of the Santals, lies on the extreme eastern edge of the tableland of Eastern India, where it slopes down into the Ganges valley of lower Bengal, extending southward from the Ganges at Bhagalpur. In this region two distinct aboriginal tribes reside. The Paharis, of Dravidian origin, live on the hill tops, and were a terror to the whole country until the closing decades of the 18th century, when they were subdued and tamed by the young civil officer, Augustus Cleveland. As, however, the Hindus were still afraid to occupy the valleys below the Pahari, the government in 1832 encouraged the Santals, who lived further south, to occupy them and the adjoining lowlands, marking off for their use the territory 23° 48' to 25° 19' latitude, and 86° 30' to 87° 88' longitude, called the Santal Parganas, which became the home of the race. Colonization has taken place to Assam and to the Santalpur district, at the foot of the Himalayas, 250 miles northward.

The Santals have very dark skins, round faces, flat noses, large mouths, with protruding lips, and straight black hair. They wear almost no clothing. They are strongly built, simple, tractable, devoid of caste, and, judged by the standards of India, honest and truthful. They are nomadic farmers and are in demand as laborers on the indigo plantations and railways of Bengal, and the tea plantations of Assam. The women are notable, if not for beauty, for grace of limb, tho laden with brass rings. They are on a higher plane socially than most heathen women. It is customary for each family to live by itself within an enclosure of intertwined hedge. Santali is a more developed speech than the other Kolarian dialects, but was first reduced to writing by the missionaries. Bengali is taught in the schools. Their religion is ancestor and nature-worship, human sacrifices being offered until the extinction of the brutal custom by the British Government in 1835.

The earliest mission in Santalia was that begun in 1850 among the Pahari, by the Church Missionary Society, under Rev. E. Droese, who continued at Bhagalpur for 36 years. Attention was especially drawn to the Santals by their terrible insurrection in 1855 against the extortions of the Hindu money-lenders, which proved a turning-point in their history. Commissioner George Yule, who restored order, encouraged Droese to open schools among them, obtaining grants for this purpose, and he and his successors did much for their material and moral improvement. The CMS opened a mission to the Santals in 1859. The following year, E. L. Puxley, a British officer and Oxford graduate, who had volunteered for India, was interested in the Santals by officers whom he had met *en route*. He opened a station and erected buildings at Taljhari, which he presented to the CMS. In 1868 H. M. Shackell resigned the principalship of St. John's College at Agra to undertake the same work at Godda. This repeated voluntary effort for the Santals is proof of the hopefulness of this field. New stations were opened in 1878 at Baharwa and Baghara. The stations named, all in the N. E. of Santalia, together with Santalpur, where 880

Christian colonists are settled, constitute the centers of the CMS Mission to the Santals, which in 1901 reported, including Paharis, 4,130 Christians.

"The Home Mission to the Santals," founded in 1867, and led for 35 years by Boerreson, the Danish missionary, at Ebenezer, in eastern Santalia, reported in 1902 11,345 Christians, who are already trained to a considerable degree of independent activity.

The Free Church of Scotland entered the field in 1871, and has three centers in the S. W. (Pachamba, Tondee, and Chakai), reporting, in 1901, more than 1,300 Christians. The Bethel Mission, in the southern section, had enrolled, in 1900, 1,500 Christians. According to Warneck (1902) there are, in connection with these and other small Santal missions, 18,000 Christians. *Imperial Gazetteer of India*, Art. Santals.

SANTAL LANGUAGE: The Santals inhabit a considerable section of Bengal, India, lying northwest of Calcutta. Their language is not of the Aryan family, and is commonly classified with the Kolarian group of Dravidian languages.

SANTIAGO DE CUBA: A town and seaport on the E. coast of Cuba, W. I., formerly capital of the island. Population (1902), 43,090. Station of the Am. Baptist Home Missionary Society (1899), with (1900) 2 missionaries and their wives, 3 women missionaries, 3 native workers, 4 outstations, 1 place of worship, 5 Sunday schools, 1 industrial school, 1 kindergarten, and 109 professed Christians. Station also of the MES, with (1903) 2 missionaries, 2 women missionaries, 1 native worker, 1 day school.

SANTO DOMINGO; Republic of: A country in the island of Haiti, W. I., also called the Dominican Republic. It has an area of about 18,000 square miles, comprising about two-thirds of the whole island, the republic of Haiti occupying one-third in the western part. It was separated from the republic of Haiti in 1844, after a bloody struggle. Spain held it from 1861 to 1865. In 1869 a treaty was signed with the President of the United States for its annexation to the great republic, but the treaty failed of ratification by the United States Senate. It has suffered from wars and revolutions, and is very backward in its civilization. Its government is after the model of that of the United States, with a President chosen by an electoral college, who holds office for four years. Its population is estimated (1888) at 610,000, chiefly of mixed Spanish and Indian blood, with some pure negroes and mulattoes and a certain number of whites. The language is Spanish. French and English are also spoken in towns. The religion is Roman Catholic, but all religions are tolerated. From the time of the revolt of Haiti against French control until 1864, the Roman Catholic clergy withdrew from the island, which was placed under the ban of the Church. The people reverted in many instances to ancient heathenish superstitions, which have considerable sway in the smaller settlements. Protestant missions in the Dominican Republic are represented by the Protestant Episcopal Church of the U. S., who have one station in charge of a colored minister from Haiti, and by the Wesleyan Methodists of the West Indies, who have four stations; these latter stations were passed over to the charge of the WMS in 1903.

Missionary Review of the World, September, 1903; Hazard (S.), *Santo Domingo, Past and Present*, London, 1873.

SANTURCE: A town in Porto Rico, W. I., situated about 20 miles W. of San Juan. Station of the American Missionary Association (1898), with 4 women missionaries, 1 Sunday school, 1 day school.

SÃO JOÃO DEL REI: A town in Brazil, situated in the state of Minas Geraes, about 130 miles N. W. of Rio de Janeiro. Station of the PS (1895), with (1903) 1 missionary and his wife, 1 native worker, and 40 professed Christians.

SÃO PAULO: Capital city of a province of the same name in Brazil. It is an important city, and has developed much within recent years, being the most active and enterprising town in the country. It is the center of the railway system of the province, and is distant only 36 miles from Santos, and 220 miles S. W. from Rio de Janeiro. Tho the streets are narrow, they are well paved, and are lighted with gas. Sewers and watermains have been constructed. It stands on a high, but not quite healthful, plain. Altitude, 2,393 feet. Population (1900), 125,000. Station of the MES (1884), with (1903) 1 missionary and his wife, 1 woman missionary, 2 native workers, 2 outstations, 2 places of worship, 6 Sunday schools, and 953 communicant Christians. Station also of the PN (1863), with (1903) 1 missionary, 1 woman missionary, 4 native workers, 2 outstations, 3 Sunday schools, 1 day school, 1 college. Station of the PS (1895), with (1903) 1 missionary and his wife. Also station of the Southern Baptist Convention (1899), with 2 missionaries and their wives, 3 native workers, 2 outstations, 1 Sunday school, 1 theological class, and 73 communicant Christians.

SÃO PEDRO, or **RIO GRANDE DO SUL:** A town in Brazil, situated in the state of Rio Grande do Sul on the sea coast, about 40 miles S. E. of Pelotas. Station of the American Church Missionary Society (1891), with (1900) 1 missionary and his wife, 1 woman missionary, 2 native workers, 1 outstation, 3 places of worship, 1 Sunday school, 1 theological class, and 106 professed Christians. Also station of the Seventh Day Adventists Church, with 1 missionary and his wife. Church statistics included in Rio de Janeiro.

SAPPORO: A town in Japan, situated near the W. coast of Hokkaido Island and about 350 miles N. by E. of Tokio, 95 miles N. N. E. of Hakodate. It is connected with Otaru, its port, by railway. Its streets are wide. Climate cold. Population, 13,800. Station of the CMS (1893), with (1903) 1 missionary and his wife, 1 woman missionary, 22 native workers, 1 outstation, 1 place of worship, 5 day schools, 1 boarding school, and 1,612 professed Christians, of whom 358 are communicants. Also station of the ME, with (1903) 1 missionary and his wife, 2 women missionaries, 11 native workers, 5 outstations, 7 places of worship, 7 Sunday schools, and 468 professed Christians, of whom 305 are communicants. Station also of the ABCFM (1895), with (1903) 1 missionary and his wife, 1 woman missionary, 10 native workers, 2 places of worship, 5 Sunday schools. Station also of the PN, with (1903) 3 women missionaries, 3 outstations, and 1 boarding school.

SARAWAK: A district on the northwestern coast of Borneo, ruled by Rajah Sir Charles Brooke, under protectorate of the British Government. The population is about 600,000, composed of Malays, Dyaks, Kayans, and other tribes, together with Chinese and other settlers. The SPG has (1902) 5 stations in Sarawak, with about 2,500 baptized Christians.

SARENGA: A village of Bengal, India, situated in the Suri district, N. by E. of Bankura. Station of the WMS (1901), with 1 missionary, 19 native workers, 2 Sunday schools, 4 places of worship, 6 day schools, 1 boarding school, and 76 professed Christians, of whom 66 are communicants.

SAREPTA: A village in Cape Colony, South Africa, situated about 20 miles N. E. of Cape Town. Station of the Rhenish Missionary Society, with (1903) 1 missionary and his wife, 6 native workers, 1 outstation, 1 Sunday school, 2 day schools, and 565 professed Christians, of whom 200 are communicants.

SARGEANT, John: Born at Newark, N. J., 1710; died July, 1749; graduated at Yale College 1729; was tutor 1731-1734. He was contemporary with David Brainerd, and taught him the Algonquin language. In July, 1735, he was settled as a missionary to the Indians on the Housatonic River and the next month ordained at Deerfield in presence of the governor and council and a large number of English and Indians. Mr. Sargeant acquired the native language with facility, and so well that the people said he spoke it better than themselves. He translated into their language parts of the Old Testament, and all the New except the Book of Revelation. He introduced many of the arts of civilized life, interested them in singing, taught them Biblical history and doctrine, and brought into the mission school many Mohawk and Oneida children from the province of New York. Regarding the education of the youth as essential to his success, he had formed the plan of a manual-labor school, in which the pupils should contribute to their own support. Provision had been made for the education of several boys, land procured, a school-house built, and some boys were collected; but the death of Mr. Sargeant prevented the consummation of the plan. Mourned by the Indians, who loved him as a father and friend, he died at the early age of 39. Their improvement through his labors had been great. He found them but 50 in number, living miserably and viciously in wigwams, widely scattered, and roving from place to place. He left them 218 in number, settled in a thriving town, with twenty families in frame houses, and many having farms cultivated, fenced, and well stocked. He had baptized 182, and 42 were communicants.

SARGENT, Edwin: Born at Paris, France, 1815. Died October 10, 1889. Spent the early part of his life at Madras; went in 1835 to Palamcotta, Tinnevelly, as a missionary of the Church Missionary Society; in 1839 he went to England, studied three years in the Church Missionary College at Islington; was ordained in 1842, and the same year returned to his work in Tinnevelly. The first eight years he was located at Suviseshapuram, having charge of a missionary district. In 1850 he was transferred to Palamcotta, and two years later appointed principal of the Preparandi Institution, which had a high character for proficiency while he was at the head of it. More than 500 young men were instructed by him, many of whom are now pastors of native Christian churches in the towns and villages, and many more are catechists and schoolmasters. In 1874 he was nominated a suffragan or coadjutor bishop to the Bishop of Madras, and on March 11, 1877, consecrated in Calcutta by Bishop Johnson, assisted by the bishops of Madras, Bombay, and Colombo. He had charge of eight of the ten districts into which the Society's Tinnevelli Mission was divided. In these districts were 51,000 Christians, 66 native pastors, and many catechists and schoolmasters, all under his care. During the first fifty years of the bishop's missionary service, the number of villages containing Christians in the Church Missionary Society's portion of Tinnevelli rose from 224 to 1,018, the Christians and catechumens from 8,693 to 56,287, and the native clergy from 1 to 68. In the earlier period native Christians did nothing for the support of the Gospel among themselves; at the later period their contributions for church work amounted to over 33,000 rupees annually. The affairs of the church are now managed to a very large extent by the Christians themselves, and no native clergyman draws his stipend from the Missionary Society. The success of church work is due very largely, under God, to the practical wisdom, untiring zeal, and loving labor of Bishop Sargent. He had a remarkable knowledge of the vernacular.

SARON: A settlement in Cape Colony, South Africa, about 25 miles S. E. of Piquetburg. Station of the Rhenish Missionary Society, with (1903) 1 missionary and his wife, 14 native workers, 1 day school, 1 Sunday school, and 1,879 professed Christians, of whom 876 are communicants.

SARON (Dutch Guiana): Part of **Paramaribo.**

SART LANGUAGE: A dialect of the Eastern Turkish, spoken by the dwellers in cities of the parts of Central Asia S. of the Aral Sea. It is but little different from the Uighur, or Turkish of culture, in these Eastern regions.

SATTANAPALLI: A town in Madras, India, situated in the Kistna district, about 63 miles N. by E. of Ongole. Station of the ABMU (1895), with (1903) 1 missionary and his wife, 1 woman missionary, 15 native workers, 9 outstations, 5 places of worship, 6 day schools, and 2,940 professed Christians, of whom 1,112 are communicants.

SATTELBERG: A settlement in German New Guinea, situated on high land near the E. coast and about 10 miles N. W. of Simbang. Station of the Neudettelsau Missionary Society (1892), with (1903) 4 missionaries, 1 of them with his wife; 1 woman missionary, 1 day school, and 1 place of worship.

SATTHIANADHAN, William Thomas: A native of India, of the Vishnuvite Sudras. Died at Sinthupunthurai, Tinnevelli, February 24, 1892. Educated at the native English school and Palamcotta Preparandi Institution. He was stationed in North Tinnevelli, and afterward had charge of the Southern pastorate at Madras, and was Chairman of the Madras Native Church Council. In 1881 he formed the Chintadrepetta Christian Association; in 1884 he was elected Fellow of the University of Madras, and in 1885 he received B.D. degree from the Archbishop of Canterbury, on the recommendation of the Bishop of Madras, in recognition of his linguistic and other labors. He was the author of a *Church History in English and Tamil*, and he edited a *Tamil Commentary on the New Testa-*

ment. He also ably conducted two periodicals, and the power of his pen was felt among a large circle of readers. Mrs. Satthianadhan had the superintendence of a large school for high-caste women, and carried on Zenana work for many years in connection with the CEZMS and Female Education Society.

SATUPAITEA: A settlement in the Samoan Islands, situated on the S. side of Savaii. Station of the Australia Wesleyan Missionary Society, with (1901) 1 missionary and his wife, 164 native workers, 7 outstations, 24 places of worship, 28 Sunday schools, 28 day schools, 1 boarding school, and 1,050 professed Christians.

SAVAGE ISLAND. See NIUÈ.

SAVAII: The westernmost of the Samoan Islands. Area, 700 square miles. Population, 13,000. Station of the LMS (1830), with (1903) 1 missionary, 44 native workers, 1 outstation, 63 Sunday schools, 63 day schools, 2 boarding schools, and 5,555 professed Christians, of whom 2,539 are communicants.

SAVAS: An island of the East Indies, southwest of Timor Island, southeast of Java; has estimated population of 16,500, more than half of whom are nominally Christians. They are visited twice a year by the Dutch Government assistant pastor residing at Kupang, Timor.

SAWYERPURAM: A village in Madras, India, situated in Tinnevelli district, a short distance S. of Palamcotta. Founded in 1814 by Mr. Sawyer, an English trader, who bought the land in order to make a refuge for persecuted converts. Station of the SPG (1826), with (1903) 1 missionary, 57 native workers, 21 places of worship, 10 day schools, 1 boarding school, and 2,789 professed Christians, of whom 1,027 are communicants

SCHAUFFLER, William Gottlieb: Born in Stuttgart, Germany, August 22, 1798. Died January 26, 1883. His early life was spent at Odessa, in Russia, where he worked at his father's trade as a turner. At the age of twenty-two he confessed his faith in Christ. He early became interested in foreign missions; and in 1826, meeting the famous missionary, **Dr. Joseph Wolff,** his enthusiasm was further kindled. Finding, however, the plans of Dr. Wolff impracticable, he went to Constantinople, and thence to Smyrna, where he met **Rev. Jonas King,** who induced him to go to America for an education. He entered the Andover Theological Seminary, where he remained five years, studying often fourteen and sixteen hours a day. He says: "Aside from the study of Greek and Hebrew, and general classical reading, I studied the Chaldee, Syriac, Arabic, Samaritan, Rabbinic, Hebrew-German, Persian, Turkish, and Spanish; and, in order to be somewhat prepared for going to Africa, I extracted and wrote out pretty fully the Ethiopic and Coptic grammars. For some years I read the Syriac New Testament and Psalms for my edification, instead of the German or the English text." He also aided the professors in their translations. He was ordained November 14, 1831, a missionary of the ABCFM to the Jews of Turkey. He studied Arabic and Persian with De Sacy, and Turkish with Prof. Kieffer in Paris, and then went to Constantinople. There he preached in German, Spanish, Turkish, and English. In 1838 he visited Odessa, chiefly on Mrs. Schauffler's account, and was much engaged in evangelistic work, resulting in many conversions. He translated the Bible into Hebrew-Spanish, that is, Spanish with a mixture of Hebrew words and written with Hebrew characters, for the Jews in Constantinople, descendants of those who had been driven from Spain. Dr. Schauffler, besides being a translator, was an earnest evangelical preacher, his Sunday services in English and German for local residents being greatly blessed. He delivered in Constantinople a series of discourses, which were published in a volume by the American Tract Society, entitled "Meditations on the Last Days of Christ." In 1835 the first Jewish convert, a German whom he had known sixteen years before in Russia, not being allowed by the Government to profess Christianity except as a member of the Greek Church, went to Constantinople and was by him baptized. In 1839 he went to Vienna to superintend the printing of the Hebrew-Spanish Old Testament. There he resided three years, and many striking conversions occurred through his labors. He presented to the emperor, in a private interview, his printed Bible, on which he had bestowed great labor. The Jews having pronounced a favorable verdict upon it, a second and larger edition was printed. Journeying from Vienna he spent ten days in Pesth, where many of the better class of Jewish families embraced the Christian faith. The Jewish Mission having been relinquished in 1855, he was requested by the Scotch Free Church, to which it had been transferred, to take charge of the work, but he declined. He declined also the proposal to enter the Armenian field. About this time he was appointed by the Mission to lay before the Evangelical Alliance, soon to meet at Paris, the great question of religious liberty in Turkey, and to urge the Alliance to memorialize the sovereigns of Europe to use their influence with the Sultan to secure the abolition of the death penalty for Muslim converts to Christianity. The result was seen in the triumph of Sir Stratford Canning. The morning he left Paris the news of Sebastopol's fall was proclaimed on the streets, and in Stuttgart, his native city, he addressed an immense audience on the Crimean War. After this war the way seemed open for missionary work among the Turks, and Dr. Schauffler, with the approval of the mission, decided to enter that field. To fit himself for this new work, he applied himself to the Turkish language anew. In 1857 a paper on the Turkish and Bulgarian work, prepared by Drs. Schauffler and Hamlin, was sent to the Prudential Committee, and Dr. Schauffler was deputed by the mission to present, in America and England, the claims of the new mission to the Turks. After thirty-one years of absence he set sail for home. His appeals met with a generous response. The Prudential Committee, however, decided, after the Turkish Government refused liberty of conscience to Muslims, not to continue the separate mission to Mohammedan Turks, but to have the Armenian Mission cover the whole field. This decision, and the entrance of the SPG into Turkey, led Dr. Schauffler to resign as a missionary of the Board, but he pursued his Bible translation in the employ of the American and British and Foreign Bible Societies. His great work was the translation of the whole Bible into the literary Turkish, the language of the books as distinguished from that of the common people. This occupied him eighteen years. He published an ancient Spanish version of the Old Testament, revised by himself, with the Hebrew original in parallel columns, a popular translation of the Psalms into Spanish, a grammar of the Hebrew language in Spanish, a Hebrew-Spanish Lexicon of the Bible. He contributed also articles in Spanish to a missionary periodical in Salonica. He was a remarkable linguist, able to speak ten languages and read as many more. His rare scholarship, and especially his translation of the Bible into literary Turkish, led the Universities of Halle and Wittenberg to confer upon him the degrees of D.D. and Ph.D., and Princeton College the degree of Doctor of Laws. For his great services to the German colony of Constantinople the King of Prussia conferred upon him a decoration. He left Constantinople in 1874, and went to New York with his wife to live with his two youngest sons. He was in the active missionary work for nearly fifty years.

SCHEMACHI: A large and important city of Eastern Transcaucasia, Russia. Population about 25,000, of whom a large number are Armenians. As a result of the work of the Basel Missionary Society, a congregation of evangelical Armenians was organized here, which did not lose its power after the missionaries were obliged to leave. Its leader received some education at Basel Seminary, and, by his rare skill and earnest piety, succeeded in keeping his little band together. Notwithstanding the law of Russia, which insists that proselytes shall join the Greek Church, the Protestants grew in numbers and in strength, until they became one of the most influential communities in that section of the Caucasus. From Schemachi the work spread to Shusha, Lenkaran, and Baku, in each of which places congregations were gathered, which now form a recognized body of Christians.

SCHIALI. See SHIYALI.

SCHLESWIG-HOLSTEIN Missionary Society in Breklum. See GERMANY; MISSIONARY SOCIETIES OF.

SCHMELEN, John Henry: Missionary of the LMS in South Africa. Born in Germany, 1777; died at Komaggas, Little Namaqualand, July 26, 1848. Mr. Schmelen arrived at his field of labor in 1811, and opened the stations at Steinkopf and Pella, south of the Orange River, spending some time in exploring the regions about the mouth of the river, and on its north side, toward Damaraland. In 1814, on invitation of the Namaquas, he crossed the Orange River and opened a new station at Bethany, 200 miles north of Steinkopf. Here he laboriously carried on his most difficult work of reducing the Namaqua speech to writing, and translating the Gospels into that language. In one of his long tours he encountered Mr. Barnabas Shaw, of the WMS, who was sent out to establish a mission in the Namaqua country. It was characteristic of the man that he at once put himself at the disposal of the new missionary, took him to the Kamiesberg country, introduced him to the tribesmen there, and then, having seen him properly settled, went on to his own field, distant four weeks' journey. In 1824 he visited Cape Town to see his Namaqua Gospel through the press, and, that accomplished, he spent some time exploring the coast regions of Little Namaqualand, finally establishing a new station at Komaggas. There he completed the translation of the Gospels, and took them to Cape Town to be printed. In the meantime he was growing old, and called in vain for an associate to take up his work. His associate came at last in 1840, a missionary of the Rhenish Missionary Society, the LMS having transferred its Namaqua work to that Society. The closing years of his life were thus gladdened by the privilege of helping with his experience and counsel the missionaries of the new group, who were to press forward the work for his beloved Namaqua people.

SCHNEIDER, Benjamin: Born at New Hanover, Pa., January 18, 1807. Died September 14, 1877. Graduated at Amherst College, 1830; Andover Theological Seminary, 1833; ordained October 2; sailed for Turkey as a missionary of the ABCFM December 12, 1833, tho supported by Reformed (German) Churches. He was stationed first at Brousa, where he preached the first evangelical sermon ever preached in the Turkish language. In 1849 he removed to Aintab, where he laid the foundation of two flourishing churches. After the death of his wife in 1856 he visited the United States, and on returning to Turkey in 1858, was again stationed in Brousa. His health failing, he made a second visit home in 1872. A call for help in Turkish and Greek work in the theological seminary at Marsovan induced him, tho advanced in years and in feeble health, to return, reaching Marsovan March, 1874. But from nervous prostration he was compelled to relinquish the work, and in 1875 he left first for Switzerland, thence for his native land.

For more than forty years he was connected with the Turkey missions, laboring in almost every department of missionary service—preaching, translating, preparing young men for the ministry. Few have traveled more extensively as pioneers; few have more cheerfully endured the privations of the service; few are the native churches in Turkey where his name is not known and revered. Even amid the intense sufferings of the last two years of his life his eye would brighten and glow with delight at the bare mention of the missionary life. He acquired languages with great facility. He spoke German, Greek, and Turkish, almost as if each were his vernacular, the latter with an ease and fluency seldom equaled by foreigners. Even natives wondered at his marvelous flow of thought in idiomatic phrases, easily understood by all; for he chose simplicity of style, tho at home in the higher and more complicated forms of expression.

He received the degree of D.D. from Franklin and Marshall College, Lancaster, Pa., 1850.

SCHREIBER, August: Born at Bielefeld, Westphalia, August 11, 1839; died at Barmen, Germany, May 22, 1903. After graduating at Gutersloh, he studied theology at Halle and Erlangen, returning to Gutersloh for two years' further study, and for theological examinations. Having decided to become a missionary in the foreign field, he spent a year in London and Edinburgh, studying church organization and missionary methods used by the different societies. He also took a short course in medicine. In 1865 he offered himself to the Rhenish Missionary Society and was appointed missionary to Sumatra by that Society, in 1866. Since he had found means, before going out, to study the Batta language he was able to enter the active work almost as soon as he arrived on the field. He was compelled to leave Sumatra and return to Germany by his wife's illness in 1873. During the seven years of his missionary career in Sumatra he was occupied with organizing a better system of training native helpers, and also with translating the Scriptures into Batta. He completed the translation of almost the whole New Testament before he returned to Germany. On arriving at Barmen, Dr. Schreiber was usefully occupied in the Rhenish Mission House, and, in 1884, he became second "Inspector" of the Rhenish Missionary Society. In 1889 he was made first "Inspector" (Foreign Secretary) of the Society. Dr. Schreiber represented his Society at the London Interdenominational Conferences of 1878 and 1888. He made extended visits to the fields of the Society in South Africa and the Dutch East Indies, and China. In 1900 he represented sixteen German Missionary societies at the Ecumenical Conference on Foreign Missions, held in New York. Many who were present at that Conference long carried in their memory the spare figure of Dr. Schreiber, with his bright, genial manner, and the lucid and effective method of his addresses, as he took part in several of the discussions of the Conference. Dr. Schreiber was a man of learning, of good judgment, and of the broadest sympathies. He believed in missions most heartily as the great practical proof of the vigor and, therefore, of the sincerity of Christendom.

SCHWARTZ, Christian Friedrich: Born in Sonnenburg, Prussia, October 28, 1726. Died February 13, 1798. At the age of twenty he went to the Halle University, where he became established in the faith of Christ, and resolved to devote himself wholly to Him. Dr. Schultz, who had left India from failure of health, was at this time preparing to print the Bible in Tamil, and advised Schwartz to learn that language in order to assist him. Professor Francke, hearing of his great success in acquiring the language, proposed to him to go as a missionary to India. He decided to go, declining an advantageous position in the ministry at home. He was ordained at Copenhagen, with the view of joining the Danish Mission at Tranquebar, where he arrived July 30, 1750. In four months he preached his first sermon in Tamil in the church of Ziegenbalg. From the first he devoted much time and attention to the religious instruction of the young.

In twelve years Schwartz had baptized 1,238 in the city. He labored also faithfully for the English garrison, for which no religious instruction was provided. The salary of £100 which he received as chaplain of the garrison, from the Madras Government, he devoted the first year to the building of a mission house and an English Tamil school, and afterward gave a large part of it in charity.

In 1776 he went to Tanjore to found a new mission, and here he spent the remaining twenty years of his life. Even in this favorite abode of the Hindus, where was the most splendid pagoda of India, he had great success, two churches having been established in 1780. He won the high esteem of the English Government, which employed him in important political transactions with the native princes. When the powerful and haughty Hyder Ali of Mysore refused to receive an embassy from the English, whom he distrusted, he said he would treat with them through Schwartz. "Send me the Christian," meaning Schwartz; "he will not deceive me." Urged by the government, he consented to undertake the mission. Through his intercession Cuddalore was saved from destruction by the savage hordes of the enemy. On his return a present of money was forced upon him by Hyder, which he gave to the English Government, requesting that it be applied to the building of an English orphan asylum in Tanjore. Tho a Mohammedan, Hyder's regard for Schwartz was so great that he issued orders to his officers, saying: "Let the venerable padre go about everywhere without hindrance, since he is a holy man, and will not injure me." While Hyder was ravaging the Carnatic with an army of a hundred thousand, and multitudes were fleeing in dismay to Tanjore, Schwartz moved about unmolested. In the famine caused by the war more than 800 starving people came daily to his door. He collected money and distributed provisions to Europeans and Hindus. He also built there a church for the Tamil congregation. The rajah a few hours before his death requested Schwartz to act as guardian to his adopted son Serfogee. The trust was accepted and faithfully discharged.

After a protracted and severe illness, during which he delighted to testify of Christ and to exhort the people, he expired in the arms of two of his native converts. At his funeral the effort to sing a hymn was suppressed by the noise of the wailing of the heathen, who thronged the premises. Serfogee lingered, weeping, at the coffin, covered it with a cloth of gold, and accompanied the body to the grave. The small chapel in which he was interred outside of the fort has been demolished, and a large one erected. The grave is behind the pulpit, covered with a marble slab bearing an English inscription—

> To the memory of the
> REV. CHRISTIAN FRIEDRICH SCHWARTZ;
> Born Sonnenburg, of Neumark, in the kingdom of Prussia,
> The 28th October, 1726,
> And died at Tanjore the 13th February, 1798,
> In the 72d year of his age.
> Devoted from his early manhood to the office of
> Missionary in the East,
> The similarity of his situation to that of
> The first preachers of the gospel
> Produced in him a peculiar resemblance to
> The simple sanctity of the
> Apostolic character.
> His natural vivacity won the affection
> As his unspotted probity and purity of life
> Alike commanded the reverence of the
> Christian, Mohammedan, and Hindu:
> For sovereign princes, Hindu and Mohammedan,
> Selected this humble pastor
> As the medium of political negotiation with
> The British Government;
> And the very marble that her records his virtues
> Was raised by
> The liberal affection and esteem of the
> Rajah of Tanjore,
> Maha Rajah Serfogee.

Another beautiful monument was erected to his memory by the East India Company in the Church of St. Mary, Madras, part of the inscription on which is as follows:

> On a spot of ground granted to him by the Rajah of Tanjore, two miles east of Tanjore, he built a house for his residence, and made it an Orphan Asylum. Here the last twenty years of his life were spent in the education and religious instruction of children, particularly those of indigent parents—whom he gratuitously maintained and instructed; and here, on the 13th of February, 1798, surrounded by his infant flock, and in the presence of several of his disconsolate brethren, he closed his truly Christian career in the 72d year of his age.

SCHWIFAT. See SHWIFAT.

SCIENCE; Contributions of Missions to: It has been the custom of the old and thoroughly established Mission Boards to send out, for the most part, only men of the broadest university training. These have gone into regions of the earth where educated Americans or Europeans have but seldom if ever penetrated. The earlier missionaries were in many countries, and in some sections of all countries, the pioneers. Not a few of these regions were entirely unexplored.

Moreover, the missionaries entered these countries for permanent residence. There they established their homes. They mastered the vernacular of the country and thus put at their disposal, to aid in their investigations, all the wisdom the people themselves possessed. In this way they became identified with the people and the country. The facilities of the missionaries, therefore, for careful, accurate, and continuous investigation of the scientific phenomena all about them were unsurpassed. Many missionaries have been in regular correspondence with the leading scientists, who have made suggestions which the missionaries have carried out, and in turn the missionaries have reported the results of their observations and investigations to scholars connected with American and European universities, who have sent back their interpretations.

The missionaries have not given their time and strength to scientific pursuits as an end in themselves. In some cases a particular branch of investigation has been the recreation of a hardworking missionary; in other cases, independent scientific investigation has been a part of the regular work in the training in the missionary colleges abroad, while in a majority of instances perhaps the most valuable scientific results have come from the observations and investigations made in the interests of positive missionary operations, or are the direct results of different phases of missionary work.

In this article space does not permit of citation to any extent of specific cases. Such exhaustive citations would greatly increase the value of the article, but it would also necessarily add to its length many fold. We can but state the facts, leaving the illustrations to be supplied by the reader.

Geography: Probably no other department of science owes more to the missionaries than does geography. The missionaries have been the pioneers in most countries. The interests of their work, as well as the necessity of making intelligent reports to their committees, boards and constituencies, demanded that accurate information be given regarding the physical condition of the countries occupied. The first communications of the exploring missionaries in all countries have been full of geographical data, which have necessarily been the beginning of all the concrete information we to-day possess about these countries.

Franciscan and Jesuit missionaries, more than six centuries ago, traveled through Central and Eastern Asia, and even into China, and described the topography of the country. They prepared the best maps of those countries then known. Spanish and Portuguese missionaries contributed much of the first knowledge of Africa and America. They wrote the first accounts of the Congo and Abyssinia. The Danish missionaries gave us our first and best accounts of Greenland and Iceland. It is impossible even to catalog the names of the societies and distinguished missionaries who, previous to the beginning of the 19th century, made large and important contributions to the science of Geography.

During the 19th century the missionaries have been not less active in their explorations. The Sandwich or Hawaiian Islands were opened to the world and explored and mapped out by them. The South Sea Islands are known to us largely through the initial work of missionaries who explored for the sake of missionary operations. Africa and Australia were first made known to the scientific world through the report of missionaries published in missionary magazines, in independent books or in the columns of the various geographical societies. The most valuable contributions to the geography of Syria were made by a missionary, and the interiors of Asia Minor, Mesopotamia and Persia were explored for us by resident missionaries. During the first half of the last century the world was introduced to India as a country, apart from its resistance to foreign invasion and its value to commerce, through the extended reports of missionaries regarding the country, its outlines, products and people. China was a missionary country in its first introduction to the world. In 1856, when the British fleet bombarded Canton, its action was directed by a map of the city and suburbs prepared by a missionary. The best work on China, which is still a classic on the Middle Kingdom, was prepared by a missionary.

Undoubtedly the files and libraries of the missionary societies which have been in operation for half a century or more contain a more abundant supply of facts regarding the countries of the world, outside of North America and Europe, than can be found in the non-missionary part of the archives of all the geographical societies taken together. The missionary societies in their regular periodicals have published much of this material, so that the foreign missionary magazines really belong in the libraries of the geographical societies.

Rev. Dr. William Adams, of New York, has said: "I believe more has been done in philology, geography, and ethnology indirectly by our missionaries than by all the Royal and National societies in the world that devote themselves exclusively to these objects." The Princeton Review says (Vol. 38, p. 622): "Our missionaries have rendered more real service to geography than all the geographical societies in the world." Carl Ritter, the prince of geographers, confessed that he could not have written his *magnum opus*, the *Erd Kunde*, without the aid and material collected and transmitted by missionaries. Mr. L. H. Morgan in his Preface of the Smithsonian Contributions to Knowledge, Vol. XVII, says: "No class of men have earned a higher reputation as scholars or philanthropists than our missionaries. Their contributions to history, ethnology, philology, geography and religious literature form their enduring monument." Mr. G. M. Powell, of the Oriental Topographical Corps, in a paper read before the American Institute, 1874, says: "Probably no source of knowledge in this department has been so vast, varied and prolific as the investigations and contributions of missionaries."

Philology: The study of the languages of the people to be evangelized is the first work of the missionary. The successful missionary may have but a slight knowledge of the geography or the history of the country, but he can accomplish little or nothing unless he makes himself master of the spoken vernacular. Language—and that of the people among whom he works—is the instrument by which the race is to be won. Hence Philology is also distinctly a missionary science.

In order to make missionary effort permanent, it has been necessary to reduce to writing all languages not so reduced, and to prepare grammars and lexicons of the same in order to teach the people themselves the proper and scientific use of their own tongue. Upon this basis a literature has been built up. This is the natural and only method of missionary conquest in every uncivilized country of the world.

The cases are few, indeed, where men other than missionaries have ever mastered an unwritten foreign tongue, reducing it to writing and preparing for it a grammar and lexicon. To mention the languages so reduced by missionaries would require more space than is allotted to this part of the subject. In the first six volumes of the *Journal of the American Oriental Society* out of a total of 2,927 pages 1,215 are filled by 47 missionaries, and that, too, chiefly as to subjects connected with philology. Prof. Whitney, in his *Language and the Study of Language,* says: "The extraordinary activity of missions in Africa within a few years has directed study towards African dialects. A great mass of material has been collected and examined sufficiently to give a general idea of the distribution of races in this continent."

Next to the value of discovering and crystallizing the language of a people in a scientific classification and arrangement, is the production of a common literature in the spoken tongue. In this way dialectic differences in the language spoken by the same races in different parts of the same country have been broken down and the spoken tongue of the entire race has been unified. The philological unification of races and nations by the production of a general Christian literature in a pure form and in the spoken language of the masses of the people, has been one of the greatest scientific triumphs of the last century of modern missions. It has unified the people, made wider and more general literature possible, and opened the way for the scientific classification of the languages themselves. Comparative philology owes far more to the work of missionaries than to any other class of people. They are the masters of the science.

Ethnology: The missionary has been the discoverer of peoples. For this he was commissioned and sent out into strange lands. The limits of this article would be exceeded if an attempt were made to even enumerate and briefly describe the different races that have been introduced to the world, studied, and classified by foreign missionaries. The very work the missionary is sent to accomplish has compelled him to do this. No one else has ever had such opportunities for observation and study and no one else has been impelled to this work by such a permanent incentive. Whenever a missionary hears of a strange and unknown race or people, there he is immediately drawn. He cannot cease from his study until he learns all he can of the physical, mental, social, moral and religious characteristics of the people in his new found field of observation and operation. The chances are that he will take up his residence in the midst of that people and give his life to understanding them, in order that he may adapt to their peculiar conditions and needs the Gospel of Jesus Christ.

If we should eliminate from our English literature all that has been inspired and written by foreign missionaries in the line of descriptions of the peoples of Africa, Asia, South America, parts of Europe, and the islands of the seas, we would quickly discover how little remains upon which we can place any dependence. The missionaries have been the collectors of data, patiently recording the facts as they observed them. It has fallen to the lot of others to collect, classify, and compare this large array of material and draw conclusions more far-reaching than those reached by many missionaries. The individual missionary has observed and dealt with one, two or may be three different races or people. Beyond them his personal observations have not extended, but within these he stands without a peer. The results of his studies are given to the world and from this data the most of our knowledge of the races of the world has come. Ethnology and Philology are kindred sciences, and both, in a peculiar sense, are missionary sciences, owing almost everything to the discoveries of the missionaries.

Natural History and Geology: The contributions of missionaries to the sciences of Geology, Botany, and Natural History have been considerable. By the aid of native students extensive collections of specimens have been made, some of which can be found in the best known museums of the world. A missionary prepared the best existing work on the flora of Syria; and the collections of fresh-water mollusks of the Hawaiian Islands, which stands to-day as the most valuable collection of its kind in the world, was made by a missionary. The same is true of a collection of the moths and butterflies of Japan. Another missionary received an honorary degree for distinguished researches in geology in the Balkan Peninsula.

Archæology: Missionaries not a few have become archæologists of no little repute. There are few museums in Europe and America that do not possess objects discovered by missionaries, and in many cases these finds have been interpreted by them and given to the world. In the last fifty years a greater part of the archæological discoveries of Asia Minor have been made by missionaries who have been residents there. As discoverers of rock inscriptions, ancient cities, coins, cylinders, manuscripts, and an endless variety of other objects, all of which have a distinct archæological value, the missionaries have a place uniquely their own.

They have had facilities for doing this that is enjoyed by no one else. With their residence in the country, having under their tuition a large number of young men in collegiate training, and compelled in the regular routine of their operations to cross and recross the country by unfrequented routes, it is not strange that they should learn of the existence of inscriptions, manuscripts, and ruins, and should take pains to visit the same and make careful record of all they discovered. As soon as the people become acquainted with the fact that the missionaries are interested in these things, they bring all sorts of portable antiquities to them and report to them the location of what cannot be transported. In multitudes of cases antiquities which the natives, for superstitious reasons, conceal from a stranger seeking them, are freely exhibited to the missionary, who is well known and thoroughly trusted. There is no doubt that the contributions of missionaries to the archæological wealth and knowledge of the world are large and valuable.

Medical Science: The practise of medicine has constituted an important part of the missionary operations of all the regular Mission Boards. This has been especially true in the pioneer work of those societies. For the Medical Department of mission operations the best trained physicians, both men and women, have been sent out. These have opened dispensaries, built and equipped hospitals, and conducted a general medical practise among the natives of all countries where mission work has been carried on during the last century. The initial development of the modern science of medicine in China, Japan, India, Turkey, Africa, and the Pacific Islands has been accomplished almost entirely by the missionaries.

Medical schools have been opened and conducted according to modern principles of medical and surgical practise, and the youth of those countries have been taught the science and are to-day, by the thousands, practising the same among their own people. To accomplish this, text-books have been prepared in the vernacular of the people for the use of students not familiar with the English language. In connection with the mission hospitals, training classes for training native nurses have been opened and they constitute one of the popular departments of medical work.

Medical missionaries, owing to their location among hitherto unknown people and in climatic conditions unknown to the medical fraternity of England, Germany, France, and the United States, have made extended and continuous observations upon diseases that are entirely unknown in the countries mentioned. The reports of these observations have been widely published in the medical journals, and have added materially to the sum total of medical knowledge. While studying unknown diseases the missionary physicians have also sought for proper remedies in the countries themselves, and in cases not a few they have been eminently successful. It is well known that not a few of the common remedies now in constant use in our most civilized countries were discovered by medical missionaries and given to the world. Medical work has now been so thoroughly established that the work of the foreign medical missionary is now supplemental, and in some countries is taken up and carried on in a large measure by thoroughly trained native physicians.

Social Science: The social-settlement method of reaching certain classes of people in our larger cities is the application to English and American life of foreign missionary methods of operation that have been in vogue ever since that work began. The foreign missionary enters upon the work for life, and is usually located in a section of country where he is expected to devote his life to the civilization, education, and Christianization of the native peoples all about him. The missionary establishes his home among these people to whose elevation he has given his life. His home becomes a well-recognized place of refuge for those who want sympathy, comfort and instruction. The natives come and go freely. The missionary identifies himself with the life of the people, with their politics, and their ambitions and trials. They learn to recognize him as one who is interested in whatever interests them and as suffering under conditions that bring afflictions upon them. In famine and plague, in war, pestilence, and massacre, the missionary remains at his post, and not infrequently lays down his life in his endeavor to shield and help the people whom he serves. Civilized countries seldom witness such examples of self-surrender carried to such conclusions as we witness to-day in actual operation in every country of the world where foreign missionaries are operating. They were the pioneers of this method of reaching a people, and by them the science has been marvelously developed during the past century. In the face of what missionaries have done and are accomplishing by this means, our American and English operations seem but child's play, and the results obtained almost too meager for record. Missionaries are the masters of this science, and are in a position to demonstrate its value to the world. Because of the circumstances here outlined, questions of class, caste, poverty and wealth, employer and employed and, in fact, all questions that arise in the social life of various peoples, come before the missionaries and compel to some practical solution. They constantly aim to change for the better all social conditions and to set in operation forces that will eventuate in a completely reformed society.

Dr. James S. Dennis embodies extended observations and research in this line in his masterly work, *Christian Missions and Social Progress.* He says: "It may not be in harmony with the current naturalistic theories of social evolution, yet it is the open secret of missionary experience that the humble work of missions is a factor in the social progress of the world which it would be intellectual dishonesty to ignore and philosophic treason to deny. The entrance of missions into the modern life of ancient peoples is a fact of the highest historic, as well as ethical and religious, significance. They are the heralds of a new era of beneficent progress to the less favored nations of the earth. The social scientist who discounts Christian missions as of no special import is strangely oblivious to a force which has wrought with benign energy and unexampled precision in the production of the best civilization we have yet seen in the history of mankind."

Diplomacy: The missionaries' part in shaping the diplomatic relations now existing between the civilized and the non-civilized countries of the world has been large and important. In most cases missionaries have preceded the consul, minister, and ambassador. When later the official representative of the missionary's government appeared, the missionary of long residence, not infrequently well versed in the language and conditions of the country, has been compelled to advise, in no small measure, the official representative of his country and, in fact, shape the diplomatic relations of the two countries. The Protestant missionary influence in the settlement of diplomatic questions, and in the drafting of treaties for the control of future relationship, has always been conciliatory and liberal. They have been from the beginning, and in all countries not a few are to-day, confidential and trusted advisers of the accredited representatives of the great powers in delicate international questions. As much of the diplomatic influence of the missionary has been in the rôle of confidential adviser, it would be most undiplomatic to make any public record of the same, but it is safe to state that the work of the missionaries in aid of wise and conservative diplomatic relations among the nations of the world, civilized and uncivilized, has been emphatic and invaluable.

Philanthropy: The missionary's legitimate profession is not one that is primarily philanthropic in any limited use of the term. He does not take up his residence in distant, unknown countries for the purpose of distributing charity to the people who seem to be in need of it. And yet, during the last century of modern missionary enterprise, probably no one class of philanthropists have been called upon to administer larger relief funds than have the foreign missionaries. Famine and pestilence, plague, war, and massacre have, at different times, swept over countries where missionaries have been living, and they were the only trustworthy people upon the ground both able and willing to distribute the funds that were raised abroad for the relief of the suffering people. Consequently, missionaries have so systematized methods of benevolence as to reduce to a minimum the pauperizing effect of the same upon the people who received the aid. They have undoubtedly demonstrated to the world that relief funds can be distributed to a people desperately in need, while leaving upon the people the impression that the aid received has been earned by their own labors. The science of philanthropy must be studied largely from the standpoint of the experiences of the foreign missionary, in order to be understood in its widest and most important relations to the moral character of the people and the fullest development of industry and thrift.

Comparative Religion: One of the chief studies of missionaries has been the religions of the people among whom they live. As they have been sent out to change the religion of the people, and to lead them to accept Christianity in place of that which they had, it is clear that, in order to accomplish this, the missionaries must understand, as far as possible, their present beliefs and religious practises. All missionaries have not given the same attention to the investigation of the religious beliefs of the people for whom they are to work. But many of the most intelligent and observing of the missionaries of the leading Boards of the world, by a careful study of whatever religious literature the people may possess, by most painstaking observations of their religious customs and habits and by continual inquiries of the most intelligent devotees, have gathered together a mass of thoroughly trustworthy material that has become the basis for the general science of religion.

There are many tribes and races whose religion would not be known now were it not for the information given by missionaries living among them. The fundamental beliefs and practises of the great ethnic religions would be little known today were it not for the mass of information furnished by the missionaries who have given a lifetime, even to the second and third generation, to a thorough and exhaustive study of these religions, upon the ground and amid their daily practises. The results of these studies and observations have not always been gathered into book form, but they have been more frequently embodied in letters and reports, and in articles published in missionary, scientific, and popular magazines, and other periodicals. It is not exaggeration to say that missionary literature has done more for general education, in the line of the religious practises and beliefs of the people of the world, than all other sources combined. In fact, it is impossible for this subject to be studied now with any degree of thoroughness and accuracy without the free use of the material furnished by the missionaries. One has but to glance through missionary articles in the magazines, as well as books they have published, to be convinced of the measureless value of the contributions of foreign missionaries to the science of Comparative Religion.

But space will not permit a citation of individual cases. In short, educated missionaries in all parts of the world during the last century have been active and valued contributors to nearly every scientific subject that has attracted the attention of the scholars of the last century.

SCOTLAND; Missions in the Presbyterian Churches of: These will be considered under the four heads, viz.:

1. Established Church: Committee for the Propagation of the Gospel in Foreign Parts, especially in India. Headquarters, 22 Queen St., Edinburgh, Scotland.
2. United Free Church of Scotland: Foreign Mission Committee. Headquarters, 15 North Bank St., Edinburgh, Scotland.
3. United Original Secession Synod: Foreign Mission Committee. Headquarters, Shawlands, Glasgow, Scotland.
4. Reformed Presbyterian Church of Scotland and Ireland: Foreign Missions Committee. Headquarters, Paisley, Scotland.

General History: In contrast to Luther, John Knox, in the first confession of the Church of Scotland (1560), recognized the message of missions. In 1647 the General Assembly recorded the desire for "a more firm consociation for propagating it (the Gospel) to those who are without, especially the Jews," and on the occasion of the Scotch expedition to Darien (1699) the assembly counseled the ministers who went with it to labor among the heathen. Ten years later, the Society in Scotland for Propagating Christian Knowledge was founded, having chiefly in mind the needs of the Highlands. Later it enlarged its scope somewhat to include work in America, Africa, and India. In 1724 Robert Millar, a Presbyterian minister in Paisley, published a History of the Propagation of Christianity and the Overthrow of Paganism, in which he urged prayer as the first of nine means for the conversion of the heathen world. Then came the first Secession in 1733, followed by that of the Relief Church in 1761, while, in the meantime (1746), there went from Scotland and England to America the plea for united prayer.

The effect of Carey's sermons and the formation of the BMS and the LMS was manifest at once in Scotland, when two societies were organized in 1796, the Scottish (later called the Edinburgh) Society and the Glasgow Society. In both of them the Established and Secession churches were represented, and to the Scottish Society belongs the honor of sending out the first martyr missionary of modern times, Peter Greig, a gardener, and a member of the Secession Church of Donibristle, Inver-Keithing, who was murdered in the Fulah country in West Africa. The same society undertook a mission to the Tatars at Karass, in the Caucasus. This was stopped by the Russian Government, and the Society turned its attention to India and the West Indies, afterward, in 1835 and 1847, transferring them to the Established and the United churches, and passing out of separate existence. The Glasgow Society joined the Scottish Society in Sierra Leone, but not successfully, and in 1821 it started a work in Kafraria, which developed well. At the time of the Voluntary Controversy (1837) two presbyteries were formed, of which one, in 1844, joined the Free Church, and the other, in 1847, the United Church.

1. Missions of the Established Church of Scotland: While the Scottish (Edinburgh and Glasgow) Societies were carrying on their work, tho not very effectively, a strong effort was made, led by Thos. Chalmers and Dr. Inglis, to secure action by the Church. In 1825, Dr. Inglis, then convener, succeeded in persuading the General Assembly to appoint a foreign mission committee of ten men, but little interest was aroused until in 1829, when, largely through the influence of Chalmers, Alexander Duff was sent to Calcutta as headmaster of an educational institution of which Dr. Inglis had succeeded in persuading the Assembly to approve. From that time the interest increased. In 1835 the Mission established by the Scottish Society in Western India by John Wilson, J. Murray Mitchell, and others was taken over by the Church Mission, and on the earnest appeal of Duff work was commenced in Madras. In 1843 came the Disruption, and the entire body of missionaries, led by Duff and Wilson, gave in their allegiance to the Free Church. Thus the Established Church found itself with a large amount of property and one missionary—a lady. As soon as possible others were sent out, and before long the institutions in the three presidencies were running on the same basis as before. In 1874 the Church commenced work in East Africa, and in 1878 in China.

1. *India:* From 1845 until the Mutiny, the work in India was confined chiefly to the three centers in Calcutta, Madras, and Bombay. Then, however, as with other societies, a new impulse was given, and stations were opened in the Punjab, and afterward in Independent Sikkim, on the border of Tibet. This last work has been carried on in close affiliation with a missionary association of the four Scotch universities. The work at Bombay was afterward given up, and the educational work of higher grade developed in Calcutta, Madras, and Sialkot.

The report (1903) shows 26 missionaries (not including wives) of the Church Board and 38 of the Women's Association, a total of 64; 189 native workers (aside from teachers), 17 stations, 2,309 communicants, 3 colleges, and 185 schools, with 8,187 scholars.

2. *Africa:* In response to the earnest appeal from Livingstone the Established Church started a mission at Blantyre, south of Lake Nyasa, in 1874. Other stations near by were also occupied, and in 1884 Domasi and Zomba, while in 1901 work was commenced in the Kiku'yu country, British East Africa. In the African missions special emphasis is laid upon medical and industrial work. The report shows 25 missionaries (of both boards), 57 native workers, 623 communicants, 35 schools with 10,446 scholars.

3. *China:* A mission started in China at I-chang in 1878 has (1903) in 4 stations, 8 missionaries, 15 native workers, 857 communicants, 6 schools with 218 scholars.

The Church also has a Colonial Committee, which provides chaplains for a number of communities in Europe, as well as in the colonies; and a Jewish Mission Committee, which conducts schools in Alexandria, Beirut, Constantinople, Smyrna, and Salonica; 10 in all, with 2,337 scholars.

Church of Scotland Women's Association for Foreign Missions: In 1837 a Ladies' Association for Foreign Missions, including Zenana work, was organized. This afterward became "The Scottish Ladies' Association for the Advancement of Female Education in India;" then, in 1883, "The Church of Scotland Ladies' Association for Foreign Missions." More recently the above title has been adopted. The Association works in connection with the Church Foreign Mission Committee, employing 49 missionaries, 17 assistants, 134 native teachers, 28 Bible women, 9 nurses, and 59 other agents. It has 3,316 pupils on the rolls of 51 schools, and carries on medical work in all the fields occupied by the Church Missions.

2. *Missions of the United Free Church of Scotland. A. The Free Church:* Immediately upon the organization of the new body the missionaries set about reestablishing their work. A merchant in America sent Duff £500, a physician in Calcutta gave him £500, and other large gifts followed, and by January 4, 1845, he had a larger school building than before, free of debt, and more pupils—1,257. As gifts came to him he sought to share them with the mission stations in Bombay and Madras, but they were not needed. Even before reaching Scotland on his furlough, Wilson wrote: "We must enlarge our work," and a new mission was established at Nagpur, to which a British official in Madras gave £500. Soon after (1844) the Committee took over the South African Mission of the Glasgow Society. At a time when the resources of the Free Churches were strained to the utmost to provide for home needs they gave more liberally to missions than ever before. The very next year the gifts of the Free Church alone exceeded those of the entire church before the Disruption by about £3,600, and there has been a steady advance since.

In India, to the work in Calcutta, Bombay, and Madras was added Nagpur, with Hislop College, on a par with the institutions in the other cities, and a work among the Santals of Bengal. In Arabia the Society took charge of the Keith Falconer Mission at Aden (Sheikh Othman). In Africa it added to its work in Kafraria, received from the Glasgow Society, work in Natal and among the tribes of Lake Nyasa. It established a mission in Syria, shared with the Presbyterians of Canada work in the New Hebrides, while not neglecting work at home, on the Continent of Europe, among the English communities, and for the Jews in numerous cities of the Levant. In 1900 the Free Church joined the United Presbyterian Church in the United Free Church of Scotland, and the mission work of the united body was put in the hands of a committee of the General Assembly, representing each branch.

B. United Presbyterian Church of Scotland: In 1847 the Secession and Relief Churches united in the United Presbyterian Church of Scotland, with the exception of a few churches which retained their organization as the United Original Secession Church.

The first mission undertaken was that started by the Scottish Society in Jamaica in 1835, which had already developed so that the colored people inaugurated a work for their fellows in Africa, and helped to found the Calabar Mission on the

West Coast; and in Trinidad, where two stations were occupied. The division in the Presbytery of South Africa, started by the Glasgow Society, had resulted in one section joining the Free Church in 1844, and the other, on the organization of the United Church in 1847, identified itself with that movement. The events of the Mutiny in India (1857) led the Church to open work in Rajputana and the Northwest (United) Provinces. It prospered from the beginning, and the founding of the first station, Beawar, was followed by that of Nasirabad (1861), Ajmere (1862), Todgarh (1863), Jaipur (1866), and several others. The next step was into China. A medical missionary of the UP Church worked (1862-1870) in Ningpo, and then Dr. Alex. Williamson opened a station at Chi-fu. The great work of the Church in Eastern Asia, however, has been that in Manchuria, commenced by Rev. John Ross and Rev. John MacIntyre in 1873. The first stations, Newchwang, Hai-chung, and Liáo-yang, were followed by Mukden and several others. The work in China proper was given up that this might be strengthened. Japan also was entered in 1863, but on the organization of the United Church of Christ in Japan, and in view of the presence of so many other societies, the Church withdrew its force and focused its efforts on other fields.

C. *The United Free Church.* 1. *India:* The five missions, Bengal (with its Sarital branch), Western India, Nagpur, Madras, and Rajputana, report (1903) 158 missionaries, 257 native workers, 28 organized churches, 114 outstations, 3,076 communicants. The educational work shows 4 colleges, with 1,871 students, and 344 other schools, 899 teachers, 17,485 scholars. The colleges are Duff College, at Calcutta; Wilson College, at Bombay; Hislop College, at Nagpur, and the Madras College. There are 21 medical missionaries, with 66 assistants, 232 hospital beds, and 24 dispensaries. Over 160,000 individual cases were treated, while the number reached by preaching was over 420,000. The mission has fallen heir to a branch of the work founded by Carey in the old Dutch town of Chinsurah, and finds much encouragement in its work among the Santals and in the village districts of the other fields. Special reference is made to the excellent results of the addresses by Drs. Barrows, Fairbairn, and Cuthbert Hall, especially among the students. A feature of the Scotch Missions in India has always been the attention paid to the preparation and dissemination of Christian literature. Dr. Murdoch, as Secretary of the Madras Branch of the Christian Literature Society and the Madras Religious Tract Society, reports the issues of both societies for the year as nearly 2,500,000, while £5,608 ($28,000) was realized from the sale of books.

2. *Arabia:* The Mission in South Arabia, founded by the Hon. Ion Keith Falconer at Sheikh Othman, Aden, in 1885, works especially among the Mohammedans and Somalis in the vicinity, but has done good work for Galla captives released from the slavers. There are reported 3 missionaries and 5 native workers. The work is still, to a considerable degree, pioneer in its character, and the small number of conversions (7 communicants) has not warranted the organization of a church. The school, with its 16 pupils, is a nucleus for good; but the great evangelistic work is in the medical department, in which 4,600 patients were treated by the 2 medical missionaries and 2 assistants, while the audiences at the medical services numbered nearly 20,000.

3. *China:* The Manchuria Mission suffered heavily during the Boxer outbreak, but chiefly in the general disturbance of work. The missionaries in Hai-cheng, Liao-yang, Mukden, Kai-yuen, Lie-ling, and Mai-mai-kai reached New-chwang in safety, while those in Ashiho escaped to Vladivostock. The two native pastors escaped, tho several evangelists and a large number of the native Christians lost their lives. Churches, hospitals, mission houses, schools, and a great many private homes were destroyed, and there was much suffering, as well as complete disorganization of work. With the return of peace the missionaries were able to go back to their stations, and, after two years, the work has resumed its normal character. In the fall of 1902 the severe trial of the Church was followed by a special spiritual revival, with a new spirit of consecration.

The report (1903) shows 37 missionaries, 97 native workers, 12 organized churches, 75 outstations, 5,994 communicants. The college at Mukden has 106 students, including 16 in the theological department, and in 30 other schools there are 349 pupils. In the medical department the 10 missionaries and 8 assistants treated over 4,000 cases, reaching nearly twice that number by their services.

The future of this mission will be watched with much interest as Russian power in Manchuria grows stronger.

4. *Africa:* (1) South Africa, including 3 missions: Kafraria, Transkei, and Natal.

The first Scotch missionaries to South Africa accompanied a Glasgow colony in 1821, and started work on the Chumie River. In less than two years five Kafirs were baptized, and the work progressed, new stations being occupied, the most important being Lovedale (1830). In 1844 came the transference of the work to the Free Church, and every department received a new impulse. The Kafir war (1846) broke up the mission temporarily, but a new start was made and after some years two missions were formed: Kafraria, south of the Kei River, while that on the North was called the Transkei Mission. Still later (1847), in response to a special appeal from Dr. Duff, who visited the field, another mission was established in Natal. Among the important stations are Kafraria, Lovedale, Burnshill, Pirie, Macfarlan, etc.; Transkei, Cunningham, Paterson, Buchanan, etc.; Natal, Pietermaritzburg, Impolmeni, Gordon Memorial, etc.

The best known work of these missions is that of the Lovedale institution, which has furnished the model or the inspiration for a great many efforts in mission lands to develop industrial training in the Christian communities. Its principal, Rev. Robert Stewart, D.D., has been a leader in this department of mission activity. Lovedale, however, is far more than a mere industrial school. It is a college and a theological seminary as well, and being distinctively non-sectarian, it is a great power in all the mission fields of South Africa. The kindred institution at Blythswood, in the Transkei Mission, was established at the earnest request of the natives, who themselves contributed £4,500 for it.

The three missions reported (1903) 96 missionaries, 146 native workers, 28 organized churches, 32 outstations, 14,895 communicants,

262 schools, with 13,062 pupils. The Lovedale Institute has 830 pupils, and the Blythswood 219. Medical work is carried on to some extent, but not to the degree as in India and China.

(2) *West Africa. Old Calabar Mission:* In 1846 the Rev. Hope M. Waddell, with three associates, commenced work at Creek Town, under the auspices of the United Presbyterian Church, but specially representing the negroes of Jamaica. To some extent the hope that the West Indies would conduct this work has been realized, but the control of it came into the hands of the Scotch Society, and in the union with the Free Church it became a part of the united work. The first missionaries were made welcome by the native chiefs, reduced the language (Efik) to writing, established schools, and despite the fact that the section is one of the hardest for evangelistic work in Africa, there has been good success. There are (1903) 41 missionaries, 36 native workers, 8 organized churches, 13 outstations, 750 communicants, 32 schools, with 611 scholars. There is a training institution, with 114 pupils, and medical work is represented by 2 physicians, 4 assistants, and 4 dispensaries.

(3) *Central Africa. Livingstonia Mission:* In 1875 the Free Church responded to the appeal of Dr. Livingstone by sending a band of missionaries to occupy the lands around Lake Nyasa and half way north to Lake Tanganyika. The first settlement was made at Cape Maclear. The Livingstonia Institution was later removed to Kondowi, a more eligible site. The mission extended to Bandawe, Karonga, and particularly into Ngoniland, among a tribe of Bantus. Notwithstanding the wild character of the people there has been exceptional success in the work. There were (1903) 32 missionaries, 4 native workers, 7 organized churches, 2,027 communicants, 207 schools, with 15,765 scholars. The medical work is more fully developed than in the other Africa missions, and with excellent results.

5. *New Hebrides Mission:* Here the United Free Church reports as its share of the work of the Synod 4 missionaries, 2 native pastors, 3 churches, 7 outstations, 168 communicants, 30 schools, 348 scholars.

6. *West Indies.* (1) *Jamaica:* The first work of the United Presbyterian Church in 1847 was to take over from the Scottish Missionary Society the work commenced in Jamaica in 1835, and which had already developed until four stations were occupied. The work suffered from pestilence, hurricanes, etc., and for some little time was not pressed, owing to the demands in other fields. With the impulse to work in West Africa, there came new life into the mission, and the report (1903) shows 37 missionaries, 29 native workers, 64 organized churches, 22 outstations, 12,066 communicants, 64 schools, 7,130 scholars. There is a complete church organization, including 6 presbyteries, and the work is scarcely foreign mission work, except in its history.

(2) *Trinidad:* This island was first occupied in 1835 at Port-of-Spain. Later stations were opened at Arouca and San Fernando. There were (1903) 4 missionaries, 1 native pastor, 4 churches, 668 communicants.

In 1839 the Free Church sent some missionaries to Syria, who located at Shweir in the Lebanon, and developed a considerable educational work in connection with the Lebanon Schools Society. In 1901 this work was transferred to the Presbyterian Church (North) in the U. S. A., tho Dr. Carslaw remains on the roll of missionaries of the United Free Church.

Women's Foreign Mission of the United Free Church of Scotland: Headquarters, 15 North Bank St., Edinburgh. The Woman's Foreign Missionary Society of the Free Church of Scotland, organized in 1843 to carry on the work begun by the Ladies' Society for Female Education in India and Africa in 1837; the United Presbyterian Church of Scotland Zenana Mission (1880), and the Ladies' Kaffrarian Society, originally organized (1839) in connection with the Glasgow Society, have all been merged in the United Free Church in the one society, with title as above.

III. *The United Original Secession Church:* Headquarters, Shawlands, Glasgow, Scotland. The few churches that declined to join the United Presbyterian Church in 1847 established in 1872 a station at Seoni, in the Central Provinces of India. They report (1901) 3 missionaries, 20 native workers, 3 outstations, 20 communicants, 2 schools, 325 scholars.

IV. *Reformed Presbyterian Church of Scotland:* Headquarters, Paisley, Scotland. A few churches preserving the principles of the Covenanter Church have joined with the Reformed Presbyterian Synod of Ireland in the conduct of mission work in Syria.

SCOTLAND; NATIONAL BIBLE SOCIETY OF: Headquarters, 5 St. Andrew Square, Edinburgh, Scotland. The National Bible Society of Scotland was formed by the union, in 1861, of the Edinburgh and the Glasgow Bible societies, founded respectively in 1809 and 1812, together with other leading Bible societies of Scotland.

The Society carries on a large work both at home and in foreign countries. The Home Mission supplies large numbers of the Scriptures annually at reduced rates to the poor and to various missionary and benevolent associations; it circulates the Gaelic Bible throughout the Highlands and islands of Scotland and in the regions of North America where Gaelic is spoken, and aids the distribution of the Scriptures in Ireland. As a Colonial Mission it distributes the Scriptures throughout all the British colonies and dependencies. As a Continental Mission it works in nearly all European countries.

As a more distinctively Foreign Mission the National Bible Society of Scotland publishes in the vernacular and distributes by means of colporteurs the Scriptures in Africa, China, India, Japan, South America, and Turkey. It has distributed thousands of Scriptures among the Tatar tribes of Mongolia, and it was the first to establish regular colportage in Korea.

The Society has recently published the Bible in the Efik for Old Calabar, Africa; the New Testament in one of the Malay dialects and in Chinyanja, the language spoken by 500,000 in Central Africa; translations in the Tannese (New Hebrides), Motuan (New Guinea), and Mandarin (China) are also in preparation, and the Society has had its share in the Japanese version of the Scriptures, and in the Wen-li version in China.

This Society has not carried on its work chiefly through specially appointed agents, but has worked in connection with the various missionary societies, finding this method productive of good results, especially in view of the principle and practise of allowing its colporteurs to circulate unsectarian tracts together with the Scriptures in

Roman Catholic and heathen countries. It was, however, the first Society to appoint a special agent for Japan, Mr. Robert Lilley, who served there for ten years, and it has taken a prominent share in the arrangements by which the three Bible Societies of England, Scotland, and America carry on the work there conjointly. The circulation for 1902 was:

	Bibles.	Testaments.	Portions.	Total.
Foreign	42,382	112,828	788,605	943,815
Colonies	15,942	7,585	1,432	24,959
Home	66,331	55,166	29,119	150,566
Total	124,655	175,529	819,156	1,119,340

More than half the entire distribution was in China, 562,869, the great majority being portions. Next to China came India, 112,089; Japan, 48,844, while in Germany, 56,213 were distributed, and in Spain, 33,281.

SCOTTISH EPISCOPAL CHURCH, Foreign Mission Agency: Formerly the Episcopal Church of Scotland collected funds for the Church of England Missionary Societies, but upon the consecration of Bishop Cotterill as Bishop of Edinburgh the contributions of the churches in the seven Scottish dioceses were devoted to missions in India and South Africa through their own Society—"The Board of Foreign Missions of the Scottish Episcopal Church," the new form of their "Association for Foreign Missions." The SPG even went so far as to hand over to the Scottish Society contributions from Scotland over and above a fixed amount each year. This latter arrangement, however, was annulled in 1900. Bishop Cotterill, having labored as a missionary of the CMS in India for twelve years, and for another twelve in South Africa—Kaffraria—where he had been consecrated bishop, felt a peculiar interest in those two fields of his former efforts, and organized a permanent union with them. This board sends out contributions every year to Kaffraria for the general purposes of the diocese of Independent Kaffraria, now called St. John's, and also many sums to be devoted to special objects in connection with the various churches and schools there. The Board also provides the funds necessary for the maintenance of the missionary schools at Chanda, in Central India, which are under the direction of the Bishop of Calcutta, and forwards sums entrusted to it for any mission work being carried on by the Church of England, or any Church in communion with her.

SCOTTISH MISSION INDUSTRIES COMPANY (1903): This is not a missionary society nor a benevolent society in any sense. It is a joint stock company organized by friends of the UFS, with a capital of $50,000 ($30,000 paid in), established in order to foster industries in mission fields, by which famine orphans and persecuted converts may find a livelihood. It is not in any sense a training school, employing those whom the missions have already trained. The stockholders will receive 5 per cent. interest on their stock, and they are pledged, after a reserve has been established equaling one-half of the paid-up capital, to have all surplus profits paid over to the UFS.

Of course only such business as promises return will be taken up. The Company has commenced operations by undertaking the working of the UFS presses at Poona and Ajmere in India, which will be conducted on a business basis.

SCUDDER, Henry Martyn: Dr. Scudder was the son of the famous pioneer missionary, Rev. John Scudder, M.D., and was born on the Island of Ceylon, February 5, 1822. After graduating at New York University in 1840 and Union Seminary in 1843, he was appointed missionary of the ABCFM, and embarked, with his wife, for Madras, India, May 6, 1844. The *Missionary Herald* stated at the time that "this is the first instance in which the son of a missionary has been sent forth as a preacher to the heathen." He was connected with the Madras Mission till 1851, when, after his exploration of the Arcot district, he was assigned to work there, his medical skill giving him facility of access to the people. The Arcot Mission was detached from the Madras Mission in 1853, and was carried on wholly by the Scudder family, consisting of five brothers and their wives and one sister. In 1857 this mission was transferred to the Board of the Reformed Dutch Church. In 1864 Dr. Scudder returned to America, and was pastor of prominent churches in San Francisco, Brooklyn, and Chicago. In 1887 he joined his son and daughter in Japan and here he rendered excellent service for three years. He died at Winchester, Mass., June 4, 1895. He was a man of great abilities, of fine address, and of commanding power in the pulpit.

SCUDDER, John: Born at Freehold, N. J., September 13, 1798; graduated at the College of New Jersey in 1811, and at the College of Physicians and Surgeons of New York City in 1815. While in professional attendance on a lady in New York he took up in the anteroom and read the tract, *The Conversion of the World*, by which he was led to give his life to the missionary work. He sailed June 8, 1819, under the ABCFM, for Ceylon. He was ordained in 1821 by the brethren of the Mission, Baptist and Wesleyan missionaries taking part in the service. In 1836 he was transferred to Madras to found a new mission with Dr. Winslow. From 1842 to 1846 he was in the United States. In 1854, his health having failed, he went by medical advice to the Cape of Good Hope. When on the point of returning to Madras he was stricken with apoplexy, and died at Wynberg, South Africa, January 13, 1855, having been in the missionary work 36 years. He was constant in labors, devoting much time to evangelistic itinerancy. In his visit to America in 1843 he addressed a hundred thousand children. His eight sons, two grandsons, and two granddaughters have been members of the Arcot Mission in India.

SCUDDER, John, Jr., M.D.: Born October 29, 1835. Died May 23, 1900. Dr. Scudder came to America from Ceylon, where his parents resided, to obtain his education, studying first at Hudson, Ohio, where he united with the church, and at once determined to give his life to the missionary work. He graduated from Rutgers College in 1857, and from the Theological Seminary at New Brunswick in 1860. He was licensed to preach and ordained the same year. He received his medical degree from the Long Island Medical College, and the degree of Doctor of Divinity from Rutgers College in 1896. Having early in life decided upon his course, he had Christian service in foreign lands in view during his college life, and when he left this country as a missionary of the RCA he was well equipped for his work.

In 1861 Dr. Scudder sailed for India, arriving on the field in July. He labored successively as follows: Chittur, 1861-1863; Arni, 1863-1865;

Arcot, 1865-1876; Vellore, 1876-1877. In 1878, with Mrs. Scudder, he returned to America, after seventeen years of continuous service on the field, and took up his residence for four years in Nebraska. In 1882, returning to India, Mrs. Scudder following a year later, Dr. Scudder was stationed as follows: Arni, 1882-1885; Tindivanum, 1885-1892, building there the commodious mission house and church; Vellore, 1892-1894. In this latter year he and Mrs Scudder made their second journey to America, taking up their residence for three years in New Brunswick. In 1897 Dr. and Mrs. Scudder returned to India and were again stationed at Vellore. It was in connection with this portion of the field that Dr. Scudder's last work was done. Dr. Scudder's children have, with a single exception, followed his footsteps into the ministry, and three of them into missionary service.

SCUDDER, William W.: Born in 1823. Died March 4, 1895. Son of Dr. John Scudder, who gave seven sons and two daughters to the mission work in India. Coming to this country in his boyhood, he was converted during a revival in Springfield, Mass., in the winter of 1835-36. In 1839 he united with the Presbyterian church at Elizabeth, N. J. Entering the College of New Jersey, at Princeton, he graduated in 1841. Then, entering the Theological Seminary at that place, he pursued the regular course of study for two years. By special permission, he devoted the third year to studies most adapted to fit him for the missionary work. In 1846 he returned to Ceylon, under appointment by the American Board, where he continued until 1851, meantime being stationed at three different places. After a brief visit to America, he sailed for India in 1852, and with two of his brothers, Henry Martyn and Joseph, established the Arcot Mission of the RCA and organized the Classis of Arcot. He remained in India for twenty-two years, diligently doing his work and occupying in turn several stations of the mission. In 1873 family circumstances seemed to make a return to this country necessary, and in December of that year he accepted a call to the Congregational church at Glastonbury, Conn., which he served for eleven years. In 1885, tho over sixty years of age, the way being opened for a return to India, he sailed thither, laboring there for nine years, first at Madanapalle, relieving Dr. Chamberlain; and then at Palmaner, as General Synod's professor of theology in the seminary in the Arcot Mission.

SEAMEN; Missions to: As early as the latter part of the 17th century some sermons were preached in England on behalf of work for seamen, but it was not until 1780 that a society was organized, at first called "The Bible Society," whose special field was the army, but which soon was made to include the navy, and became "The Naval and Military Bible Society." In 1814, prayer meetings for sailors were started in London, and in March, 1817, the first Bethel flag (a white dove on blue ground) was unfurled on the "Zephyr" of South Shields. The next year saw the Port of London Society formed, and 1819 the Bethel Union Society. *The Sailors' Magazine* was started in 1820, yet still so strong was the prejudice against the work that even in 1828 the King was petitioned to abrogate an order by the Lord High Admiral prohibiting the distribution of tracts in the navy.

Existing seamen's missionary societies in the empire of Great Britain, distinct from local organizations, which limit the prosecution of work to their own ports, are: (1) The British and Foreign Sailors' Society (at Sailors' Institute, Shadwell, London, England), (2) The London Missions to Seamen (Established Church of England), whose operations are, for the most part, carried on afloat. Its chaplains are at fifty-two English and eight foreign seaports. Local English societies for seamen are at Liverpool (formed in 1821), Glasgow, and at other ports.

Evangelical Lutheran missions to seamen are prosecuted by societies with headquarters in Scandinavian countries, whence come in our day the larger number of sailors for the world's mercantile marine.

The Norwegian Society—*Foreningen til Evangeliets Forkyndelse for Skandinaviske Sömond i fremmede Havne* (or, in English, the Society for the Gospel's preaching to Scandinavian Seamen in Foreign Harbors)—was organized at Bergen, Norway, 1864, and does an extended work.

The Danish Seamen's Mission Society also has stations in different countries, employing ordained pastors; there are missions for seamen connected with several of the Swedish and Norwegian societies; and there is a specific Seaman's Society in Finland.

American Missions: The first Society for Seamen in the U. S. was formed in Boston in 1812, but did not continue long. A movement was started in New York City in 1816 which resulted in 1817 in The Marine Bible Society. The Society for Promoting the Gospel among Seamen in the Port of New York, commonly known as the New York Port Society, a local organization, was formed in 1818, and laid the foundations of the first mariners' church erected in the United States, in 1820. These movements led to similar organizations at Charleston, S. C. (1819); Philadelphia, Pa. (1819); Portland, Me., and New Orleans, La. (1823); at New Bedford, Mass. (1825), and elsewhere. In the latter year there were in the United States seventy Bethel Unions, thirty-three Marine Bible Societies, and fifteen churches and floating chapels for seamen.

In 1828 there was organized, in New York City, the American Seamen's Friend Society, which broadened the scope of such work to include, not merely the spiritual, but moral and physical, well-being of the sailors. Its object, as stated, is to secure this "by promoting in every port boarding-houses of good character, savings-banks, register-offices, libraries, museums, reading-rooms and schools, and also the ministration of the Gospel and other religious blessings." It commenced foreign work very early, sending Rev. David Abeel to Canton, China, in 1830. Since then it has extended its work all over the world, having chaplains and bethels in various ports of Europe and South America, India and Japan, as well as in the U. S.

There is also a Seamen's Friend Society in Boston, Mass., for a time auxiliary to the New York Society, but since 1888 independent. The Church Missionary Society for Seamen in the city of New York represents the work of the Protestant Episcopal Church. The other societies are undenominational. Mention should be made also of the extended work of the WCTU, and of a large number of Seamen's Rests and Bethels under private management. The various tract societies also assist in furnishing libraries for use on ships. Especially since the war with Spain the International Committee of the YMCA has had a most successful work of this kind. The YPSCE and similar organizations have also had a share in the work.

SEBAPALA: A settlement in Basutoland, South Africa, situated to the S. of the Orange River, about 53 miles S. E. of Morija. Station of the Paris Evangelical Missionary Society (1885), with (1903) 1 missionary and his wife, 31 native workers, 19 outstations, 1 place of worship, 1 Sunday school, 22 day schools, and 795 professed Christians.

SECHUANA LANGUAGE: Belongs to the Bantu family of African languages. It is used by the Bechuana tribes forming a large portion of the native population of South Central Africa, from the Orange River to the Zambesi. It is written with Roman letters.

SECUNDERABAD: A military cantonment in the native state of Haidarabad, India; situated 6 miles N. N. E. of the city of Haidarabad, and covering 19 square miles of territory. The largest military station in India. Climate during rainy season very unhealthy; at other times hot, but not insalubrious. Altitude, 1,787 feet. Population (1901), including troops, 74,000. Station of the SPG (1842), with (1903) 14 native workers, 1 place of worship, 2 day schools, 2 boarding schools, and 788 professed Christians, of whom 297 are communicants. Station also of the ABMU (1875), with (1903) 2 missionaries and their wives, 3 women missionaries, 18 native workers, 1 outstation, 1 place of worship, 6 Sunday schools, 1 boarding school, 4 day schools, and 210 professed Christians, of whom 195 are communicants. Station also of the ME, with 1 missionary and his wife. Station also of the WMS, with (1903) 3 missionaries, 1 woman missionary, 36 native workers, 3 outstations, 3 places of worship, 1 Sunday school, 8 day schools, 1 boarding school, and 368 professed Christians, of whom 213 are communicants.

SECUNDRA: A town in the United Provinces, India, situated 5 miles N. of Agra; contains many historical remains, among which is the tomb of the Emperor Akbar (1566), a grandson of Baber, Turkish conqueror of India. Station of the CMS, with (1903) 1 missionary and his wife, 28 native workers, 1 place of worship, 9 day schools, 1 industrial school, 1 orphanage, and 484 professed Christians, of whom 76 are communicants.

SEFULE: A village in British Central Africa, situated in the Barotsi region, about 15 miles N. E. of Nalolo, on the chain of hills bordering the Barotsi plain. Station of the Paris Evangelical Missionary Society (1886), with (1903) 3 missionaries and 1 dispensary. Some write the name Sefula.

SELANGOR: A state in the Malay Peninsula belonging to the group of Federal States under British protectorate. It lies south of Perak, and has an area of about 3,500 square miles of territory. The capital is Kwala Lumpur. Station of the PB, with (1900) 3 missionaries and their wives and 2 women missionaries. Station of the SPG, with (1903) 2 missionaries.

SELEPENG: A settlement in the Bechuanaland Protectorate, South Africa, situated on Fati River, about 23 miles N. W. of Francistown station on the Bulawayo Railroad. The people belong to the Baharotse tribe, who are somewhat inclined to move the sites of their villages, to the discomfort of missionaries, whose homes are less portable. Station of the LMS (1899), with (1903) 1 missionary and his wife, 4 day schools, 1 Sunday school, 11 native workers, and 487 professed Christians, of whom 115 are communicants.

SELWYN, George Augustus: Born at Hampstead, England, in 1809; died, April 11, 1878. Studied at Eaton; graduated at Cambridge University in 1831. It was the fine vigor of his life that made him one of the oarsmen in the first University boat race in 1829. He was ordained deacon in 1833, and took the curacy of Boveney; ordained priest in 1834; became curate of Windsor in 1839; was consecrated Bishop of New Zealand in 1841; received the degree of D.D. the same year, from both Cambridge and Oxford; sailed for his see December 26, 1841. He early saw a great truth, too often neglected by missionaries, which he later expressed in this form: "The surest way to spread the Gospel to the uttermost parts of the earth is by building up the Colonial churches as missionary centers." His whole heart was in the work to which he was called, and he became at once a tower of strength for the evangelization of New Zealand and all the surrounding regions. When he preached his farewell sermon before leaving England, his words deeply impressed a boy of fourteen who was present, named John C. Patteson. In 1855, when Bishop Selwyn returned to Auckland, after a visit to England, he had with him, as a missionary, the fruit of that early sermon in the person of Mr. Patteson, afterward the martyr Bishop of Melanesia.

Bishop Selwyn arrived at Auckland in 1842, and in 1843 he established there St. John's College for the education of a native ministry. On the voyage out he had spent much of his time in compiling from the Rarotonga, Tahiti, and Maori New Testament a comparative grammar of these three dialects. He was, therefore, somewhat prepared to supervise the work of educating a native ministry. Here, again, he was far in advance of many missionaries of that time, in realizing the vital necessity of using native laborers for pioneer work, who had been trained by foreigners. It was a maxim of his that in missions one must "use black nets, with white corks." From the very outset, too, St. John's College gave instruction in medicine and surgery. On the voyage to New Zealand, Bishop Selwyn's active, inquiring mind led him to study navigation, with the captain of the ship as his teacher. This stood him in good stead when, besides attending to the spiritual wants of his colonial diocese, he extended his field into Melanesia, navigating his own ship, "The Southern Cross," in his visitation voyages. When after twelve years of absence he visited England in 1854, he had made seven such voyages through the Melanesian Islands, had visited fifty islands, and from ten of these he had induced fifty youths to go to the college to prepare for work as evangelists. He was deeply impressed on finding at some of the southern Melanesian islands missionaries from Nova Scotia. The discovery filled him with zeal for carrying out his doctrine about making the colonies centers of missionary effort. He took a prominent part in organizing the Australian Board of Missions with the adoption by the Church in Australia of the Melanesian Mission as its peculiar field.

Bishop Selwyn's talents, character, and services placed him at the head of the colonial bishops at the Lambeth Conference, in 1867, which he attended. While from his social position, talents, and acquirements he might have commanded the highest ecclesiastical appointments, he chose the obscurity, peril, privation, and drudgery of a missionary life among degraded savages for the sake of his Master. He thus spent 27 years among the heathen, content if by any means he might save some. At last, on the earnest request of the Archbishop, he accepted the bishopric of Lichfield in 1868. He twice visited the United States, and exercised a powerful influence by his impressive addresses.

In 1878 he was taken ill, was soon partially paralyzed, and continued to fail until the 11th of April, when the end came. He died saying, "It is all light."

SENANGA: A settlement in British Central Africa, situated in the Barotsi region on the Zambesi, about 210 miles N. W. of Sheshekc. It stands in a picturesque region at the point where the mountains leave the river and open to view the great Barotsi plain. A great population is found in scattered villages in the region. Station of the Paris Evangelical Missionary Society (1898), with (1903) 1 missionary and his wife.

SENDAI: A town on the main island of Japan, situated on the N. E. coast, 12 miles from its port, Shiogama, and 200 miles N. of Tokio. It is the chief city of the region. Population (1898), 83,325. Mission station of the ABMU (1882), ABCFM (1885), Christian Church (1887), FCMS (1891), ME, PE, and RCUS, with all together (1903) 25 missionaries, men and women; 12 women missionaries, 70 native workers, 55 outstations, 23 places of worship, 51 Sunday schools, 4 boarding schools, and 2,366 professed Christians. The girls' boarding school of the RCUS was destroyed by fire in 1902, but has been rebuilt.

SENEGAL: A French colony in W. Africa, lying between the Sahara and the river Gambia. With its adjacent inland protectorate it has an area of about 80,000 square miles, and a population of about 1,180,000. It is a fertile country, rich in natural products. There are 4 communes and 9 "circles," all represented in the French parliament by one deputy. There is a transport service on the Senegal River for 460 miles from Saint Louis. The negro races, which form the bulk of the population, include the Wolofs, very black, brave, and superstitious, mostly Mohammedans, inhabiting most of the territory bounded by the Senegal, Faléme, Gambia, and the seacoast; the Serers, akin to the Wolofs, and on their southern borders; the Sarakoles of the Middle Senegal, akin to the Mandingans, of a wild disposition and an important element in the population. Senegal has 520 miles of railway and 1,400 miles of telegraph lines. The principal language of Senegal is the Wolof, which is the language of commercial intercourse, and has grammars, dictionaries, etc.; the related Gereres, the Mandingan, and the Fulah. The French Protestant Church and the Roman Catholics have mission work in Senegal.

SENEGAMBIA: A territory or sphere of influence of France in Western Africa, lying on the upper Senegal River, and in the bend of the Niger. The northern regions were formerly included in French Sudan, a terminology no longer used. A permanent delegate, representing the French home government, resides at Kayes. A railroad is being constructed from Kayes eastward to the Niger.

SENGELPAT. See CHENGALPAT.

SEONI: A town in Central Provinces, India, situated in the Hoshangabad district, 24 miles S. W. of Hoshangabad. Seoni contains large public gardens, a fine market-place, and a handsome tank. Climate healthful; temperature moderate. Population, 10,000. Station of the United Original Secession Church (1872), with (1903) 1 missionary and his wife, 5 native workers, 1 outstation, 16 places of worship, 2 day schools, 1 boarding school, 1 orphanage. Also station of the FFMA (1890), with (1903) 3 missionaries, one of them with his wife; 1 woman missionary, 9 native workers, 2 outstations, 3 places of worship, 5 Sunday schools, 4 day schools, 1 industrial school, 1 dispensary, and 1 orphanage. Some write the name Sioni Malwa.

SEOUL: Capital of Korea, situated about 30 miles E. by N. from its port, Chemulpo, on the right bank of the Han River, in a hollow surrounded by rocky hills. It was founded in 1392 by the first king and founder of the present ruling dynasty of Korea, who chose the site for the beauty and strength of its situation. The city in shape is an irregular oblong, and lies lengthwise in a valley whose trend is from northeast to southwest. The dimensions of the city are, roughly stated, 3 by 2½ miles. On the north is a succession of magnificent granite hills, culminating in granite peaks 3,500 feet high. On the south side is a chain of hills reaching the height of 1,500 feet. The most striking work of art in the landscape is the city wall, which crosses river, plain, and hills, and climbs the mountains on the south, encircling the whole city proper. At intervals are massive and imposing gates, all appropriately named, and through the largest of which the great highroads, starting from the royal palace, run to all parts of the kingdom. In the military system of the country this walled city is the center of a group of fortresses which, before the days of rifled cannon, were strong and trustworthy. The scenery from the walls of the city, and indeed from many points within the city, is magnificent, and the natural situation is one of the best for health and safety. An affluent of the Han River, with branches that run into nearly every part of the city, traverses Seoul from east to west, and is utilized as a drain and for washing clothes.

To most travelers the aspect of Seoul is uninteresting, shabby, and squalid. Nevertheless, the gay costumes, full of varied color, clean and brilliant with starch, and the peculiar gloss which the Korean women contrive to confer upon the male garments, make the streets in fair weather wear a very bright and animated appearance The houses are about 8 or 9 feet high, built of stone and mortar, and mostly roofed with tiles. The windows are under the eaves. A long street, about 200 feet wide, divides the city into nearly two equal portions. In the northern half are the walled enclosure containing the king's palace, and the more important public buildings. The main entrance gates face the south and are three in number. From the central and principal gate runs a street 60 feet wide into the main street, intersecting it at right angles and dividing the northern section of the city into eastern and western quarters. This point of meeting of these two streets is regarded as the center of the city. Here stands an imposing pavilion, the *Chong-kah*, or belfry, in which is hung a large bell over seven feet in height, which is rung every morning and evening. The street leading from the bell to the Great South Gate is as wide as the main street. It was at the corner of this bell-tower that the regent, in 1866, erected an inscribed stone denouncing as traitors to their country all Koreans who were friendly to European intercourse. Another feature in this center of the city is the rows of large warehouses, two stories in height, the lower portions of which are divided into small shops opening into a central court, instead of into the streets. These large storehouses are not private property, but are owned by the great trading guilds, which enjoy a notable monopoly. Along most of the main streets there are thousands of pedlers' booths erected, at which most of the retail trade of the city is done. These shabby-looking, temporary structures greatly mar the effect and narrow the space of the great thoroughfares. Outside of the buildings in the royal enclosure there are three palaces—two belonging to the king and one to his father. The dignity of the several mansions is shown in the relative amount of land occupied. The offices of the six ministries, or government departments, are small houses, differing but slightly from the better sort of dwellings. Since the residence of foreigners in Seoul a number of the native dwellings have been altered into good-looking houses, the Korean house lending itself more easily to the convenience of Western people than the Japanese. Many Japanese, apart from the legation people, and probably a larger number of Chinese, live in Seoul, engaged in commercial pursuits. No other city in Korea has so large a number of natives of the official class, including retainers of the nobles and office-holders. Nevertheless, the main part of the city is celebrated for the narrowness and filthiness of the streets. The population within the walls is estimated at 200,000, with about 50,000 living outside the walls. It was here, in the capital, that the Chinese costume and coiffure of the Ming period (1368-1628) was introduced, and became the still fashionable and national Korean dress. In June, 1592, Seoul was evacuated by the king and court, and occupied during parts of several years by the Japanese during the war from 1592-97. In 1637 the Manchu Tartars captured Seoul, compelled the king and his ministers to perform *kow-tow*, or the nine prostrations, and to set up a great memorial stone commemorating the clemency of the Manchu general. In 1653 Hawel and his fellow-Dutchmen visited Seoul as shipwrecked prisoners, finding other Hollanders there. In 1777 Christianity entered Seoul through some members of the embassy to and from Peking; in 1794 the first Chinese Jesuit priest, who was beheaded in 1801; in 1836 the first French priest, Maubant, followed by Bishop Imbert, who, in 1839, shepherded 9,000 believers, and was decapitated September 21 in that year. In March, 1866, nine French priests were executed on the river flats in front of the city, and on March 25 from the French war-vessels, "Déroulède" and "Tardif," piloted by an escaped French bishop and native Christians, the flag of France floated, causing a cessation of all business for several days. The French invasion took place in October, when two native Christians were beheaded and their blood poured into the river over the place of the anchorage of the French ships. The riot and attack on the Japanese Legation July 23, 1882, the *coup d'état* and battle of the Chinese and Japanese troops December 4 to 7, 1884, and the funeral of the ex-queen, a spectacle of unprecedented magnificence of the Korean sort, on an autumn day of 1890, are among the notable historic events in Seoul. The following missionary societies have establishments in Seoul: PN (1884), with (1903) 10 missionaries and their wives and 4 women missionaries, 20 native workers, men and women; 43 places of worship in the district, 10 day schools, 1 boarding school, 1 dispensary, 1 hospital, 1 printing house, and 1,430 professed Christians; ME (1885), with (1903) 2 missionaries and their wives, 6 women missionaries, 8 native workers, 3 places of worship, 7 outstations, 1 printing house, and 624 professed Christians, of whom 433 are communicants; SPG (1890), with (1903) 3 missionaries, 2 places of worship, and 37 professed Christians, of whom 13 are communicants; MES (1896), with (1901) 2 missionaries and their wives, 2 women missionaries, 2 native workers, 9 outstations, 7 Sunday schools and 262 professed Christians. The BFBS has an agency here employing 20 native workers. The YMCA has established an agent here (1901).

SERAMPUR: A city in Bengal, India, on the banks of the Húgli, some 13 miles above Calcutta, tho on the opposite (west) bank of the river. Serampur was long a Danish station, but in 1845 all the possessions held by the Danes in India were ceded to the East India Company. It was to Serampur that Carey, Marshman, and Ward, the great Baptist missionaries of the early part of the 19th century, retreated; and there, under the Danish flag, they found an asylum from the opposition of the English authorities at Calcutta, who, until the intervention of Parliament in 1814, were unwilling that missionaries should find a foothold in their possessions. The new charter contained a clause legalizing the residence in India of missionaries and philanthropists. The Baptist missionaries not only worked diligently in preaching the Gospel in Serampur and surrounding towns, but established a press, printed books and tracts, assembled their translators from many parts of India, prepared and published versions of the Bible in the principal languages of Hindustan, and even in Chinese. These versions were afterward found to be of comparatively small value, owing to the haste with which they were prepared, and the inadequate facilities enjoyed for correct translation into the idiom of the various Indian tongues; but nothing can better illustrate the diligence, zeal, and energy which have made the Baptist Mission at Serampur famous in the annals of modern missions than the fact that they were made at all. A church, college, schools of lower grade, and a good library were established at Serampur, and the mission is still in active and successful operation. The wide influence of this mission has been well summarized as covering the following points of development:

India owes to the Serampur mission, besides the first translation of the Bible into many of its northern dialects, the first newspaper in Bengali; the first steam-engine, paper-mill, and large printing press; the first efforts at education of native girls and women, the first savings bank, and many other benefits directly or indirectly the result of the labors of Carey, Marshman, Ward, and their associates.

Station of the BMS (1799), with (1903) 3 missionaries, two of them with their wives; 17 native workers, 3 Sunday schools, 1 day school, 1 theological class, 1 boarding school, and 222 professed Christians, of whom 62 are communicants. Also station of the BZM (1873), with (1903) 1 woman missionary, 7 native workers, 3 Sunday schools, 3 day schools   Some write the name Serampore.

SEROWE: A town in Bechuanaland, South Africa, the principal center of the Bamangwato tribe, which formerly had its chief town at Shoshong, and later at Palapye. In 1902 the tribe suddenly decided to move to Serowe and did so, abandoning Palapye. The new town is on a high upland, about 40 miles N. W. of Palapye, and 32 miles W. by N. of the Palapye road railway station. Population, 26,000. Station of the LMS (1862), with (1903) 1 missionary and his wife, 1 woman missionary, 9 native workers, 33 day schools, 25 Sunday schools, and 5,360 professed Christians, of whom 697 are communicants

SERVIA: A kingdom in Europe, bounded by Austria on the north, Rumania and Bulgaria on the east, Turkey on the south, and Bosnia on the west. In general, the surface is mountainous and covered with dense forests. The Danube and several other large rivers drain the country. Its total area is 18,855 square miles, of which over half is under cultivation. Cereals and grapes are the principal products.

The independence of Servia was secured by the Treaty of Berlin (1878), and since January, 1889, it has been a kingdom. The legislative authority is exercised by the king, together with the national assembly, which is composed of deputies elected by the people, indirectly and by ballot. Personal liberty, liberty of the press and conscience are guaranteed. Population in 1902, 2,600,000.

The Servians, or Serbs, belong to the most spirited of the Slavonic races, and are noted for the love of freedom and bravery. Poverty is rarely seen, for even the poorest have some sort of freehold property. Thus 97 per cent. of the country population are engaged in agriculture. The Greek Church is the state religion of Servia, but in 1902 there were 9,000 Catholics and 1,200 Protestants.

Education is conducted in elementary schools, maintained by the municipalities, and various technical schools and schools for higher education, which are supported entirely by the State. Attendance is compulsory, and no fees are required from the pupils. The main mission work in Servia is that which is carried on by the colporteurs of the BFBS.

Servians: The Servians form an important branch of the Eastern Slavs, or, as they are sometimes called, the South Slavs. They inhabit the kingdom of Servia, Bosnia, and Herzegovina, and part of Hungary. They number about 4,000,000, and belong to the Eastern or Orthodox Church, with the exception of about half a million Mohammedan Servians in Bosnia.

The Servians settled in the first half of the 7th century in the Balkan Peninsula, and their settlements spread over an extensive tract of land, comprising the present Servia, Montenegro, Herzegovina, Bosnia, and the Dalmatian coast. These various communities were ruled over by separate independent rulers called "Cans" or "Zhoopans," who were under the nominal authority of the "Great Zhoopan" residing at Rassa (Novi-Bazar), and all of whom originally were vassals to the Byzantine Emperor.. Christianity was first introduced among the Servians by the Roman Church in the middle of the 7th century, but this first introduction did not succeed; and it was only in about 868-870 that the Orthodox Church was established by Greek ecclesiastics sent by the Emperor Basil.

In the beginning of the 19th century the Servians revolted against the Sultan to regain their political independence, and after a great many vicissitudes and struggles they succeeded in establishing a semi-independent principality, under the suzerainty of the Sultan.

The Servian Church is ruled over by a Metropolitan residing at Belgrade, and bearing the title of "Metropolitan of all Servia." He is also the president of the Synod, who act as his councilors and advisers; but the power of the Metropolitan and the Synod does not extend beyond the limits of the Servian kingdom. Bosnia and Herzegovina are under the jurisdiction of bishops nominated by the Greek Patriarchate, subject to the approval of the Austrian Government. The Servians living in Austria-Hungary, and who also belong to the Orthodox Church, have a Patriarch residing at Carlovitz, who is chosen by a council and approved by the Austrian Government. He bears the title of Patriarch as an honorable title in continuation of the Patriarchs of Ipek, who ruled over the Servians in former days. All the Servians belonging to the Orthodox Church use the Church-Slavonic language in their churches and the alphabet invented by Cyril in their literature. Their language belongs to the Eastern branch of Slavic languages, and is akin to the Bulgarian, from which it differs, however, considerably in its vocal sounds. Many Turkish, Greek, and Albanian words have entered into the formation of the modern Servian language. Under the influence of their ecclesiastics and their ecclesiastical literature, the Servians in the beginning of the 19th century used in their literature a language called Slavonico-Servian, a mixture of Church-Slavonic and Servian, with the elements of the former predominating. But, thanks to the genius and efforts of Verk Karadjitch, a self-made man, the Servian alphabet was modified to a certain extent to suit the pronunciation of the spoken language of the people, which was raised to the dignity of a literary language. In this way the Servian orthography became the most phonetic of all Slavic orthographies, and, in spite of the opposition the reforms of Karadjitch met with, they were officially sanctioned by the government in 1868, and accepted by all the Servians who use the Cyrillian alphabet. Karadjitch translated also the New Testament into the common language of the people, while some years later Danitchitch, a well-known Servian philologian and a follower of Karadjitch, did the same thing for the Old Testament; and both these versions have been accepted and are used by the British and Foreign Bible Society.

SERVIAN LANGUAGE: The Servian, which belongs to the Slavonic branch of the Aryan family, is spoken in Servia, Bosnia, Herzegovina, Montenegro, Croatia, Slavonia, Dalmatia, etc., and is more akin to the Russian and Wend than to the Bohemian and Polish languages. It is rich in vowels, and free from the accumulation of consonants which render the other Slavonic tongues so harsh to the ear of a foreigner. Its sound is very soft, and one of the best Slavic scholars of our age, Prof. Schafarik, in comparing the different dialects of the Slavonic family, makes the following remark: "Servian song resembles the tone of the violin; Old Slavonic that of the organ; Polish that of the guitar. The Old Slavonic in its psalms sounds like the loud rush of the mountain stream; the Polish like the bubbling and sparkling of a fountain; and the Servian like the quiet murmuring of a streamlet in the valley." The Servian is written with the Slavic (Cyrillian) alphabet, and is beginning to possess a modern literature of its own.

SESHEKE: A settlement in British Central Africa, situated in the S. W. part of that region, on the Zambesi River, about 400 miles W. of Salisbury in Rhodesia. The climate is very trying to Europeans because of malaria. Station of the Paris Evangelical Missionary Society (1885), with (1903) 2 missionaries, one of them with his wife; 1 woman missionary, 1 place of worship, and 1 boarding school.

SEYCHELLES: A group of islands in the Indian Ocean; a dependency of the British colony of Mauritius. Missions are carried on by the SPG (1843), with 1 native male teacher and 136 Christians in native churches. At Mahé the CMS has a mission station, and works, mainly by its schools, among the creole negroes.

SHAFTESBURY: A settlement in the N. W. of Canada, situated on Peace River, in the S. W. part of Athabasca. Station of the CMS (1888), with (1903) 1 missionary, 1 native worker, 1 day school, and 26 professed Christians, of whom 10 are communicants.

SHAHJAHANPUR: A town in the United Provinces, India, situated in the Rohilkhand division, about 55 miles N. W. of Sitapur. Manufactures much sugar. Population (1901), 76,458, of whom 37,000 are Mohammedans and 36,000 Hindus. Station circuit of the ME, with (1903) 2 missionaries and their wives, 1 woman missionary, 42 native workers, 5 places of worship, 1 boarding school, 1 orphanage, 15 day schools, 29 Sunday schools, and 385 professed Christians.

SHANGHAI: The most important emporium in China, and the city which shows more of Western civilization than any other settlement of Europeans, except Hongkong. It is situated on the Wu-sung River in the Province of Kiang-su, about 14 miles from the sea. There are two entirely distinct parts to the city: (1) The Native City; (2) The Foreign Settlement.

(1) *The Native City* is very old. The first mention of it is found to be in 1015. In 1360 it became a district city. The British captured it in June, 1843, and it was the fifth of the treaty ports thrown open to foreign commerce. During the Taiping rebellion it was captured by the insurgents and occupied by them for 17 months, and when they were driven out in 1860 the eastern and southern suburbs were almost entirely destroyed. By virtue of its position it is the outlet for a vast territory. The Wu-sung and Hwang-pu rivers, the latter emptying into the Wu-sung at Shanghai, give it communication with Su-chow, Che-kiang, and all the region of the Grand Canal; while the Yangtse, only a few miles distant, makes it the outlet for the great Yangtse valley. The city, walled, three miles in circuit, stands in a large and fertile plain. Along the water front are vessels which carry goods to and from the interior. The streets are narrow and paved, the houses built of brick, and shops, eating-houses, and the usual temples and Buddhist shrines common to all Chinese cities are found here in abundance, but none of the public buildings or temples are peculiar to this city any more than to other cities of the empire. The population is estimated at 420,000, but probably the estimate is low. The climate varies greatly —from an intense heat in summer to freezing cold in winter, and great changes of temperature in 24 hours are common in the spring and autumn. The mean temperature, like that of Rome, is 59° (F.). Heavy rainfalls occur in the summer, but from September to May the climate is delightful.

(2) *The Foreign Settlement* is a municipality, and is divided into the English (and American) and French concessions, is governed by municipal officers, and there is a mixed court where cases involving natives and foreigners are tried before both Chinese and English officials. Spacious docks line the river front for three miles. The streets are broad, overhung with trees, lighted with electric light, and nearly all the comforts of modern civilization are to be found Jinrikishas, together with the native sedan chairs and wheelbarrows, provide abundant means of transportation, and horses and equipages of the latest European style are to be seen on the streets, especially along the Bubbling Well Road, the fashionable drive. Hundreds of native boats ply for hire on the river, and with the shipping, the steam-tugs, and small boats, the water presents a most animated appearance. The land of the concessions belongs really to the Emperor of China, to whom a mere nominal rental is paid. The domestic and foreign mails are handled at seven post offices—at the consulates—in connection with the Chinese customs. Clubs, libraries, museums, in addition to the various mission establishments, present attractions to the visitor. Telephone service is provided. The great northern line of telegraph was connected with the settlement in 1871, and the city is now in cable communication with the rest of the world. The first railroad in China was opened in 1876 between this city and Wu-sung, at the mouth of the river; the Chinese Government bought it the ensuing year, tore it up, and sent the material to Formosa; it has been rebuilt, nevertheless, and has been in use since 1898.

From this port is carried on the most important trade in China, the value of it having risen from 65,000,000 taels in 1868 to 240,000,000 taels in 1901. It is the center for the export of tea and silk.

According to the census of 1890, the population of the municipality, exclusive of the French concession, was 168,129; of the French concession, 34,722; the foreigners numbered only 4,265, of whom 444 were in the French quarter. Such a wide range of nationality is seldom found in any Oriental settlement; while the bulk of the foreign population is British, American, French, and German, yet twenty-one other nationalities are represented in varying numbers. Together with the estimated population of the native city, the total population of Shanghai is (1901) 620,000.

Shanghai is the literary center of the foreigners in China. Here is published the best English daily paper, together with a considerable number of the missionary publications in China At the Presbyterian Mission Press books are printed in

Chinese—not only religious, but scientific; and the Chinese Religious Tract Society issue from here their periodicals in Chinese, and the *Chinese Recorder* and the *Messenger* are published in English. On account of its central location, the beauty of its situation, the hospitality of the foreign community, it has been the place of meeting for the great Missionary Conferences.

Its importance as a center for religious work was early appreciated, and a larger force of missionaries, or representatives of more denominations, are probably not met with elsewhere in China. Mission societies now represented at Shanghai, with the last available statistics, are: LMS (1843), CMS (1845), PE (1848), Seventh-Day Baptists (1847), MES (1848), PN (1850), CIM (1854), WU (1881), FCMS (1891), and German General Protestant Missionary Society (1886); altogether these societies now (1903) have 106 missionaries, men and women; 180 native workers, men and women; 46 places of worship, 6 hospitals, with dispensaries; 3 printing houses, and 1,921 professed Christians. The BFBS and the ABS have each a center for their Bible work. The YMCA (1898) also has an agency here, with (1901) 2 men and their wives and a Young Men's Christian Association.

SHANGPOONG: A village and district in Assam, situated in the Jaintia Hills. Station of the Welsh Calvinistic Missionary Society, with (1903) 1 missionary and his wife, 31 native workers, 57 outstations, 57 places of worship, 52 Sunday schools, 57 day schools, and 2,683 professed Christians, of whom 677 are communicants.

SHANG-TSING: A town in Kiang-si, China, situated 68 miles S. E. of Nan-chang-fu. The Taouist pope resides here. Station of the CIM (1893), with (1903) 1 woman missionary, 5 native workers, 2 places of worship, 1 day school, and 36 professed Christians.

SHAN STATES: A name given to some of the hill provinces which lie on either side of the boundary between Burma and Siam, and are tributary to the one or to the other. They are inhabited by the Shans, Laos and other tribes.

SHANS: The Shans are now principally found on the mountain plateaus between the Salwen River and the great Burman plain. They are one division of the great Tai family, which extends from Tonquin on the east to the confines of Assam on the west, and from Southwest China on the north to the Gulf of Siam on the south. The kingdom of Siam is the only independent representative of this family. The differences of language are more of a broad dialectic character than of distinct tho cognate languages.

The original home of the Tai people was undoubtedly Southwestern China in Sze-chwan, and the country south of the Yangtsze-kiang. Until b. c. 250 the Chinese Kingdom did not have its subsequent compact character, and its rule did not have any permanent hold south of that river. Doubtless at that date the Chinese began to press southward and slowly pushed the Tai people into Yunnan, where they resisted the advance of the Chinese for a long time. As early as the first half of the 7th century a strong Tai state, Nan Chao, had arisen, which maintained itself as the kingdom of Tali until it was overthrown by Kublai Khan in the 13th century.

The migration of the Tai into Burma was by the branch which we know under the name of Shans, and probably began about 2,000 years ago, at which time the Chinese commenced to push their conquests south of the Yangtsze-kiang. Shan and Burman tradition places the beginning of the migration still earlier, and this tradition may be correct, tho of no political importance, as the restlessness of the nature of the Shans has always led them to frequent changes of residence. But the wars of Chinese aggression must be responsible for the great migration which found its first home in the valley of the Shweli River, and thence spread over plateaux southwest of China, and across the northern part of the plains of Burma to Assam, and to the headwaters of the Irawadi. As the oldest branch of the Tai family, the Shans have always been called Tai Long, or Great Shans, by the other branches of the family.

In the 7th century, out of this migration grew a large Shan kingdom, with a capital at Mong Maw Long in the Shweli valley. This kingdom maintained itself for several centuries with varying degrees of prosperity, until Anawratta, the Burman King of Pagan, by a victorious military career, established Burman supremacy for a time over much of the territory of the Shan princes. After the death of Anawratta, the Shan kingdom regained power, and later, in the times of Sam Kham Hpa and Sam Long Hpa, extensive military campaigns increased the territory of the kingdom to a size that it had never attained before. The prosperity of the Shan kingdom soon began to wane. From the 14th to the 16th century there was a gradual decadence of power. Distant dependencies shook off its suzerainty. Wars with Burma and China were frequent and weakened the central authority, and in the confusion many of the stronger principalities became semi-independent. In 1604 the Shan royal line ended. From that time Shan principalities became tributary to Burma, and Shan history merges into Burman history.

It was an evil day for the Shans when Burman suzerainty was established. In the Shan principalities west of the Irawadi and the mountains bordering on the eastern side of the Burman plain, successful efforts to Burmanize the people by the destruction of Shan books and the enforcement of study of the Burmese language in the monasteries were put forth by the Burman government for many decades. The Shan lingers as a *patois* in many country places in these regions, but the Burmese language has become so thoroughly the language of the people that mission work must be carried on in the Burmese language. The Shan language, however, maintains itself in the interior mountain regions.

Another cause of decadence was the frequent desolation of both border and interior principalities by war. The Shans, always restive under Burman rule, engaged in frequent rebellions put down by the Burmese with merciless cruelty, and also in civil wars fostered by Burman policy. These wrought such a great loss of life that the interior principalities became sparsely populated, except in a few important centers. With the decline in population, for a century the wave of Kachin migration has moved from the Himalaya region southeastward as far as Hsenwi and Mong-Mit, and has driven the Shans from much mountain country between Burma proper and China.

The Shans show their Chinese affinities in their physical characteristics and language. They have the Chinese type of face. Their complexion is light, and the eyes are almost almond-shaped. There are a goodly number of common roots in the two languages. The grammatical construction of sentences is the same as in Chinese, and has a great difference from that of the Tibeto-Burman family. There is an elaborate tonal system like that of the Chinese.

The Shans are a thrifty people. They are good agriculturists, but they excel in trading, for which purpose they visit Burma, Siam, and Western China. In this way they supply themselves with food and merchandise not obtainable in their mountainous country. In time of peace they are cheerful and hospitable, but in time of war they are cruel and vindictive, not only seeking to put to the sword all men of a hostile region, but slaughtering male children who fall into their hands.

The Shans are zealous Buddhists. Current legends about the introduction of Buddhism are manifestly untrustworthy. The looser Buddhism of the Northern Vehicle was doubtless the first form of that religion to be introduced into Upper Burma from Northern India. At the time of Anawratta's succession to the throne of Pagan, if Buddhism was so exceedingly corrupt in doctrine and in practise, it must have been as bad, if not worse, in the more northern Shan kingdom. Anawratta became a zealous religious reformer and introduced the stricter doctrine and practise of the Southern Vehicle. Wherever Burman influence has predominated in the Shan principalities, the people have become strong Buddhists, proud of their religion and tenacious in adhesion to it.

This strong adherence to their ancestral religion makes mission work among them slow and difficult. Buddhism, as held and practised by them, does not have much unpleasant restraining power over their lives. Every male child must, by religious law and by inflexible custom, be placed for a time in a monastery, where the tenets of Buddhism are diligently instilled into his mind. His mind thus becomes strongly possessed with Buddhist ideas and feelings, and when adult age is reached, there is at first little readiness to listen to a missionary, as they consider that it is one of the five great sins to do anything to bring about a schism in the body of Buddha. But when Shans become Christians they are generally decided in their attachment to their new faith.

The first missionary work for the Shans was confined to immigrants into Lower Burma, who had fled from the oppression of the native princes. It was impossible at that time for a missionary to live in the Shan country. Since the annexation of the whole of Burma to the British Empire, mission stations have been opened successfully at Hsipaw, Mongnai, Nam Kham, and Kengtung in the Shan principalities, and a goodly number of converts have been made. The Bible has been translated into the Shan language, and some Christian literature prepared. The prospect is one of quiet, steady growth, rather than one of rapid development.

Elias (N.), *History of the Shans*, Calcutta, 1876; Colquhon (A. R.), and Hallett (H. S.), *Amongst the Shans*, London, 1885.

SHAN-TAU. See SWATOW.

SHAO-HSING-FU: A city in Che-kiang, China, on the south side of the Bay of Hang-chau, about 60 miles W. by N. of Ningpo. Its climate is warm and somewhat malarious. Surrounded by a fertile and prosperous country, with a population of 150,000, it is one of the important cities of Che-kiang. Station of the CIM (1866), with (1903) 2 missionaries and their wives, 2 women missionaries, 12 native workers, 7 outstations, 8 Sunday schools, 2 day schools, 1 boarding school, and 326 professed Christians. Also station of the ABMU (1869), with (1903) 2 missionaries and their wives, 11 native workers, 7 outstations, 5 places of worship, 3 Sunday schools, 1 day school, 1 theological class, and 48 communicant Christians. Station also of the CMS (1870), with (1903) 2 missionaries and their wives, 3 women missionaries, 6 native workers, 1 outstation, 1 place of worship, 3 day schools, 1 dispensary, and 53 professed Christians. Some write the name Shaow-hing.

SHAO-WU-FU: A town in Fo-kien, China, situated 240 miles N. W. by W. of Fu-chau. Station of the ABCFM (1877), with (1903) 2 missionaries, 1 with his wife; 3 women missionaries, 28 native workers, 22 outstations, 17 places of worship, 8 day schools, 2 boarding schools, 1 theological class, 1 dispensary, and 513 professed Christians.

SHA-SHI-HSIEN: A town in Hu-pei, China, situated on the right bank of the Yangtse at the nearest point of that river to the Han-ho, with which it is connected by canal. It is an important trade center. Population, 100,000. Station of the PE (1889), with (1903) 10 native workers, 3 outstations, 3 places of worship, 3 Sunday schools, 3 day schools, and 276 professed Christians, of whom 103 are communicants. Station also of the Swedish Mission Society (1896), with (1901) 2 missionaries and their wives, 2 native workers, 1 outstation, 1 place of worship, 1 day school, and 250 professed Christians. Some write the name Shasi.

SHEBIN EL KOM: A village in lower Egypt, situated about 40 miles N. W. of Cairo. Station of the North Africa Mission (1899), with (1903) 2 missionaries and their wives, 1 day school, and 1 Sunday school.

SHEDD, John H.: Missionary of the American Presbyterian Board (N.). Died, Urmia, Persia, April 12, 1895. The first years of Dr. Shedd's missionary life were spent in pioneer work. His youthful energies seemed to know no limit in the tasks assumed. He shrank from no hardships. Given some special work to be done requiring vigorous action, self-denial, large resourcefulness, and he was pretty sure to be in it. His tours in the wild, rugged mountains of Kurdistan year after year marked well his character as a missionary, resolute, devoted, wise. Restricted as to times and seasons between the pathless winters and the fever-breeding summers, he would push in at the earliest possible moment of spring, abandoning his mule when he found the roads still closed, and with a Kurd as a porter to carry his quilt and a small change of clothing, he marched upon the snow crust, over the perilous passes and down through the valleys, visiting the little congregations, counseling and strengthening them in the name of the Lord Jesus. And scarcely had he returned home when he was ready to move with his family back again to the outer bounds of the mountains for the summer, drawing the native workers around him for additional instruction and training.

After his first ten years of service in Persia, Dr. Shedd returned to the United States on furlough. There he received a call to a professorship in Biddle University, which he accepted in view of conditions of health in his family which forbade his returning to the mission field, and for a few years he threw all his energies into the freedman's work.

Upon his return to Persia he was put at the head of the college at Urmia, taking a large share, at the same time, in the supervision of the church work. In both these relations his remarkable abilities for organization found ample scope. He came to be looked upon by the native preachers as a leader whom they could safely follow. On one occasion, when taunts were freely flung at the native Protestants because they lacked a bishop or head, one of the foremost pastors hurled back the answer, "Tell them we have in Dr. Shedd priest, bishop, and patriarch." His revised Confession of Faith and Manual of Church Worship and Government are a monument to his thorough study and broadminded views of the needs of the nascent Church of Christ in Persia.

Dr. Shedd's last year of service will be remembered by his associates as one of the most important in his life in connection with his conspicuous efforts in organizing and carrying through the Missionary Conference in Hamadan. In his comprehensive outlook upon the Persian field, with his bright faith in God's gracious purpose for the redemption of that land to Christ, he conceived it of pressing importance to gather a representative conference of the missionary workers to study the divine leadings. The high standard of spiritual interest and power which characterized the deliberations of the conference more than met his expectations. Out of his gratified soul he wrote at the close, "All are full of faith that God is to bless this land. There is an uplift in all our hearts toward a closer union with our Lord."

SHEFAMER: A village in Palestine, Asiatic Turkey, situated about 7 miles S. W. of Acca. Station of the CMS (1899), with (1903) 2 women missionaries, 1 day school, and 1 dispensary.

SHEIKH OTHMAN: A village in the southwest part of Arabia, 10 miles from Aden, and within the British lines. It is on high ground, and is used as a residence for escape from the intense heat of the town of Aden. Station of the UFS, with (1903) 2 missionaries, one with his wife; 8 native workers, 2 places of worship, 1 boarding school, 1 dispensary, 1 hospital, and 7 professed Christians.

SHELLA: A small town of 5,000 people in the Khasia hills, Assam, which gives name to a district of the mission of the Welsh Calvinistic Missionary Society, with (1903) 1 missionary and his wife, 32 native workers, 23 outstations, 37 places of worship, 34 Sunday schools, 34 day schools, and 1,631 professed Christians, of whom 614 are communicants.

SHEMLAN: A village in the Lebanon, Palestine, Turkey, situated about 10 miles S. by E. of Beirut. Station of the British Syrian Mission Schools (1858), with (1900) 2 women missionaries, 2 native workers, 2 outstations, 1 day school, and 1 boarding school.

SHEPSTONE. See NORTH AND SOUTH SHEPSTONE.

SHERBORO ISLAND: An island on the W. coast of Sierra Leone, West Africa, about 70 miles S. of Freetown. Station of the CMS (1822).

The care of this field passed to the local church in 1860. The UB also has a work here, of which statistics are given under **Bonthe**. The Sierra Leone CMS also maintains a mission here, with 8 native workers, 8 day schools, and 220 professed Christians. Also station of the WMS, with 26 native workers, 2 outstations, 6 places of worship, 3 Sunday schools, 3 day schools, and 346 professed Christians, of whom 281 are communicants.

SHERRING, Matthew Atmore: Born at Halstead, Essex, England, September 26, 1826; studied at University College, London, and Coward College; ordained December 7, 1852; sailed as a missionary of the LMS the same year for Benares. He took the superintendence of the Central School, with which he was identified during much of his life; also engaging in bazar preaching and itinerating, and the pastorate of the native church. On Sunday, August 8, 1880, he went through his usual services in Hindustani and English in apparently good health. At 2 o'clock Monday morning he was attacked with cholera, and on the 10th passed gently away. The same evening native Christians carried his body to the grave, among them his first convert, baptized twenty-four years before, a Brahman, and now vernacular headmaster in the institution at Benares. Combining high culture and strong common sense with a gentleness of disposition almost womanly, Mr. Sherring endeared himself to all with whom he came in contact. "I make it my rule," he would say, "to try to please every one if possible." In the twofold work of high-class education and of preaching in the vernacular he found ample scope for his superior talents.

SHERSHEL: A town in Algeria, situated 60 miles W. S. W. of Algiers. Station of the North Africa Mission (1890), with 2 women missionaries, 1 Sunday school, 1 dispensary. The French spelling of the name is Cherchel.

SHIGAR: A town in Kashmir, India, situated about 110 miles N. E. of Srinagar. Station of the Scandinavian Alliance of N. A. (1895), with (1900) 1 missionary and his wife, 2 women misaries, 1 day school, and 1 industrial institute.

SHIGATINI: A settlement in German East Africa, situated on the S. side of Mt. Kilima Njaro. Station of the Leipzig Missionary Society (1900), with (1903) 2 missionaries, 1 place of worship, 1 day school.

SHIH-TS' UEN. See SHI-TSUEN-HSIEN.

SHI'ITE MOHAMMEDANISM: Tho there are many different Mohammedan sects, yet these may all, or nearly all, be summed up under two heads—those which are generally known as Sunni and Shi'ah, respectively. Shi'ite doctrines are held almost exclusively in Persia, where it is rare to find anyone who will venture to confess himself as a Sunni. On the other hand, in Arabia a Shi'ite is not allowed to live unless he conceals his faith. Most Mohammedans in Oudh are Shi'ites, but in the rest of India the latter are not nearly so numerous as their rivals. In the Caucasus the Shi'ites are estimated to number about 800,000. The whole population of Persia is variously estimated at 8,000,000 or 10,000,000. Including the Babis, claimed to number 1,000,000, the total number of Shi'ites in the world probably falls below 20,000,000.

History and Origin: In earlier times Shi'ite doctrines were by no means confined to Persia. Under the Caliphs we find them again and again asserting themselves in Arabia, Egypt, and Mesopotamia. But whenever this occurred it was due to Persian influence. It is not too much to say, therefore, that Persia is the original home of Shi'ite belief, and that the enmity subsisting between Sunnites and Shi'ites is the continuation of the ancient hostility between Arab and Persian (*Arab* and *Ajem*—which may be compared with Greek and Barbarian) on the one side, and on the other, Persian and Turk (*Iran* and *Turan*), who, in the Persian traditions, have always been mortal enemies. These feelings were still more excited on both sides, and especially on that of the Persians, when the Arabian conquest of their country (642-643) compelled them to save their lives by outwardly professing Islam. Furthermore, skepticism and mysticism are natural to the Persian character, but alien to Arabian conservatism and devotion to the literal interpretation of the Koran and Tradition. It is no wonder, therefore, that the two races have developed differences in creed.

Another historical cause of the schism between Sunnites and Shi'ites may be found in the rivalry between the Hashimite and the Ommayite houses. Both Hashim and Ommayah were descended from a common ancestor, Abd-ul-Manaf, father of the former and grandfather of the latter. Even before Mohammed's time the descendants of these two men had been rivals in Mecca; and when Mohammed arose as a prophet, none of the Koreish opposed him so bitterly as Ommayah's family. When the caliphate fell to the lot of the latter, under Othman, the rivalry which had apparently been laid aside during the conquest under Abu Bekr and Omar, burst out with renewed energy, owing to the disappointment of Ali, who stood at the head of the Hashimites, at failing to be made Caliph on Omar's death (644). Othman's unfairness in conferring all important posts on the Ommayite faction, coupled with his evident weakness of character, still further aroused the enmity of the Hashimite party. Ali, on his part, tacitly encouraged the rebels who murdered Othman, and then he succeeded him as Caliph. But Mu'awiyyah, governor of Syria, representing the Ommayah party, was ultimately successful in securing Ali's deposition and obtaining the coveted dignity for himself. Ali refused to acknowledge Mu'awiyyah's claim, but was murdered by a *Khariji* assassin. His profligate son Hasan, surnamed the Divorcer, succeeded him, but after a reign of five or six months was forced to resign his pretensions in favor of his powerful rival, and some eight years later was poisoned by one of his many wives. When Mu'awiyyah died, Husein, the younger brother of Hasan, and, like him, son of Fatimah, Mohammed's daughter, laid claim to the caliphate, tho he had previously sworn allegiance to Yezid, Mu'awiyyah's son and heir. But Husein, with two of his sons, six of his brothers, two of Hasan's sons, and six other descendants of Abu Talib, Ali's father, was slain, fighting bravely at Kerbela (680) under circumstances of especial atrocity. This event forever put an end to all hope of harmony between the house of Ommayah and that of Hashim. Husein's tragic death evoked sympathy for his surviving descendants, and there gradually grew up the belief that Ali should have succeeded Mohammed as temporal and spiritual ruler of the Mohammedan world. It was natural that national and racial hostility to the Arabs should have led the Persians to adopt this view, and thus range themselves on the Hashimite side, as opposed to that of the Ommayite party. But this development was not clearly evident until some generations after Ali's death.

The more moderate Shi'ite party, which is that now prevailing in Persia, and with which this article deals except where sects are specified, gradually grew in numbers and influence until it became supreme in Persia in the 10th century of the Christian era. The Mongols in the 13th century at first showed no inclination to interfere with the religious views of the conquered Persians. Mohammed Khudabandeh (1303-1316) professed himself a Shi'ite. A period of depression afterward ensued, but Shah Ismail I., the descendant of the seventh Imam, Musa, founded the Safevi dynasty in 1499, and was a warm supporter of Shi'ite views. His war with Selim I. of Turkey was undertaken to avenge the slaughter of some 40,000 persons for rejecting the Sunnite in favor of the Shi'ite creed. The other sovereigns of the Safevi line supported the Shi'ite faith as the established religion of the country. The Afghan conqueror, Mahmud, was a Sunnite, and Nadir Shah, who delivered Persia from the Afghan yoke and founded a new dynasty, declared that the Sunnite teachings must be accepted by his subjects (1736). But the founder of the Kajar dynasty which now rules in Persia, Aga Mohammed, when he assumed the crown in 1796, undertook to uphold the Shi'ite creed, and his successors have continued to do so.

Characteristic Features: Turning now to the distinctive views of the Shi'ites, we find the great matter in which the Sunnites and Shi'ites differ to be a question as to the person who should be regarded as Mohammed's successor. The Sunnites hold that Abu Bekr, Omar and Othman, each in turn, became "Vicegerent of the Apostle of God" (generally abbreviated into Vicegerent—*Khalifah*—and corrupted in English into Caliph). The Shi'ites, on the other hand, hold that these three men usurped the position which belonged to Ali. The Shi'ites think it a sacred duty, therefore, to curse bitterly the memory of the first three Caliphs, and to refuse to acknowledge any Caliph except Ali himself. After Ali's death, his authority was transmitted, they hold, to his sons Hasan and Husein, and so on through the line of their descendants. But they style Ali and his eleven successors, not Caliphs, but *Imams*—the word Imam denoting a leader in religious worship. The twelve Imams are: 1. Ali; 2. Hasan; 3. Husein; 4. Ali-ul-Asghar (the less); 5. Mohammed-ul-Baqir; 6. Jafar; 7. Musa; 8. Ali-ur-Riza; 9. Mohammed-ul-Jawwad; 10. Ali-Askari; 11. Hasan-ul-Khamt; 12. Mohammed-ul-Mahdi.

It may be remarked in passing that rigid Shi'ites regard the government of the Shah of Persia as a usurpation, holding that all temporal as well as spiritual power should be in the hands of the Imam in this technical sense; and when there is no visible Imam, it should be given to the Mullas and other religious authorities.

Europeans are inclined to think the difference between Sunnite and Shi'ite very unimportant, since the reason for the schism is the question whether the Caliphs or the Imams were Mohammed's rightful successors, and this does not involve any real difference of doctrine. But if we wish to understand the importance of the schism from the Muslim point of view, let us imagine the way in which the two sections of the Roman Church would regard each other had the medieval schism in that body, which afforded the spectacle of rival Popes, lasted until our own time. The Sunnis speak of the Shi'ites as dogs, and the latter retort by calling their enemies swine.

The Shi'ite movement may, from an intellectual point of view, be regarded as an Aryan revolt against a Semitic faith forced upon the people of Persia at the point of the sword. Islam is utterly destitute of proof, and the Persians are naturally intellectual and skeptical, tho at the same time very much inclined to mystical and pantheistic conceptions, like their brethren, the Aryans of India. Mysticism, increasing superstition, credulity, and fanaticism have played an important part in the history of the Shi'ite system. It was largely opposition to the "orthodox" doctrines upheld by the Ommayad Caliphs that led the Persians to ally themselves with the Hashimite partisans of Ali. It was convenient to protect and to develop the Manichæan, Dualistic, Gnostic, Pantheistic, and other doctrines that still lingered in the East when Islam arose, under the form of an Islamic school of thought. Thus the strong political party, which was gradually formed to maintain the claims of Ali and his house, became committed to alliance with this whole medley of doctrines; and hence we find that the person now revered under the name of Ali is rather a mystical character than the historical person of the name. This will be especially noticeable in examining the views of the extreme Shi'ite sects.

To the ordinary Mohammedan profession of faith, "There is no god, but God; Mohammed is the Apostle of God," the Shi'ites often add the words "and Ali is (God's appointed) governor." Theoretically Mohammed should be accounted superior to Ali, but practically Shi'ites have put Ali in his place. Ali is invoked in Persia twenty times as often as Mohammed.

Obliged to make the pilgrimage to Mecca at least once in his life, if at all possible, the pious Shi'ite, when prevented from doing so, visits instead the supposed tomb of Ali at Najaf, or that of Husein at Kerbela, or that of Ali Riza at Meshhed, or that of Fatimah al Masumah, daughter of the seventh Imam, at Kum. Perhaps the Shi'ites reverence these and other saints more than the Sunnites do the saints in their own calendar. At any rate, the real religion of the great mass of Persians of the present time consists in belief in and what we might almost call adoration offered to the saints. Long caravans may frequently be seen bearing dead bodies to be buried near the tombs of such saints as those we have mentioned, in the fond hope that at the Resurrection the saint may intercede for his devotees.

The *Seyyids*, or descendants of Ali, are much more highly honored by the Shi'ites than by the Sunnites, and any one falsely claiming such descent is liable to very severe punishment. The proper dress of the *Seyyids* among the Sunnites is green, or at least their turbans are of that color, whereas in Persia the *Seyyids* may be distinguished by wearing black turbans.

The Shi'ites offer nearly the same Arabic prayers as do the Sunnites, their hours and their direction of prayer are the same, but they are far more particular in their strict observance of the Ramazan fast-month than the generality of Sunnites. Like the latter, they observe the "Feast of Sacrifice" (*Id-i-Kurban*), but the Shi'ites devote the greater part of Moharrem, and particularly the first ten days, to mourning for the deaths of Hasan and Husein. On the tenth day of that month mournful recitations (*Taziyehs*) descriptive of that sad scene are given before great crowds of people in all places where the Shi'ites are to be found in any numbers, and the wailing and beating of the breast which then take place are very moving, even to non-Muslim spectators. Religious fanaticism is easily excited on such occasions, and outbursts against Babis, Jews, and Christians are liable to occur. In Bombay the police have to take extreme care to prevent the Sunnites and the Shi'ites, both of whom have processions on that day, from attacking one another.

In recent times, and especially during the last few years, the Mullas in Persia have endeavored to increase the number of festivals observed by the Shi'ites, with a view to keep up their interest in their faith. Yet none can be said to be generally recognized, except the two already named. There is also the great secular festival of New Year's Day (*Nauruz*), on which newly appointed governors enter upon their duties. This is celebrated with pomp in Persia, and attempts have been made to give it a religious significance as the day on which Mohammed is said to have named Ali as his successor. But it is a national Persian festival of great antiquity, and the effort to connect it with Islam cannot be said to have succeeded.

The Sheikhu-'l Islam has not nearly the same authority and influence among the Shi'ites that the holder of the same title possesses among the Sunnites. In Persia every large city has such a functionary, but he is in many cases completely overshadowed by some other Mujtehid, not infrequently the Imam of the chief mosque in the city.

Properly speaking, Islam recognizes no atonement for sin. But the instinctive yearnings of the human heart are too strong to permit this great lack to remain entirely unsatisfied. The Shi'ites, therefore, hold that the deaths of Hasan and Husein were an atonement for the sins of true believers. This is a matter of no little importance, as it enables the Christian missionary, when dealing with Shi'ites, to find common ground on which to show the need of an Atonement, and to urge belief in that of Christ.

From the number of Imams the Shi'ites call their religious community that of the Twelve. The term Shi'ah, applied by their enemies to them, means a sect. Shi'ites, nevertheless, do not regard its use as an insult, and sometimes use it themselves as more convenient and more generally understood than the longer term. Tho the Sunnites derive their name from their reverence for the traditional law (*Sunnah*), yet it is a mistake to fancy that the Shi'ites reject tradition. They reject the six great collections of tradition accepted by the Sunnites, but in their stead acknowledge the following five others: 1. The *Kafi* of Abu Jafer Mohammed. 2. The *Man la Yastahzirah-ul-Fakih* of Sheikh Ali. 3. The *Tahzib* of Sheikh Abu Jafer Mohammed. 4. The *Istibsar* of the same author, and 5, the *Nahj-ul-Belaghah* of Sayyid Razi.

Morality in all Mohammedan lands is low, and

it would be hard to prove that the Shi'ites are in this respect worse than the Sunnites. But the former have two especially demoralizing doctrines which the latter repudiate, at least in words. These are the dogma known as *Kitman* and the doctrine of the legality of temporary (*mut'ah*) marriages.

The doctrine of *Kitman i din* (concealment of faith) is that a man is justified in concealing and even denying his belief, whenever confession would endanger life or property. When a Shi'ite makes the pilgrimage to Mecca he professes himself a Sunnite, and to prove it shows the greatest reverence for the first three Caliphs, whom he really believes it a meritorious act to curse every day.

The result of such a doctrine has been to change the ancient Persian reverence for truth into utter disregard for it, and to raise lying almost to the dignity of a fine art. No Shi'ite will, for a moment, dream of trusting another's most solemn assertions or oaths.

Mut'ah, or temporary marriage, for a month, a week, or even a shorter period, is sanctioned by Shi'ite religious law. Consequently, very large numbers of women make their living by contracting such unions, especially with the pilgrims who visit the "holy" cities. In Persia the term used to denote such a marriage is *Sigheh*. A great part of the wealth of the highest of the Mohammedan clergy in the places of pilgrimage is obtained by officiating at these marriages. To realize in any degree the moral degradation of Islam in this respect, we must try to force ourselves to imagine the higher clergy of the Church drawing their income in considerable measure from sanctioning such connexions, and the nation at large as being so degraded in moral sense as to have no revulsion of feeling. While the Sunnite law regards such unions as unlawful, the Sunnites of Central Asia, and of some other regions, permit them. Shi'ites and Sunnites both appeal to authoritative traditions in support of their respective views of Mut'ah marriages.

Sects: Even in Ali's lifetime a Jewish convert to Islam, named Abdullah Ibn Sauda or Ibn Saba, coming from Southern Arabia, proclaimed Ali to be an incarnation of the Deity. In 653 this man's followers, in spite of Ali's denunciation of their doctrines, were numerous enough to cause sedition in Basra, Kufa, and Syria, whence the sect spread to Egypt, as well as to Persia. Ibn Sauda taught that Mohammed, like Christ, would come again, and that, meanwhile, Ali was his representative. An allegorical interpretation began to be given to the Koran, and this is still a common feature with the Shi'ites party Even in very early times the Shi'ites divided into a number of sects, each holding one or other of Ali's descendants in peculiar reverence, but all agreed in looking forward, with large numbers of Sunnites also, to the coming of a *Mahdi* or guide to lead men back to the truth before the last day. One of the most important sects of the Shi'ites of the early times was that of the Ismailites. Its founder was a Persian called Abdullah Ibn Maimun, who appeared about the year 850. The sect took its name from Ismail, eldest son of Jafar, the sixth Imam, and Ismail's son Mohammed was declared to be the founder of the new religion. Abdullah taught that there had been six preceding dispensations, those of Adam, Noah, Abraham, Moses, Jesus, and Mohammed, each of these Prophets having been an incarnation of the Divine Reason. The last and most perfect dispensation was that of Mohammed Ibn Ismail, who was also an incarnation. All these prophets, therefore, are one and the same "Divine Reason" or "Universal Reason," conceived of as being produced by the will of God. This doctrine is almost identical with that held by the Elkhesaites in the second half of the 2d century, except that in the Book of Elkhesai no mention, of course, is made of Mohammed or of the founder of the Ismailites, Christ being called the one true prophet, who previously appeared as Adam, Enoch, Noah, Abraham, Isaac, Jacob, and Moses. The Ismailites added Mohammed and their own founder to the list, but still held to the doctrine that the Divine Immanence or Incarnation was found from age to age in the special Prophet of each time. One division of the Ismailis was the Karmati sect, called after their leader Karmat, who committed fearful excesses in the reign of the Caliph Mutazid. The Druses are also of Ismaili origin, their leading tenet being that Hakim, the notorious Fatimite Caliph of Egypt, was a divine incarnation. The sect of the "Assassins" (Hashishin) was the Ismailite body best known in Europe. It was founded by a Persian named Hasan Sabbah, who is said to have adopted Ismailite doctrines at the court of the Egyptian Caliph Mustansir (1261-1262). This sect was almost exterminated by the Mongols in the 13th century, but small numbers of Ismailites, who are generally inoffensive, still exist in India, Persia, and other countries.

Sufism can hardly be said to be connected with Islam at all, since the views of those who hold to this mystic and pantheistic system of thought—so far as it can be called a system—are utterly opposed to Mohammedanism. It has had very extensive influence in Persia, so much so that nearly every thoughtful and educated Persian is a more or less *Sufi*. Such men outwardly profess to be Shi'ites, but, in confidence, acknowledge that they absolutely disbelieve every tenet of Islam.

Less important Shi'ite sects are (1) the Akhbaris, who treat the doctrine of the resurrection and many others as merely allegorical; (2) the Ali-ilahis, who deify Ali and worship him as God; (3) the Sheikhis, who hold what is known as the *Rukn-i-Rabi* (fourth column) doctrine, to the effect that there must ever exist an intermediary between the twelfth Imam (the Mahdi) and his votaries. This Imam is said to have vanished most mysteriously in 874 and the popular belief is that he disappeared down a well, where he still lives. A message sent by him out of the well in 1892 was so universally believed, that, in accordance therewith, the Shah of Persia was obliged to abolish the Tobacco Regie monopoly, which he had granted to foreign companies. But it is believed that after his disappearance in 874 the Imam Mahdi once more appeared for a time in 940, only to vanish again for an indefinite period. During his "lesser disappearance" (874-940) he communicated with the faithful by means of four persons in succession, each of whom bore the title of *Bab* (Gate). Mirza Ali Mohammed of Shiraz, founder of the modern Babi sect (1844), claimed the title of Bab in this sense. This sect is, therefore, an offshoot of the Sheikhi sect from the then leader of whom (Sayyid Kasim of Resht) Mirza Ali Mohammed at first received instruction. But persecution has rendered the Babis so hostile to the Shi'ites that it is hardly correct to regard them as any longer Shi'ites themselves.

Missionaries and Shi'ites: It remains for us to inquire what is the attitude of the Shi'ite sect toward Christianity, and what way the Gospel may be most effectively brought to bear upon them.

Like all Mohammedans, a Shi'ite holds that the Gospel was at one time intended to be, as the Koran styles both the Old and New Testament, "a light and a guidance to mankind." But he believes that it has been abrogated by the descent of the Koran upon Mohammed, and he also holds that the Bible has been wilfully corrupted by the Jews and Christians. Neither the Koran nor the Traditions, however, give the very slightest support to such ideas, and this fact must be insisted on in urging Muslims to accept the Bible. It may be shown from the Koran itself that the Bible could not have been corrupted before or during Mohammed's time, while the existence of versions more ancient than that time proves that the Bible we now have is identical with that which the Koran mentions. Strangely enough, the Mohammedans endeavor to adduce from the present text of the Bible prophecies in support of Mohammedan claims. It is necessary for the missionary to prove that such passages do not bear the meaning thus attributed to them. In all controversy, however, it is important to remember Bengel's rule: "Never enter upon controversy without knowledge, without love, without necessity." The truths that are contained in the Mohammedan faith should be frankly and thankfully acknowledged and taken for a basis of agreement, and, in some sort, a foundation for what has to be proved; but it should be pointed out that these truths are taught in the Bible and borrowed from it by Islam, and that Christianity alone can reveal how much deeper such truths are than the Muslims conceive.

Besides the great truths of the Unity of God, the After-life, Future rewards and punishments, the fact of Revelation and others held by all true Muslims, the Shi'ite faith also recognizes (1) the need of an Atonement, and (2) the possibility of an Incarnation in some sense. In preaching the Gospel to Shi'ites, therefore, the Christian doctrine should be shown to inculcate both these truths, but in a manner more logical and more in accordance with the moral sense of humanity than their own mystical speculations. The *Sufi* longing after union with God can be shown to be provided for in the Gospel, which teaches how man may become, not identical with God, but a child of God, through spiritual union with Jesus Christ. Above all is it necessary to endeavor by prayer and teaching, under the guidance of God's Holy Spirit, to convince the inquirer of sin, the heinousness of which no Muslim realizes from the teachings of his own faith. The missionary should endeavor to remove misconceptions as to the nature of the Christian doctrine of the Trinity, to show that its foundation is belief in the Unity of God. Other misconceptions also must be met by careful reference to Holy Scripture. It must be clearly shown that we abhor idolatry and priestcraft, at least as much as Muslims do, and that we have no sympathy whatever with corruptions of Christianity.

In brief outline this is the method which experience in the Persian field has shown to be the best for the missionary to follow in preaching the Gospel to the Shi'ites. In life and word Christ must be exalted that He may draw men into Himself.

In studying the Shi'ite doctrines all so situated as to be able to do so should consult the original sources, *e. g.:* The *Koran* in the original; the five collections of *Traditions* named above; the *History* of Ibn ul Athir; *Katib ul Wakidi*, and Shi'ite commentaries and controversial works in general. For the Babi sect, one should consult the *Ikan*, the *Bayan*, and the *Kitabi Akdas*.
General readers will find the following useful: Muir (Sir W.), *The Caliphate;* Osborne (Major Durie), *Islam under the Khalifs of Baghdad;* Sell (E.), *The Faith of Islam;* Hughes (Rev.), *Dictionary of Islam;* Browne (Dr. J. P.), *History of the Bab;* Tisdall (Dr. W. St. Clair), *The Religion of the Crescent* (S. P. C. K.).
For dealing with Shi'ite inquirers, Tisdall (Dr.W. St. Clair), *Manual of Mohammedan Objections*, London (S. P. C. K.). Articles of value on Babism will be found in the *Missionary Review of the World*, Vol. XV pp. 771 and 775, and on Persian Mohammedan Women, the same. Vol. XIV. p. 886.

SHILLONG: A town in Assam, India, situated in the Khasia Hills, 42 miles E. by S. of Gauhati. It is an administrative center and a charming spot, commanding extensive views of the Brahmaputra valley. Station of the British and Foreign Unitarian Association, with (1900) 1 native worker, 1 place of worship, 1 day school, and 1 Sunday school. Station also of the Welsh Calvinistic Missionary Society, with (1903) 1 missionary and his wife, 2 women missionaries, 441 native workers, 80 outstations, 36 places of worship, 59 Sunday schools, 70 day schools, and 4,192 professed Christians.

SHILOH: A village in the southern portion of Basutoland, South Africa, about 62 miles N. E. of Aliwal North. Station of the Paris Evangelical Missionary Society, with 13 native workers, 3 outstations, 1 place of worship, 1 Sunday school, 4 day schools, and 978 professed Christians, of whom 562 are communicants. Some write the name Siloe.

SHIMOGA: A town in Mysore, India, situated on the Tunga River, 87 miles N. E. by N. of Mangalore. Population, 12,000. Station of the WMS, with (1903) 1 missionary, 1 woman missionary, 37 native workers, 6 outstations, 7 Sunday schools, 10 day schools, 1 boarding school, and 90 professed Christians, of whom 81 are communicants.

SHINTOISM: The origin of Shintoism is involved in more or less obscurity, but the translation of the Kojiki, which may be looked upon as the sacred record and exposition of the system, has thrown much light upon its doctrines. It is an embodiment of the crude superstitions of the early Japanese, their nature-worship, spirit-worship, ancestor-worship, and hero-worship, in fantastic combination. It is dimly monotheistic in its very earliest references. It presents the idea of one supreme being, from whom all things spring, but of whom nothing beyond this can be known. He was not a real Creator. This mysterious and unrevealed being is known in Shintoism as the "Central and Supreme God of Heaven."

Tradition relates that when the heavens and the earth separated from that confused relation in which they had been intermingled in the original chaos, this supreme god came forth and appeared uplifted between them, but he had existed, tho unrevealed, from all eternity. This system also presents the idea of a second and a third deity, subordinate to the first, but self-existent. From these deities two emanations proceeded, namely, Isaname (female), and Isanagi (male); from the fecundity of these sprang all things. They were the Adam and Eve of Shintoism. Several other subordinate gods were produced.

The process of creation ascribed to the divine pair was very unique: standing on a bridge of heaven and looking earthward, they stirred the ocean with a long spear. From the end of the spear dropped some fecundating substance, from which sprang up the islands of Japan, and in the islands thus composed was the potency of all things; vegetable and animal life sprang up spontaneously. Shintoism does not recognize a real creation out of nothing. It claims only a development. The universe is regarded as eternal. God and man and all things are of one essence. The system, therefore, is in a sense Pantheistic.

The development of the sun myth appears in Japan as in so many other countries. The male and female deities above named produced a daughter of most resplendent beauty, represented by the sun. While this fair maiden was embroidering beautiful textures—thus, perhaps, symbolizing the beautiful work of nature in verdure and in flowers—her churlish brother spoiled her work by covering it with defilement; the brother representing the principle of evil, and thus establishing a dualism which has been found in so many nations. The maiden, thus insulted, is represented as having withdrawn herself in sulkiness to a dark cave, leaving the world in gloom. The legends represent the forlorn inhabitants of the world as having resorted to various expedients to bring her forth from the cave. Three of these appear to have been successful. One was to gather as many cocks together as possible, from all quarters, and place them near the cave's entrance, that at the proper hour of cock-crowing their clamor might excite her womanly curiosity, and bring her out. A second expedient was to institute a dance of beautiful goddesses before the cave. Becoming jealous of the praises which she heard lavished on them, she would certainly come out and reveal her charms.

Another plan, quite as successful, was that of constructing a mirror, which was so placed before the mouth of the cave as to reflect to the goddess her own beautiful form. This threefold appeal to her curiosity, her jealousy, and her vanity succeeded. She came forth, whereupon means were immediately taken to prevent her return. The sunlight of her presence again bathed the world, and filled all nature with delight. This sun-goddess married at length, and became the mother of the whole line of mikados, and from her to the present incumbent of the throne there has never been a break; the succession for thousands of years is claimed to be complete.

There are imposing ceremonies connected with the worship of this goddess, almost wholly of a cheerful tone; and it may be said in general that of all races, perhaps the Japanese, before the advent of Buddhism, had the most light-hearted type of faith. In the springtime there are still festivals designed to hail the springing of the fruits and flowers, and ceremonies in imitation of planting and sowing are performed. Here is a vocation for the Shinto priests, and one far more grateful than offering bloody sacrifices or in any way striving to appease gloomy deities. This sun-goddess, the ancestor of the mikados, is a genial being, and she is symbolized, not by cruelty and death, as in the case of Moloch, the fiery sun-god of the Phœnicians, but by all benign influences, and her only sacrifices are offerings of rice and fish and flowers. It is scarcely necessary to say that the original supreme deity, who never revealed himself, and of whom nothing is known, is removed very remotely from the practical interests of life, and that the great mother of the mikados is the really supreme object of worship.

Shintoism in its essence is ancestor-worship combined with worship of nature as having proceeded from the earliest ancestors of the Japanese. The Emperor is the head of the religious system as a lineal descendant from the sun-goddess. The system is a vast Pantheon of demigods. The names of the heroes of Japanese history, fierce warriors and successful generals, and rulers are on the list, which is ever increasing. Dead statesmen and heroes, even in modern times, are deified by decree. A great general who won renown in the Chinese war of 1895 was given such an apotheosis by decree when he died. Every Shinto temple may thus be regarded as a sort of Westminster Abbey for perpetuating the fame of the great dead.

The literature of Shintoism is not extensive. Such as it is, it found its source in the fables and folk-lore of the earliest and rudest times. These were preserved by minstrels. In the 3d century Chinese legends were introduced, and some of these myths were committed to writing. It was in 712 that the Kojiki, or "ancient record," was compiled. This is the sacred Bible of Shinto priests. It is also the earliest Japanese history. It is most unique in its style, resembling nothing else that has ever been published in any land. It is remarkable for the agglutination of long compound names and expressions. But altho Shintoism cannot compare with Buddhism in its literature, or in its intellectual influence, yet it does not wholly neglect the instruction of the people. There is more or less preaching on ethical subjects, and the ethics thus presented are pure and salutary. Even this custom may have been borrowed from Buddhism. During the long centuries in which Shintoism and Buddhism have coexisted side by side, or rather have been more or less intermingled, the Buddhist influence has done most to promote the intellectual growth of the people, very little effort having been made by the Shinto priests to emulate the Buddhist culture. Buddhism has not only proved educational in its influence: it has inculcated a higher moral feeling, and especially in the direction of benevolence and humanity.

It is difficult to decide whether or not Shintoism is to be regarded as idolatrous: no idols appear in the temples, even of the sun-goddess. Statues of heroes are not invoked in prayer, and yet, undoubtedly, they receive something akin to worship; and the Japanese temples are never closed against any object which seems even to approach the supernatural. In every Shinto temple a mirror is seen. This may be a mere reflection from the idea which leads Chinese Taouists to make use of mirrors—that evil spirits dare not approach one, since it will show them as they are. But Shintoists explain that the mirror symbolizes the divine man that is in us, at the same time that it is a vivid representative of one's conscience and judge. The thought is that a man within the sacred temple precincts is brought face to face with himself, and that in one sense what it most concerns him to know is himself as he really is. It cannot be denied that this is a forcible conception. Next to the prayer of the Psalmist, that the Spirit of God may search the petitioner and try his heart, is that means, whatever it be, which brings a man face to face with himself in the solemn presence of real or supposed deity.

It is declared by some Japanese that Shintoism is not a religion, but simply a means of cultivating a patriotic, nationalistic spirit. The enduring tenet of the system is, nevertheless, admitted to be devotion to the Emperor. The will of the sun-goddess and of the Emperor are necessarily the same. The essential requirement of the system is perfect obedience as the essence of moral conduct. But Shintoism is a religion in so far as it recognizes the relations of man to a higher power, as is shown in the fact that prayer is a resource constantly resorted to. It is offered to a supreme something, which is supposed to cherish an interest in all creatures. At funerals and elsewhere prayers are offered for the dead as well as for the living. There is in Shintoism a resemblance to the ancient cult of the Aryans, both in its dread of death and of all that belongs to death. A corpse is looked upon as polluting, and one should have as little as possible to do with it; no people except the Zoroastrians carried this matter so far. It is closely connected with sun-worship in both cases.

Relations of Shinto to Buddhism: Buddhism entered Japan in the year 552. The Shinto levity and thoughtlessness opened the way for a system which was of a more melancholy tone and spirit, and which took a more earnest hold upon the future life. For a thousand years, according to Kodera, there existed a strange partnership between the two religions. By common consent the Shinto priests officiated at all marriages (with which Buddhist monks were supposed to be little in sympathy), while Buddhist priests took charge of the funerals, from which Shinto priests were only glad to be exempt. At the present time marriage is a civil rite only. So intimately interwoven did these two systems become, that the Government at length began to dread the influence of Buddhism, which had proved the stronger element. And in order that Shintoism, with its traditions of imperial descent and the prestige which it thus afforded, might not lose its supreme place, a decree was passed declaring it to be the religion of the State; and this is still the theory of the Government. Yet so closely had the two systems long been blended, that it is said that nine-tenths of the people consider themselves as belonging to both. Like other Oriental systems, Shintoism is easy-going, and in a negative sense charitable toward Buddhism; both have long been accustomed to represent their position by the maxim: "Men may ascend Fujiama on any one of many sides, but when once on the summit the same glorious moon is visible to all. So with the religions."

There can be little doubt that the early mythology of Shintoism exerted a disastrous influence upon the morality of the people. The legend which represents the goddesses as dancing in an almost nude condition before the cave in which the sun-goddess was hidden has presented a poor example to the generations of Japanese peasants, and one cannot greatly wonder that in decency and vice have known less restraint than in almost any other land. Under the influence of Shintoism immorality has scarcely been considered a vice. The late Dr. S. R. Brown, after years of observation, could scarcely find any element of moral restraint in the system, and was slow to accord to it the name of religion.

There can be no doubt that in comparison with this childish system of nature-worship and mere natural impulse Buddhism has been a blessing to Japan. Rev. K. C. Kurahara has summed up the beneficial influences of Buddhism in Japan as follows:

(1) It has taught the people a vivid realization of future rewards and punishments—thus ministering both inspiration and restraint, and giving to life a higher dignity and solemnity.

(2) It has presented a high conception of our common humanity, without caste or slavery.

(3) It has enjoined a higher grade of ethics, and much more of self-restraint.

(4) It taught the people temperance, even prohibition.

(5) It has emphatically enjoined benevolence and pity to all beings.

(6) It has stimulated an intellectual activity not known before. It has introduced philosophy and poetry, and all literature.

(7) From the 12th century until the year 1868 Buddhist priests were the only educators. All schools were due to their influence.

(8) The Buddhist doctrines have greatly enkindled the powers of imagination, pathos, and lofty aspiration.

(9) The introduction of Buddhism has led to increased foreign intercourse, and has brought in its train the literatures not only of China, but of India.

(10) Buddhism has given great impulse to architecture, landscaping, gardening, and all ornamental arts. Of this the peerless bronzes, lacquers, and the sweet-toned temple-bells are proofs.

(11) By its support of a priestly and yet a thoughtful class, Buddhism furnished many men of leisure, who gave themselves to literature, and were promoters of a higher national culture. Were the Buddhist element eliminated from Japanese literature, there would be but little left.

(12) Altho Buddhism weakened the divine autocracy of the Mikado, and thus perhaps facilitated the introduction of the rival power of the Shoguns, yet nevertheless it exerted a powerful restraint upon cruelty and oppression.

(13) It taught rulers the duty of respecting the claims of the people, and of promoting their good.

Confucianism has been credited with imparting to the Japanese nation a higher degree of moral earnestness than either Shintoism or Buddhism. To the ethics of Confucius, it is claimed, is due whatever of loyalty to government and to country has been found in public officials and the higher classes.

As to the special obstacles which Shintoism offers to Christianity, we see at once that a system which openly deifies men, blunts the sensibilities as to the sinfulness of wrong-doing. The Christian preacher who calls upon men everywhere to repent speaks a language unintelligible to the Shintoist. Belief that they are descended from the gods satisfies the Japanese that they can do no wrong. They require no moral code because they have it in their nature. The barrier which self-righteousness ever offers to Christianity is especially repellant in Japan.

At the same time, the weakness is clear of a religious system that becomes indistinguishable from political loyalty to a human leader. Shintoism in its modern and secularized form cannot long satisfy its adherents. The fruits already seen to result from conversion to faith in Jesus Christ must increase such dissatisfaction. For the Gospel of Jesus Christ has imparted more of noble impulse, secured a greater degree of moral and intellectual advancement, in twenty-five years than all the other religions have realized in Japan in the centuries of their dominion.

Missionary Review of the World, Vol. X., 650; Peery (R. B.), *The Gist of Japan*, New York, 1898; Griffis (W. E.), *Religions of Japan*, New York, 1895.

SHIRA: A settlement in German East Africa, situated on the W. slope of Mt. Kilima Njaro, about 190 miles N. W. of Tanga. Station of the Leipzig Missionary Society (1899), with (1903) 2 missionaries, 1 place of worship, and 1 day school.

SHIRAZ: A town in Persia, situated 100 miles N. E. of Bushire on the Persian Gulf. It is a place famous as the birthplace of many great Persians, and has considerable commercial importance. Population about 50,000. Station of the CMS (1900), with 1 missionary and his wife and 1 day school.

SHIRWAL: A town in Bombay Presidency, India, situated about 14 miles S. of Poona. Station of the Poona Indian Village Mission, with (1900) 4 women missionaries, 1 Sunday school, 1 day school, and 1 dispensary.

SHI-TSUEN-HSIEN: A town in Sze-chwan, China, situated among high mountains, about 45 miles N. W. of Mien-chau. Station of the CMS (1895), with (1903) 1 missionary and his wife, 1 native worker, 1 outstation, and 5 professed Christians. Some write the name Shih-Ts'uen.

SHIU-HSING: A town in Kwang-tung, China, situated about 30 miles W. of Canton. Station of the CMS, with 1 missionary and his wife and 5 women missionaries. Church statistics are included in Canton. Station also of the SBC, with 1 woman missionary.

SHIYALI: A village in Madras, India, situated about 16 miles N. N. W. of Tranquebar. Station of the Leipzig Missionary Society, with 2 missionaries and their wives, 48 native workers, 4 places of worship, 9 day schools, 4 boarding schools, and 1,201 professed Christians, of whom 1,027 are communicants. Some write the name Schiali.

SHIZUOKA: A town in Japan, situated on the S. coast of the main island, about 90 miles S. W. of Tokio. Population (1898), 42,172. Station of the MCC (1874), with (1900) 4 native workers, 1 place of worship, 1 Sunday school, and 322 professed Christians. Also station of the Methodist Protestant Church, with 2 women missionaries, 4 native workers, 7 outstations, 1 boarding school, 1 kindergarten, and 118 professed Christians. Also station of the SPG (1897), with (1903) 1 native worker, 1 place of worship, and 38 professed Christians. Station also of the UB (1896), with (1903) 1 place of worship, 23 native workers, 2 outstations, and 26 professed Christians.

SHOLAPUR: A town in Bombay, India, 280 miles E. S. E. of Bombay, on the Bombay and Madras Railroad. Temperature 50° to 110° F. It stands at an altitude of 1,800 feet, in the center of a wide plain. It is an important trade center and manufactures silk and cotton. Population (1901), 75,288. Languages, Marathi, Hindustani, Kanarese. Station of the ABCFM (1864), with (1903) 3 missionaries, one of them with his wife; 2 women missionaries, 48 native workers, 15 outstations, 9 places of worship, 28 Sunday schools, 18 day schools, 1 dispensary, 1 kindergarten, 1 orphanage, 2 boarding schools, and 174 professed Christians. Also station of the Mission to Lepers, which supports the leper asylum of the ABCFM.

SHOSHONG: The former capital of the Bamangwato tribe of Bechuanas, situated in Bechuanaland, South Africa, about 30 miles N. W. of the Shoshong Road station on the railroad. Station of the LMS, with (1903) 1 missionary and his wife.

SHUN-KING-FU: A town in Sze-chwan, China, situated about 90 miles N. W. of Chung-king-fu. Station of the CIM (1896), with (1903) 2 missionaries, one of them with his wife; 2 native workers, 2 outstations, 2 places of worship, and 25 professed Christians. Some write the name Shun-k'ing.

SHURMAN, John Adam: Born in Westphalia, Germany, 1810. Died October, 1852. Studied at Berlin; sailed for India, July 9, 1833, as a missionary of the LMS; stationed at Benares, February 17, 1834. He devoted himself to the educational department and to Bible translation. With others he labored in preparing the Urdu and Hindustani versions of the Scriptures. In April, 1842, he went to Calcutta to superintend the printing of the Urdu version of the Old Testament. Returned to Benares in June, 1843, and left in October for England. He arrived at Benares February 20, 1846, on his return to his work, remaining there until his death, six years later.

SHWE-GYIN: A town in Burma, on the branch of the Si-taung River, 100 miles N. E. of Rangoon. Climate, tropical. Population, 7,519. Race and language, Burmese. Religion, Buddhism. The Karens, however, predominate in the surrounding regions. Station of the ABMU (1853), with (1903) 1 missionary and his wife, 2 women missionaries, 36 native workers, 59 outstations, 50 places of worship, 10 Sunday schools, 28 day schools, 4 boarding schools, and 5,200 professed Christians, of whom 2,165 are communicants.

SHWIFAT: A village in the Lebanon district, in Syria, Turkey in Asia, situated about 3 miles S. E. of Beirut. Station of the Miss Proctor's Schools (1885), with (1900) 3 women missionaries, 11 native workers, 2 outstations, 1 Sunday school, 4 day schools, 2 boarding schools, 1 dispensary, and 22 professed Christians.

SIALKOT: A town in Punjab, India, situated in the Amritsar district, about 70 miles N. W. of Amritsar. It has some commercial importance, and is handsome and well built. Population (1901), 57,956. Station of the Church of Scotland Foreign Mission Com. and Woman's Board (1857), with (1901) 2 missionaries with their wives, 5 women missionaries, 46 native workers, 22 outstations, 2 places of worship, 29 day schools, 1 boarding school, 1 college, 1 dispensary, 1 hospital, and 257 professed Christians. Also station of the UP (1855), with 4 missionaries, two of them with their wives; 6 women missionaries, 58 outstations, 36 Sunday schools, 24 day schools, 2 dispensaries, 1 hospital; the number of Christians is not named by the Society.

SIAM: The kingdom of Siam lies at the southeast corner of Asia, occupying the central and principal portion of the peninsula of Indo-China. It has Burma on the west and northwest, and the French possessions of Cambodia, Annam, and Tonkin on the east and northeast. It stretches along the Malay Peninsula to within four degrees of the equator. The area is uncertain, but is estimated at about 236,000 square miles, of which 60,000 square miles lie in the Malay Peninsula.

Physical Features: The physical contour of the country may be best understood by remembering that both its mountain chains and its rivers have a general north and south direction. Of river systems there are two—that of the Me-nam in the west, and that of the Me-kong on the eastern frontier. In their lower courses the rivers traverse immense alluvial plains, which are, to a large extent, overflowed during a portion of the year. In the upper country the mountain walls on either side approach each other in some places so closely as to leave only a narrow gorge, while in others they recede, enclosing fertile plains varying in width from 10 to 50 miles. Nearly all the navigable streams are broken by rapids, which render water communication between the lower and upper courses difficult.

Climate: Altho Siam lies wholly within the tropics, the climate is not so hot as that of Southern India. The temperature at Bangkok ranges between 57° and 99° F., with a mean annual temperature of 80°. The periodical monsoons of the Indian Ocean divide the year into two seasons of about equal length—the rainy season, extending from May until October, and the dry season, covering the rest of the year. Owing to the tropical heat, the abundant rainfall, and the annual overflow of the rivers, Siam is a very fertile country.

Population: The population of Siam is uncertain, the latest (1899) foreign estimate placing it at 5,000,000. The Siamese and their near kinsmen, the Laos, make up three-fourths of the whole; the other fourth is composed of Chinese, Malays, Peguans, and Burmese, the first-named being the most numerous and important. The Siamese and Laos are alike members of the Shan race, which at one time (14th century) dominated the greater part of Indo-China.

Physical Characteristics: The Siamese are a people of medium stature, well formed, with brown skins, straight, black hair, which is worn short, except by the Laos women; and slightly flattened noses. Their eyes are not set obliquely, as in the Chinese and Japanese. In disposition they are gentle, lively, hospitable, kind to children and to the aged, fond of amusements, but lacking in energy; deceitful, unstable, and conceited. The Laos and Independent Shans are superior to the Siamese proper in strength of body and stability of character. The civilization of the Siamese strongly resembles that of China, but is of a lower grade, as they have not the patient industry, the inventive skill, nor the literary taste of the Chinese. Much of the trade of the country falls into the hands of the Chinese and Burmese. The Chinese in many cases marry Siamese women, and the children of such unions make one of the most promising elements in the population, combining the superior energy of the Chinese with the vivacity and quickness of the Siamese.

Language: The language is broken into several local dialects, *e. g.*, the Siamese, the Laos, and the Shan proper.

This tongue is properly a monosyllabic language, and, like the Chinese, has an elaborate system of *tones*, by which words otherwise identical are given different meanings. There are six tones in common use. The chief difficulties of the language for the foreigner lie in the recognition and accurate reproduction of the tones. The main obstacles to be overcome in translation are the lack of connective particles, the native love for multiplying synonyms, and the observance of a proper mean between the simplicity of the vernacular and the stilted style adopted in the sacred books of Buddhism. It should be added that besides the difference in written character between Siamese and Laos dialects, there are also slight but important differences of vocabulary, of tone, and of idiom—*e. g.*, so common a word as "not" is in Siamese *mi*, in Laos *baw*.

Social Customs: In their social customs the Siamese present several points of interest to the student of missions. The position of woman is high for an Oriental people. No attempt is made to seclude her, but she moves freely among men, engages in business, holds property in her own name, and is in general the equal of man. Monogamy is the rule, except among the nobility; and even among them the principle of monogamy is recognized in the preeminence given to one, generally the first, wife. Child marriage is not practised; widows may remarry; divorce is easy. The position of woman is due, in part, doubtless, to the humane teachings of Buddhism, and in part to the social custom which ordains that a man on marriage shall become a member of his wife's family. Children are kindly treated, and the adoption of children by childless couples is common. Great respect is paid to distinctions of age and rank. There are separate sets of pronouns which must be used with regard to superiors, inferiors, and equals.

Religions: Two religions obtain among the Siamese peoples—Buddhism and the worship of evil spirits. The one is a historic religion, with ancient, sacred books, costly temples, a numerous priesthood, and the support of the states; the other is an unorganized worship, without literature, priesthood, or temples, but in many portions of the country, particularly among the Laos tribes, it rivals, if it does not exceed, Buddhism in its hold upon the popular mind and its influence over the affairs of life. Buddhism, as held and practised in Siam, constitutes a formidable barrier to the progress of Christianity. Simply as the ancient religion of the country, it is strongly entrenched in the popular regard. "It is not the custom of our ancestors" is often considered a sufficient reply to the best-constructed argument for Christianity. Buddhism, too, is interwoven with the whole social life of the people—scarcely a family but has or has had a member in its priesthood. Its fêtes furnish the principal opportunity for social pleasures. Vast sums of money have been invested in its temples, pagodas, and monasteries, and in support of its priests. It makes strong appeal to the self-righteous tendencies of the human heart. It operates powerfully to deaden the conscience, and to discredit the possibility of a vicarious atonement for wrongdoing.

Side by side with Buddhism, and to a large degree intermingled with it, is the religion of demon-worship. This is but one form of that Shamanism which prevails so largely in Asia and Africa. What gives it interest is the extent to which it affects the lives of the people. The spirits or demons, some of which may be said to correspond to the elves and fairies of Western superstitions, but the majority of which are believed to be in greater or less degree malevolent, are of several different kinds. Some are local genii—spirits of the forests, the mountains, the streams, the caves. Others preside over certain natural phenomena—as thunder, rain, wind; or over particular operations—as plowing, sowing, reaping, house-building, or certain situations in human experience—notably birth, marriage, sickness, death. A vast multitude also are spirits of deceased persons. This burdensome superstition finds its natural climax in the belief which refers misfortune or sickness to witchcraft. Persons adjudged to be witches are driven from their homes, their houses burnt, and their gardens uprooted. There are in the Laos provinces cities where the whole population consists of such persons and their families.

Potent as this demon-worship is in its influence upon the people of Siam, and especially of the Laos provinces, it is less serious than Buddhism as a hindrance to the progress of the Gospel. Since disease in its various forms is largely attributed to the influence of demons, medical missionary practise does much to weaken this superstition. So does the mission school, with its rational explanations of natural phenomena. And so heavy is the incubus of fear which this belief lays upon its adherents, that they are prepared to hail as good tidings a religion that promises relief.

Early Missionary History: It was as a possible door of entrance to China that Siam first attracted the attention of Protestant Christians. In the year 1828, Dr. Karl Gutzlaff, who had gone to Singapore under the Netherlands Missionary Society, accompanied by Rev. Mr. Tomlin of the London Missionary Society, visited Bangkok. Convinced that here was an open door for missionary effort, these brethren sent an appeal to the American churches for men to occupy the field. This appeal was brought to America by the same trading vessel which brought the famous "Siamese Twins." In response the American Board instructed the Rev. David Abeel, then stationed in Canton, to visit Siam, with a view to the establishment of a mission there. Meanwhile Gutzlaff and Tomlin had been earnestly at work. While their attention was principally given to the Chinese, whom they found numerous in Bangkok, Dr. Gutzlaff prepared a tract in Siamese, and made a translation of one of the Gospels. But the death of his wife compelled him to leave, and Mr. Tomlin shortly went away also.

Besides the appeal to the American churches, Gutzlaff and Tomlin had sent one also to the American Baptist Mission in Burma. It is interesting to note in this connection that the very earliest effort on the part of a Protestant for the evangelization of the Siamese was made by Mrs. Ann Hasseltine Judson, who had, by the help of a Siamese resident in Rangoon, learned something of the Siamese tongue, and had translated into it the catechism just prepared by Dr. Judson for the Burmans, also a tract and the Gospel of Matthew. The catechism was printed (1819) on the mission press at Serampur, and is believed to be the first Christian book ever printed in Siamese. The Baptist missionaries in Burma sent Rev. J. T. Jones to Siam in answer to Gutzlaff's appeal. He labored there from 1833 until his death in 1851.

The attempt of the ABCFM to establish a mission in Siam began with the dispatch of Rev. David Abeel, in 1830, and ended with his breaking down in health, and consequent departure in 1832. It was renewed by the sending out of Messrs. Johnson and Robinson, who reached Bangkok in 1834. They were joined a year later by **Daniel B. Bradley, M.D.**, who arrived in the same vessel with **Mr. Dean** of the Baptist Mission. These two men were destined to enjoy long periods of missionary service. Dr. Dean continued his labors for the Chinese, with sundry interruptions, until 1885. Dr. Bradley was ordained to the ministry in 1838. He was a man of versatile powers, and left an abiding mark on the Siamese nation. Like the Baptists, the missionaries of the American Board at first carried on missions both to the Chinese and the Siamese, but with the opening of China proper the laborers engaged among the Chinese were withdrawn. The mission to the Siamese was maintained until 1849, when it was brought to a close by the departure of Rev. Asa Hemenway, the Board's only remaining missionary.

As yet but slight results had been obtained, either by the missionaries of the American Board or by their Baptist brethren, in the conversion of the Siamese. But much had been accomplished in other directions. The missionaries, by their blameless and self-denying lives, and especially by their success in healing the sick, had won the esteem of the native community. By preaching and teaching, and by translating, printing, and distributing portions of the Scriptures and Christian tracts, they had brought the truth into contact with a multitude of minds; and especially ought we, in estimating their labors, to be mindful of the influence which one of their number, the Rev. James Caswell, was permitted to exercise when the providence of God threw into his hands the daily instruction during eighteen months of the future king of the country.

One other of the American churches was to have a share in the work of missions in Siam. This was the Presbyterian Church (North). In 1848 the Presbyterian Board of Foreign Missions sent to Bangkok the Rev. William Buell and his wife. After three years of service they were compelled by the ill-health of Mrs. Buell to leave the field. The work was then suspended until 1847, when it was renewed by Rev. Stephen Mattoon and Samuel R. House, M.D. This mission continues until the present, and is now the only Protestant agency for the evangelization of the Siamese. The first convert, Nai Chune, was baptized in 1859—twelve years after the permanent establishment of the mission. In 1902 the number of church members among Siamese and Laos together was over 4,000.

In 1861 the Mission opened a new station in Petchaburee, which has now become a center of Christian influence, not only for the province in which it is situated, but also for the provinces lying to the south, along the Gulf of Siam.

Another important step was taken in 1867 in the establishment of a mission to the Laos tribes. Interest in the evangelization of these tribes was first awakened through the presence in the neighborhood of Petchaburee of a large colony of Laos, whose ancestors in a time of political disturbance had put themselves under the protection of the King of Siam, who had assigned them a residence in the province of Petchaburee. In 1863 Messrs. McGilvary and Wilson of the Petchaburee Mission made a tour of exploration to Chieng Mai, the capital of the most powerful Laos province. This important city is situated on the river Me Ping, about 500 miles north of Bangkok. In 1867 Mr. McGilvary removed thither with his family, and Mr. Wilson and his wife followed him a year later. The labor of the missionaries was soon rewarded by the baptism of their first convert, Nan Inta, a man of more than usual ability, and learned in the Buddhist religion. His faith in Buddhism was first seriously shaken by the verification of the prediction made by the missionaries of the eclipse of August 18, 1868. His conversion was followed within a few months by that of six others.

The Laos converts at first suffered persecution, but since the issue, in 1878, of a proclamation of religious liberty for the Laos, the persecuting spirit has been held in check. The edict of toleration was issued in response to an appeal from the missionaries in Chieng Mai on behalf of two native Christians who wished to be married in Christian fashion, without making the offerings to spirits customary on such occasions. Their heathen relatives attempted to prevent the marriage, and were supported in their attempt by the authorities; so there was nothing left for the missionaries but to appeal to Bangkok.

Medical missionary work was begun in Chieng Mai in 1875, with the opening of a dispensary, since developed into a hospital. A boarding school for girls was opened in 1878, and one for boys in 1888.

In the Laos states the people have shown great readiness to accept the Gospel, and here we find seven times as many Christians as in Siam, tho the field has been occupied only a little more than half as long. The PN has sole care of the work among the Laos. The press and medical missions are agencies of great usefulness in this field, and the training of the native Christians and the encouragement of the churches toward self-support are among the leading features of the Laos Mission.

SIANG-CH'ENG. See HSIANG-CHENG-HSIEN.

SI ANTAR: A village in Sumatra, Dutch East Indies, situated near the S. E. extremity of Toba Lake. Station of the Rhenish Mission Society, with (1902) 2 missionaries, one of them with his wife; 25 native workers, 4 outstations, 1 Sunday school, 6 day schools, and 705 professed Christians, of whom 217 are communicants.

SIAO-MEI. See HSIAO-MEI.

SIAR: A village in German New Guinea, situated on the coast near Prinz Heinrich Hafen. Station of the Rhenish Missionary Society, with (1903) 1 missionary and his wife and 1 day school.

SIBOGA: A town of Sumatra, Dutch East Indies, situated on the W. coast, about 210 miles N. W. of Padang. Station of the Rhenish Mission Society, with (1903) 2 missionaries and their wives, 37 native workers, 14 outstations, 4 Sunday schools, 15 day schools, and 1,804 professed Christians, of whom 647 are communicants.

SIBSAGAR: A town in Assam, India, situated about 40 miles S. S. W. of Dibrugarh, at an altitude of 333 feet on the Dikhu River, nine miles from the Brahmaputra; the seat of the river trade; once a very important place, as proved by the ruins of a magnificent tank, with temples and palaces along its border, and still interesting on account of its tea-gardens. Population, 5,200, of whom 3,000 are Hindus and 1,500 Muslims. Station of the ABMU (1841), with (1903) 2 missionaries and their wives, 11 native workers, 11 outstations, 5 places of worship, 5 Sunday schools, 4 day schools, 1 boarding school, and 1,200 professed Christians, of whom 639 are communicants.

SIDAMBARAM. See CHILAMBARAM.

SIDON: A town and seaport mentioned in the Bible as a port of Phœnicia, and now called Saida in the local languages. It is situated on the coast of Syria, Asiatic Turkey, about 30 miles S. of Beirut, standing in a plain encircled by mountains. The population is about 11,000. Station of the PN (1851), with (1903) 4 missionaries, one of them with his wife; 2 women missionaries, 52 native workers, 27 outstations, 16 places of worship, 20 Sunday schools, 26 day schools, 2 boarding schools, 1 industrial school, 1 orphanage, and 805 professed Christians.

SIENG-IU, or SIENG IU. See HSIEN-YU-HSIEN.

SIERRA LEONE: A colony and protectorate of Great Britain, on the west coast of Africa, lying between French Guinea on the north and Liberia on the south and east. The area of the colony proper, which extends from the coast inwards from 7 to 20 miles, is about 4,000 square miles, with a population of 76,665, of whom 40,790 were reported as Protestants (1901). The protectorate has an area of about 30,000 square miles, and a population estimated at 1,000,000.

The peninsula of Sierra Leone, which is completely surrounded by water in the rainy season by the junction of Waterloo and Calmont creeks, covers an area of about 290 square miles. It is mostly occupied by a range of gently rounded hills rising in places to a height of 3,000 feet. The rainfall in the whole territory is heavy; copious streams, rising in the Niger watershed, flow south and west. The climate is equable, ranging from 78° to 86°. The rainy season commences in April or May and declines in October, November, and December. January, February, and March are almost rainless. The mean annual rainfall is 134 inches. The marshy exhalations during the rainy season render the climate insalubrious. The death rate is high. Vegetation is luxuriant.

Freetown, on Cape Sierra Leone, is the capital. The dominant race is the Timne (about 200,000), on the plains between the Rokelle and Little Sarcie rivers. Their language is wide-spread. Several books, religious and educational, have been translated. The people are very superstitious and suspicious. The Los Islands and adjacent coasts north of the Mallecory River are occupied by the Bagas and the courteous Su-Sus, whose speech, a Mandingan dialect, is the dominant one in the whole region, and possesses the Bible and several other translations.

The Church Missionary Society undertook its mission in Sierra Leone in 1804, and has enjoyed encouraging success. The Wesleyan Methodist Missionary Society comes next, with nearly equal statistics; the United Methodist Free Churches, the United Brethren of Ohio (American), the Wesleyan Methodists of America, the CA, and the Roman Catholics also pursue missionary work there. The Christian schools are denominational, conducted by the missionary societies. There are also Mohammedan schools subsidized by the Government.

Crooks, *A Short History of Sierra Leone*, Dublin, 1901; Ingham, *Sierra Leone after a Hundred Years*, London, 1894; Pierson, *Seven Years in Sierra Leone*, London, 1897; Poole, *Life, Scenery and Customs in Sierra Leone and the Gambia*, London, 1850; Sibthorp, *History of Sierra Leone and Geography of Sierra Leone*, London, 1881.

SI-GAN. See HSI-NGAN-FU.

SIGOMPULAN. See NAHORUOP.

SI GUMPAR: A village in Sumatra, Dutch East Indies, situated on the W. coast of Toba Lake. Station of the Rhenish Missionary Society, with 2 missionaries and their wives, 82 native workers, 13 outstations, 14 day schools, and 1,997 professed Christians, of whom 953 are communicants.

SIH-CHAU. See HSI-CHAU

SI-HSIANG. See HSI-HSIANG-HSIEN

SIKHS: A sect of British India, numbering (in 1901) 2,195,268, of whom 2,102,896 were resident in the Punjab, where they form about 8 per cent. of the population, and where six tributary states are under Sikh rulers. Their founder, Baba Nanak (1469-1539), born near Lahore, was a contemporary of Luther, and, like him, a religious reformer. As a youth he was of a pious, contemplative disposition, and devoted his early manhood to a study of the rival creeds prevailing in India: the Hindu and Mohammedan. Not finding satisfaction, he became a pilgrim in search of truth, but returned to his own country in the conviction that he had failed to find God in any of the creeds. Laying aside the character of an ascetic, he led an ordinary life, reared a family, and preached the one invisible God, the Creator, calling upon people of all religions to seek knowledge of God, to worship Him, to find salvation in living righteously, and in doing good works, as God desires, and to be tolerant of the failings of others. By what he deemed unimportant concessions, he endeavored to reconcile the essentially diverse Monotheistic and Pantheistic creeds of Muslim and Hindu, thus showing that he had never really mastered either. He left behind him an unsullied reputation, and a company of zealous followers, whom he called Sikhs, *i. e.*, Disciples, mostly of Jat origin, like himself, but with an admixture of Hindus and Mohammedans. He was succeeded by nine other Gurus, or teachers, the first of whom, Angad, was of Nanak's own choosing, and was the author of the first of the sacred books of the Sikhs, the Adi Grunth, made up of the life and sayings of Nanak, with additions by Angad. The fourth Guru, Ram Das, gave permanent expression to Sikhism by establishing Amritsar as its central seat, and building there its Golden Temple in the midst of the Tank or Pool of Immortality. So far the counsel of Nanak, to avoid political complications, had been followed, but Arjun, the fifth Guru, systematized the theocracy, collected taxes, and assumed something of the state of a secular ruler. The unity of the Sikhs was further cemented and strengthened by the growing enmity with the Muslim power, which persecuted them bitterly. Finally, their tenth and last Guru, Govind, at the close of the 17th century, organized the Sikhs into a military brotherhood, the Khalsa, and said his followers should no longer be called Sikhs, but Singhs, *i. e.*, lions, or fighters. He relaxed the restrictions regarding food, permitting them to eat meat, instituted an initiatory rite of baptism, forbade the cutting of hair or beard, gambling and smoking, taught disregard of Hindu and Mohammedan Scriptures, priests, and ceremonies, and instilled into the people a spirit of hostility which made the Punjab, during the next hundred years, an arena of bloodshed. The fortunes of the Sikhs were various until the decline of the Mogul dynasty, and the rise, at the beginning of the 19th century, of their great leader, Runjeet Singh, who brought all the region from the Sutlej to the Himalayas under his sway. He abandoned fierce intolerance for indifference to religion, except in so far as religious zeal was useful to his political ends. Every male Sikh was enrolled as a soldier. He was ever true to his alliance with the English, and the Sikh regiments were an invaluable aid in putting down the Sepoy rebellion. After Runjeet Singh's death, the Sikhs entered upon war with the English, and, being defeated, Sikh dominion disappeared in English sovereignty over the Punjab. The Sikh regiments, true to their history, now constitute the best and bravest soldiers in the Anglo-Indian army, but the majority of the Sikhs have returned to agriculture and other peaceful pursuits, and are the most industrious race in the Punjab, where, despite their relatively small numbers and their lagging behind other races in taking advantage of educational opportunities, they exercise a leading influence. They are a people marked by their symmetry, comeliness, and courage; simple, sincere, and warm-hearted; lovable, receptive to kindness, and they render loyal service to those whom they trust. They are on a par with the rest of the population in morality, and are free from caste prejudice. Drunkenness is a prevalent vice, especially among the upper class. The subjugation and pacification of the Punjab, which ended the Sikh dominion, was accomplished by that company of great Christian soldiers and civilians, Hardinge, Edwardes, Cust, William Martin, and the brothers John and Henry Lawrence. It presents the one conspicuous instance in Indian history of a body of British rulers going to work definitely as Christian men, confessing Christ before the world, and not shrinking from energetic action for the evangelization of the people, tho never false to those great principles of religious tolerance which the government professes. It was they who first established the Church Missionary Society in the Punjab, the officers raising a subscription as a thank-offering for victory, and supporting, with large contributions, their appeal to the CMS to enter the field. Amritsar was occupied as a station in 1852, and other points soon after, the officers building church, school, and mission house, and two converted Sikhs being employed as evangelists. At the time of the mutiny, Lawrence sent to the siege of Delhi a regiment made up of Sikhs of the sweeper caste, much despised by their coreligionists, and usually of a turbulent, degraded character. When the city was taken, some of them found Christian books among the spoils, and on reading them, asked the English officers for Christian instruction. They were referred to the CMS missionaries at Amritsar, and as a result several received baptism. It looked at one time as tho a whole regiment, and perhaps two, would become Christians, but the opportunity was lost through the interference of the Calcutta authorities, who forbade the officers to further the conversion of natives. After the first Sikh war the mission of the Presbyterian Church (North) in the U. S. advanced from its Cis-Sutlej station at Ludhiana to Jullundur and Lahore in the Punjab, and other societies followed. There are, however, no missions specifically to the Sikhs, and cannot be, since they are thinly scattered among the other populations, especially in the country districts, and are indefinitely divided among themselves into various kinds of Sikhs. They are often, however, not separated by a very sharp line from other Hindus. The breaking of their national unity and their wide dispersion, the diminishing grants by the government for the support of their temples, their reverence for the Brahman priests, who are employed to officiate at birth, marriage, and death, coupled with the fact that Sikhism is not a hereditary but an elective religion, being entered by a rite of baptism, seldom taken till adult years, are influences tending steadily to lessen the number of Sikhs, and bring about a general reversion to dominant Hinduism. In districts remote from Amritsar there is now little to distinguish Sikh from Hindu. This transition period is an opportunity that should be made the most of in the effort for their evangelization. Baptisms among them have not been frequent, tho probably as large in proportion to their numbers as among other classes. They average well as Christians in comparison with other converts, and have produced some fine specimens of Christian manhood.

Cunningham, *History of Sikhs*, 1849; Hughes (T. P.), *Dictionary of Islam* (article on Sikhs), London, 1885.

SIKKIM: One of the Indian feudatory states, lying in the Himalayas, on the north of the British district of Darjiling. It is bounded on the E. by Bhutan, on the W. by Nepal, and on the N. by the Chumbi district of Tibet. The estimated area is 2,818 square miles, and the population (1901) is 59,401. The Bhutias are the masters of the land. They are of Mongol race, and have come into the country from Tibet. The Lepchas are of quite another type, and have a language of their own. They seem to be the aborigines of the country, and call themselves "Rong," the name Lepcha being given to them by their neighbors. They are treated almost as serfs by the Bhutias. The Church of Scotland Foreign Missions Committee established a mission in Sikkim in 1886, of which the working force consisted in 1901 of 2 missionaries, with 22 native workers, 14 day schools, and 94 professed Christians.

SIKONGE: A settlement in German East Africa, situated in the district of Ngulu, about 100 miles S. E. of Urambo. Station of the Moravian Missions (1902), with 1 missionary and his wife and 1 place of worship.

SI LAITLAIT: A village in Sumatra, Dutch East Indies, situated a little S. of Toba Lake. Station of the Rhenish Mission Society, with (1903) 1 missionary and his wife, 52 native workers, 10 outstations, 1 Sunday school, 11 day schools, and 1,490 professed Christians, of whom 639 are communicants. The station headquarters have been transferred to Butar.

SILCHAR: A town in Assam, India, situated on the lowlands, about 60 miles E. of Sylhet. Connected by railroad with Chittagong. Station of the Welsh Calvinistic Methodist Missionary Society, with 2 missionaries and their wives, 2 women missionaries, 7 native workers, 1 place of worship, 4 Sunday schools, 5 day schools, 1 dispensary, and 108 professed Christians, of whom 58 are communicants.

SILOAM. See TIRUKOVILUR.

SILOE. See SHILOH (BASUTOLAND).

SI MANOSOR: A village in Sumatra, Dutch East Indies, situated near the W. coast 23 miles S. E. of Siboga. Station of the Rhenish Mission Society, with (1903) 1 missionary and his wife, 11 native workers, 8 outstations, 3 day schools, and 155 professed Christians, of whom 40 are communicants.

SI MATORKIS: A village in Sumatra, Dutch East Indies, situated near Padang Sidempuan, about 23 miles S. E. of Siboga. Station of the Java Committee (Netherlands), with 1 missionary and his wife and 1 day school.

SIMBANG: A village in Kaiser Wilhelmsland, New Guinea, situated on the sea coast, on the easternmost point of the German colony. Station of the Neuendettelsau Mission Institute (1886), with (1901) 3 missionaries, two of them with their wives, and 1 day school.

SIMLA: A town in the Punjab, India, 170 miles north of Delhi, situated in the Ambala division, among the foot-hills of the Himalayas. Chief sanitarium and summer capital of India. A very pleasant place, except for its inadequate water supply. Climate cool, exhilarating, healthful, tho for several reasons the difficulties of drainage are considerable. Population averages 12,000, changing with the season. Station of the CMS (1899), with (1903) 1 missionary and his wife, 3 native workers, and 87 professed Christians, of whom 29 are communicants. Station also of the Moravian Missions (1900), with (1903) 1 missionary and his wife and 1 day school. Also station of the SPG, with (1903) 3 women missionaries, 3 native workers, 2 day schools. Station also of the YWCA, with 2 women agents of the Society.

SIMONTON, Ashbel Green: Born at West Hanover, Pa., January 20, 1833. Died December 9, 1867. Graduated at Princeton College, 1852; taught two years, and graduated at Princeton Theological Seminary 1858; ordained by the Presbytery of Carlisle; appointed the first missionary of the PN to Brazil, and reached Rio de Janeiro August 12, 1859. While acquiring the language he preached in English to Americans and other foreigners. He soon became an effective preacher in Portuguese, and his ministry was remarkably blessed. At almost every communion additions were made to the church, mostly from the Church of Rome. He knew how to use the press as an important auxiliary. He translated the Shorter Catechism and other works into Portuguese. He edited also the "Imprensa Evangelica," a religious monthly, in which his own articles, which were often of rare value, attracted the attention of readers among the educated classes. As he had been pioneer in this mission, so to the end he was one of its leading members. Master of the language, and possessing unusual prudence in planning and tact in executing, he was relied upon by his associates. Necessity alone could lead them to take any important step without first hearing his counsel.

SIMORANGKIR: A village in Sumatra, Dutch East Indies, situated in the Silindung Valley district, about 5 miles E. of Pea Radja. Station of the Rhenish Missionary Society, with (1903) 1 missionary and his wife, 1 woman missionary, 44 native workers, 6 outstations, 5 Sunday schools,

8 day schools, and 3,191 professed Christians, of whom 1,599 are communicants.

SIN-AN. See HSIN-AN-HSIEN.

SINCHANG. See HSIN-CHANG-HSIEN.

SIND: A part of the Northwest Frontier Province of India. It occupies the lower part of the Indus valley, including the delta of that river. West of it lies Baluchistan, east Rajputana, and south the Arabian Sea and the Rann of Kachchh. It has an average density of population of only about 50 to the square mile. The country is largely destitute of trees, flat and uninteresting in appearance. Its soil is, in many places, strongly impregnated with salt. Mohammedans preponderate, over three-quarters of the population being of that faith. Hindus constitute only an eighth, Sikhs about 5 per cent., aboriginal tribes about 3 per cent., Christians over 7,000, Jains and Parsees a thousand or more each. The Sindis represent the original Hindu population, but are now Mohammedans, having been converted under the reign of early Mohammedan rulers. The history of the province is complicated, and not of special interest. For many centuries it was ruled alternately by Hindu and by Mohammedan dynasties. As English power on the coast became stronger, entanglements with outlying native rulers were inevitable. At times the use of armed force against them was necessary for self-defense or for retaliation; and at other times treaties for trade and commerce would be made, and very likely broken, which again was supposed to render necessary military measures. As a result of such relationships, Sind was conquered in 1843 by an army under Sir Charles Napier, and formally annexed to British dominions. Karachi is the chief town; it lies at the northern end of the Indus delta, and by the erection of elaborate harbor works it has been made one of the most important seaports in Western India.

The Church Missionary Society occupied Karachi in 1850 and Haidarabad in 1857. The success has been small. The American Methodists began work in Karachi, largely among unevangelized Europeans, in 1872 or 1873. Education has made rapid progress since the advent of British power. In 1859-60 there were only 20 government schools; in 1883-84 there were 340, with 23,273 pupils. There are also private schools, not included in the government figures. The last census shows a gratifying number of men and women who can read and write. The language in principal use is Sindhi, one of the Sanskrit family.

SINDHIA'S DOMINIONS: A name sometimes applied to the state of Gwalior, India; ruled under British protection by one of the old Mahratta families known as that of the Maharaja of Sindhia.

SIN-FENG. See HSIN-FENG-HSIEN.

SINGAN, or **SI-NGAN-FU.** See HSI-NGAN-FU.

SINGAPORE: An island about 27 miles long by 14 wide, containing an area of 206 square miles; situated at the southern extremity of the Malay peninsula, from which it is separated by a strait about three-quarters of a mile wide. It is a part of the crown colony of Great Britain named the Straits Settlements. A number of small islands adjacent to it are also included in its territory. The population is composed of Europeans, Malays, Chinese, and natives of India. Singapore town, at the southeastern part of the island, is the seat of government for the Settlements, has a well-defended harbor, and has $12\frac{1}{4}$ miles of tramway. The climate is warm, but not unhealthful.

SINGAPORE: A town in the Straits Settlements, Malaysia, situated on the S. side of Singapore Island. It is a depot for commerce E. and W., and is the most southern point of Asia. The streets are wide, except in the Chinese and Malay quarters. Population, 186,600, of whom 1,200 are Europeans. Station of the SPG (1861), with (1903) 1 missionary, 15 native workers, 2 places of worship, 1 day school, and 350 professed Christians. Also station of the PCE, with (1900) 2 missionaries, one of them with his wife; 10 native workers, 10 outstations, 10 places of worship, and 419 professed Christians, of whom 240 are communicants. Station of the PB, with 2 missionaries and their wives, 2 women missionaries. Also station of the ME, with (1903) 8 missionaries, five of them with their wives; 4 women missionaries, 49 native workers, 2 places of worship, 4 day schools, 2 boarding schools, 1 college, and 283 professed Christians. Station also of the CEZ (1900), with (1903) 2 women missionaries, 1 native worker, and 1 boarding school. Also agency of the BFBS, with 2 men and 4 women engaged in Bible work.

SING-IU. See HSIEN-YU-HSIEN.

SINKUNIA: A village in Sierra Leone, West Africa, situated near the N. border of the Protectorate, in the region of the Yalunka tribes. Station of the CMS (1897), which is temporarily without a resident missionary, with (1903) 6 native workers, 2 outstations, 2 day schools.

SI-NING. See HSI-NING-FU.

SIN-TIEN-TSI. See HSIN-TIEN-TSZE.

SIN TU. See HSIN-TU.

SINYONG. See HSIN-YANG-CHAU.

SIOKE: A town in Fo-kien, China, situated about 40 miles W. of Amoy. Station of the RCA (1887), with 2 missionaries and their wives, 15 native workers, 7 outstations, 11 places of worship, 3 day schools, 1 boarding school, 1 dispensary, 1 hospital, and 367 professed Christians. Some write the name Sio-khe.

SIONI MALWA. See SEONI.

SIPAHUTAR: A village in Sumatra, Dutch East Indies, situated in the Toba Lake region. Station of the Rhenish Missionary Society, with (1903) 1 missionary and his wife, 31 native workers, 8 outstations, 9 day schools, 1 Sunday school, and 995 professed Christians, of whom 446 are communicants.

SIPIONGOT: A village in Sumatra, Dutch East Indies, situated in the Batang Toru district, about 62 miles E. by N. of Siboga. Station of the Rhenish Missionary Society, with (1903) 1 missionary and his wife, 14 native workers, 11 outstations, 9 day schools, and 551 professed Christians, of whom 138 are communicants.

SIPIROK: A village of Sumatra, situated in the valley of the Batang Toru, about 40 miles S. E. of Siboga. Station of the Rhenish Missionary Society, with (1903) 1 missionary and his wife, 26 native workers, 6 outstations, 10 day schools, 2 Sunday schools, and 1,102 professed Christians, of whom 442 are communicants.

SIPOHOLON: A village in Sumatra, Dutch

East Indies, situated in the Silindung region S. of Toba Lake, and about 5 miles N. W. of Pea Radja. Station of the Rhenish Missionary Society, with (1903) 3 missionaries and their wives, 2 women missionaries, 68 native workers, 9 outstations, 10 day schools, and 4,269 professed Christians, of whom 1,723 are communicants.

SIROMBU: A village on Nias Island, Dutch East Indies, situated on the S. W. coast, about 25 miles S. by W. of Gunong Sitoli. Station of the Rhenish Missionary Society, with (1903) 1 missionary and his wife, 7 native workers, 1 outstation, 1 day school, 1 Sunday school, and 636 professed Christians, of whom 350 are communicants.

SITAPUR: A town in the United Provinces, India, situated in Oudh, about 55 miles N. by W. of Lucknow. Station of the ME, with (1903) 1 missionary and his wife, 2 women missionaries, 39 native workers, 3 places of worship, 35 Sunday schools, 2 day schools, 2 boarding schools, and 449 professed Christians. Some write the name Sitapore.

SITKA: A town and seaport in Alaska, situated on the W. coast of Baranoff Island. Capital of Alaska Territory. Population, 1,200. Station of the Presbyterian Home Missionary Society (1877), with (1900) 6 missionaries and their wives, 6 native workers, 1 place of worship, 1 day school, 1 boarding school, and 349 professed Christians. Station also of the PE, with (1903) 2 missionaries, 1 place of worship, 1 Sunday school, and 60 professed Christians.

SIUT. See ASYUT.

SIVAS: A town in Asiatic Turkey, capital of the province of Sivas; situated on the Kizil Irmak (*anc. Halys*) River, at an altitude of about 4,000 feet, and 500 miles E. by S. of Constantinople. Population about 43,000, of whom 30,000 are Muslims. Station of the ABCFM (1851), with (1903) 3 missionaries and their wives, 2 women missionaries, 39 native workers, 11 outstations, 5 places of worship, 10 Sunday schools, 26 day schools, 3 boarding schools, 2 orphanages, 1 dispensary, 1 industrial school, and 320 communicant Christians.

SKAGUAY: A town in Alaska, situated at the head of Lynn channel. Terminus of a railroad over the mountains to Whitehorse. Station of the Peniel Missionary Society, with (1900) 3 women missionaries. Also station of the PE, with (1903) 1 missionary, 2 women missionaries, 1 place of worship, 1 hospital, and 41 professed Christians.

SKIDEGATE: A settlement on Graham Island, British Columbia, N. W. America, situated on the southern coast of the island, on the inlet separating it from Queen Charlotte's Island. Station of the MCC (1883), with (1900) 1 missionary and his wife, 1 place of worship, 1 Sunday school, and 141 professed Christians.

SLAVE TRADE AND MISSIONS: One would fain forget the unspeakable horrors of "the middle passage," where, in the stifling hold of a small vessel, human beings were packed like dead freight, that neither eats, nor drinks, nor breathes. Yet it is worth while to recall that missionaries have exerted no small influence in bringing to an end the traffic in human flesh in its last strongholds of Africa. The system is not dead, but great expanses of territory have been forever closed to the Muslim slave-raider. The voice of the missionary has ever been powerful to arouse the public to the duty of holding the slaver in check, because, as a pioneer of a religion of love, he notes and reports the horrors practised where pure selfishness rules.

Livingstone, in his *Last Journals*, gives some account of brutalities which he saw on the road. June 19, 1866, he passed a woman tied by the neck to a tree and dead; she could not keep up with the rest, and in order that she should not become the property of another she was thus despatched, Dr. Livingstone saw others tied up in the same way, and one lying in the path in a pool of blood. June 26 he passed another woman lying dead in the road. Bystanders told how an Arab had killed her early that morning, in anger that he must lose the money paid for her, because she was too exhausted to walk any further. His *Last Journals* gives an account of a merciless and unprovoked massacre of hundreds of native women and others.

We learn something from the pages of other modern travelers of the slave trade as carried on by Muslim Arabs. November 24, 1883, H. M. Stanley was steaming up the Congo on his way to Stanley Falls, not far from the mouth of the Werre, as it comes in from the north; he looked for the town of Mawembe, which he had passed in his first voyage down the river. The site was there, the clearing in the forest, and the white paths up the banks, but not a house or living thing was to be seen. The palisade had disappeared. The leaves of the banana trees were scorched and their stems blackened, showing the effects of the fire that had wiped out the town a few days before. Three days later he sent a boat to ascertain what slate-colored object was floating down stream, and found the bodies of two women bound together with cords. This tragedy had taken place only twelve hours before. Soon after he came in sight of the horde of banditti, 300 strong, with a like number of domestic slaves and women. Sixteen months had they been engaged in their work of slaughter. They had desolated a region of 34,570 square miles, 2,000 square miles larger than Ireland; 118 villages in 43 districts had been destroyed, containing at least 118,000 people, and all they had to show as the result of these sixteen months of slaughter over so extensive a region was a wretched, ragged, and starving crowd of 2,300 women and children, with not one grown-up man among them. Five expeditions in all had already carried as many captives away as these possessed. To obtain these 2,300 they must have shot 2,500 men, while 1,300 more had perished by the way from hunger and despair. On an average, six persons had been killed to obtain each puny child in the encampment. The slaves were fettered in groups of twenty chained together; such fruits as could be found were thrown down before each gang, to fight for as they might, and the odors and abominations of the crowded camp were simply horrible. The bones of many stared through the skin, that hung in flabby wrinkles. He adds, "How small a number of them will see the end of their journey, God only knows!" The process of their capture was as horrid as their condition, when Mr. Stanley saw them, was full of misery. The Arab stole up stealthily at midnight through the darkness to the doomed town: no sound save the chirping of insects disturbs the sleepers, till suddenly the torch was applied on all sides, and in the light of the flames of the grass roofs of the houses the deadly musket shot down the men as fast as they appeared. Many might succeed in reaching the shelter of the woods, but the women and children were seized and carried off. Mr. Stanley estimated that the gain of the Arabs from the slaughter was only 2 per cent. of the previous population, and that even that was reduced to 1 per cent. before the raiders reached their destination.

This account of the great explorer is supported by masses of testimony from the missionaries of the Nyasa region, who had many terrible experiences with the slave dealers. Rev. J. A. Bain, at Maindu, 35 miles northwest of Lake Nyasa, on the Kiwira River, wrote as follows in 1889: "At daybreak, March 15, we were awoke by a number of shots fired in rapid succession; we were told it was Mereri with two bands of Arabs. The surprise was complete. More than thirty women with babes and several girls were captured. The men, only half awake, tried to defend their wives and children, but were driven back by the murderous firing. The Arabs entrenched themselves in a bamboo stockade, then glutted their lust on their captives. Two children, whose weeping over the dead bodies of their mothers disturbed the orgies, were flung into the flames of a burning house. The two following days were spent in plundering and destroying the villages. The cattle are Mereri's. The women are claimed by the Arabs, who will sell them when they tire of them. They left, after burning everything that could be burned."

Another English missionary at Kibanga, on Lake Tanganyika, wrote in 1888: "At night we could see the villages everywhere in flames, the people fleeing for refuge to the lake, and the brigands leading away the women and children in long files. A poor old woman as she was led away caught hold of the clothing of the missionary and begged him to save her, but she was hauled away by the rope that was round her neck; another received a wound from the butt end of a pistol. Where yesterday we sought to impart instruction and comfort, now reigns the silence of a desert."

The Rev.(afterward Bishop) Chauncey Maples, of the Universities Mission, during a residence of six or seven years never went 70 miles from Masasi without meeting a caravan of slaves. One of them numbered 2,000, and, according to Mr. Stanley, that number must represent an amount of butchery and an extent of territory turned from populous villages into a desert that is appalling to think of.

Dr. Kerr Cross wrote from Karonga in April, 1889: "For five weeks the Arabs have harassed us constantly. They hide in the woods and murder men as they pass to and from their gardens. A few days since a party of Wankondè were thus attacked; one was killed and another wounded. The Arabs cut off the head of their victim and fled home, and it is now stuck on a pole in their stockade. Another was in the woods cutting trees for a house, when Arabs fired on him, piercing his shoulder. Again a band of our men were fired on by Arabs hidden in the long grass; only one was shot, and he was brought in and soon died. A week ago we were awoke at midnight by a volley fired quite near our home. In a few minutes every man was at his post on the stockade, but only one old woman was killed; three bullets had gone through her body. What would be the fate of these poor villagers should the missionaries be driven off?"

The turmoil in Uganda before British control was established, and the insurrection of the Sudanese troops in which Pilkington lost his life, may be traced directly to the Arab slave-raiders, whose business was hampered by the presence of Christians and missionaries. The same is in some degree true of the career of Mahdism in the Sudan. Each was a clash of the system that now stands alone in fostering slavery with the system which proclaims the brotherhood of man as taught in the Gospel. Because Christianity spoiled their trade, the Arabs attempted to crush out the rising Christian power in the upper Nile region.

As to the guilt of Mohammedans in connection with the slave trade, Cardinal Lavigerie was very outspoken, and for years he was in constant intercourse with them. He once remarked: 1. "I do not know in Africa a Muslim state whose ruler does not permit, and often himself practise on his own subjects, and in ways barbarously atrocious, the hunting and sale of slaves.

2. "It is only Muslims who ravage Africa by slave raids and slave-trading.

3. "Where the slave trade is prohibited by Christian powers, I do not know a Mohammedan who does not advocate slavery and declare himself ready to buy or sell negro slaves.

4. "I know personally in Asiatic Turkey and in that part of Africa under the Ottoman Sultan, many places where the slave-trade and the passage of the sad caravans take place with the complicity of Turkish authorities.

5. "Never to my knowledge has any mufti or teacher of the Koran protested against this infamous traffic. On the contrary, in their conversation they recognize it as authorized by the Koran for true believers as regards infidels.

6. "Never to my knowledge has any cadi or Muslim judge pronounced a judgment which implied the condemnation of slavery, but all have sided with the teachers and expounders of the Koran."

In conclusion, we cannot more than barely allude to the unutterable beastliness, as well as cruelty, of these Muslim slave-traders, in connection with the mutilation of boys, for tho the vast majority die after the operation, yet, as the market value of the survivors is greater on account of it than would have been the price of the whole, the horrid work goes on wherever the Muslim power is still unchecked.

The great center of the slave-trade is now in the regions of the Niger, in the Fulani territories, and the Sokoto Empire. British power is slowly advancing and enforcing its prohibition of slave-raiding in those regions, and this infamous commerce must soon come to an end, never to be revived while Christianity lives.

SLAVS: The Slavs belong to the Aryan or Indo-European family, and the group in which they are classed is commonly called the Slavo-Germano-Lithuanian group.

The primitive history of the Slavs and date of their immigrations into Europe are covered with the veil of darkness, like those of many other nations. It is generally supposed that they appeared in Europe after the Germans, and that their original settlements extended between the sources of the rivers Don and Dnieper, and beyond the Dnieper toward the eastern shores of the Baltic Sea and the river Vistula, and toward the south, not farther than the River Pribet. But in the 3d and 4th centuries they are found occupying a district the approximate boundaries of which were: from the river Niemen, as far as the mouth of the river Duna; from the Gulf of Riga over the Valdai Heights as far as the mouth of the Oka; on the east, a line stretching from the Oka to Kieff, and from there to the River Boug, while on the west the line extended to the Carpathian Mountains and the upper Vistula. Toward the end of the 5th or beginning of the 6th century the Slavs occupied the northern banks of the Danube; they soon crossed over and took possession of its southern banks, whence they spread themselves as far down as Albania, Thessaly, Epirus, and even the Peloponnesus.

The introduction of Christianity among the Slavs is the epoch from which their history takes a more definite form. This momentous event was brought about by the combined efforts of two brothers, Cyril and Methodius, natives of Salonica, whom all the Slavs venerate as their apostles and "illuminators," and whom they worship as saints. Cyril, the younger brother, was a man well versed in all the learning that Byzantium, at that time, could impart, and on account of his erudition he was honored with the title of "philosopher." Giving up all the honors and emoluments to which they might have easily attained, the two brothers went to Pannonia at the request of Prince Rostislav, to preach Christianity among the Slavs of Pannonia.

Here they devoted themselves to the spreading of the Gospel and the translation of the Scriptures, and the most essential liturgical books. Cyril devised a Slavic alphabet, constructed on the basis and model of the Greek, which is still known by the name of "Kyrillitza" (Cyril's alphabet). It consisted of 38 letters, 24 of which were the 24 letters of the Greek alphabet, while 14 others were devised by Cyril to express sounds peculiar to the Slavic speech, and for which there were no corresponding Greek letters. In spite of the opposition of the German clergy, Cyril and Methodius succeeded in obtaining the approbation of the Pope, and he allowed them to use the Slavonic language in the church services. During a visit to Rome, in 869, Cyril died, aged 43 years; while Methodius returned to Moravia, having been appointed its bishop by the Pope. But he soon found his position shaken by the virulent opposition of the German clergy, was dispossessed of his bishopric, and died, it is said, in prison, in 885.

The total number of the Slavs is estimated at about 90,000,000, distributed in round numbers as follows; Russians, over 60,000,000; Bulgarians, 4,000,000; Serbo-Croats and Slovenes, about 7,000,000; Czecho-Moravians and Slovaks, 7,-000,000; Poles, about 10,000,000; and Serbo-Lansatians, about 150,000. According to their religious denominations, about 68,000,000 Slavs belong to the Eastern Church, 20,000,000 to the Roman Catholic, 1,500,000 to the Protestant, and about 800,000 are Mohammedans. To the Eastern Church belong the Russians, the Bulgarians, and the Servians; to the Catholic Church belong the Poles, the Czecho-Moravians and Slovaks, the Croats, and the Slovenes. The Protestant Slavs are distributed as follows: Slovaks, 640,000; Poles, 500,000; Czecho-Moravians, 150,000; Serbo-Lansatians, 130,000; Slovenes, 15,000; Servians, 13,000; Bulgarians, 5,000. The Mohammedan Slavs are found chiefly in Bosnia and Herzegovina (500,000), and Bulgaria (about 250,000), who, however, have retained and speak their respective Slavic dialects. The Slavic languages are divided into two branches: (1) Southeastern, including the Russian, the Bulgarian, the Servian, the Croat, and the Slovene, with all their local dialects. (2) Western, including the Bohemian, the Polish, and the Serbo-Lansatian, with all their local dialects. The Roman Catholic Slavs use the Latin language in their church services and the Latin alphabet in their literature, while the Slavs of the Eastern Church use the *Kyrillitza*, with some partial modifications, in their writing, and the "Church-Slavonic" in their churches. This "Church-Slavonic" language is the paleo-Slavonic of Cyril's translation of the Scriptures, modified according to Russian orthography and grammatical construction. The most ancient manuscript of the *Kyrillitza* which bears any certain date is the "Ostromirov Gospel," written in 1053 for a Russian prince named Ostromir. Other manuscripts, written in another alphabet, known as the "Glagolitza," however, probably date as far back as this, or perhaps are even older.

There can be no doubt that even in the 9th and the 10th centuries various Slavic dialects existed, just as we find them now; but these dialects were nearer to each other than at present. This explains how the work accomplished by Cyril and Methodius was accessible to all the Slavs in the 9th century, and how the literary productions of one Slavic tribe could be very easily transcribed and appropriated by another. But in the course of time these various Slavic dialects have tended to diverge more and more from each other, until at the present time they form quite distinct languages. The common Bulgarian or Servian of to-day can hardly understand the spoken or literary language of the Pole or the Bohemian, nor can the Slovak or the Slovene comprehend the Russian. In grammatical forms and construction all the modern Slavic dialects, with the exception of the Bulgarian, have retained a close resemblance to the paleo-Slovenic language, and one well acquainted with the latter will not find much difficulty in mastering and understanding the various Slavic dialects.

In conclusion, we may say that many fanciful derivations and examples of the word "Slav" have been given. The most probable one is that the word is derived from *Slovo*, which means "word" or "speech," and the name in its ancient orthography is *Slovyanin*. *Slovyanin* means "man of speech," while the Germans, the nearest neighbors of the Slavs in olden time, were and are still called by the Slavs, Nyemtzi, from "nyem," meaning "dumb."

SLOVAKS: The Slovaks are, strictly speaking, only a branch of the Bohemian race, and their language may be considered as a dialect of the Bohemian language. But of late years a separatist movement has arisen among them, and they are trying to form a literature of their own and to be treated as a nation apart from the Bohemians.

The Slovaks inhabit the northwest of Hungary, and number over two millions. The greater mass of them (1,583,000) belong to the Roman Catholic, and 640,000 to the Protestant Church. They settled in the territory they now occupy toward the end of the 5th century, and shared the fate of the Bohemians and Moravians in many historical catastrophes. Christianity was introduced among them before the first half of the 9th century by German preachers; and later on in the same century Methodius, the Slavic apostle, introduced among them the doctrines of the Eastern Church, together with the Slavic liturgy. But this form of Christianity could not be maintained for long, and after the death of Methodius (885) it was replaced by Latin Christianity and the Latin liturgy. In 907 the Hungarians put an end to the existence of the great Moravian kingdom, which had united under one scepter the Slavs of Bohemia and Moravia and the Slovaks. In 999 the country of the Slovaks was conquered by the Poles, but soon after they fell again under the Hungarians, who practically put an end to their political independence. They preserved, however, their local liberties and national immunities for a long time, and in the 15th century the doctrines of Huss found warm adherents and followers among them. The dispersion of the Hussites and the emigration of the Bohemian and Moravian brethren strengthened still more the Slovak reformed party; and the Bohemian language, along with Bohemian books, was established among them. Luther's reformation likewise found an entrance among the Slovaks—not only among the common people, but also among the nobility. But a Roman Catholic reaction, which manifested itself as far back as the 16th century, gradually put down Protestantism among the larger part of the Slovaks. The efforts of the Hungarians to impose upon the Slovaks the Hungarian language, about the end of the 18th century, provoked a counter-movement on the part of the Slovaks, who defended their nationality and language against the encroachments of the Hungarians by developing a national literature of their own.

SLOVENES: The Slovenes inhabit the districts of Carinthia, Kraina, Styria, and Istria in Austria, and number about one and one-third millions. They are classed among the Southeastern Slavs, and their language is one of the South Slavic dialects. It bears a strong relationship to the Serbo-Croatian language, and in its lexicology has a great resemblance to the Bulgarian. The Slovenes belong to the Roman Catholic Church, with the exception of about 15,000 Protestants, and they all use the Latin alphabet, with some slight modifications, in their literature. The Slovenes settled in these parts of Europe in the 6th century, and about the end of the 8th they fell under the dominion of the Franks in the reign of Charlemagne. Their petty princes were allowed to rule over them as vassals of the Franks until, in the course of time, the country was entirely subjugated to German rulers, and ever since has formed a part of Austria. Christianity was introduced among the Slovenes in the 7th century by preachers who came to them from Aquilea (in Italy) and from Salzburg; but in the second half of the 8th century, and especially after the Frankish conquest of the country, the Archbishop of Salzburg, Virgilius (known as the apostle of the Slovenes), succeeded in establishing Christianity among the Slovenes through his German preachers. That the Slavic apostles, Cyril and Methodius, ever labored among the Slovenes is doubtful; still there are some very high authorities on the Slavic languages who claim that the language in which the original translation of the Scriptures was made by SS. Cyril and Methodius was the language of the Slovenes, and not that of the Bulgarians. Hence they call it paleo-Slovenic in distinction from the neo-Slovenic. The most ancient linguistic remains of this old Slovenic language are the so-called "Freisinger Extracts," found in an old Latin manuscript, and referred to the 9th century. Up to the 16th century the Slovenic language seems to have been almost lost, and to have been replaced by the Latin and German. This was due to the fact that literature was exclusively in the hands of the clergy. But when the Reformation found its way among the people a movement was made to bring the vernacular of the people to the front as a means of their enlightenment and instruction. Primus Truber (1508-1586) was the most active laborer for the spread of the new ideas among his people, and for the elevation of the national idiom. He found many followers and adherents, and, thanks to his labors and theirs, a translation of the whole Bible, the first one in Slovenic, was published in 1584, the New Testament having been translated by Truber himself. Unfortunately this reformatory movement did not last long, and in the first half of the 17th century it was suppressed by a Roman Catholic reaction, which violently raged against the reformed party, banishing those who refused to return to the Roman Church, confiscating their property, and burning the books and publications of Truber and his followers with such zeal that few are now to be found. This persecution put a stop to religious and literary progress among the Slovenes, so that literary activity remained at a standstill till the end of the 18th century. But in the general revival of the Slavic dialects and nationalities that began early in the 19th century the Slovenes also have cultivated a national literature in their national tongue, and this movement has gone on increasing, especially since 1860.

SMITH, Azariah: Born at Manlius, N. Y., February 17, 1817; died June 3, 1851, at Aintab, Turkey Graduated from Yale College in the class of 1838. After studying medicine and theology, he was sent to Turkey, November, 1842, as missionary of the ABCFM. After learning the Turkish language he spent five years in visiting the various stations of the Board in Turkey, giving to each the advantage of a "medical department" for a time. Wherever cholera appeared, there Dr. Smith also appeared; and in many a city in Asia Minor, Armenia, and Mesopotamia, Muslims and Christians learned to bless the missionary who seemed miraculously to heal. The preparation widely used in the United States in 1849 as "Dwight's Cholera Mixture," and more lately famous as "Hamlin's Cholera Mixture," was a prescription devised by Dr. Azariah Smith. In 1848 Dr. Smith was definitely stationed at Aintab, and to the people there he became deeply attached. He published valuable papers on the archeology, meteorology, and natural history of Turkey at a time when such papers were rare.

SMITH, Eli: Born at Northford, Conn., September 13, 1801; graduated at Yale College, 1821; taught in Putnam, Georgia, for two years; graduated at Andover Theological Seminary, 1826; ordained May 10, same year; left for Malta under appointment of the ABCFM, May 23, 1826, as superintendent of a missionary printing establishment. In 1827 he went to Beirut to study Arabic. The missionaries being obliged to leave Syria on the general outbreak of the war, after the battle of Navarino, Mr. Smith, in 1828, returned to Malta. He traveled through Greece in 1829, with Rev. Dr. Anderson. In 1830, with Rev. H. G. O. Dwight, he set out from Constantinople for an extended and adventurous exploring tour of Asiatic Turkey, Western Persia, and the Caucasus. The tour occupied a whole year, and secured the information on which was based the establishment of the Board's missions to the Armenians and the Nestorians. Returning to the U. S. in 1832 he published the report of these explorations under the title *Researches in Armenia* (2 vols., Boston, 1833), also a small volume of *Missionary Sermons and Addresses*. In 1833 he embarked for Syria, accompanied by Mrs. Smith, formerly Sarah Lanman Huntington, whose brief but bright missionary career of only three years was terminated by her death at Smyrna, September 30, 1836. In 1837-38 and 1852 he was the companion and coadjutor of Prof. E. Robinson in his extensive explorations of Palestine. By his experience as an Oriental traveler, his tact in eliciting information, and his intimate knowledge of Arabic he contributed largely to the accuracy, variety, and value of the discoveries of Biblical geography recorded in Dr. Robinson's celebrated *Researches*. At the same time these travels, in close relations with the people of the country, added to his own information, and prepared him for the literary work in Arabic which was the great and enduring fruit of his missionary career. He visited the United States again in 1838 and 1845, for reasons of health. During these visits he traveled extensively in the United States, speaking on "Missions" and preaching with great acceptance. He also took the opportunity while passing through Europe to study the methods of Arabic typography there in use, and gathered information which enabled him to make his printing house as complete as possible. For he was all this time pressing on the work of publication of books and tracts. Among his qualifications as translator as well as editor was his ripe scholarship. His learning was extensive and accurate. To the ancient classics he added an acquaintance with French, Italian, German, and Turkish. With the Hebrew he was very familiar, and the Arabic, the most difficult of all, was to him a second vernacular. Not only did his learning fit him for the difficult office of editor, but by long practise and close attention to the business of printing in all its branches, he acquired an unusual skill in managing the minutest details. He not only wrote himself in Arabic, but devoted much time and labor to correcting and editing works written or translated by others. For many years he carefully read the proof-sheets of nearly everything that went through the mission press. He spent also much time and intense labor in superintending the cutting, casting, and perfecting of various fonts of new type made from models which he had himself drawn with the utmost accuracy. This work was done at Leipzig in the celebrated establishment of Tauchnitz. It was in 1847 that Mr. Smith devoted himself to the translation of the Bible into Arabic. To this task all his studies and all his previous work had been made to serve as preparation. After eight years of incessant toil he completed the translation of the New Testament, the Pentateuch, the minor Prophets from Hosea to Nahum, and the greater part of Isaiah.

In 1856 failure of health compelled Dr. Smith (he had received the degree of Doctor of Divinity from Williams College) to suspend his labors for a time. He prayed often and earnestly that he might recover and be permitted to complete his work of translating the Scriptures. But it was not to be. He died at Beirut January 11, 1857.

During all his labors in the literary branch of the mission, Dr. Smith never forgot that he was a messenger of Jesus Christ, and he entered with all his heart into every plan for the spread of divine truth. Being a fluent speaker of colloquial Arabic, it was ever his delight to preach the Gospel in the family, by the wayside, and in public assemblies.

His work of Bible translation was taken up by his associate, Rev. C. V. A. Van Dyck, D.D., and carried to a full and admirable completion.

SMYRNA: A city in Asiatic Turkey, at the head of the Gulf of Smyrna, about 200 miles southwest of Constantinople. Population about 150,000, of whom a little more than half are Mohammedans and the remainder Greeks (40,000), Armenians (10,000), Jews (15,000), and Europeans. The climate is hot and trying, the summer being very oppressive. The general appearance of the city from the sea and also from the Acropolis is very attractive, many of the houses, especially in the Christian quarters and along the quay, being of stone and well built. As a business center Smyrna has grown rapidly in importance, especially since the establishment of two lines of railway connecting it with the interior of Asia Minor. European customs and influence have also been largely predominant, and the intimate connection of the large Greek population with Greece and the islands of the Ægean has helped to make it a center of far greater commercial activity even than Constantinople. It has also derived considerable importance from the fact that it is the only Turkish city which the fleets of Europe and America can visit, and during the cooler months there is seldom a time when one or more warships are not anchored in the roadstead. The colloquial Turkish name of the city is *Giaour Izmiri* (Infidel Smyrna).

As a center for missionary work Smyrna has been prominent from the earliest times. The interest of its name as the home of Polycarp, and as one of the Seven Churches addressed by the Apostle John, naturally drew attention to it; but even more was probably due to the fact that at the commencement of the 19th century it was the only city of Turkey that was really open to missionaries, and with which there was direct communication from European and American seaports. The British and Foreign Bible Society early established an agent here, and the first missionaries of the ABCFM to the Levant were located here.

At present the missionary societies working in Smyrna are as follows: ABCFM (1820), with (1903) 3 missionaries, two with their wives; 6 women missionaries, 46 native workers, men and women; 5 outstations, 7 day schools, 1 kindergarten, 2 boarding schools, 1 college, and 203 professed Christians; London Jews Society (1829), with (1903) 1 missionary and his wife and 4 native workers; Church of Scotland Jewish Mission, with (1900) 6 missionaries, men and women; 2 schools, a dispensary, and a hospital; Kaiserswerth Deaconesses' Institute (1853), with (1903) 14 deaconesses and assistants, 1 boarding school, 1 orphanage, and 1 sanitarium for deaconesses; FCMS (1891), with (1901) 1 missionary and his wife, 1 woman missionary, 1 place of worship, 1 day school, and 14 professed Christians. There is also a Sailors' Rest, which serves as a center for work among foreign sailors, and also for native inquirers.

One of the most interesting developments of missionary work has been the formation and the growth of the Greek Evangelical Alliance. It originated in the effort of Rev. Geo. Constantine, D.D., a native Greek educated in America, to place the work among the Greeks on a firm basis of self-support. Dr. Constantine commenced a series of sermons in the hall connected with "The Rest," and by his eloquence drew large crowds. A profound impression was made, and the hierarchy saw that they were in danger of losing their power. The volatile nature of the Greeks rendered it easy to stir a tumult. Threats were uttered, stones were thrown at the windows of the hall, and on one Sunday a mob attacked the place, seeking especially for Dr. Constantine. Not finding him, they turned and went to his house, which they assaulted.

The priests soon saw that such proceedings chiefly injured their own church. The result was a greater interest in Christian life than at any time before. The Alliance grew until it has become a most potent influence, not only in Smyrna, but in many other Greek communities of Asia Minor.

SMYTHIES, Charles Alan: Bishop of Zanzibar and Missionary Bishop in East Central Africa. Born August 6, 1844. Died, 1894. He was consecrated in St. Paul's Cathedral in 1883, and left England the first of the following year for his work in Africa, arriving in Zanzibar on February 25, 1884. In 1885 he paid his first visit to Lake Nyasa, and during this visit he secured a site on the island of Likoma, a convenient and comparatively healthful center for the Universities Mission work on the lake. This mission settlement on the lake showed a steady increase; in four years the staff had more than doubled; and the little steel vessel, built in England and sent out in four hundred packages, enabled the missionaries to found station after station on the lake shore. Under the supervision of the bishop, the work at Zanzibar steadily grew in power. At Kiungani, where Bishop Smythies resided, a theological college was formed, which was the heart of the mission. In 1889, and again in 1891, the bishop visited every station under his jurisdiction; and in 1890, on his trip home, he conferred with the German Chancellor, in order, if possible, to remove the possibility of friction with the German agents on the East Coast of Africa, since by a recent treaty the Magila stations remained within the sphere of German influence. The interview was entirely successful, and the effect of this visit was most beneficial to the cause of missions in and around Zanzibar. In the completion, equipment, and opening of the hospital at Zanzibar, Bishop Smythies saw the fruit of years of earnest labor, and it has proven to be an institution of increasing usefulness. Bishop Smythies was buried at sea, May 7, 1894.

SOCIETY FOR PROMOTING CHRISTIAN KNOWLEDGE: This Society is the oldest organization for Christian work in the Church of England. It was founded in 1698, and has since carried on its work in ever-widening spheres of activity, and with ever-increasing expenditure of funds. Its history has not been furnished us, and the meager outline which can be gained from its report must suffice instead of the lengthy notice which is its due, both on account of its age and its wide-spread usefulness.

The Society is composed of persons who must, of necessity, be members of the Church of England or some church in full communion with it. New members are received on recommendation of the existing members, after which they are elected, and on payment of a certain annual sum are entitled to full privileges. Persons who make subscriptions are entitled to some privileges in the form of receiving books and tracts; thus the Society is a close, self-perpetuating organization, with intimate connection with the Church of England, tho apparently responsible to no one except its own elected authorities.

His Majesty the King of England is the patron of the Society. The Archbishop of Canterbury is the president, and there are numerous vice-presidents, comprising mainly the other archbishops and bishops of the Church of England, together with like dignitaries of any church in full communion with the Church of England, who may be members of the Society. There are four treasurers, two general secretaries, and two who are designated organizing secretaries. A general committee of administration called the Standing Committee is assisted by special committees, such as the Committee of Finance, of Foreign Translation, of General Literature, the Tract Committee, etc.

Under one broad comprehensive title, the Society combines the work of many departments, each of which might well be the work of a single society. In its endeavor to aid Christian work of any kind throughout the world it is:

1. *The Bible and Prayerbook Society of the Church of England:* In this branch of the work is included the producing and circulating of these books or portions of them not only in England but throughout the world. The publication is in seventy-five or more different languages. By grants of money or books; by supplying these publications at cost or less; by assisting translation and publication committees in various foreign lands, the work is carried on, and during the year 1900 about 60,000 books and tracts were circulated in non-Christian lands.

2. *A Tract and Pure Literature Society:* It produces and circulates distinctively religious works, together with works by able writers, on science, history, and topics of general interest and utility, including fiction of an elevating character. In connection with this branch of the work, grants of books are made to churches, reading-rooms, missions of every kind, seamen, soldiers, etc.

3. *A Home Church Mission and Education Society:* In addition to the general Home Missionary work carried on along the lines already mentioned, there are the following distinctive objects of its care:

(a) A college (St. Katherine's) at Tottenham, England, where school-mistresses are trained. (b) A training college for lay-workers maintained in the east of London. (c) Money is given toward the building and fitting up of church institutes, and the building and renting of Sunday schools, together with other purposes in connection with church education, such as the providing of lecturers on church history, the preparation of lectures, and magic-lantern slides, to be rented out at low rates to churches or districts desiring such means of educating the masses, and many other plans along the same general lines.

4. *A Foreign and Colonial Missionary Society:*

This work is accomplished in various particular ways:

(a) Churches, chapels, and mission-rooms are built or aided in dioceses of the Church the world over. (b) Native clergy and lay mission agents are trained for the work. (c) Medical missions are maintained or established, and medical missionaries, both men and women, are trained. (d) Funds are provided for the support of clergymen called to work in destitute regions. (e) As mentioned above, Bible translation and other work of similar character has been aided, and books of many varieties have been donated, or the work of publication assisted. In connection with this work, the Translation Committee is assisted by vernacular sub-committees in Madras (Tamil and Telugu), Punjab, Sind, Bombay, and Calcutta. Depots for the Society's publications have been established at many places on the Continent of Europe.

5. *Emigrants' Spiritual Aid Society:* An important and, in some respects, unique feature of the work of the Society is the care which it exercises over the many emigrants who annually leave the shores of Great Britain for other lands. These emigrants are watched over both spiritually and temporally; chaplains attend them on their departure, and letters are given to the Society's representatives in foreign lands, who meet the emigrants on their arrival, give them aid in locating in their new homes, besides protecting them from the wiles of those who are ready to take advantage of their ignorance and strangeness. In many cases chaplains are deputed to accompany a shipload of emigrants, and a matron is sent to look after the single women. During the voyage—a long one when Australia, New Zealand, or South America is the objective point—the Gospel is preached, church ordinances are administered, and the weary days whiled away by lectures which deal with the country of their destination, in regard to which many of the emigrants are sadly ignorant. At the principal ports of the United States, Canada, Tasmania, Australia, South Africa, South America, and New Zealand representatives of the Society meet emigrants on arrival to render any needed service.

These, briefly stated, are the various branches of the important work of the Society. Two facts of this work should be borne in mind by all interested in Foreign Missions: 1st. This Society aided, and at last entirely supported, during nearly one hundred years, the Mission (Danish-Halle) in South India, founded by the King of Denmark at the beginning of the 18th century. 2d. The Society has furnished translations of Holy Scripture and other religious literature—particularly the Prayer Book—in many insignificant or transitory dialects of obscure tribes. The number of volumes or copies of tracts issued at home and abroad by the Society, each year, is about 14,000,000.

SOCIETY FOR THE PROPAGATION OF THE GOSPEL IN FOREIGN PARTS: From the time of Cranmer (1534) the different movements for English colonization recognized, more or less clearly in principle, the necessity of Christian work, but the performance fell so far short that, in 1675, an inquiry was instituted by the authorities of the Church of England into the situation. One result was the organization, in 1698, of the Society for Promoting Christian Knowledge. The limited scope of this Society did not meet all the need, and in 1701 a special committee was appointed in the Lower House of the Convocation of the Province of Canterbury to inquire "into ways and means for Promoting Christian Religion in our Foreign Plantations." The result was a petition to the King, granted by William III., on which a charter was drawn up, and, in its turn, granted by the King. The first meeting was held at Lambeth Palace, June 27, 1701, the "letters patent" presented, officers elected, and steps taken for full organization of the Society for the Propagation of the Gospel in Foreign Parts.

The organization of the Society, as completed by supplemental charter in 1882, includes: 1. Incorporated members (1900), about 6,000 in number, elected by the corporation, in virtue of donations to the Society's funds, or special service rendered.

2. A Standing Committee, including certain members *ex officio* (the President, Vice-President, Treasurer, and Secretary), 24 members elected by the Society out of the incorporated members (six retiring annually), and Diocesan Representatives (two for each diocese in England and Wales, and four each for Armagh and Dublin, in Ireland) also elected from resident incorporated members.

3. The President is the Archbishop of Canterbury, and the Archbishop of York and the Bishops of the Church of England holding sees in England and Wales are Vice-Presidents. The Lord Almoner and Dean of Westminster, the Dean of St. Paul's and Archdeacon of London, and the two Regius and two Margaret Professors of Divinity of Oxford and Cambridge are members *ex officio.*

Aside from certain special duties reserved for the Society, the entire management rests with the Standing Committee, ten members forming a quorum. The Society meets once a month, but, aside from some routine business, these meetings are distinctly missionary in their character. At the annual meeting of the Society for the election of members, officers, etc., all incorporated members are entitled to vote, absentees being allowed the use of voting papers. Only once has a poll of the entire Society been taken in this manner (1894).

The Society depends for most of its support upon the regular diocesan and parish organizations of the Church of England, but it has kept pace with modern development by the formation of children's associations, and has also junior clergy missionary associations. The most efficient agency, however, is the Women's Mission Association. This was first suggested in 1866, approved by the Society, and the complete organization effected on May 11 of that year.

The original title was "Ladies' Association for Promoting the Education of Females in India and other Heathen Countries in Connection with the Missions of the Society for the Propagation of the Gospel." This was altered in 1895 to "Women's Mission Association for the Promotion of Female Education in the Missions of the SPG," and its objects defined: "(1) To provide missionary teachers for the Christian instruction of native women and girls in such countries by supporting abroad and selecting and preparing in this country, Church women well qualified for the work; (2) to assist female schools; (3) to employ other methods for promoting Christian education; (4) to assist generally in keeping up an interest in the work of the Society." Tho independent of the Society as regards its funds, its methods of work were in entire harmony with the plans of the Society, and it entered no fields without its approval. The development, however, was so rapid, and its system of diocesan and parochial associations so parallel with that of the Society, that it was deemed best, in 1903, to secure a still closer arrangement. This went into effect January 1, 1904. (1) The WMA Committee became the Committee of Women's Work (SPG); (2) WMA branches became local associations of SPG; (3) WMA workers became SPG workers; (4) the WMA general fund was amalgamated with the SPG general fund; (5) where a special interest is preferred contributions may be so designated. Provision was also made for increased representation of subscribers, and each diocese has the right to send a representative to the committee, also every woman subscriber to SPG may vote at the election of new members to succeed those retiring, under the by-laws, at the annual meeting of the Society.

By the terms of the charter the object of the Society was (1) to provide maintenance for an orthodox clergy in the plantations, colonies, and factories of Great Britain beyond the seas, for the instruction of the King's loving subjects in the Christian religion; (2) to make such other provision as may be necessary for the propagation of the Gospel in those parts; (3) to receive, manage, and dispose of the charity of His Majesty's subjects for those purposes. The first action was an inquiry as to the religious state of the colonies; the second the raising of a fund. As to the scope of the Society's work, it was interpreted at first as being primarily the interests of "our own people," then the "conversion of the natives;" but in 1710 it was laid down by the Society that that branch of its design which related to the "conversion of heathens and infidels ought to be prosecuted preferably to all others." While this exclusive policy was not pursued, the Society has never, even from the beginning, lost sight of this part of its missionary character and duty.

North America: For the greater part of the 18th century the colonies of Great Britain in America, together with the negroes and Indians, constituted the principal field of the Society. Its first missionary, Rev. Geo. Keith, originally a Presbyterian, afterward a Friend, and then a member of the Church of England, landed in Boston June 11, 1702. The next move was to South Carolina, where Rev. S. Thomas landed at Charleston, December 25, 1702. Other sections were occupied, and considerable work was done among the Indians, as well as for the colonists. In the political disturbances, in 1776, the Society's missionaries, numbering 77 in all, were loyal to the Crown, and were nearly all forced to retire from their missions, altho a few eventually took the oath of allegiance to the republic. The result of the war, "while it almost destroyed the Church in the 'United States,' set her free to obtain that gift of the Episcopate so long denied." In 1785 the Society formally withdrew from the mission field in the United States, in which it had employed 309 missionaries among 6 European-Colonial races, negroes, and 14 Indian tribes, conducting its work in 8 languages.

Other fields were taken up in North America as follows: Newfoundland, 1703-5, again in 1726; the Bermudas, 1822; Nova Scotia, 1728-43, 1749; Quebec, 1759-64; New Brunswick, 1783; Ontario, 1784; Cape Breton, 1785; Prince Edward Island, 1819; Manitoba and Northwest Territories, 1850; British Columbia, 1859.

In all of these, 921 central stations have been occupied, and 1,597 ordained missionaries (European and Colonial) employed among the 12 European-Colonial races, 31 Indian tribes, as well as negroes, Chinese, Japanese, and mixed races, using 12 languages. At the time of the organization of the Society there were 500 (estimated) church members and 2 clergy. In 1900 there were 666,175 members of the Church of England, and 1,310 clergy, including 169 in the employ of the SPG.

In 1902 the General Synod of a Missionary Society, consisting of members of the Church of England in Canada, was formed for the special prosecution of missionary work among the Indians, Eskimos, etc.

West Indies: The SPG made grants of books and passage money to clergymen going to the West Indies as early as 1703, but did not undertake special work in that field until 1712, when it came into possession of the Codrington estates in Barbadoes, willed to the Society for the special purpose of maintaining "Monks and Missionaries to be employed in the Conversion of Negroes and Indians." Plans were immediately made for a college, but the building was not completed until 1745. On the abolition of slavery the compensation money was invested by the Society for the benefit of the college. The income of late years has considerably fallen off, but there are still several scholarships, and there is also connected with it a Mission House for training workers for Africa. It has been affiliated with the University of Durham. The hurricanes that have devastated the islands, and more recently the terrible eruption at St. Vincent, have heavily taxed the Society's ability to help the weak churches.

The Bahamas were occupied by a representative of the Society in 1733, but the work was chiefly among the settlers, and it was not until the abolition of slavery in 1835 that any special forward movement was made. In that year work was commenced, with special reference to the negroes in Tobago, the Leeward Islands, and Jamaica, and the next year in Trinidad. The Society has been specially interested in the Jamaica Church Theological College, founded in 1883.

Central America: In 1742 the Society's attention was drawn to the needs of the Indians of the Mosquito Coast, and six years later a missionary was sent, but comparatively little was done there or in British Honduras, occupied temporarily in 1844, and again in 1877, and 1892. In 1883 the Society sent a chaplain to Panama to care for the laborers who went in companies from Jamaica and other islands, and in 1896 it sent a chaplain to Costa Rica.

South America: The Society's labors in South America have been chiefly in British Guiana, tho a missionary was maintained for a few years (1860-7) in the Falkland Islands. In Guiana the work has been chiefly among the aboriginal Indian tribes, Arawaks, Waranos, etc., and among the Chinese and East Indian coolies. Especially successful has been the work in the Pomeroon River, where there are good schools, churches, and parsonages. The Church of England chaplaincies in South America are under the general supervision of the South American Missionary Society.

Africa: The Society entered the African field on the West Coast in 1752; South Africa, 1820; the Seychelles, 1832; Mauritius, 1836; St. Helena, 1847; Madagascar, 1864. In all these sections the work embraced native as well as European races. In North Africa it has had some chaplaincies among the English communities.

West Africa: The Royal African Company, in 1720, made application to the Society to recommend chaplains for their factories, but it was not till 30 years later that an accredited representative went as a missionary. Rev. Thomas Thompson, a graduate of Cambridge, who had served in New Jersey, resolved to devote himself to work in Guinea, and, receiving appointment, arrived at the river Gambia in January, 1752. He went to Sierra Leone, passed into the interior and met with not a little success, sending three boys to London for training, one of whom, Philip Quaque, returned to work among his people, being the first of a non-European race to receive Anglican ordination (1765). There were no great results of the work, and he remained the sole missionary for a considerable part of the time, serving as chaplain. After his death (1816) for eight years two chaplains were commissioned to superintend the free schools, but from 1824 to 1851 the Society had no permanent connection with West Africa, altho it gave some assistance at Bathurst and Fernando Po.

In 1851 the churches in Barbados turned their attention to Africa. and organized a society in connection with the SPG, which the Society assisted with funds. Care was taken to avoid collision with other societies in the region, and, finally, a location was decided upon at Rio Pongas, 130 miles north of Sierra Leone, among the Susus and Mohammedans. Since 1864 the entire work has been in the hands of native missionaries, and has not developed largely.

South Africa: The first work of the Society in South Africa was specially directed to the needs of the English colonists, by the appointment of three chaplains in 1820, supported chiefly by the Government, but directed by the Society. Schools were established, some with special reference to the children of emancipated slaves. The first Bishop of Cape Town was appointed in 1847, and then commenced a more aggressive work for the different classes, especially the Kaffirs. Then two more dioceses, Grahamstown and Natal, were created, the scattered, individual efforts became united, and work among the natives was extended, until it assumed the first place in the Eastern section, the colonists being able to provide for themselves. Thus, while in Cape Town the SPG clergy are all working among colonists, in the dioceses of St. John's and Zululand all (47) are missionaries, working among the natives; in Grahamstown, 14 out of 21; in Natal, 11 out of 21; in Mashonaland, 7 out of 9; in Bloemfontein, 9 out of 16 are missionaries to the heathen. This work has been very successful. Special attention has been paid to education, the institutions of the Society including a college at Zonnebloem, an institution at Grahamstown, a normal college at Keiskama Hoek, a training college at Maritzburg, a college for boys at Balgowan, Natal; St. John's College, Umtata; McKenzie Memorial College at Isandhlwana, St. Mary's Training College in Basutoland, and others at Pretoria and Bloemfontein.

The policy of the Society in educating and ordaining natives and placing them on a par with the white clergy has given it a certain advantage, and has drawn to the Church of England a considerable number who have felt that the other denominations, particularly the Dutch Church, did not recognize them to the full.

A survey of the special fields shows that in Western Cape Colony (1821-1900) the Society employed 112 ordained European missionaries in 57 stations among the colonists; in the Eastern Division (1830-1900), 95 European and 10 native missionaries in 56 stations among the colonists, Kaffirs, and Basutos; in Kaffraria (1855-1900), 52 European and 19 native missionaries in 30 stations among the colonists, half-castes, Kaffirs, Basutos, Fingoes, Hottentots, Griquas, etc.; in Griqualand West (1870-1900), 21 European missionaries in 6 stations among colonists, Kaffirs, Zulus, Matabeles, etc.; in Natal (1849-1900), 85 European and 9 native missionaries in 38 stations among colonists, Kaffirs, East Indians, etc.; in Zululand (1859-1900), 13 European and 1 native missionaries, in 9 stations, among colonists and Zulus; in Swaziland (1879-1900), 4 European missionaries at 1 station, among colonists and Swazis; in Tongaland (1895-1900), 2 European missionaries, itinerants, among the Zulu-Kaffirs; Portuguese E. Africa (1894-1900), 6 European missionaries in 6 stations, among colonists and natives; in the Transvaal (1864-1900), 49 European missionaries, in 32 stations, among colonists, Africans, and East Indians; in Orange River Colony (1850-1900), 23 European and 1 native missionaries, in 6 stations, among colonists and natives; in Basutoland (1875-1900), 16 European missionaries in 5 stations, among colonists and natives; in Bechuanaland (1873-1900), 5 European missionaries in 5 stations among colonists and natives; in Matabele and Mashonaland (1893-1900), 24 European and 1 native missionaries, in 6 stations among colonists and natives; in Central Africa (1879-1881), 1 European and 1 native missionary at 1 station among natives.

The Society has carried on work also in Mauritius and the Seychelles (1832-1900), in St. Helena (1847-1900), in Tristan d' Acunha (1850-56, 1881-9), and in Madagascar (1864-1900). With the exception of Madagascar the work has been chiefly for colonists and for coolies—East Indians, Chinese, etc.

In Madagascar the entire force of 12 European and 22 native missionaries are primarily engaged in work for the Malagasy and creoles, tho they do not neglect the foreign population. St. Paul's College at Ambatoharanana is a flourishing institution.

Australasia: The work of the SPG in this section of the world commenced in 1793 with the appointment of four schoolmasters to New South Wales, two for Sydney, and two for Norfolk Island, where a penal colony had been established. Application was made for a clergyman, especially for work among the convicts, but for one reason and another none was sent until 1841. References were made at different times to the needs of the natives, but practically the entire effort of the Society has been directed to the colonists. The same is true in regard to Victoria (occupied 1838), tho something there was done for the Chinese coolies. In Queensland, on the contrary (1840), considerable attention was paid to the South Sea Islanders, who came there in numbers, as well as to the aborigines and Chinese coolies. The same is true of the work in South and West Australia (1836). In Tasmania (1835) the Society's work has been entirely colonial. Moore College, Sydney; Christ's College, Tasmania, and St. John's Theological College, N. S. W., have been assisted by the Society.

To New Zealand the SPG sent chaplains in 1840 to take up work among the colonists, some of which was the direct result of the labors of the Rev. Samuel Marsden and of the CMS. As the Maori Christian community developed, the Society gave assistance in the local and missionary work until 1880, since which time it has limited its aid to grants in favor of the theological college and a few churches. The connection between the SPG and the Melansian Mission (*q. v.*) was very close from the time of the appointment of Bishop Selwyn in 1841; but its special work is dated from 1849 and continued until 1885, when the Australasian church assumed responsibility, except so far as the Melanesian Mission itself carried on the work. Closely associated with this was the care, for a few years (1853-6), of the Pitcairn Islanders.

Asia: The great work of the SPG in Asia has been in India, dating from 1820. It has also, however, maintained missions in Borneo (1848), Straits Settlements (1856), China (1863), Korea (1889), Japan (1873), and at different times and for limited periods in Western Asia.

India: While the first direct work of the Society in India commenced in 1820, the influence exerted by its organization largely influenced the starting of the Danish-Tamil Mission of Ziegenbalg and Plütschau in 1705. When grants in aid of that mission were later made by the SPCK, the SPG shared in making them, subsequently, as in America, assuming the place of principal. Until early in the 19th century, however, little interest seems to have been felt in England for missions in that land. Commencing with 1806, emphasis began to be laid at the Society's anniversaries on the need of work in India, and as the first step it was urged that a bishopric be established. Finally, through the urgent representations of the SPCK, and of Mr. Wilberforce, the Rev. T. F. Middleton was consecrated the first bishop of Calcutta in the chapel of Lambeth Palace on May 8, 1814. It is significant of the power of the opposition to Christian work in the East that, altho the change in the charter of the East India Company had been made the previous year, and missionaries of other organizations were already in the field, this consecration was private, and the sermon was suppressed. It was four years later that the SPG decided to take up work in India, and it was not until 1820 that Bishop's College was founded at Calcutta. The Bible Society, SPCK, CMS, and SPG united in securing scholarships, and the development of the college in the direction of Bible translation, the preparation of Christian literature, and the education of students for Christian work.

The work of the SPG in the Madras Presidency dates from 1825, when, in response to a special appeal by Bishop Heber, it took up the work which the **Danish Mission** had commenced, but which had been suffered to languish. Here, as in Calcutta, the first efforts were educational. "Bishop Heber's Seminary" was not long-lived, but subsequent efforts were more successful. The first appointment of a missionary to Bombay was in 1830, but it was several years later that work was really inaugurated. The Northwest Provinces were entered at Cawnpore (1833) in response to a special request from the English residents, and Debroghur, in Assam, was occupied by a missionary in 1851, as the result of the appointment of a government chaplain to Assam in 1842. The work of the Society in the Punjab, commenced at Delhi in 1854, was in response to the urgent request of residents, supported by the influences of the lieut.-governor.

The general work of the Society in India, as in Africa, combines the interest of the foreign residents, the conversion of natives, the establishment of the ecclesiastical organization of the Church of England, and of education for all classes in various directions. The diversity of these enterprises makes it practically impossible to do more than give summaries. These, again, in the absence of certain statistics, lose much of their value.

In Bengal (1820-1900) the Society was represented by 75 European and 44 native ordained missionaries in 32 stations; in Madras (1825-1900), by 112 European and 127 native missionaries, in 78 stations; in Bombay (1830-1900), by 42 European and 7 native missionaries in 15 stations; in the United (NW) Provinces (1833-1900), by 28 European and 6 native missionaries, in 5 stations; in the Central Provinces (1846-1892) by 2 European missionaries in 2 stations; in Assam (1851-1900), by 9 European and 2 native missionaries in 4 stations; in Punjab by 32 European and 4 native missionaries in 5 stations; in Kashmir (1866-7, 1893-1900) by 1 European and 1 native missionary at 1 station; in Burma (1859-1900) by 35 European and 21 native missionaries in 17 stations; in Ceylon (1840-1900) by 39 European and 31 native missionaries in 31 stations.

Among the more important educational institutions are: Bishop's College, Calcutta; St. Stephen's College, Delhi; St. John's College, Rangoon; Trichinopoly College; St. Peter's College, Tanjore; Christ Church College, Cawnpore; St. Thomas' College, Colombo, besides a number of training institutions, seminaries, etc.

The statistics from the different dioceses not being prepared with reference to any comparison of the tables, it is difficult to summarize them. There appear to be not far from 50,000 communicants and about 100,000 baptized persons connected with the missions of the SPG in British India.

Borneo: Mr. James Brooke, a naval cadet, who, while traveling for health became interested in the suppression of piracy in the Malay Archipelago, fitted out a ship, and in 1838 landed at Kuching in Sarawak, in Borneo, and made himself master (or Rajah) of the province. As soon as he had established his rule, he invited the Church of England to establish a mission. The SPG felt unable to assume the work, but contributed to a committee which was organized for the purpose in 1846. The first missionaries went out in 1851, and two years later the SPG took charge of the mission. The mission suffered severely at different times, from rebellions and wars, but on the whole its work among the Dyaks prospered, and subsequently (1861) it extended its efforts to the Straits Settlements. In all 41 European and 7 native missionaries have worked in 28 stations. Among the stations occupied in the Straits Settlements are Singapur, Penang, and Perak; in Sarawak, Kuching, Quop, Skerang, and Undup, and in North Borneo, Labuan, Kudat, and Sandakan. In 1902, 15 clergymen conducted work in 78 villages; there were 12 churches and 32 chapels; 1,781 communicants and 4,850 baptized persons, 21 schools, with 35 teachers and 913 scholars.

China: In 1843 the Society appealed for funds for a chaplain for the English residents in Hongkong, but it was not until 1863 that its first missionary, specially commissioned for work among the Chinese, reached Peking. Other stations have been occupied as follows: Chefu, 1874; Taiyuen-fu and Ping Yin, 1879; Yung-ching (originally founded by CMS, 1869), and Lung-hualien, 1880; Tien-tsin, 1890; Pei-tai-ho and Weihai-wei, 1900. In all, 24 European and 1 native missionaries have been employed in 9 stations, their work being distinctively for the Chinese.

Japan: As early as 1859, when Japan was first opened to missions, the Society reserved a sum of money for work there, but placed its first missionaries in Tokio in 1873. Other stations occupied were Kobe (1876), Awaji (1878), and Yokohama (1889). There is also some work on the Bonin Islands. There have been in all 21 European and 10 native missionaries in 14 stations. In 1902 there were 12 clergy, 11 churches, 606 communicants, and 1,170 baptized persons.

Korea: One of the founders of the SPG Mission in Japan urged, in 1880, that work be taken up in Korea. At that time it was deemed premature, but some years later Bishop Scott of North China and Bishop Bickersteth of Japan pressed the matter, and in 1889, Rev. C. J. Corfe was consecrated the first missionary bishop of Korea. He reached Seoul in 1890 with several associates. The plan of work contemplated several years of preparation before direct evangelistic work should be undertaken; but in 1896 aggressive work was indicated by the enrollment of a class of catechumens. Other places occupied are: Chemulpo (1891), Mapo and Kanghoe (1893). In 1902 the reports showed 5 clergy, 4 churches, 117 communicants, and 204 baptized persons.

Western Asia: The Society's work has been chiefly confined to occasional assistance to the Anglican Bishop of Jerusalem, the English communities in Smyrna and Cyprus, and to work among the Assyrian Christians (see Archbishop's Mission).

Europe: In its early history the Society assisted in the building of churches in various places, and in providing service for English communities, but to no great extent until 1841, when the see of Gibraltar, including the English congregations of Southern Europe, was founded, a grant in aid being made from the Society's fund. After the Crimean War (1854-56) it assisted in erecting the Crimean Memorial Church in Constantinople, and maintained a chaplain in charge of it. Since then it has added a number of chaplaincies in different parts of Europe.

The Society has always paid special attention to the preparation and dissemination of literature, including not only Bibles and prayer-books, but general religious literature. It has assisted to establish libraries in the different colleges in which it has been interested, and among its gifts is noted one to Harvard College, Boston, Mass., in 1764, on the occasion of a disastrous fire. Its list of publications includes the entire number of languages which its missionaries have used in their labors.

ORGANS: *The Mission Field*, monthly; *The East and the West*, quarterly.
Pascoe (C. F.), *Two Hundred Years of the SPG*, London, 1901.

SOCIETY, or TAHITI, ISLANDS: A group in the South Pacific, between latitude 16° and 18° south and longitude 148° to 155° west. There are 13 islands and several small islets, divided by a channel 60 miles wide into two groups, originally called the Georgian Islands and the Society Islands. The principal islands are Tahiti, Moorea or Eimeo, Titiaroa, Maitea, Raiatea, Tubuai, Moru, Huahine, Tahaa, and Bora-Bora. Tahiti, by far the largest of these islands, has an area of 600 square miles. Moorea has 50 square miles. The general physical characteristics are the same for nearly every one of the group. There is a mountainous interior, with low, rich plains sloping down to the coast. Coral reefs surround them. The water supply is abundant, tropical fruits and vegetables grow in great abundance, and a salubrious, temperate climate is universal. The natives belong to the Malay race, and resemble the Marquesans and Rarotongans in appearance, but differ greatly from them in their customs. The dialect is one of the softest languages in Oceania. Agriculture is in a rather backward state, except in Tahiti and Moorea, where 7,000 acres are under cultivation, producing cotton, sugar, and coffee. The population is about 15,000.

The Society Islands, together with the Marquesas, Tuamotu, Gambier, Tubuai, the island of Rapa the Wallis or Uea, and Howe Islands, form what is called the French Establishment in Oceania, under the control of a commandant-general, who resides in Tahiti. Tahiti was taken possession of in 1844, and the various other islands were gradually encroached upon by the French until, in 1880, they became French possessions.

Missions in the Society Islands: In 1797 the LMS sent out its missionary ship "Duff," and the missionaries arrived at Tahiti in March of that year. From that time until the French occupation in 1844 great success attended the labors of the missionaries, whose influence over the converted islanders was exerted for their best temporal and spiritual good. In 1818, the anniversary of the LMS, the Christian king Pomare originated and formed a Tahitian Missionary Society. In 1839, just previous to the introduction of the French protectorate, the following testimony to the good effects of missionary labor was given by the captain of a whaling vessel: "This is the most civilized place that I have been at in the South Seas. It is governed by a dignified young lady, about 25 years of age. They have a good code of laws, and no liquors are allowed to be landed on the island. It is one of the most gratifying sights the eye can witness on a Sunday to see in their church, which holds about 5,000, the queen, near the pulpit, with all her subjects around her, decently appareled, and in seemingly pure devotion." With the institution of the French protectorate the people were corrupted by the combined influence of rumsellers and other foreigners. The LMS Mission was embarrassed and broken up, and withdrew from Tahiti and Moorea in 1852. At that time there were 1,870 church members in those two islands. Huahine was first reached by the missionaries in 1808, and the history of the mission there is similar to that of Tahiti and Moorea. The islands were practically Christianized, missionary societies were organized, and in 1852 there were 962 church members in Huahine, Raiatea, Bora-Bora, and Maupiti. Since the French occupation of the islands the work in Tahiti and Moorea has been under the care of the Paris Evangelical Society, which has continued the good work done by the LMS in the face of two great difficulties—the traffic in liquors and the Romish propaganda. Tahiti is divided into two sections, north and south, and in the former, which includes the town of Papeete, there are several missionary stations which are under the care of native pastors, and in the latter there are eight stations, each with a native pastor, all under the supervision of European missionaries. Bora-Bora and Maupiti have each one native ordained pastor under the LMS.

SOEMBER PAKEM: A village in Java, Dutch East Indies, situated 105 miles S. E. of Surabaya. Station of the Java Committee's Mission, with 1 missionary and his wife and 1 day school.

SOGAE ADU: A village on the Island of Nias, Sumatra, Dutch East Indies, situated on the N. E. coast, about 20 miles S. E. of Gunong Sitoli. Station of the Rhenish Missionary Society, with 2 missionaries and their wives, 8 native workers, 1 outstation, 2 day schools, and 401 professed Christians, of whom 231 are communicants.

SOH-P'ING. See So-PING-FU.

SOLOMON ISLANDS: A group in the South Pacific, consisting of a double chain extending from northwest to southeast, between 5° and 10° 54′ south latitude, and 154° 40′ and 162° 30′ east longitude. They were first discovered in 1567, but as yet have not been explored to any great extent. Since 1886 the northerly part of the group, including the islands of Bougainville, Choiseul, Isabel or Mahaga, together with various smaller islands, with a total area of 57,000 square miles, has been seized by Germany. The population of this part is estimated at 80,000. The principal other islands are San Cristoval, Guaddalcanal, Malanta, and Bouro. The climate is damp and unhealthful on the coast, tho the high lands are probably more salubrious. The natives belong to the Melanesian race, and the language is of Melanesian type, but with dialects differing in different islands. Of their religion, habits, and customs little is known, tho they resemble the other Melanesians in most things, and are known to be cannibals to some extent. Mission work is carried on in these islands by the Melanesian Mission.

SOMALILAND (French): An African possession of France, including the colony of Obock, lying between Abyssinia and the Strait of Bab-el Mandeb, bounded north by Eritrea and south by Italian Somaliland, touching also British Somaliland on the east. It has 46,000 square miles of area and 200,000 inhabitants (estimated). The natives are Gallas or Danakil. The capital and chief port is Jibutil, where two French mission schools, one for boys and one for girls, were opened in 1902, under government grants.

SOMALILAND (Italian): A protectorate of Italy in Africa, lying on the Indian Ocean and bounded landward by Abyssinia, French Somaliland and British Somaliland on the north, by British East Africa on the southwest, and by the Egyptian Sudan on the west. The area is about 100,000 square miles, the population about 400,000, chiefly Somalis. The country away from the coast is mountainous, and largely unexplored by Europeans. As a mission field it is thus far unoccupied. The Mohammedan faith and the pagan religions still wholly prevail.

SOMALILAND Protectorate: A British protectorate in Africa. It adjoins Abyssinia on the southwest of that state, having Italian Somaliland on the south; comprises 68,000 square miles, with a population of about 500,000, all Mohammedans, and largely nomadic. This territory has been the scene of operations of "The Mad Mullah," as he is called. Military operations by Great Britain for the pacification of the interior of the country have been going on for some years. Some account of the "Mad Mullah" is of interest in connection with the problem of introducing and maintaining missions in this region. The name of the man is Mohammed Abdullah. He belongs to a section of the Ogaden tribe in the southwest of Somaliland, and married a girl of the Ali Gheri, one of the Dolbahanta tribes in the southeast of the British protectorate. By his marriage he extended his influence from Abyssinia on the west to the borders of Italian Somaliland on the east. The Ali Gheri were his first followers. These were presently joined by two sections of the Ogadens. He set himself forward as a champion of Mohammedan puritanism, paying great attention to the rites of religion, making several pilgrimages to Mecca, and, as is the custom with religious revivalists in Islam, advocating the free use of the sword to purify the earth. Every visit to Mecca added to his reputation and increased his influence.

In 1899 the Mullah openly incited the tribes to rebellion against the British authority, and soon afterward he began to resort to force to gain supporters. His methods were primitive but effective, and he continued to gain adherents.

It was in August, 1899, that the first serious alarm over the activity of the Mullah was felt. He appeared at Burao with 5,000 men, marched to within fifty miles of Berbera, where, tho the two British gunboats kept him from the city, he was clever enough to use them, for he told his followers their searchlights were the eyes of God looking on them with favor.

Since then it has been frequently reported that he has met with "crushing defeat," but he has always turned up again as strong and menacing as ever.

Besides the bravery and fanaticism of the Mullah's followers, the British officers have also had to contend against the cowardice of the native Somali levies.

It has been found necessary to bring Indian troops to carry on the war against this redoubtable fanatic. Meanwhile the devastation of the country by the Mad Mullah and his followers continues, and there is as yet no possibility of missionary enterprise in that region.

SOMERSET EAST: A town in Cape Colony, Africa, 80 miles northwest of Grahamstown. Population, 2,231. Station of the UFS (1869), with (1903) 1 missionary and his wife, 5 native workers, 2 outstations, 14 Sunday schools, 3 day schools, and 149 professed Christians. Station also of the South African Wesleyan Methodist Church, with (1901) 25 native workers, 15 outstations, 4 places of worship, 4 Sunday schools, 7 day schools and 335 professed Christians.

SOMERVILLE: A town in Cape Colony, S. Africa, situated in the Transkei region, 18 miles E. by S. of Maclear. Climate sub-tropical. Station of the UFS, with (1903) 1 missionary and his wife, 28 native workers, 17 outstations, 1 place of worship, 14 day schools, and 695 communicant Christians.

SONG-CHIN: A town in Korea, in the district of Phyeng-yang, about 50 miles W. of Wen-san. Station of the PCC (1901), with 2 missionaries and their wives, 3 native workers, 1 dispensary, 1 hospital and 60 professed Christians, of whom 14 are communicants.

SONGDO: A town in Korea, also called Kaiseng, situated 40 miles N. W. of Seoul. Population, 60,000. Station of the MES (1897), with (1903) 1 missionary and his wife, 2 women missionaries, 3 native workers, 9 outstations, 2 Sunday schools, and 279 professed Christians, of whom 79 are communicants.

SONG-YANG. See SUNG-YANG-HSIEN.

SOOCHOW. See SU-CHAU-FU.

SO-PING-FU: A town in Shan-si, China, situated about 220 miles W. of Peking. Station of the CIM (1895), but the work has not been reorganized since the Boxer rising, when all the missionaries were killed. Some write the name Soh-p'ing.

SOPO: A mission station of the German Baptists of Berlin, situated in Kamerun, Africa, about 10 miles S. E. of Buea, with (1900) 1 missionary and his wife, 1 woman missionary, 1 native worker, 1 place of worship, 1 day school, 1 boarding school, and 67 professed Christians.

SORABJI KHARSEDJI: Died August 14, 1894. A Parsee of Bombay. Amid the bitterest persecutions he confessed his faith boldly and clearly at the police-office, where he was under police protection; before the magistrates and a great company of Hindus, Parsees, and Mohammedans. To escape from the abuse to which he was exposed in Bombay, he accepted service under the SPG at Ahmedabad in the summer of 1842. Later he entered the CMS divinity class at Nasik, and was engaged in conducting the orphanage and building the Christian settlement of Sharanpur. In 1878 he was admitted to deacon's orders at Agra; and from 1882 he resided at Poona, serving as an honorary missionary. He was familiar with the two great Zoroastrian languages, the Zend and Pehlevi, to the mysteries of which only Parsee high priests are admitted. And this has made his book on *The Comparison of Zoroastrianism and Christianity* a valuable addition to Parsee literature. His works, entitled *Zoroaster and Zoroastrianism*, and *Life of Christ*, were left by him unfinished. He was a member of the Gujarati Bible Revision Committee; and the New Testament portion of his work, and all of his work on the Old Testament, except one book, were finished just before his labors ceased. His heroic death, as well as his consecrated life, was the means of the spiritual awakening of many Parsees and Hindus of Poona. The booklet (CMS), *How a Native Clergyman Died*, written by his daughter, is an impressive work.

SOUTH AFRICA DUTCH REFORMED CHURCH MISSION TO BRITISH CENTRAL AFRICA: Headquarters: Sea Point, Cape Town, Cape Colony.

In 1884 the ministers of the Dutch Reformed Church of the Cape Colony decided to form a Ministers' Mission Union, with a view to supporting their own ordained representative in the foreign mission field. They undertook to contribute each from $25 to $50 per annum, out of their private salary, for this purpose. While looking out for a field in which to work, they were generously invited by the Livingstonia Mission of the Free Church of Scotland to come to the region west of Lake Nyasa, and share their extensive field there. In 1888 the Rev. A. C. Murray, an ordained minister of their church, after an eighteen months' course of medical training in Scotland, left South Africa as their first representative in that field. The following year he was joined by another missionary from South Africa, and they selected the district to the S. W. of Lake Nyasa as their sphere of labor.

The first station was Mvera, in what is now the British Central Africa Protectorate. Gradually the work extended, until in 1899 the staff consisted of sixteen workers (including three missionaries), working at three main stations—Mvera, Kongwe, and Mkoma.

In 1897 the Synod of the Dutch Reformed Church of the Orange Free State decided to start their own mission work in Central Africa, and sent out two men, who proceeded from Mvera farther to the west, and planted their first station at Magwero, in the district of N. E. Rhodesia, near Fort Jameson. This work, altho carried on uninterruptedly all the time, could not be extended owing to the South African war, but within a year after peace was made the Orange River Colony Synod decided to send out three more men (one being an agriculturist), and a new station was started at Madzimoyo. In 1899 the chairman of the Cape Colony Mission, Dr. Andrew Murray, urged upon the committee definitely to pray for a doubling of the stations and workers in Nyasaland within five years. To many friends of the Mission this seemed too much to ask for, the more as within six months the devastating war broke out. But within four years there were thirty-four workers instead of sixteen, and six stations instead of three. The first two converts were baptized in 1894, but no others were admitted into the Church till 1897, when thirty adults were baptized. Since then the number has steadily increased, till in 1901 there were in all close upon three hundred church members, and at the end of 1903 over seven hundred. The district occupied by the above Mission in Nyasaland (not counting N. E. Rhodesia) contains about 300,000 natives. With two more stations it will be sufficiently occupied and can then be worked by means of native evangelists and catechists. There are over one hundred outschools under native teachers, with an attendance of 7,000 children, while about 10,000 natives are continually under religious influence and instruction. The conditions of baptism are rather strict, as the candidate must have been at least one year in the catechumen class, and have manifested a thorough breaking with all heathen customs during that time. Consequently cases of discipline are rare.

There are seven unmarried women workers in this field, who are supported by the Women's Mission Union (*Vrouwen Zending Bond*) of the same church. This union also supports women workers in other mission stations in the Cape Colony, Transvaal, Bechuanaland, and Mashonaland. Headquarters: Huguenot College, Wellington, Cape Colony.

SOUTH AMERICAN MISSIONARY SOCIETY: Captain Allen Gardiner, the founder of the South American Missionary Society, first visited South America with a view of establishing a mission in 1838. For years the great aim of his life had been to become "the pioneer of a Christian mission to the most abandoned heathen." With this object steadily in view, he went through a series of travels and adventures for some years, taking his wife and children with him on long, perilous journeys. After repeated disappointments in other countries, he was led to direct all his efforts toward the natives of South America. His attempts to reach the mountain tribes were defeated by the jealousy of the Roman Catholic priests. At last he thought that not even the Spanish priesthood would consider it worth while to interfere with anything he might attempt among the poor savages at the desolate southern corner of the great continent, and by beginning with them he hoped to reach in time the nobler tribes.

In 1830 Captain (afterward Admiral) Fitzroy had been sent by the British Government to survey the coasts of Tierra del Fuego. On his return to England he took with him, for a visit, three native lads and a girl of nine years. They were kindly treated, and found capable of learning a good deal. When, a year later, Captain Fitzroy took them back to their own land, he was accompanied by a Mr. Williams, who hoped to remain in Tierra del Fuego as a missionary. A very few days sufficed to show the danger of this attempt; he returned to the vessel, and all thought of missionary work in this region was abandoned until Captain Gardiner took it up. His hope was that the natives who had visited England might be still alive, and that one of them—called "Jemmy Button"—if he had not forgotten all his English, might act as interpreter and friend. But he found great difficulties in the way. England, while warmly supporting missions to other parts of the world, seemed utterly indifferent to the fate of South America. After much effort he succeeded, in 1844, in forming a society called the Patagonian Missionary Society; soon after, he, with a few companions, attempted to establish a mission in Tierra del Fuego. Owing to the hostility of the natives it was a complete failure. The Society in England was much discouraged; "not so the brave captain." The funds necessary were secured and on September 7, 1850, he again sailed from England. With him were Mr. Richard Williams, a surgeon in good practise; Mr. Maidment of the Church of England YMCA, a ship carpenter who had gone on the previous expedition, and who volunteered his services for this second attempt, saying that to be with Captain Gardiner was "like a heaven upon earth," and three Cornish fishermen, Christian men, who readily offered themselves for the "forlorn hope," tho plainly warned of its dangers. They took with them provisions for six months, and arranged that more should be sent by the first opportunity.

On the 5th of December the "Ocean Queen" anchored in Banner Cove, Tierra del Fuego, and on the 18th she sailed away, with many cheerful messages to friends at home from the brave men left behind. The journals of Gardiner and Williams, preserved almost by miracle, tell the painful story of the next nine months. Misfortunes and disasters rapidly succeeded one another. In a heavy storm an anchor and both small boats for landing were lost; by an oversight almost the whole supply of powder and shot had been left on board the "Ocean Queen," leaving them without the means of obtaining game, and also without power to defend themselves from the attacks of the natives. Later, a terrible gale made a complete wreck of the "Pioneer." At Garden Island they buried several bottles, placing above them boards of wood on which were written, "Look underneath." Each bottle contained a written paper: "We are gone to Spaniard Harbor; we have sickness on board. . . . Our supplies are nearly out, and if not soon relieved we shall be starved." They also painted on the rocks in two places, "You will find us in Spaniard Harbor." Then, with the last remaining boat they succeeded in reaching Spaniard Harbor. The frightful Fuegian winter began in April, and from the terrific storms of wind and snow the deep caverns in the rocks formed their best refuge. Their efforts to catch game and fish met with little success; they grew weaker and weaker; the sailor, John Badcock, was the first to die. Mr. Williams seems to have realized that the still expected "ship" would arrive too late for his relief, and his journal contains many farewell messages to beloved friends at home. One by one the little band passed away; it is probable that the brave Gardiner himself was the last survivor. The last entry in his diary is September 5; a little note was also found, dated September 6. The long-looked-for vessel, owing to strange mistakes and delays, did not reach the coast until the end of October. Following the directions written on the rocks, the boat was found, with one dead body on board, and another on the shore, while books, papers, etc., lay scattered around. "The captain and sailors cried like children at the sight." A violent gale arising, they dared not remain longer, but put out to sea at once, carrying the sad news to Montevideo. By this time friends in England, greatly alarmed, had applied to the government for aid, and the frigate "Dido" was sent to search for the lost missionaries, reaching the coast in January. Guided by the writings on the rocks, the officers soon completed the sorrowful discoveries. In Spaniard Harbor they saw on a rock the verses from Psalm lxii: 5-8, "My soul, hope thou in God, for my expectation is from Him," etc., with the drawing of a hand pointing to the spot where the wreck of the "Pioneer" and the bodies of Maidment and Gardiner were found. All the remains of the martyrs were reverently collected, and, after the reading of the burial service of the Church of England, were buried in one grave beside the "Pioneer." The colors of the "Dido" were lowered, and three volleys fired, as in honor of an officer's funeral. The heroic death of Gardiner and his companions accomplished what in life they had failed to do. The Christian public of England soon resolved that the dying wishes and prayers of the martyrs should not have ascended to heaven in vain. The last directions of Captain Gardiner, so wonderfully preserved, were acted upon; the Society was re-formed according to his plan, and a Christian mission firmly established in Tierra del Fuego, and the South American Missionary Society is rapidly extending its agencies over many regions of the great continent.

According to the plan of Captain Gardiner, the South American Missionary Society should have the threefold object of supplying the spiritual wants of "his own fellow-countrymen," the Roman Catholics, and the heathen in South America. On this general basis, the work of the Society has now four departments: 1. Missions to the heathen. 2. Evangelistic (including educational) work. 3. Chaplaincies. 4. Work among seamen.

I. Missions to the Heathen. (1) *Southern Mission:* This is the direct successor of Capt. Gardiner's work, and is especially for the Yahgans of Tierra del Fuego. It was commenced in 1854, when the missionary schooner "Allen Gardiner" sailed for the Falkland Islands. The place discreetly chosen for a base of operations was Keppel Island, a small uninhabited island lying north of the west island of the Falklands. From there, in 1856, a cautious intercourse was commenced with the Fuegians, and they were encouraged to visit the mission station at Keppel in small parties. After much toil of preparation a Fuegian family from one of the larger islands near Cape Horn was brought to Keppel by Mr. Allen Gardiner, son of Capt. Gardiner, in 1858. The man was Jemmy Button; he was still able to speak broken English, and from him, at this early date, the missionaries learned something of the Yahgan language. Much pains were taken to gain the confidence of these natives, and to impart to them some religious knowledge. So friendly did they seem that in 1859 the missionaries thought they might venture to take the first step toward the establishment of a missionary station in their island home. Forming their judgment partly from their visitors at Keppel Island, and partly from others on the Fuegian coast, they believed that the ferocity of the natives had been overstated. Accordingly, they sailed for Woolya, in Navarin Island. Mr. Philips was the leader of the little band of missionaries, and he was fearlessly supported by Captain Fell of the "Allen Gardiner." Their first reception was friendly, and on Sunday, the 6th of November, they went ashore to conduct divine worship. While thus engaged they were attacked and massacred. One Yahgan was taken back by the ship which went in search of the missionaries, and through him the language was learned, so that when another attempt was made in 1863, by Bishop Stirling, it proved more successful. The people, however, gradually dwindled in numbers, until there is now (1903) but a handful left. The "Allen Gardiner" was sold (1900) and lost (1902). There remained three stations, Tekenika, on Hoste Island, Ushuáia, on the mainland, and Keppel Island, each under care of a missionary.

(2) *The Paraguayan Chaco:* The mission to this, in the western part of Paraguay, was commenced in 1888. There are (1902) 2 central and 4 outstations, 19 missionaries (including wives). The work is carried on by itinerating and by schools for the Indians. The report of Bishop Every (1902) speaks of the spiritual results among the Indians as most encouraging, as also the progress in the schools. A significant event was the assembling of the first native church council in August, 1902. The prayer services conducted by the natives were very impressive.

(3) *The Araucanian Mission:* This was begun in 1894 as a Jubilee Memorial. The first station occupied was Cholchol, and the second, Quepe. The staff (1902) consisted of one clergyman, 7 laymen, 8 women and 1 Mapuche chief. The work is chiefly among the Mapuche tribe of Indians, who have not as yet, except some of the younger men, come under the influence of the Roman Catholic Church. They seem anxious to learn, and the schools, particularly the industrial school at Quepe, are crowded. Medical work, as elsewhere, is an invaluable adjunct in winning the sympathy of the people.

II. Evangelistic Work: This is carried on at Palermo, Buenos Aires (1898), and Alberdi, Rosario (1896). At Palermo there are a boys' school, with 6 teachers, a girls' school, with 7 teachers, an infant school, with 4 teachers, an older girls' school, with 3 teachers, and an industrial and trades' institute, with 3 teachers. Connected with this station, at Maldonado, are two schools, one for boys and one for girls, and at General Urquiza, a mission hall and schools, the latter not directly under the superintendence of the missionary. At Alberdi there is a home and school. The whole number of employed workers is 54, besides 9 honorary helpers and several physicians, who render gratuitous service.

III. Chaplaincies: These are located at São Paulo and Santos, Brazil; Fray Bentos, Uruguay; Welsh Colony, Chubut, Patagonia; Sandy Point (Punta Arenas), Straits of Magellan; Villa Rica, Paraguay; Quino and Coquimbo, Chile. In connection with several of these there are schools, and not a little general evangelistic work is done.

IV. Work for Seamen: This includes a Sailors' Home, Rio de Janeiro; a Seamen's Mission, Santos, and sailors' homes at Buenos Aires and Rosario.

In all, the Society occupies 19 stations and 35 outstations, with 12 clergy, 61 laymen, and 58 female workers.

SOUTHERN BAPTIST CONVENTION: The Southern Baptist Convention was organized in the city of Augusta, Georgia, in May, 1845. It originated in a withdrawal of the Southern churches from union and cooperation with "the General Convention of the Baptist Denomination in the United States," popularly known as the Triennial Convention. (See article on American Baptist Missionary Union.) The constitution of this convention, as well as the history of its proceedings from the beginning, conferred on all the members in good standing of the Baptist denomination, whether at the North or the South, eligibility to all appointments emanating from the convention of the Board. Unmistakable indications, however, led the Alabama Baptist State Convention in 1844 to adopt a preamble and resolutions which were submitted to the Board of Foreign Missions of the Triennial Convention, to which a frank and explicit answer was returned, that "if any one having slaves should offer himself as a missionary, and insist on retaining them as his property, we could not appoint him. One thing is certain, we can never be a party to any arrangement that would imply approbation of slavery."

When this reply was made known, the Board of the Virginia Foreign Missionary Society addressed a circular to the Baptist churches of Virginia, suggesting that a convention be held at Augusta, Georgia, for conference as to the best means of promoting the Foreign Mission cause, and other interests of the Baptist denomination in the South. Both at the North and the South a separation seemed inevitable. At the North it was desired by many, regretted by a few, and expected by all.

Before the proposed convention in Augusta could meet, the Home Mission Society at its meeting in Providence, in April, had virtually declared for a separation, and recommended that as the existing Society was planted in the North, and had there its Executive Board and charter, which it seemed desirable to preserve, it be retained by the Northern churches, and those sympathizing with them as to the appointment of slave-holders.

At the call of the Board of Managers of the Virginia Foreign Mission Society, there assembled in Augusta, May 8, 1845, 310 delegates from the States of Maryland, Virginia, North and South Carolina, Georgia, Alabama, Louisiana, Kentucky, and the District of Columbia. Owing to the short notice of the meeting, other States were represented only by letter. The committee appointed for the purpose presented a resolution, "That for peace and harmony, and in order to accomplish the greatest amount of good, and for the maintenance of those Scriptural principles on which the General Missionary Convention of the Baptist Denomination of the Untied States was formed, it is proper that this convention at once proceed to organize a society for the propagation of the Gospel." Then followed the adoption of a constitution which was "precisely that of the original union; that in connection with which, throughout his missionary life, Adoniram Judson lived, under which Ann Judson and Boardman died. We recede from it no single step. We use the very terms, and we uphold the true spirit and great object of the late General Convention."

Thus the Southern Baptist Convention claims to be the real and proper successor and continuator of that body which "at a special meeting, held in New York, November 19, 1845, was 'dissolved,' and the American Baptist Missionary Union, with an entirely new constitution and a different basis of membership, was organized in its stead."

A Board of Foreign Missions was appointed, to be located in Richmond, Virginia, and one for Domestic Missions, to be located in Marion, Alabama. In 1882 the location of this Board was changed to Atlanta, Georgia, and its name was changed to the Home Mission Board. It has had a career of great usefulness.

A Sunday-school Board was organized in 1891, with the Rev. J. M. Frost, D.D., as corresponding secretary. The work of this Board, or publishing house, located at Nashville, Tenn., has steadily grown.

Thus the Southern Baptist Convention has gathered around itself the enthusiastic support of the Baptist churches of the South; and the wisdom of its formation is evidenced by the fact that while Southern Baptists contributed to the Triennial Convention in 31 years, from 1814-1845, $212,000, during the 34 years, from 1845-1879 (covering the period of the war), their contributions for Foreign Missions alone were $939,377. From 1880 to 1890 the contributions were $812,662, and from 1890 to and including a part of 1903, contributions to the Foreign Mission Board were $1,778,583; for the single year 1902-3, $218,752.62, or more than the contributions of the entire Southern States to the "Triennial Convention" prior to its dissolution.

Development of Work: Immediately after the organization of the Board they were instructed to correspond with the Boston Board with regard to mutual claims; and were authorized to make any equitable and prudent arrangement with that Board, to take a portion of its missions under the patronage of the Convention. At the suggestion of the Boston Board, through Dr. Francis Wayland, it was agreed that "the property and liabilities of the General Convention should remain with that body," and that "the missionaries should have the choice of the associations with which they would be connected."

Under this arrangement Rev. J. L. Shuck, the first American Baptist missionary to China, and Rev. I. J. Roberts, who had followed Mr. Shuck in 1836, gave in their adherence to the Southern Convention. Rev. S. C. Clopton and Rev. George Pearcy were commissioned to join them, and the missions of the new Board were fairly inaugurated.

Coincident with the establishment of the China mission, it was determined to commence work on the coast of Africa, where missions of the Northern Board were already in operation, and in 1847 stations were formed in Liberia and in Sierra Leone, and in 1850 in Central Africa.

As early as 1850 the attention of the Board was directed to South America as an important field, but it was not until 1860 that the opportunity was afforded for carrying out the plans of the Board. The Rev. T. J. Bowen, who had been obliged to leave Africa on account of ill-health, volunteered for the South American field; he was gladly sent, and a station was founded at Rio de Janeiro, from which point the work has rapidly spread.

In 1859 the needs of Japan attracted the attention of the Board, and in 1860 four missionaries, two ministers and their wives, were sent. All were lost at sea before reaching their field of labor. The enterprise, tho deferred, was never abandoned. In 1889 four missionaries were sent out, who founded the present mission.

The duty of Baptists to send the pure Gospel into the Catholic countries of Europe was felt by the Board from the very beginning, and France was chosen as a field for missionary labor; but the occupation of Rome by Victor Emmanuel in 1870 opened Italy to missionary work, and drew attention thither, and in 1871 Rome became a center of operations, which have spread throughout the peninsula, Sicily, Sardinia, and a portion of Austria.

In 1903 the Board began a new mission in Buenos Aires, Argentine Republic, sending thither several missionaries.

Statement of the Missions. China: The work of the Southern Convention in China is carried on under three missions, South China, with Canton as a center, but extending to the interior; Central China, with Shanghai as a center, and the Shantung province. In 1846 the work was begun in Canton by the Rev. George Pearcy and Rev. Samuel Clopton. The work has progressed since that time with little or no interruption, and Canton has been the largest center of the work in China. The Mission now includes 13 churches and 46 stations, in which labor 20 foreign missionaries and 50 native helpers; the church membership is 2,464.

Shanghai was chosen as a station at the same time as Canton, being situated in a central position on the coast. It is a city of great importance for missionary operations, since the Chinese come here from all parts of the empire, the number of transient inhabitants being estimated at above 100,000. During the Tai-ping rebellion in 1854 the mission property was destroyed, but on the seizure of the city by the Imperialists, full restitution was made, and the work renewed. The Tai-ping movement was strictly religious and iconoclastic in its origin, and proved in the end a benefit to the mission, for it roused the moral sense of the people and offered a blow at the great curse, idolatry, and the preaching of the missionaries was decidedly more effective after than before the insurrection. The Shanghai, or Central China, mission has now 6 churches, 6 outstations, 21 missionaries, 8 native helpers, and 204 members.

The mission in Shantung, a northern province of China, was begun in 1860, immediately on the conclusion of the treaty of Tien-tsin, the stations chosen being Tung-cho and Chi-fu. Some opposition was experienced at first from the gentry of Tung-cho, but the common people showed great interest. At the outset the Shantung reports and statistics were included in those of the Shanghai mission, altho the fields were 500 miles apart; but in 1866 Tung-cho was set off as an independent mission, and has continued to be so regarded. There are now in the North China Mission, Shantung, 22 stations, 22 foreign missionaries, 10 churches, and 733 church members.

Africa: One of the first fields chosen by the Southern Convention was Africa. In 1846 work was begun by Rev. John Day in Liberia, where the Northern Board had already established a mission, but in 1856 they withdrew, and the Southern Board alone carried on the work of Baptists in the Dark Continent. The field was found to be one of great promise, and in 1850 the work was extended by the formation of a mission in the Yoruba country, and in 1855 a station was opened in Sierra Leone in connection with the Liberian mission. For four years, from 1860 to 1864, war raged among the native tribes of Central Africa, and the missionaries of the Yoruba country were driven to the coast, and the mission had to be suspended. Soon after this, the money pressures and panics attendant upon the Civil War at home rendered it necessary to withdraw support from the African mission for a time, and from 1866 to 1874 the work was carried on by the missionaries without aid from the Board. In 1875, the native war being terminated and the Yoruba country again opened to missionary operations, and the finances of the Board by this time permitting, laborers were sent to occupy that field. The Liberian mission was closed and Lagos chosen as a center from which work could be extended to Central Africa. The report of the Board for 1902 gives the following statistics: 6 stations, Lagos, Abeokuta, Ogbomosho, Shaki, Oyo, and Salate, with a number of outstations, 10 foreign missionaries, 21 native assistants, 389 pupils in schools, and 544 church members.

South America: The mission in South America was begun in 1860 at Rio de Janeiro by the Rev. T. J. Bowen and his wife. The health of the former, which had caused his transfer from Central Africa, compelled him to again give up his work, and with his return the mission in South America was suspended. For twelve years nothing was done, at the end of which time, at the urgent request of a church of settlers in Brazil from the Southern United States, the Board again renewed its operations. The Board has many stations in Brazil, including Rio de Janeiro, on the coast, in the southeast; Pernambuco, on the coast, in the northeast; Bahia, midway between Rio de Janeiro and Pernambuco; Maceio, south of Pernambuco; the city of Juiz de Fora in the mining district of Minas Geraes, in the southeastern part of the country; Para, near the mouth of the Amazon, and Manaos, more than a thousand miles interior. There are 21 foreign missionaries at work, 18 native preachers, 16 native assistants, 48 churches, and 75 stations; church membership over 3,000.

As previously stated, the Board has begun very recently operations in the Argentine Republic. At the time of this writing (January, 1904) four missionaries have been appointed, but only one has reached his field of labor. Indications point to a prosperous mission.

Italy: In 1850 the Board began deliberations with regard to work in the Catholic countries of Europe, but no mission was begun until 1870, when Rev. Wm. N. Cote, M.D., who was secretary of the YMCA of France, was appointed missionary of the Southern Convention. On the opening of Italy for evangelistic work, by the victory of Victor Emmanuel, operations were immediately begun in that city, and from there have spread throughout Italy. There are now 25 churches and 37 stations of the Southern Convention on the peninsula, including Rome, Milan, Venice, Modena, Carpi, Bari, Naples, and, besides others, as Cagliari and Iglesias—on the island of Sardinia; and a station in Trieste, Austria, and Cannes, France, operated in connection with the Italian Mission. There are 4 foreign missionaries, 27 native workers, and a total membership of 661.

Mexico: The missions of the Southern Baptist Convention in Mexico are divided into two groups, North Mexico and South Mexico. North Mexico takes in the cities of Saltillo, Torreon, Durango, and Chihuahua, besides outstations, and the South Mexican Mission includes the cities of Guadalajara, Morelia, Toluca, and Leon, besides outstations. There are in all Mexico 17 missionaries, 12 ordained and 7 unordained native helpers, 43 churches, with 1,251 members, 32 stations, 13 houses of worship, 18 schools, including both Sunday schools and day schools, with 628 pupils. A number of the Mexican churches are self-supporting in whole or in part.

Japan: In 1860 the Board appointed three missionaries to Japan; two of them were prevented by the outbreak of the war from going out. The third, J. Q. A. Rohrer, with his wife, set sail from New York on August 3, 1860, in a vessel which was never heard of afterward, and the mission to Japan was then abandoned until November, 1889, when two missionaries and their wives were sent out. There are now 12 missionaries doing successful work. Their fields of labor are confined for the most part to the island of Kiushiu, but include such cities as Fukuoka, Nagasaki, Kokura, Kumamoto, and Kagoshima.

The work of the Foreign Mission Board has steadily advanced, through all the years since its birth in 1845, and that, too, in spite of the desolations of the Civil War in this country and the disheartening years that followed. During more than fifty years, J. B. Taylor, D.D., and H. A. Tupper, D.D., were the able secretaries. In all the great countries where its missionaries are laboring the work is going forward with quickening pace, and in the homeland the spirit and liberality of Southern Baptists give evidence of a day of even greater things.

SOUTH SYLHET. See SYLHET.

SOUTH VILLAGES: Name applied by the BZM to a group of a score or more villages in Bengal, India, lying south of Calcutta, in the district occupied by the BMS between Port Canning (Mutlah) and Diamond Harbor, and including the 24 Pargannas. Lakikantopur is the village where the 2 women missionaries of the BZM reside (1903), giving regular religious instruction in 11 other villages. They have 31 native workers and 9 day schools under their care.

SPALDING, Henry H.: Born at Bath, N. Y., 1804; graduated at Western Reserve College, 1833, and Lane Theological Seminary, 1835; ordained August the same year; appointed by the ABCFM in 1836 missionary to the Nez Perces Indians, with his wife, Dr. and Mrs. Whitman, and William B. Gray. In a company of fur-traders they traveled on horseback nearly 2,200 miles beyond the Missouri River, to Fort Walla-Walla, a trading post of the Hudson Bay Company, which they reached September 3, 1836, being four months and six days on the journey from Liberty, Mo., to that place. The mission was broken up by the massacre of Dr. Whitman and others in 1847. Mr. Spalding, who was in the vicinity, providentially escaped. The murderers were on his track. Hiding by day, he made his way night after night, bare-footed, over sharp rocks and thorns, until, almost dead, he reached a place of safety. Then, with his family, he left the mission field for a time. In 1862 he resumed his work, but remained only a few years. In 1871 he renewed his labors under the Presbyterian Board of Foreign Missions, in which he continued till his death, which occurred at Lapnor, Idaho, August 3, 1874. Tho his labors were interrupted, he accomplished a great work among the Indians. Over 900 of the Nez Perces and Spokanes were added to the church through his instrumentality. He prepared a translation of the Gospel of Matthew and a collection of Nez Perces hymns. At the time of his death he had a translation of the Acts well advanced.

SPAULDING, Levi: Born at Jaffrey, N. H., August 22, 1791. Died June 18, 1874. Graduated at Dartmouth College, 1815, and Andover Theological Seminary, 1818; sailed for Ceylon, June 8, 1819, under the ABCFM. He labored at Manepy for several years. In 1833 he removed to Oodooville, and with Mrs. Spaulding took charge of the girls' boarding school, which was under their care for nearly forty years. He was one of the most accurate Tamil scholars in Southern India, having so mastered the language as to use it with great facility and power. More than twenty Tamil tracts were prepared by him, and many of the best lyrics in the vernacular hymn-book were from his pen. He prepared two dictionaries, one Tamil, the other English and Tamil, and took a prominent part in the revision of the Scriptures. He furnished an excellent translation of Pilgrim's Progress, and compiled a Scripture History, which is used in the schools. School-books, hymnbooks, tracts, and Gospels passed through his hands for revision and proofreading. But he was far from being chiefly occupied with these tasks. In season and out of season, to merchants on their verandas, or seated with way-farers under the hedge, to the poor and the maimed, in lanes and highways, and to the children in the school or the street, wherever he met a native, he ceased not to preach and to teach Jesus Christ. His fluency in the colloquial language, his apt quotations from Hindu books, his original illustrations, and ready and racy sallies, combined with his genial humor, gave him great influence with the natives.

Mrs. Mary Chrystie Spaulding, his wife, rendered equally conspicuous services to the mission in another line. The care of the girls' boarding school was her special duty for almost forty years. Her sympathetic services to natives and to missionaries alike, when there was suffering to be alleviated or sorrow to be borne, gave her the affectionate title of "Mother Spaulding." She died at Batticotta one year after her husband finished his labors.

SPRINGFONTEIN: A village about 40 miles N. W. of Bethulie, in Orange River Colony, S. Africa. Station of the Berlin Missionary Society (1894), with (1903) 1 missionary, 13 native workers, and 639 professed Christians.

SRINAGAR: Capital of Kashmir, India, situated in the beautiful valley of the Jhelum River, about 175 miles due N. of Amritsar in the Punjab. It lies on both sides of the river, boats on which are a principal means of conveyance between different parts of the town. Canals extend this use of boats. The place is picturesque in general, but indescribably filthy in detail. Population (1901), 122,618. Station of the CMS (1863), with (1903) 5 missionaries, three of them with their wives; 2 women missionaries, 3 native workers, 1 day school, 1 boarding school, 1 industrial school, 1 dispensary, 1 hospital, 1 lepers' asylum, and 35 professed Christians, of whom 10 are communicants. Station also of the CEZ (1888), with (1903) 3 women missionaries, 6 native workers, 2 day schools, 1 boarding school, and 1 dispensary.

Mrs. Bishop (better known as a traveler and writer by her maiden name of Isabella Bird) has given money to build a woman's hospital here, as a memorial to her late husband, Dr. John Bishop. The Maharajah gave an excellent site.

SRIPERUMBUDUR: A village in Madras, India, situated in the N. Arcot region, about 22 miles S. E. of Chittur. Station of the Leipzig Missionary Society (1898), with (1903) 2 native workers, 8 outstations, 8 places of worship, and 10 day schools. Station also of the UFS with (1903) 1 missionary, 20 native workers, 9 outstations, 1 place of worship, 11 day schools, and 105 professed Christians.

STACK, Matthew: Born at Maukendorf, Moravia, March 4, 1711. Died, December 21, 1787. In his early youth he had deep religious impressions, and, leaving Moravia, he went to Herrnhut, in Saxony. Soon after his conversion he received from Count Zinzendorf an impression of the condition of the Greenlanders which led him to devote himself to work among the heathen. He set out with his cousin, Christian Stack, and Christian David for Copenhagen, January 19, 1733. On their arrival they found that the mission under Egede was about to be abandoned, communication with Greenland closed, and their project was regarded as romantic and ill-timed. They applied to Count Von Pless, the king's chamberlain, who fully stated the difficulties. "How will you live?" he asked. "We will cultivate the soil, and look for the Lord's blessing." "There is no soil to cultivate—nothing but ice and snow." "Then we must try to live as the natives do." "But in what will you live?" "We will build ourselves a house." "But there is no wood in that country." "Then we will dig holes in the ground and live there." "No," said the Count, seeing their faith, "you shall not do that. Here are $50 to help you: take wood with you."

Other persons aided them. The king decided to reopen communication with Greenland, and gave them a letter to Egede, commending them to his kind attention.

Matthew Stack embarked with his two friends April, 1733, and after a six weeks' voyage reached Ball's River, where he selected a place for a mission and called it New Herrnhut. In commencing his work Matthew Stack encountered great obstacles. The language was difficult of acquisition; the natives not only refused to listen to him but were positively hostile, in various ways annoying and persecuting him. They mimicked his reading, praying, and singing; interrupted his devotions by hideous howling and beating of drums. They stoned him, destroyed his goods, attempted to send his boat out to sea, and even sought to take his life. He was often in straits for provisions, and obliged to buy seals from the Greenlanders, who sometimes refused to sell them at any price. Often he had to live on shell-fish and sea-weed, a little oatmeal mixed with train oil, and even old tallow-candles. But, nothing daunted, he toiled on, when, after five years of privation and suffering, he had the reward of his patient endurance. As one of his associates was copying a translation of the Gospel of Matthew some natives from South Greenland passing by, stopped, and asked what was in that book. On the missionary's reading the story of God's love and the sufferings of Christ to save us, Kajarnak, one of the savages, said with much earnestness: "How was that? Tell me that once more, for I, too, would fain be saved." He became a Christian, was baptized, labored faithfully for Christ, and died in the faith the following year. His companions through his efforts were converted, and soon three large families pitched their tents near the missionary, that they might hear more of the Gospel. After forty years spent in the Greenland Mission, he went, in 1771, to Wachovia, in North Carolina, and for years devoted himself to teaching the children in Bethabara, N. C. In 1783 he united with the Salem Congregation in celebrating the semi-annual centennial jubilee of the Greenland Mission. In 1785 he was rendered helpless by a fall. When told that the Master would soon come and call for him, he raised his clasped hands and said, with deep emotion, "Yes, dearest Savior, come soon, come soon." He died December 21, 1787, in the 77th year of his age.

STALLYBRASS, Edward: A missionary of the LMS to Siberia from 1817 to 1839. His first station was Irkutsk. In 1819 he commenced a station at Selenginsk. The early time of his residence here was spent in exploring the southeast of Lake Baikal with Mr. Rhamn, and later with Mr. Swan among the Chorinsky Buriats. On his return from a visit to England he made his home at St. Petersburg, and for some time was engaged in the revision of the Mongolian Scriptures. In 1840 the Siberian Mission was suppressed by the Russian Government, and he returned to England. He died at Shooter's Hill, Kent, July 25, 1884, aged 91.

STANLEY: A settlement in the N. W. of Canada, situated in the S. E. part of Athabasca. Station of the CMS (1850), with (1903) 1 missionary, 1 native worker, 2 outstations, 1 day school, and 731 professed Christians, of whom 190 are communicants.

STANLEY POOL: A settlement in the Congo Free State, Africa, situated at the expansion of the Congo, just above the rapids. Altitude, 920 feet. Station of the BMS (1882), with 1 missionary and his wife, 1 native worker, 1 Sunday school, 1 day school, and 5 professed Christians. Some use the name Arthington for this station.

STANN CREEK: A town in British Honduras, situated on the coast, 40 miles S. of Belize. Station of the SPG (1894), with 2 missionaries and 450 professed Christians, of whom 100 are communicants. Also station of the WMS, with 13 native workers, 2 outstations, 4 places of worship, 4 Sunday schools, 4 day schools, and 277 professed Christians, of whom 200 are communicants.

STEINKOPF: A town in Cape Colony, Africa, a little south of the Orange River, 56 miles E. of Port Nolloth. Station of the Rhenish Missionary Society, with (1903) 1 missionary and his wife, 14 native workers, 2 outstations, 2 day schools, 1 Sunday school, and 1,171 professed Christians, of whom 375 are communicants.

STELLENBOSCH: A town in Cape Colony, South Africa, 25 miles by rail east of Cape Town. Population, 3,173. Station of the Rhenish Missionary Society, with (1903) 2 missionaries and their wives, 1 woman missionary, 18 native workers, 1 Sunday school, 1 day school, and 2,915 professed Christians, of whom 1,260 are communicants.

STERN, Rev. Henry Aaron, D.D.: Born in 1820 at Unterreichenbach. Died in 1885. His parents were zealous and orthodox in the Jewish creed. It was their hope that he might become a doctor, and to that end they sent him to a school at Frankfort. While there he developed a taste for commerce. When seventeen years old he got a situation in Hamburg. While there he used to pass the house of Mr. Moritz, one of the missionaries of the London Society for the Jews, who had a glass case by his door in which were open Hebrew and German books. Through reading these from time to time he became convinced that Christianity was more rational than Judaism. In 1839 he went to London, and one Sunday a young friend suggested they should go to Palestine Place Chapel to see the "apostates." Dr. McCaul was preaching, and his words impressed him so much that he began to read the New Testament, which led him to exclaim, "If there be a Savior, it must be Jesus." Now came the struggle, as he gradually came out of death into life. He had to suffer for Christ's sake and the Gospel. At last he was baptized, March 15, 1840. For two years he remained in the Operative Jewish Converts' Institution, when he entered the training college of the London Society for the Promotion of Christianity among the Jews. In 1844 he began missionary work at Baghdad, previously being ordained in Jerusalem by Bishop Alexander. His great work in Persia was done by means of long missionary journeys, distributing the Scriptures, reaching Jews who had rarely or ever been visited by Christians.

Later on his dauntless nature and Christian zeal led him to undertake, dressed as a native, a most perilous journey throughout Arabia Felix, where his terrible experiences were similar to those of St. Paul as told in II. Cor. xi. 23-27. But his greatest work was that among the Falasha Jews of Abyssinia in 1859, and again in 1862. Owing to political difficulties between England and the King of Abyssinia, the latter determined to vent his rage on Mr. Stern, and for four years and a half kept him and his fellow-workers in prison and in chains. Nothing but the mighty power and faithfulness of God could have sustained them during those years of agony and suspense. When Lord Napier of Magdala relieved them, some of his officers brought the captives into a tent, and all knelt down and thanked God for their wonderful deliverance. He then became head of the London Mission. In 1881 the Lambeth degree of Doctor of Divinity was conferred upon him. His deeply lamented death, in 1885, closed a life of faithful service.

STEWART, Robert Warren: Born March, 1850. Died August 1, 1895. He was accepted by the CMS Committee for service abroad in 1875, and in 1876, at St. Paul's Cathedral, he was ordained. In the September following his ordination he sailed for China. For several years he was principal of the divinity school at Fuchau, where Chinese evangelists and pastors are trained. Mr. and Mrs. Stewart called forth, almost entirely by their personal influence, a noble band of women from England and Ireland, who worked in the Fu-kien province, in connection with the Church of England Zenana Society. Some years before his death Mr. Stewart left the college and took charge of the interior district of Kucheng; but severe illness drove him home. While at home he supervised the printing of the Romanized edition of the Fu-chau Colloquial New Testament; and in 1891 he was appointed by the CMS to accompany Mr. Eugene Stock to the colonies. On his return to China, in 1893, he was appointed to Ku-cheng city; and he threw himself energetically into the opening of day schools—a form of mission work that was very dear to his heart. His ideal of a native church was one entirely supported by the natives; and to this end he exerted his potent influence. This devoted missionary of the Cross was murdered at Hwa-sang.

STODDARD, David Tappan: Born at Northampton, Mass., December 2, 1818. His early education was at Round Hill Academy. He studied at Williams College; graduated at Yale College, 1838, taking high rank as a scholar, especially in the physical sciences. In 1843 he sailed for Turkey as a missionary of the ABCFM, assigned to the Nestorian mission in Persia. Before going to Urmia he visited several mission stations in Turkey. After learning Turkish he, on reaching his station, commenced Syriac, that he might preach and also might assist Dr. Perkins in his translation of the Scriptures into modern Syriac. In five months he was able to instruct a class of Nestorian youths, and the male seminary was reorganized and committed to his care. Into this work he threw himself with intense delight. In 1847, Mr. Stoddard's health being impaired, he went, by medical advice, to Erzerum and Trebizond, where his wife died of cholera in 1848. With consent of the Board he took his orphan children home, returning to his field in 1851. Soon he began to instruct his older pupils in theology, to prepare them for preaching to their countrymen. Besides his other work, he prepared a grammar of Modern Syriac, published in the *Journal of the American Oriental Society* in 1855. His theological lectures, embracing a full course of doctrinal theology, were delivered in Syriac. His labors were arduous, and for recreation he turned to astronomy and meteorology, making observations which brought him into relations with Sir John Herschel and other eminent scientists of that period. His varied talents, his energy and activity, his devoted piety, his winning, genial manner, made Mr. Stoddard a man of mark, respected by all and loved by those who knew him. In 1856 the Persian authorities undertook to hamper the liberties of the mission, and Mr. Stoddard was the one naturally chosen to go to Tabriz to secure redress. On his return from this successful errand he was attacked by typhus fever and died January 22, 1857.

STONE, Seth Bradley: Born at Madison, Conn., April 30, 1817. Died June 27, 1877. Graduated at Yale College, 1842, Union Theological Seminary, 1850; embarked as a missionary of the ABCFM for Africa, October 14, 1850; was stationed among the Zulus. His health having failed, he returned to the United States in 1875. He was a faithful, hard-working missionary for twenty-four years among the Zulus. A close student of the Zulu language, he translated portions of the Old and New Testaments. He published an edition of church history in Zulu; also a summary of general history. Thirty-nine of the hymns in the Zulu hymn-book were translated or composed by him.

STRAITS SETTLEMENTS: A crown colony of Great Britain, comprising Singapore, Penang, and Malacca, all of which are treated of in separate articles. In 1886 the Keeling or Cocos Islands, a small group 1,200 miles southwest of Singapore, owned by an English family, were placed under the government of the Straits Settlements, and in 1888 an uninhabited island, 200 miles southwest of Java, named Christmas Island, was also added to the Straits Settlements.

STRONACH, John: Born at Edinburgh, Scotland, March 7, 1810; studied at Edinburgh University and Theological Academy, Glasgow; was ordained August 10, 1837, with his elder brother Alexander, and sailed as a missionary of the LMS for China, reaching Malacca March 2, 1838. In May, 1847, Mr. Stronach removed to Shanghai, having been appointed one of the delegates for the revision of the Chinese version of the New Testament. On the completion of that work he returned to Amoy in 1853. On March 17, 1876, he left Amoy, and, after visiting Japan, proceeded via America to England, arriving January 6, 1877. In 1878 he retired from foreign missionary service. He died in Philadelphia, U. S. A., October 30, 1888, after forty years' uninterrupted labor in China. His powers were of no common order. He stood well in his university, and made a great mark in the translation of the Bible into Chinese, known as the Delegates' Version. He was a most idiomatic master of Chinese, and it was a charm to hear him speak. His literary ability did not cease with Bible translation. One of his tracts called the "Hek bun" (Inquirer) was a masterly setting forth of the difficulties felt by a literary Chinaman, and the answers of the missionary. He assisted in revising Dr. Douglas' dictionary of the Amoy dialect. He was greatly blessed as an evangelist in Amoy, and labored indefatigably in starting stations, appointing native ministers and working with them. With all this he was overflowing with high spirits and had an unfailing fund of humor, which served him well when opposers became annoying during his street preaching.

STUDENT VOLUNTEER MOVEMENT for Foreign Missions: *I. Origin:* The Student Volunteer Movement originated at the first international Conference of Christian college students, which was held at Mount Hermon, Mass., in 1886. Of the 250 delegates who attended, twenty-one had definitely decided to become foreign missionaries when the conference opened. Of this number, Wilder of Princeton, Tewksbury of Harvard, and Clark of Oberlin had come with the deep conviction that God would call from that large gathering of college men a number who would consecrate themselves to foreign missions. Before the conference closed one hundred of the delegates put themselves on record as being "willing and desirous, God permitting, to become foreign missionaries." At the Conference it was decided that a deputation should be sent among the colleges, and four students were selected for this purpose. Of the four selected, Robert P. Wilder of Princeton was alone able to go, and John N. Forman, also of Princeton, was induced to join him. Messrs. Wilder and Forman visited 176 institutions, including a majority of the leading colleges and divinity schools of Canada and the United States. During the second year, 1887-88, the movement was left to itself, it was unorganized and had no leadership or oversight.

II. Organization: About fifty volunteers attended the student conference at Northfield in the summer of 1888. It was then decided that some organization was necessary in order to conserve the results, and a committee was appointed by the volunteers present to effect such an organization. This committee met in December, 1888, and an organization was effected, taking the name of the Student Volunteer Movement for Foreign Missions. An Executive Committee of three, consisting of John R. Mott, Robert P. Wilder, and Miss Nettie Dunn, was appointed, each member representing one of the three then existing Christian organizations among students. In January, 1889, the new Committee began its work. In 1898, the work having assumed so much larger proportions, it was found desirable to enlarge the membership of the committee to six members, so that it now consists of John R. Mott, J. Ross Stevenson, W. Harley Smith, H. P. Andersen, Miss Susie Little, and Miss Bertha Condé. John R. Mott is the chairman, J. Ross Stevenson the vice-chairman, and Fennell P. Turner the general secretary and treasurer. In order to transact the ordinary business of such an organization, it is incorporated under the laws of the State of New York. There is a Board of Trustees and an Advisory Committee.

III. Purpose: The Student Volunteer Movement is in no sense a missionary board. It never has sent out a missionary, and never will. Those who become student volunteers are expected to go out as missionaries of the regular missionary organizations of the Church. The Student Volunteer Movement is simply a recruiting agency. It does not usurp or encroach upon the functions of any other missionary organization. It is unswervingly loyal to the Church, and has received the endorsement of every leading missionary board on the continent. Its purpose, as stated by the Executive Committee, is as follows: "(1) To awaken and maintain among all Christian students of the United States and Canada intelligent and active interest in foreign missions; (2) to enroll a sufficient number of properly qualified student volunteers to meet the successive demands of the various missionary boards of North America; (3) to help all such intending missionaries to prepare for their lifework and to enlist their cooperation in developing the missionary life of the home churches; (4) to lay an equal burden of responsibility on all students who are to remain as ministers and lay workers at home, that they may actively promote the missionary enterprise by their intelligent advocacy, by their gifts and by their prayers."

IV. Membership: The membership is drawn from those who are or have been students in institutions of higher learning in the United States and Canada. Only those are entitled to become student volunteers who sign the "declaration" of the Movement, which is as follows: "It is my purpose, if God permit, to become a foreign missionary." The meaning of this declaration, as interpreted by the Executive Committee, is as follows:

"This declaration is not to be interpreted as a 'pledge,' for it in no sense withdraws one from the subsequent guidance of the Holy Spirit. It is, however, more than an expression of mere willingness or desire to become a foreign missionary. It is the statement of a definite life purpose, formed under the direction of God. The person who signs this declaration fully purposes to spend his life as a foreign missionary. Toward this end he will shape his plans; he will devote his energies to prepare himself for this great work; he will do all in his power to remove the obstacles which may stand in the way of his going; and in due time he will apply to the Boards to be sent out. Only the clear leading of God shall prevent his going to the foreign field. While it is the duty of every Christian to face this question, no one should decide it without careful thought and earnest prayer. Having confronted the question, no one should leave it until a decision pleasing to God has been reached. 'Understand what the will of the Lord is.'"

V. Watchword: The watchword of the Volunteer Movement is "The Evangelization of the World in this Generation."

VI. Field: The field for the cultivation of which the Movement considers itself responsible embraces all colleges, universities, and other institutions of higher learning in the United States and Canada. There are fully 1,000 such institutions, in which are matriculated over 200,000 students. From these institutions come the leaders in all the influential walks of life. No work, therefore, can be more important than that of making the student centers strongholds and propagating centers of missionary intelligence, enthusiasm, and activity.

VII. Methods of Cultivation: The secretaries of the Movement are a General Secretary, an Assistant Secretary, an Educational Secretary, and the Traveling Secretaries. The position of traveling secretary is usually held for one year by a student volunteer ready to go to the mission field. Returned missionaries also have been employed. In a few cases the secretaries have held the position two years. The size of the staff of traveling secretaries is determined by the funds at the disposal of the Executive Committee, and by the number of available candidates. The traveling secretaries visit the colleges and deliver addresses on missions, meet with missionary committees and volunteer bands, organize mission study classes, and in every way possible promote the missionary activities of the colleges—but the chief object of their work is by public address and personal interview to lead students to give their lives to missionary service. The student volunteers in an institution are organized into a volunteer band. The objects of the volunteer band are to deepen the missionary purpose and spiritual lives of the members, to secure other volunteers, and to promote missions in the college and in the college community. Connected with each Young Men's or Young Women's Christian Association in the college there is a missionary committee whose duty is to cultivate the missionary life of the institution. The educational department of the Movement, under the direction of the Educational Secretary, has to do with the conduct of the mission study classes in the colleges. The Movement in conjunction with the Student Young Men's Christian Association publishes during the academic year a magazine called *The Intercollegian*, which circulates among the students and is a valuable agency in keeping the volunteers in touch with the aims, methods and results of the Movement, and in keeping the Movement before the Church. The Movement publishes pamphlets, mission study text-books, and such other literature as may serve its purpose. The sales of these publications amount to more than 25,000 copies per year.

The volunteers in cities which are large student centers, and in some States, are organized into unions. The purpose of these Unions is to promote the missionary interest in the different colleges represented in them. In the United States and Canada there are held each year seven student conferences for men and five for women. At each one of these conferences special attention is given to developing the missionary life and activity among students. At these conferences, missionary institutes are held to train the leaders of volunteer bands, of mission study classes, and other missionary activities of the institutions represented. Once in four years an international convention is held. Four such conventions have been held, the attendance being as follows:

Year	1891	1894	1898	1902
Total Number Delegates	680	1,325	2,221	2,957
Institutions Represented	150	294	461	465
Student Delegates	558	1,082	1,598	2,225
Members of Faculties	...	37	119	247
Foreign Missionaries	32	63	89	107
Representatives Mission Boards	33	54	87	82

VIII. Results: 1. The work of the Movement, through visitation, summer conferences, conventions and correspondence, has reached more than 800 institutions. In more than half of these institutions nothing was being done in the interests of missions prior to the effort put forth by this Movement, or, at its initiative, by the Student Young Men's or Young Women's Christian Associations. In many colleges where there has been for years more or less missionary interest, it has been the testimony of professors and of others who are in a position to know that the Movement has greatly increased that interest. Each year the traveling secretaries bring to the attention of thousands of students the needs of the non-Christian world and the claims of missionary service.

2. The Movement has been a principal factor in the recent remarkable development in the scientific study of missions, not only in the colleges and theological seminaries, but also in churches and young people's societies. In its early years the Movement simply recommended subjects and books for study; later it outlined courses of study. In 1894 the Educational Department was organized, and D. Willard Lyon was appointed Educational Secretary. He was succeeded by Harlan P. Beach in 1895. When the department was organized, there were about a score of mission study classes in all the colleges, universities, and theological seminaries in North America. Since then the text-book literature of the Movement has been created, and the reports for the year 1902-1903 show that there were 6,700 students enrolled in 544 classes in 319 institutions.

3. Since its inception the Movement has never ceased to press upon students the claims of foreign missionary service as a life work. Up to the beginning of 1904 the names of over 2,400 student volunteers have been reported as having reached the mission field, going out in connection with more than fifty different missionary agencies, and scattered throughout all parts of the non-Christian world. A large number of volunteers who have been hindered from going to the foreign mission field have taken up mission work in the home field.

4. As a result of the work of the Movement, the gifts of students for missions have steadily increased; in the academic year 1902-03 over $68,000 was contributed for missions by institutions reporting. The Movement has exerted a mighty reflex influence on the religious life of the colleges and theological seminaries. If the volunteers and all that pertains to the work of the Movement were taken from the institutions of higher learning they would suffer great loss. The traveling secretaries, through their addresses and conversations, exert a great spiritual influence. The missionary idea has been emphasized in meetings and in mission study classes, thus widening the horizon, enlarging the sympathies, and stimulating the zeal of students. Missionary intelligence, missionary activity, and the missionary spirit have done far more than is generally realized to counteract the evil and subtile influences of pride, selfishness and rationalism, as manifested in student communities.

5. The Movement has been an increasing factor in promoting the missionary life of the churches, confining its activities chiefly to work among the young people. The volunteers in all parts of the continent have taken a leading part in the work of local societies of young people in their vicinity. The principal result in this direction has been in the organization of the student campaign in connection with different denominations. The first and most successful effort of this kind was made by the Methodist Church of Canada.

Within the past few years the students of twelve other denominations have inaugurated similar movements, with varying degrees of success. The leaders of the Volunteer Movement have helped by counsel at every stage of this development. In most cases the leaders of these movements have been volunteers. In the pathway of the work of student campaigners thousands of young people have been stirred, missionary committees have been organized, missionary libraries have been established, mission study classes and reading circles have been instituted, and the young people have been influenced to form the habit of systematic giving.

Many churches have been led to support their own missionaries. Intercession on behalf of missions has been greatly promoted, and the spiritual life of young people's societies has been quickened and strengthened. The recent organization of the Young People's Forward Movement, the purpose of which is to promote missionary activities among the young people of all denominations, is a direct outgrowth of the work of the Student Volunteer Movement among young people.

IX. The Volunteer Movement in Other Countries: The Volunteer Movement has, under different names, become world-wide, largely as a result of its direct influence on the students of other lands. In Great Britain the Student Volunteer Missionary Union commands the confidence of the British missionary societies. They have held three missionary conferences, which have been the largest and most notable student conventions ever held in Europe. The Volunteer Movement in Germany and the one in Scandinavia have made most encouraging progress. They have materially increased the number of missionary candidates, and have done much to promote the scientific study of missions. A conference of the German Movement was held at Halle in April, 1901. The Movement in France and French-speaking Switzerland has not made as marked progress as the other European Movements, but it has, nevertheless, accomplished a most useful work. An organization has also been effected in Holland. The Movement in Australasia received a great impetus from the missionary conference held in Australia and in New Zealand in 1903. An organization has been effected in India and Ceylon, which gives much promise for the cause of missions in India, and a similar Movement will soon develop in China and in Japan. The organizations in different countries are related to each other through the World's Student Christian Federation.

STUDY CLASSES on Missions: Henry Venn, Secretary of the Church Missionary Society, defined the aim of Foreign Missions as to plant a native church that should be self-supporting, self-governing, and self-extending. Such a consummation cannot be hoped for abroad, unless supported in the Church at home by an interest that shares the three qualities named. We need an interest that is self-sustaining—not a smoldering spark that bursts into flame only after protracted use of the bellows; an interest that is self-directing—that understands where to find and how to use its own fuel; an interest that is self-propagating—that spreads and kindles the brushheaps all about it.

It is surprising, in view of this obvious need, that the systematic and wide-spread study of Missions has been so long delayed. The methods upon which we have relied in the past—an occasional sermon or address, a meeting once a month, desultory mention in the home—would in secular work be trusted to bring forth only the poorest kind of wild grapes. We do not trifle with the subject of American history in any such way. For that we admit the need of well-prepared and adapted text-books, of trained teachers, of serious study, of many and frequent recitations. To grasp definitely and permanently the vastness, variety, and perspective of any subject, its problems and lessons, we judge painstaking work a necessity.

The study of Foreign Missions by individuals and isolated groups has existed for many years. Suggestions for didactic meetings have been published. But the first attempt to provide a systematic course of study for classes was in connection with the Student Volunteer Movement. It had become increasingly apparent to the leaders of this organization that the effects of their stirring appeals would be short-lived unless nursed and fed. From the Volunteer Bands came the demand for guidance in systematic study. Altho Prof. Wood, of Smith College, had previously published a series of suggestions, the present system may be said to have been inaugurated by outlines published in *The Student Volunteer*, beginning in February, 1893, prepared by Messrs. Lyon, Beach, Wishard, and Adams, and Miss Wilson. In the winter of '94-'95, text-books were for the first time taken up, the first being George Smith's *Short History of Missions*. In the spring of 1895, Mr. D. Willard Lyon prepared the first text-book written specially for this course, a sketch of the *History of Protestant Missions in China*. In the fall of the same year, Rev. Harlan P. Beach, now Educational Secretary of the Movement, published the first of those text-books to which the student world owes so much, *The Cross in the Land of the Trident*, a study of India. Since that time the Movement has prepared or provided text-books every year, usually issuing courses on three different subjects. The reason for this has been the demand that as many phases of the subject as possible should be presented within the short college generation. Special mention should be made of Beach's *Geography and Atlas of Protestant Missions*, a unique presentation of the mission field at the present day. Every year these courses have been studied by an increasing number of college men and women, non-volunteers as well as volunteers.

At the Ecumenical Conference of 1900, representatives of the Women's Boards of North America planned a course for their constituencies to be known as the United Study of Missions Series. In the fall of 1901, the first text-book was published, written by Miss Louise M. Hodgkins—*Via Christi*, an introduction sketching missions from apostolic times down to Carey. The sale of 35,000 copies during the first year showed that the time was ripe for such a plan. The second volume, *Lux Christi*, published a year later, treats India; the third takes up China. Among the young people's societies a desire was expressed for something more elementary in character than the text-books of the Student Volunteer Movement, which were written with the college sophomore in view. This has led to the Forward Mission Study Series, the first of which, *The Price of Africa*, by Mr. S. Earl Taylor, was out in July, 1902. This tendency to adapt to specific needs is a very hopeful sign, but there is still much to be done. We need as many grades in text-books for the study of Foreign Missions as for that of geography or history.

In addition to these courses several of the denominations have prepared or recommended text-books, or have furnished outline studies in magazines.

The methods of the mission study class have varied. The college classes have, for the most part, met weekly, and employed prevailingly the question method. Many classes outside the colleges have followed the same plan. Among the women the tendency is stronger to meet only monthly, and to have the subject presented by papers. The lecture method is, fortunately, least in vogue, altho it has its preparatory uses in sluggish communities. In general, the effort to include an entire church organization in the study class tends toward less frequent sessions and less thorough work. The best quality of work has been obtained in small groups meeting, at least, weekly, which is only what the laws of pedagogy would lead us to expect. It is also obvious, especially where the course is traversed in a few sessions, that the profit of the class depends largely on the leader. A skilful teacher will discover means of impressing a very few of the most important points permanently, of implanting an interest in the subject, a desire to study it further and an enthusiasm to bring others under its influence. No need is more urgent than that for prayerful *trained* leaders. For some years the Student Volunteer Movement has corresponded with its class leaders, and furnished them with printed suggestions on methods of leading. In this it has been followed by several of the denominations, so that the helps grow yearly in volume.

As the most effective way of collecting a class has been found to be personal solicitation, so that of propagating classes is the personal contact of traveling secretaries, student campaigners or district workers. The growth resulting in some of the metropolitan centers from well organized efforts along this line has been very marked.

We may confidently look for a great extension in the quantity and improvement in the quality of this work during the next few years, and for a consequent broadening and deepening of missionary interest.

STURGES, Albert A.: Born at Granville, Ohio, November 5, 1819. Died, September 4, 1887. Graduated at Wabash College, 1848; Yale Divinity School, 1851; embarked January 11, 1852, as a missionary of the ABCFM for Micronesia, reaching Ponape the following September. He labored most happily for thirty-three years at his missionary station on Ponape. He showed great tact in his relations with the natives, and skill in drawing out the activities of the church members. Much of his time was given to the translation of the Scriptures, and he had the joy of seeing the New Testament completed and in the hands of the people. In 1885 his health required him to return home, where, tho in much physical weakness, he carried on the work of translation.

SUA-BUE: A town in Kwang-tung, China, situated on the S. coast about 80 miles W. by S. of Swatow. Station of the PCE (1893), with (1903) 2 missionaries and their wives. Other statistics are included with Wu-king-fu.

SUCHAU: A town in Kiang-su, China, regarded by the Chinese as one of the richest and most beautiful in China. It is situated on a cluster of islands in Ta-hu, "Great Lake," 70 miles northwest of Shanghai, with which it is connected by a network of streams and canals. Its walls are 10 miles in circuit, and the suburbs extend for many miles around, while an immense population lives in boats. The rebels captured it in 1860, and left it, when recaptured, in 1865, a ruined city. The beauty of the women, and the picturesqueness of its location, with the many fine buildings, cause it to be celebrated in proverb and poetry. Its silk manufactures are of especial note, but all Chinese manufactures are produced in great abundance and of superior quality. Several channels connect it with the Yangtszekiang, and small steamers at high tide reach the many important villages and towns in the surrounding districts. The population is estimated at 500,000, and from the top of one of the high pagodas can be seen an area containing a population of 5,000,000. Station of the Methodist Episcopal Church (South), (1863), with (1900) 7 missionaries, six of them with their wives; 6 women missionaries, 24 native workers, 4 places of worship, 3 Sunday schools, 2 boarding schools, 1 theological class, 1 college, 1 dispensary, 1 hospital, 1 medical class, and 101 professed Christians. Station also of the PN (1871), with (1903) 4 missionaries, three of them with their wives; 17 native workers, 2 outstations, 5 places of worship, 3 Sunday schools, 4 day schools, 1 boarding school, 1 hospital, 1 dispensary, and 68 professed Christians. The name is also written Soochow.

SU-CHIEN. See SU-TSIEN-HSIEN.

SUDAN: A territory in Africa adjacent to the Sahara. Taken in its broader dimensions, or as spoken of by the Arabs and earlier European geographers, together with the additions claimed by Egyptian rulers in late years, Beled-es-Sudan, or the "Country of the Blacks," extends from west to east along the southern border of the Great Desert from the Atlantic and Senegal to the Red Sea and Abyssinia, and southward from the desert to Upper Guinea on the west, and to the equatorial and lake regions on the east, being some 3,500 miles in length, from east to west, and in its broader parts on the east some 1,600 in width, and comprising a population estimated at 50,000,000. It is thus almost a fourth of Africa, both in extent of country and in the number of its inhabitants.

The Western Sudan from Wadai to the Atlantic is now comprised and described as belonging to the more recently created colonies and protectorates and spheres of influence of France, or to Northern Nigeria, which has fallen to Great Britain. The extreme northern part of Kamerun also falls in this general region.

Eastern or Egyptian Sudan, to which the eyes of the world have been chiefly turned during recent years, lies along each side of the Nile, from Assouan or the first cataract to Uganda and the Congo Free State, extending some 1,100 miles or more from north to south, while its width, from the Red Sea to the eastern limits of Wadai, is from twelve to fourteen hundred miles.

The extensive additions to his own territories, which the distinguished viceroy of Egypt, Mehemet Ali, made, more than half a century since, included all the country on the Blue and White Niles, for great distances east and west of them, and for several degrees south of the equator; and in after years his grandson, Ismail, the first Khedive of Egypt, claimed that he had a right to extend his borders as far as the Juba River on the Indian Ocean. The Sudan as now constituted (1903) comprises eight provinces, viz.: Khartum, Gezira, Dongola, Berber, Kassala, Sennar, Kordofan, and Bahr el Ghazal, and three administrative districts, Wadi Halfa, Suakin, and Fashoda. The present area is about 950,000 square miles; the population is estimated roughly at 3,500,000. Khartum, the capital of this vast region, is situated at the junction of the two

Niles, Blue and White; and Suakin, on the Red Sea, is its chief seaport.

This section of Africa is chiefly inhabited by two distinct races. From the eleventh degree of latitude northward the people are almost wholly Arab in their origin. They are chiefly nomads, and are professedly Mohammedan. Being exceedingly emotional and superstitious, they have the greatest regard for their sheikhs or spiritual guides, ascribe to them a kind of supernatural power, and venerate them almost more than they do the Prophet himself. The country south of the 11th degree of latitude is peopled by negroes, chiefly of a sedentary and agricultural mode of life, who, while classed as Mohammedans, are in reality but slightly changed pagans. The mingling of Arab and negro blood has produced a third, hybrid, Arab-speaking class, who are found in the more fertile parts of the Sudan, especially in Darfur. A small yet very distinct race, said to have descended from the ancient Nubians, is found in the northern province of Dongola; and between the Nile and the Red Sea, not far from Suakin, there is still another distinct and ancient tribe, who speak a language of their own.

The history of the Sudan, since the expulsion of the French from Egypt by the English in 1801, has been turbulent and more or less dramatic. Mehemet Ali, a poor fisherman of Greek descent, a shrewd and active leader, who, with a band of followers, had aided the English and Turks in expelling the French, succeeded in securing the appointment from the Porte, in 1806, as viceroy of Egypt. He proved himself to be a general, a statesman, and man of affairs, and met with great success for many years. Finding the Mamelukes, whom he had used as a stepping-stone to power, a hindrance to his rule, and a plague to the country, he massacred a great part of them in 1811; others escaped and fled to New Dongola, but they were followed and finally exterminated in 1820. Mehemet Ali then made himself master of Upper Egypt, and by him the Egypt of to-day was virtually founded. His rule extended from the Mediterranean to the equator, and hereditary succession was established forever, according to Mohammedan law, in the eldest of his blood. Ismail, the fifth viceroy of Egypt, and a grandson of Mehemet Ali, enlarged his army, extended his sway southward over regions which Mehemet Ali had nominally taken, so as to recover and include the Upper and White Nile, together with the equatorial and lake provinces, and pushed his victories into the Darfur regions. But in levying enormous taxes upon the people he laid the train for revolt. The revolt took definite form in the summer of 1881. It was led by Ahmed Mohammed, an Arab of African birth. An air of mystery surrounded Mohammed, and he styled himself the Mahdi, claiming to be that prophet or reformer of Islam whose coming had been awaited for many centuries. Emerging from seclusion, he and his motley army took several large towns, and in July, 1882, he overpowered and massacred a force of about 6,000 Egyptian soldiers, together with the commanders of the army. An English officer, General Hicks, was now sent to take command of the Egyptian forces at Khartum. After some successes, he marched in pursuit of the Mahdi with an Egyptian force of about 10,000 men in the autumn of 1883. Through the treachery of a guide he was led into a defile not far from El Obeid, where the Mahdi fell upon him and left "not a man" of all his army to tell the tale.

The fate of General Hicks' expedition aroused in England a deep interest in the Sudan war. The Mahdi's lieutenants appeared with strong forces before Suakin on the Red Sea. England's route to India was in danger; a fleet was sent to Suakin, and troops were sent thence to drive off the Sudanese. Defeat of the English enterprise and massacre was the only result. Stung to action by these disasters, the British Government dispatched troops to Suakin, and having now become concerned for the safety of Egypt, proposed to abandon the Sudan. As a first step to carrying out this policy, Gen. Gordon, who had formerly been Governor-General of the Sudan, was sent to Khartum in 1884. He was to tranquilize the hostile tribes and prepare a means by which English and Egyptian officers, civil functionaries, and soldiers might withdraw from that turbulent and unprofitable region. But the Mahdi won over Gordon's trusted Egyptian troops, found entrance to Khartum, and killed Gen. Gordon, so that the English forces, sent tardily in the latter part of 1884 to his relief, found naught, on arriving near the city, but desolation dominated by the green flag of Islam.

For eleven years after the fall of Khartum the Sudan was ruled by the Mahdi, and after his death, in 1885, by his successor (*Khalifa* or Caliph). These new rulers held the country under a desolating and blood-thirsty despotism, for they considered themselves divinely appointed reformers. Prosperous districts were reduced to barren wastes. The river populations, reduced to small numbers, were little better than slaves.

In 1898, however, the increasing power of the *Khalifa* led to a serious interposition on the part of Great Britain, and under Lord Kitchener's direction the combined British and Egyptian forces broke the power of the *Khalifa*, recovered Khartum and finally destroyed the last vestige of Mahdism, by the death in battle of all its most prominent leaders.

The Sudan is now a condominion of Egypt and Great Britain, an arrangement having been made, in January, 1899, between the two governments for the appointment of a Governor-General by Egypt, with the assent of Great Britain, who rules under general principles agreed upon by both governments.

The prosperity of the Sudan is slowly reviving. A primary school system is now in operation. Gordon College, an institution proposed by Gen. Kitchener for teaching Western sciences to Mohammedans, by Mohammedans, or, at least, without Christian taint, was opened at Khartum in 1902, with an endowment of about $500,000.

Direct missionary work for Mohammedans is under prohibition (1903) in the Sudan, the military authorities fearing its results upon the fanaticism of the people. Medical missions have been authorized, under certain restrictions, and the CMS has a station at Omdurman, and the UP a station at Khartum. The last-named Society has also undertaken missionary work among the pagan population (Shillahs) on the Sobat River, 540 miles south of Khartum. The British Government will probably consent to the opening of schools by missionaries without much more delay.

Alford (H. S.) and Sword (W. D.), *The Egyptian Sudan: Its Loss and Recovery*, London, 1898; Bennett (E. N.), *Downfall of the Dervishes*, London, 1898; Boulger (D. C.),

Life of Gordon, London, 1897; Churchill (W. C.), *The River War: The Reconquest of the Sudan*, London, 1902; Lady Duff Gordon, *Letters from Egypt*, new ed., London, 1902; Fenn (G. M.), *In the Mahdi's Grasp*, London, 1899; Fowler (M.), *Christian Egypt*, London, 1900; Mardon (H. W.), *Geography of Egypt and the Egyptian Sudan*, London, 1902; Neufeldt (C.), *A Prisoner of Khaleefa*, London, 1899; Steevens (G. W.), *With Kitchener to Khartoum*, Edinburgh, 1898; Slatin Pasha, *Fire and Sword in the Sudan*, New York, 1895. Also the *Travels of Schweinfurth* (1868–71), Speke (1863), Grant (1864), Jephson (1887–88), Baker (1867–68), etc.

SUDAN PIONEER MISSION. See GERMANY; MISSIONARY SOCIETIES IN.

SUDHARAM: Town in Bengal, India, situated in Noakhali district, in the eastern portion of the Ganges Delta, and about 60 miles N. W. of Chittagong. It has some commercial importance, but is unhealthful and disagreeable as a residence. Population about 5,000. Station of the Queensland Baptist Missions (1889), with (1901) 1 woman missionary, 6 native workers, 1 outstation, 1 day school, and 10 native communicants. Also called Noakhali.

SUFISM: A theosophy or mystical philosophy found among Mohammedans, altho branded as of heretical tendency by the Ulema or regular hierarchy of Muslim theologians. Upon it is based the "secret" or "mystery" of the orders of Dervishes, each order having its own practise and method of applying the philosophy of man's relation with God proposed by Sufism.

The name *Sufi* is variously derived by Persian and Turkish writers, some holding that it comes from *Sof*, wool; woolen garments being worn by ascetics. Others, more correctly, perhaps, connect the word with the Greek *sophos*, a sage. The body of doctrine and rules as to practise followed by Sufis is called the science of *tesawwuf*, a word formed by regular Arabic rules from "Sof." It is perhaps worth noting, however, that this word is spelled with the letters which might be used (with different vowel points) to represent the word "Theosophy."

Sufism has been chiefly taught, and most extravagantly also, in Persia, where the stimulus of its aspirations has fostered imagination, clothed its teachings in beautiful literary garb, and changed every philosopher into a poet.

Sufism first attracts attention in the 9th century. Under the Abbaside Caliphs, at Baghdad, it flourished among the men of genius brought together to grace the Golden Age of Mohammedan intellectual activity. The time was a critical one both for Islam and for the principle of free thought which theologians sought to suppress. The assimilation by Islam of the mass of men of various religions and philosophies who had been forced into Mohammedanism, was not complete. It had produced in Islam itself various heretical schools of thought. These schools of philosophy were gradually crushed out, and Sufism, with its careful reverence for Mohammedanism in teaching secret and inward explanations of visible and outward things, seems to have become a refuge for all who revolted against chaining the mind to dogmas and formulas. It gave hospitable welcome to everything in the way of doctrine that the world has ever heard, since "all paths lead to God."

The "Sincere Brethren," found in Baghdad in the 10th century, seem to have been imbued with the principles of Sufism. Their mysteries made their bond of union, and in the secrecy with which they surrounded their real creed they resembled some orders of the Dervishes of to-day.

So far as can be gathered from their literary remains, the chief subject of their investigation was that knowledge of divine things which is taught imperfectly by all religious systems. They held the central Sufi doctrine, that the essence of every existing thing is derived from one supreme mind. All knowledge, therefore, aids understanding of the One Source of all, and everything may turn to the benefit of the soul in leading it to the knowledge of God. The highest attainment is such separation from worldly things as will permit life with God and knowledge of His counsels. In this pursuit the poorest may be the richest, and all seekers may recognize a brotherhood bond which makes each ready to aid the other.

Sir William Jones gives the central idea of the Sufis as follows: "Nothing exists absolutely but God. The human soul is an emanation from His essence, and will finally be reunited with it. The highest possible happiness will arise from this reunion, and the chief good in this world consists in as perfect a union with the Eternal Spirit as the encumbrance of a mortal frame will allow."

The great Sufi writers give telling illustrations of their view of the nature of the essential unity of the spirit of man with God. Says one (translation by Ubicini): "You say 'the sea and the waves,' but in this utterance you do not signifiy distinct objects; for the sea when it heaves produces waves, and the waves when they settle down again become sea. In the same way men are the waves of God, and after death return to His bosom. Or, you trace, with ink upon paper, the letters of the alphabet, '*a, b, c;*' but these letters are not distinct from the ink with which you write them. In the same manner the creation is the alphabet of God, and is lost in Him."

Sufism has features which recall the doctrines of the Gnostics, who had not yet vanished from Asia when Islam put forth its sword to rid the world of all formulas of belief save the formula of allegiance to the Prophet of Mecca. Like the Gnostics, the Sufis attach an important mystic meaning to light, as symbolizing the Supreme Power. So, too, the Sufis believe in Aeons ruling the world through a whole hierarchy of under dignitaries (the *Kutb*, the *Ghaws*, etc.), and showing the power of God in thaumaturgic displays. Like the Gnostics, too, the Sufis divide mankind into two classes: on the one hand are spiritual men, understanding all things, initiated into the councils of God—thoroughly ripened souls who are free from all law, and, on the other hand, are fleshly men—immature creatures still struggling with the desires of the body and burdens of law, and of the endless rites of religious observance.

Neo-Platonism, too, is preserved like a fossil in its matrix by Sufism in the use which it makes of the doctrine of man's unity of essence with the Creator. Sufis hold that man may cease to be himself—that is to say, individual—while in the body; and he may thus identify himself with the Absolute and Infinite Truth. This intuitive grasp or vision of the Infinite is not subject to any effort of will. But by an effort of will man can concentrate his mind for the contemplation of God to such an extent that God gives, in return, the inspiration or enthusiasm of vision which is infinitely precious, altho transient in consequence of the mortal frame in which the soul of man is chained.

Sir William Jones translates from *Ferhad and*

Shirin a passage illustrating various allegories in nature which invite the soul to desire to approach God: "There is a strong propensity which dances through every atom and attracts the individual particles to some particular object. Search the universe from base to summit, from fire to air, from water to earth, from all below the moon to all above the celestial spheres, and you will not find a corpuscle destitute of natural attractability. The very point of the first thread in this apparently tangled skein is no other than the principle of attraction, and all principles beside are devoid of real basis. From such a propensity arises every motion perceived in heavenly or in terrestrial bodies; it is the disposition to be attracted which taught hard steel to rush from its place and rivet itself to the magnet; it is this quality which gives every substance in nature a tendency toward some other, and an inclination forcibly directed to a determinate point."

The Sufis speak in very warm terms of their devotion to God. "We are not afraid of Hell," says one, "neither do we desire Heaven." Asked by a scandalized follower what he meant by so blasphemous a speech, he replied, "Our devotion is for love of God only. To God belongs the right to put us either in Heaven or in Hell. And may God's commands be executed agreeably to His blessed will!"

M. Garcin de Tassy brings the attractive utterances of the Sufis to their true level by the following remarks in his translation of one of their finest poems: "Placed between the Pantheism of the Indian Yogis and the Koran (which is sometimes an informal copy of the Bible) the Mohammedan philosophers called Sufis have established a Pantheistic school appropriate to Islamic ideas—a sort of esoteric doctrine of Islamism, which must be distinguished from Indian Pantheism, tho, indeed, it presents only errors of the *Vedanta* and the *Sankhya*. Pantheism as a moral doctrine leads to the same conclusions as materialism—negation of human liberty, indifference to actions, and the legitimatizing of temporal enjoyments. In this system all is God except God Himself, for He thereby ceases to be God. The spiritualism of the Sufi, tho contrary to materialism, is in reality identical with it. But if this doctrine is not more reasonable it is at least more elevated and more poetical."

There is a special Sufi vocabulary of the experiences of the seeker after God. God is the Truth— *Hakk*. The devotee's attraction to God is called *Jezb*. The intuitive knowledge of Divine things, which the soul seeks to acquire, is *marifeh* (knowledge—*gnosis*). That state of self-effacement, which removes the obstacle of individuality from the path of union with God, is called *ifna* (annihilation) and the attainment of the sense of union with God is *visal* (the term used in speaking of a lover's gaining access to his mistress). The resulting ecstasy of joy is *Wejd*. A special meaning attaches to many other words in the mouths of Sufis. This must be borne in mind in order to avoid reading Christian or other preconceptions into the writings of these philosophers, as has been done by the one seductive translator of Omar Khayyam. The meaning conveyed to a Sufi by the name of God has already been hinted. He furthermore considers God to be the author of evil as well as of good. Hence there is no moral quality in God, and moral distinctions are obscured for men. "Love of God,"

"Desire for God," "Union with God," entrain no moral responsibility in the man who has them for his object in life. "Knowledge of God," too, is merely apprehending His existence by some mechanical or other means which concentrates attention upon the fact. The aim of the seeker after knowledge of God is neither a clearing of the mind nor a purification of the affections and desires. It is simply personal enjoyment of an ecstasy, artificially produced and transitory, whose highest value, aside from the nervous orgasm, is its power to make the Sufi oblivious of the closely linked relations to other men which characterize life. In social matters the Sufi holds an attitude like that of the stylite monks of early Eastern Christianity who could perceive nothing in the world more worthy of effort than personal advancement in what they were pleased to call "saintliness."

Sufism has never been free from the attacks of Mohammedan theologians. The heretical sects of the early centuries of Islam have disappeared. The "Sincere Brethren" have likewise gone. Sometimes one gets a glimpse of the methods of this removal of heresy in the record of the flaying alive of a poet or a teacher for some pantheistic utterance; and in modern times the persecution of Babism in Persia (which is but one of the manifestations of Sufism) is familiar to all. Such practical obstacles to free development have led the Sufis to announce loudly, and some of them honestly, their dependence upon the Mohammedan faith. They draw from the Koran proof texts which they use at their full value. One of such texts is, "It is not given to man that God should speak to Him; if he does, it is by inspiration, or through a veil." By this text the Sufis prove that their teachings are authorized; they merely follow the Koran in making strenuous efforts to raise the veil by annihilation of the individuality which separates man from the Divine essence. Another text which they use to justify their doctrine is the fourth verse of the Vth Sura of the Koran: "God made all creation as an emanation from Himself, and will afterward cause it to reenter within Himself."

Ubicini points out, however, the essential antagonism between Sufism and the Mohammedanism to which it professes to conform. It has "two schools, the one public, which precedes initiation; and the other secret, for adepts only. A strict observance of religion and all the social virtues is required of the candidate for initiation. Later, when, by a long suite of proofs and mortifications (under a teacher to whom absolute obedience has been vowed) and, above all, by the absolute annihilation of his individuality the novice is supposed to have arrived at the desired degree in which he may behold the truth face to face, the veil, until then spread over his vision, suddenly falls, and the teacher makes known to his pupil that the Prophet in his book has only presented under the veil of allegory maxims and political precepts; that the Koran without mystical interpretation is only an assembly of words void of sense; and that once the habit of mental devotion acquired, one can abandon all forms and outward ceremonies of religion, and reduce worship to a purely inward and spiritual exercise." But a Mohammedanism which has abandoned its forms of worship has ceased to be Mohammedanism. Great injustice is done to Islam by hasty writers, who represent Sufism as an emanation from Mohammedanism that explains its essentials. In fact, Sufism is a force opposed to Islam, which will one day destroy it by substituting pantheism for monotheism in the Mohammedan theology. The strength of Islam resides in its truth, tho that be linked to a phenomenal falsehood. When that truth of one personal God has been replaced by the pagan conception which Sufism seductively offers, the religion of Mohammed will be found to have vanished from the face of the earth.

On perceiving the pantheistic taint in every utterance of the more advanced Sufis respecting God, one cannot avoid a sense of disappointment, for many of their really beautiful sayings seem to offer a bridge by which the system may be connected with mystical Christianity. The Christian as well as the Sufi may join with the Hindu in saying "There is One only—and there is none else." But the Sufi parts company with the Christian to follow his Hindu teacher. The great poet Jellal-ed-din Rumi said, in a moment of exaltation, "Oh, my master, you have completed my doctrine by showing me that you are God—that all things are God!" Because the Christian finds Scripture teaching that the Spirit of God will lead him who consents to be led, and that he who is led by the Spirit of God is a son of God, he can join with the Sufi in declaring that, "To lose self in God is the one object toward which men should strive." But this the Christian understands as a call to subject self-will to the control of God, with a change of desires that places him in harmony of purpose and action with God, enabling him to make kindly helpfulness to others the God-like characteristic of his life. The Sufi, however, finds in his desire to seek God no stimulus toward moral elevation; and his brotherly feeling toward others is but the bastard kindliness of the mutual admiration society which rates the masses—those who do not belong to the aristocracy of the instructed ones—as accursed. Even for his own brethren he gains little from his quest after the Divine. Saadi sets forth the barrenness of this quest, so far as benefit to others is concerned, in one of his quaint parables in the Gulistan: "A Dervish being questioned as to what gift he had brought back to his brethren out of the garden of delights to which he had gone, replied, 'I intended on arriving at that rose-tree (the vision of God) to fill the skirt of my robe with roses, so as to offer them to my brethren. But when there, the scent of the roses so intoxicated my senses that the skirt of my robe escaped from my hands.' The tongue of that man is silenced who has known God."

Setting on the one hand this conception, that God countenances a man's content to bless himself tho his fellows are left without participation; and placing upon the other side John's great elucidation of the purpose of God's revelation of Himself to men—"He that abideth in me and I in him, the same beareth much fruit"—we touch the central point in the contrast between the two systems. Sufism, like all error which has power to enthrall men, is based on a great truth, misunderstood and elaborated by darkened minds. The missionary's approach to the Sufi, then, should be cautious until he has mastered this curious eclectic philosophy, and has prepared in some way to show clearly the truth which it has obscured and perverted.

Ubicini (M. A.), *Letters on Turkey;* Misiri (Mohammed), Turkish: *Ilm i Tesawwuf* (The Science of Sufism), Constantinople, 1854; translated also by Brown (J. P.), in *The Dervishes,* London, 1868; Gobineau (J. A. de), *Les Religions et les Philosophies dans l'Asie Centrale,* Paris, 1865; Blochet (E.), *Études sur l'esoterisme Mussulmane,* in *Journal Asiatique,* Vols. 19 and 20, Paris, 1902; Tholuck (F. A. D.), *Ssufismus,* Berlin, 1821; *Wafa ibn Mohammed Wafa,* Refutation of the ignorant follies of the Sufis (Arabic), Cairo, 1876; Bjerregard (C. H. A.), *Sufi Interpretations of the Quatrains of Omar Khayyam and Fitz-Gerald,* New York, 1902;. Safi of Samarcand, *Reshihat i Ain i Hayat* (Rills from the Fountain of Life), 1504; Turkish translation from the Persian by Arifi, 1585; printed Constantinople, 1850.

SUHIN STATION: A station of the SAMS in the Grand Chaco of Uruguay, South America, situated near the Pilcomayo River, about 150 miles N. W. of Asuncion. Station established (1899), with (1903) 4 missionaries.

SUI-CHAU: A town in Hu-pei province, China, situated about 110 miles N. W. of Wu-chang-fu. Station of the WMS, with (1903) 2 missionaries, 8 native workers, 7 outstations, 8 places of worship, 2 day schools, and 157 professed Christians, of whom 127 are communicants. Some write the name Sui-chou.

SUI-FU. See Hsu-chau.

SUI-TING-FU: A town in Sze-chwan, China, situated in the N. E. part of the province. Station of the CIM (1899), with (1903) 2 missionaries with their wives, 2 women missionaries, 1 place of worship, 1 dispensary.

SUIYANG. See Sui-chau.

SULTANPUR: A town in the United Provinces, India, situated about 30 miles S. by W. of Faizabad. Station of the ZBM, with (1903) 5 women missionaries, 5 native workers, 1 day school, and 1 orphanage.

SULU ISLANDS: An archipelago lying between Mindanao, the southern island of the Philippines, and the northeast extremity of British Borneo. By the treaty of peace, December, 1898, these islands were ceded to the United States by Spain, and they are included in statistical reports with the **Philippine Islands.** There are over fifty islands, the largest of which is thirty-six miles long and twelve broad. The population of the Sulu Islands is entirely Mohammedan in religion, and no missionary work has, as yet (1903), been attempted among them.

SULURPETA: A town in Madras, India, situated near the coast, about 50 miles N. by W. of Madras city. Station of the Hermannsburg Missionary Society (1866), with (1903) 1 missionary and his wife, 8 native workers, 2 outstations, 1 place of worship, 5 day schools, and 206 professed Christians, of whom 197 are communicants.

SUMATRA: One of the largest and richest islands of the Dutch East Indian Archipelago. It extends 1,047 miles from northwest to southeast, lying between latitude 5° 40' north and latitude 5° 59' south. Its area is estimated at 160,000 square miles, and the population (1900) at about 3,000,000. The island belongs to the Dutch Government, tho some of the interior districts have not been brought under complete subjection. Throughout the whole length of the island extends a range of lofty mountains, which lies nearer the western coast than the eastern; hence on the eastern slope there are several large rivers, but the watercourses on the western slope are comparatively short. Sugar-cane, coffee, rice, and spices are the principal products, tho much fine timber and many tropical fruits are found in abundance. The greater part of the population are Mohammedan in religion and belong to the Malay race, but it is probable that they have absorbed many aboriginal tribes, a few remnants of which are found in the interior, such as the Kubus, who seem to have a mixture of Negrito blood, and the Battaks. These latter are pagans and differ in many points from the Malay type. They are somewhat undersized, with broad shoulders and rather muscular limbs. Their eyes are large and black, with heavy brown eyebrows. These people inhabit a region running northward from Padang on the W. coast of the island to Toba Lake, and beyond, as far as Deli on the E. coast of the island. Their language contains words of Sanskrit origin, and has evidently been affected by Javanese, Malay, Macassar, Sundanese, and Tagal influence. Another peculiar tribe are the Redjangers, who use distinctive characters, which they cut on bamboo with their short kreeses or daggers. The possessions of the Dutch Government in the island of Sumatra are divided into the Residencies of the West Coast, the East Coast, Benkulen (the extreme southwestern coast), Lampongs (southeastern coast), Palembang (southeastern and central), and Atjeh, the northern extremity. The principal towns are: Padang, on the west coast, about latitude 1° south, the residence of the governor, with a population of 14,000, including a Chinese settlement and a European quarter; Benkulen, the capital of the Residency of that name, with 11,000 inhabitants; Palembang, in the Residency of Palembang, has 52,000 inhabitants, with barracks, hospitals, one of the finest mosques in the Dutch Indies, and a tomb, said to be that of Alexander the Great. Included in the Dutch possessions of Sumatra are various islands which are contiguous to it. On the west coast, under the Residency of that name, are the Banyak Islands, Nias, Butu Islands, Nassau Islands, and Engano. On the east are Bengkalis, Rhio-Lingga Archipelago, and Banka. The latter is separated from Palembang by Banka Strait, and has an area of about 5,000 square miles and a population of 106,305.

Missionary operations in the interior of Sumatra have been chiefly among the Battak tribes. The Battak tribes hold to a belief in demons, their religious rites showing traces of ancestor-worship, and being accompanied by cannibalism. The BMS sent Messrs. Burton and Ward to Sumatra about 1820, but the mission was shortly afterward given up. The ABCFM attempted a mission among these people in 1834. The enterprise came to an end, however, with the murder of its two missionaries, Munson and Lyman. A private enterprise in Ermelo, Holland, sent out missionaries in 1856, and the Netherlands Bible Society, in 1859, published a translation of the Gospel of John in one of the Battak dialects. Two years later (1861) the Rhenish Missionary Society took up this enterprise, and has had a marvelous success. It now has 32 stations in the Battak country (1903), 101 missionaries, men and women; 1,153 native workers, men and women; 207 outstations, 242 schools, and 51,585 professed Christians. The larger part of the converts are from the heathen Battaks, and the Silindung district is entirely Christianized. But the missionaries are pressing forward among the Mohammedan Battaks, and some 6,000 of the number of converts given above have been won from the Mohammedans. Besides the Rhenish Society, the Netherlands Missionary Society, the Java Committee (Holland), and the Netherlands Mennonites have opened stations on the east coast and in the interior.

SUNDANESE LANGUAGE: This is a difficult and even perplexing language of the Malayan family, and is spoken by about 4,500,000 of the inhabitants of Java, in the Dutch East Indies. It is less polished than the Javanese, but has long been written, the Javanese alphabet being used for the purpose. Arabic letters are also used for writing Sundanese, and some of the Dutch missionaries have tried to introduce the Roman alphabet for the purpose among the unlettered sections of the people.

SUNDAY SCHOOL UNIONS: The different Missionary Societies, with few exceptions, include the organization of Sunday schools as part of their regular work. The M. E. Church Missionary Society particularly emphasizes this feature. Early in the 19th century, about the same time as the Bible societies, societies were organized for the specific purpose of extending the Sunday school work. The first of these was The Sunday School Union, formed in England in 1803, which, however, devoted itself distinctively to home work. In 1817 a similar society was formed in Philadelphia, Pa., which developed in 1824 into the American Sunday School Union. That, however, like the English Society, gave its special attention to the home field, and it was left to a layman, Mr. A. Woodruff, to give the impulse for the foreign phase of this branch of Christian effort. As early as 1856 he commenced the efforts which resulted in the organization of the Foreign Sunday School Association, incorporated in 1878. Meanwhile, during a visit to England in 1864, Mr. Woodruff pleaded the cause of the Sunday School as a missionary agency so effectively before the Sunday School Union that a separate department was created, called The Sunday School Union's Continental Mission. Of these three organizations, the largest, the American Sunday School Union, still does very little for the foreign field except occasionally by grants to Sunday schools or publishing societies on the foreign field. The Sunday School Union's Continental Mission (headquarters, 56 Old Bailey, London, England,) carries on work in Norway, Holland, Belgium, France, Germany, Bohemia, Italy, Spain and Portugal, and even to a limited degree in Russia. In Sweden its missionaries have organized over 2,000 Sunday schools; in Norway one formed 160 new schools in four years; in Germany the 750,000 Sunday school scholars are very largely the fruit of the Society's labor.

The Foreign Sunday School Association (headquarters, 67 Schermerhorn St., Brooklyn, N. Y., U. S. A.) is more distinctly a foreign missionary organization. It emphasizes work among the Spanish-speaking peoples, and in connection with the foreign mission societies, especially assisting in the publication of Sunday school papers. Among them are six illustrated papers for children: *Glad Tidings*, in Japanese; *El Amigo*, in Spanish; *O Amigo*, in Portuguese; *La Feuille du Dimanche*, in French; *Die Sonntag Schule*, in German; and *Il Amico*, in Italian. Last year 13,000 subscriptions were paid for these papers. Several books have been published. One, *Christie's Old Organ*, will illustrate the diffusion of this work. First published in 1877, it has been translated into sixteen different languages, and more than 30,000 copies were circulated in Germany, Hungary, Bulgaria, Belgium, Portugal, Greece, Syria, Japan, Bombay, Ceylon, Bohemia, France, Italy, Asia Minor, and China.

SUNG-YANG-HSIEN: A town in Che-kiang, China, situated 25 miles W. of Chu-chau. Station of the CIM (1896), with (1903) 2 missionaries, 4 native workers, 3 outstations, 2 places of worship, and 20 professed Christians. Some write the name Song-yang.

SUNTH: A town in Bombay, India, situated in the district of Rewa, Kantha, about 75 miles E. by N. of Ahmadabad. Station of the PCI (1899), with (1900) 1 missionary and his wife and 1 orphanage.

SUPPORT OF MISSIONS; Principles and Methods used: It is proposed in the first place to indicate the total and per capita contributions of the churches for foreign missions; second, to partially account for the smallness of the contributions; third, to suggest an effective financial system and describe the working of the same in a local church; fourth, to discuss the policy of the support of specific objects which has been adopted by many churches in a number of leading denominations and which has been endorsed by some of our largest and most representative Missionary Boards.

I. The Contributions of the Churches: The most recent, reliable and complete exhibit of the contributions of the churches of Christendom for foreign missions is the compilation of the Rev. James Dennis, D.D., in his remarkable encyclopedic work entitled *Christian Missions and Social Progress.* From this exhibit it appears that at the close of the century the annual income from home sources of the 537 denominational and independent societies and their auxiliaries was $17,284,363, a little more than three and one-half million pounds sterling. It is next to impossible to ascertain the per capita gifts represented by this amount, but they are not far from 30c. a year. The per capita gifts of American Christians are more certainly ascertainable because our church census returns are more complete than those of most countries. The annual income from home sources of all American Missionary Societies at the close of the century was $5,199,497. The total membership of the Evangelical Churches of the United States in the year 1900 was 17,837,147, from which it appears that after a century of missionary appeal the average American Christian has become interested in the greatest work in the world only to the extent of an investment of 29c. per year. He is still settling his missionary obligations in small silver and copper coin. This pitiable showing would be rendered even more pitiable were we able to compile the large gifts of a small number of generous wealthy persons with the legacies and the product of endowment funds, and then compare this total with the total gifts of the rank and file of our church membership.

Another illustration of the low scale of missionary giving is furnished by the following table of the contributions of the living members of four of our greatest and wealthiest American denominations during the twenty-five years closing with 1901:

Year.	Aggregate Membership.	Aggregate Amount.	Per Capita.
1877	4,527,262	$1,204,177	$0.27
1878	4,666,015	1,254,442	.27
1879	4,759,362	1,094,884	.23
1880	5,002,252	1,373,915	.27
1881	4,976,517	1,378,234	.27
1882	5,126,869	1,396,488	.27
1883	5,161,180	1,531,346	.29
1884	5,360,684	1,581,457	.29
1885	5,460,650	1,715,098	.31
1886	5,662,902	1,893,685	.33
1887	5,981,924	1,931,728	.32
1888	6,271,105	1,955,191	.31
1889	6,479,991	1,950,645	.30
1890	6,636,735	1,972,270	.29
1891	6,882,669	2,316,045	.33
1892	7,085,337	2,785,000	.39
1893	7,323,933	3,168,608	.43
1894	7,666,584	2,656,195	.34
1895	7,929,538	2,263,941	.28
1896	8,110,933	2,421,957	.29
1897	8,264,070	2,166,116	.26
1898	8,553,800	2,235,371	.26
1899	8,631,833	2,430,772	.28
1900	8,752,398	2,487,605	.27
1901	8,858,563	2,482,293	.28

It is worthy of special remark that the extraordinary fluctuations which characterize the above annual incomes cannot be accounted for by the financial conditions prevailing in the different years, because it will be noticed that the per capita contributions in 1893, the first year of the panic, were 43c., and in 1894, the second year of the panic, 34c., whereas in 1899, 1900 and 1901, three of the most prosperous years in the country's history, the per capita contributions were respectively 28c., 27c. and again 28c. It would probably be impossible to account for the decrease of 16c. per capita from 1893 to 1900 by the decreased financial ability of the churches.

II. Explanation of Fluctuations in Contributions: There seems to be a general agreement among those who are engaged in supplying the missionary treasuries that the most widely tested of all financial methods has run its course. Reference is made to the annual church collection. It is evident that however efficient this method may have been in other days when there were very few causes appealing for support, it can no longer compete successfully with the definite, persistent, ingenious methods of financial appeal which are now resorted to by the legion of causes whose advocates make their appeal every week by letter and in person. The weakness of the annual collection consists in its infrequency, its indefiniteness and its unexpectedness. A man who is appealed to only once a year cannot be made to believe that the cause is as important as one whose claims are repeatedly urged. The vague, all-embracing indefiniteness which marks the two minutes' appeal from the pulpit on the day of the annual offering has no chance whatever in competition with the earnest, direct, persistent appeal of the financial representative of an educational or philanthropic institution. Moreover, the annual offering is in very many cases entirely unexpected and therefore unprepared for. Even if it was announced the preceding Sabbath the announcement was only one of a half-dozen or more reminders and notices and was probably not carried with the hearer through the church door; so the collection basket found him unprepared the following Sunday and he was obliged to choose between the stray piece of silver or copper on the one hand or the smallest bill in his pocketbook on the other, which happened on that occasion to be $5.00, and his decision had to be made while the collection basket made its way from the front of the church to his pew. A man thus hedged in will settle with the Board upon the silver or copper basis ninety-nine times out of a hundred, whereas if he had been given a fair opportunity, such as is given men every day in business and other philanthropies to make a pledge to be discharged in instalments, or even in one payment six months or a year hence, he would very likely have pledged the $5.00, and probably much more. The time fails to fully discuss this method in an encyclopedia article; it is sufficient that it be judged by its fruits, that is, by the depleted treasuries of the churches and the failure of the Church after a hundred years of modern missions to get more than one-tenth of the way around the population of the non-Christian world.

III. The Successful System: It is that which is elastic enough to adapt itself to the great variety of people who compose the membership of any single congregation. Such a system must take account of those who meet their benevolent financial obligations upon the same principles which daily characterize their commercial dealings, who do not hesitate to "promise to pay;" who will, in other words, make a pledge. It must also adapt itself to those who wish to meet their pledges in instalments semi-annually, quarterly, monthly or even weekly. It must also recognize those who will not at the outset consent to be troubled with instalment payments, but who insist upon paying their pledges in one lump sum at some subsequent time. It must also reckon with those who "will not make a pledge from principle" (notwithstanding they do it daily in business), or will not make a pledge because they are ashamed to put down in black and white the small sum they intend to contribute and therefore insist on making a cash contribution. Moreover, the system must have regard for all the various lines of beneficence which run out from the church and it must not push one cause to the detriment of others. Furthermore, it must satisfy those who prefer to apportion their own contributions, and also those who magnify the policy of supporting specific persons or objects on the home and foreign mission fields; also those who know so little or care so little about the missionary enterprise in detail that they prefer for this or some other reason to have a committee apportion their gifts. In a word, the system must be as many sided as possible. Such a system as the above is in successful operation in a well-known suburban church, and it is worth remarking in describing the system that it has increased the city, home and foreign mission contributions of the church over tenfold. The method is as follows:

(1) The Church Committee decides to raise a definite minimum amount during the year, say $10,000.

(2) On the first Sunday in December the pastor announces the budget recommended by the Committee and urges the people to give universally, weekly and proportionately. He urges the necessity of some large gifts like $20, or $10 or $5 a week. This is Scriptural, see I. Cor. xvi., 1-2.

(3) Pledge cards are put into the hands of the people immediately and all are asked to make definite pledges to be paid in weekly instalments through the year. Fully three-quarters of the people are now using the pledge card.

(4) Envelopes are placed in the people's hands and are returned every Sunday with the contributions.

(5) The Church Committee recommends a system of apportionment to those who prefer not to make their own apportionment, but concedes to each person this privilege.

(6) Every month a special free-will offering is taken over and above the foregoing contributions. A special envelope handsomely embossed is distributed the preceding Sunday with the object printed thereon. These monthly collections are devoted to the various church boards and a few other important causes. In this way the person who will not make a pledge but will make an annual contribution has his opportunity. Moreover, many persons who have made pledges, but who, because of increased prosperity or other reasons, wish to make a special thank offering have the opportunity to do so.

(7) Once a year a specific foreign missionary appeal is made for the support of the church's missionary in the Philippines. The appeal is made the Sunday before the offering and special envelopes are furnished for use on the following Sunday. This offering constitutes the third opportunity given the church to contribute to foreign missions, inasmuch as one of the monthly offerings is devoted to this cause, and 25 per cent. also of the money collected in the weekly envelopes.

(8) Considerable loose cash is contributed every Sunday. On the annual missionary day this is applied to the church's missionary; on freewill offering day, once a month, it is devoted to that cause; the balance of the Sundays it is added to the fund composed of the weekly instalment contributions.

(9) A collection is never taken for a special cause the day the appeal is made, but on the following Sunday. While an immediate collection may enlist more from those who are easily stirred by an appeal, experience has shown that those who give after reflection and prayer more than offset what is lost from the former class.

Would not the universal adoption of this system fill the mission treasuries, fill our fields with missionaries and overfill our church members with the blessing of giving, which is more blessed than that of receiving?

IV. The Support of Specific Objects: More than fifty years ago President Wayland warned the churches against a peril which to-day assails the foreign mission enterprise, when he declared "the tendency will be more and more for churches to turn over their missionary obligations to societies, for societies to turn it over to boards, for boards to turn it over to executive committees, and executive committees to secretaries, so that in the last result the chief responsibility for the great work will rest on the shoulders of a dozen men." The late Rev. Dr. A. J. Gordon, one of the foremost missionary pastors of his generation, corroborated the opinion of President Wayland when he said: "The greatest problem that confronts us for the opening century is that of distributing the missionary responsibility which has become congested in official centers." That this peril and problem are actually upon us no one will deny who is engaged in trying to rally the churches and their individual members for the discharge of their obligation to the missionary cause. The discovery of a method which will create a spirit of individual obligation for the success of missions will constitute the capital event in the final era of world evangelization. There is ground for hoping that such a method is in sight.

The method is simply this: That every church which is able to do so extend its parish boundary so as to embrace a definite section of some mission field and support a missionary there who shall sustain to the home pastor the relation of associate or co-pastor; in other words, let the church have its foreign mission and sustain its foreign missionary, just as many churches have their own city mission and sustain their own city missionary. This method has been a distinguishing feature in the splendid work which the women of several leading denominations are doing. Every one of the nearly 200 unmarried women on the Congregational mission field is supported by funds specifically pledged. The same is true of practically every woman, both single and married, connected with the mission fields of the Presbyterian Church of the United States.

This policy has been adopted by several of the leading missionary societies in Great Britain, the Dominion of Canada, and the United States. This method is one of the most notable features which characterize the marvelous advance movement which the Church Missionary Society made during the last decade of the 19th century. Fully four hundred missionaries were specifically provided for by churches, families, individuals, and societies in response to the appeal of that missionary society.

The Board which follows closest upon the record of the Church Missionary Society is that of the Presbyterian Church of the United States, which has approximately 650 of its force of 800 missionaries supported by funds specifically contributed by churches, young people's societies, Sunday schools, women's auxiliaries, and individuals.

The Congregational Churches of the United States and Canada are supporting a larger proportion of ordained missionaries by specific funds than any other denomination. After testing the method for years in several representative churches the American Board unanimously recommended the adoption of the policy as a permanent educational and financial measure at its annual meeting in Grand Rapids, Mich., in 1898, and appointed a committee which it empowered to elect representatives to exploit the movement throughout the denomination. The reports of the committee have led the Board for four successive years to recommend the continuance of the policy. It is an interesting fact that not a single Congregational Church in which the representative of the Board has had a suitable opportunity to present the method has failed to subscribe money sufficient for the salary of a missionary.

The third most notable illustration of this policy is furnished by the Missionary Committee of the Southern Presbyterian Church, under whose direction over 75 salaries were provided by specific churches within a year, and over 100 other churches made pledges for the support of specific phases of work in the different foreign missionary fields occupied by the denomination.

The Missionary Society of the Canadian Methodist Church has also endorsed the policy and commended its Young People's Movement, whose work has largely consisted in enlisting young people's societies in the support of missionaries.

Among other notable endorsements of the policy may be mentioned that of the American Baptist Missionary Union, as well as the action of certain congregations of the Church of the Disciples, the United Brethren, etc.

Experience has fully shown that the churches which have their own representatives on the foreign fields are better informed than the average church concerning the work of missions, this information being secured from correspondence and also by the home visits of the missionary.

It is perfectly obvious that this policy enlists a church in assuming and maintaining a specific obligation. Long experience and extended inquiry have failed to discover a better method of persuading a church which is giving $100 or $200 a year, and is well able to give $800 or $1,000, to give the large sum and renew it annually.

The financial significance of this policy is forcibly set forth in the last report of the Forward Movement Committee of the American Board. In the report a comparison is made between the increased contributions of the 144 churches which the committee had enlisted in assuming the salaries of missionaries or the expenses of other special objects on the one hand, and the increased contributions of all the balance of the contributing churches in the denomination on the other. This comparison shows that the Forward Movement churches contributed in 1902 $32,988 more than in 1898, the year before the Movement was launched, whereas the balance of the churches, about 3,400 in number, only contributed $24,372 more in 1902 than in 1898. In other words, the Forward Movement churches, which constitute one-twenty-fourth of all the contributing churches, made an increase of over $7,000 above the increase of the remaining twenty-three-twenty-fourths of the churches; the average increase of the 144 Forward Movement churches was $229, whereas the average increase of the balance of the contributing churches was only $8, or one-twenty-seventh of the average increase of the former. This exhibit is considered a final argument in favor of contributions for specific objects. In the light of this report the question may well be raised whether or not every church should not constitute itself a mission station and support its own outstation.

SURAT: A town in Gujarat, Bombay, India, situated on the Tapti River, about 15 miles from its mouth. In the center, facing the river, is an old castle (1540), now serving as a public office building. An ancient moat encloses the city on the land side. Among its interesting features are old Parsee temples and the tombs of the earliest European settlers. In the 17th and 18th centuries Surat was of more commercial importance than Bombay. Its population in 1797 was 800,000, but it had fallen to 80,000 in 1847. The city has revived again; it received its stimulus to growth from the American Civil War of 1861-65, and it now (1901) has a population of 119,306, of whom about 80,500 are Hindus, 21,000 Muslims and 5,000 Jains. The climate is hot, malarious, and unhealthful. Station of the PCI (1846), with (1903) 1 missionary and his wife, 3 women missionaries, 29 native workers, 2 outstations, 1 place of worship, 3 Sunday schools, 1 printing house, 15 day schools, 3 orphanages, and 86 communicant Christians.

SURINAM: A name sometimes applied to Dutch Guiana, S. America.

SUSA: A town in Tunis, North Africa, situated on the E. coast about 23 miles E. by N. of the sacred city of Kairwan. Station of the North Africa Mission (1896), with (1900) 2 missionaries and their wives, 4 women missionaries, 1 native worker, 1 outstation, 1 place of worship, 1 dispensary.

SUSAKI: A town in Japan, situated on Tosa Bay, on the S. side of Shikoku Island, about 20 miles S. W. of Kochi. Station of the PS (1898), with (1900) 1 missionary and his wife.

SUSU LANGUAGE: The Susu is spoken by some of the negroes living near the coast of French Guinea in West Africa. It belongs to the negro group of African languages and has been reduced to writing with use of Roman letters.

SUTO LANGUAGE: This language, also called Lesuto, belongs to the Bantu family of African languages. It is the language of the Basuto tribes. It is spoken in Basutoland, South Africa, and is also found in adjacent regions in the Transvaal and Orange River Colonies and among some of the tribes northward toward the Zambesi. It has been reduced to writing with use of Roman letters.

SU-TSIEN-HSIEN: A town in the province of Kiang-su, situated on the Grand Canal, about 40 miles N. W. of Hwai-ngan-fu. Station of the PS (1894), with (1900) 2 missionaries and their wives and 1 woman missionary. Some write the name Su-chien.

SUTTON, Amos: Born at Sevenoaks, Kent, England, 1798. Died August 17, 1854, at Cuttack, Orissa. Having studied theology with Rev. J. G. Pike, he was ordained at Derby, and sailed in 1824 for Orissa, India, as a missionary of the General Baptist Missionary Society. He was stationed most of the time at Cuttack. He preached in Uriye and in English, taught in the mission academy, and was superintendent of the orphan asylums. He translated the whole Bible into Uriye, and made a second revision of the New Testament. He visited England and America. He returned to his mission from America in 1835, in company with Rev. Dr. Phillips, who was sent to the same field by the American Free Baptist Missionary Society. Dr. Sutton, besides translating the Scriptures, published an Uriye dictionary, grammar and lessonbook, wrote three volumes of tracts in that language, and translated many English books for his scholars and converts.

SUVA: A town in the Fiji Islands, Polynesia, situated on the S. coast of Viti Levu Island, of which it is the capital. European population, 1,073; native population uncertain. Station of the SPG (1880), with 1 missionary and a chaplain. Also station of the Seventh Day Adventists (1895), with (1900) 2 missionaries and their wives, 1 woman missionary, 2 native workers, 2 outstations, 1 place of worship, 1 printing house, 1 day school, and 23 professed Christians. Also station of the Australian Wesleyan Missionary Society, with (1900) 1 woman missionary, 1 day school, and 1 Sunday school.

SWAHILI LANGUAGE: Among the people inhabiting the parts of East Africa adjoining Zanzibar, where the Arab influence has been very strong, and extending northward to Somaliland, a mixed language has been developed, called the Swahili or coast language. It belongs to the Bantu family and has a wide range westward from the coast toward Equatorial Africa. At the same time it has adopted a large number of Arabic words and forms because it has served as a means by which Arabs of the coast and negro tribesmen from the interior could understand each other. It is written with Arabic letters, but missionaries have succeeded to some degree in introducing the Roman letters for the purpose. Quite a beginning of Christian literature exists in Swahili.

SWAN, William: Born June 21, 1791, at Balgonie, New Brunswick. Died January 1, 1866. Studied at the Theological Academy of Glasgow; sailed July 1, 1818, for Siberia as a missionary of the LMS. His chief work was among the Buriat Tatars found on the frontiers of Siberia and Chinese Tatary, east of Lake Baikal. For eight years he itinerated with Mr. Stallybrass in the Selinginsk region, but in 1828 made his permanent home at Onon. During these years he, in conjunction with Mr. Stallybrass, completed the Mongolian version of the Scriptures. For the printing of this version Mr. Swan succeeded, by personal entreaty, in obtaining permission from the Russian Government. After twenty-two years of arduous service in the inhospitable wastes of Transbaikalia Mr. Swan and his companion were summarily informed one day in 1840 that their mission was suppressed by order of the Czar. Mr. Swan therefore returned to Scotland in 1841, and shortly afterward withdrew from the service of the Society.

SWAROE: A town in Java, situated 130 miles S. E. of Samarang. Station of the Netherlands Missionary Society (1869), with 1 missionary and his wife, 4 native workers, 6 outstations, 1 place of worship, 5 day schools, and 2,093 professed Christians, of whom 169 are communicants.

SWATOW (Shan-tau): A seaport town of Kwang-tung province, China, situated on the left bank of the Han River, about 5 miles from the sea. Its houses are mostly built of concrete, which has been rammed between molding boards, the boards being afterward taken away. It is a treaty port and has some foreign trade. The climate is healthful. Population about 30,000. Station of the ABMU (1843), with 13 missionaries, men and women; 62 native workers, men and women; 58 outstations, 32 places of worship, 11 day schools, 2 boarding schools, 1 theological school, and 2,050 professed Christians, of whom 128 are communicants. Station also of the Presbyterian Church of England (1856), with (1903) 17 missionaries, men and women; 73 native workers, men and women (in district); 51 day schools, 2 boarding schools, 1 woman's training class, 1 theological class, 1 medical class, 1 printing house, 2 dispensaries, 2 hospitals, and 3,466 professed Christians, of whom 2,250 are communicants.

SWEDISH MISSIONS: The first missionary work undertaken by Protestant Sweden was among the Lapps, or Finns, who in scattered nomadic tribes occupy the whole northern part of the country. That mission has on its records several names, as for instance that of Peer Fjellström (1697-1764), which are still remembered with gratitude; but unorganized and unsystematized as it was, all its exertions and sacrifices were of no avail for a thorough success.

In 1630 a Swedish colony, "Nya Svearike," afterward called "Vinland," now Pennsylvania, was founded on the Delaware in North America, and the Swede Campanius, who in 1642 began to preach to the Delaware Indians and compiled a dictionary of their language, was the first Protestant missionary to enter the new world.

The colony was afterward transferred to Holland, then to England, and finally to William Penn; but up to 1831 it continued to be served by Swedish pastors.

Meanwhile the powerful impulse which Protestant missions received from England in the beginning of the 19th century made itself felt also in Sweden. In 1818 a mission paper was established, and in 1829 the first small mission society was founded at Göteborg. It was followed in 1835 by the Swedish Mission Society, and in 1845 by the Mission Society of Lund. In 1855 the latter was absorbed by the former, and in 1876 the Swedish Mission Society united with the Swedish Church Mission (founded in 1874), tho it was not wholly absorbed by it. Two other large societies were organized—the Evangelical National Institution in 1856 and the Swedish Mission Union in 1878. Besides these four great associations, quite a number of minor ones, still in their infancy, have sprung up.

I. The Swedish Mission Society (Svenska Missionssälskapet): Headquarters, Stockholm, Sweden. Very soon after its foundation, January 6, 1835, the Society was able to send out its first missionary to the Finns, Carl Ludwig Tellström, a painter, whose cordial interest in the people was aroused by his summer visits to their camps. Next year he was joined by two other young men, and they visited the tents, preached, and gave some general instruction.

A young Finnish girl, Marie Magdalene Madsdaughter, through the preaching of the missionaries, had come to see and understand the misery in which her race lived. She learned Swedish that she might be able to speak to the king, and in 1864 walked two hundred miles to Stockholm. She picked out in the street the first lady who to her eyes seemed to look trustworthy, and in a short conversation she made that lady her patroness. Next day she had an audience with the king, and after talking with a number of influential men during a stay of a few days, walked back to her native place with money enough to build a house or an asylum, or, as it is called, a "Children's Home," to which she could invite the children of her race to come and stay for some time and be instructed in that which is necessary, and also in something of that which is useful. The Society provided her "Home" with teachers, and so successfully did the plan work that it has now a number of such institutions among the Finns.

A considerable portion of its annual revenue the Society draws from the so-called Five-cents Circles. It also has invested funds to the amount of about 150,000 kroner. Its missions to the Finns it directs independently, and since its union with the Swedish Church Mission in 1876 pays the surplus to that Society, and partakes proportionally in the direction of its mission to the heathen.

II. The Evangelical National Society (Den Evangeliska Fosterlandsstiftelsen): Headquarters, Stockholm, Sweden. The Evangelical National Institution was founded in 1856 by Pastor H. I. Lundborg, as a consequence of a revival within the Swedish Church, produced by the lay-preacher Rosenius. Propositions of union were made to it in 1875 by the Swedish Church Mission, but declined. It preferred to make itself the organ of all such free and spontaneous mission movements as may arise among the Swedish people. It consists of a great number of minor societies, generally called "Ansgar Societies," or "Evangelical Lutheran Societies," having a common head in their annual conference, which assembles in Stockholm.

In 1863 it established a missionary seminary at Johannelund, on Lake Mälar, a little outside of Stockholm, originally intended only for home mission work. In 1861 it extended its activity also to foreign missions, and it now works in two different fields—among the Gallas in East Africa and among the Gonds in Hither India.

The mission to the Gallas in East Africa was begun in 1865, on the advice of Dr. Krapf and Bishop Gobat, but the great sacrifices and enormous exertions it has cost do not seem to have brought proportional results. The difficulties do not arise from the character of the people, for the Gallas have on many occasions showed some sympathy for Christianity, but from difficulty of access. From the north, through Abyssinia, the door is closed. To the east, and along the coast, live the Somalis, and they and the Gallas are instinctively enemies. Notwithstanding these obstacles there were reported in 1900, 32 missionaries and 28 native workers, 7 stations, 5 outstations, 206 communicants, 502 adherents, 14 schools, 305 pupils, 1 physician and 1 hospital.

The mission to the Gonds, begun in 1877, on the advice of Dr. Kalkar, in the Central Provinces of India, reported (1900) 36 missionaries, 37 native workers, 8 stations, 9 outstations, 257 communicants, 826 adherents, 9 schools, 500 pupils, 1 higher school and considerable medical work.

III. The Swedish Church Mission (Svenska Kyrkans Mission): Headquarters, Stockholm, Sweden. In 1868 the General Assembly of the Swedish Church (*Kyrkomötet*) laid before the king a petition that the whole missionary activity should be organized by law as a function of the Church, the state institution; and September 11, 1874, the king authorized the establishment of the Swedish Church Mission, under a board of seven directors, with the Archbishop of Upsala as its permanent president. Negotiations for a union with the other mission societies already existing did not succeed, but the Church Mission, nevertheless, immediately began work. It draws its revenue from a general collection taken up on a certain day in all Swedish churches, and maintains a mission among the Zulus in Africa, and a mission among the Tamils in India.

The Zulu Mission was begun in 1876, on the advice of Bishop Schreuder, who had long wished to see the whole energy of all Scandinavian mission societies united into one common effort, made possible by the close relation between the languages and the fundamental unity of the confessions. An estate, "Rorke's Drift," was bought in Natal, just on the boundary of Zululand, and the Mission had in 1900 25 missionaries, 28 native workers, 5 stations, 34 outstations, 631 communicants, 19 schools, 281 pupils, and 1 hospital.

The Tamil Mission, also begun in 1876, in close connection with the Leipzig Mission, in Tranquebar, was located at Madura, but has become practically identified with the Leipzig Mission.

IV. The Swedish Mission Union (Svenska Missionsförbundet): Headquarters, Christinehamn, Sweden. The Swedish Mission Union was formed August 2, 1878, in Stockholm, as the representative of the Waldenström faction, which separated from the Evangelical National Society because the latter clung rigorously to the Augsburg

Confession. The Union consists of over 900 minor associations and is managed by a committee of seven, which has its seat in Stockholm and is elected by the annual assembly of delegates from the associations.

The Union maintains a mission school at Christinehamn and carries on work in Africa (Congo and Algeria), Russia (Ural), Persia, China, and Chinese Turkestan. Work commenced in Alaska has been handed over to the Swedish Mission Union in America.

A mission was begun in 1880 among the Finns, and in the same year in Russia. The latter mission, however, has principally the character of revival work, tho at the station on the southeastern frontier the missionaries come in close contact with heathendom. The Congo Mission was started in 1881 and labored for some time in connection with the Livingstone (see Regions Beyond Missionary Union) Inland Mission. There were reported (1900) 40 missionaries, 62 native workers, 1,573 communicants, 8 stations, 62 outstations, 101 schools, 3,606 pupils, 7 dispensaries, and 20,000 patients. These figures seem to include the work in Algeria among the Jews, which, however, is not large.

Similar in character to this last movement are a number of minor societies, most of them affiliated with the China Inland and Christian Alliance Missions. These include the Swedish Mission in China (*Svenska Missionen Kina*), founded in 1887 by E. Folke; The Holiness Union (*Helgelseförbundet*), founded in 1890 by a mill owner in Nerike, and which sends missionaries to China and South Africa; a Scandinavian Alliance Mission, on the same lines as the Christian Alliance, which has sent out a number of untrained workers to China, Japan, the Himalayas, and Swaziland, but with little evident result. There are also the Jönköping Society for Home and Foreign Missions, which aids other societies; Friends of the Lapps Mission; the Female Missionary Workers (*Kvinriliga Missions Arbetare*), organized in 1894, which absorbed a Swedish Women's North Africa Mission, and is practically the foreign department of the Swedish YWCA. It carries on work, particularly for children, in a great variety of fields, including Lapland, the Caucasus, Tibet, India, China, Mongolia, North Africa, the Congo, and France.

SWITZERLAND (French); Mission of the Free Churches of: (*Mission des Églises Libres de la Suisse Romande*).

In the year 1874, the Synod of the Free Evangelical Churches of the Swiss Canton of Vaud (Presbyterian) resolved to create a mission of its own among the heathen, and accordingly two young missionaries, Messrs. Ernest Creux and Paul Berthoud, were sent to South Africa. They remained for some time with the missionaries of the Paris Evangelical Missionary Society in Basutoland, and in 1875 chose a mission field for themselves in the northern part of the Transvaal Republic, among the Tonga negroes. The work has extended to the Ronga tribes living to the east of the Transvaal, on the Limpopo River, and on the coast of Delagoa Bay. The New Testament and portions of the Old have been translated into the Tonga and Ronga languages, and the work at all the stations has been very successful.

For nine years this mission was under the care of the Free Church in the Canton of Vaud; in 1883 the Free Churches of Neuchatel and Geneva (both Presbyterian) formed a federation with the Free Church of the Canton of Vaud, and the mission has since been under their joint direction.

The report (1902) shows 53 missionaries, 50 native workers, 9 stations, 30 outstations, 958 communicants, 46 schools, with 1,604 pupils.

SYLHET: A town and capital of a district in Assam, India, situated about 62 miles W. of Silchar. It is the terminus of the railway to Cherrapunji, in the hill country. Station of the Welsh Calvinistic Methodists, with (1903) 2 missionaries and their wives, 2 women missionaries, 8 native workers, 6 outstations, 5 places of worship, 3 Sunday schools, 4 day schools, and 43 professed Christians.

SYN-YIN: A mission station of the Berlin Missionary Society in Kwang-tung, China, about 140 miles N. E. of Canton (1893), with (1903) 1 missionary, 18 native workers, 9 outstations, 1 day school, and 493 professed Christians, of whom 452 are communicants.

SYRIA: The geographical term "Syria" seems to have originated with the early Greek traders, who designated by it the land whose chief commercial city was Tsur, Sur, or Tyre. When the Arabs came into the land in the 7th century they called Damascus Dimishk esh-Sham, and named the provinces of which they made it the capital Bar esh-Sham. The Christian inhabitants of the land still call it "Suriyeh." The term "Palestine" comes from Pelesheth (פְּלֶשֶׁת—"land of wanderers"), and refers probably to the nomadic tendencies of the early inhabitants. No form of the word "Palestine" (Philistia, Palestina, etc.) is at present in common use in the country. The term is historical rather than political, and defines that part of Syria which stretches from Dan (near Mount Hermon) to Beersheba, and from the Mediterranean to the Syrian desert.

Geography: Syria in its widest extent, not now locally recognized, however, extends about 400 miles from the Taurus mountains on the north (latitude 37°) to Egypt (latitude 28°), and from the Mediterranean to the Syrian desert, an average width of less than 200 miles, and contains 70,000 square miles. It is nearly conterminous with the "Promised Land" and the kingdom of David. It is about the size of New England, Palestine east and west of the Jordan being of the size of Vermont and New Hampshire, and very similarly situated. Mountains on the north, the sea on the west, and deserts south and east give the land a somewhat remarkable geographical unity. The mountain ranges and river basins run parallel with the coast, rendering access easy from north to south. The Taurus Mountains send a spur off to the south not far from the coast. This is broken by the deep gorge of the Orontes (El-'Asi) River. The range takes a new start in the beautiful peak of Mount Casius, near Antioch, and stretches down along the coast, receiving various names at different points. Between Antioch and Tripoli it is called from the people who inhabit its slopes the "Nusairiyeh" range, which terminates in Jebel el Husn. A low saddle in the hills comes next, and then the Lebanon range springs suddenly up to the height of over 10,000 feet; and twenty miles across the plain to the east the almost equally massive Anti-Lebanon starts off to follow its mate down the coast for a hundred miles. Lebanon gradually tapers down from 10,000 feet to 8,000, to 5,000, to 2,000, until it drops into the hills of Galilee, and reaches almost sea-level in the Esdraelon plain. Anti-Lebanon holds its own for over half its length, then drops; but gathering in power, as a final effort, throws up its southern peak of Mount Hermon (Jebel esh Shaykh) 10,000 feet into the air. Between these two magnificent ranges runs the fertile valley of Cælo-Syria (El Bukaa), from ten to twenty miles in breadth and averaging over 2,000 feet above sea-level. The Orontes drains the northern part of the Bukaa, while the Litany (rising not far from the sources of the Orontes) flows southward and breaks through to the sea in the latitude of Mount Hermon. At the foot of this mountain rises the Jordan ("the descender"). This strange stream is delayed in the great marsh called El Huleh (Lake of Merom) at about sea-level. Breaking away from this it tumbles down in a few miles over 600 feet below sea-level into the sea of Galilee (Bahr Tabariyeh). After lingering for 16½ miles at this level it next plunges down 667 feet in a distance (as the crow flies) of 66 miles, but winding about 200 miles until it throws its muddy waters into the Dead Sea (Bahr Lut), 1,300 feet below the Mediterranean. To this phenomenal sea (46 miles long and 5 to 15 miles broad) there seems to be no outlet. Altho there is a geological depression from its southern end to the Akabah Gulf of the Red Sea, and altho there are indications that its waters were once on a higher level, the Dead or Salt Sea could not have been connected with the ocean, because there is a rise of ground of 781 feet above sea-level in its way.

West of the Jordan and south of the Esdraelon valley the hills of Ephraim slowly rise, forming the great backbone of Palestine. A sharp spur is thrown off to the northwest, which ends in the rocky headland of Mount Carmel. But to the south the trend is continually upward past Samaria, Nablous, Shiloh, Bethel, Jerusalem, Bethlehem, until Hebron is reached. Thence the hill-country of Judea falls away into the Sinaitic desert. Deep wadies run off gradually to the Mediterranean, but to the east sharp gorges plunge precipitately down into the Jordan valley a thousand or so feet below sea-level.

South of Mount Hermon and to the east of the Jordan, Anti-Lebanon gives place to a moderately high mountain wall, for the most part precipitous on its western side, but sloping away into the Hauran region and toward the desert beyond. The mountains of Gilead merge into the mountains of Moab and are continued southward to the Arabian border. The Hauran has indications of volcanic action, and has a number of interesting mountain peaks. A few oases in the desert, such as Tadmor (Palmyra), belong geographically to Syria.

Population: The population of Syria is in the neighborhood of 2,000,000, and may be roughly divided as follows:

Mohammedans (Sunnites and Metawileh)	1,000,000
Nusairiyeh	250,000
Maronites	250,000
Orthodox Greeks	235,000
Papal Sects	80,000
Jews	40,000
Ismailiyeh, Gypsies, etc	30,000
Armenians	20,000
Jacobites	15,000
Druzes	100,000
Protestants	7,500
Bedouin Arabs	60,000

The larger cities are Damascus (200,000), Aleppo (120,000), Beirut (100,000), Jerusalem (35,000), Tripoli (with its port, 25,000), Homs (20,000), Hamath (20,000), Zahleh (15,000), Nablous (15,000), Sidon, Nazareth, Acre, Hebron, Jaffa (each 10,000), and Antioch (6,000). The western slopes of Mount Lebanon are the most densely populated parts of the country outside of cities.

Race: From the earliest times there has been a notable mixture of races in Syria, yet all along the Semitic type has prevailed with a persistence truly remarkable. Flood-tides of Egyptians, Greeks, Romans, Kurds, Armenians, Persians, Teutons and Mongols have swept the country repeatedly, only to be as repeatedly driven out. The bad blood of many nations has soaked into the soil, and reappears in many channels; but the original race type, tho modified, has absorbed the remnant of many nationalities so effectively that there is a typical Syrian resultant, which differs widely from the surrounding peoples. With the exception of the Bedouin Arab of the southeast, the Kurds of the northeast, the Turkish officials, the Armenian merchants, and the so-called Franks, or foreign residents, the Syrian type is universal, modified, it is true, by hereditary religious customs and convictions, but holding its own through the centuries. It is characterized by a certain calculating shrewdness covered with an exterior of extreme politeness. The race-type is saturated with the despotic idea, which appears in every grade of society. Manual labor is counted ignoble. Religious differences have bred a mutual suspicion. Credit is almost unknown. Trade is a matter of sharp haggling over prices. The typical Syrian is proud, ambitious, loves display of ornament, cannot be trusted to obey to the letter, has a temerity of action on the basis of slight information, quickly yields to fear in the face of real calamity, and is thoroughly immersed in a gross materialism. A millennium of Muslim dominion and centuries of Turkish oppression have accentuated these faults. But wherever an opportunity has been given, a native force of character has come to the surface, so that even the precipitous slopes of Lebanon have been terraced thousands of feet above sea-level, and a restless desire to better their condition has sent whole colonies of Syrians across the oceans to Australia, South America and to the United States. Common school and higher education is having a marked effect upon the country, but the seeds of disunion and mutual hatred were planted too long ago to be materially affected during the short period, comparatively, in which Western Christian influences have been brought to bear on Syria.

Languages: With the Arabs in the 7th century came the Arabic tongue, which immediately became the language of trade. It was thus inevitable that it should become universal in the land. The older Syriac, a closely-allied Semitic dialect, slowly succumbed, leaving behind broad marks of influence in the colloquial Arabic, so that a man's speech betrays the locality from which he comes. In the extreme north of Syria, in the region of Aleppo, the Turkish language begins to be heard among the common people, and Arabic is not generally used north of that city. The official language for the whole country is Turkish, while everywhere Muslims of all nationalities use Arabic as their language of worship. Syriac remains the liturgical language of the

Maronites and the Jacobites. North of Damascus there are several villages in which Syriac is still the vernacular. Hebrew is heard frequently in Jerusalem. Linguistically, then, Syria is a unit and is closely allied in this particular with the Euphrates region, Arabia, and Egypt.

Commerce: The centers of commerce in Syria are Damascus (which means "seat of trade"), Aleppo, Alexandretta, Tripoli, Beirut, Haifa, Nablous, and Jaffa. Homs, Hamath, and Jerusalem might also be mentioned. The Hauran is the granary of the country. Olives, figs, licorice, oranges, grapes, and apricots are important crops. Maize, tobacco, and white potatoes are freely raised—America's gift to Syria. Soap from olive oil is made in quantities at Haifa and elsewhere. The silk-worm is busy all over. Mt. Lebanon and the villages on the eastern slopes are alive with domestic weaving establishments. Bethlehem is the seat of work in olive-wood and pearl utensils (souvenirs). Jerusalem is now, as it always has been, a caravansary for pilgrims from every clime.

Political Divisions: Syria (in its widest extent) is divided by the Turkish government into three vilayets — Adana, Aleppo, Syria (proper; called in Turkish *Suriyeh*), and two *mutassarifliks* or districts—Jerusalem and the **Lebanon**. Since 1860 the **Lebanon** region has been under the protection of foreign powers and is governed by a Christian mutassarif under special foreign oversight. The center of political danger to the Turk in Syria is in the Hauran district, where the Bedouin Arabs, settled and nomadic, have never consented to do military service in the Turkish army and are exceedingly jealous of official interference. However, the telegraphic service has been extended everywhere, even to these remote districts, and Turkish soldiers have easily put down incipient revolts. The Porte has ruled Syria by skillfully playing off one religious sect against another, so that there is not the remotest danger of Nusairiyeh and Maronite and Druze striking hands. French influence since 1860 has been pervasive in the land. Trade has been opened, schools have been fostered, and religion has been watched by the French officials in the land with a care that betokens a desire at some time to control the country. Russia is jealous of this French propaganda, and under Muscovite auspices Jerusalem is being surrounded by towers, churches and hospices, and at present Russian schools are being founded in all the coast cities. The Turkish method of governing Christian sects is to use the church organization in administering them. Each sect commits its affairs into the hands of the head man of the body, who intermediates between the people and the Turkish officials. Woe to a man who falls out with his church! In effect he becomes an outlaw. Hence, when the missionaries entered the country in 1821, hoping to regenerate the decayed Christian Churches, they were compelled to start a **Protestant Community** so that those who accepted evangelical truth could have the protection of the law, such as it was. For when a Maronite was led to accept the Gospel statement of redemption through Christ alone he was not allowed to remain in that communion. He was driven forth. His neighbors could wantonly take his property and maltreat him without let or hindrance.

Socially: The feudal system has not entirely disappeared from Syria, and princely families have until lately exercised great influence. The prince is patriarchal in his relations to his house, and thus many of the evils of the system are mitigated. But the mass of the people are plebeian. The clergy exercise great social power, as would be gathered from the preceding paragraph. The marriage of the secular clergy is almost universal among the Oriental Christian sects; and in the cases where these sects have been won over to the Roman Catholic faith this custom has, by special stipulation, been retained. The status of woman has been low.

History: Syria has been from time immemorial the battle-field of nations, and it will be impossible to give in this statement even a chronicle of the great events that have taken place within its boundaries. It and its people have had a mission to perform for the civilized world, second to the mission of no other land and people. The Phœnician and the Hebrew stand for the two important elements in all civilization—commerce and religion. As history dawned, the Phœnicians were the traders of the world, and had a strong rule along the coast. Innumerable warring tribes divided up the rest of the land among themselves. The Hebrews appeared as a nation in the 15th century B.C., and in the 11th century, under David, conquered the whole of the territory called Syria to-day, with the exception of Phœnicia. After the division of the Hebrew kingdom (975 B.C.) the new power of Syria arose, with its capital at Damascus. In the 8th century (721 B.C.) Assyria conquered Northern Syria and overwhelmed the northern tribes. Later Jerusalem fell before the Babylonian power (583 B.C.) and Judah went into captivity. Persia absorbed Babylon, and, until the conquests of Alexander the Great (323 B.C.), controlled the land along the eastern Mediterranean. After the death of the great conqueror, Ptolemy and the Seleucidæ were rivals in Syria, the power of the latter from their capital of Antioch being finally successful. The Jews rose in rebellion against the attempt to Hellenize their nation, and the heroic era of the Maccabees resulted (168-37 B.C.). The Romans were irresistibly being pushed eastward, and were obliged to add Syria to their growing empire. The country was ruled by native kings and Roman governors until it was thoroughly amalgamated in the Eastern or Byzantine empire. The grand duel between Byzantine and Persian (Sassanidæ) under the Emperor Heraclius weakened the Roman power, so that in the 7th century the armies of Islam made easy work in conquering the land. The Ommeiad dynasty from Damascus ruled the Muslim world from 661 to 750. Several centuries later, as the Abbasside dynasty was breaking up at Baghdad, Syria was a prey to factions. The Seljuk Turk appeared, reversing the mild treatment the Christians had received at the hands of the Saracens hitherto, and persecution, imprisonment, and butchery aroused the knighthood of Christian Europe to undertake the Crusades (1095-1291). After the failure of the Crusades, Syria was again the scene of Muslim misrule at the hands of the Mameluke sultans of Egypt, and of fiercer raiders from Tatary. Early in the 15th century Tamerlane carried his annihilating hordes as far south as Damascus. In 1517 the whole land was conquered by Selim I., the Ottoman Turk, and, with the exception of the brief time during which Ibrahim Pasha held

Syria (1832-1841), has been controlled successfully by the Porte.

The first Christian church was at Jerusalem, and at Antioch the name "Christian" arose. The Apostles and their followers carried the Gospel to every portion of Syria, and the faith took root everywhere. The scattering of the Jews, as a result of the great rebellions against Roman dominion in 70 and 130, changed the type of Christianity in Syria materially, but the Faith advanced successfully and at the time of Constantine we find the land dotted with Christian churches.

Some of the greatest church fathers either were born or lived in Syria,—Ignatius, Justin Martyr, Eusebius, and Jerome,—missionary influences went out on every side, the Bedouin Arabs were reached, and Frumentius, a Syrian, was the apostle of the Abyssinians. Constantine and his mother, Helena, were drawn to the land made sacred by so many associations. Jerusalem became attractive to pilgrims. The ascetic spirit, so widespread in those days, took possession of this veneration for the sacred places. Monasteries sprang up all over the land. Hermits swarmed among the wild gorges of the Judean desert, and when Chosroes, the Persian conqueror, swept over the country he slaughtered Christian monks by the thousands. Then came the Arab, who treated the Christians mildly. The Church of St. John in Damascus, it is true, was converted into a mosque; but Omar at Jerusalem left the Church of the Holy Sepulchre to the Christians, as well as the Church of the Nativity at Bethlehem. But Christianity dwindled. Islam attracted many Syrians into its ranks. At the time of the Crusades the whole number of Christians in the land was probably not more than half a million. The Roman pontiff had long been desirous to win the Oriental churches, which for the most part refused to acknowledge the universal supremacy of the Pope. During the Crusades the **Maronites** threw in their lot with the Western Christians, and formed an alliance with the Church of Rome, which has grown closer every century.

Protestantism: Into this seething little world of fierce religious propaganda—Mohammedan, Oriental, and Papal—the new force of Protestantism came in the third decade of last century. The Turkish Government rather favored it than otherwise—considering it a new tool by which it could work confusion to its enemies. Rev. Pliny Fisk and Rev. Levi Parsons landed at Smyrna in 1819. In 1821 Mr. Parsons went to Jerusalem to make that the headquarters for the work in Syria. In 1823 Mr. Fisk and Dr. Jonas King summered on Mt. Lebanon, and later made Beirut the center for work. In the same year Rev. Wm. Goodell, Rev. Isaac Bird, and their wives landed at that city. Shortly after both Mr. Parsons and Mr. Fisk died, but the work moved on. In 1828 violent persecution (ending in the death of Asaad Esh Shidiak, "the martyr of Lebanon"), political and warlike agitations, the forcible closure of schools at Beirut, Tripoli, and elsewhere, led the missionaries to go to Malta and wait until the storm should blow over. In 1830, however, they returned and took up their labors with redoubled energy. A printing press was established at Malta, and later removed to Beirut by Rev. Eli Smith; tracts and books were published, a translation of the Bible undertaken, and the land was more fully explored for favorable stations. In 1843 it appeared that greater concentration would make the work more effective, and Jerusalem was handed over to the Church Missionary Society of England. As already stated, the missionaries were compelled to organize a separate church to give protection to their followers under Turkish laws. Abeih and Hasbeiya were special centers for work. The translation of the Bible into Arabic (see Arabic Version) went on. The **Syrian Protestant College** was founded at Beirut in 1865, having been incorporated in 1863 by the Legislature of New York. A medical class was formed in 1867. In 1873 the present buildings, situated on Ras Beirut, were first occupied.

But before this, in 1870, when the Old and New School Presbyterians of the United States were united, the American Syrian Mission was handed over by the ABCFM to the PN, because up to this date the New School Presbyterians had contributed largely to the ABCFM. The missionaries found that the work would not be materially affected by the change. In fact, a new impetus came to the mission, and the progress since 1870 has been very great, in twenty years more than trebling the resources of the mission as well as the number of native adherents. The translation of the Bible was carried on to completion by Dr. Van Dyck after the death of Dr. Eli Smith. Stations are located at Beirut, in the Lebanon, Tripoli, and Sidon.

During these years a large number of native Syrian Protestants have arisen who have done a great work for their land. Among them, besides the martyr Asaad Esh Shidiak, may be mentioned Gregory Wortabed, Butrus Bistany, Dr. Meshakah of Damascus, and a large number of men are to-day taking the places of these good and learned men whose names will never be forgotten.

The CMS commenced work in Palestine in 1851. It occupies the field from Acre to Hebron and Gaza and from Mt. Hermon to Moab east of the Jordan. It has pushed forward under great discouragements, but has made steady progress. It has stations at Jerusalem, Nablous, Jaffa, Gaza, Ramleh, Nazareth, Haifa, Es Salt, etc. It has a number of successful schools. In 1899 education among women received the special attention of the CMS, and medical missions have been fostered.

The London Jews' Society has missions at Jerusalem, Jaffa, Damascus, Aleppo and other places. The Established Church of Scotland has a mission to the Jews at Beirut. At Tiberias there is another Scotch mission to the Jews.

The Irish Presbyterian Mission in Damascus was founded in 1843. The United Presbyterian Church of the United States was interested in this work for many years, but has of late concentrated its mission endeavors in Egypt.

The press at Beirut, under Presbyterian management, is of great importance in the Arabic-speaking world, as may be inferred from the following report: The number of pages printed during the year 1900 was 24,882,680, making the total since the beginning, 667,974,597, and of these pages, 17,884,000 were Arabic Scriptures, and of these, 58,500 were bound; 8,193 copies were sold in Syria and 34,657 in Egypt. The entire number of books and tracts sold was 83,749, notwithstanding the fact that, owing to alterations and repairs, the presses were idle for more than two months. The total number of

Scriptures sold to the Russian schools in Syria and Palestine during 1900 was 4,026. In addition to these they have bought 7,893 volumes of scientific and educational works.

The British Syrian schools and Bible Mission were established in 1860 by Mrs. Bowen Thompson. Since her death her sister, Mrs. Mott, has had charge of the work. It comprises about 30 schools, mostly for girls, in which over 3,000 pupils are gathered. The principal schools are at Beirut, Damascus, Zahleh, Baalbec, Hasbeiya, and Tyre. The Free Church of Scotland has a mission in the Metn district of Mt. Lebanon under the care of Rev. W. Carslaw, M.D.

The Society of Friends in England has mission work at Brumana, on Mt. Lebanon, and the American Friends at Ramallah, northwest from Jerusalem. The German Evangelical missions include the German Deaconesses of Kaiserswerth, the Jerusalem Verein of Berlin, and the work of German chaplains in Beirut and Jerusalem. The Kaiserswerth Deaconesses came to Syria after the terrible Druze massacres in 1860, established orphanages in Jerusalem and Beirut, and soon became connected as nurses with the Johanniter Hospital in the last-named city. The Jerusalem Verein has work in Jerusalem and also in Bethlchem. There are girls' schools at Bethlehem, Nazareth, and Shimlan under the care of a society of English women. Miss Taylor's (Scotch) school at Beirut for Druze and Muslim girls is very successful.

There are also a number of special societies or private enterprises.

Bible work is carried on in Syria by the American Bible Society, with its headquarters at Beirut, whence it sends Arabic Scriptures over the whole world. Palestine is occupied by the British and Foreign Bible Society. The tract societies of America and England have given most substantial help to the mission in its effort to supply the whole Arabic-reading world with Christian literature. The interesting item about all these numerous Protestant societies at work in Syria and Palestine is the fact that they are all working in substantial harmony. There is no more difficult mission field in the world. Jerusalem is the worst city in the world, not because of gross licentiousness, but because of spiritual pride; and the whole land partakes of the same spirit. Syria is at present in a most depressed state, agriculturally and commercially. The last fifty years have seen a leap ahead intellectually, and roads and the telegraph are binding the country together. In the end, the simple Gospel must prevail in the land that gave it birth, but many generations must come and go before Islam will yield, and before the stubborn oriental rites, as well as the papal votaries, will give up the meaningless and injurious human elements that have entered into their worship.

SYRIAC LANGUAGE: It belongs to the Semitic family of languages. The *ancient* Syriac, as used in the Peshito and other ancient versions of the Bible, is at present a purely ecclesiastical and literary language, tho of great importance to the Biblical scholar.

The *modern* Syriac, a much corrupted form of the ancient language, is the spoken tongue of the Chaldean, Nestorian, and Syrian Christians living in Turkey and Persia. It is written with Syriac letters, but is found in many different dialects. A version of the Arabic Bible has been printed with Syriac letters and is known as the Karshuni version. It is intended for those Syrians who have lost their own language. The scattered condition of the Syriac-speaking peoples has led to the growth of dialects, some of which present marked peculiarities.

Little was known of the modern Syriac among Western scholars until 1826, when versions of some books of Scripture were brought to Europe by Dr. Joseph Wolff.

When the American missionaries began their labors among the Syrian Christians in Urmia in 1834, no literature was known to exist in this language, and Dr. Perkins, with his colleagues, proceeded to reduce it to writing and to issue from the press religious and educational works. Later on a few manuscripts were discovered, dating a hundred years back, written in the Elkosh dialect spoken in the vicinity of Mosul. These proved to be unscholarly paraphrases of the Gospels, or rude poetical renderings of Gospel history. They possess little interest save as throwing light on the development of the language. The whole number of people now using the modern Syriac is estimated at about 100,000.

SYRIAN PROTESTANT COLLEGE: This college, established at Beirut, Syria, in 1866, is one of a number of important educational institutions in non-Christian lands which are the outgrowth of successful missionary effort. It is chartered under the laws of the State of New York, its corporate name in America being "The Trustees of the Syrian Protestant College." Morris K. Jesup of New York is president of the Board of Trustees. This Board owns the college buildings and the land on which they stand, consisting of about forty acres in the most prominent situation in the city of Beirut.

The work of the College commenced in the autumn of 1866, a preparatory class having been formed the previous year. A medical department was opened in 1867, a preparatory department in 1871, and a commercial in 1900. The number of students in 1866 was 16; in 1903 it was 650. The number of teachers in 1866 was 6; in 1903 it was 40. During the 37 years of its existence the college has had under its instruction 2,763 students; it has graduated 203 bachelors of art, 189 physicians, 87 pharmacists and 462 preparatory students. Many of these students graduated elsewhere, but remain loyal to their *Alma Mater.*

The College draws its students from all the Christian sects of the East, and not a few from the Druzes, the Jews, and the Muslims. The geographical area from which the 650 young men now in the College have come extends from the Black Sea to the Sudan and from Greece to Persia—a region as large as the United States east of the Mississippi. The languages spoken by the students are Arabic, Turkish, Persian, Coptic, Hebrew, Yiddish, Armenian, Greek, English, German, and French. Their instructors are, in nationality, American, English, Arab, German, Swiss, and French.

The College is Christian but non-sectarian. It educates young men from numerous denominations, and from the fields of a score of different missionary societies. There is a flourishing YMCA among the students which occupies itself with the culture of the student body, neighborhood teaching, and close study of the Bible.

This Association affords a ground on which members of liturgical and non-liturgical churches can meet and engage together in religious work. The graduates of the College, as well as students who have taken a partial course only, occupy positions of commanding influence as civil functionaries, merchants, ministers, teachers, civil and military physicians, lawyers, judges, editors, and authors. A number of them are in the military and consular service of the United States Government.

The influence of such a body of men, educated according to American methods, on the progress and elevation of the East is obvious. The significance of this great college as an illustration of the existence and zeal of Protestant missions is also worthy of note. The fact that these missions seem to culminate in such institutions of admitted utility has stirred the Roman Catholic and Greek Churches to great activity. France, Italy, and Austria have poured in men and lavished money that they also may found churches and schools, printing presses and publishing houses, primarily, doubtless, for the benefit of those of their own communion, but also for the promotion of their national and ecclesiastical interests. Russia has done the same in the interests of its politics and the religious advancement of the Orthodox Greek Church. All these efforts unite with those of Protestant missions in contributing effectively to the general advancement of a higher civilization.

The same fact as to the relation of the college to the general missionary movement from which it sprang is seen in the healthy stimulus which it becomes to all native communities. This is seen not only in the praiseworthy efforts of native Protestants in the support of the institutions of the Gospel and the educational work inseparable from these institutions. It can be noted in all the native Christian, and after a little while in the non-Christian sects, taking the form of a general rivalry in matters of humanitarian and educational enterprise. The existence of the college stimulates the increase of Protestant schools. The example of Protestant schools has caused the Greeks and the Maronites to found common schools and, subsequently, colleges. It has led the Jesuits to found the University of St. Joseph at Beirut, with preparatory, collegiate, commercial and medical departments. It has stirred the Turkish Government to establish and enlarge primary and higher schools for boys, culminating in the Rushdîyeh and Idadîyeh Turkish Colleges of Beirut. But the most surprising result has been the general diffusion of female education. Each of the Christian sects has its complete series of girls' schools, with a collegiate institution at its head. And, most wonderful of all, this has led to the foundation of a society of Muslim men to promote female education and the establishment of schools for Muslim girls in the principal cities of Syria.

SYU-YIN. See SYN YIN.

T

TABASE: A village in Cape Colony, South Africa, situated on the Umtata River, 16 miles S. W. of Tsolo. Station of the Moravian Missions (1873), with (1903) 1 missionary and his wife, 7 native workers, 1 place of worship, 3 day schools, and 57 professed Christians.

TABRIZ: One of the oldest and most important cities of Persia, capital of the Province of Azerbaijan, situated in a valley 4,000 feet above the sea, about 360 miles W. N. W. of Teheran. A large commerce is carried on here, as it is the center of the trade between Persia, Russia and Turkey, and it is on the line of the Indo-European telegraph from London to Bombay. There are few noteworthy public buildings, tho numerous mosques, baths and shops are found throughout the city, and one mosque is especially noted. The population is 180,000, chiefly Turks and Armenians, the true Persians being very few in number.

Station of the PN (1873), with (1903) 4 missionaries, three of them with their wives; 5 women missionaries, 7 native workers, 9 outstations, 2 places of worship, 1 day school, 2 boarding schools, 2 dispensaries, 1 hospital, and 65 professed Christians. Also station of the Swedish Mission Society, with 1 missionary, 1 woman missionary and 1 day school.

TA-CHIEN-LU. See TA-TSIEN-LU.

TAHITI. See SOCIETY ISLANDS.

T'AI-AN, or TAI-AN-FU. See TAI-NGAN-FU.

TAI-CHAU-FU: A town in Che-kiang, China, situated about 70 miles S. S. W. of Ningpo. Station of the CIM (1867), with (1903) 2 missionaries, one of them with his wife; 13 native workers, 13 outstations, 14 places of worship, 1 boarding school, 1 hospital, and 504 professed Christians. Also station of the CMS (1892), with (1903) 3 missionaries and their wives, 33 native workers, 13 day schools, and 1,222 professed Christians, of whom 449 are communicants. Some write the name T'ai Chow.

T'AI CHOW. See TAI-CHAU-FU.

TAI-HO-HSIEN: A town in Ngan-hwei, China, situated in the N. W. part of the province about 20 miles N. W. of Yeng-chau-fu. Station of the CIM (1892), with (1903) 2 missionaries and their wives, 5 native workers, 1 place of worship, 1 day school, 1 dispensary, and 19 professed Christians. Some write the name T'ai-ho.

TAI-KANG-HSIEN: A town in Ho-nan, China, situated about 25 miles N. of Chen-chau-fu. The missionaries having been driven out in 1900, a Chinese layman acted as leader of the Christians and kept the church together until it was safe for the missionaries to return. Station of the CIM (1895), with (1903) 1 missionary and his wife, 1 place of worship, 1 day school, 1 Sunday school, and 43 professed Christians. Some write the name T'ai-k'ang.

TAI-KU: A town in Korea, situated about 100 miles N. W. of Fu-san, on the Naktung River. Former capital of the southeastern kingdom, and the chief city of a most fertile and prosperous region. Station of the PN (1898), with (1903) 4 missionaries, three of them with their wives; 3 native workers, 2 outstations, 1 dispensary, 1 hospital, and 4 professed Christians.

TAI-KU-HSIEN: A town of Shan-si, China, situated 10 miles S. of Tai-yuen-fu. The Christians hereabouts were attacked, and many, together with almost all the native workers, were killed in 1900. Station of the ABCFM (1883), with (1903) 1 missionary and his wife, 3 native workers, 1 Sunday school, 1 day school, 1 dispensary, 1 boarding school, and 40 professed Christians. Some write the name Tai-ku.

TAINAN: A town and seaport in Japan, situated on the island of Formosa, on the S. W. coast. Population, 100,000. Station of the PCE (1865), with (1903) 7 missionaries, four of them with their wives; 3 women missionaries, 1 boarding school, 1 theological class, 2 dispensaries, 1 hospital, 1 medical class, 38 places of worship, 58 native workers, and 4,331 professed Christians. This includes the church statistics of Tai-chu. Some write the name Tainanfu.

TAINANFU. See TAINAN.

TAI-NGAN-FU: A town in Shantung, China, situated 35 miles S. S. E. of Tsi-nan-fu. Station of the North China Mission (SPG auxiliary) (1878), with (1900) 2 missionaries, one of them with his wife, and 1 native worker. Also station of the ME, with (1903) 1 missionary and his wife, 2 women missionaries, 19 native workers, 8 outstations, 10 places of worship, 4 Sunday schools, 3 day schools, 2 boarding schools, 1 dispensary, and 304 professed Christians, of whom 100 are communicants. Station also of the Independent Baptist Mission Movement, with 7 missionaries, five of them with their wives, and 1 woman missionary. Some write the name Tai-an or Tai-an-fu.

TAI-PING-FU: A town in Ngan-hwei, China, situated on the Yangtse River, about 35 miles S. S. W. of Nan-king. Station of the Hauges China Mission (1897), with (1900) 1 missionary and his wife, 4 native workers, 1 place of worship, 1 day school, 1 outstation. Also station of the ME, with 1 native worker, 1 place of worship, 1 Sunday school, and 30 professed Christians. Some write the name Tai-ping-tien.

TAI-PING-FU: A town in Kwang-si, China, situated in the S. part of the province on the Tso River. Station of the Rhenish Missionary Society, with (1903) 1 missionary and his wife, 3 native workers, 3 outstations, 3 day schools, and 177 professed Christians, of whom 156 are communicants. Some write the name Taiping.

T'AI-P'ING. See TAI-PING-HSIEN.

TAI-PING-HSIEN: A town of Che-kiang, China, situated near the E. coast, about 50 miles N. E. of Wen-chau. Station of the CIM (1898), with (1900) 1 missionary and his wife, 4 native workers, 7 outstations, 8 places of worship, 2 day schools, 2 boarding schools, 1 dispensary, and 368 professed Christians. Some write the name T'ai-p'ing.

TAI-PING-TIEN. See TAI-PING-FU.

T'AI-YUAN-FU. See TAI-YUEN-FU.

TAI-YUEN-FU: A town in Shan-si, China, capital of the province and important for manufactures. Situated in the center of the province about 250 miles S. W. of Peking. Station of the BMS (1878), with (1903) 4 missionaries, three of them with their wives; 6 native workers, 6 outstations, 3 day schools and 130 professed Christians. Also station of the BZM (1898), with (1903) no occupant. Agency also of the BFBS, with 1 agent. Some write the name T'ai-yuan-fu or Tai Yuen Fu.

TAKAMATSU: A town on the island of Shikoku, Japan, situated on the inland sea, N. W. of Tokushima. Population, 34,625. Station of the PS (1893), with 2 missionaries and their wives.

TAKARMA: A village in Chota Nagpur, Bengal, India, situated in Lohardaga District, 55 miles S. W. of Ranchi. Station of the Gossner Mission Society, with (1903) 2 missionaries, 46 native workers, 26 places of worship, 22 Sunday schools, 2 day schools, 1 boarding school, and 5,389 professed Christians, of whom 3,646 are communicants.

TAKASAKI: A town in Japan, situated on the main island, about ten miles S. W. of Mayebashi. Station of the PE (1900), with (1903) 1 native worker and 1 woman missionary.

TAKAYAMA: A town in Japan, situated on the main island, about 40 miles S. of Toyama. Station of the Scandinavian Alliance, with 1 missionary and 1 woman missionary.

TAK-HING-CHAU. See TE-TSING-CHAU.

TA-KU-SHAN: A town in Manchuria, China, situated in the district of Liao-tung, on the coast of Korea Bay, about 35 miles W. of the Yaku River. Station of the Danish Missionary Society (1896), with (1903) 2 missionaries, one of them with his wife; 1 woman missionary, 1 place of worship, 1 dispensary, and 8 professed Christians. Some write the name Da-gu-san.

TA-KU-TANG: A town in Kiang-si, China, situated on the Yangtse River, about 10 miles E. of Kiu-kiang-fu. It is used as a sanitarium for missionaries working in the Yangtse valley. Station of the CIM (1873), with (1903) 1 missionary and his wife, 1 native worker, 1 place of worship, 1 day school, and 8 professed Christians.

TALAGOUGA: A village in the French Congo State, West Africa, situated on the Ogowe River, about 175 miles from its mouth. The people in the country about are chiefly Fangs, or Pahouin, as they are called by the French. Station of the Paris Evangelical Mission Society (1892), with (1903) 4 missionaries, three of them with their wives; 2 women missionaries, 21 native workers, 11 outstations, 2 day schools, and 341 professed Christians, of whom 72 are communicants.

TALAUT ISLANDS: A group of small islands belonging to the Dutch East Indies, lying N. E. of Celebes and about 150 miles S. E. of the Philippine Islands. Cabruang and Carkelang are the two largest of the group. The Talaut and the Sangir Islands are being evangelized through a missionary committee formed at Batavia, Java, for the purpose. There are about 45,000 professed Christians on the two groups taken together.

TALATSCHERI. See TELLICHERRI.

TALCA: A town in Chile, South America, and the capital of the province of the same name, about 180 miles by railroad N. of Concepcion. Population (1901), 29,112. Station of the PN (1876 and 1897), with (1903) 1 missionary and his wife, 1 woman missionary, 1 native worker, 3 outstations, 1 place of worship, 1 day school, 1 boarding school, 1 dispensary, 1 hospital, and 61 professed Christians.

TA-LI-FU: A prefectural city in the northern part of Yunnan, China, northwest of Yunnan City. Station of the CIM (1881), with (1903) 3 missionaries and 1 place of worship.

TALJHARA: A town in Bengal, India, situated in the Raj-mahal region, about 45 miles east of Bhagalpur. The people are mostly Santals. Station of the CMS (1861), with 3 missionaries, one of them with his wife; 46 native workers, 1 place of worship, 9 day schools, 1 boarding school, 1 theological class, and 997 professed Christians, of whom 352 are communicants. Some write the name Taljhari.

TALLAPUDI: A town in Madras, India, situated in the Godavari District, near the right bank of the Godavari River, W. of Rajahmahendri. Climate, hot and malarious. Station of the Evangelical Lutheran General Council (U. S.), with 1 missionary, 1 place of worship, 1 day school, 1 Sunday school, and 192 professed Christians.

TAMAR: A village in Chota Nagpur, Bengal, India, situated 30 miles S. E. of Ranchi. Station of the Gossner Mission Society, with 1 missionary, 27 native workers, 2 day schools, 10 Sunday schools, and 1,546 professed Christians, of whom 1,497 are communicants.

TAMATAVE: The principal port of Madagascar, situated on the east coast, on a point about 350 yards wide. It is quite cosmopolitan in its character, as representatives of some of the principal European and Asiatic nationalities live within its limits. A low estimate of the foreign residents make their number 1,200. Most of them are creoles from Mauritius, and natives of India of various religions and castes. Not more than 50 are pure British and French. French influence prevails, as there is a French Resident, controller of the customs, and Roman Catholic priests, who teach and preach in French. The native population of about 4,000 is composed of Hovas from the interior, Taimoro from the south, Tanosy from St. Marie, and Betsimisaraka from the surrounding districts. The latter are an exceptionally ignorant, superstitious tribe, who have been further debased by contact with the cargoes and crews of the various trading vessels from Mauritius and Réunion which stop at the small ports.

Station of the SPG, with 3 native workers. Church statistics included in Andovoranto, where the missionary resides.

TAMEANGLAJANG: A village in Borneo, Dutch East Indies, situated about 120 miles N. N. E. of Banjermassin. Station of the Rhenish Missionary Society, with (1903) 1 missionary and his wife, 4 native workers, 3 outstations, 4 day schools, 1 Sunday school, and 192 professed Christians, of whom 104 are communicants.

TAMI: An island off the E. coast of German New Guinea. Station of the Neuendettelsau Mission Society (1889), with (1903) 1 missionary and his wife and 1 day school.

TAMPICO: A town and seaport in the state of Tamaulipas, Mexico, situated on the River Paranco, near its mouth, and 220 miles N. of Mexico City. Population, 5,000, Indians, Spaniards, Creoles. Station of the Associate Reformed Presbyterian Synod of the South (1880), with (1901) 1 missionary and his wife, 2 women missionaries, 5 native workers, 10 outstations, 4 places of worship, 1 boarding school, 1 day school, 1 industrial school, and 253 professed Christians.

TAMSUI: A town and treaty port in Japan, situated in the island of Formosa, on the W. coast and in the N. part of the island. Population, 100,000. Station of the PCC (1872), with (1901) 2 missionaries and their wives, 79 native workers, 56 outstations, 5 places of worship, 6 day schools, 1 college, 1 hospital, and 1,891 professed Christians.

TANABE: A town in Japan, situated in the N. of the main island, about 40 miles N. E. of Aomori. Station of the Cumberland Presbyterian Missionary Society (1885), with (1901) 1 woman missionary, 1 native worker, 1 place of worship, 2 Sunday schools, and 64 professed Christians.

TANAH-ABANG: A settlement in the island of Java, Dutch East Indies, situated about 12 miles W. of Batavia. Station of the Netherlands Missionary Union (1902), with the outstations formerly connected with Tang-geran. It has (1903) 1 missionary, 5 native workers, 7 outstations, 1 day schools, and 170 professed Christians, A considerable proportion of the Christians here are Chinese coolies.

TANANA: A settlement in Alaska, situated on the Yukon River, at the confluence of the Tanana. Station of the PE, with (1901) 1 missionary, 1 native worker, 1 place of worship, 1 day school, 1 printing house, and 52 professed Christians.

TANDIL: A town in the Argentine Republic, South America, situated about 180 miles S. by W. of Buenos Aires. Station of the Missionary Pence Association (1895), with (1900) 1 missionary and his wife, 1 Sunday school, 1 boarding school, and 32 professed Christians.

TANDSCHAUR. See TANJORE.

TANETTEIJA: A town on the island of Celebes, Dutch East Indies, situated on the S. coast about 40 miles S. E. of Macassar. Station of the Utrecht Missionary Society (1897), with (1903) 1 missionary and his wife, 2 native workers, 1 day school, and 8 professed Christians.

TANGA: A town and seaport in German East Africa, situated 30 miles N. of Pangani. It is the terminus of the railroad to Korogwe. It has a German Government School. Population, 5,000. Station of the German East Africa Missionary Society (1890), with (1903) 3 missionaries and their wives, 1 native worker, 2 outstations, 1 place of worship, 1 day school, and 66 professed Christians.

TANGAIL: A town in Bengal, India, situated near the Madhupur jungle and about 50 miles N. W. of Dacca. Station of the Victorian Baptist Foreign Mission Society (1895), with (1900) 1 missionary and his wife, 2 women missionaries, 5 native workers, 1 place of worship, 1 day school, 1 theological class, and 8 professed Christians.

TANGIER: A town and seaport of Morocco, situated on the south shore of the Strait of Gibraltar, 38 miles southwest of the Rock. Population, 10,000. Station of the NAM (1884), with (1903) 3 missionaries, one of them with his wife; 5 women missionaries, 4 native workers, 1 place of worship, 3 day schools, 2 hospitals, and 12 professed Christians. Station also of the Mildmay Mission to the Jews (1889), with (1900) 2 missionaries and 1 woman missionary. The BFBS also has an agent and book depot here, with 5 colporteurs.

T'ANG-SHAN. See TONG-SHAN.

TANG-TAU: A town on the island of He-tan, China, situated in the N. E. part of the island. Station of the CMS (1902), with 2 women missionaries, 7 native workers, men and women, and 4 schools.

TANG-TAU. See ANG-TAU.

TANG-UN. See TUNG-NGAN-HSIEN.

TA-NING-HSIEN: A town in Shansi, China, situated about 50 miles W. N.W. of Ping-yang-fu. Station of the CIM (1885), with (1900) 2 women missionaries, 5 native workers, 2 outstations, 3 places of worship, 1 boarding school, and 145 professed Christians.

TANJORE: A town in Madras, South India, and the capital of Tanjore District, situated about 46 miles W. of Negapatam. It contains a pagoda which is rated by some as the finest in India. It is noted for artistic manufactures of repoussé work, copper ware, jewelry and curious models in pith. Population (1901), about 57,870. Station of the SPG (1825), with (1903) 1 missionary, 1 woman missionary, 24 native workers, 5 places of worship, 12 day schools, 2 boarding schools, 1 college, and 883 professed Christians, of whom 534 are communicants. Also station of the Leipzig Missionary Society (1858), with (1903) 2 missionaries, one of them with his wife; 2 women missionaries, 38 native workers, 13 outstations, 12 places of worship, 11 day schools, 7 boarding schools, and 1,029 professed Christians, of whom 559 are communicants. Germans write the name Tandschaur.

TANNA. See NEW HEBRIDES.

TANTA: A town and railway junction in lower Egypt, situated 60 miles N. N. W. of Cairo. Population, 33,725. Station of the UP (1893), with (1903) 1 missionary and his wife, 3 women missionaries, 23 native workers, 1 dispensary, 1 hospital, 2 boarding schools, 9 day schools and 1 Sunday school. The number of professing Christians is commonly omitted from the published station reports of this Society.

TAOISM: Laotze the philosopher is said to have been born in the year 604 B. C., tho there has been some question whether he was or was not a real character. The fact that the names of his village and county and state or province seem to be allegorical, like the names in Pilgrim's Progress, has led to a doubt on this subject. But some allowance should be made, probably, for the tendency among the Chinese to deal in allegorical names. Even the shops of the chief cities sometimes bear upon their signs names which excite a smile in a foreigner.

Laotze's history, all things considered, seems real. It is said that he left a son, who won distinction in public office.

Laotze's birth occurred about a half century before the birth of Confucius; they were therefore contemporaries. Both are said to have been the sons of very old men.

The condition of China, or of that particular province in which Laotze lived, corresponding to a portion of the present Shantung province, was greatly disturbed by border wars and intestine revolts and intrigues. There was scarcely a vestige of morality, and the political condition of the country was chaotic. Both Laotze and Confucius aimed at reform. Both appear to have been disinterested and high-minded. Both were rather impatient, however, with the stolidity and degradation of the people, and with the vices and corruption of the reigning princes.

Laotze appears to have held for a time an office as keeper of the archives, as the old records express it; but his mind drifted toward philosophy and political reform, and the position he held was far from meeting his ambition: political engagements were irksome to him.

Comparatively little is known of this truly profound thinker or reformer. He is supposed to have been poor, and for that reason perhaps the more keenly conscious that his nation and his age failed to appreciate him. He was, in short, too morbid in spirit to make the best use and secure the greatest results of his rare gifts. He formed no school of followers, and wrote no books. On the contrary, he withdrew himself from men, was too proud to teach or write, disliked display of any kind, and was in fact a recluse.

Confucius, on arriving at manhood and entering upon his career, sought an interview with Laotze, with a hope of profiting by his great ability, his observation and his experience. He was received coldly, however, and with severe criticism instead of sympathy. Much as the two men were alike, they had wide differences of character, and these were increased by the fact that Laotze was already an old man when Confucius appeared before him. He was in no attitude of mind to approve or even tolerate what he considered the gushing enthusiasm and crudity of Confucius. He looked upon him as an ambitious, blustering agitator, sounding brass and a tinkling cymbal, and he predicted the failure of his pretentious efforts at reform.

Confucius, on the other hand, was astonished at the churlishness of the old reformer, was perplexed at his involved and incomprehensible theories and mystical speculations, and he could only compare him to the "incomprehensible dragon."

At last, in old age, Laotze's despair at the condition of the country became overmastering. He had dire forebodings of calamity, revolution, bloodshed, political chaos, and destruction. He had become more and more unpopular as he had grown more and more reproachful toward his countrymen.

He dreaded to witness the ruin which he was sure was coming upon the land, and he fled into voluntary exile, passing westward through the Hankow Pass into the province of Honan. He was induced to stop for a time with the keeper of the Pass, and instruct him in the principles of his philosophy. This gate-keeper seems to have realized that no ordinary person was before him, and he was unwilling that a man who was too morbid and impracticable to write any book or organize any class of disciples should pass from the knowledge of men without leaving some substantial results of his thinking. He appears to have taken down from dictation the main principles of the reformer's teaching. This record is known as the Tao Teh King. It embraces all that is known of Laotze's doctrines.

After leaving the Hankow Pass for the west, Laotze passed into obscurity, and, so far as is known, nothing was ever heard of him afterward. Many legends sprang up around the history of Laotze like the young shoots at the root of a dying tree. One of these relates that upon leaving the Pass for his voluntary exile he parted with his servant. The latter, learning the plan of his master, was unwilling to accompany him, and in the settlement charged an exorbitant sum as back wages; but as Laotze had by a spell kept him alive far beyond his appointed time, he withdrew the spell, and the servant became a dry skeleton. However, at the request of the gate-keeper, who interceded for the servant, he restored him to life, and then found him reasonable in his price. Other absurd legends are preserved, one of which is that Laotze was miraculously born at the age of eighty, and that he was known as the "Old Boy." He was gray-haired at birth. Certain legends similar to those which are related of Gautama, and which may have been copied, are also given—as that Laotze leaped into the air as soon as he was born. Some of his followers have claimed that he was a spiritual being, and not an actual, ordinary man.

The Character of Laotze: Laying aside all legends, and contemplating the actual life of Laotze, so far as scanty materials enable us to do, we find him a man above reproach in morals, tho living in a dissolute age. The parallels between his severe type of philosophy and that of the great names of Greece are quite remarkable. He was uncompromising and exacting in his standards of right and wrong, morose and despondent in temperament, proud and impracticable in his relations to men, and having little tact in approaching them. He was too much of a quietist to be a successful reformer. He had been soured by disappointment and he died in despair. His system had brought him no comfort, he had seen no improvement in the condition of society. He regarded his life as a failure, and yet he seems to have come very near to the truth in many respects.

He approached the sublime ethics of our Savior more nearly than any of his contemporaries, tho they were among the greatest names in history, for Laotze, Confucius, Pythagoras, Gautama, and, according to Monier Williams, Zoroaster, are supposed to have lived within a century of each other. Laotze taught that real virtue is a spiritual and interior excellence, and not outward doing or speaking. In this respect he fought much the same battle with the objectivity of mere formal and immovable customs as our Savior did in His dealings with the Pharisees, and, like Him, he urged the law that is written within, and of which the outward world knows nothing. He taught also that he who foregoes and yields up and forbears is the one who really finds and succeeds, and that he who humbles himself is really exalted.

In general, like our Savior, he exalted the quiet and passive virtues, and he taught the duty of doing good even to those who injure us. In this respect he stood in strong contrast with Confucius, whose position more nearly resembled that of the old Jewish dispensation, which required "an eye for an eye, and a tooth for a tooth." The justice of that dispensation was as high as Confucius felt called to go in his dealings with men; no one placed greater emphasis than he upon justice, but he could not understand the duty of doing good in return for evil. Some terse expressions from the lips of Laotze show the deep subjectivity of character as he conceived it. "It is not necessary," he said, "even to peep through the window to see the celestial Tao." At another time he said, "There is a purity and quietude by which one may rule the world." Again, "Lay hold of Tao (wisdom) and the whole world will come to you." Again, "One pure act of resignation is worth more than one hundred thousand exercises of one's own will." The moral elevation of character that is set forth in these utterances is certainly remarkable. It is worthy of a place in Christian ethics.

There were some points in which Laotze seemed to be at one with Gautama. He taught that even in this life it is possible to completely possess Tao, and that thus the creature may become one with the creator by the annihilation of self, it being understood that to possess Tao is in another sense to be possessed by Tao, as an indwelling principle or life, all of which implies a near approach to the Pantheistic absorption in deity which Hinduism also teaches. A general difference between the spirit of Laotze's teaching and that of Confucius may be expressed thus: Confucius would say, "Practise virtues, and call them by their right names." Laotze would say, "Practise them and say nothing about it." Altho he had great reverence for the ancients, he did not idolize them as did Confucius, and as he has led the Chinese nation to do.

There seems to have been in the interviews of the two sages some little controversy on this point in which Laotze told Confucius, by way of subduing his romantic enthusiasm, that the "ancients were only so many bundles of dry bones; wisdom did not die with them." He illustrated the grace of quietness and the safety which it secures by saying that "the leopard by his brilliant colors, and the monkey by his frivolous activity, only draw the arrows of the archer," and to the loud-mouthed reformer he would say, "You are like a man who beats a drum while hunting for a truant sheep."

One point in which Laotze was far in advance of his age, and abreast with some of the best political thinking of whatever age, was his maintenance of the theory that kings exist for the good of the people and not for their own selfish ends, which ends the people, like so many dumb beasts, are designed to subserve. "Kings," according to Laotze, "should rule so quietly, and hold the reins so lightly, that the people may forget them as kings, and only think of them as superiors." There should in all government, as he insisted, be a minimum, and not a maximum, of government. Surely these practical and lofty political principles stamped Laotze as a man of prophetic genius.

Confucius said much more than he concerning government: more, certainly, in the number of details; but no counsels of his are so laden with sublime principles as those of his rival, and none of his teachings are more in accord with the truth.

The Philosophy of Laotze: It is as a philosopher that Laotze most inspires our respect and honor. Tao, which was his ideal of the all-comprehending and eternal essence of things, means Reason, as nearly as it can be translated; but it means more than that word represents to us. It is the Infinite Reason, in such a sense that it embraces all excellence and glory; it corresponds very nearly to the word Wisdom as it is used in the Book of Job and the Ecclesiastes. Tao was deified by Laotze, tho in no superstitious sense; and yet it was impersonal; it was apprehended by him in a pantheistic sense. Thus he says: "All things originate with Tao, conform to Tao, and return to Tao."

Tao exerts its influence in a very quiet manner; its influence is still and void, and yet it "encircles everything and is not endangered;" it is ever inactive, and yet leaves nothing undone; nameless, it is the origin of heaven and of earth. It is not strange, perhaps, that with so vague a conception of the supreme force in the world the Chinese mind should have lapsed into a mere general conception of Deity, and that the prayers of the emperors have for ages been addressed to heaven.

Professor Douglas, of the London University, has summarized the elements of Tao as follows: (1) "It is the Absolute, the Totality of Being and Things. (2) The Phenomenal world and its order. (3) The ethical nature of the good man, and the principle of his action." One is reminded of various philosophic schools of ancient and modern times. The "totality of being and things" is about equivalent to the pantheistic conception of the Indian Vedanta. It does not differ materially from the "absolute substance of" Spinoza or the "absolute intelligence" of Hegel. It must be confessed that Laotze was a profound philosopher. He has rarely been excelled in the history of philosophy, for in view of his comparatively isolated position we must regard him as eminently original. His system was wholly his own; he was the father of Chinese philosophy. In profundity of thought he far exceeded Confucius, tho he was less practical. Confucius was not a philosopher in the strictest sense; he was only a skilful and eminently practical compiler of ancient wisdom. He did not claim to be more than this, and with laudable modesty he spoke of himself as only an editor. But the Tao Teh King of Laotze came from his own brain.

There is a seeming contradiction in the teachings of Laotze in reference to the past. While Confucius carried his reverence for ancient authorities to an extreme which scarcely seemed to admit the possibility of anything new in the world, Laotze took issue with him sharply, and even poured a degree of contempt upon his extreme reverence. At the same time, tho he admitted no age of antiquity as necessarily authoritative, he looked back, in a general way, to a golden age of simplicity and virtue which had passed away, and his whole idea was to return from the complex wisdom and civilization which he regarded as only a curse, to the better days when men had few wants and lived quietly.

He was in accord with Confucius on one point, namely, the uprightness and dignity of man's original nature. They recognized no doctrine of human apostasy which assumed hereditary form. In logical consistency they both maintained that every man is born without evil bias, and is sound at the core. The continued influences of demoralizing example were supposed to account for the evils which these great sages found in the world about them.

Like the ancient Druids, Laotze propounded his great principles of life in triads, and the three precious virtues which he cherished were compassion, economy and humility, all of a quiet type. He did not believe in intellectual brilliancy of any kind, much less in any show and pomp of conscious power, and he had little to say of prowess; his ideals were not the great and ambitious and mighty, as men are reckoned to be mighty, but those, rather, who represented the passive virtues, the gentle and retiring graces of human life.

There is a difference of opinion as to Laotze's idea of God. Professor Douglas thinks that he had no conception of a personal divine being, at least that he recognized no such being; but on the other hand, Professor Legge of Oxford seems confident that the supreme "heaven" or God in heaven was involved in his idea of Tao. He maintains that Laotze often spoke of heaven in a non-material sense, and that in one instance he calls the name of God itself.

One thing is certain: whether Laotze regarded Tao as personal or not, he assigned to it providential oversight and care and all forms of beneficent interest. Says Professor Legge: "Tao does more than create. It watches over its offspring with parental interest. It enters into the life of every living thing. It produces, nourishes, feeds, etc."

Laotze's doctrine of creation seems a little vague. He says: "That which is nameless is the beginning of heaven and earth. Tao produced One, the first great cause; One produced Two, the male and female principles of nature; Two produced Three, and Three produced all things, beginning from heaven and earth." This strikingly resembles the Shinto notion of the origin of all things, according to which there is one absolute tho unknown being, from whom emanated two, male and female, and from these the world of beings was produced. Both Confucius and Laotze speak of heaven both as material and as personified.

According to Professor Douglas, Laotze would agree with the Darwinians as to the creative indifference of the Deity or deified influence which is characterized as heaven. "It has," he says, "no special love, but regards all existing beings as 'grass dogs' made for sacrificial purposes." "Yet," he adds, "it is great, and compassionate, and is ever ready to become the Savior of men."

If the question whether Laotze was really religious in his thought were dependent on such statements as this, we should be compelled to answer in the affirmative, for the being or power which is regarded as "great and compassionate and ever ready to become the Savior of men" is an object of religious contemplation, surely.

As to the physical laws of the world, Laotze maintained that the earth is held together, not by gravitation, but by Tao. In a sense this was true, supposing Tao to represent the infinite force, for gravitation is but a second cause. The expression "the earth is held together by Tao" is nearly equivalent to the declaration that "God holdeth the earth in His right hand." Something like the Buddhist idea of an eternal round of life and death seems to be intended by Laotze's doctrine that existence and non-existence constantly originate each other.

We have alluded to some similarities between the teachings of Laotze and those of Christ, especially in the gentle virtues of kindness, humility, forbearance, etc. The differences, however, which appear are more striking than the resemblances.

Christ showed a balance of truth. He taught the passive virtues, but also the active ones, which Laotze did not. He commended modesty and secrecy in prayer, and yet the duty of active influence. "Let your light so shine," etc. This was not for self, but for others. Confucianism was active, Taoism passive, Christianity was both. The fatal defect in Taoism was its lack of divine recognition and divine power. Its ethics were high, but it had no love for God, and therefore none for man.

The Tao Teh King: This is a short treatise, already referred to, embracing the sayings of Laotze which were recorded by the keeper of the Hankow Pass as the great teacher was about to go into exile. It is very brief, only about the length of the Sermon on the Mount. In its general character it is exceedingly intricate, and often obscure. The best scholars feel little confidence in their interpretations of it. Here is a specimen: "There was something chaotic and complete before the birth of heaven and earth. How still it was and formless, standing alone and undergoing no change, proceeding everywhere, and in no danger of being exhausted. It may be regarded as the mother of all things." In its real spirit and meaning this passage corresponds remarkably with one found in the Rig Veda, in which the original chaos is described as being brooded over by the infinite Brahm, the "Only Existing One," breathing quietly. The vagueness of the philosopher's conception is well set forth in this passage: "I do not know the name, but designate it the Tao (the way) and forcing myself to frame a name for it, I call it the Great. Great, it passes on in constant flux; so passing on it becomes remote; when remote it comes back."

Modern Taoism: There could hardly be a stronger contrast than that which is presented between the ancient and the modern Taoism. Laotze was virtually rationalistic, but the present system is the most irrational of the great existing religions; it is a mass of superstitions of the lowest type. It is only the name of Taoism applied to a mixture of Buddhism and the ancient ancestor-worship and other superstitions of China. Speculation seems to have spent itself in the few centuries which followed the life of Laotze. Having first run wild in theories, it degenerated into low superstitions. The principle in Laotze's teachings which seems to have suggested the prevalence of spirits and ghosts in all nature, animate and inanimate, was his declaration that the presence of Tao is universal. He gave it a pantheistic omnipresence and indwelling in all beings and things. He little thought, probably, that this would lead to the notion that every object in nature is haunted, and thus cause the land to swarm with polytheism. A Taoist is afraid of his shadow. In the woods or in dark ravines he imagines he is about to be pounced upon by sprites or demons. The trees have souls, the very air is laden with a mysterious influence. Telegraph wires cannot pass through the open spaces nor steeples be reared without disturbing "fung-shui," nor can the earth be excavated for the purpose of mining or the introduction of any modern improvement without great risk that this omnipresent something shall be disturbed.

Taoism continued to be a philosophy for some time after the death of Laotze, but it was a changed and ever-varying series of speculations. In the opinion of Dr. Legge, it did not become a religion, strictly speaking, until after the introduction of Buddhism in the 1st century. It had a priesthood and abundant superstitions, but it was sorely in need of being reenforced by something higher. So far as history informs us, no successor of Laotze seemed to correctly interpret or propagate his teachings. His standard was too high, his theories were above the reach of his successors, his ethics and his transcendentalism alike failed to be appreciated. Professor Douglas has a very different estimate of the followers of Laotze from that ascribed to the immediate successors of Confucius. While the latter drew multitudes of the best men of the age about him, Laotze's camp was a Cave of Adullam to which the discontented and erratic resorted. His teachings, therefore, were left in the worst of hands.

Among the most influential Taoists in the next generation was Leitsze, who argued Laotze's quietism into a general Epicurean license. "Lay aside aspiration, and live for to-day; live in the freedom of the beast," would express his general view. Laotze had said: "Lay aside pomp and circumstance; live simply and with little pretense." Leitsze carried the idea to extremes. He also gave a licentious interpretation to the pantheism of Laotze, assuming that "if Deity lives and acts in us, then we are Deity, and are above restraint; we are as free as the gods."

The development of this extreme logical sequence of pantheism has not been confined to Taoists or to any particular country. The Upanishad pantheism of the Hindus led to the same results by the same logical process; men came to regard the soul as beyond the reach of sin or stain. Even in the extreme fanaticism which sometimes attaches to Christian doctrine, notions of liberty and perfection lead to the abandonment of law, and to general laxity of life.

Leitsze attached great importance to dreams. They constituted one mode of his teaching. He represented the emperor Hwangte as dreaming that he was in a world where men lived in the freedom of perfect indifference; nothing troubled them. These wonders led to the art of conjuring, and Leitsze wrung from Yin He, the Hankow gate-keeper, his assent to these arts, and his endorsement of them on the alleged authority of Laotze. In all this Leitsze wholly misrepresented the great philosopher and his principles. As a result of these frauds there swept in that flood-tide of juggleries which swamped the principles of Taoism, and opened the way for the old national superstitions.

Leitsze did not fail to encounter the rising Confucianism. He tried the old tactics of his master Laotze; he endeavored to put down Confucianism with ridicule. He had no better weapons than those of borrowed sarcasm. As it seemed necessary to his prestige that he assume the rôle of a philosopher, he developed a theory of the universe, but it was puerile and failed to win respect. His favorite method of argument was that of dialogue, in which his view was always made to triumph. He was forever fighting men of straw of his own manufacture. In one of these the superior wisdom of pursuing sensual enjoyments while one can is shown to the best advantage. Yet this man, by his intellect and vigor, won great influence for a time.

He was followed by Chwangtze. He was inclined to return from Leitsze to a position more like that of Laotze. He discoursed on the vanity of life, and bitterly opposed the superfluous homilies and showy benevolences of Confucianism. "Sages," he said, "turn round and round to be benevolent and kick and struggle to become righteous, and the people suspect their very earnestness. They bow and distort themselves in their endeavors to act with propriety, and the empire begins to break up." The satire which underlies all this is keen, and has a measure of truth.

There are some resemblances between the theories of Chwangtze and the Vedanta philosophy of India. He treated wakeful and conscious life as an illusion, and doubted the substantial reality of all things. And to this day there is a belief among Taoists that there is an inner and invisible soul in all objects; the unseen appears to be quite as real as the visible. As an illustration of this doubt as between the tangible and the invisible, he related a dream in which he seemed to be a butterfly, flitting about in the air, and he felt no little surprise on waking to find that he was no butterfly, but Chwangtze. "But then," he says, "the thought came to me, on the other hand, was that really a dream, or am I now dreaming that I am Chwangtze and not a butterfly?"

In the 3d century before Christ, Taoism had gained such influence that the reigning emperor ordered a general conflagration of all sacred books except those of the Taoists, but the doctrine as then held was not that of Laotze. It had undergone successive changes until it had become a system of childish superstitions. It was believed that immortality might be gained by charms and spells. The emperor Chwangtze believed this, and also that in the western seas there were happy isles where genii dispensed the elixir of immortality to all who came. This emperor sent expeditions to these imaginary isles to bring back the elixir. The period of his reign was a great harvest-time for all Taoistic frauds. The priests claimed the most astonishing of occult arts.

Taoism was now neither a philosophy nor a religion; it was a system of jugglery. Under the reign of the emperor Wu of the Han dynasty, who also became an implicit believer, the system still flourished, even down to about 100 B. C. This emperor also sent expeditions to the happy islands; alchemy and the quest for the elixir of life were at their height. It will be remembered that in Europe, also, similar fanaticisms have at various times been rife; but the wildest of them never equaled that of the Taoists of China in the reign of Wu. From the emperor down, all classes were seeking this elixir. Business of every kind was for a time neglected and the fields were untilled. Only the astrologists and priests were thrifty. The emperor lavished fortunes on their wild schemes.

Under these fanatical emperors Confucianism was bitterly persecuted. Many distinguished Confucian philosophers were burned alive, and all their books were burned. But at the death of Wu a great reaction took place and Confucianism was revived and reinstated.

In the 1st century the first high-priest or pope of the Taoists was appointed, and the office has descended in his clan to this day. He is elected by the priests of the clan; he is not bound by rules of celibacy or any particularly ascetic requirements.

Taoism became a religion, strictly speaking, soon after the advent of the Buddhists, somewhere about the close of the 1st century. Like Buddhism, it had great powers of absorption, and from having been at first a philosophy and then a system of jugglery it now borrowed certain religious elements from Buddhism. The two systems, both of which were rather absorbent than catholic and charitable, entered into kindly relations with each other. They at length came to have so much in common that their priests united in the same services, and it is stated by Prof. Legge that an emperor of the Chi dynasty strove to unite them by ordering Taoist priests to adopt the practise and the habit of the Buddhists. Some were put to death for refusing to conform. Taoists have persistently refused to submit to the full ritual of Buddhism, and their monks have withstood the requirement of celibacy. Low and degraded as Taoism had long been, it never sank into idol-worship until it came into contact with Buddhism. Neither had the followers of Confucius or Laotze ever worshiped an image until the custom was borrowed from the Buddhists. Now the temples of Taoists vie with those of the Buddhists in this respect.

One of the most noticeable effects of Buddhism upon the Taoist system is seen in the adoption by the latter of a trinity. Buddhism had images in its temples representing Buddha, the Law and the Sangha, tho at a later day they came to be regarded as representing Buddha past, present and to come. At length there appeared in the Taoist temples a trinity of colossal images, representing the Perfect Holy One, the Highest Holy One, and the Greatest Holy One. Monasteries and nunneries were unknown among the Taoists until after the introduction of Buddhism; the doctrine of transmigration was also derived from the same source. The Buddhist notion that women distinguished for virtue and character shall be rewarded at the next birth by being born as men, was also adopted by Taoists.

In one view a doctrine of eschatology seems out of place in Taoism, since it maintains that rewards and punishments are received in the present life. For example: the so-called "Book of Rewards" makes punishments consist almost invariably in shortening the period of the present life; immortality is spoken of, but it is something treated as of little account. Nevertheless, in each provincial temple of the Taoists may be seen what is called a Chamber of Horrors—a Purgatory. This, doubtless, is an esoteric conception, and is borrowed from Buddhism.

The real spirit of Taoist superstition is seen in the writings of an old author of the 4th century named Ko Hung. He says that "mountains are inhabited by evil spirits who are more or less powerful, according to the size of the mountain. If a traveler has no protection he will fall into some calamity. He will see trees move, tho not by the wind, and stones will fall from impending rocks without any apparent cause; he will be attacked by sickness or pierced by thorns," etc. A mirror should be carried, since the mischievous elves are afraid to approach him thus equipped, lest their true character should be discovered.

Taoism has experienced great vicissitudes.

During the reign of the emperor Whan, 147-165, great favor was shown to this system, and the custom of offering imperial sacrifices to Laotze at Kocheen, his birthplace, was begun. Many attempts were made to save life by charms, and in order to increase their power, legends borrowed from Buddhism were assigned to Laotze. Among other things it was claimed that after he left the Hankow Pass he spent three nights under a mulberry tree under temptation of the Evil One; lovely women, also, were his tempters.

The system again sank into neglect in the reign of Taikeen, 569-583. Orders were issued against both Taoist and Buddhist monasteries, and no doctrine could be taught but Confucianism. Again, under the Wei dynasty, Buddhism and Taoism were reinstated. In the reign of Tai Wute there was a return to the notion of an elixir of life, and the emperor became a Taoist. In this reign Buddhist asceticism began to be copied by Taoists. The emperor Tai Ho, 477-500, built temples and monasteries for this sect.

The emperor Wu, 566-578, abolished Buddhism and Taoism because their jealousies and strifes created disturbance, but Teing, 580-591, reinstated the two religions on equal grade. Under the Tang dynasty Taoism again held for a century the ascendancy over Buddhism, and Laotze was canonized. In 625-627, the Taoists, having become insolent, were banished to the provinces of Kwang-tung and Kwangsi, but under Hwuy Chang they were reinstated, and Buddhism was stigmatized officially as a foreign religion. Under the Sung dynasty, 960-976, Taoist priests were forbidden to marry. Hweitsung ordered the Buddhist priests to adopt Taoist names for their orders. The Manchu dynasty, following next in order, persecuted the Taoists, but Jenghis Khan promoted them; also Kublai Khan, in the 13th century. Hung Che, 1488-1506, was very hostile. The present Manchu dynasty has also been hostile, and has passed various edicts against Taoist jugglery.

The sacred book of Taoism, known as the "Book of Rewards," inculcates ethics which are on the whole commendable. The precepts are generally in negative form, but notwithstanding the morality of the "Book of Rewards," the moral grade of modern Taoism is extremely low.

Among the virtual deities at the present time are, first of all, Laotze, who is supremely reverenced. But a god of providence having general charge of human affairs is found to be necessary, and, accordingly, Yunwang Shangti, or the Precious Imperial God, is assigned to that place. The constellation of the Great Bear is also worshiped as a representative of the sidereal powers; also various forces of nature, as the Mother of Lightning, the Spirit of the Sea, the Lord of the Tides, etc. The dragon is a great object of worship with Taoists. His images are everywhere; serpents are his living representatives. Even Li Hung Chang, great statesman as he was, worshiped a serpent which crept into a temple in Tientsin in time of a flood in 1874. Chang Chun, a disembodied sage of the past, is now worshiped as a god of literature; a great hero of the past is worshiped as the god of war, and a third deity is the god of medicine. But altogether the most popular is Tsaichin, the god of wealth. Every store and shop has a little altar for burning incense to him. This suits the average Chinaman better than the transcendentalism of Laotze, or the lofty ethics of Confucius, or the nirvana of Buddhism. The boasted millions of Buddhists in China all believe supremely in Tsaichin.

The polytheism of China is still further ramified under the influence of Taoism, embracing gods of the sea, of the village, of the hearth, of the kitchen, and demigods to represent all virtues; in other words, deified men, heroes, scholars, etc.

A remarkable influence has been produced by these superstitions upon the Buddhism of China, as shown in the fact that the Buddhist temples are full of the same images of ideals, of virtues, and of heroic men. In the great Buddhist temple of Honan in Canton there are hundreds of full-sized figures of deified men.

The facts of Taoism which press most weightily upon the missionary are: (a) Its vague ideas of a Supreme God, which leave the people practically without such a conception; (b) Its substitution for God of a multitude of spirits of various qualities and purposes, and endowed with knowledge, activity and power; (c) The absence of the idea of Divine love in any form or of human love to the Creator and Preserver, and the certainty which it cultivates that the spirits to whom the worshiper looks are without sympathy even when they are not malicious toward man; (d) The concentration of attention upon devices for thwarting or placating the spirits so as to make ingenuity more important than conduct; (e) The filling the future life with an anarchy of spirits that repels as much as death itself. With all this there is an occasional help to moral excellence in men in the wise saws that contain principles of right intended for immediate use.

Chalmers (J.), *The Speculations of the Old Philosopher, Laotze*, London, 1868; Douglas (R. K.), *Confucianism and Taoism*, New York, 1879; Legge (J.), *Religions of China*, New York, 1881.

TARKASTAD: A town in Cape Colony, South Africa, situated in Tarka district, Kaffraria, about 40 miles W. of Queenstown. Station of the UFS (1869), with (1903) 1 missionary and his wife, 3 outstations, 1 day school, 1 Sunday school, and 96 professed Christians.

TARN TARAN: A town in the Punjab, India, situated about 15 miles S. S. E. of Amritsar. It is a very sacred place to the Sikhs and a holy fair is held there every month. Population, 6,000. It was terribly visited by the plague in 1902. Station of the CMS (1885), with (1903) 1 missionary and his wife, 9 native workers, 1 place of worship, and 521 professed Christians, of whom 44 are communicants. Station also of the CEZ (1888), with (1903) 5 women missionaries, 12 native workers, 3 day schools, 1 boarding school, 1 dispensary and 1 hospital.

TARPUM BAY: A station of the WMS, on Eleuthera Island, Bahamas, with (1903) 1 missionary, 15 native workers, 3 Sunday schools, 3 places of worship, and 539 professed Christians.

TARSUS: A city of Asiatic Turkey, situated in the province of Adana, 20 miles from Mersine. The birthplace of the apostle Paul. Population, Turks, Armenians and Nusairiyeh. In 1889 an institution called St. Paul's Institute was founded here with the financial support of Mr. Elliott F. Shepard of New York, and has done good work in educating young men for business and for service as teachers, etc. The institute is now under care of the ABCFM, and serves as a preparatory school for the Central Turkey College at Aintab.

TARTAR: A corruption of the name Tatar, a

word derived, according to some, from the Mongol tribal name, Ta-ta. Turks accept this derivation, merely adding that the tribal name should be followed by *ar* or *er* (man) so as to make full sense. The word Ta-ta-ar (man of the Ta-ta tribe) would thus be the identical word now in use. The form Tartar is a play-on words introduced by those sufferers of the Middle Ages who could imagine no source but Hell or Tartarus for the hordes who stripped them. The term has been loosely applied to any inhabitants of Central Asia, and does not carry with it any ethnological or political significance. Many writers discard it altogether. It seems better, however, to use it in a wide sense, including both Mongol and Turkish tribes, since these are allied, yet not the same. As things now are the term Mongol is made to do double duty, describing the genus as well as the species. Silence were better than loose speech that confuses. The word "Tartars" as applied by popular writers to the Tatars of Western Asia (the Kazan, Astrakan, Kipchak, Nogai and Crimean Tatar) means neither more nor less than "Turks." As applied to the Siberian nomads and those of North Turkestan, it means "Mongols." See Mongols and Turks.

TASIK MALAJA: A town in Java, Dutch East Indies, situated about 50 miles S. by W. of Cheribon. Station of the Netherlands Missionary Union (1898), with (1903) 1 missionary, 1 native worker, 1 day school, and 24 professed Christians.

TASMANIA: A British colony in Australasia, formerly called Van Diemen's Land, and including the island of that name and several smaller ones lying, for the most part, in Bass Strait. Area, 26,215 square miles. The estimated population, about 150,000, is composed of Tasmanians, English, Australasians, Chinese and Germans. The island is traversed by mountain ranges with fertile valleys. The climate is mild and not subject to extremes. It was made a penal settlement in 1804, but transportation of criminals ceased in 1853. The aborigines are entirely extinct. Hobart, the capital, had a population of 21,118 in 1881, and Launceston had 12,752.

The people are now nominally Christian, the majority belonging to the Church of England, the remainder being Roman Catholics, Wesleyan Methodists, Presbyterians and others.

The SPG maintains a mission here, and the Wesleyan Methodists have several hundred churches in Victoria and Tasmania together.

TA-TSIEN-LU: A town in Sze-chwan, China, situated 68 miles W. of Ya-chau-fu. Station of the CIM (1897), with 3 missionaries and 1 place of worship. Also written Ta-chuen-lu.

TA-TUNG-FU: A town in Shan-si, China, situated on a branch of the Pai-ho, 170 miles W. of Peking. All the missionaries in this region were killed in 1900 and the work is slowly being taken up again. Station of the CIM (1886), with (1903) 1 missionary and his wife, 2 native workers, 1 place of worship, 1 Sunday school, 1 day school, 1 dispensary, and 18 professed Christians. Some write the name Ta-T'ung.

TAUNG-NGU: A town in Burma, India, 170 miles from Rangoon by railroad. It has very extensive suburbs and a sheet of water more than a mile long lies within its walls. It was formerly the seat of an independent king. Altitude, 181 feet. Population, 17,500, nearly all being Buddhists.

Station of the ABMU (1853), with (1903) 3 missionaries and their wives, 2 women missionaries, 255 native workers, 87 outstations, 161 places of worship, 73 Sunday schools, 68 day schools, 5 boarding schools, 1 dispensary, 1 hospital, and 17,000 professed Christians, of whom 4,849 are communicants. Also station of the SPG (1873), with (1903) 4 missionaries, one of them with his wife; 108 native workers, 6 day schools, 4 boarding schools, and 2,903 professed Christians, of whom 2,868 are communicants. Station also of the ME, with (1903) 1 missionary and his wife. Some write the name Toongoo.

TAUNGS: A town in Bechuanaland protectorate, South Africa, situated on the Hart River, 40 miles S. of Vryburg. Station of the LMS (1868), with (1903) 1 missionary and his wife, 8 native workers, 5 day schools, and 2,000 professed Christians, of whom 130 are communicants. Some write the name Taung.

TAURANGA: A town in New Zealand, situated on North Island on the N. coast, about 90 miles S. E. of Auckland. Station of the CMS, with (1903) 1 missionary and his wife, 29 native workers, and 1,100 professed Christians, of whom 158 are communicants. Grants of the CMS to the New Zealand native congregations ceased in 1902.

TAVETA: A settlement in British East Africa, situated S. E. of Mt. Kilima Njaro, about 60 miles S. W. of Tsavo on the railroad from Mombasa to Uganda. It is a wild country where a part of the missionary's duties consists of shooting the lions and leopards that attack the people. Station of the CMS (1893), with (1903) 2 missionaries and their wives, 1 woman missionary, 6 native workers, 1 outstation, 121 professed Christians, of whom 41 are communicants; 1 place of worship, 3 day schools, 1 industrial class, 1 dispensary, and 1 printing house.

TAVOY: A town in Burma, India, situated in Tenasserim, on the Tavoy River, 30 miles from its mouth. The town lies low, and its northwestern and southern portions are flooded at high tide and swampy during the rains. It is laid out in straight streets, and the houses are generally built of timber or bamboo, thatched with palm-leaves. Its trade is of little importance. Population, 13,372, mostly Buddhists. Station of the ABMU (1828), with (1903) 2 missionaries and their wives, 1 woman missionary, 50 native workers, 23 outstations, 24 places of worship, 24 Sunday schools, 20 day schools, 1 boarding school, and 1,172 professed Christians.

TA-YE: A village in Hu-pei, China, situated about 45 miles S. E. of Wu-chang-fu. Station of the WMS, with (1903) 1 missionary, 11 native workers, 7 outstations, 2 day schools, 11 places of worship, and 130 professed Christians, of whom 105 are communicants.

TE AUTE: A settlement in New Zealand, situated on the North Island in the Hawkes' Bay district, about 24 miles S. W. of Napier. Station of the CMS, with (1903) 2 missionaries, one of them with his wife; 29 native workers, 1 college, and 1,450 professed Christians, of whom 130 are communicants. The native congregations in this region are under the charge of the local church, grants to which ceased in 1902.

TEGWANI: A settlement in Rhodesia, Africa,

situated about 70 miles S. W. of Bulawayo. Station of the WMS, with (1903) 1 missionary, 5 native workers, 15 outstations, 15 places of worship, 4 day schools, and 130 professed Christians, of whom 22 are communicants.

TEHERAN: The capital of Persia, situated due S. of the Caspian Sea in latitude 35° 40' north, longitude 51° 25' east. It is a walled city, with narrow, ill-paved streets, tho here and there Parisian boulevards and European houses present striking contrasts to the native quarters. The water supply is good and abundant, and public baths are numerous. The population of 250,000 consists of Persians, Turks, Armenians, and a few Jews and Parsees. The government established a polytechnic school here in 1849, with a certain number of European professors. Its students receive a liberal education. There is also a military school and Civil Service school, the latter opened in 1900.

The Imperial Bank of Persia has its chief offices in Teheran. It is an English establishment. Russian capital has also established two banking houses there. There is a railway of six miles length leading out of the city, and two carriage roads of about ninety miles length each.

Station of the London Jews' Society (1888), with (1903) 1 missionary and his wife, 4 native workers, 2 day schools, Also station of the PN (1872), with (1903) 4 missionaries, three of them with their wives; 17 native workers, 3 outstations, 1 place of worship, 2 day schools, 2 dispensaries, and 40 professed Christians.

TEKENIKA: A settlement on Hoste Island, about 65 miles N. W. of Cape Horn. This is almost the last existing settlement of the Yahgans, who are becoming extinct. Station of the SAMS (1892), with (1903) 1 missionary and his wife, 1 place of worship, 1 boarding school, 1 orphanage, and 50 professed Christians.

TEKKALI: A town in Madras, India, situated in the district of Vizagapatam, about 30 miles N. E. of Chicacole. Station of the BMP (1898), with (1902) 1 missionary, 16 native workers, 1 outstation, 5 Sunday schools, 5 places of worship, 7 day schools, and 72 professed Christians.

TELLICHERRI: A town and seaport on the Malabar Coast, Madras, India, 43 miles north-northwest of Calicut. A healthful and picturesque town built upon a group of wooded hills running down to the sea, protected by a natural breakwater of rock. It has a good harbor and an excellent trade. Population, 26,410, Hindus, Muslims, Christians.

Station of the Basel Missionary Society (1839), with (1903) 4 missionaries, three of them with their wives; 52 native workers, 6 outstations, 8 day schools, 3 boarding schools, and 591 professed Christians, of whom 324 are communicants. The name is written by Germans Talatscheri.

TELUGUS: A non-Aryan or Dravidian race inhabiting the east coast of the peninsula of Hindustan, India, north of the city of Madras and south of the Godavari River, and extending nearly 200 miles westward from the coast of the Bay of Bengal. The language of the Telugus is refined and has been called the Italian of Hindustan. The number of Telugus is placed at about 20,000,000 by the census of 1901.

TEMBE: A settlement in Portuguese East Africa, situated on the Tembe River, about 20 miles S. of Lourenço Marques. Station of the Swiss Romande Mission (1898), with (1903) 1 missionary and his wife, 1 woman missionary, 7 native workers, 7 places of worship, 7 Sunday schools, 7 day schools, and 417 professed Christians, of whom 102 are communicants. This place is sometimes spoken of as The Tembe.

TEMOHON: A village in the island of Celebes, Dutch East Indies, situated in the Minahassa district near Menado. Station of the Netherlands Missionary Society (1819), with (1902) 1 missionary and his wife and 1 theological class.

TEMPLE, Daniel: Born December 23, 1789, at Reading, Mass. Died August 9, 1851. The perusal of Dr. Buchanan's *Christian Researches in India* at his conversion led him to the decision to become a missionary to the heathen. He studied at Phillips Academy, Andover; Dartmouth College, and Andover Theological Seminary. He was ordained October 3, 1821, and embarked January 2, 1822, as a missionary of the ABCFM for Syria, reaching Malta February 22. Here he remained till 1833, the political condition of Turkey and Syria rendering it unsafe for a missionary family to settle there. He prepared books and tracts for circulation in Italy, Greece, and Turkey, which were printed on the press he took with him, widely distributed, and well received. In 1828, by invitation of the Prudential Committee, he visited the United States, and engaged in an agency for the Board for two years, returning to Malta in 1830. In addition to the superintendence of the press, he had during almost his whole residence here two services on the Sabbath in English in his own house, a Sabbath school which he taught himself, and also a lecture Friday evening. In 1833, by direction of the Society, he removed the Greek and Armenian part of the press plant to Smyrna. From 1822, when the press was established in Malta, to the time of its removal, were issued 350,000 volumes containing 21,000,000 pages. Nearly the whole had been circulated, and additional supplies of some of the works were urgently demanded. The arrival at Smyrna of a vessel with presses and printing materials, and an ordained missionary, aroused the fanaticism of the Greeks, and Mr. Temple was ordered by the governor to leave the city in ten days. But after some correspondence with the consul the storm passed away. The Greek Ecclesiastical Committee broke up eight schools, containing from six to eight hundred children, and forbade the teachers to remain with the missionaries, threatening them with imprisonment or banishment if they refused to obey. In 1837 Mr. Temple commenced the publication of a monthly magazine in Greek, *The Repository*, which met with much favor. The Greek patriarch forbade all his church members to read any of the missionaries' translations of the Scriptures in Turkish, Arabic, Servian, Bulgarian or Slavonian. During this year the plague raged with terrific violence at Smyrna. The Board shortly afterward decided to abandon the specifically Greek department of the mission. This left Mr. Temple no option but to return to the United States, which he did in 1844. He preached in Concord, N. H., and at Phelps, N. Y., but resigned his pastorate on account of ill-health December 27, 1849.

TE-NGAN-FU: A town in Hu-pei, China, situated about 60 miles N. W. of Han-kau. Station of the WMS, with (1903) 1 missionary, 1 woman missionary, 7 native workers, 1 outstation, 6 places of worship, 1 day school, and 160 professed Christians, of whom 120 are communicants. Some write the name Tehngan.

TE-TSING-CHAU: A town in Kwang-tung, China, situated on the Hsi-kiang, about 90 miles W. of Canton. Station of the Reformed Presbyterian Missionary Society (1897), with (1900) 1 missionary and his wife and 2 native workers. Some write the name Tak Hing Chau.

TETUAN: A town belonging to Spain, in Morocco, situated on the N. coast, about 50 miles S. of Gibraltar. Station of the NAM (1889), with (1903) 4 women missionaries, 1 Sunday school, 2 day schools, 1 dispensary, and 10 professed Christians.

TENG-CHAU-FU: A city in Shantung, China, on the coast of the Gulf of Chi-li, 55 miles northwest of Chi-fu. This city is one of the most healthful places for Europeans in China. Station of the PN (1861), with (1903) 8 missionaries, seven of them with their wives; 2 women missionaries, 55 native workers, 19 outstations, 10 places of worship, 20 Sunday schools, 1 printing press, 20 day schools, 2 boarding schools, 1 college, 1 dispensary, 1 hospital, and 1 medical class, and 657 professed Christians. The college is to be removed to Wei-hsien. Also station of the SBC (1860), with (1903) 3 missionaries with their wives, 2 women missionaries, 6 native workers, 5 outstations, 4 places of worship, 2 Sunday schools, 3 day schools, 1 boarding school, and 220 professed Christians.

TEZPUR: A town of Assam, India, on the Brahmaputra, 75 miles above Gauhati. The town is built on a plain between two low ranges of hills, upon which the houses of the European residents are built. It is an important seat of trade, where the river steamers touch to take on board tea, and to leave stores of various kinds to be distributed among the neighboring tea-gardens. Of late years the character of the houses and sanitary condition of the town have been much improved. Population, 2,910. Station of the SPG (1862), with (1903) 1 missionary, 24 native workers, 6 places of worship, 17 day schools, 1 boarding school, and 783 professed Christians, of whom 110 are communicants. Some write the name Tezpore.

THABA BOSIGO: A village in Basutoland, South Africa, situated 18 miles N. E. of Morija. Station of the Paris Evangelical Missionary Society (1837), with (1903) 1 missionary and his wife, 3 women missionaries, 20 native workers, 13 outstations, 14 day schools, 1 boarding school, and 2,029 professed Christians, of whom 1,379 are communicants. Some write the name Thaba-Bossiou.

THABA MORENA: A village in Basutoland, South Africa, situated about 20 miles S. of Morija. Station of the Paris Evangelical Mission Society (1862), with (1903) 1 missionary and his wife, 21 native workers, 10 outstations, 11 places of worship, 10 day schools, and 1,382 professed Christians, of whom 896 are communicants. Some write the name Thabana-Morena.

THABA' NCHU, or THABA NCHU: A settlement in the Orange River Colony, South Africa, situated about 30 miles E. of Bloemfontein. Station of the South African Wesleyan Methodist Missionary Society, with (1901) 1 missionary, 105 native workers, 6 places of worship, 6 Sunday schools, 12 day schools, 57 outstations, and 2,774 professed Christians.

THABOR: A town in Madras, India, situated in the district of Salem, about 15 miles N. of Salem. Station of the Danish Mission Society (1883), with (1901) 1 missionary and his wife, 1 place of worship, 1 Sunday school, 1 outstation, and 35 professed Christians.

THARAWADI: A town in Burma, situated in the district of Pegu, about 20 miles E. of Henzade. Station of the ABMU (1876), with (1903) 2 women missionaries, 64 native workers, 37 outstations, 27 places of worship, 10 Sunday schools, 15 day schools, 1 boarding school, and 1,924 professed Christians, of whom 962 are communicants. Some write the name Tharrawaddy.

THARRAWADDY. See THARAWADI.

THAYETMYO: A town on the Irawadi River, Burma, 25 miles from Prome. In the rains the place looks fresh and green, but during the dry season it presents a dreary appearance. Climate healthful, but excessively hot. Population, 8,379, who are mostly Chins. Station of the ABMU (1887), with (1903) 1 missionary and his wife, 7 native workers, 2 places of worship, 1 Sunday school, 2 day schools, and 170 professed Christians.

THLOTSE HEIGHTS: A settlement in Basutoland, South Africa, in the district of Leribe, near the Orange River, and about 15 miles E. of Ficksburg. Station of the SPG (1876), with (1903) 2 missionaries, 1 college, and 154 professed Christians.

THOBURN, Miss Isabella: The first missionary appointed by the Woman's Foreign Missionary Society of the ME Church after its organization in March, 1869. She was appointed to India and assigned to Lucknow, where she opened a boarding school for girls, beginning with one pupil. Before she died she saw completed and paid for the commodious building which now houses the great college for girls which has grown out of that humble beginning

Altho Miss Thoburn's work was largely educational, her energies were not limited to that department. She was a born leader, encouraged and aided Zenana work, Sunday school work, and other forms of city missions, and made her home a place of recourse to the tired worker and the poor, the weak and the fallen She had a mighty influence among all classes, Christian and non-Christian, and through this influence on her scholars she impressed upon them her own spirit in a marked manner.

THONG-THAU-HA: A village in Kwang-tung, China, situated about 50 miles S. E. of Canton. Station of the Rhenish Mission Society, with (1903) 1 missionary and his wife, 1 woman missionary, 2 native workers, 1 day school, and 125 professed Christians, of whom 110 are communicants.

THONZE: A town in Burma, India, situated in the district of Pegu, about 6 miles S. of Tharawadi. Station of the ABMU (1855), with (1903) 1 woman missionary, 7 native workers, 3 outstations, 4 places of worship, 1 Sunday school, 1 day school and 379 professed Christians. Some write the name Thongze.

THURSTON, Asa: Born at Fitchburg, Mass., October 12, 1787. Died at Honolulu March 11, 1868. Graduated at Yale College 1816, Andover

Theological Seminary 1819; embarked as a missionary of the ABCFM 1819, with others, who formed the first band of missionaries for the Sandwich Islands. As a missionary Mr. Thurston ever labored with great usefulness and success. His knowledge of the native language and character was most thorough; and as a preacher he was much beloved by the native Hawaiians. In the early years of the mission his labors as a translator were arduous and successful. He was stationed at Kailua, the ancient residence of the Hawaiian kings, and there for more than 40 years he continued to reside and to labor as the honored pastor of a large and very important parish. He was the instructor for a time of both Kamehameha II. and Kamehameha III., and his influence over them, especially the latter, was great. Never once leaving the islands for 48 years, he was honored by natives and foreigners alike as a faithful, patient, persistent worker. Only when advanced age and repeated strokes of paralysis had rendered him incapable of service did he consent to resign his pastorate at Kailua, that he might spend the closing years of his life in Honolulu.

TIBERIAS, or TUBARIYÈ: A village in Palestine, Asiatic Turkey, situated on the W. shore of the Sea of Tiberias, about 35 miles E. by S. of Acre. Station of the UFS Mission to the Jews (1884), with (1901) 2 missionaries, 13 native workers, 1 Sunday school, 2 day schools, 1 dispensary, and 1 hospital.

TIBET: One of the possessions of China, claimed to be an integral part of the Chinese Empire. It is a country of which very little is definitely known. Surrounded by high mountains, it has been to a great degree isolated from the rest of the world. Tibet is a corruption of the Chinese name; the people themselves call it the "land of Bod." The Kwanlun Mountains bound it on the north; on the east are the Chinese provinces of Sze-chwan and Yunnan; the Himalaya Mountains bound it on the south, and Kashmir on the west. Little Tibet does not properly belong to Tibet, tho it is claimed by Chinese geographers. The greater part of the surface consists of high tableland (elevation 11,510 feet), divided into three parts by mountain ranges: the valley of the Indus on the west, between the Hindu Kush and Himalaya Mountains; the high desert land, almost uninhabitable and wholly unknown, lying between the Kwanlun and Himalaya Mountains; and the basin of the Yaru-tsangbu on the east, consisting of high ridges and deep gorges, mountains and valleys. Numerous peaks of perpetually snow-capped mountains are here found, of which Mt. Kailasa (26,000 feet) is the highest.

The principal river, the Yaru-tsangbu, drains the whole of southern Tibet between the first and second ranges of the Himalayas, and is supposed to empty into the Brahmaputra, tho explorations have not yet been extensive enough to decide the truth. The Indus, the Yangtse, the Brahmaputra and other large rivers of Southern and Eastern Asia find their source in Tibet. In the central part are numerous lakes. The climate is varied, but in general the air is pure and excessively dry. Snow and ice last for most of the year, but in the middle of summer the valleys, even between the snowy mountains, are excessively hot. In the southern part moisture and vegetation are found, and sheep, goats and yaks are raised.

The government is conducted by two high commissioners appointed at Peking, but these confer with and are guided by the two grand officers of the Tibetan hierarchy, the Dalai-Lama and the Teshu-Lama: the former, known generally as the Grand Lama, is usually a child (supposed to be a reincarnation of the soul of the last Grand Lama) who is not suffered to live more than seven or eight years in his high office; and the latter being a regent who rules during the minority of the little Dalai-Lama. The power is practically in the hands of the priests or lamas, whose number is so great as to give Tibet the name of the "kingdom of priests." The southern frontier is strongly fortified, and communication between Tibet and India or the intervening states is forbidden. On the Chinese frontier the same strictness is exercised, for the policy of exclusion is fostered alike by the lamas and the Chinese—the one because they wish to preserve their religious supremacy and fat offices, the other because they wish to retain their political power, faint tho it be. The present Dalai-Lama, as an exception to the policy of the last hundred years, has been permitted to live to maturity and to rule without a regent. He seems to desire independence of Chinese control, and for this reason to foster political relations with Russia. Both Russia and the British Indian Government have tried to open relations with Tibet for some fifteen years past. In 1901 it became known that Russia had secured from the Grand Lama rather exclusive privileges by a secret treaty. The British then demanded execution of a commercial agreement with India to which China and the lamas had already agreed. The British Commissioner was, however, refused a hearing and was sent back to India. Late in 1903 he went to Tibet again to insist upon a favorable answer. This time he was escorted by troops. The Tibetans refused to negotiate, and finally in March, 1904 attacked the embassy with armed force. Thus began a war with the British which can only result in destroying, at last, the barriers erected by this strange people against the world.

Lhassa, the capital, has only once been visited by an Englishman—Thomas Manning, in 1811—and its location has but recently been agreed upon to be approximately in latitude 29° 45' N. and longitude 91° 55' E. It stands in a fertile plain, at an altitude of 11,700 feet, encircled by mountains. It is noted for the number of its monasteries, bonzes and lamas, filthy streets and mean buildings. The population is estimated at from 40,000 to 80,000, and the population of the whole of Tibet, while unknown, is estimated at 6,000,000. The people belong to the Mongol race, and they are intensely religious. Their religion is of two kinds: the old original religion called the "Bon," of which little or nothing definite is known, and that form of Buddhism called Lamaism. The social customs of the people differ greatly from that of their neighbors on the east and south, particularly in the position which women hold. Here polyandry is the custom instead of polygamy, the wife being usually espoused by brothers. In general, education is restricted to the priests, but the women, who conduct most of the traffic, learn writing and arithmetic. In some of the northern provinces the chieftainship is held by the women.

The language of Tibet is derived from the Sanskrit. It is alphabetical, and reads from left to right. Thirty consonants are recognized, with four additional vowel signs. Tibetan literature, as well as Tibetan customs, have been influenced to a great degree by China.

Missions are not permitted in Tibet. In former times the Roman Catholic Church made noble efforts to enter the forbidden land, and was for a time successful. In 1330 the apostle of Tartary, Odoric Forojuliensis, traveled in Tibet and found missionaries already in the city of Lhassa, who had gone there, it is supposed, early in the preceding century. In the 17th century a mission was commenced from India, and the reigning prince was favorable to the new religion; but his apostasy was made the pretext for his overthrow. Various attempts at evangelization have been made since that time. The most noteworthy one was in 1845, when Fathers Gabet and Huc penetrated to Lhassa after a journey of eighteen months, only to be arrested by the Chinese officials, who sent them prisoners to Canton. From that time the Roman Catholic Missions have made numerous attempts both by way of India and China to enter the kingdom; but after suffering persecution and the massacre of their priests they have given up the effort, and occupy now only the confines of Tibet, where they work among the Chinese and such Tibetans as are there found.

The Moravian Brethren occupy three stations in Little Tibet—Leh, Poo and Kailang—where they are waiting for opportunity to enter Tibet. One or two attempts have been made at great risk, but have proved ineffectual. They have studied the Tibetan language, and there are now several works which will aid the future missionaries to Tibet when the country is opened. A Tibetan-English grammar, a Tibetan grammar, and a New Testament in Tibetan have all been published. A prayer union has been formed among the Moravians, whose object is to pray for the opening of the land of priests to the preaching of the Gospel. The members of the Tibetan band of the China Inland Mission, working on the eastern frontier, in the province of Sze-chwan; the Christian and Missionary Alliance, located in Kansu, on the northeastern border; the Scandinavian Alliance Mission of North America; the Church of Scotland, the LMS, the CMS, and the Assam Frontier Mission have all made preparatory efforts to enter this field. There is now some prospect that the Forbidden Land may soon be open to missionary enterprise.

Huc (L'Abbé E. R.), *Travels in Tibet, Tartary and China* (Translated from the French), 2 vols., London, 1898; Bower (H.), *Diary of a Journey Across Tibet*, London, 1894; Waddell (L. A.), *The Buddhism of Tibet*, London, 1895; Landor (A. H. S.), *In the Forbidden Land*, London, 1899; Rijnhart (S. C.), *With the Tibetans in Tent and Temple*, London, 1891; Cary (W.), and Taylor (Miss A.), *Travel and Adventure in Tibet*, London, 1902; Das (Sarat Chandra), *Journey to Lhassa and Central Tibet*, London, 1902.

TIEN-TAI-HSIEN: A town in Che-kiang, China, situated about 18 miles N. by W. of Tai-chau-fu. Station of the CIM (1898), with (1903) 1 missionary and his wife, 8 native workers, 4 places of worship, 1 Sunday school, 2 day schools, and 107 professed Christians.

TIENTSIN: One of the most important cities of North China, situated at the junction of the Grand Canal with the Pei Ho, 30 miles from the sea and 80 miles southeast of Peking. It is the port of and "key" to the capital, and is famous as the place where in 1858 the treaties were made, and where in 1900 the allied forces encountered long and fierce resistance on attempting to move for the relief of the Legations in Peking. As a result of the fighting at this place a considerable part of the native city was destroyed. The walls of the city were razed to the ground and fine roads constructed in their place. Since the restoration of peace the foreign settlements at Tientsin have been much increased, and the place made into quite a handsome town. Climate healthful and pleasant; maximum temperature 100° Fah. Population, 900,000.

Foreign missions entered the town in 1859, when the Methodist New Connexion sent their first representatives there. These were followed by the ABCFM (1860); LMS (1861); ME; CIM (1888); Church of England (SPG); North China Mission (1890); the Scandinavian Alliance, and the Christian and Missionary Alliance. These two societies last named do not publish clear statistics. The other societies named above have (1903) in Tientsin and dependencies 37 missionaries, 45 native workers, 25 places of worship, 12 day schools, 7 boarding or special schools, 2 hospitals, 5 dispensaries, and 718 professed Christians. The YMCA has an agency here, and the BFBS and the National Bible Society of Scotland have agents and a large force of colporteurs.

TIERRA DEL FUEGO: An archipelago at the extremity of South America, separated from the mainland by the Strait of Magellan. The islands are divided into three groups: East Fuegia, including one large island 200 miles long from north to south; South Fuegia, a triangle of numerous small islands, with Cape Horn at the apex; and West Fuegia. The climate of most of the archipelago is cold and disagreeable, and fogs and high winds make navigation difficult. A line from Cape Espiritu Santo due south to Beagle Channel divides the archipelago between the Argentine Republic on the east and Chile on the west. Three races are recognized among the inhabitants: the Onas, the Alacalufs, and the Yahgans. They are all on a low scale of mental and moral life; they wear little or no clothing, kill the old women and eat them, throw their children overboard to propitiate the storm spirits, and indulge in other barbaric customs. The language has been reduced to writing by the missionaries, and is said to contain 30,000 words. The South American Missionary Society works among the Yahgans almost exclusively, from Ushuaia, a station on Beagle Channel, on both sides of which this race is found. The Yahgans are rapidly dying out, and while there are many interesting cases of conversion and many promising children in the mission schools, the future does not seem to offer permanency of results.

TIFLIS: A town in Asiatic Russia and capital of Transcaucasia, on the Kur River. It is a mixture of Asiatic and European architecture, the old part being built of sun-dried brick, and containing all the bazars and business life of Tiflis, the modern part resembling any European city. Tiflis was for centuries a stronghold of refuge for Eastern Christianity when attacked first by the Persians and later by Islam. Its population is now (1903) largely made up of Armenians. Its situation is extremely picturesque, forming a depression surrounded on all sides except the north by mountains. Altitude, 1,350 feet. Population (1892) 146,790. Station of the Swedish National Missionary Society (1882), with 2 missionaries and their wives, 1 place of worship, 3 day schools, and 1 Sunday school. The restrictions of Russian law against missionary effort prevent much work outside of the recognized Protestant families. Climate hot and unhealthful, but the place is popular on account of the warm mineral springs in the vicinity.

TIFOE: A village on the island of Buru, Moluccas, Dutch East Indies, situated on the S. coast of the island. Station of the Utrecht Mission Society (1888), with (1903) 1 missionary and his wife, 9 native workers, 11 outstations, 10 day schools, and 1,748 professed Christians.

TIKARI: A town in Bengal, India, situated in the Gaya district, 50 miles S. W. of Patna. Station of the BZM (1885), with (1903) 2 women missionaries, 10 native workers, 2 Sunday schools and 3 day schools.

TILLIPALLY: A large town in Ceylon, East Indies, on the north shore of the peninsula of Jaffna, at the northern extremity of the island. Climate tropical, damp, but very healthful for young children. Population, 21,698. Caste rule is rather relaxed here, so that one is not expelled from his class on becoming a Christian. Station of the ABCFM (1831), with (1903) 1 missionary and his wife, 54 native workers, 5 outstations, 29 day schools, 1 boarding school, and 365 professed Christians.

TINANA: A settlement in Cape Colony, South Africa, situated in Griqualand East, about 12 miles N. W. of Fletcherville. Station of the Moravian Mission Society (1875), with (1903) 1 missionary and his wife, 20 native workers, 2 outstations, 3 places of worship, 2 Sunday schools, 5 day schools, and 338 professed Christians.

TINDIVANAM: A town in Madras, India, lying about 25 miles N.W. of Pondicherri and 75 miles S. W. of Madras. Station of the RCA (1868), with (1901) 1 missionary and his wife, 89 native workers, men and women; 39 common schools, 34 Sunday schools, 1 high school, 38 outstations, and 629 professing Christians.

TINNEVELLI: A district in the southern part of the Madras Presidency, in India. It contains an area of 5,381 square miles, at the southeastern point of Hindustan, bounded on the south and east by the sea, on the west by the Ghats, which separate it from Travancore, and on the north by the district of Madura. The history of the district is involved with that of Madura. After centuries of Hindu rule the Mohammedans came, and after them came a half-century of anarchy, which was ended in 1801 by the cession of the whole region to the English. The population of the district (1891) is about 1,916,000. Christianity has taken firmer root here than in any other district in India. Statistics show that between 1871 and 1881 the Hindus lost 2½ per cent., while the Mohammedans gained nearly 6 and the Christians over 37 per cent. The number of baptized Christians connected with the SPG and CMS missions was 59,203 at this time, of whom 13,265 were communicants. There were also about 40,000 more under instruction for baptism. Ninety-five per cent. of them belong to the Shanar caste, who live by the culture of the Palmyra palm. Protestant missionary work was begun in the town of Tinnevelli about 140 years ago, by the Danish missionaries at Tranquebar, who, with their native preachers, made occasional tours to the south. But no Christian preacher seems to have resided there permanently before 1771, when a native preacher took up his residence in Palamkotta, three miles from the town of Tinnevelli; no European missionary was stationed there until the year 1788, when Rev. J. D. Jaenicke was sent there. He died in 1800. The missionary Schwartz also traveled in the district. The SPCK maintained the mission at Palamkotta until 1816, when it was passed over to the Church Missionary Society, and in 1825 it transferred its work in the town of Tinnevelli to the SPG. These two societies have since divided the work in the district between them. Christianity had begun to exert no small degree of influence at the time the work was transferred to the societies that now conduct it, and since then the work of conversion has proceeded with great vigor. About the year 1877 Rev. R. Caldwell, D.D., of the SPG, and Rev. E. Sargent, D.D., of the CMS, were consecrated bishops assistant to the Bishop of Madras, for the purpose of affording better episcopal supervision to the work of their respective societies in that district. In 1896 the Bishopric of Tinnevelli and Madura was instituted, and the supervision was thus simplified.

The CMS (1816), the SPG (1825) and the CEZ (1874) are working in the Tinnevelli district, with (1903) 38 missionaries, men and women; 1,497 native workers, men and women; 607 day schools, 26 boarding schools, 1 orphanage, 1 theological training school, 2 colleges, and 80,813 baptized Christians. Among the special lines of work may be mentioned the schools for the blind carried on by the CMS and the Palamkotta School for the Deaf and Dumb, established by the CEZ.

TINNEVELLI: A town in Madras, India, the capital of Tinnevelli district, situated about 40 miles W. S. W. of Tuticorin. Population, 23,221. Station of the CMS (1820), with (1903) 1 missionary and his wife, and in the district 681 native workers, 413 day schools, 1 college, and 54,970 professed Christians, of whom 13,493 are communicants. The congregations in the surrounding district are united in a Native Church Council, of which the chairman is the CMS missionary.

TIRUKOVILUR: A town in Madras, India, situated in the S. Arcot district, 50 miles N. W. of Cuddalore. Station of the Danish Mission Society (1869), with (1903) 2 missionaries and their wives, 1 woman missionary, 9 native workers, 2 places of worship, 2 day schools, 1 boarding school, and 402 professed Christians. Some give to this place the name Siloam.

TIRUMANGALAM: A town in Madras, India, situated about 10 miles S. W. of Madura. Station of the ABCFM (1838), with (1903) 1 missionary, 59 native workers, 50 outstations, 24 places of worship, 29 Sunday schools, 19 day schools, 1 boarding school, and 1,560 professed Christians.

TIRUPATI: A town in Madras, India, situated about 77 miles S. E. of Cuddapa. Station of the Hermannsburg Missionary Society (1877), with (1903) 1 missionary and his wife, 36 native workers, 2 outstations, 1 place of worship, 3 day schools, 1 boarding school, and 160 professed Christians, of whom 144 are communicants.

TIRUPATUR: A town in Madras, India, situated in Salem district, about 65 miles N. E. of Salem. Population, 14,278 (Tamil). Station of the LMS (1861), with (1903) 1 missionary, 26 native workers, 11 outstations, 5 Sunday schools, 11 day schools, and 197 professed Christians, of whom 123 are communicants. Some write the name Tripatoor.

TIRUVALUR: A town in Madras, India, situated in the North Arcot division, about 24 miles W. of Madras. Station of the Leipzig Missionary Society, with (1903) 26 native workers, 15 places of worship, 20 day schools, 14 outstations, and 1,914 professed Christians, of whom 707 are communicants. Also station of the WMS, with (1903) 2 missionaries, 2 women missionaries, 118 native workers, 27 outstations, 44 places of worship, 64 Sunday schools, 72 day schools, 2 boarding schools, 1 hospital, and 920 professed Christians, of whom 484 are communicants.

TIRUVANNAMALAI: A town in Madras, India, situated in the S. Arcot district, about 50 miles S. of Vellore. Station of the Danish Missionary Society (1899), with (1903) 1 missionary, 5 native workers, 1 day school, and 32 professed Christians.

TIRUWALLUR. See TIRUVALUR.

TIRUWELLA: A town in Travancore, India, situated 20 miles S. E. of Allepie. Station of the CMS (1849), with (1903) 1 missionary and his wife, 62 native workers, 40 day schools, 2 boarding schools, and 7,000 professed Christians, of whom 1,997 are communicants. The churches in this vicinity are joined in a Church Council of their own.

TJIDERES: A village in Java, Dutch East Indies, situated about 50 miles S. E. of Cheribon. Station of the Netherlands Mission Union (1878), with (1903) 1 missionary, 3 native workers, 1 outstation, 1 hospital, and 191 professed Christians, of whom 79 are communicants.

TOBAGO: An island in the West Indies, lying northeast of Trinidad, of which it is a dependency. It is a rocky mass rising abruptly to a height of 900 feet. There are several good harbors. It was settled by the Dutch in 1654, taken by the French and finally by the English in 1763. Area, 114 square miles. Population (1892) 19,594. Missions are carried on in the islands by the Moravians (1790).

TOBELO: A village on the island of Halmaheira (Jilolo), Moluccas, situated in the N. part of the island. Station of the Utrecht Missionary Society (1897), with (1901) 1 missionary and his wife, 14 native workers, 10 day schools, and 21 professed Christians.

TODAS: These people, who live in the Nilgiri hills in India, are generally looked upon as a remnant of the primeval race of Mysore, existing, like driftwood, on the heights above a changeful world. They belong to the Dravidian race which has peopled the land from time immemorial. A description of their characteristics is given by one of the missionaries as follows: The Toda is striking in appearance, with well-marked features, hazel eyes, and an abundant growth of wavy hair, hanging to its full length in well-oiled ringlets. The single unbleached cloth which envelops him often presents a study in sepia, as he never washes his cloth, and rarely himself, from birth to death. Tho fine in physique, the tribe is numerically small; yet not so small as to preclude the existence of at least five castes, observing the usual social restrictions. The form of marriage known as polyandry is still prevalent, one woman marrying all the brothers of a family. Only eighty years have passed away since the barbarous custom of female infanticide was discontinued, through the moral influence of the first English who penetrated these benighted regions.

The odorous abode of the Todas consists of scattered "munds" or villages of from three to five pent-roofed huts, fashioned after a style of architecture peculiar to the tribe. The hut, twelve feet square, has a capacity which is truly marvelous, for the accommodation of relatives of both sexes and all ages. The only ventilation is derived from the diminutive doorway, two-and-a-half feet by one-and-a-half; and the mode of ingress and egress can scarcely be called dignified.

It has been said, in regard to the religion of the Todas, that there exists "a partiality to the regard of light—apart from fire—as, par excellence, the manifestation of deity." The bell worn by a succession of sacred cows is revered as the "chief god." Only members of the priestly clan are permitted to tend the sacred buffalos, and officiate as "pujaris" or priests to the Bell-god, assuming the title of "sons of the gods." Of recent years the simple faith of their forefathers has become adulterated with Hinduism and assumes the form of the worship of spirits which are feared as capable of evil.

Content if he may know enough to tend his father's buffalos in the pastures, the Toda recks not of personal improvement or social duties. In true Eastern placidity he lives, in hope that, at the end, the "Lord of life" will receive him into "the other district," as he calls the unseen world. There he believes he will dwell under conditions similar to the present, for the buffalos slain at his decease are supposed to supply him with milk and ghee in the new life; and the coins burnt with the body are intended for the keeper of the thread-bridge, which the soul must pass on its pilgrimage—tho they mostly fall into the hands of the more mundane village sweeper.

A curious feature of the Toda social system is their custom, still preserved in some degree, of demanding and receiving a dole of grain at harvest from the surrounding farmers. The grain is demanded as tribute for the use of the land. But it is now given as charity.

The name of this curious people is sometimes written Todar and Todawar.

TOGOLAND: A German possession in West Africa, lying on the Gulf of Guinea, and having an area of 33,160 square miles and a population estimated at from one to two millions. The coast line is but 32 miles, the country widening to several times that dimension in the interior. It is situated between the French colony of Dahomey on the east and the British Gold Coast Colony on the west, and extends back from the coast some 250 miles. It was declared a German protectorate in 1884. The coast climate is unhealthful for Europeans; the interior hilly and well watered with streams. Good roads connect Lome, now regarded as the capital, with Misahohe and Atakpame, and there is a narrow gage railway between Lome and the Little Popo. Telegraphs connect the chief towns and extend into Dahomey and the Gold Coast Colony, thus providing cable communication with Europe. The German Government is represented by the Hamburg and Bremen traders, settled in the seaports, who cannot as yet vie with the village chiefs and fetish priests in influence over the people.

The tribes between the Ogun and Volta Rivers belong to the Ewe family, and from them the region takes the name "Eweme."

The North German Missionary Society has 4 stations in Togoland and the Basel Society 1 and the WMS 1. The whole force of missionaries and native workers is 170, with 69 schools and about 3,500 communicants.

TOKAT: A town in the province of Sivas, Asiatic Turkey, situated about 70 miles S. of Samsun. Henry Martyn died and was buried here. Population, 10,000. Outstation of the ABCFM. Statistics given under Sivas. Station of the FCMS (1884), with (1900) 1 missionary, 4 native workers, 5 outstations, 3 places of worship, 4 day schools, 5 Sunday schools, and 233 professed Christians. Some write the name Tocat.

TOKELAU ISLANDS: A group of small islands in Polynesia, N. of the Samoan Islands, southeast of the Ellice group. These islands, together with the Ellice and Gilbert groups, are visited annually by missionaries of the LMS at Samoa. Native ministers are doing excellent work among a church membership of 3,374 (1903) in the three groups, and several thousand pupils are in the Sunday and day schools.

TOKIO: Capital of Japan, formerly called Yeddo. It is situated in the center of a great plain, which extends back from the water to the mountains for a distance varying from twenty to sixty miles, and borders the shores of the Bay of Tokio for about a hundred miles. There is thus no want of land over which the city may extend. Already it occupies about 28 square miles, and as far as the extent is concerned, it is second only to London. The city lies at the northwest end of the Bay of Tokio. Through the city runs the O-gawa, or Great River, dividing it into an eastern and a western part. Numerous canals penetrate the city at various points, and on the east is another river, Naka-gawa. The city is divided into various sections for purposes of government and postal delivery. Here are found the numerous palaces and public buildings of the government; the temples of Buddha, Confucius, and various Japanese deities representing the old civilization and the old religion; but side by side with these stand the distinctively Christian buildings, together with the Imperial University, School of Engineers, and the numerous other institutions of learning, whose influence is rapidly lessening the number of worshipers at the ancient shrines, so that a few years from now they will probably be museums of antiquities rather than temples to which worshipers are drawn through fear and superstition. The rapid strides which European civilization is making in Japan can be seen nowhere better than in this city. Alongside the old stone wall, surrounding the palace grounds, with its moat—one tortuous ribbon of variegated colors from the lotus flowers, which bloom there in summer-time—are seen the electric wires for the telegraph and telephone. The puffing smoke of the railway-engine overcomes the pungent odor of the incense in the temples; gas is used for lighting streets and shops, and each year civilization, with its attendant conveniences and luxuries, is thoroughly permeating the life and habits of the citizens. Not only is Tokio within easy reach of Yokohama, 10 miles away by rail, but it is an important railway center. One of the numerous bridges which span the watercourses of the city is considered the topographical center of the empire, from which all distances are reckoned. The population (1898) is 1,440,121.

Missionary societies commenced their work in Tokio almost as soon as the empire was opened to the outside world. At present the societies engaged in work in Tokio and its surroundings are the following, with the date of their entrance upon work in the city: PN (1869); ME (1872); PE (1873); SPG (1875); ABMU (1874); CMS (1874); RCA (1876); Evangelical Association (1877); MCC (1879); RCUS (1880); General Evangelical of Germany (1885); AFFM (1885); Christian Church (1888); PB (1888); Universalist, U. S. (1890); ABCFM (1890); FCMS (1891); UB (1895); SDA (1896); Methodist Protestant (1900); ELUS; Scandinavian Alliance; Synod of the Norwegian Evangelical Lutheran Church of N. A. The YMCA also has an agency here, with two men and their wives; the Salvation Army has a post, and the Mission to Lepers in India and the East cares for a leper hospital. Connected with these societies there are (1903) in the aggregate in Tokio and its outstations 168 missionaries, men and women; 361 native workers, men and women; 102 places of worship, 23 day schools, 25 boarding or special schools, 2 hospitals and dispensaries, 4 publishing houses and 7,937 professed Christians, including baptized children.

TOKUSHIMA: A town in Shikoku Island, Japan, situated on the E. coast. Population, 59,969. Station of the CMS (1888), with (1903) 2 women missionaries, 7 native workers, and 205 professed Christians, of whom 103 are communicants. Also station of the PS (1889), with (1903) 2 missionaries and their wives and 2 women missionaries.

TOKYO. See TOKIO.

TOLEDO: A village in British Honduras, situated on a small bay about 60 miles S. by W. of Belize. Station of the WMS, with (1903) 1 missionary, 8 native workers, 2 outstations, 6 places of worship, 4 Sunday schools, 2 day schools, and 72 professed Christians, of whom 69 are communicants.

TONG-AN. See TUNG-NGAN-HSIEN.

TONGA ISLANDS (Friendly Islands): A group in the South Pacific, extending from 18° 5' to 22° 29' south latitude, and from 173° 52' to 176° 10' west longitude, was discovered by Tasman in 1643, and named Friendly Islands by Captain Cook, but is now called Tonga, after the principal island. There are about 150 islands in three separate groups, comprising a total area of 374 square miles. Part of these are of volcanic nature, but a majority of the islands are level and covered with rich, productive soil. The principal island is Tonga or Tongatabu, 128 square miles in area, on which is situated the capital, Nuku-alofa. Earthquakes are frequent, and at times volcanic eruptions have taken place. The climate, like that of Fiji, is warm and humid. Southeast trade-winds blow except for a few months in the winter. The islands are now Christianized, and are governed by a Christian king under the protectorate of Great Britain. Formerly Tonga was noted for cannibalism, infanticide and other crimes characteristic of savages. The people are intellectually far in

47

advance of most of the Polynesian race, and have at one time and another conquered many of the surrounding islands. Nearly every one can read, and they are industrious farmers, as well as skilful sailors. They number (1901) 19,000, of whom 300 are Europeans. The triumphs of the Gospel in Tonga, the devoted zeal of the king, and the proud position which Tongan converts have held as pioneers of Christianity to Fiji and other Polynesian groups are striking testimonials to the civilizing and regenerating power of Christian missions. In these islands colleges have been established, where young men and women are being trained for Christian service.

The evangelization of the Tonga Islands is one of the fruits of the effort of the WMS. The Tonga churches are now, however, a district in connection with the Australasian Methodist Missionary Society.

TONGAREVA, or PENRHYN ISLAND: A small island in Polynesia, east of the Tokelau Islands, west of the Marquesas, and north of the Society Islands. It is visited from Rarotonga.

T'ONG-CHI. See TUNG-CHI-HSIEN.

TONGOA: A settlement in the S. W. part of the island of Espiritu Santo, New Hebrides. Station of the New Hebrides Missionary Society, with (1901) 2 missionaries, one of them with his wife; 1 woman missionary, 28 native workers, 3 outstations, 2 places of worship, 1 day school, 1 theological class, and 730 professed Christians.

TONG-SHAN: A town in Chi-li, China, situated about 70 miles N. N. E. of Tientsin, on the road to Manchuria. Station of the Methodist New Connexion Society (1884), with (1901) 2 missionaries and their wives, 25 native workers, 43 outstations, 44 places of worship, 8 day schools, 1 boarding school, 1 hospital, and 541 professed Christians. Also station of the PB, with (1901) 3 missionaries, two of them with their wives, and 1 woman missionary. Some write the name T'ang-shan.

TONKIN (Tonquin): A French colony in Asia, on the borders of the Gulf of Tonkin, lying between the Chinese provinces of Kwang-tung and Yunnan on the north and Annam on the south and west. It was annexed by France in 1884, and is divided into fourteen provinces, with an estimated population of 9,000,000. Hanoi, the chief city, is a union of many villages, with an aggregate population of 150,000. The Roman Catholics are at work in Tonkin, and claim a large membership.

TOONDEE: A village in Bengal, India, situated about 40 miles S. of Mandhupur. Station of the UFS, with (1903) 1 missionary, 12 native workers, 1 boarding school, 7 day schools, 1 dispensary and 1 printing press. The church statistics are included under Santalia.

TOONGOO. See TAUNG-NGU.

TORREON: A town and railroad junction in Mexico, situated in the State of Coahuila, close to the border of Durango, near Lerdo. Station of the SBC (1890), with (1903) 1 missionary and his wife, 5 native workers, 22 outstations, 6 places of worship, 6 Sunday schools, 1 theological class, and 471 professed Christians.

TOTTORI: A town in Japan, situated near the N. coast of the main island, about 90 miles N. W. of Kioto. Station of the ABCFM (1890), with 2 missionaries, one of them with his wife; 5 native workers, 2 outstations, 2 places of worship, 3 Sunday schools, 1 boarding school, and 62 professed Christians.

TOY, Robert: A missionary of the LMS to Madagascar from 1862 to 1880; stationed at Antananarivo. In 1863 he took charge of the native church at Ambohipotsy, in the capital, and of the connected country churches. In November, 1868, the Memorial Church at Ambohipotsy was opened, of which he took charge, and besides his other duties was occupied in a revision of the Malagasy version of the Bible and other literary work in the Malagasy language. The theological seminary for native ministers was founded by Mr. Toy in 1869, with the efficient aid of Mr. G. Cousins. His health failing, he went to England in 1870. Returning in 1873, he resumed his work in the theological institution, and in addition assisted in the revision of the Malagasy Bible. In 1877 the church at Faravohitra and its surrounding districts was added to his college work. In 1879, his health having seriously failed, he again sailed for England, and died on the voyage, April 19.

TOYOHASHI: A town on the main island, Japan, situated on a bay of the S. coast and on the railroad between Nagoya and Shizuoka. Station of the CMS (1896), with (1903) 1 missionary and his wife, 1 woman missionary, 2 native workers, and 38 professed Christians, of whom 14 are communicants. Also station of the ME, with (1903) 1 native worker.

TOZER, William George: Universities' Mission; Bishop of Central Africa. Born in Devonshire, 1829. Died, 1899. He was consecrated on February 2, 1863, in Westminster Abbey, and in the summer of that year he arrived in the Shiré district. Zanzibar was selected as the most favorable point from which to carry the Gospel to the tribes of Central Africa.

All the principal towns of the East African coast are situated on islands; and Bishop Tozer appreciated the fact that Zanzibar, the chief commercial center of East and Central Africa, would afford special advantages for a settlement of European missionaries. He arrived here in August, 1864, and from the beginning of his work he foresaw the necessity of training up a native ministry in Central Africa, where, in less than forty years, the mission lost six bishops, twenty-seven members of the clergy and forty-six lay workers. To this work he addressed his best energies. Having somewhat organized the work on the island, Bishop Tozer turned his attention to the mainland, and there he had the privilege of first planting the Church. The country of Usambara, north of Zanzibar, with its ports of Pangani and Tanga, seemed to be the most accessible and favorable district, and here he established flourishing mission stations. The success of the mission at Zanzibar was interrupted in 1868 by cholera, and in 1872 a terrible hurricane "left everything a complete wreck." All the mission party were safe, and, led by the Bishop, order was soon restored, and the mission work resumed. For six years Bishop Tozer, enfeebled in health, made his home in London; in 1879 he attempted episcopal work in the dioceses of Jamaica and Honduras, and in 1888 he became vicar of South Ferriby, with the hope of regaining his health. The end came after two strokes of paralysis.

TRACY, William: Born at Norwich, Conn.,

June 2, 1807; studied at Williams College and at Princeton Theological Seminary; was ordained April 12, 1836; sailed November 23, 1836, for India as a missionary of the ABCFM, and, after spending a few months at Madras, reached Madura October 9, 1837. He visited the United States in 1851 and 1867. At Tirumangalam he opened a boarding school for boys. From that day he was largely engaged with the educational work of the district. By 1842 the boarding school had grown to a high-grade seminary. In 1845 it was removed to Pasumalai, where twenty-two years of Mr. Tracy's life were spent. More than 250 young men passed through the course of study. Few classes left him in which nearly all were not Christians, a large number of them engaging in evangelistic work and others occupying honorable posts in government service. Mr. Tracy was an efficient member of the Revision Committee of the Tamil Bible. He died at Tirupuvanam, South India, November 28, 1877, aged seventy, and in the forty-first year of his missionary service.

TRAINING SCHOOLS for Missionaries: Every young man and woman who is physically fit to be sent to the mission field has, upon a life insurance basis, reason to expect at least twenty-five years of active service. How to make every one of these years most effective is the problem both for the individual and the society which commissions him. His preparatory work must be done partly at home and partly after his arrival at his station. The whole of his equipment cannot be secured before reaching the field. But it is surely advisable to get in the homeland as thorough a training as possible in those subjects and methods which are essential to the best work.

Adequate Preparation is a needed watchword in the missionary movement. It is easily conceivable that a year of special training may double the missionary's power in every one of those twenty-five or more years of service; two years may quadruple it. To neglect or belittle this truth is foolish and hurtful. That it has been too lightly esteemed in the past is admitted by those most skilled in the science of missions and most experienced in their operation. Dr. Gustav Warneck said in the Ecumenical Conference of 1900: "What we need beside expert mission directors is, above all, missionaries really capable for their great work. * * * * The petition that the Lord of the harvest should send forth laborers into His harvest has also reference to their quality."

If appeal be made to the missionaries now in action, most of them will complain that however much general education they may have received, they lacked training to meet most effectively the conditions existing in their fields of labor.

In order to raise materially the standard of missionary qualifications two things are essential: *stimulus* and *machinery*. The former must be furnished mainly by the societies which decide upon the qualifications of candidates. These may, at will, raise the standard of requirements for obtaining commissions. The latter must consist of schools managed and equipped according to the best science and strength of the Christian Church.

Missionary training schools are numerous. A comprehensive list of them may be found in Dr. Dennis' *Centennial Statistics*. Most of these are of great service to the men and women who seek their aid to qualify for mission work, city, home or foreign. Do these meet the requirements of the time and the cause? No invidious distinctions shall here be drawn nor dogmatic opinion expressed. A noted secretary of one of the largest American Foreign Mission Boards writes: "The ideal school that we have in our minds has not as yet been realized. * * * We feel the need of some institution that will train our young women and laymen satisfactorily and also give some opportunities for finishing off young men from the theological schools."

An attempt is here made to indicate what "the ideal school" must give to those purposing to join the missionary ranks. All will agree with Dr. Warneck when he says: "Spiritual equipment is, of course, the chief consideration." This is a matter that cannot readily be included in a scheme of subjects. In one sense too much emphasis cannot be placed upon the preparation of heart; yet this further statement from the same eminent authority is no less weighty: "The experience of more than a hundred years should prevent us from falling into the mistake of thinking that this alone suffices without a thorough training."

Quality of the Preparation: The special training needed by missionaries is indicated by the abnormal conditions of the masses of the people to whom they are sent. Asia and Africa are the great missionary continents; most of the world's people inhabit them. In what respects are they abnormal, differing from the masses of Christendom? (1) They are *religiously* misguided, debased and lost, *i. e.*, they cannot find the way to their Father and their Home. They cannot find righteousness. (2) They are *socially* dwarfed and demoralized. Tested by their treatment of the weak—women, children, the aged, the sick—by their domestic, civic and international relations, they are in or near barbarism. (3) They are *educationally* illiterate. Leaving out Japan, probably not five per cent. of them can read books. Their science is false, their minds warped. (4) *Medically* they are ignorant. Their treatment of diseases and wounds is distressingly inadequate. (5) *Hygienically* they are unsanitary. Cholera, plague and smallpox run along avenues of uncleanly living. (6) *Industrially* and *economically* they are backward. Famine is a common condition. Poverty is the general state, because land is overpopulated; improved methods and machinery are lacking and thrift is very feebly possessed. The true missionary cannot help striving to cure all of these abnormal conditions. In his preparation he should take them definitely into account and fit himself as far as possible to handle them. These conditions indicate generally the following special requirements for the missionary candidate:

The candidate should have special training in:

1. *His own religion* and *non-Christian religions*. (1) Comprehensive Bible study, including introduction. (2) The Christian system of theology and evidences. (3) History and comparison of religions. Is there any sufficient reason why all women, male physicians and other lay workers should not, as well as ordained men, obtain a good knowledge of these subjects?

2. *Elementary and practical Sociology:* A study of the origin and growth of society with its various institutions; of the perversions of marriage, family life, social intercourse, labor conditions, government, etc., and of the remedies for these ills.

3. *History of Missions* and the principles on which they are conducted.

4. *Psychology and Pedagogy:* Most missionaries teach or supervise schools. Many must train native teachers. There are 100,000 pupils in mission boarding and training schools, most of whom are preparing to be teachers. They should have the best training. All who deal with the abnormally ignorant classes have special need of acquaintance with the laws of mind and of teaching. *Kindergarten* training is most helpful. Rev. J. L. Barton, D.D., Secretary ABCFM, has said: "I heartily believe in a pedagogical course for the most of our missionaries."

5. *Elementary medicine, surgery and nursing:* There are special schools for regular physicians and nurses. The Missionary Training School should give to all other students such training as will fit them to render intelligent "first aid" to the sick or injured.

6. *Principles of Hygiene*, or Health Lectures.

7. *Technical crafts and business methods:* Women should learn domestic economy; men should have training in carpentry, photography and stereopticon management, agriculture or at least gardening, book manufacture, and even in blacksmithing. Both men and women should have drill in bookkeeping and in modern methods of filing correspondence and other documents.

8. *Music.*

9. *Language of the people to be reached:* It is not practicable to teach many oriental vernaculars in the home schools. But such comprehensive languages as Arabic, Chinese, Hindustani and Turkish might be given. As showing that such a scheme is not impracticable two actual courses are here given, one for men, the other for women.

I. Church Missionary Training College at Islington. In addition to regular instruction, university and theological, a course is given in (1) Elementary Medicine and Surgery; (2) Principles and Practise of Teaching; (3) Vocal Music; (4) Carpentering, Bookmaking, Printing, Tinsmithing and Blacksmithing; (5) Religious Systems of the pagan world;

II. The Training Institute for Women of the UFS, Edinburgh, gives instruction in (1) The Study of Scripture; (2) Christian Doctrine; (3) Introduction to the Bible; (4) The Hindustani Language; (5) Theory of Education, Kindergarten Principles, Nature Studies, Class Teaching and School Visiting; (6) Voice Culture and Singing; (7) Account Keeping; (8) Drill Exercises; (9) Nursing; (10) Care of Health; (11) History of Missions; (12) Non-Christian Religions; (13) Sociology, from the missionary standpoint; (14) Evangelistic Theology.

"Missionaries must be weighed, not merely counted," says Dr. Warneck. "Thorough training" is his prescription for their need. The vital question presses: have the 17,000 missionaries in the foreign mission service the weight obtainable through a practicable preparation? The ordained men number more than 6,000. Has the theological school given a training specific enough for their needs? The physicians, men and women, are more than 700. Have they been fitted most effectively to minister to the darkened spirits in the sick bodies? Unordained men, not physicians, to the number of about 3,500 are in the ranks; unmarried women, an equal number; married women, more than 4,000. How many of these are lamenting the lack of "thorough training?" The best preparation is none too good for the missionary; it will not be wasted upon the Master's work for the heathen.

TRANSVAAL COLONY: A colony of Great Britain in S. Africa, conquered from the Boers, who governed it as the South African Republic prior to 1900. At the date of annexation the area was 119,139 square miles, but in 1903 about 7,000 square miles, constituting the provinces of Vryheid and Utrecht and a part of the Wakkerstroom district, were annexed to Natal. The State Almanack of the Transvaal for 1898 gives the population at 1,094,156, of which 245,397 are returned as whites. The population has undoubtedy decreased in consequence of the war.

The colony lies between Matabililand on the north and Natal and the Orange River Colony on the south, and extends east and west from Portuguese East Africa to Bechuanaland. It lies about 50 miles from the ocean at Delagoa Bay, and has a mean altitude of over 3,000 feet. The upland region drained by the Vaal River (Hooge Veld), from 4,000 to 7,000 feet high, includes most of the richest mineral districts, and has a healthful climate. The eastern terrace lands (Banken Veld) include Swaziland and the Upper Maputa Valley. These lands are lowlying, some being not more than 2,000 feet high. Bosch Veld, the inner plateau, 3,000 to 4,000 feet high, is largely steppe land, and suitable for grazing. On the whole, the climate is invigorating. Along the river valleys and in the low-lying districts fever is endemic. The rainfall is unequally distributed. The land is fertile. The settlers have chiefly busied themselves with stock raising, tho the tsetse fly proves very destructive in the river tracts and terrace lands. A tsetse belt 40 miles wide along the Limpopo bars the progress of settlement in that direction.

The missionary societies operating in the Transvaal are the Berlin Mission Society, the Mission Romande (French Switzerland), the Hermannsburg Missionary Society, the WMS, the SPG, the African Methodist Episcopal Church, the National Baptist Convention, the South African Baptist Society, and the ABCFM. These societies occupy 35 stations, of which 24 are stations of the Berlin Society. The aggregate working force is 611 missionaries and native workers, men and women, with 61 schools of various grades and about 5,000 communicants.

Bryce (J.), *Impressions of South Africa*, 3d ed., London, 1899; Cloete (H.), *History of the Great Boer Trek*, London, 1899; Colquhon (A. R.), *The Renaissance of South Africa*, London, 1900; Amery (L. S.), *"The Times" History of the War in South Africa*, London, 1903.

TRANQUEBAR: A town in Madras, India, on the shore of the Bay of Bengal, about 150 miles south of Madras. It is situated in the delta of the Caveri River, 22 miles N. of Negapatam. The town, with a small area of country, was obtained by the Danish East India Company in 1616, and held by the Danes until 1845 (with the exception of a few years), when, with Serampur in Bengal, it was sold by them to the English. Under Danish rule it was a place of some political and commercial importance, which in recent years, by the diversion of business to other centers, it has almost wholly lost. The population is about 5,000, chiefly Hindus. The great interest which Tranquebar possesses for us consists in the fact that it is the earliest Protestant Missionary station in India. Here Bartholomew **Ziegenbalg** and Henry Plutschau, the pioneers of the great army of Protestant evangelists, settled in 1706. They labored under the greatest difficulties, and yet within three and a half years a Christian community had been gathered, numbering 160 persons, which rapidly grew. The publication of books was begun at once. Ziegenbalg completed the translation of the New Testament in 1711, and when he died in 1719 he left behind him a translation of the Old Testament as far as the Book of Ruth. A church was built by his efforts, which is no longer in existence, its site having been undermined by the sea. The mission was manned for many years by men of superior attainments and character, among whom was the great **Schwartz**, and exerted a profound influence in South India. For a long time it received pecuniary aid from England through the Society for Propagating Christian Knowledge. In 1847 the mission passed into the hands of the Leipzig Evangelical Lutheran Mission. Station of the Leipzig Missionary Society (1841), with (1903) 6 missionaries, 4 of them with their wives; 28 native workers, 4 outstations, 4 places of worship, 4 day schools, 1 boarding school, 1 printing house, and 759 professed Christians, of whom 411 are communicants. The name is also written Trankebar.

TRAVANCORE: A native state in India, occupying the extreme southwestern portion of the peninsula. Its limits of north latitude are 8° 4' and 10° 22', and of east longitude 76° 12' and 77° 38'. Its boundaries are, on the north, the native state of Cochin; on the east, the British districts of Madura and Tinnevelli, belonging to the Madras presidency, from which districts it is separated by a mountain range; on the south and west, the Indian Ocean. The length of Travancore from north to south is 174 miles, and its greatest breadth 75. It embraces an area of 6,730 square miles, with a population of 2,952,157 in 1901; 73 per cent. were Hindus, about 21 per cent. Christians, and a trifle over 6 per cent. were Mohammedans. The Christian population includes a large number of adherents of the old Syrian Church of Malabar—more than half of the whole; nearly a third are Romanists and the remainder Protestants. As to language, Malayalim—a Dravidian tongue allied to Tamil—is used by about four-fifths of the people, and Tamil by the rest. The chief town and capital is Trivandrum, with a population of 41,173. Travancore has been ruled from time immemorial by Hindu princes of approved orthodoxy. It has never—like all the rest of India—come at any time under the sway of the Mohammedans. In the latter part of the 18th century it was attacked by Tippu, Sultan of Mysore, but, with the aid of the English, it successfully resisted him. Treaties, made early in the 19th century with the English, have firmly cemented this old connection and made English influence powerful within its borders, tho there was armed opposition in 1809. An English resident is maintained at the court of the Maharajah of Travancore, and an annual tribute is paid to the "paramount power." The Government of Travancore, tho Hindu, is intelligent, efficient, and progressive. Its native rulers have studied to good advantage the example set them by the English rulers of adjacent regions. There is a good system of education in vogue, as a result of which the people of Travancore show about as high an average of intelligence and as large a proportion of persons able to read and write as many British provinces in India. The people are chiefly agricultural; rice, the coconut palm, and pepper are the principal productions, and the exports are largely derived from the coconut tree, tho pepper, ginger, cardamom, timber, and some other articles are included among them.

The forms of Hindu worship usual throughout India are practised in Travancore, mingled, however, to a greater or less extent, with the rites of demon-worship, which prevail extensively in South India and Ceylon, especially among the aboriginal tribes. Missionaries in Travancore have had to encounter among their converts far more of the degrading power of these old habits and associations, rooted in this ancestral demonolatry, than their fellow-laborers among Hindus in other regions.

Mission work was commenced in this state in 1816 by the CMS. The plan was to work in alliance with the old Syrian Church of Malabar, but the plan failed, and twenty-five years later the Society turned its attention to the people at large, with great success.

The London Missionary Society's operations in Travancore began in 1806. Rev. Mr. Ringeltaube, a German, joined one of the first companies which this Society sent to India. He labored in Travancore until 1816, when a Christian community of 900 persons had been formed. Mr. Ringeltaube's health then broke down and he left the country.

In 1818 the Society sent out other missionaries. Col. Munro was then resident, and continued the aid of the mission which his predecessor had begun; without such aid from the representative of British power it is hard to see how the mission could have started in the face of Hindu opposition on the part of the Brahmans and the Hindu Government. The converts rapidly increased—largely from among the low-caste Shanars. From 1827 to 1830 violent persecution was experienced, and the low-caste people in Travancore have never, unless perhaps recently, been admitted to the privileges of the public schools maintained by the government. The progress of the mission in late years has been rapid and its usefulness great. In 1838 it was allowed to begin a station at Trivandrum, the capital; and since 1844 it has drawn many converts from the higher castes. Rev. Samuel Mateer, one of its most distinguished members, published, in 1871, a full account of the country and people of Travancore, with historical sketches of missionary work within its borders, under the title "The Land of Charity."

TREBIZOND: Seaport and capital of a province in Asiatic Turkey, situated on the Black Sea. By reason of its location, it has been an important center for the trade from Persia and Central Asia to Europe. The climate is temperate, and its location is picturesque. The city is divided into the old quarter, inhabited by Mohammedans; the more modern, or Christian, quarter; and the commercial quarter. Behind the city is the rocky height with flattened top which gave the place its ancient name of Trapezus. At this point Xenophon reached the Black Sea on his retreat with the famous ten thousand. From 1203 until nearly the end of the 15th century Trebizond was an independent and autonomous power. Population said to be about 35,000, of whom 18,000 are Mohammedans and 15,200 Christians. Station of the ABCFM (1835), with (1903) 11 native workers, 1 day school, and 148 professed Christians.

TRICHINOPOLI: A town or municipality in Madras, India, on the Caveri River, 56 miles from the sea, 186 miles southwest of Madras City. It is a place of much historic interest, having been the scene of many sieges. Besides the fort and cantonment it consists of seventeen separate villages. Inside of the fort is the holy rock of Trichinopoli, which rises 273 feet above the street at its foot and which has on its summit a small temple. Numbers of pilgrims always attend the annual festival. It is well known for its cigars, and for its peculiar and beautiful gold jewelry. Heber, the Protestant Bishop of Calcutta, is buried here (1826), and the place is the scene of great missionary activity. Population (1901), 104,721, of whom about 72,000 are Hindus, 17,000 Christians and 10,000 Muslims.

Station of the SPG (1825), with (1903) 1 missionary, 1 woman missionary, 28 native workers, 5 places of worship, 7 day schools, and 301 professed Christians. Also station of the Leipzig Missionary Society (1864), with (1903) 1 missionary and his wife, 14 native workers, 6 outstations, 7 places of worship, 6 day schools, 2 boarding schools, and 745 professed Christians. Station also of the WMS, with (1903) 1 missionary, 1 woman missionary, 52 native workers, 5 outstations, 1 place of worship, 15 Sunday schools, 16 day schools, and 267 professed Christians, of whom 168 are communicants. Germans write the name Tritschinopoli.

TRICHUR: A town in Cochin, India, situated at the head of a chain of canals and inland waterways which give safe navigation for small boats as far as Trivandrum. It is a great stronghold of Brahmanism. Station of the CEZ (1881), with (1903) 2 women missionaries, 35 native workers, 7 day schools, and 1 female helpers' training class. Also station of the CMS (1842), with 1 missionary and his wife, 47 native workers, 8 day schools, and 3 boarding schools.

TRINIDAD: An island belonging to Great Britain in the West Indies, at the mouth of the Gulf of Paria, off the northeast coast of Venezuela, north of the mouth of the Orinoco. Area, 1,754 square miles. Population, 255,148 (1901). Temperature, 70° to 86° Fahrenheit. Soil, fertile. Capital, Port-of-Spain. Mission field of the UFS, the PCC, the SDA, and the Moravian Missions, with stations at Port-of-Spain, Arouca, and San Fernando—3 churches, 379 church-members, 600 scholars. There are 191 schools, 16,000 pupils, under the Government grant of £16,783. The Queen's Royal College has 65 students. The Roman Catholics have also a college with 220 students.

TRINITARIAN BIBLE SOCIETY: Headquarters, 7 St. Paul's Churchyard, London, E. C., England. The Trinitarian Bible Society was organized in 1831, for the circulation of the Word of God, translated from the originals only, to the exclusion of all versions from the Vulgate. No person is admitted to the management of the Society who denies the doctrines of the Trinity and the Atonement. The work of the Society is chiefly in those countries in which the Vulgate or Roman Catholic versions most abound. It has prepared a Spanish Bible in several editions, and a Portuguese Bible with references. The first translation of the Bible into the Breton language for the Breton Evangelical Mission was printed by the Society; also Salkinson's Hebrew translation of the New Testament, of which 100,000 copies have already (within three years) been distributed among Jews in all countries.

The Society avoids colportage as far as possible, its work of distribution being mainly carried on by agents of other societies.

TRIPOLI: A province of the Turkish Empire in North Africa. It is bounded on the northwest by Tunis, on the east by the Nubian Desert, which separates it from Egypt, and it includes within its southern border the oases of Kufra, Fezzan, etc. It covers an area of about 400,000 square miles, and has a population variously estimated at from 800,000 to 1,300,000. The dervish order of the Senoussis, whose capital used to be Jarabub, in the Fared Ghah Oasis, in the Libyan Desert, is the dominant power in the whole country. It has 15 stations in Morocco, 25 in Algeria, 10 in Tunis, 66 in Tripoli, and 17 in Egypt. The Sultan of Wadai is one of the most fervent adherents of the sect. It does not confine itself to the white race; the blacks have also been drawn into its numerous schools, founded in the Sudan, which have extended their influence from Senegambia to Timbuktu, Lake Tchad, Bahr-el-Ghazel, and even to the country of the Danakils, the Gallas, and the Somalis.

Tripoli is naturally divided for administrative purposes into four provinces. The country is made up of vast sandy plains interrupted by rocky ranges, with a fertile strip adjacent to the sea, and here and there in the desert a depression, where the springs of water are sufficient for a few inhabitants and their groves of date palms. The principal products are corn, barley, olives, saffron, figs, and dates. The climate is variable, resembling that of southern Europe, and generally salubrious. The population consists of Arabs, Berbers, Negroes (brought from the interior as slaves), Turks, and Jewish and European (Maltese) traders. A few uninfluential Coptic groups are found. The North Africa Mission has 1 station in Tripoli.

TRIPOLI: A seaport town of Syria, situated 2 miles from Mina its seaport, on the Mediterranean, 40 miles N. N. E. of Beirut. It owes its name to its three separate sections distinguished in remote history. Many remains of ancient buildings are still found there. It was taken by the Crusaders in the 12th century, at which time its library was burned. It is one of the neatest towns of Syria, and is surrounded by many gardens and groves of orange and other fruit trees, but the ground in the neighborhood is marshy, and the climate is unhealthful at certain seasons. Population, 26,000, one-half Greek Catholics. Station of the PN (1848), with (1903) 3 missionaries and their wives, 2 women missionaries, 43 native workers, 18 outstations, 13 places of worship, 20 day schools, 2 boarding schools, 1 dispensary, 1 hospital, and 724 professed Christians.

TRIPOLI: Capital of the Turkish province of T. in Africa, called by Turks *Tarabulus-i-Gharb*. It is the starting point of caravans for the Sudan as far west as Timbuktu and a center of a flourishing slave-trade which is protected by Turkish officials. It is a picturesque town; population (estimated), 40,000. Station of the North Africa Mission (1889), with (1903) 2 missionaries with their wives, 2 women missionaries, and 1 dispensary.

TRIVANDRUM: A town and capital of Travancore, India, situated about 38 miles S. E. of Quilon. It is a stronghold of Brahmanist influence, which centers in the fort where the palaces of the reigning family are found, besides the chief pagoda and the residence of many high-caste people. The English resident and other foreigners live among gardens outside the fort. Population (1901), 57,882. Station of the LMS (1838), with (1903) 2 missionaries and their wives, 127 native workers, 64 outstations, 50 Sunday schools, 74 day schools, 2 boarding schools, 1 hostel, 1 dispensary, 1 lepers' asylum, and 14,751 professed Christians, of whom 1,975 are communicants. Also station of the CEZ (1862), with (1903) 2 women missionaries, 28 native workers, 1 dispensary, 1 hospital, and 1 boarding school, which is in an old palace in the fort, the gift of the Maharajah. Some write the name Trevandrum.

TROWBRIDGE, Tillman Conklin: Born in Michigan, January 28, 1831. Died at Marash, Turkey, July 20, 1888. Studied at Romeo, Mich.; the University of Michigan, and Union Theological Seminary. Appointed missionary of the ABCFM in 1856, and sailed for Constantinople. After learning the language he engaged in itinerating among the Armenians of Eastern Turkey. Returning to Constantinople in 1861, he married a daughter of Dr. Elias Riggs. He had charge of the city work of Constantinople for six years, and in 1868 was transferred to Marash to assist in the instruction of the Theological Seminary. In 1872 he visited England and America to raise funds for the Central Turkey College at Aintab. In 1876 he was appointed president of the college. From that time to his death, with the exception of a brief visit to England, he devoted himself with energy to promoting its interests, as well as to the material, moral, and religious improvement of the people of Turkey. His well-known good judgment, his quick and contagious sympathy, his unfailing cheerfulness and optimism, his ready pen and persuasive tongue, united to give him a wide influence, and the Central Turkey College owes to his energetic labor a large share of its present position and power.

TSAKOMA: A settlement in the Transvaal, South Africa, situated in Zoutpansberg District, about 100 miles N. E. of Pietersburg. Station of the Berlin Missionary Society (1874), with (1903) 2 missionaries, 9 native workers, 3 outstations, 1 day school, and 206 professed Christians, of whom 89 are communicants. Some write the name Tschakoma.

TSAO-SHIH: A town of Hu-pei, China, situated about 50 miles W. of Han-kau on a little lake connected with Han River. Station of the LMS (1880), with (1903) 2 missionaries, 1 of them with his wife, and 1 dispensary. Church statistics are included with Han-kau.

TSCHAKOMA. See TSAKOMA.

TSCHI-CHIN: A town in Kwang-tung, China, situated about 130 miles N. by E. of Canton. Station of the Berlin Missionary Society (1898), with (1903) 1 missionary, 14 native workers, 11 outstations, 1 day school, and 803 professed Christians, of whom 359 are communicants.

TSCHOMBALA. See CHOMBALA.

TSCHONGHANGKANG. See TSONG-HANG-KUNG.

TSCHONGSTSHUN. See TSONG-SHUN.

TSCHOU-TONG-AU: A town in Kwang-tung, China, situated about 80 miles E. by N. of Canton. Station of the Berlin Missionary Society (1891), with (1903) 2 missionaries, 18 native workers, 8 outstations, 1 day school, and 352 professed Christians, of whom 356 are communicants.

TSHABO. See BERLIN, CAPE COLONY.

TSIAFAHY: A town and district of Madagascar, situated in the Imerina province about 15 miles S. of Antananarivo. Station of the Paris Evangelical Mission Society (1897), with (1903) 1 missionary and his wife, 113 native workers, 4 Sunday schools, 55 day schools, 2 boarding schools, and 900 professed Christians.

TSI-HO: A town in the province of Hu-pei, China. Station of the Hauges Synod's China Mission (1900), with (1903) 1 missionary and his wife, 1 place of worship, 2 day schools. Some write the name Tsze-ho.

TSI-NAN-FU: A town in Shan-tung, China, situated 175 miles S. of Tien-tsin. It is walled. Its trade is in silks and in imitation precious stones. Temperate, healthful. Population, 150,000, Mongolian Chinese chiefly. Station of the PN (1872), with 4 missionaries, three of them with their wives; 3 women missionaries, 1 native worker, 2 outstations, 2 places of worship, 12 day schools, 2 boarding schools, 2 hospitals, and 573 professed Christians. Some write the name Chinanfu.

TSIN-CHAU: A prefectural city in the province of Kan-su, China, situated 62 miles S. E. of Kung-chung-fu. Station of the CIM (1878), with (1903) 1 missionary and his wife, 2 women missionaries, 4 native workers, 1 place of worship, 2 day schools, 1 dispensary, and 51 professed Christians.

TSING-CHAU-FU: Town in the province of Shantung, China, 160 miles W. S. W. of Chi-fu. It was formerly the capital of the province, and has still a large silk industry. Station of the BMS (1877), with 7 missionaries and their wives, 82 native workers, 98 outstations, 1 dispensary, 1 hospital, 24 day schools, 2 boarding schools, and 1,618 professed Christians. Also station of the BZM (1893), with (1903) 4 women missionaries, 1 boarding school, and 15 day schools. Some write the name Ching-chow.

TSING-KIANG-PU: A town in Kiang-su, China, situated on the Grand Canal about 10 miles N. W. of Hwei-ngan-fu. Station of the CIM (1869), with (1903) 2 women missionaries, 5 native workers, 1 place of worship, 1 Sunday school, 2 day schools, and 26 professed Christians. Also station of the PS (1887), with (1900) 3 missionaries and their wives.

TSING-NING-CHAU: A town in Kan-su, China, situated about 100 miles E. S. E. of Lanchau-fu. Station of the CIM (1897), with 1 missionary and 1 place of worship.

TSI-NING-CHAU: A town in Shantung, China, situated on the Grand Canal in the S. part of the province, 150 miles S.W. of Tsi-nan-fu. Station of the Independent Baptist Movement Mission, with (1901) 2 missionaries and their wives. Also station of the PN (1892), with (1903) 3 missionaries, one of them with his wife; 21 native workers, 2 day schools, 1 dispensary,

1 hospital, and 159 professed Christians. Some write the name Chining Chow.

TSING-TAO: A town in Shan-tung, China, situated in the German district at the N. side of the entrance to Kiao-chau Bay. It is the terminus of the German Shan-tung Railway. Station of the General Evangelical Protestant Missionary Society (German) (1898), with (1903) 3 missionaries, 2 of them with their wives; 1 outstation, 10 native workers, 1 day school, 1 dispensary, 1 hospital, and 1 place of worship. Also station of the Berlin Missionary Society, with (1903) 2 missionaries, 22 native workers, 1 woman missionary, 2 outstations, and 233 professed Christians, of whom 186 are communicants. These statistics include Kiao-chau. Station also of the PN (1898), with (1903) 2 missionaries, 1 of them with his wife; 2 outstations, 2 places of worship, 17 day schools, and 100 professed Christians. Some write the name Tsingtau or Tsing Tau.

TSIN-YUN-HSIEN: A town in Che-kiang, China, situated 55 miles N. W. of Wen-chau. Station of the CIM (1898), with 1 missionary and his wife, 4 native workers, 1 outstation, 1 place of worship, 1 Sunday school, and 2 professed Christians.

TSIVORY: A town in Madagascar, situated in the S. part of the island, about 55 miles N. W. of Port Dauphin. Station of the Lutheran Free Church (U. S. 1901), with 1 missionary and his wife, 2 native workers, and 2 outstations. Some write the name Tsivoro.

TSOLO: A town in Cape Colony, South Africa, situated in Pondoland West, 50 miles N. W. of Port St. John's. Station of the Episcopal Church in Scotland (1865), with (1903) 6 missionaries, 2 missionary women, 46 native workers, 27 outstations, 4 places of worship, 23 day schools, 1 boarding school, and 1,673 professed Christians. Statistics are also included in the SPG. Some use the name St. Cuthbert's for this station.

TSOMO: A town in Cape Colony, South Africa, situated in the Transkei region, about 55 miles S. E. of Queenstown. Station of the Episcopal Church in Scotland (1899), with (1903) 1 missionary, 17 native workers, 17 outstations, 17 day schools, and 753 professed Christians. Statistics are included in the SPG also. Station also of the NBC, with (1900) 1 missionary, 1 woman missionary, 1 place of worship, 1 Sunday school, and 80 professed Christians. Also station of the South African Wesleyan Methodist Missions, with (1900) 1 missionary, 111 native workers, 16 outstations, 26 places of worship, 6 Sunday schools, 21 day schools, and 1,462 professed Christians.

TSONG-HANG-KUNG: A town in Kwangtung, China, situated about 50 miles S. E. of Canton. Station of the Basel Missionary Society (1883), with (1903) 2 missionaries, 1 of them with his wife; 9 native workers, 5 outstations, 3 day schools, and 388 professed Christians, of whom 262 are communicants. Some write the name Tschong-hang-kang.

TSONG-SHUN: A village in Kwang-tung, China, situated about 100 miles N.W. of Swatow. Station of the Basel Missionary Society (1864), with (1903) 2 missionaries, 1 of them with his wife; 16 native workers, 7 outstations, 8 day schools, and 676 professed Christians, of whom 380 are communicants. Some write the name Tschongtshun.

TSOU-PING-HSIEN: A town in Shan-tung, China, situated about 45 miles E. by N. of Tsinan-fu. Station of the BMS (1889), with (1903) 8 missionaries, 7 of them with their wives; 54 native workers, 208 outstations, 13 Sunday schools, 2 dispensaries, 1 hospital, and 2,117 professed Christians. Also station of the BZM (1894), with (1903) 2 women missionaries, 3 outstations, 3 day schools, and 4 native workers. Some write the name Chow Ping.

TSO-YUN-HSIEN: A town of Shan-si, China, situated 18 miles S. S. E. of So-ping-fu. Station of the CIM (1895), with (1903) 4 missionaries, 3 native workers, 1 place of worship, 1 day school, 1 Sunday school, and 14 professed Christians. Some write the name Tso-yuin.

TSU: A station in Japan, of the Cumberland Presbyterian Board, with (1903) 2 missionaries and their wives, 2 native workers, 3 outstations, 2 places of worship, 2 Sunday schools, 1 boarding school, 1 theological class, and 172 professed Christians. Also station of the PE, with (1901) 2 missionaries, 3 places of worship, 2 Sunday schools, and 22 professed Christians.

TSUEN-CHAU-FU: A town in Fo-kien, China, situated near the coast about 45 miles N. E. of Amoy. Station of the PCE (1866), with (1903) 10 missionaries and their wives, 2 dispensaries, 2 hospitals, and 1 medical class. Some write the name Chinchew.

TSUN-I-FU: A town of Kwei-chau, China, situated 85 miles N. by E. of Kwei-yang-fu. Station of the CIM (1902), with 2 missionaries, 1 of them with his wife, and 1 dispensary.

TUAMOTU ISLANDS: A cluster of small islands east of the Society Islands, Polynesia. They were acquired by France in 1880, together with the Gambier Islands, and form part of the French establishments in Oceania. The two groups have an area of 390 square miles and a population of 5,946. The people are many of them Roman Catholics, and there are a few Mormons at Anaa. The Paris Evangelical Society missionaries tour among the islands in their missionary cruiser, *The Southern Cross*, and they have stationed a preacher at Anaa.

TUBETUBE: An island of the D'Entrecastreaux group, about 50 miles off the S. E. point of New Guinea. Station of the Australian Wesleyan Methodist Missionary Society, with (1901) 1 missionary and his wife, 6 native workers, 1 outstation, 6 places of worship, 6 day schools, 5 Sunday schools, and 55 professed Christians.

TUCAMAN: A town in the Argentine Republic, South America, situated about 700 miles N.W. of Buenos Aires. Population 50,000. Station of the PB, with 2 missionaries, 1 of them with his wife. Some write the name Tucuman.

TUCKER, Miss Charlotte Maria: Born in 1821. Died at Amritsar, India, December 2, 1893. Miss Tucker (better known as A. L. O. E.) was famous as a writer of captivating stories before 1875, when, at the age of fifty-four, and at her own expense, she went to India as a missionary. She studied Urdu before going out to India, and almost from the first day of her arrival there she turned her thoughts to writing parables and stories for the natives; with wonderful ease adopting their modes of thought and style of language, and entering into their prejudices and difficulties. Thousands of her tracts and books were soon circulating in many parts of India. At the special request of the Christian Vernacular Education Society for India, she wrote a volume, explanatory of our Lord's Parables, entitled "Pearls of Wisdom," and it was published also in separate tracts, to enable the poorest to purchase it. She first entered upon her missionary work at Amritsar, but soon went to Batala, where she labored among the large Mohammedan population. She did much evangelistic work from house to house. She would find her way to a zenana, and, on gaining admittance, would seat herself on the floor with true Oriental ease and grace, the native occupants of the dwelling gathering round, curious and expectant; and then she would fix their attention by a pleasing story or beautiful pictures, until she drove home some helpful Gospel truth. She took a special interest in the High School for Boys, and for some years she lived in the school-building, which was formerly the palace of Maharaja Sher Singh. She taught the boys the Bible, literature, and history; and from her own private resources she extended the influence of this and other institutions of learning. Miss Tucker showed active pity for the Mihtars (sweepers), who are the very lowest caste in society—the opposite end of the social scale to the Brahmans; and she made an effort to carry the Gospel to the thousands of convicts on the Andaman Islands, but the plan had to be abandoned, as the Government could not sanction religious proselytising among the political prisoners. One of the last projects in Batala which received Miss Tucker's sympathy and aid was the new CEZMS Dispensary. For eighteen years this consecrated woman, who resolved to spend the "sunset of her life" among the women of the Punjab, labored far from her earthly home until she entered her heavenly home.

TUCUMAN. See TUCAMAN.

TUH-SHAN. See TU-SHAN-CHAU.

TULBAGH: A town in Cape Colony, S. Africa, 75 miles northeast of Cape Town. Population, 660. Station of the Rhenish Mission Society, with (1903) 1 missionary and his wife, 12 native workers, 1 Sunday school, 2 day schools, and 881 professed Christians, of whom 350 are communicants.

TULLIAR: A town in Madagascar, situated on the W. coast, north of St. Augustin Bay. Station of the Norwegian Missionary Society (1874). Some write the name Tulear.

TUMKUR: A town in Mysore, India, situated 40 miles N. E. of Bangalore. Population, 11,170. Station of the WMS, with (1903) 1 missionary, 2 women missionaries, 98 native workers, 11 places of worship, 8 Sunday schools, 24 day schools, 1 boarding school, and 253 professed Christians, of whom 232 are communicants.

TUNAPUNA: A village in Trinidad, situated 10 miles E. of the Port of Spain in the plantation district where East Indian coolies are found in numbers. Station of the PCC (1881), with (1903) 1 missionary and his wife, 1 woman missionary, 11 native workers, 2 outstations, 16 day schools, 1 boarding school, and 150 professed Christians. Also station of the SPG, with (1903) 1 missionary, 2 native workers, 3 outstations,

and 3,500 professed Christians, of whom 657 are communicants.

TUNG AN. See TUNG-NGAN-HSIEN.

TUNG-CHAU: A city in Chi-li, China, at the head of navigation on the Peiho, 13 miles east of Peking. Population, 50,000. Station of the ABCFM (1867), with (1903) 7 missionaries, 6 of them with their wives; 2 women missionaries, 9 native workers, 2 places of worship, 4 day schools, 2 boarding schools, 1 theological class, 1 college, 1 dispensary, 1 hospital, and 213 professed Christians. Some write the name Tung-cho.

TUNG-CHAU-FU: A town of Shen-si, China, situated about 65 miles N. E. of Hsi-ngan-fu. Station of the CIM (1891), with (1903) 1 missionary and his wife, 4 women missionaries, 5 native workers, 1 outstation, 2 places of worship, 1 Sunday school, 1 boarding school, 1 dispensary, and 25 professed Christians.

TUNG-CHI-HSIEN: A town of Kan-su, China, situated in the E. part of the province, about 50 miles E. N. E. of Ping-liang-fu. Station of the CIM (1899), but there has been no resident missionary since the troubles of 1900. Some write the name T'ong-chi.

TUNG-CHO. See TUNG-CHAU.

TUNGKUN. See TUNG-KWAN-HSIEN.

TUNG-KWAN-HSIEN: A town in Kwang-tung, China, situated about 35 miles S. E. of Canton. Station of the Rhenish Mission Society, with 4 missionaries, 3 of them with their wives; 6 native workers, 3 day schools, and 314 professed Christians, of whom 250 are communicants. Some write the name Tungkun.

TUNG-LU: A town of Che-kiang, China, situated about 30 miles S. W. of Yen-chau-fu. Station of the CIM (1902), with 1 missionary.

TUNG-NGAN-HSIEN: A town in Chi-li, China, situated about 30 miles W. N. W. of Tien-tsin. Station of the LMS (1897), with (1901) 1 missionary and his wife, 12 native workers, 2 places of worship, 1 dispensary, and 180 professed Christians. Some write the name Tung An.

TUNG-NGAN-HSIEN: A town in Fo-kien, China, situated about 25 miles N. by E. of Amoy. It is a walled town, with a large population in its suburbs outside the walls. Station of the RCA (1895), with (1903) 1 woman missionary, 11 native workers, 9 outstations, 11 places of worship, 2 day schools, and 290 professed Christians. Some write the name Tong-An.

TUNI: A town in Madras, India, situated in the district of Vizagapatam, about 40 miles N. E. of Cocanada. Station of the BOQ (1878), with (1903) 1 missionary and his wife, 1 woman missionary, 22 native workers, 7 outstations, 3 places of worship, 16 Sunday schools, 7 day schools, 1 boarding school, and 183 professed Christians.

TUNIS: A protectorate of France in Africa, lying on the Mediterranean, which bounds it north and east, with Algeria on the west and Tripoli on the east. It has an area of about 51,000 square miles and a population of about 1,900,000, mostly Bedouin Arabs and Kabyles. The French population (1901) is 38,889, including soldiers and sailors of the ships and garrisons. There are about 60,000 Jews. The physical and climatic conditions are much the same as in Algeria. Protestant missions are carried on in

Tunis by the North African Mission and the London Society for Promoting Christianity among the Jews, with 4 stations.

TUNIS: Capital of the country of the same name in Africa, is situated on the western side of a very shallow lake which separates it from its port, Goletta. A deep-water canal 7 miles long runs through the lake, allowing sea-going vessels to come up to Tunis. The ancient city of Tunis contains several historically interesting buildings, as the Kasba, a castle formerly used as a prison for Christian captives and now occupied by the French garrison, and the palace of the Bey, etc. This part of the city is separated by the Bab el Bahr (sea gate) from the European quarter, known among foreigners as La Marine. Tunis is commonly called a healthful town, but typhoid fever and diphtheria are very common. Population, 145,000, of whom 45,000 are Jews, 11,000 French, and 8,000 Maltese and other foreigners. Station of the London Jews' Society (1833), with 1 missionary and his wife, 2 women missionaries, 8 native workers, 1 place of worship, 1 Sunday school, and 2 day schools. Also station of the NAM (1885), with (1903) 2 missionaries and their wives, 5 women missionaries, 1 native worker, 1 place of worship, 1 day school, 1 Sunday school, and 12 professed Christians.

TURA: A village among the Garo Hills, Assam, 73 miles S. E. of Kuch Behar. Climate hot and unhealthful. Altitude 1,300 feet. Station of the ABMU (1876), with (1903) 5 missionaries and their wives, 2 women missionaries, 125 native workers, 92 outstations, 93 places of worship, 63 Sunday schools, 87 day schools, 1 boarding school, 1 dispensary, 1 hospital, 1 printing house, and 5,545 professed Christians, of whom 3,835 are communicants.

TURKESTAN AND TARTARY: These are terms which have been loosely applied to all that part of Central Asia which lies east of the Caspian Sea, south of Siberia, west of Manchuria or China, and north of Tibet, India, Afghanistan, and Persia. The name Tartary is a barbarism which is gradually falling into disuse as the formerly unknown plateaus and steppes of Central Asia are being more thoroughly explored, but the term Turkestan can still be retained as applying to that part of Central Asia which includes three divisions: (1) West Turkestan, (2) East Turkestan, and (3) Jungaria.

West Turkestan includes in its territory the highlands of Thian Shan, the plains of the Balkash, and the lowlands between the Aral and the Caspian Seas. It comprises Russian Turkestan, the provinces of Samarcand, Fergana, Semirechensk, Syr-Daria, Khiva, Bokhara, and Kokhand; the Chinese oasis of Kulja, and some parts of Afghan Turkestan. It includes an area of about 1,600,000 square miles, with a population estimated at 8,500,000, of which 793,032 square miles are in the Russian provinces or dependencies, having a population of over 3,500,000. The physical features of this large area vary greatly—from mountain peaks of perpetual snow to deep gorges and valleys, with every variety of climate and vegetation. Prairies and lowlands alternate with deserts, over which the dry winds, at times scorching hot and then again icy cold, blow sand or snow, and blight all vegetation. The population of this territory is very mixed. Aryans and Mongols are both found, the former principally in the cities, while the latter are wandering tribes. To the Turanian group belong the Turcomans, Kirghiz, Uzbegs, and Sarts. The Mongolians include the Kalmucks and Torgoutes. To the Aryan race belong the Tajiks, who are Sunnite Mohammedans, Persians, British Indians, and Russians. The principal cities are Kokhand, Marghilan, Tashkend, Khojend, Bokhara, and Khiva. The two latter have each from 30,000 to 100,000 inhabitants.

East Turkestan includes that large depression in the plateau of Eastern Asia which lies between Western Turkestan and those parts of Asia which have received distinctive names, and whose boundaries have been defined. Its boundary on the northwest is the Thian Shan range; on the southwest and south the Kuenlun mountains; on the southeast to Lake Lob-nor, the Altyn-Dagh, and on the northeast the mountains which run east-northeast from the Thian Shan range. It includes a territory of about 465,000 square miles, with a population of 1,000,000, of which 431,800 square miles, with a population of 580,000, is part of the Chinese Empire. The climate is severe; there is no great fertility of the soil, and consequently the whole district is very sparsely populated. The few inhabitants are representatives of both the Aryan and Turanian groups of the human race. The Mongol element predominates toward the northeast. Turkish mixed with Chinese is the prevailing tongue. Yarkand and Kashgar, in Chinese Turkestan, are the chief towns, and here the Swedish Society (*Svenska Missionsförbundet*) has stations. Tho the first representatives of the Swedish Society came in 1891, work was not regularly organized until 1894. The Bible has been translated into the Kashgarian language, medical work has begun, and the good seed is bringing forth fruit.

Jungaria or Songaria lies to the north of East Turkestan, and is a deep valley leading from the lowlands to the central plateau. It includes 147,950 square miles, with a population of 600,000, and is a dependency of the Chinese Empire.

There are no missionary societies at work in West Turkestan. The only Protestant work that is carried on is that by the BFBS. The Scriptures in whole or in part have been translated into several local dialects of Turkish which are very nearly alike but have different names on the Bible Society lists.

TURKEY: The Turkish, or Ottoman, Empire covers extensive territories of Southeastern Europe, Western Asia, Northern Africa, and the islands of the Eastern Mediterranean and Ægean Seas. Certain of the provinces in Europe and Africa, however, are only nominally a part of the Empire, being either autonomous or under the general supervision of European governments.

Taking first the Empire in its fullest sense, we notice,

Turkey in Europe: This extends from the Adriatic Sea on the west, across the Balkan Peninsula, to the Black Sea on the east, and includes Albania, the three provinces corresponding in general with ancient Macedonia, Adrianople, and the Principality of Bulgaria, with Eastern Rumelia.

Turkey in Asia is bounded on the north by the Black Sea, on the east by Russia (Trans-Caucasia) and Persia, on the south by Arabia and the Gulf of Aden, and on the west by the Mediterranean and Ægean Seas and the straits of the Dardanelles and Bosphorus. Both eastern and southern boundaries are somewhat vague, the former because the two empires have not succeeded in drawing a satisfactory line through the mountains of Kurdistan, the latter because of the uncertain limits of the Sultan's authority in Arabia outside of the coast provinces of Hejaz and Yemen.

Turkish Possessions in Africa: These consist of Tripoli with the Fezzan, and Egypt, which is Turkish by virtue of paying an annual tribute to the Sultan.

Islands in the Eastern Mediterranean include the islands of the Archipelago, Crete and Cyprus. All the islands of the Archipelago, except Crete and Samos, are included in the tables among the Asiatic possessions. Samos is a tributary principality, with an area of 210 square miles. Cyprus, with 3,670 square miles, is under the British Government, which, however, pays an annual tribute to the Turkish Government. Crete, with an area of 3,326 square miles, is ruled by a prince under supervision of the European powers, altho still (1903) nominally a province of Turkey.

Tabulating the whole we have the following:—

IMMEDIATE POSSESSIONS OF THE EMPIRE:

	Square Miles.	
Europe,	63,850	
Asia,	729,170	
Africa,	398,873	
		1,191,893
TRIBUTARY STATES:		
Europe,	37,860	
Africa,	400,000	
Mediterranean,	3,880	
		441,740
Total,		1,633,633

It should be remembered that estimates as prepared by different authorities differ very widely, owing partly to the diverse views held in regard to the political relations of the various sections, and partly to the absence of absolutely accurate measurements.

Population: Following the same general divisions as above, we find the totals as follows:

IMMEDIATE POSSESSIONS OF THE EMPIRE:

Europe,	4,790,000	
Asia,	16,133,900	
Africa,	1,000,000	
		21,923,900
TRIBUTARY STATES:		
Europe,	3,154,375	
Africa,	6,817,265	
Mediterranean,	276,156	
		10,247,796
Total,		32,171,696

Here, too, mere estimates are possible. A census in the East is in a great degree an anomaly, and altho the Turkish Government has taken two, its efforts have not been crowned with the greatest success. The fact that in some provinces, especially in Asiatic Turkey, the males were reported as 20-50% in excess of the females, indicates the great difficulty of the census-taker. For a division of these totals among the different races and religions, see below.

Physical Characteristics: Albania, Arabia, Bulgaria, Egypt, and Syria are described under their several heads.

European Turkey is for the most part a mountainous region belonging to the same physical system as Albania. The province of Adrianople, however, includes the great plains extending from the Rhodope to Constantinople.

Asiatic Turkey is largely occupied by the western extremity of the vast belt of mountains and high plateaus which extends from east to west through the whole continent of Asia. South of this region lie the great plains of Mesopotamia with the highlands of Syria shutting them off from the Mediterranean. In the northern Asiatic provinces the country is mostly a high tableland, covered with ranges of mountains. The tableland is highest on its eastern and southern sides, diminishing in altitude as it approaches the Mediterranean on the west and the Black Sea on the north. Egypt is one unbroken plain, and in Tripoli the rocks and desert seem to vie with each other as to which shall possess the land.

Climate: The Turkish Empire has every variety of climate, from the severe cold of the Balkans and the highlands of Armenia to the almost equatorial heat of the Red Sea and Baghdad. In the greater portion, however, it is temperate, not varying very much from that of corresponding sections of the United States. In general, Mesopotamia and the Syrian coast may be called hot, and the sections bordering upon them are affected in a great degree by the winds that blow over their plains. Central Asia Minor is temperate, its great plains being warm in summer and cold in winter, but day and night generally equalizing the temperature. The same is true of European Turkey, where the coast regions about Salonica are the only parts that have a notably warm climate.

The climate is undoubtedly greatly affected by the almost entire absence of trees over the great plains and even most of the mountains. The soil having to a great degree been washed down into the plains and valleys, the hills and mountain sides are barren, and the reflection of the sun from them in summer is intense. Especially is this true in some places, as Aintab, Urfa, Mardin, and Erzerum, where the summers are very hot.

Soil and Productions: The Turkish Empire includes probably some of the most fertile land on the globe. From the plains of Bulgaria to the valleys of the Nile and the Tigris the soil is wonderfully rich. The people of a section of the great central tableland of Asia Minor near Cesarea have a proverb: "If the world is hungry, the Bozok region can satisfy it, but if the Bozok is hungry the world is not sufficient." The wheat of Bulgaria and Rumelia is well known in the markets of Europe, and America is finding rivals in Asia Minor and Mesopotamia, as improvements in means of communication give these regions an outlet. Mesopotamia is especially rich, and any one who goes down the Tigris by raft and watches the line that marks the depth of the rich loam in the river banks will not wonder that empires succeeded each other with such rapidity in that whole section, or that the mountaineers of Persia looked with such longing eyes on the fields of Assyria. Aside from wheat there is a large amount of barley raised, and in Eastern Turkey a good deal of millet. Near the coast in Northern Syria, and within Asia Minor, cotton is raised to some extent, and on the plains of Western Asia Minor there are large fields of poppies for the opium trade. The common vegetables are rice, cabbage, onion, turnip, and okra, but the potato is being widely introduced. Tobacco is cultivated everywhere, the best coming from Northern Syria, the eastern parts of the Black Sea coast and Macedonia.

Turkey is especially rich in fruits, many of which originate in that territory. Grapes, melons, figs, olives, peaches, pears, quinces, pomegranates, dates, etc., are of the finest.

In European Turkey and the western parts of Asiatic Turkey are large vineyards, and a considerable amount of wine is made. This is generally pure, and is very largely exported to Italy, France, and Austria, where it is fortified, and exported again under French and German names.

Olive groves are especially abundant along the shores of the Mediterranean, and the fig orchards of Smyrna are famous. Oranges abound in the islands of the Archipelago and on the coast of Syria. Dates are not found in any quantity north of Egypt.

The only forests in Turkey are on the Rhodope and Balkan mountains in Europe, the shores of the Black Sea, the Zagros mountains about Bitlis and Van, and a portion of the Taurus. In these forests there is still much fine timber—oak, walnut, and sycamore—but elsewhere almost the only trees, aside from the fruit trees, are the cypresses of the Muslim cemeteries, and the poplars and willows that line the streams and watercourses near cities and villages.

By far the greater part of Asiatic Turkey is pasture-land, and wherever one goes he sees immense flocks of sheep and goats.

The mineral wealth of Turkey is very great, but has never been developed, so that it remains still an unknown, scarcely even an estimated, quantity. Iron, copper, silver, baryta, coal, etc., are mined to a greater or less degree, but mostly in a crude, imperfect way. Foreign capital would gladly take up the business, but the hostility, not only of the government, but of the people, is an almost insurmountable obstacle.

Means of Communication: Previous to the Crimean war, almost the only roads in Turkey were bridle paths, trodden smooth by the caravans of centuries. In a few places remnants could be seen of old Roman causeways, but the huge blocks of stone and the intervening pitfalls were shunned by all, except as the mire by the side was so deep as to be really impassable. In a few instances the Sultans, both Seljuk and Ottoman, made efforts to repair these causeways, but they were seldom successful, and caravans were forced to find their own way over plains and mountain passes as best they might. Everything was carried on horses, mules, or camels, and such a thing as a cart or carriage was unknown. As the country, however, was opened up to foreign enterprise, one of the first things attempted was the building of roads over the great routes of travel. Of these there were five, four connecting the western coast with Baghdad, and one from Trebizond, on the Black Sea, to Persia. The course they took was 1. Constantinople, via Nicomedia, Angora, Sivas, Diarbekir, Mardin, and Mosul. 2. Samsoon (on the Black Sea) via Amasia, Sivas, etc. 3. Smyrna, via Konia, Cesarea, Diarbekir. 4. Alexandretta, via Aleppo, Urfa, Diarbekir. 5. Trebizond, via Erzerum and Van, to Khoi, and Tabriz. Along all of these lines work was commenced in sections, but the sections seldom connected, owing to the difficulty and expense of carrying the roads over the mountain passes, and the result was that the paths remained. Then a new element came in. After the overthrow of Schamyl (1859), the great Circassian leader, multitudes of Circassians found their way into Asia Minor, bringing with them the rough carts they had used in the Caucasus. These made roads for themselves, and gradually, as renewed pressure was brought to bear upon the Turkish Government, road building was recommenced, so that now there are fairly good carriage roads from Trebizond to Erzerum, and from Samsoon to Diarbekir and Mardin, with branches to all important cities.

The first railroad in Asiatic Turkey was from Smyrna to Aidin. That was followed by one from Smyrna to Manisa, and from Constantinople to Nicomedia, and one from Mersine to Adana. The railway from Constantinople to Nicomedia has been extended to Angora and Konia (Iconium), with branches connecting with the lines running out of Smyrna. It is shortly to be carried on toward the Euphrates valley and Baghdad. In European Turkey the first railroad connected the Danube with the Black Sea at Kustendji; that was followed by one between Varna and Rustchuk, connecting with one to Bucharest and Vienna; one from Constantinople to Adrianople and Philippopolis, now extended to Sofia, Pirot, Alexinatz, Belgrade, Pesth, and Vienna; and one from Salonica to Uscup, and so joining the last named line.

Postal and Telegraph Arrangements: These are entirely in the hands of the Turkish Government, so far as the interior is concerned, the mails being carried in wagons, under the escort of an armed guard. Both mail and telegraph are under a rigid censorship, which sometimes violates letters, and always refuses "code" or cipher telegrams.

The foreign postal service is a curious anomaly resulting from the peculiar treaty relations between Turkey and the various powers. So long as there was no regular Turkish postal service an independent foreign postal service was an absolute essential, and the English, French, Austrian, Russian, Italian, and Greek Governments established post-offices of their own in the various seaports, and sent their own bags of mail matter. As the international postal system came into vogue, each post-office took mail matter for every country in the Postal Union. By that time the Turkish Government also had organized a complete postal system, and, as it had been admitted to the Postal Union, it pressed its claim that the foreign post-offices should retire. This has not been found possible, owing to the Turkish claim of a right to read letters passing through the mails.

Social Conditions: To describe in detail the mode of life of the people of Turkey is scarcely within the province of this work. The city life approaching so nearly in its buildings, its customs, its dress, and food to that of Europe; the country life, with its adobe houses, sometimes with a single room, sometimes more pretentious with its upper chambers; the tent life of the Kurds,—have all been described over and over again. A few general statements will suffice here.

Except in the poorest parts of the Kurdish mountains and in some of the villages of northern Syria or Mesopotamia, the people live in comparative comfort. To be sure, what is ample for them seems to the foreigner a very meager supply, but it is still true as a rule that they are in comfort so far as the supply of bodily needs is concerned. Their food is simple, but it is wholesome, and there is ordinarily enough of it. It is rarely the case that they suffer from hunger, except as drought and poor transportation cause famine. It is very seldom that the traveler fails to find bread, rice, milk, and some meat in even the smallest hamlet or the poorest hut. The houses are rough, the furniture scanty, the bedding and clothing coarse, but they serve usually to keep the people warm. It is when sickness and old age bring weakness and distress that the discomforts principally appear. Taken as a class, the Turkish peasant, whether Muslim or Christian, probably fares as well as the peasant class of any non-Christian land; in some respects he is better off. There are few, if any, in Turkey, even in the great cities, as wretched as are the miners of Europe or many of the poor of London.

If we look now to the relations of the different classes, we find them exceedingly democratic. There is no hereditary aristocracy in Turkey. There is absolutely nothing to hinder a farm-hand or a pedler from becoming Grand Vizier, if he be a Muslim; or Patriarch, if he be Armenian or Greek; and should he thus rise he will never find his low birth a cause of shame or regret. The castes of India are unknown. In every part of the Empire there is the freest inter-communication between the different races, and between the different parts of the same race. Not that this inter-communication involves good feeling. The Turk despises the "dog of a Christian;" the Armenian hates the Greek; and the Jew, Nusairiyeh and Yezidi are the contempt of all. Intermarriage between Muslims and Christians is unknown, except as Christian girls are drawn into the harems of wealthy Turks. There is no social intercourse of the families of different races, yet business relations and social courtesies between the men are common, and in that one is in most cases just as good as another.

Races: The population of the Turkish Empire presents some very interesting features to the student and especially to the missionary. To trace back through the centuries the influences that have converged from all the surrounding countries, and have resulted in the races of to-day, would be beyond the limits of this article. We can only give the barest sketch of the peoples now before us.

In a general sense, the inhabitants of Turkey are either Mohammedan or Christian, and if we assume the population of the direct possessions of the empire to be about 22,000,000, we shall have about 16,000,000 Mohammedans and 6,000,000 Christians. Both Mohammedans and Christians, however, include widely different races. Greeks and Armenians are hardly more diverse than are Turks and Albanians; Jacobites and Bulgarians are as little alike as are Kurds and Kabyles. This great diversity gives rise to much of the misconception in regard to the country, its history, and its political relations. We note now these different races very briefly.

I. The Mohammedans comprise the Turks proper, or Ottomans or Osmanlis, as they cal themselves. The word Turk is a general term applied almost indiscriminately to the general Tatar races that from different sections of Central Asia, and at different periods, have poured in upon the richer countries of Asia Minor and southeastern Europe. They include the Ottomans, Seljuks, Turkomans, etc. We have to do now with that tribe called Ottomans or Osmanlis, from their first sovereign, Othman or Osman, whose tomb is one of the sacred places of the city of Broosa. As has been said, only estimates are possible, but if the number of Ottoman Turks be put at 9,000,000, it is probably not far from the truth. They are found chiefly in Asia Minor, comparatively few living in European Turkey, or in Kurdistan, Mesopotamia, or Syria. The so-called Turks of European Turkey are mostly Albanians or Slavs who have accepted Islam; those of Kurdistan are Kurds, or Christians forced to become Muslims in one of the massacre periods, and the same is true of "Turks" in Syria. This fact should be distinctly kept in mind in forming an estimate of the Ottoman Turk. "The unspeakable Turk" of the Batak massacres in Bulgaria was a Muslim Bulgarian (Pomak); of the Druze massacres of Syria, an Arab. The Ottoman peasant of Asia Minor is a man far different from the ordinary conception. As a rule quite peacefully inclined, a hard worker, a faithful servant, courteous and dignified in his bearing, rather proud of his assumed superiority to the "meannesses of his Christian fellows," there is still an inherent element of ferocity in his nature, and when religious fanaticism is roused, he is a most dreaded enemy. The Ottoman of the city is, however, quite a different man; with as much Christian as Tatar blood in his veins, influenced by the strife of Western with Eastern civilization, studiously polite, easily adapting himself to the circumstances of his associates, he develops a power of intrigue, a facility for deception, an unblushing delight in bribery that makes him the scorn of his sturdy compatriot of Anatolia. There are notable exceptions, but as a rule, and this is the testimony of those who have traveled most in the interior of Asiatic Turkey, the native unadulterated Ottoman Turk is a man with many noble characteristics, and presenting great possibilities for Christian influence. Of the other elements making up the Muslim population the most important races in Asia are the Arabs and Kurds, in Europe the Albanians. These races have been described under separate heads. As a rule they are hostile to the Turks, feeling that the latter are oppressors, and even their recognition of the Sultan or Caliph is weakened by race enmity and the sense of subjection. Next to them in importance are the Circassians, including the Circassians proper and the Abkhazes who have emigrated from the Caucasus to Asia Minor. They furnish a most turbulent element of the population, and by far the greater amount of the depredations committed in Asia Minor are by them. There are also large numbers of Turkomans (another Turkish race), chiefly found in northern Syria. The Druzes and **Nusairiyeh** of Syria and the **Yezidis** of Mesopotamia probably represent the small remnant of the ancient paganism of the Levant which has accepted the form, tho not the spirit, of Mohammedanism. The original races of Asia Minor are represented among the Mohammedans by a number of tribes, of somewhat uncertain extent and character, found chiefly in the mountains of the western part. Such are the Yuruks of Bithynia, and the Zeibeks of the region of Smyrna. The Kabyles of Tripoli in Africa, of the Berber race, are scarcely recognized as Turkish subjects.

II. The Christians include the Armenians, Greeks, Syrians, Jacobites, Copts, Bulgarians and Protestants. The Armenians are a race by themselves, as distinct to-day as at any time in their history. Formerly occupying the northeastern part of Asiatic Turkey, they have spread until they are found all over Asia Minor. The Greeks are found chiefly in Western Asia Minor and along the shores of the Black Sea. They, too, have kept their race distinction, and retain many of the characteristics of their ancestors who founded the Pontic and Doric colonies. Sharp, keen in enterprise and speculation, the commerce of Turkey is largely in their hands, while the traders and bankers are chiefly Armenians. The Greeks of the interior are of a higher grade of character than those at the seaboard. The term Jacobite is distinctive of the remnants of the Monophysite sects found in northern Syria about Urfa (Edessa) and through Mesopotamia. The term Syrian is often a very indefinite one, applied generally to all the Christians of Syria and Mesopotamia. Specifically it refers to those churches in communion with the Roman Catholic Church, such as the Maronites, the United Greeks of Syria, and sometimes the Chaldeans, who are Jacobites that have left their old communion for the Romish Church. The term Syrian is also applied, tho incorrectly, to the Assyrians or Nestorians who are found in the mountains of Kurdistan. The Copts are found only in Egypt. The Bulgarians are a Slavic people inhabiting European Turkey. They belong to the Orthodox or Greek Church, but are independent of the Patriarch. Of the Christian peoples of Turkey the only ones whose race distinctions have been preserved are the Armenians, Greeks, and Bulgarians. The rest are not races, properly speaking, but religio-political divisions of the descendants of those of the original inhabitants who accepted Christianity under the rule of the Byzantine Empire. The religions of the Turkish Empire have been specially noticed under the articles **Armenian Church, Greek Church, Maronites, Mohammedanism, Nusairiyeh, Yezidis.** It remains here to add a few words as to the political relations of the Greek, Roman Catholic, and Protestant Churches.

The Greek, or "Orthodox," Church is the direct descendant of the Byzantine Church. In general doctrine, as found in the creeds and confessions, it is in sympathy with the Protestant Church, and only separated from the Armenian by a distinction so shadowy that it is claimed by some Armenians that the theological difference was a pretext, rather than an occasion, for the separation, the real reason lying in the effort of the Byzantine church to compel the Armenians to use the Greek liturgy. However that may be, it is certain that the age of theological controversy between the different Oriental churches has passed. The question now is not of "one Nature or two," "one Will or two," but of nationality. Under the rule of the Muslim Caliph every Christian sect has become a nationality, and every apostate is also a traitor. The position of the Greek Church in Turkey is thus primarily political. In its religious aspect it is practically on a par with its fellows, and a stranger could hardly tell the difference between the services of any two sects.

Ecclesiastically, the Patriarch of Constantinople is the head of the Church in all its different branches, but the Holy Synods of Russia, Greece, and Servia practically ignore him, while the Exarch of Bulgaria is ignored by him. In fact, the Greek Church of to-day is split up into fragments, each fragment claiming absolute independence, and each characterized by the same formalism and absence of spiritual life.

The Roman Catholics of Turkey, aside from the Maronites, include sections of the Armenians, Greeks (Uniats), and Syrians or Chaldeans, who, chiefly for political reasons, have made their peace with the Papacy. They have succeeded, by special dispensation from the Pope, in preserving the use of their national language in their liturgy, in return for their political allegiance to Rome, and, except in the dress of their priests, are not distinguishable from their fellows of the old faiths. France is the recognized protector of all Roman Catholics in Turkey.

The Protestanism of Turkey needs no special description, following as it does closely in the lines of the evangelical churches of America and England. Except in rare cases there is little emphasis laid upon creeds. Of the doctrines, perhaps the one that is most prominent is the one that Luther pressed so hard—Justification by Faith—and for the same reason. There has been no effort to establish new dogmas. The new church was a civil even more than a religious necessity. See **Protestant Community.** In most cases every effort has been made to avoid antagonism to the old churches, in the belief that the emphasis laid upon truth would crowd out the error. The Protestant Churches of Turkey are distinguished from the old churches rather by their conception of sin, its character and heinousness, the absolute necessity of a change of heart, and the idea of individual communion with Christ, as a personal Redeemer and Savior, than by elaborate creeds or confessions. Church services take on the non-liturgical form, partly because that has been the habit of the missionaries, partly because of the natural repulsion of the soul, awakened to a sense of its personal need, to a ritual where personality was lost in forms that had practically lost their meaning.

Government: The Government of Turkey is often called "Theocratic." In the sense that the Sultan as Caliph is the head of the Muslim religion, as well as of the Turkish Empire, and that all civil authority centers in the ecclesiastical, this is correct. Mohammed claimed to derive his power from God by special dispensation through the archangel Gabriel, and committed his authority to the Caliphs. The Sultan, as Caliph or "successor" of the Prophet, has for one of his titles "the Shadow of God on Earth." But as for any personal relations between the Sultan and Deity, they are no more than those of the meanest of his subjects. He is the representative of divine authority, but by no means its medium.

Both theoretically and practically the Sultan is the head of the government. He has the usual number of Ministers, but none is independent in responsibility for the minutiæ of his special department of Foreign Affairs, the Interior, Finance, Commerce, War, Marine, Public

Instruction, or Evkaf. The Cabinet meetings are presided over by the Grand Vizier; but any question must be referred to the Sultan, and he keeps his eye on all the different lines of governmental policy. So, too, the Sheikh ul Islam and the Ulema guide the affairs of the church, but, whether in civil or ecclesiastical affairs, the Palace is constantly the most potent factor, liable at any moment to interfere with the best-laid plans of subordinates, and assume direct control even of the minutiæ of administration. That administration, in its civil department, is in general on much the same plan as that of the European governments, at least in the cities of the seaboard. The interior is divided into provinces, whose boundaries are constantly modified to suit political exigencies of many kinds.

Side by side with the civil administration are the judicial and ecclesiastical, and the three are often so intermingled that it is impossible to distinguish between them. The judicial is based in some respects upon the Code Napoleon, but in others on the Canon Law derived from the Koran. Where one ends and the other begins it is often impossible to decide. The Canon Law alone applies in questions affecting real estate. Landed properties in Turkey are divided into three categories, the *miri*, or royal domain, the *mulk*, or unlimited, and the *vacouf*, or dedicated property. *Mulk* property corresponds very nearly to freehold, but the *vacouf*, which comprises a very large per cent. of all real estate in cities, is dedicated to some mosque or other "pious foundation" to which it pays a small annual rent, and to which it reverts on the failure of direct heirs of the holder. Title to *mulk* property is transferable in full, but that of *vacouf* property only on condition of perpetual payment of the annual rent and perpetual obligation to surrender the title on the failure of direct heirs. It will readily be seen that this arrangement prevents the transfer of such property to corporations, since such a transfer would prevent ultimate reversion of the land to the mosque. It also gives for the same reason opportunity for local officials to hinder or prevent the erection of church or school upon *vacouf* land. That so many such buildings have been erected in Turkey is a marked evidence of the wisdom and patience of the missionaries who have gained the permission for their construction.

Relations of the Turkish Government with its Christian subjects and with unbelieving foreigners residing in Turkey are peculiar. When the Mohammedan conqueror captured Constantinople the question became grave of the attitude which it was most expedient for him to take toward those of the vanquished population who refused to accept his creed. To put them to the sword was quite proper under the Canon Law, if he thought best. But to do this would depopulate the land, and would deprive the Government of much income as well as of the services of useful artisans whose places could not be filled by Turks. Yet aliens in religion could not be admitted to the privileges of citizenship in a divinely guided nation whose laws are an expression of divine justice.

In this emergency the Sultan adopted the practise of the Roman Empire toward religious dissenters and aliens. The unbelievers were told that in all relations between themselves and in matters of which their ecclesiastical law took cognizance they must get along as best they could under the jurisdiction of their own church authorities. Their religious chiefs thus received recognition as civil functionaries of the empire and responsible representatives of their spiritual flocks. With them the sovereign held communication through the officials charged with the management of foreign affairs. The result was that the Christian subjects of Turkey became nationalities distinct from each other and from the Muslim population whose privileges were denied to them. As relations with foreign nations became more frequent, the same rule was applied to the relations of foreign residents in Turkey to the Turkish Government. Such residents were not entitled to the privileges of Mohammedan law, and were left under the control of their own laws, being made amenable to their own consular officials only. This system, which places the persons and property of foreign residents in Turkey beyond the jurisdiction of Turkish officials, was consecrated in agreements and treaties known as "the Capitulations" in the 17th century and later. The resulting condition of "extra-territoriality" protects foreign residents in Turkey in some degree from the inequitable religious partisanship of Mohammedan Canon Law, and especially from the arbitrary and lawless exactions of corrupt officials. It is in fact an essential condition of business stability and even of personal safety to foreign residents in Turkey. This "extra-territoriality," first applied as a stigma of inferiority to foreigners and to Christian subjects living under the rule of the Sultans, has become a precious privilege which it is the constant effort of recent Turkish rulers gradually to obliterate that all, like the Muslims, may be under control of the Canon Law courts and may be forced to satisfy the greed of Turkish officials.

History: The history of Turkey is of the utmost importance to the student of Christian missions. Only by a careful survey of it from the time when the Byzantine Empire commenced to decay can he understand how the present condition is but the crystallization of conditions that existed many centuries ago. The capture of Constantinople by the Turks, and the establishment of the internal regulations of the empire on the basis of an absolute union of church and state, or rather of an absorption of the state by the church (for not only the Muslim, but the Christian) acted upon the social, civil, and religious condition of the land, as Mohammedanism always acts upon the lands that it conquers, like a sudden petrifying power. When the 19th century opened it found a country which had practically slept for nearly four centuries. The modern era of Turkish history, which is all that space and the general purpose of this article will allow, commences with the reign of Mahmoud II. (1808). More than any of his predecessors, Mahmoud realized the value of modern progress, and he understood very clearly the situation in which he found his empire. Napoleon had just uttered his famous prediction that Europe was destined to be either all Cossack or all republican. The French Revolution on the west, Russian aggression on the east, were influences that must be fatal unless they could be checked. Internally there was commotion. The Janissaries had ruled so long that the upturning of their kettles was a more serious affair than a death in the Palace. The feudal chiefs of Asia Minor were growing more and more arrogant, and the army was in danger of disorganization, through their refusal to send recruits to the order of the Sultan. Greece was feeling the impulse of the strife for freedom. Mohammed Ali was laying the foundation of his power in Egypt, while Albania was practically independent under Ali Pasha of Janina. A less vigorous, clear-headed man would have succumbed, and the Cossack would have carried the day. Mahmoud set himself to his task with courage, but the forces against him were too strong. He succeeded in overpowering the Janissaries, reorganized his army, and successfully withstood an attack from Russia; but England and France interfered and forced upon him the Treaty of London, 1827, and the Treaty of Adrianople, 1829. Greece was declared free, and the Danubian principalities of Moldavia and Wallachia were placed under the protection of Russia. Meanwhile Mohammed Ali was increasing in power. The traditional hostility of England and France manifested itself more and more in the Mediterranean. France espoused the cause of the Pasha, while England supported the Sultan. The rivalry became open war, and the Albanian leader threatened the very existence of the Turkish Empire. Just at this crisis Mahmoud died (1839), leaving the Caliph's sword to his oldest son, Abd ul Medjid, an amiable but weak and irresolute man. England and France saw at once that the danger foreseen by Napoleon was upon them. The "Cossack" was an immediate probability, the "republican" (Louis Philippe was then reigning) a remote possibility. Accordingly they united their forces, and by the treaty of 1841 confirmed Mohammed Ali in the possession of Egypt as vassal to the Sultan, and assumed a European protectorate over the Turkish Empire.

No sooner was this settled than intrigues opened again. England, realizing the necessity of the situation as affecting her relations with India, placed one of her strongest men at Constantinople. Sir Stratford Canning (afterward Viscount Stratford de Redcliffe) was an able, far-sighted, Christian man. Not only did he comprehend the general political bearings of the situation, but he understood clearly their social, civil, and religious relations. He realized that for the Christian races of Turkey it was in a sense a choice between two evils—the despotism of a weak Sultan amenable to influence and under obligation to Christian nations, or that of the Czar, secure in his position and utterly beyond the reach of any motives except those of aggrandizement and supremacy. With marvelous patience and skill he set himself to his task of strengthening his hold upon the Sultan. French and Russian ambassadors alike had to yield to the great "*Elchi*," as he was called. One after another, reforms were introduced. The Hatti Sherif of Gulhané announced the speedy establishment of institutions "which should insure to all the subjects of the Sultan perfect security for their lives, their homes, and their property, a regular method of collecting the taxes, and an equally regular method of recruiting the army and fixing the duration of service." But proclamation was one thing, enforcement another. Palace intrigues supplemented those of Russia. The Turkish officials saw their opportunities for oppression and bribery disappearing, and offered to the new reforms an Oriental shrug when they did not positively refuse obedience. Genuine advance was, however, made. Torture and the death penalty for apostasy from Islam were abolished, and the bastinado was forbidden in the schools and finally in the army. Christian evidence in courts of law was rendered legal, if not always actual, and there appeared possibilities for the future where hitherto there had been absolutely no hope. Then came the stirring scenes of 1848 and 1849. Kossuth and some associates took refuge with the Porte, which refused to give them up to the power that had crushed the Magyar Government. Nicholas, flushed with his victory, looked forward to the speedy extinction of Turkey, and in 1853 proposed to the British ambassador at St. Petersburg a plan for the division of "the Sick Man's" inheritance as soon as he should expire, and claimed the right of a protectorate over the Greek Christian subjects of the Sultan. This was naturally objected to by the Porte, and was followed by the entrance of the Russian army into the Danubian principalities. England took up the side of Turkey, and France, angered by the effect of Russian championship of the Greek Church in a contest between Latin and Greek priests in Jerusalem, added her forces to those of the Sultan, while Sardinia took her place for the first time as one of the powers of Europe. The victory of the allied powers in the Crimea resulted in the Treaty of Paris, which affirmed the neutrality of the Black Sea, the independence and integrity of Turkey, abolished the Russian protectorate over the Danubian principalities, closed the Bosphorus and Dardanelles to foreign ships of war, and reasserted and emphasized the principles of the Hatti Sherif of Gulhané, guaranteeing complete religious liberty and the execution of the reforms already promulgated.

The most fruitful result of the Crimean War, however, was its destruction for a large part of the Turkish people of the illusion that a Mohammedan nation must be superior in knowledge and power to all Christian nations. Scientific knowledge possessed by the masterful allies of Turkey was seen to be good, notwithstanding the Mohammedan dogma that all useful knowledge centers in the Koran. Government schools were established to instruct Mohammedans in Western science out of books translated from Western languages, and to teach the languages of the infidels which gave young Muslims access to the literature of the West. By such iconoclastic results the Crimean War undertaken by Europe in order to bolster up for selfish reasons the failing Mohammedan power, must be regarded in its outcome as the most deadly blow ever given to Mohammedanism.

England and France and Italy now made the mistake of ceasing to try to lead Turkey into a wise use of the opportunity which they had won for the Sultan at the point of the bayonet. Formal interference with Turkey in its execution of the promised reforms was forbidden by the Treaty of Paris. The Western powers desisted from informal influence, and left the field clear for Russia, whose one policy since that day has been to encourage Turkey in following every path that leads to national suicide.

In 1858 Lord Stratford was replaced by Sir Henry Bulwer, and English influence at the Porte rapidly lessened. Then commenced a time of national extravagance. Hitherto Turkey had been an almost unknown factor in the stock markets of Europe, but now investors began to crowd in. The adoption of the Code Napoleon in civil courts, and the introduction of customs revenues, etc., necessitated the employment of numbers of Europeans, who looked upon the Turks as legitimate prey. Financial propositions of every sort were made; loans were offered upon Treasury bonds, and the government was launched upon a financial career to the management of which it was an utter stranger. When Abd ul Medjid came to the throne he had reversed the usual custom of his ancestors, and spared the life of his brother, Abd ul Aziz; and he, on the death of Medjid, in 1861, became Sultan. A morose, selfish man, bent upon gratifying every whim of the moment, he lent a ready ear to the adventurers that thronged Constantinople. Palaces and public buildings of various kinds sprang up on every hand. A fleet was necessary and it was furnished, while contractors in every department grew rich at the expense of the government, which, elated by the hitherto unheard of possibility of borrowing unlimited sums of money, went into the wildest extravagances. Meanwhile the Druze massacres of 1860 had resulted in the French occupation of Syria. Wallachia and Moldavia united in the principality of Roumania, and, like Servia, became autonomous provinces. The Russian Embassy was practically supreme, Sir Henry Bulwer, Sir Henry Austin Layard, and Sir Henry Elliott being utterly unable to cope with Count Ignatieff. The year 1869 saw the completion of the Suez Canal, intensifying England's interest in keeping her connections with India clear, and the collapse of France in the war of 1870 made it possible for Lord Beaconsfield to secure from the spendthrift Khedive a controlling money interest in that great waterway.

The internal administration of Turkey became worse and worse. Two parties became clearly developed, the Young Turkey party, favoring reform and looking to England for moral support, and the Old Turkey party, opposed to reform and warmly supported by Russia because a reactionary policy must destroy the Turkish Empire. Numerous efforts were made by the Western powers to secure real reform, but in vain. Revolt broke out in Bosnia and Herzegovina (1875), and produced disquietude and plots of sedition in Bulgaria, which were repressed by terrible massacres that aroused all Europe (1876).

Mithad Pasha, a leading member of the Young Turkey party, now contrived a plot to replace the Sultan Abd ul Aziz by his nephew Murad. The Sultan had proved himself by his senseless extravagance to be incapable, and the revolution was easily carried through. Sultan Murad V. was placed upon the throne in May, 1876, and was pledged to introduce constitutional government in the Empire with real equality of civil rights for Christians. He was quickly adjudged insane, perhaps because of his liberal views, and three months later was deposed, giving place to his brother Abd ul Hamid II., the present (1903) Sultan. Mithad and his companions were promptly exiled, conveniently dying shortly after, and the Old Turkey party remained in triumphant ascendancy.

48

Servia now declared war upon Turkey, and the European powers consulted together in conference at Constantinople as to a means for pacifying the Balkan provinces. The Sultan in vain proclaimed a constitution, and later convoked a parliament. Neither measure satisfied Europe, and both were promptly abolished when the hope of that result was seen to be vain. The objections of Turkey to real reform gave Russia a pretext for declaring war in 1877. England held aloof, stipulating the neutrality of Egypt. Austria had received her price in a promise of Bosnia and Herzegovina, and Russia met Turkey alone. The campaign of the Balkans resulted in placing Constantinople at the mercy of the Czar, and the Treaty of San Stefano made Russia supreme in the Balkan peninsula, and gave her a strong hold on Eastern Turkey. This was more than England and Austria could stand. The British fleet entered the Marmora, covering with its guns the Russian camp at San Stefano. Austria gave tokens of hostility, and Russia, ill prepared for a general European war, consented to the Conference of Berlin. This granted the independence of Roumania and Servia, each under a king of its own; made Bulgaria an autonomous principality with a relation of tribute only to the Sultan, handed over Bosnia and Herzegovina to Austria, enlarged the borders of Greece, and guaranteed internal reforms, especially for the Armenians.

Since then there have been no great territorial changes except that Eastern Rumelia was joined to Bulgaria in 1885, and Prince Alexander, who proved not as amenable to Russian influence as was desired, was seized, forced to abdicate, and was replaced by Prince Ferdinand. Later, Crete followed the manifest destiny of abused Turkish provinces and was given autonomy under a prince of Greece.

The "Eastern Question," which after all is nothing more than the question of securing some means of living in peace while a Turkish neighbor holds to religious principles that demand war, still exists in all of its disturbing aggressiveness. The present (1903) situation in Turkey may be briefly summed up:

Ruling influences among the Turks represent neither of the parties of a few years ago. Taking as his motto "Muslim Turkey for Muslim Turks," the Sultan, with a persistence, patience, and skill that place him among the greatest of the rulers of Turkey, is endeavoring by every means in his power to strengthen the Mohammedan and weaken the Christian elements of the population. Every concession of political equality or civil rights not contemplated by the Koran for unbelievers living under Muslim rulers has been wrung from Turkey by force. The principle followed by a Muslim ruler in such a case is to serve the interests of Islam by granting the demand when he cannot meet force with force, and then to serve Islam again by withdrawing the concession so soon as circumstances permit. In obedience to this rule many of the concessions granted by the Hatti Humayoun of 1856 (formally recognized by the Treaty of Paris in that year) have been gradually withdrawn. Christian Pashas have been allowed to die out, Christian officials have been weeded out from all positions of administrative responsibility. Since the argument for Christian representation in government office has been the large proportion of Christians in certain sections, a feverish activity has been shown in introducing Mohammedan colonists into Christian districts in Asiatic Turkey. Circassians from Russia, Pomaks from Bulgaria, Tatars from Roumania, and Kurds from Persia have been offered inducements to remove to points in Turkey where their presence will affect the balance of power. The right to establish schools at will, which was guaranteed to Christians by the Hatti Humayoun, has been quietly withdrawn, and existing Christian schools are restricted in their course of study and closed on trivial pretexts. At the same time the greatest energy is displayed in increasing the number of fanatically Mohammedan schools whose expenses are largely borne by special taxation of Christians "for education," in which they cannot participate. The number of outrages committed by Muslims upon Christians has been notably increased, and the punishment of such outrages is more than ever difficult. In fact, capital punishment for murder of Christians by Muslims has been done away, an imprisonment for fifteen years having taken its place, with the understanding that at least one-third of such a sentence will be remitted by imperial clemency.

It is not a matter of surprise that the Christian populations of Turkey have become restive under such conditions. In 1895 the European powers undertook to interfere in behalf of the six provinces of Asiatic Turkey where Armenians are most numerous. The Sultan granted the demands of Europe. That very week a series of massacres began which destroyed the flower of the Armenian population of every city and of many of the villages in each one of the six provinces. Insurrectionary tendencies were alleged as a reason for these massacres, in which at least 40,000 Armenians fell victims. It has not, however, been shown that anything worse than deep dissatisfaction, or at most plans for organization which might have been checked by a few arrests, existed among the Armenians. The massacres ended every pretense at reform. An attempt of Bulgarian patriots to excite insurrection in Macedonia in 1903, for the sake of compelling Turkey to grant reforms long since promised, led to similar demands on the part of European powers, and the granting of these demands was followed by a similar systematic and terrible massacre of Bulgarian inhabitants of Macedonia. Whether this, as in the case of Armenia, will be allowed to terminate the validity of the promise of reforms, it is not our province to prophesy. All that can be said is that the same internal conditions which have kept the Eastern Question alive in the past remain active to-day in Turkey, and are likely to remain so until Mohammedans are willing to admit that their mission in the world is other than the subjugation and plunder of unbelievers. Meanwhile, certain influences are at work among all classes, modifying each, sometimes silently, but not the less surely; often unnoticed, yet which at no distant day may be most potent factors in the political situation.

Of these the most prominent perhaps is education. The presence of Robert College on the Bosphorus, the American College for Girls in Scutari, the Syrian Protestant College at Beirut, and the many American and European colleges through Asia Minor have had a mighty influence in stirring the popular demand, until there is not a city in the Empire, scarcely a town or village, where there is not a certain amount of education. This education is not always thorough or complete, but it is opening the eyes of the people to truths that have hitherto been unrecognized, and no efforts of ecclesiastics or government officials can close them. The wide use of the French language has occasioned a great influx of French literature and French phrases, and it is not infrequent to hear some Armenian, Greek, or even Turk, boast of being a "libre penseur." Free-thinking is spreading, and with it the ideas of modern socialism. As yet confined chiefly to the cities of the seaboard, these are spreading into the cities and towns of the interior, and are exerting an influence which it is impossible to measure, but which is not less potent.

Next to education as a very positive element in influencing the political condition of all classes of the Empire is the introduction of European modes of life. The change in this respect is most marked; and tho detailed notice is out of place here, the fact that the Oriental simplicity of manners, from which has come in no small degree the vigor of the Ottoman race, is fast becoming a thing of the past is of most practical import. Parallel with these is the growth of infidelity. This will be especially noticed below, under the head of Mission Work, but it should be mentioned here as a most important element in politics. The condition of the Turkish Empire, as regards both Muslim and Christian inhabitants, is rapidly assuming the complexion of the later Roman Empire. Religion is a good thing for the masses, but for the educated, the leaders, it continues only as a political bond. In the consciousness of this among the more sincere Mohammedans of Kurdistan, Arabia, and Africa lies the ground for such movements as those of the Mahdi, and of the rebellious Arabs of Yemen, who declare that the Caliph has fallen from his high estate and no longer deserves to hold his position.

The subject races, divided among themselves, grasping at anything that seems to offer them any help, are waiting, sometimes patiently, sometimes impatiently, for the action of the European powers, or for the action of this slow, disintegrating force in Islam itself.

Mission Work: The general history of missions in the Turkish Empire is sufficiently noted in the articles on the missionary societies named below. It is needful here to give merely an outline of the work as a whole, and show its relations to the peculiar problems, political, social, and religious, of this interesting field of foreign missions.

The territory of the Turkish Empire is well covered by the mission societies. The ABCFM, the oldest in the field, also occupies the largest territory—the whole of European Turkey, together with Bulgaria south of the Balkans, Asia Minor, Eastern Turkey, and Mesopotamia. These fields have constituted for many years about one-fourth of the entire territory occupied by this Board throughout the world. The Presbyterian Church (North) occupies Syria and a portion of Eastern Turkey, where Nestorians are found in Kurdistan. The Methodist Episcopal Church has its work in Bulgaria, north of the Balkans. The Reformed Presbyterian (Covenanter) Church of America has its stations in Northern Syria and Southern Asia Minor. There are also some congregations under the care of the Foreign Christian Missionary Society (Disciples) in Asia Minor, and a few Baptist churches, at one time under the care of the American Baptist Publication Society. The Church Missionary Society has a flourishing work in Palestine, the Friends of England have a mission in Syria, and a single medical missionary among the Armenians of Constantinople. The Reformed Presbyterian Church of Ireland has a station at Damascus and one at Idlib, near Antioch, and the North Africa Mission one at Hums in Syria. There are also a number of schools in Syria supported by the Lebanon Schools Committee and British Syrian Schools Association. The missions to the Jews of the various English and Scotch societies at Constantinople, Smyrna, Adrianople, and in Palestine, are specially noted in the article on the **Jews.**

The Bible work of the Empire is carried on by the American and the British and Foreign Bible Societies, and the National Bible Society of Scotland. The American Bible Society occupies the territory covered by the American mission societies, except Bulgaria, while the BFBS works in European Turkey, the western coast of Asia Minor, and Palestine. Constantinople and Smyrna are shared by the two societies. The National Bible Society of Scotland has a depot at Salonica in European Turkey. In Asiatic and European Turkey there are thirty-one societies at work. Nine of these are American, nineteen are British and two are German.

If we turn now to the population, we find that the work for the Armenians is carried on chiefly by the ABCFM; for the Greeks by the ABCFM; for the Bulgarians by the ABCFM and the Methodist Episcopal Church; for the Maronites and Syrians by the Presbyterian Church (North) and the various English and Scotch societies and committees; while the Nusairiyeh are the chosen field of the sturdy Scotch Covenanters. The Turks, Arabs, Kurds, Yezidis, etc., have been the care of all the societies, tho the CMS is the only one that has made a special effort to establish mission work distinctively for Muslims.

Not merely is the territory thus provided for as a whole, but it is well covered in its different parts. True to the best policy, the missionaries have from the beginning sought the centers. Not always the largest cities on the basis of a census, but those which for one reason or another furnish most opportunities for reaching the widest circle of people.

There are of course sections where there is comparatively little accomplished, but those are few. In the main, the Turkish Empire is well covered, and it may be truly said that there is scarcely a village, except in the mountains of Kurdistan and some parts of Mesopotamia and Syria bordering on Arabia, that does not have at least occasionally the opportunity to hear the Gospel, while in some cities, notably Aintab, Marash, Harpoot, the evangelical element is so strong as to be a very important factor in the general life of the people. Mission work in the Turkish Empire thus has passed the exploring, introductory stage and reached that of development. It is no longer experimental; it has settled down to the same problems that meet the Church in other lands, affected yet by the fact that it is still rejected totally by the immense majority of the people, and looked upon with varying degrees of distrust by the greater part of the remainder.

We will look now at the relations that mission work in Turkey holds to the different classes of people whom it seeks to influence.

I. The Jews: When the first missionaries entered the Levant in 1819, their special message was to the Jews. Not many years passed, however, before that branch of the work was given up by them as manifesting less opportunity for success than others. At present it is chiefly educational. Large schools are supported by the Scotch and English societies, especially in Constantinople, Smyrna, Salonica, and Jerusalem. There are also numerous preaching services, and there is enough of success manifested in the Christian life of converts to keep the laborers from being discouraged in their work or giving up the hope of a redeemed Israel, apart from their faith in the promises of the Scriptures. Mission work among the Jews is, however, so distinctively sectional, and confined to them as a race, that it enters as a comparatively unimportant factor into the question of the conversion of the Empire as a whole.

II. The Oriental Churches: When missionaries first turned their attention to the Christian churches of Turkey, their one idea was to secure reform within the churches themselves. So close to the creeds and confessions of the Reformation were those of the Armenians, Greeks, Nestorians, that it seemed to them a comparatively easy task to show the incompatibility between those confessions and the actual practises of the church. Thus every effort was made to come into cordial relations with the people, and all idea of a separate communion was specially disclaimed. This course was favored also by the eagerness with which these churches looked for foreign sympathy and aid in their bitter struggles with their Muslim rulers.

It was not long, however, before the ecclesiastics saw that the new ideas would inevitably result in loosening and ultimately destroying their control over their followers. Then they massed their power against the new doctrines. An excommunicated man had no rights that a Turkish court could recognize. He was nobody; could neither marry nor be buried; could not buy, sell, or employ. He had absolutely no status as a citizen. The result was that the formation of a Protestant civil community became absolutely essential to the very life of Protestants. Then other influences began to come in. The introduction of Europeans into the commercial and governmental affairs of the Empire brought with it the introduction of French and German thought. With increased ease of access to Europe more and more the Armenian and Greek youth sought education in Paris and Vienna. Returning, they brought with them the free-thinking of the day, and the grip of the Church, not only on their belief but their life, began very perceptibly to loosen, and the ecclesiastics began to think that perhaps they had not been absolutely wise in their repulsion of evangelicalism. In the meantime it became evident that these Protestants were no less national in their feeling than the orthodox: indeed, had an even clearer conception of what a true national life was. Here was clear proof that the study of the Bible did not make a man or woman less capable of good work for his people. The result has been that in very many sections of the Empire there is a constantly growing cordiality between the evangelical and the orthodox communities. Bishops and priests are preaching Gospel sermons; in some cases Sunday-schools and Bible classes are started, in order to satisfy the growing desire for religious instruction. With infidelity staring them in the face, the leaders of the old churches are coming more and more to look upon the missionaries and the native evangelical churches as allies rather than enemies.

The problem of missions in Turkey, in their relations to the old churches, is, on the one hand, so to establish the evangelical churches in faith and life that when a reunion with the others comes they shall not be borne away and swallowed up; on the other, to convince the old churches that their one aim is to establish the kingdom of God, not a temporal organization, and at the same time to set forth in the evangelical churches as clear and accurate an idea as possible of what constitutes a true church life.

III. *Mohammedanism:* The general relations of evangelical missions to Mohammedanism are fully set forth in the article on that subject. It is needful here to note only such points as are specially brought out in the Turkish Empire.

The first feeling of the Muslims of Turkey toward the new sect was one of amused and rather tolerant indifference. Indeed, in not a few instances Turks who saw the simplicity of the evangelical worship, the absence of ritual, of pictures and priestly rule, the stress laid upon spiritual worship, said: "Why, these are Muslims." The use of the Bible in distinction from the creeds of the Church compared favorably in their eyes with the position they accorded to the Koran, and a Kurdish chief once said: "Why do not the Bible Societies print and bind the two books together? then we should have the complete revelation." For a while this cordial feeling for Protestants as distinct from the Eastern Church rather increased, except when the influence of ecclesiastics secured special hardships for those who had dared to brave the power of the Church. The missionaries had great influence, because the Turkish officials recognized, in many cases, their freedom from political motives. Little by little, however, this changed. Shrewd Mollahs saw, as Armenian and Greek bishops had already seen, that these new people were exerting an influence for stimulating mental processes among the people, and that an intellectual awakening must in time cut the ground entirely from under their whole system of belief and government. Then commenced a most determined and bitter opposition. Not in appearance,—that was in most cases friendly, —but in the form of hindrance. Censorship of publications was made increasingly stringent. The necessary permits for buildings, churches, schools, and even private dwellings were refused or delayed as long as possible. Any Turks who manifested a leaning toward or an interest in the Bible were quietly arrested on some fictitious charge and spirited away. Spies were everywhere. Occasionally some Mohammedan more bold than his fellows, or feeling more secure in his position and relations with Porte or Palace, would give expression to his feeling that the work of the missionaries was really a good thing for the Empire, but means were generally found to neutralize the effect of such a statement. In not a few instances laws were promulgated especially directed against the missionaries. Vexations upon vexations were put upon them.

The result has been that there have been very few conversions of Muslims to Protestant Christianity. There have come, however, from every side constantly increasing testimonies to the hold that Christianity is getting upon the people of the land. The number of Scriptures sold to Muslims indicates a profound interest in the Bible, which cannot fail to bring forth fruit in Christian life.

Islam in its historic inception was in a great degree a protest against a devitalized polytheistic Christianity. If Muslims are to be brought to Christ, it must be largely through the example and influence of a living Christian church. The problem of missions in Turkey in their relation to Mohammedanism is that of developing a native church freed from the political quality of the old churches, strong in its belief in the unity of God, manifesting in its daily life an educated Christian faith.

In meeting this problem, missions in Turkey rely upon five special agencies: (1) Evangelical preaching; (2) Bible distribution; (3) Education; (4) Publication; (5) Social influence.

1. *The Evangelical preaching* of Turkey is very largely, in most cases almost entirely, in the hands of the native pastorate. The pastors, educated in the different seminaries and colleges, are taking a position of constantly increasing importance. Men of large views, earnest Christian spirit, they have done much, not only to build up the native evangelical churches, but to convince others that Protestant Christianity is a genuine power in the world for good. Not only in the larger cities but in the smaller places they are doing a great tho often unheralded work, laying foundations in Christian character for future building.

2. *Bible Distribution:* There is probably no mission field where this department of mission work is more thoroughly organized so as to reach periodically every portion of it than the Turkish Empire. This has been already spoken of in the articles on the American and the British and Foreign Bible Societies.

3. *Education* in connection with the missionary work has been a normal growth. Free primary schools were first started. Schools, called theological, to educate native ministers and teachers soon followed, and were free to the class for which they were designed. Girls' boarding-schools were also established early, the first in 1840. All this work was rudimentary. In 1863 **Robert College** was opened on the Bosphorus, and, almost simultaneously, the **Syrian Protestant College** at Beirut. These institutions mark the beginning of serious educational work in Turkey on the basis of requiring pupils to pay reasonably for their instruction, and on a plan of thorough training with an ample and well-prepared curriculum.

They had much to contend against in the as yet feebly developed desire among even the people of the seaboard for a college education. They had also to meet the opposition of many Christian men—missionaries and supporters of missions—who, in their zeal for the largest development of the evangelistic work, were jealous of an elaborate course of collegiate training. The first years of those colleges were marked by a slow growth. Classes of five, three, two, in one case of only one, were graduated.

In the course of a decade of years the increase was abnormal. There was a plethora of raw material which had to be in part eliminated that what remained might be assimilated.

The institution at Scutari, Constantinople, now known as the American College for Girls, was started at this time, and struggled, in its inception, through difficulties and limitations similar to those from which the college on the Bosphorus had emerged.

Between 1871 and 1875 two colleges in the interior of the country were projected, and in the latter year were opened, viz., the Central Turkey College, at Aintab, south of the Taurus Mountains, and the Armenia—now Euphrates—College, at Harpoot, east of the Euphrates River. These colleges show points of resemblance and of unlikeness to each other and to Robert College. Their course of study is not quite so full as that of the colleges on the seaboard. German and Italian are not needed in the interior, and much better work is done at Robert College in the physical sciences and in chemistry than is yet possible in an interior college. But the colleges of the interior have the advantage of being in closer touch with the races to be reached and molded by them.

This growth of education, especially within the last seven or eight years, has developed the following noteworthy results:

a. The youth of Turkey *can pay* for their education, where terms are made light, according to location of the college, and such proportion of aid is given, through scholarships and by furnishing work, as is done in the colleges of this country.

b. This securing of the privilege of Christian education through strenuous exertion on the part of pupils and their friends is one of the most essential conditions of realizing that growth in manly, self-reliant, aspiring character and that establishment of a vital, self-propagating Christianity, without which education is nowhere a blessing. The plan of education now adopted has already yielded excellent results in this way. The more men, or races of men, are held down by the incubus of poverty, the more urgent is the necessity of rousing the will-power to self-help, by every right device and pressure.

c. It is the stand taken and the work done by Americans in the recent years in the matter of education which has won the confidence of the best men of all races in Turkey.

d. It is this influence alone which can fit the several races for their future, and hold in harmonious relation one to another all those whose vital interests are identical.

e. These American colleges furnish in large part the models in education for all the Christian communities in Turkey, and train large numbers of the teachers. It was after Americans gave the signal that Armenians, Greeks, and Bulgarians established for themselves any schools worthy of the name. The Turks have ideal capacity for establishing excellent schools on paper, and ideal incapacity for establishing them in any other way. They also are already recognizing the American leadership.

f. All discussion among missionaries and their supporters relative to the utility of education and to the *comparative* value of educational and evangelistic work has ceased.

4. *Publication:* There are two centers of missionary publication in the Turkish Empire: Constantinople and Beirut. The work at Beirut is entirely Arabic; that at Constantinople includes Turkish, Armenian, Greek, Bulgarian, Judæo-Spanish, Kurdish, etc. In each place some of the best of missionary strength has gone into the work of providing not only the Bible and religious books, but periodical literature, educational works, and such general literature as a growing Christian community is constantly demanding, and in ever-increasing quantity. Aside from the work of Bible translation in these different languages, the work done in Turkey is telling all over the Empire in the correction of erroneous views, not by antagonizing their errors, but by presenting the truth.

5. *Social Influence:* This is an ever-increasing power in Turkey. The ready access gained to all classes of people, the power of personal presence and actual acquaintance, has done and is doing a great deal toward preparing the way for the entrance of the Gospel. Many old-time prejudices against those that "having turned the world upside down, are come hither also," have quietly but absolutely disappeared before the presence in an Armenian, Greek, Maronite, and Turkish home of a simply dressed, unassuming Christian lady. Many an ecclesiastic has found it impossible to harangue against one whom he knew from personal acquaintance to be a Christian gentleman.

In the Turkish Empire the gates are open. It is only necessary to hold the vantage-ground gained and to make steady advance, in order to solve the deepest problems of the Eastern Question, by building up the kingdom of God in the lands where it was first established.

As we dwell upon past achievement and present encouragement, we feel that the future of Christian missions in Turkey is hopeful. The words of Dr Jessup point to the light in the cloud: "Protestant missions have given the entire population the Bible in their tongue; have trained hundreds of thousands of readers; published thousands of useful books; awakened a spirit of inquiry; set in motion educational institutions in all the sects of all parts of the Empire, compelling the enemies of education to become its friends, and the most conservative of Orientals to devote mosque and convent property to the founding of schools of learning. Protestantism has forced Oriental patriarchs, bishops and priests to modify, if not abandon, their arbitrary oppressions and exactions. Protestantism has made ignorance unfashionable and persecution disgraceful. It has broken the fetters of womanhood, created directly and indirectly the system of female education spreading over the Empire and let light into unnumbered homes where women before had been consigned to ignorance and inferiority. . . . Every evangelical church is a provocation and stimulus to the old sects, a living epistle to the Mohammedans with regard to the true nature of original apostolic Christianity. The Protestant translation of the Bible into Arabic by Drs. Eli Smith and Cornelius Van Dyck forced the Jesuit Father Von Ham to make another translation based on the Vulgate. Encouraged by the spirit of reform and modern progress, even the Mohammedan doctors of Constantinople have issued orders that all editions of old Mohammedan authors which recount the fabulous stories of Muslim saints and Welys are to be expurgated or suppressed and not to be reprinted."

The number of foreign missionary workers in the Ottoman Empire is 637. Proportion of these missionaries to the population is 1:37,416.8. The statistical summary for 1903 is as follows: Ordained men, 128; unordained men, 108; missionaries' wives, 123; other missionary women, 278; native workers, both sexes, 1,805; stations where missionaries reside, 122; outstations or substations, 526; communicants, 18,367; adherents not communicants, 51,244; day schools, 767; pupils, 36,719; higher institutions, 51; students in same, 3,251; foreign male physicians, 35; foreign women physicians, 3; hospitals or dispensaries, 63; patients reported during year, 189,737.

Creasy (Sir E. S.), *History of the Ottoman Turks*, new ed., London, 1882; Freeman (E. A.), *The Ottoman Power in Europe*, London and New York, 1887; Haurmer-Purgstall (J. von), *Geschichte des Osmanischen Reiches*, 1st ed., 10 vols., Pesth, 1827-35 (a translation in French can also be had); Poole (S. L.), *Turkey* (in Story of the Nations series), London, 1889; Holland (T. E.), *The European Concert in the Eastern Question*, Oxford, 1897; Garnett (Lucy), *The Women of Turkey and their Folk Lore*, London, 1890; Doris (G.), *Abd ul Hamid* (translation), New York, 1901; Amicio (E. de), *Constantinople* (translation), New York, 1896; Hamlin (C.), *My Life and Times*, Boston, 1893; Dwight (H. O.), *Constantinople and its Problems*, New York, 1901; Cuinet (V.), *La Turquie d'Asie* (Geography and Statistics), 5 vols. Paris, 1900, 1901; Harris (J. R. and H. B.), *Letters from the Scenes of the Recent Massacres in Armenia*, London, 1897; *Turkey in Europe*, by Odysseus, London, 1900.

TURKISH LANGUAGE: This is an important member of the Ural-Altaic family of languages. It is thoroughly typical of the family (1) in tolerating no change or obscurement of the root through inflection, (2) in adding syllables or particles to the root for purposes of inflection, and (3) in giving the leading vowel of the root domination over the vowels and even consonants of such added syllables so as to secure euphony in the whole combination.

In etymology the Turkish is remarkable for the regularity of its declensions and conjugations, and for the abundance of the forms of the verb, especially in the Osmanli Turkish. There is, properly speaking, but one conjugation of verbs. The verb is conjugated in great fullness of moods and tenses, with abundance of participial forms and verbal nouns. Moreover, by the incorporation of certain particles the simple verb may give rise to new verbs signifying a reflexive and a reciprocal quality of action. Another particle gives causative significance to the original or the derived verbs. And, finally, by use of the appropriate particle with each of the verbs of the three series, each one is made to produce a new verb with a negative and one with an impossible signification. Each verb may be conjugated in all the moods and tenses and in the active and passive voices exactly on the model of the simple verb, producing some 20,000 tense, number, and person forms from each simple verb. The variety and compactness of expression thus secured is extraordinary.

The principle of agglutination has its application also in the formation of adjectives, adverbs, and nouns, giving great breadth of expression in the use of the somewhat limited vocabulary. Most pronouns and all prepositions in Turkish are used in accordance with the same principle, following the noun which they limit as suffixes and having a regular place in the building of the word.

The Turkish language lacks the relative pronoun and the article. It has neither gender nor declension of adjectives, and is defective in the comparison of adjectives.

In syntax the characteristic of Turkish is that while the subject occurs at or near the commencement of a paragraph, the sense is held in suspense while qualifying phrases and particulars of the most diverse description are brought in, the verb of the predicate, which stands at the very end of the paragraph, serving as the key to the whole enigma.

The Eastern Turks of Turkestan and Mongolia once had an alphabet derived, perhaps, from the Syriac taught by early Nestorian missionaries. At present, however, Arabic letters are used for writing Turkish, a dot or two being added to five of them in order to express consonant sounds not found in Arabic. This alphabet, being without vowels, is quite unsuited to writing Turkish. Various attempts have been made without success to introduce Western alphabets. The Bashkir Turks of the Volga have adopted the Russian alphabet to some extent. Christians living in Turkey who have adopted the Turkish language use the alphabets of their ancestors in writing. Hence we meet with *Greco-Turkish* and *Armeno-Turkish*, which are merely Turkish written with Greek or with Armenian letters.

The Turkish vocabulary is of limited extent, suggesting the limited range of ideas of pastoral peoples. All the dialects borrow freely from the Persian and Arabic languages. In the *Osmanli* Turkish, used in the Turkish Empire, this appropriation of Persian and Arabic words has been carried to a greater extent, and in the literary usage has borrowed phrases and grammatical forms to a degree which has raised its literature far above the comprehension of the unlearned, and has even threatened to destroy the very basis of the language.

Of late years, however, a strong movement has set in at Constantinople for rejecting the use of unnaturalized Persian and Arabic words and phrases. This tends to bring the literary Turkish back within the comprehension of the masses, and promises important results.

The domain of the Turkish language is remarkable for its extent. Turkish is spoken in varying universality of use in a wide belt extending from Chinese Mongolia westward to the Adriatic Sea. Its dialects are numerous, but on the whole may be classed as Eastern and Western, the dividing line being the Caspian Sea. The Eastern Turkish shows the language in its earlier stages of development, still preserving in Chinese Turkestan the words added to roots in lieu of declension of nouns, which have become in the Western Turkish mere case endings. The *Uighur* of Kashgar and the *Uzbek* or *Jagatai* of Bokhara and Khiva are dialects closely related to the *Osmanli* or Ottoman Turkish, but not easily intelligible to the Ottomans because of grammatical differences and a curious substitution of related consonants, as "f" and "b" in the west for "p" and "m" in the east, etc. The *Azerbaijan* Turkish, found in Persia on the south of the Caspian Sea, and the Nogai Turkish and the Krim- (Crimean) Tatar dialect spoken in Russia between the northern end of the Caspian and the Black Sea, are so closely allied to the *Osmanli* or western language that Turkish newspapers published in the Crimea have subscribers in Constantinople. The *Kumukhi* dialect, spoken in Daghestan, and the *Kazan* Turkish, spoken in the plains of the Volga, belong rather to the eastern type. At

Kazan, by the way, is the present center of literary activity in the Eastern Turkish. As we proceed northward we find in the Ural mountain regions the *Bashkir* Turkish and the *Chuvash*, which are strongly tinged with Finnish words. In the extreme northeast of Siberia, along the Lena River, the *Yakut* Turkish is strongly Mongolian in its affinities. The same is true of the *Kirghiz* dialects used by the nomads of the steppes.

Shaw, *Sketch of the Turkish Language as Spoken in Eastern Turkestan*, Calcutta, 1878–80; De Courteille, *Dictionnaire Turc-Orientale*, Paris, 1870; Radloff, *Die Alt-Turkische Inschriften der Mongolei*, St. Petersburg, 1879; Wells, *Practical Grammar of the Turkish Language*, London, 1880; Redhouse, *Lexicon of the Ottoman Turkish Language*, Constantinople, 1884; also *English-Turkish Dictionary*, Constantinople, 1861; also *Turkish-English, English-Turkish Dictionary*, London, 1880; Gibb, *History of Turkish Poetry*, 2 vols., London, 1902; Turkish Literature in *World's Great Classics*, London, 1901; Poole, *Story of Turkey*, New York, 1888.

TURNER, Rev. George: Born January 22, 1818. Died May 19, 1891. A prominent missionary of the LMS. His heroic labors in the South Seas, amid the daily peril of life among the people who had recently been the murderers of John Williams, form a thrilling chapter in the annals of missions. In 1882 he left Samoa. The establishment of the Malua Institution for training native evangelists was mainly due to his influential labor; and from this institution have gone forth many well-equipped preachers of the Gospel of Christ. Dr Turner was not only a devoted missionary of the Cross, but from his pen the people of the South Sea Islands received a large supply of Christian literature. After his retirement his literary labors for the benefit of Samoa continued until his last brief illness, when he left a manuscript on the claims of this people, which was printed by the LMS.

TURTON, William: A native of Barbados, who, after serving for a time as a minister in the colonies on the American continent, returned to the West Indies in 1785, and devoted his life to working for the negro slaves, first at St. Bartholomew and afterward at New Providence in the Bahamas. He encountered bitter opposition from planters and from clergy of the established Church because he was a Methodist. Having collected a congregation in St. Bartholomew he induced the WMS to place it on their list of stations. He then, in 1801, began a similar work in New Providence, and, notwithstanding the influence of those who sought to impede his labors, met with great success until, worn out with exposure and privation, he was obliged to call on the WMS to send men to his aid. Thus this humble worker was the founder of two of the stations of that society in the West Indies.

TU-SHAN-CHAU: A town of Kwei-chau, China, situated in the extreme S. E. of the province near the borders of Kwang-si. Station of the CIM (1893), with (1903) 1 missionary and his wife, 1 place of worship, 1 woman missionary, and 10 professed Christians. Name also written Tuh-shan.

TUTICORIN: Town on the coast of Madras, India, 35 miles E. by N. of Tinnevelli. The appearance of the place and its neighborhood is very unattractive, since in parts the subsoil is so shallow that no plants or trees will grow, and elsewhere there is nothing but heavy sand, with palmyra palms and a few bushes. During the southwest monsoon the dust is intolerable. In value of its foreign trade Tuticorin is second in Madras and sixth in all India. Its harbor, tho shallow, is secure. Population, 25,100, of whom 15,000 are Hindus. Station of the SPG (1878), with (1903) 22 native workers, 6 places of worship, 6 day schools, 2 boarding schools, and 1,590 professed Christians, of whom 504 are communicants.

TUTUILA: An island of the Samoan group belonging to the United States. Station of the LMS (1836), with (1903) 1 missionary and his wife, 2 women missionaries, 38 native workers, 2 boarding schools, 42 Sunday schools, 34 day schools, 1 dispensary, and 3,841 professed Christians, of whom 1,525 are communicants.

TUTURA: A village in Cape Colony, South Africa, situated in the Transkei region S. of Butterworth. Station of the UFS (1885), with (1903) 1 missionary and his wife, 29 native workers, 12 outstations, 5 places of worship, 10 Sunday schools, 13 day schools, and 500 professed Christians.

TYLER, Josiah: Born July 9, 1823. Died in 1896. Entered Amherst College in 1841, where he graduated in 1845. While he was taking his theological course at East Windsor Seminary he decided to enter the foreign field. He was ordained in 1849, and soon afterward, with his wife, he sailed from Boston for Cape Town. He was associated with Messrs. Wilder, Lindley, Aldin Grout and Lewis Grout in the Zulu Mission. Dr Tyler labored forty years in Natal, and his "Forty Years Among the Zulus" is a standard and most interesting record of missionary life and labor. He founded the Esidumbini station, the fiftieth anniversary of which was celebrated in 1901.

TYRE, or ES SUR: A town in Syria, situated on the coast of the Mediterranean Sea, 20 miles N. by E. of Acre. Station of the British Syrian Mission Schools (1869), with (1903) 2 women missionaries, 9 native workers, 4 outstations, 1 place of worship, 4 day schools, 1 dispensary.

U

UDAIPUR: A town and capital of the state of the same name in Rajputana, India, situated about 140 miles S. of Ajmere. Population, 38,143. Station of the UFS (1877), with (1903) 2 missionaries, one of them with his wife; 30 native workers, 1 outstation, 4 day schools, 1 dispensary, 1 hospital, 1 orphanage, and 124 professed Christians.

UDAPI. See UDIPI.

UDAYAGIRI: A town in Madras, India, situated in the district of Nellore, about 50 miles W. of Kavalli. Station of the ABMU (1885), with (1903) 1 missionary and his wife, 19 native workers, 11 outstations, 1 place of worship, 2 Sunday schools, 1 day school, 1 boarding school, 1 dispensary, and 334 professed Christians, of whom 325 are communicants.

UDIPI: A town in South Kanara, India, situated near the W. coast, about 35 miles N. of Mangalore. Station of the Basel Missionary Society (1854), with (1903) 6 missionaries, four of them with their wives; 44 native workers, 10 outstations, 10 day schools, and 1,857 professed Christians, of whom 1,040 are communicants. Some write the name Udapi.

UDUPITTY: A settlement in the Jaffna district of Ceylon, about 12 miles N. of Chavakacheri. Station of the ABCFM (1847), with (1903) 1 missionary and his wife, 43 native workers, 2 outstations, 18 day schools, 1 boarding school, and 165 professed Christians.

UEN-CHAU. See YUEN-CHAU-FU.

UE-WU. See YU-WU-HSIEN.

UGANDA: A British protectorate in Central Africa, lying at the northern end of Lake Victoria Nyanza. It is bounded on the south by German East Africa and by the 1st degree of S. latitude (on the lake); on the east by a line drawn through the middle of Lake Rudolf and by the British East African Protectorate; on the west by the Congo Free State, and on the north by the 5th degree of N. latitude, at the frontier of the Egyptian Sudan. It has an area of about 80,000 square miles, and a population of about 4,000,000 natives, one-fourth of whom belong to the Bantu race, who call themselves Baganda. There are about 300 Europeans in the protectorate. For administrative purposes it is divided into five provinces, of which the kingdom of Uganda forms the southernmost. This kingdom is recognized by the British as a native kingdom under a ruler called a *Kabaka*, and entitled to be addressed as "Highness." The present *Kabaka* is a grandson of Mtesa, and is a baptized Christian named Daudi Chua. Since he is a minor, a regency rules the land. In all five of the provinces the British encourage the native chiefs to govern their own subjects. Mengo is the capital of the kingdom of Uganda, and Entebbe, about 20 miles from Mengo, is the seat of the British administration. Uganda is connected by railway with Mombasa. Steamers on the Nile ascend from Khartum to Gondokoro, in the northern part of the protectorate, and the Uganda post office has been admitted to the universal Postal Union. The soil is very fertile, for the most part, and the climate agreeable. The altitude of the Lake Victoria Nyanza is 3,800 feet.

The history of Uganda illustrates in some degree the service rendered by missions in pioneer work for civilization. The country was first visited by Henry M. Stanley, who, in 1875, sent word to England that King Mtesa of Uganda was anxious to have missionaries sent there. The CMS at once sent a party of missionaries, who landed in East Africa in 1876. The leader and one other member of the party were killed almost at once, but the mission was established in Uganda in July of 1877. There is no question that their arrival decided the destiny of the land. In 1879 a party of Roman Catholic missionaries arrived, and the Arab traders and slave-dealers endeavored to thwart both parties by inducing the king to become a Mohammedan. The situation was one suited to rivalries and intrigues, and these did not fail to appear. In 1884 King Mtesa died, and his successor, Mwanga, was soon taught suspicion of the CMS missionaries. He caused Bishop Hannington to be murdered in 1885, and persecuted the Protestant native Christians with great cruelty. The Mohammedans saw an opportunity in these proceedings, and in 1888 they drove Mwanga and the Roman Catholic, as well as the Protestant, missionaries out of the country. The Christians, however, stood firm, and one year later drove off the Mohammedans, and brought Mwanga back by armed force. The missionaries returned with Mwanga, and the power of the Christian party increased, and its peaceful development made steady progress. The British East Africa Trading Company now appeared on the scene, where mission influence had so far been the sole civilizing force. A sort of supervision of the government was established by the Trading Company in 1890, but failed to prevent intrigues and strife among the three religious denominations, and a condition of anarchy threatened, owing to the time-serving vacillations of the King Mwanga. A British protectorate was declared in 1894. In 1897 King Mwanga fled from his capital with the intention of freeing himself from British control. He was at once declared deposed, and the infant Chua was proclaimed king. In the same year the Sudanese Mohammedan troops in British employ mutinied and for a time the whole foreign colony was in the greatest danger. After some sharp fighting, in which the Christian Ugandans rendered efficient aid, the mutiny was quelled. The British Government now maintains an armed force in Uganda of Indian troops and native levies under British officers.

During the whole of this period the CMS mission has been making steady growth. It now (1903) has, in Uganda, 24 stations, 76 missionaries, men and women; 2,221 native workers of all grades and of both sexes, 49 schools, an industrial school, a printing house, a hospital, 5 dispensaries, and 38,844 professed Christians, of whom 11,145 are communicants. The characteristic of the Uganda Christians is their readiness to labor for the extension of the Kingdom of Jesus Christ, and their eagerness to possess and read the Bible. Of course, among so large a number of professed Christians many are in a low stage of development. Yet the development of Christian character is remarkable, seeing that the first convert was baptized only in 1882.

Ansorge (W. J.), *Under an African Sun*, London, 1899; Ashe (R. P.), *Two Kings of Uganda*, 2d ed., London, 1897; Johnson (Sir Harry), *The Uganda Protectorate*, 2 vols., London, 1902; Kollman (P.), *The Victoria Nyanza*, London, 1900; Stanley (H. M.), *Through the Dark Continent*, London, 1878.

UGANDAN LANGUAGE: Belongs to the Bantu family, and is spoken by the people of Uganda, Central Africa. It has been reduced to writing by missionaries of the CMS, and is written with Roman letters. The beginnings of a literature have already been created. Some writers speak of this language as the "Ganda" or the "Luganda." Since Uganda has become the accepted name of the protectorate, there appears to be no reason for confusing English readers by forcing them to form the name of the language of that country by Bantu, instead of by English, grammatical rules.

UIN-HO. See YUN-HO-HSIEN.

UJJAIN: A town in Central India, situated about 35 miles N. by W. of Indore. A very sacred city to the Hindus, who reckon longitude from here. Population, 32,932. Station of the PCC (1893), with (1903) 1 missionary and his wife, 2 women missionaries, 7 native workers, 1 place of worship, 5 day schools, 1 boarding school, 1 dispensary, 1 hospital, and 27 professed Christians.

UKHRUL. See UKRUL.

UKRUL: A village in Assam, India, situated in the state of Manipur, in a salubrious position among the lower Naga hills about 40 miles S. E. of Kohima. Station of the ABMU (1896), with (1903) 1 missionary and his wife, 1 native worker, 1 day school, 1 place of worship, and 16 professed Christians. Some write the name Ukhrul.

ULU: A settlement on Duke of York's Island, in the Bismarck Archipelago. Station of the Australian Wesleyan Methodist Missions, with (1901) 1 missionary, 99 native workers, 7 outstations, 28 places of worship, 40 Sunday schools, 41 day schools, 1 theological class, and 822 professed Christians.

ULUBARIA: A town in Bengal, India, situated W. of Calcutta, and in its suburban region. Station of the Churches of God (1889), with (1901) 1 woman missionary, 5 native workers, 5 outstations, 1 day school, and 5 professed Christians.

UMBALLA. See AMBALA.

UMHLANGENI: A settlement in Natal, South Africa, situated in the southern part of the colony, about 8 miles S. W. of S. Shepstone. Station of the Hannover Lutheran Free Church (1900), with (1901) 2 missionaries, 1 place of worship, 1 day school, and 100 professed Christians.

UMSINGA: A settlement in Natal, South Africa, situated in the N. part of the colony, about 35 miles E. of Ladysmith. Station of the UFS, with 3 missionaries, 2 women missionaries, 49 native workers, 22 outstations, 1 place of worship, 21 day schools, 1 dispensary, 1 hospital, and 642 professed Christians. Some use the name Gordon Memorial for the station.

UMTALI: A town in Rhodesia, Africa, situated on the railroad, about 160 miles N. W. of Beira and 170 miles S. E. of Salisbury. The present is the second new Umtali, the town having been twice removed by the Government. Station of the SPG (1891), with (1903) 1 native worker and 54 professed Christians. Also station of the ME, with 6 missionaries, four of them with their wives; 1 woman missionary, 2 native workers, 1 place of worship, 1 industrial school and farm, 1 dispensary, 1 hospital, and 16 professed Christians. Some use the name New Umtali.

UMZINTO: A village in Natal, South Africa, situated near the coast about 45 miles S. W. of Durban. Station of the South Africa General Mission (1899), with (1901) 1 missionary and his wife, 3 native workers, 2 outstations, 1 place of worship, 1 day school, 1 dispensary, and 40 professed Christians. Some use the name Dumisa for this station.

UMZUMBI: A settlement in Natal, South Africa, situated about 70 miles S. W. of Durban, on the Umzumbi River. Station of the ABCFM (1861), with (1901) 2 women missionaries, 19 native workers, 1 place of worship, 6 day schools, and 1 boarding school. Some write the name Umzumbe.

UNALAKLIK: A settlement in Alaska, situated on the W. coast of Norton Sound, about 170 miles S. E. of Cape Nome. Station of the Swedish Evangelical Mission Covenant (1888), with (1901) 2 missionaries and their wives, 1 woman missionary, 3 native workers, 1 place of worship, 1 day school, and 87 professed Christians.

UNDUP: A settlement in Sarawak, Borneo, situated on the Batang lupar River, about 40 miles from its mouth. Station of the SPG (1863) with (1903) 1 missionary, 5 native workers, 9 places of worship, 1 boarding school, and 1,164 professed Christians, of whom 481 are communicants.

UNG KUNG. See YANG-KANG.

UNITED BRETHREN IN CHRIST; Home, Frontier, and Foreign Missionary Society of the: The first missionary work undertaken by the United Brethren in Christ was in the home field, but in 1853 a society was organized for the prosecution of home, frontier, and foreign work. Its first foreign mission field was Shengeh, on the west coast of Africa, in the colony of Sierra Leone, where work was begun in 1855. Later a temporary mission was commenced in China, and in 1895, after the disastrous revolt in Sierra Leone, work was begun in Japan, which has developed into a most successful mission. In 1900 the Society established a station in Porto Rico.

The Mission in Africa from the first had many trying experiences, as did also the Mendi Mission of the American Missionary Association, also in Sierra Leone. The trying climate, the unsettled political conditions combined to hinder the work, but notwithstanding everything, it prospered. In 1883 the American Missionary Association withdrew from its foreign work, and transferred the Mendi Mission to the United Brethren. A revolt on the hut tax question, by the interior tribes, brought heavy loss, and for a time there was question as to the Society's continuing its African work. It decided to do so, and as a result (1903) 4 missionaries and 16 native workers report 8 organized churches, with 321 communicants in 9 stations, each one of which has a circuit subjoined. There are 8 day schools, with 464 scholars, and every department shows decided gain.

In Japan there are 6 missionaries, 11 native workers in Tokio and Kioto, 1 organized church, 130 communicants. A considerable amount of evangelistic work has been carried on in the district about Kioto, special emphasis being laid upon temperance, in connection with representatives of the World's Woman's Temperance Union.

In Porto Rico a commodious church building has been dedicated, and the four missionaries speak very hopefully of the outlook. The Woman's Missionary Association of the United Brethren in Christ has its headquarters at Dayton, Ohio, and is a most efficient organization. The Young People's Union is also a strong auxiliary.

UNITED METHODIST FREE CHURCHES' FOREIGN MISSIONS: The Missionary Society of the United Methodist Free Churches of England was formed in 1857, by a union of the Wesleyan Association with certain churches of the Wesleyan Reformers. The Wesleyan Association had, at the time of the union, several missions in Jamaica and the Australian colonies, continued by the united body, which also opened in a few years missionary operations in the new fields of New Zealand, East and West Africa and China.

In the West Indies, after the abolition of slavery, the work progressed, and in 1902 there were in Jamaica and at Bocas del Toro 11 missionaries, 379 native workers, 3,559 church members, 10 stations, 37 schools. The work in Australia and New Zealand has been merged in that of the Australian Wesleyan Missionary Society.

The admission, in 1859, of a body of native Christians of Sierra Leone into the missionary connection turned the attention of the Society to Africa. Accordingly the Rev. Joseph New was sent out, and shortly afterward Rev. Charles Worboys. The work of these two men was of short duration, but their places in the mission were not long left vacant, and many noble men have been found willing to risk the climate, so unfavorable to Europeans, and have carried on the work with much success. The report (1902) shows 7 missionaries, 276 native workers, 3,358 church members, 8 stations, and 5 outstations in the Mendi field.

The Rev. Chas. Cheetham of Heywood brought before his denomination the necessities of East Africa, as represented by Dr. Krapf, and so interested his brethren in the object of his own attention, that in 1861 the Methodist Free Churches, who were then seeking to send out missionaries to a heathen field, applied to Dr. Krapf for advice as to a sphere of labor. He promptly replied, suggesting the Ribè region, and volunteered to conduct thither and establish firmly there four young missionaries, if the church would send them; and so, in that same year, the Revs. Thomas Wakefield and James Woolner, accompanied by two young Swiss, sailed for Africa. Ere long the failing health of Drs. Krapf and Woolner made their return home necessary, and the two Swiss shortly followed them. Thus Dr. Wakefield was left alone until the latter part of 1862, when he was joined by the Rev. Charles New. In 1874 Mr. New attempted to open a mission on the Tana; was cruelly treated by a savage chief, and died alone, when trying to return to Ribè, before any one could come to his assistance. Then followed an attempt to work among the Wa Nyika race, dwelling near Ribè and along the coast of the Indian Ocean, which met with disaster, but others took the place of those who had fallen, and on the Tana the mission among the Gallas was pushed forward, notwithstanding the unsettled state of the country.

The East Africa work is now carried on in two districts, Ribè and Tana, in 6 stations, with 3 missionaries, 11 native workers, and 361 church members.

The China mission was opened in 1864 by the Rev. Wm. Fuller, at Ningpo. Here he was joined after a short time by Rev. John Mara and the Rev. F. W. Galpin. Later a station was opened at Wenchow, and altho there was much hostility, through fear of foreign influence, the work was pushed until 5 outstations were occupied. The report (1902) shows 6 missionaries, 200 native workers, and 5,257 church members.

Headquarters of the Society, 4 Newton Grove, Leeds, England.

UNITED PRESBYTERIAN CHURCH; Board of Foreign Missions: The Board of Foreign Missions of the United Presbyterian Church dates from the organization of that Church by the Union of the Associate and Associate Reformed Churches in the city of Pittsburg, Pa., May 26, 1858. It had its beginnings in the Board of Foreign Missions which each of these churches had before the union. Its constitution was issued by the General Assembly in May, 1859. It was formally organized in Philadelphia, June 15 of that year, and was incorporated by the Legislature of the State of Pennsylvania April 12, 1866, under the title of "The Board of Foreign Missions of the United Presbyterian Church of North America."

This Board consists of nine members, each elected by the General Assembly of the church for a term of three years. The Corresponding Secretary, who is also appointed by the Assembly for a term of four years, is a member of the Board *ex officio*.

For a number of years this Board had under its care missions in Trinidad, Syria, China, Egypt, and India. At length it concentrated, under the direction of the General Assembly, its whole foreign work upon the latter two of these fields—Egypt and India.

India: This mission was commenced at Sialkot in 1855 by Rev. Andrew Gordon. The work (1902) occupies 12 districts: Sialkot, Pasrur, East and West Gujranwala, Gurdaspur, Pathankot, Jhelum, Zafarwal, Khangah Dogran, Bhera, Rawal Pindi and Lyallpur. There are 69 missionaries, 303 native workers, 23 organized congregations, 209 other preaching places, 9,493 church members, 13,810 adherents. There is a theological seminary at Jhelum and a college at Rawal Pindi; also 4 boarding schools, 2 industrial and 134 day schools, with a total of 8,752 scholars; 7 dispensaries and hospitals, and 2 sanitariums. Zenana and other departments are fully equipped.

Egypt: The mission was begun by the arrival in Cairo of the Rev. Thomas McCague and his wife, on November 15, 1854, and in December of the same year they were joined by Rev. James Barnet, who had been laboring in Damascus for several years in connection with the same Church. It was a favorable time for establishing a mission in Egypt, as Said Pasha was well disposed toward European civilization, and seemed not the least afflicted with that jealousy and hatred of Europeans so common among Mohammedan officials. For some years little was accomplished in mission work, except the opening of a school for girls and another for boys, and the conducting of regular divine services on the Sabbath, at which, however, very few attended. In 1856 Rev. Julian Lansing and Miss Sarah B. Dales also removed from Damascus to Egypt. Later, the work carried on at Alexandria, under the United Presbyterian Church of Scotland, and Miss Pringle's girls' school, supported by the Ladies' Society of Paisley, Scotland, both passed over to the American United Presbyterian Mission, together with two missionaries, Dr. Philip and Mr. John Hogg. Up to the year 1860 the missionary operations of the United Presbyterian Mission were, for the most part, confined to Cairo and Alexandria. A few evangelistic trips for the sale of Scriptures and other religious books, and for preaching the Gospel in an informal way, had been made both north and south of Cairo, and unsuccessful attempts had been tried to open regular mission work at Benisouef, Luxor, and Assiout. At Assiout, Muslim hatred broke out against the mission's native agent there, and thirteen Muslims were imprisoned a year for beating him in open court. The Coptic hierarchy had begun to traduce and malign the missionaries and decry their labors; while excommunication was threatened against any Copts who were disposed to read Protestant books, or meet with those who had joined the little Protestant church, and all who had professed openly their belief in Protestant principles were made the subjects of the church's anathemas. In 1860, and from that time onward for several years, other recruits from America joined the mission. The work began to prosper, the schools grew in the number of pupils and in efficiency; the attendance at divine service on Sabbath steadily increased, the property at the "mouth" of the Mooski, given by Said Pasha, was repaired and fitted up as mission premises, containing residences for the missionaries and rooms for the schools, and a comfortable and commodious place for religious services. The central position of these premises, separated but not distant from the Coptic quarter, and in the very line of traffic and travel, helped to swell the number of visitors and inquirers; persons from all parts of the country visited the mission book-depot on the Mooski on week-days, and the mission chapel on the Sabbath. Additions by profession of faith were made every few months. A commencement was made in training young natives for mission service. Sabbath-school work was prosecuted with vigor and success, and the organization of the first native Protestant church was effected in Cairo in the year 1863.

Assiout was occupied in 1865; Koos, near Luxor, in 1865; Medinet el Fayoom, and Mansura, in the Delta, in 1866; Esneh and Erment, south of Luxor; Kosair, on the Red Sea, in 1876; Manfaloot in 1878; Minieh and Tanta, in 1880; Benisouef, in 1882; Zagazig, in 1885; Assouan, at the First Cataract, in 1887. With the capture of Khartum by the British, the mission sought to enter the Sudan. For a time they were much hindered by the refusal of the Government to allow any mission work in that region. Still Mr. and Mrs. Giffen were located at Omdurman, and found work in caring for their own people who had come for trade, and gradually the restrictions were removed, and in February, 1902, permission was given to occupy a station on the Sobat River, in the Fashoda district of Sudan.

Special emphasis is laid upon school work, book distribution, evangelistic and Zenana work. It has been the policy of the mission to leave to the natives themselves the primary education of their children, and in consequence a large number of parochial or free schools have been established, supported entirely, superintended, and taught by them. The mission restricts its operations in the line of education for the most part to the training of teachers, and to giving instruction in the higher branches. Most of the teachers in the parochial schools were taught in the Mission Training-school or College at Assiout. There are also academies and seminaries for boys and girls at Alexandria, Mansura, Cairo, and Assiout, where instruction and training are given sufficient to enable pupils to prepare for school-teaching, or for taking positions in the government service. In these, as in all the mission schools, an hour every day is devoted to religious instruction, in addition to the opening exercises in the morning. The Training-school or College at Assiout has a good corps of American and native professors. The theological classes are taught in Cairo. The mission has given a good deal of attention to the distribution of religious literature, educational, practical, and controversial, and to this end has opened depots for the sale of books in a number of places, and employs a large number of colporteurs, making special arrangements with the British and American Bible Societies.

The general type of the Mission's educational work has won from Lord Cromer, the British resident, the heartiest commendation, and was probably the basis of the permission to establish stations in the Sudan.

The report for 1902 shows 74 missionaries, 495 native workers, 52 organized congregations, 171 other preaching places, 6,800 church members, 25,000 adherents, 170 schools, 12,942 scholars, 3 hospitals and dispensaries.

The Women's General Missionary Society of the United Presbyterian Church of North America is auxiliary to the General Board of the church. It was organized in 1883 and has done a notable work in Zenana, educational, and medical missions. It is represented in India by 30 missionaries and in Egypt by 19.

UNITED PROVINCES: One of the great divisions or provinces of the Anglo-Indian Empire. Its ruler is a lieutenant-governor, who is appointed by the viceroy and governor-general of India, to whom he is directly subordinate. The former kingdom of Oudh is included in the United Provinces. The territory extends from north latitude 23° 52′ to 31° 7′, and from east longitude 77° 5′ to 84° 41′. It reaches from Bengal on the southeast to the Jumna River on the northwest. On the northeast the independent kingdom of Nepal forms part of the boundary, while farther west the area extends clear up into the Himalayas themselves, and impinges at last on Tibet. Near the southern edge runs the great Ganges, tho some of the territory of the province lies south of that river. Thus a vast extent of the Upper Ganges valley is included in these provinces, and the great tributaries of that river flow through them. The area of the provinces is 107,164 square miles. The population is (1901), 47,691,782. The country is largely flat, sloping gradually toward the southeast. In the extreme northwest, however, it becomes mountainous as it approaches the Himalayan region, and several mighty peaks of that great range lie within the limits of these provinces, the highest being Nandi Devi (25,661 feet). In this vicinity are located several sanitaria and favorite places of European resort and residence. In this same region also, at the locality known as Haridwar, far among Himalayan defiles, the Ganges takes its rise. This is a famous point of Hindu pilgrimage, as being the source of their most sacred river. On the mountain slopes hereabouts tea is grown in large quantities; this industry is mainly in the hands of Europeans and supported by European capital. The Jumna River has its rise, like the Ganges, in the Himalayas; and, after describing a southerly, takes a southeasterly, course, nearly parallel to the Upper Ganges, tho gradually approaching it; and farther west it joins the greater river at Allahabad, which is now the capital city of the province. This point of union is another famous place of Hindu pilgrimage. The district enclosed between these two rivers (known as the "Doab," or Two Waters), is the granary of the Northwest. The rainfall of the whole territory is only twenty-five inches a year, and confined within three or four months. This fact renders artificial irrigation necessary to ensure the fertility of the soil. The government has supplemented the smaller labors of the native husbandmen in this direction by establishing large canal systems fed by the great rivers of the provinces, and often large enough to be of use for navigation as well as for irrigation. Besides wheat and the other cereals usual to Indian agriculture, large quantities of opium are grown near Benares, and in other parts of the provinces, and in Oudh. Two hundred and fifty thousand acres, or six per cent. of all the land under cultivation, was reported a few years since as devoted to opium. It is a government monopoly here, as elsewhere in India.

The population is largely Hindu.

Historically, these provinces present many points of great interest. Of the very earliest inhabitants few remnants now are left; the aboriginal tribes (Kols and others of this and adjacent regions) are almost certainly their representatives. The Aryan invasion, pouring in from the northwest through the Punjab, dispossessed the former dwellers on the soil, founded great cities, of which the ruins of some remain (such as Hastinapur and Kanauj), and established kingdoms and dynasties, whose wars and achievements form the basis of fact for the great Hindu poem of the Mahabharat. At Kapila, in Oudh, Gautama Buddha was born early in the 6th century before Christ, and at Kasia he died half a century later. The territory of this province formed a part of the realms of the great King Asoka, who, in the 3d century before Christ, gave his political support to Buddhism, and made it the prevailing religion of Hindustan. In the 11th century after Christ, the Mohammedans began to invade the land, through the same northwestern door as the Aryans before them. The upper portion of these provinces became a few centuries later the central seat of their power; tho the city of Delhi, their greatest capital, once just within the northwestern boundary of the Northwest Provinces, has more recently been transferred to the Punjab. Late in the last century, when the great Mogul power had sensibly declined, and was disintegrating into weak and petty principalities, the English authority, then firmly established in Bengal under Warren Hastings, began to creep up the Ganges. Benares became theirs in 1775; a part of Oudh was ceded in 1801; other districts followed; but the details we need not here repeat. A British cantonment was established at **Cawnpur** as early as 1778, which became the nucleus of the present great city. The districts thus annexed to the English territory were first governed from Bengal; but in 1833 the plan was formed of erecting them into a fourth presidency; this plan was abandoned two years later in favor of that still in force, by which they constitute a province of similar rank to the province of Bengal, and, like that, governed by a lieutenant-governor, subject to the governor-general. In 1856 the continued misgovernment of the King of Oudh caused that territory to be annexed and placed under the charge of a chief-commissioner.

The great Indian mutiny of 1857 raged more fiercely within the borders of this province than elsewhere in all India. It was at Mirat, in its northwestern part, that a native regiment of cavalry broke into open and violent rebellion on the 10th of May, 1857. After massacring their officers and many others, they started for Delhi. There the native infantry joined them. The city was seized by them, the old Mogul Empire was proclaimed, and the fire of rebellion spread rapidly over the whole province. In September of the same year Delhi was recaptured, and Lucknow was relieved the next March. The rebellion was wholly quelled before the end of 1858. But the siege of Delhi, the defense of Lucknow, under Lawrence and his little band, with its subsequent relief by Havelock, and the massacres at Cawnpur, are destined to perpetual memory.

Hindi is the principal language, subject in different localities to marked dialectic variation. The Mohammedans mostly use Urdu or Hindustani, as they do generally throughout India—a fact which constitutes that form of speech the *lingua franca* of India.

Christian missionary work dates back to 1807, when Rev. Mr. Corrie, chaplain of the East India Company, was stationed at Chunar, and undertook a little evangelistic work in addition to his regular duties; and to 1809, when Henry Martyn, also a chaplain, residing at Cawnpur, made full proof of his ministry among the natives. But no regular missionary work by any agency specially existing for that purpose was undertaken until 1811, when the Baptist Society undertook to occupy Agra.

The BMS, CMS, American Presbyterian, American Methodist, and the LMS have been actively at work for years; and a German mission has accomplished great good. Education, promoted by government and mission, is making progress.

UNITY OF BRETHREN (Brüder-Unität). See MORAVIAN.

UNIVERSITIES' MISSION to Central Africa: The Universities' Mission to Central Africa was proposed by David Livingstone in 1857, and undertaken in 1859, after a second appeal by Robert Gray, Bishop of Cape Town. In 1861 Charles Frederick Mackenzie, Archdeacon of Natal, was consecrated bishop of the mission, and by him, under the guidance of Livingstone, the mission was started at Magomero, south of Lake Nyasa, a colony of released slaves forming its nucleus. The place chosen being found unsuitable, on account of the climate, the site was twice changed, but both places proving too unhealthful for the European missionaries, Bishop Tozer, who succeeded Bishop Mackenzie in 1862, then resolved to settle in Zanzibar, and there to devote himself to the training of released slave children, in the hope of forming with them Christian settlements on the mainland at a later date.

About ten years of quiet preparatory work was carried on in Zanzibar, under Bishop Tozer and Dr. Steere, in the education of rescued slaves, the preparation of grammars and dictionaries, and the translation of portions of the Scriptures.

In 1874 Bishop Steere succeeded Bishop Tozer, and in 1875 a station was opened at Magila (Msalabani), in the Usambara region, on the mainland northwest of Zanzibar, by a colony of released slaves trained by the mission. With a view to the formation of stations in the interior, a half-way station was made at Masisi, in the Rovuma region far to the south of Magila, in 1876, and in 1879 the Rev. W. P. Johnson settled alone on the south shore of Lake Nyasa, but was expelled in 1881 by the chief of the district. In 1882 a station was opened on the east shore of Lake Nyasa, at Chitiji's, and was maintained for eighteen months under great danger, owing to the repeated attacks of the natives.

In 1883 Charles Alan Smythies was appointed bishop. In 1884, owing to the efforts of the Rev. W. P. Johnson, a steamer was purchased for the use of the mission on Lake Nyasa, and in 1885 a station was begun on the island of Likoma, in the lake, where are now the headquarters of the Nyasa Mission.

The work is now carried on in two dioceses— Zanzibar and Likoma—and in the two outlying districts of Usambara and Rovuma, in German East Africa. The two dioceses are in constant relations with those of Mombasa and Uganda, and there is in anticipation the formation of a West African province, which shall more thoroughly unify the work of the Church of England in that section.

Educational work is kept well provided, a new industrial house having been established at Zanzibar, completing the general scheme, with St. Marks Theological College at the highest grade. A new steamer has been added to the lake service, and special attention is paid to evangelistic work on the shores of the lake. In providing for the boys and girls in the schools, so far as practicable, native customs are preserved. Considerable difficulty is experienced from the unfriendliness of the Portuguese officials and their disregard of justice in dealing with the natives. The Mission staff (1902) consists of two bishops, 33 English and 16 African clergy, 22 laymen, 52 women, and 204 native readers and teachers. In the schools, homes, and workshops there are gathered nearly 5,000 children, 800 being supported by the Mission. The number of communicants is over 3,700, and of adult catechumens baptized, etc., over 12,000.

UNOCCUPIED FIELDS: This phrase is misleading, since there is, on the one hand, no land in which evangelical religion has not some representatives, while on the other, scarcely a country among those where many missionary societies are found has more than a handful of workers,—so meager a proportion of laborers that not more than the corners of great harvest fields are being touched.

I. Considering first the lands where work is established but in which few, comparatively, are affected by it, the following countries may be placed, the order being that of populations as yet unreached. Lowest in the list are such countries as Persia, Mexico, Central America, and the islands of Borneo, New Guinea, Sumatra, and Madagascar. For years, or in some cases decades, these countries have been the objects of missionary endeavor, but for various reasons few have heard the Gospel message. Save in New Guinea there is no sufficient excuse for such a state of affairs. South America is truly a "Neglected Continent," yet the portion of its inhabitants that is most neglected is the one which in a sense most needs the Gospel, viz., the more than six millions of Indians, who constitute about sixteen per cent. of the entire population. These are usually open to the missionary, so far as any governmental opposition is concerned. As for the Spanish and Portuguese-speaking populations of South America, they, too, have been largely neglected, except for the presence of a few mission stations along the coast; so that the number of missionaries of the Protestant faith are in the proportion of 1 to 54,985 of the entire population. The Dark Continent comes next in the number of those who are unreached by missions. Neglecting the vast expanse of the Sahara, which is so sparsely inhabited that it need not be considered, there are the adjacent stretches of the Sudan, in most sections densely peopled, where a population two-thirds as great as that of the United States cannot reach a Protestant mission station. In other sections of the continent there are extensive regions without a single missionary or native Christian. India, the oldest mission field of the world of any great size, comes next in the numbers that are beyond the influence of the missionary. Here there are about seventy-four thousand to every Protestant worker from foreign lands. While in most cases the nearness of mission stations, especially in South India, and the ease of reaching a Christian center because of railroads, etc., seem to place a larger responsibility on the unevangelized, it should be remembered that poverty and the obstacles due to the caste and to the village system militate against such a quest. As China is the most populous empire in the world, so within her confines is found the largest number practically beyond the pale of Christian influence. One Protestant missionary to 146,260 Chinese, and the fact that the province where mission stations were nearest together in 1898 gave each station a territory larger than Rhode Island, suggest how largely unoccupied this great empire is, and that, too, when there exists no governmental obstacle, nor any serious difficulty in the way of climate, or in the attitude of religions and the people.

II. Turning to those fields where scarcely a beginning of missionary effort has been made, the most extensive area is found in Siberia. In a territory of nearly five million square miles, or about as much as would be contained in forty United Kingdoms, the population is so sparse as to lack nearly a million of equaling that of Greater London. It is true that the Russian Church is nominally active, but its influence is *nil* on that portion of the population most needing the Gospel. Shamanism is the practical religion of the people in the north, and vices are hurrying the aboriginal peoples to their grave. Such characteristics as the burial alive of widows or motherless children, the exposure of helpless old people, who in exceptional cases have been eaten by their own offspring, and the fearful cruelty of men who slay their enemies in revenge, are by no means universal; but they display a nature which sadly needs the principles of love and common humanity, not to speak of other virtues. Southward from this Russian territory lies Central Asia, including Turkestan. All this territory is under Russian influence, tho in the eastern portion China is a more prominent factor in the life of the inhabitants. Mohammedanism and a weak form of Confucianism are the main religious stays of the people. As these races are nomadic and predatory, they constitute a confessedly difficult population to reach. Tibet, the almost inaccessible pinnacle of Asia, is even more isolated because of the exclusive policy which for decades has succeeded in keeping from her territories all save a mere handful of adventurous travelers and equally brave missionaries. Lamaism, which even in Mongolia has proven so great an obstacle to missions, is here found entrenched against all other religions, and the serious problem of living at so great an altitude, added to the isolation which must always be the lot of missionaries in that land, will further work against the missionary occupation of Tibet. The adjacent countries of Afghanistan and Baluchistan are as fanatically Muslim as Tibet is Lamaistic, even in that portion of the territory under British influence or control. Hatred of Christianity is the prime article in the creed of the bulk of the people, and this will always be a serious difficulty; tho mission work along the India boundary has shown that even the Afghans are open to its benevolent and salvatory influences. Arabia is sufficiently cut off by sandy wastes on the north to merit the appellation of the natives, who call it "The Island of the Arab." Its area, equaling one-third that of Europe, or that part of the United States east of the Mississippi, is contained in the world-zone of maximum heat, and it boasts the two great high-places of the Muslim world,—both facts constituting serious obstacles to missionary occupation. The southern and southeastern seaboard, however, are so largely under British influence that Muslim interference and persecution are not much to be feared. As containing the Holy Land of the Mohammedans, this peninsula in a peculiar manner challenges the Christian Church, despite the fact that it has but little more than eight million inhabitants. Asia's southeastern peninsula, French Indo-China, while under European control, is yet in great religious need. Upward of twenty-two millions of people are without any regular Protestant missionary work, except as Bible colporteurs and a few individuals bring the Gospel to their knowledge. India's earlier influence, which at one time was so dominant, is yielding to the ancestor-worship and Confucian ethics from China.

A little is being done for these lands; yet what are the labors of four societies and their twenty-seven representatives among populations aggregating nearly fifty millions? Naturally most of the work done has been of an elementary character, or else has been very limited in its territory. The Bible, particularly in Russian and French possessions, has been the great dependence. Unaided by any human factor, this book has proven the power of God unto the salvation of a few, thus planting the tree of healing in lands of death. Russian non-conformists in Siberia are an evangelical factor that counts for more than all that is being done by missionary societies elsewhere in the lands here under consideration. If Professor G. Frederic Wright's estimate in 1901 is correct, the half million non-conformists will do much for Siberia's various provinces, and this portion of his prophecy may be realized: "The conditions of a new country rapidly filling up with settlers are so favorable to the adoption of new customs and the reception of new light that the coming century may see Siberia leading the whole Empire into purer and more spiritual religion." Medicine in Kashgaria and Arabia is proving an entering wedge of great value. It leads to not a few cases of "double cure," as it does also at the Tibetan outpost of Leh. Tibet is becoming encircled with missions, which are able to send in through natives of the country the Tibetan Scriptures and the still better gift of a few lives charged by the dynamics of the Gospel. Were it not for the recent Russo-Chinese treaty, hope for Tibet's future would be bright. Its third article, however, is ominous, not merely for this country, but also for all other regions, especially North China, where Russia's influence is felt. The first sentence reads thus: "Entire liberty in what concerns Russian Orthodox, as well as Lamaist, worship will be introduced in Tibet; but all other religious doctrines will be absolutely prohibited." In that portion of French Indo-China adjoining the Laos country, the work is being taken up by the native church, a fact of considerable significance and hope.

III. Some of the obstacles to missionary enterprise in the lands named are serious, tho some of them are not insurmountable. Not considering the countries which contain numerous missionaries but whose territory is far from occupied, the health obstacles in the others are not to be compared with what has been overcome in certain coastal regions of South America and Africa, where fevers have been exceedingly deadly. Even Indo-China is healthful compared with some other sections of the missionary world fully occupied. Sparsity of populations is characteristic of some of the unoccupied fields; but this is not more than has confronted missionaries in Greenland, in some portions of British America and Alaska, in the southern extremity of South America, and elsewhere. The ferocity of the inhabitants of these lands is no more marked than it has been in many parts of Oceania, notably New Guinea and the New Hebrides, where missionaries have brought the work to a happy stage of progress. Religious fanaticism, it is true, is a problem in such countries as Afghanistan, Baluchistan and Arabia, while the attitude of the state religion in Siberia, Indo-China, and Tibet is an obstacle which is most serious. In the last named countries a widespread missionary movement is at present impracticable.

A serious question may be raised here, namely, that of the wisdom of expending force in overcoming the difficulties connected with all these lands, except possibly Arabia, when the missionary contingent is so meager and is needed so sorely in countries where there is perfect freedom of action and greater numbers without the Gospel. Thus the Malay Archipelago, Persia, and China are really far more strategic and actually needy fields than are the practically unoccupied lands where it is so difficult to carry on missionary work. It is not to be forgotten that parts of a great continent having in other regions a goodly number of missionaries may be more truly an unoccupied field than is French Indo-China, or Arabia. Such an instance is found in the Sudan, already spoken of, which is really the greatest unoccupied field of the present day, and one, too, which has in it nearly all the elements called for in a strategic position of the highest importance. While these counter considerations are not to be forgotten, the world-encompassing commission of Jesus Christ demands that the less important unoccupied fields should not be entirely forgotten. The angel of God still calls upon men to turn away from white harvest fields and "go toward the south unto the way that goeth down from Jerusalem unto Gaza: the same is desert." To minister, as did Philip, unto a single man, has a place in the Divine purpose which cannot be neglected in the wide scheme of preaching the Gospel to the whole world.

IV. It should not be forgotten, in considering the unoccupied fields, that there are certain portions of the population that are often unreached, tho scattered widely in lands where missionaries are laboring in force. Thus the Mohammedans are scarcely thought of in China, where, according to the "Statesman's Year-Book," some 30,000,000 of them are found, mostly in the northeast and southwest. The same is largely true of Mohammedans in Africa. While there may be a valid excuse for neglecting these religionists in the Turkish Empire and Persia, there certainly is even less reason for passing by those resident in China than in British India, where Mohammedan missions are so fruitful. Neglected classes are no less worthy of special consideration than are unoccupied lands.

UNTUNJAMBILI: A settlement in Natal, South Africa, situated N. of Tugela River, about 25 miles N. W. of Eshowe. Station of the Norwegian Church Mission of Schreuder, with (1901) 2 missionaries and their wives, 2 women missionaries, 3 native workers, 1 place of worship, 1 day school, 1 boarding school, and 118 professed Christians.

UNWANA: A settlement in Southern Nigeria, West Africa, situated on Cross River, about 85 miles N. by W. of Creektown. Station of the UFS (1888), with (1903) 2 missionaries, 2 women missionaries, 4 native workers, 1 place of worship, 1 day school, 1 dispensary, 1 hospital.

UPOLU. See SAMOAN ISLANDS.

URAMBO: A district in German East Africa, situated in the Unyamwezi country, about 175 miles E. of Ujiji on Lake Tanganyika. It was formerly a station of the LMS, but was transferred to the Moravians after they opened stations in German East Africa. Station of the Moravian Missionary Society (1897), with (1903) 2 missionaries and their wives and 1 place of worship. Some use the name Kilmani for this station.

URAWA: A town in Japan, situated on the main island, about 10 miles N. of Tokio. Station of the PE (1903), 1 missionary, 1 native worker, 1 Sunday school, and 23 professed Christians.

URDU LANGUAGE: A language which arose from the mingling of races produced by the Mohammedan conquest of India. It is closely allied to the Hindi, but, being used by the Mohammedans, where Hindi is the language of the Hindus, it is very much farther from the Sanskrit than even the Hindi. It has a large number of Arabic and Persian words. It is the official language in Western India, and serves as a medium of general intercourse between different races. It is written with the Arabic letters. The name Urdu means "camp" and is applied to the language as the "language of the camps" of the time of the Mogul conquerors of the 11th century and their followers. It is also called Hindustani.

URIPIV: A mission station of the New Hebrides Missionary Society, on Mallicolo Island.

URIYA LANGUAGE: The language of about 8,000,000 inhabiting the province of Orissa, India. It belongs to the Indic branch of the Aryan family of languages, and is closely related to the Bengali. Sometimes, in fact, it has been classed as a dialect of Bengali. Reasons exist, however, for regarding it as a distinct language. It is written with the Uriya character.

URMIA: A town in Persia, situated in the N. W. part of the country near Lake Urmia, 480 miles W. by N. of Teheran. It is the reputed birthplace of Zoroaster. Population, 35,000. Station of the PN (1835), with (1903) 8 missionaries, four of them with their wives; 4 women missionaries, 164 native workers, 112 outstations, 53 places of worship, 63 Sunday schools, 86 day schools, 2 boarding schools, 1 theological class, 1 college, and 2,719 professed Christians; 1 dispensary, 1 hospital, 1 printing house. This station was founded by the ABCFM in 1835 and transferred in 1871. Also station of the Archbishop's Mission to the Assyrians, with (1903) 1 missionary, 2 native workers, 1 boarding school, and 1 theological class. Some write the name Urumia.

URUGUAY: The smallest republic of South America, is situated on the east coast, and is bounded by Brazil on the northeast, the Atlantic Ocean and the La Plata River on the south, and on the west by the Uruguay River, which separates it from the Argentine Republic. The country is divided into 19 provinces, with a total area of 72,110 square miles and a population of about 750,000. Seven per cent. of the population are native-born, consisting principally of half-breeds; the remainder are Spaniards, Italians, French, Brazilians, and Argentines. Montevideo, the capital, situated at the entrance of the river La Plata, has a good harbor and roadstead, and a population of nearly 150,000. Uruguay was formerly a part of the vice-royalty of Spain, then became a province of Brazil, but declared its independence in 1825, which was recognized by the treaty of Montevideo (1828). By the terms of the constitution, adopted 1830, a president, elected for four years, and a parliament, composed of two houses, constitute the government of the republic.

The territory is one vast pasture-land. On the rolling plains great numbers of cattle and sheep are raised, and the principal wealth and exports of the country consist of live stock and the resulting products. Agriculture is carried on to a limited extent. The climate is in general healthful. In the coast districts there are no great extremes of heat and cold; in the interior the thermometer ranges from 86° in summer to 35° in winter. Extensive roads, more than a thousand miles of railway, an active commerce, and a good climate are doing much for the advancement of Uruguay.

The state religion is Roman Catholic, but there is complete toleration, and the general condition of education is very satisfactory.

Uruguay is blessed with a prosperous branch

of the Waldensian Church, and pastors in German and Swiss colonies are caring for the religious needs of their countrymen. The Methodist Board North is doing most of the regular missionary work, with its headquarters in Montevideo. In different parts of the city is a group of six churches, and from these there is a chain of interior stations, which are themselves centers of usefulness.

USHUAIA: A settlement in Tierra del Fuego, S. America, situated on the S. coast, on Beagle Channel. Station of the SAMS (1869), with (1903) 1 missionary and 1 place of worship.

UTAKAMAND: A village and sanitarium in the Nilgiri Hills, Madras, India, situated about 12 miles N. by W. of Coonoor, its railroad station. It is the resort of the Madras Government during several months of the year. Population, 12,000. Station of the CMS (1870), with (1903) 1 missionary and his wife, 39 native workers, 2 outstations, 13 day schools, 1 boarding school. Also station of the CEZ (1885), with (1903) 4 women missionaries, 24 native workers, 1 outstation, 7 day schools, 1 boarding school. Also station of the WMS, with (1903) 1 missionary, 9 native workers, 1 outstation, 1 place of worship, 1 Sunday school, 1 day school, and 120 professed Christians, of whom 109 are communicants. Some write the name Ootacamund.

UTENGULE: A settlement in German East Africa, situated about 60 miles N. W. of the N. extremity of Lake Nyasa. Station of the Moravian Missionary Society (1895), with (1903) 1 missionary and his wife, 1 place of worship, 1 day school, and 4 professed Christians.

UTUROA: A village on the island of Raiatea, Society Islands. Station of the Paris Evangelical Association (1893), with (1903) 1 missionary and his wife, 1 native worker, 1 outstation, 1 place of worship, 1 printing house, 1 day school, 181 professed Christians.

UVEA: One of the **Loyalty Islands**.

UWAJIMA: A town in Japan, situated on the island of Shikoku, about 45 miles S. W. of Matsuyama. Station of the MES (1888), with (1903) 1 missionary and his wife, 1 native worker, 2 outstations, 1 place of worship, 2 Sunday schools, and 80 professed Christians, of whom 53 are communicants.

V

VACAOS: A town in Mauritius, situated about 25 miles by railway S. of Port Louis. Station of the CMS, with (1903) 1 woman missionary.

VAKADU: A town in Madras, India, situated in the District of Nellore, about 16 miles E. of Gudur. Station of the Hermannsburg Missionary Society (1871), with (1903) 1 missionary and his wife, 5 native workers, 1 place of worship, 3 day schools and 90 professed Christians, of whom 76 are communicants.

VALDEZIA: A settlement in Transvaal, South Africa, situated in the Zoutspansberg District, about 80 miles N. E. of Pietersburg. Station of the Swiss Romande Mission (1875), with (1903) 2 missionaries and their wives, 1 woman missionary, 10 native workers, 5 outstations, 6 places of worship, 6 Sunday schools, 6 day schools and 505 professed Christians, of whom 120 are communicants.

VALPARAISO: An important city of Chile, S. America, situated on a bay of the same name. It is the chief Chilean seaport. It has many institutions of learning; the streets are narrow, but usually well paved, and the houses present a gay appearance with their bright colors and overhanging balconies. A railroad connects it with Santiago. Population (1895) 122,435. Station of the PN (1873), with (1903) 2 missionaries and their wives, 2 native workers, 3 outstations, 1 place of worship, 1 Sunday school, 1 printing press, 1 day school and 133 professed Christians. Also station of the SDA (1894), with (1903) 3 missionaries, 3 women missionaries, 5 native workers, 12 outstations, 11 Sunday schools, 1 printing press and 160 professed Christians. Also station of the ME, with (1903) 1 missionary and his wife, 7 native workers, 7 Sunday schools and 517 professed Christians.

VAN: A town in Asiatic Turkey, on the east shore of Lake Van, 145 miles southeast of Erzroom, 350 miles southeast of Trebizond. Climate mild, healthful; elevation 5,500 feet. Population, 30,000, Armenians, Kurds, and Turks. It is now, as it always has been, the center of Armenian influence in Eastern Turkey. On the picturesque rock behind the city are a large number of inscriptions in cuneiform, dating back even earlier than many of the Assyrian inscriptions, and relating to a kingdom that preceded the Armenian occupation. Near Van is the island of Aghtamar, the seat of an Armenian Catholicos, whose spiritual rank is equal to that of the Catholicos of Etchmiadzin. His influence, however, is small. Station of the ABCFM (1872), with (1903) 2 missionaries and their wives, 1 woman missionary, 25 native workers, 2 outstations, 2 places of worship, 2 Sunday schools, 3 day schools, 2 boarding schools, 1 industrial school, 1 hospital, 1 dispensary and 63 professed Evangelical Christians. It has not been the policy of the missionaries to advise Armenians to join the Evangelical Church if they adopt evangelical ideas.

VANDERKEMP, John T.: Born in 1747 at Rotterdam, Holland, where his father was pastor of the Dutch Reformed Church; studied at the University in Leyden; spent 16 years in the army, where he was captain of horse and lieutenant of dragoons. After leaving the army he went to Edinburgh, where he became distinguished for his attainments in the natural sciences and modern languages. He then returned to Holland and practised medicine with great success. He was converted as a result of the death of his wife and child by a shocking accident. He then offered himself to the LMS for service in

South Africa, was ordained, and in 1798 he sailed with three others for Africa, in a convict ship. On the voyage he and his companions ministered to the spiritual as well as the temporal wants of the convicts. Arriving at Cape Town in March, 1799, Dr. Vanderkemp commenced at once to labor among the natives, while at the same time he awakened a deep interest in missions among the Europeans. In May he left Cape Town for the interior. After some weeks he reached the Great Fish River, where he obtained permission from the native king Geiha to open a school. The king ordered him to leave a year later, and with some 60 followers he retired to Graaf Reinet, arriving there early in 1801. His work was especially among the Hottentots, of whom he soon collected a congregation of over 200. His efforts in behalf of this despised race aroused the enmity of the colonists, but by his wise conciliatory policy they were pacified, and he continued his work unmolested. Buildings were erected and Graaf Reinet was made a permanent station, but the privileges afforded to the natives at that station bade fair to stir up another rebellion, and Dr. Vanderkemp saw the necessity of removing the Hottentots to a place of safety, where they would form a colony by themselves. The governor gave the mission a grant of land near Algoa Bay, to which the missionaries removed in 1802. The station of Bethelsdorp was founded in 1803, and in 1810 the number of people who assembled there for worship was fully a thousand.

The cruelties which the Hottentots had so often suffered at the hands of their Boer masters excited the deepest pity in the heart of the doctor, and it is said that in the course of three years he paid no less than $5,000 for the redemption of slaves from bondage, and by his exertions, with the help of other missionaries, the Hottentots were finally set free. Almost the last public service which the doctor was able to render that people was in testifying in the courts at the Cape to the wrongs practised upon the Hottentots.

He died on the 15th of December, 1811, in the midst of active preparation to enter upon a new field of work in Madagascar. It was said of him that as combining natural talents, extensive learning, elevated piety, ardent zeal, disinterested benevolence, unshaken perseverance, unfeigned humility, and primitive simplicity, Dr. Vanderkemp has perhaps never been equaled since the days of the Apostles. As Mr. Moffat wrote about him: "He came from a university to teach the alphabet to the poor, naked Hottentot and Kafir; from the society of nobles to associate with beings of the lowest grade of humanity; from stately mansions to the filthy hovel of the greasy African; from the army to instruct the fierce savage in the tactics of a heavenly warfare under the banner of the Prince of Peace; from the study of medicine to become a guide to the Balm of Gilead and the Physician there; and, finally, from a life of earthly honor and ease to be exposed to perils of waters, of robbers, of his own countrymen, of the heathen, in the city, in the wilderness."

His period of service was short. His work was the most difficult sort of pioneer's work, for its enemies were nominal Christians quite as often as heathen savages. But his work remained. Those who later built on the foundations prepared by Vanderkemp were the first to acknowledge the value of the influence of this devoted man.

VAN DYCK, Cornelius Van Alan: Born in Kinderhook, Columbia County, New York, August 13, 1818. Died November 13, 1895. He secured a medical education at Jefferson Medical College in Philadelphia, and at the age of twenty-one was appointed medical missionary of the ABCFM in Syria. Only one medical missionary, Dr. Asa Dodge, had preceded him in Syria, and Dr. Dodge, who arrived in February, 1833, died in Jerusalem January, 1835, so that for five years, until the arrival of Dr. Van Dyck, there was no American physician in this land.

Dr. Van Dyck arrived in Beirut April 2, 1840, and spent the month of May in a tour in Northern Syria with Messrs. Thomson and Beadle, going to Tripoli, Hums, Hamath, Antioch, Latakia and Aleppo.

In July he went to Jerusalem with three of the missionary families, and in his absence Beirut was bombarded by the allied English and Austrian fleets. In January, 1841, he returned to Beirut and spent the summer in Deir el Komr, with Dr. Eli Smith and Mr. Wolcott, opening a school for the sons of the Druze chiefs. In June, 1843, he removed to Abeih, with Dr. Thomson, remaining there for eight years, teaching in the newly-founded Abeih Seminary, making journeys to Southern Lebanon, Merj Aiyun, and Hasbeiya, attending the sick in all parts of the field, translating and writing text-books for the schools in Arabic, and studying the Arabic language with constant assiduity and enthusiasm. In the wars of 1840 and 1845 he was called to attend the wounded and suffering.

On January 14, 1846, he was ordained in Abeih to the Christian ministry.

During the year 1847 a committee on behalf of the mission prepared and sent to the United States an appeal in behalf of undertaking the translation of the Bible in the Arabic language, the work to be entrusted to Dr. Eli Smith. The document is long, and now of great historical value.

The work of Bible translation was begun in 1848-49 by Dr. Eli Smith, who continued the preparatory work for eight years, until his death, January 11, 1857, but stated before his decease that he was only willing to be responsible for the translation of the first ten chapters of Genesis, which had been corrected and printed under his own direction.

In 1851 Drs. Thomson and Van Dyck were transferred to the Sidon station, having the care of the Hasbeiya and Tyre districts. Dr. Van Dyck stated that he wished to "give himself now more fully to the ministry of the Word." For the following six years his labors were abundant, and Dr. Thomson stated that their "station was on horseback." A church was organized in Hasbeiya, a Bible class was maintained in Sidon, attended by large numbers of the people. At this time his well-known Arabic geography was published.

In 1853 he visited the United States with his family. In July, 1854, he returned to Syria, and on the decease of Dr. Eli Smith, in January, 1857, he was called by the unanimous vote of his mission and the Missionary Board to take up the great work of the Arabic translation of the Scriptures.

God, in His wise providence, had been preparing him for seventeen years for this work. He had read and mastered a whole library of Arabic books, poetry, grammar, rhetoric, logic, history, geography and medicine; had published Arabic books on algebra, geometry, higher mathematics, geography, logic and prosody, besides religious tracts and sermons; and in the colloquial Arabic he was without an equal. Using Dr. Smith's work as a basis he began the work *de novo*, and after two and a half years of labor the Reference New Testament was printed, March 29, 1860. The printing of the Old Testament was finished on August 22, 1864, and the printing of the whole Arabic Bible was finished in March, 1865.

The event was celebrated in the old American Press building, and in the upper room where Dr. Smith had labored on the translation eight years, and Dr. Van Dyck eight years more, the assembled missionaries gave thanks to God for the completion of this arduous work.

The printing of the Arabic Scriptures was now carried on, but the press could not keep up with the demand, and Dr. Van Dyck went to New York in 1865 and spent two years in electrotyping the royal octavo edition of the Bible, and during his stay gave instruction in Hebrew in the Union Theological Seminary.

On his return to Beirut, in the fall of 1867, he superintended the electrotyping of various editions of the Arabic Bible, conducted the weekly Arabic journal, and entered upon his duties as professor in the medical department of the Syrian Protestant College, continuing his connection with it in abundant labors, in teaching the theory and practise of medicine and chemistry, founding the Astronomical Observatory, and witnessing the growth and development of the institution, and the graduation of 12 medical classes, until his resignation.

His labors in the St. John's and the Greek hospitals are too well known to need more than mere mention here. He labored in Syria over 55 years.

VANIYAMBADI: A town in Madras, India, situated in the N. Arcot District, about 40 miles S. E. of Vellore. Station of the German Evangelical Lutheran Synod of Missouri, etc. (1897), with (1901) 1 missionary and his wife, 3 native workers, and 3 day schools.

VAN LENNEP, Henry John: Born at Smyrna, Turkey, April 18, 1815. Died, January 11, 1889. He came from an old Dutch family long connected with the Levant trade. At the age of fifteen he was sent to America for an education. He graduated at Amherst College in 1837, and Andover Theological Seminary in 1839; was ordained at Amherst, and embarked for Turkey the same year as a missionary of the ABCFM. He was stationed first at his native city, removed in 1844 to Constantinople, and in 1854 was sent as a pioneer missionary to Tokat, Asia Minor. In 1863 he was again stationed at Smyrna, where he remained till his final departure for America. His main work was preaching and education. He was distinguished as a linguist, preaching acceptably in four foreign languages—French, Armenian, Greek, and Turkish. He was a proficient in music, drawing, and painting, which were his favorite sources of recreation. He excelled as an instructor of youth. Numbers of the most successful professional men among the evangelical Armenians and Greeks of Constantinople and Asia Minor—ministers, physicians, and instructors of youth—were his pupils. After retiring from his work abroad he secured to twenty-five Asiatics facilities for education in the United States. His warm sympathy with the people among whom he worked won their respect and love to a marked degree.

Dr. Van Lennep was honored with the degree of D.D. by his *Alma Mater*, Amherst College, in 1862.

VATÉ LANGUAGE. See EFATÉ LANGUAGE.

VATORATA: A settlement in British New Guinea, situated on the S. W. coast, about 40 miles S. E. of Port Moresby. Station of the LMS (1894), with (1903) 2 missionaries, 11 native workers, 4 outstations, 6 day schools, and 169 professed Christians.

VAYYURU: A town in Madras, India, situated in the Kistna delta, about 16 miles N. W. of Masulipatam. Station of the BOQ (1891), with (1903) 1 missionary and his wife, 1 woman missionary, 32 native workers, 12 outstations, 23 places of worship, 24 Sunday schools, 15 day schools, 1 boarding school, and 1,234 professed Christians. Some write the name Vuyyuru.

VELLORE: A town in Madras, India, situated in the N. Arcot district, 82 miles W. of Madras. It was the scene of a massacre of English soldiers by native mutineers early in the 19th century. The SPCK founded a Christian Church here in 1796. This was neglected after 1803 during about 20 years, until the care of the district was transferred to the SPG in 1835. In 1855 the chapel was sold to the RCA, and since 1885 the SPG has had no mission there. Population, 38,032. Station of the RCA (1854), with (1903) 1 missionary and his wife, 3 women missionaries, 142 native workers, 24 outstations, 27 places of worship, 30 Sunday schools, 28 day schools, 1 boarding school, 1 college, and 1,397 professed Christians, of whom 504 are communicants. Also station of the Loventhals Mission (Danish), (1872), with (1903) 1 missionary and his wife and 3 native workers.

VENEZUELA: The most northerly of the South American republics, lies between British Guiana and Colombia on the east and west, with Brazil to the south and the Caribbean sea to the north. In size it is larger than France and Germany taken together, and is about equal to the Gulf States plus Kentucky, Arkansas, and Tennessee, and is divided into eight states, two national settlements, and eight territories. In 1899 it was decided to restore a former division into twenty states, and this work is still in progress (1904). Its estimated population is between 2,000,000 and 3,000,000. The government is modeled after that of the United States of America, with more freedom given to the provincial and local governments. Education is compulsory and gratuitous, and illiteracy is fast decreasing. The state religion is Roman Catholic, and tho other religions are tolerated, they are not permitted any external manifestations. The people are engaged in agriculture, cattle and sheep raising, and mining; there are very rich deposits of gold and silver, copper and iron. Caracas, the capital, has a population of about 75,000. Altho the American Bible Society commenced the work of the distribution of Bibles in Venezuela in 1876, but little progress was made until 1886, when Mr. Milne and Mr. Penzotti canvassed the republic. Emilio Bryant, who came from Spain to Caracas in 1884, may be called the pioneer of missions in this land; and his heroic life did much for the cause of truth. Workers of the Brethren and of the Christian and Missionary Alliance have accomplished much good by their faithful ministrations. The PN and the Scandinavian Alliance of America also have missionaries in Venezuela.

VENGURLA: A town in Bombay, India, situated in the Konkan region, about 30 miles N. by W. of Goa. Station of the `PN (1900), with (1903) 1 missionary and his wife, 4 women missionaries, 1 native worker, 1 day school, 1 dispensary, 1 orphanage, and 15 professed Christians. Some write the name Vengurle.

VENKATAGIRI: A town in Madras, India, situated about 30 miles S. W. of Gudur. Station of the Hermannsburg Missionary Society (1869), with (1903) 1 missionary and his wife, 10 native workers, 3 outstations, 1 place of worship, 4 day schools, and 198 professed Christians, of whom 104 are communicants.

VERBECK, Guido Fridolin: Born January 23, 1830, in the province of Utrecht, Netherlands. Died March 9, 1898. On May 7, 1859, he sailed from New York for Japan as a missionary of the RCA, and on the following November he arrived at Nagasaki. From this time until his death, nearly forty years afterward, his life was identified with the progress of Protestant Missions in Japan. It was while living in Nagasaki that he came in contact with Wakasa, the Japanese officer who, while commander-in-chief of the forces at Nagasaki in 1854, picked up a floating copy of the New Testament in English, became interested in the life and teachings of Christ, and, in 1866, was baptized by Dr. Verbeck.

During a part of his residence in Nagasaki he taught two classes of young Samurai, the "two-sworded." These young men afterward became prominent in the new government which succeeded the revolution of 1868. Remembering their instructor, they summoned him from Nagasaki and sought his aid and advice in framing their new institutions, and in 1869 he removed to Tokio, or Yedo, as it was then called. For nine years thereafter he remained in close connection with the government, giving shape to and supervising the government university and the system of education as at first established. He accompanied the first deputation of Japanese to the outside world, on their tour among the nations of Europe. In recognition of his services in this and other directions, he received from the government the decoration, of the third class, of the Rising Sun, which entitled him to appear at all public and court receptions.

In 1889-90 Dr. Verbeck visited the United States, and his addresses on the evangelization of Japan made a deep impression. In the translation of the Old Testament he bore a conspicuous part; but he took most pleasure in lectures and evangelistic preaching. He did much toward the planting of Christianity and the development of a new civilization in the "Sunrise Kingdom."

VICTORIA (Kamerun): A trading station on the coast of the Kamerun Colony, West Africa, situated about 35 miles W. of Kamerun River. It has a botanical garden, is connected with Buea, the capital, by telephone, and is the terminus of the railway to Lisoka. Station of the Basel Missionary Society (1886), with (1903) 2 missionaries and their wives, 5 native workers, 5 outstations, 6 day schools, and 115 professed Christians, of whom 85 are communicants. Also station of the German Baptists of Berlin (1891), with (1903) 1 native worker and 1 place of worship.

VICTORIA (Mexico). See CIUDAD VICTORIA.

VICTORIA FALLS: A settlement in Rhodesia, situated on the Zambesi at Victoria Falls. Station of the Paris Evangelical Missionary Society (1898), with (1903) 1 missionary and his wife. The station, also called Mosi oa Thunya, is merely a place of transit for all the upper river country.

VIKARABAD: A suburb of Haidarabad, the capital of the native state of Haidarabad, India. Station of the ME, with (1903) 1 missionary and his wife, 14 native workers, 5 Sunday schools, 2 day schools, and 158 professed Christians, of whom 79 are communicants.

VIKTORIA. See VICTORIA (KAMERUN).

VILLUPURAM: A town and railroad junction in Madras, India, situated in South Arcot, about 35 miles by railway from the French port of Pondicherri. Station of the Leipzig Missionary Society (1875), with (1903) 2 missionaries, one of them with his wife; 17 native workers, 7 outstations, 11 places of worship, 8 day schools, 2 boarding schools, and 669 professed Christians, of whom 322 are communicants. Some write the name Wulupuram.

VINTON, Justus Hatch: Born at Willington, Conn., February 17, 1806. Died at Rangoon, Burma, March 31, 1858. Graduated at Hamilton Literary and Theological Institution, 1828; appointed in 1832 missionary to Burma by the ABMU; studied with Dr. Wade and two native converts, a Burman and a Karen, who were then in the United States; sailed with Mrs. Vinton July, 1834, reaching Maulmain in December. Having studied the language at home and on the voyage, they began their work at once. Within a week they left for the jungles, traveling for three months from village to village, making known the Gospel of Christ. Mr. Vinton's labors were not confined to the Karens. He studied Burmese that he might preach to the Burmans. During the rainy season, when travel is impossible, he labored among the English soldiers in garrison, preaching and distributing tracts among the Burmans, and translating the New Testament into Karen, or writing his commentary. In six weeks he distributed 8,000 tracts, and his labors among the troops resulted in the conversion of many, both among the common soldiers and the officers. In Maulmain Mrs. Vinton had in her school pupils who had come 200 miles for the sake of learning to read God's Word in their own language, threading the forests by night, not daring to travel by day.

The failure of Mrs. Vinton's health made a visit to America necessary in 1847. On their return to Burma in 1850 Rangoon was chosen as the center of his operations. War between Burma and England broke out in 1852, and the Burmans wreaked their vengeance for defeat upon the Karen Christians. As soon as the English had captured Rangoon, Mr. Vinton went there and took a leading part in the work of aiding the persecuted Karens, and restoring confidence among them. During this work Mr. and Mrs. Vinton had to provide for the sick in an epidemic of smallpox. All this devotion to the interests of the needy won the hearts of the Karens, and ensured the success of the new station established at Kemmendine, in the outskirts of Rangoon. In 1854, at Mr. Vinton's suggestion, the Karens of the Rangoon district organized the Karen

Home Missionary Society, the first of the kind ever formed in Burma, designed for aggressive work among the heathen, the natives already supporting their own pastors and schools. In May, 1855, the corner-stone of a church was laid by Mr. Vinton in the presence of a large assembly of native and English friends. A substantial church of brick was erected, with funds contributed in America, England, and Burma, at Kemmendine, on land given to the mission by Lord Dalhousie, Governor-General of India. In the mission premises at Kemmendine Mr. Vinton now had the work of training young men for the ministry. He also toured among the villages in the mountains, and in one•of these tours contracted the fever which caused his death. Mr. Vinton is regarded as one of the most zealous and successful missionaries ever sent to heathen lands by the Baptists of the United States.

VINUKONDA: A town in Madras, India, situated in the district of Kistna about 43 miles N. N. W. of Ongole. Station of the ABMU (1883), with (1903) 2 missionaries and their wives, 1 woman missionary, 56 native workers, 49 outstations, 2 places of worship, 34 day schools, 1 boarding school, and 3,878 professed Christians. Also station of the ELGS.

VIZAGAPATAM: A town and seaport in Madras, India, situated about 100 miles N. of the Godavari delta and about half way between Madras and Calcutta. Population (mainly Telugus), 30,291. Station of the LMS (1806), with (1903) 2 missionaries, one of them with his wife; 2 women missionaries, 22 native workers, 3 outstations, 7 day schools, 3 Sunday schools, and 108 professed Christians, of whom 78 are communicants.

VOGELSTRUISKNOP: A settlement in the Transvaal Colony, S. Africa, situated in the district of Lichtenburg. Station of the Hannover Lutheran Free Church Mission, with (1903) 1 missionary and 4 outstations.

VOHEMAR: A town and seaport in the N. part of Madagascar, situated on the E. coast. Station of the Lutheran Free Church (U. S. A.) (1898), with (1903) 1 missionary and his wife, 4 native workers, 4 outstations, 1 place of worship, and 37 professed Christians. Some write the name Vohimary.

VOLUNTEERS OF AMERICA, THE: A philanthropic and religious organization, inaugurated in March, 1896, by Commander and Mrs. Ballington Booth in response to numerous requests on the part of American citizens. It is organized in military style, having as its model the United States Army, but in conjunction with military discipline and methods of work it possesses a thoroughly democratic form of government, having as its ideal the Constitution of the United States of America.

The organization is under the command of Ballington and Mrs. Booth, who are elected by its directors as President, and by its members as Commanders-in-chief. The national headquarters are at No. 38 Cooper Square, nearly opposite Cooper Institute, New York City. The Volunteers have six regiments, under the command of six territorial and regimental officers and their wives. These embrace nine companies or central societies that have met the higher requirements before becoming chartered by the corporation, and nearly 100 self-supporting posts or societies throughout the country, not including outposts. Some of the statistics gathered at the close of the fiscal year in the month of September, 1903, may furnish some larger idea of the excellent results of the Volunteers' mission to men. It has philanthropic institutions in Chicago, Joliet, Austin, Fort Dodge, Kansas City, Pueblo, Worcester, Boston, Lynn, Malden, Toledo, Erie, Pittsburg, Buffalo, New Castle, Philadelphia, Newark, Flushing, New York City, and other centers. During the year closing September, 1903, over 400 women have been cared for, and over 3,000 beds have been provided for young women in the Homes of Mercy. There have been 479 children received into and cared for in the children's homes, and 3,400 children have been helped with clothing. The Volunteer officers and workers have visited and aided 29,084 families during the year in and around the poorer sections of the large cities where they labor. No less than 180,555 persons were lodged during the year in the Homes and institutions for working and destitute men and women, not counting the many hundreds sheltered during the floods in St. Louis, Kansas City and other centers. There were 275,428 persons fed with substantial meals at a nominal cost in these institutions, and 81,900 persons were given temporary relief and food. Over 4,000 quarts of fresh milk were donated, principally to sick children.

Over 14,000 prisoners living reformed lives have been enrolled in the Volunteers' Prison League. Mrs. Ballington Booth has the entire oversight of this branch of the work. They are in touch by correspondence and services with 28,-000 men within the walls. Tens of thousands of poor people and children were given an outing into the fresh air during the year through the organization. The Volunteers attracted 1,077,-965 persons to their Sunday and week-night services inside their halls, and despite the almost unprecedented wet season 2,537,349 to their 13,664 open-air services during the year. In addition to the Volunteer Reading Rooms, thousands of copies of Christian literature are circulated in States' prisons, jails, hospitals, soldiers' homes, and children's homes. Not by any means least, as an evidence of the permanence of the work, $97,068.40 were contributed by the poor people, irrespective of the national receipts, in support of their own Volunteer societies and local cause.

If the foregoing figures, taken from the reports of the field commanders, do nothing else, they justify the existence of the Volunteers of America, and are in themselves eloquent testimony to the work accomplished in one year.

VUGA: A settlement in German East Africa, situated in the Usambara region, about 53 miles E. by N. of Tanga. Station of the German East Africa Mission (1895), with (1903) 5 missionaries, three of them with their wives; 1 woman missionary, 1 native worker, 2 outstations, 1 place of worship, 1 day school, and 108 professed Christians. Some write the name Wuga, and call the same place Ngazi.

VUYYURU. See VAYYURU.

W

WADAI: A native state of Africa under the protection of France, lying between the Egyptian Sudan and the Lake Chad basin, containing 170,000 square miles, and a population of about 2,000,000. The state is semi-civilized. It is a rigidly Mohammedan region, with a strong tendency to destroy any person dissenting from Islam. No missionary has ever visited Wadai unless in disguise or with military force.

WADAL: An ancient city in Bombay, India, 26 miles northeast of Ahmadnagar. It was formerly of some political importance. Station of the ABCFM (1855), with (1903) 1 missionary and his wife, 43 native workers, 15 outstations, 12 places of worship, 16 Sunday schools, 1 boarding school and 237 professed Christians. Some write the name Wadale.

WADE, Jonathan: Born at Otsego, N. Y., December 10, 1798. Died at Rangoon, Burma, June 10, 1872. Graduated at Hamilton Literary and Theological Institution 1822; ordained February, 1823; embarked as a missionary of the ABMU for Burma, June 22, 1823; reached Rangoon December 5 following. At the commencement of the first Burmese war, soon after his arrival, he and Mr. Hough were arrested, imprisoned, and put in irons, then dragged to the place of execution, and compelled to kneel before a Burmese executioner, who had received orders to smite off their heads at the discharge of the first British gun on Rangoon. Panic-stricken at the sound of the cannon, the executioner, alarmed for his own safety, left his prisoners and fled. They were afterward seized by the Burmese officials, but rescued by the advancing British troops. They went to Calcutta, remaining till the close of the war. Mr. Wade occupied himself during this interval in the study of the language, translation of books, and superintending the printing of useful works. He preached also in English in the Circular Roads Baptist Chapel. At the close of the war he returned to Burma, making Amherst his home until the transfer of the mission to Maulmain, where he labored thirteen years. In 1830 he returned to Rangoon. In 1831 he visited Kyouk Phyoo in Arrakan, and began the work which was continued by Mr. Comstock and others. He received the degree of D.D. in 1852 from Madison (now Colby) University. In the absence of Dr. Binney in the United States he had charge of the theological seminary for Karens at Maulmain. In addition to preaching the Gospel, he reduced to writing the two Karen dialects, Sgau and Pwo, and prepared important theological and educational works—among them a Karen Thesaurus, a work in 5 volumes, the last volume completed in 1850. This he designed to be for the Karen language what Dr. Judson's Dictionary was for the Burmese, and to its revision he devoted his powers as long as he was able to work. He visited the U. S. twice, returned to Maulmain from the second of these visits in 1852, and during twenty years more, tho suffering from an incurable malady, he continued his literary labors for the Karens. Only six days before his death did he lay down his pen.

WADHWAN: A town in Bombay, India, situated in the Gujarat region, about 65 miles S. W. of Ahmadabad. Station of the PCI (1895), with (1901) 1 missionary and his wife, 6 native workers, 2 Sunday schools, 2 day schools, 1 orphanage and 17 professed Christians.

WAHIAJER: A settlement in Assam, India, situated in the Jaintia Hills, S. E. from Jowai, and giving access to the Mikir and Bhoi hill tribes. Station of the Welsh Calvinistic Methodist Mission, with (1903) 1 missionary, 22 native workers, 17 outstations, 28 places of worship, 18 Sunday schools, 32 day schools and 1,055 professed Christians, of whom 344 are communicants.

WAI: A town in Bombay, India, situated about 20 miles N. N. W. of Satara. Station of the ABCFM (1872), with (1903) 2 women missionaries, 14 native workers, 1 outstation, 3 places of worship, 6 Sunday schools, 1 boarding school and 22 professed Christians.

WAIKTHLATINGMANGYALWA: A station of the SAMS (1892) in the Chaco, Paraguay, South America, situated about 57 miles W. of the Paraguay River and 140 miles N. W. of Asuncion. It has now (1903) 4 missionaries with their wives, 1 place of worship and 1 day school. It is also called the Central Station of the Chaco Mission.

WAKAYAMA: A town and seaport in Japan, situated on the main island about 40 miles S. W. of Osaka. Station of the Cumberland Presbyterian Mission (1877), with (1903) 1 missionary and his wife, 4 native workers, 1 outstation, 2 places of worship, 2 Sunday schools, 1 dispensary and 142 professed Christians. Also station of the PE, with (1903) 1 missionary, 1 place of worship, 1 Sunday school, 1 day school and 28 professed Christians.

WAKEFIELD, Thomas: Born at Derby, England, June 23, 1836. Died December, 1901. In the year 1861 he was accepted by the Methodist Free Church for pioneer missionary service in Eastern Africa. The district of Ribé, eighteen miles from Mombasa, was decided upon for the first mission station; and here, for six months, Mr. Wakefield bravely grappled with the difficulties of a pioneer missionary in the Dark Continent entirely alone. Besides acquiring the Kiswahili and Kinyika languages, and preaching the Gospel among the scattered peoples around Ribé amid many discouragements, Mr. Wakefield in 1865 made a most interesting journey across the plains to the Galla country, and his experience on this trip was published in a work entitled *Footprints in Eastern Africa*. The Galla Mission was established at Golbanti in 1884; but the Masai warriors came down upon the station on May 3, 1886, and besides putting to death Mr. and Mrs. Houghton, the missionaries settled there by Mr. Wakefield, massacred several native Christians, who had volunteered to reside there that they might assist in the establishment of the mission. In 1887, having completed twenty-five years of service for the East Africa Mission, he returned to England, and during the following year he received the highest honor his denomination could confer upon him, being elected to the Presidency of the Assembly at its annual gathering. For many years he was a member of the

Missionary Committees, and he was elected a Fellow of the Royal Geographical Society and of the Royal Historical Society. In the year 1891 he reoffered himself for Eastern Africa, and he would have returned to his adopted land if his medical advisers had consented for him to do so. The Annual Assembly of his Church in an Appreciation on his life gave utterance to these words: "He not only laid the foundation of our East African Mission; he also lifted the missionary ideal of our churches to a high standard."

WALAJABAD: A town in Madras, India, situated in Chingleput Division, about 6 miles W. S. W. of Conjeveram. Station of the UFS, with (1903) 1 missionary, 80 native workers, 10 outstations, 72 professed Christians, 1 place of worship, 10 day schools, 1 dispensary and 1 hospital.

WALFISH BAY: A settlement on the coast of German S. W. Africa, which belongs to Great Britain, together with the land immediately commanding the bay. Population, 31 Europeans and 700 negroes. Station of the Rhenish Missionary Society, with (1903) 2 missionaries, 3 native workers, 2 outstations, 2 day schools, 1 Sunday school and 512 professed Christians, of whom 216 are communicants. Some write the name Walfischbei.

WALLINGER, Miss Amelia Anne: Born in England, November 13, 1839. Died in India, March 3, 1894. Miss Wallinger was the only daughter in a home of refinement and wealth, and after the death of her parents, having an abundant income at her command, she commenced her home charitable work among the orphan daughters of professional men. From 1870 to 1882, entirely at her own expense, she made her house the home and school for a large number of girls of gentle birth, whose means were not sufficient to educate them for the position to which they belonged. Afterward, she entered into active home mission work, and under her supervision were held mothers' meetings, children's sewing classes, and missions for the lowest classes of society. Altho advanced in years, she decided to give up her English home and its ties of friendship, and go to the foreign field. She set out, as a missionary of the CEZ, for Utakamund, South India, in 1886. Not only did she go at her own charges, but she bore the expense of another missionary who accompanied her. After remaining in Utakamund for a year, she and her colleague, Miss Ling, made a tour in the Wynaad, a wild country inhabited largely by Malayalim, Tamil, and Kanarese-speaking people, and having as its principal towns Gudalore and Devala. Plans were formed, not only to do missionary work in the lower plateau of the Wynaad, but also among a remnant of an ancient race in the heights of the Nilgiri Hills. The chief tribe of this race, the Todas, are believed to have been the Lords of the Hills, and Miss Wallinger and Miss Ling were the first women evangelists to these neglected men of the jungles. She and her companion would creep on hands and knees through the entrance-holes of the houses of these wild tribes; and amid indescribable degradation, they would tell the story of Divine love. During a visit to England, the year before her death, she awakened a new interest in the Nilgiri work, and almost all of the developments of this mission were at her instigation and largely assisted by her means. Her last two periods of residence in India were spent in Coonoor, and by the special request of the native Christians, they were allowed to carry her body to its last resting-place in the Coonoor churchyard.

WANGEMANNSHOH: A settlement in German East Africa, situated in the Konde region N. of Lake Nyasa. Station of the Berlin Missionary Society (1891), with (1903) 8 missionaries, of whom 5 are laymen and colonists to be stationed later; 7 native workers, 2 outstations, 1 Sunday school, 1 day school, and 53 professed Christians.

WAN-HSIEN: A town in Sze-chwan, China, situated on the Yangtsze River, 65 miles E. S. E. of Sui-ting-fu. Station of the CIM (1888), with (1903) 1 missionary and his wife, 1 woman missionary, 1 native worker, 1 outstation, 1 place of worship, 1 Sunday school, 1 day school, and 23 professed Christians. Some write the name Wan-hien.

WANICA: A station of the Moravian Mission (1886) in Paramaribo, Dutch Guiana, South America. Statistics are included under Paramaribo.

WANIYANKULAM: A town in Madras, India, situated in Malabar, 20 miles W. of Palghat. Station of the Basel Missionary Society (1886), with (1903) 2 missionaries, one of them with his wife; 27 native workers, 4 outstations, 1 Sunday school, 3 day schools, and 170 professed Christians, of whom 94 are communicants.

WANNARPONNAI: A station of the WMS Missionary Society in Jaffna, Ceylon.

WARD, William: Born at Derby, England, October 20, 1769; died at Serampur, India, March 7, 1823. Mr. Ward was a printer by trade. Having studied for the ministry, he was appointed missionary to India of the BMS, and sailed in May, 1799, with the second party sent out by that Society. Owing to the opposition of the East India Company, the missionaries established themselves at the Danish settlement of Serampur, on the Hugli River above Calcutta. Here they were joined by Carey and Thomas, who had preceded them to India, and in March, 1800, Mr. Ward printed the first page of Carey's Bengali translation of the New Testament. The work of giving the Bible to the people proceeded with astonishing rapidity. According to Mr. Ward's report in 1809, besides the whole Bengali Bible, parts of the Bible had been printed in Sanskrit, Uriye, Hindustani, Marâthi, Sikh, and blocks had been cut for the Gospel of Matthew in Chinese. The printing office was finely equipped with type for Arabic, Persian, Hebrew, Greek, and English, besides the languages named above. The building used for the printing house was 200 feet long.

The tremendous energy of this first of missionary printing offices was shown when, in March, 1812, the whole establishment, with twelve fonts of Indian type, stores of books, printed sheets, paper, etc., was destroyed by fire. Fifty thousand dollars was a low estimate of the loss. The matrices for casting type were saved. Recovering the melted type-metal from the ruins, the missionaries began casting type at once. In two weeks' time Mr. Ward was able to begin printing the Scriptures again in one language. In two months the fonts of type were so far restored that the printing was resumed on a large scale, with presses going day and night.

This catastrophe was, in fact, a blessing to the mission. It not only won instant sympathy for the men who could derive new energy from misfortune, but it made the mission and its beneficent work widely known, and brought help from every quarter.

Mr. Ward was not a mere printer, but a historian of the mission, and a true missionary in the general work. After twenty years of such service his health became impaired, and he returned to England for rest in 1819. In 1821 he was again at his post in Serampur, but his work was done, and two years later he passed away.

WARDHA: A town in the Central Provinces of India, and capital of the district, situated about 50 miles by railway S. W. of Nagpur. Station of the Mission to Lepers (1896), with (1903) 1 lepers' institute. Also station of the UFS, with (1903) 1 missionary and his wife, 18 native workers, 4 outstations, 5 day schools, 2 dispensaries, and 1 hospital.

WARMBAD: A village in German S. W. Africa, situated in the S. part about 25 miles N. of the Orange River, and 70 miles N. E. of Steinkopf; terminus of the railway to Port Nolloth. It was first occupied as a mission station by Dutch missionaries in 1806. Station of the Rhenish Missionary Society, with (1903) 1 missionary and his wife, 1 native worker, 1 outstation, 1 day school, 1 Sunday school, and 310 professed Christians, of whom 156 are communicants.

WARREN, Charles Frederick: Born at Margate, Kent, 1841. Died at Fukuyama, June 8, 1899. In 1873 was sent to the Osaka Mission, Japan, under the CMS. The first missionary at Osaka, he was principal of the theological college at that place. For a year he was appointed to the ministry of St. John's, Ashbourne, on account of the illness of Mrs. Warren; but after her death he returned to Japan, in 1888, as Secretary of the Mission. He was appointed Archdeacon of Osaka and Central Japan. Mr. Warren exerted a great influence in the Foreign Concession of Osaka, in the municipal council of which he was, for years, the president; and his ability was recognized, more or less, throughout the Japanese Empire, and, owing to his previous residence and work in China, in the Far East generally. He was a prominent member of several committees for the translation or revision of the Bible, prayer-book, and hymn-book; and as one of the originators of the Christian Conference (on Keswick lines) at Arima, his ripe experience and wise counsel proved most helpful. Under the blessing of God he lived to see the fruit of his twenty-five years' life at Osaka in the organized work of the CMS, in the development of the Osaka Settlement into the model of a Christian civilized community, and in the better understanding of all Christians for the redemption of Japan. He was author of *Family Prayers for a Week*, in Chinese; *Scripture Catechism of Faith and Duty*, in Japanese; *Book of Prayers for Family and School Use*, in Japanese; and he was one of the translators of the prayer-book into Japanese, and a member of the revising committee for translation of the Old Testament into Japanese.

WARTBURG: A town in Cape Colony, situated in Kaffraria, about 10 miles N. of Stutterheim. Station of the Berlin Missionary Society (1855), with (1903) 1 missionary, 8 native workers, 3 outstations, 1 day school, 1 Sunday school, and 387 professed Christians, of whom 163 are communicants.

WATERBERG: A village near the railway, between Pretoria and Pietersburg, at the foot of the Waterberg Mountains, on the S. slope of which is Warmbad, with its hot spring. The mountains give name also to a mission of the WMS, of which statistics are given under Makapan. Station of the Berlin Missionary Society (1867), with (1903) 1 missionary, 16 native workers, 7 outstations, and 498 professed Christians. Some call the station Modimolle.

WATERLOO: A town in Sierra Leone, West Africa, situated 15 miles S. E. of Freetown. Station of the CMS (1819), with (1903) 23 native workers, 10 outstations, 1 place of worship, 1 Sunday school, 9 day schools, and 1,374 professed Christians, of whom 600 are communicants. Also station of the UMFC (1879), with (1903) 1 missionary and his wife, 32 native workers, 3 places of worship, and 283 professed Christians, of whom 192 are communicants. Also station of the WMS, with (1903) 12 native workers, 3 outstations, 8 places of worship, 3 Sunday schools, 3 day schools, and 434 professed Christians, of whom 345 are communicants.

WATERLOO: A settlement in Dutch Guiana, South America, situated about 10 miles S. of Nickerie. Station of the Moravian Mission Society (1859), with (1903) 1 missionary and his wife, 22 native workers, 2 places of worship, 1 day school, and 224 professed Christians.

WATHEN. See NGOMBE.

WAZIRABAD: A town in the Punjab, India, situated about 30 miles E. by S. of Sialkot. The town is comparatively new, and has only recently risen to importance. It is much better and more regularly built than most native towns, altho the houses are mostly made of sun-dried or kiln-burned bricks. Population, 16,462. Station of the Church of Scotland Foreign Missions (1863), with (1901) 1 missionary, 15 native workers, 8 outstations, 4 day schools, and 25 professed Christians.

WEASISI: A station in the northern part of Tanna, New Hebrides.

WEI-HAI-WEI: A seaport and military post in Shan-tung, China, situated at the entrance of the Straits of Chili, and temporarily occupied by Great Britain under lease. Station of the PB, with (1900) 3 missionaries, two of them with their wives.

WEI-HSIEN: A town in Shan-tung, China, situated about 150 miles S. W. of Teng-chau-fu, an important center, which will be a station on the German road from Kiao-chau. Population, 100,000. Station of the PN (1882), with (1903) 4 missionaries and their wives, 4 women missionaries, 88 native workers, 124 outstations, 20 places of worship, 48 day schools, 9 boarding schools, 1 dispensary, 1 hospital, and 3,000 professed Christians. The college from Teng-chau-fu is to be removed to this place. Some write the name Wei Hien.

WEI-HWEI: A town in the province of Ho-nan, China, situated on the Wei River, about 50 miles S. by W. of Chang-te-fu. Station of the PCC (1903), with 3 missionaries, 1 place of worship, 1 dispensary, and 37 professed Christians. This town takes the place of Hsin-cheng in the list of the Society's stations. This latter place is now an outstation of Wei-hwei.

WEIPA: A settlement on the W. coast of Cape York Peninsula, Australia. Station of the Mission of Federated Churches of Australia and Tasmania, with (1901) 2 missionaries, one of them with his wife, and 1 woman missionary. Station of the Moravian Missionary Society, with (1903) 1 missionary and his wife, 1 woman missionary, and 1 place of worship.

WELSH CALVINISTIC METHODISTS, Foreign Missions of the: The Calvinistic Methodists of Wales began to take an interest in missionary work at the time when the London Missionary Society was established. They contributed liberally to its funds, and several of the most useful missionaries of that Society had been trained in their churches. But the growing desire that the connection should have a mission of its own led ultimately to the organization of the Welsh Calvinistic Methodist Foreign Missionary Society in Liverpool in January, 1840. In 1834 the British Government completed a treaty with the chiefs of the Khasi Hill tribes in the extreme northeastern part of Hindustan, and a military post was to be established at Cherrapunji, and a road made across the Khasi Hills to the British territory in the Brahmaputra valley. When the Welsh Foreign Missions were planned in 1840 the attention of the directors was called to the Khasi Hills as a new and promising field. Accordingly, the plan seeming wise, the first missionary of the Society, the Rev. Thomas Jones, left for Cherrapunji in November, 1840. Missionaries were also sent out in 1842 and again in 1845; but at times, owing to various circumstances—defection, illness, and death—only one or two men were left to carry on the work, and the progress for some years was but small, if reckoned by the number of converts, which reached but fourteen in the first decade.

In 1846 a new station was established at Jowai, the chief village in the Jaintia Hills, and in subsequent years the work was extended to various other parts of the hill country. In 1849 the Rev. W. Pryse commenced operations at Sylhet, in the plains of the Barak River region. Tho the work was carried on vigorously, and not without some degree of success, circumstances occurred which made it advisable to limit the operations of the mission to the hill country, and until 1887 the large district around Sylhet was left unoccupied, when in that year the mission was again enabled to resume its work there. The mission field in India is divided into 15 districts: 10 in the hills, and 5 in the low country to the southward, which was transferred from Bengal to Assam in 1879. Day schools, evangelistic work, publishing, and medical work are all features of the mission.

An indication of the growth of the work is given by the fact that the districts have doubled since 1890. There are now (1902) 439 preaching stations, against 136; 331 Sunday schools and 16,161 scholars, against 140 schools and 7,294 scholars. There are now 5,616 communicants, while the total attendants at churches number 16,659. There are 10 ordained missionaries in the hills and 2 women missionaries, and in the plains, 5 ordained and 5 women missionaries.

Recently work has been commenced in the Lushai Hills, in the extreme southwest of Assam. Two missionaries are located here, but their enterprise is still in its infancy. There are 13 native ministers, and 48 preachers who have been admitted to the presbytery, some of them being pastors and others in charge of schools. There is a theological institution at Cherra, and there are 401 day schools, with 8,241 scholars (2,809 girls), and a medical mission in the Jaintia Hill district.

In 1842 the Society organized mission work among the Bretons in Western France, and still has a small mission work in Brittany. There are 3 stations, each with 1 missionary, 5 churches, 74 converts, and 71 adherents not admitted to membership. The influence of the work, however, extends far beyond the immediate Protestant community.

There is also a woman's branch of this Society, with headquarters at 20 Sherlock Street, Liverpool, which aids in the collection of funds, but does not carry on independent work.

WEN-CHAU-FU: A town and treaty port in Che-kiang, China, situated about 160 miles S. S. E. of Hang-chou, China. Population (1901) 80,000. Station of the CIM (1867), with (1903) 2 missionaries and their wives, 4 women missionaries, 17 native workers, 22 places of worship, 1 day school, 1 boarding school, and 448 professed Christians. Also station of the UMFC (1877), with (1903) 5 missionaries, three of them with their wives; 156 native workers, 6 outstations, 6 day schools, 7 Sunday schools, 1 dispensary, 1 hospital, and 3,294 professed Christians, of whom 1,294 are communicants. Some write the name Wenchow.

WEN-LI: Name applied to the classical or book language of China, as distinguished from the colloquial. To write in the same natural way as one would talk is contrary to Chinese teaching and practise; and the classical book style so abounds in stilted, condensed, epigrammatic phrases, that a man who has not mastered the literary style is unable to understand the sense, even tho he may be able to recognize the characters or ideograms. A variation of the Wen-li is the Easy Wen-li, which is not so severely independent of the spoken dialect.

WEN-SAN, or GEN-SAN: A town and seaport in Korea, situated on the E. coast, about 120 miles N. E. of Seoul. Station of the PCC (1893), with 2 missionaries and their wives, 2 women missionaries, 1 native worker, 1 outstation, 1 place of worship, 2 day schools, 1 Sunday school, and 125 professed Christians, of whom 77 are communicants. Also station of the MES (1900), with 1 missionary and his wife, 2 women missionaries, 1 dispensary, and 205 professed Christians, of whom 55 are communicants. The station of the ME was transferred to the MES in 1902.

WEN-TENG-HSIEN: A town in Shan-tung, China, situated about 12 miles S. of Wei-hai-wei. Station of the PB, with (1900) 1 missionary and his wife.

WESLEYAN METHODIST MISSIONARY SOCIETY: *History:* The first distinctively foreign missionary of Wesleyan Methodism was Dr. Coke. As early as 1744, through the efforts of Whitefield, special hours of prayer for the outpouring of the spirit of God upon all Christian churches and upon the "whole inhabited earth" were observed, and John Wesley went to North America to preach. From that time onward missions in the British possessions in North America were carried on, and numerous preachers were sent out. These missions, however, were mainly intended for the benefit of British colonists, and missions to the heathen were not undertaken until 1786, when Thomas Coke, destined by the Methodists in England for Nova Scotia, was driven to the British West Indies, where a mission to the negro slaves was at once commenced. In his hand the conduct of the Wesleyan missions was mainly placed until 1804, when, upon his departure for America, a committee of three was appointed by the Conference to undertake the management of the work. It was at Dr. Coke's instigation that a mission to West Africa was undertaken in 1811, and after crossing the Atlantic eighteen times, when he was 76 years old, he again sailed, with six other missionaries, December 31, 1813, to Ceylon to found there the third Methodist mission. His death, early in the following year, made necessary other arrangements for carrying on the work; the Society was accordingly reorganized, and in the course of a few years was placed on its present permanent footing.

The management of the missions and the collection and disbursement of funds are entrusted to a committee appointed annually by the Conference, as are also the general secretaries and two treasurers, a minister and a layman.

Development of Work: Before the death of John Wesley, his teachings had been extended into Ireland, Scotland, the Shetland Isles, and the Channel Islands; and the first years of the new century saw the Methodists at work among the French prisoners in England and in the French prisons. As early as 1807 a society of seventy persons was reported at Arras, France, and Methodism rapidly extended to other parts of the country. Work was begun in Germany in 1830 by Christopher Gottlob Müller, who had been converted through the instrumentality of a Wesleyan minister; in Switzerland in 1839, by the Wesleyan missionaries already at work in the south of France; at Gibraltar in 1809, from whence Spain and Portugal were reached; and in Italy in 1860, after the revolution in the civil government had allowed a measure of religious liberty to the people. In 1766 the first Methodist sermon was preached in America by a Mr. Embury at his house in New York City. In 1780 Methodism was carried to Canada by a local preacher, and not long after missions were established among the Indians in Canada, and, later, in Hudson Bay Territory, British Columbia, Nova Scotia, New Brunswick, Prince Edward's Island, and Newfoundland. Upon Dr. Coke's recommendation a missionary was sent to the Bermudas in 1799. The mission to India at Ceylon was undertaken by Dr. Coke in 1813. The first scheme for the establishment of a mission to West Africa, devised by Dr. Coke in 1769, proved a failure, but in 1811 a second attempt was made at Sierra Leone, which was eventually successful; in 1821 a second station was opened on the river Gambia, and in 1834 a mission to the Gold Coast was undertaken. In the year 1814 the Society sent the Rev. John McKenny to Southern Africa as its first missionary. A little later a station was established in Little Namaqualand, and from this point the work extended by degrees throughout Southern Africa. In 1812 the committee received an appeal from two schoolmasters who were teaching in New South Wales, by order of government, to send out Wesleyan preachers to undertake a mission among the convicts, and the Rev. Samuel Leigh went for this purpose to Sydney in August, 1815. Missionaries were sent to Tasmania in 1821, to Victoria in 1838, and to Queensland in 1850. The mission to the cannibals of New Zealand was commenced in 1822; in the same year a missionary was also sent to the Friendly Islands, but it was not until 1826 that a mission was established there. As soon as this work was on a firm basis, the missionaries endeavored to do something for Fiji, but some years elapsed before the mission to Fiji became an actual fact. Work in China was undertaken in 1853.

As a result of this development the Foreign Missions of the Wesleyan Methodist Missionary Society are classed in three departments:

A. Missions originated by the Society but now entirely independent and under the direction of Colonial Conferences: Canada, Australia, New Zealand, and the South Sea Islands.

B. Missions under the immediate direction of local Conferences but aided by the Society: Ireland, France, West Indies, and South Africa (Cape Colony, Natal, Orange River Colony).

C. Missions still under the immediate direction of the British Conference: Europe (Italy, Spain, Portugal, Gibraltar, Malta, Cairo); Ceylon; India (North and South); China; South Africa (Transvaal, Swaziland, Rhodesia); West Africa (Sierra Leone, Gold Coast, Lagos); Western Hemisphere (Bahamas, Honduras and the West Indies).

A. Missions originated by but now independent of the WMMS.

Canada: The work in this country was from the first chiefly colonial, and the organization of the Canadian Methodist Missionary Society in 1824 early took the care of the work among the Indians from the parent Society.

Australia: It is perhaps doubtful whether a mission was ever commenced in any part of the world under more discouraging circumstances than was that of the Wesleyan Society to Australia. New South Wales was chiefly a community of convicts, with wandering tribes of savage natives on its borders. The free settlers and squatters, widely scattered and entirely destitute of religious instruction, were only a few degrees above the convict population. Up to the time of the arrival of the first Wesleyan missionary the government had been occupied in erecting jails, barracks, and other public buildings necessary for the civil, military, and convict establishment, but very little had been done for the religious and moral improvement of the people. Indeed, the whole aspect of affairs—the state of society, the mode of government, the discipline adopted in the management of convicts, and the temper and spirit of everything and everybody—appeared cold, cruel, and repulsive in the extreme. Nevertheless, Mr. Leigh (1815), having secured the countenance and protection of the colonial government, began to arrange his plans, and mapped out a wide circuit in which to itinerate. From Sydney he extended his labors to Paramatta, where he met the Rev. Samuel Marsden, one of the four chaplains appointed to minister to the troops and convicts, and afterward identified with missions to New Zealand. Assistance was given by Methodists in Australia, reenforcements were sent from England and the work prospered. In 1864 funds were secured for a Wesleyan College at Sydney, and the formation of the Australasian Methodist Missionary Society (organized in 1822 as an auxiliary and in 1855 as a separate Society) relieved the parent Society of responsibility for work in that section of the world. The fields specially under the care of this Australasian Society are Samoa, Fiji, New Britain, New Guinea, China, the Chinese in Victoria, New South Wales, and Queensland; and the Indian Coolies of Fiji. In 1900 the Bible Christians of Australia united with the Methodist churches, and the combined forces (1898) represented 55 missionaries, 3,903 native workers, in 22 principal and 1,411 outstations, with 100 organized churches and 35,275 communicants.

New Zealand: In 1818 the Rev. Samuel Marsden persuaded Mr. Leigh to take a trip to New Zealand, and as a result on a visit to England he laid before the committee a proposal for the commencement of a mission to the cannibals of New Zealand. The Society was at that time laboring under a heavy debt, but Mr. Leigh, by forcible appeals to the friends of missions in many parts of England, obtained contributions of goods of various kinds, which in New Zealand would be more valuable than money itself, and the Society undertook to commence the new mission without delay. About this time two Maori chiefs arrived in London with Mr. Kendall of the Church Missionary Society; their appearance gave a new impetus to the plans for New Zealand; the necessary preparations were soon completed, and the party of missionaries—consisting of Mr. and Mrs. Leigh, Mr. and Mrs. Horton, appointed to Tasmania, and Mr. Walker—sailed from England on April 28, 1821. Work was commenced at Wangaroa in 1822. Up to 1830 the mission met with no success, and for a time the work was broken up. Then there came a change and the advance was most marked, and when in 1855 the work was passed over to the Australian Conference there was a large community of European and Maori Wesleyans. Subsequently the Maori church was greatly depleted, but after the establishment of the New Zealand Conference (1874) it revived.

South Seas: These missions include those in the Friendly Islands, Samoa, Fiji, and New Britain (Neu Pommern). In June, 1822, about twenty-two years after the last surviving agent of the LMS had escaped from the Tonga or Friendly Islands, the Rev. Walter Lawry, with his family, sailed from Sydney, and in the following August anchored off Tonga. Among the hundreds of natives who came off from the shore in their canoes was one Englishman, named Singleton, who had lived sixteen years on the island, being one of the survivors of the ill-fated "Port-au-Prince," whose crew had been massacred in 1806. He had become a thorough Tonga man in manners and language, but became very useful to Mr. Lawry as an interpreter and in other ways, and before long himself accepted the Gospel. Mr. Lawry was kindly welcomed by chiefs and people, and tho the habitual fickleness of the people manifested itself, there was some success and in 1826 other missionaries were sent out by the Society. Urgent calls come from other islands, and at Vavau, Hapai and Mau the progress was phenomenal. Special attention was paid to education and the preparation of Christian literature, and in 1870, it was affirmed that not a single heathen remained in the Tonga Islands.

One of the results of the revival in the Friendly Islands in 1834 was the commencement of a mission to Fiji, which was undertaken by the missionaries (one of whom, Mr. Watkin, went to England to plead there the cause of "poor Fiji"), seconded by King George and some other zealous disciples from Tonga. The Fijians at that time were atrocious cannibals, even exceeding the people of New Zealand, the New Hebrides, and other islands in this and in war, polygamy, adultery, murder, suicide, deception, fraud, theft, and many other crimes. In October, 1835, Messrs. Cross and Cargill, with their families, several converted Friendly Islanders, and a few Fijians returning to their own country, embarked in a small schooner, the "Blackbird," and, landing at Lukemba, commenced the work destined to be so hard and perilous, but also so blessed. Perhaps there never was a harder struggle between light and darkness, truth and error, than that which took place in the course of the Fiji Mission, but the missionaries persevered and pushed forward, and had their reward in the victory which crowned their efforts at last. The cession of the islands to Great Britain in 1874 facilitated the work, which has been continued under the auspices of the Australasian Society.

As the mission to Fiji was the outgrowth of the work in the Friendly Islands, so that in New Britain resulted from the work in Fiji. Commenced in 1875 by a company largely made up of native teachers from Fiji, there were the usual experiences of hostility and bloodshed, but the courage of the little band never faltered, the places of those who had fallen were soon filled and the work has grown under the care of the Australasian Society. The Society has also some work in Savaii and the adjacent islands, commenced in 1835, tho never developed as fully as that of the LMS.

B. Missions aided by the Society: Those in Ireland and France are chiefly among Roman Catholics, altho the English communities are not neglected.

West Indies: In January, 1758, Mr. Wesley preached in the house of Nathaniel Gilbert, Esq., the Speaker of the House of Assembly in Antigua, who was at that time residing in England. Several of Mr. Gilbert's negro servants were also present and appeared much affected by the sermon. Later on, two of these slaves were baptized by Mr. Wesley. Mr. Gilbert, too, became identified with the Methodist people, and upon his return to Antigua commenced at once to hold religious meetings for his own people and those of the surrounding estates, and in every possible way labored for their good until his death. Two of the slaves kept up the work, and a Mr. Baxter, a shipwright and a Methodist local preacher, did what he could. Repeated appeals were made to England, but it was not until 1786 that Dr. Coke, driven out of his course to Nova Scotia by a storm, landed at Antigua, became interested in the situation there and in the neighboring islands. The result was that missionaries were sent out in 1787 and in the course of a few years almost every colony was reached.

In 1885 the British Conference, contrary to the judgment of the Missionary Committee, decided that the time had come for a West Indies Conference, and accordingly the entire work of the Society in that section, excepting Bahamas and Honduras, was so set apart. Two conferences were found, a Western, including Jamaica, Haiti, San Domingo, Panama and Costa Rica, and an Eastern, including Antigua, St. Kitts, St. Vincent, Barbados, Trinidad, and British Guiana. All of these sections have suffered heavily in recent years, and while the churches, notably in Guiana, have been ordinarily prosperous, the general situation is such that (1903) it has been decided to bring them back under the care of the British Conference.

South Africa: In 1815 the Rev. Barnabas Shaw was appointed to commence a Wesleyan Mission in Cape Colony. Permission to preach was refused, but he took matters into his own hands and preached without the governor's sanction. His congregations, however, were composed principally of soldiers, and his greatest desire being to preach Christ to the heathen, he gladly availed himself of an opportunity which offered, through Mr. Schmelen of the LMS, to go to Great Namaqualand. In September, 1815, Mr. Schmelen and Mr. Shaw, with their families, attendants, and supplies, set out on their long journey. On the 4th of October, after crossing the Elephant River, Mr. Shaw unexpectedly found his sphere of labor in meeting the chief of Little Namaqualand, accompanied by four men, on his way to Cape Town to seek for a Christian teacher, so that his tribe, like others, might have the advantages which he had seen follow the introduction of the Gospel. Mr. Shaw agreed to go with the chief to his mountain home and to remain with him and his people, while Mr. Schmelen continued his journey to his own station in Great Namaqualand. About three weeks later the chief and his party reached Lily Fountain, on Kamiesberg, the principal home of the chief of the tribe of Little Namaquas. They were met by a party of natives who had come out to welcome them, and from that introduction the work prospered, and was extended by tours into Great Namaqualand and Damaraland. An attempt to establish a mission north of Orange River resulted in the murder of the company of missionaries and native teachers, but another effort was more successful. Subsequently, on the entrance of German societies, the work beyond the Orange River was transferred to the Rhenish Society.

In the year 1820 a second attempt was made to start a Wesleyan Mission in Cape Colony, and Mr. Edwards was directed to proceed thither from Little Namaqualand. With the cordial permission of the governor to preach to and instruct the slave population of the town and neighborhood, he began his work, which he for some time prosecuted with success, and in which he was succeeded by other missionaries sent out from England. Chapels were built in various parts of Cape Town, with which were connected prosperous day and Sunday schools. The work has extended also into the Grahams Town and Queenstown districts. Mission work was commenced in Bechuanaland in 1822, tho it was some little time before it was successful. In 1841 a Wesleyan missionary accompanied the British troops into Natal, and after a time of service for the English and Dutch inaugurated a work for the natives. The churches in the whole section, English and Kafir, grew rapidly, and in 1882 the South African Conference was organized and assumed the entire care of the mission work in South Africa, excepting that in the Transvaal, Swaziland, and Rhodesia, which remained under the direction of the parent Society.

C. Missions under the British Conference. 1. *Western Hemisphere.* (1) *Honduras:* In British Honduras four stations are occupied: Belize, Corozal, Stann Creek, and Toledo. In Spanish Honduras the stations are Roatan and San Pedro Sula. The work is among the foreign population and among the natives, including the mahogany and logwood cutters. There are (1903) 32 chapels, 17 other preaching places, 8 missionaries and assistants, 41 teachers, 48 catechists and local preachers, 1,737 communicants, 26 schools, 1,453 scholars (including S. S. scholars, 2,254), attendants on services, 6,180.

(2) *Bahamas:* The work here was commenced in 1803 by Rev. William Turton, a native of the West Indies, at New Providence. It has been extended until there are stations at Nassau, Rock Sound, Tarpum Bay, Governor's Harbor, Harbor Island, Great Abaco, Andros and Bimini, and Key West. The report shows (1903) 29 chapels, 9 other preaching places, 12 missionaries and assistants, 7 teachers, 111 local preachers, 3,561 communicants. The number of day schools is small—4, but special attention is paid to Sunday schools, which number 30, with 3,795 scholars; attendants on services, 11,520.

(3) *West Indies:* As mentioned above, the British Conference is now taking charge of this work, for some time cared for by local Conferences.

2. *Ceylon:* Notwithstanding repeated appeals, the Society did not feel willing to undertake work in India, until Dr. Coke offered to lead the enterprise and to provide the necessary initial expense, to the amount of £6,000. In 1813 he and six young missionaries started. Dr. Coke died on the voyage, but his colleagues resolved to carry through the undertaking. They reached Colombo, Ceylon, were kindly received by the governor, and several places were named to them as greatly in need of the Gospel and of schools for the training of native children. It was decided to open stations at Colombo, Galle, and Matura in the south, among those of the native population who speak Sinhalese, and at Jaffna and Batticaloa in the north, where the Tamil language is in common use. In a very short time the missionaries were able to preach to the natives, and also to Dutch and Portuguese colonists. Schools were organized, a printing-press was set up at Colombo, a Sinhalese grammar and dictionary were prepared, and the work flourished in all its departments—literary, evangelical, and educational. In addition to those already mentioned, important stations were established in Southern Ceylon, at Negombo, Kandy, Caltura, Pentura, Seedua, Morotto, Wellewatta, and other places; while in North Ceylon, where the Tamil language had been conquered and several native teachers trained for the work, chapels and schools were established, not only in the villages adjacent to Jaffna, but also at places at a considerable distance, which were afterward occupied as separate stations. As at present organized the work is divided into four districts: Colombo, Kandy, Galle, and Jaffna.

There are two colleges, Wesley College, at Colombo, and Richmond College, at Galle. There are also several industrial schools and medical work is developed, while the system of day schools is well arranged. Considerable attention is paid to the needs of the English and Portuguese communities, but the chief work is in the Tamil and Sinhalese languages. The report (1903) shows for the four districts 69 chapels, 245 other preaching places, 68 missionaries and assistants, 4,738 communicants, 986 day school teachers in 379 schools, with 29,031 pupils, and about 15,000 attendants on services.

3. *India:* The first Wesleyan mission work in India was begun in Madras in 1817. It has since developed until there are eight districts, Madras, Negapatam, Haidarabad, Mysore, Calcutta, Lucknow, Bombay, and Burma. Special attention is paid to education: witness Royapettah College, in Madras, and Findlay College, at Mannargudi; also training institutions and general schools in the different districts. Street preaching in Madras and tours through the villages of Haidarabad have brought good results. Medical work, too, has been pressed. In Burma the chief work is at Mandalay. In all, work for the English residents takes an important place. The report shows for the 8 districts 152 chapels, 267 other preaching places, 130 missionaries and assistants, 224 local preachers, 8,035 communicants, 570 day schools, with 27,886 scholars, and more than 20,500 attendants at services.

4. *China:* In 1852 Mr. Piercy, who had for some time labored in China at his own expense, offered his services to the Wesleyan Society, was accepted by them, and appointed to Canton, where he remained until the war between England and China forced him, with other missionaries, to take refuge in Macao. During the two years spent there he continued the study of the language with unabated zeal, and upon the restoration of peace, in 1858, reoccupied Canton, as a station of the Society. In 1860, upon the receipt of a legacy intended expressly for the India and China missions, the Committee was enabled to largely extend its work. The staff of workers was increased in numbers, and a new station was commenced at Fat-shan. In 1862 a mission for North China was established at Hankau. Later Wu-chang, Han-yang, Sui-chow, Wu-hsueh and other stations were occupied, and more recently a station has been opened in Hunan at Chang-sha. In this work the Society has the assistance of the Central China Wesleyan Lay Mission. In the two districts, Canton and Wu-chang, including Hu-nan, the report (1903) shows 79 chapels, 27 other preaching places, 34 missionaries and assistants, 51 local preachers, 2,597 communicants, and 52 teachers in 42 day schools, with 1,011 scholars.

5. *South Africa:* The missions in South Africa, retained under the care of the British Wesleyan Conference and thus controlled by the Missionary Society, include the Transvaal and Swaziland, and Rhodesia districts. The former is divided into the central section, Johannesburg, Pretoria, Middleburg, etc.; the northern and eastern section, Zoutpansberg, Swaziland, Delagoa Bay, etc.; the southwestern section, Potchefstroom and Klerksdorp; British Bechuanaland section, Mafeking. The Rhodesia district is divided into the Mashonaland and Matabililand sections. The report (1903) shows in the two districts 151 chapels, 282 other preaching places, 53 missionaries and assistants, 559 local preachers, 51 catechists, 9,683 communicants, 61 day schools, with 56 teachers and 2,970 scholars. Especially in the Transvaal section it is impossible to distinguish between the work for English and Dutch and that for the natives.

6. *West Africa.* (1) *Sierra Leone and Gambia:* Dr. Coke's first scheme (1769) for the civilization of the Fulas, in the neighborhood of Sierra Leone, proved a failurc. Some of the company sent out died of fever before reaching their destination, others absconded, and the rest returned home. In the year 1811 the Rev. George Warren and three school teachers were sent to Sierra Leone. Upon their arrival in the colony they found about one hundred persons, chiefly free blacks from Nova Scotia, who had received the Gospel at the hands of Wesleyan missionaries there. They had already built a chapel, and had sent repeatedly to England for a missionary. After eight months of labor Mr. Warren died of fever, and for many years there was much loss of life from the climate. Eventually, however, this was to a good degree overcome, the work was developed into the surrounding country, including a settlement at the mouth of the Gambia. The principal stations are Freetown, Wellington, Waterloo, Sherbro, etc., in Sierra Leone, and Bathurst, in the Gambia section.

(2) *Gold Coast:* The work of the Society in this section commenced in an effort to provide for some native boys who had learned to read the Bible in the Government school. In 1845 the Rev. Henry Wharton, a native of the West Indies, went out, and, with the help of several native missionaries and some Europeans, the foundations for a successful work were laid. Stations were formed at Cape Coast Castle, Accra, and a number of other places, while the Lagos region, including Abeokuta, Yoruba Interior, Porto Novo, etc., was set apart as a separate mission district. The report (1903) shows in the three districts 212 chapels, 787 other preaching places, 61 missionaries and assistants, 109 catechists, 777 local preachers, 214 teachers in 159 day schools, with 11,748 pupils, and 19,180 communicants.

7. *Europe:* (1) *Italy:* The work of the Society is carried on in three sections: the northern at Rome, Spezia, Parma, Bologna, Padua, Milan, Luino, Simplon, etc.; the southern at Naples, Salerno, Potenza, etc.; the Sicily at Palermo, Messina, Catania, etc.

(2) *Spain:* Barcelona, Palma de Mallorca and Minorca.

(3) *Portugal:* Lisbon and Oporto.

(4) *Mediterranean:* Gibraltar, Malta, and Cairo.

A considerable amount of the European work is for English residents, and of that at Malta and Gibraltar for the soldiers.

The report for the European Missions (1903) shows 24 chapels, 75 other preaching places, 44 missionaries and assistants, 19 catechists, 62 teachers in 42 day schools, with 2,325 scholars, and 2,199 communicants.

The Wesleyan Society emphasizes Sunday school work, and in most cases the number of Sunday school scholars exceeds the number of those in the day schools.

The' Women's Auxiliary of the Wesleyan Methodist Missionary Society, organized in 1858, carries on its work in closest connection with the general society.

The Central China Wesleyan Lay Mission, which for some years represented a number of independent workers along the lines of the CIM, was, in 1899, merged in the general Society, tho in some cases the funds remain distinct.

WEST, Henry S.: Born at Binghamton, N. Y., January 21, 1827. Died at Sivas, Turkey, April 1, 1876. He studied at Yale College and the College of Physicians and Surgeons in New York City. After practising medicine for some time, he was appointed by the ABCFM a missionary to Turkey and sailed in January, 1859. He was stationed at Sivas, at the western edge of the Armenian highlands; but he journeyed far in every direction to heal the sick. In fact his missionary career of 17 years was remarkable. His surgical skill, combined with his willingness to ride a hundred miles to help a desperately sick man, made him famous. The blind eyes which he opened were past counting; the deformed, the crippled, the diseased who were relieved or cured by him would make a great host if assembled together. His operations in lithotomy alone were 150 or more, with barely half a dozen unfavorable results. Wherever he went the diseased, the halt, the blind thronged him, for they thought his powers miraculous, like those of Jesus. Probably no physician in the Turkish Empire enjoyed an equal reputation among the whole people. In addition to ceaseless labors of this sort he trained quite a body of skilled native physicians, who in the main did credit to their teacher. While Dr. West treated the poor with great and sympathetic liberality, he always insisted on proper payment from Pashas and others able to pay. But for himself he received nothing but his missionary salary, paying over all his professional earnings into the treasury of the mission. In all of his career he was a warm-hearted, sincere and earnest Christian and a faithful missionary. He never showed nervousness in the most difficult operation, and he never flinched from duty. His devotion to duty cut short his life. It was while attending one of the very poor in Sivas that he contracted the typhus fever which resulted in his death.

WEST, Maria Abigail: Miss West was born in Palmyra, New York, March 27, 1827. She embarked from Boston under the ABCFM for Turkey December 22, 1852, being appointed to Constantinople. She had charge of the female boarding school at Hasskeuy in that city for about ten years. After a visit to America she was stationed at Constantinople, at Marsovan, and at Harpoot, engaged in all of these places in work for women and girls, and for a time was in charge of a female seminary at Harpoot. She was a woman of great energy and rare ability. Her book on the *Romance of Missions; or, Life and Labor in the Land of Ararat*, is based upon her experiences in various parts of Turkey, and has had great influence in developing missionary zeal on both sides of the Atlantic. The first primer in the Armenian language for children in the mission schools was written by Miss West, and has been widely used for more than a generation in many of the schools using Armenian in different parts of Turkey. After leaving the service of the ABCFM she organized coffee-houses in Smyrna and Constantinople for sailors and others. She was preeminently a pioneer, with great power of initiative in all of her missionary life. Miss West died in London June 28, 1894.

WEST INDIES: This group of islands extends in a rude bow-like form from the coast of Florida, U. S. A., to the coast of Venezuela in South America. The larger and more important islands belong to one or other of the great European nations, with the exception of Haiti, and this political division will be followed in the more detailed account of the islands, while some facts which are true of all will serve as a preface to the specific description of them as English, Danish, Dutch, Spanish, or French possessions.

The population of these islands is composed of Europeans and Americans, together with negroes and other Africans, Hindus and Chinese. Diversity of tongue, of character, and of life is consequently so great that there is little attempt at cohesion or federation, even where the islands are under the same flag. In the years just subsequent to their discovery, evil of the most pronounced character was the business of the men who invaded these shores, and all that selfish greed and fiendish cruelty could suggest was done to exterminate the mild aborigines. Hardly a trace of them is now to be found.

Then the islands became the battlefields of the rival powers of Europe. Piracy was rife, and the commerce of Europe suffered from the marauding buccaneers, who smarted from the wrongs they suffered and retaliated on the innocent as well as the guilty. The slave trade had its origin here, and the hardly less cruel importation of coolies has left its curse on the lands. The occupation of the West Indies has afforded the material for a black chapter in the history of the conquests of European nations. Harmless savages were put to death in the name of Christ. Into this moral sewer was swept the refuse of Europe. Hundreds of Hindus and Chinese were lured to this region of faithless promises. The African was dragged here to die of pestilence. No wonder that the burden of debt which weighs down the different administrations is the despair of statesmen.

Patient and heroic hands early planted the Gospel in this miry soil. From the earliest time when Christians saw the image of God in the sable body, to the present day, the conflict between the forces of good and the powers of evil has been fierce and bitter. Prejudices of the white and superstitions of the black races united to render the work excessively difficult. The faithful preacher of Christ was never free from all the persecutions that malignity and hatred could devise or ignorance and superstition suggest. Even his own race insulted, beat, and imprisoned the missionary, and the people he came to succor betrayed him into the hands of his enemies.

The results now seen in the islands are but additional proof that the Gospel is suited alike to the moral and the immoral, to the wise and the foolish, to the black as well as to the white man.

Porto Rico: This island lies at the Eastern extremity of the chain of the Greater Antilles. It was ceded to the United States by Spain in 1998. It has an area of about 3,668 square miles and its population (1899) is 953,243.

Cuba is the largest and one of the richest of the islands in its natural resources.

The island of **Haiti** is divided between the two republics of Santo Domingo and Haiti. The republic of **Santo Domingo** was founded in 1844, and includes the eastern portion of the island. The religion of the state is Roman Catholic, but other forms of worship are permitted.

Haiti became a republic in 1867. It occupies the western portion of the island, with an area of 10,204 square miles. The inhabitants are negroes and mulattoes. The capital, Port au Prince, has a fine harbor. The religion is nominally Roman Catholic.

British West Indies.—THE BAHAMAS: These are twenty inhabited and many uninhabited islands off the southeast coast of Florida. The total area is 5,450 square miles. The principal islands are New Providence, which has been notorious as the home of buccaneers, pirates, and blockade-runners, and San Salvador, supposed to be the island first discovered by Columbus. On the west side of the island are quite a number of intelligent Africans. Eleuthera is over 200 miles long. Great Abaco is the most northerly island. Andros is the largest of the group, with a length of 90 miles and a breadth of 40 miles at its widest part. The remaining islands are: Great Bahama; Harbor Island, Long Island, Mayaguana, Great Inagua, Ragged Island, Rum Cay, Fortune Island, Exuma, Crooked Island, Bimini, Acklin's, and Berry. The population is (1901) 54,358. The government is in the hands of a governor assisted by an Executive Council of 9, a Legislative Council of 9, and an Assembly of 29 representatives.

JAMAICA: The island of Jamaica is about 150 miles long, with an average width of 50 miles. On account of its mountainous character the scenery is beautiful, and there is abundance of fresh water. The sagacity of Oliver Cromwell saw the future value of this island, and secured it to the British Government. Its area is 4,200 square miles, with a population (1902) of 770,242, of whom 500,000 were blacks. The capital is Kingston (46,542), and some of the other principal towns are Spanish Town, Montego Bay, and Port Maria. Attached to Jamaica for administrative purposes are the following smaller islands: Turk's and Caicos Islands, area 224 square miles, population 5,000; Cayman Islands—Grand Cayman, Little Cayman, and Cayman Brae—with a total population of 3,500, the Morant Cays and Pedro Cays.

BARBADOS lies to the east of the Windward Islands, and has an area of 166 square miles. It abounds in varied and beautiful scenery, and almost the entire island is under cultivation. Population (1901) 195,000, of whom 115,000 were blacks. Bridgetown, the capital, has a population of 30,000, and is beautifully situated on the shores of the bay. The English began to exercise authority here in 1645. Since 1885 it has been separated from the Windward Islands, to which administration it formerly belonged, and has now a government of its own.

LEEWARD ISLANDS lie to the north of the Windward Group and southeast of Porto Rico. The islands are: Antigua, 170 square miles; Barbuda and Redonda, 62 square miles; Virgin Islands, 58 square miles; Dominica, 291 square miles; St. Kitt's or St. Christopher, 65 square miles; Nevis, 50 square miles; Anguilla, 35 square miles; Montserrat, 32 square miles. Population (1901) 127,434.

WINDWARD ISLANDS: These islands, with their area and population, are: Grenada, 120 square miles, 64,288; St. Vincent (*q. v.*), 122 square miles, 41,000; and the Grenadines. The principal cities are: Kingston, the capital of St. Vincent; Castres, the chief town of St. Lucia, and St. George, the capital of Grenada.

TRINIDAD lies immediately north of the mouth of the Orinoco. It is an island of extreme beauty and great fertility. In 1802 it was finally handed over to British rule by the peace of Amiens. Its area is 1,754 square miles, with a population of (1901) 255,148. Port-of-Spain is the capital (54,100). Tobago was annexed to Trinidad on January 1, 1889. It has an area of 114 square miles, with a population of 18,750.

The chain of the Lesser Antilles includes, besides the British Islands already mentioned, St. Thomas and its dependencies, belonging to Denmark, Guadaloupe and Martinique, with several smaller islands, belonging to France. These islands collectively have an area of 1,207 square miles, and a population (1901) of 416,420. Like the other islands of this chain these are of volcanic origin. Martinique was the scene of the terrible eruption of Mt. Pelée in May, 1902.

In addition to the lines of missionary work actively prosecuted by the Moravians and British and American societies among the three races on the islands, those of European birth or descent are not being neglected. The Wesleyans and the Jamaica Church of England Home and Foreign Missionary Society are especially interested in this growing class; and the latter is largely doing this work through the agency of catechists, superintended by about 100 clergy, who are one-third Englishmen-born and two-thirds Jamaica-born. The past and present influence of Romanism among the peoples of these islands is one of the greatest hindrances to the spread of evangelical truth; but as in Protestant Jamaica, we may hope that ere long the Bible may be the book most commonly found throughout the islands.

WHATELY, Mary L.: Born at Halesworth, Suffolk, England, the second daughter of Archbishop Whately. Died March 9, 1889. After the father's appointment to the See of Dublin the family removed thither. She was given the highest educational training, mental, moral, and religious, by her parents, and from her childhood was distinguished for uncommon activity, energy, and intelligence. She early gave herself to the service of Christ in works of kindness to the needy. After the Irish famine, she and her mother and sisters spent most of their time in the ragged schools in Dublin. Subsequently, having acquired Italian, she was much occupied with teaching and visiting the poor Italians, who were numerous in that city. In 1858 she visited Cairo and the Holy Land, and in 1860 was ordered by her physician for her health to a southern climate. In Cairo she opened a school for neglected Muslim girls, the first attempt of the kind in Egypt. Taking with her a Syrian Protestant matron, she went into the streets and lanes near her home, and, persuading the mothers to let their girls come to learn to read and sew, she gathered nine little ones into her school. Later, home duties required her return, and while at home she read to her father the proof-sheets of her second volume of *Ragged Life in Egypt.* Her father having died, she returned to Cairo. She soon opened a boys' school also. In 1869, at the suggestion of the Prince of Wales, Ismail Pasha gave her a site just outside the city walls, and friends in England aided her in the erection of a spacious building. The school increased to six hundred, half the boys and two-thirds of the girls being Muslims, the rest Copts, Syrians, and Jews. All were taught to read and write Arabic, and all learned the Scriptures and Christian doctrine. In addition the boys received an excellent secular education, and the girls were taught plain and fancy needlework. Two branch schools have also been established. Pupils of the boys' school are found all over the country, filling important positions in the railway and telegraph offices, mercantile houses, places under government, and in other situations of trust. In 1879 a medical mission was added to the schools, and with her own private means Miss Whately built a dispensary and patients' waiting-room, where several thousands of sick and suffering poor have been treated gratuitously and where she herself daily read and expounded the Scriptures to such as were willing to listen.

Miss Whately's schools are now carried on by the CMS.

WHEELER, Crosby Howard: Born September 8, 1823. Died October 11, 1896. Entered Bowdoin College in 1843; graduated in 1847; entered Bangor Theological Seminary in 1849, completing his course in 1852. In 1857 he and his wife sailed for Turkey as missionaries of the ABCFM. In July, 1857, Mr. Wheeler and Mrs. Wheeler, with Mr. and Mrs. O. P. Allen, entered upon their work at Harpoot, and there they labored, with Mr. and Mrs. H. N. Barnum, for thirty-nine years. After the Turkish massacres in 1895 the circle was broken, Mr. and Mrs. Wheeler returning to the homeland. Dr. Wheeler mastered the Armenian language with unusual speed; shortly after entering the Harpoot field he mingled freely among the Turks, Armenians, Syrians, and Kurds, scattering the seeds of truth; and he was early impressed by the need of schools for boys and girls. In the basement of their hired house Dr. and Mrs. Wheeler began a school, and immediately discussions and controversies arose on every side, and much bitter opposition was shown, especially by the Gregorian clergy; but the pupils increased in number. For nearly twoscore years he worked for the multiplication of schools, and the improvement of their grade, and when, broken in health, he returned to this country, he was president of Euphrates College, which had grown up under his leadership, in which there were over five hundred pupils of all grades, over one hundred of whom were in the collegiate department, and about half of whom were girls. At this time there were in Harpoot alone over eleven hundred pupils, and in the territory covered by the station nearly five thousand. Soon after reaching Armenia, Dr. Wheeler insisted that "native pastors must be ordained over native churches and supported by them, and native churches must be ultimately self-governing and self-perpetuating." He gave the best thought and effort of his long missionary life to this policy; and by his book, *Ten Years on the Euphrates*, he did much toward impressing this important principle upon the mission boards in all parts of the world. Dr. Wheeler was a man of remarkable versatility. He was a preacher of unusual power; he possessed fine executive ability; he was an impressive teacher, and successful organizer of schools; and as a practical man of affairs he proved to be a most useful factor in the pioneer work at Harpoot. He planned and erected some thirty different buildings during his missionary experience; and he did on a small scale a publishing business, preparing himself a variety of text-books in both English and Armenian for the schools. As Dr. Creegan well says of his work for Harpoot: "He found chaos and disorder; he left a fairly well-organized Christian school system for both boys and girls; a group of self-supporting, self-governing, self-propagating Christian churches; a strong Home Missionary Society among the native churches for work in Kurdistan, and a college that is deeply entrenched in the confidence and affection of all classes, crowded with students, and yet unable to meet the demands that come from all sides for teachers in the lower schools."

Creegan (C. C.), *Pioneer Missionaries*, New York, 1903.

WETI: A village on Pemba Island, East Africa. Mission station of the University Mission.

WHAI-AN-FU. See HWAI-NGAN-FU.

WHITMAN, Marcus: Born at Rushville (Gorham), N. Y., September 4, 1802. Died November 29, 1847. Studied with private tutors and at Berkshire Medical College; appointed by the ABCFM missionary physician to Oregon. He left home February, 1835, on an exploring tour with Rev. Samuel Parker, arriving at St. Louis in April, Council Bluffs, May 30; crossed the Rocky Mountains, reaching Green River, a branch of the Western Colorado, a rendezvous of the fur-traders, previous to August 17. The prospect for missionary labor among the Nez Percés and Flathead Indians seemed so favorable that it was deemed expedient for Dr. Whitman to return and procure associates before establishing a mission among them. For this purpose he directed his way homeward August 27. Dr. Whitman established himself at Waiilatpu, among the Kayuses, 25 miles from Walla Walla. Having frequent occasion to visit the post of the Hudson's Bay Company at that place, he perceived that it was designed to hold that immense and valuable territory as a British possession. In part to forestall that design, and in compliance with a resolve of the mission, he, in October, 1842, crossed the Rocky Mountains in midwinter on horseback, arriving at St. Louis February, 1843, with fingers, nose, ears, and feet frost-bitten, in spite of furs and buffalo robes. He visited Washington, called on Mr. Webster, Secretary of State, and President Tyler, and by his earnest representations prevailed upon them not to cede Oregon to the British Government. A personal friend of Mr. Webster remarked: "It is safe to say that our country owes it to Dr. Whitman and his associate missionaries that all the territory west of the Rocky Mountains, and as far south as the Columbia River, is not now owned by England, and held by the Hudson's Bay Company." A sharp controversy has arisen over the verity of the incidents which give this importance to Dr. Whitman's foresight. The balance of evidence, nevertheless, favors the substantial correctness of the statements made above. Dr. Whitman wrote from Fort Walla Walla November 1, 1843: "I do not regret having visited the States, for I feel that this country must be either American, or foreign and mostly papal. If I never do more than to establish the first wagon-road to the Columbia River, and prevent the disaster and reaction which would have followed the breaking up of the present emigration, I am satisfied." While at the East he published a pamphlet describing the climate and soil of the Western region, and its desirableness for American colonies. After a hurried visit to Boston, he was back again on the Missouri in March, and conducted more than a thousand emigrants in wagons over the Rocky Mountains.

Dr. Whitman, Mrs. Whitman, two adopted children, and ten other persons, American emigrants, who had stopped at the station to winter there, were cruelly murdered by the Kayuse Indians, November 29, 1847, and the mission was thus broken up.

WILDER, Royal Gould: Born at Bridport, Vt., October 27, 1816; graduated at Middlebury College, 1839; graduated at Andover Theological Seminary, 1845; sailed for India as a missionary of the ABCFM in 1846. He was stationed for six years at Ahmadnagar. The seminary, containing from 50 to 80 boys, was put under his care by the mission. In 1852 he went to Kolhapur. On his arrival the Brahmans petitioned for his banishment, but he continued at his post, and after five years had one convert. When he went there he found in a population of 44,000 only one school, in a back street, with twelve boys. When he left in 1857 there was a government college, costing $200,000, and he was requested to make the opening address. In the years 1854-56 occurred a controversy between Dr. R. Anderson and the missionaries concerning the place of education in the missionary enterprise. Mr. Wilder, in common with all his associates, was a strong advocate of schools for the Hindus; was in favor of employing even heathen teachers, if Christians could not be obtained, and refused to abandon his schools, or curtail educational work, as required by Dr. Anderson. Mr. Wilder's health having failed from the severe labor and exposure involved in founding the new station at Kolhapur, he embarked in 1857 for America, the day after the Sepoy mutiny broke out. His health having improved, he offered in 1858 to return to his station, but was informed by Dr. Anderson that the Prudential Committee had voted to discontinue the Kolhapur Mission. His Presbytery and friends approving his course, he returned to Kolhapur in 1861, and established an independent mission. On reaching his Indian home he found his beautiful church had been sold and turned into a Mohammedan mosque. He received generous aid for a second church. There he continued to labor for twelve years, receiving no aid from any society, but sustained by voluntary gifts, Sir Bartle Frere, Governor of Bombay, and other English people, as well as natives, contributing to the work. From 1861 to 1869 he contributed many articles to the Bombay *Times and Gazette* on the subject of the system of national education. He also took a prominent part in memorializing Parliament, and inducing the Indian Government to establish the present system. In 1871 he transferred the Kolhapur Mission to the Presbyterian Board of Foreign Missions, and was a missionary of that Board till 1875, when, partly for his health and partly to educate his children, he left India and returned home, having been engaged in mission work for thirty-two years. During that time he had preached in 3,000 cities, towns, and villages, had distributed 3,000,000 pages of tracts, had gathered into schools 3,300 pupils, of whom 300 were girls. Besides this, he had served on committees for the translation and revision of the Bible, and had written and published commentaries on three Gospels, and had edited and translated many books. The vessel which brought his luggage by sea was wrecked off the Cape of Good Hope, and among his goods that were lost was his manuscript history of the Kolhapur kingdom, with full diary of his missionary work. His later years were spent at Princeton, N. J. In 1877 he started the *Missionary Review*, which he edited with ability and success. He longed to return to India, and when the *Review* was provided for, he determined, tho a great sufferer from an internal malady, to sail for Kolhapur. But his work was done, and on the day when the *Review* was transferred to other hands, and he had sent to the printers proofs of the closing number of the last volume, he was called away. He died in New York October 8, 1887.

WILLIAMS, John: Born at Tottenham, near London, England, June 29, 1796. Died at Erromanga November 20, 1839. At the age of fourteen, while an apprentice to an ironmonger, he showed great taste for mechanics, and acquired considerable experience in mechanical work. At the age of twenty he offered himself to the London Missionary Society as a missionary, and, after some special training, was ordained, and sent with his wife, November, 1816, to the South Sea Islands. He was first stationed at Eimeo, one of the Society Islands, where he soon acquired a knowledge of the native language. Thence he went to Huahine, where he found the natives had generally renounced idolatry. At the invitation of the King of Raiatea, the largest of the Society group, he went to that island, which became his permanent headquarters. His success here was remarkable, not only in Christianizing the people, but with Christianity introducing the arts and habits of civilization. In 1823 he visited, with six native teachers, the Hervey Islands, and after several days' search discovered Rarotonga, the largest of this group. Remaining here for some time, he founded a mission, which was greatly successful, not only Rarotonga, but the whole group of the Hervey Islands being Christianized. He helped the people at their own request to draw up a code of laws for civil administration. He made great use of native teachers whom he had trained. The work accomplished by him on both of these islands for the secular as well as the religious welfare of the natives was useful and permanent. He reduced the language of Raiatea to writing, translated with Pitman and Buzacot the New Testament into it, and prepared books for the schools he had established. Rarotonga being out of the way of vessels, he built one in which he might visit other islands. The boat was named the "Messenger of Peace." In this vessel, during the next four years, he explored many groups of the South Sea Islands. In 1830 he set out in his vessel to carry the Gospel to the Samoan Islands, which he had planned to do in 1824, but was deterred by the great distance—2,000 miles—and the ferocious character of the people. In 1832 he made a second visit to the Samoans, and found the people waiting for the Gospel. In less than twenty months an entire change had taken place in the habits and character of the Samoans. Chapels had been built, and everywhere the people seemed waiting to receive instruction. Having completed the object of his voyage, and visited all the islands of the Samoan group, he returned to his family. With health impaired, after seventeen years of toil and hardship, he sailed in 1833 for England, where he remained four years. During this time he had the Rarotongan New Testament published by the Bible Society, raised £4,000 for the purchase and outfit of a missionary ship for Polynesia, wrote and published a *Narrative of Missionary Enterprises in the South Sea Islands*, and prepared plans for the establishment of a college for the education of native teachers, and for a high school at Tahiti. In 1838 he and his wife again embarked, accompanied by ten other missionaries. After visiting the stations already established by him, and several new groups, he proceeded with one companion to the New Hebrides with the view of establishing a mission, but was met by hostile natives at Erromanga, by whom he was killed. A portion of his bones was recovered from the cannibals. It is supposed they were provoked to the deed by the ill treatment they had received from the crew of a vessel which a short time before had landed there.

WILLIAMS, Samuel Wells: Born at Utica, N. Y., September 22, 1812. Died, February 16, 1884. Graduated at the Rensselaer Institute in Troy, 1832. While there, he was, at the age of twenty, invited by the ABCFM to join a party about to start for China, as superintendent of the mission press, having learned to some extent the art of type-setting in his father's publishing house. He accepted the invitation, and June 15, 1833, sailed in the ship "Morrison" for Canton, China. Drs. Abeel and Bridgman were the only Americans to welcome him. He rapidly gained a knowledge of the Chinese language, and became editor of *The Chinese Repository*, begun the year before by Dr. Bridgman, to which many able writers contributed, he himself furnishing 140 distinct articles. The *Celestial Empire*, published in Shanghai, says: "The *Repository*, extending through 20 volumes, is looked upon as of pricelesss worth, and the name of the editor will be long and honorably remembered by sinologues in connection with it." In 1835 he completed at Macao Medhurst's *Hokkeen Dictionary*. In 1837 he was one of a party sent to Japan to restore seven shipwrecked seamen to their home. They were fired upon from batteries of two ports, and returned with the men to Canton. Taking some of these sailors into his own house, he learned their language, translated for them the Book of Genesis and the Gospel of Matthew, and had the joy of seeing them embrace Christianity. This knowledge of the language thus providentially acquired led to his being appointed interpreter for Commodore Perry, who was sent by the United States Government to Japan fifteen years later. Soon after the press was established at Canton, Chinese interference with his native helpers compelled him to remove it to Macao; thence, later, it was transferred to Hongkong, and established again afterward in Canton, where, in December, 1856, his own dwelling and the entire establishment, comprising three presses and many fonts of type, with 7,000 printed books, were destroyed by fire. In 1844 he returned to the United States. During the three years spent at home he delivered a course of lectures on Chinese subjects, which were afterward enlarged and published under the title of *The Middle Kingdom*. With the proceeds of the lectures he secured from Berlin a font of movable Chinese type. Soon after the publication of *The Middle Kingdom* the trustees of Union College conferred upon him the degree of LL.D.

Restrictions forbidding foreigners to bring their wives to Canton having been removed, he was married, and with his wife sailed in 1848 for Canton, taking with him the new font of type. On arriving at Canton he found to his great joy regular public services in Chinese. His remarkable success as an interpreter led to his appointment to the diplomatic service of the United States, with which he was connected from 1858 to his resignation in 1876. In 1857 he was Secretary of the United States Legation in Japan. In 1858 he aided William B. Reed in negotiating the treaty of Tientsin. In 1860-61 he revisited the United States, and delivered lectures before the Smithsonian Institution and elsewhere, returning to China in 1862 as Secretary of the United States Legation at Peking. Besides the *Chinese Repository*, which for twenty years occupied much of his time, he published *Easy Lessons in Chinese* (1841); *An English and Chinese Vocabulary in the Court Dialect* (1843); *The Chinese Commercial Guide* (1844); *A Tonic Dictionary of the Canton Dialect* (1856); *A Syllabic Dictionary of the Chinese Language* (1874), containing 12,527 characters. On this dictionary, a work of great philological value, he spent eleven years. His *Middle Kingdom*, the best work extant on Chinese government, geography, religion, and social life, reappeared in 1883 in a revised and enlarged edition. Retiring from the service of the government in 1876, he returned to the United States, took up his residence in New Haven, was appointed professor of Chinese at Yale College, and in 1881 was elected president of the American Bible Society. To the end of his life he was, by himself and in his words, a witness of the dignity and inspiration of the missionary calling.

WILLIAMS, William Frederic: Born at Utica, N. Y., January 11, 1818. Died at Mardin, Turkey, February 14, 1871. Studied at Yale College, and was subsequently engaged in various employments, mostly in engineering, till 1844, when he entered Auburn Theological Seminary to prepare for the ministry. In November, 1846, he offered himself to the ABCFM for the missionary work, in which his elder brother, Samuel Wells Williams, was engaged in China. Was ordained in 1848; sailed January 3, 1849, for the Syria Mission. In the summer of 1850 he was designated to Mosul. There he remained till 1859, when he commenced the station at Mardin.

He had a fine knowledge of Arabic. His clear mind had been carefully cultivated and his acquisitions were very exact. However much he distrusted his own judgment, his associates confided in it largely. Few missionaries have secured the affection of the people for whom they labor as he did. He was, in a sense, the mainstay of the mission work among the Arabic-speaking peoples of Northern Mesopotamia during years of trial and perplexity when it seemed often as if the mission would be compelled to withdraw, and to his patient, wise perseverance is very largely due the success that is now attending the labors of the missionaries in that field.

WILLIAMS, Rev. S. T.: A missionary of the Southern Baptist Convention; born in Floyd Co., Va., February 12, 1862; died in Canton, China, April, 1903. His work lay among the Hakka people, where his labors were greatly blessed. His was pioneer work, done amid great difficulties. It extended the missions of his society in the South China field some 250 miles into the interior.

WILLIAMSON, Alexander: Born at Falkirk, Scotland, December 5, 1829. Died at Shanghai, China, August 28, 1890. Studied at Glasgow; ordained April, 1855; sailed as a medical missionary of the LMS May 21 for China, arriving at Shanghai September 24; was stationed for two years at Shanghai and Ping-hu. His health failing, he returned to England in 1858, and his connection with the Society soon terminated. After some years spent in Scotland, he returned to China as the agent of the Scottish Bible Society, and in connection with the United Presbyterian Mission. He was at first stationed at Chefu, and traveled extensively, making adventurous journeys into unknown and distant regions. Much valuable information was obtained, which in 1879 was published in two volumes. He was afterward settled in Shanghai, where he established the Society for the Diffusion of Christian and General Knowledge among the Chinese. He was a frequent contributor to the *North China Daily News.*

WILLIAMSON, Thomas S.: Born in Union District, S. C., March, 1800. Died at St. Peter, Minn., June 24, 1879. He graduated at Jefferson College, Penn., and at Yale Medical School, and practised medicine for ten years in Brown County, Ohio. After spending one year in Lane Theological Seminary, he was licensed and ordained by the Presbytery of Chillicothe, and in 1835 left Ripley, Ohio, as a missionary of the ABCFM, with his family, reaching Fort Snelling, in the country of the Dakotas, in May. He remained in connection with the ABCFM for thirty-six years, until 1871, when he and his son, Rev. John P. Williamson, transferred themselves to the care of the Presbyterian Board.

He fully believed in the capability of Indians to become civilized and Christianized, and also that God had by special providences called him to this work. His great life-work—that of translating the Bible into the language of the Sioux Nation—was continued through more than twoscore years, and was only completed in 1889. In this, as in most things, he worked slowly and carefully. He lived to read the plate-proofs of all, and to know that the Scriptures of the Old and New Testaments were in the language of the Dakotas.

WILSON, John: Born at Lauder in Berwickshire, Scotland, December 11, 1804. Died December 1, 1875. At the age of fourteen he went to the Edinburgh University, where he graduated in 1828, taking a high place in the classes of physical science, and in the last two years studying anatomy, surgery, and the practise of physic. The reading of the reports of the Bible Society, he said, first awakened him to the importance of missions, and led him to resolve to devote himself to a foreign field He was ordained in 1828, and sailed August 30 of the same year for India, under the Scottish Missionary Society, reaching Bombay February, 1829. He gave himself to the acquisition of the vernaculars of a varied population—the Marâthi, Gujarati, Hindustani, Hebrew, Portuguese, with Persian, Arabic, and Sanskrit in reserve for the learned classes. All these he acquired and fluently used. Almost his earliest work in Bombay was the preparation of a Hebrew and Marâthi grammar for the Jews, known there as Ben Israel. He also spoke the Portuguese with fluency. He was thus able early to influence the Hindu, Mohammedan, Parsee, Jewish, and Portuguese communities. His advance in Sanskrit was parallel with his acquisition of Marâthi, so that he was able to confute the Brahmans out of their own sacred books. He soon commenced a series of discourses on Christianity with Hindus, Mohammedans, and Parsees. Having mastered the languages, he mingled with the people who spoke them, and made many tours to Nasik, Poona, the caves of Ellora, and other prominent places. Tho aware that for some time his toil must be that of preparation, he worked for and expected converts from the first. So in February, 1831, he formed in Bombay a native church of eight members. In 1833 was established in Bombay an English college for the Christian education of native youth among Parsees and Hindus, and Dr. Wilson threw the whole weight of his culture and energy into the new institution. Organizing this college was the great work of his life, and its effectiveness caused him to be reckoned one of the great benefactors of India. In 1836 he received the degree of Doctor of Divinity from Edinburgh University. In 1839 he baptized two Parsee youths,—the first proselytes from the faith of Zoroaster,—who afterward became ordained ministers in the Free Church of Scotland and the Baptist Church. In 1842 he resigned the presidency of the Bombay branch of the Royal Asiatic Society, which he had filled for seven years. In 1843, after fourteen years of hard work in India, Dr. Wilson left for his native land.

In the disruption of the Scottish Church Dr. Wilson joined the Free Church and on his arrival he was received with great honor. In September, 1847, he returned to India. In 1857 he was appointed by the government Vice-Chancellor of the University of Bombay, and was examiner in Sanskrit, Persian, Hebrew, Marâthi, Gujarati, and Hindustani. He was twelve years secretary to the different translation committees of the Bombay Bible Society. The fortieth anniversary of his arrival in India was made the occasion of a remarkable demonstration of the respect and gratitude felt for him by all classes of the people. The Governor presided at a great meeting in the Town Hall to present him with a token of regard. The citizens of Bombay in general also presented him with an address, and the Asiatic Society reviewed, with high commendation, his great services for India. The same year he returned to Scotland. While there he was elected Moderator of the General Assembly of the Free Church. In his closing address before the Assembly on the foreign mission work, he said that notwithstanding his forty-one years' connection with India, if he lived to the age of Methuselah he would consider it a privilege to devote his life to its regeneration. He returned to India in 1871. Increasing ill-health compelled him finally to give up work in 1875, and to go for recuperation to a health resort. But it was too late; he died on the way.

WILSON, John Leighton: Born in Sumter Co., S. C., March 28, 1809. Died July 13, 1886. Graduated at Union College 1829, and Theological Seminary of Columbia, S. C., 1833; ordained the same year by Harmony Presbytery, and set apart as a missionary to Africa. In the summer of 1833 he studied Arabic at Andover Seminary, and in the autumn went to Western Africa to explore the coast, returning in the spring, and on the 24th of November, 1834, sailed as a missionary of the ABCFM for Cape Palmas, Liberia, arriving in December. He was received with demonstrations of joy by the natives, and found the frame house which he had taken out on his first visit erected on the spot he had selected. In 1836 he made three tours of exploration in the interior, journeying mostly on foot. He had, while at Cape Palmas, where he remained seven years, a boarding-school numbering fifty, a fourth of whom were females; a church of forty members, 180 youths had been educated, the Grebo language was reduced to writing, a grammar and dictionary of the language published, the Gospels of Matthew and John translated and printed, besides several other small volumes. In 1842 he removed to the Gabun River, 1,200 miles south of Cape Palmas, and commenced a new station among the Mpongwe people. This language also he reduced to writing, and published its grammar and vocabulary; he also translated and published portions of the Bible. In 1853 he returned home on account of failing health, and became Secretary of the Presbyterian Board of Foreign Missions in New York, editing also the foreign department of the *Home and Foreign Record*. He served as Secretary till the commencement of the civil war. when, returning to his Southern home, he organized for the Southern Church a Board of Foreign Missions, of which he was appointed Secretary, holding the office till 1885. He established and edited *The Missionary*, a monthly magazine. He organized also the Board of Sustentation. In 1854 he published a volume of 500 pages on Western Africa, its history, condition, and prospects, which was pronounced by Dr. Livingstone the best work on that part of Africa ever written. He published also many articles in the *Southern Presbyterian Review*. He received the degree of D.D. from Lafayette College in 1854.

WINSLOW, Miron: Born at Williston, Vt., December 11, 1789. Died at Cape Town, S. Africa, September 1, 1864. Studied at Middlebury College, Vermont, and at Yale College; studied theology at Andover Seminary. He was appointed missionary to Ceylon by the ABCFM. At his ordination on November 4, 1818, in the Salem Tabernacle, in company with Messrs. Spaulding, Woodward, and Fisk, Professor Moses Stuart preached the sermon, which was widely circulated among the churches. In the same edifice, February 6, 1812, had been ordained the initial band of American foreign missionaries—Messrs. Judson, Hall, Newell, Nott, and Rice. With Messrs. Spaulding, Woodward and Scudder he sailed for India June 8, 1819, arriving at Oodooville, Ceylon, on July 4. He remained there till 1833, conducting the boarding and day school, laboring and preaching in the neighborhood, and performing a large amount of literary work. He was the pioneer American missionary of his day in championing the idea that education must go hand in hand with preaching in missionary operations. He carried out this idea in the Batticotta Seminary (1823). After the death of Mrs. Winslow in 1833 he returned to the United States, where he remained two years. In August, 1836, he established the ABCFM Mission in Madras, the scene of his labors for the remaining twenty-eight years of his life.

At an early period of his labors in Madras Mr. Winslow was engaged in translating the Bible into Tamil, and as late as 1850 he was much occupied with improvements and revisions of portions of the translations. When not thus engaged, he was occupied three hours daily on the Tamil and English dictionary. In November, 1850, he announced that the printing of the new version of the Tamil Scriptures was completed. He published "occasional reports" of the Madras Mission. He received from Harvard College the degree of D.D., which his *Alma Mater* supplemented with LL.D. upon the reception in this country of copies of his Tamil lexicon, which was the great literary work of his life. Its title-page reads thus: "A Comprehensive Tamil and English Dictionary of High and Low Tamil, by the Rev. Miron Winslow, D.D., etc., assisted by competent Native Scholars: in part from manuscript materials of the late Rev. Joseph Knight and others. Madras: Printed and Published by P. R. Hunt, American Mission Press." The splendid quarto of 976 pages, three colums to a page, with 11 additional pages, attested the ability of the mission press to execute the highest grade of printing. With the exception of Wilson's Sanskrit lexicon, this work is the most elaborate and complete dictionary of the languages of India, containing 67,452 words with definitions, of which 30,551 for the first time take their place in Tamil lexicography. The publication of the dictionary called forth hearty expressions of commendation and of gratitude from scholars and missionaries, as well as from the government officials of India.

Dr. Winslow sailed for the United States, very much broken in health, in August, 1864, but his strength was not equal to the long voyage, and he was obliged to stop at Cape Town, where he found a grave.

WITTE BERGEN: A district in Orange River Colony, South Africa, situated about 120 miles N. E. of Bloemfontein. Station circuit of the South African Wesleyan Methodist Missionary Society, with 1 missionary, 44 native workers, 14 outstations, 8 places of worship, 5 Sunday schools, 7 day schools and 825 professed Christians.

WODEHOUSE (Forests): A district in Cape Colony, South Africa, situated in the Transkei region between the Great Kei and Tsomo Rivers. Station of the South African Wesleyan Methodist Missionary Society, with (1901) 44 native workers, 28 outstations, 10 places of worship, 10 Sunday schools, 8 day schools and 443 professed Christians.

WOGENTHIN: A village in the Transvaal, S. Africa, situated about 15 miles S. of Heidelberg. Station of the Berlin Missionary Society (1884), with (1902) 1 missionary, 11 native workers, 3 outstations and 919 professed Christians, of whom 395 are communicants. Some write the name Woyentin.

WOGUL LANGUAGE: One of the Finnish group of the Ural-Altaic family of languages, rather closely allied to the Hungarian and spoken by a small group of the inhabitants of Western Siberia. It is written with the Russian character. The name is also pronounced Vogul.

WOLFF, Joseph: Born in Bavaria, Germany, 1795, of Jewish parentage, the son of a rabbi; early became a Christian; was baptised in 1812 at Prague by a Benedictine monk, taught Hebrew for a time at Frankfort and Halle, studied at Munich, Weimar, and Vienna; went to Rome in 1815, to be educated as a missionary. He entered first the Collegio Romano and in 1817 the College of the Propaganda. While in Rome he spent his time in studying the Oriental languages. Suspected by the Inquisition of heresy, he was sent in 1818 to Vienna, then to a monastery in Switzerland, and finally dismissed as incorrigible. He went to London, joined the Church of England, and through the influence of Charles Simeon and others, who perceived his fitness for mission work among the Jews, he entered Cambridge University, where for two years he continued his Oriental studies under Professor Lee. He then commenced his career as a traveler, visiting Malta, Egypt, Palestine, Mesopotamia, Armenia, Bassorah, and Persia, and returning home by the way of Circassia, Constantinople, and the Crimea, reached Dublin, May, 1826. In these travels he became acquainted with learned men of all ecclesiastical relations, everywhere professing Jesus as the Christ, and, altho he had been imprisoned and his life often endangered, showing in all undaunted courage and great presence of mind. In 1827 he married Lady Georgiana Walpole, daughter of the Earl of Oxford, who accompanied him on his second missionary tour as far as Malta. In April he proceeded to Smyrna, the Ionian Islands, and Jerusalem, where he was poisoned by some Jews, and just escaped death. On recovering he set out for Bokhara by way of Persia, encountering on the journey the plague; was repeatedly robbed, taken prisoner, and sold as a slave, but finally reached Bokhara. After laboring there three months in mission work among the Jews, he went to India, visited the Punjab, Lahore, Ludhiana, Simla, Delhi, Benares, Lucknow, and reached Calcutta March, 1833. He preached everywhere in different languages, distributed the Scriptures, and interested the most prominent men and women in his behalf. From Calcutta he went to Haidarabad, visited the Jews at Cochin and Goa, proceeded to Bombay, whence he sailed for Arabia, and returned to England in 1834. In 1836 he made a second visit to Abyssinia, whence he sailed for Bombay, and there embarked for America, reaching New York August, 1837. He was ordained as deacon in the Protestant Episcopal Church by Bishop Doane of New Jersey, visited the principal cities, preached before Congress, and returned to England January 2, 1838. Having received priest's orders, he was settled as curate in Lengthwaite, and then for his wife's health he went to York, where he remained five years. In 1843, the news of the imprisonment of Colonel Stoddart and Captain Conolly at Bokhara having reached England, Dr. Wolff set out to attempt their release or ascertain their fate. Before reaching Bokhara he learned that they had been beheaded. He himself was made a prisoner and condemned to death, but through the intervention of the Persian Ambassador he made his escape. Reaching England in 1845, he was settled in the parish of Isle Brewers, Somersetshire, where he labored till he died, May 2, 1862. The most interesting of his publications are *Travels and Adventures of Rev. Joseph Wolff* (2 vols. 1861).

WOLKENBERG, Rev. Marcus: Born of Israelite parentage in Russia in 1834, he was converted to Christianity in 1856, and educated in the Malta Protestant College. In 1862 he was appointed by the London Society for the Jews to labor at Jassy (in Roumania), and subsequently at Bacan and London. In 1876 he was placed in charge of the Northern division of the Home Mission, which post he continuously held for a quarter of a century and up to the time of his death. Mr. Wolkenberg will be remembered as one of the ablest missionaries of the London Society for Promoting Christianity among the Jews in the present age. Bishop Ryan, at one of the anniversaries, gave him a most remarkable public testimonial; and Pastor de le Roi, in his history of Jewish missions, speaks of him as possessing a more sober and better judgment concerning the needs and the operations of the Jewish mission than many of his contemporaries. He was certainly distinguished for good intellectual powers, sound classical and Hebrew learning, and a masterly ability in preaching special sermons to the Jews and for the Jews. In private conversations or controversies with individual Jews, he had the talent of winning the attention and respect and often the admiration and love of his hearers. Had he enjoyed better health, he would have been considered a great preacher. Mr. Wolkenberg rendered good service to the Missionary Publications' Sub-Committee in their preparation of new tracts and pamphlets, his keen, critical intellect being of the greatest value. His English literary works testify to his learning and ability as an author, especially *The Pentateuch according to the Talmud* (a translation of Hebrew with a very learned introduction). Mr. Wolkenberg wrote also the following tracts: *Alienation of Jews from Judaism; General Aspect of Judaism; Israel's Mission to the World, When and How Fulfilled; Judaism and Christianity on the Threshold of Eternity; Theory and Practice of Judaism and Christianity;* and also contributed excellent papers to the Conferences on Jewish Missions held in Southport, 1875, and in London, 1899.

WOMANHOOD; its debt to Missions: To Rev. David Abeel, D.D., an American missionary to China, must be conceded the honor of suggesting to Christian women the importance of a distinctive mission for heathen women. During his missionary career he realized that the greatest hindrance to the spread of the Gospel lay in the fact that heathen homes were the strongholds of Satan. Womanhood itself, synonymous with ignorance and superstition, was trampled under brutal feet. Women throughout the Orient were unwelcomed at birth, unloved and oppressed in life, and unwept at death. Hoary customs precluded the possibility of reaching them through ordained ministers, and only by the undivided efforts of Christian women aglow with gratitude for their elevation through Christ, could they be approached.

Dr. Abeel's burning zeal awakened a responsive chord in the hearts of consecrated women in England and America, resulting in 1834 in the organization of the *Society for Female Education in the East* in England, and, seconded by the appeals of Mrs. Francis B. Mason of Burma, in the establishment in 1860 of the *Woman's Union Missionary Society of America for Heathen Lands.* Thus these two Societies in England and America were the pioneers of woman's organized distinctive work for women.

Pitiful as is the position of all Oriental women, in no land is it so peculiarly painful as in India. Since the Mohammedan dominion in 1001 A.D. the custom of the *zenana* has prevailed (*zen* means woman), whereby millions of women having no contact with the outside world become literally prisoners. Missionaries give these results of wide experience:—"The more I see of woman's lot in India, the more I know that no account of her degradation, darkness and suffering can be exaggerated." "No one realizes the depths of suffering borne by the women of India, and the longer I am here the more terrible I see it is. As they often tell us, we do not begin to suspect what goes on behind the scenes, even in the shelter of their own homes. We know their only hope is in the Savior's redeeming love, of which they know nothing."

Pundita Ramabai, the foremost Hindu reformer of Indian women, states: "Distrust and a low estimation of woman's character is at the root of the custom that secludes women. I have never read any sacred book in Sanskrit literature without meeting this deplorable sentiment."

Among many questions on this subject transscribed by Manu, the law-giver of the Hindus, these occur: "What is the chief gate to hell? A woman. Who is the wisest of the wise? He who has not been deceived by women, only to be compared to malignant fiends."

This low estimate of woman induced the deplorable custom of *child marriage*, whereby girls of tender years are doomed to responsibilities for which immaturity unfits them. Following in the ascending scale of misery is the condition of *child widows*. A recent census gives 38,-000,000 girls under fifteen, of whom 24,000,000 are widows; nearly 14,000 are four years of age. Rigid custom forces these tiny children to undergo all the penalties of widowhood. The luxuriant hair, the pride of the Oriental woman, is forever shaved, and one white, coarse garment is the badge of the household drudge, for whom nothing is too severe. Allowed but one meal a day of the simplest character, often obliged to observe rigorous fasts, is it any wonder that death is eagerly sought, to end untold misery and often manifold temptations?

In such conditions began what may be called a *social and religious revolution* in India. Attractive fancy work was the bait which opened the doors sealed for generations. Visiting where the patriarchal system of living pertains, large numbers of women were reached. Children from this same secluded class were gathered into schools, where the vital truths of the Gospel formed the prominent teaching. Native Bible women were trained as evangelists to reach the masses in 718,000 Indian villages, orphanages were established to rescue the victims of famines, and hospitals were endowed, where gifted women physicians could, while mitigating suffering, lead to Christ—the only remedy for the ills accumulated under ages of heathenism. Books also have been written or translated especially suited to women and girls, thus creating a Christian literature for a class hitherto excluded from every avenue for mental culture. Richest results have followed these varied methods of service, and thousands of heathen women have emerged from utter darkness and degradation, to become in Christian homes centers of light and influence.

Often is the flippant comment made—"The religions of the East are well suited to the people—why disturb their belief?" What can be said of religions which doom half of the human race to degradation inconceivable, dwarf aspirations and stifle sympathies, robbing life of every joy, and the future of every hope?

We hear from a gifted missionary in China, "One-fifth of all the women of the world are waiting in China for the Savior, Who so long has waited for them. What a burden of responsibility does this lay on the women of Christendom!"

Through girls' schools established by Christian women in Japan has the Empire realized the possibilities of women trained and elevated through education. The establishment of Government schools from which religion is excluded does not diminish the obligation in this direction resting on Christian women. Elevated solely by the Cross of Christ to the enviable position which they as Christian women occupy in the Occident, and believing that the Redeemer died for the *whole world*, and not for a favored few, can they dismiss responsibility without an effort to mitigate a doom incident on heathen birth which but for the grace of God might have been theirs?

It is not only individual women in Asia and Africa who have been blessed by Christian Missions: it is Womanhood as a whole which is being lifted up and given a position of dignity and influence. The very first effect of a mission in any Mohammedan or pagan community has ever been to force into the minds of men the fact that Christians consider girls and women capable of absorbing book knowledge altho they themselves have classed them with cows. Upon the one enterprise of the education of women, Christian philanthropy has applied a peristant energy which has amazed, aroused, perplexed and at last won the support of men who are neither Christians nor philanthropists. What it means for womanhood in India, for instance, to have a large section of the population now stand forth as ardent defenders of the capacities and rights of women, needs not to be detailed. Such a change in the place given womanhood in the thoughts of men is the direct outcome of Christian teaching and practise gradually and insensibly permeating the community.

The same is true of the abolishment of debasing customs and crimes against womanhood in both Asia and Africa. Long after the African slave-trade had been abolished by Europe and America, Mohammedan activity in slave-raids continued. The object of these raids was not to secure laborers, but to capture women. This determined and brutal purpose to degrade and destroy womanhood was revealed to the world, and the passion to end it was aroused by Christians, and in great measure by Christians who were missionaries. The abolition of the *Suttee* in India was but languidly pressed until Carey and his companions and many later missionaries made the halls of Parliament ring with their indignant protests.

The successful agitation in Travancore (1827-30 and 1858-59) against degradation of womanhood through caste denials of the right of low-caste women to cover their persons, is another instance of the debt of womanhood to missions. So, too, is the strong sentiment now seen among progressive Hindus against child-marriages and the oppression of widows. The same is true of the growing sentiment of Chinese against foot-binding. Wherever we look, the effect of Gospel-teaching is to loose the bands of the captives and to lift up those who stand in the mire that they may sit among the princes of the people.

WOMAN'S UNION MISSIONARY SOCIETY of America, for Heathen Lands: Headquarters, 67 Bible House, New York, N. Y., U. S. A. This Society was organized in New York City January 15, 1861, as the result of an address by a missionary from Burma at a parlor meeting the week previous. Its first membership included representatives of six denominations, and it has remained strictly undenominational. Its immediate conduct is in the hands of an executive committee of women representing the different denominations residing in or near New York City. In May, 1861, a Philadelphia branch was organized, and branches and auxiliaries have been established in different parts of the country.

The first missionary, Miss Marston, went in November, 1861, to Burma, and in 1863 Miss Brittan (Episcopalian) went to Calcutta. Later work was commenced in Shanghai, China, and Yokohama, Japan. The work in Burma has been dropped.

In India the great work of the Society has from the first been Zenana work. It is carried on in Calcutta, where it is known as "The American Doremus Mission," in honor of Mrs. Doremus, the first President and really the founder of the Society. Other stations are Allahabad, Cawnpore and Jhansi. In Calcutta there are 15 missionaries and 57 native workers; in Allahabad, 12 missionaries and 24 native workers; in Cawnpore 9 missionaries and 21 native workers; in Jhansi 4 missionaries and 2 native workers, a total in India of 40 missionaries and 104 native workers. The Broadwell Memorial School at Calcutta, the Woman's Home at Allahabad, and the Mary A. Merriman Orphanage at Cawnpore, besides other homes and rescue work, supplement the Zenana work.

In Shanghai the work of the Union includes the Margaret Williamson Hospital, with 4 physicians, and the Bridgman Memorial School, besides the evangelistic work, in which there are engaged 2 missionaries and 5 native workers. The work for 1902 shows 472 patients admitted to wards and 34,743 cases at the dispensary, of which 22,570 were new. There were in addition 208 visits to homes, while over 47,000 prescriptions were filled.

At Yokohama the boarding school has 58 pupils, and the 3 missionaries find excellent openings for educational and evangelistic work.

WOMAN'S WORK FOR WOMEN: The activity of Christian women in support of early foreign missions is a fact often overlooked. The records of the missionary movement at the beginning of the 19th century show that an astonishing proportion of the necessary money was collected by societies of women. These early societies were separate local bodies differing from the modern woman's missionary society in lacking provision for permanence, in taking no responsibility for definite work, in assuming an auxiliary position to the general missionary societies as collectors of money only, and especially in undertaking no enterprises of their own in the mission field.

The following list of the operations of Women's Foreign Missionary Societies in America in the first half of the 19th century shows the character of these early missionary efforts by women. The list was derived, like the most of the material used in this article, from a paper by Miss Ellen C. Parsons, editor of *Woman's Work* (PN).

1800 "Boston Female Society for Missionary Purposes." (Baptist and Congregational.)
1801 "Boston Female Society for Promoting the Diffusion of Christian Knowledge." (Congregational.)
1808 "Female Mite Society," Beverly, Mass. (Baptist.)
1811 "Salem Female Cent Society," Massachusetts. (Baptist.)

About this time, 1808-1812, "Cent a Week" societies were common among women of different denominations in Eastern Massachusetts.

1812 The "Female Foreign Missionary Society" of New Haven, Conn., contributed to the American Board $177.09.
1813 First legacy to the American Board $345.83 out of an estate of $500, left by Sally Thomas, of Cornish, N. H., a domestic, whose wages had never exceeded fifty cents a week.
1814 April 11, a woman's missionary society was organized in the Fayette Street Baptist Church in New York City.
1815 Legacy from Mrs. Norris of Salem, Mass., was realized to the American Board—$30,000, the largest received up to that time or for many years thereafter.
1816 "Female Charitable Society" of Tallmadge, Ohio, contributed $20 to the American Board—the first received by the Board from west of the Alleghenies, save one dollar from a pastor's pocket.
1818 Woman's Missionary Society formed in Derry, Pa. (Presbyterian.)
1819 July 5, a society was formed in the Wesleyan Seminary, Forsyth Street, New York City. It issued its last annual report in 1861. During forty years it had contributed to the missionary treasury of the Methodist Episcopal Church the sum of $20,000.
1821 There were 250 societies in existence (formed from 1812-1820), all contributing to the American Board; many of them were composed exclusively of women.
1823 A society "For the Support of Heathen Youth" was organized in Philadelphia, Pa., and existed until 1874. (Presbyterian.)
1835 A society "For the Evangelization of the World" was organized in the First Presbyterian Church, Newark, N. J. During the first ten years it contributed $2,344.76 to the American Board. The Society still lives (having joined the new movement), and celebrated its jubilee in 1885, one of its original members and 20 descendants of members participating on that occasion.
1838 A society was formed in the First Church, Allegheny, Pa. (United Presbyterian),

and has celebrated its jubilee. The original secretary was still holding the position.

1839 More than 680 "Ladies' Associations," having nearly 3,000 local agents of their own membership, were collecting funds for the American Board. One of these associations met in Brookline, Mass., at the house of Mr. Ropes, and made regular contributions for Japan, altho that empire was then sealed against foreigners. The amount which they forwarded expressly for Japan was $600, which, with the accruing interest, became $4,104.23 before the American Board opened its mission to Japan, of which the first expenses were paid from the Brookline fund.

1847 "The Free Baptist Female Mission Society" was formed in Sutton, Vermont. It continued in operation for over twenty years, and was never formally dissolved.

1848 The "Ladies' China Missionary Society" (Methodist) of Baltimore, Md., was formed. It was a thriving Society in 1871, when it merged itself as a branch of the wider organization of the Methodist Episcopal Church.

The modern uprising of women in behalf of foreign missions must be emphasized as an epoch in the history of missions. It had its motive in the social systems of the East. It was primarily the *purdah* and the latticed window, the zenana and the harem, that roused the women of Christendom to attempt an errand of mercy to their sister-women of the heathen world. Experience proved that no nation can be elevated until its women are regenerated; also that no man, whether clerical missionary or even physician, can carry the Gospel to the jealously-guarded women of Oriental households. When the degradation and sufferings of Asiatic women and the darkness of their future were revealed to the Western world the conscience of Christian women was aroused. The Gospel had developed them and given them honor, security, moral power, and intellectual freedom. They recognized the claim of their less happy sisters to the same blessings.

David Abeel, missionary of the American Board, was the first to suggest action for this end. On his way home from China in 1834 Mr. Abeel told the people of England the facts, which had hitherto been imperfectly known, concerning the condition of women in India and China. He showed that the missionaries' wives, who had always done what they could for women and children about them, were neither sufficient in numbers nor sufficiently free to assume the burden of lifting up their sex. Effort so strenuous and continuous would be necessary as to demand the entire consecration of many lives, and he urged unmarried women to volunteer in Christ's name for this new form of service. He also declared that women of the Church at home should organize to render their labors permanent. Little did Mr. Abeel know what a force he was evoking. The Spirit of God winged his words. That same year the first society was formed in England, The Society for Promoting Female Education in the East; and upon whatever others, in the progress of years and under divine control, the burden of leadership may seem to fall, this Society is ever to be had in reverence, as the one that ventured first and led the way. Others followed speedily in Great Britain: those connected with the Free Church and the Established Church of Scotland in 1837, the Indian Female Normal School and Instruction Society in 1852, and the Wesleyan Auxiliary in 1859; the German Society for Christian Education of Women in the East in 1842, but none of these was much known across the Atlantic.

Meanwhile Mr. Abeel had brought his plea to America, but hearts were not ready for it. At last, in 1861, Mrs. Doremus, of New York City, was able to carry out her cherished longing, and the Union Missionary Society was launched. Women of six denominations composed its membership, and it stood alone in America for eight years. This was the period of the Civil War in the republic, and in the absorbing demands of that struggle Christian women had no leisure to undertake new departures in missions, but at the same time they were acquiring a training for it in the future. By combining as they did, on a large scale, for work in soldiers' hospitals and in the Sanitary Commission, they learned the possibilities and the power of organization. In 1868 the Woman's Board of Missions (Congregational) of Boston was organized. From that time the process of organization went on until nearly every denomination has its Woman's Home and Foreign Missionary societies, working in cooperation with the general missionary societies of the denomination.

Organization: All the main features of organization necessary in each separate Woman's Board of Missions may be included in three, and in England two are often made to answer.

First: There is the local or parish society, made up of individuals from a single local church, or, as often occurs in America, women of two or more churches of the same denomination in one large town unite to form one Missionary Society. This local society is usually called an Auxiliary. It has its own constitution and officers, and is independent in its management; but when it undertakes to carry out its purpose of sending forth missionaries and funds to sustain various forms of missionary work at a distance, it does not try to act alone, but under its Woman's Board, of which it thus becomes an "auxiliary," or helper. An annual fee is the usual requisite for membership.

Second: These auxiliaries are grouped, and thus constitute what are usually called Branches. This relation is sectional. Adjacent auxiliaries, sometimes to the number of not more than 20, sometimes covering a county, sometimes a whole State containing several hundred auxiliaries, combine, with a set of officers elected from the whole territory represented by the Branch. This stands between the Board and its auxiliaries. It voices the wishes of the Board to the auxiliaries, and expresses the sentiment of the latter to the Board. A Branch assumes the responsibility for some missionary enterprise, and its auxiliaries share it among themselves proportionally.

Third: The Board includes all the Branches, and requires its own officers. A legal charter is requisite for a Board, but not for auxiliaries and Branches. Auxiliaries usually hold their meetings monthly or oftener; Branches quarterly; but the Board meets annually, or, at most, two or three times a year. Business of the Board is transacted throughout the year by its officers, who are elected by the delegates of annual meeting. The delegates are chosen, not from auxiliaries, but from Branches. The Board or Society (whichever name is given to the inclusive organization) has supervision over an area which varies according to circumstances. If the Society is undenominational, like the English Society for Promoting Education in the East, or the Woman's Union Missionary Society in America, it may have its constituency in any part of the country. If the Society cooperates with a Board of some denomination, its territory will depend upon the form of organization of that Church. The Society within the Protestant Episcopal Church in America, for reasons which are apparent, is indivisibly one all over the country. But the geographical spaces are so great in America that in many cases it is found more practicable to have several coordinate boards in one church. The area of each Board is geographically determined. The Congregational women are massed distinctly under Eastern, Middle, and Western Boards, the Baptist women under the East, the West, and the Pacific Coast Boards.

The advantage of one great undivided Board is offset in the case of several coordinate Boards by the following results:

a. A far greater number of responsible, official workers are secured.

b. The work of each Board does not become unmanageably large for its officers.

c. Interest throughout the constituency is augmented by nearness to headquarters.

d. It is possible for a vastly greater number of members to afford the expense of the journey to attend the annual meeting where the Board is a local center than where it is a national center.

While organization always begins at the top, with the Board the real germ is the auxiliary, and this is the place of growth. Enlargement of an auxiliary by addition of members, one at a time, an auxiliary formed in a local church by gathering a few picked individuals into a little monthly meeting—this is the unobtrusive way in which Boards grow. Societies of young ladies and children's bands are regarded as only phases of the auxiliary, but the officers of the Branch are responsible for the work undertaken both by young ladies and children within its domain.

The existence of more than 30,000 auxiliaries and bands in America, with a membership of several hundreds of thousands, speaks volumes for the patient, persevering, enthusiastic efforts of the women of the Church for foreign missions; but it after all represents the efforts of only a fraction of them. Many of the Societies cover not more than one-fifth of the church membership of the denomination.

Terms Employed: In Great Britain the name "Ladies Association," or "Ladies Society" is employed, while in America "Woman's Board" or "Society" is preferred. Also many societies in Great Britain dispense with the "auxiliary" and appoint "collectors" of funds from the churches; others do not use the term "Branch," but "District Auxiliary" instead. "Presbyterial societies" and "Associations" and a variety of other terms take the place of those explained above.

In the Presbyterian Church in America "Presbyterial Society" corresponds to the term "Branch," tho "Synodical Society" is introduced in some places. The Protestant Episcopal Society is itself called, not a Board, but "Auxiliary;" and its constituent societies, not auxiliaries, but, respectively, diocesan and parish branches.

In Great Britain, societies often have long lists of honorary officers. Such are scarcely known in America, where names heading the official list are those of the actually responsible leaders, who conduct public meetings and control the affairs of their societies. The committees of gentlemen which some societies in the old country appoint are also unknown in America, the office of Auditor of Accounts being the only one ordinarily filled by a man.

Meetings: Under the auspices of a single one of many of these women's societies hundreds of meetings are held every year. Meetings for both business and prayer are convened at the headquarters of most Boards, at stated times, besides farewell meetings upon the departure of missionaries, and other meetings specially called; and an annual meeting is universal; but in both character and conduct of them great diversity exists.

Breakfast and tea meetings, and working parties for the purpose of making clothing for native children in orphanages and schools, for filling Christmas boxes and preparing embroidery patterns for classes—all these are much mentioned in English reports, but are comparatively infrequent in America. In Europe a limited number of Christmas boxes are sent to the missions, but the general purpose of meetings in America is either the transaction of business or the imparting of information in order to arouse interest in missions. Whatever its object, the missionary meeting is always partly a devotional service and sometimes strictly such. Many societies have a by-law requiring the opening of all meetings with devotional exercises; and altho many printed reports make no allusion to prayer meetings, it is not supposable that societies often exist without them. Where the organization extends to parishes the number of meetings is vastly multiplied. An "auxiliary" is generally understood in America to mean a company of ladies, who, among other things, hold a meeting every month, in the morning, in cities, for prayer and deliberate study of missions; in the afternoon in the country; and perhaps, on Sunday, in rural districts where people live widely scattered.

A Branch, or Presbyterial meeting, means a quarterly meeting, often lasting all day, which is held in one or another town by invitation. It is thus brought at some time within the reach of every member of the Branch. Those of adjacent towns who can conveniently attend go by carriages or train to the quarterly meeting, and a hearty sight it is on pleasant days, in a country town, to see the ladies driving up from every direction, all their horses' heads pointed toward the church. There they spend the day. A little Branch business, Scripture-reading, and frequent prayer and song, wideawake, practical papers, inspiring talks, often from missionary ladies on a furlough, with a hospitable lunch between morning and afternoon sessions—these are quarterly meetings. Perhaps their place is most nearly filled in Great Britain by "deputation meetings," where some speaker is sent out to a certain locality by the secretary and holds an appointed meeting, generally in connection with one managed by the parent society.

In the old country, also, annual meetings are

often, but not always, presided over by gentlemen, and sometimes no ladies speak on their own platforms. Such a thing is unknown in America. It is there very exceptional for a gentleman to preside, altho occasionally one is invited to speak; and while in the early days of the societies they were rigorously excluded from the audience, gentlemen are now absent chiefly because there is not room for them. Annual meetings of the larger Boards now occupy two or three days, and attendants upon them are quite familiar with the sight of a large church packed with women.

Children's Societies: Beyond occasional mention of contributions from "pupils" of some lady, or "from a Bible-class" or "Sunday-school," the reports of women's societies in the old country seldom have anything to say of the children's part in the modern missionary crusade. But in America they are a great factor—both in the United States and Canada. The children are organized into Bands, of which they are themselves officers, altho superintended by some skilful leader; and they read their little reports with quite as much gravity, accumulate their offerings with equal enthusiasm, and, in general, march to the music, if with a somewhat broken step, as happily as their seniors. One of the first momentous duties of a band is to name itself, and the English language has been explored for the purpose. There are the Carrier Doves and Lookout Guards, Snowflakes and Mayflowers, Busy Bees, Steady Streams, Mustard Seeds, King's Cadets, Up and Readys, Little Lights, Pearl Seekers, Acorns, The Drum Corps, Do What You Can Band, and so on, in endless variety. As one has said, "Each dainty or suggestive name looks out from the record like the growing face of a child." And no mean sum in hard cash do these children send to the foreign mission treasury.

And what have the children not done to fill their mite-boxes? They have tithed what was given for Christmas and Fourth of July; they have hemmed towels by the mile, and practised scales by the half day; they have foregone sweets and even butter; they have picked blackberries in the sun; they have "minded" baby, and submitted to have their teeth drawn, and "buttoned papa's boots, who can't stoop over because he's so fat;" they have bunched flowers and shoveled snow; raised vegetables and poultry; and after earning their money some of them have divided with little brother, so that he might share the glory of giving. One little girl had her music-box, "which plays with a handle, right by my bank, and I play a tune whenever I put some money in, so I like to put the pennies in oftener than before."

Meetings of these Bands are held statedly, and the inventiveness of the most skilful leader is taxed to arrange programs which are at once instructive and entertaining. The children are taught numerous hymns and Scripture passages and many learn to pray in the meetings. They draw maps, recite dialogues, hold African palavers, and Indian pow-wows in costume, and give facts about missionary lands in one-minute reports or five-minute papers. They quiz their parents and teachers, and ransack the library and search the atlas for information, because they are "on the committee." Sometimes exercises take a different turn, and they make scrap-books or dress dolls for a missionary school, or pick lint and roll bandages for a hospital. In a great variety of ways their childish energies and sympathies are directed into missionary channels, and they are becoming both grounded in the principles of giving, and through graphic stories and letters, exhibitions of curios, and talks from missionaries, they are growing up in the churches of America, familiarized with missions as their parents never were; so that, much as the little people now accomplish, it is as nothing compared with what may be expected from them when they come to years of maturity.

Results of the active entrance of women into Missionary work: What has already been said of the influence of the women in cultivating the missionary spirit among children suggests one important branch of these results. Christian women have taken a leading place in arousing interest in missions and in securing systematic study of this branch of the work of the Church. Theirs is the scheme for united study which has brought forth in America a series of valuable works used by study classes in all denominations. The first three volumes of this series have found sale for 120,000 copies. To the activity of the women, also, must be ascribed a notable increase of funds devoted to the missionary enterprise. Without the women's societies there would always be devout women in the churches desirous of contributing to the support of missions. But the mass of women, without these societies and the methods which they use, would never be sufficiently in touch with missions nor sufficiently informed upon the details of their beneficent influence to make sacrifices for their support. Through the energy of the women's societies it has come to pass, however, that a very large proportion of the funds which they collect must be reckoned as a gain, not otherwise possible, to the resources of foreign missions.

The most far-reaching and weighty result of the entrance of women upon the mission enterprise is found on the mission field. The missionary woman is not a preacher, but she is an evangelist. She is also a teacher, and often she is a physician of the highest ability. She may be also a skilled writer, and a linguist of talent that finds its field even in translation of the Bible. Missionary women not only thus reenforce other workers in all the great departments of the missionary enterprise, but, being women, they gain effective access to that half of the population which no man can hope to reach in any but the most superficial and unsatisfactory way. It is their entrance among the women of non-Christian lands and their many-sided activity for the culture of true womanliness that has made the period of the uprising of the women of Christendom in behalf of missions the dawn of a new era in missionary history.

WONG-BUANG: A village in Fo-kien, China, situated 30 miles N. of Fu-chau-fu. Station of the CEZ (1893), with (1903) 3 women missionaries, 6 native workers, and 4 day schools.

WONSAN. See WEN-SAN.

WOOD, George W.: Born in Haverhill, Mass., February 14, 1814. Died in Geneseo, N. Y., July 17, 1901. He was educated at Dartmouth College and Princeton Seminary; ordained by the Presbytery of Elizabeth, N. J., in 1837; missionary of the American Board, Singapore, 1838; transferred to Constantinople, 1842; returned home, 1850; corresponding secretary of the American Board, resident in New York, 1852-1871; then reentered upon missionary work in Constantinople and continued for fifteen years until his state of health required his return to America, after 48 years of service of the Board. Dr. Wood was accomplished in the art of dealing with men, and was the author of tracts, periodical articles, and books in Armenian, the latter including commentaries on several of the New Testament epistles and on the Book of Revelation.

WOODSTOCK. See LANDAUR.

WOOSUNG. See WU-SUNG.

WORCESTER: A town in Cape Colony, 60 miles N. E. of Cape Town. Station of the Rhenish Missionary Society, with (1903) 2 missionaries, one of them with his wife; 32 native workers, 2 outstations, 2 day schools, and 4,000 professed Christians, of whom 1,680 are communicants.

WORCESTER, Samuel Austin: Born at Worcester, Mass., January 19, 1798; graduated University of Vermont, 1819; Andover Theological Seminary, 1823; ordained August 25, 1825; left as a missionary of the ABCFM, August 31, for the Cherokees, reaching Brainerd, Ga., October 21, 1825. Through his labors and those of other missionaries, the Indians made great progress in Christian knowledge and the arts of civilized life. They had become largely a nation of farmers and artisans, had organized, with the advice of the United States Government, a regular and creditable government, were to a considerable extent supplied with schools and religious institutions, and many were members of Christian churches. In 1831 the missionaries became involved in a controversy with the State of Georgia in consequence of the passage of a law restricting their privileges, and which they deemed unconstitutional. Mr. Worcester and his two companions were arrested. After sixteen and a half months' imprisonment they were released, January 14, 1833, returned to their stations, and resumed their missionary work. Mr. Worcester removed in April, 1835, with the mission press to Dwight, and spent the summer among the Cherokees of Arkansas, mostly in making arrangements for printing. He afterward was stationed at Park Hill, in the Indian Territory, to which the Cherokees had been removed. Here he died April 20, 1859.

WORLD'S WOMAN'S CHRISTIAN TEMPERANCE UNION: The United States Woman's Christian Temperance Union was organized at Cleveland, O., in 1874, as a result of the great Woman's Temperance Crusade of the previous winter. Soon after the completion of the national organization the suggestion was made of an International Union. At the Detroit Convention (1883) Miss Frances E. Willard urged the project, and in 1884 the Union was fully established, with Mrs. Margaret Bright Lucas, of England, as first President. From 1890 to 1898 Miss Willard was President, and since then Lady Henry Somerset has held the office.

At the first delegated convention of the World's Union at Boston, 1891, the following Declarations of Principles and Pledge were adopted:

"We believe in the coming of His Kingdom, whose service is the highest liberty, because His laws, written in our members, as well as in nature and in grace, 'are perfect, converting the soul.'

"We believe in the Gospel of the Golden Rule, and that each man's habits of life should be an example safe and beneficent for every other man.

"We therefore formulate, and for ourselves adopt, the following pledge, asking our brothers of a common danger and a common hope to make common cause with us, in working its reasonable and helpful precept into the practise of every-day life:

"I hereby solemnly promise, God helping me, to abstain from all Alcoholic Liquors as beverages, whether distilled, fermented, or malted; from opium in all its forms, and to employ all proper means to discourage the use of and traffic in the same."

In pursuance of this pledge, the plan includes education of the young, the development of public sentiment, the reform of drunkards, and the general work for the establishment of the Kingdom of Christ.

The conduct of the Union is in the hands of an executive committee, consisting of the officers, Presidents of National Societies, Superintendents of World's Departments, and others who may be selected. There are two secretaries, one in England and one in the U. S. A., and the headquarters of the U. S. Union are practically those of the World's Union.

According to the report (1903) there are auxiliaries in 60 countries (including 6 in Australia), scattered all over the world: 11 in Asia, 15 in Europe, 7 in Africa, etc. There are 37 departments, including a Young Woman's Branch, Scientific Education, Systematic Giving, Anti-Narcotics, Opium—Gambling; Penal, Charitable and Reform work; Purity, Franchise, Peace and International Arbitration, etc.

Statistics of such a work are scarcely possible. An idea of its extent is given by the fact that official papers are published in the U. S. A., England, Canada, Australia, New South Wales, South Australia, Transvaal, Japan, Tasmania, India, Burma, Cape Colony, and New Zealand. An extensive work is carried on also among soldiers and sailors. Cordial cooperation is given by missionaries of all societies in every land, who look upon the organization as an effective agency for advancing the Kingdom.

WOTYAK LANGUAGE: One of the Finnish group of the Ural-Altaic family of languages, spoken west of the Ural Mountains and in the provinces of Viatka and Orenburg, in Eastern Russia. It is written with the Russian alphabet. The name is also pronounced Votyak.

WOYENTIN. See WOGENTHIN.

WRAY, John: Missionary of the LMS to British Guiana, South America, from 1807 to 1837. He was sent to Demerara in 1808, at the request of a wealthy planter, and made his home on the plantation. Here his labors were so much blessed that a great reformation took place among the negroes, not only on this estate, but also on the surrounding ones. They changed their ways of living, and became earnest and attentive listeners to his preaching. The local government of Demerara was not in sympathy with the religious work among the negroes, and it placed so many obstructions in the way of the missionaries that Mr. Wray was sent to England to obtain, if he could, a modification of the laws of the country. He partially succeeded, and returned to Demerara in 1811.

In 1813 he began work among the crown negroes at the stations of Georgetown and

Berbice. The laws which he had secured for the amelioration of the condition of the negroes being misunderstood, or not carried out, he found it necessary to go a second time to England in their behalf. Still negroes were hindered in their religious worship. Their books were taken from them, and overseers accompanied them to the meetings "to judge of the doctrines held forth to the negroes."

Such persecutions irritated them beyond endurance, and a serious insurrection broke out, many of them leaving the plantations and going into the back country. On Mr. Wray's return to Berbice he was requested by the governor to explain to the slaves the new laws, so that there might be no further trouble. He seems to have succeeded, and quiet was restored in his mission, where he remained for 13 years, when, worn out with his work, he with his wife sought rest and health in England. In 1832 he returned to Berbice and continued his work for eight years longer, when he died of yellow-fever at New Amsterdam.

WRIGHT, Austin H.: Born at Hartford, Vt., November 11, 1811. Died January 14, 1865. He studied at Dartmouth College and Union Theological Seminary, N. Y., and in the medical department of the University of Virginia, Charlotteville, preaching during his term of study to the destitute population of the "Ragged Mountains;" sailed March 9, 1840, as a missionary of the ABCFM for the Nestorians, to take the place in Urmia of Dr. Grant, whose impaired health and large plans for the Mountain Nestorians led him to seek a residence in one of the mountain districts of Kurdistan. His perfect acquaintance with the Turkish, Syriac, and Persian languages, coupled with his knowledge of medicine and his kind, gentle courtesy of manner, gave him much influence among all classes of the people, and the business connected with the authorities, and intercourse with the higher classes, was to a great extent in his hands, or carried on through him. The Persian officials and other gentlemen appreciated very highly the courteous, dignified, yet simple ease and grace with which he met them.

In 1860 he returned to the United States, but, tho feeble, he engaged in labors for the Nestorians. In the early part of 1863 he began the revision of the New Testament in Syriac, preparatory to its being electrotyped and printed by the ABS in pocket form. To this the Psalms were added, and he took back with him on his return in 1864 the first few copies, which were hailed with delight by the people. A short time before this it was determined to undertake the translation of the Bible into Turkish for the Mohammedan population of Azerbaijan. This work was assigned to Dr. Wright in conjunction with Mr. Rhea, and he entered upon it with great enthusiasm. But in three months he was called to a higher service.

WU-CHANG-FU: A town and capital of Hupei, China, situated on the Yangtsze, opposite Han-kiang and Han-kau. Population about 100,000. With the other two cities together the population is estimated at 1,200,000. It is a great center of Chinese culture, and there are also manufactures. The following societies have mission stations there: LMS (1867); PE (1868); WMS; Swedish National Society (1890); Scandinavian Alliance; CA; with, altogether (1903), 32 missionaries, men and women; 22 native workers, men and women; 12 places of worship, 10 day schools, 2 boarding schools, and 314 professed Christians.

WU-CHAU-FU: A town in Kwang-si, China, situated in the E. part of the province, on the West River, about 125 miles E. of Canton. Population (1901), 52,000. Station of the WMS, with (1903) 1 missionary, 6 native workers, 1 place of worship, 3 day schools, 1 hospital, 1 dispensary, and 22 professed Christians. Station also of the CA. The BFBS has an agency and book room here. The place is sometimes called Wu-chow.

WUCHEO and **WU-CHOW**. See WU-CHAU-FU.

WUCIEH. See WU-HSI-HSIEN.

WUGA. See VUGA.

WU-HSI-HSIEN: A town in Kiang-su, China, situated on the Grand Canal, about 30 miles N. W. of Su-chau-fu. Station of the MES, with 1 missionary. Also station of the PE, with 1 native worker, 1 day school, 1 boarding school, 2 Sunday schools, and 10 professed Christians. Some write the name Wu-sih.

WU-HSUEH: A town in Hu-pei, China, situated on the Yangtsze River, about 35 miles W. N. W. of Kiu-kiang. Station of the WMS, with (1903) 1 missionary, 8 native workers, 4 outstations, 6 places of worship, and 102 professed Christians, of whom 69 are communicants. Some write the name Wusueh.

WU-HU-HSIEN: A town and treaty port in Ngan-hwei, China, situated on the Yangtsze River, about 60 miles S. W. of Nan-king. Population (1901), 102,116. Station of the FCMS (1890), with (1903) 1 missionary and his wife, 1 woman missionary, 4 native workers, 1 outstation, 2 places of worship, 1 day school, and 90 professed Christinas. Also station of the CIM (1893), with (1903) 2 missionaries and their wives, 3 native workers, 1 outstation, 2 places of worship, 1 day school, and 61 professed Christians. Station also of the ME, with (1903) 3 missionaries, two of them with their wives; 1 woman missionary, 6 native workers, 5 Sunday schools, 5 day schools, and 384 professed Christians, of whom 184 are communicants. Also station of the PE (1894), with (1903) 1 missionary, 5 native workers, 3 outstations, 1 day school, 1 boarding school, 4 places of worship, and 53 professed Christians. Also station of the CA. Some write the name Wuhu.

WU-KING-FU: A town in Kwang-tung, China, situated about 45 miles W. N. W. of Swatow, among the Hakka people. Station of the PCE (1865), with (1903) 3 missionaries and their wives, 2 women missionaries, 16 native workers, 2 boarding schools, 1 dispensary, 1 hospital, 1 medical class, 1 theological seminary, 1 printing house, and 1,304 professed Christians.

WULUPURAM. See VILLUPURAM.

WUN-CHAU. See WEN-CHAU-FU.

WUPPERTHAL: A village in Cape Colony, South Africa, situated in the Doorn River district, about 70 miles N. of Tulbagh. Station of the Rhenish Missionary Society, with (1903) 1 missionary, 8 native workers, 3 outstations, 3 day schools, and 1,721 professed Christians, of whom 355 are communicants.

WU-SIH. See WU-HSI-HSIEN.

WUSUEH. See WU-HSUEH.

Y

YA-CHAU-FU: A town in Sze-chwan, China, situated about 70 miles S. W. of Chen-tu-fu. Station of the ABMU (1894), with (1903) 3 missionaries, two of them with their wives; 3 outstations, 1 place of worship, 1 day school and 52 professed Christians. Some write the name Yachau.

YAFA. See JAFFA.

YAKUSA: A village on the upper Congo River, Congo Free State, 70 miles N. W. of Stanley Falls. It has trade relations with five different tribes. Population 1,200. A railroad is now being built thence to Lake Tanganyika. Station of the BMS (1895), with (1903) 4 missionaries, one of them with his wife; 1 outstation, 1 dispensary, 1 industrial school, and 1 day school. The name is sometimes written as Yakusu, or Sargent is used to indicate the same place.

YANG-CHAU-FU: A town in Kiang-su, China, situated on the Grand Canal, about 15 miles N. of the Yangtsze River. Population about 150,000. Station of the CIM (1868), with (1903) 2 missionaries and their wives, 3 women missionaries, 8 native workers, 1 outstation, 2 places of worship, 1 Sunday school, and 36 professed Christians. The main work of the station is the training home for newly appointed missionary women. Also station of the SBC (1891), with (1903) 1 missionary and his wife, 2 outstations, 1 place of worship, 1 Sunday school, 1 dispensary, and 23 professed Christians. Some write the name Yang-chow.

YANG-HSIEN: A town in Shen-si, China, situated in the S. part of the province on the Han River about 51 miles E. by N. of Han-chung-fu. Station of the CIM (1896), with (1903) 2 women missionaries, 1 outstation, and 18 professed Christians. Some write the name Yang-hien.

YANG-KANG: A town in Kwang-tung, China, situated in the northern environs of Swatow, about 10 miles from the city. Station of the ABMU (1893), with (1903) 2 missionaries and their wives, 2 women missionaries, 31 native workers, 20 outstations, 8 places of worship, and 618 professed Christians. Some write the name Ung-kung.

YANG-KAU-HSIEN: A town in Kiang-si, China, situated a little to the S. E. of Kwan-hsin-fu, in the N. E. part of the province. Station of the CIM (1890), with (1903) 3 women missionaries, 3 native workers, 1 place of worship, 1 Sunday school, and 68 professed Christians. Some write the name Yang-k'eo.

YANG-KIANG-HSIEN: A town in Kwang-tung, China, situated on a little bay about 150 miles S. W. of Canton. Station of the PN (1893), with (1903) 3 missionaries, two of them with their wives; 20 native workers, 4 outstations, 11 places of worship, 1 day school, 1 hospital, 1 dispensary, and 279 professed Christians. Some write the name Yueng-kong.

YAO LANGUAGE: One of the Bantu family of African languages, spoken by a number (not yet ascertained) of tribes inhabiting the Eastern shores of Lake Nyasa, in Portuguese East Africa, and found also in the Shirè region south of the lake. It has been reduced to writing by missionaries with use of the Roman letters.

YARKAND: A town in Chinese Turkestan, situated on the Yarkand River, about 200 miles S. E. of Kashgar. Population about 60,000, mostly Turks, who speak Turkish of the Eastern dialect. They are Mohammedans in religion. Station of the Swedish National Missionary Society (1895), with 1 missionary and his wife, 1 place of worship, and 1 day school. Some write the name Jarkend.

YATES, Rev. M. T.: Missionary of the Southern Baptist Convention, born in Wake County, N. C., January 8, 1819; died in Shanghai, China, March 18, 1888. He was born of humble but intelligent and pious parents. Their poverty forbade them to give him the education they desired him to have, and for which his own soul yearned. He therefore made his own way through school and college with the assistance of his brethren who at various times became interested in his struggles. His remark to his father upon setting out to prepare himself for college has been an inspiration to many lads in the Southern States:—"I will go to school if I have to make bricks by moonlight to pay my way." It was also characteristic of the steady determination and self-reliance of the man.

He graduated from Wake Forest College, N. C., in 1846, was appointed a missionary August, 1846, married Miss Eliza Moring of Chatham Co., N. C., September 27, 1846, sailed for China April, 1847, and arrived in Shanghai Sept. 13, 1847, shortly after it had been made a treaty port by the treaty of 1846. There in Shanghai and its environs he labored for more than forty years, in spite of wars, famines, perils, sickness, and manifold trials. Always he was cheered and supported by his devoted wife and at intervals by other missionaries sent out to reenforce him. A part of the time he supported not only himself, but also other missionaries by his labor as Vice-Consul and his judicious investments of frugal savings and the small patrimony of his wife. Largely in this way the Central China Mission of the Southern Baptist Convention was preserved, during the great Civil War in America and for some years after, when the Board which sent him to China was crippled and all but destroyed. He grew in power and usefulness in spite of overwhelming difficulties, until he became a master missionary.

His work was that of laying good and true foundations. He made himself such a master of the spoken Chinese language and so thoroughly learned the Chinese manners, modes of thought and customs that he was regarded by the Chinese—like Verbeck in Japan—as one of their own number. Besides useful religious works he translated the New Testament into the Shanghai dialect, he organized churches and built houses of worship, established schools, and otherwise built up what has come to be the Central China Mission of the SBC.

His personality was great and inspiring. The man had a tremendous influence both in China

and America and among all Christian people. By some, if not all, of his compeers he was regarded (as a Presbyterian brother expressed it) as "head and shoulders above any missionary in China." Certainly his towering form, his learning, force, manners, and all that goes to make personality—all conspired to make him a mighty factor in the world's evangelization. Tho his body has slept in the grave for more than fifteen years, his influence is powerful in all the Southern States to-day. Once in the dark hours of war and reconstruction his imposing influence inspired the hearts of the brethren with fresh courage and enthusiasm, and that influence "still in the world endures."
Taylor (C. E.), *Life of M. T. Yates*, Sunday School Board SBC, Nashville, Tenn.

YATES, William: Born at Loughborough, Leicestershire, England, December 15, 1792. Died July 3, 1845. Educated for the ministry at Bristol College; ordained August, 1814, and sailed for Calcutta as a missionary of the Baptist Missionary Society April 16, 1815. He joined the mission at Serampur, devoting himself to preaching and assisting Dr. Carey in the translation of the Scriptures. Because of the controversy of Dr. Carey and his companions at Serampur with the BMS, Mr. Yates, with three associates, separated from the Serampur Mission. They established themselves at Calcutta in 1817. His special work at Calcutta was the preparation of books and the organization of the new printing establishment, which was soon self-supporting. Mr. Yates visited England and the United States in 1827-29, and while he was in England the unhappy breach was healed between the Serampur mission and the BMS. On his return to India he was again stationed at Calcutta. He translated the whole Bible into Bengali, the New Testament into Hindi and Hindustani, and the New Testament and large portions of the Old Testament into Sanskrit. He was engaged in preparing the latter for the press, and a large part had been already printed. He hoped by the close of another year to complete the translation of the Scriptures into this sacred and learned language of the East. But, his health failing, he sailed for England in 1845, and died on the passage up the Red Sea.

YELAMANCHILI: A town in Madras, India, about 35 miles by railway S. W. of Vizagapatam. Station of the BOQ (1890), with (1903) 1 missionary and his wife, 9 native workers, 1 outstation, 1 place of worship, 7 Sunday schools, 1 day school, 1 dispensary, and 50 professed Christians.

YELANDUR: A town in Central India, situated S. of Raipur and in the vicinity of Jagdalpur. Station of the ME, with (1903) 1 missionary and his wife, 5 native workers, 6 Sunday schools, 1 day school, 1 place of worship, 1 outstation, and 77 professed Christians, of whom 64 are communicants. Some write the name Yellandu.

YELLAMANCHILE. See YELAMANCHILI.

YELLANDU. See YELANDUR.

YEN-CHAU: A town in Che-kiang, China, situated on the river, about 60 miles S. W. of Hang-chau. Station of the CIM (1902), with 1 missionary and 1 place of worship.

YEN-CHENG: A town in Ho-nan, China, situated on the Hoang-ho, and destined to become an important center, as the railroad is to pass through it. Station of the CIM (1902), with 1 missionary and his wife and 1 place of worship.

YEN-SHAN-HSIEN: A town in Chi-li, China, situated about 80 miles S. by E. of Tien-tsin and 35 miles from Tsang-chau. Station of the LMS (1878), with (1903) 2 missionaries and their wives. The station residences have now been transferred to Tsang-chau. Some write the name Yen-san.

YEOTMAL: A town in Berar, Central India, about 55 miles S. E. of Amraoti. Station of the Free Methodist Church in America (1892), with (1900) 2 missionaries and their wives, 2 women missionaries, 5 native workers, 1 place of worship, 2 Sunday schools, 2 day schools, 1 industrial school, and 20 professed Christians.

YEZD: A town in Persia, situated in the central part of the country, about 300 miles S. E. of Teheran. Population about 53,000. There is a small Parsee colony here, and many of the Mohammedans belong to the Babi sect. Station of the CMS (1898), with (1903) 2 missionaries and their wives, 3 women missionaries, 9 native workers, 2 day schools, 1 hospital, 1 dispensary, and 42 professed Christians, of whom 12 are communicants.

YEZIDIS: The Arabs who accepted Mohammed called those who did not *el johaleen, i. e.*, the ignorant ones. Among the latter was Yezid ben M'awe, who refused to accompany M'awe, his father, who, as an attendant upon his person, followed the fortunes of Mohammed. Many of "the ignorant ones" rallied around Yezid, and he became the nucleus of the sect which appropriated his name. The Yezidis possess a lineage tree by means of which they trace their religious origin back to him.

They seem to have existed as a very loose organization until about 1106, when there arose among them an elder called Sheikh Hadi, from the region of Damascus. He removed to the district of Hakkiari in Kurdistan, and dwelt in Mount Lalish, which is eleven hours from Mosul. He died in 1162, and his tomb, called Sheikh Adi, is hard by the village of Ba'adri, where also is the temple of the Yezidis. This place, as their religious center, is by them esteemed superior to Mecca.

Sheikh Hadi gave more consistency to their religious system—still very confused and illogical —and greater stability to its organization, by commiting to writing its tenets and traditions. His work, which is the authority for their belief, is named *El Jilweh* (the Revelation). The original is the only copy existing, and it is esteemed as most holy, and is guarded at Sheikh Adi with the most scrupulous care. It is in Arabic, and speaks in this wise of the origin of the Yezidis: " 'O angels,' said the great God, 'I am going to create Adam and Eve. They will become mankind, and from the lines of Adam's palm (?) shall proceed Shehr ben Jebr, and of him a separate community will appear upon the earth, that of Azazael, *i. e.*, of Melek Taous, which is the sect of the Yezidis.' Then he sent Sheikh Hadi ben Musaffer from the land of Damascus, and he came and dwelt in Mount Lalish." Sheikh Hadi was an Arab, and was held in high repute for his piety and devotion. He holds among the Yezidis the same place that is given to Moses by the Jews, and that is claimed by the Muslims for Mohammed.

This degraded yet interesting people number

probably about 200,000 souls, but they are scattered over a belt of territory 300 miles wide, extending in length from the neighborhood of Aleppo in Northern Syria to the Caucasus in Southern Russia. The mass of them, however, are to be found in the mountains of Northern and Central Kurdistan, and among the Sinjar hills of Northern Mesopotamia.

Tho the mysteries of their religion are in the Arabic language, Kurdish is more generally spoken by the Yezidis than Arabic, both languages being used by those living in the Sinjar hills and in the region of Mosul.

The Yezidis are an agricultural people and live in fixed abodes. As a rule they are neater and cleaner in their homes, and in respect to person and dress, than either Arab or Kurd; while their style of dress follows the fashions of the people by whom they are surrounded, except that the shirt has a square-cut opening in front.

Generally speaking they are quiet and industrious, but in the regions of Redwan and Midyat they are given to house-breaking and highway robbery, and also hire themselves to Muslims and Christians for the commission of deeds of blood, so that they are the terror of those districts. In the Sinjar hills, where they constitute almost the entire population, they are restive and refractory. Everywhere they entertain a deep-seated hatred of Muslims, whether Arabs or Kurds, who treat them in return with contempt and oppression. Polygamy is allowed among them to the limit of six wives, but its practise is not so general as with the Muslims, limited to four wives. The drinking of *raki* (a mild arrack) is enjoined as a religious rite in connection with the worship of Melek Taous, and accordingly intemperance is common.

They are recognized by the Turkish Government as a distinct religious community. Their civil head is an Emir whose title is hereditary, and who is of royal blood, if *El Jilweh* is to believed. It says: "Then Melek Taous came down to earth for our sect, *i. e.*, the Yezidis, the disturbed, and appointed kings for us, besides the kings of ancient Assyrians, Nisroch, etc. . . . And after that we had two kings—Shaboor (Sapor) First and Second—who reigned 150 years; and our Emirs, until this day, have descended from their seed."

The Emir never marries outside of this royal line. He is lord of the persons and affairs of the Yezidis, and his power over them is absolute. His person is considered holy, and all his acts are regarded as righteous. To him belongs administrative power and dignity, as well as ecclesiastical, and all the dealings of the Turkish Government with the Yezidis are through him. For this reason he resides most of the time in Mosul.

The Yezidis have written laws and statutes which are read and interpreted only by the members of one family—that of Mella Haider, surnamed El Bussowi. The secretary of the Emir is always chosen from this family.

Doctrine: The Yezidis believe in God as the supreme deity and the first cause of all things; but they have nothing to do with Him either in the way of worship or service.

They believe in one Melek Taous (King Peacock), who is eternal, an emanation from God, became incarnate as Lucifer, deceived Adam and Eve as Satan, is one of the seven gods who, in turn, rule the world for 10,000 years, and he, having now governed it for the 6,000 years, has yet 4,000 years in which to reign.

They believe in one Sheikh Hadi, called also in *El Jilweh* 'Abd Taous (servant of Taous). They say that he is the god of that which is good, of day and of life; that he is descended from the divine nature, or, at least, is so honored of God that whatever Sheikh Hadi wills comes to pass; and that he revealed to his disciples revelations, secrets, a knowledge of the unseen and of prophecies. In his book he claimed to be sent both of God and of Melek Taous. The second assertion of *El Jilweh* is: "He (Melek Taous) sent 'Abd Taous to this world that he might separate truth from error, and make it known to his people; and the first step to that is by tradition, and afterward by this book *El Jilweh*, which the uninitiated must neither read nor behold." His claim to have been sent of God is made farther on in the sentence quoted at length when stating the origin of this sect. They also say of him, "The Yezidis' god descended in this era and both taught and established us." Sheikh Hadi associated himself with God in stating farther on in his book that "He afterward came and dwelt in Lalish." Is there in Sheikh Hadi an effort at the reconciliation of God and Melek Taous, or the union of the two eternal principles (according to Zoroaster) of good and evil, in order to secure a reconciliation of man with each, and with both together, through worship at the shrine of one who stood for both?

They believe in six other gods. *El Jilweh* says: "He created six gods from himself and from his light; and their creation was as one lights a light from another light." This recalls the Zoroastrian doctrine of Ahura Mazda and his six gifts.

They accept Christ as the "Light of God," and say that He cannot die; also that He is a Savior and will come again. But all these are evidently accommodations to the Christian sects with whom they are brought into contact. In the same way the Yezidis about Redwan have attempted to accommodate their tenets to the Christian doctrine of the Trinity.

They hold to the Transmigration of Souls, but subject to the caprice of Melek Taous, for *El Jilweh* says: "I (Melek Taous) will not allow one in this wretched world longer than the time determined by me; and if I desire it I send him a second or a third time into this world, or some other, by the transmigration of souls." When righteous souls return they enter into men, but wicked spirits are sent back to reside in the beasts. Yet along with this they hold to a Resurrection, when Sheikh Hadi will carry all the Yezidis to paradise on a tray borne upon his head. They hold to a future judgment and punishment for all—except the Yezidis. *El Jilweh* says: "I (Melek Taous) punish in other worlds those who do contrary to my laws." They have Islamic notions of paradise as a place of eating and drinking, together with the pleasures of physical love. They claim to receive the Old Testament, the New Testament, and the Koran, but reverence the Old Testament more than either of the others. This acceptance is, however, a qualified one, for *El Jilweh* says: "The books of those who are without I accept in a sense, *i. e.*, those that agree with and conform to my statutes. Whatsoever is contrary to these they have altered."

The Yezidi ecclesiastical polity has the form of a religious oligarchy, is composed of six orders besides the Emir, which are chiefly hereditary and confined to as many distinct families. These orders are:

(1) *The Sheikh:* He is called Sheikh Mengah, which is the name of a district comprising the regions of Mosul, Amadieh, and Zakho. He is the chief ecclesiastic of the sect. He ranks next to the Emir, who is the religious as well as political head, even as the Sheikh ul Islam in Turkey ranks next to the Sultan, who is the Caliph. The Sheikh is the guardian of the tomb of Sheikh Hadi. The insignia of his office are a kind of girdle which is worn about the body and a netting of catgut which is carried in the hand. He is supposed to prophesy, and has paradise in his flowing sleeves, sections of which he is willing to dispose of to purchasers according to the sums received. Whenever the Sheikh appears among the people they submit themselves to him in lowly reverence and humility.

(2) *Sheikhs:* This order was founded by Sheikh Hadi. Every Sheikh traces his lineage back through a regular succession to a Patriarch who is regarded not only as the bestower of the office of Sheikh, but also as the assistant and advocate of those in his line who exercise the office, and as the avenger of all injuries inflicted upon them. For this reason no Yezidi dares to return the smiting of an ecclesiastic. Each Sheikh has the privilege of doctoring a special disease. The Sheikhs frighten their followers into giving presents and alms according to their will by threatening to punish them, upon refusal, with pestilence, fever, distress, sickness, and pains, or the control of their enemies over them—such power being supposed to reside in each Sheikh.

From this order comes the Mella, who is the instructor of youth, the guardian of "the book," of religious mysteries, and of the interests of the sect. He is also the secretary of the Emir, and in his family alone are reading and writing allowed. The office is hereditary.

(3) *Pirs:* They are the Nazarites, who take vows of celibacy and devote themselves and their property to Sheikh Hadi. To them appertains the conduct of hair-dressing and of the fasts and feasts. They are also intercessors, and perform their function upon certain heaps of stones in the neighborhood of Sheikh Adi, where they continually reside.

(4) *Kuchiks:* The word is Kurdish and signifies dancer. These attend to the service of the tambourines, praises and songs. They order and conduct the sacred dance upon the feast-days. They praise the gods Hadi and Taous with tambourine and fife until they swoon in a trance, when they utter strange sounds and language. They declare what is revealed to them in dream, trance, and vision, and are reckoned as prophets. They are said to have the power of life and death—probably through the influence of magic.

(5) *Kowals:* These are the priests proper, to whom pertain the duties of imparting religious instruction to the people, and of sepulture. All instruction is oral, in which they profess to be guided by an "inner light" to which all, even the Emir, must give heed. Whenever a Yezidi is about to die he is visited by a Kowal, or his agent, who removes the dying man's sins by transferring them to himself. They divide with the Pirs the function of intercessors, and to them belongs the privilege, each year, of bidding for the concession of conducting the "Sanjak Taous" among the Yezidi villages. They never use a razor upon their heads.

(6) *Fakirs:* These constitute the lowest order of the priesthood. They are entrusted with the instruction of boys and girls in the tambourine, in dancing, and religious evolutions. They are married, have a salary, live in Sheikh Adi, and are the janitors of that holy place.

The Yezidis worship Melek Taous through his "Sanjak," or symbol, which is a sacred brazen cock, one eye of which is marked over by a cross. They also adore Sheikh Hadi, who is still a god tho his body be dead, and who receives divine honors at his tomb in Sheikh Adi. Forasmuch as he was also sent of Melek Taous, the sacred cock stands for him also, so that he is worshiped at the same time with Melek Taous, and at his tomb the "Sanjak" of Melek Taous is revered equally with the tomb. The two eternal principles have thus equal honor, and by this arrangement no one can worship the one without equally worshiping the other. Here again there seems to be an attempt to accommodate something to their needs from the Parsee religion. In the Vendidad the cock is a sacred bird—the bird of Sraosha, who is Obedience to the law of Mazda and chief of the Yazatas and their leader against the leader of the demon host, Æshna Dæva. The Yezidis seem to combine the two principles and so make the cock represent both.

These two gods are the chief objects of their worship, and the tomb of one and the *sanjak* of the other are the symbols employed to bring them before the worshipers.

The sun is regarded as an exalted spirit without whom there would be no stability to the universe, and, therefore, also worthy of respect and worship. Fire, more especially as lightning and flame, is considered a sacred element, and is worshiped by adoration. They have also a bronze image of an ox which they worship at a festival in November.

The tombs of departed Sheikhs are regarded as holy, and in religious rites conducted at them the assistance of those entombed therein is specially invoked.

The Yezidi worship has a certain fixed ritual difficult to understand. When the "Sanjak Taous" is carried to a village it is accompanied by *Kowals*, who march before it with timbrel and pipe. It must remain in the village over night, and the Yezidis must drink "raki" in its presence. Its worshipers approach it upon their knees, kiss it, mutter prayers, deposit their contributions in a box by its side, rise and walk away with their face toward it. Meanwhile a candle burns on either side of the holy bird. They have no liturgy, nor do they pray audibly, believing that all prayer should be with the heart only. They say God does not require them to fast, save during Ramazan, when they fast three days instead of thirty. This fast must be begun and ended in the presence of either Sheikh or Pir. It is ended by a participation in holy wine that is considered to be the blood of Christ. The cup containing it is held in both hands, after the sacrificial manner of the East, and if a drop should fall it is gathered with religious care.

The Yezidi feasts are the following: 1. On the first Wednesday in April, which is the beginning of their year. 2. August 1, continuing three days, in honor of Melek Fukhr ed Deen. 3. September 22, continuing eight days, to Sheikh Hadi. This is called "et towafat"—*i. e.*, the floods. 4. November, called the Naheevi. (This feast is especially observed by the Yezidis of Jebel Toor, at which the sacred ox is worshiped in connection with Babylonian orgies.) 5. January 1, lasting three days, in honor of Shems ed Din At all these feasts there is much singing in connection with the religious dances. They have a hymn-book called "Zemboor," the hymns of which are in Arabic. They have also songs which are in Kurdish, and are sung to Kurdish tunes. So long as the Turkish Government continues to draft Yezidis into the army it will not allow them to be Christianized. Another formidable obstacle is found in a requisition of their religion that no one shall learn to read or have any dealing with books except the family of Sheikh ul Bussowi, as stated above, the custodians of the sacred book. Nevertheless, there have been instances where Yezidis have seemed to be touched by the Gospel, and there is reason to believe that, with freedom to learn, the Yezidis may yet come forth from their strange superstitions to follow Him who is the Light of the World.

YING-CHAU-FU: A town in Ngan-hwei, China, situated in the N. W. part of the province, on the Sha-ho. Station of the CIM (1897), with (1903) 3 missionaries, one them with his wife; 2 native workers, 1 place of worship, 1 day school, 1 Sunday school and 3 professed Christians. Some write the name Ying-chow-fu.

YING-SHAN-HSIEN: A town in Sze-chwan, China, situated about 40 miles S. E. of Pao-ning-fu. Station of the CIM (1898), with (1903) 3 women missionaries, 1 native worker, 1 place of worship and 15 professed Christians.

YO-CHAU-FU: A town in Hu-nan, China, situated a little S. of the Yangtsze River, used by the LMS as a point of entrance to the province. After a short period of observation the station residences were transferred to Heng-chau.

YOH-YANG. See YO-YANG.

YOKOHAMA: One of the most important of the treaty ports of Japan. It is situated on a plain by the side of the bay of Tokio, on the S. coast of the main island, and is shut in by hills. It occupies an area of a square mile, about one-fourth of which is a foreign settlement. The climate is variable, the thermometer ranging from 95° to 43° F., and the rainfall is quite great. The harbor is a wide and commodious one, well protected by a breakwater. Yokohama is a port of call for the lines of steamers between San Francisco and Hongkong. Other lines connect it with Shanghai, as well as numerous steamers which run from it to points in Japan and China. A line of steamers from Vancouver to Hongkong stops there regularly. A railway connects it with Tokio, and was the first railway opened in Japan (1872). It is also the terminus of a railroad which runs to Kioto.

Population (1898) is 193,762; many Europeans and numerous Chinese are included in the total. The following Societies have mission stations here: RCA (1859), PN (1859), WU (1871), ABMU (1872), ME, Methodist Protestant (1879), Salvation Army, Hephizabah Faith Mission, Zion Catholic Christian Church. All together they have 44 missionaries, men and women; 155 native workers, men and women; 22 native workers, 8 day schools, 10 boarding schools and 1,921 professed Christians. The ABS (1876) and the BFBS each have an agency and a book depot in Yokohama.

YORK: A town in Sierra Leone, West Africa, situated on the seacoast at the mouth of the Whale River 16 miles S. by E. of Freetown. Station of the CMS (1822), with (1903) 4 native workers, 3 outstations, 1 place of worship, 1 Sunday school, 2 day schools, and 261 professed Christians, of whom 83 are communicants. Also station of the UMFC (1860), with (1903) 1 missionary and his wife, 36 native workers, 1 outstation, 2 places of worship, 2 Sunday schools, and 430 professed Christians, of whom 217 are communicants. Station of the WMS also, with (1903) 25 native workers, 4 outstations, 7 places of worship, 3 Sunday schools, 3 day schools and 355 professed Christians, of whom 316 are communicants.

YORUBA: Name of a people inhabiting the country inland from Lagos, West Africa.

YORUBAN: A language belonging to the Negro group of African languages. It is found in several dialects among the tribes occupying the Lagos protectorate and the terrritory from Dahomey to the west bank of the Niger, behind the seacoast belt. The people are intelligent and enterprising and the language is suited to the development of the people. It was reduced to writing by CMS missionaries in the early part of the 19th century, and is written with Roman letters.

YOUNG MEN'S CHRISTIAN ASSOCIATION: Organizations of Christian young men for mutual improvement, and for more or less of religious activity, have probably existed in almost every age of the Church. There is historical record of such societies in Great Britain and Ireland as early as the reign of Charles I. They maintained a continuous existence for nearly one hundred years, through the revolutions under Cromwell and King William, attaining their highest prosperity in the reign of the latter. The chief object of these societies was the promotion of personal piety among their members, but they gave rise in 1691 to the "Societies for the Reformation of Manners," which had for their aim the suppression of vice through legal means. These were called into being by the low state of public morals, which, notwithstanding the better attitude of the court of William and Mary, had little mended since the dissolute reign of Charles II. The early efforts of these reform societies were favored by the civil courts, and they flourished for about forty years. They had become extinct, however, in 1757, and an effort to revive them by members of Wesley's and Whitefield's congregations was defeated through the indifference if not actual hostility of the authorities. In the 19th century, between 1823 and 1838, David Nasmith, of Glasgow, formed about seventy Young Men's Societies in as many cities of the United Kingdom, France, and America. In Germany, as early as 1832, similar associations of young men were formed, closely connected with the established churches and their pastors. But while all these were societies for young men, with a distinctively Christian purpose and activity, they did not seek broadly to promote the physical, intellectual and social as well as the spiritual welfare of young men; develop or train a special class of executive officers or acquire property in the form of buildings which made them locally permanent. They did not band themselves together in district, national, international and world's conferences, altho some of them, notably those of Germany, are now part of the brotherhood forming the World's Conference of the Associations. The present Glasgow and Cincinnati Associations claim to have originated quite independently of suggestion from London; but it seems beyond dispute that the movement which has resulted in the present world-wide brotherhood can be traced to the parent English-speaking association which was organized in London by George Williams, June 6, 1844.

But while the origin and early growth of the movement took place in Great Britain, the larger development and expansion of the work has been wrought out by the American Associations. A knowledge of the London Association and its work led to the formation of Associations in Montreal, Canada, December 9, 1851, and in Boston the 29th of the same month, neither city having any knowledge of the other's action. Other cities followed, till some twenty-five similar organizations were known to be in existance at the date of the first convention, which met in Buffalo, June 7, 1854, followed by the first World's Conference in Paris, August 19, 1855. Here the following declaration, since known as the Paris Basis, or the Basis of 1855, was adopted: "The Young Men's Christian Association seeks to unite those young men, who, regarding Jesus Christ as their God and Savior, according to the Holy Scriptures, desire to be His disciples in their doctrine and in their life, and to associate their efforts for the extension of His kingdom among young men." Upon this rests the affiliation of the Associations of all lands, represented since 1855 by a triennial World's Convention, and since 1878 by a Central International Committee, with headquarters at Geneva, Switzerland. This declaration was ratified by the American International Convention at Montreal in 1856, and at Detroit in 1868 was added what is known as the "active membership test," by which in the American Associations only those in full communion with an evangelical church are admitted to voting and office-bearing membership. At the Portland Convention the following year this action was unanimously reaffirmed, the meaning of the term "evangelical" was defined, and representation at the International Convention, from all Associations thereafter organized, made conditional upon this test being embodied in their constitutions.

In April, 1860, the Associations of North America had about 25,000 members. At the breaking out of the civil war large numbers of their young men entered the armies on both sides, and the Associations naturally followed them with efforts for their welfare and that of their comrades. At the instance of the New York Association a special convention was called November 14, 1861, which resulted in the organization of the United States Christian Commission, the work of which largely absorbed the energies of the Northern Associations during the remainder of the war. With the return of peace, however, the Associations took up their old work with renewed zeal, advanced ideas, and better methods. From about this time dates the beginning of that unparalleled growth which has marked the past three decades. The formal adoption of the evangelical test secured the active sympathy of the churches; a clearer conception of the work, as distinctively for and by young men, focalized thought and effort, and rapidly developed both methods and men; this called for better facilities, which were readily furnished as the practical character of the work was recognized; the work demanded systematic supervision, and the paid secretaryship was developed; the Associations increased in number, spread over the country, and grew multiplex in their departments of work, and State organization and a comprehensive general supervision became a necessity; broadened methods and appliances in the local work asked for larger, better adapted and permanent quarters, and buildings sprang up by the score, till to-day the Associations are a universally acknowledged force in the religious, educational, and social life of the country.

In government the individual Associations are independent, except as to the single item of the active-membership test, each society conducting its business affairs through a board of directors as the corporate management, and with a paid executive officer styled a general secretary; but they are united in a thorough system of general organization, embracing delegated conventions, executive committees, and visiting agents, the decisions and advice of which, tho in the main only advisory, are very generally accepted and followed. With the Associations of the United States and Canada this system embraces:

1. *A Biennial Convention* (annual previous to 1878), composed of delegates from all the Associations, representation being based upon the active membership. The *ad interim* powers of this convention are vested in an executive board, the members of which are elected by classes at the biennial sessions. Since 1866 the headquarters and a working quorum of this body have been located in New York, and in 1883 it was incorporated as the International Committee, a name by which it had for years been known. The scope of the committee's work is broad, including (*a*) supervision and extension—generally of all the work, in full when there is no State organization, and very largely of such special departments as the college, railroad, German, and foreign work; the State organizations owe their existence and early nurture to the act and care of the International Convention and its committee; (*b*) securing, training, and recommending general secretaries; (*c*) advising and assisting regarding the plans, location, and methods of building and the management of property; (*d*) securing funds for its own work and aiding State and local Associations in raising money for State work, for new buildings, to place secretaries in new fields, and in special financial emergencies; (*e*) arranging for the International meetings, assisting in planning many State and special conventions, and sending official representatives to all; (*f*) conducting an extensive correspondence; (*g*) a publication list of tracts and books, several annuals and periodicals, including the "Year-Book;" (*h*) through the systematic efforts of the committee, the American Associations have observed annually, since 1866, a day and week of prayer in November, and since 1875,

by act of the World's Conference, the Associations of other lands have joined in this observance; (i) in times of overwhelming calamity by fire, flood, fever, or disaster, the Associations have often rendered communities effective help through this committee, as their agent, in gathering and distributing such relief.

2. *State Organizations:* modeled after the international, and doing a like work, so far as needed, in their respective fields.

The organization and work of the typical American Association may be thus described: (a) A dual membership: (1) Active—men who are members of evangelical churches, and who constitute its voting, office-bearing, and working force; (2) Associate—young men of good moral character, who join usually for the secular privileges. The total membership of the 1,736 Associations reporting in 1903 is 350,455. (b) A business organization, with constitution, legal incorporation, officers, board of management, and well-ordered system of committees. (c) A paid secretary, to supervise and direct, under the local board, and to develop workers, rather than to attempt too much detail work himself, leaving that mostly to assistants. The total number of general secretaries, physical directors, and assistants in the various departments of the local work is 1,729. A school devoted chiefly to the training of young men as general secretaries and gymnasium instructors, opened in Springfield, Mass., in 1885, has (1903) an enrollment of about 100, while a school of like character organized in 1891 at Chicago has about 150 students, and there are several well-constituted summer schools, notably those at Lake Geneva, Wis., and at Silver Bay, Lake George, N. Y. (d) A building of its own, usually comprising reading-room, library, parlors, recreation-room, offices for secretaries and directors, large and small lecture-rooms, class-rooms, gymnasium, including bowling-alley, baths, and dressing-rooms; a kitchen and janitors' quarters. There are 460 such buildings, valued at $24,016,415—a good index of the estimate put upon the work by Christian business men, and a strong guarantee of its permanency. (e) An organized work: (1) Religious—consisting of Bible-classes, evangelistic and for Christian young men; workers' training-classes; evangelistic and devotional; meetings for young men; special work in the interests of personal purity, temperance, etc.; systematic invitation work; the distribution of religious literature; and a directly personal work, which is specially emphasized. (2) Educational—reading-rooms; circulating and reference libraries; evening classes in practical and liberal branches, book-keeping, penmanship, stenography, mathematics, drawing, languages, history, literature, political science, music, etc.; literary societies, and educational lecturers. (3) Social—attractive rooms for resort, with companionable supervision, music, recreative games, and a variety of social gatherings and entertainments. (4) Physical—facilities for artificial exercise of every description, and under instructors competent, from both a scientific and practical training, to make physical examinations and prescribe safe and helpful work; baths and open athletic grounds for field-sports, and clubs for boating, swimming, rambling, etc. (5) Economics—employment bureau, boarding-house register, savings-bank, medical club, visitation of the sick, and similar service. (6) Junior department, in which, under special supervision and with separate rooms, a more or less full line of work is carried out for boys, and from which they graduate into the senior departments.

The International Committee, with headquarters at 3 W. 29th St., New York City, has 43 members aside from the officers, and 15 advisory members, besides Board of Trustees of 15 members. Most of the members live in New York or vicinity, but there are representatives from different parts of the United States and Canada. There are also 52 corresponding members representing different States and foreign countries.

For active work the staff is divided into 14 departments:

The Office, Publication, and Business Departments have charge of the general correspondence, literature, and financial management. *The Field Department*, occupied with the extension, development, equipment and trained leadership of the Association work in the cities and towns, and also the strengthening of the work of the State and provincial organizations. There are 7 secretaries, 1 in New York, the others in other parts of the country. *The Railroad Department* organizes Associations among railroad men, provides rooms, libraries, buildings, and all the usual features of an Association. For a time it was rather frowned upon by railroad authorities, but of late years they have come to recognize its value and have aided materially in its development, contributing liberally in the erection of buildings and assisting in many ways to make it easy for men to attend the meetings, etc. An illustration is the Missouri Pacific system, where 13 well-equipped Associations were organized within four years. There were in 1903, 198 Associations, with a membership of 63,000, an increase of 50 per cent. in two years. There are 79 buildings, valued at $1,129,050, owned by Associations, 8 under construction valued at $159,500, and 35 others set apart by the companies for their use, valued at $541,000. Work among street employes is being organized and plans are under consideration for extending the system into the countries of Europe. *The Industrial Department* is the most recently organized (1902) and resulted from a study of Association work among the 4,500,000 men employed in the various industrial enterprises of the continent. It looks forward to the erection of buildings or the equipment of rooms in connection with the great factories.

The Students' Department has (1903) 635 Associations among students (exclusive of colored and Indian departments); of these, 48 are in the theological seminaries, 72 in the medical and other professional schools, and the remainder in universities, colleges, and normal and preparatory schools. Special emphasis is placed on Bible study, and in 1902 there were 16,042 enrolled in the Student Bible Classes, while the secretary in charge was in correspondence with 1,808 Bible class leaders. Student Conferences for the training of leaders are held at Northfield, Mass.; Lake Geneva, Wis.; Asheville, N. C.; Pacific Grove, Cal.; Gearhart, Oregon, and Lakeside, Ohio. The spiritual effect of the work is seen in the conversion of over 3,000 young men in the year. Ten student secretaries are employed by the International Committee, some in office and superintendence work and others in visiting colleges, etc.

The *Army and Navy Department* received a special impulse during the war with Spain and has been developed steadily. It has received the most cordial support of officials, and the membership of enlisted men steadily increases. A Soldiers' Bible and Prayer League and a Temperance Union have added over 1,000 names in a single year. There are 150 traveling libraries in constant circulation, and 75 tons of stationery, reading matter, games, etc., were shipped from the office in New York for the different posts. There are 31 buildings in the U. S., 14 in Cuba, 1 in Porto Rico, 4 in the Philippines, 1 in China, and 4 in Alaska. Bible classes, religious meetings, and entertainments are held at 269 different points.

In the *Naval Department* branches are open in Brooklyn, N. Y.; Norfolk, Va.; Newport, R. I.; San Juan, Porto Rico, and at Manila, Cavite, and Olongapo, in the Philippines. Over 1,000 sailors and marines are members. A striking feature is the savings department, which in six months handled nearly $150,000 for the men. Over 1,600 men joined the Naval Temperance League during the year (1903).

The Colored Department: Of the 103 Associations in this department 69 are in educational institutions and 34 in cities, with a membership of over 7,000. Two Conferences at Danville, Va., and Montgomery, Ala., were well attended. Seventeen secretaries give their entire time, 2 in New York and 15 in the Associations.

Boys' Department: The growth in this department has been very great. The 576 Associations report 45,000 members, or if those holding senior tickets were included, 80,000. There are over 100 boys' work specialists, 1,500 rooms used, 120,000 in attendance on Bible classes, while between 3,000 and 4,000 are admitted to the evening classes.

The Indian Department: This reports 47 Associations, with a membership of over 2,000, in Manitoba, Ind. Ter., Kansas, Nebraska, North Dakota, Oklahoma, Oregon, Pennsylvania, and South Dakota.

Religious Work Department: In this the special effort has been to secure quality rather than quantity, yet 8,016 volunteer workers have been registered in the year, while 31,300 have attended the 1,711 Bible classes, and the total attendance at religious meetings of all kinds was 3,230,000. In 1903, 18,613 conversions were reported.

The Educational Department: In the different schools, clubs and lectures, 30,600 students were enrolled, while 1,200 more men reached the Physical Department. This, too, has had great success, 634 Associations reporting attention to it, 93,983 men making use of the gymnastic and athletic features. There are 545 gymnasiums, while 464 Associations report out-door games and sports.

Foreign Department: This organization represents the foreign missionary interests of the American Associations. It arose as a result of investigations begun by Mr. Luther D. Wishard, who, in 1889, began a three years' tour of mission lands with the purpose of studying the conditions of young manhood in non-Christian countries. As a result of that tour and of the subsequent study and experience of Mr. John R. Mott and others, work has been established in India, Japan, China and Hongkong, Ceylon, Brazil, Argentina, Mexico, and Korea. A total of 31 secretaries, most of them with families, are laboring in the countries named. These men have organized or aided in the organization of some 300 Associations in those fields, about one-half of which are what are known as Student Associations in institutions of higher learning. They have a total membership of 14,000, of whom 3,600 are active. Eight periodicals are published in their interest abroad, and they have 14 buildings, valued at $400,000.

The reasons which have led to the inauguration and prosecution of this enterprise are as follows: (1) In non-Christian lands, where moral ideals are largely wanting and where temptations are omnipresent, there is no class which so much needs the oversight and religious incentives of Christianity as the young men. (2) In some of these countries, notably Japan and India, young manhood holds a strategic relation to the progress of their countries. (3) Most of the young men reached are educated and the process of education has alienated them from the superstitions of their fathers, thus leaving them a prey to the skepticism of the West and to the materialism of a semi-foreign environment. (4) The achievements of the Association in Christian countries have led missionaries in all the lands where the foreign Associations are doing their work to strongly appeal to the initiation of the enterprise. They have done so because they believe that an Association fosters Christian unity, deals with a difficult class in a most effective way, and trains them for Christian discipleship, as no other agency is able to do. (5) The achievements of the Association, tho not reducible to any large statistical exhibit, have more than justified the anticipations of the missionaries who have urged the foundation of these asylums for the tempted, and training schools for an active evangelical propaganda. The branches of the World's Student Christian Federation established in India, China, and Japan owe their existence and effectiveness to the foreign Associations. Those in China, India, and Japan are associated as national organizations, under committees consisting of prominent missionaries and Christian workers long resident in those lands.

The following is a general summary of Y. M. C. A. organizations in all lands:

AMERICA: United States and Canada, 1,736; Mexico, 1; West Indies, 3; Bermuda, 2; Argentina, 1; Brazil, 7; Chile, 1; Guiana (Dutch), 2; Uruguay, 3.

EUROPE: Austria, 87; Belgium, 34; Bulgaria, 3; Denmark, 270; England, Ireland and Wales, 935 (including some church Associations); Finland, 28; France, 103; Germany, 1,784 (including 540 Associated Unions); Greece, 1; Hungary, 27; Iceland, 5; Italy, 58; Luxemburg, 1; Netherlands, 314; Norway, 30; Portugal, 10; Rumania, 1; Russia, 11; Scotland, 243; Spain, 5; Sweden, 125; Switzerland, 470; Turkey (European), 6.

ASIA: Asia Minor, Syria and Palestine, 13; Ceylon, 14; China, 43; Dutch Archipelago, 1; India, 151; Japan, 54; Persia, 2; Tonkin, 2.

AFRICA: Madagascar, 1; North, West and Central Africa, 11; South Africa, 8.

Oceania: Australia and Tasmania, 15; New Zealand, 3.

YOUNG PEOPLE'S SOCIETY OF CHRISTIAN ENDEAVOR in Mission Fields: Immediately upon the founding of the Christian Endeavor society by Rev. Francis E. Clark, February 2, 1881, the missionary cause was placed in the forefront of its interests. Missionary committees were organized, regular missionary meetings were held and books were written for the use of the committees planning for missionary meetings. Many societies established missionary libraries and organized mission study classes. The missionary giving of the Endeavorers has largely increased. The two-cents-a-week plan has added largely to the treasuries of the boards, and the Tenth Legion (the Christian Endeavor organization for the promotion of tithe-paying) has enrolled more than twenty thousand members. The missionary sessions of Christian Endeavor conventions are always rich with instruction and emotion. Hundreds of Endeavorers have been led to give their lives to missionary service. The principle of the support of some definite missionary worker, in addition to the general gifts, has been widely adopted, societies and individuals adopting the plan being enrolled in what is known as the Macedonian Phalanx. The various boards have, almost without exception, recognized the young people by applying their gifts to the support of certain missionaries, the building of certain churches, and the carrying on of other enterprises. Some denominations have thus built dozens of Christian Endeavor churches and sent out scores of Christian Endeavor missionaries. All these activities, when multiplied by the 64,380 societies now in existence (January, 1904), attain a very large and influential aggregate, more important in their promise for the future than even in their present accomplishment.

The strongest missionary influence that has come to Christian Endeavor societies, however, is a result of their wide spread among all nations and races. Endeavor conventions are cosmopolitan, and Endeavorers have become familiar with the thought that all men are their brothers through the knowledge, brought to them in many ways, that their own society, its prayer-meeting subjects, its committees, its pledge, its constitution, is beloved by Japs and Germans, Hindus and Hottentots, Brazilians and Norwegians, New Zealanders, Chinese, Armenians and Copts. In many ways this world-wide bond of Christian Endeavor has proved itself a very real tie, and the power it may exercise in coming years is illustrated by the following brief survey of Christian Endeavor around the globe:

In the *United States* there are now 44,360 societies, and hundreds of these consist wholly of foreigners, including German, Chinese, Indian, Japanese, Greek, Swedish, Bohemian, French, Italian, Armenian. Societies are found in many parts of *Alaska*, even at Point Barrow, where is the most northern society in the world, and some of them have served for months, before the arrival of missionaries, as the only religious centers for Indians and white miners in wide regions. In *Canada* there are 4,047 societies, and here also many of the societies are formed of Endeavorers from other lands, especially, in the West, from China and Japan.

Mexico has 111 societies, banded together in a strong national union, and possessing a Spanish Christian Endeavor organ, *El Esforzador Mexicano*. The Mexicans are very earnest in the work; two of them, for instance, once walked more than 200 miles to attend an Endeavor convention. They are evangelistic in their temper always, and at one session of a Mexican Endeavor convention thirty Catholics were converted.

Many islands of the *West Indies* have received the Christian Endeavor movement. Porto Rico, where the society was introduced by an American soldier, now has 4 societies; the Bermudas 7, Trinidad 10, the Barbados and Grenada 2 each, Cuba 11. An American soldier founded the first society in Cuba, leading, with two Cubans, the first meeting, which lasted two hours and three-quarters. In Jamaica the society was started through the influence of a copy of *The Christian Endeavor World* sent by a Boston lady to a sick sailor in a Jamaica hospital, and now there are 236 societies in the island, organized in flourishing unions, and conducting their own paper, *The Christian Endeavor Gem*.

Guatemala formed in 1896 the first Christian Endeavor society in *Central America*—the "Lone Star" society. There are now two others in the country, and Costa Rica has 10. One Spanish society in Guatemala City, with only thirty-five members, prints tracts on its own press, has circulated many, and has sent into the home mission field seven of its own number.

Half of the 43 societies in *South America* are in Brazil, where there is a National Christian Endeavor Union, which is rapidly growing, and a National Endeavor paper, *O Esforco Christao*. The meetings are conducted in Portuguese, and the native name for the society, translated, is "the Society of Christian Effort." One Brazilian society meets in an old Catholic Inquisition hall, and one of its first fruits has entered the Protestant ministry. Christian Endeavor meetings often take an evangelistic turn, and these gatherings are often held in the open air where many Catholics can be reached with the Gospel. Elsewhere in South America the society is flourishing; in Chile, where a Christian Endeavor paper is published and where the Spanish Protestants have enjoyed the society for many years, tho at first they had much difficulty in finding any one who would rent them a room for their meetings, there are 6 societies, 11 in British Guiana, and 5 in Colombia.

In *Hawaii* was organized the first Christian Endeavor society formed outside of the United States, the date being 1884. Now there are 28 societies, organized in a union which holds vigorous conventions and reaches out among the Chinese, Japanese, Hawaiians, English, and Americans on the Island.

In all parts of the *Pacific* the society has found a home. There are some 12 societies in the Loyalty Islands, where the organization was introduced in order to safeguard the results of a revival. There are in the Marshall Islands 21 societies, with 3,000 Endeavorers, who take the name "Imitators of Christ." There is a notable society in the New Hebrides, established by Dr. Paton's son. New Zealand has a strong Christian Endeavor union, which in three years sent out from their number 15 ministers and 39 foreign missionaries. The Gilbert Islands have

4 societies, the Tokelaus 2, the Carolines 3, the Ellice Islands 6, Samoa 19. The pioneer society in Samoa was a remarkable one, having established sixteen others. It has 250 corresponding members, and has sent out from its own number more than 100 missionaries, more than half of them to the deadly climate of New Guinea. Since the United States has gained possession of the Philippines, Christian Endeavor has been introduced, and already there are 6 societies on the islands. One society has 130 corresponding members among the soldiers. The first native society had 12 members at the start, and they all took part at the very first meeting. Christian Endeavor has also made a beginning in Guam, where the society consists wholly of converted Catholics.

Australia possesses 3,960 Christian Endeavor societies, and has a very active union which supports two papers, *The Golden Link* and *The Roll Call*. Its conventions are among the most important religious gatherings held in the southern hemisphere. The Australian Endeavorers are greatly interested in missions. Large numbers of the young people have become missionaries, and their money and time are spent with especial liberality on behalf of the aboriginals.

The first Christian Endeavor society was formed in *Japan* in 1891, in the Girls' School at Okayama. Two years later the National Christian Endeavor Union was formed, which now numbers 115 societies, and supports a national magazine and a paid secretary, who gives his whole time to the organizing of societies. The president of the Japanese Union, Rev. Tasuké Harada, renounced his hereditary privileges as a *samurai* and became a commoner, the better to preach Christ. Japan has a number of especially interesting societies, such as those in the navy, that among the employes of the Sendai post-office, those in the Okayama Orphan Asylum. At Nagasaki is an admirable institution, the Christian Endeavor Seaman's Home—a Christian place of entertainment for sailors whose ships touch at that port. Christian Endeavor marines on board the U. S. S. Charleston established the home, and now it has become self-sustaining.

In *Korea* the first Christian Endeavor society was formed in 1900, and now there are twelve of these societies, tho Korea, on account of the earnestness of the native Christians, has less need of the society than many mission lands, for, as Dr. Underwood declares, "Every church in Korea is a church of Christian endeavor."

After Hawaii, the first country to take up Christian Endeavor outside of the United States was *China*, where the first society was formed in 1885, in Fu-chau. It was called the "Drum-around-and-rouse-up Society." Now there are in China 188 societies, organized in a national union, which holds conventions that have brought together as many as 1,000 native Christian Endeavorers. There are also local unions, such as that of Canton. Just before the Boxer massacres the North China Union was formed, and during that terrible time it lost half of its members. In one society 53 out of 65 members were murdered. Many deeds of heroism are recorded of these brave Endeavorers. The World's Christian Endeavor Union supports a traveling Christian Endeavor secretary for China—Rev. Geo. W. Hinman.

In southern *Siam* we know of only two societies, but among the *Laos* there are 29. These Laos Endeavorers hold rousing conventions, and publish a paper in the native language. *Burma* has 15 societies. It belongs to the India Christian Endeavor Union—a vigorous body with 600 societies. There are sectional unions, such as those for South India and the Punjab. Large and enthusiastic conventions are held, and *The India Endeavourer* is published. An organizing secretary is supported, with the aid of the World's Christian Endeavor Union, and he gives all his time to the work, greatly aiding the missionaries of all the denominations. In India, as everywhere else, the missionaries find the Christian Endeavor society an invaluable auxiliary in their labors among the natives, as it furnishes precisely the training school needed for undeveloped Christians. Indeed, some of the missionaries in India have formed Endeavor societies (we cannot call them *Christian* Endeavor societies) among those that are still unbelievers in Christianity, but are being led by their Endeavor work into close acquaintance with our religion. Ceylon has many zealous Endeavorers. Christian Endeavor literature has been translated into all the great languages of India. Much evangelistic work is done by the native Endeavorers—outdoor preaching with the magic lantern, personal work on the railroad trains, going from coach to coach, outdoor services for beggars, and similar endeavors.

Persia has 35 societies, most of them springing from a single earnest society in a boarding-school, whose members carried the Christian Endeavor seed as they returned home. In 1902 a national union was formed, which held its first convention three days long. In one Hamadan society, Jews, Armenians, and Muslims are mingled. One Teheran society uses in its meetings English, Persian, Armenian, and Hebrew. During a terrible plague of cholera in 1893, when the Jewish and Muslim doctors fled and 20,000 died in the city, the members of this society bravely aided the American missionaries in their hospital work, serving as nurses.

Turkey has 75 societies, in spite of Turkish oppression, which will not allow constitutions to be signed, badges to be worn, or even the word "society" to be used. The Cæsarea Society was obliged at one time to burn its records. The members are all Armenians, and they suffered terribly during the Armenian massacres. The young men and young women meet in separate societies, as everywhere throughout the Orient. Some of the most active societies are in Macedonia. In addition to these 75 societies, there are 16 in Syria. Jerusalem itself has an active Christian Endeavor society.

Of *Africa's* 141 societies, Egypt has only 5, but they are decidedly cosmopolitan. One of them has among its members Italians, Syrians, Armenians, Copts, Hindus, Germans, English, and Americans. There are some societies on the west coast of Africa, especially a vigorous one in Yorubaland, which started out with five members and now numbers 200. Most of the African societies are in the south, where there is a strong South African union, publishing a paper, *The South African Endeavourer*. Andrew Murray is active in the work there. There are many Zulu societies, especially in Cape Colony and Natal. The Boers have entered heartily into Christian Endeavor activities. During the war there were 8 societies in the Boer prison camp on St. Helena, with 800 members; 700 Endeavorers in 8 societies in the Ceylon camp, 600 in the Bermudas, and others in the Portugal camp. After their return from prison, 200 Boer Endeavorers took up active service as missionaries.

In 1892, 30 Christian Endeavor societies were reported to Christian Endeavor headquarters from *Madagascar*, tho previous to that time it was not known in America that a single society existed. When last heard from, the Madagascar societies numbered 93. Christian Endeavor has also got a start in the Island of Mauritius.

Passing to Europe, we find Christian Endeavor, at least in its initial stages, in all European countries, while in some of them it is very flourishing. *Portugal* possesses only 3 societies, for the movement is a new one there. The pioneer society is in Lisbon, the capital. One of its endeavors was the opening of a mission in the slums. In *Spain* the first society was founded in 1888 in the American Girls' School conducted by Rev. and Mrs. W. H. Gulick, and as the girls returned home, new societies were started in many places, until now Spain has 47 societies, and more Mothers' Christian Endeavor Societies than any other country. The Spanish Christian Endeavor paper, *Esfuerzo Cristiano*, is published in Madrid. It has been assailed by much Catholic persecution. The first Spanish national convention was held in 1900 in Madrid in spite of persecution. There were 200 delegates.

There are 96 societies in *France*, most of them in Paris and its vicinity and in Southern France. Paris has a large and flourishing Christian Endeavor union. The French societies are found chiefly in the Reformed churches and the McAll missions.

Switzerland has 13 societies, chiefly in the western or French-speaking cantons. These Endeavorers publish an attractive Christian Endeavor paper, *L'Activité Chrétienne*. Geneva has a Christian Endeavor union.

The beginning of Christian Endeavor interest in *Germany* was Dr. Clark's visit in 1894. The first societies were refused the churches as meeting places, and compelled to meet in barns and inns. Now there are 252 societies, largely in the national, or Lutheran, churches. There is a national union, which supports two secretaries, each German Endeavorer contributing half a mark (12 cents) a year. There are 6 provincial unions, and admirable conventions are held. There is an able Christian Endeavor organ, *Die Jugend-Hilfe*. The United Society of Christian Endeavor helped the work by annual grants of money for years, but now the German Endeavorers are independent and contribute to the work in newer countries. They are also supporting German missionary work in the Caroline Islands. The German name for the Christian Endeavor Society, translated, is "The Society for Decided Christianity."

There are seven *Italian* societies, with a regular Christian Endeavor department in a leading paper, *L'Italia Evangelica*. There are societies in Rome, Florence, and other famous cities. *Bulgaria*, with its five societies, has already formed a union. The same step has been taken by *Hungary's* three societies. In *Austria* there are six societies, found in Bohemia and Moravia. *Sweden* has 70 societies, one of them fifty-five miles within the Arctic Circle, with an evening, once a year, fourteen days long in which to hold a meeting. *Norway* has 5 societies, *Denmark* 4 and *Belgium* and *Holland* each have 3. *Russia* also has 3, the first society having been formed by a young Scotch drygoods clerk in St. Petersburg who went home on a visit, and on his return brought Christian Endeavor with him. *Finland* has 7 societies. When Dr. Clark visited that land, expecting to find it virgin soil, to his amazement he learned that 4 societies already existed there.

In *Great Britain* the first society was formed in August, 1887, being inspired by the account of a young Englishman who had visited Dr. Clark's society in Portland. Now Great Britain has a national union next in strength to that of the United States, and numbering 9,716 societies. Branch unions with vigorous conventions are found in Ireland, Scotland and Wales. Three able Christian Endeavor papers are published—the national organ, *The Christian Endeavour Times*, with *The Irish Endeavourer* (printed patriotically on green paper), and *The Church of England Endeavourer*, which represents the rapidly growing societies of the Anglican Church. The largest city Christian Endeavor union in the world is that of London, with its more than 700 societies. Philadelphia comes next, with 625 societies.

In the majority of the lands thus passed in review, Christian Endeavor is young, the society having been established only four or five years. Everywhere, however, it is full of energy and enthusiasism, and it is certain that this great international brotherhood, laboring together "for Christ and the Church," will prove year after year a constantly growing power for the upbuilding of Christ's Kingdom.

YO-YANG: A town in Shan-si, China, situated 35 miles N. E. of Ping-yang-fu. Station of the CIM (1896), with (1903) 2 missionaries, 4 native workers, 1 outstation, 2 places of worship and 51 professed Christians. Some write the name Yoh-yang.

YUEN-CHAU-FU: A town in Hu-nan, China, situated in the E. part of the province on the Yuen River about 80 miles S. W. of Chen-chau-fu. Station of the CMS (1903), with 1 missionary and 1 place of worship. Some write the name Yuin-cheo.

YUENG-KONG. See YANG-KIANG-HSIEN.

YUH-SHAN. See YU-SHAN-HSIEN.

YUIN-CH'ENG. See YUN-CHENG.

YULU: A settlement in Nicaragua, Central America, situated in the N. part of Mosquito Reserve about 30 miles from the E. coast. Station of the Moravian Missionary Society (1884), with (1903) 1 missionary and his wife, 11 native workers, 1 outstation, 1 place of worship, 1 day school, 1 Sunday school and 80 professed Christians.

YUN-CHENG: A town in Shan-si, China, situated in the S. W. part of the province about 15 miles N. E. of Kiai-chau. Station of the CIM (1888), with (1903) 3 missionaries, two of them with their wives; 5 native workers, 1 place of worship, 1 Sunday school and 40 professed Christians. Some write the name Yuin-ch'eng.

YUN-HO-HSIEN: A town in Che-kiang, China, situated in the S. part of the province about 70 miles W. of Wen-chau-fu. Station of the CIM (1895), with 4 women missionaries, 3 native workers, 1 place of worship, 1 Sunday school and 6 professed Christians. Some write the name Uin-ho.

YUNG-CHING. See YUNG-TSING-HSIEN.

YUNG-CHUN-CHAU: A town in Fo-kien, China, about 80 miles S. W. of Fu-chau-fu. Station of the PCE (1894), with (1903) 2 missionaries, one of them with his wife; 3 women missionaries, 16 native workers, 12 outstations, 2 dispensaries, 1 hospital and 1 boarding school. Some write the name Engchhun.

YUNG-HSIN-HSIEN: A town in Kiang-si, China, situated on a branch of Kan River, 45 miles W. by S. of Ki-ngan-fu. Station of the CIM (1899), with (1903) 3 women missionaries and 1 place of worship. Some write the name Yung-sin.

YUNG-KANG-HSIEN: A town in Che-kiang, China, situated about 25 miles S. E. of Kinhwa-fu. Station of the CIM (1882), with (1903) 1 missionary and his wife, 3 native workers, 1 place of worship and 40 professed Christians. Some write the name Yung-k'ang.

YUNG-SIN. See YUNG-HSIN-HSIEN.

YUNG-TSING-HSIEN: A town in Chi-li, China, on the Hun River, about 40 miles N. W. of Tien-tsin. Station of the SPG (1880), with 2 missionaries and 2 native workers. Some write the name Yung-ching.

YUN-NAN-FU: A town in Yun-nan, China, capital of the province, situated about 650 miles W. by N. of Canton. Station of the Bible Christian Missionary Society (1885), with (1903) 2 missionaries and their wives, 2 native workers, 1 dispensary and 2 professed Christians. Also station of the CIM (1882), with 8 missionaries, three of them with their wives; 2 places of worship and 3 professed Christians.

YU-SHAN-HSIEN: A town in Kiang-si, China, situated in the E. part of the province near the border of Che-kiang, and about 40 miles S. W. of Ku-chau-fu. Station of the CIM (1877), with (1903) 7 women missionaries, 10 native workers, 2 outstations, 3 places of worship, 1 boarding school and 101 professed Christians. Some write the name Yuh-shan.

YU-WU-HSIEN: A town in Shan-si, China, situated about 65 miles E. N. E. of Ping-yang-fu. Station of the CIM (1896), with (1903) 2 missionaries, one of them with his wife; 2 native workers, 1 place of worship, 1 Sunday school and 71 professed Christians. Some write the name Ue-wu.

Z

ZACATECAS: A town in Mexico, capital of the state of the same name. The place is not attractive in its appearance, owing to its wild, arid surroundings, and the streets are uneven and badly paved. Population (1900), 32,856, pure-blood Indians, mixed Indians and Spaniards. Station of the PN (1873), with (1903) 1 missionary and his wife, 1 woman missionary, 5 native workers, 4 Sunday schools, 1 day school, 5 outstations and 984 professed Christians. Also station of the SBC, with (1900) 5 native workers, 3 places of worship, 1 day school and 193 professsed Christians.

ZAFARWAL: A town in Punjab, India, situated about 20 miles S. E. of Sialkot. Station of the UP (1866), with (1903) 1 missionary and his wife, 2 women missionaries, 29 Sunday schools, 9 day schools, 8 outstations and 1 boarding school.

ZAGAZIG: A town in lower Egypt, situated 50 miles E. of the Suez Canal at Ismailieh. Population (1897) 35,715. Station of the UP (1894), with (1903) 1 missionary and his wife and 1 woman missionary. Some write the name Zakazik.

ZAHLEH: A town in Syria and mission station of the PN (1872), with (1903) 2 missionaries and their wives, 2 women missionaries. Church statistics included under **Mt. Lebanon.** Also station of the British Syrian Schools, with (1901) 2 women missionaries, 8 native workers, 5 outstations, 1 place of worship and 5 day schools.

ZAKAZIK. See ZAGAZIG.

ZANZIBAR: A town on Zanzibar Island, E. coast of Africa. Station of the Universities Mission (1864), with (1903) 7 missionaries, 14 women missionaries, 1 outstation, 2 places of worship, 1 printing house, 2 day schools, 2 dispensaries and 256 professed Christians. Some use for this place the name Mkunazini, which is a suburb where missionaries reside.

ZANZIBAR PROTECTORATE: A British protectorate comprising the island of Zanzibar off the east coast of Africa in the Indian Ocean and about 30 miles from the mainland, having an area of 640 square miles and a population of 150,000, and the island of Pemba, a little further from the coast and to the north of Zanzibar, having an area of 380 square miles and a population of 50,000. The ruler of the islands under British protection is the Sultan Ali bin Hamoud bin Mohammed. The authority of the Sultans formerly extended to the coast of the mainland and indefinitely into the interior, but leases and arrangements with Germany and Great Britain have resulted in the transfer of sovereignty of all the mainland to those powers, and they are now included in **German East Africa** and **British East Africa.**

The religion of the country is Mohammedan, the natives being mostly Sunnis of the Shafi school, tho many are still pagans. The town of Zanzibar is a station of the Universities Mission, which also has some work on Pemba I. The BFBS and the Anti-Slavery committee of the Friends also have missionary enterprises on the islands.

ZAZEGA: A town in Eritrea, N. E. Africa, situated about 95 miles W. of Massaua. The people are Tigré-speaking Abyssinians. Station of the Swedish Evangelical National Society (1891), with (1900) 1 missionary, 2 native workers, 1 outstation, 1 place of worship, 2 day schools and 58 professed Christians.

ZEHNDER, J. L.: Died at Lundu, Borneo, February 10, 1898. Missionary of the SPG for nearly thirty-three years. In the report of the SPG he is spoken of as an accomplished linguist, writing and conversing in many European and Oriental languages. In translation work his services were specially valuable. At Lundu, where several races meet after the services on Sunday, the people who had come from a distance would congregate in the veranda of the mission-house for refreshment and conversation; and an eye-witness declares it was a sight to be remembered to see the old missionary going from group to group—Sebuyaus, Selakaus, Laras, Chinese and Malay—with words of cheer and inspiration for each in his own tongue. Thus "speaking to every man in his own language," his influence was wide-spread, and the impressions left by the spoken and written Word were deep and lasting.

ZEISBERGER, David: Born at Zauchtenthal, Moravia, April 11, 1721; died November 17, 1808. His progenitors belonged to the ancient Church of the Bohemian Brethren, founded sixty years before the Reformation by the followers of John Huss. When David was five years old, his parents fled to Herrnhut, in Saxony, a colony of Moravian emigrants. In 1736 his parents joined the colony in Georgia, which James Oglethorpe had established three years before, leaving their son at Herrnhut to be educated by the Moravians. From thence he went to Holland and lived in a Moravian settlement called Herrendyk, joining his parents in America in 1738. In 1740 he went North, and with others founded Bethlehem and Nazareth in Pennsylvania. In 1745 he began his work among the Indians, and was soon arrested as a spy of the French by the colonial government of New York, and was imprisoned for seven weeks. Released by Governor Clinton, he labored till 1750 among the Delawares at Shamokin (Sunbury, Pa.) and the Iroquois at Onondaga, where the Six Nations made him a sachem, and "keeper of their archives." In 1750 he visited Europe in behalf of the mission. In 1752 he returned to Onondaga, but was compelled to retire to Bethlehem at the opening of the French and Indian war. Between 1755 and 1762 he visited North Carolina and the New England Provinces, labored among the Indians of Canada, and acted as interpreter for Pennsylvania in the treaty with Teedyuseung and his allies. In the time of the Pontiac conspiracy he ministered to the Christian Indians who had found refuge in Philadelphia, and at the close of the war he led the survivors of the converts to Wyalusing, Bradford County, Pa., on the Susquehanna. In 1767 he established a mission among the Monsey Delawares on the Allegheny River, Venango County, and three years later began the station which he called Friedenstadt, on Beaver Creek, in what is now Lawrence County. In 1772 he went to Central Ohio, and commenced a town called Schoenbrunn, on the Tuscarawas, ten miles from the site of Canal Dover, where he was soon joined by all the Moravian converts from Pennsylvania. He built two more towns, other missionaries came, and many converts were added. Early in the Revolution the Delawares were accused of favoring the American side, and the converts were forced to leave their towns and come within the British lines. In 1781 the settlements were destroyed by a band of Wyandotte warriors at the instigation of the commandant of the British post at Detroit; the missionaries were tried as spies, and the Christian Indians removed to Sandusky. The next year ninety-six of them returned from Sandusky to the Tuscarawas to gather their corn, and were massacred at Gnadenhütten by a party of colonial militia. Disheartened by this catastrophe, Zeisberger in 1782 led a small remnant to what is now Michigan, and built an Indian town on the Clinton River. In 1786 he went back to Ohio, and founded New Salem, one mile from Lake Erie. Thence the hostility of other Indians, after four years' rest, compelled them to emigrate to Canada, where they founded Fairfield. In 1798 he returned to the Tuscarawas valley, where Congress had granted to his Indians their former lands, and built a town, calling it Goshen. There he labored for ten years, to the close of his life. He was a missionary among the American Indians for sixty years. He established thirteen Christian towns, and tho scarcely one remained, yet he had many converts, and his character, motives, and efforts are "an honor to the Moravian Church, and to our common humanity." Zeisberger was a thorough scholar. He mastered several native tongues, especially the Delaware and Onondaga. He left in manuscript a German and Onondaga lexicon in seven volumes quarto, a grammar of the Onondaga language in German and English, a Delaware grammar and dictionary, and several vocabularies. All of these are deposited in the Library of Harvard College, and in the Library of the American Philosophical Society in Philadelphia. His Diary, translated by Eugene H. Bliss, was published in two octavo volumes in 1885.

ZENANA BIBLE AND MEDICAL MISSION, or Indian Female Normal School and Instruction Society: Headquarters: 2 Adelphi Terrace, London, W. C., England. This society was first organized under the second name in 1852, as a general missionary society, with the special purpose of cooperating with other societies, particularly the CMS, BFBS, and others. Later there was a distinction made between Zenana and educational work, and the scope of the society was enlarged and its present organization was effected. Its special object is to help the women of India by sending female missionaries to relieve sickness, promote education, establish hospitals, schools and such other institutions as may be needed. The Executive Committee, of not more than 24 nor less than 18 members, is self-perpetuating. While more closely connected with the Church of England, it cooperates with any orthodox Protestant Missionary Societies; holding that the work which it does need not be denominational.

Its work is in India, at 32 stations in the Bombay and Madras Presidencies, the United Provinces, and the Punjab. According to the report (1903) there were 104 European and 53 assistant missionaries, 275 native workers, 64 schools with 3,208 pupils and 226 under training in Normal Schools. The hospital shows 1,892 in-patients and 21,083 out-patients in 5 hospitals and dispensaries, with a total of 72,921 attendances at dispensaries. In the Zenana work 4,375 houses were visited and 2,728 pupils instructed.

ZENANA MISSIONARY SOCIETY (Church of England). See CHURCH OF ENGLAND.

ZIEGENBALG, Bartholomew: Born June 24, 1683, in Pullsnitz, Saxony. Died at Tranquebar, India, in 1719. King Frederick IV. of Denmark, aroused to his duty to give the Gospel to those under his sway in India by his chaplain, Dr. Lütken, directed him to seek men suitable for missionary service. Ziegenbalg and Plutschau, then students at Halle, young men of talent, learning, and Christian zeal, were appointed, and embarked at Copenhagen in 1705. After a long and dangerous voyage they arrived, July, 1706, at Tranquebar, a Danish possession on the Coromandel coast of Hindustan. After several day's delay the governor received them with great harshness. Ziegenbalg obtained a room near the heathen and Portuguese quarters, and began his work not only among hostile heathen, but with a government openly opposed, and a European population absorbed in business, addicted to vice, and determined at all hazards to be rid of these earnest men. Ziegenbalg, having no grammar or dictionary to help him in learning the language, persuaded a native schoolmaster to bring his school to the mission room, and, sitting down with the children, he imitated them in making the letters in the sand till he had become familiar with their form. He then found a Brahman who knew a little English, and with his help was able in eight months to speak Tamil intelligibly. The teacher, however, was loaded with irons by the rajah and thrown into prison. Some of the Europeans owning slaves, Ziegenbalg obtained their consent that "these poor outcasts might meet for two hours daily for instruction." In less than a year five slaves were baptised. A native built a church at his own expense, and at the dedication Ziegenbalg preached in Tamil and Portuguese to a large congregation of Christians, Hindus, and Mohammedans. In the second year he made extensive preaching tours. In 1708 he visited Negapatam, and the Dutch magistrate invited the most learned Brahmans to a friendly conference with the missionary on religious subjects. The discussion lasted five days, and much information concerning the origin, history, and doctrines of Christianity was diffused among the native population.

Ziegenbalg had so far mastered the language that in two years after his arrival he began Scripture translation, and a year later could speak Tamil with as much facility as his native German. He soon began the preparation of a grammar and two lexicons—one of prose, the other of poetical words. In 1711 he finished the translation of the New Testament into Tamil —the first into any language of India—and a large part of the Old Testament. Not only to Hindus, but to the half-breed Portuguese and to the slaves of Tranquebar he preached the Gospel. He had also a German service weekly, which was largely attended.

In 1714 his translation of the New Testament, the Danish Liturgy, and German hymns, with thirty-three Tamil works, including a dictionary he had prepared, were printed. His health failing, he returned to his native land in 1715. His account of the Hindus and his missionary work created great interest in Germany and England, vast crowds being moved by his glowing appeals, and kings, princes, and prelates giving liberally to the cause. He returned to India in 1719, but died soon after, at the early age of thirty-six, having in the brief period of thirteen years as the pioneer of modern missions in India accomplished a remarkable work. Three hundred and fifty converts and a large body of catechumens mourned his death.

ZINZENDORF, Count Nicolaus Ludwig: Born in Dresden, May 26, 1700. Died May 9, 1760. While a school boy at Halle he heard of the mission established in the East Indies by the King of Denmark, and occasionally he met missionaries returning from the field. His young heart was fired by the missionary spirit, and, moved by the desire of aiding the work of the world's evangelization, he founded the famous "Order of the Grain of Mustard Seed," composed originally of five lads, who pledged themselves to "give the Gospel to all, Jews and heathen alike." In 1715 he joined with his friend, the Baron Frederick von Watteville, in a covenant to introduce the Gospel of salvation especially among those heathen to whom no one else would go. Hoping that he would fit himself for a diplomatic career, his relatives matriculated him as a student of law at the University of Wittenberg; and there, amid worldly-minded associates, he made a deep religious impression. His passion for souls became more intense as he grew toward manhood; and despite the efforts made by his family to "take the nonsense out of him," he never swerved from his noble purpose. While on his travels he visited the gallery at Dusseldorf, and as he looked upon the *Ecce Homo* of Sternberg, under which was the inscription:

"Hoc feci pro te;
Quid facis pro me?"

he renewed his consecration vows and determined, without reserve, to dedicate himself to the service of his Lord. On September 7, 1722, he was married to the Countess Erdmuth Dorothea, and on their wedding day they covenanted to put aside all favors of rank, to win souls, and to hold themselves in readiness to go, without delay, wherever the Lord might call them. Soon after he attained his majority, he waived his rights to large estates rather than go to law, and modestly settled at Berthelsdorf, near Gross-Hennersdorf, hoping to make it a model Christian village. In 1723, with Rothe, Schaefer and Frederick von Watteville, he formed the "League of the Four Brethren," which had as its object the promulgation of the Gospel among all peoples, and soon new channels of service were opened before him. The Moravian Church, founded in 1457 by the proscribed followers of John Huss, seemed nearly extinct at the close of the 17th century, but there remained, scattered through Bohemia and Moravia, little communities of secret disciples known as the "hidden seed." When Zinzendorf and Watteville made their memorable covenant (1715), these heroic Christians were entering upon new life, under the quickening influence of the Holy Spirit; and soon afterward the great Protestant awakening occurred, followed by bitter persecutions. Driven from Moravia and led by **Christian David**, these refugees found an asylum in Berthelsdorf. Soon after Zinzendorf settled in his estate, he came in sympathetic touch with these heroes of the faith; and under his guidance they adopted certain rules and regulations for their government. Zinzendorf was now impressed that he was called of God to become the leader of this people; and he formed bands and societies, from among them, for effective and systematic Christian work. As the communion grew in spiritual power, unmistakable signs of divine approval were placed upon it; and on August 13, 1727 (regarded as the spiritual birthday of the renewed Moravian Church), while the people were assembled to partake of the Communion, the Holy Spirit manifested Himself in a wonderful way, and the power of the revival that followed this awakening is felt until now. Zinzendorf now gave his life entirely to the one work of the development and organization of this "Church within the Church," fitting it, under God, for its world-wide mission. To quote another: "Under his guidance a firm and stable form of government was established in Herrnhut. Men of loose views and worldly tastes were weeded out, and none but true-hearted Christians allowed to remain. The women gave up their brilliant Bohemian dress and adopted a simple costume, consisting of a plain dress and cap tied with ribbons, the color of which indicated their position in life—widows wearing white, wives blue and maidens red. And order of worship, with many beautiful customs, including the far-famed Easter service, was introduced, and the constant use of sacred song became one of their marked characteristics. Under the new regime, life at Herrnhut became grave and serious, but happy and prosperous, combining joyous religious experience with the faithful performance of daily tasks." Before Zinzendorf and the brethren God was unfolding plans for the evangelization of peoples in distant lands. In 1731, while Zinzendorf was attending the coronation of Christian VI. at Copenhagen, he met two Eskimos who had been converted through the influence of Hans Egede, and he learned that Egede was about to abandon his mission. During the same visit, the attendant of Zinzendorf became acquainted with Anthony, a negro servant of Count de Laurwig, who told them of the slaves in the West Indies, who had no one to tell them of the true God. Count Zinzendorf's appeal to his people at Herrnhut and the visit of the negro Anthony stirred mightily the congregation, and two young men offered themselves as missionaries to the West Indies, and two others decided to carry the Gospel to Greenland. Thus was begun Moravian Missions; and at the time of their first jubilee in 1782, ten years before Carey preached his epoch-making sermon, they occupied 27 stations and supported a force of 165 missionaries. In the meantime, under the direction of Zinzendorf, the Brethren at home were indefatigable in their work. They visited the countries of Europe, founded new settlements, and began the Diaspora work, the object of which was to awaken and foster spiritual life by the formation of societies of prayer. Relentless opposition and persecution followed Zinzendorf as his influence arose and his work increased in power, and in 1736, owing to the misrepresentations of his enemies, he was banished from Saxony. In 1739 he visited the mission at St. Thomas, and in 1741, accompanied by his daughter, the Countess Benigna, he visited the English colonies in North America. For more than a year he labored among the North American Indians and others in the colonies and established the church at Bethlehem, Pa. Before returning home, he did missionary work in England and Holland; and in all of his travels he sought to quicken the zeal of Christians in the cause of missions. In 1749 Zinzendorf was entirely vindicated of all charges preferred against him, and the Saxon Government repealed the edict of banishment and requested him to form other communities like Hernnhut in Saxony. The last years of his life were spent peacefully at Berthelsdorf; and his body was borne to the grave by thirty-two missionaries and preachers from Holland, England, Ireland, North America, and Greenland.

Bovet (F.), translated by J. Gill, *The Banished Count*, London, 1865; Tietzen (H.), *Der Graf von Zinzendorf*, Gutersloh, 1888; *Missionary Review of the World*, Vol. XIII., pp. 329, 647, 715, New York, 1900.

ZITACUARO: A town in Mexico, situated 70 miles W. of Mexico City. Station of the PN (1893), with (1901) 1 missionary and his wife, 7 native workers, 5 day schools, 6 Sunday schools and 464 professed Christians.

ZOROASTRIANISM: The form of religion supposed to have been inculcated by Zoroaster (Persian, *Zardusht*), long the state religion of Persia, but now professed by a mere handful of followers in two districts in Persia (Kirman and Yezd), and by the **Parsees** of India, whose name bears witness to their Persian origin. If Zoroaster was a historical character, as seems to have been the case, he probably lived in the east of Iran, in the region known as Bactria, now sometimes called Balkh. His date cannot be ascertained; some Greek writers put him 5,000 years before the siege of Troy! Modern scholars place him, some 1,000 years before Christ, and some 1,500; at the best all is conjecture, but he certainly lived before Cyrus. Monier Williams thinks that he was nearly contemporary with Confucius. That he was the leader of schism in the old Aryan race seems to many probable. As the result of this the religion of one branch of the race developed into Vedism and Hinduism in India, and that of the other, which settled in Persia, into the dualistic system which still bears the name of Zoroaster.

According to this system, the world is the battle-field of two contending spirits, eternal in their origin and possessing the power of creation. The one is *Ahuro-mazda* (the wise god), who is the source and author of all that is good; the other is *Angro-mainyash* (the spirit enemy), who, evil in his nature, ever strives to neutralize the beneficent activities of the first. These two names have become corrupted by long use into the shorter forms now common, Ormuzd and Ahriman. But the conflict between these two powers, tho now conducted on terms which are apparently pretty nearly equal, is not hopelesss, and is not destined to be perpetual. In due time Ormuzd is to summon all his power, and enter upon the last and decisive phase of the struggle. The might of Ahriman is to be broken forever, and the supremacy of the good established; Ahriman with his defeated followers is to be cast into hell, and to remain there, destitute of power to disturb the progress and enjoyment of the good, who are to be rewarded and to prosper, unvexed by evil, as citizens of the good kingdom.

Modern Zoroastrianism recognizes the existence of vast hierarchies of good and evil spirits, doing the will and fulfilling the purposes respectively of Ormuzd and of Ahriman. To what extent these elaborate systems of angelology and demonology influenced Jewish thought, and through them Christian thought, is a question still undetermined. The sacred books of Zoroastrianism are spoken of collectively as the Zend-Avesta. The term is not wholly accurate: the proper designation is *Avesta*, the word *Zend* signifying "interpretation," with reference to the commentaries on the original books. The Avesta itself is written in an ancient form of Aryan speech, allied to the Sanskrit, known popularly as the *Zend*, and possessing no other extant literature. The "interpretation" is in Pahlavi, a more modern (tho ancient and now dead) language, which prevailed formerly in Persia. The Avesta, as at present known, is but a fragment, and not a large fragment, of the original sacred literature of Zoroastrianism. Like the Old Testament, it is not a book, but a collection of books—a literature developing in and with the life of the people. Parts of it may date back to Zoroaster, but much of it consists of the accretions of later years. A collection of hymns or "Gâthâs" is the oldest part of it, and may be said to form the kernel of the whole; these alone claim to be the *ipsissima verba* of Zoroaster. The remainder consists of liturgical matter, and, what is called by some (borrowing a phrase from Old Testament scholarship), the "priestly code" of Zoroastrianism.

The light, the sun, the fire, are considered by the Zoroastrians the symbols of Ormuzd. Therefore in their temples the sacred fire is continually burning, night and day, year after year. For this reason at evening, when they recite the prayers of the Avesta, the faces of Zoroastrian worshipers are turned westward, toward the setting sun. Hence they are often spoken of as "sun-worshipers" and "fire-worshipers," tho they themselves reject the imputation which is thus involved; they do not pray to the sun or to the fire, they say, but to that good and shining one whose presence and character are symbolized by the light, and the sources of it.

The Zoroastrian religion developed and flourished in Persia, through the vicissitudes of declension and revival incident to all religious history, from the time of its origin to the Mohammedan invasion. During that time it saw and survived the political changes and dynastic revolutions to which Persia was subject, but which need not be recounted here. Mohammed died in 632. It was but a few years after his death that Persia was invaded by armies of his followers, who, under the fierce lead of the early caliphs, were just beginning that astonishing career of conquest which within a century carried the crescent over Western Asia, Northern Africa into Spain, across the Pyrenees, and almost to the shores of the British Channel. The Persian army was ignominiously defeated, the king dethroned, and his realms taken possession of in the name of the Prophet. The people embraced the new religion. The fire went out on the Zoroastrian altars, and the Avesta was dropped for the Koran. A handful merely of the Persians refused to be converted and sought refuge among the mountains. There for a time they were suffered to remain, but soon after the year 700 they were subjected to such a violence of Muslim persecution that many of them were constrained to abandon Persia and look for a refuge beyond the sea. The story of the wanderings and sufferings of this company of Zoroastrians forms a pathetic episode in the religious history of the race.

Through all their wanderings and shipwrecks the sacred fire was studiously kept alive. About the year 720 of the Christian era they landed on the western coast of India near the city of Surat, some 150 miles north of where Bombay now stands, and craved permission from the Hindu prince then ruling in that region to settle among his people, and to practise the religion of their fathers. The permission was granted,—so tradition says,— with a few easily observed conditions, among which was this, that they should adopt the dress and language of the country where they were to make their home. These conditions were accepted, and ever since the language of this Indian branch of the race has been the Gujarati, the vernacular of the district where they landed, with such dialectic variations as would naturally arise in the use of a new tongue by foreigners whose customs and religion differed so greatly from those of the land where the language had developed. The Parsees— as these Persian dwellers in India came in course of time to be called—do not appear prominently in Indian history until the English era. They faithfully maintained the practise of their religion, jealously guarded the sacred fire, and preserved inviolate the purity of their race. When, under English rule, the city of Bombay grew from a cluster of fishermen's huts into a great commercial mart, the Parsees appear as keen-eyed men of business, and founded great commercial houses. There are said to be about 8,500 Zoroastrians still remaining in Persia.

Darmesteter (J.), *In Sacred Books of the East*, Vols. 4 and 23, *The Zend Avesta*, London, 1879; ditto, *Ormazd et Ahriman*, Paris, 1877; Murray (J. M.), *The Zend Avesta and the Religion of the Parsis*, London, 1884.

ZULUS: The Zulus, according to tradition and the testimony of generations that have but lately passed away, came, something more than a century since, from the north and took up their abode, first on the Imfolosi and Umhlatusi rivers, and then farther south as far as the Umzimkulu, and farther east in the vicinity of Delagoa Bay. Not to go back beyond a somewhat definite knowledge of them, we find them a small tribe under the chieftain Usenzangakona, son of Jama, and father of Chaka. Chaka, born in 1787, was a chieftain of great enterprise in his way, of great ambition, military prowess, and success. Starting out at the head of a small army, he assailed and subdued tribe after tribe, and incorporated all into his own, till he had mastered a considerable territory and made himself feared by the Dutch and English at the Cape, the tribes on the west, and other far-distant tribes on the north and east. Finally, in 1828, he was assassinated through the jealously of two brothers, one of whom,

Dingan, took his place in power. During Dingan's reign, or rather at the close of it, which came through a war with the Boers, as a result of which he was chased out of the country and died of his wounds in the wilderness, his kingdom was divided, in 1840, and the southern half of it, called the Natal District, came into the hands of the Dutch, and then, in 1842, into the hands of the English, and so became a British colony; while the northern half, which has since gone by the name of Zululand, came under the rule of Umpande, brother of the two previous kings. Umpande continued nominally at the head of affairs till the day of his death, in October, 1872, when his son Ketchwayo was installed king. He held office till the English-Zulu war in 1879, when he was taken captive and carried to Cape Town and thence to England. The British Government, now professing to have a kind of moral protection and authority over the Zulu realm, divided it into thirteen sections, and over each appointed a kind of petty chief or kinglet, the result of which was confusion, strife, and anarchy. Then Ketchwayo was carried back to Zululand and reinstated king, January 31, 1883, over at least a part of his former realm, but soon died, some say of heart disease, some of grief and disappointment, while others think he was poisoned by his late antagonist.

The division of the country into sections under native chiefs continued for some years in Zululand proper. But in 1897 Zululand was made a part of Natal, with the Governor of Natal in control, and with Zululand represented in the legislative body of the Province. The negro population of Natal, including Zululand and the recently annexed districts of Vryheid and Utrecht, in 1901 amounted to 836,912 souls.

The Zulu is a man of many marked and ready parts, self-respecting, sometimes haughty, of a martial spirit, quick-witted, a studious and keen observer of men and things, and, within all lines of his own observation and experience, a good judge, a good logician, a good reader of character, and a good narrator of facts and events. One of them, having heard his missionary tell of the great power and goodness of God, how He hates sin, and how the race was beguiled to their ruin through the temptations of the adversary, promptly challenged his teacher with the sharp inquiry, "But why didn't God kill the devil at once and stop all that mischief in the beginning?" Another Zulu, being once asked by his missionary, "What is the best color for man?" replied, "For you Americans no doubt white is the best, but for us Africans there is nothing better than a good, clear, shiny black, with just a little of the red in it." The famous Zulu chief Pakade, who used to come now and then into sharp collision with the English, was once visited by Bishop Colenso, who tried to interest him in his translation of the Lord's Prayer into Zulu; but right in the midst of the Bishop's laborious effort, he was suddenly pulled up by his pupil's breaking in upon him with the remark, "Yes, yes, that is all very good, but how do you make gunpowder?"

The dress, habitations, and pursuits of the Zulus are all in accord with what should be looked for among a people living for ages in a tropical climate and without refining, quickening influences.

In their untutored condition the woman's dress is a half cow-hide, tanned soft, dyed black, bound about the loins, and coming down about to the knees. And when it is old, and worn, and torn, as it will be in time, she goes to one bush and tears off the bark, and to another for a thorn, punches a hole here, another there, puts in the string and sews up the rent. The man's wardrobe is only about a fourth part as much as that of the woman, and the little he has is generally from the fur of wild beasts; while the children are left to go for some years as on the day they were born. But all—men, women, and children, young men and maidens—are fond of ornaments, such as beads and brass bangles or charms, of wood or bark, bones, horns, hoofs, teeth, and claws of birds and beasts. The distinguishing mark of the married man is a head smooth shaved, all but a ring of blackened hair around the crown; while the married woman's head is also smooth shaved, all but a tuft of hair on the crown colored with red ochre. Under pure native rule the Zulu could never marry or build himself a house or kraal till he had served his king as a soldier for a term of years, got his discharge, and with his discharge a piece of ground on which to build. Having a right to build, he selects a dry, oval spot for his *kraal*, which consists of a circular enclosure for his cattle; and around this a circular row of houses, one for himself and one for each of his wives and her children. The house is hemispherical in shape, seven or eight feet high, with a diameter of fifteen or twenty feet. The frame consists of wattles about the size and length of fishing-rods, over which is laid a thick coating of long thatch grass for covering. On one side is a door two feet high and eighteen inches wide. The floor is made of hardened clay or earth from the ant-heap; near the center is a shallow basin, saucer-like in shape, for the fire. There is no chimney, nor is there any opening for light and air, save the door. A portion of the border of this one room is set apart for a calf or goat for the night, and the rest is used as a place for stowing wood, bedding, millstone, calabashes, earthern pots, and spears and shields for hunting and fighting. The rest of the hut, or central portion, serves as a place for cooking, eating, sitting, and sleeping.

The house is built chiefly by the women, the enclosures by the men. In times of war the men are engaged in war. In times of peace they are expected to prepare the fields, if need be, for the pick, and either fence them or watch them against cattle and wild beasts. The men tan the hides for their wives' dresses; they and the boys herd the cattle and milk the cows; they hunt, smoke, bask in the sun, drink beer, make offerings to their divinities, the shades of the dead, and institute interminable suits at law. In their heathen state the women keep the house, so far as it is kept at all, do all the drudgery, carry the burdens, and cultivate the fields. With their baskets and heavy, clumsy picks they do the digging, planting, harvesting—the work of the plow, harrow, cart, ox, and horse. When the corn or other grain is gathered and dry, they do the threshing, winnowing, and grinding; or if the grain must go to the market ten or twenty miles away, they must carry it there in baskets on their heads.

The matrimonial affairs of the Zulus are based upon a belief in polygamy and correspond to their faith. Native law prescribes no limit to the number of wives a man may have, provided he can find them, and has the means—five or ten head of cattle each—with which to obtain them.

The Zulu who would woo has great confidence in the subduing, winning potency of certain medicinal preparations. The more common way would be to prepare a delicate powder and send it by the hand of some unsuspected person, to be given in a pinch of snuff or sprinkled upon the person whose will is to be changed or affections won. The engagement made and the wedding at hand, the parents and friends of the bride, all in their best attire, make up a party and escort her to the home of the bridegroom. Arriving there, they begin to sing and dance; nor is it long before the young men of the kraal join them. At length the master of the kraal slaughters an ox, and all give up dancing and singing for feasting and carousing. And so, after an exchange of presents and other exercises of a joyous character, the man and woman become husband and wife after the manner of a Zulu marriage.

Missionary Work for Zulus: The first missionary enterprise among the Zulus was that of Capt. Allen Gardiner, who afterward lost his life in an attempt to establish a mission in Patagonia. He went to Zululand in 1835 and obtained permission from the Zulu chief Dingan to establish a mission near Port Natal (now Durban). He then induced the CMS to send the Rev. Mr. Owen to Natal. Mr. Owen, established himself at Dingan's kraal in 1847, but the outbreak of a war of reprisals between Zulus and Boers forced him to retire. Work has been carried on by the Church of England diocesan initiative among the Zulus ever since, aided by the SPG to some extent. The SPG now has in Natal 16 missionary stations, with 8,588 professed Christians, of whom 2,714 are communicants. It also has in Zululand proper 5 stations, with 4,982 professed Christians, of whom 1,522 are communicants.

The ABCFM was urged by Dr. Philips of the LMS as early as 1833 to open a mission to the Zulus. It sent out six missionaries, Rev. Messrs. Alvin Grout, Champion and Adams, M.D., for Zululand, and Rev. Messrs. Lindley, Venable and Wison, M.D., for the Matabili. The two parties reached Cape Town in 1835, and the party for Matabililand established themselves in 1836 at Mosiga Valley, about 100 miles west of the spot where Pretoria was afterward built. Within six months, however, an irruption of Boers destroyed the people of Mosiga Valley and compelled the missionaries to withdraw. The missionaries made their way to the coast and joined their colleagues, who meanwhile had become established near Port Natal with the consent of the chief, Dingan. In 1838, however, the war between Dingan and the Boers broke up the mission and drove the missionaries to less troubled regions. Altho work was resumed when the country became more quiet, the Board decided in 1844 to close the mission, and was only prevented from doing so by the conviction of its missionaries on the ground, led by Dr. Adams and supported by official and clerical opinion at Cape Town, that this would be a mistake. In 1847 the mission was reenforced and the stations of Amanzimtote, Ifume and Inanda in Natal were permanently occupied. It was only about this time, ten years after the work began, that the first Zulu convert, an old woman, was baptised. Connected with the ABCFM mission are now (1903) 23 self-supporting churches of Zulus, with 14,000 professed Christians, of whom 3,256 are communicants. These churches support their own pastors and carry on home missionary work at their own expense.

The WMS was the next to establish a mission among the Zulus. Rev. Mr. Archbell of that Society came from Kaffraria into Natal in 1841. The mission grew and prospered until, with changed conditions, the whole work was passed over in 1882 to the South African Wesleyan Conference as an indigenous church. There are at hand no data for separately enumerating the Zulu members among the 95,000 members who form the Wesleyans of South Africa to-day.

The Norwegian Missionary Society under Schreuder established a station near Verulam in Natal in the year 1845. At present this Society has three stations and 988 professed Christians, of whom 323 are communicants.

The Berlin Evangelical Missionary Society commenced its work in Natal in 1847, Messrs. Posselt and Dohne being its first missionaries. Mr. Posselt founded the station of Emmaus, near the sources of the Tugela River, and Christianenburg, near Pinetown, ten miles west of Durban. The mission afterward opened stations in the northern part of Zululand, but were driven out, and changed the line of their expansion to the Orange Free State and the Transvaal. The society has now four stations in Natal, with 2,752 professed Christians and 1,457 communicants. It has in the Transvaal and the Orange River Colony 38 stations, with 28,704 professed Christians, of whom 13,804 are communicants.

The Hermannsburg Missionary Society opened a station at Hermannsburg in Natal in 1854 and afterward extended its work into Zululand and westward to the Transvaal Marico region, among the Bechuanas. This Society now has in Natal and Zululand 15 stations, with 3,709 professed Christians, of whom 2,092 are communicants.

The Free Church of Scotland began its permanent establishment in Natal in 1857, taking up the work at Pietermaritzburg and Empolweni commenced by the Rev. Mr. Allison, who had been laboring under the WMS. The UFS has now in Natal 4 stations, with a full complement of workers, both native and foreign, and with 2,241 communicant church members.

The Swedish Church Missionary Society has two stations in Natal and Zululand, where it has gathered about 350 communicants.

The Boers have often been charged in mass with hostility to mission work among the negroes. It is a case of judging the mass by the conduct of some. As a body they are working earnestly for the evangelization of the Zulus who live with and around them. They do this not by organized missionary societies, but as individuals, families, committees, ministers, and laymen. Quite a number of Zulus have been formed into churches in connection with the Dutch Church, but statistics on this point are not at hand.

Brooks (H.), *Natal,* London, 1887; Russell (R.), *Natal, the Land and Its Story,* 6th ed., London, 1900; Baynes (A. H.), *My Diocese during the War,* London, 1900; Tyler (J.), *Forty Years in Zululand,* Boston, 1891; Stewart (J.), *Dawn in the Dark Continent,* London and New York, 1903; *Missionary Review of the World,* Vol. II., p. 738.

APPENDICES

APPENDICES

		PAGE
I.	DIRECTORY OF FOREIGN MISSIONARY SOCIETIES	817
II.	CHRONOLOGICAL TABLE OF THE EXTENSION OF PROTESTANT MISSIONS FROM THE TIME OF CAREY	824
III.	LIST OF BIBLE VERSIONS	826
IV.	MISSIONARIES WHO HAVE MADE TRANSLATIONS OR REVISIONS OF HOLY SCRIPTURE	830
V.	STATISTICAL TABLES	835
VI.	ROMAN CATHOLIC FOREIGN MISSIONS	848

APPENDIX I

DIRECTORY OF FOREIGN MISSIONARY SOCIETIES

Aborigines Protection Society (1837); Headquarters: Broadway Chambers, Westminster, London, S. W., England; Secretary, H. R. Fox Bourne, Esq.
African (South) Dutch Reformed Ministers Union (Predikanten Zending Vereeniging). See South African Dutch Reformed Ministers Union.
African Methodist Episcopal Zion Church; Home and Frontier Mission Society of the; Headquarters: Birmingham, Ala.; Secretary: Rev. A. J. Warner.
African Training Institute (1889); Headquarters: African Institute, Colwyn Bay, North Wales; Secretary: Rev. W. Hughes.
Africa Association. See Germany.
African Methodist Episcopal Church (1847); parent Home and Foreign Missionary Society of the; Headquarters: 61 Bible House, New York; Secretary: Rev. H. B. Parks; Treasurer:
American Advent Missionary Society (1866); Headquarters: 160 Warren Street, Boston, Mass.; Secretary: Mr. A. C. Johnson; Organ: *Prophetic and Mission Quarterly*.
American Baptist Missionary Union (1814); Headquarters: Tremont Temple, Boston, Mass.; Secretaries: Rev. H. C. Mabie, Rev. T. S. Barbour; Treasurer: C. W. Perkins, Organ: *Baptist Missionary Magazine*. "Woman's Baptist Foreign Missionary Society;" Headquarters: Tremont Temple, Boston, Mass.; Secretaries: Mrs. H. G. Safford, Mrs. N. M. Waterbury; Treasurer: Miss A. E. Stedman. "Woman's Baptist Foreign Missionary Society of the West;" Headquarters: 1535 Masonic Temple, Chicago, Ill.; Secretaries: Mrs. F. Clatworthy, Miss J. L. Austin; Treasurer: Mrs. M. E. Kline; Organ of the Woman's Societies: *The Helping Hand*.
American Bible Society (1816); Headquarters: Bible House, New York; Secretaries: Rev John Fox, Rev. W. I. Haven; Rev. E. P. Ingersoll; Treasurer: William Foulke; Organ: *Bible Society Record*.
American Board of Commissioners for Foreign Missions (1810); Headquarters: Congregational House, 14 Beacon Street, Boston, Mass.; Secretaries: Rev. Judson Smith, Rev. J. L. Barton, Rev. E. E. Strong; Treasurer: F. H. Wiggin; Organ: *Missionary Herald*. "Woman's Board of Missions;" Headquarters: 14 Beacon Street, Boston, Mass.; Secretaries: Miss E. H. Stanwood, Miss Kate G. Lamson, Miss A. M. Kyle; Treasurer: Miss S. Louise Day. "Woman's Board of Missions of the Interior;" Headquarters: 40 Dearborn Street, Chicago, Ill.; Secretary: Miss M. D. Wingate; Treasurer: Mrs. S. E. Hurlbut; Organ: *Mission Studies*. "Woman's Board of Missions of the Pacific;" Headquarters: 1275 Sixth Avenue, Oakland, Cal.; Secretary: Mrs. W. J. Wilcox; Treasurer: Mrs. S. M. Dodge; Organ of the Women's Boards of Missions: *Life and Light for Women*.
American Christian Convention. See Christian Church.
American Church Missionary Society (1860); Aux. to P. E. Dom. and For. Miss. Soc.; Headquarters: 281 Fourth Avenue, New York; Secretary: Eugene M. Camp.
American Friends Foreign Mission Society (1894); Headquarters: Richmond, Ind.; Secretary: Mrs. Mahalah Jay; Treasurer: James Carey, Jr., 838 Park Avenue, Baltimore, Md.; Organ: *The American Friend*. "Woman's For. Miss. Union," Carmel, Ind.; Secretary: Sarah K. King
American Missionary Association (1846); Headquarters: 287 Fourth Avenue, New York; Secretaries: Rev. A. F. Beard, Rev. F. P. Woodbury, Rev. C. J. Ryder; Treasurer: H. W. Hubbard; Organ: *American Missionary*.
American Ramabai Association. See Ramabai Association.
American Tract Society (1825); Headquarters: 150 Nassau Street, New York; Secretaries: Rev. G. W. Shearer, Rev. John H. Kerr, Rev. Wm. W. Rand; Treasurer: Louis Tag; Organ: *American Messenger*.
American Unitarian Association (1825); Headquarters: 25 Beacon Street, Boston, Mass.; Secretary: Rev. Samuel A. Eliot.
Anglo-Continental Society (1853); Secretaries: Rev. H. J. White, Weston College, Oxford England, and A. Larpent, Esq., Vicarage, Kensing, Sevenoaks, England.
Arabian Mission; Under Foreign Mission Board of the Reformed Church of America.
Archbishop's Mission to Assyrian Christians (1884); Secretary: Rev. A. H. Lang, Church House, Dean's Yard, Westminster Abbey, London, S. W., England.
Arnots' Garenganze Mission. See Christian Mission (Brethren).
Asia Minor Apostolic Institute (1892); Headquarters: 1301 Divinity Place, West Philadelphia, Pa.; Principal: Rev. H. S. Jenanyan; Treasurer: G. S. Hickok, National Pa`k Bank, New York.
Associate Reformed Presbyterian Synod of the South (1875); Board of Foreign Missions of the: Headquarters: Due West, South Carolina; Secretary: Rev. W. L. Pressly, D.D.
Australian Wesleyan Methodist Missionary Association; Headquarters: 381 George Street, Sydney, New South Wales; Secretary: Rev. George Brown.
Australian Board of Missions; Secretary: Rev. John Dixon, St. Thomas' Rectory, Balmain West, Sydney, New South Wales.
Balaghat Mission (1893); Secretary: Miss Adelin Lampard, 114 Clapham Common, London, N. E.
Baptist Conventions of Canada. See Canada; Baptist Conventions of.
Baptist Industrial Mission of Scotland. See Scotland; Baptist Industrial Mission of.
Baptist Missionary Society; Headquarters: 19 Furnival Street, Holborn, London, E. C., England; Gen. Secretary: Alfred Henry Baynes; Treasurer: William Richard Rickett; Organ: *The Missionary Herald*.
Baptist Mission: Strict. See Strict Baptist.
Baptists, German, in Berlin. See German Baptists, etc.
Baptist Zenana Mission (1867); in connection with BMS; Hon. Secretaries: Miss Angus, Miss E. A. Angus, Miss H. C. Bowser, 5 Ellerdale Road, Hampstead, London, N. W., England; Treasurer: Mrs. A. Pearce Gould, 10 Queen Anne Street, Cavendish Sq., London, W., England.
Baptists in Berlin, Missionary Society of the. See Germany.
Basel Evang. Miss. Society. See Switzerland.
Bengal Evangelistic Mission (1874); Headquarters: Calcutta, India.
Berlin Ladies' Miss. Society for China. See Germany.
Berlin Missionary Society (1824). See Germany.
Bethel Santal Mission (1875); Secretary: Mrs. J. Morris, care Gostling & Morris, 9 Meadow Street, Bombay, India.
Bible Christian Home and Foreign Missionary Society (1821); Headquarters: 44 Brandram Rd., Lee, Lewisham, London, S. E., England; Secretary: Rev. I. B. Vanstone. The Woman's Missionary League is auxiliary to the above.
Bible Lands Missions' Aid Society (1856); Headquarters: 7 Adam Street, Strand, London, W. C., England; Secretary: Rev. W. A. Essery.
Bible Translation Society (1840); Headquarters: 19 Furnival Street, Holborn, London, E. C., England; Secretary: Rev. F. D. Waldock.
Blind in China, German Mission to. See Germany.
Breklum Missionary Society. See Germany.
Brethren in Christ (River Brethren); For. Miss. Bd. of (1896); Secretary: Elder W. O. Baker, Louisville, Ohio.
Brethren Church, Gen. Mission and Tract Com. See German Baptist Brethren Church.
Brethren; Mission of the. See Christian Mission.
Brethren's Society (Moravian) for the Furtherance of the Gospel among the Heathen. See Moravian Missions.
British and Foreign Bible Society (1804); Headquarters: 146 Queen Victoria Street, London, E. C., England; Secretaries: Rev. John Sharp, Rev. J. H. Ritson; Organ: *Bible Society Reporter*.
British Society for Prop. of Gospel among Jews (1842); Headquarters: 9 Great James Street, Bedford Row, London, W. C., England; Secretary: Rev. Isaac Levinson.
British Syrian Schools Society (1860); Headquarters: 29a

High Street, Wimbledon, London, S. W., England; Secretary: Miss Wilmot.

Calvinistic Methodist Church of America; Miss. Society of the (1869); Secretary: Rev. W. Machno Jones, Lake Crystal, Minn.

Cambridge Mission to Delhi (1867); Secretary: G. M. Edwards, Esq., Sidney Sussex College, Cambridge, England.

Canada: Baptist Convention of the Maritime Provinces (1846); Foreign Mission Board of the; Headquarters: 85 Germain Street, St. John, New Brunswick; Secretary and Treasurer: Rev. J. W. Manning. Women's Baptist Missionary Union; Headquarters: St. John, N. B.; Secretary: Mrs. C. H. Martell, Great Village, N. S.

Canada: Baptist Convention of Ontario and Quebec (1873); Foreign Mission Board of the; Headquarters: 177 Albany Avenue, Toronto, Ontario; Secretary: Rev. J. G. Brown; Treasurer: Rev. E. T. Fox; Organ: *Canadian Missionary Link*. Women's Foreign Missionary Society of Ontario; Headquarters: 165 Bloor Street, E., Toronto; Secretary: Miss Jane Buchan. Women's Foreign Missionary Society of Eastern Ontario and Quebec; Headquarters: Montreal; Secretary: Mrs. H. H. Ayer, 350 Olivier Avenue, Westmount, Montreal.

Canada: Congregational Foreign Missionary Society (1881); Headquarters: 2367 St. Catherine Street, Montreal, Canada; Secretary, Rev. Edward Munson Hill.

Canada: Domestic and Foreign Missionary Society of the Church of England in (1883); Headquarters: Kingston, Ontario; Secretary: Rev. Canon Spencer.

Canada: Foreign Missionary Committee of the Presbyterian Church in (1844); (Western Division) Headquarters: 89 Confederation Life Building, Toronto, Ontario; Secretary: Rev. R. P. Mackay; (Eastern Division) Headquarters: 108 Granville Street, Halifax, N. S.; Secretary: Rev. E. A. McCurdy. Woman's Foreign Missionary Society; (Western Division) Headquarters: Toronto, Ontario; Secretary: Miss B. MacMurchy, 133 Bloor Street, E., Toronto, Ontario; (Eastern Division) Headquarters: Halifax, N. S.; Secretary: Miss B. McGregor.

Canada: Mission. Society of the Methodist Church in (1824); Headquarters: 33 Richmond Street, W., Toronto, Ontario; Secretary: Rev. A. Sutherland; Organ: *Missionary Outlook*.

Canada: Presbyterian Mission to East Indians in Trinidad (etc. in W. I.); Under Foreign Mission Committee of the Presbyterian Church in Canada, Eastern Division.

Canada: Missionary Dept. of the Sunday School and Epworth League Board; Secretary: Rev. A. C. Crews, 9 Wesley Buildings, Toronto, Ontario, Canada.

Canadian Church Missionary Association (1894); Secretary: Rev. T. R. O'Meara, 467 Parliament Street, Toronto, Ontario, Canada.

Central American Mission (1890); Secretary: Rev. C. I. Scofield, Dallas, Texas.

Central Morocco Medical Mission (1894); Secretary and Treasurer: Mr. Grahame Wilson, 191 Meadowpark Street, Dennistown, Glasgow, Scotland.

Ceylon and India General Mission (1893); Secretary and Treasurer: Mr. David Gardiner, 46 Beresford Road, Highbury, London, N., England. Organ: *Darkness and Light*.

Children's Special Service Mission (1868); Headquarters: 13a Warwick Lane, Paternoster Row, London, E. C., England; Secretary: Mr. Henry Hankinson; Organ: *Our Own Magazine*.

China Inland Mission (1865); Headquarters: Newington Green, Mildmay, London, N., England; Secretary: F. Marcus Wood; Organ: *China's Millions*. U. S. Branch; Secretary: Rev. W. J. Erdmann, D.D., 702 Witherspoon Building, Philadelphia.

China Mission, Hauge's Synod. See Hauge's Synod.

China, Murray's Mission to the Blind and Illiterate in (1887); Secretary: John Grant, Esq., care Grant & Wylie, 204 St. Vincent Street, Glasgow.

Chinese; Soc. for the Diffusion of Christian and Gen. Knowledge among the (1887); Rev. Timothy Richard, 41 Kiangse Road, Shanghai, China; British organization (Christian Literature Society for China); Hon. Secretary: Rev. J. Cumming Brown, Balgonie, Hampstead Sq., London, N. W.; Organ: *China*, quarterly.

Chota Nagpur; Dublin University Mission to. See Dublin University, etc.

Christian Church (1886); Mission Board of the; Headquarters: 1231 West Fifth Street, Dayton, Ohio; Secretaries: Rev. J. G. Bishop, Rev. W. H. Dennison; Treasurer: Mr. A. M. Kerr; Organ: *Christian Missionary*. Woman's Board for Foreign Missions: Headquarters: Dayton, Ohio; Secretaries: Miss A. E. Batchelor, Miss Annie Libby; Treasurer: Miss Mary J. Batchelor.

Christian and Missionary Alliance (1887); Headquarters: 692 Eighth Avenue, New York; Secretary: Rev. A. E. Funk; Treasurer: Mr. David Crear; Organ: *Christian and Missionary Alliance*.

Christian Endeavor Society. See United Society C. E.

Christian Literature Society for India (1858); Headquarters: 7 Adam Street, Strand, London, W. C., England; Secretary: Rev. George Patterson.

Christian Faith; Soc. for Advancing the (1691); Secretary: Harry W. Lee, Esq., The Broad Sanctuary, Westminster, London.

Christian Knowledge, Society for Promoting (1698); Headquarters: Northumberland Ave., London, W. C., England; Secretaries: Rev. W. O. B. Allen, M.A., Rev. Edmund McClure.

Christian Mission: (England; Mission of the Brethren) (1827); Treasurer: J. L. McLean, M.D., 10 Widcombe Crescent, Bath, England; Organ: *Echoes of Service*.

Christian Unity Association (1896); Secretary: Rev. W. D. Fowler, Hawleyville, Conn.

Christian Woman's Board of Missions (Disciples) (1874); Headquarters: 152 East Market Street, Indianapolis, Ind.; Secretary and Treasurer: Mrs. Helen E. Moses; Organ: *Missionary Tidings*.

Church Missionary Society, American. See American Church Missionary Society.

Church Missionary Society for Africa and the East (1799); Headquarters: Church Missionary House, Salisbury Sq., London, E. C.; Secretaries: Rev. Prebendary Henry Elliott Fox, Mr. Eugene Stock, Rev. B. Baring-Gould, Rev. George Furness Smith, Mr. David Marshall Lang; Medical Department Secretary: H. Lankester, M.D.; Women's Department Secretaries: Miss G. A. Gollock, Miss M. C. Gollock; Organ: *Church Missionary Intelligencer*; *Church Missionary Gleaner*; *Mercy and Truth* (Medical Missions).

Church of England Zenana Missionary Society; Headquarters: Lonsdale Chambers, 27 Chancery Lane, London, W. C., England; Secretaries: cleric l, Rev. G. Yonge; Cent. Association, Miss Mulvany; lay, J. B. Braddon, Esq.; Organ: *India's Women*.

Church of Scotland For. Miss. Com. See Scotland, Ch. of.

Churches of God; Woman's Gen. Miss. Soc. of (1890); Miss Ella Jeffries, El Pasco, Woodford Co., Ill.

Colonial and Continental Church Society (1823); Headquarters: 9 Serjeants Inn, Fleet Street, London, E. C., England; Secretary: Rev. Canon Hurst.

Colonial Miss. Society (1836); Headquarters: 22 Memorial Hall, Farringdon Street, London, E. C., England; Secretary: Rev. D. Burford Hooke.

Colwyn Bay Training Institute. See African Training Institute.

Congo Balolo Mission. Now Regions Beyond Miss. Union.

Countess of Huntingdon's Connexion Sierra Leone Mission (1842); Secretary: Rev. Joseph Bainton, Ashbourne, Derbyshire, England; Treasurer: Mr. E. Dolby Shelton Ely, Cambridgeshire.

Cumberland Presbyterian Board of Foreign Missions and Church Erection (1852); Headquarters: Holland Building Annex, St. Louis, Mo.; Secretary: Mr. J. M. Patterson; Treasurer: Mr. J. C. Cobb; Organ: *Missionary Record*. Woman's Board of Missions; Headquarters: Evansville, Ind.; Secretaries: Mrs. M. E. Dyer, Mrs. D. F. Clarke; Treasurer: Miss L. M. Durham; Organ: *Missionary Record*.

Danish Evangelical Lutheran Church (United) in America (1896); Headquarters: Blair, Nebraska; Secretary: Rev. A. M. Andersen.

Danish Missionary Society (1821) (Danske Missionsselskab); Secretary: Rev. T. Loegstrup, Fredericia, Denmark; Organ: *Danske Missions-Blad*.

Danish Løventhal's Mission. See Løventhal's Mission.

Danish Mission to the Santhals. See Indian Home Mission to the Santhals.

Deaconess' Society: Rhenish Westphalian. See Germany.

Delhi, Cambridge Mission to. See Cambridge Mission to Delhi.

Disciples of Christ. See For. Ch. Miss. Society; also Christian Woman's Board of Miss.

Dublin University Mission to Chota Nagpur (1891); Secretary: Rev. Newport J. D. White, Marsh's Library, St. Patrick's, Dublin.

Dunkards. See German Bapt. Brethren Church.

Dutch Mission Societies. See Netherlands.

Dutch Reformed Church of S. Africa. See South Africa Ministers' Union.

Edinburgh Medical Missionary Society (1841); Headquarters: Mission House, 56 George Sq., Edinburgh, Scotland; Secretary: E. Sargood Fry; Organ: *Quarterly Paper*.

Egypt: Association for Furtherance of Christianity in (1883); Headquarters: 7 Dean's Yard, Westminster Abbey, London, S. W., England; Secretary: Rev. R. Milburn Blakiston.

Egypt General Mission (1898); Headquarters: Kingscourt, Belfast, Ireland; Hon. Secretary: Mr. Wm. J. Roome; Organ: *E. G. M. News*, occasional.

Egypt: Mission for the Propagation of the Gospel in. See Netherlands.

England: Foreign Missions Com. of the Presbyterian Church of (1847); Headquarters: 7 East India Avenue, London, S. E., England; Secretary: Rev. W. Dale, New Barnet, London; Organ: *Monthly Messenger*. Women's Missionary Association; Secretaries: Mrs. Matthews, 25

Christ Church Avenue, Brandesbury, London, N. W.; Mrs. Voelcher, 20 Upper Philimore Gardens, Kensington, London, W.; Organ: *Our Sisters in Other Lands.* Mission to the Jews; Headquarters: 7 East India Avenue, London, E. C.; Gen. Secretary: Rev. J. Thoburn McGaw; Financial Secretary: Mr. John Leggat.

Epworth League of the Methodist Episcopal Church (1889); Headquarters: 57 Washington Street, Chicago, Ill.; Office Secretary: Mr. R. E. Diffendorfer.

Epworth League of the Methodist Episcopal Church South (1889); Headquarters: Nashville, Tenn.; Secretary: Rev. H. M. DeBose.

Ermelo Missionary Association. See Netherlands.

Evangelical Association (1876); Missionary Society of the; Headquarters: 265 Woodland Avenue, Cleveland, Ohio; Secretaries: Rev. H. Mattill, Rev. T. C. Meckel; Treasurer: Rev. Yost; Organ: *Evangelischer Missionsbote.* Woman's Missionary Society; Headquarters: Cleveland, Ohio; Secretaries: Miss A. E. Rickert, Miss M. Grimm; Treasurer: Mrs. H. Mattill; Organ: *Missionary Messenger.*

Evangelical Lutheran Churches. See Lutheran Churches.

Furreedpore Mission (Australian Baptist) (1864); Headquarters: King William Road, Hyde Park, South Australia; Secretary: Rev. John Price; Treasurer: A. S. Neill, Palmer Place, North Adelaide, South Australia; Organ: *Missionary Echo.*

Female Education in Eastern Countries; Woman's Society for. See Germany.

Finnish Missionary Society (1859); (Finska Missions-Salskapet); Headquarters: Observatoriigatan 18, Helsingfors, Finland; Secretary: Director Rev. Lector Jos Mustakalir.

Foreign Christian Missionary Society (Disciples) (1875); Headquarters: 15 East Seventh Street, Cincinnati, Ohio; Secretaries: Rev. A. McLean, Rev. F. M. Rains; Treasurer: S. M. Cooper; Organ: *Missionary Intelligencer.* See also for Woman's Work, Christian Woman's Board of Missions.

Foreign Missions Industrial Association of America; Headquarters: 105 East 22d St., New York; Secretary and Treasurer, C. N. Talbot, 34 Pine St., New York; Organ: *Industrial Missions Magazine.*

Foreign Sunday School Assoc. of the U. S.: Secretary: Rev. H. C. Woodruff, 67 Schermerhorn Street, Brooklyn, N. Y.

France: French Methodist Mission among the Kabyles (Mission Methodiste Francaise en Kabylie) (1886); Secretary:——

France: French Young Men's Christian Association (Alliance des Unions Chrétiennes de Jeunes gens de France-Comité National) (1867); Headquarters: 14 Rue de Trevise. Paris; Secretary: Mr. Emmanuel Sautter.

France: McAll Mission (Mission Pouplaire Évangélique de France, 1872); Headquarters: 36 Rue Godot de Mauroy, Paris, France; Secretary: M. W. Soltau; Gen. Secretary for the United States: Miss M. Harvey, 759 St. Nicholas Avenue, New York.

France: Paris Evangelical Missionary Society (Société des Missions Évangéliques chez les Peuples non-Chrétiens, établie à Paris, 1822); Headquarters: Maison des Missions, 102 Boulevard Arago, Paris, France; Secretary: M. le Pasteur A. Boegner; Organ: *Le Journal des Missions Évangéliques,* monthly.

Friends. See also American Friends For. Missions.

Friends' Foreign Mission Association (1886); Headquarters: 15 Devonshire Street, Bishopsgate, Without, London, E. C., England; Secretary: Dr. William Wilson; Organ: *Our Missions.*

Free Baptists (1833); General Conference of; Headquarters: Auburn, Rhode Island; Secretaries: Rev. Arthur Given, Rev. H. M. Ford; Treasurer: Rev. Arthur Given. The Free Baptist Women's Missionary Society; Secretary: Mrs. S. C. S. Avery.

Free Methodist Church of North America (1882); General Missionary Board of the; Headquarters: 14-16 North May Street, Chicago, Ill.; Secretary: Rev. Benjamin Winget; Treasurer: S. K. J. Chesbro. Woman's Foreign Missionary Society of the Free Methodist Church; Headquarters: 14 N. May Street, Chicago, Ill.; Secretaries: Mrs. E. L. McGeary, Greenville, Ill.; Mrs. H. H. Jones, Jackson, Mich.; Treasurer: Mrs. L. C. Jensen, Chicago, Ill.; Organ: *Missionary Tidings.*

Friends: Woman's Foreign Missionary Union. See American Friends.

Friends of Augsburg, Board of Foreign Missions. See Lutheran Free Church, Board of Foreign Missions.

Garenganze Mission: Under Christian Brethren Mission (England).

German Baptist Brethren Church (Dunkers) (1884); General Mission and Tract Committee; Headquarters: Elgin, Ill.; Secretary: Mr. G. B. Royer; Organ: *The Missionary Visitor.*

German Baptist Mission (England) (1845); Secretary: Rev. Wm. Sears Oncken, Wragby Road, Lincoln, England.

German Evangelical Lutheran Synod of Ohio and Other States: India Mission of the (1896); Headquarters: Reedsburg, Wisconsin; Secretary: Rev. A. Rohrlach.

German Evangelical Synod of North America (1867); Headquarters: 1920 G. Street, N. W., Washington, D. C.; Secretary: Rev. Paul A. Menzel; Treasurer: P. L. Kohlmann, 1135 Gath Avenue, St. Louis, Mo.; Organ: *Deutscher Missions Freund.*

Germany: Africa Association (*Evangelischer Africaverein*); Headquarters: Blucher Strasse 53, Berlin, S.; Gen. Secretary; Pastor Erich Otto; Organ: *Afrika.*

Germany: Berlin Missionary Society (*Gesellschaft zur Beförderung der evangelischen Missionen unter den Heiden zu Berlin, Berlin I,* 1824); Headquarters: Georgenkirchstrasse 70, Berlin, N. O., Germany; Missions Director: Past Superintendent Genischen; Mission Inspector: Pastor F. Wendland; Past Superintendent A. Merensky; Pastor Sauberzweig-Schmidt; Organ: *Berliner Missionsberichte,* monthly; *Missionsfreund,* monthly.

Germany: Berlin Woman's Mission Society (*Berliner Frauen Missionsverein,* 1850); Headquarters: Berlin, Germany; President: Fr. ulein Julie von Buddenbrock; Inspector: Pastor Sauberzweig-Schmidt, Georgenkirchstrasse 70; Organ: *Mitteilungen des Berliner Frauenvereins für China,* quarterly.

Germany: Blind in China: German Mission to the (*Deutsche Blindenmission unter dem weiblichen Geschlecht in China,* 1890); Headquarters: Hildesheim, Germany; President: Pastor Fr. Borchers, Sibbesseb, Hildesheim; Lady President and Acting Treasurer: Frl. Luise Cooper, Sedanstrasse 33, Hildesheim; Organ: *Tsaukwong,* quarterly.

Germany: Breklum Missionary Society (*Schleswig-Holsteinische evang. luth. Missionsgesellschaft zu Breklum,* 1877); Headquarters: Breklum, Reg-Bez, Schleswig; President: General Superintendent D. Wallroth, Kiel; Inspector: Pastor Bahnsen; Secretary: Pastor Dittmer; Professor of Missions: Pastor Bracker; Organ: *Schleswig-Holsteinisches Missionsblatt,* monthly. (In Danish) *Vort Missionsblad,* monthly.

Germany: Woman's Society for Education of Women in the East: (*Frauen Verein fur Christliche Bildung des Weiblichen Geschlechts im Morgenlande,* 1842); Headquarters: Berlin, Germany; President: Fraulein Julie von Buddenbrock; Organ: *Missionsblatt des Frauenvereins,* etc.

Germany: German Baptists in Berlin, Missionary Society of the (*Missionsgesellschaft der Deutschen Baptisten in Berlin,* 1890); Headquarters: Schutzenstrasse 53, Stegletz bei Berlin; Inspector: K. Mascher; Organ: *Bluten und Fruchte,* quarterly; *Unsere Heiden Mission,* monthly.

German East Africa: Evangelical Missionary Society for (*Evangelische Missionsgesellschaft für Deutsch-Ost-Afrika,*—Berlin *III,* 1886); Headquarters: Grosslichterfeld bei Berlin, Germany; Inspectors: Pastor W. Michaelis, Pastor W. Trittelvitz; Organ: *Nachrichten aus der Ost-Afrikanischen Mission.*

Germany: General Evangelical Protestant Missionary Society (*Allgemeine Evangelische-Protestantische Missionsverein,* 1884); Headquarters: Berlin, Germany; President: Prediger D. Kind, Kronenstrasse 70, Berlin W., 8, Germany; Inspector: Prediger Lempfuhl, Scharrnstrasse 11, Berlin C.; Organ: *Zeitschrift für Missionskunde und Religionswissenschaft,* monthly; *Missionsblatt der Allg. ev.-Prot.,* etc., monthly.

Germany: Gossner Missionary Society (*Gossnerische Mission—Berlin II,* 1836); Head uarters: Handjerystrasse 19-20, Friedenau-Berlin, Germany; President: Gen. Sup. D. Braun; Inspector: Dir. P. Kausch, P. Romer; Organ: *Die Biene,* monthly.

Germany: Hannover Free Evangelical Lutheran Church Missionary Society (*Mission der Hannoverischen ev.-Luth. Freikirche in Hermannsburg,* 1892); Headquarters: Nettelkamp, Hannover, Germany; President: Pastor Heutze; Organ: *Missionsblatt der Hannoverischen ev.-Luth. Freikirche,* monthly.

Germany: Hermannsburg Missionary Society (*Hermannsburger Missionsgesellschaft,* 1849); Headquarters: Hermannsburg, Hannover, Germany; Director: Egm. Harms; Assoc. Director: Pastor Georg Haccius; Organ: *Hermannsburger Missionsblatt,* fortnightly.

Germany: Jerusalem Society (*Jerusalem-verein in Berlin,* 1852); Headquarters: Berlin; President: Count von Zieten Schwerin, Wustrau, Kreis Ruppin; Secretary: Pastor D. Weser, Bischofstrasse 4-5, Berlin C., 2, Germany; Agent: Pastor Pflanz, Neu Ruppin; Organ: *Neueste Nachrichten aus dem Morgenlande,* annual.

Germany: Kiel China Mission (*Kieler-China-Mission,* 1879); Headquarters: Missionshaus, Kiel, Germany; Conductor: Pastor Witt, at present in China; Organ: *Er Kommt,* semi-monthly.

Germany: Leipzig Missionary Society (*Evangelisch-Lutherisch Mission zu Leipzig,* 1836); Headquarters: Carolinenstrasse 19, Leipzig; President: Geh. Oberkirchenrat D. Bard; Mission Director: D. V. Schwartz; Inspector: Dr Siedel; Organ: *Missionsblatt;* Women's Auxiliary: (*Frauen Hilfs Vereine*), same address.

Germany: Neu Dettelsau Missionary Society (*Missions-Anstalt in Neuen Dettelsau;* also called *Bayerische Missions-Gesellschaft,* 1886); Headquarters: Neuen-Dettelsau, Bavaria; President: Pastor Stirner, Rothenburg; Inspector: Mr. Deinzer; Organ: *Freimund's Kirchliches und Politisches Wochenblatt,* with Supplement on Church work in N. America, Australia, and British Guinea.

Germany: Neukirchen Missionary Institute (*Neukirchener Missions Anstalt,* 1881); Headquarters: Neukirchen bei Mörs, Dusseldorf, Germany; Inspector: Pastor Stursberg; Organ: *Der Missions-und Heidenbote,* monthly, with supplement.

Germany: North German Missionary Society (*Norddeutsche Missions Gesellschaft*); Headquarters: Ellhornstrasse 26, Bremen, Germany; President: I. Schroeder; Inspector: Aug. W. Schreiber; Organ: *Monatsblatt der Nordd. Miss. Gesellschaft,* monthly.

Germany: Rhenish Missionary Society (*Rheinische Missions Gesellschaft*); Headquarters: Rudolfstrasse 129, Barem, Germany; President: Th. Gundert; Inspector. Pastor I. Spiecher; Organ: *Missionsblatt, Barmen,* monthly.

Germany: Sudan Pioneer Mission (*Sudan Pionier Mission,* 1900); Headquarters: Eisenach, Germany; President: Pastor Ziemendorf, Emserstrasse 12, Wiesbaden, Germany; Treasurer: P. em. Dammann, Eisenach; Organ: *Der Sudan Pionier,* monthly.

Germany: Unity of Brethren, or Brüdergemeine. See Moravian Missions.

Gospel in Foreign Parts: Society for the Propagation of. See Society for the Propagation of the Gospel.

Gossner's Evang. Missionary Society. See Germany.

Gospel Missionary Union (1891); Mr. George S. Fischer, 415 East, Kansas City, Mo.

Hannover: Evang. Lutheran Free Church of. See Germany.

Hauge's Synod China Mission (*Hauges Synodes China Mission,* 1891); Headquarters: 298 Williams Street, St Paul, Minn.; Secretary: Rev. Charles O. Brohaugh.

Hawaiian Evangelical Association (1863); Headquarters: Honolulu, Hawaiian Island; Secretary: Rev. O. P. Emerson; Treasurer: Theodore Richards; Organ: *The Friend.* Woman's Board of Missions; Secretary: Miss M. S. Seelye.

Hephzibah Faith Home Association (1892); Secretary: Mrs. H. W. Kelley, Tabor, Iowa; Organ: *Sent of God.*

Hermannsburg Evangelical Lutheran Missionary Society. See Germany.

Highways and Hedges Mission. See South Arcot Highways, etc.

Holiness Union. See Sweden.

Ikweci Lamaci Mission (1877); Secretary: Rev. Samuel Aitchison, Harding, Alfred County, Natal, South Africa.

India: Christian Literature Society for. See Christian Literature Society.

Indian Home Mission to the Santhals (1867); Treasurer: J. Shroeder, Copenhagen, Denmark; Secretary: Rev. L. O. Skrefsrud, Ebenezer, Bengal, India.

Industrial Missions Aid Society; Secretary: Mr. W. H. J. Hatch, 10 Paternoster Row, London, E. C., England.

Industrial Missions Association of America. See Foreign Missions Industrial Association.

International Medical Missions and Benevolent Association. See Seventh Day Adventist General Conference.

International Medical Missionary Society (1881); Headquarters: 288 Lexington Avenue, New York; Secretary: George D. Dowkontt, M. D.; Treasurer: J. E. Giles, M. D.

Ireland: Foreign Missions Com. of the Reformed Pres. Church of (1871); Secretary: Rev. Wm. Russell, Reformed Presbyterian Manse, Balla, Ireland.

Ireland: Presbyterian Church in, Foreign Missions of the (1840); Secretary: Rev. George McFarland, 12 May Street, Belfast, Ireland.

Ireland: Jewish Missions of the Presbyterian Church in (1841); Secretary: Rev. George R. Buick, Culleybackey, County Antrim, Ireland.

Ireland: Presbyterian Church in; Mission to the Jungle Tribes (1890); Secretary: Rev. Henry Montgomery, Upper Crescent, Belfast, Ireland.

Jaffa Medical Mission and Hospital (1878); Secretary: C. E. Newton, Esq., Mickleover, Derby, England.

Jaffa Tabeetha Mission. See Tabeetha Mission.

Jamaica Baptist Union (1849); Secretary: Rev. P. Williams, Bethel Town P. O., Jamaica; Secretary Missionary Society (1855); Rev. E. J. Hewett, Anchovy P. O., Jamaica.

Jamaica Church of England: Home and Foreign Missionary Society (1861); Secretary: I. R. Latreille, Esq., 3 Duke Street, Kingston, Jamaica.

Jamaica: Congregational Union of (1876); Secretary: Rev. Jas. Watson, Whitefield, Porus, Jamaica.

Jamaica: Foreign Missions Com. of the Presbyterian Church of (1824); Secretary: Rev. W. Y. Turner, M.D., Christiana P. O., Jamaica.

Jamaica: United Methodist Free Church, Missionary Committee; Secretary: Rev. Francis Bavin, Kingston, Jamaica.

Java Committee, Amsterdam. See Netherlands.

Jerusalem and the East Mission (1888); Secretary: Rev. W. Sadler, Dembleby Rectory, Folkingham, England.

Jerusalem: Union for the Syrian Orphange at (1889); Secretary: Mr. Adolf Mess, Cologne, Germany.

Jerusalem Company (Jerusalem-verein). See Germany.

Jews: Church of Scotland Conversion of the. See Scotland Church of, etc.

Jews, London Soc. for Promoting Christianity among. See London Soc., etc.

Jews, Pres. Church of England's Mission to. See Presbyterian Church of England, etc.

Jews. See Brit. Soc. for Prop. of Gospel among.

Kabyles, French Methodist Mission among the. See France.

Kaiserswerth Deaconesses. See Germany.

Keswick Mission (1896); Secretary: Rev. John Harford-Battersby, Ridley Hall, Cambridge, England.

Kurku and Central Indian Hill Mission (1890); F. W. Howard Piper, Beechwood, Highgate, London, N., England.

Lebanon Hospital for the Insane, London Committee for the (1896); Headquarters: 35 Queen Victoria Street, London, E. C., England; Secretary: Mr. Francis C. Brading; Treasurer: Sir Richard Tangye.

Leipzig Evangelical Lutheran Missionary Society. See Germany.

Lepers in India and the East, Mission to (1874); Headquarters: 17 Greenhill Place, Edinburgh; Secretary: Wellesley C. Bailey, Esq.; Organ: *Without the Camp.*

London Society for Promoting Christianity among the Jews (1809); Headquarters: 16 Lincoln's Inn Fields, London, W. C., England; Secretaries: Rev. W. T. Gidney and Rev. F. L. Denman.

London Missionary Society (1795); Headquarters: 30 Gray's Inn Road, London, W. C., England; Secretaries: Rev. R. Wardlaw Thompson, Rev. George Cousins.

Löventhal's Mission: Pres. of Com. Rev. P. J. St. Riemann Faxe, Prastegaard, Denmark.

Lutheran Church in America (Danish). See Danish Evangelical Lutheran Church, etc.

Lutheran Church: Foreign Mission Board of the Evangelical Lutheran Synod of Iowa and other States (1854); Headquarters: Charles City, Iowa; Secretary: Rev. E. H. Casselmann.

Lutheran Church: Foreign Missions Committee of the Evangelical Lutheran Joint Synod of Ohio and other States (1884); Headquarters: 48 E. Frankfort Street, Columbus, Ohio; Secretary: Rev. J. H. Schneider.

Lutheran Church: Foreign Missions Committee of the German Evangelical Lutheran Synod of Missouri, Ohio and other States. See German Evangelical Lutheran Synod, etc.

Lutheran Free Church: Board of Foreign Missions of (1895); (formerly called Friends of Augsburg); Headquarters: Minneapolis, Minn.; Secretary: Prof. Geo. Sverdrup; Treasurer: J. H. Blegen.; Organ: *Gasseren.*

Lutheran General Council: Board of Foreign Missions of the Evangelical Council of the Evangelical Lutheran Church in North America (1867); Headquarters: 1522 Arch Street, Philadelphia; Secretaries: J. M. Snyder, Conrad Itter, Rev. W. Ashmead Schaeffer; Treasurer: William H. Staake; Organ: *Missions-Bote.* Woman's Board of Foreign Miss. Soc.; Secretary: Mrs. A. Woll, 33d and Diamond Streets, Philadelphia.

Lutheran General Synod: Board of Foreign Missions of the General Synod of the Evangelical Lutheran Church in the U. S. (1841); Headquarters: 19 W. Saratoga Street, Baltimore, Md.; Secretaries: Rev. M. J. Kline, Rev. George Scholl; Treasurer: O. F. Lautz; Organ: *Lutheran Mission Journal.*

Lutheran Church in the South (1886); Board of Foreign Missions and Church Extension of the United Synod of the Evangelical Lutheran Church in the South; Headquarters: Strasburg, Va.; Secretary: Rev. L. L. Smith; Treasurer: J. W. Eberly.

Lutheran Church in America (Norwegian). See Norwegian Evangelical Lutheran Church, etc.

McAll Mission. See France.

Medical Missionary Association, London (1878); Headquarters: 49 Highbury Park, London, N., England; Secretaries: Henry Soltau, L. R. C. P. and S., Edin., James L. Maxwell, M.D.; Organ: *Medical Missions at Home and Abroad.*

Melanesian Mission (1849); Secretary: Rev. Geo. MacMurray, St. Mary's Vicarage, Auckland, New Zealand.

Mennonite Mission Board (1882); Headquarters: Quakertown, Pa; Secretary: Rev. A. B. Shelly.

Mennonite Union, etc., for the Netherlands Possessions beyond the Sea. See Netherlands.

Methodist Church in Canada. See Canada; Miss Soc. of Meth. Church in.

Methodist Episcopal Church: Missionary Society of the (1819); Headquarters: 150 Fifth Avenue, New York; Secretaries: Rev. A. B. Leonard, Rev. H. K. Carroll, Rev. G. O. Benton; Treasurer; Homer Eaton; Organ: *World Wide Missions.* Woman's Foreign Missionary Society of the Methodist Episcopal Church; Headquarters: 150 Fifth Avenue, New York; Secretary: Mrs. J. T. Gracey.

Methodist Episcopal Church (South); Board of Missions of the (1846); Headquarters: Nashville, Tenn.; Secretaries: Rev. Walter R. Lambuth, Rev. J. H. Pritchett; Treasurer: J. D. Hamilton; Organ: *Review of Missions.* Woman s Board of Missions; Headquarters: Nashville, Tenn.; Secretaries: Mrs S. C. Truehart, Nashville, Tenn.; Mrs. M. L. Hargrove, Kansas City, Mo.; Treasurer, Mrs. H. N. McTyeire; Organ: *Woman's Missionary Advocate.*

Methodist Free Church. See United Methodist.

Methodist New Connexion Miss. Soc.: Secretary: Rev. George Packer, 3 St. John's Ter ace, Belle Vue Road, Leeds, England; Organ: *Gleanings in the Harvest Field.* Woman's Auxiliary for China; Miss Stacey, Ranmoor, Sheffield, England.

Methodist Protestant Church: Board of Foreign Missions of the (1888); Headquarters: Greensboro, N. C.; Secretary and Treasurer: Rev. T. J. Ogburn. Woman's Foreign Missionary Society Methodist Protestant Church; Headquarters: Greensboro, N. C.; Secretaries: Mrs. D. S. Stephens, Kansas City, Kansas: Mrs. H. Hupfield, Baltimore, Md.; Treasurer: Mrs. J. D. Anderson, Bellevue, Pa.; Organ: *Woman's Missionary Record.*

Mildmay Institute and Missions (1856); Headquarters: The Conference Hall, Mildmay Park, London, N., England; Treasurer and Superintendent: Col. J. F. Morton. Mildmay Mission to the Jews (1876); Headquarters: 79 Mildmay Road, London, N., England; Secretary: Rev. John Wilkinson.

Missionary Pence Association: Headquarters: Rooms 21-22 Exeter Hall, Strand, London, W. C., England; Secretary: Mr. William Roger Jones.

Miss Taylor's Schools, Beyrout (1868); Headquarters: 35 Great King Street, Edinburgh, Scotland; Secretary: Mrs. Sandeman.

Moravian Missions (*Missions-Werk der Evangelischer Brüder Unität,* 1732); Headquarters: Berthelsdorf, Herrnhut, Saxony; Director: Rev. Dr. C. Buchner; Secretaries of Missions (in Berthelsdorf): Rev. Leonard Tietzen; (in London) Rev. C. J. Klesel; (in Bethlehem, Pa., U. S.) Rev. Paul de Schweinitz; Organ: *Missionsblatt der Brüdergemeine.*

Morocco: Medical Mission in, Central; See Central Morocco Medical Mission.

National Baptist Convention: Foreign Mission Board of the (1880); Headquarters, 718 W. Walnut Street, Louisville, Ky.; Secretary: Rev. L. G. Jordan; Treasurer: Rev. C. H. Parrish; Organ: *Mission Herald.*

National Bible Society of Scotland. See Scotland; National Bible Society of.

Netherlands Bible Society (1814); Rev. C. F. Gronemeijer, Vossiusstraat 15, Amsterdam, Holland.

Netherlands: Committee in support of the Salatiga mission in Java (*Comité tot understeuning van de Zendelingen der Salatiga- Zending op Java, gevestigd te Utrecht,* 1887); Secretary: Rev. M. Mooij, Varsseveld, Holland.

Netherlands: Ermelo Missionary Association (*Ermelosche Zendingsgemeente,* 1856); Secretary: Mr. H. W. Mooij, Ermelo, Holland.

Netherlands: Java Committee (*Java Comité,* 1855); Headquarters: Boerhaavestraat 5, Amsterdam, Holland; Secretary: Rev. L. Kooperus; Organ: *Het Geillustreerd Zendings blad; Medeaeelingen van het Zendingsveld.*

Netherlands: Mennonite Union for Propagation of the Gospel in the East Indian possessions of the (1847); Secretary: Rev. W. I. Leendertz, Reizersgracht 194, Amsterdam, Holland.

Netherlands Missionary Society (1797); Headquarters: Rechter Rottekade 57, Rotterdam, Holland; Secretary: Rev. J. W. Gunning, Jr.; Organ: *Maandberichten,* monthly; *Mededeelingen,* quarterly.

Netherlands: Mission of the Reformed Churches in the (1892); Dr. J. Hania, Steenwijk, Netherlands.

Netherlands Missionary Union (1858); Headquarters: Stationweg 7, Rotterdam, Holland; Secretary: Rev. F. A. van der Heijden.

Netherlands: Union for the Propagation of the Gospel in Egypt (*Vereeniging tot uitbreiding van het Evangelie in Egypt,* 1886); Secretary: Rev. J. H. Van Noort, Nassaukade, 82, Amsterdam, Holland.

Netherlands: Utrecht Missionary Union (*Utrechtsche Zendingsvereeniging,* 1859); Headquarters: Utrecht, Holland; Secretary: Rev. M. A. Adriani, Janskerhof, Utrecht.

Neukirchen Missionary Society. See Germany.

New England Company (1649); Headquarters: 1 Hatton Garden, Holborn, London, E. C., England; Secretary: W. W. Venning, Esq.

New Jerusalem in U. S. A.: Board of Home and Foreign Missions of the General Convention of; Headquarters: 16 Arlington Street, Boston, Mass.; Secretary: Rev. Willard H. Hinkley; Treasurer: Dr. E. A. Whiston.

New South Wales, Baptist Foreign Missionary Society of (1892); Secretary: Rev. F. Hibberd, "Sarum," Carlingford, New South Wales, Australia.

New South Wales, Pres. Church in; Secretary: Rev. John Walker, Woollahra, Sydney, New South Wales, Australia.

New Zealand Baptist Miss. Society: Secretary: Mr. H. Driver, "Chaucer's Head," Book-room, Dunedin, New Zealand.

New Zealand, For. Miss. Com. of the Pres. Church of (1869); Convener: Rev. Wm. Hewitson, Dunedin, New Zealand. Maori Missions Committee of the same; Convener: Rev. D. Gordon, Marton, N. Z.

North Africa Mission (1881); Secretary: Dr. C. L. Terry, 34 Paternoster Row, London, E. C., England; Organ: *North Africa.*

North China Mission (1874); Secretary: Rev. Mackwood Stevens, Addington Rectory, Winslow, Bucks, England.

North German Missionary Society. See Germany.

North India School of Medicine, London Committee for (1894); Secretary: Miss Mabel W. Brown, 120 St. James Road, West Croydon, Surrey, England.

Norwegian Board of Missions (1889); Secretary and Treasurer: Mr. Gustave Andersen, Kronprinsensgade No. 1, Christiania, Norway.

Norwegian Church Mission of Schreuder (1877); Secretary: Rev. Paul Vilhelm Skaar, Helgesensgo 44, Christiania, Norway; Organ: *Missionsblad.*

Norwegian Lutheran China Mission Association (*Det Norske lutherske Kina missions forbund*), 1891; Secretary: Mr. Johannes Brandtzaeg, Framnes, Norheimsund, Norway.

Norwegian Lutheran Church in America: Board of Foreign Missions of the United (1858); Secretary: Rev. Peter Dreyer, Harmony, Fillmore County, Minnesota.

Norwegian Missionary Society (1842); Secretary: Rev. L. Dahle, Stavanger, Norway.

Nyassa Industrial Mission (1893); Headquarters: 4 Paternoster Buildings, London, E. C., England; Secretary: Rev. Alfred Walker, Sandrock, Sevenoaks, Kent.

Nyassaland Mission. See South Africa Ministers Union.

Open Brethren, Garenganze Mission. See Christian Mission (England).

Palestine and Lebanon Nurses' Mission (1865); Hon. Secretary: Miss Lloyd, 22 Al ert Square, Clapham Road, London, S. W.; Organ: *Open Doors,* quarterly.

Paris Society for Evangelical Missions. See France.

Pentecost Bands of the World (1897); Secretary: Mr. Geo. E. Bula, Indianapolis, Ind.

Pilibhit Industrial and Evangelistic Mission (1902); Superintendent: Rev. J. C. Lawson, Pilibhit, U. P., India.

Pongas Mission. Under S. P. G.

Poona and Indian Village Mission (1895); Director: Chas. F. Reeves; Secretary: A. Leigh, Nasarapur, Bhor State, Bombay.

Presbyterian Church in the U. S. (North): Board of Foreign Missions of the (1837); Headquarters: 156 Fifth Avenue, New York; Secretaries: Rev. F. F. Ellinwood, Mr. R. E. Speer, Rev. A. J. Brown, Rev. A. Halsey; Treasurer: Chas. W. Hand; Organ: *Assembly Herald.* Woman's Board of Foreign Missions of the Presbyterian Church (North); Headquarters: 156 Fifth Avenue, New York; Treasurer: Miss H. W. Hubbard. Woman's Foreign Missionary Society of the Presbyterian Church (North); Headquarters: Witherspoon Building, Philadelphia, Pa.; Treasurer: Miss E. H. Eldridge. Woman's North Pacific Presbyterian Board of Foreign Missions; Headquarters: Portland, Oregon; Treasurer: Mrs. H. C. Campbell. Woman's Occidental Board of Foreign Missions; Headquarters: 920 Sacramento Street, San Francisco, Cal.; Treasurer: Mrs. E. G. Dennison. Woman's Presbyterian Board of Foreign Missions of the Southwest; Headquarters: 1516 Locust Street, St. Louis, Mo.; Treasurer: Mrs. Wm. Burg. Woman's Presbyterian Board of Missions of the North West; Headquarters: LeMoyne Block, Chicago, Ill.; Treasurer: Mrs. C. B. Farwell. Woman's Presbyterian Foreign Missionary Society, Northern New York; Headquarters: 78 First Street, Troy, N. Y.; Treasurer: Mrs. B. Arnold; Organ of these seven Societies: *Woman's Work for Woman.*

Presbyterian Church in the U. S. (South): Executive Committee of Foreign Missions of the (1861); Headquarters: Chamber of Commerce Building, Nashville, Tenn.; Secretary: Rev. S. H. Chester; Treasurer: Mr. Erskine Reed; Organ: *The Missionary.*

Presbyterian Church of England. See England, Pres. Church of.

Primitive Methodist Church in the U. S. (1896); Headquarters: Plymouth, Luzerne Co., Pennsylvania; Secretary: Rev. Daniel Savage. Auxiliary to the Prim. Methodist Miss. Society of London.

Primitive Methodist Miss. Soc. (1842); Secretary: Rev. R. W. Burnett, 71 Freegrove Road, Holloway, London, N., England; Organ: *Primitive Methodist Missionary Magazine.*

Promoting Christian Knowledge, Soc. for. See Christian Knowledge, Soc. for, etc.

Propagation of the Gospel in Foreign Parts, Society for the. See Society for the Propagation of the Gospel.

Protestant Episcopal Church in the U. S. A.: Domestic and Foreign Mission Society of the (1835); Headquarters: 281 Fourth Avenue, New York; Secretaries: Rev. A. S. Lloyd, Rev. J. Kimber, Mr. John W. Wood; Treasurer: George C. Thomas; Organ: *Spirit of Missions.*

Pundita Ramabai Mission (1887); (See Ramabai Association); Directors: The Pundita Ramabai, Sharada Sadan, Poona, India.

Pure Literature Society (1854); Secretary: Mr. R. Turner, 11 Buckingham Street, Adelphi, Strand, London, W. C., England.

Qua Iboe Mission (1887); Secretaries: Mr. H. B. Niblock, Mr. James Hamilton, Scottish Provident Building, Belfast, Ireland; Organ: *Occasional Paper*.

Queensland Baptist Association Foreign Missions (1887); Secretary: Mr. Sidney G. Martin, 295 Queen Street, Brisbane, Queensland.

Queensland Pres. Church Mission to the Heathen (1882); Rev. D. F. Mitchell, The Manse, So. Brisbane, Queensland, Australia.

Ramabai Association, American (1898); Secretary: Mrs. George H. McGrew, 715 Case Ave., Cleveland, O.; Treasurer: Mr. Curtis Chipman, 222 Boylston St., Boston, Mass.

Ranaghat Medical Mission (1893); Director: C. G. Monro, Ranaghat, Nuddea, Bengal.

Reformed Church in America: Board of Foreign Missions of the (1832); Headquarters: 25 East 22d Street, New York; Secretaries: Rev. C. L. Wells, Rev. J. L. Ferris, Rev. H. N. Cobb, Rev. J. W. Conklin; Treasurer: Chas. H. Harris; Organ: *Mission Field*. Woman's Board of Foreign Missions; Headquarters: 25 East 22d Street, New York; Secretaries: Miss O. H. Lawrence; Treasurer: Mrs. F. S. Douglas; Organ: *Mission Gleaner*.

Reformed Church in the U. S. (German): Board of Commissioners for Foreign Missions of the (1881); Headquarters: 1306 Arch Street, Philadelphia; Secretary: Rev. Allen R. Bartholomew; Treasurer: Rev. J. S. Lemberger.

Reformed Episcopal Church in the United States: Board of Foreign Missions of the (1894); Headquarters: 2630 North 12th Street, Philadelphia, Pa.; Secretary: Mr. H. S. Sinamon; Treasurer: Rev. C. F. Hendricks.

Reformed Episcopal Church in the United Kingdom: Punjab Mission of the (1900); Secretary: Rev. John Anderson, 20 Minet Avenue, Harlesden, London, N. W., England.

Reformed Presbyterian Church in N. A.: Board of Foreign Missions of the General Synod of the (1836); Headquarters: 2102 Spring Garden Street, Philadelphia, Pa.; Secretary: Rev. David Steele.

Reformed Presbyterian Church in N. A.: Board of Foreign Missions of the Synod of the (1856); Headquarters: 325 West Fifty-sixth Street, New York; Secretary: Rev. R. M. Sommerville, D.D.; Treasurer: ———; Organ: *Olive Trees*.

Reformed Pres. Church of Ireland and Scotland, For. Miss. Com. of. See Ireland, Scotland etc.

Regions Beyond Missionary Union (1899); Headquarters: Harley House, Bow Road, London, E. England; Secretary: Rev. H. Grattan Guiness, M.D.; Organ: *Regions Beyond*.

Religious Tract Society (1799); Headquarters: 56 Paternoster Row, London, E. C., England; Secretary: Rev. R. Lovett.

Rhenish Missionary Society. See Germany.

River Brethren. See Brethren in Christ.

Romande Mission. See Switzerland; Mission Romande.

Sacred Mission, Society of the (1891); Director, Rev. Herbert Kelley, House of the Sacred Mission, Kelham, Newark, England.

Saint Chrischona Pilgrim Mission. See Switzerland.

Salatiga Mission in Java. See Netherlands.

Salvation Army (1865); International Headquarters: 101 Queen Victoria Street, London, E. C., England; Director, Rev. William Booth.

Santals, Indian Home Mission to. See Indian Home Mission to Santhals.

Scandinavian Alliance Mission in North America (1891); Headquarters: 81 Ashland Boulevard, Chicago, Ill.; Secretary: Rev. C. T. Dyrness; Treasurer: Prof. F. Risberg.

Scotland; Baptist Industrial Mission of (1895); Secretary: Rev. W. J. Millar, 40 St. Enoch Square, Glasgow, Scotland.

Scotland; Conversion of the Jews Committee of the Church of (1840); Secretary: John A. Traill, Esq., 17 Duke Street, Edinburgh, Scotland.

Scotland; Foreign Missions Committee of the Church of (1829); Headquarters: 22 Queen Street, Edinburgh, Scotland; Secretary: Rev. John McMurrie. Woman's Association for Foreign Missions (1837); Secretary: Miss Rutherfurd.

Scotland; National Bible Society of (1860); Headquarters: 224 West George Street, Glasgow; Edinburgh office: 5 St. Andrew Square; Secretaries: Wm. J. Slowan, Esq., Glasgow; Rev. J. S. Nisbet, Edinburgh; Organ: *Record*.

Scotland; Foreign Missions Committee of the Reformed Presbyterian Church of (1871); Secretary: Rev. John McKee, Wishaw, Scotland. See also Ireland.

Scotland, United Free Church of, Foreign Missions (1900); Headquarters: 15 North Bank Street, Edinburgh; Secretaries, Rev. James Buchanan, George Smith; Organ: *Monthly Record*.

Scottish Episcopal Church Foreign Missionary Society (1872); Secretary: Mr. W. W. Farquharson, 13 Queen Street, Edinburgh, Scotland.

Scripture Gift Mission (1862); Secretary: Mr. W. Waters, 15 Strand, London, W. C., England.

Scriptures, Association for Free Distribution of the (1874); Secretary: Mrs. A. E. Pridham, 6 Cannon Place, Hampstead, London, N. W.

Seventh Day Adventist General Conference; Foreign Mission Committee of the (1887); Headquarters: 222 N. Capitol Street, Washington, D. C.; Secretary: W. A. Spicer; Treasurer: I. H. Evans; Organ: *The Advent Review and Sabbath Herald*. International Medical Mission and Benevolent Association: Headquarters: The Sanitarium, Battle Creek, Michigan; Secretary: John F. Morse, M.D.

Seventh Day Baptist Missionary Society (1842); Headquarters: Westerley, R. I.; Secretary: Rev. O. U. Whitford; Treasurer: ———.

Society for the Propagation of the Gospel in Foreign Parts (1701); Headquarters: 19 Delahay Street, Westminster, London, S. W., England; Secretary: Rt. Rev. H. H. Montgomery, D.D.

South Africa General Mission (1889); Secretary: Arthur Mercer, Esq., 17 Homefield Road, Wimbledon, London, S. W., England.

South African Dutch Reformed Church Ministers' Missionary Union (Predikanten Zending Vereeniging; also called "Nyasaland Mission" (1886) Chairman: Rev. Andrew Murray, D.D.; Secretary: Rev. J. du Plessis, Sea Point, Cape Colony, South Africa.

South African Missionary Society of the Wesleyan Methodist Church (1883); Secretary: Rev. Geo. Weaver, Cape Town, South Africa.

South American Evang. Mission (1895); Secretary: Mr. Bryce W. Ranken, 23 Overton Street, Edgehill, Liverpool, England.

South American Missionary Society (1884); Headquarters: 1 Clifford's Inn, Fleet Street, London, E. C., England; Secretary: Capt. Edward Poulden; Organ: *South American Missionary Magazine*.

South Arcot Highways and Hedges Mission (1885); Secretary: Miss C. M. S. Lowe, 8 Childevert Road, Upper Tooting, London, S. W., England.

South Australia, Foreign Missions Com. of the Presbyterian Church of (1872); Secretary: Rev. James Lyall, Adelaide, South Australia.

Southern Baptist Convention (1845); Foreign Mission Board of the; Headquarters: 1103 Main Street, Richmond, Va.; Secretaries: Rev. R. J. Willingham, Rev. E. E. Bomar; Treasurer: J. C. Williams; Organ: *Foreign Mission Journal*. Woman's Missionary Union; Headquarters: 233 N. Howard Street, Baltimore, Md.; Secretaries: Miss A. W. Armstrong, Miss Nellie Martein; Treasurer: Mrs. W. C. Lowndes.

Southern Morocco Mission (1888); Director: Mr. John Anderson, 64 Bothwell Street, Glasgow, Scotland. Organ: *The Reaper*, monthly; Ladies' Auxiliary; Secretary, Miss Kerr, Paisley.

Stirling Tract Enterprise (1848); Manager: Mr. John Macfarlane, Drummond's Tract Depot, Stirling, Scotland.

Strict Baptist Mission (1860); Secretary: Mr. W. S. Millwood, Edward House, Leison Grove, London, N. W., England.

Student Volunteer Missionary Union (1893); Headquarters: 22 Warwick Lane, London, E. C., England.

Student Volunteer Movement (1888); Headquarters: 3 West 29th Street, New York; Secretary: H. P. Turner; Treasurer: ———.

Sunday School Union (1803); Headquarters: 55 and 56 Old Bailey, London, E. C., England; Secretary: Rev. Carey Bonner; Secretary of India S. S. Mission, and Chairman of Continental S. S. Mission: Charles Waters.

Sweden; Evangelical National Society in (*Evangeliska Fosterlands-Stiftelsens*, 1856); Headquarters: Stockholm, Sweden; Director: Rev. A. Kolmodin, Johannelund, Stockholm; Organ: *Missionstidning*.

Sweden; Female Mission Workers (*Kvinliga Missions-Arbetare*, 1894); Headquarters: Stockholm, Sweden; Secretary: Miss Ellen Palmstierna, Birga Jarlsgatan 14.

Sweden; Holiness Union (*Helgeseförbundet*, 1890); Secretary: Rev. A. Kihlstedt, Kumla (auxiliary to CIM).

Swedish: Baptist Missionary Society (*Sallskapet Svenska Baptist Missionen*, 1889); Headquarters: Stockholm, Sweden; Secretary: Rev. Wilhelm Lindbloom Walhallavagen 57, Stockholm; Organ: ———.

Swedish; Church Mission (*Svenska Kirkans Missionstyrelse*, 1874); Headquarters: Upsala, Sweden; Secretary: Rev. Gudmar Hogner; Organ: *Missionstidning*. Women's Missionary Society, auxiliary to the above.

Swedish Evangelical Mission Covenant of America (1885) Headquarters: North Park College, Chicago, Ill.; Secretary: Prof. D. Nyvall.

Swedish Missionary Union (*Svenska Missionsförbundets*, 1879); Headquarters: Stockholm; Secretary: Rev. E. J. Eckman, Hollandaregatan 27.

Swedish Mission in China (*Svenska Missionen i Kina*, 1887); Secretary; Rev. Josef Holmgren, Lastmakaregatan 30, Stockholm, Sweden (associated with CIM).

Switzerland: Basel Evangelical Missionary Society (*Evangelische Missionsgesellschaft zu Basel*, 1815); Headquarters: Basel, Switzerland; President: Pfarrer Ernest Miescher; Inspector: Th. Oehler; Organ: *Der Evangelische Heidenbote*, monthly.

Switzerland; St. Chrischona Pilgrim Mission (*Pilger-*

Mission auf St. Chrischona, 1840 and 1895); Headquarters: St. Chrischona, Basel; Inspector: Rev. C. H. Rappard (auxiliary to China Inland Mission); Organ: *Der Glaubensbote*, monthly.

Switzerland; Romande Missionary Society (*Mission Romande, oeuvre d'evangelisation chez les paiens, dirigée par les Eglises Libres de Vaud, Neuchatel et Genève*, 1875); Headquarters: Lausanne, Switzerland; Secretary: Rev. A. Grandjean, Chemin des Cédres, Lausanne, Switzerland; Organ: *Bulletin*.

Syrian Schools Soc., British. See British Syr. Schools Soc.

Tabeetha Mission, Jaffa (1863); Secretary: Miss E. Walker Arnott, 24 St. Bernard's Crescent, Edinburgh.

Trinidad; Canadian Pres. Mission to E. Indians in. See Canadian Pres., etc.

Unitarian Association, American. See American Unitarian Association.

Unitarian Assoc., British and Foreign (1825); Headquarters: Essex Hall, Essex Street, Strand, London, W. C., England; Secretary: Rev. W. Copeland Bowie.

United Brethren in Christ; Home, Frontier and Foreign Missionary Society of the (1853); Headquarters: Cor. Main and Fourth Streets, Dayton, Ohio; Secretaries: Rev. Wm. Bell, Rev. C. Whitney; Treasurer: Rev. W. McKee; Organ: *The Searchlight*.

Unity of Brethren (Brüder Unität). See Moravian Missions.

United Danish Evang. Lutheran Church in America. See Danish Ev. Luth., etc.

United Evangelical Church Missionary Society (1899); Headquarters: Myerstown, Pa.; Secretary: Rev. A. M. Sampsel, Reading, Pa.; Treasurer: ——; Organ: ——. Woman's Missionary Society; Headquarters: ——; Secretary: Mrs. S. P. Remer, 628 Market Street, Williamsport, Pa.; Treasurer: Mrs. W. E. Detuhler, Carlisle, Pa.; Organ: *Missionary Tidings* (of Harrisburg, Pa.).

United Free Church of Scotland For. Mission Board. See Scotland; United Free Church.

United Methodist Free Ch., Home and Foreign Miss. (1857); Secretary: Rev. H. T. Chapman, 4 Newton Grove, Leeds, England.

United Presbyterian Church of North America (1859); Board of Foreign Missions of the: Headquarters: Witherspoon Building, Philadelphia, Pa.; Secretary: Rev. Chas. R. Watson; Treasurer: Mr. R. L. Latimer; Organ: *United Presbyterian Church Record*. Woman's General Missionary Society; Secretaries: Mrs. S. Yourd, Carnegie, Pa.; Mrs. W. J. Reid, Pittsburg, Pa.; Mrs. E. M. Hill, Pittsburg, Pa.; Treasurer: Miss E. J. Sloan, 5150 Liberty Avenue, Pittsburg, Pa.; Organ: *Women's Missionary Magazine*.

United Society for Christian Endeavor (1885); Headquarters: Tremont Temple, Boston, Mass.

Universalist Gen. Convention (1890); Secretary: Rev. G. L. Demarest, Manchester, N. H.

Universities Mission to Central Africa (1858); Headquarters: 9 Dartmouth Street, London, S. W., England; Secretary: Rev. Duncan Travers.

Utrecht Mission Union. See Netherlands.

Victorian Baptist Foreign Mission (1885); Secretary: Rev. J. H. Goble, Footscray, Melbourne, Victoria, Australia.

Welsh Calvinistic Methodists' Foreign Missions (1840); Headquarters: 10 Pearl Buildings, St. John's Lane, Liverpool, England; Secretary: Rev. R. J. Williams.

Wesleyan, Central China Lay Mission. See Central China.

Wesleyan Methodist Connection of America; Missionary Society of the (1890); Headquarters: 316 E. Onondaga Street, Syracuse, N. Y.; Secretary: Rev. W. H. Kennedy.

Wesleyan Methodist Missionary Society (1813); Headquarters: Wesleyan Miss. House, 17 Bishopsgate Street, Within, London, E. C., England; Secretary: Rev. W. H. Findlay; Organ: *The Foreign Field*, monthly. Woman's auxiliary of the W.M.S.; Hon. Foreign Secretary; Mrs. Wiseman, 25 Queens Ave., Muswell Hill, London N.; Home Secretary, Miss A. M. Hellier, 20 Gloucester Road, Finsbury Park, London, N., England.

West Indies; Eastern Annual Conference, Wesleyan Methodist Missions; Secretary: Rev. E. Donald Jones, Port of Spain, Trinidad.

West Indies; Wesleyan Methodist Home and Foreign Missionary Society of the Western Annual Conference (1884); Secretary: Rev. John A. McIntosh, Wesley House, Duncans, Jamaica.

Woman's Union Missionary Society of America for Heathen Lands (1860); Headquarters: 67 Bible House, New York; Secretary: Miss S. D. Doremus; Assistant Treasurers: Miss M. S. Stone, Miss E. B. Stone; Organ: *Missionary Link*.

Young Men's Christian Association; International Committee of the (1889); Headquarters: 3 West 29th Street, New York; Secretaries: Rev. Richard C. Morse, Mr. H . A . Black; Organ: *Association Men*.

Young Men's Christian Assoc., Colonial and International Dep't of Eng. National Council of (1890); W. H. Mills, Esq., Exeter Hall, Strand, London, W. C., England.

Young Men's Christian Assoc., Students' Theol. Section of, Mr. S. Earl Taylor, 3 West 29th Street, New York.

Young Men's For. Miss. Society (1877); Mr. Edwin A. Page, Y. M. C. A., Needlers Alley, Birmingham, England.

Young People's Missionary Movement; Headquarters: 156 Fifth Ave., New York City; Secretary: Charles V. Vickery.

Y. P. S. C. Endeavor. See United Soc. Chr. Endeavor.

Young Women's Christian Assoc., American Dep't (1894); Headquarters: 74 W. 124th Street, New York; Secretary: Miss R. F. Morse.

Young Woman's Christian Assoc., World's; Miss Ethel Stevenson, 26 George Street, Hanover Square, London, W., England.

Zambesi Industrial Mission (1892); Headquarters: 6 Colonial Avenue, Minories, London, England; Secretary: Mr. Robert Caldwell.

Zenana Bible and Medical Mission (1852); Headquarters: 2 Adelphi Terrace, Strand, London, W. C., England; Secretaries: Rev. A. R. Cavalier, Mrs. Firth.

Zenana Missionary Society. See Church of England Zenana Miss. Society.

APPENDIX II

CHRONOLOGICAL TABLE OF THE EXTENSION OF PROTESTANT MISSIONS FROM THE TIME OF CAREY

NOTE.—There is not a little confusion of dates in the records. It is not always practicable to distinguish between the date when a mission was decided upon, and that when the missionaries started, or actually commenced the work. The object of this table is not so much scientific accuracy as the attainment of a bird's-eye perspective of the stages by which the missionary enterprise of the Church has reached out to cover the earth. Extension from one district to another in the same country is not noted unless some special feature seems to call for mention.

Year	Location	Society
1793	India, Serampore	BMS
	New South Wales	SPG
1796	Pacific Islands, Tahiti	LMS
1789	South Africa, Zulus	LMS
	India, Calcutta	LMS
1804	West Africa, Sierra Leone	CMS
1806	Ceylon	BMS
1807	China, Hongkong	LMS
1813	Java	Netherlands MS
	West Indies	BMS
	India, Calcutta	CMS
	India, Bombay	ABCFM
	Burma	ABMU
1814	South Africa, Zulus	WMS
	New Zealand	CMS
	Ceylon	CMS
1815	Levant, Malta	CMS
	Levant, Malta	LMS
1816	India, Bengal	Gen. Baptist (now) BMS
	Ceylon	ABCFM
1817	India, Bengal	WMS
1818	Ceylon	CMS
	Madagascar	LMS
1819	Syria	ABCFM
	Egypt	CMS
	Hawaiian Islands	ABCFM
1820	West Indies	ME
	South Africa, Cape Colony	SPG
1821	India, Calcutta	SPG
	South Africa, Zulus	Scottish M. S. (now) UFS
	West Africa, Liberia	ABMU
1822	India, Calcutta	Scottish M. S. (now) UFS
	New Zealand	WMS
1827	West Africa, Liberia	B
1828	Greece	ABCFM
	Siam	LMS
1829	Persia	Basel
	India, Bombay	CSFM
	South Africa, Zulus	Rhen.
	South Africa, Zulus	P
1830	China, Canton	ABCFM
	West Africa, Liberia	PE
	East Africa, Abyssinia	CMS
	Greece	PE
1831	Turkey, Constantinople	ABCFM
1832	Mauritius	SPG
1833	China, through Bangkok	ABMU
	India, Northwest Provinces	PN
	Persia	ABCFM
	West Africa, Liberia	ME
1834	India, Madras	B
	Siam	ABCFM
	Java	Rhen.
	South Africa, Zulus	ABCFM
	South Africa, Bechuanas	Ber.
1835	China, Shanghai	PE
	India, Bengal	Free Bapt.
	West Africa, Liberia	PN
	West Indies, Trinidad, Scottish M. S. (now)	UFS
	Australia	WMS
1836	Borneo	RCA
	India, Telugus	ABMU
	India, North	PB
	South America, Buenos Aires	ME
1837	India, Northwest Provinces	RP
	Borneo	SPG
1838	Malaysia	PN
1839	New Hebrides	LMS
1840	India, Central Provinces	Luth. MS., U. S. A.
	Madras	Leipz.
	Siam	PN
	New Zealand	SPG
1841	India, Bombay	PCI
	India, North	WCM
	New Hebrides	LMS
1842	China, Shanghai	CMS
	China, Amoy	RCA
	Ceylon	SPG
	Borneo	Rhen.
	New Hebrides	PCC
1843	South Africa, Zulus	Norweg.
	India, Telugus	N. Ger.
1844	China, Canton	PN
	East African Coast	CMS
	India, Central	GM
	South America, Tierra del Fuego	SAMS
1845	China, Shanghai	CMS
	Tahiti	P
1846	China, Canton	Rhen.
	West Africa, Gold Coast	UFS
1847	China, Fuchau	ME
	China, Amoy	PCE
	China, Canton	Ber.
	China, Canton	SBC
	West Africa, Angola	No. Ger.
	West Africa, Congo	SBC
	Melanesia	MM
1848	China, Shanghai	MES
	Malaysia, Singapore	SPG
1849	Central America, Mosquito Coast	Mor.
	Syria	RP
1850	India, Punjab	CMS
1851	China, Canton	WMS
	Borneo	SPG
1852	Palestine	JU
	Micronesia	ABCFM
1853	India, Arcot	RCA
1854	Egypt	UP
1855	India, N. W. Province	ME
	India, N. W. Province	UP
	Ladakh (Little Tibet)	Mor.
	West Africa, Liberia	UB
1856	Dutch East Indies	Erm.
	Madagascar	CMS
	South America, Colombia	PN
1857	Bulgaria	ME
	West Africa, Nigeria	CMS
1858	Bulgaria	ABCFM
1859	China, Shantung	BMS
	Japan	PE
	Japan	RCA
	Japan	PN
	Burma	SPG
	New Zealand	Mor.
1860	Japan	FB
	West Africa, Liberia	ELGS
1861	Siam	SPG
	India, Tamils	DM
	Straits Settlements	SPG
	East Africa, Mombasa	Utr
	West Indies, Haiti	PE
1862	India, Bengal	PCE

Year	Location	Society
1862	Sumatra	Rhen.
	Australasia	SPG
	West Africa, Senegambia	P
1863	China, Manchuria	UFS
	China, Peking	SPG
	Siam, Laos	PN
	India, Calcutta	WU
	Java	Neth
	Tahiti	P
1864	Dutch East Indies	Utr
	Madagascar	SPG
	China, Che-kiang	UMFC
1865	China	CIM
	Japan	PCE
	Formosa	PCE
	South Africa, Zulus	Swed.M
1866	India, N. W. Provinces	FFMA
	Straits Settlements	PB
1867	China, Canton	PS
	China, Peking	ME
	India, Central Provinces	GES
	Madagascar	FFMA
	Madagascar	Nor.
1868	India, Telugus	BOQ
	German Southwest Africa	FMS
1869	China, Manchuria	PCI
	Japan	ABCFM
	Japan	CMS
	India, Central Provinces	ELGC
	India, North	Mission to Lepers
	Persia, Ispahan	CMS
	Syria	FFMA
	South America, Brazil	PS
1870	South Africa, Cape Colony	PMMS
	Mongolia	LMS
	West Indies, Trinidad	PCC
	Mexico	PE
1871	Japan	MCC
	Japan	WU
	New Guinea	LMS
	Mexico	AFFM
1872	Japan	ABMU
	Japan	ME
	Formosa	PCC
	West Indies	MES
	Mexico	ABCFM
	Mexico	PN
1873	Japan	SPG
	Mexico	ME
	Mexico	MES
1874	New Guinea	LMS
	British East Africa	CMS
	British Central Africa	UFS
	Congo Free State	Swed. N
	Mexico	PS
	China, Hongkong	SPG
	Turkey (Greeks)	PS
1875	Burma	CIM
	Siam	PCE
	South Africa, Zulus	MR
1876	Japan	EA
	West Indies	FCMS
	South America, Brazil	MES
1877	India, Madras	PCC
	Japan	CP
	Turkey	SDA
	British Central Africa	LMS
1878	West Africa, Liberia	AME
	Congo Free State	RBMU
1879	Japan	Reformed (German) U.S.
	Turkey	FCMS
	Congo Free State	BMS
1880	Japan	MP
	Portuguese West Africa, Benguella	ABCFM
	Mexico	SBC
	Mexico	Associate Reform (South)
1881	China, Shanghai	WU
	Algeria	NAM
	Congo Free State, Garenganze	PB
	West Indies	AFFM
1882	China, Hongkong	Ber.
	India, Central Provinces	FCMS
	Java	Neukirchen Inst.
	Central America, Guatemala	PN
	South America, Brazil	SBC
1883	Japan	FCMS
	Congo Free State	ABMU
	East Equatorial Africa	ABCFM
1884	India, Central Provinces	Breklum MS
	Korea	PN
1884	Congo Free State	CA
1885	India	UMFC
	Siam	ME
	China	UB
	Korea	ME
	Japan	PS
	Japan	AFFM
	Japan	GES
	Japan	MES
	South Africa, Cape Colony	UMFC
	South America	PCC
	New Guinea	Neuendettelsau
1886	China	AFFM
	China	FCMS
	Japan	MES
	Persia, Nestorians	Archbishop's Mission
	Arabia, Aden	UFS
	Central America	SDA
	German East Africa	German E. Africa Soc.
1887	Japan	CC
	New Guinea	Rhen.
	South America	SDA
1888	China, Honan	PCC
	Japan	PB
	Mexico	CP
	South America, Paraguay	SAMS
1889	China	UB
	India, Central Provinces	CA
	Korea	SPG
	Malaysia	ME
	West Africa, Gabun	P
1890	China	AFFM
	China, Hunan	CA
	Japan	SBC
	Japan	Universalist
	Turkey, Syria	CA
	Arabia, Bahrein	RCA
	Mexico	PB
	Central America	Cent. America Miss. Soc.
	South America, Brazil	PE
1891	China	MCC
	China	Miss. to Lepers
	Congo Free State	PS
1892	Japan	ELGS
	Japan	Canada Ch. of Eng.
	Korea	PS
	Madagascar	Norwegian Luth. (U.S.)
	German East Africa	Leipz.
1893	Japan	Miss. to Lepers
	Korea	PCC
	India	SDA
1894	Japan	CA
	Mexico	SDA
	Central America	West Indies Wesleyans
1895	India	German Bapt. Breth
	Japan	UB
	Japan	UMFC
	Syria	PCC
	South America	RBMU
1896	China	DMS
	Japan	SDA
	Korea	MES
	India	AFFM
	Ceylon	AFFM
	Madagascar	ME
	Madagascar	P
1897	China	RP
	Mexico	FCMS
1898	China	CP
	India	ECS
	Burma	Leipz.
	West Indies	UB
	South America	BOQ
1899	Philippines	PN
	Porto Rico, W. I.	PN
	Porto Rico, W. I.	PS
	Porto Rico, W. I.	AMA
	Porto Rico, W. I.	FCMS
	Porto Rico, W. I.	ELGC
1900	China	MP
	China	UE
	Philippines	ABMU
	Philippines	ME
	Philippines	PB
	Philippines	SDA
	Philippines	Miss. to Lepers
1901	Philippines	UB
	China North	FMS
	West Indies	CC
1902	Philippines	ABCFM

APPENDIX III

LIST OF BIBLE VERSIONS

LANGUAGE DIALECT	LOCALITY	SOURCE OF TRANSLATION
AIMARA	Bolivia, S. America	BFBS
AINU	Japan	BFBS
AKKAWAY	Dutch Guiana, South America.	SPCK
AKRA, or GA.	Basin of Volta, W. Africa.	BFBS
ALBANIAN:	Albania, Turkey	
1. Tosk, or S.		BFBS
2. Gheg, or N.		BFBS
ALIEUT	Aleutian Is., Alaska	RBS
ALIFUR	Celebes Island	Neth. BS
AMHARIC	Abyssinia	BFBS
AMOY DIALECT	Fo-kien, China	ABS
ANEITYUM ISLAND	New Hebrides	BFBS
ANIWA ISLAND	New Hebrides	BFBS
ANNAM	Indo-China	BFBS
API	New Hebrides	BFBS
1. Baki		
2. Bieri		
3. Lævo		
4. Tasiko		
ARABIC:	Turkey, Syria	
1. Standard	Mesopotamia, Arabia Egypt, Tripoli, Algeria, Morocco, Zanzibar,	ABS, BFBS
2. Malta	Maltese	
ARAPAHOE	U.S.A.	ABS
ARAWAK	S. America	ABS
	Dutch Guiana	SPCK
ARMENIAN:		
1. Ancient		OV
2. Ararat (E.)	Trans-Caucasia	BFBS
3. Modern (W.)	Turkey (Asia Minor)	BFBS, ABS
ASHANTI:	W. Africa,	
1. Fanti	Cape Coast Castle Colony	BFBS
2. Akwapem	Ashanti	BTS, BFBS
ASSAMESE	Assam	BTS, BFBS
AZERBIJAN	See Turkish.	
BADAGA	Mysore, S. India	BFBS
BALI	Java	Neth. BS
BALUCHI	Baluchistan	BFBS
BASHKIR	See Turkish.	
BASQUE:	France, Spain.	
1. French	Prov. of Pyrenees (France)	BFBS
2. Spanish	Prov. of Biscay	BFBS
3. Guipuscoa	Prov. of Guipuscoa	BFBS
BATTA:		
1. Toba	Sumatra	Neth. BS, BFBS
2. Mandailing		BFBS
Beaver	Canada, Athabasca	BFBS, SPCK
BENGA	W. Africa	ABS
BENGALI:	Gabun Colony	
1. Standard	Bengal, India	1. Serampur, 2. BFBS
2. Mohammedan		
BERBER	Algeria	BFBS
BERBER	Rifian	BFBS
BICOLAN	Philippine Islands	BFBS
BILIN, or BOGOS	Abyssinia	BFBS
BLACKFOOT	Canada, Prov. Alberta	BFBS
BOHEMIAN, or CZECH	Austria, Bohemia	OV
BONDEI	German East Africa, Usambara	BFBS
BRETON	France, Brittany	BFBS
BUGI	Celebes Island	Neth. BS, BFBS
BULGARIAN	Turkey in Europe, Bulgaria	BFBS, ABS
BULLOM	Sierra Leone, W. Africa	BFBS

LANGUAGE DIALECT	LOCALITY	SOURCE OF TRANSLATION
BUNDA, or MBUNDA, or KI-MBUNDA	Angola, Africa	BFBS
BURMESE	Burma, Brit. India	ABMU
CAKCHIQUEL	Central America	BFBS
CAMBODIAN	Cochin China	BFBS, ABS
CHAGGA	German E. Africa	BFBS
CHAMBA	Punjab, India	BFBS
CHAU-CHAU, or SWATAU DIALECT	Kwang-tung, China	BFBS
CHEREMISI	Russia (European), Kazan and Simvirsk	RBS
CHEROKEE	United States	ABS
CHIPEWAN	Canada, Athabasca	BFBS
CHOCTAW	U. S. America	ABS
CHUANA	S. Africa, Bechuanaland and Matabeleland	BFBS
CHUVASH	Russia (European), Kazan, Nijni-Novge, and Orenburg	RBS
CREE:		
1. E., or Hudson Bay	Canada	BFBS
2. W., or Moosonee	Hudson Bay Ter.	BFBS
DAKOTA, or SIOUX	U. S. America	ABS
DELAWARE	U. S. America	ABS
DIKELE	See Kele.	
DOBU	Brit. New Guinea	BFBS
DUALLA	Kamerun, W. Africa	BTS
DUKE OF YORK'S ISLAND	Bismarck Archipelago	WMS
DUTCH	Holland and Cape of Good Hope Col.	OV
DYAK:		
1. Standard	Island of Borneo	Neth. BS
2. Sea		SPCK
EBON ISLAND	Marshall Islands	ABS
EFIK	Old Calabar, W.Africa	NBS
ENGLISH:	Gt. Brit. and Ire., and	
1. Standard	Brit. Subject-Dominions	OV
	U. S. of N. America	OV
2. Negro of Surinam	West Indies	BFBS
EROMANGA	New Hebrides	BFBS
ESKIMO:	Greenland,	DBS
1. Greenland	Labrador, and Provs.	BFBS
2. Labrador	of Hudson Bay	BFBS
3. Hudson Bay.		
ESTHONIAN	Russia (European),	
1. Dorpat, or Werro	Provs. Esthonia	BFBS
2. Reval	and Livonia	OV
ETHIOPIC, or GIZ	Abyssinia	OV
EWE:		BFBS
1. Anlo	Dahomey, W. Africa	BFBS
2. Popo		
FALASHA-KARA (Di. of Agau)	Abyssinia (Jews)	BFBS
FANG	Gabun, W. Africa	BFBS
FANTI	See Ashanti	
FANTING	Ambrym, New Hebrides	BFBS
FATÉ:		
1. Erakar	New Hebrides	BFBS
2. Havannah Har.		
FIJIAN	Fiji Islands	BFBS
FINN	Finland, Russia (European)	OV
FIOTI	Congo F. S.	BFBS
FLEMISH	Belgium	OV
FLORIDA ISLAND	Solomon Islands	SPCK
FORMOSA	Formosa (Japan)	PCC
FRENCH:	France, French Cols.	
1. Standard	Channel Isl.	Can-OV
2. Vaudois	ada, Belgium, Switzerland (French Cantons), Italy (Submontane Prov.)	BFBS
3. Provençal		
4. Mauritius	Mauritius Isl.	BFBS

LANGUAGE DIALECT	LOCALITY	SOURCE OF TRANSLATION
FRIS.	Holland	BFBS
FU-CHAU DIALECT	Fo-kien, China	BFBS
FUTUNA	New Hebrides	BFBS
GAELIC	Highlands of Scotland	OV
GALLA:	E. Africa,	
1. Shoa	Gallaland	} BFBS
2. Ittu		
3. Bararetta		
GALWA	French Congo, W. Africa	BFBS
GANDA	Uganda, Africa	BFBS
GARO	Assam	{ BTS / BFBS }
GEORGIAN	Russia (Asia) Trans-Caucasia	OV
GERMAN:	Germany, Austria,	
1. Standard	Switzerland, Russia,	
2. Judæo—German (Yiddish)	France	OV
		BFBS
GILBERT ISLANDS	Micronesia	ABS
GIRYAMA	East Africa	BFBS
GITANO, or SPANISH GYPSY	Spain	BFBS
GOGO	Ugogo, E. Africa	BFBS
GOND	Cent. Provs., India	BFBS
GREBO	Liberia, Africa	ABS
GREEK:		
1. Ancient		OV
2. Modern, or RomaicGreece, Turkey		BFBS
GUARANI	Paraguay, S. America	BFBS
GUJARATI:		
1. Standard	Bombay, India	{ BFBS / BFBS }
2. Parsee		
HAI-NAN	Hai-nan, China	BFBS
HAKKA	Kwang-tung, China	BFBS
HAUSA	Upper Basin of the Niger, W. Africa	BFBS
HAWAIIAN	Sandwich Islands	ABS
HEBREW		OV
HERERO	German East Africa	BFBS
HINDI:	North India	
1. Standard		{ BFBS / BMS }
2. Hindustani, or Urdu		BFBS
3. Dakhani		BFBS
4. Kumaoni, or Pahari		BFBS
5. Marwari, or Central		ABS
6. Guhrwali		BFBS
HING-HWA	China	ABS
HYDAH	Brit. Columbia, Queen Charlotte Island	CMS
IBO	S. Nigeria, W. Africa	BFBS
1. Lower		
2. Upper		
ICELANDIC:		
1. Standard	Iceland	} DBS
2. Faroe	Faroe Island	
IDZO	S. Nigeria, W. Africa	CMS
IGARA	S. Nigeria, W. Africa	CMS
I'GBIRA	S. Nigeria, W. Africa	BFBS
IJO, see IDZO		
ILOCANO	Philippine Islands	ABS
IRISH, or ERSE	Ireland	OV
IROQUOIS	N. America, Quebec and Ontario	BFBS
ISABEL, or BOGOTU ISLAND	Solomon Islands	SPCK
ITALIAN:	Italy; the Levant;	
1. Standard	Ionian Islands; Island of Malta; Adriatic Provs.(Aus.)	OV
2. Piedmont	Italian Cantons (Switzerland)	BFBS
JAGHATAI	See Turkish	
JAPANESE	Japan	{ ABS / BFBS / NBS }
JATKI, see PUNJABI		
JAVANESE	Java	{ Neth.BS / BFBS }
JOLOF	Senegambia, W. Africa	BFBS
KABYLI	Algeria	{ BFBS / Ba. BS }
KAFIR, or XOSA	Kaffraria, S. Africa	
KAGURU	Usagara, German EastAfrica	BFBS
KANARESE	Mysore, S. India	BFBS
KARA-KIRGHIZ	See Turkish	
KAREL	Russia (Asia), Prov. of Tver	RBS
KAREN:	Burma, Brit. India	{ ABMU / ABMU / ABMU }
1. Bghai		
2. Sgau		
3. Pwo		
KARIB	Dutch Guiana, S. Am. Cent. America	Edin.
		BFBS
KARSHAN	Mesopotamia	BFBS
KASHGAR, TURKISH	See Turkish	
KASHMIRI	Kashmir, N. India	BFBS
KATCHI, see SINDHI		
KAZAK-KIRGHIZ	See Turkish	
KAZAN-TURKISH	See Turkish	
KELE	Gabun, W. Africa	ABS
KHASI	Assam	BFBS
KIKUYN	British E. Africa	BFBS
KIN-HWA DIALECT	Prov. Che-iang, China	BFBS
KOI	Madras, India	BFBS
KOL	Chota Nagpur, India	BFBS
KONGO	Kongo Free State, Africa	BMS
KOPTIC	Egypt	OV
KORANKO	Sierra Leone	BFBS
KOREAN	Korea	{ ABS / BFBS }
KROAT	Austria Provs. Kroatia and Dalmatia	BFBS
KUANYAMAN	German S. W. Africa (Ovambo)	BFBS
KUMUKI-TURKISH	See Turkish	
KURDISH	Turkey (Asia), Persia	{ BFBS / ABS }
KUSAIAN	Strong Island, Micronesia	ABS
KWAGUTL	Brit. Columbia, Vancouver Island	BFBS
KWANG-TUNG, or CANTON DIALECT	Kwang-tung, China	{ BFBS / ABS / PN / ABMU }
LAOS	Siam	
LAPP:		
1. Norse, or Quan.	Lapland, Norway, and	
2. Russian	Sweden	
3. Swedish		
LATIN	Rom. Cath. Ch.	OV
LEPCHA	Sikkim, Brit. India	BTS
LETT	N. Russia (Europe), Livonia and Courland	OV
LIFU	Loyalty Islands	BFBS
LITHUANIAN	Russia, Germany, Baltic Prov.	OV, RBS
1. Standard		
2. Samoghit, or Zemait		RBS
LIVONIAN	Prov. W. Courland, Russia (Europe)	BFBS
LOLO	Congo Free State	BFBS
LUCHU	Luchu Islands, Japan	{ SPCK / BFBS }
LUSHAI	Assam	BFBS
MACASSAR	Celebes Island	Neth.BS
MADURESE	Madura, Dutch E. Indies	BFBS
MAFUR	New Guinea	Neth.BS
MAGHADI	Prov. Behar, India	BFBS
MAGYAR, or HUNGARIAN	Hungary	OV
MAKUA	Portuguese East Africa	UMS
MALAGASI	Madagascar	BFBS
MALAY:		
1. Standard	Pen. of Malacca,	OV
2. Low Malay, or Surabaya	Sumatra	BFBS
MALAYALAM	Travancore, India	BFBS
MALISEET	New Brunswick, Can	BFBS
MALLIKOLLO ISLAND	New Hebrides	BFBS
MALO	New Hebrides	BFBS
MALTO, PAHARI, or RAJMAHALI, or MALER	Hill tribes of Rajmahal, Bengal, India	BFBS
MAMBWE	N. E. Rhodesia, Africa	BFBS
MANCHU	Manchuria, N. China	BFBS
MANDARI, or KOL	Cent. Provs., India	BFBS
MANDARIN:		
1. N., or Peking	China	{ BFBS / ABS }
2. S., or Nanking		
MANDÉ, or MANDINGO	Gambia, W. Africa	{ BFBS / ABS }
MANIPUR	Cent. Provs., India	BFBS
MANX	Isle of Man, Gt. Britain	OV
MAORI	New Zealand	BFBS
MARATHI:		
1. Standard	Bombay, India	{ ABS / BFBS }
2. Konkani		
MARÉ	Loyalty Islands	BFBS
MARQUESAN	Marquesas Islands	BFBS
MARWARI, see HINDI		
MASHONA	So. Africa	BFBS
MAYA	Yucatan, Cent. Amer.	BFBS

Appendix III — THE ENCYCLOPEDIA OF MISSIONS

LANGUAGE DIALECT	LOCALITY	SOURCE OF TRANSLATION
MBUNDU, see BUNDU and UMBUNDU		
MENDÉ	Sierra Leone, W. Africa	BFBS
MER	Murray Islands, New Guinea	BFBS
MEXICAN, or AZTEC	Mexico	BFBS
MIK-MAK:		
1. Standard	Nova Scotia	BFBS
2. Abenaqui	N. America	ABS
MOHAWK	U. S. America	BFBS
MON, or PEGU	Burma, Brit. India	BFBS
MONGOL:	Russia (Europe),	
1. Literary	Basin of Volga;	
2. N. (Buriat)	Russia (Asia),	
3. S. (Kalkhas)	China,	
4. W. Kalmuk	Provs. Mongolia	BFBS
MORDWIN:	Provs. of Nijni-Nov-	
1. Erza	gorod and Kazan,	
2. Moksha	Russia (Europe),	RBS
MORTLOCK ISLAND	Mortlock Island	ABS
MOSQUITO	Mosquito Coast, Nicaragua	Mor.
MOTA ISLAND	Banks Islands	BFBS
MOTU	New Guinea	BFBS
MUSKOKI, or CREEK	U. S. America	ABS
NAHUATL	Mexico	ABS
NAMA, or HOTTENTOT	S. Africa, Cape Colony and Namaqualand	BFBS
NARRINYERI	S. Australia	BFBS
NEPALI	Nepal, Brit. India	BFBS
NEW BRITAIN ISLAND	Bismarck Archipelago	BFBS
NEW GUINEA, SOUTH CAPE DIALECT	New Guinea	BFBS
NEZ PERCES, or SAHAPTIN	U. S. America	ABS
NGUNA ISLAND	New Hebrides	BFBS
NIAS	Nias Island	BFBS
NICOBAR	Nicobar Island, Brit. India	BFBS
NING-PO DIALECT	Che-kiang, China	BFBS
NISHKAH	British Columbia	CMS
NIUE	Savage Island	BFBS
NKONDI	Nyasaland	BFBS
NOGAI-TURKISH	See Turkish.	
NOGOGU	New Hebrides	BFBS
NORWEGO-DANISH	Norway and Denmark	OV
NUBIAN	Sudan, Nubia	BFBS
NUPE	Nigeria, W. Africa	BFBS
NYAMWEZI	German E. Africa	BFBS
NYANJA	Nyasaland, Africa	NBS
NYIKA	E. Africa, Wa-Nyika Tribe	BFBS
NYORO	Uganda Protectorate	BFBS
OJIBWA, or CHIPPEWA	Canada W. of Lake Superior and U. S. A.	ABS / SPCK / BFBS
OSSET	Prov. Cis-Caucasia, S. Russia (Asia)	RBS
OSTYAK	Provs. Tobolsk and Tomsk, Russia (Asia)	BFBS
OVAMBO	German S. W. Africa	BFBS
PAHOUIN (Fang)	French Congo, W. Africa	BFBS
PALI	Ceylon	BFBS
PALITYAN (Paulician)	Hungary	NBS
PAMPANGAN	Philippine Islands	ABS
PANAICTI	New Guinea	BFBS
PANGASINAN	Philippine Islands	BFBS
PASTU	Afghanistan	BFBS / BVS
PEDI	Transvaal, S. Africa	BFBS
PERM	Provs. Perm and Archangel, Russia, (Europe)	RBS
PERSIAN	Persia; Afghanistan	OV
PIEDMONTESE. See ITALIAN.		
POKOMO	British East Africa	BFBS
POLE	Polish Provinces of Russia, Germany and Austria	OV
PONAPÉ	Caroline Islands	ABS
PONGWÉ	Gabun, W. Africa	ABS
POPO. See DAHOMEY.		
PORTUGUESE:		
1. Standard	Portugal; Brazil;	OV
2. Indian	Ceylon	BFBS
PUNJABI, or SIKH	Punjab, India	
1. Standard		
2. Dogri		
3. Chambali		BFBS
4. Multani, or Jatki		
QUECHUA	Peru, S. America	ABS
QUICHE	Central America	BFBS
RAROTONGAN	Hervey Islands	BFBS

LANGUAGE DIALECT	LOCALITY	SOURCE OF TRANSLATION
ROMANSCH, or LADIN	Switzerland, Engadine.	
1. Upper		OV
2. Lower		
3. Oberland		Coire BS
RONGA	Portuguese E. Africa	BFBS
ROTUMAN	Rotuma Island	BFBS
ROUMAN:	Roumania:	
1. Standard	Austria, Hungary	BFBS
2. Macedon	Transylvania Bukowina	BFBS
RUSSIAN	Russia (Europe)	OV
RUTHENIAN	N. Russia (Europe), Austria, Galiciakowina, Transylvania	OV
SAIBAI ISLAND	N. Guinea, Torres Sts.	BFBS
SAMBARA	Ger. E. Africa	BFBS
SAMOAN	Samoa Islands	BFBS
SAMOGITIAN. See LITHUANIAN.		
SANGIR ISLAND	Dutch E. Indies	BFBS
SANSKRIT	India	BTS
SANTAL	Santalia, Bengal, India	BFBS
SENA	Port. E. Africa	BFBS
SENECA	U. S. America	ABS
SERVIAN	Austria, Hungary, Bosnia, Herzegovina Servia; Montenegro	BFBS
SHAN	Indo-China, Shan States	BTS
SHANG-HAI DIALECT	Kiang-su, China	BFBS
SHEETSWA	Port. East Africa	ABS
SHILHA, RIFF	Morocco	BFBS
SHIMSHIAN	British Columbia	CMS
SIAMESE	Siam	ABS
SINDHI:	Prov. of Sindh, India	BFBS
1. Standard		
2. Katchi		BFBS
SINHALESE	Ceylon	BFBS
SLAVE	Canada, Mackenzie River	BFBS
SLAVONIC	Greek Church, Russia, Austria Northern Balkan Peninsula	OV
SLOVAK	Austria-Hungary	BFBS
SLOVEN	Austria, Provs. Karniola and Karinthia	BFBS
SOGA	Uganda Protectorate	BFBS
SPANISH:	Spain, Cent. and So.	
1. Standard	America (except Brazil); W. Indies	OV
2. Catalan		BFBS
3. Judæo-Spanish		BFBS
4. Curaçoan		Neth.B
SU-CHAU DIALECT	Kiang-su, China	BFBS
SUKUMA	Ger. E. Africa	BFBS
SUNDANESE	Java	Neth.B
SUSU	Senegambia, W. Africa	SPCK
SUTO	Basutoland, So. Africa	BFBS
SWAHILI	E. Africa	BFBS
SWEDISH	Sweden	OV
SYRIAC:		
1. Peshito, or Ancient	Syria	OV
2. Syro-Chaldaic, or Modern	Persia	ABS
SYRYIN, or ZIR	Vologda, Russia (Europe)	RPS
TABILI	Rhodesia	BFBS
TAGALOG	Philippine Islands	BFBS
TAHITAN	Society Islands	BFBS
TAMIL	India, Madras, Ceylon	BFBS / DBS
TANNA-KWAMERA	Tanna, New Hebrides	BFBS
TANNA-WEASISI	Tanna, New Hebrides	BFBS
TAVARA	New Guinea	BFBS
TEKE	Congo Free State, W. Africa	ABMU
TELUGU	Madras, India	BFBS
TEMNE	Sierra Leone, W. Africa	BFBS
TIBETAN	Tibet, Lahul, N. India	BFBS
TIGRE	E. Abyssinia	BFBS
TINNE	Hudson Bay, Canada	BFBS
TOARIPI	New Guinea	BFBS
TODA	S. India	BFBS
TONGA	Portuguese E. Africa and North Transvaal	SPCK
TONGAN	Tonga, or Friendly Is.	BFBS
TUDUKH	Alaska	BFBS
TULU	Madras, India	BFBS
TURKISH:		
Azerbaijan	N.W. Persia, Russian Trans-Caucasia	BFBS
Bashkir	Ufa, Russia (Europe)	BFBS
Jaghatai	Trans-Caspian regions, Russia in Asia	BFBS
Kara Kirghiz	S. Siberia	BFBS

LANGUAGE DIALECT	LOCALITY	SOURCE OF TRANSLATION
TURKISH:		
Kashgar	Chinese Turkestan	BFBS
Kazak Kirghiz	Orenburg, European Russia	BFBS
Kazan	Kazan, European Russia	BFBS
Kumukhi	Daghestan, European Russia	BFBS
Nogai, East	Cis-Caucasia, Russia	BFBS
Nogai, Crim.	Crimea, Russia	OV
Osmanli Arabic letters	Turkish Empire	BFBS
Armenian letters		
Greek letters		ABS
Uzbek	Khiva, Bokhara, Turkestan	BFBS
Yakut	N. E. Siberia	BFBS
ULAWA	Solomon Islands	BFBS
UMBUNDU	Benguella, W. Africa	ABCFM
URDU. See HINDI.		
URIYA	Orissa, India	BFBS
UVEAN	Loyalty Islands	BFBS
UZBEK	See Turkish.	
VAUDOIS. See FRENCH.		
VISAYAN: Cebu	Philippine Islands	ABS
VISAYAN: Iloilo	Philippine Islands	ABS
VOGUL	W. Siberia	BFBS
VOTYAK	Viatka and Orenburg, European Russia	RBS
WEDAU	New Guinea	BFBS
WELSH	Wales	OV
WEND: Saxon	Germany	Pruss.BS
Prussian		
WEN-LI: Standard	China (book language)	BFBS
Easy		ABS
		BMS
WIND: anc. Slovenian	Hungary Styria	BFBS
WUN-CHAU, DIALECT	Che-kiang, China	BFBS
YAHGAN	Tierra del Fuego	BFBS
YAKUT	See Turkish.	
YALUNKA	W. Africa	BFBS
YAO	Brit. Cent. Africa	BFBS
YORUBA	Lagos Protectorate, W. Africa	BFBS
ZULU	Natal and Zululand, S. Africa	ABS

APPENDIX IV

MISSIONARIES WHO HAVE MADE TRANSLATIONS OR REVISIONS OF HOLY SCRIPTURE

Non-Christian nations will one day know their peculiar indebtedness to missionaries whose laborious scholarship brought the Holy Scriptures within their reach. It has seemed worth while to gather from the records of the 19th century and to preserve from oblivion the names of such missionaries of all nations. We have now to admit, however, that difficulties of compilation mark the following list as merely tenative. We give it in hope that it may serve as a foundation on which a permanent and accurate record will be built up.

NAME	SOCIETY	LANGUAGE	DATE
Abel, Rev. C. W.	LMS	Suan, N. Guinea	1901
		Tavara, N. Guinea	1898
Adams, Rev. Thos.	WMS	Tonga or Friendly I.	1851–60
Adger, Rev. J. B.	ABCFM	Armenian	1842–45
Ainslee, Rev. Geo.	PN	Nez Perces	1876
Allégret, Rev. E.	P	Pahouin (Fang-Congo)	1900
Alley, Rev. J. A.	CMS	Temnè	1895
Alvarez, Rev. T. S.	CMS	Yalunka, W. Africa	1902
Ammann, Rev. F.	B	Tulu	1847–58
Anderson, Rev. W. G.	ZIM	Nyanja	1900
		Sena (Brit. Cent. Afr.)	1897
Andrews, Rev. L.	ABCFM	Hawaiian	1828
Andrus, Rev. A. N.	ABCFM	Kurdish	1892
Appenzeller, Rev. H. G.	ME	Korean	1885–1902
Arbousset, Mr.	P	Suto (Basutoland)	1881
Armour, Rev. Andrew		Indo-Portuguese	1819
		Sinhalese	1817
Ashe, Rev. R. P.	CMS	Ganda (Uganda)	1888
Ashmore, Rev. Wm.	ABMU	Swatau (Chauchau)	1879
Avederanian, Rev. Hohannes	Swed. U.	Kashgar-Turkish	1898
Bailey, Rev. Thos.	BMS	Uriya (Orissa)	1899
Bain, Rev. J. A.	FCS	Wanda (Lake Tanganyika)	1897
Ballentine, Rev. H.	ABCFM	Marathi-Standard	1845
Barff, Rev. Chas.	LMS	Samoan	1850
Bassett, Rev. J.	PN	Jaghatai-Turkish (Tekke Turcoman)	1880
Batchelor, Rev. J.	CMS	Ainu (Japan)	1887
Bate, Rev. J.	BMS	Hindi	1883
Bateman, Rev. R.	CMS	Punjabi Urdu (Musalmani)	1894
Bau, Rev. Andreas	Mor.	Negro-English (Surinam)	1846
Baumann, Rev. C.	CMS	Bengali	1883–96
Beauchamp, Rev. E. B.	CMS	Canton	1896
Bell, Miss	CMS	Manganja (Nganja)	1897
Bentley, Rev. W. H.	ABMU	Congo Free State	1893–96
Bettelheim, Dr.	Neth	Japanese	1855
		Luchuan	1849
Betz, Rev. M.	Rhen.	Batta or Battak Mandaling	1873
Beverley, Rev. J. S.	CMS	Gogo (Ger. East Africa)	1900
Bicknell, Rev. James	HEA	Marquésan	1853–57
Bingham, Rev. Hiram	ABCFM	Hawaiian	1828
Bingham, Rev. Hiram, Jr.	ABCFM	Gilbert Islands	1860–93
Bink, Rev. G. L.	Utr.	Mafur (N. Guinea)	1888
Bishop, Rev. A.	ABCFM	Hawaiian	1856
Blaich, Rev. J.	CMS	Santali	1888
Blodget, Rev. H.	ABCFM	Chinese Mandarin-Peking	1872–90
		Easy Wenli	1886 1900
Boardman, Mrs. Sarah	ABMU	Talaing (Pegu)	1847
Bodding, Rev. P. O.	DS	Santali	1900
Bomford, Rev. T.	CMS	Punjabi-Urdu (Musalmani)	1894
Bompas, Rt. Rev. W. C.	CMS	Tinne (Slave)	
		N. Am	1871
Bowen, Rev. A. J.	RBMU	Mongo (Congo Balolo)	1897
Bower, Rev. H.	SPG	Tamil	1868
Bowley, Rev. W.	CMS	Hindi	1826
Braches, Rev. F. E.	Rhen.	Dyak (Standard)	1858
Bradley, Dr. D. B.	PN	Siamese	1846
Brayton, Rev. D. L.	ABMU	Pwo Karen	1853–62
Brett, Rev. W. H.	SPG	Akkaway	1864
		Arawak	1856
Bridges, Rev. Thos.	SAMS	Yahgan	1881
Bridgman, Dr. E. C.	ABCFM	Wenli-Classical Chinese	1852–62
Brincker, Rev. H.	Rhen.	Herero (German S. W. Africa)	1877
Brincker, Rev. P. H.	Rhen.	Kwanyama (German S. W. Africa)	1893
Bromilow, Rev. W. E.	AWM	Dobu (N. Guinea)	1895–98
Brower, Rev. D.	Neth.	Malay, Java	1688
Brown, Rev. Geo.	AWM	Duke of York Island	1882
Brown, Rev. J.		Chuana, S. Africa	1901
Brown, Rev. Nathan	ABMU	Assamese	1850
		Japanese	1878
Brown, Rev. S. R.	RCA	Japanese	1888
Bruce, Rev. R.	CMS	Persian	1871–81
Bruckner, Rev. G.	Neth.	Javanese	1831
Brunton, Rev. Henry	CSFM	Nogai Turkish (Eastern)	1807–13
Bryer, Miss	CEZ	Kien-ning Chinese	1896
Buckley, Rev. J. B.	ABMU	Uriya (Orissa)	1844
Buckner, Dr. H. F.	ABHMS	Muskokee (Muskoki or Creek)	1867
Budd, Rev. H.	CMS	Cree-Western	1876
Bührer, Rev. A.	B	Tulu (Mysore)	1847
Burdon, Rt. Rev. J. S.		Chinese Mandarin-Peking	1872
		Easy Wenli-Low	1890
Burn, Rev. A.	CMS	Sindhi-Standard	1883–89
Burton, Rev. R.		Batta or Battak (Toba)	1820
Bushnell, Rev. Albert	ABCFM	Dikele (Kele)	1879
		Mpongwe	1850
Buzacott, Rev. A.	LMS	Rarotongan	1830
Cain, Rev. J.	CMS	Koi (Godavari region, India)	1891
Cain, Mrs. J.	CMS	Koi	1891
Caldwell, Rt. Rev. Robert.	SPG	Tamil	1890
Calvert, Rev. Jas.	WMS	Fiji	1883–92
		Rotuma	1885
Campbell, Rev. Andrew	FCS	Kortha (Bengal, India)	1894–97
Campbell, Rev. Wm.	PCC	Formosan	1889
Carey, Dr. Felix	BMS	Burmese	1817
Carey, Rev. Dr. Wm.	BMS	Bengali	1801
		Hindi-Standard	1809–18
		Khasi	1824
		Marathi-Standard	1820
		Palpa (Obsolete)	1832
		Uriya (Orissa)	1811–19
Carmichael, Rev. T.	CMS	Hindi-Garhwali (Tehri)	1895–1901
Carter, Rev. Chas.	BMS	Sinhalese	1860–98
Chalmers, Rev. J.	LMS	Motu, New Guinea	1882

NAME	SOCIETY	LANGUAGE	DATE
Chalmers, Rev. Jno		Chinese, Wenli (Classical or High)	1890
Chamberlain, Rev. Jno.	BMS	Bruj-bhasa (Obsolete)	1822–32
Chater, Rev. J.	BMS	Burmese	1815
		Sinhalese	1817
Christalles, Rev. J. G. B.		Ashanti-Otshi	1870
Christie, Rev. Dr. J.	CSFM	Judæo-Spanish	1878
Clark, Rev. E. W.	ABCFM	Hawaiian	1833–39
Clark, Rev. Jno.	BMS	Fernandian (Adiyah)	1846
Clark, Rev. R.	CMS	Pashtu	1857
Clough, Rev. Benj.	WMS	Indo-Portuguese	1827
		Sinhalese	1823
Codding, Mr. R. C.	CA	Koranko, Sierra Leone	1899
Codrington, Rev. R. H	MM	Florida, SolomonIs.	1882
		Isabel, or Bogotu	1887
		Motu, Banks Is.	1885
Cole, Rev. F. T.	CMS	Santali	1881–88
Cole, Rev. H.	CMS	Gogo (Ger. East Africa)	1890
Coles, Rev. S.	CMS	Sinhalese	1865–1901
Coolsma, Rev. S.	Neth	Sundanese	1878–82
Copeland, Rev. Jos.	NHM	Futunese	1869–76
Copleston, Rt. Rev.	SPG	Sinhalese	1901
Cosh, Rev. James	NHM	Faté or Efatese	1871–75
Cousins, Rev. W. E.	LMS	Malagasy	1888
Cowie, Rev. H.	PCE	Amoy dialect, Chinese	1853–73
Cran, Rev. Geo.	LMS	Telugu	1812
Creagh, Rev. and Mrs. S. M.	LMS	Maré, Loyalty Is.	1866–1902
Crowther, Rt. Rev. Sam.	CMS	Yoruban	1850
Culbertson, Rev. M.S.	PN	Wenli-Classical Chinese	1859
Cushing, Dr. J. N.	ABMU	Shan (Burma)	1871–1902
Danks, Rev. B.	AWM	Duke of York Island	1887
Dawson, Rev. J.	FCS	Gond	1872
Dean, Rev. Wm.	ABMU	Wenli-Classical Chinese	1865
Deas, Rev. E.	UPS	Umon (S. Nigeria)	1895
Dencke, Rev. C. F.	Mor	Delaware-Munsee	1818
Denniger, Rev. E.	Rhen	Nias	1875
Dennis, Rev. T. J.	CMS	Ibo (Nigeria)	1893–1901
Desgranges, Rev. Aug	LMS	Telugu	1828
De Silva, Rev. C. W.	WMS	Sinhalese	1860
Dibble, Rev. S.	ABCFM	Hawaiian	1828
Dittrich, Rev. A. H.	B	Armenian-Ararat	1835
Dixon, Rev. R.	WMS	Jolof Gambia, West Africa	1882
Doane, Rev. E. T.	ABCFM	Ebon (Marshall Islands)	1860–63
		Ponape	1887
Dobinson, Archdeacon H. H.	CMS	Ibo, Nigeria	1893
Drake, Rev. J.	KIM	Kurku	1900
Droesce, Rev. E.	CMS	Malto (Pahari, Rajmahali or Maler)	1880–89
Duffus, Rev. Wm.	PCE	Swatow dialect, Chinese	1877
Dunlap, Rev. E. P.	PN	Siamese	1846
Dwight, Rev. H. O.	ABCFM	Turkish	1886
Edkins, Rev. J.	LMS	Mongol-Southern or Kalkhas	1872
		Wenli-Classical Chinese	1890–1900
Edwards, Rev. J.	ABCFM	Choctaw	1852
Egede, Paul	DMS	Eskimo-Greenland	1766
Ella, Rev. Sam	LMS	Uvea	1868–79
Ellenberger, Mr.	P	Suto (Basutoland)	1880
Elliott, Rev. W. A.		Tabele—Matabele tribes	1901
Ellis, Rev. R. J.	BMS	Bengali-Musalmani	1877
Esser, Dr. J. P.	Neth	Madura Island (Java)	1895
Fabricius, Johann Phil	DMS	Malayalam	1813
		Tamil	1782
Fanggidaej, Rev. Johannes		Rotti	1894
Farler, Archdeacon, Rev.	UM	Bondei	1888
Fellows, Rev. S. B.	AWM	Panaieti(N.Guinea)	1895
Fielde, Miss A. M.	ABMU	Swatau Chauchau dialect, Chinese	1879
Fitch, Rev. G. F.	PN	Suchau dialect, Chinese	1881
Fletcher, Rev. R.	WMS	Maya (Yucatan)	1865–70
Fletcher, Rev. Wm.	WMS	Rotuma	1870
Fountain, Rev. Jno.	BMS	Bengali-Standard	1832
Fox, Rev. W. B.	WMS	Indo-Portuguese	1826
Frazer, Rev. Chas.	CSFM	Kazak or Orenburg Turkish	1818
Fraser, Rev. R. M.	NHM	Epi-Baki	1886
Freeman, Rev. Mr.	SPG	Mohawk	1700–41
Fyson, Rt. Rev. P. K.		Japanese	1878–88
Fyvie, Mr. Wm.	LMS	Gujarati	1820–23
Gale, Rev. J. S.		Korean	1895
Garrioch, Rev. A. C.	CMS	Beaver	1886
Geddie, Rev. John	NHM	Aneityum	1854
Geissler, Rev. J. G.	Utr	Mafur (N. Guinea)	1871
Genähr, Rev. J.		Chinese Easy Wenli	1890
Gericke, Rev. Dr. C.	Neth	Javanese	1831
Gibson, Rev. J. C.	PCE	Chinese Swatou	1879
		Easy Wenli	1900
Gill, Rev. N. Wyatt	LMS	Rarotongan	1884
Gillan, Rev. John	NHM	Mallikolo	1893
Goddard, Rev. Josiah	ABMU	Ningpo Chinese	1853
Goddard, Rev. J. K.	ABMU	Ningpo Chinese	1860–1900
		Classical Wenli	1865
Goldie, Rev. Hugh	UPS	Efik	1862
Gomes, Rev. W. H.	SPG	Malay-Standard	1890
Good, Rev. A. C.	PN	Bulu Gabun, West Africa	1895
Goodell, Rev. W.	ABCFM	Turkish	1819–31
Gordon, Rev. E. C.	CMS	Sukuma (Southern coast of Lake Victoria Nyanza)	1895
Gordon, Rev. John	LMS	Telugu	1828
Gordon, Rev. G. N.	NHM	Eromangan	1865
Gordon, Rev. J. D.	NHM	Eromangan	1865
Gough, Rev. F. F.	CMS	Ningpo dialect, Chinese	1868
Grashius, Rev. G. J.	Neth	Sundanese	1866
Graves, Rev. R. H.	SBC	Canton dialect	1895–1900
		Wenli-Simple or Low	1900
Gravius, Rev. Mr.	NSM	Formosa	1661
Gray, Rev. Wm.	NHM	Weaisi, Tauna (New Hebrides)	1889–96
Green, Rev. J. S.	ABCFM	Hawaiian	1839
Greene, Rev. D. C.		Japanese	1878–88
Greiner, Rev. G. B.	B	Tulu, Mysore	1834
Griffiths, Rev. David	LMS	Malagasi	1835
Grunwald, Mr.	Mor	Moskito (Nicaragua)	1864
Guilford, Rev. E.	CMS	Punjabi	1899
Gulick, Rev. L. H.	ABCFM	Ponape (Micronesia)	1862
Gundert, Rev. H.	B	Malayalam	1868
Gunn, Dr. Wm.	NHM	Futuna (N. Hebrides)	1888–94
Gurney, Dr. A. K.	ABMU	Assamese	1889
Gutzlaff, Dr. Karl	Neth	Wenli-Classical or High	1835
		Siamese (Tai)	1828
		Japanese	1839
Gybbon-Spilsbury, Rev. J. H.	SAMS	Quechua	1880
Hadfield, Rev. J.	LMS	Uvean (Loyalty Is.)	1897
Hahn, Rev. F.	GM	Kurukh (Chota Nagpur)	1895–96
Haigh, Rev. H.	WMS	Kanarese, Mysore	1898–1901
Hall, Rev. A. J.	CMS	Kwagutl (Vancouvers Island)	1882
Hall, Rev. Gordon	ABCFM	Marathi	1826
Hall, Rev. Sherman	MCC	Ojibwa (Chippewa)	1856
Hamlin, Rev. J.	CMS	Maori, N. Zealand	1868
Hands, Rev. John	LMS	Kanarese, Mysore	1821–32
Hanson, Rev. Ola	ABMU	Kachin, Burma	1896–1901
Hardeland, Dr. A.	Rhen	Dyak, Borneo	1846–58
Harris, Rev. T. S.	ABCFM	Seneca Indians	1829
Harrison, Rev. C.	CMS	Hydah, Queen Charlotte's Isl., Brit. Columbia	1891
Haswell, Rev. Jas.	ABMU	Talaing (Pegu), Burma	1847
Hay, Rev. J.	LMS	Telugu, Madras	1874–91
Hazelwood, Rev. David	WMS	Fiji	1854
Henderson, Rev. Alex	BMS	Moskito	1846
		Carib, Honduras	1847
Hepburn, Dr. J. C.	PN	Japanese	1881
Herbert, Rev. E. P.	CMS	Gond	1899
Hermann, Rev. H.	Neth	Alifur (Celebes)	1852
Herrick, Rev. G. F.	ABCFM	Turkish	1883–1902
Hetherwick, Rev. A.	CMS	Yao, Brit. Central Africa	1889–1901
Heyde, Rev. A. W.	Mor	Tibetan	1901
Hill, Rev. S. J.	LMS	Bengali-Musalmani	1856
Hinderer, Rev. David	CMS	Yoruba, W. Africa	1880
Hoare, Rev. J. C.	CMS	Ningpo dialect, China	1900
Hödberg, Rev. L. E.	Swed. U.	Kashgar Turkish	1898
Hodgson, Archdeacon F. R.	UM	Swahili	1892
Holmes, Rev. J. H.	LMS	Toaripi	1901
Howe, Rev. Wm.	LMS	Tahiti	1848
Hubbard, Rev. E. H.	CMS	Sukuma, Victoria Nyanza	1895

NAME	SOCIETY	LANGUAGE	DATE
Hughes, Rev. Griffith.	WCM	Khasi, Assam	1892
Hughes, Rev. T. P.	CMS	Pashtu, or Afghani	1874
Hunt, Rev. John.	WMS	Fiji	1843
Hunter, Archdeacon Jas.	CMS	Cree-Western	1876
Hutchison, Rev. J.	CSFM	Punjabi (Chamba)	1878
Inglis, Rev. John.	NHM	Aneityum, N. Hebrides	1854
Isenberg, Rev. C. W.	CMS	Tigré, Abyssinia	1842
Isenberg, Rev.C.W.H.	CMS	Sindhi	1864
Ivens, Rev. W. G.	MM	Ulawa, Solomon Is.	1900
Jaeger, Rev. G.	B	Accra, Gold Coast Colony	1901
Jansz, Rev. P	Neth.M.	Javanese	1885–90
Janvier, Rev. L.	PN	Punjabi	1902
Jaschke, Rev. H. A.	Mor.	Tibetan (Bhutian)	1859
Jens, Rev. W. L.	Utr.	Mafur, N. Guinea	1883
Jeremiassen, Mr. C. C.	PN	Hainan, China	1891–96
Jewett, Rev. Lyman	ABMU	Telugu	1885
John, Rev. Griffith.	LMS	Mandarin-Nanking or South	1886
		Wenli-Easy	1883–86
Johnson, Archdeacon H.	CMS	Nupè, W. Africa	1886
Johnson, Archdeacon W. P.	UM	Nyanja (Brit. Cent. Africa)	1895
Johnson, Rt. Rev. Jas.	CMS	Yoruba	1900
Jones, Rev. David	LMS	Malagasi	1835
Jones, Rev. D. P.	LMS	Mambwe, Tanganyika	1894
Jones, Rev. G. H.	ME	Korean	1902
Jones, Rev. J.	LMS	Maré (Loyalty Is)	1867
Jones, Rev. J. T.	PN	Siamese (Tai)	1846
Jones, Rev. Thos.	WCM	Khasi, Assam	1846
Joseph, Rev. Thos.	LMS	Tahiti	1838
Jowett, Rev. W.	CMS	Maltese	1822
Judd, Rev. C. H.	CIM	Mandarin (Shantung)	1894
Judson, Mrs. A.	ABMU	Siamese (Tai)	1819
Judson, Rev. A.	ABMU	Burmese	1817
Jukes, Dr. A	CMS	Jakti	1894
Junod, Rev. H.	MR	Tonga, Delagoa Bay	1894
Keasberry, Rev. B.P.	LMS	Malay-High	1863–75
Keen, Rev. J. H.	CMS	Hydah	1899
Kelling, Rev. F.	GM	Sangir, Dutch E. Indies	1879
Kellogg, Rev. S. H.	PN	Hindi-Standard	1883–99
Kennedy, Rev. Jas.		Hindi-Standard	1855
King, Rev. C.	ACM	Wedau, N. Guinea	1897
King, Rev. T.	CMS	Yoruba, W. Africa	1850
Kingdon, Rev. J.	JB	Maya, Yucatan	1862
Kirby, Arch. W. W.	CMS	Chipewan (Chipewyan)	1878
Klinkert, Rev. H. C.	Neth	Malay-High or Standard	1872–89
		Malay-Low	1888
Knowles, Rev. J. H.	CMS	Kashmiri	1900
Knudsen, Rev. Mr.	Rhen	Namaqua Hottentot	1860
Koelle, Rev. C.	B	Accra, Gold Coast Colony	1901
Konym, Rev. W.	NSM	Sinhalese	1739
Kraft, Rev. A.	Neuk	Pokomo (Brit. E. Africa)	1900
Krapf, Rev. J. L.	CMS	Amharic (Abyssinia)	1879
		Galla-Shoa	1872
		Kamba	1851
		Nyika(Mombasa)	1848
		Tigrai (Tigre)	1865
Kronlein, Rev. G.	Rhen	Namaqua, Hottentot	1866
Krothe, Rev. C.	Ber	Pedi (Transvaal)	1888
Kugler, Mr. C.	CMS	Tigre	1865
Laman, Rev. K. E.	SwedM	Fioti (Congo Free State)	1901
Lamb, Rev. R.	NHM	Fanting, Ambrym	1899
Lambert, Rev. J. A.	LMS	Hindi	1885–99
Lambrick, Rev. J. D.	CMS	Sinhalese	1833–34
Landels, Rev. S.	NHM	Malo, N. Hebrides	1896
Last, Rev. J. F.	CMS	Kaguru, Ger. E. Africa	1885
Laughton,Rev. J. F.	SPG	Carib-Honduras	1896
Laws, Rev. W. G.	LMS	Motu-N. Guinea	1882
Laws, Rev. R.	FCS	Nyanja, Brit. Cent. Africa	1886
Lee, Rev. W.	LMS	Telugu	1812–28
Leggatt, Rev. T. W.	NHM	Mallicolo, N. Hebrides	1894–97
Leupolt, Rev. C. B.	CMS	Hindi-Standard	1855
Lewis, Rev. A.	CMS	Baluchi	1885
Lewis, Rev. C. B.	BMS	Bengali-Standard	1867
Lewis, Rev. Edwin.	LMS	Telugu	1891
Lewis, Rev. W.	WCM	Khasi, Assam	1870
Ling, Miss C. F.	CEZ	Toda	1896
Loewenthal, Rev. I.	PN	Pashtu (Pushtu or Afghani)	1863
Logan, Rev. R. W.	ABCFM	Mortlock	1880
		Ruk	1893
Long, Rev. A. L.	ME	Bulgarian	1864
Lord, Rev. E. C.	ABMU	Wenli-Classical or High	1859
Lorrain, Rev. J. H.	Ind	Lushai	1899
Louis, Rev. C. W	Rhen	Canton dialect	1867
Lowndes, Rev. I.	LMS	Greek-Modern	1808
Luke, Rev. Jas.	UPS	Akunakuna	1897
Lund, Rev. Eric.	ABMU	Visayan or Iloilo (Bisayan)	1899
Lütze, Rev. W.	B	Kanarese-Badaga	1852
Lyth, Rev. R. B.	WMS	Fiji	1854
Mabille, Mr. A.	P	Suto (Basutoland)	1837
Macbrair, Rev. R. M.	WMS	Mandingo (Mande)	1837
McClure, Rev. W. G.	PN	Siamese (Tai)	1846
McCullagh, Rev.	CMS	Neshga(Niskkah)	1900
Macdonald, Rev. Dav.	NHM	Faté, Havannah Harbor	1877
McDonald, Archdeacon Rob't.	CMS	Ojibwa, Mackenzie River	1875–86
		Tukudh, Alaska	1874–84
MacFarlane, Rev. Dr. S.	LMS	Lifu, Loyalty Is.	1868
		Murray Island, Torres Straits	1886
		Saibai	1883
McGilvary, Mrs.Danl.	PN	Laos	1887–91
McGilvary, Rev. E.B.	PN	Laos	1895
Macgowan, Rev. J.	LMS	Amoy	1887–1901
Macgregor, Rev. J.		Amoy	1853–73
MacIntyre, Rev. J. L.		Nupè, Nigeria	1886
Mackay, Rev. Alex.	CMS	Ganda (Uganda)	1888
McKean, Dr. J. W.	PN	Laos	1901
Mackenzie, Rev. H. L.	PCE	Swatow dialect	1882
Mackenzie, Rev. J. W.	NHM	Faté or Efatese	1866
Mackichan,Rev.Dr.D.	FCS	Marathi	1883–93
Maclagan, Rev. P. J.	PCE	Swatow dialect	1882
Maclay, Rev. R. S.		Japanese	1878–88
Macmahon, Miss.	ME	Malay-Low	1891
McMinn, Rev. R. D.	FCS	Chitonga, Brit. E. Africa	1900
Maddox, Mr. H. E.	CMS	Toro, Uganda	1900
Maples, Bp.Chauncey	SPG	Nyanja	1895
Marling, Rev. A. W.	PN	Fang	1893
Marshman,Rev.Josh.	BMS	Wenli-Classical	1822
Marten, Rev. J. L.		Malay-Low	1878
Martin, Rev. W. A. P.	PN	Mandarin-Peking	1872
Martyn, Rev. Henry.	SPG	Hindustani	1814
		Persian	1812
		Arabic	1816
Mason, Dr. Francis.	ABMU	Karen-Sgaw-Karen	1843
Mason, Rev. M. C.	ABMU	Garo, Assam	1875–1900
Mason, Rev. W.	CMS	Cree-Eastern	1860
Mateer, Rev. C. W.	PN	Mandarin-Peking	1895
Mather, Dr. R. C.	LMS	Hindi-Hindustani	1870
Mattoon, Rev. S.	PN	Siamese	1860
Maunsell, Rev. Robt.	CMS	Maori	1858–68
Maxwell, Dr. James L		Amoy dialect	1853–84
Mayer, Rev. T. J. Lee.	CMS	Baluchi	1893
		Pashtu, Afghan	1880
Medhurst, Rev. W. H.	LMS	Shanghai	1846
		Wenli-Classical	1835–52
		Malay-Low	1833
Meeker, Mr. Jonathan	ABHMS	Ottawa	1841
Meller, Rev. T. W.	WCM	Khasi, Assam	1870
Michelsen, Rev. O.	NHM	Epi, N. Hebrides	1892
Miller, Dr. W. R. S.	CMS	Hausa-Gierko in N. Nigeria	1900
Milne, Rev. Peter.	NHM	Nguna	1882–99
Milne, Rev. Wm.	LMS	Shanghai	1846
		Wenli-Classical	1814–22
Moericke, Rev. Wm.	B	Kanarese-Badaga, Mysore	1852
Moffat, Rev. Robt.	LMS	Chuana, Bechuanaland	1831–56
Moffett, Rev. S. A.	PN	Korean	1902
Molony, Rev. H. J.	CMS	Gond	1899
Moody, Rev. Andrew	FCS	Palityan (Paulician) Hungary	1899
Moore, Rev. Joseph.	LMS	Tahiti	1848
Morrison,Rev.Donald	NHM	Faté or Efatese	1866
Morrison, Rev. Robt	LMS	Wenli-Classical	1814–23
Morton, Rev. Alex.	NHM	Mallicollo	1894
Moulton, Rev. Jas. E.	WMS	Tonga, Friendly Is	1851
Muirhead,Rev.W.	LMS	Shanghai dialect	1886
Murray, Rev. Chas.	NHM	Ranon, N. Hebrides	1899
Murray, Rev. A. W.	LMS	Samoan	1841–70
Murray, Rev. W. B.	NHM	Ranon,N.Hebrides	1899
Newcombe, Miss B.	CEZ	Kien-ning, Chinese	1896
Newell, Rev. Saml.	ABCFM	Marathi-Standard	1826
Newstead, Rev. Robt.	WMS	Indo-Portuguese	1826
Newton, Rev. John	PN	Punjabi (Gurmukhi character)	1850

NAME	SOCIETY	LANGUAGE	DATE
Newton, Rev. E. P.	PN	Punjabi (Gurmukhi character)	1894-99
Niebel, Rev. C. J.	Ind	Lepcha, Sikkim	1874
Nihill, Rev. Wm.	SPG	Lifu, Loyalty Is.	1855
		Mare, Loyalty Is.	1867
Nommenson, Rev. R. J. L.	Rhen	Batta, Toba, Sumatra	1875-79
Nott, Rev. Henry	LMS	Tahiti	1818-38
Nottrott, Rev. C. A.	GM	Mandari (Kol)Chota Nagpur, India	1876-96
Noyes, Rev. Eli	BMS	Uriya (Orissa)	1844
Nylander, Rev. G R.	CMS	Bullom	1815
O'Meara, Rev.Dr.FA.	SPG	Ojibwa	1854
Ormerod, Rev. R. M.	UMFC	Galla-Southern or Bararetta	1890
Ott, Rev. P.	B.	Marathi-Konkani	1886
Ousley, Rev. Benj.	ABCFM	Sheetswa, Port, E. Africa and N. Zululand	1891
Owen, Rev. Joseph	LMS	Hindi-Standard	1855
Parker, Rev. A. P.	ME	Suchau dialect	1881
Parsons, Rev. J.	BMS	Hindi-Standard	1868
Paterson, Rev. J.	LMS	Bengali-Musalmani	1855-56
Paton, Rev. F. H. L.	NHM	Lenakel, N. Hebrides	1900
Paton, Rev. F. J.	NHM	Mallicollo, Pangkumi	1891
Paton, Rev. John G.	NHM	Aniwa, N. Hebrides	1877
		Tanna, N. Hebrides	1869
Patteson, Rt. Rev. J. C.	CMS	Lifu	1868
Payne, Rev. John	PE	Grebo	1848-56
Pearse, Rev. A.	LMS	Keapara,N.Guinea	1892
Pease, Rev. E. M.	ABCFM	Ebon (Marshall Is.)	1862
Peck, Rev. E. J.	CMS	Eskimo, Cumberland Sound	1897
Pelissier, Rev. J. P.	P.	Suto,Basutoland	1837
Penny, Rev. A.	MM	Florida, SolomonIs.	1862
Percival, Rev. P.	WMS	Tamil, India	1868
Perham, Arch. J.	SPG	Malay-High	1890
Perkins, Rev.H. E.	CMS	Hindustani	1892
		Punjabi Gurmukhi	1899
Perkins, Rev. Justin.	ABCFM	Syriac-Modern	1846
Pershore, Mr.		Dyak-Sea, Borneo	1879
Pettigrew, Rev. W.	ABMU	Manipuri, Assam	1896
Pfander, Rev. C. G.	B.	Turkish-Azerbaijan	1826
Phillips, Rev. E. G.	ABMU	Garo, Assam	1875
Phillips, Rev. H. S.		} Kien-yang dialect	1899
Phillips, Mrs. H. S.			
Pierson, Rev. G.	ABCFM	Ebon (Marshall Islands)	1862
Pike, Rev. J. G.	BMS	Uriya (Orissa)	1899
Pilkington, Mr. G. L.	CMS	Ganda, Uganda	1896
		Sukuma	1895
Pitman, Rev. Chas.	LMS	Rarotonga	1830
Pratt, Rev. George.	LMS	Niue	1863
		Samoan	1837
Pratt, Rev. A. T.	ABCFM	Turkish	1870
Preston, Rev. I. M.	PN	Dikele, Gabun	1877
Price, Rev. F. M.	ABCFM	Ruk, Micronesia	1893
Price, Rev. J. C.	CMS	Gogo, Ger. E.Africa	1887
Price, Rev. Roger.		Chuana, So. Africa	1901
Pritchett, Rev. E.	LMS	Telugu	1828
Puckey, Rev W. G.	CMS	Maori, New Zealand	1868
Puxley, Rev. E. L.	CMS	Santali	1868
Ramsay, Rev. J. R.		Muskokee, or Creek	1893
Rand, Rev. S. T.		Maliseet	1870
Rattray, Dr. P.	UPS	Ibo, Old Calabar	1899
Rebmann, Rev. John	CMS	Swahili-Zanzibar	1862
Reed, Rev. G. C. H.	LMS	Kalana, Rhodesia	1902
Reeve, Rt. Rev. W.D	CMS	Tinne, Slave	1871
Reeve, Rev. Wm.	LMS	Kanarese, Mysore	1821-32
Reynolds, Rev. W. D.		Korean	1898
Rhenius, Rev. C.T.E	CMS	Tamil	1813
Richards, Rev. E. H.	ME	Tonga, Port E. Af.	1888-90
Richards, Rev. W.	ABCFM	Hawaiian	1828
Richards, Rev. R. H.	AWM	Duke of York Is.	1887
		New Britain	1893
Ridley, Rt. Rev. Wm	CMS	} Shimshi, or Tsimshi	1885
Ridley, Mrs. Wm.			
Riggs, Rev. Elias	ABCFM	Armenian-Modern	1835-45
		Bulgarian	1855-64
		Turkish	1883-86
Riggs, Rev. S. R.	ABCFM	Dakota (Sioux)	1839
Rinnooy, Rev. N.	Utr.	Mafur, N. Guinea	1873
Robb, Rev. A.	UPS	Efik, Old Calabar	1862
Roberts, Rev. H.	WCM	Khasi, Assam	1846
Robertson,Rev.H.A.	NHM	Eromanga	1879
Robin, Rev. L. P.	MM	Torres	1900
Robinson, Rev. Canon C. H.	CMS	Hausa, N. Nigeria	1899
Robinson, Rev. Wm.	BMS	Malay-Low, Java	1814
Roehl, Rev. Karl		Shambala, Ger. E. Africa	1901
Roepstorff, Rev. F.A.		Nicobar	1879
Rood, Rev. I.	ABCFM	Zulu	1889(R)
Rooney, Rev. I.	AWM	Duke of York Is.	1882
Rose, Mrs. A. T.	ABMU	Pwo-Karen	1853
Roskott, Mr.		Malay-High	1877
Ross,Rev. John	UPS	Korean	1885
Rouse, Rev. G. H.	BMS	Bengali-Standard	1867-1900
Rowling, Rev. Frank.	CMS	Uganda	1900
		Usogan	1899
Rudland, Rev .W. D.	CIM	Tai-chau	1892
Ruskin, Rev. A. E.	RBMU	Lolo, Congo Free State	1901
Saker, Mr. A.	BMS	Dualla, Kameruns, W. Africa	1870
Savidge, Mr. F. W.	Ind	Lushai, Assam	1899
Saville, Rev. A. T.	LMS	Tahiti	1879
Schaub, Rev. M.		Wenli-Classical	1900
Schauffler, Rev. W. G.	ABCFM	Judæo-Spanish	1843
		Turkish	1873
Schereschewsky, Rt. Rev. S. I. J.	PE	Mandarin-Peking	1872
		Wenli-Simple, or Low	1900
Schlenker, Rev. C. F.	CMS	Temnĕ, Sierra Leone	1866
Schmelin, Rev. Mr.	LMS	Nama (Namaqua-Hottentot)	1825
Schmidt, Dr. Jas.	Mor.	Mongol (Western or Kalmuk)	1815
		Mongol (Northern or Buriat)	1824
Schneider, Rev. F. E.		Hindi-Standard	1855-66
Schon, Rev. J. F.	CMS	Hausa	1857
Schopf, Rev. J.	B.	Accra, Gold Coast Colony	1901
Schuler, Rev. Eugen.	B.	Dualla,Kameruns	1896-1901
Schultze, Rev. Benj.	Danish-Halle.	Tamil	1721
		Hindustani	1741
		Telugu	1727-32
Schütz, Rev. C.	Rhen	Batta, Mandailung, Sumatra	1889, 1889-1901
Scott, Rev. D. C.	CSFM	Nyanja	1897
Scott, Rev. H. (and Mrs)	LMS	Murray Is., N. Guinea	1885-1902
Scranton, Dr. W. B.		Korean	1885
Seaman, Rev. Wm.	CSFM	Nogai Turkish	1666
Shaw, Rev. T. F.	LMS	Nyamwezi, Ger. E. Af ica	1896
Sheffield, Rev. D. Z.	ABCFM	Wenli-Classical	1890-1900
Shellabear, Rev. W.G	ME	Malay-High	1890-1900
Shirt, Rev. G.	CMS	Sindhi-Standard	1868-89
Sieboerger, Rev. W.	Mor.	Moskito	1890
Sikemeier, Rev. W.	B.	Kanarese-Badaga	1852
Skinner, Rev. Jas.	LMS	Gujarati-Standard	1821-25
Skrefsrud, Rev. L. O.	DS.	Santali	1868
Sleigh, Rev. Jas.	LMS	Lifu, Loyalty Is.	1868
Smaill, Rev. T.	NHM	Epi-Baki or Western	1896
Smith, Rev. Eli	ABCFM	Arabic	1857
Smith Rev. G.	PCE	Swatow	1882
Smith, Rev. H. C.	CA	Koranko, Sierra Leone	1899
Snow, Rev. B. G.	ABCFM	Ebon (Marshall Islands)	1862
		Kusaien	1869
Soothill, Rev. W. E.	UFMC	Wenchau	1891-95
Sparham, Rev. C. G.	LMS	Mandarin-Peking	1895
Spaulding, Rev. H.H.	ABCFM	Nez Perces Indians	1845
Spence, Rev. D. B.	CSFM	Judæo-Spanish	1896
Stallybrass, Rev. Ed	LMS	Mongol (Northern or Buriat)	1840
Start, Rev. Wm.	Ind	Lepcha (Sikkim)	1874
		Nepali	1850
Steere, Rt. Rev. E.	UM	Swahili-Zanzibar	1864-82
Steggall, Rev. A. R.	CMS	Taveta, Brit. E. Africa	1892
Steller, Miss Clara		Sangir, Dutch E. Indies	1880
Stenberg, Rev. Dr.	Scand.	Mongol-Southern or Kalkhas	1899
Stewart, Rev. R. W.	CMS	Fuchau	1892
Stronach, Rev. J.	LMS	Mandarin-Nanking	1856
		Wenli-Classical	1859
Sturges, Rev. A. A.	ABCFM	Ponape	1862
Sunderland, Rev. J. P.	LMS	Mare, Loyalty Is.	1867
Sundermann, Mr. H.	Rhen.	Nias, Dutch E. Indies	1875
Sutton, Rev. A.	ABMU	Uriya (Orissa)	1844
Swan, Rev. Wm.	LMS	Manchu	1834
		Mongol-Northern or Buriat	1840
Swanson, Rev. W. S.		Amoy dialect	1868
Sykes, Rev. W.	LMS	Matabele, Rhodesia	1884

NAME	SOCIETY	LANGUAGE	DATE
Talmage, Rev. Dr. J. van N.	RCA	Amoy dialect	1853
Taplin, Rev. Geo.		Narrinyeri	1865
Taylor, Dr. John		Marathi-Standard	1819
Taylor, Rev. J. Hudson	CIM	Ningpo dialect	1868
Taylor, Rev. W. E.	CMS	Swahili-Mombasa	1900
Teissers, Rev. U.	P.	Galwa, French Congo	1901
Thomas, Mrs. B. C.	ABMU	Chin, Burma	1896
Thomas, Mr. John	BMS	Tamil, India	1818
Thomas, Rev. T. Morgan	LMS	Matabele, Rho'sia	1897
Thomas, Rev. W. F.	ABMU	Chin, Burma	1896
Thompson, Rev. M.		Malayalam	1813
Thomson, Rev. Edw.	CMS	Tai-chau	1892
Thurston, Rev. A.	ABCFM	Hawaiian	1828
Tims, Rev. J. W.	CMS	Blackfoot, Alberta	1890
Tisdall, Rev. W. St.C.	CMS	Kurdish, Persia	1896–99
Tomlin, Rev. Jacob	LMS	Siamese	1828
Torrey, Rev. C. C.	ABCFM	Cherokee	1832
Tracy, Rev. W.	ABCFM	Tamil	1870
Trollope, Rev. M. N.		Korean	1899
Turnbull, Rev. A.	CMS	Nepali	1892
Turner, Rev. Geo.	LMS	Samoan	1850
Underwood, Rev. H. G.	PN	Korean	1885
Van der Vorn, Petrus	Neth	Malay-High	1701
Van Dyck, Rev. C. V. A.	PN	Arabic	1884–86
Van Dyke, Rev. J. W	PN	Siamese (Tai)	1846
Van Eck, Rev. R.	Utr	Bali, or Balinese	1877
Van Hasselt, Rev.J.L.	Utr	Mafur, N. Guinea	1878–83
Verbeck, Rev. G. F.	RCA	Japanese	1888
Vreede, Dr. A C.		Madura Island, Dutch E. Indies	1895
Wade, Rev. T. R.	CMS	Kashmiri	1884
Wakefield, Rev. T.	UMFC	Galla-Southern	1890
		Nyika	1882
Walker, Rev. F. W.	LMS	Suan, N. Guinea	1886
Walker, Rev. W.	PN	Mpongwe	1850
Ward, Rev. N. M.	ABMU	Batta, Toba	1826
Waterhouse, Rev.Jos.	NHM	Rotuma, N. Hebrides	1870
Watkins, Rev. E. A.	CMS	Chipewan (Chipewyan)	1878
Watsford, Rev. John.	LMS	Fiji	1854
Watt, Rev. Wm.	NHM	Tanna	1890
Weakley, Rev. R. H.	CMS	Turkish-Osmanli	1883
Weigle, Rev. G.	B.	Kanarese, Mysore	1860
Weitbrecht, Rev. H. U.	CMS	Hindustani	1898
Welchman, Rev. H.	MM	Bugotu, Solomon Islands	1901
Welton, Rev. W.	CMS	Fuchau	1867
Wenger, Rev. Dr.	BMS	Bengali-Standard	1867
		Sanskrit	1873
Went, Rev. Thos.	WMS	Tonga	1851
Wertz, Rev. C.	B.	Accra, Gold Coast Colony	1901
Westlind, Mr. N.	Swed.U	Fioti, Congo Free State	1897
Wherry, Rev. J.	PN	Wenli-Classical	1890
White, Rev. John.	WMS	Mashona, S.Africa	1897
Whitmee, Rev. S. J.	LMS	Samoan	1850
Whitney, Rev. J. F.	ABCFM	Ebon (Marshall Islands)	1885
Wigram, Rev. B.	CMS	Toro, Uganda	1900
Wilder, Rev. G. E.	ABCFM	Zulu	1861–66
Wilkinson, Rev. A. B	BMS	Khondi	1893
Williams, Rev. John.	LMS	Rarotonga	1830
Williams, Rev. P. J.	CMS	Igbira	1891
Williams, Rev. R. H.	WMS	Mandingo, Gambia	1837
Williams, Rev. Thos.	LMS	Fiji	1854
Williams, Rev. Wm.	CMS	Maori	1837
Williamson, Rev. H. D.	CMS	Gond	1872
Wilson, Rev. D. A.	PN	Mpongwe, Gabun	1850
Wilson, Rev. J.	PN	Laos, Siam	1891
Wilson, Rev. Sam'l.	LMS	Samoan	1850
Wimbush, Rev. J. S.	UM	Nyanja	1895
Winquist, Dr. K.	Swed.N	Tigrai, Abyssinia	1901
Winslow, Rev. Miron	ABCFM	Tamil	1840–50
Withey, Mr. H. C.	ME	Mbundu, Angola	1900
Wood, Rev. A. N.	CMS	Kaguru	1885
Wookey, Rev. A. J.	LMS	Chuana, S. Africa	1901
Worcester, Rev. S. A.	ABCFM	Cherokee	1832
Wray, Rev. J. A.	CMS	Sagalla, Taita, Brit. E. Africa	1892
Wright, Rev A.	ABCFM	Choctaw	1831
Wright, Rev. Asher.		Seneca	1875
Wright, Rev. J N.	PN	Turkish-Azerbaijan	1882
Wurtz, Rev. L.	Neuk	Pokomo, Brit. E. Africa	1894
Yates, Rev. Dr. W.	BMS	Bengali Standard	1833
		Hindustani	1847
		Sanskrit	1818
		Sanskrit	1840–46
Zaremba, Rev. Mr.	B.	Turkish-Azerbaijan	1836
Ziegenbalg, Bartholomew, Danish	Halle	Tamil	1714

APPENDIX V

STATISTICAL TABLES

INTRODUCTORY NOTE

All Christendom is home to the Christian. To him the non-Christian lands, alone, are foreign lands. The statistics of "foreign missions" given in the following tables, therefore, relate to Missionary work in non-Christian lands. Exceptions to this rule are made, however, in the case of, (1) Protestant Missions in Roman Catholic countries whose statistics are reported by some Societies in the tables of their foreign Mission work; and (2) of Missions in those parts of North America and in South America where pagans still form an important element in the population. Consistency would require the exclusion from these tables of statistics of Christian work in lands that have become Christianized by colonization or otherwise, and maintain their own Missionary Societies. Such are the Protestant islands of the West Indies and parts of South Africa, Australasia, etc., where local Christianity is thoroughly organized and established. But this consistency has not been possible, because some Societies do not separate statistics of Missionary work among East Indian coolies or other pagans from those of the regular ministrations to the local Churches under settled pastors.

The plan of this work has required us to exclude from the tables of statistics work for European soldiers, colonists or seamen. It has also seemed necessary in order to avoid reduplication of statistics to omit mention of purely auxiliary Societies.

The column "Professed Christians" is intended to show the whole number publicly known as Christians, whether communicants, probationers, or children of Christian parents. This intention has been very imperfectly executed because many societies continue to give in reports the number of communicants only, just as was the usage before the rise on the Mission field of families and even communities which have never been pagans.

The statistics given are intended to represent the condition of the Foreign Missions on January 1, 1903, except in the case of Societies whose names are followed by an asterisk (*). The figures in such cases show the status of 1900, and for them we are under obligation to Beach's Atlas of Protestant Missions.

Notwithstanding close application and exhausting labor, we find ourselves forced to crave indulgence for the faults of the tables. Such tables can be no more than relatively exact, and they require so much time in compilation that they are already out of date before publication.

A. THE OPERATIONS OF PROTESTANT MISSIONARY SOCIETIES IN NON-CHRISTIAN LANDS.

Names of Societies.	No. of Missionaries, Men and Women	Native Workers, Men and Women	Places of Regular Worship	Elementary Schools	Higher or Special Educational Institutions	Hospitals and Dispensaries	Publishing Houses or Printing Establishments	Professed Christians
Africa Inland Mission	5		3	1				
African Training Institute (Colwyn)*		172		29	1			
African Meth. Episcopal Church	21	300	348	126	1			20,000
American Advent Miss. Society	7	8	5	3				
American Baptist Missionary Union 1	541	3,595	1,312	1,322	78	2	6	152,481
American Board of Com'rs for Foreign Missions	544	3,919	1,668	1,240	128		9	59,585
American Friends Foreign Missions	80	138	33	27	10	4	3	5,516
American Missionary Association	2	2	2	2				
American Norwegian China Mission	5	7	3					36
Archbishop's Miss. to Assyrian Christians	2			46			1	
Associate Ref'd Pres. Synod of the South	11	11	5	5	1			573
Australian Presbyterian Mission	9	17	10	5	1			268
Australian Wesleyan Meth. Mission	51	1,436	1,116	2,110	20	1		43,715
Balaghat Mission	8	2	4	2	1	2		180
Baptist Missionary Society 2	244	1,153	752	385	13	20	6	15,195
Baptist Zenana Miss. Society	65	236		98	5	4		
Basel Evang. Missionary Society	333	1,266	505	535	24	2	2	45,204
Bengal Evangelistic Mission		21	5	9	1	1		117

Names of Societies.	No. of Missionaries, Men and Women	Native Workers, Men and Women	Places of Regular Worship	Elementary Schools	Higher or Special Educational Institutions	Hospitals and Dispensaries	Publishing Houses or Printing Establishments	Professing Christians
Bengali Mission Union*	3	5	1	1	1			
Bethel Santal Mission	5	17	3	8	5	8		1,480
Bible Christian Home and For. Mission	7	3	2	1		2		19
British and For. Unitarian Association	1	2	2	1				
British Syrian Schools*	18	103	1	50	3	4		
Canada; Baptist Convention, Maritime Provinces	24	46	21	17				495
Canada; Baptist Convention, Ontario and Quebec	41	197	113	78	13			4,605
Canada; Methodist Miss. Society	112	30	41	49	10	4	1	2,436
Canada; Presbyterian Church in	178	267	135	98		8	2	6,358
Central American Mission*	26	25	16					1,425
Central Morocco Mission	4					1		
Ceylon and India Gen. Mission	24	36	16					
China Inland Mission	763	741	476	83		25	2	7,774
Chinese Blind, Murray's Mission to	1			1				
Christian and Missionary Alliance	159	10	62					
Christian (Brethren) Mission	271							
Christian Church Miss. Board (U. S. A.)	11	11	27		1			382
Christian Women's Board of Missions (Disciples)	50	26	5	9	4	3	1	317
Church Missionary Society	1,330	8,076	580	2,325	53	22	15	270,053
Church of England's Zenana Missionary Society	200	930		248	37	31		
Cumberland Presbyterian Missionary Society	25	42	20	3	1	1		843
Danish Missionary Society	23	35	13	10	5			911
(See also Indian Home Mission to Santhals and Loventhal's Mission.)								
Edinburg Medical Missionary Society	6	10			1	2		
Egypt General Mission	9	10	3	3				
Evangelical Association	6	24	1		1			
Finnish Missionary Society	13	39	20	10				1,235
Foreign Christian Missionary Society (Disciples) 3	93	222	68	32	3	15	1	2,874
Free Baptist Gen. Conference	28	67	12	36	2	3	1	1,831
Free Methodist Church in N. A.	23	30	14	6	2			396
Friends For. Miss. Association (British)	94	978	274	239	16	11	1	31,052
Furreedpore Mission	5	9	2	3		1		39
German Baptist Brethren Church (Dunkard)	11	20	11					45
German Evang. Lutheran Synod of Ohio, etc.*	9	9			8			9
German Evang. Synod of N. A.	15	109	44	24	3	5	1	4,499
Germany: German Baptists in Berlin	14	80	45	47				2,170
" Berlin Missionary Society (Berlin I.)	138	924	331	85	3	1		43,240
" Berlin Women's Society for China	4	3			1			
" Breklum Missionary Society	23	70	8	34				7,026
" Deaconesses' Inst. at Kaiserswerth	102			2	4	5		
" General Evang. Prot. Miss. Society	12	23	8	2	1	2	2	172
" Gossner's Missionary Society (Berlin II)	44	746	460	178	27		2	83,237
" German East Africa Mission (Berlin III)	24	26	9	6				900
" Hannover Luth. Free Church	9	64	8	17				4,050
" Hermannsburg Missionary Society	62	303	124	122				50,163
" Jerusalem Union	1	22		8	2			370
" Kiel China Mission	6	3		1				33
" Leipzig Missionary Society	72	774	237	268	18		1	21,815
" Miss. to Chinese Blind	2	2		1				
" Neudettelsau Missionary Society	15		7	6				30
" Neukirchen Missionary Institute	17	54	55	16				1,067
" North German Missionary Society	24	82	27	49	5			3,545
" Rhenish Missionary Society	285	498	180	388		3		91,124
" Sudan Pioneer Mission	2	3	2					
" Women's Soc. for Education of the Female Sex in the East	11			2	1			
Gospel Mission Union	16	1						
Hauge's Synod China Mission	12		5	12				
Hawaiian Evang. Association	21	54	57	4	6		1	2,183
Ikwezi Lamaci Mission (Young Men's For. Miss. Soc. Birmingham)	15	14	8	6				110
Indian Home Mission to the Santhals (Danish)	6	87	27		2		1	11,345
International Medical and Benevolent Assoc. (Seventh Day Adventist)*	71					22		
Ireland; Presbyterian Church in*	76	488	128	164	9	6	1	14,902
" Ref. Presbyterian Church in*	3	8	1	3	1			61
Jaffa Medical Mission*	11	5				4		
Jamaica Baptist Union	7	12						1,129
Jerusalem and the East Mission	19	6				2		
Kurku and Indian Hill Mission	18	8	5		3	2		
Labrador Medical Mission	5		2			2		
London Missionary Society	435	6,465	1,448	1,922	19	40	8	196,026
Loventhal's Mission (Danish)	1	3	1					
Lutheran (Evangelical) General Council (U.S.A.)	16	142	122	120	3	1		6,189
" " General Synod (U.S.A.)	37	518	172	240	4	1	1	26,458
" " Church in the South (U.S.A.)*	10	6		3		1		77
" Free Church Board of Missions (U.S.A.)	9	37	12	13	1			230
Melanesian Mission*	28	400	15	170	2	2	1	13,000
Mennonite Mission Board (U.S.A.)								
Methodist Episcopal Missionary Society 3	13	7	3	1	2	2		100
Methodist Episcopal Miss. Society, Home Missions	603	4,819	1,109	1,112	61		18	91,184
	8	1	1					63

Names of Societies.	No. of Missionaries, Men and Women	Native Workers, Men and Women	Places of Regular Worship	Elementary Schools	Higher or Special Educational Institutions	Hospitals and Dispensaries	Publishing Houses or Printing Establishments	Professing Christians
Methodist Episcopal (South) Miss. Society 4	228	463	103	83	28	8	1	11,713
Methodist New Connexion (England)	18	102	211	2	1	2		3,479
Methodist Protestant Church (England)	17	15	17	2	2			619
Missionary Pence Association	14	7	6	1	1	2		87
Miss Taylor's Schools*	2	6			1	2		
Miss Trotter's Mission*	5		1					
Moravian (*Brüder Unität*) Missions 5	402	1,863	212	230	7		2	94,769
Netherlands; Ermelo Missionary Society	2							
" Java Committee	6	11		8				500
" Lutheran Home and Foreign Mission Society*	5	1	3	1		1		28
" Mennonite Miss. Union (*Doopgezinde Vereeniging*)	11	26	12	8	1	1		1,657
" Missionary Society (*Nederlandsch Zendeling genootschap*)	26	13	12	18	1	1		5,620
" Mission of the Reformed Church in	16	12	14	4	1	1		718
" Missionary Union (*Nederlandsche Zenlings Vereeniging*)	17	42	21	21				1,844
" Society for Propagation of the Gospel in Egypt	2	7	2	2				42
" Utrecht Missionary Union	12	26	23	26				3,452
New England Company	14	13	7		2			100
New Hebrides Mission Synod*6	39	341	46	203	1	1	1	2,603
New Zealand Presbyterian Church	15	1	4	3	1	1		
North Africa Mission	92		16	11	2	12		
North India School of Medicine for Christian Women*|	10	6			1	7		
Norwegian Missionary Society	115	1,836	778	982	5	2	1	53,431
" Church Mission of Schreuder*	13	8	10	3				665
" Evang. Lutheran Church (U. S.)	2		1					
Nyasa Industrial Mission	6							
Palestine and Lebanon Mission	3	2		1		1		
Paris Evangelical Missionary Society	135	1,243	490	1,142	9	4	1	43,693
Peniel Missionary Society*	20	1	7	1				
Pentecost Bands of the World*	27		2	1		1		
Poona and Indian Village Mission	36		12		2	1	1	
Presbyterian Church in U. S. (North) 7	773	2,029	1,554	765		57	13	63,488
Presby. Church in U. S. (North) Home Mission Society	35	11	14	4		1		868
Presbyterian Church in U. S. (South)	165	141	210	15	9	3	2	13,295
Presbyterian Church of England (see also Canada, Ireland, Scotland)	110	203	61	100	23	8	3	12,951
Primitive Methodist Miss. Society*	39	12	21	5	1	1		4,063
Protestant Episcopal Church in U. S. A. 1	224	97	256	138	11	20	2	5,908
Qua Ibo Mission	10	12	11	12	1			100
Queensland Baptist Association, For. Missions	3	9	6	4				
Ramabai Association		9	2		2			
Ranaghat Medical Mission	13	20	1	1		2		90
Reformed Church in America (Dutch)	85	571	273	173	23	7	1	4,932
Reformed Church in U. S. (German)*	19	50	41	0	2			5,430
Reformed Episcopal Church	5	17	4	5	1	1		131
Reformed Presby. Church in N. A. (Gen. Synod)*	2	50	4	2	1		1	1,130
Reformed Presby. Church in N. A. (Synod)	21	40	17	15				328
Regions Beyond Missionary Union	59	10	19	9		5		
Scandinavian Alliance in N. A.*	87	8	34	13				247
Scotland: Church of (For. Miss. Com.) 4	143	466	188	281	9	17	3	4,270
" United Free Church of 5	409	3,228	423	957	8	45	9	39,644
Seventh Day Adventist Society	174	107	165	24	1	7		3,548
Seventh Day Baptist Missionary Society	6	18				1	1	66
Society for the Propagation of the Gospel	509	2,864	919	746	106	4	7	127,477
Sierra Leone Mission (Countess of Huntington's Con)								
South Africa Minister's Mission Union (Dutch Reform	34	0	5	100				700
South Africa General Mission	29	16	15	9		3		140
South African Wesleyan Methodist Missions*	11	3,531	1,770	581	10			209,627
South American Evangelical Mission	16		5			1		
South American Miss. Society	54	32	17	9	2	1	1	
South Arcot Highways and Hedges*	1							
Southern Baptist Convention	127	190	170	62			1	8,880
Southern Morocco Mission	18		5	1		5		
Sweden: Church of Missionary Soc. (*Kyrkans*)	30	48	71	56	1			3,262
" Evang. National Society (*Fosterlands*)	78	71	33	26			1	1,514
" Holiness Union (*Helgeseforbundet*)	11	7	9					
" Missionary Union (*Missionsforbundets*)	68	72	58	109	1	7		1,873
" Y. W. C. A.*	2		1					
Swedish Evang. Mission Covenant in U. S. A	19	8	10	7		2		223
Swedish Mission in China	Statistics	included	in CIM					
Switzerland: Romande Mission (See also Basel Missionary Soc.)	41			10	14	1	2	1	4,581
Tabeetha Mission in Jaffa	3	7		3	1			
United Brethren in Christ	14	31	36	8	1			501
United Evangelical Church	7	3	1	1				8

Appendix V   THE ENCYCLOPEDIA OF MISSIONS   838

Names of Societies.	No. of Missionaries, Men and Women	Native Workers, Men and Women	Places of Regular Worship	Elementary Schools	Higher or Special Educational Institutions	Hospitals and Dispensaries	Publishing Houses or Printing Establishments	Professing Christians
United Methodist Free Church	27	848	211					12,555
United Presbyterian Church of N. A.	104	1,496	432	281	31	10		16,293
Universalist Gen. Convention*	5	19	10					
Universities Mission	28	39	46	115	7	5	3	8,336
United Norwegian Lutheran Church of N. A.*	23	51	37	34	4			200
Victorian Baptist Foreign Missions	9	35	23	22	2			543
Welsh Calvinistic Methodist Missions	26	253	306	401	2	2	1	16,931
Wesleyan Methodist Missionary Society	371	5,270	2,445	1,282		2	3	66,276
Woman's Union Missionary Society	43	87	6	16	5	3		
Zambesi Industrial Mission	27	50	19	34		2		
Zenana Bible and Medical Mission	104	328		64		6		
Total	13,371	69,670	24,337	23,527	960	553	147	2,219,291
THE BIBLE SOCIETIES IN THE NON-CHRISTIAN LANDS.								
American Bible Society	21	384						
British and Foreign Bible Society	55	1,134						
Scottish National Bible Society	14	217						
Netherlands Bible Society	2	1						
Total	92	1,736						

Notes.— * From Beach's Atlas of Protestant Missions.
1 Contains items rated by the Society as Domestic Missions.
2 Work in West Indies (now Independent) is not included.
3 Work in Protestant Europe not included.
4 Including work of Women's Societies.
5 Christian establishments in Protestant islands of the West Indies figure in this report.
6 Probably duplicated in other society reports.
7 Schools not classified in reports of this Society.

B. THE FOREIGN MISSIONARY FIELDS OF THE PROTESTANT SOCIETIES.

Names of Societies.	Date of Entrance into this Field	No. of Missionaries, Men and Women	Native Workers, Men and Women	Places of Regular Worship	Elementary Schools	Higher or Special Educational Institutions	Hospitals and Dispensaries	Publishing Houses or Printing Establishments	Professed Christians
AFRICA.									
Society for the Propagation of the Gospel	1752	101	18	105				1	25,081
Moravian (Brüder Unität) Missions	1792	127	500	59		2		1	16,916
Wesleyan Methodist Missionary Society	1796	114	1,872	1,432	220				35,688
London Missionary Society	1799	50	155	57	89			1	15,763
Church Missionary Society	1804	259	2,709	125	266	5	5	5	63,177
United Free Church of Scotland	1821	169	1,169	198	489	2	13	5	17,672
Basel Missionary Society	1828	130	414	202	302	6		1	22,675
Rhenish Missionary Society	1829	91	96	37	76				29,325
Paris Evangelical Missionary Society	1833	84	364	113	186	3	1	1	29,770
Methodist Episcopal Missionary Society	1833	63	102	72	40	3		2	3,632
Berlin Missionary Society	1834	115	758	241	80	2	1		39,616
American Board of Commis'rs for Foreign Missions	1834	66	590	182	87	7		1	4,566
Protestant Episcopal Church of U. S.	1836	27	18	88	56			1	1,767
Presbyterian Church in U. S. (North)	1842	34	49	46	22		2		1,716
Norwegian Missionary Society of Schreuder	1843	13	8	10	3				665
North German Missionary Society	1847	24	82	27	49	5			3,545
Norwegian Missionary Society	1849	27	41	28	32	1			2,060
Southern Baptist Convention	1850	10	21	9	5				544
Hermannsburg Missionary Society	1854	50	182	105	85				47,822
United Presbyterian Church	1854	71	862	223	147	23	3		6,800
United Brethren in Christ	1855	4	16	18	8				321
Pongas Mission	1855	Included in statistics of SPG							
United Methodist Free Churches	1859	10	287	27					3,739
Evangelical Lutheran Church (U.S.) Gen. Synod	1860	10	12	8	8	2			96

Names of Societies.	Date of Entrance into this Field	No. of Missionaries, Men and Women	Native Workers, Men and Women	Places of Regular Worship	Elementary Schools	Higher or Special Educational Institutions	Hospitals and Dispensaries	Publishing Houses or Printing Establishments	Professing Christians
AFRICA—*continued*									
Universities Mission	1861	28	39	46	115	7	5	3	8,336
Swedish National Missionary Society (*Fosterlands*)	1865	35	33	15	15			1	566
Netherlands Soc. for Prop. the Gospel in Egypt	1870	2	7	2	2				42
Primitive Methodist Missionary Society	1870	39	12	21	5	1	1		4,063
Finnish Missionary Society	1871	11	39	20	10				1,235
Church of Scotland For. Miss. Committee	1874	36	72	16	33	1	2	2	544
Romande Mission	1875	41		10	14	1	2	1	4,581
Church of Sweden Missionary Society (*Kyrkans*)	1876	19	38	48	31				1,579
Ikwez; Lamaci Mission (Young Men's Society of Birmingham)	1877	15	14	8	6				110
American Baptist Missionary Union	1878	33	217	50	107	3		1	3,104
African Methodist Episcopal Church	1878		300	300	120	1			11,000
Baptist Missionary Society (England)	1879	61	236	87	50		10	3	764
Christian (Brethren) Missionary Society	1881	55							
North Africa Mission	1881	92		16	11	2	12		
Swedish Missionary Union (*Missionsförbundets*)*	1882	40	62	48	101	1	7		1,573
Central Morocco Mission	1886	4					1		
Neukirchen Missionary Institute	1887	8	8	9	5				142
German East Africa Missionary Society	1887	24	26	9	6				900
Qua Ibo Mission	1887	10	12	11	12	1			100
Christian and Missionary Alliance	1887	31	8	11					
Southern Morocco Mission	1888	18		5	1		5		
Miss Trotter's Mission*	1888	5		1					
Regions Beyond Missionary Union	1889	35	6	13	6		5		
South Africa General Mission	1890	29	16	15	9		3		140
Presbyterian Church of U. S. (South)	1891	9	20	8	2		1	1	2,454
German Baptists in Berlin	1891	14	80	45	47				2,170
Swedish Holiness Union	1891	10	7	9					
Scandinavian Alliance of U. S.	1892	9	4	4					
Leipzig Missionary Society	1892	27		20	20				218
Hannover Free Church Mission	1892	9	64	8	17				4,050
Zambesi Industrial Mission	1892	27	50	19	34		2		
African Tr. Institute (Colwyn Bay)*	1893		172		29	1			
Gospel Mission Union	1894	8							
Africa Inland Mission	1895	5		3	1				
Seventh Day Baptist Missionary Society	1895	1	2						
Peniel Missionary Society	1895	3	1	1	1				
Foreign Christian Missionary Society	1896	8	1	1	1		1		
Int. Medical and Benevolent Miss. Society	1896	14					3		
Egypt General Mission	1898	9	10	3	3				
Swedish Young Women's Christian Assoc.*	1899	2		1					
Free Methodist Church	1899	10	11	8	4				235
American Friends Foreign Missions		10		1					402
Sudan Pioneer Mission		2	3	2					
South Africa Wesleyan Methodist Miss. Soc		11	3,521	1,770	581	10			209,627
Nyasa Industrial Mission		6							
South Africa Ministers' Mission Union		34		5	100				700
Deaconess' Institute Kaiserswerth		24					2		
Total Africa		**2,572**	**15,426**	**6,081**	**3,812**	**90**	**85**	**31**	**31,591**
MADAGASCAR AND OTHER AFRICAN ISLANDS.									
London Missionary Society	1818	56	3,323	440	630	2	3	1	47,264
Society for the Propagation of the Gospel	1843	38	35	17					12,984
Friends Foreign Mission Association	1867	23	830	220	180	8	2	1	28,383
Norwegian Missionary Society	1867	88	1,795	750	950	4	2	1	51,371
United Norwegian Lutheran Church of N. A.	1892	23	51	37	34	4			200
Lutheran (Free Church) Board of Missions U. S. A.	1895	9	37	12	13	1			230
Paris Evangelical Missionary Society	1896	34	842	322	950	4	2		9,182
American Advent Missionary Society	1900	1		1					
Total Madagascar		**272**	**6,913**	**1,793**	**2,757**	**23**	**9**	**3**	**49,614**
Total Africa and Madagascar		**2,844**	**22,339**	**7,880**	**6,569**	**113**	**94**	**34**	**781,205**
AMERICA—ALASKA.									
Presbyterian Church (North) Home Missions	1877	35	11	14	4		1		868
Moravian Missions	1885	18	11	3	2				596
Amer. Friends Foreign Miss. Association	1887	9	15	4	3				1,058
Swedish Evang. Mission Covenant of America	1887	13	3	6	3		1		186
Amer. Missionary Association	1890	2	2	2	2				
Amer. Baptist Home Missionary Society	1893	1		2					30
Peniel Missionary Society*	1895	8		3					
Methodist Episcopal Church in U. S. 1	1897	8	1	1					63
Protestant Episcopal Church in U. S., Dom. and For. Missions 1	1898	29	8		7		4		
Norwegian Evangelical Lutheran Church (U. S.)*		2		1					
Total Alaska		**125**	**51**	**36**	**21**		**6**		**2,801**

Names of Societies.	Date of entrance into this field	No. of Missionaries, Men and Women	Native Workers, Men and Women	Places of Regular Worship	Elementary Schools	Higher or Special Educational Institutions	Hospitals and Dispensaries	Publishing Houses or Printing Establishments	Professing Christians
AMERICA—Canada and Labrador.									
New England Company	1649	14	13	7	2				100
Moravian Missions	1771	44	38	9	6				1,379
Methodist Church in Canada	1822	87	4	25	45	9	2		
Church Missionary Society	1822	106	133	70	92	3	1	1	14,471
Presbyterian Church in Canada	1866	73	8	22	16			1	425
Labrador Medical Mission*	1892	5		2			2		
Total Canada and Labrador		329	196	135	159	14	5	2	16,375
AMERICA—Mexico.									
American Baptist Home Missionary Society 1	1870	20		43				1	474
Protestant Episcopal Church in U. S. (Dom. and For. Missions) 1	1870	1	1						
Presbyterian Church in U. S. (North)	1871	23	81	72	29			1	3,902
American Friends Foreign Missions	1871	16	29	10	7	3		2	1,532
American Board of Com. for Foreign Missions	1872	17	23	74	4	4		1	1,193
Cumberland Presbyterian Board	1872	4	7	1	3				105
Methodist Episcopal Church (South) 4	1873	55	174	27	16	7	2		5,814
Methodist Episcopal Church in U. S.	1873	31	185	93	51	7		1	5,592
Presbyterian Church in U. S. (South)	1874	5	11	53		2			1,522
Associate Reformed Presbyterian Ch. of the South*	1880	11	11	5	5	1			573
Southern Baptist Convention	1880	17	19	43	4				1,251
Christian Missions (Brethren)	1890	4							
International Medical and Benevolent Assoc.(S.D.A.)	1894	15					2		
Seventh Day Adventists Missions	1894	10	1	3	1		1		32
Christian Woman's Board of Missions (Disciples)	1897	7	3		3			1	20
Total Mexico		236	545	424	123	24	5	7	22,010
AMERICA—Central and Southern.									
Moravian Missions	1776	127	492	62	38	1			35,555
London Missionary Society	1808	2	3	4		1			
Wesleyan Missionary Society	1825	7	91	49	26				2,017
Society for the Propagation of the Gospel	1835	21							
Methodist Episcopal Church in the U. S.	1836	72	181	67	14	10		3	5,563
South American Missionary Society	1844	54	32	17	9	2	1	1	
Presbyterian Church in U. S. (North)	1856	54	50	52	46			2	4,362
Presbyterian Church in U. S. (South)	1869	30	18	17	2	2		1	3,289
Methodist Episcopal Church in U. S. (South)	1876	40	58	29	7	6		1	3,343
Southern Baptist Convention	1882	21	32	48	11			1	2,903
Presbyterian Church in Canada	1885	4	6	6					20
Seventh Day Adventists	1887	57	49	80	15		1		1,598
Jamaica Baptist Missionary Union	1887	5	10						957
Central America Mission*	1890	26	25	16					1,425
African Methodist Episcopal Church	1893	1		20	3				5,000
Regions Beyond Missionary Union	1894	18		4	3				
Missionary Pence Association	1895	5		2	1	1			32
International Medical and Benev. Assoc. S. D. A.	1895	4					1		
South American Evangelical Mission Society	1895	16		5			1		
Gospel Mission Union	1896	8	1						
Sweden: Holiness Union	1898	1							
Baptist Conventions of Ontario and Quebec (Canada)	1898	9	1	2		4			5
Christian and Missionary Alliance		16							
Christian (Brethren) Missions		39							
Total South America		637	1,049	480	175	27	4	9	66,069
AMERICA—West Indies.									
Moravian Missions 5	1732	52	813	68	108	3			40,107
Wesleyan Missionary Society	1786	11	120	38	4				3,913
African Methodist Episcopal Church	1820	20		28	3				4,000
United Free Church of Scotland 5	1835	41	709	26	64	1			12,734
United Methodist Free Church	1838	11	379	46					3,559
Protestant Episcopal Church in U. S.	1861	1	12	22	9				537
Presbyterian Church in Canada	1870	14	66	4	59				917
Jamaica Baptist Missionary Union	1872	2	2						172
Methodist Episcopal Church in U. S. (South)	1872	18	13	3	3	2			454
Christian Woman's Board of Missions (Disciples)	1876	2			1				
American Friends Foreign Missions	1881	20	25	11	5	3		1	1,668
Seventh Day Adventists Missions	1890	26	37	39	3				1,339
International Medical and Benevolent Society(SDA)	1895	1					1		
American Baptist Home Missionary Society	1898	15		11					218
United Brethren in Christ	1898	4	4	8					50
Evang. Lutheran Church in N. A., Gen. Council	1899	3		2					30
Presbyterian Church in U. S. (South)	1899	7	2	3	1	1			213
Foreign Christian Missionary Society	1899	5	1	4	1				21
Christian Church, Mission Board	1901	4	1	9					

Names of Societies.	Date of Entrance into this Field	No. of Missionaries, Men and Women	Native Workers, Men and Women	Places of Regular Worship	Elementary Schools	Higher or Special Educational Institutions	Hospitals and Dispensaries	Publishing Houses or Printing Establishments	Professing Christians
AMERICA—WEST INDIES—contd.									
Christian and Missionary Alliance............		8		3					
Peniel Mission Society....................		2		1					
Christian (Brethren) Mission.............		10							
Total West Indies...............		277	2,184	326	261	10	1	1	69,932
Total America..................		1,604	4,025	1,401	739	75	21	19	177,187
ASIA—CHINA.									
London Missionary Society	1807	106	326	239	104	6	20	1	7,799
Amer. Board of Com. for Foreign Missions........	1830	95	398	214	134	22		2	6,410
Prot. Episcopal Domestic and Foreign Missions.....	1835	72	27	56	50	4	12	1	1,469
Reformed Church in America...............	1842	19	79	50	13	8	3		1,407
Germany: Women's Society for Educa. Female Sex..	1842	2				1			
Amer. Baptist Mission Union...............	1843	77	232	151	35	2		1	10,275
Presbyterian Church in U. S. (North)............	1844	214	548	300	162		18	3	12,033
Southern Baptist Convention................	1845	63	79	32	41				3,401
Methodist Episcopal Church in U. S.............	1847	148	717	438	203	23		3	22,646
Seventh Day Baptists.....................	1847	5	16				1	1	66
Presbyterian Church in England.............	1847	85	122	12	86	19	4	2	8,316
Rhenish Missionary Society................	1847	23	22	12	18		2		1,185
Methodist Episcopal Church in U. S. (South).......	1848	59	157	22	47	9	5		934
Berlin Women's Mission for China............	1850	4	3			1			
Wesleyan Methodist Missionary Society.........	1851	34	173	106	42				3,267
Basel Missionary Society..................	1852	50	173	57	73	4	1		7,060
China Inland Mission....................	1853	763	741	476	83		25	2	7,774
Baptist Missionary Society................	1859	43	187	328	18		4	1	4,503
Methodist New Connexion Miss. Soc...........	1859	18	102	211	2	1	2		3,479
Church Missionary Society................	1863	230	527	49	248	5	5	2	14,329
United Free Church of Scotland.............	1863	37	156	75	30	1	4	1	5,994
United States Methodist Free Church...........	1864	6	182	138					5,257
Presbyterian Church in U. S. (South)............	1867	68	46	30	7	3	2		759
Berlin Missionary Society.................	1867	23	166	90	5	1			3,624
Presbyterian Church in Ireland..............	1869	28	195	94	32	1	5		9,212
Society for the Propagation of the Gospel.........	1874	19	15	17				1	777
Church of Scotland, Foreign Missions Committee 4....	1878	10	24	4	6		1		206
Woman's Union Missionary Society...........	1881	4		1		1	1		
Church of England Zenana Missionary Society......	1884	43	102		50	11	5		
General Evang. Prot. Miss. Society (German).......	1885	6	10	6	2		2	1	32
Christian (Brethren) Mission................	1885	55							
Bible Christian Home and For. Missionary Society....	1885	7	3	2	1		2		19
Foreign Christian Missionary Society...........	1886	26	72	18	10	2	4	1	648
Friends For. Mission Association.............	1886	18	24	15	4	2	1		349
Murray's Mission to the Chinese Blind...........	1888	1			1				
Seventh Day Adventists Mission..............	1888	1		1					
American Friends Foreign Missions............	1890	10	16	2	4	1	3		164
Christian and Missionary Alliance............	1890	43		19					
Swedish Missionary Covenant in America 6.......	1890	6	5	4	4		1		37
Sweden: Missionary Union (Missionförbundets).....	1890	22	10	8	4				300
Germany: Mission to the Blind in China..........	1890	2	2		1				
Scandinavian Alliance Mission in N. A...........	1891	55		12	12				95
Methodist Church in Canada................	1891	10	5	4	2		2	1	62
Hauge's Synod China Mission...............	1892	12		5	12				
Presbyterian Church in Canada..............	1893	32	12	8	3		2		215
Baptist Zenana Mission...................	1893	6	4		18	1			
Meth. Protestant Women's Society............	1894	2							
Danish Missionary Society.................	1896	9	2	2					57
American Advent Missionary Society*...........	1897	4	5	1	1				
Kiel China Mission.....................	1897	6	3		1				33
Cumberland Presbyterian Church.............	1898	5		1			1		36
American Norwegian China Mission...........	1899	5	7	3					8
United Evangelical Church.................	1900	7	3	1	1				
Reformed Pres. Church Synod (U. S.)*..........	1900	2	2	1					
Presbyterian Church in New Zealand...........	1900	6		1					
Finnish Missionary Society................	1901	2							
Total China....................		2,708	5,700	3,316	1,570	129	138	24	144,237
ASIA—FARTHER INDIA.									
Amer. Baptist Miss. Union.................	1813	173	1,756	780	511	35	1	1	74,706
Presbyterian Church in U. S. (North)...........	1840	69	53	61	23		8	2	3,145
Society for the Propagation of the Gospel.........	1859	37	381	17	75	15		1	6,906
Methodist Episcopal Church in the U. S.........	1885	13	38	1	5	1			583
Missionary Pence Association..............	1892	2	4	1					40
Church of England Zenana Miss. Society.........	1900	2	1			1			
Wesleyan Methodist Missionary Society.........		8	67	24	22				288
Christian Missions (Brethren)...............		2							
Total Farther India...............		306	2,300	884	636	52	9	4	85,668

Names of Societies.	Date of Entrance into this Field	No. of Missionaries, Men and Women	Native Workers, Men and Women	Places of Regular Worship	Elementary Schools	Higher or Special Educational Institutions	Hospitals and Dispensaries	Publishing Houses or Printing Establishments	Professed Christians
ASIA—INDIA AND CEYLON.									
Baptist Missionary Society	1793	124	704	285	312	13	6	2	9,045
London Missionary Society	1798	163	1,863	394	835	5	17	3	93,885
Church Missionary Society	1813	498	4,014	238	1,625	38	2	6	152,670
American Board of Com. for For. Missions	1813	90	1,587	520	484	32		2	13,454
Wesleyan Methodist Missionary Society	1817	190	2,812	709	936		2	3	18,912
Society for the Propagation of the Gospel	1821	215	2,199	691	655	78	3	2	75,049
United Free Church of Scotland	1829	155	1,143	113	343	4	23	3	3,069
Church of Scotland Foreign Missions	1829	97	370	168	242	8	14	1	3,520
Presbyterian Church in the U. S. (North)	1834	149	469	295	173		15	2	3,935
Basel Missionary Society	1834	153	679	246	160	14	1	1	15,469
Free Baptist General Conference (England)	1836	28	67	12	36	2	3	1	1,831
Christian (Brethren) Missions	1836	74							
Reformed Presbyterian Church in N. A., General Synod	1837	2	50	4	2	1		1	1,130
Amer. Baptist Mission Union	1840	153	1246	239	663	32	1	2	61,145
Presbyterian Church in Ireland	1841	43	251	31	113	7	1	1	5,483
Welsh Calvinistic Methodist Mission	1841	24	251	301	401	2	2	1	16,659
Leipzig Evang. Missionary Society	1841	45	774	217	248	18		1	21,597
Lutheran Church (Evangelical) in U. S., Gen. Synod	1842	27	506	164	232	2	1	1	26,362
Gossner Missionary Society	1844	44	746	460	178	27	2	2	83,237
Zenana Bible and Medical Missionary Society	1852	104	328		64		6		
Reformed Church in America (Dutch)	1853	26	450	165	159	10	2		2,442
United Presbyterian Church in the U. S.	1855	33	634	209	134	8	7		9,493
Methodist Episcopal Church in the U. S.	1856	199	3,221	271	781	7		4	34,558
Moravian Missions (Himalaya Mission)	1856	22	9	7	10	1		1	110
Presbyterian Church of England	1862	5	13		5	3			35
Women's Union Missionary Society	1863	35	87	4	16	3	2		
Danish Missionary Society	1864	14	33	11	10	5			854
Hermannsburg Missionary Society	1865	12	121	19	37				2,341
Friends Foreign Missionary Association (England)	1866	40	77	28	39	4	5		1,850
Baptist Zenana Mission	1867	59	232		80	4	4		
Furreedpore Mission	1867	5	9	2	3	1	1		39
Baptist Convention of Ontario and Quebec	1868	32	196	111	78	9			4,600
Lutheran Church (Evangelical) in the U.S., General Council	1869	13	142	120	120	3	1		6,159
Loventhal's Mission (Danish)	1872	1	3	1					
Bengal Evangelical Mission	1874		21	5	9	1	1		117
Baptist Convention of the Maritime Provs. (Canada)	1875	24	46	21	17				495
Bethel Santhal Mission	1875	5	17	3	8	5	8		1,480
Presbyterian Church in Canada	1877	47	88	11	12	0	4	1	1,318
Swedish National Miss. Society (*Fosterlands*)	1878	43	38	18	11				948
Church of England Zenana Mission	1880	155	827		198	25	26		
Edinburgh Medical Mission	1881	1				1			
Pentecost Bands of the World*	1881	27	1	2	1	1	1		
Foreign Christian Missionary Society	1882	23	104	10	11	1	10		501
Christian Woman's Board of Missions	1883	41	23	5	5	4	3	1	297
Breklum Missionary Society	1884	23	70	8	34				7,026
Victorian Baptist Foreign Missionary Society	1886	9	35	23	22	2			543
American Advent Missionary Society*	1886	2	3	3	2				
Reformed Episcopal Church	1888	5	17	4	5	1	1		131
Christian and Missionary Alliance	1889	50		21					
Kurku and Central Indian Hill Mission	1889	18	8	5		3	2		
Queensland Baptist Missionary Society	1889	3	9	6	4				
Free Methodist Church in N. A.	1891	9	13	3	2	2			80
Scandinavian Alliance of N. A.	1892	15		3	1				
Missionary Pence Association	1892	4	1	2			2		15
Seventh Day Adventist Missions	1893	15	5	3	1		1		39
Balaghat Mission	1893	8	2	4	2	1	2		180
Poona and Indian Village Mission	1893	36		12		2	1	1	
North-India School of Med. for Christ. Women	1894	10	6			1	7		
Lutheran (German Evangelical) Synod of Ohio, etc.*	1895	9	9			8			9
Lutheran (German Evang.) Synod of N. A.	1895	15	109	44	24	3	5	1	4,499
German Baptist Brethren	1895	9	20	11					45
Amer. Friends Foreign Missions	1896	4		1					
Peniel Missionary Society*	1896	3		1					
International Medical and Benevolent Missionary Society (SDA)	1897	10					1		
Mennonite Mission Board in U. S.*	1899	13	7	3	1	2	2		100
Regions Beyond Missionary Union	1900	6	4	2					
Ramabai Association			9	2		2			
Ranaghat Mission		13	20	1	1	2	2		90
Indian Home Mission to the Santhals (Danish)		6	87	27		2		▲	11,345
Swedish Church Mission (*Kyrkans*)		11	10	23	25	1			1,683
German, Woman's Education Society (for women in the East)		9			2				
Ceylon and India General Mission		24	36	16					
Bengali Mission*		3	5	1	1	1			
British and Foreign Unitarian Association		1	2	2	1				
South Arcot Highways and Hedges Mission*		1							
Total India and Ceylon		3,584	26,938	6,341	9,574	408	200	46	699,874

Names of Societies.	Date of Entrance into this Field	No. of Missionaries, Men and Women	Native Workers, Men and Women	Places of Regular Worship	Elementary Schools	Higher or Special Educational Institutions	Hospitals and Dispensaries	Publishing Houses or Printing Establishments	Professed Christians
ASIA—JAPAN (Including Formosa).									
Presbyterian Church in the U. S. (North)	1859	61	136	99	16				5,825
Reformed Church in America (Dutch)	1859	30	30	52		5			1,083
Protestant Episcopal Church in U. S., Dom. and Foreign Miss.	1859	66	21	74	13	6	4		2,035
Presbyterian Church of England	1865	17	58	38	9	1	4	1	4,331
Church Missionary Society	1869	103	152	24	17	1	3		5,499
Amer. Board of Com. for Foreign Missions	1869	70	109	216	3	8		1	10,693
Woman's Union Missionary Society	1871	4		1		1			
Amer. Baptist Missionary Union	1872	58	137	33	6	6			2,157
Presbyterian Church in Canada	1872	4	57	53	2		1		2,037
Methodist Episcopal Church in U. S.	1872	67	161	51	9	3	2	2	6,561
Society for the Propagation of the Gospel	1873	26	121	22	2	2	1		1,626
Cumberland Presbyterian Board	1877	16	35	18		1			738
Evangelical Association	1877	6	24	1		1			
Reformed Church in the U. S. (German)	1879	19	50	41		2			5,430
American Friends Foreign Missions	1880	7	22	3	1	2			542
Methodist Protestant Church	1880	15	15	17	2	2			619
Methodist Church in Canada	1882	15	21	12	2	1			2,374
Foreign Christian Missionary Society	1883	20	26	13	3				1,011
Presbyterian Church in U. S. (South)	1885	28	35	80		1			3,958
Germany: Gen. Evang. Prot. Miss. Society	1885	6	13	2		1		1	140
Methodist Episcopal Church, South (U.S.)	1886	39	28	9	8	2			744
Christian Church Foreign Mission Board (U. S.)	1887	7	10	18		1			382
Southern Baptist Convention (U. S.)	1890	12	12	13					120
Universalists General Convention*	1890	5	19	10					
Scandinavian Alliance (U. S.)	1891	8	4	15					152
Lutheran (Evangelical) Church, South	1892	10	6	3			1		77
Christian and Missionary Alliance	1894	3		4					
United Brethren in Christ	1895	6	11	10		1		1	130
Seventh Day Adventist Mission Society	1896	8	4	3	2				24
Free Methodist Church of North America		4	6	3					81
Christian (Brethren) Missions		2							
Total Japan		742	1,323	938	95	47	15	5	58,369
ASIA—KOREA.									
Presbyterian Church in the U. S. (North)	1884	64	182	374	75	4	5	1	22,662
Methodist Episcopal Church in the U. S.	1885	26	26	47		1		1	5,855
Presbyterian Church in Australia	1889	9	17	10	5	1			268
Society for the Propagation of the Gospel	1889	16	7	6	3	1		1	204
Presbyterian Church in U. S. (South)	1892	12	9	19	3				1,100
Presbyterian Church in Canada	1893	10	30	26	6		1		941
Missionary Pence Association	1896	3	2	1					
Methodist Episcopal Church in the U. S. (South)	1896	17	33	13	2	2	1		424
Total Korea		157	306	496	94	9	7	3	31,454
						1			
ASIA—MALAYSIA (Including Malay Peninsula, Singapore, Dutch East Indies, Borneo, New Guinea and Philippines).									
Netherlands Missionary Society (*Genootschap*)	1831	26	13	12	18		1		5,620
Rhenish Missionary Society	1836	171	380	131	294		1		60,614
Society for the Propagation of the Gospel	1848	29	88	44	11	10			4,850
Netherlands Mennonite Missionary Society (*Doopgezinde*)	1852	11	26	12	8	1	1		1,657
Java Comité	1855	6	11		8				500
Netherlands Missionary Union (*Vereeniging*)	1863	17	42	21	21				1,844
Utrecht Missionary Society	1866	12	26	23	26				3,452
London Missionary Society	1871	23	112	12	6			1	969
Netherlands Reformed Church Missions	1878	16	12	14	4	1	1		718
Netherlands Lutheran Home and Foreign Missionary Society	1883	5	1	3	1		1		28
Neukirchen Mission Institute	1884	9	46	46	11				925
Neudettelsau Missionary Society	1886	15		7	6				30
Christian and Missionary Alliance	1899	2		1					
Presbyterian Church in the U. S. (North)	1899	15	32	24	2		2		469
Foreign Christian Missionary Society	1899	4		2					23
Amer. Baptist Missionary Union	1900	11	7	3					372
Netherlands Ermelo Missionary Society	1900	2							
Methodist Episcopal Church in U. S.	1900	38	75	22	6	2		1	3,413
Seventh Day Adventist Missions	1900	2		1	1				
Christian (Brethren) Missions	1900	30							
Protestant Episcopal Church in U. S.		13		3					
Presbyterian Church of England		1	10	11					269
American Board of Commis'rs for Foreign Missions	1902	4							
Total Malaysia		462	881	392	423	15	7	2	85,753

Appendix V — THE ENCYCLOPEDIA OF MISSIONS

Names of Societies.	Date of entrance into this Field	No. of Missionaries, Men and Women	Native Workers, Men and Women	Places of Regular Worship	Elementary Schools	Higher or Special Educational Institutions	Hospitals and Dispensaries	Publishing Houses or Printing Establishments	Professed Christains
ASIA—PERSIA AND THE CAUCASUS.									
Presbyterian Church in the U. S. (North)	1835	52	222	137	105		6	1	2,897
Church Missionary Society	1875	40	44	5	7		3	1	262
Archbishop's Mission to the Assyrians		2			46			1	
Swedish Missionary Union (Forbundets)		6		2	4				
Total Persia		100	266	144	162		9	3	3,159
ASIA—TURKEY (Including Arabia, Syria and the European districts).									
American Board of Com. for Foreign Missions	1819	172	1,003	265	405	45		2	14,901
Presbyterian Church in the U. S.(North)	1823	38	207	94	108		1	1	2,542
Methodist Episcopal Church in U. S.	1858	4	42	15	1	1		1	324
Presbyterian Church in Ireland*	1843	5	42	3	19	1			207
Church Missionary Society	1851	76	132	21	64		3		2,288
Deaconess' Institute at Kaiserswerth	1851	78			2	4	3		
Reformed Presbyterian Church in N. A. (Synod)	1857	19	38	16	15				328
British Syrian Mission Schools*	1860	18	103	1	50	3	4		
Edinburgh Medical Missionary Association	1861	5	10				2		
Germany: Jerusalem Union	1861	1	22		8	2			370
Tabeetha Mission	1863	3	7		3	1			
Miss Taylor's Schools	1868	2	6			1	2		
Friends Foreign Missionary Association	1869	13	47	11	16	2	3		470
Amer. Friends For. Missions	1869	4	31	1	7	2	1		150
Reformed Presbyterian Church of Ireland*	1876	3	8	1	3	1			61
Seventh Day Adventist Missions	1877	7	7	18					223
Jaffa Medical Mission	1878	11	5				4		
Foreign Christian Missionary Society	1879	5	18	17	6				670
Baptist Missionary Society	1885	2	8	4	2				129
United Free Church of Scotland	1886	3	8	1	1		2		7
Palestine and Lebanon Mission	1887	3	2		1		1		
Reformed Church in America (Dutch)	1890	10	12	6	1		2		
Christian and Missionary Alliance	1895	6	2	3					
Jerusalem and the East Mission Fund		19	6				2		
German Baptist Brethren		2							
Total Turkey		509	1,766	477	712	63	30	4	22,670
Aggregate Asia		8,568	39,486	12,988	13,266	723	415	90	1,131,184
AUSTRALASIA (Including Australia and New Zealand).									
Church Missionary Society	1814	18	365	48	6	1			17,357
Moravian Missions	1859	12		4	3				106
Australian Wesleyan Meth. Miss. Soc	1891	14	53	16	28		1		625
International Medical and Benevolent Assoc. (SDA)	1896	19					10		
New Zealand Presbyterian Mission		4	1	2					
Total Australasia		67	419	70	37	2	11		18,088
OCEANIA.									
London Missionary Society	1797	35	683	302	258	5		1	30,346
American Board of Commis'rs for For. Missions	1819	25	166	180	108	9			6,603
Hawaiian Evangelical Association	1823	21	54	57	4	6		1	2,183
Australian Wesleyan Meth. Missionary Society	1835	37	1,383	1,100	2,082	19			43,090
New Hebrides Mission* 6	1842	39	341	46	203	1	1	1	2,603
Melanesian Mission	1849	28	400	15	170	2	2	1	13,000
Society for the Propagation of the Gospel	1862	7							
Paris Evangelical Missionary Society	1863	17	37	55	6	2	1		4,741
Seventh Day Adventist Missions	1886	48	4	17	1	1	3		293
International Medical and Benevolent Assoc. (SDA)	1893	8					4		
Peniel Missionary Society	1899	4		1					
Foreign Christian Missionary Society	1899	2		3					
Prot. Episcopal Church in U. S. 1		14	10	13	3	1			100
New Zealand Presbyterian Church		5		1	3	1	1		
United Free Church of Scotland		4	43	10	30		3		168
Presbyterian Church of Canada		6		3					400
Total Oceania		3,300	3,121	1,803	2,868	47	15	4	103,527
ROMAN CATHOLIC EUROPE.									
AUSTRIA.									
American Board of Com. for For. Missions		4	19						1,414
FRANCE.									
Baptist Missionary Society		4	4	7					57
Welsh Calvinistic Methodist Missionary Society		2	2	5	2				272

Names of Societies.	No. of Missionaries, Men and Women	Native Workers, Men and Women	Places of Regular Worship	Elementary Schools	Higher or Special Educational Institutions	Hospitals and Dispensaries	Publishing Houses or Printing Establishments	Professed Christians
ROMAN CATHOLIC EUROPE—*continued*								
ITALY.								
Methodist Episcopal Church in the U. S.	12	71	32	2	3			2,457
Southern Baptist Convention	4	27	25	1				661
Baptist Missionary Society	10	14	41	1				697
Wesleyan Methodist Missionary Society	3	87	67	9				1,866
PORTUGAL.								
Wesleyan Methodist Missionary Society	2	21	7	5				199
SPAIN.								
American Board of Commis'rs for For. Missions	4	24	17	15	1			351
Wesleyan Methodist Missionary Society	2	27	13	18				126
Total in Roman Catholic Europe	47	296	214	53	4			8,100
Aggregate	13,371	69,670	24,337	23,527	960	553	147	2,219,291

Notes.—* From Beach's Atlas of Protestant Missions.
1 Contains items rated by the Society as Domestic Missions.
2 Work in West Indies (now Independent) is not included.
3 Work in Protestant Europe not included.
4 Including work of Women's Societies.
5 Christian establishments in Protestant islands of the West Indies figure in this report.
6 Probably duplicated in other society reports.
7 Schools not classified in reports of this Society.

Names of Societies.	No. of Missionaries, Men and Women	Native Workers, Men and Women	Places of Regular Worship	Elementary Schools	Higher or Special Educational Institutions	Hospitals and Dispensaries	Publishing Houses or Printing Establishments	Professed Christians
THE BIBLE SOCIETIES.*								
AMERICA, including Alaska, N. W. Canada, Labrador and Latin America.								
American Bible Society	9	78						
British and Foreign Bible Society	5	23						
Total	14	101						
ASIA.								
American Bible Society	12	281						
British and Foreign Bible Society	43	1,087						
Netherlands Bible Society	2	1						
Scottish National Bible Society	14	217						
AFRICA.								
American Bible Society		25						
British and Foreign Bible Society	6	24						
NEW ZEALAND.								
British and Foreign Bible Society	1							
Aggregate	92	1,763						

*Note.—These statistics do not include superintendents, colporteurs or Bible Women who are supported by local Missions or Auxiliaries.

C. PROTESTANT MISSIONS TO THE JEWS (by Rev. Louis Meyer, Hopkinton, Ia.).
Statistics brought down to March, 1904.

Note.—The CMS, the CA, the PN, the ZBM, the British Syrian Schools, the Swedish Missionary Union, the Swedish Evangelical National Society, and some others of the Foreign Missionary Societies come in contact with Jews and labor for them in the course of their general work, of which the statistics are reported in Tables A and B. Table "C" contains work that is not reported in the other tables. The heading "schools" includes Sabbath Schools and all of distinctly Christian influence.

Names of Societies.	No. of Missionaries	Unordained Workers	Stations	Schools	Hospitals and Dispensaries	Publishing Houses or Printing Establishments
BRITISH ISLANDS						
London Soc. for Promoting Christianity among Jews—London—(1809) (A)	29	185	51	10	1	1
Philo-Judæan Society—London—(1828) (A)						
Operative Jewish Converts' Institution—London—1829 (A)						
British Soc. for the Propagation of Gospel among Jews—London—1842 (U)	10	24	18			4
Jewish Mission of the Presbyterian Church of England—London—1871 (P)	1	19	2	2		1
London City Mission, Jewish Branch—London—1874 (U)		7	7			
Wild Olive Graft Mission—London—1874 (U)		3	1			
Parochial Missions to the Jews at Home and Abroad—London—1876 (A)	9	3	10			
Mildmay Mission to the Jews—London—1876 (U)	7	60	9	2		1
East London Fund for the Jews—London—1878 (A)	1	7	1			
Barbican Mission to the Jews—London—1879 (A)	2	4	2	1		
Prayer Union for Israel—London—1880 (U)						
East End Mission to Jews—London—1881 (U)		4	1			1
Jerusalem and the East Mission Fund—London—1887 (A)	7	12	5			2
Hebrew Christian Testimony to Israel—London—1894 (U)	2	11	2			
Church Medical Mission for Jewish Women and Children—Birmingham—1894—(A)		6	1			
Kilburn Mission to the Jews—London—1896 (A)	1	7	1			
Brick Lane Mission—London (A)	1	1	1			
Messiah's Witnesses—London—1902 (U)		5	1			
Gospel Mission to Jews in Algiers—Wimbledon—1902 (U)		1	1			
Jewish Mission of the Church of Scotland—Edinburgh—1840 (P)	5	57	5		3	
United Free Church of Scot. Mission to the Jews—Edinburgh—1843 (P)	5	65	5	8	6	
Jewish Medical Mission in Edinburgh—Edinburgh—1900 (P)		2	1		1	
Glasgow Jewish Evangelical Mission—Glasgow—1893 (P)	1	2	1			
Bonar Memorial Mission to the Jews—Glasgow—1893 (U)		1	1	1		
Church of Ireland Auxiliary to London Jews Society—Dublin—1818 (A)*	2	5				
Jewish Mission of the Presbyterian Church in Ireland—Belfast—1841 (P)	4	36	2	33		
Irish Mission to the Jews—Belfast—1896 (U)		1				
EUROPEAN CONTINENT						
Esdras Edzard Fund—Hamburg—1667 (L)						
Soc. for Promoting Christianity among the Jews—Berlin—1882 (L)	3	4	3			
Soc. for Christian Care of Jewish Proselytes—Berlin—1836 (L)	4	4	3	2		
Central Organization of Lutheran Church for Work among Jews—Leipzig—1871 (L)**						
West German Association for Israel—Cologne—1842 (L)	3	1	3			
Society of the Friends of Israel—Strasburg—1835 (L)						
Society of the Friends of Israel—Lubec—1844 (L)						
Institutum Judaicum Delitzschianum—Leipzig—1880 (L)						
Institutum Judaicum (Strack)—Berlin—1883 (L)						
Society of the Friends of Israel—Basel—1830 (R)						
Penny Collection Fund for Israel—Geneva—1898 (R)	2		2			
French Soc. for Promoting Christianity among Jews—Paris—1888 (F)		1	1			
Netherlands Soc. for Promoting Christianity among Jews—Amsterdam—1844 (A)†	2	2	3	1		
Netherlands Society for Israel—Amsterdam—1861 (R)		3	1			
Netherlands Reformed Ch. Miss. to the Jews—Ryswyk—1875 (R)		1	2			
Norwegian Central Committee for Jewish Missions—Christiania—1865 (L)	1	3	2	1		
Society for Missions to Israel—Stockholm—1875 (L)	1		2			
Society for Missions to Israel—Copenhagen—1885 (L)	5	7	6			
Rabbi Lichtenstein's Work among the Jews—Budapest—1885 (U)	1		1			
Asylum for Jewish Girls—St. Petersburg—1864 (L)		1	1			
Jewish Mission of the Baltic Lutheran Church—Riga—1865 (L)		2	1			
Finland Missionary Society—Helsingfors—1859 (L)		1	1	1		
AFRICA AND THE ORIENT						
Asylum Rudolph—Alexandria—1880 (U)	1		1	1		
South Africa Mission to the Jews—Cape Town—1897 (U)		1	1			
Jewish Mission of the Dutch Ref. Church of the Transvaal—Johannesburg—1903 (R)						
Old Church Calcutta Hebrew Mission—Calcutta (A)		1	1			
Calcutta Jewish Mission—Calcutta—1901 (U)		5	1	1	2	
Bombay Jewish Mission (M's. Cutter)—Bombay—1895 (U)		1	1			
Friends of Israel Prayer Union—Melbourne—1896 (U)		1	1			

Names of Societies.	No. of Missionaries	Unordained Workers	Stations	Schools	Hospitals and Dispensaries	Publishing Houses or Printing Establishments
UNITED STATES OF AMERICA						
Church Soc. for Promoting Christianity among the Jews—New York—1878 (E) (1842)		10	2	2		
New York City Mission and Tract Society, Jewish Work—N.Y.,1827 1878(U)	1	3	1	1		
Zion's Society for Israel of the Norwegian Lutherans in America—Minneapolis—1878 (L)	3		3			
Jewish Mission of the Evangelical Lutheran Synod of Missouri, Ohio and other States—New York—1883 (L)	1		1	1		
New York City Church Extension and Missionary Society, Jewish Mission—New York—1886 (M)		7	1		5	1
Chicago Hebrew Mission—Chicago—1887 (U)	3	19	1		2	
Hebrew Messianic Council—Boston—1888 (U)		1	1			
Gospel Mission to the Jews—New York—1892 (U)			1			1
Brooklyn Christian Mission to Jews—Brooklyn—1892 (U)		10	1		3	
Jewish Mission of the Joint Synod of Ohio—Alleghany—1892 (L)	1					
Reformed Presbyterian Mission to Jews—Philadelphia—1894 (RP)	1	6	1		3	1
Brownsville and Williamsburg Christ. Miss. to the Jews—Brooklyn—1894(B)	1	15	2		2	1
San Francisco Hebrew Mission—San Francisco—1896 (U)		2	1			
Emmanuel House Hebrew Mission of South Jersey Hebrew Colonies—Rosenhayn, N.J.1897 (U)		2	2			
New Covenant Mission to Jews and Gentiles—Pittsburg—1898 (U)		6	1			
Immanuel Mission to Jews—Cleveland—1898 (U)		3	1		1	
Jewish Bible Mission—Philadelphia—1898 (U)	1	11	2		2	
Presbyterian Hebrew Mission—San Francisco—1898 (P)		1	1			
The People, the Land, and the Book (Schapiro)—Brooklyn—1900 (U)	1					
Central Union Mission, Hebrew Branch—Washington, D.C.—1902 (U)		1	1			
Union Gospel Mission (Ragowski)—Cincinnati—1902 (U)	1	1	1			
Friends of Israel Union Mission—St. Louis—1902 (U)		6	1		1	1
Nathan Missionary Society—Butler, Pa.—1902 (U)	1	1	1			
Anglo-American Board of Missions to the Jews—New York—1903 (U)						
New York Hebrew Christian Association—New York—1903 (U)			1			
Postal Mission to the Jews—Chicago—1903 (U)						
Society for the Advancement of the Gospel of the Circumcision—Richmond, Va.—1903 (U)		1	1			
Christian Catholic Church in Zion Jewish Work (Warszawiak)—Zion City—1903 (Dowiite)		3	1			
The World's Gospel Union—Kansas City—1894 (U)						
CANADA						
Toronto Jewish Mission—Toronto—1894 (U)		1	1			
Hamilton Jewish Mission (Fretz)—Hamilton—1902 (U)	1		1			
Total Jewish Mission Statistics	**126**	**677**	**196**	**87**	**34**	**1**

* This work independent.   **Has 9 or more contributary organizations.
† Auxiliary to the London Jews Society.
Note.—The denominational relation of the above-named Jewish Missions is shown as follows: A—Anglican; B—Baptist; E—Episcopal; F—French Protestant; L—Lutheran; M—Methodist; P—Presbyterian; RP—Reformed Presbyterian; R—Reformed; U—Undenominational.

APPENDIX VI

ROMAN CATHOLIC FOREIGN MISSIONS

A.—THE MISSIONS

The following statistics, borrowed from the "Annals of the Propagation of the Faith," were compiled from the Directory of Missions issued by the Congregation of the Propaganda (*Missiones Catholicæ*: Romæ, 1901), supplemented by the publications of the Society for the Propagation of the Faith.

This list includes the greater part of the mission field of the Roman Catholic Church; but it is not claimed that the figures are exact. In some cases they are only approximative.

Dioceses	Catholics	Priests Missionary	Priests Native	Schools	Charities
AMERICA.					
Canada.					
Athabasca-Mackenzie	13,000	28	..	10	2
Indian Missions	6,500	26	..	..	?
New Westminster	28,000	30	5	18	3
Pembroke	40,000	14	24	86	4
St. Albert	16,000	37	8	25	6
St. Boniface	39,000	57	52	112	7
St. George's (Newfound'd)	7,000	8	..	20	..
Saskatchewan	9,800	23	1	28	2
Vancouver (Ecclesiastically in U. S.)	9,000	14	..	11	4
United States.					
Alaska	1,000	18	..	5	2
Boise, Idaho	10,000	9	15	8	4
Brownsville, Texas	63,000	20	2	14	1
Cheyenne, Wyo	6,000	13	2	8	1
Helena, Mont	50,000	..	46	19	12
Indian Territory	19,000	49	..	46	1
Natchez, Miss	20,000	32	5	28	2
Natchitoches, La	30,000	19	2	18	..
Rocky Mt. Mission	20,000	84	..	1	?
Santa Fe, N. M	133,000	60	7	20	3
Tucson, Ariz	40,000	25	..	16	5
West Indies.					
Roseau, Virgin Islands	50,000	24	..	29	3
Jamaica	13,000	11	..	19	2
Curaçao	38,000	32	..	22	5
Central America.					
British Honduras	19,000	13	1	28	?
South America.					
Dutch Guiana, Surinam	17,000	26	..	18	2
French Guiana, Oyapok	29,000	22	..	5	..
N. Patagonia	90,000	40	..	33	8
S. "	13,000	16	..	11	2
EUROPE.					
Balkan States.					
Antivari	12,900	11	2	12	?
Armenian Missions	270,000	480	..	..	..
Athens	17,000	5	17	15	4
Banialuka	53,000	4	45	11	4
Bukharest	120,000	42	5	39	1
Candia	800	10	..	6	1
Constantinople	45,000	100	180	80	20
Corfu	4,000	3	5	5	1
Durazzo	2,300	2	15	6	?
Jassy	74,460	38	11	6	2
Nicopolis	13,000	18	1	9	1
Philippopolis	15,000	15	12	32	5
Salonica	10,000	58	1	9	7
Santorin	500	..	6	2	1
Scopia (Uskup)	15,000	3	14	10	?
Scutari	27,000	30	30	8	2
Serajevo	170,000	156	22	1	13
Syra	8,000	7	15	14	?
Tine	4,000	6	21	13	1
British Isles.					
Menevia (Wales)	8,000	42	18	22	2
Plymouth	14,000	55	56	36	3
Ross	52,662	..	26	14	2
Denmark.					
Copenhagen	7,926	29	16	31	11
German Empire.					
N. German Mission	34,000	20	8	20	5
Saxony	150,000	39	12	21	19
Norway.					
Christiania	1,575	24	2	18	11
Sweden.					
Stockholm	1,800	10	4	9	7
AFRICA.					
Abyssinia	1,955	7	18	2	?
Benin	16,400	27	..	24	16
Cimbebasia, Lower	120	8	..	1	..
Dahomey	5,200	22	..	15	11
Delta of the Nile	8,000	35	..	11	7
Egypt	56,180	94	11	84	20
Erythraea	7,900	53	..	4	8
Galla	7,000	20	7	9	2
Gold Coast	5,650	16	..	13	9
Guinea, French	1,100	8	..	8	2
Ivory Coast	380	16	..	7	4
Kabyles Mission	582	40	3	24	21
Kamerun	2,420	9	..	30	..
Niger, Lower	1,200	9	..	5	8
Niger, Upper	450	14	..	10	4
Sahara	561	30	..	5	2
Senegambia-Senegal	15,000	52	6	53	36
Sierra Leone	2,800	7	..	6	3
Sudan	2,000	14	..	10	4
Togoland	1,300	12	..	20	5
Tripoli	5,750	11	..	11	2
Cimbebasia (Upper)	7,000	17	..	7	?
Congo (Lower French)	1,500	20	3	12	6
Congo (Upper French, Ubangi)	2,000	23	..	11	18
Congo Free State	3,516	62	..	14	3
Congo (Lower)	5,689	21	..	16	?
Congo (Upper)	2,376	16	..	14	6
Cunene	3,450	20	2	22	8
Gabon	12,000	35	1	25	6
Nile (Upper)	3,530	11	..	3	1
Nyassa	190	10	..	2	?

AFRICA—Continued.

Dioceses.	Catholics.	Priests. Missionary.	Priests. Native.	Schools.	Charities.
Tanganyika	1,689	17	..	34	2
Uelle	600	12	..	4	2
Unyanyembe	1,133	14	..	6	2
Victoria Nyanza (North)	39,586	32	..	8	4
" " (South)	1,290	14	..	5	?
Zambesi	1,200	17	..	20	9
Zanzibar (North)	7,860	38	..	22	3
" (South)	700	6	..	2	2
Basutoland	6,000	14	..	12	?
Cape of Good Hope (Cent)	762	7	..	6	2
" " " (East)	6,830	25	..	38	2
" " " (West)	6,240	16	..	26	2
Natal	12,000	50	7	55	6
Orange Free State	5,600	14	1	13	2
Orange River	500	10	..	7	5
Transvaal	6,200	15	..	16	3

African Islands.

Fernando Po (Annoban)	3,400	28	..	12	?
Madagascar (Central)	61,500	49	7	930	15
" (North)	6,000	10	..	10	5
" (South)	?	8	..	?	?
Mayotte-Nossi-Be, Madagascar	4,600	4	..	6	2
Seychelles	17,370	16	..	30	5

ASIA.

Arabia.

Aden	1,500	12	..	6	4

Chinese Empire.

Amoy	4,800	23	2	29	44
Che-kiang	10,500	13	13	64	?
Chi-li, North	40,000	24	40	133	31
" East	3,000	3	2	30	?
" S. East	50,000	42	16	418	8
" S. West	52,000	13	19	97	12
Fu-chau	41,000	26	20	61	?
Ho-nan, North	3,000	9	3	11	3
" South	10,300	14	8	51	4
Hongkong	9,000	13	7	36	8
Hu-nan, North	250	6	2	3	?
" South	5,600	4	10	7	5
Hu-pei, N. West	11,600	10	11	20	5
" East	18,000	14	22	28	5
" S. West	5,200	15	9	18	6
Ili Mission	112	3	..	1	1
Kan-su	3,000	17	..	8	4
Kiang-si, North	5,070	9	2	16	7
" East	10,800	10	10	91	7
" South	5,500	17	6	19	4
Kwei-chau	19,000	38	8	118	10
Kwang-si	1,350	17	..	31	11
Kwang-tung	42,500	58	12	150	5
Manchuria North	17,000	23	8	147	?
" South	8,900	10	8	60	14
Mongolia, Central	17,300	29	14	65	15
" East	9,000	27	7	38	7
" S. West	5,600	27	1	52	4
Nanking	124,000	115	45	959	100
Shan-si, North	13,150	9	15	70	5
" South	9,600	21	3	21	?
Shan-tung, North	18,200	13	15	39	4
" East	12,000	12	2	45	6
" South	16,190	31	11	41	5
Shen-si, North	20,400	16	23	26	9
" South	10,200	13	9	74	4
Sze-chwan, East	34,000	43	33	137	6
" West	40,000	35	42	234	6
" South	19,500	35	10	67	9
Tibet	1,560	18	1	11	4
Yun-nan	10,300	29	8	58	20

Corea.

Seoul	32,200	39	9	60	3

India.

Assam	1,340	9	..	9	?
Bettiah	4,000	15	..	13	11
Bombay	16,000	51	22	23	2
Calcutta	54,200	77	27	127	7
Changanacerry	107,200	..	277	234	?
Coimbatore	35,800	36	8	59	8
Colombo	198,000	80	14	661	10
Dacca	11,000	8	..	15	8
Ernaculum	80,900	..	115	167	?
Haidarabad	12,590	19	..	30	5
Jaffna	42,500	34	10	108	2
Kandy	21,150	10	19	24	5
Krishnagar	4,050	8	..	18	6
Combaconum	85,000	19	17	54	4
Lahore	3,590	23	..	22	4
Madras	49,000	23	22	76	6
Madura	206,000	51	24	239	10
Mangalore	83,600	34	47	64	15
Mysore	41,000	47	10	71	15
Nagpur	8,000	20	5	15	11
Point de Galle	6,300	12	..	34	?
Pondicherry	134,000	77	27	80	19
Poona	13,000	21	10	98	2
Quillon	87,000	16	28	96	3
Rajputana	3,600	12	2	5	5
Trichur	69,800	..	76	165	?
Trincomali	7,150	8	..	20	?
Verapoly	60,000	13	52	149	5
Vizagapatam	12,915	18	..	25	4

Indo-Chinese Peninsula.

Bangkok	22,000	36	14	43	23
Burma, East	9,600	10	1	72	14
" North	6000	21	3	39	25
" South	41,000	39	9	75	26
Cambodia (Prom-Penh)	28,400	33	21	104	5
East Cochin China	68,000	48	29	20	4
North " "	59,800	46	33	27	4
West " "	63,800	57	68	168	37
Laos (Nangsen)	9,430	21	4	20	10
Singapore	19,800	32	2	25	43
Central Tongking	204,000	17	78	681	10
East "	49,900	15	38	200	22
North "	27,600	13	26	40	11
South "	118,000	34	68	183	6
Upper "	18,410	24	14	?	3
West "	201,700	66	119	645	7

Japan.

Hakodate	4,600	21	1	3	3
Nagasaki	37,100	31	27	4	8
Osaka	4,650	27	2	8	5
Tokio	9,050	36	2	13	4

Malaysia.

Batavia	49,800	50	..	29	6
Borneo	1,200	12	..	10	?

Persia.

Ispahan	14,000	12	65	47	3

Turkish Empire.

Bagdad	5,000	6	15	25	2
Brusa	3,000	3	5	4	2
Chios	400	10	..	3	?
Cyprus	30,000	160	120	20	?
Jerusalem	15,000	24	24	67	20
Kurdistan	4,500	10	21	6	?
Marash	6,000	6	10	8	?
Mesopotamia	66,000	50	155	84	20
Mush	6,000	?	6	?	?
Sebasteia (Sivas)	3,000	..	10	11	..
Smyrna	15,500	40	17	15	5
Syria	40,000	43	50	30	?
Trebizond	5,000	7	7	4	?

OCEANIA.

Australasia.

Auckland, N. Z.	23,500	42	..	33	5
Christchurch, N. Z.	25,000	32	..	8	2
Port Augusta, Aust.	11,160	15	..	12	?
Wellington, N. Z.	28,000	58	..	37	4
Wilcannia, Aust.	16,000	16	..	16	?

Polynesia.

Fiji Islands	10,200	32	..	8	?
Gilbert Islands	11,000	11	..	67	?
Marquesas Islands	3,100	7	..	7	?
Navigators Islands, Samoa	6,000	18	1	67	?
New Caledonia	34,500	61	..	30	?
New Guinea	4,000	18	..	29	?
New Pomerania	6,600	20	..	15	5
Central Oceania	9,450	19	4	51	?
Sandwich Islds. (U.S.)	28,000	24	..	17	4
Solomon Islds. North	?	4	..	?	?
" " South	?	3	..	?	?
Tahiti	7,200	18	..	52	1
Wilhelmsland	?	3	..	?	?

The following dioceses, tho not under the jurisdiction of the *Propaganda*, and therefore not strictly speaking missionary dioceses, have for special reasons been aided by the "Propagation of the Faith" during the year 1900.

Germany.—Breslau, Cologne, Fulda, Hildesheim, Limburg, Mainz, Münster, Paderborn, Pomerania and Brandenburg. Posen and Gnesen, Treves. Warmia (Ermeland).

Switzerland.—Basel, Chur, Lausanne-Geneva, Sion.

Africa.—Algiers, Carthage, Constantine, Oran, Bourbon Island.

B.—ROMAN CATHOLIC RELIGIOUS ORDERS AND SOCIETIES ENGAGED IN MISSION WORK

		Founded.	Headquarters.	Mission Fields.
1	African Missions, Lyons	1856	Lyons.	Benin, Dahomey, Gold Coast, Ivory Coast, U. Niger, Egypt.
2	African Missions, Verona	1867	Verona.	Central Africa.
3	Algerian Missionaries	1868	Algiers.	Algeria, Upper Congo, Jerusalem, Nyassa, Unyanyembe, Sahara, Sudan, Tanganyika, Tunis, Victoria Nyanza.
4	Augustinians	1256	Rome.	Cooktown (Australia), Northern Hu-nan, Philippines, United States.
5	Augustinians of the Assumption	1851	Paris.	Turkey, United States.
6	Basilians	1822	Annonay (Fr.)	Canada, United States, Algeria.
7	Basilians of Bavaria		Munich.	Southern Zanzibar.
8	Benedictines	520	Monte Casino.	United States, Australia, England.
9	Benedictines (Sylvestrian)		Rome.	Kandy.
10	Benedictines (St. Ottilien)	1884	Bavaria.	Zanzibar.
11	Carmelites	1528	Rome.	Bagdad, Quillon, Verapoly, United States.
12	Carthusians	1086	Grande-Chartreuse.	England.
13	Children of Mary Immaculate	1820	Vendée.	Antilles.
14	Children of the Immaculate Heart of Mary		Spain.	Fernando Po.
15	Cistercians (Trappists)	1098	Rome.	Africa, Australia, Canada, China, England, Palestine, United States.
16	Company of Mary	1710	St. Laurent, sur Sevre, France.	England, Africa, Haiti, Canada.
17	Dominicans	1215	Rome.	Amoy, Canada, Curacao, Fokien Mesopotamia, Philippines, Central, Eastern and Northern Tongking, United States.
18	Eudist Fathers	1643	Rennes.	Canada.
19	Fathers of Mercy	1802	Paris.	United States.
20	Foreign Missions, Belgian	1865	Scheut-lez Bruxelles.	Congo Free State, Ili, Kan-su, Mongolia.
21	Foreign Missions, English	1866	Mill Hill.	Borneo, Kafiristan, Madras, Upper Nile.
22	Foreign Missions, French	1663	Paris.	Burma (Southern and Northern) Cambodia, Cochin China, Coimbatore, Korea, Japan, Kwang-si, Kwang-tung, Kuichau, Malaysia, Mysore, Pondicherry, Siam, Si-chuan, Tibet, Tongking, Yun-nan.
23	Foreign Missions, German-Holland, (Society of the Divine Word)	1875	Steyl, Hol.	Southern Shan-tung, Togoland, Williamsland, United States.
24	Foreign Missions, Milan	1850	Milan.	Eastern Burma, Ho-nan, Hongkong, Southern Hu-nan, Haidarabad, Krishnagar.
25	Foreign Missions, Rome	1874	Rome.	Southern Shen-si.
26	Franciscans, Minor	1209	Rome.	America, Egypt, Southern Hu-nan, Hu-peh, Philippines, Shan-si, Northern and Eastern Shantung, Northern Shen-si, Syria, Tripoli, etc.
27	Franciscans, Minor, Conventuals	1507	Rome.	Adrianople, Constantinople, Moldavia, United States.
28	Franciscans (Minor Capuchins)	1528	Rome.	Aden, Agra, Allahabad, Canada, Candia, Erythræa, Galla, Lahore, Mardin, Seychelles, Sophia, United States.
29	Holy Cross	1821	Le Mans.	Dacca, United States, Canada.
30, 31	Holy Ghost (1703) and Sacred Heart of Mary (1841)	1848	Paris.	French Colonies; Cimbebasia, French Congo, Lower Congo, Guinea, French Guiana, Kunene, Lower Niger, Senegambia, Sierra Leone, Zanzibar, and small Madagascan Islands, United States.
32	Jesuits	1540	Fiesole near Florence.	Alaska, Armenia, Australia, Western Bengal, Bombay, British Guiana, Canada, Kotayam, Jamaica, Madagascar, Mangalore, Eastern Chile, United States, Poona, Trichinopoli, Zambesi, etc.
33	Josephite Society	1892	Baltimore.	United States (Missions for the colored people).
34	La Salette	1852	La Salette.	Canada, Madagascar, United States.
35	Lazarists	1632	Paris.	Abyssinia, Adrianople, Bulgaria, Constantinople, Kiang-si, Madagascar, Persia, Chi-li, Syria, Che-kiang, U. S., etc.
36	Marists	1836	Lyons.	Fiji Islands, New Zealand (Wellington and Christchurch), New Caledonia, New Hebrides, Navigators Islands, Central Oceania, Solomon Islands, America.
37	Mechitarists (Benedictines)	1700	Venice.	Armenia.
38	Oblates of Mary Immaculate	1826	Paris.	Athabasca-Mackenzie, British Columbia, United States, Colombo, Jaffna, Natal, Orange Free State, St. Albert, St. Boniface, Saskatchewan, Transvaal, United States.
39	Oblates of the Sacred Heart		Pontigny, Yonne, Fr.	United States.
40	Oblates of St. Francis de Sales	1850	Troyes, Fr.	Greece, Orange River.
41	Oratorians	1577		England.
42	Passionists	1737	Rome.	England, Bukharest, Nicopolis, United States.
43	Paulist Fathers	1858	New York.	United States.
44	Pious Society of Missions (Pallotins)	1850	Rome.	Kamerun, Kimberly (Australia), Brazil, South America, United States.
45	Precious Blood	1814	Rome.	United States.
46	Premonstratensians (Norbertins)	1119	Rome.	Canada, Norway, United States, Madagascar.
47	Redemptorists	1732	Rome.	Dutch Guiana, United States.
48	Resurrectionists		Rome.	Adrianople, Canada, United States.
49	Sacred Heart Missionary Fathers	1854	Issoudun.	Micronesia, New Guinea, New Pomerania, United States.
50	Sacred Heart of Jesus		Rome.	Belgian Congo; (Stanley Falls).
51	Sacred Hearts of Picpus	1817	Paris.	Marquesas Islands, Sandwich Islands, Tahiti.
52	St. Charles Missionary Fathers		Piacenza.	United States.
53	St. Francis de Sales of Annecy	1833	Annecy.	Nagpur, Vizagapatam.

		Founded	Headquarters	Mission Fields
54	Salesians of Turin	1855	Turin	North and South Patagonia, United States
55	Servites	1233	Rome	England, United States
56	Society of the Divine Savior		Rome	Assam, United States
57	Sulpicians	1642	Paris	Canada, United States

Auxiliaries to the Missionary Priests: The chief auxiliaries in mission works are communities of Brothers and Sisters. Not to mention the lay-brothers accompanying Religious Orders of Priests nor the catechists and other missionary helpers, in almost every quarter of the globe where the priest has planted the faith, Brothers and Sisters have followed to help sustain it. These are represented in various countries approximately as follows:

	Number of Orders			Number of Orders	
	Brothers	Sisters		Brothers	Sisters
AMERICA.			Arabia	..	2
United States	9	75	Persia	..	1
Canada	8	33	India	10	31
Antilles (except Cuba, Porto Rico, etc.)	1	11	Indo-Chinese Peninsula	2	16
Guiana	1	10	Malaysia	1	4
Patagonia	..	1	China	4	13
			Japan and Korea	1	4
EUROPE.					
British Isles	9	49	**AFRICA.**		
Gibraltar	1	3			
Holland	15	30	Egypt	1	10
North German Mission	..	7	North Africa (except Egypt and Barbary States)	2	18
Denmark	1	4	Equatorial Africa	3	12
Norway and Sweden	..	6	South Africa and Islands	4	13
Balkan States	1	18			
ASIA.			**OCEANIA.**		
Turkish Empire (including the Holy Land and Syria)	1	17	Australia	3	28
			Other Oceanic Islands	4	18

It is impossible to furnish satisfactory figures as to the whole number of missionaries, because of the different views people may take as to what is understood by missionary countries and by missionaries. In the popular sense, those are missionaries who have gone to distant regions, and especially to heathen countries for the purpose of spreading the faith among unbelievers.

Taking these distinctions into consideration we may safely assert that there are at least 15,000 priests and others dedicated to the religious life, 5,000 teaching brothers, and 45,000 sisters laboring as missionaries, not to speak of the priests, brothers and sisters native to the regions where they work, catechists and others who make up the personnel of a mission, and the laborers among the Oriental Rites. Probably the estimate is much too small, but we may conclude that there are in the field about 65,000 missionaries of the Roman Catholic Church.